ENCYCLOPAEDIA JUDAICA

ENCYCLOPAEDIA JUDAICA

SECOND EDITION

VOLUME 6
DR–FEU

FRED SKOLNIK, *Editor in Chief*
MICHAEL BERENBAUM, *Executive Editor*

MACMILLAN REFERENCE USA
An imprint of Thomson Gale, a part of The Thomson Corporation

IN ASSOCIATION WITH
KETER PUBLISHING HOUSE LTD., JERUSALEM

THOMSON
GALE

Detroit • New York • San Francisco • New Haven, Conn. • Waterville, Maine • London

THOMSON GALE™

ENCYCLOPAEDIA JUDAICA, Second Edition

Fred Skolnik, *Editor in Chief*
Michael Berenbaum, *Executive Editor*
Shlomo S. (Yosh) Gafni, *Editorial Project Manager*
Rachel Gilon, *Editorial Project Planning and Control*

Thomson Gale
Gordon Macomber, *President*
Frank Menchaca, *Senior Vice President and Publisher*
Jay Flynn, *Publisher*
Hélène Potter, *Publishing Director*

Keter Publishing House
Yiphtach Dekel, *Chief Executive Officer*
Peter Tomkins, *Executive Project Director*

Complete staff listings appear in Volume 1

For more information, contact
Macmillan Reference USA
An imprint of Thomson Gale
27500 Drake Rd.
Farmington Hills, MI 48331-3535
Or you can visit our internet site at
http://www.gale.com

LIBRARY OF CONGRESS CATALOGING-IN-PUBLICATION DATA

Encyclopaedia Judaica / Fred Skolnik, editor-in-chief ; Michael Berenbaum, executive editor. -- 2nd ed.
v. cm.
Includes bibliographical references and index.
Contents: v.1. Aa-Alp.
ISBN 0-02-865928-7 (set hardcover : alk. paper) -- ISBN 0-02-865929-5 (vol. 1 hardcover : alk. paper) -- ISBN 0-02-865930-9 (vol. 2 hardcover : alk. paper) -- ISBN 0-02-865931-7 (vol. 3 hardcover : alk. paper) -- ISBN 0-02-865932-5 (vol. 4 hardcover : alk. paper) -- ISBN 0-02-865933-3 (vol. 5 hardcover : alk. paper) -- ISBN 0-02-865934-1 (vol. 6 hardcover : alk. paper) -- ISBN 0-02-865935-X (vol. 7 hardcover : alk. paper) -- ISBN 0-02-865936-8 (vol. 8 hardcover : alk. paper) -- ISBN 0-02-865937-6 (vol. 9 hardcover : alk. paper) -- ISBN 0-02-865938-4 (vol. 10 hardcover : alk. paper) -- ISBN 0-02-865939-2 (vol. 11 hardcover : alk. paper) -- ISBN 0-02-865940-6 (vol. 12 hardcover : alk. paper) -- ISBN 0-02-865941-4 (vol. 13 hardcover : alk. paper) -- ISBN 0-02-865942-2 (vol. 14 hardcover : alk. paper) -- ISBN 0-02-865943-0 (vol. 15: alk. paper) -- ISBN 0-02-865944-9 (vol. 16: alk. paper) -- ISBN 0-02-865945-7 (vol. 17: alk. paper) -- ISBN 0-02-865946-5 (vol. 18: alk. paper) -- ISBN 0-02-865947-3 (vol. 19: alk. paper) -- ISBN 0-02-865948-1 (vol. 20: alk. paper) -- ISBN 0-02-865949-X (vol. 21: alk. paper) -- ISBN 0-02-865950-3 (vol. 22: alk. paper)
1. Jews -- Encyclopedias. I. Skolnik, Fred. II. Berenbaum, Michael, 1945-
DS102.8.E496 2007
909'.04924 -- dc22

2006020426

ISBN-13:

978-0-02-865928-2 (set)
978-0-02-865929-9 (vol. 1)
978-0-02-865930-5 (vol. 2)
978-0-02-865931-2 (vol. 3)
978-0-02-865932-9 (vol. 4)
978-0-02-865933-6 (vol. 5)
978-0-02-865934-3 (vol. 6)
978-0-02-865935-0 (vol. 7)
978-0-02-865936-7 (vol. 8)
978-0-02-865937-4 (vol. 9)
978-0-02-865938-1 (vol. 10)
978-0-02-865939-8 (vol. 11)
978-0-02-865940-4 (vol. 12)
978-0-02-865941-1 (vol. 13)
978-0-02-865942-8 (vol. 14)
978-0-02-865943-5 (vol. 15)
978-0-02-865944-2 (vol. 16)
978-0-02-865945-9 (vol. 17)
978-0-02-865946-6 (vol. 18)
978-0-02-865947-3 (vol. 19)
978-0-02-865948-0 (vol. 20)
978-0-02-865949-7 (vol. 21)
978-0-02-865950-3 (vol. 22)

This title is also available as an e-book
ISBN-10: 0-02-866097-8
ISBN-13: 978-0-02-866097-4
Contact your Thomson Gale representative for ordering information.
Printed in the United States of America

10 9 8 7 6 5 4 3 2 1

TABLE OF CONTENTS

Initial letter "D" for "Dixit," the first word of Psalm 53, from the Angoulême Psalter, *France, 13th century. The illustration shows King David and a fool who, in accordance with medieval iconography, is represented holding a club and eating cheese, Besançon, Bibliothèque Municipale, Ms. 140, fol. 62 v.*

Dr–Dz

DRA (Draa), river valley region in southern Morocco on the borders of the Sahara. Many well-known scholars have ethnic regional names such as Dar'i, Edrei, etc., meaning "from Dra." According to an ancient legend, Dra was an independent Jewish state which was overthrown in wars with the Christians. In the Middle Ages active communities in the region corresponded with the Babylonian *geonim*. The Jews of Dra were the first to suffer during the *Almohad persecutions. The geographer Yaqut (1179–1229) stated that most tradesmen in the Dra valley were Jews. Dra is a fertile area with gardens and date-palm groves and until the mid-1950s Jews owned land farmed by "haratin," descendants of black slaves. As late as 1930, there were *mellahs* in the villages of Tamnugalt, Qasbat al-Makhzan, Rabat-Tinzulin, Arumiyat, Mansuriya, Amzru, Alhammid, and Mhamid, containing about 500 families. Some Jewish notables participated in the political life of the region as delegates to the 'councils' which governed this Berber-Arab society.

BIBLIOGRAPHY: J.M. Toledano, *Ner ha-Ma'arav* (1911), 13, 26, 47, 109–10; *Villes et tribus du Maroc*, 9 (1931), 94–95, 127, 178, 181; Hirschberg, Afrikah, 1 (1965), 90–91, 101, 236, 302; 2 (1965), 27; idem, *Me-Ereẓ Mevo ha-Shemesh* (1957), 105–13; Corcos, in: *Sefunot*, 10 (1966), 75–79.

[David Corcos]

DRABKIN, ABRAHAM (1844–1917), rabbi, born in Mogilev, Belorussia. After studying at the yeshivah of Volozhin and the rabbinical institute in Vilna, he was sent by the *Society for the Promotion of Culture among the Jews in Russia to the rabbinical seminary in Breslau, completing his dissertation, *Fragmenta Commentarii ad Pentateuchum Samaritano-arabicum*, in 1875. From 1876 to 1908 he served as *Kazionny Ravin* (government-appointed rabbi) of St. Petersburg. Drabkin was a member of the Provisional Committee for the Promotion of Crafts and Agriculture among the Jews in Russia. He took part in the conferences convened after the pogroms of 1881. He was editor of the rabbinical section for the first eight volumes of the *Yevreyskaya Entsiklopediya* (Russian Jewish encyclopedia).

DRACH, PAUL-LOUIS-BERNARD (David; 1791–1865), French apostate. Drach, who was born at Strasbourg, received a traditional rabbinic education. In 1813 he went to Paris, married a daughter of E. Deutz, chief rabbi of France, and, in 1819, was appointed head of the Paris Jewish School. At this time he published a Passover *Haggadah* (1818) and a *siddur* (1819), both with translation, a Jewish calendar (1821), and other works. On Easter 1823, to the consternation of French Jewry, Drach had himself baptized, with much pomp and circumstance, into the Catholic church, and he spent a year and a half in obtaining paternal control of his three children whom his wife had secretly taken to London. For a time he worked in

Paris as an expert in Hebrew and took part in the publication of the Venice Bible (27 vols., 1827–33). From 1832 to 1842 he served as librarian of the Congregation for the Propagation of the Faith in Rome, and published Hebrew poems in honor of the pope and the cardinals. Returning to Paris, Drach collaborated with the Abbé J.P. Migne in the publication of his *Patrologia*. He also edited the fragments of Origen's *Hexapla* (1857–60), and translated into French the anonymous work **Sefer ha-Yashar* (1858), wrongly attributed to Jacob *Tam who wrote another work similarly entitled. He also wrote a number of books and pamphlets to justify his apostasy and to prove to his former coreligionists the truth of Christianity. He succeeded in winning over his brother-in-law Hyacinthe (Simon) Deutz, the man who denounced the Duchess of Berry to the police; and his children, too, grew up as Christians and took Holy Orders.

BIBLIOGRAPHY: P. Klein [= M. Catane], in: *Revue de la Pensée Juive*, 7 (1951), 87–103.

[Moshe Catane]

DRACHMAN, BERNARD (1861–1945), U.S. Orthodox rabbi, first of the modern English-speaking Orthodox American rabbinate. Drachman was born in New York and reared in Jersey City. His early Jewish education was at a Reform institution, the Hebrew Preparatory School, sponsored by Temple Emanu-El Theological Seminary. He graduated from Columbia College, and was sent to study at Breslau and Heidelberg by New York's Temple Emanu-El (Reform). In Europe, much to the chagrin of his patrons, for the first time he came into personal contact with the deep piety of East European Jewry, and was so influenced by it that he became entirely committed to Orthodoxy, of which he later became one of the leading spokesmen in the United States. Drachman served as rabbi of Oheb Shalom in Newark until it introduced mixed seating, and in several New York City pulpits, including Zichron Ephraim (1889–1909) and Oheb Zedek (1909–22). His background was unusual. American-born, he shared none of the East European experiences of his Orthodox colleagues; Reform-trained, he shared none of the enthusiasm for Reform of those who first taught him. He was the first ordained Orthodox rabbi to preach in the vernacular in the U.S. and was one of the founders of the *Jewish Theological Seminary, where he taught Bible, Hebrew, and Jewish philosophy from 1887 to 1902. After Solomon Schechter's arrival, he continued as assistant reader in Codes from 1902 to 1908. There are two versions of his decision to sever his service at the Jewish Theological Seminary. Some believe that Drachman was not sufficiently scholarly for the institution that Schechter was rebuilding and others believe that he left the Seminary when it gradually started to diverge from Orthodoxy; he later taught at Yeshiva College. He served as president of the *Union of Orthodox Jewish Congregations during 1908–20. He was a candidate for the Chief Rabbinate of England in 1912 but withdrew when one of his first pupils, J.H. *Hertz, a graduate of the Jewish Theological Seminary, put forward his candidacy. Drachman was a founder of the Jewish Endeavor Society and Jewish Sabbath Alliance, which sought to repeal the Blue Laws that prohibited businesses from being open on Sunday and thus imposed a great economic hardship on Sabbath-observing Jews. In the 1920s, together with the labor movement they advocated a five-day work week. He translated Samson Raphael Hirsch's *Nineteen Letters of Ben Uziel* into English (1899). His autobiography, *Unfailing Light* (1948), is a vivid portrait of American Jewry during his lifetime.

BIBLIOGRAPHY: M. Davis, *Emergence of Conservative Judaism* (1963), 335–6. **ADD. BIBLIOGRAPHY:** J. Gurrock, "Bernard Drachman and the Evolution of Jewish Religious Life in America," in: *American Jewish History*, 76:4 (June 1967).

[Michael Berenbaum (2nd ed.)]

DRACHSLER, JULIUS (1889–1927), U.S. sociologist. Drachsler was born in Austro-Hungary, taught at Smith College and at the City College of New York. He served in the Bureau of War Risk Insurance (1918–19), was assistant secretary of the Jewish Big Brother Association (1913–15), assistant executive director of the Bureau for Jewish Social Research (1919–20), secretary of the faculty of the School for Jewish Communal Work (1915–18), president of the Conference on Immigration Policy (1921–22), and consultant of the Bureau of Jewish Social Research (1921–22). In addition, he served as director of the training courses for community center workers of the National Jewish Welfare Board. In his organizational as well as in his scholarly work, Drachsler's interest was centered on topics relevant to the sociology of Jews, then in its infancy. His major published works are *Democracy and Assimilation* (1920) and *Intermarriage in New York City* (1921). The latter is considered a classic in the demography of the Jews, and has been frequently quoted in subsequent studies on intermarriage.

[Werner J. Cahnman]

DRAGUIGNAN (Heb. דרגינ״א), capital of Var department, S.E. France. Toward the end of the 13th century, when the poet *Isaac b. Abraham Ha-Gorni visited Draguignan, there was already an important community of wealthy Jews, who gave an unfriendly welcome to the poet, mistrusting his licentious behavior. The ancient synagogue, no longer standing, a beautiful building with a 23-m.(75.4-ft.)-long facade and a single spacious hall without the support of columns, was built during the same period. During the middle of the 14th century the community of 200 to 250 persons was governed by an administrative council and two bailiffs. In the 15th century, the number of Jews in Draguignan had increased so much that the accommodation in the Rue Juiverie had become inadequate. There were numerous Jewish physicians, one of whom received a salary from the municipality. In 1489 the Jews in Draguignan were among the first victims of the edict of expulsion from Provence. Five accepted baptism to avoid being expelled. During World War II, there were about 12 Jewish families living in Draguignan. A new community of Jews of

North African origin established there numbered approximately 100 in 1968.

BIBLIOGRAPHY: Gross, Gal Jud, 170–1; F. Mireur, *Les rues de Draguignan*, 1 (1921), 134; Monore and Mireur, in *Bulletin de la Société d'Etudes scientifiques et archéologiques de… Draguignan*, 60 (1941); Boyer, in: *Evidences*, 64 (1957), 23–24; Blumenkranz, in: *L'Arche*, 76 (1963), 48–51; Z. Szajkowski, *Analytical Franco-Jewish Gazetteer* (1966), 281.

[Bernhard Blumenkranz]

DRAGUNSKI, DAVID ABRAMOVICH (1910–1992), Soviet army officer. Born in Sviatsk, Btyansk district, Russia, he started his army career in 1933. During World War II he commanded a tank battalion and a tank brigade. He was twice awarded the title Hero of the Soviet Union and finished the war as a colonel. After studying in the Military Academy he was promoted to major-general in 1953, lieutenant-general in 1961, and colonel-general in 1970. During World War II he was a member of the Jewish *Anti-Fascist Committee, and in 1947 his biography was published by the Committee in Yiddish. He represented Soviet Jewry at the opening of the Holocaust museum in Paris and in other places. He was used by the Soviet authorities to attack Israel, Zionism, and the movement to immigrate to Israel. He appeared at an anti-Zionist press conference in Moscow in March 1970 and headed the delegation of Soviet Jewry in Brussels in February 1971 for an international conference to defend Soviet Jews' rights. In 1968 he published his war memoirs.

[Shmuel Spector (2nd ed.)]

DRAÏ, RAPHAËL (1942–), French political scientist, sociologist, religious thinker. Born in Constantine, Draï had to leave Algeria at the age of 19, in 1961, and always considered the fate of Algerian Jews after the war of independence, and his own exile, as a great injustice. Nevertheless, he consistently refused to blame anyone for these events, which he saw as a result of the "hardships of history," leaving the door open to a process of "reconciliation"; he thus remained an advocate of trans-Mediterranean, intercultural, and inter-religious dialogue, and in 2000, after Algerian president Bouteflika acknowledged for the first time, in a speech in Constantine in 1999, the importance of Jewish culture to the history of Algeria, he tried to move forward and, together with the singer Enrico Macias and other Jews from Constantine, traveled to Algeria to pray at the tomb of Algerian-Jewish singer Sheikh Raymond Leyris, assassinated in 1961 and a symbol of the involvement of Jews in the shaping of Arab-Algerian classical culture. Intended to be the beginning of a reconciliation process, the journey left a harsh impression of unrelieved misunderstanding and alienation, but was still a remarkable step forward. In the wake of this journey, Draï voiced the complexity of his feelings in an open letter to President Bouteflika, *Lettre au président Bouteflika sur le retour des Pieds-Noirs en Algérie* (2000). In France, he had a successful academic career in which he tried to apply a broad perspective to political science, taking into account the results of diligent juridical analysis as well as new developments in the social sciences; he was one of the first social scientists to fully internalize and use the tools provided by psychoanalysis, joining the Psychanalyses et pratiques sociales research unit at the University of Aix-Marseille, where he taught. A former dean of the University of Amiens, Draï also wrote a number of books on social, juridical, administrative, and political subjects, including *Le temps dans la vie politique* (1981), *Sous le signe de Sion: L'antisémitisme nouveau est arrivé* (2001), *Science administrative, éthique et gouvernance* (2002), and *Le Droit entre laïcisation et néo-sacralisation, Instabilités européennes: recomposition ou décomposition?* (2000). Taking part in official think tanks on bioethics, Draï is also a recognized expert in Talmud and *halakhah*, using his knowledge of Jewish Law to deepen his ethical, social, and political analysis, so that his work can be described as an unusual attempt to combine a classical juridical approach to political science with the progress of the modern social sciences, psychoanalytical elements, and Jewish tradition. This original endeavor culminated in *Identité juive, identité humaine* (1995), a discussion of Jewish identity and universal values. Other works related to Judaism were *Lettre au Pape sur le pardon au peuple juif* (1998), *L'Economie chabbatique* (1998), *Freud et Moïse – Psychanalyse, loi juive et pouvoir* (1997), *La pensée juive et l'interrogation divine* (1996), and *La sortie d'Egypte, l'invention de la liberté* (1986).

[Dror Franck Sullaper (2nd ed.)]

DRAMA, city in Macedonia, Greece. *Benjamin of Tudela found 140 Jews in Drama in c. 1165. Documentation points to the settlement of a small Jewish community of merchants in Drama from the beginning of the 17th century who brought their legal problems to the Salonikan *bet din*. During the years 1671–68, the Hebron emissary Rabbi Moses ha-Levi *Nazir visited the community. After the fall of Ottoman Hungary in 1689, Jews from Buda settled in Drama. Jewish merchants carried goods in caravans from Drama to other towns. In 1900 the Jewish community numbered 45 families, or 150 people. Many Jews from Serres settled in Drama in 1913 after a large fire erupted under Bulgarian occupation. Before World War II the Jews were engaged in commerce (especially in tobacco); some were craftsmen or in the liberal professions. In 1934, the Zionist Geula organization was founded. In 1940 there were 1,200 Jews in the town. In 1941 Drama was occupied by the Bulgarians, who requisitioned all the Jewish enterprises. Jewish-owned capital in the banks was also confiscated. On March 4, 1943, the Jews of the community were arrested by the Bulgarian police and army, held in tobacco warehouses in the Agia Barbara quarter for three days, and then sent to the Gorna Djumaya camp in Bulgaria, where they were kept in extremely harsh conditions. From there, young men in their teens and early twenties were sent to forced labor in Bulgaria and 113 families (589 people) were dispatched by train to Lom and from there put on a boat to Vienna, where they were reloaded on trains to Treblinka and gassed upon their arrival.

In 1948 there were 39 Jews in Drama and in 1958, 17. A Holocaust memorial plaque was inaugurated in 1999.

BIBLIOGRAPHY: Rosanes, Togarmah, 3 (1938), 77; H. Pardo, in: *Fun Letstn Khurbn*, 7 (1948), 88–90. **ADD. BIBLIOGRAPHY:** B. Rivlin, "Drama," in: *Pinkas Kehillot Yavan* (1999), 93–97.

[Simon Marcus / Yitzchak Kerem (2nd ed.)]

DRANCY, small town near Paris where an internment camp was established by the Germans late in 1940. It became the largest center for the deportation of Jews from France. Beginning on August 20, 1941, it was reserved exclusively for Jews. They were deported from there "to the East" from July 19, 1942, until the camp was liberated on August 17, 1944. On that date some 1,500 internees were still there. The camp was directed by high Gestapo officers stationed in France. More than 61,000 persons were sent from Drancy to the death camps. The camp has been transformed into an apartment complex for low-income families. At the site, there are a number of memorial plaques and a small museum housed in a cattle car that was used to transport Jews during World War II.

BIBLIOGRAPHY: G. Wellers, *De Drancy à Auschwitz* (1946); Z. Szajkowski, *Analytical Franco-Jewish Gazetteer 1939–1945* (1966), 262 (includes bibliography).

[Shaul Esh / Michael Berenbaum (2nd ed.)]

DRAPKIN (Darom), ABRAHAM S. (1908–1993), criminologist and Israeli diplomat. Born in Argentina, Drapkin studied in Chile and from 1935 to 1940 was secretary-general of the Chilean Department of Prisons. In 1936 he founded the journal *Revista de Ciencias Penales*, and a year later helped establish the Chilean Institute of Penal Sciences. He published *Jurisprudencia de las Circunstancias Eminentes de Responsabilidad Criminal* (1937) and *Relación de Causalidad y Delito* (1943). In 1948 he immigrated to Israel and entered its foreign service. He represented Israel in Greece, Yugoslavia, Thailand, Mexico, and at the United Nations.

DRAPKIN (Senderey), ISRAEL (1906–1990), Israeli criminologist and physician. Drapkin, who pioneered criminological studies in Latin America, was born in Rosario, Argentina. In 1936 he established the first Criminological Institute in Chile, and in 1950 the chair of criminology at the University of Chile. He advised on the establishment of other national institutes of criminology, particularly in Venezuela, Costa Rica, and Mexico. Drapkin settled in Israel in 1959 and established the chair of criminology and the Institute of Criminology at the Hebrew University. His publications include *Manual de Criminología* (1949) and *Prensa y Criminalidad* (1958).

[Zvi Hermon]

DRAY, JULIEN (1955–), French politician. Born in 1955 in Oran, Algeria, Dray was first active in far-left movements after his family had to move to France at the end of Algeria's war of independence. During the 1970s, he was a member of the Trotskyite Ligue communiste révolutionnaire and the left-wing student union Mouvement d'action syndicale, which merged in 1980 with the newly created UNEF-ID, a radical faction of the mainstream socialist UNEF union. At the time, Dray himself moved from the far-left to the mainstream left and joined the Socialist Party (PS) in 1980, shortly before the socialist François Mitterrand was elected France's president. Dray was in charge of managing the Socialist Party's youth movements, and in 1984 was a founding member of SOS-Racisme, an anti-racist youth association affiliated with the PS and aiming at promoting the social integration of the immigrants, federating French youth around anti-racist values, and countering the rise of the anti-immigration far-right Front National party. In 1986, Dray also helped create the FIDL, a high-school student union. In 2003, he was involved in the creation of Ni putes ni soumises, a feminist organization that worked in the neglected, impoverished suburbs and among immigrant youth to promote the advancement of young women and lead the fight against sexual discrimination and violence. Dray was a member of Parliament from 1988 and in 1997 and 2002 was elected vice president of the Ile-de-France Regional Council. Acting as a spokesman for the party, Dray also participated in its internal ideological debates and headed one of the ideological clubs within the PS, the Club de la Gauche Socialiste. Julien Dray was widely seen as one of the most promising young leaders of the Socialist Party.

[Dror Franck Sullaper (2nd ed.)]

DREAMS.

In the Bible

The biblical view of dreams agrees substantially with that held by almost all ancient peoples. Dreams are visions of things actually transpiring on an ultramundane plane, where persons are not bound to bodies or events to specific moments and places. This plane is indistinguishable from that of the gods (or God), and dreams are therefore considered to be divine communications (Gen. 20:3, 6; 31:10–11). What is thus revealed may subsequently be actualized in historical fact. Accordingly, dreams are regarded as presages or omens. They are best understood by visionaries, i.e., by prophets, mantics, and ecstatics, who, in their suprasensory states, are in rapport with the "divine dimension," and it is to such persons that God vouchsafes dreams when He wishes to communicate with mankind (cf. Num. 12:6). In the Bible, "dreamer," "prophet," and "magician" are related terms (cf. Jer. 23:28; 27:9; 29:8; see *Divination). The final interpretation of dreams rests with God (Gen. 40:8).

Dreams are usually symbolic, and their interpretation (known as oneiromancy) revolves around the unraveling of their images. Dreambooks, in which such images are codified, feature in Egyptian and Mesopotamian literature. Biblical examples of such symbolic dreams are those of Joseph (Gen. 37:5ff.), of Pharaoh's butler and baker (*ibid.* 40:1ff.), and of Pharaoh himself (*ibid.* 41:1, 5); in Judges (7:13ff.) a man's dream that a cake of barley rolls onto the Midianite camp and bowls it over is taken to portend the imminent discomfiture of that people. Ancient Near Eastern parallels are afforded by a series of prophetic dreams related in the Babylonian "Epic of Gilgamesh" and in the Hittite "Legend of Kessi."

Dreams that occur in sacred places are considered to be revelations from the resident deity. People in search of divine direction resort to such shrines and sleep on the premises. This widespread practice, called incubation, is attested for the ancient Near East by a Sumerian inscription of Gudea of Lagash and a Hittite text of King Mursilis II of Hatti. The only clear instance in the Bible is the story of Jacob at Beer-Sheba (Gen. 46:1ff.), though some scholars claim that the narratives of the infant Samuel at Shiloh and of Jacob at Beth-El fall within the same category. It is necessary, however, to distinguish between incubation, which involves a purposeful visit to a shrine, and more general revelation through dreams, such as is described, for example, in I Kings 3:5–15 (Solomon at Gibeon). In sundry passages (e.g., Jer. 23:25; Zech. 10:2), the Bible speaks of false dreams. There appear to be two criteria for this designation, as there are also for false prophecy: a dream may be deemed false either because it is not subsequently realized, or because it never occurred at all. In the future Golden Age, says the prophet Joel (3:1), the gift of prophetic dreaming will be bestowed on all men, young and old alike. In the Greco-Roman age, apocalyptic visions were thought to be vouchsafed in dreams. Literary works inspired by this idea are the Book of Daniel and the Apocalypses of Ezra and Baruch. There is evidence of a pious protest against oneiromancy; both Ben Sira (31:1ff.) and the Letter of Aristeas (213–216) denounce belief in dreams.

[Theodor H. Gaster]

In the Talmud

Diametrically opposed views on dreams were expressed by the sages. Jonathan stated that "a man is shown in a dream only what is suggested by his own thoughts" (Ber. 55b). This statement is similar to Freud's views that certain thoughts which during the day are suppressed to the unconscious, reappear in a dream, where they find gratification. It is told of Meir and Nathan that after behaving unbecomingly toward Simeon b. Gamaliel the *nasi*, "they were told in their dreams to go and pacify him. Nathan went, but Meir did not, saying, 'Dreams are of no consequence'" (Hor. 13b; see also Git. 52a). The extent to which the sages did not set store by dreams is attested by Hanan's statement that "even if the genius of dreams informs a man that on the morrow he will die, he should not desist from prayer, since it is said (Eccles. 5:6): 'For through the multitude of dreams and vanities there are also many words; but fear thou God'" (Ber. 10b). There were sages who believed in dreams, however, and regarded them as being in the nature of prophecy; Ḥanina b. Isaac declared that "a dream is a variety of prophecy" (Gen. R. 17:5), and R. Joseph said, "If one was placed under a ban in a dream, ten persons are necessary for lifting the ban" (Ned. 8a). Some fasted on account of a bad dream, the *fast being known as *ta'anit ḥalom* ("dream-fast"). Thus Rav asserted: "Fasting is as potent against a dream as fire is against tow. Ḥisda said: Provided it is on the same day. R. Joseph added: Even on the Sabbath" (Shab. 11a).

The Talmud contains a prayer which originated in the last generation of the *amoraim* and which, said during the priestly benediction, reads as follows: "Sovereign of the Universe, I am Thine and my dreams are Thine. I have dreamt a dream and do not know what it is. Whether I have dreamt about myself, or my companions have dreamt about me, or I have dreamt about others, if they are good dreams, confirm and reinforce them like the dreams of Joseph, and if they require a remedy, heal them, as the waters of Marah were healed by Moses our teacher, and as Miriam was healed of her leprosy and Hezekiah of his sickness, and the waters of Jericho by Elisha. As Thou didst turn the curse of the wicked Balaam into a blessing, so turn all my dreams into something beneficial for me" (Ber. 55b). The Talmud records that there were 24 professional interpreters of dreams in Jerusalem (*ibid.*), an indication of how deep-rooted a belief in dreams was among the masses. (Extensive material on dreams and their interpretation is given in Ber. 55a–57b.) A third view, midway between these two extremes, regarded dreams as composed alike of truth and of incidental features. This was stated by Johanan in the name of Simeon b. Yoḥai: "Just as there can be no grain without straw, so can there be no dream without meaningless matter." A similar view was expressed by Berechiah, "While part of a dream may be fulfilled, the whole of it is never fulfilled," and by Ḥisda: "Neither a good dream nor a bad one is wholly fulfilled" (Ber. 55a). Some sages distinguished between one dream that lacks all substance and another that is fulfilled. This was the view of Johanan, who declared that "three dreams are fulfilled: an early morning dream, a dream which a friend has about one, and a dream which is interpreted within a dream" (Ber. 55b).

[Abraham Arzi]

In Medieval Thought

Interest in dreams continued through the Middle Ages to modern times, especially among the kabbalists and Ḥasidim. The Zohar discusses the problem of the admixture of truth and falsehood in dreams, and distinguishes between the dreams of the wicked, which derive from the forces of impurity, and the dreams of the righteous, which contain the visions, images, and prophecies seen by the soul in the higher worlds. Nevertheless, even the dreams of the righteous are infected by the false notions of the *sitra aḥra*. The angel in charge of the dreams of the righteous is Gabriel. These dreams, while they are not as great as prophecy, are close to prophecy (Tishby, *Mishnat ha-Zohar*, 2 (1961), 136–43). Maimonides developed a conception of dreams, based on his psychology and epistemology, as an integral part of philosophical anthropology, which totally rejects all supernatural categories. The religious significance of Maimonides' conception lies in his identification of dreams and prophecy in terms of their essence, and their distinction in terms of their content (*Guide of the Perplexed*, 2:36–38; cf. *Shemonah Perakim*, 1; Yad, Yesodei ha-Torah 7:2). Maimonides attributes no cognitive significance to dreams in the sense of a spiritual process which introduces new ideas or knowledge which was not previously known. Dreams are a function of the imagination only, not of the senses or the intellect. What one learns in dreams is not a new product of one's soul or a new idea from the outside, but is rather brought up from the imaginative faculty, the storehouse of sensual and intellectual impressions: "The thing which engages greatly and earnestly man's attention while he is awake and in the full possession of his senses forms during his sleep the object of the action of his imaginative faculty." The prophetic dream is unique in that "his [the prophet's] attention must be directed to the knowledge of God.... There must be an absence of the lower desires and appetites." If the prophet fulfills these requirements while he is awake, of necessity he will, in his dreams, "perceive things very extraordinary and divine, and see nothing but God and His angels." The experiences of the dream, those of both the prophet and the ordinary person, occur only "when the senses are at rest and pause in their action." In his dreams a person apprehends ideas which he previously had and which left their impression in his imaginative faculty, which "sees the thing as if it came from without and perceives it as if through the medium of bodily senses." It thus appears as if these are new ideas which have never before been experienced. From this conception of the essence of dreams it can be seen that Maimonides avoids the traditional interpretation of the "dream-fast" as a means of protection from an anticipated danger or for the purpose of abolishing a harmful decree, and sees the fast as an obligation which has a didactic-psychological purpose: "that he may reexamine his actions and analyze them and repent" (Yad, Ta'aniyyot 1:12). A later attempt to promulgate a belief in dreams and their interpretation on a "philosophical" basis was made by Solomon Almoli, whose book *Mefasher Ḥelmin* or *Pitron Ḥalomot* ("The Interpretation of Dreams") was very popular among eastern European Jews. Some medieval thinkers would rely on dreams even in matters of religious law, as, for example, Jacob of Marvège in his responsa. Other scholars, however, strongly opposed this practice: "We do not require the dream of R. Jacob ... nor his interpretation based on a dream ... and one should take no notice of dreams, because we know that it is not in the heavens" (Zedekiah b. Abraham Anav's *Shibbolei ha-Leket* (1896), no. 157). Nevertheless, there were people in later generations who made decisions on the basis of dreams.

[*Encyclopaedia Hebraica*]

BIBLIOGRAPHY: A. Lowinger, *Der Traum in der juedischen Literatur* (1908); A. Kristianpoller, *Traum und Traumdeutung* (*Monumenta Talmudica*, 4, 1923); J. St. Lincoln, *Dream in Primitive Culture* (1935); E.L. Ehrlich, in: BZAW, 73 (1953), 1–170; H.L. Oppenheim, *Interpretation of Dreams in the Ancient Near East* (1956); Jacob of Marvège, *She'elot u-Teshuvot min ha-Shamayim*, ed. by R. Margoliouth (1957), introduction, 3–20; S. Lieberman, *Yevanit ve-Yavnut be-Ereẓ Yisrael* (1962), 204–9; M. Harris, in: PAAJR, 31 (1963), 51–80.

DREBEN, SAM (1878–1925), U.S. soldier of fortune. Born in Russia, Dreben immigrated to the United States in 1898 and volunteered for the army. He fought in China during the Boxer Rebellion of 1900 and later in Nicaragua, where he became known as the "fighting Jew." In 1916 he volunteered as a colonel in the Mexican army and in 1918 fought in France, where he won the Distinguished Service Cross. Dreben donated a large sum of money to the *American Jewish Joint Distribution Committee and helped fight the Ku Klux Klan in Texas in the 1920s.

DREIFUSS, RUTH (1940–), Swiss politician. Born in St. Gall, she spent her youth in Geneva. Her father was active on behalf of Jewish refugees in Switzerland. After receiving a diploma in commerce, she became editor of the consumer association's magazine *coop* in Basle (1961–64). She joined the Social Democratic Party in 1965 and studied economics at the University of Geneva, beginning her academic career there as assistant professor (1972–74). She was engaged by the Federal Foreign Ministry (1972–81) and was elected secretary of the Swiss Labor Union (Berne, 1981–93). She also served on the city council of Berne as a member of the Social Democrats. In 1993 she was elected by the Federal Assembly (Parliament) as a Federal councilor, becoming the first Jewish member of the Swiss government. As minister of the interior, she fought to cut welfare spending and was broadly perceived as fighting for women's equality in Swiss private industry. Her vision of social justice had roots in Jewish tradition, even if she declared herself an agnostic and did not become a member of a Jewish community.

In 1998 she was elected vice president of the Swiss Confederation and in 1999 she became president for the one-year term, serving in effect as the Swiss head of state. As such, she reiterated Switzerland's official apology to the victims of the Holocaust, acknowledging that Swiss asylum policy had been "marred by errors, omissions, and compromises." In 2002 she resigned from the government after being reelected councilor twice. In 2004 she contributed to the jubilee volume of the Swiss Federation of Jewish Communities, describing the changes in the position of Swiss Jewry from pre-emancipation times until the present.

BIBLIOGRAPHY: I.M. Fischli, *Dreifuss ist unser Name* (2002); U. Altermatt, *Conseil fédéral* (1993), 611.

[Uri Kaufmann (2nd ed.)]

DRESDEN, capital of Saxony, Germany. A Jewish community existed there in the early 14th century, and its members were massacred in the *Black Death persecutions of 1349. Jews are not mentioned in Dresden again until 1375. They were expelled in 1430. Jewish settlement was renewed in the early 18th century when the *Court Jews Behrend *Lehmann and Jonas Mayer, with their retainers, were permitted to settle in Dresden. A synagogue and cemetery were opened in the middle of the 18th century. A society for caring for and visiting the sick was established which formed the nucleus for communal organization. During this period the Jews in Dresden were subjected to strict regulations and their rights of residence were limited. Nevertheless there were about 1,000 Jewish residents by the end of the 18th century. Their situation improved in the 19th century. Active in the communal leadership were R. David Landau of Lissa, who settled in Dresden in 1803, and Bernhard *Beer, founder of the "Mendelssohn-Verein" for the advancement for crafts, art, and science among Jewish youth (1829). As communal leader for 30 years, Beer was active in efforts for improvement of the civil status of the Jews in Dresden and the rest of Saxony. A new synagogue was built and consecrated on his initiative in 1840 and Zacharias *Frankel officiated as its first rabbi (1836–54). Frankel succeeded, among other achievements, in obtaining the repeal of the more humiliating portions of the Jewish *oath in 1840. During this period a Jewish elementary school was founded (1836) and complete civil equality attained (1869). Emil Lehmann (d. 1898) followed Beer as leader of Dresden and Saxon Jewry. Frankel was succeeded by the teacher Wolf Landau (1854–86) and the scholar of Midrash Jacob *Winter (1887–1941). The community numbered approximately 2,300 in 1886, 4,300 in 1913, and over 6,000 in 1925.

A number of Jews from East Europe settled there after World War I. A prosperous and well-endowed community, it owned a valuable library and maintained numerous social and charitable organizations. A group of Orthodox Jews seceded and founded the "Shomerei ha-Dat" congregations. In October 1938, 724 Jews of Polish citizenship were deported from Dresden. On *Kristallnacht*, 151 Jews were arrested and shipped to Buchenwald. The synagogues were burned and the Jewish community was presented with a bill for their demolition. By May 1939, the community had been reduced to 1,600 people as a result of emigration, deportation, and arrests. There were 12 deportations, dispatching 1,300 Jews, between January 1942 and January 1944. The final deportation was scheduled for February 1945. The Allied bombing of Dresden allowed the deportees to escape.

A synagogue seating 200 was opened in 1950. Subsequently the Dresden community declined, numbering 100 in the late 1960s. From 1962 to 1990 Dresden was the seat of the Association of Jewish Communities in the GDR. Owing to the immigration of Jews from the Former Soviet Union, the number of community members rose to 618 in 2005. A new synagogue was inaugurated in 2001. Dresden is the seat of the Association of Jewish Communities in Saxony.

BIBLIOGRAPHY: E. Lehmann, *Aus alten Acten…* (1886); idem, *Ein Halbjahrhundert in der israelitischen Religionsgemeinde zu Dresden* (1890); MGWJ, 1 (1852), 382–5, 421–6; Germ Jud, 2 (1968), 175; Gruen, in: AUJW, 9 (1954/55), 3; B. Beer, *Geschichtliche Darstellung der 50 – jaehrigen Wirksamkeit des Krankenunterstuetzungs – Institutes fuer Israeliten zu Dresden* (1857). **ADD. BIBLIOGRAPHY:** U. Ullrich, *Zur Geschichte der Juden in Dresden* (2001); *Der alte juedische Friedhof in Dresden* (2002).

[Akiva Posner / Annegret Nippa (2nd ed.)]

DRESDEN, SEM (1881–1957), composer and teacher. Born in Amsterdam, Dresden studied there and with Pfitzner in Berlin. In 1914 he founded a choral ensemble which gave concerts of the works of the great Dutch composers and of Renaissance and modern works. He was director of the Amsterdam Conservatory (1924–37) and of the Royal Conservatory at The Hague (1937–40; 1945–49), and for a number of years president of the Society of Dutch Composers and of the Dutch section of the International Society of Contemporary Music. His compositions include *Chorus Tragicus* for choir, wind instruments, and percussion (1928, after Vondel's *Hierusalem verwoest*); Psalm 84 for choir "based on an old Hebrew prayer"; concertos for various instruments; orchestral and chamber works; and an opera, *Toto* (1945). He also wrote and edited books on music history and theory.

DRESNER, SAMUEL HAYIM (1923–2000), U.S. Conservative rabbi, activist, scholar, and author. Dresner was born in Chicago and began his education at the University of Cincinnati (B.A., 1945) and Hebrew Union College. He left HUC to study with his mentor Abraham Joshua *Heschel, who went to the Jewish Theological Seminary after World War II, where Dresner was ordained (1951) and subsequently earned his D.H.L. degree (1954). Dresner began his career as associate rabbi of Congregation Har Zion in Philadelphia, Pennsylvania; in addition, in 1955, Dresner and several colleagues revived the quarterly magazine *Conservative Judaism*. For 10 years, Dresner almost single-handedly kept the magazine alive. In 1957, he became the rabbi of Congregation Beth El in Springfield, Massachusetts, where he also joined the civil rights struggle as chairman of the Massachusetts Human Relations Commission. He used his positions in the Conservative movement to promulgate a code of Jewish living, promoting Sabbath observance, and establishing an adult Leadership Training Institute. As part of his lobbying efforts for Jewish funeral reform, Dresner co-chaired the Committee on Funeral Practices of the non-denominational *Synagogue Council of America. In 1969, Dresner became rabbi of North Suburban Synagogue Beth El in Highland Park, Illinois (1969–77). In 1977, Dresner joined the faculty of Spertus College in Chicago and moved to Deerfield, Illinois, where he assumed the pulpit at Congregation Moriah. Following his retirement from the congregational rabbinate in 1984, he taught at the Hebrew University of Jerusalem (1985), at Hebrew Union College (1986–88), and at the Jewish Theological Seminary (1989–2000).

Dresner contributed hundreds of articles to such periodicals as *Judaism, Commentary, Forum,* and *Jewish Digest,* and wrote and edited numerous books, including *Prayer, Humility and Compassion* (1957), *The Jewish Dietary Laws* (1959, 1966), *Three Paths of God and Man* (1960), *The Zaddik* (1960; reissued as *The Zaddik: The Doctrine of the Zaddik According to the Writings of Rabbi Yaakov Yosef of Polnoy,* 1994), *The Jew in American Life* (1963), *God, Man and Atomic War* (1966), *The Sabbath* (1970), *Between the Generations: A Jewish Dialogue* (1971), *Levi Yitzhak of Berditchev: Portrait of a Hasidic Master* (1974; reissued as *The World of a Hasidic Master: Levi Yitzhak of Berditchev*, 1985, 1994), *Agenda for American Jews: Federation and Synagogue* (1976), *Judaism: The Way of Sanctification* (with Byron Sherwin, 1978), *Rachel* (1994), *Can Families Survive in Pagan America?* (1995), *Abraham J. Heschel: Prophetic Witness* (Vol. I, with Edward Kaplan, 1998), and *Heschel, Hasidism and Halakha* (2000).

BIBLIOGRAPHY: P.S. Nadell, *Conservative Judaism in America: A Biographical Dictionary and Sourcebook* (1988); Contemporary Authors Online, Gale, 2005.

[Bezalel Gordon (2nd ed.)]

DRESS.

In the Bible

The biblical terms for clothing (Heb. בֶּגֶד, *beged;* כְּסוּת, *kesut;* לְבוּשׁ, *levush*) and the corresponding verbs are employed in connection with the cover of the body for warmth or reasons of modesty. Extensive use is also made of the terms in figures of speech: "Put on thy beautiful garments" (Isa. 52:1), as an emblem of greatness; "He put on garments of vengeance for clothing" (Isa. 59:17), as a symbol of revenge; "For he dressed me in clothes of triumph," as a metaphor for victory and good fortune (Isa. 61:10); "They shall wear shame" (Ps. 35:26), as a metaphor for failure and defeat; and "Let your priest be clothed with triumph" (Ps. 132:9), as a metaphor for success and prestige; and so forth. On many occasions, clothing emphasizes a person's status, position, clothing, or particular situation or task: "Royal apparel (*levush malkhut*)... which the king is accustomed to wear" (Esth. 6:8), with which another man (Mordecai) would be honored or favored. A hairy cloak was probably a hallmark of Nazirites and ascetics: "Neither shall they wear a hairy mantle (*adderet se'ar*) to deceive" (Zech. 13:4). During the period of mourning widows wore a characteristic garment: "She put off from her garments of widowhood" (Gen. 38:14). Prisoners apparently also had special clothing: "He changed his prison garments" (II Kings 25:29). The official uniform (holy garments) worn by priests in the service of God was of great importance: "And Thou shalt make holy garments for Aaron" (Ex. 28:2). Just as the beauty of a garment symbolized a man's greatness, tearing the clothing or wearing poor and dirty clothing or sackcloth indicated a lowered station or mourning.

The Bible mentions articles of clothing appropriate to specific parts of the body: a cloth miter or turban (*ẓenif, miẓnefet*) to cover the head (Ex. 29:6; Zech. 3:5); metal or leather helmets (*kova*ʿ), and head coverings used in warfare for protection (I Sam. 17:5; II Chron. 26:14); a dress-like garment (*simlah*), apparently with closed seams used by both men and women to cover the entire body from the shoulders to the ankles (I Kings 11:30; Ex. 12:34; Y. Yadin, et al., *Hazor*, 3–4 (1961), pl. cccxxxix: 1, 2); the tunic (*ketonet*), a short, closed garment, covering the top part of the body, worn by both men and women (Gen. 37:3; Lev. 16:14; Song 5:3); the coat (*me*ʿ*il*), a long outer garment open at the front (I Sam. 15:27; 24:5; II Sam. 13:18); breeches (*mikhnasayim*), covering the loins, worn by the priests (Ex. 28:42; Ezek. 44:18); the girdle (*ʾavnet*), a belt for fastening the coat or dress around the waist (Ex. 29:9; Lev. 8:7); and the shoe, made of skin and attached with laces, strings, or straps (Gen. 14:23; Isa. 5:27).

Clothes, particularly the dress-like garment and the tunic, were considered essential though expensive articles, both because of their value, which of course was related to the work that went into producing them, and by reason of their importance in indicating a man's status, position, character, and living style. It is for this reason that the Bible and royal documents frequently list the quantities of clothing given as gifts (Gen. 45:22) or taken in war (Judg. 14:12). Kings had keepers of the wardrobe (II Kings 22:14), and the Temple in Jerusalem had a special wardrobe room.

Types of Garment Shown on Monuments

A common garment worn by men, which is often depicted on monuments in Egypt and Mesopotamia, was a piece of cloth covering from the waist to the knees or below (N. de Garis Davies, *The Tomb of Puyemrê at Thebes*, 1 (1922), pl. xxxiii, A), gathered around the waist and held in place by a belt fastened either in front or at the back or tied near the navel (L. Borchardt, *Das Grabdenkmal des Koenigs Sahu-Re*, 2 (1913), pl. 6; M.G. Lefébure, *Le tombeau de Séti I*, 4 (1886), pl. V). Occasionally this garment was patterned and multicolored, but more often it was a solid color, usually white. It was sometimes held in place by a leather or cloth suspender, passing diagonally over one shoulder from the upper part of the garment (Y. Yadin, et al., *Hazor*, 3–4 (1961), pl. ccxxvi). A more complex garment, made of a wide piece of cloth, covered the body from shoulder to ankle; it was worn by both men and women and was most common in Mesopotamia, though in other places it was worn as a festive garment (N. de Garis Davies and A.H. Gardiner, *The Tomb of Ḥuy*, 1926). This garment could be both in single color or in multicolored patterns. While it usually covered only one shoulder, it was occasionally worn covering both. In addition to the patterns woven into the cloth, a decorative border was common (W. Wreszinski, *Atlas zur altaegyptisehen Kulturgeschichte*, 2 (1935), pl. 46).

A garment more characteristic of the lower classes consisted of two shrunken cloths which were suspended from the waist in front and back by a belt or string, thus covering the loins (P.A.A. Boeser, *Die Denkmaeler des Neuen Reiches* (1911)). A sewn dress-like garment with sleeves covered the entire body; it had a large opening for the head, somewhat resembling a collar. The pictures on several monuments show that the stitches were prominent, serving also as a kind of decoration. The more elegant classes wore two garments: a sewn, short- or long-sleeved dress over which was worn a sheath covering the shoulder or sometimes the entire dress (E.F. Schmidt, *Persepolis*, 1 (1953, pls. 31, 32). Another such two-piece ensemble in the luxury category was made up of a length of cloth extending from the waist to the knees or trousers over which was worn a wide decorated cloth covering the body from shoulder to ankles. Typical of the colder, northern countries was a sleeved coat fastened all the way down

(F. Thureau-Dangin, *Arslan Tash* (1931), 111–2, pl. 33:43; N. de Garis Davies, *The Tombs of Menkheperrasonb…* (1933), pl. iv). Pieces of cloth were frequently added to the basic garment in order to cover the shoulders (Boeser, op. cit., pl. xxiv). The tunic was a short, sewn garment, usually with short sleeves. It was made of one piece of cloth specially woven for this purpose with an opening for the head in the center. The cloth was folded along the shoulder line and sewn along the edges, thus making a garment which covered the upper part of the body. The tunic was often made with a woven decoration or later embroidered.

The clothing shown on early Mesopotamian and Egypt monuments emphasizes ethnic differences. Most apparent are the shorter lengths, relatively lighter weights of the materials (including translucent cloth) – especially in the case of women's wear – and the head coverings worn in Egypt, while the northern countries used longer and heavier clothing. The materials from which the garments were made also show ethnological differences. The garments depicted on a number of Mesopotamian monuments of the third millennium B.C.E. are made of heavy wool strands, fastened with large laces, or sewn with strips of animal skin. Noticeable ethnological differences also appear in head coverings. Wigs seem to have been widely worn by both men and women. A common style was a band circling the hair, tied at the back or side. On the majority of the Egyptian monuments feathers worn on the head depict Ethiopian captives. Headgear crowned with feathers is characteristic of the Sea Peoples (T. Dothan, *Ha-Pelishtim ve-Tarbutam ha-Ḥomrit* (1967), figs 1–7). Skullcaps resembling cones and cylinders decorated with ribbons and lacing were common in Babylonia and Assyria. Covering the head with a kerchief was customary in Egypt and Canaan. The most common sandal had a leather sole held in place by straps. Sandals could be partly closed, covering half the foot, or completely enclosed. However, the figures on monuments are usually shown barefoot.

[Ze'ev Yeivin]

Talmudic Times

Talmudic and midrashic literature is replete with information on matters of dress and clothing, usually supplied incidentally as part of a comment on biblical themes or in connection with religious law and custom which often concern matters of dress.

The importance of clothing in adding to the confidence and dignity of man is stressed in the Talmud: "fine garments" are among the things which "enlarge man's mind" (Ber. 57b), and "a man's dignity is seen in his costume" (Ex. R. 18:5). Apart from the special and distinctive garments which characterized the scholar, he was enjoined to be spotless and neat in his dress: "A scholar on whose garments a stain is found is worthy of death" (Shab. 114a), and he should not go out in patched shoes (Ber. 43b). An incident related in the Midrash is based upon the fact that *Yannai mistook an ignorant man for a scholar because he was elegantly dressed (Lev. R. 9:3).

As many as 90 different articles of clothing are listed by Krauss, but the Talmud enumerates the 18 articles of clothing which were regarded as indispensable and which could therefore be rescued from a fire on the Sabbath. The lists given both in the Babylonian (Shab. 120a) and the Jerusalem (Shab. 16:5, 15d) Talmuds, apart from some differences in spelling, are practically identical, affording a picture of a man's complete apparel. On the upper part of the body, next to the skin, he wore a sleeveless tunic which was covered by a shirt (*ḥalluk*). Over this came an outer tunic, and the top garment was a cloak. A hollow money belt was worn. The lower part of the body was covered by breeches, over which trousers were worn; on the feet were socks and shoes. A girdle was tied round the waist and an apron was also worn. A felt cap covered the head and a hat was worn over this. A scarf completed the attire. Even the order of donning the clothes was laid down (DER 10). Apart from the shirt and the girdle, all these garments were worn by the Greeks, and this raises the question of whether there was a distinctive Jewish dress in talmudic times.

There is evidence that there was. With regard to men, the Midrash states that Moses was called an Egyptian (Ex. 2:19) because he was dressed as such and not as a Jew. In one version of a well-known Midrash, one of the reasons given for the redemption of the children of Israel from bondage is "that they did not change or substitute their [distinctive Jewish] dress" and on the verse "Lo, it is a people that shall dwell alone," a Yalkut (Num. 768) states, "they are distinguished from the other peoples in everything, in their dress…" Generally speaking, however, it would appear that apart from the **ẓiẓit* enjoined by the Bible, the dress of the ordinary people was similar to that of non-Jews. The scholar however wore distinctive garments. The scarf worn by ordinary people, which was probably fringed, became the **tallit* of the scholar. The Talmud indicates its severe displeasure of the common person who wore the *tallit* of the scholar (BB 98a). The scholar's shirt covered his whole body, so that his skin was invisible, and his *tallit* completely covered the shirt (BB 57b), so that "the scholar was recognized by the manner in which he wrapped himself in his *tallit*" (DEZ 5). He wore a distinctive hat, a kind of turban (Pes. 111b). Judah b. Ilai used to wrap himself in his fringed shawl and he looked like an angel of the Lord (Shab. 25b).

It was regarded as immodest and against Jewish custom for a married woman to wear her hair loose. The difference between the costume of women in Ereẓ Israel and Babylon is noted; in Babylon the women wore colored garments, while in Ereẓ Israel they wore starched white linen garments (Pes. 109a). Black clothing was worn as a sign of mourning, trouble, or distress (Ḥag. 16a), or when appearing as a defendant in a lawsuit (TJ, RH 1:3, 57b). When R. *Akiva had to break to R. Eliezer b. Hyrcanus the news of his excommunication he "clothed himself in black" (BM 59b). A complete change of garments was enjoined for the Sabbath, and this was regarded as so important that biblical sanction was found for it (Shab. 113a, 114a).

Hellenistic and Persian Periods

The frescoes of the third-century synagogue at *Dura-Europos, depicting a number of biblical scenes, portray costumes reflecting the Hellenistic and Persian cultures, both of which influenced this frontier city. The more common type of dress-tunic or gown (*chiton, colobium,* or *dalmatica*) with purple stripes (*clavi*), shawl (*himation orpallium*), and sandals – is assigned to prophets, elders, civilian leaders, and laymen. In certain cases, the *pallium* has *ẓiẓit* attached to the corners. The Persian costume, which includes a short belted tunic, trousers, and soft white boots, is assigned to royalty, courtiers, and Temple personnel. The high priest wears a long cloak; he alone has a head covering. Women wear a plain *chiton* with elbow-length sleeves and a shawl, one end of which is fastened over the shoulder and the other draped over the head. The two distinct traditions in Jewish dress, Hellenistic and Persian, are represented by a group of Jews portrayed in the sixth-century mosaics in the church of San Vitale, Ravenna, and by the sixth-century wall painting from Wadi Sarga, Egypt, of the "Three Children in the Furnace," now in the British Museum. These two works are probably based on much earlier types. The pronged ornaments known as *gams* shown on many of the costumes at Dura-Europos are similar to those found on garments discovered in the Judean Desert caves used as refuge by Bar Kokhba's followers in the second century.

The Post-Talmudic Era

In the post-talmudic period Jewish costume was greatly influenced by various halakhic, moral, and social principles laid down in rabbinic literature. The prohibition against following the custom of the Gentiles in the manner of dress and mode of cutting hair (Lev. 18:3; 20:23; Deut. 12:30; Zeph. 1:8) became an important factor behind many of the communal dress regulations and *sumptuary laws. The garb of a Jew should reflect propriety and humility and he should therefore avoid wearing expensive clothes. He must observe the laws regarding *ẓiẓit* and *sha'atnez* (see *mixed species) and decency requires him to wear a belt. Women must be modest in their attire, and married women should always cover their hair. Fine clothes should be worn on the Sabbath and even finer ones on the festivals. These rabbinical regulations served to keep Jewish dress conservative and outmoded. Discriminatory laws passed against the Jews had a similar effect. The earliest example of these, decreed in Egypt in 849 by the caliph al-Mutawakkil, required Jews and Christians to wear a yellow Persian mantle (*tailasan*) and a cord belt (*zunnar*). If they wore the Persian hat (*kalansuwa*) they were restricted to certain colors, and if they wore a turban it had to be yellow. Later, they also had to wear a *badge of the same color. In the Christian world, the first legislation of this kind was enacted in 1215 by the Fourth Lateran Council, which ordered Jews to wear a distinct type of dress on the grounds that in some regions they could no longer *be* distinguished from Christians. All these different influences combined to create a specifically Jewish dress, which, however, varied from one country to another.

Early Middle Ages

Little is known of Jewish costume in the early Middle Ages. Certain pottery figures of peddlers with Semitic features discovered in some of the Chinese T'ang Dynasty tombs (618–907) are believed to represent Jews, particularly those with pointed Persian hats, caftans, and girdles. There are no paintings or descriptions of European Jews from this period, and only two obscure references to their attire. In 839, when *Bodo became a convert to Judaism he allowed his hair and beard to grow, and also put on a military belt. This may be an early reference to the practice of wearing a girdle, later laid down in the Shulḥan Arukh. In the ninth century, Pope Nicholas I (858–67) attacked Arsenius, bishop of Orta, for introducing Jewish furred garments (*judaicae peluciae*).

The Orient

In many Muslim countries, Jews were restricted to black clothing, in North Africa practically up to our times. During the 16th century in Turkey, a native Jew wore a yellow turban, while the Sephardi Jew wore a red hat, shaped like a sugar loaf. The *ḥakhamim* of the Spanish expulsion wore the *capos* ("cape") on the Sabbath, which had been the distinctive dress of the Jews in Spain. In spite of the strict ruling of R. Elijah *Mizraḥi the *capos* was used as a festive garb. By the 18th century, the common dress for all Jews in Turkey was a violet *kaveze* ("turban"), a black or violet habit, *mest* ("socks"), and violet slippers. The same dress was worn in Mesopotamia, Syria, and Ereẓ Israel. Women developed various regional styles of dress with marked Jewish distinctions. During the 19th century, in Smyrna and Salonika, a woman's costume included full Turkish trousers, over which two or three gowns slit open from the hips to hem were worn. The different cloths had wide contrasting stripes with flower patterns printed over them. Outdoors, a woman wore a long, dark red pelisse, lined and trimmed with fur, and she covered her head with a fine white Turkish towel with fringed ends. In Constantinople, a short, loose jacket replaced the red pelisse. The Turkish Jewish woman's headwear included a *hotoz*, an enormous cushion-like headdress covered by a white muslin veil; this reached such fashionable extravagances at Constantinople that the chief rabbi banned it at the request of the grand vizier. The *feradje* ("cloak") worn by Jewish women was distinctive in color and shape. Peculiar to Aleppo was a high-domed cap of striped silk, from which hung a quantity of false hair.

The characteristic costume of Moroccan, Algerian, Tunisian, and Tripolitanian Jews was black; it consisted of a skull cap, a tunic, drawers, a *burnous* ("cloak"), and slippers. In Morocco, for ceremonial occasions, the women wore the *keswa el-kbira*, a costume that had elaborate gold embroidery for which the Jewish needlewomen of Tetuan were renowned. They also wore characteristic wigs which had many regional variations. In Algeria and Tunisia, the tall headdress, known as the *çâma*, was retained by Jewish women as part of their ceremonial dress, after it had ceased to be fashionable during the 19th century. In Tunisia women's ordinary dress consisted of a baggy chemise reaching down to the hips, a small gold-embroidered velvet jacket, a pair of white, very tight pantaloons, and a velvet *kufia*, shaped like a sugar loaf, worn on the head. No information is available on the Jewish dress in Turkestan, Kurdistan, South Arabia, or India prior to the 19th century. In recent times, some elaborate Jewish costumes have emerged from Bukhara, Yemen, and Aden, most of which reflect local influence. (See also *Bukhara; Costume.)

In India, the distinctive feature of the Bene Israel was their *pe'ot* (side curls). They wore Hindu-style turbans and shoes, and Muslim-style trousers. The Iraqi Jews of India retained Turkish dress; for festive occasions their women wore a long, silk brocade gown with a white plastron, probably also Turkish in origin. In the middle of the 19th century, the White Jews of Cochin wore a white cotton skullcap, a jacket, a waistcoat with 12 silver buttons, and trousers. The synagogue dress included a turban and a *djubba* ("Turkish gown"). The distinctive feature of the dress of the Black Jews of Cochin was a round embroidered cap.

Western Europe

In medieval Spain, Jews were obliged at times to wear a full length black gown with a cape and a pointed hood. They were also forbidden to shave their beards. Other distinctive features were the badge and the pointed Jewish hat. By the 13th century, in Germany, France, England, and other parts of Europe, the pointed hat, known as the *Judenhut*, had become distinctly Jewish; it was worn voluntarily and was accepted as a Jewish symbol. Later, however, the *Judenhut*, like the *badge, was also sometimes imposed by law. The hat was not worn after the 15th century, by which time a new type of hat with a tassel on its crown was prescribed by the laws of Frankfurt; other garments also acquired a distinctively Jewish significance. The medieval *chaperon* ("hood") known in Germany as the *matran, gugel*, or *kappe* as well as the *liripipe* ("tailed hood") was still being worn among the Jews of Nuremberg in 1755. Elsewhere in Germany and many parts of Central Europe, it had been replaced by a *barrette* (a black round hat made of felt or wool). Together with the *Judenkragen* (the 16th-century ruff), it became a distinctive feature of Jewish costume.

In the Papal States and elsewhere in Italy, the church canon requiring Jews to wear a yellow hat remained in effect until the French Revolution. Elsewhere in Western Europe, most Jewish distinctive dress had by then disappeared, except for synagogue and ceremonial occasions. The Jew, however, could still be identified by his beard and until the beginning of the 19th century even in England and Holland it remained a distinctive feature among Ashkenazi Jews.

The Sabbath *barrette*, known as *schabbes deckel*, and the *schulmantel* ("synagogue cloak") worn with a ruff, remained the accepted synagogue attire until the end of the 18th century; the whole costume was black. The *schulmantel*, or Sabbath *sarbal*, was a long cloak closed on the right side to prevent anything being carried on the Sabbath. During the 19th century, a new style for synagogue wear became the accepted garb: a three-cornered hat, a tail coat, knee breeches, and buckled shoes.

From the 13th century onward, in many parts of Europe, Jewish women were obliged to have two blue stripes in their veil (*oralia* or *orales*). The *oralia* was replaced by a pointed veil (*cornalia* or *cornu*) and, in the middle of the 18th century, it, together with the Jewish ruff and a special synagogue cloak, was still part of the Jewish woman's synagogue apparel. Other distinctive clothes worn by Jewish women were the *sivlonot* ("marriage belt") and the *kuerse* (a kind of blouse worn by brides). The *sheitel* ("wig") worn by Jewish women is a relatively recent custom (see Wig; Covering of the *Head).

Rabbinical Dress

There is no traditional rabbinical dress but among the Ashkenazim the distinctive features of Jewish lay dress were retained much longer by the rabbis. In 1705, at Fuerth, the rabbi wore a plain collar, a long tunic buttoned down the front, and a *barrette*. In 1755 the *Judenmeister* of Nuremberg wore the medieval *kappe* (hood) with a deep fringed collar and a long sleeveless gown. By the 19th century, the typical European Ashkenazi rabbi had a heavy beard and wore a Polish-style costume which included a fur-trimmed gown and a fur-trimmed hat; the latter was exchanged for a *streimel* (a wide-brimmed hat made of fur) on the Sabbath. The rabbinical *streimel* was made of 13 sable-tails. In the middle of the 19th century at Mattersdorf, Hungary, the rabbi wore a *streimel* on the Sabbath and a boat-shaped hat on weekdays. In England and America, Christian dress was adopted much earlier and in the 18th century Isaac Polack, *ḥazzan* of London's Great Synagogue, was clean-shaven, wore a three-cornered hat, a wig, and clerical robes with white bands.

The European Sephardi rabbis were even less subject to traditional influences. In the 15th-century painting by Nuno Goncalves, in the Lisbon National Museum, the rabbi wears a tall, black circular hat and a black gown with the Jewish badge shaped as a red six-pointed star. By the 17th century, the Sephardi rabbis of Holland and England, with their stiletto beards, skullcaps, wigs, and clerical gowns with white bands, were indistinguishable from the Christian clergy. In Oriental countries, a few instances of distinctive dress can be cited. In 1781, in Morocco, the rabbi's habit had very large sleeves and he usually had a blue kerchief around his cap. In the 1860s in Constantinople, the rabbis wore a dark blue felt cap, bound around the base with a white kerchief or turban with fine blue stripes. In 1873, at Smyrna, the rabbi wore a *bonneto*, a type of turban reserved for doctors and priests. At the present time, there are no distinctive features in rabbinical dress either in Eastern countries or in the West.

[Alfred Rubens]

Eastern Europe

The earliest Jewish costume from Poland, depicted on a 12th-century miniature, is an exact copy of the Byzantine tunic and *paludamentum* ("cloak") worn by men, though usually the Jews of Eastern Europe were less influenced by Christian fashions in dress than in the West. The first intervention of the authorities occurred as early as the 13th century; a church council held in Breslau in 1266 ordered the Jews in the bishopric of Gnesen in western Poland to wear a special hat. Soon the Council of Ofen (1279) specified the distinction to a greater extent by requiring the Jews to wear a red badge. Late medieval costumes seem to have been influenced by Central European gentile and Jewish garb, like the dress cut like a kimono, called a *cotte*, worn by men and women, the female kerchief, and the Jewish conical hat worn by men. Later the Jews adopted from the East their most characteristic garment – the *caftan*, which is still in use in certain extreme Orthodox circles. This Persian coat, cut open in the front, was so widely worn throughout the Turkish Empire that it was found in Yemen and Morocco under the same name. In the eastern areas of Poland and Russia the *caftan* was girdled by a wide Oriental sash and in the western regions by a cord.

Like other European regional costumes, the characteristic Jewish dress evolved during the 16th century, incorporating some features of the attire no longer worn by the Polish nobility or upper classes. The authorities in several parts of Eastern Europe reacted independently but with the same aim: to restrict the splendor of Jewish costume and to preserve some form of distinction. Thus the Piotrkow diet of 1538 reproved the Jews for adopting Christian attire and compelled them to wear a yellow hat. The Lithuanian statute of 1566, as well as the southern Polish statutes of 1595, laid down minute specifications restricting the sumptuousness of female dress and jewelry. The Lithuanian statute ordered yellow hats to be worn by men and yellow kerchiefs by women. On the other hand in times of special calamity, like the *Chmielnicki massacres (1648–49), the Jewish communities themselves imposed sober dress on their members. In the 18th and 19th centuries the Jews in Eastern Europe clung to their distinctive wear. Local differences continued paramount; in Russia and Lithuania clothes revealed an Oriental influence shown in the multicolored silks of the women, the halfmoons printed on materials, and an immense turban with three tails made of white starched linen.

The most widely known garments worn by Jewish men in Poland were the *bekeshe* and the *kapote*. The latter, both in name and shape, was derived from the Persian *caftan*. The *kapote* was generally made of very expensive cloth, such as velvet or *atlas* (a glossy silk or satin). Besides a shirt, knee-length trousers, and white stockings, the men also wore velvet waistcoats (Yid. *vestel* or *speneer*), a black silk belt with tassels called a *gartel*, and a small prayer shawl. Special headcoverings were the skullcaps (Yid. *keppel, yarmulke*), the fur hats (*soibel-heet* and *streimel*), the immense sable *kolpak*, adopted from the Gentiles, and the fur-trimmed *spodek* ("saucer") with a plush base. Most of these types of clothing, as well as female costumes, appear in the pictures and engravings of Polish types drawn by several artists (Norblin, Le Prince, Dave, Piwarski, Kilisinski, Kruszewski, Andrioli, and Debucourt).

The most important item of clothing was the white woolen prayer shawl, the *tallit*. Its central neckpiece *(atarah)* was decorated with an appliqué of knit embroidery, executed in flat, silver threads, in a style called by Polish Jews *spanier* ("Spanish style") or *shikh*, which was probably brought to Poland by Jewish craftsmen from Spain during the reign of King Sigismund Augustus. A similar type of Spanish embroidery was also used on Torah curtains and Torah mantles.

WOMEN'S COSTUME FROM THE 18TH TO THE BEGINNING OF THE 20TH CENTURY. Although the woman's dress was more colorful, her finery was not meant to be displayed out-of-doors, for it is written: "In all glorious things the king's daughter is within" (Ps. 45:14). However, the sumptuary decrees regulating women's clothing made an exception for the Sabbath. The dress of the Jewish woman was generally in the fashion of the period, but rather more subdued. The Jewish woman of the late 18th and 19th centuries wore on top of her dress a kind of bodice, the *vestel* or *kamisol*, usually made of brocade with black passementerie trimmings. At a later stage these trimmings were sewn on to the dresses themselves, or even on to separate plastrons, called *brust-tukh, brist-tikhel*, or *bristekh*. The *brust-tukh* was initially a wide strip of brocade adorned with silver stitching and occasionally ornamented with semiprecious stones. Later, this rectangular strip was almost covered with silver stitching, but in the 20th century it lost its regular shape and was made of velvet and adorned with various trimmings. The very Orthodox woman always wore an apron (Yid. *fartekh* or *fartukh*), usually trimmed with lace, embroidery, and ribbons, and serving no practical purpose.

WOMEN'S HEADDRESS. A distinctive form of headcovering for Jewish women did not emerge until the 17th century. At first the forms of headgear varied through the different regions of the area. In western Poland during the 18th century, it was customary to wear on the Sabbath a bonnet made of brocade trimmed with lace and silver stitching. On the other hand, in the east – Lithuania and parts of Russia – the earliest form of headcovering consisted of lace trimmed with colored ribbons, glass baubles, and beads. In time pearls and diamonds gradually replaced the simpler popular ornaments, and not only among rich women. In central Poland, Galicia, and Hungary the headcovering was made up of three separate parts: the *harband*, which covered the hair above the forehead; the *grint*, which served as the background; and the *kupke*, made of cloth or lace. Floral trimmings or ribbons were placed over all three. The headdress for very Orthodox women had to be made up from seven different parts assembled in strict order (in an implicit reference to the seven species of crops). The elaborate trimmings for these headcoverings were made by an expert hat-trimmer called *pitzikel* (derived from *putz*, "adornment").

For the Sabbath a woman put on a sort of tiara, the *binde*, consisting of two strips of velvet (recalling the two tablets of the Law), decorated with gold chains, pearls, and diamonds.

One such tiara, belonging to a Jewish woman of the late 18th or early 19th century, was acquired by the well-known Polish painter Jan Matejko, and he used it in several of his paintings as a headdress for Polish princesses. After the beginning of the 19th century the *binde* gradually disappeared and was replaced by the *sterntikhel, sternbindel*, or *bindalikh* worn on top of the *kupkeh*. The *sterntikhel* consisted of pearls and diamonds, strung on iron wire, set off against a cloth background, and later on with no background. Fixing the jewels on the *sterntikhel* was the job of an expert craftsman (which gave rise to the family names Perlherfter and Perlsticker ("pearl-fixer," "pearl-embroiderer"). From the *sterntikhel* (and other pieces of jewelry) a pearl or a segment was deliberately removed to indicate that there can be no complete joy as long as the Temple is in ruins. From the beginning of the 20th century the *sterntikhel* ceased to be worn almost entirely. In Lithuania where the *sterntikhel* was never worn, the headdress consisted of a white *binde* wound around the head like a turban, called a *patshaile;* it was often adorned with a decorative pin, the *knopp*.

Various forms of the *harband* and of the *kupke* continued to evolve in Poland throughout the 19th and early 20th centuries, most of them trying to suggest a woman's hair (with a white line of parting, the *kvishel*). The wig or *sheitel* (made of natural hair) was never considered proper wear for the very Orthodox woman, but many imitations, made of brown satin, were in use. Eventually the *kupke* took on the shape of a hat, the *hitel*, topped by flowers, ribbons, peacock feathers, and a *tsitenadel* ("trembling pin"). Two pairs of earrings were sometimes attached to the *kupke*, one at the level of the temples, the other at the level of the earlobes. Exhibitions of Jewish clothing may be seen at the Israel Museum (Jerusalem), the Museum of Ethnography and Folklore (Tel Aviv), and the Ethnological and Folklore Museum (Haifa).

[Miriam Nick]

Modern

Distinctive Jewish costume largely disappeared from the early 20th century. Among the influences of ancient dress that have survived in synagogue wear is the Roman *pallium*, in the form of the *tallit*, and the **kitel* (*sargenes*) worn by some on the Day of Atonement and for the *seder*. Distinctive features are still found in the everyday dress of Oriental Jews. In addition, the wearing of a headcovering at all times has become *de rigueur* as the external sign of the Orthodox Jew; among the modern element this has developed as the small embroidered *kippah*. The ultra-Orthodox groups, concentrated mostly in Jerusalem and Bene Berak in Israel, and in limited areas in other parts of the world, still wear the characteristic *streimel* on Sabbaths and festivals (including the intermediate days) and the long *caftan*, yellow and white striped, is sometimes still retained. The custom of married women covering their hair, obligatory according to the Mishnah, is no longer widely observed, except in Orthodox circles where the *sheitel* is also sometimes worn as a substitute.

BIBLIOGRAPHY: IN THE BIBLE: EM, 4 (1962), 1034–49 (incl. bibl.); IDB, s.v., *cloth* (incl. bibl.); A. Rosenzweig, *Kleidung und Schmuck in Bibel und talmudischen Schrifttum* (1905); H.F. Lutz, *Textiles and Costumes…* (1923), 40–72; C. Singer, et al. (eds.), *A History of Technology*, 1 (1955), 413ff.; W.F. Albright, in: AASOR, 21–22 (1941–43), 55–62, Pl. 53; Y. Yadin, in: *Eretz Israel*, 4 (1956), 68ff; idem, *The Finds from the Bar Kokhba Period in the Cave of Letters* (1963), 169ff. OTHER PERIODS: A. Rubens, *A History of Jewish Costume* (1967), includes bibliography; Krauss, Tal Arch, 1 (1910), 127ff.; M. Grunwald, in: JJV, 25 (1923); H. Munic, in: *YIVO-Bleter*, 12 (1937), 463–73; E. Fuchs, *Die Juden in der Karikatur.*

DRESSLER, WILLIAM (1890–1969), U.S. cardiologist and electrocardiographer. Born and educated in Austria, Dressler went to the United States as a refugee in 1938. From that year until 1967 when he became consultant, Dressler served as chief of the Cardiology Clinic and head of the Electrocardiographic Laboratory at Maimonides Medical Center. Dressler's major contribution to medicine was his recognition and description of the post-myocardial infarction syndrome, also known as the Dressler syndrome. He wrote six cardiology texts, three in German and three in English. His *Clinical Cardiology* (1942) became the classic book of cardiological diagnosis.

[Fred Rosner]

DREUX (Heb. דרו"ש), town in the Eure-et-Loire department, France, 53 mi. (86 km.) S.W. of Paris. During the Middle Ages, the Jews of Dreux were numerous enough to occupy their own quarter, which was remembered as the rue des Juifs up until the 19th century. Many figures previously associated with Dreux, like R. *Solomon b. Judah ("the saint") are now believed to have been active in Rouen. According to W. Bacher (REJ, 17 (1888), 301), Abraham *Ibn Ezra stayed there for a time.

BIBLIOGRAPHY: Gross, Gal Jud, 171–85; E. Lefèvre, *Documents historiques… Dreux* (1859), 398–9.

[Bernhard Blumenkranz]

DREXLER, MILLARD S. ("**Mickey**"; 1944–), U.S. merchant. Born and raised in New York City, Drexler spent all his professional life as an apparel retailer. He rose from humble beginnings to become chief executive officer of the publicly owned Gap Inc., whose focus on affordable basics made it the biggest specialty clothing store chain in the U.S. and an internationally familiar name. While attending the Bronx High School of Science, Drexler worked in New York City's garment center with his father, a buyer of buttons and textiles for a coat manufacturer. In 1966, he earned a business degree at the State University of New York at Buffalo and two years later received an M.B.A. at Boston University. He entered retailing with posts at Bloomingdale's, Macy's, and Abraham & Straus. In 1980, he was appointed president of Ann Taylor and within three years turned the women's apparel chain into a success. He joined Gap in 1983 as deputy to Donald *Fisher, founder and chairman, was named president of the Gap division, and went about reinventing the company. He hired new designers, strengthened quality control, and invested in store renovation. In 1986, he launched GapKids, an immediate success. He was named president of Gap Inc. in 1987 and CEO in 1995. In his almost two decades at the company, he cemented a reputation as a master merchandiser. When Drexler joined Gap, it had 550 stores filled with clothes that were not selling and $80 million in sales. When he left 19 years later, it had more than 4,000 Gap, Old Navy, and Banana Republic stores and more than $14 billion in sales. In 1994, when Gap's business was feeling the effects of increased competition from high-end designers as well as mass merchandisers, Drexler launched Old Navy, a discount chain that grew to 282 stores in less than three years. In 1998, *Fortune* magazine called him "possibly the most influential individual in the world of American fashion," pointing out that he had transformed Gap from a national retail chain into a global brand. A soft economy and tougher competition contributed to a two-year sales slump that began to reverse itself in 2002, the year Drexler left Gap. In January 2003, he became head of the smaller, privately held J. Crew Group, another specialty chain.

BIBLIOGRAPHY: *Fortune* (Aug. 1998).

[Mort Sheinman (2nd ed.)]

DREYFUS, family of bankers originating from Sierentz in Alsace. ISAAC DREYFUS (1786–1845) founded the firm Isaac Dreyfus, Soehne, Basle, with his sons as partners, as one of the few Jews the city magistrate allowed to settle within the walls (1813). His son SAMUEL (1820–1905), who remained with the firm, was president of the Basle Jewish community (1865–96) and founder of the Jewish orphanage and old-age home. A second son, JACQUES (1826–1890), moved to Frankfurt where he established the Dreyfus-Jeidels bank in 1868, which became J. Dreyfus and Co. in 1890, to which a Berlin branch was added in 1891. His son ISAAC (1849–1909) and grandson WILLY (1885–?) developed the bank into one of the largest investment banks in Germany, but the Nazis forced it into liquidation in 1937. Samuel Dreyfus was succeeded by his son JULES DREYFUS-BRODSKY (1859–1941) and his nephew ISAAC DREYFUS-STRAUSS (1852–1936). The family banking tradition was further maintained by Jules's son PAUL (1895–1967), who considerably expanded the firm's activities. Members of the Dreyfus family worked for the Jewish community. In Switzerland, Jules was president of the Swiss Union of Jewish Communities (1914–36) and of the community of Basel (1906–36) and Paul, who was a founder of *ORT in Switzerland, campaigned for the admission of Jewish refugees from Germany during World War II. In Germany Jacques, Isaac, and Willy Dreyfus were all active in communal affairs. Katjy Guth, née Dreyfus, was the director of the Jewish Museum of Switzerland in Basel (est. 1968).

BIBLIOGRAPHY: R.M. Heilbronn, *Das Bankhaus J. Dreyfus & Co.* (1962). **ADD. BIBLIOGRAPHY:** H. Haumann, *Acht Jahrhunderte Juden in Basel. 200 Jahre Israelitische Gemeinde Basel* (2005).

[Hanns G. Reissner / Uri Kaufmann (2nd ed.)]

DREYFUS, ALFRED (1859–1935), officer in the French army, involved in a treason trial. His court-martial, conviction, and final acquittal developed into a political event which had repercussions throughout France and the Jewish world. Born in Mulhouse, Alsace, Dreyfus was the son of a wealthy, assimilated family which settled in Paris after the Franco-Prussian War. He studied at the Ecole Polytechnique and entered the army as an engineer. In 1892 he became a captain on the general staff, where he was the only Jew. He was overwhelmed by the drama (see below) in which he played the central role, but failed to grasp its deeper significance: its Jewish, general humanitarian, and political aspects. After his final exoneration he was reinstated in the army as major and served a further year. He reenlisted in World War I and was promoted to lieutenant colonel at its conclusion. Dreyfus published his *Lettres d'un innocent* (1898; *The Letters of Captain Dreyfus to his Wife*, 1899) written from Devil's Island, and his memoirs *Cinq ans de ma vie* (1901; *Five Years of my Life*, 1901). Additional *Souvenirs et correspondence* were published posthumously (1936; *Dreyfus: His Life and Letters*, 1937).

Dreyfus Affair

In the fall of 1894 a secret military document (the *bordereau*) sent by a French officer to the military attaché of the German embassy in Paris, Col. von Schwartzkoppen, fell into the hands of the French Intelligence Service. On the basis of a certain similarity of handwriting, and probably out of anti-Jewish prejudice against Dreyfus, the heads of the Intelligence Service – among whom Major H.J. Henry was conspicuous – threw suspicion upon Dreyfus. He was arrested and tried before a court-martial. The trial took place *in camera* and the testimonies were insufficiently verified. It was also not disclosed that contrary to all legal procedure the ministry of war had placed a file of secret documents (part of which were forgeries) before the tribunal, a fact concealed even from Dreyfus' attorney. The court unanimously found Dreyfus guilty of treason, and he was sentenced to life imprisonment. On January 5, 1895, Dreyfus was publicly demoted in a degrading ceremony, during which he continued to proclaim, "I am innocent." The mob, which had been incited by the antisemitic press, especially by E.A. *Drumont, accompanied the ceremony with fulminations against Dreyfus and the Jews. Dreyfus was exiled to Devil's Island (French Guinea, off the coast of South America), even though in the meanwhile, the German ambassador had declared formally that Germany had had no contact with Dreyfus.

Dreyfus' brother turned to the writer Bernard *Lazare, who now led the struggle against the verdict. In November 1896 Lazare published a pamphlet, "The Truth about the Dreyfus Affair," and sent it to members of the senate and public figures. The new head of the French Intelligence Service, Lt. Col. Georges Picquart, had independently sensed something suspicious in the Dreyfus trial. In March 1896, Intelligence Service personnel seized a letter which Schwartzkoppen had written to a French major, Ferdinand Walsin Esterhazy, an adventurer of aristocratic Hungarian origin. This made it clear that Esterhazy was a German agent. Picquart concluded that the *bor-*

dereau incriminating Dreyfus had been written by Esterhazy. Henry forged additional documents to prove to his superiors that the court-martial had not erred. Picquart was dismissed from his position and dispatched to serve in Africa.

Before leaving Paris he transmitted the facts to his friends. Through them they reached the ears of the left-wing senator, Auguste Scheurer-Kestner, who announced in the senate that Dreyfus was innocent, and openly accused Esterhazy. The right-wing prime minister, F.J. Méline, refused to accept his statement and tried to hide the facts. The Dreyfus case increasingly became the focus of the political struggle centering round the regime, its image and principles, and fought in all strata of French society, including circles close to the government. Esterhazy was tried and acquitted, while Picquart was punished with 60 days imprisonment. On January 13, 1898 *L'Aurore*, Georges Clemenceau's newspaper, published an open letter from the novelist Emile *Zola to the president of the republic, captioned "*J'accuse!*," which accused the denouncers of Dreyfus of malicious libel. The article made a powerful impression; 200,000 copies were sold in Paris. Zola was found guilty of libel in February 1898. Officers of the general staff threatened to resign if Dreyfus was acquitted and antisemitic riots occurred in different parts of the country. In the meantime confidence in the justice of the verdict was waning. The affair aroused lively interest abroad and in France it became a public issue. Parties, social circles, and even families were split. The antagonistic groups formed two camps – the *Ligue des Droits de l'Homme*, which spearheaded the fight for Dreyfus, and the *Ligue de la Patrie Française*, led by Paul Déroulède. Many of the supporters of the latter camp considered that a single case of injustice involving one Jew was not sufficient grounds for staining the honor of the army.

In summer 1898 the protestations of Picquart and others induced the new war minister, Cavaignac, to reopen the case and re-investigate the documents. Henry's forgeries were detected. He was arrested and subsequently committed suicide in his cell. Public opinion moved in Dreyfus' favor and the controversy divided the government. At last the government decided to request an annulment of the verdict and a retrial for Dreyfus from the Supreme Court. The political agitation continued, and after several crises René Waldeck-Rousseau formed a cabinet whose avowed aim was to restore the rule of law and justice and reestablish democracy.

THE SECOND TRIAL. The second trial took place in Rennes. The army officers adhered to their original testimony. Finally, on September 9, 1899, the court-martial decided by a majority that Dreyfus had committed treason – but because of "extenuating circumstances" he was sentenced to only ten years' imprisonment, five of which he had already served. Anti-Semites and reactionaries viewed the verdict as a justification of their position. Differences of opinion developed between Dreyfus' defenders: those to whom the Dreyfus affair was a political issue and a matter of principle wanted him to appeal and continue the struggle, while Dreyfus and his family were interested only in securing his release. At Waldeck-Rousseau's suggestion, Dreyfus withdrew his appeal and was finally granted a "pardon" by the president of the republic. In 1904, with the Leftist government firmly established, Dreyfus demanded a fresh investigation. The Court of Appeal reexamined the case, and in 1906 pronounced that the evidence against Dreyfus was completely unsubstantiated and that it was unnecessary to order a further trial to exonerate him.

The Dreyfus affair was a turning point in the history of the Third Republic. It embittered the struggle between the opponents and partisans of the republican regime. The Waldeck-Rousseau cabinet succeeded in enacting a number of anti-clerical measures, and in 1905 it passed a law separating the church from the state. This also influenced the status of the Jewish Consistory in France. The Dreyfus affair made a powerful impact on the attitude of the socialist parties toward the Jews. The radical Marxist wing under Jules Guèsde, which identified Jews with the capitalists and viewed the affair as an internal concern of the bourgeoisie, retreated before the socialist-humanitarian wing led by Jean-Léon Jaurès. Proletarian antisemitism weakened. The Dreyfus affair made a strong impact on the outlook of world Jewry and the atmosphere in their respective countries. Jews everywhere were shocked that the affair could take place in France, the "homeland of liberty and the Great Revolution," and that hatred of the Jews could still prejudice the behavior of a considerable part of the French people, in particular when the Jewish victim was completely assimilated. This seemed to prove clearly that assimilation was no defense against antisemitism. Theodor *Herzl's confidence in liberalism was shaken when he personally observed the French mass reaction and the uproar that the Dreyfus case aroused. The experience led him to Zionism.

Echoes of the Dreyfus affair continued to reverberate in France for over a generation. Its consequences were still recognizable in the line that divided the Vichy government from the Free French during World War II.

BIBLIOGRAPHY: Shunami, Bibl, 268–9; J. Reinach, *Histoire de l'affaire Dreyfus*, 7 vols. (1901–11); *Le procès Dreyfus...*, 3 vols. (1900); *La revision du procès de Rennes*, 3 vols. (1908); P. Dreyfus (ed.), *Dreyfus: His Life and Letters* (1937); Tcherski, in: E. Tcherikower (ed.), *Yidn in Frankraykh*, 2 (1942), 155–92 (Eng. abstract: 332); J. Kayser, *The Dreyfus Affair* (1931); R.F. Byrnes, *Antisemitism in Modern France*, 1 (1950); G. Chapman, *The Dreyfus Case: A Reassessment* (1955; revised as *The Dreyfus Trials*, 1973); N. Halasz, *Captain Dreyfus: The Story of a Mass Hysteria* (1957^2); M. Baumont, *Aux sources de l'affaire* (1959); P. Boussel, *L'Affaire Dreyfus et la presse* (1960); L. Derfler (ed.), *Dreyfus Affair: Tragedy of Errors?* (1963); D. Johnson, *France and the Dreyfus Affair* (1967); B. Schechter, *The Dreyfus Affair: A National Scandal* (1965); M. Paléologue, *My Secret Diary of the Dreyfus Case* (1957); L. Blum, *Souvenirs sur l'Affaire* (1935). **ADD. BIBLIOGRAPHY:** J.-D. Bredin, *The Affair: The Case of Alfred Dreyfus* (1986); A.S. Lindemann, *Jews Accused: Three Anti-Semitic Affairs (Dreyfus, Beilis, Frank), 1894–1915* (1991); M.P. Johnson, *The Dreyfus Affair: Honor and Politics in the Belle Epoque* (1999); M. Burns, *France and the Dreyfus Affair: A Documentary History* (1999).

[Moshe Catane]

DREYFUS, STANLEY A. (1921–), U.S. Reform rabbi. Dreyfus was born in Youngstown, Ohio, and received his B.A. from the University of Cincinnati and his B.H.L. from Hebrew Union College in 1942. Ordination and his M.H.L. followed in 1946, when he also won the Heinsheimer Fellowship for graduate study at HUC, where he began teaching liturgy and served as director of the Reference Department. Subsequently (1948–50), he became counselor to the Hebrew Union College's Interfaith Program, working with Christian clergymen who were studying Hebrew, Bible, and Jewish thought to teach in their own seminaries. In 1951, Dreyfus was awarded his Ph.D. from HUC-JIR, which later conferred on him an honorary D.D. (1971). While pursuing his graduate studies, Dreyfus served as rabbi of Congregation Beth-El in Beaver Falls, Penn. (1946–50), and West London Synagogue in London, England (summer 1949). He went on to pulpits at Congregation Beth Shalom, East Liverpool, Ohio (1950–51), and United Hebrew Congregation of Terre Haute, Ind. (1951–66), where he also served as chaplain of the U.S. penitentiary (1951–53). His term as rabbi in Terre Haute and visiting professor at the Indiana School of Religion in Bloomington was interrupted by active service as chaplain for the United States Army in Colorado and Germany (1953–55). Subsequently, as rabbi of Congregation B'nai Israel in Galveston, Texas (1956–65), Dreyfus was president of the Association of Texas Rabbis and chairman of Home Service for the Galveston Red Cross, in addition to serving on the Galveston County Biracial Committee and the Human Relations Committee. In 1965, Dreyfus was appointed rabbi of Union Temple in Brooklyn, N.Y., where he remained until 1979, when he became emeritus and was named director of the Rabbinic Placement Commission of the Central Conference of American Rabbis, becoming emeritus in 1991.

From 1969 to 1973, Dreyfus was chairman of the Liturgy Committee of the *Central Conference of American Rabbis. He played an instrumental role in compiling *Gates of Prayer: The New Union Prayerbook* (the standard text for synagogue use on Sabbaths and Festivals); *Gates of the House* (for home prayer); and *Gates of Repentance* (for the High Holidays). In this role, he also oversaw and contributed to the publication of *Gates of Understanding*, a volume of lengthy introductions to the series of Reform Jewish prayerbooks. In addition, Dreyfus served on the CCAR's Committee on Homosexuality and the Rabbinate – which ruled that homosexuality *per se* was not to be considered a disqualifying factor when it comes to candidacy for the rabbinate – and the Committee on Patrilinear Descent, which established that Jewish lineage may be passed on to children through the father alone, breaking from Orthodox and Conservative tradition that only the mother determines the religion of the offspring. Dreyfus was also a member of the CCAR's Committee on Reform Jewish Classics, the Admissions Committee, the Responsa Committee, the Rabbinic Population Committee, and the Reform Jewish Practice Committee.

At different periods during his career, Dreyfus also served as president of the Association of Reform Rabbis of New York, of the Brooklyn Board of Rabbis, of the Association of Jewish Chaplains of the United States Armed Forces, and of the National Association of Retired Reform Rabbis. Additionally, he was a member of the Governing Body of the World Union for Progressive Judaism, the Board of Governors of the New York Board of Rabbis, and the Commission on Jewish Chaplaincy of the National Jewish Welfare Board as well as co-chairman of the Catholic-Jewish Relations Committee of Brooklyn and Queens. Dreyfus was an instructor in the Active Reserve on the faculty of the Army Chaplain School for 21 years, attaining the rank of lieutenant colonel.

[Bezalel Gordon (2nd ed.)]

DREYFUS BROTHERS, pioneers of the cellulose acetate rayon industry. The brothers, HENRY (1876–1945) and CAMILLE (1878–1956), were born in Basle, Switzerland. They developed quality cellulose fiber soluble in acetone and manufactured noninflammable cellulose film, used by the Allies in World War I for treating fabric wings of airplanes. After the war they developed in England processes for spinning this film into man-made fiber, Celanese. Henry headed British Celanese Ltd.; Camille became president of Celanese Corporation of America and Canadian Celanese Ltd. Henry took out over 1,000 patents, the greatest number ever held by a single individual.

DREYFUSS, BARNEY (1865–1932), owner of the Pittsburgh Pirates baseball team from 1900 to 1932, founder of the World Series, builder of baseball's first modern stadium. Born in Freiberg, Germany, to Samuel Dreyfuss, an American citizen living in Germany, Dreyfuss came to the United States in 1881 to avoid being drafted into the German army. He settled in Paducah, Kentucky, and found work at the Bernheim whiskey distillery, at first cleaning whiskey bottles and eventually becoming head bookkeeper. Advised that outdoor activity would cure his poor indigestion, headaches, and general poor health, he organized and played second base on a semiprofessional baseball team that he formed.

The distillery moved to Louisville in 1888, and there Dreyfuss became part owner, secretary-treasurer, and eventually team president and owner of the National League Louisville Colonels. At the same time, he bought into the Pittsburgh Pirates, and as the National League was dropping the Louisville Colonels, Dreyfuss became sole owner of the Pirates, where he remained until his death. Considered the best judge of baseball talent in his time, Dreyfuss' outstanding ability as a scout made it possible for the Pirates to win the National League pennant six times (1901, 1902, 1903, 1909, 1925, 1927) and the World Series in 1909 and 1925. Indeed, many of his star players were elected to Baseball's Hall of Fame, and it was said by the president of the National League upon Dreyfuss' death, "He discovered more great players than any man in the history of baseball."

In 1903, Dreyfuss approached Henry Killilea and proposed that his American League champion Boston Pilgrims

(Red Sox) meet the National League champion Pirates in a nine-game interleague series, with the winner taking 60 percent of the gate receipts and the loser 40 percent. Dreyfuss believed a post-season contest would establish better relations between the two squabbling leagues and create additional interest in baseball. It did, beyond anyone's imagination, and thus was born the first World Series, a permanent American icon that achieved almost mythic proportions. In a gesture of goodwill, and contrary to the treacherous, greedy image of the typical owner, Dreyfuss put his club's $6,699.56 gate receipts into the players' pool, which earned the 16 Pirates $1,316 each, more than the victorious Boston players' $1,182.

In 1909, Dreyfuss built Forbes Field, the first modern steel-frame triple-tier stadium and the first baseball park capable of seating 25,000 fans. The stadium represented a visionary statement, for up until then no one believed that a game of baseball could attract that many people. Dreyfuss was also instrumental in having the spitball pitch banned from baseball in 1920.

Dreyfuss was also a pioneer in the formative years of professional football. He was co-owner and manager of the Pittsburgh Athletic Club, winners of the pro football championship in 1898, professional football's fourth organized season.

[Elli Wohlgelernter (2nd ed.)]

DREYFUSS, RICHARD (1948–), American actor. Dreyfuss was born in Brooklyn, New York, where his father was an attorney, but the family moved to Los Angeles, where he was educated. He joined the West Side Jewish Center and at the early age of nine showed his penchant for acting, taking part in all the plays produced there. Even as a high school student he was engaged to play professional parts, and from 1963 to 1973 acted on Broadway, in repertory and comedy. He first gained his reputation as a film actor in George Lucas' *American Graffiti*, playing the part of Curt Henderson, and from then went from strength to strength. In 1974 he went to Canada, and *The Apprenticeship of Duddy Kravitz*, a film with a Jewish theme in which he starred, won first prize at the Berlin Film Festival. In 1974 he starred in Steven Spielberg's film adaptation of Peter Benchley's best-selling novel *Jaws*, which became the biggest box-office hit to that date. A year later he played the part of Yonatan Netanyahu in the TV film *Victory at Entebbe*, about the Israeli commando action that freed hostages held in a plane hijacked to Uganda. In 1977 he starred in another highly successful Spielberg film, *Close Encounters of the Third Kind*. In 1977 he was awarded the Academy and Golden Globe awards for best actor for his performance in *The Goodbye Girl*. At the time, at age 29, he was the youngest performer ever to have won a Best Actor Oscar. Dreyfuss went on to act in such films as *The Big Fix* (1978), *Whose Life Is It Anyway?* (1981), *Down and Out in Beverly Hills* (1986), *Tin Men* (1987), *Stakeout* (1987), *Nuts* (1987), *Moon over Parador* (1988), *Lost in Yonkers* (1983), *Always* (1989), *Postcards from the Edge* (1990), *Rosencrantz and Guildenstern Are Dead* (1990), *What about Bob?* (1991), *Silent Fall* (1994), *Mr. Holland's Opus* (Oscar nomination for Best Actor, 1995), *Mad Dog Time* (1996), *Krippendorf's Tribe* (1998), *The Crew* (2000), *The Old Man Who Read Love Stories* (2001), and *Silver City* (2004).

Dreyfuss has also performed in many stage and television productions. He starred in the 2001 TV drama series *The Education of Max Bickford* as well as such TV movies as *Prisoner of Honor* (1991), *Oliver Twist* (1997), *Lansky* (1999), *Fail Safe* (2000), *The Day Reagan Was Shot* (2001), *Coast to Coast* (2004), and *Copshop* (2004). On Broadway he has appeared in *But Seriously* (1969), *Total Abandon* (1983), *Death and the Maiden* (1992), and *Sly Fox* (2004). In 2000 Dreyfuss was awarded a Lifetime Achievement Award at the Hollywood Film Festival. With Harry Turtledove, Dreyfuss co-authored the novel *The Two Georges* (1996).

BIBLIOGRAPHY: J. Phillips, *You'll Never Eat Lunch in This Town Again* (1991).

[Jonathan Licht / Rohan Saxena and Ruth Beloff (2nd ed.)]

DREYZL, LEAH (second half of 18th century), composer of *tkhines* (Yiddish prayers). Dreyzl lived in Stanislav, Poland, and came from a distinguished family. Her great-grandfather was Ḥakham Ẓevi *Ashkenazi (1660–1718) and several of her male relatives were rabbis and scholars. Leah Dreyzl married Rabbi Aryeh Leib Auerbach, who became the rabbi at Stanislav and was closely associated with the burgeoning Ḥasidic movement. He was believed to be an intimate of the Baal Shem Tov.

It is clear from her own writings that Leah Dreyzl was educated. The two *tkhines* she is known to have written are filled with biblical references and lines from the prayer book, and are permeated with mystical overtones. They were published posthumously, probably during the 19th century, and were named (by the publisher) "Tkhine es rotsn" ("Tkhine of a Time of [Divine] Favor") and "Tkhine Sha'arei Teshuvah" ("Tkhine of the Gates of Repentance"). An introduction to the published edition credits "Mistress Hena...widow of the departed...Rabbi David Tsvi," with passing down these writings "from her mother-in-law, the righteous, pious, renowned rabbi's wife, Mistress Leah Dreyzel." Both of these poems, written for the penitential month of Elul, easily lend themselves to oral recitation. This has led literary analysts to conclude that Leah Dreyzl was a *firzogerin* in the Stanislav synagogue, leading the women's congregation in prayer.

BIBLIOGRAPHY: E. Taitz, S. Henry, and C. Tallan, *The JPS Guide to Jewish Women: 600 B.C.E.–1900 C.E.* (2003), 143; C. Weissler, *Voices of the Matriarchs: Listening to the Prayers of Early Modern Jewish Women* (1998), 26–28.

[Emily Taitz (2nd ed.)]

DREZNER, YEḤIEL DOV (1922–1947), Jew executed by the British in Palestine. Drezner was born in Poland and came to Ereẓ Israel with his parents who settled in Jerusalem, where Drezner joined the Betar movement. In 1940 he moved to Netanyah, where he joined I.Ẓ.L. under the pseudonym of Dov Rosenbaum. In 1945 I.Ẓ.L. retaliated for the flogging inflicted on one of their members who was captured by the British, by seizing British officers and subjecting them to the same humiliating punishment. Drezner was in command of one unit, the other four members of which were Mordekhai Alkaḥi, Eliezer Kashani, Abraham Mizraḥi, and Ḥayyim Golavski. The whole unit was captured. Mizraḥi was wounded and died before the trial (one version is that he was murdered) and the other four put on trial. Golavski was sentenced to life imprisonment in view of his youth, while the other three were sentenced to death. An attempt to rescue them by an assault on the Jerusalem central prison where they were held was foiled by their removal to Acre on the very morning of the intended assault. All four, together with Dov *Gruner, were hanged on the same day, Apr. 16, 1946.

BIBLIOGRAPHY: Y. Nedava, *Olei-ha-Gardom* (1966); Y. Gurion, *Ha-Nizzaḥon Olei Gardom* (1971).

°**DRIVER, SAMUEL ROLLES** (1846–1914), Bible scholar and Hebraist; from 1883 Regius Professor of Hebrew at Oxford. Driver's chief work, *An Introduction to the Literature of the Old Testament*, appeared in 1891 (1913[9]). Among his early publications was *A Treatise on the Uses of the Tenses in Hebrew* (1874, 1892[3]). He was a practicing Christian ordained as a priest in the Anglican Church and held various offices in that church. Nevertheless, he wrote his books in the spirit of the critical method established by J. *Wellhausen, at the same time stressing that his conclusions did not impugn the sanctity of the Bible or attribute literary forgeries to it. He was therefore attacked from both sides. Conservative theologians condemned his views as "dangerous," while some of his fellow Bible critics accused him of making concessions to orthodox extremism. Driver was alert to every new potential source of information on the Bible, as may be seen by the fact that he was among the first to write a book on archaeology and the Bible, *Modern Research as Illustrating the Bible* (1909). Driver was one of the editors of the "International Critical Commentary" series of scholarly editions of biblical books, and also contributed commentaries on Deuteronomy (1895, 1902[3]), and Job (with G.B. Gray, 1905). His other works include commentaries on Genesis (1911[9]), Exodus (1911), Daniel (1900), and other books of the Bible, and papers on specific points in the prophetic writings, as well as researches into the Masoretic text of Samuel (*Notes on the Hebrew Text and the Topography of the Books of Samuel*, 1890, 1913[2]). He also participated in the compilation of *A Hebrew and English Lexicon of the Old Testament* (with F. Brown and C.A. Briggs, 1907). This work, based on the lexicon of William *Gesenius, and popularly known as BDB (from the initials of its authors), remains in widespread use. Together with A. *Neubauer, he published *The "Suffering Servant" of Isaiah According to the Jewish Interpreters* (1877). All of Driver's books were well written and carefully researched and three of them are so basic that for all the progress that has been made since then the specialist still has occasion to consult them (his *Introduction…*, his *Tenses*, and his *Notes on the Hebrew Text*).

His son SIR GODFREY ROLLES DRIVER (1892–1975), Bible and Semitic scholar, gained knowledge of the Middle East with the British Egyptian Expeditionary Force in 1919 for which he wrote *A Report on Kurdistan and the Kurds* (1919). Later he also published *A Grammar of the Colloquial Arabic of Syria and Palestine* (1925). From 1919–28 he taught classics at Oxford and from 1928 lectured there on Hebrew and comparative Semitic philology, becoming professor of Semitic philology (1938–62) and intermittently professor of Hebrew (1934, 1953–54, and 1959–60).

One of his important early works was "The Modern Study of the Hebrew Language" in *The People and the Book* (ed. A.S. Peake), 73–120. In 1935 he collaborated with J.C. Miles in editing *The Assyrian Laws*, which aimed to serve as a textbook for scholars of the Old Testament as well as of comparative law (revised as vol. two of *Assyrian Laws and Babylonian Laws*, 1952, 1955). The following year Driver published *Problems of the Hebrew Verbal System* in which he explained the peculiarities of the Hebrew tense system and other features of Hebrew as resulting from the origin of Hebrew as a mixture of Canaanite and the original language spoken by the Israelites. In 1948 he published his Schweich Lectures of 1944 under the title *Semitic Writing* where he examined the origin and development of the Semitic alphabet and in which he was one of the first to realize the significance of Ugaritic. In 1954 he edited and translated the Borchardt Aramaic documents in the Bodleian Museum under the title *Aramaic Documents of the Fifth Century B.C.* (revised 1957). These were official and semiofficial documents from the court of the Persian satrap in Egypt. The following year he published *Canaanite Myths and Legends*, in which he translated Ugaritic legends and included an Ugaritic glossary.

His *Judean Scrolls* (1965) discussed the problem of the identity and date of the community of Qumran, which he identified with the *Zealots. On his seventieth birthday a volume of *Hebrew and Semitic Studies* (1963) was dedicated to him. It contains a selected bibliography of his works. He was joint director of the committee that prepared the translation of the Old Testament in the New English Bible (1970). He wrote numerous articles on Hebrew lexicography, in which, by the use of cognate languages, he uncovered hitherto unrecognized meanings of biblical words. Much of these he incorporated into the New English Bible and into his work on a new edition of F. Brown, S.R. Driver, and C.A. Briggs' *Hebrew Lexicon*.

BIBLIOGRAPHY: T.K. Cheyne, *Founders of Old Testament Criticism* (1893), passim (esp. chs. 11–13). **ADD. BIBLIOGRAPHY:** J.A. Emerton, DBI, 308–10.

DROB, MAX (1887–1959), U.S. Conservative rabbi. Drob was born in Mlawa, Poland, and was taken to the United States in 1895. He graduated from Columbia University (1908) and received rabbinic ordination from the Jewish Theological Seminary (1911), and served congregations in Syracuse, New York (1911–13), Buffalo, New York (1913–19), New York City

(1919–27), and Philadelphia (1927–29). From 1929 he was rabbi of the Concourse Center of Israel, Bronx, New York, where he remained for the rest of his career. Drob was president of the Rabbinical Assembly of America from 1925 to 1927, and chairman of its *bet din* from 1923 to 1941. He was regarded as belonging to the traditionalist wing of Conservative Judaism seeking to transmit traditional religious practice in a manner more decorous and more American. He was actively involved in the professionalization of the rabbinate with such issues as rabbinic placement and pension determined by regulations and procedures. He was president of the non-denominational New York Board of Rabbis 1933–34 and also served as a member of the commission set up by New York State to supervise the enforcement of *kashrut* laws, at a time before the Orthodox Union had established its domination of *kashrut*. He was a founder of the United Synagogue of America and on the board of the Jewish Theological Seminary.

ADD. BIBLIOGRAPHY: P.S. Nadel, *Conservative Judaism in America: A Biographical Dictionary and Sourcebook* (1988).

[Michael Berenbaum (2nd ed.)]

DROBNER, BOLESLAW (1883–1968), Polish socialist politician. Born in Cracow into an assimilated family, Drobner joined the Polish Social Democratic Party of Galicia and Silesia in 1898, attaching himself to the radical left wing. He took part in the revolution of 1905 and during World War I fought in Pilsudski's Legion. After Polish independence, Drobner joined the Socialist Party and in 1922 became one of the founders of the Independent Socialist Party. When the two parties reunited in 1928 he was appointed to the supreme council of the united party. He represented the left wing of the party calling for cooperation between socialists and communists. Drobner was frequently arrested for organizing strikes and following the outbreak of World War II left Poland for the U.S.S.R., where he was a founder of the Soviet-sponsored Union of Polish Patriots. He became minister of labor and social care in the Committee of National Liberation and at the conference of the Polish Socialist Party in 1944 was elected party chairman.

Drobner returned to Poland after the war and was a member of the Polish delegation at the Russo-Polish frontier negotiations of August 1945. In 1947 he was elected to the Sejm (Polish parliament) and in the following year joined the ruling communist United Workers Party. He had a great love for his native Cracow and did much for the preservation of its historical relics. He also initiated the restoration of Jewish culture there, particularly the 15th-century Jewish synagogue.

BIBLIOGRAPHY: *New York Times* (March 23, 1968), 31 (obituary). **ADD. BIBLIOGRAPHY:** C. Kozlowski, *Zarys Dziejow Polskiego Ruchu Robotniczego …* (1980), index.

[Abraham Wein]

DROGOBYCH (Pol. **Drohobycz**), city in Ukraine, formerly in Poland and Austria. Information about individual Jewish contractors of the salt mines in Drogobych dates from the beginning of the 15th century. Some of them settled in the city, eventually forming a small community (*kehillah*). In 1578, however, Drohobych obtained the privilege *de non tolerandis Judaeis* authorizing the exclusion of Jews from its precincts. Although a number of Jews were subsequently found living in the vicinity, their settlement was not permanent until the end of the 17th century, enabled by royal patronage. All commerce and crafts were then concentrated in Jewish hands. Jewish guilds were formed and the records evidence the friction that existed between them and the Christian guilds of the city, as also between the citizens of Drogobych and the Jewish inhabitants. The Drohobych *kehillah* was represented on the provincial council of *Rzeszow (see *Councils of the Lands). In the middle of the 18th century a wealthy, despotic farmer of the taxes and customs revenues, Zalman b. Ze'ev (Wolfowicz), seized control of communal affairs. He appointed his son-in-law rabbi, and for his ruthless treatment of both Jews and non-Jews he was finally denounced to the authorities; in 1755 he was arrested, tried, and condemned to death, but as generous assistance was contributed by his coreligionists the sentence was commuted to life imprisonment. He subsequently adopted Christianity and died a member of the Carmelite order in 1757.

After Drogobych passed to Austria in 1772, economic oppression, heavy taxation, and government interference in communal affairs had an adverse effect on the Jewish position. It improved in the 19th century, however, especially with the exploitation of the mineral resources of Drogobych; the salt industry was also a Jewish enterprise. The first attempts to prospect for oil and its extraction were made in Drogobych by a Jew, Hecker, in 1810, and in 1858–59 a refinery was constructed by A. Schreiner in nearby *Borislav at the same time as the industry was developed in the United States. Drogobych Jews took a prominent part in oil extraction and refining, and its export was mainly in Jewish hands. Many families made fortunes in this sector. The takeover of the smaller companies by big enterprises at the end of the 19th century, however, badly hit the Jewish concerns, and the economic position of the community began to deteriorate. After World War I it became impoverished. *Ḥasidism and the *Haskalah movement spread to Drogobych at the end of the 18th century. A German biweekly printed in Hebrew characters, the *Drohobitzer Zeitung*, was published between 1883 and World War I, and brought out several Hebrew supplements entitled *Ẓiyyon* (1886–87, 1897). Toward the end of Hapsburg rule the constituency of Drogobych was represented in the Austrian parliament by a Jewish deputy, an assimilationist with sympathies for Poland, who had the backing of the authorities. He was opposed by a Zionist-supported Jewish national candidate in 1911. The authorities were accused of ballot-fixing during the elections, and the army was called out to disperse a demonstration. Shots were fired into the crowd. Thirteen Jews were killed and many injured. Drogobych remained the center of the Galician *kolel* from the 1890s until the Holocaust. Ḥayyim Shapira, the last *ẓaddik* in Drogobych, was the first of the ḥasidic *ẓaddikim* to join officially the Zionist movement. He went to Ereẓ Israel in 1922. The Jewish population of Drogobych totaled 1,924 in 1765, 2,492 in 1812, 8,055 in 1865, 8,683 in 1900, and 11,833 (about 44% of the total population) in 1921.

[Nathan Michael Gelber]

Holocaust and Postwar Periods

When World War II broke out, the town with its 17,000 Jews came under Soviet occupation. The authorities arrested the Zionist leaders and closed the Hebrew schools. Jewish refugees from western Poland found shelter in Drogobych, but most of them were deported to the Soviet interior. The Germans entered Drogobych on June 30, 1941, and immediately staged a pogrom with the help of the local Polish and Ukrainian population. About 400 Jews were brutally murdered outside the courthouse and at the Jewish cemetery. Another 300 were executed in the nearby Bronice forest in November. In March 1942 some 2,000 Jews were sent to the *Belzec extermination camp. The second mass deportation took place on August 8, with the dispatch of 2,500 Jews to the same destination, while another 600 were shot in the town itself. The ghetto was established in September. The remaining 9,000 Jews, some of whom were refugees from the nearby villages, were crowded into it. Toward the end of October an additional group consisting of 2,300 Jews was sent to Belzec, and 200 hospital patients were murdered. The surviving Jews began building hideouts or sought shelter in the nearby forest. However, the Germans thwarted their efforts by continuing the *Aktion* for the whole month of November 1942 and by ordering the death sentence for all non-Jews caught sheltering Jews. For a while the process of extermination did not affect those Jews conscripted for forced labor in the local petroleum industries. The Bronice forest became a mass grave for the Jews of Drogobych and vicinity, including all members of the Judenrat. On February 15, 1943, 450 were executed there, including 300 women. In March 800 from the labor camps were murdered. The remnants of the Jewish community tried to save themselves by hiding or by escaping to Hungary via the Carpathian Mountains, while a few tried to obtain "Aryan" papers. When the Soviet army entered Drogobych in August 1944, some 400 Jews were still alive.

After the war, Drogobych was ceded to the Ukrainian S.S.R., and most of the Jews left for Poland in transit to Israel and other countries.

[Aharon Weiss]

BIBLIOGRAPHY: N.M. Gelber (ed.), *Sefer Zikkaron le-Drohobich, Boryslav ve-Hasevivah* (1959); M. Balaban, *Z historji Żydów w Polsce* (1920), 129–46.

DROPKIN, CELIA (1887–1956), Yiddish poet. Born Zipporah Levine in Bobruisk, Belorussia, daughter of a lumber merchant, Dropkin was raised by her widowed mother. Taught Jewish subjects by a rabbi's wife, she graduated from the Novosybko (Russian) gymnasium. She tutored in Warsaw, before continuing her studies in Kiev. There, the Hebrew writer Uri Nissan *Gnessin encouraged her writing of Russian poetry. Returning to Warsaw, then to Bobruisk, Dropkin married Samuel Shmaye Dropkin in 1909. She and their first child (born 1910) joined him in New York in 1912. Five of their six children survived into adulthood. In New York, Dropkin wrote Russian poems which she translated into Yiddish (1917) and published in *Di Naye Velt* and *Inzikh* (1920). Throughout the 1920s and 1930s, her works appeared in avant-garde publications of *Di *Yunge* and the *Inzikhistn*: *Onheyb*, *Poezye*, and *Shriftn*. Dropkin's poems – notable for their explicit sexuality, whether about love, motherhood, or death – earned her a reputation as a leading woman poet. Her short stories and poems also appeared in Abraham *Liessin's **Tsukunft*. Only a single volume of Dropkin's poems appeared during her lifetime: *In Heysn Vint* ("In the Hot Wind," 1935). Widowed in 1943, she spent her last years painting in oils and water colors. Her last published poem appeared in *Tsukunft* (April 1953).

Three years after Dropkin's death, her children published an expanded edition of her poetry, short stories, and paintings: *In Heysn Vint* (1959) includes the poems of the 1935 edition, as well as uncollected and previously unpublished poems, selected by Sasha Dillon. Another poem, "Shvere Gedanken" ("Heavy Thoughts"), was later discovered on a tape recording and appeared in *Yidishe Kultur* (1990). Poems and stories in English translation appeared in I. Howe and E. Greenberg (eds.), *A Treasury of Yiddish Poetry* (1969); I. Howe et al. (eds.), *Penguin Book of Modern Yiddish Verse* (1987); F. Forman et al. (eds.), *Found Treasures: Stories by Yiddish Women Writers* (1994); R. Whitman (ed.), *Anthology of Modern Yiddish Poetry* (1995); J. Chametzky et al. (eds.), *Jewish American Literature: A Norton Anthology* (2001); S. Bark (ed.), *Beautiful as the Moon, Radiant as the Stars: Jewish Women in Yiddish Stories* (2003).

BIBLIOGRAPHY: LNYL, 2 (1958), 540–1; Rejzen, Leksikon, 1 (1926^2), 742–3; Y. Yeshurin, in: *In Heysn Vint, Poems, Stories, and Pictures* (1959), 271–3; S. Dillon, in: *ibid.*, 263–9; G. Rozier and V. Siman, in: *Dans le vent chaud: Bilingue yiddish-francais* (1994); J. Hadda, in: N. Sokoloff et al. (eds.), *Gender and Text in Modern Hebrew and Yiddish Literature* (1992), 93–112; K. Hellerstein, in *ibid.*, 113–43.

[Kathryn Hellerstein (2nd ed.)]

DROPSIE, MOSES AARON (1821–1905), U.S. attorney, businessman, philanthropist, and patron of Jewish learning. Dropsie was born in Philadelphia to a Dutch-Jewish immigrant father and a Christian mother. He embraced Judaism at the age of 14, and ultimately became a vigorous proponent of traditional Judaism in America. Dropsie made his livelihood in the jewelry business until he was 28, when he began the study of law. He was admitted to the bar in 1851. Although his practice was largely in business law, Dropsie became a scholar in legal history and published a number of works on Roman law, including one on the trial of Jesus. Dropsie invested very early in streetcar ventures and became the president of two traction companies. He served as chairman of the commission that supervised the construction of the South Street bridge across the Schuylkill River in 1870. An early organizer of the

Republican Party of Pennsylvania, Dropsie ran for public office only once. He became leader and officer of many Jewish communal activities, and was an admirer and disciple of Isaac *Leeser. Their sense of mutual understanding was disturbed only by their divergent sympathies in the early days of the Civil War. Dropsie was an active supporter of Leeser's short-lived Maimonides College from its inception in 1867, the first Jewish theological seminary in America. Dropsie believed that one of the major reasons for its failure was the refusal of New York Jewish leaders to give it their full support; when the Jewish Theological Seminary was organized in 1886 in New York City, he refused to lend a hand. This resentment was one of the factors which motivated his establishing a bequest for a totally new institution for higher Jewish learning. Another factor was his anger, which he also expressed in a number of pamphlets, against what he considered to be the extremism of Reform Judaism. Dropsie's will was written in 1895, while he was serving as president of *Gratz College. He assigned his fortune to the creation of Dropsie College.

BIBLIOGRAPHY: C. Adler, *Lectures, Selected Papers, Addresses* (1933), 43–64; B.W. Korn, *Eventful Years and Experiences* (1954), 187–9; H. Morais, *Jews of Philadelphia* (1894), 255–8.

[Bertram Wallace Korn]

DROPSIE COLLEGE, independent, nontheological, academic institution dedicated to graduate instruction and research in Jewish studies and related branches of learning. It was founded in Philadelphia, Pennsylvania, in 1907 as Dropsie College for Hebrew and Cognate Learning. The establishment of the institution was provided for in the will of Moses Aaron *Dropsie, dated September 17, 1895. Dropsie stated: "The increasing need in the United States for a more thorough and systematic education in Jewish lore has long been felt, and is a matter of solicitude to true Israelites, who cherish the religion of their ancestors.... [Hence] I order and direct that there be established and maintained in the City of Philadelphia a college for the promotion of and instruction in the Hebrew and cognate languages and their respective literatures and in the Rabbinical learning and literature." The will directed "that in the admission of students there shall be no distinction on account of creed, color, or sex." The college offered the Ph.D. and, from 1952 onward, the M.A. degrees in areas such as Hebrew, Arabic, and other Semitic languages, biblical and rabbinic studies, medieval Jewish philosophy, Assyriology, and Middle Eastern studies. In 1962 it instituted a program in Jewish education leading to the Ed.D. The original president of Dropsie was Mayer Sulzberger, who directed the Board of Governors selected to execute Dropsie's will. The first operating president was Cyrus *Adler, who served from the opening of the college in 1909 until his death in 1940 while holding other important positions including the chancellorship of the Jewish Theological Seminary. He was succeeded by Abraham A. *Neuman (1941–66), Abraham I. *Katsh (1968–76), Joseph Rapaport (1979–81), and David M. Goldenberg (1981–86). In 1986 the college closed its doors as a graduate school and reopened two years later as the Annenberg Research Institute for Judaic and Near Eastern Studies, a postdoctoral research center and fellowship program in Judaic and Near Eastern studies. In 1993 the institution was incorporated into the University of Pennsylvania as the Center for Judaic Studies.

The college's importance lies in that fact that when it was founded, and for several decades afterwards, it was the only non-theological institution in the United States that offered the Ph.D. in Judaic studies. As such, it attracted many distinguished scholars to its faculty (such as Cyrus H. Gordon, Benzion Halper, Leo L. Honor, Henry Malter, Max L. Margolis, Ben-Zion Netanyahu, Moshe Perlmann, Solomon L. Skoss, Bernard D. Weinryb, and Solomon Zeitlin). The faculty produced close to 250 Ph.D.s, many of whom filled positions in Judaic and related studies throughout the United States, thus spurring the growth of Jewish studies programs in the country. From its beginnings the college published the *Jewish Quarterly Review*, continuing the publication begun in England in 1888 under the editorship of I. Abrahams and C.G. Montefiore. As the only American Ph.D.-granting school in Judaic studies for several decades, Dropsie acquired an important library collection (including manuscripts and incunabula) in biblical, rabbinic, and medieval Jewish literature, as well as early American Jewish imprints.

Ironically it was the success of the college that, to a significant extent, spelled its demise. With the burgeoning of Jewish studies programs in U.S. universities during the 1950s and 1960s, Dropsie found that with its limited resources it could not compete with the larger and well-endowed universities. By the early 1980s it appeared that the college would eventually be forced to close. An attempt at a revival was made in 1981 with the appointment of David Goldenberg to the presidency of the institution. Goldenberg, a recent Dropsie graduate and then faculty member, rebuilt the faculty with young promising scholars, revived the languishing *Jewish Quarterly Review*, attracted funding for the conservation of *genizah* manuscripts, and hired professional library staff to convert the collection to the Library of Congress cataloguing system and provide online access to the library's holdings. However, the general financial situation of the College did not much improve and, finally, in 1986 the Dropsie closed.

By this time, Albert J. Wood, a member of the Board of Trustees, had induced the American Jewish philanthropist and former ambassador to Great Britain, Walter H. Annenberg, to become involved with Dropsie's future. Wood saw that while a small graduate school was no longer feasible, a postdoctoral research center in Jewish studies would fill a need. Annenberg embraced the plan, funded the construction of a new building near historic Independence Hall in Philadelphia, and supplied the new institution's annual budget. Thus Dropsie was transformed into the Annenberg Research Institute for Judaic and Near Eastern Studies. Under its first president, Bernard Lewis, the scholar of Islamic studies, the Institute opened it doors in 1988 with an annual program of invited scholars from throughout the world to work on various themes in Jewish and related studies. This program continues today as the University of Pennsylvania's Center for Judaic Studies.

BIBLIOGRAPHY: A. Neuman, *Landmarks and Goals* (1953), 255–356, passim; idem, in: *Seventy-fifth Anniversary.*

[Meir Ben-Horin / David M. Goldenberg (2nd ed.)]

DROSDOFF, MATTHEW (1908–1998), U.S. soil chemist. Born in Chicago, Drosdoff received his Ph.D. in soil science from the University of Wisconsin at Madison in 1934. He joined the U.S. Department of Agriculture and was adviser on mineral nutrition and coffee production to Colombia (1951–53), soils adviser to Bolivia (1954), soils adviser to Peru (1955–60), and chief of the Agricultural Division of the U.S. Agency for International Development (AID) in Vietnam (1960–64). From 1964 to 1966 he was the administrator of the International Agricultural Development Service, and in 1966 he became professor of soil science at Cornell University, remaining emeritus professor until his death.

Drosdoff was active in B'nai B'rith in various capacities and from 1944 to 1947 was director of the Hillel Foundation at the University of Florida.

Many of Drosdoff's contributions to scientific journals were concerned with foliar analysis of tropical tree crops. Other topics were soil composition, genesis and morphology, colloidal clays, soil surveys, and agricultural development generally. He was a fellow of the American Society of Agronomy and was honored with its international award for his many overseas services to the U.S. government.

[Samuel Aaron Miller / Ruth Rossing (2nd ed.)]

DRUCKER, DANIEL CHARLES (1918–2001), U.S. structural engineer. Drucker was born in New York and studied engineering as an undergraduate and postgraduate at Columbia University, where he obtained his Ph.D. in 1940. He taught at Cornell University in 1940–43 before serving in the U.S. Army Air Corps, after which he joined Brown University in 1946, becoming professor in 1950. He was Dean of Engineering at the University of Illinois in 1968–83. His main interests were the theory of plasticity and its application to designing metal structures. He introduced the universally accepted concept of material stability termed "Drucker's stability postulate" which governs the plastic behavior of metals in response to strain and has wide academic and practical applications. Among many honors and awards he received the National Medal of Science (1980) and was the first recipient of the American Society of Mechanical Engineers' Daniel C. Drucker Medal bestowed for outstanding contributions to mechanical engineering (1998). While at Brown University, he was active in the Providence, Rhode Island, Jewish community.

[Michael Denman (2nd ed.)]

°**DRUMONT, EDOUARD-ADOLPHE** (1844–1917), leader of the antisemitic movement in France. Originally holding strongly leftist opinions, while still an unknown journalist Drumont contributed to a number of publications, including *La Liberté* owned by the Jewish Saint-Simonist, Isaac *Péreire. In the 1880s, however, Drumont's views changed and he became associated with the activities of ultra-Catholic circles, although adhering to certain remnants of his radical social philosophy. It was on this foundation that he developed a rabid antisemitism, which became his consuming passion. His book *La France juive*, first published in 1886, describes France as subjugated to the Jews in the political, economic, social, and cultural spheres; in a short time it ran to over a hundred editions. Drumont continued his anti-Jewish propaganda in further books. In 1889 he founded the Antisemitic League (see *Antisemitic Political Parties and Organizations) and *La Libre Parole* whose policy veered between the Catholic right and social radicalism, but was invariably violently antisemitic in tone. Drumont and his paper had a considerable share in exacerbating the *Dreyfus Affair. In 1898 Drumont was elected to the chamber of deputies, but after the victory of Dreyfus' supporters he was not returned a second time; in 1909 his application for membership of the French Academy was rejected.

BIBLIOGRAPHY: L. Daudet, *Les oeuvres dans les hommes* (1922); I. Schapira, *Der Anti-semitismus in der franzoesischen Literatur: Eduard Drumont und seine Quellen* (1927); G. Bernanos, *La Grande peur des bien-pensants* (1931); R.F. Byrnes, *Anti-semitism in Modern France* (1950); *Dictionnaire de biographie française*, 11 (1967), 852–4. **ADD. BIBLIOGRAPHY:** M. Winock, *Edouard Drumont et Cie: antisémitisme et fascisme en France* (1982); F. Busi, *The Pope of Antisemitism: The Career and Legacy of Edouard-Adolphe Drumont* (1986).

[Moshe Catane]

DRUNKENNESS (Heb. שִׁכָּרוֹן, *shikkaron*).

In the Bible

Biblical, apocryphal, and ancient Near Eastern references make it clear that, far from being condemned, the use of alcoholic beverages was regarded by Jews and others as a necessary (Ecclus. 39:26; Pritchard, Texts, 598, line 89; 602, line 32) and distinctive (Ps. 104:15; Pritchard, Texts, 77c, line 12ff.) feature of human life. A feast was inconceivable without wine, and Proverbs 9:1ff. speaks of Wisdom personified offering food and wine. Indeed, complete abstinence was associated with a turning away from civilization (Jer. 35; see *Rechabites). Likewise, the *Nazirite avoidance of alcohol is of a piece with their refraining from cutting the hair and from participating in the burial of the dead, two other hallmarks of civilization (Numbers 6). *Wine was valued for bringing joy and banishing sorrow (Judg. 9:13; Ps. 104:15; cf. Pritchard, loc. cit., line 21; Prov. 31:6–7; Eccles. 10:19; Ecclus. 31:27–28; 40:20) and was used cultically in libations (Ex. 30:40–41) and the festive sacral meal (Deut. 14:26).

Intoxication, however, was deprecated (cf. Ecclus. 31:25–31; 39:27), both in the cult – in keeping with the biblical rejection of the Dionysiac element of other ancient religions (Lev. 10:8–11; 1 Sam. 1:13–16; Ezek. 44:21) – and in daily life. Wisdom literature warns that drunkenness brings poverty, woes, quarrels, wounds, strange visions, etc. (Prov. 20:1; 21:17;

23:19–21:29–35; 31:4–5; cf. I Esd. 3:19–24) and causes kings to err in judgment (Prov. 31:4–5; cf. Lev. 10:8–11 (priests); Isa. 28:7 (priest and prophet)). Several narratives depict the disgrace and sometimes death of drunkards (Noah, Gen. 9:20–27; Lot, Gen. 19:31–38; Nabal, I Sam. 25:36; Amnon, II Sam. 13:28–29; Elah, I Kings 16:9; Ben-Hadad, I Kings 20:16; Ahasuerus, Esth. 1:10; cf. Holofernes, Judith 13:2). The prophets frequently condemn drunkenness, particularly among the wealthy and the leaders (Isa. 28:1ff.; 56:11–12; cf. Prov. 31:4–5), associating it with moral insensitivity (Isa. 5:11–12, 22–23; Amos 2:8), licentiousness (Hos. 4:11–12, 18), and forgetting God (Hos. 4:11–12; cf. Job 1:4–5). Drunkenness and gluttony are among the charges against the insubordinate son (Deut. 21:20). However, Isaiah 51:17–18, like the Ugaritic Aqhat epic (in Pritchard, Texts, 150b, line 32–33), reflects a view that filial duties include helping a parent made unsteady by alcohol to walk. The occasion of drunkenness might be private drinking (Noah, Lot) or group celebration (Nabal, Amnon, Ben-Hadad, Ahasuerus), including carousing on religious festivals (Hos. 4:11ff.). Drinking songs and music are mentioned at such celebrations (Isa. 24:7–9; Amos 6:5–6; Ps. 69:13). One type of gathering that appears, especially in the light of extra – and post – biblical attestations, to have been conducive to drunkenness is the *marzeaḥ*, referring at times to a joyous banquet (Amos 6:7), at others to a mourning meal (Jer. 16:5)

[Jeffrey Howard Tigay]

In the Talmud

Basing himself on the fact that the death of Nadab and Abihu is followed by the injunction against priests drinking wine or strong drink when officiating, R. Simeon attributes their death to the fact that they entered the sanctuary while in a state of intoxication (Lev. R. 12:1). Judges must not render decisions after drinking wine (Er. 64a). As a result, judges were forbidden to eat dates because of their possible intoxicating effects (Ket. 10b). The judges of the *Sanhedrin had to abstain from wine during the entire hearing of a capital case (Sanh. 5:1; Sanh. 42a). The criterion for drunkenness is whether the person affected is capable of addressing himself properly to a king. A quarter of a "log" (approx. 3.2 oz., 100 milliliters) of wine was regarded as sufficient to cause intoxication, but it was not a rigid rule. If he later walked a mil (approx. 3,300 ft., 1,100 meters) or slept, a drunken person was considered sober, unless he drank strong Italian wine, in which case he must walk at least three mils (Er. 64a–b). A drunken person is forbidden to conduct a service. Based upon High Priest Eli's reprimand of Hannah (I Sam. 1:13–15), the Talmud lays down that if a person prays in a state of drunkenness, his prayer is an abomination (Ber. 31b). A person under the influence of alcohol is legally responsible for his actions unless he has reached the state of oblivion attributed to Lot (cf. Gen. 19:31–36; Er. 65a). The Bible adopted an ambivalent attitude toward wine, and there are several statements in the Talmud concerning the virtues of wine and its beneficial effects on health (cf. Er. 65a–b). There are many traditions that relate to the negative effects of drink on everyday life. One example that may be cited is the legend that when Noah was about to plant his vineyard, Satan buried in the soil carcasses of a sheep, a lion, a pig, and a monkey. As a result when a person indulges mildly he becomes sheepish, further indulging makes him feel like a lion. Overindulgence causes him to befoul himself like a pig, and when he becomes roaring drunk he literally "makes a monkey of himself" (Tanḥ., Noaḥ, 14). In one chapter of the Midrash (Lev. R. 12:1) there are three statements with regard to drunkenness. One interprets Proverbs 23:31 homiletically to mean that "while the drunkard has his eyes on the cup, the publican has his eyes on his pocket." The second tells of the despairing attempt on the part of the sons of a drunken addict to rid him of his vice, while the third is an account of a drunkard who was determined to make up the absence of one bottle from his daily quota of 12. Some scholars have assumed that drunkenness was not a serious problem in the talmudic period, and so have understood these traditions to reflect a lighthearted, almost jocular attitude toward the phenomenon. Others have suggested that these traditions may reflect not the rarity of drunkenness, but rather its frequency. While the Talmud states a positive injunction that a person shall get so drunk on *Purim that he cannot distinguish between "Blessed be Mordecai" and "Cursed be Haman," the disastrous results of an actual incident in which two famous amora'im, Rabbah and R. Zera, were involved (Meg. 7b), would seem to represent a serious criticism of this tradition. As a result, later rabbinic authorities were at pains to point out that this talmudic permissibility was not to be taken literally.

[Louis Isaac Rabinowitz / Stephen G. Wald (2nd ed.)]

Modern Times

Interest in contemporary drinking among Jews stems from the mystery of drinking not being a problem. Writers in many countries during recent centuries have commented on the comparative sobriety of the Jews. Multinational statistics of arrests for drunkenness, incidences of alcoholic psychosis, and alcoholic admissions to hospitals have consistently revealed a marked underrepresentation of Jews. From the 1940s, social scientists in the United States have systematically studied drinking patterns of Jewish youth and adults. The consistent finding has been that proportionately more Jews than other ethnic or religious segments of the population drink wine, beer, or spirits, but proportionately fewer Jews are heavy drinkers or alcoholics. Sophisticated socio-cultural-psychological hypotheses, rejecting rational blame-avoidance as an adequate explanation, relate Jewish sobriety to the early initiation of children in a family-centered, religiously oriented, moderate drinking pattern. The attitudinal values thus engendered are presumed to prevent later excess in drinking. An alternative but untested hypothesis proposes a genetic immunity to alcoholism.

Leading studies through the late 1960s suggested that the more acculturated Jewish youth tended to adopt the drinking patterns of the general population. Thus the frequency of drinking was highest among Jews whose religious orientation is Orthodox, lower among those whose orientation is Conservative, lower still among the Reform, and lowest among the secular, i.e., those who deny any feeling of religious association. But the frequency of drinking large amounts on an occasion, of getting drunk, or of getting into trouble on account of drinking ran in the opposite direction, from highest among the secular to lowest among the Orthodox. This suggested to some sociologists that alcoholism among Jews may increase as acculturation proceeded. But two antithetic findings reported that Jews who ostensively drink in the acculturated style consider themselves to have overindulged or "been drunk" after substantially smaller quantities than non-Jews; and the acculturated drinking style tends to be abandoned on settling down and starting to raise children. Only in the United States has Jewish drinking been studied extensively and systematically, but observers in many countries continue to report the pattern of sobriety. Some theorists speculated that the pattern may change in a Jewish state and, that drunkenness is more common among some Eastern Jews than among Westerners. However, although statistics on admission of alcoholics to mental hospitals in Israel in former years are not known, in 1966 78 new cases were admitted (2% of all new cases; in some countries alcoholism accounts for up to 25% of admissions to mental hospitals). The total admission of alcoholics was 154 in 1966 (2% of all admissions); and during a six-year period, only 23 deaths were attributed to alcoholism or its complications. Recent data on Jews in the United States are not available, but in New York State in 1950 0.2% of new cases were alcoholics. There was some evidence of greater alcoholic indulgence by Oriental-born Jews in Israel (but not in those of Oriental descent). Asian and African-born male Jews had twice the rate of first admission for alcoholism to mental hospitals than European-born men did. Israel-born Jews, of whatever descent, had only a third of the rate of the European-born. The rates in women of all origin groups were negligible. Thus there were no signs at the time of serious alcohol problems developing in Israel. However, with the development of a "pub" and "disco" culture among Israeli youth through the 1980s and 1990s and the influx of immigrants from the former Soviet Union with its more marked drinking tradition, not to mention growing disaffection in the economic underbelly of Israeli society, drinking has come to be perceived as more of a problem, though still not reaching the proportions characteristic of other societies.

[Mark Keller]

BIBLIOGRAPHY: IN THE BIBLE: Kaufmann Y., Religion, 321, 374; B. Porten, *Archives from Elephantine* (1968), 179–86; G.R. Driver, in: *Words and Meanings, Essays... D.W. Thomas* (1968), 47–67; L. Milano (ed.), *Drinking in Ancient Societies* (1994). MODERN TIMES: D. Cahalan, I. Cisin and H.R. Crossley, *American Drinking Practices* (1970); V. Efron and M. Keller, *Selected Statistical Tables on the Consumption of Alcohol and on Alcoholism* (1963); Keller, in: *British Journal of Addiction*, 64 (1969); King, in: *Quarterly Journal of Studies on Alcohol*, 22 (1961), 321; Knupfer and Room, *ibid.*, 28 (1967), 676; C.R. Snyder, *Alcohol and the Jews* (1958); Shuval and Krasilowsky, in: *Israel Annual of Psychiatry*, 1 (1964), 277; 3 (1965), 249.

DRUSILLA (b. 38 C.E.), daughter of *Agrippa I and *Cypros. Drusilla had been promised in marriage by her father to Epiphanes, son of King Antiochus of Commagene. The agreement was canceled, however, when Epiphanes refused to convert to Judaism, after originally agreeing to do so. Drusilla was later married by her brother *Agrippa II to Azizus, king of Emesa, who had consented to be circumcised. Shortly afterward, a Jewish magician from Cyprus persuaded Drusilla to leave her husband and marry his friend *Felix, the procurator of Judea. Out of this marriage a son was born, named Agrippa. Josephus alludes to the disappearance of this son and his wife during the eruption of Vesuvius in 79 C.E.

BIBLIOGRAPHY: Jos., Wars, 2:220; Jos., Ant., 18:132; 19:354–5; 20:139–44; Acts 24:24; Schuerer, Hist, 573.

[Isaiah Gafni]

°DRUSIUS (Van Der Driesche), JOHANN CLEMENS (1550–1616), Dutch theologian, Hebraist, and Bible scholar. A native of Oudenarde (East Flanders), he was professor of Oriental languages at Oxford (from 1572) and later in Leiden, Ghent, and Franeker. Drusius wrote several books on Hebrew grammar, including *Alphabetum ebraicum vetus* (1587) and *Grammatica linguae sanctae nova* (1612). He also edited Elijah *Levita's Hebrew-Yiddish dictionary, *Shemot Devarim* (*Nomenclator Eliae Levitae*, 1652), adding to it the Arabic; his son Johann added the Greek. He wrote several works of biblical exegesis.

BIBLIOGRAPHY: Zunz, Gesch, 11; Steinschneider, Handbuch s.v.; Steinschneider, Cat Bod, 895, no. 4877; Abel Curiandez, *Vita Joannis Drusii* (1618).

DRUYA (Pol. **Druja**), town in Molodechno district, Belarus. The Jewish community is mentioned in the late 16th century. Many Jews there were occupied in the local soap industry and others traded in farm products, like flax, grain, and hides. They dominated trade. In the late 18th century a beautiful synagogue was constructed. The community numbered 1,305 in 1766; 2,366 in 1847; 3,006 in 1897 (out of a total population of 4,742); 1,011 (41%) in 1921; and 1,800 in 1925. The author Alter *Druyanow was born in Druya. After WWI, Jewish merchants resumed their trade in agricultural products; others were artisans. The center of cultural life was the Bund-dominated Yiddish school.

[Shmuel Spector (2nd ed.)]

Holocaust Period

On the eve of World War II the Jewish population of Druya numbered about 1,500. Between October 1939 and June 1941 Druya was occupied by the Soviets. On July 6, 1941, after the outbreak of the German-Soviet war, the Germans entered the town. During the first days of the war many people accused of allegiance to the Soviets were killed. In April 1942 two ghettos were created, one for workers, the second for non-workers. On

July 2, 1942, the Germans surrounded the ghettos in order to liquidate them. The inhabitants tried to break out and some groups succeeded in reaching the forests. In order to prevent a mass escape, the Germans shot at Jews and set the ghettos aflame. Some of those who escaped to the forest joined the partisans around the village of Balnia and participated in activities against the Germans. About 50–60 persons survived.

[Aharon Weiss]

BIBLIOGRAPHY: I. Schipper, *Dzieje handlu żydowskiego na ziemach polskich* (1937), index; B. Wasiutiński, *Ludność żydowska w Polsce…* (1930), 84; O. Hedemann, *Dzisna i Druja* (1934); A. Druyanow, in: *Reshumot*, 1 (1925), 437–49; Yad Vashem Archives.

DRUYANOW, ALTER (**Asher, Avraham Abba**; 1870–1938), Hebrew writer, editor, and Zionist leader. Born in Druya, in the district of Vilna, he studied at the Volozhin yeshivah in his youth and then turned to commerce. In 1890 he published his first essay in *Ha-Meliẓ*, under the pen name "Alef, Beit, Gimmel, Dalet," and from then on was a frequent contributor to the Hebrew press (*Mi-Mizraḥ u-mi-Ma'arav; Ha-Shilo'aḥ*, etc.), using various pen names. From 1900 to 1905 he was the secretary of the Committee for the Settlement of Ereẓ Israel in Odessa. In 1906 he immigrated to Palestine, but returned to Russia in 1909 and until 1914 was editor of *Ha-Olam*, the official organ of the World Zionist Organization. In 1921 he settled permanently in Palestine. Together with *Bialik and *Ravnitzky, he edited the first four volumes of *Reshumot*, a periodical devoted to the study of folklore (1919–26). His literary work includes Zionist articles, descriptive writing, and literary criticism. He is best remembered for two compilations: *Ketavim le-Toledot Ḥibbat Ẓiyyon ve-Yishuv Ereẓ Yisrael* ("Writings on the History of Ḥibbat Zion and the Settlement of Palestine," 3 vols., 1919–32 (re-edited by Shulamit Laskov, 1982)) and *Sefer ha-Bediḥah ve-ha-Ḥiddud* ("The Book of Jokes and Witticisms," enlarged 3-vol. edition, 1935–38), a collection of Jewish folk humor with notes on the origin and history of the contents. A two-volume selection of his essays was published in 1943–45.

BIBLIOGRAPHY: J. Fichmann, *Be-Terem Aviv* (1959), 371–6; Kressel, Leksikon, 1 (1965), 564; ABGD: *Yad la-Kore*, 9 (1968), 116–8, a bibliography.

DRZEWIECKI, HENRYK (**Hercel Rosenbaum**; 1902–1937), Polish novelist and critic. An avowed Communist, Drzewiecki wrote essays and reviews advocating revolution in order to abolish Poland's economic misery. His controversial novel *Kwaśniacy* (1934) greatly influenced Polish proletarian literature and the writer only escaped imprisonment by fleeing first to Paris and then to the U.S.S.R. He was executed during the Stalinist purges of the late 1930s. He was rehabilitated in 1956.

DUALISM, the religious or philosophical doctrine which holds that reality consists, or is the outcome, of two ultimate principles which cannot be reduced to one more ultimate first cause. Dualistic systems have appeared in philosophical (metaphysical) as well as moral forms, both of which have exerted considerable influence on the history of religions, including the history of Judaism.

Philosophical Dualism

In the history of Western thought, philosophical dualism goes back to *Platonism and *neoplatonism which developed and spread the idea of an opposition between spirit and matter, spirit being the higher, purer, and eternal principle, whereas matter was the lower and imperfect form of being, subject to change and corruption. Applied to the understanding of the nature of man, this meant that man was composed of a lower, material part (the body), and a higher, spiritual part (the soul). This dualism could, and not infrequently did, lead to a contempt for the body and for "this world" in general, and encouraged a moral outlook which held *asceticism (or, in its more extreme forms, total renunciation of the world) to be the way by which the soul could liberate itself from the hold of the body and, purifying itself of the bodily passions, render itself worthy again of returning to its celestial and spiritual home. This view exerted considerable influence on Jewish thinking in the Hellenistic period (see *Philo) and in the philosophy and *Musar literature of the middle ages, though its more radical forms were partly inhibited by the rabbinic tradition which considered the physical universe and its enjoyment as essentially good, provided they were hallowed in the service of God.

Moral Dualism

Although moral dualism generally tended to express itself in the forms of a thoroughgoing metaphysical dualism, the term is justified inasmuch as it reflects the basic doctrine that good and evil were the outcome or product of two distinct and ultimate first causes. The best known form of this dualism is the ancient religion of Persia (Zoroastrianism), according to which history is a cosmic struggle between the powers of good, i.e., light, and evil, i.e., darkness. This system has the logical advantage of accounting for evil in terms of a separate, independent principle, and thus exonerating the "good" creator and God from responsibility for the existence, in the world, of evil and sin. On the other hand it raises many other problems and was unacceptable to any form of *monotheism. Some commentators see in the declaration that God "formed the light and created darkness, is the maker of peace and the creator of evil" (Isa. 45:7) the prophet's polemic against this dualism (a polemic, the harshness of which is mitigated by the wording in which this verse appears in the daily morning prayer: "the maker of peace and creator of all" Hertz, Prayer 109). The two types of "philosophical" and "moral" dualism were capable of fusing and merging in various combinations. The body, matter, and "this world" could become identified, or at least associated, with darkness and evil, and the soul, with goodness and light. Another pair of opposites, "spirit" and "flesh," though not identical with Platonic dualism, was yet sufficiently similar to combine with it in various ways. It is this dualism which underlies the theology and anthropology of the *Dead Sea (*Qumran) sect, and of the epistles of Paul in the New Testament. *Gnosticism presents a peculiar combination of the two types of dualism: this world and our bodily existence, being characterized by evil, are the work of a lower, imperfect deity (the "demiurge" or creator), above whom there is a completely distinct, more transcendent and spiritual, good and "true" god. This higher deity intervenes and "saves" the elect from the power of the evil creator who holds them imprisoned in matter and in this world. Some of the gnostic sects equated this lower and evil demiurge with the god of the Hebrew Bible, i.e., with the Jewish God and giver of the law. Gnostic dualism has therefore been described as a metaphysical antisemitism. The gnostic rejection of creation and the cosmos, as well as of the biblical law, as the work of a lower, evil, or at least imperfect, power led in some cases to manifestations of *antinomianism, and in others to a very rigorous asceticism and rejection of this world.

Dualism in Jewish History

Whether or not Isaiah 45:7 is a polemical reference to Persian dualism (see above), it is evident that dualistic tendencies asserted themselves in the Second Temple period and in the first centuries of the common era. These were of a neoplatonic, later also of a gnostic, character. In a general way it can be said that apart from the "heretical" dualistic doctrines of some gnostic sectarians (see **Minim*), Judaism could accommodate a "mitigated dualism," i.e., doctrines and attitudes which express metaphysical or moral contrasts in a dualistic manner, but without attributing to them an ultimate character or calling in question the sovereignty of the one omnipotent and good Creator God. This mitigated dualism can be found in some of the biblical *Apocrypha (e.g., *Jubilees or the Testaments of the *Patriarchs) and especially in the writings of the Dead Sea sect, whose doctrines of the spirit and the flesh, of the spirits (or angels), of purity and impurity, i.e., of light and darkness, come as near to a dualistic system as Judaism could tolerate. Yet even these beliefs can be characterized as a "dualism under God," since the spirits of light and darkness were held to exist through God's inscrutable will and to be subject to him. The Platonic dualistic spirit-matter (i.e., the realm of ideas as against the material world) penetrated rabbinic Judaism in the form of the soul-body dualism (cf. Plato's *Phaedo*, 67), and the belief in the preexistence of the soul. The doctrine of the immortality of the (spiritual) soul reflects, in this respect, a more dualistic anthropology than the doctrine of the resurrection of the body (see *Eschatology, Immortality of *Soul, *Resurrection). Rabbinic theology in general tended to reject or at least to mitigate dualistic tendencies. Thus the doctrine of the good and evil *yeẓer* (see Good and Evil *Inclination) is a transposition onto a more psychological (and hence theologically more harmless) level of what, for the Qumran covenanters and others, were metaphysical opposites. Talmudic literature has many polemical references to those who believe in *shetei reshuyyot* ("two powers"). Other polemical references are directed at the gnostic distinction between the supreme God on the one hand, and the Creator-Lawgiver on the other. Thus the *kofer ba-ikkar* (one who denies the essence of the faith) is said to be one who denies his creator and the giver of the Law (cf. Tosef. Shav. 3:7).

Dualism in Jewish Mysticism

The esoteric discipline and ecstatic visionary practices of the early *Merkabah mystics, while exhibiting certain gnostic traits, certainly did not share the basic dualism of the great gnostic systems. Dualistic elements, however, were not absent, as, e.g., in the doctrine of *Metatron (originally Javel) as the "lesser YHWH." In fact, the term *yozer bereshit* ("Creator") was deprived of any possible gnostic connotation by being used, in the **Shi'ur Komah* literature, for the manifestation of God on the Throne of Glory. Another kind of dualism is involved in the radical distinction made by the kabbalists between the hidden, inaccessible *deus absconditus* (the *Ein Sof*), and the godhead as manifested in the **Sefirot*. The latter two are occasionally described in a dualistic manner (right-left, male-female), but the essential point of the kabbalists was precisely the ultimate mystical unity behind the multiple manifestations.

The dualistic tendency is, perhaps, most marked in the kabbalistic treatment of the problem of evil. The profound sense of the reality of evil brought many kabbalists to posit a realm of the demonic, the *sitra aḥra* (or "*aẓilut* of the left"), a kind of negative mirror image of the "side of holiness" with which it was locked in combat. Nevertheless, here too it is necessary to distinguish between dualistic tendency and dualistic theory. It is precisely because kabbalistic doctrine does not know an ultimate dualism, that it is forced to seek the origin of the demonic realm of the *kelippot* somewhere in the sphere of divine emanation – whether in the *sefirah gevurah* (*din*) or (as in Lurianic kabbalism) in even more hidden aspects of the godhead. More than anything else, it is this awareness of the reality of evil, coupled with an essentially monotheistic rather than dualistic theology of the Zoroastrian type, which gives kabbalistic speculation such an audacious and indeed all but "heretical" quality. In medieval philosophy, the solution proposed for the problem of evil and its possible dualistic implications was the theory that evil had no substantial existence of its own but was a negation of good, even as darkness was the absence of light (cf. *Maimonides, *Guide*, 3:8; see also *Good and Evil). The first Jewish philosopher to argue systematically and at length against dualistic notions was *Saadiah Gaon in his *Beliefs and Opinions* (treatise 2).

Prophetic Dualism

While Judaism can thus be said to have been consistently anti-dualistic in the sense of recognizing only one ultimate cause and source of all being – including the opposites characteristic of being – there is another sense in which biblical and prophetic religion can be said to be dualistic. It assumes a radical distinction between the absolute being of God and the contingent being of all other (i.e., created) things. Contact and communion with God is possible in love, obedience, or mystical contemplation, but no identity of the creature with the creator is possible. Systems of thought which assert that all being is ultimately one and that the duality of God and the world (or God and the soul) can be transcended in a more profound unity have not been able to maintain themselves in any significant measure in Judaism. Pantheism and other forms of metaphysical or mystical monism (see *God, Conceptions of) have never been dominant Jewish philosophies.

BIBLIOGRAPHY: S. Pétrement, *Le dualisme chez Platon, les gnostiques et les manichéens* (1947); Guttmann, Philosophies, index; D. Flusser, in: *Scripta Hierosolymitana*, 4 (1958), 215–66; G.R. Driver, *The Judean Scrolls* (1965), 550–62; A.C. Leaney, *The Rule of Qumran and its Meaning* (1966), index; M. Burrows, *More Light on the Dead Sea Scrolls* (1958), index; I. Tishby, *Mishnat ha-Zohar*, 1 (1949), 285–343.

[R.J. Zwi Werblowsky]

°**DU BARTAS, GUILLAUME DE SALLUSTE** (1544–1590), French poet and diplomat. Du Bartas served Henry of Navarre as ambassador to England and Scotland. A Gascon Protestant, he opposed the paganism of the Pléiade group of poets and wrote baroque verse imbued with the spirit of the Bible. *Judith* (1573) commemorates the apocryphal Jewish heroine. The epic *La Semaine* (1578), which retells the Creation story of Genesis, and its sequel, *La Seconde Semaine* (begun in 1584, but never completed), set out to unfold the history of mankind to the beginning of the Christian era. The *Semaines* are outstanding for their lofty tone and moral purpose, though the style and imagery are often grotesque. Their encyclopedic conception betrays the influence of Du Bartas' erudite contemporary, Guy *Le Fèvre de la Boderie. Du Bartas' Hebrew scholarship may have been modest but his respect for and interest in Hebrew studies and the *Kabbalah (typical of the French humanists) may be deduced from the lengthy "Hommage au langage hebrieu" in the *Seconde Semaine.* Du Bartas made a powerful impression in the 16th and 17th centuries and probably influenced Hugo, as well as Milton and Goethe, in translation.

BIBLIOGRAPHY: U.T. Holmes (ed.), *Works of Guillaume De Salluste Sieur Du Bartas* (1935–40); A.M. Schmidt, *Poésie scientifique en France au 16è siècle* (1938), 247–69; F. Secret, in: *Studi francesi*, 7 (1959), 1–11.

[Godfrey Edmond Silverman]

DUBERMAN, MARTIN B. (1930–), U.S. historian and playwright. Duberman, who was born in New York City, entered Yale University in 1948 and received his M.A. and Ph.D. from Harvard University. From 1957 to 1961, he was history instructor at Yale. He then became an assistant professor at Princeton University and full professor in 1967. Duberman's research centered on the "middle period" of American history, with special attention given to the Civil War and Reconstruction, American radicalism, and intellectual history. His publications include *Charles Francis Adams, 1807–86* (1961) and *James Russell Lowell* (1966). Duberman, himself an advocate of dissent and deeply concerned with the advancement of human rights, edited *Antislavery Vanguard: New Essays on the Abolitionists* (1965). He also wrote a number of plays, notably *In White America* (1964), a documentary on the American black.

After exposing glaring instances of homophobia in his history *Black Mountain: An Exploration of Community* (1971), Duberman himself became the target of homophobic attacks from his academic peers. Subsequently, he became involved in gay activism on academic, public, and private levels. With fellow gay scholars, he founded the Gay Academic Union (1973) and joined the National Gay and Lesbian Task Force.

In 1971, Duberman resigned from Princeton to become Distinguished Professor of History in the field of gay and lesbian studies at Lehman College, the City University of New York (CUNY), where he continued to teach. He was the founder and first executive director of the Center for Lesbian and Gay Studies (CLAGS) at CUNY. The Martin Duberman Fellowship is a CLAGS endowment awarded to a senior scholar (tenured university professor or advanced independent scholar) from any country doing scholarly research on the lesbian/gay/bisexual/transgender/queer (LGBTQ) experience.

Other publications by Duberman include *The Uncompleted Past* (1969), *The Memory Bank* (1970), *Visions of Kerouac: A Play* (1977), *About Time: Exploring the Gay Past* (1986), *Paul Robeson* (1989), *Hidden from History: Reclaiming the Gay and Lesbian Past* (1989), *Cures: A Gay Man's Odyssey* (1991), *Mother Earth: An Epic Play on the Life of Emma Goldman* (1991), *Stonewall* (1993), *Midlife Queer: Autobiography of a Decade, 1971–1981* (1996), *A Queer World: The Center for Lesbian and Gay Studies Reader* (1997), *Left Out: The Politics of Exclusion: Essays 1964–2002* (2002), and the novel *Haymarket* (2003).

[Mark D. Hirsch / Ruth Beloff (2nd ed.)]

DUBIN, MORDECAI (1889–1956), *Agudat Israel leader in Latvia. Dubin represented his movement in the Latvian houses of representatives (1919–34). From 1920 until 1940 he was also the chairman of the Jewish community in Riga. He acquired a reputation among all sectors of the Jewish population as a negotiator and mediator (*shtadlan*) with the government on Jewish public matters and particularly for Jewish individual needs. An adherent of *Chabad Ḥasidism, in 1927 he played a decisive part in obtaining permission for Joseph Isaac *Schneersohn (the "Lubavitcher rabbi") to leave the Soviet Union. Even after the liquidation of the democratic regime in Latvia, Dubin, who was personally close to the dictator Ulmanis, continued to intercede with the government to obtain alleviation of anti-Jewish economic measures. With the incorporation of Latvia into the Soviet Union in June 1940, Dubin was arrested with other communal leaders and deported. He was released in 1942 and subsequently lived under police supervision and extreme poverty in Kuibyshev and Moscow. In spite of his personal plight he succeeded in extending help to many Latvian Jews who passed through these cities. In 1946 he returned to

Riga, but was forced to leave after attacks against him were published in the local Communist press. Again arrested in 1948, he died in a concentration camp near Moscow. His remains were buried in the Jewish cemetery in Malakhovka, a suburb of Moscow.

BIBLIOGRAPHY: *Yahadut Latvia* (1953), index; M. Bobe, in; *He-Avar*, 14 (1967), 250–61.

[Yehuda Slutsky]

DUBINSKY, DAVID (1892–1982), U.S. labor leader. Born in Brest-Litovsk, Belorussia, Dubinsky was brought up in the Polish city of Lodz, where he became a master baker and secretary of the militant Lodz Bakers Union organized by the *Bund. He was arrested and imprisoned for organizing strikes against his father's bakery, and was exiled to Siberia in 1909 for making inflammatory speeches. He managed to escape en route, however, and at the end of 1910 immigrated to the United States. He joined his elder brother in New York and obtained work through the International Ladies Garment Workers' Union (ILGWU) becoming an apprentice in Cutters' Local 10. He devoted more of his time to the Socialist party than to trade union affairs until larger numbers of East European Socialist Jews entered Local 10, but in 1918 he was elected to its executive board. In 1921 he was chosen president of the Cutters' Local. Dubinsky also rose rapidly in the ILGWU, where he joined the anti-Communist majority. He was elected to its general executive board in 1923. In 1928 he played a leading part in bringing back Benjamin *Schlesinger as a compromise candidate for president to avoid a split in the union, and in the following year was himself elected secretary-treasurer. On Schlesinger's death in 1932 he became president, a position he held until 1966.

During the 1930s Dubinsky dominated the ILGWU and was a powerful force in the American labor movement. He favored cooperation with the employers in rationalizing the complex structure of the garment industry and made his union a symbol of progressive unionism. In 1934 he was elected a vice president of the AFL. Almost immediately he became embroiled in the controversy between the proponents of industrial unionism and the supporters of the old-style craft union. He played a leading part in the CIO which he helped to found in 1935, his union being the second largest in the country. In 1936 he resigned his vice-presidency of the AFL in protest against their support of the craft unions against the industrial unions, and persuaded the ILGWU to give their backing to the latter. For two years from 1938 the ILGWU was isolated from the American labor movement, but in 1940 Dubinsky brought it back into the AFL. In his capacity as president of the ILGWU for more than 30 years, he transformed the union from a struggling entity to one with assets in the hundreds of millions of dollars. Under his guidance, the union took on issues such as the provision of health insurance, severance pay, retirement benefits, and a 35-hour workweek. He also worked to abolish the sweatshops that were prevalent in the industry.

An influential figure in United States politics, Dubinsky refused to endorse Tammany Hall, New York's political machine, and supported Franklin D. *Roosevelt for president in 1932 and 1936. To this end he helped to create the American Labor Party (ALP) in 1936. In 1944, when Communists began to dominate the ALP, he helped to form the Liberal Party. After World War II Dubinsky was one of the founders of the anti-Communist International Confederation of Free Trade Unions. In 1945 he served once again as a vice president and member of the executive council of the AFL, even after it merged with the CIO in 1955. Due largely to his efforts to eliminate corrupt union leaders, the AFL-CIO adopted the anti-racket codes in 1957.

In 1969 U.S. President Lyndon Johnson awarded Dubinsky the Presidential Medal of Freedom, which cited him as "a national leader of foresight and compassion. He has advanced the cause of the workingman in America – and the broader cause of social justice in the world, with unfailing skill and uncommon distinction." In 1993 Dubinsky was inducted into the Labor Hall of Fame.

As a self-styled "Jewish worker," Dubinsky was concerned with the special problems facing the Jewish community as a consequence of events in Germany and World War II. He was a member of the executive council of the Jewish Labor Committee founded in 1933, engaged in relief efforts on behalf of refugees, and became a staunch supporter of Israel and in particular of the *Histadrut, Israel's General Federation of Labor. A hospital in Beersheba, financed by his union, carries his name. Dubinsky wrote *David Dubinsky: A Life with Labor* (1977).

BIBLIOGRAPHY: M.D. Danish, *The World of David Dubinsky* (1957); J. Dewey, *David Dubinsky, a Pictorial Biography* (1951); C.A. Madison, *American Labor Leaders* (1962), 199–231; R. Cook, *Leaders of Labor* (1966), 102–12.

[Melvyn Dubofsky / Ruth Beloff (2nd ed.)]

DUBISLAV, WALTER ERNST OTTO (1895–1937), German philosopher. Born in Berlin, he studied mathematics with Hilbert at Goettingen, served on the Russian front in World War I, and took his degree in philosophy at Berlin after the war. He became professor at the Technische Hochschule in Berlin in 1931, and fled in 1936 to Prague. Dubislav was a logical positivist and conventionalist, influenced by Aristotle, Bolzano, and Frege. He was critical of Kant and a supporter of Fries, and was, with Reichenbach, a leader of the "Gesellschaft fuer empirische Philosophie." Dubislav participated in *Das systematische Woerterbuch der Philosophie* (1923) and wrote *Ueber die Definition* (1925, 1931^3), *Die Friessche Lehre von der Begruendung* (1926), *Die Philosophie der Mathematik in der Gegenwart* (1932), and *Naturphilosophie* (1933).

BIBLIOGRAPHY: NDB, 4 (1959), 145.

[Richard H. Popkin]

DUBLIN, capital of the Republic of Ireland. A small Jewish group apparently lived there in the Middle Ages since the Exchequer of the Jews at Westminster had an Irish branch. In the middle of the 17th century, some Spanish and Portuguese Marranos settled in the city, including Francisco and Manuel Lopes Pereira and Jacome Faro. According to tradition, a synagogue was founded in Crane Lane around 1660. Military operations in Ireland after the revolution of 1689 attracted a few more Sephardi Jews, and the community knew a short period of relative prosperity. In 1718 a cemetery was purchased with the assistance of the London Sephardi community, which advanced the Dublin congregation money to meet its debts and lent it some scrolls of the Law. During the 18th century, the original Sephardi element died out, and was replaced by Ashkenazi immigrants. By 1791 the congregation had fallen into complete decay and the borrowed scrolls were returned. The community was revived in 1882 by East European immigrants. It increased considerably with the Russo-Jewish immigration at the close of the century. Many of the Jews of that time engaged in peddling, small business, and small financial transactions (moneylending and pawnbroking). In the course of time the Jews moved into shopkeeping, manufacturing, and the professions. There has been considerable emigration over the years, especially among the younger generation. In 1968 the Jewish population numbered approximately 3,600 and maintained seven synagogues (including one Progressive) with the usual congregational institutions. James Joyce's *Ulysses* depicts certain elements of Jewish life in Dublin at the beginning of the century. Paradoxically, many literary visitors to today's Dublin come to see the route taken on "Bloomsday" by James Joyce's Leopold Bloom. Isaac *Herzog, later chief rabbi of Israel, was chief rabbi of Dublin 1919–36. Immanuel *Jakobovits was chief rabbi from 1949 and Isaac Cohen from 1959. Robert *Briscoe was lord mayor from 1956–57 and from 1961–62, and his son in the 1980s. In the mid-1990s the Jewish population numbered approximately 1,300. In 2004, after some renewed growth, it was estimated at about 1,500.

BIBLIOGRAPHY: B. Shillman, *Short History of the Jews in Ireland* (1945), passim; Shillman and Wolf, in: JHSET, 11 (1924–27), 143–67; Huehner, *ibid.*, 5 (1902–05), 224–42; C. Roth, *Rise of Provincial Jewry* (1950), 56f; L. Hyman, *Jews of Ireland* (1972). **ADD. BIBLIOGRAPHY:** D. Keogh, *Jews in Twentieth Century Ireland* (1998); R. Rivlin, *Shalom Ireland: A Social History of the Jews in Modern Ireland* (2003).

[Cecil Roth]

DUBNO, city in *Volhynia, Ukraine. Jews in Dubno are first mentioned in documents of 1532 in connection with the ownership of cattle. The oldest tombstone inscription in the Jewish cemetery dates from 1581. At the beginning of the 17th century Isaiah ha-Levi *Horowitz, author of *Shenei Luḥot ha-Berit*, was rabbi in Dubno. The community was represented on the council of the province (*galil*) of Volhynia (see *Councils of the Lands). On the eve of the *Chmielnicki uprising there were about 2,000 Jews in Dubno. In 1648–49, most of the Jews were massacred because the Poles refused to permit them to take refuge in the fortress. According to tradition the graves of the martyrs were located near the eastern wall of the great synagogue, where it was customary to mourn them on the Ninth of Av.

The Jewish community was reestablished shortly afterward under the patronage of the owners of the town, the princes Lubomirski, who accorded it special privileges in 1699 and 1713. By the beginning of the 18th century Dubno had become the largest Jewish community in Volhynia, being represented on the Council of the Four Lands and earning the sobriquet "Dubno the Great" (*Dubno Rabbati*). Its delegate, R. Meir ben Joel, was chosen to be head (*parnas*) of the Council of the Four Lands in the late 1750s. As many blood libels occurred then in Poland, R. Meir sent his relative R. Eliokim-Zelig of Yampol to the pope in Rome, to get bull against the libels, which he published in Latin and Polish. Jewish poll tax payers numbered 1,923 in 1765. The great fair of *Lvov was moved to Dubno between 1773 and 1793, and the city became an important commercial center. The most famous of the 18th-century Jewish preachers of Lithuania, Jacob *Kranz, was known as the Maggid of Dubno after the city with which he was most closely associated. In the 19th century Haskalah (Enlightenment) activists like the physician and writer Reuben Kalischer, the lexicographer and poet Solomon *Mandelkern (author of a monumental Bible concordance), and the poet and writer Abraham Baer *Gottlober lived there. In 1780 the Jewish population numbered 2,325, in 1847, 6,330, and in 1897, 7,108 (about half the total). A main occupation was dealing in grain and hops. During World War I and the civil war in Russia (to 1921), the city changed hands a number of times and the community suffered extreme hardship, mainly of an economic nature. In March 1918 the Cossacks staged a pogrom killing 18 Jews. While Dubno belonged to Poland (1921–39), the community maintained many cultural institutions and there was an active Zionist and pioneer movement. In 1921 they numbered 5,315 (total population 9,146), and in 1931, 7,364 (total population 12,696).

[Yehuda Slutsky / Shmuel Spector (2nd ed.)]

Holocaust and Postwar Periods

After the outbreak of World War II Dubno was occupied by Soviet forces (Sept. 18, 1939). The Soviet authorities liquidated the Jewish community institutions, made all political parties illegal, transferred Jewish welfare institutions to the municipality, and allowed only one Jewish activity – the public kitchen for refugees from the West. All Jewish economic enterprises and buildings were nationalized. Jewish leaders, among them David Perl, president of the Zionist Organization, were arrested. When the German-Soviet war broke out (June 1941), hundreds of young Jewish men escaped from Dubno to the Soviet interior. After the Germans entered Dubno (June 25), the local Ukrainian population indulged in acts of murder and robbery, while the Germans extracted 100,000 rubles ($20,000) from the Jewish community. On July 22, 1941, 80 Jews were executed by the Nazis in the local cemetery; one month later 900 were killed. The Germans organized a Judenrat headed by Konrad Tojbenfeld. The Jewish population was conscripted for forced labor and many succumbed to the unbearable conditions. The winter that followed (1941–42) was marked by hunger and disease, despite the attempts to provide relief by organizing public kitchens. Two ghettoes were established at the beginning of April 1942, one for the workers and their families and the second for the rest of the Jews. On May 26–27, 1942, the Germans murdered all the Jews in the second ghetto, burying them in mass graves on the outskirts of the city. In August 1942 Jews from the environs and survivors were brought to the first ghetto. On October 5, 1942, about 4,500 inhabitants of the ghetto were murdered. The remaining 353, needed as artisans, were murdered on October 23, 1942, and the last 14 Jews escaped. Two partisan groups were formed by Dubno escapees. One headed by Isaac Wasserman was wiped out by the Germans, the other suffered losses in battles and the last 16 fighters joined the Polish self-defense units which fought the Ukrainian UPA. When the war was over only about 300 Jews from Dubno remained alive, including those who had returned from the Soviet Union. No Jewish community was reestablished after the war.

[Aharon Weiss / Shmuel Spector (2nd ed.)]

Hebrew Printing

The first Hebrew printing press was set up in Dubno in 1794 by Jonathan b. Jacob of Wielowies, Silesia. Jonathan's partner was M. Piotrowsky, a non-Jew, and the business was under the patronage of Prince Lubomirski, the ruler of the town, whose escutcheon and initials appeared on the title pages. The press was active for nine years and produced 22 books. Another press was founded in 1804 by the printer Aaron b. Jonah, who owned a similar business in Ostrog, in partnership with Joseph b. Judah Leib. During the four years Aaron was in Dubno ten books were published. Dubno's rabbi, Ḥayyim Mordecai Margolioth, established a press in 1819, printing works by his brother Ephraim Zalman of Brody, and a Shulḥan Arukh with his own commentaries (*Sha'arei Teshuvah*) and those of his brother (*Yad Ephraim*). The press was closed after a fire.

BIBLIOGRAPHY: P. Pesis, *Ir Dubno ve-Rabbaneha* (1902); H.S. Margolies, *Dubno Rabbati* (1910); H.D. Friedberg, *Toledot ha-Defus ha-Ivri be-Polanyah* (1950²), 119–20; A. Yaari, in: KS, 9 (1932/33), 432; Rivkind, *ibid.*, 11 (1934/35), 386–7. **HOLOCAUST PERIOD:** M. Weisberg, in: *Fun Letstn Khurbn*, 2 (1946), 14–27; Elimelekh, in; *Yalkut Volhyn*, 1 (1945), index; Fefer, *ibid.*, index; *Dubno* (1966), memorial book (Heb. and Yid.). **ADD. BIBLIOGRAPHY:** PK.

DUBNO, SOLOMON BEN JOEL (1738–1813), Bible scholar and Hebrew poet. Dubno took his name from his birthplace in the Ukraine and studied in Lemberg (Lvov) under Solomon b. Moses *Chelm, whose *Sha'arei Ne'imah* on the masoretic accents he published in 1776 with annotations and an introductory poem (also appended to some editions of Judah Leib Ben-Ze'ev's *Talmud Leshon Ivri*, 1886). From 1767 to 1772 he lived and studied in Amsterdam and then in Berlin, where he was engaged by Moses *Mendelssohn as private tutor for his son Joseph. On Dubno's suggestion Mendelssohn undertook his famous German translation of the Bible and Hebrew commentary, known as the *Biur*. For that work Dubno prepared the prospectus with a lengthy introduction, *Alim li-Terufah* (1778), and contributed the commentary on Genesis (except ch. 1) and part of Exodus as well as annotations to the Masorah of Genesis and Exodus, *Tikkun Soferim*. Dubno, however, left Berlin in 1781 for Vilna before the *Biur* on the Pentateuch, *Netivot ha-Shalom*, appeared in 1783. He had been prompted, apparently, by his friends in Russia such as Zalman Volozkin, who disapproved of his association with Mendelssohn and his circle, and who encouraged him to write his own Bible commentary. Nevertheless, Mendelssohn paid generous tribute to Dubno's work in his introduction to the *Biur*. In 1786 he returned to Germany and finally to Amsterdam, where he lived in penury, though he possessed a valuable library of over 2,000 books, some of them very rare, and over 100 manuscripts, for which he prepared a catalog, *Reshimah* (1814). In Amsterdam he published a commentary on the Masorah of the whole Pentateuch, *Tikkun Soferim* (1803). Dubno also wrote a good deal of Hebrew poetry, e.g., *Yuval ve-Na'aman* (n. d.); *Evel Yaḥid* (1776), a eulogy on the death of Jacob Emden; and *Kol Simḥah* (1780), in honor of the wedding of Simḥah Bunim b. Daniel Jaffe (*Itzig). He published M. Ḥ. Luzzatto's drama *La-Yesharim Tehillah* (1780 or 1799) with an introduction and wrote a preface, interspersed with poetry, to Heidenheim's edition of the Shavuot *maḥzor* (1805). Dubno also wrote a geography of Palestine, *Kunteres Aharon* (Berlin, n.d.).

In his Bible commentary Dubno followed mainly the medieval exegetes, but added historical and geographical explanations as well as defending his own traditional position. He was the first Jewish commentator to dwell on the structure and didactic style of the Bible stories. In his notes on the masoretic accents, he stressed their exegetical importance as well as their antiquity.

BIBLIOGRAPHY: I. Zinberg, *Geshikhte fun der Literatur bay Yidn*, 7 pt. 1 (1936), 53–62, 82, 134, 256; P. Sandler, *Ha-Be'ur la-Torah shel Moshe Mendelssohn ve-Si'ato* (1941), 16–30; Zobel, in: KS, 18 (1941/42), 126–32; R. Mahler, *Divrei Yemei Yisrael*, 4 (1956), 30–33; Beit-Arié, in: KS, 40 (1964/65), 124–32; A. Marx, *Studies in Jewish History and Booklore* (1944), 219–21; F.J. Delitzsch, *Zur Geschichte der juedischen Poesie* (1836), 118; Kressel, Leksikon, 1 (1965), 524–5.

[Jacob S. Levinger]

DUBNOW, SIMON (1860–1941), historian and political ideologist. Born in Mstislavl, Belorussia, Dubnow received a traditional Jewish education from his grandfather, but early in his life ceased to observe religious practices. He was self-taught, having achieved his general education at "the home university," as he put it. Between 1880 and 1906 Dubnow lived, first illegally, in St. Petersburg; in his home town; in Odessa, where he joined the *Aḥad Ha-Am circle; and Vilna, writing all the time for the Jewish press. He finally settled in St. Petersburg, this time legally, teaching Jewish history, which from then on became his dominating interest; from 1908 at the Institute of Jewish Studies (established by Baron David *Guenzburg); and from 1919 at the government-supported "Jewish

People's University." Dubnow was one of the founders and directors of the Jewish Historico-Ethnographical Society and from 1909 to 1918 editor of its quarterly *Yevreyskaya Starina*. When the Bolsheviks came to power, Dubnow was asked to participate in the work of various committees appointed to prepare publications on Jewish themes; none of this work was ever published.

In 1922 he left Russia. A proposal for him to become professor of Jewish history at the University of Kovno met with the opposition of the Lithuanian professors, and Dubnow settled in Berlin, where he stayed until 1933. When Hitler came to power, Dubnow found refuge in Riga, the capital of Latvia. There the aged scholar continued his work in solitude, but with undiminished vigor. Riga was captured by the Germans in July 1941, and in a night of terror, on December 8, 1941, when the Jewish community was deported to a death camp, Dubnow was murdered by a Gestapo officer, a former pupil of his.

Dubnow's lifework was the study of Jewish history, of the relevant source material, and its "sociological" interpretation. He began with the evaluation of such men as I.B. *Levinsohn, *Shabbetai Ẓevi, and Jacob *Frank and his sect (*Razsvet*, 1881; *Voskhod*, 1882). This he followed by a study of *Ḥasidism (*Voskhod*, 1888–93; *Ha-Pardes*, 1894; *Ha-Shilo'aḥ*, 1901). Dubnow then published a series of documents and studies on Jewish life in Eastern Europe (*Voskhod*, 1893–95). He translated H. Graetz's *Volkstuemliche Geschichte der Juden* (1881) into Russian, with an introduction on the philosophy of Jewish history. When the censor prohibited the publication of the translation, Dubnow published his introduction separately (*Voskhod*, 1893; also in German, 1897, 1921^2; in English, *Jewish History*, translated by Henrietta Szold, 1903; and Hebrew, 1953). In 1896, he published in two volumes an adaptation in Russian of S. Baeck's *Geschichte des juedischen Volkes und seiner Literatur* (1878), and of M. Brann's book of the same title (1893), adding a chapter on the history of the Jews in Poland and Russia. In his introduction, for the first time, Dubnow stated his main thesis of Jewish history as a succession of "centers" and their "hegemony" (see below).

In 1898, he began writing his series of works on Jewish history, based on the works of Baeck and Brann: *An Outline of Jewish History* (3 vols., 1925–29; Russian, 1901–05, 1910^2, and translated into many languages); *History of the Jews in Russia and Poland* (3 vols., 1916–20; Russ., 1914, and translated into several languages); and finally his world history of the Jewish people, first published in German (*Die Weltgeschichte des juedischen Volkes*, 10 vols., 1925–29), then in Hebrew (1923–38) and Yiddish (1948–58). A version in the Russian original was published between 1934 and 1938. In 1940 an 11th volume was published in Hebrew, updating the work to World War II. An English translation by M. Spiegel began to appear in 1967. Although engaged in the writing of general Jewish history, Dubnow did not neglect research into its details. Thus, in 1922, he published the *pinkas* of the Council of Lithuania for the years 1623–1761. At the age of 70 Dubnow summarized his lifelong study of Ḥasidism in his history of Ḥasidism (Hebrew, 1930–32, many reprints; German, 2 vols., 1931). He also served as an editor of the Russian and English Jewish encyclopedias. Dubnow's activities in the field of journalism began with the foreign editorship of *Razsvet* (1881–83), and from 1883 to 1908 he was the literary critic of *Voskhod*.

Dubnow believed that his study of history gave him the key to the understanding of the past, enabled him to work for the improvement of the present, and even provided the solution for the future of the Jewish people. According to him the Jewish people in the Diaspora lost some of the attributes which normally ensure the continuous existence of a people. As a "natural" compensation it developed instead a special social system and communal ideology. Through these the Jewish people was able to exist in foreign countries in a state of judicial autonomy and spiritual independence. In every period there had been a Jewish community which had been more successful than others in maintaining self-rule and national creativity, and it was this community which became the "center" and exercised "hegemony." In the early Middle Ages it was Babylon, taking over from the Palestinian "center"; this was followed by Spain and the Rhineland; in the late Middle Ages and the beginning of the Modern Age it was the *Councils of the Lands of Poland-Lithuania. During the Middle Ages, the Jews became a "European" people, and they have remained one. Dubnow believed that not only was it possible to establish in modern times a regime of internal independence within the framework of a foreign country, but also that such a regime would rest on firmer foundations and would be more highly developed than during the Middle Ages. At this point he showed the influence of ideas, prevalent in his time, for a "State of Nationalities," which could preserve the unity of the Russian and Austro-Hungarian empires while satisfying the demands for self-rule of the various peoples living in them. The exceptional situation of the Jewish people during the Middle Ages could become a rule of life for many peoples and states in Europe. In this new period of Jewish history, the "center" would be Russian-Polish, with its spiritual strength and aspirations for self-rule. It was Dubnow's hope that under the new conditions Jewish creativity would lose the religious character which it had acquired in the talmudic period and the Middle Ages. Yiddish would be the language in which the new Jewish culture would express itself.

Dubnow's ideas placed him in strong opposition to both Zionism and the various forms of assimilation. In the course of time he became less outspoken in his anti-Zionist attitude but did not give up his basic stand (cf. the amended and "expurgated" Hebrew version of his "Letters on the Old and the New Judaism," 1937, with the original Russian version, 1907). In a series of articles published during World War I in *Novy Voskhod*, he outlined his position on the Jewish problem, demanding an international solution. In *Istoriya yevreyskogo soldata* ("History of a Jewish Soldier," 1918; French, 1929), he described the tragic situation of a Jew serving in a non-Jewish army.

Dubnow took an active part in a number of Jewish activities. In the Society for the Promotion of Culture he joined the Zionists in their struggle for the establishment of national Jewish schools. After the *Kishinev pogrom in 1903, he was among those who called for an active Jewish self-defense. Opposing the policy of the socialist-Marxist *Bund, he strongly supported Jewish participation in the elections to the Duma in 1905, established a Jewish section of the Constitutional Democrat party, and asked the Jewish deputies to join it. Dubnow also took part in the work of the Society for the Full and Equal Rights of the Jewish People in Russia in 1905, but later seceded and founded the Jewish People's Party in 1906. This "Folkist" party never exercised much influence and was weakened by internal dissension. It continued to exist until 1918.

The principal source on Dubnow's life is his autobiography, *Kniga moey zhizni*. The first two volumes appeared in Russian (1930–34; partial Heb. trans., 1936; Yid., 1962; Ger., 1937). A third volume, completed in 1940, was published in Riga shortly before the German conquest; the entire edition was destroyed by the Nazis. A single copy, however, rediscovered in 1956, made it possible to publish a new complete edition in 1957. Portions of Dubnow's private archives are in the possession of the Central *Archives for the History of the Jewish People in Jerusalem. A festschrift on the occasion of his 70th birthday was published in 1930; a memorial volume appeared in 1954, edited by S. Rawidowicz; and a centenary volume, edited by A. Steinberg, appeared in 1963 (all three with bibliographies).

[Joseph Meisl]

Historian and Political Ideologist

In his youth, Dubnow was influenced by the positivism of Comte and his followers, and especially by the philosophy of J.S. Mill, the "Gospel of Individualism" and the "Absolute Freedom of Thought and Speech." For several years Dubnow remained faithful to the teachings of these masters and attacked Judaism sharply in the name of the individual, of scientific thought, and of liberty.

Subsequently he was captivated by the historical world of Judaism. In 1887, having gone through a severe physical and spiritual crisis, he began to strive for a synthesis of "my self-acquired general knowledge and my universal aims… with my inherited treasures of Jewish wisdom and national ideals." To this synthesis he added a profound knowledge of the life and history of Russia and Russian Jewry, and a tremendous capacity for the uncovering of obscure sources of Jewish history. There was, too, the influence of Renan and Taine. Like Taine – who emphasized the importance of *petits faits significatifs*, from which the general principles are evolved – Dubnow placed the stress upon detail, which in its true form can only be found at the source. Both historians taught Dubnow the organic concept of the nation (which they termed "race"), and from Taine, in particular, he took over the idea that the situation of a people and its aspirations are faithfully reflected in the spiritual creations of its great men. Renan's historical concepts made it easier for Dubnow to change his adverse criticism of the Jewish religion into a positive evaluation of it as the revelation of the national spirit. "A mixture of the teachings of Renan and Tolstoy" was "the main element in his state of mind" when he embarked upon the study of Ḥasidism and of Jesus and the Apostles. In theory Dubnow always remained a radical individualist, while as a historian, he admired the national unit and the requirements of its life, though these may put restrictions upon the individual. Again, in theory he was a confirmed rationalist, yet he valued religion and religious movements for their role in serving as the nation's shield and as the expression of its spirit. In the writing of history, Dubnow preferred describing "objective" processes and circumstances, based upon a study of detailed events, to the portrayal of personalities, their feelings, and desires; and he noted with pride that in later editions of his works "many lyrical passages were omitted."

Dubnow viewed Jewish history on the assumption that a people is an organism whose life and development depend upon its environment, the conditions under which it lives, and upon the manner in which it chooses to react to them. "In the course of the centuries, the nation passed from the embryonic stage and achieved its own identity… assumed a certain national form, created a state and forfeited it…, the form of the national type reached its perfection when and, perhaps, because its first statehood was destroyed." Diaspora, as it were, is a fate preordained for the Jewish people, from the moment it entered Ereẓ Israel. Even toward the end of his life – on the eve of the destruction of European Jewry in 1939 – Dubnow restated in precise terms his conviction that "in the view of historism, as opposed to dogmatism, the diaspora was not only a possibility, but a necessity. A people small in numbers but great in quality, situated on the crossroads of the giant nations of Asia and Africa, could not preserve both its state and its nationality, and had perforce to break the barrel in order to preserve the wine – and this was the great miracle in the history of mankind." From this follows his definition of the Jewish people as "a people whose home is the entire world"; and his belief that what is known as Jewry is the result of the growth of a people and its adaptation to the conditions under which it lived; though of a special nature, these do not transcend the general laws of history. "… Ancient tribes combine to form a national entity, a state or kingdom. The kingdom is destroyed and the national entity splits into parts, which reconstitute as the communities." Here lies the source of the "unbroken chain of autonomy… of Jewish communities everywhere." Dubnow was convinced that in this respect the Jewish people was a pioneer of national development far wider in scope and much earlier in time than many nations of the 20th century.

As for the religion of Israel, Dubnow held that until the 19th century it was part of Jewish nationalism, a means of self-defense used by a people which possessed none of the normal defenses of other nations. When the Jewish people, by virtue of its belief in monotheism, became a special group within the pagan (and later Christian) world, having to fight against assimilation, its leaders were forced to make use of religion for the defense of its existence. In the 19th century, however, a Jewish "renaissance" set in, in which, on the one hand, the individual was liberated, and, on the other hand, there arose a new secular interest in the national life. In the development of the Wissenschaft des Judentums in Germany in the 19th century, Dubnow saw one of the manifestations of the Jewish renaissance. He went so far as to try to justify the Jewish converts in the period of the *salons (an observation not included in the Hebrew version of the "World History"). Religion was a discipline imposed upon the national organism, necessary only so long as Jewish culture stood isolated, unrelated to the culture of other peoples, i.e., to the time of *Emancipation. Once Emancipation had taken place, this discipline was no longer desirable. In Ḥasidism Dubnow saw a fresh manifestation of the creative power of Jewish religion among East European Jewry, which had preserved tradition and had not yet entered the era of cooperation with the nations of the world. Such cooperation would enable Jewry to exist as a European people with a secular culture, a people destined to remain a permanent minority in the countries of Europe. Basing his work upon such a concept of history, Dubnow regarded the attempts of Zionism to renew the Jewish State in its ancient land as a pseudo-messianic adventure. He put forth a program for the Jews' future based on these theories which he called *autonomism.

[Haim Hillel Ben-Sasson]

BIBLIOGRAPHY: A.S. Steinberg (ed.), *Simon Dubnow, the Man and His Work* (1963), 225–51, 254–5 (autobiography); S.W. Baron, *History and Jewish Historians* (1964), index; I. Friedlaender, *Dubnow's Theory of Jewish Nationalism* (1905); J. Fraenkel, *Dubnow, Herzl, and Aḥad Ha-am* (1963); Pinson, in: S. Dubnow, *Nationalism and History* (1961^2), 1–65; J. Meisl, in: *Soncino-Blaetter*, 1 (1925/26), 223–47; idem, in: *Festschrift zum siebzigsten Geburtstag* (1930), 266–95; S. Brieman, *Ha-Pulmos bein Lilienblum le-vein Aḥad Ha-Am ve-Dubnow ve-ha-Reka shello* (1951); B.Z. Dinaburg-Dinur, in: *Zion*, 1 (1936), 95–128; E.R. Malachi, in: *Sefer Shimon Dubnow* (1954); S. Niger, in: YIVOA, 1 (1946), 305–17; S. Goodman, in: *Commentary*, 30 (1960), 511–5.

DUBNOW, ZE'EV (1858–1940?), *Bilu member. Dubnow, who was born in Mstislavl, Belorussia, was the elder brother of Simon *Dubnow, the historian. He tended to assimilation in his youth and became interested in the Russian radical movement. After the 1881 pogroms he joined Bilu and went to Ereẓ Israel with its first group in 1882. After working at *Mikveh Israel, Dubnow moved with several friends to Jerusalem, where he was one of the founders of Shaḥu (Hebrew initials for the words "return of the craftsmen and the smiths"), an artisans' association. In his letters to his brother he expressed the ultimate aim of the Bilu movement: "to acquire Ereẓ Israel and return to the Jews their political independence." In 1885 he returned to Mstislavl, "disappointed in the hopes of quick success in settling Ereẓ Israel," but still "a fervent nationalist in his belief." He became a teacher, and assisted his brother in examining historical documents. Dubnow remained in contact with the Biluim in Ereẓ Israel and corresponded with them. Eventually he settled in Moscow, where he died.

BIBLIOGRAPHY: A. Druyanov (ed.), *Ketavim le-Toledot Ḥibbat Ẓiyyon*, 3 (1932), index; A. Hurwitz, in: *He-Avar*, 8 (May 1961), 102–5; I. Klausner, *Be-Hitorer Am* (1962), index.

[Yehuda Slutsky]

DUBNOW-ERLICH, SOPHIA (1885–1986), poet, political activist, critic, translator, and memoirist. Born in Mstislavl, Belarus, she was the eldest child of Ida (Friedlin) and historian Simon *Dubnow. The family moved to Odessa in 1890, where Sophia entered a gymnasium in 1899; upon graduation in 1902, she studied at the Bestuzhev Higher Courses in St. Petersburg. Dubnow-Erlich began her foray into the literary and political worlds in 1904, when her first poem, "Haman and his Demise," appeared in the Russian-Jewish weekly *Budushchnost'* (Future). This satire of the czar's minister of interior, Plehve, was immediately confiscated by the censors. That same year, university officials expelled her from her courses for participating in a student protest. Undeterred, she entered the history-philology department of St. Petersburg University in 1905 and later studied comparative religion and the history of world literature at the Sorbonne (1910–11). Rejoining her family in Vilna, the hotbed of Jewish politics in the Russian Empire, Dubnow-Erlich became an active member of the Social Democratic Labor Party and the Jewish Labor Party and an antimilitarist propagandist.

In 1911 Sophia married Henryk *Erlich (1882–1941), a prominent leader of the leftist Bund in Poland with whom she worked to promote the ideals of Jewish cultural autonomy and socialist internationalism. By 1918, the political situation drove the Dubnow-Erlichs to relocate to Warsaw, where they remained for over 20 years with their two sons. When Warsaw fell to the Nazis in 1939, Erlich was arrested by Soviet authorities and Dubnow-Erlich moved her family to Vilna, where they lived until 1941. She reached the United States in 1942 where she learned of her husband's death and her father's murder by the Nazis. Dubnow-Erlich remained politically active throughout her life, advocating for civil rights and protesting the Vietnam War. She died in New York City.

Dubnow-Erlich contributed over 50 poems, essays, and translations to Russian and Yiddish-language journals and newspapers. She wrote three volumes of symbolist poetry (*Osenniaia svirel': stikhi*, 1911; *Mat'*, 1918; rep. Tel Aviv, 1969; and *Stikhi raznykh let*, 1973); several histories on topics relating to the Bund, including co-editing *Di geshikhte fun 'bund'* (5 vols., New York, 1960–81); a biography of her father (*The Life and Work of S.M. Dubnov*, transl. J. Vowles, ed. J. Shandler, Bloomington, Indiana, 1991; Russian original, 1950); and a memoir, *Khleb i Matsa* ("Bread and Matzah," 1994). Her papers are at YIVO.

BIBLIOGRAPHY: G. Ia. Aaronson, "Dubnov-Erlikh, Sofie (March 9, 1885)," in: *Leksikon fun der nayer yidisher literatur*, 1 (1958), 466–67; C.B. Balin, *To Reveal Our Hearts: Jewish Women Writers in Tsarist Russia* (2000), 156–94; K.A. Groberg, "Sophie Dubnov-Erlich," in: J.B. Litoff (ed.), *European Immigrant Women in the United States: A Biographical Dictionary* (1994); idem, "Dubnov and Dubnova: Intellectual Rapport between Father and Daughter," in: A. Greenberg and K. Groberg (eds.), *Simon Dubnov 50th Yortsayt Volume* (1994).

[Carole B. Balin (2nd ed.)]

DUBOSSARY, town on the Dniester River, E. Moldova. Founded at the end of the 18th century as a Russian fortress, Dubossary developed as a nearby settlement. The inhabitants were employed in the timber trade and log rafting. Jews traded in grain, wine, and prunes. They also grew tobacco. There were 2,506 Jews living in Dubossary (about 1,000 in the town itself) and its vicinity, including the towns of Grigoriopol and Ananyev, by 1847. In 1897 there were 5,220 Jews in Dubossary (43% of the total population). In April 1882 a pogrom was staged, and two Jews were killed, and much property was looted and destroyed. In the beginning of the 20th century the community operated a *talmud torah*, nine *ḥadarim*, and four private schools. An attempt to resuscitate the *blood libel was made in 1903. During the civil war of 1918–20 Jewish *self-defense was organized and the community remained relatively free from the pogroms that occurred at the time. Thousands of refugees making their way to Romania in 1920–22 passed through the town, and many from Dubossary itself also crossed the border. There were 3,630 Jews in Dubossary in 1926 (81% of the total population), dropping to 2,198 (total population 4,250) in 1939. In the 1930s there were about 400 Jewish artisans organized in nine cooperatives, and 227 farmers raising tobacco, while others worked as laborers and clerks.

The Germans occupied Dubossary in mid-July 1941. At the end of August a ghetto was set up, and on September 1 the town was annexed to Romanian Transnistria. On September 11, 1941, the Jews were ordered to assemble. By September 28 about 6,000 Jews had been murdered. In September 1943 thousands of Jews were brought to Dubossary from Bessarabia and Moldavia and "liquidated" there. Some managed to join the partisans in the neighborhood. After the liberation of Dubossary on August 14, 1944, the Soviet Commission for Investigation of Nazi Crimes found that about 18,000 Jewish victims were buried in mass graves near the town. Approximately 100 to 150 survivors returned after the war.

BIBLIOGRAPHY: I. Rubin (ed.), *Dubossary* (Heb., and Yid., 1965); Dubnow, Hist Russ, 3 (1920), 70–1. **ADD. BIBLIOGRAPHY:** PK.

[Yehuda Slutsky / Shmuel Spector (2nd ed.)]

DUBROVNIK (Ragusa), port in S. Dalmatia, Croatia; oligarchic maritime city-state, autonomous until 1808, mainly under Venetian or Turkish protectorate. Jewish merchants from Durazzo (Albania) are mentioned in Ragusan archives in 1368. French Jews living in Apulia (south Italy) after the expulsion from France temporarily resided and traded in Dubrovnik in the second half of the 15th century. After the Spanish expulsion in 1492 Dubrovnik became an important transit center for refugees traveling to Balkan cities under Turkish rule. In 1502 there were many refugees staying in Dubrovnik. When an old woman was found murdered, a dozen of them were arrested and tortured; several were declared guilty and burnt at the stake.

After the expulsions from Aragonese possessions in south Italy in 1514 and 1515, many more refugees went to Dubrovnik. Their success in commerce, together with the local clergy's zeal to have the city follow the example of other Christian states, resulted in several expulsion decrees (1514, 1515, 1545) which were revoked on the sultan's intervention. When wars against Turkey in the second half of the 16th century made the Mediterranean insecure for commerce, trade was re-routed through the Adriatic to Dubrovnik and thence by caravan to Turkey. Jews were allowed to settle in Dubrovnik and were given customs privileges to encourage transit trade. Jews dealt mainly in textiles, silk, wool, leather (Hananel-Eškenazi, 1 (1958), 264), and spices. They were allowed to live inside the walls in 1538, but in 1546 a ghetto was established in a small street (still called the Jewish street) enclosed by walls, and the gate was locked at night. A monthly tax was levied per person for residence and per bale for storage of wares. The synagogue is said to date from 1532. The Jewish cemetery was first mentioned in 1612 when it had to be enlarged; it was still in use in 1910. Two more streets were added to the ghetto in 1587, when there were 50 Jews in Dubrovnik, some with their families. Most of the trade with Turkey and much of the transit trade with Italy was in Jewish hands. At this time some Jewish intellectuals found temporary or permanent refuge there, such as the physician *Amatus Lusitanus and the humanist Didacus Pyrrhus. Many Jewish physicians were in the service of the republic, which had to obtain from Rome the authorization for them to treat Christians.

The most important Jewish family in the 16th and 17th centuries was that of *Aaron b. David ha-Kohen; arriving from Florence in the 16th century, they established connections with Sarajevo and Sofia, and also acted as agents for many Jewish traders throughout Europe. To induce more Jewish merchants to settle in Dubrovnik, the senate issued in 1614 a letter of safe conduct for five years, guaranteeing Jewish merchants freedom from arrest and from seizure of their wares for payment of previously incurred debts. There was a notorious blood libel in 1622, in which Isaac Yeshurun was accused of murdering a small girl: he stoically maintained his innocence, but was sentenced to 20 years imprisonment (he was released after 32 months). As a result of the restrictions imposed on the Jewish community at the time of this libel, most Jews left for Venice or Turkey; only four families remained in Dubrovnik, among them that of Aaron b. David ha-Kohen, rabbi of Dubrovnik. The Jewish population increased again after Aaron had obtained another letter of safe conduct in 1637. Since many restrictions imposed in 1622 were disregarded, the Church renewed its attacks and obtained from the senate the enforcement of several of them. But in many instances, the senate refused to pass anti-Jewish measures as Dubrovnik was a Turkish protectorate and the sultans had always protected the Jews.

In the 18th century the Jewish population increased; there were 218 Jews out of a total population of around 6,000. Ragusan archives mention Jewish schools, teachers, weddings, and a Jewish bookseller; Jews participated in maritime ventures as co-owners of ships that went as far as Scandinavia and America, or supplying loans for equipment of such ships; they also played a part in establishing the first maritime insurance companies. With the economic decline of Dubrovnik, however, restrictions were imposed on all foreigners. Jews could not engage in commerce and could only be teachers, physicians, or help in commerce, and some were tax farmers. In 1755 they were again forbidden to live outside the ghetto or to leave it at night. Although it had supported the French against the Russians, Dubrovnik was annexed in 1808 to the French vice kingdom of Illyria, which abolished all Jewish disabilities. When Dubrovnik passed to Austria in 1815, laws applied to Jews in Austria became valid in Dubrovnik too; e.g., Jews had to obtain permission from Vienna to get married. Full emancipation was granted only in 1873. When after World War I Dubrovnik became part of Yugoslavia, the Jewish population had decreased. There were 308 Jews in 1815, and 250 in 1939.

Holocaust and Contemporary Periods

Dubrovnik was occupied by the Italian army in April 1941; administratively however it belonged to the Independent Croatian State of the Croat quisling Pavelić, whose *ustashi* were allowed to persecute Jews. Jewish property was confiscated or put under "caretakers," and a few Jews were sent to concentration camps in Croatia. The Italians, however, did not allow mass deportations, so that many refugees from other parts of Yugoslavia went to Dubrovnik. At the bidding of the Germans, in November 1942, the Italians interned all Jews (750) in Gruž and on the island of Lopud, near Dubrovnik. There they remained until June 1943, when they were transferred to the big Italian internment camp on Rab in northern Dalmatia, together with most Jews from the Italian-occupied territories in Yugoslavia. During the brief interregnum in 1943 between the capitulation of Italy and the German occupation, most of them were transported by the partisans to the liberated territory on the mainland. Some joined the Jewish battalion formed on Rab, and others served as physicians or nurses. The 180–200 Jews who could not leave Rab were taken by the Germans to extermination camps. After World War II, 28 Jews immigrated to Israel. The Jewish community in Dubrovnik had 31 members in 1969. The rabbi of Dubrovnik served as the chief rabbi for the regions of southern Dalmatia, Herzegovina, and Montenegro. Services in the old synagogue were held irregularly. During the Yugoslav War of Secession of 1991/2 the synagogue suffered slight damage from artillery shells and its roof had to be repaired. Ceremonial objects from this synagogue, built c. 1510, were loaned to New York's Yeshiva University in 1964 and returned only in 1988 following a court order. A small community is now affiliated to the Coordination Committee of Croatian Jewish Communities, headed by Zagreb. It maintains a museum showing the synagogue artifacts and other items belonging to the past. The well-preserved cemetery contains 200 old gravestones, including that of Rabbi Jacob Pardo, who died there in 1819.

BIBLIOGRAPHY: J. Tadić, *Jevreji u Dubrovniku do polovine XVII. stoljeća* (1937); C. Roth, *The House of Nasi: Dona Gracia* (1948), 85–86; M. Levi, in: *Recueil jubilaire en l'honneur de S.A. Rosanes* (1933), 47–53 (Sp.); Hananel-Eškenazil, 1 (1958), 39, 110, 199, 335; 2 (1960), 264; J. Subak, *Judenspanisches aus Salonikki... Ragusa* (1906); Aaron b. David ha-Kohen, *Il Processo di Isach Jeshurun*, ed. by I.A. Kaznačić (1882). **ADD. BIBLIOGRAPHY:** *Zbornik*, 1 (1971), Dubrovnik issue; B. Stulli, *Zidovi u Dubrovniku* (1989).

[Daniel Furman / Zvi Loker (2nd ed.)]

DUBROVNO, city in the Vitebsk district, Belarus. Jews are first mentioned there in 1685. There were 801 Jewish taxpayers in Dubrovno and its environs in 1766. During the 18th century Dubrovno became a center for weaving prayer shawls in Eastern Europe. Conditions were difficult for the weavers, who worked on handlooms, and were harshly exploited by the merchants who supplied them with the yarn and afterward bought their products and marketed them through agents in Jewish settlements throughout Russia and Galicia, and even exported them to Western Europe and America. From the mid-19th century the industry, which had about 660 workers in 1847, encountered competition from the factories in the big cities where prayer shawls were woven by machine, and Jews began to leave the town. The plight of the weavers in Dubrovno aroused the attention of the Jewish community in Russia. In 1902, the Aktsionernoye Obshchestvo Dneprovskoy Manufaktury (Dnieper Textile Industry Ltd.) was founded with the help of the *Jewish Colonization Association (ICA), which held two-thirds of the shares, the rest being subscribed by wealthy Jews in St. Petersburg and Moscow. A large weaving factory, whose directors, staff, and workers were Jews and where Saturday was kept as the day of rest, was established. Near the factory, a public school and a cooperative store were opened. Dubrovno was also a center for scribes of Torah scrolls, phylacteries and *mezuzot*, who received permission to form a professional union in the early period of Soviet rule. A trainload of 30,000 phylacteries which had accumulated in Dubrovno after the war was permitted to be dispatched to Berlin. The manufacture of prayer shawls ceased in the 1920s. Around 1930, the weaving factory employed about 1,000 workers, of whom a considerable number were Jews. The community numbered 4,481 in 1847, 4,364 in 1897 (57.5% of the total population), 3,105 in 1926 (about 39%), and 2,119 (21%) in 1939. Dubrovno was the birthplace of the Zionist leader M. *Ussishkin and the brothers *Polyakoff. The Germans occupied the town on July 16, 1941. Soon the Jews were collected in a ghetto. In December 1941 the Germans murdered 1,500 Jews. The remaining 300 skilled workers and their families were executed with the help of Belorussian police in February 1942.

BIBLIOGRAPHY: Lurie, in: *Voskhod*, 9 (1889), 1–8; 10 (1890), 1–16; Zeitlin, in: *He-Avar*, 6 (1958), 70–72.

[Yehuda Slutsky / Shmuel Spector (2nd ed.)]

DUCKESZ, EDUARD (Yecheskel; 1868–1944), rabbi and scholar. Duckesz was born in Szelepcsény, Hungary, and studied at the Pressburg (Bratislava) yeshivah. In 1889 he became rabbi at the Klaus synagogue and *dayyan* in Altona, Germany. His scholarly efforts were devoted to the history of the three sister communities Altona, Hamburg, and Wandsbeck (אה"ו). He fled to Holland in 1939 but was interned in Westerbork by the Nazis in 1943 and sent to the Auschwitz extermination camp in 1944 where he perished. Among Duckesz' published works are *Ivah le-Moshav*, the first volume of which contains biographies and tombstone inscriptions of the rabbis who served in the three communities, with annotations by S. Buber, and the second, entitled *Chachme Ahu*, biographies of the *dayyanim* and rabbinical authors of these communities, partly in German (2 vols., 1903–08); and *Zur Geschichte und Genealogie der ersten Familien der hochdeutschen israelitischen Gemeinden in Hamburg-Altona* (1914).

BIBLIOGRAPHY: T. Preschel, in: N.Y. Institute of Religious Jewry, *Elleh Ezkerah*, 4 (1961), 58–64; H. Schwab, *Chachme Ashkenaz* (Eng., 1964), 47.

DUDA, VIRGIL (Rubin Leibovici; 1939–), Romanian writer. A lawyer by profession, Duda chose a literary career in the mid-1960s, working also as a producer at the Bucharest Film Studio. After a first volume of short stories, he published several novels demonstrating his remarkable talent for psychological analysis: *Catedrala* ("The Cathedral," 1969), *Anchetatorul apatic* ("The Apathetic Interrogator," 1971), and *Măştile* ("The Masks," 1979). The following novels, published during the 1980s, made his reputation as one of the more important Romanian prose writers: *Războiul amintirilor* ("The War of Remembrances," 1981), which received the prize of the Writers Association); *Hărţuiala* ("The Harassment," 1984); and *Oglinda salvată* ("The Saved Mirror," 1986). Autobiographical elements going back to his life as a teenager in the Moldavian town of Bârlad became more obvious in these works. Settling in Israel in 1988, he continued his literary activity, publishing (in Romania) novels with a preponderance of Jewish themes, including the impact of the Holocaust and the Communist period: *România, sfârşit de decembrie* ("Romania, End of December," 1991), *Alvis şi destinul* ("Alvis and the Destiny," 1993), *A trăi în păcat* ("To Live in Sin," 1996), *Viaţă cu efect întârziat* ("Life with Belated Effect," 1998), and *Şase femei* ("Six Women," 2002). A volume of essays, *Evreul ca simbol* ("The Jew as a Symbol," 2004) includes many subtle reflections on Jewish intellectuals and writers (Franz Kafka, Isaac Babel, Benjamin Fondane, Mihail Sebastian). Duda's brother, Lucian Raicu, is a well-known Romanian literary critic.

BIBLIOGRAPHY: A. Mirodan, *Dicţionar neconvenţional al scriitorilor evrei de limbă română* II (1997), 180–89; *Dicţionarul general al literaturii române*, 2 (2004), 768–70.

[Leon Volovici (2nd ed.)]

°**DUEHRING, KARL EUGEN** (1833–1921), German economist and philosopher, born in Berlin; one of the initial proponents of modern racial antisemitism. He studied economics, law, and philosophy at the University of Berlin. Although totally blind at 30, Duehring made significant contributions to philosophy and the theory of national-autarkic economics. A quarrelsome disposition, however, caused him to give up academic teaching in 1864. Eventually he developed a pathological aversion to such *bêtes noires* as academicians, Social Democrats, and all cosmopolitans, "whether Jews or Greeks." He propounded his theories on racial antisemitism in such scurrilous pieces as his *Die Judenfrage als Rassen-Sitten-und Kultur-Frage* (1881), *Die Ueberschaetzung Lessings und dessen Antwaltschaft fuer die Juden* (1881), *Sache, Leben, und Feinde* (1882), *Der Ersatz der Religion durch Vollkommeneres und die Ausscheidung alles Judenthums durch den modernen Voelkergeist* (1883). To Duehring, Karl Marx was the personification of evil, both because of his theories and his race. He had "taken his system from the Mosaic Law." Baptism had not prevented him from associating with his own kin (*Sippe*), namely "the descendants of Judas," in order to form a kind of international "Alliance Israélite." As to Social Democracy, its aim was to exploit and enslave the people in the interests of Jewry. Duehring had a paramount influence on the development of German antisemitism in the 1880s, whether indirect or active, and continues to inspire "voelkisch" elements to this day. In his *Der Wert des Lebens* (1865), Duehring rejected Zionism for strengthening Jewish "world power." Instead he recommended solving the Jewish question "by killing and extirpation" (*durch Ertoetung und Ausrottung*).

BIBLIOGRAPHY: F. Engels, *Herrn Eugen Duehring's Umwaelzung der Wissenschaft...* (1878) (= *Anti-Duehring*); E. Silberner, *Sozialisten zur Judenfrage...* (1962), 150, 155ff.; A. Voelske, *Die Entwicklung des rassischen Anti-semitismus zum Mittelpunkt der Weltanschauung Eugen Duehrings...* (1936). **ADD. BIBLIOGRAPHY:** B. Mogge, *Rhetorik des Hasses – Eugen Dühring und die Genese seines antisemitischen Wortschatzes* (1976); R. Kirchhoff and T.I. Oisermann, *100 Jahre Anti"Dühring" – Marxismus, Weltanschauung, Wissenschaft* (1978).

DUEÑAS, city in Castile, central Spain. Its Jewish community began to flourish in the 13th century. In 1221, Ferdinand III transferred to the monastery of Huelgas near Burgos the Jews settled on lands belonging to the monastery in Dueñas. The first document referring to the Jews of Dueñas is from 1225. At the end of the 13th century the Jewish community of Dueñas was one of the smallest in Castile. In 1290 the community paid taxes amounting to 2,427 maravedis. The Jews of Dueñas owned land and vineyards; in 1346, the king's surgeon Don Judah, an inhabitant of Dueñas, leased several gardens belonging to the local church. The community was evidently impoverished by the Black Death (1348–49), since in 1352 it paid only 300 maravedis in tax. Among those who engaged in tax farming in Dueñas were Don Çag Merdohay of Sahagún and his sons David and Shem Tob (1365). During the Civil War in Castile, the Jewish quarter of Dueñas was attacked and sacked, around 1368. The Hebrew chronicler Samuel Zarza, who gives this information, writes that the members of the community were learned and righteous. Considering the tax paid, the community remained small in the 15th century. Following the edict ordering Jews and Christians to live in separate quarters, Ferdinand and Isabella gave instructions in 1483 that the *alcabalá* ("indirect taxes") should not be collected from houses owned by Christians which were situated in the new Jewish quarter. In May 1492 the Jews of Dueñas complained that they would not be able to leave the city on the date fixed by the decree of expulsion, as they were being hindered in selling their possessions and collecting their debts and the townspeople kept presenting them with claims dating back for generations.

The Jewish quarter was near the castle.

BIBLIOGRAPHY: Baer, Urkunden, index; Suárez Fernández, Documentos, index; León Tello, in: *Instituto Tello Téllez de Meneses*, 25 (1966), index. **ADD. BIBLIOGRAPHY:** J.M. Lizoain Garrido (ed.), *Documentación del Monasterio de las Huelgas de Burgos* (1985).

[Haim Beinart / Yom Tov Assis (2nd ed.)]

DUENNER, JOSEPH ẒEVI HIRSCH (1833–1911), rabbi and talmudist. Duenner was born in Cracow. He studied in the yeshivah there and subsequently at the University of Bonn. In 1862 Duenner was appointed director of the rabbinical seminary in Amsterdam and in 1874 chief rabbi of the Ashkenazi community there. Regarded as the spiritual leader of Orthodox Jewry in Holland, Duenner nevertheless combined traditional learning with a critico-historical approach. The results of his researches and his new interpretations were published as glosses to 19 tractates of the Talmud (1896–1929). His main work is *Die Theorien ueber Wesen und Ursprung der Tosephta* (1874). Duenner became a supporter of the early movement for settlement in Ereẓ Israel in consequence of his contacts with Moses *Hess while studying in Bonn. He later became a leader of the *Mizrachi party.

BIBLIOGRAPHY: B. de Vries, in: *Shai li-Yshayahu… Wolfsberg* (1955), 247–83; idem, in: L. Jung (ed.), *Guardians of our Heritage* (1958), 337–44; idem, in: L. Jung (ed.), *Men of the Spirit* (1964), 624–44; EẒD, 1 (1958), 652–5.

[Jacob S. Levinger]

DUEREN, city near Aachen, Germany. Jews from Dueren are mentioned in 13th-century records. In 1238 Anselm of Dueren and his wife, Jutta, acquired some property in the Jewish quarter of Cologne. In 1241 the Jews of Dueren paid ten marks imperial tax. Judah of Dueren was involved in a famous controversy over a marriage mentioned in a responsum of Meir b. Baruch of Rothenburg. During the second half of the 13th century Isaac ben Meir *Dueren lived in the city.

The community was annihilated during the Black Death (1348–49), and was not reconstituted until the 19th century. The modern community, which had its own elementary school, numbered 252 in 1880, 268 in 1905, and 358 in 1933, but was reduced to 184 in 1939. During *Kristallnacht* (November 10, 1938) the synagogue and community center were burned down by the Nazis. One hundred Jewish men from Dueren were interned in Buchenwald. In July 1941 the remaining Jews were deported to the death camps. After the war, 15 Jews returned there, but subsequently left, and Jewish community life was not resumed.

BIBLIOGRAPHY: W. Bruell, *Chronik der Stadt Dueren* (1895); Germ Jud, s.v.; A. Kober, *Grundbuch des Koelner Judenviertels* (1920); I. Kracauer, *Geschichte der Juden in Frankfurt a.M.*, 1 (1925); Salfeld, Martyrol; A. Schoop, *Quellen zur Rechts- und Wirtschaftsgeschichte der rheinischen Staedte: Juedische Staedte*, 1 (1920); A. Wedell, in: *Geschichte der Stadt Duesseldorf… zum 600-jaehrigen Jubilaeum* (1888); H.J. Zimmels, *Beitraege zur Geschichte der Juden in Deutschland* (1926); Hoeniger-Stern, *Judenschreinsbuch*. **ADD. BIBLIOGRAPHY:** N. Naor, *Erinnerung. Eine Dokumentation ueber die Juedinnen und Juden in Dueren* (1994).

[Ze'ev Wilhem Falk]

DUEREN, ISAAC BEN MEIR (second half of 13th century), German halakhic authority on the laws of **issur ve-hetter*. Isaac's surname Dueren derives from the town of that name in Germany. In his youth he studied under Tobias b. Elijah of Vienne in France. The period of Dueren's activity has hitherto been uncertain owing to the possibility of his having been confused with other contemporary local scholars of the same name. His date however can now be determined with some precision. Not only does Israel Isserlein state (*Pesakim u-Khetavim*, no. 215) that *Meir b. Baruch of Rothenburg is to be regarded as a *batrai* ("a later authority") compared with Dueren, but the recent discovery that the *issur ve-hetter*, in which Dueren is already referred to as an accepted authority, was written by a disciple of *Perez b. Elijah of Corbeil, and not, as previously accepted, by *Jeroham b. Meshullam, fixes his dates as the latter part of the 13th century. The statement therefore that he was the teacher of Alexander Suslin ha-Kohen, the author of the *Sefer Aguddah*, is erroneous. Dueren is chiefly known for his *Sha'arei Dura (Issur ve-Hetter shel Rabbi Yiẓḥak mi-Dura, She'arim mi-Dura, Dura*, etc.), which deals with the laws of forbidden food and of menstruant women. This book, based wholly upon the traditions of Germany and France, became the basis of *halakhah* in this difficult sector, exerting a decisive influence upon all Ashkenazi halakhic authorities after him from the *Aguddah* of Alexander Suslin ha-Kohen through *Terumat ha-Deshen* of Israel Isserlein until *Torat Ḥattat* of Moses Isserles. The early halakhic authorities guided themselves by the rule that Isaac was to be followed in *issur ve-hetter* even when he was lenient, although the rule did not apply to *terefot* (*Pesakim u-Khetavim*, no. 215). *Sha'arei Dura* was first published in Cracow in 1534. Since then it has been republished ten times with the addition of many glosses and commentaries by the greatest talmudists in each generation, among them Israel Isserlein, Solomon Luria, Elijah Loans, and Nathan Spiro. These glosses, as well as those of the scholars who preceded Israel Isserlein, were sometimes indiscriminately incorporated into the text, so that it is difficult, without the aid of manuscripts, to determine the original content of the book, a critical edition of which is still lacking. The book was regarded with such sanctity that Ḥayyim

b. Bezalel, brother of Judah Loew of Prague, complains about Moses Isserles' daring to deviate in his *Torat Ḥattat* from the order of *Sha'arei Dura*. Another of Dueren's books, *Minhagim mi-Kol ha-Shanah*, was published by Elfenbein (see bibliography). He also wrote *tosafot* to *Gittin* and *Kiddushin*.

BIBLIOGRAPHY: J. Freimann, in: *Festschrift… D. Hoffmann* (1914), 421 n. 4; A. Freimann, in: JJLG, 12 (1918), 244 n.4, 248 n.7, 272; Elfenbein, in: REJ, 105 (1940), 107–19; idem, in: *Horeb*, 10 (1948), 129–84; Ta-Shema, in: *Sinai*, 64 (1969), 254–7.

[Israel Moses Ta-Shma]

DUESSELDORF, city in Germany, capital of North Rhine-Westphalia. Jews are first mentioned there in 1418; the cemetery of the community then served the whole region of *Berg. They were expelled from Duesseldorf in 1438. In 1582 permission was granted to one *court Jew to settle there. The community numbered 14 families in 1750 and 24 in 1775. Of these the most distinguished was the wealthy *Van Geldern family, one of whose members, the court Jew Joseph (d. 1727) in the service of the duke of *Juelich-Berg, was head (*parnas u-manhig*) of the Jewish community of the duchy. He donated a synagogue to the community in 1712, where services were held until 1772. Joseph van Geldern's son and grandson followed him in these communal offices. During the 19th century Duesseldorf Jews achieved importance in trade and banking. The community increased from 315 in 1823 to 5,130 in 1925. A seminary for Jewish teachers functioned from 1867 to 1874. Leo *Baeck served as district rabbi from 1907 to 1912.

The events of November 10, 1938, were particularly calamitous for the Duesseldorf community since the diplomat Vom Rath, who had been assassinated by Herschel *Grynszpan at the German embassy in Paris a few days earlier, was a native of Duesseldorf. The main synagogue, built in 1905, and two Orthodox synagogues were burned down. Seven Jews were killed or died from the effects of their wounds, and about 70 were injured. In May 1939, 1,831 Jews remained in Duesseldorf, dropping to 1,400 in 1941. Most were deported to Minsk, Lodz, Riga, and Theresienstadt. Only 25 Jews remained in Duesseldorf in 1946. The community was reconstituted after the war, and in 1951 the Central Council of Jews in Germany was established in Duesseldorf. The main German Jewish newspaper, the *Allgemeine Wochenzeitung der Juden in Deutschland* (today *Juedische Allgemeine*), founded in 1946, was published there until 1985. A synagogue was inaugurated in 1958. The community numbered 1,585 in 1969. Owing mainly to the immigration of Jews from the Former Soviet Union, the number of community members rose to 7,237 in 2003. A Jewish elementary school was opened in 1993.

BIBLIOGRAPHY: A. Kober, in: *Festschrift… Martin Philippson* (1916), 293–301; A. Wedell, in: *Geschichte der Stadt Duesseldorf… zum 600 jaehrigen Jubileum* (1888), 149–254; M. Eschelbacher, *Die Synagogengemeinde Duesseldorf, 1904–1929* (1929); FJW (1932–33); B. Postal and S.H. Abramson, *Landmarks of a People…* (1962); H. Lachmanski, *Duesseldorf und Heinrich Heine…* (1893); E.G. Lowenthal, in: *Die neue Synagoge in Duesseldorf* (1958), 3–12. **ADD. BIBLIOGRAPHY:** A. Genger (ed.), *Aspekte juedischen Lebens in Duesseldorf* (1997); *Juden in Duesseldorf* (1998); H. Schmidt, *Der Elendsweg der Duesseldorfer Juden* (2005).

[Zvi Avneri / Stefan Rohrbacher (2nd ed.)]

°**DUGDALE, BLANCHE ELIZABETH CAMPBELL** (1890–1948), British Zionist; a niece of Arthur James *Balfour. Blanche Dugdale was employed in the British Naval Intelligence Department and became a member of the League of Nations Union and the British government's delegation to the League of Nations Assembly (1932). Described by Chaim Weizmann as "an ardent, lifelong friend of Zionism," "Baffy," as she was affectionately called, constantly tried to influence cabinet ministers and high commissioners by personal contact and in writing, stressing the justice of the Jewish cause in Palestine. She also addressed public meetings, Zionist conferences, and even World Zionist Congresses and advised Weizmann in his political dealings with the British. From 1940 until a few months before her death she worked daily in the political department of the Jewish Agency. During World War II she served on various committees to aid Jewish refugees. She regularly published articles in the *Zionist Review* and authored a pamphlet *The Balfour Declaration: Origins and Background* (1940) and a two-volume biography, *Arthur James Balfour* (1936). Her diary is preserved in the Weizmann archives in Reḥovot. Before she died, on May 15, 1948, relatives and friends told her that the State of Israel had been established. Extracts from her diaries, covering the period 1936–47, were edited and published by Norman Rose in 1973. One of the most committed of British "gentile Zionists," it has been said that she "thought of [Jewish] Palestine as her second country."

BIBLIOGRAPHY: Locker, in: *Davar* (May 9, 1958). **ADD. BIBLIOGRAPHY:** B.E. Dugdale and N. Rose (eds.), *Baffy: The Diaries of Blanche Dugdale, 1936–1947* (1973); ODNB online.

[Josef Fraenkel]

°**DUHM, BERNHARD** (1847–1928), German Protestant biblical scholar. Born in Bingum on the Ems, East Friesland, Duhm studied at Goettingen (chiefly under H. Ewald). In 1877 he was appointed professor at Goettingen University and in 1899, at Basle University. His activities in Basle, which included teaching in secondary schools and lecturing (*Das Geheimnis in der Religion*, 1896; *Das kommende Reich Gottes*, 1912; Eng. trans., *The Evercoming Kingdom of God*, 1914), extended beyond the academic sphere. His main works were devoted to the study of the Prophets. His early work *Die Theologie der Propheten…* (1875) reflects a somewhat dogmatic understanding of the prophets, whom Duhm regarded as analogous to the writers and orators of other ancient peoples, in particular the Greeks. In this work Duhm (simultaneously with Wellhausen, with whom he was friendly) rejects the presupposition of an older "Mosaic" law. His last work on the prophets, *Israels Propheten* (1918), is an overall exposition of the Israelite religion, based on his previous exegetical studies in his commentaries on Isaiah (1892), Jeremiah (1901), and Minor

Prophets (1911), all of which contain impressive translations. His outstanding capacity for understanding the prophets, especially the irrational aspects of prophetic vision and audition and their subsequent expression, enabled him to set forth a frequently violent (e.g., in conjectural criticism of texts), but profound and imposing, portrayal of the prophetic personalities. Duhm isolated the Servant Songs of Isaiah 40–55 from Deutero-Isaiah. He proposed the separation of Isaiah 56–66 (as "Trito-Isaiah") from Isaiah 40–55 and the rejection of the authenticity of Jeremiah's prose orations. Of less importance are his commentaries on Job (1897) and Psalms (1899). The latter work contains exaggerated historical criticism (e.g., he dates most of the psalms to the Hasmonean period).

ADD. BIBLIOGRAPHY: W. Thiel, DBI, 1, 310–11.

[Rudolf Smend]

DUISBURG, city in Germany. A small Jewish settlement existed there from the second half of the 13th century whose members were massacred in the wake of the *Black Death (1350). No Jews lived there subsequently until the 18th century, when a few families are mentioned. A few Jewish students studied medicine at the university between 1708 and 1817. In 1793 there were ten families living in the town, who formed an organized community. A small synagogue was consecrated in 1826 and replaced by a more impressive edifice in 1875. The Jewish population increased during and after World War I as a result of immigration from Poland and Galicia. The community (united with Hamborn) numbered 2,560 in 1933. In October 1938, 144 Polish Jews were expelled. On *Kristallnacht*, the synagogue was set on fire; 40 Jewish homes and 25 stores were vandalized and 25 Jews were sent to Dachau. In December 1938 Jewish youngsters were sent to Holland on a *Kindertransport*; some later reached England, where they survived the war. The remaining 809 Jews were crowded into 11 Jewish houses from which they were deported in 1941 to ghettos in the East and later to death camps.

In 1969, 75 Jews lived in Duisburg and Muelheim an der Ruhr, which constituted one community. In 1989 the joint community of Duisburg, Muelheim, and Oberhausen had 118 members; due to the immigration of Jews from the Former Soviet Union, their number rose to 2,653 in 2003. The new synagogue, designed by Zvi Hecker and inaugurated in 1999, is an architectural hallmark of the city.

BIBLIOGRAPHY: I.F. Baer, *Protokollbuch der Landjudenschaft des Herzogtums Kleve* (1922), 54–55; Kober, in: MGWJ, 75 (1931), 118–27; Germ Jud (1934, repr. 1963), 90–91; 2 pt. 1 (1968), 178. **ADD. BIBLIOGRAPHY:** G. von Roden, *Geschichte der Duisburger Juden* (1986); F. Niessalla, K.-H. Keldungs, *1933–1945: Schicksale juedischer Juristen in Duisburg* (1993); M. Komorowski, in: *Juden im Ruhrgebiet* (1999), 541–54.

[Zvi Avneri / Michael Birenbaum and Stefan Rohrbacher (2nd ed.)]

DUJOVNE, LEON (1899–1984), Argentine lawyer, philosopher, and community leader. Dujovne was born in Russia and went to Argentina as a child. In 1966 he settled in Israel and in 1973 returned to Argentina. For many years Dujovne was a member of the Faculty of Philosophy and Letters of the University of Buenos Aires. He published many books, the most important of which are *Baruj Spinoza – Su vida, su época, su obra y su influencia*, 4 vols. (1941–44); *Martín Buber – sus ideas religiosas, filosóficas y sociales* (1966); *La Filosofia y las teorías científicas* (1930); and *Teoría de los valores y filosofía de la historia* (1959), which received the First National Prize of Argentina. Dujovne also translated into Spanish Dubnow's *History of the Jewish People*, Maimonides' *Guide of the Perplexed*, and works by Ibn Gabirol, Saadiah Gaon, Baḥya ibn Paquda, and others. He was for many years president of the Sociedad Hebraica Argentina and of the Instituto de Intercambio Cultural Argentino-Israelí as well as editor in chief of the Jewish weekly, *Mundo Israelita*.

[Lawrence H. Feigenbaum and Kenneth R. Scholberg]

DUKAS, PAUL (1865–1935), French composer. Born in Paris, Dukas studied at the Conservatory and taught there from 1909 until his death. In French music, his style formed a bridge between the school of César Franck and that of Debussy. He achieved fame in 1897 with his brilliant orchestral scherzo *L'Apprenti sorcier* ("The Sorcerer's Apprentice," inspired by Goethe), which, it was later suggested, was actually intended as a satire on the fashion of "symphonic poems." The most important of Dukas' works is the opera *Ariane et Barbe-Bleue* (1907, with text by Maeterlinck), symbolizing the struggle for emancipation from dictatorship. His other works also include a symphony, several overtures, the ballet *La Péri*, chamber music, and piano works. After 1912, Dukas, who had become increasingly self-critical, gave up composition almost entirely. He devoted himself to teaching at the Conservatory. Before his death he destroyed his unpublished works.

BIBLIOGRAPHY: G. Samazeuilh, *Un musicien français, Paul Dukas* (1913); V. d'Indy, *Emmanuel Chabrier et Paul Dukas* (1920); G. Favre, *Paul Dukas, sa vie, son oeuvre* (1948); Riemann-Gurlitt; Baker's Biog Dict; Grove's Dict; MGG.

[Chanan Steinitz]

DUKER, ABRAHAM GORDON (1907–1987), U.S. educator and historian. Duker, who was born in Rypin, Poland, went to the U.S. in 1923. He served on the library staff at the Jewish Theological Seminary (1927–33) and was research librarian at the Graduate School of Jewish Social Work (1934–38). From 1938 to 1943 he was on the staff of the American Jewish Committee, serving inter alia as the editor of the *Contemporary Jewish Record* (1938–41). He was also an editor of the *Universal Jewish Encyclopedia* (1939–43), *Reconstructionist*, and *Jewish Social Studies*, a quarterly. Duker was president of the Chicago Spertus College of Judaica (1956–62) and from 1963 director of libraries and professor of history and social institutions at Yeshiva University. His works include education surveys, books, and articles in his main fields of interest, Polish-Jewish relations and American Jewish sociology.

His books include *Jewish Emancipation under Attack: Its Legal Recession until the Present War* (with B. Weinryb, 1942) and *Emancipation and Counter Emancipation* (with Meir Ben Hurin, 1974). He also wrote about religious trends in American Jewish life (1949), Jewish community relations (1952), socio-psychological trends in the American Jewish community since 1900 (1954), and the impact of Zionism on American Jewry (1958).

[Sefton D. Temkin / Ruth Beloff (2nd ed.)]

DUKES, LEOPOLD (**Judah Loeb**; 1810–1891), historian of Jewish literature. Dukes was born in Pressburg, Hungary. He was a student of R. Moses *Sofer and of R. Ḥayyim Joseph Pollak; the latter introduced him to secular study. An inveterate, though poor, traveler, Dukes visited most of the important libraries in Europe, researching Jewish manuscripts and uncovering many hitherto unknown medieval works. His research covered various aspects of language and literature: aggadic literature, Bible exegesis, medieval Jewish literature, Hebrew grammar and the masoretic text, and talmudic maxims and truisms. Frequently, however, his research was unsystematic and his edited texts in need of correction. Dukes' translation of Rashi's Pentateuch commentary into German was published with Sofer's imprimatur in Prague during 1833–38 (*Ḥamishah Ḥumshei Torah im Ha'takah Ashkenazit al Perush Rashi [Raschi zum Pentateuch]*, 5 vols.). Dukes produced various studies on the poetry of Solomon ibn Gabirol and Moses Ibn Ezra. His autobiography appears in AZDJ, 56 (1892).

BIBLIOGRAPHY: Zeitlin, Bibliotheca, 1 (1891), 69–71; I. Davidson, in: PAAJR, 1 (1928), 43.

[Jacob S. Levinger]

DUKHAN (Heb. דּוּכָן; "platform"), an elevated platform. According to talmudic literature, the word was used in four instances.

(1) The place in the Temple where the levites sang while the sacrifice was being offered (Ar. 11b). According to the Mishnah (Mid. 2:6), this *dukhan* was placed upon a step one cubit high, which was situated between the court of the Israelites and the court of the priests. It had three steps, each half a cubit high. Hence the height of the *dukhan* was one and a half cubits, or, together with the step, two and a half cubits.

(2) The place where the priests stood while reciting the *Priestly Blessing. The Talmud quotes R. Tarfon as saying "I once ascended the *dukhan* [for the Priestly Blessing]" (Kid. 71a). The Mishnah (Tam. 7:2) implies, however, that the priests stood on the 12 steps between the porch and the altar when blessing the people and not on the *dukhan* (cf. Tosef. Sot. 7:7). The explanation, apparently, is that the steps of the porch were the main site for the Priestly Blessing, but when there were too many priests to fit on the steps, the others took up this position on the *dukhan* (cf. *Tiferet Israel* on Middot 2:6).

(3) After the destruction of the Temple, the meaning of the word was extended to apply to the place in the synagogue where the Priestly Blessing was recited (Shab. 118b; Sot. 38b; et al.), and still later, to the Priestly Blessing itself. Hence the familiar phrase "to *dukhan*" was used for "to recite the Priestly Blessing."

(4) The platform where teachers sat while teaching children (BB 21a).

BIBLIOGRAPHY: S. Krauss, *Synagogale Altertuemer* (1922), 393.

[Jehonatan Etz-Chaim]

DULCEA OF WORMS (d. 1196), wife of R. *Eleazar ben Judah of Worms. Dulcea came from medieval German Jewry's elite leadership class. Married to a leading figure in the *Ḥasidei Ashkenaz, the German-Jewish pietist movement, she was the economic support for an extensive household, including children, students, and teachers. A capable businesswoman, she was apparently entrusted with the funds of neighbors which she pooled and lent out at profitable rates of interest on which she received commissions. Among R. Eleazar ben Judah's surviving writings are two Hebrew accounts, one in prose and one in poetry, recounting the murders of Dulcea, and their daughters, Bellette and Hannah, by intruders in November 1196. Both documents are important sources of information about medieval Jewish women's activities. Although many scholars have assumed the attackers were Crusaders, there were no massed Crusader forces in Germany at this time. While the two miscreants may have worn Crusader markings, they appear to have attacked the family out of criminal motives, probably prompted by Dulcea's business reputation. These assaults did not go unpunished; the local authorities, in accordance with the German emperor's mandate of protecting the Jews of his realm, quickly captured and executed at least one of the men. R. Eleazar's elegy, an expanded alphabetic acrostic, links numerous details of Dulcea's domestic, religious, and communal endeavors with the praise of the "woman of valor" in Proverbs 31. R. Eleazar designates Dulcea as *ḥasidah* (pious or saintly) and *ẓadeket* (righteous); in addition to noting her domestic management and business finesse, he praises her needlework, recounting that she prepared thread and gut to sew together books, Torah scrolls, and other religious objects. Unusually learned for a woman of her milieu, Dulcea is said to have taught other women and led them in prayer. As a respected investment broker, Dulcea may have been involved in arranging matches and negotiating the financial arrangements which accompanied them. She is also said to have bathed the dead and to have sewn their shrouds, meritorious endeavors in Jewish tradition. More than anything, R. Eleazar reveres his wife for facilitating the spiritual activities of the men of her household; the reward he invokes for Dulcea at the conclusion of his lament is to be wrapped in the eternal life of Paradise, a tribute to her deeds, on which so many depended.

BIBLIOGRAPHY: J.R. Baskin, "Dolce of Worms: The Lives and Deaths of an Exemplary Medieval Jewish Woman and Her Daughters," in: L. Fine (ed.), *Judaism in Practice: From the Middle Ages through the Early Modern Period* (2001), 429–37; idem, "Women Saints in Judaism: Dolce of Worms," in: A. Sharma (ed.), *Women*

Saints in World Religions (2000), 39–69; I.G. Marcus, "Mothers, Martyrs, and Moneymakers: Some Jewish Women in Medieval Europe," in: *Conservative Judaism*, 38:3 (Spring 1986), 34–45.

[Judith R. Baskin (2nd ed.)]

DULZIN, ARYE LEIB (1913–1989), Zionist leader and Israeli politician. Born in Minsk, Belorussia, he immigrated with his parents to Mexico in 1928, where he was educated and was for many years active in commerce. From 1931 to 1937 he acted as the honorary general secretary of the Zionist Federation of Mexico and in the years 1938–42 was president of the federation. From 1944 to 1946 he was chairman of the Mexico branch of the World Jewish Congress and member of the General Zionist Council at the 23rd Zionist Congress in 1951, and at the 24th Zionist Congress in 1961 was elected to the Zionist Executive of the World Zionist Organization (WZO), as representative of the Union of the General Zionists. He thus became the first Latin-American member. In 1965 Dulzin settled in Israel, acting as head of the Economic Department of the Jewish Agency and later head of the Aliyah and Absorption Department. From 1968 to 1978 he was treasurer of the Jewish Agency and the WZO and in this capacity traveled widely throughout the Jewish world to raise funds and to bring the message of Israel to the Jewish world. In 1970–71 on behalf of the Liberal Party, he was cabinet minister without portfolio in the Israeli government but later returned to the Zionist Executive. In 1973–74 and again in 1975 he was acting chairman of the Jewish Agency and the WZO. He was the president of the World Union of the General Zionists, chairman of the Central Actions Committee of the Liberal Party, and a member of the Likud Executive. Among his many other functions he was a governor of Bank Leummi, governor of the Land Development Company (Hachsharat ha-Yishuv), member of the board of directors of Keren Hayesod, president of the Israel-America Society as well as a member of a number of cultural and arts institutions in Israel. In 1978 he was elected chairman of the Jewish Agency and the WZO.

[Benjamin Jaffe]

DUMA, Imperial Russian legislature, in existence between 1906 and 1917. The electoral law establishing the First Duma included no specific restrictions on the Jewish franchise. Although the Jewish socialist parties, and primarily the *Bund, boycotted the elections to the First Duma, the majority of Jews took an active part, voting for candidates of the Russian Constitutional Democratic Party (the Kadets). Twelve Jewish deputies, including five Zionists, were elected: L. *Bramson, G. *Bruk, M. Chervonenkis, S. Frenkel, G. Jolles, Nissan *Katzenelson, Shemaryahu Levin, *M. *Ostrogorski, S. *Rosenbaum, M. *Sheftel, M. *Vinawer, and B. Yakubson. Nine of the deputies were affiliated to the Kadet fraction and three to the Labor group (Trudoviki). On May 15, 1906, a bill to grant civil equality to the Jews and repeal all discriminatory legislation on the ground of religion or nationality was brought in. When news of the pogrom in *Bialystok reached the Duma at the beginning of June 1906, it sent an investigating commission there. The commission's report placed the responsibility for the pogrom on the Russian authorities, and the debate on this burning issue terminated with the dissolution of the First Duma by the Russian government in July. The Jewish representatives took part in the subsequent convocation of protest held by Duma deputies in Vyborg, Finland, and joined in signing the "Vyborg Manifesto," which called on the Russian people to register passive resistance by refusing to pay taxes or enlist in the army. Jews were also among the deputies who were sentenced to three months' imprisonment for signing the manifesto and deprived of their elective rights.

The Second Duma, which met in February 1907, included only four Jewish deputies, and they were hardly known to the Jewish public: S. Abramson, L. Rabinovich, Y. Shapiro – affiliated to the Kadets – and V. *Mandelberg (Siberia), affiliated to the Social Democrats. The small number of Jewish members was the result of the organization and activities of the antisemitic groups who opposed the election of Jewish deputies on principle. Since the Jews were in the minority throughout the country they were unable to return Jewish deputies without the support of the non-Jewish electorate. A bill was laid before the Second Duma by the government abrogating all denominational restrictions in Russia excepting those imposed on the Jews. The premature dissolution of the Second Duma in June 1907 interrupted the debate on the bill.

The Third Duma (1907–12) was returned by a new electoral law which restricted *ab initio* representation of the national minorities and increased that of the landowners and clergy. It was overwhelmingly composed of right-wing elements. There were two Jewish deputies, N. *Friedman and L. *Nisselovich. The Jews were constantly attacked, especially by representatives of the extreme right such as Purishkevich and Zamyslowsky. A bill to abolish the *Pale of Settlement signed by 166 deputies met with ridicule and abuse from the antisemites. On the other hand, the assassination of Premier Stolypin and the *Beilis blood libel case provided an opportunity for scurrilous anti-Jewish attacks. The antisemites also proposed excluding Jews from the army.

Three Jews were elected to the Fourth Duma (1912–17), N. Friedman, M. Bomash, and E. Gurewich. A political office was established by a number of non-socialist Jewish parties to assist the Jewish deputies and provide guidance. The members of this bureau included Y. *Gruenbaum and I. Rosow (Zionists), S. *Dubnow and M. *Kreinin (Jewish Populist Party, *Folksspartei*), M. Vinaver and H. *Sliozberg (Jewish Peoples' Group), L. Bramson and A. *Braudo (Jewish Democratic Group), and O. *Grusenberg. During World War I the Jewish deputies were assigned to counteract the anti-Jewish vilification campaign spread by the army general staff and the restrictions introduced in its wake. It was on the initiative of the political office that deputy A. Kerensky paid a visit to the war zone: on his return he denied the libels from the podium of the Duma. The political office also appealed to the Duma to protest against the government memoranda of 1916 which accused the Jews of sabotaging the Russian war effort. After the February 1917 Revolution the Jews were granted equal rights and the "Jewish question" disappeared from the agenda of the Duma.

BIBLIOGRAPHY: Y. Maor, in: *He-Avar*, 7 (1960), 49–90; J. Frumkin, in: *Russian Jewry (1860–1917)* (1966), 47–84; Dubnow, Hist Russ, 3 (1920), 131–42, 153–6.

[Yehuda Slutsky]

DUMUH, village near Cairo, thought to be on the site of the ancient Memphis. In the Middle Ages there was an ancient synagogue called *Kanīsat Mūsā* after Moses, because according to legend this was where he lived when he went on his mission to Pharaoh. Al-Maqrīzī (d. 1442), an Arab historian, mentions the miracles observed there and writes that the Jews of Egypt customarily visited the synagogue on Shavuot. Joseph Sambari (17th century) says that they came there on the seventh of Adar, the anniversary of Moses' death. Regulations were initiated to ensure proper conduct and, especially, that men and women should be separated. The leaders of Egyptian Jewry issued appeals for donations for the upkeep of the synagogue.

A 12th-century document reports that the elders of the Cairo community rented a plot of land in the vicinity of the synagogue to a Jew who wished to erect a building there so that the synagogue would not be isolated. Obadiah of *Bertinoro (end of 15th century) reports that there were two synagogues, one belonging to the Rabbanite Jews and the other to the Karaites. On Sabbaths and festivals, Jews went specially there to pray; thus it seems that Jews were still not living there. At the beginning of 1498 the sultan al-Malik al-Nāṣir Muhammad II ordered that the synagogue should be destroyed and this order was carried out in his presence; the synagogue may have been rebuilt, however. Sambari mentions some families who were named "Dumūhī," because of their origin.

BIBLIOGRAPHY: Mann, Texts, 2 (1935), 206; Ashtor, Toledot, 1 (1944), 245–6; 2 (1951), 385, 503; Assaf, in: *Melilah*, 1 (1944), 18–25; Goitein, in: *Homenaje a Millás-Vallicrosa*, 1 (1954), 718.

[Eliyahu Ashtor]

DUNAJSKA STREDA (Hung. **Dunaszerdahely**), town located on the largest island of the Danube River in S.W. Slovakia, now Slovak Republic. Towns and villages of the region had dense Jewish populations and most were supervised by the Dunajska Streda rabbinate.

The first Jews probably settled in the area around 1700. Count Palffy granted the community legal rights in a charter of 1739. The Jewish population rose from 16 families in 1700 to 1,874 people in 1880 (44.8% of the entire population) and around 2,700 in 1930.

From the outset, both the royal treasury and the Palffy family burdened the Jews with heavy taxes. The Jews were occupied in crafts, agriculture, and trade in grain and spirits. Rabbi Simeon David officiated in the mid-18th century and by 1780 the community already had a second synagogue and such communal institutions as a ritual bath, kosher butcher, matzah bakery, *talmud torah*, and primary school (a *Beth Jacob school for girls was opened in the 1920s). The Great Synagogue was constructed in 1865. The earliest tombstones in the old cemetery were from 1755. (All Jewish religious installations, with the exception of a small synagogue, were pulled down by the Communist regime in 1950 and 1960.) In 1780 the Jewish community of Dunajska Streda was the second largest in the Hungarian kingdom, after Pressburg (Bratislava).

The community was a center of Orthodoxy and important yeshivot were also located there. Among the celebrated rabbis who officiated in Dunajska Streda were Alexander Meislisch (1784–1800), David b. Menachem Mendel Deutsch, and Judah b. Israel Aszód.

In the late 1880s there was an outburst of severe antisemitism. After an extended anti-Jewish campaign the synagogue was set on fire in June 1887. In the same year the Jewish quarter was sacked and hooligans attacked Jews in the street and in their homes. Not until military units were alerted did the attacks stop. In World War I, 220 Jewish men enlisted in the army; 46 of them died. During the war a large number of Polish Jews settled in the town. With the end of the war, the town was hit by another wave of pogroms and robberies.

The Zionists were active in the town along with the Orthodox political bodies. Jews were well represented in the municipal council, including Jewish members of the Communist Party.

With the entry of the Hungarian army in 1938, persecution increased. Budapest would not forgive Dunajska Streda Jewry its loyalty to Czechoslovakia. Anti-Jewish laws in existence in Hungary were applied to the conquered territories. Jews were left with no source of income, and lived on the charity of Hungarian Jewish organizations. In 1940 Jews were recruited into the labor brigades of the Hungarian army, where many perished. Around 200 Jews who were not able to prove their Hungarian citizenship were assembled in the late summer of 1942 and deported to the vicinity of Kamenets-Podolski in Poland, where they were executed by the Germans. During the years 1942–44 Dunajska Streda was one of the centers for smuggling Slovakian and Polish Jews into Hungary.

In March 1944 German forces occupied Hungary. A new wave of persecutions started immediately. On March 29, the property of local Jews was sequestered. The community institutions were closed down and in their stead a Judenrat was organized. On June 8, all Jews were ordered to assemble in the Great Synagogue and on June 13–15 around 3,000 were deported to Auschwitz.

In 1947 there were 404 Jews in Dunajska Streda. In 1948–49, most of the Jews immigrated to Israel and elsewhere. A community of around 20 families established regular services in the small synagogue in the 1990s and the congregation organized social activities, including a yearly memorial service.

The well-known Orientalist Arminius *Vambery (1832–1913) was born in the town.

BIBLIOGRAPHY: *Magyar Zsidó Lexikon* (1929), 208.

[Yeshayahu Jelinek (2nd ed.)]

°**DUNANT, JEAN HENRI** (1828–1910), Swiss Protestant philanthropist. Dunant was the founder of the Geneva Convention and the International Red Cross. Among his humanitarian causes was the settlement of Jews in Ereẓ Israel, which he regarded as essential for reviving the Middle East. During the early 1860s he tried to arouse the interest of Napoleon III and leaders of West European Jewry in his Jewish settlement plan. He established an association for the colonization of Palestine, and in a letter to the *Jewish Chronicle* of December 13, 1867, described its basic principles: the acquisition of land by the association; the building of a Jerusalem-Jaffa railroad; and the development of agriculture "aided by the cooperation of Israelites." He traveled throughout Europe in an attempt to interest such personalities as Adolphe Crémieux and Moses Montefiore. Dunant was unsuccessful in his efforts, and his contention was that the indifference of the Jews was to blame. Herzl, in his closing speech at the First Zionist Congress (1897), referred to Dunant as a Christian Zionist.

BIBLIOGRAPHY: *Die Welt*, 1:22 (1897), 6f.; N. Sokolow, *History of Zionism*, 2 (1919), 259–61, 265–7; A. François, *Aspects d'Henri Dunant: le bonapartiste, l'affairiste, le sioniste* (1948).

[Getzel Kressel]

DUNASH BEN LABRAT (mid-tenth century), Hebrew poet, linguist, and exegete. Most medieval scholars believed that he and Adonim ha-Levi were the same person. Moses Ibn Ezra described him as a Baghdadi by origin and a man of Fez by education. He could have been born around 925, in Baghdad or in Fez, and was one of the last students of *Saadiah in Baghdad. After the death of his master (942) he established himself first in Fez and later on in Córdoba, where he was teaching around 960. Some years later, after having had problems with *Ḥisdai ibn Shaprut, he abandoned Andalusia; in 985 he wrote a poem in honor of a prominent Andalusian Jew. We have no more concrete references about the rest of his life or about his death.

Dunash as a Poet

It was Dunash who applied the Arabic poetic forms, genres, and meters to Hebrew, adapting them to the biblical language and thus laying the foundation of medieval Andalusian Hebrew poetry. Though initially there was some opposition in Córdoba, in the circle of Menahem ben Saruq, the innovation was immediately accepted and developed. Ibn *Gabirol speaks of Dunash as the greatest poet of his generation and imitates his style in one of his compositions. Only some of Dunash's poems have been discovered and a few of them are known only by the lines quoted in his philological work. As was common at the time, his secular poems include panegyrics (in honor of Ḥisdai ibn Shaprut and other Jewish notables), songs of friendship and love, with praise to nature, the good life, and wine, and also didactic and wisdom poetry. The ambivalence of Jewish life in a Muslim atmosphere left deep traces in his verses. He expressed his sadness for the situation of his people, among Muslims and Christians, and for the ruins of Jerusalem. His religious poems include the Sabbath song *Deror yikra* and *Devai hasser,* which has become part of the Grace said after the wedding meal. He also wrote *piyyutim* as is clear from the remains of a *kerovah* for the Day of Atonement and other fragments. *A genizah* fragment indicates that ten rhymed riddles, previously thought to be the work of Ibn Gabirol, were written by Dunash. E. Fleischer published a short poem possibly written by Dunash's wife when her husband was leaving Andalusia.

Collections of Dunash's poems were published by D. Kahana in 1894 and by N. Allony in 1947 (see Mirsky, in: KS, 24 (1947/48), 16–19; *Shir u-Fulmus*, ed. by Y. Zmora, 1944); M. Zulay, in *Sinai*, 29 (1951), 36ff.; E. Fleischer, in *Tarbiz*, 39 (1970), 33ff., and in *Jerusalem Studies in Hebrew Literature*, 5 (1984), 189–202; in 1988 C. del Valle published 56 poems by Dunash with Spanish translation and commentary (*El diván poético de Dunash ben Labraṭ: la introducción de la métrica árabe*).

Dunash as a Linguist

When Dunash arrived in Córdoba, *Menahem b. Jacob ibn Saruq, Ḥisdai ibn Shaprut's secretary, was working on his dictionary of Biblical Hebrew and Aramaic in Hebrew, the *Maḥberet.* Dunash, worried about some possibly heterodox interpretations and dissenting from him in basic grammatical views, wrote some replies against Menahem and presented them, with praise and thanks, to Ḥisdai (shortly after 958). The grammatical and lexical study of the language of the Bible became for Menahem and Dunash a passionate question that gave rise to one of the hottest debates that took place in the Middle Ages. Dunash claimed to have disputed 200 items, but in the text which has been preserved there are 180 entries. Sixty-eight are included in the poem *Le-doresh ha-ḥokhmot* which is explained by parallel prose paragraphs, a literary form borrowed from technical Arabic literature. Many of Dunash's comments deal with those grammatical or lexical explanations which, in his opinion, are likely to lead to error in matters of *halakhah* and belief. This religious factor may explain the severity of his attack. From our perspective, it is not easy to understand that the meaning of a word or its appropriate grammatical classification could give rise to such vicious and scornful attacks. But it was not a mere question of words: upon this discussion depended the entire Jewish conception of God and his relation to the world, the way of understanding the moral obligations of mankind, and the confirmation of rabbinic tradition over sectarian views. Therefore, his could not be just a cold and objective science. For Dunash the meaning of the biblical text and theology could never be at odds. In some cases Dunash criticized interpretations of his adversaries which seemed to be close to Karaism. Though Menahem was relieved of his position as a result of accusations of heresy, there is no proof that Dunash deliberately caused his downfall or that he benefited from it in any way. Three of Menahem's students, Ibn Kapron, Isaac ibn Gikatilla (Ibn Janaḥ's teacher), and Judah Ḥayyuj, came out against Dunash though Ḥisdai was still alive. They wrote responsa dealing with 50 items, which imitated Dunash's poem in their form. Dunash's student, *Yehudi b. Sheshet, answered sharply in the same manner. Rashi, who knew of the argument between the school of Menahem and the school of Dunash, quotes Dunash about 20 times, and many more times Menahem. R. Tam wrote "decisions" on the disagreements between Dunash and Menahem, and Joseph Kimḥi, in his *Sefer ha-Galui*, wrote against these decisions in favor of Dunash. Although Dunash was correct in many of the points under discussion, his grammatical method is no more advanced than that of Menahem. Both shared, for example, the search for the "bases" of Hebrew words and verbs, a set of firm consonants very different from the diachronic concept of "root" used in later philology. However, while Menahem rejected for ideological reasons the comparison of Hebrew with other languages, Dunash accepted the comparatist method, in particular in relation to Arabic.

The book *Teshuvot 'al Rav Sa'adyah Ga'on* ("Responsa on R. Saadiah Gaon") is also attributed to Dunash, but many scholars doubt if he was the author, since it is written in prose full of Arabisms and, moreover, dissents on several points from the opinion of Dunash in his dispute with Menahem and recognizes that hollow roots are also triliteral. There are some who believe that Dunash wrote this work when an old man, perhaps after being influenced by Ḥayyuj, whom all consider to be the founder of the new method in Hebrew grammar.

Dunash's responsa were edited by Filipowski in 1855, and in a critical edition with new materials by A. Sáenz-Badillos in 1980; the arguments, written in verse by students of Menahem and Dunash, were edited by S.G. Stern (1870); S. Benavente published the answers of the students of Menahem (1986); the replies by Yehudi ben Sheshet were published by E. Varela (1981); the *Teshuvot 'al Rav Sa'adyah Ga'on*, by R. Shroeter (1866).

Dunash as an Exegete

Dunash did not write complete commentaries to biblical books, but practiced, like Menahem, a kind of grammatical analysis that was a true literal exegesis. For Dunash philology was not an end in itself, it was an instrument for the adequate comprehension of the Bible, the only correct way of interpreting the Scriptures. Dunash was very respectful toward the interpretations of the Targum and the Masorah, remaining faithful to the literal meaning of the text. This did not mean disregarding the fact that the Scriptures uses metaphors and analogies that should be understood as such, above all in the case of the anthropomorphisms and anthropopathisms in Scripture. Dunash applied linguistic knowledge to the interpretation of the Scriptures, complementing it with "the 13 rules by which most of the precepts, laws, norms, and instructions are governed and measured." He made moderate use of the methods of permutation or metathesis applied by some traditional interpreters, and continued the comparative methods initiated by Saadiah and other grammarians in North Africa in order to understand the most difficult words of the Bible.

BIBLIOGRAPHY: W. Bacher, *Die hebraeische Sprachwissenschaft…* (1892), 27–33; idem, in: ZDMG, 49 (1895), 367–86; idem, in: MGWJ, 46 (1902), 478–80; H. Hirschfield, *Literary History of Hebrew Grammarians and Lexicographers* (1926), 26–31; Davidson, Oẓar, 4 (1933), 378; Englander, in: HUCA, 7 (1930), 399–437; 11 (1936), 369–89; 12–13 (1937–38), 505–21; Brody, in: *Sefer ha-Yovel… S. Krauss* (1936), 117–26; Yellin, *ibid.*, 127–35; idem, in: *Sefer Zikkaron… Gulak ve-Klein* (1942), 105, 114; idem, *Toledot Hitpatteḥut ha-Dikduk ha-Ivri* (1945), 67–93; D. Herzog, in: *Saadya Studies*, ed. by E.J. Rosenthal (1943), 26–46; N. Allony, in: JQR, 36 (1945), 141–6; idem, in: *Leshonenu*, 15 (1946/47), 161–72; idem, in: Dunash ben Labrat, *Shirim* (1946), 5–46 (introd.); idem, *Torat ha-Mishkalim* (1951). **ADD. BIBLIOGRAPHY:** E. Ashtor, *The Jews of Moslem Spain*, 1 (1973), 252ff.; Schirmann-Fleischer, *The History of Hebrew Poetry in Muslim Spain* (Heb., 1995), 119–143; A. Sáenz-Badillos and J. Targarona, *Gramáticos Hebreos de al-Andalus (Siglos X–XII). Filología y Biblia* (1988), 39–89; idem, *Los judíos de Sefarad ante la Biblia* (1996), 55–76; A. Sáenz-Badillos, in: M. Saebo et al. (eds.), *Hebrew Bible. Old Testament. The History of Its Interpretation*. Vol. 1, Part 2 (2000), 96–109.

[Chaim M. Rabin / Angel Sáenz-Badillos (2nd ed.)]

DUNASH IBN TAMIM (c. 890–after 955/6), North African scholar, known also as **Adonim**, the Hebrew form of Dunash, and by the Arabic surname **Abu Sahl**. (The descriptive adjective *shaflagi* appended to his name by Moses *Ibn Ezra is inexplicable.) Dunash was from Kairouan, and studied with Isaac *Israeli, to whom he undoubtedly owed the greater part of his intellectual development. The philosophical and theological parts of his commentary on the *Sefer *Yeẓirah* reflect the neoplatonism of Israeli's philosophical thinking. Dunash probably also received from Israeli his medical knowledge, displayed authoritatively especially in the last pages of his commentary. Dunash also demonstrates a thorough knowledge of certain theories of Arabic grammar, chiefly theories of phonetics. In addition to astronomy, of which he had made a special study, this commentary shows that he had read treatises derived from Greek sources on physics and the natural sciences. Dunash is thought to be the author of several works (all probably in Arabic). The following three are no longer extant: (1) a comparative study of Arabic and Hebrew, in which the author tries to prove the antiquity of Hebrew, and which is mentioned or quoted by Judah *Ibn Bal'am, Abu Ibrahim Isak *Ibn Barun, Moses *Ibn Ezra, and Abraham *Ibn Ezra, but in deprecatory terms; (2) a book on Indian calculus, probably bearing the title *Ḥisab al-Gubar*; and (3) a treatise on astronomy in three parts (structure of the spheres, mathematical astronomy, and astrology, probably critical). The last was written at the request of *Ḥisdai ibn Shaprut; another edition or copy was dedicated by Dunash to the Fatimid caliph al-Mansur Ismail ibn al Qayyim. Extant in manuscript is a treatise on the armillary sphere, an astronomical instrument, dedicated to a high Fatimid dignitary and written in Arabic characters (as opposed to other Arabic writings in Hebrew script; Hagia Sophia Ms. 4861). There are vague allusions to a commentary on the first chapter of Genesis. The Arab physician Ibn al-Baytar (d. 1248) refers to a medical work by Dunash, and there are other references to a "Book on Urine" as well.

The commentary on the *Sefer Yeẓirah*, mentioned above, was written in 955/6. Attempts made to attribute this work to Isaac Israeli or Jacob b. Nissim may be disregarded. To date, the Cairo *Genizah* has yielded only about one-third of the Arabic original of this text; it has been preserved fully in four Hebrew versions: the first by Nahum ha-Ma'aravi (c. 1240); the second by Moses b. Joseph b. Moses (somewhat earlier), based on the complete Arabic editions; the third by an anonymous author, probably of the 14th century, from a shorter Arabic text of perhaps the mid-11th century; and the fourth by another anonymous author of unknown date, from an Arabic abridgment, possibly of 1092.

Dunash's exegetical method in *Sefer Yeẓirah* is scientific. He succeeded in incorporating in his commentary much of the knowledge of his day without losing sight of the influence of philosophic and scientific truths on religion. He dealt with such truths as an incorporeal God, creator of a perfectly regulated universe, a hierarchy of souls of the spheres, and prophetic inspiration, said to coincide in its highest degree, as in the case of Moses, with Plotinian ecstasy. Dunash did not hesitate to criticize *Saadiah Gaon's commentary on the *Sefer Yeẓirah*; however, these criticisms have been attenuated or suppressed in some of the Hebrew versions. Dunash's commentary enjoyed some renown in the 12th century when *Judah b. Barzillai, Joseph ibn *Ẓaddik, and perhaps *Judah Halevi made use of it. It is mentioned several times in the 13th century, particularly by Abraham *Abulafia; it was copied with slight alterations c. 1370 by Samuel ibn Motot, and traces of it are found among 15th-century authors, such as Ẓemaḥ Duran, Isaac Halayo (unpublished sermons on the Song of Songs, Paris, Ms. Heb. 228), and *Moses b. Jacob (*Oẓar Adonai*, Oxford, Bodleian Library, Ms. Opp. 556). However, Dunash's work, like that of Isaac Israeli, his teacher, played only a secondary role in the history of Jewish thought.

BIBLIOGRAPHY: Poznański, in: *Zikkaron le-Harkavy* (1903), 190–2; H. Malter, *Saadia Gaon, His Life and Works* (1921), index; Vajda, in: REJ, 105 (1939), 132–140; 107 (1946–47), 99–156; 110 (1949–50), 67–92; 112 (1953), 5–33; 113 (1954), 37–61; 119 (1961), 159–61; Goldziher, *ibid.*, 52 (1906), 187–90; G. Vajda, in: *Annuaire de l'Institut de Philologie et d'Histoire Orientale et Slaves*, 13 (1953), 641–52; Stern, in: *Homenaje a Millás Vallicrosa*, 2 (1956), 373–82 (Eng.); A. Altmann and S.M. Stern (eds.), *Isaac Israeli* (1958), index; Baron, Social², index.

[Georges Vajda]

DUNAYEVSKI, ISAAC OSIPOVICH (1900–1955), Soviet Russian composer. Born at Lokhvitsa, near Poltava, Ukraine, he began to learn the piano at the age of four and studied at the Kharkov Conservatory, with Joseph *Achron. In 1919 he settled in Leningrad. Dunayevski was one of the leading popular composers of Soviet Russia, and in 1937 was made president of the Union of Soviet Composers. His works include light operas, dance music, songs, choruses, and incidental music to plays and films, as well as a string quartet, a *Song of Stalin* for chorus and orchestra, a *Requiem* for reciter and quintet, and one work for jazz orchestra, the *Rhapsody on Song-Themes of the Peoples of the U.S.S.R.* (1931). Among his operettas were *The Golden Valley* (1934) and *The Road to Happiness* (1939). His 12 scores for films include *Circus* (1935) and *Volga-Volga* (1938) which made a permanent contribution to Soviet popular song. For a time after 1933 he experimented with jazz idioms. He was awarded the Stalin Prize in 1941. Dunayevski died in Moscow, and the collection *Vystupleniya, statyi, pisma, vospominaniya* ("Appearances, Articles, Letters, Memoirs") was published posthumously in 1961.

BIBLIOGRAPHY: L. Danilevich, *I.O. Dunayevski* (1947); I. Nestyev, in: *Sovetskaya Muzyka*, 19: 11 (1955), 35–48; L.V. Mikheyeva, *I.O. Dunayevski, 1900–1955: kratki ocherk zhizni i tvorchestva* (1963).

DUNAYEVTSY, town in Khmelnitski district, Ukraine. The Jewish community numbered 1,129 in 1765, but by 1775 was reduced to 484 as a result of the *Haidamak uprising of 1768. From the beginning of the 19th century many Jews found employment as workers, dyers, and traders in the flourishing textile industry there. Dunayevtsy was the scene of a trial lasting from 1838 to 1840 in which a number of Jews were accused of the murder of two informers. The Jewish population numbered 2,020 in 1847 and approximately 10,000 before the outbreak of World War I (about two-thirds of the total population). Dunayevtsy became known as a center of Hebrew and Zionist literary and educational activity. The scholars and writers Yeḥezkel *Kaufmann, Ẓevi *Scharfstein, S.L. *Blank, and Abraham *Rosen were born and educated there. After the establishment of Soviet rule the town became impoverished. Many Jews immigrated or moved to the cities of the Russian interior. There were 5,186 Jews in Dunayevtsy in 1926 (60.5% of the total), dropping to 4,478 (68.23% of the total) before World War II. The Germans occupied Dunayevtsy on July 11, 1941. They concentrated the Jews into a ghetto. On May 2, 1942, about 3,000 were murdered by the Nazis.

BIBLIOGRAPHY: *Kamenetz-Podolsk u-Sevivatah* (1965), 103–52; Z. Scharfstein, *Hayah Aviv ba-Areẓ* (1953), 11–163.

[Yehuda Slutsky]

DUNEDIN, city in Otago, New Zealand. Five Jewish families had settled in Dunedin, the most southern Jewish community in the world, before the discovery of gold in Otago in 1861. In 1862, the congregation had a membership of 43, including the poet and novelist Benjamin *Farjeon. Jacob *Saphir of Jerusalem, then visiting Dunedin, wrote a *megillah* for reading on Purim. The first synagogue was consecrated in 1864. A number of congregational activities were initiated while B. Lichenstein was minister, from 1875 to 1892. A synagogue was built in 1881. From 1884 D.E. Theomin headed the community for almost 30 years. Wolf Heinemann, professor and examiner in German and Hebrew at Otago University from 1895, lectured in the synagogue and founded the Dunedin Zionist Society in 1905. Other ministers included A.T. Chodowski, who officiated from 1898 to 1909 and later founded the *Australian Jewish Chronicle*, and A. Astor (1926–30). Although a small community, it produced four notable members of the legislature – Sir Julius *Vogel, Samuel Shrimski, Bendix Hallenstein, and Mark Cohen. In the present century it dwindled and numbered only 100 in 1968 and about the same number in 2004.

BIBLIOGRAPHY: L.M. Goldman, *History of the Jews in New Zealand* (1958), index; *Journal and Proceedings of the Australian Jewish Historical Society*, 1 (1943), 154–60; 2 (1948), 202–12, 269–80, 394–400; *New Zealand Jewish Review and Communal Directory* (1931), 19, 47, 69. **ADD. BIBLIOGRAPHY:** S. Levine, *The New Zealand Jewish Community* (1999), index; JYB 2004.

[Maurice S. Pitt]

DUNKELMAN, BENJAMIN (1913–1997), Canadian manufacturer and volunteer soldier in World War II and Israel's War of Independence. Dunkelman was born in Toronto. His father, David, was a wealthy Toronto clothing manufacturer and retailer and his mother, Rose Miller (see *Dunkelman, Rose), was a leading figure in Canadian Hadassah. After finishing at Toronto's elite Upper Canada College, he visited Palestine in 1932 as a teenager and worked for several months at Tel Asher, with the intention of joining a kibbutz. He returned again in 1935 hoping to stay on and establish a new settlement but returned to Canada and in 1939 – believing that he had a personal score to settle with the Nazis – tried to join the Royal Canadian Navy. Rejected, he enlisted in the Canadian Army and served in combat with great distinction, earning the prestigious Distinguished Service Order as a company commander in the Queen's Own Rifles for, among other achievements, leading his men under fire through the heavily mined Hochwald forest. He was recognized as an expert in mortars. Arriving back in Palestine in April 1948, Dunkelman joined Haganah forces battling on the roads to keep Jerusalem supplied and commanded one of the units in the fight for control of Galilee. Troops under his command captured Nazareth. He also organized and trained a heavy mortar support brigade. He returned to Canada after Israel's War of Independence and took over the family clothing manufacturing business. In Toronto he was active also in many Jewish and non-Jewish organizations and later wrote a revealing autobiography, *Dual Allegiance: An Autobiography* (1976), which reflects the tension he felt between his commitment both to Israel and Canada.

[Gerald Tulchinsky (2nd ed.)]

DUNKELMAN, ROSE (1889–1949), Canadian Jewish communal leader and philanthropist. Rose Dunkelman (Miller) was born in Philadelphia and moved to Toronto at age 13. She married David Dunkelman, a major Toronto clothing manufacturer, in 1910. They had six children. Rose Dunkelman was a formidable force in a number of Jewish causes, including the Toronto Talmud Torah and Hebrew Free Schools, the Toronto YMHA and YWHA, and the Jewish Federated Charities. A passionate Zionist, however, her prime organizational focus was in support of Canadian Hadassah and in her forthright manner she was partly responsible for making the organization an independent and powerful Canadian Zionist force during the interwar and immediate postwar years. At her Toronto home and summer estate, "Sunnybrook Farm," she often entertained visiting Zionist leaders who kept her informed of unfolding events in Palestine. Outraged by the exclusion of Jews from nearby vacation resorts, she founded Balfour Beach on Lake Simcoe north of Toronto, where she had 30 cottages built which welcomed Jewish vacationers. A veritable whirlwind of energy and activity, she also worked for the Canadian Red Cross and was awarded the King's Coronation Medal in 1937. Miffed by the anti-Zionist editorials in the Toronto-based *Canadian Jewish Review*, in 1931, together with her husband, she founded the *Canadian Jewish Standard*, and recruited the talented Meyer *Weisgal, who briefly served as editor. This monthly magazine reflected her deep commitment to the Zionist cause. When she died in 1949 Rose Dunkelman was buried in Israel at *Deganyah Alef. Her son, Benjamin *Dunkelman, fought in Israel's War of Independence.

[Gerald Tulchinsky (2nd ed.)]

°DUNS SCOTUS, JOHN (1265–1308), Catholic theologian and philosopher. Scotus opposed many of the views of Thomas *Aquinas. Against Aquinas he affirmed the limitations of philosophy, and argued that the will is superior to the intellect, because the will is free while the intellect is bound by necessity, insofar as one is constrained to believe what the intellect recognizes to be true. He objected to Aquinas' contention that attributes are applied analogically to man and God, holding that if man is to know anything at all about God, the attributes applied to God and man must, in some sense, be univocal. He affirmed the existence of individualized forms, maintaining that every object has its own unique form, its "thisness" (*haecceitas*), which differentiates it from other objects. Scotus is known for his support of the forcible baptism of Jewish children, and his contention that a sovereign has the right to have Jewish children educated in the Christian faith without parental consent. In this he opposed Aquinas who had argued against forcible baptism on the ground that it violates the right of parenthood which is a principle of natural law. Scotus held that conversion supersedes natural law, for nothing should stand in the way of enabling man to achieve eternal salvation. In the case of conflict between the right of parenthood and the will of God, the right of parenthood ceases to be binding. He did maintain that forcible baptism, when carried out by a private individual, violates natural law; however, when carried out by a sovereign it is legitimate (L. Wadding (ed.), *Opera Omnia*, 8 (1639), 275).

In a polemical passage directed against infidels Scotus characterized the Jews in exactly the same terms as had Aquinas: the laws of the Old Testament have become "tasteless" (*insipidi*) with the appearance of Christ (*Opus Oxoniense* Prolog., pt. 2, in *Opera*, 1 (1951), 71ff.). His negative attitude toward Judaism did not prevent Scotus from utilizing the views of Solomon ibn *Gabirol, author of *Fons Vitae* (*Mekor

Ḥayyim; "The Fountain of Life"), whom he knew under the name of Avicebron, and did not identify as a Jew, and *Maimonides. He defended Ibn Gabirol's theory that even spiritual beings are composed of form and matter, a view which was traditionally upheld by the Franciscans and rejected by the Dominicans. Scotus refers to Maimonides' discussion of the relation of reason and revelation, and to his doctrine of divine attributes, which he finds similar to that of Avicenna, and follows Maimonides in his doctrine of prophecy. He argues against the view that the temporal creation of the world cannot be proved – a view which Aquinas adopted from Maimonides – but does not mention Maimonides in this connection. While there are no direct references to Scotus in their writings it had recently been suggested that Scotus and his school exerted an influence on late medieval Jewish philosophers. Thus reflections of Scotus' theory of individuation are found in *Ma'amar ha-Dan ba-Ẓurot ha-Peratiyyot o Ishiyyot* ("A Treatise Upon Personal Forms," Paris Bibliothèque Nationale, Ms. Heb. 984) written by *Jedaiah ha-Penini. *Levi b. Gershom, in his view that man's freedom of the will is a deviation from the determinism that prevails in the universe, and in his rejection of negative attributes, appears to have been influenced by Scotus. There are distinct similarities to Scotus in Ḥasdai *Crescas' criticism of the physical proofs of God's existence, in his theory of divine attributes, and in his seeing a compulsory element in the activity of the intellect. (For further details on Scotus' influence on Jewish philosophy, see S. Pines, in PIASH, 1 (1967), 1–51.)

BIBLIOGRAPHY: E. Gilson, *History of Christian Philosophy in the Middle Ages* (1955), 454–71; idem, *Jean Duns Scot. Introduction à ses positions fondamentales* (1952); F. Copleston, *A History of Philosophy*, 2 pt. 2 (1962), 199–275; idem, *Medieval Philosophy* (1952), 107–17; *Encyclopedia of Philosophy*, 2 (1967), 427–36; JE, 5 (1907), 14–15; J. Guttmann, *Die Scholastik des* dreizehnten *Jahrhunderts in ihren Beziehungen zum Judenthum und zur juedischen Literatur* (1902), 154–67. **ADD. BIBLIOGRAPHY:** E. Bettoni, *Duns Scotus* (1961); J.K. Ryan and M.M. Bonansea (eds.), *John Duns Scotus 1265–1965* (1965).

°DUPONT-SOMMER, ANDRÉ (1900–1983), French Bible scholar. Dupont-Sommer was director of studies at the Ecole des Hautes Etudes from 1938, professor at the Sorbonne from 1945, professor of Hebrew and Aramaic at the Collège de France from 1963, and president of the Institut d'Etudes Sémitiques of the University of Paris from 1952. He undertook archaeological excavations in the Near East from 1925 to 1934.

Dupont-Sommer was one of the first interpreters of the Dead Sea Scrolls. He published many articles and a number of books on them, including three that have been translated into English under the titles *The Dead Sea Scrolls: A Preliminary Survey* (1952), *The Jewish Sect of Qumran and the Essenes* (1954), and *The Essene Writings from Qumran* (1961). His *Les Araméens* (1949) is an outstanding contribution on the Arameans. His publication of an important collection of several hundred Aramaic ostraca discovered in the French excavations at Elephantine, conducted by C. Clermont-Ganneau, has increased the knowledge of the Aramaic of the Book of Ezra and of the culture of the Jews of Egypt in the Persian period. His other published works include *La doctrine gnostique de la lettre "Waw" d'après une lamelle araméene inédite* (1946), *Les inscriptions araméennes de Sfiré* (1958), and *Observations sur le commentaire d'Habacuc découvert près de la Mer Morte* (1950).

[Zev Garber]

DU PRÉ, JACQUELINE (1945–1987), British cellist. Du Pre was born in Oxford and began studying the cello at the age of six. In 1968, she graduated from the Guildhall School of Music, London, with a gold medal, then studied with Tortelier (in Paris), with Casals, and with Rostropovich (in Moscow). After her London debut at the Wigmore Hall (March 1961), she steadily acquired an international reputation as one of the most naturally gifted musicians England has ever produced. In 1967, she met Daniel *Barenboim, the Israeli pianist, and they were married in June of that year after her conversion to Judaism (she was previously an Anglican). She and her husband made many tours together and performed frequently all over Israel, playing chamber music with Itzchak *Perlman and Pinchas *Zuckerman and appearing in concerts with conductor Zubin *Mehta. In 1973, however, her career tragically ended when she was stricken by multiple sclerosis.

[Max Loppert (2nd ed.)]

DUQUE, SIMON DAVID (1897–1945), one of the last two *ḥazzanim* of the Portuguese Synagogue of Amsterdam, Holland. Born in Amsterdam, Duque was appointed *ḥazzan* in 1923. He was chosen from among three candidates because of his adherence to the Amsterdam tradition. He also aimed at an operatic style and had a beautiful voice. Among his many moving *ḥazzanut* features are his *Kedushah* for Sabbath *Musaf* and *Ve-Hu Raḥum* for the evening service. His falsetto was famous. He was deported by the Nazi occupiers of Holland and died at the Dachau concentration camp.

[Amnon Shiloah (2nd ed.)]

DURA-EUROPOS, ancient city on the Euphrates River in Syria. It was long known from the writings of the first-century geographer Isidore of Charax/Bosra, but its exact whereabouts, a site known as el-Ṣalihiye, was discovered only accidentally by a British patrol in the aftermath of World War I while they were digging military installations. A brief excavation was conducted at the site by F. Cumont in 1922–23. A major Franco-American expedition carried out work at the site between the years 1928–37. The city was founded in about 300 B.C.E. by Seleucus I Nicator. It served as a transfer post where goods brought up the river from India were put on camels and carried to Palmyra and the Mediterranean. Dura-Europos was taken by the Parthians in 114 B.C.E. but it retained its autonomy and Greek character. After being held briefly by the Romans at the time of Trajan in 116 C.E., it was restored to the Parthians in 118 C.E., and captured once again by the

Romans in Lucius Verus' campaign of 168 C.E. The Romans ruled it until its conquest and destruction by the Sassanids under Shapur I in 256 C.E. Throughout its history the city contained a mixed population and judging from its temples it was largely eastern in orientation, with strong cultural ties with Palmyra. In addition to a synagogue the excavators also found a Mithraeum for the Roman soldiers and a small Christian chapel. The relative sizes of the pagan temples and the synagogue seem to indicate that Dura-Europos' Jewish population was a small minority in the city. Thus although the city was only about 250 miles (400 km.) north of Nehardea, the great center of Babylonian Jewry, the Jews of Dura-Europos must have lived as an isolated group in a pagan center rather than as a fully Jewish community.

The synagogue at Dura-Europos, discovered in 1932, was found in a remarkable state of preservation. It lay just inside the western city wall within an insula of ten houses (block L7) and when the inhabitants, judged expendable by the shrinking Roman Empire, attempted to strengthen the wall against the advancing Sassanid army, they tore off the roofs of the buildings just behind the wall and filled them with sand from the desert. The synagogue was accordingly as securely buried and protected as at Pompeii. The paintings, completed only some five years before the city fell, emerged from the sand nearly as fresh as when painted. The synagogue was built in c. 244–45 C.E. by remodeling a private house and followed the plan of the inner shrines of the pagan temples of the city. Since it contained benches around the room, often found in synagogues elsewhere, it evidently served for group worship. The benches, however, could accommodate only a small part of the congregation and wooden stools were probably used as well. Beneath the synagogue the remains of another smaller and more modest one was found, dating to the last quarter of the second century C.E. The entrance to the earlier synagogue was on the side adjoining the city wall through a narrow corridor which led to a courtyard with porticoes on two sides. The prayer room, 25 × 14 ft. (10.85 × 4.60 m.), contained a niche (the Torah Shrine?) in its west wall, a bench along the walls of the room, and two doorways, one of which may have served as the women's entrance (no sign of a women's gallery was found at Dura-Europos). The walls of the building were painted in geometric designs and fruit and floral motifs. In one corner of the court was a pool; adjoining it was a large room with benches (*bet midrash*?).

The second (upper) synagogue has an inscription written in Aramaic indicating the date of the completion of its construction in 245 C.E. Its entrance was on the street side far from the wall; the entrance was well hidden and the prayer room itself was accessible only through various passageways. The courtyard of the synagogue was expanded and surrounded by porticoes on three sides and the prayer room was also enlarged (to 45 × 25 ft. (13.65 × 7.68 m.)). Benches were extended along all the walls and a stepped *bimah* ("platform") built near the niche. A Greek inscription commemorates the building of the synagogue by Samuel b. Idi "elder of the Jews" with the assistance of several members of the congregation. All the walls of the second synagogue were covered with paintings, most of them representing scenes from the Bible, and these must have been executed within only a few years of the renovation. Into these scenes were incorporated pagan figures, forms, and symbols (see *Symbolism, Jewish, in the Greco-Roman Period). The biblical paintings, and others, which only by a flight of the imagination can be associated with any specific biblical incident, were arranged in variously proportioned rectangles separated by borders of running grapevines. Pilasters painted with vines occupy the corners and support the ceiling which seems originally to have been made of square coffers decorated with painted tiles and probably with plaster wreaths at the intersections of the beams. The paintings around the bottom row of the room show masks and harnessed felines holding fragments of their victims. Both the masks and the felines are of the kind generally associated with Dionysus and also with other deities, e.g., the felines with Cybele, the Great Mother of fertility. The many tiles preserved from the ceiling show a large number of fertility symbols: bunches of fruit and grain, and many representations of female heads which Kraeling identified with the "ubiquitous Demeter-Persephone of the eastern Mediterranean," i.e., Cybele. This goddess also appears with the felines and the masks in the dado. Other ceiling tiles show birds, fish, running gazelles, and centaurs holding out a fish. Several tiles bear dated donor's inscriptions in Greek and Aramaic; the congregation was presumably bilingual. Since the ceiling was about 23 ft. (7 m.) high, the inscriptions, written in relatively small letters, could have been read only by the sharpest eyes and thus they were possibly designed to suggest the donors' destiny in the heavenly setting of the ceiling itself, and not as plaques for conspicuous notice.

The room was oriented for worship toward Jerusalem by placing the niche, presumably for the Torah, in the long west wall. On a panel above the niche were painted a *menorah*, *etrog*, and *lulav*, the temple facade, and a crudely drawn scene of the sacrifice of Isaac (the *Akedah*), which was apparently used to represent a *shofar* ("ram's horn"). This decoration, and the first stage of the high vine painted above the niche, seem to have been executed even before the other paintings had been planned. The high panel (the reredos) above the niche was repainted several times; this makes it the most important design in the room. After being exposed to light for a few hours, the underpaintings came through the upper ones, rendering the whole scene one of utter confusion. The various stages of painting, however, can be fairly well reconstructed, and show that the master directing the decoration planned it during the execution of the paintings and did not merely copy conventional models. First a great tree, rising nearly to the ceiling, was painted with grape leaves and tendrils but without grapes (and thus called a "tree-vine") growing out of a large crater. How many times this design was altered cannot be determined but at a later stage a king in Persian dress seated on a throne and two throne guards were inserted at the top of the tree-vine since leaves show through the white Greek robes of the guards. Several other alterations were also made. The crater at the bottom was painted out and the trunk awkwardly extended downward to leave spaces on either side of the trunk. In the space at the left a table was painted with a bread symbol, and on the right a crater with rampant felines facing each other above it. Halfway up the vine a figure of Orpheus was added playing his lyre to an eagle and a lion, and perhaps other birds and a monkey. This group was not part of the original design since the vine leaves show through the bodies of Orpheus and the lion. These alterations were apparently made to indicate more clearly the meaning of the tree-vine, namely, through the salvation of music, bread, and wine, the tree led to the great throne above. The design apparently still did not seem specific, or specifically Jewish enough, for the lower table and the crater with felines on either side of the trunk were painted out and replaced by two new scenes. On the left Jacob on his deathbed was represented blessing his twelve sons, while on the right he blesses Ephraim and Manasseh in the presence of Joseph. Representatives of the 13 tribes were also painted standing around the throne above. The alterations in the design were made to show explicitly what seems to have been originally implied by the tree-vine alone, i.e., the salvation of Israel. Orpheus was left in as he was apparently identified with some Jewish figure such as David who saved Israel through his music.

On each side of the reredos two standing figures were painted. The upper two clearly represent Moses at the burning bush and receiving the tablets of the Law on Sinai. Of the lower two figures one depicts a man in a white Greek pallium (as Moses was dressed in the upper two figures) reading a scroll on the model of readers in scenes of mystery religions, and the other an old man in similar garb standing under the arc of heaven with its sun, moon, and stars. The reader seems to be Moses giving the Law to the Israelites after his descent from Sinai, and the old man, the dying Moses, who in Philo's account of his life was taken at his death to join in the song of the heavenly bodies to God. Other identifications, however, have been suggested for the latter two figures and no positive judgment can be made. The painters now continued to cover the walls with scenes based mainly on biblical incidents, all of which are stylized and given midrashic or allegorical interpretation. On the bottom left side of the west wall Elijah is represented reviving the widow's son, an infant dead and without features who is held out to the prophet by his mother; next the prophet holds up the baby alive but still with no features, and lastly he is again in his mother's arms, glorified, and finally with features. Beside this scene a longer painting shows three groups of people. On the right Ahasuerus, enthroned with Esther, is humiliated as a messenger brings him news of the massacre of his subjects. At the left Mordecai in full regal splendor rides on a horse led by Haman in slave's dress. Between these two scenes, in the dramatic center of the painting, stand four large figures dressed in pallia with three of their hands raised in blessing. These are apparently angelic figures representing God's intervention in the Persian crisis. On the same row to the right of the niche Samuel anoints David, who stands with his hands folded under a dark pallium, while a large Samuel in a white pallium pours oil from a horn onto David's head. Jesse and five brothers stand behind in a hieratic row wearing white or light-colored pallia. To the right of this scene is the last painting on the bottom row of the west wall, a large work based on the infancy of Moses. At the right Pharaoh enthroned and in Persian dress orders the midwives (the mother and the sister of Moses) to kill all male Jewish babies and a woman stoops apparently to put Moses into the ark. In the center of a group at the left Moses is taken out of the ark by a naked woman who stands knee-deep in the river. She is identified as Aphrodite-Anahita by her peculiar necklace. She holds the baby up to three women standing on the bank; these are identified by the emblems they carry as the three nymphs who were the nurses of all divine babies, actual gods, and divine kings. As Aphrodite-Anahita holds the baby up to the nymphs it has no features, but in the last scene the baby is in the hands of the mother and sister and at last fully formed with features. At the far left of the row above, Moses again stands in the pallium, parts of which have a peculiar checked design. He touches a well with his rod and from it 12 streams flow out toward 12 tents surrounding the well. In each tent stands a short figure in Persian dress. A gabled doorway with only darkness behind it occupies the back center of the painting; a *menorah* and incense burners stand before it. It is generally agreed that the scene is based on Moses' bringing water from the rock in the desert, and that the 12 tribes here, as often in Jewish tradition, are equated with the Zodiac.

Adjoining this scene on the right, the artist depicted a temple with Aaron in priestly dress dominating the scene. Aaron is identified by his name written in Greek beside him. Five much smaller men in Persian dress attend him, one holding an ax as if to strike a reddish bovine before him, and the others carry horns (not like *shofars*). Another bovine, probably a bull, stands with a ram on the right. The main interest is the temple itself, which instead of the curtained tabernacle of Aaron's priesthood, is a temple of stone, an outer wall forming a court around an inner porticoed sanctuary. In the outer wall are three closed doorways; a pink-lined curtain blows back from the central one. Aaron stands in the court along with a large *menorah*, two small incense burners, and an altar with an indistinguishable animal on it for sacrifice. The *menorah* is the central object, but behind it, through the open door of the inner shrine, can be seen the veiled Ark of the Covenant. The Ark stands in front of the veil after the ancient custom for revealing veiled objects. The form of the temple was taken from a common design which the Dura painter spaced out so as to indicate the inner court with its objects. Even the winged Victories bearing wreaths as acroteria for the inner shrine were retained. This painting seems to represent the values of the Aaronic priesthood in general. Balancing this on the other side of the reredos is a basically similar temple, but with the design altered to express a more abstract idea. Again three closed doors pierce what was meant as the outer wall and above it is the inner shrine still with its winged Victories. The outer wall, however, has become a series of seven stone walls, each a different color, which rise from the bottom to the top and from side to side of the painting. Thus the three doors and the inner shrine seem to be artificially superimposed upon the walls. The inner shrine has ten columns instead of the five in the Aaron scene, and like the three doors, it is closed. The temple does not stand on the ground and no ritual is indicated (and so it is called the "Closed Temple"). On each of the two doors in the lower central doorway are three panels. These depict, from top to bottom, a bull lying in the position of sacrifice; a herculean figure standing naked and flanked by a small naked figure; and the figure of Tyche.

To the right of the "Closed Temple" is the last painting on this register of the west wall which depicts a third temple, open and empty, with cult objects and the fragments of two Persian deities strewn on the ground before it. Beside it is the Ark on a cart pulled by two bovines that are being whipped and led by two men in Persian costume. Three dignified men in light-colored pallia walk abreast behind the Ark. The painting was without doubt suggested by the biblical incident in which the idol of Dagon collapsed before the Ark and the Ark itself was returned to the Israelites on a cart. The left side of the top register of the west wall is almost totally destroyed although the base of a throne with "Solomon" written on it in Greek and the bottom of various figures can be seen. Nothing, however, can be identified. Opposite this, a long painting presents the drama of the Exodus from Egypt. Egypt is depicted as a walled town at the far right with figures of Ares and two Victories above the open gate through which the Israelites march out. They advance in four columns. In the upper three columns two bands of armed troops guard both sides of a row of 12 men in white pallia, presumably the 12 heads of tribes. The bottom row is made up of ordinary people wearing only the belted chiton. Leading them is Moses as a great heroic figure. In a white dotted pallium Moses strides vigorously toward the Red Sea, which he is about to strike, not with the rod expected from the biblical narrative, but with the knobby mace of Heracles. The sea before him is already closed in the economy of narrative art and Moses is again depicted closing it on its other side; the sea is filled with drowning people. Beyond this Moses again touches water with his rod; this time the water is a pool filled with numerous leaping fish to indicate its vitality. The armed guards of the first scene stand behind the pool with the 12 heads of the tribes; they hold banners like those carried in mystic processions. When the sea was divided, according to Jewish legend, 12 paths were made, one for each tribe, and these are apparently indicated by a tier of horizontal lines behind the third Moses. The other walls of the room present biblical scenes in a similar vein but, since they are only partially preserved, their overall plan, if any existed, cannot be reconstructed. Of the east wall only the lowest register and dado remain; one scene shows a few birds and part of a table. Another apparently shows David and Abishai approaching the sleeping Saul and Abner in the wilderness; half the painting is occupied by an army on white horses led by a captain. In the Esther scene the artist seems to have represented divine intervention and this apparently also appears in two scenes on the south wall. There, below a badly preserved procession of the Ark of the Covenant are three scenes from an Elijah cycle which first depicts Elijah coming to the widow, and then the sacrifice of the prophets of Baal. The sacrifice is being vitiated by a great serpent that attacks the small figure of Hiel according to the legend in which Hiel was hidden behind the altar to set fire to the sacrifice but was killed by a snake. Beside this, in the corner adjoining the west wall, Elijah offers his sacrifice while servants pour on water and three great figures dressed in pallia bring down heavenly fire. Although Elijah reviving the widow's son should have preceded the two scenes of sacrifice, it instead adjoins them on the wall where it was apparently part of the original plan and the cycle on the south wall, an afterthought probably intended to show the lesser triumphs of the prophet as preparation for his final power to raise the dead.

The north wall is better preserved but still only part remains. In the single scene left at the top Jacob dreams of the ladder. The design is identical with that in the catacomb of Via Latina in Rome except that in the catacomb the angels wear white pallia and at Dura-Europos, Persian dress. As the pallium is the original form, the change to Persian dress in the East must be of significance, but nothing suggests what prompted it. The register beneath this contains only unidentifiable fragments on the right; beside it is a fine representation of a great battle centering on two champions attacking each other with lances as in other scenes of Eastern art while warriors in identical armor fight above and below them. One champion rides on a black horse and the other on a white. In the same painting a group of six warriors guard the Ark of the Covenant while four men in Greek chitons carry it away from the battle. The scene must be based on the battle of Ebenezer where the Ark was captured but it also shows the turmoil of the conflict between light and darkness (the two horsemen) as against the triumphant reality embodied in the Ark. As in the Elijah cycle the scene seems to be related to the one adjoining it on the west wall where the heathen idols crash before the Ark after the same battle. The scene on the side wall again seems to amplify the one on the west wall but the artist's exact intention cannot be determined. Below this in the longest painting in the room is a great pageant of Ezekiel. He is first depicted being brought into the valley, then preaching to the bones, and supervising their restoration to life. The continuation depicts either the legendary beheading of Ezekiel or Mattathias the Hasmonean slaying the faithless Jew.

The paintings at Dura-Europos were executed by at least two artists. One, influenced by Hellenistic art, portrayed the major biblical personages (Moses, Jacob, Joseph, etc.) as Roman citizens dressed in the tunic and pallium, and the Israelite host as Roman soldiers. The other drew his inspiration from Persian art and portrayed his figures as horsemen in Parthian dress (Mordecai, Ezekiel, the sons of Aaron, the Israelites fighting the Philistines, etc.). The women (such as Queen Esther, Pharaoh's daughter, etc.) are dressed like the Hellenistic city-goddesses (Tyche). Particularly forceful and vivid in artistic execution are the imaginative paintings, such as the vision of dry bones which contains three episodes of the story of Ezekiel in one painting, and the souls of the dead are portrayed as Greek Psyches with wings of butterflies. The Dura-Europos paintings contain a wealth of material from the *aggadah*, which was also apparently derived in part from the early Targum, such as the descriptions of the miracle of the battle of Meribah where water was sent through channels to each of 12 tents which symbolize the camps of the tribes. Solomon's throne and the sacrifice of the prophets of Baal on Mt. Carmel are depicted according to the legends of the Midrash and thus they contain details not present in the biblical narratives, as for example, Hiel bitten by a snake on the altar of the prophets of Baal (cf. Yal., I Kings 18:25 [214]). The architecture in the paintings generally follows Hellenistic style but Jewish tradition can be recognized in several details, such as the Ark of the Covenant in the desert as a wheeled chariot (similar to a relief from Kefar Naḥum). This tradition is also evident in the dress of the high priest Aaron and other details.

From the social and religious historical standpoint it is significant that in the third century a Jewish community in the Diaspora did not hesitate to decorate the walls of a synagogue with the human form, with the major figures of the Bible (although this was later on also done in synagogues in the Galilee). The discovery of Dura-Europos is of primary importance for the history of art: until then this Jewish-Hellenistic art style was known only from the paintings of early Christians in the catacombs of Rome. Dura-Europos provided a Jewish source of this art. Its paintings present a blending of Eastern and Western – Persian and Hellenistic – elements (notably in the frontal pose of the figures and the Hellenistic style dress) which predates by centuries the same fusion which is the basis of Byzantine art. The paintings provide a focal point in ancient art in which influences of the past converge with developments of the future. The Dura-Europos paintings were later transferred to the Damascus Museum. A complete copy was reconstructed at Yale.

[Erwin Ramsdell Goodenough / Michael Avi-Yonah]

Later Scholarship

The synagogue paintings (approximately 29 panels are preserved) are thought to have been the work of Jewish artists, perhaps hailing from Palmyra (Kraeling), utilizing pattern books of artistic renderings of biblical stories available to them, as well as inspired by Jewish liturgy, customs, and legends prevalent in Palestine at that time. Wright wrote in 1980 that the paintings "are too clumsy and provincial in execution to have been invented independently, without an iconographic model, in that desert outpost" (quoted in Gutmann 1987). Among the questions that scholars have been dealing with in regard to the paintings are the following: What are their stylistic and iconographic sources? Why was the Second Commandment (Ex. 31:45–: "You shall not make for yourself a sculptured image or any likeness") ignored? Does the cycle of murals have an overall purpose and meaning? Do they reflect a set form of theological Judaism of that time? Did they exert any influence on subsequent Jewish and Christian art? Goodenough dedicated three volumes of his *Jewish Symbols of the Graeco-Roman World* to a detailed analysis of the Dura-Europas synagogue paintings. Goodenough's attempts to read Jewish mysticism into many of the details of the paintings, especially in regard to the type of garments worn by the various figures, and the absence of certain symbols next to the representation of the *menorah*, and so forth, have met with much criticism by scholars, notably by Avi-Yonah (1973) and Smith (1975). Although Jewish religious symbolism and imagery undoubtedly existed in antiquity, and much of it was clearly influenced by Graeco-Roman artistry, what remains unclear is the extent of the values that Jews attached to these symbols and images as they appeared in the Dura-Europas paintings. Most scholars are in agreement regarding many of the painted scenes, but a lack of agreement still prevails as to whether these scenes were connected to a central organizing theme or whether they were made at random to enshrine various events in the destiny of the Jewish people. Grabar was of the opinion that the paintings in the synagogue had explicit messianic associations; Flesher has recently shown this to be misguided. Gutman commented in 1987 that "the Dura Europas synagogue paintings have opened up hitherto unforeseen horizons in ancient religious art and history."

[Shimon Gibson (2nd ed.)]

BIBLIOGRAPHY: Mayer, Art, index; F. Cumont, *Les Fouilles de Doura-Europos, 1922–1923* (1926); *The Excavations at Dura-Europos… Preliminary Report of Sixth Season of Work, October 1932–March 1933* (1936), 309–96; T. Ehrenstein, *Ueber die Fresken der Synagogue von Dura Europos* (1937); M.I. Rostovtzeff, *Dura-Europos and its Art* (1938); R. Du Mesnil du Buisson, *Les peintures de la synagogue de Doura Europos* (1939); H.F. Pearson, *A Guide to the Synagogue of Doura Europos* (1939); Grabar, in: RHR, 123 (1941), 143–92, 124 (1941), 5–35; N. Schneid, *Ẓiyyurei Beit ha-Keneset be-Dura Europos* (1946); Sonne, in: HUCA, 20 (1947), 255–362; E.L. Sukenik, *Beit ha-Keneset shel Dura Europos ve-Ẓiyyurav* (1947); R. Wischnitzer, *The Messianic Theme in the Paintings of the Dura Synagogue* (1948); R. Meyer, in: *Judaica*, 5 (1949), 1–40; CH Kraeling, *The Synagogue* (*The Excavations at Dura-Europos. Final Report*, 8 pt. 1, 1956; 8, pt. 2, 1967); Eissfeldt, in: *Reallexikon fuer Antike und Christentum*, 4 (1959), 358–70; E.R. Goodenough, in: IEJ, 8 (1958), 69–79; idem, in: JBL, 81 (1962), 113–41; Goodenough, Symbols, vols. 9–11 (1964). **ADD. BIBLIOGRAPHY:** M. Avi-Yonah, "Goodenough's Evaluation of Dura: A Critique," in: J. Gutmann (ed.), *The Dura-Europas Synagogue: A Re-evaluation (1932–1972)* (1973), 117–35; M. Smith, "Goodenough's Jewish Symbols in Retrospect," in: J. Guttman (ed.), *The Synagogue: Studies in Origins, Archaeology and Architecture* (1975), 194–209; C. Hopkins, *The Discovery of Dura-Europas* (1979); L.I. Levine, "The Synagogue of Dura-Europas," in: L.I. Levine (ed.), *Ancient Synagogues Revealed* (1981), 172–77; J. Guttman, "The Dura Europas Synagogue Paintings: The State of Research," in: L.I. Levine (ed.), *The Synagogue in Late Antiquity* (1987), 61–72; L.M. White, *Building God's House in the*

Roman World (1990); P.V.M. Flesher, "Rereading the Reredos: David, Orpheus, and Messianism in the Dura Europas Synagogue," in: D. Urman and P.V.M. Flesher (eds.), *Ancient Synagogues: Historical Analysis and Archaeological Discovery*. vol. 2 (1995): 346–66.

DURAN, family which originated in Provence, settled in Majorca in 1306, and after the persecutions of 1391 in Algiers. ẒEMAḤ ASTRUC DURAN (d. 1404), a grandnephew of Levi b. *Gershom, was respected as a scholar by both the Jews and non-Jews of Majorca. He died in Algiers. His son was Simeon b. Ẓemah *Duran (14th–15th century). Until the end of the 18th century, the descendants of Simeon b. Ẓemaḥ provided uncontested lay and spiritual leaders among Algerian Jewry. His son was Solomon ben Simeon *Duran whose three sons were *dayyanim* in Algiers. They were AARON (d. c. 1470), a rabbinical authority consulted by such distant communities as Constantinople; Ẓemaḥ ben Solomon *Duran who was married to the daughter of the illustrious Rab (rabbi) Ephraim al-Nakawa of Tlemçen; and Simeon ben Solomon *Duran. ẒEMAḤ BEN SIMEON BEN ẒEMAḤ (d. 1590) wrote a commentary on the poem for Purim by Isaac b. Ghayyat which was published in *Tiferet Yisrael* (Venice, 1591?) by his son SOLOMON (d. c. 1593). The latter wrote notes on the works of his grandfather Simeon b. Ẓemaḥ, *Yavin Shemu'ah* and *Tashbaẓ*, which are followed by his casuistic responsa *Ḥut ha-Meshullash*, part 1. In addition, Solomon wrote a collection of sermons, a commentary on the Book of Esther, and a treatise on temperance. All of these are included in his *Tiferet Yisrael*. He is also the author of a commentary on Proverbs, *Ḥeshek Shelomo* (Venice, 1623). His son ẒEMAḤ (d. 1604) was a talmudist whose death inspired Abraham *Gavison to write an elegy. AARON DURAN (d. 1676), *dayyan* in Algiers, was probably his grandson.

Ẓemaḥ ben Benjamin (d. 1727) was a prominent authority in religious matters. He also was active in Algerian commerce and left a large fortune to his sons: JOSEPH BENJAMIN (d. 1758), whose responsa were published in the works of Judah Ayash, together with whom he was *dayyan* in Algiers; and ḤAYYIM JONAH (d. c. 1765), who settled in Leghorn, where he published the first part of *Magen Avot* (1763). MOSES BEN ẒEMAḤ, one of the notables of Leghorn, had a previously unpublished part of *Magen Avot* printed in 1785 from an original manuscript which was in the possession of his family. DAVID DURAN (18th–19th centuries), whose father JUDAH (d. c. 1790) was a direct descendant of Simeon b. Ẓemaḥ and one of the wealthiest merchants of Algiers, himself held a distinguished position in Algerian commerce from 1776. He became a rival of the *Bakri-*Busnach merchant families who were then at the height of their power. After the assassination in 1805 of Naphtali Busnach and, two months later, of the dey himself, David was appointed *muqaddim* (leader of the Jewish community) by the new ruler of Algiers, Aḥmad Dey, but was replaced in the same year owing to the intrigues of Joseph Bakri. He continued representing the interests of England in Algiers as against those of France and Spain, whose side was taken by the Bakri-Busnach families. David Bakri was appointed *muqaddim* in 1806 and held the position for over four years but Duran's machinations evidently caused his execution. Although David Duran was again appointed *muqaddim* he was himself executed the same year (October 1811) for no apparent reason, immediately after bringing the annual tax, or presents, to the dey.

The descendants of Simeon b. Ẓemaḥ who had established themselves in Leghorn settled in London before 1826.

BIBLIOGRAPHY: Benjacob, Oẓar, 203 (no. 875), 222 (no. 215), 659 (no. 699), 674 (no. 995); I. Epstein, *Responsa of Rabbi Simon ben Zemah Duran as a Source...* (1930), 1–5, 16, 102; I. Bloch, *Inscriptions tumulaires...* (1888), nos. 7, 17, 27, 37, 46; A. Devoulx, *Le Livre d'or des Israélites algériens* (1872), 4ff., 34, 65ff.; Hirschberg, Afrikah, index.

[David Corcos]

DURAN, PROFIAT (**Profayt**; d.c. 1414), scholar and physician, one of the outstanding anti-Christian polemicists of Spanish Jewry. Duran was probably born in Perpignan and later moved to Catalonia. He was the son of Duran Profiat, himself the son of Profiat de Limos, both Jews of Perpignan. His Hebrew name was Isaac b. Moses ha-Levi, and he signed his books and letters with the pseudonym אפד ("Efod"), the Hebrew acronym of אני פרופיאט דורן, *Ani Profiat Duran* ("I [am] Profiat Duran"). Duran acquired an extensive knowledge of sciences and languages and associated with Ḥasdai *Crescas. He was the author of two polemical tracts against Christianity, the dates of which are not known with certainty: *Al Tehi ka-Avotekha* and *Kelimat ha-Goyim*. The decisive event in his life was the wave of anti-Jewish persecutions in Spain in 1391. According to R. Isaac *Akrish's introduction to *Al Tehi ka-Avotekha* (Constantinople, 1570), Duran himself had been forcibly converted to Christianity in 1391 but reverted to Judaism. However, documents recently discovered in the archives of Perpignan show that Duran lived there as a Christian, under the name of Honoratus de Bonafide, for about 12 years after 1391/2, serving as astrologer to Juan I of Aragon. This presents obvious difficulties, as it is certain that he continued his Hebrew literary activity throughout this period. Tradition has it that he wrote the *Al Tehi ka-Avotekha* when his friend David Bonet *Bonjorn, who was compelled to undergo conversion with him, became a sincere Christian. Duran apparently considered that the other should have remained like himself a Christian only in name, continuing to believe and act like a Jew. Nevertheless, how he managed to do this remains a mystery.

Al Tehi ka-Avotekha is a penetrating satire on Christianity, its tenets, and the affairs of the Church (the schism between Rome and Avignon), and especially on the Jewish converts attracted by the Church. Duran emphasizes the irrationality of Christian doctrine and its insistence on feelings and on "faith" alone. In contrast, he presents the view of Judaism in accordance with the approach of the Jewish philosophers that salvation is attained by faith that does not contradict the demands of the intellect, combined with the performance of the practical *mitzvot*. Because of its witty ambiguities several Christians of the period understood the epistle as a panegyric of Christianity and it was cited by Christian authors, who referred to it as *"Alteca Boteca"* a distortion of the opening words of the letter. When its real intention was recognized, the epistle was condemned to public burning.

Kelimat ha-Goyim, an attack on the tenets of Christianity by historico-critical method, was written by Duran at the initiative of Ḥasdai Crescas. Duran reviewed the writings of the Church Fathers and clarified inaccuracies and fabrications in the translations of Jewish writings by those who attacked Judaism. *Kelimat ha-Goyim* served as a source for subsequent Jewish apologetic literature.

Duran's grammatical work, *Ma'aseh Efod* (Vienna, 1865), shows his extensive knowledge of Semitic and Romance languages and Greek. More than a methodical presentation of grammatical rules in the conventional manner, the work is outstanding in its original approach to grammatical problems and its incisive logical analysis of a number of principles in the same field through an impartial critique of his predecessors. Duran arrived at a new evaluation of the conjugations of the verb by a system resembling that of modern Semitic linguistics. His discussion of the theory of pronunciation reveals exact observation of the functions of the organs of speech and describes in passing the accepted pronunciation of the Hebrew of his time in Spain. He emphasizes the social function of language and stresses that writing is a matter of convention. Unique to *Ma'aseh Efod* is the discussion of the essence of Jewish music, to which Duran attributes two basic styles: chant, such as the cantillation for the reading of the Bible, which is addressed to the mind and understanding, and free melody which arouses the feelings, such as used by supplicants in prayer and by righteous men. Duran regards Jewish melody as having a spiritual object and thus different from the music of other nations, which aspires to aestheticism for its own sake.

Important historical details and an outline of his philosophical ideas are found in a letter of condolence which Duran wrote in 1393 to his friend Joseph b. Abraham on the death of his father, R. Abraham b. Isaac ha-Levi of Gerona, a leader of Catalonian Jewry. In the letter, Duran describes the desperate plight of the Jews in his day whose sufferings had increased to such an extent that the loss of their leaders and scholars was not even felt. He blames the people for not observing the *mitzvot* with proper care and for being concerned only for personal benefit. On the other hand he comforts Jews who had been converted under duress and encourages them to repent.

The other works by Duran include replies on philosophical subjects; elucidation of various parts of the commentary on the Pentateuch by Abraham *Ibn Ezra and of some of his poems; works on astronomy including *Ḥeshev ha-Efod* on the Hebrew calendar (1395); explanations to the commentary of *Averroes on the *Almagest;* a criticism of the *Or Olam* of Joseph ibn *Nahmias; *Ma'amar Zikhron ha-Shemadot*, a history of the persecutions and expulsions from the destruction of the Second Temple until his own times (mentioned by Isaac *Abrabanel but now lost). The work was used by Jewish historians of the 16th century such as Solomon *Ibn Verga, *Joseph *ha-Kohen, and Solomon *Usque. Many of his writings remain in manuscript; some were published as supplements to *Ma'aseh Efod*. New editions of *Al Tehi ka-Avotekha* were published by A. Geiger in *Kovez̩ Vikkuḥim* (Breslau, 1844) and in some copies of *Melo Chofnaim* (Berlin, 1840); by P.M. Heilperin in *Even Boḥen* (Frankfort, 1846); and J.D. Eisenstein in *Oz̩ar Vikkuḥim* (1928), which also includes *Kelimat ha-Goyim*. His commentary on the *Guide* of Maimonides appeared after 1500 together with other commentaries.

[Jacob S. Levinger / Irene Garbell]

Philosophy

The introduction to *Ma'aseh Efod* contains Duran's philosophical views. The Torah, he writes, is perfect, and its study is the only means of attaining eternal, supreme felicity as well as happiness on earth. There are those who maintain that only the observance of *mitzvot* can lead to eternal life. However, while Duran does agree that the observance of the *mitzvot* is very beneficial, he maintains that only knowledge can lead to eternal felicity. He criticizes the talmudists, who reject the study of anything other than the Talmud, refusing even to study the Bible. The philosophers, on the other hand, are also misled. In attempting to reconcile two contraries – Aristotelian philosophy and the Bible – they attribute only a moral function to the Torah. In reality, Duran states, philosophy too is consonant with Jewish teachings, since gentile philosophers borrowed extensively from Jewish sources. However, when Maimonides places the philosopher closest to the throne of God, he is speaking of philosophy in the sense of true knowledge, which is the privileged property of Israel alone. The kabbalists, whose aim is to achieve communion with God, also realize that the worship of God can reach perfection only in the Land of Israel, since the commandments are in harmony with the stars which guide the destiny of that land. Thus the Kabbalah, too, conforms to the Torah and the prophetic books. Nonetheless, since the principles of the Kabbalah are not easily demonstrable and the dissensions among its adherents clearly indicate its dangers, Duran concludes that the surest course is the study of the Torah. The Bible, like the Temple of Jerusalem, has virtues which preserve Israel's physical existence; for example, the Jews of Aragon were saved from persecution as a reward for having recited the Psalms continually. In addition, the Torah has intellectual virtues: it is only the Torah which contains both moral precepts and all of true philosophy. The *sine qua non* of Jewish survival and of eternal life is to preserve the Torah, its text, and its grammar. Thus, for Duran, the real doctrine of Judaism, which he ardently defended, encompasses both philosophy and the whole range of the human sciences, without being limited as are the latter. His commentary on Maimonides' *Guide* (first published 1553) is quite literal. He rejects any interpretations of Maimonides which would portray the latter as a philosopher who holds the Torah in contempt. Nevertheless, he also emphasizes the dangers inherent in certain Maimonidean doctrines. He is very close to the astrological teachings of Abraham ibn Ezra. In response to questions raised by his student, Meir Crescas, he wrote commentaries on various passages of ibn Ezra's commentaries.

[Colette Sirat]

BIBLIOGRAPHY: Baer, Spain, index s.v. *Profet Duran;* F. Cantera Burgos, *Alvar Garcia de Santa Maria* (1952), 318–20; R.W. Emery, in: JQR, 58 (1967/68), 328–37; Renan, Ecrivains, 395–407.

DURAN, SIMEON BEN SOLOMON (**RaShBaSh**, Heb. acronym of **R**abbi **Sh**imon **b**en **Sh**elomo ha-Sheni ("the Second"); 1438–after 1510), rabbi and author. Simeon, son of Solomon b. Simeon *Duran (called RaShBaSh ha-Rishon, "the First"), was born in Algiers and succeeded his brother Ẓemaḥ *Duran as rabbi there. In 1499 he was active in the ransoming of 50 Spanish Jews who had been brought as slaves to Algiers (see Zacuto in bibl.). His attitude toward the Marranos from the religious point of view was lenient (his responsa *Yakhin u-Vo'az* pt. 2 nos. 3, 19, 31), regarding them as Jews. In his old age he had to flee from Algiers when the Spanish army was approaching Bougie and Tunis. He wrote responsa which are printed as the second part of *Yakhin u-Vo'az* (Leghorn, 1782), the first part being by his brother Ẓemaḥ. They are quoted by Joseph *Caro. He has been confused with Simeon (ha-Sheni) b. Ẓemaḥ.

BIBLIOGRAPHY: Abraham Zacuto, *Sefer Yuḥasin ha-Shalem*, ed. by Z. Filipowski (1925^2), 227; S.P. Rabinowitz, *Moẓa'ei Golah* (1894), 32; H.J. Zimmels, *Die Marranen in der rabbinischen Literatur* (1932), index.

[Hirsch Jacob Zimmels]

DURAN, SIMEON BEN ẒEMAḤ (**RaSHBaẒ**, Hebrew acronym of **R**abbi **Sh**imon **b**en **Ẓ**emaḥ; 1361–1444), rabbinic authority, philosopher, and scientist. He was born in Majorca to R. Ẓemaḥ Astruc Duran. In his youth Simeon studied in Palma (Majorca) at the yeshivah of Ephraim Vidal, who was martyred in the year 1391, and in Aragon at that of Jonah *Desmaestre, whose daughter he later married. Educated in accordance with the old Spanish method, he acquired a thorough knowledge of mathematics, astronomy, science, logic, and particularly medicine, which was to become his profession. After his return to Majorca, Simeon practiced as a physician and surgeon in Palma, and he seems to have been in comfortable circumstances. He was also highly esteemed as a rabbinic scholar and even his teacher Ephraim Vidal sought his advice. His prestige there can be gauged from the fact that 44 years after he had left the island he addressed a letter to the Jews of the island reproaching them for negligence in some religious practices and admonishing them to change their way of life.

After the massacre of 1391 in which he lost all of his fortune, Simeon left Majorca for Algiers together with his father and family. Jews from other parts of Spain also immigrated to North Africa, and the arrival of the immigrants had a beneficial effect upon the native Jews there. It caused a revival of knowledge and scholarship, which had been neglected and was in a state of great decline. Spanish rabbis now became religious leaders of African communities. In Algiers the aged *Isaac bar Sheshet was appointed chief rabbi and was also nominated a supreme judge of the Jews by the king. Simeon seems to have joined his *bet din*. Having lost all his fortune and being unable to earn his livelihood from his medical profession, since the native population resorted to superstitious practices rather than to medical help, he was forced to accept a salaried office of rabbi. As Maimonides had prohibited the acceptance of a salary for a rabbinical office, and since in Algiers only Maimonides' decisions were regarded as authoritative, Simeon later found it necessary to justify his action.

The nature of Simeon's official activity during the lifetime of Isaac b. Sheshet can be seen from the following examples. In 1394 a commission to deal with matrimonial laws was appointed, consisting of Bar Sheshet, Isaac *Bonastruc, a rabbi in Algiers, and Simeon, who was asked by the other members to draft the ordinances; his draft was accepted in its entirety. Originally intended for the Spanish immigrants, the ordinances were soon adopted by some of the native Jews as well and were authoritative for African Jewry for centuries. A ban against informers issued about that time was also signed by Bar Sheshet, Bonastruc, and Simeon. From the very fact that Simeon signed third, it is obvious that he was not assistant chief rabbi as some scholars believe (at least not at that time).

Much has been written about the relationship between Bar Sheshet and Simeon. On the one hand Simeon respected the older rabbi, but on the other hand the latter bitterly complained of Simeon, who himself also confesses "I was childish and behaved impudently toward a rabbi who was very old and distinguished in learning" (*Tashbeẓ*, 1, no. 58). In view of this there can be no doubt that a certain tension had existed between the rabbis, the active party being Simeon. The reason for this animosity is not quite certain; it may have been the appointment of the chief rabbi which annoyed Simeon, who although much younger, regarded himself no less worthy of the post owing to his secular and rabbinical knowledge. It seems that Isaac bar Sheshet, being good-natured and peace-loving, succeeded in the course of time in dispelling the greater part of the unfriendly atmosphere. Soon after Bar Sheshet's appointment as judge by the king, Simeon wrote a responsum in which he tried to prove that such an appointment was not permitted, but he did not publish it (*ibid.*, 162). Bar Sheshet often consulted Simeon on various matters, asking him to deal with them and to write responsa. After Isaac bar Sheshet's death (1408) Simeon was appointed chief rabbi (he himself says *dayyan*) with the request that his appointment not be confirmed by the king. (According to the report of the Algerian rabbis in the introduction to *Tashbeẓ*, Simeon's appointment already took place during the older man's lifetime.) During his period of office Simeon was very active. While he had to fight some practices not in accordance with Jewish religion current among the native Jews, he had to raise his voice against his own countrymen who criticized the doctrines of *terefah* and were lax in the observance of some commandments. As judge, Simeon was regarded as an undisputed authority, and interesting facts have become known of his legal proceedings. From various communities, questions were sent to him about religious and legal matters. He had to deal with the problem of the Marranos from the religious and legal points of view. Of his pupils only Abraham ha-Kohen Sholal is known by name, but he may have been his pupil when he was still in Majorca.

Simeon was against adopting stringent practices (*ḥumrot*) which had no foundation in the Talmud; he said that one should be stringent with oneself, but lenient with others. There were some contradictions in him, however, which can also be found among other Spanish scholars. On the one hand he was meek, but on the other he praised himself for his wisdom. Although he greatly admired Maimonides and followed his philosophical views, he believed in astrology which Maimonides so strongly opposed, and he quoted Abraham *Ibn Ezra in connection with astrology, calling him "*he-Ḥasid.*"

A characteristic feature of the method employed in his decisions as *posek* is given by Simeon himself: "In reaching my decisions I do not grope like the blind grope along the wall, for I give a decision only after studying the case carefully. I have never given a decision which I later retracted" (*Tashbeẓ*, pt. 3, no. 189). His decisions were indeed always correct; they exhausted all existing sources and discussed all opinions, leaving no possibility of controverting them. His decisions became authoritative in North Africa (see introduction to *Tashbeẓ*). The *takkanot* he drafted were in vogue among the Jews in North Africa for centuries, and his responsa were a guide to later *posekim* who frequently quote them (e.g., Joseph *Caro, *Beit Yosef* EH 119, 122, 126, 130, 134, 140, 141, 143; they became known to Caro through Jacob *Berab; see introduction to *Tashbeẓ*). Ḥayyim *Benveniste established the principle that in cases in which Simeon's decisions contradict those of Solomon b. Abraham *Adret, the decision is according to the former (*Keneset ha-Gedolah*, ḤM 386). Preference should also be given to Simeon when he is contradicted by Israel *Isserlein.

Philosophy

As in his halakhic decisions, Simeon also respected the opinions of Maimonides in the area of philosophy, but often differed with him, even on important issues. He accepted Maimonides' naturalistic views on prophecy but with added emphasis on the role of divine grace. Like Ḥasdai *Crescas, he disagrees with Maimonides' theory that eternal bliss depends on how much knowledge one has acquired. He accepts the Aristotelian conception of the soul, but adds to it another, immaterial part of man, his *neshamah*, which is derived from God and bears the intellective faculty, and which is eternal. Thus eternal bliss is not proportioned only according to one's acquired intellect, as Maimonides claimed, but human felicity, both in this world and the next, depends on one's observance of the *mitzvot*, as Naḥmanides had shown. Further, Simeon disagrees with Maimonides' theory that superior intellect determines the amount of divine providence to which one is subject. According to Simeon, divine providence is contingent upon one's performance of God's commandments. Simeon's most important contribution (later repeated by Joseph *Albo) was his fixing the boundaries of philosophical speculation in order to safeguard the principles of traditional Judaism. Thus he reduced the fundamental dogmas of Judaism to three, which, according to him, must be accepted by everyone: the existence of God, revelation, and divine retribution. In doing so, he was not disagreeing with Maimonides but only commenting on Maimonides' system of 13 principles of faith. He insisted that "Every Jew must believe that the Holy Scriptures, and in particular the Torah, come from God and he must accept their contents as the absolute truth" (*Ohev Mishpat*, Introd.). Although, as has been mentioned, Simeon believed in astrology (*Magen Avot*, 4:21), he defined himself primarily as a disciple of the "masters of the truth," the kabbalists (*Ohev Mishpat*, Introd. to ch. 19), whose doctrines he often quoted in his works.

Among Simeon's writings as an exegete were a commentary on Job and glosses on Levi b. Gershom's commentary on the Bible (see list of his works). Only the former has been preserved, and shows that he was an adherent of the *peshat* ("simple meaning") and strongly opposed allegories such as those developed in the school of southern France in the 13th century. He often quoted Targum, *Saadiah Gaon, Abraham Ibn Ezra, Rashi, Naḥmanides, and Levi b. Gershom. When citing the Zohar he generally added "by R. *Simeon b. Yoḥai." He adopted some doctrines from the Kabbalah (e.g., transmigration of the soul, *Magen Avot*, 88a). In his responsa he quotes and uses *gematriot, notarica* (see *Notarikon), and letter mysticism. Sometimes he says (*Tashbeẓ*, 3 no. 54): "I can only explain what I have been permitted" and warns "You should give only a plain interpretation and consider what is permitted."

Simeon's philosophy is included mainly in his *Magen Avot*. However, his commentary on Job also contains several of his philosophic teachings. In it he refers to many philosophic sources, constructs his exposition lucidly, and takes a clear position on the philosophical problems which he treats. His philosophical ideas and writings did not have much influence on subsequent generations, except for Joseph *Albo, who in turn did make a significant impact on later philosophers.

As an apologist, Simeon deals with the *Karaites when seeking to prove the divine origin of the *Oral Law. He shows how important the Oral Law is for understanding Torah and fulfilling the commandments and states that many actions of Jewish leaders and institutions can only be explained as being based on oral tradition. He then attacks the doctrines of the Karaites (e.g., their explanation of Ex. 16:29 which contradicts Isa. 66:23). Simeon was very well acquainted with Christian literature (it has to be studied, he says, in order to be refuted). He had a dispute with a Christian theologian (*Keshet u-Magen*, 14a) who had to admit that Simeon was right. He quotes Saadiah Gaon, *Judah Halevi (*Kuzari*), the disputation of *Jehiel b. Joseph of Paris, and Naḥmanides. It is doubtful, however, whether he used Ḥasdai Crescas' *Bittul Ikkarei ha-Noẓerim* and the work of Profiat *Duran, since they are never mentioned. He first refutes the attacks of the Christians and then counterattacks. The Christians, he says, admit that the Torah is of divine origin, but maintain that it is superseded by the Gospels. He shows that Jesus and his disciples strictly observed the Law and that Jesus declared that he had come not to destroy the Law or the teaching of the prophets but to fulfill them. His death was not due to his negligence of the Law but to his assertion that he was "the son of God and Messiah" (*Keshet u-Magen*, 2b). Simeon points out the various contradictions regarding the origin of Jesus, his claim to be the Messiah (refuted by the fact that the criteria of the Messianic age had still not occurred), and the assertion that the Torah had been superseded by the Gospels, since the Torah, being of divine origin, is unchangeable. He draws attention to the many mistakes and forgeries contained in Jerome's Bible translation. He also enumerates 21 misquotations from the Bible by Jesus and his disciples. Simeon tries to prove that the Koran cannot be of divine origin owing to the great number of contradictions found in it (e.g., in regard to free will), to its many unintelligible passages, and to its sensual views on the world to come. What is good in it had been borrowed from the Midrash. Regarding Islam as a whole, Simeon did not consider Islam as idolatrous, however, he did consider the pilgrimage to Mecca as an idolatrous practice.

Simeon was also active as a poet and composed many *piyyutim, kinot, seliḥot*, and *teḥinnot*, some of which have been printed (see below). He was a prolific writer, and there is no subject with which he did not deal. His *Magen Avot* is more than a philosophical treatise. It covers human and animal physiology and pathology, psychology, science, phonology, etc., and has the character of an encyclopedic work. Perhaps the intention of its author was to write a book which should serve as a source of knowledge and information particularly for the Jews of North Africa. His responsa not only treat religious and legal problems, but also deal with grammar, philology, exegesis, literary history, philosophy, Kabbalah, mathematics, and astronomy.

The following list of his writings is given in the same order as mentioned by the author in *Tashbeẓ*, end of pts. 2 and 3: (1) *Perush Hilkhot Berakhot le-ha-Rif*, commentary on Alfasi's laws on *Berakhot*; (2) *Piskei Massekhet Niddah*, decisions on the tractate *Niddah*; (3) *Sefer ha-Hashgaḥah*, called *Ohev Mishpat*, commentary on Job, printed together with *Sefer Mishpat Ẓedek* by R. Obadiah *Sforno (Venice, 1589); (4) *Zohar ha-Raki'a*, commentary on Solomon ibn Gabirol's *azharot* (Constantinople, 1515); (5) *Tashbeẓ* (תשב״ץ, abbreviation of *Teshuvot Shimon ben Ẓemaḥ*), responsa in three parts (the fourth part is called *Ḥut ha-Meshullash*, containing responsa of three rabbis of North Africa, including Simeon's descendant Solomon b. Ẓemaḥ Duran; Amsterdam, 1738–41); (6) *Magen Avot*, four parts, philosophical work; the first three parts, without the fourth chapter of the second part (Leghorn, 1785); the fourth part is (7) *Magen Avot*, a commentary on the tractate *Avot* (*ibid.*, 1763); (8) *Keshet u-Magen* (fourth chapter of the second part of *Magen Avot* (see above no. 6)), polemics against Christianity and Islam, printed together with *Milḥemet Mitzvah* of his son Solomon (*ibid.*, c. 1750); the sections dealing with Christianity and Islam were published separately; (9) *Perush Massekhet Eduyyot*, commentary on *Eduyyot* mentioned by Simeon in his list; (10) *Ḥiddushei ha-RaSHBaẒ*, novellae on *Niddah, Rosh ha-Shanah*, and *Kinnim* (*ibid.*, 1745); the novellae on *Kinnim* were also printed with those of Solomon b. Abraham Adret on *Niddah* (Metz, 1770); (11) *Perush Keẓat Piyyutim*, commentaries on various poems, as well as poems composed by Simeon: (a) a *piyyut* by Isaac *Ibn Ghayyat for the Day of Atonement with Simeon's commentary appeared in B. Goldberg's *Ḥofes Matmonim* (Berlin, 1845, pp. 85ff.); (b) a commentary on the *Hoshanot* (Ferrara, 1553); (c) an elegy on the destruction of the Temple appeared with Profiat Duran's letter *Al Tehi ka-Avotekha* (Constantinople, c. 1575–78); (d) an elegy on the persecution in Spain was printed in *Magen Avot* (Leipzig, 1855); (e) some *piyyutim* published by I. Mar'eli appeared in *Kobez al Jad*, 7 (1896–97) under the title *Ẓafenat Pa'ne'aḥ* (see also A. Gavison, *Omer ha-Shikhhah* (Leghorn, 1748, 125); (12) *Or ha-Ḥayyim*, polemics against Ḥasdai Crescas (mentioned by Simeon in his list); (13) *Livyat Ḥen*, glosses on the commentary of Levi b. Gershom and four discourses against Ḥasdai Crescas mentioned by Simeon in his list; (14) *Yavin Shemu'ah* on *Hilkhot Sheḥitah u-Vedikah*, on the laws of slaughtering and porging; (15) *Ma'amar Ḥameẓ*, commentary on the *Haggadah*; (16) *Tiferet Yisrael*, on the calendar; (17) *Perush Eizehu Mekoman*, commentary on *Mishnah Zevaḥim* ch. 5, and commentary on the *Baraita* of R. Ishmael in the beginning of *Sifra*. Nos. (14), (15), (16), and (17) were published together with (18) *Tikkun Soferim* of his son Solomon (Leghorn, 1744); (19) also appeared in the Roedelheim *Haggadah* edition of 1882; novellae on *Bava Meẓia*, quoted in *Shitah Mekubbeẓet* of Bezalel *Ashkenazi; (20) *Sefer ha-Minhagim*, on customs, in the responsa of Abraham Tawwah in *Tashbeẓ*, pt. 4 no. 32; (21) *Sefer Tikkun ha-Ḥazzanim* (*ibid.*, no. 31); (22) commentaries on the *ketubbah* and *get* ("divorce document") and regulations about divorce and *ḥaliẓah* (Constantinople, 1516; cf. also *Tashbeẓ*, pt 3 no. 301); (23) *Takkanot*, see *Tashbeẓ*, pt. 2 no. 292.

BIBLIOGRAPHY: Michael, Or, 601–5; Weiss, Dor, 5 (1904), 187–98; Graetz, Hist, 4 (1949²), index; E. Atlas, in: *Ha-Kerem*, 1 (1887), 1–26; H. Jaulus, in: MGWJ, 23 (1874), 241–59; 24 (1875), 160–78; D. Kaufmann, *ibid.*, 41 (1897), 660–6; J. Guttmann, *ibid.*, 52 (1908), 641–72; 53 (1909), 46–79; I. Epstein, *The Responsa of Rabbi Simon b. Ẓemaḥ Duran* (1930); Davidson, Oẓar, 4 (1933), 487; A.M. Hershman, *Rabbi Isaac b. Sheshet Perfet and his Times* (1943); Guttmann, Philosophies, 242ff.; M.M. Kasher and J.B. Mandelbaum, *Sarei ha-Elef* (1959), index; Hirschberg, Afrikah, index. **ADD. BIBLIOGRAPHY:** M. Shapiro, in: *Judaism*, 42:3 (1993), 332–43; M.M. Kellner, in: PAAJR, 48 (1981), 231–65; J.D. Bleich, in: JQR, 69:4 (1979), 208–25; N. Arieli, "*Mishnato ha-Filosofit shel Rabbi Shimon ben Zemach Duran*," dissertation, Hebrew University (1976).

[Hirsch Jacob Zimmels]

DURAN, SOLOMON BEN SIMEON (known as **RaShBaSh**, Hebrew acronym of **R**abbi **Sh**elomo **b**en **Sh**imon; c. 1400–1467), North African rabbinical authority; son of Simeon b. Ẓemaḥ *Duran. He was born in *Algiers, but no details are known of his youth. His education embraced not only rabbinical knowledge but also science, medicine, and philosophy. It appears from his responsa that he joined his father's *bet din* at an early age and was the head of the yeshivah. Some of his responsa were written during the lifetime of his father. His apologetical work *Milḥemet Mitzvah* (1438) was written with his father's authorization. In it Solomon repulsed the accusations against the Talmud made by the apostate Joshua *Lorki (Geronimo de Santa Fé) and even made counterattacks against the Christian clergy. He showed that Lorki's accusation that the Talmud favored immorality was wrong, and on the contrary that it teaches a high standard of morality and chastity; and that it was the Christian clerical circles who indulged in immoral conduct to such an extent that it became known by the name "peccato dei frati." After defending the halakhic parts of the Talmud he proceeded to explain the *aggadot* attacked by Lorki. In Solomon's view (as expressed already by *Jehiel b. Joseph of Paris and by Naḥmanides in their disputations) they had no binding force.

In his youth he wrote a rhetorical epistle (*meliẓah*) to Nathan Najjar in Constantine (Rashbash, no. 259) using talmudic idioms, style, and language (the use of this kind of *meliẓah* is characteristic of him). His letter made a deep impression upon Najjar as can be seen from his reply in which the following passage occurs: "My son, my son, my heart was filled with anxiety for I said 'Who will sit on the throne of my master the rabbi, your father?'… Now, however, I know that Solomon, his son, will reign after him and will sit upon his throne" (cf. I Kings 1:13, 17, 30). After his father's death Solomon was appointed rabbi of Algiers. He seems to have also been the head of a yeshivah and some of his pupils were mentioned by name. His religious and general outlook can be derived from his responsa. Thus when asked whether the dialogue of *Balaam and his ass (Num. 22:28), Jacob's wrestling with the angel (Gen. 32:25), and the visit of the angels to Abraham (Gen. 18:1ff.) took place in reality or were dreams, his reply was that all were real events, as Naḥmanides had already stated (Rashbash, no. 44). In responsum no. 3 he strongly criticized Haggai b. Alzuk in Mostaganem, who maintained that perfection of the soul could be achieved by perfection of the intellect and that *aliyah* to Ereẓ Israel had no effect. In his view settling in Ereẓ Israel is a great *mitzvah*, particularly as many religious commands concern only Ereẓ Israel. With regard to the question whether the world will be destroyed or not, he showed that the Talmud and Naḥmanides decided in the affirmative, while Maimonides' view was in the negative. Solomon thought that while the belief in creation *ex nihilo* is binding, belief in the ultimate destruction of the world is not; it is left to one's own discretion (responsum no. 436). Concerning the Kabbalah he said of himself (no. 36): "I am not one of its members" and expressed his indignation at the doctrine of the ten *Sefirot (no. 188). His decisions were quoted by later authorities (including Joseph *Caro and Moses *Trani).

His works are (1) *Teshuvot Ha-Rashbash* (Leghorn, 1742), cited above, which deal not only with the legal matters but also with some philosophical problems and contain explanations of some biblical and talmudic passages; (2) *Milhemet Mitzvah*, in *Keshet u-Magen (ibid.*, 1750); (3) *Tikkun Soferim*, dealing with contracts together with *Yavin Shemu'ah* of his father (*ibid.*, 1744); (4) the elegy *Shamayim Laveshu Kadrut*. The bibliographers mention also *Meliẓah le-ha-Rashbash;* in fact, this *meliẓah* is contained in his responsum no. 259 (*Kerem Ḥemed*, 9 (1856), 110ff.).

BIBLIOGRAPHY: H.J. Zimmels, *Die Marranen in der rabbinischen Literatur* (1932), index; A.M. Hershman, *Rabbi Isaac ben Shesheth Perfet and his Times* (1943), index; Hirschberg, Afrikah, index.

[Hirsch Jacob Zimmels]

DURAN, ZEMAḤ BEN SOLOMON (15th century), North African rabbinical authority. Ẓemaḥ, the second son of Solomon b. Simeon *Duran, acted together with his brothers Aaron and Simeon as *dayyan* in *Algiers. It appears from the sources that he was the most active of them and the greatest scholar of the three. In an admonishing responsum written to a certain rabbi he says of himself: "I do not boast of my distinguished ancestry, of my sermons, and of my responsa, of my learning – that I am familiar with all the tannaitic literature and the whole of the Talmud, of the accuracy and profundity of my legal tradition, of my rational reasoning, though my paternal grandfather [Simeon b. Ẓemaḥ *Duran] praised and eulogized me from my childhood for my readiness to grasp the truth." Being rather sickly he went for a cure to Majorca, returning in 1468. He had some knowledge of medicine and a great knowledge of philosophy and Kabbalah, and his attitude toward the latter was positive. His ideology and piety are reflected in the responsum in which he tries to refute the views expressed to him by R. Abraham Conque of Malaga, who, following other philosophers, maintained that perfection and immortality do not depend on fulfilling the commandments and studying the Talmud but rather on the study of sciences and philosophy. Ẓemaḥ tries to show that perfection can only be achieved through the fulfillment of the *mitzvot*. The seven sciences (see Ibn Ezra on Prov. 9:1; Klatzkin, *Thesaurus Philosophicus*, I, 292ff.) serve only to teach fear and love of God. They are not the end but only the means. He writes that Maimonides wrote his *Guide of the Perplexed* to refute the philosophers with philosophical arguments (cf. also his father's responsum, Rashbash no. 3). Ẓemaḥ dealt with the problem of the Marranos (*Yakhin u-Vo'az*, pt. 1, nos. 75, 125), whom he regarded as Jews from the religious point of view. He wrote responsa which form the first part of his brother Simeon's collection *Yakhin u-Vo'az*. Some of them are quoted by Joseph *Caro.

[Hirsch Jacob Zimmels]

DURAZZO (Durrësi, Durrës), chief port of Albania. There may have been Jews in Durazzo during the Roman period. The community, referred to as Durachi(um), is mentioned however for the first time in 1204 in a responsum of R. *Isaiah b. Mali di Trani. An English traveler found a group of Jews in Durazzo in 1322. Documents of 1368 mention the community leader (*magister Yudayce*) David, his business associates, and the communal scribe. The Jewish merchants traded with Italy, Serbia, and Dubrovnik exporting salt and importing textiles. In 1401 the representatives of the Jews appealed to the Senate of Venice, which then ruled over Durazzo, to exempt or partly exempt them from the obligation of presenting to the civic authorities annually 16 cubits of finest velvet, in addition to a sum of money in cash. During the 16th century a few Spanish refugees settled in Durazzo, but they do not seem to have had a communal organization. In 1939, refugee families from Vienna settled in Durazzo.

BIBLIOGRAPHY: H. Bernstein, in: *Jewish Daily Bulletin* (April 17–18, 1934); J. Starr, *Romania…* (Eng., 1949), 81–83; A. Milano, *Storia degli ebrei italiani nel Levante* (1949), 64–65.

[Simon Marcus]

DURBAN, port in KwaZulu-Natal, third largest city in the Republic of South Africa. The relatively small Jewish population has always played a prominent part in the life of the city. One of the founders of Port Natal (Durban's original name) was Nathaniel *Isaacs, who came as a youth in 1825. Important contributions to the port's early development were made by Jonas *Bergtheil and by Daniel de *Pass. The first *berit milah* in Natal, for the son of a former Durban resident D.M. Kisch, was performed in 1876 by the Rev. S. Rapaport, who came from Port Elizabeth for the ceremony. In 1880 a Jewish burial ground was laid out. Three years later a congregation was formed and in 1884 a building which had been a Methodist chapel was converted into a synagogue, with Bernard Lipinski (d. 1907) as the first president. Outstanding services were rendered by Felix C. Hollander (1876–1955), who was mayor of Durban (1910–13), a member of the Natal provincial executive committee (1914–23 and 1926–39), a senator (1939–48), and the head of the Jewish community. Charles Phineas Robinson (d. 1938) was a member of the Natal legislature and later of the Union parliament. His son Albert also sat in parliament and later became London high commissioner for the Central African Federation. Other leading communal personalities were Philip Wartski (1853–1948) and Solomon Moshal (1894–1986).

Less affected by Eastern European immigration than other communities of the Republic, Durban Jewry has at the same time an active communal life. There are four synagogues (one Reform) and the usual fraternal and welfare organizations. Diminishing numbers, however, led to the closure of the city's Jewish day school, Carmel College, in 1997. The Durban Jewish Club, the only institution of its kind in the Republic, has played a major role in the community's development. The Council for KwaZulu-Natal Jewry is a coordinating body and also functions as the provincial office of the South African Jewish Board of Deputies. Zionist activity is directed by the KwaZulu-Natal Zionist Council. The Jewish population of Durban in 2004 was 2,750.

BIBLIOGRAPHY: G. Saron and L. Hotz, *Jews in South Africa* (1955), index; *South African Jewish Year Book* (1929), 107–10; M. Gitlin, *The Vision Amazing* (1950), index.

[Louis Hotz / Gustav Saron]

DURHAM, city in North Carolina, U.S. Jewish communal life formed in the late 1870s as the agrarian village grew into a New South industrial town. The Jewish population, with neighboring Chapel Hill, rose from 40 in 1880 to 305 in 1910. As the region evolved into a Sunbelt academic, research, and retirement center, the Jewish population reached 5,000 in 2005.

In 1874 the first permanent Jewish settlers, Polish-born brothers Abe and Jacob Goldstein, opened a general store, which served as a way station for peddlers. By 1880, ten more Jewish merchants, all of German origin, had arrived from Virginia to establish dry-goods stores. In the early 1880s tobacco magnate James B. Duke contracted with a young Ukrainian immigrant, Moses Gladstein, to bring more than a hundred East European proletarians from New York to roll cigarettes in his factory. These Jewish rollers formed a chapter of the Cigarmaker's Progressive Union and later an assembly of the Knights of Labor. In 1884 Duke automated the factory and dismissed the Jewish workers. Most returned north although several, including Gladstein, opened Durham stores.

Immigrant peddlers, artisans, and storekeepers, mostly of Latvian-Lithuanian origin, created a viable community. Durham was a typical New South mill and market town. Jews provided mercantile services to workers, farmers, and industrialists. Durham's appeal was enhanced by the educational opportunities of Duke University and the University of North Carolina at Chapel Hill. Jewish faculty began establishing themselves in the 1930s. They included European émigré scholars, notably Polish law professor Raphael *Lemkin, author of the Genocide Convention. In 1943 Duke became the first southern campus to institute Jewish studies with the hiring of Judah *Goldin.

East European Jews resided first in a ghetto near the African-American "Bottoms" and then in a middle-class neighborhood near Main Street. The community supported chapters of B'nai B'rith, Hadassah, Mizrachi, and the Zionist Organization of America. In 1951, E.J. Evans, running on a progressive platform with black support, was elected to the first of six terms as Durham mayor, and in 1991 Kenneth Broun was elected Chapel Hill mayor.

Religious services were held as early as 1878, and a burial society formed in 1884, under Myer Summerfield, a Prussian-born Orthodox merchant. Two years later the Durham Hebrew Congregation organized, and by 1892, when it received a state charter, it had evolved into an East European shul. After meeting in rented halls, the congregation purchased a wooden house in 1905. In 1921 it built a brick, downtown cathedral-style synagogue, renaming itself Beth El. Evolving into a Conservative congregation, it dedicated a new suburban synagogue-center in 1957. Beth El also housed an Orthodox Kehilla.

In 1961 Judea Reform Congregation formed, and it built a temple in 1971. Growing into the area's largest congregation with 550 members, it built a new campus in 2003. The Lubavitcher movement established Chabad houses in Durham and Chapel Hill. In 1996 the Chapel Hill Kehillah, a Reconstructionist congregation, organized, and it purchased a synagogue five years later. The area also accommodated a Triangle Congregation for Humanistic Judaism. The communities are united by the Durham-Chapel Hill Jewish Federation and Community Council, founded in 1977, which supports Jewish Family Services, and Midrasha, a supplemental high school. In 1995 the Lerner Jewish Community Day School opened with a religiously pluralistic program. Both Duke and UNC erected new Hillel centers and expanded their Jewish studies programs.

Durham-Chapel Hill's growth reflects the national Jewish population movement toward the Sunbelt. With two major universities and the creation of the Research Triangle Park in 1959 it also reflects the Jewish demographic movement into the professions. Scientists Martin *Rodbell and Gertrude *Elion won Nobel Prizes at the Park. The moderate climate and college-town ambience also draw retirees.

BIBLIOGRAPHY: E. Evans, *The Provincials: A Personal History of Jews in the South* (2005); L. Rogoff, *Homelands: Southern Jewish Identity in Durham and Chapel Hill, North Carolina* (2001).

[Leonard W. Rogoff (2nd ed.)]

DURKHEIM, ÉMILE (1858–1917), French sociologist. Born in Epinal (Lorraine), France, of a long line of rabbinical ancestors, Durkheim initially prepared himself for the rabbinate. Although he never wrote directly on a Jewish topic, the interest in law, ethnology, and the ethical implications of social relations, which were aroused by his early training, stayed with him throughout his life. To be a sociologist always meant for him, essentially, to be a moral philosopher as well as a scientist of moral behavior; and although he became a free thinker early in life he remained conscious of his rabbinical heritage. Durkheim studied in Paris, where he was a pupil of the philosophers Emile Boutroux and Jules Monod and of the historian Fustel de Coulanges. He was also influenced by the French neo-Kantian Charles Renouvier and by his fellow students Lévy-Bruhl, *Bergson, and Jaurès.

Durkheim is a towering figure in the history of *sociology. The first chair in social science in Europe was established for him at the University of Bordeaux in 1887. In 1902 he became professor of sociology and education at the Sorbonne; a separate department of sociology, under his chairmanship, was established in 1913. Durkheim was a founder and editor in chief of *L'Année Sociologique*, which was published from 1898 until the beginning of World War I. Durkheim attempts to demonstrate that it is possible to trace regularities of behavior in human action regardless of the subjective motives of individuals. The physical, biological, and psychological factors operative in the social life of man must be taken into account. Yet, as soon as attention is focused on the interpersonal relationships characterizing group life, the special nature of "social facts" becomes apparent: group products, such as art, morals, and institutions are in the mind of the individual, and yet entities apart from him. These group products are irreducible facts which must be studied in their own right. Society's "collective representations" have an objective existence outside the individuals and, at the same time, exercise a constraining power over them. Even conceptual knowledge may be said to consist of collective representations having their roots in society.

The best exemplification of the fruitfulness of Durkheim's approach is his concept of social solidarity, as employed in his studies on the division of labor, religion, morality, conscience, and suicide. Because society, at the same time, is above man and penetrates man, it is ultimately the only thing that has the power to inspire awe and reverence in individuals and to submit them to rules of conduct, to privations, and to the kind of sacrifice without which society would be impossible. But society, on which the individual is absolutely dependent, is not sufficiently concrete to be an object of direct reverential submission. Instead, the individual experiences his dependence indirectly, by focusing his attention on everything essential to the maintenance of society: its principal norms, values, institutions, its sacred symbols. Especially, the notion of divine authority is a sublimation of society. Thus religion springs not from the nature of individual man, but from the nature of society. According to Durkheim, the effect of beliefs and acts with respect to essential norms and symbols is to create a more effective society. Similarly, suicide is not a function of race, climate, religious doctrine, and economic conditions, however close the correlations between any of these facts and the phenomenon of suicide itself may be. The clue, says Durkheim, lies in crucial social facts, that is, the breakdown of social solidarity and the ensuing normlessness, or "anomie." Groups with little social cohesion tend to have higher suicide rates than those providing strong psychic support to their members in the various crises of life.

Durkheim stresses the concept of "collective consciousness" (or "conscience"). Durkheim initially explained social control mainly in terms of external constraints. In his later work, however, he stressed the internalization of culture, the fact that social norms are "society living in us." On his conception of education he places no less heavy a burden. Through education, he holds, society implants general social values and discipline in the individual. "Discipline," he writes, "has its justification in itself." Yet, the nature of the discipline is not wholly a matter of indifference. It depends not only on society in general, but on the particular society in question. Not every society values the kind of individualism and democratic pluralism which Durkheim espoused in his personal and political thought.

Durkheim's early work, *De la division du travail social* (1893), still shows traces of evolutionary thought; but his opposition to the utilitarianism of the economists is clearly marked there. In his subsequent works, especially in *Les règles de la méthode sociologique* (1895; *The Rules of Sociological Method*, 1950) and in *Le suicide: étude de sociologie* (1897; *Suicide*, 1951), as well as in numerous scholarly papers published chiefly in *L'Année Sociologique*, he increasingly emphasized scientific method and the combination of empirical research with sociological theory. His major work, cast largely in the language of functionalism, is *Les formes elémentaires de la vie religieuse: le système totémique en Australie* (1912; *The Elementary Forms of the Religious Life*, 1965). Other treatises with a strongly historical and philosophical bent are *Education et sociologie* (1922; *Education and Sociology*, 1956), *Sociologie et philosophie* (1929), *L'éducation morale* (1925), *Le socialisme: sa définition, ses débuts, la doctrine Saint Simonienne* (1928; *Socialism and Saint-Simon*, 1958), *L'évolution pédagogique en France* (1938), and *Montesquieu et Rousseau; précurseurs de la sociologie* (1953).

BIBLIOGRAPHY: Analyses of Durkheim's approach to sociology abound. The most influential of these are contained in G. Gurvich, *Essais de sociologie* (1936), and in T. Parsons, *Structure of Social Action* (1937). Among book-length evaluations the best known are C.E. Gehlke, *Emile Durkheim's Contributions to Sociological Theory* (1915); P. Faconnet, *The Durkheim School in France* (1927); R. Lacombe, *La Méthode sociologique de Durkheim* (1926); E. Conze, *Zur Bibliographie der Durkheim Schule* (1927); and H. Alpert, *Emile Durkheim and His Sociology* (1939). A complete bibliography is found in K. Wolff (ed.), *Emile Durkheim, 1858–1917* (1960).

[Werner J. Cahnman and Joseph Maier]

DUSCHAK, MORDECAI (**Moritz**; 1815–1890), rabbi, teacher, and writer. Duschak was born in Triesch, Moravia. He studied under Moses *Sofer in Pressburg, and later was appointed rabbi in Aussee and in Gaya, both in Moravia. From 1877 he occupied the post of preacher and teacher in Cracow. Toward the end of his life he moved to Vienna, where he remained until his death. Duschak published many studies on talmudic topics and Jewish scholarship in both Hebrew and German.

His noteworthy books in German are *Umriss des biblisch-talmudischen Synagogen-Rechtes* (1853), *Das mosaisch-talmudische Eherecht* (1864), *Geschichte und Darstellung des juedischen Cultus* (1866), *Das mosaisch-talmudische Strafrecht* (1869), *Zur Botanik des Talmud* (1870), *Die biblisch-talmudische Glaubenslehre* (1873), and *Tor Esier* (against the Blood *Libel, 1883). In Hebrew he published *Yerushalayim ha-Benuyah* (1880, combining the Babylonian and Jerusalem Talmuds in order to explain the *mishnayot* of tractates *Eruvin, Pesaḥim, Megillah*, and *Yoma*).

BIBLIOGRAPHY: Zeitlin, Bibliotheca, 39, 71; M. Schwab, *Répertoire des Articles…* (1914–23), 106f., s.v.; A. Bauminger et al. (eds.), *Sefer Cracow* (1959), 103f.; Kressel, Leksikon, 1 (1965), 546, s.v.

[Yehoshua Horowitz]

DUSCHINSKY, CHARLES (**Jacob Koppel**; 1878–1944), historian. Duschinsky was born in Námestovo, Czechoslovakia; he served as rabbi in Kostel, Moravia, from 1904 to 1907, and thereafter settled in London, where he engaged in business. He continued publishing monographs in scholarly journals on Anglo-Jewish history and other topics. His most important work was *The Rabbinate of the Great Synagogue, London, from 1756–1842* (1921).

[Cecil Roth]

DUSCHINSKY, JOSEPH ẒEVI BEN ISRAEL (1868–1948), Hungarian rabbi, and later rabbi of the separatist Orthodox community of Jerusalem. Duschinsky was born in Paks, Hungary, where his father was the *sofer* ("scribe"). He studied first under Moses Pollak, rabbi of Paks, and later under Rabbi Simḥah Bunim Sofer (Schreiber, the *Shevet Sofer*) in Pressburg. In 1892 he married the only daughter of R. Mordecai Leib Winkler of Brezovanad Bradlom (Slovakia) and spent the next three years in his house. The years spent at Pressburg and his father-in-law's fine personality were the main formative influences in his life. In 1895 he was elected rabbi to a congregation in Galanta established in opposition to the existing one, and in 1921 went to Khust (Carpatho-Ruthenia). In 1932 he visited Palestine and on the death of R. Joseph Ḥayyim *Sonnenfeld was elected in 1933 to succeed him as rabbi of the Edah Ḥaredit ("Orthodox Community") of Jerusalem. He founded a yeshivah, Bet Yosef, which had hundreds of pupils. Duschinsky, an active supporter of *Agudat Israel, appeared before various commissions of inquiry of the British mandatory government, and although he did not normally cooperate with the official rabbinate, during the siege of Jerusalem in 1948 he endorsed their permission to undertake defense and fortification work on the Sabbath.

Duschinsky was a discerning bibliophile of refined taste and amassed a fine library of rare books. None of his own works was published in his lifetime. From his literary legacy two volumes of responsa, *She'elot u-Teshuvot Mahariẓ* (pt. 1, 1956; pt. 2, 1966), and three volumes of his homiletic commentary to the Bible (pt. 1, 1956; pt. 2, 1961; and pt. 3, 1965) have been published. His responsa in particular reflect his immense learning and wide range of reading (e.g., vol. 2, no. 51 adduces proof for a halakhic point of view from Emden's anti-Shabbatean tract *Mitpaḥat Soferim*, Altona, 1768). He died during the siege of Jerusalem. His yeshivah continued to function under the direction of his only son, Moses Israel.

BIBLIOGRAPHY: A. Katzburg, *Temunat ha-Gedolim* (1925–); S.Z. Tennenbaum, *Nata Sorek* (1899), 167b–174b (HM 1–5).

[Abraham Schischa]

DUSHKIN, ALEXANDER MORDECHAI (1890–1976), educator. Born in Suwalki, Poland, Dushkin was taken to the United States in 1901. He was associated with J.L. *Magnes' Kehillah experiment in New York City (1910–18) and with its Bureau of Jewish Education under Samson *Benderly, and in

1916 went to Europe as a secretary of the American Jewish Relief Committee. In Palestine in 1919, he was inspector of Jewish schools and taught at David *Yellin's Teachers' Seminary in Jerusalem. Returning to the United States, Dushkin was appointed secretary of *Keren Hayesod (1921–22). From 1923 to 1934 he was director of Chicago's Board of Jewish Education and founded that city's College of Jewish Studies (1924). In 1934 he was called by the Hebrew University in Jerusalem to organize and conduct its Department of Education (since 1952, the School of Education). He was lecturer in educational methods and administration and also the principal of Bet ha-Kerem High School, Jerusalem (1934–39). Upon his return to the United States he became executive director of the Jewish Education Committee in New York City (1939–49). In 1949 Dushkin was invited by the Hebrew University to establish and direct its undergraduate studies and to teach education and education administration. From 1962, he headed the Department of Jewish Education in the Diaspora in the Hebrew University Institute of Contemporary Jewry. Dushkin wrote the first doctoral dissertation on a Jewish educational theme (Columbia University, 1917), *Jewish Education in New York City* (1918), and was the editor of the first educational journal in English in the United States, *The Jewish Teacher* (1916–19); edited and co-edited its successor, *Jewish Education* (1929–35, 1939–49); was coauthor of *Jewish Education in the United States* (1959); edited the third volume of the *Enzyklopedyah Ḥinnukhit* ("Educational Encyclopedia"); and wrote many monographs and articles. In his educational philosophy Dushkin recognized the validity of pluralism in American Jewish education, but saw its bases in common elements and values. He saw Jewish education in the Diaspora as being one of the main responsibilities of Jewish communal efforts. As a student of Kilpatrick and disciple of the progressivist concepts, he strove to base education on science and experience; he had, however, a positive attitude to Jewish tradition, seeing it as the unique force in the preservation of the Jewish people. Dushkin was awarded an Israel Prize in 1968.

BIBLIOGRAPHY: J. Pilch and M. Ben-Horin, *Judaism and the Jewish School* (1966), 60f.

[Nathan Greenbaum and Leon H. Spotts]

DUSHKIN, SAMUEL (1891–1976), violinist. Dushkin was born in Suwalki, Poland, and studied with Guillaume Remy (violin) and Ganaye (composition) at the Paris Conservatoire, and with *Amar and *Kreisler in New York. After his Paris début in 1918, he toured widely and gave many important first performances, notably of Ravel's *Tzigane* (Amsterdam, 1925) and Stravinsky's *Violin Concerto* (Berlin, 1931). Stravinsky, who composed it with technical advice from Dushkin, often accompanied him in it at subsequent performances. Dushkin also collaborated with Stravinsky in making transcriptions from *Pulcinella* and *Le baiser de la fée* and recorded the *Duo concertant* with him. He gave the first performances of a considerable amount of chamber music by Prokofiev, *Milhaud, Poulenc, and others. Dushkin edited, and in some cases transcribed, virtuoso music for the violin. Some are in fact his own compositions attributed to earlier composers, such as Johann Benda and Boccherini. He also published teaching manuals for the violin.

ADD. BIBLIOGRAPHY: Grove online; MGG[2]; R. Ellero, *Le Composizioni Violinistiche di Stravinskij per Dushkin*, Tesi di laurea Univ. degli Studi di Venezia (1991/2).

[Max Loppert / Israela Stein (2nd ed.)]

DUSHMAN, SAUL (1883–1954), U.S. chemist and physicist. Dushman was born in Rostov, Russia, and was taken to Canada as a child of nine. He obtained a doctorate at the University of Toronto in 1912 and in the same year joined the General Electric Company Laboratory at Schenectady, N.Y., where he worked for 40 years, from 1928 as assistant director. For a period he was also director of research at the Edison Lamp Works. Dushman's published books and papers were mainly concerned with the development and use of high vacuum with which his name is firmly associated. He introduced, with Langmuir, the suffix *-tron* for equipment in which high vacuum was used; later the suffix was used in words such as cyclotron, magnetron, etc. His books included *High Vacuum* (1923), *The Elements of Quantum Mechanics* (1938), *Scientific Foundations of Vacuum Technique* (1949), and *Fundamentals of Atomic Physics* (1951).

BIBLIOGRAPHY: Langmuir, in: *Vacuum*, 3 (1953–54), 113f.

[Samuel Aaron Miller]

DUSTAN (**al-Dustān**; Dositheans), Samaritan sect (or sects), followers of Dusis or Dustis, which is probably the Aramaic form of the Greek name Dositheos. In a somewhat different form – Dosa or Dostai – it is quite common in Jewish sources such as Mishnah, Tosefta, and Midrash. A Dostai and a Sabbai are mentioned in the Midrash as the priests sent by the Assyrian king to Samaria to teach the new settlers the laws and customs of the country. In a legend told by Josephus about a religious dispute between Jews and Samaritans before Ptolemy IV Philometer, Samaritan representatives are called Sabbeus and Theodosius (Theodosius being another form of Dositheos). But in all probability there is no connection between these and the founder of the Dosithean sect. Information about this sect is found in the *Samaritan Chronicles* and in patristic and Islamic writings. The relation between this sect and the 11th-century C.E. al-Dustan of the Samaritan liturgy has not yet been clarified. The accounts about the Dosithean sect (or sects) differ in many ways and contradict each other in some places. The Samaritan sources, the *Annals* of *Abu al-Fatḥ and the *New Chronicle*, speak of two sects: one called al-Dustān, which arose shortly before the time of Alexander the Great, i.e., in the fourth century B.C.E., and a sect mentioned in the *Tolidah* as founded by Dūsis or Dustis in the days of the high priest Akbon, the brother of *Baba Rabbah, i.e., in the second half of the fourth century C.E. Patristic sources from the second–seventh centuries mention a founder of a Samaritan sect, Dositheos, who claimed to be the messiah prophesied by Moses in Deuteronomy 18:15. The dating of the sect is vague, generally given as before or after the time of Jesus.

The Islamic writer al-Shaharastānī (1086–1153) describes a Samaritan sect al-Dustāniyya, also known as al-Īlfāniyya. Their founder, al-Ilfān, is said to have lived approximately 100 B.C.E. Al-Shaharastānī explains the name al-Dustāniyya to mean the dissenting, mendacious sect. It is difficult to tell from these accounts whether they render different traditions about one and the same sect which became blurred in the course of time, or whether there existed two or more sects at different times. The main source for the account of the fourth-century B.C.E. sect is the *Annals* of Abu al-Fatḥ. There the sect is said to have been called al-Dustān because they abolished the lawful festivals and the traditions of their ancestors. Their most important deviations were: changing of the Samaritan combined solar-lunar *calendar, counting all months as 30 days; ceasing to recite the formula "Blessed be our Lord in eternity" and to pronounce the Tetragrammaton, substituting *Elohim*; counting the 50 days between Passover and Pentecost from the day after the first day of Passover, as the Jews do; and altering the laws of ritual purity. Because of the above differences and others outside the sphere of belief and religious rites, they started to build their own synagogues and to appoint their own priests. The first to become their high priest was the son of the then high priest. He was called Zarʿa, perhaps an allusion to Ezra, and was banned from the community for infamous conduct. He composed a compendium of laws for them – a new Torah, derided the high priests, and was esteemed the most learned of his time. The account concerning the Dosithean sect of the fourth century C.E., found in the *Tolidah*, the *Annals* of Abu al-Fatḥ, and the *New Chronicle*, is centered on the person of Dustes b. Pilpeloy, who went to Shechem in the time of Akbon, Baba's brother. He was not of Samaritan extraction but descended from the Aravruba (*Erev rav*), the mixed multitude who left Egypt together with the Israelites. The Tolidah does not go beyond this brief statement, whereas the other two chronicles, especially that of Abu al-Fatḥ, elaborate their story with much detail.

Dusis b. Fufti (or in the *New Chronicle*, Dusis) was living in Jewish territory, committed adultery there, and was sentenced to death. However, when he proposed to the Jewish elders the founding of a heretic sect in Samaria, they consented to release him. He went to Qaryat ʿAskar, where he won the friendship of a very learned and pious man called Yaḥdū. Together they spent two years abiding by a vow of asceticism. When their vow ended, they ate, drank, and became intoxicated. When Yaḥdū was still sleeping off his drunkenness, Dusis took away his hood, gave it to a harlot, and bribed her to testify on the Day of Atonement before the community, gathered for prayer on Mt. Gerizim, that Yaḥdū had sinned with her. But his plot was discovered by the high priest Akbon, who sought to kill him. Dusis fled to Shuwayka or Socho and hid in the house of a widow called Amintū, whom he told that he was the son of the high priest. During his stay there, he occupied himself with writing. When he had finished, he heard that the high priest was still looking for him, so he left the house of Amintū and went to hide in a cave, where he eventually died of hunger and was devoured by the dogs. Before leaving, he had ordered Amintū to allow his writings to be touched only by those who had purified themselves in a nearby pool. Soon afterward the high priest's nephew, Levi, with seven companions, arrived at the house of Amintū in search of Dusis. She told them faithfully all Dusis had taught her. Levi then sent one of his men to immerse in the pool. Upon rising, the man cried out, "My belief is in Thee O Lord and in Dusis Thy servant and in his prophetic mission." Levi shouted at him and struck him. However, the same happened to all of the seven and at last to Levi himself. Then they read the books of Dusis and learned that he had changed much of the Torah, similar to Ezra and even more so. They kept all this to themselves and returned to Shechem. On the first day of the Passover festival, when Levi was called upon to recite the Law, he substituted the word "zatar" for "ezov," according to the books of Dusis. When the community tried to correct his reading, Levi insisted on it and blamed them for having rejected the prophetic mission of Dusis; he changed the days of the festivals, the mighty name of YHWH, and sent pursuers after the second prophet sent by God from Mount Sinai. Thereupon, Levi was stoned, and his followers went to a place near Jerusalem, from where they continued to win disciples from among the Samaritans. They venerated Levi as a martyr, kept a palm leaf dipped in his blood in the books of Dusis, and allowed only those who had fasted for seven days to approach and study them. They believed that the dead would soon rise; they cut their hair, prayed with their body immersed in water, did not go from one house to another on the Sabbath, and observed all the festivals on the Sabbath only. When one of the followers died, they put a belt around his waist, sandals on his feet, and a rod in his hand so that he could rise from his grave in haste. Some of them believed that as soon as the dead were buried they rose from their graves and went to Paradise. After a short story about Simeon the Sorcerer (Simon Magus, who, according to most scholars, belongs to the first century C.E.) there is an enumeration of seven subsects that succeeded each other and the fate that befell each of them. The narrative ends with the words: "All these came forth from the *Books of Dusis* and caused the Samaritans much hardship and great sinning."

Especially interesting is one of the sects, founded by Shaliyah ibn Ṭīrūn ibn Nīn, because his followers are once called al-Dustān. That is the only occurrence of this name in the narrative about the sect founded by Dusis. In this report antisectarian polemics are intermingled with the legend about Levi, which is obviously borrowed from the literature of the sect. The short notes speaking of Dositheos in the patristic sources all agree that he was a Samaritan heretic and founder of a messianic sect. But they differ in details. Thus Pseudo-Tertullian (second century C.E.) mentions the Samaritan Dositheos as the first Jewish heretic from whom the heresy of the Sadducees developed. He was the first to reject the prophets, deny belief in resurrection, angels, and the last judgment. According to the Pseudo-Clementines (third century C.E.), Dositheos and Simon Magus were pupils of John the Baptist. The Samaritans, awaiting a prophet predicted by Moses, had been prevented by the depravity of Dusis from believing in the prophetic mission of Jesus. Origen (second and third centuries C.E.) mentions Dositheos several times. After the time of Jesus, Dositheos tried to convince the Samaritans that he was the messiah prophesied by Moses, and he succeeded in winning some of them over. Then he adds that these are the Dositheans, still extant in his time, who own scriptures of Dositheos and recount myths about him that he had never died and was still alive somewhere. Similar to the above is the account of Eusebius (third and fourth centuries C.E.), who states that Dositheos appeared after Jesus' time and was acknowledged by the Samaritans as a prophet like Moses. Epiphanius (fourth century C.E.) gives a report resembling that of Abu al-Fatḥ in some basic points about Dusis and his sect. According to him, the Dositheans were a Samaritan sect; kept circumcision, the laws of the Sabbath, and the Pentateuch; refrained from eating meat; venerated abstinence; and believed in resurrection. Dositheos was of Jewish origin and had retired to a cave. However, out of an exaggerated desire to gain knowledge, he fasted so that at last he died of starvation. Eulogius (seventh century C.E.) tells of two rival Samaritan parties, one believing that the expected prophet of Deuteronomy 18:15 was *Joshua son of Nun, the other claiming that it was someone called Dosthes or Dositheos, who was a disciple of Simon Magus, cast blame on the prophets and the patriarch Judah, left scriptures, and did not believe in resurrection. Even from this scanty material, it becomes obvious that the Dosithean sect must have had considerable influence in the beginning of the common era or even before it. It seems quite plausible that several subsects branched off from an original major sect in the course of time. This may account for the double report of the Samaritan chronicles, including that of the seven subsects, and the discrepancies found in patristic and Islamic sources.

BIBLIOGRAPHY: J.A. Montgomery, *Samaritans* (1907; repr. 1968), 253–64; K. Kohler, in: *American Journal of Theology*, 15 (1911), 404–35; T. Caldwell, in: Kairos: *Zeitschrift fuer Religionswissenschaft und Theologie*, 4 (1962), 105–17; J. Macdonald, *Theology of the Samaritans* (1964), index; B. Lifshitz, in: RB, 72 (1965), 98–107; A.D. Crown, in: *Essays in Honour of G.W. Thatcher* (1966), 63–83; idem, in: *Antichthon*, 1 (1967), 70–85; Z. Ben-Ḥayyim, *Ivrit ve-Aramit Nusaḥ Shomeron*, 3 pt. 2 (1967), 17–18; H.A. Kippenberg, *Garizim und Synagoge* (1971) 122–37. TEXTS: E. Vilmar (ed.), *Abulfathi Annales Samaritani…* (1865), lxxi–lxxiii, 82–83, 151–7, 159–64 (Arabic, with Latin notes and introduction); E.N. Adler and M. Seligsohn (eds.), *Une nouvelle Chronique Samaritaine* (1903), 37, 64–67; P. Koetschau (ed.), *Origines*, in: *Die griechischen christlichen Schriftsteller der ersten Jahrhunderte*, 2 (1899), 108, lines 25–28; E. Preuschen (ed.), *Origines, ibid.*, 10 (1903), 251, lines 15–19; H. Grossmann (ed.), *Eusebius, ibid.*, 11 (1904), 33, lines 24–27; K. Holl (ed.), *Epiphanius, ibid.*, 25 (1915), 205, 206, lines 11–13; B. Rehm (ed.), *Pseudo-Clementines, ibid.*, 51 (1965), 39, lines 9–19; E. Kroymann, *Pseudo-Tertullian*, in: *Corpus Scriptorum ecclesiasticorum Latinorum*, 47 (1906), 213, lines 4–8; J. Bowman, *Transcript of the Original Text of the Samaritan Chronicle Tolidah* (1957), 18a (Heb., with Eng. notes).

[Ayala Loewenstamm]

DUTCH LITERATURE.

Influence of the Bible

The arrival, on October 27, 2004, of the Nieuwe Bijbelvertaling, a completely new translation into Dutch of the Bible and the Christian Apocrypha, initiated a fierce debate in Dutch literary circles. At the core was the major influence of the Bible on Dutch culture and linguistics. Many participants in the discussion lamented the sometimes radical choices the translators had made to rephrase the biblical stories into a modern vernacular. They stated their desire to protect the language and imagery of the Statenbijbel, the official translation of the Bible which was commissioned by the Dutch Reformed Church in the early 17th century. It was completed during the years 1627–37. Similar to its English-language counterpart, the King James Version, the Statenbijbel has enriched the Dutch language with countless beautiful and poetic similes, expressions, and metaphors, most of which are still in use in present-day Dutch.

The original Statenbijbel translation project was one high point in the cultural revolution that brought Calvinism and Humanism to Holland. The Eighty Years' War (1568–1648) led to a new and powerful interest in the Bible as a source of inspiration for a national Dutch identity, which was at that time beginning to assert itself. In a famous poem which later became the Dutch national anthem, "Wilhelmus van Nassouwe," Prince William of Orange was compared to David, king of Israel. The war against Spain was likened to Israel's war against her enemies. Among the many poetic adaptations of the Psalms composed in these times were those of authors such as Philips van Marnix van Sint Aldegonde (1540–1588), and the poets Pieter Corneliszoon Hooft (1581–1647) and Constantijn Huygens (1596–1678).

Humanists and Reformers promoted the study of Hebrew in the Low Countries during the 16th century, particularly in such circles as that of the humanist Antwerp printer Christophe *Plantin (1514–1589), who at one time was obliged to move to Leiden. During the 15th century, biblical drama flourished in the many chambers of rhetoric (*Rederijkerskamers*) and later poets such as Carel van Mander (1548–1606) and Dirck Volkertszon Coornhert (1522–1590) wrote a number of biblical plays. Outstanding among these authors was Joost van den Vondel, who wrote *Joseph in Dothan* (1640), *Joseph in Egypten* (1640), *Salomon* (1648), *Jephta* (1659), *Samson* (1660), and *Adam in Ballingschap* ("Adam in Exile," 1664). The last work can be compared to *Milton's *Paradise Lost*.

After the 17th century there was a sharp decline in interest in biblical subjects. In the late 18th century, Willem Bilderdijk wrote some biblical poetry, while Arnold Hoogvliet composed an epic entitled *Abraham de Aartsvader* ("Abraham the Patriarch," 1729). In the 19th century, Allard Pierson published *Israel*, the first part of his study *Geestelijke Voorouders* ("Spiritual Ancestors," 1887–91) and J.L. ten Kate wrote *De Schepping* ("The Creation," 1866).

Dutch biblical dramatists of the 20th century include H. van den Eerenbeemt, the author of *Judith* (1916); F. Rutten, who wrote *Hagar* (1917); and the Flemish poet René de Clercq, the author of biblical stories in verse form such as *Thamar* (1917). The poet Albert Besnard composed an epic poem about the history of the Jewish people called *Drama* (1959). In 1945 a Protestant author, H. de Bruin, published *Job*, a dramatic adaptation of the Book of Job. The Bible and the land of the Bible provide the themes of some of the writing of Roman Catholic poet Bertus Aafjes, notably his poem *In den Beginne* (1949) and his novels, *Vorstin onder de landschappen* ("Empress Among Landscapes," 1952) and *Arenlezers achter de maaiers* ("Gleaners Behind the Reapers," 1952).

During the 20th century Protestant religion lost its prominence in Dutch society. In mainstream fiction, Biblical themes have almost disappeared, the work of author and artist Jan Wolkers (1925–) being the most notable exception. In 1990 Wolkers published *Op de vleugelen der profeten* ("On the Wings of Prophets"), essays on the beauty of the Bible. As a literary topos, the Bible can be found in the works of novelists Maarten 't Hart, Nicolaas Matsier, and Desanne van Brederode. From the 1960s onwards, poet and novelist Gerard Kornelis van het Reve (1923–) created an original poetic aesthetic, mixing the language and imagery of the *Statenbijbel* with Roman Catholic mysticism and explicit references to homosexuality. This literary style is known as Revisme ("Revism").

Hebraic Influences on the Dutch Language

The influence of the *Statenbijbel* on the Dutch language can not be overestimated. Expressions deriving from this translation are still current in literature and colloquial usage. Besides such common words as *Satan, cherubijn*, etc., there are expressions like "*met de mantel der liefde bedekken*" ("to cover with the coat of love"), borrowed from the story of Noah (Gen. 9:23). The influence of Yiddish began to be felt with the appearance of Dutch books by Jewish authors, which contained Yiddish expressions. Some Yiddish words that have become part of standard Dutch are *Mokum*, the popular nickname for Amsterdam ("place," from *makom*); *bajes* ("prison," from *bayit*); *gabber* ("friend," from *ḥaver*); *stiekem* ("in secret," from *shetikah*); and *lef* ("courage," from *lev*). Many more are to be found in popular speech and thieves' slang – *jatten* ("to steal," from *yad*), and *kapoeres* ("gone to pieces," from *kapparah*). Others which were mainly used by Jews are disappearing with the dwindling of the Jewish community in Holland.

The Jewish community has coined some Dutch words for its specific linguistic needs. By subtly changing the prefix of verbs and nouns, meaning has shifted – predominantly in the verbs *aanbijten* (lit. "to bite onto," to break the fast after Yom Kippur) and *uitkomen* (lit. "to come out," to convert to Judaism), and the noun *voorzanger* (lit. "singer in front," Cantor), which are not in use outside the Jewish community.

The Figure of the Jew in Dutch Literature

The physical presence of Jews in the Netherlands is not reflected in medieval Dutch literature. The Jew is made to symbolize the forces of evil, and his sufferings are pointed to as proof of the Christian concept of history. Examples of this are to be found in the *Rijmbijbel* of Jacob van Maerlant (c. 1235–1300), in the same writer's *Spieghel Historiael*, in *Van den Levene Ons Heren* ("On the Life of Our Lord") by an unknown 13th-century author, and in various other sources. A literary record of the pogroms following the plague of 1350 occurs in *Brabantse Yeesten* by Jan van Boendale. The alleged use of the blood of Christian children for healing purposes was described in the *Bienboek*, a medieval Dutch version of the *Liber Apum* by Thomas de Cantimpré. Van Boendale's *Van den Joden ende van haren Wesen* ("Of the Jews and Their Nature") was a more rational work. The secular morality poem *Der minnen Loep* ("The Course of Love") by Dirck Potter (c. 1370–1428) denounces sexual intercourse with Jews. The Shylock motive appears in the fragmentary rhetorical play *Van den Gedinge tusschen eenen Coopman ende eenen Jode* ("On the Case Between a Merchant and a Jew," c. 1515).

Despite the increase in the number of Jews in Holland during the 17th century, none of the great authors of the Golden Age dealt with Jewish themes, with the exception of Joost van den Vondel, who wrote the poem *Aan de Joodsche Rabbijnen* as an addendum to the play *Hierusalem verwoest* (1620). On the other hand, many chronicles deal with Jews, mostly from a Christian, antisemitic point of view. An exception is the treatise on Jews and the Jewish religion in *Bewijs van den waren godsdienst* ("Proof of the True Religion") by the great Dutch jurist Hugo *Grotius. After a speculation scandal in 1720, Jews began to appear in low comedy, satirical poetry, and scurrilous writings. Examples are to be found in the unfinished comedy of manners *De Spiegelder Vaderlandsche Kooplieden* ("Mirror of Native Merchants," 1720) by Pieter Langendijk. Two periodicals founded by Justus van Effen, *Spectatoriale Geschriften* and *De Hollandsche Spectator*, were influenced in their attitude toward the Jews by the ideas of the Enlightenment.

In the 19th century, too, the number of literary works dealing with Jewish themes was very small. They include the poem *De Israelitische Looverhut* by Antonie Christiaan Wynand Staring; descriptions of middle-class Jews in the *Camera Obscura* (1839) of Hildebrand (pen name of Nicolaas Beets); descriptions of the Amsterdam ghetto in the novel *Woutert e Pieterse* (2 vols., 1865–77) by Multatuli (pen name of Eduard Douwes Dekker); and the antisemitic novel *Jeanne Colette* by W. Paap. At the beginning of the 20th century, Jewish types appear in the short stories collected in *Vluchtige begroetingen* ("Casual Greetings," 1925) by Aart van der Leeuw. An exotic Jewish girl figures in the novel *Tobias en de dood* ("Tobias and Death," 1925) by Jan van Oudshoorn (pen name of J.K. Feylbrief). The *Wandering Jew motif is to be found in the novel *De wandelende Jood* (1906) by the Flemish author August Vermeylen. The poet Johan Andreas dèr Mouw was the only writer who tried to analyze his attitude toward Jews.

The first writer to react to rising Nazism and the persecution of the Jews was the outstanding essayist Menno ter Braak, who had a great influence on Dutch literature. The change of attitude to Jewish themes brought about by World War II can be gauged by a comparison of two novels by Simon Vestdijk (1898–1971): *Else Boehler, Duits dienstmeisje* ("Else Boehler the German Maid," 1935) and *De rimpels van Esther Ornstein* ("The Wrinkles of Esther Ornstein," 1958). A writer who often used Jewish themes was Ferdinand Bordewijk, whose novels show a progressively antisemitic tendency. His works include the collections of short stories *Fantastische vertellingen* ("Fantastic Stories," 3 vols. 1919–24), and the novels *Noorderlicht* ("Northern Lights," 1948) and *Bloesemtak* ("Blossoming Branch," 1955).

In the years immediately after World War II, there was a remarkable increase in literary works dealing with Jewish themes and fictional characters. Some writers, like August Defresne in his play *De naamloozen van 1942* ("The Nameless of 1942," 1945), tried to prove the unequivocally sympathetic attitude of the Dutch people toward the Jews. The theme of other works is the absence of differences between Jews and non-Jews, as in *Volg het spoor terug* ("Follow the Track Back," 1953), an essay by J.B. Charles (pseudonym of W.H. Nagel), and in the novel *De ondergang van de familie Boslowits* ("The Ruin of the Boslowits Family," 1946) by Gerard Kornelis van het Reve. Nel Noordzij deals with collective guilt feelings as a personal experience in *Variaties op een moederbinding* ("Variations on a Mother Attachment," 1958), and with Jewish self-hate in her novel *Het kan me niet schelen* ("I Don't Care," 1955).

The difficulties arising in mixed marriages as a result of traumatic war experiences form the theme of several novels, including *De donkere kamer van Damocles* ("The Dark Room of Damocles," 1958) by Willem Frederik Hermans, *Het wilde feest* ("The Intruder," 1952) by Adriaan van der Veen, *Allang geleden* ("A Long Time Ago," 1956) by W.G. van Maanen, and Jan Wolkers' *Kort Amerikaans* ("Short American,"1962). A worthy attempt to draw an authentic Jewish portrait is that by the Flemish writer Marnix Gijsen (pseudonym of Jan-Albert Goris), who went to live in New York in 1939, in his short stories "Kaddisj voor Sam Cohn" and "De school van Fontainebleau" in the collection *De Diaspora* (1961).

During the 1960s and 1970s, Dutch literature shifted direction as a result of rising tides of realism and early postmodernism. Also, many Jewish writers came into their own, with a staggering growth of publications on Holocaust and post-Holocaust themes. As a result, Jewish experience and the place of the Jew in Dutch society became almost a taboo subject for non-Jewish writers. Jews all but vanished as characters in fiction by non-Jewish authors, with the exception of Erik Hazelhoff Roelfzema's *Soldaat van Oranje* ("Soldier of Orange"), which was published in 1971, a picaresque autobiographical novel about his travails during 1940–45 that included a Jewish love interest. The crime fiction that Jan-Willem van de Wetering wrote during the 1970s and 1980s features a minor character who is a Sephardi Jew.

It took until the late 1980s for a Jew to return to Dutch fiction. The novel *Mystiek Lichaam,* published in 1986 by acclaimed author Frans Kellendonk (1951–1990), caused a major literary scandal. Kellendonk uses the relationship between two siblings in a Roman Catholic family as the backdrop for an exposition of the intrinsic Otherness of homosexuality and Jewishness in Dutch society. Some critics denounced the novel as antisemitic. Since then, not many non-Jewish writers have dared touch the subjects of Jewish history, Jewish identity, and Judaism.

The Jewish community in the former Dutch colony of *Surinam has a long history. Cynthia Macleod-Ferrier (1936–), a writer from Surinam, described the experiences of a fictional Jewish family at an 18th century plantation in *Hoe duur was de suiker* (1987, "How Expensive Was the Sugar"). In children's fiction Karlijn Stoffels' novel about two friends during the Holocaust, *Mosje en Reizele* (1996, "Moshe and Reizele"), attracted a large audience.

The Jewish Contribution to Dutch Literature

17TH AND 18TH CENTURIES. The Sephardi Jews, arriving in Amsterdam toward the end of the 16th century, were the first Jewish writers in Holland. Although they wrote in Latin, Spanish, and Hebrew, they made a significant contribution to Dutch literature. Prominent among them were poets such as Jacob Israel *Belmonte; Paulo de Pina, author of the biblical morality play *Dialogo dos Montes* (1624); the satirist Abraham (Diego) Gómez Silveyra; and the dramatist and poet Antonio Enríquez *Gómez. A vast but inaccurate source for the history of the Amsterdam Sephardi Jews is the poetry of Miguel (Daniel Levi) de *Barrios. Other important cultural figures were the scholar and statesman Manasseh Ben *Israel and the philosophers Uriel da *Costa and Baruch *Spinoza (see also Spanish and Portuguese *Literature).

The literary production of the Ashkenazi Jews did not cross over into Dutch society in general. Until the 1750s Ashkenazi Jews mainly wrote in Yiddish. In addition to translations of religious books, they made adaptations of secular literature, such as the *Bove-Buch, Josef Maarsen's *Sjeine artliche Geschichten* (1710) translated from *Boccaccio's *Decamerone*, and a translation of the *Travels of Benjamin of Tudela* (1691) by Ḥayyim ben Jacob.

During the second half of the 18th century, the elite of the Jewish community slowly gained entrance into Dutch society through their growing ease with the Dutch language. A handful of young Amsterdam Jews actively participated in the revolutionary movements of 1787 and 1795. Some Jewish revolutionaries contributed to magazines and pamphlets in Dutch, marking the entrance of Dutch Jewry into Dutch letters. The emancipation of the Jewish nation, as declared by the French in 1796, officially opened the doors for their entrance into Dutch society.

FROM THE 19TH CENTURY TO WORLD WAR II. The 19th and early 20th centuries saw a gradual entry of a growing number of educated Jews into most walks of Dutch life. Jews went into law, medicine, commerce, and the fine arts. They entered journalism, the theater, and the entertainment industry. The advent of liberalism and socialism profoundly influenced Jewish intellectuals. Jewish writers reflected upon social inequality and depicted scenes of squalor and misery in the poorer Jewish communities and working-class neighborhoods of the major cities. Also, many explored Jewish self-hatred, assimilation, and, to an extent, Zionism.

The first writer of Portuguese-Jewish descent to contribute to Dutch literature proper was the poet Isaac da *Costa, who at first worked for Jewish emancipation but converted to the Reformed Church in 1822 under the influence of the poet William Bilderdijk. Da Costa was active in the Protestant Réveil movement, which strove for a deepening of religious experience. His works include a collection of poetry, *De Chaos en het Licht* ("Chaos and Light," 1850–53); the biblical drama *Hagar* (1848); and studies on various Jewish themes. Da Costa's friend Abraham Capadose (1795–1874), who also converted, was another early contributor to Dutch literature. He wrote several conversionist works, including *Rome en Jeruzalem* (1851). Other 19th-century authors were the satirist Mark Prager Lindo, the poetess Estella Hijmans Hertzveld, and the novelist Arnold Aäron Aletrino.

Herman *Heijermans, who is generally considered the most important playwright of his time, wrote naturalistic works reflecting the struggle with Jewish identity and social involvement. His many outstanding books include the novel *Diamantstad* ("Diamond City," 1904); *Ghetto* (1898), a drama of Amsterdam Jewish life; and a play about the life of fishermen, *Op hoop van zegen* ("The Good Hope," 1900), which is generally considered one of the best plays ever written in Dutch. The Sephardi author Israël *Querido wrote a number of novels on "ghetto" life, as well as several biblical works. His brother, the publisher Emanuel Querido (1871–1943), was also an author. Other writers of the time were Samuel C. Goudsmit; Willem Schürmann (1879–1915), the author of the "ghetto" play *De Violiers* (1912); and the anti-assimilationist rabbi Meyer de Hond (1873–1943), author of *Kiekjes* ("Snapshots," 1926).

Jewish national feelings dominate the works of M.H. van Campen and a few other writers. A.B. Kleerekoper (1850–1943), who was a minor Hebrew poet, wrote a Dutch adaptation of Song of Songs, *Het Hooglied Zangen van Liefde* (1903). A. van Collem (1858–1933), the first president of the Dutch Zionist Organization, wrote *Russische melodieën* (1891), the story of a pogrom, and the lyrical poem *God* (1930). Outstanding for his religious poetry was Jacob Israël de *Haan, a controversial figure who was assassinated in Jerusalem. His collection *Het Joodsche Lied* ("The Jewish Song," 2 vols., 1915–21) is among the finest religious poetry of modern times. De Haan's sister, the novelist Carry van *Bruggen, whose writing was mainly autobiographical, often dealt with the rift between Jewish parents and children. Sebastian Bonn (1881–1930) wrote some fine poems in both Dutch and Yiddish on Jewish and socialist themes, notably those collected in *Gewijde Liederen* ("Sacred Songs," 1926). The literary critic and poet Victor Emanuel van *Vriesland published an essay on Jewish literature, *De cultureele noodtoestand van het Joodsche volk* (1915). An important impressionistic poet was Herman van den *Bergh. The Catholic convert Herman de Man (1898–1946) wrote regional novels such as *Het wassende water* ("Rising Water," 1926). Jewish themes play a large part in the works of the novelist and literary critic Siegfried Emanuel van *Praag. Among his books were *Jerusalem van het Westen* ("Jerusalem of the West," 1961), an account of vanished Amsterdam Jewish life, and the monograph *De West-Joden en hun letterkunde sinds 1860* ("The Western Jews and Their Literature Since 1860," 1926). The novelist Maurits *Dekker wrote on Jewish and socialist themes, his works including *Brood* ("Bread," 1933) and *De laars op de nek* ("The Jackboot on the Neck," 1945), an account of the German occupation of Holland. Another writer with strong socialist leanings was David de Jong (1898–1963), whose collection of poems, *Eenzame opstandigheid* ("Lonely Revolt," 1925), displays deep melancholy. Dola de Jong (1905–2003), who settled in New York and Los Angeles, wrote the novel *En de akker is de wereld* ("And the Field Is the World," 1947).

EARLY POSTWAR PERIOD. World War II and the Holocaust are generally seen as the watershed in Dutch history. Since 1945, all Jewish novelists, poets, and playwrights have in one way or another reflected on the Holocaust. Some have published their prewar memoirs, others have written about their experiences in hiding or in the Nazi death and concentration camps. A younger generation has taken on the subject of the wartime and postwar experiences of their relatives. This contemplation has taken shape in many different genres. Some authors pursued careers in academia, commerce, journalism, or the stage before turning to writing fiction. Others were already well-established writers when they finally found the courage to give an autobiographical account of their wartime experiences.

War journals are headed by the world-famous diary of Anne *Frank, *Het Achterhuis* (1946; *The Diary of a Young Girl*, 1952). Others are *Brieven uit Westerbork* ("Letters from Westerbork," 1961) by Etty Hillesum (1914–1943), whose letters and diaries were rediscovered and reprinted in the 1970s, with dazzling commercial success. The diary *In Depot* (1964) by Philip Mechanicus (1899–1944) was also rediscovered by a younger audience in the 1970s and again in the 1990s.

Jacob *Presser wrote prose and poetry inspired by World War II experiences, and the two-volume historical study *Ondergang. De vervolging en verdelging van het Nederlandse Jodendom 1940–1945* (1965; *Ashes in the Wind: The Destruction of Dutch Jewry*, 1969). The prominent Zionist and lawyer Abel *Herzberg wrote factual stories on the Bergen-Belsen concentration camp, such as *Amor Fati* (1946) and *Brieven aan mijn kleinzoon* ("Letters to My Grandson," 1964).

A fine autobiographical novel on the war is *Het bittere kruid* (1957; *Bitter Herbs*, 1960) by Marga *Minco. She has continued publishing one novella per decade, in a sober, washed-out style.

Clara Asscher-Pinkhof (1896–1984), who settled in Israel, wrote about children in Bergen-Belsen in her novel *Sterrekinderen* ("Starchildren," 1946; Hebrew, *Yaldei ha-Kokhavim*, 1965); Meyer Sluyser (1901–1973), a popular radio commentator, wrote several novels on vanished Jewish life in Amsterdam, notably *Voordat ik het vergeet* ("Before I Forget," 1956). Another war writer was Salvador Hertog (1901–1989), author of the novel *De Tuin* ("The Garden," 1957) and *Meijer en ik* ("Meijer and I," 1980).

Early postwar poets include Maurits *Mok, author of *Aan de Vermoorden uit Israel* ("To the Murdered of Israel," 1950); Leo Vroman (1915–), who settled in New York and wrote in Dutch and English; and Hannie Michaelis (1922–). Novelist Josepha Mendels (1902–1995), who settled in Paris, tasted literary success only late in life, when her novels about Jewish family life *Rolien en Ralien* (*Rolien and Ralien*, 1947), and *Als vuur en rook* (1950; *Like Ashes and Smoke*) were rediscovered by an eager young readership.

1970–2005

Judith Herzberg (1934–), the youngest daughter of Abel Herzberg, made her literary debut as a poet with *Zeepost* ("Seamail," 1963). She developed into the most important poet and playwright of her generation. She is revered for her clarity of style and her use of seemingly simple language. She based *27 liefdesliedjes* (1971, "27 Love Songs") on the biblical Song of Songs. She succesfully translated and adapted classics of the Yiddish theater *The Golem* and *The Dybuk* for the Dutch stage. Her play *Leedvermaak* (1982) was chosen the best play of the 1980s by her peers. It deals with the unspoken trauma of a family of Holocaust survivors and the younger generations of child survivors and Jews born after 1945. Herzberg subsequently wrote two more plays revolving around the Leedvermaak characters, *Rijgdraad* (1995) and *Simon* (2003).

The literary career of Harry *Mulisch (1930–) has spanned decades. He broke new ground in the early 1980s with his highly successful *De aanslag* ("The Assault," 1981). In 1985, the film by Dutch director Fons Rademakers based on the novel won an Academy Award for Best Foreign Film. Mulish had dealt with Jewish themes in his novel *Het stenen bruidsbed* ("The Stone Bridal Bed," 1959) and wrote an account of the *Eichmann trial, *De zaak 40/61* (1968). His major epic on the world's redemption, as seen from a Jewish perspective through the unwitting ministrations of a Dutch boy, *De ontdekking van de hemel* (1992; *The Discovery of Heaven*, 1996), established his reputation worldwide.

A generation after the Holocaust, Dutch Jews who had pursued non-literary careers started putting their wartime experiences on paper. This has resulted in some exquisite fiction that has reached a large international audience. Andreas Burnier, the pen name of criminologist Catharina R. Dessaur (1931–2002), published *Het jongensuur* (*The Boys' Hour*, 1969), the first of many novels and essays on Judaism, ethics, and religion. Physicist Jona Oberski (1938–) wrote *Kinderjaren* (1978; *Childhood*, 1983), a memoir of his experiences in the Bergen-Belsen concentration camp as a small boy. Sociologist Gerhard Durlacher (1928–1996), a prewar refugee from Baden-Baden in Germany, did not dare to start writing fiction until the 1980s. His small body of work includes *Strepen aan de hemel* (1985; *Stripes in the Sky*, 1992), *Drenkeling* (1985, *Drowning: Growing up in the Third Reich*, 1993), and *De zoektocht* (1991; *The Search: The Birkenau Boys*, 1998). Lisette Lewin, who had previously worked as a journalist, published her semi-autobiographical novel *Voor bijna alles bang geweest* ("Having Been Afraid of Almost Anything," 1989). Eli Asser, a popular writer for television and the stage, changed direction in the early 1990s, which resulted in his war memoir *Rembrandt was mijn buurman* ("Rembrandt Was My Neighbor," 1995).

The autobiographical novel *Brief aan mijn moeder* ("Letter to My Mother," 1974) by journalist and theater critic Ischa (Israel Chaim) Meijer (1943–1995) is credited with shattering the taboo that children of Holocaust survivors have no cause to complain. Meijer luridly described his troubled childhood amongst Holocaust survivors. In Meijer's wake many new, younger writers have emerged who have grappled with the Holocaust "as part of their mental history, if not their own physical history," in the words of author Marcel Möring. This intense inner search has led to a large body of novels, poetry, and plays.

Leon de Winter (1954–) is both a novelist and a screenwriter. He started out as the highly literary author of *De (ver)wording van de jonge Dürer* ("The Corruption of Young Dürer," 1979), *Place de la Bastille* (1981), and *Zoeken naar Eileen* ("In Search of Eileen," 1981). With the publication of *Kaplan* (1986) De Winter seemed to have changed his pace. His Jewish characters, bitter humor, and use of literary techniques often used in crime fiction have made him a bestselling novelist, both in Holland and abroad, with *Hoffman's Honger* ("Hoffman's Hunger," 1990), *SuperTex* ("SuperTex," 1991), *De ruimte van Sokolov* ("Sokolov's Space," 1992), *Zionoco* (1995), *De hemel van Hollywood* ("The Heaven Above Hollywood," 1997), and *God's gym* (2002). Many of his novels were adapted for film or television.

Marcel Möring's (1957–) highly accomplished novels *Mendels Erfenis* ("Mendels Heritage," 1990), *Het grote verlangen* (1995; *The Great Longing*, 1995), *In Babylon* (1997; *In Babylon*, 1999), and *Modelvliegen* (2001; *The Dream Room*, 2002) seriously explore the emotional entanglement of children of Holocaust survivors, a theme also explored by Wanda Reisel (1955–) in her novel *Het beloofde leven* (1995).

Arnon Grunberg (1973–) has been called the most interesting young author in the Dutch language. He made his debut with the novel *Blauwe Maandagen* (1994; *Blue Mondays*, 1996). Grunberg moved to New York in the 1990s, but has continued to write in Dutch and concern himself with Dutch society. His novels *De figuranten* ("The Extra's," 1997), *Fantoompijn* (2000; *Phantom Pain*, 2002), *De asielzoeker* (2002; "The Asylumseeker"), and *De Joodse Messias* (2004, "The Jewish Messiah") gained him prominence. He has published poetry and essays, made a new version of Desiderius Erasmus' *Lof der Zotheid* (1509, *The Praise of Folly*), called *De mensheid zij geprezen.* ("Humanity Be Praised," 2001). Grunberg also makes use of the not overtly Jewish pseudonym Marek van der Jagt. Both Grunberg and Van der Jagt have won many Dutch and international literary prizes.

In fiction for children and young people, the novel *Chaweriem* ("Hawerim" (Hebrew for "Friends"), 1995) stands out as a modest Dutch classic. In this tale of a group of young Jews wanting to immigrate from Holland to Israel, Leonard de Vries (1919–2002) caught the hopes of young child survivors for a better future. Child survivor Ida Vos (1931–) has gained prominence with her many novels for children: *Wie niet weg is wordt gezien* (1981; *Hide and Seek*, 1995), *Dansen op de brug van Avignon* (1989; *Dancing on the Bridge of Avignon* 1995), *Anna is er nog* (1991; *Anna Is Still Here*, 1995), *Witte Zwanen, Zwarte Zwanen* ("White Swans, Black Swans," 1992), *De sleutel is gebroken* (1996; *The Key Is Lost*, 2000), and *De lachende engel* ("The Laughing Angel," 2000).

Dutch literary critics include Joseph Melkman (1914–), who settled in Jerusalem and wrote *Geliefde Vijand* ("Beloved Enemy," 1964), a book about the Jew in postwar Dutch literature. Historian Jaap Meijer (1912–1993) published a study on poet Jacob Israël de Haan, *De zoon van een Gazzan* ("The Son of a Cantor," 1967). Meijer, the father of Ischa Meijer, also became known by his pen name Saul van Messel, a poet who distinguished himself from his peers in the literary world by writing in the Saxon dialect of Groningen province.

A few Jews have also written in Afrikaans, a dialect of Dutch containing other elements and spoken mainly by the South African Afrikaners; see *South African Literature.

BIBLIOGRAPHY: S.E. van Praag, *De West-Joden en hun letterkunde sinds 1860* (1926); J. Meijer, *Zij lieten hun sporen achter* (1964); P. Kat, *Bijbelsche uitdrukkingen en spreek wijzen in onze taal* (1926); H. Beem, *Jerôsche, Jiddische spreekwoorden en zegswijzen uit het Nederlandse taalgebied* (1959); idem, *Resten van een taal, woordenboek van het Nederlandse Jiddisch* (1967); C.G.N. de Vooys and G. Stuiveling, *Schets van de Nederlandse letterkunde* (1966); J. Melkman, *Geliefde Vijand* (1964). **ADD. BIBLIOGRAPHY:** S. Dresden, *Vervolging, vernietiging, literatuur,* (1991); J. Snapper, *De wegen van Marga Minco*(1997); D. Meijer, *Levi in de Lage Landen* (1999), J. Vos, *Het geschrevene blijft te lezen* (2004).

[Gerda Alster-Thau / Daphne Meijer (2nd ed.)]

DUTY, an action that one is obligated to perform; a feeling, or sense, of obligation. In Judaism man's duties are determined by God's commandments. The entire biblical and rabbinic conception of man's role in the world is subsumed under the notion of *mitzvah* (meaning simultaneously "law," "commandment," "duty," and "merit"). The term *ḥovah*, meaning "obligation" or "duty," which came into use later, is used interchangeably with *mitzvah*. To perform a divine commandment is to fulfill one's duty, *laẓet yedei ḥovah* (Ber. 8b). The translator from the Arabic original into Hebrew of *Baḥya ibn Paquda's major work *Ḥovot ha-Levavot* ("Duties of the Hearts") used the term *ḥovah* as a synonym for commandment, and the term was taken up by other writers of **musar* literature (for a discussion of the relationship between "*mitzvah*" and "*ḥovah*" see ET, vol. 12, s.v. *ḥovah*). Duty is the incentive to moral action, and a morality-based duty is evidently different from one that is based on pleasure. According to a talmudic dictum "Greater is he who performs an action because he is commanded than he who performs the same action without being commanded" (BK 38a). The pleasure derived from the performance of a commandment is irrelevant to its nature (cf. RH 28a "the commandments were not given to be enjoyed"), and conversely dislike of an action is no sufficient reason for abstention from it, cf. the saying of R. Eleazar b. Azariah: "Say not, 'I do not like to eat pork'... but say, 'I would like, but I will not for it is God's prohibition'" (Sifra 20:26; cf. Mak. 3:15). One should not perform an action in order to gain a reward, but because it is a divine commandment, and hence one's duty: "Be not like servants who work for the master on condition of receiving a reward..." (Avot 1:3).

The morality of an action is determined more by the motivation of the one who performs it than by its consequences: "You must do what is incumbent upon you; its success is up to God" (Ber. 10a). The notion of intention (*kavvanah*) is central in Jewish ethics: "Whether it be much or little, so long as the intention is pure" (Ber. 17a; Sif. Deut. 41); "God demands the heart" (Sanh. 106b). That is not to say that an action performed without the proper motivation is worthless. The fact that its results are beneficial does give it some worth. Moreover, through performing an action without the proper motivation, one may come to perform it with the proper motivation: "From doing [good] with an ulterior motive one may learn to do [good] for its own sake" (Pes. 50b; cf. Maim., Yad, Teshuvah, 10:5).

The major problem in modern Jewish thought in connection with the concept of duty is posed by the Kantian notion of autonomy, according to which an action to be moral must be motivated by a sense of duty, and must be autonomous (I. *Kant, *Fundamental Principles of Ethics*, trans. by T.K. Abbott (1946[10]), 31ff.). This appears to conflict with the traditional Jewish notion that the law is given by God, that is, that it is the product of a heteronomous legislator. Moritz *Lazarus in his *Ethik des Judentums* (1898, 1911; *The Ethics of Judaism*, trans. by H. Szold, 1900) attempts to show that rabbinic ethics are based on the same principles as Kantian ethics, the basic underlying principle of both being the principle of autonomy (*ibid.*, 1 (1898), no. 90–105). In so doing he somewhat distorts the Kantian notion of autonomy. Hermann *Cohen, in *Die Religion der Vernunft aus den Quellen des Judentums*, in his attempt to deal with the problem of heteronomy and autonomy, interprets *mitzvah* to mean both "law" and "duty," the law originating in God and the sense of duty in man. Man, of his own free will, must take upon himself the "yoke of the commandments." Franz *Rosenzweig approaches the question of the duties imposed by Jewish law from a somewhat different consideration. Distinguishing between "law" (Ger., *Gesetz*; Heb., *ḥukkah*) and "commandment" (Ger., *Gebot*; Heb., *mitzvah*), he holds that the individual is confronted by the body of Jewish law which is impersonal (*Gesetz*) and that he must make a serious effort to transform it into commandments (*Gebot*) by appropriating whatever is meaningful to him in the situation in which he finds himself (F. Rosenzweig, *On Jewish Learning* (1955), 83–92, 109–24).

BIBLIOGRAPHY: J. Heinemann, *Ta'amei ha-Mitzvot be-Sifrut Yisrael*, 2 (1956), index s.v. *heteronomiyyut*.

DUVDEVANI, SHMUEL (1903–1987), Israel botanist. Duvdevani was born in the Ukraine. He studied botany in England and went to Palestine in 1921. He was an instructor at the Hebrew University in Jerusalem and beginning in 1935 he taught at the agricultural school at Pardes Ḥannah. In 1936 he turned his attention to research on *dew. He invented an optical method of measuring the amount of dew precipitation which has been accepted all over the world. The international meteorological organization, accepted the Duvdevani Dew Recorder as a standard method for the international measuring of dew. Duvdevani was instrumental in setting up a network of observation stations throughout Israel for recording dew precipitation, the first such network in the world. In connection with his meteorological work, Duvdevani carried out research on plant physiology, especially on the absorption of water by the foliage of the plant. In 1946 he participated in the publication of *Magdir le-Ẓimḥei-Bar* (1946), which is a systematic definition of flora, according to vegetative qualities alone.

DUVEEN, family of British art dealers. The famous firm of Duveen Brothers was founded by Sir JOSEPH JOEL DUVEEN (1843–1908), who was born in the Netherlands, the son of a Jewish blacksmith, and migrated to Hull, where he opened a curiosity shop dealing in china. Duveen developed a deep knowledge of Nanking china, which he imported successfully, and, in 1879, moved to London. There he opened an impressive gallery. With the help of his brother Henry in New York, Duveen then specialized in selling paintings and other art works to nouveau riches millionaires, especially Americans and South Africans. He increasingly employed the renowned American-born art expert resident in Italy, Bernard *Berenson, to authenticate the works he sold. Duveen also built luxury houses for his wealthy clients. He received a knighthood in 1902 for his gift of £20,000 to build the Turner Gallery at London's Tate Museum.

Sir Joseph's eldest son, Joseph *Duveen, first Baron Duveen of Millbank (1869–1939), with whom he is often confused, became head of the firm after the death of his father and uncle (in 1919), and continued to maintain the firm as a leading international art house.

BIBLIOGRAPHY: ODNB online; DBB, II, 213–17; S.N. Behrman, *Duveen* (1972); E. Fowles, *Memories of Duveen Brothers* (1976).

[William D Rubinstein (2nd ed.)]

DUVEEN, JOSEPH, LORD (1869–1939), English art dealer. His grandfather was a Dutch Jewish blacksmith, and his father a dealer first in lard, then in Delft pottery, furniture, and objets d'art. Duveen was born in Hull, and later moved to London. He began to deal in paintings in 1901 and by 1906 was buying famous collections. In the same year he engaged Bernard *Berenson as his authenticator of Italian art. Duveen's chief clients were a relatively small number of American millionaires. He encouraged in his clients a taste for the luxurious surroundings in which great works of art could be shown, sometimes even going so far as to build and furnish their houses. At the same time he "educated" them in an appreciation of the old masters and fostered in them a desire to achieve lasting fame through the formation of important collections. He then met their requirements by supplying the most magnificent examples available of the Italian, Dutch, French, and English schools at the highest prices. His specialty was the English masters of the late 18th and early 19th centuries. The collections he thus brought into existence were often donated to the public on their owners' death. Lord Duveen received many honors. Most controversially, he was appointed a Trustee of London's National Gallery, National Portrait Galley, and the Wallace Collection. The apparent conflict of interest of an art dealer having a potential role in deciding which works of art England's leading art museums might purchase was widely debated, and led to Duveen's dismissal from these posts shortly before his death. Duveen received a knighthood in 1919, a baronetcy in 1929, and was awarded a peerage in 1933 – the first ever awarded to an art dealer – in large part for paying for the building of the famous gallery at the British Museum which houses the Elgin Marbles.

BIBLIOGRAPHY: S.N. Behrman, *Duveen* (Eng., 1952); J.H. Duveen, *The Rise of the House of Duveen* (1957).

DUVERNOIS, HENRI (pen name of **Henri Simon Schwabacher**; 1875–1937), French author and journalist. Duvernois' popular melancholy and ironical stories of everyday life in Paris, influenced by Maupassant, include the novels *Crapotte* (1908), *Faubourg Montmartre* (1914), *Edgar* (1919), and *Maxime* (1927). Duvernois also published a volume of one-act comedies (1928).

DUWAYK (**Doweik ha-Cohen**), family of rabbis and authors in Aleppo, Syria. SIMEON BEN SAMUEL (first half of the 18th century) was the author of *Rei'aḥ Sadeh* (Constantinople, 1738). ABRAHAM (d. 1900) was an author and presided over the Jewish community of Aleppo for many years, until his dismissal in 1896. His wealthy brother SAUL (d. 1874 in Aleppo) wrote *Emet me-Ereẓ* (Jerusalem, 1910). JACOB SAUL (d. 1919 in Aleppo) was acting chief rabbi of Aleppo beginning in 1906 and wrote *Derekh Emunah* (1914) and *She'erit Ya'akov* (1925), sermons. The family was also found in India, Calcutta and Bombay, and in the latter they had a certain influence on the *Bene Israel community.

[Haim J. Cohen]

DVIR, Hebrew publishing house, founded in 1922 in Berlin by Ḥayyim Naḥman *Bialik, Shemaryahu *Levin, and Yehoshua Hana *Rawnitzki as a successor to the *Moriah publishing firm of Odessa. Bialik expressed Dvir's program as: "Not just books, but basic books; books bequeathed from generation to generation that provide light for our people." The firm began publishing books in Tel Aviv in 1924. Dvir's publications covered all areas of publishing: reference books, dictionaries, handbooks, anthologies, belles lettres, humanities, sciences, social sciences, art, children's books, and textbooks. Its list included many basic works in Judaica and the classics of modern Hebrew literature. Its *Sefer ha-Mo'adim* ("Book of Festivals," 9 vols., 1956 on, ed. Y. Lewinsky) contains a wealth of material about each holiday. A new edition of the Mishnah, vocalized by Hanoch Yalon and annotated by Hanokh Albeck, was published in cooperation with Mosad Bialik. Dvir also began publishing the Babylonian Talmud with a Hebrew translation. Authors published by Dvir, in addition to the founders, include *Shalom Aleichem, Sholem *Asch, Yiẓḥak Dov *Berkowitz, Simon *Dubnow, Isaac Leib *Peretz, Moshe *Smilansky, Benẓion *Dinur, and Yeḥezkel *Kaufmann. Later Dvir merged with the Zemorah-Bitan Kinneret publishing house.

[Israel Soifer]

DVORETZKY, ARYEH (1916–), Israeli mathematician. Born in Chorol, Russia, Dvoretzky went to Palestine in 1922 and studied at the Hebrew University, Jerusalem, where he became professor of mathematics in 1951. As dean of the faculty of science (1955–56) and as vice president (1959–61) he adopted a policy of fostering basic research designed to keep pace with advances in contemporary mathematics. He was also chief scientist to the Israel Defense Forces. His special fields of study were mathematical statistics, the theory of probability, and functional analysis. In 1973 Dvoretzky was awarded the Israel Prize in exact sciences, and in 1974 he was appointed president of the Israel Academy of Sciences and Humanities, after serving as chairman of its science section (1963–68) and vice president (1968–74). In 1975 he established the Institute for Advanced Studies at the Hebrew University of Jerusalem and from 1985 to 1988 he was president of the Weizmann Institute.

[Bracha Rager (2nd ed.)]

DVORZETSKY, MARK MEIR (1908–1975), writer, communal worker, and partisan fighter. Dvorzetsky was born in Vilna, where he graduated in medicine in 1935 and received his rabbinical diploma in 1938. He was active in Vilna in student affairs and a member of the Jewish Students' Self-Defense Organization. He was also a permanent contributor to the Jewish press in Poland. In 1939 he was elected to the Executive of the municipality of Vilna.

An officer in the Polish Army in World War II, he was taken prisoner by the Germans but escaped and returned to Vilna, where he took part in the Jewish self-defense against the Lithuanian pogromists. In 1941–43 he was one of the founders of the Jewish underground in the ghetto of Vilna and wrote a diary which is now in the historical archives of the city. During this period he did research on ghetto life during the Middle Ages on the basis of responsa existing in the ghetto library. In 1943 he was transported to a concentration camp in Estonia, where he formed an underground group called She'ar Yashuv, and where he also kept a diary. In 1944 he was transferred to concentration camps in Germany. In 1945 he organized the escape of Jewish internees from the camp during a death march and was finally freed by the French army. He organized and headed a displaced persons organization and served as editor of the Yiddish daily *Unzer Vort*. From 1945 to 1949 he resided in Paris, where he was active in the rescue of Jewish children who had been hidden in monasteries.

From this time Dvorzetsky devoted himself entirely to research on the Holocaust, publishing numerous papers and books on the subject in Hebrew, Yiddish, French, and English. Immigrating to Israel in 1949, he was a member of the executive of Yad Vashem from its establishment, and an active member of all the organizations of ex-partisan fighters and ex-inmates of the concentration camps, as well as literary organizations, including the Israeli branch of PEN.

He was instrumental in founding the chair for research into the Holocaust at Bar-Ilan University and lectured there from 1960. He received the Israel Prize for social sciences. in 1953.

[Benjamin Rivlin]

DWORKIN, RONALD (1931–), U.S. legal philosopher. Born in Worcester, Massachusetts, Dworkin received a B.A. degree from Harvard in 1953 and another B.A. degree in 1955 from Oxford. Two years later he received his law degree from Harvard. After admission to the New York bar, he joined the law firm Sullivan and Cromwell as an associate. In 1962 he joined the faculty of Yale Law School, where he was named Hohfeld Professor in 1968. In 1969 he was appointed professor of jurisprudence and Fellow at University College, Oxford; in 1977 he became professor of law at New York University without resigning his position at Oxford.

Dworkin is recognized as a leading philosopher of law. His best-known works are *Taking Rights Seriously* (1977), *A Matter of Principle* (1985), and *Law's Empire* (1986). In his work Dworkin has contended against the philosophy of legal positivism, identified with Jeremy Bentham, John Austin, and more recently H.L.A. Hart. Legal decisions, he maintains, should be based on principles and pre-existing rights, rather than on discretion or policy. While rights may be controversial, Dworkin holds that nonetheless there is always only one right answer in hard cases. Rights, he holds, are inherent in the Constitution and in the precedents that interpret it. Judges make moral judgments as they apply precedents to factual situations – precedents on which principles are based and which are the bases of decisions.

In *Ronald Dworkin and Contemporary Jurisprudence* (1984), the editor – Professor Marshall Cohen – states, "In the opinion of the editor, the jurisprudential writings of Ronald Dworkin constitute the finest contribution yet made by an American writer to the philosophy of law."

Despite Dworkin's close association, as student and as teacher, with Oxford, he is basically an American thinker. Much more than would be true of a British jurist, Dworkin has been influenced by American constitutional law and constitutional jurisprudence. His emphasis on principle is a reflection of this influence.

Dworkin holds the positions of professor of philosophy and Frank Henry Sommer Professor of Law at NYU and chair at University College, London. He is a fellow of the British Academy and a member of the American Academy of Arts and Sciences, as well as co-chairman of the Democratic Party Abroad, a member of the Council of Writers and Scholars Educational Trust and of the Programme Committee of the Ditchley Foundation, and a consultant on human rights to the Ford Foundation.

Other works by Dworkin include *Philosophical Issues in Senile Dementia* (1987), *A Bill of Rights for Britain* (1990), *Life's Dominion: An Argument About Abortion, Euthanasia and Individual Freedom* (1993), *Freedom's Law: The Moral Reading of the American Constitution* (1996), and *Sovereign Virtue: The Theory and Practice of Equality* (2000).

ADD. BIBLIOGRAPHY: S. Guest, *Ronald Dworkin* (1991); M. Cohen (ed.), *Ronald Dworkin and Contemporary Jurisprudence* (1984), A. Hunt (ed.), *Reading Dworkin Critically* (1992).

[Milton Ridvas Konvitz / Ruth Beloff (2nd ed.)]

DWORKIN, ZALMAN SHIMON (1911–1985), Lubavitch rabbi. Dworkin was born in Rogotchov, White Russia. At the age of 11, he arrived in the city of Lubavitch, then the center of activities of the *Chabad-Lubavitch movement, to study in the Yeshivah Tomchei Tmimim Lubavitch. In late 1915, when the fifth Lubavitcher Rebbe, Shalom Dov Baer, relocated from Lubavitch and settled in Rostov, Dworkin also settled there. As the need for additional Chabad grade schools and yeshivot across Eastern Europe became apparent to the Rebbe in Rostov, Dworkin was one of the students that served as the seed group in establishing many of them, as the Rebbe's emissary. He received rabbinic ordination from the Rogotchover Gaon, Rabbi Joseph *Rozin.

Following his marriage, Dworkin became the rabbi of the city of Stardov, Russia. He also served as a *rosh yeshivah* in Yeshivah Tomchei Tmimim Lubavitch in Samarkand and in later years in Paris, France. During World War II, he oversaw the *kashrut* of meat in Ireland. After the war, he arrived in the United States and settled in the Lubavitch community in Crown Heights, Brooklyn, N.Y. In the mid-1960s, he was appointed to the position of "*rav*" and "*av bet din*" in the Lubavitcher community.

The Lubavitcher Rebbe, Menachem Mendel *Schneersohn, was very fond of Dworkin and would refer many people with complicated halakhic questions to him, but also those with personal dilemmas that needed a bright and caring individual to assist them. The rabbi was exemplary in treating every individual, no matter who he was, with great sensitivity and understanding. He was a renowned expert on *sheḥitah* (ritual slaughter) and many other issues. After his death his responsa were published in book form as *Koveẓ Razash*.

[Michoel A. Seligson (2nd ed.)]

DYATLOVO (Pol. **Zdzięciol**; Yid. **Zhetl**), town in Grodno district, Belarus. Jews first settled there around 1580, and by 1670 a community was formed. Rabbi Ḥayyim ha-Kohen Rapoport served there in 1720–29, and then moved to Lvov, where he was an important participant in the dispute with the Frankists in 1759. The number of Jews in the town steadily increased; of the total population of 3,979 in 1897, 3,033 (75%) were Jews. Personalities associated with Dyatlovo include Aryeh Leib ha-Levi Horowitz and Ḥayyim ha-Kohen *Rapoport. Dyatlovo was the birthplace of Jacob of Dubno (the "Dubner Maggid") and Israel Meir ha-Kohen (the "Ḥafeẓ Ḥayyim"). Zalman *Sorotzkin was rabbi of the community from 1912 to 1929. There were 3,450 Jews (75% of the total) in 1926, comprising 621 Jewish families. Of these, 303 earned their livelihoods from crafts, mainly as tailors and shoemakers, while 210 lived from trade. The community had a hospital and an old age home. Two schools were in operation: a Hebrew Tarbut school and a Yiddish CYSHO school.Communal and Zionist activities continued until the outbreak of World War II. The Germans occupied the town on June 30, 1941. A hundred and twenty prominent Jews were executed on July 25 and 400 were sent to the Dworzec labor camp on December 15. On February 22, 1941, a ghetto was created, housing together with refugees 4,000 Jews. On April 30 around 1,200 were murdered and on August 6, 1942 another 1,500–2,000. About 800 succeeded in escaping into the forests and joined the Soviet partisans or later the Red Army. A hundred of them died in the battles.

BIBLIOGRAPHY: B. Kaplinski (ed.), *Pinkas Zhetel* (1957); PK.

[Shmuel Spector (2nd ed.)]

DYCHE, JOHN ALEXANDER (1867–1939), U.S. labor leader. Dyche was born in Kovno, Lithuania. He went to New York City in 1900 after 14 years in England, where he was active in trade unionism. Dyche soon became involved in the newly founded International Ladies' Garment Workers' Union, and from 1904 was its secretary-treasurer. Dyche defended the principles of "pure and simple" trade unionism, including the sanctity of contracts, the use of the strike only as a last resort and only under the strict control of a national union, and the basic interest of the worker in self-advancement rather than solidarity and socialism. He strongly supported the Protocol of 1910, arguing that this collective bargaining agreement in the cloak and suit trade, with its unusual provision for arbitration, would aid the large clothing concerns at the expense of the small contractors, and allow the union and the employers to move toward a single wage schedule in the industry. He stressed that employers were prepared to raise wages if their competitors did likewise. However, the Protocol produced bitter disputes within the union, and Dyche refused to seek another term in office in 1924. He subsequently left the labor movement and became the owner of a small business in the garment industry. He wrote *Bolshevism in American Labor Unions* (1926).

BIBLIOGRAPHY: L. Lorwin, *Women's Garment Workers* (1924); L.P. Gartner, *Jewish Immigrant in England, 1870–1914* (1960), 66.

[Irwin Yellowitz]

DYEING.

Biblical Period

The preparation of cloth for clothing required several operations. After the cleaning of the wool or flax, it was dyed the necessary color, usually light blue or purple, with animal or vegetable dyes mixed with minerals and salts by chemical processes unknown today. Special dyeing plants and implements were used in Ereẓ Israel. Dye tools were found at Tel Beth-Mirsim, Gezer, and other places. They were made of stone, like hollow barrels: on the upper surface a groove was carved, which was connected to the inside by means of a hole. With the introduction of the material to be dyed into the dye-filled barrel, the liquid would rise, overflow through the hole, and be collected in the groove. Upon the removal of the wet garment, the overflow would return through the reverse process thus permitting the material to be dyed again and preserving the precious dyes. Some operations required heating or boiling, and portable earthenware vessels, which could be placed over a fire, were used for these purposes.

Mishnaic and Talmudic Periods

The craft had developed considerably by the mishnaic and talmudic periods, both in the preparation of dyes and in the dyeing of materials and clothes. The sources describe the dyer's workshop (MK 13b) and his equipment, such as the coverings which protected his hands (Kelim 16:6); before he cast the ingredients into the crucible, the dyer made a small sample for himself which was known as the "taste" (Men. 42b); the ingredients were ground with a special handmill (Tosef. Shab. 9 (10):19). During this period, some places were known as centers of dyeing: Migdal Zevaya on the eastern bank of the Jordan, which was noted for the production of cloth; *Haifa, which was also called Purpurin (Purple); and a place called Luz where the **tekhelet* was manufactured (Sot. 46b). After the Bar Kokhba War (132–135 C.E.) dyeing was developed in *Lydda and *Beth-Shean, both important weaving centers.

Middle Ages

As the Jews had been masters of the techniques of the craft from ancient times, in some districts, especially in the Mediterranean region, the preparation of dyes and dyeing of cloth was considered mainly a Jewish occupation. Such occupations were generally despised and their practice by Jews was seen as part of the general humiliation of the Jewish people. However, some sources indicate that dyeing was a highly respectable profession. The apparent contradiction points to a difference in social and economic standing between the artisan engaged in the craft and the merchant who dealt in the ingredients (though this distinction was not always clearly expressed in the sources). During this period, Jewish trade in dyestuffs expanded extensively. Jewish merchants imported reseda from eastern India, via Egypt and Tunisia, to Italy and Spain, and exported saffron from Tunisia to southern Europe. Those trading in indigo between Egypt and Europe were known as *al-nili* (nil = indigo). Contemporary letters illustrate the range of the undertakings: a Jewish merchant of Kairouan wrote to his friend in Egypt that in Sicily only indigo of the best quality could be sold; another merchant, head of the Babylonian congregation of Fostat (Old Cairo), wrote to an associate in Tyre in the 11th century, "The price of indigo has risen over the last fortnight because it was in great demand among the people of Syria and the West…." Documents also point to the high prices of these commodities: 270 pounds of indigo cost from 100 to 300 quarter dinars.

Jews also developed the manufacture of dyes, especially in Greece and Italy, where they were most active in the south, and in Sicily; important dyeing centers existed in *Brindisi, *Benevento, Salerno, Agrigento, Trani, and Cosenza. In these localities, the dyehouse was sometimes the center of the Jewish quarter, along with the synagogue.

*Benjamin of Tudela found Jews engaged in dyeing in several localities in Ereẓ Israel, notably in Jerusalem, Jezreel, Lydda, Bethlehem, and Bet Nubi. In Jerusalem, their shops were situated in a special building which they had obtained from King Baldwin II. In 1231, Emperor Frederick II created a crown monopoly of the silk and dyeing industries and Jewish firms in Trani were appointed to administer it. When the monopoly came to an end with the death of the emperor in 1250, the Jews continued to engage in this industry, which also spread to the north of Italy. In *Montpellier, France, Jews were prominent in the manufacture of dyes, while in Spain they had engaged in the craft from the Muslim period, especially in *Seville and *Saragossa. After the Christian reconquest, the Jews continued in this occupation, in particular in Saragossa where they owned special workshops. Among the responsa of Solomon b. Abraham *Adret are clear allusions to the existence of dyers' guilds. During the 16th century, the occupation expanded after *Safed had become the Jewish center of the wool weaving industry.

During this period, dyeing was highly developed in a number of Jewish communities in the Ottoman Empire, especially in *Salonika and *Constantinople. During the 17th century, the Salonika dye industry declined, along with weaving, mainly as a result of competition from Venice and Ancona. Jews of *Brest-Litovsk are often mentioned as experts in manufacture in Poland and Lithuania. Responsa literature contains numerous accounts of the craft of dyeing, the tools employed, and the various methods used in the preparation of dyes. There are descriptions of a dyeing shop where the work was carried out (Responsa of Abraham, the son of Maimonides, no. 117); of a dye-pit (*ibid.*, no. 101); and of barrels in which wool was dyed (Responsa of Samuel b. Moses di Medina, ḤM 462). Documents also mention dyers who were expert in a given color: *Samāk*, the expert in preparing dyes from the sumac shrub; *quirmizini*, the expert in crimson, etc.

Modern Times

In the Near East, the Jews continued to practice this profession during the 19th century. The surname Zebag (dyer), still widespread among Oriental Jews, is evidence of the fact. In Damascus in the middle of the 19th century, 70 of the 5,000 Jews were dyers. Jews also played an important part in the development of dye ingredients in the Americas. Planting of indigo was introduced in Georgia during the 17th century and Moses *Lindo from London invested large sums in the cultivation of indigo in South Carolina in 1756. The development of modern chemistry and the *chemical industry, in which Jewish scientists and entrepreneurs played a considerable role, brought to a close the traditional methods in the manufacture of dyes and dyeing.

BIBLIOGRAPHY: Demsky, in: IEJ, 16 (1966); G. Caro, *Sozial- und Wirtschaftsgeschichte der Juden*, 2 vols. (1908–20), index, s.v. *Farben*; R. Strauss, *Die Juden im Koenigreich Sizilien* … (1910), 66ff.; A.S. Hershberg, *Ḥayyei ha-Tarbut be-Yisrael bi-Tekufat ha-Mishnah ve-ha-Talmud*, 1 (1924), 207–316; I.S. Emmanuel, *Histoire de l'industrie des tissus des Israelites de Salonique* (1935), 16ff.; J. Starr, in: *Byzantinisch-neugriechische Jahrbuecher*, 12 (1936), 42–49; Ashtor, Toledot, 1 (1944), 176ff.; R.S. Lopez, in: *Speculum*, 20 (1945), 23f. (Eng.); Roth, Italy, index; J.R. Marcus, *Early American Jewry*, 2 vols. (1951–53), index, s.v. *Dyeing Industry, Indigo;* S. Avitsur, in: *Sefunot*, 6 (1962), 58ff.; Hirschberg, Afrikah, 1 (1965), 200ff.; M. Wischnitzer, *History of Jewish Crafts and Guilds* (1965), 127ff., 203f., and index; S.D. Goitein, *Mediterranean Society*, 1 (1967), index.

DYE PLANTS. The dye materials that were used in ancient times were many and varied and were obtained from various mineral, plant, and animal sources. The last gave fast and beautiful colors, but these were so costly that only the wealthy could afford them. Of these the most famous were the "blue and purple and scarlet" mentioned frequently in the Bible in connection with the construction of the Sanctuary and the Temple (see *Crimson, **Tekhelet*). In mishnaic times cheaper dyes were obtained from such common plants as the carob and the sumac (*og*; Tosef. Shev. 5:7). Green walnut and pomegranate shells were used to produce a brown-black dye (Shev. 7:3).

In the Bible three plants are mentioned from which dye was obtained: *karkom* (*saffron), *kofer* (*henna), and *pu'ah* (madder). The saffron provided an orange dye, the henna a reddish orange one, and the madder a red-colored dye. *Tola* (crimson) and *puvah* (or *puah*) are mentioned in the Bible as proper names (Gen. 46:13; I Chron. 7:1; Judg. 10:1). These names, which were borne by the sons of Issachar, suggest that this tribe was skilled in the production of these dyes or in using them for dyeing cloth. Madder is obtained from the plant *Rubia tinctorum* which was grown in large quantities before the discovery of synthetic dyes. It is indigenous to Edom, and many species grow wild in Israel. The plant was cultivated in the mishnaic period and there is a discussion on the methods to be employed in uprooting it in a sabbatical year (Shev. 5:4).

Other dyestuffs are mentioned in rabbinic literature. *Isalis, koẓah*, and *rikhpah* are mentioned together (Shev. 7:1). *Isalis* is obtained from a plant, *Isalis tinctoria*, from whose leaves a blue dye was extracted. It grew in abundance until the end of the 19th century; some 2,000 kg. (about 4,400 lbs.) of leaves per dunam were harvested, from which four kg. (about 8¾ lbs.) of dyestuff was produced. *Koẓah* is the *Carthamus tinctorius* whose top leaves provide a dye of a reddish orange shade. The seeds of this plant served both as a food and as a source of dye. In the Mishnah it has the additional name *ḥari'a* (Kil. 2:8; Uk. 5:3). In the Talmud it is also called *morika, kurtemei* (i.e., *carthamus*), and *dardara*. The latter means a thistle, hence its mishnaic name *koẓah* as it is a thorny plant of the family *Compositae. Rikhpah* is dyer's reseda, the *Reseda luteola* that grows wild in the arid areas of Ereẓ Israel. Its leaves and flower provide a yellow dye. *Leshishit* (turnsole, *Chrozophora tinctoria*) grows wild among the summer crops in many parts of the country. The various parts of the plant produce a blue dye which is used for dyeing textiles and is used in Europe for coloring food to this day. This plant is mentioned in the Tosefta (Shev. 5:6). *Kalilan* (indigo, indigotin) was imported from India during Roman times, and a dye of bluish shade was obtained from it. It was not easy to distinguish it from the true blue (see **Tekhelet*) permitted for the ritual fringes, and the rabbis therefore warned against the use of ritual fringes dyed with it.

BIBLIOGRAPHY: Loew, Flora, 1 (1924), 394ff., 493ff., 595ff.; 4 (1934), 117f.; B. Ẓizik, *Oẓar ha-Ẓemaḥim* (1944), 329–34; J. Feliks, *Olam ha-Ẓome'aḥ ha-Mikra'i* (1957), 301–2; idem, *Kilei Zera'im ve-Harkavah* (1967), 225ff., 259ff.

[Jehuda Feliks]

DYHERNFURTH (Pol. **Brzeg Dolny**), town in Lower Silesia; from 1945 in Poland, near Wroclaw (Breslau). Its Jewish community dates from 1688, when Shabbetai *Bass, founder of modern Hebrew bibliography, leased printing privileges from the local magnate who, in turn, held them from the emperor. The first work he printed in Dyhernfurth was *Samuel b. Uri Shraga Phoebus' *Beit Shemu'el*, a commentary on Shulḥan Arukh *Even ha-Ezer* (1689). A community was formed by 13 families, all employed in Bass's printing works. Both Bass and his son Joseph had to contend with the hostility of the Jesuits, but printing continued until 1762, from 1717 under Berel Nathan, husband of Bass's granddaughter Esther, and later under Esther herself. Other printing houses were established by Samuel b. Abraham Katz (until 1767), Abraham Lewin (until 1771), Solomon Koenigsberg (1774–75), M.L. May (until 1819), H. Warschauer & Co., and lastly D. Sklower whose press closed in 1834 when he moved to Breslau. The Dyhernfurth productions, which included a complete Talmud and Maimonides' *Mishneh Torah*, were very popular at the time, but business declined due to outside competition. A Yiddish newspaper, serving the Breslau community, was printed there in 1770. The cemetery of Dyhernfurth was used by Breslau Jews until 1765; a *Memorbuch* was started before 1700. The synagogue, consecrated in 1847, was sold in 1926. The numbers of the community declined from 191 in 1833 to 42 in 1885, and 5 in 1910, and it was dissolved in 1916.

BIBLIOGRAPHY: M. Gruenwald, *Zur Geschichte der juedischen Gemeinde Dyhernfurth* (1881); I. Rabin, *Aus Dyhernfurths juedischer Vergangenheit* (1929); D. Weinbaum, *Geschichte des juedischen Friedhofs in Dyhernfurth* (1903); Landsberger, in: MGWJ, 39 (1895), 120–33, 187–92, 230–38; Brann, *ibid.*, 40 (1896), 474–80, 515–26, 560–74; Brilling, in: ZGJB, 7 (1937), 109–12. **ADD. BIBLIOGRAPHY:** M. Marx, in: C. Berlin (ed.), *Studies in Jewish Bibliography ... in Honor of I.E. Kiev* (1971), 217–36; H.C. Zafren, *ibid.*, 543–80.

DYKMAN, SHLOMO (1917–1965), translator and literary critic. Born and educated in Warsaw, he fled to Bukhara during World War II and taught Hebrew there. In 1944 he was arrested for "counterrevolutionary Zionist activities" and sentenced to 15 years' hard labor in the Vorkuta coal mines in the far north. He was released in 1957 and repatriated to Warsaw. In 1960 he immigrated to Israel. He translated Bialik's collected poems into Polish, and his translations of the Greek and Roman classics into Hebrew include Virgil's *Aeneid* (1962); Lucretius' *On the Nature of the Universe* (1962); Ovid's *Metamorphoses* (1965); Sophocles' *Tragedies* (1963); and Aeschylus' *Tragedies* (1965). He was awarded the Israel Prize posthumously in 1965. Autobiographical notes on his years in Vorkuta appeared in *Ha-Ummah* (1 (1963), 531–46; 2 (1963), 60–67, 230–45, 375–89; 3 (1965), 375–85).

BIBLIOGRAPHY: Elḥanani, in: *Moznayim*, 20 (1964/65), 529–32; Ben-Shamai, *ibid.*, 21 (1965), 415–25.

[Getzel Kressel]

DYLAN, BOB (Robert Allen Zimmerman; 1941–), U.S. folk singer, composer. Probably the most significant folk artist in the last half of the 20th century, Dylan was born in Duluth, Minn., and grew up in the small town of Hibbing. He started writing poems at ten and taught himself piano and guitar in his early teens. He fell under the spell of the music of the country, rock, and folk performers Elvis Presley, Jerry Lee Lewis, Hank Williams, and Woody Guthrie. Dylan dropped out of the University of Minnesota and went to New York to be part of the burgeoning folk-music scene, and to meet Guthrie, who was hospitalized with a rare, incurable disease of the nervous system.

Dylan spent all his time with other musicians and began writing songs, including a tribute, "Song to Woody." He began to perform at local nightclubs, honing his guitar and harmonica work and developing the expressive nasal sound that would become the hallmark of his distinctive style. Around this time he adopted the stage name Bob Dylan, presumably in honor of the Welsh poet Dylan Thomas. In 1961, a reviewer for the *New York Times* said he was "bursting at the seams with talent." Columbia Records soon signed him to a contract, and in 1962 his first recording, *See That My Grave Is Kept Clean*, offered the sound of an aging black blues man in the voice of a 21-year-old from Minnesota. His next album, *The Freewheelin' Bob Dylan*, in 1963, contained two of the most important and durable folk anthems, "Blowin' in the Wind" and "A Hard Rain's A-Gonna Fall," and two influential ballads, "Girl From the North Country" and "Don't Think Twice, It's All Right" as well as nine other originals, marking the emergence of the most distinctive and poetic voice in the history of American popular music.

Dylan's next album, *The Times They Are A-Changing*, provided more of the same: the title cut, the protest song "The Lonesome Death of Hattie Carroll," and "Boots of Spanish Leather," a sad but graceful love song. In 1965, as he grew tired of the folk genre, Dylan recorded *Bringing It All Back Home*, a half-electric, half-acoustic album of complex biting songs like "Subterranean Homesick Blues," which featured the line "You don't need a weatherman to know which way the wind blows." (It was a line that inspired the name, the Weathermen, an American antiwar protest group.) Also on the album were "Mr. Tambourine Man" and "It's All Over Now, Baby Blue." When Dylan introduced his move from folk to rock at the 1965 Newport Folk Festival, he was booed off the stage. Nevertheless, he released the album *Highway 61 Revisited*, which contained the monumental single "Like a Rolling Stone," an angry six-minute-long song that found a huge audience.

Dylan had brought a new, literate standard to rock music writing. In *Blonde on Blonde*, a two-record set recorded in Nashville, Tenn., in 1966, he offered the now-classic "Stuck Inside of Mobile With the Memphis Blues Again," "Visions of Johanna," and "Sad Eyed Lady of the Lowlands."

After a near-fatal motorcycle accident on July 29, 1966, Dylan retreated to his home in Woodstock, N.Y., to reevaluate his career. He produced more recordings: *The Basement Tapes*, *John Wesley Harding*, *Nashville Skyline* (which included "Lay Lady Lay"). Over the years he dabbled, unsuccessfully, as a film actor and toured extensively with various groups. In the mid-1970s, one rock promoter said there were mail-order requests for more than 12 million tickets, though only 658,000 seats were available for 40 shows in one period. Dylan's pain after his marriage ended resulted in the album *Blood on the Tracks*, a moving and profound examination of love and loss that included the songs "Tangled Up in Blue," "Idiot Wind," and "Shelter from the Storm." His religious explorations led him to profess to be a born-again Christian in 1978, but in

1983 he reportedly returned to his Jewish roots and was said to have observed the Jewish holidays.

Widely regarded as America's greatest living popular songwriter, Dylan was inducted into the Rock and Roll Hall of Fame in 1988. In 1990 he received France's highest cultural award, the Commandeur dans l'Ordre des Arts et des Lettres. In 2001 he won an Academy Award and a Golden Globe for Best Original Song, "Things Have Changed," for the film *Wonder Boys*.

The 1967 documentary *Don't Look Back* chronicles Dylan's 1965 tour of England, which includes appearances by Joan Baez and Donovan. Martin Scorsese's 1978 film *The Last Waltz* is a documentary about Dylan and The Band performing their last concert after 16 years on the road. Among Dylan's publications are *Bob Dylan in His Own Words* (with C. Williams, 1993); *Tarantula,* a book of poetry (1994); *Younger Than That Now: The Collected Interviews with Bob Dylan* (with J. Ellison, 2004); and his autobiography, *Chronicles, Vol. 1* (2004).

Beginning in the mid-1980s Dylan hit the road full-time, performing all over the world. His albums were not as successful as those of his early years, but he continued to perform and sing in his nasal twang through the early years of the 21st century. He rarely granted interviews, refused to explain the meaning of his songs, and remained a significant but enigmatic figure. He had millions of fans – he played in Rome at the behest of Pope John Paul II – and inspired hundreds of articles, books, and websites. In December 2004 he was one of five recipients of one of the highest awards for artistic excellence, the Kennedy Center honors.

[Stewart Kampel (2nd ed.)]

DYMOV, OSSIP (pen name of **Joseph Perelman**; 1878–1959), Russian and Yiddish author and playwright. Dymov was born in Bialystok, attended a Russian gymnasium and the Forest Institute in St. Petersburg, and at 16 began publishing humoresques in Russian satiric journals. The first collection of his stories, *Solntsevorot* ("The Sun Cycle," 1905), artistically blending symbolism, irony, and wit, placed him in the mainstream of Russian literature. The motif of Jewish suffering became predominant in his plays *Slushay, Izrail!* ("Hear, Israel!" 1907; Heb., 1913) and *Vechny strannik* ("Eternal Wanderer," 1913), which were staged in Russian, Hebrew, Yiddish, and other languages in Europe and in the U.S., bringing Dymov substantial fame. He settled in New York in 1913 and over decades contributed hundreds of stories and humoresques to the Yiddish press and wrote dramas and comedies for the Yiddish theater. He also reworked classical texts for Yiddish screenplays, published two volumes of memoirs, and worked in Yiddish radio. His most popular play, *Yoshke Muzikant* ("Yoskhe the Musician") is included in the volume *Dramen un Dertseylungen* ("Dramas and Stories," 1943).

BIBLIOGRAPHY: LNYL, 2 (1958), 502–4. **ADD. BIBLIOGRAPHY:** Z. Zylbercweig, *Leksikon fun Yidishn Teater,* 1 (1931), 557–62; *The Encyclopedia of Russian Jewry,* 1 (1994), 448–9.

DYMSHYTS, VENIAMIN E. (1910–1993), Soviet economist and engineer who became a deputy premier of the Soviet Union in 1959. He was a grandson of the Hebrew writer A.A. Rakowski. Born in Theodosia (Crimea) he qualified as an engineer at the Moscow Technical Institute and began working as a construction engineer in 1931. By 1950 he was deputy minister of construction enterprises in the metallurgical and chemical industries. Later he went to India as chief engineer of the Bhilai steel plant which was erected with Soviet aid. Dymshyts became chairman of the State Planning Committee in 1959 and simultaneously was appointed deputy premier, the only Jew in the upper echelon of the regime. He was promoted to head of the National Economic Council in 1962, with responsibility for dealing with the daily problems of overall economic management. Later he assumed the leadership of the new state committee to centralize the distribution of industrial products. Dymshyts was a member of the Communist Party Central Committee for 1961 and a deputy to the Supreme Soviet. He was awarded the Stalin Prize twice (1946, 1950). On March 4, 1970 he was the main representative of Soviet Jewry in a press conference about the situation and strongly criticized the State of Israel.

[Shmuel Spector (2nd ed.)]

DYNOW, ẒEVI ELIMELECH (1785–1841), ḥasidic *ẓaddik* in Dynow, Galicia, often known after his main work as "the author of *Benei Yissakhar*" (Zolkiew, 1850). He was a disciple of Ẓevi Hirsch of *Zhidachov, *Jacob Isaac "ha-Ḥozeh" ("the seer") of Lublin, and the *Maggid* Israel of *Kozienice. Ẓevi Elimelech served as rabbi in Strzyzow, Halicz, Dynow, and Munkacs. His total opposition to Haskalah and philosophy was evidenced in both his devotion to Kabbalah as the essence of Judaism and his statement that "there is no knowledge, either in the realm of science or philosophy, which is not alluded to in the Torah [which is higher than the intellect]" (*Benei Yissakhar,* Sec. 2:88). He considered philosophical enquiry a waste of time and of soul. Rational reason should not be sought for the *mitzvot*, but they should be observed with love, as divine decrees, whether rational or not, without questioning or seeking proofs. Man must have faith "even in two opposite [commands of God] where the intellect cannot solve the contradiction" (*ibid.*, Sec. 1, 73). The task of the *ẓaddik* is of utmost importance since by means of the high spiritual level he attains he may help to unite the upper and lower worlds. Ẓevi Elimelech differentiated between two types of *ẓaddikim:* the perfect one, "the servant of God" (*eved adonai*) and the one who only "worships God" (*oved Adonai*). Worship of God must combine both love and fear. Fear corresponds to *ẓimẓum* and love corresponds to *hitpashetut* ("expansion"). Just as there can be no stability or survival for worlds without *ẓimẓum*, so if it were not for fear, man would dissolve in ecstasy "and the light of the soul would depart from its earthly container." Fear of Divine Majesty – in contradistinction to fear of punishment – is the acme of faith. A man "to whom God gives knowledge (*binah*) is enabled to retreat within himself directing his thought to his Creator also while in the company of other men." Dynow thus reformulates *Naḥmanides' thesis (commentary on Deuteronomy 11:20).

Dynow's writings comprise (1) kabbalistic: glosses to the commentary of *Eleazar of Worms on Sefer *Yeẓirah (Przemysl, 1888); commentary on the beginning of Eleazar's *Sefer Ḥokhmat ha-Nefesh* (Lemberg, 1876); glosses to the *Zohar* (Przemysl, 1899); *Ma'yan Gannim*, a commentary on *Or ha-Ḥayyim* (1848) by Joseph Jabetz; *Regel Yesharah* (Lemberg, date of publication not known), an alphabetical commentary on names and concepts on the basis of the kabbalistic system of Isaac *Luria. (2) Homiletic and exegetical works which became popular among Ḥasidim, among them *Derekh Pikkudekha* (Lemberg, 1851), homilies on the mitzvot; *Igra de-Kallah* (Lemberg, 1868), homilies on the Torah; *Igra de-Pirka* (Lemberg, 1858); *Likkutei Maharẓa* (Przemysl, 1885), on the Torah and the Prophets; *Keli ha-Ro'im* (Lemberg, 1808), commentary on Obadiah; *Devarim Neḥmadim* (Przemysl, 1885); *Maggid Ta'alumah* (Przemysl, 1876), novellae to tractate *Berakhot; Rei'aḥ Duda'im* (Munkacs, 1879), on tractate *Megillah; Ve-Heyeh Berakhah* (Przemysl, 1875), commentary on Mishnah Berakhot; *Berakhah Meshulleshet* (Przemysl, 1896, commentary on the Mishnah); *Tamkhin de-Oraita* (Munkacs, 1926).

BIBLIOGRAPHY: Horodezky, Ḥasidut, 2 (1953^4), 201–18; idem, in: *Meẓudah* (1948), 284–9; Berger, *Eser Ẓaḥẓaḥot* (1909), 106–118; M. Bodek, *Seder ha-Dorot* (1927), 67; L. Grossmann, *Shem u-She'erit* (1943), 21–23; R. Mahler, *Ha-Ḥasidut ve-ha-Haskalah* (1961), index; N.Z. Horowitz, *Ohel Naftali* (1964), 98–99.

DZIALOSZYCE, town in S. central Poland; passed into Austria in 1795 after the third partition of Poland, and to Russia after 1915; from 1919 in Poland. From 1765 it had a considerable Jewish majority. The community numbered 651 in 1765; 2,514 (83% of the total population) in 1856; 3,526 (76.5%) in 1897; 5,618 (83.3%) in 1921; and about 7,000 (80%) in 1939. Tanning, brickmaking, and tailoring were the principal occupations of the community. After World War I Jews in Dzialoszyce owned about 78 clothing stores, six tanneries, and brick kilns. In 1930 the artisans established an authorized union to protect their status and assist their members in obtaining recognized technical diplomas. Although efforts were made to reconstruct life in 1937, it had not returned to normal before the German occupation in World War II.

[Shimshon Leib Kirshenboim]

Holocaust Period

The German army entered on September 7–8, 1939, and the anti-Jewish terror began. In 1941 about 5,000 Jews from *Cracow, *Warsaw, *Lodz, *Poznan, and Lask were deported to Dzialoszyce, swelling the population to 12,000. In June 1941 Jews were forbidden to leave the town, but no closed ghetto was established. On September 2, 1942, the Germans carried out the first *Aktion* against the Jews. At least several hundred succeeded in fleeing to the surrounding forests and 800 were selected for the labor camps, but up to 2,000 unfit to travel were murdered in the local cemetery and about 15,000 were sent to Michow en route to Belzec. Several hundred Jews were allowed to remain in Dzialoszyce.

RESISTANCE. Those Jews from Dzialoszyce who fled into the woods joined other Jewish runaways from Pinczow and other places in the vicinity. A number of Jewish partisan groups were formed to resist actively the German police search units and Polish antisemitic gangs. The biggest partisan units were those organized by Zalman Fajnsztat and Michael Majtek. They united to form the guerrilla unit "Zygmunt," which was recognized by the Polish People's Guard. This unit fought the Nazis and provided armed cover for hundreds of Jews hiding in the forest until February 1944, when it suffered great losses in a battle near the village of Pawlowice. The surviving Jewish partisans joined different Polish guerrilla units, but only a few of them were still alive by the time of the liberation of Dzialoszyce region from the Germans (January 1945). The Jewish community in Dzialoszyce was not reconstituted after the war. The town retains a 19th-century synagogue built in the classic style.

[Stefan Krakowski]

BIBLIOGRAPHY: Yad Vashem Archives; *Sefer Yizkor shel kehilath Dzialoszyc ve-ha-Seviva* (1977).

DZIGAN, SHIMON (1905–1980), Yiddish satirical actor. Dzigan began his career in Lodz, Poland, where he was born. He became popular in comic dialogues with Israel Schumacher, who played the sedate know-all to Dzigan's quick-witted ignoramus. When World War II broke out, they escaped to Russia and gave performances for the Polish Jewish refugees. After the war, Dzigan and Schumacher performed in Western Europe and North and South America, before settling in Israel in 1952. When the two parted as a result of personal differences, Dzigan staged his own revues.

Initial letter "E" of the word Ecclesia, *from the* Sacramentary of Gellone, *E. France, eighth century. The illumination shows the afflicted Job sitting down among the ashes, and his wife urging him to "curse God and die" (Job.2:8–9), Paris, Bibliothèque Nationale, Ms. Lat. 12048 fol. 143.*

Ea–Ez

EAGLE, bird of prey of the genus *Aquila*, in particular the *Aquila chrysaetos*, the largest of the birds of prey. The eagle has been identified by the translators of the Bible with the biblical *nesher*, rendered by the Septuagint as *aetos* and by the Vulgate as *aquila*. Biblical passages, however, ascribe to the *nesher* characteristics that do not belong to the eagle, such as its feeding on carcasses (in the manner of Ugaritic *nšr*.; the biblical dictionaries notwithstanding, there is no native Akkadian *našru* for comparison) and having a bald head, and already R. Tam pointed out the mistake of regarding it as the eagle (Tos. to Hul. 63a). The biblical *nesher* is the griffon vulture (see *vulture), although its traditional identification as an eagle was accepted by the sages of the Talmud who applied the word to the Roman eagle. Ezekiel also apparently understood it in this sense when he compared the king of Babylonia to the *nesher*, which has "great wings and long pinions, full of feathers" (Ezek. 17:2–3). This is not the usual biblical *nesher*, the griffon vulture, which has no feathers on its neck.

The biblical name for eagle is apparently *ayit* (cf. Gr. *aetos*), described by Jeremiah (12:8–9) as carnivorous like the lion and as *ẓavo'a*, the latter in reference, it seems, to its middle talon (*eẓba*) which is especially long for clutching its prey. The powerful king, the conqueror of Babylonia, is compared to an *ayit* (Isa. 46:11); the bird's keen sight is referred to by Job (28:7). It is also mentioned several times in the Bible as a general term for carnivorous birds of prey (Ezek. 39:4; Isa. 18:6; and apparently also Gen. 15:11). In Israel there are six species of eagle of the genus *Aquila*, but they are rare. The largest of the eagles, the *Aquila chrysaetos*, is seldom seen in Israel.

BIBLIOGRAPHY: J. Feliks, *Animal World of the Bible* (1962), 66; M. Dor, *Leksikon Zo'ologi* (1965), 246f. **ADD. BIBLIOGRAPHY:** CAD N/II, 79.

[Jehuda Feliks]

EARTH.

In Biblical Literature

The earth is portrayed in the Bible as a flat strip (Isa. 42:5; 44:24) suspended across the cosmic ocean (Ps. 24:2; 136:6). It is supported on pillars (Ps. 75:4; Job 9:6) or props (Isa. 24:18; Prov. 8:29) and is evidently surrounded by a mountain range like the *qār* of Arabic folklore, to keep it from being flooded (Prov. 8:29; Job 26:10). The ultimate bounds of the earth known to the ancient Hebrews were India and Nubia (Esth. 1:1; cf. Zeph. 3:10). A similar conception of the earth was held by Herodotus (3:114) and is found in the Persian inscriptions of Darius. Sometimes, too, its furthermost inhabitants were thought to be the peoples who resided in remote lands north of Palestine – *Gog and Magog – a concept which finds a parallel among the Greeks. It was believed that the fertility of the earth could be affected by the misconduct of men. It was then said to be "polluted" (Heb. *ḥanefah*; Isa. 24:5). As a result of Adam's sin, the earth yields grain only when man puts heavy labor into it (Gen. 3:17–19), and for receiving the blood of Abel it was forbidden to "yield its strength" to Cain under any circumstances (Gen. 4:11–13). The idea that the land could be rendered infertile by having innocent blood shed upon it is widespread in other cultures, and probably stems from the notion that "the blood is the life" and, therefore, represents the outraged spirit of the murdered man who exacts vengeance until the crime is redressed or expiated. Bloodshed could likewise cause lack of rainfall (II Sam. 1:21). Since it is usually a particular land, especially the Land of Israel, that is affected by misdeeds committed in it, such misconduct includes not only moral turpitude but also disobedience to divine commandments. For example, a famine ensued for several years as a result of David's taking a census, against the orders of God. According to Exodus 23:10–12, the land of Israel had to lie fallow every seventh year; according to Leviticus 25, every 50th year as well. This may be explained as a survival of the ancient belief that life is vouchsafed in seven-year cycles. Deuteronomy, which speaks of the seventh year only as one of debt remission (Deut. 15) and enjoins a public reading of the Torah to the pilgrims assembled in Jerusalem on the festival of Tabernacles of that year (Deut. 31:10–13), is believed to represent a late development. Among the gentiles particular lands were regarded as the estates, or inheritances, of their tutelary gods; in the Bible YHWH is the Lord of what would later be known as the universe, yet the land of Israel is the object of His special care (Deut. 11:12; 32:8–9; II Sam. 20:19; Jer. 2:7; Ps. 79:1). In the apocryphal book of Ben Sira (17:17), the Lord parcels out the earth among "rulers," i.e., celestial princes, as an emperor might apportion his dominion among satraps. Conversely, waste places were deemed the natural habitat of demons (Isa. 34:13–14), and the winds which sweep the wilderness were depicted as howling monsters, just as in Arabic folklore the desert is called "howl-place" (*yabāb*; cf. Deut. 32:10). Earth, like sky, was sometimes called to serve as a witness in prophetic denunciations of the people (Deut. 4:26; 30:19; 31:28). This reflects a common ancient Near Eastern practice of invoking the earth and sky, along with the national and local gods, to witness covenants and treaties. There is no clear evidence in the Bible of any worship of the earth, even by apostate Israelites. However, a goddess named Arṣay, i.e., Ms. Earth, is mentioned in the Canaanite texts from Ras Shamra (Ugarit) as one of the brides of Baal, and the Phoenician mythographer Sanchuniathon (second quarter of the sixth cent. B.C.E.) speaks of a primordial woman, called Omorka, who was cut asunder by Belus (Baal) to make earth and heaven respectively. In the six-day scheme of creation described in the first chapter of Genesis, earth is said to have emerged on the third day (Gen. 1:9–11). It was originally watered not by rain but by a subterranean upsurge (Heb. *ed*; Gen. 2:5–6). It is not impossible that this picture was inspired by conditions that actually obtain in parts of Palestine where, before the onset of the early rains and the beginning of the agricultural cycle in autumn, the soil is moistened only by springs which burst forth at the foot of the hills. It is possible – though this must be received with caution-that the Hebrews shared with the Babylonians the notion that the geography of the earth had its counterpart aloft and that the portions of the heavens corresponded to terrestrial domains, for it is in terms of such a view that it may perhaps be possible to interpret the words of Balaam (Num. 24:17) about the star which is stepping out of Jacob (i.e., the region of the sky answering to the Land of Israel) and which is destined to smite the borders of Moab. It was held that at the end of the present era of the world, when a new dispensation was to be ushered in, the soil of the Land of Israel would undergo a miraculous renewal of fertility. A stream, like that which flowed through Eden, would issue forth (Zech. 14:8), and there would be a prodigious increase in vegetation and livestock.

Post-Biblical Literature

Ideas about the earth are elaborated in post-biblical literature. The earth is represented as resting on a primal foundation stone, which also forms the bedrock of the Temple. The navel, or center, of the earth is located at Zion, just as among the Samaritans it is located at the sacred Mt. Gerizim, and among the Greeks, at Delphi. Earth, like heaven, consists of seven layers superimposed upon one another. Its extent is reckoned in one passage of the Talmud (Ta'an. 10a) as equivalent to (roughly) 190 million square miles, and it is 1,000 cubits thick. In IV Ezra 6:42 it is said that six parts of it are habitable, and the seventh is covered by water. According to post-biblical sources, the earth is sheltered from the blasts of the south wind by the gigantic bird ziz, and, as in the Bible, it will become miraculously fertile in the messianic age (Ginzberg, Legends, s.v.). Earth's pristine fertility, it is said, was diminished through the sin of Adam, and its smooth surface was made rugged by mountains as a punishment for its having received the blood of Abel. When the new age dawns, it will again become level. Just as in the Greek myth the earth opened to rescue Amphiaraus, so in Jewish legend it hid the tender babes of Israel hunted by Pharaoh. It likewise swallowed up the vessels of the Temple, to conceal them when that edifice was destroyed. On the other hand, it engulfed the four generations of the offspring of Cain as an act of punishment; it also swallowed up the army massed against Jacob, the unfinished part of the Tower of Babel, and the city of Nineveh. However, it refused to receive the body of Jephthah who, as the result of a rash vow, had sacrificed his own daughter (*ibid.*, s.v.).

BIBLIOGRAPHY: A.J. Wensinck, *Ideas of the Western Semites Concerning Navel of the Earth* (1916); R. Patai, *Adam ve-Adamah* (1943); T.H. Gaster, *Myth, Legend and Custom in the Old Testament* (1969), 5, 6, 98(d), 103(c), 144, 188, 294.

[Theodor H. Gaster]

EARTHQUAKE, ground vibrations produced generally by a sudden subterranean occurrence. Accounts of destructive earthquakes extend far into antiquity. In biblical times earthquakes, like thunder and other natural cataclysms, were regarded as demonstrations of God's unlimited power. It was believed that the phenomenon preceded divine manifestations (I Kings 19:11–12; Isa. 6:4; Ezek. 3:12–13), the revelation at Sinai (Ex. 19:18), divine wrath (Ps. 18:8; 104:8), and collective punishment (I Sam. 14:15; Isa. 5:25; Nah. 1:5; 16:32; Amos 9:1), and it was also envisaged as heralding the end of the world (Ezek. 38:19–20). The descriptions of earthquakes in the Bible – especially by prophets – indicate that such cataclysms occurred from time to time and that people were therefore familiar with their consequences. The almost scientific description of the phenomenon of earth dislocation and cracking related in a prophecy of wrath (Zech. 14:4–5) might be based on a personal experience of an earthquake. Because of its powerful impact, the major earthquake which occurred toward the end of King Uzziah's reign (about 800 B.C.E.) was referred to for some time in date references (Amos 1:1; Zech. 14:5). In 31 B.C.E. a disastrous tremor in Judea claimed 10,000 to 30,000 victims (Jos., Ant., 15:122). In 749 a powerful earthquake, thought to be 7.3 on the Richter scale, hit northern Israel, destroying *Bet(h)-Shean, *Tiberias, Kefar Naḥum (*Capernaum), and *Susita. The earthquake caused a huge tidal wave that led to the death of thousands. Another series of earthquakes occurred in 1033, striking Tiberias and its environs. During the last 2,000 years, earthquakes in Palestine and its neighborhood have been recorded in greater detail (see bibl. Amiran, 1951; Shalem, 1951; Arieh, 1967). These records reveal that, on the average, several damaging earthquakes have occurred in each century, but usually only one reached disastrous proportions. Seismological observatories have been operated by the Geological Survey of Israel since 1955 and by the Weizmann Institute of Science since 1969. Recent seismographic measurements indicate that most earthquake epicenters are situated in or near the Jordan Rift Valley, an area where the two most destructive earthquakes since the 19th century originated. The earthquake on Jan. 1, 1837, whose epicenter was near Safed, took about 5,000 victims, ruined much of the old city, and was strongly felt from Beirut to Jerusalem. This earthquake was preceded by one in 1759 in which the walls of *Safed were ruined and many were killed. On July 11, 1927, an earthquake occurred north of *Jericho violently affecting vast areas from Lebanon to the Negev, and in Transjordan killing about 350 persons and ruining some 800 structures (mainly in Shechem). This earthquake stopped the flow of the Jordan River for a few years owing to rock collapse. The last significant earthquake in Israel was in 1995 in Eilat (*Elath), when the epicenter was in the Red Sea, therefore causing minor damages. In 2004 a series of tremors struck Israel, mainly in the Dead Sea area. Experts argue that such earthquakes are a warning sign of a bigger one yet to come in the next few years. The extent of damage caused by an earthquake depends not only on magnitude, focal depth, and proximity to the epicenter, but also, and sometimes mainly, on local ground features, topographic conditions, type of foundation and construction, and density of population. In areas with long-standing earthquake records, seismic risk can better be evaluated than in areas without such records. Cities which have suffered relatively much from earthquakes are Safed, Tiberias, Shechem (all near the epicenter zone, and partly built on slopes and unconsolidated ground with poorly built structures), Lydda, and Ramleh (unstable ground conditions). Jerusalem, with its rocky fundament, has remained during its long history relatively undamaged by earthquakes, as if to justify the psalmist's verse: "Those who trust in the Lord are like Mount Zion, which cannot be moved, but abides for ever" (Ps. 125:1).

BIBLIOGRAPHY: C.F. Richter, *Elementary Seismology* (1958); N. Shalem, in: *Jerusalem Quarterly*, 2 (1949), 22–54 (Heb.); idem, in: *Bulletin of the Research Council of Israel*, 2:1 (1952), 5–16; D.H.K. Amiran, in: IEJ, 1 (1950–51), 223–46; 2 (1952), 48–62; E.J. Arieh, in: *Geological Survey of Israel*, 43 (1967), 1–14.

[Eliyahu Arieh]

EAST LONDON, port in Eastern Cape province, South Africa. East London was founded in 1836 as a landing stage and proclaimed a town in 1847. W. Barnett acquired a grant of land in 1849, but the first known permanent Jewish resident was Gustave Wetzlar, who arrived in Cape Town in 1861 from Germany and settled as a merchant in East London in 1873. A town councilor in 1881, he became mayor in 1889. John Lewis Norton, a descendant of the British settlers of 1820, became chief constable and messenger of the court. The growth of the Jewish population resulting from immigration and an influx during the Boer War of 1899–1902 led to the establishment of a Hebrew congregation in 1901. Julius Myers and G.G. Deal, both immigrants from England, took the initiative and continued to be active in communal life. Emmanuel Lipkin, later of Oudtshoorn, arrived from England in 1903 as minister and a small synagogue was opened. A larger synagogue was built 20 years later. A small Reform congregation was established in 1958. In the heyday of the community, which at its height in the mid-1960s numbered some 1,200 people, there was an active Jewish communal life, with Hebrew schools, Zionist and other organizations, regional branches of national bodies, and a country club. By 2004, however, it had dwindled to fewer than 150, mainly elderly individuals, though the main communal organizations continued to function. Jews have been prominent in civic affairs, the mayors including (besides Wetzlar) David Lazarus, 1947–48 and 1966–68, Abraham Addleson, 1957–59, and Leo Laden, 1962–64.

BIBLIOGRAPHY: G. Saron and L. Hotz, *Jews in South Africa* (1955), 311–13.

[Abraham Addleson / David Saks (2nd ed.)]

EATON, JOSEPH W. (1919–), U.S. sociologist and educator. Born in Nuremberg, Germany, Eaton went to the United States in 1934. After graduating in 1948, he directed the study of the Hutterites, an isolated Mennonite sect of northwestern U.S. and Canada who lived in communities and held property in common. The results were published in 1955 in *Culture and Mental Disorders* (J. Eaton and R.J. Weil). Eaton published an analysis of prison reform and treatment programs in California (*Stone Walls Not a Prison Make*, 1962). In 1961 he published *Measuring Delinquency* and in 1964 *Prisons in Israel.* He directed a long-range study of Israel's youth organization and national service program financed by the U.S. Office of Education (*Influencing the Youth Culture: A Study of Youth Organizations in Israel*, 1969). His academic interests were in evaluative research, applications of social theory, and the sociology of social work. He also wrote *Card-Carrying Americans: Privacy, Security, and the National ID Card Debate* (1986) and *The Privacy Card: A Low Cost Strategy to Combat Terrorism* (2004).

Eaton became professor emeritus at the Graduate School of Public and International Affairs at the University of Pittsburgh, in the field of economic and social development and sociology. He remained actively involved in studying the Hutterites and was a consultant for a University of Pittsburgh research project on the causes of schizophrenia.

[Zvi Hermon / Ruth Beloff (2nd ed.)]

EBAN, ABBA (Aubrey) SOLOMON (1915–2002), Israeli statesman, diplomat, and writer, member of the Fourth to Eleventh Knessets. Born in Cape Town, South Africa, Eban was brought up in England. He studied Oriental languages and classics in Queens College at Cambridge University, where he was research fellow and lecturer in Arabic in 1938–40. Eban was noted for his mastery of several languages. As an undergraduate, he was a founder of the University Labor Society and became president of the Students' Union.

During World War II Eban held the rank of major, serving on the staff of the British minister of state in Cairo from 1941. In 1942 he served as liaison officer on behalf of the Allied Command with the leadership of the Jewish *yishuv* in Palestine, and in 1944 as chief instructor in the Middle East Center for Arab Studies in Jerusalem, for the purpose of training Jewish volunteers. At the end of the war he took up residence in Jerusalem and in 1946 was appointed by the Jewish Agency political information officer in London, and the following year served as its liaison officer with UNSCOP. After serving as a member of the Jewish Agency delegation to the UN General Assembly, Eban was appointed representative of the newly established State of Israel to the UN, and in the years 1949–59 as Israel's permanent delegate, serving in 1952 as deputy president of the General Assembly. In the UN Eban was known for his eloquence and superb presentation of Israel's case in the face of Arab hostility. In 1950–59 he also served as Israeli ambassador to the United States. In 1958–66 Eban was president of the Weizmann Institute in Rehovot and initiated the International Rehovot Conferences on "Science in the Advancement of New States." In 1959 he was elected to the Fourth Knesset on the *Mapai list. He served as minister of education and culture in the years 1960–63, deputy prime minister in 1963–65, and minister for foreign affairs in 1966–74. As minister for foreign affairs, Eban sought to consolidate Israel's relations with the United States and to secure association status for Israel in the European Economic Community. In May 1967 he paid dramatic visits to Paris, London, and Washington in an effort to avert the outbreak of war. Throughout the Six-Day War in 1967 and the Yom Kippur War in 1973 he led Israel's diplomatic campaigns in the UN. Eban was reappointed minister for foreign affairs in the short-lived government formed by Golda *Meir after the Yom Kippur War and participated in the negotiations with Henry *Kissinger which led to the Disengagement Agreement with Syria on May 31, 1974. However, after Meir's resignation, following the publication of the *Agranat Commission report on the background to the outbreak of the war, he was not included in the government formed by Yitzhak *Rabin. Though continuing to serve in the Knesset, Eban started to teach at Haifa University and at Columbia University in the U.S. as a visiting professor. In September 1974 he was appointed chairman of the Board of Governors of Bet Berl, which was the ideological center of the Labor Party. In the Eleventh Knesset he served as chairman of the Knesset Foreign Affairs and Defense Committee and as chairman of a subcommittee that dealt with the Pollard Affair. In the primaries held in the Central Committee of the Labor Party for a place in the party's list for the Twelfth Knesset, Eban failed to be elected. Eban then withdrew from the political arena and concentrated on the production and presentation of TV programs in the U.S. on Jewish tradition and the history of the State of Israel. His writings include *Voice of Israel* (reprinted speeches, 1957), *The Tide of Nationalism* (1959), *The Final Solution: Reflections on the Tragedy of European Jewry* (1961), *Chaim Weizmann – A Continuing Legacy* (1962), *My People: The Story of the Jews* (1968), *My Country: The Story of Modern Israel* (1972), *An Autobiography* (1977), *Heritage: Civilization and the Jews* (1984), *The New Diplomacy: International Affairs in the Modern Age* (1983), *Personal Witness: Israel Through My Eyes* (1992), and *Diplomacy of the Next Century* (1998).

ADD. BIBLIOGRAPHY: R. St. John, *Eban* (1972); A. Ron (ed.), *Abba Even: Medina'i ve-Diplomat: Sefer le-Zikhro shel Sar ha-Ḥuẓ le-She'avar* (2003).

[Edwin Samuel, Second Viscount Samuel / Susan Hattis Rolef (2nd ed.)]

EBEN-EZER (Heb. אֶבֶן הָעֵזֶר). (1) Site of the Israelite camp facing the Philistine army at *Aphek before the battle in which the Philistines captured the Ark of the Covenant (I Sam. 4:1). It is generally identified with Majdal Yābā, which was still known in the first century C.E. as Migdal Aphek. (2) Name of the stone set up as a victory monument by Samuel between *Mizpah and Shen after the Israelites had "pursued the Philistines and smote them, until they came under Beth-Car" (I Sam. 7:11–12). Most scholars consider the two Eben-Ezers identical and locate it on the Israelite-Philistine border.

BIBLIOGRAPHY: Albright, in: BASOR, 11 (1923), 7; Abel, Geog, 2 (1938), 309; EM, S.V.

[Michael Avi-Yonah]

EBER (Heb. עבר, **Ever**). (1) Great-grandson of *Shem, son of Noah and ancestor of Abraham (Gen. 10:21ff.; 11:14ff.; I Chr. 1:17ff.); presumably (but nowhere explicitly) intended as the eponymous ancestor of the *Hebrews (*Ivrīm*). "All the children of Eber" (Gen. 10:21), a phrase which appears – possibly unintentionally – to include Arabian and other tribes as well as Israelite, may or may not be related to the term "Hebrews"; certainly there is no solid evidence that the Bible understood any but Israelites to be Hebrews. The names appearing in the genealogies of Genesis 10 and 11 are, as in other ancient West Semitic genealogies, personifications of tribes, nations, cities, and lands rather than individuals (see *Genealogy; *Nations, The Seventy). In view of this, many scholars consider the name Eber to be derived from Ivri, rather than vice versa, while others suggest that the term refers to the region known as *ever hanahar* ("beyond the river [Euphrates]"; Josh. 24:2; cf. Num. 24:24). Such usage of the name was facilitated by the fact that Eber was probably also the name of a clan or a personal name. (2) The head of a Gadite family (I Chron. 5:13). (3 & 4) The heads of two Benjaminite families (I Chron. 8:12, 22). (5) A post-Exilic priest (Neh. 12:20). (In nos. 2–5 some Hebrew and/or LXX manuscripts read עבד (*ebed*).)

BIBLIOGRAPHY: A. Malamat, in: JAOS, 88 (1968), 165–8.

[Jeffrey Howard Tigay]

EBLA, archaeological site in northern Syria, present-day Tell Mardikh, located 35 mi. (60 km.) south of Aleppo and excavated by an Italian team of archaeologists starting in 1964. In the 1970s thousands of cuneiform texts dated to the second half of the 3rd millennium B.C.E. (in archaeological terms, EB IV, or Early Bronze Age IV) were discovered at the site. The language reflected in these texts was neither Sumerian nor Akkadian, two well-known languages of the period written in cuneiform, but rather was determined to be a previously unattested language, called "Eblaite" by scholars.

Scholars continue to debate the specific date of these texts. The main issue is whether they are pre-Sargonic (i.e., from a time before the reign of Sargon of Akkad (2270–2215 B.C.E. according to one standard opinion)), or whether they are contemporary with the Sargonic period. The discovery of an object bearing the cartouche of the Egyptian pharaoh Pepi I is an important find – attesting to trade relations between Ebla and Egypt, though perhaps only indirectly, through the intermediation of Byblos (see below) – but unfortunately the date of Pepi I (and all the 6th Dynasty monarchs) is not fixed (2333–2283 B.C.E. is one approximation), and thus this artifact cannot help answer the chronological question definitively. The issue of whether the heyday of Ebla is pre-Sargonic or Sargonic hinges in the main on who or what caused the destruction of Ebla (well attested in the archaeological record) during this period. Was the city destroyed by Sargon, by his grandson Naram-Sin, or by accidental fire that simply could not be controlled? Without attempting a definitive answer to these questions, for our present purposes we will side with those scholars who view the Ebla texts as pre-Sargonic. Accordingly, we proceed with the statement that Eblaite is the earliest attested Semitic language, antedating the oldest Akkadian material by about a century, though perhaps by only a few decades.

Another scholarly debate concerns the exact identification of the Eblaite language. Some scholars hold that the language reflected in the Ebla texts is nothing more than a dialect or variation of Old Akkadian; according to this opinion it would be incorrect to speak of a separate language called Eblaite. Other scholars, meanwhile, hold that Eblaite is sufficiently distinct from Old Akkadian to merit the identification as a separate Semitic language. Among the latter, though, there is still no consensus: some hold it to represent an independent branch of Semitic to be called North Semitic, while others group Eblaite in the West Semitic branch. To be sure, there are quite a few lexical and grammatical links between Eblaite and the later attested Amorite (early second millennium) and Aramaic (first millennium), thus suggesting a Syrian *Sprachbund* incorporating these three languages. An important piece of evidence is the first person singular independent pronoun *ana ana* 'I', exactly as in Amorite and Aramaic (in contrast to Akkadian *anāku*).

The debate over the language is due in part to the nature of the texts written in Eblaite. The Eblaite texts use a very high percentage of Sumerograms, that is, words written as Sumerian signs though meant to be read as Eblaite words. Often, however, we do not know what Eblaite words lie behind these Sumerograms. For example, in the expression *si-in i-li-lu* A-MU DINGIR-DINGIR-DINGIR, appearing in an incantation text, we can understand the words to mean "to Elil father of the gods." But the only Eblaite words that we learn are the preposition *si-in*, to be normalized as *sin*, "to," and the name of the deity *i-li-lu*, to be normalized as *ilîlu*, "Ilil" or "Elil." The remaining words are A-MU and DINGIR-DINGIR-DINGIR, whose meanings are clear as "father" and "gods," respectively. But these are the Sumerian forms. When the Eblaite scribe read this text aloud, he would have pronounced these words as their Eblaite equivalents. And while we can be almost certain that the former was based on the root *ab* and that the latter was based on the root *il* (as in all the Semitic languages), we lack the precise information in this case. When one multiplies this example several hundredfold, it becomes clear how scholars can differ over the issue of the exact identification of Eblaite.

Most of the Ebla texts were found in several rooms of Palace G from the 24th century B.C.E. (as per the statement above that the tablets are pre-Sargonic). The total number of texts is about 2,000 complete or nearly complete tablets and about 10,000 fragments. The discovery of this archive in 1974 came as a complete surprise to scholars. No one had imagined that a city in northern Syria might be home to such a literate culture. Even for the heartland of Mesopotamia at this time, the discovery of such a large archive would have been astonishing. Moreover, the previous scholarly consensus held that the Tigris and Euphrates valley at one end of the Near East and the Nile valley at the other end were the two great centers of culture, already in the third millennium B.C.E., but that the vast area in between, including Syria, was a cultural backwater, populated mainly by pastoralists with their flocks, with no great urban centers of the type found in Egypt or Mesopotamia. The excavations at Ebla and the discovery of this large archive changed everyone's conception.

The corpus of Ebla texts includes a wide variety of documents. The greatest number by far are administrative texts, recording in great detail the activities of the palace, the economy of Ebla centered mainly on textile production and the growing of barley and other grains, the far-reaching trade with cities throughout Syria and Mesopotamia, and so on. The second group consists of texts of a historical nature; these include some important treaty texts. The best preserved of the treaty texts is a highly detailed pact with Abarsil on the upper Euphrates; it includes about two dozen articles regulating commerce, taxation, emissaries, and the like. The third group is made up of lexical texts, the most important of which are the bilingual dictionaries providing us with the Sumerian and Eblaite equivalents of hundreds of words. While these dictionaries do not give us the words in literary contexts, they provide us with very valuable information about the Eblaite vocabulary (see further below). Finally, there is a series of incantation texts (a line from one was quoted above). (There have been some reports about literary texts found at Ebla; but at present only one such text has been published, and that composition is a duplicate of a document known from Abu Salabikh in southern Mesopotamia.)

The administrative and historical texts reveal that Ebla had contacts with hundreds of cities throughout the region. Many if not most of these cannot be identified with any confidence, but the toponyms that can be identified give us an indication of Ebla's power and influence. Here we may mention important urban centers such as Gublu (= Byblos) on the Mediterranean (though not all scholars agree with this reading); Emar and *Mari, both on the middle Euphrates; and Kish, situated between the Tigris and Euphrates near Babylon; as well as KURKi *la-ba-na-an*, "the mountain-country of Lebanon." (When the Ebla tablets first were discovered, there were reports that the five cities of the plain listed in Genesis 14 appear at Ebla as well; but there is no substance to this claim.)

The quantity of materials appearing in the administrative texts is sometimes staggering. One text (ARET 2:20) gives a total of 548,500 barley measures distributed (and of this amount 360,400 appears in one line and 182,600 appears in a second line). Eblaite, in fact, attests for the first time in any Semitic language a word for 100,000, namely *ma-i-at* (obviously based on the pan-Semitic word for "hundred"; cf. Hebrew מאה).

The deities attested at Ebla are better known from later West Semitic sources than from East Semitic sources. Important gods are Dagan, Hadd/Baal, Rashap, Ashtar, Kamish, Malik, and Qura, as well as the sun and moon deities, though their Eblaite names are unknown since the Sumerograms UD ("sun") and ITI ("moon") respectively, are used consistently. (There is absolutely no validity to the claim (reported in the early days of Ebla studies) that Ya (a shortened form of Yahweh) appears in personal names.)

Of particular interest is the god Kamish: the name appears in the city name Kar-Kamish (Carchemish) in northern Syria; it is attested in the pantheon of *Ugarit on the Syrian coast from the Late Bronze Age, spelled alphabetically as *kmt* and syllabically as *ka-ma-ši* (= /kamāt/); and most prominently it appears much later as the national god of the Moabites, spelled כמוש and vocalized *kəmôš* in the Bible. Note, however, that in one passage, Jer 48:7, the name of the Moabite god occurs as כמיש in the Ketiv. While previous scholars typically assumed a confusion between *waw* and *yod* in the scribal transmission of this text, we now must consider another possibility, that the Ketiv in Jer 48:7 preserves an ancient alternative pronunciation, Kamish, harking back to the Early Bronze Age as attested at Ebla.

An important deity hitherto unknown is Qura (typically spelled Kura in Ebla studies), clearly a major god given the number of times the name occurs, including some prominent contexts. Apart from Ebla, we know nothing about this deity. The name resurfaces, however, about 3,000 (!) years later as the first element in the name of the angel Quriel, attested in Aramaic, Syriac, and Greek magical texts of the first millennium C.E. In one passage Quriel occurs as the father of a demoness; this invites comparison with the demotion of *Baal, worshipped throughout the Bronze and Iron Ages as a major deity, but appearing in the New Testament as ruler of the demons in the form Baal-zebul.

Whenever a new Semitic language is uncovered, the natural tendency among Hebraists and Biblicists is to mine the new source for information that can help elucidate problems in the Bible and can supply cognates for Hebrew lexemes. Several examples of this process were noted above. The remainder of this entry will present additional instances of contributions from the study of Eblaite to the study of Hebrew (notwithstanding the temporal and geographical distances between Eblaite in third millennium northern Syria and Hebrew in first millennium southern Canaan).

A number of Hebrew words, which hitherto had no cognates within Semitic (see the standard dictionaries), now gain etyma from the Eblaite lexicon. Examples include the following: *ni-zi-mu* (to be normalized as *nizmu*), "a type of jewelry" ≈ נזם, "nose-ring, earring"; *a-a-tum* (to be normalized as *ayyatum*), "a type of bird" ≈ איה, "a bird of prey"; *bar-su-um* (to be normalized as *parsum*), "a type of bird" ≈ פרס, "a bird of prey." The first of these items appears in an administrative text; the latter two appear in the bilingual lexical lists as the Eblaite equivalents of Sumerian forms classified as birds due to the presence of the MUŠEN determinative.

The common Hebrew word for "cedar" is ארז, but a unique feminine form ארזה occurs in Zephaniah 2:14. This now has a parallel in Eblaite *ar-za-tum*, presented in the bilingual dictionary as the equivalent of Sumerian GIŠ-NUN-SAL (the GIŠ determinative indicates a type of tree).

The above represents but a handful of Hebrew lexemes with parallels in Eblaite. In truth, however, the very large Sumerian-Eblaite dictionary (attested in multiple copies at Ebla) affords the scholar of ancient Hebrew much fodder for lexical exploration. We permit ourselves one further example here. The root גדד, "cut, incise, divide," yields the *hitpael* form התגודד, "make incisions upon oneself" (Deut. 14:1; I Kings 18:28, etc.) and the noun גדוד, "troop" (cf. English "division" in a military sense). Cognates to this word occur in various Aramaic dialects (Biblical, Samaritan, Jewish Babylonian, Syriac). The verb *gadādu*, "separate off," occurs in Akkadian, but only in Neo-Assyrian and Neo-Babylonian, and thus scholars conclude that the word is a borrowing from Aramaic. The bilingual dictionary from Ebla glosses Sumerian TAR-TAR with Eblaite *ga-da-dum*; since Sumerian TAR means "cut," it is clear that Eblaite *ga-da-dum* represents an Early Bronze Age forerunner of later Hebrew and Aramaic גדד.

We move now from the realm of lexicon to the realm of grammar, with one representative illustration. Already prior to the discoveries at Ebla, Francis Andersen opined that ancient Hebrew included a morpheme ומ-, that is, conjunctive *waw* + enclitic *mem*. Andersen's insight was strikingly confirmed by the presence of *ù-ma* in Eblaite, composed of the same two elements. Biblical passages which include this morpheme are Gen. 41:32, Num. 23:10, Judg. 13:19, I Kings 14:14, Ezek. 48:16, 48:22 (twice), Amos 6:10, Nah. 2:13, Ps. 147:3, Ruth 4:5, Neh. 5:11. A study of these passages reveals that Hebrew ומ- has a specific syntactic function: it serves as an emphasizing conjunction to be translated "indeed, even, verily, yea." The recognition of this form impacts most of all on the analysis of Ruth 4:5, where the phrase ומאת רות does not mean "and from Ruth" (note the *etnaḥ* on the previous word), but rather is to be analyzed as the emphasizing conjunction ומ- followed by the direct object indicator את and then the proper name רות, thus yielding a translation for the entire verse as follows: "Boaz said, 'On the day you acquire the field from the hand of Naomi – ; verily, Ruth the Moabitess, the wife of the deceased, I have acquired [reading with the Ketiv] to raise the name of the deceased on his estate.'"

Our last instance of the interconnections between Eblaite and Hebrew returns us to the world of magic. One of the incantation texts is directed against a demon named ḫa-ba-ḫa-bi, normalized as *ḫabḫabi*, who is bound and rendered powerless by the magician. This name is the reduplicated form of the demonic figure *Ḥby* attested in Ugaritic (Mesopotamian cuneiform has no symbol for [ḥ] and here substitutes [ḫ]; where he gains the epithet "lord of the horns and tail," that is, the traditional imagery of a devilish character), and appearing in the Bible in two passages in variant forms (one the basic form, the other with suffixed *-ôn*): חבי in Isa 26:20 and חביון in Hab 3:4. The occurrence of *ḫabḫabi*/*ḥby*/חבי in Early Bronze Ebla, Late Bronze Ugarit, and Iron Age Israel attests to the tenacity of magical praxes throughout the epochs (see also the discussion above concerning Qura and Quriel).

Finally, we may note that Ebla was rebuilt after the major destruction noted above and achieved a second floruit c. 2050–1950 B.C.E., that is, during the Ur III period. We possess very few Eblaite literary remains from this period, however. Most of our evidence comes from other sites, including, for example, references to Ebla in inscriptions of Gudea, famous ruler of Lagash, whose great building projects necessitated his men to travel to the region of Ebla in order to procure quantities of timber and stone.

BIBLIOGRAPHY: A. Archi, (ed.), *Eblaite Personal Names and Semitic Name-giving* (1988); R.D. Biggs, in: ABD 2, 263–70; G. Conti, *Il sillabario della quarta fonte della lista lessicale bilingue eblaita* (= *Miscellanea Eblaitica* 3 = *Quaderni di Semitistica*, 17; 1990); C.H. Gordon and G.A. Rendsburg (eds.), *Eblaitica*, vols. 1–4 (1987–2002); P. Matthiae, *Ebla: An Empire Rediscovered* (1980); P. Matthiae, *Ebla, la città rivelata* (1995); L. Milano, in: CANE, 2:1219–30; G. Pettinato, *Ebla: A New Look at History* (1991); idem, *Ebla, nuovi orizzonti della storia* (1994); idem, *Testi lessicali bilingui della bibliotheca L. 2769* (1982).

[Gary A. Rendsburg (2nd ed.)]

EBNER, MEIR (**Meyer**; 1872–1955), Jewish leader in Bukovina and Romania, active Zionist. Born in Czernowitz, he participated in the establishment of the Jewish national student association, Hasmonea, in 1891. He earned the degree of jurist doctor from the university in his native city. With the advent of Herzl, Ebner joined the Zionist Organization, attending the First Zionist Congress and many succeeding ones. He was active in Jewish affairs in Bukovina, at the same time working to obtain Jewish representation in the local *Landtag* and at the *Reichsrat* in Vienna. He was exiled to Siberia by the Russian conquerors in 1915 and returned in 1917. In 1918–20 he was head of the Jewish National Council of Bukovina. When Bukovina was annexed to Romania in 1918, he led the struggle for Jewish rights and in 1919 founded the German language periodical *Ostjuedische Zeitung* in which he advocated Zionism and a Jewish national policy in the Diaspora. It was published until the end of 1937, when it was banned by the government. Ebner attended the international Congresses of National Minorities in Geneva, becoming vice president of the organization after the death of Leo *Motzkin in 1933. In May 1926 (until July 1927) he was head of the Czernowitz Jewish community and was elected to the Romanian parliament, where he frequently spoke with great courage, undeterred by threats from antisemites. In 1928 Ebner was elected to the Romanian Senate and became head of the Jewish faction of four members. He helped found the Jewish Party of Romania in 1930 and was elected on its behalf to the Romanian parliament. In 1934 his election was prevented through the machinations of the government. Ebner immigrated to Palestine in the beginning of 1940, where he became a regular contributor to Zionist publications in Palestine and abroad and was active in associations of immigrants from Romania and Bukovina. He died in Israel.

BIBLIOGRAPHY: M. Kleinman (ed.); *Enziklopedyah le-Ẓiyyonut*, 1 (1947), 3f.; M Reifer, *Dr. M. Ebner* (1947); J. Gruenbuam, *Penei ha-Dor*, 2 (1961), 176–80; S. Bickel, *Yahadut Romanyah* (1978), 326–31; *Parlamentari evrei* (1998); D. Schaari, in: SAHIR, 4 (1999), 148–77; Z. Yavetz, in: *English Historical Review* (1998).

[Yehuda Slutsky]

EBONY, heartwood of certain trees. The Hebrew word *hovenim*, which occurs in Ezekiel (27:15) in a reference to Tyre's commerce in "horns of ivory and *hovenim*," is identified by most translators and exegetes as ebony, called *hbn* in Egyptian. Several tropical trees supplied the ebony used in ancient times, the most important being the *Diospyros ebenum*, which grows in India. Other species of the same genus grow in Africa. Ebony was extensively used with ivory ornamentation (as described by Ezekiel) for the effect given by the contrast of black and white.

BIBLIOGRAPHY: Loew, Flora, 1 (1928), 588–9; J. Feliks, *Olam ha-Ẓome'aḥ ha-Mikra'i* (1968²), 126.

ECCLESIA ET SYNAGOGA, the name given to the symbolic representations in Christian art of the Middle Ages of the victorious Church and defeated Synagogue, symbolizing the triumph of Christianity. The representation is often found in medieval Christian manuscript art. It also became a conventional decoration in many medieval churches, especially in France, England, and Germany, and took the form of two graceful female figures, usually on the outside of the building. The Church is shown erect and triumphant, bearing a cross; the Synagogue is usually blindfolded and dejected, bearing a broken staff and sometimes decorated with the Tables of the Ten Commandments symbolizing the Old Testament. The best known statues of this type are on the exterior of the cathedrals of Strasbourg and Bamberg. They are also found in Rheims, Paris, and Bordeaux. In England, they figure, generally in a mutilated condition, in Rochester, Lincoln, Salisbury, and Winchester. The representation of the blindfolded synagogue was paradoxically reflected even in Jewish manuscript art: as for example in the miniature of the blindfolded Torah with her spouse, the People of Israel, in a 14th-century manuscript prayer book (Hamburg, Cod. Lev. 37; possibly having a symbolic meaning, representing the Torah and the People of Israel).

BIBLIOGRAPHY: W.S. Seiferth, *Synagoge und Kirche im Mittelalter* (1964); B. Blumenkranz, *Juden und Judentum in der mittelalterlichen Kunst* (1965); E. Roth, in: AWJD, 18:1 (1963); L. Edwards, in: JHSET, 18 (1958), 63–75; P. Hildenfinger, in: REJ, 47 (1903), 187–96.

[Helen Rosenau]

ECCLESIASTES (Heb. קֹהֶלֶת, הַקֹּהֶלֶת), one of the group of minor writings of the Hagiographa known as the Five Scrolls (*Megillot*). The name Ecclesiastes is Greek and probably means "member of the assembly." It renders the Hebrew word *kohelet* (*qohelet*, or *ha-qohelet* = the Qohelet; 1:1, 2, 12; 7:27; 12:8, 9, 10). Qohelet is not a proper name but means something like "one who acts in the assembly" or "teaches the public" – see the description of his activities in 12:9. Qohelet is usually thought to be the author, but he may be a fictional persona, the author's "mouthpiece." Though Qohelet never claims to be Solomon, he does describe himself in Solomon-like terms: He is "king in Jerusalem" (1:12) and "son of David, king in Jerusalem" (1:1). Traditionally, therefore, he was identified with Solomon. Solomonic authorship, however, is ruled out by evidence of language and content.

Language and Date

The Hebrew of the book represents the latest stage in the evolution of biblical Hebrew. An example of the indicators of late biblical Hebrew is the root *tqf* (4:12; 6:10), which can only be borrowed from Aramaic, and not before the seventh century B.C.E. Also, the nouns *pardes* "orchard" (2:5) and *pitgam* "decree" (8:11) are both borrowed from Persian. Persia only emerged from obscurity in the middle of the sixth century B.C.E., and no words are known to have been borrowed from its language before that. Moreover, *pardes*, from the Persian *piridaēza* ("rampart," a domain of the king) was also borrowed by the Greeks (*paradeisos*) in the sense of "orchard," the sense it has in Ecclesiastes 2:5. The word *avadeyhem* "their deeds" in 9:1 is Aramaic, not Hebrew. So too, *ʾillu*, the Aramaic and post-biblical equivalent of the classical *lu*, occurs in the Bible only in Ecclesiastes 6:6 and in *Esther 7:4 (the latter being obviously post-exilic and probably third century B.C.E.). There are, in fact, Aramaisms in Qohelet at a much greater frequency than we would expect in a pre-exilic work. Indeed it has been argued – see the items by Ginsberg in the Bibliography – that the book was written in Aramaic and later translated into Hebrew. This theory has not been accepted by other scholars, but it calls for further examination. On the linguistic background of the book, see especially the books by Schoors and Seow.

The content too points to a Hellenistic dating. There is reason to think that the author was influenced by Stoic philosophy (see Rudman in Bibliography). Also, competitive foot races, alluded to in 9:11, entered the Near East only in the third century B.C.E. A deeper indicator of Greek influence (which would scarcely be possible before the Hellenistic period) is the book's display of the mindset of Greek philosophy. This enterprise tried to determine the good by the application of human reason alone, without appeal to tradition or revelation. Qohelet, alone of the Bible, follows this path.

Contents

The book of Ecclesiastes is a reflection on life together with advice on making one's way through it. Qohelet introduces himself as a wise king who sought to examine all that happens on earth (1:12–18), including toil, wisdom, and pleasure. His goal is to determine "what is good for man to do under the heavens during the few days of his life" (2:3). He amassed wealth and belongings, and this accomplishment seems to have given him pleasure; but ultimately he found it senseless (2:4–2:26). As Qohelet proceeds on his investigation, he observes a variety of values and typical events. Most of these he finds senseless and "bad," but he does suggest various ways of maneuvering through life and, from time to time, does praise certain modes of behavior and experiences. Still, he begins and concludes with a judgment that recurs throughout the book, "All is *hevel*," a keyword usually translated "vanity" or "transient" but that might be better translated "senseless" or "absurd."

Recurring topics include injustices (3:16–22); social oppressions (4:1–3; 5:7–11); the futility of toil and pleasure (2:18–26; 4:4–8; 5:12–6:9); the failure of wisdom and the frailty of its achievements (4:13–16; 6:10–12; 7:13–14, 23–24; 8:16–9:10; 9:1–3). Occasionally he grants wisdom's (limited) value (9:13–18; 10:1–3). He more emphatically affirms life's goodness and the importance of grasping life's pleasures when they present themselves (9:4–10; 11:7–12:1) – an imperative made all the more urgent by the incessant awareness of death's grim certainty (9:7–10; 12:1–8). He concludes with a mysterious description of the path to death (12:2–7). The opening declaration "All is *hevel*" concludes his words. An epilogue (12:9–14) speaks about Ecclesiastes from the standpoint of a later sage.

Teaching

The book of Ecclesiastes is written in an unusual, difficult Hebrew, and its thought is self-contradictory and sometimes opaque. Hence its interpretation has been marked by sharp disagreement among the commentators.

Traditional commentators, following the Midrash (especially *Kohelet Rabbah*), regard the book to be King Solomon's words in old age. Having experienced both the world's glories and its disappointments, he realized the futility of mundane strivings and the insignificance of earthly goods – matters "beneath the sun" (1:3 and often). These he deemed *hevel* (understood to mean "trivial"). In contrast, matters that are *not* "beneath the sun" but rather belong to the transcendent, spiritual realm, have great and everlasting value. These are, above all, the eternal life and study of Torah. The book teaches that one must resign oneself to God's will, for all his works are good. Injustices will eventually be rectified and righteousness rewarded, if not in this life then in a blessed eternity, the "world to come."

Most modern commentators understand the book to express skepticism about traditional beliefs, especially the verities of the book of Proverbs and similar wisdom literature, in particular the axioms of God's justice and the efficacy of wisdom and hard work. An example of a negative reading is that of Crenshaw, according to whom Qohelet directs a radical, unrelenting attack on the traditional beliefs of the sages and denies the reality of a moral order. All that is left, Qohelet concludes, is the pleasure of the moment, which may soothe the troubled spirit. A more positive reading is advocated by Fredericks, who argues that Ecclesiastes is only commenting on the human realm. This is characterized by transience, to be sure, but man can find ways to cope, namely by simple pleasures, wisdom, the joy of work, and resignation to God's will. Similarly, Seow argues that "all is *hevel*" does not mean that everything is meaningless or insignificant, but that the meaning of life and the rationale of its inequities transcend human comprehension. Humans must accept whatever happens, while making the most of life's possibilities.

Fox (1999, 2004) argues that the underlying issue that Qohelet addresses is the question of meaningfulness in life. For events to be meaningful, they would have to cohere in a comprehensible picture, with deeds securely and predictably producing the appropriate consequences. The righteous should be rewarded and the wicked punished; the one who toils should get to enjoy the full fruits of his work while the foolish should suffer penury; the wise should have a life the polar opposite of the fool's; and something should distinguish them in death.

Qohelet sees that these things do not happen, at least not consistently (see 6:2; 8:11; 9:11), and he is weighed down by the collapse of meaning, which is revealed by the contradictions that pervade life. These he repeatedly calls *hevel* – "absurd" or "senseless." Qohelet is frustrated that life does not make sense. The irrationality of the world is his fundamental grievance, and his other complaints – such as the brevity of life, the futility of effort, the triviality of worldly goods, the vulnerability of wisdom, and the anomalies in divine justice – are secondary to this one and serve to confirm it.

Qohelet believes, or at least tries to believe, that God will eventually execute justice (3:17; 11:9b). The righteous, in principle at least, live long and the wicked die young (8:11–12a, 14). But Qohelet does not see this happening at present and fears that justice will come too late (8:10–11, 14). Qohelet sees injustices but insists that God is just. Qohelet does not eliminate this contradiction but is just frustrated by it.

God for Qohelet is an absolute, unpredictable autocrat. He is a distant and all-powerful force who can be feared but not loved (3:14b; 5:1, 2, 4; 6). But, though rather steely and remote, He is not uniformly hostile. If (for unpredictable reasons) God should grant someone good things, He wants the fortunate man to enjoy these gifts (5:20; 9:7).

For all his complaints, Qohelet is not a nihilist. "Everything is absurd" is to be understood as expressing a general characterization of life, not an absolute negation of the value of all activities and values. Qohelet shows how humans can recover and reconstruct meanings. He does not arrive at a grand logic or theology that makes sense of everything, but he does recommend modest adjustments and small-scale accommodations in our individual lives.

Some things Qohelet does find worthwhile, such as moderate work, temperate enjoyment of the pleasures that come to hand, love and friendship, gaining and using whatever wisdom is within our capacity, being reasonably righteous, and fearing God. Though their benefits are brief, imperfect, and uncertain, they are enough to make life worth living. Qohelet comes to realize that despite all its unfairness and absurdity, life itself is good, to be grasped all the more eagerly for death's finality.

Qohelet's affirmations all look inward, to each individual's benefit, and his concerns are internal as well: what troubles people, what cheers them up, how they can get along in a world in which much is predetermined and opaque. Though there are practical things we can do to reduce the risks, the only real realm of real freedom and control is the human heart – the domain of emotions, thoughts, and attitudes. We are to enjoy whatever pleasures God makes possible and avoid whatever sorrow we can. This, we may note, is Stoic doctrine as well.

A different theology emerges in the epilogue, 12:9–14. This is commonly considered an addition by a later scribe, but it may well be the words of the anonymous author. The epilogue evaluates Qohelet from a more conventional standpoint. It assures the reader that Qohelet was a wise and eloquent teacher, but also warns that the words of the wise hold certain dangers. What is of ultimate importance is to fear God, obey His commandments, and live in awareness of His ultimate judgment.

BIBLIOGRAPHY: EARLY COMMENTARIES: MIDRASH QOHELET RABBA 8th–10th C. B.C.E.; ENGLISH TRANS. A. Cohen, *Midrash Rabbah*, 8 (1983); Saadiah Gaon; Rashi; Abraham Ibn Ezra; Samuel b. Meir; Samuel ibn Tibbon; Obadiah b. Jacob Sforno; Yosef Ibn Yaḥyah; Moshe b. Hayyim Alsheikh. MODERN COMMENTARIES: G.A. Barton (ICC, 1908); C.D. Ginsburg (1861; with extensive survey of older literature); E. Podechard (Fr., 1912); H.W. Hertzberg (Ger., 1932, 1963²); R. Gordis (1951, 1967³); H.L. Ginsberg (Heb., 1961); J.L. Crenshaw (OTL, 1987); R.L. Murphy (WBC, 1992); M.V. Fox (JPS Commentary, 2004); C.L. Seow (AB, 1997); T. Longman III (NICOT, 1998); N. Lohfink (Continental Commentaries, 2003). STUDIES: H.L. Ginsberg, *Studies in Kohelet* (1950); E. Bickerman, *Four Strange Books of the Bible* (1967), 139–67. **ADD. BIBLIOGRAPHY:** A. Schoors, *The Preacher Sought to Find Pleasing* Words (1992); idem, *Qohelet in the Context of Wisdom* (1997); M.V. Fox, *A Time to Tear Down and a Time to Build Up* (1999); D.C. Fredericks, *Coping With Transcience* (1993); E. Christianson, *A Time to Tell: Narrative Strategies in Qoheleth* (1998); S. Burkes, *Death in Qoheleth* (1999); R. Sandberg, *Rabbinic Views of Qohelet* (1999); D. Rudman, *Determinism in the Book of Ecclesiastes* (2001).

[Harold Louis Ginsberg / Michael v. Fox (2nd ed.)]

ECCLESIASTES RABBAH (Heb. קֹהֶלֶת רַבָּה, *Kohelet Rabbah*), *aggadic Midrash on the book of *Ecclesiastes, called "*Midrash Kohelet*" in the *editio princeps*. (On the term "*Rabbah*," see *Ruth *Rabbah*.)

The Structure

Eccelesiastes Rabbah is an exegetical Midrash which gives a chapter by chapter and verse by verse exposition of the Book of Ecclesiastes. In the *editio princeps*, it is divided into three *sedarim* ("orders"): (a) Chapters 1–6; (b) 6:1–9:6; (c) 9:7–the end of the book of Ecclesiastes. In later editions however it is also divided into 12 sections, corresponding to the biblical chapters. The Midrash opens with an anonymous proem of the classical type found in amoraic Midrashim. It begins with an extraneous verse from the Book of Proverbs which is then connected with the opening words of the Book of Ecclesiastes. It bears, however, a few signs of lateness, including its (introductory formula): "This is what the Scripture declared in the holy spirit by Solomon king of Israel."

The Language

Ecclesiastes Rabbah is written for the most part in mishnaic Hebrew. Galilean Aramaic is also used, and there are numerous Greek words.

The Date of its Redaction

The redactor used tannaitic literature, the Jerusalem *Talmud, **Genesis Rabbah*, **Leviticus Rabbah*, **Lamentations Rabbah*, and **Esther Rabbah*. The work also incorporates material taken from the Babylonian *Talmud, some of which, however, was added later. Several factors indicate that *Ecclesiastes Rabbah* is of a comparatively late date, having been redacted apparently not earlier than the eighth century C.E. It was used by the *paytan* *Solomon b. Judah ha-Bavli, who flourished in the second half of the tenth century C.E., and it is quoted by *Nathan b. Jehiel in his *Arukh* (c. 1100). *Ecclesiastes Rabbah* contains much important material of the tannaitic and amoraic periods, and also numerous *aggadot* of a polemical character, some with anti-Christian references.

Editions

Ecclesiastes Rabbah was first published at Pesaro in 1519, together with Midrashim on the four other scrolls (Song of Songs, Ruth, Lamentations, and Esther) to which, however, it is entirely unrelated. The many subsequent ones are based on this edition. Although several manuscripts of *Ecclesiastes Rabbah* are extant (the earliest dating from the 14th century), a complete scholarly edition has yet to appear. M. Hirshman edited the four first chapters of the book in his dissertation

(1983). An English translation by Abraham *Cohen appeared in the Soncino Midrash (1939).

BIBLIOGRAPHY: Zunz-Albeck, Derashot, 128–9. **ADD BIBLIOGRAPHY:** J. Wachten, *Midrasch-Analyse: Strukturen im Midrasch Qohelet Rabba* (1978); M. Hirshman, in: *Jerusalem Studies in Jewish Thought*, 3 (1982), 7–14; G. Stemberger, *Introduction to the Talmud and Midrash* (1996), 317f.

[Moshe David Herr]

ÉCIJA, city in Seville, S. Spain. We have no information on the Jews of Écija in the Muslim period. The earliest information concerning Jews there dates from the 13th century. Following its conquest by Ferdinand III, Zulema, a Jewish courtier, was given substantial property. The size of the Jewish community can be judged from the fact that for the year 1293 its tax amounted to 5,000 maravedis. Its most prominent member was the wealthy Don Yuçaf (Joseph) de *Écija (Joseph ha-Levi ibn Shabbat), who distinguished himself in the service of Alfonso XI of Castile. In 1332 he endowed a yeshivah in Écija, and provided stipends for the scholars who studied in it. The persecutions of 1391 struck Écija and its synagogue was destroyed by order of Fernando *Martínez, who was archdeacon of Écija. However, when in 1396 the archbishop of Toledo demanded from the vicar of Écija an account of the destruction of the synagogue, he was told that it was razed by the mob. It is not known when the community was reconstituted, but its tax assessment in 1439 was 6,800 maravedis, in old coin. The community apparently lasted until the expulsion of 1492. There was also an organized group of *Conversos, which in 1477 had as its leader a New Christian named Fernando de Trujillo.

BIBLIOGRAPHY: Baer, Urkunden, index; Baer, Spain, index; H. Beinart, *Anusim be-Din ha-Inkvizizyah* (1965), 62; Ballesteros, in: *Sefarad*, 6 (1946), 253–87; R. Menéndez Pidal, *Documentos linguísticos de España*, 1 (1966²), 475–7; F. Cantera Burgos, *Sinagogas Españolas* (1955), 203–12. **ADD. BIBLIOGRAPHY:** J. Aranda Doncel, in: *Boletín de la Real Academía de Córdoba*, 104 (1983), 5–18.

[Haim Beinart]

ÉCIJA, JOSEPH (Yuçaf) DE (Joseph b. Ephraim ha-Levi ibn Shabbat; d. 1339/40). Écija was born in Écija, Andalusia, and was chief tax farmer (*almoxarife mayor*) of Alfonso XI of Castile. He played a major role within the Jewish community and cooperated with R. *Asher ben Jehiel, then the leading halakhic authority in Castile. He was advanced in the royal service through the patronage of Infante Felipe, son of Sancho IV. By 1322 he was *almoxarife mayor* and a member of the royal council, besides two other Christians. In 1326 he was sent by Alfonso XI to meet his betrothed, the daughter of the Portuguese king. While at Valladolid, some of the knights who accompanied him stirred up the populace against him, but he was saved through the intervention of Dona Leonor, the king's sister. He was dropped from the royal council in 1328 as a concession to the Cortes, which had been summoned to approve extraordinary taxes. A year later, however, he was again high in royal favor, conducting negotiations with Alfonso IV of Aragon. He gained the latter's favor as well and appealed to him to relieve the Aragonese Jews from the obligation to wear the Jewish *badge. In a letter of 1329 the Aragonese king expressed his regret over his inability to grant Joseph de Écija's request at that time. At court Joseph's rival was the royal physician, Samuel ibn Waqar of Toledo. The two competed for the farming of various royal revenues. Gonzalo Marténez de Oviedo, a protégé of Joseph, became royal major-domo and commander of the Order of Alcántara. Marténez turned against his benefactor and brought about the imprisonment of both Joseph and Samuel. Joseph appears to have died in prison. Solomon *Ibn Verga in his *Shevet Yehudah* emphasizes the fact that Joseph, for all his high rank at court, was a loyal and devoted son of his people. He built a synagogue in Seville and endowed a house of learning in his native Écija, providing for the maintenance of the dean and students. In 1342, the king asked Pope Clemens VI to permit the Jews of Seville to worship in the synagogue that was built by Joseph. He was also a lover of music, an interest which he shared with Alfonso IV of Aragon, who asked Joseph to send him his favorite Castilian musicians.

BIBLIOGRAPHY: Amador de los Ríos, *Historia de los Judíos de España y Portugal*, 2 (1876), 128f.; Y. Baer, in: *Minḥah le-David* (*Yellin*) (1935), 198f.; Baer, Urkunden, 1 (1929), 262f.; 2 (1936), 141f., 163f.; A. Ballesteros, in: *Sefarad*, 6 (1946), 253–87; A. Shochat (ed.), *Shevet Yehudah* (1947), 52f., 181; Samuel ibn Sason, *Sefer Avnei ha-Shoham*, ed. by A. Ḥamiel (1962), 22f.

[Haim Beinart]

°ECKARDT, ROY A. (1918–1997), theologian and Methodist minister. Born in Brooklyn, New York, Eckardt, a prolific writer and a leading figure in the field of Jewish-Christian relations in the U.S., was from 1955 president of the American Academy of Religion and, from 1956, chairman of the department of religion at Lehigh University (Bethlehem, Pennsylvania). His books on the Jewish-Christian dialogue (*Christianity and the Children of Israel*, 1948, and *Elder and Younger Brothers: The Encounter of Jews and Christians*, 1967), and his many articles on the subject, center upon three themes: the meaning of antisemitism; the theological and moral relations between Christians and Jews; and the understanding of the State of Israel. He interprets Christian antisemitism as the pagans' war against the people of God, and the Gentiles' war against Jesus the Jew. The Jewish people, whether conceived in religious or in secular terms, belongs to the unbreakable covenant between God and Israel. In Jesus the Jew, the covenant is opened to the world, but not in any way that annuls the election of the original Israel. Because the Christian has been brought into the family of Jews, the fate of Israel, including the State of Israel, is also his fate. Together with his wife, Alice, he wrote *Encounter with Israel: A Challenge to Conscience* (1970), which analyzed the distortion of facts related to Israel frequently favored by antisemites, and *Long Night's Journey into Day: A Revised Retrospective on the Holocaust* (1982). Regarded as one of the most powerful and prolific teams working in the area of Christian-Jewish relations, they traveled the globe to challenge Christians in the way they related to Jews, Judaism, and Israel. The couple made a point of encouraging young people who worked in the field of Christian-Jewish relations.

Eckardt was an active member of the National Christian Leadership Conference for Israel (NCLCI) since its establishment in 1979. That same year, President Carter appointed him special consultant to the President's Commission on the Holocaust. From 1981 to 1986 he served on the United States Holocaust Memorial Council as a special advisor to its chairman, Elie *Wiesel. Eckardt was also a senior associate fellow of the Center for Postgraduate Hebrew Studies and a Maxwell Fellow at Oxford University.

Other publications by Eckardt include *The Surge of Piety in America, an Appraisal* (1958), *Your People, My People: The Meeting of Jews and Christians* (1974), *Jews and Christians, the Contemporary Meeting* (1986), *For Righteousness' Sake: Contemporary Moral Philosophies* (1987), *Long Night's Journey into Day: Life and Faith after the Holocaust* (1988), *Black-Woman-Jew: Three Wars for Human Liberation* (1989), *Reclaiming Jesus of History: Christology Today* (1992), *No Longer Aliens, No Longer Strangers: Christian Faith and Ethics for Today* (1994).

[Yona Malachy / Ruth Beloff (2nd ed.)]

°ECKHART, MEISTER (c. 1260–c. 1327), theologian and mystic. Born Johannes Eckhart at Hochheim, Thuringia, he joined the Dominican Order in his youth. Although some of his propositions were condemned as heretical by Pope John XXII, Eckhart exerted a great influence on medieval mysticism. Because Eckhart wrote little about the Jews, and, unlike other Christian theologians, did not discuss the question of the continued existence of the Jewish people, it was generally assumed that he had nothing to do with Judaism. The pioneers in the study of the influence of Jewish philosophy on Christian scholasticism, Manuel *Joel and Jacob *Guttmann, did not even bother to analyze Eckhart's writings. However, in 1928, Josef Koch advanced the thesis that Eckhart was influenced by Jewish philosophy, in particular by *Maimonides. According to Koch, Eckhart first came into contact with the writings of Jewish philosophers in 1313, when he began to prepare a comprehensive collection of doctrinal statements to serve as authorities for his own interpretation of religious doctrines. Koch suggests that Maimonides' method of biblical exegesis, found in the *Guide of the Perplexed*, influenced Eckhart to change the direction of his work and to begin to write biblical commentaries instead of the collection of doctrinal statements he had originally begun. Maimonides' doctrine of negative attributes had a profound influence on Eckhart, in that it showed him that it was possible for man to describe God without obliterating the distinction between God and His creatures, a distinction which Eckhart regarded as fundamental. While it was a matter of routine by the last decades of the 13th century for Christian philosophers to refer to Maimonides, Eckhart was more dependent on Maimonides than other Christian philosophers of the period. It should be emphasized that Eckhart's interest in Judaism always remained purely intellectual, and that he was not at all interested in the social role of the Jews in a Christian society.

BIBLIOGRAPHY: Meister Eckhart, *Die deutschen und lateinischen Werke*, ed. Deutsche Forschungsgemeinschaft (1936); J.M. Clark (ed. and tr.), *Meister Eckhart: an Introduction to the Study of his Works* (1957); R.B. Blakney (ed. and tr.), *Meister Eckhart, A Modern Translation* (1941); N. Smart, in: *Encyclopedia of Philosophy*, 2 (1967), s.v.; J. Koch, in: *Jahresbericht der Schlesischen* NDB, 4 (1959), s.v.; E. Gilson, *Christian Philosophy in the Middle Ages* (1955), index.

[Hans Liebeschutz]

ECKMAN, JULIUS (1805–1877), U.S. rabbi. Eckman was born in Rawicz, Posen. He began a mercantile career in London at the age of 14, but after three years left for Berlin to resume his studies. In 1846 he was appointed rabbi in Mobile, Alabama, and subsequently in New Orleans, Richmond, and Charleston. In 1854 he was appointed rabbi of Congregation Emanu-El, San Francisco, but his appointment was terminated after one year. A man of high principles and constant devotion to scholarship, Eckman was in demand on account of his ability to preach in English as well as in German, but the reclusive bachelor lacked the temperament to cope with the conditions of congregational life in pioneer America. Eckman remained in San Francisco for the greater part of his life. He took over the congregational school as a private venture and devoted himself to the education of Jewish children. In 1856 he established a periodical *The Gleaner*, which he published until 1862 and resumed in 1864. Shortly thereafter he merged it with the *Hebrew Observer*. Eckman served as rabbi of congregations in Portland, Oregon, during 1863–66 and 1869–72.

BIBLIOGRAPHY: J. Voorsanger, *Chronicles of Emanu-El* (1900), 141–51; O.P. Fitzgerald, *California Sketches* (1880). **ADD. BIBLIOGRAPHY:** F. Rosenbaum, Visions of Reform (2000).

[Sefton D. Temkin / Fred S. Rosenbaum (2nd ed.)]

ECOLOGY. This survey deals with those Jewish sources which have particular reference to environmental matters, and the restrictions upon the actions of the individual both in his own private domain and in public places, to the extent that they affect his nearest neighbors and the community in general. Four general observations may be made:

(1) According to the Bible, the earth has not been given over to man's absolute ownership to use and abuse as he wishes; he merely acts as a custodian to maintain and preserve it for the benefit of his contemporaries and future generations; stress is laid on the influence exerted by the environment on the mind and spirit of man. The special talmudic approach to the individual's duty to protect and preserve public property is illustrated by the story told in the Tosefta of the man who threw boulders from his land onto the public highway. A pious person (*ḥasid*) chided him: "Dolt, why are you throwing stones from a place which does not belong to you to one which does?" The man was scornful of the *ḥasid*. Eventually,

the man sold his land. One day, as he walked along the highway adjoining the land, he stumbled over the boulders. Only then did he realize the wisdom of what the *ḥasid* had told him (Tosef. BK 11:10; BK 50b).

(2) Protection of the public is a constant motive.

(3) Although the regulations in the Talmud are cast in typical casuistic form, a number of general principles or basic guiding rules may be inferred, which are capable of extended application in the light of existing conditions.

(4) Although many of the rules fall within the specific context of what may be termed tort concepts, such as private nuisance, they have clear public law projections because of the religious character of Jewish law.

The Protection of Nature

THE FALLOW YEAR. The idea of preserving nature clearly inspires the biblical command concerning the fallow year (Lev. 25:1–5).

Maimonides in his *Guide of the Perplexed* (3:39) explains as one of the reasons for the fallow year "that the earth shall increase its yield and recover its potency." The clearly religious nature of the commandment extends its immediate utilitarian purpose and turns it into a general overriding principle of the widest application to the natural environment as a whole.

THE PROHIBITION OF WASTE. The peculiarly Jewish religious attitude towards nature is also to be seen in the rule forbidding the purposeless destruction of things from which human beings may derive benefit. The prohibition covers the destruction of animal and vegetable life as well as inanimate objects.

The reason for the prohibition in connection with fruit-bearing trees (see below) is given by the author of *Sefer ha-Ḥinnukh* in the following words: "to inculcate in our hearts a love of the good and the beneficial so that it becomes part of us and we separate ourselves from evil and destructiveness. That is the way of the pious, of those who observe religious practice – they love peace and rejoice in the well-being of their fellow-men, not even a mustard seed will they destroy" (Commandment 529).

THE FELLING OF FRUIT-BEARING TREES. The Bible prohibits the felling of fruit-bearing trees in time of war (Deut. 20:19), and the halakhic Midrash to this verse extends the prohibition to failing to irrigate the trees. The rule, however, is not confined to destruction in time of war, but is of more general application. Maimonides states it in the following terms: "Fruit-bearing trees growing in the countryside are not to be cut down, nor are they to be deprived of water so that they dry up and wither. Whoever cuts down (such trees) is liable to the penalty of flogging, and this not only during times of siege, but whenever they are wantonly destroyed. They may, however, be cut down if they damage other trees or a neighbor's land, or because it is too costly to maintain them. The Torah only forbids wanton destruction" (Yad, *Melakhim* 6:18; cf. *Talmudic Encyclopaedia*, s.v. *Bal Tashḥit*).

The rule is further extended to all objects, including buildings, unless their demolition is necessary for essential human needs. A case of the destruction of trees in the Bible which appears to contradict the clear proscription contained in Deuteronomy (II Kings 3:19) is regarded by Rashi and Kimḥi as exceptional in view of the special circumstances, in which higher national considerations were involved.

THE REARING OF SMALL CATTLE IN EREẒ ISRAEL. The Mishnah proscribes the breeding of small cattle except in Israel (BK VII:7), and the Talmud comments that it refers to "small cattle, but not to large, since intolerable restrictions are not imposed on the community, and whereas small cattle can be imported, large cattle cannot" (BK 79b). Rashi *ad locum* explains the prohibition by saying that the purpose of the regulation was to encourage settlement of Ereẓ Israel, and small cattle crop the soil so closely that it is impaired; they are also inclined to stay and trespass on the land of others.

The seriousness with which the prohibition was regarded from a religious (public) viewpoint is illustrated by the following incident related in the Talmud: There was once a pious person who suffered from heart disease. His doctors advised him to drink warm milk each morning, and for this purpose he acquired a goat which he tied to his bedpost. Some days later, friends came to visit him and when they saw the goat tied to the bedpost they said: "An armed robber is in the house of this man. How can we go in to him?" When on the point of death, he himself declared: "I know that I have not sinned except as regards the goat, when I transgressed against what my colleagues had said." Further it is reported that R. Ishmael said: "My father's family belonged to the landowning class in Upper Galilee. Why were they ruined? Because they pastured their cattle in the forest… but there was also a small field nearby (belonging to another) and they led their cattle on to it." In the talmudic period the regulation was extended to the Jewish settlement in Babylon (BK 80a).

Environmental Pollution

SEWAGE AND ODOR.

Human waste. The injunction of the Bible providing for the sanitary disposal of human waste (Deut. 23:13, 14) is formulated in a more comprehensive fashion by Maimonides: "It is forbidden to withdraw within the camp or to any chance place in the open fields, but it is a positive precept to set aside a special place for the purpose.… Likewise it is a positive precept that each one shall have with him a spade as part of his military equipment so that he can dig a hole for his needs and thereafter cover it up" (Yad, *Melakhim* 6:14, 15). In his comment upon this command, the author of *Sefer ha-Ḥinnukh* stresses in a still wider perspective the importance of cleanliness as a means for promoting the life of the spirit. "It is very well known that cleanliness is one of the virtues that conduces to holiness of mind" (Commandment 566). The precept is not confined to military camps, but applies to all human settlements (TJ Eruvin 5:1). Within the context of the Jewish law of torts, there is an injunction against the construction of privies too close to human habitation, and their removal may be ordered.

Sewage. The rabbis were stringent about public places being made insalubrious. They distinguished between summer and winter. "Nobody has the right to open up his drains or clear his cesspits in the summertime; that may only be done during winter" (BK 6a). Rashi explains that during summer it is pleasant out of doors and therefore wrong to make the place unsightly and malodorous, whereas this consideration does not apply to the rainy season.

The same passage also provides that although the disposal of sewage may be permitted, any injury caused thereby must be compensated for. The same rule is laid down by the Codes (Maim., Yad, Nizke Mammon 13:13; Sh. Ar., HM 104:31).

The Mishnah also prohibits pollution by industrial effluent. "Flax water must be kept away from vegetables" (BB 11:10), and the principle underlying it is naturally of general application.

Odors. The ruling of the Mishnah (BB 2:9) that "carrion, graves, and tanneries must be 50 cubits from a town" is ascribed to the bad odor which they emit, and for the same reason the Mishnah states that a tannery may be sited only on the east of a town, since the winds prevailing in Israel are northwesterly. The odors of privies are also included (BB 23a). These instances given by the Talmud are merely examples, and all like instances are comprehended in the prohibition. Thus R. Asher b. Yehiel (1250–1327, Germany-Spain), replying – inter alia – upon a geonic responsum regarding water pollution, gave a ruling about stagnant water which penetrated a neighbor's house and gave off an offensive smell (Responsa 108:10; cf. Tur HM 155:20–26; Sh. Ar. 155:20).

On the other hand, the rabbis composed a special benediction on fragrant odors "which give enjoyment to the soul and not to the body" (Ber. 34b).

AIR POLLUTION. Air pollution is also the subject of a number of mishnaic provisions. "A permanent threshing floor must be kept at a distance of 50 cubits from a town. One should not set up a permanent threshing floor on his own property unless there is a space of 50 cubits in every direction" (Mishnah BB 2:8). Rashi explains that the prohibition is because of the chaff which is injurious to humans and is also liable to affect sown fields. The same applied to all industrial waste, and Maimonides states that it applies to any operations which create dust, whatever the direction of the prevailing winds (Yad, Shekhenim 11:1).

SMOKE. Among the ten regulations enacted on entering Ereẓ Israel is one which, in order to preserve the amenities of Jerusalem, proscribed the erection of kilns which emit smoke and blacken the surrounding buildings (BK 82b). R. Nathan in the Tosefta generalized this rule by providing that kilns must be kept 50 cubits from any town (BB 1:7), and smoke damage is included among those injurious acts to which no legal title can be acquired by prescription (BB 23a). The *geonim* later did not prescribe a specific minimum distance for removal, but insisted that kilns must always be kept at such a distance that the smoke will not be a source of injury or give rise to any nuisance or annoyance (cf. S. Assaf, *Teshuvot ha-Geonim* 10:32).

The particular significance of smell, smoke and similar sources of damage are explained by Naḥmanides in the 13th century: "Since they cause injury to the person no prescriptive right can arise, for that only applies to pecuniary damage. Pools of water, lime, stones, and debris will affect only the fabric of a person's house and he may well acquiesce therein, even if real damage is done. Smoke, however, and privies give rise to damage and annoyance to the person, and no prescriptive right can be acquired" (Novellae to BB 59b).

WATER POLLUTION. According to the Tosefta, a person who digs a cistern or water hole for public use may wash his face and hands and feet there, unless there is mud or excrement on his feet. If the cistern and water hole, however, provide drinking water, he may not wash himself at all (Tosef. BM 11:31).

The fear of polluted drinking water is also manifested in the talmudic prohibition against drinking water which has been left uncovered for any length of time, since insects or other harmful matter may have contaminated it (AZ 12b; see also 30a and b).

The protection of water from pollution served as a cause of action against anyone who dug a cesspit close to a neighbor's well. The geonic responsa cite an instance which came before R. Samuel bar Ḥofni of Sura in the early tenth century. Reuven had a well adjoining the boundary of his land. Shimon came along and built a privy nearby at the prescribed distance of three *tefaḥim*. Reuven sued Shimon for the damage caused to his well water. Shimon defended by claiming that in accordance with rabbinical precept his privy did not adjoin the pit. R. Samuel was asked whether Shimon came along and built a privy nearby at the prescribed distance of three *tefaḥim*. Reuven sued Shimon for the privy must be removed from the well to a distance even up to 20 *amot*, at which the well water would not be affected. It was no argument, he added, that the privy had already been built, since no prescriptive right can be acquired when serious damage is suffered.

NOISE. Noise is an actionable civil wrong. According to the Talmud, millstones which create noise and vibrations must be kept at a prescribed distance (BB 18a and 20b). The Shulḥan Arukh extends the principle by making the distance vary with the size of the millstones, and making it apply to noises from other sources (HM 155:7).

An exception is made in the case of a school where the convenience of neighbors must give way to the needs of education (*ibid.*). This exception is again extended by the Shulḥan Arukh to all activities connected with the performance of religious precepts. In the case of a large school having at least 50 pupils, Rashi and Naḥmanides would, however, enable neighbors to prevent its continuance on account of excessive noise, when it is possible to moderate the noise by conducting the school in smaller classes (Rashi to BB 21a; *Naḥmanides Novellae, ibid.*).

AMENITIES OF PROSPECT. The Bible prescribes for an open space to be left surrounding the levitical cities (Num. 35:1–5). Maimonides, in summarizing the law, adds that it applies equally to other towns and cities in Ereẓ Israel (Yad, Shemittah 13:1–2, 4–5). Rashi explains that the reason for this open space, uncultivated, without trees or buildings, is to allow for free passage of air (Sotah 27b). The *Sefer ha-Ḥinnukh* suggests that since the levitical cities served national requirements (the levites were chosen to conduct divine services and people always came to consult them), they were to be kept pleasant and attractive to add to the luster of the people as a whole (Commandment 342). The same consideration lies behind the mishnaic rule that trees generally are to be kept at a distance of 25 cubits from a town, and carob and sycamore trees up to 50 cubits. R. Solomon b. Adret went further and introduced the rule that townspeople cannot forgo or waive anything which has been prohibited in the interest of the town's amenities.

Conclusions

Major environmental protection problems which concern us today are dealt with extensively in old Jewish sources. They indicate various ways in which spoiling of the environment in its various aspects may be prevented. Rules are laid down with some degree of particularity to control and inhibit the abuse of private rights to the detriment of others, both neighbors and local inhabitants.

Biblical passages dealing with the preservation of nature were elaborated in the Mishnah and Talmud to circumscribe and even remove possible sources of environmental damage. Its importance was emphasized by the fact that the rabbis were not merely content to rely upon the sanctions of the general law, as the law of torts but promulgated enactments specifically devoted to the environment and its protection, such as regulations relating to Jerusalem because of its special status, which were subsequently in part given wider application. Of utmost significance in this regard was the rule that while a particular injury might not be actionable according to the letter of the law, it was, nevertheless, forbidden. Equally important was the rule that no prescriptive right could be acquired in respect of any environmental tort of a serious nature which resulted in injury to the person, individual or collective, as distinct from injury to property, on the basis that no real acquiescence obtains in such cases.

The precise standards imposed by the Talmud to measure and control the injurious effects of the various sources of environmental injury were treated not as absolutes, but according to prevailing conditions, and thus were (and still are) adaptable, as times change. Injury to the environment included not only cases of proximate causation, but also those in which conditions were created which might reasonably give rise to nuisance.

[Nahum Rakover]

For the Jewish contribution to the environmental sciences, see *Environmental Sciences. See also *Conservation.

BIBLIOGRAPHY: E.C. Freudenstein, in *Judaism*, 19, 406; N. Lamm, *Faith and Doubt* (1971), ch. 6; *Talmudic Encyclopaedia*, s.v. *Bal Tashḥit, Behemah Dakah, Gilui, Harḥakat Nezikin*; B. Yashar, *Ha-Torah v'ha-Medinah*, 2 (1950) 59–64; M.Z. Neriah, *Shevilin*, 1 (1962), 47–49.

ECONOMIC HISTORY.

This article is arranged according to the following outline:

First Temple Period

Reconstruction of ancient Jewish economic conditions is greatly hampered by the paucity of available documentation. The main source of information still is the Bible; but its general orientation is either normative in the legal sections, exhortatory in the prophetic enunciations, or romanticizing in some of the historical descriptions. Thus a great deal may be learned of what the leaders believed the economic conditions ought to be rather than what they really were, the *Sollen* rather than the *Sein*. Archaeology, on the other hand, which has greatly enriched our knowledge about such *realia* as the utensils employed in agricultural and industrial production, the size and shape of buildings, sudden devastations by earthquakes or wars, and the like, has proved wholly inadequate in reflecting the daily economic relationships or the dynamics of economic evolution. More informative have been the documents found in the archaeological mounds, such as the el-Amarna and the Lachish Letters and the Samarian ostraca. But these documents are too few and limited to certain localities which may not warrant generalization from them to other areas and periods. Much can also be learned, however, from the vaster accumulation of materials in the neighboring civilizations (including the more recently explored Mari, Nuzi, and Ugaritic collections), provided one does not lose sight of the great differences prevailing between the respective countries and the many unique features which characterized the economy of ancient Israel as also Israelite society and culture at large. Utilizing these and other sources, as well as the combined results of many generations of intensive research by scholars, often of high competence, one may perhaps obtain some approximation of the actual economic evolution of ancient Israel after its entry into Canaan and the formation of its monarchy.

One conclusion which seems clearly to emerge from the state of knowledge today is that we must abandon the long-held assumption of both traditionalists and critical scholars that the historic evolution of ancient Israel must be explained in terms of a gradual emergence of a nomadic people into an agricultural society which was later combined with an urban civilization characterized by an increasing division of labor. This evolution, it was believed, required several centuries of slow growth. Such gradualism was used to explain not only the changing economic trends but also the general societal and religious transformations; it supposedly proved helpful even in the dating of biblical sources. It is now known, however, that the ancient Middle East, including the land of Canaan, had a fairly advanced civilization more than 2,000 years before the appearance of Israel on the historical scene. Even according to the biblical narratives, the first patriarch, Abraham – now widely accepted as an historic personality of prime magnitude – combined in his career an intimate acquaintance with his native Babylonian city of *Ur (the excavation of which has revealed its rich and ramified social stratification at the beginning of the second millennium B.C.E.) with that of Egypt, which he visited for a time and of Canaan, in which he settled. The segment of the Canaanite people which appears under the name of Phoenicians was soon drawn into the orbit of a maritime empire extending all the way to Spain. Hence even a primitive, nomadic tribe conquering one Canaanite city after another could quickly learn its methods of production and adopt its mode of living, skipping many stages of the accepted economic evolution.

It may be assumed, therefore, that very early Israel replaced nomadic cattle raising by agriculture as its dominant source of livelihood. Settlers in the formerly Canaanite cities also turned to crafts and even commerce as their primary occupation. With the establishment of a monarchy and the building of the Temple in Jerusalem there also arose a substantial royal and priestly bureaucracy. The new capitals of Jerusalem and Samaria, especially, revealed many characteristics of major urban centers where upper classes indulged in considerable luxuries in dwellings and personal attire, such as are described by Isaiah in his censure of the ladies of Jerusalem (Isa. 3:18ff.). At the same time, the old occupations of cattle raising and even the still more "primitive" activities of fishing and hunting – the latter was never a mere sport even among the Israelite kings – were never completely given up. They flourished particularly in the peripheral areas of the south and Transjordan.

This great diversity of pursuits was aided by both climatic and hydrographic conditions in the country. Despite its relatively small size, it has been found that ancient Palestine consisted of no less than 40 distinct geographic units, each with a different set of natural conditions, which not only affected the type of production but also colored the entire system of political and social life by promoting local independence, even tribalism. That is also why throughout the First Temple period Israel continued to share its land with Edomites, Moabites, Ammonites, Philistines, and some Arameans, while, beginning with a sort of "amphictyonic" alliance, its own 12 tribes gradually built up whatever unity existed later in their divided kingdom.

Although the country was dotted with many localities called cities (*arim*), these settlements did not resemble, as has often been assumed, the medieval and modern cities in being primarily centers of industry and commerce. While no less than 400 such "cities" existed in the territory of Israel and Judah, their population, as a rule, numbered no more than 1,000 persons and consisted principally of farmers who had banded together to live behind city walls for protection against raiders. Their livelihood was derived from cultivating their fields, vineyards, and orchards, for the most part located outside the city walls, to which they proceeded in the morning and from which they returned in the evening (note this sequence in Ps. 121:8; II Kings 19:27). Beyond their fields and vineyards there also were some pastures where the farmers could maintain some sheep and goats, particularly for the purpose of producing milk.

Nutrition of the ancient Palestinian population was about equally divided between grain and fruit. Barley was a particularly important staple which, if the prices are deduced from better known Babylonian parallels, was at times more in demand, and even more costly, than dates. Among the fruits grapes, dates, olives, and figs loomed very large in the popular diet. Meat was always considered a luxury and was consumed by the majority of the population only on festive occasions. The cultivation of vineyards and orchards often required intensive irrigation – already practiced in the pre-Israelitic period – and years of waiting for actual production, further aggravated by certain ritualistic taboos and imposts (*orlah, kilayim, bikkurim*). This system presupposed investment of much capital and human labor. But the ultimate returns were quite rewarding in produce yielded by small plots of land. The quality of some ancient Israel fruits seems to have been as high as that of similar products of the Second Temple era (see below).

Industrial production, on the other hand, was usually in the hands of artisans who were often organized in clans or guilds or both. We know of villages dedicated to single crafts (I Chron. 4:14). Entire families or clans served as scribes. While there is no evidence of guild monopolies, it appears that admission to certain crafts depended on a fairly long apprenticeship and hence was beyond the reach of ordinary laborers. At the same time we also learn about royal enterprises employing, for instance, numerous potters. The frequent occurrence of potsherds bearing the imprint of *la-melekh* ("to the king") suggests that it might have been a trademark of royal potteries. Some scholars, however, interpret that mark as a fiscal receipt for a certain quantity of wine or oil delivered to the royal treasury in payment of taxes. No final decision can be made on this score, since the entire subject of ancient Jewish taxation is shrouded in obscurity, deepened by many unresolved controversies.

A certain number of Israelites also entered mercantile occupations. Some of them did this as "the king's merchants," especially in the days of King Solomon (I Kings 10:28). At that time the international trade of ancient Israel made rapid strides both because it was fostered by the concentrated royal power and because, ever since David's conquest of Edomite territory, Israel had gained access to Ezion-Geber-Eloth on the Red Sea (I Kings 9:26). The new open route to the Indian Ocean made Israel a very welcome ally to Hiram, king of Tyre. Even earlier some northern Israelites seem to have hired themselves out as sailors to Phoenician shipowners (this seems to be the meaning of "Dan, why doth he sojourn by the ships?" in the Song of Deborah; Judg. 5:17). But now the two kings could collaborate in sending ships both to the Indian Ocean and the western Mediterranean where the Phoenicians had long been exploiting the copper mines of Sardinia and were ultimately to establish a colony in Tartessus, Spain. A combined Phoenician-Israelite expedition to Ophir, probably located on the west coast of India or even further east, was a landmark in the history of eastern navigation.

This condition did not last, however. After Solomon's death and the ensuing partition of the country into two kingdoms, Israel lost its overlordship over the Edomites, not to regain it except for a short time under Jehoshaphat. Nor could Israel any longer exploit the copper mines and use the refinery built by Solomon in Ezion-Geber. These losses contributed to the overall decline in both the commercial and political activities of Northern Israel and Judah, which often became tributary to foreign monarchs and occasionally indulged in internecine struggles. As a result, most of the country's mercantile activities were now conducted by strangers, mainly Phoenicians and other Canaanites. The term *kena'ani* now became a synonym for merchant in popular parlance.

All through that period Israelite commerce was abetted by a more or less stable system of weights and measures which the country shared with other Middle Eastern nations. There was also an increasing demand for money to facilitate mercantile transactions, and even in his day Abraham purchased the cave of Machpelah for "four hundred shekels of silver, current money with the merchant" (Gen. 23:16). At first the currency circulated in the form of silver bars which had to be weighed, but soon their weight was standardized and officially marked. By the end of the First Temple era regular coins, whether first introduced in Lydia or in Babylonia, gained the ascendancy. Curiously, gold never became the main instrument of exchange. Down to the Roman period it was often considered a mere commodity, valued at so-and-so many silver shekels, although its price was steadily gaining.

Another effect of the political weakness of the two kingdoms was the relative absence of *slaves from the productive processes in the country. Even Solomon's ambitious public works, including the building of the royal palace and the Temple, required more manpower than could be supplied by slaves. Hence the royal imposition of corvée labor on hundreds of thousands of free Israelites. After Solomon's death the supply of unfree labor must have further dried up, since the country now was rarely victorious in battle and thus could recruit only a small number of slaves from among prisoners of war. On the other hand, to purchase slaves in the Phoenician slave market became increasingly unremunerative. As early as the early days of the Book of the Covenant (ninth century or before) the indemnity for a male or female slave was set at 30 shekels of silver (Ex. 21:32). Later on the price seems to have gone up to 50 or more shekels. With the prevailing high rates of interest throughout the ancient Middle East, which ranged from a minimum of 20–25% on cash loans and of 33⅓% on grain loans, up to 100% and more for more risky credit or in periods of scarcity of capital, it simply did not pay for a landowner or craftsman to acquire a slave and maintain him to the end of his life while free day laborers were readily available at very low cost. "Hebrew" slaves probably originated only from debt bondage or a condemned criminal's inability to pay the fine. But the legal restrictions on the treatment of Hebrew slaves, the enforced manumission at the end of a six-year term, and the (probably utopian) demand of the Deuteronomist that a manumitted slave should be provided by his master with means for earning a living (Deut. 15:13–14), made the possession of a Hebrew slave very irksome. It was, therefore, not for productive purposes but rather for domestic service or concubinage that a few slaves were acquired by better situated masters. However, unemployment among free labor was often so great that one or another Hebrew slave may have chosen voluntarily to forego freedom and stay on after the expiration of the six-year term.

Surplus of free labor must have grown toward the end of the First Temple period as a result of the sharp inequalities which the prophets denounced. At that time many small farmers fell into debt and, unable to earn enough to pay the high rates of interest (probably collected under some subterfuge to avoid the even more far-reaching laws against usury), lost their land. Isaiah was not alone in exclaiming: "Woe unto them that join house to house, that lay field to field, till there be no room and ye be made to dwell alone in the midst of the land" (5:8; see also Hos. 5:10; Micah 2:1–2). The ensuing social unrest gave rise to the immortal calls for social justice by the great Israelite prophets. It also stimulated much idealistic social legislation (see below), the practical implementation of which left much to be desired. The rumblings of discontent among the masses helped to undermine the existing social order, particularly in Northern Israel with its constant revolts and assassinations of reigning monarchs. Of its ten ruling dynasties in the relatively short period of 931–721 B.C.E. all but two were replaced after the reign of one or two kings. Such instability was also ruinous for the country's economy and helped to bring about the disastrous fall of Samaria in 721 and of Jerusalem in 586 B.C.E. which spelled the end of the First Temple period.

Exile and Restoration

The fall of Jerusalem marked a turning point also in the economic history of the Jews. Not only was Palestine severely devastated – the reservations voiced by some modern scholars were disproved by the widespread desolation evidenced by archaeological diggings – but a large segment, perhaps the majority, of the Jewish population either perished during the war, was deported by the Babylonians, or emigrated voluntarily. The removal of the most active members of the community, including the royal house, the priests, the great landowners, and the artisans, further aggravated the effects of the depopulation and material destruction. Like the Philistine overlords of the early Israelite tribes, many ancient conquerors saw in the exile of smiths, the main suppliers of weapons as well as of industrial and agricultural tools, the best method of disarming the conquered population. Deprived of their leadership, the Israelites who remained behind were prone to adopt some of the more primitive ways of life and thought of their pagan neighbors.

On the other hand, the exiles to Babylonia joined the ever-growing Jewish dispersion. There are reasons to believe that a number of those deported from Northern Israel by the Assyrians in 733–719 B.C.E. had continued to profess their ancestral religion on the foreign soil. Their descendants, as well as those of the Judeans deported by Sennacherib in 702, now joined the groups of the new arrivals to form a powerful new community. (Only thus can we explain why those returning from the exile half a century later included descendants of families who had lived in Northern Israelite localities before the fall of Samaria; see Ezra 2:2ff. and the commentaries thereon.) They developed a new center in and around Nippur, the second largest city in Babylonia, which was located on the "river" Chebar, or rather the canal connecting the Euphrates and the Tigris. Here, both the new and old settlers now enjoyed the distinguished leadership of Ezekiel and many former Palestinian elders. They were also supported by surviving members of the royal family after Amel Marduk ("Evil-Merodach") released the imprisoned king of Judah, Jehoiachin, and restored him to a high position at the royal court of Babel. This release, narrated in the Bible (II Kings 25:27ff.) and confirmed also by Babylonian sources (E.F. Weidner in *Mélanges Dussaud*, 2 (1939), 923–35), seems to have laid the foundation for the development of the exilarchate, a remarkable institution which lent the dispersed Jews a focus of leadership, with few interruptions, for the following 2,000 years.

Besides Babylonia, Egypt also accommodated a number of Jewish communities; the best known being the Jewish military colony of *Elephantine in Upper Egypt, established perhaps as early as the seventh century by Psammetichus I to help defend the southern frontier of Egypt against Nubian raiders. Before long, Jewish settlers spread throughout the Middle East, especially after 549 B.C.E. when Cyrus and his successors founded the enormous Persian Empire, territorially exceeding in size even the later Roman Empire at the height of its grandeur. The author of the Book of Esther did not hesitate to place in the mouth of Haman, the anti-Jewish courtier in the capital of Susa, the accusation against "a certain people scattered abroad and dispersed among the peoples in all the provinces of thy kingdom; and their laws are diverse from those of every people" (3:8). Nor was Deutero-Isaiah guilty of vast exaggeration when he prophesied that "I [God] will bring thy seed from the east and gather thee from the west; I will… bring My sons from far and My daughters from the end of the earth" (Isa. 43:5–6).

This multitude of Jewish settlers appears to have been rather speedily integrated into the environmental economic structures. Despite their vivid messianic expectations, their majority followed Jeremiah's advice and built houses, took wives, and generally established themselves in their new countries on a semipermanent basis. In Babylonia, particularly, which at that time marched in the vanguard of a semicapitalistic civilization, Jews entered the stream of advanced mercantile exchanges. The people who at home had devoted itself largely to agriculture and small crafts now assumed an important role in *banking and far-flung commerce. Whether or not Jacob, the founder of the leading banking house of Egibi, was Jewish – there is some support for this hypothesis in the fact that loans were formally extended without interest, though the bankers collected the revenues from the mortgaged properties including slaves and cattle – there is no question that some Jewish landowners and businessmen wrote significant contracts with leading Babylonian capitalists. In the archives of the House of *Murashu, an important banking and warehousing firm, no less than 70 Jewish names have been identified. Some of the Jewish contracting parties, to be sure, merely undertook to raise sheep and goats in return for a specified annual delivery of cattle, butter, wool, and hides. Others obligated themselves to deliver to the firm 500 good fish within 20 days if they were provided with five nets and permits to fish in the firm's waters. But some major contracts were signed by wealthy Jewish landowners in their own right who traded with the Murashu Sons on a basis of equality.

In contrast, the Aramaic papyri of the Elephantine colony include business contracts representing rather small amounts, as was to be expected from a typical soldiers' camp which derived its main livelihood from cultivating the soil. Other Egyptian localities, particularly Migdol, Taphanhes, and Noph – mentioned by Jeremiah (44:1) and identified by scholars with Magdalos, Daphne, and Memphis in Lower Egypt – doubtless offered the Jewish settlers and other arrivals from the Asiatic mainland much wider business opportunities. Certain glimpses of such "higher" activities may be obtained from a number of other papyri which have come to light in recent decades.

In short, by acclimatizing themselves to their surroundings many Jews, especially those living in Babylonia, acquired considerable wealth and extensive political as well as business contacts with the ruling classes in the empire. They now could undertake the ambitious program of resettling thousands of their coreligionists in Palestine and to secure from the friendly Persian regime charters guaranteeing full autonomy to the reestablished community. In his original proclamation, *Cyrus himself provided that the Jews remaining behind should equip the returning exiles "with silver, and with gold, and with goods, and with beasts, beside the freewill offering for the house of God which is in Jerusalem" (Ezra 1:4). As a result, some 50,000 Jews, including approximately 7,000 slaves, left with Zerubbabel and another 5,000 later on under Ezra.

Not surprisingly, the returning Jews found the country in a chaotic state; they also encountered considerable hostility on the part of their new neighbors. To begin with, those families which, on the basis of their excellently kept genealogical records, started reclaiming the landed possessions of their ancestors evoked, as has often been the case elsewhere, the staunch resistance of the new owners. Before very long their "theocratic" leadership (a term later coined by Josephus to describe the new form of government in the Second Temple period) had to fight a protracted battle to stave off both the hostile actions of neighbors and excessive assimilation to them. For several centuries the Jewish autonomous area covered no more than some 1,200 square miles in and around Jerusalem. Cut off from the coastal region occupied by Phoenicians (as evidenced by the so-called Eshmunazarid inscriptions), they engaged in small-scale farming and petty trade and crafts. The socioeconomic difficulties encountered in the First Temple period now returned with increased severity because of the greater yoke of taxation imposed by the Persian bureaucracy, made doubly burdensome by the numerous gifts, bribes, and other "voluntary" contributions extracted by the Persian officials.

Once again the economic shortcomings brought about a state of unrest which boded ill for the future of the country. The complaints of the masses to the new governor, Nehemiah, were eloquently restated by him in his memoirs. They claimed:

> "We, our sons and our daughters, are many; let us get for them corn, that we may eat and live." Some also there were that said: "We are mortgaging our fields, and our vineyards, and our houses; let us get corn, because of the dearth." There were also that said: "We have borrowed money for the king's tribute upon our fields and our vineyards. Yet now our flesh is as the flesh of our brethren, our children as their children; and, lo, we bring into bondage our sons and our daughters to be servants, and some of our daughters are brought into bondage already; neither is it in our power to help it; for other men have our fields and our vineyards" (Neh. 5:2–5).

We are told, to be sure, that Nehemiah succeeded in persuading the upper classes to renounce their claims, to restore the fields to their rightful owners, and thus to reestablish for a while the social equilibrium. But the activities of this disinterested high official, who emphasized that he "demanded not the bread of the governor, because the service was heavy upon the people" (5:18), undoubtedly could offer but temporary relief. The conditions in the city of Jerusalem were no more satisfactory. Nehemiah actually had to take measures to prevent the flight of Jerusalemites, particularly the Temple personnel, to the countryside. Yet, the prolonged era of peace within the borders of the Persian Empire made life more or less bearable in the long run, and the country could look forward to better times.

Second Temple Period

The boundaries of the autonomous Jewish state, as established under Ezra and Nehemiah, did not expand, but there was a possibility for some Jews to settle in other parts of the country on both sides of the Jordan. While fertile Galilee was still called the *gelil ha-goyim* ("the district of gentiles"), the Jewish minority there was becoming a substantial factor. Transjordan, too, had a growing number of Jewish settlers. Alexander the Great's conquest of western Asia and the replacement of the Persian domination by that of Ptolemies and Seleucids opened up vast new opportunities for both Palestinian and Diaspora Jews. The new pervasive Hellenistic civilization greatly encouraged exchanges between the various provinces, including those between the Jews of Palestine and their ever growing Diaspora. Legally, too, under Alexander, Ptolemy I, and Antiochus the Great, Jewish self-government, with its implied economic freedoms, received a favorable interpretation. If, in time, the new Hellenistic culture began attracting many Jewish individuals, fostered their assimilation to Greek ways of life, and thereby created deep internal cleavages within the Jewish people, the ultimate result was the Hasmonean revolt and the establishment of a new and enlarged sovereign Jewish state. In the century between 165 and 63 B.C.E. the Hasmoneans conquered all of Palestine and Transjordan, converted most of the subject population to Judaism, and established a strong and populous Jewish country with but a few enclaves of Samaritans and Hellenistic city-states along the coast and in Transjordan.

Because the Temple of Jerusalem now served as a focal point for millions of dispersed Jews, the country benefited greatly from the influx of the half-shekels, imposed annually upon all adult male Jews, and from additional gifts voluntarily added by benefactors in various lands. A wealthy Egyptian Jew by the name of Nicanor, for example, provided the Temple with a brass gate named after him which allegedly required 20 men to open or close. In addition, thousands upon thousands of pilgrims from all lands considered it a high religious duty to visit the Temple and offer their sacrifices there at least once in a lifetime. Even Egyptian Jewry, which, for historic reasons, had built an independent Jewish "Temple of Onias" in the district of Leontopolis after the outbreak of the Maccabean revolt, continued to send to Palestine groups of pilgrims, including their spiritual leaders such as the Alexandrine philosopher Philo. Some pilgrims brought along with them substantial funds they had collected for Palestine in their home communities. Naturally, the coins collected by these cosmopolitan groups, as well as those spent by them during their stay in the Holy Land, greatly differed from one another in weight and value since many municipalities issued currencies of their own. To facilitate exchanges, the Palestinian authorities arranged for the opening of money-changing establishments in all parts of Palestine, including the Temple Mount, several weeks before Passover at the height of the pilgrim season. When Jesus "overthrew the tables of the money changers" in the Temple precincts (Matt. 21:12), he merely removed a facility which the visitors from many lands greatly appreciated.

Not surprisingly some large collections aroused the cupidity of Roman officials. One of them, Lucius Valerius *Flaccus, governor of Apamea, confiscated a local collection of 100 pounds of gold on the excuse that gold was not to be transferred to what in 59 B.C.E. still was a foreign country (despite Pompey's conquest of Palestine four years before). But in fact he merely sought to line his own pocket with the seized amount. However, he was promptly accused before the Roman senate of having committed a "sacrilege" on property belonging to a temple. He escaped severe punishment only after an effective defense by Cicero, whose eloquent plea, mixing Jew-baiting with purely legal arguments, still serves as a Latin textbook in many schools today. Later, Roman legislation, however, clarified the issue by placing all funds destined for the Jerusalem Temple, and later for the Palestinian patriarchs, under the protection of the laws governing sacrilege.

Domestically, too, the economy was surging upward. Agriculture still was the mainstay of the entire social structure. Benefiting from the accumulated energies of many generations, irrigation systems were installed in new areas, stimulating the annual output. True, in time, the needs of a quickly expanding population forced the farmers to put many marginal lands under cultivation. Probably for this reason R. Yose (second century) spoke of the seed yielding on the average a fivefold return in finished products (Ket. 112a), which contrasted with much higher yields in earlier periods. But some areas still produced the ten- or fifteenfold return characteristic of ancient Italy and even higher than ones recorded both in the First Temple era and in the talmudic period (see the exaggerations cited *ibid.*). Once again it was barley rather than wheat which was the mainstay of the bread diet. Dates, grapes, olives, and figs continued to furnish major ingredients for both domestic consumption and the export of surpluses. Remarkably, despite the growing population and the excessive costs of transportation, Palestine was able to export both cereals and fruits. Some of its choice fruits were served at the imperial tables in Rome, notwithstanding the competition of Italy, Spain, and Greece, all of which yielded similar products. A rarer plant was the papyrus grown in the Negev, the high price of which, however, maintained by the Egyptian state monopoly, made it noncompetitive as writing material with the far less expensive parchment, and still less costly ostracon. For its part Palestine had a sort of monopoly on the balsam tree, the growing of which was largely limited to the "fat lands of Jericho." Balsam was often sold for its weight in gold. During the Roman-Jewish War of 66–70, Pliny informs us, the Jewish defenders cut down the balsam trees lest they fall into the hands of the enemy; and "there have been pitched battles in defense of a shrub" (*Historia naturalis*, 12, 54:113).

It is small wonder that plants were considered a vital social asset of the country and cutting them down wantonly was treated as a serious crime. The term for cutting down plants was extended metaphorically to cover infringement on the fundamentals of the Jewish law and religion. To be called a "cutter, son of a cutter" became a superlative insult. The vine, palm, and olive trees were often used as symbols of the Jewish people; they still adorn many extant Jewish graves in ancient cemeteries and catacombs. Compared with agriculture, cattle raising played a rather minor role. While sheep were still needed to provide wool and milk products, meat was a relatively minor article of consumption. According to a second-century rabbi, "a man who owns 100 shekels shall buy a pound of vegetables for his stew; 1,000 shekels, shall buy a pound of fish; 5,000 shekels, a pound of meat [it is later explained: for the Sabbath]. Only if he owns 10,000 shekels, he may put his pot on the stove every day" (Ḥul. 84a). A major consumer of cattle was the Temple with its sacrificial worship, particularly on Passover when thousands of families lined up to offer their paschal lambs. However, the total production could probably be provided by the outlying steppes in Transjordan and the south, where more intensive cultivation was impeded by the shortage of water. With this geographic differentiation also went a cultural disparity, since the cattle-raising areas were removed from the main center of learning. As a result we may understand the transition from the high esteem of the shepherd in the First Temple period to the low status he held before and after the second fall of Jerusalem. Although conscious that in the Hebrew Bible God Himself was often compared to the "good shepherd," the rabbis now deprecated the shepherd not only as an illiterate person but also as a man untrustworthy to testify in court. Pigeon fanciers were likewise rejected as witnesses because they often engaged in aleatory games which were very popular throughout the Greco-Roman world.

In trade and industry the changes created by the new opportunities consisted in the main of the intensification of existing trends rather than of any change of direction or basic innovation. During most of the period the Jewish population remained cut off from the coastal area, the old Philistines and Phoenicians having been replaced by the Hellenistic city-states. Josephus' observation, "Ours is not a maritime country; neither commerce nor the intercourse which it promotes with the outside world has any attraction for us" (*Against Apion*, 1:60) was generally true, in spite of the Maccabeans' determined drive to the sea, which was blocked by the Roman conquest, and the presence of substantial Jewish minorities in Jaffa and Caesarea, the harbor newly founded by Herod. Yet some Jews engaged in maritime commerce, owned ships, and even participated in Mediterranean piracy. During the Jewish War of 66–70, the pirates actually threatened to reduce the supplies to the Roman legions by blockading the port of Jaffa. But the majority of Jewish merchants consisted of shopkeepers, agents, and other petty traders.

Industry, too, was conducted on a very small scale. As before, Jews often organized guilds of their own. This movement was stimulated by the growth of Greco-Roman guilds which were often endowed with special privileges by the administration. As before, some crafts were concentrated in special villages or had assigned to them special quarters in the cities. In the battle for Jerusalem, the Romans stormed "that district of the new town, where lay the wool shops, the braziers' smithies, and the clothes market" (Jos., Wars, 5:331). While the country was poor in metals, almost all of which had to be imported, it distinguished itself in the production of textiles, particularly linen. In the later price list of Emperor Diocletian the highest price was assigned to the linen produced at Beth-Shean (Scythopolis). The Dead Sea region supplied the country with a variety of minerals; it was renamed by the Romans the "Lacus Asphaltitis." Another series of industrial opportunities was created by the Temple. Because of its holiness and partial inaccessibility to laymen some tasks had to be performed by priests, so that we hear of 1,000 priests serving as skilled craftsmen at one time.

In general, the economic situation in the country might have been tolerable, were it not for the excessive fiscal exploitation by both Herodians and Romans and their corrupt bureaucracies. Ancient governments usually placed the main tax burdens on the farmers. As a major concession Caesar reduced the state's share in the farm produce from one-third to one-quarter. However, in actual practice the publicans, who farmed the taxes against lump sums, as a rule exacted more than their due. In Jewish Palestine, moreover, according to biblical law, the farmer was also expected to set aside a first tithe to the levite, a heave offering averaging 2% to the priests, and an additional second tithe to be consumed in two out of three years in Jerusalem, and to be distributed among the poor every third year. Through the observance of the year of fallowness the farmer not only lost the crop of the seventh year but often had no incentive to cultivate the soil in the preceding year. There also was much chicanery in the collection of tithes. The total number of priests and levites seems not to have exceeded 3% of the population – it may not have exceeded 1% of the world Jewish population – and hence the 12% of the produce should have provided sufficient income for all of them. Yet the powerful priestly families used their political power to the disadvantage of their fellow priests. Josephus states that the servants of High Priest Ananias (47–59 C.E.) "went to the threshing floors and took away tithes that belonged to the priests by violence, and did not refrain from beating such as would not give these tithes to them… so that priests that of old were wont to be supported with those tithes died for want of food" (Ant., 20:181).

As a result many farmers, crushed by these combined burdens and unable to resist the state-supported publicans, often disregarded the law of tithing altogether. In consequence, they appeared suspect to the orthodox leadership. Because of the prohibition on consuming untithed food there was practically no conviviality between observant Pharisees (or Sadducees) and the *am ha-areẓ* ("people of the land"), creating an almost unbridgeable class division (see Ber. 47b, and the exaggerations in Pes. 49b). Economically, too, the farmers were often unable to meet their obligations and lost their properties to better situated neighbors. Although Palestine never developed *latifundia* comparable with those existing in contemporary Italy, the number and size of "large estates" grew from generation to generation. The concomitant evils of absentee landlordism became even more manifest now, since after the Maccabean expansion the capital, Jerusalem, was located at a considerable distance from those estates.

The great difficulties confronting the small farmer and his ensuing migration to the cities resulted in a rapid increase of the urban proletariat. Although many small towns continued to engage in a mixed economy in which agriculture still played a predominant role, the larger cities, especially Jerusalem, developed into centers of trade, industry, and governmental bureaucracy. Into such cities streamed thousands of landless peasants seeking employment as unskilled laborers at below-subsistence wages. Understandably, the role of slavery constantly diminished. Not being a conquering country, Palestine had few prisoners of war, while purchasing slaves at the prevailing high prices was even less remunerative now that a vast army of underpaid free laborers was readily available. Hebrew slavery, in particular, hedged around by a variety of legal restrictions, to all intents and purposes disappeared completely. The rabbis phrased it metaphorically: "The Hebrew slave existed only when the Jubilee Year was in force" (Kid. 20a, 69a). Gentile slavery, too, played a small role in the agricultural and industrial production and was largely limited to domestic service.

Once again economic disarray combined with other socioreligious and political conflicts to bring about a social turmoil in the country which prepared the ground for its ultimate downfall. The great Roman-Jewish War of 66–70 was an almost unavoidable consequence. With it came the destruction of the Temple and the end of its hierarchy as well as of whatever residua of national independence had still remained after

6 C.E. when Judea was incorporated into the Roman Empire as a mere subdivision of the Syrian province. Thenceforth the center of gravity of the whole people shifted more and more to the Diaspora lands.

Talmudic Era

Before the fall of Jerusalem the majority of the Jewish people had long lived outside Palestine. Yet the course of Jewish history was largely determined by the Palestinian leadership and society. Only Egypt acted in a more independent way and Alexandria, its great emporium of trade and culture, served as Jerusalem's counterpart, as it was designated by the Palestinian leaders in their letter to Judah b. Tabbai (TJ, Ḥag. 2:2). Even Babylonia, upon which soon descended the mantle of leadership of the whole people, was rather inarticulate about its Jewish life until the third century C.E., when it came under the neo-Persian domination. Outside these two centers there is some information about the Jews of *Rome, owing to the preservation of numerous catacomb inscriptions, as well as occasional references, mostly in an anti-Jewish vein, in contemporary Latin letters. As to the multitude of Jews inhabiting Syria, Asia Minor, the Balkans, and North Africa west of Egypt, we are limited to stray flashes of light thrown by a few surviving inscriptions, the Pauline Epistles, and other sporadic sources. Before long, the distinction between Palestine Jewry and those of other countries became increasingly blurred as the former gradually lost their position as a majority of the Palestinian population.

Minority status understandably affected also the Jewish economic structure. Many Mediterranean communities may have owed their origin to Jewish prisoners of war taken by the Romans and sold into slavery. This was particularly true of the capital itself. To be sure, the Jews did not long remain in bondage. Because many Jewish slaves insisted upon observing the Sabbath rest commandment and abstained from consuming ritually forbidden food, they must have been uncomfortable workers and domestic servants. On the other hand, Jewish families and communities bent every effort to redeem captives, a commandment placed high in the hierarchy of values by the ancient rabbis. Roman law facilitated manumission inasmuch as freedmen retained certain connections with their patrons – whose family names they usually assumed – and performed important economic services for them. According to law, moreover, freedmen enjoyed a limited Roman citizenship, while their descendants were treated as full-fledged citizens with rights far superior to those of other citizens in the complex political structure of the empire before 312 C.E. Economically, however, such privileged citizens at first joined only the vast group of landless proletarians. Especially in Rome many of them joined the estimated 200,000 welfare clients (about a fourth of the population). In fact, Augustus singled out the Jewish welfare recipients for special favors. Taking into account their religious scruples, he allowed them to demand a double portion of the grain due them on Friday so that they would not have to violate the Sabbath. He also gave them the option of refusing oil, the other major article of consumption given away free, and to ask for money instead. In this way the Roman emperor decided a question still controversial among Palestinian rabbis as to whether "the oil of gentiles" was prohibited for Jewish consumption.

Nevertheless some former slaves and many free immigrants found ultimate employment in agriculture. Most of them had been engaged in farming at home and, wherever given the opportunity, they tilled the soil either as small farmers or as hired hands. In the major countries of their settlement, particularly Egypt and Babylonia, many of them cultivated vineyards, which they and the Greeks seem to have introduced into Egypt, and olive groves, in the planting of which their ancestors appear to have pioneered in Babylonia. They also helped produce dates and other fruits, as well as grain. Dates were particularly plentiful and inexpensive. The Palestinian rabbi Ulla upon arriving in Babylonia exclaimed: "A whole basket of dates for a *zuz* [28 cents] and yet the Babylonians do not study the Torah!" But after overindulging in dates, which caused him a stomach upset, he varied his epigram by saying: "A whole basket of poison for a *zuz*, and yet the Babylonians study the Torah!" (Pes. 88a). To facilitate their coreligionists' agricultural pursuits in competition with non-Jewish farmers, the Babylonian sages quite early suspended the obligation of Diaspora Jews to observe the years of fallowness and even the payment of levitical tithes. They included these requirements among "commandments dependent on the land" of Israel, that is, as being binding only for Palestine. Later on, under the pressure of Roman taxation and particularly after the reform of Diocletian (who instituted the collection in kind of the land tax from territorial groups (so-called *iugera*) regardless of the ethnic or religious differences among the owners of particular parcels of land) R. Yannai ordered even the Palestinian farmers to "go out and sow during the Sabbatical Year because of the tax" (Sanh. 26a).

Certain industrial activities, such as the brewing of beer, were also connected with *agriculture. Unlike Palestine, whose population preferred table wines, Babylonia had from ancient times consumed much beer, one variety being brewed from a mixture of barley and dates. No less than three distinguished Babylonian rabbis, *Huna, *Ḥisda, and *Papa, are recorded as having amassed considerable wealth from brewing. Jews were also active in many other crafts, and at times organized specific Jewish guilds. The crafts of tanners (see *Leather), collectors of dog dung, and copper miners were, however, considered so malodorous that the law permitted wives to sue for divorce on this ground. Nevertheless everybody knew that they were socially necessary and all that Judah ha-Nasi could say was that "the world cannot get along without either a perfumer or a tanner. Happy is he whose occupation is perfuming. Woe unto him who must earn a living as a tanner" (Kid. 4:14; 82a-b). Complaints of unethical practices by craftsmen were also heard; an example of such prejudices was the popular adage that "the best of surgeons belongs to Hell, and the most conscientious of butchers is a partner of Amalek." Judah bar Ilai, who reported this saying, also drew a line of demarcation between different types of transport workers. He contended that "most of the donkey drivers are evildoers, most of the camel drivers are honest, most of the sailors are pious." The latter's reputation may have been owing to the fact that *shipping had now become an even more important occupation than in earlier centuries. The Alexandrian Jewish guild of *navicularii* had become so important that even the hostile Roman administration had to extend it important privileges in 390 C.E. (*Codex Theodosianus*, 13, 5, 8).

Perhaps the most significant economic change, resulting from the transfer of the center of gravity to the dispersion, occurred in the much larger Jewish participation in commerce. It is a well-known sociological phenomenon that alien immigrants often turn to mercantile endeavors because they have no attachment to the foreign soil, shun isolated living among native majorities, are familiar with two or more languages and cultures, and hence are able the better to mediate between distant localities. If, as seems to have been the case, a large number of former Phoenicians and Carthaginians had joined the Jewish community via conversion, they must have brought some of their commercial skills and contacts into their new communities. Jewish slaves, if employed in their masters' businesses, must also have acquired certain aptitudes which they put to good use upon obtaining freedom. For all these reasons the number of Jewish traders, ranging from peddlers to big merchants, must have greatly increased. Yet their ratio in the Jewish population of the Diaspora need not have greatly exceeded the general mercantile ratios among the majority of peoples.

Even banking began to assume a certain role in Jewish economic life. True, would-be Jewish moneylenders faced the tremendous obstacles of the traditional Jewish anti-usury laws. In fact, some rabbis tried, on segregationist grounds, to forbid their coreligionists to lend money with or without interest even to gentiles, unless they found absolutely no other means of earning a living (BM 70b). However, there were always legal subterfuges which made loans profitable, such as high conventional fines for missing the repayment date, intervening in utilization of mortgaged properties, and the like (see, e.g., *The Tebtunis Papyri*, 3, 1902, ed. by B.P. Grenfell et al., 315ff., nos. 817–8; E.N. Adler, introd. to his ed. of *The Adler Papyri*, 1939, 5f.). In Alexandria Jewish banking may have played a certain role even in nurturing the anti-Jewish animus of the population. This is, at least, the interpretation given by some scholars to an Alexandrian merchant's warning to a friend "to beware of the Jews" recorded in a single papyrus dated 41 C.E. (*Aegyptische Urkunden aus… Berlin, Griechische Urkunden*, 2, no. 1079). But this explanation has been cogently disputed. There is no question, however, that Philo's relatives, Alexander and Demetrius, holding the high position of *alabarchs* (the meaning of this term is still controversial), could enter banking on a large scale. For example, Alexander extended to Agrippa I the substantial loan of 200,000 sesterces (about $30,000), the bulk of which he paid out to the Jewish king from his Italian branch office in Putoli-Dikaerchia (Jos., Ant., 18:160). But these were exceptions confirming the rule that the majority of Jews were still very poor and eking out a living by hard work in various occupations.

On the other hand, in the talmudic age Jewish slavery played even less of a role than before. Jewish masters, rigidly circumscribed by law, did not enjoy employing coreligionists as slaves. A popular adage had it that "he who buys a Hebrew slave acquires a master unto himself" (Kid. 20a). Certainly, as aids in production, even gentile slaves could not compete with the readily available free laborers. The Roman *colonate* with half-free sharecroppers tilling the soil for the landlords only developed toward the end of antiquity. Characteristically, the new Christian empire after Constantine I, which totally outlawed Jewish ownership of Christian slaves and encouraged pagan slaves to obtain freedom by conversion to Christianity, was prepared to tolerate the employment of Christian *coloni* by Jewish farmers (Gregory I, *Epistolae*, 4:21, 9:38). Even Jewish slave trading (see *Slavery and the *Slave Trade), which was to play a certain role in the early Middle Ages still, was quite insignificant.

In all these activities Jews depended even more than before on the general economic transformations which took place during the first centuries of the Christian era. The Roman Empire's semicapitalistic economy of the first two centuries increasingly gave way to a semifeudal system. The Sassanian Empire never reached the stage of relative economic freedom of the early Roman Empire. Jews, as well as their intellectual leaders, had to make constant adjustments to both economic systems through the adaptation of traditional laws by way of interpretation. As a consequence of this pliability, rabbinic legislation was to prove quite useful to the Jewish communities in their medieval pioneering. One result of the growing state controls in both empires was a certain regimentation in occupations and price structures, which also induced the Jews to organize their own zoning tariffs in transportation, supervision of weights and measures, and even setting maximum prices. Even the unfriendly Theodosius I decreed in 396 that "no one outside the Jewish faith should fix prices for Jews" – a principle upheld by his successors (*Codex Theodosianus*, 16, 8, 10). On the other hand, because of the ensuing commercial restrictions, customs barriers, and innumerable official fees, the exchanges between the provinces of the Roman Empire were now severely hampered. This reduction in imperial and international commerce greatly stimulated the local and regional autarky and helped to create in many parts of the empire highly diversified occupational structures, providing for most of the needs of the local populations. These developments account also for the greater diversity of occupations among Jews from the third century onward.

Economically perhaps even more important was the sharp decline in the class struggle within the Jewish community. Confronted with indiscriminate hostility on the part of many neighbors, Jews, whether rich or poor, employers or employees, had to close ranks. Since the hostile state legislation often interfered with their ability to earn a livelihood, many Jews now depended on the ramified Jewish welfare system. The economic effects of anti-Jewish riots also were quite significant. Although far from resembling medieval massacres, the occasional anti-Jewish outbreaks in the Middle Eastern cities seriously interfered with Jewish business activities. The first major anti-Jewish riot, staged by the Alexandrian mob with the support of the Roman governor Avilius Flaccus, is well described by Philo, an eyewitness. In his indictment of Flaccus, the philosopher wrote:

> But cessation of business was a worse evil than plundering. The provision merchants had lost their stores, and no one was allowed, either farmer or shipper or trader or artisan, to engage in his normal occupation. Thus poverty was brought about from both quarters, both from plunder, for in one day they were dispossessed and stripped of their property, and from inability to earn a living from their normal occupations (*In Flaccum*, 7:57).

Even in less stormy periods the Jewish masses required the intercession of their leaders to counteract inimical measures by unfriendly officials. Under these harsh conditions the old ritualistic animosities between the learned and the illiterate *am ha-areẓ* paled into insignificance. In any case, the main obstacle to rapprochement between the two classes was eliminated when the levitical tithes were discontinued in the Diaspora. Differences in the study of Torah were likewise toned down by the leading Palestinian rabbi Johanan's declaration (in the name of R. Simeon b. Yoḥai) that the biblical commandment, "This book of the law shall not depart out of thy mouth" (Josh. 1:8), could be fulfilled by the mere recitation of the *Shema* in the morning and evening. If, because of fear that the disclosure of this statement might discourage study, the rabbis forbade its being given wide currency; the fourth-century Babylonian Raba, however, insisted that it be divulged to the public (Men. 99b; see also the anecdote about Judah ha-Nasi's reconsideration in BB 8a). In short, even illiterate Jews could now fulfill their religious duties to the satisfaction of their more learned brethren.

Muslim Middle Ages

After the rise of Islam and its speedy expansion from southern France to India, Jewish economic life took a drastic turn. Together with the simultaneous developments in Christian Europe, *Islam's perennial antagonist, the new political and socioeconomic evolution for the first time converted a predominantly agricultural Jewish population into a people of merchants, moneylenders, and artisans. This lopsided economic stratification carried over into the modern period and was only slightly rectified in the emancipation era.

A major cause of this epochal change was the new treatment of Jews by the host nations as primarily an indispensable source of fiscal revenue for the respective governments and bureaucracies. In the declining Roman Empire and, still more, in Sassanian *Persia, Jews were often considered important objects of fiscal exploitation. This, however, was largely done by administrative chicanery within the generally oppressive taxation systems in the two empires. Jews and pagans in the Christian Roman Empire and Byzantium, and Jews and Christians in Zoroastrian *Iran may have been mere defenseless victims of arbitrary acts by rapacious officials; or, for special historic reasons, they may have been forced after the fall of Jerusalem to pay for a time a special tax, the so-called *fiscus judaicus* (in lieu of the old Jewish Temple tax); but they were not singled out, as a matter of principle, as a separate class of taxpayers on whose shoulders was supposed to rest the main burden of financially maintaining the existing governmental structures.

It was left to the founder of Islam to enunciate the broad general commandment: "Fight those who do not practice the religion of truth from among those to whom the Book has been brought, until they pay the tribute by their hands, and they be reduced low" (*Qur'an* 9:29). Later Muslim jurists and statesmen, constantly invoking this injunction of their messenger, interpreted it to mean that Jews, Christians, and for a time also Zoroastrians, as "people of the book," that is as adherents of scriptural religions, be tolerated in Muslim countries, provided they pay "tribute," that is taxes of all kinds, and are kept in a low social status without exercising any control over faithful Muslims. The latter provision (similar to Christian Rome's denial to Jews of the *honos militiae et administrationis*) was supposed to entrust all responsibility for the defense of the country and its administration to the Muslims, while delegating the entire fiscal burden and the task of keeping the economy alive to the infidel or "protected" peoples. Though *Muhammad himself left the details open, some extremists, such as Ash-Shafiʿī, founder of one of the four influential schools of Muslim jurisprudence, contended that a Muslim state could exact tribute to the extent of two-thirds of all his possessions from a Jewish or Christian subject.

The prevailing practice was to collect from these religious minorities a land tax of 25% of the crops and a poll tax from adult and able-bodied males. According to Abu Yusuf, Caliph Harun al-Rashid's chief fiscal expert, the Christians and Jews were divided into three income classes and paid 1 dinar, 2 dinars, and 4 dinars, respectively (*Kitab al-Kharaj*, 69ff. (Ar.), 187ff. (Fr.); a dinar was valued about $4 by its weight in gold, but had many times that value in purchasing power). Despite the great inflationary changes in the following three centuries, *Obadiah (Johannes), the Norman proselyte, recorded an increase by only half a dinar for each of these classes. He added that if a delinquent Jewish taxpayer died his body could not be buried unless his family or the Jewish community paid up all tax arrears (*Fragment*, ed. by A. Scheiber, in: KS, 30 (1954/55), 98). These basic imposts were augmented by a variety of local and individual taxes, enforced "gifts" and loans, and other services which made the life of the Jewish masses very difficult. But at least in periods of rapid economic progress, as in the ninth century, some Jews of the upper classes were able to amass sizable fortunes.

Methods of tax collection aggravated the generally arbitrary and unpredictable forms of fiscal exploitation. They were also designed to demonstrate the taxpayers' inferiority. A description preserved in an old papyrus gives an inkling of the deliberately humiliating ceremony accompanying the delivery by a representative Jew or Christian of a sum collected from his community. "Then the emir," we are told, "gives him a blow on the neck, and a guard, standing upright before the emir, drives him roughly away… The public is admitted to enjoy this show" (J. Karabacek, in *Mitteilungen aus der Sammlung der Papyrus Erzherzog Rainer*, 2–3, 1962, 178). Occasionally, following an old Babylonian custom, the tax receipt was stamped on the taxpayer's neck in a more or less indelible form. Needless to say, the Jews resented such excesses. However, they realized that their special taxation was the main justification for their being allowed to live in Muslim countries altogether. A Jewish family chronicle mentions that the prominent Baghdad Jewish banker, Netira, on being told by Caliph Al-Mutaḍid (c. 892) that the administration wished to eliminate all special Jewish taxes, allegedly dissuaded the ruler from such drastic action. He agreed that a reduction of the tax to its original size would be a blessing for his community, but he added, "Through the tax the Jew insures his existence. By eliminating it, you would give free rein to the populace to shed Jewish blood" (A. Harkavy, in: *Festschrift Berliner* (1903), 36 (Ar.), 39 (Heb.)). In the back of Netira's mind may also have loomed the danger that anyone of Al-Mutaḍid's successors might not only reinstate the taxes but also demand from the Jews the instantaneous repayment of all arrears thus accrued.

One effect of this discriminatory fiscal pressure was the constant diminution of the Jewish share in agriculture. Even after the extension of the land tax to the growing Muslim majority, many farmers were unable to meet their obligations to the state. Jewish farmers had the additional burden of the heavy poll tax paid in produce at a price arbitrarily set by the tax collector. The requirements of Jewish law, too, particularly the Sabbath rest commandment, which was much more stringent than the rest precepts of the Muslim Friday and Christian Sunday, generally made Jewish agricultural endeavor less competitive. There is evidence that in the days of Harun al-Rashid (766–809) the land flight of Palestinian farmers was so severe that the government was forced to appeal for their return under the promise of permanent tax abatement. The chances are that fewer Jews returned after having found shelter in one or another urban Jewish community. The growing disorders in the great caliphate from the tenth century on must also have induced many Jewish villagers, whose defenselessness invited attacks by marauders, to leave their landed properties – despite their great attachment to their ancestral soil attested by some geonic sources – and settle in a somewhat more secure urban Jewish quarter. Beginning in the 12th century the increasingly powerful trends toward semifeudalism throughout the Middle East further militated against Jewish farming as they did, on a larger scale, in contemporary Christian Europe.

On the other hand, new opportunities beckoned to Jews in the commercial area. The general upsurge of the Middle East economy during the first centuries of Muslim rule, the rise of great metropolitan areas such as *Baghdad and *Cairo, and, for a time, uniformity and stability of currency and relative security in travel and transportation, all stimulated the expansion of mercantile activities on the part of merchants of various nationalities. Commerce was generally held in higher esteem than agriculture among Middle Eastern Muslims, Christians, and Jews. Al-*Farabi voiced the prevailing notions that "villages are in the service of cities." While in the internal exchanges within the caliphate the Jews encountered severe competition on the part of several equally gifted mercantile groups, including Greeks, Armenians (increasingly muslimized), Syrians, and even Arabs – a popular Middle Eastern adage was to state later that one Greek could cheat two Jews, and one Armenian could cheat two Greeks – Jewish merchants had certain advantages in domestic and, even more, in international trade.

In the first place their competitors often came from regions of diverse legal systems. Most of the Christian merchants followed deep-rooted customs and traditions of the former provinces of the Byzantine Empire. The Muslims, too, were divided in their mercantile and other civil laws through the disparate teachings of their four major schools of Muslim jurisprudence and the great variations of local and regional customs. These factors were far less pronounced in the case of Jews. Although the Babylonian and Palestinian laws often differed in many significant details, a growing majority of Jews, settled in the great caliphate and adjoining countries, increasingly came under the sway of the Babylonian Talmud and its official interpretation by the geonic academies of Babylonia. At the same time the presence of Jewish communities throughout the far-flung empire and in many neighboring countries, both east and west, assured Jewish merchant travelers a brotherly reception and help in emergencies wherever they went. They could also readily establish branch offices, and engage a number of dependable local agents. Examples like those recorded in the documents preserved in the Cairo **Genizah* have shown the vast geographic extension of the mercantile dealings of certain Cairo-Fostat firms. In 1115–17 one Abu ʿImran gave a power of attorney to an agent surnamed "the candle maker" to look after all his business undertakings in Sicily, *Morocco, and other localities, as well as to manage his houses in Spain and Sicily. Another businessman, Ḥalfon b. Nethanel, after returning to *Aden in 1134 from a prolonged stay in India, soon thereafter traveled to Cairo. In the following year we find him in Morocco and *Spain before his return home (H. Hirschfeld, in: JQR, 16 (1925/26), 280f.; S.D. Goitein, *Speculum*, 29 (1954), 186f.)

An even greater advantage accrued to Jewish merchants in the burgeoning international trade with Western Europe. Although the Carolingian Empire and its successor states were still economically quite backward, their growing landed aristocracy furnished many customers for the luxury articles imported from Eastern lands. Here Jewish traders served as important mediators in a world divided between Islam and Christendom. Few Western merchants traveled to the Middle East, despite occasional Christian pilgrimages to the Holy Land, while even fewer Arabs dared to enter the hostile Christian countries for any length of time. Jews were tolerated under both civilizations. The legal advantages arising from the uniformity of their law were even greater in this area, since Christian and Muslim laws diverged very greatly and familiarity with each other's legal systems was extremely rare. The Jews also had a linguistic advantage in being able to communicate with one another, whereas few Christians knew Arabic and still fewer Arabs could converse in Latin or any local dialect. But a few polyglot individuals could occasionally serve as interpreters. We hear of a ninth-century Jewish linguist named Sallam, apparently a native of Spain or Khazaria, who in 845 reached the "wall of Gog and Magog" in China and who allegedly was able to converse in 30 languages. Multilingual documents were also found in the Cairo *Genizah*. When Charlemagne decided to send an embassy to Harun al-Rashid he had to add a Jewish interpreter, named Isaac, to the mission. It turned out that the chief noble envoys died on the journey and Isaac alone returned from Baghdad, bearing gifts from the Eastern potentate to the Western emperor. In general, however, Hebrew could easily serve as the regular medium of communication among Jewish merchants under both Islam and Christendom, and by the ninth century it had become a leading international language.

In his oft-cited *Kitab al-Masalik* ("Book of Routes"), written in 846 and revised some 40 years later, Ibn Khurdadhbah, who held in the caliphate an office approximating that of a modern postmaster general, described the routes taken by the Jewish *Radaniya (Radhanites; a word of uncertain etymology and meaning) from northern France and southern Morocco to India and China. He wrote:

> These merchants speak Arabic, Persian, Roman [Greek and Latin], the Frank, Spanish, and Slav languages. They journey from West to East, from East to West, partly on land, partly by sea. They transport from the West eunuchs, female slaves, boys, brocade, castor, marten and other furs, and swords. They take ship from Firanja [France] on the Western Sea, and make for Farama [Pelusium]… On their return from China they carry back musk, aloes, camphor, cinnamon, and other products of the Eastern countries… Some make sail for Constantinople to sell their goods to the Romans; others go to the palace of the King of Franks to place their goods… These different journeys can also be made by land (pp. 153ff.; E.N. Adler, *Jewish Travellers*, 1966, p. 2).

There is some reason to believe that Western Jewish merchants quite early reached even Korea and Japan.

Ibn Khurdadhbah's statement helped support what soon became a Christian ecclesiastical myth, adopted by some modern historians, about an extensive Jewish slave trade in the Middle Ages. Medieval and modern controversialists from St. Agobard, archbishop of Lyons, onward, often pointed a finger at the medieval Jews as the main slave traders who transported Christian slaves, especially from Slavonic countries, to the ever more manpower-hungry Middle East and Muslim Spain. They readily overlooked the staggering legal barriers erected against that trade by both Jewish and gentile laws. Islam and Christendom severely outlawed the possession by Jews of Muslim or Christian slaves respectively. On its part, the Talmud had long demanded that a slave acquired by a Jewish master should be circumcised, made to observe the seven Noachide commandments, and live an essentially Jewish life. If a slave refused to be converted within 12 months, he was to be freed or sold to a gentile master. Female slavery, mainly intended to serve sexual purposes, was made difficult for Jewish slaveholders by the strict prohibition on sexual relations with slave girls. Typical of the provisions of Jewish law was the following statement by the ninth-century Babylonian teacher Natronai Gaon: "If a son of Israel is caught with his slave… she is to be removed from him, sold, and the purchase price distributed among Israel's poor. We also flog him, shave his hair, and excommunicate him for 30 days" (*Sha'arei Ẓedek*, fol. 25a, attributed to Amram Gaon). The trade in eunuchs, so much in demand for Oriental harems, depended on whether the Jewish slave trader could acquire castrated males. Otherwise talmudic law had long included castration among the physical mutilations which entitled the slave to seek immediate release. Responsibility for a slave's hidden blemishes, both mental and physical, was greatly delimited by talmudic law and hence anyone acquiring a slave ran considerable risks. If some Jews, defying these legal difficulties, were attracted to this extremely lucrative commercial branch, they must have constituted but a minority among the international slave traders and doubtless played an even smaller role in the various domestic slave markets throughout the world of Islam. It is not surprising, therefore, to find that in the vast, populous, and affluent North African lands, hardly any reference to Jewish slave traders appears in the extant Muslim and Jewish sources of the time.

Under the rule of medieval Islam Jews also entered the money trade in all its ramifications in an important way. Some of them played a considerable role in the very *minting of coins. Under Caliph Abd al-Malik (695–96), for example, one Sumeir helped set up a very important monetary reform which so impressed a Jewish homilist that he placed it among the signs of the approaching Messiah (PDR, XXIX, ed. by Michael Higger, in: *Horeb*, 10 (1948) 193f.; in G. Friedlander's English trans., p. 221). Other Jewish minters are recorded in various Muslim and Christian countries, though not in Byzantium where minting was an effective state monopoly. Some of the first coins issued by Poland in the 11th and 12th centuries bore inscriptions in the Hebrew alphabet, probably because the minter was most familiar with that script. Money changing likewise became a very widespread and profitable trade, particularly after the dissolution of the caliphate when diverse coins from various lands began appearing in all large mercantile centers. Considerable expertise was required in order to recognize defects, whether inflicted by coin clippers or by the admixture of undue amounts of alloy. Here, too, internationally experienced Jewish dealers were often in a favored position. Deposit banking also assumed a major economic role. Unlike the ancient temples and medieval churches, neither mosques nor synagogues ever served as important depositories of funds. Because of the relative absence of expulsions and large-scale massacres of Jews in Muslim countries, Jewish bankers were considered a fairly secure outlet for surplus funds which, if profitably invested, could yield substantial profits to both depositors and depositaries. To be sure, in unstable periods an arbitrary official (for instance, Al-Baridi, governor of Al-Aḥwaz) could seize the bankers' possessions, including deposits held by them for other accounts, without compensation. But the depositors running afoul a dignitary's personal greed or whim found keeping their funds at home no less risky. In general, however, the frequency and usefulness of the new methods were so great that the rabbis had to relax some ancient restrictions and alter the areas of responsibility on the part of the depositaries in order to facilitate their operations.

Similarly, the transfer of large amounts from one province to another in the vast empire and beyond its boundaries became the more imperative as carrying cash to a distant locality by land or sea became increasingly hazardous. Gangs of robbers on land were far exceeded in number and efficiency by both Mediterranean and Indian Ocean pirates. The North African coast and the extended coastline of the Arabian Peninsula served as particularly useful hideouts for corsairs. If the Talmud had objected to the method of transferring money through a deed called *dioqni* (derived from sign), and some medieval rabbis still opposed the bearer instrument called *suftaja* in Arabic (which Jews apparently helped develop jointly with the Arabs), the economic realities were such that the *geonim* had to yield and recognize its employment as a legitimate mercantile usage, "lest the commercial transactions of the people be nullified" (*Teshuvot ha-Ge'onim*, 1887, ed. by A.E. Harkavy, nos. 199, 423, 467). Ultimately, Samuel b. Hophni, head of the academy of Sura, felt impelled to write a special legal monograph on "Letters of Authorization" (*Sefer ha-Harsha'ot*). Nor did the *Kairouan scholar Nissim b. Jacob hesitate to use a *suftaja* in forwarding a gift for the support of the Babylonian academies.

Even more important, of course, was the large-scale Jewish participation in the increasingly vital credit system. Although all three major religions tried to outlaw usury – the Muslim *riba* being even more broadly defined than the Christian *usura* or the Jewish *ribbit* – the economic needs of credit became overwhelming. Since most loans were now extended not to impoverished farmers but rather to businessmen or government officials for use in trade or public administration, the outlawry of any kind of increment over the amounts lent lost its moral justification. Jews were in a strategic position to overcome the legal obstacles, as they were the relatively smallest group in the population and, even if observing the prohibition of charging interest to coreligionists, could engage in profitable *moneylending with the large majority of borrowers of other denominations. All sorts of legal evasions, moreover, were conceived by jurists of all groups, although this system was never quite so refined as it was to become in medieval Europe. One of the simplest expedients appeared to be a fictitious sale of income-producing property with the right of repurchase which gave the lender the opportunity of collecting the revenue of that property during the interim. The widespread *commenda* contract, in which the investor appeared as a partner in the enterprise, likewise offered him the opportunity of exacting the pledge that he would participate in the ultimate sale with a specified profit regardless of possible losses. It was this form of purported silent partnership with a guaranteed revenue which was most widely used to secure for the lender an income agreed upon in advance. Until today, some pious Jews still enter on a bond of indebtedness the words *al ẓad hetter iska* (often in abbreviated form, see *Usury) to indicate their mental reservation against the transgression of the biblical commandment.

During periods of quiet, profits derived from banking could be enormous. As a result there emerged a number of wealthy Jewish bankers, especially in the metropolitan areas of Baghdad, Cairo, *Alexandria, Kairouan, *Fez, and *Córdoba. These banking firms did not limit their activities to loans but usually engaged in related businesses such as trade in jewelry and precious metals, investment in real estate, and the like. They often had at their disposal large funds deposited with them by high government officials secreting away illicit income from briberies. Ibn al-Furat, a leading vizier of early tenth-century Baghdad, admitted having had large deposits with the two Jewish bankers Aaron b. Amram and Joseph b. Phinehas. In return, the bankers had to perform services for these officials which went much beyond ordinary business risks. For example, ʿAli ibn ʿIsa, Ibn al-Furat's more virtuous rival, did not hesitate to force his Jewish banker to advance him monthly the equivalent of $40,000 in gold for the wages of the imperial infantry. This loan was to be covered by the banker's revenue from tax farming in the province of Al-Aḥwaz. Another Jewish tax farmer, Ibn ʿAllan al-Yahudi of Baṣra, who had lent both the sultan and the famous Persian statesman Nizam al-Mulk the equivalent of $100,000, was assassinated in 1079. Sometimes the whole Jewish community was held responsible for a banker's refusal to lend money to a dignitary. In one such case, in 996, the mob attacked the entire Jewish quarter.

Less dramatic, but equally significant, was the expansion of Jewish activities in the traditional fields of handicrafts and professions. Needless to say, these occupations offered vast opportunities to many more Jews than did commerce and banking. Regrettably no exact occupational statistics can be offered, but a few extant lists show that the proportion of craftsmen considerably exceeded that of merchants, even including the petty shopkeepers and peddlers. Three such *genizah* lists show percentages ranging from 38.4 to 52.1 for industrial occupations, compared with 17.3 to 37.5 for commerce and banking. According to Al-Jaḥiẓ, Jews predominated in the industries of dyeing and tanning in Egypt, Syria, and Babylonia and formed the majority among the Persian and Babylonian barbers, cobblers, and butchers. Another contemporary Arab observer, Muqaddasi, contended that "for the most part the assayers of corn, dyers, bankers, and tanners are Jews; while it is usual for physicians and scribes to be Christian" (J. Finkel, ed., in: *Journal of the American Oriental Society*, 47, 311–34; Muqaddasi, *K. Aḥsam at-taqasim*, p. 183; in Le Strange's English trans. in his *Description of Syria*, p. 77). In fact no less than 265 different crafts are mentioned in the *genizah* records, showing both the extensive Jewish participation in industrial occupations and their great specialization. Gradually Jews also penetrated the medical profession, some of them achieving considerable fame as medical theorists and writers (Asaph, Israeli, *Maimonides, and others). One must add, of course, a considerable number of Jews who were employed by their own communities as rabbis, teachers, cantors, *shoḥatim*, sextons, and in administrative capacities, forming a sort of Jewish civil service.

This occupational diversification was greatly facilitated by the openness of Muslim society and the relatively large measure of economic equality for subjects of all faiths. The latter included much freedom of movement, except in Egypt where the traditional state-capitalistic order presupposed governmental controls over the influx of foreigners and the exit of natives. Only Egypt enacted strict regulations concerning passports. In industry, too, there was much freedom of choice. Even where industrial *guilds existed, they were neither so monopolistic nor so discriminatory in the admission of Jewish members as their counterparts in Europe. It was also possible for the autonomous Jewish communal organs to use considerable discretion in enforcing their own price controls whenever needed, supervising weights and measures, and generally policing the markets in the Jewish quarters.

It was unfortunate for the Jews and non-Jews alike that this flourishing commercial-industrial civilization sharply declined after the tenth century as a result of the caliphate's dissolution and its constant foreign and civil wars. By the time of the 13th-century *Mongolian invasions much of the grandeur of that great civilization had given way to a slow process of decay. Coming on top of the Christian *Crusades, these invasions dealt further severe blows to both the international and local commerce of the eastern lands. While Christian Europe was marching ahead on the road toward a flourishing economic structure, the eastern lands began to stagnate. Among the numerous departures were Jews, fleeing from foreign invaders as well as domestic enemies and seeking whatever uncertain shelter they could secure in Western lands. The center of world commerce now began shifting westward, with the various Italian merchant republics taking over the offensive, establishing colonies in the eastern Mediterranean and later in the Indian Ocean, and ultimately displacing the East even in the Levantine trade.

Medieval Christendom

At first, to be sure, far fewer Jews lived under Christendom. Only from the 13th century on, as a result of the general upsurge of the Western nations, the Spanish reconquest, and the simultaneous sharp decline of the Eastern countries, did the center of gravity of the Jewish people slowly move to the European area. Here the far better accumulation and preservation of archival materials and the concerted efforts of generations of scholars have yielded much reliable and detailed information about general and Jewish economic developments. Jewish documents, too, such as the "starrs" of England, the records of the Laurenz parish in Cologne, the vast collection of Arabic and Hebrew documents in Toledo and other parts of Spain, the numerous notarial records, and even occasional private archives of Jewish firms, have made the study of economic Jewish history much more reliable and concrete.

Clearly, the existing trends toward the alienation of Jews from agriculture were much stronger in Europe than in the Muslim Middle East and North Africa. In certain areas the insecurity of Jewish life and the ever-present danger of massacres, expulsions, and forced conversions made landholdings far less attractive for Jews. Whenever a landowner had to depart suddenly or was otherwise obliged to dispose of his property within a very short time, forced liquidation, if not total confiscation, resulted in enormous losses. For example, two years after the expulsion of Jews from France in 1306 a Christian landlord was able to acquire 50 Jewish houses in the old and venerable community of Narbonne for the mere pittance of 3,957 livres. This transaction so aroused the ire of both the viscount and the archbishop, each of whom had special feudal rights in the city, that, to appease them, the purchaser gave an additional 5,000 livres, two houses, and a plot of land to the viscount and an unspecified, but undoubtedly large, amount to the archbishop (S. Luce, REJ, 2 (1881). Of course, the Jewish exiles received nothing. Similarly, according to the court historian Andrés Bernáldez, after the promulgation of the Spanish decree of expulsion in March 1492, anyone could acquire a Jewish vineyard for a piece of cloth or linen (*Historia de los Reyes Católicos* (1870), 338f.). In addition to such countrywide expulsions, there were local and regional forced exiles of varying frequency. For instance, the city of *Speyer, to which Jews had originally been admitted in 1084 by Bishop Ruediger-Huozmann "in order to enhance the city's honor," subsequently often ousted them on short notice. To mention only the events of the 15th century: Jews were expelled from Speyer in 1405, readmitted in 1421, banished again in 1430, and allowed to return in 1434, to be once more evicted a year later. Yet they were there again in 1465. They became objects of renewed Episcopal legislation in 1468–72.

The first major blow of this kind came to the Jews of Byzantium as a result of Emperor *Heraclius' decree of 632 forcing all Jews to become Christians. Although incompletely carried out even in the areas which remained Byzantine after the expansion of Islam soon after, such Byzantine decrees were repeated in the following three centuries. It was truly amazing, therefore, that during his visit to the Balkans in the 1160s Benjamin of Tudela found an entire Jewish community of 200 families in the village of Crissa who "sow and reap on their own land" (Travels, pp. 12 (Heb.), 10 (Eng.)). Similar forced conversions occurred in Visigothic Spain, Merovingian Gaul, and Langobard Italy in 613–61, and were replaced in Spain by many sharply discriminatory laws against the Jews who survived or were allowed to return before the Muslim conquest of 711–2. To all intents and purposes these hostile actions put an end to all forms of organized Jewish life there and only a small Jewish remnant remained under Catholic domination in central and southern Italy. Even if not all the Jews left these countries, their ownership and cultivation of land must have practically ceased, while returning Jews may have had little incentive or opportunity to acquire new agricultural property. Similar effects were later produced by the successive expulsions of Jews from royal France, England, Spain, Portugal, various Italian states, and other parts of Christian Europe between 1182 or 1290 and 1600.

An equally important factor was the growth of European feudalism. Land now not only became the source of economic power but also the mainstay of political and military force. He who owned land exercised dominion over a multitude of peasants whether they tilled the soil as half-free sharecroppers so long as the Roman *colonate* persisted, or as villeins furnishing parts of their produce and corvée labor to their masters. While since Pope Gregory the Great the Church had allowed Jews to maintain Christian *coloni* on their land, it became increasingly awkward for Jews to be either vassals taking oaths of fealty to Christian lords, or seigneurs administering such oaths to Christian barons. Remarkably, this system persisted in Provence up to the 12th century and beyond. In Angevin England, kings also protected Jewish feudal holdings through decrees such as that issued by Richard the Lion Heart in 1190 in favor of one Isaac, son of R. Joce, and his sons or, more broadly, through the generic decree by John Lackland in 1201. It was in the royal interest to protect the Jewish holding of a "baronial state, claiming for themselves wardships, escheats, and advowsons," as did Henry III. Even the antagonistic Edward I had to allow Jews to acquire feudal possessions if their noble owners defaulted on the payment of their debts. But the antagonisms aroused in such cases contributed to the baronial revolt against the crown in 1264–66. The barons argued that the kings selfishly promoted feudal acquisitions by Jews because through the royal overlordship over Jews noble property was thus indirectly transferred to the royal domain. Ultimately, beginning in 1269, the kings themselves had to oblige Jewish creditors to dispose of such foreclosed estates to Christian owners within a year. In short, feudalism and Jewish landholdings appeared incompatible in the long run and it was the weaker Jewish side which had to yield ground.

On the other hand, unlike under Islam, Jewish landowners were not subjected to a special land tax. "In our entire realm," declared *Meir b. Baruch of Rothenburg, "[Jews] pay not tax on land. Sometimes capitalists have tried to change this system, but when the matter was brought before us, we disallowed it" (Responsa (Prague, 1607), 50c no. 452). In other areas, however, the general land taxes became so burdensome that the Barcelona rabbi Solomon b. Abraham *Adret complained that "frequently the very best fields yield insufficient harvests to pay the royal taxes" (Responsa, 3 (Leghorn, 1778), no. 148). More universal and irksome was the ecclesiastical drive to force the Jews to pay tithes on property they acquired from Christian owners, lest the parish priests or monasteries lose the income from such lands. Finally, the Fourth Lateran *Council of 1215 insisted that these contributions be universally collected from Jews, riding roughshod over the religious scruples of some Jewish pietists who saw in such payments subsidies for the erection of churches and monasteries devoted to the worship of another faith.

Employment of Christian agricultural workers by Jews became another important issue, anti-Jewish agitators of all kinds clamoring that Jews be forced to cultivate the land with their own hands. The nobles, on the other hand, even in Mediterranean countries, often tried to eliminate Jewish landholdings altogether. Such a proposal was advanced, for instance, by the Castilian Cortes in 1329. These opponents readily overlooked the early medieval Jewish pioneering contributions to European agriculture. Coming from the more advanced Eastern countries, Jewish groups settling in the West are often still remembered in such names as Terra Hebraeaorum, Judendorf, Żydaczów, and the like. Even a Spanish name like Aliud is probably a derivative of *Al-Yahud*. As late as 1138 three Jews of Arles bought from Abbot Pontius of Montmajour the entire output of *kermes* of the district of Miramar, thus stimulating the farmers to produce that dyestuff. They were also very active in introducing the silkworm into Sicily and other Mediterranean countries.

Yet it was only the opposition of the crown which prevented general prohibitions of Jewish land ownership. Wherever such were enacted, they usually bore a local character and even these were not always fully implemented. Even in fervently anti-Jewish Germany after the *Black Death of 1348–49, the assertion of the author of the *Rechtsbuch nach Distinctionen* (iii. 17, 1) that "Jews are not allowed to own real property in this country" was a clear exaggeration. In the Mediterranean lands, especially, Jews continued to own and cultivate landed properties; this they did to the very end of their sojourn in Spain, Portugal, Provence, Sicily, and Naples. Their endeavors were particularly flourishing in those areas where extensive orchards and vineyards, located in the neighborhood of towns, enabled them to combine fruit production with other occupations. Queen Maria of Aragon was not wrong when in 1436 she upheld the right of *Huesca Jewry to dispose of the grain and wines produced on its property, "since the Jews of the said city for the most part live as workers and cultivators of fields and vineyards and derive a living from the latter's produce" (Baer, Urkunden, 1 (1929), pt. 1, 858f. no. 535). The city council of Haro (Faro), close to the Navarrese border, complained that Jewish and Muslim landowners in the district had in 1453 signed a covenant not to sell any land to Christians. In the council's opinion this created a threat that before long the entire land of the area would fall into the hands of infidels (N. Hergueta, in: *Boletin de la Real Academía de Historia*, 26, 467ff.). Less exaggeratedly, a modern scholar of the rank of F. de Bofarull y Sans claimed (in his *Los Judíos en el territorio de Barcelona*) that between the 10th and 12th centuries one-third of all the land around Barcelona was owned by Jews. In short, Jewish agriculture never completely disappeared from the European scene and the alleged complete outlawry of Jewish landholdings throughout medieval Europe is another example of a widely accepted historical myth.

Jewish land ownership was particularly frequent in urban settlements, particularly in Jewish quarters. Understandably, wherever the Jewish population grew rapidly and its quarter could not enlarge its area, the real estate owned by a family was often subdivided into small parcels by the numerous progeny. In the Laurenz parish of Cologne a Jewish couple sold in 1322 a one-eighth and one-96th portion of "a large house" in which two other coreligionists owned another quarter and one-16th part. Thirteen years later another Jewish couple acquired a share of one-third and one-60th minus one-700th of a house from a Christian neighbor. For the most part, however, in Europe north of the Alps and the Loire Jews were rarely allowed to live long enough to create many such subdivisions over several generations.

In Europe, too, Jewish industrial occupations were far more significant. In this area early Jewish immigrants from the Middle East and North Africa, often in possession of an advanced technology, could perform many pioneering services. In 1147 Roger II of Naples attacked Byzantine Thebes, a major center of the silk industry, and evacuated "all" Jews to southern Italy, where they helped establish a flourishing silk industry. Another trade in which Jews played a considerable role since ancient times was that of dyeing. When Benjamin of Tudela arrived in Brindisi he found there ten Jewish dyers. A particular "Jewish" dye existed in the Neapolitan kingdom. Weaving, too, had long been a prominent Jewish craft. It was partly stimulated by the biblical prohibition on **sha'atnez* (mixing wool and linen) which, carried down through the ages, became an important factor in preserving Jewish tailoring and other branches of the clothing industry in many lands. Another religiously stimulated industrial craft was that of slaughtering animals according to the Jewish ritual. Even where, as in most German areas, the Christian guilds tried to suppress Jewish competition, they had to make some exceptions in favor of Jewish butchers and tailors who were permitted to produce such ritually restricted goods for the Jewish customers. Many Jewish crafts were stimulated by Jewish pawnbroking. Since most pledges consisted of articles of clothing, furniture, or jewelry which, upon the debtor's default, became the property of the pawnbroker, it was natural for him to try to refurbish the pawns for sale to the public at a higher price.

In fact, many restrictive ordinances inspired by Christian merchants made a special allowance for Jewish trade in used articles (see *Secondhand Goods). For instance, in Rome during the Counter-Reformation Jews performed a major service by acquiring secondhand clothing from the luxury-loving high clergy and nobility for resale to the masses of the population. Indirectly, such business furnished employment also to tailors, dyers, and other craftsmen.

Beyond these specially Jewish areas there were also Jewish craftsmen in almost all domains of industry, although specialization here was far less developed than in the contemporary Islamic world. In Cologne, for example, where the guilds succeeded in ultimately barring Jews from almost all industrial occupations, they still allowed them to become glaziers, probably because no other qualified personnel was available. This exception was reminiscent of the Greek glassblowers in seventh-century France who claimed to be able to produce glass as well as the Jews did. The few extant Spanish occupational statistics are very enlightening indeed. For example, the 20 Jewish families in the small town of Valdeolivas near Cuenca embraced, in 1388, six shoemakers, three tailors, one weaver, one smith, and one itinerant artisan. Some of the wealthiest of the 168 Jewish taxpayers in Talavera de la Reina shortly before the expulsion in 1492 consisted of 13 basketmakers and three goldsmiths. Jewish cobblers, tailors, blacksmiths, and harness makers also seem to have made a reasonable living there. True, in 1412–13 Castile and Aragon, in sharply anti-Jewish decrees, forbade Jews to serve as veterinarians, ironmongers, shoemakers, tailors, barbers, hosiers, butchers, furriers, rag pickers, or rag dealers for Christians. Yet the very man who inspired that legislation, Anti-Pope Benedict XIII, himself employed a Jewish bookbinder, two Hebrew scribes, and even a Jewish seamstress-laundress for his ecclesiastical vestments. A Roman list of 1527 recorded the presence of 1,738 Jews in a population of 55,035 in the city. The more than 80 Jewish families whose occupations were recorded included about 40 Jewish tailors and a substantial number of other craftsmen. Twelve years earlier Cardinal Giulio de' Medici had urged his cousin Lorenzo to attract some of the Jewish manufacturers of saltpeter from Rome to Florence or Pisa, since "such opportunities do not occur every day." Although similar detailed data are not readily available elsewhere, it appears that wherever Jews lived in larger numbers their majority derived a livelihood from one or another craft.

In some Spanish cities there were enough Jewish craftsmen to form independent guilds. The statutes of the Jewish cobblers' guild in *Saragossa, approved by Pedro IV in 1336, offer mute testimony to the continuity of Jewish craftsmanship from the ancient associations of Jewish master artisans. When the Spanish decree of expulsion was extended to Sicily on June 18, 1492, the Christian leaders of Palermo and other cities protested that "in this realm almost all the artisans are Jews. If all of them will suddenly depart there will be a shortage of many commodities, for the Christians are accustomed to receive from them many mechanical objects, particularly iron works needed both for the shoeing of animals and for cultivating the soil; also the necessary supplies for ships, galleys, and other maritime vessels." In the north, of course, there was no opportunity for Jews to organize guilds of their own, whereas the Christian guilds in their constant drive for monopolistic control of their trades and political power in their municipalities not only sought to suppress Jewish competition but, if possible, to get rid of the Jews completely.

At the same time Jewish commercial activities played an ever-increasing role in Western Europe. There are relatively few records of Jewish *peddlers. Apart from the insecurity of roads in most European countries, aggravated by the hostility toward Jews on the part of many peasants and townsfolk – even hostile legislators often freed Jews from wearing their badges on journeys for this reason – the majority of the villeins had little cash available to purchase goods from itinerant merchants. Most of their needs were provided for by their own agricultural production and the home work of their wives and daughters in spinning, weaving, and tailoring. With the growth of the urban centers, Jewish shopkeepers increased in number wherever Jews were tolerated at all. Of course, there was a constant struggle with the growing burghers' class which wanted to monopolize whatever trade was available locally or regionally. In many cities these commercial rivals sooner or later succeeded in ousting Jews completely and even in obtaining from the royal power, whose self-interest dictated protection of Jewish tradesmen, special privileges *de non tolerandis Judaeis*. In England, for instance, where Henry III's exorbitant fiscal exploitation depended on the presence of a prosperous Jewry, there was a wave of such enactments in favor of many cities in the 1230s and 1240s. In many continental localities the law restricted Jewish shopkeeping to the Jewish quarter and often forced the Jewish merchants to abstain from displaying their wares on Sundays and Christian holidays – a major burden indeed for observant Jewish shopkeepers who kept their stores closed on the Sabbath and Jewish festivals. Nevertheless economic necessity forced Jews to use all means at their disposal to earn a living from merchandising.

Jewish international trade, which in the Carolingian age had been a major incentive for Christian regimes to invite Jewish settlers, later suffered greatly from the competition of the Italian merchant republics, the prevalence of Mediterranean piracy, highway robbery on land routes, discriminatory tolls at the multitude of feudal boundaries, and special Jewish taxation. Nevertheless, many rulers still tried to maintain freedom of movement and trading for their Jewish "serfs." The major imperial privileges for German Jewry often repeated, with minor variations, the provision in the 1090 privilege for the Jews of Speyer given by Emperor Henry IV: that they "should have the freedom to trade their goods in just exchange with any persons, and that they may freely and peacefully travel within the confines of Our kingdom, exercise their commerce and trade, buy and sell, and no one shall exact from them any toll or impost, public or private" (Aronius, Regesten, 71ff., no. 170, etc.). Similar sweeping provisions were enacted by John of England in 1201 and other monarchs (J.M. Rigg, *Select Pleas*, 2). If in practice Jews often suffered from attacks and despoliation by local barons and arbitrary officials, this was the effect of the poorly organized governmental systems in most European countries rather than of the rulers' intent. In this respect Jews had plenty of fellow sufferers among their gentile competitors.

International fairs in particular (see *Markets and Fairs) offered many opportunities for Jewish traders to profitably exchange goods with other merchants, Jewish and non-Jewish. Even in the less hospitable northern lands they played a considerable role in the famous Champagne fairs and those of Cologne. When in the last three medieval centuries most of these fairs lost their international character and catered more to regional needs, Jews still appeared as welcome visitors even in areas from which they were generally barred. They enjoyed the special protective devices developed by many communities seeking to attract foreign trade without discriminating among the visitors according to their faith or country of origin. One important concession generally granted at fairs was the suspension of the group responsibility of merchants of the same origin for each other's misdeeds or insolvency. Such mutual responsibility affected non-Jewish burghers as well as Jews, but the process of generalization in blaming all Jews for the misconduct of any coreligionist was generally much more prevalent. Even in Mediterranean commerce, where group responsibility was less strongly stressed, Pedro III of Aragon felt obliged to intervene in 1280 on behalf of many Jewish Levant traders, when one of their coreligionists, Isaac Cap of Barcelona, had been accused of unethical business dealings in the Middle East. The main argument advanced by the king in his epistle addressed to the Templars and Hospitalers in Jerusalem, the consuls of Pisa and Venice, and the representative of the king of Cyprus was not that other Jews should not be held responsible for Cap's actions, but that Cap had long since left Aragon. It so happened that in time Cap was able to return to Barcelona, settle his debts, and again become an honored member of his community.

Another major concession to Jewish traders was the acceptance by many regimes of the prevailing Jewish practice in respect to the so-called law of concealment. In the talmudic age the rabbis had already come to the conclusion that a merchant who had unwittingly acquired some stolen object was not to suffer complete loss in returning that object to its legitimate owner. They provided, "for the benefit of the market," that if the acquisition was proved to have been made in good faith, the owner had to compensate the merchant to the full amount of his investment. The more primitive Teuton laws, which dominated many European legislative systems, had made no such provisions in favor of the bona fide merchant. Jews, especially in areas where they were largely restricted to dealing in secondhand merchandise or lending on used pledges, could not carefully investigate the title of each seller or borrower. At times fraudulent borrowers might actually scheme to offer, through impecunious intermediaries, pledges for loans and subsequently as owners reclaim these objects without paying their debts. There were antecedents for such protection of legitimate merchants in other laws. Yet Jewish traders were in the vanguard of those clamoring for redress. Ultimately, this provision, which German antisemites often denounced as a *Hehlerecht* (privilege for "fences"), became a widely accepted principle in most modern mercantile laws.

Despite these and other legal safeguards, the general insecurity of Jewish life affected the Jewish merchants as well. A remarkable illustration is offered by the business ledgers kept during the years 1300–18 by the important mercantile firm of Héliot (Elijah) of Vesoul in Franche-Comté. These extant ledgers reveal both the firm's effective method of bookkeeping and its far-flung business interests. Principally a banking establishment endowed with vast resources, it also bought and sold merchandise of all kinds either through *commenda* agreements with Christian or Jewish traders, or by direct shipment of its own. It dealt in cloth, linen, and wine produced in its own vineyards. Héliot also served as a tax collector for the government. Characteristically, the ledgers also include entries relating to horses and carriages used by members of the firm for business travel as far as Germany and Flanders. Héliot was also very precise in delivering the ecclesiastical tithes to the churches, notwithstanding scruples he may have had in thus contributing to the upkeep of non-Jewish religious institutions. His career was cut short, however, when in 1322 Philip the Tall extended his decree of expulsion of the Jews from France to Burgundy as well. Two years later Héliot's house was given away to a lady-in-waiting of the queen.

In spite of all these difficulties Jewish commerce, particularly in the more friendly Mediterranean lands, frequently flourished and became another mainstay of the Jewish economy. In the 12th century a German rabbi, Eliezer b. Nathan, could assert that "nowadays we are living on commerce only" (*Sefer Even ha-Ezer* (Prague, 1610), 53d no. 295).

Commerce included money trade in its various ramifications, particularly moneylending. Because of their general insecurity and frequently enforced mobility, Jews under Christendom were not good risks for deposits. Unlike the Jews under Islam, they could not compete with the stability of deposits in churches or such major banks as the Banco di San Giorgio in 12th-century Genoa. Their rabbis, therefore, fell back on the talmudic regulation that treasures should be buried in the soil, which was not always feasible in the crowded Jewish quarters. Burying them out of town subjected the owner to the risk of some stranger accidentally discovering the place of burial and appropriating the treasure trove. Moreover, even accumulations of savings by Jewish communal bodies were subject to seizure by unfriendly rulers. In 1336 King John of Bohemia not only confiscated the communal "treasure trove" kept in the old synagogue of Prague but also fined the Bohemian elders for concealing its presence from him. Minting could occasionally help support a Jewish individual, especially in backward areas. But generally the manufacture of coins was a governmental enterprise, even if exercised by some local baron or city council (there were, indeed, many kinds of coins and even scrip circulated by such local rulers). On the other hand, coin clipping, whether for the purpose of reminting or for that of using the gold or silver in the fabrication of some industrial objects, was considered a major crime if indulged in by private individuals, although it was accepted as a perfectly legitimate performance on the part of governments. One such accusation of coin clipping, real or alleged, supposedly resulted in 1278–79 in the execution of 293 English Jews and was partially responsible for the decree of expulsion of 1290 (H.G. Richardson, *English Jewry*, 218ff.). Finally, notwithstanding the great variety of coins in circulation, money changing likewise seems to have been only a minor sideline of Jewish banking, if we are to judge from the paucity of references thereto in the extant sources.

Moneylending, however, increasingly became the lifeblood of the Jewish economy at large. It was abetted by the increasing Christian prohibition on usury which was broadly defined by Richard, son of Nigel, as "receiving, like the Jews, more than we have lent of the same substance by virtue of a contract" (*Dialogus de Scaccario*, trans. by C. Johnson, 99f.). It was an uphill struggle for the Church because, down to the 12th century, the clergy themselves often indulged in moneylending on interest, a practice surreptitiously pursued by some priests even later. Jews also encountered stiff competition from Lombards and Cahorsins, often styled the papal usurers for their major services in transferring ecclesiastical dues to Rome. However, Jews had the advantage of being able openly to engage in this legally obnoxious business; as a matter of fact they did it as a rule with considerable governmental support.

In fact, kings considered Jewish gains via moneylending as an increase of their own resources. This was basically the meaning of "belong to the imperial chamber," a stereotype phrase referring to Jews found in many imperial privileges in German, implying that the Jews were the "king's treasure," as they were designated in Spanish decrees. When in 1253 Elias of Chippenham left England and took along his own bonds, Henry III prosecuted him because he had "thievishly carried off Our proper chattels." This nexus did not escape the attention of hostile observers who often blamed the princes for the excesses of their Jewish usurers. In his letter of 1208 to the count of Nevers the powerful Pope Innocent III complained that while certain princes "themselves are ashamed to exact usury, they receive Jews into their hamlets [*villis*] and towns and appoint them their agents for the collection of usury" (S. Grayzel, *The Church and the Jews in the 13th Century*, 126f.). Although in a special pamphlet *De regimine judaeorum* Thomas Aquinas tried to appease the conscience of Princess Aleyde (or Margaret) of Brabant for deriving benefits from Jewish taxation largely originating from usurious income, one of his most distinguished commentators, Cardinal Tommaso Vio Cajetan, sweepingly declared that "the gain accruing to a prince from a usurer's revenue makes him an accessory to the crime." The better to control Jewish revenues, the English administration introduced in 1194 the system of public chests (**archae*) into which all bonds had to be deposited, supposedly to avoid controversies between lenders and debtors. Philip II in France tried in 1206 and 1218 to emulate the English example, as did Alfonso IV of Aragon in 1333, and in a somewhat different way Alfonso XI of Castile in 1348. But outside of England this system broke down, apparently because neither lenders nor debtors wished to comply. In any case, the Protestant clergy of Hesse was not wrong when, in its memorandum of 1538 to the landgrave, it compared the role of Jewish moneylending with that of a sponge, used by the rulers to suck up the wealth of the population via usury ultimately to be squeezed dry by the treasury.

Despite all opposition, Jewish moneylending was an imperative necessity in many areas. Because of the prevailing high rates of interest it also was a lucrative business. Emperor Frederick II's Sicilian constitution of Melfi of 1231 restricting the permissible interest rate to 10% remained a dead letter even in his own kingdom. Somewhat more effective were the maximum rates of 20% set by certain Aragonese kings and Italian republics. But for the most part the accepted rates ranged between 33⅓ and 43⅓%, although sometimes they went up to double and treble those percentages, or more. Upon their readmission to France in 1359–60, Jews were specifically allowed to charge up to 86⅔%. Even some Silesian princes are recorded to have paid 54% to their Jewish moneylenders. In the case of the innumerable small loans by petty pawnbrokers, these high rates were justified by the lenders' overhead in receiving weekly interest payments, slow amortization, and much bookkeeping. But the Lombards who, for the most part, dealt in large credit transactions nevertheless likewise charged what the trade could bear.

So long as the economy was on the upswing the resentment against these high rates of interest was moderate. But when the European economy entered a period of deceleration in the late 13th century, further aggravated by recurrent famines and pestilences, such exorbitant charges, though economically doubly justified because of the increased risks, created widespread hostility. They were an important factor in the growing intolerance aimed at the English, French, and German Jews. Of course, expelling the Jews from the country, as England did in 1290 and France in 1306, merely meant replacing one set of moneylenders by another. Christian creditors, as a rule, charged even higher rates, partly to compensate for the increased opprobrium and sinfulness connected with their trade. As a result, Philip IV's successor, Louis X, in 1315 revoked the decree of expulsion and called the Jews back to the country as he claimed, in response to "the clamor of the people." Yet when the Jews returned under the royal pledge that they would be tolerated for at least 12 years, the popular outcry became so vehement that Philip the Tall broke his predecessor's promise and banished the Jews again in 1322. At the same time in neighboring Italy, where the grandeur of the Florentine and Genoese bankers was on the decline, Jews began to be invited by various republics to settle in their midst and to provide credit "to the needy population." These *condottas*, resembling formal treaties between the governments and groups of Jewish bankers, extended to the latter a variety of privileges for specified periods of time, subject to renewals. The city of Reggio (Emilia) went so far as to guarantee to the incoming Jewish bankers that, if they ever were to sustain losses from a popular riot, the city would fully indemnify them. This significant chapter in Jewish economic history, however, began drawing to a close in the latter part of the 15th century on account of the emergence of the new, rivaling institution of *monti di pietà*. These charitable loan banks were supposed to extend credit to the poor without any interest and thus make Jews wholly expendable. In itself this was a laudable idea and spread quickly into countries such as France from which Jews had long disappeared. At times the *monti* were supported by Jewish bankers themselves (for instance, by Isaac b. Jehiel of Pisa). But most of them assumed from the outset a strongly antisemitic character. They were propagated by outspoken anti-Jewish agitators and rabble rousers, especially *Bernardino da Feltre. Only in Venice, which refused admission to Da Feltre, did the Serenissima reach a compromise with the Jews by persuading them to establish the so-called *banchi del ghetto* which, financed entirely by Jews, were to serve an exclusively Christian clientele at nominal rates of interest. These institutions lasted until the emancipation era when, upon the entry of the French army into Venice in 1797, the Jewish community voluntarily transferred the assets of its five banks to the new republic.

Connected in many ways with banking was Jewish public service. As under Islam, the Christian rulers could not scrupulously adhere to the demands of their religious leaders to keep "infidels" out of any public office lest they exercise dominion over the faithful. Governments often had to rely on the religious minorities to provide fiscal experts whose specific experiences as taxpayers as well as businessmen could be put to good use by the treasuries for tax collection and necessary cash advances. In his petition to Alfonso IV of Aragon (before 1335), requesting the king's assistance in the collection of loans from Hospitalers, the Navarrese Jewish banker, Ezmel b. Juceph de Ablitas, boasted that Alfonso "had never received so great a service from either a Christian or a Jew as you have received from me at a single stroke" (M. Kayserling, "Das Handelshaus Ezmal in Tudela," in: *Jahrbuch fuer Israeliten*, 1860, 40–44).

Most widespread was the Jewish contribution to tax farming. The medieval regimes, as a rule, aided by only small, inefficient, and unreliable bureaucracies, often preferred to delegate tax collection to private entrepreneurs who, for a specified lump sum they paid the treasury, were prepared to exact the payments due from the taxpayers. Of course, the risks of undercollection were, as a rule, more than made up by considerable surpluses obtained, if need be, by ruthless methods. So indispensable were the Spanish Jewish tax farmers that the Catholic Monarchs signed such four-year contracts with Jewish entrepreneurs as late as 1491, only a year before the expulsion. Among their most prominent collectors was Abraham Seneor, officially the "rabbi of the court" or chief rabbi of Castilian Jewry, and Don Isaac b. Judah *Abrabanel. In the early days of the Christian reconquest, the services of able Jewish financiers and administrators were even more indispensable. Members of the Cavalleria and Ravaya families were particularly prominent in 13th-century Aragon. For one example, Judah b. Labi de la Cavalleria served from 1257 on as bailiff of Saragossa, from 1260 on as chief treasurer to whom all royal bailiffs had to submit regular accounts, and finally in 1275 also as governor of Valencia. Jews were also active in diplomatic service, for which their familiarity with various lands and languages made them especially qualified. In vain did Pope Honorius II address a circular letter to the kings of Aragon, Castile, Navarre, and Portugal, warning them against dispatching to Muslim courts Jewish envoys who were likely to reveal state secrets to the Muslim enemies, since "you cannot expect faithfulness from infidels." Yet his successor, Gregory IX, generally even more insistent on the observance of all canonical provisions, conceded in 1231 and 1239 that the Portuguese and Hungarian monarchs had no workable alternative.

In other countries Jews exerted political influence more indirectly. Even in some antagonistic German principalities of the 14th and 15th centuries some Jews were called upon to provide the necessary funds for raising mercenary forces as well as to supply them with food, clothing, and other necessities. Such a combination of large-scale financing and contracting was performed, for example, by a Jewish banker, Jacob Daniels, and his son Michael for the archbishop-elector Baldwin of Trier in 1336–45. This adumbration of the future role of *Court Jews in helping build up the modern German principality was cut short, however, by the recurrent waves of intolerance which swept Germany in the last medieval centuries and resulted in the expulsion of the Jews from most German areas.

Economic Doctrines

Notwithstanding these constant changes in the Jewish economic structure and the vital role played by the Jewish economic contributions for the general society, no ancient or medieval Jewish scholar devoted himself to the detailed interpretation of these economic facts and trends. No Jew wrote economic tracts even of the rather primitive kind current in Hellenistic and early Muslim letters. All Jewish rationales must therefore be deduced indirectly from the legal teachings. Even Maimonides who, in his classification of sciences, recognized the existence of a branch of science styled domestic economy, or rather the "government of the household" (a literal translation of the Greek *oikonomia*), did not feel prompted to produce a special monograph on the general or Jewish economic life. Speaking more broadly of political science which included that branch of learning, he declared: "On all these matters philosophers have written books which have been translated into Arabic, and perhaps those that have not been translated are even more numerous. But nowadays we no longer require all this, namely the statutes and laws, since man's conduct is [determined] by the divine regulations" (*Treatise on Logic [Millot ha-Higgayon]*, Arabic text, with Hebrew and English translations, by Israel Efros, 1937, 18f.). In consonance with this conception, the great codifier devoted the last three sections of his *Mishneh Torah* to economic matters regulated by civil law. He also often referred to economic aspects in the other 11 books, following therein the example of both Bible and Talmud. None of these normative sources, however, which always emphasized what ought to be rather than what is or was, can satisfactorily fill the lacuna created by the absence of dispassionate analytical, theoretical, and historical economic studies. From the outset we must, therefore, take account of the idealistic slant of our entire documentation. The emphasis upon ethics and psychology far outweighs that of realistic conceptualism. Only indirectly, through the use of the extant subsidiary factual source material, can we balance that normative slant by some realistic considerations.

Typical of such idealistic approaches is the biblical legislation. For example, the commandment of a year of fallowness may have resulted from the practical observation that land under constant cultivation was bound to deteriorate and to yield progressively less produce. Similar experiences led other agricultural systems to adopt the rotation of crops and other methods. But there is no hint to such a realistic objective in the biblical rationales. The old Book of the Covenant justifies the commandment by stating that in this way "the poor of the people may eat" (Ex. 23:11). The more religiously oriented Book of Leviticus, on the other hand, lays primary stress on the land keeping "a Sabbath unto the Lord" (25:2) so that it provide "solemn" rest for servants, foreign settlers, and even cattle. Similarly, the Jubilee Year was conceived as a measure of restoring the landed property to the original clan, envisaging a more or less static agricultural economy, at variance with the constantly changing realities of the then increasingly dominant urban group. No less idealistic were the provisions for the poor, particularly widows and orphans. We also recall the extremely liberal demand that, upon manumitting his Hebrew slave, the master should also provide him with some necessaries for a fresh start in life.

That these and other idealistic postulates did not represent the living practice in ancient Israel we learn from the reverberating prophetic denunciations of the oppression of the poor by the rich and other social disorders. But here again we deal with even more extravagant idealistic expectations than had been expressed by the lawgivers. In the main, the Bible reflects in part the "nomadic ideals" carried down from the patriarchal age and in part the outlook of the subsequently predominant agricultural population. But the landowning aristocracy, as well as the priesthood and royal bureaucracy often residing in Jerusalem and Samaria, and the impact of foreign relations, especially wars, shaped the actual affairs of the people to a much larger extent than normative provisions or prophetic denunciations, although the latter's long-range effects far transcended in historic importance the immediate realities.

Even the far more realistic legal compilations of the Mishnah, the Talmud, and other rabbinic letters are still in the main ethically and psychologically oriented. This remains true for most periods of Jewish history until the emancipation era. Certain economic factors are simply taken for granted. Not even Maimonides, who tried to find rationales for many biblical rituals, considered it necessary to offer any justification for such a fundamental economic fact as private versus public ownership. There only was common agreement that good fortune is bestowed upon man by God's inscrutable will, while poverty is to be borne with patience and submission to fate. Asceticism never became a major trend in Jewish socioreligious life, although certain groups and individuals practiced it as a matter of supererogation. Similarly, the postulates of communal ownership raised by the *Rechabites in the days of Jeremiah and the *Essenes toward the end of the Second Temple period were only part of their rejection of alleged departures from the purity of the old law. But they remained rather ineffectual fringe movements.

At the same time the "normative" Judaism of the majority subjected private ownership to severe limitations because of ethical requirements. From the restatement by Maimonides of talmudic law, as modified by the subsequent rabbinic literature, the following categories of property clearly emerge: "(1) public property belonging to no one and accessible to everybody for free use, e.g., deserts; (2) public property belonging to a corporate group, but open to general use, e.g., highways; (3) potentially private property belonging to no one, but available for free appropriation, namely all relinquished and some lost objects; 4) private grounds belonging to the ownerless estate of a deceased proselyte, equally open to free appropriation; (5) private grounds not yet taken over by a Jew from a gentile, open to appropriation against compensation; (6) private grounds in a walled city, open to everybody's use but not to appropriation." To these must be added the "sacred property" (*hekdesh*) of the Temple of Jerusalem, which, however, did not apply to the later synagogues; objects placed outside ordinary use or sale by ritualistic law; as well as the theoretical claim of every Jew in the world to the possession of four ells of land in Palestine. Based on the assumption that forcible deprivation of land never eliminates the rights of the real owner, the latter legal fiction was of practical significance only in connection with certain technical restrictions on the formal transfer of property.

With all their emphasis on private ownership the rabbis recognized its limitations necessary for the common good. To begin with, they did not acknowledge the riparian rights of owners, but considered four ells along all shores as belonging to the community at large. They also accepted the right of expropriation for purposes of roadbuilding, the erection of city walls, and other necessary public works. A city also had a right to banish certain odiferous trades, such as that of tanning, outside its walls. Even individuals trying to sell land had to respect the neighbors' right of preemption at the price offered by strangers. In general, referring to an old tradition going back to the agricultural economics of Palestine and Babylonia, Jewish leaders placed land outside the range of ordinary commodities. During the very era of semicapitalistic prosperity under Islam, they still believed in the stability of land ownership as against the fluctuations in the value of any other property. Going beyond the advice of talmudic sages that prudent men should invest one-third of their funds in land, one-third in commerce, and keep one-third in ready cash, Maimonides, perhaps inspired by the severe business losses sustained by his own family on account of his brother David's shipwreck on a voyage to India, counseled his readers not to sell a field and purchase a house, or to sell a house and acquire a movable object. They should rather generously "aim to acquire wealth by converting the transitory into the permanent." The rabbis also greatly stressed the responsibility of relatives for one another, not only in such dire emergencies as the redemption of captives but they also generally taught that "a relative may prove to be extremely wicked, but he nevertheless ought to be treated with due compassion."

Other ethical and psychological criteria were employed in the rabbinic approximation of the doctrine of the just price, later extensively debated by the medieval Christian scholastics. No one questioned the community's right to supervise weights and measures. Any deficiency, if purely accidental, called for restitution, but if it was premeditated it was to be punished severely. Maimonides waxed rhetorical on this subject: "The punishment for [incorrect] measures is more drastic than the sanction on incest, because the latter is an offense against God, while the former affects a fellow man. He who denies the law concerning measures is like one who denies the Exodus from Egypt which was the beginning of this commandment" (Yad, Genevah 7:1–3, 12; 8:1, 20 with reference to BB 89b). The community also had the right as well as the duty to set maximum prices whenever conditions demanded it. Of course, under the general rabbinic doctrine of *dina de-malkhuta dina* ("the law of the kingdom is law") all market regulations by the state, including the maximum prices set by it, were to be respected by the Jews too, except when they specifically conflicted with the divinely revealed Torah. Conversely, in many areas (for instance in Majorca in 1344) the government specifically forbade the local market supervisors to interfere in any business dealings in the Jewish quarter. In any case, with their inveterate conservatism the rabbis were reluctant to accept the law of supply and demand as the determining factor in controlling prices.

A convenient psychological expedient was found in the theory of "misrepresentation" (**ona'ah*). To prevent overcharges by sellers and, to a lesser extent, the taking of excessive advantage of an existing "buyers' market," the ancient sages had already established the principle that if the price paid for an object exceeded or was below its market value by one-sixth, the sale could be nullified by the injured party. This rabbinic doctrine of "misrepresentation," which seems to have inspired some related teachings of the Church Fathers and, through them, the Code of Justinian, could prove to be a serious obstacle under the freer economy of medieval Islam or modern Europe. An escape clause was opened by the rabbis, however, through their emphasis on psychology. They taught that if a seller openly declared to the purchaser that he had overcharged him by so and so much and the purchaser accepted the deal, there was no redress. Also by removing such important areas as land, slaves, and commercial deeds – the latter particularly important in transferring properties from one individual to another – from the operation of this principle, the economic realities could reassert themselves without formally altering the law. The same exception facilitated barter trade. A man could trade, for example, a needle for a coat of mail if, for some psychological reason, he preferred the needle. This was particularly true in the case of jewelry where emotional preferences might well have outweighed purely market considerations.

Among the transactions also not subject to the law of "misrepresentation" was free labor. Although the economic importance of hired workers was much greater than that of slaves, there was no comprehensive labor legislation in rabbinic law (see *Labor Law). Generally, the leaders preferred the employment of Jewish workers as a matter of ethnoreligious policy. Typical of the rabbinic attitude was Maimonides' contention that "he who increases the number of his slaves from day to day increases sin and iniquity in the world, whereas the man who employs poor Jews in his household increases merits and religious deeds" (Yad, Mattenot Aniyyim 10:17). This doctrine implied a general right to work for Jewish laborers, just as it conversely stressed everybody's duty to work in order to make a living. "Skin a carcass on the streets [the lowest type of labor], rather than be dependent on other people" was an old rabbinic watchword. Because of the primarily psychological interpretations, an employer could overtly arrange with a free laborer to do work which he could not impose upon a slave, since this was but a voluntary agreement on both sides. Similarly, the ancient protective regulation in the Bible that the payment of a daily worker's wages must not be delayed overnight could be modified by mutual agreement if a labor contract extended over a longer period. On his part, the employee was obliged to do an honest piece of work and not waste any time. Following ancient precedents, however, the rabbis allowed agricultural workers to partake of some of the grapes or grain on which they were working, though not of the fruit from orchards or vegetables from truck gardens. There also were many specific regulations concerning different categories of labor, such as shepherds. Each category had its own regulations, largely derived from age-old customs prevailing in particular localities.

The most difficult problem confronting the Jewish leaders was that of moneylending on interest. From biblical times there existed the outright prohibition, "Unto thy brother thou shalt not lend upon interest" (Deut. 23:21). Once again the approach of the ancient and medieval interpreters to that passage was based on ethics and psychology rather than economics. We are told in the same verse that "unto a foreigner [or stranger] thou mayest lend upon interest," but it did not occur to any of these interpreters to look for an economic rationale for this distinction. Under the conditions of ancient Palestine, lending money to a fellow Israelite usually meant extending credit to a needy farmer or craftsman for whom the return of the original amount plus the prevailing high interest was an extreme hardship. At the same time the foreigner, that is, the Phoenician-Canaanite merchant, as a rule borrowed money to invest it in his business for profit. Such a productive form of credit fully justified the original lender to participate in some form or other in the profits derived by the borrower.

Instead, the interpretation was always purely moralistic, namely a demand that lending to a fellow Jew had to be purely charitable, while extending credit to a non-Jew could be a businesslike proposition. Without going to the extreme of St. Ambrose who considered lending to a stranger a legitimate hostile act against an enemy (*ubi ius belli ibi ius usurae*), nor sharing the equally extreme view of some Jewish jurists who considered the biblical phrase, *la-nokhri tashikh* a commandment: "thou shalt," rather than "thou mayest," lend on interest to a stranger, most rabbis followed the talmudic rule that for segregationist reasons all but well informed scholars should abstain from moneylending to gentiles altogether. Yet they admitted that many Jews could not make a living any other way. Remarkably, not even the medieval Jewish Aristotelian philosophers quoted, as did their Christian counterparts, Aristotle's doctrine of the essential sterility of money. Whatever the theoretical justification of this point of view was, it ran counter to the daily experience of most Jewish sages that money could, in fact, earn greater increments than did land or any other movable property.

In their extremist ethico-psychological bent of mind the rabbis even outlawed such external forms of "usury" as nonmonetary gains. They taught, for example, that, unless the borrower used to do so before securing the loan, he was not entitled to greet the lender first or even to teach him the Torah. Echoing talmudic teachings Maimonides insisted that "it is forbidden for a man to appear before, or even to pass by, his debtor at a time when he knows that the latter cannot pay. He may frighten him or shame him, even if he does not ask for repayment" (Yad, Malveh ve-Loveh 1:1–3). Needless to say, only a few pietistic moneylenders could live up to these high expectations. On the other hand, economic realities, particularly in countries like medieval England, France, northern Italy, and Germany, where banking became the very economic foundation of many Jewish communities, forced the Jews to make some theoretical concessions. In his apologetic tract, *Milḥemet Mitzvah* of 1245, Meir b. Simon of Narbonne argued that "divine law prohibited usury, not interest... Not only the peasant must borrow money, but also the lords, and even the great king of France... The king would have lost many fortified places, if his faithful agent, a Jew of our city, had not secured for him money at a high price" (cited by Adolph Neubauer from a manuscript in *Archives des missions scientifiques*, 3d ser., 16, 556). Addressing his own coreligionists, a German rabbi, Shalom b. Isaac Sekel, insisted that "the reason why the

Torah holds a higher place in Germany than in other countries is that the Jews here charge interest to gentiles and need not engage in a [time-consuming] occupation. On this score they have time to study the Torah. He who does not study uses his profits to support the students of the Torah" (cited by Israel Isserlein's disciple, Joseph b. Moses of Hoechstadt, in his halakhic collection, *Leket Yosher*, ed. by J. Freimann (1903–10), 1, 118f.).

Like their Muslim and Christian colleagues, the rabbis had to legitimize many practices aimed at evading the prohibition of usury. The ingenuity of businessmen and jurists invented a variety of legal instruments which, formally not reflecting borrowings, nevertheless secured sizable profits for the capitalist advancing cash to a fellow Jew. Called in Europe the *contractus trinus, contractus mohatrae* (the purchase of rents, and the like), these instruments were also employed by Jewish lenders with telling effect. It was also easy to circumvent the law by the purchase of bonds. Since deeds were generally exempted from the prohibition of usury and could be discounted below their nominal value, a lender could extend a profitable loan to a third party by using an intermediary. Agents, too, were entitled to charge a commission for securing credit for any borrower. Most importantly, the various forms of the *commenda* contract, which enabled a lender to appear as a silent partner in the enterprise, opened the gate very widely for "legitimate" profits by the "investor." The permission of that type of *iska* ("deal") became quite universal and served as the major instrument for credit transactions among Jews.

These examples of the rabbis' economic teachings, which can readily be multiplied, must suffice here. They give an inkling of the great power of halakhic exegesis which made it possible for scholars to read into the established texts of Bible and Talmud provisions, as well as limitations, to suit the changing needs of Jewish society. In this way the people's intellectual leaders were able to preserve a measure of continuity within a bewildering array of diverse customs and usages. At the same time ample room was left for individual opinions, which often sharply differed. Some interpretations were derived from the simple operation of juristic techniques which had an autonomous vitality of their own. However, in many cases the communal leaders, rabbinic and lay, often personally immersed in a variety of economic enterprises and thus acquiring much practical experience, consciously made interpretive alterations to reflect genuine social needs. Since the entire system of Jewish law operated through inductive reasoning on the basis of cases rather than the deduction from juristic principles, as advanced by Roman jurists and their medieval disciples, the sages of various countries and generations were able to maintain a certain unity of purpose and outlook among the different segments of the Jewish dispersion. They thus lent the Jewish economic rationales the same kind of unity within diversity that permeated the entire Jewish socioreligious outlook on life.

[Salo W. Baron]

Early Modern Period

The variety of place, social condition, and economic development puts any review of the economic aspects of Jewish life since the end of the 15th century beyond the reach of a simple unified framework. For this variety to be seen in a meaningful way, for an analysis of the leading features of the subject, there must be some preliminary, if crude, divisions of the subject. Yet even a simple temporal division of the developments of almost 500 years is not free from difficulty. The pace and pattern of Western economic development differed markedly from country to country and from region to region, and as a matter of course the economic situation and activities of the Jews in those countries and regions differed widely also. The striking event, the momentous date, that might symbolize a qualitative change in Western economic structure is not to be found. If there is some basis for separating the early modern economic history of the Jews from the later modern developments, it must be sought in other criteria: the basic structure and leading characteristics of the economy and the goals of the society.

If we accept these criteria, it is not difficult to divide the whole period into two phases. During the first, economic development and economic policy were clearly and rigidly subordinated to noneconomic considerations of the society, and there was relatively little room for activity prompted by considerations of economic rationality as determined by the individuals concerned. In the second phase economic interests were articulated more openly and clearly, and the idea of freedom of economic activity was accepted as leading to results generally beneficial to the community as a whole. The transitional period between the two phases saw fundamental changes occurring throughout society: the legal and social framework had to be adjusted to the new demands, as symbolized by the substitution of the voluntary contract for traditional, customary relationships or for relationships hitherto determined and regulated by the usage of special privileges and governmental orders. Equality before the law was established as a principle that overrode the predominant institutionally ingrained system of legal and social inequality.

This transformation took place slowly and unevenly. Decades and even centuries apart in the various regions of Europe, the process nevertheless was continued and was accompanied by major differences in the legal status, pattern of employment, and other characteristics of the various Jewish communities at each point in time. Thus, the study of the economic aspects of Jewish life over the 500 years is basically the study of the participation of the Jews in the process of economic change and of the impact of the changing conditions upon the economic and social structure of the Jews. Even within the first period, which for reasons of convenience and convention will be called the early modern one, the conditions of the Jews living in the economically advanced regions must be distinguished from conditions in the economically less developed regions of Europe. Examples of the advanced regions are the city-states and major commercial centers of Italy and the Low Countries; examples of less developed regions are the countries of Central and Eastern Europe.

The discussion here of the early modern period will be confined almost exclusively to Europe because most Jews lived there (although Jews of course lived within the boundaries of the Ottoman Empire, in the Middle East, and other areas). Although the variety and heterogeneity of the European situation make generalization hazardous, much of what was done in one part of the continent to the Jews was more or less emulated in other parts, because of the cultural affinities within Christian Europe.

SEPHARDIM AND ASHKENAZIM. The Jewish communities in Europe at the end of the 15th century were not homogeneous in the cultural sense. The two mainstreams or dominant groups were the *Sephardim, originating from the Spanish-Portuguese Jews, and the *Ashkenazim, originating from the French and German Jews. These two branches grew apart, especially from the time of the Crusades. By the end of the 15th and beginning of the 16th century, when the Sephardi Jews were finally expelled from the Iberian Peninsula, the two major "tribes" of European Jewry came into a much closer contact, one resulting not in integration of the two, but in tolerable coexistence and peripheral cross-cultural interchange. The intellectual impact of the Sephardim was noticeable primarily in one area, namely that of religious mysticism. In other areas the Ashkenazim excelled the Sephardim in the creative development of what could be termed Jewish culture.

In the area of economic and social activity, the difference between the Sephardim and Ashkenazim was profound. The Sephardim were on the average much more affluent, skilled, and better educated (at least in the secular sense) than the Ashkenazim. In comparison the Ashkenazim were not only less prosperous but less culturally influenced by the gentile environment and less successful in any attempts at finding an intellectual symbiosis between their own and the surrounding culture. Therefore, the elements of the resource endowment of the Sephardi Jews made them the more attractive group of the two for settlement and employment in any European country. The Sephardi Jews were able to bring into the new areas of their settlement highly developed skills and craftsmanship in the areas of luxury consumption and were therefore highly valued by the influential consumers of such products and services, by the nobility, gentry, and patricians – the ruling classes of the contemporary societies. From available direct and circumstantial evidence it becomes clear that some of the Sephardi Jews were able to transfer portions of their capital out of Spain and Portugal, and thus their settlement in an area was accompanied by a capital import. It is interesting to note that in most cases, as far as the Christian countries are concerned, the Sephardi Jews were attracted to and sought opportunities in the more economically advanced regions, areas with both developed trade and crafts and with a legal framework that did not hinder the economic activities of a developed money economy. These were areas actively engaged in foreign commerce in which the knowledge of commodity and money markets possessed by Sephardi Jewish merchants could be profitably utilized. An additional asset of some Sephardi Jews was their knowledge gained from family and former business connections in the Iberian Peninsula and the overseas empires of Spain and Portugal. The Jewish participation in trade with Spain, Portugal, and their colonies never ceased, contrary to the myth of a worldwide Jewish boycott of the Iberian Peninsula.

ECONOMIC ENVIRONMENT. Thus it could be roughly assumed that the "territory" of the Sephardim, at least during the 16th and 17th centuries, was the city-states and commercial centers of Europe, while the "territory" of the Ashkenazim was the interior, the landmass or hinterland of Central and Eastern Europe.

The economy of city-states like Genoa, Venice, and Dubrovnik (Ragusa), or of commercial centers like Antwerp, Amsterdam, and Hamburg, was based on international and interregional trade and the exploitation of politically dependent territories where trade was carried on or which were administered by corporate bodies either in the form of trading companies or governmental agencies acting on behalf of organized mercantile interests. The main problem for the Jews, as for any group of outsiders, and even more so because of some peculiar restrictions or prejudices, was to gain entry into the organized institutions of economic activity, whether registered partnerships, trading companies, or later the commodity and money exchanges. It was difficult, if not impossible, for the Jews as newcomers to operate outside the institutional framework except in areas where their specialized skills or professions (such as medicine or science) would be recognized as exceptionally useful for the polity or economy. Thus, each outsider, including the Jews as individuals, had to fit into the preexisting economic structure and social fabric, upon neither of which he could expect to make any significant impact. The process by which the Jews were economically integrated in the city-states and commercial centers was therefore primarily the sum total of adjustments by individuals in these occupations and activities. Much depended on individual skill or wealth, with very limited room left for the collectivity of the Jews, the autonomous and organized Jewish community, to influence significantly the pattern of economic activity of its members.

The economic environment of the majority of the Ashkenazi Jews in the areas of Central and Eastern Europe differed from that in the city-states and in the major commercial areas. In the latter the Jews were restricted in terms of numbers, place of habitat, and areas of gainful employment, and formed almost exclusively an urban element concentrated in the major cities and confined largely to trade, some specialized skills, and money and lending operations. The situation of the Jews in Central and Eastern Europe, by contrast, can be described as characterized by both greater opportunities and more severe constraints. The peculiar combination is a paradox of underdevelopment and discrimination, both operating simultaneously.

There is an inherent conflict in societies with a high propensity to have rigid institutional arrangements in their economic sphere, even if within the institutions there may be provisions and conditions enabling the exercise of individual initiative. This is the conflict between such a propensity for institutional stability and the need to innovate, for it is only through innovation that the economy can grow. Within such societies it is particularly difficult for newcomers, who have to be integrated and accepted, to innovate. Outsiders are often forced to follow a circuitous road and assume greater risks to achieve their objectives. An interesting case in point is presented by the penetration of the Jews into the international *sugar trade. Apparently finding it initially difficult to enter via trade activity, Jews of Amsterdam entered the sugar plantation business in Brazil, Surinam, and the West Indies. The result was beneficial for many parties: for Amsterdam, a widening of its foreign trade; for the Jews, entrance into sugar production and sugar trade; for Europe, presumably a decrease in the price of sugar as a result of a rapid increase in supply.

In the predominantly agrarian economies of this period, a very large sector of the population was on a subsistence level and for all practical purposes outside the exchange and money economy. The money economy included the court, the nobility, gentry, and the urban classes, but only to a very limited extent the majority of the rural population, the peasants or serfs. While the areas of traditional or routine economic activity were circumscribed and regulated to an extent that made it virtually impossible for the Jews to enter the established institutions, there was a relatively wide spectrum of activities that were not institutionalized or controlled and that broadened the market or money economy. This presented a range of opportunities for individuals who possessed or were forced to have a lesser-than-average risk aversion for activities in which returns proved to be higher and for whom accordingly the returns could be higher than average.

The Jews suffered from discriminatory legislation; very seldom did their legal or social status as individuals depend upon their individual skills or the size of their personal wealth. There was no institutional arrangement by which a Jew could be integrated into his economic class or professional group. In a sense, he was the eternal outsider regardless of the economic function he performed, operating under conditions of discrimination and extreme uncertainty, dependent upon the arbitrary decisions of the rulers, and paying a high price (in the form of high taxes, bribes, ransom, etc.) for his right to be employed. Thus with the environmental conditions differing between the more advanced and less advanced countries, the ranges of opportunities and the areas of economic activity of the Jews differed, which in turn influenced the patterns of utilization of their resource endowment and their social structure.

JEWISH MIGRATION. One of the chief characteristics of Jewish economic activities in Europe during the early modern period was the relative (for this period) mobility of both capital and labor of the Jews. Even if we could consider exclusively voluntary mobility, the two other outstanding groups, the Italians and the Dutch, are in quite a different class when compared with the Jews. Thus, the migration phenomenon can be considered as one of the most significant dynamic elements of the economic and social history of the Jews. Jewish migration from the end of the 15th century was from Western to Central and Eastern Europe; this continued as the main vector until the second half of the 19th century. The eastward movement overshadowed in its intensity the "return" of the Jews to the countries of Western Europe from which they were exiled in the earlier centuries and to which they gradually returned between the 17th and 19th centuries.

The process of migration did not take the form of an even, continuous flow but proceeded through spurts and movements differing in intensity, with interruptions, reversals, and resumptions that defied regularity. It is also difficult to ascertain, apart from the general vector of the migration movement and the main routes, the average distances and time periods of the earlier phases of the migration. For the Sephardi Jews two general directions can be established: one from the Iberian Peninsula to the areas adjacent to the Mediterranean toward Italy, the Balkans, and Asian Turkey; the other toward southern France, the Netherlands, Hamburg, and England. For the Ashkenazim the direction of migration was from Western Germany over Austria toward Bohemia and Hungary, with another branch through Bohemia leading toward Poland, Lithuania, Belorussia, and the Ukraine, while the Jewish population of eastern and northern Germany consisted of primarily Austrian and Bohemian Jews and to a lesser extent of western German Jews. Many aspects of Jewish migration still await thorough investigation. Nevertheless, certain generalizations can be made on the basis of available evidence:

(1) By and large the eastward migration was in fact a movement of labor and capital from more highly developed to less economically developed countries and regions, from areas of greater availability of skilled labor and capital to areas of greater scarcity of these factors of production.

(2) The mobility of labor and capital and thereby the migration process was facilitated not only by religious identity but also by the cultural affinity of common customs and language, by the availability of established and organized Jewish communities not far from the destination of the migration route, and by the relatively high level of liquidity of capital on the part of capital owners.

(3) The significance of the migration process for the economy of the Jews was due to a large extent to the fact that through migration and mobility a more remunerative distribution of human and capital resources could be achieved over a large territory, while both cultural and economic intercourse

could be maintained thanks to the continuing ties between the older and newer communities.

(4) Some of the benefits of the process of mobility accruing to the Jewish communities were congruent with the benefits to the economies of countries that absorbed the Jewish migrants, namely the import of skilled labor and capital resources to meet a strong demand.

(5) The migration process of the Jews in the eastward direction, although caused to a very large extent by economic considerations, even by the differential of economic well-being or differences in the rates of return to skills, had significant effects in other areas as well. It became a part of the "strategy for survival" either in cases of mass expulsions and exile or under conditions of a clear worsening of the legal status. Moreover, the absence of effective internal barriers supported the prevailing notion of a single, general Jewish community in Central and Eastern Europe. Leading schools drew students from far afield; famous scholars and rabbis were not bound to a particular locale; mystics and messianic claimants attracted multitudes from all over the continent.

The first reversal of the direction on a larger scale in the eastward migration took place around the middle of the 17th century during the times of the *Chmielnicki massacres in the Ukraine, the Swedish and Muscovite invasions of Poland, and the subsequent worsening of the economic situation there. The flow of refugees from Eastern Europe reached western Germany and even the Netherlands. From the middle of the 18th century, there was a small but continuous flow of Central and Eastern European Jews trying to settle in Western Europe and North America. But this early ebb of migration had a minimal effect upon the economic life of the communities that they left or the ones that they joined. It only indicated that change was possible if not imminent.

PATTERNS OF EMPLOYMENT. Any systematic insight into the economic activities of the Jewish population in Europe during this period requires an examination of the patterns of employment. If the chief economic characteristic of Jewish migration was the movement from more developed to less developed countries one would expect the Jews to be employed primarily not in areas of an abundant labor supply but in the economic sectors with a scarcity of labor and capital, namely trade and highly skilled crafts. Only when the employment in such areas had reached a level of saturation or was encountering barriers would we expect the migrants to turn to less remunerative employment. The great majority of the Jews was employed in sectors of the economy that were directly connected with the market. Very few operated outside the exchange and money economy, while most derived their incomes from the production and sales of goods and services. It is true that the markets differed, but it is important to bear in mind that the market psychology affected the activities of the great majority. It is therefore appropriate to begin the review of the patterns of employment with the type of employment and activity most intimately connected with the organized markets and also yielding the highest returns. The "big business" of that period was carried on by a small group of enterprising individuals who either combined or fulfilled separately the functions of wholesale merchants, bankers, and industrial entrepreneurs. Such individuals in the economically advanced countries acted mostly in their private capacity, in the economically backward countries mostly in conjunction with the government, and were termed *Court Jews.

It is impossible to measure directly the volume of international trade carried on by Jewish wholesale merchants from the 16th to the 18th century, or the share of Jewish trade in the countries they inhabited, or even the share of these countries in the total volume of international trade. Such data are not as yet available, but it should be clear that, for example, a 10% share in the Dutch trade would probably be more than a 50% share in Poland's international trade, because of the relative sizes of the trade volume of the two countries. Direct and indirect evidence indicates that the Jews were involved in the trade of precious metals, the colonial trade, and trade of products possessing a high value per unit. Only later, with the improvement of shipping technology and cheapening of transportation costs, did Jews enter the trade in grain and other bulk products, thus expanding the trade with the agrarian economies of Central and Eastern Europe.

As bankers and bill brokers in the economically developed countries, their operations did not differ from others of the profession. The two advantages that they might have possessed over some of their competitors were their ability to transfer money rapidly from one locality to another, as they had either family or business connections with members of other Jewish communities, and the extension of credits by using the savings deposited with them by members of the community. Jewish bankers' preference for short-term over long-term credit could perhaps be explained by the desire for a quicker turnover of their capital and the unwillingness to accept land or real estate as security for loans outstanding. Industrial entrepreneurship of the Jews in the developed areas was due to the availability of technical skills and business expertise in a number of craft and industry branches that the incoming Jews had brought with them.

In the less developed countries the Court Jews played a significant role, and the gradual transformation of their functions reflected the economic development of such countries as well as the contribution such individuals made to the development process. The shortage of money and the low credit standing of most European rulers and their governments were notorious. Accordingly, the initial role of the Court Jews, as the title implies, was to serve the rulers in a double capacity, as lenders of money and as suppliers of precious metals to the mint, precious stones, and other luxury items for consumption of the court. The form of payment and security given were often tax farming, toll collection, and other privileges that provided for the principal and interest of the transaction. Thus the Court Jews not only provided credit for the rulers but also performed functions in the revenue collection of the states. Two major factors contributed to the transformation of the nature of the service of the Court Jews. The first were the wars of the 17th and 18th centuries which called not only for greater monetary outlays and thus expanding demand for credits, but also for the organizational talent to supply the numerous armies in the field with weapons, ammunition, clothing, food, and fodder. The need to contract and pay for, and to deliver large bulks of necessary supplies at great distance, called for new and substantial organizational talents. The Court Jews performed well when requested to carry out the above tasks, and in the process of doing so gained new knowledge in large-scale operations requiring greater efficiency in mobilizing vast resources in relatively backward economies. In so doing the Court Jews were assisting the political interests of the rulers or of the state.

Another factor contributing to the transformation of their service was the entry of the Jews into the ranks of industrial entrepreneurs. The setting-up of mining and manufacturing industries in the economically backward countries was not a market response to a demand for such products. It was in most cases either a direct result of government action or an indirectly induced development as a result of a conscious government policy. Government policies in those countries pursued two goals: first, to develop armament industries to strengthen the countries militarily and politically in their struggles for hegemony or for the restoration of a power balance in Europe; secondly, to develop industry branches that produced import-substitutes, which meant primarily products used by the wealthy upper classes of society. The military needs on the one hand and the maintenance of a positive balance of payments on the other were mainly responsible for the state initiative and support given to early mining and manufacturing industries. Given the government financial or tax support for the industrial establishments, the critical factors were skilled labor and entrepreneurial and managerial talents. In providing technical skills the contribution of the Jews was probably inferior to the possibilities of importing skills from the advanced countries, so the primary area of their contribution, by no means exclusively Jewish, was that of entrepreneurial and managerial talent. Their previous experience in large-scale banking, military contracting, etc., provided the necessary background. The involvement in previous services for the state gave them the knowledge and political connections necessary for obtaining licenses, privileges, and often the labor force for the budding industrial enterprises. Thus the former Court Jew became an industrial entrepreneur, continuing social innovation, creating new types of economic organization, and helping to break old patterns and traditional systems. The economic significance for the Jewish community of this group of wholesale merchants, bankers, and industrial entrepreneurs consisted not only in their role in the accumulation of capital, but also and primarily in their collective role in creating employment opportunities for other Jews. The relatively large-scale operations of this entrepreneurial class gave rise to a demand for services that could be performed by other members of the community. For example, in such enterprises as supply-contracting, a system of subcontracting was established that provided income for a relatively large number of smaller-scale merchants, and even the administration of large landed estates provided employment for many innkeepers, alcohol distillers, and other self-employed members of the Jewish community.

A second area of employment, which was represented by a massive participation of the members of the Jewish community, was that of smaller-scale and retail trade and of commercial intermediaries operating with limited capital resources, in many cases not their own. In the economically more advanced centers the economic activities of this employment group were rather specialized, with heavy concentration in limited areas of the retail trade and specialized services as commercial and financial intermediaries. Here too their activities were limited by the existing institutional structure of the commercial centers. In order to compete with the more established firms or individuals, the Jewish merchants tried to deviate from the standards of goods being marketed and provided a greater variety in terms of quality for a broader range of prices. The economic effect of such – for that period – unorthodox behavior was a broadening of the market and an increase in the number of consumers attracted by a wider range of quality. In the less advanced economies of that period, the Jewish merchants had to overcome both the power of the urban guilds and the customary location of actual markets in the cities. Therefore a major area of the trade of the Jewish merchants consisted in reaching the social circle beyond the orbit of the exchange economy, the peasants. The merchants sought out the areas of a marketable surplus of agricultural products. By increasing the size of shipments from the outlying areas it was possible to decrease the costs of transportation that previously had made it unprofitable to bring these products to market.

A number of varied and interesting phenomena attended this Jewish mercantile activity. First, through their penetration of the rural areas Jewish merchants and peddlers supplied both the manor and the peasant huts with manufactured goods that were in demand, and simultaneously collected the marketable surplus of grains, flax, wool, and livestock. This two-way trade enabled the Jews to compete relatively successfully with the local merchants who conducted their trade at fixed points, primarily in the cities, and were relatively protected by their status as city dwellers and merchants. Secondly, the penetration of Jewish peddlers and merchants into the countryside enabled them to organize early, still primitive forms of a putting-out system, making use of and helping in the further development of cottage industries in the rural areas, and thus organizing and supporting a form of production in competition with the urban crafts controlled and protected by the city guilds (see *Peddling). Thirdly, the employment of Jews in innkeeping, alcohol distilling, and livestock production in the rural areas helped further to inject into the agricultural sector the elements of an exchange and money economy. The result of the activity of the Jewish small merchants in the rural areas was to encourage the production of an agricultural surplus, to stimulate the consumption of nonagricultural goods, and to foster the alienation of some part of the former agricultural labor force from the land and to channel it into the cottage industries and into transportation services, thus helping to create a nonagricultural labor force in the rural areas that depended upon wages rather than upon returns from land.

The second largest employment group within the Jewish community was that of the artisans. Given the limited size of the market and the degree of organization of the craft guilds, the Jewish artisans faced a constant struggle for the right to compete. Since they were refused admittance to the craft guilds, they suffered from the constraints imposed on nonmembers of the guilds and at best could count on a compromise that would allow them to continue their activity at the price of compensatory payments to the guilds. The alternative was to be restricted to the very narrow market for craft production provided by the Jewish community. Faced with this choice, the Jewish artisans accepted the conditions of higher costs of production, including the payment of compensation to the guilds, until such time as the burden of discrimination could be lessened or alternative arrangements could create new opportunities. The range of Jewish crafts was very wide, beginning with highly specialized gold- and silversmiths and jewelers, ranging to masons, carpenters, and blacksmiths, but with a heavy concentration in the clothing crafts like tailoring, cap-making, furriery, and shoemaking. This concentration indicates a reliance upon a mass market. Through this orientation toward an expanding market the survival of Jewish artisans was guaranteed and new arrangements for production and marketing were developed. The new arrangements took the form of what amounts to a putting-out system organized by Jewish merchants who provided the artisans with raw materials and occasionally with advance payments for their work. Thus, the artisans were converted almost into wage laborers. The arrangement, however, freed them from the necessity of having their own or borrowed capital tied up in stocks of raw material or finished goods and also from involvement in the process of distribution, these functions being performed by the merchants. From the end of the 16th century the artisans started to organize Jewish craft guilds. Although there is still much debate about the actual effectiveness of these Jewish guild activities, there is no doubt that their establishment was a response to a deeply felt need for collective action and for articulating their interests at least within the Jewish communities. Under such arrangements Jewish artisans were better able to survive at least until the time when modern industry posed new threats to the positions of small crafts and the putting-out system.

A description of the various employment categories within the Jewish milieu would be incomplete if it did not note that a certain part of the economically active population was employed within the Jewish community itself. This general area of employment can be divided into two groups: (1) the occupations that served the Jewish community exclusively; (2) those providing services for which an assured demand existed within the Jewish community but of which outsiders also could avail themselves. Among the first category were rabbis, schoolteachers, ritual slaughterers, scroll scribes, employees of the ritual bathhouse, and keepers of synagogues and cemeteries. The demand for the services of this group was determined largely by religious laws and customs and therefore was not very flexible. Among the other category were butchers, candlemakers, bookdealers, and prayer-shawl weavers. The demand for their employment could have been a joint demand since they were capable of providing services for non-Jews as well. Nevertheless the Jewish community had to sustain the costs of maintaining the bulk of their services when outside demand proved insufficient. The percentage of all these intracommunity services in the total of gainful employment varied for the particular communities according to their size; but there was less variation if the Jewish population of each of the countries was viewed as a unit. While smaller communities could have shared in some of the services that none alone could afford, the combined percentage of intracommunity employment, when standardized for size, was not much different from that of the larger communities. As a rule of thumb it would probably be correct to assume that at least 10% of total employment was devoted to the internal community services.

These various categories of employment constituted a wide spectrum within the Jewish communities and absorbed much of the energy of its members. In terms of the percentage of gainful employment or actual volume of labor input within the year they were probably greater than the average for the population at large for whom seasonality of agriculture reduced the volume of labor input. Apart from them, however, there existed a numerous group of unemployed or unemployable members of the community. It would be fair to assume that the primary responsibility for the support and maintenance of the unemployed or unemployable rested with the extended family which was the basic social unit within the community. Whenever the family was unable to provide such support, the community accepted such people as public charges. The three major ways in which the community met its responsibilities were through private charity; institutionalized voluntary associations organized for the purposes of providing assistance through institutions, such as hospitals, homes for incurables or the aged, and loan-societies; and through direct community support out of the taxation levied upon the tax-paying members. In accord with traditional beliefs, private charity was not only considered a responsibility but also an opportunity for the more prosperous members of the community. The activities of voluntary associations concerned with this type of welfare and social services prevented a full bureaucratization of functions, which would otherwise have been taken over entirely by the community authorities, and left thus much room for individual initiative and energy. Needless to say, neither private charity nor the work of the voluntary associations sufficed to meet the problem. Since the number of unemployed and unemployable also depended upon general economic conditions, in times of relative prosperity the economy would tend to absorb the unemployed and the community would be in a better condition to support the unemployable, while the reverse was true during periods of economic decline. Thus the role of community taxation increased at times when the tax burden was already felt most heavily. Nevertheless, the communities accepted this "welfare responsibility" either out of a sense of moral obligation or in order to mitigate the social friction and conflicts that a refusal would have entailed. It is difficult to estimate the proportion of unemployed or paupers within the Jewish communities for this period, but depending upon the economic and legal conditions of the Jews, it would be no exaggeration to estimate their number as between 15 and 25%, with a secular tendency to rise since the second half of the 17th century.

It is likewise difficult to document the employment distribution within the Jewish communities for countries scattered all over the map of Europe, although there are data for separate local communities either for irregular intervals or for single years. The employment distribution for the largest Jewish community in Europe – Poland-Lithuania – in the middle of the 18th century can roughly be reconstructed. The employment distribution differed markedly among the Jews settled in the larger cities, among those inhabiting the small towns, and among those scattered in the rural areas. In addition, the peculiarity of the settlement pattern of the Jews in Poland-Lithuania during this period was the large proportion of Jews living in rural areas, about one-third of the total Jewish population. While in the rural areas leaseholding (see **arenda*), innkeeping, alcohol distilling, and ancillary agriculture were the main occupations, the mass of Jewish artisans inhabited the larger cities and smaller towns. The social structure which emerges from the approximate data reflects the following employment distribution of the Polish Jews by the middle of the 18th century: wholesale merchants, financiers, etc. – about 2–3%; small traders, including leaseholders and innkeepers – less than 40%; artisans and other urban wage earners – more than 33%; employed in intracommunity services – about 10%; unemployed and paupers – at least 15%. The most obvious conclusions that could be drawn from this employment distribution is that the vast majority of the Jews earned their livelihood from physical labor and that a substantial proportion of the population was either already living on charity or on the threshold of poverty.

RESOURCE ENDOWMENT AND SOURCES OF INCOME. The consideration of the employment distribution within the Jewish community sheds some light on the problem of the sources of Jewish income and on one particularly interesting aspect, that of resource endowment and returns to labor and capital, the factors of production. For a long time the prevailing view among historians of the period has been that capital was the more important component of the resource endowment of the Jewish community and that returns to capital were also quantitatively the more significant component of the income earned by the Jews. Needless to say, this view was more congruent with popular images than with documentary calculations. Both progress in historical research and increased sophistication of economic analysis have led to serious questioning of this view. There is no doubt that a substantial part of the capital with which the Jews operated was borrowed from non-Jews, as evidenced by the bankruptcy of the Jewish communities in Poland during the 18th century and their large debts to the nobility and clergy. It is also increasingly clear that the return to skills in the pre-industrial period was relatively higher than was initially assumed. If first the labor income derived from the goods produced by Jewish artisans and craftsmen is calculated and then the labor component of the earning in retail trade is added, the result arrived at would be a very substantial share of the total income earned by all employed. The vast majority of the Jews during this period earned the bulk of their income from labor services. The profit rate of owners of capital could be maintained only by using capital in new areas of trade and industry, thus counteracting the secular tendency of the profit rate to decline while capital was becoming relatively more abundant. The capital earnings of the members of the Jewish community were in part used, through a process of income redistribution, to maintain intracommunity services and to aid the poorer members of the community.

The income position and income level of the Jewish community depended upon prevailing economic conditions and their changes. If the Jewish community is considered as being involved in an exchange of goods and services with the community at large, the economic well-being of the Jewish community would depend not only upon its employment composition and resource endowment, but also upon the "terms of trade" of its production of goods and services with the products for which it traded with the community at large. If, for simplicity's sake, it is assumed that the Jews were producing manufactured goods and consuming food and raw materials, their prosperity or lack of it would depend to some extent upon the terms of trade between manufactured goods and raw materials. In fact, the income of the Jews depended upon the economic situation of the various countries and particularly upon conditions in the agrarian sector which provided the bulk of the consumers of the products and services produced and marketed by the Jews. Since the goods sold by the Jews were more sensitive to the income position of consumers and since prices tended to vary with regard to relatively small changes in the demand or supply of such goods, their income probably fluctuated even more than that of the primary product producers. At the same time the volume of consumption of the Jews was less liable to fluctuate, thus tending to underscore even more the vulnerability of their net income position.

The secular trend of the economic well-being of the Jewish community in Europe varied from country to country, making it difficult to establish a general trend that would fit all countries during identical periods. The most general trend in the economic conditions of the Jews, and one that helps to explain the historical direction of the migration process, is the continuous improvement of their economic status and income level in Eastern Europe until the middle of the 17th century when the decline set in. About the same time, actually after the recovery following the Thirty Years' War in Germany (1618–48), a slow process of improvement of the economic conditions favorable to the Jews started in Central and Western Europe. While the 18th century reinforced the two diametrically opposed tendencies, the reversal of the migration pattern became discernible. The dependence of the Jews upon the economic conditions of the country and the particular society is self-explanatory. What is less clear, however, is the existence of significant differences in the attitude of different social groups toward the Jews behind the facade of a generalized "attitude."

ATTITUDES OF AND RELATIONS WITH THE SOCIETY AT LARGE. The pattern of economic and especially social relations between Jews and non-Jews remained almost unchanged throughout most of the early modern period. These relations were initially established to a very large extent upon the basis of the expected or actual utility of the Jews to the interests of particular social groups. The similarities and differences of economic interests of the social groups and their relative political strength played a decisive role in shaping the constraints upon the economic activity of the Jews. The following social groups might be differentiated: the crown and the nobility; the gentry; the merchants, with differentiation between the more advanced and backward countries; the craftsmen; and the peasants. From the outset it should be noted that the Jews had no economic counterpart to some of the social groups (crown and nobility, gentry, peasants) and thus no problem of economic competition could enter into the relationship. In the cases of the craftsmen and merchants, however, the problem of direct competition created almost an a priori presumption of an antagonistic relationship.

For the crown, the Jews were either a source of revenue or a vehicle of economic development in the areas of foreign trade, money and credit, and later manufacturing industry. The dependence of the Jews upon the crown allowed them to be considered both as a pliable instrument of government policies and as an important source of money income, fully compensating for the distaste or religious resentment generally felt toward the Jews. In the countries where the upper nobility shared in the power of the government, the economic convenience and money incomes from the Jews derived by the nobles employing them on the large private estates or in the discharge of the nobility's public offices rivaled the gains derived by the crown. The attitudes of the gentry toward the Jews were somewhat more ambiguous than that of the nobility. The Jews served the gentry as middlemen in the sale of their agricultural surplus and as suppliers of manufactured goods on terms more favorable than other merchants would customarily offer. In addition they often served as a source of credit for the money-hungry, debt-ridden gentry. Like the nobility, the gentry preferred in many cases to have the Jews act as a buffer between them and the peasantry, so that for the opportunity of employment and income the Jews often assumed the role of the gentry's agent in the economic exploitation of the peasantry and in effect became the scapegoat of the justified wrath of the peasants. The presence of the Jews as a threat of competition to the urban dwellers was useful to the gentry in resisting the merchants' demands for economic and political privileges, which the gentry were loathe to give up or to share. The gentry, therefore, appeared as a defender of the Jews and of their activities as traders and craftsmen. The ambiguity in the gentry's position arose mainly in connection with their role as debtors who were quite unwilling to live up to their obligations.

With respect to the merchants, a distinction has to be made between the advanced and the economically backward countries. In the economically advanced countries, the merchants during this period had already given up many of their special privileges in exchange for the legal protection of the business contract. The existing institutions and organizational forms of trade allowed a certain degree of competition; and the merchants as a group did not feel terribly threatened by an influx of newcomers, as long as the newcomers subscribed to the generally accepted rules of business conduct, were subject to the common jurisdiction, and were contributing to the expansion of trade. Therefore, even if the Jewish merchants were not socially accepted, they were tolerated as performing the same social function as the merchants in general. In contrast, the merchants in the economically backward countries were hostile for a number of reasons: (1) the occupation of merchants was circumscribed by sets of special privileges and regulated by the guild organizations in the areas of entry, business behavior of the guild members, and the nature of the markets; (2) the merchants in those countries subscribed very strongly to the erroneous notion that there is at each point in time a given volume of business, and the admission of more people into the profession will only reduce the share everyone already enjoys; (3) the fear of competition, which might lead to a decrease of the profit rate, made the merchants hostile to newcomers in general and particularly to the Jews who were outside their jurisdiction; (4) many of the merchants in the less developed countries were themselves ethnically of foreign stock and by keeping the conspicuous Jews out they tried to mollify the popular impression that trade was almost exclusively in the hands of foreigners. Thus the merchants in such countries did their best, wherever they could, to limit the occupations of the Jews, trying to eliminate competition from the most lucrative areas of trade and from the conventional channels of trade.

The social group that felt subjectively most threatened by competition from the Jews were the artisans who relied even more than the merchants upon benefits derived from old privileges and the guild organization. They tried to augment their incomes by following monopolistic practices, by regulating entry into guilds, setting a long time period for apprenticeship, prescribing the production process in detail, and trying to control the market. The artisan guilds in urban areas were relatively powerful, closed corporate bodies, quite effective in controlling urban crafts. As a social group the artisans had a much narrower outlook than the merchants, were much more under the influence of the Church, and resentful and suspicious of outsiders. During this period the Jewish artisans did not succeed in being incorporated into the general guilds and had to operate outside the Christian guild organization. Attempts to set up guilds of Jewish artisans were numerous and always argued for on the basis of the need for organization for successful competition or income maintenance. Needless to say, the artisans, the plebeian masses of the cities, quite often linked their struggle against competition from Jewish craftsmen and traders to the social struggle against the gentry and urban patricians. Thus anti-Jewish sentiment often accompanied particular forms of the class struggle of the urban plebeians.

The attitudes of the peasantry to the Jews did not matter in terms of the policies toward the Jews, except in cases of peasant wars and uprisings. Nor could the peasants prevent Jews from acting on behalf of the crown, gentry, and nobility. Nevertheless they affected some of the economic activities of the Jewish traders and artisans and were of importance in the social sphere since the peasants constituted the vast majority of the population. There is no doubt that in the situations in which the Jews acted as economic agents for the landowners they were strongly resented by the peasants. But even in the many instances when the Jews helped to bring the peasants into the money economy the attitude was not one of unqualified gratitude. This was due to the fact that the peasants' entry into and participation in the money economy was accompanied by rising demands for incomes on the part of both the landowners and the state at the expense of the peasants. In a sense, with peasant incomes rising, rents and taxes tended to rise accordingly. It would probably not be incorrect to conclude that in spite of tangible benefits provided for the peasants by some economic activities of the Jews, the peasants did not differentiate among the various roles played by the Jews in the rural economy. They were certainly either unable or unwilling to distinguish between different categories of Jews, a trait which they share with other social groups. The Jew was the stranger who, in the eyes of the peasants (as well as of the artisans), was suspected of undermining the traditional order. That old order was one that the peasants did not like, but they were too conservative to substitute another for it because of all the accompanying uncertainties. The Jews, in turn, especially those that settled in the rural areas, were perhaps only a notch above the peasants economically, but they were separated from the peasants by a cultural gulf that could not be bridged. Thus suspicion on the one side was reciprocated by contempt from the other.

ROLE OF THE JEWISH COMMUNITY ORGANIZATION. To the extent that the relations between some groups of the general community and various social groups within the Jewish community appeared to the contemporaries as antagonistic, and to the extent that the legal framework and policies of many European states were discriminatory, there existed a strong tendency within the Jewish community to engage in self-defense. In addition, there manifestly existed a desire to free themselves of the fetters of restrictions and controls imposed by the state, guilds, and other existing corporate bodies. But the latter attitude did not lead necessarily to a laissez-faire attitude even in areas of autonomous choice. The Jews' demand for freedom of trade or for the free exercise of one's skills in crafts and manufacturing did not include a demand for the abolition of regulations by the Jewish community itself of the economic activity of its members. The adoption of such an attitude would clearly clash with existing economic realities and with the basic tenet of governmental policy toward the Jews, which was accepted, willingly or unwillingly, by the Jewish communities. The point of departure of governmental policies was the principle, explicitly stated or implicitly assumed, of collective responsibility of the community for the acts of its members. In order for the Jewish community to discharge this responsibility at least a modicum of autonomy had to be granted in areas of taxation and civil law.

Seen in historical perspective, the measures of self-regulation and control by the autonomous authorities of the Jewish community over the economic activities of their members were perhaps only minor alterations in the general framework of the economic life of the Jews, which was determined largely by the conditions of the economy and major policies of the state. Nevertheless, the details and alterations seem to have been important since they apparently influenced the well-being of many and helped minimize some effects of discrimination. In general the spirit in which particular adjustments and arrangements were made was one of pragmatic realism. Broadly it coincided with the abolition of the restriction upon Jews charging interest to their coreligionists, a move that officially sanctioned a usage originating much earlier than the beginning of the 17th century. The basic criteria for community control appear to be in the same spirit: (1) maximum economic effectiveness for the community, the collectivity as the sum of its members; (2) conformity with traditional standards of justice and welfare; (3) minimal interference with individual initiative; and (4) continuity of religious traditions and maintenance of the existing authority structure, social order, and economic stratification.

Among the most outstanding examples of community activity as a self-regulatory agency influencing the economic life of its members, the following may be mentioned: (1) The right to accept new settlers enabled communities at least to some extent to regulate and direct the flow of migration. By granting or refusing the "right of entry" in the community (which was tantamount to the right of habitat and employment in a certain locality; see *Ḥerem ha-Yishuv*), the communal authorities were able to exercise a degree of control upon the supply of labor and the extent of competition for employment and business opportunities. (2) The community had the right of enforcing the principle of *ḥazakah – of seniority or preferential option granted in the bidding or negotiation of a new contract to the previous partner over his competitors. This was a rule that benefited the previous or current party over any new entrant and effectively limited competition among Jewish businessmen. (3) There was a right and obligation to guarantee the solvency of the members of the community in business transactions whenever such guarantee were required or requested. In practice such guarantees helped members of the community avail themselves of business opportunities and strengthen their credit position, but in some cases the community, by indicating the limits of credit, was both protecting itself and preventing its members from engaging in high-risk operations. (4) There was a right to distribute the tax burden of the community among its members both for the purposes of poll tax payments and for its intracommunity needs (see *Taxation).

The paradox of the situation is that most of the cited examples appear to be in conflict with the liberal idea of granting freedom of economic activity to individuals. It is, however, congruent with the conviction that for a minority to survive as a distinct group it has to place the interests of group survival above the short-run interests of the individual members. It is also plausible that when the state was regulating economic life and practicing economic discrimination, an autonomous group could not afford a laissez-faire practice and still maintain its identity and internal cohesion. In fact, when during a later period the state started to withdraw from the positions of control and regulation, the Jewish communities also had to give up most of their regulatory functions under the pressure of the individual members in order to survive at least as voluntary associations. But during the period under consideration the Jewish community organization was still very strong in enforcing its control over an economically heterogeneous and socially stratified population.

SOCIAL STRATIFICATION WITHIN THE JEWISH COMMUNITY. Since the Jewish community was differentiated in respect to economic functions, it would be well to inquire into the pattern of social stratification among the Jews during this period. The society at large was hierarchically organized, and the social conditions of its members were largely predetermined either by birth (by hereditary status) or by the role and functions assigned to them by prevailing custom or by the state. There was no perfect identity, however, between the stratification of the society at large and the Jewish community for the simple reason that the Jews were excluded from land ownership and were therefore lacking the equivalent of the nobility, gentry, and serf-peasantry. Within the Jewish community there was the equivalent of three large groups which had their counterparts in the society at large, namely: the equivalent of the urban patricians, the equivalent of the small producers (craftsmen) and middlemen (merchants), and the wage earners and paupers.

The first group, in terms of wealth, was represented by rich merchants and entrepreneurs engaged in international and interregional trade, in ownership of industrial establishments, in banking and moneylending, as court factors, tax farmers, etc. In terms of social prestige this group also included famous rabbinical scholars and book publishers, although the last two categories were far inferior in terms of wealth. The second group, representing the majority of the Jewish population, included all the owners of some capital, in the form of tools or stocks of goods, to which their own or family labor was applied and who employed a small number of workers. They were the ones who, like the vast majority of the first group, came into direct contact with the market and were exposed to all the irregularities of the early, imperfect markets of the time. Although social mobility from this group into the upper stratum was not prevented by any legal means, the dichotomy between the two groups was noticeable both in the economic and the social spheres, and the grievances voiced by this group against the upper stratum are a clear witness to the cleavage existing between them. The third group included wage earners engaged in crafts, trade, transportation, services (including domestics), and a large number of unemployables for whom the community had to provide a livelihood. While social mobility from the third group into the second was a possibility, the "plebs" of the community constituted a distinct group, inferior not only in terms of income, but also in education and skills and separated by many social and cultural barriers from the ones who were economically independent.

While the intergroup mobility was limited by economic factors and perhaps also by some cultural factors, intragroup mobility was much more free and frequent; and in this respect the Jewish community was ahead of its times in comparison with the society at large. There were also special reasons why the tensions among the various groups and social classes were dampened and less explosive than in the society at large. Two reasons were especially significant: first, the generally oppressive attitudes of the society at large, which apart from exceptional cases and special situations was hardly in a mood to differentiate among the various categories and groups within the Jewish community; secondly, the institutionalized system of welfare within the Jewish community acted as a form of income redistribution and provided for the most basic needs of its indigent members. But even this mitigation of the internal tensions could not eliminate the intensity of the discord and the deep resentment that existed among the various social groups within the community, contrary to the superficial impressions of casual outside observers who were convinced that the Jewish community was a model of internal harmony and solidarity. The internal conflicts were at times so intense that external, governmental authorities were called upon to take sides and intervene either to strengthen the forces of authority within the community or to curb the arbitrariness of the decisions and limit the authority of the ruling bodies. The various intellectual and religious movements within the Jewish community also exhibited strong social overtones and in some cases revealed the strength of subterranean resentments and open protest on the part of the lower classes of the community.

The real power in the community was located in the hands of the upper social group, and the wealthy occupied offices of consequence and social prestige. Although Jewish communities strongly resented the appointment of officers by government authorities – which guaranteed office-holding for the wealthiest – as an interference in community affairs, the system of electing officers (who were often personally responsible for the fiscal obligations of the community) no less favored the election of the rich, the ones who could afford the burden of office. Wealth became almost a prerequisite for office and could be augmented by holding office, since offices provided access to information and opportunities that could be turned to business advantage by their holders. In part, some of the power of the wealthy elite was exercised because of the economic dependence of members of the community directly employed or indirectly influenced by the elite. The relatively large-scale business operations by the members of the elite provided employment opportunities for agents, salesmen, domestics, etc., which assured the elite of the support of the dependents in community affairs. The symbol of the autonomy of the Jewish communities was their right to elect their spiritual leaders, the rabbis. The communities viewed any attempt by governmental authority to appoint rabbis as an assault on their right of religious autonomy. Nonetheless, the power of the spiritual leaders was more important in maintaining the continuity of tradition and is to be seen more in their role as mitigators in internal conflicts than in the internal policies or the routine economic activities of the community. It was left to the business elite to regulate and supervise the economic activities of the community. In cases where a conflict arose between the spiritual leaders and the upper stratum in the community, the real power, that of the elite, usually asserted itself. In the communities in which the power of office was shared by the upper stratum with representatives of the middle group, the important decisions were usually left to the "patrician" families. An important result of the existing social stratification during this period was the degree of stability provided by community leadership recruited basically from one social group. In a period when all other societies were hierarchically organized, the Jewish community could hardly afford to be organized according to any other principle.

Transition Period

The transition between the "old" conditions and the "new" was neither smooth nor short. It spanned two distinct periods, which differed markedly from one another in respect to the general framework of economic activity, the prevailing ideologies, and the social groups that made the important decisions. The transition reflected the change in social and economic development, in this sense exhibiting both its revolutionary aspects regarding some institutions and individuals and its evolutionary aspects of piecemeal transformation of other institutions, habits, and activities. The major characteristics of the transition in the economic sphere included acceleration in the accumulation of tangible assets (capital) as well as the possibility and willingness to transfer increasing amounts of capital from one area of economic activity to another. This phenomenon was accompanied by the development of technology, which provided labor-saving mechanical devices for the production of goods, and in turn became a strong force in creating the demand for new capital and for new skills.

Concurrent with these economic changes were new developments in generally held beliefs and opinions. Among the many, some must be singled out for their significance. Especially important was the rise of secularism at the expense of traditional religious and theological views. The turn toward secularism put man in the center of the universe and assumed that he was able and willing to subordinate the forces of nature to serve him. This led both to the development of a more generalized utilitarian approach and, with the weakening of earlier dogmatic attitudes, to the development and penetration of scientific thought, thus providing the basis for innovations and inventions in the field of technology. The spread of the idea of egalitarianism was another important element in the change of social thought. While not a characteristic feature of the period, the fact that man in the abstract was now at the center of the universe, led egalitarianism to challenge the basic premises of a hierarchical society in which the accidents of birth largely determine the social position of individuals. Though egalitarianism was not yet successful during the period of transition in securing the political and social participation of a broad spectrum of the populace, it at least achieved the legitimization of merit and achievement rather than birth as the leading criteria for joining the social elite. The change of criteria was of utmost importance, while the implementation of the principle could proceed only slowly if the social fabric was not to be torn by revolution. If ideas of secularism and egalitarianism are to be intellectually tenable and socially effective, equality before the law is perhaps the first necessary step. Thus the establishment of a new legality based not upon divine law or the will of the sovereign but upon the consensus of the governed led to new forms of individual freedom and to social responsibilities or disciplines being shared by all citizens or inhabitants of the particular countries. That social discipline required the resolution of conflicts within a legal framework was obvious, and for the framework to be effective it had to approach universality and offer equitable treatment to all.

The transition period in Western Europe dates from about the middle of the 18th century until after the Napoleonic Wars, and in Eastern Europe runs from the Napoleonic Wars until the third quarter of the 19th century. The distinction and the lack of overlap in time is important to the extent that the Western European experience could have been considered as a model of the future economic and social development of Eastern Europe. However, if a comparison were made of the situation in Western Europe with that of Eastern Europe during a particular point in time, more striking contrasts than similarities would be found. At a time when the economies of Western Europe were caught up in the process of economic growth, those of Eastern Europe during the same period were in a state of relative stagnation in which the process of economic development either did not get off the ground or was arrested by the prevailing political regime. While in the West the end of the 18th and the beginning of the 19th century witnessed new economic opportunities for its indigenous population and for immigrants, the Jews included, the wholesale bankruptcy of the Jewish community organizations of Poland in the second half of the 18th century and the economic plight of the majority of the Polish and Russian Jews around the turn of the 19th century were examples of the different situations of the Jewish communities in various countries at those times.

How did the Jews fare under the conditions which were defined as the transition period? There is no doubt that the initial benefits were considerable since they signified the changed status of the Jews. Even in the absence of equal civil rights or true emancipation they meant an increased sense of personal security, a decrease in arbitrariness, and a greater recourse to the prevailing law of the land. It is possible to describe, rather than measure, the economic effects of these transitional changes upon the activities of the Jews in two distinct areas, labor and capital.

The loosening of restrictions affecting places of habitat or work made it possible for labor to move more freely in search of markets with higher earnings. Thanks to the relaxation of restrictions, on entering particular professions Jews could avail themselves of training opportunities or enter educational institutions with hopes for upward social mobility and higher incomes. The rising demand for new types of employment, spurred by the accelerated pace of economic development, provided possibilities for absorption of at least a part of the relatively large groups of unemployed members of the Jewish communities in the labor market. The greater degree of personal safety and security of their assets had a number of effects upon Jewish owners of capital. There was a reduction of the size of reserves previously kept as personal insurance against various emergencies. The size of such reserves for Jewish merchants was variously estimated as up to a third of their wealth. By reducing the reserve it was possible to devote a larger part of the total wealth to productive use. The improvement of the legal position of the Jews increased the amount of credit that could be extended to them without excessive risks on the part of the lenders. This development in turn probably led to a decrease in the rates of interest at which Jews could borrow. Added security and new opportunities enabled the Jewish owners of capital to use it in a number of areas (real estate, industry) hitherto closed to them, thus increasing both the returns and effectiveness of capital. The removal of some discriminatory regulations (such as double taxation), which previously increased the costs for Jews of carrying on economic activities and affected the size of their income, had the effect of increasing their disposable income and could have led to simultaneous growth in, or to a redistribution of the shares of, consumption and savings. In some cases an increase of savings (or investment) could be expected; in other cases an increase of consumption or an increase in family size could follow. With regard to the last, it is clear that even partial removal of some discriminatory rules applied to the Jews, like restriction on settlement, on marriage, and the like (see, e.g., *Familiants Laws), resulted in an increase in the birth rate and population growth.

The transition period can be characterized as the beginnings of consideration of the "Jewish problem" as a matter of social and national policies for the states and societies in Europe, in contradistinction to earlier preoccupation with fiscal interests, Church concerns, or narrowly defined group competition. The growing concern of the state with the economic activity of the Jews was exhibited in various attempts by governments to influence such activity. Some attempts could be classified as representing a policy of "productivization" of Jews and attempts to change the social composition of the Jewish population. Interesting examples of such policies, perhaps in part also inspired by physiocratic thought, were the attempts to settle Jews on the land by "enlightened absolutist" regimes such as those of *Joseph II in Austria and Alexander I in Russia. It is immaterial here that such attempts were completely unsuccessful, either because the schemes were insufficiently prepared and financed or because they were sabotaged by the bureaucracy that was to administer them. The disappointments of tens of thousands of Jews and the sufferings of thousands who participated in the failing experiments are also not at issue. The important feature was the clearer realization that in part, at least, government policies were responsible for the peculiarities of Jewish economic activities or social structure and that state policies – as a part of the social and legal framework of Jewish activity – had to be brought in line with or adjusted to the economic changes that were taking place. Therefore, while during the transition period, government-sponsored agricultural colonization in southern Russia resulted in settling on land only a few thousand Jewish families and failed abysmally in Austria, it nevertheless raised by implication the problem of legal tenancy and ownership of land for Jews. This in turn resulted in the subsequent development of a small but socially diverse farming element in the Jewish communities of Eastern Europe during the 19th century.

Whatever the impact of the changing economic and social conditions on the economic activities of the Jews, during the transition period the Jewish communities had to face an imminent, fundamental change. For the Jewish communities the problem was how to continue as a distinct group in the general society, not under conditions of forced separation but under those of free choice by their members. For the first time within the general period under consideration, it became possible for larger numbers of Jews to break away culturally and socially from the Jewish community, even while maintaining their religious beliefs, and to be accepted by the community at large. Social acceptance was offered to a small but influential minority of the Jews as remuneration for cultural assimilation. The price to pay was basically severance of their relations with the rest of the Jewish community and the abandonment of the active desire to perpetuate this community. Under the circumstances, the offer of social acceptance was a tempting one since it involved social advancement by the criteria of the community at large. That not every social group would accept its Jewish counterpart even at the price of cultural assimilation was obvious, but during the transition period personal or narrow group interests were strong and the fight for universal civil rights still very much ahead. The situation presented a challenge to the Jewish communal authority and called for surrender of its traditional power of exclusive representation of the Jews and of its power of *taxation. The weakening of the authority of the Jewish community organization could also be traced to the growing unwillingness of the more affluent groups in the community to subject themselves to income redistribution in favor of the poor. Poor relief was "scaled down" from a duty concept to one of discretionary charity, and paupers were "encouraged" to find employment. Although the full impact of the newly created situation of defining one's identity, under conditions of relatively free choice, was to be felt during a later period, the difficulties and problems thus created – psychological and social – were already becoming apparent during the transition period.

Modern Period

The main features of the development of the economy of the Jews during the modern period are patterns of migration, penetration into areas of industry, maintenance of a strong position in the area of services, and very limited involvement in agriculture. Decades ago economic historians were engaged in a debate about the role of the Jews in the development of capitalism, some trying to define the historically objective role of the Jews as active agents of capitalist development. Now with historical hindsight the discussion would probably be conducted and conclusions reached within a different framework. The implicit notion that capital was abundant in the Jewish sector of the economy would now be refuted and therefore the logic of portraying the Jews as "objectively acting" on behalf of a capitalist order would be rejected. It would probably be accepted, however, that an order of economic liberalism is one that provides greater opportunities for any minority, the Jews included, than an alternative economic system based upon a different ideology and set of political principles. An impersonal market and a high degree of division of labor may create alienation and other social ills, but by not requiring that the commodities produced have any other labels than the price tag, the free market works against discrimination. A competitive market may injure high-cost producers or cause unemployment, but its principles were compatible with the ideas of social and cultural pluralism. The relatively favorable response of Jews and other minorities to the liberalization of the economic order was based primarily on an expected reduction in discrimination. However, while a liberal economic order provided the Jews with opportunities, it could not provide them with a right to work, to compete on equal terms, to the same extent that such a "right" was traditionally enjoyed by the various classes of the majority population. In addition, the phase of economic liberalism as a chief characteristic of the capitalist system was neither a permanent feature nor a very long-lasting one, nor even one universally followed in all countries experiencing the capitalist type of economic growth.

In most countries of Eastern Europe the capitalist stage of development coincided with a rise of nationalism, which at various points exhibited a discriminatory attitude toward the Jews in general or toward some social groups within the Jewish community, in attempts to promote the interests of the ethnic majority. Tariff policies against foreign goods were accompanied not infrequently by discriminatory taxation imposed upon "foreigners" within the country, meaning national minorities. In the multi-national states of Eastern Europe there were ample opportunities for labeling various minorities as "foreign," "alien," and so on. Under such conditions it could hardly be expected that the Jewish masses, who were adversely affected by discriminatory policies, would consider the capitalist economic system as more desirable or attractive than an alternative promising them the "right to work."

JEWISH MIGRATION. It is against the background of insufficient employment opportunities and discrimination that the process of migration has to be viewed. The pattern of Jewish migration, of spatial mobility of labor, during the modern period differed in many respects from previous migration patterns. The general direction was westward, from Eastern Europe to the West, and from Europe overseas. As a matter of fact, the migration from Western Europe overseas was more than made up for by an influx of Jews from the East. This general direction of the migration was significant as a movement from less rapidly developing countries to more rapidly developing ones. In terms of its time dimension the inter-country migration was intensified during the 19th century and reached its peak during the decade prior to World War I. But apart from the inter-country migration, of very considerable significance was the intra-country migration from the less urbanized areas to the more urbanized areas, a development that increased the degree of concentration of the Jewish population in large urban and metropolitan areas, with their developed industry, trade, and other social or cultural characteristics. Both the domestic and international migration and the pattern of settlement of the Jews contributed to urban concentration and had an impact upon the social and economic structure of the Jewish population. While it is tempting to assign the role of prime mover in Jewish migrations to purely economic causes, it would be erroneous to omit political elements such as discriminatory legislation, violent antisemitism, pogroms, and revolutions. Political upheavals and governmental policies influenced the pace of the migration process, but could not stop it for any appreciable length of time (the case of the Soviet Union being an exception).

What were the characteristic features and effects of the migration process as a whole and of its various forms? The migration process started as soon as the Jewish population could rise above the level of poverty and isolation to which it had deteriorated in Eastern Europe by the end of the 18th and first half of the 19th century and regain its age-old habits of mobility. In terms of numbers, the migration stream from continental Europe during the 100 years preceding World War II accounted for approximately 4,000,000 individuals, of which over 70% went to the United States, about 10% each to South America and Palestine, and the rest to Britain, Canada, South Africa, Australia, and other countries. Thus, in view of the fact that the North American continent absorbed three-quarters of the total international (or overseas) migration, the characteristics of this migration may be assumed as the most typical.

The available data indicate that the migration was a family one (of whole families, even if separated by a one- or two-year period) rather than of single individuals; that it was a migration for settlement and not for work, saving, and return; and that it was a migration involving a relatively very high percentage of skilled workers. With respect to the last characteristic, only the data can be relied upon and little investigation beyond these can be done: the explanation of this phenomenon can only be surmised. It is logical to assume that the process of overseas migration required payment of transportation costs, in other words some amount of savings, and thus could not involve paupers. Therefore, it is logical to assume that the migrants were either members of the industrial labor force, or entrants into the labor force who already had acquired skills, or individuals who acquired particular skills in anticipation of their migration, having made an investment over and above their transportation costs or borrowed in anticipation of future returns. It was in large measure due to the industrial skills and some working habits of the migrants that their future relative success can be explained.

Three further points need to be emphasized in connection with the migration problem. First, given the nature of the family ties within the Jewish community, the financing of migration took place within the extended family of the immigrants and was later also subsidized by the earnings of the immigrants, often virtually out of their first savings. Secondly, prior to the end of the 19th century there were already in operation well-organized voluntary associations that assisted in the migration process. In their absence the economic and psychological costs of migration would have been considerably higher. Thirdly, by organizing voluntary associations of mutual assistance, in part copying the models from Eastern Europe, the immigrants were able to help the new arrivals more effectively. Some relatively small part, probably not more than about 3% of the total of the migration movement, was financed and assisted by funds donated or collected on behalf of the migration, especially in the presence of an ideological or programmatic background. The two most outstanding examples were Palestine and the agricultural settlements in Argentina.

The primary effect of both the intraregional and international migration of the Jews was to decrease the competition for employment opportunities where such were scarce and provide a higher return for the migrants where their labor and skills were in greater demand. Thus while the income of the migrants increased in comparison with their previous income level, the income level of those who remained behind did not fall. However, it must be admitted that the movement of millions of people within a few generations deprived the established Jewish communities of a young, enterprising, and skilled element. This movement had a number of demographic, economic, and cultural repercussions on the European Jewish communities. It is difficult to pinpoint such effects, but it certainly affected the age structure of the European communities by removing some of the middle groups (age groups 20–40 in particular). It also perhaps affected adversely the growth rate of the Jewish population in Europe, although it would be difficult to predict what that rate would have been under worse economic conditions in the absence of migration. In terms of its impact upon the social structure, it probably increased the economic polarization within the Jewish communities since neither the rich nor the very poor contributed to the migration stream. In another sense the migration movement contributed to a greater stability within the Jewish communities since it absorbed much of the unruly and nontraditionally inclined element of the community. Last but not least, the migration movement contributed to an activated exchange among Jewish communities, with a money transfer to Eastern Europe that not only subsidized further migration but supported relatives and community institutions, and that was in part compensated by an export of cultural and spiritual services from Europe to the areas of new settlement.

PENETRATION INTO INDUSTRIAL EMPLOYMENT. Some assessment must be made of the conditions that enabled Jews to penetrate into industrial employment and maintain their position in the areas of services under conditions of modern industrialization. What adjustment was required on their part to attain their goals? Here we are concerned with entrepreneurial activities in the industrial sector as well as the transformation of handicraft employment into small-scale and larger-scale industrial employment. This entrepreneurial activity is not being considered here in terms of "Jewish contributions" to the development of this or that country, or the amassing of wealth by individuals of Jewish descent. It is beyond the purview of this account to dwell upon the Rothschilds in England and France, on the German-Jewish bankers, or on mining magnates in Africa or South America. In addition, a distinction should be made between large-scale and small-scale entrepreneurs. While a few Jews entered industrial entrepreneurship via high finance, the banking system, etc., the multitude consisted of small-scale industrial entrepreneurs who were recruited mostly from the ranks of craftsmen and merchants, previously engaged in the putting-out system. They were subordinate to and dependent upon the large-scale industrial establishments because they could hardly compete with large-scale industrial firms in the production of goods and had therefore either to become suppliers to the large firms of some specialized goods or producers of market goods that were outside the assortment manufactured by large-scale industry. Given the scarcity of capital in the social milieu from which the small-scale producers or entrepreneurs were recruited, their proximity to industrial centers and markets was absolutely crucial. Small-scale industrial firms did not possess the capital to carry large stocks, and a quick turnover was their only mode of survival. A great deal of flexibility in product-mix and in assuring sources of demand was required to keep the enterprises in operation. They also required a labor force skilled but not overly specialized and with relatively few employment alternatives to accept a less-than-regular employment. This was a typical solution for economic branches that operated with a basically backward technology at low levels of productivity, low wages, and long hours of work, in what were fringes of the consumer goods industries. It was due to the declining role of handicraft production, which was suffering from industrial competition, that this type of industrial employment was acceptable to Jewish industrial job seekers.

Jewish entrepreneurs did, however, play an important role in providing gainful employment for large numbers of Jews. It may be assumed that for a Jewish entrepreneur there existed a "psychological income" in providing employment for other Jews, whether he did so for reasons of greater familiarity and cultural affinity or because it was considered a "good deed" in cases when discrimination in favor of Jewish employees increased his operational costs. Those costs, in turn, depended upon the nature of the labor supply and the distribution of skills within the Jewish labor force and within the total population. If the costs of hiring Jewish labor were less than or equal to those of hiring other members of the labor force, it can be assumed that there were no costs in the discrimination in favor of employing Jews. As will be seen from a number of examples, the employment pattern of Jewish labor by Jewish entrepreneurs did not in fact impose additional costs upon the employers. There were, however, two other obstacles that had to be overcome in order to have the employment of a Jewish labor force reach a significant level. The first constraint was the assumed or real strength of the religious taboo against work on the Sabbath, regardless of whether the taboo was expressed in the behavior of workers or in the attitudes of the entrepreneurs. The second constraint was the assumed animosity of non-Jewish workers and foremen toward Jewish co-workers. There is no doubt that such constraints upon the entrepreneurs were real, especially in the later part of the 19th century in Eastern Europe.

The cases of a few industries in Europe and one in the U.S. are instructive since they provide a broad spectrum of employment opportunities created by Jewish entrepreneurs for Jewish workers. One is the *textile industry in Russian Poland in which Jewish spinners, weavers, and other textile workers were predominantly employed in the smaller-scale enterprises, while the larger-scale factories refrained from employing them. Second is the case of the forestry trade, in which few Jewish workers and laborers could compete successfully with the low-paid peasants seeking off-season employment in lumbering. Therefore, thousands of Jews were employed in this industry by Jewish firms as overseers in the forests, sawmills, and transportation of the products, much of the output being destined for export or railroad construction. Thus, the demand for trained personnel with a degree of familiarity with the operation and quality standards in forestry and with some clerical skills attracted many Jewish workers and employees. While such a combination of skills was rare in the general labor force, and the wages and salaries accepted by the Jewish workers were generally low, there was hardly any cost of discriminating in favor of Jewish employment in the forestry trade. In the third case, the sugar and oil industries may be subsumed under one type of employment. Neither in sugar-beet growing nor in the processes of sugar refining were Jews represented. The same is true for the oil industry located outside the Jewish *Pale of Settlement. The Jews could compete neither with the peasants and local oil-workers nor with the highly skilled specialists in sugar and oil refining. The areas of employment for Jews provided for them by Jewish entrepreneurs were those of distribution and trade. Thus, thousands of Jews were employed as clerical personnel, salesmen, and sales agents in the trade networks of both the sugar and oil industries. The outstanding case of industrial employment provided by Jewish entrepreneurs for Jewish workers in the U.S. is the garment industry. The levels of skill brought over by the Jewish immigrants, the relatively low wage schedule of the garment industry, and the relatively small scale of the operations of the firms led to a high concentration of Jewish workers, with the industry as a whole serving as a massive source of employment.

The above examples illustrate some of the patterns of the penetration by Jews into areas of industrial employment. They are indicative of the manner in which masses of former artisans and pauperized elements of the Jewish community could join the ranks of industrial workers and employees. As in other societies, child labor and long-term apprenticeship were the chief means of skill-acquisition for the poor. Although the capital-goods industries were virtually closed for both Jewish entrepreneurs and workers alike, industrial employment concentrated in consumer goods industries signified the adjustment to modern, industrial society and injected a new dynamism both in the social relations within the Jewish communities and with the community at large.

MAINTENANCE OF POSITIONS IN THE SERVICE SECTOR OF THE ECONOMY. The service sector includes employment in trade, transportation and communication, public and private services, and the liberal professions. For the huge segment of the Jewish population previously employed in it, largely in trade and particularly commodity trade, the problem of economic survival within this sector became absolutely essential. During the early period of industrialization when massive investments are made in the build-up of physical industrial capital – primarily in construction and equipment and in some of the services of the social overhead type such as railroad and road building – the majority of the services are not recipients of capital. It is only when the basic capital in industry is created, and both the producers' goods and consumers' goods branches are producing at relatively high levels of productivity, that the demand for services increases on the part of a population whose general level of income has risen very substantially. The fact that Jews were heavily concentrated in the service sector in countries whose pace of development was slow, whose market growth was sluggish, and whose levels of personal income were among the lowest in Europe, did not augur well for service employees. It was, therefore, not so much a matter of historical foresight but a lack of viable alternatives that kept large masses of Jews within this sector during the early stages of industrialization. It was the gradual process of commercialization of agriculture that provided outlets for the commodity trade and thus for service employment for the Jews who were living in rural areas or small towns. Urbanization provided other opportunities for employment in trade and also in other services; but paradoxically the process of urbanization and the development of service opportunities in the large cities significantly undercut or substituted the service functions previously performed in small towns. The process of urbanization was accompanied by the development of a more dense transportation network which created direct links between the big cities and the hinterland, decreasing transportation and travel costs and making the big city and rural areas accessible to one another. The result was that many of the services concentrated in the small towns could no longer be performed at the prices offered in the big cities where economies of scale were more likely; and the decline of small towns under the conditions of a competitive market followed. The problem for Jewish service employment was whether the opportunities available to Jews in the big cities were sufficient to compensate or substitute for the disappearance of such opportunities in the small towns and also allow for the rate of Jewish population increase. The answer for Eastern Europe appears to have been negative, for Western Europe positive. In the U.S. there was a secular trend of employment growth in the service sector for the Jews. In Eastern Europe the crisis of the small towns remained a continuous problem, especially exacerbating for the Jews when coupled with discriminatory policies of limiting access or prohibiting the influx of Jewish service employees in such branches as the civil service, central government or municipal services, and public transportation. In countries that did not openly follow discriminatory policies, the solution of the service employment problem for the Jews became very much dependent upon both the general pace of economic development and the urbanization process.

The diversity of service employment makes it very difficult to estimate the degree of substitution of one type of employment for another or the mobility of individuals from one category to another within this sector. The required educational background differed substantially; and substitution or transfers were possible probably at the lower levels of skills in which literacy could be considered the predominant, if not the universally sufficient, prerequisite. Internal mobility within the service sector was much less frequent at higher levels of specialization and especially when the specific training presupposed a higher level of schooling. The explanation of the continuity of a high proportion of Jewish employment in the area of services would be incomplete if two other factors were overlooked. The first was the opening up of opportunities in the liberal professions; the second was the continued demand for special services generated within and performed expressly for the Jewish communities. The first phenomenon, entry into the free professions, was a result of the reduced effectiveness of discriminatory policies toward Jews in the area of secondary and higher education relative to the areas of the public services. Educational opportunities that provided employment possibilities in the free professions became attractive avenues of social and economic advancement for the Jewish middle class, previously employed primarily in commodity trade. Therefore, with employment in the public sector and in the civil service very much restricted and curtailed for eligible Jewish candidates, the typical employment pattern was in the private service sector, including health services, educational services, and legal services. In addition, the private service sector provided employment opportunities for a certain number of educated individuals as salaried employees, such as bookkeepers, legal clerks, and pharmacist's assistants.

The demand for services by and for the Jewish communities continued during this period, although the process of secularization tended to shift the demand from the purely religious areas to those of education, health, and social services. Attempts to maintain a general cultural and not only an exclusively religious identity helped to sustain the demand for educational services. Meanwhile, the pattern of settlement in urban and metropolitan areas created a demand for the development of a communication network by which some of the cultural needs could be met and thus supported the activities of the press, theater, literary activities, and the like. Given the fact that public services in the area of health for the total population were highly inadequate and that the Jewish population received even less than a proportionate share of those, the demand for health and social services provided within and by the Jewish community was very strong. This stimulus was instrumental in the provision of such services either on a private basis or as a part of the welfare activities carried on by the community authorities for needy members.

EMPLOYMENT IN THE AGRICULTURAL SECTOR. Farming played a very subordinate role in the employment structure of the Jewish population during this period and its share in total employment was relatively small. It is not difficult to provide an explanation for this phenomenon. During the 19th century and later, agriculture in Europe was a declining industry, releasing rather than attracting labor. In addition, previous discriminatory policies prevented land ownership and restricted land tenure for Jews to the extent that farming as a skill did not develop within the Jewish milieu. Although the lifting of some of the most severe restrictions rendered farming a plausible alternative to the precarious positions of small-town traders or artisans, a number of circumstances mitigated against a mass influx of Jews into farming. Land was becoming relatively expensive in Eastern Europe, and the returns to both capital and labor in agriculture were relatively small. Settlement on large land tracts and the establishment of colonies required sizable capital outlays and a degree of organizational effort beyond the available resources and authority of the organized Jewish communities. The pattern of individual settlement in a dispersed manner was discouraged on the one hand by religious and traditional attitudes, since it typically involved a high degree of cultural isolation, and on the other hand by an often hostile rural environment, suspicious of any aliens settling in its midst. Within the Jewish milieu or as part of Jewish folklore, the stigma of boorishness or coarseness was associated with Jewish farmers, characteristics of a low prestige status, not so much in economic terms as in general cultural ones.

Outside of Europe, however, two types of development have to be considered: (1) countries of rapidly developing agriculture in which the employment of Jews in this sector of the economy was not significant, the United States and Canada being prime examples; (2) countries in which the employment share of agriculture was higher than in most of Europe, the specific cases being Palestine and Argentina.

With respect to the first group, two factors might explain the relatively low share of agriculture in the employment distribution. The foremost was the greater attraction that employment opportunities had for immigrants in the industrial and service sectors coupled with the preference for urban settlement, which provided additional security to the immigrants as members of their own ethnic communities. The second was the timing of the large migration streams, which took place after the closing of the so-called "agricultural frontier." In the case of Palestine and Argentina there was an induced process in which some noneconomic variables were of utmost importance. In Palestine the ideological aspect, the Zionist idea, motivated a relatively high percentage of the immigrants to settle on land, beginning with the last decades of the 19th century; farming became as much a way of life as a profession. In Argentina a substantial segment of the immigration was sponsored by adherents of agricultural colonization schemes who induced agricultural employment by paying the transportation costs and providing land for agricultural group settlement in the name of ideas of "productivization" of unskilled and unemployed members of the Jewish community. However, the long-term trend both in Palestine, later the State of Israel, and in Argentina was the relative decrease of farm employment under the impact of industrialization and urbanization.

INCOME. Given the employment structure of the Jewish population during the modern period, what could be said about the level and distribution of income within this population?

At the beginning of the period, and in a number of countries during most of the period, the average income of the Jews was below that of the population at large, including the peasants. However, the level of income increased both as a result of the total increase of incomes in Europe in general and because of the impact of migration, which, given its direction from economically less prosperous areas to economically more prosperous ones, had a net impact of increasing the average income level of the Jewish population. In addition, because of its composition as an increasingly urbanized population and one concentrated in the industrial and service sectors of the economy, its income during the 100 years preceding World War II probably increased at a higher rate than the average income of the total population of the countries they lived in. As a rule of thumb it would not be incorrect to assume that the average income level of the Jewish population by the end of the period reached a level that was higher than the average for farmers and industrial workers, although probably not above the level of the skilled stratum of industrial workers and salaried employees. Another way of saying this is that Jewish income was at about the average level of the urban population. The level of Jewish income fluctuated around the general upward trend. The fluctuations were pronounced, first because of the relatively large proportion of self-employed, a social group whose income is less stable than that of salaried workers and employees; secondly, because of the impact of exogenous factors such as wars and major upheavals during which the property of the Jews was much more vulnerable than that of other population groups (e.g., the forced mass exile of Russian Jews from the war zones in World War I and the wave of pogroms in the Ukraine (1918–21), during which property was either destroyed, expropriated, or simply taken away by force from its rightful owners). Thirdly, during the downturns of the business cycle, Jews as a minority group usually suffered more than the average member of the society at large. But notwithstanding such fluctuations, the general trend of Jewish income growth on a global scale was upward.

How was this income distributed, and what were the basic determinants of its distribution? Both tendencies to increase and to decrease the income inequality were at work, and it would be very difficult to measure the separate effects with any degree of precision. Following intuitive judgment it would be sensible to assume that in the countries in which the impact of discrimination against Jews was the strongest, income inequality within the Jewish community was probably more pronounced than in the countries that followed a more liberal policy toward the Jews. That income inequality within the Jewish community led to tensions, internal struggle, and organized activities of one social group against the other is obvious. That the divergency of interests led to the development of different ideologies and as such intensified the divisive tendencies in the community is no surprise, being a reflection within the Jewish milieu of what was taking place within the population at large. It is also true that the internal struggles within the Jewish communities during the last decades of the 19th century and beginning of the 20th century made a considerable contribution toward reforming the community authorities toward their democratization and modernization. They thereby became much more responsive to the needs of their members. But whatever generalizations are attempted in order to bring under a common denominator the economic and social trends prevailing during the modern period, the significant differences of the developmental patterns of the Jewish communities can be better understood only upon a closer examination of at least the major Jewish communities. The ones selected for further scrutiny are the Western European, the Eastern European, the U.S., and the Palestine Jewish communities.

WESTERN EUROPE. The economic development of Western European Jewish communities during the modern period can be generally characterized by their successful attempt to join the middle class. Their problems roughly paralleled the problems of the middle class in Europe, in the sense that they enjoyed apparent well-being and security under normal conditions and discovered the precariousness of their position in times of crisis. Western Europe, following the example of England, experienced the industrial revolution around the middle of the 19th century and was busily involved in adjusting its institutional structure to fit the new economic order. Since the institutional adjustment was more complicated while vestiges of the older order had to be destroyed, eliminated, or transformed, and the state played a much more decisive role in the process of economic transformation on the European continent than in England, there was a greater degree of politization of economic issues than in England. The politization of economic issues provided a specific impetus for the activities of the middle class and had a profound impact upon the activities and attitudes of the Western European Jews.

At a time when new economic opportunities were being created in Western Europe, the Jewish population of those countries was relatively sparse and the Jews constituted a negligible percentage of the total population. Therefore, there was within the Jewish communities very little of the fierce competition for relatively scarce economic opportunities which characterized the situation of the Eastern European Jews. The process of urbanization and concentration of the Jewish population in Western and Central Europe started relatively early, but proceeded gradually, largely undisturbed by outside political factors. Migration, both internal and overseas, by the less prosperous members of the Jewish communities helped to achieve the aims of both the migrants as economic opportunities in the new centers of industry and the drive to penetrate into the middle class. The gradualism of the process of economic growth resulted in strengthening commerce, helped to develop among the Western European Jews a preference for independent economic activity. Economic integration of the Jews in Western European society meant self-employment in trade, finance, industry, and the free professions and not in manual labor. This process was facilitated by their utilization of the opportunities provided by the educational system and the marked decrease in discriminatory attitudes and policies.

The groundwork for the development of more liberal attitudes toward the Jews and for the readiness of the Jews to take advantage of the new economic and social opportunities was laid by the Enlightment (*Haskalah) and its impact on the Jewish milieu. Originally the new opportunities and social acceptance were offered to the upper strata of Jewish communities for the price of language assimilation and severance of their ties with the Jewish community. The upper strata of the Jews found the conditions acceptable and acted accordingly. When the opportunities to join the middle class became available to a larger number of Western European Jews and after they joined the political struggle of the middle class for broader suffrage, the problem of emancipation and of their civil rights was raised by the members of the Jewish middle class. Emancipation and civil rights for Jews meant a further integration of the Jews with the society, not within the concept of a Christian state but within a modern, secularized state. In the latter case language assimilation of the Jews was considered an insufficient prerequisite. The existence of Jewish Orthodoxy both as a symbol and major characteristic of their culture was considered a serious obstacle to real integration. Thus at the roots of the religious Reform movement which spread from Germany, there were both the changing patterns of employment among the Jews and the desire for cultural assimilation. As a result the gradual adjustment of religious rituals to modern conditions and some relaxation of the Orthodox law, which previously supported the exclusiveness and guarded the separation of the Jews from their environment, gained in appeal to the majority of the Western European Jews. An interesting by-product of the changes in the social position and cultural attitudes was the growing gulf between the Western European and East European Jews. The cultural ties were becoming looser and the sense of a common destiny weaker.

The penetration of the Jews into the middle class was a slow process which marked the second half of the 19th century. Its success over the period was unmistaken, but not necessarily continuous and certainly not without problems. It was challenged first by a wave of nationalism at the end of the century, when it became clear that the new social order in Europe could not guarantee the universal fulfillment of the rising expectations in the short run. The new wave of nationalism exhibited antisemitic aspects which gained currency among members of the European middle class. The *Dreyfus affair and other manifestations of antisemitism had a profound impact upon some members of the Western European Jewish communities and forced them to rethink and revise their notions of social and cultural integration. Although the majority continued to behave according to previously established patterns, a minority turned to solutions of either cultural pluralism or Jewish nationalism as the more satisfactory for the long run. A greater need was also felt for the maintenance of Jewish cultural (including religious) continuity and for closer ties with other Jewish communities. The net result was a somewhat decreased atomization of the Western European Jewish communities and their activities as well as the development of new cultural and economic institutions which strengthened the sense of Jewish identity and were instrumental in the moments of crises that lay ahead.

EASTERN EUROPE. To explain the economic activities of the Jewish communities in Eastern Europe during the third quarter of the 19th century and until World War II in purely economic terms, in terms of the market opportunities, demand for products, and labor supply would not only be a difficult task but provide incomplete and sometimes misleading answers. Since so much more is known about the economic conditions of this period, the interaction of the economic and extra-economic factors, be they political, legal, or psychological, is keenly felt. The outstanding characteristic of the other factors was the existence of a measure of discrimination against the Jews that was much more intense in this part of the world than elsewhere. Thus, in spite of the progress of a modern market economy, in spite of the process of industrialization that took place there, there was a strong residue of discrimination that limited the benefits of economic progress for the Jews and affected their economic activities. One rather striking example is to be found in the exile of Jews from the rural areas of Russia in the 1880s. The process of urbanization that took place as a result of industrial development is a familiar phenomenon and one that affected Jews in the rural areas. But there is a qualitative difference between a process that creates new opportunities in urban areas and draws labor away from the rural areas, and a mass exile that uproots tens of thousands and forcibly transplants them in a new economic and social environment with no visible means for their economic survival and with no economic alternatives since the demand for their labor or service is absent. Apart from such major catastrophes, the conditions of discrimination included a whole chain of minor calamities which created an atmosphere of uncertainty and determined the behavior of large masses of the Jewish population in Eastern Europe. Thus, the development of a capitalist society in Eastern Europe, while creating new economic opportunities was, as far as the Jews were concerned, accompanied by unsettling features that were constantly threatening to destroy the benefits bestowed by the economic progress. It is, therefore, proper to emphasize that the economic and social conditions of the majority of the Jews in Eastern Europe were influenced by a number of external constraints, one of which was the Pale of Settlement in Russia. The existence of the Pale limited the mobility of most of the Jews and virtually excluded them from some of the more important regions and dynamic centers of industry, trade, and public life and often forced them to accept opportunities that could be described as second best. The existence of legal and economic discrimination made the process of social mobility much more difficult and expensive for the Jews. The limitations on entering areas of employment, professions, public service, and education decreased their chances of fully contributing to the process of economic development and benefiting from it. While the advancement of the industrialization process destroyed some of the traditional areas of Jewish economic activity and created new ones, the process itself was erratic and did not allow for the formation of long-term expectations or less costly adjustments. Thus, while on the whole the Jewish population benefited from the process, growing in size and slowly improving in income position, the accompanying hardships were burdensome and unsettling. Given the relatively slow pace of economic progress of the regions of concentrated Jewish population in Eastern Europe (western part of the Russian Empire, northeastern part of the Hapsburg Empire, and Romania), coupled with the existence of discriminatory policies, these regions were primarily involved in the migration of Jews to Western Europe and America. But although emigration had the function of a safety valve, it could not counteract the impact of the industrialization process, which, while injecting a new dynamism in the economic and social sphere, affected the life of the Jewish communities by creating new areas of internal conflicts and threatening to destroy the traditional values built up through centuries of relative cultural isolation. To the extent that they represented breaks with previous traditions and emphasized the existence of new opportunities, the very processes of industrialization and urbanization raised the level of expectations of the Jewish masses and made them more aware of their relationship to the outer world. This led to the development of new patterns of thought, increased sensitivity to the conditions of discrimination, and a more intensive search for new solutions to the specific problems of the Jews. The awareness of common specific problems was demonstrated not only in the economic but also in the cultural sphere. In spite of some tangible returns to the cultural assimilation of groups of Jews, until the end of the period a cultural homogeneity of the Jewish population in Eastern Europe was preserved. This culture embraced the basic elements of traditional moral and religious values with an addition of modern elements developed during the period following the Enlightenment in Eastern Europe. While the symbiosis of the elements of the traditional culture with those of a secular, modern, and nationally oriented one was by no means harmonious, the tensions had a culturally stimulating effect. It was a period of very intensive cultural activity and creativity by the Eastern European Jews, marked by the revival and modernization of Hebrew literature and development of modern Jewish literature in Yiddish. Cultural activities, in addition to rudimentary religious training and bare literacy, penetrated and affected the Jewish lower classes which had previously been excluded from most of their cultural heritage.

The period between the two world wars witnessed a number of new developments in Eastern Europe that were of major significance for the Jewish population. The most important events were the Russian Revolution and the establishment of new national states in the region on the ruins of the two large empires that had long dominated the political scene in Eastern Europe prior to World War I. The positive effect of the political changes was the granting of citizenship and civil rights to the Jews in the new states. On the negative side were the growth of nationalism of the dominant ethnic groups and the continuation of de facto discrimination against the Jews in most countries. Coupled with the difficult economic conditions in those countries, which were even more aggravated by government interference in the economic sphere, the precarious power balance in Europe, and the impact of the economic depression of the late 1920s and 1930s, this worsened rather than improved the economic conditions of the Jewish population.

In the Soviet Union, after an initial gain resulting from the granting of civil rights and the abolition of the Pale of Settlement by the democratic government of 1917, the period of the civil war inflicted heavy population losses upon the Jews, particularly in the Ukraine. The three outstanding features of Soviet policy toward the Jews were the following: (1) The isolation of Soviet Jews from the Jewish communities abroad and the slow but consistent policy of destruction of their cultural autonomy, institutions, and organized forms of communal life, leaving cultural assimilation as the solution to their problems as individuals. (2) The destruction of the small town, the former locus of economic activity of the majority of Russian Jews as a result of the forced industrialization drive and the mobilization of human resources to build up the industrial base of the country. This policy led to a mass migration from the western parts of the Soviet Union (Belorussia and the Ukraine) to the metropolitan areas and new centers of industrial activity. (3) Since education became one of the major vehicles of social advancement and was made available in the first instance to the urban population, a large proportion of the Jewish population took advantage of the opportunities and a marked shift in the employment pattern as well as in the professional composition took place. The Jews entered en masse into industrial employment and various service branches, all of which were nationalized and under the centralized control of the government. Although the social and economic advancement of the Jews in the Soviet Union should not be disputed, it raised two grave issues: one of cultural assimilation and the loss of group identity of the Jews, of their existence as a distinct cultural or religious entity; and the second, of their dependence as a group or as individuals upon the decisions lodged in the hands of the supreme policy makers of the country. The gravity of both issues arose, however, in a later period, following World War II.

THE UNITED STATES. The chief characteristic of the development of the Jewish community in the United States during the late 19th and early 20th century was its rapid numerical growth by comparison with other Jewish communities. The growth occurred primarily as a result of the immigration of the Jews, rather than because of the birth rate of the Jewish population per se. The attraction of the U.S. for Jewish immigrants could be explained both in terms of a wage level relatively higher than in Europe as well as an open immigration policy, and the lack of specific anti-Jewish discrimination. However, the pace of immigration cannot be explained only in terms of increasing attraction. The impetus to immigration of the Jews can be traced to events in the European countries of their origin, and the influence of the turns of the business cycle in the United States on the size of the immigration stream can be demonstrated. During the modern period there were two streams of Jewish immigration, one of Western European Jews and the other involving almost entirely Eastern European ones. Each of these streams, although different in terms of its occupational or professional endowment, was faced by similar problems of economic integration and general acculturation with the environment.

While the German Jews arrived with the experience of language assimilation, a weakened sense of culture traditions, and the articulated desire to join the middle class, the Eastern European Jews arrived with industrial skills and the expressed willingness to be employed in any sector of the economy where opportunities were available, but without the experience of previous cultural assimilation. In addition, they transferred some of their habits of group behavior from their European environment. There was, therefore, among Jewish immigrants from Eastern Europe a strong preference for settling in compact masses for reasons of economic and psychological security. At the time of the first waves of mass immigration from Eastern Europe, the Western European Jews (mostly immigrants from Germany) had already acquired in the U.S. a basically middle-class or quasi-middle-class status and their pattern of employment reflected a high percentage of self-employment and concentration in the area of services. The mass influx of Eastern European Jews changed for at least two generations the social composition of the Jewish community in the United States. It became a predominantly industrial and labor-oriented community concentrated in major cities. The symbiosis of the two elements, the German and the East European, was ridden by conflicts and prejudices, by distinctions in wealth and status, the latter being derived from the degree of "Americanization" or the duration of residence in the U.S. The German Jews, often in the role of employers of the recent immigrants, especially in the garment industry, tried to maintain the social distance between themselves and the immigrants arriving from the culturally most backward areas of Europe. Faced with the model of success presented by the German Jews, the East European immigrants could not avoid aspiring to positions of social and economic advancement. While they accepted their status as manual workers and laborers as inevitable, and drew from it a number of conclusions, expressed by their political orientation, trade union activities, and so on, they actively sought an improvement in the economic position and status for their offspring. Thus, while the process of acculturation of the immigrants took time, the gradual social advancement of some was counterbalanced by the successive waves of immigration swelling the ranks of the Jewish industrial working population. It was not until after World War I and the harsh restrictions against East European immigration that the process of penetration into the service sector and self-employment category became much more visible.

The rapid growth of the economy, the decline of agriculture, and changes in industrial structure, accompanied by a sustained, relatively high level of income, made it possible for the service sector to develop. Aided by the availability of educational opportunities, the almost exclusively urban Jewish population found outlets for its employment in the service sector, and the percentage of employment as unskilled labor, domestic service, or low-paid industrial employment declined. It would be wrong to assume that the shift in employment and the resulting improvement in the income position of the Jews in the United States before World War II took place in the total absence of discrimination. There was in fact a whole range of discriminatory attitudes operating against the Jews, as against many other ethnic groups representing relatively recent immigration. There was, however, a major difference between the U.S. and Europe in that discrimination was a de facto attitude rather than a de jure, statutory, or legal arrangement; that it was a private matter rather than one of public policy. Like other groups of European origin, the Jews were relatively successful in minimizing the effects of discrimination, first by improving their economic position and second by using political power derived from their numbers and concentration in some major urban centers of the country. In addition, discrimination was met by the Jews with an almost atavistic reflex of communal activity. The Jewish community developed a time-honored self-defense mechanism against discrimination in the form of institutions designed to meet specific needs of individuals or groups within the community. In the absence of organized communal authorities, recognized either by the outside world or by the Jews themselves, or representing their collective interests, the role of voluntary associations and institutions was even more significant for the discharge of group responsibilities and for the maintenance of whatever cohesion was possible within the Jewish community.

The numerical growth and economic advancement of the United States' Jewish community resulted in a change in the relationships among Jewish communities in the world, the U.S. Jewish community becoming an important source of economic assistance for the others. In a certain sense the bonds between American and European Jews provided a community of interest and purpose for the various groups of American Jewry, giving expression to their Jewish identity. At a time when the process of language assimilation was in progress, and the commonalty of cultural concerns was diminishing, the "foreign aid" of American Jews provided them with a much-needed psychological satisfaction and helped to maintain their identity. This process turned out to be of particular importance for the subsequent developments during and after World War II.

PALESTINE. While the first systematic attempts of organized mass colonization in Palestine go back to the 1870s and 1880s, a marked acceleration of the immigration stream occurred at the beginning of the 20th century, primarily as a result of the growth of a modern nationalist movement making immigration and settlement in Palestine the cornerstone of its ideology. The more organized manner of immigration and settlement, in part directed by a long-term national vision, led to the establishment of a social infrastructure within and for the Jewish population in Palestine, and to the establishment of modern social, economic, and educational institutions in an otherwise primitive and backward country. The introduction of modern institutions was accompanied by a striking attempt to modernize agriculture, a successful undertaking that integrated the need for economic modernization with the ideological factor of the need to recover the land, producing a sizable agricultural sector within the Jewish community in Palestine. The fact that the agricultural sector embraced a variety of organizational forms of production, that alongside private agriculture a cooperative and even a communal network of farms was created, was of considerable importance for the further development of the economy. The ideas of cooperation were also applied to other sectors of the economy: in industry, construction, and the services. Such enterprises had to reconcile private and social criteria in their decision-making and had to accept procedures for social control, arrangements that provided a particular atmosphere for economic activity within the Jewish community.

The continuous numerical growth of the Jewish population, resulting from successive immigration waves and natural population increase, and the emotional intensity of the issues connected with its development and its role among Jewish communities in the world often obscured the interesting pattern of economic and social development of the Jewish community in Palestine. An important feature of the Jewish population in Palestine was its relatively homogeneous cultural background since the majority of immigrants came from Eastern Europe. It possessed or created a full array of industrial, agricultural, and service skills at various levels, coupled with a level of education that was compatible with, if not excessive of, the existing level of skills. The economic activities of the Jewish population were conducted under conditions of virtual absence of discriminatory policies, apart from restrictions on immigration, particularly during the interwar period. This in turn created a basically stable economic structure; the employment distribution did not change drastically with time. There was relatively less income inequality than within other Jewish communities because skills were distributed differently. The level of income of the Jewish population in Palestine provided for the consumption needs of the population, with investment funds either imported by private investors from abroad, borrowed abroad, or provided as a form of nonreturnable transfers (gifts) from other Jewish communities to the Jewish community in Palestine.

While the above characteristics appear to portray the main features of economic and social conditions of the Jewish community in Palestine until World War II, they obviously do not convey the dynamics of the process of economic development per se. A more detailed treatment of this subject would have to include the economic relationships with the majority of the population, the Arabs; the extent of self-sufficiency achieved within the Jewish community; and the economic relations with the foreign markets to which some of the products of Jewish labor, land, and capital were exported and from which income was derived (see *Israel, State of, Economic Affairs).

Epilogue

The interwar period that ended with the catastrophe of World War II, an event in the history of the Jews whose dimensions and consequences our present generation is still unable to perceive let alone define, was marked by the following characteristics: (1) the forced separation and isolation of one of the largest Jewish communities, namely that in the Soviet Union, from the rest of world Jewry; (2) the growth of the Jewish population in the United States and its relative economic strength in comparison with Jewish communities elsewhere created a new element in the balance and relationship between Jewish communities and indicated a future trend; (3) the economic situation of the European Jews, and especially of the East European communities, which worsened since economic and political uncertainty had become the norm even before the rise of Fascism and Nazism; (4) the rise of Nazism which created a direct danger to Jewish life and property in Central Europe, and the spread of discriminatory policies modeled upon the early legislation of Nazi Germany which became a real threat to a large part of European Jewry; given the limited opportunities for migration, the European Jewish population did not possess any real alternatives; (5) the growth of the Jewish community in Palestine which became an important cultural factor in the life of other Jewish communities, but its small relative size and the severe limitations imposed by the British upon Jewish immigration kept it from having a larger impact and from contributing toward a solution of European Jews' distress.

Therefore, prior to World War II, the Jewish communities found themselves at a crossroad, with the direction of their future fate and development depending upon exogenous, primarily political forces. The tragic results of World War II have left most of Europe virtually without Jews. There are now two major communities: that of the United States and that of the State of Israel, to shape the future of the Jews as a national entity. This situation of the Jewish communities, recovering from the physical disaster and psychological shock of World War II, made the economic relationship between the American Jewish community and the State of Israel one of the cornerstones of a policy of survival. The economics of the Jews, apart from the parochial interests of economists and economic historians, was geared toward the survival of the group during most of its recorded history.

[Arcadius Kahan]

BIBLIOGRAPHY: GENERAL: Baron, Social², with extensive documentation. FIRST TEMPLE PERIOD – EXILE AND RESTORATION: M. Weber, *Ancient Judaism* (1952); A. Bertholet, *A History of Hebrew Civilization* (1926); M. Lurie, *Studien zur Geschichte der wirtschaftlichen und sozialen Verhaeltnisse im israelitisch-juedischen Reiche* (1927); D. Jacobson, *The Social Background of the Old Testament* (1942); Pedersen, Israel; E. Ginzberg, *Studies in the Economics of the Bible* (1932 = JQR, 22 (1910/11)); I. Mendelsohn, in: BASOR, 80 (1940), 17–21; S. Daiches, *The Jews in Babylonia in the Time of Ezra and Nehemiah* (1910). SECOND TEMPLE PERIOD–TALMUDIC ERA: S. Yeivin (ed.), *Ha-Mishar ve-ha-Ta'asiyyah* (1937); V. Tcherikover, *Hellenistic Civilization and the Jews* (1966); L. Herzfeld, *Handelsgeschichte der Juden des Altertums* (1894²); Juster, Juifs; A. Buechler, *The Economic Conditions of Judaea after the Destruction of the Second Temple* (1912); Krauss, Tal Arch; E. Lambert, in: REJ, 51 (1906), 217–44; 52 (1906), 24–42; D. Farbstein, *Recht der unfreien und der freien Arbeiter nach juedisch-talmudischem Recht* (1896); Neusner, Babylonia; J. Newman, *The Agricultural Life of the Jews in Babylonia between the Years 200 C.E. and 500 C.E.* (1932). MUSLIM MIDDLE AGES: S.D. Goitein, *A Mediterranean Society*, 1: *Economic Foundations* (1967); Fischel, Islam; Hirschberg, Afrikah; Ashtor, Toledot; Ashtor, Korot; M. Wischnitzer, *A History of Jewish Crafts and Guilds* (1965); R. Levy, *An Introduction to the Sociology of Islam*, 2 vols. (1929–31); C. Cahen, in: *Studia Islamica*, 3 (1955), 93–115. MEDIEVAL CHRISTENDOM: G. Caro, *Sozial-und Wirtschaftsgeschichte der Juden im Mittelalter*, 2 vols. (1908 [1924]–1920); Schiper, *Yidishe Geshikhte*, 4 vols. (1930); idem, *Toledot ha-Kalkalah ha-Yehudit*, 2 vols. (1935–36); idem, *Wirtshaftsgeshikhte fun di Yidn in Poyln* (1926); M. Hoffmann, *Der Geldhandel der deutschen Jude bis zum Jahre 1350* (1910); I. Abrahams et al. (eds.), *Starrs and Jewish Charters Preserved in the British Museum*, 3 vols. (1930–32); H.G. Richardson, *English Jewry under Angevin Kings* (1960); Baer, Spain; Roth, Italy; A. Milano, *Vicende economiche degli Ebrei nell'Italia meridionale ed insulare durante il medioevo* (1954); J. Starr, *Jews in the Byzantine Empire, 641–1204* (1939). ECONOMIC DOCTRINES: S.W. Baron (ed), in: *Essays on Maimonides* (1941, photo-offset, 1966), 127–264; S. Bernfeld et al. (eds.), *Die Lehren des Judentums* (excerpts from primary sources), 3 vols. (n. d.); S. Ejges, *Das Geld im Talmud* (1930); E. Cohn, in: *Zeitschrift fuer vergleichende Rechtswissenschaft*, 18 (1905), 37–72; S. Eisenstadt, *Ein Mishpat* (1931), lists numerous, economically relevant, juristic monographs.

ECSTASY, from Greek *ekstasis*, "displacement," "movement outwards," "distraction of mind," "drunken excitement," "entrancement," or secondarily, "astonishment." (See Mark 5:42.) In Greek religion two fundamental types of ecstasy, dionysiac and contemplative, are well attested; the former is induced by means of narcotics, alcohol, music, and dance; the latter by contemplation and prayer. Only the dionysiac is represented in the Bible. Several scholars have maintained that ecstasy was the fundamental experience of all prophecy. This view ultimately can be traced back to *Philo who maintained that no prophecy is without ecstasy (see Spec. 4:49). Some scholars have distinguished between two groups: the classical prophets, or literary prophets, allegedly did not suffer from loss of identity, but maintained their consciousness and were aware of a divine encounter to which they responded. The second group, the pre-classical prophets, sometimes manifested group prophecy, which was ecstatic and contagious (cf. Num. 11:16ff., where the 70 elders "speak in ecstasy" after the spirit of the Lord rests upon them – the Hebrew verb used is *hitnabbe'*). Thus, when Saul meets "a band of prophets coming down from the high place with harp, tambourine, and lyre before them," he, too, is overwhelmed: "A spirit of God came mightily upon him and he spoke in ecstasy among them" (I Sam. 10). Similarly, when Saul sends men to capture David, who was staying with Samuel, they find Samuel at the head of a group of ecstatic prophets. The messengers are overcome by the spectacle and begin to rave. After this has happened to three sets of messengers, Saul goes himself, and, in a violent ecstatic fit, strips off his clothes and lies naked a whole day and night (I Sam. 19:18–24). Both these incidents are cited as the origin of the proverbial expression "Is Saul among the prophets?" Scholars who maintain the pre-classical ecstatic/classical non-ecstatic distinction also cite I Kings 22, where some 400 prophets rave in ecstasy before kings Jehoshaphat and Ahaz on the eve of their united attack against Ramoth-Gilead. They note, correctly, as well that this feature of collective dionysiac frenzy is not confined to early Israelite prophets. In I Kings 18:28–29, 450 Canaanite prophets of Baal and 400 prophets of Asherah "cried aloud and cut themselves after their manner with swords and lances till the blood gushed out upon them ... They prophesied in ecstasy until the time of the evening offering. ..." Individual prophets, too, might fall into an ecstatic trance. Thus, Elijah ran before Ahab's chariot when the hand of the Lord was upon him (I Kings 18:46). An extra-biblical example, in addition to the Canaanite prophets of Baal just mentioned, is found in the 11th-century Egyptian tale of Wen-Amon, which relates that while Zakar-Baal, king of Byblos, was offering a sacrifice, "the god seized one of his youths and made him possessed" (Pritchard, *Texts*, 26). In such a state the person turns into "another man" (e.g., Saul, I Sam. 10:6) and may behave madly (I Sam. 18:10ff.). This is doubtless why a disciple of the prophets is referred to as "the madman" (II Kings 9:11). But a careful reading of the classical prophets shows that they too manifested odd behavior. Jeremiah is referred to as "madman" and "ecstatic" (*mitnabbe'*) in the same breath (Jer. 29:26; cf. Hos. 9:7). Isaiah walked about barefoot and naked for three years (Isa. 20:3). Ezekiel lay on his left side for 390 days and 40 days on his right. From Zech. 13:4–6 we learn that a prophet might be expected to wear a hairshirt and have sores on his back, perhaps from some ritual beating. Indeed, the Hebrew word for madman, *meshugga'*, may be a *terminus technicus* for a type of god-inspired individual who is called in the *Mari letters a *muḫḫu* (fem., *muḫḫutum*), "frenzied," "mad," "ecstatic." Such an ecstatic seizure may be induced by external means: music (cf. Elisha, II Kings 3:15, and the musical instruments carried by the bands of prophets, I Sam. 10:5 and II Chron. 35:15) or dancing (mentioned in connection with the prophets of Baal, I Kings 18:26). Sometimes this ecstatic seizure is described as caused either by "the hand of God" (I Kings 18:46; II Kings 3:15; Jer. 15:17) or by "the spirit of God" (I Sam. 10:6, 10; 18:10; 19:23), an indication that seizure and strange behavior might lend credibility to claims of prophecy.

BIBLIOGRAPHY: G. Hoelscher, *Die Propheten* (1914); T.H. Robinson, *Prophecy and the Prophets* (1923); C.J. Lindblom, *Prophecy in Ancient Israel* (1962); A.J. Heschel, *The Prophets* (1962). **ADD. BIBLIOGRAPHY:** R. Wilson, in: JBL, 98 (1979), 329–37; G. André, *Ecstatic Prophecy in the Old Testament* (1982); S. Geller, *Sacred Enigmas* (1996); J. Roberts, *The Bible and the Ancient Near East* (2002), 95–101, 157–253.

[Shalom M. Paul / S. David Sperling (2nd ed.)]

ECUADOR, South American republic; population 13,363,593 (2005); Jewish population 900.

Unlike most other Latin American countries it was only in the wake of the Nazi persecution in Europe that a considerable number of Jews arrived in Ecuador. With the Spanish conquerors Jews, too, had in fact come to Ecuador, but their number was small. Also after independence from Spain comparatively few Sephardi Jews immigrated; these assimilated or at least did not practice their tradition in public. Certain family names among established Ecuadorian families attest until today to their Sephardi descent. At the end of the 19th century, and in the 1920s and 1930s, Jews emigrated mainly from Eastern Europe and settled chiefly in Guayaquil but did not become visible as a group. It is related that the first meeting for a New Year's celebration took place in 1934 in a private apartment. In 1914 Vienna-born Julius Rosenstock was appointed by the Ecuadorian government to head the construction of the Sibambe–Quito highland railway. Because of his excellent connections in government circles he successfully fought for the entry of persecuted Jews to the country. The stream of refugees to Ecuador began in 1938, reaching its peak in 1939. On Rosenstock's initiative a HICEM Committee was founded and the government negotiated the conditions of immigration with him. Because of his personal intervention, he succeeded in obtaining the repeal of the 1937 decree by the dictator Alberto Enríquez Gallo ordering Jews who did not work in agriculture or industry to leave the country within 30 days.

A relatively small number of Jews, 3,500–4,000, found refuge in Ecuador through 1942. Settlement projects from the mid-1930s, including the plan for long-term settlement of 50,000 families in mostly remote areas, were supported neither by the Ecuadorian public nor by the Jewish settlers and proved to be untrustworthy and impractical. For most of the Jews who found refuge in the country until 1942, Ecuador, with its three million inhabitants, was a second-choice place of exile, since they had failed to find asylum in another, preferred country. The majority came from Germany and Austria after the pogrom of November 1938 (**Kristallnacht*) having lost hope that they could stay in their native country. Part of them settled in Guayaquil, the biggest city of the country, which was a real trading center with a population of about 180,000.

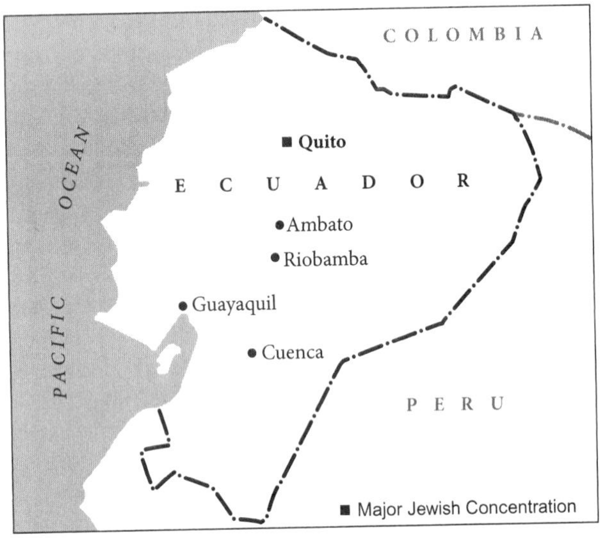

Major Jewish communities in Ecuador.

Located near the Pacific coast, it had a tropical climate. The vast majority, however, preferred the capital, Quito, situated in the Andes at an altitude of 9,200 ft. (2,800 m.). Few settled in small towns like Ambato (100), Banos, Cuenca (30), and Riobamba, or in the jungle around Puyo.

In Quito as in Guayaquil they were concentrated in several streets in the city center or not far from it. Quito with 150,000 inhabitants had no industry and only one multi-story building. Compared to middle-class European standards the living conditions were cramped and primitive, with no infrastructure and with infectious diseases and a lack of hygiene threatening their health. Many of the immigrants had only meager financial means, though many of them had brought their household goods and other possessions. Since the authorities returned the deposits that the immigrants had made to receive their visas (a few hundred dollars each), most of them had money to invest. Many had to earn their livings in unfamiliar occupations. But wherever it was possible they tried to continue in their former professions or similar ones.

Despite the regulations restricting immigration to industrial or agricultural laborers, only a minority worked in agriculture. Because of the difficult living and working conditions and their lack of knowledge such onerous attempts were given up. The project of HICEM and the Joint in 1937 to settle 60 families in the area of Ambato for chicken farming was among those failed attempts. A considerable number of the immigrants were active in trade, as peddlers, in retail and wholesale, and in the import and export trade. While the majority of the enterprises in the first years required hard work by all family members to reach a subsistence level, some of the enterprises reached a considerable size by 1942 and exist until today. The most successful were those that found a niche in the market, offering services and goods unknown in the country or absent from the market because of the war. In the field of food and textile production, in the metallurgical (El Arco, Ideal, Siderúrgica SA.) and pharmaceutical industries, in services and the hotel trade, they played an important role and brought a dynamic element into business life. Names like Rothschild, Seligmann, Neustätter, Di Capua, and Ottolenghi stand out.

The fact that the authorities as a rule did not enforce industrial or agricultural employment made it easier for the immigrants to integrate into the economic process but soon led to anti-Jewish pressure on the part of the local population. While the presidents José Maria Velasco Ibarra (1934–35, 1944–47) and Carlos Arroyo del Rio (1940–44) approved the immigration of Jews, some circles espoused an antisemitic line with recourse to the German-based press and deep-seated Christian prejudices. Also textile merchants of Arab origin, especially from Lebanon, who had lived in Ecuador for decades, considered the Jews undesirable competitors. In August 1944 Velasco Ibarra rescinded the regulations that restricted immigration to industrial or agricultural employment, but already at the end of the 1940s the authorities stepped up the control of Jewish enterprises and in 1952 another law was passed requiring proof that a foreigner was engaged in the occupation stipulated in his entry visa. This legislation was counteracted by the intervention of the World Jewish Congress. Within these limited political and social limitations the immigrants were free to do whatever they wished. There was no bar to practicing their religion or founding associations.

The biggest group among the refugees was in Quito. Its nucleus was the above-mentioned HICEM Committee founded in 1938. In the same year the Asociación de Beneficencia Israelita was founded, reaching its peak with over 540 members (heads of families) in 1945. Unlike most Latin American countries, where Jewish communities already existed and the newcomers founded their own separate organizations according to their countries of origin, the "Beneficencia" united Jews from Germany, Austria, Italy, Poland, Hungary, Czechoslovakia, Romania, the Soviet Union, and the Baltic states.

Though there was some religiously motivated separation this was of minor significance. While in Guayaquil differences of opinion about Zionism were a greater potential cause of discord than in Quito, in religious matters the situation was quite the opposite. In Guayaquil the strongest organization, Comunidad de Culto, with more than 140 members, combined the Sociedad de Beneficencia, founded in 1939–40, and the Centro Israelita, which had split off in 1944, both competing for cultural primacy. Under the impression of the foundation of the State of Israel all organizations in Quito united under the umbrella of the "Beneficencia" while in Guayaquil it took almost 20 years more to reach such unity.

The "Beneficencia" did a great deal to create a center of religious, social, and cultural life for its members. A bulletin called *Informaciones para los Inmigrantes Israelitas*, in the first period mainly written in German, informed readers about the community, the host country, and international affairs. Based on the model of their European countries a court of arbitration, a *ḥevra kaddisha*, a women's association, a cooperative bank, Maccabi, and B'nai B'rith were established. In

Quito and in Guayaquil Zionist organizations were founded that succeeded in winning the support of public figures in the host country for the objectives of Zionism. The Ecuadorian representative cast his vote in the UN General Assembly resolution of November 29, 1947, in favor of the partition of Palestine. Ecuador and Israel established diplomatic relations. From the late 1960s a network of technical cooperation and assistance was developed between the two countries, especially in the fields of agriculture, water development, youth training, and technology.

Jews achieved prominence in Ecuadorian society beyond the economic field. They contributed to cultural development in music, painting, theater, arts and crafts, architecture, literature, science, journalism, and publishing.

In the 1940s the Kammerspiele theater was established on a high artistic level, directed by Karl (Carl) Loewenberg, co-founder of the Juedischer Kulturbund of Berlin. In the 1950s the theater continued to perform in Spanish before appreciative local audiences. An international reputation was achieved by the painter Olga Fisch-Anhalzer, co-founder of the Instituto Ecuatoriano de Folclor. The painter and sculptress Trude Sojka, who had survived Auschwitz, arrived in 1946. Paul Engel, a physician and writer (pen name Diego Viega), who immigrated to Ecuador in 1950 from Colombia, became known as an endocrinologist. Benno Weiser (Benjamin Varon) made a name for himself as a journalist. Like his brother Max Weiser, who was the first Israeli consul to Ecuador, he entered the Israeli diplomatic service.

As the majority of the immigrants had regarded their stay in Ecuador as a temporary episode, emigration after the end of the war was considerable. By 1948 about half the Jews in Quito had emigrated, mainly to the U.S. On the other hand, a considerable number of survivors of the Holocaust arrived in the early postwar years. Because of continuous emigration, mortality, and partial assimilation of the following generation, which considered Spanish its mother tongue, the immigrant organizations lost their pivotal role as preservers of social and cultural identity. However, the Jews continued to form a small middle-class group largely cut off from the strong Catholic upper class and the masses of mestizos and the indigenous population.

In 1972 the *Informaciones* ceased publication. Different attempts to revive tradition did not persevere. The small communities of Ambato and Cuenca disbanded. At the beginning of the 1970s, in the course of the oil boom and thanks to easier-to-obtain entry permits, Jewish families from other Latin American countries arrived. As a result of political developments under the presidency of Salvador Allende a large number of families preferred to exchange Chile for Ecuador as a domicile. Towards the end of the 20th century many Jews from Argentina settled in Quito.

In 2005 the Jewish community (Comunidad Judía del Ecuador) of the city of Quito with its 2 million people numbers 200 families, or 550–600 members (the community of Guayaquil has 20 families, or some 70 members). The community has modern facilities for its social, recreational, and administrative needs. There is a synagogue and a rabbi for religious services. A *ḥevra kaddisha* and a home for the aged continue to function as well as the women's association as an independent organization. About 75 children go to the Colegio Alberto Einstein, a private school founded in 1973 by members of the community where the great majority of the pupils are non-Jews. The community is in contact with other Jewish organizations in Latin America and worldwide.

BIBLIOGRAPHY: M.L. Kreuter, *Wo liegt Ecuador? Exil in einem unbekannten Land 1938 bis zum Beginn der fuenfziger Jahre* (1995); *Dónde queda el Ecuador? Exilio en un país desconocido desde 1938 hasta fines de los años cincuentas* (1997); Organizaciones Israelitas en el Ecuador, *La Colonia Israelita en el Ecuador* (1948).

[Marie Luise Kreuter (2nd ed.)]

EDAH, U.S. grassroots organization comprised of rabbis, laity, intellectuals, and communal leaders who joined forces to revitalize a distinctive Modern American Orthodoxy. By the late 1960s, most observers had abandoned earlier predictions of the imminent demise of American Orthodoxy. Champions of Orthodoxy, as well as more neutral observers, pointed to the growth of day schools, the strength of the Orthodox family, and the intensity of Orthodox commitments as markers of sustained vitality. Generally, however, these commentators pointed to Modern Orthodoxy as the wave of the future. Ḥaredi Orthodoxy remained in retreat and on the defensive. Israel's victory in the 1967 war signaled the ascendancy of religious Zionism. Yeshiva University, the flagship institution of Modern Orthodoxy, was experiencing unprecedented growth. High-profile Modern Orthodox intellectuals – notably Emanuel *Rackman, Irving *Greenberg, David *Hartman, and Eliezer *Berkovits – were eagerly probing the bold and exciting challenge of defining the shape of a Judaism that would wed modern values with the teachings of Torah.

By the end of the 1980s, much had changed. Although increasingly vibrant, American Orthodoxy seemed decreasingly modern. Some pointed to a Ḥaredi ascendancy. Others underscored the widespread Orthodox practice of attending year-long post-high school programs in Israel, which had intensified Orthodox commitment and attachment to Israel, but whose faculties loudly proclaimed the bankruptcy of Modern Orthodox culture and values. Historians pointed to a new wave of Ultra-Orthodox immigration to America. Survivors of the Holocaust, these individuals spared no effort to rebuild Ultra-Orthodoxy on American shores. Lastly, Modern Orthodox parents, unlike their Ḥaredi counterparts, generally failed to perceive Jewish education as a suitable profession for their children, thereby creating a vacuum that Ḥaredi educators eagerly filled.

Thus, within short order, Modern Orthodoxy appeared to be more in danger of eclipse than on the cusp of renewal. Interdenominational programs, such as the Joint Chaplaincy Board and the Synagogue Council of America, were closed down in 1987 and 1994, respectively. The very nomenclature

"Modern Orthodoxy" was dropped in favor of the more neutral and less ideologically-charged "Centrist Orthodoxy," a change that Dr. Norman *Lamm, then president of Yeshiva University, for one, publicly regretted by the close of the century.

In this context, it was easily understandable that some sought to restore the "modern" in American Orthodoxy. In the late 1990s, a group of Orthodox intellectuals and lay leaders established Edah under the banner of "the courage to be modern and Orthodox." Launched initially as a grassroots initiative, with Rabbi Saul Berman as president, Edah's founding conference in February 1999 attracted over 1,500 participants. At stake were the questions on which the founders of Edah maintained that Modern Orthodoxy has ceded leadership. These included the challenge of feminism and women's equality, the hijacking of religious Zionism by *Gush Emunim, the pursuit of secular education as a value in itself rather than purely for utilitarian or instrumental reasons, and the continuing need for cooperation with the non-Orthodox religious movements and their leaders. More specifically, Edah hoped to redress women's inequality, notably in Jewish divorce law, to train a cadre of Modern Orthodox educators, to help define religious Zionism for the 21st century, and, perhaps above all, nurture an atmosphere of open dialogue and freedom of exchange that was so sorely lacking in an Orthodox world dominated by *roshei yeshivah*. Significantly, during these years, one of the most prominent of Yeshiva University Talmud faculty had pronounced Modern Orthodoxy to be the "Amalek of our time."

Yet Edah's hope to reclaim Yeshiva University as Modern Orthodoxy's stronghold remained unfulfilled. For one thing, notwithstanding Edah's impressive turnout of supporters and intellectual leadership, Yeshiva University faculty generally were absent. At best, Yeshiva University remained neutral towards Edah if not outright dismissive. Rabbi Aharon Lichtenstein wrote from Israel that he was certain that his late father-in-law, Rabbi Joseph B. *Soloveitchik, upon whose memory as Modern Orthodox scholar and communal leader Edah had sought to build, would today have little identification with Edah and its program. More generally, Yeshiva University leadership dismissed Edah as unnecessary, pointing to Y.U.'s Orthodox Forum which claimed the virtue of continuing dialogue between Orthodox intellectuals and *roshei yeshivah*. Nonetheless, Edah, under Rabbi Berman's leadership, persisted into the 21st century. By 2005, it had held four national conferences and several regional ones. Five volumes of the Edah journal had appeared, containing impressive scholarship and dialogue on critical issues, e.g., *aliyot* for women, generally not found elsewhere in the Orthodox world. Other institutions, notably the Jewish Orthodox Feminist Alliance (JOFA), Rabbi Avi Weiss' Yeshivat Chovevei Torah, proclaiming its commitment to an "open Orthodoxy," and, in Israel, the Lavi Conference, all loosely aligned with Edah in an effort to spearhead a Modern Orthodox renewal.

In the final analysis, however, the struggle for the Orthodox future remained open. Most observers agreed that Yeshiva University, given its enormous resources and prominence inside the Jewish community, would continue to set the tone for Modern Orthodoxy in America. To be sure, Yeshiva's direction, under the presidency of Richard Joel, who was appointed in 2003, remained unclear. Yet the purposes for which Edah had come into being in the late 1990s remained as compelling in the 21st century.

[Steven Bayme (2nd ed.)]

EDEL, YIẒḤAK (1896–1973), composer and teacher. Edel was born in Warsaw and from 1924 to 1927 he taught music in the orphanage of Janusz *Korczak, in Warsaw. In 1929 he immigrated to Palestine where he worked as a music teacher in teachers' colleges. His works include orchestral and piano music, quartets for strings and wind instruments, songs, and cantatas. His musical style shows the influence of Eastern European Jewish tradition.

EDELMAN, GERALD MAURICE (1929–), U.S. biochemist and immunologist, Nobel Prize laureate. Edelman was born in New York. He originally studied as a violinist but turned to biochemistry and received his M.D. from the University of Pennsylvania in 1954 and his doctorate from the Rockefeller University in 1960, where he was appointed associate professor of biochemistry, and associate dean of graduate studies in 1963. One of the leading immunologists in the United States, he devoted himself to research in the elucidation of the structure of antibody molecules and established the complete chemical structure of gamma globulin, which defends the body against foreign bodies and disease. In 1977 Edelman and his colleagues discovered cell adhesion molecules. Subsequently he turned his attention to neuroscience, becoming director of the Neurosciences Institute in San Diego, California. He has proposed a global brain theory called Neural Darwinism, which provides the basis for understanding the origin of consciousness. Edelman is a member of numerous scientific bodies, including the National Academy of Sciences, the American Academy of Arts and Sciences, the American Association for the Advancement of Science, and the American Chemical Society. In 1972 he was awarded the Nobel Prize for Medicine and Physiology together with Dr. Rodney Porter.

EDELMAN, MAURICE (1911–1975), author and politician. Born in Cardiff and educated at Cambridge, Edelman was a Labour M.P. from 1945 until his death. He was president of the Anglo-Jewish Association in 1963. His works include *France: The Birth of the Fourth Republic* (1945); *David Ben-Gurion* (1964), a biography; and political and other novels, including *A Trial of Love* (1951), *Who Goes Home* and *A Dream of Treason* (both 1953), *A Call on Kuprin* (1959), *The Fratricides* (1963), *The Prime Minister's Daughter* (1964), and *Shark Island* (1967). Edelman's best-known work was probably the novel *Disraeli in Love* (1972). Although a Labourite, Edelman was such an admirer of Disraeli that, in 1972, he leased and lived in a wing of Hughenden manor, Disraeli's country house. Once a leftist supporter of the Soviet Union, by the end of his life Edelman was active in the movement for Soviet Jewry.

BIBLIOGRAPHY: ODNB online.

[William D. Rubinstein (2nd ed.)]

EDELMANN, RAPHAEL (1902–1972), Danish scholar and librarian. Born in Latvia, Edelmann immigrated to Copenhagen as a child. In 1933 at the recommendation of David *Simonsen he began working in the newly established Jewish department of the Royal Library of Copenhagen, which consisted of the rich library of Simonsen; from 1938 he headed the department. From 1948 he lectured at the University of Copenhagen, where he was in charge of Judaic studies, including Yiddish. In 1955 he founded the Association of Libraries of Judaica and Hebraica in Europe and in this capacity organized training courses for Jewish librarians. Edelmann published extensively in several scholarly fields and made important contributions to the dissemination of Jewish scholarship in Denmark. Among his works are *Bestimmung, Heimat and Alter der synagogalen Poesie* (1932), and *Zur Fruehgeschichte des Machzor* (1934), important works on the early history of liturgical poetry. He compiled the catalog of Hebrew incunabula of the library of L. *Goldschmidt, now at the Royal Library (in *Fund og Forskning*, 3 (1956), 82–90); edited the series *Corpus Codicum Hebraicorum Medii Aevi* (1954–); and edited the *Subject Concordance to the Babylonian Talmud* by L. Goldschmidt (1959). He also arranged successful exhibitions of the treasures of the Royal Library in Paris, Strasbourg, Milan, and New York.

[Menahem Schmelzer]

EDELMANN, SIMḤAH REUBEN (Sar ha-Adulammi; 1821–1893), Lithuanian Hebrew scholar. Edelmann was born in Vilna and studied at the Volozhin yeshivah. He tried his hand in various branches of Jewish scholarship, and also wrote poetry and was one of the first to "discover" J.L. *Gordon, whom he befriended.

Among his published books are *Shoshannim* (1860); *Ha-Mesillot* (1875); *Ha-Tirosh* (1871), on *Genesis Rabbah;* and *Doresh Reshumot* (1893), on I.H. *Weiss' historical work *Dor Dor ve-Doreshav*, which Edelmann criticized for its liberal views. Edelmann also contributed to Hebrew periodicals. Part of his literary remains were used by A.D. Lebensohn and I. Benjacob in their edition of the Bible (1849–53) and published by Edelmann's son Mordecai Isaac in his *Me'arat Adullam* (1922) and *Tovim ha-Shenayim* (1913). An autobiographical fragment was published by the son in his biography of his father, *Hakḥam ve-Sar* (1896).

EDELMANN, ẒEVI HIRSCH (1805–1858), Hebrew scholar, printer, and publisher. Edelmann, who was born in Svisloch, Belorussia, published books at Danzig, Koenigsberg, and London. In England, in particular, he carefully searched the libraries for Hebrew manuscript material. Edelmann published editions of hitherto unpublished medieval Hebrew literature such as Estori Ha-Parhi's *Kaftor va-Ferah* (1851, repr. 1959); *Ginzei Oxford* (translated into English by M.H. Bresslau and published in *Treasures of Oxford*, 1851), a collection (with L. Dukes) of liturgical and secular poetry by Spanish-Jewish poets; *Derekh Tovim* (also translated into English by M.H. Bresslau and published in *Path of Good Men*, 1852), varia by Maimonides, Judah ibn Tibbon and others; *Ḥemdah Genuzah* (1856), an important collection of philosophical writings and letters, mainly by, to, or about Maimonides; *Divrei Ḥefeẓ* (1853), another collection of philosophical and poetical material; and also M.Ḥ. Luzzatto's *La-Yesharim Tehillah* (1854). Edelmann also published a number of important liturgical items: *Seder Haggadah* (1845), with critical notes; *Haggadah Le-Leil Shimmurim* (1845), with commentaries and notes; and *Siddur Hegyon Lev* (1854) containing Edelmann's critical notes and emendations, *No'am Megadim* by J. Teomim, and *Mekor Berakhah* by E. Landshuth. Edelmann's first publications, which were purely talmudic, were *Haggahot u-Vi'urim li-Me'irat Einayim* (1839) and *Alim le-Mivḥan*, including *Megillat Sefer Iggeret ha-Purim* (1844) on Esther. He also wrote an historical study on Saul *Wahl, the alleged one-day king of Poland, *Gedullat Sha'ul* (1854), with an appendix *Nir David*. His considerable publishing ventures were carried out under conditions of great financial stringency. Edelmann lived in Berlin from 1852 and died in the ward for the insane in a Berlin hospital.

BIBLIOGRAPHY: *Jewish Chronicle (1841–1941)* (1949), 55; A. Berg, *Birkat Avraham* (1882); Kressel, Leksikon, 1 (1965), 24–25.

EDELS, SAMUEL ELIEZER BEN JUDAH HA-LEVI (known as **MaHaRShA** – **M**orenu **Ha-R**av **Sh**emu'el **A**dels; 1555–1631), one of the foremost Talmud commentators. Born in Cracow, he moved to Posen in his youth, where he married the daughter of Moses Ashkenazi Heilpern. His mother-in-law, Edel, by whose name he was later known, was a wealthy woman and supported him and his numerous disciples for a period of 20 years (1585–1605). After her death, Edels took up a rabbinic position in Chelm. In 1614 he was appointed rabbi of Lublin, and in 1625 of Ostrog, where he founded a large yeshivah. On the lintel of his house (burned down in 1889) was inscribed the verse: "The stranger did not lodge in the street; but I opened my doors to the traveler" (Job 31:32). His commentary on the Talmud is one of the classical works of talmudic literature included in almost every edition of the Talmud. The commentary is divided into two parts. In his *Ḥiddushei Halakhot* he explains the talmudic text with profundity and ingenuity. In his introduction to the work he writes that "out of love for terseness" he would refrain from elaboration. He ends most of his comments with the phrases: "And weigh carefully" or "And the meaning is simple," although in reality it is far from clear and many later scholars often found difficulty in understanding his point. Often he poses a difficulty and says: "And this may be solved," leaving it to the students to find the answer. He was fond of talmudic casuistry, and used to say: "No one can arrive at the root and depth of a talmudic problem without a master who teaches him *pilpul*"; but he vehemently opposed the kind of casuistry which, in his time, came to be known as *ḥillukim*, where students would engage in fruitless debate to try to demolish one another's arguments. In his *Ḥiddushei Halakhot*, Edels' explanations of talmudic problems are generally in accordance with the view of Rashi and the tosafists. His book gained such wide currency that an understanding of Edels' comments came to be regarded for many generations as one of the qualifications of the average talmudic scholar. The second part of his commentary is called *Ḥiddushei Aggadot*, in which he attempts to explain the difficult talmudic *aggadot* in a rational manner, sometimes taking them as parables with interpretations which are at variance with their literal meaning. He criticized, however, the prevailing tendency of preachers to distort the plain sense of biblical and talmudical passages. Although censuring "those people who in the present generation give all their time to the study of Kabbalah," he nonetheless quotes extensively from kabbalistic literature. He also made use of his acquaintance with Jewish philosophy in his interpretation of talmudic *aggadot.*

He adopted a positive attitude toward the secular sciences, considering them important for a fuller understanding of Torah, and their acquisition as vital for learned Jews in their disputations with non-Jews. His statements are sometimes marked by a spirit of critical inquiry. He decides, for example, that the Targum to the Pentateuch ascribed to Jonathan b. Uzziel is not by him. He senses that the *tosafot* to the tractate *Yoma* are different in style from those to other tractates. He established that some statements or passages in Rashi's commentary and in the *tosafot* had originated as marginal comments by students who had not understood the passage, and in the course of time these comments had come to be interpolated in the text. Edels reproved his contemporaries for making light of certain precepts, e.g., those who drink to excess at the *melavveh malkah* meal on Saturday night and so neglect the recitation of the *Shema* upon retiring, and rise too late the following morning for the statutory time for the reading of the *Shema* and the recital of the morning prayers. He was a sharp critic of social evils in the communities, such as the dishonesty and egotism of some rich *parnasim.* He reproached the rabbis of his time with overawing their communities for motives which were not purely altruistic, and was irked by the fact that "in these times, whoever possesses wealth is appointed to public office for a price and is in constant pursuit of honor." In 1590 he participated at a session of the *Council of the Four Lands which pronounced a ban on those who purchase rabbinic office. Edels was held in high esteem by the scholars of his day. Joel *Sirkes in his address to the leaders of the Council of the Four Lands in Lublin, said: "You have in your midst the greatest man of the present generation … with whom to consult and deliberate." On his tombstone, Edels is described as "a holy man … exemplary in his generation … whose fame traveled far and wide. His great work was a light to the eyes of the Sages of Israel." He was also highly regarded by later generations. Jonah *Landsofer enjoined his sons to pay close attention to the works of Edels, "because his writings are amazingly terse and plumb the depths of Torah's truth … The spirit of God spoke through him, for without divine inspiration it would have been impossible for a man to write such a book." Edels' other works are *Zikhron Devarim*, novellae of the group of scholars at Posen (published by his mother-in-law in 1598); a penitential prayer beginning with the words: "*El Elohai Dalfah Einai*"; and a penitential prayer written in memory of the Warsaw martyrs (1597).

His brother's son, whose name has not been preserved, made his way to Morocco, and apparently settled there. His work *Sha'arei Ḥokhmah*, on *aggadah* and homiletics, is extant in many manuscripts. In it he quotes his uncle and many of the other great 17th-century scholars of Poland, including Israel Spira, son of Nathan *Spira, whom he calls "my teacher," and Abraham Abele *Gombiner. He died before 1674.

Modern rabbinic teachers lament the forsaking of Edels' talmudic commentary. In addition to the profundity of his ideas, Edels' work is instrumental in teaching the correct analysis of the talmudic text.

BIBLIOGRAPHY: Dubnow, Hist Russ, 1 (1916), 129–30; R. Margulies, *Toledot Adam* (1912); S.A. Horodezky, *Le-Korot ha-Rabbanut* (1914²), 183–90; H.H. Ben-Sasson, *Hagut ve-Hanhagah* (1959), index; J.M. Toledano, *Sarid u-Falit* (1945), 74f. **ADD. BIBLIOGRAPHY:** Y. Barka'i, "*Shitato ha-Parshanit shel ha-Maharsha be-Ḥiddushei Aggadot*," dissertation, Hebrew University (1995).

[Shmuel Ashkenazi]

EDELSTADT, DAVID (1866–1892), Yiddish poet. Edelstadt was born in Kaluga, the son of a cantonist. After the Kiev pogrom of 1881, he immigrated to the U.S. as part of the agricultural *Am Olam movement but settled in Cincinnati to work in the garment industry, joined the anarchist movement (which at the time wielded great influence among Jewish workers), and became one of the first Jewish socialist poets, initially composing radical poetry in Russian. In 1888 he moved to New York and continued working in sweatshops, writing increasingly in Yiddish. In works such as "In Kamf" ("In Struggle"), "Vakht Uf" ("Awaken"), and "Mayn Tsavoe" ("My Last Will and Testament"), Edelstadt called upon his working-class audience to revolt against the upper classes and seize the means of production. In 1890, he became a regular contributor to and, a year later, editor of the newly founded anarchist weekly *Fraye Arbeter Shtime.* His lyrics, sung in sweatshops and on picket lines, depict the world's imperfections and the wondrous life to come after a social revolution. After he contracted tuberculosis in 1891, he traveled to Denver to recuperate but died there the following year at the age of 26, becoming a romantic legend to the young Jewish labor movement and a central figure, along with Joseph *Bovshover, Morris *Rosenfeld, and Morris *Vinchevsky, of the *Sweatshop Poets. His collected works were published in London in 1910 and in Moscow in 1935.

BIBLIOGRAPHY: Rejzen, Leksikon, 2 (1927), 718–21; LNYL, 6 (1965), 554–63; K. Marmor, *Dovid Edelstadt* (1950), incl. bibl.; B. Bialostotsky (ed.), *Dovid Edelstadt Gedenkbukh* (1953); N.B. Minkoff, *Pioneren fun Yidisher Poezye in Amerika* (1956), 89–128; H. Leivick, *Eseyen un Redes* (1963), 195–207. **ADD. BIBLIOGRAPHY:** S. Liptzin, *A History of Yiddish Literature* (1972), 94–96; I. Howe, *World of Our Fathers* (1976), 420; O. Kritz, *The Poetics of Anarchy* (1997).

[Sol Liptzin / Marc Miller (2nd ed.)]

EDELSTEIN, JACOB (d. 1944), Czech Zionist leader and head of the *Theresienstadt ghetto. Born in Horodenka, Galicia, Edelstein went to Bohemia as a refugee during World War I. He first joined the Social Democrat youth movement there, and then the Zionist movement. From the early 1930s he was one of the leaders of the Labor Zionist movement in Czechoslovakia, a member of the presidium of the nationwide Zionist Federation, and director of the Palestine Office of the Jewish Agency in Prague. After the invasion of Bohemia and Moravia by Nazi Germany in 1939, Edelstein became the central figure of the Zionist movement and of Jewish life in the Nazi Protectorate. In the autumn of 1939, he visited the group of Jewish deportees at Nisko, in the Lublin region, and reached the conclusion that in most cases deportation of Jews to the East meant their death. In order to avoid deportation of the Protectorate's Jews, he suggested establishing a labor camp for them within the Protectorate that would employ the Jews to further the economic needs of the occupying power.

The establishment of the ghetto in Theresienstadt (Terezin) was apparently due to Edelstein's initiative. He was appointed its first *Judenaeltester* (Jewish Elder), serving in this post from December 1941. His courageous stand on behalf of the ghetto inmates made him the object of hatred of several heads of the *Gestapo. His jurisdiction was restricted, and in November 1943 he was arrested for having falsified the lists in order to rescue several inmates. He was sent to *Auschwitz, where he was kept in a punishment cell and shot on June 20, 1944, after having been forced to witness the execution of his wife and young son. He went proudly to his death. Opinions are divided in the evaluation of his activities during the Holocaust. Some (such as H.G. Adler) contend that Edelstein misunderstood the situation and thus engaged in a measure of cooperation with the Nazis; others, particularly survivors from the Zionist pioneering movement, see in him a tragic martyr, who fought the enemy for the rescue of Jews until his defeat. The liberated inmates of Bergen-Belsen named their camp school for him.

BIBLIOGRAPHY: Y. Ereẓ (ed.), *Theresienstadt* (Heb., 1947); H.G. Adler, *Theresienstadt, 1941–45* (Ger., 1965); idem, *Die verheimlichte Wahrheit* (1958); Ch. Yahil, *Devarim al ha-Ẓiyyonut ha-Czekhoslovakit* (1967). **ADD. BIBLIOGRAPHY:** R. Bondy, *Edelstein neged ha-Zeman* (1981).

[Chaim Yahil]

°**EDEN, SIR ANTHONY, EARL OF AVON** (1897–1977), British Conservative statesman, foreign secretary (1935–38, 1940–45, 1951–55), secretary for war (1940), and prime minister (1955–57). Eden resigned in 1938 in protest against Neville Chamberlain's policy of "appeasement" to the Axis and became Churchill's right-hand man during World War II. In 1936 Eden signed the Anglo-Egyptian Treaty of Friendship and Alliance, which was unilaterally denounced by Egypt in 1951. During World War II he increasingly advocated Arab unity, which in 1945 took the form of the *Arab League that eventually turned against Britain. Eden was aware of the Holocaust and, indeed, made a famous statement in the House of Commons in 1942 confirming that the Nazis were exterminating Europe's Jews, but that Britain could do little or nothing to thwart it apart from winning the war. In 1955 Eden led Britain into the Baghdad Pact, an additional source of friction with Egypt. In November 1955 he suggested a compromise between the Arab demand that Israel withdraw to the boundaries of the UN Partition Plan of 1947 and Israel's stand on the borders of the armistice agreements of 1949. In October 1956, after the nationalization of the Suez Canal by Egypt, he and Guy Mollet, the prime minister of France, mounted the Suez Expedition, the object of which was to gain control of the Canal. The Suez campaign had the secret backing and cooperation of David *Ben-Gurion and the Israeli government. (See *Sinai Campaign.) Under the extraordinary agreement reached between Britain, France, and Israel, Israeli forces were to take control of the Sinai – which they proceeded to do in short order – at which point Britain and France were to intervene to keep the belligerents apart but also to retake the Suez Canal for themselves. The Suez Campaign failed, thanks in large measure to American opposition. It aroused fierce hostility from the British Labour party and left-wing sources, but also marked the first time in which Israel's military prowess was displayed successfully. Soon afterwards, Eden became seriously ill and retired from the prime ministership and from political life early in 1957. In retirement, he wrote *Full Circle* (1960), *Facing the Dictators* (1962), and *The Reckoning* (1965). In 1961, Eden was given an earldom. He had been made a knight of the Garter in 1953 and was known as Sir Anthony Eden during his prime ministership.

BIBLIOGRAPHY: R. Churchill, *Rise and Fall of Sir Anthony Eden* (1959). **ADD. BIBLIOGRAPHY:** R. Lamb, *The Failure of the Eden Government* (1987).

[Sh.Be / William D. Rubinstein (2nd ed.)]

EDEN-TAMIR, Israeli piano duo. Bracha Eden was born in Jerusalem (1928) and Alexander Tamir (1931), a native of Vilna, settled in Jerusalem after World War II. Both studied with Alexander Schroeder (a pupil of A. Schnabel) at the Rubin Academy of Music in Jerusalem. After graduating in 1952, they formed a piano duo. In 1955 they continued their studies with Vronsky and *Babin at Aspen. They made their debut in Israel in 1954 and appeared in New York (1955) and Rome (1956), where they won the 1957 Vercelli Competition. Eden and Tamir founded the Max Targ Music Center in Ein Kerem, near Jerusalem (1968), and taught as senior professors at the Rubin Academy. During the 1990s they began to perform and teach regularly in China, Russia, and Poland, and in 1997 they became directors of the International Duo Piano Seminary. Well known for their artistry, virtuosity, and immaculate ensemble playing, the duo made an important contribution to the revival of works for two pianos and piano duet.

Among their recordings are the complete works for two pianos and piano duet of Mozart, Schubert, and Rachmaninoff, and works by Bach, Brahms, Debussy, Ravel, Bartók, and Poulenc. They gave the American première of Lutoslawski's *Paganini Variations* (1955) and, at the suggestion of Stravinsky (1968), were the first to perform and record the piano duet version of *The Rite of Spring*. Tamir has made several transcriptions for piano duo and duet and has written a few works for piano duo.

ADD. BIBLIOGRAPHY: Grove online.

[Uri Toepliz, Yohanan Boehm / Naama Ramot (2nd ed.)]

EDER, MONTAGUE DAVID (1865–1936), Zionist leader, psychoanalyst, and physician. Born in London into an assimilated family, Eder devoted himself to the medical care of the poor in London's slums and mining villages, becoming a member of the Labour Party. One of the first British psychoanalysts and protagonists of Sigmund Freud, together with Ernest Jones he founded the Psychoanalytical Association in England in 1913. Eder also established a children's clinic and founded and edited the journal *School Hygiene*. His interest in Jewish affairs was aroused by his cousin, Israel *Zangwill, and his brother-in-law, Joseph *Cowen. Eder joined the Jewish Territorialist Organization (JTO) and participated in a mission on its behalf to Cyrenaica to evaluate the possibilities for Jewish settlement there. In 1918 he was invited by Chaim *Weizmann to join the *Zionist Commission for Palestine, as a representative of JTO and as medical officer. He arrived there in 1918 and stayed for over four years, becoming an enthusiastic Zionist. He played a key role in the Commission, being its only member to extend his stay after 1918. He conducted the negotiations with the military and civil administration of Palestine and helped actively in the absorption of the first groups of immigrants of the Third *Aliyah, displaying great understanding for their pioneering spirit. Eder was a member of the Zionist Executive 1921–23 and 1922–28, first in Jerusalem and later in London. His kinship with the Soviet diplomat Maxim *Litvinov (to whom he was related through his wife) enabled him to visit the Soviet Union in 1921, where he tried, unsuccessfully, to achieve some degree of legal status for the work of the Zionist Organization there. Upon his return to Britain, Eder was active on behalf of the Hebrew University, the Political Department of the Zionist Executive, and the British Zionist Federation, which he headed for a short time in 1930. An agricultural farm for the training of Palestine pioneers, established in 1935 in Ringelstone, Kent, was called the David Eder Farm.

BIBLIOGRAPHY: David Eder, *Memoirs of a Modern Pioneer* (ed. by J.B. Hobman, with foreword by S. Freud, 1945). **ADD. BIBLIOGRAPHY:** ODNB online.

[Getzel Kressel]

EDESSA, a city in the upper Euphrates Valley (today Urfa in Turkey). Archaeological remains are known in the area of the city going back to the second millennium B.C.E., and Edessa may very well have been a Hurrian city alternatively known as Orrhoe, Orhai, or Osrhoene. Until 11 C.E. Edessa was part of the border area that passed on various occasions from Parthian to Roman hands. The city was conquered in August 116 by Lusius Quietus, and remained a Roman possession until 216, when it was officially incorporated into the Roman Empire. The suppression of the Parthian resistance against the Romans meant also the subjugation of the Jews of the city (see Segal). By the end of the second century C.E. Edessa had become the center of Christianity beyond the Euphrates, and this development suggests a Jewish influence in the area during that period. It is known, for instance, that the local king during the early second century, Abgar VII, was a son of *Izates of Adiabene, a monarchy already converted to Judaism. Eusebius, a primary source regarding the establishment of Christianity in Edessa, relates that Abgar V had corresponded with Jesus himself, and as a result immediately accepted the teachings of the first Christian disciple to arrive at Edessa, the preacher Addai. The story is also given in the "Doctrine of Addai," which claims that the conversion involved, among others, Jewish silk merchants. The story is a Christian invention. The Palestinian Targum identifies the Erech of Genesis 10:10 with Edessa and refers to it, together with Ctesiphon and Nisibis, as one of the three Babylonian cities ruled by *Nimrod. In the Talmud the name of the community is Hadass.

[Isaiah Gafni / Shimon Gibson (2nd ed.)]

The Edessa chronicles mention an order issued by the emperor in 411, to erect a convent on a spot occupied by a synagogue; other reliable sources, however, describe the bishop who was then in office, and was alleged to have built the convent, as a friend of the Jews (see Overbeck, *Opera Selecta*, 195; reports on Jews in Edessa are also available for the year 499: REJ, 6 (1883), 137). The participation of Edessa Jews in the wars between Heraclius I, the Byzantine emperor, and the Persians (610–42), on the side of the latter, gives reason to believe that their number was quite substantial.

For a considerable period after its capture by the Arabs (who renamed it al-Ruha), the town remained predominantly Christian. Islam, of course, spread in the town, at the expense of Christianity and Judaism. There is a source about a false Messiah in c. 735, who was a native of Edessa. According to Bar-Hebraeus, Muḥammad b. Ṭāhir built a mosque in 825 on a site previously occupied by a synagogue. In the 9th century the physician Yizhaq Ben Ali Al-Rohawi (Odessa man) was born in Edessa. In 1098 the town was conquered by the Crusaders and the Jews were expelled. There is a document from December 1101 in Ruzafa (150 km. south of Edessa) which notes the Jews of the castle of Ruzafa (one of the names of Edessa); probably these Jews were the refugees from Edessa who had fled to Ruzapa. When ʿImād al-Dīn Zengi captured the town in 1144, he settled 300 Jewish families there; and in 1191 when

R. Samuel b. Ali, head of the Baghdad Academy, addressed a circular letter to the communities in northern Babylonia and Syria, he included the al-Ruha community among those addressed. *Al-Ḥarizi (13th cent.) also mentioned the Jewish community and noted that the local Jews were polite and cultured. He noted the *Ḥazzan* Joseph and another person, Hasan. He mentioned that the origin of the Jews in Ruha was from Al-Ein. Maybe he referred to the settlement of 300 Jewish families in Edessa two generations earlier which had been organized by the Mamluk Ruler Zengi I in 1144. From the 12th century the Karaite scholar Yehuda Hadassi (from Edessa) is known. Jews continued to live there during the Ottoman rule, when the town's name was changed to Urfa. In the 17th century, the traveler Pedro de Texeira found many Jews there. In 1834, 500 Jews lived there and the general population was 50,000. *Benjamin II, who visited the town in 1848, wrote of a community of 150 families, whose economic standard was very good, but their cultural standard was so low that only about a third was able to read the prayerbook. Benjamin also gave details of the local legends relating to biblical figures; the Syriac name of the town, Orhai, for some reason appears always to have been identified with Ur Kasdim (Ur of the Chaldees), and thus the town came to be regarded as the scene of various events in the life of Abraham. Among the sights pointed out to Benjamin II was a cave which was regarded as Abraham's birthplace and the oven into which Nimrod had been thrown. These places were venerated by both Jews and Muslims. In 1876 the Jews of the place spoke Aramic. In 1880 the Jews survived a big fire that had spread in the city. In 1893, 1,000 Jewish families lived in Urfa. At the end of the 19th century and the beginning of the 20th, the number of Jews in Urfa dwindled steadily; in 1904 there were 322 Jews there, and thereafter their number was further reduced. Many of the town's Jews settled in Jerusalem, where they formed a separate community, that of the "Urfalis." During World War I most of the Jews in Urfa were merchants. Following a blood libel many of them were murdered and the survivors fled to Syria, Lebanon, Istanbul, and Ereẓ Israel, where many of the immigrants settled in Jerusalem. There have been no Jews in Urfa since the late 1960s.

[Eliyahu Ashtor / Leah Bornstein-Makovetsky (2nd ed.)]

BIBLIOGRAPHY: R. Duval, *Histoire politique, religieuse et littéraire d'Edesse* (1892); J.J. Benjamin, *Acht Jahre in Asien und Afrika* (1858), 49–53; H. Pognon, *Inscriptions semitiques de la Syrie…* (1907), 7; Krauss, in: *Zion Me'assef*, 3 (1929), 17–21; J. Obermeyer, *Landschaft Babylonien* (1929), 132f., 261, 280 n. 1, 299 n. 4; A. Ben-Ya'acov, *Kehillot Yehudei Kurdistan* (1961), 129–30; Neusner, Babylonia, 1 (1965), 62 n. 1, 89, 166–9. **ADD. BIBLIOGRAPHY:** A. Sharf, *Byzantine Jewry from Justinian to the Fourth Crusade* (1971), 51, 133, 181; J.B. Segal, *Edessa: The Blessed City* (1970), 41–43, 100–5, 182; M. Gil, *Be-Malkhut Yishma'el*, 1 (1997) 42, 152, 209, 296, 367; M. Yona, *Enẓyklopedya shel Yehudei Kurdistan*, 1 (2003), 70, 82.

EDINBURGH, capital of *Scotland. No trace of Jews is to be found in medieval Scotland generally. Apart from individual Jews, a community possibly existed in Edinburgh at the close of the 18th century, but the present congregation was established in 1816 with 20 families. The first minister was Moses Joel of London, who served in the office for 46 years. With the influx of Russian and Polish Jews at the close of the 19th century, the community grew and many communal institutions were founded. For many years Salis *Daiches was the rabbi. In 1968 the community numbered approximately 1,100 out of a total population of 468,770. There was one synagogue and extensive communal and Zionist activity. In the mid-1990s the Jewish population numbered approximately 500. According to the 2001 British census, 763 Jews lived in Edinburgh. There is an Orthodox synagogue.

BIBLIOGRAPHY: Daiches, in: *Publications of the Scottish Church History Society* (1929); C. Roth, *Rise of Provincial Jewry* (1950), 57–59; Levy, in: JHSET, 19 (1960), 129–62. **ADD. BIBLIOGRAPHY:** K.E. Collins, *Scotland's Jews: A Guide to the History and Community of the Jews in Scotland* (1999); JYB, 2004.

[Cecil Roth]

EDINGER, LUDWIG (1855–1918), German neuroanatomist and neurologist; considered the founder of modern neuroanatomy. Edinger was born in Worms on the Rhine, Germany, and began his academic studies at Heidelberg University. He completed his medical studies at the University of Strasbourg and became a licensed physician in 1877. In 1879 he began teaching at the University of Giessen and in 1883 he moved to Frankfurt to practice neurology. That same year he started lecturing on the structure of the central nervous system. In 1885 he joined the Senckenberg Research Institute in Frankfurt and conducted further studies in neurology, particularly in brain anatomy. That year marked the appearance of *Zehn Vorlesungen ueber den Bau der nervoesen Zentralorgane*, later translated into English as *Twelve Lectures on the Structure of the Central Nervous System,* his most famous text on the structure of the nervous system.

By 1907 his division had become one of the most modern neurological departments of the time and he became professor of neurology at Frankfurt University. In his research Edinger described the ventral and dorsal spinocerebellar tract, clarified polioencephalon and neoencephalitis, as well as the paleo-cerebellum and the neo-cerebellum. His studies and research appeared in many publications, and his name became associated with several parts of the human brain that he elucidated, including "Edinger's nucleus," "the Edinger fibers," and "Edinger's tract."

Edinger was also a gifted artist and achieved considerable notoriety in the field of hypnosis.

BIBLIOGRAPHY: S.R. Kagan, *Jewish Medicine* (1952), 381f.; *Biographisches Lexikon der hervorragenden Aerzte* (1932), 349–50.

[Suessmann Muntner / Ruth Rossing (2nd ed.)]

EDINGER, TILLY (1897–1967), vertebrate paleontologist. Born in Frankfurt on the Main, Edinger received her doctorate in paleontology from Frankfurt University. Her main research interest was brain development and she created the field of paleoneurology. She was fascinated by the disproportionate growth of the forebrain in many mammals and the implications for the emergence of Homo sapiens. She worked initially at Frankfurt University's Geological Institute but, under antisemitic pressure, left for London in 1939 before moving to the U.S. in 1940. She joined Harvard University's Museum of Comparative Zoology and became a research associate in paleontology. Her classic works are *Fossil Brains* (1929) and *The Evolution of the Horse Brain* (1948).

[Michael Denman (2nd ed.)]

EDIRNE (**Adrianople**), town in Turkey located in eastern Thrace near the Turkish-Greek-Bulgarian frontier. According to the 2000 census, the city's population was recorded as 119,316. The city was named after the Roman emperor, Hadrian (125 C.E.). Individual Jews went to Adrianople even before the destruction of the Second Temple, but certain knowledge of a Jewish settlement comes only from the beginning of the *Byzantine period. The Adrianople Jews then traded in textiles, leather goods, and wine. The community is mentioned in connection with the opposition to the messianic ferment in the Byzantine Empire at the time of the First Crusade (1096), and the synagogue of the Greeks (or Romaniots), burnt down in 1905, probably dated back to that period. After the Ottoman capture (1361) the city, now renamed Edirne, became the new Ottoman capital and the main administrative and military base from where the *Ottomans set off to conquer the Balkans. The city maintained this latter position even after the capital moved to Constantinople/*Istanbul following the conquest of the Byzantine city in 1453. The Ottomans populated Edirne with many immigrants; among them there were a large number of Jews arriving from the newly conquered lands in the Balkans. The community developed further following the influx of immigrants from Hungary after the expulsion of 1376 and from France after 1394. R. Isaac Zarefati, the leader of the Ashkenazi community, issued an appeal to West European Jews to settle in the *Ottoman Empire (after the capture of Constantinople in 1453). He and his descendants held office until 1722. The Ottomans transferred some of the local Jews to Constantinople. After 1492 many exiles from Spain came to Edirne followed by refugees from Portugal, and Italy as well. These new immigrants, who had different customs from the Romaniots, established their own congregations (*kahal*, pl. *kehalim*) according to their place of origin. In 1656 there were 15 different *kehalim*, most of them named after locations in Spain, Portugal, and Italy. On the basis of Ottoman fiscal registers, we can estimate that the city's population in 1580 was around 30,000 inhabitants. During the second half of the 17th century, the general population grew to about 100,000; many of them arrived in Edirne following the temporary transfer of the sultan's residence to the city (until 1703). At the time the Jewish population of the city grew from 2,500 people to about 5,000. *Shabbetai Ẓevi was brought to Edirne for questioning before the sultan in September 1666, and after his apostasy, some of his disciples in Edirne also converted to Islam. Shabbetai lived another ten years after his conversion, mostly in Edirne. His influence lingered in the city: Samuel *Primo (d. 1708), the leading rabbi of Edirne, was a secret adherent of Shabbatean mysticism, covertly giving instruction in it to small groups of followers. The decline of the Ottoman central authority brought new burdens on the local Jewish community, which had to accommodate itself to the changing local political circumstances. Nineteenth-century developments, encouraged by the new policy of reforms (*tanzimat*) led to the emergence of a new bourgeoisie in the non-Muslim communities of Edirne. The Jewish economic elite was composed of moneylenders and traders. The 19th century was also marked by a deterioration in the relations between the Jews and their Christian neighbors: the Jews suffered, for example, from *blood libels, spread by the Armenians (1871–72). The rise of nationalism in the Balkans was another and much more menacing threat to the community: when the Bulgarians temporarily occupied Edirne during the First Balkan War (March 1913), following a six-month siege, the Jews suffered and many of them found temporary shelter in Istanbul.

The Ottoman census of 1831, which counted only the adult male population, registered 1,541 Jewish men in the city. In 1873 there were approximately 12,000 Jews in the city; a report submitted to the *Alliance Israélite Universelle in Paris in 1897 on the various handicrafts and occupations in the Jewish community mentioned some 815 workers in 47 different categories. The community developed further following the arrival of refugees from the newly established Balkan states. The Ottoman census of 1906–7 put the number of the Jews in Edirne at 23,839. They lived in various neighborhoods according to their professions. Each neighborhood maintained its own community organization, synagogue, and *bet din* under the general supervision of the city's chief rabbi (the first chief rabbi, *ḥakham bashi*, was appointed in 1836 as part of the formal recognition of the Ottoman Jewish community as an official one). Before World War I their numbers rose to 28,000 but thereafter they declined in 1921–22 to 13,000, in 1927 to 5,712 Jews, the community being reduced by 1943 to 2,000. The decline can be explained in part by the changed status of the city which became a border town, in part by the impoverishment due to the wars, which resulted in immigration to *Salonica, France, and America, and later to Palestine. Apart from the Rabbanite community there was also a *Karaite community dating from the Byzantine period; among its members was the *Bashyazi family which became famous in Karaite history. For a time, Edirne was one of the important Karaite centers in Europe. At the beginning of the 20th century no trace of the Karaites remained.

The Jews of Edirne played an important part in the city's economy. They traded with Jewish and Christian merchants in other countries, either directly or through the latter's Jewish agents in Edirne. Local Jews held at times the lease (*iltizam*) of the import taxes and manufactured glass. Government taxes were paid on the basis of a fixed assessment which took into account one hundred families, although the number of Jews had increased. These taxes were imposed on the 13 congregations. In accordance with a special *firman* of 1783, the Jewish community was allowed to collect the *gabela*, a tax on meat which covered the poll tax (**kharaj*), the clothing of the poor, and other communal needs. Tax collectors appointed by the general body apportioned the taxes among the congregations making evaluations every three years. Edirne was long a center of learning. In the 15th century Mordecai *Comtino lived there and at the beginning of the 16th century R. Joseph *Caro wrote most of his famous *Beit Yosef* commentary there. In the 16th century there lived in Edirne the *Ibn Verga family and the poet R. Avtalyon b. Mordecai (see Avtalyon *Modena). In the court of Sultan Mehmet II (1451–81) there was a famous Jewish physician, Hekim Ya'akub, with widespread diplomatic connections. He later converted to Islam.

The printers Solomon and Joseph *Jabez set up a Hebrew printing press in Edirne in 1554 when they fled from the plague in Salonica but returned a year later. During this short period they produced *She'erit Yosef* by Joseph ibn Verga; *Shevet Yehudah* by Solomon ibn Verga; and Joseph Jabez's own commentary on *Avot*. A press reappeared in Edirne only in the late 19th century.

The last of the rabbis of the Zarefati family was Abraham (d. 1722). After his death the jurisdiction of the Edirne rabbinate was divided between Abraham Gheron, Zarefati's son-in-law, and Menahem b. Isaac Ashkenazi (Bekhemoharar), each of whom had his adherents; the Bekhemoharar family officiated for approximately 180 years and counted among its descendants halakhists and authors, and the Gheron family officiated for approximately 170 years. Each family maintained its own **bet din*. In the 18th century R. Isaac Molkho, author of *Shulhan Gavoha* (1756), a popular handbook on the laws of *shehitah*, lived in Edirne. In the middle of the 19th century, the haskalah movement penetrated Edirne through the philologist Joseph *Halevy (1827–1917). While the role of Edirne's *maskilim* in diffusing these new ideas was only secondary when compared to the role of Istanbul or Salonica, we can still recognize some of their contributions: on the request of the *maskilim*, the *Alliance Israélite Universelle opened a school for boys in 1867 and one for girls in 1870. The writer, historian, and poet Baruch b. Isaac Mitrani (1847–1919) taught at the Alliance schools. He endeavored to implement new methods of education. To achieve these aims he established a new school – Akedat Yitzḥak – and published books on education in Hebrew and a grammar of spoken Judeo-Spanish. He edited the first newspaper that was published in Edirne: *Karmi* (1871–81) and *Kerem Sheli* (1890; in Hebrew and Ladino), calling for Jewish colonization in Palestine and national revival. Abraham *Danon (1857–1925), a pupil of Joseph Halevy, established under the latter's influence the *Doreshei Haskalah* group and in 1888 edited the historical periodical *Yosef Da'at* (in Hebrew and Ladino) in order to collect and publish Jewish historical studies. The periodical was closed down by the government after a short time. In 1891, Danon opened a rabbinical seminary that taught both secular and religious subjects. The teaching was partly in Turkish – a major innovation for the period. The seminary moved to Istanbul in 1898 with its 11 students. In his writings, he attempted to reconcile traditional and Western knowledge. The Ladino press was the major printed product of the period: Joseph Barishak edited the major political-literary Jewish journal of Edirne: *La Boz de la Verdad* ("The Voice of Truth") in 1911–22. Nissim Behar published the weekly *L'Echo d'Adrianople* in French in 1921–22. Many of the graduates of the Alliance joined the newly founded alumni associations. A B'nai B'rith lodge was established in 1911. These associations – including reading clubs and mutual-aid fraternities – were chiefly meant to support and propagate the new trends of modernization among the community's members. In this capacity they contributed to the Westernization and secularization of the local community. Following the great fire of 1905 in which all the 13 synagogues of Edirne were burned to the ground, the community constructed a new synagogue in 1907 which was modeled on the synagogue of Vienna. It could accommodate 1,200 worshipers – 900 men and 300 women – and was designated to demonstrate the community's achievements and modernity.

[Simon Marcus / Eyal Ginio (2nd ed.)]

The demise of the Ottoman Empire and the foundation of the Turkish republic put unprecedented pressure on all the Jewish communities of Turkey. They were required to assimilate linguistically and culturally into Turkish society. This pressure must be seen as part of the overall anti-minority attitude in public opinion in the republic's first years. It seems that the lot of the Jewish community in Thrace (including Edirne) was the harshest. Living in a sensitive border area and remaining the only non-Muslim minority following the transfer of the Bulgarian, Greek, and Armenian populations, the Jews of Edirne suffered from verbal and sporadically physical assaults as well as from legal restrictions on their economic activities. The local Turkish press played a major role in inciting the local population against their Jewish neighbors. This reached its peak with the outbreak of assaults on Jews in the major towns of eastern Thrace in 1934. The agitation of mobs in Edirne, which involved physical attacks on the Jews and threats against the community, caused panic among Edirne Jewry. Thousands moved permanently to Istanbul, although the government intervened to stop the attacks and assured the Jews of their safety. The community never recovered from this blow. The conscription to labor battalions and the imposition of a discriminatory head tax caused impoverishment and further decline in the community. The town suffered economic crises after World War II. The community diminished through migration to Israel and other countries and also to Istanbul. In 1948, 2,750 Jews remained in Edirne, while by 1960 their number dwindled to 438, and in 1977 there were only 72 Jewish inhabitants in the city. In 1948 the community was still well organized and levied dues from its members. Its council maintained charitable institutions, a Bikkur Holim society (which then provided medical care for 730 patients), a Mahazikei Torah association (which provided Hebrew and religious education), the 'Ozer Dallim association (which cared for the needy), and several synagogues. By 1969 most of the institutions had closed and the community was left with only one synagogue. In 1971 the municipality prohibited the community from using its cemetery and in 1975 it confiscated it altogether. Subsequently the cemetery was destroyed. The shrinking community used the synagogue until 1983. In 1998 there were only three Jews living in Edirne.

[Hayyim J. Cohen / Eyal Ginio (2nd ed.)]

Music

Edirne was also a center of Jewish music. A choral society of Maftirim was founded in the seventh century. It sang every Sabbath at dawn from a book of religious hymns which were locally called *jonk* (the Persian-Arabic designation of "harp"). A great number of able cantors and assistant singers (*maftirim, mezammerim*) came from Edirne. Congregations from as far away as Bulgaria and Romania appealed to this community whenever there was need of a good synagogue singer. The activity and reputation of the Maftirim Society helped Edirne become a center for hymn writers. Among the best known were Aaron b. Isaac *Hamon (18th century; possibly the composer called Yahudi Harun by the Turks), Abraham Zemah (late 19th century), and Joseph Danon (d. 1901). A large repertoire of Ladino folksongs from Edirne was collected and published by A. Danon in 1896. Danon contended that the proficiency of the local Jews in Eastern music had been stimulated by, and modeled after, the style of the Muslim Dervish brotherhoods.

[Hanoch Avenary]

BIBLIOGRAPHY: Rosanes, Togarmah, passim; A. Hananel and E. Eshkenazi, *Fontes hebraici… balcanicarum…*, 2 (1960), index (Hebrew text with Bulgarian translation, summaries in Russian and French); Nathan, in: JJSO, 6 (1964), 180ff.; Marcus, in: *Sinai*, 21 (1947), 48–63; 29 (1951), 7–23, 318–44; 45 (1959), 376–86; idem, in: *Mizraḥ u-Ma'arav*, 5 (1930), 173–84; W. Reich, in: *Oesterreichische Wochenschrift*, 30 (1913), 7–26; M.S. Goodblatt, *Jewish Life in Turkey in the 16th Century* (1952), index; Rosanes, in: B. Joseph (ed.), *Shirei Yisrael be-Ereẓ ha-Kedem* (1921), preface; Danon, *ibid.*, 8–10; Behar, in: YIVO *Bleter*, 31–32 (1948), 400–5; Ch. D. Friedberg, *Toledot ha-Defus ha-'Ivri* (1956^2), 144; M. Benayahu, in: *Reshumot*, 2 (1946), 144–54; Cowen, in: *Jewish Life* (July-Aug. 1969), 24–30. **ADD. BIBLIOGRAPHY:** R. Bali, "Edirne Yahudileri," in: E.N. İşli and S. Koz (eds.), *Edirne, Serhattaki Payitaht* (1998), 205–27; E. Benbassa and A. Rodrigue, *Sephardi Jewry: A History of the Judeo-Spanish Community, 14th–20th Centuries* (2000); P. Dumont, "Jewish Communities in Turkey during the Last Decade of the Nineteenth Century in the Light of the Archives of the Alliance Israélite Universelle," in: B. Braude and B. Lewis, *Christians and Jews in the Ottoman Empire*, 1 (1982), 209–42; M.A. Epstein, *The Ottoman Jewish Communities and their Role in the Fifteenth and Sixteenth Centuries* (1980); H. Gerber, "*Yehudim be-Edirne (Adrianople) ba-Me'ot ha-Tet Zayin ve-ha-Yud Zayin*," in: *Sefunot*, 18 (1985), 35–51; A. Levy, "The Siege of Edirne (1912–1913) as Seen by a Jewish Eyewitness: Social, Political, and Cultural Perspectives," in: A. Levy (ed.), *Jews, Turks, Ottomans: A Shared History, Fifteenth Through the Twentieth Century* (2002), 153–93; idem, *The Sephardim in the Ottoman Empire* (1992); A. Rodrigue, *French Jews, Turkish Jews: The Alliance Israélite Universelle and the Politics of Jewish Schooling in Turkey, 1860–1925* (1990); S.J. Shaw, *The Jews of the Ottoman Empire and the Turkish Republic* (1991); A. Levy, "*Ha-Pra'ot bi-Yehudei Trakya, 1934*," in: *Pe'amim*, 20 (1984), 111–32; Shaul Tuval, "*Ha-Kehillot ha-Yehudiyot be-Turkiyah ka-Yom*," in: *ibid.*, 12 (1982), 114–39; A. Yerolympos, "A Contribution to the Topography of 19th Century Adrianople," in: *Balkan Studies*, 34:1 (1993), 49–72.

EDMAN, IRWIN (1896–1954), U.S. philosopher. He was born in New York, earned his Ph.D. at Columbia in 1920, and taught there until his death. He was appointed full professor in 1935. Edman wrote poetry, essays, and philosophical works. He was greatly influenced by John Dewey and American naturalism, while drawn to the philosophical classics. He once called himself "an empiricist homesick for Platonism." Edman was interested in aesthetics, social and political philosophy, and the philosophy of religion. He published many works, including *Human Traits and Their Social Significance* (1920); *The Mind of Paul* (1935), on St. Paul's religious outlook; *Philosopher's Holiday* (1938), a popular presentation of philosophical anecdotes from his own life; *Arts and the Man* (1939); and *Philosopher's Quest* (1947). Edman also edited English editions of Plato, Boethius, Schopenhauer, and Santayana. An anthology of his writings, *The Uses of Philosophy*, was published in 1955.

[Richard H. Popkin]

EDMONTON, capital of Alberta, Canada. Edmonton was first incorporated as a town in 1892. At that time, there were about 700 permanent residents. Founded on the banks of the North Saskatchewan River on the site of the former Hudson's Bay Company's Fort Edmonton, it gradually began to attract settlers. Abraham and Rebecca Cristall, Edmonton's first Jews, arrived in 1893. Their children, George and Rose, were the town's first Jewish-born children. Abe became a successful businessman and encouraged Jews from his native Bessarabia to come. By 1901, there were 17 Jews in Edmonton. In 1904, Edmonton became incorporated as a city, and in 1905 Alberta officially became a province and the Canadian Pacific Railway arrived.

In 1905, William "Boss" Diamond came to Edmonton from Calgary, where his businessman brother Jacob had been Alberta's first Jewish citizen. William set up in the clothing business in competition with Abe Cristall, but the two competitors worked together to establish Edmonton's Jewish community. Together with eight other men they formed the Edmonton Hebrew Association in 1906. They hired Rabbi Hyman Goldstick of Pilton, Latvia, to be rabbi, *shoḥet*, and *mohel* to serve both the Edmonton and Calgary Jewish communities.

In 1907, Abe Cristall purchased land on the south side for a Jewish cemetery and the *ḥevra kaddisha* was formed. In 1912, the foundations were laid for the Orthodox Beth Israel Synagogue. Cristall served as its first president, and William Diamond its second president, a position he held for 31 years. In 1912, the newly founded Edmonton Talmud Torah Society organized classes in the synagogue basement. In 1925, the Society erected its own building and in 1933 it was incorporated as the first Hebrew day school in Canada.

In 1928, a second congregation was started in the basement of the Talmud Torah building, which in 1932 became the Conservative Beth Shalom Congregation and engaged Rabbi Jacob Eisen, who became one of the first English-speaking rabbis west of Winnipeg. Also at that time, the Peretz or New Yiddish School was organized and opened its own building. An offshoot of the Arbeiter Ring, which started in Edmonton in 1922, it had its heyday in the early 1930s, but had to close in 1939 due to declining enrollment. By 1941, Edmonton's population had increased to 93,817, and the Jewish population stood at 1,449. Of the 120 men and women from Edmonton's Jewish community who served during World War II, 11 were killed in action.

The postwar years saw rapid growth in both the Jewish and general population of Edmonton. With prosperity and a shift by Jews into the city's West End, a new Beth Shalom Synagogue was built in 1951. A new Beth Israel Synagogue building was also constructed as well as a new Talmud Torah building. In 1954, the Edmonton Jewish Community Council was formed as a community-wide umbrella organization and served as such for 28 years. On September 20, 1982, the Community Council merged with the Edmonton United Jewish Appeal to become the Jewish Federation of Edmonton.

Alberta's booming oil-based economy brought increased immigration to Edmonton including that of Jews from other provinces in Canada, as well as from Hungary, Russia, and South Africa. From a Jewish population of 1,748 in 1951, the community grew to 2,910 in 1971 and 5,430 in 1991. In 2001 it stood at about 6,000.

All these new immigrants contributed to Edmonton's vibrant Jewish community life. Local branches of prominent Jewish organizations thrive, including the Canadian Zionist Federation, Edmonton Hadassah-WIZO, chapters of ORT and Na'amat, B'nai B'rith and Emunah, all of which are actively working for the welfare of the State of Israel. Local offices of the Jewish National Fund are located at the Edmonton Jewish Community Centre, founded in 1970. The now defunct Edmonton chapter of the National Council of Jewish Women was responsible for founding the city's Jewish Seniors' Drop-in Centre (formerly the Golden Age Club) in 1954, as well as Jewish Family Services.

The community's third congregation, Temple Beth Ora Reform Congregation, was founded in 1979, and incorporated in 1980. It rented space at the Jewish Community Centre. In 1996 Congregation Beth Tzedec, a breakaway from Beth Shalom, incorporated and began to hold services at the Talmud Torah. Chabad Lubavitch arrived in Edmonton in 1991, and in 1993 a second Hebrew day school, the Orthodox Menorah Academy, was founded. In 1999, a new building for Edmonton Talmud Torah was erected and the next year a new Beth Israel Synagogue was opened reflecting a further westward shift in population.

In the fall of 2004, Edmonton elected its first Jewish mayor, Stephen Mandel. Mandel had previously served as a city councilor, continuing a long tradition of Jewish city councilors, including Dr. Morris Weinlos, Helen Paull, Mel Binder, Tooker Gomberg, and former MLA Karen Leibovici. There has also been a strong tradition of Jewish civic involvement in the larger Edmonton community, with members serving on the boards and executives of many local arts, cultural, educational, and fundraising organizations, as well as on the judiciary.

The Jewish Archives and Historical Society of Edmonton and Northern Alberta (JAHSENA) was founded in 1996 to preserve and promote the history of this vibrant Jewish community.

BIBLIOGRAPHY: U. Rosenzweig (ed.), *The First Century of Jewish Life in Edmonton and Northern Alberta, 1893–1993* (2000).

[Debby Shoctor and Ed Mickelson (2nd ed.)]

EDOM (Heb. אֱדוֹם), a land in the south of eastern Transjordan, the southeastern neighbor of Palestine.

The Country

"The land of Edom" is the most common name for the Edomite territory. It had, however, other names and appellations, both prosaic and poetic, i.e., "the field of Edom" (Judg. 5:4), "Seir" (*ibid.*), "Mount Seir" (Deut. 1:2), "the land of Seir" (Gen. 36:30, "the lands of Seir," cf. *mâtâti*^{d} *še-e-ri*^{ki}, in el-Amarna letter no. 288, line 26; Pritchard, Texts, 488; J.A. Knudtzon, *Die El-Amarna-Tafeln*, 2 (1915), 1340), and a combined name, "the land of Seir the field of Edom" (Gen. 32:3). There are also in Egyptian sources the equivalents of two names: Seir (Pritchard, Texts, 262) and Edom (Papyrus Anastasi VI, Pritchard, Texts, 259). It is possible to establish, according to the Egyptian and Akkadian sources, that the name Seir is chronologically first, since it is mentioned at the beginning of the 14th century B.C.E. in the Tell el-Amarna document, as well as in an Egyptian list from the time of Ramses II, i.e., from the first half of the 13th century B.C.E. On the other hand, the first mention of the name Edom in Egyptian sources occurs only at the end of the 13th century B.C.E.

The name Seir is apparently related to the Horites; this is especially evidenced by Genesis 36:20: "These were the sons of Seir the Horite, who were settled in the land" (cf. Deut. 2:12). The name Edom is related to the Western Semitic settlers who came after them.

It appears that the Edomite territory consisted of the mountain which extends from the Dead Sea in the north to the Red Sea in the south. The northern border of Edom was the Zered River (Wadi al-Hesa), which was also the southern border of Moab (Deut. 2:13). Its eastern border was the desert and its inhabitants were the Kedemites. Its southern border was Elath and Ezion-Geber (Deut. 2:8), i.e., the gulf of Elath. There was probably no fixed western boundary; during the Exodus from Egypt, the Israelites who requested permission to pass through Edom said to the king of Edom: "Now we are in *Kadesh, the town on the border of your territory" (Num. 20:16). Another place mentioned as being on its western border is "Mount Hor on the boundary of the land of Edom" (Num. 20:23). The western border is described more comprehensively as "the boundary of Edom to the wilderness of Zin at the farthest south" (Josh. 15:1), and in an abbreviated manner as "south, toward the boundary of Edom" (Josh. 15:21).

In later periods there was an Edomite expansion beyond Mount Seir, especially after the fall of the kingdom of Judah (see below). Ezekiel thus terms the Edomite territory "Mount Seir and all Edom" (Ezek. 35:15). The capital of Edom was probably Bozrah (see especially Amos 1:12, "the palaces of Bozrah," similar to the palaces of other capital cities mentioned in this prophecy). Bozrah was the principal city, the other cities of Edom being called Bozrah's cities: "For I have sworn by myself, says the Lord, that Bozrah shall become a horror, a taunt, a waste, and a curse; and all her cities shall be perpetual wastes" (Jer. 49:13). Among the other cities of Edom mentioned in the Bible are Teman, which is used as a parallel for Bozrah (Amos 1:12), and Dedan (Jer. 49:8). The principal cities of Edom, which were also the royal cities, can be learned from the list of kings, who reigned "before any king reigned over the Israelites" (Gen. 36). In this list, Bozrah and Teman are mentioned with other towns such as Avith, Rehoboth Hanahar, Masrekah, and Pau, about which nothing is known from the Bible or from other sources.

The People

In the biblical tradition about the origin of the Edomites or, more precisely, in accounts about the eponym "Esau who is Edom" (Gen. 36:1), the Edomites are related to the Hebrews. Esau was the grandson of Abraham the Hebrew and the son of Isaac. The close relationship of *Esau to Israel is especially emphasized in the narratives which point out his closeness with Jacob-Israel, and describe their birth as twins. In parenthetical narrative comments and especially in genealogical lists, the complexity of the Edomites' ethnic composition is demonstrated. In the accounts of Esau's marriages, which should be viewed as etiological-ethnological stories, it is told that Esau married Canaanite-Hittite women (Gen. 26:34; cf. 36:2). It is likewise told that he married Ishmaelite women (Gen. 28:9; cf. 36:3). He also took Hivite wives (Gen. 36:2). These parenthetical narrative remarks substantiate and confirm the contents of the genealogical lists of Edom. The ethnic composition appears to be even more heterogeneous when in addition to the Canaanite-Hittite, Hivite, and Ishmaelite elements, Kenazite (Gen. 36:15), Amalekite (36:16), and especially Horite (36:20, 21, 29, 30) elements are found in the genealogical list of Esau's descendants and in the list of the chiefs of Esau. A similar picture is reflected in the names appearing in the genealogical lists of Edom. West-Semitic names are listed side by side with Horite names. It is possible to distinguish earlier and later elements in the ethnic composition of Edom. Traditions, whose authenticity is beyond doubt, have been preserved in the Bible about the antiquity of the Horites in Edom. In the Deuteronomic tradition about the ancient settlers of eastern Transjordan before the advent of the Hebrews, it is stated: "Seir was formerly inhabited by the Horites; but the descendants of Esau dispossessed them, wiping them out and settling in their place" (Deut. 2:12). This tradition is reported in brief also in the chapter specifically dealing with Edom, Genesis 36, where a parenthetical remark is made: "these were the sons of Seir the Horite, who were settled in the land" (36:20). Thus, the ancient ethnic element of Edom is the Horites, to whom were later added those descendants of Esau who were from a Western-Semitic origin. This is corroborated by epigraphic sources and archaeological findings. From Akkadian and Egyptian epigraphic sources it is known that toward the first half of the second millennium B.C.E. "Horite" (Akk. *ḫurru*) tribes penetrated all the areas of the Ancient East and settled in these areas including Canaan and eastern Transjordan. There is also information about waves of migration of Western-Semitic elements who infiltrated western Asia, including Transjordan, and apparently conquered these territories and defeated the Horite population. According to biblical tradition, Esau and his descendants first inhabited the land of Canaan (Gen. 36:5), and when "the land in which they sojourned could not support them because of their livestock," Esau, together with Jacob and his children, "took … all the members of his household … [and] settled in the hill country of Seir" (36:6–8). From the archaeological survey of eastern Transjordan conducted by Nelson Glueck the same picture emerges. It appears that the settlement which existed from the 23rd to the 20th centuries B.C.E. was highly civilized, but the 19th century B.C.E. saw a steep decline and the total extinction of all the great fortresses and settlements. The blow was final and the destruction, total. The cities were not rebuilt and most of Transjordan became a camping spot for shepherds and nomads until the end of the 14th century B.C.E. The archaeological survey demonstrated that at the end of the 14th and the beginning of the 13th centuries B.C.E., there was a revival of an agricultural civilization among the Edomites, the Moabites, the Ammonites, and the Amorites, who quickly divided into national groups within defined territorial boundaries. Thus, Transjordan was divided into the kingdoms of Edom, Ammon, and Moab, which were separated mainly by the deep and wide natural boundaries of the Zered, Arnon, and Jabbok rivers. These kingdoms underwent a fast development of prosperity and growth, primarily material, from the 13th to the 8th centuries B.C.E. There followed a period of decline which ended in utter destruction in the sixth century B.C.E.

Biblical Sources

These latter comments would have exhausted our knowledge about Edom had the Bible not preserved much information about this kingdom, more so than about any of the other kingdoms neighboring Israel. This great amount of material in the Bible is very valuable from both the historical and historiographical points of view. Biblical information about Edom may be divided into two types, which are distinctly separable. The first type is the original and authentic material, which apparently originated in Edom itself and somehow made its way to Israel, and which is found mainly in Genesis 36. The second type is information about Edom which is connected with the history of Israel. These two types of material give a chronological coverage of the two periods of Edom's history (see below). The original and authentic material about Edom is from the period before the monarchy was established in Israel (it is not intended here to discuss R.H. Pfeiffer's Edomite-Seirite, or Southern source (s); for its scope, character, and time see *Pentateuch). This material describes the history of Edom until its conquest by David. On the other hand, the material about Edom which is contained in the Israelite history covers the period of the monarchy in Israel and Judah, and, in fact, beginning with the time of David, the history of Edom is contained within the history of Israel.

History until Its Conquest by David

From the information contained in Genesis 36, it may be learned that the Edomites were governed by chiefs (*allufim*) and kings in the period which preceded its conquest by David. The question arises as to whether chiefs and kings ruled at one and the same time, the kings being only the most powerful of the chiefs, or whether there were two periods, a first of chiefs and a subsequent one of kings. It appears that two periods should be distinguished, the "period of the chiefs" and the "period of the kings," typologically paralleling the "period of the judges" and the "period of the monarchy" in Israel.

THE PERIOD OF THE CHIEFS (*Allufim*). It appears that the chiefs were the heads of the thousands (*alafim*), which were tribes or clans (in the broad sense of the word), and later, heads of regions. This form of organization was prevalent among nomadic tribes. Actually, only 11 chiefs of Edom are mentioned, but there is reason to accept the opinion that a 12th name, which is found in the Septuagint, was left out. The tradition of the 12-fold organization in Edom is based on, and confirmed by, the organization of other tribes which are closely related to Edom in terms of race and origin. This 12-fold organization is found among the Nahorites (Gen. 22:20–24), the Ishmaelites (25:13–15), and the Israelites, and it is M. Noth's opinion that this system is based on "principles such as were customary in tribal societies which were still lacking settled political institutions" (Noth, Hist Isr, 87; for details). Taking as a starting point the conclusion of Nelson Glueck's survey that the Edomites arrived in Edom at the end of the 14th and the beginning of the 13th century B.C.E., it may then be assumed that the rule of the chiefs lasted approximately 150 years, until the middle of the 12th century B.C.E. Actually, the Bible appears to contain information to the contrary, since in the narrative on the Exodus from Egypt and the penetration of Canaan it is told that the Israelites had dealings with the king of Edom (Num. 20:14; if it is assumed, as is the accepted opinion today, that the Exodus was during the second half of the 13th century B.C.E.). It is known, however, that the source for the narrative (Num. 20) is late and "the king of Edom" is an anachronism. More authentic evidence from a very early poetic source, the Song of the Sea, testifies that at the time of the Exodus the chiefs were ruling in Edom: "Now are the chiefs of Edom dismayed" (Ex. 15:15). There are also sources outside the Bible which confirm this. In the Papyrus Anastasi VI from the time of Merneptah (end of the 13th century B.C.E.) the population of Edom and its adjuncts is divided into "tribes" or *shasu*: "[We] have finished letting the Shasu (*š*'*sw*) of Edom (*'idm*) pass the Fortress [of] Merneptah" (in Pritchard, Texts, 259). Ramses III (beginning of the 12th century B.C.E.) boasts: "I destroyed the people of Seir among the nomad tribes. I razed their tents: their people, their property, and their cattle as well, without number, pinioned and carried away in captivity, as the tribute of Egypt" (see Papyrus Harris I, in: Pritchard, Texts, 262). In any event, it becomes evident from these two Egyptian sources that there was a tribal organization, the population was nomadic, and there was no monarchy.

THE PERIOD OF THE MONARCHY. The genealogy of Edom in Genesis 36 contains a list of the kings of Edom who ruled "before any Israelite king reigned" (probably meaning "before any Israelite king ruled over Edom"). It is not certain whether "kings" were merely judges or tribal chiefs, or whether they were literally kings. Those scholars who hold that they were judges point to the following supporting evidence: the absence of succession, the absence of a fixed capital city, the parallelism of *melekh*/*shofet* ("king"/"judge") in Ugaritic and the Bible, as well as the formula "in those days there was no king over the Israelites," which recurs repeatedly in the Book of Judges in reference to the period of the judges. Thus, king here means judge (this opinion has been expressed by S. Talmon). It appears that the second opinion is the correct one, however, and that kings is meant literally.

The list of the Edomite kings (36:31–39) resembles a "royal chronicle" in that it includes various details found in the Judean and Israelite chronicles contained in Kings and Babylonian Chronicles. Details given in this list – though not all the details are given for every king – are the name of the king, his father's name, the name of his city (or place of origin), and an informative comment. This list includes eight kings. The names of the fathers of four of them are given, and the city (or place of origin) of seven out of the eight is mentioned. An informative comment is made about two of them. The informative comment about Hadad son of Bedad is distinctly historical. It is stated that he "defeated the Midianites in the country of Moab" (36:35), while the comment about Hadar, the last king, refers to his wife's genealogy: "and his wife's name was Mehetabel daughter of Matred daughter of Me-Zahab" (36:39). This list has been analyzed by numerous scholars in an attempt to derive from it information about the history of Edom, its chronology and the possibility of synchronization, its monarchy, and its character. It is clear from this list that the monarchy in Edom was not dynastic. Not one of the kings of Edom is said to be son of the former king. However, it should not be deduced from this, as has been done by several scholars, that the monarchy was not consistent. The formula: "when … died, … succeeded him as king" attests to the consistency and continuity of the monarchy. Further, it should be pointed out that there was no central authority based in one capital city. The fact that the king's capital or place of origin is mentioned shows that there was no common ruling city for even two of the kings (cf. the absence of a regular capital city in the kingdom of Israel until the establishment of Samaria by Omri). The two informative statements were variously interpreted by scholars. From the statement about Hadad son of Bedad E. Meyer tried to establish a synchronistic connection with events in Israel, namely that Hadad, who defeated the Midianites, was a contemporary of Gideon who defeated the Midianites. On the basis of this they attempted to derive chronological conclusions with regard to the history of the kings of Edom. There is no certainty, however, about Gideon's time, and even less about the time of the kings of Edom, concerning whom there is no chronological information. From the information about Hadar's wife's lineage on her mother's side, and from the naming of her mother and grandmother, W.F. Albright attempted to deduce the existence of a royal dynasty in Edom which passed in succession on the side of the mother and not the father. Thus, the king's son-in-law because he marries the queen's daughter is heir to the throne. A general conclusion of this nature, derived from a single comment, is, however, difficult to maintain. Moreover, there are no examples of such a custom in the ancient Near East to support this hypothesis (the example of Saul-Michal-David cannot be explained in this way).

It is most difficult to assess the dating of Edom's kings since, as has been stated, there is no chronological information given in regard to this period. It is only known that it ended at the time of David's conquest of Edom. If this assumption is correct, namely, that at the time of the Exodus, Edom was ruled by chiefs and not by kings, then the period of these kings can be set from the middle of the 12th century to the end of the 11th century B.C.E., i.e., a period of around 150 years, and an average of approximately 20 years per king.

During this period of chiefs and kings, Edom was strong and its borders well-fortified by a series of border fortresses which prevented the penetration of nomadic tribes from the desert. A series of fortresses was discovered during the archaeological survey in eastern and southern Edom, and some also in western Edom. (In the north, Edom shared a common border with Moab, with which it apparently had close and good neighborly relationships.) There is almost no biblical information in regard to contacts between Israel and Edom during this period, except that Edom is listed among the nations oppressing Israel which Saul defeated at the end of this period (I Sam. 14:47; it is possible that this refers to Amalek which is related to Edom). In Psalm 83, which is assumed by B. Mazar and S. Feigin to be from the period of the judges, Edom (as well as Amalek and Gebal which belong to Edom) is also mentioned as joining with Israel's other neighbors against Israel. It appears, however, that these two mentions are schematic and it is difficult to arrive at historically valid conclusions from the appearance of Edom in these lists.

From David until the Destruction of Judah

THE TIME OF DAVID AND SOLOMON. In David's wars of expansion, Edom was conquered after a decisive defeat in the Valley of Salt. This is echoed in three biblical sources – actually three accounts of the same battle. According to II Samuel 8:13 it was David who defeated Edom (this should be read instead of Aram) in the Valley of Salt, slaying 18,000 Edomites. According to I Chronicles 18:12, "Abishai son of Zeruiah slew 18,000 Edomites in the Valley of Salt," while according to Psalm 60:2, it was Joab who defeated Edom, and here there is a different number given for Edom's casualties – 12,000. While a few scholars held that these are accounts of battles led by the different people mentioned, it appears that they are, in fact, different accounts of the same event, and the numbers are schematic. In any event, in order to clarify the historical aspects, it appears that the original historical version is that Joab defeated Edom. The introduction of Abishai in Chronicles is aimed against Joab and is based on the wars in eastern Transjordan in which Joab and Abishai led the armies. The war was attributed to David because it appears that the victories of Joab, his military commander, were credited to the king, David, as was the case in the defeat of Rabbath-Benei-Ammon (II Sam. 12:26–31). Edom suffered a decisive defeat, apparently after a difficult battle. Contrary to his custom with regard to the other nations of Transjordan, David did not leave the Edomite monarchy in power but made Edom into an Israelite province ruled by appointed governors (II Sam. 8:14; I Chron. 18:13). There is additional information about this battle in I Kings 11:15–16 which states that "For six months did Joab remain there with all Israel, until he had cut off every male in Edom." His reasons for turning Edom into a province which rendered tribute and was ruled by governors were probably primarily economic, since Edom controlled the trade routes, both overland – the "King's Highway" – and maritime – the port of Ezion-Geber-Elath. Israel's rule of Edom by means of governors lasted throughout David's reign and apparently also through most of Solomon's time, until Hadad, a descendant of the last Edomite king, rebelled against Solomon. (It is difficult to determine whether Hadad was the son or the grandson of the last king of Edom. Actually, this was the introduction of a dynastic monarchy in Edom. In the opinion of Edward Meyer the Edomites were loyal to their last king.) This Hadad, who fled to Egypt during the conquest of Edom, received personal aid and political support in Egypt, and returned to Edom after David's death (I Kings 11:14–22). According to the Septuagint, what is said about Aram in I Kings 11:25 refers to Edom, and it thus turns out that this Hadad rebelled at the beginning of Solomon's reign and ruled Edom. It is difficult to accept this version, however, since it would mean that at the beginning of his reign, a time of prosperity and growth, of the development of the Negev and Arabah, and of maritime and inland trade, Solomon did not have absolute control over Edom and over the routes which crossed its territory. It would therefore appear that Edom's liberation was possible only at the end of Solomon's reign.

FROM JEHOSHAPHAT TO AHAZ. There is no information about Edom from the end of Solomon's reign until Jehoshaphat's, either from the Bible or from other sources. It may be assumed that after the collapse of Solomon's kingdom and its division, and especially after Shishak's campaign in Judah and Israel, Edom finally overthrew the yoke of Israel's rule and established an independent kingdom, which lasted around 50 years, until the time of Jehoshaphat. With the expansion of Judah southward in the time of Jehoshaphat, the submission of the Arabian tribes (II Chron. 17:11), and the institution of a mercantile fleet at Ezion-Geber (I Kings 22:49), Edom was probably conquered. In fact, there is an explicit statement in this regard from which it can be understood that not only was Edom conquered by Jehoshaphat but he dealt with it as did David and turned it into a province ruled by governors. Chronicles writes in connection with Jehoshaphat that "there was no king in Edom; a deputy was king" (I Kings 22:48 (47)). The conquest of Edom probably stemmed from the same economic motivations which existed at the time of David and Solomon. Edom became subject to Judah, and, during the period of subjection, "the king of Edom" (probably the "deputy" mentioned above) joined the campaign of Joram king of Israel and Jehoshaphat king of Judah against Mesha, the rebellious king of Moab, which passed "through the wilderness of Edom" (II Kings 3:8). The participation of the "king of Edom" angered the king of Moab, who attempted first and foremost "to break through opposite the king of Edom" (3:26). The failure of this campaign led to the weakening of the rule of Judah and Israel in eastern Transjordan, as well as Judah's rule in Edom. It is explicitly stated that during the time of Joram, Edom rebelled against Judah: "In his days Edom revolted from under the hand of Judah, and made a king over themselves" (II Kings 8:20). Joram attempted at the beginning of his reign (probably in 848 B.C.E.) to reinstate Israel's hegemony over Edom in a great campaign including "all the chariots" (8:21–22), which apparently failed (the biblical text is corrupt here), and Edom was completely liberated from the domination of Judah. Edom maintained its independence for about 60 years, until the middle of Amaziah's reign. At the time of Amaziah, Judah recovered from the pressure of Aram, to which it paid heavy taxes. This recovery is expressed in the undertaking of a military campaign against Edom in order to renew the rule of Israel there. It is said of Amaziah that "He slew of Edom in the Valley of Salt 10,000, and took Sela by war, and called the name of it Joktheel unto this day" (II Kings 14:7). The battle was waged in northern Edom, the Valley of Salt (as in David's time), and in Sela. Amaziah (like Joab) treated the Edomites with cruelty, as is recounted in II Chronicles 25:11–12: "...and [Amaziah] smote 10,000 men of Seir. The men of Judah captured another 10,000 alive and took them to the top of a rock and threw them down from the top of the rock; and they were all dashed to pieces." It seems that the changing of Sela's name can be interpreted not only as a symbol of renewed domination but perhaps also as the introduction of Judahite settlers in the new important town Joktheel which "on account of its geographic conditions, its distinctly strategic location, its close proximity to the capital Bozrah which lay south of it, and its control over the approach to the mines of the Arabah, ... was subject to a violent controversy between Israel and Edom" (S. Abramsky). With the conquest of Sela, Amaziah assured Judah of control over northern Edom and the copper mines of the Punon area. It appears that Uzziah son of Amaziah completed his father's activity by conquering Edom. Uzziah, who expanded his kingdom in the direction of south and the Negev, "built Elath and restored it to Judah" (II Kings 14:22); this was the climax of his activity in the Negev and the Arabah, in developing agriculture, industry, and commerce, which has been confirmed by archaeological excavations and surveys. Apparently, in the days of Jotham son of Uzziah as well, Judah ruled over Edom. The "ליתם" (*lytm*) seal found at Ezion-Geber may have belonged to Jotham. This period of Judah's rule over Edom did not last long, and ended with the establishment of the Aramean-Israelite coalition between Rezin king of Aram and Pekah king of Israel: "At that time the king of Edom recovered Elath for Edom (the MT text reads Aram instead of Edom) and drove the men of Judah from Elath; and the Edomites came to Elath, where they dwell to this day" (II Kings 16:6). The Edomites took the opportunity to penetrate Judah itself: "For again the Edomites had come and smitten Judah, and carried away captives" (II Chron. 28:17). There was probably a final attempt on the part of Judah, during the time of Hezekiah, to renew its hegemony over Edom. In the genealogical list of Simeon's descendants, it is stated parenthetically that "some of them, 500 men of the Simeonites, went to Mount Seir ... and they destroyed the remnant of the Amalekites that had escaped, and they have dwelt there to this day" (I Chron. 4:42–43). This attempt, however, was probably limited to the western border district of Edom and had no real results since Edom, like Judah, was subjugated by Assyria.

FROM AHAZ UNTIL THE DESTRUCTION OF JUDAH. From the time of Ahaz, Edom became an Assyrian vassal state, like the other nations of Palestine and Syria. Tiglath-Pileser III (745–727 B.C.E.) mentions, together with the kings of Palestine and Syria, Qosmalaku, king of Edom, who surrendered to him (Pritchard, Texts, 282). Sennacherib mentions the king of Edom, Aiarammu (*ibid.*, 287), who surrendered to him in his campaign against Jerusalem (701 B.C.E.). Esarhaddon (680–669 B.C.E.) mentions Qosgabri king of Edom together with the 22 vassal kings whom he swore to loyalty at Nineveh (*ibid.*, 291). In addition to its subjugation to Assyria, Edom was, beginning with the eighth century B.C.E., under pressure from the Arabian tribes that impoverished the land and brought about its decline in material culture. Toward the end of the kingdom of Judah (beginning of the sixth century B.C.E.), when Judah was rising up against Babylonian rule, Edom was among the peoples preparing to rebel against the Babylonian king. The king of Edom sent messengers to a meeting of rebels called in Jerusalem by Zedekiah king of

Judah (Jer. 27). Later, however, during the destruction itself, Edom was on the other side, sending its troops against Judah (II Kings 24:1; "the bands of Edom" should be read in place of "the bands of Aram"), and even participating in its destruction. This is verified from the recently discovered Arad letters, in which Judah is guarding itself against Edom's penetration into the land (Y. Aharoni). Edom's participation in the destruction of Judah aroused the great anger and strong condemnation of the poets (Ps. 137; Lam. 4:21–22) and prophets (Isa. 34, which is to be dated to this period; Jer. 49; Obad.) of Judah. The anger and condemnation continued in the following generation in the prophecies of Deutero-Isaiah (Isa. 63).

Edom, too, was subject to destruction in the sixth century B.C.E. Nomadic tribes infiltrated Edom and exerted pressure on the Edomites, who turned toward Judah and settled in its southern region. This settlement was long known in Hellenistic sources as *Idumea.

Religion and Culture

The gods of Edom were mainly fertility gods, as is evidenced by the numerous clay figures found in Edom. Like Ammon and Moab, Edom had one chief god, Qos. This name is known to be a theophoric element, both from the names of the Edomite kings mentioned in the inscriptions of the Assyrian kings (see above) and from names which are preserved in the Bible (e.g., Barkos, Neh. 7:55). This name also appears as a first name in a seal in Hebrew-Edomite script on oil jugs from the eighth and seventh centuries B.C.E. which were found at Tell al-Khalayfa "לקוסענל עבד המלך," "*lqwsʿnl* servant of the king." There are some scholars who read instead of the unclear name *Alqum* in Proverbs 30:31, *Alqus*, on the assumption that the name is included here in the context of Edomite wisdom. Although Edom had one national god, it cannot be described even as monolatry. Biblical evidence emphasizes Edomite polytheism. It is told of Amaziah after "he came from the slaughter of the Edomites, he brought the gods of the men of Seir, and set them up as his gods, and worshipped them, making offerings to them" (II Chron. 25:14).

Apparently there was an early connection between the religion of the men of Seir and the early religion of Israel, a connection deduced from an Egyptian list from the time of Ramses II (13th century B.C.E.) from a statement in which there is the unusual juxtaposition "the land of the Shasu of JHW" (see Herrmann in bibl.). In the same list there is the equivalent juxtaposition "the land of the Shasu of Seir." (The connection between YHWH and Seir can be learned from a number of early biblical verses, e.g., Deut. 33:2; Judg. 5:4.) Of course, one cannot speak of the identification in this period of this name with YHWH but rather about the origin of YHWH from the same area and ancient contacts between the people of Israel in its early period and the sons of Seir. In this way the biblical tradition is confirmed.

From the archaeological excavations and surveys in Edom it appears that its material culture was developed. The only evidence with regard to its spiritual culture is biblical. The wisdom of Edom was held in esteem by the prophets. Jeremiah asked in amazement: "Is wisdom no more in Teman? has counsel perished from the prudent? has their wisdom vanished?" (49:7); Obadiah 8 repeats the same idea: "destroy the wise men out of Edom, and understanding out of the mount of Esau."

In Second Temple Times

The geographical conception of Edom during the Second Temple period differs radically from that at the time of the First Temple. Following the movement of Edomites from southern Transjordan and into southern Palestine, across the Arabah, in the late seventh and early sixth centuries B.C.E. (II Kings 24:2; Ezek. 35:6), the area to the south of the territory of Judah came to be referred to as Edom/Idumea. The territory of "Darom" ("south") in Talmudic literature usually refers to Idumea. Idumea in Second Temple times was further north than in the previous period and covered a considerable part of the territory of the tribe of Judah, including Hebron. The border with Judea passed south of Beth-Zur. This change came about on the one hand in consequence of the invasion of Old Edom by new tribes from the desert and the establishment there, in the course of time, of the Nabatean kingdom; and secondly through the weakening of Jewish resistance during the time of the destruction of the Temple and the Babylonian exile. The return only changed the situation slightly; in general the returning exiles did not settle south of Beth-Zur. Even in the list of those who built the walls of Jerusalem in the days of Nehemiah, there is no mention of men from places south of the line Tekoa-Beth-Zur-Keilah-Zanoah.

During the Hellenistic period the Idumean region formed a separate administrative district and is mentioned as such by Diodorus in connection with the period of the Didache (*Bibliotheca Historica*, 19, 98, 1). Marissa and Adorah were the main Idumean settlements in the Hellenistic era. Marissa became an important junction during the Ptolemide era and served, as can be inferred from one of the Zenon papyri (C.C. Edgar, *Catalogue général des antiquités égyptiennes du Musée de Caire*, 1 (1925), 34, no. 59015 *verso*), as the seat of the government administration. From the inscriptions and painted designs in one of the tombs, it is possible to follow in great measure the process of Hellenization of Marissa during the Ptolemide era. Among other things, a Phoenician settlement, which was the standard-bearer of the Hellenistic movement in Idumea, existed in the town, and had organized itself as a *politeuma* of Sidonians in Marissa (W. Dittenberger, *Orientis Graeci Inscriptiones Selectae*, 2 (1905), 284–5 no. 593). The Ptolemide government of the country also helped in the migration of many Idumeans to Egypt. Hostile relations between the Idumeans and the Jews persisted throughout the Hellenistic period. Ben Sira enumerates the Edomites among the "nations whom his soul abhorred" (50, 25–26). The same enmity is reflected in the quotation from the Greek writer Mnaseas given by Josephus (*Apion* 2:112ff.) describing how Zabidus of Dorii fooled the people of Jerusalem. During the

Hasmonean wars the Idumeans assisted the Seleucids against the Jews. Judah Maccabee fought the Idumeans, and was particularly active against Hebron (I Macc. 5:65).

A decisive change in the relations between the two nations took place in the days of John *Hyrcanus (end of second century B.C.E.). Hyrcanus conquered the whole of Idumea and undertook the forced conversion of its inhabitants to Judaism (Jos., Ant., 13:257ff.). Thenceforth the Idumeans became a section of the Jewish people, Idumea becoming one of the ordinary administrative districts of the Hasmonean state. It appears that the Hasmonean dynasty used some of the respected families of Idumea to establish its dominion in that country. During the reigns of Alexander Yannai and his wife Alexandra Salome, *Antipas, who was an Idumean, served as ruler of Idumea on behalf of the Hasmoneans (Ant., 14:10). *Herod, appointed king of Judea by the Romans in 40 B.C.E., was his grandson. During the reign of Herod, Idumea served in general as the firm basis of his authority. He considered the Idumeans to be much more loyal to him than the Jews, and also depended upon them for the military settlement in Transjordan; three thousand Edomites being settled in Terakhan (Ant., 16:285). Despite this, even during his reign, an attempt was made to sever the link between Idumea and Judea. The king's brother-in-law, Costobar, entered into a conspiracy with Cleopatra, queen of Egypt, for the purpose of annexing Edom directly to Egypt, but the plot was foiled by Herod. After the death of Herod in 4 B.C.E. Idumea was included with Judea and Samaria in the ethnarchy of Archelaus. When the latter was deposed in 6 C.E., Idumea became part of the Roman province of Judea. Furthermore Gaza was severed from any administrative connection with Idumea and added to the province of Syria. Consequently, the size of Idumea was reduced – and in view of the fact that by degrees the differences between the Idumeans and their northern neighbors became blurred – the Roman government decided to abolish the separate status of Idumea as an administrative district equal in status to Judea or Samaria. Toward the end of the Second Temple era, Idumea appears as one of the 11 ordinary toparchies of Judea (Jos., Wars, 3:55).

The Idumeans participated in the Roman War of 66–70 C.E. They were organized into their own detachments and, at the time of the fratricidal war in Jerusalem between the Zealots and their opponents under the leadership of Anan b. Anan, hastened to the help of the Zealots, on the assumption that Anan and his associates intended to deliver the city into the hands of the Romans. The Idumeans were led by four commanders. They penetrated into Jerusalem on a rainy night and freed the Zealots who were besieged in the Temple, thus triumphing over their enemies. During the siege of Jerusalem by Titus they constituted a special division, numbering 5,000 men. They were led by ten officers, the most prominent among them being *Jacob b. Sosas and Simeon b. Katala. They acted under the high command of Simeon b. Giora (Jos., Wars, 5:249). Johanan, the brother of Jacob, was killed during the siege (6:290), and the Idumeans were prominent in the defense of Jerusalem (9:358–6:92, 148). Titus, too, regarded them as an important element of the Judean military force (8:379). It is not known which were the most important Idumean centers of settlement at the end of the days of the Second Temple. At the time of the Parthian invasion in 40 B.C.E., Marissa had already been destroyed, and Adorah no longer appears in the sources of the period. On the other hand Hebron is mentioned (4:529, 554).

Idumea is frequently mentioned in Latin poems of the period, usually as a synonym for Judea.

[Isaac Avishur]

In the *Aggadah*

Edom appears sometimes in the *aggadah* as referring to the actual Edomites and sometimes to the Romans, who are identified with them (see *Esau *aggadah*).

THE HISTORICAL EDOM. The historical Edom is chiefly discussed from the point of view of its relations with the Israelite people as these are reflected in the books of the Bible. Beside the enmity and hatred already stressed there, the *aggadah* emphasizes that Edom oppressed the people most closely akin to him. There are interesting *aggadot* which discuss, for example, the legal aspects of Israel-Edom relations in the time of King David (Gen. R. 74:15; ed. Theodor-Albeck, p. 872ff.), and also attempt to justify David's wars against Edom despite the biblical command laying down that Edom was not to be a heritage of the people of Israel (Deut. 2:5).

EDOM AS ROME. The identification of Edom with Rome is never found in the literature of the Second Temple period. It appears for the first time close to the Bar Kokhba revolt (cf. Margolioth, p. 610/2). R. Meir even connects it with the verse (Isa. 21:11), "The vision of Dumah" = the vision of Dome (דומי = רומי, Rome, TJ, Ta'an. 1:1, 64a see ed. princ.); also "The *re'emim* [wild-oxen] shall come down with them" (Isa. 34:7) is read as "The Romans shall come down with them" (PdRK 7, 11, ed. Mandelbaum, p. 134). The previous verses (5–6) speak of Edom (cf. also Targ. Jon. ed. Sperber, Isa. 9, "The streams thereof shall be turned into pitch": "The streams of Rome shall be turned into pitch"). Many scholars are of the opinion that the source of this identification lies in the connection between *Herod, a descendant of Edomite proselytes, whose evil rule over Judea left a harsh impression and the intensification of Roman rule in Judea, especially as Herod was virtually a vassal of Rome. However these conjectures cannot be accepted. Not only are substantial proofs lacking, but the identification appears only in the second quarter of the second century C.E., more than four generations after the death of Herod. It seems, therefore, that its source is to be sought elsewhere.

In the Bible Edom is described as the eternal enemy of Israel (and Judah, Amos 1:11; Ezek. 35:5) who not only always oppressed Israel, but at the time of the destruction of the First Temple took advantage of the situation and seized control of parts of Judah (Ezek. 25:12; 35:5, 10, 2; Obad. 11–16), and it is hinted that Edom also took part in the destruction of Jerusalem (Ps. 137:7; Obad. 11) and even in that of the Temple itself (Obad. 16). In consequence, during the Second Temple period there spread a belief that it was actually the Edomites who burned the First Temple (I Esdras 4:45; Ethiopian Enoch 89:66), and also interfered with the building of the Second Temple (*ibid.*, 72). Hence the intense enmity toward Edom which grew stronger in the course of time (Ecclus. 50:25–26), until the conquest of Edom and its conversion to Judaism in the time of John Hyrcanus – a conquest which is the background to the descriptions of the wars of Jacob and his sons with Esau and his sons in the Book of Jubilees (37–38) and in the Testament of the Twelve Patriarchs (Judah 9). Edom is even compared to a black boar (I En. 89:12, 42–43, 49, 66; Jub. 37:20, 24). The intense hatred of Rome after the cruel crushing of the revolt of the Diaspora in the time of Trajan and still more after the harsh suppression of the Bar Kokhba revolt and the decrees of persecution in Hadrian's days; the fact that Rome, like Edom, had destroyed the Temple; the similarity of Edom, compared to a pig, with Rome, for whom the pig (or, more correctly, the sow) was a most important symbol; the allusions to Edom dwelling on high like an eagle and the fact that the eagle, too, was an important Roman symbol; and perhaps finally even the similarity to the name Rome and Romans in several verses that speak of Edom, Seir, and Esau – all these apparently combined to cause the application to Rome of the biblical references to Edom, the eternal enemy of Israel.

At the end of the tannaitic period, and still more in the amoraic, the identification became very widespread, and the overwhelming majority of homilies about Edom speak explicitly of Rome. Thus it was stated that Rome was founded by the children of Esau, and Rome was identified as one of the cities of the chiefs of Esau enumerated at the end of Genesis 36 (these identifications occur not only in the Midrashim and the Talmuds but also in the Palestinian *Targums of the Torah and in the Targums to Lamentations and Esther). At a still later period the term became a synonym for Christian Rome and thence for Christianity in general, and allusions were even found to *Constantinople among the cities of Edom (and see *Caesarea).

[Moshe David Herr / Carl Stephen Ehrlich (2nd ed.)]

BIBLIOGRAPHY: F. Buhl, *Geschichte der Edomiter* (1893); M. Noth, *Das System der Zwoelf Staemme Israels* (1930); N. Glueck, *The Other Side of the Jordan* (1940); R.H. Pfeiffer, *Introduction to the Old Testament* (1952^2), 159–67 (on the S. Document); S. Abramsky, *Mesillah ba-Aravah* (1959); J. Liver (ed.), in: *Historyah Ẓeva'it shel Ereẓ Yisrael...* (1964), 190–205; S. Herrmann, in: *Fourth World Congress of Jewish Studies, Papers*, 1 (1967), 213–6 (Ger.); Y. Aharoni, in: *Eretz Israel*, 9 (1969), 10–21 (Heb. pt.), 134 (Eng. summ.). SECOND TEMPLE PERIOD: Klausner, Bayit Sheni, index; S. Klein, *Ereẓ Yehudah* (1939), 249–54. IN THE AGGADAH: M. Gruenbaum, in: ZDMG, 31 (1877), 305–9; A. Epstein, *Kol Kitvei*, ed. A.M. Habermann, 2 (1957), 33; Ginzberg, Legends, 5 (1947^6), 272–3; Schuerer, Hist, 3 (1909^4), 320–11; I. Heinemann, *Darkhei ha-Aggadah* (1954[2]), index, s.v. *Esau*; H. Fuchs, *Der geistige Widerstand gegen Rom* (1964^2), 69ff., 78. **ADD. BIBLIOGRAPHY:** A. Kasher, *Jews, Idumeans, and Ancient Arabs* (1988).

EDREHI (Heb. אדרעי), **MOSES BEN ISAAC** (c. 1774–c. 1842), Moroccan scholar. Edrehi was born in *Agadir, Morocco, but when the Jews were expelled from that city Moses, while still a boy, was taken with his parents to *Mogador, and after 1784 to Rabat. He began to preach in public at the age of 14, and became an itinerant preacher in North Africa. In 1791 he reached London, where he studied for a time in the *bet ha-midrash* Eẓ Ḥayyim and was accustomed to preach every Sabbath. In 1792 he published his *Torat Ḥayyim* readings for Friday nights according to the custom of the Jews of Morocco. In 1802 he proceeded to Amsterdam, where he published his *Yad Moshe* (1809), consisting of sermons preached in various places; and *Ma'aseh Nissim* (1818), tales of the ten tribes, with a Yiddish translation. An English edition of this somewhat preposterous work was published in London in 1834 under the title, *Book of Miracles... With... an Account of Many Millions of Israelitical Children... Dwelling Beyond that River*, later expanded as *An Historical Account of the Ten Tribes Settled Beyond the River Sambatyon in the East* (1836) which was prefaced by letters of commendation from Dutch, French, and English scholars and clergymen. About 1829 he met the writer John Wilson ("Christopher North") in Edinburgh who described him in his series *Noctes Ambrosianae* in Blackwood's Magazine. Edrehi finally left for Ereẓ Israel, traveling by way of France, Italy, Malta, and Smyrna and taking four years on the journey. While in *Izmir in 1841, his belongings and manuscripts – among them a grammar of the French and English language with a translation in Spanish – were destroyed by fire. In 1842 he published in *Jerusalem the *Azharot* of Isaac b. Reuben *al-Bargeloni. After his death his son Isaac published his *History of the Capital of Asia and the Turks, together with an Account of the Domestic Manners of the Turks in Turkey*, 3 vols. (1855).

BIBLIOGRAPHY: Slouschz, in: *Revue du Monde Musulman*, 7 (1909), 53–68; J.M. Toledano, *Sarid u-Falit*, 1 (1945), 79–80; A.M. Hyamson, *Sephardim of England* (1951), 263; Yaari, in: KS, 33 (1957/58), 521–8; 35 (1959/60), 269–72; Raphael, *ibid.*, 34 (1958/59), 526–7; Roth, Mag Bibl, index.

EDREI (Heb. אֶדְרֶעִי).

(1) A biblical town in Transjordan. It may be recorded among the towns captured by Thutmosis III in c. 1469 B.C.E., but that reference may be to (2) below. In all likelihood the toponym is found in Ugaritic (KTU 1.108:3). It is first mentioned in the Bible as the city of *Og, king of Bashan, whom Moses and the Israelites defeated before entering Canaan (Num. 21:33; Deut. 1:4; 3:1; Josh. 12:4; 13:12). Og's lands were allotted to the half-tribe of *Manasseh (Num. 32:33ff.; Josh. 12:6; 13:7–12, 29–31; cf. Deut. 3:5; I Kings 4:13). In Roman times, as Adraene, it was a well-known town in Provincia Arabia, located on the highway leading from Bozrah to Bet Reshah (Capitolias) 24 mi. (40 km.) from the former and 16 mi. (26 km.) from the latter. Edrei contained a Jewish community up to the 14th century. It is identified with the modern town of Darʿā in Syria, near the Jordanian border, 1,887 ft. (575 m.)

above sea level, with a population of about 8,000 Muslims. Potsherds ranging from the Early Bronze Age to the Arab period have been found on an adjacent tell. Within the town were discovered fragments of an early medieval Hebrew inscription. As a junction on the Hejaz Railway, Darʿā had great strategic importance during World War I and played a part in T.E. *Lawrence's campaign.

(2) A town in the territory of *Naphtali in Upper Galilee (Josh. 19:37). Aharoni identified it with the Edrei mentioned in Thutmosis III's list.

BIBLIOGRAPHY: S. Klein (ed.), *Sefer ha-Yishuv* (1939), s.v.; G. Schumacher, *Across the Jordan* (1886), 121–48; Albright in: BASOR, 19 (1925), 16; Alt, in: PJB, 29 (1933), 21; Abel, Geog, 2 (1938), 310; Noth, in: ZDPV, 61 (1938), 56; Aharoni, Land, index; Press, Ereẓ, 1 (1951), 10; T.E. Lawrence, *Seven Pillars of Wisdom* (1935), index, s.v. *Deraa*. **ADD. BIBLIOGRAPHY:** B. Margulies (Margalit), in: JBL, 89 (1970), 293–94.

[Michael Avi-Yonah]

EDUCATION. The Jewish people has an educational tradition as old as history (see *Education, Jewish). From the very beginning of their identification as a distinct entity, Jews have contributed not only to the advancement of their own education, but also to that of the world at large. The educational principles of the Bible found their way into the educational thought of Christians and Muslims. As an example one might cite the moral, spiritual, and character education through the family and community described in the Book of Proverbs. Compulsory teaching, incumbent upon the father in the first instance, is ordained in Deuteronomy 6:6–9 and 11:18–20. Compulsory school attendance was decreed by *Simeon b. Shetaḥ in 75 B.C.E. and by *Joshua ben Gamla in 64 C.E. In recent years, educators have come to recognize that ancient Jewish education anticipated, and no doubt indirectly and remotely influenced, modern education. Thus the National Education Association of the United States cited the Babylonian Talmud as authority for a maximum class size of 25 pupils (BB 21a). The same source requires, under Joshua ben Gamla's ordinance, that children start school at six or seven, the age at which children all over the world traditionally enter school. Adult education is sometimes traced by educational historians, such as I.L. *Kandel, to the *bet ha-midrash* of Second Temple times. The importance of the teacher in the learning process is repeatedly emphasized in the Talmud (*Avot*), as is the significance of motivation in teaching and of vocational training-principles, which are basic to effective instruction and a modern educational system. The practice of "each one teach one," inaugurated by Frank C. Laubach in teaching literacy to the people of developing nations, has a talmudic prototype.

For most of their history, Jews educated their children in their own institutions and expressed their educational ideas in their own languages, until the late 18th century. There was little contact between Jewish and non-Jewish pedagogues. Jews made few, if any, contributions to general education during the greater part of the development of education from ancient times. One outstanding exception may be Constantinus Afer or Africanus (d. 1087), believed by some historians to be Jewish. He influenced the course of medical education at the University of Salerno and other medieval universities, chiefly through his Latin translations of Greek and Arabic medical works, many of the latter of Jewish origin. Africanus had learned Hebrew and Kabbalah from a Jewish teacher and transmitted his inspiration to the German humanist Johannes *Reuchlin. Reuchlin then learned his Hebrew from Jacob Loans, physician to the emperor Frederick III, and from R. Obadiah *Sforno, the biblical exegete. Reuchlin went on to introduce the study of Hebrew as a learned subject in German universities. In this way Jews exercised an impact on the development of the European university curriculum.

The Edict of Tolerance issued by Emperor Joseph *II of Austria in 1782 applied the principles of the Enlightenment to the Jews of his empire. Among other reforms, Jews were permitted to enroll their children in government schools and to establish secular schools of their own. Young Jews could now attend institutions of higher education. These changes were hailed by Naphtali Herz *Wessely, a disciple and collaborator of Moses *Mendelssohn, in his *Divrei Shalom ve-Emet* (Berlin, 1782). The separation of Jews from the general stream of education was now beginning to be bridged. This German Haskalah *period ushered in a growth of interest among Jews in the secular pedagogical theories and practices of their Christian neighbors. Especially of interest to Jewish educators were the new ideas and methods of Johann Bernhard Basedow, Johann Friedrich Herbart, and Friedrich Froebel of Germany, Johann Heinrich Pestalozzi of Switzerland, and Andrew Bell and Joseph Lancaster, founders of the mutual or monitorial method of instruction in England.

Among the Jewish contributors to education in the early 19th century was the Austrian philanthropist Joseph Ritter von *Wertheimer who, among other things, was responsible for the development of Austrian kindergartens, the first of which he founded in Vienna in 1830. Another was Sir Isaac Lyon *Goldsmid, the first Jewish baronet in England, who helped to finance the establishment of University College in London (1825). The list of Jewish philanthropists in education is long. It covers many types of institutions in many countries. Among the men who made munificent and influential benefactions to education were Julius *Rosenwald, who contributed huge sums for the founding of schools for Blacks in the Southern states of the U.S.; James *Loeb, patron of the Loeb Classical Library; Sir Ernest *Cassel, founder of the Anglo-German Institute for the advancement of cultural relations between the two countries through the encouragement of mutual studies; and the Baroness Mayer de *Rothschild, who founded the Association for the Oral Instruction of the Deaf and Dumb in London on the basis of the lip-reading method practiced by William van Praagh. The kindergarten movement received much attention from Jewish educators and philanthropists. Adolf Pick (1829–1874) founded a pioneering kindergarten in Italy on the German model. In Germany, the original home of the kindergarten, the well-known feminist Lina *Morgenstern-Bauer was an ardent propagandist of the movement through her writings on childhood development, as well as a founder of kindergartens and seminaries for training kindergarten teachers. In still another branch of education there was a Jewish pioneer in the 19th century. Otto Salomon (1849–1901) promoted the teaching of manual skills in Swedish schools. In 1875 he established the Sloyd Seminarium at Nääs, where he trained teachers of manual crafts from all over the world. His impact on education was extensive not only in Sweden, but in other countries as well. A notable educator in the specialized field of teaching deaf-mutes was the Frenchman Jacob Rodrigues *Péreire. The first teacher of deaf-mutes in France, Péreire was to influence Maria Montessori a century later in her teaching of handicapped children. The international authority Edouard Séguin has also testified to the significance of Péreire's work. Perhaps the most long-lasting contribution to general education was the opening in 1805 of a school in Seesen, Germany, by Israel *Jacobson, an initiator of the Jewish Reform movement and an ardent advocate of closer Christian-Jewish relations. Among German historians this type of school is known as a "Simultanschule," an institution where religious instruction is given to different religious groups within the same school building. For 30 years, between 1838 and 1867, there was an equal number of Jewish and Christian pupils in the school, but because of the shortage of Jewish teachers of secular subjects, especially the sciences, as a result of the earlier limitations on higher education for Jews, there was a much larger proportion of Christians on the staff. Jacobson's school remained in existence until the advent of the Nazis in 1933. Few other Jews in the 19th century made any recognizable mark on general education. Félix Hément (1827–1891) rose from elementary teaching in France to become inspector of primary schools in the department of the Seine and, upon his retirement, honorary inspector-general of public instruction. Naphtali Herz *Imber, author of *Ha-Tikvah*, contributed bulletins on ancient Jewish education to a series published by the U.S. Bureau of Education.

In the 20th century, the liberalization of the position of Jews in the Western world made it possible for more of them to participate in the educational thought and work of the world at large. Ferenc Kemény (1860–1944), a Hungarian convert to Christianity who served as teacher, principal, school inspector, and professor at the University of Budapest, was active in promoting plans for international education toward world peace. Emile *Durkheim, professor of sociology and education at the universities of Bordeaux and Paris, won an international reputation not only as a sociologist, but also as author of a number of influential and scholarly works on education. International figures in education included William *Stern, an émigré from Hamburg to Duke University in the U.S., whose *Psychologie der fruehen Kindheit* (1914; *Psychology of Early Childhood*, 1924) and interpretation of the nature of intelligence were most helpful to teachers on both sides of the Atlantic. Also of international interest was Kurt Hahn (1886–1974), another refugee from Nazi Germany, who moved his Salem progressive school to Gordonstoun, Scotland, where Prince Philip and his son Prince Charles received their education.

To obtain a balanced view of the Jewish contribution to education the subject should also be considered from the standpoint of particular nations.

In Germany, Clara Stern, the wife of William Stern, wrote on and put into practice principles of child development in relation to education. Erich *Stern, a doctor of medicine and philosophy, was a professor at the universities of Giessen and Frankfurt before leaving for the University of Paris after 1933. His educational work was concerned with intelligence tests and with the application of child psychiatry. Curt *Bondy, who returned to Germany after World War II to become professor of social and educational psychology at the University of Hamburg, planned a system of education for juvenile prisoners. In the theoretical aspects of education, Jonas *Cohn, the neo-Kantian philosopher, wrote several works on educational philosophy, among them *Geist der Erziehung* (1919). Like Cohn, Richard *Hoenigswald approached pedagogy by way of his philosophical specialty, and wrote books on the theoretical foundations of education. He left Germany for the U.S. in 1933 after having been professor of philosophy at the universities of Breslau and Munich. There were many German Jewish educators who were concerned with the education of girls and women. Susanne *Engelmann wrote on the psychological foundations of girls' education, as well as a study of the teaching of German literary history. Ulrike Henschke (1830–1897) and her daughter Margarete (1859–?) were active in the promotion of secondary and vocational education for girls. Higher education for women was the special interest of Henriette Goldschmidt (1825–1920), who also made significant contributions, as a follower of Froebel, to the development of the kindergarten movement. This movement benefited immensely from the activities and writings of Clara Morgenstern and Johanna Goldschmidt. Eugen Pappenheim (1831–1901) opened kindergartens and seminaries, edited *Der Kindergarten*, and founded the Deutscher Froebelverband (1873). Among the other prominent German Jewish educators were Kurt Levinstein, author of research on the history of education and the teaching of literature; Leo *Kestenberg, author and editor of books on musical education; and Fritz *Karsen, head of the Karl-Marx-Schule in Berlin, a specialist in experimental schools and later professor of education at Brooklyn College, New York. August Homburger (1873–1930), a psychiatrist, founded in Heidelberg in 1917 the first German counseling center for the education of the mentally handicapped.

In Austria, Theodor *Heller pioneered in the teaching of the blind and the mentally handicapped, wrote and edited works in these fields, and organized societies. Alfred *Adler founded kindergartens and experimental schools, and edited and published works on education from the standpoint of individual psychology. Ferdinand Birnbaum (1892–1947), a psychologist, promoted through his teaching, writing, editing, and organizational work, the education of mentally handicapped children on an international basis. Siegfried *Bernfeld, a Freudian psychoanalyst, was active in youth psychology and education. In Denmark, Ernst Trier (1837–1893) founded the Vallekilde Folk High School (1865) in accordance with the principles of Grundtvig. Sofie *Elkan, a novelist, translated the writings of Comenius, Salzmann, and Pestalozzi into Swedish, thus making pedagogical classics available to the teachers of Sweden.

Jean *Zay, a youthful minister of education in France in 1936–39, introduced a school reform involving careful guidance of 11-year-old pupils before classification in secondary education. Among contemporary educators have been Lamberto *Borghi, professor and director of the Istituto di Pedagogia, University of Florence, and author and editor of pedagogical works and journals; Leon van Gelder, professor of education at the University of Groningen and former director of the Dutch teachers' association; and Joseph Katz, professor of comparative education at the University of British Columbia, founder-president of the Comparative and International Education Society of Canada, and author and editor of significant writings on Canadian and international education.

Jews have played a significant role in general education in the U.S.S.R. Moses M. Rubenstein wrote extensively on the applications of psychology to education. Sergey L. *Rubinstein, of the Academy of Pedagogical Sciences, worked along similar lines. Moses M. Pistrak (1888–1940), author of the first textbook on education for pedagogical institutes (1934), also wrote works on educational theory. Yevgeni Y. Golant, professor at the Hertsen Pedagogical Institute in Leningrad, became a leading figure in the historical and methodological aspects of education. Sholom Izrailovich Ganelin, of the Academy of Pedagogical Sciences, is recognized as a specialist on the theory and history of education. Alexander R. Luria, a psychologist in the Academy of Pedagogical Sciences, won an international reputation as an expert on the education of the mentally handicapped. Elye I. Monoszon, another of the many Jews in the Academy of Pedagogical Sciences, wrote important works on didactics. Distinction in editorial work was attained by M.S. Epstein, coeditor of the pedagogical encyclopedia (1927–30), and by David A. Epshtein, an editor of the new children's encyclopedia.

In England, Sir Meyer A. Spielman (1856–1936) served as inspector of schools for juvenile delinquents and as a pioneer in the Borstal movement for their rehabilitation. Sir Philip J.H. *Hartog was a well-known specialist on higher education and on education in India. Susan *Isaacs applied psychoanalytic methods in early childhood education, published important studies on the social and intellectual development of children, and headed the department of child development at the University of London's Institute of Education (1933–43). A refugee from Nazi Germany, where he was professor of psychology at the University of Frankfurt, Karl Mannheim enhanced his international reputation when he was professor at the University of London's Institute of Education by his publications on the sociology of knowledge and education.

In the United States, the Jewish contributions to general education in the 20th century have been varied, frequent, and profound. Probably the single most influential force in changing American education was Abraham *Flexner, the author of reports on medical education (1910) and universities (1930). The arguments of Louis *Marshall, the lawyer on behalf of private schools, influenced the U.S. Supreme Court's Oregon decision (1925) upholding the constitutionality of parochial schools. Lillian D. *Wald, a social worker, pioneered in public school nursing in New York City. Vice Admiral Hyman G. *Rickover emerged as a widely read critic of the U.S. educational system. Of particular value was the analysis by Fred M. Hechinger, who replaced Benjamin Fine as education editor of the *New York Times*. In the professional field of education, numerous Jews have distinguished themselves: Isaac B. *Berkson, Harry S. *Broudy, and Israel *Scheffler in the philosophy of education; Bernard Bailyn, Lawrence A. *Cremin, and Saul Sack in the history of education; Isaac L. Kandel and Harold J. Noah in comparative education; David P. *Ausubel, Bruno *Bettelheim, Benjamin S. *Bloom, Frank S. Freeman, Kurt *Lewin, and Irving *Lorge in educational psychology and research; Jacob Greenberg, Mark M. Krug, Morris Meister, Paul C. Rosenbloom, and Joseph J. *Schwab in methods of teaching various subjects; Harold H. *Abelson, Paul *Klapper, and Harry N. *Rivlin as deans of university schools of education; and Myron *Lieberman as specialist on the professional status of teachers. Abraham A. *Ribicoff and Wilbur J. *Cohen both served as U.S. secretary of health, education, and welfare; David H. Kurtzman was superintendent of public instruction in Pennsylvania. Rose Shapiro was elected president of New York City's Board of Education in June 1968. Most of these experts exercised considerable influence on education in other countries. Another powerful force in education was the mostly Jewish United Federation of Teachers in New York with over 140,000 members. Throughout the 1960s and 1970s, with the controversial Albert *Shanker serving as president 1964–74, it led a number of major strikes to improve the conditions of the city's teachers.

Two Israelis have won international recognition in education. The philosophical and educational writings of Martin *Buber have had a profound impact in educational theory and on teaching in Protestant theological seminaries in various countries. Ernst A. *Simon pioneered in the teaching of general educational history and theory in Israel, in research in these fields, and in advancement of comparative education.

BIBLIOGRAPHY: S. Kaznelson (ed.), *Juden im deutschen Kulturbereich* (1959^2), 307–22; C. Roth, *The Jewish Contribution to Civilisation* (1956^3), 37–53 (bibl.), 281–2.

[William W. Brickman]

EDUCATION, JEWISH. This entry is arranged according to the following outline. Bibliography at the end of a section is indicated by (†).

IN THE BIBLICAL PERIOD

The Nature of the Sources

The Bible is the primary source for an understanding of the process of education in ancient Israel. Since there is no biblical text that formulates a philosophy, methodology, or curriculum of education such information must be pieced together from occasional admonitions and narrative references and episodes supplemented by known facts about ancient Near Eastern institutions. Additional information is contained in the growing amount of ancient Hebrew epigrapha and relevant artifacts from archaeological digs.

Because of geographic proximity and cultural contact, extra-biblical Near Eastern material can be used to clarify the nature of biblical educational institutions. However, this material must be used judiciously, with an eye to the particular limitations of each society. For example, higher education or book learning in Mesopotamia and Egypt was formal and limited to the scribal class, which does not seem to have been the case in Israel. The difference was no doubt due to the simpler alphabetic system of writing used by the Hebrews.

Any description of education in the biblical period is necessarily incomplete and must ultimately rely on general impressions of what was applicable to most levels of society, as it is reflected in the Bible and later Jewish sources.

Historical Survey

The sources at hand do not allow for a precise, chronological description of the development of pedagogical institutions or methodology. Three major periods may be discerned, each displaying a distinctive political, social, and economic order in ancient Israel.

THE PATRIARCHAL PERIOD AND THE SETTLEMENT. During this crucial but sparsely documented period, the Israelites developed national-religious institutions that were to have a profound influence on them and on the world at large. For most of this period, they were seminomadic, residing in the great cultural centers of the ancient world, from Ur in Babylonia to the eastern Nile Delta in Egypt. Politically they were subject to greater and lesser powers in the Fertile Crescent.

The family or *bet av* was the basic socioeconomic unit tending to the communal needs of its members, including educating the young. In matters of war and external affairs the families acted concertedly with related groups to form the tribe and nation. There was little economic diversity. As the need arose, other clans that had specialized as scribes joined the confederation of shepherds and farmers (I Chron. 2:55).

The character of the Israelite nation was shaped during this period. Central to the religion of Israel were the promise to Abraham (Gen. 15), the exodus from Egypt (Ex. 7ff.), and the theophany at Sinai (Ex. 19–20). These historic moments welded the tribes into a nation related through blood and history. Guided by prophets and priests, they set upon the united goal of the conquest and settlement of the Land of Canaan. The revolutionary ideals of monotheism were later crystallized in the laws of the Torah and the historical narratives of the lives of the Patriarchs.

THE KINGDOM. Through the genius of David, the Israelite tribal union was reshaped into a politically independent, centralized monarchy. Over the following 400 years, and in spite of the internal split into two kingdoms, Israel and Judah were able, at times, to control politically and influence their neighbors (David-Solomon, Ahab, Jeroboam II, Uzziah, and Hezekiah). To serve the needs of this society, new institutions evolved. Tribal allegiances were subordinated to the new order. The country was redivided into administrative areas, not always along tribal lines (I Kings 4:7–20). A bureaucracy, patterned after local Canaanite models, came into existence, introducing new administrative forms (I Sam. 8:11–18).

The portable tabernacle and local shrines were overshadowed by the Jerusalem Temple, which was patronized by the king and officiated at by his appointees. The king's conquests and military establishment superseded the tribal holy wars. Professional soldiers and mercenaries now fought the battles of Israel (Song 3:8).

The centralized monarchy and subsequent urbanization directly affected all aspects of education. The need was felt for trained professionals and skilled artisans. Religious ideals of the covenant were transmitted to the people at the Temple and sanctuaries by a recognized priesthood. In reaction to the increased social injustice found in urban society, the classical prophets appeared in the eighth century to interpret the social implications of the election of Israel to the people.

THE BABYLONIAN EXILE AND HELLENISTIC TIMES. The Jewish people successfully overcame the trauma of the Babylonian Exile. The small province of Judah that was established subsequently was politically part of the Persian Empire and economically dependent upon the gifts of wealthier Jews in exile.

Ezra the Scribe and his colleagues were empowered to teach the Torah to the Jews (Ezra 7:25), and under his guidance the Torah became the accepted basis of individual and community life. Beginnings of a program of mass education (Deut. 31:12–13; II Chron. 17:7–9) matured under Ezra into new institutions, intensifying the study of Torah and raising the quality of popular knowledge. Recognized instructors, called *mevinim*, were appointed to teach publicly. The Torah was read out and explained (Neh. 8:7–8). It was the beginning of the regular public lection of the Torah, later connected with the synagogal liturgy and ascribed anachronistically to Ezra (BK 82a). The internal tensions between stipulations of the Torah, on one hand, and between the Torah and the reality of the period on the other, led to a search for new meaning in the biblical text, thereby creating Midrash (Dan. 9:23–27; Neh. 8:13–15). In Hellenistic times there began to appear schools for public instruction (Eccles. 12:9; Ecclus. 39:1–3). Ben Sira, the late third century B.C.E. pedagogue, seems to have introduced tuition-free education (51:28–30). It was not uncommon for an informal study session to take place even at a student's house (Avot 1:4). Finally, toward the end of the second century B.C.E., *Simeon ben Shetaḥ inaugurated the first known system of community-supported public education. A new intellectual model had emerged: the biblical *ḥakham*, or wise man, gave way to the rabbinic *talmid ḥakham*, or scholar.

The Goals and Orders of Instruction

The goals of education may be broadly summed up: (1) To transmit knowledge and skills from one generation to another or from one person to another; (2) To broaden the range of man's knowledge and skills; and (3) To concretize cultural values into the form of accepted group and individual behavior.

In each of the three main orders of study in ancient Israel – religious education, the learning of occupational skills, and military training – these goals were pursued to varying degrees. Each type of instruction had its own specific goals, methods of study, and pedagogic institutions.

Occupational and military training were subject to social and technological changes. For example, with the appearance of professional soldiers, military training for the average man became less important and at times nonexistent. On the other hand, religious education was conservative, retaining its goals and some of its methods well after the biblical period.

RELIGIOUS EDUCATION. The goal of religious education was to produce "a kingdom of priests, a holy people" (Ex. 19:6). Wisdom literature stated the corollary, *reshit ḥokhmah yirat adonai* ("The essence of knowledge is fear of the Lord"; Ps. 111:10; Prov. 1:7).

The means of achieving this goal were twofold: first, the recognition of the divine will in the laws of the Covenant; and second, the study of Israel's history, which reflected God's concern for His chosen people. Learning God's law and Israel's history became the basic means of receiving a peculiarly Israelite religious education.

The law was regarded as the conditions of the *berit*, or covenant, between God and Israel (Ex. 24:7). Near Eastern vassal and parity treaties help to clarify many aspects of the *berit* as it is found in the Bible (see *Covenant). Since the covenant at Sinai was accepted by all those present when they said "We will do and obey" (Ex. 24:7), it followed that the whole nation would have to be taught the laws incumbent upon them. It is for this reason that Moses, Israel's first teacher, is repeatedly commanded to "Speak unto the Children of Israel saying …."

How were the laws to be taught? Some Near Eastern treaties contained a "document clause," i.e., a clause providing either for the public display of the treaty document or for its deposit in a temple, where it was read at regular intervals before the vassal king and citizens. Parallels are found in the Torah. The text of the covenant was read at the time of the agreement (Ex. 24:7) and an authentic copy was kept in the holy ark guarded by the priesthood (Deut. 31:9, 26). The covenant was to be reread publicly once every seven years during the Feast of Tabernacles (31:10–11); this was the earliest prescription for mass education in ancient Israel: "Gather the people – men, women, children and the strangers in your communities – that they may hear and so learn to revere the Lord your God and to observe faithfully every word of His Teaching. Their children, too, who have not had the experience, shall hear and learn to revere the Lord your God as long as they live in the land which you are about to cross the Jordan to occupy" (Deut. 31:12–13; II Kings 23:1–3; Neh. 8:1–8; Sot. 7:8).

The second means of acquiring a religious education was through the study of Israelite history. The belief in a God acting in events, coupled with a high regard for oral tradition, made the telling of history a most effective pedagogical method. These collective memories took the literary forms of song and story that made up so large a part of biblical literature.

In the words of the psalmist:

> Give ear, O my people, to my teaching;
> Incline your ears to the words of my mouth.
> I will open my mouth with a parable;
> I will utter riddles concerning days of old.
> That which we have heard and known,
> And our fathers have told us,
> We will not hide from their children,
> Telling to the generation to come the praises of the Lord,
> And His strength and His wondrous works that He has done
>
> (Ps. 78:1–4; cf. 44:2).

A periodic reading of a written covenant in addition to the recital of an oral tradition of sacred history were the distinctive features of the Hebrew religious education. If the laws specified man's duty, it was history that revealed God's concern. Together, they instilled in the Israelite a sense of identification with his God and people.

Educational Institutions

During the biblical period various social and religious institutions served to disseminate the ideals and the amassed knowledge of society. Some of these were relatively short-lived, already disappearing during the biblical period, e.g., the monarchy and prophecy. Others, like the Temple itself, lasted through the Second Temple period.

One institution, the *family, has remained a vital educational influence in Israel from biblical times to the present. The family educated the whole man, only delegating some of its responsibilities in periods of technical specialization. While it is true that in most societies the family plays the key role in the child's socialization, in Israel new emphases were developed.

INTRA-FAMILY RELATIONSHIP. The ancient Israelite family was characterized as having respect and awe for parents (Ex. 20:12; Lev. 19:3) and love and responsibility toward the children (Mal. 3:24). The parents were allowed almost complete control over the lives of their offspring, except where the Torah limited their authority, as in cases of dispensing capital punishment (Deut. 21:18–21) or in disallowing the birthright of the eldest son (21:15–17). Fatherly love, even for the disobedient child, is a favorite prophetic image (Jer. 31:20).

Disciplinary measures were an expression of concern for the child's well-being (Prov. 13:24; 22:15; 29:15) and were to help him control the inherent evil inclination (Gen. 8:21; Ps. 51:7). At the same time, the child's natural abilities were to be encouraged (Prov. 22:6).

An especially close relationship between mother and son seems to have existed in the polygamous family. This motif plays a major part in the patriarchal stories (Sarah and Isaac; Hagar and Ishmael; Rebekah and Jacob; Rachel and Joseph; Leah and Reuben). While sibling rivalry was a decisive factor in these and later narratives, fraternal concern is also not lacking (Reuben for Joseph; Judah and Joseph for Benjamin; Miriam, Aaron, and Moses; Eliab for David; Absalom for Tamar).

OCCUPATIONAL TRAINING. It was a simple matter for the child to learn the rudiments of herding and farming by observing his elders and taking on these responsibilities at an early age (I Sam. 16:11). Girls learned the basic home trades necessary to make the family self-sufficient.

During the nomadic period some families may have specialized as merchants along the trade routes of the Fertile Crescent (cf. Gen. 37:25), while others were wandering smiths, as represented in a 19th-century B.C.E. picture from an Egyptian tomb. After they settled in Canaan, extended families and even whole villages were employed in a single trade (I Chron. 4:21–23).

Some families became artisans, eventually developing into professional societies. The terminology employed by these "guilds" was drawn from family life. The founder was called "father" and the members were "sons." The biblical term for these groups was, among others, the *mishpaḥah*, or "family" (I Chron. 4:21; cf. *lehakah (lehaqah)* and *ḥevel*).

This same system seems to have been common among Israel's neighbors: "Adah bore Jabal, he was the father of those who dwelt in tents and amidst herds. The name of his brother was Jubal; he was the father of all who play the lyre and the pipe. As for Zillah, she bore Tubal-Cain, who forged all implements of copper and iron" (Gen. 4:20–22). In Israel the noted craftsmen Bezalel son of Uri and Oholiab son of Ahisamach taught their skills to others (Ex. 35:30–34). Even the courageous Shiphrah and Puah may have become eponyms of "households" or professional midwives (Ex. 1:21).

MILITARY TRAINING. Before the establishment of the Davidic monarchy, the tribes were beset by continual local wars, necessitating general military training (Judg. 3:2).

The boys learned agility (II Sam. 22:34, 37) and courage in face-to-face combat (II Sam, 2:14ff.). They traveled with their warrior fathers and took active part in warfare (Judg. 8:20–21). They learned to handle the simple weaponry of the tribesman – sling, bow, sword, and spear.

The youth's training was probably supplemented by the telling of heroic exploits (Judg. 14–16; II Sam. 21:15–22), including tactical blunders that were not to be repeated (Judg. 9:50–53; II Sam. 11:20–21).

The tribes fought as units, each under its own banner (Num. 1:52). Some tribes seem to have developed their own military specialty. The tribe of Benjamin was noted for what seems to be the ambidextrous use of the sword (Judg. 3:15ff.) and the sling (Judg. 20:16), whereas the tribe of Judah was practiced in the bow (II Sam. 1:18). The monarchy probably exploited these local talents in homogeneous units in the organization of the national army (I Chron. 27:1–22; II Chron. 17:14–18). At that time, though, foreign mercenaries, professional Israelite soldiers, and sophisticated arms and defense systems were introduced, ultimately reducing the importance of the tribal warrior.

RELIGIOUS EDUCATION. The Israelite home was consciously employed for the religious education of the young (Deut. 4:9; 6:7). The content of this education centered on the telling of family, tribal, and national history:

> Remember the days of old,
> Consider the years of ages past;
> Ask your father, he will inform you,
> Your elders, they will tell you
>
> (Deut. 32:7).

The many prophetic allusions to bygone generations assume a wide popular knowledge of Israel's early history.

Deuteronomy makes a particular point of ensuring that the child be instructed orally in the laws of Israel. The head of the household was put under obligation to teach his own children (Deut. 6:6–7). The naturally inquisitive boy might himself initiate such lessons (6:20–25). Copies of appropriate sections of the Torah were to be attached to the doorposts (6:9; 11:20) or (so literally the scriptural phrases were later interpreted) worn on the person (6:8; 11:18; cf. Prov. 1:9; 3:3; 6:21; 7:3).

An outstanding innovation of biblical pedagogy was the religious home ceremony, which became the primary means of conveying cultural values from one generation to another. The Passover home ritual is found at the very inception of Israel's national history (Ex. 12:21–27) and other home rituals were associated with other holidays of the Hebrew calendar (Deut. 16:10–12; I Sam. 20:5–6). The home as an educational institution would become the hallmark of the Jewish people.

Specific Training

THE EDUCATION OF ROYALTY. The young prince grew up in the harem where he was raised by his mother. She was his first teacher and continued to exert her influence on him after he reached his majority (I Kings 1–2; Prov. 31:1–9). In the event that her son became king, her influence was enhanced when she assumed the title and privileges of queen mother or *gevirah*.

As an infant the prince was placed in the hands of a wet nurse, who was responsible for his physical well-being (Ex. 2:7–10; II Kings 11:2). After being weaned, the child was given over to a governess (*'omenet*) until he reached the age of five, approximately (II Sam. 4:4). Childhood and youth were spent at court in the company of aristocratic contemporaries (II Sam. 8:10; 13:3; II Kings 14:14). Due to accident or intrigue, the eldest son did not always succeed his father. To prepare for this eventuality, all the young princes received the same education. Upon maturing, they assumed positions of political responsibility, either as advisors to their brother (I Kings 12:8) and/or as governors of key cities in the kingdom (II Chron. 11:23).

Already in Davidic times, provision was made for the formal instruction of the king's sons (I Chron. 27:32). Ahab's 70 sons were educated by leading men of the northern capital of Samaria, no doubt with specialized training by professional tutors (II Kings 10:1ff.). Neo-Babylonian administrative documents show that the exiled Judean king Jehoiachin had a Hebrew attendant, perhaps a tutor, for five of his sons (Pritchard, Texts, 308).

Some princes had personal tutors. Solomon benefited from the prophet Nathan's guidance (II Sam. 12:25; I Kings 1); the young Joash was raised under the eye of his influential uncle (according to II Chron. 22:11), Jehoiada, the high priest (II Kings 11–12). Similarly, Isaiah took great interest in the young Hezekiah, over whom he was to wield a strong influence (Isa. 9:5–6; 11:1ff.).

The king himself also had influence over his son's upbringing. His own personality played a major part in their relationship. Some, like Saul, tended to harshness, while others, like David, were over-lenient. Both extremes led to family tragedies. In general, the king supervised the transfer of responsibilities to his sons (II Kings 15:5; II Chron. 21:2–3). On his deathbed, the king gathered his royal progeny to deliver his last testament, charging them in religious and diplomatic matters (I Kings 2:1–9; Isa. 38:1; cf. Gen. 48–49).

Drawing on the Former and Latter Prophets, it is possible to reconstruct broadly the curriculum of a prince's education. To fulfill his duties properly, he had to be trained in three main areas: physical and military training, diplomacy and government, and the national religion of Israel.

The first kings, Saul and David, were famous for their military prowess; some later kings rose to power through the army ranks (Omri, Jehu, and Pekah son of Remaliah). However, not only soldier-usurpers but also princes must have learned the art of warfare. Kings Jehoshaphat, Uzziah, and Josiah, to mention a few, took an active part in leading their soldiers. They trained with the bow (I Sam. 20:19–20, 35ff.; II Sam. 22:35), could handle horse and chariot, and probably learned the fundamentals of military strategy (I Kings 20:13–14; II Kings 3:6–8). Some were known for bravery and on more than one occasion a king died from battle wounds (I Kings 22:34–35; II Chron. 35:23–24).

In contrast to ancient Near Eastern descriptions of contemporary royalty, the Bible is silent in regard to hunting expeditions. This pastime, which is mentioned in connection with the non-Israelite Nimrod and Esau, was usually a basic part of physical training.

DIPLOMACY AND GOVERNMENT. Because of the ever-present foreign influences at court, the prince had a good measure of familiarity with the larger world. Through the many foreign wives, sons of vassals, and frequent diplomatic envoys (II Kings 5:5ff.; 20:12ff.; Isa. 18), he learned of the customs of the gentiles and learned to appreciate their political strength in relation to that of his father. In the later monarchy the prince may have acquired some fluency in Aramaic, which was during the eighth century B.C.E. the lingua franca of the ancient Near East.

The prince had also to learn the workings of government. Upon reaching his majority, he went through a period of practical training, when he accepted responsibilities in the royal bureaucracy. Jotham, Uzziah's heir apparent, held the high position of *'al ha-bayit* or "chamberlain" (II Kings 15:5). A personal seal inscribed only with *lytm* was discovered in the excavations of ancient Ezion-Geber, and possibly belonged to the prince. The absence of his father's name reflects his high administrative position. That other princes held minor administrative positions is suggested by several *ben ha-melekh* ("son of the king") seals found in and around Palestine.

RELIGIOUS EDUCATION. The king was patron and administrator of the Temple and national cult (II Kings 12). Like all other kings of antiquity, he demonstrated his piety by lavish donations to the cult (I Kings 8:63).

On the other hand, the prophets demanded of the king allegiance to monotheism and the religious values of the Torah, expressed in acts of justice (Isa. 9:5–6) and humility (Deut. 17:14–20). It was by these criteria that the Israelite kings were judged by the authors of the books of Kings and Chronicles. These values were imparted to the princes by the court prophets and priests, not always successfully.

From the very inception of the monarchy in Israel, the king was conceived to be the highest judge in the land (I Sam. 8:5–6). Most of the famous cases mentioned in the Bible are ad hoc decisions demonstrating the king's legal sagacity in finding a just solution (II Sam. 14:5–11; I Kings 3:16–28). In order to fulfill this primary function of kingship, the prince must have received a thorough education in common law and in the written law collections (II Sam. 15:1–6; II Kings 14:6).

Though there are no actual records, some kings may have promulgated laws of their own (cf. Micah 6:16). Jehoshaphat is said to have reorganized the judicial system, dividing it into local courts and a high court of appeal, and appointing supervisors for religious and royal interests (II Chron. 19:5–11). Such familiarity with Hebrew law assumes that the princes had training in jurisprudence. Indeed, the Deuteronomic ideal entailed a literate king, well versed in the Torah (Deut. 17:18–19; cf. II Kings 5:7; 19:14).

Not only in his judicial capacity, but in setting the tone of court life, the king patronized the literary arts. The more talented among Israelite royalty were accredited even with composition in the various genres. David's musical talent was still proverbial in the Kingdom of Israel two centuries after his death (Amos 6:5). His religio-national poems inspired later religious poets to see in him their own spiritual forebear (II Sam. 1:17–27; 22; 23:1–7, and 74 of the 150 psalms).

Solomon was the proverbial wise man, mastering all forms of wisdom literature (I Kings 5:9–14). This literature was edited from time to time by the court savants (Prov. 25:1). Such was the case in the time of Hezekiah, who was also credited with poetic talents (Isa. 38:9–20).

The importance of alphabetic writing for the history of education must not be overlooked. It ushered in a break with the traditional scribal cultures of Egypt, Mesopotamia, and second-millennium Canaan. To be literate was no longer the identifying and exclusive characteristic of a class of professional scribes and priests, versed in the abstruse cuneiform and hieroglyphic scripts.

SCRIBAL EDUCATION. The etymology of the term *sofer*, "scribe," has not been conclusively determined. It may be derived from the Canaanite root *spr*, "to count," "to tell." The rabbis suggested a similar origin (Kid. 30a). Others derive the word from the Assyrian, *šaparū*, "to send," "to deliver a message." Whatever the origin, it seems clear that in the Bible a distinction should be made between a scribe, in the usual sense, and a Scribe who because of personal ability or family ties was appointed a minister or secretary of state. Both, however, received the same basic training.

As in the ancient Near East, the scribal class (or "guild") in Israel was originally organized along family lines. An early example is found in I Chronicles 2:55. Under the Davidic monarchy, the same principle of kinship is found in the position of "the king's scribe" (II Sam. 8:17; I Chron. 18:16; I Kings 4:3; cf. Ezra 2:55 and Neh. 7:57). This was probably the case toward the end of the kingdom of Judah. The family of Shaphan dominated the bureaucracy and held the position of king's scribe from the time of Josiah until the Exile (II Kings 22:3; Jer. 36:11, 12, 20, 21; 40:9).

Most professional scribes served the administrators of the central government, city councils, and Temple bureaucracy. These institutions set up their own schools which taught the specific scribal skills demanded.

Perhaps the youth of Judges 8:14 was a local scribe: "And he [Gideon] caught a young man of the men of Succoth, and inquired of him; and he wrote down for him the princes and elders of Succoth, seventy-seven men."

CURRICULUM. Scribal education everywhere was the conservative study of traditional methods and subjects. The Israelite scribe had the easy task of learning the 22-letter alphabet, whereas his Egyptian and Mesopotamian counterpart had to master at least one system of hundreds of signs.

The alphabet was invented and developed by the Canaanites during the second millennium B.C.E., probably in one of the major Phoenician cities. Indicative of the conservative nature of the scribal art is the fact that the form of the letters in the three main alphabetic branches (Phoenician, Hebrew, and Aramaic) did not differ radically during the period between 1200 and 600 B.C.E. While mastering the forms, the apprentice scribe learned their order. The standard order of the characters is found already in the 30-letter abecedaries of the scribal schools of Ugarit (15th century B.C.E.). Minus eight letters, the series reappears in biblical acrostics (Ps. 119, 145; Lam. 1–4) and is almost identical with the sequence of the modern Hebrew alphabet. Probably in the ninth century B.C.E. the form and order of the letters were exported to the Greek islands as well.

It seems that Isaiah refers to an elementary class learning the alphabet in one of his prophecies (28:9–13): he describes the "first grade" lesson for the day when the children learned the letters *ẓadi* (צ) and *kof* (ק). During the excavations at Lachish, a list of the first five letters was found incised on one of the steps of an Israelite building, perhaps the work of a child practicing his alphabet.

The second stage of a scribe's training was the copying of short texts that may have been learned by heart and practiced at home. The *Gezer Calendar (tenth century B.C.E.) is a possible example of such an assignment. It divides the year into eight agricultural seasons, noting the main characteristics of each. Gezer had been an important Canaanite city, and during the tenth century it housed a levite community serving the Jerusalem administration. Perhaps it was in cities like Gezer that the Canaanite scribal traditions were conveyed to the Israelites.

The young student next learned epistolary and other administrative formulae. After much practice, he could easily produce the names of the city elders (Judg. 8:14). During the monarchy there was a standard tax form, as found in the Samaria Ostraca (mid-ninth or according to others mid-eighth-century B.C.E.), and as more recently noted in the inscribed jar handles from Gibeon (late seventh century B.C.E.).

The local scribe had also to master the forms of deeds of sale (Jer. 32:10–14), marriage contracts (Tob. 7:13 (14) and Elephantine Papyri), bills of divorce (Deut. 24:1–3; Isa. 50:1; Jer. 3:8) as well as court pleas (ostracon from Meẓad Ḥashavyahu; Job 31:35). The latter, however, may have been part of the responsibilities of the *shoṭer* or "court secretary." This term is derived from the Akkadian *šaṭāru* ("to write") and related to the later Hebrew *sheṭar* ("a written document").

The king's scribes received a broader and more cosmopolitan education. They had to be competent in diplomacy and the exact sciences. Their knowledge of international diplomacy began with the study of Aramaic, the lingua franca of the period (II Kings 18:26; Dan. 1:4).

Because of the involvement of all the Israelite kings, from Ahab to Zedekiah, in regional politics, it was necessary that the royal scribes know the workings of the Assyrian, Egyptian, Aramean, and Phoenician courts. Several kings even appeared in person before their Mesopotamian suzerains. International law and treaty formulae (II Chron. 20:35–37) as well as far-reaching trade agreements (Ezek. 27) were the scribes' normal business.

Simple arithmetic was probably learned in all formal systems of education (Isa. 10:19). The Israelite court scribe, like his Egyptian and Mesopotamian counterparts, mastered the higher mathematics needed for solving problems of logistics and engineering (II Kings 20:9–11; II Chron. 26:15; 32:30). While astronomy is not specifically mentioned in Israelite sources, it was needed for the calendrical intercalations decreed by the central government (II Chron. 30:2–4; Pes. 4:9; cf. Jub. 4:7; I En. 8:3). Cartography as well was a well-known ancient art (Josh. 18:9; Ezek. 4:1).

In addition to diplomacy and the exact sciences, the court bureaucracy developed what might be termed a "scribal ethic." Wisdom literature, more specifically the collections now found in the Book of Proverbs, served as a primary text for character education: they focused on the individual's rather than on the national interest.

Like the comparative Egyptian material, and the Book of *Ahikar (Aramaic), the Book of Proverbs was an outstanding example of court literature. The book was meant to serve in educating king and courtier (8:15–18) but especially the bureaucracy (22:29). The virtues stressed by these pedagogues were, among others, religious piety, proper family relations, honesty, industry, sagacity, responsibility, social virtues, and loyalty to the king.

Various literary methods were used as memory aids for the student. Key words (Prov. 25:4–5; 30:11–14) and common ideas (25:2–3, 5–6) tied together independent statements. Similarly alliteration (*rash, rasha*ʿ, *ra*ʿ, 28:3–5) and repetition of the same or similar roots (25:18–20) served as learning devices. Other units might be formed as number series (30:15–33). Another mnemonic device was the alphabet acrostic (31:10–31).

Foreign material was freely borrowed: Proverbs 22:17–24:22 bears a great resemblance to the "Thirty Sayings of Amen-em-Opet," a famous Egyptian wisdom text (Pritchard, Texts, 421ff.).

The Book of Proverbs may be the closest thing to an actual school text from the biblical period. Its explicit pedagogic goal, as well as its employment of mnemonic devices, supports this contention. The centrality of secular, royal figures (Solomon, Hezekiah, King Lemuel of Massa, "The Wise") and its affinities to non-Israelite wisdom literature further argue for its role in the education of the officialdom.

EDUCATION OF PRIEST AND PROPHET. The nature of the priest's education can be determined through an inductive analysis of his manifold functions in biblical society.

Foremost were the cultic duties centered on the elaborate and complicated sacrificial rites. Later, the sacrifice was accompanied by music and song, performed by levitic families, versed in liturgical composition (I Chron. 25).

Giving rulings on questions of ritual law and ritual purity was intrinsic to the priest's responsibilities (Lev. 10:8–11; 12–15; Jer. 18:18; Haggai 2:11ff.; Mal. 1:4–8). The necessary knowledge for these decisions was no doubt acquired by training and study, including the study of the body and its diseases. Professional secular physicians are mentioned in II Chronicles 16:12 (cf. Ecclus. 38:7; Pes. 4:9, a "book of medicines").

It was to the priests that Moses delivered the official copy of the Torah (Deut. 31:24–26; Jer. 2:8). They authenticated and supervised the writing of subsequent copies (Deut. 17:18–19; II Kings 22:8) and became the authoritative teachers of the Torah (Deut. 31:10–13; II Kings 17:28; II Chron. 17:8–9; Ezra the Scribe was a priest).

The priesthood, though ultimately subject to the king administratively, supervised the Temple finances (II Kings 12:8–17). (The Chronicler even has the priests assume trusted positions in the centralized government system of David and Solomon, I Chron. 26:30–32.) Their religious and secular functions demanded that they be literate. This is apparent also in the centrality of the written word in the cult (Ex. 34:27–28; Num. 5–23) and upon the sacred vestments (Ex. 28:21, 36).

Though there are no actual records, the clergy must have received formal training. As was the case elsewhere, schools probably were part of the Temple complex.

The clerical census counted priests only from the age of 30 (Num. 4:3) and levites from the age of 25 (8:24), when they began to assume their cultic functions. This relatively late age indicated a long period of apprenticeship necessitated by their complex duties.

Unlike the priesthood, there were no qualifications for joining the prophetic orders. Even women achieved renown as prophetesses (Miriam, Deborah, Huldah).

The prophets attracted a following known as *bene hanevi'im*, "sons (i.e., disciples) of the prophets." Some encouraged only a selected group of disciples (Isa. 8:18) or only a single protégé (Moses-Joshua; Elijah-Elisha; Jeremiah-Baruch). The disciple did not always succeed the master since true prophecy was not a skill to be learned but rather a result of divine election (II Kings 2:9–10).

The disciple's education was acquired through his ministering to the needs of the prophet. This type of training resembled the rabbinic concept of *shimmush*, attendance upon a master (Avot 1:3). This, of course, is not to say that there was no formal or literary side to the novices' education. Several prophets may have been trained in the court schools (Isaiah and possibly Zephaniah); others had a priestly education (Jeremiah, Ezekiel, and possibly Malachi). Both schools provided a thorough knowledge of the national-religious literature and more.

The prophetic order no doubt preserved and studied the words and deeds of their illustrious predecessors (Elijah and Elisha cycles; cf. II Kings 8:4; Jer. 26:17–18). The writings of the prophets show unmistakable signs of their acquaintance with the writings of their predecessors (Isaiah of Amos', Zephaniah of Isaiah's, Deutero-Isaiah with those of Isaiah, Zephaniah, and Jeremiah) as well as with the older psalms and other literature.

There must have been some training in prophetic oration, and musical accompaniment (II Kings 3:15). An enlightening passage, reflecting prophetic training, in addition to the general popularity of the prophets' presentation, is found in Ezekiel 33:30–33: "… the children of thy people that talk of thee by the walls and in the doors of the houses and speak one to another … Come, I pray you and hear what is the word that cometh forth from the Lord … and, lo, thou art unto them as a love song of one that hath a pleasant voice, and can play well on an instrument …."

THE EDUCATION OF WOMEN. Women's education was conditioned by several cultural factors which limited and set the goals of their training. Before marriage, the woman was protected by her father or older brothers; afterward, by her husband who represented her interests in the community. Her dependent status is reflected in her being called by the name of her husband, be she ever so illustrious in her own right (Deborah, the wife of Lappidoth; Huldah, the wife of Shallum). Likewise her personal seal always refers her to some male: Elsegov, daughter of Elishama; Ne'ehevet, daughter of Remaliah; Abigail, wife of Asaiah; Aḥotmelekh, wife of Yesha; Menaḥemet, wife of Gadmelekh.

Her protected status was based on a religious and moral outlook, sharply contrasting local Canaanite custom, as well as on economic and social interests that predated the Settlement. These generally limited her activity to that of the home and kindred occupations and provided the goals and limitations of her education, contingent upon her father's position in society.

The mother was naturally the girl's primary teacher and model (cf. Ezekiel's epigram "Like mother like daughter," 16:44). Besides her religious obligations, the young girl learned the domestic chores and special skills of her mother through observation and imitation in the informal atmosphere of the home. She performed other tasks dictated by the family's work – attending the flocks (Gen. 29:6) or helping at harvest time (Song 1:6; Ruth 2:8). She played in the streets and markets (Zech. 8:5). Recently discovered artifacts have demonstrated that she also possessed an assortment of games and dolls.

The upper-class maiden was raised by her nurse, who sometimes accompanied her to her husband's house (Gen. 35:8). If orphaned at an early age, she was raised by a close relative (Esth. 2:7). If there were no brothers, she could inherit her father's property, though in order to protect tribal interests she would have to marry paternal relatives (Num. 27:1–11).

She was brought up on the virtues of sexual innocence and chastity. Violation of her body demanded retaliation by her menfolk (Gen. 34:25ff.; Judg. 21:22) and was considered a great personal and family tragedy (II Sam. 13:11ff.).

Woman was created to be a helpmate to her husband (Gen. 2:18). A good wife was regarded as a gift of God and worth great riches (Prov. 31:10). Her subordinate social and economic status did not diminish the affection in which she was held. A mother's guidance was highly regarded by sons and daughters, influencing them long after they had matured.

She was taught to be industrious and to take an active interest in the economics of her home. The paean to a good wife (Prov. 31:10–31) is an extraordinary celebration of woman's industry. Other virtues lauded are foresight, thrift, good judgment, devotion to her husband's interests, and, above all, piety. It has been suggested that this passage served as a guide to a formal course of study in home economics for upper-class girls.

If a woman had a profession or skill, it was passed on to her daughters. The usual skills were midwifery (Ex. 1:21), weaving and cooking (I Sam. 8:13), and professional mourning (Jer. 9:19). In the pre-Israelite period a musical profession, associated with the pagan cult, was regarded as a proper alternative to marriage. In a letter to a Canaanite nobleman living in 15th century B.C.E., Taanach, a friend, advises "As for your daughter … let me know concerning her welfare; and if she grows up you shall give her to become a singer or to a husband" (Pritchard, Texts, 490).

While Israelite women did not participate in the Temple choirs at Jerusalem, they did sing at the royal court (II Sam. 19:36; Eccles. 2:8). Others were known for gifts of prophecy and poetic expression (Ex. 15:20–21; Judg. 5). There were wise women able to compose fables; still others practiced the black arts and magic (I Sam. 28:7). Such skills indicate a formal training, learned from experts.

Women raised at court later assumed positions of importance. Political marriages were not infrequent in Israel; such women must therefore have received some formal education befitting their future positions. Since some women had personal property (II Kings 4:8ff.) and seals of their own (see above), they may have known writing and calculation.

BIBLIOGRAPHY: GENERAL: F.H. Swift, *Education in Ancient Israel from Earliest Times to 70 AD* (1919); L. Duerr, *Das Erziehungswesen im Alten Testament und im antiken Orient* (1932); B. Dinur, in: EM, 3 (1958), 114–21; S. Greenberg, in: L. Finkelstein (ed.), *The Jews*, 2 (1960), 1254ff.; S. Talmon and M. Weinfeld, in: *Enẓiklopedyah Ḥinnukhit*, 4 (1964), 144–68; J. Kaster, in: *Interpreters' Dictionary of the Bible*, 2 (1962), s.v. *Education, O.T.* ON GOALS AND ORDERS OF INSTRUCTION: D.J. Mc-Carthy, *Treaty and Covenant* (1963). ON EDUCATIONAL INSTITUTIONS: I. Mendelsohn, in: BASOR, 80 (1940), 17–21; A. Demsky, in: IEJ, 16 (1966), 211–5. ON SPECIFIC TRAINING: W.F. Albright, in: BA, 5 (1942), 49–55; idem, *Yahweh and the Gods of Canaan* (1968), 179–80; M.B. Crook, in: JNES, 13 (1954), 137–40; J. Katzenstein, in: IEJ, 10 (1960), 149–54; B. Uffenheimer, in: *Oz le-David Ben-Gurion* (1964), 291ff.; U. Simon, in: *Biblica*, 48 (1967), 207–42; A.F. Rainey, in: EM, 5 (1968), 1010–17; S. Aḥituv, *ibid.*, 554–66; J. Liver, *Perakim be-Toledot ha-Kehunnah ve-ha-Leviyyah* (1968).

[Aaron Demsky]

IN THE TALMUD

General

While the sages regarded education as a central instrument in the preservation of Judaism, talmudic sources, characteristically, nowhere deal with the subject systematically in a comprehensive halakhic exposition. Instead, statements on education are scattered throughout talmudic literature, not as normative *halakhot*, but rather as incidental philosophical or psychological ideas, which in the main express the educational aspirations of spiritual leaders during about 600 years (c. 100 B.C.E.–500 C.E.). It is possible to derive a good idea, however, of the actual state of education at that time, which, when compared with the ideal, presents a unique cultural phenomenon – the approximation of pedagogical achievement to the ideal, not only in the attainments of exceptional individuals but also in the numbers of outstanding contemporary personalities. Here would seem to lie one answer to the riddle of the continued existence of Judaism despite the catastrophe which overwhelmed it in the first century C.E. History has revealed the profundity of *Joḥanan b. Zakkai's insight in his plea to the Roman ruler at the time of the destruction of the Second Temple: "Give me Jabneh and its sages" (Git. 56b). It was the study of the Torah which filled the breach left by the loss of the Temple service and which instilled new vigor into the nation.

Character and Aims

The basis of education is, according to talmudic sources, the study of the Torah, an all-embracing concept which includes means and ends alike. Two basic educational principles followed from the sages' regarding Torah as the very substance of their lives: (1) Education is not to be treated as distinct from the inner content of life but as one with it; (2) accordingly, Torah study is not to be limited to a certain age but to continue throughout one's life under the guidance of a teacher. The prompting of Rabban *Gamaliel, "Provide yourself a teacher" (Avot 1:16; cf. also 1:6), was intended for everyone, without regard to age or social standing. The unique character of Jewish education finds expression in the phrase "Torah for its own sake," a concept which sets before the student of Torah two goals: the disinterested fulfillment of the commandment itself – as it is written (Josh. 1:8): "Thou shalt meditate therein day and night" (Maim., Yad, Talmud Torah 1:8) – and the orientation of his studies to observance of the *mitzvot*. Torah study was actually regarded as greater than observance in that the first, aside from its intrinsic worth, led to the second by its very nature (Kid. 40b). The sages, in what was apparently designed to serve as a model for educators in all generations, defined the ideal man as one who studies the Bible and the Mishnah, attends upon scholars, is honest in business, and speaks gently to people (Yoma 86a).

Even as the supreme goal of study was Torah for its own sake, so was the general aim of education, "Let all your actions be for the sake of Heaven" (Avot 2:12), an epitomization which brings all actions, even those seemingly removed from Torah and *mitzvot*, into the sphere of man's central purpose – the service of God. To the end that a man support himself by his own labors and not become a burden on society, the sages declared: "All study of the Torah that is unaccompanied by work is ultimately futile" (*ibid.* 2:2). Accordingly, the permission granted parents to make arrangements on the Sabbath for the education of their children was extended to include arrangements "for teaching him a trade," both activities being regarded as "the affairs of Heaven," i.e., religious duties (Shab. 150a). One sage even declared that whoever fails to teach his son a trade, encourages him to become a brigand (Kid. 29a). A child was also to be taught swimming, undoubtedly for the preservation of life. As for other subjects, astronomy and geometry were regarded as aids to the study of the Torah, philosophy ("the wisdom of the Greeks") was not approved, and foreign languages, though discouraged for fear of contaminating cultural influences, were apparently, in view of the number of non-Hebrew words that found their way into talmudic literature, not entirely prohibited (see *Greek and Latin Languages, Rabbinical Knowledge of). Moreover, *Abbahu allowed girls to be taught Greek as "a social accomplishment" (TJ, Pe'ah 1:1, 15c), while Rabban Gamaliel established a school in which 500 pupils were taught philosophy so that they might be able to maintain contacts with the ruling authorities.

Age Levels

A child's education commences when he begins to speak, whereupon the duty devolves upon the father to teach him to repeat selected biblical verses, such as "Moses commanded us a law, an inheritance of the congregation of Jacob" (Deut. 33:4). This reveals the sages' appreciation of the cultivation of a child's imitative, mechanical faculties even before the attainment of understanding. They were aware of the value of inculcating in young children the habit of observing the *mitzvot*: "A minor who knows how to shake a *lulav* is obliged to observe the laws of the *lulav*; a minor who knows how to wrap himself in the *tallit* is obliged to observe the law of the *ẓiẓit*" (Tosef. Hag. 1:2). The pedagogical rule in *Judah b. Tema's statement: "At five years the age is reached for studying the Bible, at ten for studying the Mishnah, at thirteen for fulfilling the *mitzvot*, at fifteen for studying the Talmud" (Avot 5:21) was not always rigidly adhered to. At variance with it is *Rav's statement to *Samuel b. *Shilat, a schoolteacher: "Do not accept a pupil under the age of six; but accept one from the age of six and stuff him [with knowledge] like an ox" (Ket. 50a). At Usha it was laid down that up to the age of 12 gentle means were to be used to induce a child to study (*ibid.*, loc. cit.). A girl and a boy on reaching the age of 12 and 13 respectively were regarded as "adults," whereupon the father was no longer obliged to teach them Torah and the observance of *mitzvot*, the obligation now devolving upon the "new adults." The studies of adolescents did not thus represent a unique pedagogical stage. The obligation to study Torah under their teachers for the rest of their lives applied to them as it did to all other adults. Having learned Bible and Mishnah, they attended lectures on the Mishnah together with the young scholars and were present at the talmudic discussion centering around the *mishnayot*. In this "yeshivah" no distinction was made on grounds of age or status. Even those engaged primarily in earning a livelihood took part in the studies during the month of **kallah*, the special lecture series given by the academy head during the months of Adar and Elul when the studies of the intervening periods were summarized.

The Educational Framework

THE FAMILY, THE SCHOOL, THE TEACHER. In biblical times, as mentioned, the family, particularly the father, was the source of education. After that time, however, the growing demands of life and the expanding boundaries of Torah study made an institutional framework necessary. At an early stage it was apparently the custom to assemble children in the synagogue, where they were taught reading from the biblical scrolls. The first regulation that children be sent to school was introduced by Simeon b. Shetaḥ, the brother-in-law of King Alexander Yannai (c. 100 B.C.E.). The Talmud provides a more explicit statement on the establishment of schools at the end of the Second Temple period (the beginning of the common era) in which are noted the various stages in the development of institutional education: "Rav Judah said in the name of Rav: 'Truly the name of that man is to be blessed, namely, *Joshua b. Gamla, since but for him the Torah would have been forgotten in Israel. At first, if a child had a father, his father taught him; if he had no father, he did not learn at all... They then introduced an ordinance that teachers of children be appointed in Jerusalem ... Even so, if a child had a father, the father would take him up to Jerusalem and have him taught there; but if he had no father, he would not go up there to learn. They therefore ordained that teachers be appointed in each district and that boys enter school at the age of 16 or 17. But because a boy who was punished by his teacher would rebel and leave school, Joshua b. Gamla at length introduced a regulation that teachers of young children be appointed in each district and town, and that children begin their schooling at the age of six or seven'" (BB 21a). The basis of organized schooling for all ages was laid by Joshua b. Gamla's regulation. Most of these schools were in synagogues and were under the supervision of beadles (see Shab. 1:3). "There were 480 synagogues in Jerusalem, each of which had a Bible school (*bet sefer*) for the study of the Bible and a Talmud school (*bet talmud*) for the study of the Mishnah" (TJ, Meg. 3:1, 73d). At a later period, the patriarch, as the chief spiritual leader, was concerned with education and with the quality of teachers. *Judah III (third century C.E.) sent emissaries throughout Ereẓ Israel to ascertain whether each town had teachers of the Bible and of the Mishnah (TJ, Ḥag. 1:7, 76c). *Rava, a leading *amora* of the fourth century C.E., introduced, on the basis of Joshua b. Gamla's regulation, several important educational ordinances: (1) No child was to be sent daily from one town to a school in another, but could be sent from one synagogue to another in the same town. (2) The number of pupils to be assigned to a teacher was 25. If there were 40, an assistant was to be appointed. Whether one teacher could be replaced by a better one was the subject of a difference of opinion between Rava and *Dimi of Nehardea, who also differed on which teacher was to be preferred, one who taught a great deal but inaccurately, or one who taught less but without mistakes. Dimi's view, favoring the more careful teacher, was adopted (BB 21a).

All these institutions – the *bet sefer* for the study of the Bible, the *bet talmud* for the study of the Mishnah, and the yeshivah – had as their purpose not only the imparting of knowledge but also education for a life of Torah. This aim was achieved thanks to the personal example set by the teachers, who were held in awe by their students, as witness the statement of *Joḥanan b. Nappaḥa and *Simeon b. Lakish (prominent *Ereẓ Israel amoraim* of the third century C.E.): "We succeeded in the Torah only because we were privileged to see *Judah ha-Nasi's finger projecting from his sleeve" (TJ, Beẓah 5:2, 63a).

Methods of Instruction

Instruction was two-pronged in intent – improvement of the memory by accurate transmission and frequent repetition of material, and, at a later stage, the development of creative thought. Pupils learned to transmit statements in the same phraseology used by their teachers ("one is obliged to use the language of one's teacher"). Since the Oral Law, which could not be committed to writing, was continually expanding, accuracy in learning it was attainable only through endless repetition; hence the dictum, "He who has repeated his chapter a hundred times is not to be compared to him who has repeated it a hundred and one times" (Ḥag. 9b). The pupils thus acquired proficiency in recitation and a knowledge of the language of Scripture and the basic equipment required for participation in the creative study of the Talmud, essentially an incisive analysis of the *mishnayot* and the *beraitot*. The sages were strikingly modern in their practice of the pedagogic art. When *Tarfon's pupils said to him: "Tell us, teacher, by what virtue did Judah merit the kingdom? he answered, 'You tell'" (Mekh., Be-Shallaḥ 5). On one occasion *Akiva deliberately stated a *halakhah* incorrectly "to sharpen the wits of his pupils" (Nid. 45a). Every possible mnemonic device was employed – *notarikon*, association of ideas, and many others. Only in this way could the vast body of talmudic thought have been transmitted intact from generation to generation until the end of the fifth century C.E., when it was finally redacted.

Discipline played a vital role in this system (see Shab. 13a, and Rashi, ad loc., s.v. *ve-eimat rabban aleihem*). Although corporal punishment was inflicted when deemed necessary, the sages sought to curtail it as much as possible and warned against injuring a child. Rav's directives to Samuel b. Shilat the school teacher included the following: "When you punish a pupil, hit him only with a shoe latchet. The attentive student will learn of himself; the inattentive one should be placed next to one who is diligent" (BB 21a). This counsel applied to younger students; with those who were older the teacher might introduce the lesson with a humorous remark to create an atmosphere congenial to learning. But the teacher's most valuable asset was the example he set for his students. Well aware of this, the sages sought to impress upon teachers the need for circumspection in speech and deed. Thus *Ze'eira, a leading *amora* of the end of the third century, stated: "One should not promise something to a child and then fail to give it to him, for he thereby teaches him to lie" (Suk. 46b). Though the sages were remarkable pedagogues, the greater part of their achievement doubtless resulted from the atmosphere generated by their personalities, an atmosphere of unbounded love for the Torah and of supreme self-discipline in the observance of *mitzvot*.

BIBLIOGRAPHY: *Enẓiklopedyah Ḥinnukhit*, 4 (1964), 144–68, includes bibliography; J. Ster, *Die talmudische Paedogogik* (1915); H. Gollancz, *Pedagogics of the Talmud and that of Modern Times* (1924); N. Morris, *Toledot ha-Ḥinnukh shel Am Yisrael*, 1 (1960); M. Eliav and P.A. Kleinberger, *Mekorot le-Toledot ha-Ḥinnukh be-Yisrael u-va-Am-*

mim (1960), 48–70; A. Berman, *Toledot ha-Ḥinnukh be-Yisrael u-va-Ammim* (1968²), 25–35.

[Yehuda Moriel]

IN THE MIDDLE AGES

Babylonian, Pre-Geonic, and Geonic Periods

By the end of the fifth century, the time of the completion of the Babylonian Talmud, the Jewish community in Babylonia had become the leading Diaspora Jewry, a position it was destined to maintain for another five hundred years. This leadership expressed itself also in its educational system and in its high level of scholarship. Many synagogues had both a *bet sefer* for elementary study, and a *bet talmud* for advanced study. At the peak of this network of educational institutions were the two major academies of *Sura and *Pumbedita that contributed so richly to Jewish scholarship and, through the interpretation of the *halakhah*, set the pattern for Jewish religious life and the place of study in it. The heads of these academies – known at first as *rashei ha-yeshivot*, and later as *geonim* – were accepted as the authorities on religious law not only in Babylonia but also in the other lands of the dispersion. In the seventh century, Babylonia's influence was enhanced by the Arab conquests of many Mediterranean countries, extending as far as Spain, which united them with Babylonia in the bonds of a common language, Arabic. This last factor facilitated personal contact and communication between the Jewries of the geonic period and helped establish and solidify a more or less uniform style of Jewish life.

One of the chief components of this style of life was the upbringing of children. Their education was started at home where at a very early age they noted numerous observances, learned some of the benedictions and simple prayers and began participating, on their level, in many traditional practices, especially on Sabbaths and holidays, where they became acquainted with the synagogue rituals and celebrations. The home and the synagogue were effective educational agencies from the child's very infancy.

While some children were instructed by their fathers, starting school at age six was the more common practice. The school was usually in the synagogue or in a building near it, and the pupils were accordingly referred to as "synagogue children" (*tinokot shel bet keneset*). It was a community institution. However some affluent parents preferred private schools for their sons.

The elementary school's chief aim was to prepare the boy for participation in the synagogue service. The ability to read was therefore the first objective. Books being rare and expensive, children learned the alphabet by copying its letters on parchment, or paper or slate. In the early stages of learning, the teachers often outlined block letters which the children filled out, and sometimes colored. On the more advanced level, scrolls or sheets with biblical texts were available, or Torah scrolls that were unfit (*pesulim*) for synagogue use. Prayers and sections from the Pentateuch came next on the program, often starting with Leviticus. The Torah was studied assiduously in an attempt to cover the *sidra* ("portion of the week"). Afterward the pupils delved into the books of the Prophets and Hagiographa, but a later tendency was to neglect these works in favor of Talmud. In some schools the native language and arithmetic were also taught. *Hai ben Sherira (10/11th century), the last *gaon* of Pumbedita, permitted teaching these secular subjects, recognizing the need for them in daily life. However, their inclusion in the school's curriculum probably preceded Hai's dictum.

Widespread and effective elementary education continued in Babylonia's Jewry for a thousand years or so. Surely *Pethahiah of Regensburg exaggerated when he recorded in his travel diary (of 1180) that "there is no one so ignorant in the whole of Babylonia, Assyria, Media, and Persia, that he does not know the twenty-four books [of the Hebrew Bible] with their punctuation and grammar. …" This statement, however, reinforces information from other sources indicating that basic instruction was the lot of nearly all boys during the centuries of the gaonate.

The elementary teachers at this period were known as *melammedei tinokot*, or simply *melammedim*. Their economic position was relatively low, as was also apparently their social status. Hai Gaon, who, in his didactic poem *Musar Haskel* ("Wise Instruction"), urged the people not to be miserly in educational matters and engage good teachers for their children, also advocated generosity in the matter of teachers' remuneration. Teachers enjoyed extra presents on special occasions and on gift-giving holidays, particularly from parents pleased with their children's achievements.

The elementary schools were also preparatory institutions for more advanced studies. There were two levels of such study that may be characterized in the modern terms of secondary and higher learning but this division did not reflect so much the age of the students as the level of studies. In the intermediate stage, those engaged in *Midrash Mishnah* (study of the Mishnah) or *Midrash Talmud* (study of the Talmud) still needed the assistance of a *rav* – a teacher. On the upper level students proceeded with their learning independently. The subject was almost exclusively Talmud. The stress on Talmud brought about a nearly complete elimination of Bible and Mishnah from schools beyond the elementary. *Natronai b. Hilai Gaon (nineth century) expressed the opinion that adults, being pressed for time because of the need to earn their living, should concentrate on the study of the Talmud, since the Talmud contains much of the other two works. This same logic was later expressed by Rabbenu Jacob b. Meir *Tam in France.

The Babylonian academies served substantial numbers of students, some of them from distant lands: Egypt, Tunisia, Italy, Spain. During the pre-holiday months of Adar and Elul, the *kallah* assemblies in the academies attracted many students. In Babylonia there thus developed a system of talmudic learning also for the broader circles of the Jewish population, something on the order of peoples' universities or, to use still another modern term, extension courses.

This entire educational enterprise, however, was restricted to the male population. Girls did of course learn a great deal at home and were taught those observances that applied to their function as housekeepers. They knew the benedictions and prayers related to these activities. Some of them also learned to read and attended synagogue services. There are references to an organized girls' class, to a girl that attended school together with her brother, and even to some women teachers. But these were exceptions. By and large the Jewish women of that period were untutored and either completely or partially illiterate.

The West Mediterranean Lands

In the West Mediterranean countries of Spain, southern France, and Italy, one finds in the eighth and ninth centuries the same basic educational pattern that prevailed in Babylonia. But in the course of time a substantial network of elementary schools and important academies for advanced study were established in Spain, which inherited Babylonia's place as the Diaspora's leading Jewry, and the dependence on Babylonian scholarship lessened considerably. The elementary Judaic program remained much the same as in earlier centuries in Babylon. On the more advanced levels, however, many new books were introduced, most of them by Spanish authors, but including the commentaries of northern France's *Rashi. There was also a tendency to engage less in *pilpul* (the casuistry of excessive arguing pro and con on all halakhic matters, which was supposed also to sharpen one's mind) and concentrate instead on works of such codifiers as Isaac *Alfasi and, later, *Maimonides.

Another innovation was the introduction into the curriculum of Hebrew language and grammar, a more serious study of the Prophets and Hagiographa, and of contemporary Hebrew poetry. Judah *Al-Ḥarizi (c. 1200, Spain) speaks of the "inspiration that descended upon the Jews of Spain … in the year 4700 (940 C.E.) to train their manifold tongues in the style of poems," which was very poor at first but improved in the course of a century until "they learned to construct a stanza in meter and proper form." In Spain also the curriculum expanded, especially in the upper classes, to include general, secular instruction. The language of the country, Arabic, was studied in order to improve one's professional or business opportunities. Judah ibn *Tibbon (1120–1190, Spain and France), in his "testament" to his son, stated that "as you know, the great men of our people did not achieve their high position except through their knowledge of Arabic." Some students found it feasible to combine the study of Bible and of Arabic, and Ibn Tibbon advised his son to review the weekly *sidra* every Sabbath both in the original and in Arabic translation, "as this would be of benefit to you [in understanding] the vocabulary of Arabic books." Good writing, too, was taught: fine penmanship to the young, proper language and good style to the more advanced.

The progression in the Judaic program of studies was, as elsewhere, reading the Pentateuch, then Mishnah and Talmud. Obviously, not everyone continued through all these stages of learning. *Baḥya ibn Paquda, in a classification of educational accomplishments, describes the person on the lowest level of achievement as able to read a biblical verse without understanding its content, without even knowing the meaning of the words, as "comparable to an ass carrying books." There were then some, perhaps many, who remained ignorant. Others advanced to substantial levels of knowledge.

During this period there appeared for the first time in Jewish literature treatises on education, mostly chapters in various books, testaments, or commentaries, some of which are quite informative about the educational practices of the time. A school curriculum was fully outlined by Joseph ibn *Aknin who lived mostly in North African lands, but whose opinions represent typical Spanish views. Besides Torah, Mishnah, and Talmud, he advocated the study of grammar, poetry and continuation to logic, rhetoric, arithmetic, geometry, astronomy, music, physical science, and metaphysics. Ibn Aknin also expressed definite opinions about teacher qualifications and prerequisites for the good student. The teacher must be well versed in the subject he instructs; must practice what he teaches or preaches; should be patient with students and consider their learning abilities; should stress ethical behavior, etc. The good student is to acquire habits of cleanliness and good manners; should not be too bashful to ask questions; should pay attention and subject himself to his teacher's discipline; must never be idle; should study for the sake of knowledge and not in order to acquire wealth or for any other ulterior purpose. The mature student should seek out communities that have good schools and try to learn from qualified teachers rather than exclusively from books. Other writers give programs of study similar to Ibn Aknin's or to parts of it, suggesting that in all likelihood some such programs were actually followed in many communities. An even more detailed and ambitious outline by Judah ibn *Abbas (13th century, Spain) offers curriculum guidance for virtually a lifetime. At the age of three or three and a half the child learns the alphabet, reading, and proper vocalization. He is then taught the weekly portions of the Torah, with stress on correct reading and cantillations; the translation of the Torah into Aramaic, which will prepare him for the language of the Talmud; the Former Prophets, with emphasis on accurate meaning, syntax and writing, to be followed by the Latter Prophets and the Hagiographa. This program should be covered by about the age of 13. The boy will then study grammar and language. Only after such well-grounded preparation does one begin studying the Talmud with commentaries. The *halakhah* requires separate attention, and is taken up next, culminating in Maimonides' *Mishneh Torah*. When the young man reaches the age of 18 or so, he studies medicine, mathematics, astronomy, logic, and natural sciences. Specific works are named in textbooks for the various subjects. Ibn Abbas warns that at all times the scholar must observe the commandments, and the more he delves into the various subjects (*ḥokhmot*), the more must he strengthen his fear of the Lord and the observance of the *mitzvot*. This program may have been followed by a few of high intellectual abilities who could afford to devote themselves entirely to study. But the unexceptional too, especially among the wealthy, followed a rich curriculum of both the sacred and profane subjects. Even music and sports were learned in affluent families, though most likely not in the schools, but privately. King Affonso of Portugal is reported to have asked some Jewish scholars why they taught their sons music and fencing when they are obligated to weep over the destruction of the Temple and they do not go into battle.

Such Spanish curricula, with extension into languages and secular studies, were not universal. There were always those who concentrated almost exclusively first on the Pentateuch (*Ḥumash*), then on Talmud, to the neglect even of Hebrew and of the post-Pentateuch Bible books. A compromise view was that "extraneous" subjects were permissible for God-fearing and observant adults who had already become thoroughly versed in Jewish lore. Jacob *Anatoli (1200–1250, Marseilles) expressed the opinion that those who prohibited the study of "Greek wisdom" on the basis of the talmudic injunction not to teach "your sons" *higgayon* (meaning "Greek wisdom") erred in interpretation, and the word "sons" should be understood to mean young boys who were not ready to assimilate it.

This issue of advanced "extraneous" studies stirred Jewish communities repeatedly in both Spain and southern France and led to serious controversies. In Montpellier (southern France) it resulted in a violent split between the proponents and opponents of philosophy and in mutual excommunication by and of the two groups. Solomon b. Abraham *Adret, rabbi of Barcelona and prominent leader of Spanish Jewry, wrote a decision which prohibited "extraneous" teachings to those below the age of 25, on threat of excommunication. However, he permitted the teaching of medicine which was needed to heal the sick.

The fear of the effects of broad general education was not without foundation in reality. Spanish Jewry of the 12th and 13th centuries experienced a weakening of the faith in some of its best-educated circles. M. *Guedemann states that Jews of Spain became in large measure "Arabized," or, through Arabic learning of Greek philosophy, Hellenized (Guedemann's term in German is "*graecisiert*"). This resulted in a countertendency on the part of many leaders troubled by the phenomenon. They gained strength by the arrival from Germany in 1305 of *Asher b. Jehiel who became rabbi in Toledo. R. Asher never studied "Greek wisdom" and rather gloried in that fact. His opposition to this area of scholarship was resolute and effective. Talmudic study gained greatly due to his efforts and influence, and as a result Jewish education in Spain took a turn away from the trend of the two or three previous centuries, and by and large restricted itself to Torah and Talmud. In certain groups, particularly those in the higher economic and social strata, the practice of engaging in secular studies persisted.

The Jewish settlements in Provence, southern France, resembled those of Spain in their educational and cultural development. Here too, learning had developed to a high level. *Benjamin of Tudela, who traveled in the area in 1165, listed a string of towns that had important academies and scholars. Lunel is mentioned as a city with "about three hundred" Jews, where the "holy community of Israel" is engaged in studying Torah day and night and "people that come there from afar to study are maintained by the community as long as they stay in the house of study." Posquières, with only "about 40 Jews," has "a great yeshivah." Marseilles, with "about 300 Jews," is "a city of *geonim* and sages." Narbonne and Arles were centers of Jewish medical learning in the 13th century. Some Jewish schools in the French cities must have been substantial institutions, as reflected in documents of the sale of Jewish properties that accrued to the royal treasury after the expulsion of the Jews in 1306. While ordinary houses were sold for 5–20 livres and big houses for somewhat higher prices, Jewish school structures realized 350 livres for the building of the *Midrash Katan* and 620 livres for the *Midrash Gadol*, both in Narbonne, and similarly for buildings in other cities. In Toulouse there was a street named *Rue des Ecoles Juives*, suggesting more than one school. These houses were sold for 700 livres.

The educational picture in Italy resembled that in Spain and southern France. A cultural spurt in Italy during the eighth century contributed to a parallel development in the Jewish community. Apparently there were at that time well-established Jewish communities and schools in the south of Italy. Abraham *Ibn Ezra, who visited Italy in mid-12th century, expressed little respect for Italian Jewish scholarship. Hebrew, however, was in use, at least in certain circles. Solomon b. Abraham *Parḥon (12th century, Spain and Italy) observed that Italian Jews spoke Hebrew better than those of Spain. His explanation was that since all the "lands of Ishmael" used one language (Arabic), the Jews understood each other without resort to Hebrew, but it was a necessity in the Christian lands that used diverse languages, and Jewish travelers from these lands used Hebrew among themselves. From the 13th century on, Italian Jews were active in the study of Hebrew poetry, Bible, and Talmud, but in all of these pursuits Italian Jewry more or less followed the paths paved in Spain and in southern France.

Northern France and Germany

The educational aims of the Jews in northern France and in Germany during the first half of the previous millennium differed from those in Spain and Provence. Knowledge of Torah, strict observance of the commandments, and complete devotion to God and to Israel, even to the point of readiness to be martyred, were the exclusive objectives in the rearing and teaching of the young generation. Philosophy did not hold any lure for them and they delved into the study of the Scripture and Talmud without the need to reconcile them with Greek philosophy. The teacher's task was thus to teach and not to speculate; the scholar's task to elucidate and explicate the law where it was obscure and difficult, as did Rashi (Troyes, France), the explicator par excellence whose commentaries helped the young boy and fascinated the adult. With such an attitude deeply implanted in the Jewish communities, Judaic knowledge was quite widespread. Guedemann states his conviction that the study of the Bible in the original was so widespread in 11th-century France, that there was hardly a Jew there who did not know Hebrew and learned Jews spoke Hebrew out of preference.

The Franco-German educational literature of this period, both fragments found in various works as well as several documents dealing primarily with learning, provides a fairly complete picture of education in the Jewish communities. The home, the rearing institution of early childhood, was saturated with a motivating atmosphere and with practices that would later lead to effective Jewish learning. Some of these were performed long before the child could appreciate their meaning. Thus, the *Maḥzor* *Vitry, a compilation of Jewish laws, prayers, and customs for the cycle of the year, written by Simḥah of Vitry (d. about 1105), tells of a custom that "some short time after circumcision, ten men would be gathered [in the home of the infant], a *Ḥumash* (Pentateuch) placed over the infant" in his cradle and the wish would be expressed "may this [boy] observe what is written in this [book]." As he was growing up the boy heard prayers and benedictions on many occasions at home, and was taught to repeat many of them. He soon began to carry his father's prayer book to the synagogue and sat there during services on low benches provided for children. On Fridays after the *Minḥah* service he would run home to notify his mother of the arrival of the Sabbath and of candle-lighting time. On Passover eve children were given nuts or chestnuts to play with, and wine glasses to arouse interest in their role at the *seder* ceremony. Similarly there were various practices in which children participated on other holidays: noisemakers on Purim, bows and arrows on Lag ba-Omer, etc.

The start of formal schooling was a special event. The boy was sent to a "*ḥeder*" (the word meaning room), a term which came into use in the 13th century, suggesting that certain rooms in the synagogue were designated especially for study. According to the *Maḥzor Vitry*, "when a person introduces his son to the study of Torah, the letters are written for him on a slate. The boy is washed and neatly dressed. Three cakes (*ḥallot*) made of fine flour and honey are kneaded for him by a virgin and he is given three boiled eggs, apples, and other fruits. A scholarly and honorable man is invited to take him to school … The boy is given some of the cake and eggs and fruit, and the letters of the alphabet are read to him. Then the letters [on the slate] are covered with honey and he is told to lick it up … And in teaching him, the child is at first coaxed and finally a strap is used on his back. He begins his study with the Priestly Code and is trained to move his body back and forth as he studies." This description is followed by an explanation of the rationale of each of these details. R. Eleazar b. Judah of Worms lists some of the same details in his version of school enrollment, as does also an anonymous document, *Sefer Asufot*, written probably around the year 1300. This initiation into school was usually made when the boy was five years old, in some cases earlier, at the time of the festival of Shavuot, which celebrates the giving of the Torah. Another source gives the month of Nisan as a suitable time weatherwise, "neither cold nor hot," for such a start.

The curriculum of the elementary school was the traditional one consisting, as R. Eleazar of Worms summarized it, of first learning the letters, then combining them into words, then biblical verses, to be followed by Mishnah and Talmud. But there was no need for pedagogues to outline this curriculum, since most Jews knew it quite well. The document *Hukkei ha-Torah* ("Rules of the Study of Torah") instructs the father to bring his child to a teacher at the age of five and tell the teacher what he expects of him: "… you are to teach my son knowledge of the letters during the first month, vocalization in the second, combination into words in the third and afterwards this 'pure' child will take up the 'purities' of the book of Leviticus. …" Later, the boy is to learn the weekly *sidra*, first in Hebrew and then in the vernacular and the Targum (the Aramaic translation of the Pentateuch) and its translation into the vernacular. At the age of ten the boy starts Mishnah and certain tractates of the *Gemara*. By 13 he has completed his course in the *Midrash Katan* and then continues in the *Midrash Gadol* (terms probably taken from the French *petite école* and *grande école*.)

These *Ḥukkei ha-Torah*, written in 1309, are unique in that they constitute a complete set of regulations dealing with community responsibility, school administration and supervision, course of studies, and other administrative and instructional elements. According to these regulations, teachers should not instruct more than ten children in any one group. The pupils should be trained to discuss their lessons with each other, and thus sharpen their minds and increase their knowledge. "On Fridays teachers should review with their students what they had studied during the preceding week, at the end of the month what they studied during the past month, in the month of Tishri what they had studied during the summer, and in the month of Nisan what they had studied during the winter." A supervisor is to be appointed to observe the pupils' diligence or indolence. Should the supervisor note a slow-learning, dull child, he should bring him to his father and say: "May God bless your son, and may he be brought up to perform good deeds, because it is difficult to bring him up for study, lest on account of him brighter students be retarded." Seven more years of talmudic study were to follow the elementary and intermediate schooling. This did not apply to the masses (*hamon*). However, the numerous references in the literature to yeshivot suggest that there were many bright boys who did continue with such an advanced program.

*Judah b. Samuel he-Hasid of Regensburg in his *Sefer Hasidim* advocated continuation of studies until the students no longer need their teacher and "are already teaching others." He, too, felt that talmudic studies were not for everyone: "if you see that [the boy] can study Bible but not Talmud, do not pressure him to study Talmud." For Talmud was practically the exclusive subject in the yeshivot, and talmudic erudition was the highest educational objective. The starting of a new tractate of the Talmud was an occasion for a minor celebration and a feast in which community leaders often participated. Hours of study were long, even for the young children, but especially for the talmudic scholars. When the young boys (*baḥurim*) arrived at an independent age, some of those who sought further knowledge wandered off to towns that had renowned yeshivot. This practice seems to have become fairly widespread in the 14th and 15th centuries during the decline of the Jewish communities in Germany that followed the severe persecutions associated with the *Black Death. Many schools closed their doors and young men in search of Torah wandered about the land. Occasional yeshivot arranged accommodations for these nomadic scholars and communities helped provide for their maintenance.

Here, as elsewhere, the educational program was aimed at the male population only. Women were not taught Torah, although a few of them managed to learn some of it. *Sefer *Ḥasidim* states that girls should be taught to pray, and also those commandments that fall within their realm of activities, "for if she does not know the regulations of the Sabbath, how will she observe the Sabbath?" The education of girls was thus quite limited in France and Germany as elsewhere.

Eastern Europe and Asia

The Jews from Byzantium who settled in southern Russia and the Crimea around the turn of the millennium at first had no rabbinic authorities of their own and maintained a correspondence with scholars in Germany in matters religious. They also sent there some of their young men who desired a talmudic education. There is thus a suggestion that some elementary schooling, or elementary instruction, was available at home. Hebrew was not unknown in the region. One Crimean Jew, Khoza Kokos, an influential agent of Ivan III Vasilievich, grand duke of Muscovy, used to write reports to the duke in Hebrew, causing the latter some difficulties in finding an interpreter for them. In Poland and Lithuania Jewish communities were formed in the 12th and 14th centuries, mainly by refugees from German persecution. Among these were some rabbis, teachers, and cantors. The new communities continued for some time importing these functionaries from Germany, so that the Jewish educational efforts in these lands were shaped in the German-Jewish style of the period. The advanced scholarship of East European Jewry did not begin to flourish until later times.

In the Asiatic lands the Jewish communities could not, because of poverty and the extremely primitive conditions of life in their physical and social environment, develop the type of educational institutions that evolved in Western Europe. However, elementary instruction was imparted among the Jews in *Yemen and occasionally scholarly talmudists were found among them. In Iran, during the geonic period, elementary study of the Torah seems still to have been popular. In the ninth century a deviationist tendency appeared in the work of *Ḥiwi al-Balkhi, who apparently wrote an abbreviated version of the Pentateuch, omitting portions that he considered unsuitable for children, and criticizing many biblical passages and teachings. His book and opinions gained popularity also in *Afghanistan, his land of birth, and in other countries, so that *Saadiah b. Joseph Gaon found it necessary to attack it severely. Jewish learning in Persia was already then on the decline, but the Jews, some of whom were active in Persian cultural life, retained their Hebrew alphabet for the Persian language in whatever writing they had to resort to. A number of Persian language manuscripts of the 12th to the 16th centuries authored by Jews, including poetry and fiction, were written in Hebrew characters. Most of this literature was not Jewish in content, but at least one major poet *Shahin wrote on Jewish themes and authored a poetical version of the Pentateuch. There were Jewish communities also in other Asiatic lands or cities that preserved their Jewish identity, but their education was mostly quite rudimentary.

Community Responsibility

With the demand for education so widespread in the Jewish population and with the heavy burden borne by parents for the schooling of their sons, it was only natural that the organized community too undertook certain responsibilities in the educational field. As far back as the geonic period teachers used to be appointed by the communities, paid by them, and considered community functionaries. Later, community support of education was best organized in Spain. Various responsa that deal with this problem refer to community taxes and to the handling of bequests for education. Meir ha-Levi *Abulafia (13th century, Spain) ruled that "communities must engage teachers for young children; and in smaller villages ... it is the duty of the entire community, and not only of the children's parents, to pay [the teachers]." A revealing document on the subject is the set of ordinances of the Valladolid synod, convened by Abraham *Benveniste in 1432. Part I of these ordinances dealt with education, including its financing. It imposed taxes on meat and wine, and imposts on circumcisions, weddings, and funerals, for education expenditures. These taxes were not to be used for any other purpose than education or "support of students who received maintenance from the aforementioned *talmud torah* contributions." Each community of 15 householders was obligated to maintain a qualified elementary teacher who had to be paid according to the number of his dependents. Where the tuition fees from the pupils' parents were insufficient for his needs, the community had to supplement his income. The community also exercised a measure of supervision as seen from rulings about school practices, such as a limit on the number of children to be taught by one teacher (25), and other such administrative regulations.

Essentially the same type of responsibility obtained also in North European countries. Rabbenu Tam (12th century,

Troyes, France) in his ordinances referred to communities paying or supporting teachers' salaries as established practice, and ruled that in cases of shortage of educational funds, moneys designated for other purposes might be diverted to meet educational needs. These ordinances were accepted by the Rhenish communities in the year 1220. Even very small Jewish communities in many German towns managed to maintain schools, or at least a teacher. Reference is also made to such practices and to support of advanced students in *Ḥukkei ha-Torah.* Guedemann, who first published this document, expressed the opinion that while there can be no certainty that it represents the exact reality of its period, he was inclined to believe that it did reflect prevailing practices. Nor was financial support the only responsibility undertaken by the community. Mention was made above of regulations dealing with size of classes, supervision, reviews of material covered, and similar practices. Large schools were even required to have non-teaching supervisors, akin to the modern principals, who were to manage the business aspects of the school as well as assure proper instruction by the teachers (*Ḥukkei ha-Torah*). These may have been concomitants of financial support, since in education, as in other endeavors, subvention is often linked with at least some regulation and supervision. In any case, Jewish communities of the Middle Ages, even in extremely difficult times and circumstances, undertook a substantial measure of responsibility for the education of their young.

BIBLIOGRAPHY: Assaf, Mekorot (1925–47); Baron, Community, 2 (1942), 169–207; S.M. Blumenfield, *Masters of Troyes; a study of Rashi the Educator* (1946); W.J. Fischel, in: L. Finkelstein (ed.), *The Jews*, 2 (1960^3), 1149–90; Graetz, Hist, 3 (1949); 4 (1949), passim; Guedemann, Gesch Erz (3 vols. 1966^3), index; N. Morris, *Toledot ha-Ḥinnukh shel Am Yisrael*, 2 (1964); Weiss, Dor, 4–5 (1924^7).

[Elijah Bortniker]

JEWISH EDUCATION – 16TH–18TH CENTURIES

General

Jewish education during the 16th–18th centuries continued as a virtually universal practice. It was greatly facilitated by the then recently developed process of printing which made reasonably priced books readily available. There was, of course, one negative factor that interfered with Jewish life and hence also Jewish learning. The constant prejudice and persecution, the repeated expulsions, the frequent minor and occasional major pogroms, reduced the numerical strength of the world Jewish community which reached its lowest ebb in the 17th century. However education seemed to persist in high priority in the Jewish family and in the Jewish community of the period.

Europe – North and East

Elementary Jewish schooling in the German lands and in Poland, Lithuania, and Russia was given either in the private *ḥeder* or in the community *talmud torah.* The former was in many places a rather shabby institution. Moses Moravchik, in a pamphlet entitled *Keiẓad Seder Mishnah* ("How to Organize Learning"), published in Lublin in 1635, listed among the causes for the poor state of the *ḥeder* the tendency of many parents to change teachers each half-year term, low instruction fees and difficulties in collecting them, the *melammed*'s inclination to promote pupils for fear of losing them, the difficulties of proper instruction in the *melammed*'s home, and improper program and methods of instruction. The *talmud torah*s, maintained primarily for the poor, were often better organized, because they were supervised by the community, usually by a Talmud Torah Society (Ḥevrah Talmud Torah). At periods and in places of community strength the *talmud torah*s too benefited. In the 16th and early 17th centuries, many Jewish communities in Eastern Europe enjoyed considerable autonomy and authority in their internal affairs, and they regulated both *talmud torah*s and private *ḥadarim.* The Cracow community ordinances (1594) are typical of those in many communities. They imposed penalties on parents who failed to pay the teacher in prescribed time and prohibited teachers to accept children for whom tuition fee was owed to another teacher. A "truant officer" was to see that boys were not out in the streets or market place during their school hours. Supervision of the schools was likewise quite common. It was the duty of *talmud torah* officials to visit the schools, to ensure adherence to the program of studies, to test the pupils at specified times, and to select those pupils who merited awards.

The age of school entrance was usually five, but many three- and four-year-olds were sent to the *melammed*, even if merely to sit in his *ḥeder* and thus absorb some fragments of knowledge or get into the habit of accepting learning. They were referred to as "sitting children." School attendance was obligatory in most communities to age 13, in 16th-century Moravia "even for boys who did not do well in their studies." In Metz (1690) education was compulsory to age 14, and the community announced that it "will pay out of its tuition fee fund for all the children whose parents request it … without inquiring into the applicants' economic position." Those aged 14–18 who did not continue attendance in a yeshivah were required to study at least one hour daily. Amsterdam regulations (1738) obligated the community to provide orphans with the best teachers, to keep them in school until they were 13, and good students to age 15. A 1750 revision changed these ages to 14 and 17. The Sephardi community of the same city placed even greater stress on equal quality of instruction for the rich and for the poor. Similar specific concern for the poor and the orphans is found in many towns across Europe, from Amsterdam to Belaya Tserkov in the Kiev region of Russia (1764). Some regulations fixed the number of students per class: up to 40 pupils, with two boys as assistants (*behelfers*), in Cracow; or 25 in Dubno. However, Talmud classes in Dubno were limited to 15; in Fuerth to 10; in Mikulov to 14. In Mogilev-Podolski a limit of 15 was set on Talmud groups, but of only ten for those studying Talmud with Rashi's commentary and *tosafot.*

Education of girls remained very limited during this period as in previous centuries. A few of them received some instruction in reading the prayers and no doubt some girls, not tutored formally, managed on their own to acquire reading skills at home, where book learning was highly regarded and assiduously practiced. From the 17th century on, after the publication in 1620 of *Ẓe'enah u-Re'enah by Jacob Ashkenazi of Janow, the Yiddish work which became immensely popular among women, many girls learned biblical and later stories, aggadic and midrashic homilies, comments on Jewish life, customs and morals, as told by a remarkable raconteur. Private instruction was given to girls in some affluent families, which in the German and Western lands in the late 17th and in the 18th century often included French and German as well as music and dancing.

The elementary curriculum consisted, as in previous generations and periods, of reading, prayers, and *Ḥumash.* A new development was the widespread use of Yiddish as the language into which *Ḥumash* lessons were translated, in most cases word by word. Textbooks appeared of such translations, or of commentaries, some of which were based mostly on the popular commentaries of Rashi, like the *Be'er Moshe* of Moses ha-Levi (Prague, 1605) that became very popular, and other similar works. The weekly portion constituted the week's *Ḥumash* curriculum, but it was seldom completed. The stress on talmudic learning was so great that it was started at age seven or eight, the Prophets, the Hagiographa, and Mishnah being completely omitted. R. Joseph Yuspa *Hahn (d. 1637) of Frankfurt wrote that "in our generation there are rabbis who never studied the Bible." Even less interest, or rather no interest whatever, was evinced in any area of study that was not directly related to the Jewish religious lore. Secular subjects were completely excluded from the curriculum.

In the yeshivot of Central and Eastern Europe the aim was to produce scholars with a thorough knowledge of the Talmud and its commentaries, the *tosafot*, and the major halakhic codes. The talmudic *pilpul* method, a thorough dialectical examination of all possible arguments pro and con, was further elaborated in this period and transformed, mainly under the influence of Rabbi Jacob b. Joseph *Pollak of Prague, Cracow, and Lublin, into the "*ḥilluk*," extra-keen hairsplitting sophistry and ability to come forward with innovations (*ḥiddushim*) used in disputations and learned discourses, a sort of impressively complicated mental gymnastics, no matter how odd or absurd, which led to neglect of genuine search for understanding and even to distortion of original meanings. Although time consuming and apparently lacking in any practical purpose, it became very popular and highly valued in itself, to the neglect of more worthwhile scholarly pursuits.

Both the elementary and yeshivah programs and methods of study were severely criticized by R. *Judah Loew b. Bezalel of Prague and a number of his disciples. He advocated a graded program in accord with the child's readiness and in response to actual needs, greater stress on the commandments and practices taught in the Pentateuch rather than on Rashi's commentaries which were in his opinion a waste of time, and a further study of Hebrew, Bible, and Mishnah. He also sought the introduction into the school of certain secular subjects, particularly natural science. In the Talmud, according to him, children need not engage in study of tractates that are meaningless to them, and the overly refined pilpulistic method should be avoided at any stage since "it distorts one's intelligence." A number of prominent rabbis and scholars followed Loew's ideas and an elementary teacher, Moses Moravchik of Moravia (quoted above), wrote a pedagogic pamphlet based on them. But except for a few followers in several localities, these progressive ideas did not gain popularity.

The 17th century saw a decline of Jewish schools and of Jewish learning. In Germany the cities suffered decimation of population and impoverishment due to the Thirty Years War (1618–48). In Poland many Jewish communities were completely destroyed or reduced in the pogroms (1648–49) perpetrated by the *Chmielnicki rebellion, and the Jewish community organizations that flourished there broke down. After a slow and gradual recovery another development, mainly in the German lands, was the rise among the Jews of a substantial body of wealthy financiers, merchants, and *Court Jews, who lost interest in the traditional scholarship and observance. Their business required the use of local European languages, and "culture" decreed knowledge of French and Latin. Jewish learning was reduced in these circles to mechanical reading of ideas, and fragments of the Pentateuch. These attitudes and practices spread slowly into wider groups. Jonathan *Eybeschuetz (1690–1764), who served as rabbi in Metz, Hamburg-Altona, and Prague, and everywhere had many students and disciples, nevertheless complained about this decline in traditional learning and, in the lessened community, lack of support for it at a time when there seemed to be sufficient means for many other purposes, "some of them quite useless."

The second half of the 18th century brought about further changes in Jewish education in Germany and in the Austrian empire, which included, besides Austria proper, also Bohemia, Moravia, Hungary, Galicia, and parts of the Slavic Balkans. Emancipation of the Jews in these and other North and West European countries and the removal of many disabilities that afflicted them for centuries encouraged the spread of Moses *Mendelssohn's "Enlightenment" and of the educational views of Naphtali Herz *Wessely. Himself well educated both in traditional Jewish and general lore, Wessely advocated modernization of the Jewish school, through improved educational methods in the Jewish traditional subjects, which are God's law, and the introduction of secular subjects like the country's language, arithmetic, geography, history, and good manners, which are man's lore, into the Jewish school. Many prominent rabbis bitterly fought Wessely's proposals. But the desire for liberation from the old ghetto atmosphere and the slogans of enlightenment appealed to many in Germany and in parts of Austria. The governments too helped strengthen these tendencies.

In Germany, a high official, Christian Wilhelm von *Dohm, a friend of Mendelssohn, proposed reforms for the "civic improvement of the Jews" through modernized education. The very next year (1782) Emperor Joseph II of Austria issued a Toleration Edict that lifted some of the restrictions on

Jewish occupations and mobility, but also demanded "reform" of some of their practices including educational ones. The frank statements or implications that Jews needed "improvement" in order to merit improved civil status did not seem to offend and were in fact accepted by many of the Jewish seekers of emancipation and enlightenment. New schools were established by them in German and Austrian cities, where things soon took a very different turn from what Mendelssohn and Wessely intended, and Jewish studies in them suffered a serious decline. However, the Jews of Galicia, whose background and sentiments resembled more those of their fellow Jews in Poland and Russia to the east of them, remained refractory to the educational modernization efforts and only a few sent their children to the many schools opened for them, on government instruction, by the Jewish educator Naphtali Herz *Homberg.

Throughout this period, education of the youth in the Jewries of Poland, Lithuania, and Russia was most nearly completely traditional. During the period of the *kahal*'s ("community") greatest autonomy, traditional learning flourished. German cities exploited the scholarship of Polish and Lithuanian communities by employing rabbis and teachers who came West upon invitation or on their own. These East European Jews were influenced much less than their Western coreligionists by their environment, perhaps because this environment was much more primitive. Neither political emancipation nor cultural enlightenment and modern educational ideas had yet had a serious impact on the Jewries of the Russian lands at the end of the 18th century.

Italy

After the expulsion of the Jews from Spain and Portugal, Italian Jewry became the major Jewish community of the Mediterranean lands. Here, too, education was the earmark of the Jew. Even towns with only a few Jewish families, or for that matter a single one, had their local teachers. Nearly all the *condottas* (contractual agreements) drawn up with Jewish loan bankers allowing them to conduct business in towns where no other Jews resided included permission to have a teacher brought by the family to instruct their children. In larger communities, too, there was a tendency by the affluent to engage private instructors. The *talmud torahs*, originally established for the benefit of the poor, eventually as they became well organized were generally placed in the service of all members of the community. The management of the schools was left to Talmud Torah Societies that operated them according to carefully formulated regulations. The manner and rate of assessment for the maintenance of the schools was usually distributed to all community members. In some towns, as in Casale Monferrato in the 16th century, school funds were raised mainly from obligatory contributions made by those called to the Torah. Minimum obligatory contributions were fixed in Ancona (1644) for those called to the Torah, for men getting married, for families celebrating the birth of a male child, and for the School Society members on specified holidays. House-to-house collections were practiced in some places, as in Modena (TT Society, 1597). Schools had overseers and supervisors. The Talmud Torah Society regulations of Ancona (1644) and of Verona (1688) specified the physical facilities of the building, the authority of the trustees, number of teachers, teachers' duties and salaries, discipline, the program of studies, and supervision. The Modena regulations, as well as several others, state that the school is open to all comers, whether rich or poor, whether local residents or out-of-towners. A number of these sets of regulations spell out in detail not only the manner of collecting funds but also of their disbursement, occasionally specifying that teachers, both men and women, must sign receipts for the books given them, that these receipts are to be handed over to the accountant and must be properly recorded, and so forth.

While the schools were primarily for boys, it appears that girls learned a great deal at home through private instruction, and in the early years some of them seem to have attended the schools as well. Women were knowledgeable enough to instruct children of pre-school level, i.e., below age six, and perhaps some of the school children as well, in reading and prayers. The woman teacher (*melammedet*) was popular in Italy and her functions and salary are set down in some of the TT Societies' regulations. David *Reuveni wrote in his travel notes that in Pisa (in 1524) he met a young lady who "read" the Bible and prayed daily the morning and the evening prayers. He also met there a wealthy woman who served as a schoolteacher. Later, in 1745, a *talmud torah* for girls was opened in Rome.

Children attended school generally from age 6 to 14, a practice that was virtually obligatory. Study to age 18 was strongly encouraged. The six-year-old who started school could usually read, having been taught previously by the *melammedet* who in some cases was also a community functionary, like the teachers in the *talmud torah*.

The program of study in the early grades was the Pentateuch, the Prophets and Hagiographa, prayers, Hebrew and its grammar. The weekly portion of the Torah was stressed, and the Torah with Rashi's commentary was continued in several grades. In the third or fourth year, the Code of Maimonides was introduced or Caro's Shulḥan Arukh, then Mishnah with Obadiah of *Bertinoro's commentaries. The Talmud, burned in 1553 and by decree not printable in Italy, was for nearly two centuries practically eliminated from the curriculum and replaced by the various Codes, particularly Isaac Alfasi's *Halakhot*, a codified compendium of the Talmud.

An important feature of the Jewish schools in Italy, which distinguished them from the *ḥadarim* in Central and Eastern Europe, was the inclusion in the program of general subjects – Italian, arithmetic, good writing and style. Following an educational trend that had its origins in the West Mediterranean European lands in the Middle Ages (see above), the schools aimed to train individuals to be at ease in Italian life and society as well as faithful Jews, rather than talmudic or halakhic scholars. The teachers of the secular subjects in the *talmud torahs* and the yeshivot were often Christian. In affluent families private teachers also taught music, dancing, and dramatic reading.

Higher learning was provided in the yeshivot which were established in the larger Jewish communities, such as Venice, Mantua, Padua, Modena, Ferrara, Leghorn, and elsewhere. Jewish students also attended general higher schools, mainly medical colleges. Reflective of the cultural tendencies among the Jews of Italy during the Renaissance period is a proposal circulated in all Italian Jewish communities by one David Provenzale of Mantua in 1564, to establish a Jewish university. It was to be a sort of combination yeshivah and university for advanced study of Hebrew, Bible, the Oral Law, Jewish philosophy, good speech and good writing, as well as Italian, general philosophy, mathematics, astrology, and medicine. In such an institution, the proposal stated, Jewish students would feel at ease and would not be influenced by their Christian environment, a comment suggesting that there was at the time some concern about assimilation and possibly conversion. The stress on good speech and good language, applied to both Hebrew and Italian, is particularly illuminating. Good, grammatical, and well-styled Hebrew seems to have been highly valued. The period's Hebrew documents evince great care in writing and editing. Fondness for Hebrew language and literature was widespread. Shabbetai Ḥayyim *Marini, a physician, must have been convinced that he would have a substantial reading audience when he translated Ovid's *Metamorphoses* into Hebrew. Moses Ḥayyim *Luzzatto, one of the earliest pioneers of modern Hebrew literature, learned his Hebrew in his native town of Padua. But, Luzzatto's work excepted, the bulk of Hebrew writing in Italy in this period seems to have been that of poetasters, altogether lacking substance and originality. In the 18th century, with restrictions somewhat relaxed, the Talmud became once more the main subject of study in the yeshivot, and there seems to have been a lessening of the emphasis on general secular studies. But when, toward the end of the 18th century, new trends in Jewish education rocked Jewish communities in Germany and Eastern Europe (see next section), they caused only a ripple of controversy in Italy. When after the French Revolution emancipation and liberation from the ghetto came to Italy's Jewry, it was on the one hand quite ready for their concomitant educational and cultural "enlightenment," and on the other hand quite unable to withstand their corollary assimilating powers.

East Mediterranean and North African Lands

In the other Mediterranean lands traditional Jewish education continued in all sizable Jewish communities and moreover there was some intensification in Jewish life and schooling due to the influence of the expellees from Spain who settled in North Africa, the Balkans, and *Turkey. The Turkish cities *Constantinople and *Izmir had substantial Jewish communities in the 16th and 17th centuries and there is a reference to Constantinople as "a city of sages and scribes." A report from the mid-18th century by a Constantinople rabbi speaks of about 1,600 children in that city's *talmud torahs* of whom about 1,000 received community assistance in the form of clothing. Izmir had a Talmud Torah Society and a *talmud torah* in which *Shabbetai Ẓevi received his schooling. *Damascus in the first half of the 16th century had about 500 Jewish families and three synagogues. There was no yeshivah there but several teachers were teaching 30 or so pupils each. In 17th-century *Alexandria boys apparently studied to age 13, mostly the Pentateuch, and at their bar mitzvah they held forth on the portion of that week. There is reference to a yeshivah in Arta, Greece, in mid-16th century. *Aleppo in the 17th century had a *ḥeder* or *ḥadarim* maintained by two communities, one of which was composed of "*Francos," West European Jews who settled there. A large and important Jewish community in the eastern Mediterranean was that of *Salonika, which had a number of private *ḥadarim* in the early 16th century. These were later merged to form a central community school. A Talmud Torah Society was organized, buildings were put up, and the institution apparently flourished. In 1564 the *talmud torah* opened a clothing manufacturing shop, mainly to produce clothes for its pupils. In 1694 the Society also opened a printing press to supply textbooks for the *talmud torah* and for the yeshivah. This *talmud torah* and the yeshivah of Salonika became popular in the Balkan area and attracted students from other Greek towns, from Albania, and from some of the Greek islands. Out-of-town Jews contributed toward their support.

In the Maghreb countries the Jews spoke Arabic and Spanish but also taught their children in accord with established tradition, first at home – various phrases, benedictions, and prayers, and even reading. Later, in school, they learned the Torah, prayers, and some of the Oral Law as well. The Bible was studied much more than in the Ashkenazi lands. The majority of the Jewish population, however, was very poor and could not afford adequate schooling. A 1721 document from *Meknes, Morocco, bewails the fact that poverty drives many families to send children of six and seven into trade apprenticeship, appeals for the cessation of the practice, and enjoins tradesmen from accepting for employment children below the age of 13. Even under these difficult conditions Jewish literacy seems to have been impressive to the non-Jew. A Christian minister, Lancelot Addison, in describing the life of Maghreb Jews in his book *The Present State of the Jews* (London, 1675), states that early in life children are taught at home some Hebrew terms of daily use and from age 5 to 13 they attend school. According to Addison, "there is no boy in the world who can at the age of thirteen give such an accurate account of the laws of his faith as can the Jewish boy."

BIBLIOGRAPHY: Dubnow, Hist Russ, 1 (1916), 114–39; I. Fishman, *The History of Jewish Education in Central Europe, from the End of the 16th to the End of the 18th Century* (1944); Graetz, Hist, 5 (1941) passim; Roth, Italy, index; M. Szulwas, *Ḥayyei ha-Yehudim be-Italyah bi-Tekufat ha-Renaissance* (1955).

[Elijah Bortniker]

THE MODERN PERIOD, 1800–1939

General

The political emancipation of Jews in 19th-century Europe was associated with the so-called "Enlightenment" (Haskalah), in the educational and cultural spheres. Its effects differed in the various European lands, depending upon the local culture and politics, and on the numerical strength and the social and economic status of the Jewish populations.

Italy and Western Europe

The small French Jewry, formally organized as a consistory, opened two schools in Paris, one for boys (1819) and one for girls (1821), which were shortly afterward taken over by the municipality. Besides the general, secular subjects they offered a very limited program of Jewish studies. Additional schools of the same type came into being as the Jewish population increased, in Paris and in several other cities, particularly in southern France. After mid-century, however, most Jewish families began sending their children to the government schools. Supplementary religious instruction was at a minimum. In Alsace and Lorraine Jewish education was more intensive, but here too it became mainly supplementary by the beginning of the 20th century. Even more precipitous was the decline of Jewish education in Italy, where for centuries prior to the French Revolution a well-organized system of both elementary and advanced Jewish schools was in operation. Many small communities were virtually depleted of Jews by their migration to bigger cities, but here too a desertion of the Jewish schools took place, especially by those in the upper economic strata. About 1,600 pupils attended Jewish schools in 1901, mainly four-year elementary schools (some with two-year kindergartens, known in Italy as "*asili*"), accepted by the government authorities as fulfilling the legal requirements of elementary education. Jewish instruction was given in these schools for about one hour daily and consisted of reading, prayers, selections from the Torah, and a Jewish catechism in Italian. Older pupils received "religious instruction."

The rabbinical seminaries in France and Italy were similarly weak. The years 1827 and 1829 saw the establishment of such higher institutions of learning in Metz and in Padua. The Ecole Rabbinique moved to Paris in 1859, but continued to attract some students from the Alsace and Lorraine areas, and later, in the pre- and post-World War I periods, also from the East European Jews who settled in France. The Italian seminary, in its early years under the direction of Samuel David *Luzzatto, attracted a small group of eager young students, but declined after Luzzatto's death (1865). Removal of this Collegio Rabbinico to Rome (1865) did not improve its status. It was reinvigorated when it was again transferred, this time to Florence (1899), and came under the directorship of Samuel Hirsch *Margulies, chief rabbi of that city, who raised its level of scholarship and who introduced a Jewish nationalist spirit into it and into Italian Jewry.

In England, prior to the introduction of compulsory education (1870), Jews maintained schools of their own, some of which continued in existence for many years. When immigration brought many Jews from Eastern Europe, philanthropists established Jewish Free Schools for them in several cities. One of those in London was toward the end of the 19th century the largest school in England, with 3,000 pupils. Jewish studies were allotted limited time, no more than one hour a day. Some of the immigrants, displeased with this meager Jewish program, opened *ḥadarim* for supplementary instruction. Jews' College, for the training of ministers, was established in 1855. It had at all times a very limited enrollment.

The few Jewish schools that were founded in the 19th century in the Scandinavian countries closed their doors after the introduction of general compulsory education. Religious instruction preparing for confirmation became the accepted form of Jewish education. In Holland too, Jewish education was converted into this type of schooling, but here the Jewish community took it rather seriously, as did also the Dutch people their Christian religious instruction. After the enactment of the law of 1889, which permitted various religious groups to organize schools of their own to be supported by the government, Jewish full-time schools were opened in Amsterdam. Their program of Jewish studies was limited, but Jewish practices were strictly observed, and a Jewish spirit prevailed in them. Some private schools offered a more solid Jewish education. A rabbinical seminary, founded in 1808, began to train teachers as well as rabbis. A small Sephardi *bet midrash* likewise trained teachers and occasionally a rabbi.

Germany and Austria

The German lands present a more complex picture. Here emancipation and the "Enlightenment" brought about major changes in Jewish style of living and education, strong assimilationist tendencies, and considerable conversion. The old style *ḥadarim* were replaced by modern Jewish schools for those who did not wish to send their children to the general schools where an anti-Jewish attitude often prevailed. The number of these modern Jewish schools was rather small. Besides, their Jewish program was very meager: reading of prayers, some portions of the Bible translated into German, bits of Jewish history, mostly biblical, and religion and ethics. The traditional study of Mishnah and Talmud was abandoned, even in the secondary schools. After mid-century, when larger numbers began to enroll in the general educational institutions, supplementary schools came into being, from which students usually withdrew after the age of 13. Some religious instruction was also given in the general schools to Jewish students.

There was, however, a movement in Germany that countered these tendencies. Samson Raphael *Hirsch opened a coeducational school in Frankfurt (1855) offering a substantial program of Jewish studies, including Hebrew, Bible, and some Talmud, as well as the general subjects programmed after the pattern of the government or private German schools. A similar institution was opened in Fuerth (1862) after the previously existing Jewish school in that city was made nonsectarian. The Orthodox element, following Hirsch's approach, proved an anti-assimilationist force of considerable strength throughout the 19th century and in the early 20th. Germany also was a haven for many Jewish young men from Poland and Russia who, unable to gain admittance into the Russian universities, came for their higher education to Germany whose language they partly knew via Yiddish. Waves of emigration from Russia to the United States likewise passed through Germany. The students and migrants contributed to an ideological ferment that made Germany, in spite of the decline of its Jewish educational system for the many, a forum for live debates and discussions and study of Jewish religio-cultural life and Jewish issues.

On the higher level of Jewish studies German Jewry made a substantial contribution to scholarship through the establishment in the 19th century of several outstanding rabbinical seminaries. In 1854 the Jewish Theological Seminary was established in Breslau with Zacharias *Frankel at its head. It was a modernly organized institution, open to critical scholarship, yet traditionally oriented, in accord with Frankel's theory of "positive historical Judaism." The historian Heinrich *Graetz was one of the institution's early teachers, and many important Judaic scholars received their higher education in it.

The Higher School for Jewish Science (Hochschule fuer die Wissenschaft des Judentums) was opened in Berlin in 1872 and under Abraham *Geiger's influence came to represent Reform Judaism. However not all of its scholars were followers of Geiger's views, and it included among its teachers strictly observant talmudists and Zionist nationalists. An Orthodox rabbinical seminary (Rabbiner Seminar fuer das orthodoxe Judentum) was also established in Berlin in 1883 by Azriel *Hildesheimer, and it, too, soon became a school of high scholastic standing. These three rabbinical seminaries continued in existence until World War II.

In the German-speaking areas of the Austrian Empire, Jewish education resembled that of Germany. Although the Vienna Jewish community became numerically large, Jewish education declined. Again as in Germany, a rabbinical seminary was established in Vienna in 1893 which maintained high standards of scholarship. This, too, existed until the eve of World War II. The Hungarian part of the Empire had two paths of development, an assimilationist tendency in one section of the population and a strong Orthodox one in another. The latter elements gave their children an intensive Jewish education of the traditional type, as reflected in many yeshivot, some in rather small communities. A modern rabbinical seminary was established in Budapest in 1877.

The situation was different in Polish-Ukrainian Galicia, home of about half of the Empire's Jewish population. Here developments resembled those in Poland and Russia. Most of the government schools for Jewish children which were organized under the directorship of Herz *Homberg at the end of the 18th century closed in the first decade of the 19th. The only remaining modern type Jewish schools were the one founded by the esteemed educator Joseph *Perl in Tarnopol which was supervised by rabbis and gained the confidence of many traditional Jews, and a high school in Brody. The number of Jewish children attending government general schools increased slowly and reached some 78,000 in 1900. A new type of Jewish nationalist school (see below, Eastern Europe) made its appearance in the last decades of the century. However most Jewish boys continued receiving their instruction in the old style *ḥadarim*.

Eastern Europe

Western ideas began penetrating into the Polish-Russian domain after a lag of some decades. In Poland, contiguous to Germany and with many German contacts, the "Enlightenment" first reached the more prosperous and worldly Jewish circles who believed that talmudic training was obscurantist, that the educational system maintained by the communities was backward, and that the cure for these ills was stress on the Polish language and a school program similar to that in the Polish schools. The government, too, was interested in this educational issue, its aim being polonization. A similar situation obtained somewhat later in Russia where the government attempted a russification of the Jewish school and tried to destroy the *ḥeder* and the yeshivah. Many Jewish assimilationists in both Poland and Russia supported the government efforts. Even some of the non-assimilationist *maskilim* cooperated with the government, often not realizing its ulterior motives. Isaac Baer *Levinsohn advocated a revolutionary change in Jewish life, with return to such occupations as agriculture and manual trades, and, educationally, a modernization of the program of Jewish studies, and the introduction of secular subjects, particularly the Russian language and civics. He believed that the government intended to improve the status of the Jews. The government exploited this trend of thought and tried to change the *ḥeder* system under the direction of the rabbi and educator Max *Lilienthal, who was invited from Germany, first to administer a modern school in Riga (1840) and soon (1841) commissioned by the government to establish a chain of modern schools throughout the Pale of Settlement. Most of the Jewish population opposed Lilienthal's enterprise. After a few years Lilienthal himself became convinced of the government's ulterior objective of russification of Jewry and he immigrated to the United States. A number of these new schools continued to function but the majority of the Jews resisted the attempt to convert the *ḥeder* into a school and the *melammed* into a teacher and remained faithful to their traditional style of schooling.

The "enlighteners" nevertheless were gaining ground, even if slowly. Levinsohn's ideas of better organized and graded curricula and Lilienthal's modern practices and organization proved attractive to many groups. Westernized Jewish elementary and secondary schools began to appear in various communities. In the 1860s the newly formed "Society for the Promotion of Culture among the Jews of Russia" became influential in limited circles. At first this Society stressed knowledge of the Russian language and Russian culture, but toward the end of the century it came under the influence of the movement for the revival of the Hebrew language that was spreading among the Ḥovevei Zion and the intelligentsia. The revival of Hebrew as a national tongue became a passionate ideal in numerous nuclei of the large Diaspora of Russian Jewry. Limited though they were in numbers, these small groups soon began to exercise considerable influence in their communities. The search for effective ways to spread the knowledge of Hebrew led to the evolution at the turn of the century of a new type of Jewish school known as the *ḥeder metukkan* (improved *ḥeder*) that derived its inspiration from Jewish nationalism, and which rapidly developed into an educational movement. Its leadership included active Zionists, like *Weizmann and *Dizengoff, the poet *Bialik and others of similar stature and status in the Russian Jewish community. *Aḥad ha-Am spoke of the "invasion" of the school by Hebrew, the national language. The early *ḥadarim* of this "improved" kind were founded in the south of Russia – in the Kiev area, in Bessarabia, and in Odessa – and soon spread throughout the Pale of Settlement as well as in Austrian Galicia and sections of Romania. The movement proved a powerful intellectual and administrative stimulus. Men, and women, began studying educational programming and method and successfully organized and taught in the new schools. Ḥayyim Aryeh *Zuta authored a curriculum for this type of school. Isaac Epstein, linguist and psychologist, pioneered in the method of instruction which became known as *Ivrit be-Ivrit* (also referred to as the "natural method"). Samuel Leib *Gordon, later to gain renown as a popular biblical commentator, opened a *ḥeder metukkan* in Warsaw in 1903, and soon afterwards a similar school was opened by Ḥayyim Kaplan which continued in existence until the eve of World War II. Some of the "improved" *ḥadarim* were coeducational, but new schools for girls also made their appearance following the example of Pua Rakovsky's school in Warsaw, which gained considerable repute. A pioneer of the movement, Jehiel *Heilprin, organized a Hebrew kindergarten in Warsaw (1909), and as this enterprise was soon emulated in many other communities, Heilprin opened "Froebel courses" for the training of kindergarten teachers. Efforts to establish a training institution to provide teachers for the "improved" schools were made as early as the 1880s. These failed due to government opposition, but finally, in 1907, the Society for the Promotion of Culture succeeded in opening "Pedagogic Courses" in Grodno under the direction of Aaron Cohenstam in which all subjects were taught, at least partly, in Hebrew. The students were recruited in large part from the circles of yeshivah young men caught in the nationalist spirit. A more limited program of teacher training, including summer seminars, was later started in Odessa. The teachers themselves began to organize under the leadership of P. Shifman in 1906 for educational as well as for professional-economic purposes. A teachers' association was also formed in Galicia under the leadership of S. *Schiller, with the aim of strengthening and guiding the "improved school." Many new textbooks appeared during this period as well as Hebrew publications for children, youth, and adults. The Hebrew language was being revived as a modern language, even if in limited circles. Some Orthodox elements opposed this trend, maintaining that the sacred tongue (*leshon kodesh*) must not be turned to "profane" use. Assimilationist elements were likewise critical, as they were of the entire nationalist-Zionist movement. The revival of Hebrew however kept gaining ground. The term Hebrew School (*bet sefer ivri*) that crept into use reflected the new educational trend.

While the old style *ḥadarim* in Eastern Europe declined in quality, though not in enrollment, during the 19th century, some of the yeshivot saw a remarkable development, this in spite of government interference and of the indifference to them of the modern, so-called enlightened Jewish groups. Many of the leaders of Russian Jewry during the period under discussion were products of these yeshivot, in which high scholarship and originality raised the repute of talmudic studies and added dignity to those engaged in them. The community of the small country of Lithuania pioneered in this respect when the Volozhin yeshivah was established in 1803 and from the very start introduced innovations in the method of study, considerable freedom in students' choice of tractates to be covered, and later the introduction of some general subjects as well, such as history and mathematics. Yeshivot were founded in the following decades in Mir, Telz, Grodno, Radin, and elsewhere. A number of these were centers of distinctive Jewish philosophies, like the yeshivah of Slobodka (a suburb of Kovno), founded by Rabbi Israel *Lipkin, where his views on ethics (*Musar*) became a major subject, or the Tomkhei Temimim yeshivah of the Lubavitch ḥasidim where ḥasidic ideology was stressed. Modern type yeshivot too made their appearance, which included general studies as an integral part of the program, like the yeshivah in Odessa, founded in 1865 and reorganized in 1906 under the directorship of Rabbi Chaim *Tchernowitz (Rav Tza'ir) into an important institution of Jewish scholarship. The poet Bialik and the historian Joseph *Klausner served for brief periods as instructors in this Odessa yeshivah. Another prominent yeshivah, traditional but modernized in its program and organization of studies, was the Torah v'Daas, founded by Rabbi Isaac Jacob *Reines in Lida in 1905; it included in its program Hebrew grammar, Bible, Jewish history as well as Russian, and several general subjects in the humanities. On the eve of World War I the enrollment in some 30 yeshivot in Russia, which at the time included the Baltic states, much of Poland and Bessarabia, was about 10,000 students.

The Balkans and the Lands of Islam

In the Balkans, and in the Muslim lands of the Eastern Mediterranean and North Africa, an important factor in modernization of Jewish education appeared in the second half of the 19th century, that of the *Alliance Israélite Universelle (AIU). This organization was an expression of the Jewish group consciousness of French Jews, who, while themselves strongly assimilationist, yet felt the responsibility incumbent upon them to help their coreligionists in these underdeveloped lands. The AIU began its activities in the political field but after about 1860 concentrated mainly on education. It was instrumental in westernizing to a great extent some of the Oriental-style primitive *kuttabs* and *talmud torahs* of the old *Ottoman Empire and the Maghreb countries as well as in *Persia and the Balkans. Its first schools were established in *Tetuán, Morocco, in 1862, in *Tangiers in 1864, in *Damascus and *Baghdad in 1865. Soon a large network of schools, numbering on the eve of World War I more than 100, came into being. To train teachers for these schools the AIU founded the Ecole Normale Israélite Orientale in Paris (1867). Students were recruited from the AIU schools in the various countries and their study in Paris was subsidized. The AIU educational institutions stressed the French language and culture, but Hebrew, Bible, and other Jewish subjects were taught in them as well, the extent of the latter varying in different communities and sometimes depending on the personal opinions and sentiments of the local school directors. Other Jewish schools in the communities where the AIU operated were influenced by this educational enterprise. Old *ḥadarim* underwent considerable modernization. In Izmir, Turkey, a society was formed (1869) to help the education of the poor, mainly in order to ward off the influence of the missionary schools. In the same city regulations were passed earlier in the century prohibiting craftsmen from employing boys who do not know the three daily services. School societies came into being in many other cities of the Muslim lands. One of the largest schools, modern in its organization and program, was founded in *Baghdad in 1865. Recognizing that withdrawal into Jewish studies alone is disadvantageous, it introduced the study of the languages of the country, Arabic and Turkish. In Bulgaria, Hebrew as a spoken language gained a foothold in some schools. The trend reached also some non-Alliance schools in the North African lands of *Egypt, Tripolitania, *Tunisia, and *Algeria. Education of girls, too, became acceptable practice during this period. A girls' school was established in *Mogador, Morocco, as early as 1840. Later in the century a number of such schools, as well as several kindergartens, were opened in Egypt and in *Turkey.

A German society, the *Hilfsverein der deutschen Juden, founded in 1901, also entered the educational area of activities in the Balkan countries and in the Middle East. On the eve of World War I it maintained some 50 schools in these regions, including 29 in *Palestine.

The Period between the Two World Wars

The political upheavals that followed World War I brought about radical changes in the fate of the Jews of Eastern Europe. The Russian Revolution cut off Russian Jewry from the rest of the world and suppressed both Jewish religious and Hebrew-nationalist education. Yiddish was recognized as the language of the Jews in Russia, but in fact Yiddish schooling too was discouraged and was rapidly reduced to near the vanishing point (see below).

A second major outcome of the war was the establishment in Eastern Europe of a chain of new or enlarged states from the fragments of the broken Austrian and reduced Russian empires. The majority of Europe's Jews lived in these states, and they were recognized as national minorities entitled to national-minority status and to specific rights in the educational and cultural spheres. But the new states, as yet uncertain of, and jealous of their new national sovereignty, did not treat their minorities generously, and, steeled in the old tradition of antisemitism, the Jews found themselves a discriminated group. At the same time the Zionist ideal, which in the pre-War period inspired only narrow strata of the Jewish population, suddenly became, on the heels of the Balfour Declaration (1917) and the British Mandated National Home authorized by the League of Nations, a hope inspiring near-reality. This conjuncture of circumstances strengthened the Hebraist-Zionist trend in Jewish education both in the secular and religious groups. (It also encouraged the creation by the radical circles of a nationalist Yiddish movement.) The extreme Orthodox, non-Zionist elements resorted to a passive withdrawal into the traditional life and education, slightly modified to meet contemporary needs. During this period the cultural life of Jewry became strongly politicized, the schools and various courses having come under the auspices or sponsorship of Jewish political parties.

The Orthodox Agudat Israel maintained or supported a network of schools, "Ḥorev," which included *ḥadarim, talmud torahs*, and yeshivot, some of them full day schools in which both general subjects and Jewish subjects were taught. In the mid-1930s, "Ḥorev" schools in Poland numbered about 350 and had an enrollment of over 47,000 pupils. Another network, of schools for girls, grew out of the activities of a Cracow seamstress, Sarah Schnirer (1883–1938). Having noted the neglect of Jewish education for girls, she organized a group of girls into a class which eventually developed into a school. Its success encouraged the establishment of similar institutions, designated as Beth Jacob Schools, in many other communities. In 1938 they numbered 230 in Poland including several day schools, with about 27,000 pupils. In 1929 Agudat Israel took over the sponsorship of these institutions. The Mizrachi Zionist religious party sponsored the Yavneh network of schools. These included kindergarten and elementary day schools and, on the secondary level, mostly supplementary schools. In 1938 the Yavneh system had 235 schools of all types with an enrollment of over 23,000. A major difference between the Agudah and Mizrachi school systems was the attitude to and the use of the Hebrew language. The extreme Orthodox elements had not yet made peace with Hebrew as a modern language. In their view the language of conversation and instruction was to be Yiddish, the language of the majority of Jews in Eastern Europe and the one in which many prominent rabbis had preached. The Mizrachi leaders, on the other hand, with their Zionist philosophy, accepted Hebrew as the language of the National Home in Ereẓ Israel and the desired language of the people in daily life everywhere as well as the language of the sacred lore.

Another large school system was that of Tarbut. In these schools students were imbued in the Jewish nationalist spirit and were oriented towards *ḥalutziyyut* (pioneering) in Palestine. The Bible was the core of the Hebrew traditional program, and modern Hebrew literature provided the contemporary nationalist orientation. The Tarbut educational institutions included many day schools, both elementary and secondary. By and large the students came from the middle and upper middle classes, the poor being unable to afford them. Nevertheless the Tarbut schools, which in 1918 numbered 50 with 2,500 pupils, grew by 1935 to 270 with about 38,000 students, scattered throughout the Baltic states, Poland, and Romania.

There were also some schools not formally identified with these major trends in Poland and Lithuania, but that were actually under the same type of religious or secular sponsorship. Thus in Latvia Agudat Israel schools were known as "Moriah" and the Mizrachi schools "Tushiah" were similar in their Hebraic-religious program to the "Yavneh" schools in Poland. In several Bessarabian towns and elsewhere there were secondary schools not associated with the Tarbut network, but following virtually the same program. Aside from these major organized groups of schools private unaffiliated *ḥadarim* of the traditional type continued to function, mostly in Poland. These had, in the mid-1930s, an enrollment of some 50,000 boys.

The above school systems all had their teacher-training schools: the Beth Jacob school in Cracow (established 1925); the *bet midrash* "Taḥkemoni" in Warsaw (1920), which trained rabbis and teachers for the Mizrachi's Yavneh schools, and a similar institution in Vilna; and three Tarbut teacher seminaries, in Vilna (1921), Lvov (1922), and Grodno (1926). In Warsaw there was also a government school for teachers of the "Mosaic Faith" which became Hebraically oriented during this period.

The decline in the economic positions of the Jewish communities brought about considerable enrollment in Jewish trade schools and the study of agriculture in preparation for Palestine. One of the Tarbut schools offered courses in agriculture as did some of the yeshivot of Yavneh. The *Ort trade schools too were popular. In Poland alone in 1934 Jewish trade schools had an enrollment of about 5,000.

The yeshivot suffered greatly from the war, some having closed and others being forced to move. To recover from this decline a Va'ad Yeshivot (Yeshivot Committee) was organized under the leadership of R. Ḥayyim Ozer *Grodzinski, and numerous yeshivot and "junior yeshivot" (*yeshivot ketannot*, preparatory to the yeshivot proper) were established within a few years by this committee as well as by other groups or individual rabbis. In 1937 there were in Poland 136 yeshivot with some 12,000 students. Outstanding among these new institutions in its organization, physical facilities, and scholarship, was the Yeshivat Ḥakhmei Lublin (the Yeshivah of the Lublin Scholars) founded in 1930 by R. Meir *Shapira, who had previously established yeshivot in several towns in which he served as rabbi and who gained renown for his passionate advocacy of "the page a day" idea (*daf yomi*), that every Jew study one page of the Talmud daily.

In Central and Western Europe the Jewish educational trend continued much in the same direction as it did before World War I. Here and there new schools were founded, and some old schools closed their doors. In Antwerp there were two large day schools. A new day school was opened in Paris. In Gateshead, England a yeshivah was founded in 1927 which attracted students from the West European countries, especially after the beginning of the flight of Jews from Germany and the other lands threatened by the Nazis. Most Jewish learning however was in supplementary schools of limited hours and programs. In the general schools for Jewish students that continued functioning in Germany, England, Austria, and elsewhere time allotted to Jewish studies also remained minimal. On the eve of and immediately after the Nazi rise to power, study of Hebrew became widespread among the Jewish youth of Europe.

In the Muslim lands the Alliance Israélite continued to maintain or support schools, although their number began to decline in the 1930s. There still were 65 AIU schools in 1938, of which 33 were in one country, Morocco. In *Iraq certain restrictions were imposed on Jewish education after the country gained its independence in 1932, but a substantial number of schools continued functioning in *Baghdad and in several other cities. In the East Mediterranean Arab lands the schools took on a more modern Western character while the old style *ḥadarim* declined. In the Maghreb lands the *ḥadarim* and yeshivot remained numerous and popular.

All these educational activities of the period between the two world wars – modest in some of the countries discussed above, extensive and vibrant with vitality in others – were terminated in 1939 or soon after when the Germans invaded nearly all of Europe and gained control of North Africa. Even where the Jews were not physically destroyed as in Italy and the North African lands, the restrictions imposed upon them and the dread and uncertainty in which they lived during the German occupation suppressed their educational and cultural functions. The largest and most creative Jewries of Eastern Europe were almost totally destroyed and with them disappeared centuries-old centers of Jewish life, culture, and scholarship. While about two and one half million Jews remained alive in the Soviet Union after the Nazi Holocaust, the discriminatory regime deprived them of opportunities for the free exercise of their religio-cultural life. In this country there was practically no Jewish education of any kind. Fortunately the other large Jewish population centers on the American continent were unaffected by the ravages of World War II. One-half of the world Jewish population of 13 million was to be found on the American continent. The United States became the largest Jewish population center with 5,750,000 Jews who have created institutions for Jewish learning for both young and old.

BIBLIOGRAPHY: A. Chouraqui, *Between East and West: A History of the Jews of North Africa* (1968), 133–5, 204–13; Elbogen, Century, index; A. Levinson, *Ha-Tenu'ah ha-Ivrit ba-Golah* (1935); Z.

Scharfstein (ed.), *Ha-Ḥinnukh ve-ha-Tarbut ha-Ivrit be-Eiropa bein Shetei Milḥamot ha-Olam* (1957); idem, *Toledot ha-Ḥinnukh be-Yisrael ba-Dorot ha-Aḥaronim*, 5 vols. (1960–65²); M. Eliav, *Ha-Ḥinnukh ha-Yehudi be-Germanyah bi-Ymei ha-Haskalah ve-ha-Emanzipazyah* (1960), includes bibliography.

[Elijah Bortniker]

JEWISH EDUCATION IN EUROPE (WAR & POSTWAR)

The War Years

In Nazi-occupied Europe normal Jewish education practically ceased to exist. In Western Europe the Germans initially insisted that Jewish children be removed from general schools and educated in Jewish schools. Later, however, when the "Final Solution" was initiated, Jewish education was completely disrupted, particularly in Eastern Europe, where it was officially prohibited. In spite of this ban, clandestine classes in Hebrew and Yiddish were held, under highly dangerous conditions, in most larger ghettos such as Lodz, Warsaw, Vilna, and others. They continued until the liquidation of the ghettos themselves (see *Holocaust). Jewish schools developed during these years in Italy, where all Jewish children had to leave government schools.

The Period Since World War II

The survivors of the war gathered in Displaced Persons camps. About 250,000 Jews from Eastern and Central Europe were in D.P. camps in Italy, Austria, and Germany. Few children had survived, but for those who did come back from their various hiding places, schools were opened. An education board consisting of representatives of the Jewish Agency, the Joint Distribution Committee, and the DPs was set up in 1947. Work had to start from scratch. Books were reprinted, teachers were brought from Palestine, a complete network of schools was set up, serving all the camps and Jewish communities in the larger towns. Soldiers of the *Jewish Brigade played an important role in this work.

The camps were emptied with the establishment of the State of Israel in 1948. The vast majority of the Jews in the D.P. camps left for Israel. Those that remained behind settled in various communities in Central and Western Europe. By that time Jews in Eastern European countries could no longer freely leave their place of residence. New Jewish communities grew up in Eastern Europe, whose educational program depended on policies of the governments in their respective countries of residence. No serious educational program was developed in any of the Communist countries except for Hungary and, for a short period of time, in Poland. The Theological Seminary was reopened in Budapest. A primary and secondary Jewish day school was also started, which continues to function to the present time. The total number of children involved in Hungary, however, never exceeded 200–300 out of a total Jewish population of 80,000.

The education program in Poland developed after the era of Stalin and with the return of Jewish refugees from the Soviet Union. Four Yiddish schools were opened for the returning refugees. The language of instruction was Polish, but Yiddish and Yiddish culture were taught. These schools were closed with the reduction of the Jewish community in Poland through emigration and because of a change in government policy after 1967.

There were no Jewish schools in Romania, Czechoslovakia, or Yugoslavia. Very few children received a supplementary Jewish education in any of these countries.

With the collapse of Communism and the dissolution of the Soviet Union, Jewish communal life in Eastern Europe underwent a marked revival in parallel with mass emigration. Community organizations now offered a wide range of religious, social, and cultural services, including Jewish education. In 2005 the Federation of Jewish Communities of the Former Soviet Union operated 54 kindergartens, 72 elementary day schools, 15 high schools, and five universities in 65 cities, with a total enrollment of over 15,000 youngsters. In addition it had 15 yeshivot with 700 students and over 100 Sunday schools in 13 countries. The Federation also operated a teacher training institute and a resource center turning out educational materials.

In Hungary there were just three Jewish day schools and a high school in Budapest in 2005, serving a population of around 80,000 Jews countrywide, of which only a few thousand were affiliated to the Orthodox or Neolog community. However, it continued to operate the only rabbinical seminary in Eastern Europe. In Bulgaria formal Jewish education was received at a state secondary school where Hebrew and Jewish history studies were compulsory, while a few Sunday schools were also in operation. Other countries of Eastern Europe, with their small Jewish populations, were also making efforts, whether in *talmud torah* or Sunday schools, to perpetuate Jewish education.

In postwar Western Europe a new awareness spread among the surviving leadership that education is the foundation of Jewish communal life.

Several factors contributed toward the achievements in cultural reconstruction.

a) The respective governments were sympathetic to the Jewish communities and many helped in the maintenance of the schools. The Swedish government provided grants for the day schools and so did the governments of France, Belgium, Holland, Denmark, Finland, Germany, and Italy.

b) American Jewish aid, through the Joint Distribution Committee, heavily subsidized educational reconstruction in all Western European countries. The German government paid compensation channeled through the *Conference on Jewish Material Claims against Germany. These funds made it possible to build new schools or to renovate old ones in practically all larger Jewish communities.

c) The creation of the State of Israel was an enormous stimulus for Jewish education.

d) The Jewish Agency through its emissary-teachers played an important role in upgrading the level of education throughout Western Europe.

As a result of all these factors there were in 1969 over 40 day schools, some in communities where none existed before the last war, such as Stockholm, Madrid, Zurich, and Basle.

Parallel with the building program went an effort to train teachers and to prepare textbooks. Individual teachers were sent for training to Israel or to England and teacher-training programs were set up in Italy, Holland, and Belgium, the last one recognized by the Belgian government.

The Claims Conference encouraged the printing of textbooks, some of which were translated and adapted into various European languages.

Israel educators provided in-service training for European Jewish teachers.

Jewish education in 1970 embraced approximately 50% of all children of school age in Western Europe. Out of every four children receiving some Jewish education, three attended supplementary schools and one a Jewish day school. The underlying approach in all these schools was based on religious teaching. Only one day school in Western Europe (Brussels) declared itself to be non-religious. Even this school had to introduce the teaching of festivals and Jewish practices because of the demand of parents. Almost all schools taught Hebrew as a language and were Israel oriented.

The day school system continued to thrive into the 21st century, but with varying levels of enrollment. In Paris there were over 20 such schools, including kindergartens, primary and secondary schools, and religious seminaries, but only 4% of French Jewish children were enrolled in these frameworks, despite the influx of tradition-minded North African immigrants that made France the third largest Jewish community in the world. There was also a rabbinical seminary ordaining rabbis. In Antwerp, most of the community's children were enrolled in seven Jewish schools, receiving an intensive religious education, while another four such schools operated in Brussels.

There were three Jewish primary schools in Germany in 2005, but with low enrollment, and a Jewish high school in Berlin (opened in 1993). In Switzerland, nine schools were operating in five cities. Two Jewish day schools operate in Amsterdam, one each for the traditional communities (primary and secondary school) and the ultra-Orthodox community (primary and secondary school). Furthermore, there are three institutes of higher learning – a *kolel*, a seminary, and the Institute of Jewish Studies in Leiden. In Italy Jewish schools were to be found in Rome, Milan, Florence, Genoa, Livorno, and Trieste.

For Education in Israel see *Israel, State of.

BIBLIOGRAPHY: *Enẓiklopedyah Ḥinnukhit*, 1–4 (1964). **WEBSITES:** www.fjc.ru; www.worldjewishcongress.org/communities.

[Stanley Abramovitch / Fred Skolnik (2nd ed.)]

YIDDISH EDUCATION

In Czarist Russia

Yiddish had been the language of instruction in the *ḥeder* and the *talmud torah* for as long as it had been the vernacular. However, in recent centuries the language itself was introduced into those institutions as a new subject, i.e., the art of writing. The instructor in this subject bore the designation of "*Shrayber*" (scribe). Ordinances of communities and societies determined his duties and assigned specific periods of time during which he was to "write" with his boys. This was a new tendency in Jewish education, a sort of secularism, since the "*Brifnshteler*" (as the textbooks were known) introduced new content into the subject of writing.

In the first quarter of the 19th century several of these *Brifnshteler* were stereotyped reprints of older editions. There is a list of 60 such letter composers. In 1826 there appeared a *Brifnshteler* by Abraham Leon Dor which was reprinted in 1843, 1861, 1868, 1870, 1873, 1876, and 1882. In 1850 his son, Hirsh Leon Dor, issued "letter learning," a new *Brifnshteler*, in which he included various kinds of letters, customs, business letters, and arithmetic. This work, too, appeared in several editions. Gradually these works acquired the character of reading textbooks. They introduced anecdotes and fables, ideas for entertainment and humor that made reading "enjoyable," even some elements of arithmetic and geography. These scribes gained entry into all types of schools and in small towns they organized groups and conducted systematic instruction for girls. The method of instruction of these groups carried the name *Shura Greizel*. In this manner the study of "Yiddish writing" became an attempt at secular education in Yiddish. At first the Russian school authorities tolerated this study, but after 1863 they began to oppose it and finally prohibited it.

A further development in the study of Yiddish was the establishment of the "Sabbath and Evening Schools" for the young (1859). In the 1860s such schools existed in Vilna, Berdichev, Zhitomir, Minsk, and other cities. The official language in these schools was Russian, but lectures were also given in Yiddish on nature study, geography, and Yiddish literature. The Russian government mistrusted these schools, closed some of them promptly, and authorization of new schools was obtained with great difficulty. Nevertheless the number of these Sabbath and evening schools grew and toward the end of the 19th century such schools were found in Vilna, Homel (Gomel), Grodno, Kovno (Kaunas), Yekaterinoslav, Kishinev, Kharkov, Lodz, and elsewhere. Some of these bore a cultural-philanthropic character; but there were also schools on which the teachers and leaders bestowed an ideological character, and they valued the role of the Yiddish language in the program. In the officially required Russian subjects Yiddish was used as an aid language. In this fashion did the Sabbath and evening schools prepare the ground for schools for secular studies in the mother tongue of the children. Schools in the Yiddish language were not legalized by the education authority, and this led to the opening of schools under disguised designations (as in Mir, Dokshitsy, Warsaw). Under various legal excuses the study of the Yiddish language was carried on in the authorized schools. Out of the 53 schools which the Society for the Diffusion of Enlightenment (*Mefiẓei Haskalah*) subsidized in 1909, there were 27 schools that included Yiddish in their programs, of which 16 were girls' schools, 3 boys', and 8 coeducational. In 1910 there was a school in Kremenchug which conducted instruction of all the subjects in Yiddish. In 1911, in the town of Demievka (a suburb of Kiev) a collective *ḥeder* established by several progressive teachers, who obtained certificates of *melammedim*, was legalized, and all the subjects of study were taught in Yiddish. In 1912 teachers and community leaders converted the Warsaw school *Ḥinnukh Yeladim* into one of general studies in the Yiddish language. Also the modernized *talmud torahs* in the country gradually introduced Yiddish into their program.

When World War I broke out, Jewish refugees from Poland and Lithuania flooded the cities of central Russia and the Ukraine. The Yiddishist teachers and the Progressive Democratic organizations began establishing schools for the refugees' children where instruction was carried on in Yiddish, under the approval of the new law of 1914. By 1916 there were several dozens of schools in which Yiddish was the language of instruction. Teachers adopted new methods of instruction, and they created suitable textbooks for the pupils and pedagogic literature for the teachers. The Russian Revolution of 1917–18 brought about great changes in Jewish education.

The Ukraine and Belorussia

During the brief existence of the "Jewish Ministry" and after its liquidation there were under the leadership of the "*Kultur Lige*" 63 active elementary schools, three secondary, and dozens of kindergartens and evening schools, all conducted in Yiddish. In 1920 the Ukraine experienced the Bolshevik upheaval and the People's Commissariat for Nationalities of the Soviet regime became the school authority over the Jewish educational institutions in the Ukraine, Belorussia, and Russia proper.

The next decade, 1921–31, was very productive in the Soviet Yiddish schools. In the Ukraine there were in 1931 a total of 831 schools with 94,000 students; Belorussia had 334 schools with 33,000 students; and there were also a number of high schools; in all, 160,000 children were given schooling in Yiddish. In the year 1933–34 the attitude of the authorities to Yiddish underwent a radical change and a decline set in; the number of schools diminished annually, reaching a catastrophic low level on the eve of World War II.

Poland

With liberation and unification of the Polish Republic a strong school movement developed among the Jews of that country. In 1920 Warsaw already had 14 all-Yiddish schools with 49 classes and 14 kindergartens, with a total of 2,000 children. Similar developments took place throughout the provinces. At a conference in 1921 attended by 376 delegates, the Central Yiddish School Organization (CYSHO) was formed, which included as its affiliates Yiddish schools of all trends. In 1921 there were, in 44 Polish cities, 69 Yiddish elementary schools and 35 kindergartens, having altogether 381 classes with 13,457 children.

The Polish government took a hostile position to these new secular Yiddish schools, but nevertheless freed their pupils from the obligation of attending other schools to meet the requirements of compulsory education. Various absurd police accusations were leveled against the schools. Schools were closed and teachers arrested or removed. Nevertheless the network of these CYSHO schools grew. In 1925 their numbers reached 91 elementary schools with 455 classes and 16,364 pupils; 3 secondary schools with 780 pupils. In 1929 there were 114 elementary schools with 17,380 pupils, 46 kindergartens, 52 evening schools, 3 secondary schools, and 1 teachers' training seminary, a grand total of 216 institutions with 24,000 pupils. The Polish government became ever more reactionary and antisemitic, which resulted in a quantitative decline in the schools, but their quality kept improving. The character of the CYSHO school became crystallized; its educational approach included also the social and national upbringing of the child, attachment to his people, and an attitude of social responsibility. The methodology of instruction was in consonance with these objectives. The pride of the CYSHO school movement was the children's sanatorium named after V. *Medem. This was a great creative institution with many pedagogic achievements. On the eve of World War II it had 250 children, and the institution was open the entire year. The children and teachers were all killed by the Nazis.

The Educational and Cultural Union (Shul un Kultur Farband) of the right-wing Poale Zion and of the nonpartisan organizations tried to open Yiddish schools with a stress also on Hebrew and *Yiddishkeit*. In 1934–35 they had in Poland seven elementary schools with 818 children. The ideological and programmatic effect of this movement was minimal. The number of the religious schools was large, 2,560 schools with 171,000 pupils. These schools too conducted their program in Yiddish. Thus, over 200,000 children received their schooling in the Yiddish language.

Borderlands

The 1917–18 upheaval in Russia freed the countries of the borderland areas: Lithuania, Latvia, Estonia and, in part, also Romania. In these countries the Yiddish language schools went through the same development as in Poland. In 1934 there were in Lithuania 16 elementary schools with 1,555 pupils and 3 secondary schools with 420 students. In 1933 Latvia had 122 Yiddish schools with 6,000 children (45% of the total Jewish child population). The Fascist revolution destroyed these school systems in both lands. In 1934 Estonia had one Yiddish school with 80 children. For a time the Yiddish schools in these countries enjoyed the same status as government schools and were maintained by the state. In Bessarabia (Romania) there were 62 Yiddish elementary schools with 5,757 pupils. The decreed Rumanization of education gradually brought about their liquidation.

United States and Canada

The October 1910 conference of the Poale Zion formulated a policy for Yiddish National Radical Schools and soon afterward the first such school was opened in New York. In 1911 the National Workers' Farband formed a committee to organize and maintain these National Radical schools. This school program was also supported by the Socialist-Territorialists and by non-partisan groups. However, differences of opinion arose on the place of Hebrew in the curriculum. One school in the Bronx seceded from the National Radical movement and, after the death of *Shalom Aleichem, took on the designation of Sholem Aleichem School. In 1918 several schools of this type organized the Sholem Aleichem Folk Institute. The Farband likewise changed the designation of its schools to Jewish Folk Schools.

In 1915 a new type of school made its appearance. Members of the Jewish Socialist Federation opened a school in Harlem, New York, and a year later, one in Chicago. In 1916 the Conference of the Workmen's Circle decided to "demand of all its branches that they support the Socialist Yiddish Schools"; and in 1918 their convention declared that the school enterprise was the duty of the entire organization and of its Education Committee. Thus there came into being three different school organizations. The schools of the Workmen's Circle and of the Sholem Aleichem Institute put the stress on Yiddish language and literature and Jewish history; the Farband stressed Hebrew and national traditional upbringing. At the end of 1927 there were 103 Workmen's Circle schools with 6,000 pupils. In 1928 the Farband opened in Montreal a day school vis-à-vis the Folkshulen, which operated as an institution for supplementary education. By 1919 it had 559 pupils; the Peretz schools in Winnipeg had 600 pupils. In 1929 the Sholem Aleichem Institute conducted three schools in Chicago, three in Detroit including a secondary school, and the New York schools with an enrollment of 1,400 pupils. World War II upset the whole school system. In 1956 the picture was as follows: Workmen's Circle, 85 elementary and six secondary schools; the Farband, 57 elementary schools and seven day schools; Sholem Aleichem Institute, 16 elementary schools and five kindergartens. The International Order, a left-wing organization (no longer in existence), maintained a number of schools with an enrollment of approximately 4,000 as of 1939. In 1969 the various organizations had the following numbers: Workmen's Circle, a total of 50 institutions (kindergartens, elementary, and secondary) with 2,500 pupils; Farband, 21 schools with 1,700 pupils; Sholem Aleichem Institute, nine schools (five of them with pre-school educational programs) and, jointly with the Workmen's Circle, one secondary school.

All these schools faced extraordinary social and pedagogic problems in the early postwar period. The differences in the educational ideologies of these organizations were substantially reduced. Yet each continued its work on its own (with the exception of the joint secondary school and the teachers' seminary). Since that time the large majority of these schools have disappeared.

Latin American Countries

In most of the countries of Latin America with any appreciable Jewish community there were Yiddish schools of which the majority were secular. Such schools were established in Argentina (1917–1921), Brazil (1945), and Mexico (1924) and originally the language of instruction was Yiddish. The schools were oriented to a Yiddish Bundist ideology and in Argentina a teachers' seminary was also established which by 1955 had graduated 265 teachers to work in such schools and had 170 pupils in 1967. However, with the steady acculturation of the Jews the vernacular, by and large, replaced Yiddish as the language of instruction although the schools still styled themselves as Yiddish. The establishment of the State of Israel and particularly the Six-Day War in 1967 gave tremendous impetus to the study of Hebrew.

General

A few Yiddish language schools, all of them supplementary, are to be found in cities throughout the world under both ultra-Orthodox and secular auspices. In Israel, particularly in Jerusalem, there are many *ḥadarim* in which the language of instruction is Yiddish and in which the curriculum is hardly different from that of Eastern European *ḥadarim* of the Middle Ages. In most of the major yeshivot in Israel the language of instruction is Yiddish; the students, however, speak mainly Hebrew among themselves. In England, both in London and Manchester, there were Yiddish language schools associated with the ultra-Orthodox ḥasidic groups. In these schools a minimum of instruction in secular subjects was given in order to accord with the Compulsory Education Act.

BIBLIOGRAPHY: H.S. Kazdan, *Fun Kheder un "Shkoles" bis Tsisho* (1956), 452; idem, *Di Geshikhte fun Yidishn Shulvezn in Umophangikn Poiln* (1947); Z. Yefroikin, in: *Algemayne Entsiklopedye Yidn*, 5 (1957), 166–219, includes bibliography; N. Mayzel, *ibid.*, 415–9; S. Rojansky, *ibid.*, 359–47, includes bibliography; E.H. Jeshurin, *100 Yor Moderne Yidishe Literatur* (1965), 260–458, a bibliographical list.

[Chaim S. Kazdan]

JEWISH EDUCATION IN THE UNITED STATES OF AMERICA

Early National Period

During the colonial and early national periods, Jewish education was not regarded as a communal responsibility. Congregational life was led by volunteer trustees and non-ordained religious functionaries (*ḥazzanim*). Indeed, the first rabbi to settle in the United States did not arrive until 1840. While Jews acquired burial grounds, built synagogues for public worship, and established mechanisms for aiding the poor, education was not treated as a public concern. Tutoring in Hebrew language, prayers, and Torah (primarily reading and translating) was provided for a fee, most commonly by independent teachers. On occasion, congregations would contract with an instructor to provide education to indigent children.

In the generation that the American colonies became a nation, the most prominent Jewish religious figure in the United States was Gershom Mendes *Seixas. Congregation Shearith Israel in New York, at which Seixas received his education and which he served as religious leader, conducted an all-day school from 1755 to 1776 and, intermittently, through the early decades of the 19th century. The aim of this initiative was to provide both Hebrew and general studies under Jewish auspices, as an alternative to secular training under non-Jewish, sectarian auspices.

In the early national period, almost all schools in New York City, as elsewhere, were religious in character. "Common pay" (i.e., private) schools generally assumed the religious identity of their headmaster; charity or "free schools," supported by churches, could draw funds from the state. Through a bequest, Shearith Israel established a charity school named Polonies Talmud Torah, in 1803. Starting in 1811, the school achieved equal footing with the Protestant and Catholic schools in the city, benefiting from state financial assistance. In New York, state support of religiously sponsored charity schools continued until 1825; public schools were, gradually, to achieve a monopoly over state funding of education throughout the country.

Shearith Israel's inability to maintain a school on a continuing basis was not only a function of uncertain state financial support, but of an apparent disinclination of its members to enroll their children. This may, in part, have resulted from the lack of educational leadership on a sustained basis. For example, when Emanuel N. Carvalho, a well-qualified teacher who had come to New York from London, served as the school's headmaster, 1808–11, there was a well-subscribed, full day instructional program. When Carvalho moved to Charleston, the school experienced years of intermittent openings and closings, depending on the availability and ability of teaching personnel. The Polonies Talmud Torah eventually turned to the provision of supplementary education, holding sessions on Sunday morning and Tuesday and Thursday afternoons. Primary attention was given to prayers, Bible, preparation for bar mitzvah, and elements of Hebrew language and grammar.

In Charleston, home to the largest population of Jews in America in the early 19th century, the Jewish community allocated no funds for a school – parents had to rely, exclusively, on private tutors. Savannah's Mikveh Israel offered no congregationally sponsored religious education before 1853. With a modest population, rapid acculturation, and a negligible educational infrastructure, Jewish learning in the early national period was at a low ebb.

Emergence of Sunday Schools

As public, non-sectarian schools became increasingly predominant, many Christian Sunday schools, initially established by "benevolent societies" to provide poor children with general as well as Christian religious educational opportunity – and to keep them off the streets on Sunday – became strictly religious institutions. By 1838, there were 8,000 Christian schools of this kind in the United States. Consistent with this trend, American-born Rebecca *Gratz (1781–1869), member of a prominent Jewish family of merchants and community leaders in Philadelphia, aided in founding the Female Hebrew Benevolent Society (1819) and the Hebrew Sunday School Society (1838). Rebecca Gratz was convinced that religious instruction for all Jewish children was imperative, particularly in the face of Christian proselytizing.

One month after securing the approval of the Female Hebrew Benevolent Society for this initiative, the Hebrew Sunday School opened with 50 students and six teachers (including Gratz, who served as superintendent). The volunteer faculty consisted of women respected for their moral character and intelligence. From its inception, the Jewish Sunday School movement was, as its Protestant counterpart, a women's movement. Women founded, directed, and taught at the schools, starting with the Philadelphia prototype, and girls attended alongside boys. In America, children's religious education was considered part of the domain of women, and women thus required religious education to properly educate their children. Financial support came from the FHBS, private donors, and Mikveh Israel (Philadelphia's well-established Sephardi congregation). Parents who could afford to do so paid $2 per year, and an annual appeal was held at a festive public exam.

Gratz's Philadelphia-based efforts benefited from the assistance of the *ḥazzan* of Mikveh Israel, Isaac *Leeser. By 1845, Jewish Sunday schools had been established in a number of communities, including New York, Charleston, Cincinnati, and Richmond. As in the Philadelphia model, Saturday and Sunday schools established in other locales were conducted on a coeducational basis. Jewish Sunday schools reinforced the middle class values of public schools and Protestant Sunday schools: obedience, order, punctuality, cleanliness, and self-discipline. They embraced the Protestant division between universal morality (the domain of public education) and particularistic forms (the province of supplementary religious education).

Leeser, who championed Jewish traditionalism throughout his career, authored a *Catechism for Younger Children* (1839), used in many of the schools. The catechism opened with reflections on religion in general, before turning to the "Mosaic Religion" in particular. He affirmed the divine origin of the Torah and its correct interpretation by the sages; hence, the enduring imperative of both the moral and ceremonial law. The catechism concluded with Maimonides' 13 principles of faith.

Leeser also published a Hebrew Reader, "Designed as an Easy Guide to the Hebrew Tongue, for Jewish Children and Self-Instruction," in 1838. The text devotes 23 pages to the development of skills for Hebrew reading, with the ensuing 25 pages applying those skills to such recurring prayers as *Adon Olam, Shema, Ma Tovu, Modeh Ani*, the opening paragraph of *Birkat ha-Mazon*, and *Yigdal*. While the work was reprinted a number of times, Leeser lamented, in his preface to the 1856 (fourth) edition, that though the book "has met with approbation, still the sale has been very slow, the demand for the various schools being quite small." Leeser, who founded a short-lived Jewish Publication Society in 1845, produced dozens of printed works, along with a widely disseminated periodical

(*The Occident*). Improvements in print technology and the declining cost of printed material led, at mid-century, to expanded publications of all kinds, including evangelical literature. Consequently, Jewish education and Jewish educational materials were essential both to strengthen the faith and to protect against proselytizing missionaries.

Even as he expressed the highest regard for the work of Rebecca Gratz and her assistants, Leeser urged the establishment of an all-day Jewish school for two basic reasons. First, it was impossible to achieve Hebrew literacy in "extra" hours. Second, the public or private schools were, in Leeser's view, essentially Christian. Where it was impracticable to conduct day schools, supplementary education needed to be strengthened – hence, Leeser's support of Rebecca Gratz's Sunday School initiative.

Educational Currents in the Era of Heightened German-Jewish Immigration, 1840–1880

During the period 1840 to 1880, the American Jewish community grew from 15,000 to 250,000, primarily bolstered by the immigration of Jews from German-speaking lands. German Jews spread through the length and breadth of the expanding nation and, with their geographic diffusion, the number of congregations grew from 18 to 277 by 1877. As in the colonial and early national periods, congregations typically progressed from establishing a burial society to forming a synagogue and, only later, providing some form of Jewish education.

In the 1840s and 1850s, many American schools were still conducted by churches, and instruction in the Christian religion was part of the curriculum. Many public schools had a distinctly Protestant tone. Within this context, Jewish day schools were established by immigrant Jews in a number of communities.

By the 1850s, seven Jewish day schools had been established in New York, enrolling more than 1,000 students. Similar schools were initiated in other cities, including Philadelphia, Baltimore, Chicago, Boston, Albany, Cincinnati, Detroit, Essex County, New Jersey, Pittsburgh, and Washington, D.C. A typical school of this kind was the one organized by Kehillath Anshe Maariv Congregation, in Chicago in 1853. The school was patterned on similar schools in Germany, where the curriculum included general studies supplemented by instruction in Jewish religion, Hebrew prayers, and Bible reading in German translation. At KAM, in addition to English, German, arithmetic, geography, drawing, and singing, prayers and readings from the Pentateuch, as well as catechism relating to Jewish religion and history, were part of the curriculum. The "common" school branches were taught by non-Jewish instructors, with a rabbi or cantor responsible for Jewish studies. The commitment of German-Jewish immigrants to maintaining German culture is reflected in the fact that of the 17 mid-19th century Jewish day schools with extant curricular information, all schools included German.

Several private boarding schools teaching Jewish and secular subjects also operated in the middle of the 19th century. The creation of this variety of day school reflected their founders' interest in the Jewish education of their children, an interest in preserving German culture, a desire for "quality assurance" in their children's schooling (the developing public schools were not, uniformly, seen as centers of educational excellence), and concern about sectarianism in public schools. Intensive Hebrew education was, not always, of paramount interest; often, one hour per day was devoted to Jewish studies.

In the 1840s, Hebrew literary associations, maintaining libraries and conducting lectures, were founded in several cities. From references in Jewish newspapers, it appears that literary discussion groups typically were conducted separately by and for men and women. During the 1860s and 1870s, a new type of organization – the Young Men's Hebrew Association (YMHA) – was established in a number of communities (the first YMHA had been organized in Baltimore in 1854 but suspended its activities in 1860–68). The YMHA aimed to foster improved knowledge of the literature, history, and doctrines of Judaism. The "Y" often included a library of Jewish reading matter and offered lectures and classes for young men and women in Jewish history and Hebrew language. Y's thus met the need of young adults for a congenial social and intellectual milieu.

During the 1860s, Christian missionaries operating on New York's East Side operated a school teaching Jewish children Bible in Hebrew. Mission schools, with conversionary aims, appeared in other poor Jewish neighborhoods. In 1864, several congregations organized the Hebrew Free School, as a countermeasure. Five branches were established and, in addition to Jewish education, pupils were supplied with clothing and other necessities. Similarly, Jewish Y's introduced gymnasiums and sports as a counterinfluence to Christian missionaries, and in imitation of YMCAS.

While, in the development of American Jewry, the period 1840–80 was, primarily, an era of Western and Central European Jewish settlement and institution building, a trickle of Eastern European Jewish immigration was already apparent by the 1850s. New York's first East European congregation, Beth Hamidrash Hagodol, founded in 1852, established a *talmud torah* (supplementary Jewish school) for the instruction of children attending New York City public schools. This school was, in the 1880s, to become a communally supported *talmud torah* known as Mahazikai Talmud Torah.

As public schools, through exclusive state funding, came to be viewed as superior educational settings, Jews (unlike Catholics) increasingly opted for public education. For the American-born generation of parents with children of school age in the 1870s – by which time public education had become well established throughout the country – public schooling was a "given." By 1875, no Jewish day schools remained in operation.

Though, by 1860, there were 150,000 Jews in the United States, there was no institution of higher Jewish learning. All American rabbis were foreign-born and -trained immigrants.

An attempt to create an academy of higher Jewish learning, spearheaded by Isaac Leeser, was initiated, in 1867, with the founding of Maimonides College in Philadelphia. Leeser died in 1868, and the College disbanded in 1873.

An enduring college for the training of American rabbis was established by Isaac Mayer *Wise, the institution-builder of Reform Judaism in America. The Bohemian-born Wise, who had immigrated to the U.S. in 1846, succeeded in forming a "Union of American Hebrew Congregations" in 1873, with 34 participating synagogues. In turn, the Union, in 1875, sponsored the establishment of the *Hebrew Union College for the training of rabbis. The college, based in Cincinnati, with Isaac M. Wise as its president, was to take root and grow. Though Wise's vision of the possibility of a "Minhag America," an "American Way," among the Jews of the U.S. was not realized, the UAHC and HUC were destined to become pillars of American Reform Judaism.

It is estimated that, in 1880, there were 40,000–50,000 Jewish children of school age in the United States. Of this number, no more than 15,000 received some type of Jewish education in "Sabbath school" one or two days a week (Saturday afternoon and/or Sunday morning) or through private lessons. "Sabbath school" was generally of three to five years' duration. The curriculum consisted of Bible stories, religious thought (through catechism), and a few Hebrew verses used in worship. The first Jewish children's magazine in America, *The Hebrew Sabbath School Visitor,* founded and edited by Dr. Max Lilienthal, was initiated as an instructional aid for such schools, in 1874. Commonly, the rabbi served as "Superintendent," and volunteers taught the classes at these very part-time schools. In a paper on "Pedagogics in the Sabbath-School," presented in 1880, Moses Mielziner, professor at the HUC, reported that of 118 congregations affiliated with the UAHC (representing more than 40% of the then existing congregations), only 12 did not have a Sabbath school.

Educational Responses to Mass Migration from Eastern Europe, 1881–1910

Though East European Jews were to be found among the immigrants of earlier generations, a rising "wave" of such immigrants came to the shores of the U.S. in 1881–1910. The new immigration resulted not only from political persecution but from lack of economic opportunity, exacerbated by a fivefold increase in East European Jewish population in the 19th century. Swelled by immigration, primarily (though certainly not exclusively) from Eastern Europe, the American Jewish population reached two million by 1910.

East European immigrants transplanted to the United States the traditional educational institutions of their native lands. The immigrants' readiness to adjust to American life was manifest in their adoption of the public school for their children. On the Lower East Side of New York City, where Jewish immigrants were most heavily concentrated, 38 elementary schools, serving a total population of 65,000 students, included 60,000 Jews by 1905. The most prevalent form of Jewish education established by the new immigrants (primarily for boys) was the *ḥeder,* a private one-room school, open every weekday of the year. The teachers in most cases were ill-educated men untrained in pedagogy. Parents were too busy with their jobs in the sweatshops or small businesses to have the time to consider the quality of their children's education, or to exercise some control of the *ḥeder,* as was the case in their country of origin. The "curriculum" consisted of mechanical reading of prayers, study of the Torah portion of the week, recitation of portions of liturgy, and bar mitzvah preparation.

The *talmud torah*, an educational framework maintained in Eastern Europe for the children of the poor, developed as a promising alternative to the *ḥeder* in America. It was, typically, founded and managed by residents of a given neighborhood, financed by a paid membership and through synagogue appeals. These schools tended to be staffed by more competent teachers, among them nationalist Jews, products of the Russian *Haskalah and the *Ḥibbat Zion movement. The curriculum of most *talmud torah* schools approximated that of the East European elementary *ḥeder*: Hebrew reading (of the prayerbook), word by word translation – typically, into Yiddish – of the Pentateuch, and the commentary of Rashi on the Torah.

Concomitant with the onset of mass migration was an "awakening" in Jewish life among young, American-born Jews who, by the late 1870s, had lost confidence in the liberal, universalist visions of the era. This awakening expressed itself in initiatives for the revitalization of Jewish education. One manifestation of this agenda was the Jewish Chautauqua Society, launched by Henry *Berkowitz, one of the four men in the initial (1883) graduating class of HUC, in 1893. The Chautauqua Society had been developed by Bishop John H. Vincent of the Methodist Episcopal Church in 1874. Begun as an intensive training program for Sunday school teachers (with a summer assembly at Lake Chautauqua, New York), the society established local reading circles and adult correspondence courses. By the 1880s, it had become a forum for the discussion of politics, literature, science, economics, and religion. Dozens of local Chautauqua assemblies were launched; hence, Rabbi Berkowitz's initiative in launching the Jewish Chautauqua Society in Philadelphia (where he served as rabbi of Rodeph Sholom Temple) was also part of a national phenomenon.

The Jewish Chautauqua Society held its first summer assembly in 1894. By 1908, it had 125 circles, with 2,500 members. Starting in 1909, it sent scholars to teach summer courses on Jewish topics at universities (a function which, by the 1930s, was to become the society's central focus), and, in 1915, it initiated a correspondence school. This adult education project sprang from the sense of its leaders and supporters that Jewish education was sorely lacking.

While the Jewish Chautauqua Society focused on adults, the Jewish education of children was, likewise, a significant concern. Indeed, the first book published by the newly established Jewish Publication Society, in 1890, was a revised edition of a work (initially published in England, in 1886) by

British children's author Lady Katie Magnus, titled *Outlines of Jewish History*. The book sold tens of thousands of copies and went through numerous printings.

The first yeshivah day school in the U.S., Yeshivat Etz Chaim, an all-day Jewish school for elementary school boys, was established in New York in 1886. The school's constitution averred that "the purpose of this Academy shall be to give free instruction to poor Hebrew children in the Hebrew language and the Jewish religion – Talmud, Bible and Shulhan Aruk – during the whole day from nine in the morning until four in the afternoon. Also from four in the afternoon, two hours shall be devoted to teach the native language, English, and one hour to teach Hebrew – Loshon Hakodesh – and jargon [Yiddish] to read and write. The Academy shall be guided according to the strict Orthodox and Talmudic law and the custom of Poland and Russia." The general studies program also included grammar, arithmetic, reading, and spelling. Though called a "yeshivah," this elementary school, as others later to be established, differed significantly from its European predecessors, both with regard to the age of its students and to the breadth of its curriculum (which included general education).

In the ensuing decades, additional yeshivah schools, including the Rabbi Jacob Joseph Yeshiva (1900), the Yeshiva Rabbi Chaim Berlin (1906), and the Talmudical Institute of Harlem (1908), were established. To meet the continuing Jewish educational needs of Etz Chaim graduates and of teenage immigrants at advanced levels of talmudic study, the Rabbi Isaac Elchanan Theological Seminary (RIETS) was founded in 1897, creating a framework for the training of (Orthodox) rabbis. RIETS combined with Yeshivat Etz Chaim in 1915; the expanded institution was headed by Lithuanian-born Bernard *Revel (1885–1940), a scholar who had studied at the yeshivah of Telz and who, after emigrating, had earned a doctorate from the recently established Dropsie College in Philadelphia.

The Reform Pittsburgh Platform of 1885 had led established ("Americanized") traditionalists to band together to create a more traditionalist seminary than the HUC. The driving force behind the founding of the *Jewish Theological Seminary, which opened its doors in New York in 1887, was Sabato *Morais (1823–1897), who had succeeded Isaac Leeser as *ḥazzan* of Mikveh Israel in Philadelphia. Among the seminary's founders, in addition to Morais, were American-born, European-ordained Rabbis Bernard *Drachman and Henry Schneeberger, recently arrived Hungarian-born Rabbi Alexander Kohut, and the British-born *ḥazzan* of Shearith Israel (New York), Henry Pereira Mendes. In the early years of the 20th century, the seminary received significant financial support from such well established (Reform) German Jews as Jacob *Schiff, Felix M. *Warburg, David *Guggenheim, and Louis *Marshall, who hoped that it would attract Russian Jews and prepare them to be leaders in the Americanization of immigrants.

Under the leadership of Solomon *Schechter (1847–1915), reader in rabbinics at Cambridge University, who assumed the presidency of the fledgling Seminary in 1902, JTS became a center of Jewish scholarship and a core institution in the emerging Conservative stream of Judaism. Of great significance in the unfolding history of Jewish education in the United States was the establishment at JTS of a Teachers Institute (1909). Mordecai *Kaplan (1881–1983), himself a JTS rabbinical graduate, was appointed dean of the new Institute by Schechter.

The Teachers Institute, which was to play an important role in training a cadre of Jewish educators in the decades that followed, was the second Jewish institution for the preparation of teachers to be founded in the United States. The first, *Gratz College, had been launched in Philadelphia in 1893 through a bequest of Philadelphia merchant and philanthropist, Hyman Gratz, brother of Rebecca Gratz. Both of these teachers' colleges, as others established in the ensuing years, were open to and attracted significant numbers of women.

While an organic process of Jewish educational development was in evidence, an "external" event served as the catalyst for a pivotal, communal educational initiative in New York City. In the September 1908 issue of the *North American Review*, New York Police Commissioner Theodore A. Bingham commented that half of the city's criminals were "Hebrews" and that Hebrew juveniles were emulating the adults in this regard. This accusation served to galvanize hundreds of New York Jewish organizations – synagogues, federations, fraternal lodges, and professional societies – to establish the "New York Kehillah" in 1909. The Kehillah was headed by San Francisco-born, HUC-ordained Judah *Magnes (1877–1948), rabbi at New York's Temple Emanu-El. Magnes was close to the premier German-Jewish banking families who formed the leadership of Emanu-el and was the brother-in-law of the prominent Louis Marshall. At the same time, he was attracted to the Yiddish intellectual milieu of the East Side Russian immigrants, among whom he enjoyed a broad-based following.

One response to the Police Commissioner's charge was the establishment by the Kehillah of a Committee on Jewish Education to survey the state of Jewish education and to develop appropriate responses to needs that would be identified. The survey was undertaken by Professor Mordecai Kaplan of the Jewish Theological Seminary and Dr. Bernard Cronson, a public school principal.

The report identified six frameworks within which Jewish education was being conducted:

(a) *talmud torah* schools
(b) institutional schools
(c) congregational schools
(d) Sunday schools
(e) Chedorim (*ḥadarim*)
(f) private tutors

The *talmud torah* schools, opined the researchers, "instill more Jewishness into the lives of the children" than any of the other educational settings; and this, despite the facts that: "homework is never allotted; the discipline is poor; the attendance is very irregular and seldom kept up for any length of time."

The institution schools (operated by orphan asylums and social work agencies – often sponsored by German-Jewish-supported charitable groups) – had the benefit of good pedagogy and materials, but lacked the confidence of the population it aimed to serve, "because they do not regard it as Jewish enough insofar as it makes Hebrew only secondary." The congregational school, holding sessions three or more times per week, was typically sponsored by a Conservative or Orthodox synagogue. Here, "the work covered is not very extensive, and is usually confined to the reading and translation of the prayers, and of a few passages in the Bible, with a smattering of a few rules of grammar." Sunday schools, reported the survey, engaged a cadre of public school teachers, mostly women, many of whom volunteered their services. However, these teachers lacked "the knowledge necessary for a Jewish school," and carried out "a vague kind of curriculum...." As to the *ḥeder,* the researchers described it in the following, critical terms:

> A cheder is a school conducted by one, two or three men, for the sole purpose of eking out some kind of livelihood which they failed to obtain by any other means. It generally meets in a room or two, in the basement or upper floor of some old dilapidated building where the rent is at a minimum....The instruction, which seldom goes beyond the reading of the prayer book, and the teaching of a few blessings by rote, is carried on only in Yiddish. The method of instruction is quite unique. It consists of about fifteen minutes of individual instruction, with seldom or never any class work. Each pupil, not knowing when he is needed, straggles in at random, and waits for his turn to come, in the meantime entertaining himself with all sorts of mischief. When his turn comes and the teacher has given him the fifteen minutes, he runs off. There is hardly an ideal aim in the mind of the teacher, except in some cases it is the training for the Bar Mitzvah feat of reading the Haftorah.

The survey could not gauge the number of students who might have been receiving private tutoring, nor did the tally include the handful of day schools and their several hundred students. It was estimated that 21–24% of 200,000 Jewish children of school age were in the *talmud torah*, institutional, congregational and Sunday schools, and the various *ḥadarim*.

Ready to undertake communal action to address these challenges, the Kehillah of New York initiated a response which was to be replicated in the decades ahead in scores of American Jewish communities. It established a Bureau of Jewish Education. The Bureau was to provide educational guidance and service, and organize and coordinate activities beyond the capacity of any one school unit to conduct. In the ensuing generation, the concept of community responsibility in the domain of Jewish education was to be embraced by federations and central Jewish philanthropies in cities across the country. The BJE, launched through a $50,000 contribution from Jacob Schiff and $25,000 from the New York Foundation, was, initially, to perform the following specific functions:

> 1. To study sympathetically and at close range all the Jewish educational forces in New York City, including alike those that restrict themselves to religious instruction and those that look primarily to the Americanization of our youth, with a view to cooperation and the elimination of waste and overlapping.
> 2. To become intimately acquainted with the best teachers and workers who are the mainstay of these institutions, and organize them for both their material and their spiritual advancement.
> 3. To make propaganda through the Jewish press and otherwise, in order to acquaint parents with the problem before them and with the means for solving it.
> 4. To operate one or two model schools for elementary pupils, for the purpose of working out the various phases of primary education, these schools to act also as concrete examples and guides to now existing Hebrew schools, which will undoubtedly avail themselves of the textbooks, methods, appliances, etc. worked out in the model schools....

Dr. Samson *Benderly, of Baltimore, who had served as a consultant to the Kehillah on the Kaplan-Cronson survey and its analysis, was engaged as director of the new Bureau. Having worked with the Kehillah's education committee for a year, Benderly's educational and ideological positions were clear to Judah Magnes and to the Board which hired him. Benderly's ideas were to shape the work of the New York Bureau and influence scores of Jewish educators summoned to leadership in communities throughout the country.

Samson Benderly (1876–1944) was born and raised in Safed. At age 15, he traveled to Beirut to study at the American University. After completing a B.A., he began medical studies. In 1898, Dr. Aaron Friedenwald, professor of ophthalmology in Baltimore, visited Beirut, and encouraged Benderly's interest in coming to the United States. By September 1898 Benderly had moved to Baltimore, where he completed his medical studies at the College of Physicians and Surgeons (he earned his degree and began residency, in June 1900). Concurrently, he undertook to teach Hebrew and direct a Jewish school.

Having, because of the demands of time, to choose between medicine and Jewish education, Benderly chose the latter. His Hebrew immersion program (*Ivrit be-Ivrit*) included not only Hebrew language, but also Bible, holidays, history, and activities designed to nurture strong connection to Israel. In 1905, he initiated a youth group called "Herzl's children." He used visual aids and incorporated music, dance, and drama as instructional tools.

Though having begun his Baltimore career at a synagogue school, Benderly left, early on, to head the "Hebrew Free School for Poor and Orphaned Children." Interestingly, early in his Baltimore stay, Benderly served as Hebrew tutor to his "patron" Dr. *Friedenwald's son, Harry, then in his thirties, who was to become president of the Federation of Zionists in America – later known as the Zionist Organization of America. At the same time, he tutored Henrietta *Szold (also an adult learner) who was soon (1912) to found Hadassah.

Benderly's "Zionist-nationalist" bent was not unknown to the Kehillah committee that enlisted him. His pedagogic approach, centering on children and the development of a school-based society, was rooted in the progressive education ideals of John Dewey. For Benderly, as for Dewey, all human association – and most assuredly, the intentional constructs of schools – were educative, ensuring cultural continuity. The executive committee to which Benderly reported in New York consisted of five individuals, four of whom were Zionists (Israel *Friedlaender, Judah L. Magnes, Mordecai Kaplan, and Henrietta Szold). The fifth, Louis Marshall, was close to Jacob Schiff, and was likely keeping a watchful eye on the project for Schiff.

Modern Zionism had, already, expressed itself in two "*aliyyot*" to Palestine, several Zionist Congresses, and numerous Zionist ideologies. For Benderly and his committee, it was the cultural Zionism of *Aḥad Ha-Am combined with a commitment to Americanism, which shaped an emerging approach to Jewish education. In the modern era, the Zionist center (Palestine) would, it was supposed, serve as a spiritual hub of renewed Jewish cultural creativity, nurturing Jewish life in the Diaspora. Consistent with the findings of the Kaplan-Cronson report, the vehicle which Benderly and his supporters saw as best suited to furthering Jewish consciousness and commitment to Jewish ideals was the *talmud torah* school.

Institutional Development, 1910–1945

The New York BJE, created as a mechanism for improving and expanding Jewish education in a burgeoning community, undertook a vigorous program of federating and supporting *talmud torah* schools, providing in-service professional training to educators, writing modern textbooks, and recruiting pupils. *Talmud torah* curricula – typically, Hebrew-based (consistent with cultural Zionist nationalism) – included Hebrew language and literature, Bible, festivals, Palestine (as the source of Jewish creativity), selections from Midrash and the Talmud, Jewish history, and some degree of synagogue ritual familiarity (customs and ceremonies). Among the curricular innovations of the BJE was the use of arts and crafts and of music and dramatics in the instructional program. The BJE also gathered together graduates of the various *talmud torahs* and organized a Hebrew High School. A Board of Teachers' License and a Hebrew Principals' Association were organized; a summer camp was opened; the League of Jewish Youth was organized. Benderly successfully encouraged a group of young American Jews to study both Judaica and education, in preparation for professional careers in Jewish education.

Bureau-supported communal *talmud torah* schools had a decidedly Hebraic-Zionist emphasis, with much of the instructional program conducted *Ivrit be-Ivrit* (in Hebrew). Communal sponsorship and the Hebrew language emphasis (a cultural unifier) established the *talmud torah* as a community, "non-denominational" program. With few exceptions, *talmud torah* schools operated on a coeducational basis, consistent with the prevailing practice in public schools and Sabbath schools. As in Sabbath schools and public schools, women were well represented in the teaching force.

Yiddish (secular) schools offered a significant alternative. Starting in 1908, in Brownsville, New York – an area with a large, working class population noted for socialist leanings – Yiddish schools of various kinds were founded in every major locus of Jewish settlement. Among the larger networks of Yiddish schools were those of the Arbeiter Ring (Workmen's Circle), grounded in secularism and radicalism. Such schools were essential, their sponsors believed, both because the public schools were largely controlled by capitalists and because education in "*Yiddishkeit*," the culture of the immigrant generation, would bridge the disaffection between immigrant parents and their American-born and educated children. By the mid-1920s, the peak period of Yiddish secular education, 10,000 to 12,000 children attended *folkshuln* which centered on the study of Yiddish. At the other end of the spectrum, Orthodox day schools continued to be established in the early decades of the 20th century, though at a slow pace. In 1928, 4,290 students were enrolled in 17 such schools. Immigration restrictions, implemented in 1925, put an end to the massive influx of immigrants; by that time, more than 4 million Jews called America home.

A noteworthy structural opportunity for part-time Jewish study presented itself, beginning 1913, with the spread of the "Gary Plan" initiated in Gary, Indiana. The "Gary Plan," among other innovations, authorized release time during the school day for religious instruction, off campus. In New York, the plan was supported by the Reform movement and opposed by supporters of the *talmud torah* system. Reform educators were finding Sunday-only instruction insufficient to meet their Jewish educational goals. Release time might have represented a "slot" for additional instructional time. The Gary Plan, on the other hand, lengthened the school day. Supporters of the 5-days-per-week *talmud torah*, which drew children from multiple public schools, were concerned about negative impact on scheduling and enrollment in the established, more intensive Jewish educational programs. While the Gary Plan did not long survive, it evoked varying pronouncements within the Jewish community on church-state considerations relating to education. Discussions of "strict separation" of church and state were to become a matter of considerable debate later in the 20th century surrounding the issue of public funding in support of education in non-public schools.

Non-Formal Education

In 1913, many of the country's YMHAS and YWHAS (which had come into being starting in 1888) organized to form the Council of Young Men's Hebrew and Kindred Associations. The Y's cooperated with the Jewish Welfare Board, established in 1917, to provide Jewish chaplains and support services (starting with meeting religious needs) for Jews serving in the armed forces. In 1921, the Council of Young Men's Hebrew and Kindred Associations merged with JWB. Many mergers of YMHAS and YWHAS ensued, with most of the "new" institutions taking the name Jewish Community Center. In 1990, the JWB itself was to be renamed the Jewish Community Centers Association of North America. From their inception, the centers inherited from the Y's a culture of Americanizing Russian Jewish newcomers.

The first Jewish residential camps date to the closing decade of the 19th century, and a 1936 directory of Jewish camps sponsored by Jewish communal organizations listed 88 such camps in the U.S. and Canada. In the "fresh air" camps, Jewish experiences were, by no means, paramount; rather, good health and Americanization were emphasized. Under the influence of progressive educational thinking which recognized the rich possibilities for individual and group development inherent in camping, Jewish educational camping was launched starting in 1919 by Dr. Albert P. Schoolman. Schoolman, a disciple of Samson Benderly, founded CEJWIN (Central Jewish Institute) camps, to use the summer months to continue and strengthen the educational program of the Institute's *talmud torah* program. Jewish camps of diverse ideologies, both communal and private, were soon operating.

In the early decades of the 20th century, informal Jewish youth movements were formed, including such Zionist youth groups as Young Judaea (1909), Hashomer Hatzair (1923), AZA (1924), and Habonim Dror (1935). The (Reform) North American Federation of Temple Youth – NFTY (1939) and (Conservative) Leadership Training Fellowship (1945) followed suit. By 1940, there existed 30 American, nationally organized Jewish youth groups. Many served young people ages 18 to 25 or 30; only four (Young Israel, Agudat Israel Youth, Young Judea, and Hashomer Hatzair) served children under 12 years of age. Tabulation of membership in 26 of the 30 national Jewish youth organizations for the year 1939–40, showed 61,019 males and 99,262 females participating.

As young immigrants and the children of immigrants proceeded in increasing numbers to colleges, Jewish campus organizations were initiated. The Menorah movement began with the founding at Harvard University of the Harvard Menorah Society for the Study and Advancement of Jewish Ideals, in 1906. Jewish student organizations were, similarly, founded at several other universities. At a convention at the University of Chicago, the Intercollegiate *Menorah Association was launched, in 1913. The object of the IMA, as articulated in its constitution, was "the promotion in American colleges and universities of the study of Jewish history, culture and problems, and the advancement of Jewish ideals." Basic elements of any Menorah Society were lectures and study circles. By 1917, there were more than 60 such societies.

The exclusively intellectual focus of the IMA made it less appealing to many collegiates than the *Hillel Centers, which emerged in the 1920s. Hillel, which began at the University of Illinois in Champaign in 1923, encouraged social and cultural as well as scholarly programs. B'nai B'rith undertook sponsorship of Hillel in 1925, and Hillel Foundations were soon established at Wisconsin, Ohio State, West Virginia, California, Texas, and Cornell. The Intercollegiate phase of the Menorah Association ended by the late 1920s.

Institutions of Higher Learning, National Organizations, New Initiatives

In addition to Gratz College and the Teachers Institute of JTS, institutions for the education of Jewish teachers were established in New York, Baltimore, Boston, Pittsburgh, Cleveland, and Chicago between 1917 and 1929. The communal model of *talmud torah* education seemed headed for ascendancy in the American environment, and Hebrew teachers colleges, it was anticipated, would train the necessary faculties for a growing educational system. Moreover, these institutions were centers of higher Jewish learning, and their instructors often saw their mission as nothing less than ensuring the continuity of Jewish life.

As the teaching profession grew – in number of practitioners and level of training – several teachers' organizations were established, including a Hebrew Teachers Union. To link the efforts of communities across the country, the National Council for Jewish Education was created in 1926, as a forum for Jewish educational leaders. This organization became a catalyst for the establishment (1939) of the American Association for Jewish Education (AAJE) as a national service agency in the field of Jewish education. The AAJE served, in part, as a link among and between local bureaus of Jewish education which were, increasingly, becoming educational service providers to synagogue schools, rather than *talmud torah* operators.

An enrollment shift towards synagogue-based schools (as Jews moved from urban centers) was, already, in process after World War I. In the generation of 1910 to 1935, the percentage of children enrolled in synagogue-based Jewish schools rose from 35% to 60%. While *talmud torah* schools commonly met 4–5 days, 10–12 hours per week, congregational schools typically provided no more than 6 weekly hours of instruction and often lacked clear, curricular goals. In a notable resolution (1923) which, very gradually, came to be mirrored in practice, the Commission on Jewish Education of the Union of American Hebrew Congregations, headed by Emanuel *Gamoran, a disciple of Benderly, urged that UAHC schools add a weekday session to the existing Sunday program. The Conservative movement's Commission on Jewish Education of the United Synagogue was established in 1940, and urged an educational program of no fewer than 6 hours per week.

Despite the decline of the communal, Hebraic-Zionist-oriented *talmud torah*, the supplementary schools operated by congregations of the growing Conservative movement continued to emphasize Hebrew language, and were commonly known as "Hebrew schools." While Hebrew had, at one time, been seen as a means to accessing classical Jewish texts ("*talmud torah*" in the sense of studying Torah), Hebrew proficiency – both in communal and congregational schools – gradually assumed paramount status, with classical (Hebrew) texts studied with the aim of improving Hebrew language proficiency.

Beyond the earlier-established HUC, JTS, and RIETS, a number of academies and yeshivot of higher Jewish learning were established in the early decades of the 20th century, as East European immigration continued. These included Tifereth Yerushalayim of New York (1908), Torah V'daath of New York (1918), Hebrew Theological College of Chicago (1921),

Ner Israel of Baltimore (1934), and the Jewish Institute of Religion, organized in New York, in 1922 (JIR, founded by Stephen S. Wise, was to become part of HUC in 1950). JIR, a liberal rabbinical seminary, was – unlike HUC – pro-Zionist and welcoming of the immigrant East European Jews. Through a bequest of Moses Aaron Dropsie, *Dropsie College, an independent, non-theological institution dedicated to research in Jewish studies and related branches of learning, was established in Philadelphia in 1909.

In 1928, the Rabbi Isaac Elchanan Theological Seminary (RIETS) opened a College of Liberal Arts and Sciences, alongside its rabbinical school. Yeshiva President Bernard Revel recruited Rabbi Moses *Soloveitchik, scion of a world-renowned rabbinic family, to head the RIETS faculty in 1929. On the death of Rabbi Soloveitchik (1941), his son, Rabbi Joseph *Soloveitchik, talmudic scholar and Ph.D. in philosophy from the University of Berlin, became head of the RIETS Talmud faculty. The "Rav," as Soloveitchik came to be known, was to emerge as the "towering ideologue" of American Orthodoxy in the 1940s and beyond.

At Hebrew Union College, Kaufman *Kohler served as president in 1903–21. Kohler, whose religious ideology was expressed in the Pittsburgh Platform of 1885, expanded the faculty, brooking no tolerance of Zionist leanings. He was succeeded as president by Julian *Morgenstern, an HUC alumnus, and professor of Bible. During Morgenstern's tenure (1921–47), a dozen European Jewish scholars found a haven at the College, largely through his efforts.

At the Jewish Theological Seminary, Solomon Schechter was succeeded as president by Cyrus *Adler, who served until his death in 1940. Adler, an American-born, Hopkins-trained semiticist, took part in founding the Jewish Publication Society of America (1888), was a founder of the American Jewish Historical Society (1892), served on the staff of the Smithsonian Institution, played a leading role in the reorganization of the Seminary and its engagement of Solomon Schechter, was President of Dropsie College, and edited numerous publications, including the first seven volumes of the *American Jewish Yearbook* and the *Jewish Quarterly Review* (1916–40). Consistent with Adler's personal interests, it was during his tenure that JTS developed a pre-eminent library collection. Adler's successor was Louis *Finkelstein, a JTS alumnus. Both HUC and JTS had thus succeeded in educating leaders who could carry forward the spiritual-religious mission articulated by these institutions' founders.

Between 1917 and 1939, four "progressive" Jewish day schools were established; these schools aimed to synthesize progressive and Jewish education. Limited time was devoted to Hebrew studies. Three of these schools closed their doors after brief periods of operation for lack of pupils and financial support. The fourth of the progressive schools (Brandeis "bi-cultural" school) eventually affiliated with the Conservative movement.

In 1937, the Ramaz School in Manhattan and Maimonides School in Boston were established. These Orthodox day schools aimed at providing outstanding general education alongside excellent, classical Jewish education. Each of these schools was to grow and develop (continuing into the 21st century), serving as a model to future generations of modern Orthodox day schools. In 1939, an experiment in Jewish pre-school education was initiated in New York, with the establishment of Beth Hayeled (House of the Child) School. Children entered the program at the age of three, remained at Beth Hayeled five years, and transferred to public school (and a neighborhood *talmud torah*) in third grade. Soon after this program began, additional such early childhood "foundation" schools were established.

Though, by the beginning of World War II, there were 7,000 students in 30 day schools (almost all of which were in New York), most Orthodox leaders shared the view that, when it came to formal Jewish schooling, the congregationally sponsored *talmud torah* was to be the primary institutional framework for religious education. In 1942, the Union of Orthodox Jewish Congregations published a curriculum guide for *talmud torah* education. The curriculum was designed, ideally, for a ten-hours-per-week school. Interestingly, as in the educational programs developed and promoted by Samson Benderly and his protégés, the Orthodox "Model Program" called for *Ivrit be-Ivrit* (Hebrew-based) instruction. Though influenced by the pedagogic approach of the Benderly "school," the UOJC manual made it clear that it brooked no tolerance for deviation from traditional Jewish belief and practice.

With the relocation of several leading personalities of Jewish educational life from Europe to the United States before and during World War II, a number of new institutions appeared on the American scene. These included Lubavitcher schools, established with the arrival of the Lubavitcher Rebbe in 1940, the creation of Bais Yaakov (*Beth Jacob) girls schools in the early 1940s, and the establishment, in 1941, of the Telshe Yeshiva in Cleveland and, in 1943, the Beth Medrash Govoha in Lakewood, New Jersey. In 1944, under the impetus of Shraga Feivel Mendlowitz, an immigrant from Austria-Hungary, who had studied with noted European rabbinic scholars and significantly expanded Brooklyn's Torah V'daath yeshiva, an ambitious Orthodox day school initiative was launched.

Mendlowitz, who had devoted himself to Jewish education in the U.S. since his arrival in 1913, aimed to "jump start" and unite a national network of (Orthodox) yeshivah day schools. Towards that end, Mendlowitz enlisted Samuel *Feuerstein, a successful business executive, to serve as president of the "Torah Umesorah Society for the Establishment of Torah Schools." The articles of incorporation of the society firmly established the ideological authority of a body of Orthodox rabbis in all matters of religious life appertaining to its functions; indeed, the Rabbinical Supervisory Council would determine the very scope of its jurisdiction, since it would decide what constituted a religious matter. A group of Orthodox rabbinical leaders was enlisted, and Torah Umesorah launched into the work of advocating the establishment of hundreds of Jewish day schools, nationwide.

Jewish Education in a World Transformed, 1945–1975

The dominant motifs of American Jewish life in the period 1945–75 were suburbanization and institutional growth. In the 1950s and 1960s, at least a billion dollars were spent building a thousand new synagogue buildings. Many of the young families who relocated to new suburban areas had not previously been involved in synagogue life. The synagogue, however, represented an expression of Jewish group feeling and was seen as a primary vehicle – particularly with the decline of "Jewish neighborhoods" – for the Jewish education and socialization of the younger generation. The Union of American Hebrew Congregations grew from 334 member congregations in 1948 to 664 in 1966, while the United Synagogue grew from 350 affiliates at the close of World War II to 800 by 1965. With the growth of Los Angeles Jewry – from 160,000 to 480,000, in the period 1945–65 – a West Coast branch of the Jewish Theological Seminary (*University of Judaism) was established (1947), as was a branch of Hebrew Union College (1954). In the 1950s and 1960s, the rate of synagogue affiliation climbed from the 20% of the 1930s to nearly 60%. American society validated Sunday school attendance as an expression of wholesome, middle class values.

One hundred forty thousand Holocaust survivors came to the United States after World War II, joining more than 200,000 refugees who had been admitted to the U.S. between Hitler's rise to power in 1933 and America's entry into the war, late in 1941. Among the most recent arrivals were Jews from traditional Jewish societies, who served as a "cultural booster shot," advancing demand for more substantial Jewish education. At the same time, the establishment of the State of Israel heightened Jewish identification among many American Jews, and excitement surrounding the founding of the State of Israel seemed to validate the teaching of modern Hebrew.

The post-World War II baby boom, combined with heightened synagogue and Jewish (largely synagogue-sponsored) school attendance brought about a trebling – in one generation – of students enrolled in Jewish schools, from 200,000 in 1937, to 588,955 in 1962. While, in the 1930s, only an estimated 10,000 students (5% of total enrollment) were in high school programs of Jewish education, by 1959, closer to 10% of the expanded population of students was to be found in Jewish secondary schools. Conservative congregational schools aimed to meet 6 hours per week (typically divided among three sessions) and the curriculum included Hebrew, prayerbook, history, Bible, customs and ceremonies, current events, and songs. By the late 1940s, 25% of Reform congregational schools had introduced weekday (in addition to Sunday) sessions. Instruction included holidays, biblical and post-biblical heroes, Jewish history and literature, Hebrew, prayers, Bible selections, singing, current events, and modern Jewish problems, and Jewish contributions to civilization.

Growth of Day Schools

Spearheaded, often, by Orthodox refugees who had found asylum in the United States, Jewish day schools, which had been rare phenomena before 1940, rapidly proliferated. From 30 day schools with 7,000 students in 1940, the "system" grew to 95 schools with 14,000 students in 1946, to 330 schools with 67,000 students in the early 1970s. By 1975, there were 425 Orthodox day schools (including 138 high schools) with a total enrollment of 82,200.

Although most Torah Umesorah schools devoted half of the school day to "Torah studies" and half of the day to general education, there was considerable diversity in outlook. While some schools emphasized the complete subordination of all study to a "Torah mindset," "integrationists" sought to achieve "synthesis" of Judaism and Americanism. Such ideological differences influenced the apportionment of time between Torah studies and general studies, the language of religious studies instruction, the choice of texts (within the "sea" of classical Jewish sources), and the structure of the school day.

Writing in 1973, Alvin Schiff distinguished between Orthodox Hebrew day schools, traditional yeshivot, and ḥasidic schools, noting that in the latter two categories – accounting for one-third of U.S. day schools – 30–40 hours per week were dedicated to Jewish studies and 10–15 hours (frequently less) to general education. From the 1940s to the 1960s, significant numbers of Torah studies educators were European immigrants. As Orthodox rabbinical seminaries grew and yeshivah day school enrollment escalated, American-educated teachers – themselves yeshivah graduates – became, increasingly, common. While the great majority of day schools were under Orthodox sponsorship, it was estimated, in the 1960s, that one-third of the students enrolled in yeshivah day schools were from other than Orthodox homes.

A number of Conservative congregations launched day schools under synagogue sponsorship, in the years after World War II. In 1946, Congregation Anshe Emet (Chicago) opened a day school, followed in 1950 by Temple Beth El in New York. By 1958, there were 14 Conservative day schools. Additional Conservative day schools were founded in the late 1950s and 1960s; in 1964 the (Conservative) Solomon Schechter Day School Association was formed. By 1977, nearly 10,000 students were enrolled in 50 Solomon Schechter schools.

Notwithstanding movement opposition to the establishment of day schools, two Reform temples – Congregation Rodeph Sholom in New York and Temple Beth Am in Miami – opened such schools in 1970. The emergence of Reform day schools – in 1970, and subsequently – represented a coalescence of parental concern for quality secular education and the interest of rabbinic leadership in quality Jewish education. Of great significance was the fact that, as confidence in public education eroded, private schooling was undergoing "democratization" in the eyes of many Reform Jews. By 1981, there were nine Reform day schools. Not until 1985, however, were day schools approved by the UAHC, and, subsequently (1990), a Reform day school network (PARDeS – Progressive Association of Reform Day Schools) established.

During the period of mass Jewish migration to the United States, the public school had been a key agent of Americanization. By the closing decades of the 20th century, at a time of increasing acceptance of ethnic and religious diversity and, among Jews, of greater openness to and the economic means of accessing private education, many children and grandchildren of Americanized immigrants chose to send their children to Jewish day schools. For many of these students and their families, the school experience now served a Judaizing function, nurturing intensive knowledge of and commitment to a Jewish way of life.

Congregational Education in the 1960s and 1970s

Notwithstanding the rapid growth in enrollment and the proliferation of congregational schools, curricula had not developed, substantially, for decades. Responding to this reality, and to the sense that congregational schools were missing the mark, a flurry of curriculum initiatives was launched in the 1960s and 1970s. The Melton Center (at the Jewish Theological Seminary) published curricular materials on Bible and holidays. Experimental editions of the UAHC's Shuster Curriculum began appearing in 1977, and the United Synagogue produced its Menorah curriculum in 1978. Behrman House published textbooks at all levels, utilized by both the Conservative and Reform congregational schools.

One of the noteworthy additions to the new curricula was the study of "comparative religion."

The National Conference of Christians and Jews had been established in 1928, and the interfaith "goodwill" movement gained strength after World War II. In 1955, Will Herberg published his classic *Protestant, Catholic, Jew.* On this backdrop, the UAHC published *Our Religion and Our Neighbors*, in 1963, and Behrman House published *Judaism and Christianity: What We Believe*, in 1968. Students who mastered the information in these texts could recognize certain similarities and differences between Jewish and Christian beliefs about God, human nature, sin, and salvation. They would also learn about various life cycle events, calendars, and liturgies. The textbooks encouraged their readers to view themselves as no different from their neighbors in values and citizenship, while suggesting the maintenance of boundaries between Jews and Christians in a narrowly circumscribed religious sphere.

In 1959, the AAJE published the "Report of the Commission for the Study of Jewish Education in the United States." The report estimated that 40–45% of Jewish children ages 5–14 were, in 1959, receiving Jewish schooling – though upwards of 80% were enrolled in Jewish education at some time during their elementary school years. It "pegged" the average stay at 3–4 years.

With regard to the profile of teachers teaching in various school types, the report distinguished between Sunday school, weekday (supplementary) school, and day school faculties. It found that, among day school faculty members, 69% were men/31% women, and that 62% of teachers were foreign-born; among weekday Hebrew school teachers, the data showed 64% women/36% men – 61% foreign-born; among Sunday school teachers, 64% women / 36% men – 90% U.S.-born. With reference to the qualifications of teachers, the report (which was based upon an extensive survey) noted that of the "pool" of Sunday school teachers, 58% claimed nothing beyond elementary Jewish education of some sort, and 9% claimed no Jewish education.

In 1950, the Jewish Educators Assembly of the Conservative Movement was established, followed by the (Reform) National Association of Temple Educators in 1954. Yet, with the collapse of the *talmud torah* system, there were few full-time teaching positions outside of day schools in Jewish education, and a lack of qualified personnel. There was a decided tendency, in the 1960s and 1970s, to embrace pedagogic trends in public education, including audio-visual technology, programmed instruction, values clarification, and cooperative learning. A 1967 study conducted by the American Association for Jewish Education showed that 42.2% of students enrolled in Jewish schools were in one-day-per-week programs; 44.4% in 2 to 5-days-per-week programs; and 13.4% in day schools.

New Settings of Jewish Education

A much different educational phenomenon, first emerging on a modest scale in the 1940s, was the *kolel*. The *kolel*, a full-time program of advanced talmudic study for adult men (supported by stipends) of outstanding scholarly ability, was introduced to the U.S. by Rabbi Aaron *Kotler at the Beth Medrash Govoha in Lakewood in 1943. The Lakewood *kolel* began with 12 graduates of American rabbinical schools. In 1945, 15 men who had been Rabbi Kotler's students in Europe joined the *kolel*.

A second *kolel*, Beth Medrash Elyon of Monsey – an extension of Brooklyn-based Mesivta Torah Vodaath – soon followed. While, in 1950, there were no more than 50–100 persons studying in American *kolelim*, by the end of the 1970s the number of *kolel* participants exceeded 1,000. Beyond the numerical growth, a cultural transformation had occurred over the course of a generation: the latter-day *kolel* was no longer exclusively for the elite, most outstanding students.

Yet another Jewish educational development which came into full flower in the 1940s was the Jewish residential summer camp. Early Jewish residential camps, dating back to the years before World War I, had been sponsored by philanthropic agencies to provide relief from tenement conditions and to teach immigrant children "American ways." As earlier noted, camping as a Jewish educational vehicle was first explored by Albert P. Schoolman, principal of the Central Jewish Institute in New York (an educational center influenced by the theories of Mordecai Kaplan) in 1919. Schoolman's Camp CEJWIN, originally envisioned as a bridge between the school year and the summer months, provided enveloping experiences in Jewish living and served as a training ground for young adults entering careers in Jewish education and social service.

In the 1920s and 1930s, a number of Yiddish and Zionist camps were launched, including camping initiatives by Hashomer Hatzair, Habonim, Young Judea, and B'nei Akiva (then known as Hashomer Hadati). The first Hebrew-speaking camp, Camp Achvah, was established by Samson Benderly in 1927. Though it provided a rich educational experience, the Depression dashed its early promise.

A more enduring Hebrew-based, Zionist camp, Camp Massad, opened in 1941, led for many years by founding Director Shlomo Shulsinger. In 1944, the Boston Hebrew Teachers College opened Camp Yavneh to advance the knowledge of students of the Hebrew Teachers College and to encourage the use of Hebrew outside the classroom. The Conservative movement entered the arena of Jewish educational camping with the opening of Camp Ramah in Wisconsin in 1947. NFTY held its first encampment at the UAHC's newly purchased camp in Wisconsin in 1951. In the 1940s and 1950s, scores of Jewish residential camps were established, coast to coast. While, prior to 1947, Jewish camping had been avowedly pluralistic, the opening of Ramah and, subsequently, of the Union Institute (Oconomowoc, Wisconsin), represented a move to a denominational agenda within the universe of Jewish educational camping. Within a few years, both Ramah and Union Institute became full-scale camping movements, often serving as training grounds for the development of the movements' leadership, lay and rabbinic.

Jewish youth groups continued their growth and development after World War II. Among the "new entries" were (Conservative) United Synagogue Youth (1951) and (Orthodox) National Conferences of Synagogue Youth (1959). Educators often encouraged students to participate in school, youth group, and residential summer camp, to maximize Jewish educational opportunity.

During the first half of the 20th century, a variety of Jewish community centers were created. In the settlement house era, such centers often focused on "Americanization" of Jewish immigrants. In the course of the Great Depression of the 1930s, JCC services to the broader community became common; many of the centers' professionals saw JCCs as agents in the mission of social reconstruction. During World War II, many Jewish centers had organized nursery schools and kindergartens to provide care for the children of working mothers. These early childhood programs became an integral part of the centers' "menu" of activities.

With increasing suburbanization, new Jewish community centers were built in emerging areas of Jewish population. In the two decades after World War II, $125 million were invested in new JCC facilities. In an effort to clarify the mission of the JCC in the new era, the Jewish Welfare Board, umbrella organization of the Jewish Community Centers, commissioned a study (1945–47) aimed at articulating the direction to be taken by Jewish centers at mid-century. Summarizing the data, the author of what came to be known as the "Janowsky Report" noted that very few centers provided an atmosphere reflecting intensive Jewish interest or activity. While the report called upon centers to promote Jewish activity, it did not offer guidance as to how the program of centers was to move towards this outcome.

Though Harry *Wolfson and Salo *Baron had, by the 1930s, achieved scholarly eminence in Jewish studies at Harvard and Columbia, respectively, it was the ethnic studies current of the late 1960s that brought courses in Jewish studies to hundreds of American universities. The number of full-time university positions in Jewish studies had risen from 12 in 1945 to 65 in 1965, and increased even more dramatically in the ensuing decades. In addition to the availability of and mounting interest in university-level Judaic studies courses, the aftermath of the June 1967 Six-Day War saw a proliferation of and enrollment in Israel programs for high school students and collegiates.

While the "Foundation Schools" of the 1940s for students ages three through eight (combining Jewish and general education) were being supplanted by day schools, early childhood ("nursery") centers for pre-school children, which had expanded significantly during and after World War II, continued to grow. As more women entered the work force, such programs served not only a Jewish educational function, but assumed an essential child care role. Synagogues, Jewish centers, and elementary day schools were among the primary providers of burgeoning early childhood education services.

In the 1940s, adult Jewish education began a generation of renewed growth. The Conservative Movement's National Academy for Adult Jewish Studies was established in 1940, followed in 1948 by the founding of the Department of Continuing Education of the UAHC. B'nai B'rith launched adult "Institutes of Judaism" in 1948. Another adult educational initiative destined to have a significant impact was the Brandeis Camp Institute for college-age young adults, initiated by Shlomo Bardin in 1941. In 1965, the AAJE convened the first national conference on Jewish adult education in the United States. There was ample evidence that programs of adult Jewish learning were on the rise. This was consistent with the expansion, during the 1950s and 1960s, of adult education generally, as a result of increased leisure time and an escalated level of education.

Despite the many positive trends in the Jewish educational landscape, there were some ominous signs of challenge to continuing Jewish vitality. In 1957, the U.S. Census Bureau reported the following regarding birthrates among Catholics, Protestants, and Jews: Catholics, 3.1; Protestants, 2.8; Jews, 2.1. Indeed, with the end of the post-World War II baby boom, Jewish school enrollment declined to under 400,000 (from a peak of nearly 590,000 in 1962) by the mid-1970s. Perhaps most shocking was the dramatic rise in intermarriage. The National Jewish Population Study of 1971 reported that the rate of intermarriage had risen from under 7% in the 1950s to 31% between 1966–70.

The vision of integration articulated by Benderly, Kaplan, and generations of educators was, it was beginning to appear, less tenable than once imagined. As Jewish communal leaders increasingly spoke the language of "Jewish survival," the focus of congregational education became Jewish identity – "to make young people feel more Jewish." Adding to concern about the success potential for ensuring Jewish survival in the United States were two studies, published in 1975 and 1976, which "scientifically" demonstrated that a minimum threshold of instructional hours of Jewish schooling (3,000 according to one study and 1,000 according to the second) was required to impart adult religious identification. These thresholds exceeded the level of Jewish education received by all but a small minority of Jewish students.

Educational Trends at the Close of the 20th Century

The last quarter of the 20th century, particularly its closing decade, saw Jewish education emerge as a centerpiece of Jewish communal and philanthropic efforts to address the perceived challenges to "Jewish continuity" in the United States. During this period, Jewish day schools came to serve nearly 200,000 students from the four-year-old pre-school level through high school, participation in "Israel experience" programs by teens and collegiates was defined as a "birthright" and heavily subsidized, a Foundation for Jewish Camping sought to expand the availability of residential camping as a Jewish educational option, initiatives aimed at recruiting and training recent college graduates for service as Jewish educators were launched, programs of systematic, comprehensive adult learning were created and embraced by significant numbers of participants, and congregational change strategies aimed at nurturing communities of Jewish learning were conceived and piloted. Philanthropic foundations and individual funders with interest in Jewish life came to play an increasingly more substantial role in shaping Jewish educational projects. Evidence of intensification of Jewish learning and living was readily available, as was evidence of declining Jewish population and the diminishing Jewish involvement – at least on a communal level – of many Jews. Sociologists aptly noted that, notwithstanding the plans and prescriptions of Jewish community leaders and organizations, the story and extent of individual Jewish involvement was, increasingly, a function of the "sovereign self."

Among the educational trends of note towards the close of the 20th century were the following:

1. The growth of early childhood education programs
2. The "boom" in Jewish studies programs on college campuses and the revitalization of Hillel
3. A more "holistic" approach to Jewish education, embracing both formal and informal educational experiences
4. Family education in a variety of settings (including Jewish community centers, schools, and retreat centers)
5. The proliferation of adult study opportunities
6. The impact (albeit touching a modest percentage of the population pool) of Jewish residential camping
7. Expanded Israel trips, including Birthright Israel (a partnership between North American Jewish philanthropists, Jewish Federations, and the Israeli government to make it possible for American Jewish college students to experience Israel on organized, ten-day trips, at no charge)
8. Foundation initiatives in funding broad issues in a systemic fashion

Many of these initiatives were responses to the findings of the 1990 National Jewish Population Survey, indicating inter alia that the intermarriage rate had reached 52% (a figure challenged by some as overstating a rate which stood "only" at 43%). Even before release of the NJPS, the Commission on Jewish Education in North America, convened by respected philanthropist Mort Mandel, had issued its report, *A Time to Act*, giving expression to the malaise of American Jewry, and suggesting Jewish education as the antidote.

As growing numbers of school-age children of the "echo" of the post-World War II baby boom were enrolled in private schools, including Jewish day schools, "community" (i.e., pan-denominational) Jewish day schools were among the expanding educational venues. Alongside the Torah Umesorah, Solomon Schechter, and PARDeS School networks, there emerged networks of pluralistic day schools, representing approximately 10% of day schools and of student enrollment. Community elementary schools were organized as RAVSAK: the Jewish Community Day School Network. In 1999, the North American Association of Jewish High Schools (NAAJHS) was formed. Consisting chiefly of community day high schools, this network had more than 20 member schools within three years of its establishment. Its programs included joint student activities, in addition to collaboration among educational professionals. The American Association of Jewish Education was, in 1981, reconstituted as JESNA (Jewish Education Service of North America), and undertook to work with federations, bureaus, and school networks for the advancement of Jewish education, nationally.

With the growth of non-Orthodox day schools – and the enrollment in such schools of students whose families, in many cases, represented the element within Conservative and Reform congregations most interested in a more intensive Jewish life style – the primary focus of part-time congregational education came to be "Jewish identity" development. Consistent with this change in emphasis, and responding to member families' expressed needs, many schools sponsored by Conservative congregations modified their "traditional" 3 days /6 hours per week standard in favor of two weekly sessions.

Concern about the efficacy of congregational schooling was expressed not only by earlier research reporting on the inadequacy of instructional hours, but by a major study conducted by the Board of Jewish Education of New York in the mid-1980s. Findings of the study were released in a report titled "Jewish Supplementary Schooling; An Educational System in Need of Change." The report urged that family education and informal education became integral to supplementary education and that training and the provision of educational career opportunities be made available to attract and retain qualified personnel for the type of instruction proposed.

The 1980s and 1990s saw significant growth in family education initiatives. Early childhood Jewish education programs, in particular, were increasingly understood as portals of entry offering the possibility of Jewish educational engagement with parents and families. At the same time, there were those who argued that not only the family but the communities of families comprising congregations needed to "re-imagine" themselves. In the 1990s, Joseph Reimer chronicled a model of effective, school-based Jewish education in a congregation which had apparently transformed itself into a community of learning. Isa Aron led a systematic project, "The Experiment in Congregational Education," aimed at facilitating a reconceptualization of congregational education. In Dr. Aron's vision, synagogues needed to re-engineer themselves into congregations of learners. On a parallel track, adult education frameworks such as Boston's Meah program, the Wexner Foundation Heritage program, and the Florence Melton Adult Mini-School, each serving thousands of participants over a two-year period of intensive study, aimed at effecting sociocultural transformation through Jewish learning.

An Avi Chai Foundation study of day school enrollment, released in the year 2000, showed that 80% of the 185,000 students (pre-K–4-years-old–through 12th grade) enrolled in the country's 670 day schools were in Orthodox schools; more than half of the total number of day school enrollees were in the state of New York. Ḥasidic and yeshivah day school enrollment – estimated at 33% in 1973 – had, a generation later, grown to nearly 50%. That the day school phenomenon, however, was not exclusively the concern of Orthodox institutional leadership was reflected in the emergence of PEJE (Partnership for Excellence in Jewish Education) – a consortium of mainly other-than-Orthodox philanthropists organized to promote access to and the quality of day school education – as a prominent advocacy group in support of day school education. The end of the 20th century saw an escalating number of day high schools established, many of them "community" (non-Orthodox) schools. Within the Orthodox sector, an Association of Modern Orthodox Day Schools and Yeshiva High Schools (AMODS) was established, affiliated with Yeshiva University.

The 1990s saw the emergence of "Partnership 2000," a series of "twinning" linkages between Israeli municipalities and various American Jewish Federations. Within those partnerships, educational initiatives between Israeli schools and American Jewish schools (typically, day schools) were launched. These joint ventures commonly brought faculty (and, sometimes, students) together, often around the question of the nature and meaning of Jewish peoplehood and core Jewish values. A century after Aḥad Ha-Am suggested that, somehow, a critical mass of Jews constituting a majority population in the land of Israel might resolve the malaise of Judaism in the modern world, the legatees of his thinking – both in Israel and in the U.S. – were working jointly to meet the continuing, complex challenge of articulating the very meaning of Jewish identity. On both sides of these partnerships, Jewish communities aggregating 75% of world Jewry sensed the need for such definition, knowing that, in the case of Jewish education as with any other educational matter, coherent purpose is essential for effectiveness.

The 1990s saw renewed declarations regarding the importance of Hebrew language literacy. The Statement of Principles for Reform Judaism, for example, adopted at the 1999 Pittsburgh Convention of the Central Conference of American Rabbis, affirmed "the importance of studying Hebrew, the language of Torah and Jewish liturgy, that we may draw closer to our people's sacred texts." It remained to be seen what impact the "new" Pittsburgh Platform might have on emphases in curriculum and instruction in the educational settings of Reform Judaism. Similarly, in the mid-1990s, the chancellor of the (Conservative) Jewish Theological Seminary of America, Ismar *Schorsch, issued a pamphlet describing the seven "core" values of Conservative Judaism. Schorsch identified recognition of the importance of Hebrew as a core value of Conservative Judaism, urging that Hebrew must emerge as the unifying language of the Jewish people. Writing at a time when Conservative congregational education was, for increasing numbers of students, being restructured from three weekly sessions to two weekly contacts, it remained to be seen in which settings this sentiment might be "translated" to an action program.

By 1998, Jewish civilization was being taught or researched at over 700 American institutions of higher learning. While the 2000–1 NJPS indicated that 41% of Jewish undergraduates took at least one course in "Jewish studies" during their college years, it is important to keep in mind that the academic analysis of aspects of Jewish civilization is neither designed nor presented as an exploration which should, in any way, inform the learner's identity. A revitalized Hillel Foundation sought to meet – and, for many, to create – Jewish educational needs of an estimated 400,000 Jewish collegiates.

By the year 2000, an estimated 18,000 post-high school young men – in addition to the 150,000 students of both genders in Orthodox Jewish day schools – were enrolled in yeshivot and *kolelim*. Of this number, approximately 2,350 studied at the Beth Medrash Govoha in Lakewood and 1,500 were at the United Talmudical Seminary of the Satmar ḥasidim. An emerging phenomenon was the establishment of small, "activist" *kolelim* in cities from Boca Raton to Atlanta to Pittsburgh, Chicago, Los Angeles, and elsewhere, in which full time, deeply Orthodox talmudists devoted significant time to community education, engaging in study with non-traditionalist segments of Jewry. In addition to the growing number of *kolel* participants, thousands of American Jewish young men and women were studying in yeshivot and seminaries in Israel each year. Yet, even the Orthodox population was by no means impervious to acculturating tendencies. The estimates for dropouts by youth from Orthodoxy, though not from Judaism, ran as high as one-third.

The 2000–1 NJPS indicated that, among students ages 6 to 17 in once per week programs, 2–3 times per week, or Jewish day schools, the day school group represented a plurality of students, with 29% of school age students receiving day school education, 24% part-time (but more than once per week) Jewish education, and 25% attending once-per-week classes, during the course of their educational "career." Day school enrollment had become ubiquitous in Orthodox circles and PEJE was undertaking a series of initiatives designed to double – over the ensuing decade – day school enrollment in the non-Orthodox sector (this at a time of a shrinking potential student pool owing to the end of the "echo" of the post-World War II baby boom). Issues such as government financial support for the education of students attending (day) schools, whether through voucher programs or funding of assorted educational services, continued to be vigorously debated within the Jewish community. The growing number of "community" (non-denominationally affiliated) day schools, combined with the emergence of two new non-denominational rabbinical schools (Academy for the Jewish Religion, California, and the Rabbinical School of Hebrew College, Newton, MA), suggested a growing strand of "post-denominational" American Judaism in the making.

The notion of Jewish education as "enculturation" gave rise, in the closing decades of the 20th century, to increased attention to "beyond the classroom" experiences engaging children and families. Influenced perhaps by public discussion and government action in the matter of providing appropriate educational services and opportunities for students with special learning needs, expanded initiatives to provide Jewish education for students with special needs were launched. Programs built on "inclusion" and self-contained models were established in schools, camps, and youth groups.

The trend towards maximizing the Jewish educational effectiveness of Jewish community centers continued at the turn of the century, as did "synagogue transformation" projects. If the Pittsburgh Platform of 1885 was a statement of late 19th-century American Jewish acculturation, the Pittsburgh Platform of 1999 reflected revitalized interest in the "whole array" of Jewish teaching. Kaplan's vision of Jewish organizations as vehicles for promoting Jewish learning and fostering Jewish consciousness was being realized in many settings.

Thus, by the end of the 20th century, trends of intensified engagement in Jewish education stood alongside diminishing numbers of Jews, and the spirit of individualism – long a distinguishing feature of the American ethos – was pervasive in Jewish life. The structures of Jewish corporate society, ruptured by modernity, never held sway on American soil. Through the first half of the 20th century, however, immigrant ties, the specter of antisemitism, and support of the emerging State of Israel had served to nurture and sustain strong communal bonds. By the latter part of the 20th century, the "sovereign self" reigned fiercely supreme. Individual "journey" had, for increasing numbers of Jews, supplanted community-centered Judaism. A growing array of Jewish educational frameworks aimed to respond to diverse needs and interests.

Challenges at the Beginning of the 21st Century

Within the many domains of Jewish educational activity, the issue of goal clarification, or educational vision, is an increasingly recognized focus. Articulating a vision (or multiple visions) of Judaism and its significance must, as generations of concerned observers have noted, be the starting point of Jewish educational activity. One significant model of building education on a "platform" of vision and clearly defined purpose was a pioneering school accreditation program developed by the Bureau of Jewish Education of Greater Los Angeles for Jewish day, supplementary, and early childhood education centers in the 1990s. This comprehensive program, as the Experiment in Congregational Education, called for institutional articulation of the mission and goals of each Jewish educational community as an essential starting point. Towards the same end, the Mandel Foundation, prior to and since publication of its *Visions of Jewish Education* (2003) – a work which "unpacks" the educational implications of alternative visions of Jewish education – has sponsored training programs aimed at encouraging more careful reflection on educational vision.

The challenge of personnel recruitment, training, and retention has been part of the "story" of Jewish education since the earliest period of American Jewish life. The Mandel Commission report of 1990 highlighted personnel as key to addressing Jewish educational challenges in every domain – early childhood through adulthood; in 2004, JESNA convened a national "Summit" focused on addressing the personnel needs of Jewish education. This heightened attention to the essential need for personnel has "translated" to a proliferation of fellowship and in-service programs, both preparing new recruits and strengthening the skills of those already in the field.

In addition to clarity of vision and the training of educational personnel, the cost of providing and accessing Jewish education is a third, critical issue, early in the 21st century. Having developed such outstanding – and costly – frameworks as day schools and residential camps, to name but two examples, the need for ensuring student access is compelling. If seats or beds, as the case may be, cost thousands or tens of thousands of dollars per child per session, what is to be the "standing" of the majority of American Jews who are unable to sustain the costs involved? The engagement of increasing numbers of private foundations in the cause of Jewish education and the example of "Birthright Israel" represent "promising prospects," but the challenge of financial access to Jewish education remains considerable. The organic inter-relationship of the above issues is clear. Attracting and retaining qualified personnel surely has cost implications. A sense of vision and mission relates to attracting personnel and funds, and will be rooted in notions of the very nature of Judaism and the purpose of Jewish education.

If American Jews are to continue to flourish and contribute to the world as Jews, intensive and extensive Jewish educational opportunity must, surely, be available and accessible. Though Jewish population is declining (because of low birthrates) and many Jews lack rudimentary Jewish education or more than an ephemeral sense of Jewish identity, the percentage and numbers of American Jews involved in serious Jewish study have never been greater. An Avi Chai report released in 2005, for example, showed that, over the five-year period 1998–99 to 2003–4, day school enrollment had increased from 185,000 students to 205,000 students.

At the start of the century, new initiatives were also underway aimed at strengthening early Jewish education and engaging parents of early childhood students in Jewish experiences. The challenges of creating, sustaining, and providing access to frameworks of meaningful Jewish educational engagement to nurture and facilitate lifelong Jewish learning and living are considerable. It is, however, the commitment and sense of urgency of those who care deeply about the advancement of Jewish education and act accordingly in each generation that ensures the vitality of Jewish life in the United States, as elsewhere.

BIBLIOGRAPHY: W.I. Ackerman, "Jewish Education for What?," in: *American Jewish Yearbook*, 70 (1969); H.W. Bomzer, *The Kolel in America* (1985); A. Dushkin, *Jewish Education in New York City* (1918); A. Dushkin and U. Engleman, *Jewish Education in the United States: Report of the Commission for the Study of Jewish Education in the United States* (1959); S. Fox, I. Scheffler, and D. Marom, *Visions of Jewish Education* (2003); A.P. Gannes, *Central Community Agencies for Jewish Education* (1954); L.P. Gartner, *Jewish Education in the United States* (1969); S.A. Ginsburgh, "A Study of Nationally Organized Jewish Youth Groups in America as Educational Agencies for the Preservation of the Jewish Cultural Heritage," Diss., Massachusetts State College (1940); W. Helmreich, *The World of the Yeshiva* (2000); O.I. Janowsky, *The Jewish Community Center: Two Essays on Basic Purpose* (1974); D.Z. Kramer, *The Day Schools and Torah Umesorah* (1984); J.B. Krasner, "Representations of Self and Other in American Jewish History and Social Studies School Books: An Exploration of the Changing Shape of American Jewish Identity," Diss., Brandeis University (2002); J. Pilch, *A History of Jewish Education in the United States* (1969); E.L. Rauch, *The Education of Jews and the American Community: 1840 to the New Millenium* (2004); J.D. Sarna, "American Jewish Education in Historical Perspective," in: *Jewish Education* (Winter/Spring, 1998); M. Schick, *A Census of Jewish Day Schools in the United States, 2003–2004* (2005); A.I. Schiff, *The Jewish Day School in America* (1966); L. Sussman, *Isaac Leeser and the Making of American Judaism* (1995); J. Wertheimer, "Jewish Education in the United States: Recent Trends and Issues," in: *American Jewish Year Book*, 99 (1999); J. Wertheimer, "Recent Trends in American Judaism," in: *American Jewish Year Book*, 89 (1989); N.H. Winter, *Jewish Education in a Pluralistic Society* (1966); M. Zeldin, "The Promise of Historical Inquiry: 19th Century Jewish Day Schools and 20th Century Policy," in: *Los Angeles* (1987).

[Gil Graff (2nd ed.)]

GREAT BRITAIN

Early Period

Jewish education was quickly reorganized after the readmission of the Jews in the mid-17th century. The London Sephardi congregation established a boys' school, *Sha'arei Tikvah* ("Gates of Hope"), in 1664, where instruction was at first given in Spanish, Portuguese, and Ladino, although English was one of the secular subjects taught. A talmudical college (Beth Hamedrash Heshaim, 1664) was also sponsored by the Sephardim, and in 1730 the Villareal girls' school was founded to provide a training in Judaism, languages, and domestic science. During the 17th century, the haham of the London Sephardim had to devote several hours of his day to teaching the children of his congregants. Jewish educational standards among the British Ashkenazim were uniformly lower. Although the Great Synagogue in London established a *talmud torah* school in 1732, records of the mid-18th century show that the more recent Ashkenazi community had managed to organize only two small "*ḥadarim*" in which the language of instruction was Yiddish. An anonymous publication of the late 18th century, *Sefer Giddul Banim* (London, 1771), discussed contemporary teaching methods and syllabi in the spirit of the Haskalah. Despite its Hebrew title, this work was written in Yiddish and its approach reflects the critical views of English *maskilim* of the time.

The 19th Century

By the beginning of the 19th century, English had replaced Portuguese and Yiddish as the language of instruction in Jewish congregational schools, which were reorganized and broadened. The Sephardi "Gates of Hope" school was reconstituted in 1821 and the Villareal girls' school merged with the National and Infant Schools in 1839. Meanwhile, the Ashkenazim had overtaken the Sephardim in numbers and importance and this development was reflected in the comparatively large number of educational projects established during the first half of the century. In London, various "free schools" came into being: the Westminster Jews' Free School (1811); the (East End) Jews' Free School (1817); and the Jews' Infant Schools, founded to combat missionary activities. The Western Metropolitan Jewish School flourished during the years 1845–97 and, from the 1860s, other schools were established in the Bayswater, Borough, and Stepney districts. "Hebrew endowed schools" were also founded in the major cities of the Provinces, such as Manchester (1838), Liverpool (1840), Birmingham (1840), and Hull. By 1850, some 2,000 Jewish children attended schools of this type in Britain, representing a remarkably high proportion of the total Jewish school age population at a time when the Jews of Britain numbered no more than about 35,000.

The "free schools" did not, however, enjoy a complete monopoly of Jewish education at this period. Some children attended religion classes after spending the day at non-Jewish schools, and their educational needs were catered for by the Jewish Association for the Diffusion of Religious Knowledge (1860). Other children attended Jewish fee-paying schools run by private individuals and these were often of vastly differing educational standards. Among the best known were those of the Hebraist Hyman Hurwitz (Highgate, c. 1800), whose pupils included many who later attained eminence in Anglo-Jewry; Solomon Lyon (1754–1820), whose Jewish boarding school at Cambridge was the first of its type in Britain; the writer Grace *Aguilar (Hackney, 1842–47); and the Orientalist Louis *Loewe, who was secretary to Moses Montefiore.

Jewish educational institutes of an advanced type also came into existence during the early and mid-19th century. A chair of Hebrew was established at the non-sectarian University College of London in 1828 and attracted Jewish teachers and students; while the Jews' General Literary and Scientific Institution, inspired by the popular "mechanics institutes," was founded in 1845. Ten years later, Jews' College was established in London to train Jewish ministers and preachers. During the 1870s a Society for Hebrew Literature also flourished in London. Boys intending to enter the Jewish ministry were educated at the Jews' College Preparatory School (1855–79), a forerunner of Aria College in Brighton.

Following the Education Act of 1870, which established free primary schooling for children in Great Britain, no new Jewish "free schools" came into being and the private, fee-paying establishments suffered a sharp decline. Toward the end of the 19th century, when Jewish immigration from Eastern Europe swamped the old-established communities in London and the provinces, dozens of Yiddish-speaking *ḥadarim* and *talmud torah* schools were set up throughout the country. Though despised by many of the anglicized Jews, these provided Jewish youngsters with a far deeper basic training in Judaism. The Association for the Diffusion of Religious Knowledge was reorganized as the Jewish Religious Education Board (1893) and, by the turn of the century, the Jews' Free School in London's East End with its 3,000 pupils (2,000 boys and 1,000 girls) was the largest school in Britain and reputedly the biggest Jewish teaching center in Europe, if not in the whole world. Many of its own teachers were former pupils and it provided the staff for many other Jewish schools in Great Britain and the British Empire. However, as Israel *Zangwill observed in *Children of the Ghetto* (1892), the school's primary aim was to neutralize the more fiery Judaism of "alien" immigrants by the process of anglicization; and by 1901 Solomon *Schechter was already deploring the ignorance prevalent in the Anglo-Jewish community.

The 20th Century

As early as the first decade of the 20th century, the established Jewish educational organizations were feeling the pressure of the more Orthodox bodies set up by, or on behalf of, the immigrant population. The process had a synagogal parallel in the rivalry between the United Synagogue and the Federation of Synagogues in the London area, and there were similar repercussions in the major Jewish centers in the Provinces. A Talmud Torah Trust (known in later years as the London Talmud Torah Council) was founded in London in 1905; while bodies of the same type came into being in Leeds (1879) and Liverpool (1893) and in Manchester and Glasgow. The Redmans Road Talmud Torah in Stepney (1901) first introduced instruction in Hebrew on the Zionist pattern ("*Ivrit be-Ivrit*"), the same system being adopted by the Liverpool Hebrew Higher Grade School of Jacob Samuel *Fox. However, the overwhelming proportion of Jewish children attended state primary and secondary schools and acquired their meager knowledge of Hebrew and Judaism in "withdrawal classes" or in the religious schools administered by the various synagogue groups. Although an amalgamated Union of Hebrew and Religious Classes was founded in London (1907), there was little concerted effort to train teachers, standardize textbooks, or inspect classes in the Provinces. Those Jewish parents sufficiently interested could request the withdrawal of their children from Scripture ("Divinity") lessons and their exemption from attendance on Saturday mornings and Jewish festivals, wherever non-Jewish head teachers were agreeable. Only a small minority of youngsters enjoyed the benefit of a more intensive course of instruction.

After World War I, a fresh attempt was made to reorganize Jewish education through the "Jewish War Memorial" project, which led to the establishment of the Central Committee for Jewish Education (1920). This worked with limited success for the next two decades. More strenuous efforts were made by Zionist educators such as Jacob Koppel *Goldbloom in London's East End and Izak *Goller in Liverpool, as well as by the more strictly Orthodox Jews of London, led by Rabbi Victor (Avigdor) *Schoenfeld. In 1929, the latter established the Jewish Secondary Schools Movement, which was reinforced by Orthodox teachers and scholars from Central Europe who sought refuge in Britain during the 1930s. Other immigrants helped to fortify and improve the religion classes and standards of the Reform and Liberal movements. In the sphere of rabbinic training, Jews' College – the British Empire's only seminary from 1855 – continued to prepare ministers and a few rabbis under the direction of Adolf *Buechler; while the more recent yeshivot (talmudical colleges) founded by immigrants from Lithuania and Poland endeavored to produce "learned laymen" capable of influencing the religious direction of the community and of raising its Jewish educational sights. By 1939, there were flourishing yeshivot in London (Etz Chaim – Tree of Life College, 1903; Law of Truth Talmudical College, 1938, etc.), Manchester (1911), and Gateshead (1927), and smaller yeshivot in Liverpool (1915), Leeds, and Glasgow.

At the outbreak of World War II, the Jewish educational picture in Great Britain showed signs of improvement. Apart from the two old-established Sephardi schools and the London and provincial "free schools" of the 19th century, there were some 3,000 pupils at the Jews' Free School, over 2,000 at the 19 institutes run by the Talmud Torah Trust, and nearly 5,000 boys and girls enrolled in the 57 classes of the Union of Hebrew and Religious Classes, with many more at *talmud torah*s and religion classes in the Provinces. In 1939, the Central Committee for Jewish Education merged with the Joint Emergency Committee for Jewish Religious Education in Great Britain and, led by educators such as Nathan *Morris, grappled with the urgent problem of maintaining a Jewish educational program for children and young people uprooted from their homes by wartime evacuation. A series of regular publications and correspondence courses was devised for the teaching of Hebrew, Bible, Mishnah, Jewish history, and religious subjects; and supplementary aid was provided by the *Habonim, *Bnei Akiva, and *Torah va-Avodah Zionist youth movements, all of which published material of an educational nature during the war years. The Education Act of 1944 first gave formal sanction to the withdrawal of Jewish children from state or state-aided voluntary (i.e., denominational) schools for the purpose of worship or religious instruction in accordance with parents' wishes.

Early Postwar Developments

A Communal Conference on the Reconstruction of Jewish Education in Great Britain was held in London in 1945, as a result of which two major coordinating bodies came into being: the London Board of Jewish Religious Education and the Central Council of Jewish Religious Education, which had the harder task of organizing schools and classes in Jewish communities throughout the British Isles. In London and the Provinces, the old "*ḥeder*" and *talmud torah* institutions gradually gave way to the Jewish day school system, and increasing emphasis was laid on combating ignorance, apathy, and assimilation. In this battle much inspiration was obtained from the emergence of the State of Israel, which has enlivened the Jewish calendar and added a new zest to the learning and teaching of Judaism and Jewish history as well as the Hebrew language.

During the late 1940s and the 1950s many new Jewish day schools were founded in London and the major cities, this movement gaining added impetus and encouragement after the Ministry of Education granted recognition to several such schools in 1951. Most of them provide primary education (ages 5–11) in general subjects and Jewish studies, but there are also some secondary and grammar schools which receive state aid. Progress was at first slow after the devastation of the war years and in 1953 less than 19,000 Jewish children in the Greater London area (with a total Jewish population of 285,000) received regular religious instruction, as compared with slightly more than that number in 1924, when there were only 175,000 Jews in the British capital. By 1954, there were ten Jewish schools in Britain receiving state aid and 13 others operating on a private basis. One important development was the revival of the old Jews' Free School as the JFS Comprehensive School in Camden Town, North London (1958). The postwar years also saw the growth of the Jewish Secondary Schools Movement and of two other Orthodox networks: the right-wing Yesodey Hatorah schools (1943) and the Lubavitch Foundation (1959). A few schools were also sponsored by the British Mizrachi Federation in conjunction with the Jewish Agency Torah Department (North-West London, Dublin) and many more in London and the Provinces by the British Zionist Federation. Schools of the Zionist type run in conjunction with the London Board or local Jewish education authorities were founded in the London suburbs of Clapton (1956), Willesden (1945, 1947), Hampstead Garden Suburb, Golders Green (1959), Edgware (1956), and Ilford (1970), and older schools refounded in Bayswater and Stepney. The same trend was maintained in the Provinces with Jewish primary schools in Birmingham, Leeds, Liverpool, Manchester, Newcastle, Southend, Sunderland, and in Dublin and Glasgow.

The rate of educational progress may be gauged from the fact that, while only a little more than 4,000 Jewish children attended day schools in 1953, nearly 9,000 were enrolled in schools of this type by 1963. In 1961, it was estimated that 13% (approximately 8,000 children) out of the total Jewish school population attended 18 kindergartens, 23 primary, and 9 secondary schools under various Jewish auspices in Great Britain (of which 16 were state-aided); while 22,000 Jewish youngsters were enrolled in "withdrawal classes," "*ḥadarim*" and *talmud torah* and synagogue schools throughout the country. Nevertheless, only a little over half of the Jewish population of school age received regular Jewish education. Attendance in the day schools compared with the national average, whereas boys enrolled in synagogue and similar classes tended to abandon their Jewish studies after the critical age of 13, when they had reached their bar mitzvah. The same was true of girls once they reached their early teens. By 1970 there were 50 Jewish day schools in Great Britain (a little over half of them in the London area), with about 10,000 pupils in all, including 4,000 in the Provinces.

Secondary and Higher Education

During the 1950s and 1960s there was a gradual, but significant, increase in the number of Jewish youngsters in full-time attendance at Jewish secondary and grammar schools. In the Provinces, the two principal mixed grammar schools were both in Lancashire – the Liverpool King David School (part of a local network with a total enrollment of 700, not all of whom were, however, Jewish children) and the Manchester King David High School, which also had associated infants' and junior schools. The Glasgow Hebrew College taught youngsters over the age of 13. There were also a number of voluntary schools in Manchester, where about half the Provincial day schools were concentrated, including the Manchester Jewish Grammar School (Boys) and the Manchester Jewish High School for Girls. The most novel experiment in Jewish education of the postwar years was Carmel College at Wallingford, near Oxford, founded by Rabbi Kopul Rosen in 1948. This was a highly successful Jewish "public school" combining a high level of secular and traditional Jewish studies. It appealed to parents frustrated by the public school "quota" system operating against Jewish boys, but also attracted students from abroad. Whittingehame College in Sussex, run on a Zionist pattern, was, unlike Carmel College, based on a secular program, which may account for the lack of public support which led to its closure in the late 1960s.

The Jewish institutions of higher learning were headed by Jews' College which, under the direction of Isidore *Epstein, was reorganized from 1958 as a seminary for the training of rabbis, ministers, and cantors, with an associated teachers' institute. The Judith Lady Montefiore College (1869) in Ramsgate was reestablished in 1952 as the result of an agreement between the London Sephardim and the Jewish Agency Torah Department to train teachers and cantors mainly recruited from North Africa. In 1960 the college was transferred to London. Leo Baeck College (1956), a Reform foundation, was later reorganized in conjunction with the Liberal and Progressive movement to train non-Orthodox rabbis and teachers. By 1967, there were a dozen yeshivot in Great Britain with a total enrollment of some 400 full-time students – about four times as many as those attending the two London seminaries. Four of the yeshivot (Etz Chaim, Law of Truth, Horomo, and Chaye

Olam) were in the Greater London area; and there were three major yeshivot in Gateshead, Manchester, and Sunderland, each of which had an associated *kolel* (institute for higher rabbinic studies). Gateshead, an island of strict Orthodoxy, had a yeshivah population of 160 in 1962 and also housed two Jewish schools. There were smaller yeshivot in Ilford, Leeds, Liverpool, and Glasgow. Advanced Hebrew studies were also pursued by degree students at the universities of London, Leeds, Manchester, and Oxford, and at Dublin and Glasgow.

Jewish education was promoted in Great Britain by various communal and other bodies, including the National Union of Hebrew Teachers (1945), which fought a long campaign to raise the status and remuneration of the Jewish teacher; the B'nai B'rith Hillel Foundation (1953); the Inter-University Jewish Federation (1919); the Central Council's Jewish Youth Study Groups (1946); and Ḥovevey Torah (1951), a voluntary organization of young adults conducting a weekly program of advanced Torah study in London. Other important educational bodies included the Society for Jewish Study (1946), whose members ranged from the Orthodox to the Liberal; the Jewish Book Council (1949), which organized an annual Book Week of lectures and exhibitions in London; and the Institute of Jewish Studies (1953), established in Manchester by R. Alexander *Altmann and later transferred to University College, London. One notably successful educational scheme was the Hebrew Seminar movement initiated by Levi Gertner, director of the Jewish Agency Education Department, which drew hundreds of participants to its weekend and vacation courses in the countryside and abroad.

Hebrew Teaching

The cost of maintaining the fabric of Jewish education in Great Britain is borne by the most committed, and derives from communal taxation, voluntary donations, Zionist grants, *kashrut* supervision fees, and synagogue seat rentals. Additional sums are obtained from fees paid by a minority of parents, and a proportion of the budget is also paid by the state.

In order to improve the general standard of Hebrew teaching, salaries were increased (this was not necessary in state-recognized schools) and a number of teachers' training colleges established. These included the Teachers' Institute attached to Jews' College, whose students sat for degree and diploma examinations; an evening institute run by the London Board; the Lady Judith Montefiore College; the Salford Training College in Manchester; and two women's colleges administered by the Beth Jacob movement in London and Gateshead. In most, if not all, of these the minimum training period was three years; and in 1960 there were close to 250 men and women enrolled. There were active Jewish education boards in Glasgow, Leeds, Manchester, and Sheffield, and a communal education officer in Birmingham.

Subsequent Developments

While estimates of the Jewish child population (and of those receiving part-time Jewish education) fell with the decline of the general child population in Britain, the number enrolled in Jewish day schools reached some 13,000 at the end of the 1970s, representing over 20% of the estimated Jewish child population. New Jewish day schools continued to be founded and there were positive developments in Jewish adult education in various aspects involving synagogues of different religious affiliation, the Lubavitch movement, and courses for younger Jewish leaders. Enrollment continued to rise through the 1980s and 1990s reaching 30% in 1992 and 51% in 1999. The United Synagogue Agency for Jewish Education operated 14 primary and nursery schools and five secondary schools in the early 2000s and had trained over 150 teachers since 1997. The Leo Baeck College Center for Jewish Education offered an M.A. program in Jewish education from 2002.

BIBLIOGRAPHY: Z. Scharfstein, in: *The Jewish People*, 2 (1948), 178–88; V.D. Lipman (ed.), *Three Centuries of Anglo-Jewish History* (1961), 53–54, 85–89, 179–80; I. Fishman and H. Levy, in: J. Gould and S. Esh (eds.), *Jewish Life in Modern Britain* (1964), 67–85; S. Stein, in: *Remember the Days. Essays … Cecil Roth* (1966), 145–79; L. Gertner and B. Steinberg, in: *Jewish Education*, 38:1 (1968), 34–45; A. Eisenberg (ed.), *World Census on Jewish Education* (1968), 95–97; I. Mehlman, *Ha-Ḥinnukh ha-Yehudi ba-Golah* (1969), 46–55. **WEBSITES:** www.brijnet.org; www.lbc.ac.uk.

AUSTRALIA

In 1968 there were 40 school units of which 12 were day schools with an enrollment of 3,580 and 28 supplementary schools with a total registration of 3,335.The programs of all-day schools included secular subjects as prescribed by State authorities. In most of these schools 12 hours per week were allocated for Jewish study of traditional subjects, including modern Hebrew. These schools served children from grades 1 to 6 (ages 5–13 primary) and grades 7 to 12 (ages 14–17 secondary). The percentages of pupils on the secondary level were satisfactory (about 690 out of the total 3,580).

In the supplementary schools or part-time schools, based on a six-year program, the children attended four days a week as well as once-a-week classes. The educational program of the supplementary schools conducted by synagogues varied with the type of sponsorship. The Orthodox placed more stress on traditional subjects (prayers, Bible, customs, and Hebrew), the classes conducted by the Zionist Council emphasized the study of Hebrew, the liberal synagogue-schools, especially in the one-day-a-week classes, employed the vernacular in all teaching, and the Yiddish schools taught almost exclusively Yiddish language and literature and some Hebrew for bar mitzvah purposes. In addition to children receiving an education in the Jewish schools, there were in 1968 about 3,700 pupils in the religious instruction classes of the government schools. Since the education departments in all states of Australia permit denominational teachers to conduct weekly lessons, the Jews made full use of this opportunity. Thus a total of approximately 10,600 children received a Jewish education: a little more than a third having had a maximum program, and about two-thirds a minimal education. Most schools lacked adequate text materials and instructional aids. Most textbooks were imported from England, the U.S.A., and Israel.

The teacher situation was very grave in the 1960s. There was a shortage of competent, qualified teachers. In 1968 the day schools employed Israeli teachers; they constituted 35% of the instructional staff. Of the teachers of general subjects in the Jewish day schools more than 50% were non-Jewish.

The schools in each state were affiliated with its State Board of Jewish Education, a community representative body headed by competent educational leadership. In addition, there was in the 1960s an Orthodox United Education Board and a Board for the Schools of the Liberal Congregations. Hebrew classes were also conducted under Zionist auspices. All schools received regular supervisory services by educators engaged by the central educational agencies. In 1968 the Jewish education budget for all Australia was 1,700,000 Australian dollars.

[Judah Pilch]

Several full-time Jewish day schools were founded in the subsequent decades, bringing the total up to 18 in the early 1990s: nine in Melbourne, six in Sydney, and one each in Perth, Adelaide, and Brisbane. These represented the various streams in Australian Jewish life, with three schools in Melbourne, for instance, representing strict Orthodoxy, and the other schools associated with the Mizrachi movement, mainstream Orthodoxy, and with the Progressive movements, with secular Yiddish culture, and with secular Zionism. Enrollments continued to climb at these schools through the 1980s and into the 1990s. In Melbourne, they rose from 4,840 at all schools in 1982 to 5,492 in 1989, and about 6,000 in 1992. In Sydney, the rise was even more spectacular, from 1,594 in 1982 to 3,041 in 1988. During the severe recession of the early 1990s, doubts were widely expressed about the continued viability of several Jewish schools, all of which were fee-paying although they each received some state government assistance. Nevertheless, though their rate of growth fell off, absolute numbers continued to increase, with especially strong growth in the Strictly Orthodox schools, and enrollments at Jewish day schools in Australia probably represented a higher percentage of the local Jewish community than in any other significant Diaspora community, with over 50 percent of Jewish school-age children attending one or another school. Indeed, Australia's Jewish-day-school system has been termed "the jewel in the crown" of Australian Jewish life, with Melbourne's Mount Scopus College, with 2,700 students, long claiming to be the largest Jewish day school in the world. Growth, though slight, continued into the 2000s despite the fact that tuition had become prohibitive for many Jewish families, who were increasingly sending their children to state schools.

Advances were made in this period in tertiary Jewish education, long an area of neglect, especially in comparison with the well-developed day school movement. By 1992, the University of Sydney and three universities in Victoria – Melbourne, Monash, and Deakin – were offering or actively planning Jewish studies programs, a notable advance on the situation a decade before. Lecturers in Modern Jewish History were appointed at Melbourne and Monash universities in, respectively, 1988 and 1992. An Australian Association for Jewish Studies was established in 1987 and held annual conferences since then; hundreds of scholarly papers, representing all facets of Jewish studies, were presented. Several Orthodox *kolelim* also existed.

BIBLIOGRAPHY: U.Z. Engelman, *Jewish Education in the Diaspora* (1962), index; A. Eisenberg (ed.), *World Census of Jewish Education* (1968); P.Y. Medding, *From Assimilation to Group Survival* (1968), index.

CANADA

Jewish education in Canada began as formal schooling, using models that were familiar to the early immigrants arriving from Europe. These modes of instruction were slowly adapted to public school models that were developing at the same time in late 19th-century and early 20th-century Canada. What began, then, as *ḥadarim* in private homes soon became classrooms in a synagogue, and then, later on, modern school buildings. Early schooling was supplemental to the public system, in the afternoons and on Sundays, but day schools eventually became the dominant system. In the large communities of present-day Montreal, Ottawa, Toronto, Winnipeg, Calgary, and Vancouver day school students outnumber supplementary school students, a phenomenon which distinguishes Canadian communities from those in the United States.

This distinguishing characteristic is due, in part, to the fact that early in the history of Canadian public schooling, religion separated different school systems. This remains the case in certain provinces. As a result, Jewish day schools are government-assisted in some provinces, the great exception being Ontario, with the largest Jewish population. Many attempts have been made to right this injustice in the Ontario system where Catholic schools receive full funding, and for a brief period a tax credit did exist in the early years of the 21st century.

There are a number of modes of Jewish education currently operating in Canada. These include full day schools and supplementary congregational or independent schools; Jewish pre-schools linked to day schools, JCC's, or associated to congregational or independent supplementary schools; educational programs organized by denominational, community-, or Zionist-based youth groups; educational programs at denominational, community, Zionist, or private summer camps; adult educational programs offered by congregations and community organizations as well as Jewish teacher training programs and Jewish studies courses and programs available through different Canadian universities. With the exception of a few secular schools, youth groups, and camps, almost all Jewish education in Canada is religious education and is divided by denominations: Ḥasidic, Ḥaredi, Modern Orthodox, Reform, Conservative, Reconstructionist, and Ḥavura communities. Of course, university-based Jewish studies are conducted in the secular settings of Canada's largest academic institutions.

Day schools across Canada offer the typical full day of studies with varying proportions of general studies vis-à-vis Jewish studies, based on the ideology of the school. A typical Ultra-Orthodox school might have a morning and early afternoon of intensive holy studies followed by a late afternoon period of general studies. Another denomination will emphasize high-quality general studies for two-thirds of the day and a Jewish studies curriculum for the remaining third. Most day schools teach both textual and modern Israeli Hebrew, while some teach Yiddish for varied ideological reasons. Jewish curricular content and emphases are determined by the ideology of each particular school.

Pedagogical methodology is also case-specific to each school. The approaches range from rote recitation of texts to Montessori, multiple intelligence instruction, and arts-based techniques.

Supplementary schools are even more varied in their content and form. They range from volunteer-taught Sunday or Sabbath schools to three-day-a-week institutions with full-time directors and professional teachers. There are schools linked to synagogues and temples, community schools, Orthodox *kiruv* schools for non-Orthodox children, and for-profit commercial establishments. In Canada, supplementary schools account for the minority of children in Jewish schooling, but have demonstrated great potential for outreach to peripheral and marginal Jewish families.

Youth groups and summer camps are divided by religious denominations or Zionist movements, with some community-wide groupings. BBYO, Beitar, Bnei Akiva, Habonim-Dror, Hashomer Hatzair, NFTY, NCSY, Tzofim, USY, and Young Judea all have chapters and groups in various communities across Canada. Zionist camps, community camps, denominational camps, and private camps are active near most of the larger communities.

Teacher education has a unique character in Canada due to two university-based programs at McGill University in Montreal and at York University in Toronto, respectively. The McGill program was established in 1973, with York opening its version soon after in 1977. These are Jewish teacher training programs based on an undergraduate degree and a teaching diploma, using faculties of general education and Jewish studies programs in both institutions. York University has an agreement with western Canadian communities to train teachers for the schools of the western provinces. Other teacher training takes place either in pre-service seminaries of Ultra-Orthodox systems or in in-service professional development offered by central agencies such as Toronto's Board of Jewish Education or Montreal's Bronfman Jewish Education Centre.

Aside from teacher training, which is professionally oriented, there are multiple modes of adult education sponsored by a variety of synagogues, temples, service organizations, and community federations. They range from *kolelim* in the Orthodox community, sporadic lectures in a JCC, home study groups, on-line courses, synagogue *shiurim*, Daf Yomi classes, to the *kolel* in Toronto's liberal community.

It should be noted that although several provinces provide partial funding for day schools, all other Jewish educational activities are funded by users, voluntary organizations, and federated communities. In two such federated communities, Montreal and Toronto, there are central agencies for Jewish education, which provide a variety of services to Jewish schools, youth groups, camps, and Israel experiences such as the March of the Living and Birthright for Israel. In Toronto, where there is no provincial aid to day schools, the UJA Federation's Board of Jewish Education grants millions of dollars annually to subsidize day school tuition for parents in need. Over 200,000,000 Canadian dollars are spent annually on all aspects of Jewish education across Canada.

Data from the 2001 Canadian census, coupled with statistics provided by Jewish schools across the country, provide us with a snapshot of the status of Jewish education in Canada.

Of the 61,000 school-age children (those between the ages of 6 and 17) in Canada, 87% lived in the six largest Jewish communities, communities with more than 7,000 Jews. A review of enrollment in day elementary, day high school, and supplementary schools demonstrates the following: In 2001, of the 53,300 children aged 6–17 in the six largest Jewish communities, 25,446 children or 48% were receiving some form of Jewish education. In 2001, of the 34,215 Jewish students aged 6–13 in these communities, 13,767 or 40% attended day elementary schools; by comparison, in 1970, 30% of Jewish students aged 6–13 in all Jewish communities with more than 25 families attended day elementary schools. In 2001, of the 19,085 Jewish students aged 14–17 in the six largest Jewish communities, 4,889 or 26% attended day high schools; by comparison, in 1970, only 10–14% of Jewish students aged 14–17 attended day high schools, so there clearly has been a marked increase in high school attendance. In 2001, of the 53,300 children aged 6–17 who might have enrolled in supplementary schools, 6,790 or 13% were in attendance.

An examination of the figures for individual communities reveals that enrollment statistics vary widely:

	Total Jewish population (2001 Census)	Student population ages 6–17 (2001 Census)	Total enrollment in Jewish education	Total % enrolled in Jewish education
Toronto	179,100	30,365	14,569	48
Montreal	92,975	13,585	7,733	57
Vancouver	22,590	3,140	993	32
Winnipeg	14,775	2,240	875	39
Ottawa	13,130	2,650	913	34
Calgary	7,950	1,320	363	28

In Calgary, Ottawa, and Vancouver, approximately 30% of the children aged 6–13 were enrolled in Jewish schools, with 5–7%

of the students continuing through high school and 6–14% attending supplementary school programs.

Winnipeg's Jewish elementary day schools also service close to 30% of children ages 6–13. However, the situation in Winnipeg is somewhat different. In addition to those students enrolled in Jewish schools, a significant number were enrolled in Hebrew bilingual programs at two public schools, where they study Hebrew language, culture, holidays, etc. In total, then, some 48% of students ages 6–13 were enrolled in Jewish programs. Another difference: in Winnipeg, 20% of students ages 14–17 were enrolled in Jewish high schools. A very small percent attended supplementary school programs.

Montreal and Toronto, with the largest Jewish populations, attracted a larger percentage of the students than the smaller communities. Montreal had the highest percentage of enrollment, with 55% attending elementary schools and 46% attending high schools. Supplementary schools in Montreal attracted some 5% of students ages 6–17. Toronto had 36% of 6–13-year-olds in elementary day school and 21% of 14–17-year-olds in high schools. Toronto had the highest percent of students in supplementary school settings – 17% of 6–17-year-olds. (School population data provided by Federations and schools.)

BIBLIOGRAPHY: B.G. Sack, *History of the Jews in Canada* (1965); United Jewish Welfare Fund of Toronto, *Study on Jewish Education* (1975); J. Kutnick, "Jewish Education in Canada," in: H.S. Himmelfarb and S. DellaPergola (eds.), *Jewish Education Worldwide Cross-Cultural Perspectives* (1989); H.M. Waller, "Canada," in: *American Jewish Year Book*, 103 (2003); Statistics Canada, 2001 Census, special order tabulations for UIA Federations Canada (2003).

[Joyce Levine and Seymour Epstein (2nd ed.)]

SOUTH AFRICA

The outstanding feature of South Africa Jewish education is the predominance of all-day schools over supplementary classes. This is a development that followed World War II. Whereas in 1948 there were only seven pupils in a pioneering day school, in 1968 there were 17 schools with an enrollment in elementary and high school departments of a total of 5,632 pupils. The early post-World War II supplementary schools consisted of several types: one hour daily, five days a week in the morning prior to classes, on public school premises, for secondary school pupils; one hour each day, or two hours twice a week in the afternoon, meeting mostly in Orthodox congregational buildings. These classes had a total enrollment in 1968 of 4,275 pupils. In Johannesburg and its environs the afternoon Hebrew schools, or *talmud torahs*, were organized in a regional body called the United Hebrew Schools. Apart from these Orthodox part-time classes, the Reform congregations under the aegis of the South African Union of Progressive Judaism also maintained such Hebrew schools with a total enrollment of about 1,300 pupils. Finally, 3,406 children studied in 1968 in 53 Jewish nursery schools established and maintained by various women's groups. In 1967 Johannesburg had an Orthodox Yeshiva College and a *Folkshule* where instruction was given in Yiddish.

All these schools, except the Reform, were administered by two separate bodies, the South African Board of Jewish Education based in Johannesburg, and the Cape Board of Jewish Education in Cape Town. This division of labor was due to the distance between the two cities. The South African Board provided various services to scattered small settlements of Jews in rural areas, such as visiting teachers, correspondence courses, syllabi, and supervisory visits.

The South African Jewish community provided especially lavish support for its ever expanding system of day schools. All these schools were accommodated in magnificent, modern structures, usually surrounded by spacious sports fields. Expenditures were covered by tuition fees, fundraising campaigns, grants by Jewish communal organizations, and by private bequests, trust funds, and endowments. To accommodate pupils from outlying country districts, hostels, or dormitories, were provided. In 1968 more than 100 pupils were housed in such hostels of the King David schools in Johannesburg. The hostel of the Herzlia school in Cape Town was also quickly filled with over 50 out-of-town boarders. Sustained living in a richly Jewish atmosphere, especially on the Sabbath, provided a lasting influence on the character of students in these hostels. A further salutary effect upon the development of student Jewish consciousness was afforded by an ulpan scheme whereby groups of secondary school pupils from day schools spent annually over three months in Israel, learning Hebrew and touring the country.

Crowning the Jewish educational system was the Rabbi Judah Leib Zlotnik Seminary in Johannesburg for the training of Hebrew teachers. From the year of its foundation in 1944 to 1968 it produced more than 100 graduates. These teachers served not only the day schools but also the widespread country communities. Every graduate was sent for a year's further study in Jerusalem. The seminary did not meet the demand for teachers. A number of students, mainly women, took courses in Hebrew at the universities of Witwatersrand and Cape Town. Bursaries (stipends) were provided for by the community for those who studied for teaching. The severe shortage of Hebrew teachers was partly filled by arrivals from Israel. In addition to the formal schooling the community provided informal cultural activities, as well as sports and recreational facilities for both youth and adults.

[Isaac Levitats]

In 2003, over 80% of school-going Jewish children in Johannesburg, Cape Town, and Port Elizabeth (whose Theodor Herzl school by then had a mainly non-Jewish enrollment) were attending one of the Jewish day schools. The total pupil enrollment in the day schools was about 8,000, substantially more than the 1970 figure of nearly 6,000 even though the overall Jewish community declined by more than a third. Those still in government schools had their Jewish educational requirements catered to by the United Hebrew Schools (under the SABJE) in Johannesburg and the Religious Instruction Department of the SAJBD in Cape Town. Jewish pupils in Pretoria and Durban received Jewish education through a special department at the Crawford College branches. This arrangement came about following the takeover of the Carmel College Jewish day schools in those cities by Crawford during the 1990s.

The mainstream schools in Johannesburg were the three King David schools, located in Linksfield, Victory Park, and Sandton. The first two provided Jewish education from preschool to matriculation level while the third went up to primary school level. King David's counterparts in Cape Town were the Herzlia schools.

The ideological basis of the King David, Herzlia, and Theodor Herzl schools was officially described as "broadly national traditional," a formula intended to indicate both the religious and the Zionist character of the education. Pupils received a full education following a state syllabus and a Jewish studies program, including religion, history, literature, and Hebrew language. However, many demanded more intensive religious instruction and greater religious observance. Thus Johannesburg's Yeshiva College developed into a full-time day school from nursery school up to matriculation and steadily grew from an initial few dozen pupils to well over 800 by the turn of the century. In 1995, the school received the Jerusalem Prize for Jewish Education in the Diaspora. Yeshiva College could be regarded as centrist Orthodox in its approach. More right-wing Orthodox schools that subsequently were established included Torah Academy and Cape Town's Hebrew Academy (both under Chabad's auspices), Yeshivas Toras Emes, Shaarei Torah, Bais Yaakov, Hirsch Lyons, and Yeshiva Maharsha.

The Progressive movement also maintained a network of supplementary Hebrew and religious classes at its temples. These schools are affiliated with the Union for Progressive Jewish Education.

At the tertiary level, university students were able to take Jewish studies through the Semitics Department of the University of South Africa (UNISA); the Department of Hebrew and Jewish Studies of Natal University; and the Department of Hebrew and Jewish Studies (including the Isaac and Jessie Kaplan Centre for Jewish Studies and Research) at the University of Cape Town. Programs of adult education continued to be provided by the South African Board of Jewish Education, the South African Zionist Federation, and the various affiliates, including most particularly the Union of Jewish Women, the Women's Zionist Council, and the South African Zionist Youth Council.

[David Saks (2nd ed.)]

BIBLIOGRAPHY: B. Steinberg, in: *Jewish Education*, 39 (1969), 14–22; A. Eisenberg (ed.), *World Census on Jewish Education* (1968).

ARGENTINA

Jewish education was sponsored and supervised by the Central Board of Education, an affiliate of the Va'ad ha-Kehillot. This Board represented a consolidation in 1956–57 of two formerly independent educational boards, one for Buenos Aires, the other for the provinces. It included the Agudah-oriented Heikhal ha-Torah school with 500 students in 1970. Only the Yieuf (Peoples Democrats, Communist) schools with some 2,000 students remained out of this national Jewish school network. In the past the Argentine Jewish educational system consisted of supplementary schools. The first day school was opened in Buenos Aires in 1948; it took a long time for these schools to spread. Supplementary education was facilitated by the fact that the public schools meet on a four-hour two-shift basis. This enabled Jewish children to attend either morning or afternoon Jewish classes. The predominant element in the program was national rather than religious. Yiddish was given preference over Hebrew, although both languages were taught. Each of the many ideological groupings had its own program of instruction. In the 1960s these curricula began to coalesce and to gravitate toward more traditional and broadly national common elements. There were many inherent weaknesses in the system. As late as 1965 it was pointed out that only 17% of the Jewish school age population was enrolled in Jewish schools. Of those who did attend the first grade in Buenos Aires in 1960 only 4.2% stayed until the sixth grade. Small schools predominated; most buildings were inadequate. European-trained teachers were gradually replaced by native-born, most of them female and inadequately prepared for teaching. Since schools were often initiated and administered teaching by lay individuals, supervision left much to be desired. The general apathy of parents and the assimilatory factors in the community resulted in cultural deprivation of the children.

In the late 1960s there was a turn for the better. Many school buildings were modern, airy, and roomy. The well-organized community supplied a considerable proportion of the school budgets for operational and capital expenditures and strove toward a general upgrading of curriculum and supervision. There were four types of schools: purely Hebraic, Yiddish–Hebrew, Hebrew–Yiddish, and religious. Israel was a most important element of the course of study.

In addition to in-service training courses for teachers there were a number of teachers' seminaries. The oldest among them was the Midrashah, or Seminario Docente para Escuelas Israelitas, established in 1940. In the course of the first 25 years it enrolled some 3,000 students; 900 teachers were graduated. Close to 70% of the teachers in Buenos Aires and neighboring schools were graduates of Midrashah, recognized for the higher Jewish learning it offered, and the requirement was that high school teachers must be graduates of that school. In 1966 it had 350 students enrolled. The Moisesville Teachers Seminary trained many of the teachers for the interior of the country. In 1949 it graduated its first class of ten primary and kindergarten teachers. In 1966 it had 120 resident and 85 local students. Ninety-nine percent of the teachers were native-born. Many spent a year in Israel. In 1964–69, 281 Buenos Aires graduates of teacher training schools enjoyed such an experience. Special courses were offered also for administrative personnel.

In addition to opportunities for formal schooling Argentina offered many informal programs. Thousands of students attended summer day and sleep-away camps. Evening courses for adults were offered at the spacious community center named Hebraica in Buenos Aires. Sports activities were popular among the recreational facilities which provided a means of identification with the Jewish group. Widely ramified communal and Zionist efforts further enhanced such identification. These positive factors were outweighed by the large sectors of the unaffiliated, the unschooled, and those bent on the road to assimilation.

[Isaac Levitats]

The institution of a longer school day in Argentina's public educational system in the late 1960s worked a revolution in Jewish education. With no time left for complementary education Jewish schools were transformed into day schools offering both a general and a Jewish curriculum. To keep their students the general curriculum was upgraded, often at the expense of Jewish studies, but the strategy succeeded. A survey carried out in 1997 found that nearly half of all Jewish children aged 13–17 and two-thirds of children aged 6–12 attended Jewish day schools. A total of 19,248 students attended classes in 56 kindergartens, 52 elementary schools, and 29 high schools.

By 2002, however, the numbers had dropped to just 14,700 students in 40 elementary schools and 22 high schools. The difference was the natural result of low birthrate, assimilation, and emigration. The high tuition rates in these private schools were also a deterrent under Argentina's grim economic conditions, even though local Jewish institutions, the Jewish Agency, and Israel's Ministry of Education, together with the Joint Distribution Committee and World Jewish Congress, established financial aid programs.

To reach Jewish youngsters not in day schools, the community, in cooperation with the Jewish Agency, established a supplementary program called *Lomdim* for secondary level (with about 1,200 students in 2004) with classes two or three days (6–9 hours) a week. A second supplementary program, for elementary-school children, called *Chalomot*, with 4–12 hours a week had approximately 600 children. Chabad developed a similar strategy, offering children attending public school an enriched after-school program in computers, English, and other subjects, together with Jewish studies.

There were also no teacher training institutions in Argentina after Michlelet Shazar was closed in the late 1990s. The only institutions of higher Jewish studies were Orthodox yeshivot and the Seminario Rabínico Latinoamericano of Conservative orientation, in which there was also a section for non-rabbinic studies.

[Efraim Zadoff (2nd ed.)]

BIBLIOGRAPHY: I. Janasowicz (ed.), *Pinkas fun der Kehilla in Buenos Aires 1963–68* (1969); U.Z. Engelman, *Jewish Education in the Diaspora* (1962), 64–71; Z. Sohar, *Ha-Ḥinnukh ba-Tefuẓot* (1953), 155–67.

BRAZIL

On the assumption that the children of elementary and secondary school age constitutes 20 percent of the Jewish population in most countries, there should have been a Jewish school enrollment in Brazil of 28,000. Actually only a little more than 10,000 pupils attended the Jewish schools of Brazil in the late 1960s. The number of schools supervised by the central office for education consisted of kindergartens, elementary and secondary schools, a yeshivah, a college, a seminar, and a teacher training institute. Altogether 10,409 students attended these 33 schools.

The Jewish educational system combined both Jewish and general studies in the same school. The Jewish program included the study of both Hebrew and Yiddish. In schools where Jewish studies were taught two or three hours a day, there was still the possibility of teaching both languages; many of the schools, however, allowed only 40–50 minutes a day for Jewish studies, making the study of two languages in those schools to all intents and purposes impossible. The 20 Jewish day schools in the country had small enrollments, and thus had difficulties in grading the children adequately, in providing an adequate staff, and in financing. Among the Jewish teachers in Brazil there still were a number of teachers who came from abroad equipped with pedagogic skill, Jewish knowledge, experience, and deep commitment to Jewish education. But the number of those teachers was gradually diminishing. To meet in some manner the pressing need for classroom teachers, the community organized seminars for teachers in Rio and Sao Paulo, which in reality were secondary schools, applicants entering upon completion of the primary school. The Sao Paulo seminar, founded in 1950, had an enrollment of 84 students in 1968. A considerable number of the teachers were Israelis. In addition to maintaining the teacher training school, the Council of Education and Culture conducted periodically, especially during the summer, in-service teacher training programs for kindergarten and grade teachers. During the winter, the Council also conducted special courses for teachers in Bible, Jewish history, Hebrew literature, and educational psychology. In the early 21st century the Sao Paulo community had four Orthodox and four traditional schools, with 3,000 students at the Educacio Hebraico Brasileiro Renscenca. There were several Jewish schools in Rio de Janeiro, including the 500-student Bar-Ilan School, which also had a kosher dining room and a synagogue.

URUGUAY

The enrollment in Montevideo's 11 Jewish schools (seven of them day schools) was about 3,000 in 1968. Most of the schools offered elementary Jewish education, beginning with kindergarten. With the exception of the Sholem Aleichem school, Hebrew had replaced Yiddish in all schools. Many of the teachers and principals were Israelis or had studied in Israel. All the schools were affiliated with the Board of Education of the Montevideo *kehillah*, which acts as a central coordinating supervisory community agency for Jewish education. In the early 21st century there were four Jewish schools in all of Uruguay, with studies both in Spanish and Hebrew. A comprehensive school was the largest, going from pre-school through high school. The Chabad Center also ran a comprehensive school. About a third of the country's Jewish children attended these schools.

BIBLIOGRAPHY: U.Z. Engelman, *Jewish Education in the Diaspora* (1962), index; A. Eisenberg (ed.), *World Census on Jewish Education* (1968); A. Spolinsky, in: *Bi-Tefuẓot ha-Golah* (1964), 45–55.

[Judah Pilch]

MEXICO

After World War I large numbers of Jews from Eastern Europe and their families came to Mexico with the intention of staying temporarily while waiting for visas to the U.S.A. American immigration laws did not relax and they lost hope and decided then to make Mexico their permanent home. The married couples began to worry about the education of their children. Fortunately for Jewish education in Mexico there were among the immigrants a few young men with a good Jewish background who could not adapt themselves to the hard and humiliating occupation of peddling and consequently took upon themselves the organization of a school for Jewish children. The desire of the parents was to open a day school authorized by the Mexican Board of Education in accordance with the programs of the Mexican government schools, but with a substantial part of the schedule to be devoted to Jewish studies. Thus in 1924 an all-day Jewish school with 24 students was established in Mexico City.

By 1969, 45 years later, it had developed to nine all-day schools with a population of approximately 5,000 boys and girls between the ages of 3–18 in spacious modern buildings with up-to-date equipment, libraries, laboratories, workshops, and assembly halls. It has been claimed that as many as 90% of Jewish children in Mexico attended these Jewish schools, and still did at the outset of the 21st century in a country where the intermarriage rate is just 10 percent. In Mexico City there were at least a dozen Jewish schools in 2005. The schools in existence in 1969 were (1) Colegio Israelita de Mexico – from kindergarten to college with about 1,500 students; (2) Colegio Yavne – from kindergarten to college with about 700 students; (3) Colegio Tarbut – from kindergarten to college with about 1,000 students; (4) I.L. Peretz school – from kindergarten to high school with about 400 students; (5) Colegio Tarbut Sephardi – from kindergarten to college with about 800 students; (6) Colegio Monte Sinai – from kindergarten to college with about 700 students; (7) Yeshivah de Mexico – from kindergarten to high school with about 100 students; (8) Colegio Israelita de Monterrey – from kindergarten to high school with about 80 students; (9) Colegio Israelita de Guadalajara – from kindergarten to sixth grade elementary school with about 50 students; (10) The Yiddish-Hebrew Teachers Seminary in Mexico City – with about 70 students.

In all the schools the Jewish subjects were compulsory. The majority of them did not admit students in the higher grades without a proper preparation in Yiddish or Hebrew or both. Some schools were more lenient and special groups for Jewish studies were formed to prepare the newcomers for their respective classes.

In Colegio Israelita de Mexico, Colegio Yavne, I.L. Peretz school, and in the Yeshivah de Mexico, Yiddish and Hebrew were compulsory. In all the other schools only Hebrew was taught. Three hours daily were devoted to the Jewish subjects up to high school and two hours in high school and college. In the schools where both languages were taken the time was divided equally between Yiddish and Hebrew.

All the schools were authorized by and incorporated with the Board of Education of Mexico. The colleges were under the jurisdiction of the autonomous University of Mexico. In the colleges, after successful completion of the curriculum, the students were granted the degrees of B.A. or B.S. which entitled them to be admitted to the professional schools at the university without any additional examinations.

The Jewish subjects were Yiddish language and literature, Hebrew language and literature, Jewish history, Bible, and geography of Israel. The State of Israel occupied a very prominent place in the curriculum. In the higher grades study about Israel was included and in the lower grades starting from kindergarten the teachers made use of all available material to develop in the children a sense of national identity and common fate with the people and State of Israel.

Mexican Jewry has continued to be a tight-knit mostly Orthodox community into the 21st century, enfolding its young in a comprehensive educational system that ensures a strong Jewish identity.

[Bezalel Shachar]

NORTH AFRICA

Modern Jewish education in North Africa started with the opening of the first Alliance Israélite Universelle (AIU) School in *Tetuán in 1862. This French-Jewish organization through its schools and through its educators inspired with missionary zeal saved a significant number of Jewish children in North Africa and Asia from misery and prepared the new generation for modern professions and techniques.

The first schools were opened for boys, often against the opposition of the rabbis. Slowly the population was won over and schools were opened for girls in the larger cities. In 1878 the first school was opened in *Tunis. *Algeria, being a French *département* and its Jews having been declared French citizens, had government schools for the French population, including Jews, and did not require AIU schools.

Once the advantages of a modern education were understood, the parents clamored for more AIU schools. By 1914, when the French Protectorate was established, there were 14 schools in *Morocco with an enrollment of 5,500 pupils.

In 1928 an agreement was reached with the Protectorate authorities which assigned primary education for Jewish children to the AIU. The Protectorate agreed to subsidize the schools and to provide buildings. This enabled the AIU to develop further the network of its schools in North Africa. In 1939 there were 45 schools with an enrollment of 15,800.

The basis of programs was the teaching of the French language as a channel for Western and particularly French culture. This education enabled the Jews to leave the mellahs, to enter commerce and certain professions, and to become the intermediaries between the Protectorate authorities and the Arab population. Hebrew education was given by local rabbis in the age-old tradition and with the ancient methods which had neither influence nor any relevance to the emerging new generation of AIU students.

French influence in Algeria brought about speedy assimilation, to the extent that the AIU intervened to set up *talmud torahs* and to ensure some Jewish education.

Jewish communities in North Africa assumed new importance after the loss of the six million Jews in the Holocaust. American Jews, through the Joint Distribution Committee, became interested in Muslim countries. The AIU, with the help of the Protectorate authorities, developed a large network of new schools. By 1960 there were about 30,000 Jewish pupils in AIU schools. Two new agencies started working in North Africa after World War II. *Oẓar ha-Torah, an Orthodox organization for Jewish education in Muslim countries, opened schools for boys, girls, yeshivot, and teacher training colleges. The Lubavitch Ḥasidim opened yeshivot for boys and Battei Rivkah for girls.

The creation of the Jewish state, the independence of *Tunisia in 1955, Morocco in 1956, and Algeria in 1962 completely changed the Jewish map. On the one hand greater stress was laid on Hebrew and Jewish subjects. The AIU opened the Ecole Normale Hébraïque in Casablanca to train Hebrew teachers for its schools. On the other hand there was the rise in Muslim countries of anti-Jewish sentiment as a result of the wars in Israel. The independence of these countries and political events in the Middle East reduced through emigration the number of Jews in Tunisia, Algeria, and Morocco to about 50,000 by 1969. By the mid-1990s only Morocco had a substantial Jewish population of around 5,500, with only the AIU, Oẓar ha-Torah, Lubavitch, and ORT schools still in operation.

BIBLIOGRAPHY: A. Chouraqui, *Between East and West* (1968), 204–215.

[Stanley Abramovitch]

IRAN

*Iran, unlike Jewish communities in other Muslim countries, did not preserve through the centuries a high standard of Jewish learning. The arrival of the Alliance Israélite Universelle (AIU) in 1898 was, therefore, very important for the preservation of the Jewish community. AIU schools opened the doors of the "*mahaléh*," the Jewish quarter in *Teheran, for the Jews. In many towns the schools served as a safeguard against the inroads of Christian and Bahai missionaries. The French language provided wider commercial possibilities for Jews in a developing country.

The revolution of *Reza Shah in 1925 and his reforms weakened the influence of Muslim priests and introduced state schools for the entire population including Jews. AIU schools were opened in the larger cities. By 1939 there were 17 schools with an enrollment of 6,000. The schools provided a basic Iranian education with French as first foreign language. Hebrew was taught by local teachers and was generally on a low level. The flow of refugees through Iran during World War II drew the attention of American Jewry to Iran. The Joint Distribution Committee (JDC) opened an office in Teheran and Oẓar ha-Torah (OH) sent a representative. New schools were opened in Teheran, *Shiraz, and provincial cities, where no AIU schools existed. OH assumed responsibility for Jewish education in all AIU and OH schools. Teachers were trained in Iran and in Israel, and Israeli teachers were brought to Iran. Hebrew textbooks, suitable for Muslim countries, were printed. A first attempt was made to produce a Jewish history book in Persian for school children.

In 1969 there were 11,000 pupils in AIU, OH, and communal schools. On the basis of statistics available, it can be assumed that half the Jewish school population was in Jewish day schools and the other half in government and Christian schools. The AIU and OH developed secondary schools in the larger cities. There was emphasis on Hebrew language and Jewish religion. The level of Jewish education progressed in the 1960s and 1970s with the increasing wealth of the Jews in a period of general economic prosperity and was effective in containing assimilation trends in a community which had not known profound Jewish scholarship for many generations.

In 1977/78 there were in Teheran 11 OH, 7 AIU, and 6 community schools, including an ORT vocational school and a school belonging to the Iraqi Jews in the city. This picture drastically changed with the mass exodus of the Jews after the Islamic revolution in Iran. By the end of the 20th century there were reportedly three Jewish schools in Teheran, one in Shiraz, and one in Isfahan.

[Stanley Abramovitch]

EDUYYOT (Heb. עֵדֻיּוֹת; "Testimonies"), tractate of the Mishnah in the order *Nezikin*. *Eduyyot* is different from all other tractates in the Mishnah, in that it does not focus on a particular subject matter but rather contains a number of relatively small collections of *halakhot* dealing with various topics, and organized around the names of the particular sages who transmitted them. These *halakhot* often "bear witness" to the disputes and controversies of earlier authorities and frequently involve an attempt by contemporaries or by later sages to decide or to resolve these disputes and controversies. This general tendency of the tractate as a whole, together with the repeated use in the later chapters of the phrase "rabbi so-and-so testified" (הֵעִיד, *he'id*), probably explains the tractate's title. The tractate is also referred to in the Talmud (Ber. 27a; Kid. 54b; Bek. 26a) by the name *Beḥirata*, i.e., the "select" or "chosen" *halakhot*. This name seems to reflect an assumption that the traditions included in *Eduyyot*, having been reviewed and adjudicated by the sages, possess some special authority, as the Talmud itself explicitly states (Ber. 27a; Kid. 54b; Bek. 26a): "The *halakhah* of R. Judah (or Meir) is accepted as normative since his view was included in *Beḥirata* (i.e., in *Eduyyot*)."

Ḥ. Albeck argued that *Eduyyot* differs from the rest of the Mishnah because it represents an earlier stage – in fact the earliest stage – in the redaction of the Mishnah. In his opinion later redactors of the Mishnah then took most of its *halakhot* and included them in the various tractates and orders arranged according to subject matter, each in its own proper place. Epstein, however, argued vigorously against this view (Tanna'im, 428), and it is fair to say that no consensus had been reached concerning the date and purpose of the redaction of *Eduyyot* (Stemberger, 131). According to one tradition (Ber. 28a), these testimonies were pronounced on the day when *Eleazar b. Azariah was elected president of the Sanhedrin, but Epstein effectively refuted this view.

The Content of *Eduyyot*

The first chapter puts on record three items of controversy between Shammai and Hillel, and further items of controversy between their respective schools. There are instances where the school of Shammai disapproved of the view of Shammai, and instances where the school of Hillel eventually accepted the view of the rival school. Reasons are given why opinions which were finally rejected are nevertheless recorded in the Mishnah.

The second chapter opens with a testimony of *Ḥanina, Segan Ha-Kohanim, on four items of *halakhah* followed by mnemotechnical triads of sayings. R. Ishmael propounded three laws before the sages. They in their turn discussed another three laws before him. Again a halakhic pronouncement of Ishmael concerning three things is mentioned, with which R. Akiva disagreed. Then come three laws discussed before R. Akiva, and the chapter ends with two sets of five aggadic sayings by R. Akiva, and a concluding one by R. Johanan b. Nuri.

The third chapter records ten items of controversy between *Dosa b. Harkinas and the sages as well as other controversies between single scholars (Joshua, Zadok, Rabban Gamaliel, and Eleazar b. Azariah) and the majority of the sages. The fourth chapter lists items of law in which the House of Shammai was, contrary to custom, more lenient than the House of Hillel.

The fifth chapter puts on record further halakhic items in which, according to several named scholars, the House of Shammai was more lenient than its rivals. It includes one of the most beautiful aggadic passages of the Mishnah concerning the moral and intellectual integrity of *Akavyah b. Mahalalel. He gave testimony on four items of *halakhah* on which the majority of the sages had a different tradition. The sages urged him to retract, promising to appoint him *av bet din* if he did, and threatening him with excommunication if he did not; he remained steadfast. Before his death, however, he told his son to follow the majority ruling, as halakhic discipline required it. When his son, as a last favor, asked that he commend him to his colleagues, he refused, saying, "Your own deeds will bring you near or your own deeds will remove you far."

The rest of the tractate (chapters 6–8) gives a great variety of *halakhot* in which the word העיד ("testified") is consistently used and concludes with an *aggadah* to the effect that at the end of time Elijah the Prophet, in accordance with Malachi 3:23f., will settle the controversies between the sages and make peace in the world. There is no *Gemara* either in the Babylonian or the Jerusalem Talmud, since the various *mishnayot* are included in the other tractates, where they are duly discussed. There is, however, a Tosefta.

BIBLIOGRAPHY: P. Blackman (ed. and tr.), *Mishnayot*, 4 (1954), 385ff., Eng. tr. and notes; Danby, *Mishnah* (Eng., 1933), 422–37; H. Albeck, *Mavo la-Mishnah* (1959), 82–84; idem, *Shishah Sidrei Mishnah*, 4 (1959), 275ff.; Epstein, Tanna'im, 424–44, includes bibliography. **ADD. BIBLIOGRAPHY:** G. Stemberger, *Introduction to the Talmud and Midrash* (1996), 122, 131.

[Arnost Zvi Ehrman / Stephen G. Wald (2nd ed.)]

EDWARDS, PAUL (1923–2004), U.S. philosopher and editor of the eight-volume *Encyclopedia of Philosophy* (1967), the first comprehensive work of its kind in English since 1901. Edwards was born in Vienna, took his doctorate at Columbia University, and taught at New York University and Brooklyn College. In later years, he taught at the New School for Social Research in New York City.

A leading exponent of Bertrand Russell's philosophy and an atheist, Edwards was an aggressive opponent of religious philosophy and theological argumentation. He wrote *The Logic of Moral Discourse* (1955), in which he held that ethical predicates such as "good," "right," and "should" generally have two major functions: to describe something as having a certain property or properties and to express the speaker's pro or con attitude. Hence, he postulated, ethical predicates have, for the most part, descriptive as well as emotive meaning.

He also wrote *Heidegger on Death: A Critical Evaluation* (with Eugene Freeman, 1979), *Equiano's Travels* (1989), *Reincarnation: A Critical Examination* (1996), and *Heidegger's Confusions* (2004).

Among the many books Edwards edited are *A Modern Introduction to Philosophy: Readings from Classical and Contemporary Sources* (1967); and *Immortality* (1997).

[Richard H. Popkin / Ruth Beloff (2nd ed.)]

°**EERDMANS, BERNARDUS DIRKS** (1865–1948), Dutch Protestant Bible scholar. He was privatdocent of Semitic languages from 1896 to 1898 and professor of Bible from 1898 in Leiden. His *Alttestamentliche Studien* (4 vols., 1908–12), a collection of writings on the composition of Genesis, Exodus, Leviticus, and the early history of Israel, are uniform in their complete rejection of the starting points of modern Pentateuchal criticism. Unlike the advocates of the Documentary Hypothesis, Eerdmans posits a fragmentary-supplementary hypothesis that views J, E, and P as redactors and supplementers, rather than composers. According to Eerdmans, material found particularly in Genesis belongs to various stages of religious development of which the earliest is polytheistic and the latest monotheistic, the earlier material referring to God by the plural form Elohim and the later as Yahweh. He argued for the cultural historicity of the patriarchs and for the advanced state of ritual in the Mosaic period. He maintained that most of the legal codes of Leviticus were Mosaic, thus rejecting the commonly accepted J. *Wellhausen–K.H. *Graf hypothesis. He was one of the earliest scholars who advanced an Exilic date for sections of the book of Daniel. He wrote *Der Ursprung der Ceremonien des Hosein Festes* (1894); *The Religion of Israel* (1947), a new treatment of his earlier *De godsdienst van Israeel* (2 vols., 1930); *The Covenant at Mt. Sinai* (1939); *Studies in Job* (1939); and *The Hebrew Book of Psalms* (in: *Oudtestamentische Studieen*, 1947).

BIBLIOGRAPHY: H.F. Hahn, *The Old Testament in Modern Research* (1956), 23–26, 97–98; Eissfeldt, in: ZDMG, 85 (1931), 172ff. **ADD. BIBLIOGRAPHY:** S. Devries, in: DBI, 1, 318.

[Zev Garber]

EFRAT (Heb. אפרת), urban community with municipal council status, located in the *Gush Etzyon area south of Jerusalem. Its area is 1.5 sq. mi. (4 sq. km.). Efrat was established in 1983 after planning by an Israeli group and an American group led by Rabbi Shlomo *Riskin of New York, who settled in Efrat and became the town's rabbi. When the first families arrived the Shevut Yisrael Yeshivah, one of the *hesder* yeshivot, was functioning on the site. Efrat was unique among the West Bank settlements in that settlers moved immediately into permanent housing. Neighborhoods are named after the seven species for which the Land of Israel was famous in biblical times (Deut. 8:8). In 2002 the population of Efrat was 6,810, mainly religious people. Many of its inhabitants are Anglo-Saxons.

WEBSITE: www.efrata.muni.il.

[Shaked Gilboa (2nd ed.)]

EFRAT, YAACOV (1912–1977), agricultural researcher. Born in Poland, Efrat immigrated to Israel in 1936. He specialized in field agriculture, particularly in the various breeds of wheat used in Israel. He developed special systems for winter agriculture. Efrat received the Israel Prize in 1977 for services to agriculture.

EFRON, ILYA (1847–1915), Russian publisher. Efron was born in Vilna. In 1880 he founded a printing press in Peterburg and in 1890 he and the well-known German encyclopedia publisher F. Brockhaus founded the Brockhaus-Efron publishing house in St. Petersburg. It became one of the leading publishing houses in Russia, responsible for a number of historical and literary reference works, including an 86-volume Russian encyclopedia, the Library of Famous Writers, and the multi-volume Library for Self-Education and Library of Natural Sciences. It also published, in cooperation with the Society for Jewish-Scientific Publications, the Russian-Jewish encyclopedia *Yevreyskaya Entsiklopediya* in 16 volumes (1907–13). In the field of Jewish history it published, among other works, Renan's "History of the Jewish People" with commentaries by S. Dubnow and others, and two works on the Inquisition. After 1917 it transferred its activities to Berlin, operating there until the 1930s.

[Shmuel Spector (2nd ed.)]

EFROS, ISRAEL ISAAC (1891–1981), Hebrew educator, poet, and scholar. Born in Ostrog, the Ukraine, he went to the United States in 1905. He served for a time as rabbi and in 1918 founded the Baltimore Hebrew College and the Teachers Training School. He was professor of Hebrew at Johns Hopkins University (1917–28), rabbi of Temple Beth El in Buffalo (1929–34), professor of Semitics at the University of Buffalo (1935–41) and Hunter College, N.Y.C. (1941–55), where he founded the Hebrew Division; in 1945 he was appointed professor of Jewish philosophy and modern Hebrew literature at Dropsie College, Philadelphia. Efros served as president of the *Histadrut Ivrit of America (1938–39). He settled in Israel in 1955 and served as rector of Tel Aviv University. In 1960 he was elected honorary president of the university.

His works on Jewish philosophy include *The Problem of Space in Jewish Medieval Philosophy* (1917), *Philosophical Terms in the Moreh Nebukim* (1924), *Judah Halevi as Poet and Thinker* (1941), *Ha-Pilosofyah ha-Yehudit ha-Attikah* (1959), *Ancient Jewish Philosophy: A Study in Metaphysics and Ethics* (1964), *Studies in Medieval Jewish Philosophy* (1974), and studies on Saadiah Gaon and Abraham B. Ḥiyya. Among his volumes of poetry are *Shirim* (1932); *Vigvamim Shotekim* (1932), a poem about the American Indians with echoes of American epic poetry; *Zahav* ("Gold," 1942) about the California Gold Rush of 1849; *Anaḥnu ha-Dor* (1945). A four-volume collection of his poetry was published in 1966. His spiritual world is rooted both in tradition and in critical philosophy; thus tension is felt in his poetry between the antipodes of feeling and cerebration. Efros' diction is both poetic and precise. A pessimistic vision dominates his post-World War II works. Efros translated Shelley's poetry and Shakespeare's *Hamlet* and other works into Hebrew, and some of Bialik's poetry into English. He also collaborated with Judah Even-Shmuel (Kaufman) and Benjamin N. Silkiner in compiling an English-Hebrew dictionary (1929). For translations of his poetry, see Goell, Bibliography, p. 21.

BIBLIOGRAPHY: A. Epstein, *Soferim Ivrim ba-Amerikah*, 1 (1953), 66–91; J. Kabakoff, in: *Jewish Book Annual*, 28 (1970), 105–109; Kressel, Leksikon, 1 (1965), 135–6; Waxman, Literature, 4 (1960^2), 1065–67, 1115, 1188; J. Kabakoff, in: JBA, 28 (1970/71).

EGALITATEA ("Equality"), Romanian-language periodical (1890–1916, 1919–40), edited, directed, and published in Bucharest by Moses Schwarzfeld with Elias *Schwarzfeld (from his exile in France) as chief editor in the first years. It was the longest-running Jewish periodical in Romania, at first calling itself a "weekly journal." The editor stated his aim in a letter sent to potential subscribers before the publication of the first number, explaining that it was an Israelite journal intending to inspire Romanian Jews with strength, courage, conviction, and moral force, and to give them guidance in their individual trials. The journal described Jewish life and the struggle for emancipation in Romania, condemned discrimination and antisemitism, and also published literary material. Although an independent journal, as its owner and manager involved himself in the Zionist movement it became the official publication of the Jewish National Fund of Romania (1907) and also published Zionist propaganda. In the fall of 1916, when Romania entered World War I and Bucharest was occupied by the German army, the journal ceased publication. It reappeared in 1919, also as a weekly, but with only four pages, and included popular historical articles promoting Jewish identity and the Zionist idea. In July 1931, when Moses Schwarzfeld was ill and in financial difficulties, he began to publish *Egalitatea* every two weeks, in double numbers, up until July 3, 1940, when its publication was banned by the government. Many articles in *Egalitatea* were written by Moses Schwarzfeld himself, sometimes signed with pen names. Among the contributors were Elias Schwarzfeld, Wilhelm Schwarzfeld, I.H. Fior, M. Braunştein-Mibashan, Carol Drimer, J.I. Niemirower, Leon Feraru, Adolphe Ştern, A.L. Zissu, E. San-Cerbu, and others.

BIBLIOGRAPHY: S. Podoleanu, *Istoria presei evreieşti din România* (1938), 108–17; I. Bar-Avi, *Familia Schwarzfeld* (1969), 105–11; H. Kuller, *Presa evreiasca bucureşteana* (1996), 51–58; M. Mircu, *Povestea presei evreieşti* (2003), 69–80; E. Aczel, *Periodicele evreieşti din România 1857–1900* (2005).

[Lucian-Zeev Herscovici (2nd ed.)]

EGER (Ger. **Erlau**), city in N. Hungary. Although Eger is mentioned in 1660 as a Jewish community it was only in 1841 that Jews obtained the right of residence there. A community organization was set up in 1843. By 1858 there were 861 Jews living in the city and an additional 680 in the district. Its first rabbi was Joseph Zevi Weiss. After his death the Orthodox members established a community – separate from the existing status quo community – whose first rabbi was Simon Schreiber, son of Abraham Samuel Benjamin *Sofer. Many Jews in Eger engaged in the wine trade. There were 2,559 Jews living in Eger in 1920, and 1,787 in 1941. They were deported to *Auschwitz by the Nazis on June 8, 1944. By 1946, only 215 Jews remained in Eger.

BIBLIOGRAPHY: E. László, in: *Hungarian-Jewish Studies*, 2 (1969), 137–82.

EGER (Eiger), AKIVA ("The Younger") BEN MOSES GUENS (1761–1837), German rabbi. Born in Eisenstadt, Eger went to Breslau at an early age to study under his uncle, Benjamin Wolf Eger, and Ḥayyim Jonah Teomim-Fraenkel. In 1780, he went to live with his father-in-law in Lissa, where for about ten years he engaged in study, free from financial stress. Impoverished as a result of the losses suffered in the fire of 1791, he accepted a position as rabbi in Maerkisch-Friedland, where he established a yeshivah. As his reputation grew, his decisions were sought in many matters. The thought of reaping material benefit from the Torah was repugnant to him, and on several occasions he thought of leaving the rabbinate and devoting himself to teaching. In 1807 he led a deputation of Jewish leaders who negotiated with the French authorities on Jewish rights in the newly established duchy of Warsaw. In 1814 he was prevailed upon to accept the position of rabbi in Posen, which was offered to him over the objections of the **maskilim* and the followers of the Reform movement, who, fearing his great influence, sought the intervention of the secular authorities, on the grounds that he had no command of the German language and was opposed to all innovations. They were eventually obliged to accept Eger's appointment, but they attempted to minimize his influence by the insertion of certain restrictive clauses in his letter of appointment. Eger, as unofficial chief rabbi of the Posen district, labored on behalf of his own and other Jewish communities. He established a large yeshivah, whose students included Ẓevi Hirsch *Kalischer, Jacob *Levy (author of the dictionaries of the Talmud), and Julius *Fuerst. He waged a constant struggle against the Reform movement. The *maskilim* opposed him and drew attention to what they considered bizarre and unreal questions discussed in his responsa. Eger was not blind, however, to the spiritual and educational needs of his time. He made certain concessions to meet official demands for a more modern curriculum in Jewish schools, and he encouraged Solomon Plessner's pioneer efforts to propagate traditional Judaism using German instead of Yiddish, which was until then the medium of instruction. He received a royal message of thanks from Frederick William III for his services during the cholera epidemic of 1831, during which he framed a number of helpful *takkanot* and cared for many of the sick. A number of welfare institutions established by him were in existence until World War II. He was the father-in-law of Moses *Sofer and the ancestor of many prominent scholars, scientists, and writers. His son Solomon *Eger was elected rabbi of Posen on his father's death. Many popular legends surrounded Akiva's person. His exemplary humanity and beneficence earned him universal admiration, even among his adversaries. A story typifying his sensitivity to others tells of a Jew who asked Akiva before Passover if he could use milk for the Seder rituals. When asked why, the Jew answered that he did not have enough money to buy wine. Akiva promptly gave him 20 rubles for purchasing wine. When rebuked by his wife for giving too much, Akiva answered that he deduced from the question that the Jew also did not have enough money to buy meat for the holiday. His modesty was proverbial, and he was sternly opposed to the titles of honor common in rabbinical circles. Of his works, the following were published in his lifetime: *Ḥilluka de-Rabbanan* (1822); *Haggahot* to the Mishnah (1825–30); *Gilyon ha-Shas*, notes to the Prague edition of the Babylonian Talmud (1830–34), and later to the Vilna edition; responsa, together with decisions, etc. (1834). After his death there appeared responsa, part 2 (1839); *Ḥiddushei R. Akiva Eger* (1858); *Tosafot* (1841–48 in the Altona edition of the Mishnah); *Haggahot*, glosses to the Shulḥan Arukh (1859); responsa (1889); *Kitvei R. Akiva Eger* (letters; 1929). In addition many of his letters and responsa were printed in talmudic journals and in numerous other works. Much of his work has remained in manuscript and some has been lost (e.g., his glosses to the Palestinian Talmud).

BIBLIOGRAPHY: L. Wreschner, *R. Akiba Eger* (Ger., 1906); idem, in: JJLG, 2 (1904), 27–84; 3 (1905), 1–78; S. Blum, *Gedolei Yisrael* (1938); A. Ovadyah (Gottesdiener), *Ketavim Nivḥarim*, 2 (1944), 77–115; idem, in: *Sinai*, 1 (1937), 511–50; Posner, in: *Koveẓ … Unna* (1940), 147–57; S. Sofer, *Iggerot Soferim* (1928, pref. 1929), 1–95 (1ˢᵗ pagination); Leiman, in: L. Jung (ed.), *Jewish Leaders* (1953), 99–113. **ADD. BIBLIOGRAPHY:** J.S. Sinasohn, *Gaon of Posen: A Portrait of Rabbi Akiva Guens-Eger* (1990).

[Akiva Posner]

EGER, AKIVA BEN SIMḤAH BUNIM (c. 1720–1758), rabbi and author, known as R. Akiva Eger the Elder. A native of Halberstadt, he was a pupil of Ẓevi Hirsch *Bialeh (Ḥarif) of Halberstadt and Jacob ha-Kohen Poppers of Frankfurt. Around 1747, he served as rabbi of Zuelz (Upper Silesia). He conducted a yeshivah in Halberstadt even during the lifetime of his teacher Bialeh, and in 1756, became head of the yeshivah of Pressburg. Eger, who was among the foremost talmudic scholars of his generation, carried on halakhic correspondence with Jonathan *Eybeschuetz, Meir *Eisenstadt, and other prominent rabbis. His novellae on the Talmud, *Mishnah de-Rabbi Akiva*, to which are appended a number of his responsa, were published posthumously (Fuerth, 1781). Eger had two sons, Judah Loeb, who served as rabbi in Halberstadt, and Wolf, rabbi of Leipnick.

BIBLIOGRAPHY: B.H. Auerbach, *Geschichte der israelitischen Gemeinde Halberstadt* (1866), 33, 71; I. Weiss, *Avnei Beit ha-Yoẓer* (1900), pt. 2, 35b–37b; L. Wreschner, in: JJLG, 2 (1904), 32f.; P. Frankl, in: *Nachlat Z'wi*, 7 (1937), 320; S. Weingarten, in: *Arim ve-Immahot be-Yisrael*, 7 (1960), 38.

[Jacob Haberman]

EGER, JUDAH LEIB OF LUBLIN (1816–1888), ḥasidic *ẓaddik*, son of Solomon *Eger, grandson of Akiva *Eger the Younger. Born in Warsaw, Judah studied in Posen under his grandfather, whom he regarded as an example of moral virtues. He also studied at the yeshivah of Isaac Meir Alter (later the founder of the ḥasidic Gur dynasty) in Warsaw, through whose influence Judah became a Ḥasid. After his marriage Judah settled in Lublin, and visited Menahem Mendel of *Kotsk (Kock), continuing as his disciple despite opposition from his family. When Menahem Mendel secluded himself from society, Judah became a disciple of Mordecai Joseph Leiner of Izbica. After his father's death in 1852 Judah declined the position of rabbi of Posen. Following the death of the Izbica *ẓaddik* in 1854 Judah led his own ḥasidic congregation in Lublin. It was not until after the death of Menahem Mendel of Kotsk in 1859, however, that Judah assumed the role of

ẓaddik and propounded his own teachings. Judah Leib's moral integrity and conduct won him esteem even from people who opposed Ḥasidism. He spent a long time over prayer, devoting himself to it with concentration and fervor, accompanied by weeping and loud cries. His manner of prayer, which was contrary to the tradition of his preceptors, aroused severe criticism. Judah's teachings on the portions of the law and the festivals were arranged by his son Abraham in *Torat Emet* (3 vols., 1889–90) and *Imrei Emet* (2 vols., 1902–3). Judah corresponded on halakhic questions with his relatives Abraham Samuel Benjamin *Sofer in Pressburg and Simeon *Sofer in Cracow. Abraham succeeded Judah as leader of his disciples from 1882 to 1914. He was the author of a work on Ḥasidism, *Shevet mi-Yehudah* (1922–38). Judah Leib's grandsons Solomon and Ezriel Meir continued to lead their congregation until they perished in the Holocaust.

BIBLIOGRAPHY: A.I. Bromberg, *Mi-Gedolei ha-Ḥasidut*, 13 (1958), 91–158.

EGER, SAMUEL (Perez Sanwel) BEN JUDAH LOEB (1769–1842), German talmudic scholar and author. Eger, the grandson of Akiva *Eger the Elder, was born in Halberstadt. After studying at his father's yeshivah, in 1809 he became rabbi of Brunswick where he served until his death. He had one of the most acute minds of the talmudic scholars of the time, engaging in halakhic correspondence with his cousin, Akiva *Eger (the Younger) of Posen, and with Moses *Sofer, who was related to him by marriage. A staunch opponent of the Reform movement, he took a firm stand against the innovations of the Kassel Consistory. Although in principle he was opposed to changes in the liturgy, he stated that he would not oppose those changes which were not contrary to the Shulḥan Arukh. His insistence on the retention of Hebrew in prayer was motivated by his belief that it was a necessary link uniting all Jews throughout the world. His published works include *Ateret Paz* and *Rimmon Parez*, novellae on the tractates *Beẓah* and *Ketubbot* (both Altona, 1823); and homiletic discourses delivered on Sabbath *Devarim* (1837) and Sabbath *Mishpatim* (1829). The bulk of his work, talmudic novellae and responsa, comprising an extensive correspondence with the rabbis of Eastern and Western Europe, remains in manuscript.

BIBLIOGRAPHY: Herzfeld, in: AZDJ, 6 (1842), 412, 460f., 762–64; B.H. Auerbach, *Geschichte der israelitischen Gemeinde Halberstadt* (1866), 103, 216–22; L. Wreschner, in: JJLG, 2 (1904), 33.

[Jacob Haberman]

EGER, SIMḤAH BUNIM BEN MOSES (1770–1829), Hungarian talmudist, younger brother of Akiva *Eger the Younger. Eger was also known by the family names of Guens and Schlesinger. After studying under his brother Akiva and then continuing his studies in Krotoszyn, he was appointed rabbi of Rogasen and in 1810 of Mattersdorf, where he remained until his death. Some of his novellae are printed in his brother's *Ḥiddushei Rabbi Akiva Eger* (1858) which also includes their halakhic correspondence. Eger was also in correspondence with his relative Moses *Sofer, with Mordecai Michael Jaffe, author of *Beit Menaḥem*, and with Israel Moses b. Aryeh Loeb, author of *Rishmei She'elah*. His novellae were later published as an appendix to his brother's responsa (2nd part; 1938). His sons were JOSEPH GINZ of Vienna, founder of the well-known publishing firm of Schlesinger; SAMUEL GENZ, rabbi of Abrany (Hungary), who published many of his novellae in the talmudic periodical *Tel Talpiyyot* (ed. D. Karzburg); and MOSES, rabbi and preacher in Hamburg. His daughter married Zalman Ulman, rabbi of Makow.

BIBLIOGRAPHY: Wreschner, in: JJLG, 2 (1904), 34; Moses, *ibid.*, 18 (1927), 313f.; P.Z. Schwartz, *Shem ha-Gedolim me-Ereẓ Hagar*, 1 (1913), 20b no. 1; 2 (1914), 39b no. 63 (Samuel Ginz); I. Kunstadt, *Lu'aḥ Ereẓ he-Ḥadash* (1915), introd.; B. Wachstein, *Die Inschriften des alten Judenfriedhofes in Wien*, 2 (1917), 168; S. Sofer, *Iggerot Soferim* (1929), 2nd pagination, 42–44, 55; J.J. (L.) Greenwald (Grunwald), *Maẓẓevat Kodesh* (1952), 140–2.

[Itzhak Alfassi]

EGER, SOLOMON BEN AKIVA (1786–1852), rabbi and *rosh yeshivah*. Born in Lissa, he was the son of R. Akiva *Eger the Younger, under whom he studied. Eger became a merchant in Warsaw, but after losing his fortune in the Polish rebellion in 1831, he accepted the rabbinate of Kalisz. In 1839 he was appointed to succeed his father in Posen. Active in communal affairs, Eger sought to direct the Jews from commerce to farming, and in 1844 appealed to Frederick William IV, king of Prussia, to assist Jews in founding an agricultural village in the province of Posen. The request was granted, and Eger took active steps to implement the plan. In 1846 he founded an organization for agricultural settlement with the consent and formal support of 21 local communities, with promises of support. The project was, however, brought to an end by the disturbances of 1848. Eger was also active in soliciting contributions for Ereẓ Israel and in assuring their fair disbursement. He also took a prominent part in the campaign for emancipation of the Jews in his country. A strong advocate of traditional Judaism in its strictest interpretation and an outspoken opponent of the Reform movement, he sided with G. *Tiktin of Breslau in his controversy with A. *Geiger and was influential in restoring Tiktin to his position. Many of his responsa are included among those of his father, particularly those which he published together with his older brother, Abraham. His own published works include *Gilyon Maharsha*, notes on the Talmud and on Alfasi's Code appended to the Vilna Talmud (1859); *Gilyon Rasha*, notes on *Yoreh De'ah* (Koenigsberg, 1859) and republished with additions in the Vilna Talmud. His letters were published in *Iggerot Soferim* (1929), pp. 62–86.

BIBLIOGRAPHY: Bloch, in: *Jeschurun*, ed. by B. Koenigsberger, 1 (1901), 5–8, 75–79, 104–8; Wreschner, in: JJIG, 2 (1904), 47–48; L. Lewin, *Geschichte der Juden in Lissa* (1904), 245–8.

[Akiva Posner]

EGGED (Heb. "bundle"), Israel public transport cooperative. In the 1930s small groups of drivers, each numbering between 50 and 100, constituted themselves into cooperatives to avoid duplication by abolishing parallel routes, and to increase efficiency. Egged was founded in 1933 and established branches all over the country. With the large increase in public transport that followed the establishment of the State of Israel, two other cooperatives, Shaḥar, which operated in the Haifa area, and Drom Yehuda, which operated in Tel Aviv and the south, merged with Egged, the merger being completed in 1951. The Jerusalem transport cooperative, Ha-Mekasher, joined in 1967.

Egged is one of the largest public transport cooperatives in the world. In 1968, the company operated 2,200 buses, which traveled about 620,000 mi. (1,000,000 km.) daily on 1,100 routes. At that time, Egged members numbered about 4,400, and there were also 2,200 hired workers. In 2004, Egged employed 6,309 workers, 2,452 of whom were Egged members. It owned 3,332 buses, traveling on 1,308 routes, and served about a million people a day.

Egged owns four subsidiary companies: Egged Transport offers personalized transport services, including VIP limousines, company transport, a messenger service, and so on. Egged Tours is an inland tourist company operating 300 tourist buses. Derech Egged offers air and recreation services. Egged Investments develops new sources of employment for Egged. The cooperative is governed by a general assembly, composed of all members, which biennially elects a council of 80, an executive of 20 from the members of the council, and a secretariat with five members elected by the executive, which runs the cooperative.

WEBSITE: www.egged.co.il

[Leon Aryeh Szeskin]

EGGS. One of the few references to the egg in the Bible, and the only injunction connected with it, is the command to drive away the dam before taking the eggs from the nest (Deut. 22:6). The only other references to birds' eggs are in Isaiah 10:14 and the hatching of the egg of the ostrich through the heat of the sun (Job 39:14). Viper's eggs are mentioned in Isaiah 59:5. In contrast, the egg figures prominently in rabbinical literature, both in *halakhah* and *aggadah*.

Halakhah

The egg belongs to two spheres of *halakhah*: as permitted food and as a standard measure of volume (the tractate of the Talmud called *Beẓah* ("egg") deals with the laws of the festivals and is so called merely because of the first word of its first Mishnah, which deals with the question of the permissibility of eating an egg laid on the festival).

(1) Although it is nowhere clearly stated in the Bible that eggs are permitted for food (the Talmud sees a reference to it in Deut. 22:6; see Ḥul. 140a), on the principle that "that which emerges from a clean animal is clean and that from an unclean animal unclean" (Bek. 1:2) it is established that the eggs of clean birds are permitted for food, and those of unclean birds, forbidden (Ḥul. 122a). With the formation of the hard shell of the egg, however, even before the egg has been laid, it is regarded as independent and no longer part of its dam,

with the result that the prohibition of eating a part of a living animal does not apply to it, nor the law prohibiting the eating of meat with milk (Beẓah 6b). Nevertheless fully formed eggs in a bird which is *terefah or *nevelah are forbidden (Maim., Yad, Maakhalot Asurot, 3:19). The Talmud (Ḥul. 64a) gives the signs of the eggs of permitted and forbidden birds. The former have one end oblate and the other pointed and the white surrounds the yoke, while if both ends are oblate or pointed and the yellow surrounds the white it is the egg of a forbidden bird. The egg is regarded as beginning to form the embryo when a bloodspot appears on the yoke, from which time it is forbidden as food, but the custom has been generally adopted of forbidding eggs if the bloodspot appears even on the albumen (see *Blood).

(2) The bulk of an egg is one of the most common of all the measures of volume in the *halakhah*. It constitutes the usual quantity of volume to establish liability, e.g., for ritual uncleanness, for the size of the *etrog, for the amount of bread from which *ḥallah must be separated, and many others. It is also the standard whereby all other measurements are calculated, a *log* being equal to six eggs, a *kab* to 24, and a *se'ah* to 144 (see Er. 83a and *Weights and Measures). It is evident however that these relative measurements do not accord with the normal size of an egg. It is accepted that the "egg" is that of the chicken (Yoma 80a) and recourse has had to be made to the theory that the egg thus referred to is a "desert egg" which was much larger than the present day one, and to be on the safe side the standard adopted in the *halakhah* for the egg of the Talmud is two present-day eggs (*Ḥatam Sofer*, OḤ, Tesp. no. 127).

Aggadah

The egg is regarded both as having laxative qualities and of bringing about sexual stimulation. The egg, being "round and having no mouth" (opening), is regarded as a symbol of mourning which "is like a wheel which continually revolves in the world, and one must not open one's mouth in complaint" (BB 16b; YD 378:9 of Gen R. 63:14). It is therefore given to mourners at the meal given to them on the return from the burial (*se'udat havra'ah*) and is eaten at the meal before undertaking the fast of the Ninth of *Av. On the *seder* night of Passover there has developed the custom of eating an egg dipped in salt water before beginning the festive meal. There is no authority for this custom in the sources; various explanations have been put forward, and Moses Isserles connects it with its mourning aspect. According to him it is in commemoration of the destruction of the Temple with which the paschal sacrifice was discontinued, and it happens that the first day of Passover always falls on the same day of the week as the Ninth of Av of each year (OḤ 476:2). A roasted egg, in memory of the festival offering (*ḥagigah*), forms part of the Passover plate at the *seder*.

BIBLIOGRAPHY: Krauss, Tal Arch, 1 (1910), 124–6; Eisenstein, Yisrael, 3 (1951), 37–40; ET, 3 (1951), 131–45.

[Louis Isaac Rabinowitz]

°EGIDIO DA VITERBO (c. 1465–1532), Italian ecclesiastical statesman and humanist. He entered the Augustinian order in 1488. The papal Curia utilized his diplomatic talents and in 1517 Leo X made him a cardinal; he was also bishop of Viterbo. For many years he maintained Elijah *Levita in his entourage in Rome, Levita instructing the cardinal in rabbinics and Jewish mysticism and himself obtaining instruction in Greek. He was also among *Reuchlin's correspondents (*Illustrium ... epistolae ... ad ... Reuchlin*, Hagenau, 1519, 97–98) and entertained the false messiah David *Reuveni. Egidio's interests in Jewish (particularly kabbalistic) studies were very considerable. In addition to projecting a plan for translating David Kimḥi's dictionary he translated (or sponsored translations of) extracts of the Zohar and various esoteric tracts (*Ginnat Egoz, Razi'el*, etc.; also portions of Menahem Recanati's commentary), and composed a treatise on the Ten *Sefirot (all preserved in manuscript: Paris Mss. 527, 596–8, 3363, 3367, Angelica Ms. 3).

BIBLIOGRAPHY: Vogelstein-Rieger, 2 (1896), passim; G. Signorelli, *Il Cardinale Egidio da Viterbo* ... (1929); G.E. Weil, *Elie Lévita* ... (1963), 203–11 and passim; C. Astruc and J. Monfrin, in: *Bibliothèque d'humanisme et renaissance*, 23 (1961), 551–4; A. Palmieri, in: *Dictionnaire Theologique Catholique*, 6 (1920), 1365–71; F. Secret, *Le Zôhar chez les Kabbalistes chrétiens de la Renaissance* (1958), index.

[Raphael Loewe]

ʿEGLAH ʿARUFAH (Heb. עֶגְלָה עֲרוּפָה), an expiatory ceremonial for an untraceable murder prescribed in Deuteronomy 21:1–9, in which the elders of the settlement nearest the corpse bring an unworked heifer to an uncultivated area in a watered wadi, break the heifer's neck, wash their hands over it, and profess their innocence to the bloodshed. This ceremonial of the *ʿeglah ʿarufah*, "the broken-necked heifer," is unique to the Bible, but it is elucidated by prior Hittite and subsequent rabbinic law codes. The *ʿeglah ʿarufah* is not a sacrifice. It is not slaughtered ritually on an altar, but is killed like a nonsacrificial animal (Ex. 13:13) away from the altar; it need not be unblemished like a sacrifice (Sot. 9:5), but it must never have been subjected to the yoke, a stipulation attested only in rituals never incorporated into the sacrificial system (Num. 19:2; see *Red Heifer; cf. I Sam. 6:7). Above all, its death does not make expiation for the life of the murderer (nor does any sacrifice; see *Atonement, *Sacrifices), for if the murderer is subsequently discovered, he is still put to death (Sot. 9:7; see Ket. 37b).

The key to this rite is its underlying postulate that the blood of the innocent does not "remain on his head" (e.g., Josh. 2:19; see *Bloodguilt), but pollutes the earth on which it is shed (Num. 35:33). The earth, having received the blood involuntarily, withholds its strength (Gen. 4:11–12), bringing drought and famine upon its inhabitants (II Sam. 21:1, LXX; cf. also II Sam. 1:21; Ezek. 22:24). This belief is not peculiar to Israel, but is part of its heritage from the cultures along the Mediterranean littoral (e.g., Ugarit: Aqhat 1:42–46; Asia Minor (Hittites), Proclamation of Telepinus,

20). That the blood of the slain must come into contact with the ground is confirmed by the rabbinic dictum that if the murder was perpetrated by some other means, e.g., hanging, the heifer ceremonial is not required (Sot. 9:2; TJ, Sot. 9:2, 23c). In rabbinic law, just as in the Hittite Code, paragraph 6 (earlier version, cf. Pritchard, Texts, 189), the corpse is interred on the spot where it was found (BK 81b), and the original owner loses his rights to a set area circumscribing the corpse.

According to biblical law, "the land shall have no expiation for blood that is shed except by the blood of him who shed it" (Num. 35:33b). However, what if the murderer is unknown: will the land be permanently blighted? The *ʿeglah ʿarufah* is the cultic prophylactic to avert this contingency. Its purpose is to transfer the land polluted by the corpse to an uncultivated plot, removed from the settled area. Thus it closely resembles the rites of the **azazel* goat and of the purification of the healed *leper, whereby sin and impurity, respectively, are exorcised from the afflicted and banished to the wilderness. Here, however, the fact that land and not man needs to be expiated necessitates the use of another method, not banishment, but transference. Through the killing of the heifer, the murder is, in effect, reenacted; the blood of the heifer (*ha-dam ha-zeh*, "this blood," Deut. 21:7) becomes identified with the blood of the slain, and the pollution is transferred from the area of the corpse to the area of the heifer. This rite of reenactment and transference explains why the ceremonial must take place at a perennial stream: the blood must not come into contact with the earth again and trigger the fatal polluted soil-drought syndrome, and it is thus drained off to some distant sea. Also explained is the need for the elders of the nearest settlement to wash their hands and recite a confessional over the broken-necked heifer: since the blood of the heifer represents the blood of the slain, they must purify themselves and declare their innocence of either committing or witnessing the crime (Deut. 21:6–7). Finally, the rabbinic law that the land surrounding the heifer is forever forbidden to be cultivated further underscores that the purpose of the ritual is the transference of land impurity from the human to the animal corpse.

According to this interpretation the Torah has incorporated an ancient rite, whereby land pollution due to an untraceable murder is transferred from a desirable area to an undesirable one. At the same time, it should not be overlooked how an act of pure sympathetic magic was transformed by the Torah to conform to its basic spiritual and ethical outlook. First, the ritual was placed in the hands of the priests, those "chosen by the Lord to serve Him" (21:5), and removed from the authority of the lay-elders, who might be addicted to its pagan origins. Then, the declaration was given an appendix (21:8–9), whereby the automatic, magical expiation presumed by the ritual was abolished, and the expiation and, indeed, all forgiveness of sin attributed solely to the Lord.

[Jacob Milgrom]

In the Talmud

No less than nine *mishnayot* (Sotah 9:1–9) and six folios of the Babylonian Talmud (Sotah 44b–47b) are devoted to the laws of the *ʿeglah ʿarufah*, despite the fact that the rite was abolished at the beginning of the first century (see below). Unless otherwise stated, the details that follow are derived from those passages. According to the rabbis, this act of expiation and disavowal by the elders was not for the murder itself, of which no one could possibly accuse them, but for failure to create conditions which would make such a crime impossible. "He [the victim, or possibly the murderer?] did not appeal to us for help and we dismissed him without providing him with food; we did not allow him to depart without an escort." The measurement of the distance between the corpse and the nearest town was performed by three or five elders from the Great Sanhedrin of Jerusalem. When they had finished their task and had decided to which city the murder was to be ascribed, they returned to Jerusalem, and the rite of breaking the heifer's neck (from behind with a hatchet) was performed in the presence of all the elders of that city. The rite was performed only when it was presumed that the undetected murderer was a Jew, and it was therefore not performed in a city near the border or where the majority of the inhabitants were gentiles. Nor did the rite apply to Jerusalem. It was limited to a murder executed with a lethal weapon and therefore did not apply in the case of hanging or strangulation. The heifer had to be less than two years old. The ceremony took place by day, and the carcass was buried *in situ*. The rite of the *ʿeglah ʿarufah* was discontinued "when murderers increased in number." Its discontinuation is connected with *Eleazar b. Dinai, also called Tehinah b. Parishah, a notorious murderer who is probably identical with the Zealot leader of the same name (c. 35–60 C.E.) mentioned by Josephus (Ant. 20:121 and 161; Wars, 2:235–6, 253).

[Louis Isaac Rabinowitz]

BIBLIOGRAPHY: H.J. Elhorst, in: ZAW, 39 (1921), 58–67; R. Patai, in JQR, 30 (1939), 59–69; S.H. Hooke, in: VT, 2 (1952), 2–17; A. Rofé, in: *Tarbiz*, 31 (1961/62), 119–43.

EGLON (Heb. עֶגְלוֹן), Canaanite royal city. According to the Bible, Debir, king of Eglon, joined the confederation of Amorite kings, led by *Adoni-Zedek of Jerusalem, against *Gibeon. They were defeated by Joshua at Aijalon and slain near the cave of Makkedah, where they had sought refuge (Josh. 10). Eglon was subsequently captured, sacked, and destroyed (*ibid.* 10:34–35). The king of Eglon is again mentioned in the list of conquered cities (*ibid.* 12:12). The city was allotted to the tribe of Judah in the Lachish district (*ibid.* 15:39). It does not appear in later sources; Eusebius mentions an Agla, present-day Khirbat ʿAjlān, 12 mi. (19 km.) west of Bet Guvrin (Eleutheropolis) (Onom. 48:19). Scholars are divided as to the location of Eglon; the identification generally accepted is that of Tell al-Ḥasī proposed by Albright. This tell is situated 7 mi. (11 km.) southwest of Lachish, at the edge of the foothills that extend into the Coastal Plain. Elliger has suggested the more westerly Tell Beit Mirsim, and recent studies have shown that this identification is no less probable (cf. *Debir).

BIBLIOGRAPHY: Albright, in BASOR, 17 (1925), 7ff.; Elliger, in: PJB, 30 (1934), 67f.

[Michael Avi-Yonah]

EGLON (Heb. עֶגְלוֹן; lit. "calf"), king of Moab in the period of the Judges, apparently in the first half of the 12th century B.C.E. The Bible relates that Eglon assembled the *Ammonites and the *Amalekites and with them attacked Israel, subduing the land for 18 years (Judg. 3:12–14). It is likely that Eglon had previously conquered the plain north of the Arnon, a region disputed by Israel and Moab. Eglon and his allies crossed the Jordan, captured the city of Jericho, and from there penetrated to the center of the country and subdued the tribes of Benjamin and Ephraim. It is natural, therefore, that a Benjaminite, the "judge" *Ehud, son of Gera, assassinated Eglon by a ruse and freed Israel from Moabite rule. The events related in Judges 3 appear historically plausible although some scholars have argued that the mention of Eglon's gross obesity (vs. 17, 22) and the chapter's apparent scatological references (vss. 21–25) are indications that the story is fictional political satire.

[Bustanay Oded]

In the *Aggadah*

Eglon is identified as the grandson of Balak (Yal. 665). Because of the respect he showed to God through rising from his throne when Ehud told him that he had a message from the Lord, he was rewarded: Ruth was his granddaughter (Naz. 24b) and her descendant David "sat on the throne of the Lord" (Ruth R. 2:9).

BIBLIOGRAPHY: E.G. Kraeling, in: JBL, 54 (1935), 205–10; K. Galling, in: ZDPV, 75 (1959), 1–13; A.H. van Zyl, *The Moabites* (1960); Y. Kaufmann, *Sefer Shofetim* (1962), 104–11; W. Richter, *Traditionsgeschichtliche Untersuchungen zum Richterbuch* (1963), 1ff.; A. Malamat, in: B. Mazar (ed.), *Ha-Historyah shel Am Yisrael, ha-Avot ve-ha-Shofetim* (1967), 229–30. **ADD. BIBLIOGRAPHY:** B. Halpern, *The Bible's First Historians* (1980), 39–75; idem, in: ABD, 2, 414; M. Brettler, in: HUCA, 62 (1991), 285–304; Y. Amit, *Judges* (1999), 71–79.

EGOZI, Turkish family, members of which served as rabbis of Constantinople in the 16th and 17th centuries. MENAHEM BEN MOSES EGOZI (second half of 16th century) was a rabbi, preacher, and poet. His sermons, *Gal shel Egozim*, were published in the printing press of Gracia *Nasi in Belvedere between 1593 and 1599. *Ginnat Egoz*, a manuscript collection of his letters and poems, some showing considerable talent and of historical importance, is in the British Museum (Or. 11.111). A responsum by him is included in the responsa of Elijah b. Ḥayyim (no. 38). ḤAYYIM, a contemporary of the former, was a member of the *bet din* of Elijah b. Ḥayyim in Constantinople, their signatures appearing together in a document of 1601. A manuscript of his book on the laws of divorce is in the Jerusalem National Library (no. 119, 8°). DAVID (d. c. 1644) was rabbi of the indigenous Turkish community of Constantinople. He was appointed to be in charge of the congregational property and was in halakhic correspondence with Ḥayyim and Moses *Benveniste. NISSIM BEN ḤAYYIM, rabbi and *dayyan*, was involved in the Shabbatean controversy which engaged the Constantinople rabbis in 1666.

BIBLIOGRAPHY: Rosanes, Togarmah, 3 (1938), 33; Scholem, Shabbetai Ẓevi, 2 (1957), 416–7; A. Yaari, *Ha-Defus ha-Ivri be-Kushta* (1967), 140–1, no. 228, 147.

EGYENLÖSÉG, a political weekly newspaper, its title meaning "Equality," which was published in the Hungarian language in Budapest from 1881. The official mouthpiece of the Neolog (non-Orthodox) sector of Hungarian Jewry, it circulated among Hungarian Jewry as a whole. Its founder was Moritz Bogdányi, who published daily editions during the proceedings of the *Tiszaeszlár blood libel trial of 1882–83. Miksa *Szabolcsi headed the editorial staff from 1884, later becoming its owner, and after the Tiszaeszlár trial took up the struggle anew for religious equality of the Jews of Hungary. Some of the best-known Hungarian Jewish writers were among its contributors, such as Adolf *Agai, Hugo *Ignotus, József *Kiss, Tamás *Kóbor, Emil *Makai, and Péter Ujvári. The declared policy of the paper was assimilationist, aiming at moderate religious reform but complete integration in the life of the state. With the appearance of organized Zionism, the paper took up an anti-Zionist stand. After the death of Miksa Szabolcsi in 1915, his son Lajos Szabolcsi edited the paper and took a bold stand against the "numerus clausus" and the excesses of the "White Terror" after the revolution of 1918–19. The paper was banned in 1938.

BIBLIOGRAPHY: *Magyar Zsidó Lexikon* (1929), 213–4.

[Baruch Yaron]

EGYPT, country in N.E. Africa, centering along the banks of the River Nile from the Mediterranean coast southward beyond the first cataract at Aswan. The ancient Egyptians named their land "Kemi," the "Black Land," while the neighboring Asiatic peoples used the Semitic word "Miṣr" which is still the country's name in both Hebrew (Heb. מִצְרַיִם; *Miẓrayim*) and Arabic. Geographically Egypt consists of two areas, Lower Egypt, the northern part of the land, which contains the Delta, and Upper Egypt, the south, which comprises the narrow strip of cultivable land on both sides of the river as far south as Aswan.

Ancient Egypt

Ancient Egyptian history can be divided into seven periods that correspond to the major dynastic ages of Pharaonic history:

1. Predynastic – (prehistory)
2. Early Dynastic Period (Archaic) – Dyn. 1–3, 2920–2575
3. Old Kingdom – Dyn. 4–8 (Pyramid Age), 2575–2134
4. First Intermediate Period – Dyn. 9–10, 2134–2040
5. Middle Kingdom – Dyn. 11–12 ("Classical" Period), 2040–1640

6. Second Intermediate Period – Dyn. 13–17 (including the Hyksos Period), 1640–1532
7. New Kingdom – Dyn. 18–20 (Empire Period), 1550–1070

PREDYNASTIC – EARLY DYNASTIC PERIOD. The Predynastic history of Egypt refers to the period before the unification of Upper and Lower Egypt. It is the unification of the two kingdoms that heralds the national consciousness of Egypt; therefore, her history as a nation cannot start before the Early Dynastic Period. Egyptian tradition traced its historical beginnings to the time when King Menes of Upper Egypt (as recorded by Manetho, and transmitted with slight variations by Herodotus, Josephus, and Diodorus Siculus) conquered Lower Egypt and unified the two lands. By this action, he became the ruler of both Upper and Lower Egypt, thereby establishing the First Dynasty. Menes' unification came to symbolize the nation and its conception of itself. The earliest representation of the unification of Egypt is the Narmer Palette (+/–3150 B.C.E., now in the Cairo Museum). The legendary Pharaoh Narmer has been identified with Menes, and the Narmer Palette apparently represents the Pharaoh of Upper Egypt conquering Lower Egypt and subduing the enemy. The obverse of the palette shows the ruler wearing the White Crown of Upper Egypt, while the reverse has him wearing the Red Crown of Lower Egypt. Throughout dynastic history the unification represented the potency of the land, a potency recalled in a variety of ways, from the titles of the kings, through the representations in the artistic canon.

The most important legacy of the Early Dynastic Period is the foundation of what we view as the civilization of ancient Egypt. The national economy, political ideology, and religious philosophy all developed in this period, and the administrative seat of Egyptian government moved north to Memphis. Much of the contact between Egypt and the Levant during the Early Dynastic Period was in the area of trade. Grain, timber for construction, precious and semi-precious materials, including lapis lazuli copper and turquoise, were imported to Egypt from Southwest Asia.

THE OLD KINGDOM. The Old Kingdom is also known as the Pyramid Age. During this period Egypt's power revolved around her resources, human and natural, and the Pharaoh's ability to utilize them. One of the results of the successful harnessing of resources was monumental architecture; the first complexes built from fully dressed stones are from this period. These large structures seem to represent the physical manifestation of the Pharaoh's godhead and authority. The strong centralized government of the god-king that had developed earlier underwent decentralization during the 5th dynasty and resulted in a new class of officials: The vizier no longer had to be a prince, and the nomarchs began to reside in the nome that they administered rather than in the royal residence or capital.

Foreign relations during the Old Kingdom were generally peaceful, and foreign expeditions were related either to defense or, more frequently, to trade. A 6th dynasty official named Weni inscribed his autobiography on a wall in his tomb-chapel. He reports that at the behest of the Pharaoh he led five expeditions into the Southern Levant to defend against the "Sand-dwellers" (Lichtheim 18 ff.). At least two stone vessels bearing Old Kingdom royal names have been discovered at *Tel Mardikhi*, *Ebla, in central Syria. There is no certainty as to how the vessels got to Ebla (one, bearing Pepy I's name, is thought to have come through Byblos, and the other with Kephren's name may have come directly from Egypt), but their existence attests to far reaching diplomatic connections between Egypt and the Levant.

THE FIRST INTERMEDIATE PERIOD. In Egyptian chronology, the term "Intermediate" refers to the periods when there was no strong centralized government unifying the Two Lands. During the first Intermediate Period there was dynastic rule both in the North (at Herakleopolis), and in the South (at Thebes). The attempts to reunify the land fostered sporadic internal conflicts and civil wars.

THE MIDDLE KINGDOM. The detailed origins of the Middle Kingdom are unknown, but in a political sense the Middle Kingdom may be said to begin when the ruler of Upper Egypt becomes the sole Pharaoh and the two lands are again united. During the 11th Dynasty the seat of rule remained at Thebes in the South, but the first Pharaoh of the 12th Dynasty moved the capital North to a new capital called *Itjtawy*, "Grasper of the Two Lands"; the capital remained there for more than 300 years. The 12th Dynasty is the "Classical Period" in the art and the literature of Ancient Egypt.

The literature and the art of this period were used to promote the royal and elite values and interests. Many of the literary texts of this period have a propagandistic flavor and were circulated to the literati though the temples and schools. The monumental royal inscriptions on temples and other buildings were also used to address the public, to inspire loyalty, and to tell the people of the grandeur of their rulers.

For the most part Egypt's foreign relations remain peaceful during this period as witnessed by the famous tomb painting in the tomb of Khnumhotep II at Beni Hasan. Part of this painting depicts 37 Asiatics (men, women, and children) bringing eye-paint to Khnumhotep. But there is evidence of international strife during the Middle Kingdom in the Execration Texts. The Execration Texts were a class of formulas that functioned as destructive magic; they were designed to counteract negative influences, and they are attested from the Old Kingdom through the New Kingdom. The performance of execration rituals centered on objects inscribed to identify the target of the magical act; they were then destroyed or symbolically neutralized. These texts include figures made of unbaked clay and crudely formed into the shape of a bound prisoner. There are three lots of execration texts that deal with Western Asia containing standard formulae with the names of Asiatic chieftains and their related toponyms (place names), after which follows a comprehensive statement of curse along the lines of "all Asiatics of Gns, and their mighty runners ... who may rebel ... etc."

THE SECOND INTERMEDIATE PERIOD AND THE PERIOD OF THE HYKSOS. The Second Intermediate Period began toward the end of the 13th Dynasty when the centralized government began once again to falter, leading to the rise of local rulers in the eastern Nile Delta. The period reached its culmination when the *Hyksos invaded from Western Asia and usurped the throne. Originally these Near Easterners were referred to as "Shepherd kings" or "captive shepherds" by the scholarly community. These titles are based on an incorrect folk-etymology attested to as early as Josephus. The term Hyksos is the Greek rendering of the Egyptian appellation for these foreigners. But the Egyptian that underlies the Greek is best translated as "rulers of the foreign countries." In Egypt it became the official designation of the first three kings of the 15th Dynasty. The capital of the Hyksos was at Avaris, modern Tel ed-Dab'a in the Delta, on the eastern most of the Delta branches. The population there seems to have been composed of Asiatics, especially those who spoke Amorite, a West Semitic dialect.

Much of the Hyksos's power resulted from good trade relations with Cyprus, Nubia, and the Levant, and it was during this period that the horse, and wool-bearing sheep were introduced into Egypt. The archaeological record indicates that the Hyksos were not the first Near Easterners to live in the Nile Delta, but it was under the Hyksos that Egypt became more involved with the eastern Mediterranean (Bietak).

The reign of the Hyksos ended when the Theban ruler Ahmose finally expelled them and reunited the Two Lands. After this expulsion the capital shifted south again to Thebes.

THE NEW KINGDOM. The New Kingdom is the period of Egyptian expansion and imperialism. In the earlier periods Egypt's contact with, and control over, foreign areas was limited to her desire for trade and resources; during the New Kingdom Egypt's foreign policy became more aggressive. The Hurrian kingdom of Mitanni became a threat to Egypt, and the New Kingdom rulers responded to Mitanni's rising power in the area. The 18th Dynasty ruler Thutmose I led a campaign into northern Syria. Later, Thutmose III led 14 campaigns into Western Asia (one of which included a seven-month siege at Megiddo), and eventually subdued the Levantine coast, increasing Egyptian hegemony into the interior of Syro-Palestine. Under Thutmose III the rulers of the conquered Asiatic city-states became vassals to Egypt who had to send tribute and swear an oath of loyalty to the Pharaoh. True peace was not realized until the reign of Thutmose IV, who married one of the Mitannian princesses (Murnane 2001).

The Egyptian Empire reached its height during the reign of another 18th Dynasty Pharaoh, Amenhotep III. By this time the empire was firmly established, so that Egypt was able to keep her troops in just a few areas and to send garrisons only to regions that threatened revolt. But this relative ease of imperialism was short lived, and the Empire began to falter under the reign of Amenhotep IV whose internal policies caused him to be labeled the "heretic king." Amenhotep IV devoted much of his energy to religious reform. Traditionally, the established cults of Egypt's gods were under the care of the Pharaoh. Amenhotep IV neglected the traditional gods of Egypt and showed strict devotion to a new conception of the sun god the "Aten" (solar orb); he eventually withdrew his patronage from the capital at Thebes (which was the "city of Amun"), he changed his name to reflect his religious preferences to Akhenaten (*Akhenaton; "effective on behalf of the orb"), and established a new capital city named Akhetaten ("horizon of the orb"). Akhenaten weakened the power of the royal family to such an extent that that even when the traditional cult was re-established in the land, the last kings of the 18th Dynasty (including Tutankhamun) had no real power. The entire balance of power in the Near East changed during this period when the Mitannians lost control of most of their vassals to the Hittites and Egypt lost control of her vassal Kadesh to these same Hittites. The resulting hostilities between Egypt and Hatti only increased when a Hittite prince died on his way to Egypt with the intent to marry Tutankhamun's widow. Egypt's borders continued to recede south for the next three generations.

The Ramesside kings of the 19th and 20th Dynasties attempted to regain Egypt's past glory. These attempts met with varying levels of success. Ramesses II successfully defended Egypt against the invasions of the Sea Peoples, but his "victory" against the Hittites at Kadesh is not the unqualified "victory" portrayed on his temple walls. In addition, the balance of power achieved by Egypt in the south, and the Hittites in the north changed as Assyria emerged as a major force in Western Asia. Ramesses III was the strongest ruler of the 20th Dynasty, and he too defended Egypt against the Sea Peoples, and defeated two Libyan invasions. But the end of his reign is marked by a series of strikes by craftsmen who were working on the royal tombs at Thebes. These strikes were the beginning of the economic difficulties that helped bring about the end of the 20th Dynasty and Egypt's Empire period.

The New Kingdom saw Egypt rise to become an international superpower ruling territories from Nubia to Asia. But by the end of this period Egypt was a nation overwhelmed by internal troubles, which had lost control of all of her foreign territories; never again would Egypt regain her splendor.

For the biblical depiction of events in this period, see *History; *Exodus; *Pentateuch.

[Sharon Keller (2nd ed.)]

After the shortlived 21st Dynasty, the 22nd Dynasty, of Libyan origin, came to power in Egypt. Sheshonk I (the biblical *Shishak) gave refuge to the Israelite pretender *Jeroboam and, after the latter had returned to Israel, invaded first Judah, thoroughly ravaging and looting the country, and then Israel, treating it in like manner. Returning with vast plunder, and leaving a weakened Palestine behind him, Sheshonk retired to Egypt. Henceforth the Libyan rulers of Egypt, having shown their power, left West Asia alone.

By the end of the eighth century B.C.E. the Egyptianized Nubian rulers of *Cush had displaced the Libyans in control of Egypt, while the Assyrians under *Tiglath-Pileser III made their presence felt in Syria and Palestine. During the last revolt of Israel against Assyria (724–721 B.C.E.) Hosea wrote to So, the king of Egypt, for support against the Assyrians. This otherwise unknown king has been plausibly identified recently as Tefnakht, the ruler of Sais (So), a vassal of the Nubians. However, Egyptian support was to no avail; Tefnakht was repulsed and Samaria fell. Nevertheless Egypt still appeared to be powerful, and in the following decades *Hezekiah, king of Judah, again relied on Egypt. Although the biblical account names *Tirhakah (Taharka), king of Cush (Nubia; II Kings 19:35) as Jerusalem's ally, there are chronological problems involved, since the decisive battle of this campaign, that of Elteke, took place in 701, and Taharka's rule began only in 689.

*Sennacherib's successors subjugated Egypt, expelled the Cushites, and installed puppets who managed to regain Egyptian independence under the twenty-sixth Dynasty. The founder of this dynasty, Psammetichus I (c. 664–610 B.C.E.) strengthened Egypt by the widespread employment of foreigners – Greek and Jewish mercenary troops and Phoenician sailors and merchants. During his reign or that of Psammetichus II (c. 595–89 B.C.E.) the famous colony of Jewish mercenary soldiers was established at *Elephantine to protect the southern frontier of Egypt. After the fall of the Assyrian capital of Nineveh in 612 B.C.E. to the Neo-Babylonians and Medes, the king of Egypt, Neco II, "went up against the Babylonians," but found his way barred by *Josiah, king of Judah, whom he defeated and killed at Megiddo in 609. Four years later, the Babylonians decisively defeated him at the battle of Carchemish. The subsequent Babylonian invasion of Egypt, preceded by the siege and sack of Ashkelon, was, however, beaten back, although Palestine remained under Babylonian control.

In 589 *Nebuchadnezzar besieged Jerusalem, whose king, *Zedekiah, had rebelled at the instigation of the pharaoh Apries (*Hophra). The latter invaded Syria in an attempt to relieve Jerusalem, but again Egyptian support proved ineffectual, and in 587 Jerusalem fell. Most of the city's population was deported to Babylon; some, however, took refuge in Egypt, including the prophet *Jeremiah.

[Alan Richard Schulman]

Egyptian Literature in the Bible

Egypt has a long and full literary history and tradition, and as such, there is ample evidence of both literary and nonliterary genre of texts. These texts serve many functions and come in a variety of forms each with its own established conventions and styles. The technical aspects of Egyptian literary forms are not generally paralleled in biblical literature, yet it is well recognized that there is a commonalty in content between some biblical narrative motifs and those found in various Ancient Egyptian texts. Direct links in the prose literature are difficult to establish, but there is a scholarly consensus that relates the two bodies of literature. Wisdom texts fall in their own category; the consensus maintains that the biblical wisdom tradition is dependent, at least in part, upon the Egyptian. Questions of borrowing and/or primary derivation notwithstanding, there is no doubt that the Egyptian material antedates the biblical.

Egypt plays an important part in the narrative setting of the Torah. From the time that Joseph is sold into servitude through the Exodus and the crossing of the Sea of Reeds, the central location of the story is Egypt. It is in these stories, the ones set in Egypt, that the majority of narrative parallels are to be found. The most frequently cited example is the biblical tale of Joseph and Potiphar's wife (Gen 39) and the New Kingdom *Tale of Two Brothers*. The Egyptian tale is the first known example in ancient literature of the Temptress motif. The details and purposes of each of the stories differ greatly, but there is no serious doubt that the structure of the motif is essentially the same. In such stories an older woman (or a woman of higher social status) develops an ill-advised passion for a younger man (or one of a lesser social status). This "temptress" makes her desires known to the young man (Gen 39:7) who refuses her advances on moral grounds (verses 8–9); thus spurned, the "temptress" accuses the young man of violating her, and the "wronged" husband then seeks retribution. The standard versions of this tale eventually vindicate the youth and punish the mendacious wife. In the biblical account Joseph is punished for his supposed actions by being imprisoned (verses 19–20). Eventually he is pardoned by Pharaoh and released from prison because, after interpreting Pharaoh's dreams, Joseph is rewarded and made viceroy of Egypt (41:14–45). The biblical version deviates from the pattern in two significant ways: First, the narrator never tells us that Joseph is ever publicly declared innocent. (He is pardoned not exonerated). Second, the fate of the temptress is not revealed. Potiphar's wife disappears from the story right after she accuses Joseph (Gen 39:18–19), because she is no longer important to the progress of the narrative.

Although the *Tale of Two Brothers* is the most frequently cited example of biblical and Egyptian narrative parallels, it is by no means the only one. Some literary tales present us with a picture of Syria-Palestine that is reminiscent of the description of the area in the Patriarchal Narratives of Genesis and also show some parallel values. The prime example is the Middle Kingdom *Tale of Sinuhe*, which depicts the environment of the Levant in detail and shows it much the same as described in the Torah narratives. Both the Hebrew and Egyptian sources describe pastoral nomadic clans who travel among the settled urban population centers. Sinuhe was an attendant to Princess Nefru, daughter of Amenemhet I and wife of Sesostris I. After Amenemhet I dies, Sinuhe overhears plans for a palace coup. Fearing that he will be caught up in the civil-war that will inevitably follow, he flees Egypt and wanders through the Nile Delta and throughout Canaan. Sinhue becomes very successful in Canaan, but always longs to return to his native land. Ultimately, he is reunited with Sesostris I and urged to return to Egypt. As with most Egyptian tales, this one ends happily when Sinhue returns to Egypt and is welcomed back into the royal household, His wish that he be allowed to returned to Egypt so he may die and be buried there is fulfilled. Sinuhe's flight from political danger may be compared to Moses' flight from Egypt to avoid Pharaoh's wrath (Ex. 2:15). Sinuhe's subsequent wanderings though the Egyptian Delta and into Canaan along with his new found prosperity in a foreign land may be compared with the accounts of Abraham's peregrinations. Another frequently cited parallel is that Sinuhe very much wants to be buried in his native Egypt, just as Jacob desires that his body be returned from Egypt to Canaan (Gen. 47:29–30). Similarly, Joseph adjures the children of Israel to carry his bones out from Egypt when they leave (Gen 50:25, Ex. 13:19).

Narrative parallels are not limited to the Torah. One of Sinuhe's exploits has been compared to David's slaying of Goliath. "He came toward me while I waited, having placed myself near him. Every heart burned for me; the women jabbered. All hearts ached for me thinking: 'Is there another champion who could fight him?' He [raised] his battle-axe and shield, while his armful of missiles fell toward me. When I had made his weapons attack me, I let his arrows pass me by without effect, one following the other. Then, when he charged me, I shot him, my arrow sticking in his neck. He screamed; he fell on his nose; I slew him with his axe. I raised my war cry over his back, while every Asiatic shouted. I gave praise to Mont, while his people mourned him" (Lichtheim in COS) Both Sinuhe and David are underdog warriors who surprisingly vanquish the enemy champion with his own weapon (I Sam 17:51).

Scholarly consensus recognizes that the biblical Wisdom tradition, and much of the poetic and instructional literature related to that tradition, has very close associations with Egyptian Wisdom Literature. Within the Bible there is a conception of Egypt as a source of great wisdom (I Kings 4:30, "Solomon's wisdom was greater than the wisdom of all the Kedemites and than all the wisdom of the Egyptians"), but this "wisdom" is not that of the Wisdom Literature. Egyptian Wisdom Literature deals with "truth," "justice," and especially "order," the "cosmic order" as ordained by the gods. Biblical Wisdom focuses primarily upon Wisdom personified and the "fear of God" associated with it. So the larger conceptions that inform the genre are not identical, but the Egyptian material most certainly has influenced the biblical.

Psalm 104 is frequently viewed in light of "The Great Hymn to the Aten." Both texts venerate the solar aspects of the deity and use similar language in so doing. Song of Songs is widely recognized as having significant parallels to Egyptian love poetry (Fox) There are parallels of phraseology: In the Song of Songs "sister" is used as a term of intimacy between the two lovers (4:9, 10–12, "…my sister, my bride…"; also 5:1, 2), and in the Egyptian Love Songs both "sister" and "brother" are used as terms of love and intimacy. In both literatures there is an alternation between the speech of the girl and that of the boy, but with a difference; In the Bible the lovers engage in dialogues, whereas in the Love Songs from Egypt the lovers are given alternating soliloquies. Another common feature is found in the so-called "Praise Song," where the physical beauty of the beloved body is described limb by limb. (4:1–7; 5:10–16; 7:2–10a).

Even more striking parallels are to be found in instructional literature; these connections were first recognized in the early 20th century, and are regularly noted in modern commentaries. The prime example is the "Instruction of Amenemope." Proverbs 22:17–24:22 and Jeremiah 17:5–8 are both thought to be inspired by "Amenemope." Of particular interest is Proverbs 22:20 and the difficulty surrounding the Hebrew word traditionally written both *shlshwm* (*ketiv*) and *shlyshym* (*qere*) and vocalized to mean either "officers" or "the day before yesterday." Neither makes any sense in the context of the pericope. Accordingly, many scholars vocalize this word as *sheloshim*, "thirty" ("Have I not written for you thirty sayings of counsel and wisdom") especially since there are 30 chapters in the "Instruction of Amenemope" and that text ends "Look to these thirty chapters, They inform, they educate …."

The points of contact between biblical and Egyptian literature go beyond content, and include linguistic borrowings as well. There are close to six dozen agreed upon Egyptian loan words in the Bible, not including personal names and toponyms (place names); some of these words are Hebraized, whereas others are used in forms that are close to their Egyptian form. Understandably, there is a remarkable clustering of these loan words in the biblical accounts relating to Egypt. We have come to expect Egyptian words used to describe the natural environment of Egypt, so the biblical words for "reeds" (Ex. 13:18, 15:4, 22, 23:31; passim), "Nile" (Gen. 41:1–3; passim), "papyrus" (Ex. 2:3; Isa. 18:2, 35:7; Job 8:11), and "marsh grass" (Gen. 41:2, 18; Job 8:11) all are Egyptian loans. The same goes for specifically Egyptian offices like the *hartumim* typically translated as "magicians" (Gen. 41:8, 24; Ex. 7:11, 22, 8:3, 14–15, 9:11; Dan. 1:20, 2:2, 10, 27, 4:4, 6, 5:11). Pharaoh is a royal title (literally "big house" / "palace") used in the Bible both as a royal title with a specific royal name following (Pharaoh RN – II Kings 23:29, 33–35; Jer. 46:2), or alone as a virtual royal name or specific appellative (this usage is consistent in the Torah text). Attempts have been made to date biblical passages according to the usage of the word "Pharaoh," but such arguments are speculative at best, and ignore the literary aspects of the text.

[Sharon Keller (2nd ed.)]

The Hellenistic Period

THE PTOLEMAIC PERIOD. Egyptian Jewry traced its history back to the time of Jeremiah (Letter of Aristeas, 35), but it was not until the conquest of *Alexander the Great in 332 B.C.E. that the second great wave of Jewish emigration to Egypt began. Alexander's successors in Egypt, the Ptolemid dynasty, attracted many Jews early in their reign to settle in Egypt as tradesmen, farmers, mercenaries, and government officials. During their reign Egyptian Jewry enjoyed both tolerance and prosperity. They became significant in culture and literature, and by the first century C.E., accounted for an eighth of the population of Egypt. The majority of the Jews of Egypt lived,

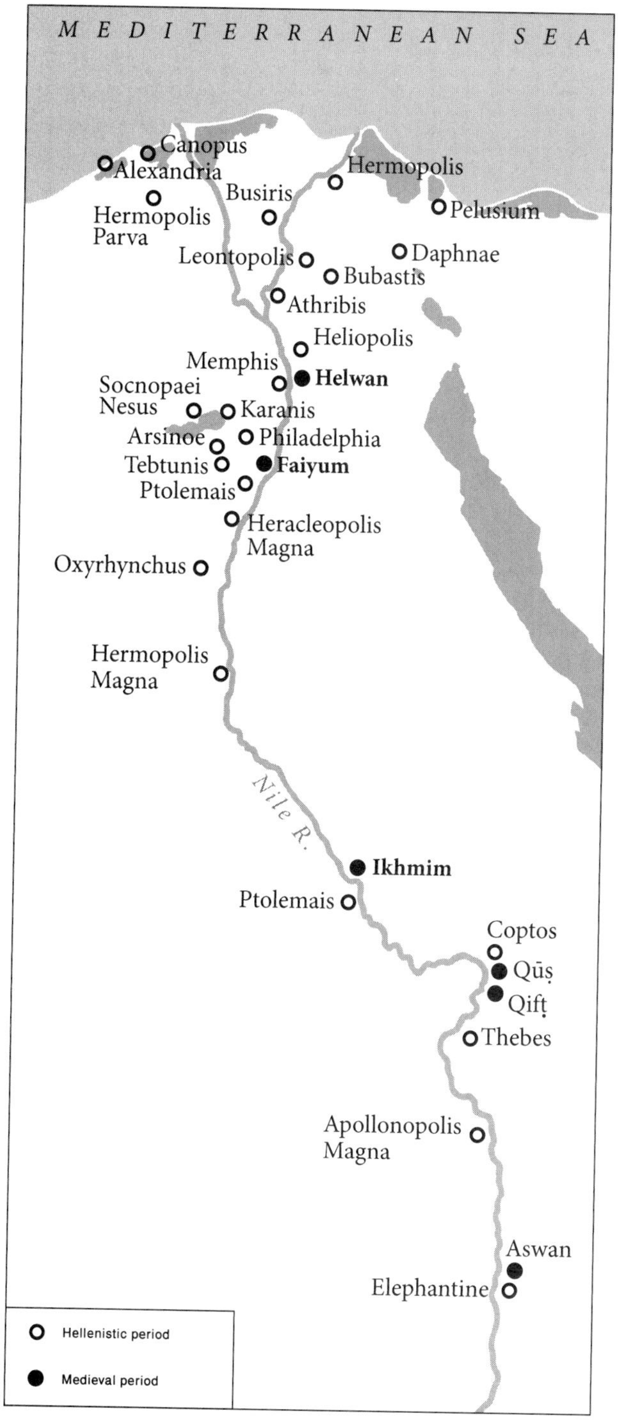

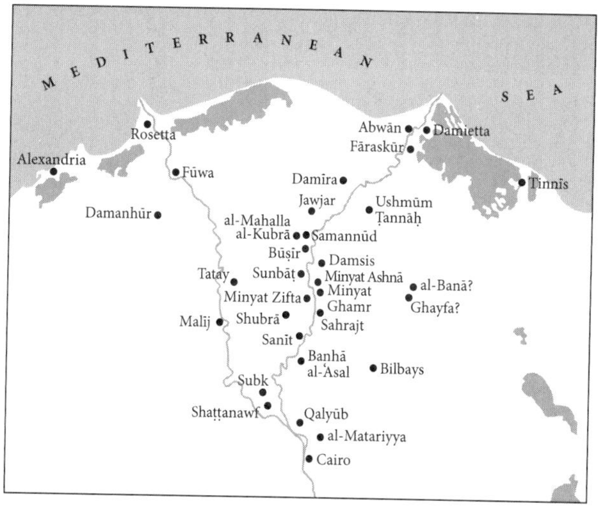

Map 1. Main Jewish communities in Egypt during the Hellenistic period and during the Middle Ages; the enlarged section of the Delta region (right) gives medieval communities only.

as the Greeks, in *Alexandria, but there were also very many in the *ehora*, the provincial districts outside Alexandria.

*Ptolemy I Soter (323–283) took a large number of Jewish prisoners of war in Palestine and forcibly settled them as mercenaries in Egypt to hold down the native Egyptians (*ibid.*, 36). On Ptolemy I's retreat from Palestine many Jews fled with him to Egypt, where they found a haven of tolerance. *Ptolemy II Philadelphus (283–44) emancipated the Jews taken captive by his father and settled them on the land as cleruchs or in "Jew-Camps" as Jewish military units. He was remembered by the Jews of Egypt as having instigated the translation of the Septuagint (see Letter of *Aristeas; *Bible: Greek translation). Since *Manetho's antisemitic work was written in his reign there must have been a fair number of Jews already in Egypt.

*Ptolemy III Euergetes (246–221) was said to have been favorably disposed toward the Jews and to have respected their religion. Two facts confirm this. One is the number of Jews who settled in the nome of Arsinoe (*Faiyum) in his reign, and the other is the synagogue inscription dedicated to him, declaring that he granted the rights of asylum to the synagogues (Frey, Corpus 2 pp. 374–6). There is also a synagogue inscription from Schedia, which was also probably dedicated to him (Reinach in REJ, 14 (1902), 161–4).

*Ptolemy IV Philopator (221–203) attempted to institute a massacre of the Jews of Alexandria in 217 B.C.E., but was later reconciled with them (III Macc. 5–6). During the reign of *Ptolemy VI Philometor (181–145) a marked change took place. Ptolemy VI won Jewish favor by opening up the whole of Egypt to the Jews, on whom he relied, as well as by receiving Jewish exiles from Palestine such as *Onias IV, to whom he granted land to build a temple at Leontopolis (c. 161 B.C.E.; Jos., Wars 1:33). The Jewish philosopher *Aristobulus of Paneas was said to have advised him on Jewish affairs, and he appointed two Jews, Onias and Dositheos, to high military posts (Jos., Apion, 2:49). During the struggles of Cleopatra *III (116–101) with her son *Ptolemy IX Lathyros (116–80) the Jews of Egypt sided with the Queen, thus earning her esteem but alienating the Greek population from them (Ant. 13:287). She appointed two Jewish brothers, *Ananias and Helkias, as commanders of her army.

SOCIAL AND ECONOMIC DEVELOPMENTS. Most of the Jews who settled in the *chora* were either farmers or artisans. The

Ptolemies did not generally trust the native Egyptians and encouraged the Jews to enter three professions:

(a) the army, where, as other nationalities in Egypt, they were allowed to lease plots of land from the king (called cleruchies), and were granted tax reductions;

(b) the police force, in which Jews reached high ranks (cf. the Jewish district chief of police in Frey, Corpus, 2, p. 370); and

(c) tax collecting (a government executive job) and sometimes in the *chora*, tax farming (a government administrative post; see Tcherikover, Corpus nos. 107, 109, 110).

Others were managers in the royal banks or administrators (*ibid.*, nos. 99–103, from middle of second century B.C.E.). In Alexandria there was a greater diversity of occupations and some Jews prospered in trade and commerce.

Early in the third century B.C.E. synagogues were founded in Egypt. They are known to have existed at Alexandria, Schedia (third century B.C.E.), Alexandrou Nesou (third century B.C.E.), Crocodilopolis-Arsinoe (three: third century B.C.E., second century B.C.E., and second century C.E.), Xenephyris (second century B.C.E.), Athribis (two: third or second century B.C.E.), and Nitriae (second century B.C.E.). They were usually called προσευχή or εὐχεῖον (from the Greek *euche* = prayer), and tablets were often erected dedicating the synagogue to the king and the royal family.

At first the Jewish immigrants spoke only Aramaic, and documents from the third century and the first half of the second century B.C.E. show a widespread knowledge of Aramaic and Hebrew (cf. Frey, Corpus 2, pp. 356, 365). But from the second century on there was a rapid Hellenization. Documents were written in Greek, the Pentateuch was read in the synagogue with the Septuagint translation, and even such a writer as *Philo probably knew no or little Hebrew. At first the Egyptian Jews transliterated their names into Greek, or adopted Greek names that sounded like Hebrew ones (e.g., Alcimus for Eliakim, or Jason for Joshua), but later they often adopted Greek equivalents of Hebrew names (e.g., Dositheos for Jonathan, Theodoras for Jehonathan). Gradually Egyptian Jewry adopted any Greek name (even those of foreign gods), and among the *Zeno Letters only 25% of the names are Hebrew.

In the *chora* the Hellenization was not so strong, but there the Jews were influenced by the native Egyptians. Documents testify to Egyptian names among the Jews, and sometimes to an ignorance of Greek (presumably these Jews spoke Egyptian). However, the *chora* Jews were more observant of the Sabbath and dietary laws than those of Alexandria.

The relations between Greek and Jew was on the whole good under the Ptolemies. The Jews often sought to explain Judaism to the Greeks (cf. Aristobulus of Paneas, Philo, and others). They tried to enter the Greek gymnasium which was a sign of the cultured Greek. Cases of actual apostasy were rare; that of Dositheos, son of Drimylos, who renounced Judaism to enter court, was exceptional (III Macc. 1:3).

CONSTITUTION. It used to be thought that the Jews were given equal rights with the Greeks by Alexander the Great, and that they called themselves Macedonians (Wars, 2:487–88). This has been disproved by papyri where it appears that only Jews or Jewish military units, who were incorporated into Macedonian units, were termed "Macedonians" (compare Tcherikover, Corpus nos. 142 line 3 with no. 143). Since the population registered its name and racial origin, each nationality in Egypt formed a separate group through the Ptolemid period. The Jews, unlike the Greeks, were not granted a *politeia* (rights of free citizenship), but received a *politeuma* (a constitution by which they had the right to observe their ancestral laws). Individual Jews were granted citizenship occasionally by the polis or the king, or by managing to register in a gymnasium. These, however, were exceptions. From the papyri of Faiyum and Oxyrhynchus it seems that the majority of Jews did not use the right of recourse to Jewish courts, but attended Greek ones even in cases of marriage or divorce. The head of the Jewish community in Alexandria was the *ethnarch, while in the *chora* elders held sway.

Toward the end of the Ptolemid period Jewish-Greek relations steadily worsened. The Greeks, supported by the Egyptians, were struggling to strengthen the power of the polis, while the Jews supported the Ptolemids, first Cleopatra III (see above), and then *Ptolemy XIII and *Gabinius in 55 B.C.E. Papyri of 58 B.C.E. recorded some unrest in Egypt of an antisemitic nature (e.g., Tcherikover, Corpus no. 141). Josephus records that *Julius Caesar was aided by Jewish cleruchs in Egypt when *Antipater brought reinforcements from Palestine. In return for this Caesar is said to have reaffirmed the citizenship of the Alexandrian Jews in 47 B.C.E. (Ant., 14:131, 188–96).

Roman Period

EARLY ROMAN EMPIRE. The new administration under *Augustus at first was grateful to the Jews for their support (cf. the stele of their rights set up in Alexandria; Jos., Ant. 14:188), but generally it relied on the Greeks of Alexandria for help, which fact caused a great rift between the Jews and the rest of the population early in their rule. Augustus disbanded the Ptolemaic army and abolished the tax-collection system about 30 B.C.E. Both of these acts caused great economic hardships for the Jews. Few of them joined or were permitted to join the Roman army in Egypt (an exception being a centurion of 116 C.E., in Tcherikover, Corpus no. 229). Jewish tax collectors were mostly replaced by Greek government officials. The *cursus honorum* was closed to Jews unless they renounced their religion, which most refused to do (an exception being *Tiberius Julius Alexander, prefect of Egypt). Jewish civil rights (*politeuma*) were endangered by Augustus' revision of the constitution of Egypt. Three classes were created:

(a) the upper class of Romans, priests, Greek citizens of Alexandria, Naucratis, and Ptolemais, and those who had registered in the gymnasium;

(b) Egyptians, the lowest class, who paid a burdensome poll tax; and

(c) the middle class *metropolitae* (i.e., half-Greeks who lived in the *chora*), who paid the poll tax at a reduced rate.

Augustus placed the Jew in the lowest class, forced to pay the tax. This was a blow to Jewish pride, for besides those few individual Jewish families who had received the distinction of Greek citizenship, the vast majority of Jews could no longer register in the gymnasia and had to pay the poll tax.

From that time began a long struggle by the Alexandrian Jews to confirm their rights. The works of writers such as Josephus (*Contra Apionem*) and Philo (Vita Moysis 1:34) contain a defense of Alexandrian Jews' rights. The Greeks in turn approached Augustus suggesting that they would keep all non-Greeks out of the gymnasia, if he, in turn, would abolish the privileges of the Jews. Augustus refused and confirmed the Jewish ancestral rights, to the intense anger of the Greeks. Augustus abolished the post of ethnarch of Alexandria in 10–12 C.E., replacing it by a *gerusia* of elders.

The Greeks of Alexandria seized their opportunity with the rise of the pro-Hellenic emperor, Caius *Caligula in 37 C.E. The following year they stormed the synagogues, polluted them, and set up statues of the emperor within. The prefect, Valerius *Flaccus, was embarrassed and dared not remove the images of Caesar. The Jews were shut up in a ghetto and their houses plundered. Philo, who wrote *In Flaccum* and *De Legatione* on the affair, headed a Jewish delegation to Caligula to complain, but was dismissed with derision. On the assassination of Caligula in 41 C.E. the Jews of Alexandria took vengeance by instigating a massacre of the Greeks.

The new emperor, *Claudius, issued an edict in favor of the Jews in 41 C.E., abolishing the restrictions imposed at the time of the pogrom of 38 C.E., but he banned the Jews from entering the gymnasia, and refused them Greek citizenship. Much antisemitic material was written at this period in Egypt, e.g., *Apion's works, and the *Acts of the *Alexandrian Martyrs*.

Consequently the Jews closed their ranks and became more self-conscious of their Jewish heritage. Such works were written as III *Maccabees and the Wisdom of *Solomon. The Jews also tended to live closer together, though no ghettos were imposed.

In 66 C.E. the Alexandrians, in debating about a delegation to be sent to Nero, presumably to complain about the Jews, discovered several Jewish spies among themselves. Three were caught and burnt alive. The Jews rose in revolt and tried to burn the Greeks in their amphitheater, and Tiberius Julius Alexander, the prefect, crushed them mercilessly, killing more than were slain in the pogrom of 38 C.E. After the destruction of the Jerusalem Temple in 70 C.E. Onias' Temple at *Leontopolis was destroyed and the **fiscus judaicus* imposed. However, the Egyptian Jews had to pay more than other Jews, because the Egyptian calendar provided that they pay in the first year of the fiscus (71 C.E.), two years in arrears instead of one year, as other Jews. It is estimated that they paid that year 27 million Egyptian drachmae in taxes.

In 115 the great revolt of the Jews of Egypt, Cyrene, and Cyprus occurred (see *Trajan). The revolt was immediately crushed in Alexandria, by Marcus Rutilius Lupus, but it continued in the *chora* with the help of the Jews of *Cyrene (in centers as Thebes, Faiyum, and Athribis). Marcius Turbo was sent by the emperor to deal with the situation, and crushed the revolt in 117. Much of Alexandria was destroyed and the revolt resulted in the virtual annihilation of Egyptian Jewry. From that time on Jews almost vanish from the *chora*. In Alexandria the great synagogue was destroyed, large tracts of Jewish-owned land in Heracleapolis and Oxyrhynchus were confiscated, and Jewish courts were suspended. The causes of the revolt suggested are the antisemitism of the local Greeks, and the "messianic" movement centered around *Lucuas of Cyrene. The revolt spelled the end of Jewish life in Egypt for a long time. From 117 to 300 only a few Jewish names occur among the peasants in the *chora*.

From the End of the Second Temple Period to the Muslim Conquest

The defeat suffered by the Jews, both in Ereẓ Israel under Bar Kokhba and in the quelling of the rebellion in Egypt during the years 116–117 C.E. almost crushed the Jewish communities in Egypt, especially in Alexandria. The evidence from the papyri of the presence of a large, cohesive community in Egypt, found rather abundantly before 70 C.E, diminishes, until after the year 200 C.E. it becomes almost negligible. The territory of Egypt was still a marked battleground for imperial ambitions and rebellions during this later period of the Roman Empire. The revolt of the Βουκολοι (herdsmen) and its aftermath, finally settled by the emperor Septimus Severus (194 C.E.), left the country with its agriculture almost ruined and burdened with heavy taxes. During the latter half of the third century Egypt was again racked with internal dispute. Finally, Diocletian brought a period of relative peace to the land, reorganizing the territory into three, and later four, provinces. The later history of Egypt under the Byzantine emperors is closely tied up with the growth and predominance there of hitherto persecuted Christianity.

Centered as it was in Alexandria, Christianity in Egypt inherited some of the classical antisemitism of the city. Clement of Alexandria mentions (*Stromata*, 3:63; 2:45.5) the fact that there existed in the primitive church there two "Gospels," an "Egyptian Gospel" and a "Hebrew Gospel" – evidence of the dichotomy in the early church between gentile and Jewish Christianity, the latter being characterized in Egypt by a Gnostic tendency. By 150 C.E., however, both Orthodox and Gnostic Christianity found themselves allied with regard to the Jews. Basilides, an Alexandrian Gnostic at the end of the second century, tried to stress in Gnostic terms that Christianity is to be completely dissociated from its Jewish ancestry. An early work called the *Epistle of Barnabas* (c. 135 C.E.) argued for the abrogation by God of the Old Covenant (Old

Testament) and the preference for an allegorical and "spiritual" interpretation of the Jewish Scriptures, a tendency later adopted by Clement of Alexandria and the exegetical school of the Alexandrian, *Origen (d. 253 C.E.). Another early work, found only in citations, the *Kerygma Petrou*, accused the Jews of angel and star worship.

Some of the knowledge of the Jews in these times is derived from Christian sources. The martyrologies of the time, as a matter of style, brought in the Jews as the accusers. Generally though, as Baron reports (Social², 2 (1952), 188), the early Christians got along with their Jewish neighbors. Indeed, toward 300 C.E., Jewish names begin to appear more frequently in the papyri, giving witness to a renewal of activity. There are even some Hebrew fragments found at Oxyrhynchus which speak of *rashei* ("heads"), *benei* ("members"), and *ziknei* ("elders") of the *keneset* ("the community"; Cowley, *Journal of Egyptian Archaeology*, 2 (1915), 209ff.). An interesting feature of the Greek papyri of this period is the appearance of the name "Sambathion" among both Jews and non-Jews, giving testimony to the great respect given the Sabbath among the Egyptians (for a fuller discussion cf. Tcherikover, Corpus, 3 (1964), 43–56). It is true that the Jews did support the Arians in their disputes with orthodox Christianity, and patristic literature placed the Jews together with the heretics and pagans as the hated enemies of the church. This attitude later became codified into law by the *Codices* of the emperors Theodosius and Justinian. A pogrom and expulsion of the Jews from Alexandria by the patriarch Cyril occurred in 415 C.E. Whether or not this expulsion was fully carried out is still a moot point, since later Christian literature points to the fact that Jews were still living there (M. Chaine, in *Mélanges de la Faculté orientale de l'Université Saint-Joseph*, Beyrouth, 6 (1913), 493ff.). The Persian conquest seemed to be especially helpful to the Jews in Egypt, since they were able to receive those Jews persecuted in Syria by the emperor Heraclius. The Arab conquest in 632 saw the beginning of a new regime.

[Evasio de Marcellis]

Arab Period

There is little information available concerning the condition of the Jews from the Arab conquest in 640 until the end of the tenth century. In Fostat, founded by the conqueror of Egypt, ʿAmr ibn al-ʿĀṣ, a relatively large community was established, while the Jewish population probably also grew in other Egyptian cities. Ahmad ibn Ṭūlūn (ninth century), the first independent ruler of Egypt under the Muslims, seems to have favored the Jews. The historian al-Masʿūdī relates that he had a Jewish physician. Documents found in the *Cairo *Genizah* of Fostat give evidence of the commercial ties between the Jews of Egypt and those of *Kairouan (Tunisia) during the second half of the tenth century. The Jews of Egypt also renewed their relations with the major academies of Babylonia. It is significant for the high standard of Jewish learning in Egypt itself that *Saadiah Gaon (born in Faiyum in 882) acquired his widespread culture there. At that time many Babylonian Jews settled in the principal Egyptian cities and established communities with their own synagogue and *bet din*. They also maintained a close relationship with the academies in their country of origin. Students traveled there to study, and religious and judicial queries were addressed to the heads of the Babylonian academies. The Palestinian and Syrian Jews who settled in Egypt acted in the same manner. They established Palestinian communities and synagogues, and they recognized the heads of the Palestinian academies, to whom they gave their material support, as their spiritual leaders. The activities of Saadiah Gaon prove the presence of large numbers of *Karaites in Egypt at the time. It seems that during the ninth and tenth centuries, there was still a variety of sects in Egypt. The work *Kitāb al-Anwār wa-al-Marāqib* ("The Book of Lights and Watch Towers") by al-*Kirkisānī, in 936 (L. Nemoy (ed.), 1 (1939), 12), mentions a sect which observed Sunday as a day of rest instead of Saturday. Members of this sect lived on the bank of the Nile, some 20 miles from Fostat (Bacher, in: JQR, 7 (1894/95) 704).

THE *FATIMIDS. A change in the condition of the Jews occurred with the conquest of the country by the Fatimids in 969. After the conquest by this dynasty of Shiʿites which was in rivalry with the *Abbasīd caliphs, Egypt became the center of a vast and powerful kingdom, which, at the end of the tenth century, included almost all of North Africa, *Syria, and *Palestine. The union of all these countries brought a period of prosperity in industry and commerce from which the Jews also benefited. Of even greater importance was the characteristically tolerant attitude adopted by the Fatimids toward non-Muslim communities. They did not insist on the observance of the decrees of discrimination, such as the wearing of a distinctive sign on the garments; they permitted the construction and repair of non-Muslim houses of prayer, and they even accorded financial support to the academies in Palestine. In the court of al-Muʿizz (d. 975) and his son al-ʿAzīz (975–996), a Jew converted to Islam, Yaʿqūb *Ibn Killis, occupied an important position and was finally appointed vizier. He was the first to hold this post under the reign of the Fatimids in Egypt. There were also Jewish physicians in the service of al-Muʿizz. The third Fatimid caliph, al-Ḥākim (996–1020), founder of the *Druze sect and a controversial personality, departed from the policy of tolerance toward non-Muslims, which was characteristic of his dynasty, during the second half of his reign. At first, he ordered that the Christians and Jews mark their clothes with the *ghiyār* ("distinctive sign"; see Jewish *Badge); later, he issued orders for the destruction of their houses of prayer. He also prohibited Christians and Jews from riding horses and purchasing slaves and maidservants. Many Christians and Jews converted to Islam in order to escape these degrading decrees, while others emigrated to different countries, such as Yemen and *Byzantium. However, after some time, al-Ḥākim revoked his decrees and authorized the converts to return to their former religion.

In 1036 the grandson of al-Ḥākim, al-Mustanṣir, ascended to the throne. A Jewish merchant, who had previously sold al-Mustanṣir's mother to the caliph al-Ẓāhir, then wielded much influence in the court. This merchant Abu Saʿd (in Hebrew, Abraham b. Yashar) was also named "al-Tustari" after his city of origin in Persia. He and his brother, Abu Naṣr Ḥesed, endeavored to protect their coreligionists by all available means. According to one opinion, Abu Saʿd and his brother were Rabbanites, while according to another they were *Karaites. In 1047 Abu Saʿd was killed, as was his brother, Abu Naṣr, some time later. The economic stratification of Egyptian Jewry during the Fatimid period was very diversified. According to the lists of taxpayers and of charitable donators (such as the one published by E. Strauss in *Zion*, 7 (1941/42), 142ff.), the majority were engaged in various trades and a minority in commerce. At that time, the transit trade of products from India and the Far East became an important source of income in Egypt and the Jews played an active role in this commerce. The Fatimid government encouraged these commercial ties with India and protected the seaways and overland routes. The friendly attitude of the Fatimids was also expressed by the granting of a large degree of autonomy to the merchants.

At the beginning of their rule, the office of **nagid* was established. The first *nagid* seems to have been a physician in the service of the caliph al-Muʿizz. In later generations, the office of *nagid* was also filled by men employed in the court, especially as court physicians. The Fatimid dynasty began to weaken at the end of the 11th century, but the condition of the Jews did not worsen. A Jewish family which during several generations produced scholars and physicians held high positions at the royal court at that time. Judah b. Saadiah was probably court physician and from 1065 acted as *nagid*. He was followed by his younger brother *Mevorakh, who was also court physician and *nagid* from 1079–1110. During his period of office *David b. Daniel b. Azariah, a scion of a family of Babylonian exilarchs, arrived in Egypt. David made an effort to secure the leadership of the Jewish population and succeeded in deposing Mevorakh for a short while. Moses, the elder son of Mevorakh, was *nagid* from 1110–1140. At that period a Christian favorite of the regent al-Afḍal endeavored to remove the Jews from government service (see Neubauer, in JQR, 9 (1896/97), 29–30). Fragments from the **Genizah* mention another enemy who plotted against the Jews until Yakhin b. Nethanel, who was influential in the royal court, succeeded in saving them. On the other hand, *Abu al-Munajjā, one of the Jewish courtiers, was responsible for the administration of the "Eastern" province. In the middle of the 12th century *Samuel b. Hananiah was court physician. He was a distinguished scholar and also acted as *nagid* from 1142 to 1159. His poems in honor of his guest, *Judah Halevi, are well known.

During this period the Jews of Egypt prospered in every sphere. *Benjamin of Tudela, who was in Egypt in c. 1171, gives much information concerning the prevailing conditions in the communities he visited. On the basis of his information and other relevant data, the number of Jews in Egypt at that time has been estimated at between 12,000 and 20,000 (see Neustadt-Ayalon in *Zion*, 2 (1937), 221; Ashtor, in JQR, 50 (1959/60), 60 and JJS, 18 (1967), 9–42; 19 (1968), 1–22). After the death of Samuel b. Hananiah, there was a crisis within the Jewish community of Egypt. An ambitious individual named *Zuta, who succeeded in being appointed *nagid* for a short while during the lifetime of Samuel b. Hananiah, exploited his connections to secure the office for a second time, after Samuel's death, and later a third time. As a result of Zuta's activities, the prestige attached to the office of *nagid* declined and for a long time there was no new appointment. At that time the heads of the Fostat academy became the leading authorities of Egyptian Jewry; an academy had existed in Fostat from at least the end of the tenth century. During the reign of al-Ḥākim the academy in the Egyptian capital was headed by *Shemariah b. Elhanan, who had studied in Babylonia in his youth. He was succeeded by his son, *Elhanan b. Shemariah. During the first half of the 12th century, *Maẓliʾaḥ b. Solomon Ha-Kohen, a member of the family of the Palestinian academy heads, arrived in Egypt. He founded an academy in Fostat, whose leaders were referred to as *geonim*. They appointed *dayyanim* and gave authority to their activities. The authority of these *geonim* was recognized even outside Egypt, especially in South Arabia and *Aden. In the early 1150s Abu Saʿīd Joshua b. Dosa headed the academy in Fostat.

With the end of the Fatimid dynasty, orthodox Islam again became the official religion in Egypt. Saladin (Salāḥ al-Dīn) and his successors made their religiosity conspicuous and, among other actions, Saladin renewed the discriminatory decrees against the non-Muslim communities. However, both he and his successors were by no means fanatical and they did not persecute non-Muslims. His successors, the *Ayyubids, who reigned in Egypt until 1250, followed the same policy. Communal life was well organized and cultural activities were maintained. During this period a number of scholars from Christian countries settled in Egypt and took an active part in the communal life. They included *Anatoli b. Joseph and Joseph b. Gershon from France, who became *dayyanim* in Alexandria. Moses *Maimonides spent most of his life in Cairo, where he played a leading role in the life of the community. His son, *Abraham b. Moses, acted officially as *nagid* after the death of his father in 1205 until his own death in 1237. He had an independent mind and was also a halakhic authority, as can be seen from the numerous legal questions which were addressed to him.

THE MAMLUKS. In the middle of the 13th century the *Mamluks came to power in Egypt. The entire political regime was changed and a decisive change in the condition of the Jews also took place. These rulers were the leaders of the foreign Turkish soldiery of which the army was exclusively composed, and they tried to enhance their position and to curry favor with the Muslim native population by emphasizing their piety and by introducing a series of measures directed against the non-Muslim communities. The first Mamluks declared total war against the Crusaders. They found it necessary to encourage religious fervor in order to succeed in their efforts. Thus, the Mamluk rule was accompanied by a series of decrees and persecutions against the Christians and Jews, which continued until the Mamluks were deposed by the Ottomans. The ancient discriminatory laws were brought back into prominence and new ones were also instituted. These activities were primarily directed against the Copts, the most powerful non-Muslim community in the Mamluk kingdom, but even so the Jews suffered considerably. On the other hand, Jewish communal organization in Egypt was not abolished and its autonomy was mostly maintained. The decrees against non-Muslims were introduced during the first generation of the Mamluk rule. In 1290 Sultan Qalāwūn issued an order which prohibited the employment of Jews and Christians in government and ministerial departments. This order was reissued during the reign of his son and successor, al-Malik al-Ashraf Khalīl (1290–1293).

In 1301 there was a large-scale persecution. The Christians were compelled to cover their turbans with a blue cloth, the Jews with a yellow one, and the Samaritans with a red one. The authorities renewed the prohibition of riding horses and also forbade the building of houses higher than those of the Muslims. On this occasion the Jewish and Christian houses of prayer in *Cairo were closed down. In 1354 there was an even graver persecution. The cause for it was again attributed by Arab historians to the haughtiness of the Christian officials. There were attacks on non-Muslims in the streets of Cairo and the government instituted a severe control over the habits of Muslim converts. At that time the economic situation of the Jews took a turn for the worse; under the Mamluks the system of monopolies was consolidated. Private industry was generally ruined and the commerce of spices, the most important part of Egypt's external trade, was taken over by the monopolized "Kārimī" merchant company in which only a few members were Jews. During this period the Jewish population was led by *negidim* of Maimonides' family. Maimonides' grandson, R. *David b. Abraham, was *nagid* from 1238 to 1300. In various documents the *negidim* are referred to as heads of academies but the exact nature of the academy is in question. During the second half of the 13th century, the literary activities of Egyptian Jewry continued to flourish, as in the Fatimid and Ayyubid periods. *Tanḥum ha-Yerushalmi, the well-known Bible commentator, and his son *Joseph, a competent Hebrew poet, lived in Egypt at this time.

At the end of the 14th century, a second dynasty of the Mamluks, the Cherkess, came to power. The Mamluk rule then increased in violence and the anti-Jewish and anti-Christian decrees grew in frequency. The oppression and extortions of the sultans were severer than in former times. There often were internal conflicts within this Mamluk faction, and as a result the soldiers, unrestrained, rioted in the streets and attacked the citizens. In order to appease the embittered people, the sultans issued a multitude of decrees against the non-Muslims. While the first sultan of the Cherkess Mamluks, Barqūq (1382–1399), as well as his son and successor Faraj (1399–1412), acted leniently toward the non-Muslims, the third sultan, al-Mu'ayyad Sheikh, oppressed the non-Muslims by various means. The discriminatory decrees were renewed, and there were searches for wine in the non-Muslim quarters. During the reign of the Cherkess Mamluks the autonomous organization of the communities in Egypt remained unharmed and as previously, they were led as before by the *negidim*. The last of Maimonides' descendants to act as *nagid* was R. *David b. Joshua. For reasons that are not known R. David was compelled to leave Egypt in the 1370s. He was replaced by a man named *Amram. At the end of the Mamluk period, Egyptian Jewry was led by the *negidim* R. Nathan *Sholal and his relative R. Isaac *Sholal, who emigrated to Palestine after the conquest of Egypt by the Ottomans.

The travelers Meshullam of Volterra, who arrived in Egypt in 1481, and R. Obadiah of *Bertinoro, who came there seven years later, provided information about the size of the communities in the descriptions of their travels. The numbers which are found in their writings emphasize the decrease in the Jewish population, which was concomitant with the general depopulation and was partly a result of the oppression under Mamluk rule. According to Meshullam there were 650 families, as well as 150 Karaite and 50 Samaritan families, in Cairo, 50 families in Alexandria, 50 in Bilbeis, and 20 in al-Khānqā. Obadiah mentions 500 families in Cairo, besides 150 Karaite and 50 Samaritan families, 25 families in Alexandria, and 30 in Bilbeis. From this it can be deduced that there was probably a total of 5,000 persons in all the communities visited by the two travelers. By then the immigration of Spanish Jewry to the oriental countries had begun. Even before the expulsion, groups of forced converts arrived in Egypt. Immediately after the expulsion, the Jews who had not converted arrived and the Jewish population in Egypt increased. In those centers where an important number of newcomers settled separate communities were established. The arrival of the Spanish immigrants had a beneficial effect on the cultural life of Egyptian Jewry. Their numbers included scholars of renown who engaged in educational activities and who were appointed as *dayyanim*. Among the scholars who arrived in Egypt during the first generation after the Spanish expulsion were R. *Samuel ibn Sid, who was a member of the *bet din* of the *nagid* in 1509, R. Jacob *Berab, who is mentioned in a document of 1513 as a *dayyan* of this same *bet din*, and R. Samuel ha-Levi *Ḥakim, who was a prominent halakhic authority and acted as *dayyan* at the beginning of the 16th century in Cairo. The *negidim* welcomed the Spanish refugees.

THE OTTOMAN TURKS. When Egypt was conquered by the Ottomans in 1517, there was a decisive turn in the history of the country and the Jews living there. A wide choice of commercial possibilities was offered to the Jewish merchants, as well as an introduction to a variety of other trades. At the height of their power, the Ottomans were very tolerant and the Jews held key positions in the financial administration and in the collection of taxes and customs duties. Almost all the Turkish commissioners and governors who were sent to Egypt turned over the responsibility of the financial administration to Jewish agents, who were known as *ṣarrāf-bashi* ("chief treasurer"). It is evident that the agents greatly profited by holding these positions. After two generations of prosperity, the political and economic decline of the *Ottoman empire manifested itself and affected the rank and file of the Jewish population who sank into poverty and ignorance. Thus, Ottoman rule caused a distinct polarization in the status of Egyptian Jewry. The corruption of the governors, who were often replaced and whose ambition was to enrich themselves or to rebel against the sultan in Constantinople, and their acts of violence, extortion, and cruelty brought suffering on the Jews. One of the first Turkish governors, Ahmad Pasha, who was appointed in 1523, extorted a large contribution from Abraham *Castro, director of the mint. He then ordered him to mint coins carrying his name, as if he were an independent ruler. When the Jewish official fled to Constantinople, Ahmad imposed an enormous contribution on the Jews, who were fearful of his vengeance if they did not provide the sum by the appointed time. However, on the day of payment, Ahmad Pasha was killed by soldiers loyal to the sultan and the anniversary was thereafter celebrated as *Purim Miẓrayim ("Purim of Egypt," i.e., Cairo).

In 1545 the governor Dā'ud Pasha ordered the closure of the central synagogue of Cairo. All the efforts to obtain its reopening were in vain; the synagogue remained closed until 1584. After the conquest of Egypt by the Turks, Jews of Constantinople were sent to Egypt to act as *negidim*. The first of them was R. Tājir, who was followed by R. *Jacob b. Ḥayyim Talmid. When this *nagid* came to Egypt, a dispute broke out between him and R. Bezalel Ashkenazi, who was then the leading rabbi in Egypt. As a result of this dispute, the office of *nagid* came to an end in about 1560. From then onward the Jewish finance minister in the service of the governor was recognized as the leader of the Jewish community in Egypt. He was referred to by the Turkish title of *chelebi* (*çelebi* = "gentleman"). Many of these Jewish ministers were executed by despotic governors. Masiah Pasha, who was appointed in 1575, chose Solomon *Alashkar, a well-known philanthropist whose efforts were directed toward the amelioration of Jewish education among the Jews of Egypt, as *chelebi*. His activities continued for many years, until Karīm Hussein Pasha executed him in 1603.

The standard of Jewish learning improved with the arrival of the expelled Spanish Jews. During the first generation of the Turkish rule, the leading rabbi in Egypt was R. *David b. Solomon ibn Abi Zimra. He instituted several regulations in the Jewish communal life, and, among others, he abolished the system of dating documents according to the Seleucid era, which was still in practice in Egypt. In the 1520s the renowned halakhic authority R. Moses b. Isaac *Alashkar also lived in Egypt, where he acted as *dayyan*. However, he emigrated to Palestine and died in Jerusalem in 1542. Later David b. Solomon Abi Zimra also emigrated to Palestine and Bezalel Ashkenazi became the spiritual leader of Egypt's Jewish communities. During the second half of the 16th century, R. Jacob *Castro was the most prominent Egyptian rabbi. These rabbis acted as *dayyanim*, gave responsa, and educated distinguished pupils. R. Isaac *Luria, the famous kabbalist, was one of Bezalel Ashkenazi's pupils.

The Jews of Cairo and Alexandria were at that time divided into three communities – the Musta'rabim (Arabic-speaking i.e., indigenous Jews), the Spanish (immigrants), and the Mograbim (settlers of North African, Maghreb origin). There were occasional disputes between the communities and the rabbis and communal leaders exerted themselves to restore peace.

During the 17th and 18th centuries, the Ottoman government became harsher and the upper class of wealthy Jews, who were employed by the governors and ministers, suffered especially. About 1610 the position of *chelebi* was filled by Abba Iscandari, a physician and philanthropist. In 1620 with the arrival of a new governor, the Albanian ("Arnaut") Husain, the Muslim enemies of the *chelebi*, jealous of his wealth, slandered him before the governor and he was executed. Jacob Tivoli replaced him as *chelebi* until he was executed by Khalīl Pasha. In 1650, when Silihdar Ahmad Pasha was appointed governor of Egypt, he brought with him Ḥayyim Perez, a Jew, whom he appointed *chelebi*. In the same year natural catastrophes and a plague occurred in Egypt; the sultan summoned the commissioner and the *chelebi* to Constantinople and had them both executed. A year later another governor, Muhammad Ghāzī Pasha, was sent to Egypt. He appointed Jacob Bibas as *chelebi*, but after a time became jealous of his wealth, killed him with his own hands and buried him in the garden of his palace. In 1661 the governor Ibrāhīm Pasha appointed the exceedingly wealthy Raphael b. Joseph Hin as his *chelebi*. The latter actively supported *Shabbetai Ẓevi, the pseudo-messiah, who had visited Cairo twice. In 1669 Karākūsh Ali Pasha was appointed governor of Egypt, became jealous of Raphael Hin's wealth, accused him of various crimes, and had him publicly executed. The title of *chelebi* was then abolished and the Jewish agent of the Egyptian governor, who stood at the head of his community, was henceforth known as *bazīrkān* (from Persian *bāzargān* "merchant"). In 1734–35, a serious popular riot killed many of Cairo's Jewish community which, as a result, became much less effective in Egypt's administration and economy. The severity of Ottoman rule and the economic decline lowered the cultural level of Egyptian Jewry. During this period the community ceased to be led by renowned rabbis, as in the 16th century, even though some of them were excellent talmudic scholars such as Abraham Iscandari, Samuel *Vital, the son of R. Ḥayyim *Vital, *Mordecai ha-Levi, and his son Abraham during the 17th century, and Solomon Algazi during the 18th century. Nevertheless, the Shabbatean movement brought some activity to the stagnant community. In 1703 the Shabbatean propagandist Abraham Michael *Cardoso settled in Egypt, where he became physician to the Turkish governor

Karā Ahmad Pasha. At times scholars and authors came to Egypt from other countries and acted as *dayyanim* and rabbis for a number of years. Such was the case of David *Conforte, author of *Kore ha-Dorot* who came in 1671.

The transition from an Ottoman province to a virtually independent unity was accompanied by a difficult struggle during which Jews also suffered considerably. In 1768 when Turkey became embroiled in war with Russia, Ali Bey, the governor of Cairo, proclaimed himself the independent governor of Egypt. He also made an effort to impose his authority on Palestine, Syria, and the Arabian Peninsula. In order to provide for the tremendous expenses of his wars, he levied a heavy contribution on the Jews, which they were compelled to pay within a short period (see Ben-Ze'ev in *Zion* (1939), 237–49). The reforms of *Muhammad (Mehmet) Ali (1805–1848) and later the opening of the Suez Canal (1863) brought a new prosperity to commerce and the other branches of the Egyptian economy. As a result of the changes in all spheres of life, the Jewish population grew. Jews from European countries settled in Egypt and schools where education was dispensed along modern lines were introduced. Alexandria again became a commercial center and its Jewish community expanded until it was equal to that of Cairo. The census of 1897 showed that there were 25,200 Jews in the country. Of these, 8,819 (including approximately 1,000 Karaites) lived in Cairo, 9,831 in Alexandria, 2,883 in *Tanta, 400 in Port Said, and 508 in al-*Manṣūra. There were also small communities in other provincial towns, numbering a total of 4,600 Jews. The immigrants from European countries founded their own communities, even though they recognized the authority of the rabbis of the existing ones. Thus, in the middle of the 19th century there were communities of Italian and Eastern European Jews in Alexandria, while in Cairo the immigrants from Italy and Turkey united in one community. The relations between Muslims and Jews were normal and there were only rare cases of disturbances resulting from religious hate. In 1844 there was a blood libel against the Jews of Cairo and this was repeated in 1881 and in 1901–1902. In 1840, after the blood libel of *Damascus, Moses *Montefiore and Adolphe *Crémieux came to Egypt and established Jewish schools in cooperation with R. Moses *Algazi. In Alexandria, rabbis who distinguished themselves by their western education were appointed, and social activities were encouraged in the community. The numerical increase, the improvement of cultural standards, and the development of social activities continued throughout the first half of the 20th century.

After World War I Sephardi Jews from *Salonika and other Ottoman towns, as well as Jews from other countries, settled in Egypt. According to the census of 1917 there were 59,581 Jews in Egypt, of which 29,207 lived in Cairo, and in 1937 their numbers reached 63,550, of which 34,103 lived in greater Cairo and 24,829 in Greater Alexandria. With the improvements in the economic and intellectual standards, the Jews took an active part in public life. Some financiers were appointed as members of Parliament and ministers. Joseph *Cattaui was a member of parliament in 1915 and minister of finances and communications in 1923 (the year Egypt became officially independent), and Aslan Cattaui was a member of the Senate during the 1930s. Some, such as Yaʿqūb (James) *Ṣanūʿ, had even been associated with the Egyptian nationalist movement. On the other hand, Zionist organizations were created at the end of the 19th century in the larger towns such as Cairo, Alexandria, Manṣūra, *Suez, *Damanhūr, and al-Maḥalla al-Kubrā. As a result of the expulsion of large numbers of Palestinian Jews to Egypt during World War I, the attachment of Egyptian Jewry to the Palestinian population and to the national movement strengthened. The reinforcement of Jewish consciousness found expression in the publication of Jewish newspapers in various languages. In 1880, a Jewish weekly in Arabic, *al-Ḥaqīqa* ("The Truth"), began to appear in Alexandria. In 1903, a weekly in Ladino, *Miẓrayim*, was founded in Cairo. From 1908 to 1941 a French weekly, *L'Aurore*, appeared in Cairo, and in 1919 another weekly, *Israël*, was founded in Cairo. This newspaper was amalgamated in 1939 with the Alexandria weekly *La Tribune Juive*, which was first published in 1936. It appeared until 1948, as did the Arabic weekly *al-Shams* ("The Sun"), founded in 1934.

[Eliyahu Ashtor]

Contemporary Period

According to the Egyptian census of 1947, 65,600 Jews lived in Egypt, 64% of them in Cairo, 32% in Alexandria, and the rest in other towns. Egyptian Jewry was thus among the most urban of the Jewish communities of Asia and Africa. In 1947 most Egyptian Jews (59%) were merchants, and the rest were employed in industry (18%), administration, and public services (11%). The economic situation of Egyptian Jewry was relatively good; there were several multi-millionaires, a phenomenon unusual in other Jewish communities of the Middle East.

Most Egyptian Jews received some form of education, and there were fewer illiterates among them than in any other Oriental community in Egypt then. This was due to the fact that Jews were concentrated in the two great cities with all kinds of educational facilities. There were no restrictions on accepting Jews in government or foreign schools. In November 1945 riots, organized by the "Young Egypt" group led by Aḥmad Ḥusayn, ended in attacks on the Cairo Jewish quarter. A synagogue, a Jewish quarter hospital, and an old-age home were burned down and many Jews injured or killed. This was the first disturbance of its kind in the history of independent Egypt.

The year 1947 was the beginning of the end of the Egyptian Jewish community, for in that year the Companies' Law was instituted, which required that not less than 75% of employees of companies in Egypt must be Egyptian citizens. The law affected Jews most of all, since only about 20% of them were Egyptian citizens. The rest, although in many cases born in Egypt and living there for generations, were aliens or stateless persons. After the State of Israel was established, perse-

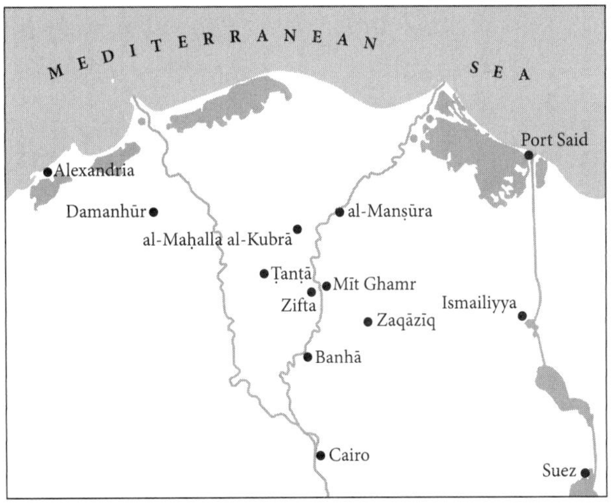

Map 2. Main Jewish communities in Egypt at the end of the 19th century.

cution of Jews began became more severe. On May 15, 1948, emergency law was declared, and a royal decree forbade Egyptian citizens to leave the country without a special permit. This was applied to Jews. Hundreds of Jews were arrested and many had their property confiscated. In June through August 1948, bombs were planted in Jewish neighborhoods and Jewish businesses looted. About 250 Jews were killed or wounded by the bombs. In 1949, when the consular law courts which tried foreign citizens were abolished, many Jews were affected. The condition of the Jews gradually worsened until, in July 1949, the new government headed by Ḥusayn Sirrī Pasha began to release detainees and return some of the frozen Jewish assets which had been confiscated, also allowing some Jews to leave Egypt, In January 1950, when the Wafd government under Nuqrāshī Pasha was overthrown, all Jewish detainees were released and the rest of their property restored to them. The condition of the Jews slightly improved, although they were forced to donate large sums of money to the soldiers' fund, and leaders of the community were coerced into publishing a declaration against the State of Israel. During the anti-British riots on Black Saturday (January 26, 1952), many foreign citizens were injured, and the loss of Jewish property on that day was estimated at EL9,000,000 ($25,000,000). About 25,000 Jews left Egypt between 1948 and 1950, some 14,000 of them settling in Israel. When persecution lessened, Jewish emigration decreased.

After the deposition of King Farouk in July 1952, the new government headed by General Muhammad Naguib was favorably inclined toward Jews, but when Naguib was overthrown and *Nasser seized power in February 1954 there was a change for the worse. Nasser immediately arrested many Jews who were tried on various charges, mainly for Zionist and communist activities. In 1954 about 100 Jews were arrested, but most attention was attracted by the trial of the 13 charged with being members of an Israel intelligence network. Two of those charged died, and Moses Leo *Marzuk, a Karaite surgeon and Samuel Bekhor Azar, a teacher, were sentenced to death, while the rest were condemned to various terms of imprisonment (see. *Cairo Trial).

Arrests of Jews continued. They were also forced to donate money to arm the military forces, Chief Rabbi Haim *Nahoum explaining that it was a national duty. In addition, strict supervision of Jewish enterprises was introduced; some were confiscated and others forcibly sold to the government.

Immediately after the Sinai Campaign (November 1956), hundreds of Jews were arrested. About 3,000 were interned without charge in four detention camps. At the same time, the government served notice on thousands of Jews to leave the country within a few days, and they were not allowed to sell their property, nor to take any capital with them. The deportees were made to sign statements agreeing not to return to Egypt and transferring their property to the administration of the government. The International Red Cross helped about 8,000 stateless Jews to leave the country, taking most of them to Italy and Greece in chartered boats. Most of the Jews of Port Said (about 100) were smuggled to Israel by Israel agents. The system of deportation continued into 1957. Other Jews left voluntarily, after their livelihoods had been taken from them, until only 8,561 were registered in the 1957 census. Most of them lived in Cairo (65.3%) and Alexandria (32.2%). The Jewish exodus continued until there were about 3,000 in 1967 of whom only about 50 were Ashkenazim, since most members of this community had left or been deported.

With the outbreak of the Six-Day War in June 1967 the few remaining Jewish officials holding public posts were discharged and hundreds of Jews were arrested. They were beaten, tortured, and abused. Some were released following intervention by foreign states, especially Spain, and were permitted to leave the country. Among the detainees were the chief rabbi of Egypt, R. Ḥayyim Duwayk, and the rabbi of Alexandria, who were held for seven months. Several dozen Jews were held in detention until July 1970. Less than 1,000 Jews still lived in Egypt in 1970, when they were given permission to leave Egypt but without their possessions. Subsequently, only some four hundred Jews (1971) remained in Egypt. Thirty-five thousand Egyptian Jews live in Israel and there are about 15,000 in Brazil, 10,000 in France, 9,000 in the United States, 9,000 in Argentina, and 4,000 in Great Britain.

Egypt was the only Arab country in which the Zionist shekel was clandestinely distributed for the Zionist Congress of 1951 after the establishment of the State of Israel. There was a well-developed Zionist underground movement in Egypt, and some of its members were arrested. After the mass exodus from Egypt, most of the synagogues, social welfare organizations and Jewish schools were closed; the Jewish newspaper, *La Menora* (published in French and edited by Jacques Maleh from February 1950 to May 1953), was closed down after Maleh had been deported. The Jewish representatives in the Senate and the House of Representatives (Aslan *Cattaui and his brother René) lost their seats. The Cairo and Alexandrian communities had official committees, but there was no nationwide organization, the chief rabbi of Cairo simply being recognized as the chief rabbi of Egypt.

The peace negotiations between Israel and Egypt brought some information and a certain renewed activity with regard to the small Jewish community remaining in Cairo. The total number of Jews in Egypt was approximately 400, and it was an aging community.

There was only one synagogue in Cairo, the 70-year-old Shaarei Ha-Shamayim synagogue, normally attended by a handful of old men and women. There was no rabbi, the last having left in 1972. In December 1977 over 120 persons, Israeli citizens and Jewish journalists who had come to cover the peace talks in Cairo, attended the services. The members of the Israeli delegation were unable to attend, but they attended the services the following Friday night. There was also a synagogue in Alexandria, the Eliyahu Ha-Navi synagogue. With only 150 Jews remaining in the city they succeeded with difficulty in holding services on Sabbaths and Festivals only.

In May 1977, at the request of Lord Segal of Wytham, 11 scrolls of the Torah from the Great Synagogue of Alexandria – of the 50 in the synagogue – were sent to Great Britain through the good offices of President Anwar *Sadat.

Jewish rights were restored in 1979 after the Camp David Peace Accords. Only then was the community allowed to establish ties with Israel and World Jewry. However, these ties remained weak, despite Israeli tourism to Egypt, because the community is almost extinct.

Egypt was one of the Arab countries that invaded Israel upon its establishment in May 1948. After the defeat of the Egyptian forces, an Armistice Agreement was signed between the two states at Rhodes on Feb. 24, 1949; however, Egypt still regarded itself as at war with Israel, and there was no improvement in the relations after the Egyptian officers' 1952 revolution and the accession to power first of Muhammad Naguib and, later, of Gamal Abdel *Nasser. Egypt participated in the Arab economic *boycott of Israel, did not permit passage of Israel shipping and cargoes to and from Israel through the Suez Canal, and obstructed the passage of Israel shipping and cargoes to and from Israel through the Straits of *Tiran. It occupied the *Gaza Strip after the 1948 war and encouraged an increase in armed infiltration and sabotage against Israel beginning in 1955, which led to the Sinai Campaign (October–November 1956). After the Sinai Campaign and the stationing of the United Nations Emergency Force (UNEF) in the Gaza Strip and Sharm el-Sheikh, there was an almost complete cessation of fedayeen activity on the Gaza Strip-Sinai border and no interference with shipping to the port of Eilat until the withdrawal of the UNEF at Egyptian demand in May 1967, which was one of the factors that precipitated the Six-Day War (June 1967). Throughout the period that followed the Israel War of Independence, Egypt was the leading force in Arab opposition to Israel and the threat to its existence. It attacked Israel again in October 1973 ("the Yom Kippur War") and, although defeated, President Anwar Sādāt felt the war's results were honorable enough for Egypt to initiate a peace process. The Camp David Peace Accords of November 1978 normalized relations between Israel and Egypt.

For subsequent political developments, see *Israel, State of: Historical Survey; *Arab World.

[Hayyim J. Cohen / Jacob M. Landau (2nd ed.)]

BIBLIOGRAPHY: ANCIENT EGYPT: A.H. Gardiner, *Egypt of the Pharaohs* (1961); J.A. Wilson, *The Burden of Egypt* (1951 = *The Culture of Ancient Egypt*, 1958); J. Wilson (tr.), in: Pritchard, Texts, passim. **ADD. BIBLIOGRAPHY:** M. Lichtheim, *Ancient Egyptian Literature*, vol. 1 (1973); J. Baines and J. Malek, *Atlas of Ancient Egypt* (1980); D.B. Redford, "Egypt and Western Asia in the Old Kingdom," in: JARCE, 23 (1986), 125–143; N. Grimal, *A History of Ancient Egypt* (1992); K. Kitchen, "Egypt, History of (Chronology)," in: ABD, vol. 2 (1992), 321–31; D.B. Redford, *Egypt, Canaan and Israel in Ancient Times* (1992); D. Franke, "The Middle Kingdom in Egypt," in: J.M. Sasson (ed.), *Civilizations of the Ancient Near East*, vol. 2 (1995), 735–38; W.J. Murnane, in: *ibid.*, 691ff; J. Assman, *The Mind of Egypt: History and Meaning in the Time of the Pharaohs*, trans. Andrew Jenkins (1996); M. Bietak, "Hyksos," in: D.B. Redford (ed.), *The Oxford Encyclopedia of Ancient Egypt*, vol. 2 (2001), 136–43; W.J. Murnane, "New Kingdom: An Overview," in: *ibid.*, 519–25. HELLENISTIC PERIOD: Frey, Corpus 2, 356–445; Tcherikover, Corpus; idem, *Hellenistic Civilization and the Jews* (1961), index s.v. *Egypt:* E.R. Bevan, *The Legacy of Israel* (1953), 29–67; idem, *House of Ptolemy* (1969); M. Radin, *The Jews Among the Greeks and Romans* (1915), index s.v. *Egypt;* Baron, Social^2, index s.v. *Egypt, Alexandria;* J. Lindsay, *Daily Life in Roman Egypt* (1968). FROM END OF SECOND TEMPLE TO MUSLIM CONQUEST: Baron, Social^2, 2 (1952), index; Graetz, Gesch 3 (1905–65), index, s.v. *Alexandrien*, 4 (1908), index, s.v. *Alexandrien.* JEWS IN EGYPT FROM ARAB AND OTTOMAN CONQUEST: Mann, Egypt; Mann, Texts; idem, in: HUCA, 3 (1926), 257–308; Rosanes, Togarmah; Zimmels, in: *Bericht des juedisch-theologischen Seminars, Breslau* (1932), 1–60; Neustadt, in: *Zion*, 2 (1937), 216–55; S. Assaf, *ibid.*, 121–4; idem, *Be-Oholei Ya'akov* (1943), 81–98; Noury Farhi, *La Communauté juive d'Alexandrie* (1946); Ashtor, Toledot; idem, in: HUCA, 27 (1956), 305–26; idem, in: *Zion*, 30 (1965), 61–78, 128–157; idem, in: JJS, 18 (1967), 9–42; 19 (1968), 1–22; S.D. Goitein, in: JQR, 53 (1962/63), 93–119; idem, *Studies in Islamic History and Institutions* (1966), 255–95, 329–60; idem, *A Mediterranean Society*, 1–6 (1967–1993), passim; Lewis, in: *Eretz Israel*, 7 (1964), 70–75 (Eng. pt.); idem, in: *Bulletin of the School of Oriental and African Studies*, 30 (1967), 177–81; Abrahamson, Merkazim, passim; J.M. Landau, *Ha-Yehudim be-Miẓrayim* (1967, Eng., *Jews in Nineteenth Century Egypt*, 1969); S. Shamir (ed.), *The Jews of Egypt: a Mediterranean Society in Modern Times*, (1987); N. Robinson, in: J. Fried (ed.), *Jews in the Modern World*, 1 (1962), 50–90; J.M. Landau, "Abū Naḍḍāra an Egyptian Jewish Nationalist," in: JJS, 3 (1952), 30–44; 5 (1954), 179–180; idem, "Ritual Murder Accusations in Nineteenth-Century Egypt," in: A. Dundes (ed.), *The Blood Libel Legend*, 197–232; idem (ed.), *Ha-Yehudim be-Miẓrayim ha-'Othmanit 1517–1914* (1988); CONTEMPORARY PERIOD: D. Peretz, *Egyptian Jewry Today* (1956). **ADD. BIBLIOGRAPHY:** J. Hassoun, *Juifs du Nil* (1981); idem, *Juifs d'Egypte; images et textes (1984);* G. Kraemer, *Minderheit, Millet Nation? Die Jueden in Aegypten, 1914–1952* (1982) T. Mayer, *Egypt and the Palestine Question, 1936–1945* (1983); M.M. Laskier, *The Jews of Egypt, 1920–1970* (1992); V.D. Sanua, *A Guide to Egyptian Jewry in the Mid-Twentieth Century* (2005).

EGYPT, BROOK OF (Heb. נַחַל מִצְרַיִם, *Naḥal Miẓrayim*), the natural border of the land of Canaan and the Kingdom of *Judah on the south and the southwest according to the Bible (Num. 34:5; Josh. 15:4; cf. II Chron. 7:8; Isa. 27:12; Ezek. 47:19;

48:28). It is also described as the southern border of Solomon's kingdom: "from the entrance of *Hamath unto the Brook of Egypt" (I Kings 8:65) and the eastern extremity of Egypt (II Kings 24:7). Assyrian inscriptions of *Sargon and *Esarhaddon also refer to it as the Muṣur or Muṣri River. Its identification with Wadi el-Arish is found in the Septuagint (Isa. 27:12), which translates it "Rhinokoroura," the Greek name of the city near its mouth.

The river, about 150 mi. (240 km.) long, drains about 12,500 sq. mi. (32,500 sq. km.) in the northern part of the *Sinai Peninsula. It absorbs part of the heavy flood waters inundating it, and the area near its mouth is rich in wells.

BIBLIOGRAPHY: Abel, Geog, 1 (1933), 301; Pritchard, Texts, 286, 290, 292; Aharoni, Land, index. **ADD. BIBLIOGRAPHY:** S. Ahituv, *Joshua* (1995), 243.

[Moshe Kochavi]

EḤAD MI YODE'A (Heb. אֶחָד מִי יוֹדֵעַ; "Who Knows One?"), song incorporated in the Ashkenazi rite among the concluding songs of the Passover **Haggadah*, whose aim was "to keep the children awake" until the end of the *seder* (cf. Pes. 108b–109a). The song consists of 13 stanzas, made up of questions (Who knows One?.. Two?.. Three?.. etc.) and their corresponding answers. The reply to each succeeding question also repeats the previous answers. The last verse reads: Who knows thirteen? I know thirteen. Thirteen are the attributes of God; twelve the tribes of Israel; eleven the stars (in Joseph's dream); ten the Commandments; nine the months of pregnancy; eight the days of circumcision; seven the days of the week; six the books of the Mishnah; five the books of the Torah; four the matriarchs (Sarah, Rebekah, Leah, and Rachel); three the patriarchs (Abraham, Isaac, and Jacob); two the tables of the Covenant; One is our God in heaven and on earth. (Some *Haggadot* have substituted other answers for the eighth and ninth questions of the traditional form. They read: nine are the Jewish holidays of the year, eight the Ḥanukkah lights.) In some places the song is chanted responsively: one person, usually the leader of the *seder*, asks the questions, and the whole company answers, each person responding as quickly as possible in an effort to finish the answer first. *Eḥad Mi Yode'a* is first found in *Haggadot* of the 16th century and only in those of the Ashkenazi ritual. Many scholars believed that it originated in Germany in the 15th century. Perles showed its similarity to a popular German pastoral song, "Guter Freund Ich Frage Dich" (one of the "Hobelbanklied" German folk songs), the first stanza of which ends with the same words as the Passover song. In fact, the identical words of this line of the pastorale are given as the German translation of the first answer of *Eḥad Mi Yode'a* in many early *Haggadot*. The Christian theme of the original was changed to one of Jewish content. Zunz discovered that the Hebrew song was used in Avignon as a festive table song chanted on other holidays as well, and Geiger noted other German counterparts. Since then it has been found among the liturgical music of Jews from Ceylon and Cochin, where it forms part of their Sabbath songs for the entertainment of bride and groom. Some scholars have even traced it to Greek or English church songs and Scottish nursery songs.

BIBLIOGRAPHY: D. Goldschmidt, *Haggadah shel Pesaḥ, Mekoroteha ve-Toledoteha* (1960), 98; C. Zibrt, *Ohlas obradnich pisni ...* (1928).

EHRENBERG, VICTOR LEOPOLD (1891–1976), German historian. Born in Altona, Ehrenberg was professor of ancient history at the German University in Prague (1929–39). The Nazi regime forced his immigration to Great Britain (1939), where he was visiting lecturer at several universities, and from 1949 to 1957 lecturer and reader in ancient history at the University of London. He was joint founder of the London Classical Society and joint founder and editor of the journal *Historia*. The bulk of Ehrenberg's work was in ancient Greek history. These include *Neugruender des Staates* (1925); *Alexander und Aegypten* (1926); and *Alexander and the Greeks* (1938). The *People of Aristophanes* (1943, 1951^2) is a sociological account of life in ancient Athens, based upon the surviving works of old Attic comedy; *Sophocles and Pericles* (1954) deals with the spiritual trends of the fifth century B.C.E.; *From Solon to Socrates* (1968) describes Greek civilization of the sixth and fifth centuries B.C.E. Many of his numerous articles were gathered in *Aspects of the Ancient World* (1946) and *Polis und Imperium* (1965).

BIBLIOGRAPHY: H. Schaefer, in: *Historia*, 10 (1961), 387–408 (includes list of works); *Ancient Society and Institutions, Studies Presented to Victor Ehrenberg on his 75th Birthday* (1966). **ADD. BIBLIOGRAPHY:** P.R. Franke, "Victor Ehrenberg – Ein deutsches Gelehrtenschicksal," in: R. Schneider (ed.), *Juden in Deutschland* (1994), 309 ff.

[Irwin L. Merker]

EHRENBURG, ILYA GRIGORYEVICH (1891–1967), Soviet Russian writer and journalist. Born to an assimilated middle-class Jewish family in Kiev and, with no ties to Jewish religion or culture, Ehrenburg is typical of many Jewish left-wing intellectuals of this century, whom Hitler and Stalin would not allow to forget their origins. A feeling of outrage at antisemitism recurs in Ehrenburg's books and journalistic output throughout his career and was a major factor in his youthful revolt against Czarist and, at the end of his life, against Stalinist injustice. Forced to flee Russia because of participation in revolutionary activities, he lived abroad, mainly in Paris, between 1908 and 1917. Ehrenburg returned to Russia after the February Revolution, criticizing sharply in his essays the October Revolution and its leaders, Lenin, Kamenev, Zinoviev, and others. He left again in 1921 and lived mainly in Berlin, where he witnessed the rise of the Nazis to power. Understanding that Nazi ideology was a danger to the world, he proposed to Stalin in September 1934 to turn the International Organization of Revolutionary Writers into a movement against Fascism and in support of the Soviet Union. His proposal was accepted. He did not permanently settle in the U.S.S.R. until shortly before the Nazi attack on the U.S.S.R. in the summer of 1941. On the eve of the Molotov-Ribbentrop agreement, the publication of his poems and essays was stopped, but renewed on the eve of the German attack on the Soviet Union. From 1948 he was active in the pro-Soviet World Peace Movement, serving as its vice chairman.

Of the nearly 30 volumes of Ehrenburg's literary and journalistic output, including collections of poems, the most successful was his first novel, *Neobychaynye pokhozhdeniya Khulio Khurenito* (1922; *The Extraordinary Adventures of Julio Jurenito*, 1958), an all-out sardonic attack on different aspects of modern civilization, including its persecutions "of the tribe of Judah." A series of rather undistinguished novels dealing with different subjects followed in rapid succession. These include *Zhizn i gibel Nikolaya Kurbova* (1923; "The Life and Death of Nikolai Kurbov"), the story of the undoing of a Soviet secret policeman; *Lyubov Zhanny Ney* (1923; "The Love of Jeanne Ney"), an account of a love affair involving a Russian Communist and a "bourgeois" French woman; *Rvach* (1925; "The Grabber"), a typical tale of a Soviet revolutionary corrupted by peacetime prosperity; and *Zagovor ravnykh* (1928; "The Conspiracy of Equals"), which tells the story of Babeuf, one of the heroes of the French Revolution.

Closest in spirit to *Julio Jurenito* is Ehrenburg's "Jewish" novel, *Burnaya zhizn Lazika Roytshvantsa* (1927; *The Stormy Life of Lazik Roitschwantz*, 1960) a biting lampoon of injustice, hypocrisy, and pretense both under capitalism and in the new Soviet republic. Its hero, a pathetic Jewish tailor, is a direct descendant of the ne'er-do-wells and *Luftmenschen* of *Shalom Aleichem. Try as he may, Lazik Roitschwantz cannot understand why both the Reds and the Whites consider harmless folk like himself dangerous enemies of the State. Though outwardly a rogue, all Lazik Roitschwantz really desires is to earn a livelihood and to be left alone by the authorities. Though liberated by the revolution from the yoke of official Czarist antisemitism, he is now suspect to the Soviet bureaucrats as a petty bourgeois individualist artisan. Escaping to Western Europe, he finds himself mistaken for a Communist agent and is packed off to jail as a Jewish Bolshevik. When he finally makes his way to Palestine, fate decrees that he die of starvation in the land of his ancestors.

There are no grounds to doubt Ehrenburg's assurances that the main reason he opposed reprinting the novel in the post-Stalin nine-volume set of his works brought out in the 1960s was his feeling that the old caricature of the "little Jew" should not be revived only a few years after millions of real-life "little Jews" were murdered in Nazi crematoria. Ehrenburg's loyalty to the Soviet regime did not waver during Stalin's bloodiest terror as well as during the Nazi-Soviet pact, and for years he was a most vocal apologist for some of the most abhorrent features of the Soviet regime. His activities in the latter capacity frequently smacked of cynical opportunism, just as his later championing of freedom might have been dictated by a desire to expiate his guilt as a verbal accomplice in Stalin's crimes. There is, however, one aspect of Ehrenburg's activity in which the writer's sincerity is beyond all questioning, namely his opposition to Nazism. His novel *Padeniye Parizha* (1941; "The Fall of Paris"), written during the period of Nazi-Soviet friendship, was published in its entirety only after Hitler's armies had invaded Russia. Ehrenburg had become the leading Soviet journalist on the strength of his reports in *Izvestia* on the Spanish Civil War and, during World War II, his impassioned diatribes against the German invaders were distributed to millions of Soviet soldiers. A member of the Jewish *Anti-Fascist Committee, he stressed his Jewish identity during the war. On the assignment of the Committee he prepared together with Vasily Grossman the "Red Book" on the heroism of Jewish fighters and the "Black Book" on the Holocaust of Soviet Jewry. The first book was banned outright by the authorities. The second was even typeset, but during the liquidation of the committee in 1948 it was halted by the KGB. Parts of the book were then published in Yiddish (1944) and Romanian (1946), and it was fully published in Russian in 1980 in Jerusalem by Yad Vashem.

Ehrenburg's usefulness as the Soviet Union's foremost anti-German ideologist came to an end with the defeat of Nazism, but he was soon to achieve eminence in the propaganda onslaught on the West, which is also much in evidence in his two novels of that period, *Burya* (1947; *The Storm*, 1949) and *Devyaty val* (1952; *The Ninth Wave*, 1958). In the fall of 1948 he played a significant part in the Soviet Union's swing away from outright support for the State of Israel. In an article in *Pravda* he opposed Jewish nationalism and warned Soviet Jews against cultivating any special attachment to Israel more than any other capitalist land.

A controversy that is not likely to be solved for years to come relates to Ehrenburg's role during the sinister antisemitic purges which claimed the lives of scores of Ehrenburg's friends and colleagues, such as the actor Solomon *Mikhoels, the poets Itzik *Fefer and Peretz *Markish, the novelist David *Bergelson and others. Not only did Ehrenburg escape their tragic fate, but in 1952, the year when the others were executed, Ehrenburg was awarded the Stalin Prize. However, he detached himself from the official line over the "*Doctor's Plot."

Almost immediately after Stalin's death in March of 1953 Ehrenburg became a spokesman for those Soviet intellectuals who demanded liberal reforms. His novelette *Ottepel* (1954–56; "The Thaw") was a major event in the struggle for a more humane Soviet society: it was an indictment of many aspects of Stalinism, including crudely propagandistic art and the antisemitic campaigns. Yet in retrospect Ehrenburg's crowning achievement may well prove to be his memoirs *Lyudi, gody, zhizn* (1961; *People and Life 1891–1921*, 1962; *Memoirs: 1921–41*, 1964), which were serialized in the monthly *Novy Mir* between 1960 and 1965. In spite of all the evasions and distortions, these presented a relatively truthful picture of Russia's and Western Europe's artistic and literary intelligentsia during the 1920s and 1930s and included several loving portraits of Yiddish cultural figures. Ehrenburg's memoirs constitute, in fact, the closest Soviet approximation to date of cultural history.

On the occasion of his 70th birthday celebrations, Ehrenburg stated: "Even though my passport declares me to be a Jew,

I am a Russian writer," implying that Soviet Jews were allowed entry into Russian culture, but not into the Russian people.

Toward the end of his life Ehrenburg frequently clashed with Soviet official spokesmen, stubbornly championing the cause of a greater degree of artistic and personal freedom and, whenever the opportunity presented itself, heaping scorn on Soviet antisemites. Thousands took part in his funeral, many of them young Jews who saw him as a liberal and a fellow Jew.

A major biographical study of this Soviet Jewish writer in English appeared in 1984: *Ilya Ehrenburg: Writing, Politics and the Art of Survival* by Anatol Goldberg, with an introduction, postscript, and additional material by Erik de Mauny.

BIBLIOGRAPHY: M. Friedberg, in: G.W. Simmonds (ed.), *Soviet Leaders* (1967), 272–81; M. Slonim, *Soviet Russian Literature* (1964), 208–17; T. Trifonova, *Ilya Ehrenburg* (Russ., 1952); V. Alexandrova, *A History of Soviet Literature* (1964), 127–42.

[Maurice Friedberg / Shmuel Spector (2nd ed.)]

EHRENFELD, family of Hungarian rabbis. The founder was DAVID ZEVI EHRENFELD (d. 1861), a son-in-law of Moses *Sofer. He wrote no books of his own, but some of his writings are included in the books of his son Samuel. Ehrenfeld had five sons, four of whom served in the rabbinate of Hungary. Samuel *Ehrenfeld served as rabbi of several communities. SIMEON (b. 1860) was rabbi of Szinna (Snina) and Nagymihaly (Michalovce), both of which places became part of Czechoslovakia after World War I. He laid the foundation of the central bureau of Orthodox rabbis in Czechoslovakia. SAUL (1835–1905), who was born in Pressburg, succeeded Samuel at Szikszo and served there until his death. ISAIAH (1850–1902) was rabbi in Berzavicze, Sarospatak, and Nagysurany and wrote *Shevet Sofer* (1903, 1938^2) on the Pentateuch. He fought vigorously against every form of religious innovation. Abraham Glazner was his son-in-law.

BIBLIOGRAPHY: A. Stern, *Meliẓei Esh:* Tishri and Marḥeshvan (1933), 153a no. 435 (on David Ẓevi), Av and Elul (1932), 7a no. 6 (on Samuel), 111a no. 284 (on Saul), Sivan (1931), 149a no. 197 (on Isaiah); P.Z. Schwartz, *Shem ha-Gedolim me-Ereẓ Hagar*, 1 (1914), 266 no. 54 (on David Ẓevi), 52b no. 260 (on Isaiah); 2 (1914), 40a no. 71 (on Samuel), 366 no. 1 (on Saul); (A.S.) B. Sofer-Schreiber, *Ketov Zot Zikkaron* (1957), 262–7.

[Naphtali Ben-Menahem]

EHRENFELD, NATHAN (1843–1912), chief rabbi of Prague. He was a pupil of Azriel *Hildesheimer both at the yeshivah in Eisenstadt and at his seminary in Berlin. In 1890 he was appointed chief rabbi of Prague. While strictly Orthodox himself, he managed to keep the peace between the divergent factions in the Prague community. He gave particular attention to religious instruction and founded a college for teachers of religion. He acted as trustee for the charitable foundations in Austro-Hungary of the Orthodox Karl Wilhelm Rothschild. His son-in-law, Heinrich (Ḥayyim) *Brody, succeeded him in office.

BIBLIOGRAPHY: *Der Israelit* (Feb. 29, 1912), 7–8; AZDJ, 76 (March 1, 1912), 3.

EHRENFELD, SAMUEL BEN DAVID ẒEVI (1835–1883), Hungarian rabbi known from his works as the "Hatan Sofer," ("son-in-law of Sofer" to indicate his connection by marriage with the famous Moses *Sofer, and in assonance with the title of Sofer's responsa *Ḥatam Sofer.* Actually it was his father who was the son-in-law of Moses Sofer). Ehrenfeld was born in Pressburg. He studied under his father and in the yeshivah of Pressburg under Abraham *Sofer, his maternal uncle. At first he engaged in business, but when this failed he accepted the rabbinate of Betlen (now Beclean, Romania) in 1866. In 1868 he became rabbi in Szikszo, because of the opportunities which a larger yeshivah there afforded him. In 1877 he moved to Mattersdorf where his grandfather and other members of his family had served before him. He was able to devote himself completely to the interests of the community and the large yeshivah there. He died at Kierling, where he had gone to recuperate after a long illness. As a teacher he was able to impart his own approach to Talmud and *halakhah*, based on the clear understanding of the talmudic text and its relevance to the ultimate *halakhah*.

His clarity and complete mastery of all branches of *halakhah* is evident in his published works: *Ateret Baḥurim, Ḥatan Sofer* (only one part, 1874), on various topics from *Ḥoshen Mishpat*, and *Ḥatan Sofer* on the Shulḥan Arukh, *Oraḥ Ḥayyim* (one part, 1878; 2 vols., 1963^2), both having long aggadic introductions. He printed the biography of his grandfather as well as other historical matter. *Ḥatan Sofer* was edited with an introduction by his son, Simḥah Bunim Ehrenfeld (1912), and contains a biography of his father. *Misped Mar* (1874) was his next work. A Passover *Haggadah* (1884) with his own commentary and that of his grandfather was edited by Rabbi Joseph Baumgarten (later *rosh bet din* of Vienna).

Ehrenfeld was succeeded in Mattersdorf in 1884 by his son SIMḤAH BUNIM (1856–1926) who had from 1876 been rabbi in Sarvar. He is the author of *Ma'aneh Simḥah*, part of which is printed in the introduction to his father's *Ḥatan Sofer.* He was succeeded by his son SAMUEL, who served that community until 1938/39, when he immigrated to New York and there reestablished the Mattersdorf yeshivah (1939). In 1958 he founded Kiryat Mattersdorf, a religious suburb in Jerusalem. He re-edited all the above-mentioned works with copious notes and added much new material.

BIBLIOGRAPHY: Samuel b. David Ẓevi Ehrenfeld, *She'elot u-Teshuvot Ḥatan Sofer* (1912), introd.; P.Z. Schwartz, *Shem ha-Gedolim me-Ereẓ Hagar*, 2 (1914), 40a no. 71 (on Samuel I); 47 no. 179/1 (on Simḥah Bunim); J.J. (L.) Greenwald (Grunwald), *Maẓẓevat Kodesh* (1952), 127, 149–50; S.N. Gottlieb, *Oholei Shem* (1912), 251 (on Simḥah Bunim); A. Stern, *Meliẓei Esh al Ḥodshei Av-Marḥeshvan*, 2 (1962^2) 7 no. 6; (A.S.) B. Sofer-Schreiber, *Ketov Zot Zikkaron* (1957), 262–5, 269f. (Samuel I), 273–80 (Samuel II); S. Sofer (Schreiber; ed.), *Iggerot Soferim* (1968), introd. and pt. 4, 99–103, 106–8 (Samuel I).

[Abraham Schischa]

EHRENFEST, PAUL (1880–1933), Austrian physicist. Born in Vienna, Ehrenfest studied under Ludwig Boltzmann, the

Austrian physicist, and later went to Goettingen. He and his wife, Tatiana Afanashewa, carried out a critical investigation of kinetic theory, and collaborated in an extensive article on statistical mechanics which is still one of the classics on that subject. From 1912 until his death Ehrenfest was professor of physics at Leiden. His work in that period included papers on the adiabatic hypothesis and invariants (a term he coined), propagation of wave pockets, and ferromagnetic Curie points. Ehrenfest was a masterful teacher, infecting his students with his own enthusiasm for physics. He was a merciless critic of unclear and superficial expositions and in his own work stressed clarity and fundamentals. Ehrenfest became a symbol of a period in physics characterized by two great advances, the quantum theory and the theory of relativity, where fundamental enquiry was the rule.

BIBLIOGRAPHY: H.A. Kramers, in: *Nature*, 132 (Oct. 28, 1933), 667; G.E. Uhlenbeck et al., in: *Science*, 78 (Oct. 27, 1933), 377–8.

[Gerald E. Tauber]

EHRENKRANZ, BENJAMIN (WOLF) ZEEB (1819–1883), popular Yiddish and Hebrew poet known as **Velvl Zbarzher**. Born in Zbarazh, Galicia (now Ukraine), Ehrenkranz had a traditional Jewish education. He composed and sang folk songs, and as a singing bard traveled to various European cities, spending his last years in Galata, a district in Istanbul. He performed his songs in Yiddish, shifting to Hebrew when appearing before a maskilic audience. His songs spread quickly, gradually changing until their original versions were forgotten. The major themes of his poetry were nature and people, poverty and wealth, and the fight of light against darkness, i.e., as he viewed it: *maskilim* against ḥasidim. Much of his work, only a fraction of which he published, is comprised of satires and parodies. His collected poetry, *Makkel No'am* (Hebrew and Yiddish), appeared in 1865–78 in four parts. He also wrote *Makkel Ḥovelim* (1869), in Hebrew and Yiddish, as well as *Siftei Yeshenah* (1874). B. Wachstein published three of Ehrenkranz' long Yiddish poems (*YIVO-Bleter*, 1938), and a selection of his letters in 1928. Although most of his improvised songs were never published, some were issued by L. Morgenstern, the Warsaw publisher, but were not attributed to the poet.

BIBLIOGRAPHY: S. Niger, in: *Tsukunft*, 1 (1925); Tiger, in: *Yidish*, 3–4 (Vienna, 1928), 1–6; D.I. Silberbusch, *Mi-Pinkas Zikhronotai* (1936), 81–9; Rejzen, Leksikon, 2 (1927), 832–40; LNYL, 3 (1960), 580–3, s.v. *Zbarzher, Velvl*; L. Wiener, *History of Yiddish Literature* (1899); S. Liptzin, *Eliakum Zunser* (1950), 74.

[Mordechay Zerkawod]

EHRENPREIS, MARCUS (Mordecai; 1869–1951), rabbi and author. Ehrenpreis, who was born in Lemberg where his father was a Hebrew printer, combined a traditional East European Jewish upbringing with a Western education, attending the *hochschule fuer die Wissenschaft des Judentums in Berlin as well as German universities. He officiated as rabbi in Djakovo, Croatia, from 1896 to 1900, and later became chief rabbi of Sofia, Bulgaria, and from 1914 of Stockholm. As the chief rabbi of Sofia, Ehrenpreis labored to ameliorate the condition of minorities in the Balkans, and in 1913 went on a mission to several European capitals on behalf of King Ferdinand I of Bulgaria. His contributions to the early Hebrew periodicals *Ha-Maggid* which first appeared in 1884 and in *Ha-Shilo'ah* among others make him one of the pioneers of modern Hebrew literature. At the request of Theodor *Herzl he translated the invitation to the First Zionist Congress into Hebrew, personally setting the type. There, and at later Zionist congresses, Ehrenpreis acted as a consultant on cultural matters. Like *Berdyczewski he criticized *Aḥad Ha-Am's view that Hebrew literature confine itself to Jewish themes and demanded that it fulfill all the spiritual needs of Jews living within the boundaries of European culture (*Ha-Shilo'aḥ*, no. 1, 1896/97). However, in his article *Ha-Sifrut ha-Illemet* ("The Silent Literature") in *Ha-Shilo'aḥ*, 17 (1908), he expressed the view that the Hebrew literature of his generation was not capable of creating "the redeeming synthesis between Judaism and Europeanism." From then on he abandoned almost totally his interest in Hebrew literature and the Zionist movement (for which he was severely criticized by the Zionists), and devoted himself to his rabbinic and public work, writing in Swedish and other languages. He published many translations of modern Hebrew literature into Swedish; and his own essays "De som byggt Israel" ("The Builders of Israel," 3 vols., 1929–43); "Landet mellam öster och vaster" ("The Country Between East and West," the journey of a Jew to Spain, 1927); *Österlandets Själ* (1926; *The Soul of the East*, 1928), impressions of a journey to the Middle East; and his autobiography, *Mitt liv mellam öster och väster* ("My Life Between East and West," 1946). His books were translated into several European languages and his autobiography (1953) into Hebrew. He founded the Jewish-Swedish journal *Judisk Tidskrift* (1928), and edited a Jewish encyclopedia in Swedish. Although first a political Zionist, he became an advocate of spiritual nationalism, believing that dispersal and assimilation were the true way of life for the Jewish people, enabling them to fulfill their spiritual mission among the nations.

BIBLIOGRAPHY: *Judisk Tidskrift*, 17 (1944), no. 1, on Ehrenpreis' 70th birthday with bibl. (special suppl.); M.J. Berdyczewski, *Ma'amarim* (1960), 223–5; J. Klausner, *Yoẓerei Tekufah* (1956), 126–32; Gelber, in: *Zion*, 3 (1953), 45–51; Waxman, Literature, 1 (1960^2), 155–6.

[Gedalyah Elkoshi and Hugo Mauritz Valentin]

EHRENREICH, BERNARD COLONIUS (1876–1955), U.S. Reform rabbi. Ehrenreich was born in Hungary and immigrated to the United States as a young child in 1879. He attended New York University, where in 1898 he was one of the founders of the Zeta Beta Tau American Jewish Fraternal Organization as a forum for exchanging ideas and promoting Zionism. Ehrenreich earned his B.A. degree from NYU in 1900, the same year he was ordained at the Conservative movement's Jewish Theological Seminary. He became rabbi of Congregation Beth Israel in Atlantic City, New Jersey (1901–2) and served as recording secretary of the Federated Zionists of America. In 1903, he assumed the pulpit of Congregation Adath Jeshurun of Philadelphia, where he was one of the nucleus of founders of the Alumni Association of the Jewish Theological Seminary (the forerunner of the Rabbinical Assembly). In 1906, after affiliating with the Reform movement's Central Conference of American Rabbis, he became rabbi of Kahl Montgomery in Montgomery, Alabama, where he was also active in the Jewish Welfare Board, the Montgomery Chamber of Commerce, the Graduate Menorah Society, and the American Jewish Congress. During World War I, he served as a welfare worker in the military base at Camp Sheridan, Alabama.

Devoted to the education, character building, and leadership development of young people, Ehrenreich purchased a summer camp in Minocqua, Wisconsin, in 1915, named it Camp Kawaga, and directed it as a Jewish boys' camp – albeit heavily influenced by Native American culture – from 1916 to 1951. His philosophy was that he could teach boys the Great Outdoors (GOD), as well as skills to turn them into men. Over the years, Kawaga attracted (and continues to attract) thousands of campers, winning the approval and endorsement of rabbis and educators from states throughout the Midwest, the South, and the Southwest. Ehrenreich's voluminous correspondence shows that many men stayed in close touch with "Doc E." into adulthood and attributed their lifelong allegiance to Judaism and Jewish values to his influence. Ehrenreich also became a civic leader in the town of Minocqua, where he eventually chose to reside for most of the year. During World War II, although in his late sixties, Ehrenreich traveled as far afield as Columbia, South Carolina, and Stockton, California, to volunteer as a replacement for congregational rabbis who were away serving as military chaplains.

BIBLIOGRAPHY: Guide to the Papers of Bernard C. Ehrenreich, American Jewish Historical Society (http://www.cjh.org/academic/findingaids/ajhs/nhprc/Ehrenreichf.html); *Journal of the 66th Annual Convention of the Central Conference of American Rabbis* (1955).

[Bezalel Gordon (2nd ed.)]

EHRENREICH, ḤAYYIM JUDAH BEN KALONYMUS (1887–1942), Hungarian rabbi. Ehrenreich served as rabbi of Holesov, Moravia; Deva, Transylvania; and Humenne, Slovakia. In this last community, to which he was appointed in 1930, he devoted himself to a study of talmudic literature. Ehrenreich planned a scientific edition of the Babylonian Talmud together with a new commentary of his own, and a similar one of the Jerusalem Talmud, but nothing was published. Immersed in this scholarly activity, he hardly engaged in communal activity, but in 1920 published an important pamphlet *Yisrael bein ha-Amim* ("Israel Among the Nations") dealing with Jewish survival. His works include *Saadiah Gaon's Shelosh Esreh Middot* (1922); *Sefer ha-Pardes* (1924); parts of *Sefer Abudarham* (1927); *Abraham Klausner's Minhagim* (1929); and *Givat ha-Moreh* (1936), sermons. From 1920 he published parts of *Seder Rav Amram Ga'on* with his own commentary and edited a monthly journal, *Oẓar ha-Ḥayyim*, from 1924–38. He and his family were killed by the Nazis in Lublin in 1942.

BIBLIOGRAPHY: Ehrenreich, in: *Oẓar ha-Ḥayyim*, 2 (1926), 47; 5 (1929), 260; Wininger, Biog, 6 (c. 1930), 555; S.K. Mirsky (ed.), *Ishim u-Demuyyot...* (1959), 432–7; EẒD, 1 (1958), 194–7.

[Naphtali Ben-Menahem]

EHRENSTAMM, family of pioneering textile manufacturers in the Hapsburg Empire in the 18th–19th centuries. Solomon Jacob, a son of Phinehas *Illovy, was first known by the family name of Kolin. He settled in *Prostejov (Prossnitz) in 1752 as a textile importer, but twice went bankrupt because of the unfavorable government policy on imports. In 1787 he adopted the family name of Ehrenstamm. His son Feith (d. 1827), who from 1786 had acquired wealth as an army contractor, took over the firm in 1790. In 1801 he founded a textile factory with modern imported machines, initially employing 3,000 workers, for supplying the army and export. He later added dyeing departments. In 1812 he accepted a contract for supplying the quota of textiles for army uniforms imposed on Moravia, and in 1820, in partnership with Simon von *Laemel, for supplying the entire Hapsburg army. He took up residence next to his factory, becoming the first Jew at this time to live outside the Jewish quarter of a Moravian town. After his death, the privileges he had received were transferred to his four sons. They became known for their extravagance, and gave a lavish reception in honor of Archduke Franz Karl. The firm built additional factories, but in 1833 went bankrupt. The factories were liquidated, the bankruptcy proceedings continuing until 1856. One of the brothers committed suicide, and another immigrated to Hungary in 1852.

BIBLIOGRAPHY: Hellig, in: BLBI, 3 (1960), 101–22; R. Kestenberg-Gladstein, *Neuere Geschichte der Juden in den boehmischen Laendern* (1969), 103–15.

EHRENSTEIN, ALBERT (1886–1950), German poet and author. Born in Vienna of Hungarian parents, Ehrenstein lived until 1932 mostly in Vienna and Berlin as a freelance writer. Studying history and geography in Vienna, he published his first poems in Karl Kraus' *Die Fackel* (e.g., "Wanderers Lied"). The publication of the novel *Tubutsch* (with drawings by Oskar Kokoschka, 1911) made Ehrenstein an important exponent of the expressionist movement. His texts were guided by a new diaspora politics and aesthetics, understanding modernity as the overcoming of the bourgeois concept of nation and art. Ehrenstein's work is populated by exterritorial figures who suffer from homelessness and at the same time stand for a modern, aesthetic cosmopolitanism which transcends the 19th century concept of nationalism. This constant subject is found in Ehrenstein's novels (*Der Selbstmord eines Katers*, 1912; *Nicht da nicht dort*, 1916; *Bericht aus einem Tollhaus*, 1919; *Zaubermerchen*, 1919; *Die Nacht wird*, 1921; *Briefe an Gott*, 1922; *Ritter des Todes*, 1926) as well as in his poetry (*Die weisse Zeit*, 1914; *Die Gedichte*, 1920; *Wien*, 1921; *Herbst*, 1923; *Mein Lied*,

1931). In his essays, collected in *Menschen und Affen* (1926), Ehrenstein legitimized this programmatic extraterritoriality as a new "ahasverism" with social-revolutionary aspects, criticizing both assimilation and Zionism as throwbacks to old-European nationalism (cf. *Zionismus, Vom deutschen Adel juedischer Nation, Nationaljudentum*). He spent World War I in exile in Switzerland, vehemently criticizing the war (cf. *Der Mensch schreit*, 1916; *Die rote Zeit*, 1917; *Den ermordeten Bruedern*, 1919). After the war he turned to rewriting old Greek and Chinese works (cf. *Lukian*, 1918; *Longos*, 1924; *Schi-King*, 1922; *Pe-Lo-Thien*, 1923; *China klagt*, 1924; *Raeuber und Soldaten*, 1927; *Das gelbe Lied*, 1933). With the three cultural spaces of Hellas, Zion, and China, Ehrenstein constructed an antique world as a medium for contemporary criticism. In 1929, Ehrenstein together with Kokoschka visited Palestine, describing his impressions in a series of articles. In 1932, Ehrenstein moved to Switzerland. Even though the Swiss authorities prohibited him from writing, Ehrenstein praised Switzerland as a liberal and pancultural community within barbarian Europe (*Tessin*, 1938; *Switzerland*, 1942). In 1941 he settled in New York, where he died in poverty. After selected editions by Karl Otten and M.Y. Ben-Gavriel, the work and letters of Ehrenstein were published in a complete edition (ed. H. Mittelmann). Ehrenstein's manuscripts are at the Hebrew University.

BIBLIOGRAPHY: A. Beigel, *Erlebnis und Flucht im Werk Ehrensteins* (1966); J. Drews, *Die Lyrik Ehrensteins* (1969); A. Beigel, *Erlebnis und Flucht im Werk Albert Ehrensteins* (1972); K.-M. Gauss, *Wann endet die Nacht* (1986); U. Laugwitz, *Albert Ehrenstein* (1987); A.A. Wallas, *Albert Ehrenstein* (1994); A. Kilcher, "Jenseits von Zionismus und Assimilation," in: *Kirche und Israel*, 18 (2003).

[Andreas Kilcher (2nd ed.)]

EHRENTREU, HEINRICH (1854–1927), Orthodox German rabbi and author. Ehrentreu was born in Alt-Ofen (Obuda), Hungary. Considered a brilliant talmudist in the yeshivah of Pressburg, he later pursued Semitic studies at the University of Heidelberg (from 1877) and was a tutor in Mainz. Ehrentreu became preacher at the Ohel Jakob synagogue in Munich where he supervised and greatly developed the religious institutions of the Jewish community over a period of 42 years. He was a member of the German chapter of the Rabbinical Council of Agudat Israel. In 1897 Ehrentreu edited the last volume of R.N. *Rabbinovicz's *Dikdukei Soferim*, 16 (1897). He also published *Heker Halakhah* ("Halakhic Research," 1904), and *Minḥat Pittin*, halakhic essays published in 1927/28. Together with Rabbi Jacob Schor of Kuty, he wrote *Ẓidkat ha-Ẓaddik* (1910), a defense of Z.H. *Auerbach's edition of *Sefer ha-Eshkol*, which had been attacked as a forgery by S. *Albeck. His responsa and numerous articles were published in Jewish scholarly journals. Ehrentreu's son, ERNST (JONAH) EHRENTREU (1896–?), succeeded him. Escaping from Germany to England, Ernst Ehrentreu became rabbi of a small congregation (Adath Yeshurun) in London. He published *Untersuchungen ueber die Massora* (1925), and *Jewish Thought in the Modern World* (1947).

BIBLIOGRAPHY: S. Levi, in: L. Jung (ed.), *Men of the Spirit* (1964), 375–87.

[Jacob Hirsch Haberman]

EHRLICH, ABEL (1919–2004), composer and teacher. Born in Crantz, Germany, Ehrlich went to Zagreb to study with Vaclav Huml at the academy of music (1934–38). In 1939 he settled in Palestine and studied composition at the Jerusalem Academy of Music with Solomon *Rosowsky. He taught theory and composition in various music institutions such as the Oranim Teachers College and at the Rubin Academy of Music in Tel Aviv. His works before 1953 were influenced by Arab music. In the late 1950s he began to use serial procedures, after attending the courses of Stockhausen and Pousseur at Darmstadt in 1959. He was awarded the Lieberson Prize three times (1969, 1971, 1980), won the Israel Composers and Authors Association Prize in 1974, 1980, and 1994, the Israel Prime Minister's Award in 1990, the ACUM Prize for life achievement in 1994, and the Israel Prize for music in 1997. Ehrlich was one of the most prolific Israeli composers – he wrote more than 3,500 pieces and as a result appeared in the Guinness Book of Records as the world's most prolific contemporary composer. Among his early compositions are *Bashrav* for violin solo (1953) and *Symphonic Bashrav* for orchestra (1958), in which he explored the fusion of Near Eastern and Western musical elements. His later works include *I Will Sing in Praise* for chamber orchestra (1977); *Will It Work?* suite for guitar (1985); *Enkhah Yode'a* for youth choir and violin solo (1986); *Our Modest Friend Avraham* for chamber ensemble (1992); *The Jubille,* chamber opera in 16 scenes (1995); *Another Exercise: Four Dreams: May 1997*, for four tenors and chamber ensemble (1997); and many pieces for solo instruments.

BIBLIOGRAPHY: Grove online; A. Wolman and Y. Shaked, *Abel Ehrlich* (1995).

[Israela Stein (2nd ed.)]

EHRLICH, ARNOLD BOGUMIL (1848–1919), biblical exegete. Ehrlich was born in Wlodawa in Russian Poland. As a youth he studied in a *ḥeder* and then a yeshivah, married at an early age, and had two daughters. Despairing of his narrow Jewish world, Ehrlich, still quite young, divorced his wife, and, in 1865, went to Germany. There he worked as a librarian in the Semitics department of the Berlin Royal Library. In Leipzig, under the influence of Christian missionaries and tempted by the greater opportunities available to Christians, Ehrlich converted to Christianity. He worked with Franz *Delitzsch (1813–99) in the missionary Institutum Judaicum, helping to translate the New Testament into Hebrew (1877) for the purpose of a Christian mission to the Jews. At the age of 30, Ehrlich migrated to the U.S., married again, and raised a family under difficult economic conditions, working at various jobs including social work, portraiture, and Hebrew teaching. According to Richard J.H. *Gottheil, when Ehrlich reached New York in 1876 he called on Rabbi R. Gustav Gottheil of Temple

Emanu-El (Richard's father), confessed that he had been converted to Christianity at the age of 23 while working for Delitzsch, and expressed a desire to be reaccepted formally into the Jewish faith. He accordingly appeared before a *bet din* on March 7, 1876, and was readmitted to the Jewish community after making the necessary declarations in both German and English (which are quoted by Richard in his biography of his father). The proceedings were duly recorded. Ehrlich, who weighed three hundred pounds, never obtained a real academic post. On the one hand, Jews with academic influence suspected his Christian connections, while on the other hand Christians probably saw him as too much of an East European Jew. In 1884 he published a chrestomathy containing selections from the Talmud and the Midrashim, "for youths and students." His main work, however, was devoted to biblical exegesis. From 1899 to 1901 his Hebrew commentary on the Bible *Mikra ki-Feshuto* was published in Berlin in three volumes (of the four he planned; repr. 1969). He subscribed the title page with the pseudonym "Shabbetai b. Yom Tov ibn Boded." In the introduction he explained that he had written the commentary in Hebrew so that the Hebrew reader would study his words and comments. His book, however, received only scant attention. The Jewish press on the whole reacted to the book with exceptionally sharp criticism (also because of his skeptical attitude to tradition and his attacks on the medieval commentators), and the Christian scholars, who had great difficulty with Modern Hebrew, almost completely disregarded the commentary. The publication of his German commentary on the Book of Psalms (1905), which included a new translation, was a turning point in his life. It served as an introduction to his German commentary on the Bible, which like his Hebrew one consists of notes on the Bible, *Randglossen zur hebraeischen Bibel* (7 vols., 1908–14). Ehrlich included part of the material from his Hebrew commentary, but in an expanded form, as well as new interpretations arrived at since its publication; many of his earlier opinions are changed here. Although Ehrlich does not mention the Documentary Hypothesis, he employs evidence from language, religious concepts, and institutions to assign relative "late" and "early" dates to specific passages. Historical assessments such as the denial of Egyptian enslavement and of the Exodus are buried in comments to individual verses. He concentrates on textual criticism and reconstructions, and his very numerous emendations (especially in his German commentary) are at times conjectural (such as haplography or dittography, letters having a similar appearance in the ancient or in the square script, the use of abbreviations, glosses, etc.), and in most cases are not based on ancient translations. His comments, which are distinguished by their originality, at times have the quality of homiletics and are derived from Ehrlich's innovating spirit; yet through his sound linguistic instinct and fine linguistic differentiations he succeeded in illuminating and explaining, with great acumen and profundity, many verses and linguistic usages. Ehrlich's exegetical work is an important contribution to modern biblical exegesis. Ehrlich's work was highly influential on the Jewish translation produced by the Jewish Publication Society in 1917 and its successor of 1962–82.

BIBLIOGRAPHY: S. Bernfeld, in: *Ha-Shilo'aḥ*, 5 (1899), 547–52; B.Z. Halpern, in; *Miklat*, 2 (1920), 417–26; T. Friedlaender, in: *The Nation*, 110 (1920), 41; M. Haran (Diman), in: *Bitzaron*, 22 (1950), 190, 193–196; J. Bloch, in: JBA, 12 (1953–5), 23; A.B. Ehrlich, *Mikra ki-Feshuto*, 1 (1969^2), introd. by H.M. Orlinsky; R.J.H. Gottheil, *The Life of Gustav Gottheil: Memoir of a Priest in Israel* (1936), 75–77; R.M. Stern, in: AJA, 23 (1971), 73–85; G. Kressel, in: *Hadoar* (Sept. 17, 1971), 665–6. **ADD. BIBLIOGRAPHY:** S.D. Sperling, *Students of the Covenant* (1992), 45–47; E. Greenstein, in: DBI, 1, 323–24.

[Raphael Weiss / S. David Sperling (2nd ed.)]

EHRLICH, EUGEN (1862–1922), jurist. Born in Czernowitz, Ehrlich was associate professor of Roman Law in the university there from 1899 to 1914. In this capacity he made an important contribution to the study of the sociology of law, his thesis being that the law of society was the only "living law" and that the norms of a legal system must conform with the laws of society. Ehrlich was removed from all teaching posts in 1919 following antisemitic attacks by the student body in the nationalist press. His main works were translated into English and had a profound influence on American legal and sociological thought in the 20th century. These include *Grundlegung der Soziologie des Rechts* (1913, *Fundamental Principles of the Sociology of Law*, 1936). Although Ehrlich renounced Judaism in his youth he became interested in Jewish affairs in his later years and his treatise *Die Aufgabe der Sozialpolitik im oesterreichischen Osten* (1916) discusses the question of the Jews and the peasants.

BIBLIOGRAPHY: H. Sinzheimer, *Juedische Klassiker der deutschen Rechtswissenschaft* (1938), 231–55.

[Guido (Gad) Tedeschi]

EHRLICH, GEORG (1897–1966), graphic artist and sculptor. Born in Vienna, he studied at the Arts and Crafts School in Vienna under Oscar Strnad and Franz Cizek from 1912 to 1915. During World War I he served in the Austrian Army until 1918. In 1919 at his first exhibition Ehrlich became known for lithographs revealing the influence of Oskar Kokoschka. After he had been exhibited along with other modern artists such as Barlach, Beckmann, and Kokoschka in Munich, Paul Cassirer approached him with a commission for an album of lithographs entitled "Biblical Portfolio." The lithographs of this album reflect a deeply conscious Jewish identification and an intensely Jewish upbringing. At the same time, Ehrlich also painted watercolors of landscapes. He took up sculpture in 1926, in the graceful, elongated style of Lehmbruck, who remained a lasting influence. He cast numerous small-scale sculptures and busts in bronze, his favorite material. Ehrlich was already a prominent artist when in 1937 he was forced by the Nazis to leave Austria. He settled in England where he soon became established. His heads of the composer Benjamin Britten (1950) and the singer Peter Pears are among the finest works of this period. His work appears in leading museums in Britain, the U.S., and Israel.

ADD. BIBLIOGRAPHY: G. Kreuter (ed.), *Georg Ehrlich – graphische Arbeiten* (2002); A. Hoerschelmann (ed.), *Georg Ehrlich. 1897–1966* (1997); R. Oberbeck (ed.), *Georg Ehrlich (1897–1966). Von der Zeichnung zur Bronze – gestaltgewordene Suche nach Versöhnung* (2004); E. Tietze-Conrad, *Georg Ehrlich* (1956).

[Charles Samuel Spencer / Sonja Beyer (2nd ed.)]

EHRLICH, JACOB (1877–1938), Austrian Zionist leader. Born in Bistrica, Moravia, Ehrlich studied at Vienna University and joined the Jewish student association "J.A.V. Ivria." Encouraged by Theodor *Herzl, he toured Moravia and Bohemia to propagate Zionism. In 1908 he settled in Vienna, where he became a lawyer, and in 1912 he was one of the first Zionists to be elected as a member of the Board of the Jewish Community (Israelitische Kultusgemeinde). As a high officer of the Austro-Hungarian army during World War I he saved a number of Russian Jews from false accusations, among them the son of Abraham Menachem Mendel *Ussishkin. From 1919 to 1923 Ehrlich was a member of the Vienna city council. In the 1920s, and also during the Zionist Congress of 1925, he was president of the Zionist Federation in Austria. He helped to obtain a Zionist majority at the Israelitische Kultusgemeinde in December 1932, and in February 1936 became its vice president. In 1934, after the defeat of the Austrian Socialists in the civil war and the establishment of the Austrian corporate state, he became the representative of the Jewish community (councilor of the city of Vienna) in the "Buergerschaft," which replaced the city council, and an outspoken defender of Jewish rights. After the annexation of Austria by Nazi Germany (March 1938) Ehrlich was arrested, beaten daily by the Gestapo, and deported with the first transport to the Dachau concentration camp. He was murdered on May 17, 1938, the first prominent Austrian Jewish victim of the Nazis. His body was sent to Vienna, but the Nazis forbade all speeches and obituaries. His widow, Irma, and his son, Paul, immigrated to the United States via England.

The society of Jews from Austria in England and a B'nai B'rith Lodge in Tel Aviv bear his name.

[Josef Fraenkel / Evelyn Adunka (2nd ed.)]

EHRLICH, LUDWIK (1889–1968), Polish international lawyer. Born in Tarnopol, Ukraine, Ehrlich became professor of international law at the University of Lwow in 1924 and professor at the University of Cracow in 1945. He was recognized as an authority on international law and in 1928 and 1962 lectured at the Hague Academy. Ehrlich's writings include textbooks on general international law, and the law of treaties and sovereignty.

EHRLICH, PAUL (1854–1915), German chemist, pioneer of modern histology, immunology, and chemotherapy; Nobel Prize winner. Ehrlich was born in Strehlen near Breslau. He studied at German universities and began his scientific work in 1878 in Berlin University as an assistant, becoming an associate professor in 1890. In 1896 he became director of the Royal Institute for Serum Research in Steglitz (Berlin) and three years later director of the Institute of Experimental Therapy in Frankfurt on the Main, which was subsequently amalgamated with the Georg Speier Institute for Chemotherapeutic Research. In 1904 Ehrlich was appointed honorary professor at the University of Goettingen and in 1914 became a professor at Frankfurt University. He was awarded the Nobel Prize for Medicine in 1908. Ehrlich began his scientific work in the fields of hematology and histology. From methods of staining dead blood cells he progressed to staining living cells, and discovered methods of staining living nerve fibers. His research work on the staining of microorganisms led to the method of staining TB bacilli and he discovered the diazo reaction in urine for the recognition of aromatic compounds, which serves to diagnose typhoid fever.

From 1890 onward Ehrlich concentrated mainly on problems of immunization. He proved the specificity of immunity to toxins, and established the basic concepts of applied immunology: active and passive immunization. He laid the foundation for standardization of therapeutic sera by employing as standard serum a stable antitoxic serum capable of long-term preservation. On the basis of this method he developed, in 1897, the evaluation of the antitoxic sera and its theoretical basis, one of the vital practical achievements in the history of immunology.

Recognizing the particular specific affinity of dyes, active organic compounds, and toxins to certain cells, Ehrlich started to search for chemical compounds which would specifically attack the microorganisms causing disease without damaging the body cells. He first treated syphilis with the poisonous organic arsenic compound atoxyl and in 1909, after years of investigation, he discovered, together with his Japanese assistant Hatta, the compound "606," Salvarsan, which can inactivate the treponema causing syphilis, as well as other treponemas causing various tropical diseases. This was the greatest achievement in the fight against syphilis since its appearance in Europe four centuries earlier and marked the beginning of modern systematic chemotherapy.

Developments in theoretical and applied medical biology since Ehrlich's day have thrown new light on certain of his concepts and some of his theoretical assumptions have been modified. But his basic concepts and methods remain firm and still serve as fundamentals for research in the fields of hematology, immunology, and chemotherapy.

Ehrlich was interested in Jewish affairs all his life. He was an active member of Le-Ma'an Zion, and was also associated with and supported the Nordau Institute, one of the nuclei of the Hebrew University of Jerusalem.

BIBLIOGRAPHY: A. Lazarus, *Meister der Heilkunde, Paul Ehrlich* (1922); M. Marquard, *Paul Ehrlich als Mensch und Arbeiter* (1924); W. Bulloch, *The History of Bacteriology* (1938); F. Himmelweit (ed.), *The Collected Papers of Paul Ehrlich* (1956–57); S. Munther, *Paul Ehrlich, Founder of Chemotherapy* (1966); C.E. Dolman (ed.),

Paul Ehrlich and William Bulloch: A Correspondence and Friendship (1896–1914); Clio Medica, 3 (1968), 65–84.

[Aryeh Leo Olitzki]

EHRLICH, SIMḤA (1915–1983), Israeli politician, leader of the Liberal Party, and first non-Labor minister of finance, member of the Seventh to Tenth Knessets. Ehrlich was born in Poland. He studied at the Hebrew Gymnasium in Lublin and was active in the General Zionist youth movement prior to his immigration to Israel in 1938. In Israel he worked at first as an agricultural laborer in Nes Ẓiyyonah. Ehrlich studied optics and in 1961 established a firm for the manufacture of lenses and applied optical instruments. He joined the General Zionist Party and was elected to the Tel Aviv Municipal Council in 1955, serving as deputy mayor in 1962–65. In 1965 he ran in the municipal elections at the head of the *Gaḥal list. In 1969 he ran for the Seventh Knesset on the Gaḥal list.

In 1970, Ehrlich was appointed chairman of the Liberal Party Executive, and after the founding of the *Likud in 1973 he became a member of its Executive. In June 1977 he was appointed by Menaḥem *Begin as minister of finance, in which position he introduced a policy of economic liberalization, first of all in the field of foreign currency. However, his policy resulted in a serious deterioration in Israel's balance of trade and a rapid rise in the rate of inflation. As a result he was forced to resign in October 1979, remaining in the government as deputy prime minister. In Begin's second government formed after the elections to the Tenth Knesset, Ehrlich served as minister of agriculture and deputy prime minister.

ADD. BIBLIOGRAPHY: Y. Ben Porat, *Siḥot* (1981).

[Fern Lee Seckbach / Susan Hattis Rolef (2nd ed.)]

EHUD (Heb. אֵהוּד), son of Gera the Benjaminite, referred to as "a left-handed man" (Judg. 3:15). Ehud delivered Israel from *Eglon, the king of Moab, to whom they had been subject for 18 years. According to I Chronicles 8:3, Gera was the son of Bela, Benjamin's firstborn. If this is the same person, it would imply that Ehud belonged to one of the chief families of the tribe. Apparently, this family lived in the region of Geba, which may have been associated with the ancient Gibeonites. Possibly, this was the reason that some of its members were driven to the western slopes of the mountain (Manahath; see I Chron. 8:6). In early Israel's pre-monarchic period, some of the adjoining kingdoms, notably Moab, attempted to extend their dominion over the Jordan Valley and the hill country on the western bank of the river. They encountered resistance only in Mt. Ephraim, the territory of the Rachel tribes, who did not suffer foreign rule until the Philistine hegemony.

Ehud headed a tribute-bearing delegation to *Eglon, king of Moab (Judg. 3:15ff.). Being left-handed, he wore a sword under his garments on his right thigh, where guards were not in the habit of looking for a suspicious bulge, and no one noticed it. Under the pretext of having a "secret word" for the king, he succeeded in gaining a private audience with him. When he said "I bring you a word of God, your Majesty" the heavy-fleshed monarch rose to hear it; Ehud drew his sword, thrust its entire length into the belly of the corpulent king, and fled. Returning to his country, he sounded the ram's horn for the armies to gather, captured the fords of the Jordan, and defeated all the Moabite garrisons on the western bank of the river. This ended the Moabite rule over Israel for several generations. Ehud is not actually called a judge, although he is usually numbered among the "judges."

BIBLIOGRAPHY: Bright, Hist, 157; Kittel, Gesch, 1 (1922), 27; Albright, Stone, 216; M. Noth, *Geschichte Israels* (1956), 144–5; Y. Kaufmann, *Sefer Shofetim* (1962), 104–6; Kraeling, in: JBL, 54 (1935), 205–10; Yeivin, in. *Zion Me'assef*, 4 (1930), 8; idem, in: *Ma'arakhot*, 26–27 (1945), 65–66. **ADD. BIBLIOGRAPHY:** Y. Amit, *Judges* (1999), 71–79; See also the bibliography under *Eglon.

EIBESCHUETZ, SIMON AARON (1786–1856), Danish philanthropist. He bequeathed the major part of his property, which amounted to about 700,000 Danish thalers, to various municipal institutions in Copenhagen, but especially to Jewish institutions. Among other bequests, he donated an annual grant to the University Library of Copenhagen in order to purchase ancient Hebrew works and books dealing with Oriental culture. The condition that two Jewish students be admitted annually without payment was attached to his bequests to the Polytechnic and the Academy of Arts of Copenhagen.

BIBLIOGRAPHY: AZDJ, 21 (1857), 104; *Dansk Biografisk Leksikon*, s.v.

EICHELBAUM, SAMUEL (1894–1967), Argentine playwright and short-story writer. Born in a Jewish agricultural colony in Domíguez, Entre Ríos, he lived most of his life in Buenos Aires. Though in his psychological plays Eichelbaum deals mostly with the Argentinian middle class and is not especially concerned with Jewish life, Jewish themes and characters (both urban and rural) appear in his plays *El Judío Aarón* (1942), *Nadie la conoció nunca* (1926), and *Divorcio nupcial* (1941); and in some of his short stories such as "La buena cosecha," "El señor Lubovitzky depositario" (1925), and "Lo que la luna vio." He is considered one of the principal architects of Argentinian drama. Two of Eichelbaum's plays were awarded the municipal prize of Buenos Aires: *Tormenta de Dios* (1930) and *Señorita* (1937); but his best-known plays, also adapted for the screen, are *Un guapo del 900* (1940) and *Un tal Servando Gómez* (1942), which deal with the suburban cultural environment of Buenos Aires.

BIBLIOGRAPHY: D.W. Foster, *Cultural Diversity in Latin American Literature* (1994); N. Glickman and G. Waldman, *Argentine Jewish Theatre: An Anthology* (1996); D.B. Lockhart, *Jewish Writers of Latin America. A Dictionary* (1997); L. Senkman, *La identidad judía en la literatura argentina* (1983).

[Florinda Goldberg (2nd ed.)]

EICHENBAUM, BORIS MIKHAILOVICH (1886–1959), Russian literary scholar. Eichenbaum was born in Krasnoye (Smolensk district) to a Jewish father and a Russian mother, both physicians. His father, who became a Pravoslav Christian, was the son of Jacob *Eichenbaum (Gelber), a well-known Hebrew poet and scholar. After finishing the First Voronezh Gymnasium, Boris Eichenbaum entered the Military-Medical Academy of St. Petersburg in 1905. In 1907, he published his first essay on Russian literature ("Pushkin and the Rebellion of 1825," *Vestnik znaniya*, 1 and 2), and during the following year he was admitted to the Philological Faculty of St. Petersburg University, where he studied Slavic and Romano-Germanic philology, graduating in 1912 and joining the faculty of the university in 1918. From 1912, Eichenbaum regularly published scholarly and critical essays in *Russkaya Mysl, Apollon*, and other literary journals, as well as some poetry (in Gumilev's *Giperborey*). In 1919, Eichenbaum joined the Society for the Study of Poetic Language (OPOYAZ) and soon became one of the foremost exponents of the so-called "Formal Method" in literary scholarship, an early structural trend that laid the foundation of modern scientific poetics. Between 1922 and 1931, Eichenbaum published nine books, which are generally considered classics and have almost all been reprinted in the West: *Melodika stikha* ("Melodics of Verse," 1922); *Molodoy Tolstoy* ("Young Tolstoy," 1922; reprinted 1968); *Anna Akhmatova* (1923); *Lermontov* (1924; reprinted 1967); *Skvoz literaturu* ("Through Literature," Collected Essays, 1924; reprinted 1962); *Literatura, Teoriya. Kritika. Polemika* (1927; reprinted 1969); *Lev Tolstoy* (vol. 1, 1928; vol. 2, 1931; 1–2 reprinted 1968); *Moy vremennik* ("My Chronicle," 1929) (the latter collection includes an essay on Jacob Eichenbaum and his long poem "*Ha-Krav*").

In the late 1920s Eichenbaum attempted a synthesis of the purely intrinsic and the sociological approach to literature. However, this attempt, as well as Eichenbaum's earlier books, evoked official criticism, which found some support in retrograde academic and literary circles. Forced to abandon theoretical research, Eichenbaum devoted himself to textual work, preparing exemplary critical editions of such classic Russian authors as L. Tolstoy, Lermontov, Gogol, and Leskov. In 1933, he published a novel, *Marshrut v bessmertiye* ("A Route to Immortality"), about the lexicographer N. Makarov. In his diary he mentioned that his spiritual-genetic ties to his Jewish grandfather had an affect on him. When in 1924 his grandfather's Hebrew poem "The Battle" appeared in Russian anonymously, he wrote an essay speaking among other things about the forgotten author.

In 1947, in the course of the official campaign against the great Russian comparative philologist Aleksandr Veselovsky, Eichenbaum and his colleagues *Zhirmunsky and Tomashevsky "were taken to task for perpetuating Veselovsky's 'bourgeois cosmopolitanism,' i.e., drawing parallels between Russian and Western literature" (V. Erlich). In September 1949, an officially inspired article about Eichenbaum's "reactionary militant idealism," abundantly interspersed with antisemitic allusions, appeared in the magazine *Zvezda*, virtually silencing Eichenbaum for five years. He did not resume his scholarly activity until 1954.

The third volume of his great monograph on Tolstoy appeared posthumously in 1960. Following the revival of the study of poetic language in the U.S.S.R., two volumes of Eichenbaum's selected writings appeared in 1969 in Leningrad, *O poezii* ("On Poetry") and *O proze* ("On Prose"). The following works of Eichenbaum have been translated into English: "Theory of the Formal Method," in: *Russian Formalist Criticism*, transl. and ed. by L.T. Lemon and M.J. Reis (1965); "On Tolstoy's Crises," in: *Tolstoy* (20th Century Views series; 1967); "O. Henry and the Theory of the Short Story," transl. with notes and postscript, by I.R. Titunik, in: *Michigan Slavic Contributions* (1968); *Young Tolstoy* (1972).

BIBLIOGRAPHY: V. Erlich, *Russian Formalism* (1965); R. Jakobson, in: *International Journal of Slavic Linguistics and Poetics*, 6 (1963), 159–67; *ibid.*, 7 (1963), 151–87 (a complete bibliography of Eichenbaum's writings).

[Omri Ronen (2nd ed.)]

EICHENBAUM (Gelber), JACOB (1796–1861), Haskalah poet, educator, and mathematician. Born in Krystianopol, Galicia, he was married at the age of 11, but divorced when his father-in-law suspected him of secular leanings. He married again in 1815 and settled in Zamosc where he developed his interest in mathematics and translated Euclid from German into Hebrew (unpublished). Here he adopted the name Eichenbaum in order to obtain a resident's permit. Later he served as a private tutor, traveling from place to place, and finally settling in Odessa where he established a private Jewish school in 1835. He was appointed director of the Kishinev Jewish school in 1844 by the Russian government and in 1850 inspector of the newly established Zhitomir Rabbinical Seminary. Eichenbaum contributed poetry to Hebrew journals of the period. *Kol Zimrah* (1836), his collection of poems (and some translations), was one of the first books of poetry published in the Haskalah period. He also wrote *Ha-Kerav* ("The Battle," 1839), a book in verse describing the game of chess, and *Hokhmat ha-Shi'urim* (an adaptation of a French arithmetic book, 1857). His grandson Boris *Eichenbaum was a well-known Russian literary scholar.

BIBLIOGRAPHY: Zinberg, Toledot, 6 (1960), 229–30; A. Zederbaum, in: *Ha-Meliẓ*, 2 (1961/62), nos. 49, 50; 3 (1862/63), nos. 1, 3, 6; Kressel, Leksikon, s.v.

[Getzel Kressel]

EICHHORN, DAVID MAX (1906–1986), U.S. Reform rabbi, chaplain, and author. Eichhorn was born in Columbia, Pennsylvania, and received his B.A. from the University of Cincinnati in 1928. He was ordained at Hebrew Union College in 1931 and earned a D.D. degree from the same institution in 1938. In 1956, he was awarded an honorary D.H.L. from HUC-JIR. He served as rabbi of Sinai Temple in Springfield, Massachusetts (1932–34), and Mt. Sinai Temple in Texarkana, Arkansas (1935–38), before becoming the first rabbi of Temple Israel in Tallahassee, Florida, in 1939. He also became the first state director of Florida Hillel Foundations (1939–42). In 1942, he enlisted as a chaplain in the U.S. Army and was the first Jewish chaplain to enter Dachau, conducting the first religious service inside the liberated concentration camp on April 30, 1945. The service was captured on film and is commonly seen in liberation films. He was made supervisor of displaced persons for the Austrian Zone of the U.S. occupation, working with survivors of several concentration camps. For his service in combat zones, he was awarded the Bronze Star and eventually promoted to the rank of lieutenant colonel. After the war, the demobilized Eichhorn remained in the U.S. Army Reserve and was appointed director of field operations for the Committee on Army and Navy Religious Activities, as well as director of religious activities at the *National Jewish Welfare Board – a position he retained until he retired in 1968. He was also president of the Association of Jewish Chaplains of the Armed Forces (1953–55).

During his retirement, Eichhorn served as rabbi of Temple Israel in Merritt Island, Florida, and chaplain of the Kennedy Space Center and Patrick Air Force Base. In 1973, he founded the Jewish Community Center of Brevard County. In the field of scholarship, Eichhorn was renowned as an expert in the history of conversion to Judaism as well as Christian attempts to convert Jews in the United States. He wrote *Conversion to Judaism: A History and Analysis* (1965), *Evangelizing the American Jew* (1978), and *Jewish Intermarriage: Fact and Fiction* (1974). He was chairman of the Central Conference of American Rabbis' Committee on the Unaffiliated (1950–58), and a liberal who favored rabbinic participation in the wedding ceremonies of mixed marriages. He also wrote *Cain, Son of the Serpent* (1957); *Joys of Jewish Folklore* (ed., 1981; reprinted as *Jewish Folklore in America*, 1996); and *Musings of the Old Professor: The Meaning of Koheles* (1973). His posthumously published letters home from World War II provide a vivid depiction of Jewish life: *The GI's Rabbi: The World War II Letters of David Max Eichhorn* by Greg Palmer and Mark S. Zaid (2004).

BIBLIOGRAPHY: K.M. Olitzky, L.J. Sussman, and M.H. Stern, *Reform Judaism in America: A Biographical Dictionary and Sourcebook* (1993); Contemporary Authors Online, Gale, 2005.

[Bezalel Gordon (2nd ed.)]

°EICHHORN, JOHANN GOTTFRIED (1752–1827), German historian and biblical scholar. Eichhorn was professor of Oriental languages at Jena (1775–87) and of philosophy at Goettingen (1788–1827), where he succeeded his teacher, J.D. *Michaelis. He was one of the pioneers in the modern study of the Bible. He shares the credit with G. *Herder for freeing biblical studies from the shackles of church dogma and making biblical literature accessible to a wider public. Some of his work attempts to explain biblical myth naturalistically. In his *Einleitung in das Alte Testament* (3 vols., 1780–83; a partial translation: *Introduction to the Study of the Old Testament*, 1888), which ran into four editions (the 4th edition including 5 vols., 1820–24) and several reprints, he summed up the results of research in the field of biblical literature up to his day and endeavored to give a just appreciation of the poetic and religious elements in the Hebrew Bible. This was the first introduction to the Bible to be written, and through its vivid style and wide scholarship made a deep impression upon the scholarly world. Eichhorn's *Einleitung* exerted great influence on the biblical studies of Moses *Mendelssohn and his fellow commentators, especially *Ben-Ze'ev. Eichhorn also wrote an introduction to the Apocrypha (*Einleitung in die apokryphischen Schriften des Alten Testament*, 1795) as well as translations of Job and the prophetical books of the Bible (*Die hebraeischen Propheten*, 3 vols., 1816–19). He edited *Repertorium fuer biblische und morgenlaendische Litteratur* (18 vols., 1777–86) and *Allgemeine Bibliothek der biblisehen Literatur* (10 vols., 1787–1801).

BIBLIOGRAPHY: T.K. Cheyne, *Founders of Old Testament Criticism* (1893), 21–26; H.J. Kraus, *Geschichte der historisch-kritischen Erforschung des Alten Testaments* (1956), 120–40; ADB, 5 (1877), 731–7. **ADD. BIBLIOGRAPHY:** J. Rogerson, in: DBI, 324.

[Moshe Zevi (Moses Hirsch) Segal]

EICHLER, MENAHEM MAX (1870–1927), U.S. Conservative rabbi. Eichler was born in Hungary and immigrated to the United States in 1892. In 1899, he earned a B.A. degree from the City College of New York and was ordained at the Jewish Theological Seminary. Eichler became rabbi of Congregation Beth Israel (1899–1905) in Philadelphia, Pennsylvania, where in 1901 graduates of the *Jewish Theological Seminary met in his home to discuss the impending financial collapse of the Seminary. Their plan of action led to the formation of the Alumni Association of the Jewish Theological Seminary, which quickly evolved into the *Rabbinical Assembly. Eichler was elected the second president of the Rabbinical Assembly (1904–7) and served on the financial committee that planned the Seminary's million dollar campaign. From 1905 to 1916, he was rabbi of Congregation Ohabei Shalom in Boston, where he also attended law school at Boston University. After receiving his LL.B. degree in 1914 and being admitted to the Bar in 1916, Eichler began the practice of law and devoted much of his time to Jewish communal causes. He founded the Central Jewish Organization of Boston – which he also served as president – and was director of the Federated Jewish Charities of Boston, as well as the Zionist Bureau of New England. Eichler returned to the rabbinate in 1920, moving to Temple Beth El in Buffalo, New York, where he remained until his death. He wrote two books: *What Makes Life Worth Living* (1904) and *Jewish Home Prayers* (1913).

BIBLIOGRAPHY: P.S. Nadell, *Conservative Judaism in America: A Biographical Dictionary and Sourcebook* (1988).

[Bezalel Gordon (2nd ed.)]

°EICHMANN, ADOLF OTTO (1906–1962), SS officer and head of the Jewish Department of the Gestapo. He became one of the people most identified with "the Final Solution of the Jewish Problem" during his trial, which took place in Jerusalem in 1961, and a synonym in all discussions dealing with human evil.

Eichmann was born in Solingen, Germany, to Adolf Karl, an accountant, and Maria, a housewife, both of whom were devout Protestants. When Eichmann was seven years old, the family moved to the city of Linz, Austria, a mostly Catholic city. In 1916, Eichmann's mother died and, shortly thereafter, his father remarried.

Eichmann's childhood was a usual bourgeois one, very different from the commonly accepted image of what is thought to be the childhood of Nazi war criminals, as if they had usually experienced traumas in childhood and were on the fringes of society. No social rejections can be found in his childhood nor any outstanding expressions of hatred of Jews.

Eichmann's achievements as a student were low, and at age 19, he became a traveling salesman for the Vacuum Oil Company in Upper Austria. In 1933, he was promoted to the Salzburg area, but in the same year was fired because of staff downsizing in the company. His joining the ranks of the Nazi Party of Austria was the result of several factors. The general context was that Eichmann had grown up in an Austria where there was a long history of anti-Jewish movements and public discourse full of Jewish stereotypes. Eichmann was surrounded by an atmosphere and environment within which Jews were thought, as a matter of course, to be despised, foreign, and suspect as to their loyalty, as well as different in their religion and culture. Jews and non-Jews belonged to different societies. That is, there was a background of antisemitism, but not outright and aggressive. As to the street, there was a desire to eradicate the shame of Versailles and that, too, was thought to have been caused by the Jews. The strengthening of the National Socialist Party in Austria during the 1932 local elections gave it, besides strength, an increasing size and public respectability. To all this was added personal background. It was Ernst Kaltenbrunner, who later became the commander of the Head Office of the Security of the Reich, an acquaintance of the Eichmann family, who suggested to Eichmann that he join the ranks of the party and the SS. On April 1, 1932, Eichmann became a member of the Nazi Party. His number was 899895. Seven months later, he also swore allegiance to the SS, which at the time, numbered about 2,000 members in all of Austria.

The strengthening of the Nazi Party in Austria after 1933 resulted in its persecution by the government, and this, in addition to the fact that Eichmann was unemployed, caused him to immigrate to Germany in August 1933. Once in Germany, he received military training in one of the SS camps. In 1934, Eichmann served as a colonel in the Austrian unit of the SS in the concentration camp at Dachau. At the end of the year, he volunteered for the SD, the Secret Service, and was transferred to Berlin. This was extremely important because in a few years the SD became the driving force of the implementation of Jewish policies in Nazi Germany and an influence on the determiners of that policy.

Initially, Eichmann's main job in the SD was in Intelligence. At the beginning, he dealt with the Freemasons; later he gradually became an expert in the subjects of Judaism, Jews, Jewish organizations, Zionism, Herzl, and Jewish immigration. In appreciation of his efforts and achievements in the field of Jewish policy, he was promoted to *Untersturmfuhrer* (second lieutenant) in January 1938.

Now he had real standing and prestige. In the same year, he was requested by *Heydrich to prepare a memorandum about the international effort to encourage Jewish emigration from Europe. This was the beginning of a great advancement in Eichmann's career. This matter dealt with the future of the Jews in Austria, which had been annexed to the German Reich in March 1938. The SD made Eichmann responsible for the Jewish Emigration Office and, for the first time, he had real power. He had enactment authority in the security force and dictatorial authority over the helpless Jews. The summit of his achievements was the establishment of the Main Office of Jewish Emigration. The success of this office hinged on four factors: the ambitions of the SD and the despair of the Jews, together with the great effort of Eichmann to implement the emigration according to the SD doctrine, along with Eichmann's burning desire to achieve promotion. Moreover, in Vienna, Eichmann added a new twist to emigration by having the Jews themselves finance it and enlisting their cooperation, an action which was a precedent for the formation of the Judenrat.

Despite Eichmann's contentions that his efforts to encourage Jewish emigration were in the spirit of Zionism, the reality was that forced emigration was the realization of Nazi policy and that by forced, brutally implemented emigration the Nazis also got hold of Jewish possessions. Eichmann bragged that within a year of the annexation of Austria, about 100,000 Jews had emigrated from Austria legally and a few thousand Jews to Palestine illegally, and in total by November 1941, 128,000 Jews had left Austria. Eichmann's achievement was quickly rewarded by his promotion to *Obersturmfuhrer* (first lieutenant). Eichmann's activities in Vienna became the model for policy that was enacted in Germany beginning in January 1939, when the Main Office of Emigration within the Reich was established. Heydrich was appointed commander and Heinrich Mueller was appointed his second in command.

A few weeks later, Czechoslovakia was conquered and Eichmann was asked to come to Prague to establish an additional emigration center. At this point, Eichmann had formed a staff from the Austrian Nazis, which included Frantz Novak, Anton Burger, Karl Rohm, and Alois Brunner as well as the Gunther brothers. Fritz Gunther was to be his deputy. Theodor Dannecker and Dieter Wisliceny were also among the group. These were to be at the heart of activities in the years to come. To Bohemia and Moravia, which became a German Protectorate, Eichmann took Brunner and Hans Gunther.

All of Eichmann's activities seemed to be quite efficient until September 1939, when Germany invaded Poland and World War II began. At this point, Eichmann's command changed radically.

With the outbreak of war, *Himmler established the Main Office for the Security of the Reich (RSHA) commanded by Heydrich. Eichmann was appointed to chair the Jewish Department with Heinrich Mueller at the head. Consequently, Eichmann was serving under Heydrich.

During October 1939, Eichmann and his men were responsible for the expulsion of thousands of Jews from Germany, Austria, and the Protectorate of Bohemia-Moravia to a remote place in Poland called Nisko. Most of them perished; only about 300 of them survived. These deportations and those that came immediately afterwards became the basis for the development of methods of mass expulsions during the entire period of Nazi rule on the entire continent. It was Eichmann who at that time translated the German Foreign Office's plan to deport the Jews to the tropical island of Madagascar into a viable plan. The plan was never put into action.

In February 1940, the RSHA began a series of reorganizations. Eichmann's unit was renamed IVB4, the name by which it would become known forever: the "Department of Jewish Matters and Deportation." It was formally listed under the authority of the Gestapo. It was a victory for the SD in the struggle for control of anti-Jewish policy. Eichmann was now formally a Gestapo officer.

Now Eichmann worked furiously. As head of the Department of Emigration in Vienna, Prague, and Berlin, he had to evacuate hundreds of thousands of people to Poland to make room for ethnic Germans who had been evacuated from the Baltic countries. The deportation was carried out from the areas of Stettin and Posen, causing great chaos in the General Government and strong protests from Governor Hans *Frank. This crisis crossed wires historically with the preparations for the invasion of the U.S.S.R. It seems that at this point, the expert in emigration became the expert in mass murder and genocide.

The month of September 1941 marks the beginning of Eichmann's activities on a mass scale. In mid-September, *Hitler ordered Himmler to carry out a deportation of Jews from Germany, Austria, and the Protectorate. In October, Himmler officially prohibited Jewish emigration from the continent and in the same month Eichmann organized the deportation of 20,000 Jews from the Reich along with 5,000 Roma (gypsies) to the Lodz ghetto. In the same month, Eichmann was again promoted. This time, he was promoted to *Obersturmbannfuhrer* (lieutenant colonel), his highest rank. In October, Eichmann held a meeting of representatives of different institutions that were connected to the Jewish issue where he informed them of the deportation of German Jews. Likewise, they were required to report their activities in that matter. When all was ready, the trains from Germany and Austria began to move towards Poland, White Russia, and the Baltic area. Eichmann personally commanded all arrangements and traveled to Minsk, Lvov, Lublin, and Lodz, to check the progress of the preparations to receive the deportees.

At the beginning of 1942, Eichmann visited Auschwitz and Treblinka. Even so, most of his activities until then had involved deportations and their organization, and not the genocide of European Jews. His involvement in the latter phase began with the convening of the *Wannsee Conference on January 20, 1942.

At the Wannsee Conference, the coordination of all the German bodies connected with the implementation of the Final Solution was discussed. Eichmann had convened the conference, written Heydrich's speech, and written the protocol. At the end of the day, it was Eichmann, Muller, and Heydrich who joined together after all of their aims had been discussed. Eichmann had now turned from an emigration expert to one of the most important people in the implementation of the new policies against the Jews.

After Wannsee, Eichmann became the director of the largest murder project in history.

Eichmann now directed transportation from all parts of Europe to the extermination camps in Poland, and oversaw the number of deportees. He coordinated the train departure schedules with railroad authorities in different countries. In cooperation with the German Foreign Office, he organized the seizure of the huge quantity of possessions that the deported Jews left behind.

In defining Eichmann's role in this time period, it can be said that it was not Eichmann who determined the policy, yet he was an important link as an operative interpreter of the policy.

Although Eichmann was well aware of what was happening in the death camps, most of his activities were not in Poland and Eastern Europe. He was not involved in the activities of the *Einsatzgruppen*. His greatest impact was mostly in activities in Central and Western Europe. In all of those countries, except for Denmark, Norway, and Finland, representatives of his department spread out and were responsible for the deportations. In occupied France, Holland, Belgium, Greece, Slovakia, and the Protectorate of Bohemia-Moravia, as well as in the Reich, the orders were given by Hitler, Himmler, and Heydrich and carried out by the joint action of local collaborators and Eichmann's department. Yet Eichmann was informed and knew all along of the growing severity of the policy. Again and again, it can be seen how he intervened to reduce the number of Jews who received temporary exemptions from deportation orders. In Holland, for example, Eichmann fought to cancel the exemptions that were given to the country's Jewish diamond workers, who were very important for its economy.

Eichmann was a key figure in two places: in the Theresienstadt ghetto and in Hungary. The history of the Theresienstadt ghetto/camp in Bohemia is closely connected with the name of Eichmann. It begins with the order of Heydrich in October 1941 to evacuate 86,000 Jews from the Protectorate. The fear of chaos as with Nisko produced the decision to isolate them in the area of the Protectorate itself. Between January and June 1942, more than 50,000 Czech Jews were sent to the camp. In addition, Jews from Vienna and Jews of German nationality were later added. For most of them, the camp was a way station to Auschwitz.

It was Eichmann who realized the potential of Theresienstadt as a means of deceiving the world about the fate of the Jews. He made it into a "model camp," where the Red Cross Committee was allowed to visit in order to counter the reports of Nazi atrocities. The day after the Red Cross Committee's visit, one of the largest deportations was dispatched to Auschwitz.

In Hungary, which was conquered by the Germans on March 19, 1944, it was Eichmann himself who managed the deportations. Using the great experience he had acquired, Eichmann succeeded in sending off 437,402 Jews between May 15 and July 9, mostly to Auschwitz. More than 70% of them were murdered shortly after arriving at the camp. This "success" was made possible partly by the help the Nazis received from the Hungarians. Yet, at the beginning of July, the leader of Hungary, Miklos Horthy, ordered the cessation of this collaboration under international pressure. Eichmann was among those who fought most furiously to continue the deportations but was unable to continue for several months. He renewed his activities when the Hungarian Arrow Cross Fascists gained control of Hungary in October 1944. With his return, execution by gas in Auschwitz was stopped and he ordered marches of Jews to Germany through Austria to help with the German war industry. Around 76,000 Jews took part in these marches, which were called "death marches." In Hungary, Eichmann met with various attempts to save the Jews. In Budapest, Raul *Wallenberg, the Swedish diplomat, was active together with other representatives of neutral countries, against Eichmann's activities. Eichmann also played an important part in the famous "blood-for-trucks negotiations." In these, Joel *Brandt of Budapest was sent to Istanbul with the offer to exchange Jews for trucks and other goods that would be given to the Germans. The plan was apparently an instance of German duplicity, as was the involvement with Eichmann's approval of Wisliceny, a member of his department, in the "Europe Plan" in 1943, in which Jews would be exchanged for dollars. Eichmann worked to ruin two other plans in Bulgaria and Romania but had to allow the release of some of the Sephardi Jews from Greece and some Jews from the Land of Israel who had been seized in Europe in exchange for Germans who had been seized in the Land of Israel.

At the end of the war, Eichmann was captured, but managed to escape. Like thousands of escaping Nazis, in 1950, Eichmann used the "Rat Path" which led from Germany to Argentina through Italy. He lived with his family in Buenos Aires as Ricardo Klement and became a father to a third son. In 1960, he was abducted by the Israeli Mossad and brought to Israel. There his trial took place, in which he was found guilty and condemned to death.

The Eichmann Trial

On May 23, 1960, the prime minister of Israel informed the Knesset, the Israeli public, and the world, in a short announcement of 62 words that Adolf Eichmann, who had been designated one of the most important Nazis, was in Israel and would stand trial for his part in the "Final Solution of the Jewish Problem."

The Eichmann Trial was one of the biggest media trials of the 20th century and it made the name of Adolf Eichmann a synonym for the essence of human evil and its sources.

It took Israel almost a year to prepare for the trial, which began on April 19, 1961. The interrogation was carried out by a special unit of the Israeli Police Force (Department 06). Eichmann was charged with "Crimes against the Jewish People," "Crimes against Humanity," "War Crimes," and "Membership in an Enemy Organization" (SD, SS, and Gestapo). All of these were listed in Israel's Nazi and Nazi Collaborators Punishment Law (1950), on the basis of which Eichmann was brought to trial.

The trial ended in August 1961. On December 15, 1961, the verdict and sentence were read. Eichmann was convicted and sentenced to death. Eichmann appealed to the Supreme Court. A panel of five Supreme Court justices rejected his appeal and confirmed the verdict and sentence. Eichmann was executed by hanging on June 1, 1962, almost two years after he was brought to Israel. It was the only death sentence ever carried out by the State of Israel. Eichmann's body was cremated and his ashes were scattered outside the territorial waters of Israel.

Eichmann's trial revealed to the Jews and the world what had happened to the Jews during World War II. Ben-Gurion called the trial "The Nuremburg of the Jews" because during the Nuremburg trials in Germany the Holocaust had been sidelined, while this time it was at the heart of the matter. In this, Ben-Gurion also wished to emphasize that in 1961, unlike during the course of Jewish history in the Diaspora, the Jews had a sovereign state, and as a result they could call to account those who had injured them. Thus it was asserted that the State of Israel represented all the Jewish people in the world.

The prosecutor at the trial was the attorney general, Gideon *Hausner, who headed a prosecution team that numbered five people. The defense attorney was Robert Servatius of Germany, who had represented a number of German defendants in the Nuremburg trials. His co-consul was Dieter Wechtenbruch, an attorney from Munich. The panel of judges consisted of judges at two levels. The president of the court was a member of the Supreme Court, Moshe *Landau, and alongside him sat two judges from district courts, Benjamin Halevy and Yitzhak Raveh. The trial took place in front of an audience in a hall in Jerusalem, while Eichmann sat in a bulletproof glass enclosure. The beginning of the trial focused on the motions of the defense attorney, who mainly challenged the right of the court to try Eichmann. The defense attorney's main objection was that the judges, being Jews, could not judge Eichmann impartially. If that was not enough, Eichmann had been abducted from Argentina and brought to Israel illegally, in violation of international law. Finally, the defense attorney held that the law under which Eichmann was charged was retroactive and extraterritorial, in that it related to crimes committed before the State of Israel had existed and were committed outside the territory of Israel, on European soil. The judges rejected all of these arguments. They rejected the first on the grounds that a judge is bound to restrain his feelings while on the bench, and if he did not he would not even be able to sit in judgment of a felony. The issue of retroactivity did not involve a binding principle. Usually it is cited in cases where a law was not law at the time of the crime. But in the case of the current trial, laws had been passed all over the world that did not constitute new judicial norms but make it possible to bring to trial criminals who knew very well at the time of their crimes that their actions were illegal. In the matter of the abduction, the court held that it was not the court's business to deal with how the defendant had been brought to court but with the legality of the accusation and venue. Finally, in the matter of extraterritoriality, the court held that it was not relevant, for two reasons. First, the intention to murder was also to exterminate the Jews of the Land of Israel, and second, that there is an existential connection between the Land of Israel and the will to ensure that people who commit crimes against the Jewish people will be brought to trial and punished for their crimes.

With the rejection of the objections, the trial began. Eichmann's answer to each of the accusations was: "In the spirit of the indictment – not guilty."

The documentary evidence that was brought before the court included 1,600 documents, many of them with Eichmann's signature, and 110 witnesses, mostly Holocaust survivors. The trial told the story of the Holocaust as the story of European Jewry but excluded the story of the fate of the Jews of Libya and Tunisia in North Africa. The prosecution described the fate of the Jews of Europe in a wide geographic context while describing the chronological stages of the fate of the Jews in each country. The prosecution put on record the stories of the camps in Europe and the activities of the *Einsatzgruppen*, while emphasizing that in each stage one could see the fingerprints of Eichmann.

The defense attorney did not question the authenticity of the Holocaust, but the central role that the defendant had in it. The defense was not able to bring witnesses to speak for Eichmann since SS and other Nazi personnel were not offered immunity if they came to Israel and were therefore subject to prosecution. As a result a group of jurists was sent to Germany to gather testimonies from SS men who were willing to testify. Clearly this was a deviation from the commonly accepted practice in criminal trials.

The court rejected the claims of the defense that Eichmann was mainly obediently fulfilling the orders of his commanders, and claimed that Eichmann had acted in a criminal manner on his own initiative. The outstanding example was the murder of hundreds of thousands of Hungarian Jews, where the defendant had become relentless in his implementation of the "Final Solution." The court did not accept the claims of the prosecution especially with regard to Eichmann's part in the *Einzatzgruppen* murders and the murders in the camps. The main accusation against Eichmann concerned his part in what had occurred in Central Europe and in the west of the continent. The judges in their verdict did not rely on the testimony of witnesses when they came to convict Eichmann. The witnesses' testimony about their individual experiences had a powerful and enduring impact on Israel and the world, in contrast to their apparent lack of effect on the judges.

The Eichmann Trial left a lasting effect on the discourse and memory of the Holocaust as well as on Holocaust survivors, who at the time made up more than a quarter of the population of Israel.

Israel's public discourse shifted from an attitude that judged European Jews harshly and maintained that they had gone like "sheep to the slaughter," to deeper understanding of the desperate situation of the Jews at the time of the Nazi occupation and a more complex and varied insight into the essence of heroism. No longer was the latter understood only as armed combat but also as spiritual resistance. The Holocaust discourse underwent personalization. Israelis stopped speaking about "the six million" and began to speak about individuals with names and faces. Holocaust research, which until then had relied on German documents, began to focus on documents and materials that came from the victims. The Jerusalem school of Holocaust study began to flower. As a result, alternative interpretations of the behavior of the Jews, their leadership, and their choices in the Holocaust period were made. The status of Holocaust survivors in Israeli society underwent a dramatic change. For the first time, they were also seen as part of the Holocaust history, no less than the six million who were murdered. The Israelis, who perceived themselves as writing a new chapter in Jewish history, began to search for ways to rejoin the mainstream of Jewish history. The Holocaust survivors became the living bridge between the ruins of the Diaspora, its history and spiritual treasures, and the modern Israelis. It was the survivors who, in 1963, initiated the youth trips to Poland in search of the past.

Jews of the Diaspora also followed the trial with bated breath to discover the story of the Holocaust as it was revealed.

The trial's impact, however, transcended the borders of the State of Israel and the Jewish people. In Germany, the trials of Nazi criminals were sped up and, in 1963, the Auschwitz trials were held there.

The Western intellectual debate profited profoundly from the trial which introduced two ongoing controversies.

It was Yehiel Dinur (*K. Zetnick), the survivor of Auschwitz and well-known writer, who described in his testimony what he called "Planet Auschwitz." By this he excluded Auschwitz from ordinary human experience. This phrase significantly increased the danger of mystification of the Shoah. An important variation of this theme can be found in the debate about the uniqueness of the Shoah as opposed to its universalistic aspects.

In the wake of the *New Yorker* articles that later became the book *Eichmann in Jerusalem* by Hannah *Arendt, an intellectual and moral dialogue began about the essence of evil as expressed in Arendt's theory of "the banality of evil." In this she had meant to say that Eichmann did not differ from millions of people around the world. What was crucial, she claimed, is the essence of the Nazi evil, which does not lie in its sadistic manifestations but rather in its ability to undermine basic morality of humanity.

The controversy over "the banality of evil" became one of the cornerstones in the discussion of evil and the sovereignty of people in making their choices. In this connection, one must mention the title of *Righteous Among the Nations bestowed by Yad Vashem on gentiles who saved Jews during the Holocaust, a designation stemming from the need to illuminate the choice to do good.

Almost five decades after the trial, it can be said that for Diaspora Jews as well as for Israelis, the trial brought about a dramatic shift in the perception of national identity. Today it can be said that the heart of Jewish national identity is rooted in the Holocaust. Ironically, though, the result is the marginalization of the Jewish State in this identity.

BIBLIOGRAPHY: Z. Aharoni Zvi, *Operation Eichmann: The Truth about the Pursuit, Capture and Trial* (1997); H. Arendt, *Eichmann in Jerusalem: A Report on the Banality of Evil* (1963); D. Cesarani, *Eichmann, His Life and Crimes* (2004); G. Hausner, *The Jerusalem Trial*, 2 vols. (1980); H. Yablonka, *The State of Israel vs. Adolf Eichmann* (2004).

[Hanna Yablonka (2nd ed.)]

EICHTHAL, GUSTAVE D' (1804–1886), French publicist, Saint-Simonian, and Hellenist. He was the son of a family of Jewish bankers originally named Seligmann. His parents adopted Catholicism, and Eichthal himself was baptized in childhood. In 1822 Eichthal met Auguste Comte who introduced him to the doctrines of Saint-Simon. Subsequently, Eichthal became active in favor of civil rights for Jews and Negroes. In 1837 Eichthal went to Austria but was unsuccessful in enlisting official support for Jewish emancipation. He visited Algeria in 1838 and prepared a project for organizing the Jewish community there. After visiting Greece in 1832, Eichthal advocated the use of Greek as a universal language. Despite his Saint-Simonian and cosmopolitan outlook, Eichthal died a fervent Catholic. His works include *Les trois grands peuples mediterraneens et le Christianisme* (1864); *Melanges de critique biblique* (1886); and *La langue grecque* (1887).

BIBLIOGRAPHY: Loeb, in: REJ, 15 (1887), 153–5; Weill, *ibid.*, 31 (1895), 261–73.

EICHTHAL-SELIGMANN, family of German Court Jews and bankers. The family was descended from ARON SELIGMANN (d. 1744), a trader and banker of Leimen, near Heidelberg. His sons ARON and ELIAS served as Court Jews in the Palatinate and in Wuerttemberg; both died in the 1770s. Four sons of Elias – ARON ELIAS, MAYER, LIEBMANN, and LEMLE – followed their father's vocation in the Palatinate, Bavaria, Baden, and Saxonia. The eldest, Aron Elias (1747–1824), became successively court factor, court agent, court councilor, and court banker to the royal house of Bavaria. In 1814, as a reward for his services as an army supplier during the Napoleonic Wars, he was made Freiherr (Baron) von Eichthal, the changed name and status being accompanied by a change of religion. All five sons of the first Freiherr Elias von Eichthal became bankers: ARNOLD (1772–1838) in Augsburg; DAVID (1775–1850) – who was also a factory owner in Karlsruhe; LOUIS ARON (ADOLPH) (1780–1850) in Paris, where he cooperated with the *Péreire brothers and the *Rothschilds in early French railroad development; BERNHARD (1784–1839), who was a financial councilor; and SIMON (LEONHARD) (1787–1854), who was court banker in Munich. Simon initiated the first Bavarian banking legislation in 1834, was a main shareholder in and first president of the Bavarian Mortgage and Exchange Bank, and pioneered Bavaria's railroad development. Simon's son CARL (1813–1880) was one of the founders of the Bayrische Vereinsbank. He was also a member of the "Zollparlament," composed of South-German delegates and the North-German Reichstag. A street in Munich is named after the family to mark their achievements in many community affairs.

BIBLIOGRAPHY: H. Theiss, *Die Bedeutung der Hoffaktorenfamilie Seligmann-Eichthal* (1966); F. Steffan, *Bayerische Vereinsbank* (1969); H. Schnee, *Die Hoffinanz und der moderne Staat*, 4 (1963), 213–41; L. Huemmert, *Die finanziellen Beziehungen juedischer Bankiers und Heereslieferanten zum bayerischen Staat* (1927).

[Joachim O. Ronall]

EIDLITZ, LEOPOLD (1823–1908), U.S. architect. Eidlitz was probably the first Jewish architect to practice in the United States. Born in Prague, he immigrated to America in 1843, and went into partnership with the German architect Otto Blesch. He was a versatile designer, known for his banks, his work on the Capitol at Albany, New York, and churches, including the Christ Church Cathedral in St. Louis (1867). The synagogue Shaaray Tefila in New York was erected by Blesch and Eidlitz in 1847. It was built in the Romanesque style, and represented a break with the classical style of synagogue design previously current in America. In 1868 Eidlitz built Temple Emanu-El, on Fifth Avenue, New York. The basic plan was Gothic, as were some of the decorative details such as the rose window, but the Moorish element was given particular prominence. Eidlitz wrote *The Nature and Function of Art* (1881).

BIBLIOGRAPHY: Roth, Art, 726–8; R. Wischnitzer, *Synagogue Architecture in the United States* (1955), 43–44, 74–76.

EIDLITZ, (Abraham Moses) ZERAH BEN MEIR (fl. c. 1720), rabbi and preacher in Prague. An orphan, he was educated in the home of Jonathan *Eybeschuetz and was one of his outstanding pupils. He was a member of the *bet din* presided over by Ezekiel *Landau, and headed a yeshivah for over 30 years. At first wealthy, he supported numerous scholars. Later becoming impoverished, however, he would not accept support; it is related that a sum he had received from the head of the community was found sealed up after his death with instructions to return it. Fourteen of his sermons were printed under the title *Or la-Yesharim* (1785, reprinted 1942). His novellae on *Beẓah* were published in Jerusalem in 1960, and further manuscripts exist. Eidlitz appreciated the value of secular sciences, considering them necessary for both scholars and layman but inferior to the Torah. He therefore wrote a textbook on mathematics, in Hebrew and Yiddish on facing pages, entitled *Melekhet Maḥashevet*, of which only the first part appeared (Prague, 1785; the Hebrew section was reprinted in Zolkiew (Zholkva), 1837 and 1845, and an abridged Yiddish version in Warsaw, 1837). Some of his responsa were printed in works by his contemporaries. Jacob *Emden listed Eidlitz among those suspected of *Shabbateanism.

BIBLIOGRAPHY: Zinberg, *Sifrut*, 4 (1958), 173, 201; Klemperer, in: HJ, 13 (1951), 65f.; *Ḥiddushei R. Zeraḥ Eidlitz al Massekhet-Beẓah* (1960), 1–2, 7–20; I. Ta-Shema, in: *Ha-Sefer*, 9 (1961/62), 47; *Literaturblatt des Orients*, 9 (1848), 140, 524–7; Bers, in: *YIVO-Bleter*, 19 (January–June 1942), 69–79 (on *Melekhet Maḥashevet*).

EIFMAN, BORIS (1946–), Russian choreographer. He was born in Rubtzovsk, Siberia, where his parents were exiled before WW II and returned to Kishivev in the 1950s. At an early age Eifman showed a keen interest in ballet and dreamed of becoming a choreographer. He went to Leningrad where he was admitted to the ballet faculty of the conservatory. An autodidact, without taking any professional theater directing courses nor performing as a dancer, he became one of the world's prominent choreographers of his time. His first step as a choreographer was made in 1970 with his ballet *Gayane*, to the music of Kachaturian, performed in the Musorgsky Theater in Leningrad; this was a great achievement for a beginning choreographer. In 1997, he founded the theater of modern choreography named after him: the Boris Eifman Ballet Theater, which was extraordinary for Russia at that time. His theater's unusual repertoire included over 40 productions comprising tragedy, comedy, biblical story, fairy tales, and philosophical and psychological works. His theater became a laboratory where he experimented with different approaches and elaborated his own unique style, which combined modern art achievements and features of the classical school tradition. In Eifman's theater, the corps de ballet holds a place of pride and plays a role comparable to soloists. Turning to Russian literature he created in 1980 the ballet *The Idiot* based on Dostoyevsky's novel and set to the music of Tchaikovsky's 6th symphony. This performance played a very significant role in the cultural life of Russia. Another significant event was his ballet *Tchaikovsky* where Eifman used movement to penetrate the inner world of the musical genius. In 1990, he created *Don Quixote*, based on the original music of Mincus, and its original interpretations. The performance resulted in a political manifest, his creativity turned against totalitarian rule. In 1995 he returned to Dostoyevsky and created the ballet *The Karamozovs*, full of lust. A peak of his creativity is the ballet *Giselle*, based on the magical life the Russian dancer Olga Spessivtseva. Here, Eifman achieved the supreme blend of dance styles from classical to character dancing to expressionist movements. After his visit to Israel in 1997 he created a ballet *My Jerusalem*, based on Mozart's requiem. One of his most impressive works dedicated to the perverse Russian history is *Russian Hamlet* based on the sad life of Tzar Pavel I, the son of the great Yekaterina, set to the music of Beethoven and Mahler. Many of his productions were televised. Boris Eifman was a philosopher and a very sensitive person, concerned with contemporary problems. Among his numerous awards are the People's Artist Award (1995), National Prize of Russia (1995), Theater Prize (1996 and 1997), Golden Mask Prize (1996 and 1999), the prestigious prize of Peace and Consent (1998), and the chevalier of Arts in France (1999).

[Yossi Tavor (2nd ed.)]

EIG, ALEXANDER (1895–1938), botanist. Born in Minsk, Belorussia, Eig was taken to Palestine at the age of 14. During World War I he volunteered for the Jewish Legion, and after the war devoted himself to the study of botany, specializing in the vegetation of Palestine. He worked for some years as a traveling librarian, and on his travels acquired a rich and varied collection of plants and grasses which he classified. From 1926 to 1929, at the invitation of Otto Warburg, Eig headed the department of botany of the Agricultural Experimental Station, which was transferred in 1929 to the Hebrew University of Jerusalem. Eig began investigating the geobotany of Palestine, and in 1931 published the first table of phytogeographic regions and the first phytogeographical map of the country. During the same period he also compiled, with the help of his colleagues, the first Hebrew catalog of the flora of Palestine. From 1931 to 1933, he traveled in Syria, Turkey, and Iraq doing further research. In addition to his scientific work at the Hebrew University, he continued to interest himself in general botanical research and published descriptions of many new species of plants. In 1937 he was appointed lecturer in botany at the Hebrew University and devoted much of his time to the development of its botany department. His collection of plants served as a basis for the department's herbarium. His important works include *A Contribution to the Knowledge of the Flora of Palestine* (1926), *The Vegetation of Palestine* (1927), *Les elements et les groupes phytogeographiques dans la flore palestinienne* (2 vols., 1931–32), and *The Vegetation of the Light Soils Belt of the Coastal Plain of Palestine* (1939).

BIBLIOGRAPHY: M. Zohary, in: *Palestine Journal of Botany*, Jerusalem Series, 1 (1938), 114–24, includes list of his publications.

EILAT, port and resort town at the southern extremity of Israel on the Red Sea coast. Eilat is the modern spelling for the biblical *Elath, under which heading the town and its history are described.

EILBERG, AMY (1954–), first woman to be ordained as a Conservative rabbi and admitted into the Rabbinical Assembly, the international association of Conservative/Masorti rabbis. Eilberg was the daughter of a prominent Philadelphia family. Her father Joshua Eilberg served in Congress from 1967 to 1979. A product of the Conservative movement, she began her journey towards the rabbinate in the mid-late 1960s in the institutions of informal and youth education of the Conservative movement, United Synagogue Youth and Ramah Camps, where she discovered her passion for Jewish religious practice and her innate talent for Jewish leadership.

Eilberg's college and graduate school years coincided with the height of the Jewish feminist movement. She entered Brandeis University in fall 1972, the same year the Reform movement ordained its first female rabbi, Sally *Priesand. At Brandeis, Eilberg enjoyed the mentorship of long-time Hillel rabbi Al Axelrad, who encouraged several pioneering women to become rabbis. As a freshman undergraduate, Eilberg was a student leader in a successful effort to make services at the campus Jewish chapel egalitarian. During her undergraduate years, Eilberg decided to pursue a path to the Conservative rabbinate, even though the Jewish Theological Seminary was, at that time, a decade away from its decision to ordain women.

In 1976, Eilberg entered the Seminary as an MA student in Talmud. After completing the masters program, she continued her academic work as a doctoral student in Talmud, studying primarily at Neveh Schechter (the name by which the Conservative movement's seminary in Israel was then known) and also at the Jewish Theological Seminary in New York. As a Talmud student, Eilberg was taught and mentored by such luminaries as Shamma *Friedman, David *Weiss-Halivni, Seymour *Siegel, and Gordon Tucker as well as the Seminary's then chancellor Gerson *Cohen.

While Eilberg and other women hoping to enter the rabbinical school pursued graduate studies, the battles surrounding women's ordination grew more intense. Chancellor Gerson Cohen established a "Commission on the Ordination of Women," charged to take testimony from communities around the country and which encouraged Seminary faculty to write position papers on the matter. A faculty vote that was to be held on December 19, 1979, was tabled in the face of a sharply divided group. Disappointed supporters established a popular and effective grassroots organization called GROW (Group for the Rabbinic Ordination of Women) that held public rallies, gathered support, and utilized the press to draw attention to their concerns.

Despite these setbacks, Eilberg remained committed to pursuing the rabbinate. In 1982, she entered the Masters of Social Work program of Smith College in order to train in the pastoral aspects of rabbinic work. In October 1983, following heated debate at both the Jewish Theological Seminary and in the Rabbinical Assembly, a vote was taken by the Seminary faculty to admit women to the Rabbinical School beginning with the incoming class of the fall 1984. Nineteen women, including Amy Eilberg, were admitted to the Rabbinical School. Since Eilberg had already completed most of the Rabbinical School curriculum, she was able to graduate in the same academic year, becoming the first female Conservative rabbi on May 14, 1985.

Subsequent to her ordination, Eilberg was drawn to pastoral work and served as a Jewish hospital chaplain. She also served as assistant rabbi at Har Zion Temple near Philadelphia. While in the Philadelphia area, she headed the Yad L'Chaim Jewish Hospice Program of the Philadelphia Board of Rabbis. These experiences in pastoral care came to serve as the basis for Eilberg's groundbreaking work in the nascent Jewish Healing movement. In 1991, Eilberg, together with Rabbi Nancy Flam (Reform), co-founded the Bay Area Jewish Healing Center. At the height of the AIDS crisis in San Francisco, the Jewish Healing Center offered spiritual care to Jews living with illness, death, and loss, as well as support to health professionals and Bikkur Holim volunteers, and conducted educational programming to inform the Jewish community about Jewish teachings on the challenges of illness and loss. Since the founding of the Healing Center in 1991, and the creation of the National Center for Jewish Healing in 1995, dozens of Jewish communities have launched their own Jewish healing programs and countless synagogues have embraced healing as a primary focus of communal concern.

Eilberg remained at the Jewish Healing Center through 1996, when, once again in the forefront of Jewish religious innovation, she was drawn to the practice of "Spiritual Direction," a counseling practice dedicated to supporting individuals in recognizing the ways in which God is present in their everyday life experience. Eilberg was also the co-founder of Yedidya, the Center for Jewish Spiritual Direction, and continued to write and lecture widely.

[Julie Schonfeld (2nd ed.)]

EILON (Heb. אֵילוֹן), kibbutz in northern Israel, near the Lebanese border, affiliated with Kibbutz Arẓi Ha-Shomer ha-Ẓa'ir. It was founded in 1938 as a "tower and stockade" outpost by pioneers from Poland and joined by Israel-born youth. All its fields necessitated heavy reclamation work to clear the rocky ground. Fruit orchards and livestock were prominent farm branches. It also operated a metal and other factories. In 2002 the population of Eilon was 635. The name Eilon refers to the local vegetation of oak and pistachio trees ("*allon, elah*").

[Efraim Orni]

EILOT (Heb. אֵילוֹת), southernmost kibbutz in Israel, 2½ mi. (4 km.) north of Eilat, affiliated with Ha-Kibbutz ha-Me'uḥad, founded in 1963 by pioneers, the majority of whom were Israeli-born. From 1955, the members of the kibbutz maintained a camp on the Eilat shore, where its members tried fishing in the Red Sea, worked in various trades, and participated in laying the foundations of the new town of Eilat. The kibbutz planted date-palm orchards on the southernmost playa of the Aravah Valley and raises out-of-season vegetables, melons, and flowers. In 2002 its population was 286. The kibbutz continued to grow vegetables and date palms, as well as mangoes, cattle, and grapes. It had a packing house for agriculture products, a transformer factory, and a guesthouse.

About half its members worked outside the kibbutz. In 1994 the peace agreement between Israel and Jordan was signed in the kibbutz fields.

[Efraim Orni / Shaked Gilboa (2nd ed.)]

EILSHEMIUS, LOUIS M. (1864–1941), U.S. painter and watercolorist. Born in Arlington, New Jersey, to wealthy and cultured parents, Eilshemius studied at the Art Students League (1884–86) and at the Académie Julian in Paris (1886–87) in addition to taking private lessons from the landscape painter Robert L. Minor (1884–86). Influenced by painters of the Barbizon School, Eilshemius' late 19th-century landscapes are mostly traditional representations. *Delaware Water Gap Village* (c. 1886, Metropolitan Museum of Art) shows a panoramic landscape in soft focus with limited yet rich earthy hues. Recognition came early when Eilshemius had paintings accepted at the Pennsylvania Academy of Fine Arts and the National Academy of Design while in his early twenties. This initial success was followed by years of critical neglect and often derision.

Around 1910, Eilshemius' art changed drastically when he began making unsophisticated, frankly naïve images that obviously rejected his training. From this period until his death, Eilshemius most frequently painted landscapes inhabited by nude, anatomically distorted female figures, and sometimes mysterious subjects derived from his imagination. In *Three Bathers* (1918, Hirshhorn Museum and Sculpture Garden), three simplified nudes pose awkwardly in a stream against a shallow, nondescript background. From then, critics began to call his work primitive, a designation Eilshemius disdained as it indicated a lack of training rather than the artist's goal to render "a silent poem" on canvas. Marcel Duchamp discovered Eilshemius at the first annual exhibition of the Society of Independent Artists in 1917. Thereafter, Duchamp helped promote the artist; he facilitated a 1920 one-man show of Eilshemius' work at the Société Anonyme, then one of the most progressive venues in the United States, followed by a second exhibition in 1924. While some members of the avant-garde praised Eilshemius, most critics negatively reviewed his work. Frustrated with lack of recognition, in 1921 Eilshemius stopped painting.

Nonetheless, several shows ensued, and interest and praise of Eilshemius' idiosyncratic paintings increased substantially. In 1939 three leading art dealers in New York City held solo exhibitions of Eilshemius' work, and a nearly 300-page biography of the artist was published. Indeed, from 1932 until his death, over 25 one-man shows were organized in New York. Hit by a car in 1932, Eilshemius was permanently paralyzed. He spent the remainder of his days writing letters to newspapers criticizing the art establishment.

BIBLIOGRAPHY: W. Schack, *And He Sat among the Ashes* (1939); P.J. Karlstrom, *Louis Michel Eilshemius* (1978); idem, *Louis M. Eilshemius: Selections from the Hirshhorn Museum and Sculpture Garden* (1978).

[Samantha Baskind (2nd ed.)]

EINAEUGLER, KAROL (**Ḥayyim;** 1885–1952), lawyer and socialist leader, born in Lemberg. Member of a poor family, he became a socialist while still in secondary school. In 1905 he served as secretary of the founding committee of the *Jewish Social Democratic Party (ZPS; the Bund of Galicia), later becoming one of its major leaders. In independent Poland, Einaeugler won a reputation as a lawyer; he served as a member of the community council of Lvov and representative of the Bund for eastern Galicia. Between 1939 and 1948 he was interned at intervals in Soviet prisons, and returned to Poland seriously ill. He subsequently immigrated to the United States, where he maintained contact with Bundist groups there. Einaeugler wrote "Der Ershter Yidisher May Oyfruf in Galitsie" ("The First Jewish May Day Proclamation in Galicia," in: *Historishe Shriftn*, Yivo, 1939).

BIBLIOGRAPHY: LNYL, 1 (1956), 71–72; J.S. Hertz (ed.), *Doyres Bundistn*, 2 (1956), 187–90; idem (ed.), *Di Geshikhte fun Bund*, 3 (1966), index. **ADD. BIBLIOGRAPHY:** A. Reiss, *Bereshit Tenu'at ha-Po'alim be-Galicia* (1973), 210–11; J. Kisman, in: *Doyres Bundistn*, vol. 2 (1956), 187.

[Moshe Mishkinsky]

EINBECK (Heb. איינבכא, איימביק), town in Lower Saxony (formerly in Hanover), Germany. Several Jews were burned there at the stake about the year 1298. A Jewish street and synagogue in Einbeck are first mentioned in 1355. An "old" Jewish cemetery is referred to in 1454. The Jews were expelled from Einbeck around 1579 at the instance of a pastor, Johann Velius. They made several attempts to return, and are again mentioned in Einbeck in 1667. They were granted letters of protection in 1673 and 1678, and although these were opposed by the local inhabitants the duke refused to withdraw them. In 1718 the elector of Hanover, George I of England, restricted further Jewish settlement in Einbeck and few Jews were authorized to reside there in the 18th century. The number of Jewish families increased from nine in 1806–13 to 16 in 1816, and 139 persons in 1880 (2.04% of the total population). A new synagogue was dedicated in 1896. It was destroyed by the Nazis in 1938. Around 60 Jews remained in Einbeck in 1933. About half emigrated and most of the others were deported to the east. In 1968 there were two Jewish residents.

BIBLIOGRAPHY: W. Feise, *Zur Geschichte der Juden in Einbeck* (1901); Germ Jud, 2 (1968), 194–7; Salfeld, Martyrol, 163–4; MGADJ, 2 (1910), 78, 88, 91; FJW, 138. **ADD. BIBLIOGRAPHY:** F. Bertram, *Verloren, aber nicht vergessen. Juedisches Leben in Einbeck* (1998).

EIN FASHKHAH (**'Ein Feshkha, Enot Ẓukkim**), brackish springs on the western shore of the Dead Sea, just over 2 miles (3 km.) south of Kh. *Qumran. The surrounding swamp, covering 1 km. in the 1950s, was crossed by both natural and artificial channels. The Ein Fashkhah springs fed a basin of 180–240 sq. yds. (150–200 sq. m.), up to 4 ft. (120 cm.) deep, with a maximum temperature of 27 degrees Celsius. The oasis has in recent times supported tall reeds, tamarisks, and oleanders. Today a wild nature reserve, this oasis is in danger of withering away with the recession of the Dead Sea and the fresh water aquifers along its perimeter, a condition that has also inhibited seasonal sweetwater springs (e.g., Ein et-Tannur/Tanourih, Ein Ghazal) furnishing what was a relatively fertile area between Ein Fashkhah and the Wadi Qumran. The water of Ein Fashkhah, drunk by Bedouin, animals, and European visitors of the 19th–20th centuries, as well as being the former home of five species of small fish, in 2001 was tested as having a fairly high salinity of 4.5 to 23 mS/cm.

The region of Ein Fashkhah was visited by Felicien de Saulcy in 1851, who identified ancient ruins. These were excavated in 1956 and 1958 by Roland de *Vaux, following his excavations at Kh. Qumran, and again in 2001 by Yitzhar Hirschfeld.

It is now clear that the first structure at Ein Fashkhah was an Iron Age II fort, located south of the springs, associated with a string of forts (at Qumran, Kh. Abu Tabak, Kh. es-Samrah, and Kh. el-Maqari) which guarded the road from the Dead Sea to Jerusalem via the pass at the Wadi Qumran. A large isolated building (60 × 64 m.) dating to the Iron Age was discovered by de Vaux, close to the spring of Ein Ghazal.

North of the pool of Ein Fashkhah, a structure (18 × 24 m.) was constructed in the first century B.C.E. De Vaux believed there were traces from the period 100–31 B.C.E., but the entire building is now reassigned to the Herodian period (by both Magness and Hirschfeld), after 37 B.C.E. This structure comprised a courtyard with a rectangular building on three sides. The exterior walls are 1 m. thick. Later, two ground floor rooms were built in the west. These had an upper story, including a balcony. North of this structure was an installation most likely used as a date-wine press (so Netzer), though alternative proposals have identified it as being associated with tanning (de Vaux), fish farming (Zeuner), opobalsam processing (Hirschfeld), or indigo manufacture (Bélis). Water was fed to a reservoir next to this installation from a now extinct spring north of the site. In between the date-wine press and the reservoir channel was a paved area, as also to the southeast. South of the building was an animal pen (34 × 34 m.) with a stable running along the northern side.

A long wall running north from the settlement of Ein Fashkhah towards Qumran (identified east of the isolated Iron Age building by de Vaux) would suggest an estate enclosure, most likely for date-palm cultivation (cf. Pliny, *Natural History* 5:17, 4 (73)). The wall may have been begun as early as the Iron Age, though its appearance adjoining the Herodian settlement of Ein Fashkhah indicates it is contemporary here. The continuation of the wall into the area of the Qumran settlement appears to indicate a linked estate. Ein Fashkhah may have been occupied by the *Dead Sea sect, usually identified as *Essene, who could have employed the spring-pool as a natural *mikveh*. The pottery forms of Ein Fashkhah are virtually identical to forms found at Qumran during the same period of occupation, but large cylindrical jars have not been discovered here.

The Herodian complex at Ein Fashkhah was partly destroyed by fire after the Romans took control of this region in 68 C.E., though occupation continued after this on the north side of the main building. A coin of Domitian from Antioch (81–96 C.E.; locus 16) and a coin hoard of 17 coins of Agrippa II, dating from 78–95 C.E., were found, giving the *terminus post quem* for the abandonment of the settlement as 95 C.E. A single coin indicates that Bar Kokhba rebels may have camped here in 132–5 C.E.

In the Byzantine period there was occupation in the northeast corner of the stable (locus 20), probably for just one anchorite. This may be evidenced in the *Pratum Spirituale* of John Moschus (158), which testifies to a vegetable garden for the monastery of Marda (Kh. Mird), 5.5 miles (9 km.) away.

BIBLIOGRAPHY: M. Bélis, "The Workshops at ʿEin Fashkhah: A New Hypothesis," in: J.-B. Humbert, J. Zangenburg, and K. Galor (eds.), *The Site of the Dead Sea Scrolls: Archaeological Interpretations and Debates* (2005); F.M. Cross, "El-Buqeiʿa," in: NAEHL, 1, 267–29; Y. Hirschfeld, "Excavations at ʿEin Fashkhah, 2001: Final Report," in: IEJ, 54 (2004), 35–54; idem, *Qumran in Context: Reassessing the Archaeological Evidence* (2004); H. Hötzl, W. Ali, and M. Rother, "ʿEin Fashkhah Springs as a Potential for Fresh Water Extraction, Dead Sea Area," in: *Le premier colloque national de hydrogéologie et environment* (Fes, Morocco), 62 (abstract); J. Magness, *The Archaeology of Qumran and the Dead Sea Scrolls* (2002); E. Netzer, "Did Any Perfume Industry Exist at ʿEin Fashkhah?" in: IEJ, 55 (2005), 97–100; H. Steinitz, "The Fishes of Ein Fashkhah, Palestine," in: *Nature* (167/4248; March 31, 1951), 531–32; E. Mazor and M. Molcho, "Geochemical Studies on the Feshcha Springs, Dead Sea Basin," in: *Journal of Hydrology*, 15 (1972), 37–47; R. de Vaux, *Archaeology and the Dead Sea Scrolls* (The Schweich Lectures of the British Academy, 1959 (1973)); idem, "Fouilles de Khirbet Qumrân," in: Ribbentrop, 63 (1956), 532–77; F.E. Zeuner, "Notes on Qumran," in: PEQ, 92 (1960), 27–36; "Fouilles de Fashkhah," in: Ribbentrop, 66 (1959), 225–55.

[Joan E. Taylor (2nd ed.)]

EINFELD, SYDNEY (1909–1995), Australian politician and communal leader. Born in Sydney, the son of a minister at Sydney's Great Synagogue, Syd Einfeld became one of the leading Jewish politicians and communal leaders in modern Australia. He served as a Labour member in Australia's federal House of Representatives in 1961–63 and as a member of the New South Wales parliament in 1965–81. From 1975 to 1983 he was deputy leader of the state's branch of the Australian Labour Party, and was subsequently a popular minister for consumer affairs when Labour held office. Einfeld was probably the most important communal leader from New South Wales of his time, and served as president of the Executive Council of Australian Jewry, the community's national body, in 1952–54, 1956–58, 1960–62, and 1964–66. Einfeld was also president of the Australian Jewish Welfare Society, the main immigrants' aid body, and is regarded as very influential in liberalizing Australian policy towards Jewish refugees.

BIBLIOGRAPHY: W.D. Rubinstein, Australia II, index.

[William D. Rubinstein (2nd ed.)]

EIN GEV (Heb. עֵין גֵּב), kibbutz on the east shore of Lake Kinneret in Israel, situated on the narrow lowland strip between the lake and the rim of the Golan Plateau below Mt. *Susita.

It was founded in 1937 as a "*tower and stockade" settlement by a group of pioneers from Germany, Austria, and the Baltic countries who had previously worked at *Kinneret. The kibbutz, which came under frequent attack during the Arab riots before World War II, was particularly vulnerable in its initial years when it was accessible only by boat from Tiberias. In the *War of Independence (1948), Ein Gev was again isolated and suffered a severe Syrian air and artillery attack, which it repulsed. After the armistice it remained exposed to the Syrian positions on the Golan rim and on land north of it, which the Syrians held until the *Six-Day War of 1967. Early in its history the kibbutz developed fishing in Lake Kinneret as well as tourism. The kibbutz operates a holiday resort, fish restaurant, and sailing boats. The Ein Gev Music Festival is held annually during Passover, and a 2,500-seat concert hall was erected. Farming is intensive, including bananas, dairy, and ostrich breeding. Near the kibbutz is the archaeological site of Susita. In 2002 the population of Ein Gev was 521. The name ("Waterhole Spring") is Hebraized from the Arabic designation of the site, "Nuqayb."

WEBSITES: www.eingev.org.il; www.eingev.co.il/main.html.

[Efraim Orni / Shaked Gilboa (2nd ed.)]

EIN HA-EMEK (Heb. עֵין הָעֵמֶק; "Spring of the Valley"), rural community in northern Israel, in the Manasseh Hills of Samaria. Ein ha-Emek began as a moshav affiliated with Tenu'at ha-Moshavim. It was founded in 1944 by Jewish farmers from Kurdistan who had been stonemasons in Jerusalem before settling the moshav. Its hill-type farming included in 1969 mainly deciduous fruit orchards and vineyards. Farming was phased out and over the years the settlers took up other occupations. In the 1980s the moshav became an ordinary rural community and began to undergo expansion, its population increasing from 312 in 1969 to 440 in the mid-1990s and 616 in 2002.

WEBSITE: www.megido.org.il/arad/news/megidon/ein_haemek60.htm.

[Efraim Orni / Shaked Gilboa (2nd ed.)]

EIN HA-ḤORESH (Heb. עֵין הַחוֹרֵשׁ; "Plowman's Spring"), kibbutz in central Israel, in the Ḥefer Plain, affiliated with Kibbutz Arẓi ha-Shomer ha-Ẓa'ir. It was founded on April 10, 1932, by pioneers from Eastern Europe who reclaimed the land. In 1968 it had 570 inhabitants; in 2002, 715. Ein ha-Ḥoresh engages in intensive farming, in citrus and avocado plantations, field crops, and milch cattle. It also ran a factory for industrial packaging materials. A culture center put on a variety of performances.

[Efraim Orni]

EIN HA-MIFRAẒ (Heb. עֵין הַמִּפְרָץ; "Spring in the Bay"), kibbutz in Israel, south of Acre, affiliated with Kibbutz Arẓi ha-Shomer ha-Ẓa'ir. It was founded in 1938 by pioneers from Eastern Europe. In addition to defending themselves against Arab attacks from Acre during the riots that lasted until 1939, the settlers had to drain the salt swamps near the mouth of the Na'aman River. Its economy was based on intensive farming (field crops, dairy cattle, fishery, and orchards) and two industrial enterprises (plastic products and cardboard packing material). The kibbutz was also a partner in the nearby power station. In 1968 the kibbutz had 580 inhabitants. In the mid-1990s the population increased to 760, but then dropped to 674 in 2002.

[Efraim Orni]

EIN HA-NAZIV (Heb. עֵין הַנְּצִיב), kibbutz in Israel, in the Beth Shean Valley, affiliated with Ha-Kibbutz ha-Dati, founded in 1946 by pioneers from Germany. Its economy was based on intensive farming and included dates, fishery, poultry, and dairy cattle. The kibbutz also operated a polyethylene foam factory and architectural firm. In 1969, it had 347 inhabitants; in 2002, 537. It is named after R. Naphtali Ẓevi Judah *Berlin, head of the Volozhin yeshivah and one of the first Ḥovevei Zion.

WEBSITE: www.hanatziv.org.il.

[Efraim Orni]

EIN HA-SHELOSHAH (Heb. עֵין הַשְּׁלֹשָׁה), kibbutz in southern Israel, in the northwestern Negev, on the border of the *Gaza Strip, affiliated with Ha-No'ar ha-Ẓiyyoni. Ein ha-Sheloshah was founded in 1949 by former members of *Loḥamei Ḥerut Israel and originally called Neveh Ya'ir, after the underground name of their commander Avraham *Stern. They were succeeded one year later by a group of settlers from Argentina, Uruguay, and Morocco. Farm branches included citrus orchards and irrigated field crops. In 2002 the population of Ein ha-Sheloshah was 340. The settlement's name ("Spring of the Three") commemorates three South American members of the pioneer group who fell in Israel's War of Independence.

[Efraim Orni]

EIN HA-SHOFET (Heb. עֵין הַשּׁוֹפֵט), kibbutz in Israel, in the Manasseh Hills, affiliated with Kibbutz Arẓi ha-Shomer ha-Za'ir. Ein ha-Shofet was founded in 1937 by the first immigrants of Ha-Shomer ha-Ẓa'ir from the United States and by a group from Poland. A "tower and stockade" settlement, the kibbutz was set up at a site that until then had been the headquarters for Arab bands attacking Jewish villages. It became part of the "settlement bridge" connecting the Sharon and the Jezreel Valley, the two principal Jewish regions at the time. Its economy was based on intensive farming (avocado plantations, field crops, and cattle) as well as factories manufacturing screws, electrical appliances, and automotive products. In 1968 Ein ha-Shofet had 590 inhabitants; in 2002, 715. The nearby Manasseh Forest is the largest in the country. The name Ein ha-Shofet ("The Judge's Spring") commemorates the American Zionist leader, Justice Louis *Brandeis.

[Efraim Orni]

EIN HOD (Heb. עֵין הוֹד), artists' village in northern Israel, on Mt. Carmel E. of Athlit, founded on the initiative of the painter Marcel *Janco, in 1953, on the picturesque site of an abandoned

Arab village. Artists inhabit the village either permanently or seasonally. Ein Hod has workshops for ceramics, lithography, weaving, and mosaics; art galleries; and an open-air amphitheater. Courses and seminars are held in painting, sculpture, lithography, and weaving. Antiquities of the Roman and Byzantine periods have been found, and there are crusader structures. During Napoleon's campaign (1799), the village served as a vacation site for French soldiers. In the mid-1990s Ein Hod's population was 291; by 2002 it had increased to 437. The village's name, which means literally "Spring of Splendor," was adapted from the name of the abandoned Arab village ʿAyn al-Ḥawḍ ("The Garden Spring").

WEBSITE: www.ein-hod.Israel.net.

[Efraim Orni /Shaked Gilboa (2nd ed.)]

EINHORN, DAVID (1809–1879), Reform rabbi and theologian. Einhorn was born in Dispeck, Bavaria, and received his rabbinical training at Furth, near his birthplace. He studied philosophy at Erlangen, Wurzburg, and Munich. His thinking was influenced by the ideas of F.W. Schelling. In 1838 he was elected rabbi of the community at Wellhausen near Uffenheim, but the Bavarian government would not confirm his appointment on account of his liberal views. Four years later he became *Landesrabbiner* of Birkenfeld in the Grand Duchy of Oldenberg. At the Frankfurt Rabbinical Conference of 1845, he took a decided view in favor of introducing the vernacular into the service and of eliminating prayers for the restoration of sacrifices and a Jewish state. Three years earlier, in coming to the defense of the position taken up by Abraham *Geiger in his controversy with Solomon Titkin, he had rejected the divine authority of the Talmud and upheld the right to diverge from ceremonial laws.

In 1847 Einhorn succeeded Samuel *Holdheim as chief rabbi of Mecklenburg-Schwerin. There he was involved in controversy with Franz *Delitzsch, the Christian Hebraist, for having pronounced a blessing in the synagogue over an uncircumcised child. Einhorn's radical religious standpoint jeopardized his position. In January 1852 he became rabbi of the Reform congregation of Budapest, but after two months the government closed the temple. While living in Budapest, Einhorn began his work *Das Prinzip des Mosaismus*, but completed only one volume (1854).

Denied any opportunity in Europe, Einhorn became rabbi of the Har Sinai Congregation of Baltimore (1855). His arrival in the United States coincided with the Cleveland Rabbinical Conference, which, under the leadership of Isaac Mayer *Wise, adopted a platform designed to permit a broadly based union among the various tendencies in American Judaism. Einhorn regarded this platform as treachery to the cause of Reform and denounced it violently. This marked the beginning of a bitter feud between Einhorn, the uncompromising Reformer, and I.M. Wise, who was ready to moderate his Reform in the interests of unity. Einhorn expounded his ideas in his monthly magazine *Sinai* (Ger., 7 vols., 1856–62) and gave them expression in his prayer book *Olat Tamid* (1856), which was no mere shortening of the traditional liturgy, but a new work written mainly in German.

Einhorn's sojourn in Baltimore was cut short in 1861, when his unsparing denunciation of slavery placed him in danger from the mob. He became rabbi of Congregation Keneseth Israel, Philadelphia, and in 1866 moved to New York as rabbi of Congregation Adath Israel, which was later known as Temple Beth El. His was the dominant personality at the Philadelphia Rabbinical Conference which met in 1869 and adopted a thoroughgoing Reform platform.

Einhorn's farewell sermon, delivered after a quarter of a century in America, contained a plea for the cultivation of German as the vehicle for the ideas of Reform Judaism. If the dogmatic Reform upon which he insisted dominated neither the Union of American Hebrew Congregations nor Hebrew Union College at their inception, his spirit came to influence them later. Kaufman *Kohler, his son-in-law and disciple, formulated the Pittsburgh Platform of 1885, which was the basis of American Reform for a generation, and later became president of Hebrew Union College; Einhorn's *Olat Tamid* served as the model for the *Union Prayer Book*.

A letter which Einhorn wrote in 1844 summed up his theological system: "In all its stages, Judaism shows its capacity for continuous development both as to its form and its spirit, insofar as the latter became ever clearer and purer in the human consciousness; and no Israelite who knows his religion will deny it the power of perfectibility. Its essence, which is truth uniting all men, was from the beginning intended to overcome the exclusiveness attached to the form, which is national; but insofar as the latter served as an armor of protection and as the priestly garb of Israel among the nations, it cannot with impunity be cast off until the former in its entire inner force and its all-encompassing extent will have penetrated the whole human family, and Israel (Mosaism) will have fulfilled its priestly mission at the arrival of the Messianic era." Little has been published concerning the personality of David Einhorn or analyzing his thought.

BIBLIOGRAPHY: K. Kohler (ed.), *David Einhorn, Memorial Volume* (1911) (contains a selection of his sermons); idem, in: CCARY, 19 (1909), 215–70.

[Sefton D. Temkin]

EINHORN, DAVID (1886–1973), Yiddish poet and publicist. Born in Korelichi (Belorussia), his earliest poems were in Hebrew, but under the influence of socialist ideas he turned to Yiddish and made his debut in Bundist publications. His first volumes of verse, *Shtile Gezangen* ("Quiet Chants," 1909) and *Mayne Lider* ("My Poems," 1912), acclaimed by leading critics, expressed the tension between the declining traditional order and the heralded new society. In 1910 Einhorn helped organize the Boris Kletskin press, and was also the secretary of S.Y. *Abramovitsh. In 1912, after six months in prison for suspected revolutionary activities, Einhorn left Russia, moving to Paris and then in 1913 to Berne, Switzerland. There he studied at the university, wrote for *Di Yidishe Velt* and the children's periodical *Grininke Beymelekh*, and edited *Di Fraye Shtime* (1916–17). In 1917 his book, *Tsu a Yidishe Tokhter* (a present to his wife), appeared. He lived briefly in Warsaw, where he wrote for the Bundist *Lebns-Fragn*. In 1920 he moved to Berlin, and later, warning of the coming destruction of Europe, to Paris. He was among the first contributors to the *Algemayne Entsiklopedye*. In 1940 Einhorn immigrated to the U.S. and became a regular correspondent for the New York *Forverts*, publishing a weekly column (1956) "Tsvishn Tsvey Veltn" ("Between Two Worlds"), memoirs of the Yiddish literary world. Einhorn was active as a translator and editor, proclaimed a classical, coherent, and grammatically principled style (his poetry was criticized, especially by H. *Leivick, for its stylistic simplicity), and preferred traditional Jewish motifs, his work becoming progressively more national in character. He was quite popular among Hebrew authors such as *Agnon and *Brenner.

BIBLIOGRAPHY: Rejzen, Leksikon, 1 (1928), 81–86; LNYL, 1 (1956), 73–6. **ADD. BIBLIOGRAPHY:** Sh. Kuperman, in: *Khulyot*, 8 (2004), 177–88.

[Ruth Wisse / Shifra Kuperman (2nd ed.)]

EINHORN, IGNAZ (Eduard Horn; 1825–1875), Reform rabbi and leader in Hungary, economist, and politician. Einhorn, who was born in Nove Mesto, organized the Society for the Reform of Judaism in Pest in 1847. Later, as rabbi of the society's first Reform temple, he introduced several radical changes (such as observing the Sabbath on Sunday). A year later he helped to found the Society for the Propagation of Hungarian Language and Culture, and edited the first Jewish-Hungarian Yearbook. In 1848 he published his *Zur Judenfrage in Ungarn*, and established the weekly *Der Ungarische Israelit*. During the Hungarian national uprising in that year he volunteered for the national army as chaplain. After the revolt was suppressed, he fled to Leipzig, Germany, changing his name to Eduard Horn. On the publication of his treatise on *Ludwig Kossuth* (1851), the Hungarian government requested his extradition. He took refuge in Brussels, where he studied philosophy and economics, and later (1856) moved to Paris. He published several important works on economics and was made an honorary member of scientific societies in France and Belgium. In 1867 he received the Grand Prix of the French Academy for his *L'economie politique avant les physiocrates*. After the Austro-Hungarian compromise in 1867 Einhorn returned to his native country. He was elected to parliament and in 1869 was appointed deputy undersecretary of commerce, the first Jew to occupy such a high post there. During his government service he was associated with drafting the laws granting the Jews equal rights. In the conflict between Orthodox and Reform Judaism he then supported the former. By government decree, a memorial tablet was affixed to the house where he was born; a street in Budapest was named after him.

BIBLIOGRAPHY: J.J. (L.) Greenwald (Grunwald), *Korot ha-Torah ve-ha-Emunah be-Ungarya* (1921), 65–66; idem, *Li-Felagot Yisrael be-Ungarya* (1929).

[Aharon Fuerst]

EINHORN, MAX (1862–1953), U.S. internist and gastroenterologist. Born in Grodno, Russia, he immigrated to the U.S. where he became professor of medicine at the College of Physicians and Surgeons at Columbia University from 1896 to 1940. He was visiting physician at New York's Lenox Hill Hospital and consulting physician to several other hospitals. His major work was on gastric, digestive, and intestinal disorders.

EINHORN, MOSES (1896–1966), U.S. physician and editor. Born in Volkovysk, Russia, he was brought to Ereẓ Israel in 1908. In 1916 he was forced to emigrate by the Turkish authorities and after short sojourns in Egypt and the Balkans, he went to the U.S. Einhorn made several contributions to gastroenterology and headed the gastroenterological department of the Bronx Hospital in New York City. He is best known for his promotion of the use of Hebrew medical terminology. In 1926, together with Asher Goldstein, he founded the Hebrew medical journal *Harofe ha-Ivri* which appeared twice a year in New York until 1965. This journal was dedicated to the study of Hebrew medicine and Hebrew medical terminology. Einhorn contributed to the founding of various medical libraries in Israel, and in 1964 established a special fund in his name for the granting of prizes in Hebrew medical literature by the Tel Aviv municipality.

BIBLIOGRAPHY: Goldstein and Muntner, in: *Korot*, 3 (May 1966), 635–7.

[Eisig Silberschlag]

EIN IRON (Heb. עֵין עִירוֹן), moshav in central Israel, in the northeastern Sharon, affiliated with Tenu'at ha-Moshavim. It was founded in 1934 by settlers from Russia and Poland, who were later joined by a few families from Germany. The principal farm branches were citrus orchards and milch cattle. In 1969, its population was 197, increasing to 255 in the mid-1990s, and 384 in 2002.

[Efraim Orni]

EIN KE-ELOHENU (Heb. אֵין כֵּאלֹהֵינוּ; "There is none like our God"), hymn recited at the end of the Additional Service on Sabbaths and holidays in the Ashkenazi ritual and in the Sephardi ritual on weekdays after the Morning Service. This hymn is already mentioned in the prayer books of *Amram Gaon (ninth century), *Maimonides (12th century), and *Rashi (13th century), where, however, the order of its stanzas differs from their present sequence. Now the initial letters of the first three verses form the word "*Amen*" and the other two verses start with "*Barukh*" and "*Attah*," forming the phrase "*Amen Barukh Attah*" ("Amen, Blessed be Thou"). It is possible that originally there was a final verse starting with *Adonai*. Rashi states that *Ein ke-Elohenu* is recited, in the Ashkenazi ritual, on Sabbaths and holidays only, because on those days the *Amidah* consists of seven benedictions instead of the 19 on weekdays and through this hymn additional praises are recited, making up for those missing (cf. *Maḥzor Vitry*, no. 134; Zedekiah

b. Abraham ha-Rofe, *Shibbolei ha-Leket* (1966), 131f.). In the *Genizah* fragments, where the stanzas are in a different order from the present text, the hymn is followed immediately by a quotation from Psalms 90:1, which suggests that it may have been recited at the termination of the Sabbath.

BIBLIOGRAPHY: Davidson, Oẓar, 1 (1929), 142; Eisenstein, Dinim, 14f.; Abrahams, Companion, clxvi–clxvii; Sendrey, Music, 2306. 2587–92.

[Meir Ydit]

EIN KEREM (Heb. עֵין כֶּרֶם), village on the western edge of Jerusalem, identified with biblical *Beth-Cherem; since 1949 part of the Jerusalem municipality. Early Christian tradition dating back to the sixth century identifies Ein Kerem as the birthplace of *John the Baptist in the house of Zacharias (*domum Zachariae*, Luke 1:40) and with the location of the visit paid to Elizabeth, John's mother, by her relative (συγγενίς) Mary, Jesus' mother (Luke 1:39–80). Theodosius (c. 530 C.E.) referred to the "dwelling place of Saint Elizabeth" about 5 miles from Jerusalem, and Procopius of Caesarea (550–58 C.E.) speaks of a well situated at the "Monastery of Holy Zacharias [father of John the Baptist]." In the seventh century, Epiphanius referred to Ein Kerem (garbled to "Carmel") as the family home of the forerunner (i.e., John the Baptist). References to "Encharim" also exist in the Georgian Lectionary (eighth century), in the Commemoratorium de Casis Dei (c. 808 C.E.), and in a work by Eutychius (tenth century). There are two churches associated with John the Baptist at Ein Kerem today: the Church of the Nativity of John on the northern hill and the Church of the Visitation on the southern hill. Outside the village is the Monastery of John in the Wilderness (Ein el-Habis). Numerous medieval and later travelers refer to Ein Kerem and its churches. The Franciscans established their first church in 1621, and after 1674 the Franciscan presence in the village became permanent.

The Franciscans remained the only Christians in Ein Kerem until the middle of the 19th century. In 1860 the Sisters of Our Lady of Zion settled in the village, followed by the nuns of the Russian Orthodox Church (1871), the White Fathers (1882), the Greek Orthodox Church (1894), and the Rosary Sisters (1911). A mosque (maqam 'umair) and minaret was built over the spring which gave the village its name. During the Israel War of Independence (1948) the inhabitants of the village – until then all Moslem Arabs – fled and were replaced by new immigrants mostly from Oriental countries. In 1949 Raḥel Yannait *Ben-Zvi brought the training school (after 1952 the Ein Kerem Agricultural School), of which she was director, from Talpiyyot in Jerusalem to Ein Kerem. In the 1950s and 1960s many Israeli artists (such as Yitzhak Greenfield) and academics settled in the village. Many of its residents offer guest accommodations to vacationers attracted by the rural setting.

ADD. BIBLIOGRAPHY: P.F. Cangioli, *Il Santuario e Il Convento di S. Giovanni in 'Ain-Karem* (1947); M.T. Petrozzi, *Ain Karim* (1971); S. Gibson, *The Cave of John the Baptist* (2004), 26–43; M. Amirav, D. Harel, and B. Binnun, *Ein-Kerem: Voyage to the Enchanted Village* (2004).

[Walter Zanger / Shimon Gibson (2nd ed.)]

EIN SHEMER (Heb. עֵין שֶׁמֶר), kibbutz in central Israel, near the entrance to the Iron Valley. Affiliated with Kibbutz Arẓi ha-Shomer ha-Ẓa'ir, the site served as a camp for the *Ha-Shomer association before World War I. After 1918 a laborers' camp was opened there, which was taken over by a group of *Ha-Shomer ha-Ẓa'ir members in 1924. The permanent settlement was established in 1927. The kibbutz has intensive farming, with field crops, avocado plantations, poultry, and dairy cattle, and maintained several manufacturing enterprises (food, plastics, and rubber). The kibbutz operates the Old Courtyard on its premises, a theme museum showing life in the traditional kibbutz. In 1968 Ein Shemer had 545 inhabitants, increasing to 605 in the mid-1990s and 758 in 2002. The name refers to Ha-Shomer and to Ha-Shomer ha-Ẓa'ir as well as to the nearby Samaria (Shomron) Hill.

WEBSITE: www.courtyard.co.il.

[Efraim Orni / Shaked Gilboa (2nd ed.)]

EIN-SOF (Heb. אֵין סוֹף; "The Infinite," lit. that which is boundless), name given in Kabbalah to God transcendent, in His pure essence: God in Himself, apart from His relationship to the created world. Since every name which was given to God referred to one of the characteristics or attributes by which He revealed Himself to His creatures, or which they ascribed to Him, there is no name or epithet for God from the point of view of His own being. Consequently, when the kabbalists wanted to be precise in their language they abstained from using names like *Elohim*, the Tetragrammaton, "the Holy One, blessed be He," and others. These names are all found either in the Written or the Oral Law. The Torah, however, refers only to God's manifestations and not to God's own being which is above and beyond His relationship to the created world. Therefore, neither in the Bible, nor in rabbinic tradition was there a term which could fulfill the need of the kabbalists in their speculations on the nature of God. "Know that *Ein-Sof* is not alluded to either in the Pentateuch, the Prophets, or the Hagiographa, nor in the writings of the rabbis. But the mystics had a vague tradition about it" (*Sefer Ma'arekhet ha-Elohut*). The term *Ein-Sof* is found in kabbalistic literature after 1200. However, it was apparently not coined as a technical term since this was not the style in which, in the medieval period, negative terms were coined. Most probably its source is to be found in those phrases stressing God's sublimity which is infinite (*ad le-ein sof*), or which emphasize the characteristics of the (Divine) thought, comprehension of which "has no end" (*ad le-ein sof*). The use of this epithet in early kabbalistic literature proved without doubt that the term grew out of this kind of expression. It originated, apparently, in the circle of *Isaac the Blind, and his disciples. In the view of some kabbalists, the name *Ein-Sof* was likewise applicable to the first product of emanation, the *Sefirah Keter,* because of its completely concealed nature, and this double use of the word gave rise in kabbalistic literature to considerable confusion. There is no doubt that from the beginning the intention was to use the name in order to distinguish the absolute from the *Sefirot* which emanated from Him. The choice of this particular name may be explained by the emphasis placed on the infinity of God in the books of *Saadiah Gaon which had a great influence on the circle of the Provençal kabbalists. The term also shows that the anthropomorphic language in which the kabbalists spoke of the living God of faith and revelation does not represent the totality of their theosophical theological approach. At first there was no definite article used in conjunction with *Ein-Sof*, and it was treated as a proper name, but after 1300 there were kabbalists who spoke of "the *Ein-Sof*." At first, the term was used only rarely (even in the principal part of the *Zohar its occurrence is very rare), but from about 1300 its use became habitual, and later Kabbalah even speaks of several "kinds of *Ein-Sof*," e.g., the enveloping *Ein-Sof*, the enveloped *Ein-Sof*, the upper *Ein-Sof*.

[Gershom Scholem]

Another possible source for the kabbalistic theory of *Ein-Sof* is the term *aperantos*, which occurs in a Gnostic source of late antiquity in a book in which interpretations of biblical verses and themes are found. According to some kabbalists, most eminently R. *David ben Judah he-Ḥasid, within *Ein-Sof* there are ten supernal *Sefirot*, called *Ẓaḥẓaḥot*, which are described by resorting to many classical anthropomorphic terms. This view of the *Ein-Sof* reverberated in Safedian Kabbalah.

[Moshe Idel (2nd ed.)]

BIBLIOGRAPHY: G. Scholem, *Ursprung und Anfaenge der Kabbala* (1962), 233–8. **ADD. BIBLIOGRAPHY:** M. Idel, "The Image of Man above the Sefirot," in: *Daat*, 4 (1980), 41–55 (Heb.); idem, "*Al Torat ha-Elohut be-Reshit ha-Kabbalah*," in: *Shefah Tal: Studies in Jewish Thought and Culture Presented to Berakhah Sack* (2004), 131–48.

EINSTEIN, ALBERT (1879–1955), physicist, discoverer of the theory of relativity, and Nobel Prize winner. Born in the German town of Ulm, son of the proprietor of a small electrochemical business, Einstein spent his early youth in Munich. He detested the military discipline of the German schools and joined his parents, leaving school after they moved to Italy. His interest in mathematics and physics started at an early age, and he avidly read books on mathematics. Unable to obtain an instructorship at the Zurich Polytechnic Institute, from which he graduated at the age of 21, he took a post at the patent office in Berne, having become in the meantime a Swiss citizen. This position left him ample time to carry on his own research. In 1905 he published three brilliant scientific papers, one dealing with the "Brownian motion," the second one with the "photoelectric effect," and the third on the "Special theory of relativity." It was the last one which was to bring his name before the public. He demonstrated that motion is relative and that physical laws must be the same for all observers moving relative to each other, as well as his famous $E = mc^2$ equation showing that mass is equivalent to energy. Ironically, however, when he received the Nobel Prize for physics in 1921 it was for his explanation of the photoelectric effect. Immediately after the publication of that paper Einstein was offered a professorship at the University of Zurich which he at first refused, having become fond of his job at the patent office. In 1910 he joined the German University in Prague, where he held the position of professor ordinarius in physics, the highest academic rank. Despite his absorption in his scholarly pursuits he could not fail to notice the political strife and quarrels between the rival feelings of nationalism, and felt great sympathy for the Czechs and their aspirations. In 1912 Einstein returned to Switzerland, where he taught at the Polytechnic, the same place to which he had come as a poor student in 1896. His friend and colleague, Max Planck, succeeded in obtaining for him a professorship at the Prussian Academy of Science in Berlin, a research institute where Einstein could devote all his time to research. In 1916, amid a world in the throes of World War I, Einstein made another fundamental contribution to science contained in *Die Grundlagen der allgemeinen Relativitaetstheorie (Relativity, the Special and the General Theory, a Popular Exposition*, 1920). In this theory he generalized the principle of relativity to all motion, uniform or not. The presence of large masses produces a gravitational field, which will result in a "warping" of the underlying (four-dimensional) space. That field will act on objects, such as planets or light rays, which will be deflected from their paths. His prediction of the deflection of starlight by the gravitational field of the sun was borne out by the expedition at the time of a solar eclipse in 1919. When the results of the solar eclipse observations became known to the general public, Einstein's name became a household word. He was offered, but refused, great sums of money for articles, pictures, and advertisements as his fame mounted. During the early years after World War I he worked for the League of Nations Intellectual Cooperation Organization and became a familiar figure on public platforms speaking on social problems as well as his Theory of Relativity. He became more and more disappointed by the misuse of sciences in the hands of man. "In the hands of our generation these hard-won achievements are like a razor wielded by a child of three. The possession of marvelous means of production has brought care and hunger instead of freedom." In 1932, Einstein accepted an invitation to spend the winter term at the California Institute of Technology. By January 1933, Hitler had come to power. Einstein promptly resigned from his position at the Royal Prussian Academy of Sciences and never returned to Germany. Many positions were offered him but he finally accepted a professorship at the Institute for Advanced Studies in Princeton, N.J., and later became an American citizen. During World War II secret news reached the U.S. physicists that the German uranium project was progressing. Einstein, when approached by his friend *Szilard, signed a letter to President Roosevelt pointing out the feasibility of atomic energy. It was that letter which sparked the Manhattan Project and future developments of atomic energy. However, Einstein was opposed to the use of the atomic bomb, as were many other scientists, and wrote another letter which, however, arrived only after Roosevelt's death. In spite of his dislike for engaging in public affairs Einstein became chairman of the Emergency Committee of Atomic Scientists and urged the outlawing of the atomic and hydrogen bombs. During the McCarthy period Einstein advised scientists to refuse to testify before the Congressional Committee on Un-American Affairs. Despite his advanced age he continued to work on the "Unified Field Theory" which attempted as a first step to unify gravitation and electromagnetism into one theory. It is impossible to assess whether he would have succeeded in this momentous task, since he died before its completion.

Einstein was not only one of the greatest scientists of all time but also a generous person who took time and effort to help others and spoke out openly for his beliefs and principles. He never forgot that he had been a refugee himself and lent a helping hand to the many who asked for his intervention. The man who refused to write popular articles for his own benefit devoted hours to raising money for refugees and other worthwhile causes. Einstein was a Jew not only by birth but also by belief and action. He took an active part in Jewish affairs, wrote extensively, and attended many functions in order to raise money for Jewish causes. He was first introduced to Zionism during his stay in Prague, where Jewish intellectuals gathered in each other's homes talking about their dream of a Jewish Homeland. He and *Weizmann had become acquainted, and, despite different outlooks – Weizmann regarded Einstein as an unpractical idealist and Einstein in turn thought Weizmann was too much of a "Realpolitiker" – remained allies and friends. In 1921 Weizmann asked Einstein to join him on a fundraising tour of America to buy land in Palestine and seek aid for the Hebrew University. Einstein readily agreed, since his interest in the University had been growing. The tour was highly successful. He visited Palestine and was greatly impressed by what he saw. Einstein appeared before the Anglo-American Committee of Inquiry on Palestine in 1946 and entered a strong plea for a Jewish Homeland. When the State of Israel was established he hailed the event as the fulfillment of an ancient dream, providing conditions in which the spiritual and cultural life of a Hebrew society could find free expression. After Weizmann's death he was asked by Ben-Gurion to stand as a candidate for the presidency of the State of Israel, which he declined "being deeply touched by the offer but not suited for the position." When he went to the hospital for the illness which proved to be his last he took with him the notes he had made for the television address he was to give on Israel's seventh Independence Day. The notes were expanded into an article which is included in *Einstein on Peace* (ed. by O. Nathan and H. Norden, 1960). Among his works are *About Zionism* (ed. and tr. by L. Simon, 1930), speeches and letters; *Mein Weltbild* (1934; *The World As I See It*, 1934); *Evolution of Physics* (with L. Infeld, 1938); *Out of My Later Years* (1950); and *The Meaning of Relativity* (1921, 1956^{6}).

The Albert Einstein Archives at the Jewish National and University Library of the Hebrew University of Jerusalem (www.albert-einstein.org) house Einstein's personal papers. Through 1998, eight volumes of a projected 30 volumes of Einstein's Collected Papers were published by Princeton University Press.

BIBLIOGRAPHY: A. Moszkowski, *Einstein, the Searcher: His Work Explained from Dialogues* (1921); M. Born, *Einstein's Theory of Relativity* (1924, 1962^{2}); P. Frank, *Einstein, his Life and Times* (1947); L. Barnett, *The Universe and Dr. Einstein* (1948, 1950^{2}); E.E. Levinger, *Albert Einstein* (Eng., 1949); P.A. Schlipp (ed.), *Albert Einstein, Philosopher-Scientist* (1949, 1951^{2}), includes autobiographical notes and bibliography of Einstein's writings; L. Infeld, *Albert Einstein: His Work and Its Influence on Our World* (1950); A. Vallentin (pseud.), *The Drama of Albert Einstein* (1954); K. Seelig, *Albert Einstein: A Documentary Biography* (1956); N. Boni, *A Bibliographical Checklist and Index to the Published Writings of Albert Einstein* (1960); P. Michelmore, *Einstein, Portrait of the Man* (1962); H. Cuny, *Albert Einstein, the Man and his Theories* (1963); C. Lanczos, *Albert Einstein and the Cosmic World* (1965); H. Schmidt, in: *Judaism*, 8 (1959), 234–41; H. Parzen, in; JSOS, 32 (1970), 187–213; R.W. Clark, *Einstein, The Life and Times* (1971); B. Hoffmann (with H. Dukas), *Albert Einstein, Creator and Rebel* (1973); A. Moszkowski, *Conversations with Einstein* (1970). **ADD. BIBLIOGRAPHY:** A. Pais, *Subtle is the Lord. The Science and the Life of Albert Einstein* (1982); J. Stachel, *Einstein's Miraculous Year: Five Papers That Changed the Face of Physics* (1998); P.D. Smith, *Einstein* (2003); E.B. Blair, *Einstein Defiant: Genius versus Genius in the Quantum Revolution* (2004).

[Gerald E. Tauber]

EINSTEIN, ALFRED (1880–1952), musicologist. A cousin of the physicist Albert *Einstein, he was born in Munich. Einstein was a music critic in Munich and Berlin, and became editor of the *Zeitschrift fuer Musikwissenschaft* in 1918. In 1933 he left Germany for Italy, reached the U.S. in 1939, and was professor at Smith College, Northampton, Mass. Einstein combined the qualities of a music critic with those of a precise scholar and bibliographer.

In 1919 Hugo Riemann charged him with the preparation of the ninth edition of his *Musiklexicon*. Einstein subsequently edited also the 10th and 11th editions of this basic reference work. Of more popular character was his *Das neue Musiklexicon*, translated and edited by him from A. Eaglefield Hull's *Dictionary of Modern Music and Musicians* (1924). His Mozart studies culminated in his version of Koechel's catalogue of Mozart's works (3rd ed., 1937). He also enlarged and revised E. Vogel's *Bibliothek der gedruckten weltlichen Vocal-musik Italiens* (1962). A prolific writer, Einstein compiled semi-popular books, such as his *Geschichte der Musik* (1930^{4}; *Short History of Music*, 1954^{4}), *Music in the Romantic Era* (1947), and biographies of Schuetz (1928), Gluck (1936), Mozart (1946), and Schubert (1951). He produced scholarly studies on Renaissance music and edited compositions by Renaissance, Baroque, and classical composers. Also outstanding are his three volumes on *The Italian Madrigal* (1949), and the first four volumes of Mozart's *Collected Works* prepared by him.

BIBLIOGRAPHY: Haggin, in: *Music Review*, 24 (1963), 269–78; Hertzmann, in: *Musical Quarterly*, 27 (1941), 263–79, incl. bibl.; *Grove's Dict.*; Sendrey, Music, indexes; Riemann-Gurlitt; MGG; Baker, Biog Dict.

[Judith Cohen]

EINSTEIN, ARIK (1939–), Israeli pop-rock singer, actor. Einstein's initial performances were as a member of an army entertainment troupe, which he joined after his actor father encouraged him to go for an audition. Following his release from the army, in 1959, he acted and sang in a satirical theatrical show called *Sambation*. Einstein's debut four-song EP record was released the following year, and over the next four years he sang with several pop-folk bands, such as Green Onion and *Ha-Ẓe'irim* ("The Young Ones").

During this time he also furthered his acting career with parts in such acclaimed theater productions as *Little Tel Aviv* and *Irma La Douce*. Einstein's film career began with a role alongside his father in *Nini*. In 1964 he appeared in Ephraim *Kishon's *Sallah Shabati*, which took a bemused look at the difficulties faced by Jewish immigrants from Arab countries during the heyday of the Zionist movement in Israel. By 1972 he was an established star and played a lead role in the highly risqué Uri *Zohar film *Meẓiẓim* ("Peeping Toms").

Einstein's musical career took a significant leap in the mid-1960s when he joined singers Yehoram *Gaon (who was later replaced by Israel Gurion) and Benny Amdursky to form the Yarkon Bridge Trio. Over the next two years the band was the most successful act on the Israeli pop scene. In 1965 and 1966 Einstein placed first in the annual Israeli Song Festival with *Ayelet ha-Ḥen* and *Leil Stav*, respectively, and became a household name.

In 1969 Einstein revealed a rawer side to his artistic temperament when he recorded the first Israeli rock record in Hebrew, *Puzi*. It was shortly after this that Einstein joined forces with singer-guitarist Shalom *Hanokh and, together with other young artists such as Uri Zohar, American-born singer Josie Katz, and singer-songwriter Shmulik Krauss, produced a film called *Shablul* ("Snail"), which documented the making of the milestone rock record of the same name, with some loosely structured comedy sketches bridging the intervals in the music. Einstein also appeared in the comic skit series *Lul*, which was screened on Israeli television in July and September 1970, and was released as a full-length movie in 1988. In 1971 Einstein recorded an album of children's songs together with American-born guitarist Rob Huxley.

In 1973 Einstein changed musical direction, breaking away from the largely high energy rock material of the previous four years to produce a record of folk-oriented, more traditional songs called *Ereẓ Yisrael ha-Tovah ve-ha-Yeshanah* ("Good Old Israel"). Over the next decade Einstein put out more nostalgia-tinted records, collaborating with songwriter-musicians such as Shem-Tov Levi, Yitzhak Klepter, Yoni Rechter, and Miki Gabrielov.

In 1982 he was involved in a serious road accident and his next album, *Shavir* ("Fragile"), released in 1983, revealed a more vulnerable side to Einstein's character. Around this time he also stopped performing live. In the later 1980s and early 1990s Einstein produced several albums of children's songs, along with Levi and Rechter, and two video tapes called *Kemo Gedolim* ("Like Grownups") and *Kemo Gedolim 2*. In 1992, Einstein reunited with Zvi Shissel, who had produced *Shablul*, on a movie called *Kevallim* ("Cables"), a parody on cable television which had just become popular in Israel at the time. *Kevallim* also included some memorable musical collaborations, including a duet with singer Yehudit Ravitz, and comedy routines with well-known comic Moni Moshonov.

In 2001, Einstein renewed his professional relationship with Hanokh, recording a new version of *Aggadat Desheh*, written by the late Meir Ariel who grew up on the same kibbutz as Hanokh. Einstein and Hanokh also recorded a new album. In 2005 Einstein received a Lifetime Achievement Award from the Israeli artists' association, ACUM, in recognition of his songwriting and comedy sketch-writing contributions. He had maintained his position as the "prince" of Israeli pop music for four decades.

[Barry Davis (2nd ed.)]

EINSTEIN, CARL (1885–1940), German writer, art theoretician. Einstein drew philosophical inspiration from Nietzsche's apotheosis of aesthetics as well as from the reviews of causality of Schopenhauer and Mach. Intellectually challenged by the lectures of Georg Simmel during his studies at Berlin's Friedrich-Wilhelm-University, he composed his first novel, *Bebuquin oder die Dilettanten des Wunders* (1906–12), as a kaleidoscope of a world in which everything "exists only in its destruction." With its reflections on God and its somewhat preachy tone, Einstein's novel may also be regarded as a first step on the syncretistic-religious path he would follow in the years to come. Emphasizing a world of myth it also relates to the art of the primitive. The result was *Negerplastik* (1915), which was internationally acclaimed for its incorporation of a formerly ethnological field of study into the "world history of art" and constituted his theoretical contribution to Cubism.

His radical socialism brought Einstein into close contact with the "Malik" circle that grew up around George Grosz, Walter *Mehring, and John Heartfield. The product of these encounters was Berlin Dadaism, which Einstein abandoned only a year later. In 1922 he was prosecuted for the "blasphemous" representation of Jesus in his drama *Die schlimme Botschaft*. His most ambitious work, *Die Kunst des 20. Jahrhunderts* (1925), a vast compendium, proved him not only a profound connoisseur of contemporary art but also a serious theoretician and made his name widely known throughout Europe.

In 1927, Einstein settled in Paris, where he coedited the journal *Documents – Doctrines, Archéologie, Beaux Arts, Ethnographie* and came into contact with French surrealism. He called for a takeover of modernity by the "romantic generation," a term he used to characterize the messianic categories of the artistic revolutions of the 1920s. The failure of modernity in its capitulation to Fascism is the subject of *Die Fabrikation der Fiktionen*, written between 1930 and 1934.

During the Spanish Civil War, Einstein joined an anarchist militia in Aragon, fleeing after Franco's victory in 1939. Back in Paris, he was arrested by order of the French government (applying to all Germans living in France) and deported to a camp in Gurs. Released in June 1940, he attempted to escape the impending German invasion across the Pyrenees. He committed suicide near the Spanish border.

BIBLIOGRAPHY: S. Penkert, *Carl Einstein* (1969); H. Oehm, *Die Kunsttheorie Carl Einsteins* (1976); K.H. Kiefer, *Diskurswandel im Werk Carl Einsteins* (1994); L. Meffre, *Carl Einstein 1885–940* (2002); K.H. Kiefer (ed.), *Die visuelle Wende der Moderne* (2003).

[Philipp Theisohn (2nd ed.)]

EINSTEIN, LEWIS (1877–1967), U.S. diplomat and author. Einstein was born to a wealthy New York City merchant family. He entered the U.S. diplomatic service in 1903. His postings included Paris, London, the delegation to the Algeciras Conference, Peking (Beijing), Constantinople during World War I, and Prague throughout the 1920s. Einstein's score of books and nearly 100 published articles, reviews, notes, and comments embraced the diverse worlds of Renaissance art, modern biography, Tudor manners, Civil War diplomacy and, always, contemporary geopolitics, preserving the often fragile link between diplomacy and letters. One of the most prophetic of his articles, "The United States and the Anglo-German Rivalry" (*National Review*, 60 (1913)), also explained Einstein's realistic approach to international affairs. His memoir *A Diplomat Looks Back* (1968) provides insight into Einstein's deftness as a diplomat as well as an appreciation of his refined and skeptical world view. Another prominent work is *Holmes-Einstein Letters: Correspondence of Mr. Justice Holmes and Lewis Einstein, 1903–1935* (1964).

[James F. Watts, Jr.]

EIN VERED (Heb. עֵין וֶרֶד; "Rose Spring"), moshav in central Israel, in the southern Sharon. Affiliated with Tenu'at ha-Moshavim, it was founded on May 1, 1930 by settlers from Eastern Europe. Ein Vered was enlarged to absorb new immigrants after 1948. Farming was intensive, with citrus groves, field crops, beehives, and flowers as the principal branches. In 1969, there were 510 inhabitants; in the mid-1990s, 650; and in 2002, 965, as the moshav expanded.

[Efraim Orni]

EIN YAHAV (Heb. עֵין יַהַב), moshav in southern Israel, in the central Arabah Valley, affiliated with Tenu'at ha-Moshavim. It was founded in 1950 as an observation post for experiments in desert farming and later became a *Naḥal outpost. In 1967 Ein Yahav was transferred to a permanent site nearer the Jordanian border to become a moshav. In spite of its being exposed to attacks by Arab infiltrators because of its isolation, the moshav developed benefiting from a fairly abundant spring and hot climate. Its special farm branches included date palm groves, out-of-season vegetables, and flowers for export. Another specialty was turkey breeding. In 2002 the population of Ein Yahav was 457. Ein Yahav is the Hebraized version of the former Arab name "Ayn al-Wayba."

[Efraim Orni]

EIN ZEITIM (Heb. עֵין זֵיתִים), place in northern Israel, north of Safed. Jews resided in Ein Zeitim (in Arabic ʿAyn Zaytūn) from the 11th century C.E. In the 16th and early 17th centuries, 40 families of Moriscos (Arabic-speaking Jews) lived there and it was the site of a yeshivah, headed by R. Moses b. Makhir. After the 1837 earthquake in Safed, many Safed Jews fled to Ein Zeitim. A modern settlement was founded in 1891 by a Zionist group from Minsk, Russia, which planted olive groves and fruit orchards there. It was abandoned, however, before World War I. After 1918 Ein Zeitim was resettled but was again abandoned and destroyed in the 1929 Arab riots. A few families subsequently returned but were forced to leave again in the 1936 riots. A further attempt was made on January 17, 1946, when members of Ha-Kibbutz ha-Me'uḥad settled there, but it dispersed after the establishment of the State of Israel. A training farm was set up in its stead, but lacked adequate farming land and dissolved. In the 1950s a forest was planted in the Ein Zeitim area, forming part of the large *Biriyyah forest. The Ein Zeitim section has a large variety of trees, such as pine, cypress, eucalyptus, acacia, etc., as well as recreational facilities.

[Efraim Orni / Shaked Gilboa (2nd ed.)]

EINZIG, PAUL (1897–1973), British economist. Born in Brasov, Romania, Einzig was educated in Budapest and after World War I settled in London where he was the first economic reporter on East European conditions. He became foreign editor of the *Financial News* and later political correspondent for that paper and the *Financial Times*. His main field was monetary policy and foreign exchange operations. Einzig's criticism of official policy, which drew considerable public attention, brought him into frequent conflict with cabinet ministers and central bankers. He advocated closer parliamentary scrutiny of public spending. Einzig wrote more than 50 books, including *Monetary Reform in Theory and Practice* (1936), *Primitive Money in its Ethnological, Historical and Economic Aspects* (1949), *How Money is Managed* (1954), *History of Foreign Exchange* (1962), *Foreign Exchange Crises* (1967), *The Case Against Floating Exchange Rates* (1970), and *Destiny of the Dollar* (1972). In 1960 he published an autobiography, *In the Centre of Things*.

ADD. BIBLIOGRAPHY: ODNB online.

[Joachim O. Ronall]

EIN ẒURIM (Heb. עֵין צוּרִים; "Rock Spring"), kibbutz in S. Israel, 9.3 mi. (15 km.) N.E. of Ashkelon, affiliated with Ha-Kibbutz ha-Dati, originally founded in 1946 in the Hebron Hills by members of the religious youth movement Bnei Akiva. With other *Eẓyon Bloc settlements, it fought and fell during the War of Independence (1948), and its survivors were taken to Jordan as prisoners of war.

On July 6, 1949, upon their release, they established their kibbutz at its new site as part of the Shafir region of religious settlements. Besides intensive farming, which included field crops, citrus groves, fruit orchards, dairy cattle, and turkeys, the kibbutz operated the Tadmor air-conditioning plant, a catering service and holiday guest house, and the Bottle Tree company, which specialized in the development and production of gifts incorporating citrus fruit and blossoms in specially designed bottles. Two religious institutions operate in the kibbutz: a yeshivah and the Jacob Herzog Center for Jewish Studies. In 1969 the population of Ein Ẓurim was 330, increasing to 527 in 2002. A new settlement (Rosh Ẓurim) was established on the original site in August 1969 by *Naḥal Youth affiliated with Bnei Akiva.

WEBSITE: www.ein-tzurim.org.il.

[Efraim Orni / Shaked Gilboa (2nd ed.)]

EISEN, ARNOLD (1951–), U.S. professor of religious studies and author of works on Judaism in modern America. Raised in Philadelphia, Eisen received his undergraduate degree from the University of Pennsylvania; he earned a degree in the sociology of religion from Oxford University and a doctorate from the Hebrew University. He taught at Tel Aviv University and Columbia University, then was recruited by Stanford University in 1986 to help plan a program of Jewish studies. He was subsequently the Daniel E. Koshland Professor in Jewish Culture and Religion at Stanford.

Eisen is well known as an expert in modern Judaism. A trained sociologist, he considers the relationship between social and cultural contexts and religious ideas, and in particular examines the contemporary American Jewish experience. His work *The Chosen People in America: A Study in Jewish Religious Ideology* (1983) suggested that the conception of the Jews as God's chosen people faced a unique challenge in America, where Jews became integrated into the larger society to a greater extent than in Europe. Called a complex work, it nevertheless received critical praise.

Galut: Modern Jewish Reflection on Homelessness and Homecoming (1986), one of Eisen's best-known works, received the National Jewish Book Award in 1987. The work examines the concepts of exile and return, and presents the Jewish problem of living apart from and within a society of others. Eisen discusses three major aspects of Jewish life: religion (Judaism), ethnicity (Jewishness), and nationality ("Israeliness"). *Galut* has been considered an original contribution to the field of religious studies.

Eisen again won the National Jewish Book Award in 1998, for *Rethinking Modern Judaism: Ritual, Commandment, Community*. Here Eisen examines the transformation and evolution of modern Jewish religious belief and practice, considering the effects of secularization and modernity on Judaism, even among the Orthodox. Eisen's other works include *Taking Hold of Torah: Jewish Commitment and Community in America* (1997) and *The Jew Within: Self, Family, and Community in America* (with coauthor Steven M. Cohen, 2000). In *The Jew Within* Eisen and Cohen explore the new emphasis on personal Jewish identity characteristic of the Jew in the late 20th and early 21st century, an identity so different than the Holocaust-centered, Israel-centered portrayal of Jewish identity only 15 years earlier.

In 1999 Eisen received the Koret Prize for outstanding contributions to the Jewish community. He is a fellow of the American Academy for Jewish Research and also serves on its executive committee. His recent work includes the study of the increased involvement of women in modern American Judaism. In 2006 he was named chancellor of the Jewish Theological Seminary.

[Dorothy Bauhoff (2nd ed.)]

EISENBAUM, ANTONI (1791–1852), author and educator, one of the first advocates of *assimilation in Poland. In 1823 he submitted a memorandum to Czar *Alexander I, conceived from the standpoint of an assimilationist, urging measures to improve the condition of the Jews. At the end of that year he began the publication of **Der Beobachter an der Weichsel*, subsidized by the government. Eisenbaum wrote articles for other Warsaw papers, urging emancipation for the Jews. In 1826 he was appointed supervisor, and in 1835 director, of the rabbinical seminary in Warsaw. The seminary aroused vehement opposition among traditionally minded Jews. Eisenbaum also acted as censor of Hebrew books in Poland (see *Censorship).

BIBLIOGRAPHY: Linberg, in: *Perezhitoye*, 4 (1913), 119–48; J. Shatzky, *Geshikhte fun Yidn in Varshe*, 3 vols. (1947–53), index; S. Lastik, *Z dziejów Os´wiecenia Żydowskiego* (1961), 176–8; R. Mahler, *Ha-Ḥasidut ve-ha-Haskalah* (1961), 263; EG, *Varsha*, 1 (1961), 240–6.

[Nathan Michael Gelber]

EISENBERG, AHARON ELIYAHU (1863–1931), pioneer of Jewish settlement in Ereẓ Israel. Eisenberg, born in Pinsk, Russia, settled in Ereẓ Israel in 1886. He worked as a laborer in *Rishon le-Zion, later settling in Wadi Hanin (now Nes Ẓiyyonah), where he became one of the outstanding vineyard cultivators in the country. Eisenberg was one of those who acquired the land of *Reḥovot from its previous owners (1890). He was entrusted with the task of cultivating the lands of members of the Menuḥah ve-Naḥalah Association (the group of Warsaw Zionists who established Reḥovot) living abroad. He joined the *Benei Moshe association in 1893. In 1904 he established Agudat Neta'im, an association for planting and cultivating vineyards and orange groves on behalf of foreign investors. Eisenberg was instrumental in establishing small holdings for Jewish workers. He also helped settle Yemenite immigrants in Reḥovot. In 1920 he was chosen a delegate to the first Asefat ha-Nivḥarim and to the Palestine Advisory Council established by Sir Herbert *Samuel in the same year. Eisenberg was a leading member of the Va'ad Leummi and participated in various delegations to Paris and London.

BIBLIOGRAPHY: A. Yaari, *Goodly Heritage* (1958), 191–8, 217; E. Ha-Dani (ed.), *A.E. Eisenberg* (Heb., 1947); M. Smilansky, *Mishpaḥat ha-Adamah*, 1 (1953), 116–27.

[Yehuda Slutsky]

EISENBERG, SHOUL (1921–1997), industrialist and philanthropist. Born in Munich, Eisenberg fled from Germany in 1938 and eventually settled in Japan. At the end of the war he laid the foundations of his worldwide industrial empire. In Japan, his companies became principal suppliers of raw materials for the country's steel industries and partners in a number of shipping enterprises. In South Korea, Eisenberg Companies developed many of its major industries. Eisenberg was the leader of the Tokyo Jewish community and he built its synagogue. He also made many gifts for projects in Israel where he and his family settled in the 1960s. An active participant in the economic conference called by the Israeli government in 1968, he established two large exporting companies. In 1980 he gained control of the Israel Corporation, one of Israel's large investment companies, which after his death was sold to the Ofer brothers in 1999. In 1978 he began to operate in China, with projects worth around $1 billion.

[Morton Mayer Berman / Shaked Gilboa (2nd ed.)]

EISENDRATH, MAURICE NATHAN (1902–1973), U.S. rabbi and leader of Reform Judaism. Eisendrath was born in Chicago, Illinois, and received rabbinic ordination from Hebrew Union College, Cincinnati. After serving in pulpits at the Virginia Street Temple in Charleston, West Virginia (1926–29) and at Holy Blossom Toronto (1929–43), he established a towering reputation in Toronto, where he was involved in a weekly radio program at a time when radio was the dominant media of its age. *Forum on the Air* gave him prominence in Canada well beyond his own community. He used his forum to advance the ideas of prophetic Judaism, to push for anti-poverty assistance, to advocate civil rights and social justice, and to condemn the growing menace of Nazism.

In 1943, Eisendrath came to the Union of American Hebrew Congregations first as the interim director while Nelson Gleuck was away and later as the director and finally as its president, a position he held for almost three decades. During his administration the Reform movement grew in membership and changed its direction perceptibly. So too did Eisendrath. A committed pacifist at the beginning of his career, Eisendrath was forced to change his mind by Nazism, which could only be combated by force. He took Reform Judaism from an anti-Zionist movement, with some Zionist rabbis, into a more pro-Israel position, first declaring neutrality but not opposition to Israeli statehood in 1946 and later strongly supporting the new State.

He presided over the transfer of the movement's headquarters from Cincinnati to New York, and thus its integration into Jewish organizational life in the United States. He pushed for a shift in the balance of power from the South and Midwest to the East, and its ideological change from classical Reform to a new rapprochement with tradition. He was elected president of the World Union for Progressive Judaism in July 1972. Eisendrath was particularly active in interfaith activities and in social action, speaking out frequently during the 1960s for civil rights and later against the Vietnam War. With the big presence of Reform Judaism in the South, both moves took courage and spurred opposition. In protest, New York's Temple Emanu-El seceded from the Union for a time. Despite the opposition of two major congregations, New York's Emanu-El and Washington Hebrew Congregation, he established the Kivie Kaplan Religious Action Center in Washington to represent Reform Judaism in Congress and the White House, fortifying the connection between Liberal Judaism and American Liberalism. He also established the House of Living Judaism, headquarters of the Union. As a young rabbi, he was one of the founders of the Canadian Conference of Christians and Jews. Eisendrath was the author of *Spinoza* (1932), *Never Failing Stream* (1939), and *Can Faith Survive? The Thoughts and Afterthoughts of an American Rabbi* (1964), both the latter collections of essays on contemporary religious issues. He died at the biennial convention of the UAHC, on the eve of retirement.

BIBLIOGRAPHY: *Current Biography* (1950), 134f.; M.Meyer, *Response to Modernity: A History of Reform Movement in Judaism* (1988); *New York Times*, November 10, 1973. **ADD. BIBLIOGRAPHY:** K.M. Olitzky, L.J. Sussman, and M.H. Stern (eds.), *Reform Judaism in America: A Biographical Dictionary and Sourcebook* (1993).

[Jack Reimer / Michael Berenbaum (2nd ed.)]

°**EISENHOWER, DWIGHT DAVID** (1890–1969), U.S. soldier, supreme commander of the Allies' European Theater of Operations during World War II, and 34th president of the United States. During World War II, he commanded the U.S. troops in the United Kingdom, and then the Allied forces landing in North Africa. There he pressured the French authorities to annul the anti-Jewish laws of the Vichy regime. As supreme commander of the Allied Expeditionary Forces, Eisenhower led the Normandy invasion in 1944. After the German surrender one of his first acts was to void all Nazi racial and antisemitic legislation.

Eisenhower's armies liberated tens of thousands of Jews in concentration camps. Upon the discovery of the remnant who refused to return to their native lands, and after pressure from President Harry Truman, he created the unprecedented position of adviser to the commanding general on Jewish affairs to speed the handling of the Jewish survivors. Chaplain Judah Naidich first filled the post and was succeeded by a series of civilians beginning with Judge Simon H. *Rifkind. Separate *displaced persons camps were created for Jews to improve their physical, cultural, and spiritual conditions. Eisenhower also ordered the admission into these camps of tens of thousands of Jews fleeing from Poland and Eastern Europe after the war (see *Beriḥah). In October 1945 Eisenhower received David Ben-Gurion and acceded to his request for planes to bring Hebrew teachers and agricultural instructors from Palestine to the camps, thus facilitating the later immigration of the displaced persons to Palestine.

During Eisenhower's presidential terms of office (1953–61), hundreds of millions of dollars in grants-in-aid were extended to Israel. An atomic energy agreement with Israel provided for training Israeli scientists and making heavy water available. Military equipment sent to Israel included training aircraft, signal supplies, and spare parts and ammunition. Relations between Eisenhower's administration and Israel reached their lowest ebb during and after the *Sinai Campaign of October 1956, when the U.S. took the lead in the UN in demanding the withdrawal of Israeli forces, even threatening sanctions. Upon Israel's withdrawal, Eisenhower affirmed that Israel would have no cause to regret its decision, and pledged support for Israel's national existence and internal development. American policy, he stated, viewed the Gulf of Akaba and the Suez Canal as international waterways.

BIBLIOGRAPHY: H. Finer, *Dulles over Suez* (1964); J. Nadich, *Eisenhower and the Jews* (1953).

[Judah Nadich]

EISENMAN, CHARLES (1864?–1923), U.S. philanthropist. Eisenman was born in New York City. Moving to Cleveland, Ohio, he co-founded the K and E (later Kaynee) Company, manufacturing boys' clothing, in 1888. Eisenman retired as company president in 1906 and devoted himself entirely to philanthropic work. He was the founder and first president of the Cleveland Federation of Jewish Charities from 1904 until his death; he was active in the Cleveland Community Fund Council, the American Jewish Committee, the American Jewish Relief Committee, and other organizations. During World War I he was chairman of the Council of National Defense Committee on Purchases and Supplies, for which he received the Distinguished Service Medal. He advocated socially concerned business in a series of essays, *Everybody's Business* (1916).

[Edward L. Greenstein]

EISENMAN, PETER (1932–), U.S. architect. Eisenman was born in Newark, New Jersey, and studied at Cornell (B.A. 1955) and Columbia universities (M.A.), receiving a second M.A. and Ph.D. from Cambridge University in England. He taught at Cambridge, Princeton, Yale, Harvard, Ohio State, and the Cooper Union in New York, where he was founder and director of the New York Institute for Architecture and Urban Studies (1967).

Unique among modern architects, until 1980 most of Eisenman's work was in theoretical writing and teaching. During this period in his career, he was the leader of a group known as the "New York Five," which included John Hejduk, Michael Graves, Charles Gwathmey, and Richard *Meier. Eisenman Architects was established in 1980.

Eisenman's thought is often associated with that of postmodern philosophers Noam *Chomsky and Jacques *Derrida as well as Friedrich Nietzsche. Eisenman co-authored *Choral Works* with Derrida. His architecture is sometimes viewed as a text that emphasizes concepts such as fragmentation, and in the case of the *Berlin Memorial to the Murdered Jews of Europe* (Denkmal), opened in 2005, irreparable loss. His work thus avoids the use of traditional compositional elements familiar to architects as well as pure aesthetics. Eisenman has noted: "You cannot have an architecture that doesn't relate to cultural issues, whether they be philosophic, artistic, musical, filmic, psychological. I think that there is no question that architecture moves culture in the same way that other disciplines do, but it is also affected by and affects other disciplines."

Eisenman experimented with ten house designs between 1960 and 1980, each one being numbered in sequence. Eisenman, with associates Richard Trott and Laurie Olin, designed the Wexner Center for the Arts (1983–89) at Ohio State University in Columbus, Ohio. The building serves as an early example of Eisenman's concept of deconstruction in architecture. The structure contains a white spine that links pre-existing buildings with new construction and was designed on a series of grids that attempts to link symbolically the city of Columbus with the university campus. Among his other designs, which mirror the principles of deconstruction but with added computer engineering in the 1990s, can be found the Emory University Center for the Arts (1991); the Arnoff Center for Design and Art at the University of Cincinnati (1996), which mirrors the Wexner Center with a spine bringing together pre-existing structures; the Staten Island Institute of Arts and Sciences, with its use of vast curved "fluid fractals"; Cardinal Stadium in Phoenix, Arizona, which features a retractable roof, retractable side, and the field that has the capacity to move in and out of the structure in order to grow natural grass. The City of Culture of Galicia is a monumental project in the Spanish city of Santiago de Compostela. The 810,000 square feet project also includes a history museum, a library, a landscaped forest, and a theater for ballet, opera, and symphonies. From an aerial perspective, the City of Culture appears as a series of structures highly integrated into the Galician landscape.

The architect's most controversial project was the *Berlin Memorial to the Murdered Jews of Europe*, finished in 2005. The project, from its inception in 1988, featured two competitions and a long and often bitter debate in German society about the need for such a monument.

While Christine Jackob-Marks' design was selected from the 1,200 submissions of the first competition of May 1994, it was vetoed by German Chancellor Helmut Kohl. In 1997, 25 artists were asked to send in revised proposals. Among the four finalists was a joint project by Peter Eisenman and sculptor Richard Serra. The original conception of the team was to create a "field of memory," and it envisioned 4,000 concrete pylons of varying sizes, laid out like a field of wheat and progressively sinking below ground level. Serra later removed himself from the project and after an intense debate the parliament finally decided on June 15, 1999 on the revised Eisenman plan. The design reduced the number of pylons to 2,700.

BIBLIOGRAPHY: A.E. Benjamin, C. Davidson, P. Eisenman, and L. Fernandez-Galiano, *Der Denkmalstreit – das Denkmal?: Die Debatte um das "Denkmal für die ermordeten Juden Europas:" eine Dokumentation* (1999).

[Stephen C. Feinstein (2nd ed.)]

EISENMANN, LOUIS (1869–1937), French historian. Eisenmann, born in Haguenau, Alsace, moved with his family to France after the German annexation in 1871. In 1905 he became a professor of history at the University of Dijon, and in 1931 professor of Central European history at the Sorbonne. Eisenmann's special field of interest, in which he made important contributions, was Slavonic cultural history. Besides teaching, writing, and editing in this field, he served as general secretary of the Institute for Slavic Studies at the University of Paris. He was also an active director of the Center for the Study of Foreign Policy. Eisenmann's major writings deal with the Austro-Hungarian Empire. He wrote *Le compromis austro-hongrois de 1867* (1904), *La Hongrie contemporaine* (1921), *La Tchécoslovaquie* (1921), and *Un grand européen, Edouard Benes* (1934). He contributed sections to Paul Milyukov's classic work on Russian history, *Histoire de la Russie* (1932–33). Eisenmann played a prominent role as editor of two French historical journals, *Le monde slave* and *La revue historique*.

[William Korey]

°**EISENMENGER, JOHANN ANDREAS** (1654–1704), author of a work which had a formative influence on modern antisemitic polemics. Eisenmenger, born in Mannheim, studied Hebrew while at Heidelberg University. During a visit to Amsterdam in 1680–81 he was shocked when three Christians adopted Judaism, and also by the criticism of Christianity expressed by David *Lida, rabbi of the Ashkenazi community in Amsterdam. Eisenmenger therefore set out to examine Jewish writings to find material that would deter Christians from turning to Judaism. For 19 years he studied talmudic and midrashic literature with Jews, pretending that he wished to become a proselyte. In 1686 he was appointed lecturer at Heidelberg University, and, in conjunction with Johann *Leusden, published in 1694, at Frankfurt, an unvocalized edition of the Bible to which David *Gruenhut wrote an introduction describing Eisenmenger as a man of great learning. However, in 1699 the Frankfurt Jews learned that Eisenmenger was about to publish a work denouncing Judaism, titled *Entdecktes Judenthum* ("Judaism Unmasked"). As it was in German and not in Latin, they feared that it would inflame popular feelings against the Jews (especially as anti-Jewish riots occurred in Franconia, and in particular in *Bamberg in 1699). The Frankfurt Jews turned to Samson *Wertheimer in Vienna, and he and Samuel *Oppenheimer persuaded the emperor to forbid the publication of the book, which had been printed in 2,500 copies. A Protestant professor from Giessen, a Jesuit from Mainz, and six rabbis from Frankfurt were asked to study Eisenmenger's book and comment on it. In the meantime, the king of Prussia asked the emperor to allow the publication of the book and the elector of the Palatinate also intervened in Eisenmenger's favor. However the pleas of the Jews for its suppression were supported by the archbishop of Mainz, since Eisenmenger had also offended Catholic susceptibilities, as well as by the elector of Hanover. Eisenmenger, who had invested all his money in the printing, died suddenly in 1704. His heirs again induced the king of Prussia to intervene with the emperor to allow the book to be issued, but without success. The king of Prussia, therefore, permitted them to publish a second edition of 3,000 copies in Berlin in 1711. On the title page the place of publication is given as Koenigsberg, a city outside the emperor's jurisdiction. The city council of Frankfurt, the elector of the Palatinate, and the king of Prussia, meanwhile, made continual efforts to obtain permission for publication of the first edition; this was granted only in 1741. Eisenmenger's heirs claimed damages from the Jews of Frankfurt; their claim was finally quashed in 1773. In this book of two volumes, with over 2,000 pages, Eisenmenger had assembled passages to suit his argument from 182 books written in Hebrew, 13 in Yiddish, and eight written by apostates who had converted to Christianity. They were mostly extracts from talmudic literature, beginning with the Mishnah and concluding with commentaries, codes, and notes of the *rishonim* and *aḥaronim*. He cited them in the original language, providing a translation alongside. The translations are erroneous in places and often intentionally distorted. Eisenmenger's charges against the Jews include the *blood libel and poisoning of wells. Possibly Eisenmenger did believe in what he wrote, although his negotiations with the Jews, and the fact that he was prepared not to publish his book against a certain price, cast some doubt on this assumption. An English edition was published in 1732–33. Among a number of other German and Austrian antisemites, A. *Rohling quoted Eisenmenger, often inaccurately, in his venomous *Talmudjude* (1871), as Franz *Delitzsh decisively proved. *Entdecktes Judenthum* was republished in 1893.

BIBLIOGRAPHY: Graetz-Rabbinovitz, 8 (1899), 320–6; D. Kahana, *Rosh Petanim* (1883); Dubnow, Weltgesch, 7 (1928), 321–3; G. Wolf, in: MGWJ, 18 (1869), 378–84; M. Wiener, in: MWJ, 6 (1879), 48–63; L. Loewenstein, *ibid.*, 18 (1891), 209–40; S. Stern, *Der Preussische Staat und die Juden*, 2 (1962); Akten, nos. 178, 179, 181, 183, 185, 186, 216; H.L. Ehrlich, in: K. Thieme (ed.), *Judenfeindschaft* (1963), 209ff.

[Zvi Avneri]

EISENSTADT (Ger. also: **Weniger Maertersdorf**; Hung. **Kismarton**; Heb. א"ש; עיר ברזל), capital of *Burgenland, E. Austria. Its community was the leading one of the "Seven Communities" of Burgenland, and from the end of the 17th century to the middle of the 19th century one of the most important communities in Europe. Jews are mentioned in the city records in 1373, and the bishop of Eisenstadt was permitted to settle Jews there in 1388. Others came to the city after the expulsions from Austria (1421), Styria (1496), and Sopron (1526). By 1569 the community numbered 81 persons, living in eight small houses. A Jewish quarter and community institutions are mentioned for the years 1547 to 1571. Each Jew had to work eight days villenage services and pay ten florins in taxes yearly. The Jews were expelled from Eisenstadt in 1572 but returned soon afterward. In 1626 the community came under the protection of the aristocratic Hungarian Esterhazy family. The Jews had to leave Eisenstadt at the time of the expulsion from Austria in 1670 but were shortly afterward permitted to return. In 1675 Jews who had immigrated there from Mikulov (Nikolsburg), Moravia, were granted a letter of protection. The renewed version of 1690 served as model for the charters granted to all "Seven Communities" in the region. In return for yearly taxes and gifts on all possible occasions, the community was granted broad autonomy. Prince Esterhazy built near his farming estate a "Jewish street" of 20 houses, which formed a political community (see *Politische Gemeinden) as Eisenstadt-Unterberg (Hung. Alsókismartonhegy). Its leaders included the *Judenrichter,* before whom, from 1732, a mace was carried as symbol of his function. In 1900, only 38 of the 451 inhabitants on its territory were not Jewish. In 1704 and 1707, during the Kurucz revolts, Eisenstadt was destroyed, its inhabitants taking refuge in Wiener Neustadt. The community was restored with the help of Samson *Wertheimer, who also served as its rabbi. He built a house there containing a *bet midrash* (maintained by Wertheimer's endowment until the 1840s). Meir *Eisenstadt (Maharam Esh) was rabbi from 1717 until his death in 1744, and through him the local yeshivah became celebrated. This was the most prosperous period for the community because some of the wealthy Jewish families living in Vienna without residence rights paid heavily for a fictitious right of domicile in Eisenstadt. Some 35 Jewish house owners are on record in 1725. In 1735 the community numbered 113 families (24 living in Vienna), totaling 600 persons. The Jewish quarter was destroyed by a conflagration in 1795. A new synagogue was built in 1832. In 1836 the community numbered 191 families (908 persons) of whom 61 were part house owners and 12 owned their own houses. Azriel *Hildesheimer was rabbi of Eisenstadt between 1851 and 1869, and his yeshivah, at which secular studies were also taught, attracted pupils from all over Europe. After the Revolution of 1848 when Jews were able to move freely, many left Eisenstadt.

In its days of fame as a center of Jewish learning the Eisenstadt community used to be referred to as "Little Jerusalem." It had many customs peculiar to itself. The entrances to the Jewish street were closed on Saturdays and holidays by chains. Above the entrance to the synagogue a silver ball was hung containing cord for *ẓiẓit*, free of charge, supplied by a donation (*keren ẓiẓit*). Those who were called to the Torah as an obligation, such as a bridegroom on the Sabbath before his wedding, paid a special due. The *shammash* served the rabbi a cup of wine after the sermon. On the eve of Simḥat Torah it was the women's task to adorn the Torah scrolls before the **hakkafot*. At the beginning of the cherry season the first child to show the rabbi a worm in a cherry was rewarded, and the *shammash* would then proclaim in the street that henceforward it was forbidden to eat cherries without first examining them.

At the end of the 19th century, the *Wolf family, who concentrated the wine export in their hands, were prominent in local and communal affairs. Sandor Wolf founded a private museum in 1902 and published books on Jewish and general local history. After World War I, Eisenstadt remained the only Jewish community in Europe to have the status of a political community (until 1938). The Jews there suffered economically because of the disruption of their former commercial ties.

The Jews were expelled from Eisenstadt immediately after the *Anschluss* in 1938; most of them moved to Vienna. Some were among the refugees thrust onto the land strip in the Danube (see *Burgenland). On Nov. 10, 1938, the synagogue equipment and part of the houses in the Jewish street were destroyed by a mob. The synagogue building was demolished. (The trade-union headquarters was built on the site in 1952; it contains a plaque commemorating the synagogue.) Many of the tombstones in the Jewish cemetery were used to build anti-tank traps in 1945.

One hundred and nine Jews from Eisenstadt perished in the Holocaust. Five survivors returned after the war. The community was not reorganized. The Jewish collection of the Wolf museum was incorporated into the Burgenlaendisches Landesmuseum; in 1972 a Jewish museum was opened, the first of its kind in Austria. Some 23,500 documentary items are preserved in the *Juedisches Zentralarchiv der ehemaligen Judengemeinden des Burgenlandes.* Rabbi Akiva *Eger the Younger was a native of Eisenstadt; a plaque on the house where he was born was destroyed by the Nazis. Moritz *Benedikt, the professor of neuropathology in Vienna and liberal politician, was also born in Eisenstadt.

BIBLIOGRAPHY: A. Fuerst, *Sitten und Gebraeuche in der Eisenstaedter Judengasse (Minhag Asch)* (1908); idem, in: *Egyenlöség*, 40 (Jan. 8, 1921), 6–7; O. Aull, *Eisenstadt* (1931); H. Gold (ed.), *Gedenkbuch der untergegangenen Judengemeinden des Burgenlandes* (1970), 37–50, 51–55; N. Gergely, in *Új Élet*, 24 (Oct. 15, 1969), 3, 17–36; MHJ, 1 (1903)–12 (1969), index locorum s.v. *Kismarton*; H. Weiss, in: *Zikhronotai* (1895), 29–41; R. Patai, in: *Arim ve-Immahot be-Yisrael*, 1 (1946/47), 41–79, incl. bibl.; B. Wachstein, *Die Grabinschriften des alten Judenfriedhofs in Eisenstadt* (1922); idem, *Urkunden und Akten zur Geschichte der Juden in Eisenstadt…* (1926); S. Wolf, *Die Kunst im Eisenstaedter Ghetto* (1912); I. Schwarz, in: *Menorah*, 4 (1926), 705–8; M. Eliav (ed.), *Iggerot Rabbi Azriel Hildesheimer* (Heb. and Ger., 1965), passim. **ADD. BIBLIOGRAPHY:** J. Reiss, *Weil man uns die Heimatliebe ausgeblaeut hat* (2001).

EISENSTADT, ABRAHAM SELDIN (1920–), U.S. historian. Eisenstadt was born in New York City. He taught at Brooklyn College, where he was appointed professor of history. In 1998, he was one of 412 leading historians who signed an open letter deploring the proposal to impeach President Bill Clinton, on the grounds that "if successful, it will have the most serious implications for our constitutional order." Eisenstadt wrote *Charles McLean Andrews: A Study in American Historical Writing* (1956), and he edited *American History: Recent Interpretations* (2 vols., 1962) and *The Craft of American History* (2 vols., 1966), *Before Watergate: Problems of Corrup-*

tion in American Society (1979), and *Reconsidering Tocqueville's Democracy in America* (1988) as well as numerous volumes in Davidson, Harlan's American History Series.

[Ruth Beloff (2nd ed.)]

EISENSTADT, ABRAHAM ẒEVI HIRSCH BEN JACOB (1813–1868), halakhic authority. Eisenstadt, who was born in Bialystok, was appointed rabbi of Berestovitsa, district of Grodno, in 1836, and of Utina (Uttian), district of Kovno, in 1856. Eisenstadt took upon himself the task of collecting and digesting the enormous amount of halakhic material scattered throughout the responsa literature, and relating it to the relevant laws in Caro's Shulḥan Arukh, publishing his digest in *Pitḥei Teshuvah.* At the end of his introduction to *Even ha-Ezer* he enumerates 180 volumes of responsa and other works that he used. In the introduction he explains that the purpose of his book is to supply a missing link in the chain of *posek* literature, namely, the decisions to be found in responsa. In addition to establishing the *halakhah* he also gives the reasons and the essence of the arguments in the different responsa. This enabled rabbis to give decisions on matters and problems which had arisen as a result of changed conditions since Caro's code had appeared. Eisenstadt regarded the literature dealing with *Even ha-Ezer* as of supreme importance, as he believed that it was impossible to come to a practical decision on any of the laws discussed in it by relying upon the original text. As a result, his work on this section of the Shulḥan Arukh is very detailed. Since the *Sha'arei Teshuvah* (Dubnow, 1820), begun by Ḥayyim Mordecai Margolioth of Dubnow and completed by his brother Ephraim Zalman *Margolioth, already met this need with regard to the *Oraḥ Ḥayyim*, Eisenstadt confined himself to the other three sections of the Shulḥan Arukh. His own novellae on the Shulḥan Arukh are highly regarded by halakhists.

Pitḥei Teshuvah on *Yoreh De'ah* and *Even ha-Ezer* was published during Eisenstadt's lifetime (1836 and 1861) and on *Ḥoshen Mishpat* (1875) after his death. He also published *Seder Gittin va-Ḥaliẓah by* Michael b. Joseph of Cracow accompanied by his own commentary and glosses, also entitled *Pitḥei Teshuvah* (1863), in which he gave the sources of the book in the Shulḥan Arukh and among the *rishonim* and *aḥaronim.* Many of his responsa appear in the works of contemporary rabbis. Eisenstadt died in Koenigsberg where he had gone for medical treatment. His son BENJAMIN (1846–1920) was appointed to succeed him in Utina after his death, and served in this post for 52 years. He was the author of *Masot Binyamin* (1921), talmudic novellae. Benjamin's son ABRAHAM ẒEVI (1871–1939) succeeded his father in Utina and served there for 19 years. He was one of the early Zionists. Leon *Rabinovich, editor of *Ha-Meliẓ*, was also a grandson of Abraham Ẓevi Hirsch Eisenstadt.

BIBLIOGRAPHY: S.M. Chones, *Toledot ha-Posekim* (1910), 502; H. Tchernowitz, *Toledot ha-Posekim*, 3 (1947), 313, 325–30; *Yahadut Lita*, 1 (1959), 256f.; 3 (1967), 26.

[Shmuel Ashkenazi]

EISENSTADT, BENZION (1873–1951), U.S. Hebraist, rabbi, and scholar. Eisenstadt was born in Kletsk, Belorussia. He studied at Nishvitz with Rabbi Yosepoh Grodzinski. In his youth he was attracted to modern Hebrew literature and while in his teens corresponded with Jewish scholars, such as Slonimski and Buber. While still in Russia he published *Ẓioni* (Warsaw, 1895; Parts 2–4, Vilna, 1899–1902), a biographical dictionary of contemporary rabbis and scholars, and *Rabbanei Minsk va-Ḥakhameha*, on the rabbis and scholars of Minsk (Vilna, 1899), as well as *Ve-Zot li-Yehudah* (1901), annotations on *Noda bi-Yehudah*, the responsa of Ezekiel Landau.

In 1903 he immigrated to the U.S. where he served as a pulpit rabbi and continued writing biographical works on well-known rabbis, scholars, and communal leaders. They include *Ḥakhmei Yisrael be-Amerikah* (with photographs, 1903), *Dorot ha-Aḥaronim* (2 vols., 1913, 1917), *Anshei ha-Shem Be-Arẓot ha-Brit* (1933) on American rabbis and, posthumously, *Benei Ḥiyyon* (1952). He was an ardent Zionist, active in Mizrachi and in charity for the then Palestine.

ADD. BIBLIOGRAPHY: M.D. Sherman, *Orthodox Judaism in America: A Biographical Dictionary and Sourcebook* (1996), 56–58.

EISENSTADT, ISAIAH (Isay; pseudonym: **Yudin, Vitali**; 1867–1937), pioneer of the Jewish socialist labor movement in Russia; born in Vilna. He became a member of Populist Narodnaya Volya ("People's Will") circles in the 1880s and was imprisoned for revolutionary activities. He returned to Vilna and in 1889 joined the Social Democrats. A Marxist theoretician, Eisenstadt also proved an extremely able organizer among the Jewish workers in Vilna and in Odessa. In 1896 he was exiled to Siberia, remaining in prison there until 1901. After his release, Eisenstadt became one of the main leaders of the *Bund, his activities being suspended by frequent arrests; during the controversy within the party (1908–10) between those preferring the use of legal action and the "anti-legalists," Eisenstadt supported the latter. In the central committee of the Russian Social Democratic Workers' Party he endeavored to effect a compromise between the Mensheviks and Bolsheviks. After the Revolution of February 1917 Eisenstadt was active in Petrograd (Leningrad). He was elected vice chairman of the central committee of the Bund, and after its split with the Communists, became associated with the leadership of the Social Democratic Bund. He was subsequently imprisoned, and at the beginning of 1922 received permission to leave Soviet Russia. He reached Berlin, and continued his political activity among the Menshevik émigrés there and in Paris, gradually inclining to the leftist faction. His first wife LYUBA EISENSTADT-LEVINSON (1866–1903), also born in Vilna, became a Social Democrat while a student in Geneva. She was arrested at the Russian border and imprisoned for three years. From 1890 she was active as one of the leading propagandists for the party among the Jewish workers in Vilna and Bialystok. She was imprisoned with her husband in Siberia from 1896 to 1901. She died on a visit to New York.

BIBLIOGRAPHY: G. Aronson, in: J.S. Hertz (ed.), *Doyres Bundistn*, 1 (1956), 137–54; LNYL, 4 (1961), 249–52; *Sotsialisticheskiy Vestnik*, 17:14, 15 (1937), 1–4.

[Moshe Mishkinsky]

EISENSTADT, MEIR (**"MaHaRaM ESH"** – Morenu **Ha-Rav Meir Esh** [short for Eisenstadt]; c. 1670–1744), Polish rabbinical authority. After serving as rabbi in Szydlowiec in Poland, he settled in Worms, where Samson *Wertheimer appointed him head of the yeshivah. On the occupation of Worms by the French in 1701, he went to Prossnitz, Moravia, and there he was appointed rabbi. Among his disciples was Jonathan *Eybeschuetz, whom he brought up after the death of the latter's father. In 1714, with Wertheimer's support, Meir was appointed rabbi of *Eisenstadt and its "seven communities," which by then had recovered from the expulsion of 1670 and from the havoc wrought by the Kurucz uprising (1704). Students from far and near flocked to the yeshivah which he had established. He fashioned the character of the community, which became distinguished for its piety, so that men of wealth and influence in nearby Vienna sought "right of residence" in Eisenstadt. In 1723 Meir was obliged to leave the community for a short time because of "informers and calumniators." Upon his return he instituted a special prayer to be recited every Monday and Thursday, against "those who bring harm to Israel by their tongues and tear down the foundations of the community." Meir issued a ban against card playing (except on Hanukkah and Purim). His works include *Panim Me'irot*, responsa and novellae on the Talmud (Amsterdam, 1715). His responsa, containing questions addressed to him by Akiva *Eger, *Moses Harif of Pressburg, and even rabbis of Italy and Turkey, testify to his wide authority. Other works are *Kotnot Or*, a homiletic commentary on the Pentateuch and the Five Scrolls, published together with *Or Ḥadash*, the commentary of his grandson Eliezer Kallire, under the general title of *Me'orei Esh* (1766), and *Or ha-Ganuz* (1766), novellae on *Ketubbot* and on the rules concerning *yein nesekh* in the *Yoreh De'ah*.

BIBLIOGRAPHY: I.T. Eisenstadt and S. Wiener, *Da'at Kedoshim*, 1 (1898), 190f.; Pollák, in: *Sefer ha-Yovel… M.A. Bloch* (1905), 47–58 (Heb. sect.); P.Z. Schwartz, *Shem ha-Gedolim me-Erez Hagar*, 2 (1914), 153f., no. 14; 3 (1915), s.v. *Panim Me'irot*; B. Wachstein, *Grabinschriften des alten Judenfriedhofes in Eisenstadt* (1922), 47–93.

[Aharon Fuerst]

EISENSTADT, MENAHEM ẒEVI (d. 1966), Polish rabbi. Born in Warsaw, Eisenstadt studied in Brisk, Lithuania, under R. Ḥayyim Soloveitchik and his son, R. Isaac Ze'ev. For a while he served as a member of the Cracow City Council. At the beginning of World War II, Eisenstadt moved to Vilna, where he directed the exiled Yeshivat Ḥakhmei Lublin. In 1941 he immigrated to Ereẓ Israel and lived in Tel Aviv. In 1947 he moved to the United States. In New York, he began the publication of an edition of Nahmanides' biblical commentary, based on early manuscripts and early editions. His work was not completed, however, and only the commentary to Genesis appeared (2 vols. 1959–62). He died in New York, and was buried in Jerusalem.

BIBLIOGRAPHY: (A.S.) B. Sofer-Schreiber, *Ketov Zot Zikkaron* (1957), 258; N. Ben-Menahem, *Be-Sha'arei Sefer* (1967), 11; *Beth Yaakov*, 7 (1966), 7, 38.

[Naphtali Ben-Menahem]

EISENSTADT, MOSES ELEAZAR (1869–1943), rabbi, educator, and author in Russia and France. Born in Nesvizh, Belorussia, he studied at the yeshivah of *Volozhin, and from 1889 at the university and Hochschule fuer die Wissenschaft des Judentums in Berlin. He wrote his doctoral thesis on "Bible Criticism in Talmudic Literature" in 1898. From 1899 to 1910 Eisenstadt officiated as *Kazyonny Ravvin (government-appointed rabbi) of Rostov, and from 1911 to 1923 held the same position in St. Petersburg. He subsequently immigrated to France, and in 1926 was appointed rabbi of the Ohel Ya'akov community of the Russian Jews in Paris. He also lectured in modern Hebrew literature at the rabbinical seminary. When the Nazis occupied Paris, he left for New York, and in 1942 was appointed rabbi of the Merkaz Beit Yisrael community of Russian Jews there. From an early age, he published articles, reviews, and stories in the Jewish press in Hebrew, Yiddish, Russian, and German. His books include *Be-Shuvi el Ereẓ Moladeti* ("On My Return to My Fatherland," 1893), and *Me-Ḥayyei Benei Lita* ("From the Lives of the Inhabitants of Lithuania," 1893). In 1918, he was a member of the editorial board of the Jewish historical journal *He-Avar*, published in Petrograd.

BIBLIOGRAPHY: LNYL, 1 (1956), 66–67; Kressel, Leksikon, 1 (1965), 84.

EISENSTADT, SAMUEL NOAH (1923–), Israel sociologist. Born in Warsaw, and educated at the Hebrew University of Jerusalem and at the London School of Economics, Eisenstadt joined the faculty of the Hebrew University in 1948 and became chairman of the department of sociology in 1951. Eisenstadt's contributions have been chiefly in the fields of political and historical sociology, with special attention to the analysis of social structure and of bureaucracy. In 1973 Eisenstadt was awarded the Israel Prize for social sciences. His book *The Political Systems of Empires* (1963) analyzed the social structures of the major empires throughout world history; this work has been hailed as the most significant contribution to political sociology after that of Max Weber. Among his other works in this field are *Political Sociology* (1955), *The Absorption of Immigrants* (1954), and *From Generation to Generation: Age Groups and Social Structure* (1956). The latter are comparative studies based chiefly on materials referring to problems arising from mass immigration, and the integration of the many different cultures which are found in Israel. Eisenstadt brought the analysis of developmental and general social problems into the framework of sociological analysis and comparative institutional study through his *Essays on Comparative Institutions* (1965) and his *Comparative Social Problems* (1964). He also published "Bureaucracy, Bureaucratization and Debureaucratization" in *Administrative Science Quarterly*, 4 (1959), 302–20, and *Israeli Society* (1967). Other books include *Tradition, Change, and Modernity* (1983), *Transformation of Israeli Society* (1986), and *European Civilization in a Comparative Perspective* (1987).

[Werner J. Cahnman and Pearl J. Lieff]

EISENSTADTER, MEIR BEN JUDAH LEIB (d. 1852), rabbi, author, and liturgical poet (*paytan*). Eisenstadter was born in Schossberg (Sastin), but in his youth moved to Eisenstadt, from which he took his name. He was also known as "Maharam Esh" (Hebrew acronym for Morenu ha-Rav Meir Eisenshtadt – "our teacher, the rabbi Eisenstadter"). He studied under Moses *Sofer and married the daughter of David Deutsch, the rabbi of Nove Mesto in Slovakia, where Eisenstadter was appointed head of the yeshivah. After serving as rabbi in Baja, Balassagyarmat (1815–35), he was appointed rabbi of Ungvar in 1835 and was regarded, together with Moses *Schick, as the leading rabbi of Hungary. In Ungvar, too, he headed a large yeshivah and many of the future rabbis of Hungary were his pupils. He took an active part in the communal life of Hungarian Jewry and exercised a profound influence on the course it was to take. He vehemently opposed the progressives who desired to introduce religious changes and reforms. He was the author of *Imrei Esh*, responsa in two parts (1852–64); *Imrei Yosher*, sermons (Ungvar, 1864); *Imrei Binah*, novellae on a number of tractates (1866), and, with the same title, his novellae and those of his son on the laws of *shehitah*, appended to A.Z. Schorr's *Simlah Ḥadashah* (1927); *Imrei Esh*, in two parts, expositions of the Pentateuch with the novellae of his father-in-law and his son (1901); and *Zikhron Yehudah*, containing his testament and novellae (1900). The greatest rabbis of Hungary and Galicia including Solomon *Kluger of Brod, Ḥayyim *Halberstam of Neu-Sandec (Nowy Sacz), and Simon *Sofer of Cracow addressed problems to him. His son Menahem succeeded him as rabbi in Ungvar.

BIBLIOGRAPHY: M. Eisenstadt, *Zikhron Yehudah* (1900); P.Z. Schwartz, *Shem ha-Gedolim me-Ereẓ Hagar*, 2 (1914), 1b, no. 15; A. Stern, *Meliẓei Esh al Ḥodshei Kislev-Tevet* (1962²), 112b, no. 436; H.Y. Braun, *Toledot Gedolei Yisrael Anshei Shem* (1943), 1–12; J. Spiegel, in: *Arim ve-Immahot be-Yisrael*, 4 (1950), 9–12; S. Reinhasz, in: *Enẓiklopedyah shel Galuyyot*, 7 (1959), 403–10.

[Itzhak Alfassi]

EISENSTAEDT, ALFRED (1898–1995), photographer. Born in Dirschau, West Prussia (now Tczew, Poland), Eisenstaedt was the pre-eminent photojournalist of his time, whose pioneering images for *Life* magazine helped define American photojournalism. Over a career that lasted more than 50 years, Eisenstaedt became famous as the quintessential *Life* photographer, producing more than 2,500 picture stories and 90 covers for the magazine. His most famous photograph, of an exuberant American sailor kissing a nurse in a dance-like dip in Times Square on V-J Day, August 14, 1945, summed up the euphoria many Americans felt as the war came to a close. It is the most widely reproduced of the magazine's millions of photographs. Another of his best-known images shows Joseph Goebbels, the Nazi propaganda minister, in 1933, glaring at the camera. "Here are the eyes of hate," the photographer later wrote.

When Alfred was eight, his father, a merchant, moved the family to Berlin, and they remained there until Hitler came to power. At 17, Alfred was drafted into the German army and served on the Flanders front, where he was wounded in both legs. Sent home, he recuperated for a year before he could walk unaided. He used the time to visit museums and study light and composition. Although he became a belt and button salesman, he saved his money and bought photographic equipment. In 1927, while vacationing with his parents in Czechoslovakia, he took a photograph of a woman playing tennis. He was on a hillside 50 yards away, and the photo captured the long shadow the woman cast on the court. He sold it to *Der Welt Spiegel* for about $12.

By the age of 31, he became a full-time photographer, working for Pacific and Atlantic Photos, which became the Associated Press. At the time he began working with the innovative Leica 35 mm. camera, which had been invented four years earlier. His assignments included portraits of statesmen and famous artists. By 1933 he was sent to Italy to shoot the first meeting of Hitler and Mussolini. Two years after Hitler took power, Eisenstaedt immigrated to the United States, where he was soon hired with three other photographers, including Margaret *Bourke-White, to be the original photographers for the new *Life* magazine. The first issue carried five pages of Eisenstaedt's pictures. He became known for his ability to bring back visually striking pictures from almost any assignment. Among the many celebrities he photographed were Churchill, John F. Kennedy, Chaplin, Marilyn Monroe, George Bernard Shaw, and a smoldering Marlene Dietrich in top hat and tails. His mastery of the Leica allowed him to capture his subjects in unguarded moments, creating a sense of intimacy. In a 1947 picture, for example, the physicist J. Robert *Oppenheimer puffs on a cigarette as he stands in front of a blackboard covered with mathematical formulas.

Eisenstaedt became an American citizen in 1942 and traveled overseas to document the effects of the war. He received many awards and honors, including the Presidential Medal of Arts and the Master of Photography Award, given by the International Center of Photography. He continued to work until shortly before his death. In 1993 he photographed President Clinton, his wife, and their daughter on Martha's Vineyard, Mass.

He was the subject of many exhibitions and was the author of many books, including *Witness to Our Time* (1966), *The Eye of Eisenstaedt* (1969), *Eisenstaedt's Guide to Photography* (1978), and *Eisenstaedt: Germany* (1981). At age 81 he returned to Germany for the first time for an exhibition of pictures he had taken there in the 1920s and 1930s. Things in Germany seemed different, he said, from when he left. "You couldn't call it prettier, but maybe more relaxed."

[Stewart Kampel (2nd ed.)]

EISENSTEIN, FERDINAND GOTTHOLD (1823–1852), German mathematician. Eisenstein was brought up in poverty and succeeded in studying at a university despite considerable family opposition. In 1847 he became a lecturer at Berlin University. He made important contributions to algebra and to elliptic functions and their applications to number theory.

EISENSTEIN, IRA (1906–2001), U.S. rabbi and leader of the *Reconstructionist movement. Born in New York City, Eisenstein grew up in Harlem along with his friend Milton *Steinberg. Eisenstein was a grandson of Judah David *Eisenstein, a traditional scholar who compiled the anthology *Oẓer Dinim u-Minhagim*. He was ordained at the Jewish Theological Seminary in 1931. He later served as president of the *Rabbinical Assembly from 1952 to 1954. As a son-in-law and leading disciple of Kaplan, the founder of Reconstructionist Judaism, Eisenstein was associate rabbi from 1931 to 1954 of Kaplan's Society for the Advancement of Judaism in New York City, the first Reconstructionist synagogue. Eisenstein was the associate chairman and later the editor of *The Reconstructionist* from 1935 to 1982, which in the 1930s and 1940s was the premier intellectual journal of the American Jewish community and which he was instrumental in creating. In 1954, the invitation was extended for Eisenstein to become the rabbi of Anshe Emet congregation in Chicago. The relationship with Anshe Emet did not endure, and in 1959 he returned to New York to become the president of the Jewish Reconstructionist Foundation, which he had founded. The foundation continued to publish the magazine, coordinated annual conventions of Reconstructionists, expanded the Reconstructionist Press, and began to issue a series of pamphlets on Reconstructionist ideas. One of these, titled "The Havurah Idea," was the first published program for what would in the 1960s and 1970s become a new and vital form of Jewish community.

While Mordecai *Kaplan, who was deeply rooted in the Jewish Theological Seminary, was reluctant to see Reconstructionism become a separate denomination, Eisenstein advocated for the creation of institutions that could embody Reconstructionist ideas. He founded the Fellowship of Reconstructionist Congregations and Havurot in 1955. Following Kaplan's retirement from JTS in 1963, Eisenstein rallied Reconstructionist lay leaders in support of establishing a seminary for the training of Reconstructionist rabbis, and in 1968 he became the founding president of the *Reconstructionist Rabbinical College (RRC) in Philadelphia, from which he retired in 1981.

In fulfillment of Kaplan's concept that American Jews "lived in two civilizations" Eisenstein's vision of rabbinic training mandated that RRC students simultaneously pursue a Ph.D. in religious studies at nearby Temple University where they would interact with faculty and students of many different religious traditions.

Eisenstein was coeditor of the controversial *New Haggadah* (1941), which eliminated the ten plagues as "unedifying" and celebrated Moses, rather than God, as the one who had "liberated Israel." With Kaplan, Steinberg, and Eugene Kohn, Eisenstein helped edit the original Reconstructionist prayerbooks for Sabbath (1945), High Holidays (1948), and Festivals (1958). This liturgy applied Kaplan's key ideas such as eliminating the idea of Jews as the chosen people and the mention of miracles and the hope for a personal Messiah, although only Kaplan was "excommunicated" by a small sect of Orthodox rabbis upon the publication of the Sabbath Prayerbook.

Recognizing that Kaplan's major books were often seen as overly long and complex for the average reader, Eisenstein helped to popularize Kaplan's work in *Creative Judaism* (1936) and *What We Mean by Religion* (1938). He also wrote *Judaism under Freedom* (1956) and *Reconstructing Judaism* (1986) and co-edited *Mordecai M. Kaplan: An Evaluation* (1952). With his wife, the musicologist Judith Kaplan Eisenstein, he co-authored a number of cantatas based on Jewish themes.

[Jack Reimer / Richard Hirsch (2nd ed)]

EISENSTEIN, JUDAH DAVID (1854–1956), U.S. encyclopedist, anthologist, and author. Eisenstein was born in Mezhirech, Poland, and in 1872 immigrated to the United States, where he became a successful coat manufacturer. He was a founder of the first Hebrew society in the United States, Shoḥarei Sefat Ever (1880), and one of its first Hebrew writers. Although he also undertook translations, e.g., in 1891 publishing the text of the American constitution in Hebrew and Yiddish, his fame rests on his anthologies, for which he earned the epithet "master of treasuries" (as all his anthologies bore the title *Oẓar*, "Treasury"). He published a Jewish encyclopedia in ten volumes with the assistance of experts from various countries, *Oẓar Yisrael* (1907–13). His other anthologies include *Oẓar Midrashim* (2 vols., 1915); *Oẓar Dinim u-Minhagim* (1917, "Laws and Customs"); *Oẓar Derushim Nivḥarim* (1918, "Selected Homilies"); *Oẓar Derashot* (1919, "Sermons"); *Oẓar Perushim ve-Ẓiyyurim al Haggadah shel Pesaḥ* (1920), on the *Haggadah; Oẓar Massa'ot* (1926), anthology of Jewish travel literature; *Oẓar Ma'amrei Tanakh* (1925), a biblical concordance; *Oẓar Ma'amrei Hazal* (1922), rabbinic aphorisms; *Oẓar Vikkuḥim* (1928), disputations; *Oẓar Musar u-Middot* (1941), on ethics and morals.

Eisenstein was the author of *Ma'amrei Bikkoret* (1897), a criticism of Rodkinson's translation of the Talmud; *History of the First Russian American Jewish Congregation* (1901); *Development of the Jewish Casuistic Literature in America* (1904); and other works. Eisenstein's *Commentary on the Torah*, edited by B.D. Perlow and I. Eisenstein, was published posthumously (1960). His autobiography and memoirs, *Oẓar Zikhronotai* (1929), includes a bibliography of his articles.

BIBLIOGRAPHY: AJYB, 6 (1904/05), 85; *Hadoar*, 36:27 (May 25, 1956); L.P. Gartner, in: AJHSQ, 52 (1962–63), 234–43; R.L. Samuels, in: AJA, 12 (1960), 123–42.

[Abraham Meir Habermann]

EISENSTEIN, JUDITH KAPLAN (1909–1996), U.S. musicologist, educator, composer, and author. Born in New York

City, Eisenstein was the eldest of the four daughters of Rabbi Mordecai Menachem *Kaplan, the philosopher and founder of Reconstructionist Judaism, and Lena (Rubin) Kaplan. In 1922, at the age of 12, she celebrated one of the earliest known bat mitzvah ceremonies in the U.S. at the Society for the Advancement of Judaism, where her father was the presiding rabbi. Judith Kaplan Eisenstein had a second bat mitzvah at the age of 82 where she was honored by a number of Jewish and feminist leaders.

Kaplan continued her Jewish education at the Jewish Theological Seminary Teachers Institute and her secular education at Columbia University Teachers College, from which she received her B.S. in 1928 and her M.A. in 1932 in music education. Following a brief first marriage that ended in divorce, Kaplan married Rabbi Ira *Eisenstein, her father's assistant at the Society for the Advancement of Judaism, in 1934. This marriage endured for over 60 years; the couple had three children. From 1929 to 1954 Judith Eisenstein taught music education and the history of Jewish music at the Jewish Theological Seminary's Teachers Institute (now the Albert A. List College of Jewish Studies). While at the Teachers Institute she began her publishing career with a Jewish songbook for children, *Gateway to Jewish Song* (1937). She wrote several more books on Jewish music and on Jewish musical history for young readers; these include *Festival Songs* (1943) and *Songs of Childhood* (1955) with Frieda Prensky. In the years between 1942 and 1974, Eisenstein composed two song cycles and five cantatas on Jewish themes, written in collaboration with her husband. The most frequently performed of these is "What Is Torah?" (1942).

Eisenstein began doctoral studies at the School of Sacred Music of Hebrew Union College-Jewish Institute of Religion in New York in 1959. Her dissertation was entitled, "The Liturgical Chant of Provencal and West Sephardic Jews in Comparison to the Song of the Troubadours and the Cantigas." After receiving her Ph.D., she taught at HUC-JIR from 1966 to 1979. In 1978, when her husband became president of the Reconstructionist Rabbinical College, the Eisensteins moved to Philadelphia. Eisenstein taught at the RRC from 1978 to 1981. Her book, *Heritage of Music: The Music of the Jewish People*, was published in 1972 and reprinted in 1990. In 1987, she wrote and broadcast a series of 13 radio lectures on the history of Jewish music.

BIBLIOGRAPHY: I. Eisenstein, *Reconstructing Judaism: An Autobiography* (1986); P.B. Eisenstein, "Eisenstein, Judith Kaplan," in: P.E. Hyman and D.D. Moore (eds.), *Jewish Women in America*, 1 (1997), 370–71.

[Carole Kessner (2nd ed.)]

EISENSTEIN, SERGEI MIKHAILOVICH (1898–1948), Russian film director, son of a Jewish father who converted to Christianity and a non-Jewish mother. Eisenstein's work, revolutionary both in technique and in subject matter, was a major contribution to the modern art of the cinema. He was originally trained as a civil engineer, and served the Red Army in this capacity during the Russian civil war. In 1920, however, Eisenstein took up stage work, joining first the Proletkult Theater in Moscow and then the avant-garde company of V. Meyerhold. He was a disciple of Meyerhold in stage direction. After deciding that the theater was not close enough to the masses, he turned his attention to the cinema. His first film was *The Strike* (1924), followed in 1925 by *Battleship Potemkin*, which had an immediate impact on contemporary film making. It demonstrated a new approach, the dramatic handling of crowd scenes, and the use of nonprofessional actors for greater realism. Eisenstein further developed his methods in *October* (1926), a film about the Russian Revolution, and *The General Line* (1929), which extolled Soviet agriculture. He was invited to Hollywood in 1931, but his scenarios proved unacceptable there. With the assistance of the novelist Upton Sinclair he spent 14 months in Mexico making a film on the Mexican revolution but he was recalled to the U.S.S.R. before its completion. Parts were edited in Hollywood as *Thunder Over Mexico* (1933), evoking much criticism as being untrue to Eisenstein's principles. Another section of the film was issued in 1940 as *Time in the Sun*. In the 1930s he encountered difficulties with the authorities, who saw film as an important propaganda tool. They criticized his esthetic approach, and he was unable complete some of his works. In Russia, after these difficulties, he won the Order of Lenin for *Alexander Nevsky* (1938). Of his *Ivan the Terrible* trilogy, part 1 was shown in 1946, part 2 was suppressed until 1958, and part 3 was not shot. He expounded his theories in lectures and in two books, *The Film Sense* (1942) and *Film Form* (1949). Though he never affirmed his Jewish ancestry, he agreed to appear together with other known Jewish cultural activists in antifascist meetings on August 24, 1941, and in 1942. Eisenstadt's memoirs, called *Beyond the Stars* and written in 1946, appeared as volume 4 of his selected works in 1997 (published by the British Film Institute). A previous version had appeared in 1983 as *Immoral Memories*.

BIBLIOGRAPHY: M. Seton, *Sergei Eisenstein* (Eng., 1952). **ADD. BIBLIOGRAPHY:** O. Bulgakowa, *Sergei Eisenstein, a Biography* (2002); A. Nesbit, *Sergei Eisenstein and the Shape of Thinking* (2003); R. Bergen, *Sergei Eisenstein: A Life in Conflict* (1999).

EISLER, EDMUND MENAHEM (1850–1942), writer who envisioned a Zionist utopia. Born in Tyrnau, Slovakia, Eisler was active for many years in Jewish literature and journalism. He contributed Hebrew poetry to the literary annual *Kokhevei Yiẓḥak* (1877) but later wrote only in German. In 1882 he wrote a vision of a Zionist utopia in the form of a novel entitled *Ein Zukunftsbild*, which he published anonymously in 1885. The book relates the exodus of Jews from Europe and the establishment of a Jewish state under the rule of a king (the one who had conceived the idea of the exodus and the state was chosen as a monarch). It includes a detailed description of the constitution, how Hebrew functions as the official language of the country, and the division of the country into tribes according to the biblical account. There is even a description of the war that the young country must wage against those who threaten to destroy it, and its total victory followed by peace. Eisler prophesied a Europe without Jews after anti-Jewish legislation and terrible persecution and predicted the path of the German "hob-nailed boot." The novel fell into obscurity until it was rediscovered by Perez Sandler who identified its author and reprinted it in a Hebrew translation (by Y. Tolkes) in an anthology of Zionist utopias, *Ḥezyonei Medinah* ("Visions of a State," 1954), with a monograph on this utopia and its author. The work predates *Herzl's novel *Altneuland* by 17 years, and a copy of it was found in Herzl's personal library.

[Getzel Kressel]

EISLER, GERHART (1897–1968), East German Communist. Born in Leipzig, he was the son of Rudolf *Eisler and became a convinced Communist after serving with the Austrian army in World War I. In 1930 he served as political secretary in the Far East bureau of the Communist Trade Union International in Shanghai. Eisler went to Spain in 1936 and later to France, where he was interned in 1940. On his release he left for the United States where he became a leading Communist agitator. In 1949 he was sentenced to a year's imprisonment for contempt of Congress when he refused to be sworn as a witness before the House of Representatives' Un-American Activities Committee. While free on bail pending an appeal, he escaped to England on a Polish liner, after paying 25 cents to tour it as a visitor. On arrival in England he was arrested on the application of the United States Embassy, and a political storm arose when it was suggested that there was collusion between the British and American secret services. Eventually Eisler was released and flew to Prague, where he engaged in Communist propaganda activities for four years. Later he was minister of information in East Germany (until 1952) and became chairman of the East German radio authority. He died while on a mission to the Soviet Union.

BIBLIOGRAPHY: *The Times* (London, April 21, 1968). **ADD. BIBLIOGRAPHY:** C. Epstein, *The Last Revolutionaries – German Communists in their Centuries* (2003).

EISLER, HANNS (1898–1962), German composer; son of Rudolf *Eisler. Eisler, born in Leipzig, was a pupil of Arnold *Schoenberg and Anton von Webern in Vienna. His early compositions were in an advanced idiom, but Eisler soon adapted to the demands of "socialist realism." He went to Berlin in 1924 and wrote the music for some of Bertolt Brecht's plays, including *Die Rundkoepfe und die Spitzkoepfe* and the incidental music for *Galileo*. In 1937 he immigrated to the United States where he lectured at the New School for Social Research, New York, and then went to Hollywood. He was musical assistant to Charlie Chaplin (1942–47) and also composed scores for other filmmakers. He left in 1948 under "voluntary deportation" because of his political past. Settling in East Berlin, he became one of the ideological leaders of musical activity in East Germany. He taught at the Akademie der Kuenste and received a state prize for his compositions in 1950. He composed the national anthem of the German Democratic Republic (to a text by Johannes Becher). He wrote an opera, *Johannes Faustus* (1953), which was criticized for its mysticism. His works include symphonies (e.g., *Deutsche Symphonie*, 1937), chamber music, cantatas, a *Suite for Orchestra with Capriccio* based on Jewish folksongs, operas, oratorios, and songs.

BIBLIOGRAPHY: *Baker's Biog Dict*; *Grove's Dict*; MGG; *Komponisten und Musikwissenschaftler der Deutschen Demokratischen Republik* (1959^2), 47–50.

[Dora Leah Sowden]

EISLER, MÁTYÁS (1865–1931), Hungarian rabbi and scholar. Eisler was born in Paty, county of Pest, and was ordained at the rabbinical seminary of Budapest in 1891. He taught Hebrew at the *Israelitische Lehrbildungsanstalt* in 1890 and later at the University of Kolozsvar. He was chief rabbi of Kolozsvar from 1891 until his death. His scholarly interests included the history of the Jews of Transylvania and Hebrew linguistics, and among his works were *Az erdelyi zsidok mult abol...* ("From the Past of the Jews of Transylvania," 1901) and *Agyökbeli hangok interdialektikus valtozasai az aram nyelvekben* ("Interdialectal Changes of Root Sounds in the Aramaic Languages," 1889).

BIBLIOGRAPHY: *Magyar Zsidó Lexikon* (1929), s.v.

[Alexander Scheiber]

EISLER, MORITZ (1823–1902), educator and historian of Jewish philosophy. Eisler was born in Prossnitz, Moravia. In 1853 he became a teacher of religion at the Piarist high school and director of the communal school at Nikolsburg. In 1862 he founded an organization for the support of disabled Jewish teachers, their widows and orphans (which later became the "Maehrisch-Schlesischer Israelitischer Lehrerverein") and served as its president until 1898. His *Vorlesungen ueber die juedische Philosophie des Mittelalters* ("Lectures On Jewish Philosophy in the Middle Ages," 3 vols., 1870–83) became one of the first attempts to present, in popular fashion, the main systems of medieval Jewish philosophy. In addition, he published a number of essays on specific questions in the history of Jewish philosophy, including essays on *Spinoza, *Ibn Daud, and Ibn *Ẓaddik.

BIBLIOGRAPHY: H. Heller, *Maehren's Maenner der Gegenwart*, 1 (1889), 3, 28; *Kuerschners Deutscher Literatur-Kalender* (1902); Ch. D. Lippe, *Bibliographisches Lexicon*, 1 (1881), 92; 2 (1887), 52.

EISLER, RUDOLF (1873–1926), Austrian philosopher known for encyclopedic writings, especially his dictionaries of philosophy and biographies of philosophers. His works, which contributed greatly to the dissemination of philosophical ideas, include *Geschichte des Monismus* (1910), *Kritische Einfuehrung in die Philosophie* (1905), *Woerterbuch der philosophischen Begriffe und Ausdruecke* (1899), and his *Philosophen-Lexikon* (1912). He was the editor of the *Wissenschaftliche Volksbibliothek*. His *Kant-Lexikon* was published in 1930. Eisler was the father of Gerhart *Eisler, the Communist leader, and Hanns *Eisler, the composer.

BIBLIOGRAPHY: *Oesterreichisches Biographisches Lexikon 1815–1950*, 1 (1957), 238–39. **ADD. BIBLIOGRAPHY:** NDB, 4 (1959), 421f.

[Samuel Hugo Bergman]

EISMANN, MOSES (1847–1893), Hebrew journalist. Born in Tivrov, he began his literary activity in 1870 with an article in *Ha-Meliẓ*, concerning government-appointed rabbis. In *Bi-Fero'a Pera'ot be-Yisrael* (1882), he argued that there was only one solution to the "Jewish Question" – the Jewish settlement of Palestine, which in the course of time would become the home of all the scattered Jews. This was also the subject of his pamphlet *Inyanei ha-Yehudim: She'elat ha-Yeẓi'ah* ("Concerning Jewish Affairs: the Emigration Question," Jerusalem, 1887). In 1890 he participated in the founding convention of Ḥovevei Zion in Odessa. He wrote Yiddish articles in *Der Veker*, edited by *Lilienblum, as well as in other publications. He also wrote articles in Russian under a pseudonym.

His brother, DAVID EISMANN (1869–1922), wrote stories in Russian, published in seven volumes in 1911, dealing mainly with the Jewish intelligentsia, exposed to the cultural environment of Russian society.

BIBLIOGRAPHY: Z. Scharfstein, in: *Moznayim*, 43 (1964/65), 184–7; Waxman, Literature, 4 (1960^2), 403–4.

[Baruch Shohetman]

EISNER, KURT (1867–1919), German socialist leader, who was founder and first prime minister of the Bavarian Republic. Born in Berlin, Eisner became a journalist. He was a contributor to the *Frankfurter Zeitung* from 1891 to 1893, and from 1893 to 1897 to the *Hessische Landeszeitung*. In 1897 he was imprisoned for nine months for lese majesty. In 1898 he joined the social-democratic journal *Vorwaerts* as political editor. In 1905 he had to leave because of disagreements with the orthodox left (Kautsky, Luxemburg, Mehring). Two years later, he became editor of the *Fraenkische Tagespost* (Nuernberg), and from 1910 he reported on the Bavarian Landtag as official correspondent for the *Muenchner Post*. A gifted writer, he had an intellectual and moral approach to political problems. At the beginning of World War I, Eisner favored the granting of war credits to the German government. However, he objected to the imperial policy of conquest and became a bitter opponent of the government's war policies. He was arrested and imprisoned in January 1918 for participating as one of the leaders in the Munich metal workers' peace strike but was released in October, in order to stand as Independent Social-Democratic candidate for the Reichstag. On November 7, 1918, Eisner headed the revolutionary uprising in Munich and next day became prime minister of the new republic of Bavaria. To affix the blame for the war on the German government, he revealed the contents of Bavarian government reports and as a result his enemies falsely accused him of taking huge bribes from the Allies to start the revolution. In the Bavarian elections that followed the uprising, Eisner's Independent Socialist Party received only a small number of votes. On February 21, 1919, on his way to the Landtag (parliament), to announce the resignation of his government, he was shot dead by the young Count Arco-Valley. Eisner's *Gesammelte Schriften* appeared in 1919 in two volumes.

BIBLIOGRAPHY: A. Mitchell, *Revolution in Bavaria 1918–1919: The Eisner Regime and the Soviet Republic* (1965), incl. bibl.; F. Fechenbach, *Der Revolutionaer Kurt Eisner* (1929); F. Schade, *Kurt Eisner und die bayerische Sozial-Demokratie* (1961), incl. bibl.; F. Wiesemann, in: K. Bosl (ed.), *Bayern im Umbruch* (1969), 387–426; F. Eisner, *Kurt Eisner* (Ger., 1979); A.E. Gurganus, *Kurt Eisner* (1984); B. Grau, *Kurt Eisner 1867–1919* (Ger., 2001).

[Bernhard Grau (2nd ed.)]

EISNER, MARK (1886–1953), U.S. lawyer and public official. Eisner was born in New York City. After serving in the New York State Assembly (1913–15), Eisner was appointed delegate to the state's Constitutional Convention (1915). An authority on taxation law, Eisner was collector of internal revenue for the New York district from 1915 to 1919, and lectured on his specialty at New York University and New York Law School. He formed a law partnership in 1924. When the New York City Board of Higher Education was established in 1926, Eisner was appointed a member by Mayor James J. Walker, later serving as chairman (1932–38). Eisner was active in other civic, professional, and communal organizations, including service as president of the *American Association for Jewish Education (1939–47). He wrote *Lay View of Some of the Problems of Higher Education* (1936), and was an editor of *How Government Regulates Business* (1939).

BIBLIOGRAPHY: *New York Times* (March 30, 1953), 21.

[Morton Rosenstock]

EISNER, MICHAEL DAMMANN (1942–), U.S. business executive. Born in Mount Kisco, N.Y., to Lester, a lawyer and administrator for the U.S. Department of Housing and Urban Development, and Margaret (née Dammann), co-founder of the American Safety Razor Company, Eisner grew up in the family's apartment on Fifth Avenue in New York City and graduated from Denison University in 1964. Following summer jobs as a page and a first job as a Federal Communications Commission logging clerk at NBC, Eisner landed a job in the CBS programming department. Unhappy, Eisner sent his resume out to hundreds of companies. ABC head Barry Diller convinced the board to bring Eisner on as assistant to the national programming director, a position he held from 1966 to 1968. From there Eisner rose to senior vice president for prime-time production and development, creating such programs as *Happy Days*, *Barney Miller*, and *Starsky and Hutch*. When Diller took over as chair of Paramount Pictures in 1976, he offered Eisner the position of studio president. Under Eisner, the studio released such hits as *Raiders of the Lost Ark*, *Grease*, *Ordinary People*, *Terms of Endearment*, *Flashdance*, *Trading Places*, *Beverly Hills Cop*, and *Airplane*. Eisner left

Paramount to become chair and CEO of Walt Disney Company in September 1984. At the time, Disney had not had a hit film since 1969 and its profits had fallen dramatically. Eisner reinvigorated the studio on several fronts, luring new executives, making popular films for adults like *Down and Out in Beverly Hills* (1985), re-releasing classic Disney films, creating new animated films such as *Beauty and the Beast* (1991) and *The Lion King* (1994) – and launching Broadway versions of the films – as well as computer animated films in partnership with Pixar such as *Toy Story* (1995) and *Finding Nemo* (2003). He also expanded the company in TV and cable (launching the Disney Channel and acquiring ABC and the Family Channel), expanded the existing Disneyland and Disneyworld resorts and established Disneyland theme parks in Europe outside Paris, France, and in Japan, and acquired Harvey and Bob Weinstein's specialty films division Miramax Films. Although in a 20-year period Eisner increased the value of the company 2000%, his management style and inability to groom a successor led to major conflicts. Former president of production Jeffrey Katzenberg left to found Dreamworks and won a $250 million suit against Disney. Eisner hired former Creative Artist Agency founder Michael Ovitz and then a year later fired him, paying him a severance that exceeded $100 million and spurred several stockholder lawsuits. The relationships with Pixar and Miramax soured. In 2003, Walt Disney's nephew Roy Disney asked Eisner to resign as head of the company. Following a vote to remove Eisner from the board, the Disney CEO announced he would retire at the end of his contract on September 30, 2006. However, subsequently, he announced he would step down on September 30, 2005, and would be succeeded by Robert Iger. Eisner's tenure at Disney has been the subject of several books, including Eisner's own 1998 account, *Work in Progress*, and *Disney Wars* by James Stewart (2005).

[Adam Wills (2nd ed.)]

EISNER, PAVEL (**Paul**; 1889–1958), bilingual Czech-German writer, translator, and literary critic. His literary work made him a bridge-builder between Czech and German cultural circles in Czechoslovakia. Born in Prague, Eisner studied Slavic philology at the German University there and soon became known as the editor of a series of anthologies, mainly of Czech and Slovak folk literature (*Tschechische Anthologie, Slovakische Anthologie, Volkslieder der Slaven, Volksmaerchen der Slaven).* As editor of the literary supplement of the government-owned paper *Prager Presse,* he became one of the few interpreters – most of whom were Jews – of Czech literature to the German reading public. One of the most prolific writers of his time, he translated hundreds of poems and short stories by practically every modern Czech author of importance. On the other hand, he was also a tireless translator from German into Czech, acquainting the Czech reader with authors ranging from J.W. Goethe to Thomas Mann and from Heinrich *Heine to Franz *Kafka. He was the first, in his book *Německá literatura na půdě Československé republiky* ("German Literature on Czechoslovak Soil," 1933), to analyze the contribution of the German Jewish writers from Prague. Czech-German-Jewish symbiosis is also the theme of his book of essays *Milenky* ("Lovers," 1930) and of *Franz Kafka and Prague* (1950). However, the bulk of his literary studies, mainly in the fields of comparative literature, psychology of languages, and the mutual influence of national cultures, remains dispersed in a great number of Central European publications. Although prevented by a hearing defect from becoming a musician, he nevertheless kept in constant touch with musical life and not only translated foreign operas into Czech and libretti of Czech operas (by Dvořák, Martinů, Jeremiáš) into German, but also wrote several studies on the history of music, including one on Jewish music and musical instruments. Shielded by his non-Jewish wife, who was distantly related to Richard Wagner, Eisner escaped deportation during the Nazi occupation and was able to work in the Jewish Museum in Prague. Some of his last essays were published in *Věstník,* the monthly of the Jewish community of Prague. His best known work is *Chrám i tvrz* ("The Cathedral and the Fortress," 1946), an exposition on the Czech language and its riches.

ADD. BIBLIOGRAPHY: A. Mikulášek et al., *Literatura s hvězdou Davidovou*, vol. 1 (1998); *Lexikon české literatury,* 1 (1985).

[Avigdor Dagan]

EISNER, WILL (**William Erwin**; 1917–2005), U.S. comic book artist and author. Born in Brooklyn, N.Y., the son of Jewish immigrants, Eisner published his first drawings in his high school newspaper. He published his first comic in 1936 in *Wow, What a Magazine!*, where he met Jerry Iger. Together they created a comic book outfit, Eisner & Iger, that employed among other artists Bob *Kane, creator of Batman and other superheroes. (Eisner turned down a comic called *Superman* by Jerry *Siegel and Joe *Shuster.)

In 1940 Eisner created the Spirit, a hero without superpowers. Fans called the strip the "Citizen Kane" of comics for its innovation, its seriousness, and its influences. A website devoted to the Spirit described the hero as a man "with no gimmicks or powers" other than "his freedom from society" and noted that Eisner called the Spirit a "middle-class crime fighter." At the height of its popularity, the Spirit appeared in 20 newspapers, reaching 5 million readers every Sunday. In 1942, when Eisner was drafted into the army, he started drawing comics for the military. In late 1945 he went back to the Spirit, and with the help of other artists, including Jules *Feiffer, he revived and deepened it. The Spirit expired in 1952. For the next 25 years, Eisner spent much of his time running the American Visual Corporation, a producer of education, army, and government comic books. Military manuals used to be dry and virtually unreadable but Eisner used words and pictures together to show soldiers how to do everything from cleaning their tanks to putting their lives back together after the war.

The Kitchen Sink Press reprinted all of the postwar Spirit comics from 1978 to 1998. Meanwhile, in the 1970s, Eisner was reborn as a comic artist. In 1978 he wrote and drew *A Contract* *with God*, a comic book story about Frimme Hersh, a Jewish immigrant who becomes a slumlord in the Bronx when he discovers that God has forsaken him. With that book, Eisner became famous for his moody rain, which came to be called "Eisner spritz." His work over the years was also noted for wordless, emotional close-ups on characters' faces. Eisner is credited with coining the phrase "graphic novel" in 1978. Eisner's seriousness influenced the work of Art *Spiegelman, author of *Maus*. Eisner wrote two books on comic art, *Comic and Sequential Art* in 1985 and *Graphic Storytelling* in 1996.

In 2004, Eisner took on Charles Dickens in *Fagin the Jew*, challenging most characterizations in *Oliver Twist* that stereotyped Jews. In Eisner's version of events, Fagin, who is in prison awaiting the hangman, confronts Dickens and demands a recasting of his characters without the prejudice in the novel. "A Jew is not Fagin," he tells the author, "any more than a Gentile is Sikes!" another character in the story. Eisner's *Last Day in Vietnam*, a collection of the military battle stories he wrote in Korea and Vietnam, was issued in 2005. His last work, *The Plot: The Secret Story of the Protocols of the Elders of Zion*, provided a graphic history of one of the most notorious works in the pantheon of antisemitism.

[Stewart Kampel (2nd ed.)]

EISS, ALEXANDER VON (1832–1921), Austro-Hungarian soldier. Born in Piesling, Moravia, Eiss joined the army in 1848 and took part in Austria's wars against Italy (1849), France and Italy (1859), and Prussia and Italy (1866). He was one of the first Jewish officers to receive many decorations for heroism. Eiss was proud of his Jewish identity and fought more than 30 duels over insults to his people. In 1866 he was awarded the Order of the Iron Crown, which conferred hereditary knighthood upon him. After the conquest of Bosnia, Eiss was awarded the Order of Maria Theresa, after having rejected it years earlier when it entailed his conversion to Christianity. In 1896, after becoming a major-general, he retired from the army and became almost blind. He sometimes appeared in his general's uniform at Zionist meetings in Vienna. His proud Jewish stance brought him to the attention of Herzl, who made him responsible for administering the central organ of the Zionist Organization, *Die *Welt*. Later, he also headed the Vienna office of the *Jewish National Fund. Also his three sons became officers in the army; two of them fell in World War I.

BIBLIOGRAPHY: N. Agmon (Bistritzky) (ed.), *Megillat ha-Adamah*, 2 (1951), 56; H. Gold (ed.), *Die Juden und Judengemeinden Maehrens* (1929), 468. **ADD. BIBLIOGRAPHY:** E.A. Schmiedl, *Juden in der k. (u.) k. Armee 1788–1918* (1989); I. Deák, *A Social and Political History of the Habsburg Officer Corps 1848–1918* (1990).

[Mordechai Kaplan]

°**EISSFELDT, OTTO** (1887–1973), German Lutheran Bible scholar. From 1913 to 1921 he was *privatdocent* in Berlin, and from 1921, professor in Halle (Saale). In his two principal fields, literary criticism and the history of religion, he was decisively influenced by his teachers Smend, with whom he studied at Goettingen, and Baudissin, who taught him in Berlin. (At Goettingen he studied with Wellhausen as well.) Following Smend, Eissfeldt postulated instead of Wellhausen's oldest Hexateuch source, J, two originally independent sources, J^1 and J^2, or L (Lay source) and J, and also the continuation of the Hexateuch sources beyond Joshua (*Hexateuch-Synopse*, 1922; *Die Quellen des Richterbuches*, "The Sources of the Book of Judges," 1925; *Die aeltesten Traditionen Israels*, 1950; *Die Genesis der Genesis*, 1958). His comprehensive *Einleitung in das Alte Testament* (1934, 1964[3]; Eng. trans., *The Old Testament, An Introduction*, 1965) strives to preserve the heritage of Gunkel, being concerned with the smallest preliterary units and their "Situation in Life" *(Sitz im Leben)*. Eissfeldt's inaugural lecture "Jahwe and Baal" given in Berlin (1914) prefigured the development of his work in the history of religion, which, to begin with, followed in the footsteps of Baudissin (the publication of his *Kyrios*, 1929); he concerned himself with numerous problems and figures in the Canaanite-Phoenician religion (*Der Gott Bethel*, 1930; *Der Gott Thabor*, 1934; *Molk als Opferbegriff im Punischen und Hebraeischen* ("Molek as a Sacrificial Term in Hebrew and Punic"), 1935; *Der Gott Karmel*, 1953), and after the discoveries at Ras Shamra the specific study of their Ugaritic manifestations (*Ras Schamra und Sanchun aton*, 1939; *El im ugaritischen Pantheon*, 1951). His chief aim was to arrive at a better understanding of the religion of the Israelites (*Ba'alsamen und Jahwe*, 1939; *Jahwe Zebaoth*, 1950; *El and Yahwe*, 1956; *Adonis und Adona*, 1970). He edited the *Handbuch zum Alten Testament* and, together with A. Alt, the third edition of R. Kittel's *Biblia Hebraica*. Many of his shorter articles were collected in *Kleine Schriften* (5 vols., 1962ff.).

ADD. BIBLIOGRAPHY: G. Wallis, DB, 1, 327.

[Rudolf Smend]

EISSLER, KURT R. (1908–1999), psychoanalyst. Born in Vienna, Eissler worked at the Vienna Psychoanalytic Institute under August Eichhorn and applied his training to juvenile delinquents. When the Nazis took over Austria, he left Vienna and settled in the United States. On the basis of his Viennese experience he edited and contributed to the book *Searchlights on Delinquency* (1949). Eissler was the first analyst who in 1943 broke away from tradition and treated schizophrenics. He wrote *Limitations to Psychotherapy of Schizophrenics* (1943). His action at that time was considered a bold step and he attempted in his book *Objective Criteria of Recovery from Neuropsychiatric Disorders* (1947) to introduce research methods into this area of psychotherapy. Later he began research into the psychodynamics of dying. His wide scholarship was evident in works like *Goethe, a Psychoanalytic Study* (1963), *Leonardo da Vinci: Psychoanalytic Notes on the Enigma* (1961), and *Freud and the Seduction Theory: A Brief Love Affair* (2001). His wife, Ruth Eissler, also trained at the Vienna Psychoanalytic Institute, was known for her work with children.

BIBLIOGRAPHY: A. Grinstein, *Index of Psychoanalytic Writings*, 1 (1956), 435–7; 6 (1964), 3135–36.

[Miriam Gay]

EITAN, RAPHAEL (**"Raful"**; 1929–2004), Israeli soldier, 11th chief of staff of the IDF. Eitan was born in Israel and began his military career as an officer in the *Palmaḥ and was wounded in the battle for Jerusalem during the War of Independence.

In the 1956 Sinai Campaign he was one of the first to parachute into the Mitla Pass, and took a prominent part in the campaign in Sinai during the Six-Day War. He commanded the Israeli commando force which raided Beirut airport in 1968 and was later appointed chief infantry and paratroop officer. During the Yom Kippur War his unit played a key role in stemming the Syrian attack and advanced to within 25 miles of Damascus.

In 1978 he was appointed chief of staff in succession to Lt.-General Mordecai ("Motta") *Gur, taking up his appointment in April. During his service as chief of staff he initiated the "Raful Youth" project, a special program for youth from underprivileged backgrounds. In his position as chief of staff he commanded the Israeli forces in the 1982 Lebanon War. In 1983 he was criticized by the *Kahan Commission – established to investigate the causes of the killing by Phalangist forces of Palestinians in the refugee camps of Sabra and Shatilla in west Beirut – for failure to try to prevent the massacre, but was not dismissed since his term as chief of staff was by then nearly over.

In 1983 Eitan formed the *Tzomet political party, which united with the ultra-right-wing Teḥiyah party before the elections for the Eleventh Knesset in 1984. He was elected to the Eleventh on the joint slate and to the Twelfth Knesset in 1988 with Tzomet running independently, having split with Teḥiyah. Tzomet contested the 1992 elections on a hawkish, anti-religious platform and won eight seats, making it the fourth largest party in the Knesset; it remained in the opposition rather than join Yitzhak Rabin's Labor-led coalition. He was elected again to the Knesset in the 1996 elections, running on the combined *Likud-Gesher-Tzomet ticket, and was appointed minister of agriculture and environment and deputy prime minister in the *Netanyahu government. His influence on government policy was minimal, and as a result he lost public support. In 1998 he announced his candidacy for prime minister, but withdrew later on. In the 1999 elections, Tzomet failed to win any seats and as a consequence Eitan retired from political and public life. He drowned in November 2004 when he was swept off a breakwater in Ashdod port on a stormy day.

[Fern Lee Seckbach / Rohan Saxena and Susan Hattis Rolef (2nd ed.)]

EITINGER, LEO S. (1912–1996), psychiatrist and pioneer researcher in psychotraumatology. Born in Lomnice, Czechoslovakia, and graduating from medical school in 1937, Eitinger fled from the Nazis in 1939 and came to Norway as a refugee with a Nansen passport. He was given permission to work as a resident in psychiatry in Norway until the Nazi occupation of Norway in 1940. In 1942 he was deported to Auschwitz together with the Norwegian Jews and was one of the very few to survive. After the war he returned to Norway, where he specialized in psychiatry. Eitinger wrote his doctoral thesis on "Psykiatriske undersøkelser blant flyktninger i Norge" ("Psychiatric Examination among Refugees in Norway," 1958). In 1954 Eitinger was awarded the King's Gold Medal for his study of the influence of military life on young Norwegian men's mental health. He is regarded as one of the founders of victimology, the study of the effects of aggression upon the victim. After spending a year in Israel (1961–62) examining survivors of concentration camps, he published *Concentration Camp Survivors in Norway and Israel* (1964). This work, together with "Mortality and Morbidity after Excessive Stress" (1973), were his greatest achievements. He described a "concentration camp syndrome" comprising anxiety and depression in the survivors. He ascribed this to physical trauma. Eitinger, professor of psychiatry at Oslo University, was president of the Norwegian Psychiatric Association from 1963 to 1967. In 1966 he became head of the University Psychiatric Clinic. As professor emeritus, Leo Eitinger continued his research and writing uninterruptedly. He was awarded the World Veterans Federation's Prize in 1995 for his unrelenting work for war veterans. He was also appointed Commander of the Royal Norwegian St. Olav Order, an award given to him by the king of Norway for his great contribution to medical science. He and his wife, Lisl Eitinger, devoted their lives to the promotion of human rights and the fight against injustice and racism. In this spirit they established the University of Oslo's Human Rights Award, the Lisl and Leo Eitinger Prize.

BIBLIOGRAPHY: L. Weisaeth, *Echoes of the Holocaust*, 5 (July 1997).

[Inger-Lise Grusd / Lynn Claire Feinberg (2nd ed.)]

EITINGON, MAX (1881–1943), psychoanalyst. Born in Mohilev, Russia, Eitingon was raised in Leipzig, Germany, where his parents settled. He studied philosophy, first in Heidelberg and then in Marburg, where he was a pupil of Hermann *Cohen. However, he subsequently moved to the study of medicine, and qualified as a physician at Zurich in 1909. There he joined the group of psychiatrists headed by Bleuler and Jung, who tried to give Sigmund *Freud's theories a broader basis by applying them to psychiatric diseases. While still a medical student in 1907, Eitingon went to Vienna, where (as Freud himself disclosed) he was the first foreign visitor to study psychoanalysis at its source. Later he settled in Berlin. During World War I he served in the Austrian medical corps, and his encounter with war neuroses induced him to establish clinics for psychoanalytical treatment. In 1919 he was appointed a member of the so-called "Committee" – a small inner circle at the heart of the psychoanalytical movement. In 1920, together with Karl *Abraham and E. Simmel, he founded the Berlin Psychoanalytic Polyclinic to provide treatment for the underprivileged and to establish a program for the teaching of psychoanalysis. This Polyclinic was in 1924 registered as the Berlin Institute for Psychoanalysis, and became the model on which later institutes were based. Eitingon was elected president of the International Psychoanalytical Association at the Innsbruck congress in 1927. He chaired three later congresses and resigned only in 1932. After the rise of the Nazis, Eitingon immigrated to Jerusalem. In 1933 he founded the Palestine Psychoanalytical Society and a year later he established the Psychoanalytical Institute (subsequently named in his memory), of which he remained the head until his death. His move to Palestine was a natural consequence of his lifelong interest in and devotion to Zionism. He placed the Psychoanalytical Institute, as well as his own experience, at the disposal of Youth Aliyah.

BIBLIOGRAPHY: M. Wulff (ed.), *Max Eitingon: In Memoriam* (1950); E. Jones, *The Life and Work of S. Freud*, 2 (1955) and 3 (1957), indices; E. Gumbel, in: *Israel Annals of Psychiatry...*, 3 (1965), 89; S.L. Pomer, in: F. Alexander et al. (eds.), *Psychoanalytic Pioneers* (1966), 51–63.

[Heinrich Zwi Winnik]

EIZENBERG, JULIE (1964–), U.S. architect; president and founder of the architectural firm Koning Eizenberg Architects, Inc., a California corporation established in 1981 and based in Santa Monica. The vice president is Hendrick Koning. This husband-and-wife team is known in the U.S. and Australia for its imaginative, site-specific, and people-oriented approach. Both principals hold degrees in architecture from the University of Melbourne, Australia, and the University of California, Los Angeles. The firm has a reputation for its creative thinking. The postmodern approach to design results in buildings with clear, clean, straight lines applied to a variety of commercial, retail, hotel, and residential premises. The firm is also known for designing affordable housing, schools, and community buildings. Its long list of honors includes awards for such buildings as the Simone Hotel, the first new single-room occupancy to be built in Los Angeles in 30 years. This hotel, built in the "skid row" neighborhood, won the National AIA Honor Award in 1994 for providing subtle changes in the usual plans for low-cost housing. They planned especially for the safety, comfort, and dignity of the occupants. Good lighting in the rooms, kitchen, and lounges provided a cheerful atmosphere. The firm also won the national competition in 2001 for the design of two new schools for the Chicago Public Schools and for the Pittsburgh Children's Museum expansion in 2000. Julie Eizenberg has lectured widely in the United States and Australia. She was the William Henry Bishop Visiting Professor at Yale University in 2004. Later projects in Los Angeles include the downtown LA Standard, 5th Street Family Housing, P.S. 1 Elementary School expansion, RAD Clothing, the Avalon Hotel, and the 25th Street Studio.

BIBLIOGRAPHY: W.J. Mitchel, A. Betsky, and J. Eizenberg, *Koning Eizenberg Buildings* (1996).

[Betty R. Rubenstein (2nd ed.)]

EIZENSTAT, STUART (1943–), U.S. government adviser and special envoy and mediator for Holocaust property claims. Eizenstat was born in Chicago, Illinois, grew up in Atlanta, graduated with honors in political science from the University of North Carolina (1964), and received a law degree from Harvard Law School (1967). After law school, he worked in the Johnson White House as a staff aide and, in 1968, as the research director for Hubert Humphrey's presidential campaign. In 1969, he clerked for Justice Newell Edenfield of the U.S. District Court of Georgia, and in 1970, he joined the Atlanta law firm Powell, Goldstein, Frazier, and Murphy. He continued his interest in politics in 1976, joining the Jimmy Carter presidential campaign as policy and issues director, and subsequently served as domestic policy advisor in the Carter White House. At that time, he was an anomaly in public life, a high-ranking practicing Jew whose children attended Jewish school. President Carter honored Eizenstat's religious Jewish commitment by attending a Passover *seder* in his home. Since then, religiously committed American Jews have been quite comfortable in government service, comfortable as Americans and as observant Jews.

As domestic policy advisor, Eizenstat's Jewish commitment and knowledge of the Holocaust influenced two major decisions. He was instrumental in recommending the establishment of the President's Commission on the Holocaust, which led to the establishment of the United States Holocaust Memorial Museum, and in providing shelter in the United States for Iranian Jews, Bahais, and Christians who were fleeing Ayatollah Khomeini's regime in Iran in 1979. Eizenstat succeeded in establishing a special visitor's visa, which would expire only when the Shah of Iran was returned to power. This served as a measure to protect some 50,000 Iranian Jews, almost all of whom are American citizens today.

With the defeat of President Carter, Eizenstat resumed private legal practice in 1980 and also served as an adjunct lecturer at the Kennedy School of Government at Harvard University and a guest scholar at the Brookings Institution. In 1993, he returned to public service, holding several high-profile positions in the Clinton Administration. He first was named U.S. ambassador to the European Union. While serving as ambassador, he was asked to assume the role of the State Department's special envoy for property claims in Central and Eastern Europe. In 1996, Eizenstat was named under secretary for international trade at the U.S. Department of Commerce and continued his role as special envoy for property claims. Eizenstat was asked to investigate U.S. and Allied efforts to recover billions of dollars of gold stolen by the Nazis from the central banks of the conquered countries and from Holocaust victims. Eleven U.S. government agencies participated; the report documented the complicity of the Swiss National Bank in converting looted gold into hard currency for the Nazis, the centrality of Switzerland to the Nazi economic effort, the inadequacies of U.S. postwar policies, and the inadequacy of reparations from the Allied nations to victims.

After moving to the State Department in 1997 as under secretary for economic, business, and agricultural affairs, Eizenstat became more immersed in the reparations issues, as Congressional hearings (led by Sen. *D'Amato, R-NY) continued and U.S. class action lawsuits against three major Swiss banks seized the world's attention. The United States government stepped up its involvement: Eizenstat was now deputy secretary of the U.S. Treasury and became the lead U.S. mediator not just in the class action lawsuits against the Swiss banks but in negotiations between Jewish organizations, such as the World Jewish Congress and the World Jewish Restitution Organization, and the governments and companies of Germany, Austria, and France. In his book, *Imperfect Justice: Looted Assets, Slave Labor, and the Unfinished Business of World War II*, Eizenstat recounts his efforts, which led to the disclosure of more than 20,000 dormant accounts in Swiss banks; $8 billion in class action settlements against private Swiss, German, Austrian, and French companies and their governments; the negotiation with 40 countries of the Washington Principles on Art regarding the return of looted works of art; and – most importantly – the emergence of truth about the large-scale theft of property and the financial methods the Nazis used to sustain their war effort.

[Lisa Lubick-Daniel (2nd ed.)]

EKRON (Heb. עֶקְרוֹן), one of the capital cities of the Philistine Pentapolis. According to the Bible, Joshua allotted it to the tribe of Dan on its northeastern border with Judah (Josh. 15:11, 45–46; 19:43), and Judges 1:18 relates that it was captured by the tribe of Judah. In Joshua 13:3, however, and all later sources, Ekron appears as one of the five cities of the Philistine confederation. After the Ark of the Covenant, which was captured at Eben-Ezer, had brought misfortune to the Philistine cities that received it, the people of Ekron refused to admit it and proposed returning it to Israelite territory (I Sam. 5:1ff.; 6:16–17). Cities in the region of Ekron and Gath were restored to Israel by Samuel (I Sam. 7:14). In the story of David and Goliath, the Israelites pursued the Philistines to "the gates of Ekron" (I Sam. 17:52). In the ninth century messengers of King Ahaziah of Israel consulted "Baal Zebub, the god of Ekron," receiving a stern rebuke from Elijah (II Kings 1:2–16). Amos (1:6–8) reprimanded Ekron and its sister cities for their slave trade and threatened it with destruction as did Jeremiah (25:20) and Zephaniah (2:4) in King Josiah's time (640–609 B.C.E.). Zephaniah threatened Ekron with being "rooted up" (תֵּעָקֵר), a play on words.

The siege of 'amqar(r)una (Ekron), which took place in 712 B.C.E., was depicted on a wall relief in the palace of Sargon II at Khorsabad. Sennacherib captured Ekron in 701 B.C.E. during his suppression of the rebellion led by King Hezekiah of Judah. According to Sennacherib's Royal Annals, Padi, king of Ekron, who was loyal to Assyria, was deposed by a part of the populace who handed him over to Hezekiah for imprisonment. Despite the help Ekron received from the Egyptians, Sennacherib took the city, executed the rebels, and forced Hezekiah to release Padi, whom he restored as ruler of the city. Padi also received territory taken from Judah. His successor, Ikausu, however, was not so fortunate and, together with Manasseh of Judah, paid heavy tribute to both Esarhaddon (particularly materials for the palace at Nineveh) and Ashurbanipal during their campaigns against Syria, Egypt, and Cush, in the first half of the seventh century B.C.E.

In 147 B.C.E. Alexander Balas granted the city and its district to Jonathan the Hasmonean as a reward for his loyalty (I Macc. 10:89; Jos., Antiq., 13:102). Eusebius describes it as "a very large Jewish village called Akkaron" (Onom. 29:9). Jerome situates it to the east of Azotus and Iamnia, mentioning also that some equated Accaron with Straton's Tower at Caesarea; similarly in the Talmud R. *Abbahu mistakenly identifies Ekron with Caesarea (Meg. 6a). It is also mentioned in connection with a march by Baldwin I during the Crusades (c. 1200).

The biblical city of Ekron is now identified with Tel Miqne (Khirbat al-Muqanna'), a large fortified mound (75 acres), situated 22 mi. southwest of Jerusalem on the frontier zone that once separated Philistia from Judah. J. Naveh was the first to identify Muqanna' with Ekron, correcting W.F. Albright who had suggested that it should be identified as biblical Eltekeh. Naveh's identification has been borne out by subsequent excavations at the site (14 seasons) that were undertaken between 1981 and 1996 by T. Dothan and S. Gitin on behalf of the W.F. Albright Institute of Archaeological Research and the Hebrew University. Apart from ceramic finds from the Chalcolithic and Early Bronze Ages, the earliest remains of a settlement at the site date from the Middle Bronze Age (MB II), including monumental platforms – the base of a fortifications rampart, and intramural burials. The Late Bronze Age settlement was apparently unfortified and restricted to the ten acres of the northeast acropolis/upper city, while the lower city was abandoned. Finds attest to links with Cyprus, the Aegean, and Anatolia, on the one hand, and Egypt, on the other. The final LB stratum was destroyed by fire.

Ekron saw a process of re-urbanization during the Iron Age I with the founding of the first Sea Peoples/Philistine city in the second quarter of the 12th century B.C.E. This fortified urban center, encompassing upper and lower cities, was characterized by a new material culture with Aegean affinities, including megaron-type buildings and local versions of Mycenaean (IIIC:1) wares. The Iron Age I city was destroyed in the first quarter of the tenth century B.C.E., either by the Egyptians (at the time of Pharaoh Siamun) or by the Israelites. The Iron Age IIA–B city (tenth–eighth centuries B.C.E.) was limited to the northeast acropolis/upper city. Following the Assyrian conquest in 701 B.C.E., when Ekron became an Assyrian vassal city-state, the city once again expanded encompassing the lower and upper cities and a new area of 25 acres to the north of the site. During the Iron Age II period, when the Aegean affinities of the Philistine material culture had ceased to exist, the Philistines themselves did not disappear but underwent a process of acculturation. Nevertheless, throughout this period the Philistines were able to maintain their ethnic identity. Excavations have shown that in the seventh century B.C.E. Ekron achieved its zenith of economic growth, with the largest industrial center for the mass production of olive oil yet known from antiquity. Seventh century

Ekron also produced a unique temple with a royal dedicatory inscription dating from the second quarter of the seventh century B.C.E. This inscription refers to two kings of Ekron who are also attested in the Neo-Assyrian annals, namely Padi and his son Ikausu, the builder of the temple, and identifies the site as Ekron. The city was substantially destroyed by fire at the time of the campaign of the Neo-Babylonian Nebuchadnezzar (604 B.C.E.). Although it was partially resettled in the sixth century B.C.E., the mound was largely abandoned with only very few remains surviving from later periods.

BIBLIOGRAPHY: T. Dothan, "Tel Miqne-Ekron: An Iron Age I Philistine Settlement in Canaan," in: N.A. Silberman and D. Small (eds.), *The Archaeology of Israel: Constructing the Past, Interpreting the Present* (1997), 96–106; S. Gitin, T. Dothan, and J. Naveh, "A Royal Dedicatory Inscription from Ekron," in: IEJ, 47 (1997), 1–16; S. Gitin, "The Neo-Assyrian Empire and its Western Periphery: The Levant, With Focus on Philistine Ekron," in: S. Parpola and R.M.Whiting (eds.), *Assyria 1995* (1997), 77–103; T. Dothan, "Initial Philistine Settlement: From Migration to Coexistence," in: S. Gitin, A. Mazar and E. Stern (eds.), *Mediterranean Peoples in Transition: Thirteenth to Early Tenth Centuries BCE* (1998); J. Naveh, "Achish-Ikausu in the Light of the Ekron Dedication," in: BASOR, 310 (1998), 35–37; S. Gitin and M. Cogan, "A New Type of Dedicatory Inscription from Ekron," in: IEJ, 49 (1999), 193–202; T. Dothan, "Reflections on the Initial Phase of Philistine Settlement: Type Site – Tel Miqne-Ekron," in: E.D. Oren (ed.), *The Sea Peoples and Their World: A Re-Assessment* (2000), 145–58; S. Gitin, "The Philistines: Neighbors of the Canaanites, Phoenicians and Israelites," in: D.R. Clark and V.H. Matthews (eds.), *100 Years of American Archaeology in the Middle East* (2000); S. Gitin, "The Four-Horned Altar and Sacred Space: An Archaeological Perspective," in B. Gittlen (ed.), *Sacred Time, Sacred Space: Archaeology and the Religion of Israel* (2002), 95–123; T. Dothan, "Bronze and Iron Objects with Cultic Connotations from Philistine Temple Building 350 at Ekron," in: IEJ, 52 (2002), 1–27; S. Gitin, "Neo-Assyrian and Egyptian Hegemony over Ekron in the Seventh Century BCE: A Response to Lawrence E. Stager," in: *Eretz-Israel*, 27 (2003), 55*–61*; P. James, "The Date of the Ekron Temple Inscription: A Note," in: IEJ, 55 (2005), 90–93.

[S. Gitin (2nd ed.)]

ELAD (Heb. אֶלְעָד), urban community with municipal council status. It is located in the center of Israel, 2.5 mi. (4 km.) south of *Rosh ha-Ayin and occupying an area of about 1 sq. mi. (2.7 sq. km.). The town was geared to a religious population, mainly ultra-Orthodox Jews. The first settlers arrived in 1998. In 2002 its population was 15,100, about half 15 and under in age. Earnings in the town were about half the national average. An educational complex and industrial area were planned for the town's center.

[Shaked Gilboa (2nd ed.)]

ELAH (Heb. אֵלָה; 9th century B.C.E.), king of Israel in the period coinciding with the reign of King Asa of Judah; son of *Baasha. According to I Kings 16:8, Elah reigned two years (c. 883–882 B.C.E.); however, in effect it was only a few months (a short time before and a short time after the official New Year's day). Elah was murdered, while in a state of intoxication, by *Zimri, the captain of half his chariot force, in the house of Arza, who was Elah's steward, in the capital city Tirzah (*ibid.* 9–10). The murder of Elah was apparently connected with the army's dissatisfaction over his indifference to the renewed campaign against the Philistines near Gibbethon. This campaign was undertaken as a continuation of the efforts of *Nadab son of Jeroboam to ensure the security of the southwestern border of the kingdom (*ibid.* 16; cf. 15:27).

BIBLIOGRAPHY: Bright, Hist,\viv]

EL AL (Heb. "Skyward"), the State of Israel's national airline; founded in November 1948. Its original mission was to facilitate the transportation of Jewish immigrants. Using surplus World War II aircraft – DC-4 Skymasters and C-46 Curtiss Commandos – and manned by volunteers from various parts of the world, it played a decisive role in rescuing Jewish communities in the Middle East. By 1949, however, El Al was flying scheduled routes between Israel and Rome and Paris. In the following year, it obtained the more modern Constellations, and with four of these planes routes were extended to include Athens, Vienna, Zurich, London, Nairobi, Johannesburg, and New York. Shortly afterward, Istanbul, Brussels, Amsterdam, Teheran, Frankfurt, Munich, and Copenhagen were added. By 1996, it served 50 intercontinental destinations including Cairo, Beijing, and New Delhi as well as nine cities in the U.S. In December 1957, El Al was the world's second air carrier to employ turboprops (four Bristol Britannias) for transcontinental service, and in January 1961 it procured three Boeing 707–420 intercontinental jet airliners. In June 1961 it inaugurated the first nonstop service between New York and Tel Aviv – then one of the world's longest nonstop scheduled commercial flights. El Al rapidly expanded its fleet to keep pace with the increasing development of tourism. By the mid-1960s it had two Boeing 720 B intermediate range jets, three standard intercontinental 707s, and two powerful 707–320 BS; it leased additional jet planes as required. In February 1969 an eighth plane was added and later in the year the airline acquired its first 320 C mixed cargo-passenger plane. Development plans included the acquisition of Boeing 747 Jumbo jets and two Boeing supersonic airliners. In 2004 the company had 28 Boeing aircraft: five 747–200s, four 747–400s, three 737–700/800s, six 767s, six 757s, and four 777–200s.

The majority shareholder in El Al is the Israeli government. Nearly all training is carried out at the company's headquarters at Lydda (Lod) Airport. All food served aboard its aircraft is *kasher.* The airliner does not fly on Saturdays, the Jewish Sabbath. However, its subsidiary, Sundor, a charter airline company, works seven days a week. Sundor was established in 1977 for low-cost flights. In 2003 El Al employed more than 3,000 workers and had 77 offices all over the world. It flew to 40 direct destinations, and to many others by share agreements with several other aircraft companies. It carried over 1.3 million people a year and its annual turnover was about $1.2 billion. Sundor carried 250,000 passengers during the years 2001–4 in two 757–200 aircraft.

After the Six-Day War, El Al became a target for one of the Arab terrorist organizations, the People's Front for the Liberation of Palestine. A Boeing 707 was hijacked to Algeria in July 1968 but was later returned to Israel. In December 1968, an El Al plane was attacked on the ground at Athens airport and one passenger killed, and an attack on another at Zurich in February 1969 resulted in the death of one of the crew. A hijacking attempt in 1970 was foiled by the crew. A Constellation, straying off course, was shot down over Bulgaria in 1955 (all passengers were killed and Bulgaria later paid compensation).

El Al played a crucial role during the 1991 Persian Gulf conflict, acting as Israel's sole airlink with the world when all other airlines had ceased flying to Israel. It also played a vital role in the 1990s in bringing Russian and Ethiopian immigrants to Israel. In the last two decades of the 20th century, the company faced serious economic problems. The government began privatization in 2003, issuing stock to the public. In 2004 the company showed a profit due to its increased share in both passenger and cargo flights.

BIBLIOGRAPHY: *Israel Economist*, 24 (Jan. 1968), 11–19; El Al Public Relations Department, *Twenty Years History of El Al* (1969). **WEBSITE:** www.elal.co.il.

[Arnold Sherman / Shaked Gilboa (2nd ed.)]

ELAM (Heb. עֵילָם, *'eylam*; Elamite *halhatamti*; Akk. *Elamtu*), region on the edge of the southwestern part of the Iranian plateau, modern Khuzistan, including the river valley around Susa and the highlands beyond. In Elamite Elam may mean "the lord-country," but in Mesopotamian languages it was understood as "The Heights." The word Elam probably derives from the Elamite, relying on a popular etymology in Akkadian relating it to *elû*, "high." In classical sources it is referred to as Susiana, from Susa (Heb. שׁוּשַׁן, *Shūshan*), the capital of Elam.

History

Elam was closely connected with Mesopotamia, serving as a source of its raw materials, wood, stone, and metals and as the route for precious metals and stones like lapis lazuli, the blue stone prized by the Mesopotamians, which were brought from as far away as Afghanistan. The Elamites also raided the valleys of the Diyala and the Tigris, and, according to the Sumerian King List, the Awan dynasty, the most ancient royal dynasty in Elam, ruled Sumer for a time. There is a poorly understood treaty between the Akkadian ruler Naram-Sin and an Elamite ruler from around 2200 B.C.E. In the 21st century B.C.E., the kings of the third dynasty of Ur in Mesopotamia annexed Elam, and Susa became a seat of Sumerian governors.

At the beginning of the 19th century B.C.E., an independent Elamite royal dynasty reigned in Anshan in the uplands and Susa on the plain. Elam exerted a widespread influence, and trading expeditions carried raw materials from Elam as far as Hazor in Canaan. In the middle of the 18th century B.C.E., Elam was consolidated under the rule of Kutir-Nahhunte I, whose reign coincided with the later years of *Hammurapi of Babylon and with the reign of Hammurapi's son, Samsu-iluna. From about this time on, and throughout the whole period, Babylonian influence is evidenced by the use of Akkadian as the written language of economic and cultural life.

During this period three rulers held power in Elam at one and the same time: the highest ruler, called in Sumerian the "Grand Regent" (Sumerian *sukkal-mah*), and two others, who were his sons, one ruling the highlands and the other the Susiana plain. The manner in which authority was divided among the three is not clear. But the rulers of Elam were members of one family, and succession to the throne was matrilineal. The old idea that one of the rulers was a nephew should be discarded. One of the son's mothers was the regent's sister, indicating a way of keeping power within the family that to moderns looks incestuous but must not have been seen as incestuous to Elamites.

Almost nothing is known about the history of Elam during the 17th-15th centuries B.C.E., but it appears to have suffered greatly from the migrations of the peoples who descended upon the Babylonian plain from the Zagros mountains. Elam rose to prominence again at the beginning of the 13th century B.C.E. The most famous king of that period was Untash-napirisha, who reigned during the first half of the 13th century and built his capital, Dur-Untash, the modern Tchoga Zambil ("Basket Hill"), 25 mi. (40 km.) southeast of Susa. Here was found the best preserved ziggurat, or temple tower, in all of the ancient Near East, still 82 ft. (25 m.) tall. The Elamite language and pantheon became more popular around Susa in the period. Untash-Napirisha honored both the lowland god Inshushinak and the highland god Napirisha in his temple complex.

The consolidation and rise of Elam in the 12th century B.C.E. coincided with the decline of Babylon during the rule of the last kings of the Kassite dynasty. The Elamites made several raids into Babylonia, plundered Sippar and its temples, and brought as booty to Susa royal monuments including the stele of the Code of Hammurapi now in the Louvre Museum. In 1159 B.C.E. the Elamites seized the city of Babylon itself and captured the statue of Marduk, its god, and snuffed out the long-lived Kassite dynasty. Elam's military ascendancy ended, however, with the renewal of Babylonian power during the reign of Nebuchadnezzar I (1125–1104 B.C.E.), who defeated the Elamites, captured Susa, and brought the statue of Marduk back to Babylon.

The decline of Elam was rapid and there are no further records of its history until the eighth century B.C.E. During this, the last period of Elam's history as an independent state, the Elamites joined forces with the Chaldean tribes in their wars against Sargon and Sennacherib, kings of Assyria, until their final defeat by Assurbanipal (669–627 B.C.E.), who devastated Elam. In a series of bloody battles (647–646 B.C.E.), the Assyrians razed most of the cities of Elam, especially Susa, deliberately desecrating its holy places, and destroying the temple of Inshushinak.

There were attempts at the beginning of the Neo-Babylonian period to rebuild Elam, but they were never totally successful. After the fall of the Assyrian Empire (612–610 B.C.E.), Elam was incorporated into the greater kingdom of Media; and after the defeat of Astyages, king of Media, by Cyrus, the Persian king, it became an integral part of his empire. Cyrus even called himself "King of Anshan," thus adopting the ancient title of the Elamite rulers (see *Cyrus). In the administrative division of the Persian Empire, Elam became the satrapy of Uja, Huja, or Huvja (whence Huz, in Middle Persian, and modern Khuzistan). Susa was rebuilt with magnificent palaces, and became a capital city of the Persian monarchs, second only to Persepolis. The Elamite language continued as the second language after Persian and equal with Akkadian in the royal inscriptions of the kings of Persia. The name Elam was still used in I Maccabees 6:1 (Elymais, Ελυμαΐς, attacked by Antiochus IV Epiphanes) and by Greek and Roman writers (Elamitai, Ἐλαμῖται, Acts 2:9).

Language

The Elamite language does not fall into any linguistic group known today. It can be divided into three strata: (1) Old Elamite (last quarter of the third millennium B.C.E.); (2) Middle Elamite (13th–7th cent. B.C.E.), the major stratum; and (3) Achaemenid Elamite (6th–4th cent. B.C.E.), known mainly from the bilingual and trilingual inscriptions of the Persian kings and archival texts from Persepolis.

Achaemenid Elamite was deciphered in the second half of the 19th century, and since the beginning of the 20th century great progress has been made in the understanding of Middle Elamite. Nevertheless, knowledge of the language remains imperfect; and particularly in the scantily documented older strata much is still obscure.

Scripts

The most ancient Elamite script is pictographic "proto-Elamite," employed at the beginning of the third millennium B.C.E., which has not yet been deciphered. A linear script which developed from it in the second half of the third millennium B.C.E. is still being worked out. During the reign of the kings of *Akkad (24th–23rd cent. B.C.E.), the ancient scripts of Elam were superseded by the Mesopotamian cuneiform writing, which, adapted to the needs of the Elamite language, was from then on the only one in which it was written.

In the Bible

Elam, located at the edge of the eastern border of the biblical world, is mentioned only a few times in the Bible. In the "Table of Nations" Elam is listed with the sons of Shem (Gen. 10:22; I Chron. 1:17), since from a geographic point of view it was apparently considered part of the Mesopotamian world. The odd narrative of Genesis 14 mentions *Chedorlaomer, king of Elam – sometimes identified with Kutir-Nahhunte (around 1750 B.C.E. or the later one around 1200) – as head of an alliance with two other kings, those of Shinar and Goiim, meaning probably Babylonia and the Hittites.

In the "Prophecies Against the Nations" in Isaiah and Jeremiah, Elam is mentioned, together with Media, as one of the "Peoples of the North" who would destroy Babylon (Isa. 21:2; Jer. 25:25). The only prophecy that may be related directly to a specific event in the history of Elam is Jeremiah 49:34–39, perhaps about Nebuchadnezzar's encounter with Elam in his ninth year (596/5 B.C.E.). According to Ezra 4:9–10, Elamites were deported to Northern Israel in the aftermath of the Assyrian king Assurbanipal's victory in the 640s, and thus constituted part of the peoples Jews later regarded as Samaritan non-Jews. In Isaiah 11:11 Elam is seen as a place of exile, in Ezekiel 32:24 as a typical foreign nation, and in Dan 8:2 as a site of a vision. Elam also appears as a personal name among returnees from exile, but also as a clan of Benjamin in I Chronicles 8:24.

BIBLIOGRAPHY: W. Hinz, *The Lost World of Elam* (1973); M. Stolper and E. Carter, *Elam. Surveys of Political History and Archaeology* (1984); R. Zadok, *The Elamite Onomasticon* (1984); L. De Meyer, H. Gasche (eds.), *Mésopotamie et Elam* (1991); F. Vallat, in: ABD II, 424–29; G. Gragg, "Elamite," in: J. Sasson (ed.), CANE 4, 2162–67; F. Vallat, "ELAM: *haltamti/Elamtu*," in: N.A.B.U. (1996), 89; R. Henrickson, "Elamites," in: E. Meyers (ed.), *The Oxford Encyclopedia of Archaeology in the Near East* 2 (1997), 228–34.

[Hayim Tadmor / Daniel C. Snell (2nd ed.)]

EL-AMARNA, modern name of the site of Akhetaton, the capital city of Egypt, founded by Amenophis-Amenḥotep IV (*Akhenaton), the "heretical" pharaoh of the 18th Dynasty (14th cent. B.C.E.). On this site was discovered the El-Amarna archive.

El-Amarna Letters

The El-Amarna Letters comprise a collection of cuneiform tablets named after al-ʿAmārna, a plain on the east bank of the Nile about 190 mi. (304 km.) S. of Cairo, in the territory of the Beni-ʿAmrān, or ʿAmārna, tribe. (Though often referred to as Tell ʾAmārna, or Tell el-ʿAmārna, the location is not a tell, or mound.) Amarna was the site of the Egyptian capital, Akhetaton, for about 15 years around the middle of the 14th century B.C.E.; here, in 1887, through the chance discovery of a peasant, a part of the diplomatic correspondence in the royal archives was unearthed. The clandestine explorations of the natives which followed, and the later scientific excavations (1889–92, 1912–14, 1921–22, 1926–36), yielded about 355 letters – some might be better classified as lists (of gifts) – besides more than 20 other cuneiform documents (scribal exercises, vocabularies, mythological and epical texts). The entire Amarna (cuneiform) corpus numbers 379 tablets. Though incomplete and lacking nos. 359–379, the standard edition, with transliteration of the cuneiform and a German translation, remains that of the Norwegian scholar J.A. Knudtzon, *Die el-Amarna Tafeln* (1915 = EA; for nos. 359–379 and other translations, see bibl.). An authoritative annotated French translation by W. Moran appeared in 1987 followed by a revised English version by the same author in 1992.

With only three exceptions (EA 24, Hur 32, Hittite), the letters are all written in Akkadian, the lingua franca of the ancient Near East in the second millennium B.C.E. In general, the language belongs to the "peripheral Akkadian" found at Nuzi, Alalakh, Ugarit, etc. Eloquent and moving as it may be at times, it lacks all elegance; it is awkward, often barbarous, betraying the scribes' ignorance not only of Akkadian but of their own native speech. This is especially true of the letters from Phoenicia and Palestine, and for this reason they are one of the most important sources for the early Canaanite language (and therefore for the background of biblical Hebrew). From the glosses to Akkadian words, the non-Akkadian morphemes, the non-Akkadian use of morphemes common to the two languages, and the syntax in these letters, it is possible to reconstruct much of the Canaanite grammar in this period.

The Amarna letters are also an invaluable historical source. Together with contemporary Ugaritic and Hittite documents and other Egyptian records, they make the two decades or so which they cover the best known in the early history of Syria and Palestine. They span, in absolute dates, around 1385/1375–1355 B.C.E.: about the last decade of the reign of Amenophis III, the 17-year reign of Amenophis IV, and the three or four years before Tutankhaten (Tutankhamun), to whom EA 9 is addressed, abandoned the capital. (The difference of a decade in estimating the period is due to the still very mooted question of the co-regency of Amenophis IV with his father and predecessor; according as one accepts or denies a co-regency, the chronology of the Amarna letters must be lowered or raised.) Some (at least nine) of the letters, which are probably copies of the originals, have a pharaoh as author; the rest were written outside Egypt, and, with few exceptions, are addressed to the pharaoh or, less commonly, to a high Egyptian official at court. The correspondents are the kings of major states (Babylonia, Assyria, Mitanni in northern Mesopotamia, Ḫatti and Arzawa in Anatolia, Cyprus) and Egyptian vassals in Syria and Palestine. The letters (41) to and from the larger powers are in striking contrast with the vassals' correspondence, and hardly hint at the political situation which motivates so many of them. According to the custom of independent nations at peace, their majesties exchange messages of mutual friendship, which are carried by their emissaries and accompanied by gifts; often their principal concern is the discussion and working out of marriages, a conventional bond of international amity. Were it not for the vassals' letters and other contemporary sources it would be impossible to measure the real significance of the efforts of Tushratta of Mitanni to reestablish diplomatic relations with Amenophis III (EA 17) and to maintain them with his successor (EA 26); of his passing reference to a victory over the Hittites (EA 17); of the presence of Assyrians at the Egyptian court (EA 15–16), with its implications of rising Assyrian power (cf. EA 9:31–35) and Mitannian weakness; of the murder of Babylonian merchants in Palestine (EA 8); of the reported request of the Canaanites for Babylonian support in a rebellion against Egypt (EA 9), etc. The general impression these letters give is one of legendary Egyptian wealth in an era of relative peace and political stability.

This impression is dispelled by the remaining Amarna letters. The vassals from Tyre across to Damascus and northward were caught, directly or indirectly, in the struggle of the Mitannians to defend their control of northern Syria and even their own independence, and of the Egyptians to maintain their rule in the rest of Syria, against their common enemy, the resurgent Hittites under Suppiluliuma. Though their letters to the pharaoh are all filled with protests of unswerving loyalty, it is evident from the accusations against their fellow vassals that many of them were exploiting the situation to secure and expand their own power while toadying to both sides and avoiding for as long as possible an irrevocable commitment to one or the other. Most prominent in this group of letters, and most successful in this game of intrigue, sedition, and popular and palace revolts, were Abdi-ashirta and his sons, particularly Aziru, who made of Amurru an important minor state in central Syria east of the Orontes. The almost 70 letters of Rib-Adda of Byblos are a long, increasingly nervous denunciation of their advances along the coast and of Egyptian inaction. The latter is probably to be attributed, in part at least, to the tendency of the vassals' accusations to cancel each other out; but it is also likely that the court felt Egyptian interests would be safeguarded best by a strong Amurru as a buffer against the Hittite thrust. Events proved Rib-Adda right: like so many of his neighbors (Ugarit, Kadesh, etc.), Aziru became a Hittite vassal.

In Palestine the situation reflected by the vassals' letters, if less dire in its consequences for Egyptian rule, was not less chaotic. The letters reflect the same rivalries of the local rulers, the same charges against one another of perfidy, and the same signs of deep popular unrest. These petty kings are constantly at war with one another, plundering and seizing villages, at times forming small coalitions against a common enemy, which soon break up, regroup, and exchange the roles of enemies and allies. In central Palestine, in the struggles involving Gezer, Megiddo, Taanach, Acre, Jerusalem, Lachish, and (perhaps) Hebron, the main instigators were the rulers of Shechem, Lab'ayu and his sons, who in a movement comparable to that in contemporary Amurru, attempted to expand their city-state into a territorial state, with one important objective being the possession of the fertile Plain of Esdraelon. The local Egyptian administration, when not corrupt and supporting treason, was apparently really concerned only with the payment of tribute and with a few other Egyptian interests like the provisions for troops moving northward, and this policy seems to have had the court's approval.

BIBLIOGRAPHY: EXCAVATIONS: Wm. F. Petrie, *Tell el-Amarna* (1894); L. Borchardt, in: *Mitteilungen der deutschen orientalischen Gesellschaft*, 46 (1911), 1–32; 50 (1912), 1–40; 52 (1913), 1–55; 55 (1914), 3–39; 57 (1917), 1–32; T.E. Peet and C.L. Wooley, *The City of Akhenaten*, 1 (1923); D.D.S. Pendelbury et al., *The City of Akhenaten*, 1 (1923); B. Porter and L.B. Moss, *Topographical Bibliography of Ancient Egyptian Hieroglyphic Texts, Reliefs, and Paintings…* (1934), 192–239; H. Kees, *Ancient Egypt* (1961), 288ff. PRIMARY PUBLICATIONS AND COLLECTIONS: H. Winckler and F.M. Abel, *Der Thontafelfund von el Amarna*, 1–3 (1889–90); C. Bezold and E.A.W. Budge (eds.), *The Tell el-Amarna Tablets in the British Museum* (1892); O. Schroeder, *Die Tontafeln von*

El-Amarna (1915); idem, in: OLZ, 20 (1917), 105–6; F. Thureau-Dangen, in: *Revue d'assyriologie*, 19 (1922), 91–108; P. Dhorme, in: RB, 33 (1924), 5–32; G. Dossen, in: *Revue d'assyriologie*, 31 (1934), 125–36; S.A.B. Mercer, *The Tell el-Amarna Tablets*, 1–2 (1939); C.H. Gordon, in: *Orientalia*, 16 (1947), 1–21; A.P. Millard, in: PEQ (1965), 140–3; A.F. Rainey, *El Amarna Tablets* (1970), 359–79; R. Borger, *Handbuch der Keilschriftliteratur* (1967), 237–40; W. Reidel, *Untersuchungen zu den Tell el-Amarna Briefen*, 1–2 (1920); F. Bilabel, *Geschichte Vorderasiens und Aegyptien vom 16–11 Jahrhunderten*... (1927); Maisler, *Untersuchungen*, 43–46; idem, in: JPOS, 9 (1929), 80–87; W.F. Albright, in: JEA, 23 (1937), 190–203; idem, in: BASOR, 87 (1942), 32–38; 89 (1943), 7–17; 104 (1946), 25–26; idem, in: JNES, 5 (1946), 5–25; idem, in: Pritchard, Texts, 483–90; idem, in: CAH², 2 (1966), ch. 20 (incl. bibl.); W. von Soden, in: *Orientalia*, 21 (1952), 426–34; Y. Aharoni, in: IEJ, 3 (1953), 153–61; Aharoni, Land, 87, 157–64; idem, in: VT, 19 (1969), 137–45; Alt, Kl Schr, 3, 158–75; E.F. Campbell, in: BA, 23 (1960), 2–22; idem, in: G.E. Wright (ed.), *Shechem* (1965), 191–207; D.O. Edzard, in: *Journal of Economic and Social History of the Orient*, 3 (1960), 38–55; M.L. Verani, *Storia di Ugarit* (1962), 18–30; idem, in: *Revista degli studio Orientalo*, 40 (1965), 267–77; idem, in: *Revue d'assyriologie*, 61 (1967), 1–18; Ph. H.J. Houwink Ten Cate, in: BOR, 20 (1963), 270–76; M.C. Astour, in: *For Max Weinreich* (1964), 7–17; H. Klengel, in: MIO, 10 (1964), 57–83; P. Artzi, in: *Revue d'assyriologie*, 58 (1964), 159–66; idem, in: JNES, 27 (1968), 63–71; idem, in: *Bar-Ilan Decennary Volume*, 2 (1969); idem, in: *Proceedings of the 27th International Congress of Orientalists* (1969); A. Goetze, in: CAH², 2 (1965), ch. 17; H. Klengel, *Geschichte Syriens*, 1–2 (1965–68); A.F. Rainey, *Christian News from Israel*, 2 (1966), 30–38; 3 (1966), 23–24; idem, in: IEJ, 18 (1968), 1–14. LINGUISTIC STUDIES: F.-M. Th. Boehl, *Die Sprache der Amarnabriefe* (1909); E. Ebeling, *Das Verbum der El-Amarna Briefe* (1910); E. Dhorme, in: RB, 10 (1913), 369–93; 11 (1914), 37–59, 344ff.; O. Schroeder, in: OLZ, 18 (1915), 105–6; S. Smith and C.J. Godel, in: JEA, 11 (1925), 230–40; J. Friedrich, *Kleinasiatische Sprachdenkmaeler* (1932), 8–32; W.F. Albright, in: BASOR, 86 (1942), 28–31; idem and W.L. Moran, in: JCS, 4 (1950), 163ff.; B. Landsberger, *ibid.*, 8 (1954), 55–61; W.L. Moran, in: *Orientalia*, 29 (1960), 1–19; idem, in: G.E. Wright (ed.), *The Bible and the Ancient Near East* (1961), 54–72; idem, in: *Eretz Israel*, 9 (1969), 94–99; R. Youngblood, in: BASOR, 168 (1962), 24–27; E. Salonen, *Die Gruss-und Hoeflichkeitsformeln in babylonisch-assyrischen Briefen* (1967), 61–70; P. Artzi, in: *Bar-Ilan*, 1 (1963), 27–57; idem, in: JNES, 28 (1969), 261ff. CHRONOLOGY: A. Kitchen, *Suppiluliuma and the Amarna Pharaohs* (1962); E.F. Campbell, Jr., *The Chronology of the Amarna Letters* (1963); D.B. Redford, *History and Chronology of the Eighteenth Dynasty of Egypt* (1967). STUDIES ON THE HISTORICAL, POLITICAL, GEOGRAPHICAL BACKGROUND: B. Maisler, *Toledot Ereẓ Yisrael* (1938), 125–52; H. Reviv, in: BIES, 27 (1963), 270–5; P. Artzi, in: *Eretz Israel*, 9 (1969), 22–28; Z. Kalai and H. Tadmor, *ibid.*, 138–47. **ADD. BIBLIOGRAPHY:** W. Moran, *Les Lettres d'El Amarna* (1987); idem, *The Amarna Letters* (1992) (reviewed by A. Rainey, in: *Biblica*, 70 (1989), 568–72); idem, *Amarna Studies* (2003); R. Hess, *Amarna Personal Names* (1993); A. Rainey, *Canaanite in the Amarna Tablets* (1995). See also the bibliography under *Akhenaton.

[William L. Moran]

EL-ARISH (Ar. العريش, *al-ʿArīsh*), town on the Mediterranean coast of the Sinai Peninsula, near where Wadi al-ʿArīsh (the biblical Naḥal Miẓrayim: see Brook of *Egypt) reaches the sea. It was Sinai's principal center through most historic periods due to a number of geographical assets: loess soil present in patches along Wadi al-ʿArīsh and, on other stretches, loess hidden beneath a thin cover of coarse, porous sand allowing seepage of rainwater to the subsoil; an average yearly rainfall of more than 100 mm. (4 in.) which exceeds that of the rest of Sinai; an enrichment of its water supply by underground seepage and by seasonal surface flow in Wadi al-ʿArīsh; land communications leading to the east and west along the ancient *Via Maris* (sea road) and to the south, southwest, and southeast along the course of the wadi; and anchoring facilities on the beach near the wadi mouth. From the first century, it was known as a trade center by the name Rhinokoroura. Josephus mentions the town as part of Judea (Ant. 13:395) and Titus prepared his march on Palestine there (Wars 4:662). Until 1895 El-Arish served as the border town between Egypt and Palestine. Rabbi Judah *al-Ḥarizi passed through El-Arish in 1218 but does not mention any Jews who might have been there.

El-Arish Project

In the early 20th century, El-Arish and its region were sparsely settled. At that time, Davis *Trietsch proposed the El-Arish project for northern Sinai as one of several alternatives for Jewish settlement in the Middle East. On the basis of *Herzl's meeting in 1902 with Joseph *Chamberlain, the area, including the Pelusian Plain, was designated to become an autonomous Jewish settlement sponsored by the British government. Lord Cromer, then the British consul-general in Egypt, requested that a commission of experts explore the region on the prospects of settlement and its findings were positive. Nevertheless, the Egyptian government, on Cromer's insistence, rejected the report, declaring itself unable to allocate water from the Nile for the settlement's irrigation needs. Cromer's refusal came in spite of Herzl's efforts to rescue the scheme by reducing the project's scope to the El-Arish vicinity and renouncing appropriation of Nile waters for development.

From 1948

During the Israel War of Independence (1948), an Israeli army unit under Operation Ayin temporarily took up positions just south of El-Arish (December 1948). In the *Sinai Campaign, El-Arish fell to Israeli forces on Oct. 31, 1956, and was evacuated by them, according to the UN's request, in February 1957. In the *Six-Day War it was taken by an Israeli column on June 6, 1967, and remained under Israeli administration. Under the terms of Israel's peace agreement with Egypt, El-Arish was returned to Egypt.

After World War I, the town expanded gradually, numbering 7,000 inhabitants in 1932 and, according to Egyptian sources, 22,000 in 1956 and 45,000 in 1967. In the census conducted by Israel in August 1967, El-Arish had a population of 29,973. The date-palm groves near the seashore continue to constitute an important economic branch. Sea fishing and trapping of quails are additional sources of income. Since the 1950s, plantations of rhicinus bushes have gained ground in the area between El-Arish and Rafiaḥ (Rafaḥ) and rhicinus oil is produced in a factory in the town. Under Egyptian rule, administrative services to the Sinai Peninsula and especially services to the Egyptian army became important in El-

Arish's economy, although more recently tourism, based on new hotels and general development, seems to be its main source of income.

BIBLIOGRAPHY: T. Herzl, *Complete Diaries*, ed. by R. Patai, 5 (1960), index; Rabinowicz, in: JSOS, 13:1 (1951), 25–46; Press, Ereẓ, 4 (1955), 757–8; M. Medzini, *Ha-Mediniyyut ha-Ẓiyyonit me-Reshitah ve-ad Moto shel Herzl* (1934), 224–43, 320–32; J. Braslavsky, *Hayadata et ha-Areẓ*, 2 (1947), 7–12, 22–31. **ADD. BIBLIOGRAPHY:** A. Bein, in: *Shivat Ẓiyyon*, 1 (1950), 179–220; Y. Friedman, *Germania, Turkiya ve-ha-Ẓiyyonut* (1995).

[Oskar K. Rabinowicz / Efraim Orni]

ELASA (**Eleasah**, **Alasa**), a town north of Jerusalem near Beth-Horon. Judah *Maccabee encamped there before his last battle against *Bacchides, whose army was at *Beeroth, and was killed nearby in the fighting (I Macc. 9:5–18). Some scholars read Ḥadasha (Adasa) instead of Elasa. The town was apparently named after Eleasah, a descendant of Benjamin (I Chron. 2:39–40; 8:37; 9:43). It is identified with Khirbat al-Ishshī, southwest of al-Bīra.

BIBLIOGRAPHY: F.M. Abel, in: RB, 33 (1924), 383f.; idem, *Les Livres des Maccabées* (1949), 160; Avi-Yonah, Geog, 100.

[Michael Avi-Yonah]

ELASAH (Heb. אֶלְעָשָׂה; "God has made"), son of *Shaphan, and one of Zedekiah's emissaries to Nebuchadnezzar, who brought the letter written by Jeremiah to the elders in exile (Jer. 29:3). Elasah was a member of one of the most influential pro-Babylonian families in the last years of the Kingdom of Judah. Shaphan, his father, was the scribe of Josiah (II Kings 22:3ff.; et al.). His brother *Ahikam was one of the men sent by King Josiah to the prophetess Huldah (II Kings 22:12, 14; II Chron. 34:20). His other brother *Jaazaniah is mentioned in Ezekiel 8:11 among the elders of Jerusalem.

BIBLIOGRAPHY: Yeivin, in: *Tarbiz*, 12 (1940/41), 257–8.

ELATH (in modern Israel, **Eilat**; Heb. אֵילַת, אֵילֹת, אֵילוֹת), ancient harbor town in Transjordan at the northern end of the Red Sea near *Ezion-Geber. Elath is first mentioned in the account of the Israelites' wanderings in the desert during the Exodus (Deut. 2:8). Solomon built a "navy of ships" at Ezion-Geber beside Elath; from there it sailed to Ophir manned by his servants and those of Hiram, king of Tyre (I Kings 9:26; I Chron. 8:17). Later Uzziah (Azariah), king of Judah (785–733 B.C.E.), rebuilt Elath restoring it as the port of Judah on the Red Sea (II Kings 14:22) but after his reign Judahite control of the Negev ceased. In the Hellenistic period it served for a time as a Ptolemaic port called Berenice (Jos., Ant., 8:163) and it is later mentioned as a Nabatean port (renamed Aila) from which an important commercial highway led to Gaza (Strabo, *Geography*, 16:2, 30; Pliny, *Naturalis Historia*, 5:12). Aila continued to be a major commercial and military port in Roman and Byzantine times. In the third century the Tenth Legion, together with its headquarters, was transferred there from Jerusalem and it was thereafter a key point in the Byzantine defense system in the south of the country. The Jewish population in the neighborhood of Aila was augmented by Jewish tribes expelled from Arabia by Muhammad during whose time the Muslims gained control of the town, which was called in Arabic *Akaba. A Jewish community continued to exist there until the middle of the tenth century and possibly until the Crusader period. In 1116 Baldwin I, king of Jerusalem, captured the port; the fleet of Reynaud de Chatillon sailed from there to harass Arab maritime trade in the Red Sea. Saladin, who brought the Crusaders' rule to an end in 1170, erected a fortress at Akaba. By the 14th century the town was almost completely deserted and only under Turkish rule was an attempt made to develop it. The ancient site of Elath with remains from the Nabatean, Roman, Byzantine, and medieval periods has been located north of Akaba.

[Michael Avi-Yonah]

Modern Eilat

Modern Eilat is 3 mi. (5 km.) west of *Akaba along the coast. The site, a wasteland bearing the Arabic name Umm Rashrash, was included in the future Jewish state in the UN partition plan of 1947. In fact, it was occupied by Israel forces on March 13, 1949, in the bloodless "Operation *Uvdah*" ("Established Fact"), which was the last military move in the *War of Independence. A first step in establishing a civilian settlement was made in December 1949 when members of Ha-Kibbutz ha-Me'uḥad set up a temporary camp on the Eilat shore. They transferred their settlement in 1962 about 2 mi. (3 km.) further north, where it became kibbutz Eilot. The first water pipeline was laid in 1952 to Eilat to take water from the *Be'er Orah and *Yotvatah wells which, however, are strongly saline (1,500 mg. chlorine content per liter and with a strong magnesium content). In the ensuing years, the first dwellings were built. By December 1952 Eilat received local council status. As long as the Straits of Tiran were closed to Israel-bound shipping, Eilat's growth was extremely slow (275 inhabitants in 1953, 520 in 1956). A few services to excursionists, experimental coastal fishing, and mineral exploration provided the inhabitants' principal occupations. The turning point came with the opening of the straits in the *Sinai Campaign (1956). Two months later, Eilat's population increased to 926 inhabitants. In view of its outstanding importance for Israel's development, Eilat was given city status in March 1959, although it had only 3,500 inhabitants, still far from the 20,000 population mark which in Israel normally warrants the accordance of this status. In 1963, the population rose to 7,000, and by 1968 reached 12,100, 80% veteran Israelis or Israel-born and the rest immigrants who were less than five years in the country. In the mid-1990s, Eilat's population reached 33,300 and by the end of 2002 it was already 42,100, spread over an area of 30 sq. mi. (80 sq. km.). Eilat's town planning, taking the local topography into account, endeavored to direct most of the city's living quarters to the hills rising at a short distance from the beach, to altitudes of 100–400 m. above sea level, where the climate is slightly cooler than on the shore. The many narrow gorges cutting through the hilly area make planning and communications difficult.

The renewed blockade of the Tiran Straits in May 1967 by Egypt threatened Eilat's existence and future as Israel's gateway to East Africa, South and East Asia, and Australia. That move led to the *Six-Day War, in which the Egyptian plan (according to documents found in Sinai) to cut off the city from the interior of Israel by pushing through to Jordanian territory in the Aravah Valley was foiled by Israel's victory, which subsequently accelerated Eilat's progress. From time to time in the period following June 1967, Arab saboteurs made attempts to attack Eilat despite the Jordanian government's fear that Israel's countermeasures against Jordan's only port, Akaba, would constitute an incomparably heavier blow for Jordan.

Great efforts were directed to creating the city's infrastructure. In 1957 the Eilat–Mizpeh Ramon–Beersheba road was built, and opened to traffic in January 1958. In 1967, the Eilat–Sedom highway was put into use. In 1969, construction began on the road leading from Eilat southward to Sharm el-Sheikh. With the sea bottom sloping steeply from the Eilat shore, port building there is relatively easy. From 1957 the original anchorage was repeatedly enlarged to cope with the mounting sea cargo traffic, and an oil port was installed in the southwest of the city. A new port was built at an investment of IL 20,000,000 (about $ 5,700,000) and opened in 1964; in 1968, it employed 500 laborers and handled approximately 1,000,000 tons of import and export goods. Mineral exports (potash, phosphates, copper) through Eilat amounted to 110,000 tons in 1966/67. Because of Eilat's distance from Israel's central sectors, air communications are vital. The Elath airfield, situated just east of the city, was enlarged, and in 1969 10–12 daily flights (operated by Arkia Company) connected Eilat with Tel Aviv and Jerusalem. The city's water shortage was gradually reduced by seawater desalination. An experimental plant employing the freezing method, developed by Alexander *Zarchin, was closed down after a few years of operation. In 1965, a thermal distillation plant was opened, which simultaneously supplied electricity to the town; its daily capacity was 4,000 m^3 (over a million gallons) of practically salt-free water which, when blended with brackish spring water, made the latter potable. In 1970 another plant was opened with a capacity of 2,000 m^3 (c. half a million gallons) a day.

Air conditioning is an absolute necessity in the Eilat climate and the local "desert cooler," which is relatively inexpensive to operate, reduces the temperature, and increases air humidity, was gradually introduced in all buildings in the city. The first 16 in. oil pipeline connecting Eilat with Haifa was laid in 1958/59. Work on the large 42 in. pipeline from Eilat to Ashkelon began in 1968 and was finished in 1970. A decisive factor in Eilat's economic life were the *Timna Copper Works, which in 1968 employed 1,000 workers, nearly all residing in Eilat. However, in 1975 they were closed due to economic difficulties. Local industry, mostly small and medium-size enterprises, included branches connected with the local building trade, several jewelry workshops (for processing the malachite "Eilat stone"), diamond-polishing plants, fish processing, metal products, and gypsum. Tourism and recreation always constituted one of the major branches in Eilat's economy. In 1968, Eilat had a marine museum and a modern art museum, municipal libraries, a concert and lecture hall, and an amphitheater. In 1970 the city's hotels had 2,000 beds; at the turn of the 20th century around 11,000 in five hotels, with considerable income derived from tourist services. Tourism was the main reason for the great Eilat shoreline project, providing for a number of artificial lagoons and land tongues. To encourage tourism further, the city received a VAT exemption in 1985. One of the city's tourist attractions is the coral reef in the Gulf of Elath where the diversified marine species of the Red Sea can be observed. Every year Eilat hosts two major cultural events: a jazz festival and a classical music festival with international participation.

[Izhak Noam / Shaked Gilboa (2nd ed.)]

BIBLIOGRAPHY: Y. Ben-Zvi, *She'ar Yashuv* (1937), 97–119; N. Glueck, *The Other Side of the Jordan* (1940), 86–113; idem, in: AASOR, 15 (1934–35), 46ff.; A. Konikoff, *Transjordan* (1946), 80–82; The Israel Exploration Society, *Elath* (Heb., 1963); Z. Vilnay, *Guide to Israel* (1966³); Aharoni, Land, index; Avi-Yonah, Geog, index; Press, Ereẓ, 1 (1951²), 16–17. MODERN: Fenton and Steinitz, in: *Ariel*, 20 (1967), 61–72. **WEBSITE:** www.eilat.muni.il.

ELATH (Epstein), ELIAHU (1903–1990), Israeli diplomat and Arabist. Born in Snovsk, Russia, Elath was active in the Zionist movement in Russia before settling in Palestine in 1924. He worked as a laborer in a number of settlements for a few years, meanwhile making a special study of the Bedouin. From 1934 to 1945 he was director of the Middle East section in the Jewish Agency's Political Department. As head of the Agency's Political Office in Washington, D.C., during 1945–48, Elath received the U.S. government recognition of the State of Israel in May 1948. With the de facto recognition of Israel he was appointed special representative of the Provisional Council of the Government of Israel, and from 1949 Israeli ambassador to Washington. From 1950 to 1959 he was ambassador in London. He served as president of the Hebrew University (1962–68) and chairman of the board of governors of the Afro-Asian Institute (1959–62). His books include *Ha-Bedu'im* (1933); *Ukhlosei Ever ha-Yarden ve-Ḥayyeihem* (1936); *Ḥaj Amin al-Ḥusseini* (Heb., 1968); *San Francisco Diary* (Heb., 1971); *Shivat Ẓiyyon ve-Arav* ("The Return to Zion and the Arabs," 1974) which deals with the contacts made between the Zionist and Arab leaders and the attempts to arrive at an understanding with them before the establishment of the State; *The Struggle for Statehood: Washington 1945–1948* (Heb., 3 vols., 1979–82).

BIBLIOGRAPHY: D. Lazar, *Rashim be-Yisrael*, 1 (1953), 185–91.

[Benjamin Jaffe]

ELAZAR, DANIEL J. (1934–1999), political scientist. Elazar was born in Minneapolis and received his M.A. and Ph.D. from the University of Chicago. He was appointed professor of political science at Temple University in Philadelphia, where he founded and directed the Center for the Study of Federalism. A leading authority on the subject, he was a founding president of the International Association for Federal Studies. Elazar divided his time between the U.S. and Israel, where he was professor of intergovernmental relations at Bar-Ilan University. And, as founder and president of the Jerusalem Center for Public Affairs, he headed the major independent Jewish think tank concerned with seeking solutions to the pivotal problems facing Israel and world Jewry.

In 1986 he was appointed by President Reagan to be a member of the U.S. Advisory Commission on Intergovernmental Relations and was reappointed in 1991 by President Bush. He was secretary of the American Political Science Association and served as consultant to many federal, state, and local agencies, including the U.S. Departments of Education, Health and Human Services, and Housing and Urban Development, the National Governors' Association, the Education Commission of the States, and the Pennsylvania Science and Technology Commission, as well as to the governments of Israel, Canada, Cyprus, Italy, South Africa, and Spain.

Elazar was recognized as an expert on Jewish community organization worldwide, on the Jewish political tradition, and on Israel's government and politics. He was a consultant to the Israeli government, the Jewish Agency, the World Zionist Organization, the City of Jerusalem, and to most major Jewish organizations in the U.S. and Canada, Europe, South Africa, and Australia. Taking a leadership role in numerous local and national Jewish organizations, he was chairman of the Israel Political Science Association, a member of various consultative bodies of the Israeli government, active in the World Sephardi Federation, president of the American Sephardi Federation, and served on the International Council of Yad Vashem.

Elazar wrote or edited more than 60 books and many other publications, including *Community and Polity: The Organizational Dynamics of American Jewry* (1976), an in-depth study of the American Jewish community and its institutions; *People and Polity, The Organizational Dynamics of World Jewry* (1989), a study of the communities and institutions of World Jewry; *Israel: Building a New Society* (1986); *A Double Bond: The Constitutional Documents of American Jewry* (1992); *Israel at the Polls, 1992* (1994); *The Conservative Movement in Judaism: Dilemmas and Opportunities* (with R.M. Geffen, 2000); and *Israel at the Polls, 1999* (2001). Some of his books have sought a solution to the Israel-Palestinian problem based on federal principles. He was the founder and editor of *Publius*, the journal of Federalism, and the editor of the *Jewish Political Studies Review.* Together with his brother, David H. Elazar, he published *A Classification System for Libraries of Judaica.*

[Yitzhak Kerem / Ruth Beloff (2nd ed.)]

ELAZAR, DAVID (**"Dado"**; 1925–1976), Israeli soldier. Elazar was born in Sarajevo, Yugoslavia, and came to Israel in 1940, joining kibbutz Sha'ar ha-Amakim. In 1946 he became a member of the *Palmaḥ and during the War of Independence carried out reconnaissance in Syria. In 1948 he was appointed company commander of the Harel Brigade and led the forces which broke through to the Old City of Jerusalem via the Zion Gate in May of that year.

He studied economics and Middle Eastern studies at the Hebrew University of Jerusalem. After the Sinai Campaign, in which he commanded the infantry brigade which fought in Gaza, he was transferred to the Armored Corps, and in 1961 succeeded General Ḥaim Bar-Lev as its commander, being promoted to the rank of major-general in 1962. In November 1964 Elazar was appointed O.C. Northern Command and was responsible for the capture of the Golan Heights in the Six-Day War. In 1969 he was appointed chief of the General Staff Branch, and in November 1971, chief of staff and promoted to the rank of lieutenant-general.

Following the publication of the interim report of the Agranat Commission on the *Yom Kippur War, which was published early in 1974 and recommended that his term of office be terminated, Elazar submitted his resignation. Many felt he had been made a scapegoat for Israel's failures in the war. He was subsequently appointed head of the Zim Shipping Company.

A biography of Elazar, *Dado*, by Hanoch *Bartov, appeared in 1978.

ELAZAR, YA'AKOV (1912–2002), last of a generation of Sephardi historians and personalities who lived through the course of the 20th century in the Ottoman, British, and Israeli periods and were active in the Sephardi life of Jerusalem. He was the last authority on active Sephardi life in Jerusalem, his death at the age of 90 symbolizing the end of an era.

A descendant of the Salonikan Elazar rabbinic family which moved to Jerusalem in 1878 and the Abulafia family of Tiberias on his mother's side, he lived and breathed the Sephardi life of Jerusalem. He was one of the younger members of the He-Ḥalutz ha-Mizrachi movement. From 1931 to 1936, he taught Hebrew in the revived Sephardi Jewish community of Hebron. He was elected to Va'ad ha-Kehillah in Jerusalem (1937), and the Asefat ha-Nivḥarim of the *yishuv* (1944). On "Black Saturday" (June 29, 1946), after 700 leaders of the Jewish *yishuv* were arrested, he gathered some 3,000 people in Jerusalem within hours for prayer and public protest against the British authorities.

He spoke the Jerusalemite Judeo-Spanish dialect, was an active researcher and authority on the Sephardim of the Old City of Jerusalem and the Sephardi courtyards, and was active in the Sephardi community of Jerusalem. His books include *Diyyur ve-Klitah be-Yishuv ha-Yashan 1842–1919*, *Ḥaẓerot Bi-Yrushalayim ha-Atikah*, and *Yamei Avra: Ha-Shevitah ha-Aravit April–Oktober 1936*. He wrote about the Ereẓ Israel Sephardi chief rabbis, the *Rishonei le-Ẓiyyon*, and advocated that the younger generation know and follow their teachings. He received *semikhah* for *sheḥitah* from Chief Rabbi Jacob *Meir and published a bibliography of him in 1997, feeling that his former teacher was already forgotten.

As a Jerusalem Street Names Committee member, he proposed names of past Sephardi figures for streets. He received the distinction *Yakir Yerushalayim* and is buried in the section of prominent Jerusalemites in the Har Menuḥot cemetery in Jerusalem. He was the uncle of the American Sephardi leader and political scientist Daniel *Elazar and a cousin of Israel Defense Forces Chief of Staff David *Elazar.

[Yitzchak Kerem (2nd ed.)]

ELAZARI-VOLCANI (Wilkansky), YIZ̤ḤAK (1880–1955), agronomist and one of the planners of agricultural settlement in Ereẓ Israel, brother of Meir Wilkansky. Born at Eisiskes, near Vilna, Elazari-Volcani studied at European universities and in 1908 immigrated to Ereẓ Israel, where he managed the farm settlements of Ben Shemen and Ḥuldah (1909–18). He was an active member of the Ha-Po'el ha-Ẓa'ir party, which he represented at Zionist Congresses and in Zionist institutions. In 1921, he set up the experimental agricultural station of the Zionist Executive (today the Agricultural Research Station) and ran it until his retirement in 1951. He was one of the founders of the Institute for Agricultural Studies of the Hebrew University at Reḥovot, which later became the university's faculty of agriculture. In 1938, he was appointed professor of agricultural economics, and held various public and scientific posts connected with agriculture.

Volcani was also a prolific writer and polemicist. His first writings were published in David *Frischmann's journal *Ha-Dor* and he later contributed to J.H. *Brenner's *Ha-Me'orer*. Under the name of "E. Ẓiyyoni," he was also one of the main contributors to Ha-Po'el ha-Ẓair from its foundation. He was the first to give a positive evaluation of Baron de Rothschild's settlement scheme, and contended that it laid healthy foundations for the continuation of Jewish settlement in Ereẓ Israel. He also wrote literary studies and plays (under the pseudonym I. Avuyah). He published several books on agricultural subjects, settlement, etc. His collected articles on agriculture and other topics were published in ten volumes.

His brother, MEIR WILKANSKY (Elazari-Volcani) (1882–1949), Hebrew author, was born in Eisiskes, and immigrated to Ereẓ Israel in 1904. He first worked as an agricultural laborer; between 1908 and 1918, he was secretary of the *Palestine Office and, from 1918 until his retirement in 1942, head of the Palestine Land Development Company. Wilkansky was one of the first writers to depict the life of the pioneers of the Second Aliyah in Hebrew fiction. His stories include "*Be'er Ḥafarnu*," "*Baḥar*," and "*Yom Avodati ha-Rishon*." His books include *Sippurim me-Ḥayyei ha-Areẓ* (1918), *Ba-Ḥeder* (1934), *Bi-Ymei ha-Aliyyah* (1935), *Mi-Gal el Gal* (1943), and *Senuniyyot* (1963). He translated two of Goethe's works, *Die Leiden des jungen Werthers* and *Dichtung und Wahrheit* (Yefet series, 1911–12), and published two statistical pamphlets on Jewish settlement in Palestine (1918–19). Meir's son, RAANAN VOLCANI (1910–2002), became associate professor of animal husbandry at the agricultural faculty of the Hebrew University in 1960 and head of the Husbandry Department of the National and University Institute of Agriculture at Reḥovot.

BIBLIOGRAPHY: Hebrew University, *Ha-Fakultah le-Ḥakla'ut* (1958), 16–40, 261–7; A. Granott, *Ishim be-Yisrael* (1956), 225–38; I. Cohen, *Demut el Demut* (1949), 234–45; J. Fischmann, *Be-Terem Aviv* (1959), 332–56; M. Smilansky, *Mishpaḥat ha-Adamah*, 4 (1953), 282–7; Y. Keshet, *Maskiyyot* (1953), 109–21.

[Getzel Kressel]

ELBAZ, North African family noted for its rabbis. The Elbaz family originally lived in Azzaouia, *Morocco, from which it was expelled in 1668 by King Moulai Rashid along with 1,300 other families. They then settled in Fez and in Sefrou. Members of the family included MOSES BEN MAIMON *ALBAZ OF TARRODANT, author of *Heikhal Kodesh*, a kabbalistic commentary to the prayer book (Amsterdam, 1653), SAMUEL BEN ISAAC, author of *Toledot Adam*, a brief history up to the burning of the books in Italy (Venice, 1585), JACOB, author of *Toledot Ya'akov*, sermons (Venice, 1609), and SAMUEL BEN ISAAC (1698–1749), talmudist and codifier, who was head of the *bet din* of Fez. He was a friend of Ḥayyim b. Moses Attar, who would make no legal decision without his consent. Samuel is the author of *Va-Yomer Shemu'el*, talmudic novellae (Casablanca, 1929); his other works are still in manuscript. Many of his decisions were published in Jacob Ibn Ẓur's *Mishpat u-Ẓedakah be-Ya'akov* (Alexandria, pt. 1, 1894; pt. 2, 1903). Some of his *piyyutim* are in manuscript at the Ben-Zvi Institute in Jerusalem (no. 2072). JUDAH (1770–1847) was a codifier who headed the *bet din* of Sefrou. Many of his decisions were published in *Avnei Shayish* (2 pts., Jerusalem, 1930–34), and in his son's *Ḥayyei Amram*. He was one of the major fundraisers for the *kolelim* in Ereẓ Israel. His son AMRAM (1799–1857), codifier, judge, and poet, wrote *Ḥayyei Amram* (Meknes, 1949). Another son, SAMUEL (1790–1844), left behind a manuscript work on Rashi, *Ḥanokh la-Na'ar*. RAPHAEL MOSES ((1823–1896), Samuel's son, was a talmudic scholar, kabbalist, poet, and scientist. He wrote many works, including *Halakhah le-Moshe*, responsa (Jerusalem, 1901); *Shir Ḥadash*, poems (Jerusalem, 1935); and *Eden mi-Kedem* (Fez, 1940). Still in manuscript are many of his writings, including *Kisse ha-Melakhim*, a history of ancient kings and of the Jews.

BIBLIOGRAPHY: S. Bass, *Siftei Yeshenim* (Amsterdam, 1680), 400, nos. 20, 28; H. Ben-Attar, *Peri To'ar* (Lemberg [?], 1810), introduction; J.M. Toledano, *Ner ha-Ma'arav* (1911), 74, 107, 138, 142, 208; idem, *Oẓar Genazim* (1960), 88; J. Ben-Naim, *Malkhei Rabbanan* (1931), 44, 102, 107, 120–1; A. Elbaz, *Ḥayyei Amram* (1949), introduction.

[David Obadia]

ELBERG, YEHUDA (1912–2003), Yiddish journalist and novelist. Born in Zgierz, Poland, Elberg came from a rabbinical family and was ordained as a rabbi. He was a distant cousin of the literary *Singer family. He began publishing stories and journalistic articles in Yiddish and Hebrew newspapers in 1932. His wartime activity involved smuggling people through safe houses, and he himself avoided identification and deportation; he also took part in the Warsaw ghetto uprising. After the war he wrote as a correspondent for Israeli and American newspapers, and for the European Yiddish press.

Immigrating to New York via Paris, he began a lifelong friendship with Chaim *Grade. In 1948 he arrived in New York and became active in Zionist causes. Shortly after the death of his first wife in 1955 he moved to Montreal, where he remained until his death.

Although he wrote belles lettres from the beginning of his career and published a book of short stories, *Unter Kuperne Himlen* ("Under Copper Skies"), in 1951, his greatest literary works came later in life. The novel *Afn Shpits fun a Mast (Ship of the Hunted)* appeared in 1974, followed in quick succession by five more novels and two collections of short stories between 1976 and 1987. His masterwork was the 1983 *Kalman Kalikes Imperye (The Empire of Kalman the Cripple)*. In the 1990s he turned his attention to translating his work, publishing both *Ship of the Hunted* and *The Empire of Kalman the Cripple* in 1997. His short story "837" was made into a play and is frequently anthologized. These three works constitute his most important contributions to Yiddish literature. They have appeared in Spanish, Hebrew, French, and German as well as English. During the 1980s he won the Manger Prize and Israel's Prime Minister's Award for literature.

BIBLIOGRAPHY: B.E. Galli, "Yehuda Elberg's Wounded Words Unfolding: Uttering the Holocaust's Unutterability," in: *Literature and Theology*, 15:4 (2001), 396f; LNYL, 6, 587f; C.L. Fuks, *100 Yor Yidishe un Hebreishe Literatur in Kanade* (1980), 191f; *Forward* (Oct. 31, 2003).

[Faith Jones (2nd ed.)]

ELBLAG (Ger. **Elbing**), a city near Gdansk (Danzig), Poland, from 1772 to 1945 in Germany. Jews were reported to have been burned there during the *Black Death. There were no Jews living in Elblag after the first partition of Poland in 1772, but in 1783 Moses Simon was permitted to settle in the city and provide for visiting Jewish merchants, obtaining a trade license in 1800. There were 33 Jewish families in 1812 and 42 in 1816, all of whom had been granted the right of settlement despite opposition from the local merchants. The community opened a cemetery in 1811, an elementary school in 1823, and a synagogue and *mikveh* in 1824. A rabbi was engaged from 1879. In 1932 the community numbered 460 and maintained three charitable and five welfare organizations, and a school attended by 60 children. The synagogue was burned down by the Nazis on Nov. 10, 1938, and most of the homes and shops of the Jews there were looted. Part of the communal archives (1811–1936) are in the Central Archives for the History of the Jewish People in Jerusalem. There has not been an organized Jewish community in Elblag since World War II.

BIBLIOGRAPHY: Neufeld, in: *Zeitschrift fuer die Geschichte der Juden*, 2 (1965), 1–14; 5 (1968), 127–49; 7 (1970), 131f.; Neufeld, in: AWJD (March 25, 1966); Germ Jud, 2 (1968), 200.

[Ze'ev Wilhem Falk]

ELBOGEN, ISMAR (1874–1943), scholar, teacher, and public figure. Elbogen was born in Schildberg, Posen province, and studied at the Breslau Rabbinical Seminary. Israel *Lewy, the famous Talmud critic, was the teacher who most influenced him. In 1899 he began teaching Jewish history and biblical exegesis at the Collegio Rabbinico Italiano in Florence. While in Italy he perfected his knowledge in Italian Jewish history and literature. In 1903 he joined the faculty of the Hochschule fuer die Wissenschaft des Judentums in Berlin, teaching many subjects and for many years was involved unofficially in directing the institution. He was involved in the organizational life of German Jews, heading important committees and commissions. In 1938, in the wake of Nazi persecution, Elbogen immigrated to New York. He was appointed research professor simultaneously at four institutions: Jewish Theological Seminary, Hebrew Union College, Jewish Institute of Religion, and Dropsie College.

His scholarly interests were chiefly in Jewish history and the history of Jewish liturgy. His major work, *Derjuedische Gottesdienst in seiner geschichtliehen Entwicklung* (1913^3), is a comprehensive and important work on Jewish liturgy; it traces the history of the prayers said in the synagogue. His other works are devoted to Jewish history and are written in a popular style. His *Century of Jewish Life* (1944) was planned as a sequel to *Graetz's history. Elbogen devoted his attention also to the history of *Wissenschaft des Judentums and set forth a program for Jewish scholarship that, in addition to describing the Jewish past, would be a guide for the Jewish present and future. He was one of the editors for the periodical *Devir* (1923–24); *Germania Judaica* (2 vols., 1917–34); the jubilee edition of Moses Mendelssohn's collected works, of which only six volumes appeared (1929–32); *Zeitschrift fuer die Geschichte der Juden in Deutschland* (vols. 1–7, 1929–38); *Juedisches Lexikon* (4 vols. in 5, 1927–30); *Encyclopaedia Judaica* (vols. 1–9, 1928–34); *Eshkol* (2 vols., 1929–32); and *Universal Jewish Encyclopedia* (10 vols., 1939–43). He was an active participant in the Liberal movement in the German Jewish community. He took part in writing the Liberal prayer book for German Jews, *Tefillot le-Kol ha-Shanah: Gebetbuch fuer das ganze Jahr bearbeitet im Auftrage des Liberalen Kultus* (1932), which in the main reflects his spirit. He restored to the liturgy those prayers that had been removed by the reformers in their desire to eradicate the concept of Jewish peoplehood from the Jewish religion. He also wrote *Geschichte der Juden in Deutschland* (1935).

BIBLIOGRAPHY: R. Elbogen, in: HJ, 8 (1946), 69–94, a bibliography of I. Elbogen's writings; A. Marx, in: I. Elbogen, *Century of Jewish Life* (1944), xi–xx; M. Wiener, in: HJ, 6 (1944), 95–98; S.W. Baron, in: JSS, 6 (1944), 91–92; E. Rosenthal, in: YLBI, 8 (1963), 3–28; J.H. Kaplan, in: CCARY, 25 (1915), 403–13, a review of Elbogen's major work. **ADD. BIBLIOGRAPHY:** M.A. Meyer, *The Life and Thought of the Jewish Historian Ismar Elbogen* (2004).

ELCAN, MARCUS (c. 1757–1808), early settler of Richmond, Virginia. Elcan probably was born in Germany. He arrived in Richmond by 1782, when his name appeared as witness to a deed, although he was listed as a member of Philadelphia's Mikveh Israel in the same year. A founder of Beth Shalome Congregation, Elcan was a successful merchant and highly respected citizen; his will provided an endowment of $1,000 to the Richmond Charity School. A man of cultural attainments, he willed his considerable library of almost 200 volumes to Joseph Marx, a friend and one of his executors. Elcan's widow, Phila (c. 1760–1820), is buried in the cemetery of Touro Synagogue, Newport, Rhode Island.

BIBLIOGRAPHY: Rosenbloom, Biog Dict, 34.

[Saul Viener]

ELCHE, city on the east coast of Spain, near Alicante; important in the late Roman period. Greek inscriptions discovered in 1905 on a mosaic floor in Elche dating to some time between the third and fifth centuries are believed to refer to a synagogue. They seem to indicate that the community in Elche was organized along the same lines as other Jewish communities in Mediterranean countries. Nothing is known about the Jews in Elche under Muslim rule. After the capture of the city by James I of Aragon in 1263, Astruc *Bonsenyor of Barcelona served as interpreter. Alfonso X of Castile granted land to Don Isaac ibn Wakar, the physician of Don Juan Manuel, in the neighborhood of Elche. A Jewish scribe was in charge of the office registers and taxes of the Muslim community there in 1308. In a document from 1314 dealing with a case between Muslims of Elche and a local Christian, a scribe had to translate Catalan passages into Arabic. Abraham al-Behbehi, the Jewish scribe, wrote the text in Judeo-Arabic, that is, in Arabic written in Hebrew characters. Apart from its linguistic interest, the document has great historical significance. It sheds light on the role Jews, experts in Arabic, played in a multicultural and multilingual society. Abraham b. Baḥye farmed the taxes in Elche from 1381 to 1384. Nothing is known of the later fate of the community.

BIBLIOGRAPHY: Baer, Spain, index; Cantera-Millás, Inscripciones, 406–10; Vernet, in: *Sefarad*, 12 (1952), 126, 140, 142; Frey, Corpus, 1 (1936), nos. 662–4; F. Cantera Burgos, *Sinagogas Españolas* (1955), 212–6. **ADD. BIBLIOGRAPHY:** D. Romano, in: *Separad*, 29 (1969), 313–18; J. Hinojosa Montalvo, in: *Homenaje al Profesor Juan Torres Fontes*, vol. 1, (1987), 791–800; M. Guardia, in: M. Mentre (ed.), *L'art juif au Moyen Age*, (1988), 105–12.

[Haim Beinart / Yom Tov Assis (2nd ed.)]

ELDAD (Scheib), ISRAEL (1910–1996), Israeli underground leader, educator, geographer, writer, and translator from German; also known by his underground name and nom de plume Sambatyon. Eldad was born in Podvolochisk, in Eastern Galicia. In 1914 his family moved to Vilna, and finally settled in Lvov. He completed his studies at the rabbinical seminary in Vienna and studied for a doctorate in philosophy and history at the University of Vienna, writing his thesis on Schopenhauer. He returned to Poland to teach Jewish studies at the Jewish Teachers Seminary in Vilna. He was active in *Betar, and wrote literary and political articles for various Polish-Jewish publications in Yiddish. In 1938 he participated with Avraham *Stern in the World Conference of Betar. Back in Vilna he and his wife lived with Menaḥem *Begin's family.

In 1941 Eldad and his wife were allowed to leave Soviet-occupied Vilna and travel to Turkey, from which they then made their way to Palestine. In Palestine he taught Bible in Tel Aviv. He soon joined the leadership of the *Leḥi underground, becoming its ideologue, and editor of its underground publications, the monthly *He-Ḥazit*, and the weekly *Ha-Ma'as*. After Avraham *Stern was murdered by the British he became one of its triumvirate of leaders. In 1944 he was wounded in the back while trying to escape arrest by the British and was held in a prison hospital in Jerusalem, and later in the Latrun detention camp. In 1946 he managed to escape with the help of Leḥi members and continued his underground activities until the establishment of the State of Israel.

After the establishment of the State a breach occurred between the supporters of Nathan *Yellin-Mor, who sought to establish a neo-socialist party, and Eldad's supporters, who took a right-wing, nationalist line and focused on extra-parliamentary activities. The political group that Eldad founded was called Ḥazit ha-Moledet, but after Count *Bernadotte was assassinated in September 1948, the Israeli government declared the group to be illegal. Several of its members were detained while Eldad himself managed to escape detention. Eldad then started to publish a periodical called *Sulam*, which continued to appear until 1964. In *Sulam* he advocated Revisionist maximalism, according to which the goal of Zionism is a kingdom of Israel (*Malkhut Yisrael*), from the Nile and the Euphrates.

In the 1950s Eldad was frequently accused of incitement to violence and underground activities, but no concrete evidence was ever found. Upon orders from David *Ben-Gurion as minister of defense Eldad was fired from his post as a high school teacher and was prohibited from teaching in the public school system. Even though the Supreme Court decided in his favor he could not find work as a teacher. Subsequently he established a students association called the Nationalist Cells and earned a living as a translator. Later on he became a lecturer in humanities at the Haifa Technion and Beersheba (now Ben-Gurion) University.

After the Six-Day War Eldad became a leading figure of the radical right and was one of the founders of the Greater Israel Movement. In the elections to the Seventh Knesset in 1969 he ran at the head of a list called Le-Ereẓ Yisrael but failed to win a seat. In 1979 he was one of the founders of the Teḥiyya party with Geula *Cohen but did not run for the Knesset.

Eldad published articles regularly in *Haaretz* and *Yedioth Aharonoth*.

His son, Arie Eldad, was elected to the Sixteenth Knesset, on the National Union list. Among his books are *Ma'aser Rishon* (1975^3), memoirs of the underground, and *Hegyonot Mikra* (1984^2) on the Bible.

ADD. BIBLIOGRAPHY: A. Amichal-Yavin, *Sambatyon: Ideologiyah be-Mivḥan Tamid (Biografiyah shel Dr. Yisrael Eldad)* (1995).

[Benjamin Jaffe / Susan Hattis Rolef (2nd ed.)]

ELDAD AND MEDAD (Heb. אֶלְדָּד, מֵידָד), two of the elders (see *Elder) chosen by Moses to assist him in governing the people following their protests about the inadequacy of their diet in the wilderness (Num. 11:26–27). Both names are based on the root *ydd*, "to love, be in love." Thus, Eldad, "Beloved-of-El" and Medad, "Beloved." In response to Moses' complaint about the unbearable burden of administration placed upon his shoulders (verse 14), God commanded him to select 70 men known to him "as elders and officers of the people," that is, from the traditional leadership, who would share the burden with him (verses 16–17). To enable them to perform their function, God endowed them with part of the spirit that had rested on Moses, whereupon they made ecstatic utterances. Eldad and Medad, who did not go out with the others to the Tent of Meeting, but remained in the camp, nevertheless also spoke in a state of *ecstasy. When this was made known to Moses and Joshua, the latter suggested that they be restrained, but Moses answered him, "… Would that all the Lord's people were prophets" (verses 26–29). Eldad and Medad are not otherwise identified or mentioned in the Bible.

In the *Aggadah*

The enigmatic appearance of the otherwise unknown Eldad and Medad as authors of an unrecorded prophecy (Num. 11:26ff.) provided a fertile field for aggadic interpretations. It appears that at least some of these are thinly disguised references to the conspiracy of R. Meir and R. Nathan against R. Simeon b. Gamaliel (Hor. 13b), an event which gave rise to many "biblical" *aggadot* (cf. A. Buechler, *Studies in Jewish History* (1956), 160–78). Thus, according to R. Simeon b. Yoḥai, Eldad and Medad, though chosen to be among the elders of Israel, considered themselves unworthy of such high dignity. Thereupon God said, "Because you have humbled yourselves, I will add to your greatness yet more greatness" (Sanh. 17a). Hence, unlike other prophets, they never ceased to prophesy, and they were granted additional advantages (Num. R. 15:19; Tanḥ. B., Num. 29). The moral of the story seems to be that R. Meir and R. Nathan should have humbled themselves instead of plotting against the patriarch. All the sources report that Eldad and Medad prophesied, "Moses shall die, and Joshua shall bring Israel into the (promised) land." This prediction by the two prophets that the leader of Israel was to be replaced evidently alludes to the plan of the two rabbis to replace the patriarch. Other conjectures were that Eldad and Medad predicted the (imminent) arrival of the quails (cf. Num. 11:31) or else prophesied concerning Gog and Magog (Sanh. 17a; cf. Ezek. 38, 39). The latter suggestion was put forward by R. Naḥman who generally displayed a keen interest in messianic speculations (cf. Sanh. 96b–97a, 98b).

Joshua's objection to prophesying by Eldad and Medad (Num. 11:28) was attributed either to the fact that it was unauthorized – a serious offense in rabbinic times – or to the nature of the prediction (Sanh. 17a). The restraint proposed by Joshua (כְּלָאֵם, *kela'em*) was interpreted by some as implying the imposition of public office which would cause them to "cease (or "perish") of themselves" (*ibid.*), an unmistakable allusion to the ruinous burdens of the *Boule office in the amoraic age. Earlier interpretations were even harsher: "Destroy them from the world," or, according to R. Judah ha-Nasi (who many years after the plot against his father bore a grudge against R. Meir and R. Nathan (cf. Hor. 13b–14a)), "Chain them in bonds and fetters" (Sif. Num. 96).

While some late Midrashim make Eldad and Medad sons of Amram and half-brothers of Moses and Aaron, Targum Jonathan, Numbers 11:26, assigns their parentage to Jochebed and Elizaphan son of Parnach (Num. 34:25), whom she is supposed to have married during her temporary divorce from Amram. This strange Midrash may have been designed to counter in advance the charge against Moses' marriage alliance with a Cushite woman (Num. 12:1) – who is in some sources identified with Zipporah (Targ. Jon., Num. 12:1; Sif. Num. 99 et al.) – whom he had married before the giving of the Torah. At that time, Jochebed, too, could have been divorced, remarried, and returned again to her first husband, Deuteronomy 24:4 notwithstanding. (It is noteworthy that the numerical value of the letters פַּרְנָךְ (*Parnach*) is identical with that of עַמְרָם (Amram); and אֱלִיצָפָן (Eliẓaphan; "God has hidden") is reminiscent of Jochebed's hiding (וַתִּצְפְּנֵהוּ, *va-tizpenehu*) of Moses, Ex. 2:2.) Other Midrashim (Num. R. 15:19; Tanḥ. B., Num. 29) identify Eldad and Medad with Elidad son of Chislon and Kemuel son of Shiphtan (cf. Num. 34:21,24), due no doubt to the similarity or assonance of the names.

BIBLIOGRAPHY: B. Maisler, in: EM, 1 (1950), s.v.; C.H. Gordon, *Ugaritic Manual* (1955), glossary, no. 796; Ginzberg, Legends, 3 (1911), 251–3; 4 (1913), 158; 6 (1928), 88–90. **ADD. BIBLIOGRAPHY:** B. Levine, *Numbers 1–20* (AB; 1993), 315–16.

[Moses Aberbach]

ELDAD HA-DANI (late ninth century), traveler. His origins and personality remain a mystery. He professed to belong to the tribe of Dan, whence his name ha-Dani. Eldad claimed that the Danites together with the tribes of Naphtali, Gad, and Asher, while leading a nomadic existence, formed an independent kingdom under the rule of their king Addiel (or Uzziel). Their kingdom was in Havilah, the land of gold (cf. Gen. 2:11) near Ethiopia. The tribes, of whom the descendants of Samson and Delilah were outstanding for their valor, were constantly at war with their neighbors. Eldad also mentions the "sons of Moses," who lived nearby but were cut off from the world by the *Sambatyon, an impassable river of rolling stones and sand which stops only on the Sabbath when it is surrounded by fire or covered by a cloud. It is possible to see and speak with these "sons of Moses" but not to cross the river. Eldad relates how he and a companion of the tribe of Asher set out on a journey but were shipwrecked and fell into the hands of cannibals; his companion was eaten but he escaped a similar fate owing to an attack by other natives, fire worshipers, from whom he was eventually ransomed by a Jew of the tribe of Issachar. He further gives a colorful description of the Ten Tribes, their whereabouts and independent existence. Eldad's accounts are probably embroidered legends, based on Jewish rulers and kingdoms known to have existed: the Arabian king Joseph Dhu Nuwas (sixth century) of Ḥimyar who along with his subjects converted to Judaism; the Falashas (*Beta Israel) in Ethiopia, who were possibly independent in the early Middle Ages; and the *Khazar state, whose rulers along with many of their subjects converted to Judaism. His aim was probably to raise the spirits of the Jews by giving them news of tribes of Israel who lived in freedom and by creating an attractive Jewish utopia. The report of the existence of such Jewish kingdoms undoubtedly encouraged and comforted Eldad's hearers, by contradicting the Christian contention that Jewish independence had ceased after the destruction of the Second Temple. For the Jews his stories obviously had far-reaching messianic implications.

According to the 12th-century Karaite Judah *Hadassi Eldad made two journeys, the first to Egypt, and the second to Africa. *Ẓemaḥ b. Ḥayyim, *gaon* of Sura, writes that Eldad spoke to R. Isaac b. Mar and R. Simḥah in Babylonia. It seems therefore that Eldad was in the east before arriving in Kairouan (North Africa) about 880. In Africa Eldad conversed with Judah *Ibn Quraysh. In 883 he sent a letter to the Jews of Spain and it appears from *Ḥisdai ibn Shaprut's letter to the Khazar king that he also visited Spain.

The Jews of Kairouan consulted Ẓemaḥ Gaon about Eldad, especially concerning four *halakhot* of his on the laws concerning *sheḥitah* and *terefah*. The source of these laws is not known. While in parts there is some resemblance to Karaite laws, which caused certain scholars (Pinsker, Graetz) to conclude that he was a Karaite, most of the *halakhot* resemble the traditional talmudic law, both Babylonian and Jerusalem, although some Islamic influence seems discernible. The language shows traces of Arab usage. It is therefore probable that they reached Eldad from a country influenced by both the Arabic language and the Jerusalem Talmud.

Meir b. Baruch of Rothenburg and Abraham Ibn Ezra regarded Eldad as an impostor but his *halakhot*, even if mostly not accepted, were quoted by many of the outstanding scholars of the Middle Ages (Rashi, Asher b. Jehiel, the tosafists, et al.). Neither was he rejected by Ẓemaḥ Gaon, who stated that the possibility of different traditions existed. Eldad's accounts have been preserved in several versions. They first appeared in print in Mantua in 1480. Changes were made in several later editions in accordance with the manuscripts. Besides this there are also extant the *halakhot* sent from Kairouan to Ẓemaḥ Gaon (Constantinople, 1516).

BIBLIOGRAPHY: A. Epstein, *Eldad ha-Dani, Sippurav ve-Hilkhotav* (1891), introd.; idem, *Kitvei …*, ed. by A.M. Habermann, 1 (1950); Lazar, in: *Ha-Shilo'aḥ*, 9 (1902), 46ff.; 10 (1903), 42ff,; Graetz-Rabbinowitz, 3 (1929²), 267–73; M. Schloessinger, *Ritual of Eldad Hadani* (1908); Neubauer, in: JQR, 1 (1888/89), 95–114; M. Higger, *Jewish Utopia* (1932); Kupfer and Strelcyn, in: *Rocznik Orientalistyczny*, 19 (1954), 125–41 (Fr.); Ashtor, *Korot*, 1 (1966), 94–102; Hirschberg, Afrikah, 1 (1965), index; E.N. Adler, *Jewish Travelers* (1930), 1–21.

[Azriel Shochat]

ELDAR (Lederer), REUVEN (1926–), professor of medicine. Eldar was born in Osijek, Croatia, but raised in Novi Sad (Serbia), where he was active in the Zionist Ha-Shomer ha-Ẓa'ir youth movement and the Maccabi Sports Club. Eldar immigrated to Israel in 1948. He studied in Jerusalem and then specialized in clinical neurology in London and New York. As a physician he was appointed chief medical officer of the Israel Defense Forces with the rank of brigadier general, serving for eight years. After his military career ended, he became director of Rambam Hospital in Haifa, followed by a WHO (World Health Organization) Mission to the Philippines. On his return in 1981, he joined the Faculty of Health Sciences at Ben-Gurion University in Beersheba. From 1986 until his retirement in 1992, Eldar was in charge of the Löwenstein Rehabilitation Center, Raanana. After his retirement he acted as a consultant to WHO on services for disabled persons and for the elderly, and completed another mission abroad, in war-torn Yugoslavia, advising on the rehabilitation of the wounded. Eldar served on the editorial board of several medical journals and published over 100 papers as well as the book *Quality of Medical Care* (in Croatian) in 2003.

[Zvi Loker (2nd ed.)]

ELDER (Heb. זָקֵן, *zaken*). In Israel, as among all other ancient peoples, the elder is not only a person of advanced age, but also a man of distinct social grade (cf. *šībum* in Akkadian, *senator* in Latin, *geron* in Greek, and *sheikh* in Arabic). The elders were the consulting body of the city, the nation, or the king respectively, and as such were considered "the wise" (cf. Ezek. 7:26 with Jer. 18:18). As a social institution, various types of elders are named: elders of a people (Israel, Judah, Moab, and Midian, Num. 22:4, 7; Egypt, Gen. 50:7); elders of an area (Gilead, Judg. 11:5–11); elders of a tribe (Deut. 31:28); elders of the Diaspora (Jer. 29:1); elders of the priests (II Kings 19:2; Jer. 19:1); elders of the city (passim); and elders of the house (i.e., palace, Gen. 50:7; II Sam. 12:17). The most prominent are the elders of the people or the country and the elders of the city.

The Elders of the City

These elders represented their fellow citizens in local matters. Their functions are best exemplified by the pertinent laws of Deuteronomy. The city elders are involved in five laws: (1) blood redemption (19:12); (2) expiation of murder by an unknown culprit (21:3, 6); (3) the rebellious son (21:19); (4) defamation of a virgin (22:15); and (5) levirate (25:9). All these cases deal with protection of the family and local patriarchal interests. In the first, the elders tend to the appeasement of the murdered person's family by delivering the slayer into its hands; in the second, they see to it that their town atones for a homicide committed within its borders. In the next two instances, the elders protect the family against a rebellious son and defend the family against defamation. In the last instance, the elders are concerned with preventing the extinction of a family in their town. No professional judgment is necessary in such cases: the elders preside over a case, whose consequences are clear beforehand. The same applies to Ruth 4:2ff., where the elders only confirm the act of levirate. In contrast, "the judges" in the laws of Deuteronomy have functions that are altogether different from those of the elders. The judges act in connection with disputes (19:17–18; 25:1–3) and controversies in the local courts (17:8ff.) that cannot be solved by the local patriarchal representatives, but need a higher and more objective judicial authority. Furthermore, disputes and controversies involve thorough investigation (cf. 19:18), which can be made only by qualified and professional people. These judges are nominated (cf. Deut. 16:19) in contradistinction to the elders, whose dignity is as a rule hereditary. In only one case in Deuteronomy do the elders act together with the judges: the case of the unknown murderer (21:1ff.). The elders of the town nearest the spot where the corpse was found have to perform the expiation rites on behalf of their town. In order to establish which town is nearest, the distances must be measured (see **Eglah Arufah*). This has to be implemented by the judges and the elders of the country (21:2), i.e., by a higher authority. This case is important for an understanding of the composition of the courts in ancient Israel, especially since it has its antecedents in the judicial procedures of the other peoples in the ancient Near East. Among ancient Near Eastern peoples, a representative of the state joined the local authority (i.e., the elders) in order to settle disputes. In Mesopotamia the elders (*šībūtum*) cooperated with the mayor (*rabiānum* or *ḫazānum*), and in the Hittite state the commander of the garrison acted with the elders in settling disputes. In purely provincial matters, such as the returning of stray cattle, the elders themselves acted without resorting to government officials (Hittite Laws, para. 71). Only when investigation was involved was the case brought before a tribunal, which consisted of both state officials and elders. In ancient Israel, as in the Hittite state, the judges were associated or even identical with officers and military commanders (Ex. 18:21; Deut. 1:15). That the officer and the elder had much in common is evident from Isaiah 3:14, Ezra 10:8, et al. In I Kings 21:11, they act together (for the interchange of "noble" with "officer," cf. Jer. 39:6 with 52:10; Jer. 27:20 with II Kings 24:14).

The Elders of the People or Country

In the city-state, as it existed in Canaan, the elders of the city were identical with the elders of the state. In Israel, both before and during the monarchic period, the elders of the town and those of the people, country, and congregation operated separately. Matters that concerned the entire confederation or the nation were brought to the elders of the people, and after the division of the kingdom to the elders of Israel and Judah respectively, whereas the elders of the town dealt only with the local provincial problems (see above). It is not known how the elders of the country were chosen, but it is possible that they were recruited from the city elders. One might argue that the monarchy had deprived the elders of their power and authority, but this was not the case. Even as powerful a king as Ahab had to consult "the elders of the land" before proclaiming war (I Kings 20:7). It is needless to dwell here on the important role that the elders of Israel and Judah played at the time of David (II Sam. 3:17; 5:3; 17:4, 15). The elders cooperated with Elisha against the king (II Kings 6:32), and the elders of the land interfered in the trial of Jeremiah (Jer. 26:17). The "people of the land" or the "people of Judah," who took action when the dynasty was at stake, seem to be identical with the elders of Judah.

The emergence of the elders has been explained in the Pentateuch etiologically. According to Exodus 18, it was Jethro who advised Moses to establish a judicial-social organ in order to help him judge the people. (In the desert setting of the narrative there was no distinction between the elders of the town and the elders of the congregation.) In Numbers 11, following Moses' complaint that he cannot manage the people by himself, the Lord draws from some of the spirit of Moses and instills it in the 70 elders who are to assist him. In Deuteronomy 1:9ff., finally, Moses himself proposes that he pick men from the tribes in order to create the judicial body. These three traditions present different outlooks on the quality of the elder-judge in ancient Israel. In Exodus 18, the attributes of the chosen men are fear of God, trustworthiness, and honesty. In Numbers 11, it is the spirit of God, i.e., divine inspiration (cf. the judge in the period of the Judges, Judg. 3:10; 6:34; et al.), which makes a man a member of the elders' council. In Deuteronomy 1, intellectual capacity (wisdom, understanding, and knowledge) makes a man fit to judge. The description in Deuteronomy is apparently the latest, since it reflects the aristocratic approach, which places wisdom at the top of the ladder of values (cf. e.g., Prov. 8:15–16; et al).

The Functions of the Elders of the People

The functions of the elders of the people were (1) to represent the people in the sacral covenant and in the proclamation of the law (Ex. 19:7; 24:1, 9; Deut. 27:1; 29:9; 31:9; Josh. 8:33; 24:1; cf. II Kings 23:1); (2) to appoint a leader or a king (I Sam. 8:4; Judg. 11:5–11); (3) to proclaim war (Josh. 8:10; II Sam. 17:4–15; cf. I Kings 20:7); (4) to conduct political negotiations and make agreements (Ex. 3:16, 18; 4:29; Num. 16:25; II Sam. 3:17; 5:3); (5) to perform sacred ceremonies (Ex. 12:21; 18:12; Lev. 9:1; I Sam. 4:3; I Kings 8:1, 3; I Chron. 16:25); and (6) to act in times of national crisis (Ex. 17:5–6; Josh. 7:6; I Sam. 4:3; I Chron. 21:16). The elders held their meetings near the city gate (Deut. 21:19; 22:15; 25:7; Ruth 4:1ff.; Lam. 5:14), and more precisely in the square located next to the gate (Job 29:7). In the desert the assemblies were held "at the entrance of the Tent of Meeting" (see *Congregation). The place of the assembly had also been called "the threshing floor" (I Kings 22:10), because of its smooth, stamped surface and its circular shape (cf. Sanh. 4:3). In texts from Ugarit, Danel the pious judge is presented as sitting "before the gate, in the place of the mighty on the threshing floor" (Aqht A, V, lines 5ff., Pritchard, Texts, 151). Participation in the assembly of the elders was considered a great honor (Prov. 31:23; Job 29:7ff.), and appears as such also in Greek literature (*Iliad*, 1:490; 4:225; et al.).

[Moshe Weinfeld]

In the Talmud

During the mishnaic period the name *zaken* ("elder") was reserved for scholars, and particularly members of the Sanhedrin or *bet din*. The title was regarded as equivalent to a sage, and was unconnected with age, as was emphasized by regarding the word as a notarikon: "The *zaken* is none other than a sage, and the word means *zeh she-kanah ḥokhmah* ("one who has acquired wisdom"; Kid. 32b). Thus one reads of the elders of Bet Shammai and the elders of Bet Hillel (Ber. 11a), of the "elders of the *bet din*" who supervised the high priest before the Day of Atonement (Yoma 1:3 and 5), and of "Rabban Gamaliel and the elders who were traveling by ship" (Shab. 16:8; Ma'as Sh. 5:9; cf. also **Zaken Mamre*). The word *zaken* hardly occurs with regard to local government (the "elders of the city" of. Sot. 9:5 and 6 is a reference to Deut. 21:3), although in the Book of Judith, the elders of the city or of the people appear as the main authority of the beleaguered city. It seems that the institution of "the seven good men of the city" who were responsible for its affairs was confined to Babylon. The Mishnah (Meg. 3:1) states that if the people of a town sell a synagogue or other sacred object, the purchaser may not use it for purposes of lesser sanctity. Where the Babylonian Talmud (Meg. 26a, 27a) makes the reservation that this does not apply in cases where the "seven good men of the city" stipulated at the time of the sale that the synagogue or the sacred object could so be used, the parallel passage in the Jerusalem Talmud merely mentions the stipulation but has no reference to the seven communal leaders. Nevertheless Josephus (Ant. 4:214–4) refers to the seven men who ruled the city in Ereẓ Israel, and the Syriac Baruch mentions "the seven elders of the people" (II Bar. 44:1).

[Louis Isaac Rabinowitz]

Middle Ages and Modern Period

In the Middle Ages and early modern times the term "elder" or "elders" appears both as a titular synonym for scholar and sage as well as a frequent description for the unpaid lay members in the leadership on the boards of communities within the framework of the *Councils of the Lands. It can also be regarded as an honorific description for members of the ruling aristocracy of wealth and learning in the communities of the period. The designation disappears almost entirely from the middle of the 18th century for both communal leaders as well as scholars (except for the fossilized expression *zaken ve-yoshev bi-yshivah* used as a title in ultra-conservative circles). Its disuse was the natural corollary of a diminished reverence for age and the rise of a mentality that refused to equate it with wisdom and leadership qualities. It is not accidental that antisemitic vilification in modern times fastened on the term "elder" and attempted to turn it into a horror image. Exploiting the feelings of revulsion against the notion of scheming old men and recalling the use of the term in the Jewish hierarchy and tradition, it conjured up a new Jewish bogey in the shape of the *Elders of Zion ("Sages de Sion"). The Nazis in their calculated policy of fragmentation and foisting a spurious leadership on the Jews turned to the use of the name *Judenaeltestе* ("elders of the Jews") for some of the functionaries in this leadership.

[Haim Hillel Ben-Sasson]

BIBLIOGRAPHY: J.L. McKenzie, in: *Analecta Biblica*, 10 (1959), 388–400; H. Klengel, in: *Orientalia*, 29 (1960), 357–75; de Vaux, Anc Isr, 68–70; Evans, in: JRH, 2 (1962), 1–12; H. Klengel, *Zeitschrift fuer Assyriologie*, 23 (1965), 223ff.; H. Tadmor, in: *Journal of World History*, 11 (1968), 3–23; H. Reviv, in: *Journal of the Economic and Social History of the Orient*, 12 (1969), 283–97; Baron, Community, index. **ADD. BIBLIOGRAPHY:** T. Wills, *Elders of the City* (2001); A. Rof, "The Organization of the Judiciary in Deuteronomy," in: M. Daviau et al. (eds.), *World of the Arameans* (2002), 92–112.

ELDER, WILL (1921–), U.S. cartoonist. Elder, who was born in the Bronx, N.Y., attended the High School of Music and Art, where he began a lifelong friendship with a classmate and future collaborator, Harvey *Kurtzman, in stinging and hilarious cartoon art. Elder's penchant for zany humor flowered early with legendary stunts: when he failed to show up for class, he was discovered by a nervous teacher hanging by his neck in the school coat closet, his face chalked white. Another time he dressed joints of beef in clothing and spread them across train tracks, moaning, "Poor Schlomie! He fell on the tracks," horrifying passers-by.

Elder began his comic book career in 1946, writing and drawing a feature called Rufus Debree in *Toy Town Comics*. After several cartooning positions, Elder in 1952 joined Kurtzman, creator of *Mad* magazine, which gave him a chance to display his zany style of humor. Elder penciled and inked his own stories from the first issue on. He was credited with being the main creator of the early, zany Mad "chicken fat" style. His art was most notable for having numerous visual jokes hidden in the nooks, crannies, and backgrounds of the stories he drew. Elder became such a sensation at *Mad* that issue number 22 featured a book-length biography of him. Elder and Kurtzman left *Mad* in 1956 and worked together on a number of projects, including some short-lived satirical magazines. In one of them, *Help!*, Elder and Kurtzman created an innocent Candide-like character, Goodman Beaver. Inspired by a lusty spoof of the comic-book character Archie, Elder and Kurtzman turned the innocent Goodman Beaver, a man, into a sexy woman and named her Little Annie Fanny. *Playboy* magazine published the four-to-seven-page stories, written by Kurtzman and painted by Elder, from 1962 to 1988. The strip took comic art to new heights with sophisticated and savage satire and carefully painted stories.

Over the years, Elder's genres included crime, science fiction, horror, fantasy, war, and sex. In 2003, Fantagraphics published *Will Elder: The Mad Playboy of Art*, a definitive career retrospective. It contained more than 100 pages of comics and other art work.

[Stewart Kampel (2nd ed.)]

ELDERS OF ZION, PROTOCOLS OF THE LEARNED, antisemitic forgery aimed at showing the existence of international Jewish aspirations bent on world power. The specter of a worldwide Jewish conspiracy aiming at reducing the gentiles to slavery or exterminating them loomed up in the Christian imagination during the Middle Ages, growing out of legends about well-poisoning and plague-spreading. Some such stories claimed that a secret rabbinical conference had been held to work out a detailed plan for ritual genocide of the Christians. From the time of the Renaissance, at first in Spain, these legends turned on a political plot rather than a religious one; similar notions circulated in France and Germany, after Napoleon's convocation of the Great Sanhedrin (see French *Sanhedrin) in 1807. They did not gain widespread popular credence, nor at first did the versions launched during the second half of the century by French Catholic authors like *Barruel and Bailly, who associated *Freemasons and Jews in an anti-Christian plot. In its latest version, the legend of the "Elders of Zion" was concocted in Paris in the last decade of the 19th century by an unknown author working for the Russian secret police (*Okhrana*); in all probability, it was intended to influence the policy of Czar *Nicholas II toward the interests of the secret police. For his purposes, the anonymous forger adapted an old French political pamphlet by Maurice Joly attributing ambitions of world domination to Napoleon III, *Dialogue aux Enfers entre Machiavel et Montesquieu, ou la politique au xixe siècle* (1864), which does not contain the slightest allusion to Jews or to Judaism. This "dialogue" was transformed into the "protocols" of an alleged conference of the leaders of world Jewry, who stated in summing up that, under the cloak of modern democracy, they already controlled the policies of numerous European states and were therefore very close to their objective. However the calculations of the Russian police misfired on that occasion: Nicholas II, impressionable and antisemitic though he was, detected the fraud, writing "One does not defend a worthy cause by vile means" in the margin of the manuscript submitted to him. The first Russian public edition of the *Protocols*, which appeared in 1905, did not attract much attention and was taken seriously in a few mystic and sectarian circles only.

The worldwide success of the *Protocols* dates from 1919 to 1921; after the widespread slaughter in World War I, the Russian Revolution in 1917, and the risings in Germany, many people felt impelled to discover a "hidden cause" for such tragic and momentous events. The text was widely circulated during the Russian civil war by propagandists seeking to incite the masses against the "Jewish Revolution," and undoubtedly contributed to the extensive pogroms perpetrated in southern Russia between 1918 and 1920. After the defeat of the White armies, Russian émigrés publicized the *Protocols* in the West. Translations followed, but most reputable European newspapers, such as the *Times* of London, questioned their authenticity. In 1921 the English journalist Philip Graves pointed out the close similarity between the text of the *Protocols* and Joly's pamphlet; from then on, balanced and responsible circles refused to take them seriously. This was no bar to an enormous circulation of the text, which was translated into all the main world languages. In the United States it was even sponsored (until 1927) by the influential and popular Henry Ford I.

However, well before the Nazi rise to power, the *Protocols* found the largest number of adherents in Germany. The theory of the occult power of the Jews' sworn enemies of German-Christian culture, perfectly suited those reactionary propagandists who attributed Germany's defeat to "a stab in the back." Right from the start the Nazi Party propagated this theme. The Weltdienst organization of Erfurt was specially formed to diffuse it and to strengthen ties with antisemites in other countries. In Berne in 1934 the Jewish community of Switzerland brought the distributors of the *Protocols* to trial, establishing in court that the work was a forgery, but this did nothing to diminish the zeal of its propagators. During World War II, the *Protocols of the Learned Elders of Zion* became an implicit justification for the genocide of the Jews; and Nazi propaganda relied on them until the last days of the Third Reich. Although from 1945 no more than bibliographical curiosity in the majority of civilized countries, the *Protocols* were reissued in numerous Arab states and President Nasser of Egypt publicly vouched for their authenticity, as did the Jordanian delegate to the United Nations in 1980. The Arab states continued to disseminate the *Protocols* in places as diverse as Sweden and the United States, joined in the latter by black Muslim groups and the Ku Klux Klan. A Spanish edition, published in 1963, was probably an attempt to prevent the revision of the Catholic Church's traditional attitude toward the Jews at the Ecumenical Council Vatican II. The *Protocols* were also circulated in Japan, Latin America, and the Soviet Union.

Research by Colin Holmes, a lecturer in economic history of Sheffield University, has revealed the source which enabled Philip Graves to expose the *Protocols* as a forgery. They were given to Graves by a Russian émigré, Michael Raslovleff, who fled to Constantinople after the Russian Revolution of 1917. Raslovleff, a self-confessed antisemite, gave the information to Graves because he was unwilling to "give a weapon of any kind to the Jews, whose friend I have never been."

BIBLIOGRAPHY: N. Cohn, *Warrant for Genocide* ... (1967), a bibliographical note dealing with numerous early works can be found in this work; L. Poliakov, *Histoire de l'antisémitisme*, 3 vols. (1956–68), passim; Y. Harkabi, *Arab Attitudes to Israel* (1971); "Patterns of Prejudice," Institute of Jewish Affairs (London, 1977).

[Leon Poliakov]

ELEALEH (Heb. אֶלְעָלֵא, אֶלְעָלֵה), biblical town in Transjordan, northeast of Heshbon. Elealeh is always mentioned together with Heshbon. It was settled by the tribe of Reuben and later reverted to Moab (Num. 32:3, 37; Isa. 15:4; 16:9; Jer. 48:34). Eusebius refers to it in the fourth century C.E. as a large village

(Onom. 84:10). The site is occupied at present by the Arab village al-ʿĀl, 2,986 ft. (910 m.) above sea level, halfway between Amman (Rabbath) and Madaba (Medba) in a region rich in vineyards. Remains of walls from the Early Bronze (pre-patriarchal) Age have been uncovered there as well as Moabite and Hellenistic potsherds. The ruins of a settlement from the Arab period are visible on the surface.

BIBLIOGRAPHY: Horowitz, in: EI, 48f.; Press, Ereẓ, 1 (1951^2), 22; Glueck, in: AASOR, 14 (1934), 6; P. Thomsen, *Loca Sancta* (1907), 59. **ADD. BIBLIOGRAPHY:** B. Levine, *Numbers 21–36* (AB; 2000), 484.

[Michael Avi-Yonah]

ELEAZAR (Heb. אֶלְעָזָר; "God/El-has-aided"), high priest after *Aaron. Eleazar was Aaron's third son (Ex. 6:23); his older brothers Nadab and *Abihu perished after offering strange fire before the Lord (Lev. 10:1–7; Num. 3:4). During his father's lifetime Eleazar served as the "head chieftain of the Levites" (Num. 3:32) and performed some of the functions of the high priest (*ibid.* 19:4). After Aaron's death, Eleazar was appointed high priest in his father's place (*ibid.* 20:28; Deut. 10:6). Together with Moses, he concluded the census of the people on the plains of Moab by the bank of the Jordan (Num. 26:1–3) and, together with Joshua, supervised the division of the land (Num. 34:17; Josh. 14:1 and elsewhere). In the text describing the appointment of Joshua as Moses' successor, it is stated that Eleazar was to stand before Joshua when the latter inquired "by the judgment of the Urim" (Num. 27:18–22). Eleazar's burial place was on the hill of his son *Phinehas in Mount Ephraim (Josh. 24:33). The priestly family of *Zadok traced its descent from Eleazar, who was regarded as the ancestor of 16 of the 24 priestly houses (I Chron. 24:4–18).

BIBLIOGRAPHY: H. Gressmann, *Moses und seine Zeit* (1913), 213ff.; L. Waterman, in: AJSLL, 58 (1941), 50ff.; de Vaux, Anc Isr, index; EM, 1 (1950), 369f.

ELEAZAR (2nd cent. B.C.E.), martyr during the religious persecution instigated by Antiochus Epiphanes (167 B.C.E.). "Eleazar, one of the foremost scribes, well advanced in years," was compelled to eat swine's flesh, but chose "death with glory rather than life with pollution, and of his own free will was tortured" after refusing to so much as pretend to partake of the forbidden meat. The principal source of this story is II Maccabees 16:18–31, while IV Maccabees 5–6 offers an elaborated version of the original. Eleazar's martyrdom was subsequently extolled by the church fathers (Origen, Προτρεπτικὸς εἰς μαρτύριον, xxii–xxvii).

BIBLIOGRAPHY: Maas, in: MGWJ, 44 (1900), 145–56; Schuerer, Hist, 28.

[Isaiah Gafni]

ELEAZAR (**Alatzar**, **Abenalazar**), prominent Jewish family in the kingdom of Aragon in the Middle Ages. They were considered *francos* ("free") for the special services which they had rendered to the kings of Aragon during the Christian Reconquest and as such exempted from taxes. The main branch of the family lived in Saragossa. The founder of this branch was apparently ALAÇAR, treasurer of Ramon Berenguer of Aragon, who in 1135 granted him and his descendants a release from taxes. In 1212 ABULFATH ABENALAZAR, son of Alazrach, was transferred by King Pedro, together with his family, to the protection of the Knights of the Order of St. John. They were granted special protection, right of appeal to the king's court of justice, and exemption from the discriminatory Jewish *oath. This privilege was confirmed by James I in 1235 to Abulfath's grandson, ALAÇAR B. ALAZRACH, who served as *alfaquim* ("physician-interpreter") in Saragossa. The family's omission to pay their share of the communal taxes and failure to participate in communal affairs alienated them from the Jewish community. However, in 1413 the community succeeded in obtaining an order from King Ferdinand I by which the Eleazar family was compelled to share the expenses of sending a delegation to the papal court. Their release in 1425 from the tax on meat and wine finally caused their excommunication by the Jewish community.

Other members of this family include the physician MOSSE ABEN ELEAZAR (active c. 1390), as a result of whose services to the Franciscans in Saragossa the Jews were permitted in 1385 to carry their dead to the cemetery on the road which passed by their church. Other physicians of the family include EZDRA ELEAZAR, in attendance on the royal court in 1387, and TODROS ALAZAR (second half of the 15th century). The wealthy DON MAIR ALAZAR (first half of the 15th century) established a Jewish hospital. One of the gates to the Jewish quarter of Saragossa situated near his house was named after him. Maestre MOSSE ALAZAR was in the service of the court of Aragon in 1384. The richest Jewish moneylender in Saragossa at the time of the Expulsion of 1492 was SOLOMON ELEAZAR: an inventory of pledges in his possession has been preserved. A secondary branch of the family lived in Valencia. JUDAH ELEAZAR (d. 1377) was the most forceful communal leader in the city and among the signatories of the regulations of the communities of Aragon issued in 1354. He gave considerable financial help to the king in the war against Castile, and in 1370 lent 110,000 solidos for equipping the ships which conveyed Pope Urban V from Rome to Avignon. Several less influential members of the Eleazar family lived in Calatayud and Huesca.

BIBLIOGRAPHY: Baer, Urkunden, 1 (1929), index; Baer, Spain, index; Neuman, Spain, index; M. Serrano y Sanz, *Origenes de la Dominación Española en América* (1918), 12–13, 451–2; Cabezudo Astrain, in: *Sefarad*, 14 (1954), 377–9; 20 (1960), 412–3, 415–6; Lopez de Meneses, *ibid.*, 14 (1954), 109, 112, 114; Piles Ros, *ibid.*, 10 (1950), 370, 377, 378, 381, 384; A.M. Hershman, *Rabbi Isaac Ben Sheshet Perfet and His Times* (1943), 22, 159, 169.

ELEAZAR BEN ANANIAS, Zealot leader in Jerusalem during the Jewish war with Rome 66–70 C.E. Eleazar evidently already held the office of Captain of the Temple (*segan ha-Kohanim* – στρατηγός) during the procuratorship of *Albinus, 62–64 C.E., and continued to hold that position until the destruction of the Temple. Son of the high priest *Ananias and a member of the priestly circles who joined the revolt, he persuaded the priests to discontinue the practice of accepting offerings on behalf of aliens. Cessation of the sacrifice offered up for the emperor was tantamount to challenging Roman rule, and – according to Josephus – this action signaled the revolt against Rome. The Talmud attributes the action to Zechariah b. Avkulus (Git. 56a).

The discontinuation of sacrifices for the health of the emperor led to a struggle in Jerusalem between the Zealots and those favoring conciliation. Eleazar and his partisans gained possession of the Temple mount and the lower city while the peace party and troops of King *Agrippa II occupied the upper city. With the help of the extremist *Sicarii faction, however, Eleazar and his men succeeded in capturing this section too. The extremist elements then gained the upper hand, and attacked not only the Romans, but also their opponents among their compatriots. They set fire to the palaces of Agrippa, *Berenice, and the high priest Ananias, as well as to the public archives where loan bonds were deposited. Ananias and his brother Hezekiah (see *Ananias b. Nedebeus) were put to death. When *Menahem b. Judah the Galilean, a central figure among the extremists, attempted to seize the command for himself, he was foiled by Eleazar. After *Cestius Gallus was defeated, Eleazar was appointed general of Idumea by the war party in Jerusalem, together with *Jesus b. Zapphas. The appointment was evidently prompted by a desire to remove him from a key position in the command, and no more is known of him.

BIBLIOGRAPHY: Derenbourg, Hist, 472–4; Schuerer, Gesch, 1 (1901^4), 584, 602, 607; Klausner, Bayit Sheni, 5 (1951^2), 145–9; M. Stern, in: *Ha-Ishiyyut ve-Dorah* (1963), 73; Jos., Ant., 20:208; Jos., Wars, 2:17, 409, 425, 566.

[Lea Roth]

ELEAZAR BEN ARAKH (second half of the first century C.E.), *tanna*. He was one of the most outstanding disciples of R. *Johanan b. Zakkai, who described him as "an overflowing spring," i.e., an inexhaustible source of innovative interpretation and insight into the meaning of the Torah. According to one tradition, he was considered to "outweigh all the sages of Israel" (Avot 2:8). Relatively few traditions are preserved in his name in the tannaitic sources. To his teacher's question, "Which is the good way to which a man should cleave?" Eleazar answered, "A good heart," a reply which, in R. Johanan's opinion, embodied all those given by his other pupils (Avot. 2:9). In addition he is associated with two other aggadic statements: the one "Be eager to study the Torah, and know what you should answer to an unbeliever ..." (Avot 2:14); and the other that God humbled Himself by speaking to Moses from the burning bush and not from some high mountain or elevated place (Mekh. Sby, to 3:5; cf. Mid. Ḥag. to Ex. 3:2). Only two of his halakhic statements are cited in tannaitic sources (Tosef. Ter. 5:15; TJ, Yev. 2:1, 3c, and parallel passages; Sifra 2:8; Ḥul. 106a). According to two early traditions (Mech. of Rabbi Shimon, 158–159; Tos. Ḥag. 2:1), Eleazar engaged, together with his teacher, in mystical speculation concerning the Divine Chariot (see *Merkabah Mysticism). While this story may have an historical foundation, the literary figure of R. Eleazar – the "overflowing spring" – may also have been used here by later story tellers to exemplify Ḥag. 2:1, which permits mystical speculation only in the case of "a sage who understands by himself." According to the *Mech. of Rabbi Shimon*, R. Eleazar expounded the secrets of the Chariot "on the basis of his own understanding" until "a fire surrounded him" – a sign of divine confirmation of his experience. The story as related by the Tosefta is a far more sober affair, involving a form of "scholastic" mysticism, which takes place wholly on the earthly plane, and which was strictly supervised by Rabban Johanan. The Babylonian Talmud (following the lead of the Jerusalem Talmud) combines and elaborates these two traditions, relating that while they were traveling together, Eleazar asked R. Johanan to teach him the secrets of the Chariot, to which the latter replied: "Have I not taught you that such speculations may not be conveyed to an individual, unless he is a scholar who is able to think and speculate for himself?" Having obtained R. Johanan's permission, Eleazar began to expound the subject, whereupon fire immediately descended from heaven and enveloped all the trees in the field, which broke forth in song. R. Johanan then kissed his pupil and said: "Blessed be the Lord, God of Israel, who has granted our father Abraham a descendant capable of understanding, inquiring into, and expounding the Divine Chariot" (Ḥag. 14b). Later traditions tell a story of his having followed his wife's advice to go to Emmaus instead of accompanying R. Johanan from Jerusalem to Jabneh. As a result of his isolation he is reputed to have forgotten his learning in Emmaus, "a place of bath-houses and luxury" (Shab. 147b; ARN 14:30; ARN^2 29, 3; Eccl. R. 7:7). It is likely, however, that these traditions, rather than reflecting the historical truth of Rabbi Eleazar's own life, reflect an attempt to explain the paucity of traditions preserved in his name despite the lavish praise bestowed upon him by his teacher as recorded in *Avot.*

BIBLIOGRAPHY: Geiger, in: JZWL, 9 (1871), 45–49; Bacher, Tann, 1 (1903^2), 69–72; Frankel, Mishnah, 95f.; Alon, Toledot, 1 (1958^2), 63. **ADD. BIBLIOGRAPHY:** A. Goshen-Gottstein, *The Sinner and the Amnesiac* (2000); S. Wald, in: JSIJ (2006).

[Shmuel Safrai / Stephen G. Wald (2nd ed.)]

ELEAZAR BEN AZARIAH (first–second century C.E.), one of the sages of Jabneh. He was one of the most prominent *tannaim* and is quoted dozens of times in the Mishnah, the Tosefta, and the tannaitic Midrashim, his statements touching on all areas of *halakhah* and *aggadah*. A priest, it is said that he could trace his ancestry back ten generations to Ezra (TJ, Yev. 1:6, 3a–6). Like many prominent *tannaim*, events mentioned briefly or in passing in the earlier sources were expanded and elaborated in the later talmudic literature. For example, Ben Azzai mentions in three places (Zev. 1:3; Yad. 3:5; 4:2) "the day that they seated R. Eleazar ben Azariah in the yeshivah." The

Mishnah itself associates a series of important discussions and decisions with "that day" (Yad. 4:1–4). "That day" afterwards became the focus for a number of other important events mentioned or hinted at in tannaitic literature. For example, on that day the tractate *Eduyyot* was supposed to have been formulated (see however Epstein, *Tanna'im*, 422–4). "That day" was associated with the stories surrounding the removal of *Rabban Gamaliel II from office. It is told that when Rabban Gamaliel was deposed as *nasi* because of his autocratic behavior toward Joshua b. Hananiah, Eleazar was chosen to succeed him. The selection was prompted not only by his aristocratic lineage, but also by his great wealth, the *nasi* being required to bear a considerable proportion of the expenses of his office (TJ, Ber. 4:1, 7d; *ibid.* 27–28a). When appointed *nasi* he was, according to a tradition preserved in both Talmuds, only about 18 years old, but a miracle was wrought for him and his hair turned gray (Ber. 28a). This legend probably originated in Eleazar's remark (Ber. 1:5), "I am about (like one who is) 70 years old," which has been interpreted to mean that he merely had the appearance of an old man (Ber. 28a). From elsewhere in the Jerusalem Talmud (Ber. 1:9, 3d), it would seem that he made this statement in his old age. It is told that on "the day" he was appointed *nasi*, the college was thrown open to all who wished to study, without restriction, contrary to the previous ruling of Rabban Gamaliel that "No disciple whose true character does not correspond to his outer bearing may enter the *bet ha-midrash*. On that day hundreds of benches were added to the *bet ha-midrash*, and there was no *halakhah* about which there was any doubt that was not elucidated" (see Ber. 28a). After a reconciliation between the sages and Rabban Gamaliel and his reinstatement as *nasi*, it was decided that they share the discourses on alternate Sabbaths with Eleazar's known as "the Sabbath of Eleazar b. Azariah" (Ber. *ibid.*).

In another example, tannaitic literature tells of Eleazar ben Azariah's journey, together with Rabban Gamaliel and other sages, to Rome (Sif. Deut. 20:3; cf. Ma'as. Sh. 5:9; Er. 4:1). In the later literature we hear many more details of their stay there, of their meetings with the members of the Jewish community, with the authorities, and with the emperor, and with prominent Romans who had been attracted to Judaism, of their return voyage, and of Eleazar's pilgrimage, together with the *nasi* and the elders, to Jerusalem (Mak. 24a-b; et al.).

R. Eleazar was both a halakhist and an aggadist. A statement reported in the name of Judah ha-Nasi (or in that of his contemporary Issi b. Judah) praises him as being "a basket of spices" and "a spice-dealer's basket," i.e., carefully endeared by fragrant allusions to his vast, finely ordered learning, which enabled him to answer with equal facility questions on Bible, Mishnah, midrashic *halakhah*, or *aggadah* (ARN[1] 18:66; Git. 67a). Eleazar is the author of the observation that a Sanhedrin which executes a person once in 70 years is to be branded a murderous tribunal (Mak. 1:10). His exegetical practice is similar to that of the school of R. *Ishmael in keeping with the view that "the words of the Bible are to be construed literally" (Kid. 17b) and that no special significance is to be attached to the duplication of verbs in the infinitive construct since "the Bible speaks in the language of human beings" (BM 31b). He is thus at variance with the school of R. *Akiva, which felt that such duplications of the verb required an halakhic interpretation. At times Eleazar explicitly controverts the exegetical principles of Akiva (Sifra 7:12 et al.).

He was famous for his aggadic comments. After hearing one of R. Eleazar's aggadic interpretations of scripture, Joshua said, "The generation in which Eleazar b. Azariah lives is not forsaken" (Tosef., Sot. 7:12). In his aggadic interpretations he makes frequent use of two exegetical principles: the juxtaposition of biblical texts *semukhin* and the argument *a fortiori* (*kal va-ḥomer*). On the significance of the Day of Atonement he declared: "The Day of Atonement can bring forgiveness for transgressions between man and the Almighty, but not for transgressions between one man and another until the one has obtained the other's pardon" (Yoma 8:9). And again, "Where there is no Torah, there is no right conduct" (Avot 3:17). He also said: "A man should not say, 'I have no desire to eat pig's flesh' … but rather, 'I would like to do so, but how can I, seeing that God has prohibited it?'" (Sifra 11:22). Eleazar's wealth was proverbial, and it was said that "whoever sees Eleazar b. Azariah in a dream can expect riches" (Ber. 57b). He survived Rabban Gamaliel and was apparently alive at the time of the Jewish revolt under Trajan (115–117), although not at the outbreak of the Bar Kokhba revolt (131). When R. Eleazar b. Azariah died, it was stated "the crowns of wisdom have departed" (Sot. 49b).

BIBLIOGRAPHY: J. Bruell, *Mevo ha-Mishnah*, 1 (1876), 88–91; Derenbourg, in: MGWJ, 37 (1893), 395–8; Bacher, Tann, 1 (1903²), 212–32; Weiss, Dor, 2 (1904⁴), 85–91; Graetz, Gesch, 4 (1908⁴), 35ff.; Frankel, Mishnah, 96–99; Hyman, Toledot, 186–91; L. Ginzberg, *Perushim ve-Ḥiddushim ba-Yerushalmi*, 3 (1941), 168–220; Alon, Toledot, 1 (1958²), 368 (index); 2 (1961²), 273 (index); S. Lieberman, *Tosefta ki-Feshutah*, 5 (1962), 1162.

[Shmuel Safrai]

ELEAZAR BEN DAMMA (early second century C.E.), *tanna*. Eleazar is mentioned in two places in the early tannaitic sources, both in connection with R. *Ishmael. In Tosefta *Shevuot* 3:4 Ben Damma asked R. Ishmael a question concerning a *halakhah*, who in responding called him "My son!" In Tosef. Ḥul. 2:22–23 it is told that "R. Eleazar Ben Damma was bitten by a snake and Jacob of Kefar Sama came to heal him in the name of Jesus b. Pandira. Ishmael said to him, 'it is forbidden, Ben Damma.' He rejoined 'I will cite a verse to prove that he may heal me,' but he did not manage to prove it before he died. Whereupon Ishmael said: 'Happy art thou, Ben Damma, that thou hast departed from this world in peace and hast not transgressed the words of the sages'" (cf. TJ, Av. Zar. 2:2, 40d). A later Midrash (Koh. R. 1) retells the story from the Tosefta, but refers to Ben Damma as R. Ishmael's nephew, a detail lacking in the earlier tradition. He is similarly described as R. Ishmael's nephew in the Babylonian Talmud Ber. 56b, where he asked his "uncle" to interpret his dream for him. This elaboration of earlier stories, including the filling in of the family ties between earlier talmudic figures, is characteristic of the later talmudic tradition, especially the Babylonian Talmud. The Babylonian Talmud also tells of his inclination toward Greek culture, as reflected in the following passage: "Ben Damma, son of Ishmael's sister, once asked Ishmael, 'May such as I who have studied the whole of the Torah study Greek wisdom?' Ishmael thereupon read to him the verse, 'This book of the law shall not depart from thy mouth, but thou shalt meditate therein day and night' (Josh. 1:8) and added, 'Go then and find a time that is neither day nor night'" (Men. 99b). His name is cited in *Heikhalot Rabbati*, 4, as one of those arrested by the Romans, but it appears that the reference is to Judah b. Damma, one of the *Ten Martyrs enumerated in the *Elleh Ezkerah* published by Jellinek (*Beit ha-Midrash*, 2 (1967^3), 64).

BIBLIOGRAPHY: Hyman, Toledot, 161.

[Jehonatan Etz-Chaim]

ELEAZAR BEN DINAI (c. second half of the first century C.E.), Zealot leader. Josephus relates that for 20 years he ravaged Judea until, by ruse, he was captured by the procurator Felix (53–60) and sent to Rome. He is first mentioned in the period of the procurator Fadus (44–46) in connection with the conflict in the Philadelphia (Rabbath Ammon) area of Transjordan between the Jews and their neighbors, some of whom were killed. Subsequently Eleazar was arrested together with the other Jewish leaders and was banished. In the quarrel between the Jews and Samaritans arising from the murder of a Galilean pilgrim during the procuratorship of Cumanus Ventidius (48–52), the Jews called upon Eleazar, who had taken refuge in the mountains for some years, to assist them in taking vengeance. In the Mishnah, Eleazar is mentioned as a murderer in whose time the incidence of open murder greatly increased, leading to the discontinuation of the *Eglah Arufah* ceremony for an unsolved murder (see Deut. 21:1–9; Sot. 9:9), and he is mentioned elsewhere as one of those who sought to hasten the advent of the Messiah but failed (Song R. 2:7). Some are of the opinion that at first his deeds were well-intentioned but in the course of time he accustomed himself to acts of violence. It is almost certain that he was executed after being brought to Rome.

BIBLIOGRAPHY: Jos., Ant., 20:2–4, 121, 161; Jos., Wars, 2:235, 253; Klausner, Bayit Sheni, 5 (1963), 15–17.

[Lea Roth]

ELEAZAR BEN ḤALFON HA-KOHEN (12th–13th century), Hebrew poet. Eleazar lived apparently in an Oriental country. About 15 poems from his *divan* survived in the Cairo *Genizah*, where his name usually appears as "Eleazar" or "Eleazar ha-Kohen," but in one, as "Eleazar ben Ḥalfon ha-Kohen." One of the poems is a panegyric to *Maimonides composed apparently during the latter's lifetime. Eleazar, who seems to have been among the best of the Oriental Hebrew *paytanim*, adopted the Sephardi style of *piyyut* in its fullest detail. Many of his *piyyutim* were attributed by copyists to the great poets of the Spanish era, and it is possible perhaps that some of the poems of his time, signed "Eleazar ha-Kohen," should be ascribed to him.

BIBLIOGRAPHY: A. Scheiber, in: *Sinai*, 35 (1954), 183–6; idem, in: *Sefer Ḥayyim Schirman* (1970), 393–4; Ḥ. Schirmann, *Shirim Ḥadashim min ha-Genizah* (1965), 106–16.

[Abraham David]

ELEAZAR BEN HANANIAH BEN HEZEKIAH (lived shortly before the destruction of the Temple in 70 C.E.), *tanna*. His full name was Eleazar b. Hananiah b. Hezekiah b. Garon. He is quoted in Sifre Deut. 294, and Mech. Baḥodesh 7, his position in this latter source appearing elsewhere in the name of Shammai. In *Megillat Ta'anit* it is stated (p. 351) that "the group of Eleazar (Eliezer) b. Hananiah b. Hezekiah b. Garon wrote *Megillat Ta'anit*." In the Talmud (Shab. 13b), however, the compilation of *Megillat Ta'anit* is ascribed to "Hananiah b. Hezekiah and his companions" (see: Noam, 29–31). Graetz, who adopted the reading of Eleazar b. Hananiah in *Shabbat*, identified him with the Eleazar b. Hananiah mentioned by Josephus as a leader of the Zealots in the rebellion against Rome, but his view has not found wide acceptance (Noam, 335–36).

BIBLIOGRAPHY: Hyman, Toledot, 176. **ADD. BIBLIOGRAPHY:** V. Noam, *Megillat Ta'anit* (2003).

[Stephen G. Wald (2nd ed.)]

ELEAZAR BEN ḤARSOM, in the *aggadah* described as a priest and a scholar. No mention is made of him in the extant tannaitic sources. In one place in the Jerusalem Talmud (Ta'an. 4:8, 69a; cf. Lam. R. 2:2) it is stated that "there were 10,000 cities on the king's mountain; Eleazar b. Ḥarsom owned 1,000 of them, and corresponding to them he owned 1,000 ships on the sea, and all were destroyed." It would seem from the context that they were destroyed during the Bar Kokhba revolt. In another place (Yoma 3:6, 40d) the Jerusalem Talmud relates that "his mother made him a tunic worth 20,000 *minas* and his brother priests would not allow him to wear it because [it was transparent and] he looked as though he were naked." In the Babylonian Talmud (Yoma 35b) these two traditions about his wealth are joined together, and integrated with an image of Eleazar b. Ḥarsom as a wandering scholar, who took a sack of flour upon his shoulder and went from city to city and from province to province to study Torah. The moral of the story is stated explicitly at the end: "Eleazar b. Ḥarsom condemns the rich" who will not be able to justify their neglect of learning on the plea that the cares of their wealth prevented them from devoting themselves to study. In Kid. 49b he has turned into the very epitome of the wealthy man: "[If one betroths a woman] on the condition that he is wealthy, it is not necessary that he be as wealthy as Eleazar b. Ḥarsom." His status as a priest is elaborated further in *Yoma* 9a, where – according to one alternative tradition – he is accorded the rank of High Priest during the time of the Second Temple. In the list of martyrs given in *Lamentations Rabbah* (2:2) it says "…there are some who exclude Tarfon and include Eleazar b. Ḥarsom," but his name is not included in the other lists (Mid. Ps. to 9; *Piyyutei Yannai*, ed. by M. Zulay (1938), 374). It is obvious that all these different traditions cannot refer to the same historical figure, nor is it likely that a high priest would be identified as a scholar with the title "rabbi." Rather, each tradition must be seen as reflecting the narrative and moralistic concerns of each storyteller and each editor as determined by the specific context.

BIBLIOGRAPHY: Hyman, Toledot, 176–7; Klausner, Bayit Sheni, 5 (1951), 21.

[Stephen G. Wald (2nd ed.)]

ELEAZAR BEN JACOB HA-BAVLI (c. 1195–1250), Hebrew poet of Baghdad. Eleazar seems to have been a sort of house poet for the well-to-do Jewish families of Iraq. He represents himself as a disciple of Moses ben Sheshet al-Andalusi, who introduced him to the techniques of Andalusian poetry. He was probably the first young Oriental poet met by Judah *Al-Ḥarizi in his travels to the East, although he did not get a very positive evaluation. Some of Eleazar's poems were extant in various manuscript collections and in Oriental *maḥzorim* and attracted the attention of 19th-century scholars (L. Dukes, A. Neubauer, E.N. Adler, S. Poznanski). It was only with the discovery of one of the manuscripts of his *dīwān*, which comprised 281 poems, by Elkan N. *Adler in Aleppo in 1898 (Jewish Theological Seminary, New York, Ms. ENA 881), and its publication by H. *Brody (1935) that he emerged as one of the great poets of the eastern Diaspora. Thanks to other manuscripts from the Firkovitch collection of St. Petersburg and from other libraries, Y. Yahalom has been able to reproduce the possible original structure of Eleazar's *dīwān*, which contained more than 400 poems. Many of them are given over to praises and the familiar events of the notable Jews of the Iraqi community: births, circumcisions, weddings, and deaths of the families of his benefactors. Others are epigrams on secular subjects or short poems of didactic nature. He also wrote some Arabic poems, with his own Hebrew translation, and even verses with a mixture of both languages. While the *dīwān* contains mainly secular poetry, subsequent discoveries have brought to light about 50 of his religious poems. Nineteen such poems were published by S. *Bernstein; by a comparison of style and the help of acrostics, D. Jarden identified some more religious poems. They have the characteristics of the classical *piyyut* and some of the Andalusian innovations.

In addition to its importance to poetry, the *dīwān* is a historical source of utmost significance for the history of Iraqi Jews during the 13th century. It provides a glimpse into the wealthy and highly educated leading Jewish families in Baghdad, Basra, Mosul, Wasit, Hilla, and other places in Iraq. The *dīwān* is replete with the names (more than 400) of not only the contemporary *geonim* but also of eminent Jewish personalities, among them physicians, scholars, astronomers, administrators, keepers of the mint, and other state dignitaries in the service of the Abbasid caliphate in its declining years. The high-sounding titles of the Jewish notabilities indicate the social level and the great role played by them both in the community and in state and society. With the help of Arab chronicles, particularly of Ibn al-Fuwati, these personalities can be identified in their historical perspective.

Eleazar ha-Bavli also interested himself in the theory of Hebrew poetry and composed a book for teaching this theory to his Jewish audience. Substantial remnants of this work, written in Judeo-Arabic, have survived (published and translated into Hebrew by Yahalom, 2001). He studied 13 kinds of meter, the rhyme, the mistakes and deficiencies of the poets, and the figures of speech, following Arabic models. His method of studying Hebrew poetry was very different from that of his predecessor Moses *Ibn Ezra in his *Shirat Yisrael*. The situation in which Eleazar wrote was quite dissimilar, and his main goal was probably to encourage the Jews of the East to compose Hebrew poetry in consonance with Arabic poetics, reproducing the opinions of similar Arabic books and offering many examples taken from his own secular and liturgical poetic production.

BIBLIOGRAPHY: E.N. Adler, in: JQR, 11 (1898/99), 682–7; idem, in: *Livre d'hommage… S. Poznanski* (1927), 22–24 (Eng.); Mann, Texts, 1 (1931), 263–305; H. Brody, *Divan Kovez Shirei Rabbi Eleazar ben Ya'akov ha-Bavli* (1935); S.H. Kook, in: KS, 13 (1936/37), 12–13 (also in his *Iyyunim u-Meḥkarim*, 2 (1963), 194–7); W.J. Fischel, in: *Tarbiz*, 8 (1936/37), 233–6; idem, *Jews in the Economic and Political Life of Mediaeval Islam* (1969²), 127–34; S. Bernstein, in: *Sinai*, 18 (1946), 8–34; N.H. Torczyner (Tur-Sinai), in: *Leshonenu*, 11 (1941), 269–83 (also in his *Ha-Lashon ve-ha-Sefer*, 3 (1955), 366–80); D. Jarden, in: *Tarbiz*, 26 (1956/57), 317–27; idem, in: HUCA, 33 (1962), 1–26; idem, *Sefunei Shirah* (1967), 54–96; A. Ben-Jacob, *Yehudei Bavel* (1965), 32–43; Abramson, in: *Perakim*, 1 (1968), 9–28. **ADD. BIBLIOGRAPHY:** D. Yarden (ed.), *Shirim Ḥadashim le-Rabbi Eleazar ben Ya'akov ha-Bavli* (1984); Y. Yahalom, *Perakim be-Torat ha-Shir le-Eleazar ben Ya'akov ha-Bavli: Makor Arvi-Yehudi ve-Targum Ivri* (2001); idem, in: *Hispania Judaica Bulletin*, 4 (2004), 5–21; W. van Bekkum, in: *Ben Ever la-Arav*, 2 (2001), xxiii–xl.

[Walter Joseph Fischel / Angel Sáenz-Badillos (2nd ed.)]

ELEAZAR BEN JAIR (first cent. C.E.), chief of the Sicarii who captured the fortress of *Masada at the beginning of the Roman war (Jos., Wars, 2:447; 7:275ff.). Eleazar was commander of the besieged fortress from 66 until its fall in 73. According to Josephus he was a descendant of *Judah the Galilean, to whom the founding of the "fourth philosophy" (see *Sicarii) is attributed, though some identify him with Judah b. Hezekiah who, after Herod's death, raised the standard of revolt in Galilee and captured Sepphoris. Apparently Eleazar already had a connection with Masada in the time of *Menahem b. Judah, when he captured it and used the arms that he obtained there for the siege of Jerusalem. Josephus designates Eleazar, "head of the Sicarii … a valiant man," and ascribes to him a speech made to the defenders of Masada after the breach of its walls, first before a handful of fighters and afterward before all the besieged. This speech was possibly reconstructed from what Josephus heard from the woman belonging to Eleazar's family who escaped at Masada by hiding herself in the cistern there; although it has also been pointed out that the ascription of heroic speeches to the heroes of history was a literary device that characterized ancient historiography. These passages are the only sources where Eleazar is mentioned explicitly, and since Josephus is the only source for the final battle of Masada and the last days of the fighters, it should be treated with caution.

The image of Eleazar which emerges is not only multifaceted but contradictory. His colorful character made it difficult for Josephus to give a uniform or complete picture. He never fails to stress that Eleazar was one of the Sicarii, of whom he continually gives an unfavorable opinion. Yet, at the same time, when he comes to describe in detail the stand of Masada and its fall, he does not refrain from praising Eleazar. Doubts have been cast upon the reliability of Josephus' story of Masada. It has been argued (Ladouceur, but see comments by Rajak) that Eleazar's speech was written to act as a balance to Josephus' own opinions about self-inflicted death (Wars, 3:362–382). Nevertheless, the archaeological excavations at Masada – directed by Y. Yadin – even if they have not produced factual epigraphic testimony of what happened there, do not contradict the narrative. The many traces of fire throughout the whole area of the fortress are a small part of the mute testimony to the end of Masada. But the most remarkable part of the excavation was the discovery of 11 small sherds upon which names and appellations were marked (among them: "Ben ha-Naḥtom," "ha-Amki," "Yo'av," "Ben Ya'ir," etc.). These 11 *ostraka* have been tenuously connected by Yadin with the statement by Josephus (Wars, 7:395f.): "then, having chosen by lot ten of their number to despatch the rest … these, having unswervingly slaughtered all, ordained the same rule of the lot for one another, that he on whom it fell should slay first the nine and then himself last of all." The sherd bearing the name "Ben Ya'ir" strengthens the picture, unique of its kind, of Eleazar ben Jair.

BIBLIOGRAPHY: Klausner, Bayit Sheni, 5 (1951^2), 148, 287–9; S. Zeitlin, in: JQR, 55 (1964/65), 299–317; 57 (1966/67), 251–70; Y. Yadin, *Masada* (1968). **ADD. BIBLIOGRAPHY:** D.J. Ladouceur, "Masada: A Consideration of the Literary Evidence," in: *Greek Roman and Byzantine Studies,* 21 (1980), 246–47; S.J.D. Cohen, "Masada: Literary Tradition, Archaeological Remains and the Credibility of Josephus," in: JJS, 33 (1982), 385–405; T. Rajak, *Josephus: The Historian and his Society* (1983), 220; M. Stern, *Studies in Jewish History: The Second Temple Period* (1991), 313–43; D. Flusser, "The Dead of Masada in the Eyes of their Contemporaries," in: I. Gaphni et al. (eds.), *Jews and Judaism in the Second Temple, Mishna and Talmud Period* (1993), 116–46; T. Ilan, *Lexicon of Jewish Names in Late Antiquity. Part 1. Palestine 330 B.C.E.–200 C.E.* (2002), 65.

[Abraham Lebanon]

ELEAZAR BEN JUDAH OF BARTOTA (first half of the second century C.E.), *tanna*. His cognomen is derived from a place Bartota, whose exact locality is unknown. It appears that Eleazar studied under R. *Joshua for, on the authority of the latter's teachings, he challenges those of R. Akiva (Tosef., Bek. 7:6; cf. Tev. Yom 3:4–5). Among the sages who quote him are R. Simeon b. Gamaliel (Or. 1:4) and R. Simeon b. Yoḥai (Tosef., Zav. 1:5). The Talmud (Shab. 32b) ascribes to R. Eleazar ben Judah (without the additional designation "of Bartota") a statement warning about the penalties for neglecting to separate *ḥallah*.

The importance which Eleazar accorded to charity is reflected in his maxim quoted in *Avot* (3:7). "Render unto Him what is His, for thou and what thou hast are His, as David has said (1 Chron. 29:14), 'For all things come of Thee, and of Thine own have we given to Thee.'" In keeping with this maxim, the Babylonian Talmud describes him as excessively generous, which was a source of embarrassment even to the collectors of charity. The Talmud relates (Ta'an. 24a) that on one occasion, when he was on his way to purchase a trousseau for his daughter, the collectors tried to avoid him, knowing that he would give them more than he could afford. Eleazar, however, ran after them and, discovering that they were collecting to make possible the marriage of two orphans, he gave them all he had, leaving himself only one *zuz*. With this, he bought a small quantity of grain which he deposited in the granary. Miraculously, it multiplied to fill the granary to the bursting point; but when told of this by his daughter, Eleazar insisted that this, too, be consecrated to charity.

BIBLIOGRAPHY: Bacher, Tann; Hyman, Toledot, 177.

[Jehonatan Etz-Chaim]

ELEAZAR BEN JUDAH OF WORMS (c. 1165–c. 1230), scholar in the fields of *halakhah*, theology, and exegesis in medieval Germany. Eleazar was the last major scholar of the Ḥasidei Ashkenaz movement (see *Ḥasidei Ashkenaz). Born in Mainz, he traveled and studied in many of the centers of learning in Germany and northern France. He spent most of his life in Worms. Eleazar was a member of the *Kalonymus family, one of the most important German-Jewish families of that period. His father *Judah b. Kalonymus, one of the leading scholars of his generation, taught his son both *halakhah* and esoteric theology. *Judah b. Samuel, he-Ḥasid ("the Pious"), the leading figure in the Ḥasidei Ashkenaz movement, to whom Eleazar was related, was, however, his main teacher in the latter field and R. Moses ha-Kohen and R. Eliezer of Metz were his most prominent teachers in *halakhah*. Eleazar witnessed and suffered personally from the new outburst of persecution of the Jews by the Crusaders at the end of the 12th and the beginning of the 13th century. On a number of occasions in his commentary on the prayers, one of his major works, he noted the events that befell Worms, especially during the persecutions that followed the fall of Jerusalem to Saladin. In one of these persecutions, Eleazar's wife, daughter, and son were murdered, and he was severely injured. Eleazar's wife was very active in the religious and cultural life of her community. It is reported that she led the women in prayer and even gave public lectures to the women on the Sabbath. This tragedy was described by him in detail both in a story and in a poem. His personal loss and the catastrophic situation in the Jewish communities in Germany explain his pessimistic outlook concerning the prospects of German Jewry. He felt that the German Jewry of his time was but a small remnant after the disasters of 1096 and the following years, and that this remnant was continually diminishing. He expressed this feeling in his introduction to the *Sefer ha-Hokhmah* ("Book of Wisdom"), which was written in 1217 after the death of Judah the Pious. He explained in this introduction that he felt compelled to put his knowledge into writing, since oral tradition was about to die out because of the deteriorating situation in Germany.

His works may be divided into five categories: *halakhah*, liturgical poetry (*piyyutim*), theology, ethics, and exegesis. Eleazar's halakhic book *Sefer ha-Roke'aḥ* (Fano, 1505; reissued several times) followed the tradition of halakhic works of the tosafists of northern France and Germany. The book was intended to educate the common reader in the details of halakhic law. Therefore, the author did not discuss at length exegetical studies of the talmudic passages, but rather explained the law and its talmudic basis. Unlike other halakhic works written by the tosafists, Eleazar also includes recommended *minhagim* in his work, material which is not strictly halakhic. He drew extensively on the writings of his German predecessors and quoted more than 40 scholars.

Eleazar wrote many *piyyutim*. However, a reliable record of them has not yet been compiled. Many of his *piyyutim* were attributed to other writers (also named Eleazar), and some attributed to him were probably written by other writers. His poems, written in the then-current Ashkenazi tradition, express devotion to, and worship of, God. At the same time, they protest to God because of Israel's sufferings, and express hope for Israel's redemption and revenge on her tormentors.

His major theological work was *Sodei Razayya* ("Secrets of Secrets"). Four parts of this work were printed, although most of what is extant is found only in manuscripts. The first part, a study of the creation (*Sod Ma'aseh Bereshit*), describes how the earth, stars, elements, etc., were created. Eleazar wrote this part of his work as an exegesis based on the 22 letters of the Hebrew alphabet. This was in accordance with his belief (derived from *Sefer* *Yezirah*) that the alphabet, the word of God, was the source of existence. Eleazar included in this part ancient material from the *Heikhalot* and *Merkabah literature especially the *Baraita de-Ma'aseh Bereshit* and *Shi'ur Komah*. More than half of this part, the introduction and the letters *Alef* to *Nun*, was included in the *Sefer* *Razi'el* (Amsterdam, 1701). The second part of the work, *Sod ha-Merkavah* ("Secret of the Divine Chariot"), deals with the secrets of the angels, the Holy Throne, the Chariot, the Divine Voice which speaks to the prophets, the Divine Glory revealed to them, and the ways of revelation and prophecy in general. Eleazar made use here of the teachings of *Saadiah Gaon, but also included long quotations from *Heikhalot* literature. Most of this part was printed by I. Kamelhar as *Sodei Razayya* (1936). The third and largest part *Sefer ha-Shem* ("The Book of the Holy Name") contains very little theological discussion; most of it is devoted to a systematic exegesis of the names of God, using all the exegetical and homiletical methods which were used by the Ḥasidim. Eleazar defined three layers in God's manifestation: (a) the *Shekhinah* or *Kavod*, which has shape and form so it may be seen by prophets, (b) the *Borei*, which has a faint shape, hears prayers, and performs miracles and wonders, (c) *El Elyon*, which has no shape or form. The fourth part is a treatise on psychology, *Ḥokhmat ha-Nefesh* (Lemberg, 1876). The main problem analyzed is the various ways by which a connection is established between the soul and the divine world. Parts of this work discuss other problems, e.g., the meaning of dreams, the fate of the soul after death, etc. The fifth and last part of the work is a commentary on *Sefer Yeẓirah* (Przemysl, 1883) and contains detailed instructions for the creation of a *golem. Eleazar wrote one other important theological work, *Sefer ha-Ḥokhmah*, in which he described the various fields of theological study, as well as the methods used in this study. A major part of this work is concerned with exegesis of Holy Names.

Eleazar's main contribution to Ḥasidei Ashkenaz ethical literature is contained in the first two chapters of *Roke'aḥ*. In the first he discusses the central values of this Ḥasidism (love and fear of God, prayer, humility, etc.). In the second, he describes in detail the ways of repentance. A discussion of the value of ḥasidic ethics is also found in Eleazar's introduction to *Sodei Razayya*.

Eleazar wrote many exegetical works, some of which have yet to be printed, and probably quite a few are now lost. His short commentary on the Torah, another on the Passover *Haggadah*, and a few short commentaries on various *piyyutim* (e.g., *Ha-Adderet ve-ha-Emunah* and *Ha-Oḥez ba-Yad*) are extant. Eleazar's biblical commentaries have recently been published with annotations (Bene-Berak, 1985, 1988, and 2001; Los Angeles, 2004). *Abraham b. Azriel, his pupil who wrote the *Arugat ha-Bosem*, used his teacher's exegetical works extensively. Eleazar's major work in this field, extant in several manuscripts (Vienna 108, Oxford 1204), is the commentary on the prayers. In this work, he comments on every part of the usual and special prayers. He uses three methods in his commentary: explanation of the content; theological interpretation; and research for its hidden harmony with other parts of sacred literature by use of *gematriot*. This important work was edited and published by Hershler (2 vols., Jerusalem 1992). Dozens of other short treatises by him or attributed to him are scattered through manuscript libraries, and no exhaustive bibliographical study has yet been made which could describe the vast variety of his work. It seems that not one of Eleazar's pupils was able to continue his work, especially in the field of esoteric theology. His best-known disciples, Abraham b. Azriel and *Isaac of Vienna, dedicated their literary efforts to other fields.

In common with other Ḥasidei Ashkenaz, Eleazar became a legendary hero. According to a 13th-century story, Eleazar used a cloud to travel from place to place, especially when going to far-away circumcision ceremonies. As a pietist, his writings reflect a shift in emphasis away from the social-religious programs of Judah b. Samuel he-Ḥasid to a more personalized, individual pietism. He was regarded as one of the early sages of secret lore, and in later centuries many ideas and works were attributed to him.

BIBLIOGRAPHY: I. Kamelhar, *Rabbeinu Eleazar mi-Germaiza* (1930); Urbach, Tosafot, 321–41; idem (ed.), *Arugat ha-Bosem*, 4 (1963), 100–16; V. Aptowitzer, *Mavo le-Sefer Ravyah* (1938), 316–18; Scholem, Mysticism, 80–118; idem, *Ursprung und Anfaenge der Kabbala* (1962), passim; idem, *On the Kabbalah and its Symbolism* (1965), 171–93; idem, *Von der mystischen Gestalt der Gottheit* (1962), 259–65; A. Altmann, in: JJS, 11 (1960), 101–13; J. Dan, in: *Zion*, 29 (1964), 168–81; idem, in: KS, 41 (1965/66), 533–44. **ADD. BIBLIOGRAPHY:** J. Dan, *Jewish Mysticism*, vol. 2 (1999); A. Kurt, in: *Jewish Studies in a New Europe* (1994), 462–71; E. Wolfson, in: JQR, 84:1 (1993), 43–77; L. Jacobs, *Jewish Mystical Testimonies* (1977); D. Abrams, in: *Daat*, 34 (1934), 61–81; idem, in: *Jewish Studies Quarterly*, 5 (1998) 329–45; I. Marcus, *Piety and Society: The Jewish Pietists of Medieval Germany* (1981); idem, in: *History of Jewish Spirituality* (1986), 356–66; A. Farber-Ginat and D. Abrams, *Perushei ha-Merkavah le-Rabbi Eleazar mi-Worms u-le-Rabbi Ya'akov ben Ya'akov ha-Kohen* (2004).

[Joseph Dan]

ELEAZAR BEN MATTATHIAS (2nd century B.C.E.), Hasmonean; the fourth of *Mattathias' sons (I Macc. 2:2–5). He was nicknamed Auran (Αυραν; *ibid.* 2:5) which in the original source may have been written with a ḥ – i.e., Ḥauran (as in Syriac) – or with an *ayin* – i.e., Auran. Some see his nickname as derived from *ḥor* ("a hole"), with reference to his piercing the body of an elephant (see below), overlooking the fact that the name was accorded him during his lifetime. Other suggestions are equally unsatisfactory. Little is known of his role in the war of the Hasmoneans. In II Maccabees 8:23 it is stated that Judah appointed Eleazar to command part of the army, but the reading there should perhaps be Ezra instead of Eleazar. During the Syrian attack in the battle of Bet Zekharyah in 163 B.C.E., Eleazar broke through the Syrian ranks to reach an elephant on which he thought the king was riding. Thrusting his spear into its belly, he killed the beast, which fell on him and crushed him to death (I Macc. 6:43–46).

[Uriel Rappaport]

ELEAZAR BEN MATYA (first half of the second century C.E.), *tanna*. Eleazar was one of the most important of the students of Jabneh (TJ, Shek. 5:1, 48a), and was apparently a pupil of *Tarfon (Tosef., Ber. 4:16). *Ben Azzai, *Ben Zoma, Ḥanina b. Ḥakhinai, and Simeon ha-Teimani were his fellow students. He is mentioned as one of the four scholars of the Sanhedrin of Jabneh who "understood 70 languages" (TJ, Shek. 5:1, 48a). In general his halakhic and aggadic statements are based upon the interpretation of scriptural verses. This system was recognized by the *amoraim*, and Rav remarked about one of his halakhic interpretations given in the Mishnah: "Eleazar could have produced a pearl but he has produced a potsherd" (Yev. 94a). It is related of him that, together with Abba Ḥalafta and Ḥanina b. Ḥakhinai, he stood upon the 12 stones taken from the Jordan and erected in Gilgal by Joshua (Josh. 4). They discussed their weight and concluded that the weight of each stone was 40 *se'ah* (Tosef., Sot. 8:6). Among his statements are (Tosef., Shevu. 3:4): "No man has the misfortune to hear [a curse] unless he has sinned … he who sees transgressors, deserved to see them; who sees pious persons, has merited to see them," and "If my father asks me for a drink of water and at the same time there is a precept to perform, I must neglect the honor due to my father and perform the precept. For the duty of observing the precept lies both upon my father and myself" (Kid. 32a).

BIBLIOGRAPHY: Hyman, Toledot, s.v.; Frankel, Mishnah, 141.

[Yitzhak Dov Gilat]

ELEAZAR BEN MOSES HA-DARSHAN OF WUERZBURG (mid-13th century), one of the later writers of the *Hasidei Ashkenaz from the school of *Judah b. Samuel he-Ḥasid and *Eleazar of Worms. His father Moses was Judah's brother-in-law. None of his writings has been published. Two of his works, however, are found in manuscripts: a commentary on *Sefer *Yeẓirah*, cited by Abraham *Abulafia, the 13th-century kabbalist, and parts of his commentary on the Torah, which uses mainly the system of *gematria* and is known as *Sefer ha-Gematriyyot*. Probably portions of his other works are scattered in 13th-century Ashkenazi exegetical literature, and many quotations are found in the writings of later scholars, e.g., his son Moses b. Eleazar.

BIBLIOGRAPHY: M. Szulwas: in: *Alummah*, 1 (1936), 152–3; *Kitvei A. Epstein*, 1 (1950), 213–44; J. Freimann, *Sefer Ḥasidim* (1924²), 3 (introd.); Urbach, Tosafot, 445; G. Scholem, *Reshit ha-Kabbalah* (1948), 204–5.

[Joseph Dan]

ELEAZAR BEN PARTA (c. early 2nd century C.E.), *tanna*. He is mentioned only once in the Mishnah (Git. 3:4), and four times in the Tosefta. In one of his homilies, he warns against evil speech by pointing out that if the spies (Num. 12) who spoke evil only of trees and stones (*ibid.* 13:32) "died by the plague before the Lord" (*ibid.* 14:37), how much greater must be the punishment of the one who speaks evil of his neighbor (Tosef., Ar. 2:11; Ar. 15a).

In the Babylonian Talmud he is described as one of the sages arrested by the Romans for the capital offense of contravening Hadrian's decree forbidding the public teaching of Torah and observance of the commandments. While in prison, he tried to comfort Hananiah b. Teradyon, a fellow prisoner, by pointing out that while the latter only faced one charge, he himself faced five and was therefore certainly doomed. Hananiah, however, replied that for this very reason Eleazar was more worthy of Divine salvation. Hananiah's tragic death and Eleazar's miraculous deliverance proved the truth of these words (Av. Zar. 17b).

In a late Midrash (Num. R. 23:1), Eleazar shows his ability to deduce practical lessons from scriptural texts. In reply to the query of some prominent coreligionists of Sepphoris as to the legality of flight from their Roman persecutors on the Sabbath, Eleazar, not wishing to commit himself by giving them a direct answer, said: "Why do you ask me? Go and ask Jacob, Moses, and David," and referred them to biblical verses which mention distinguished leaders who had fled.

BIBLIOGRAPHY: Hyman, Toledot, 200f.; Bacher, Tann.

[Jehonatan Etz-Chaim]

ELEAZAR (in TJ usually **Lazar**) **BEN PEDAT** (d. 279), third century *amora*. He is the *amora* Eleazar mentioned without a patronymic. Scion of a priestly family (MK 28a), Eleazar was born in Babylon (Ber. 2:1, 4b). There he studied under *Samuel (Er. 66a), and more particularly under *Rav (Hul. 111b). After the latter's death, he migrated to Ereẓ Israel. It was in Ereẓ Israel that he referred to the academy of Rav as the "little sanctuary" (Meg. 29a; cf. Ezek. 11:16). He was still unmarried when he went to Ereẓ Israel, and R. Ammi and R. Assi participated at his wedding in Tiberias (Ber. 16a). He emphasizes his great fortune in having had the privilege to migrate to Ereẓ Israel and resume *semikhah* there, as well as being one of the scholars who was entrusted with the intercalation of the calendar (Kil. 112a). In Ereẓ Israel he studied under Ḥanina, the *av bet din* of Sepphoris (Kil. 9:4, 32c). He quoted so many halakhic decisions and even more aggadic sayings in Ḥanina's name (Ber. 27b; Meg. 5a; et al.) that the Talmud remarks, "Everywhere Eleazar relies upon Ḥanina" (Ter. 8:5, 45c; et al.). In Caesarea, he studied under Hoshaya Rabbah (Ber. 32b), whom he refers to as the "father of the Mishnah" (Kid. 1:3, 60a; et al.). The Jerusalem Talmud also frequently cites traditions transmitted by Eleazar in the name of *Ḥiyya b. Abba (BM 10:4, 12c), and in one instance even states that the opinions of the two scholars cannot be regarded as those of separate people since "Eleazar is the pupil of Ḥiyya Rabbah" (Kid. 1:4, 60b). It cannot mean that he was his actual disciple, since Ḥiyya had probably died by the time Eleazar migrated to Ereẓ Israel. The intensity of Eleazar's study often made him oblivious to all worldly events (Er. 54b).

Although the Babylonian Talmud describes Eleazar as Johanan's "pupil" in Tiberias (BB 135b; Tem. 25b), the Jerusalem sources see the relationship rather as that of a typical "pupil-associate" (TJ, Sanh. 1, 18b; cf. TJ, Ber. 2:4b). Moreover, the phrase "both Johanan and Eleazar say," is often found in the Babylonian Talmud itself (Yoma 9b, et al.). Eleazar was, in fact, appointed Johanan's associate in the leadership of the council after the death of Simeon b. Lakish, Johanan's previous colleague (BM 84a), but the appointment was not a happy one, Eleazar being distinguished by his extensive knowledge in contrast to the profound acumen of Resh Lakish (Sanh. 24a). He was also one of the communal leaders of Ereẓ Israel (Pe'ah 8:7, 21a), and he is sometimes referred to as serving as *dayyan*, in which capacity he consulted Johanan on difficult cases (Sanh. 3:13, 21d; BB 7b). During his last years Johanan took no active part as head of the council and it appears that Eleazar took his place (Meg. 1:13, 72b). During this period he became widely known as the "master [i.e., legal authority] of the land of Israel" (Yoma 9b), and on many occasions sent rulings and decisions to Babylon which were transmitted by the *Neḥutei* (Sanh. 63b). In fact it is stated that the words "they sent from there," i.e., from Ereẓ Israel to Babylon, refers to Eleazar (*ibid.* 17b). Among those to whom he sent his decisions were Mar Ukva the exilarch, and Judah the principal of the academy of Pumbedita (BK 1:1, 2c).

After the death of Johanan in 279, Eleazar was appointed head of the council in Tiberias, but he died in the same year (see *Iggeret Sherira Gaon).*

Private Life

Eleazar was extremely poor (Ta'an. 25a). He was, nevertheless, loath to accept any gifts from the house of the *nasi*. He excused himself by quoting the verse (Prov. 15:27), "He that hateth gifts shall live" (Meg. 28a). Moreover, despite his poverty, he sought to support other needy scholars. This he did in an honorable manner, supplying their needs in secret to save them embarrassment (BM 2:3, 8c). All but one of Eleazar's children died during his lifetime (Ber. 5b), his surviving son, Pedat, acting as an "*amora*" ("interpreter") in the *bet ha-midrash* of Assi (Meg. 4:10, 75c).

Teaching

Eleazar was one of the great exponents of the Oral Law, and the Mishnah. He quoted numerous statements of both early and late *tannaim* and several *beraitot*, particularly in *Midrash Halakhah, without indicating their source. It was with regard to one of his interpretations (Sifra 4:1) that Johanan once remarked to Simon B. Lakish, "I saw the son of Pedat sitting and interpreting the Law, like Moses in the name of the Almighty" (i.e., he expounded the verse in the manner of the *tannaim*, cf. Rashi). He was also a great halakhist who profoundly influenced the methods of mishnaic exegesis. Although he naturally preferred to follow the text of the Mishnah rather than that of the various *beraitot*, he nevertheless examined the wording of each *mishnah* in the light of the earliest sources (BB 87a). He often employed the technique of dividing the *mishnayot*, saying, "The author of this section is not the author of that section" (Shab. 92b; Ker. 24b; et al.). He would reject a *mishnah* whose source he could not find, with the words, "I do not know who taught this" (BM 51a). He thus considerably corrected and explained the Mishnah. He is the author of the rule that whenever Judah ha-Nasi transmits a case, first as subject to a difference of opinion and then in an undisputed form, the *halakhah* is in accordance with the second form (Yev. 42b) (see *Conflict of Opinion).

Eleazar was also an exceptionally prolific and profound aggadist, whose sayings are frequently quoted in the Midrash and in both Talmuds. Among them may be mentioned, "In seven places in the Bible, God equates Himself with the lowliest of creatures" (Tanḥ. Va-Yera, 3); "The performance of charity is greater than all sacrifices" (Suk. 49b); "Let us be grateful to cheats [mendicants who are not in need], for were it not for them we would sin daily by becoming unused to giving charity to the poor" (Ket. 68a); "Let my sustenance be as bitter as the olive, providing that it is from Thy hand, rather than as sweet as honey if I have to depend upon man" (Sanh. 108b); "Even when a sharp sword rests on his neck, man should not abandon hope of mercy" (Ber. 10a); "An unmarried person is less than a man ... as is he who owns no land" (Yev. 63a). Many of his sayings are devoted to fostering the sanctity and love of the Land of Israel: e.g., "Whoever resides in Israel lives without sin" (Ket. 111a); "Those who die outside Israel will not be resurrected" (*ibid.*). When told that his associate Ulla had died during one of his frequent visits to Babylon, he quoted Amos 7:17 and declared "Thou Ulla, 'shalt die in an unclean land'" (*ibid.*). He also ruled as a matter of *halakhah*, "Books which have merited to come to Israel, may not be taken out of the country" (Sanh. 3:10, 21). Although Eleazar's aggadic sayings embrace many spheres of Torah, he avoided esoteric study. He refused to receive instruction in this field from either his teacher Johanan or, many years later, from his friend Assi, who wished to attract him to the subject (Ḥag. 13a). His teachings were transmitted by numerous contemporaries and later scholars, particularly Abbahu, Rabbah b. Hana, and Zera (Shab. 12b, 134b; Suk. 43a; et al.).

BIBLIOGRAPHY: Bacher, Pal Amor, s.v.; Epstein, Mishnah, 292–307; Frankel, Mevo, 111b–113a; Halevy, Dorot, 2 (1923), 327–32; Hyman, Toledot, 192–9; Weiss, Dor, 3 (1904⁴), 76–80.

[Shmuel Safrai]

ELEAZAR BEN SHAMMUA (c. 150 C.E.), *tanna.* He is generally referred to simply as "Eleazar," without his patronymic. He is quoted frequently in the Mishnah, the Tosefta, and the Midrashei Halakhah, appearing together with R. Meir, R. Shimon, R, Johanan ha-Sandelar, and other students of R. Akiva. Many of Eleazar's *mishnayot* were incorporated into the Mishnah by Judah ha-Nasi. It is difficult, however, to determine the precise extent of this incorporation because of the repeated confusion throughout talmudic literature between Eleazar and Eliezer (b. Hyrcanus). Tannaitic sources record that when Eleazar and Johanan ha-Sandelar reached Sidon on their way to Nisibis to study under *Judah b. Bathyra they recalled Ereẓ Israel, and with tears streaming from their eyes, returned home, declaring, "Living in Ereẓ Israel is equivalent to all the *mitzvot* of the Torah" (Sif. Deut. 80). He is the author of the law that the witnesses of its delivery validate a *get* (bill of divorce) or any other document, even if the document itself is unsigned by witnesses (Git. 9:4). Among his aggadic statements is: "The Bible and the sword came down from heaven, bound together. God said to the Jews: 'If you keep what is written in this book, you will be saved from the sword, but if not, you will ultimately be killed by the sword'" (Sif. Deut. 40). According to the Babylonian Talmud he was a kohen (Sot. 39a) and one of the last pupils of R. *Akiva (Yev. 62b; cf. Gen. R. 61:3), whose views are cited on several occasions as the bases for some of Eleazar's statements (Ket. 40a; Zev. 93a; et al.). After the Bar Kokhba revolt Eleazar, among others, was ordained by *Judah b. Bava, who consequently suffered martyrdom at the hands of the Romans (Sanh. 14a). Other talmudic sources, however, do not mention Eleazar among Akiva's pupils at any of the gatherings of the sages after the period of the persecutions (TJ, Ḥag. 3:1, 78d; Song R. 2:5; Ber. 63b). Judah ha-Nasi, who was his pupil (Men. 18a), said that Eleazar's *bet ha-midrash* was so crowded that six pupils used to sit there in the space of one cubit (Er. 53a). Highly esteemed by the early *amoraim*, Eleazar was called by Rav "the happiest of the sages" (Ket. 40a), while Johanan said of him that his heart was as broad as the door of the temple porch (Er. 53a). The Talmud tells that he lived to an old age, and when asked by his pupils to what he attributed his longevity, replied: "I have never taken a short-cut through a synagogue; I have not stepped over the heads of the holy people (i.e., of other pupils to get to his place in the *bet midrash);* and I have not raised my hands (for the priestly benediction) without first reciting a blessing" (Meg. 27b). Later Midrashim include Eleazar among the *Ten Martyrs of the Hadrianic persecutions.

BIBLIOGRAPHY: J. Bruell, *Mevo ha-Mishnah*, 1 (1876), 195–7; Bacher, Tann; Hyman, Toledot, 205–10; Frankel, Mishnah, 182–4; Epstein, Tanna'im, 158–9.

[Shmuel Safrai]

ELEAZAR BEN SIMEON, Zealot leader during the Roman war of 66–70 C.E. Eleazar was a member of a distinguished priestly family of Jerusalem and a friend of *Zechariah b. Avkilus. He played an important role in the war against *Cestius Gallus, attacking the retreating Roman army and seizing military equipment, which was later to prove of great value in the defense of Jerusalem. Eleazar was not appointed a member of the governing council formed after the war against Cestius, probably because he was an extremist. The entry of Idumeans into Jerusalem, and the ensuing slaughter of those who had opposed the Zealots can be attributed to the machinations of Eleazar and his associates. Josephus attempted to exonerate Eleazar from responsibility for the massacres, putting the blame on *John of Giscala. Josephus cannot be relied on in this, since he was probably influenced by his great hostility to John. Eleazar engaged in internecine warfare with John of Giscala inside Jerusalem. Eleazar's men entrenched themselves in the Temple, which occupied the highest position in the city, affording them a significant strategic advantage over their enemies. Eleazar was thus able to maintain a defense although he had only a few men at his disposal. A peace agreement between the warring factions was not reached until Passover of 70 C.E. when the siege of Jerusalem by the Romans had already begun. Coins inscribed "Eleazar the Priest" on one side and "Year One of the Redemption of Israel" on the obverse are extant. In the opinion of some historians Eleazar b. Simeon is the subject of the inscription but it is probable that the coins date from the rebellion of Bar Kokhba, and that "Eleazar the Priest" refers to the high priest of that time.

BIBLIOGRAPHY: Jos., Wars, 2:562–5; 4:225; 5:5–10, 99, 250; Klausner, Bayit Sheni, 5 (1951²), 302 (index); Schuerer, Hist, 264ff.; F.W. Madden, *Coins of the Jews* (1967²), 35ff., 188ff.; A. Schlatter, *Zur Topographie und Geschichte Palaestinas* (1893).

[Abraham Schalit]

ELEAZAR BEN SIMEON, *tanna* of the end of the second century C.E.; son and pupil of *Simeon b. Yoḥai (Suk. 45b). He is mentioned by name very rarely in the Mishnah, though *amoraim* ascribe several anonymous *mishnayot* to him (Bek. 51b, et al.). He is quoted frequently in the *beraitot*, as well as approximately 75 times in the Tosefta, especially those of *Zevaḥim* and *Menaḥot*. His aggadic statements are few (e.g., Kid. 40b; Yev. 65b; Gen. R. 20:6). Later Palestinian sources state that after his death his contemporaries eulogized him as a biblical scholar, a student of the Mishnah, a preacher, and a poet (Lev. R. 30:1), this last remark causing him to be incorrectly identified with the *paytan* Eleazar *Kallir (Tos. to Hag. 13a). The Babylonian Talmud incorporates accounts of his youth into stories related to his father. According to the well known *aggadah*, he escaped with his father from the Romans by hiding in a cave for 13 years (Shab. 33b; BM 85a). This story, mentioned in the introduction to the *Zohar (1:11a), provided the literary framework for this pseudoepigraphic work of the 13th century, and caused its composition to be ascribed to them. According to the Talmud, Eleazar later became a noted scholar who engaged in halakhic controversy with his colleague, Judah ha-Nasi (BM 84b; et al.), as well as in halakhic and aggadic discussions with older scholars, such as Judah, Yose, and Meir (Sot. 34a; RH 4b; et al.). In contrast to his father's unyielding defiance of the Roman authorities, it is told that he accepted under compulsion a position in the Roman administration as an official responsible for the apprehension of thieves and robbers – a position that his grandfather, Yoḥai, had at one time held (Pes. 112a). Among others who reportedly censured him for this activity was his teacher, Joshua b. Karḥah, who reprimanded him by exclaiming: "Vinegar, the son of wine! How long will you continue to hand over the people of our God to be killed?" (BM 83b; et al.). It is related of his son Jose that he grew up without sufficient surveillance and was on the brink of turning to a life of crime. Judah ha-Nasi, however, placed him under the care of R. Simeon ben Issi, his maternal uncle, who directed and taught him, and he ultimately became the disciple of R. Judah ha-Nasi.

BIBLIOGRAPHY: Bacher, Tann, 2 (1890), 400–7; Krauss, in: MGWJ, 38 (1894), 151–6; Weiss, Dor, 2 (1904⁴), 165; Gutmann, in: *Zion*, 18 (1953), 1–5; Alon, Meḥkarim, 2 (1958), 88–91.

[Shmuel Safrai]

ELEAZAR BEN YOSE I (second half of second century C.E.), *tanna*. Eleazar was the second son of *Yose b. Ḥalafta of Sepphoris (Shab. 118b; TJ, Yev. 1:1, 2b). He attained distinction as a scholar during the lifetime of his father, who quotes him and praises his statements (Sif. Deut. 148; cf. Pes. 117a; Yoma 67a). He cooperated with his father in intercalating the year (Tosef., Sanh. 2:1). The Talmud counts him among the scholars of the academy of Jabneh (Shab. 33b) and reports that *Simeon b. Yoḥai held him in high esteem (Me'il. 17b). His *halakhot* are found in the Tosefta and *beraitot* but he is not mentioned in the Mishnah. Nevertheless, many statements in the Mishnah which are quoted anonymously may in fact derive from the Mishnah of Eleazar b. Yose (Kelim 11:3; cf. Tosef., Kelim; BM 1:2; Nid. 8:1). Tannaitic sources relate that he gave rulings in Rome in connection with ritual purity (Tosef., Nid. 7:1; Mik. 4:7), and while there he saw the vessels plundered from the Temple at the time of its destruction. He testified that the veil was spattered with blood from the sacrifices of the Day of Atonement (Tosef., Yoma 3 end). Talmudic tradition explains that Eleazar journeyed to Rome together with Simeon b. Yoḥai in an attempt to persuade the emperor to abrogate the edicts against Jewish religious practices that were reinstituted in the period of the Antonines (Me'il. 17a; see Alon, Toledot, 2 (1961²), 61). According to the *aggadah*, they were helped by a miracle. A demon possessed the emperor's daughter and they succeeded in exorcising it. The emperor took them into his treasure chamber and invited them to take whatever they desired. They saw the text of the edict, and consigned it to flames (*ibid.*). We are also told that while in Rome Eleazar had discussions with *Mattiah b. Heresh, the leading scholar of the capital (Yoma 84b; Me'il. id), and saw the high priest's gold plate inscribed with the words "holy to the Lord" (the Tetragrammaton) in one line (Suk. 5a; et al.). According to the *aggadah* he also saw the insect that entered the nostrils of Titus and penetrated to his brain (Gen. R. 10:7, ed. Theodor Albeck, 82, note 3), as well as fragments of Solomon's throne that had been carried off by Nebuchadnezzar and taken from one nation to another until it reached the treasure house of Rome (Esth. R. 1:12). Eleazar also was reported to have visited Alexandria where an old Egyptian showed him hair and bones reputedly of the enslaved children of Israel embedded in a building from before the exodus from Egypt (Sanh. 111a and Dik. Sof. *ibid.*). He disputed with Samaritans and Sadducees, proving to them that their copies of the Torah scroll were forged and their commentaries false (Sot. 33b; Sanh. 90b). In addition to his halakhic powers he was also a gifted aggadist. He is quoted as saying: "All the charity and kindness practiced by Israel in this world bring abundant peace and serve as powerful advocates between Israel and its Father in heaven" (BB 10a).

BIBLIOGRAPHY: Hyman, Toledot, 177–80; Epstein, Tanna'im, 178f.; Bacher, Tann. s.v.

[Yitzhak Dov Gilat]

ELEAZAR BEN YOSE II (c. early fourth century), Palestinian *amora*. He may have been the son of the *amora* Yose who, together with Jonah, headed the academy at Tiberias. In any event Eleazar discussed halakhic problems with Yose, frequently put questions to him (TJ, Ber. 1:8, 3d; TJ, Ta'an. 2:2, 65c et al.), and expounded before him (TJ, Kil. 8:2, 31c; Ned. 4:9, 38d). Eleazar frequently quotes the statements of other *amoraim* such as Avin, Rav, Tanḥum b. Hiyya (TJ, Ma'as. 1:3, 49a; 2:1, 49c; Ber. end of ch. 7, 11d; RH 4:8, 59c et al.). His own deeds and sayings are also reported. For example, he, Abba b. Mari, and Mattaniah permitted a gift (of bread) to be carried to the government representative (Ursicinus) on the Sabbath (TJ, Beẓah 1:6, 60c). In *Genesis Rabbah* (32:2), R. Menaḥemyah quotes him as saying: "No man loves his fellow craftsmen – but God does – as it is written, 'For the Lord is righteous, He loveth righteousness' [Ps. 11:7]."

BIBLIOGRAPHY: Hyman, Toledot, 177f.; Frankel, Mevo, 113b; Weiss, Dor, 2 (1904[4]), 166.

[Yitzhak Dov Gilat]

ELEAZAR (Eliezer) BEN ZADOK, name of at least two *tannaim*, both belonging to the same family, in which the names Zadok and Eleazar frequently recur.

(1) *Tanna* of the first and beginning of the second century C.E. His father was the *tanna*, *Zadok, who, in an attempt to prevent the destruction of the Second Temple afflicted himself for 40 years. When he became ill, Johanan b. Zakkai obtained a physician from Vespasian and then accompanied by Eleazar he was permitted to leave Jerusalem, then under siege, in order to recover from the effects of his lengthy fast (Git. 56 a–b; Lam. R. 1:31). Eleazar's teacher was Johanan b. ha-Ḥoranit (Tosef., Suk. 2:3). He was a priest (Bek. 36a; et al.) and transmitted information concerning the structures, procedures, and practice of the Temple (Mei. 3:7; Mid. 3:8; Suk. 49a; et al.). While living in Jerusalem he engaged in commerce and such was his honesty that he dedicated to communal use three hundred flasks of wine, which he had collected from the residue in his measuring containers (Tosef., Beẓah 3:8). He was an eyewitness of the suffering endured at the time of the destruction of the Second Temple and saw the daughter of Nakdimon b. *Guryon, one of the wealthiest men in Jerusalem, picking up barley from under horses' hooves in Acre (Tosef., Ket. 5:10), and Miriam, the daughter of Boethus and wife of the high priest Joshua b. Gamla, tied by her hair to the tails of horses and made to run from Jerusalem to Lydda (Lam. R. 1:47; cf. TJ, Ket. 5, end). After the destruction of the Second Temple he joined the sages of *Jabneh, and as frequent visitor at the home of R. Gamaliel, reported the Sabbath and festival customs he witnessed there (Tosef., Beẓah 1:24; 2:13, 14; Pes. 37a; et al.). Eleazar frequently quotes halakhic traditions heard in his father's home or from earlier sages, as well as explanations of halakhic terms and expressions gleaned from the schools in Jerusalem and Jabneh (Bek. 22a; Nid. 48b). His statements include, "Do good deeds for the sake of the Creator, for their own sake, do not make of them a crown with which to glorify yourself, nor a spade to dig with them" (Ned. 62a; cf. Avot 4:5). Some assume the existence of an earlier Eliezer b. Zadok whose entire life was spent in Jerusalem before the destruction of the Second Temple.

(2) *Tanna* of the second half of the second century C.E., apparently the grandson of Eleazar b. Zadok (1). He transmitted *halakhot* in the names of R. Meir (Kil. 7:2) and of R. Simeon b. Gamaliel (Tosef., Kelim; BM 9: end), engaged in halakhic discussions with R. Judah and R. Yose (Kelim 9:26, 2:6), and was close to Judah ha-Nasi and his household (Tosef., Suk. 2:2). Aibu (the father of Rav, according to Rashi) relates (Suk. 44b) that he once learned from Eleazar's action that the shaking of the willow-branch on Tabernacles outside Jerusalem is a custom introduced by the prophets, and that no benediction is to be made over it (see, however, the readings in Dik. Sof., Suk. 136–7). Eleazar is the author of the statement, "No restriction may be imposed on the public unless the majority of the people can endure it" (Hor. 3b). It is difficult to decide to which Eleazar b. Zadok certain *halakhot* and statements are to be ascribed.

BIBLIOGRAPHY: A. Zacuto, *Yuḥasin ha-Shalem*, ed. by Filipowski (1857), 26–27; Frankel, Mishnah, 97–99, 178; Hyman, Toledot, 201–5; Bacher, Tann, 1 pt. 1 (Heb., 1903), 36–38; S. Lieberman, *Tosefta ki-Feshutah*, 4 (1962), 850.

[Yitzhak Dov Gilat]

ELEAZAR (Eliezer) HA-KAPPAR (late second century C.E.), Palestinian *tanna*, sometimes referred to as Eleazar ha-Kappar Beribbi (i.e., the descendant of eminent scholars). It is occasionally difficult to distinguish between the statements of Eleazar and those of *Bar Kappara, who was probably his son, and who was also called Eleazar ha-Kappar Beribbi. It is improbable, as some scholars believe, that the two were identical, since the son is sometimes specifically referred to as "Eleazar ben Eleazar ha-Kappar Beribbi" (e.g., Tosef., Beẓah 1:7). The father was apparently a member of *Judah ha-Nasi's *bet ha-midrash* (Tosef., Oho. 18:18), while the son was Judah's pupil. Some of the halakhic and aggadic remarks contained in the Mishnah and the *beraitot* perhaps should be attributed to the father. Eleazar ha-Kappar (the first) may be the author of the maxim "Envy, cupidity, and the craving for honor take a man out of the world" (Avot 4:21), and of the aggadic statement: "Great is peace for all the blessings conclude with the word *shalom* [peace]" (Sif. Num. 42), since it is followed immediately by another tradition brought in the name of his son. In 1969 a stone, which was apparently the lintel over the main entrance to a *bet midrash*, was found in the Golan area, inscribed with the words: "This is the *bet midrash* of Rabbi Eliezer ha-Kappar." It is unclear whether this inscription refers to the father or to the son.

BIBLIOGRAPHY: Frankel, Mishnah, 213; Kahana, in: *Ha-Asif* (1886), 330–3; Hyman, Toledot, 215–7; Bacher, Tann; *Hadashot Archeologiyot* (April 1969), 1–2. **ADD. BIBLIOGRAPHY:** D. Urman, in: *IEJ* 22 (1972), 16–23; idem, in: *Beer-Sheva*, 2 (1985) (Hebrew), 7–25.

[Shmuel Safrai]

ELEAZAR ḤISMA (fl. first third of the second century C.E.), *tanna*, one of the sages of Jabneh. Some consider Ḥisma to have been his father's name and refer to him as Eleazar b. Ḥisma, but it appears rather to have been his byname, meaning "the strong," said to have been given to him because of the strength he displayed in overcoming his former ignorance (Lev. R. 23:4; for another interpretation, see *Midrash David on Avot* (1944), 75). A pupil of Joshua b. Hananiah and perhaps also of Akiva, he transmitted *halakhot* in the name of the former and, together with him, he gave an aggadic interpretation of a biblical passage (Tosef., Zav. 4:4; Mekh., Amalek,

176). Some of his statements are recorded in the Mishnah, *baraita*, and halakhic Midrashim. For example, on the verse (Deut. 23:25) which permits a laborer, while harvesting grapes, to eat the fruit, Eleazar commented: "A laborer may not eat more than his wage" (Sif. Deut. 266; BM 7:5). He objected to excessive demonstrativeness in prayer, applying to the person who "blinks with his eyes, gesticulates with his lips, or points with his fingers while reciting the *Shema*," the verse "thou hast not called upon me, O Jacob" (Isa. 43:22; Yoma 19:6). Though proficient in astronomy and mathematics, he did not ascribe too much importance to them; hence his statement: "(Even) ordinances concerning bird sacrifices and the purification of women constitute the essence of the law, whereas astronomy and geometry are (merely) auxiliaries to knowledge" (Avot 3:18). He remained extremely poor, as was expressed in R. Joshua's comment to Rabban Gamaliel: "Marvel at two of your disciples in Jabneh, Eleazar b. Ḥisma and *Johanan b. Nuri (this is the correct reading: see Sif. Deut. 16), who can calculate how many drops the ocean contains, but have neither bread to eat nor clothes to wear." To enable them to earn a livelihood, Gamaliel wished to appoint them supervisors in the academy at Jabneh. When, in their modesty, they declined the offer, Gamaliel sent for them a second time, saying: "You imagine that I offer you rulership? It is servitude that I offer you," whereupon they accepted the appointment (Hor. 10a–b).

BIBLIOGRAPHY: Bacher, Tann, 1 (1903²), 368–70; Weiss, Dor, 2 (1904⁴), 110; Hyman, Toledot, 217–8; Frankel, Mishnah, 142; Alon, Toledot, 1 (1958³), 143, 299, 306.

[Yitzhak Dov Gilat]

ELEAZAR OF MODI'IN (**ha-Moda'i**; end of the first and the beginning of the second century C.E.), *tanna*. He came from Modi'in, the home of the Hasmoneans, and was principally renowned as an aggadist, earning the praise of R. Gamaliel who said of him: "We still have need of [the aggadic interpretation of] the Modi'ite" (Shab. 55b; BB 10b). Defining the nature of *aggadah*, Eleazar said that it captivates men's hearts (Mekh., Va-Yassa, 5). Even the sole *halakhah* quoted in his name has an aggadic flavor about it; disputing the view that wherever "*Adonai*" is mentioned in the Pentateuch in connection with Abraham it refers to God, except in Genesis 18:3, "Adonai [my Lord], if now I have found favor in Thy sight," Eleazar is cited as saying: "This too, is sacred"; i.e., it also refers to God (Shevu. 35b). Some of his contemporaries protested against his exaggerated aggadic interpretations: "O Man of Modi'in, how long will you rake words together" (Yoma 76a). In *Avot* (3:11) he is recorded as declaring: "He who profanes the sacred things and despises the festivals and puts his fellow-man to shame in public and rejects the covenant of Abraham our father and gives the Torah a meaning contrary to its right one, even though he is learned in the Torah and has good deeds to his credit, has no share in the world to come." His reference to rejecting the covenant of Abraham – that is, to those who disguised their circumcision in order to hide their Jewish origin – is aimed at the Jews who forsook their people during the Bar Kokhba revolt (Tosef., Shab., 15:9). Most of his aggadic remarks are to be found in the *Mekhilta* on the portions dealing with the manna and with Amalek, where he is mentioned more than 40 times.

It is stated (TJ, Ta'an. 4:68d; Lam. R. 2:2) that Eleazar was the uncle of Bar Kokhba and was in Bethar during the final stages of its siege. Suspecting Eleazar's loyalty, Bar Kokhba struck him a mortal blow. "Immediately thereafter Bethar was taken and Ben Koziba was killed." It is thus probable that "Eleazar the priest," whose name occurs on coins of Bar Kokhba with that of "Simeon the prince of Israel" or by itself, refers to Eleazar of Modi'in. Although it is not stated in the sources that he was a priest, this may be taken for granted, since most of the scholars who bore this name, that of the son of Aaron the high priest, were *kohanim* (in contrast to Eliezer).

BIBLIOGRAPHY: Frankel, Mishnah (1923), 135; Bacher, Fann, 1; Alon, Toledot, 2 (1961²), 37; J. Guttmann, in: MGWJ, 42 (1898), 303–5, 337–45; L. Mildenberg, in: HJ, 11 (1949), 77–108.

[Shmuel Safrai]

ELEK (Fischer), ARTUR (1876–1944), Hungarian author and art historian. A contributor to *Nyugat* and other literary periodicals, Elek translated French and Italian classics and wrote short stories. His major works were *Álarcos menet* ("Masked Procession," 1913), *A reneszánsz festőművészete* ("Renaissance Painting," 1927), and *Ujabb magyar költők lýrai anthológiája* (1911), an anthology of modern Hungarian poetry. A convert to Christianity, he committed suicide during the Nazi occupation.

ELEPHANT. Archaeological finds of ivory objects made from elephant tusks have been found in Israel dating back to prehistoric and Chalcolithic times. It is assumed that wild elephants were still present in Syria during the second and first millennia B.C.E. until they were hunted to extinction. Alternatively, they may have been imported there from India (*Elephas maximus*) for the purposes of royal hunting, but this seems less likely. Thutmoses III is recorded as having hunted elephants during his campaign in Syria in the 15th century B.C.E.: "He [Thutmoses III] hunted 120 elephants at their mud hole. Then the biggest elephant began to fight before his Majesty. I [Amen-en-heb] was the one who cut off his hand while he was still alive, in the presence of his Majesty, while I was standing in the water between two rocks. Then my Lord rewarded me…." The lower jaws of elephants have been discovered in mid-second millennium deposits during archaeological excavations at the site of Atchana-Alalakh in Syria. While the elephant itself is not mentioned in the Bible, its ivory tusks (*Shenhabbim*) were brought from Ophir for Solomon (I Kings 10:22; II Chron. 9:21). The word "*shenhav*" means the tooth (*shen*) of the elephant (*ev* in Egyptian, hence the name of the island Yev (Jab) – *Elephantine). The word *shen* also signifies ivory, from which Solomon made his throne, overlaying it with gold (I Kings 10:18). The Bible also mentions "horns of ivory," "houses of ivory," "beds of ivory," and "ivory palaces" (Ezek. 27:15; Amos 3:15; 6:4; Ps. 45:9). Reference is likewise made to "the ivory house" which Ahab built (I Kings 22:39), the reference being to a house containing ivory vessels and ornaments. An examination of the ivory vessels, ornaments, and images uncovered at Megiddo and in Samaria shows that they were made from the African elephant *Loxodonta africana* (= *Elephas africanus*). Elephants were employed by Darius in his battle against Alexander the Great. At a later date, elephants were introduced into Ereẓ Israel being used for military purposes in the Syrian-Greek army (I Macc. 8:6; II Macc. 13:15). It was under one of these elephants that Eleazar the Hasmonean was crushed to death (I Macc. 6:43–46). A painting of an elephant appears on the walls of a Sidonian tomb found at Marissa (Maresha). In mishnaic times, elephants were kept in some rich homes and the *baraita* deals with tasks carried out for its master by an elephant (Er. 31b). It is stated that the elephant feeds on branches and is rarely to be seen (TJ, Shab. 18:1, 16c). On seeing an elephant one recites the blessing, "Blessed is He who makes strange creatures" (Ber. 58b). The elephant's period of gestation was said to be three years (Bek. 8a); it is now known, however, to be 18–22 months only.

BIBLIOGRAPHY: H.B. Tristram, *The Natural History of the Bible* (1883), 81–83; F.S. Bodenheimer, *Animal Life in Biblical Lands: From the Stone Age to the Nineteenth Century*, vol. 2 (1956), 375–77; J. Feliks, *Animal World of the Bible* (1962), 48. **ADD. BIBLIOGRAPHY:** F.E. Zeuner, *A History of Domesticated Animals* (1963), 275–98; A. Houghton Brodrick, *Animals in Archaeology* (1972); R.D. Barnett, *Ancient Ivories in the Middle East*, in: *Qedem*, 14 (1982); O. Borowski, *Every Living Thing: Daily Use of Animals in Ancient Israel* (1998), 193–95.

[Jehuda Feliks / Shimon Gibson (2nd ed.)]

ELEPHANTINE (Aram. יֵב, *yb*; Eg. *ʿibw, ʾbw*; Gr. *ieb*), "the city of ivories," situated at the eastern bank of the southern end of a small island in the Nile, just north of the First Cataract and opposite the City of Sun (the Syene of Ezek. 29:10 and opposite modern Aswan). Its name relates to the natural rock formation along the river which, from even a short distance, looks like a herd of elephants. The Greek name Elephantine (Ἐλεφαντίνη; cf. Jos., *Bellum*, 4:611; Strabo, 16) was a rendering of the Egyptian name, itself preserved in the Aramaic name. Elephantine was sacred to the ram-headed god Khnum who was believed to control the annual inundation of the Nile from the First Cataract.

During the Old Kingdom, Elephantine was known as "The Door to the South" because it was the southernmost city of Egypt, and a frontier fortress defending access to Egypt from Nubia. During the Middle and New Kingdoms it was the center of the Egyptian administration of Nubia. Under Persian rule from 525 B.C.E., it was the center of Persian military command in Egypt, and there was a large mercenary camp at Elephantine which included companies or regiments (*degalim*, "banners") of Jewish soldiers (חילא יהודה).

Elephantine became known to the modern world at the beginning of the 20th century with the discovery of the Aramaic documents known as the Elephantine Papyri, which were first published by A.E. Cowley in 1923. A second collection, edited by Emil G. Kraeling, was published in 1953.

The Jewish military colony is well known from the Elephantine Papyri. These describe the lives of the mercenaries who lived in Elephantine in the sixth and fifth centuries B.C.E. as well as their families and others.

Much of the significance of the papyri lies in their forensic detail, such as those relating to marriage and divorce or with matters relating to commerce and inheritance. Others shed light on previously unknown or obscure historical occasions.

History of the Jewish Colony at Elephantine

There are no external sources on the history of the Elephantine community. When the southern frontier was exposed to Nubian raids, Jewish soldiers were sent to defend it, perhaps as early as during the Assyrian regime. The Jewish temple at Elephantine may have been built in the second half of the seventh century or at the beginning of the sixth but was constructed, in any event, before the Persian conquest of Egypt in the days of Cambyses' rule, as mentioned in the letter of the Elephantine Jews themselves (Cowley 1923: 30). It is sometimes said that there is a connection between the building of the temple at Elephantine and Isaiah's prophecy (19:19) concerning the "altar to the Lord in the midst of the land of Egypt" and the "pillar at the border thereof."

It is not thought that the soldiers of the garrison built the temple. The description contained in the Elephantine Jews' letter to Bagoas, the governor of Yahud (Cowley 30:9–12), attests to the great magnificence of the building, and apparently the Jewish mercenaries could not by themselves afford to erect such a splendid structure. Since there were also Jewish civilians living at Elephantine, the temple was probably not built until the civilians, together with the soldiers, financed the building project. Hence the temple was presumably not built in the early days of the Jewish settlement at Elephantine, but later when the community was better established and had achieved some prosperity and local standing.

The papyri indicate that there was a developed trade in property, such as homes and land. Other types of commerce also provided the Elephantine Jews with their livelihoods, for it was not only a frontier military post but also a center of commerce with Nubia, trading especially in ivory. The elite section of Elephantine society was probably small and its wealth limited. From the contributions to the temple (Cowley 22) and also from the gifts to Mivtaḥyah the daughter of Mahseiah (Cowley 15), it can be seen that silver was both uncommon and expensive.

In general, relations between the local Egyptians and the Jewish mercenaries and civilians were strained, although there were instances of marriage between Jews and Egyptians, in which case it would seem that the Egyptian partner had to convert to Judaism. This is inferred by several scholars from the fact that the Egyptian Asḥor's sons had Jewish names (Yedonyah and Mahseiah (Cowley 20)). However, as Bohak has stated (2002: 185), it is not possible to trace a single Jewish family over several generations to accurately establish the constancy of their Judaism in the face of intermarriage with locals.

In any event, the position of the Jews declined with the ascension of Egyptian power. While they were soldiers in the service of the Persian king their position was relatively secure, but with the expulsion of the Persians from Egypt at the end of the fifth century B.C.E. and the rise of the Egyptian kingdom, the position of the Elephantine Jews worsened (cf. the fragmentary document Cowley 37, which refers to a dispute between the Elephantine Jews, who were wronged and "fear robbery because they are few," and the Egyptians).

In 410 B.C.E., the temple of the Elephantine Jews was destroyed by the priests of the adjoining temple of Khnum (Cowley 1923: 30) after it was looted for gold and silver. The most common explanation for the act of destruction is that the priests of Khnum were angered by the sacrifice by the Jews of animals sacred to Khnum, particularly the sacrifice of sheep during Passover (Cowley 1923: 21). Three years after the destruction, the Elephantine Jews applied to the Persian governor of Yehud for permission to rebuild the temple. Permission was given, but on condition that animal sacrifices would no longer be made there (Porten 1968: 292). It is not known how much longer after this the Jewish temple stood, but the account of the community in the papyri ends in 399 B.C.E.

Even after the end of Persian rule in Egypt, it is not certain whether the Jewish colony at Elephantine persisted or not. Military requirements probably made it necessary to keep an army on the frontier even after the expulsion of the Persians, and it was unlikely that even a new administration would dispense with the Jewish soldiers who, for several generations, had been trained and experienced in guarding the southern frontier. By the end of the Ptolemaic period, Egypt's eastern frontier at Pelusium was run by a Jewish guard, and the Macedonians at the beginning of the Greek period in Egypt probably did not dispense with the services of the Jewish guards on the southern frontier, although there was a fundamental change in organization.

The Legal Papyri

The legal papyri shed light on the daily life of the Jewish military colony at Elephantine. Interestingly, both a husband and a wife had apparently equal power to unilaterally dissolve their marriage (Cowley 15; Kraeling 2, 7). Thus, the prospective bride had to consent to the marriage, and the prospective bridegroom was unable to obtain the father's consent without the girl's also: if she refused, her father could not compel her to marry him. As set out in another papyri (Cowley 15), a man asked the head of the family for the hand of the woman. If both agreed, the man recited the formula: "She is my wife and I am her husband from this day for ever," and also paid a dowry to the bride's father.

The gifts presented by the bridegroom to the bride Mivtaḥyah, the daughter of Mahseiah b. Yedonyah, are also set out in Cowley 15, with a note of their value, which is explicitly given in case the marriage is dissolved. This could be effected at the request of either husband or wife by one of them declaring in public that he or she "hates" the other. The results differed depending on who initiated the divorce. According to Cowley, in the event of Mivtaḥyah's rejecting her husband Asḥor, she would have to cover the cost of the dissolution of the marriage contract, that is, seven and a half shekels but, even then, the goods and chattels which she brought into the marriage remained hers after the dissolution of that union.

However if Asḥor dissolved the marriage, he forfeited the dowry, but Mivtaḥyah had to return all that her husband had given her during their marriage. To protect a wife against her husband's capriciousness, a further regulation was laid down to the effect that if the husband arbitrarily divorced his wife with the plea that he had another wife or other children, he had to pay a heavy fine (according to Cowley 15, 20 karsah = 200 shekels) and all the conditions of the marriage agreement in whatever concerned the wife were annulled. All these stipulations refer to a marriage between free persons.

Dated 449 B.C.E., Kraeling 2 is the marriage document of Tamut, the handmaiden of Meshullam b. Zaccur. Married to Ananiah b. Azariah, she remained a handmaiden even after her marriage, but another papyrus (Kraeling 5) shows that she and her daughter Yehoyishma eventually gained their freedom after Tamut had been married for 18 years, although they both remained closely aligned to the family.

A woman's status at Elephantine could also be gauged from the gifts she received as a wife and a daughter (Kraeling 5, 9; Cowley 8). Inheritance laws were also revealed in the Elephantine papyri. It is evident that sons inherited, but less so in the case of daughters (where there were also sons in the family). It seems likely that a daughter's right to inherit existed only when there were no sons. Possibly this was the origin of the institution of the gifts made to daughters – a compensation for their being discriminated against in the matter of inheritance.

In three papyri, Cowley 15 and Kraeling 2 and 7, there are illuminating comments on the inheritance of a widow and a widower. Cowley 15 states that if Mivtaḥyah died without male or female issue, Asḥor "inherited her goods and chattels"; but if Asḥor died without Mivtaḥyah having borne his children, male or female, "she had the right to his goods and chattels." This difference in wording is explained by scholars as indicating that in such a case the widower's right to inherit the assets was established in law, but in the case of the widow it was a matter of some sort of agreement or negotiation.

The Elephantine papyri also give instances of transactions in landed and other property, the site of which was fixed according to the adjoining land or houses, a procedure familiar from many papyri of the Ptolemaic period and the days of Roman rule of Egypt. With the help of these documents it is possible to reconstruct with some degree of certainty the location of the Jewish temple at Elephantine (cf. the plan in Kraeling, p. 81).

The Religion of the Jews in Elephantine

The Elephantine Jews brought with them the religion of the early prophets shortly before the destruction of the First Temple. This religion placed the God of Judah, Yahu (a name which occurs in several variants in the papyri), at the center of faith and worship. This is revealed by the fact that those who ministered in the Elephantine Jews' temple are referred to in the papyri as *kohanim* ("priests"), while the gentile cults are said to have *kemarim* ("idolatrous priests") – exactly as in the Bible.

It is interesting to note that the Elephantine Jews saw nothing amiss in having their own temple even though a temple to the God of Israel existed in Jerusalem. They appealed to the high priest Jehohanan to take steps to rebuild their temple, destroyed by the priests of Khnum, without any thought that he might regard it as a grave sin. It is evident from the Elephantine Papyri (Cowley 30), that those who wrote the letter to the Persian governor were surprised that the high priest in Jerusalem had not answered them. However, perhaps the Jews at Elephantine were unaware of the upheaval in Jerusalem, the ousting of the temple hierarchy by the returnees from the Babylonian exile and their establishment of the old/new Temple and Torah-based cult.

The Elephantine Jews' temple was originally established to serve as a focus of worship for the Jewish military and civilian colony which, remote from the land of Judah, needed some religious center. If the Temple of Zerubbabel was built more or less according to the plan of the First Temple, the description of the Elephantine temple given in papyrus Cowley 30 shows that it had an altogether different shape. It was adorned with stone pillars and hewn stone and had a roof of cedar and five gates with bronze hinges. In the temple were also various articles of furniture as well as bowls of gold and silver.

On the altar, the full range of sacrifices were offered before the destruction of the temple (by the priests of Khnum in 410 B.C.E.) and after the rebuilding of the temple, animal sacrifice was no longer permitted. Whether the order of worship was like that observed in the Temple at Jerusalem cannot be ascertained. However, this is improbable, if only for the reason that Yahu was not the only god housed in the Elephantine temple, since a list of the Elephantine Jews' gifts to their temple (Cowley 22), totaling 31 karash and 8 shekels, states that 12 karash and 8 shekels were for Yahu (*ibid.*, p. 70:123), 7 karash for Ashambethel (*ibid.*, loc. cit.: 124), and 12 karash for Anathbethel (*ibid.*, loc cit.: 125).

It seems clear that two goddesses dwelt alongside Yahu, and may have been worshipped with Him in the Elephantine temple. The element 'Asham' in Ashambethel is to be identified with the Ashmat of Samaria mentioned in Amos (8:14), while Bethel as an element in a compound proper noun current in Judah in the days of Darius I is mentioned in Zechariah 7:2. The same applies to Anathbethel: Anath was well known in Ereẓ Israel, as is indicated by place-names such as Anathoth and Beth-Anath.

This situation in Elephantine supports the assumption that the Jewish garrison there was an ancient one, with its origins in (if not before) the days of Manasseh. In the fifth century B.C.E., the relationship between the Jews at Elephantine and Jerusalem was not close, and no remains of the Pentateuch have been discovered at Elephantine, although the finding of the "Book of Ahikar" there shows that the community contained lovers of ethical and wisdom literature. It may also explain another, more interesting fact, namely that of the festivals of Israel only the observance of Passover is mentioned at Elephantine. Passover was observed in Jerusalem in the days of Hezekiah (II Chron. 30:13–27) and Josiah (II Kings 23:21–23; II Chron. 35:1–18). During the First Temple period no mention is made of Tabernacles – the first mention of its observance in Jerusalem belongs to the Second Temple period, in the time of Ezra (cf. Neh. 8:13–18), and its reintroduction in the fifth century had not yet spread beyond the borders of Judah. As some papyri are earlier than Ezra and Nehemiah and others only a few years later, the observance of Tabernacles was therefore unknown to them. The document referring to Passover (Cowley 21) contains King Darius II's edict of 419 B.C.E. (the fifth year of his reign) to the governor Arsames that the Jewish forces (and perhaps also Jews outside Elephantine) were to celebrate Passover.

Detailed religious instructions were given on what the Jews were to do to preserve the sanctity of the festival. The document is a copy of the original edict which was brought to the attention of Yedoniyah by Hananiah, apparently a Jew influential with the authorities. The contents of the document show that the rules of eating unleavened bread and of abstaining from leaven were known and properly observed at that time, in keeping with the commandments of the Torah.

Organization of the Military Colony

With the help of the Elephantine Papyri, an extremely clear picture can be drawn of the organization of the Jewish military colony as it existed at the end of the fifth century B.C.E. The Elephantine Jews constituted a military unit known as "the Jewish force" (חילא יהודיה). There were also Jews at Elephantine who were not part of the military establishment. Every Jewish soldier belonged to a *degel* (company or regiment), and was referred to as "a man of the *degel*" (*ba'al degel*, בעל דגל), the Jewish civilian as "a man of the town" (*ba'al kiryah*, בעל קריה; Cowley 5:9, 13:10). The names of the *degalim* are not Jewish but Persian or Babylonian, and the same applies to the higher command. At the head of the Jewish force was a commander of the garrison (רב חילא), above whom was the *fratarak*, corresponding more or less to a general. These were non-Jews.

The Elephantine documents also mention "a hundred" as a military unit, apparently smaller than a *degel*. Despite the extensive civilian freedom granted to them, as attested by the

Elephantine papyri, the Jews there, being soldiers, required the Persian regime's permission for any change which interfered with their military duties. As soldiers subject to military discipline, they were tried by the military authorities at Elephantine or at Syene. Nevertheless, they enjoyed a large measure of civilian freedom in everything pertaining to their personal lives. They led a normal family life, were allowed to transact business among themselves or with non-Jews, to buy and sell landed property and houses, and to bequeath these to their children. As soldiers, however, they received their rations from the king (Cowley 24), being allotted a monthly ration in grain (usually barley) and legumes (Cowley 2; Kraeling 11:3ff.) and payment in silver (Cowley 2:16, 11:6). At Elephantine there was a "royal storehouse" (Kraeling 3:9, et al.). Accountants (Cowley 26:4ff.) and scribes (Cowley 2:12, 14) supervised the disbursement of goods and funds. One administrative document (Cowley 24) shows:

Men:	22	2	30
Ardab (c. 1 quart):	1	1½	2½

The monetary system combined the Persian karash (83.3 grams) with the Egyptian shekel (8.76 grams), a half-shekel agio being added to make 10 shekels equal 1 karash.

It is nonetheless clear that their wealth derived from commerce. The documents show that the Elephantine Jews attained a certain degree of wealth and some of them, especially the civilians, a measure of opulence. They occupied an intermediate position between a professional soldier living by his sword and a civilian engaged in a craft, in commerce, or in cultivating the soil. The same situation obtained in the Hellenistic period when, for example, the cleruchies were both soldiers and farmers. The status of the fifth-century Elephantine Jews can also be compared to that of the Babylonian Jewish military colony sent at the command of Antiochus III to Phrygia and Lydia, where the colonists were settled on the soil and in the cities and constituted a garrison loyal to the Seleucids, at the same time cultivating the land allotted to them by the king.

An active civilian life at Elephantine is attested by the various civilian officials mentioned in the papyri, such as judges (Cowley 16:4–5, 9), state scribes (ספרי מדינתא: Cowley 17:1, 6), and others. It is however probable that these officials were not Jews but Persians or other non-Jews. At the head of the Elephantine Jewish community was its most prominent personality, who represented it both internally and externally. At the end of the fifth century B.C.E. the leader of the community was Yedonyah b. Gemariah who with his colleagues sent the famous letter about the temple to Bagoas.

BIBLIOGRAPHY: Z. Ben-Ḥayyim in: *Eretz Israel*, 1 (1951), 135–9; G. Bohak, "Ethnic Continuity in the Jewish Diaspora in Antiquity," in: John R. Bartlett (ed.), *Jews in the Hellenistic and Roman Cities*, Routledge (2002); E. Bresciani and M. Kamil, in: *Atti della Accademia Nazionale dei Lincei*, ser. 8, vol. 12 (1966), 357–428; U. Cassuto, in *Qedem*, 1 (1942), 47–52; A.E. Cowley, "Some Egyptian Aramaic Documents," in: PSBA (1903), 25: 202–8, 259–63; idem, *Aramaic* (1923); G.R. Driver, *Aramaic Documents of the Fifth Century BC* (1954, 1957); A.S. Hirschberg, in: *Ha-Tekufah*, 8 (1920), 339–68; W. Kaiser, *Elephantine: The Ancient Town*, DAI: 1998; E.G. Kraeling (ed.), *Brooklyn Museum Aramaic Papyri* (1953); E.Y. Kutscher, *Qedem*, 2 (1945), 66–74; E. Meyer, *Der Papyrusfund von Elephantine* (1912); B. Porten, *Archives from Elephantine: The Life of an Ancient Jewish Military Colony* (1968); idem, "Did the Ark Stop at Elephantine," in: BAR (May/June 1995); idem (2003), "Elephantine and the Bible," in: L.H. Schiffman (ed.), *Semitic Papyrology in Context* (2003), 51–84; S.G. Rosenberg, "The Jewish Temple at Elephantine," in: NEA, 67:1 (2004); E. Sachau, *Aramaeische Papyrus und Ostraka aus einerjuedischen Militaer-Kolonie zu Elephantine*, 2 vols. (1911); A.H. Sayce and A.E. Cowley (eds.), *Aramaic Papyri Discovered at Assuan* (1906); E.L. Sukenik and E.Y. Kutscher, *Qedem*, 1 (1942), 53–56; C. von Pilgrim "The Town Site of the Island of Elephantine," in: *Egyptian Archaeology*, 10:16–18; R. Yaron, *Introduction to the Law of the Aramaic Papyri* (1961); idem, *Ha-Mishpat shel Mismekhei Yev* (1961); idem, in JSS, 2 (1957), 33–61; 3 (1958), 1–39.

[Abraham Schalit / Lidia Matassa (2nd ed.)]

ELFENBEIN, ISRAEL (1890–1964), U.S. rabbi and talmudic scholar. Elfenbein was born in Buczacz, eastern Galicia. He immigrated to the U.S. in 1906 and in 1915 was ordained at the Jewish Theological Seminary in New York. Between 1915 and 1940 Elfenbein was rabbi of congregations in Nashville, Chicago, and New York. In 1938 he became national executive director of the Mizrachi Education and Expansion Fund. Elfenbein's principal interest in scholarly research was medieval rabbinic literature. He made many contributions to scholarly periodicals and annuals. His major work was a collection of the responsa of Rashi, *Teshuvot Rashi* (3 vols. in one, 1943). Other works include *Maimonides the Man* (1946). Some of his more popular writings were collected in a volume published posthumously, *American Synagogue as a Leavening Force in Jewish Life*, edited by A. Burstein (1966).

BIBLIOGRAPHY: J.L. Maimon (ed.), *Sefer Yovel… Yisra'el Elfenbein* (1962), 9–13.

ELFMAN, DANNY (1953–), U.S. composer-musician. Born in Amarillo, Texas, to teacher Milton and teacher/writer Blossom (née Bernstein) Elfman and raised in Los Angeles, Elfman played violin in public high school and later played the conga drums and violin with the avant-garde troupe Grand Magic Circus in France and Belgium. After spending a year touring West Africa at 18, Elfman returned to Los Angeles in 1971 following a bout with malaria. His brother, Richard, asked him to join his multimedia theater ensemble, the Mystic Nights of the Oingo Boingo, and help score his film *The Forbidden Zone* (1980), which starred Elfman as Satan. Elfman taught himself composition during this time by transcribing the music of jazz great Duke Ellington. While working on the film, Elfman and other members formed the new wave group Oingo Boingo in 1979. The group released a string of albums with IRS Records – *Oingo Boingo* (1980), *Only a Lad* (1981), *Nothing to Fear* (1982), and *Good for Your Soul* (1984). Elfman recorded his first solo album *So-Lo* in 1984 for MCA. The group scored a Top 40 hit with the theme to the movie *Weird Science* (1985). That same year, the feature film *Pee-Wee's Big Adventure* debuted with

Elfman's score, and marked the first collaboration between the composer and director Tim Burton. Oingo Boingo followed Elfman to MCA, releasing *Dead Man's Party* (1986), *Boi-ngo* (1987), *Boingo Alive* (1988), and *Dark at the End of the Tunnel* (1990), but failed to break out from its local fan base. Elfman and Burton's gothic-themed creations continued with *Beetlejuice* (1988), *Batman* (1989), and *Edward Scissorhands* (1990). He won a Grammy award for best instrumental composition in 1989 for "The Batman Theme" for the film *Batman*, and was nominated for best score. In 1990, he received two Emmy nominations for his theme for the animated TV series *The Simpsons*, and in 1991 he received another Grammy nod for his Gershwin-flavored score for the 1990 film *Dick Tracy*. He released an album of his film scores, *Music for a Darkened Theater, Vol. 1: Film and Television Music* (1990), which was followed by *Music for a Darkened Theater, Vol. 2: Film and Television Music* (1996). Elfman co-wrote, scored, and sang as Jack Skellington in Burton's *Nightmare Before Christmas* (1993). Oingo Boingo shortened its name to Boingo and released a self-titled album in 1994, but called it quits a year later. Elfman, already established as a composer, went on to score such films as *Men in Black* (1997), *Good Will Hunting* (1997), *Sleepy Hollow* (1999), *Spy Kids* (2001), *Spider-Man* (2002), and *Chicago* (2002), and the TV show *Desperate Housewives* (2004). Elfman's second marriage was to actress Bridget Fonda.

[Adam Wills (2nd ed.)]

ELHANAN (Heb. אֶלְחָנָן; "God has mercy"), the name of two biblical characters: (1) the son of Dodo of Beth-Lehem and one of David's "mighty men," mentioned after *Asahel in the list of the 30 warriors (II Sam. 23:24; I Chron. 11:26); (2) the son of Jaare-Oregim of Bethlehem, one of the "servants of David." According to II Samuel 21:19 Elhanan killed *Goliath, while according to I Chronicles 20:5 (where he is called the son of Jair) he killed Lahmi, the brother of Goliath. The former verse contradicts the story of *David and Goliath in I Samuel 17. Among the various suggestions put forth to resolve this contradiction is B. Mazar's proposal that Elhanan the son of Jaare (יערי) is to be identified with David son of Jesse (ישי). Elhanan was David's true name before he ascended the throne, while Jaare is a corruption of Jesse (see *David). Some scholars believe that the Hebrew words *ʾet Golyat*, i.e., "Goliath," in the source II Samuel, was emended to *ʾaḥi Golyat*, i.e., "the brother of Goliath," in I Chronicles, in order to cover up the contradiction between the two accounts.

The *aggadah*, too, identifies Elhanan with David, and explains the word *oregim* in II Samuel 21:19 as "of those who weave (*oreg*) the curtains of the Temple" (Targum to this word).

BIBLIOGRAPHY: Goldschmid, in: BJPES, 14 (1947–49), 122; A.M. Honeyman, in: JBL, 67 (1948), 13–25; W. Pákozdy, in: ZAW, 68 (1956), 257–9; J. Stamm, in: VT supplement, 7 (1959), 165–83. IN THE AGGADAH: Ginzberg, Legends, 6 (1946), 260; I. Ḥasida, *Ishei ha-Tanakh* (1964), 62. **ADD. BIBLIOGRAPHY:** S. Japhet, *I & II Chronicles* (1993), 363–69; S. Bar-Efrat, *II Samuel* (1996), 233–34; G. Knoppers, *I Chronicles 10–29* (2004), 736.

ELHANAN (**Paulus Pragensis**?; 16th century), apostate and author of missionary works, favored by the Hapsburg emperor *Rudolf II. Born in Prague, Elhanan became converted to Christianity and was baptized in Chelm, Poland, although his wife and children did not follow suit. He received stipends from the Polish kings Sigismund Augustus and Henry of Valois. He conducted missionary activities among the Jews in Frankfurt in 1579. In 1580 at the Protestant University of Helmstaedt, he published his *Mysterium Novum*, prefaced by a poem in Hebrew, in which he attempted to prove by kabbalistic methods that Jesus was the messiah. He reached Catholic Vienna in 1581, and published a missionary treatise there. Having submitted his works to the emperor, he asked Rudolf to support him in order to publish his Hebrew translation of the New Testament. Possibly Elhanan is to be identified with the apostate Paulus Pragensis, who published a missionary pamphlet, *Symbolum Apostolicum*, in Protestant Wittenberg in 1580 and the *Jona Quadrilinguis* (Helmstedt, 1580) – the Book of Jonah in four languages: Hebrew, Greek, Latin, and German. Pragensis is said to have died after abjuring Christianity.

BIBLIOGRAPHY: Diamant, in: *Archiv fuer juedische Familienforschung*, 2:1–3 (1913/14), 17–24.

ELHANAN BEN ḤUSHIEL (first half 11th century), *av bet din* in *Kairouan, Tunisia. Elhanan went to Kairouan from Italy with his father at the end of the tenth century. His name appears in verses contained in a letter of R. Ḥushiel to R. *Shemariah ben Elhanan (publ. by S. Schechter in JQR, 11 (1899), 643–50). Scholars disagree as to whether Elhanan was the brother of R. *Hananel b. R. Ḥushiel, the well-known commentator of the Talmud, whether there were two sages by the name of Ḥushiel at the same time in Kairouan, or whether Hananel and Elhanan are the same person under different names. Only two of his responsa are extant. In one, the questioner addresses him as: "Our teacher, the great rabbi, the head of the *bet din*, the head of the schools," from which it may be concluded that as well as being the *av bet din* in Kairouan he was also the head of one of the yeshivot in that city. He also appears to have written a commentary to the tractates *Bava Kamma* and *Bava Meẓia*.

BIBLIOGRAPHY: Poznański, in: *Festschrift… A. Harkavy* (1908), 186–7 (Heb. pt.); Aptowitzer, in: *Jahresbericht der Israelitsch-Theologischen Lehranstalt in Wien (1929–1932)*, 37–39 (1933), 3–50; Mann, in: JQR, 9 (1918/19), 160; idem, in: *Tarbiz*, 5 (1933/34), 286ff.; Assaf, *ibid.*, 9 (1937/38), 22; Abramson, in: *Sinai*, 60 (1967), 149–59.

[Simha Assaf]

ELHANAN BEN ISAAC OF DAMPIERRE (d. 1184), tosafist; son of *Isaac b. Samuel the Elder of Dampierre whom he predeceased. Elhanan was martyred, but the circumstances are unknown. Although he wrote *tosafot* to many tractates, only those to *Avodah Zarah* up to p. 35a are extant (Husiatyn, 1901). His *tosafot* to *Yoma* served as the source of the *Tosafot Yeshanim* to that tractate. His father often quotes him, as do other earlier halakhic authorities. *Tosafot* also cite him frequently. Elhanan also wrote responsa which cannot, however, always be identified as his, since they were usually written together with his father and bear his father's signature. Comments on the Bible are quoted in his name and he was the author of *piyyutim*.

BIBLIOGRAPHY: Urbach, Tosafot, 211–7, 399; idem, in: *Sefer Assaf* (1953), 18–32; Davidson, Oẓar, 4 (1933), 361 (index).

[Israel Moses Ta-Shma]

ELHANAN BEN SHEMARIAH (d. 1026), head of the academy in Fostat (Old Cairo), Egypt, at the beginning of the 11th century. Elhanan studied at the Pumbedita academy during the gaonate of *Sherira with whom he later exchanged responsa as he did with the latter's son and successor *Hai, and *Samuel b. Hophni, head of the Sura academy. A number of Sherira Gaon's responsa to Elhanan are extant. Elhanan was honored by the title "the sixth" at the academy in Palestine. After the death of his father he became the head of the academy in Fostat. His academy received a grant from the royal treasury. When Caliph al-Ḥākim stopped this support, Elhanan turned for assistance to the Jewish communities, including those outside Egypt. It is believed that Elhanan wrote a talmudic commentary, and commentaries to the tractates *Bava Kamma* and *Avodah Zarah* have been attributed to him. His literary works, found in the Cairo *Genizah*, include a poem against the *Karaites following *Saadiah Gaon's approach. From a fragment of a book of Arabic sermons attributed to him, it appears he also studied philosophy.

BIBLIOGRAPHY: Poznański, in: *Festschrift A. Harkavy* (1908), 187–8 (Heb. pt.); Mann, Egypt, index; Mann, Texts, index: Assaf, in: *Tarbiz*, 9 (1937/38), 217–8; idem, *Teshuvot ha-Ge'onim* (1942), 114–6; Abramson, Merkazim, 105–55.

[Simha Assaf]

ELHANAN BEN YAKAR (first half of the 13th century), *Ḥasidei Ashkenaz theologian. Elhanan, who lived in London, seems also to have traveled on the continent. In common with the Ḥasidei Ashkenaz, his main interest was in esoteric theology and all his known writings belong to this category. His family was related to that of R. *Simeon b. Isaac ("the Great"), which also gave rise to the school of *Judah he-Ḥasid in Germany. Elhanan received some traditions from the tosafists in France, as is proved by his statement that he studied the *Sefer *Yeẓirah* with a pupil of R. *Isaac ha-Zaken, one of the most prominent tosafists. All his works are based upon the *Sefer Yeẓirah*: two of the major ones are versions of a detailed exegesis of this work, and the third, *Sod ha-Sodot* (called in a later source, probably by mistake, *Yesod ha-Yesodot*), is a theological treatise which uses the *Sefer Yeẓirah* extensively. Elhanan was well acquainted with contemporary Christian theological works, both in Latin and French, and included almost literal quotations from such works in his writings. In this he is unique, as far as is known, among the theologians of the Ḥasidei Ashkenaz movement. His writings contain, in addition to his own theology, also compilations and juxtapositions of various ideas taken from other sources and relating to problems he discussed. One such prominent source was the *baraita* attributed to *Joseph b. Uzziel and the writings of the group of Ḥasidei Ashkenaz thinkers who based their doctrines on this pseudepigraphical text. Whole pages of Elhanan's writings are found in the commentary on *Sefer Yeẓirah* attributed to *Saadiah Gaon, which was written by one or several of that group. Elhanan discussed the major problems of Ḥasidei Ashkenaz theology in his writings: the creation, the relationship between the Creator and the Divine power revealed to the prophets, the "Special Cherub" or "Holy Cherub," etc. His theories frequently contain a stronger element of mystical speculation than those found in the writings of the continental Ḥasidei Ashkenaz.

BIBLIOGRAPHY: Scholem, Mysticism, 85; C. Roth, *The Intellectual Activities of Medieval English Jewry* (1949), 62; G. Vajda, *Etudes orientales à la mémoire de P. Hirschler* (1950), 21–27; idem, in: *Archives d'histoire doctrinale et littéraire du Moyen Age*, 28 (1961), 15–34; idem, in: *Kovez al Yad*, 16 (1966), 147–97; Y. Dan, in: *Tarbiz*, 35 (1965/66), 361–73.

[Joseph Dan]

ELḤANANI (Elchanowicz), ABA (1918–), Israel architect and town planner. He was born in Warsaw, studied at the Technion, Haifa, and was in private practice from 1947. Some of his chief buildings are the Philip Murray House and the Workers' Club, Eilat, high schools in Jerusalem and Tel Aviv, a synagogue in Tel Aviv, the Civic Center in Kfar Shmuel, and the President's House, Jerusalem. He prepared large commercial projects for Tel Aviv with Oscar Niemayer, and designed Israel Trade Fairs in several countries, including the U.S. and the U.S.S.R.

ELḤANANI, ARYEH (1898–1985), Israeli architect, painter, and designer. Elḥanani was born in Russia, where he studied art and architecture in Kiev between 1913 and 1917. He immigrated to Ereẓ Israel in 1922 and began his career by designing trade fairs, and later pavilions for trade fairs abroad, designing inter alia the symbol of the Levant Fairs, a flying camel, and the Palmaḥ and IDF logos. In 1934 he sculpted *The Hebrew Worker*, located in Palmer Square, Tel Aviv. In the 1940s he undertook the planning of the buildings of the Weizmann Institute of Science in Reḥovot, and from then continued designing institutes of higher learning and other public institutes such as Bar-Ilan University. Two of his most notable designs are the Yizkor Tent at Yad Vashem in Jerusalem and the Memorial Square at Yad Weizmann in Reḥovot. His designs reflect the spirit of a nation reborn. He was awarded the Israel Prize in 1973. The Elḥanani Prize for combining art and architecture is named after him.

WEBSITE: www.imj.org.il/artcenter.

ELI (Heb. עֵלִי; "[YHWH is] exalted"), a priest in the sanctuary of the Lord at *Shiloh during the period of the Judges (I Sam. 1:9). The father of *Hophni and Phinehas, Eli's ancestry is not recorded in the Bible, but his two sons bear Egyptian names, one of them identical with the name of Aaron's grandson *Phinehas; in addition it appears from I Samuel 2:27ff. that the house of Eli was believed to have been designated by the Lord for priesthood while Israel was still in Egypt. A later speculation traces Eli to *Ithamar son of Aaron (Jos., Ant., 5:361; cf. I Chron. 24:3; Yal., Judges 68), and another connects him with the house of *Eleazar (IV Ezra 1:2–3; cf. Ex. 6:23, 25).

The fact that the *Ark was in Shiloh in Eli's day proves that at that time Shiloh was the cultic center of the tribal confederation of which Eli was the head priest. According to the narrative in the first chapters of I Samuel, *Elkanah made an annual pilgrimage to Shiloh. Here his wife *Hannah made a vow in the presence of Eli and received from him the assurance that her prayer for a son would be answered (I Sam. 1:11ff.). After her son *Samuel was weaned, Hannah brought him to Eli to serve in the sanctuary in fulfillment of her vow (1:27–28). What follows is a two-fold account of the ascent of Samuel and the downfall of the house of Eli. Hophni and Phinehas proved to be corrupt priests (2:12–17, 29; 3:13); hence the prophecy to Eli in I Samuel 2:27–36, which appears to be connected with that to Samuel (3:11–14), concerning the fall of the house of Eli and the emergence of a new priestly house. From these prophecies it appears that Eli himself had also sinned (2:29; 3:13). At any rate, his two sons were destined to die on the same day (2:34; 4:11, 17) and Eli, too, met his death when the news reached him of the tragedy at the battle of *Aphek (4:11–18). Following the death of Eli and his sons and the destruction of Shiloh, *Nob became the religious center. According to I Samuel 22:20–23, the sole survivor of Saul's slaughter of the priests at Nob was Abiathar son of Ahimelech son of Ahitub, a descendant of Eli who was deposed by Solomon (I Sam. 14:3; cf. I Kings 2:27). Clearly, the priestly house of Eli continued in importance for a long time after him.

It should be noted that the prophecies to Eli do not forecast the destruction of Shiloh; nor do they reflect the true status of the house of Eli in later times. In contrast to the promise of perpetual poverty, Abiathar was able to retire to his estate (I Kings 2:26). This indicates that the prophecies derive substantially from the time of Eli and were not adjusted to make them conform to later events.

In the *Aggadah*

When Eli accused Hannah of being drunk (I Sam. 1:13) she countered that his judging her wrongly proved him to be without divine inspiration (Ber. 31b). According to one opinion Eli was justified in his strictures, since a man who regards his neighbor as sinning is obligated to reprove him. But Hannah's retort was also in place, for one who is unjustly accused is obliged to inform his accuser of the fact (*ibid.*), for "a man must justify himself before his fellowmen just as he must do so before God" (*Mishnat R. Eli'ezer*, 129). Because Eli had suspected Hannah unjustly, he blessed her, "Go in peace" since one is obliged to appease and bless one he had wrongly suspected (Ber. 31b). The Bible brands both sons of Eli as wicked (I Sam. 2:12), although Phinehas, in fact, did not sin. The Bible censures him as it does for having failed to protest Hophni's behavior (Shab. 55b).

[Elimelech Epstein Halevy]

BIBLIOGRAPHY: Kaufmann Y., Toledot, 2 (1960), 150ff., 359ff., 370–1; S.R. Driver, *Notes on the Hebrew Text and the Topography of Samuel* (1960²), 1–50; Ginzberg, Legends, 4 (1913), 61f.; 6 (1928), 217, 220–3, 226–7.

ELIACHAR, MENACHE (1901–?), prominent Jerusalem businessman and communal worker. Eliachar, a scion of the distinguished Jerusalem family of that name, was born in the Old City of Jerusalem, the son of Isaac Eliachar, and on the death of his father in 1933 succeeded him as vice president of the Jerusalem Chamber of Commerce, becoming president in 1946, holding the position for more than 30 years. Eliachar played a prominent role in the industrial and commercial development of Jerusalem and represented Israel in the International Chamber of Commerce where he was successful in countering the Arab Boycott.

From an early age he took part in communal activity and was among the founders of the Binyanei ha-Ummah (Jerusalem Convention Center) and of the Economic Club of Jerusalem. He was instrumental in reclaiming thousands of dunams of land in Jerusalem from Arab owners which he placed at the disposal of the community, among them the land on which the Hebrew University and the Israel Museum stand.

On the occasion of his 75th birthday the title of Yakir Yerushalayim was conferred upon him and the school in the Givat Mordechai neighborhood was named in his honor.

ELIAKIM, MARCEL (1921–), physician and medical educator. Eliakim was born in Plovdiv, Bulgaria. He studied in an American high school and graduated from a French high school in Bulgaria in 1943. He then began studies at the University of Sofia Medical School (1944–49). He immigrated to Israel in 1949 and graduated from the Hebrew University–Hadassah Medical School (first class, 1949–52) with distinction. He served in the scientific corps of the Israel Defense Forces from 1952 to 1954, where he was assigned to conduct a research project on Schistosomiasis in Israel.

Eliakim started working in the Department of Medicine of the Hadassah University Hospital under Professor M. Rachmilewitz in 1954, and became full professor of medicine in 1969. He then became head of the Department of Medicine (1969–89). After retirement from Hadassah, Eliakim became head of the Department of Medicine in Bikur Holim Hospital in Jerusalem (1989–97).

During the period 1960–61 Eliakim received a grant from the American army for research in cardiovascular physiology in the Medical School of the University of Pennsylvania. Upon his return to Israel he founded and was the first director of the Institute for Postgraduate Medical Training of the Hebrew University. He also became chairman of the Board of Medicine of the Israel Medical Association in 1973. He served on the committee of higher education of the Ministry of Education (1976–79) and became dean of the Faculty of Medicine (1985–89). Eliakim founded the Israel Association for the Study of the Liver in 1973.

Eliakim published 221 scientific papers and wrote or edited four books. His research was concentrated in the field of Familial Mediterranean Fever, a disease affecting mostly Jews. Eliakim has educated a generation of physicians, many of whom have become leaders in medicine in Israel. Eliakim received many prizes, most important of which was the 75th Hadassah Anniversary prize for outstanding service in medicine (1987). He received the Worthy of Jerusalem award (1988) and the Israel Prize for medicine 2001.

[Rami Eliakim (2nd ed.)]

ELIAKIM GOETZ BEN MEIR (c. 1700), rabbi and author; grandson of R. Judah Loeb *Hanneles. He was rabbi in Swarzedz and Hildesheim. In 1700 he left Germany to travel to Ereẓ Israel, but on passing through Posen, where his father had been rabbi, he was persuaded to accept the rabbinate there, and was active until 1707. Goetz wrote (1) *Rappeduni be-Tappuhim*, a commentary on the 24 aggadic sayings of Rabba bar bar Ḥana (BB 73–74), published posthumously by his son Samvil, *dayyan* of Swarzedz (Berlin, 1712); (2) *Even ha-Shoham*, and *Me'irat Einayim*, a collection of responsa, the first part published by his son Meir (Dyhernfurth, 1733).

BIBLIOGRAPHY: Michael, Or, no. 465.

[Jacob Haberman]

ELIANO, GIOVANNI BATTISTA (1530–1589), apostate and anti-Jewish propagandist. Grandson on his mother's side of Elijah *Levita, whence the surname he adopted, he was formerly known as Solomon Romano. Born in Rome, he traveled widely with his father in the Near East and was converted to Roman Catholicism in Venice in 1551. In the following year he was admitted by Ignatius of Loyola to the newly founded Society of Jesus and thereafter taught Hebrew and Arabic at the Collegio Romano. Together with his elder brother Joseph, converted as Vittorio Eliano, he was largely responsible for the condemnation and burning of the Talmud in Rome in 1553 (see *Talmud, Burning of). Giovanni Battista subsequently returned to the Levant to spread Roman Catholic propaganda among the Copts and Maronites.

BIBLIOGRAPHY: J.C. Sola, in: *Archivum historicum Societatis Iesu*, 4 (1935), 291–321; I. Sonne, *Mi-Paolo ha-Revi'i ad Pius ha-Ḥamishi* (1954), 150–5; *Enciclopedia Cattolica*, 5 (1950), s. v., includes bibliography.

[Cecil Roth]

ELIAS, ELI (1912–2004), U.S. clothing manufacturer, Sephardi community leader. Elias was born in Rochester, N.Y., and studied drafting and machine designs while in high school. In 1929, he moved to New York City and became a plant manager at his uncle's clothing factory. It was the start of a lifelong career in the garment business, both as a manufacturer of women's sportswear and as an industry leader. In 1931, Elias left his uncle's company to become a partner in Maybro Sportswear. He opened his own business, Elias Sportswear, in 1931. By 1946, his Brooklyn plant employed 1,200 workers. Elias shifted ownership of the company to his son Richard in 1979, after being named president and executive director of the New York Skirt and Sportswear Association. At its peak, the Association had almost 300 members and was one of the biggest garment contractor groups in New York City. Elias headed the Association until he retired at the age of 86. By that time, a surge of imports had reduced the membership to 11, and when Elias was asked about the future of the New York apparel industry in the face of increasing competition from abroad, he said he felt like saying *Kaddish*, the Hebrew prayer for the dead. In addition to heading the association, Elias organized the Federation of Apparel Manufacturers and the Garment Center Economic Security Council. For many years, he was a management trustee of many union benefit funds. He was a vice chairman of the board of the Garment Industry Development Corporation and a board member of the Council for American Fashion, the Educational Foundation for the Fashion Institute of Technology, and the High School of Fashion Industries, in New York City. Elias was also a founder of the Sephardic Temple of Cedarhurst, N.Y., and an honorary president of United Sephardim of Brooklyn. He helped launch the Sephardic Home for the Aged in Brooklyn and received the Home's first Humanitarian Award, commemorating more than 55 years of service.

BIBLIOGRAPHY: *New York Times* (Sept. 28, 2004); *Women's Wear Daily* (Sept. 29, 2004).

[Mort Sheinman (2nd ed.)]

ELIAS, JOSEPH (d. 1927), Jewish community worker in Iraq. Elias graduated from the law school of Istanbul, became postmaster in the harbor of Fao (Fa'w), then an official in the judicial service of Basra and Mosul, and finally an advocate in Basra and Baghdad. From 1921 until his death he was chairman of the Arabic Literary Society in Baghdad and of the Zionist organization in Iraq. In 1924 he was elected to the Iraqi Parliament as delegate of the Jewish community of Baghdad, and the following year represented Iraqi Jewry at the opening ceremony of the Hebrew University in Jerusalem.

[Haim J. Cohen]

ELIAS, NEY (1844–1897), British explorer. Ney was born in Kent, the son of a Jewish merchant who converted to Christianity when he was a child. In 1892 he journeyed from Peking (Beijing) across the Gobi Desert by a hitherto unexplored route to St. Petersburg – a feat for which he received the gold medal of the Royal Geographical Society. He then traveled for the Indian government and in 1885 made an expedition through Central Asia. Elias defined the boundaries (1889–90) between what became Thailand and Burma. His books include *A Visit to the Valley of Sheuli* (1876) and *The Tarikh-i-Rashidi* (1895), a history of the Moghuls.

ADD. BIBLIOGRAPHY: ODNB online; G.R. Morgan, *Ney Elias: Explorer and Envoy Extraordinary in High Asia* (1971).

ELIAS, NORBERT (1897–1990), sociologist. Born in Breslau, Germany (now Wroclaw, Poland), Elias served in the German army during World War I, and then attended Breslau University. He was an active member of Blau-Weiss, the Zionist youth organization. After earning his doctorate in philosophy at Breslau in 1924, he moved to Heidelberg to work under Alfred Weber, and then to Frankfurt as Karl Mannheim's assistant. Elias fled Nazi Germany in 1933, first to Paris and then, in 1935, to London. His father died in Breslau in 1940, and his mother perished in Auschwitz around 1941.

In 1939 Elias published his seminal work *Ueber den Prozess der Zivilisation* (later translated into English as *The Civilizing Process*, 1978 and 1982). The work, largely ignored at the time, traced the process of change in standards of behavior – including those regarding acts of violence – through stages of European history, as manners and habits were transformed, in Elias' view, by changing thresholds of repugnance and increasing expectations of self-restraint. Elias linked this process to the formation of states and to the development of an interconnected society.

Elias received a senior research fellowship at the London School of Economics in 1939, but he was interred during the war as an enemy alien. In 1954 he obtained a post at Leicester University, from which he retired in 1962; he was a professor of sociology at the University of Ghana from 1962 to 1964. It was only during his retirement that Elias was acclaimed as a leading figure in his field. *Ueber den Prozess der Zivilisation* was republished in 1969, receiving international attention. The work was not, however, received without controversy; some considered it an extension of social Darwinism, overly Eurocentric, and suggested that its premise was refuted by the events of World War II and the Holocaust.

Elias wrote extensively in his later years; these works include *The Established and the Outsiders* (1965), *What Is Sociology?* (1978), *The Loneliness of the Dying* (1985), and *The Quest for Excitement* (1986), with Eric Dunning, on the sociology of sports. In 1971 he became professor emeritus of the University of Frankfurt, and in 1977 the city of Frankfurt named him the first recipient of the Theodor W. Adorno prize. In addition to other honors, he received the German Grosskreuz des Bundesdienstordens in 1986.

BIBLIOGRAPHY: R. van Krieken, *Norbert Elias: Key Sociologist* (1998).

[Dorothy Bauhoff (2nd ed.)]

ELIASBERG, MORDECAI (1817–1889), rabbi, one of the first *Ḥibat Zion (Ḥovevei Zion) in Russia. Born in Lithuania, Eliasberg studied under noted rabbis in Lithuania, became rabbi of Shishmory, Lithuania in 1853, and was rabbi of *Bauska, Latvia from 1862 until his death. Active from his youth in Jewish public life in Russia, he explained to Max *Lilienthal, who came to "enlighten" Russian Jewry, that the removal of legal restrictions on Jews was a prior condition to the achievement of this aim. Later he believed the basic principles behind Jewish demands should be the improvement of the economic situation of Russian Jewry and the achievement of equal rights. He supported the Haskalah movement, provided it did not weaken religion, and suggested the establishment of schools for commercial and vocational training. Eliasberg defended the first society for the settlement of Ereẓ Israel, founded in Germany in 1862, against attacks by ultra-Orthodox circles, who feared that messianic redemption would be delayed if the land was settled by secular efforts, and in 1879 he published articles supporting Jewish agricultural settlement in Russia and in Ereẓ Israel. After the pogroms in southern Russia (1881), Eliasberg was one of the first who vigorously supported the newly organized Ḥovevei Zion, orally and in writing, striving particularly to achieve harmony between the religious and the "free-thinking" circles in the movement. He was elected one of the leaders of Ḥovevei Zion at the movement's conference at Druzgenik (1887). During the controversy over the 1889 sabbatical year in Ereẓ Israel, Eliasberg opposed those ultra-Orthodox rabbis who demanded the cessation of Jewish agricultural work in that year and appealed to Jewish farmers not to heed their injunctions. He also strongly attacked the *ḥalukkah* methods in Jerusalem and those responsible for it, most of whom opposed the new settlement of Ereẓ Israel.

Of his more than 20 works, only one, *Terumat Yad* (1875), was printed in his lifetime. *Shevil ha-Zahav*, dealing with topical matters and the settlement of Ereẓ Israel, was published posthumously (1897) by his son Jonathan, who added a biography of his father. In 1947 a selection of Eliasberg's writings was published in Jerusalem.

[Getzel Kressel]

His son JONATHAN (1851–1898) was born in Kovno, Lithuania, and served as rabbi of Pumpian, Mariampol, and from 1886 until his death, of Volkovysk, Grodno district. His Torah novellae and ethical writings were published as a supplement to his father's *Terumat Yad* and his *Darkhei Hora'ah* was published independently (1884). In common with his father, he was one of the first rabbis to join the Ḥovevei Zion movement. Eliasberg strove to maintain harmony between the Orthodox and the progressive groups within the national movement, calling upon both sides "to be tolerant and patient with conflicting views." In 1893 he approached *Aḥad Ha-Am in connection with his essay "*Torah she-ba-Lev*," which had aroused the anger of the Orthodox. (The author replied to the charges in his essay "*Divrei Shalom.*") His Zionist articles were published in *Shivat Ẓiyyon* (ed. by A.J. Slutski, 1900). After the first Zionist Congress, he joined the Zionist Organization.

[Yehuda Slutsky]

BIBLIOGRAPHY: N. Sokolow, *Hibbath Zion* (Eng., 1935), index; A.M. Genachowski, *Ha-Rav Mordekhai Eliasberg* (1937); I. Klausner, *Be-Hitorer Am* (1962), index; idem, *Mi-Kattoviz ad Basel*, 2 vols. (1965), indexes; EZD, 1 (1958), 111–21; M. Einhorn (ed.), *Volkovisker Yizkor-Buch* (1949), 71f.; Rabiner, in: *Ba-Mishor*, 4 (1942/43), nos. 136–7; I. Nissenbaum, *Ha-Dat ve-ha-Teḥiyyah ha-Le'ummit* (1920), 81–91.

ELIASHIB (Heb. אֶלְיָשִׁיב; "may God restore"), a name attested in the Arad letters of the late seventh–early sixth century B.C.E. The Bible shows the popularity of the name in post-Exilic times, borne by three individuals married to foreign women (Ezra 10:24, 27, 36), a descendant of the Davidic dynasty (1 Chron. 3:24), and of the high priest who was the son of Joiakim (Neh. 12:10). The best known of these personalities was the high priest contemporary with Nehemiah. His house was located along the central portion of the eastern wall of Jerusalem and is mentioned in the account of the wall's reconstruction (Neh. 3:20–21). He and his colleagues were responsible for rebuilding the stretch of wall guarding the northwestern approach to the Temple Mount – the Tower of Hananel, the Tower of the Hundred, and the Sheep Gate (Neh. 3:1). An Eliashib "the priest" was in charge of the Temple storehouses and he assigned one of these chambers to Nehemiah's opponent Tobiah. This priest was somehow "related" to Tobiah (Neh. 13:4ff.), and many scholars identify him with the high priest; the lesser title, however, makes this unlikely. It is similarly unlikely that Eliashib, the father of Jehohanan, into whose Temple chamber Ezra retreated (Ezra 10:6), is identical with the high priest. A grandson of the high priest, however, did marry a daughter of Sanballat, another of Nehemiah's opponents (Neh. 13:28). During the second term of his governorship, Nehemiah expelled Tobiah from his Temple chamber and chased the high priest away from his presence.

BIBLIOGRAPHY: J.M. Myers, *Ezra and Nehemiah* (AB; 1965), 113ff., 197ff., 214ff. ADD. BIBLIOGRAPHY: A. Rainey, in: BAR, 13:2 (1987), 36–39; K. Koch, in: M. Fishbane and E. Tov (eds.), *Sha'arei Talmon* (1992), 105–10; A. Demsky, in: HUCA, 65 (1994), 1–19; M. Goulder, in: JSOT, 75 (1997), 43–58.

[Bezalel Porten]

ELIASHOV, SOLOMON BEN ḤAYYIM (1841–1926), kabbalist. Eliashov, who was born in Zagara, Lithuania, studied in the yeshivah in Telz, but spent most of his life as a private citizen in Shavli in Samogitia, Lithuania and never took a rabbinic position. In 1915 he was expelled with the rest of his community to Russia and in 1922 (or 1924) he settled in Jerusalem. Eliashov was considered one of the greatest kabbalists in Russia at the end of the 19th century. His method was influenced by the tradition of *Elijah b. Solomon, the Gaon of Vilna, and his disciples, and he generally opposed those who interpreted Kabbalah in an idealistic manner, particularly the kabbalistic commentaries of Moses Ḥayyim *Luzzatto and the Chabad Ḥasidim. All his works on Kabbalah, which he rewrote in several versions, were compiled at the end of the 19th century under the general title *Sefer Leshem Shevo ve-Aḥlamah* (Ex. 28:19). They include the following published works: *Sefer Hakdamot u-She'arim* (Piotrkow, 1908); *Sefer ha-De'ah* (an abbreviation for *Derushei Olam ha-Tohu*) in two volumes (Piotrkow, 1911); *Sefer ha-Kelalim*, on the principles of *egressus* and *digressus* in the process of emanation, two volumes (Jerusalem, 1924–26, but actually completed only in 1930); *Sefer Ḥelkei ha-Be'urim*, a commentary on Ḥayyim *Vital's *Ez Ḥayyim* in two volumes (Jerusalem, 1935–49). His glosses and additions to *Ez Ḥayyim* were also published in the Warsaw 1890 edition of that work. The works of Eliashov contain a highly detailed systematic description of the Lurianic Kabbalah concerning the doctrine of *azilut* ("emanation"). It was said that Eliashov accomplished for the works of Isaac *Luria what Moses *Cordovero had done for the *Zohar.

BIBLIOGRAPHY: A. Levin, *Toledot ha-Ga'on ha-Kadosh, Meḥabber Sifrei Leshem Shevo ve-Aḥlamah* (1935).

[Gershom Scholem]

ELIAS LE EVESKE (**Elijah ben Berechiah ha-Kohen;** before 1200–after 1259), archpresbyter of English Jewry (1243–57). Born in London before 1200, Elias Le Eveske (or l'Eveske, as he was often known) was a prominent figure in the London Jewish community by 1230. His period of office coincided with the most outrageous of the royal exactions by Henry III. In 1253 he appeared before Earl Richard of Cornwall and the Royal Council and made a pathetic appeal for permission for the Jews to leave the country. He was deposed from office in 1257 and two years later became converted to Christianity, together with his two sons. His subsequent life is unknown.

BIBLIOGRAPHY: H.P. Stokes, *Studies in Anglo-Jewish History* (1913), 12–17, 30–33; Rigg-Jenkinson, Exchequer, passim; Roth, England, index; JHSEM, 2 (1935), index. ADD. BIBLIOGRAPHY: ODNB online; J. Hillaby, "London: The Thirteenth Century Jewry Revisited," in: JHSET, 32 (1990–92), 89–158.

[Cecil Roth]

ELIASSOF, HERMAN (1849–1918), U.S. Reform rabbi. Eliassof was born in Russia, ordained in Germany, and immigrated to the United States in 1871. After serving for a year as rabbi of Congregation Rodef Shalom in Ogdensburg, N.Y., he became the first rabbi of Temple Beth-El in Chicago, where he was also editor of *The Occident*, a local religious weekly, as well as the regional correspondent for the **American Israelite*, the Anglo-Jewish weekly newspaper published in Cincinnati. For many years he served as principal of the Sabbath school of Kehillath Anshe Maarab and was a teacher in the Zion Congregation religious school. In the early 1890s, Eliassof was head of the Society in Aid of Russian Refugees, which assisted the many Jews who came to Chicago in the wake of the enforcement of the Russian *May Laws. Eliassof was the first scholar to write a history of the Jews of Illinois, which was published in a special issue of *The Reform Advocate*. He also wrote Hebrew poetry and was a frequent contributor on Jewish subjects to English, German, and Hebrew periodicals.

BIBLIOGRAPHY: *The Universal Jewish Encyclopedia* (1969).

[Bezalel Gordon (2nd ed.)]

ELIAV, ARIE LOVA (1921–), Israeli planner, educator, sociologist, politician, and peace activist, member of the Sixth to Ninth and Twelfth Knessets. Eliav was born in Moscow and was brought by his parents to Palestine in 1924. He studied at the Herzlia Gymnasium in Tel Aviv and general history and sociology at the Hebrew University in Jerusalem. He joined the Haganah in 1936 and in the years 1941–45 fought in the British army in the Middle East and Europe. In 1946–48 he was active in the organization of "illegal"*immigration to Palestine. After the establishment of the state he joined the IDF and participated in the War of Independence, reaching the rank of lieutenant colonel. In 1949–53 he served as assistant to the director of the Jewish Agency Settlement Department, and studied agricultural economics in London in 1953. In 1955–57 Eliav directed the project for the development of the Lachish region in southern Israel, where many new immigrants were settled; he participated in the planning and establishment of the town of Arad. During the Sinai Campaign in 1956 he was in charge of the project for saving the Jews of Port Said.

In 1958–60, Eliav served as first secretary in the Israeli Embassy in Moscow. In 1960–64 he headed the aid and rehabilitation mission that Israel sent to Qazvin in northwestern Iran after it had been severely hit by an earthquake. Eliav was first elected to the Sixth Knesset in 1965 on the Alignment list. In 1966–67 he served as deputy minister of industry and trade in charge of industrialization in development areas, and the following two years as deputy minister of immigration absorption under Yigal *Allon. In 1969–71 Eliav served as secretary general of the *Israel Labor Party. In this period he started to adopt dovish positions regarding the concessions that Israel might make in return for peace with its neighbors. After resigning the secretary generalship of the Labor Party, he spent the next year writing an ideological work entitled *Ereẓ ha-Ẓevi* (one of the biblical names for the Land of Israel) in which an entire chapter was devoted to a discussion of Israel's relations with the Arabs and Palestinians. It appeared in English in 1974 as *Land of the Hart.*

Following the earthquake that occurred in Managua in Nicaragua just before Christmas of 1972 Eliav headed an Israeli aid mission to help construct temporary housing there. In December 1973 he ran in the elections to the Eighth Knesset on the Alignment list, but in April 1975 left the Alignment and joined the Civil Rights Movement, forming a parliamentary group by the name of Ya'ad. In 1975 he was also one of the founders of the Israeli Council for Israeli-Palestinian Peace. In January 1976 he and MK Marsha Freedman left Ya'ad, due to a dispute about policy toward the PLO and formed the Social Democratic parliamentary faction. In 1976–77 Eliav participated in talks with representatives of the PLO.

Eliav was one of the founders of the radical party Maḥaneh Sheli, and in 1977 was elected to the Ninth Knesset on its list. In 1979 he handed his seat over to Uri *Avneri and engaged in teaching new immigrants and prisoners. In 1982–85 he participated, on behalf of Prime Minister Menaḥem *Begin, in contacts with the PLO and other Palestinian organizations in an attempt to bring about the release of four Israeli prisoners held by them in return for over 1,000 Palestinian prisoners.

In 1982 Eliav joined the International Center for Peace in the Middle East. In the elections to the Twelfth Knesset in 1988 he returned to the Knesset on the Alignment list. In 1993 he unsuccessfully ran against Ezer *Weizman for the Labor Party nomination for the presidency of Israel.

[Susan Hattis Rolef (2nd ed.)]

ELIAV (Lubotzky), BINYAMIN (1909–1974), Israeli public figure and editor. Born in Riga, Latvia, he finished his secondary education in Haifa. Returning to Europe for his higher studies, he soon became one of the outstanding figures in the Betar movement, led by Vladimir Jabotinsky, whose personality profoundly influenced him. From 1932 to 1935, he lived in Paris where he served as general secretary of Betar. In 1935 he returned to Palestine, where his political activities against the policies of the British Mandatory government earned him repeated terms of imprisonment, principally in the Acre Prison. In between, he edited the movement's newspapers *Hamashkif* and *Hayarden.*

In 1938 he was released from Acre due to ill health, on condition that he leave the country until the termination of martial law, and was in Riga until 1940. After his return he championed the cause of conciliation between the Revisionist movement and the Zionist Organization. A tentative agreement that was to be the basis of the reconciliation was vetoed by Ben-Gurion.

Eliav left Betar and formed his own political party, Tenuat Ha'am, and edited its daily newspaper, *Mivrak.* This small party attracted a wide variety of supporters. In June 1947 Eliav was again arrested, and placed in a detention camp in Latrun together with other leading figures of the *yishuv.*

After the establishment of the State of Israel he underwent a certain metamorphosis. He disbanded his party and never again played an active political role. He worked as a journalist, editor, and translator (editing the Labor Party's afternoon daily *Ha-Dor,* and translating Isaac Deutscher's biography of Stalin). From 1953 he was in the Israel Foreign Ministry, serving in South America and later as consul-general in New York.

Gradually he devoted himself exclusively to the cause of Soviet Jewry, which in the mid- to late-1950s, was a tabula rasa. To Eliav the fate of this last great Jewish community to survive in Europe was crucial to the future of the Jewish people. At the same time, he saw it as a universal human problem of minority rights.

For the next 12 years he traveled all over the world and established a veritable network of influential connections. He won the support of outstanding personalities such as Bertrand Russell, Jean-Paul Sartre, Aya de la Torre of Peru, and Senator Terracini of Italy.

After retiring from the Foreign Ministry, he served for a while as Prime Minister Eshkol's adviser on information and as acting chairman of the Broadcasting Corporation. From

1969 Eliav worked on the *Encyclopaedia Judaica*, of which he was associate editor with particular responsibility for the section dealing with Israel, Zionism, and contemporary Jewish history. *Sifriat Keter*, a series of original monographs in Hebrew on various aspects of Jewish culture and history, was launched by him, and he edited its first volumes.

[Aryeh Eliav (2nd ed.)]

ELIEL, ERNEST LUDWIG (1921–), U.S. organic chemist. Eliel was born in Germany and received his Ph.D. from the University of Illinois in 1948. He was at the University of Notre Dame in 1948–72 (professor from 1960) and W.R. Kenan, Jr. Professor at the University of North Carolina at Chapel Hill in 1972–93. He was a member of the National Academy of Sciences, U.S., and the American Academy of Arts and Sciences. He wrote *Stereochemistry of Carbon Compounds* (1962) and was co-author of *Conformational Analysis* (1965), *Elements of Stereochemistry* (1969), *Stereochemistry of Organic Compounds* (1994), and *Basic Organic Stereochemistry* (2001). He published over 300 original publications and reviews in stereochemistry, conformational analysis, synthetic methodology, physical organic chemistry, and NMR. He received the Priestley Medal (Am. Chem. Soc.) in 1996 and many other awards and was president of the American Chemical Society, 1992.

[Bracha Rager (2nd ed.)]

ELIEZER (Heb. אֱלִיעֶזֶר; "God is help"), the steward of *Abraham's household (Gen. 15:2).

In the Bible

Eliezer's name appears in the text immediately following the word "Dammesek." While English "Tokyo Rose" is syntactically unobjectionable, "Damascus Eliezer" is foreign to Hebrew. Ginsberg (in bibliography) suggests accordingly that *dammeseq eliezer* is a phantom resulting from scribal corruption. Alternatively, "Dammesek Eliezer" is simply the name of the steward, composed of two words. According to the story, Abraham complained to God that material reward would be of little use to him since, because he had no offspring, his servant Eliezer was to be his heir. God replied with the promise of a natural heir (Gen. 15:4ff.). This episode is made clear in light of the Nuzi archives, which frequently mention the filial adoption of a stranger, sometimes a slave, by a childless couple to tend them in old age and perform their funeral rites in return for being their heir. Sometimes, complications might arise where a natural son would be born after the adoption, as in the case of Eliezer. The Nuzi contracts, however, carefully set out the rights and obligations of both parties in such eventualities.

In the *Aggadah*

Although nowhere so mentioned specifically in the narrative, Eliezer is identified by the rabbis with the anonymous servant sent by Abraham to find a wife for Isaac (Gen. 24). He is thus made the prototype of the loyal and selfless servant, fulfilling his master's wish even to his own disadvantage. He had a daughter whom he hoped Isaac would marry, and the failure of his mission would have made this possible (Gen. R. 59:9). He is credited with having acquired all the virtues and learning of his master. His name, "Eliezer of Damascus" is interpreted as meaning that he drew from and provided others with his master's teachings (*Dammesek = doleh u-mashkeh*; Yoma 28b). He even resembled Abraham in his physical appearance, and Laban mistook him for his master (Gen. R. 60:7). Raised in Nimrod's court, Eliezer was presented to Abraham after his miraculous deliverance from the fiery furnace (*Sefer ha-Yashar*, Noah 42). Eliezer alone went with Abraham to rescue Lot, the *gematria* of his name being 318, the number of Abraham's servants given in the Bible as constituting his army (Gen. 14:14; Tanh. B., Gen. 73). Later, Eliezer visited Sodom where he was victim of the injustices practiced in that city (Sanh. 109b; see also *Sodom in the *Aggadah*). Despite his admirable qualities, Eliezer still remained a member of the cursed Canaanite nation. He is identified as one of the two lads who accompanied Abraham and Isaac to the **akedah* (Lev. R. 26:7), and who remained at the foot of Mount Moriah because they could not see the vision which was vouchsafed to Abraham and Isaac (Gen. R. 56:2). Eliezer was wrongly suspected of having defiled Rebekah during their journey from Haran (PdRE 16).

As a reward for successfully discharging his mission, he was emancipated by Abraham and given the kingdom of Bashan, over which he reigned under the name of Og (PdRE 16). The curse resting upon Eliezer, as upon all descendants of Canaan, was transformed into a blessing because of his loyal service to Abraham (Gen. R. 60:7). His greatest recompense was that God found him worthy of entering Paradise alive, a distinction accorded to very few (DEZ 1).

There are nine other biblical personages of the same name: (1) Moses' younger son (Ex. 18:4; I Chron. 23:15, 17; 26:25); (2)–(9) see I Chron. 7:8; 15:24; 27:16; II Chron. 20; 37; Ezra 8:16; 10:18, 23, 31.

BIBLIOGRAPHY: IN THE BIBLE: W.F. Albright, *Yahweh and the Gods of Canaan* (1970), 57–58 and note 30; L. Feigin, in: JBL, 50 (1931), 186–200; E.M. Cassin (ed.), *L'Adoption a Nuzi* (1938); M.D. Cassuto, in: EM, 2 (1954), 675–6; O. Eissfeldt, in: JSS, 5 (1960), 48–9; W.F. Albright, in: BASOR, 163 (1961), 47 and n. 54; E.A. Speiser, *Genesis* (1954), 111–2; N.M. Sarna, *Genesis* (1989), 382–83. IN THE AGGADAH: Ginzberg, Legends, index; L.I. Rabinowitz, in: JQR, 58 (1967/68), 143–61. **ADD. BIBLIOGRAPHY:** H.L. Ginsberg, in: BASOR, 200 (Albright Anniversary; 1970), 31–2.

ELIEZER BEN HYRCANUS (end of the first and beginning of the second century C.E.), *tanna*. He is sometimes called Eliezer the Great (Sot. 9:15; Tosef., Or., end) and is the Eliezer mentioned without patronymic. R. Eliezer was one of the pillars of the early talmudic tradition, and through his student R. Akiva (and Akiva's circle of disciples) he had a decisive influence on the evolution of *halakhah* during the tannaitic period and beyond. In the eyes of later talmudic tradition, the period of the *tannaim* was a heroic age, and even the slightest scrap of information about the least of the *tannaim* can develop in the later *aggadah* into a tale of epic proportions. In the case of truly heroic and significant personalities, like R. Eliezer – who was already the subject of many colorful stories in the tannaitic literature itself – this process of literary expansion and elaboration is inevitable. R. Eliezer even became the subject of an early medieval midrashic romance (**Pirkei de-Rabbi Eliezer*), while the talmudic story of his death was retold in the Zohar (1:98a), providing the literary prototype for the Zoharic masterpiece, the *Idra Zuta*. R. Eliezer remained the object of admiration and the subject of an ongoing and developing narrative tradition for over 1,000 years. As a result it is not always easy to distinguish between the earlier and more fundamental forms of the traditions relating to this historical figure, and those which reflect a later more romanticized and "fictionalized" form of these traditions. In fact it would be fair to say that up to and through the 1970s scholars rarely even made any attempt to distinguish between these different literary and historical levels. Only after Jacob Neusner's revolutionary studies of the life and legend of Rabban Joḥanan ben Zakkai did scholars begin to pay serious attention, not only to the legend, but also to the history of the legend. Below, we will first bring in outline the "legend" of R. Eliezer, as summarized by one of the finest scholars of the last generation, and then make a few brief comments about the "history of the legend."

Education

Eliezer's youth is enveloped in legend. It is said that until the age of 22 (or 28) he worked the estates of his wealthy father, but on deciding to study he left home, making his way to the school of *Johanan b. Zakkai in Jerusalem. There he studied diligently in poverty and want until he became one of the outstanding students of the academy. Some time later his father came to Jerusalem to take a vow to deprive him of his inheritance. When he entered the *bet midrash*, however, and found his son sitting at the head, with all the great scholars of Jerusalem facing him, expounding the Torah and "transcending what was said to Moses at Sinai, his countenance as luminous as the light of the sun, and beams emanating from him as the rays from Moses," Hyrcanus changed his mind and instead wished to bequeath the whole of his fortune to Eliezer, who, however, refused to accept more than his brothers (ARN[1] 6, 31; ARN[2] 13, 32; PdRE 1; 2, and parallels). According to another tradition, he was outstanding already in his youth. It was realized that he was destined to achieve great things, and the verse (Prov. 20:11), "Even a child is known by his doings," was applied to him (Gen. R. 1:11, and parallels). Johanan b. Zakkai had a very high opinion of his pupil and said of him, "If all the sages of Israel were in one scale of the balance and Eliezer b. Hyrcanus in the other, he would outweigh them all" (Avot 2:8). He also praised his phenomenal memory, calling him "a cemented cistern that does not lose a drop" and "a pitched vessel that preserves its wine" (ARN[1] 14, 58), a reference also to his intense conservatism. Eliezer followed the example of his teacher both in his method of study and his behavior. He never walked four cubits without studying and without *tefillin*; no one ever found him sitting in silence, but only sitting and learning; he never said anything that he had not heard from his teacher (Suk. 28a). During the Roman War Eliezer was closely attached to his teacher. He and his colleague, *Joshua b. Hananiah, bore Johanan in a coffin outside the walls of Jerusalem during the siege for his meeting with Vespasian (Git. 56a).

After the destruction of the Temple he was numbered among the important scholars of the great *bet din* of *Jabneh (Sanh. 17b). He also played an important part in national affairs. He was a member of a delegation to Rome headed by the *nasi* to obtain concessions for the Jews (TJ, Sanh. 7:16, 25d, et al.); and traveled to Antioch on behalf of the scholars (*ibid.*, Hor. 3:7, 48a). He married into the family of the *nasi*; his wife, *Imma Shalom, was the sister of Rabban *Gamaliel. His permanent home was in Lydda, where he established an academy. Among his outstanding pupils were *Akiva, *Ilai, *Yose b. Dormaskos, Abba Hanan, and *Aquila the proselyte. His *bet midrash* was well-known, and the verse "Justice, justice shalt thou follow" (Deut. 16:20) was applied to it: "Follow an eminent *bet din*, follow the *bet din* of Johanan b. Zakkai and the *bet din* of Eliezer [in Lydda]" (Sif. Deut. 144; cf. Sanh. 32b).

Halakhic Method and Relation to his Colleagues

In his halakhic method Eliezer is distinguished by his great attachment to early traditions and ancient *halakhot*. This tie with early *halakhah* brought him into conflict with the trends operating in the council of Jabneh to adjust the *halakhah* in the light of the changes that took place with the destruction of the Temple, and to crystallize the religious tradition into a fixed and uniform system. In his disputes with *Joshua and his associates, different attitudes to the *halakhah* found expression. Thus Eliezer endeavored to limit the use of hermeneutical rules as a basis for deriving new *halakhot*, regarding the tradition and doctrine which had been handed down as the foundation and essence of the *halakhah* (Neg. 9:3; Tosef., TY 1:8 and 10; et al.). He regarded the act as the determinant of a person's obligations and punishments, in contrast to his associates who regarded intent and purpose as the deciding factor (Ker. 4:3; Tosef., TY 2:13f.; et al.). Even the tendency to stringency which he reveals in a considerable number of his *halakhot* was grounded in the early *halakhah*, which was based on the doctrine of *Bet Shammai, as a result of which he was called "*Shammuti*" ("follower of Shammai"; Shab. 130b; TJ, Beẓah 1:4, 60c; et al.). He was very determined and unforebearing (Ta'an. 25b). The drawn-out struggle between him and the *nasi* and scholars of the Sanhedrin ended tragically. The Talmud relates that during a discussion on the ritual purity of the "oven of Akhnai" (an oven made by Akhnai) in the college, Eliezer brought every conceivable argument in favor of his view but they were rejected by his colleagues. "He said to them: 'If the *halakhah* agrees with me, let this carob tree prove it,' whereupon the carob tree was torn a hundred cubits out of its place… He then said to them: 'If the *halakhah* agrees with me, let it be proved from heaven,' whereupon a *bat kol cried out: 'Why do you dispute with Eliezer, seeing that in all matters the *halakhah* agrees with him?' R. Joshua arose and said, 'It [i.e., halakhic decision] is not in heaven' [Deut. 30:12], we pay no attention to a *bat kol*, for it is written in the Torah at Mount Sinai: One must follow the majority' [Ex. 23:2]" (BM 59b). The *aggadah* continues that on that day all objects which Eliezer had declared ritually pure were brought and burned. A vote was then taken and they excommunicated him.

This severe step affected Eliezer's status and undermined his influence in *halakhah*. He was removed from the council, his associates and pupils held aloof from him, and even refrained from quoting his *halakhot* in the assembly of the scholars (Nid. 7b; Sif. Deut. 188). Of his violent reaction it is reported: "Great was the anger on that day, for everything at which he cast his eyes was burned. Rabban Gamaliel, too, was traveling in a ship when a huge wave arose to drown him. 'It appears to me,' he reflected, 'that this is on account of none other than Eliezer b. Hyrcanus.' He arose and said: 'Lord of the Universe! Thou knowest full well that I have acted neither for my honor nor for the honor of my father's house, but for Thine, so that strife may not multiply in Israel'" (BM 59b). Rabban Gamaliel excused his action on the grounds that excommunication was designed to establish unity in the sphere of *halakhah* and to establish the authority of the council as a determining and decisive institution in a fateful period in the life of the nation.

Attitudes toward the Jewish and Pagan Worlds

Eliezer's love for Israel and his country and his hatred of pagans knew no bounds. During the Roman War he was near in spirit to the *Zealots. He considered weapons to be an adornment, permitting them to be worn on the Sabbath in public (Shab. 6:4). He forbade chapter 16 of Ezekiel to be read as *haftarah*, and sharply censured anyone who transgressed this, because it included matters that offend the honor and ancestry of the Jews (Meg. 4:10, 25b). His adverse opinion of heathens is expressed in his saying: "All the charity and kindness done by the heathen is counted to them as sin, because they only do it to magnify themselves" (BB 10b). This adverse attitude served as the basis for several of his *halakhot*, such as his disqualification of sacrifice from heathens (Par. 2:1; Av. Zar. 23a), and he endeavored as far as possible to lessen social contact between them and Jews (Ḥul. 2:7; Git. 45b). This, too, is the cause of his reservations about accepting proselytes (Yev. 48b; BM 59b).

The Tosefta relates that Eliezer was once arrested by the government for uttering heretical opinions. Though he was liberated and exempted from punishment, he was greatly distressed that he had been wrongly suspected. Akiva, in an attempt to comfort him, said to him: "Perhaps you heard a heretical opinion and it appealed to you." Eliezer remembered that in Sepphoris he had heard a *halakhah* from Jacob of Kefar Sekhania in the name of Jesus b. Pandira, which had appealed to him, thus transgressing (Prov. 5:8), "Remove thy way from her," i.e., from heresy. This may be reflected in his statement: "Keep away not only from ugly deeds but from what appear such" (Tosef., Ḥul. 2:24; Av. Zar. 16b). His bitter experience is reflected in his saying: "Let the honor of thy friend be as dear to thee as thine own; and be not easily provoked to anger; and repent one day before thy death; and warm thyself before the fire of the wise, but beware of their glowing coals that thou be not singed, for their bite is the bite of a fox, and their sting is the sting of a scorpion, and their hiss is the hiss of a serpent, and all their words are like coals of fire" (Avot 2:10).

Attitude toward his Colleagues in his Last Days

When Joshua, Eleazar b. Azariah, and Akiva came to visit him in his last illness, he expressed his severe indictment of the scholars for their withdrawal from him: "I shall be surprised if these [the scholars of the generation] die a natural death," he exclaimed bitterly; and in explanation he said, "Because they did not come to study under me." Eliezer then lifted both arms, placed them upon his breast, and said: "Woe for my two arms, that are like two scrolls of the Law and that are about to depart from the world. For were all the seas ink, and all the reeds quills, and all the people scribes they would not suffice to write all the Scripture and Mishnah I learned, and all the practice I was taught at the yeshivah ... and my pupils have taken no more than the paint brush takes from the palette" (ARN[1] 25, 80f.; Sanh. 68a).

Attitude toward Eliezer after his Death

The attitude of the scholars to Eliezer changed only after his death. "When his soul departed in purity, Joshua arose and said: 'The vow is annulled! The vow is annulled!' and he clung to him and kissed him and wept, saying, 'Rabbi! Rabbi!'" (*ibid.*; TJ, Shab. 2:6, 5b). "Akiva rent his clothes and tore his hair until blood flowed and he fell to the ground and cried out: 'Woe is me for thee, Rabbi! Woe is me for thee, Rabbi! For thou hast left the whole generation orphaned. My father! My father! the chariots of Israel and the horsemen thereof [II Kings 2:12]. I have many coins to change, but no one to accept them'" (*ibid.*). Everyone realized: "With the death of Eliezer, the scroll of the Law was hidden away" (Sot. 49b). His *halakhot* were restored to the *bet midrash*, many being cited in his name in the Mishnah and *beraitot*. When scholars wished to refute his words, Joshua said "You should not seek to refute the lion after he is dead" (Git. 83a). The *halakhah* was also decided in accordance with his views in a number of instances (e.g., Nid. 7b). Eliezer left a son Hyrcanus who, according to tradition, did not wish to occupy himself with study, whereupon Eliezer consecrated his property to heaven in order to compel him to occupy himself with Torah. The scholars later absolved him from his vow (She'iltot, Ex. 40; cf. Shab. 127b). The *Pirkei de-Rabbi Eliezer*, as well as several other minor Midrashim, are ascribed to his authorship.

[Yitzhak Dov Gilat]

Toward a History of the Legend

When approaching the history of the legends surrounding a figure like R. Eliezer, it is virtually impossible to provide a simple, synthetic overview of his life, like that presented above. Each tradition has a history of its own, often beginning with some early traditional element related in tannaitic sources, and sometimes lacking any early literary foundation whatsoever. For example, in describing R. Eliezer's early life, it is natural to begin with the most detailed and colorful versions of the story – ARN[1] 6, 31; ARN[2] 13, 32; PdRE 1; 2. But all these sources are post-talmudic, and reflect a highly romanticized version of events. Similarly in the case of the story of the "oven of Akhnai," it is tempting to begin with the "complete" version of events – including a full description of R. Eliezer's excommunication – as laid out in Babylonian Talmud BM 59b, and to set aside the fragments of information found in tannaitic sources, or the merely "partial" description found in the earlier Jerusalem Talmud. Yet what do the early sources have to tell us? Mishnah *Kelim* 5:10 reports a simple and unexceptional dispute between R. Eliezer and the Sages, over a certain kind of oven, called the "oven of Akhnai," which R. Eliezer considered pure (i.e., not susceptible to ritual impurity), while the Sages held that it was impure (i.e., susceptible to ritual impurity). In Mishnah *Eduyyot* 7:7, however, this tradition is transmitted in a somewhat different form: "They testified that an oven [of this sort] was impure, since R. Eliezer held that it was pure." From this source it sounds as if R. Eliezer's opinion about this oven had been the subject of a special debate, in which his view was dismissed as invalid. The Tosefta of *Eduyyot* (2:1) restates the more neutral formulation of Mishnah *Kelim*, but adds at the end: "and it was called the oven of Akhnai, about which there were many disputes in Israel." From this it might seem that the dispute over the oven of Akhnai did not end with the attempt of the Sages to suppress R. Eliezer's position, but rather resulted in further and more serious disputes and confrontations. The next stage in the development of this tradition is found in the Jerusalem Talmud (MK 3:1, 81d). After quoting Mishnah *Kelim*, it transmits the following description in the name of R. Jeremiah – a fourth generation Palestinian amora: "A great tribulation occurred on that day. Wherever R. Eliezer looked was stricken. Not only that, but even a single stalk of wheat was half stricken and remained half healthy, and the walls of the meeting hall began to weaken. R. Joshua said to them: 'If friends are having an altercation what concern is it of yours?' Then a heavenly voice declared: 'The *halakhah* is according to R. Eliezer, my son.' R. Joshua replied: 'It is not in heaven.'" R. Jeremiah's description contains nothing about any excommunication, and in fact this Palestinian tradition contains little more than a colorful elaboration of what could be gleaned from the tannaitic sources themselves. On the other hand, immediately prior to this discussion of Mishnah *Kelim*, the Jerusalem Talmud (MK 81c) brings two anonymous traditions beginning with the words "They attempted to excommunicate R. Meir," and "They attempted to excommunicate R. Eliezer." In the first case R. Meir objected, and it would seem that the excommunication was not put into effect. In the second case also, after R. Akiva went to inform R. Eliezer that his "friends" had excommunicated him, R. Eliezer objected, as the Jerusalem Talmud relates: "He took him and went outside, and said 'Carob, Carob! If the *halakhah* is as they say, uproot yourself!' But it did not uproot itself. 'If the *halakhah* is as I say, uproot yourself!' and it did uproot itself. 'If the *halakhah* is as they say, return!' But it did not return. 'If the *halakhah* is as I say, return!' and it did return." Here also there is no sign that the proposed excommunication was put into effect. But when all of these anonymous and attributed Palestinian amoraic traditions are brought in Babylonian Talmud BM 59b they are presented woven together into a single coherent and continuous narrative, appearing as a single tannaitic *baraita* (whose content was summarized in outline above). Does the Babylonian Talmud preserve here an early tannaitic tradition, which contains the full and authentic version of historical events as they occurred, or does the Babylonian Talmud's version represent, rather, the final stage – to use Neusner's phrase – in the "development of a legend"? Each individual case obviously needed to be analyzed and evaluated in its own right. Similar questions need to be raised and similar analyses provided with respect to the halakhic positions ascribed to R. Eliezer both in tannaitic and amoraic sources. Because of the highly technical nature of these discussions, however, we will pass over them here.

[Stephen G. Wald (2nd ed.)]

BIBLIOGRAPHY: B.Z. Bokser, *Pharisaic Judaism in Transition* (1935), biography; Schuerer, Gesch, index; Klausner, Bayit Sheni, index; Bacher, Tann, s.v.; Epstein, Tanna'im, 65–70; Halevy, Dorot, 1, pt. 5 (1923), 281ff.; H. Oppenheim, in: *Beit Talmud*, 4 (1885), 311–6, 332–8, 360–6; D. Luria, *Kuntres ha-Hakdamot ve-ha-Mavo le-Sefer Pirkei R. Eliezer ha-Gadol* (1884); G. Bader, *Jewish Spiritual Heroes*, 1 (1940), 212–25; Guttmann, in: *Memorial Volume… I. Godziher*, 2 (1958), 100–10 (English section); Y.D. Gilat, *Mishnato shel R. Eliezer ben Hyrcanus u-Mekomah be-Toledot ha-Halakhah* (1968). **ADD. BIBLIOGRAPHY:** Y.D. Gilat, *R. Eliezer ben Hyrcanus, A Scholar Outcast* (1984); J. Neusner, *Eliezer b. Hyrcanos: The Traditions and the Man* (1973).

ELIEZER BEN ISAAC (**Ashkenazi**; 16th century), Czech Hebrew printer. Eliezer was born in Prague. In partnership with others he printed Hebrew books in Lublin from 1557 to 1573. For a short while an epidemic forced him to move to Konska Wola, near Lublin, and some of the products of his press bear the name of that small town. Among the works printed by him in Lublin are some tractates of the Talmud, published with the approval and recommendation of the *Councils of the Lands. In 1574 he set out for Constantinople, taking his typographic equipment, and set up press in partnership with David b. Elijah Kashti. They printed a volume of geonic responsa (1575) and began a *Maḥzor Romania* (festival prayer book according to the Romaniot rite), in which Kashti, as a member of the old-established pre-Turkish community, was particularly interested. The partnership broke up before the *maḥzor* was finished. Then Eliezer alone issued Baruch ibn Ya'ish's commentary on the Song of Songs under the title *Mekor Barukh* (1576). The same year Eliezer went to Safed, where he entered into partnership with Abraham b. Isaac (Ashkenazi), who financed the press. Thus they established the first press in Ereẓ Israel. They produced three works in the years 1577–79. Later Eliezer returned to Constantinople, where he printed, once more in partnership with Kashti, Samuel Aripol's *Lev Ḥakham* (1586). In 1587, in Safed again, Eliezer printed three more books. Eliezer apparently died soon after.

BIBLIOGRAPHY: A.M. Habermann, *Toledot ha-Defus bi-Ẓefat* (1962), 7–15; A. Yaari, *Ha-Defus ha-Ivri be-Kushta* (1967), 30–32; idem, *Ha-Defus ha-Ivri be-Arẓot ha-Mizraḥ*, 1 (1937), 9–11, 17–20.

ELIEZER BEN ISAAC OF WORMS (also called "**Eliezer ha-Gadol**"; 11th century), German talmudic scholar. Eliezer was a pupil of his relative Simeon ha-Gadol, in *Mainz, and later of *Gershom Me'or ha-Golah, and *Judah ha-Kohen, author of *Sefer ha-Dinim*. He was a friend of *Jacob b. Jakar (Rokeaḥ, *Ha-Tefillah* 21; Joseph Solomon Delmedigo, *Maẓref le-Ḥokhmah* 14:2). After the death of R. Gershom, he and Jacob b. Yakar headed the yeshivah of Mainz, which numbered among its pupils Isaac ha-Levi and *Isaac b. Judah, the teacher of Rashi, who mentions Eliezer several times in his commentaries to the Bible (e.g., Ps. 76:11) and the Talmud (Pes. 76b) calling him "*ha-Gadol*" or "*ha-Ga'on*." A number of Eliezer's decisions and instructions have been preserved in works issuing from Rashi's school, including the *Sefer ha-Pardes*. Menahem b. Judah di Lonzano attributes to Eliezer the well-known work, *Orḥot Ḥayyim* or *Ẓavva'at R. Eli'ezer ha-Gadol*, which had previously been attributed to *Eliezer b. Hyrcanus. The suggestion that Eliezer was the father of Tobiah b. Eliezer, author of the *Lekaḥ Tov*, is without firm foundation. The *selihah* "*Elohai Basser*" recited in the *Yom Kippur Katan* service, which bears Eliezer's name in acrostic form, has been attributed to him.

BIBLIOGRAPHY: Guedemann, Gesch Erz, 1 (1880), 120–6; A. Epstein and J. Freimann (eds.), *Sefer Ma'aseh ha-Ge'onim* (1909), xv; I. Abrahams, *Hebrew Ethical Wills*, 1 (1926), 31–49; Germ Jud, 1 (1934), 192, no. 13; V. Aptowitzer, *Mavo le-Sefer Ravyah* (1938), 310f.

ELIEZER BEN JACOB, name of two *tannaim*.

(1) *Tanna* who lived during the period of the destruction of the Second Temple. He was intimately acquainted with the Temple and describes its structure, arrangements, and customs (Mid. 1:9; 2:6; Ar. 2:6; etc.). A tradition states that he was the author of the Mishnah **Middot* on the structure and dimensions of the Temple (Yoma 16a; TJ, Yoma, 2:3, 39d). It is reported that *Ben Azzai found in Jerusalem a genealogical scroll in which it was written that the opinions quoted in Eliezer's name are few "but well-sifted" (i.e., irrefutable) and that his statements everywhere represent the accepted *halakhah* (Yev. 49b). Since there was another *tanna* of the same name (see below), it is sometimes difficult to distinguish which of the two was the author of certain *halakhot*. It is, however, undoubtedly this Eliezer who is quoted in connection with laws dealing with the Temple and in discussions with R. *Eliezer b. Hyrcanus, R. *Ishmael b. Elisha, and R. *Ilai (Kil. 6:2; Kelim 7:3; Pes. 39a). One of his aggadic contributions is his interpretation of the phrase: "serve Him with all your heart and with all your soul" (Deut. 11:13), which he interpreted as an admonition to priests officiating in the Temple not to allow extraneous thoughts to enter their minds (Sif. Deut., Ekev. 41).

(2) *Tanna* of the second century. A pupil of R. *Akiva (Gen. R. 61:3; TJ, Ḥag. 3:1, 78d), he was among the sages who participated in the synod at Usha after the Hadrianic persecutions (Song Rabbah 2:5). Talmudic sources quote *halakhot* on which he differed from his colleagues R. *Meir, R. *Judah, R. *Yose, R. *Simeon b. Yoḥai, and R. *Eleazar b. Shammu'a (Neg. 10:4; Tosef., Yev. 10:5; Tosef., BK 5:7). He is reported as saying: "Whoever provides lodging in his home for a scholar and shares with him his wealth has the merit of one who offers up a daily sacrifice" (Ber. 10b). His kindness is illustrated in a story which tells that once, when a blind man came to his town, Eliezer gave him a seat of honor above his own. When the people saw this, they maintained the blind man in honor. The latter, on learning the reason for his good fortune, offered a prayer on Eliezer's behalf saying: "You have dealt kindly with one who is seen but sees not. May He who sees but is unseen accept your prayers and deal graciously with you" (TJ, Pe'ah 8:9, 21b).

BIBLIOGRAPHY: Frankel, Mishnah, 76–78; Hyman, Toledot, 181–4; Halevy, Dorot, 1 (1923), 84–86, 181–5; Bacher, Tann, 1 (1903^2), 62–67; 2 (1890), 23 n. 3, 39f. n. 5, 76 n. 2, 151 n. 1, 191 n. 4.

[Yitzhak Dov Gilat]

ELIEZER BEN JACOB HA-LEVI (Horovitz) OF TARNOGROD (d. 1806), rabbi and ḥasidic author. A descendant of a famous rabbinic family, he was a disciple of Elimelech of Lyzhansk, Jacob Isaac of Lublin, and Israel of Kozienice. He wrote *No'am Megadim* (Lemberg, 1807) and *Amarot Tehorot* (Warsaw, 1838). According to one of his sayings, even the greatest saint has to hide his own light to avoid the sin of pride.

[Adin Steinsaltz]

ELIEZER BEN JOEL HA-LEVI OF BONN (Heb. acronym ראבי"ה, *Ravyah;* 1140–1225), rabbinic scholar in Germany. His maternal grandfather was Eliezer b. Nathan. Eliezer studied under his father *Joel ha-Levi of Bonn, as well as under Judah he-Ḥasid, and Judah b. Kalonymus of Mainz. His brother Uri died a martyr's death in 1216; Eliezer's mourning for him was so great that his vision was impaired and he was compelled to dictate his novellae to his students, among them *Isaac b. Moses Or Zaru'a. In the course of his long life, Eliezer wandered from place to place: Bonn, Worms, Wuerzburg, Mainz, Metz, Cologne, Regensburg, and, apparently, through France and Lombardy. He refused to accept rabbinical office so as "neither to be glorified by, nor benefit from, the Torah" (*Ravyah*, no. 396) until he was robbed of his fortune. At his father's request, he accepted the rabbinate of Cologne in 1200. The status he then attained as spiritual leader and halakhic expert bore out the prophecy of Eliezer of Metz, "Honor will pursue you, and you will merit a lofty seat on high" (*ibid.*). In 1220 he participated in the communal synod at Mainz and was among the signatories of the enactments passed there. Nothing further is known of him after this date.

His major work, *Ravyah*, also called *Avi ha-Ezri* ("My Father is my Help"), is a compendium of articles that developed into a book. It contains *halakhot* and legal decisions according to the order of the tractates in the Talmud as well as research on halakhic subjects which he calls "responsa." Among these "responsa" are some genuine responsa written by him and his father to contemporary scholars. They are written in simple, lucid language, and are generally prefaced by rhymed introductions. In 1885 Ḥ.N. Dembitzer published tractate *Berakhot* with the relevant responsa from a manuscript of *Ravyah* to which he added his own notes, *Livyat Ḥen*. V. Aptowitzer continued the task in a two-volume critical edition (published by Mekiẓe Nirdamim, Berlin, 1913; Jerusalem, 1935) up to section 893. He later published addenda and corrigenda (1936) and an introduction (1938). She'ar Yashuv Cohen and E. Prisman revised Aptowitzer's editions in three volumes (Jerusalem, 1965) and added a fourth volume covering sections 894–919. Eliezer also wrote *Mishpetei Ketubbah*, to which *Seder Binyan Bayit Sheni* ("The Order of the Construction of the Second Temple") is an appendix. Yom Tov Lipmann Heller quotes it 15 times in his commentary on tractate *Middot*. Early authorities mention his *Avi'asaf*, a commentary on the orders *Nashim* and *Nezikin*, in addition to other material not included in *Ravyah*, which was seen by Ḥ.J.D. Azulai. He apparently also composed *tosafot* on various tractates; *likkutim*, consisting of explanations of passages of the Pentateuch; and six *piyyutim*. Although his chief purpose was the determination of the *halakhah*, Eliezer's approach to textual clarification and to the basic sources (Babylonian and Jerusalem Talmuds; *rishonim*) is reminiscent of the approach of the tosafists. His works were considered basic in halakhic literature until the publication of the Shulḥan Arukh. The great codifiers relied heavily upon him and R. Eliezer of Metz called him "the pillar of decision and the foundation of *halakhah*." He was also famous for his piety and for his ethical teaching, his contemporaries referring to him as "one who by his exhortations brought about repentance" (*Ravyah*, no. 922 in Ms.).

BIBLIOGRAPHY: Zunz, Lit Poesie, 326f.; Gross, in: MGWJ, 34 (1885), 303–20, 367–75, 505–24, 555–72; 35 (1886), 24–32, 74–81; Weiss, Dor, 5 (1904⁴), 72–73; Davidson, Oẓar, 4 (1933), 365; Germ Jud, 1 (1963), 75–78; V. Aptowitzer, *Mavo le-Sefer Ravyah* (1938); H. Tchernowitz, *Toledot ha-Posekim*, 2 (1947), 50–54; Urbach, Tosafot, 315–21; *Monumenta Judaica, Handbuch* (1963), 95, 103, 121, 122f.; S.Y. Cohen and E. Prisman (eds.), *Sefer Ravyah*, 4 (1965), 11–38.

[Yehoshua Horowitz]

ELIEZER BEN MANASSEH BEN BARUCH (mid-18th century), preacher in western Russia and author of an ethical work. In his youth, Eliezer spent some time studying in Berlin. It is not known who his teachers were or what he studied there. After some years of traveling, he was appointed *av bet din* in Rozwadow, where he probably spent most of his life. Later, at the time of the printing of his book, he was a preacher in the town of Tarnigrad. His *Ir Dammesek Eliezer* (Zolkiew, 1764) is, for the most part, a detailed homiletic and halakhic analysis of the weekly Torah portions. Each homily is divided into two parts: "*Ḥuẓot Dammesek*" and "*Penei Dammesek.*" Very often Eliezer brings lengthy sayings and rules by contemporary East European rabbis; his work is thus an important source for their teachings. The second part of this book, a short ethical work entitled "*Sha'arei Dammesek*," contains four sections called *she'arim* ("gates"). The first deals with the Torah, the second with prayer, and the third, with repentance; the fourth, "the gate of Jerusalem," deals mainly with reverence toward and fear of God. To this last section the author added, at the conclusion of the work, a collection of homilies on various ethical themes, called "*Pirkei de-Rabbi Eliezer.*" Well versed in Kabbalah, Eliezer often quotes both the Zohar and ethical kabbalistic literature, in addition to the usual rabbinic sources.

BIBLIOGRAPHY: Benjacob, Oẓar, 440.

[Joseph Dan]

ELIEZER BEN MEIR HA-LEVI OF PINSK (second half 18th century), rabbi and *darshan*. A descendant of Samuel *Edels (Maharsha), Eliezer was *rosh yeshivah* in Pinsk in the 1760s and 1770s, and, in the early 1780s, rabbi and *av bet din* in Chomsk (Khomsk). Returning to Pinsk in the late 1780s, he served as the rabbi of that city and of its *kloyz* (a type of *bet ha-midrash*). In this latter period, he became involved in a dispute in connection with a ḥasidic leader, Aaron ha-Gadol. The *Maggid* *Dov Ber of *Mezhirech sent a letter to Eliezer in which he requested that they unite in one group together with Aaron. The exact nature of this dispute is not known; some think that Eliezer was sympathetic to the Ḥasidim.

Eliezer wrote two homiletic works, *Si'aḥ ha-Sadeh* (Shklov, 1787) and *Re'aḥ ha-Sadeh (ibid.*, 1795), the first containing one sermon for each weekly Torah portion, and the second, two for each weekly Torah portion. The sermons, primarily ethical and moralistic in tone, are concerned with repentance in the realm of the *mitzvot* between man and God. Eliezer often uses kabbalistic symbols.

BIBLIOGRAPHY: Nadav, in: *Zion*, 34 (1969), 101–4; W.Z. Rabinowitsch, *Lithuanian Ḥasidism* (1970), index.

ELIEZER BEN NATHAN OF MAINZ (known as **RaBaN** = **R**abbi Eliezer **B**en **N**athan; c. 1090–c. 1170), one of "the elders of Mainz" and a leading rabbinic authority in Germany in the 12th century. Eliezer was apparently born in Germany and in his youth seems to have studied with rabbis of Mainz. Later he lived for a time in the Slavic countries, and possibly in Russia. He then returned to Mainz, where he married the daughter of Eliakim b. Joseph, of whose rabbinical court he was a member. Among his four sons-in-law were *Samuel b. Natronai and *Joel b. Isaac ha-Levi. He was also related to *Ephraim b. Jacob of Bonn and Jacob b. Isaac ha-Levi. It is doubtful whether *Asher b. Jehiel was a descendant of his. When the latter refers to *zekeni ha-Rabban*, the quotations are mainly from the *Ravyah* of *Eliezer b. Joel ha-Levi. Raban's contemporaries in France and Germany recognized his authority, and they addressed him in terms of great respect. Indeed Raban was in contact with all the major Jewish communities of his time. In 1150, together with Jacob b. Meir *Tam and *Samuel b. Meir, he drew up the famous *Takkanot Troyes* (the Troyes Ordinances).

His great work (*Sefer ha-Raban*) which he called *Even ha-Ezer* ("Stone of Help") is the first complete book that has survived emanating from German Jewry. It contains responsa and various extracts and halakhic rulings following the order of the talmudic tractates. The book appears to have come down exactly as Eliezer wrote it (but cf. *Sefer ha-Raban*, p. 106a), although there is no logical continuity from one section to the next and there are a number of omissions. The section numbers are by Eliezer himself, who used them for internal reference purposes, but in the printed editions they are deleted from §385 onward. The book contains expositions of talmudic topics and commentaries on customs, liturgical passages, including the *Kaddish*, as well as interpretations of various Midrashim and of chapter 31 of Proverbs, together with correspondence with over 20 rabbinical authorities of the day.

The book contributes much to knowledge of the way of life of the Jews of France and Germany in the 12th century and is a mine of information on the state of scholarship and religious practice in France, Germany, and Babylonia. The book functioned as a bridge between the world of the Talmud and the daily life of the Jew. *Even ha-Ezer* was a conduit for the Western dissemination of geonic literature and ideas. It is also a major source of early German customs. Special mention should be made of Eliezer's considerable use of the talmudic commentary of *Hananel b. Ḥushi'el ("Rabbenu Hananel"; often without mention of the source) only about 50 years after it appeared. Most likely Hananel's commentaries came to him from the *Arukh* of *Nathan b. Jehiel of Rome whom he also quotes. The citations from Hananel are rendered more accurately by Eliezer than by other early authorities. Eliezer is also the first to cite the anonymous *Sefer ha-Mikẓo'ot*. The Wolfenbuttel manuscript of *Even ha-Ezer* contains a sharply worded anti-Christian polemic that is based on chapter 30 of Proverbs. This is the first known polemic to emerge from medieval Germany.

There is some confusion with regard to the book *Ẓafnat Pa'ne'aḥ* ("Revealer of Secrets"), which the early authorities cite frequently, and which they attribute to Eliezer. The fact that many of the quotations appear in the *Even ha-Ezer* indicates that it may have been known by two names. Another opinion is that the reference is to a shorter edition of the book, while still another view is that there was an entirely different book, from which the copyists added to the *Sefer ha-Raban* that has been preserved. Another book ascribed to Eliezer, *Even ha-Roshah*, which is in manuscript, is merely a compilation from "*Hilkhot Dinin*" in the *Sefer ha-Raban* (pp. 92ff.), corresponding in all respects with a similar compilation printed in the **Kol Bo*. *Sefer ha-Raban* was first published in Prague (1610) and subsequently (only as far as tractate *Niddah*) by S. Albeck, who added a long introduction in Warsaw (1905). Part of it was published in Jerusalem (1915) by Leib Raskes, and the entire work was published by Solomon S. Ehrenreich (Simleul-Silvaniei, 1927), who wrote an extensive commentary to it.

Eliezer was the first commentator on *piyyut* in Germany. Part of his commentaries are preserved in manuscript, of which only fragments have been printed, often interspersed with selections from the commentaries of other early authorities in *maḥzorim* published in Ostrog (1810, 1817 et al.) and Slawita (*Maḥzor Korban Aharon*, 1826, et al.). An old manuscript, given to the editors by Ephraim Zalman Margaliot, served as the basis for this printing. Another incomplete manuscript was in the possession of Solomon Zalman *Halberstam (*Kehillat Shelomo*, Vienna, 1890). Eliezer's commentary encompassed the entire *maḥzor*, the complete *siddur* for Sabbaths and weekdays, the *Haggadah*, and *Pirkei Avot* ("Ethics of the Fathers"). He has mistakenly been credited with the authorship of the anonymous *Ma'amar Haskel* (Cremona, 1557), a commentary on his own *piyyut El Elohim ha-Shem Dibber*. The commentary was actually written more than 100 years after his time. It is also doubtful whether he is the author of the commentary on the *kinah* of Kallir, *Eikhah Yashevah Ḥavaẓẓelet ha-Sharon*, published by J.H. Schorr (see bibl.). Of Eliezer's *piyyutim*, some have been printed and others are extant only in manuscript. The horrors of the First Crusade form the theme of some of his *piyyutim*. He also devoted a special booklet to this subject, *Kuntres Gezerot "Tatnu"* ("Booklet on the Massacres of 1096," publ. Leipzig, 1854; publ. in English translation by Eidelberg, 1986). His commentary on *Avot* (also included in the above-mentioned manuscript owned by Margaliot), was in the possession of Jehiel Michael Moravchik, who made use of it "from the manuscript of the RaBaN written in 1145" in his own commentary on *Avot* (*Minḥah Ḥadashah*, Cracow, 1576). A didactic poem by Eliezer on the laws of *sheḥitah* was published in *Sefer ha-Yovel le-Rav Shimon Skop* (Vilna, 1936). In *Sefer ha-Roke'aḥ* (§319) he is credited with having written a book on customs.

BIBLIOGRAPHY: S. Albeck (ed.), *Sefer Raban* (1904), 3–27 (introd.); Davidson, Oẓar, 4 (1933), 364–5; V. Aptowitzer, *Mavo le-Sefer Ravyah* (1938), 49–57; Urbach, Tosafot, 148–58; idem (ed.), *Sefer Arugat ha-Bosem*, 4 (1963), 24–39; A.M. Habermann, *Gezerot Ashkenaz ve-Ẓarefat* (1945), 72–82; Levine, in: *Tarbiz*, 29 (1959/60), 162–75; Baron, 4 (1957), 287–8; K. Schilling (ed.), *Monumenta Judaica-Handbuch* (1963), 674, 676. **ADD. BIBLIOGRAPHY:** D. Ackerman, in: WCJS, 11, C1 (1994), 57–64; idem, in: *Proceedings of the Rabbinical Assembly*, 55 (1994), 94–104; A. Shapiro, "Jewish Life in Germany of the 12th century: A Study of Eben ha-Ezer of Rabbi Eliezer bar Nathan of Mayence as a Source for the History of the Period," dissertation, Dropsie College (1968); S. Eidelberg, *The Jews and the Crusaders* (1996).

[Israel Moses Ta-Shma]

ELIEZER BEN SAMSON (fl. 12th century), *paytan* and rabbi in Cologne; a pupil of R. Isaac b. Asher ha-Levi in Speyer. He exchanged responsa with R. *Abraham b. Nathan, who referred to him with admiration. Many of his decisions were used as precedents by early authorities (Mordecai Ket. 219, Kid. 515, Shev. 761; and R. Isaac b. Moses Or Zaru'a). He composed a number of liturgical poems including a *reshut* in Aramaic to the Sukkot *haftarah*, which described the era between the creation of the world and the revelation at Mount Sinai.

BIBLIOGRAPHY: Landshuth, Ammudei, 23ff.; Fuenn, Keneset, 133; Germ Jud, 74; Kohn, in: MGWJ, 27 (1878), 44ff.; Zunz, Lit Poesie, 176; Davidson, Oẓar, 4 (1933), 365.

ELIEZER BEN SAMUEL HA-LEVI (d. 1357), German Jew, son of Samuel b. Yakar, the *ḥazzan* of Mayence (also known as Tov Elem). Eliezer, who was not a rabbi, but was titled **ḥaver*, is known from his ethical will, which is preserved in several manuscripts and first published in 1870 in a German translation (ed. by A. Berliner in *Juedische Presse*, 1 (1870), 90f., 99). The Hebrew original was afterward published by M. Guedemann (Guedemann, Quellenschr, 295–8) and again, along with an English translation by I. Abrahams (*Hebrew Ethical Wills*, 2 (1926), 1207–18). In this touching document Eliezer requests that his children walk in God's ways, that they fulfill strictly all the *mitzvot*, that they be not mercenary, and if possible, live among Jews.

ELIEZER BEN SAMUEL OF METZ (c. 1115–c. 1198), tosafist and halakhic authority. Eliezer was a pupil of Jacob *Tam (see *Sefer ha-Yashar*, ed. by F. Rosenthal (1898), 128 n. 57), as well as of *Samuel b. Meir, and Ḥayyim Cohen of Paris. Among his disciples were some of the greatest German rabbis, such as *Eliezer b. Joel *ha-Levi and *Eleazar b. Judah of Worms, author of the *Roke'aḥ*. He thus served as an intermediary between the centers of study in France and those in Germany. Eliezer obtained his livelihood by moneylending, and was in charge of the distribution of charity. His daughters died during his lifetime. Little else is known of him. Eliezer's most important work is his *Sefer Yere'im*, written between 1171 and 1179, a work on the 613 precepts according to the enumeration of the **Halakhot Gedolot*. It was abridged by Benjamin b. Abraham *Anav, who divided it into 12 "Pillars," in which form it was published in Venice in 1566, and in many later editions. The complete book (464 paragraphs) was published from a Paris manuscript in Vilna (1892–1902) by Abraham Abba Schiff who added a commentary entitled *To'afot Re'em*. Other commentaries have also been written. Although essentially a halakhic work, *Sefer Yere'im* includes ethical maxims and homilies on the true service of God. Halakhic discussions are sometimes preceded by rhymed introductions. The rulings of *Sefer Yere'im* as well as those in Eliezer's commentaries on the Talmud were accepted as authoritative by the *rishonim*. Eliezer is also an author of *tosafot* and novellae. Mention is made of his commentary to *Berakhot, Shabbat, Zevaḥim*, and *Nedarim*. Ḥayyim Joseph David *Azulai was in possession of a manuscript by him on *Ḥullin*. Very few of his responsa have been preserved.

BIBLIOGRAPHY: Gross, in: MGWJ, 34 (1885), 506f.; V. Aptowitzer, *Mavo le-Sefer Ravyah* (1938), 246f., 312–5; H. Tchernowitz, *Toledot ha-Posekim*, 2 (1947), 78–87; M. Reich, in: *Sinai Sefer Yovel* (1958), 356–72; Urbach, Tosafot, 132–40.

[Israel Moses Ta-Shma]

ELIEZER BEN SAMUEL OF VERONA (early 13th century), Italian tosafist. Eliezer was a pupil of Isaac b. Samuel of Dampierre (*Roke'aḥ* 377) and the teacher of *Avigdor b. Elijah Kohen Ẓedek of Vienna. He was a colleague of *Eleazar b. Judah of Worms and of Abraham b. Moses of Regensburg. He wrote *tosafot* to the Talmud, and those to *Bava Batra* (from 144b ff.) in particular are attributed to him. One of his rulings gave rise to considerable controversy. He permitted the widow of a certain Solomon b. Jacob to remarry, seven years after he had disappeared when the ship in which he was sailing sank near Pesaro in 1214. He sent his ruling to "the communities of the Rhine and of Cologne," but Baruch b. Samuel of Mainz forbade the *agunah* to remarry. After Baruch's death, Abraham b. Moses of Mainz sent Eliezer's ruling to Eliezer b. Joel ha-Levi, but he confirmed the prohibition (*Sefer Ravyah*, 4 (1965), 133–43). Eliezer's responsa to *Isaac b. Moses of Vienna (Or Zaru'a) are quoted in Zedekiah b. Abraham's *Shibbolei ha-Leket* (ed. by S. Buber (1886), nos. 13, 237, and 247) and in *Sefer Issur ve-Hetter* (no. 9) by the same author (published in *Ha-Segullah*, 1, 1934). There is also mention of his biblical exegesis (Zunz, in HB, 7 (1864), 20ff.). Isaac Or Zaru'a calls Eliezer and *Isaiah di Trani the Elder "the two kings of Israel." *Hillel of Verona was his grandson.

BIBLIOGRAPHY: Zunz, Schr, 3 (1876), 250f.; S. Buber (ed.), *Shibbolei ha-Leket ha-Shalem* (1886), introd., 9; V. Aptowitzer, *Mavo le-Sefer Ravyah* (1938), 195, 311f., 429–32; Urbach, Tosafot, 357–9, 504f.

[Yehoshua Horowitz]

ELIEZER (Eleazar) BEN YOSE HA-GELILI ("of Galilee"; fl. second century C.E.), *tanna*. Eliezer is mentioned only once in the Mishnah, but more than ten times in the Tosefta, and even more frequently in the tannaitic Midrashim. Almost all of his dicta in both Talmuds, in *beraitot*, and in Midrashim are aggadic. According to the Talmud, R. Eleazar b. Simeon said of him: "Whenever you find the words of Eliezer b. Yose in the *aggadah*, bend your ear attentively" (Ḥul. 89a). The *Baraita of the Thirty-Two Rules*, which defines the hermeneutical rules for the aggadic exposition of scripture, is ascribed to him, though in its present form this is highly unlikely (see: **Baraita of the Thirty-Two Rules*). Among his statements are: "A person in distress is forbidden to pray" (TJ, Ber. 5:1, 8d); "Even if nine hundred and ninety-nine argue against a man [in the Heavenly Cause], while one argues in his favor, he is acquitted" (Shab. 32a). He applied the well-known saying of R. Eleazar b. Azariah, to the effect that the full praise of a person should not be uttered in his presence, to teach that "one utters only a portion of the praise of Him at whose word the world came into being" (Gen. R. 32:3).

BIBLIOGRAPHY: Weiss, Dor, 2 (1904[4]), 149; Hyman, Toledot, 180–1; Zunz-Albeck, Derashot, 143; Bacher, Tann, s.v.

[Alter Hilewitz]

ELIEZER FISCHEL BEN ISAAC OF STRZYZOW (end of 18th century), Galician kabbalist. Eliezer, who was born and lived in Strzyzow near Tarnopol, was close to the circle of the kabbalists of the *Klaus* of Brody, and devoted four books to the exposition of kabbalistic teaching in which the principles of Lurianic doctrine were presented in a more lucid way than in earlier works. His works include:

(1) *Sefer Olam ha-Gadol*, also called *Midrash la-Perushim* (Zolkiew, 1800); (2) *Sefer Olam Eḥad*, on the unity of God according to kabbalistic teaching (*ibid.*, 1802); (3) *Sefer Olam Barur*, on the doctrine of the elevation of sparks (*niẓoẓot*) and purification of souls (*ibid.*, 1800?); and (4) *Sefer Olam Hafukh*, homilies on morality in Kabbalah (*ibid.*, 1800?).

In addition to his works on Kabbalah, he also published *Olam Va'ed* (1849), on the calculation of the seasons and new moons (first days of months). Eliezer was nevertheless considered one of the leading opponents of Ḥasidism and several of his books contain both explicit and implicit criticism of the practices of the Ḥasidim.

[Gershom Scholem]

ELIEZER OF BEAUGENCY (fl. 12th century), biblical commentator from N. France. Nutt was of the opinion that Eliezer was a student of *Samuel b. Meir but there is no clear-cut evidence in support of this view. Few biographical details are known of him. He had a knowledge of Latin and often cited the Vulgate in his commentaries. Three of his commentaries have been preserved: on Isaiah (publ. by Nutt, 1879), on Ezekiel, and on the minor prophets (both publ. by S. Poznański, 1907–13). From references in these works and in those of other exegetes, however, it appears that Eliezer also wrote commentaries on the Pentateuch, Jeremiah, Psalms, Ecclesiastes, and Daniel. It is possible that he covered all the books of the Bible. Generally speaking Eliezer followed the literal method of interpretation of the Bible adopted by his French predecessors Rashi, Samuel b. Meir, and Joseph Kara. Although he did not cite these commentators frequently, it is quite clear that he relied upon them. Eliezer held Rashi in great esteem and called him simply "our teacher" or "our illustrious teacher."

In his attempts to give a literal exegesis of the Bible Eliezer ignored rabbinic exegesis to an even greater degree than his French colleagues. He occasionally referred to the Midrashim but adds that he would not utilize them since they were not in accordance with the plain sense of the verse (cf. his comments on Zech. 7:3; Ezek. 43:17). His comments on certain verses conflicted with the *halakhah* (e.g., Isa. 9:6). Nevertheless, he did concur at times with the homiletical interpretation. Eliezer attempted to identify the historical events alluded to by the prophets and their significance, sometimes interpreting the events to apply to the prophets' own times; on other occasions he applied them to the future. In his identifications he was greatly influenced by the *Sefer* **Josippon*. He also placed greater emphasis than did his French predecessors on the problems of dating the prophecies and the editing of the books (cf. his introduction to Isaiah). Like his contemporary, Joseph *Bekhor Shor, Eliezer attempted to give a rational explanation of the supernatural miracles (e.g., Isa. 30:26; Zech. 4:3). On the other hand he believed that the constellations influenced man's fate. Orion and the Pleiades controlled the movements of the planets and at their command the world was destined for good or evil, war or peace, famine or plenty, everything in its season (Amos 5:8 and in greater detail in Isa. 38:1). His comments were usually brief and to the point, but his comments on the building of the Temple in Ezekiel constitute an exception which he justified because of the farfetched interpretations given by other exegetes.

In its simplicity and clarity Eliezer's style was similar to that of his French colleagues. His language was studded with biblical and talmudic phrases and expressions, but he also coined new terms and expressions. Eliezer paid little attention to questions of grammar. Like Rashi, he followed the system of *Menahem b. Saruq and *Dunash ibn Labrat. In his exegesis he was usually guided by the cantillation signs (e.g., Isa. 6:3), though occasionally he disregarded them. On occasion he drew upon the Targum, but here also he did not hesitate to disagree when he felt that its interpretation was contrary to the literal meaning. In order to determine the exact biblical text Eliezer examined various manuscripts which were available to him in France. There were instances when the spelling in his text differed from the present masoretic text (e.g., Ezek. 8:16; Micah 6:7). Many of the French words (**la'azim*) of which he makes use are derived from Rashi's commentary. Eliezer resorted to the Vulgate, which he attacked together with Christological interpretations of the Bible (cf. Isa. 7:14; 9:5). At times his remarks reflect the conditions of his own times. For instance, in his commentary on Ezekiel 37:12, "I shall bring you to the land of Israel," he stated: "This verse is a great comfort to all those who die a martyr's death and even to those who do not make the supreme sacrifice since they constantly suffer shame, disgrace, and physical abuse when they refuse to acknowledge false gods."

BIBLIOGRAPHY: S. Poznański (ed.), *Perush al Yeḥezkel u-Terei Asar le-Rabbi Eli'ezer mi-Belganzi* (1913), introduction.

[Avraham Grossman]

ELIEZER OF TOUL (d. before 1234), French tosafist. Eliezer came from Toul, near the German border. He studied under *Isaac b. Samuel the Elder of Dampierre. For some time he lived in Boppard, Germany, where he served as a tutor in the household of one of the local leaders of the community. When the latter withheld his remuneration, the case was referred to the rabbis. Eliezer's talmudic discussions appear in the works of later **posekim*, the disciples of *Meir b. Baruch of Rothenburg. Zedekiah b. Abraham *Anav of Rome mentions that he consulted his *tosafot* to tractate *Beẓah*, but these have not survived.

BIBLIOGRAPHY: Urbach, Tosafot, 277f., 285.

[Israel Moses Ta-Shma]

ELIEZER OF TOUQUES (d. before 1291), one of the last tosafists and editors of tosafist literature. Only a few details of his biography are known. He was a nephew of *Hezekiah of Magdeburg and appears to be identical with the Eliezer b. Solomon who signed a well-known responsum on the question of whether the **Ḥerem ha-Yishuv* applied to the community of *Goslar. He studied under *Isaac b. Moses (Or Zaru'a) and was the teacher of Ḥayyim *Paltiel. Eliezer's contemporaries had the highest regard for him, considering him an equal of *Meir b. Baruch of Rothenburg. Isaac Joshua b. Immanuel de *Lattes looked upon him as "head of the yeshivah of France," a post later attributed to *Perez b. Elijah of Corbeil. The **tosafot* of Eliezer of Touques are primarily an adaptation of those of *Samson b. Abraham of Sens, with the addition of later novellae. He sometimes adapted the *tosafot* of other scholars, among them *Judah b. Isaac Sir Leon. The disciples of Meir b. Baruch of Rothenburg used Eliezer's *tosafot* extensively, and it was through them that they became the accepted *tosafot* of France and Germany. Consequently the publishers of the Talmud also made an effort to include them, in order to enhance the value of their publication. The *tosafot* to the tractates *Shabbat, Pesaḥim, Ketubbot, Gittin, Bava Kamma, Bava Meẓia, Bava Batra, Shevu'ot*, and *Ḥullin* in the printed editions of the Talmud, and possibly also of some other tractates, were edited by Eliezer.

BIBLIOGRAPHY: Urbach, Tosafot, index.

[Israel Moses Ta-Shma]

ELIHU (Heb. אֱלִיהוּא, once אֱלִיהוּ; "God is the one [who is to be thanked, or worshipped]"), son of Barachel the Buzite, of the family of Ram, a character – first introduced, and quite unexpectedly, at Job 32:2 – who addresses Job and his three friends from 32:6 through chapter 37. (For the literary problem this creates and an analysis of Elihu's contribution to the discussion, see *Job, Book of.) The names assigned to Elihu and to his father (Barachel, "God has [or "is"] blessed") may hint that the author of these chapters approves of the point of view that Elihu represents. The tribe and family assigned to him, however ("the Buzite, of the family of Ram"), are obviously chosen, like for example, the name and tribe of *Eliphaz the Temanite, in order to conform to the setting of the oldest stratum of the Book of Job ("the land of *Uz," Job 1:1; "the *Kedemites," 1:3b); for according to Genesis 22:21, Buz was a younger brother of Uz and an uncle of Aram, with whom the Septuagint and Symmachus, probably rightly, identify this Ram. A less likely possibility is the connection of Elihu's ancestry to Ram, grandson of Judah in the late sources (Ruth 4:19; I Chr. 2:9) that are followed by the New Testament (Matt. 1:2).

[Harold Louis Ginsberg]

In the *Aggadah*

The *aggadah* praises both the wisdom and modesty of Elihu. He was called "*buzi*" (lit. "lowly"; Job 32:2), only because he considered himself of low account in the presence of those greater than himself (Zohar, 2:166a), and showed his wisdom in never speaking until he had listened to what Job had to say (ARN[1] 37, 111–112). His wisdom is reflected in his statement: "Touching the Almighty, we can never find Him out" (Job 37:23). He would have merited to be mentioned in Scriptures had he done no more than describe the action of the rainfall (cf. Job 36:27 and 37:3; Gen. R. 36:7). Elihu was a prophet (Sot. 15b) and descended from Nahor, the brother of Abraham (SER 28, 141–2).

BIBLIOGRAPHY: Ginzberg, Legends, index; Y. Ḥasida, *Ishei ha-Tanakh* (1964), 65–66.

ELIJAH (Heb. אֵלִיָּהוּ, also אֵלִיָּה), Israelite prophet active in Israel in the reigns of *Ahab and Ahaziah (ninth century B.C.E.). In the opinion of some scholars, the designation "the Tishbite of the inhabitants of Gilead" (I Kings 17:1) supports the hypothesis that Elijah did not live in one specific place in Gilead but was a member of either the *Kenites or the *Rechabites, sects which led a nomadic existence. These scholars detect even in his resolute war against *Baal and in his zeal for Yahweh a line of conduct which they believe was characteristic of the Kenites and Rechabites but not of the nation at large. (For the role of Jehonadab son of Rechab in Jehu's purge of Baal, see II Kings 10:15–17.) But the accounts of Elijah's wanderings (I Kings 17) describe his withdrawal from society as a matter not of principle but of necessity (persecution, famine). In addition, the reading "of the inhabitants of Gilead" is suspect. It is impossible to decide whether "Elijah" was a cognomen symbolizing the prophet's mission: Eli-Jahu ("YHWH is God"), or whether he had been given that name by parents zealous for Yahweh. Elijah brought matters to a head by stressing the idea of zeal for YHWH, which unconditionally opposed the toleration of any cult (especially any official cult) other than that of YHWH in Israel. This extremist position, summed up in the sentence "I have been moved by zeal for the Lord, the God of Hosts" (I Kings 19:10, 14), was a minority opinion among Israelites, who evidently could comfortably serve Yahweh and Baal (I Kings 18:21), let alone intrinsically different from the polytheistic outlook, which never opposed in principle the blending of different religious cults, or their separate existence side by side. Even *Jezebel, who fought against zealots like Elijah and is accused of killing the Yahweh prophets (I Kings 18:13), was probably not opposed to the worship of Yahweh per se, but to the demand that he be worshipped exclusively at the expense of Baal. Ahab, in fact, gave his sons the names Ahaz-iah and Jeho-ram, which are compounded with the name of the national god YHWH. For the "Yahweh-alone" zealots, it was insufficient to worship Yahweh as the national god while tolerating others. The attitude of Elijah and those of like mind was liable to impair relations between Israel and her neighbors. Because of this, Elijah's activity encountered opposition from the royal court whose policy was to cultivate economic ties with Israel's neighbors and specifically with Tyre. Ahab saw no more harm in showing tolerance toward the religion of the people of Tyre and establishing a place of worship in Samaria than did Solomon who had acted similarly in behalf of his foreign wives (I Kings 11:7–8). But Elijah, whose attitude to the Sidonians themselves was not hostile (cf. the incident at Zarephath, which belonged to Sidon, I Kings 17:8–16), believed that it was his people's obligation to preserve within its own borders a "pure" religious cult that did not recognize any other gods but Yahweh. Hence, his vehement opposition to the cults of Baal and *Asherah of Sidon, supported by the royal court.

The most dramatic point of Elijah's activity was the confrontation on Mount Carmel. In response to Elijah's demands, Ahab assembled "all Israel unto Mount Carmel" together with 850 prophets of Baal and Asherah (I Kings 18:19). In their presence and that of the king, Elijah turned to the people: "How long will you keep limping between the two boughs? [Thus Joseph Caspi] If Yahweh is God, follow Him; and if Baal, follow him" (18:21). While the priests of Baal were offering up their sacrifices and calling "O Baal hear us," cutting themselves with knives and lances until the blood gushed out, Elijah mockingly suggested that they cry more loudly, since their god might be asleep or his attention otherwise engaged. Only after their prolonged pleas and cries proved of no avail did Elijah step forward to repair the demolished altar of Yahweh, make all the necessary preparations for the sacrifice, and offer up a short prayer. According to the biblical narrative, fire immediately descended from heaven, consuming the burnt sacrifice, and all the people of Israel present fell on their faces chanting, "Yahweh, He is the God; Yahweh, He is the God." At Elijah's command those present attacked and killed the prophets of Baal. The king showed no sign of opposition to Elijah's actions. This story is interwoven with another occurrence, which has a historical foundation, connected with the drought, the beginning and end of which were prophesied by Elijah. A short while after the events on Mount Carmel, the sky became black with clouds and heavy rain began to fall (I Kings 18:45). This was seen by Elijah and his followers as a sign that God had forgiven the repentant people their sin of Baal-worship which had been the cause of the drought (cf. I Kings 17:1). The Tyrian chronicle of Menander, which is generally reliable (Ant., 8:323–4), confirms that a drought occurred at that time, though it ascribes the rains to the prayers of Ethbaal (Ithobal) of Tyre, Ahab's father-in-law.

Elijah triumphed over the adversaries of Yahweh on the border of Tyre and Israel, and the altar on Mount Carmel remained in existence for some time (II Kings 2:25; 4:25). However, Jezebel was furious over the massacre of the prophets of Baal and launched a bloody war against Elijah and his followers, According to I Kings 19, Elijah was forced to flee to the desert south of Beersheba, where, tired and disheartened, he longed to die. However, while he was lying in a mood of despair under a broom bush, an angel appeared, strengthened Elijah with food and drink, and urged him to continue his journey. Elijah traveled 40 days until he reached Mount Horeb. There, in the place where the Lord had revealed Himself to Moses, He appeared to Elijah. The description of the revelation to Elijah differs from similar revelations which the Bible recounts as taking place on Mount Sinai. Fearful phenomena such as tempests, fire, and a general cacophony accompanied the revelation there also, but the Bible stresses specifically that these mighty forces appeared before the revelation of the Lord; that the Lord did not reveal Himself within them but rather in a still, small voice.

It is the task of the prophet to listen to the voice of God and pass on its message to the people. Since Elijah had fulfilled his prophetic task and the people had failed to stand by him in his war against Jezebel, retribution was merely a matter of time. The instruments of God's retribution were to be *Hazael, who was to assume power in Syria; *Jehu, the future king of Israel; and *Elisha, Elijah's successor. Elijah was commanded to anoint all three (I Kings 19:15–16), but the narrative makes it clear that he only appointed Elisha as a prophet and passed on to him the task of anointing Hazael and Jehu. Elisha, in turn, anointed only Hazael, and Jehu was anointed by one of the "sons of the prophets" at the behest of Elisha. All these actions, however, were carried out in the spirit of Elijah's ideals, with the aim of uprooting the worship of Baal in Israel. Despite the sharp conflict between Elijah and the royal palace over Baal-worship, there is no conclusive evidence that because of this Elijah prophesied the destruction of Ahab's house; in fact, the accusation of Baal-worship was leveled equally against the masses and the royal household. What finally caused Elijah to prophesy the complete destruction of the House of Ahab was the crime committed against *Naboth.

Elijah's last deed in the days of Ahaziah son of Ahab also reflects his zeal for the Lord. When Ahaziah fell ill and sent to inquire of Baal-zebub, the god of Ekron, whether or not he would recover, his messengers were intercepted by Elijah who asked, "Is it because there is no God in Israel that you are going to inquire of Baal-zebub the god of Ekron? Now therefore, thus says the Lord, you shall not come down from the bed which you have mounted, but shall surely die" (II Kings 1:3–4). In contrast to his relations with Ahab, on this occasion Elijah had no dealings with the king; he passed his judgment on to the king and after a short while his words were fulfilled. It seems that the difference lay in the nature of the king's fault – open consultation of a foreign god, a sin which Ahab never committed. The account in II Kings 1–2 makes it difficult to establish whether Elijah's activity ceased during the reign of Ahaziah or in that of his brother and successor Jehoram. According to II Chronicles 21:12, Elijah sent a letter to Jehoram son of *Jehoshaphat, the king of Judah. It is likely however that the letter was sent while Jehoram was acting as regent for Jehoshaphat (according to Thiele, 853–848 B.C.E.), and it is therefore possible that the event occurred in the lifetime of Ahab. By the time Jehoram of Judah was king in his own right, Elisha had succeeded Elijah. Elijah's standing was bolstered by wonder-tales. He was fed bread and meat by ravens (I Kings 17:6) at the divine command. As an *ish-elohim* ("Man of God," i.e, divine messenger, he miraculously caused a jar of flour and a jug of oil to keep on producing for the benefit of a poor woman whose son he subsequently raised from the dead (I Kings 17:7–24). It was believed that a divine wind could take him from one place to another (I Kings 18:11). He could bring rain and then, seized by the hand of YHWH, outrun the royal chariot from Mount Carmel to Jezreel (I Kings 18:46). That being the case, we should not be surprised that Elijah did not die but was carried to heaven in a chariot and horses of fire (II Kings 2:1–11). Elijah was well-known by his gait and manner of dress. Ahaziah's envoys described him as wearing "a garment of haircloth, with a girdle of leather about his loins" (II Kings 1:8). Miraculous powers were attributed to Elijah's cloak. As Elijah ascended to heaven, his cloak dropped to the ground and with its help Elisha too performed miracles (*ibid.* 2:8, 13). II Chr. 21:12–15 expands on Elijah's activity by attributing to the prophet a letter to King Jehoram of Judah prophesying dire punishment for worshipping foreign gods and for fratricide. The prophecy at the end of Malachi (3:23) that the prophet Elijah would be sent to the people before the coming of "the great and fearful day of YHWH" came within Judaism to mean that Elijah would herald the coming of the *Messiah. Some early Christians, accordingly, identified *John the Baptist with Elijah (Matt. 11:14; 17:10–13).

[Joshua Gutmann / S. David Sperling (2nd ed.)]

In the *Aggadah*

The deep impression left by Elijah's revolutionary ministry and his miraculous translation to heaven in a "chariot of fire" drawn by "horses of fire" (II Kings 2:11) had already made Elijah a legendary figure in biblical times. Malachi's final prophecy that Elijah would be sent by God "before the coming of the great and terrible day of the Lord," so that he may "turn the hearts of the fathers to the children, and the hearts of the children to their fathers" (Mal. 3:23ff.), became the point of departure for the subsequent association of Elijah with the Messianic age.

Ben Sira (c. 200 B.C.E.), in his eulogy of Elijah, attributed the future restoration of "the tribes of Jacob" to him (Ecclus. 48:10). By the first century C.E., it was taken for granted that Elijah was to be the precursor and herald of the Messiah. Jesus himself was at first believed to be Elijah, but when he revealed his own messianic claim, he proclaimed John the Baptist as having been the reincarnated Elijah (Matt. 11:10ff.; 17:10ff.; Mark 9:11ff.).

It was perhaps against this Christian and sectarian tendency to associate Elijah with religiously dubious and politically dangerous movements that attempts were made to counter the excessive veneration accorded to Elijah among apocalyptic-sectarian and Christian circles. It was, accordingly, denied that Elijah had ever gone up to heaven (Suk. 5a), biblical evidence to the contrary notwithstanding. Elijah's habit of revealing divine secrets to pious mortals (cf. BM 59b) once earned him a severe punishment of 60 lashes of fire (BM 85b). Elijah's denunciation of Israel for having forsaken the divine covenant (cf. I Kings 19:10, 14) had so angered God that He dismissed Elijah from His service and appointed Elisha in his place (Song R. 1:6, no. 1; cf. I Kings 19:16). Above all, the scope of Elijah's future tasks was limited to the solution of certain halakhic problems (Eduy. 8:7; Tosef., Eduy. 3:4). Subsequently, too, it was believed that "when Elijah comes, he will tell us" (Ber. 35b; cf. Men. 45a; Bek. 24a). He was indeed supposed to have his own court (Av. Zar. 36a), and legal problems which defied solution were to be referred to him (Shek. 2:5; BM 1:8; 2:8; 3:4–5; Men. 63a). Nevertheless, the predominant tannaitic view was that Elijah was not only to solve halakhic disputes, but also to be the great peacemaker in the world (Eduy. 8:7).

Rabbis and pious men endowed with a mystical frame of mind established a spiritual communion with Elijah and were reputed to have been guided by him in their studies (cf. *Tanna de-Vei Eliyahu*, ed. M. Friedmann, 27ff.; Ginzberg, Legends, 4 (1913), 217–23). Nine aggadic *beraitot* in the Talmud are introduced by the words "It was taught at Elijah's school" (cf. Friedmann op. cit. 44ff. for a complete list). Although these *beraitot* may have originated from a compilation by a *tanna* called Elijah (Ginzberg, Legends, 6 (1928), 330, n. 70) or from a school called after Elijah (Friedmann, op. cit., 60–61), they were soon attributed to the prophet. In post-talmudic times, the Midrash *Tanna de-Vei Eliyahu* ("It was taught at Elijah's school") was likewise believed to have emanated from the prophet's own "school."

Despite such relatively restricted rules assigned to Elijah by the rabbis, his primary task of heralding the redemption of Israel was never forgotten (cf. also the third benediction after the reading of the *haftarah*), and in the post-talmudic era it assumed primary importance in Jewish eschatology (cf. PR 35:161). Even earlier, Elijah appears almost invariably in the role of one who is deeply concerned about Israel's suffering and exile, and who does what he can to speed the day of deliverance. In a beautiful tannaitic *aggadah*, R. Yose relates how Elijah once told him that "whenever Israelites enter synagogues and houses of study… the Holy One, Blessed be He, as it were shakes His head and says: Happy is the king who is thus praised in his house! Woe to the father who exiled his children, and woe to the children who are banished from their father's table" (Ber. 3a).

R. Simeon b. Yoḥai, a relentless opponent of Roman rule who had to flee from Roman persecution, was freed from his hiding place in a cave by Elijah's announcement that the emperor had died (Shab. 33b). As the carrier of good tidings for Israel (cf. the Grace after Meals, in which Elijah is assigned the function of bringing good news to the Jewish people), Elijah inevitably became the antithesis of Rome and all it stood for. Thus, he sharply rebuked R. Ishmael b. Yose who had undertaken police work on behalf of the Romans: "How long will you deliver the people of our God for execution?" (BM 83b–84a). Similarly, when the pious R. Joshua b. Levi, who was said to have been in constant communication with Elijah (cf. Sanh. 98a; Mak. 11a; Gen. R. 35:2), persuaded a Jew sought by the Roman authorities to give himself up, thereby saving the entire Jewish community of Lydda from destruction, Elijah shunned R. Joshua for about 30 days. Later he explained that he could not be "a companion to informers": and although R. Joshua had acted according to mishnaic law, Elijah maintained that "this should have been done by others, not by you" (TJ, Ter. 8:10, 46b; Gen. R. 94:9, end).

On another occasion, Elijah told R. Joshua b. Levi that the Messiah was to be found among the beggars of Rome ready and willing to redeem Israel, although, as he subsequently explained, only if they repented and obeyed God (Sanh. 98a). A late Midrash, however, maintained that Israel would repent only when Elijah made his public appearance (PdRE 43, end).

Elijah's association with the Messiah became more pronounced in the late talmudic and post-talmudic ages. Increasingly, Elijah becomes not only a precursor, but an active partner of the Messiah. Both Elijah and the Messiah are busy recording the good deeds of the righteous, no doubt with a view to hastening the day of Israel's redemption (Lev. R. 34:8; Ruth R. 5:6). Ultimately, Elijah and the Messiah are to be among four world conquerors (Song R. 2:13, no. 4); though, according to one Midrash, Elijah himself is destined to overthrow the foundations of the heathen (Gen. R. 71:9). Elijah is, indeed, accorded the exclusive privilege of bringing about the resurrection of the dead (Sot. 9:15 end; cf. Song R. 1:1, no. 9) – no doubt because of his achievement in reviving the son of the widow of Zarephath (I Kings 17:17 ff.).

Elijah's solicitude for Israel's safety was also demonstrated in the past. Thus, when Haman was threatening to exterminate the Jews, Elijah was said to have intervened with the Patriarchs and with Moses to secure their intercession with the Almighty. At the decisive moment he appeared in the guise of Harbonah to denounce Haman (Esth. R. 7:13; 10:9). Likewise, at the time of the siege of Jerusalem by the Babylonians, Elijah was searching among those who were languishing with hunger in the hope of saving those who might renounce idolatry (Sanh. 63b).

Of equal concern to Elijah were individual pious Jews who happened to be in trouble. Among those whose lives were saved or whose health was restored by Elijah's timely appearance in various guises were Nahum of Gimzo (Ta'an. 21a; Sanh. 109a), R. Meir (Av. Zar. 18b), R. Eleazar b. Perata (Av. Zar. 17b), Judah ha-Nasi (TJ, Kil. 9:4, 32b; Gen. R. 33:3; 96:5), R. Shila (Ber. 58a), R. Kahana (Kid. 40a), and many others (cf. also Matt. 27:47 ff., and see Mark 15:35–36 for similar expectations in connection with Jesus' crucifixion). Innumerable legends and stories are still told of the poor and hopeless being aided by Elijah.

It was because of Elijah's great love for Israel that he had boldly assumed an attitude of insolence toward God, Whom he blamed for turning their hearts away from Him (cf. I Kings 18:37). God, however, eventually agreed with him (Ber. 31b–32a). The furious zeal displayed by Elijah on that occasion (cf. I Kings 18:40; 19:10, 14) was so similar to that shown by Aaron's grandson Phinehas (cf. Num. 25:7 ff.; Ps. 106:30) that in rabbinic literature the two are often identified, either expressly or by implication (PdRE 47; cf. BM 114a–b; Kid. 70a; Num. R. 21:3; Targ. Yer., Num. 25:12), and both are, accordingly, regarded as immortal (BB 121b; Gen. R. 21:5; 25:1; Num. R. 21:3).

Elijah is often associated with Moses in both rabbinic and Christian literature – first because Elijah was to inaugurate Israel's future redemption just as Moses had liberated the Israelites from Egyptian bondage; second, because his career resembled that of Moses' inasmuch as both were granted revelations at Mount Sinai in somewhat similar circumstances (Ex. 3:2; 19:16 ff.; 20:18; Deut. 4:11 ff., 33 ff.; I Kings 19:11–12); and since, moreover, Malachi's admonition to "remember the law of Moses" and his prediction of the future mission of Elijah are in close juxtaposition (Mal. 3:22–24). Elijah appears as a disciple and follower of Moses and also as a fellow prophet active in the same cause of delivering Israel, in which both are to participate on the advent of the messianic age (Tosef., Sot. 4:7; Tosef., Eduy. 3:4; Sot. 13a; TJ, Sanh. 10:1, 28a; Ex. R. 44:1; Num. R. 18:12; Lam. R. 1:2, no. 23; Matt. 17:3 ff.; Mark 9:4 ff.; Luke 9:30 ff. et al. For a detailed comparison of the careers of Moses and Elijah, see PR 4:13).

[Moses Aberbach]

In Mysticism

According to *Moses b. Shem Tov de Leon, Elijah belongs to the angels who advocated the creation of man (Cordovero, *Pardes Rimmonim*, 24:14); accordingly, Elijah is an angel who dwelt only temporarily on earth as a human being, before again ascending to heaven. Moses *Cordovero compares Elijah's life with the fate of Enoch (*ibid.*, 24:13), as the two are the only biblical personages who were carried off from earthly life in an extraordinary manner. The further fate of Elijah and Enoch in heaven is imaginatively described by Jewish mystics. While Enoch's body is consumed by fire and he himself is changed into *Metatron, the highest angel, Elijah remains after his ascension in possession of his earthly shape, which is why he can maintain his association with the human world and, when necessary, reappear on earth. Though his body is not made from dust like that of human beings but came from the tree of life, it enables him to carry out God's commands and miracles (*ibid.*; Zohar, 1:29a; 2:197a; Yalk. R. 27). Therefore, unlike Enoch who is known only as the archangel Metatron, Elijah keeps his name under which he intervenes in the fate of the Jewish people. The *Zohar, like the Talmud, tells of devout men to whom Elijah is supposed to have revealed himself. In the later mystic literature, Elijah's comments on the secrets of the Torah are extremely frequent. Elijah prophesied the births of Isaac *Luria and *Israel b. Eliezer Baal Shem Tov to their parents. He appeared frequently to Israel Baal Shem Tov, and also played an important part in the legends of the *Ẓaddikim*.

[Samuel Abba Horodezky]

In Jewish Folklore

Many of the legends and stories in written and oral Jewish folk literature are spun around biblical and post-biblical (historical) figures and legendary characters. Among these Elijah is a favorite hero and overshadows other popular folklore protagonists: e.g., Moses, King David, King Solomon, Maimonides, and such local sages as R. Shalom *Shabbazi of Yemen, R. Ḥayyim b. Moses *Attar of Morocco, R. Israel b. Eliezer Baal Shem Tov of the ḥasidic legend, and others. The redemptive motif associated with Elijah in rabbinic literature as the herald of the future redemption of Israel and of the messianic era is not stressed in folklore; he is rather portrayed as the heavenly emissary sent on earth to combat social injustice. He rewards the poor who are hospitable and punishes the greedy rich. In his attempts to right wrongs, he seeks to bridge the gap of social inequality and does not hesitate to punish the unjust, regardless of their status even if they be rabbis or respected communal leaders. In Joseph Shabbethai Farḥi's collection of folktales, *Oseh Pele* (vol. 2 (1954), 114), Elijah strangles the local rabbi while the latter rests after the **seder*. The prophet admonishes the rabbi: "You collected all the money as charity, but you distributed it according to your own will. The cries [of the needy] reached heaven and came before God, the Almighty…" Many of the stories about Elijah are outcries of the wretched and unfortunate against the proud and oppressive elements in the Jewish community and were used by the authors as a vehicle for social protest. At the same time, these legends are a type of comfort and solace to the poor. Elijah appears especially on the eve of *Passover when he punishes the misers and provides the despairing poor with the necessaries to prepare the *seder*. His activities continue late into the *seder* night; the Cup of Elijah is placed in the center of the festive table and the prophet is expected to announce the redeemer. Elijah also alleviates the burdens of Jewish communities suffering from religious and national persecution, and exposes *blood libels – mainly occurring on Passover – as absurd and perfidious calumnies.

Elijah's benign acts and the miracles he performs extend beyond the specifically Jewish sphere and have their parallel in other folklore. A recurrent theme in the Elijah legends is the prophet's ability to ward off the *Angel of Death from the young fated to die (a motif rooted in the biblical revival story); this he usually does by advising them to study the Torah. A healing agent, he also blesses the barren with fertility and is able to interpret occult events and visions described in cryptic passages in the Torah and in the Talmud. Another prevalent Elijah motif is the prophet's task to act as provider, based on his biblical endowment to make rain. He confers an inexhaustible barrel of oil on Mayer Amschel Rothschild, distributes magic money-making boxes to the poor but deprives them of this heavenly gift when they become uncharitable and stop giving alms. In the Yiddish song "God of Abraham," chanted by East European Jewish women at the termination of the Sabbath, Elijah is heralded as Israel's redeemer, but since the song is chanted at the beginning of the new week, it also stresses his role as provider. Since Elijah did not die, and is thought to wander the earth, usually disguised as a poor man, a beggar, or a gentile peasant, there are those who are eager to meet him, or at least to see him in a dream (*Gillui Eliyahu*, "Elijah's revelation"). The practical Kabbalah and Jewish folk beliefs describe ways to bring this about. His name is, therefore, also inscribed on many amulets, especially in the areas influenced by Islamic culture.

The stories and beliefs revolving around Elijah were the subject of many *chapbooks composed in Yiddish, Ladino, and Judeo-Arabic dialects. All these legends testify not only to the popularity of the prophet among all Jewish communities, but also reveal the close affinity in Jewish folklore between written and oral literature and customs (see *Elijah, Chair of; *Elijah, Cup of). Many of the customs associated with Elijah can be explained by etiological tales. Their setting is usually an Elijah cave or shrine found on Mount Sinai, at Haifa, Alexandria, Cairo, Damascus, Aleppo, etc. The miracles in these tales, which are mainly of a healing nature, often give the name and describe the origin of the cave. Elijah's role in the circumcision ceremony is not only associated with the "Chair of Elijah," but he heals and is the guardian angel of the newborn Jewish child during the "critical birth" period (lasting at least 30 days from the date of birth). Numerous religious and secular folk songs and dances testify to this fact. Many proverbial sayings and aphorisms grew around Elijah's name. The most popular among them "until Elijah arrives," used when referring to a doubtful and unsolved matter, is similar to the folk explanation of the word תיקו (*teiku*), which is actually a form of תיקום "let it stand," "stalemate," as a **notarikon* consisting of the initial letters of *Tishbi yetareẓ kushyot u-ve'ayot* "the Tishbite (Elijah) will resolve difficulties and problems." Though the main stream of the Elijah folklore is associated with his socionational and religious roles, the prophet – as is usual with popular folk heroes – is also a protagonist in witty tales, folk jokes, and humoristic stories. In these Elijah is identified with, or is the guardian angel of, the simpleminded Jew who at the end of the story is victorious; a factor which testifies to a type of wishful thinking at the root of Jewish folklore.

[Dov Noy]

In Islam

According to the Koran (Sura 37:123–130), Ilyās (Elijah) was one of the apostles sent to his people to admonish them to fear God and not worship Baal. They, however, regarded him as a liar. In Sura 6:85 he is mentioned among the righteous ones, together with figures from the New Testament who included ʿĪsā (Jesus). The commentators of the Koran and the authors of Muslim legend enlarge upon this limited information and explain that Ilyās lived during the days of Ahab and Jezebel. They also add that he was the fourth generation (!) after Aaron the Priest. In light of the Bible and the Midrashim they shaped the figure of the prophet who wages war against the worshipers of Baal and its priests, even though they occasionally change the names of the characters: Ahab becomes

Lājab, Jezebel becomes Arbil (this difference is due to omission of the diacritical mark on the letter *R*).

[Haïm Z'ew Hirschberg]

In the Arts

Elijah has inspired a wealth of literary material, mainly in the form of drama and verse. However, apart from an early appearance in the 17th-century medieval English *Stonyhurst Pageants*, he only began to receive serious attention in the late 18th century, when the Countess de Genlis included *La Veuve de Sarepta* in her sacred plays and T.S. Dupuis wrote his English dramatic poem *Elijah* (1789). These were followed in the 19th century by the U.S. writer R. Davidson's *Elijah, a sacred drama…* (1860), and by two Hebrew poems: *Tiferet ha-Tishbi* (1839) by Max E. Stern (1811–1873) and *Ru'aḥ Eliyahu ha-Tishbi* (1879) by Samuel Loeb Silbermann. The subject acquired greater popularity in the 20th century, when writers invested Elijah with fresh social or political significance. The pioneer Yiddish dramatist Peretz *Hirschbein contributed *Eliyohu der Novi* (1916), a comedy portraying the sudden arrival of Elijah at the home of a poor Jew; and Ben Jair (Moritz Golde) wrote a three-part dramatic poem entitled *Elijahu* (1914). Between the world wars the English author Clemence Dane wrote her play *Naboth's Vineyard* (1925) and John Kinmont Hart a poem entitled *Prophet of a Nameless God* (1927). During the period of World War II and immediately following it, there were further works, such as *The Vineyard* (1943), a drama about Elijah, Ahab, and Jezebel by the Earl of Longford; Norman Nicholson's verse play *The Old Man of the Mountains* (1946); and Helmut Huber's German drama *Elias* (1947). Nicholson's play set the Elijah-Ahab conflict in the North of England, the prophet here appearing as the champion of the working classes. Mid-20th century treatments of the subject include Jean Bothwell's *Flame in the Sky…* (1954); Heinrich Bela Zador's *Die Erfuellung* (1958; *Hear the Word!*, 1962), a novel about Elijah and Elisha; and a late work by Martin *Buber, *Elija; ein Mysterienspiel* (1963).

The prophet Elijah is also a prominent figure in Christian art of both East and West. From Greece, where the name was assimilated to Helios (god of the sun), his cult spread to Byzantium and Russia. In the West, the cult was propagated to some extent by the foundation of the Carmelite Order, so named because Elijah, its patron and "founder," is associated with Mount Carmel. Through this patronage Elijah acquired the attribute of a white mantle, the dress of the Order. In Christian typology, Elijah figures as the precursor of John the Baptist; like him he is an ascetic, living in the desert, and like him he is shown as emaciated and wearing a hair-tunic. Elijah, however, also prefigures Jesus: his despair in the desert parallels the Agony in the Garden; the resurrection of the son of the widow of Zarephath (I Kings 17:8–24) is seen as a prefiguration of the resuscitation of Lazarus; and his ascension in a chariot of fire is equated with the Ascension of Jesus. Even the fire of heaven which ignites his sacrificial offering is likened to the descent of the Holy Spirit at Pentecost. Elijah cycles exist in several Carmelite environments. Examples include a 12th-century storiated capital from the Carmelite cloister of Trie (now in Tarbes); paintings of the school of Jörg Ratgeb in the refectory of the Carmelite convent at Hirschhorn am Neckar (1507); 17th-century windows in the Carmelite church of Antwerp; and 18th-century paintings by Jean-Baptiste Despax in the chapel of the Carmelites in Toulouse. The beautiful Russian church dedicated to Elijah at Yaroslavl on the Volga (17th century) is painted with scenes from his life.

The important scenes in Elijah's life are Elijah fed by ravens, Elijah fed by the widow of Zarephath (Sarepta), the resurrection of the widow's son, Elijah comforted by an angel in the wilderness, the sacrifices on Mount Carmel, the massacre of the prophets of Baal, Naboth's vineyard, the smiting of the Jordan, and the ascension in a chariot of fire. These have received varying emphasis in iconographic treatment, those most favored being the ravens, the widow, the angel, and the ascension. The feeding of the ravens appears in a 14th-century fresco in a monastery on Mount Athos; in a 15th-century fresco in a church at Lublin, Poland; in a privately owned painting by Guercino (1620); and in a work by Washington Allston (1779–1843). The widow of Zarephath and her sticks and the resurrection of her son appear in the synagogue of *Dura-Europos; the widow is also depicted in a window at Chartres (12th century) and another at Bourges (13th century); in the 16th-century tapestry of La Chaise-Dieu; and in a painting by Jean Massys (1565). The resurrection of the widow's son also occurs at Bourges; in an icon of Pskov (Tretiakovskaya Gallery, Moscow; 16th century); and in a curious late 19th-century watercolor by Ford Madox Brown (Tate Gallery, London). The angel in the desert appears in a fresco in Orvieto Cathedral (14th century); in 16th-century paintings by Luini (Brera, Milan) and Tintoretto (Scuola di San Rocco, Venice); and in a Tiepolo ceiling in the archbishop's palace at Udine and a Rubens tapestry cartoon (17th century). The holocaust on Mount Carmel is represented at Athos and in a 16th-century fresco in Siena Cathedral by Beccafumi. The ascension of Elijah is, iconographically, in the strong classical tradition including Helios, Apollo, and Pluto. Some early examples are third- and fourth-century catacomb paintings and Christian sarcophagi. The Chapel of Golgotha in the Church of the Holy Sepulcher, Jerusalem, had an early mosaic representation of the scene and the subject also appears on the sixth-century wooden doors of Santa Sabina, Rome; in a ninth-century miniature of the Kosmas Indikopleustes manuscript (St. Catherine, Sinai); on the bronze door of Saint Sophia, Novgorod (1155); in Athos and Prague (14th century); in the 14th-century *Weltchronik* manuscript of Rudolf von Ems; and in paintings by Tintoretto (Scuola di San Rocco), Rubens, and Simon Vouet.

A rich and variegated selection of Elijah songs forms part of the folk and paraliturgical repertory of almost every Jewish community. In Christian music, the "History of Elijah and Ahab" occurs among Hungarian Protestant Bible songs of the 16th century (Hofgreff manuscript). Oratorio composers, from the 17th century onward, made use of the subject when the political climate was favorable, although no oratorios or cantatas about Elijah were composed for the French court. Some early examples are M. Cazzati's *Il Zelante Difeso* (Bologna, 1665), on Elijah and the priests of Baal; and the oratorios written for the Viennese court by composers such as Georg Reutter (1728) and Antonio Caldara (1729; libretto by Zeno). A comic opera after Kotzebue by Conradin Kreutzer, *Die Schlafmuetze des Propheten Elias* (1814), was by the whim of the censor retitled *Die Nachtmuetze…*, varying the term for nightcap. Felix *Mendelssohn's oratorio *Elijah*, first performed at the Birmingham Festival in 1846, has remained the outstanding musical interpretation of the prophet's character and deeds; it is also practically the only 19th-century oratorio that survives in the repertory and is most often performed in England, Germany (except during the Nazi era), and Israel. Abraham Zvi *Idelsohn's opera *Elijah* has yet to be published.

[Bathja Bayer]

BIBLIOGRAPHY: IN THE BIBLE: H. Gunkel, *Elias Jahwe und Baal* (1906); R. Kittel, *Geschichte des Volkes Israel*, 2 (1917), 312ff.; A.S. Peake, in: BJRL, 11 (1927), 296–321; R. de Vaux, in: *Bulletin du Musée de Beyrouth*, 5 (1941), 7–20; J. Morgenstern, *Amos-Studies*, 1 (1941), 291ff.; Alt, KI Schr, 2 (1953), 135–41; H. Galling, in: *Alt-Festschrift* (1953), 105–25; G. Fohrer, *Elia* (1957); R.S. Wallace, *Elijah and Elisha* (1957); Kaufmann Y., Toledot, index; D.R. ap-Thomas, in: PEQ, 92 (1960), 146–55; H.H. Rowley, *Men of God* (1963), 37–65. **ADD. BIBLIOGRAPHY:** R. Hallevy, in: JNES, 17 (1958), 237–44; K. Roberts, in: CBQ, 62 (2000), 632–44; S. Otto, in: JSOT, 27 (2003), 487–508; M. Smith, *Palestinian Parties and Politics that Shaped the Old Testament* (1971); M.A. Cohen, in: *ErIsr*, 12 (FS Glueck; 1975), 87–94; M. Cogan, *I Kings* (AB; 2000), 424–86. IN THE AGGADAH: Ginzberg, Legends, index; *Tanna de-Vei Eliyahu*, ed. by M. Friedmann (Ish-Shalom) (1904), 1–62; V. Aptowitzer, *Parteipolitik der Hasmonaeerzeit…* (1927), 95–104; M.W. Levinsohn, *Der Prophet Elia nach den Talmudim- und Midraschimquellen* (1929); D. Daube, *The New Testament and Rabbinic Judaism* (1956), 20–26; E. Margoliot, *Eliyahu ha-Navi be-Sifrut Yisrael…* (1960). IN FOLKLORE: D. Noy, in: *Maḥanayim*, 44 (1960), 110–6; B. Silverman Weinreich, in: *Field of Yiddish*, 2 (1965), 202–31; *Yeda Am*, 25 (1961); H. Schwarzbaum, *Studies in Jewish and World Folklore* (1968), 522 (index); Sartori, in: *Handwoerterbuch des deutschen Aberglaubens*, 2 (1929/30), 781–5; S. Thompson, *Motif Index of Folk-Literature*, 5 (1957), V 200–V 299; C.G. Loomis, *White Magic* (1948), index; J. Bergmann, *Die Legenden der Juden* (1919), 73–83. IN ISLAM: Kisāʾī, Qiṣaṣ, ed. by I. Eisenberg (1922), 244–50; A.J. Wensinck and J.H. Kramers (eds.), *Handwoerterbuch des Islam* (1941), s.v. *Ilyās*; H.A.R. Gibb and J.H. Kramers (eds.), *Shorter Encyclopaedia of Islam* (1953), s.v. *Ilyās*; Thaʿlabī, Qiṣaṣ (1356 AH), 212–9; H. Speyer, *Die biblischen Erzaehlungen im Qoran* (1961), 406. **ADD. BIBLIOGRAPHY:** "Ilyās," in: EIS², 3:1156 (incl. bibl.). IN ART: E. Werner, *Mendelssohn, A New Image of the Composer and his Age* (1963), 457–73, includes bibliography; A. Schering, *Geschichte des Oratoriums* (1911), 440ff.; J.Y. Rivlin, *Shirat Yehudei ha-Targum* (1959), 272–4; *Yeda Am*, 7 (1960); L. Réau, in: *Etudes Carmélitaines* (1956).

ELIJAH, APOCALYPSE OF, apocryphal work. In the *Stiehometry of Nicephorus*, a Christian list of biblical books and Apocrypha generally dated to the middle of the sixth century, there is the item, "Of the Prophet Elias, 316 *stichoi.*" Similar references are found in other early Christian lists and the *List of 60 Books* gives the title as *The Apocalypse of Elias.* The existence of such a work is confirmed by Origen's comment that the verse in I Corinthians 2:9 (Commentary to Matthew 27:9) is from the *Apocalypse of Elias the Prophet.* A similar claim is made by other Church Fathers, but Jerome, a great opponent of all apocryphal books, denies it vigorously (*Epistula LVII [ad Pammachium]*, 9). This same verse is quoted in the Ascension of Isaiah 11:34, definitely from I Corinthians and perhaps independently in Pseudo-Philo (*Antiquitatum biblicarum liber* 26:13), Clement of Alexandria (*Protrepticus* 10:94), and elsewhere. Likewise, some ancient sources attribute a quotation in Ephesians 5:14 to the same source (cf. Schuerer, Gesch, vol. 3, 361ff.).

Two Latin documents containing quotations from the *Apocalypse of Elijah* have been discovered, one of particular interest (de Bruyne, in *Revue Benedictine* (1908), 146ff.), presenting a description of the torments in Hell. A similar revelation is shown by Elijah to R. Joshua b. Levi in the *Chronicles of Jeraḥmeel* (ed. by M. Gaster (1899), 34ff.). De Bruyne published additional Latin materials relevant to the *Apocalypse of Elijah* in *Revue Benedictine* in 1925. There are also two later *Apocalypse of Elijah.* One, in Coptic, first published by G. Steindorff in 1899 (there is a 1981 edition: *The Apocalypse of Elijah, based on Pap. Chester Beatty 2018: Coptic text*, ed. and transl. by A. Pietersma and S. Turner Comstock, with H.W. Attridge), probably preserves a considerable body of older Jewish apocalyptic material, including descriptions of the Antichrist. Similar descriptions are also to be found in the Hebrew *Sefer Eliyahu*, a work edited with an explanation in German by M. Buttenwieser (1897), who discerned in it an apocalypse written about 260 C.E. with later, supplementary materials. A description of the Antichrist is also found in quotations attributed to the *Apocalypse of Elijah* in the fragments published by F. Nau in *Journal Asiatique* in 1917 (Ilesérie, tome 9, p. 453ff.).

BIBLIOGRAPHY: In addition to that cited above see M.R. James, *Lost Apocrypha of the Old Testament* (1920), 53–61; and DBI, Supplement 1 (1928), 456–8, both with bibliographies.

[Michael E. Stone]

ELIJAH, CHAIR OF (Heb. כִּסֵּא שֶׁל אֵלִיָּהוּ, *kisse shel Eliyyahu*), a special chair placed at the right of the *sandak* (godfather) at the circumcision ceremony and left unoccupied. The chair is symbolically meant for Elijah the prophet, called "The Angel of Covenant" (Mal. 3:1; covenant = *berit* = circumcision). It is usually richly carved and ornamented with embroideries. The Shulḥan Arukh (YD 265:11) prescribes the reservation of a special chair or seat for Elijah, and the *mohel* (circumciser) refers to it in the opening prayer preceding the circumcision: "This is the chair of Elijah, blessed be his memory." The chair is also mentioned in the special *piyyut* for circumcision when the rite is performed on a Sabbath. Midrashic literature links the custom to Elijah's plaint to God that "the children of Israel have forsaken Thy covenant" (I Kings 19:10, 14). According to the homiletic interpretations of this verse, Elijah had complained that the Jewish people had disregarded the commandment of circumcision and God is said to have replied: "Because of excessive zeal for Me you have brought charges against Israel that they have forsaken My covenant; therefore you shall have to be present at every circumcision ceremony" (PdRE 29; Zohar, Gen. 93a). Since "the messenger [angel] of the Covenant," spoken of in Malachi 3:1, was identified with the prophet Elijah, it was only proper that the Angel of the Covenant should be present whenever a Jewish child entered the Covenant of Abraham (i.e., circumcision). Scholars have suggested that the custom is rooted in the belief in guardian angels for the newborn; Elijah is identified as the guardian angel of the Jewish child. Most probably, the biblical story (I Kings 17:17–24) in which Elijah revived the child of the widow was instrumental in creating this concept. Elijah is also the child protector in the inscription on *amulets against *Lilith. These were placed above the bed of the mother and the newborn child.

BIBLIOGRAPHY: H. Schauss, *The Lifetime of a Jew* (1950), 34–37; Eisenstein, Dinim, 182.

ELIJAH, CUP OF (Heb. כּוֹסוֹ שֶׁל אֵלִיָּהוּ, *koso shel Eliyyahu*), term designating the cup of wine which is placed on the table of the *Passover eve ceremonial (*seder*), but which is not drunk. There was controversy among the rabbis whether the *seder* ritual required four or five cups. Since, according to traditional belief, all doubtful cases of tradition will be resolved "when Elijah comes," custom decreed that the fifth cup should be filled but not partaken of (cf. Pes. 118a; Maim., Yad, Ḥameẓ u-Maẓẓah 8:10). Later this custom became associated with the belief that Elijah had not died but had ascended to heaven in a fiery chariot (II Kings 2:11), and that he would return as the forerunner of the Messiah (Mal. 3:23). The festival of redemption from Egyptian bondage was naturally associated with the forerunner of the Messiah, who was expected in this "season of redemption" to herald the coming deliverance (cf. RH 11b). Hence the popular notion arose that the "cup of Elijah" was prepared to welcome the prophet who visited every Jewish home on the Passover night.

BIBLIOGRAPHY: H. Schauss, *Jewish Festivals* (1938), 80–82; J.L. Avida, *Koso shel Eliyahu ha-Navi…* (1958); Hoffer, in: HḤY, 11 (1927), 211–3.

ELIJAH BEN AARON BEN MOSES (also referred to as **Ibn-'Abd-al-Wālī** or *ha-dayyan*, "the judge"), Karaite author in Jerusalem; according to A. *Firkovich, he lived in the 15th century, and according to P.F. Fraenkel (see bibliography) in the 16th. He wrote the following works in Arabic: *Shurūṭ al-Dhabaḥāt*, on the laws of ritual slaughter; a key (*fihrist*) to Judah *Hadassi's *Eshkol ha-Kofer*; collectanea (manuscript in Jewish Theological Seminary, N.Y., presumably the same as *Sefer le-Eliyahu ha-Dayyan*, referred to in S. Pinsker, *Likkutei Kadmoniyyot* (1860), 192 no. 14); and a commentary on the weekly portion *Ha'azinu*. He also composed *Shevaḥ fī al-Torah*, a prayer on opening the Ark.

BIBLIOGRAPHY: Fraenkel, in: MGWJ, 32 (1883), 400–15; Mann, Texts, index, s.v. *Elijah Haddayan*.

[Jakob Naphtali Hertz Simchoni]

ELIJAH BEN ABRAHAM (first half of 12th century), Karaite scholar who may have lived in Ereẓ Israel. He wrote a polemical tract *Ḥilluk ha-Kara'im ve-ha-Rabbanim* ("The Controversy between the Karaites and the Rabbanites"). In this Elijah lists 14 Jewish sects of which there remained in his time only four: the *Rabbanites, the *Karaites, the Tiflisites, and the followers of the faith (i.e., sect) of *Meshwi al-Ukbari. Following *Kirkisānī and other Karaite writers, Elijah considers that the breach between Karaism and Rabbanite Judaism is traceable as early as the time of *Jeroboam I. Elijah was the first Karaite author to relate the questionable Karaite tradition according to which *Anan b. David and other Karaites were the first Avelei Zion ("Mourners of Zion") in Jerusalem. The list of Karaite sages in Elijah's work includes authors not known from other sources and also Rabbanite scholars such as *Judah b. Eli of Tiberias and Judah ibn Quraysh. The author states in conclusion that "although the *Rabbanim* go astray in most of the *mitzvot*, they are our brothers and our coreligionists. And our soul grieves for their errors."

BIBLIOGRAPHY: S. Pinsker, *Likkutei Kadmoniyyot* (1860), 19, 225 (first pagination); S. Poznański, *Karaite Literary Opponents of Saadiah Gaon* (1908), 72–74; Mann, Texts, 2 (1935), index; L. Nemoy, *Karaite Anthology* (1952), 4–8; Z. Ankori, *Karaites in Byzantium* (1959), index.

[Simha Katz]

ELIJAH BEN BARUCH (ben Solomon ben Abraham) THE ELDER (d. before 1712), Karaite author. Elijah lived at first in Constantinople but is included by Simḥah Isaac *Luẓki among the Karaite writers of the Crimea. Elijah subsequently visited Ereẓ Israel, and is therefore referred to as "Yerushalmi." While in Jerusalem he copied the polemic by Salmon b. Jeroham against *Saadiah Gaon, as well as the polemical tract of Sahl b. Maẓliaḥ. Elijah inserted his own comments, strongly critical of the *Rabbanites in general and Saadiah Gaon in particular. Elijah's writings, mainly polemical, include (1) *Asarah Ma'amarot*, his major work, on the differences between the Rabbanites and the Karaites; (2) *Iggeret ha-Vikku'aḥ*, in four parts, not extant (mentioned in Luẓki's *Oraḥ Ẓaddikim*); (3) *Yalkut*, a collection of 61 essays by Karaite and Rabbanite scholars, with commentary; (4) *Sippurei Massa'ot*, a description of his journey from the Crimea to Ereẓ Israel; (5) *Ẓeror ha-Mor*, a commentary on Judah Gibbor's *Minḥat Yehudah*. None of his works was published.

BIBLIOGRAPHY: A. Geiger, in: *Oẓar Neḥmad*, 4 (1863), 18; A.B. Gottlober, *Bikkoret le-Toledot ha-Kara'im* (1865), 159; S. Pinsker, in: *Likkutei Kadmoniyyot* (1860), 25, 27, 43; S. Poznański, *Karaite Literary Opponents of Sa'adiah Gaon* (1908), 86, no. 45; Mann, Texts, 2 (1935), 1426–27.

ELIJAH BEN BENJAMIN HA-LEVI (d. after 1540), rabbi and *paytan* of Constantinople. He belonged to an indigenous Turkish Jewish family. He studied under Moses *Capsali, to whose aid he came in his dispute with Joseph *Colon, and afterward under Elijah *Mizraḥi, whom he succeeded as chief rabbi of Constantinople in 1525. Elijah wrote a book of responsa called *Tanna de-Vei Eliyahu*, comprising 451 responsa (in manuscript), 221 of which were edited by Benjamin b. Abraham *Motal and published by Aaron Galimidi, one of his descendants, under the title *Zekan Aharon* (Constantinople, 1734). Some of his responsa were published in the works of his contemporaries, in the responsa *Oholei Tam* (in *Tummat Yesharim*) of *Tam ibn Yaḥya, and in the *Avkat Rokhel* of Joseph *Caro. Benjamin Motal published Elijah's article *"Kol De'i,"* on the laws of **asmakhta*, in his collection *Tummat Yesharim*. Elijah edited and published the *Maḥzor Romania*, the liturgy in use in Greece and the neighboring countries, adding to it *bakkashot, teḥinot*, and other *piyyutim*. Benjamin Motal states that Elijah wrote thousands of poems, and the following books of poetry are known to be by him: *Beit ha-Levi, Tokheḥah Megullah, Shevet ha-Musar,* and *Mei Zahav*. The book *Zekan Aharon* mentions his *Livyat Ḥen*, which deals with ethical conduct. It is divided into three parts: *Maḥaneh Leviyyah* (of which one chapter was published as no. 148 of *Zekan Aharon*), *Maḥaneh Yisrael*, and *Maḥaneh Shekhinah*. He also prepared for publication Jacob b. Asher's *Arba'ah Turim* (Constantinople, 1494 or 1504) and Alfasi's code (Constantinople, 1509).

BIBLIOGRAPHY: Motal, in: Elijah b. Binyamin ha-Levi, *Zekan Aharon* (Constantinople, 1734), introduction; Zunz, Poesie, 388–90; A. Berliner, *Aus meiner Bibliothek* (1898), 3–5; S. Wiener, *Kohelet Moshe*, 4 (1902), 441, no. 3665; Rosanes, Togarmah, 1 (1930[2]), 206–9; 2 (1938[2]), 8f.; Davidson, Oẓar, 4 (1933), 363, s.v. *Eliyahu ha-Levi;* Goldschmidt, in: *Sefunot*, 8 (1964), 205–36.

[Abraham David]

ELIJAH BEN ELIEZER PHILOSOPH HA-YERUSHALMI (fl. 15th century), scholar and Hebrew poet who lived in Crete. Elijah wrote a book on logic, *Sefer Higgayon al Derekh She'elot u-Teshuvot* (manuscripts in Leiden, Paris, and Parma), which is based entirely on Aristotelian logic, omitting the categories. He also wrote *Perush Pirkei ha-Merkavah*, a commentary on Maimonides' interpretation of Ezekiel's vision in his *Guide* (manuscript in Paris). In this work Elijah cites his commentary on the book of **Bahir*. He is also the author of a number of poems written in Hebrew and Aramaic and of prayers in prose (Mss. Parma 997; Paris 707).

BIBLIOGRAPHY: G.B. De Rossi, *Manuscripti Codices Hebraici*, 2 (1803), 163, no. 772, 3; M. Steinschneider, *Catalogue Leyden* (1858), 239ff.; Steinschneider, Uebersetzungen, 499, 523; idem, in: HB, 19 (1879), 63; 21 (1881), 27; Zunz, Lit Poesie, 518, 711; Zunz, in: ZHB, 19 (1916), 61, no. 3, 63, no. 18; S. Munk, *Manuscrits hébreux de l'Oratoire* (1911), 54–56; Davidson, Oẓar, 4 (1933), 364. **ADD. BIBLIOGRAPHY:** C. Sirat, *A History of Jewish Philosophy in the Middle Ages* (1985), 344; Sh. Rosenberg, in: *Daat*, 1 (1978), 63–71; 2–3 (1979), 127–38; 7 (1981), 73–92.

[Jefim (Hayyim) Schirmann]

ELIJAH BEN ḤAYYIM (1530?–1610?), rabbi and halakhist, known as **Maharanaḥ** or **M**orenu **ha-Rav** ibn **Ḥ**ayyim. Elijah was born in Adrianople and in about 1575 was appointed chief rabbi of Constantinople. His writings – including novellae, discussions on most of the tractates of the Talmud, and responsa – were stolen, but some were recovered and published. They comprise *Teshuvot ha-Ranaḥ* (Constantinople, 1810[2]), responsa, with an appendix consisting of novellae on tractate *Ketubbot* published by his disciple, Isaac di Leon; *Mayim Amukim* (Venice, 1647), responsa, together with others by Elijah *Mizraḥi; *Ha-Noten Imrei Shefer* (Venice, 1630), homilies on the Pentateuch (the first edition entitled *Mikhtav me-Eliyahu* (Constantinople, 1624) was probably incomplete). He was highly regarded by later rabbis, among them Akiva *Eger, who praised his *Teshuvot ha-Ranaḥ*, which he used as a source for his decisions.

BIBLIOGRAPHY: Conforte, Kore, 42a–b, 48b; Beer, in: *Literaturblatt des Orients*, 9 (1848), 805f.; Rosanes, Togarmah, 3 (1938), 32f.; Habermann, in: *Sefer Assaf* (1953), 217–22.

[Jacob Haberman]

ELIJAH BEN JUDAH OF PARIS (first half of the 12th century), French talmudist, commentator, and halakhist. Elijah is quoted in the *tosafot* and in the works of *Eliezer b. Nathan of Mainz, *Eliezer b. Joel ha-Levi of Bonn, *Moses of Coucy, *Mordecai b. Hillel, *Meir b. Baruch of Rothenburg, and others. He was considered one of the leading scholars of his time, together with R. *Tam and *Meshullam b. Nathan of Melun, who held him in great esteem. Eliezer b. Nathan of Mainz directed his question on *Ḥezkat ha-Ḥallonot* to these three scholars (Raban, 153:3); and questions were also addressed to Elijah by Isaac b. Samuel ha-Zaken (Tos. to Ket. 54b). *Moses b. Abraham of Pontoise, in a responsum to R. Tam (*Sefer ha-Yashar*, Resp. 51), refers to Elijah as "our teacher and our light." The Jews of Paris followed his customs, even in opposition to the views of R. Tam. His ruling (Tos. to Eruv. 97a) that the *tefillin* knot must be tied every day is well-known. Zunz attributes to Elijah a number of liturgical poems.

BIBLIOGRAPHY: Zunz, Gesch, 458; Gross, Gal Jud, 515f., no. 9; Michael, Or, no. 381; V. Aptowitzer, *Mavo le-Sefer Ravyah* (1938), 310–1; Urbach, Tosafot, index.

ELIJAH BEN KALONYMUS OF LUBLIN (second half of 17th century), preacher and rabbi. Little is known about Elijah, whose only extant work, *Adderet Eliyahu* (Frankfurt on the Oder, 1696), contains sermons commenting on each weekly Torah portion. They resemble short fables, each of which can stand independently, while together they form an intricate whole. In these *derashot*, written in a pleasant style, Elijah employs much kabbalistic terminology, quoting from such works as the Zohar, *Zohar Ḥadash*, and *Sefer ha-Peli'ah*, and makes use of talmudic-midrashic literature as well as Rashi. At the end of the book is appended a prayer from Ereẓ Israel, the recitation of which could ensure forgiveness for sins connected with the destruction of the Temple and the resultant Diaspora.

ELIJAH BEN LOEB OF FULDA (c. 1650/60–c. 1720), rabbi and halakhic author. Elijah was born in Wiznica (Poland), where he spent most of his life, and where he died. Toward the end of his life he moved to Fulda (southwest Germany), although there is no evidence that he became rabbi there as has been stated by some. Elijah made a special study of the Jerusalem Talmud, his fame resting principally on his commentaries to *Shekalim* (Frankfurt, 1689), the order of *Zera'im* (Amsterdam, 1710), *Bava Kamma* and *Bava Meẓia* (Offenbach, 1725), and *Bava Batra* (Frankfurt, 1742). Using manuscripts upon which he also relied for his corrections to the *editio princeps* of the Jerusalem Talmud, Elijah's commentaries deal with each topic in *halakhah* and *aggadah*. His style is generally succinct; lengthier discussions are inserted in a separate rubric. Elijah's commentary was published approximately 50 years after that of Joshua *Benveniste, the existence of which was unknown to him, and his commentary, published together with the text, exercised great influence on his contemporaries and initiated the systematic study of the Jerusalem Talmud in 18th-century Poland.

BIBLIOGRAPHY: L. Ginzberg, *Perushim ve-Ḥiddushin ba-Yerushalmi*, 1 (1941).

[Jacob Haberman]

ELIJAH BEN RAPHAEL SOLOMON HA-LEVI (end of 18th and beginning of 19th century), Italian rabbi, author, kabbalist, and liturgical poet. Elijah was both a pupil and a colleague of Isaac *Lampronti together with whom he studied under Judah *Briel in Mantua. He was at first rabbi of Finale and later worked in Alessandria. He composed a number of marriage poems and other occasional poems as well as a large work, *Seder de-Eliyahu* (Mantua, 1786). The names of all his books are connected with the name Elijah, such as *Sava Eliyahu* and *Eliyahu be-Arba*. His responsa are to be found in the *Shemesh Ẓedakah* of Samson Morpurgo, in the *Paḥad Yizḥak* of Isaac Lampronti, and in the *Givat Pinḥas* (unpublished) of Phinehas Anau. A number of talmudic and kabbalistic works, responsa, and homilies by Elijah remained unpublished. Isaac Raphael Finzi composed an elegy on his death.

BIBLIOGRAPHY: Fuenn, Keneset, 117; Ghirondi-Neppi, 13f.

[Samuel Abba Horodezky]

ELIJAH BEN SHABBETAI BE'ER (14th–15th centuries; also known as **Elia di Sabato of Fermo** and in England as **Elias Sabot**), papal physician. He attended Popes Innocent VII (1404–06), Martin V (1417–31), and Eugene IV (1431–47), as well as the duke of Milan and the marquess of Ferrara. In 1410 he was summoned to England to treat King Henry IV and was empowered to bring with him a retinue of ten persons. A teacher of medicine at the University of Pavia, he was the first Jew recorded on the faculty of a European university. In recognition of his services, he was accorded the dignity of knight, and in 1405 was awarded Roman citizenship. An enigmatic medal was struck in 1497 (or 1503) in honor of his son Benjamin.

BIBLIOGRAPHY: Gauthier, in: REJ, 49 (1904), 259; Wiener, in: JQR, 18 (1905/06), 142ff.; Simonsen, *ibid.*, 360; Milano, Italia, 155, 483, 629; Muenster, in: *Scritti... Sally Mayer* (1956), 224–58, includes bibliography; C. Roth, *Jews in the Renaissance* (1959), 39, 210, 215–6, 355.

[Ariel Toaff]

ELIJAH BEN SHEMAIAH (fl. 11th century), liturgical poet in Bari, southern Italy. He was one of the most prolific poets of the Italian school. He composed about 40 *seliḥot*, most of them strophic, which have remained in manuscripts and old editions; some were included in the German-Polish ritual. Y. David, who prepared a critical edition of Elijah's *piyyutim* (1977), commented also on their sources, meaning, and characteristics. The subject matter is mostly a variation of the same theme: grief over present misery of Israel in exile and trust in God's help. Some of his poems allude to cruel persecutions in his time, and he refers to the enemies of Israel with many allegorical names. Stylistically, the poems resemble the *seliḥot* of his contemporary *Solomon ha-Bavli, who was probably his master, but the language is more stereotyped. Zunz made a special study of his language and style. Elijah's signature is, among others, preserved in a responsum of Samuel b. Natronai. In the past scholars underlined the lack of depth and originality of this kind of *piyyutim* and the obscurity of the language. More recently, scholars have come to have a much higher opinion of the quality of Ben Shemaiah's *seliḥot*, considering him an excellent spokesperson of the Jewish community of Bari in its historical situation and a good representative of the literary tendencies of the epoch with his own individuality.

BIBLIOGRAPHY: Zunz, Vortraege, 406; Zunz, Lit. Poesie, 139, 244ff.; 616ff.; Landshuth, Ammudei, 17; Michael, Or, no. 412; Elbogen, Gottesdienst, 333; H. Brody and M. Wiener, *Mivḥar ha-Shirah ha-Ivrit* (1922), 233ff.; Schirmann, Italia, 41–47; A.M. Habermann, *Be-Ron Yaḥad* (1945), 105–7; A. Mirsky, *Yalkut ha-Piyyutim* (1958), 264ff.; Davidson, Oẓar, 4 (1933), 362; Roth, Dark Ages, 180, 258–9. **ADD. BIBLIOGRAPHY:** Y. David (ed.), *Piyyuṭei Eliyah Bar-Shemaiah* (1977); B. Bar-Tikva, in: *Sinai*, 83, 1–2 (1978), 92–94.

[Jefim (Hayyim) Schirmann / Angel Sáenz-Badillos (2nd ed.)]

ELIJAH BEN SOLOMON ABRAHAM HA-KOHEN OF SMYRNA (d. 1729), one of the outstanding preachers of his time. Born in Smyrna, Elijah spent most of his life there as a preacher, *dayyan*, and rabbi. Elijah came from a family of rabbis and writers; his grandfather, R. Michael ha-Kohen, wrote exegetical works on the Torah, and his uncle, R. Isaac ha-Kohen, was also a writer. His father, Abraham Solomon ha-Kohen, one of the rabbis of Smyrna, is known for his involvement in the rescue of Jews who had been taken captive. It would seem that he was also a scholar, as Elijah often quotes him.

Elijah was a prolific writer; about 30 of his works are extant, some in print, others in manuscript; his lost works are known only from references to them in his own writings. The following are among his extant works:

(1) *Shevet Musar* (Constantinople, 1712, and many subsequent editions), one of the most popular Hebrew works in the fields of ethics and homiletics, also translated into Yiddish. This work consists of 52 sermons, corresponding to the

weekly Torah portions and to the numerical value of his Hebrew name, "Eliyahu."

(2) *Me'il Ẓedakah* (Smyrna, 1731), an ethical work dealing with the question of charity.

(3) *Midrash ha-Ittamari* (Constantinople, 1695; Salonica, 1725), a homiletical work consisting of sermons on various subjects, many of them ethical (e.g., charity and repentance). Because of this work, Elijah became known in Hebrew literature as Elijah ha-Kohen ha-Ittamari.

(4) *Midrash Talpiyyot*, novellae on various subjects, collected, according to the author, from the 300 books listed in the preface. Only the first half of this work, arranged in alphabetical order, was printed (Smyrna, 1736).

(5) *Minḥat Eliyahu* (Salonika, 1824), 33 sermons, or chapters on ethical subjects.

The rest of his works includes several other ethical-homiletical collections, commentaries on Psalms, on other parts of the Bible, on *Pirkei Avot*, the 613 commandments, prayers, rabbinical sayings related to the various Torah portions, and on the *aggadot* of the Jerusalem Talmud. In addition, Elijah wrote several responsa, some to questions sent from far away. It is possible that he also dabbled in magic; many legends, which can be found in Ladino folktales, were related about him.

The teaching of ethical behavior, however, was Elijah's main purpose. He made extensive use of the vast ethical literature of the Middle Ages, both early and late – from *Sefer Ḥasidim* to the *Shenei Luḥot ha-Berit*, by Isaiah ha-Levi Horowitz. In the sermons, ethical writings, and exegetical works, he also used kabbalistic literature, in which he was well versed. Later writers of homiletics and ethics, the author of the famous *Ḥemdat Yamim*, for example, made use of his works.

Social problems are a basic concern in his thought. The social and economic gap between rich and poor disturbed him, and some of his sermons are devoted to the question of theodicy: Elijah dwells at length upon the heavenly rewards of the poor and the just after death while vividly describing the horrible punishment awaiting the wicked. His preaching displays a strongly negative attitude toward the benefits derived from this world, and his listeners are asked to renounce all its joys, even purposely to take suffering and hardship upon themselves.

A considerable portion of Elijah's sermons deals with messianic subjects. G. Scholem – through the aid of historical documents and theological analysis of some of Elijah's works – proved that in fact he was a Shabbatean, although not one of the extremists. He probably adhered to its theology as expounded by Abraham *Cardoso. It is possible that late in his life Elijah became detached from this movement, but he did not delete the Shabbatean portions from his earlier works.

BIBLIOGRAPHY: Steinschneider, Cat Bod, 932; Michael, Or, 188–90; M. Wunderbar, in: *Literaturblatt des Orients*, 37 (1847), 579; A. Jellinek (ed.), *Beit ha-Midrash*, 1 (1938²), 16; Rosanes, Togarmah, 6 (1945), 291; Zinberg, Sifrut, 5 (1960), 196–200; S. Werses, in: *Yavneh*, 2 (1940), 156–73; G. Scholem, in: *Sefer ha-Yovel Alexander Marx* (1950), 451–70.

ELIJAH BEN SOLOMON HA-KOHEN, Palestinian *gaon* from 1062 to 1083. His father Solomon was *gaon* from about 1020 to 1025 and was succeeded by *Solomon b. Judah, who held that office until 1051. Elijah and his elder brother Joseph, who were very young when their father died, occupied important positions during Solomon b. Judah's incumbency, Elijah being the "*shelishi*" ("third") and his brother the **av bet din*. According to the prevailing custom Joseph should have been appointed as *gaon*, and Elijah as *av bet din* after the death of Solomon b. Judah, but they were forcibly prevented by *Daniel b. Azariah who belonged to the family of the Babylonian *geonim*. Daniel assumed the gaonate, holding the office from 1051 to 1062, and the two brothers were obliged to accept his authority. Only after the death of Daniel was Elijah appointed *gaon*. After the conquest of Jerusalem by the Seljuks in 1071, Elijah moved to Tyre together with his yeshivah. About two years before his death he designated his son *Abiathar to succeed him after his death, and his second son, Solomon, as *av bet din*. A few of his responsa have survived, in which he and Abiathar reply to questions from *Meshullam b. Moses of Mainz.

BIBLIOGRAPHY: S. Schechter, *Saadyana* (1903), 80–104; Bornstein, in: *Sefer ha-Yovel… N. Sokolow* (1904), 125ff.; Marmorstein, in: REJ, 73 (1921), 84ff.; Mann, Egypt, 2 (1922), index; Mann, Texts, 2 (1935), index; Dinur, Golah, 1, pt. 4 (1962²), index; Scheiber, in: *Tarbiz*, 32 (1962/63), 273–6.

[Simha Assaf]

ELIJAH BEN SOLOMON ZALMAN (the "**Vilna Gaon**" or "**Elijah Gaon**"; acronym **Ha-GRA** = **Ha**-**G**aon **R**abbi **E**liyahu; 1720–1797), one of the greatest spiritual and intellectual leaders of Jewry in modern times. A man of iron will, Elijah combined the personal life of an intellectual hermit with active and polemical leadership in Jewish society through his overwhelming influence on a chosen circle of disciples. Born in Selets, Grodno province, he came from a well-known rabbinical and scholarly family, whose members included Moses Rivkes. From his childhood, Elijah showed unusual gifts. At the age of six and a half, he gave a homily in the synagogue of Vilna and answered with great perception the rabbi's questions on it. When he was seven, Abraham Katzenellenbogen, rabbi of Brest-Litovsk, took him to Moses Margalioth of Keidany (Kedainiai), with whom Elijah studied for a time. However he mainly studied on his own, and thus remained untrammeled by the conventional methods of talmudic education of his day. Besides the Torah and the Oral Law, Elijah also studied Kabbalah, and before the age of 13 attempted to cultivate "practical" Kabbalah and to create a *golem*. Elijah stated, however, that "while I was making it, an image appeared above me, and I ceased from making it, for I said, doubtless God is preventing me" (Ḥayyim of Volozhin, in *Sifra de Ẓeni'uta* (with a commentary by the Vilna Gaon), introd.). Elijah also acquainted himself with astronomy, geometry, algebra, and geography in order to understand certain talmudic laws and discussions. Thus his main concern with astronomy was to understand the rules of the Jewish calendar. For similar reasons he paid great attention to Hebrew grammar (see below). After his marriage around the age of 18 he would seclude himself in a small house outside the city and concentrate on learning day and night.

After staying briefly with his father-in-law in Keidany, Elijah traveled throughout Poland and Germany and visited important communities, including those of Zolkiew (Zholkva), Lissa (Leszano), and Berlin. Subsequently he settled in Vilna, where he remained until his death. He received financial support from the bequest of Moses Rivkes (who left a foundation for scholars in his family) and was additionally assisted by a sum allocated him by the community board, which also provided him with a rented apartment. In about 1785 his weekly allowance was raised by the community to 28 zlotys, which was higher than the stipend of the *av bet din*, the rabbi, or the *shtadlan*. Since there were many outstanding scholars in Vilna at the time, the financial assistance given to Elijah, although he did not hold communal office, testifies to the high esteem in which he was held, despite his extreme personal modesty.

In Vilna his exceptional diligence in study became even more pronounced. To shut out distraction, Elijah would close the windows of his room by day and study by candlelight. In winter he studied in an unheated room placing his feet in cold water to prevent himself from falling asleep (Israel of Shklov, *Sefer Pe'at ha-Shulḥan* (Safed, 1836), introd.). According to Elijah's sons he did not sleep more than two hours a day, and never for more than half an hour at a time. He noted his comments and remarks in the margin of the page he was studying. Elijah made a special study of the Jerusalem Talmud, "opening up new horizons and clarifying incomprehensible passages" (his son Abraham in his eulogy *Sa'arat Eliyahu*). When he was 40 Elijah evinced a revolutionary change in his life. According to his students, he gave up studying exclusively by himself and began to teach, giving lectures to a group of outstanding scholars. In 1768, a wealthy relative, Elijah Peseles, bought a plot near Elijah's home where the edifice he built was dedicated to prayer and study. The master's "prayer room" was later enlarged and became the *bet ha-midrash* (*Klaus*) of the Gaon. Several of Elijah's disciples, including Ḥayyim of Volozhin and the brothers Menahem Mendel and Simḥah Bunem of Shklov, recorded his observations and explanations, and hence through them and Elijah's sons his teachings were disseminated. Elijah at this time generally refrained from contact with people who were not close to him. An exception was the "Maggid of Dubno," Jacob b. Ze'ev *Krantz, whose friendship he sought, and to whom he once wrote: "Come, my friend, to my house and do not delay to revive and entertain me." Though his views had been sought earlier, only at this time did the Gaon also begin to express opinions on public issues. When in 1756 he was requested by Jonathan *Eybeschuetz's party to express his opinion on the controversy with Jacob *Emden, Elijah modestly refused to arbitrate, saying: "Who am I, a man from a distant land, a man young in years, of retiring disposition, that they should listen to me." However his intellectual and spiritual influence continued to grow, and according to the testimony of his contemporaries, "without his knowledge no important activity can be carried out" (I. Klausner, *Vilna bi-Tekufat ha-Ga'on* (1942), 237).

Elijah encouraged the translation of works on the natural sciences into Hebrew but opposed philosophy and Haskalah, seeing them as a threat to faith and tradition. He violently opposed the ḥasidic movement. Although he devoted considerable attention to Kabbalah he looked with concern on any suggestion of giving Kabbalah precedence over halakhic studies, and he also objected to changes in prayer rites and new customs that were being introduced by Ḥasidim. He was apprehensive over the possibility of the creation of a new group which would lead to a split in the community. When the first groups of Ḥasidim were organized in Belorussia and Lithuania the leaders of the Shklov community asked Elijah what policy they should adopt toward the new sect; Elijah replied that it should be fought. Etkes demonstrates that Elijah was the one who initiated the rejection of the Ḥasidim. The Vilna community decided to close the prayer rooms of the Ḥasidim, burn their works, and excommunicate them. In 1772 its leaders dispatched letters to a number of other communities urging them to combat the new movement.

Thus, under the leadership of Elijah, Vilna became the center of opposition to Ḥasidism. In 1772 and 1777 Menahem Mendel of Vitebsk and Shneur Zalman of Lyady, the heads of the ḥasidic movement in Belorussia, attempted to meet Elijah to demonstrate that the new movement did not conflict with traditional Judaism, but the Gaon refused to see them. After publication of Jacob Joseph of Polonnoye's *Toledot Ya'akov-Yosef* (1781), Elijah's fight against Ḥasidism intensified. Through his influence, the ban was again pronounced on the Ḥasidim, and emissaries were sent to rouse the communities against the movement. Around 1794 the Gaon gave instructions that the *Ẓavva'at ha-Ribash* ("Testament of R. Israel Ba'al Shem Tov") should be publicly burned in Vilna. In 1796, the Ḥasidim having spread a rumor that Elijah regretted his stand against the movement, the Gaon replied in a letter sent by special emissaries to the communities of Lithuania and Belorussia: "I will continue to stand on guard, and it is the duty of every believing Jew to repudiate and pursue them [the Ḥasidim] with all manner of afflictions and subdue them, because they have sin in their hearts and are like a sore on the body of Israel." When several Ḥasidim in Minsk cast doubts on the authenticity of Elijah's signature on the letter the community leaders sent two emissaries to Vilna to clarify the matter and Elijah responded with an even sharper condemnation of Ḥasidism. Because of the denigration of the Gaon in ḥasidic circles, the leaders of the Minsk community threatened excommunication to anyone impugning Elijah's honor. In the dispute which broke out in Vilna between the heads of the community and Samuel, the *av bet din*, Elijah opposed Samuel, although they were related. Elijah's intervention resulted in a judgment by the rabbis ruling that Samuel had broken an oath and was guilty of other instances of bad conduct. Samuel's supporters thereupon tried to persuade the state court to prevent payment of the community's weekly allowance to Elijah, since he did not hold a formal position in the communal institutions. The community leaders, however, vigorously condemned this action and imprisoned the preceptor Joel for defaming Elijah. At that time a son of one of the community leaders ran away to a monastery and became converted to Christianity. When the youth was kidnapped from the monastery to induce him to return to Judaism, the ecclesiastical and state authorities arrested several suspects and charged them with the kidnapping. Elijah was also interrogated and imprisoned for a month in February 1788; in September 1789 he was again imprisoned for 12 weeks but the term was commuted. After his death, the opposition to the ḥasidic movement abated somewhat but did not die out completely.

Elijah had decided, before 1783, to immigrate to Ereẓ Israel. He set out alone with the intention of sending for his family later, and on his way sent them a letter – a kind of spiritual testament. The missive reflects his delicate feelings toward his children, his wife, and his mother. He requested his wife not to economize on the tuition of his sons and to care for their health and diet. He also gave instructions for the education of his daughters and admonished them to refrain from taking oaths, cursing, deceit, or quarreling. He considered that vain talk was one of the greatest sins and therefore advised making few visits, even to synagogue, and praying at home, alone, in order to avoid idle talk and jealousy as much as possible. He warned them not to covet wealth and honor, because "it is known that all This World is vanity" (in his *Alim li-Terufah*, 1836). For unknown reasons Elijah did not reach Ereẓ Israel and returned to Vilna.

Over time, Elijah became known as the Gaon and Ḥasid. The first appellation is based on his enormous scholarship that spanned the entirety of rabbinic literature, including the vast world of Midrash and kabbalistic literature. In addition, the depth of his knowledge and understanding is evident in his writings. The combination of Elijah's asceticism and almost obsessive devotion to Torah study and religious observance earned him the title of Ḥasid. Through his teachings and actions Elijah did much to form the characteristics of the "Litvak" *Mitnaggedim* peculiar to Lithuanian Jewish culture whose achievements attained their pinnacle of expression in the 19th century in the many celebrated yeshivot of Lithuania, such as those of Volozhin and Mir. The semi-legendary figure of saint and intellectual giant towered over Lithuanian Jewry and influenced its cultural life in the 19th and into the 20th centuries.

[Israel Klausner]

Teachings

The importance of the spiritual activity of the Vilna Gaon stemmed primarily from the vast range of subjects with which he dealt. There is no subject relevant to Judaism on which he did not write a book or notes and glosses that at times amount to a complete book. The Bible, the Talmud, including the minor tractates, the tannaitic Midrashim, the Zohar and the *Tikkunei ha-Zohar,* the Shulḥan Arukh, Hebrew grammar, and a long list of general sciences such as geometry, measurements, astronomy, and medicine – all these occupied the Gaon of Vilna, to such an extent that it may be said of him that no Jewish or general topic which had a bearing on Judaism was alien to him. Even in the order of the prayers and in the *piyyutim* he formulated new readings that have been accepted (e.g., in the hymn for the termination of the Sabbath, instead of "our seed and wealth he shall multiply as the sand," he read, "our seed and peace").

The fundamental base of his outlook was the concept of the eternity of the Torah, with all its details and minutiae, in actual practice. He regarded the slightest attack on any single detail of the *halakhah*, or the undermining of a single precept of the Torah, as a blow at the foundations of the Torah as a whole. His outlook on the absolute eternity of the Torah he expressed strikingly in his commentary to the Sifra *de-Ẓeni'uta* (Ch. 5): "Everything that was, is, and will be, is included in the Torah. And not only principles, but even the details of each species, the minutest details of every human being, as well as of every creature, plant, and mineral – all are included in the Pentateuch." This belief also encompassed the Oral Law, whence his punctiliousness about every smallest detail of the *halakhah* which established the content and the mode of observance of the precepts of the Torah. In consequence of this outlook the Vilna Gaon came to revive many customs and early prohibitions no longer mentioned even in the Shulḥan Arukh but mentioned in the talmudic sources, or for which he found support in these sources.

The Vilna Gaon interested himself in secular sciences to the extent that he saw in them an aid to the understanding of the Torah. It was his opinion that "all knowledge is necessary for our holy Torah and is included in it." "To the degree that a man is lacking in knowledge and secular sciences he will lack one hundred fold in the wisdom of the Torah" (introduction to Baruch of Shklov's *Euclid*, The Hague, 1780). For this reason he influenced the physician Baruch of Shklov to translate into Hebrew works in such secular sciences as he found necessary for this purpose. He also desired to see the works of Josephus translated into Hebrew, "since they are in aid to the understanding of many passages in the Talmud and Midrash which deal with topics connected with the Holy Land in ancient times." According to a statement dated 1778, he regarded the lack of interest in secular sciences that was widespread in the circles of talmudic scholars as a profanation of Israel's name among the nations, "who like the roaring of many waters will raise their voice against us, saying, where is your wisdom? And the name of Heaven will be profaned" (*ibid.*).

After deeply studying many branches of science, he tried his hand at writing works on mathematics (*Ayil Meshullash*, 1833), on geography (*Ẓurat ha-Areẓ*, Shklov, 1822), on astronomy, and on the calculation of the seasons and planetary motions (in Mss.). He also greatly valued music and said that "most of the cantillation of the Torah, the secrets of the levitical songs, and the secrets of the *Tikkunei ha-Zohar*, cannot be understood without it" (Israel of Shklov, introduction to Elijah's *Pe'at ha-Shulḥan*, 1836). Similarly he greatly interested himself in medicine. However he had no knowledge of foreign languages and derived all his secular knowledge from Hebrew sources, most of which had been compiled during the Middle Ages. As a result he had no idea of Newton's theory or the theory of Lavoisier and his entire scientific thinking was bound up with the theory of the four elements. Despite this Elijah was far removed from the *Haskalah, which spread in his time in the circles of German Jewry. He imposed a severe punishment upon the preacher Abba of Glussk who identified himself with the *maskilim* when in Berlin, and in a conversation with Elijah expressed himself to the effect that "Rashi did not succeed in interpreting the Torah according to the plain meaning of the Scripture, and the authors of the Midrash as is well known are not masters of the correct literal meaning" (J.H. Lewin, *Aliyyot Eliyahu* (1856), n. 34). He did not join battle with the Haskalah movement because at that time the *maskilim* still stood within the bounds of traditional Judaism. They saw no contradiction between Elijah's attitude to secular sciences and the activities of Moses Mendelssohn and some of them had connections with both of these simultaneously.

Elijah's chief strength lay in *halakhah*. The fact that many *halakhot* and dicta in the Talmud are quoted in a fragmentary or defective form in one place, but in full or in a more correct version elsewhere, roused in him the determination to establish the correct reading of many *halakhot* by comparing the different sources. Emendations of the text not based upon investigation of the sources but the result of mere conjecture he regarded as "an absolute crime… for which excommunication is merited" (*Be'ur ha-Gra* to Sh. Ar., YD 279:2). Frequently he succeeded in explaining difficult problems in the Talmud by establishing the correct readings. His eschewal of casuistic hair-splitting, of which he said that "through it transgression increases, iniquity grows, pleasant speech is lost, and truth driven from the congregation of the Lord" (introd. by his sons Judah Leib and Abraham to *Be'ur ha-Gra* to Sh. Ar., OḤ), was also connected with this desire to clarify the readings of the *halakhot*. Hence he also demanded of the student "that he should delve into the subject with integrity, detest piling up difficulties, admit to the truth even if uttered by school children, and all his intellectual desires be nullified as against the truth" (*ibid.*). He regarded the commentary of Rashi as ideal for the study of the Talmud, since his comments "are very straightforward to the discerning" (*ibid.*). In the same spirit of this approach to the study of the Talmud he also established rules for the study of the Mishnah. The rabbis of the Talmud were accustomed in his opinion to explain the words of Mishnah as they explained the words of the Torah, i.e., both according to the plain meaning and exegetically. Expositions of the Mishnah on the basis of the assumption "there is a lacuna and this is what was taught" are exegetical. According to the Gaon, in actual fact the Mishnah lacks nothing, but Judah I occasionally cites a Mishnah which expressed the view of one of the halakhic scholars, and as the *amoraim* inclined to a different view, they understood the Mishnah as if it were defective through omissions, in order that it should conform with their view. This view of the relationship between the Mishnah and the *Gemara* is expressed with complete consistency in his commentary on the Mishnah. At times he deviates from the conclusions of the *Gemara* in connection with certain *mishnayot* and explains them in accordance with the literal meaning of the passage (see, e.g., his commentary to Ber. 4:1 and 7:2).

The Vilna Gaon included within the Torah the Zohar, the *Tikkunei ha-Zohar*, and other early kabbalistic books like the *Sefer ha-Bahir*, of which he had a profound and extensive knowledge. Here, too, he paid special attention to establishing the correct readings. His chief aim, however, was to explain the Kabbalah sources in such a way as to abolish any contradictions between them and the talmudic sources. Wherever he found such contradictions he ascribed them to error in the understanding of the Kabbalah sources or of the words of the Talmud. He applied the same thoroughness to the kabbalistic works of Isaac *Luria, in which he delved deeply, and "he brought them out of the darkness caused by copyists' errors" (Ḥayyim of Volozhin in the introduction to the commentary to the *Sifra de-Ẓeni'uta*). His method of exposition in Kabbalah literature was also directed to understanding the words in their plain sense, although pupils said that in every literal interpretation he gave there was latent the esoteric meaning of the passage. Because of his attachment to Kabbalah he took a negative attitude to philosophy, which he designated "the accursed." In particular his criticism was directed against Maimonides who rejected the efficacy of the use of Divine Names, charms, and amulets, thus denying the possibility of practical Kabbalah, which Elijah had followed from his early youth (*Be'ur ha-Gra* to Sh. Ar., YD 179:6). In his critical observations against philosophy he did not refrain from sharply attacking even Moses *Isserles. When the Gaon gives the view of Isserles who, following Maimonides, interprets *pardes* as wisdom, he comments, "Neither he nor Maimonides saw the *pardes*" (*ibid.* to YD 246:4). Despite all his vast knowledge and understanding of Kabbalah, Elijah opposed preference being given to its study over that of the *halakhah*, as he opposed changes in the text of the liturgy and new customs, in which he saw echoes of Shabbateanism. In Ḥasidism's stress on the fundamental of the love of God and the service of God in joy which it regarded as being on a higher level than Torah study, he saw contempt for the importance of Torah. Elijah's spiritual path starts with ritual observance and Torah study. Only after one has perfected these two aspects of religious life can one enter the realm of mystic experience. Mysticism is attained through perfection of the self, not by enthusiasm.

The curriculum he laid down conforms to the demands of the Mishnah (Avot 5:21). He demanded that girls should also have a certain knowledge of the Bible and laid particular importance on their acquiring a knowledge of the Book of Proverbs and conducting themselves according to its principles.

Writings

Over 70 works and commentaries are attributed to Elijah. More than 50 have appeared in print while several of his manuscripts have been completely lost. Up to the age of 40 he wrote only for his own use. Subsequently he would teach his novellae to his pupils who could take down only part of his teachings as he did not pause to allow time for this. None of his works was published during his lifetime. His commentary to the Shulḥan Arukh (OḤ, Shklov, 1803; YD, Grodno, 1806; EH, Vilna and Grodno, 1819; ḤM, Koenigsberg, 1855), *Ayil Meshullash,* fragments of a commentary on Scripture, and parts of a commentary on several *aggadot* which are extant were written by his own hand. Of his other teachings there remained notes written in haste on the margins of books and later copied – at times with errors that distort the meaning – by his sons or pupils. Of these notes, Hayyim *Volozhiner said (introduction to *Be'ur ha-Gra* to Sh. Ar., OḤ) that they are "like the stars which appear small but beneath which the whole world stands." In the scholarly circles of Vilna and beyond, several Torah novellae were also known that were transmitted in his name, and in order to make sure that everything attributed to him actually emanated from him, a proclamation was issued by the Vilna *bet din* on Kislev 19, 1798 forbidding anything to be published in the name of Elijah until it had been made absolutely certain that it was in his actual handwriting (*Shenot Eliyahu* to *mishnayot* of *Seder Zera'im*, Lemberg, 1799). The unsatisfactory external form of the Gaon's spiritual testament resulted in the fact that his great work in establishing the correct readings was not fully exploited.

The Gaon wrote commentaries to practically all the books of Scripture and to several of the books of the Mishnah. Among his expositions of the Mishnah, his commentary on that of *Arugah* (Kil. 3:1) became especially well-known in scholarly circles (*Be'ur al ha-Arugah*, in: Zerahiah Gerondi, *Sefer ha-Ẓara* (Shklov, 1803). Knowledge of geometry is necessary for its understanding, for which reason previous commentators of the Mishnah had experienced difficulty in explaining it. Israel b. Samuel of Shklov, the pupil of the Gaon, who, during the years he dwelt in Ereẓ Israel interested himself especially in the Gaon's novellae to *Zera'im* (from the standpoint of their value for agricultural work in Israel), testifies: "He toiled on the theme of *Arugah* for as long a time as it would have taken him to complete half the Babylonian Talmud, rejecting all the explanations of the early commentators and expounding it by a new and true system" (introduction to *Pe'at ha-Shulḥan*, 1836). He also wrote commentaries and glosses on the tannaitic Midrashim – *Mekhilta* (1844), *Sifra* (1911), *Sifrei* (1866) – on various parts of the Tosefta, on the Jerusalem Talmud, on the whole of the Babylonian Talmud, and on the *aggadot* of the Talmud. Among his commentaries on the sources of the Kabbalah are a commentary to the *Sefer Yeẓirah* (Grodno, 1806), the *Sifra de-Ẓeni'uta* (Vilna and Grodno, 1820), the Zohar (Vilna, 1810), the *Tikkunei ha-Zohar* (1867), the *Ra'aya Meheimna* (1858), and the *Sefer ha-Bahir* (1883). Many attempts have been made to collate his teachings and sayings. The most reliable such collection is *Ma'aseh Rav* (Zolkiew, 1808, and many more editions) by Issachar Ber of Vilna.

A singular aspect of the Gaon's writings was his constant emendation of the text. Elijah made textual emendations throughout all of rabbinic and kabbalistic literature. He combined two methods of emendation: (a) assuming that all rabbinic literature is a seamless whole, Elijah harmonized parallel sources, and (b) he corrected texts even when he had no textual sources. Rather, his amazing command of the entire literature allowed him to speculate as to the correct reading of the text. He even based some of his legal decisions on such emendations. Later historians claim that in emending the text, Elijah was a forerunner of modern scientific philological scholarship. However, what the Gaon did and how he did it is vastly different from modern scholarship. Nevertheless, he was a pioneer in thinking that many if not all of the available printed editions were filled with errors.

The Gaon's kabbalistic writing had great influence on the religious thinkers of the 19th and 20th centuries, starting with his student Ḥayyim Volozhiner, continuing through such ḥasidic giants as Abraham of *Sochaczew and *Ẓadok ha-Kohen of Lublin, to Abraham Isaac ha-Kohen *Kook. His kabbalistic ideas were explicated and expanded upon by Isaac Ḥaver and Solomon Eliashiv, author of the *Leshem Shevo ve-Aḥlamah.*

[Samuel Kalman Mirsky / David Derovan (2nd ed.)]

As Grammarian

Elijah's study of Hebrew, *Dikduk Eliyahu* ("Elijah's Grammar"), was first published by Ẓevi the grammarian (1833), and later in an edition by A.L. Gordon (*Mishnat ha-Gra*, 1874). Employing the methodology of the medieval grammarians, the study concerns itself with details from the field of phonology. It includes chapters on consonants, vowels, the *sheva*, the *dagesh*, and rules of accentuation in the Bible. In an additional list, Elijah summarizes the general principles of vocalization by means of mnemotechnical symbols and numbers. In the second part of the work, apparently authentic, are summaries of the categories of words in Hebrew (noun, verb, particle), and a short description of their morphological structure (conjugations and declensions). Here also the description is concise; at times it is summarized by numerical symbols.

Many grammatical observations are also found in Elijah's commentary on the Pentateuch (e.g., Gen. 1:1–7) and on the Prophets and Hagiographa. His entire exegesis on the first verses of the Torah is a morphological analysis, a summary of the rules of vocalization. His purism in defining the meanings of words, especially in distinguishing between synonyms, is apparent throughout his commentaries. At times he distinguishes between synonyms by using the etymology of the words (e.g., *dal,* "poor," is from *dal minneh* – "it became less for him," i.e., "his wealth was taken from him"). Similarly, linguistic and literary observations, accompanied by examples, are to be found in his commentary on the "thirty-two principles of exegesis of Rabbi Yose ha-Galili."

[Menahem Zevi Kaddari]

BIBLIOGRAPHY: S.J. Fuenn, *Kiryah Ne'emanah* (1860, 1915²), 144–70; S.J. Jazkan, *Rabbenu Eliyahu mi-Vilna* (1900), incl. bibl.; M. Silber, *The Gaon of Wilna* (1905); M. Teitelboim, *Ha-Rav mi-Ladi u-Mifleget Ḥabad* (1913); L. Ginzberg, *The Gaon, Rabbi Elijah* (1920); Dubnow, Ḥasidut, index; I. Klausner, *Vilna bi-Tekufat ha-Ga'on* (1942); idem, *Ha-Gaon Rabbi Eliyahu mi-Vilna* (1969); I. Unna, *Rabbenu Eliyahu mi-Vilna u-Tekufato* (1946); M.G. Barg, *Ha-GRA mi-Vilnah* (1948); J.I. Dienstag, *Rabbenu Eliyahu mi-Vilna, Reshimah Bibliografit* (1949; repr. from *Talpioth*, vol. 4, 1949); M.M. Yoshor, in: L. Jung (ed.), *Jewish Leaders* (1953), 25–50; B. Katz, *Rabbanut, Ḥasidut, Haskalah*, 2 vols. (1956–58); B. Landau, *Ha-Ga'on he-Ḥasid mi-Vilna* (1965); H.H. Ben-Sasson, in: *Zion*, 31 (1966), 39–86, 197–216; M. Wilensky, *Ḥasidim u-Mitnaggedim*, 2 vols. (1970); M.S. Samet, in: *Meḥkarim le-Zekher Ẓevi Avneri* (1970), 233–57. **ADD. BIBLIOGRAPHY:** A. Feldman, *The Juggler and the King: An Elaboration of the Vilna Gaon's Insights into the Hidden Wisdom of the Sages* (1990); Y.I. Herczeg (ed.), *Vilna Gaon Haggadah* (1993); E.J. Schochet, *The Hasidic Movement and the Gaon of Vilna* (1994); J. Levisohn, in: *Le'ela*, 44 (1997), 9–19; I. Lempertas (ed.), *The Gaon of Vilnius and the Annals of Jewish Culture* (1998); R. Schnold, *The Gaon of Vilna: The Man and His Legacy* (1998); E. Etkes, *The Gaon of Vilna: The Man and His Image* (Heb., 1998; Eng., 2002); Y. Vinograd, *Thesaurus of the Books of the Vilna Gaon: Detailed and Annotated Bibliography of Books By and About the Gaon Hasid R. Eliahu* (2003); M. Hallamish, Y. Rivlin, and R. Schuchat (eds.), *The Vilna Gaon and His Disciples* (2003). AS A GRAMMARIAN: Elijah b. Solomon Zalman, *Berak ha-Shaḥar* (1863), references to Elijah's commentary on synonyms by Samuel b. Abraham of Slutsk; Y.L. Maimon (ed.), *Sefer ha-GRA*, 1 (1954), 201–41; J.H. Greenstone, in: JBA, 6 (1947/48), 76–83.

ELIJAH CHELEBI HA-KOHEN OF ANATOLIA (probably 15th century), liturgical poet. Five religious poems by him are printed in the *Maḥzor Romania* and in the collection of devotional poems *Shirim u-Zemirot ve-Tishbaḥot* (Constantinople, 1545). Menahem Tamar in the introduction to his own *Azharot* (Ms. Leyden 34) claims to have seen a collection of poems by Elijah. He is also mentioned in the collection of poems by Joshua Benveniste (written in 1635).

BIBLIOGRAPHY: Dukes, Poesie, 141 (read Chelebi for Bilibi); Zunz, Lit Poesie, 519; Fuenn, in: *Ha-Karmel*, 1 (1871/72), 507; Margoliouth, Cat, 3 (1965), 251, no. 930 viii; Markon, in: *Devir*, 1 (1923), 249; Davidson, Oẓar, 4 (1933), 363.

[Jefim (Hayyim) Schirmann]

ELIJAH MENAHEM BEN MOSES (c. 1220–1284), English rabbi, physician, and financier. Elijah Menahem was the son of R. *Moses of London. From 1253, when he is first mentioned in the records, he was one of the most active English financiers. Many nobles, and even members of the royal family, were among his clients. Recent research has disclosed that he was one of the greatest and most prominent of the pre-exilic rabbis of England. Apart from various responsa, he wrote a commentary on the Mishnah (at least on the order *Zera'im*) which was frequently utilized by Yom Tov Lipmann *Heller (in his *Tosafot Yom Tov*) and also a commentary on the Passover

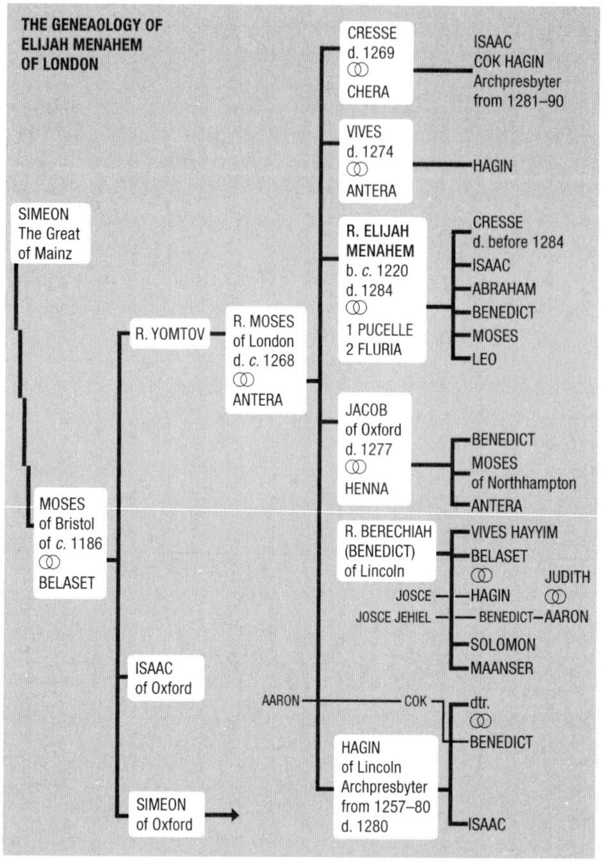

Haggadah. Elijah also achieved some reputation as a physician, on one occasion being called upon to attend the count of Flanders. One of his brothers was Hagin (Ḥayyim) of Lincoln, archpresbyter of the Jews of England from 1257 to 1280; another was the scholar Berechiah of Lincoln.

BIBLIOGRAPHY: M.Y.L. Sacks, *Peirushei Rabbenu Eliyahu mi-Londres u-Fesakav* (1956), 10–42 (introd.); idem, in: KS, 20 (1943/44), 229f.; Roth, in: JHSET, 15 (1946), 29–62; Urbach, Tosafot, 401–4; idem, in: *Essays… I. Brodie*, 2 (1966), 1–12 (Heb.); Epstein, in: *Madda'ei ha-Yahadut*, 1 (1926), 51–71; Wilhelm, in: *Tarbiz*, 22 (1951), 45–52.

[Cecil Roth]

ELIJAH OF LA MASSA (15th century), Italian rabbi and author. Elijah was head of the Padua yeshivah in the 1520s. He made a pilgrimage to Palestine via Egypt after 1433. A short while after his arrival in Jerusalem in 1437 he was appointed *dayyan*; halakhic questions were also addressed to him from neighboring countries, such as Syria and Egypt. He wrote several letters from Jerusalem to his sons via his brother in Ferrara. One of these, written after he had lived in Jerusalem for over a year, is the only known document about the Palestinian Jewish community of the first half of the 15th century. In this letter he describes his adventures and misfortunes on the way to Palestine; relates the details of the plague that struck Palestine and Syria, which was responsible for the death of 90 persons in Jerusalem; tells of his appointment as *dayyan* in Jerusalem; and mentions the occupations of the local Jews. In the last part of his letter he speaks of the rumors current in Jerusalem about the wars of Beta Israel in Ethiopia, and also of what he heard about the Ten Tribes in India from a Jew who emigrated from Iraq. These rumors were already current in Italy, and Elijah was asked to get more details about them. It is not known whether he stayed in Jerusalem or returned to Italy. An English translation was published by E.N. Adler in his *Jewish Travellers* (1966^2), 151–55.

BIBLIOGRAPHY: E. Ashkenazi, *Divrei Ḥakhamim* (1849), 61–63; A.M. Luncz (ed.), *Ha-Me'ammer*, 3 (1920), 77–80; A. Yaari, *Iggerot Ereẓ Yisrael* (1943), 86–89, 541. **ADD. BIBLIOGRAPHY:** E. Carmoly, *Itinéraires de la Terre Sainte*, Bruxelles, 1847, 323–360; Y. Haker, *Zion*, 50 (1985), 241–63.

[Avraham Yaari / Moti Benmelech (2nd ed.)]

ELIJAH OF PESARO (16th century), Italian scholar and traveler. After living for some time in Venice, Elijah set out for the Holy Land in 1563 but was obliged to stop his journey in Cyprus as there was an outbreak of cholera in Ereẓ Israel. From Famagusta he wrote a letter to his relatives in Italy describing the journey, giving advice to travelers, and including an account of Cyprus which remains a primary source for the social and economic history of the island. Elijah also wrote philosophical homilies and commentaries on the Song of Songs, Jonah, and Job (Paris, Bibliothèque Nationale Ms. Heb. 276).

BIBLIOGRAPHY: A. Yaari, *Masot Ereẓ Yisrael* (1946), 165–96.

[Ariel Toaff]

ELIJAH OF PRAGUE, rabbi and head of the yeshivah in Prague in the 15th century. Elijah was strict in applying his rabbinical authority, frequently placing his opponents under the *ḥerem* (ban), and even invoking the assistance of the secular authorities, an act for which he was censured by Israel *Isserlein. His ruling that in a case of *blood libel all the communities of the realm should be considered "one city," and obliged to share the expenses for defense was accepted under protest because he had not consulted the communities concerned. He became involved in financial affairs "not in accordance with his honor" and was summoned before a *bet din* by Isserlein. Toward the end of Elijah's life Eliezer of Passau settled in Prague and encroached upon Elijah's sphere of competence, opening a rival yeshivah, among other activities. Israel *Bruna and Perez succeeded in stopping the conflict between them which affected the whole Prague community.

BIBLIOGRAPHY: Horowitz, in: *Zeitschrift fuer die Geschichte der Juden in der Tschechoslowakei*, 1 (1930/31), 231–4; Suler, in: JGGJČ, 9 (1938), 109–11, 135–44, 167; Michael, Or, 159–60; M. Frank, *Kehillot Ashkenaz u-Vattei Dineihem* (1937), 24.

ELIJAH PHINEHAS BEN MEIR (c. 1742–1821), scholar, kabbalist, and *maskil*. Elijah was born in Vilna, but in his youth, after his father's death, he traveled extensively among the Jewish communities of Europe. In each city that he visited he furthered his Jewish learning, in particular his knowledge of Kabbalah, as well as his secular studies. Elijah became known through his work *Sefer ha-Berit*, the first edition of which appeared anonymously in Brno in 1797. This work enjoyed a relatively wide circulation and was particularly well received in Haskalah circles in Galicia and in Berlin, where, according to Elijah's own testimony, it was regarded as a kind of encyclopedia of the natural sciences, astronomy, and theology. When the work was attributed to *Elijah ben Solomon Zalman, the Gaon of Vilna, and to Moses *Mendelssohn, Elijah had the second edition published under his own name (Zolkiew, 1807, with additions and emendations; third edition, Vilna, 1818). The work is divided into two parts. The first, composed of 21 treatises, deals with science and philosophy; the second, comprising 14 treatises, deals with ethics and Kabbalah. The section on science was already outdated at the time of its composition, for, while it contains new empirical data, it embodies a conception of the universe that is based on medieval Aristotelian philosophy and on the Kabbalah of Isaac *Luria. Elijah ignores the principles of Galileo and Newton in physics, and of Lavoisier in chemistry, maintaining, for instance, that the earth is stationary. The section on ethics and Kabbalah, which Elijah intended to be the main part of the work, is modeled after Ḥayyim *Vital's *Sha'arei Kedushah*. In this section Elijah accepts *Judah Halevi's view that the Jewish people is on the fifth level in the ascending scale of creation – mineral, vegetable, animal, rational, and Israel, and he makes use of the kabbalistic concept of the five souls inherent in rational beings – *nefesh*, *ru'aḥ*, *neshamah*, *ḥayyah*, *yeḥidah*, and of the doctrine of the *Sefirot*. Turning to more practical matters Elijah discusses the means by which one can prepare oneself for communion with the holy spirit (*ru'aḥ ha-kodesh*). Since the principal requisite is "the fulfillment of the commandments for their own sake," he provides guidance for the observance of the commandments, according to the teachings of Isaac Luria. The love of one's neighbor, Elijah maintains, is one of the foundations of the service of God. However, higher than the love of human beings is the love of God, which he discusses in the final section of the work, entitled "Love and Joy," and which he defines as the soul's cleaving to God. In addition to *Sefer ha-Berit*, Elijah wrote a commentary on Immanuel Ḥai *Ricchi's *Mishnat Ḥasidim* (published in 1889); *Mitzvot Tovim*, dealing with the reasons for the commandments (*Ta'amei ha-Mitzvot*); *Matmonei Mistarim*, on the combinations of letters; and *Beit Yoẓer*, a commentary on *Sefer Yeẓirah*. These last three works are extant only in manuscript.

BIBLIOGRAPHY: *Ha-Me'assef* (1809), 68–75; Letteris, in: *Bikkurim* (1864/65), 51; S.J. Fuenn, *Kiryah Ne'emanah* (1915^2), 206; A. Walden, *Shem ha-Gedolim he-Ḥadash* (1864), s.v. *Phineḥas Elijah of Vilna*; H.D. Friedberg, *Luḥot Zikkaron* (1904), 93.

[Meir Hillel Ben-Shammai]

ELIMELECH (Heb. אֱלִימֶלֶךְ; "God [or my God] is king"), the husband of *Naomi and father of Mahlon and *Chilion, from Beth-Lehem in Judah. Due to the famine in Israel during the time of the Judges, Elimelech crossed over to Moab, where he and his two sons died. Following their deaths, his wife Naomi returned to Beth-Lehem together with her daughter-in-law *Ruth (Ruth 1:1–3; 2:1, 3; 4:3, 9). There Ruth married *Boaz, one of Elimelech's relatives. The name itself is attested in the *El-Amarna letters of the 14th century B.C.E. as Ili-Milku, a variant of the name Milk-ilu, ruler of Gezer. In Ugaritic documents of the 13th century the name is written *ʾImlk* and pronounced either Ili-Milku or Ili-Malku.

ADD. BIBLIOGRAPHY: W. Moran, *The Amarna Letters* (1992), 326; W. Watson and N. Wyatt (eds.), *Handbook of Ugaritic Studies* (1999), index, 841.

ELIMELECH OF LYZHANSK (1717–1787), popular *ẓaddik* of the third generation of Ḥasidim and one of the founders of *Ḥasidism in Galicia. Elimelech was a disciple of *Dov Baer the *Maggid* of Mezhirech and is considered the theoretician and creator of "practical ẓaddikism." Elimelech and his brother Zusya of Hanipol traveled from village to village, according to the principle of *nedudei galut* ("wanderings of exile"), i.e., their travels, symbolically expressing their identification with the wanderings of the *shekhinah* (Divine Presence). According to a later interpretation, the purpose of their wanderings was the promotion of repentance. After the death of Dov Baer (1772), Elimelech settled in Lyzhansk, Galicia, which as a result became an important ḥasidic center. He headed a court financed by *pidyonot* (lit. ransoms), i.e., a system of internal taxes paid to the *ẓaddik* usually accompanied by *kvitlakh* (lit. "receipt"), slips on which the Ḥasidim wrote their spiritual and material problems for the *ẓaddik* to solve. Letters published under his name show his attitude toward the quarrels between the Ḥasidim and the *Mitnaggedim*. Elimelech is also mentioned in the indictments against the Ḥasidim in *Sefer ha-Vikku'aḥ* and in *Zemir Ariẓim*. In his letters, he defends himself against the objections of the *Mitnaggedim* to Ḥasidim praying according to the Sephardi ritual (following the rite of Isaac *Luria). Elimelech cited as proof Joseph *Caro and even Moses *Isserles, who according to him established the Ashkenazi ritual for the general community, but not for the pious who had attained a higher plane of faith. Elimelech was ascetic, but he did not regard asceticism as the way of life for all. According to him, asceticism corresponds to the "breaking of the vessels" in Lurianic Kabbalah, whose purpose is *tikkun* ("restitution of the world"). However, it is not the only path to *tikkun*; for "one *ẓaddik* reaches *tikkun* through eating and another, through asceticism" (*No'am Elimelekh, "Va-Yikra"*).

The Doctrine of the *Ẓaddik*

Elimelech formulated the mores of ḥasidic society in the doctrine of the *ẓaddik*. In contrast with the view that the *ẓaddik* was solely a spiritual leader, Elimelech maintained that the *ẓaddik* possessed the task of leadership in all spheres of life. The *ẓaddik* had to live in the dialectical tension between the spiritual life of *devekut* (devotion) and the pragmatic, materialistic requirements of society. Apparently, Elimelech himself could not withstand the pressure of the life of a *ẓaddik*, and toward the end of his life concentrated on self-fulfillment. He withdrew from his disciples and even neglected the spiritual leadership of his community. According to Elimelech, the *ẓaddik* possesses a higher spiritual status than the *seraphim* and is the foundation of the world. He has power to influence the higher spheres, i.e., "the *ẓaddik* decrees and God fulfills" (Shab. 59b, cf. *No'am Elimelekh, "Shelaḥ"*). The authority of a ḥasidic leader comes from his direct connections with higher powers whose assistance he receives for his concerns for the individual and the community. "Every utterance of the *ẓaddik* creates an angel, and influences higher spheres" (*ibid.*). By means of reflection and contemplation, the *ẓaddik* wages a war whose ultimate purpose is *devekut* and the ascent to the absolute. He "lives below" (i.e., on earth) "but in reality he dwells in higher worlds" (*ibid., "Va-Yera"*). The *ẓaddik* faces the danger of death from an excess of enthusiasm. Therefore, God calms him in the height of his *devekut* in order that he not die from the ecstasy of the mystical experience. The condition of *devekut* is not static, but varies in its intensity, having ascents and descents.

Nefillat ha-Ẓaddik ("The Fall of the *Ẓaddik*")

Elimelech recognizes two types of falls (Heb., *nefillot*) in the status of the *ẓaddik*: descent for the purposes of *tikkun* and descent because of Satan. Descent for the purpose of *tikkun* is conceived of as a voluntary process. The *ẓaddik* knows that he is obligated to improve his community and, therefore, descends to its level in order to uplift it. Elimelech regarded the sublimation in this doctrine of descent as the inner identification and conscious comparison of the *ẓaddik* with the ordinary individual. As a result there takes place the process of the elevation or sublimation of evil thoughts (*ha'ala'at maḥashavot zarot*), the abolition of sin, and the transformation of the profane into the holy. *Tikkun* by the elevation of *niẓoẓot* ("sparks") in the Lurianic Kabbalah is transferred to the sphere of the soul in Elimelech's teachings and is interpreted as the elevation of evil thoughts, leading to personal redemption. The "fall" of the *ẓaddik* is essential, and his capacity to sin is a condition of his charismatic mission. Practical application of this doctrine, which apparently stemmed from the Shabbatean idea of sin as a source for performance of a *mitzvah*, contains a serious religious danger. Inability of the *ẓaddik* to "fall," however, interferes with the spiritual elevation of the community. The ascent of the *ẓaddik* which follows the "fall" is higher than the level he attained in his previous ascents. From this point of view, evil strengthens holiness. Elimelech's solution to the problem of evil is the sanctification of material things and the overcoming of temptation. The *ẓaddik* must abolish the dualism of coexistent good and evil by transforming evil into good, a process which will bring the advent of the messiah when all will return to their original unity. The innovations of this doctrine are the spiritual renewal of man and the revelation of the inner aspects of the Torah not revealed on Mount Sinai. These ideas appear in *No'am Elimelekh* (Lvov, 1787) arranged in the form of sermons on the weekly readings of the Torah, mostly describing how the *ẓaddik* worships God. It includes his letters, his religious testament on matters of leadership, and a treatise, *Likkutei Shoshanim*. Elimelech's disciples were Abraham Joshua Heshel of *Apta, Jacob Isaac *Horowitz, the Seer ("*Ha-Ḥozeh*") of Lublin, Kalonymus Kalman *Epstein of Cracow (author of *Ma'or va-Shemesh*), Menaḥem Mendel of *Rymanow, and *Moses Leib of Sasov.

BIBLIOGRAPHY: Schatz, in: *Molad*, 18 (1960), 365–78; M. Buber, *Tales of the Ḥasidim*, 1 (1968⁴), 253–64; Dubnow, Ḥasidut, 178–88; Horodezky, *Ḥasidut*, 2 (1953⁴), 149–273; A.H.S.B. Michaelson, *Ohel Elimelekh* (1914); B. Landau, *R. Elimelekh mi-Lyzhansk* (1963); Y. Berger, *Eser Ẓahẓaḥot* (1900), 17–41.

[Esther (Zweig) Liebes]

ELION, GERTRUDE BELL (1918–1999), U.S. pharmacologist and Nobel Prize laureate. Elion was born in New York City. She studied chemistry at Hunter College and NYU, where she obtained her master of science degree in 1941. After a series of intellectually less challenging appointments, she joined Burroughs Wellcome in North Carolina as a biochemist in 1944, becoming head of the Department of Experimental Therapy in 1967 and scientist emeritus after her retirement in 1983. Her collaboration with George Hitchings led to her lifelong interest in DNA and RNA synthesis from purine and pyrimidine precursors and the design of drugs which selectively inhibit these pathways. This led to the development of 6-mercaptopurine, a landmark drug which inhibits cell proliferation and thus has anti-cancer properties, and its derivative, the anti-leukemic drug 6-thioguanine. Later came the immunosuppressive drug Imuran (Azathioprine), used to combat graft rejection and to treat immunological diseases; acyclovir, which inhibits herpes viruses and was the first anti-viral drug; and allopurinol, which inhibits uric acid synthesis and is a mainstay of gout treatment.

In 1988 she received the Nobel Prize in medicine (jointly with George Hitchings and James Black). Other honors include the Garvan Medal (1968), the American Cancer Society's Medal of Honor (1990), election to the National Academy of Sciences (1990) with subsequent Council membership, and the National Medal for Science (1991).

[Michael Denman (2nd ed.)]

ELIONAEUS, SON OF CANTHERAS (or **Cithaerus**), high priest 43–44 C.E. Elionaeus was appointed by *Agrippa I. It is not clear whether he is to be identified with the "Cantheras" who was deposed by Herod of Chalcis and was succeeded by Joseph, the son of Camei (Kimḥit; Jos., Ant., 20:16). The Mishnah refers to him as Elioneiai b. ha-Kof (Par. 3:5), one of the few high priests who prepared the ashes of the *red heifer.

BIBLIOGRAPHY: Jos., Ant., 19:342; Schuerer, Gesch, 2 (1907⁴), 271, no. 19; Klausner, Bayit Sheni, 4 (1950²), 300ff.

[Edna Elazary]

°**ELIOT, GEORGE**, pseudonym of **Mary Ann Evans** (1819–1880), English novelist. A Christian, George Eliot was a friend of the talmudic scholar Emanuel *Deutsch, and began to study Hebrew and to show an interest in Jewish matters at an early age. *Daniel Deronda* (1874–76), her celebrated "Zionist" novel, was, however, her last great work of fiction. Possibly suggested by the career of Colonel A.E.W. *Goldsmid, the hero of this novel, after discovering his Jewish identity only in his 20s, eventually leaves for Palestine to help "revive the organic center" of his people's existence. *Daniel Deronda* influenced the early Zionist thinker Eliezer *Ben-Yehuda, and such Hebrew writers as I.L. *Peretz and P. *Smolenskin. Literary critics have severely criticized this novel complaining that the Zionist part is inflated, rhetorical, and not based on genuine observation. But it has been claimed that the author was writing a special kind of novel, dealing with the destinies of nations rather than individuals. George Eliot discussed the Jewish question again in "The Modern Hep-Hep," a strong attack on anti-Jewish prejudice published in a collection of essays entitled *Theophrastus Such* (1878).

BIBLIOGRAPHY: G. Eliot, *Daniel Deronda*, ed. by B. Hardy (1967), with introd.; D. Kaufmann, *George Eliot and Judaism* (1877); N. Sokolow, *History of Zionism 1600–1918*, 1 (1919), 209–13; idem, *Hibbath Zion* (Eng., 1934), 105–27; A. Moeller, *George Eliots Beschaeftigung mit dem Judentum und ihre Stellung zur Judenfrage* (1934); M.F. Modder, *The Jew in the Literature of England* (1939), index; F.R. Leavis, *The Great Tradition* (1948); E. Rosenberg, *From Shylock to Svengali* (1961); Fisch, in: *19th Century Fiction* (March 1965); G.S. Haight, *George Eliot, a Biography* (1968); Leavis, in: *Commentary*, 30 (1960), 317–25. **ADD. BIBLIOGRAPHY:** M. Laski, *George Eliot and Her World* (1973); G. Levine (ed.), *The Cambridge Companion to George Eliot* (2001); S. Nurbhai, *George Eliot, Judaism, and the Novels: Jewish Myth and Mysticism* (2002); W. Baker, *George Eliot and Judaism* (1975).

[Harold Harel Fisch]

ELIPHAZ (Heb. אֱלִיפַז, אֱלִיפָז; perhaps: "God is victorious"; Ar. *fwz*), the name of two biblical characters. The first is the oldest son of *Esau and his wife Adah, and the ancestor of several Edomite clans, the most important of which is Teman, since its name is employed in poetry as a synonym for "Edom" (Jer. 49:7; Obad. 9) and "Amalek" (Gen 36:2, 10–12, 15–16). The second, Eliphaz the Temanite, is the oldest of the three friends with whom the later stratum in the book of "Job the Patient" (see *Job) furnishes its hero. In his choice of a name and nationality for this friend, the author of the later stratum may have been guided by the following considerations: the older stratum locates Job himself in the land of *Uz and in the general ambience of the *Kedemites (Job 1:1, 3b). The land of Uz is identified in Lamentations 4:21 with Edom, which, in any case, included a group known by the name of Uz (Gen. 36:28), and was certainly an important Kedemite nation (Isa. 11:14). From the above data on the first Eliphaz, it is not difficult to see why within Edom the author was attracted to the tribal name of Teman and within Teman to the personal name of Eliphaz.

[Harold Louis Ginsberg]

In the *Aggadah*

Eliphaz, the comforter of Job, is identified with Eliphaz, the son of Esau (Gen. 36:4; Targ. Yer., Gen. 36:12). He had, however, few dealings with Esau (Yal. 897), and became a righteous man by virtue of the fact that he grew up under Isaac's care (Tanḥ. Va-Yera, 38). When his father sent him to kill Jacob, after the latter's flight from Haran, and Jacob beseeched him to spare his life, he agreed to do so, but, in order technically not to disobey his father completely, took all Jacob's worldly goods, since "one who has lost his possessions is regarded as dead" (Mid. Ag., Gen. 28:20). Eliphaz even attempted to avert a later tragedy by advising Amalek his son (Ten 36.12) to help Israel, because they were to inherit both this world and the world to come. In the time to come, Eliphaz will testify that Israel has observed all the Torah (Av. Zar. 3a).

BIBLIOGRAPHY: Ginzberg, Legends, 1 (1961), 421–3, 345–7; 5 (1955), 322; I. Ḥasida, *Ishei ha-Tanakh* (1964), 68–69.

ELISHA (Heb. אֱלִישָׁע; "God is salvation"), Israelite prophetic wonder-worker of the ninth century B.C.E. in the days of *Jehoram son of *Ahab, *Jehu, *Jehoahaz, and *Joash. According to I Kings 19:16, God commanded *Elijah on Mount Horeb to anoint Elisha as prophet in his place. (II Kings 19:15 is the sole biblical reference to anointing as an element of prophetic investiture.) When Elijah passed by the fields of Elisha's father and found Elisha busy plowing, "he cast his mantle upon him." The mere touch of Elijah's cloak transformed Elisha. The fact that he was plowing with 12 yoke of oxen that he slaughtered as a farewell feast before leaving his family for Elijah's service shows that he was wealthy. He became Elijah's devoted servant and outstanding disciple. Elisha came from *Abel-Meholah (19:16). On the basis of the opinion that Abel-Meholah was in Gilead (see Glueck in bibl.), certain scholars postulated that geographical proximity was one of the causes of the personal affinity between Elijah and Elisha. Elisha was given the task of continuing Elijah's general prophetic mission. He also performed certain acts which had been imposed on Elijah but which the latter did not carry out in his lifetime, e.g., the anointing of *Hazael as king of Aram and Jehu as king of Israel. The transfer of Elijah's prophetic mission to Elisha is also described in the story of Elijah's ascension. Elisha, who saw Elijah ascending and "took the mantle of Elijah that had fallen upon him," was vouchsafed two-thirds of Elijah's prophetic spirit, and the sons of the prophets said: "The spirit of Elijah rests on Elisha" (II Kings 2:1–18). In contrast to Elijah, who appears as a hermit-like prophet performing his deeds alone, Elisha in the performance of his acts avails himself of the sons of the prophets (9:1–12). He is also in need of a musician, so that the hand of God may rest upon him (3:15). Elisha's first appearance as a prophet in his own right took place during the expedition against Moab undertaken by *Jehoram king of Israel and *Jehoshaphat king of Judah (about 850 B.C.E.). Jehoram asked Elisha to reveal to him the "word of the Lord" about the outcome of the battle. Elisha did not hesitate to speak to Jehoram in the sharpest terms, and at first even refused to prophesy. Only when the king pressed him, hinting that not only was he in danger but also his allies – the kings of Judah and Edom – did Elisha agree to prophesy because of the virtues of Jehoshaphat (II Kings 3:11–19). The relations between Elisha and the kings of Israel were generally, but not always, harmonious (II Kings 6:31–3). Jehoram is described as an improvement over his parents Ahab and Jezebel because "he put away the pillar of Baal which his father had made" (3:2). The Bible has preserved an account of how the king asks *Gehazi, Elisha's young servant, to describe some of his master's deeds (8:4–6). The king listened with interest to Gehazi's narration, evidence not only of admiration for the prophet but also of complete belief in him and his prophetic powers. Nevertheless, this did not prevent Elisha from apprehending the failures of Jehoram's regime: the Moabite rebellion against Israel, defeats in the wars against the Arameans, the Aramean invasion and siege of Samaria, and the many years of famine, which Elisha saw as an indication that the sins of Ahab's house demanded atonement. In Jehu and Hazael, he saw the rod of God's wrath in the awful and terrifying events that befell Israel as a punishment for the sins of Ahab's house.

Especially noteworthy is Elisha's prophecy to the Aramean Hazael (II Kings 8:7–15) in which the prophet told Hazael that he would succeed to the throne of his ailing master *Ben-Hadad. Elisha instructed Ben-Hadad to tell Hazael that he would recover, despite Elisha's prophetic knowledge that Ben-Hadad would die. Encouraged by Elisha's prophecy Hazael hastened Ben-Hadad's death. Noteworthy as well in the same story is how Elisha wept when he told Hazael that his greatness would come at the expense of the Israelite people. Elisha is likewise depicted as playing a role in Jehu's revolution in the kingdom of Israel. It was Elisha who sent one of the disciples of the prophets (Heb.: *benei ha-nevi'im*) to anoint the army commander Jehu and instruct him: "You shall strike down the house of Ahab your master, that I may avenge on Jezebel the blood of my servants the prophets, and the blood of all the servants of the Lord" (9:1–7). Interestingly, the biblical writers do not mention any direct involvement of Elisha with Jehu in the destruction of the house of Ahab, or in Jehu's bloody purge of the worshippers of Baal. Nor do we have an account of Elisha's intervention in subsequent events of Jehu's reign. Only in the days of Jehu's grandson, Joash, more than 40 years after the bloodshed, does Elisha once again appear to prophesy future victories for the kingdom of Israel over the Arameans (II Kings 13:14–19). He died during the reign of Joash son of Jehoahaz.

Elisha was remembered as a powerful wonder-worker for both good and ill. One of his miracles rescues the son of the widow of one of the disciples of the prophets from slavery (II Kings 4). In another tale he brings fertility to a barren woman and later brings the boy back to life (*ibid.*) In another tale he heals the Aramean general Naaman of a dread skin disease (II Kings 5). In yet another case he responds to youngsters who had teased him about his baldness by cursing them in Yahweh's name with the result that 42 of them are mangled by bears. Elisha was a prophet by profession and sometimes received payments or gifts for services rendered, but refused to take them from the grateful Naaman (II Kings 5:16). In fact, when his servant Gehazi cunningly received the gift from Naaman, Elisha cursed him vehemently (II Kings 5:20–27). It appears that the stories of the wonders performed by Elisha and his master Elijah influenced the New Testament writers in their portrayals of Jesus as wonder-worker.

[Yehoshua M. Grintz / S. David Sperling (2nd ed.)]

In the *Aggadah*

Elisha was the only one of Elijah's disciples whose prophetic powers were not only not diminished after his master's ascension but were increased, as a reward for his undeviating loyalty to his master. When the angel descended to take Elijah to heaven, he found the two so immersed in a learned discussion that he had to return without accomplishing his mission (SER 5:90–91; cf. Ta'an. 10b). Elijah's promise to bestow a double portion on his disciple was realized in that Elisha performed 16 miracles compared to the eight performed by his master (David Kimḥi to II Kings 2:14). While Elijah restored one person to life, Elisha revived two – the son of the Shunammite woman and Naaman, since a leper was considered as dead (Ḥul. 7b). His washing of Elijah's hands is extolled since serving a teacher is more meritorious than being his disciple (Ber. 7b).

The Shunammite built a private chamber for him to minimize his contact with other people since any woman gazing directly at Elisha would die (PdRE 33). She discerned the holiness of the prophet since she never saw a fly on his table and because a pleasant fragrance surrounded him (Ber. 10b; Zohar, 2:44a). Elisha did not refuse her hospitality because a sage may benefit from the generosity of his followers, though Samuel refused to do so (Ber. 10b). Elisha sanctified God's name when he refused to accept any recompense from Naaman (Num. R. 7:5). The children devoured by the bears on Elisha's command were in reality disgruntled water carriers whose livelihood was affected by the miraculous healing of the waters of Jericho. They, their ancestors, and their posterity were completely devoid of virtue. Nevertheless, Elisha was punished and afflicted with severe illness because he yielded to anger and cursed his antagonists. He was also visited with illness for completely thrusting Gehazi away instead of maintaining some relationship with him (Sot. 46b–47a). When Elisha rebuked King Jehoram in anger, the spirit of prophecy departed from him and he had to resort to artificial means to arouse it again (Pes. 66b). Elisha recovered from his two illnesses and was the first person in history to survive serious illness. Before him, every illness had resulted in death (BM 87a). Even after his death a great miracle occurred when a dead man was revived by touching his bier (PdRE 33; Sanh. 47a).

In Islam

Al-Yasaʿ or Alyasaʿ is to be identified with Elisha, the disciple of Elijah. He is mentioned in the Koran twice (Sura 6:86; 38:48), once together with Ishmael, Jonah, and Lot (Sura 6:86) and the second time with Ishmael and Dhū al-Kifl, a figure who is not easy to identify (see *Ezekiel). It is, however, evident that Muhammad did not know where to place him. According to the commentators of the Koran, he lived before King Saul.

[Haïm Z'ew Hirschberg]

BIBLIOGRAPHY: H. Gunkel, *Das Maerchen im Alten Testament* (1917), index; W.W. Fereday, *Elisha the Prophet* (1924); L. Bieler, in: ARW, 32 (1935), 228–45; J. Morgenstern, *Amos Studies*, 1 (1941), 349ff.; F. James, *Personalities of the Old Testament* (1943), 187–95; N. Glueck, in: BASOR, 90 (1943), 2–23; Y. Kaufmann, Toledot, 2 (1960), index. IN THE AGGADAH: Ginzberg, Legends, 4 (1913), 239–46; 6 (1928), 343–8. IN ISLAM: A. Geiger, *Was hat Mohammed aus dem Judenthume aufgenommen?* (1833), 192; EIS², s.v.; H. Speyer, *Biblische Erzaehlungen…* (1961), 406; Thaʿlabī, *Qiṣaṣ* (1356 H), 218–9. **ADD. BIBLIOGRAPHY:** M. Cogan, *I Kings* (2000), 455; M. Cogan and H. Tadmor, *II Kings* (1988), 30–96, 147–52; Y. Zakovitch, *Every High Official* (Heb., 1986), 142–45.

ELISHA BA'AL KENAFAYIM (Heb. אֱלִישָׁע בַּעַל כְּנָפַיִם; "Elisha the man-of-the-wings"; c. second century C.E.), pious man of the tannaitic period whose name is said to reflect his miraculous escape from death during the Roman persecutions. The talmudic story reads as follows: "… the wicked state (i.e., Rome) once proclaimed a decree against Israel that whoever put on phylacteries should have his brains pierced; yet Elisha put them on and went out into the streets. A quaestor saw him; and when Elisha fled from him, the latter gave pursuit. As he overtook him, Elisha removed the phylacteries from his head and held them in his hand. 'What is that in your hand?' he asked, to which Elisha replied 'The wings of a dove.' He opened out his hand and the wings of a dove were found therein. Hence he is called 'Elisha the man-of-the-wings'" (Shab. 49a, 130a). The Jerusalem Talmud states "Whoever is not like Elisha the man-of-the-wings should not put on phylacteries" (Ber. 2:3, 4c; see *Penei Moshe, ibid.*). It seems however, that the epithet "man of the wings" is in fact a *euphemism* for "one with clean hands," i.e., that he was scrupulous with regard to the ritual washing of hands (see *Arukh ha-Shalem*, ed. by A. Kohut, 4 (1926), s.v. *Kanaf*, and S. Lieberman, *Tosefta ki-Feshutah*, 1 (1955), 215).

[Jacques K. Mikliszanski]

ELISHA BEN ABRAHAM (d. 1749), rabbi and author. Elisha was born in Leczyca, Poland. He also lived in Frankfurt and Altona in Germany and in Grodno in Lithuania. In his youth he was a pupil of Joseph Samuel of Cracow, the rabbi of Frankfurt, in whose home he was brought up. In 1697 he published in Amsterdam *Kav ve-Naki*, a short commentary to the Mishnah, which was brought out together with the text in one compact volume and has been frequently republished. He was appointed head of the *bet din* of Grodno, but in his old age returned to Germany, staying for some time in the home of Joseph Oppenheimer (son of David *Oppenheim). Oppenheimer placed at Elisha's disposal a manuscript of *Asher b. Jehiel's commentary to the Mishnah on the order *Zera'im*, which he published together with his own notes and glosses under the title *Pi Shenayim* (Altona, 1735). The work received several approbations, including that of Moses Hagiz and his opponent Jacob *Emden, who rarely gave approbations. The manuscript of Asher b. Jehiel's commentary is now in the Bodleian Library, Oxford, and an edition of *Pi Shenayim* (1966) collated anew with the manuscript was published in 1966.

BIBLIOGRAPHY: J. Emden; *Megillat Sefer*, ed. by D. Kahana (1896), 120; S.A. Friedenstein, *Ir Gibborim* (1880), 58; S.Z. Horowitz, *Reḥovot Ir* (1891), 30–32; Michael, Or, no. 472.

[Shlomoh Zalman Havlin]

ELISHA BEN AVUYAH, *tanna*, quoted once in the Mishnah as saying: "Learning in youth is like writing with ink on clean paper, but learning in old age is like writing with ink on blotted paper" (Avot 4:20). From the position of this saying toward the end of the fourth chapter (see: *Avot*, Structure) – after R. Jacob and R. Shimon ben Eleazar and before R. Eleazar Hakapar – it would seem likely that he was one of the very last of the *tannaim*. In the talmudic tradition (TJ, Ḥag. 2:1, 77b) he was identified with "Aḥer" ("the Other"), the third of the four companions who "entered the *pardes*." In the earliest form of this *baraita* (Tosef., Ḥag. 2:3, cod. Vienna), this third companion was named explicitly as "Elisha." Elisha is a relatively rare name among the *tannaim*, and this probably contributed to the identification of these two figures. From the story in Tosefta *Ḥagigah*, it seems clear that the Elisha mentioned there was a contemporary of R. Akiva. Beyond what is told in *Avot* and in Tosefta *Ḥagigah*, tannaitic sources provide no additional information on either of these two figures. Chapter 24 in *Avot de-Rabbi Natan* version A ascribes various statements to Elisha ben Avuyah. However, *Avot de-Rabbi Natan* in the forms in which we possess it is a post-talmudic work, and these specific traditions are variously ascribed to other Sages in other sources. They cannot, therefore, be viewed as reliable evidence for early traditions concerning Elisha.

Tosefta *Ḥagigah* tells us that Elisha "looked and destroyed the plants." "Destruction of plants" is a standard phrase in tannaitic sources for wanton destruction. It can refer either to damage caused to oneself or to damage caused to another (BK 8:6). In later sources it is used by extension to refer to the destructive consequences of sin (Gen. R. 19), and specifically to one who learns Torah but does not fulfill its precepts (Deut. R., ed. Lieberman, 109). In the Palestinian tradition two related interpretations of Elisha's "destruction of the plants" are suggested. According to one interpretation (TJ, Ḥag. 2:1, 77b–c; Ruth R. 6; Eccles. R. 7), Elisha himself stopped learning Torah and gave up observing the Sabbath. In this tradition Elisha is viewed as a tragic figure, who has strayed from the ways of the Torah and is convinced that there is no way back. In response to R. Meir's repeated attempts to convince him to repent, Elisha states: "Once I was passing by the Holy of Holies riding on my horse on the Day of Atonement which fell on the Sabbath, and I heard a heavenly voice coming from the Holy of Holies, which said: 'Return, O children' – except for Elisha ben Avuyah." This interchange, which provides the thematic framework for this entire narrative tradition, reflects a literary reversal of R. Meir's own position in Tosefta *Demai* 2:9, where R. Meir states that a sage who has abandoned the ways of the *ḥavurah* "can never be accepted back" into the fold, while R. Shimon and R. Joshua ben Korḥah state that he can always be accepted back, as it is written (Jer. 3:14): "Return, O repentant children." This theme of the "sinful sage" (Rubenstein, 64–104; Goshen-Gottstein, 21–229), as developed in the Jerusalem Talmud and the parallel *Midreshei aggadah*, has no obvious connection to the story of the "four who entered the *pardes*." In response to the question of what led to Elisha's apostasy, this tradition provides a number of answers. Two of them relate to the impure nature of Elisha's conception and birth, and two to Elisha's crisis of faith concerning the suffering of the righteous (e.g., seeing the tongue of R. Judah ha-Naḥtom in a dog's mouth, regarding which he commented: "Is this the Torah and this its reward?" (TJ, Ḥag. *ibid.*), cf. the parallel description of the tongue of Ḥuẓpit the Meturgeman being dragged along by a pig in the Babylonian Talmud (Kid. 39c), concerning which Elisha exclaimed: "The mouth that uttered pearls licks the dust," and see below). Since none of these reasons seem to have any connection to what Elisha may have "seen" when he entered the *pardes* (however this is understood), the later Palestinian tradition (Song R. 1) omitted the word "looked" from the original text of the *baraita*, reading instead: "Elisha destroyed the plants." According to this tradition his experience in the *pardes* was not the cause of his apostasy. Rather the underlying causes of both his apostasy and of his negative experience in the *pardes* were the flaws in his character and the weakness of his faith.

Another early Palestinian interpretation of Elisha's "destruction of the plants" is also found in the Jerusalem Talmud (TJ, Ḥag. 2:1, 77b) and echoed in Song R. 1. According to this understanding, Elisha did not merely bring damage upon himself by ceasing to learn Torah and to observe the Sabbath. He also inflicted damage upon others, by forcing them to desecrate the Sabbath, or by preventing children from learning Torah, or even – according to an extreme version of this tradition – killing children who learned Torah. Clearly this tradition does not portray Elisha as a tragic figure, but rather as an arch-villain, deserving no sympathy, but rather only contempt and hatred. It is therefore significant to note that only in this tradition does the Jerusalem Talmud use the term "Aḥer" to refer to Elisha, thus avoiding referring to him by name. R. Meir also does not appear in this tradition, nor is there any discussion of his repentance or his return to the fold (cf. Tosef., Yoma 4:11).

In the Babylonian Talmud (Ḥag. 15a–b) these two very different early aggadic traditions were combined into a single composite, but fairly continuous narrative. Elisha both sins against himself and commits crimes against others. He is simultaneously a sympathetic and tragic figure, accompanied by his still devoted disciple R. Meir, and given consideration by sages like R. Joḥanan, yet at the same time an arch-villain, never referred to by his own name, but rather only as "Aḥer" – "the Other" – and clearly despised by R. Judah ha-Nasi. As such, his complex and contradictory (or if you will: paradoxical) figure provides a profound challenge for literary critics. But the most important change in the Babylonian tradition is in fact a return, in part, to the earliest forms of the Elisha tradition, namely the connection between his apostasy and the experience of the *pardes*. No doubt basing itself on the original tradition of Tosefta *Ḥagigah*, the Babylonian Talmud assumes that Elisha's "destruction of the plants" was a direct result of what he saw when he entered the *pardes* ("Elisha looked and destroyed the plants"). Moreover, the Babylonian Talmud assumes (probably correctly) that the original story of the entry into the *pardes* as described in the Tosefta reflects a mystical journey, involving an ascension (physical or spiritual) into the heavens, and a vision of some aspect of divinity. The clarification of the precise nature of the tannaitic understanding of the mystical ascent to the divine, and of the dangers inherent in this ascent, are therefore crucial to any appreciation of the roots and development of the Elisha traditions. In their present form, the Babylonian Talmud's version of these traditions reflects a relatively late stage in the evolution of the Metatron traditions, and shows some degree of interdependence with the later strata of the *heikhalot* literature. For a powerful and profound study of these aspects of the Elisha traditions, see Liebes, *The Sin of Elisha*.

Given the composite character of the Elisha traditions, it is quite clear that any attempt to write a single consistent and coherent "biography" of this character will ultimately break down in contradiction. One extreme example of this phenomenon is reflected in the willingness of earlier scholars to accept on face value the identification of the tanna R. Jacob b. Korshai as Elisha's grandson. The textual basis of this pseudo-identification provides a good text-case both of the talmudic method of "creative historiography," and of the uncritical use of talmudic sources by some scholars. As mentioned above, one of the reasons given for Elisha's apostasy was his loss of faith in divine reward and punishment. The Jerusalem Talmud (Ḥag. 2:1, 77b) tells that Elisha once saw a man ascend to the top of a date palm, take the young birds without sending off the mother, and came down safely, despite the fact that he had transgressed the law of the Torah (cf. Deut. 22:7). The next day, Elisha saw another man ascend to the top of a date palm, send off the mother and then take the young birds, thus fulfilling the law of the Torah. When he came down, he was bitten by a poisonous snake and died. Elisha was distressed because the Torah explicitly promises that one who fulfills this commandment will be given "goodness and length of days," and so he lost his faith. To this the Jerusalem Talmud adds that Elisha lost his faith only because he was unaware of R. Jacob's interpretation of the verse: "'you shall receive goodness' – in the world to come, which is all good; 'you shall receive length of days' – in the future world, which is 'long' [i.e., unending]." This dictum is brought in the name of R. Jacob (b. Korshai) in Tosefta *Ḥullin* 10:16, a text which also includes a story about a man who ascended a tree, etc. Given the similarity between the story told by R. Jacob in the Tosefta and the story told by the Jerusalem Talmud in the name of Elisha, there can hardly be any doubt the entire passage in the Jerusalem Talmud is a free reworking and elaboration of R. Jacob's original story in the Tosefta in order to suggest an additional reason for Elisha's apostasy. In the context of the Babylonian Talmud's discussion of R. Jacob's position (Kid. 39b; Ḥul. 142a), it brings a dictum of Rav Joseph, which states: "If Aḥer had only interpreted this verse like R. Jacob the son of his daughter, he would not have sinned." This is the only evidence for any family connection between Elisha and R. Jacob. Attempts like this to provide detailed family connections between characters in aggadic narratives are very common in the Babylonian Talmud. For example, both Abba Hilkiah and Ḥanan ha-Neḥba are described in Ta'an. 23a–b as grandsons of Ḥoni Hameagel – the former as the "son of his son" and the latter as the "son of his daughter." In fact, the only substantial connection between them is that they were all miraculous rainmakers. Even the precise phrase "Jacob the son of his daughter" occurs elsewhere in the Babylonian Talmud (Sot. 49a) with regard to Rav Aha bar Jacob. "Evidence" like this is inherently weak. However in our case, the very notion that Elisha was R. Jacob's grandfather is totally implausible. R. Jacob b. Korshai's was one of R. Judah ha-Nasi's teachers. In TB Ḥag. 15b when Elisha's daughter appeared before R. Judah ha-Nasi to ask for charity, he asked her: "Whose daughter are you." She replied: "I am the daughter of Aḥer." To this he exclaimed: "Does he have any offspring still remaining in the world?" If his own teacher was the son of Aḥer's daughter, how could he be unaware that Aḥer had offspring? Moreover, how could R. Jacob b. Korshai be Aḥer's daughter's son, and still be old enough to have been R. Judah ha-Nasi's teacher? These are the sort of problems one is bound to encounter when one takes what is in effect a minor literary embellishment ("the son of his daughter") as an assertion of historical "fact."

The various legends of Elisha, who forsook Judaism to seek new paths, influenced the Jewish writers of the Haskalah period, many of whom had passed through a similar crisis. He is the central character of several historical novels and poems of that period, and is the subject of various studies, including those of M.J. Berdyczewski, Y. Liebes, J. Rubenstein, and A. Goshen-Gottstein. M. *Letteris' Hebrew adaptation of the first part of Goethe's *Faust* is called *Ben Avuyah*. Elisha b. Avuyah is also the subject of Milton *Steinberg's novel *As a Driven Leaf* (1940).

BIBLIOGRAPHY: H. Graetz, *Gnostizismus und Judenthum* (1846), 62–71; M.D. Hoffmann, *Toledot Elisha b. Avuyah* (1880); S. Back, *Elisha ben Abuya-Acher* (Ger., 1891); Bacher, Tann, 1 (1903[2]), 430–4; Weiss, Dor, 2 (1904[4]), 113, 126ff.; Hyman, Toledot, 155–7; Bin Gorion, in: *Ha-Goren*, 8 (1912), 76–83; Buechler, in: MGWJ, 76 (1932), 412–56; Yalon, *ibid.*, 79 (1935), 238–40; idem, in: *Leshonenu*, 29 (1965), 213–7; G. Scholem, *Jewish Gnosticism* (1965[2]), 14–19; Y. Liebes, *The Sin* *of Elisha* (Hebrew; 1990); J. Rubenstein, *Talmudic Stories* (1999); A. Goshen-Gottstein, *The Sinner and the Amnesiac* (2000).

[Stephen G. Wald (2nd ed.)]

ELISHAH (Heb. אֱלִישָׁה), one of the sons of Javan, a grandson of Japheth (Gen. 10:4; I Chron. 1:7), and also the name of the island from which the Tyrians obtained blue and purple dyes (Ezek. 27:7). Elishah is usually identified with the name *Alašiya* (= *Cyprus, or a part of the island) which occurs in document form in Alalakh, Tell el-Amarna, Ugarit, and in Hittite sources. The copper of Alašiya was already well-known in *Mari in the Old Babylonian period. Other forms of Elishah are Ugaritic, *Alṯy* ("from *Alṯ*"), and Egyptian *ʾá-la-sá*.

BIBLIOGRAPHY: G.F. Hill, *A History of Cyprus*, 1 (1940), 42–50; C.F. Schaeffer, *Enkomi-Alasia* (1952); EM, 1 (1955), 52–3 (incl. bibl.); J. Simons, *The Geographical and Topographical Texts of the Old Testament* (1959), 28–29; H.W. Catling, in: CAH2, vol. 1, ch. 9 (1966), 58–62; *Ugaritica*, 5 (1968), index.

ELISHA ḤAYYIM BEN JACOB ASHKENAZI (d. 1673), father of *Nathan of Gaza and emissary of the Ashkenazi community of Jerusalem. In 1650 Ashkenazi and the kabbalist Solomon Navarro were sent as emissaries to North Africa by their community. On their return, they stayed for a time in Venice where Isaac *Bing of Jerusalem published Joseph *Caro's *Maggid Meisharim* (1654), from a manuscript which Ashkenazi had brought from Jerusalem. Bing had published the first part of the work in Lublin in 1646. Ashkenazi also brought to Italy for publication Abraham *Galante's *Zohorei Ḥammah*, a commentary on the *Zohar (Venice, 1655). During his stay in Italy, Solomon Navarro converted to Christianity. The money they had collected on their mission was therefore lost, and Ashkenazi was compelled to begin anew, leaving for Germany and Poland. He returned to Italy in 1665, and in Leghorn heard of his son's prophecies in Gaza. Ashkenazi proceeded to Ereẓ Israel via Egypt, where he was received by the wealthy Raphael Joseph with honor and gifts, on account of his son, the prophet. In 1666 he again departed for Germany and Poland on a mission for the Ashkenazi community of Jerusalem, passing through Constantinople, the Balkans, Budapest, and Vienna. Toward the end of his life, Ashkenazi went to Morocco on a mission, and he died there in the city of Meknès. It is possible that he brought his son's kabbalistic writings with him on this mission, for they were circulated widely throughout Morocco at that time. Certainly the fact that Nathan's father was well known and respected in the North African communities facilitated the spread of Shabbateanism there. There is no doubt that Ashkenazi believed in the prophecies of his son, who corresponded with him notifying him of his activities, and in the messianism of *Shabbetai Ẓevi, even after the latter's conversion to Islam. Ashkenazi's other son, AZARIAH ḤAYYIM ASHKENAZI, was also sent to Morocco as an emissary of the Jerusalem Ashkenazi community. His novellae on the Torah appeared in *Mareh Einayim* (in Ms.) written by Eliezer Bahalul in 1710.

BIBLIOGRAPHY: Yaari, Sheluḥei (1951), 281–2, 331; Scholem, Shabbetai Zevi, 162–3, 188, 544, 602, 770–1.

[Avraham Yaari]

ELISHEBA (Heb. אֱלִישֶׁבַע; "[my] God is fullness"), wife of *Aaron, the daughter of Amminadab, and the sister of *Nahshon. She bore Aaron four sons, *Nadab, *Abihu, *Eleazar, and *Ithamar (Ex. 6:23).

BIBLIOGRAPHY: Noth, Personennamen, 146; Rowley, in: JNES, 3 (1944), 75–76; Koehler, in: ZAW, 55 (1937), 165–6.

°**ELISHEVA** (pen name of **Elisheva Bikhowsky** née **Elizaveta Zhirkova**; 1888–1949), non-Jewish Hebrew poet. Born in Russia, she began writing poetry in Russian in 1907, came into contact with Jewish circles, and was deeply attracted by the movement for Jewish national renaissance. Her admiration for the Jewish people and their hopes for redemption found expression in poems full of yearning for the beautiful and noble qualities of Judaism. Her Russian poems were published in two volumes in 1919: *Minuty* ("Minutes") and *Tainye Pesni* ("Hidden Songs"). She studied Hebrew, which she regarded as the "language of the heart of lights and shadow," and translated into Russian works by Judah Steinberg, J.Ḥ. Brenner, J.D. Berkowitz, G. Schoffmann, and U.N. Gnessin. Her first Hebrew poems were published in *Ha-Tekufah* (1921) no. 13. In addition to stories and poems, her Hebrew writings include articles of literary criticism on Hebrew and general European literature, particularly Russian. In 1925 she settled in Palestine with her husband Simeon Bikhowsky, whom she had married in 1920. Referred to as "Ruth from the banks of the Volga," her stories and her poems are pervaded by a deep love of everything Jewish. Her poems often have the innocence of a folk song, while her stories reflect a desire to stress the noble elements in life and to describe all that is good and exalted in man. Her Hebrew books are *Kos Ketannah* ("A Small Cup," poems, 1926); *Sippurim* ("Stories," 1928); *"Mikreh Tafel"* ("Unimportant Incident," a story, 1929); *Simtaot* ("Alleys," a novel, 1929; 1977); *Meshorer ve-Adam* ("Poet and Man," about the poetry of Aleksandr Blok, 1929); *Shirim* ("Poems," 1946). A collection of poems, *Yalkut Shirim*, appeared in 1970.

BIBLIOGRAPHY: V. Weiner, *Pirkei Ḥayyim ve-Sifrut* (1960), 74–96; *Genazim*, 1 (1961), 151–67. ADD. BIBLIOGRAPHY: *Koveẓ Ma'amarim odot ha-Meshoreret Elisheva* (1927); H. Barzel, "Essay," in: *Simta'ot* (1977); G. Shaked, in: *Maariv* (Sept. 7, 1983); idem, *Ha-Sipporet ha-'Ivrit*, 3 (1988), 87–93; O. Rav-Hon, in: *Moznayim*, 67:10 (1993), 7–11; S. Kagan, *Elisheva: "The Forgotten Poetess,"* in: *Jewish Affairs*, 52:3 (1997), 115–18; S. Kornhandler, *Ikkaron ha-Hitraḥavut ha-Zhaneristit bi-Yeẓiratah shel Elisheva* (1999); D. Miron, *"She'atah shel Elisheva,"* in: *Iyyunim bi-Tekumat Yisrael*, 12 (2002), 521–66; 13, 345–92.

[Gedalyah Elkoshi]

ELISOFON, ELIOT (1911–1973), U.S. photographer. Born in New York, the first generation of his Latvian Jewish family in America, Elisofon grew up in poverty and he later developed an immense sympathy for the victims of the cataclysms he witnessed and photographed in traveling two million miles across six continents. He became a professional photographer in 1935 after graduating from Fordham University. He depended on commercial work until 1939 when the Museum of Modern Art hired him as its first staff photographer. By the following year he had transformed himself into an energetic and committed photojournalist, artist, activist, teacher, lecturer, and writer. His still work ranged from war reportage and social photojournalism to food and glamour photography. He focused often on art and architecture of ancient cultures, and he loved Africa as a subject. He covered the London blitz, and as a staff photographer for *Life* magazine, he accompanied United States troops to North Africa. As a Hollywood color consultant, he created the mood-inducing hues of the film *Moulin Rouge*. Exhibitions of his paintings, often with his photographs, were held in leading museums and galleries throughout the world. He contributed to many books, including *The Art of Indian Asia: Its Mythologies and Transformations* (1955), *The Sculpture of Africa* (1958), and *The Nile* (1964), a work involving years of research.

[(Stewart Kampel (2nd ed.)]

ELITZUR, sports organization of the religious workers movement, *Ha-Po'el ha-Mizrachi. It was founded in 1938 at the initiative of R. Meir *Bar-Ilan. Its early years in Ereẓ Israel were devoted to mixed military and sports activities in the framework of the Haganah and Palmaḥ and also in helping "illegal" immigrants come safely ashore. Intensive sports activities only developed after World War II. Its object was to encourage sport among religious youth in a framework which would not interfere with observance, with all activities taking place on weekdays. Elitzur's membership reached 25,000 in 130 branches throughout Israel by the 1990s. Its teams played in the national leagues for basketball, volleyball, table tennis, tennis, judo, swimming, chess, athletics, badminton, squash, and handball but not for soccer where games are played on Saturdays. Outstanding has been the encouragement of sport among Ethiopian immigrant children and youth, producing several Israel champions in light athletics and winners of the Israel marathon.

Starting in 1983, the Elitzuria games were held every 4–5 years with the participation of religious Jewish youth from the Diaspora and Israel, attracting as many as 2,000 athletes from 20 countries, including Eastern Europe and the former U.S.S.R. World Elitzur has branches in North and South America, Europe, South Africa, and Australia.

BIBLIOGRAPHY: M. Michelson (ed.), *Ḥoveret Eliẓur* (1968).

[Zeev Braverman]

ELIYAHU, MORDECHAI (1929–), Israeli religious leader, kabbalist, and former Sephardi chief rabbi of Israel. Born into a Jerusalem family of little means, Eliyahu was 11 years old when his father and teacher, Ḥakham Salman Eliyahu, passed away. Eliyahu then continued his studies at Yeshivat Porat Yosef with the Rabbi Ezra Attiah. For a number of years he studied with Rabbi Abraham Yeshaya *Karelitz, the Ḥazon Ish. He graduated from the Institute of Rabbis and Religious Judges headed by Rabbi Isaac *Nissim, the former chief rabbi of Israel. Upon graduation he became the youngest *dayyan* (religious court judge) appointed to a religious court in Israel. He served on the rabbinic court in Beersheba for four years and then transferred to the court in Jerusalem. Eventually, he was elected to the High Rabbinic Court, where he continued to serve. In 1983 he was elected Sephardi chief rabbi of Israel and served one term until 1993. During his term as chief rabbi and afterwards, as well, Eliyahu, together with his colleague, Chief Rabbi Abraham *Shapira, became one of the spiritual leaders of the religious Zionist camp in Israel. For over 20 years, he spoke out on political and social issues of concern to religious Zionism. During the events leading up to the Israeli government's disengagement from Gaza in 2005, he was a vocal opponent of the removal of the Jews from their homes and the uprooting of Jewish communities in Gaza.

Eliyahu is the author of several popular works on *halakhah*, including *Darkhei Taharah*, about the laws of family purity (published in five languages); an annotated and updated edition of the *Kiẓẓur Shulḥan Arukh*; a Sephardi rite *siddur*; and various pamphlets regarding Jewish law. Every Monday Rav Eliyahu taught a *shi'ur* (lesson) that could be heard on the radio over the Internet and by satellite in 250 localities throughout Israel. He also had his own website: http://www.harav.org. Eliyahu's second son, SAMUEL, was chief rabbi of Safed. Eliyahu was recognized as a *posek* (halakhic decisor) and kabbalist, with many coming to him with their halakhic questions and for personal advice.

[David Derovan (2nd ed.)]

ELIYIA, JOSEPH (1901–1931), Greek poet, scholar, Hebraicist, and translator. Eliyia was born in Janina (Ioannina), was an ardent Zionist in 1917–18, and taught French at the Alliance Israélite Universelle school in Janina. He was a radical in defense of workers. His poem "Militarism" (1920) criticizing the role of Greece in the Asia Minor War angered the Greek authorities. He published demotic verse in various Athenian periodicals (*Noumas, Vigla*, and *Nea Estia*) and in the *Epiritikon Aghon* of Janina. His outstanding poems were love songs dedicated to Rebekah, his ideal of womanhood. Eliyia's major translations include Greek versions of Isaiah and Job, the Song of Songs, Ruth, and Jonah, the poems of Judah Halevi and Ibn Gabirol, and the works of such modern Hebrew writers as Bialik, Frishman, Shneur, Peretz, and Tchernichovsky. He also wrote articles on Kabbalah and eschatology. He was one of the first Jews to advocate liberal ideas in Ioannina. In 1924, as an anti-militarist and leftist, he was arrested. He also developed a socialist ideology. To avoid problems with the authorities, he settled in Athens in 1925, writing in *Filiki Etairia* and the *Great Greek Encyclopaedia*. In Athens he graduated from the Ecole Française d'Athènes in 1930. A teaching appointment necessitated Eliyia's move in 1930 to Kilkis, a remote town in northern Greece, where he was the only Jew in a hostile environment. By the time of his premature death from typhoid at age 29, Eliyia had written 257 poems and had contributed over 200 articles on Jewish themes to the *Great Greek Encyclopedia*. A biographical study of Eliyia (together with 90 of his poems in English translation) and a Greek edition of his poetry (sponsored by the B'nai B'rith) appeared as posthumous tributes to the writer.

BIBLIOGRAPHY: J. Eliyia *Poems*, ed. by R. Dalven (1944); G. Zographaki, *In Memoriam... J. Eliyia* (1934); Dymaras, in: *Proia* (Aug. 1, 1931); Daphnis, in: *Nea Estia*, 10 (1931), 828. **ADD. BIBLIOGRAPHY:** R. Dalven, *The Jews of Ioannina* (1990), 167–72; E. Kourmantzi-Panayotakou, "Josef Eliya and Sabbethai Kabili: Ideological Problems in Ioannina's Pre-War Jewish Community," in: I.K. Hassiotis (ed.), *The Jewish Communities of Southeastern Europe, from the Fifteenth Century to the End of World War II*, Thessaloniki: Institute for Balkan Studies (1997), 263–80.

[Rachel Dalven / Yitzchak Kerem (2nd ed.)]

ELI ẒIYYON VE-AREHA (Heb. אֱלִי צִיּוֹן וְעָרֶיהָ; "Wail, Zion and its cities"), the initial words of an acrostic elegy for the fast day of the Ninth of *Av. This dirge, written in the Middle Ages but of anonymous authorship, consists of 12 stanzas, each closing with the refrain: "Wail, Zion and its cities,/ as a woman in labor pains,/ and like a maiden that dons sackcloth to mourn for the husband of her youth." The dirge enumerates, in detail, the cruelties suffered by Judea and its inhabitants during the destruction of the Second Temple. *Eli Ẓiyyon* is sung by the congregation standing. The refrain is sung slowly (and in some traditions twice) at the beginning, and then repeated faster after each stanza. The melody is of an elegiac character, and has become, for all Ashkenazi communities, a symbol of the yearly commemoration of the Destruction. It therefore came to be used also for some other *kinot*, such as the last stanza of *Az be-ḥata'einu* ("Then, for our sins"), and for *Teraḥem Ẓiyyon ka-asher amarta* ("Have mercy upon Zion as Thou didst promise"); and also for **Lekhah Dodi* during the "Three Weeks" (17th of Tammuz to 9th of Av). It is sometimes considered one of the **Mi-Sinai Niggunim*. The origin of the melody has been discussed by Emmanuel Kirschner and Abraham Zvi Idelsohn. Kirschner related it to a 15th-century German court ballad *Die Frau zur Weissen Burg*, and to 14th- and 17th-century Catholic songs. Idelsohn related it to a 17th-century Spanish folksong, and a Czech song of the same period, both of which belong to a melodic type which he also found among the Balkan Sephardim. Since all these comparisons are based upon resemblances of isolated motives or melodic phrases, and a direct prototype has not been identified as yet, it seems more probable that it represents a particular instance of a widespread European "migrant" tune or melodic pattern. The earliest notated evidence of the melody found so far is in the manuscript manual of Judah Elias of Hanover (1743), for *Lekhah Dodi* (in a slightly varied form), and in several of the manuals of 18th-century *ḥazzanim* published in Idelsohn, Melodien, vol. 6 (1932) (Isaac Glogau, Moshe Pan, I.L. Wolf). Its earliest appearance in print is in Isaac Nathan's very free paraphrase of the melody, for his setting of "O weep for those that wept by Babel's stream" in Byron's *Hebrew Melodies* (1815). An interesting version is given by Moses Margoliouth who states that he heard it sung by Polish immigrants at the Western Wall on the Ninth of Av, 1848 (*A Pilgrimage to the Land of my Fathers*, 2 (1850), 356–9).

The melody can be found in the following publications: S. Sulzer, *Schir Zion* (1838), 188, no. 148; M. Kohn, *Vollstaendiger Jahrgang von Terzett- und Chorgesaengen*, 3 (1839), 130, no. 89; S. Naumbourg, *Zemirot Yisrael*, 3 (1864), 23, no. 25; A. Baer, *Baal T'fillah* (1883³), 90; A.S. Ersler, *T'fillah w'Zimrah*, 1 (1907), 48, no. 49; L. Kornitzer, in: *Israelitisches Familienblatt* (July 28, 1927), supplement; Idelsohn, Melodien, 6 (1932), 213, no. 35; 7 (1933), 105, no. 302 a and b; 148, no. 101. It was published in Israel in Y. Sharett (ed.), *Anot*, 5 (1938), in M. Ayali, *Ḥaggim u-Zemannim*, 1 (1953), 527, and in *Sefer ha-Mo'adim*, 7 (1957), 16–18 (music section).

In the 20th century, several composers made arrangements of the melody, including L. Zeitlin and Joseph *Achron. Its poetical and melodic structure was the inspiration for A. Luboshitzky's elegy on the death of Theodor Herzl *Eli Ẓiyyon ve-Nodedeha* ("Wail, Zion, and her dispersed ones"; *Mivḥar Shirei Amenu* (1921), 59–60). A modern *kinah*, J.L. Bialer's *Eli, Eli Nafshi, Bekhi* (Wail, wail my soul, cry"), in commemoration of the Holocaust, was approved by the Union of Synagogues in Israel for use on the Ninth of Av, and is sung to the *Eli Ẓiyyon* melody.

BIBLIOGRAPHY: Davidson, Oẓar, 1 (1924), 229; E. Kirschner, *Ueber mittelalterliche hebraeische Poesien und ihre Singweisen* (1914); A. Nadel, in: *Gemeindeblatt* (Berlin 1924), no. 9; Idelsohn, Music, 168, 171.

[Haim Bar-Dayan]

ELKABBACH, JEAN-PIERRE (1937–), French broadcast journalist. Elkabbach was born in Oran, Algeria. He was a leading figure of radio and television journalism in France. From 1970 to 1972 he was a newscaster on the first channel. In 1975 he was chief editor on the state radio network, France Inter, and he became director of the news division in 1976. During the years 1977 to 1981 he was head of the news department of the second channel of French television. Since the position at that time was based on a political appointment, he was replaced when the Socialist government came to power in 1981. He became an editor and newscaster on the main daily news report on Europe No. 1 radio station. In 1993 he reached the peak of his career when he was appointed chairman of France Television, the French public broadcasting company. His methods of dealing with the strong competition from private networks were somewhat controversial, and he was forced to resign in 1996. He wrote about his experiences and the role of public broadcasting in France in *29 mois et quelques jours* (1997).

From December 1999, Elkabbach, a dynamic reporter noted for his aggressive broadcasting style, was chairman of Public Senat, the parliamentary channel of the French Senate.

[Gideon Kouts / Dror Franck Sullaper (2nd ed.)]

ELKAN, BENNO (1877–1960), sculptor and graphic artist. Elkan was born in Dortmund, and studied art in Munich and Karlsruhe. He became a very versatile artist and could not decide whether to work as painter or sculptor. But after he had finished *The Walking* (1904, Ostenfriedhof Dordmund) he decided to specialize in sculpture. In 1905 he went to Paris where he taught himself sculpture. There he became acquainted with Paul Albert Bartholomé, whose monumental sepulcher in the Pére-Lachaise cemetery greatly influenced Elkan. A year after his marriage to Hedwig Einstein in 1907, the couple went to Rome for three years, where he immersed himself in the art of the Renaissance. In 1911 he returned to Germany where he executed a large number of stone tombstones decorated with bronze statues, and several large sculptures in colored stone. Among the busts he carved is a bronze mask of Jules Pascin (1906, Hamburger Kunsthalle), and busts of Truebner (1911, Ursula Hammil, Beverly Hills, U.S.), Alfred Flechtheim (1912, Stadtmuseum Düsseldorf), and Rathenau (1925, Museum am Ostwall Dortmund). Elkan's bas-relief portrait medals capture elements of chiaroscuro. In World War I, Elkan enlisted but was released after a bout of cholera. Elkan settled in Frankfurt for 15 years and had a profound impact on local cultural life. He published his war experiences (*Polnische Nachtstuecke)* as lithographs in 1918. The medals and busts created by Elkan are to be found in all the important museums of Europe. His most outstanding works in Germany were the freedom monument in Mainz *(Erwachende, 1930*, granite, about 17 ft., 4.5 meters, high) which was destroyed during World War II, and the memorial to the victims of war, erected in Frankfurt, which the Nazis removed in 1933, but which was restored in 1946.

In 1933 Elkan settled in London, spending the war years in Oxford. He modelled portraits of Lord Keynes, Winston Churchill, Lord Samuel, James de Rothschild, Claude Montefiore, Chaim Weizmann (on his 75th birthday), and Chief Rabbi J.H. Hertz. He created large bronze candelabra engraved with biblical figures for King's College (1934), Cambridge, New College, Oxford (*Verkündigung*, 1938), and several churches. His twin candelabra (*Old Testament*, 1931; *New Testament*, 1942, 2 × 2 meters) in Westminster Abbey depict 24 groups of figures from the Bible. Elkan's monumental bronze seven-branched candelabra (1956) decorated with biblical scenes was presented by members of the British Parliament to the Israel Knesset.

BIBLIOGRAPHY: F. Hofmann and Peter Schmieder, *Benno Elkan. Ein juedischer Kuenstler aus Dortmund* (1997); H. Menzel-Severing, *Benno Elkan* (1980); idem, "Benno Elkan – ein künstlerischer Kosmopolit aus dem Ruhrgebiet," in: J.-P. Barbian, M. Brocke, L. Heid (eds.), *Juden im Ruhrgebiet. Vom Zeitalter der Aufklärung bis in die Gegenwart.*(1999), 133–53.

[Sonja Beyer (2nd ed.)]

ELKAN, SOPHIE (1853–1921), Swedish novelist. She published some early works under the pseudonym Rust Roest, but her best-known novels, based mainly on historical themes, appeared under her own name. These include *John Hall* (1899) and two novels dealing with the Swedish king, Gustavus Adolphus IV – *Konungen* ("The King," 1904) and *Konungen i landsflykt* ("The King in Exile," 1906). Her central characters are perverted personalities, whom she analyzes with psychological subtlety. Following a voyage to Egypt and Palestine which she undertook with Selma Lagerlöf (1858–1940), she wrote an interesting book entitled *Drömmen om Österlandet* ("The Dream of the Eastern Land," 1904).

BIBLIOGRAPHY: *Svenskt Litteraturlexikon* (1964), 120.

[Hugo Mauritz Valentin]

ELKANAH (Heb. אֶלְקָנָה; "God has created"), father of *Samuel. I Samuel 1:1 names four generations of Elkanah's ancestors, thereby suggesting his important lineage. He lived in Ramathaim-Zophim (*ibid.*), which was apparently Ramah in the land of Zuph, at the southern end of Mount Ephraim. The genealogical lists in I Chronicles 6:7–12, 17–23, trace Elkanah's line to *Kohath, the son of Levi, i.e., the levites who dwelt in Mount Ephraim. But the text in I Samuel 1:1 calls him an Ephraimite, and there are some who believe that this suggests that he was a descendant of Ephrath, Caleb's concubine, whose line is associated with Beth-Lehem in Judah. Possibly the claim to his descent from Kohath was added by later sources, which concluded from Samuel's priestly service that he was a levite. Elkanah has often been praised for nobility of character attempting to comfort his barren wife Hannah (I Sam. 1:8), but in fact he negates the legitimacy of her feelings, and she is not comforted as the ensuing verses make clear. In the genealogical lists in I Chronicles several ancestors of Samuel are mentioned by the name of Elkanah.

[Samuel Ephraim Loewenstamm]

In the *Aggadah*

The good deeds of Elkanah are compared with those of Abraham (Agg. Ber. 50). He was the only pious man of his generation, and was able to overcome the problem of having two wives who hated each other (*ibid.*). He did not marry Peninah until he had been married to Hannah for ten years without offspring (PR 43, 181a). He used to encourage his fellow men to accompany him on pilgrimages to Shiloh, and himself always made four annual pilgrimages instead of the obligatory three. Because he always traveled with his kinsmen and household, his caravan invariably roused the interest of the inhabitants of the towns through which he passed. Elkanah informed them of the purpose of his journey and encouraged them to join him. By taking a different route to Shiloh every year, he was eventually responsible for all Israel going on pilgrimage (SER 8).

BIBLIOGRAPHY: Noth, Personennamen, 172; Levi Della Vida, in: JBL, 63 (1944), 8; W. Rudolph, *Chronikbuecher* (1955), 56. **ADD. BIBLIOGRAPHY:** S. Bar-Efrat, *I Samuel* (1996), 52.

ELKANN, JEAN-PAUL (1921–), French engineer, businessman, and Jewish community leader. Elkann was born in Paris; he received his engineering degree from Columbia University. In addition to his engineering endeavors, he was appointed director of important French fashion houses and director of government companies. He was the director of Christian Dior from 1983 and prior to that of Parfums Givenchy (1980–83). Elkann was the owner and director of Vanadium Steel Italiana from 1948 and of Vanadium Alloys Steel Company Canada from 1950, and vice chairman of Vanadium Alloys Steel (U.S.A.) from 1953. Among his activities in the Jewish community, he was president of the Association de la cooperation economique France-Israel and vice president of the France-Israel Chamber of Commerce. In 1982 he became president of the *Consistoire Centrale Israélite de France, holding this position for a decade. In addition, Elkann was a member of the Alliance Israélite Universelle Central Committee and the Technion's Board of Governors.

He was awarded France's highest honors: Commander of the Legion of Honor and Grand Officer of the National Order of Merit.

[Gideon Kouts / Dror Franck Sullaper (2nd ed.)]

ELKERBOUT, BEN (1940–1987), Dutch-Jewish documentary film producer. Elkerbout joined the Dutch Labor Broadcasting Company VARA as a young man, first in an administrative position but later working as a producer of television documentaries. In this capacity he made many reports from abroad – from Vietnam, Biafra, and particularly Israel, where he felt closest to the Israel Labor party. His interview with Golda Meir in 1976 won a special prize from the international press jury at the First Jewish Film and Television Festival in Jerusalem.

In 1979, together with his younger colleague Ludi Boeken, he founded the independent Belbo Film Productions Company, which specialized in documentaries on unusual subjects. The topics included the uncovering of the financial resources of the neo-Nazis throughout the world, the dumping of unlicensed medicines in the Third World, prisons in Argentina, and a reconstruction of the students' revolts in Europe in the late 1960s.

In 1986 he went over to producing full-length feature films, the first of which was *Dreamers*, on pioneers of the Third Aliyah in Palestine.

[Henriette Boas]

ELKES, ELHANAN (1879–1944), chairman of Kovno (Kaunas) *Aeltestenrat* (Council of Elders under the Nazis). Elkes was born in Kalvarija (Lithuania). He received both a traditional Jewish and a private secular education. Elkes studied medicine in Koenigsberg, Germany, was a village doctor in Belorussia, and then served as a physician in the Russian army during World War I before coming to Kovno, where he was director of internal medicine at Bikkur Holim. A respected physician, he treated prominent non-Jews as well as Jews and thus had excellent contacts, which he used when the Soviet Union occupied Kovno to assist in the emigration of Polish Jews stranded in Lithuania. Although an ardent Zionist from youth, he was not active in Jewish public life until the German occupation (June 1941), when he was unanimously elected chairman of the Kaunas *Aeltestenrat*, a position he accepted with great reluctance. Thus, he derived the legitimacy of his administration from the Jewish community and not from the Germans, who routinely appointed the Jewish leadership. Despite his failing health, Elkes guided the council for more than three years, during which time he took upon himself fateful decisions involving the future of the community while actively furthering the local resistance movement. He was a man of unquestioned integrity, who conducted the affairs of the Judenrat with equity and fairness, in marked contrast to other ghettos where corruption and the enticements of power – however limited and derivative from the German master – were rampant. Also in contrast with other Judenrat chairs, Elkes cooperated with the resistance. In Kovno the Jewish police directly assisted the partisans. In 1942, word of the fate of Polish Jews reached Kovno through Irena Adamowicz, a non-Jewish courier for the underground. From then on the members of the Jewish Council understood they would lead the battle for survival even without knowing if their efforts could postpone or prevent the day of destruction. Despite the Judenrat's best efforts, only 2,000 Jews – 8 percent of the ghetto's original population – survived, a rate little different from that of other ghettos whose internal governance was more corrupt and less benignly guided.

By his personality and dignity of bearing Elkes represents an outstanding example in the history of imposed Jewish "self-government." He wrote of his fate in a letter to his children, who were safe in England (written on October 19, 1943).

> I am writing these lines, my dear children, in the vale of tears of Vilijampole, Kovno Ghetto, where we have been for over two years. We have now heard that in a few days our fate is to be sealed. The Ghetto is to be crushed and torn asunder. Whether we are all to perish, or whether a few of us are to survive, is in God's hands. We fear that only those capable of slave labor will live; the rest, probably, are sentenced to death.
>
> We are left, a few out of many. Out of 35,000 Jews of Kovno, approximately 17,000 remain; out of a quarter of a million Jews in Lithuania … only 25,000 live … The rest were put to death in terrible ways by the followers of the greatest Haman of all times and generations …
>
> We are trying to steer our battered ship in furious seas, when waves of decrees and decisions threaten to drown it every day. Through my influence I succeeded, at times, in easing the verdict and scattering some of the dark clouds that hung over our heads. I bore my duties with head high and an upright countenance. Never did I ask for pity; never did I doubt our rights. I argued our case with total confidence in the justice of our demands.
>
> The Germans killed, slaughtered and murdered us in complete equanimity. I was there with them. I saw them when they sent thousands of people – men, women, children, infants – to their death, while enjoying their breakfast, and while mocking

> our martyrs. I saw them coming back from their murderous missions – dirty, stained from head to foot with the blood of our dear ones. There they sat at their table – eating and drinking, listening to light music. They are professional executioners.
>
> I am writing this in an hour when many desperate souls – widows and orphans, threadbare and hungry – are camping on my doorstep, imploring us for help. There is a desert inside me. My soul is scorched. I am naked and empty. There are no words in my mouth.

Following the liquidation of the ghetto, he was deported to Lansberg, where he served as a physician before succumbing to illness on October 17, 1944.

BIBLIOGRAPHY: L. Garfunkel, *Kovnah ha-Yehudit be-Ḥurbanah* (1959); A. Turai, in: *Heikhal she-Shaka*, ed. by I. Yablokowski (1962), 235–49; *Hidden History of the Kovno Ghetto*, A Project of the United States Holocaust Memorial Council (1997); W.W. Mishell, *Kaddish from Kovno: Life and Death in a Lithuanian Ghetto 1941–1945* (1988); A. Tory, *Surviving the Holocaust: The Kovno Ghetto Diary* (1990); J. Elkes, *Values, Beliefs and Survival, Dr. Elchanan Elkes and the Kovno Ghetto: A Memoir* (1997).

[Michael Berenbaum (2nd ed.)]

ELKIN, ADOLPHUS PETER (1891–1979), Australian anthropologist. Born in Maitland, New South Wales, Elkin began his fieldwork in the mid-1920s among the Australian aborigines and was one of the founders of anthropology in Australia. In 1934 he joined the faculty of the University of Sydney and became the chairman of its department of anthropology, remaining until 1956. During this time he did fieldwork in all parts of Australia, as well as in New Guinea and other areas of Oceania, and wrote on the rapidly disappearing aborigines of these areas. His books include *The Australian Aborigines* (1954³) and *Marriage and the Family in Australia* (1957). He became editor of the anthropology journal *Oceania* in 1933.

Elkin made great efforts to better the condition of the aboriginal peoples of Australia and New Guinea, and to improve relations between them and the white populations of these areas. From 1933 to 1962 he was president of the Association for the Protection of Native Races. Although Elkin's father, Reuben Israel Elkin, was Jewish, his mother was a Christian and, it should be noted, Elkin apparently regarded himself as an Anglican. He was married as an Anglican and for some years after 1919 was vice warden of St. Johns Theological College, Armadale, New South Wales, an Anglican institution.

BIBLIOGRAPHY: R.M. Berndt and C.H. Berndt (eds.), *Aboriginal Man in Australia* (1965), 453–70 (incl. bibl.). **ADD. BIBLIOGRAPHY:** *Australian Dictionary of Biography.*

[Ephraim Fischoff / William D. Rubinstein (2nd ed.)]

ELKIN, STANLEY (1930–1995), U.S. novelist and short story writer. From 1955 to 1957, he served in the U.S. Army. From 1960, he taught and wrote at Washington University in St. Louis, Missouri, where he was appointed professor of English in 1968.

Elkin has been described as a black humorist. His fiction, which dramatizes the conflicts and vulgarity of contemporary popular culture in the U.S.A., has become increasingly popular since the 1960s. His first novel *Boswell: a Modern Comedy* (1964) chronicles the post-World War II era as seen through the eyes of a cynical outside observer. His 1976 novel *The Franchiser* describes the life of Ben Flesh, who collects franchises, lives out of his Cadillac, eats fast food, and sleeps in motels. Only serious illness forces Ben to confront the sterility of his life.

Elkin's fiction is peopled by fantastically comic characters. In his third novel, *The Dick Gibson Show* (1971), Elkin utilizes a radio talk show format to recreate a set of eccentric comic personalities. His novella *The Living End* (1979) traces the lives of hold-up victims in Minneapolis-St. Paul, the cast of characters including Jesus, Mary, and Joseph and others both living and dead.

Elkin often uses the Jew and his exile as analogy for man's striving for freedom. In his first collection of short stories, *Criers and Kibitzers, Kibitzers and Criers* (1966), Elkin evokes the atmosphere of growing up Jewish in the late 1930s.

Elkin's other works have included the novel *A Bad Man* (1967) and the volume of short stories *Searches and Seizure* (1973), *George Mills* (1982), for which he won the 1983 National Book Critics Circle Award, and *Magic Kingdom* (1985).

BIBLIOGRAPHY: D. Dougherty, *Stanley Elkin* (1990); T. Pughe, *Comic Sense* (1994).

[Susan Strul]

ELKIND, ARKADI DANIILOVICH (1869–?), Russian physician and anthropometrist. Elkind was born in Mogilev. After graduating in medicine, he became increasingly involved in the scientific study of anthropometry and craniology. As a result, he was entrusted by the Imperial Society of the Friends of Natural Science, Anthropology, and Ethnography with the study of the physical anthropology of Russian Poland. His extended investigations resulted in two important monographs for the society's journal, one an anthropological and cranial sketch of the Vistula Poles, the other *Yevrei*, a study based mainly on his observations of Polish Jews. The latter, which appeared in 1903, was described by M. *Fishberg as the most comprehensive work ever published on the anthropology of a particular Jewish community. Elkind later pursued his demographic and anthropometric research in Germany and Italy. He came to the conclusion that there was a distinctive Jewish type, especially among the Jews of Russian Poland, which had been crystallized for the most part in the pre-Christian period. He published his findings in *Zeitschrift fuer Demographie und Statistik der Juden* (nos. 4–5, 1906; no. 12, 1908).

[Ellen Friedman]

ELKUS, ABRAM ISAAC (1867–1947), U.S. lawyer and public official. Elkus, who was born in New York City, practiced law there. He was appointed special United States attorney to prosecute bankruptcy in 1908, and in 1911 counsel for the New York State Factory Investigating Commission. Under the administration of President Woodrow Wilson, he was ambassador to Turkey (1916–19). Upon his return to the United States, he served briefly on the New York State Court of Appeals and as a League of Nations commissioner before resuming his private law practice. He was active in a number of Jewish organizations, especially the New York Free Synagogue, whose president he was from 1919 to 1927, and the Jewish Publication Society of America, of which he was honorary vice president until his death.

[Hillel Halkin]

ELLENBOGEN, WILHELM (1863–1951), Austrian politician. Born in Breclav (Lundenburg, Moravia), he was taken to Vienna by his family in 1870 and qualified as a physician in 1886. He was one of the first members of the newly constituted Social Democratic party, and served on its Executive Board from 1891. He was elected to the Reichsrat in 1901 and remained in the Austrian parliament also after 1918, until its dissolution in 1934. In 1907, Ellenbogen played an important part in securing the passage of the Universal Franchise Bill. At the end of World War I, he negotiated with the Hungarian government for food shipments to save Vienna from famine. In 1919 he became undersecretary for commerce, and in 1921 he succeeded Otto *Bauer as secretary for socialization, with the rank of a cabinet member. Later he headed the office for electrification of the state railroads (until 1929). After the *Anschluss* in 1938, Ellenbogen fled to France and in 1940 to New York. His publications include *Was will die Sozialdemokratie?* (1910), *Sozialisierung in Oesterreich* (1922), and *Anschluss und Energiewirtschaft* (1928).

ADD. BIBLIOGRAPHY: A. Barkai, "The Austrian Social Democrats and the Jews," in: *Wiener Library Bulletin*, 24 (1970); A. Rabinbach, *The Crisis of Austrian Socialism: from Red Vienna to Civil War, 1927–1934* (1983); R.S. Wistrich, *Socialism and the Jews: The Dilemmas of Assimilation in Germany and Austria-Hungary* (1982).

[Josef J. Lador-Lederer]

ELLENSON, DAVID HARRY (1947–), U.S. Reform rabbi and scholar of modern Jewish thought; president of Hebrew Union College. Born in Brookline, Mass., Ellenson was raised in an observant home in Newport News, Virginia. He received his undergraduate degree from the College of William and Mary in 1969, a master's degree from the University of Virginia in 1971, and his Ph.D. from Columbia in 1981. He was ordained at the Hebrew Union College-Jewish Institute of Religion (HUC) in 1977, and from 1979 to 2001 was a professor at the HUC campus in Los Angeles. In 2001, Ellenson was appointed as the president of the Hebrew Union College.

Over the course of his life, Ellenson has belonged to Orthodox, Conservative, and Reform communities. Consequently, some observers greeted his appointment as HUC president as reflective of a new post-denominational trend in American Jewish life. Ellenson's wide-ranging life experiences, broad scholarly interests, and well-known affability have enabled him to forge connections with scholars and religious leaders of differing outlooks in the United States and Israel. At the same time, his vision of a liberal Judaism balanced by ethical obligation and personal autonomy, as well as a strong commitment to Zionism and the State of Israel, have infused considerable new energy into Hebrew Union College and the American Reform movement. Since becoming president of HUC, Ellenson has been a vocal spokesperson on contemporary Jewish issues in North America and the State of Israel.

Ellenson's research has been devoted to the manifold efforts of Jews to mediate between tradition and modernity in a post-Enlightenment age, as indicated by the titles of three volumes of his collected papers: *Tradition in Transition* (1989), *Tradition and Culture* (1994), and *After Emancipation* (2004). Throughout these books, Ellenson extensively analyzes two types of Jewish sources: liturgy and halakhic responsa. In the first case, Ellenson has followed his fellow Reform scholars Jakob J. *Petuchowski and Lawrence *Hoffman in utilizing liturgical innovation and translation as a prism through which to understand the ways in which modern Jews adapt age-old ritual formulae to contemporary realities. Typical of his intellectual reach, Ellenson's study of liturgy has spanned the denominational spectrum and engaged German, American, and Israeli milieux.

The other major genre of literature that has occupied Ellenson's scholarly attention is the halakhic responsum. In a long series of studies of articles, he has sought not only to understand halakhic decision-making from within the Jewish legal tradition, but also to examine the shifting function of the responsum in modern contexts that are quite distinct from the well-guarded bounds of the pre-modern *kehillah*. His approach owes much to the historical sociological method of Jacob *Katz, with whom Ellenson studied. For Ellenson, responsa are important barometers of the struggle of observant Jews to remain true to traditional legal norms while confronting the challenges of modernity.

David Ellenson has devoted the majority of his research to Orthodox Judaism. His main monographic study, based on his Columbia doctoral dissertation, is *Rabbi Esriel Hildesheimer and the Creation of a Modern Jewish Orthodoxy* (1990) that traces the intellectual path of the founder in 1873 of the new-style Berlin Orthodox rabbinical seminar. Ellenson brings his historical sociological method to bear on a subject who, to him, personifies the central question of modern Jewish existence: "how to live in two different cultural worlds." Although their paths differ, Ellenson avers, "I have come to see much of his problem as my own."

[David N. Myers (2nd ed.)]

ELLENSTEIN, MEYER C. (1886–1967), U.S. politician. Ellenstein was born in New York City and raised in Patterson, New Jersey. He graduated from Columbia University's dental school (1912) and opened a practice in Newark, meanwhile studying law at the New Jersey Law School. Receiving a law degree in 1925, Ellenstein gave up dentistry and entered politics. In 1933 he was elected on the Democratic ticket to the five-member Newark City Commission, which chose him mayor and returned him once more to the office in 1937. During his administration Ellenstein developed Newark's airport and harbor, but his second term was marred by charges of conspiracy to defraud the city in a real estate swindle. After a three-year investigation, Ellenstein was finally acquitted in 1940, but failed in his bid for reelection in 1941. In 1945 he was voted onto the City Commission again, where he served for eight more years. After another unsuccessful mayoral candidacy in 1958, he retired permanently from politics.

ELLINGER, MORITZ (1830–1907), U.S. public official, communal leader, and journalist. Ellinger was born in Fuerth, Bavaria, and arrived in New York in 1854. He advocated Reform Judaism. Active in the affairs of B'nai B'rith, he was a member of its National Executive Committee and served as corresponding secretary between 1895 and 1905, besides being instrumental in helping to establish lodges in several European countries. Ellinger toured Europe in 1882 on behalf of American Jewish leaders in an attempt to organize the migration of Russian refugees. In addition, he edited the *Menorah Monthly*, the official organ of B'nai B'rith, from 1860 to 1901, and as founder and editor of the *Jewish Times* (1869–78) he expressed the views of David *Einhorn. In civic life, Ellinger was coroner of New York City (1876–81) and an official of the Surrogate's Court (1888–1907). He also served as secretary of the New York Medico-Legal Society.

BIBLIOGRAPHY: E. Grusd, *B'nai B'rith* (Eng., 1966), index.

[Robert Shosteck]

ELLIOT, "MAMA" CASS (Ellen Naomi Cohen; 1941–1974), U.S. folk singer, member of the rock group The Mamas and the Papas. Born in Baltimore, Maryland, to a middle-class Jewish family, Elliot was given the nickname Cass by her father. She changed her last name from Cohen to Elliot when she went to New York to try to make it as a Broadway actress in the early 1960s. Elliot joined a rock group, The Big Three, a short-lived band called the Mugwumps, and then the folk-rock band, the New Journeymen, which became The Mamas and the Papas in 1965. In December of that year the group's first album, *If You Can Believe Your Eyes and Ears*, was issued, containing the single, "California Dreamin'," which reached No. 4 on the music charts in March 1966, followed by "Monday, Monday," which in May reached No. 1 and later won a Grammy Award. Other hits included "Words of Love," "Dedicated To the One I Love," "Go Where You Wanna Go," "I Saw Her Again," and "Dream a Little Dream of Me," which became her theme song.

The Mamas and the Papas were arguably the first music act to combine both hippie and pop sensibilities, enabling Middle America to see the "safe" side of the Haight-Ashbury counterculture of the 1960s. Elliot, who had the most outgoing and appealing personality in the group, and who wore big yellow and orange flower and sun images in appliqué on a long white dress, became the poster girl for the "Age of Aquarius."

In June 1967, the group played at the prominent Monterey Pop Festival, but tensions within the band led to a break-up a year later. Eliot went solo, and had some hits with songs such as "It's Getting Better," "Make Your Own Kind of Music," and "New World Coming." In 1969 Eliot began appearing on TV variety shows doing comedy sketches and performing songs, with much success.

Eliot had health problems brought on by her obesity – she stood 5′5″ and weighed 238 lbs. – and on July 28, 1974, she died in London of a heart attack. It was initially misreported that her death was caused by choking on a ham sandwich, but despite the autopsy report by a pathologist and a London coroner a week later, the "ham sandwich" story became an urban legend.

Elliot and her fellow band mates from The Mamas and the Papas were inducted into the Rock and Roll Hall of Fame in 1998.

[Elli Wohlgelernter (2nd ed.)]

ELLIS, VIVIAN (1904–1996), British theatrical composer. Born in London, the son of a tailor, Ellis started as a concert pianist and began composing for musical shows before he was 20. He subsequently contributed music and lyrics to many revues, wrote popular songs, and was the composer for A.P. Herbert's musical plays *Big Ben* (1946), *Bless the Bride* (1947), *Tough at the Top* (1949), and *The Water Gypsies* (1955). He also wrote humorous books and two volumes of autobiography, *Ellis in Wonderland* (1939) and *I'm on a See-Saw* (1953). Ellis wrote many pieces of "light classical" music which have become well-known, such as "Coronation Scot," as well as popular songs like "Spread a Little Happiness."

BIBLIOGRAPHY: ODNB.

ELLISON, LAWRENCE J. (1944–), U.S. computer entrepreneur. Born out of wedlock in New York to a Jewish teenager and an Italian-American Air Force pilot, Ellison was raised by an aunt in a lower middle-class Jewish community in Chicago. At the University of Illinois, he was named science student of the year but dropped out of school after his aunt died. He enrolled at the University of Chicago, but also left before graduation. Ellison went to California, where, after a few jobs, he became a computer programmer. He was inspired by a paper on relational database theory, which held that if data could be stored in computers in a less "hierarchical" way, it would be easier to find and use. With two other programmers, Ellison began in 1977 what became the Oracle Corporation, now the foremost producer of computer software for corporate databases. At the time, IBM was doing pioneering research on the subject, but doubted that relational databases were commercially viable. Ellison put together a prototype and made his first sale to the CIA. Over the next few years, Oracle found itself on the cutting edge of data storage technology. IBM was wrong and Ellison was right. Relational databases were the future, and Oracle, under strong pressure from Ellison, won marquee-name clients like the National Security Agency and

Navy Intelligence before going public in 1986. Ellison turned Oracle into a world leader in producing software that runs large organizations. The initial release of Oracle was Oracle 2, even though there was no Oracle 1. The release number was intended to imply that all of the bugs had been worked out of an earlier version. Ellison was chief executive officer and a director from the time he cofounded the company. He was believed to be one of the richest people in America, with a net worth estimated at $18.7 billion.

Ellison and Oracle developed a reputation for dealing on the edge. It sold software not yet ready for use and blamed customers when things went wrong. In the early 1990s the mistakes caught up with the company and it suffered significant losses. But in 1992 Ellison brought in new leadership and Oracle regained its place in the market. At that time Ellison began focusing on the big picture. In the mid-1990s, when Microsoft was still not appreciating the importance of the Internet, Ellison pushed Oracle to switch over to web-based data storage software. It was a brilliant move, and Oracle rode the Internet to new heights.

Ellison was also the leader and principal financier of Oracle-BMW Racing, which competed for the America's Cup in 1999 and 2003 on behalf of the Golden Gate Yacht Club of San Francisco. Ellison was the winner of the disastrous 1998 Sydney to Hobart Yacht Race in his boat *Sayonara*. The storm that hit the race cost six other sailors their lives, an experience that caused Ellison to swear off ocean racing. Ellison was believed to have the biggest yacht (as of 2004) in the world, named *Rising Sun*. It was 452.75 feet long and reportedly cost more than $200 million to build.

[Stewart Kampel (2nd ed.)]

ELLMANN, RICHARD (1918–1987), U.S./British literary biographer and critic. One of the most eminent of recent literary biographers, Richard Ellmann was born in suburban Detroit, the son of a lawyer, and was educated at Yale University. When stationed in Britain during World War II he became interested in studying the lives of the leading modern Irish writers, and produced a long list of path-breaking and highly regarded studies and biographies, beginning with his life of William Butler Yeats, *Yeats: The Man and the Masks* (1948). Much of Ellmann's professional career was spent at Northwestern University in Illinois (from 1951 to 1968). From 1970 to 1982 he lived in England, where he was Goldsmiths' Professor of English Literature at Oxford University, the first American to hold this position. Ellmann returned to the United States in 1982, although he died in Oxford in 1987. Ellmann's long and distinguished list of works include his much-lauded biography *James Joyce* (1959), based on ten years of research, and *Oscar Wilde* (1987), completed immediately before his death, which received the Pulitzer Prize, as well as many other biographical works and essays. Ellmann was notable for the respect in which he held his subjects, declining, in contrast to many biographers, to concentrate on their pathologies. Ellmann was also the co-editor (with Robert O'Clair) of *The Norton Anthology of Modern Poetry* (1973), a standard collection. A posthumous *Festschrift* in his honor, edited by Susan Dick et al., *Essays for Richard Ellmann: Omnium Gatherum*, appeared in 1989.

BIBLIOGRAPHY: R.E. Johnsen, "Richard David Ellmann," in: John A. Garraty and Mark C. Carnes (eds.), *American National Biography*, vol. 7 (1999), 453–54.

[William D. Rubinstein (2nd ed.)]

ELLSBERG, DANIEL (1931–), U.S. government adviser responsible for leaking the Pentagon Papers. Born in Chicago, Ellsberg was a graduate of Columbia University, receiving both his B.S. (1952) and his Ph.D. (1959) there. A Vietnam veteran, he was a first lieutenant in the Marine Corps. He then went to work for the Rand Corporation on defense issues, ultimately becoming an important adviser to Secretary of Defense Robert McNamara. His views then were decidedly hawkish. He was assigned to study American policy toward Vietnam and in the course of that study became a fierce opponent of the war. He then took the major step of leaking a study of the history of American involvement in Vietnam to the *New York Times*. The study, commonly known as the Pentagon Papers, documented the way in which the Johnson administration had misled the American people during the Vietnam War. Although the Papers did not directly attack Richard Nixon's actions, his administration reacted with fury. Ellsberg was charged with leaking the document; a petition was filed against the *New York Times*, enjoining them from publishing the papers; and then the White House had some secret operatives, later known as the "plumbers unit" of Watergate fame, break into Ellsberg's psychiatrist's office in search of potentially incriminating information that could be used to destroy his reputation. When the *Washington Post*, which had not been enjoined from publication, printed the Pentagon Papers, the case became moot and the information became public. The break-in at the office of Ellsberg's psychiatrist became public during the Watergate hearings that led to the downfall of Richard Nixon, who resigned as president of the United States in August 1974. Having achieved his "five minutes of fame" Ellsberg remained politically active, most especially fighting against nuclear arms proliferation and becoming a prominent figure at public protests.

BIBLIOGRAPHY: D. Ellsberg, *Secrets: A Memoir of Vietnam and the Pentagon Papers* (2002).

[Michael Berenbaum (2nd ed.)]

ELLSBERG, EDWARD (1891–1983), U.S. naval officer. Born in New Haven, Conn., Ellsberg was the son of Jewish refugees from czarist Russia. The family moved to Colorado when Ellsberg was a boy. He trained as an engineer. One of very few Jews to be accepted into the U.S. Naval Academy in 1910, he ranked first in his class. After varied service on the USS *Texas*, he was ordered to the Massachusetts Institute of Technology for postgraduate work in naval architecture, receiving a master of science degree. Although he was encouraged to remain an executive officer, he transferred into naval construction. During World War I he worked in refitting confiscated German liners in the New York Navy Yard and subsequently became an authority on raising sunken vessels. In 1925 he became the first person to be awarded the Distinguished Service Medal in peacetime when he raised the submarine USS *S-51*, which had sunk after a collision off Block Island, Rhode Island. During the ten-month salvage operation, Ellsberg became the first naval officer to qualify as a deep-sea diver, understanding the importance of going down to the ocean floor with his men. He earned a reputation as an expert in submarine salvage.

In industry, Ellsberg worked as chief engineer of the Tidewater Oil Company until 1935. He patented several inventions, including a method for increasing the yield of high-octane gasoline and a process for removing water from lubricating oil.

Ellsberg organized the rehabilitation of the U.S. naval base in Eritrea (then Massawa, Ethiopia) following the entry of the United States into World War II. There, with a makeshift workforce, he restored the demolished Italian naval base and cleared the harbor of scuttled ships. At the end of 1942 he was made principal salvage officer for the Mediterranean. On the North African coast, he cleared the ports of Oran and Algiers for Operation Torch. He also took part in the Artificial Harbors project connected with the Allied invasion of France in 1944. He was released from active duty shortly before the end of World War II. Ellsberg was the recipient of many awards from the United States and British governments, such as the Legion of Merit and the Order of the British Empire. He retired in 1951 with the rank of rear admiral. He consulted for shipbuilding companies and remained on the sea, traveling and sailing on his boat.

Ellsberg was the author of books on naval topics, including *On the Bottom* (1928), *Thirty Fathoms Deep* (1930), *Pigboats* (1931), *S-54* (1932), *Hell on Ice* (1938), *Men under the Sea* (1940), *Under the Red Sea Sun* (1946), *No Banners, No Bugles* (1949), *Passport for Jennifer* (1952), *Midwatch* (1954), and *The Far Shore* (1960).

BIBLIOGRAPHY: J. Ben Hirsh, *Jewish General Officers* (1967), 96–98. **ADD. BIBLIOGRAPHY:** J. Alden, *Salvage Man: Edward Ellsberg and the U.S. Navy* (1997).

[Ruth Beloff (2nd ed.)]

ELLSTAETTER, MORITZ (1827–1905), German politician, the first Jew to become a minister in a German state. Born in Karlsruhe, Ellstaetter studied law and worked in a banking house in Berlin, where he met Karl Mathy (1807–1868), the future Baden minister of finance. When Mathy assumed office in 1866, he appointed Ellstaetter department head of his ministry. In 1868, on Mathy's death, Ellstaetter was given responsibility for the ministry. He reformed the Baden finances and introduced a new taxation policy which was followed by other German states. Ellstaetter advised the German government on fiscal and coinage legislation for 25 years. In 1881 he became director of railways. Although he took no part in Jewish affairs, Ellstaetter was, because of racial prejudice, only officially confirmed as minister of finance in 1888. He retired due to ill health in 1893.

BIBLIOGRAPHY: NDB, 4 (1959), 460.

[B. Mordechai Ansbacher]

ELLSTEIN, ABRAHAM (Abe; 1907–1963), composer, conductor, and pianist. Born in New York, Ellstein studied with Frederick *Jacobi, Rubin *Goldmark, and Albert Stoessel, and became the accompanist for Mischa Mischakoff, Michel Piastro, Isa Kramer, and Jossele *Rosenblatt. At the age of 19 he wrote the first of his 33 scores for the Yiddish musical theater. He also wrote the scores for several Yiddish films produced in Warsaw before World War II and composed over 500 Yiddish songs. In 1957 he turned to composing works for concert, stage, and the synagogue. Among his compositions are *Ode to the King of Kings*, a cantata in celebration of the tenth anniversary of the State of Israel; *The Thief and the Hangman*, a one-act opera; *Hora Fantasy*, for piano; *Haftorah*, for violin and string orchestra; *Negev Concerto*, for piano and orchestra; two *Sabbath Eve Services; Passover Service; The Redemption*, a Hanukkah oratorio for chorus, organ, and percussion; and an opera, *The Golem* (1962).

ELMALEH, family of rabbis and communal leaders in Turkey, Morocco, and Italy. The family originated in Spain. (1) ABRAHAM BEN JUDAH ELMALIK, kabbalist, settled in Pesaro in 1551. He was the author of *Likkutei Shikhḥah u-Fe'ah* (Ferrara, 1556), kabbalistic expositions of talmudic *aggadot*. In the introduction he relates his adventures on leaving his home, possibly Salonika, though some scholars took it to refer to the expulsion from Spain. (2) AARON BEN GERSHON ELMALI was an important member of the Salonika community in the first half of the 17th century. His signature occurs on a document of 1647, and members of his family were represented in the Évora congregation of Salonika (whose members originally came from *Évora). The first known member of the Turkish branch of the family is (3) MOSES BEN DON DAVID ELMALEH of Adrianople. He apparently served as *dayyan* and there is a reference to him dating from 1510. After this date the name is hardly found in Turkey, the family reappearing in Salé and Rabat in North Africa at the beginning of the 18th century. (4) JOSEPH BEN AYYUSH ELMALEH (1750–1823), kabbalist and halakhist, was considered one of the outstanding Moroccan scholars of his time. He served as rabbi of Salé and of Rabat in 1780. There he maintained a large yeshivah, which continued to function after his death. In 1809 he was in Gibraltar with the intention, according to one source, of journeying on to Ereẓ Israel, and was invited to serve as rabbi there. In the same year, however, he returned to Rabat. He introduced a special tax (*imposta*) on behalf of the poor, which is still levied. His responsa (Leghorn, 1823–55), chiefly on *Ḥoshen Mishpat* and in part on *Even Ha-Ezer*, are a valuable source for the history of the Jews of Morocco. His son (5) AMRAM (d. before 1855), a wealthy merchant, dwelt in Mogador and in Lisbon. According to one source he was once imprisoned in Lisbon, but was freed on the intervention of the British authorities. During the last years of his life, he was appointed Sicilian consul in Mogador. His protection of the Jews aroused the anger of the Muslims.

(6) AARON BEN REUBEN ELMALEH of Demnat in south Morocco settled in Rabat and studied in the *bet ha-midrash* of Joseph ben Ayyush Elmaleh, whose daughter he married. When his father-in-law went to Gibraltar, he acted in his stead. His halakhic rulings were extant in manuscript. (7) JACOB BEN JOSEPH, rabbi and poet, lived in Rabat. He was the author of poems and dirges, among them a *kinah* on the persecutions in Morocco in 1790. (8) JOSEPH ELMALEH (1788–1866), son of (7), rabbi, writer of books on Kabbalah, and merchant, was born in Rabat and married into the wealthy Gedaliah family, which had many business connections in Morocco and London. Joseph served as rabbi in Mogador for over 50 years and built a large synagogue there. His great influence with Abdul Raḥman, sultan of Morocco, enabled him to be of great assistance to the Jews. When the city was attacked by the Kabyles in 1844, hundreds of Jews gathered in his house and defended themselves against their attackers. Later he lost his wealth and immigrated to Jerusalem shortly before his death. (9) JOSEPH BEN AARON ELMALEH (1809–1886) was born in Rabat, where he later served as *dayyan*. In 1826 he went to Mogador and about 1840 was appointed rabbi there. He became Austrian consul and was decorated both by the emperor Franz Joseph and by the bey of Tunis. Joseph was active on behalf of the persecuted Jews of Morocco, opposing missionary activities, and bringing many apostates back to the fold. In 1879 on one of his numerous business visits to Europe, he was offered the position of rabbi to the Spanish and Portuguese community in London, but declined. He died in London. His son REUBEN became head of the community of Mogador as well as Austrian consul.

(10) ABRAHAM BEN JOSEPH ELMALEH, rabbi of Mogador, played an important role in the spiritual and communal life of the Jews of Morocco, and was considered one of its important contemporary poets. In 1855 he was in Leghorn as an emissary. While there he published *Sova Semaḥot*, a book of poems, a shortened version of which was published in Algiers in 1890. The poems are full of religious yearning and of longing for Zion and redemption. He also published *Tokpo shel Yosef*, responsa. (11) JUDAH BEN MORDECAI ELMALEH, rabbi of Sefrou, was also in Fez, Meknès, and Rabat. In 1833 he endorsed a responsum of the sages of Fez and in the following year, himself wrote a responsum in Tetuán. He appears to have been a bookseller, and correspondence on books and halakhic topics between him and Amir Abutbol of Sefrou are extant. (12) ELIJAH BEN ABRAHAM ELMALEH, lawyer and jurist, was the author of *Naḥalat Avot* (Leghorn, 1874) on the will of the caid, Nissim *Samama of Tunis, *Mishpat ha-Yerushah* (Leghorn, 1878), and other works. (13) ELIJAH BEN JACOB ELMALEH (1837–1908) was born in Mogador, settled in Tangiers in his early youth, and was appointed rabbi there. He was the author of *Beka la-Gulgolet* (Jerusalem, 1911) on the Bible, as well as novellae on the Talmud and the Codes.

BIBLIOGRAPHY: *The Voice of Jacob*, 4 (1844), 33–34, 50–51; JC (Jan. 5, 1886); J. Nehama, *Mikhtevei Dodim mi-Yayin* (1893), 100; Kaufmann, in: ZDMG, 50 (1896), 238–40, 335–6; idem, in: REJ, 37 (1898), 120–6; J.M. Toledano, *Ner ha-Ma'arav* (1910/11), 168–91; N. Leven, *Cinquante ans d'histoire*, 2 (1920), 81, 89; J. Benaim, *Malkhei Rabbanan* (1931), 19b, 52b, 102a; M.D. Gaon, *Yehudei ha-Mizraḥ be-Ereẓ Yisrael*, 2 (1937), 73–78; A.M. Hyamson, *The Sefardim of England* (1951), 363; Toledano, in: *Minḥah le-Avraham Elmaleh* (1959), 22–26; Benayahu, *ibid.*, 27–39.

ELMALEH, ABRAHAM (1885–1967), Hebrew author and a leader of the Sephardi community in Ereẓ Israel. Born in Jerusalem, Elmaleh fostered Hebrew education among the Sephardi Jewish communities in Palestine, Istanbul, and Damascus before World War I. He was a member of the Asefat ha-Nivḥarim and of its executive, the Va'ad Le'ummi. Elected to the Jerusalem Municipal Council, Elmaleh served as deputy mayor for some time. In 1949 he was elected to the first Knesset on the Sephardi list. A journalist and writer, he was founder and editor in chief of the daily *Ha-Ḥerut* (1909–10), served on the editorial boards of the daily *Do'ar ha-Yom*, and edited the monthly magazine *Mizraḥ u-Ma'arav* (1912–32). In addition to publishing popular works on the history of Palestine and Syria during World War I and on the Jews in Oriental countries, Elmaleh compiled the following dictionaries: Hebrew-French (1923, 1925, 1947), French-Hebrew (1935, and eight other editions), Hebrew-Arabic (1929), Arabic-Hebrew (1930), and a Hebrew-French dictionary in five volumes (1950–57). A list of his Hebrew writings is found in *Minḥah le-Avraham* (1959), 11–43 (Hebrew numerals). Elmaleh also wrote *Rishonim le-Ẓiyyon Toledoteihem u-Fe'-ulatam* (1970), containing biographies of the Sephardi rabbis of Ereẓ Israel.

BIBLIOGRAPHY: Tidhar, 1 (1947), 512–4.

EL MALE RAḤAMIM (Heb. אֵל מָלֵא רַחֲמִים; "God full of compassion"), a prayer for the departed recited at the funeral service, on the anniversary of the death (*Yahrzeit*), on visiting the graves of relatives (especially on the Ninth of *Av and during the month of Elul), or after having been called up to the reading of the Law (see *Ashkavah*). In some Ashkenazi rites it is also part of the memorial service (*Hazkarat Neshamot*) on the festivals and on the Day of Atonement. *El Male Raḥamim* originated in the Jewish communities of Western and Eastern Europe where it was recited for the martyrs of the *Crusades and of the *Chmielnicki massacres. This explains the many different versions of this prayer in various European communities (e.g., Nemirov, Lublin, Prague, etc.). At a funeral service which takes place on those days when *Taḥanun* is not said, *El Male Raḥamim* is also omitted and other appropriate prayers are substituted. In the Conservative version of *El Male Raḥamim*, the words "and in whose memory charity is offered by… so and so…" are omitted (see *Likkutei Tefillah, A Rabbi's Manual [RAA]* (1965), 120ff.). The Reform ritual has a shorter version of the traditional Hebrew and English text (*Rabbis' Manual [CCAR]* (1961[2]), 99).

Musical Rendition

The elaborate musical form of the prayer, and its – often virtuoso – rendition by a cantor, are customary only among the Ashkenazi communities. There it has become the symbolic center of the burial and commemoration ceremonies, next to the **Kaddish*. The melody is almost never featured in the standard collections of synagogal song. The version attributed originally to Joshua (Osia) *Abrass became famous when Solomon *Razumni recited it after the Kishinev pogrom.

BIBLIOGRAPHY: Davidson, Oẓar, 1 (1924), 176, no. 3808, and 3800, 3801, 3804, 3805, 3806, 3807; Elbogen, Gottesdienst, 203; *Siddur Oẓar ha-Tefillot* (Sephardi, 1916), 723ff. MUSICAL RENDITION: A. Baer, *Ba'al Tefillah* (1883[2]), no. 829; M. Wodak, *Ha-Menazze'aḥ* (1898), no. 442; J.J. Sebba, *Shirei Yosef* (1914), no. 102.

[Bathja Bayer]

ELMAN, MISCHA (1891–1967), violinist. Born at Talnoye, near Kiev, Elman received his first violin lessons from his father Saul, who later wrote a book entitled *Memoirs of Mischa Elman's Father* (1933). At the age of six he was taken to the Odessa Music Academy. In 1902 he was accepted in Leopold *Auer's class at the St. Petersburg Conservatory, having received a permit of residence by Imperial assent, since Jews were not allowed to live in that city. As a youth he made sensational debuts in St. Petersburg and Berlin (1904), in London (1905), and in New York (1908). Thereafter he made the United States his home, but traveled widely. His playing, remarkable for its sweet intonation as well as technical perfection, gave rise to the phrase "the Elman tone." Besides many transcriptions for violin, he composed several works, including a light opera.

BIBLIOGRAPHY: M. Carpenter, *Mischa Elman and Joseph Szigeti* (1955); *Grove's Dict*.

[Dora Leah Sowden]

ELMAN, ZIGGY (**Harry Finkelman**; 1914–1968), U.S. trumpeter and band leader. Elman is one of those handful of jazz musicians who has the misfortune of being known for a single recording, "And the Angels Sing," which was a huge hit for the Benny Goodman band in 1938. The song was a reworking of an Elman tune, "Frailach in Swing," that bespoke both musicians' all-but-forgotten roots in Jewish music. Elman was born in Philadelphia but raised in Atlantic City, where he flourished as a startlingly natural musician, first playing trombone with the Alex Bartha band on the Steel Pier, then joining Goodman in 1936. Elman could play any instrument he picked up, once teaching himself clarinet in a single day for a performance with the Goodman band. After leaving Goodman in 1940, he played with several other important bands, including Tommy Dorsey's and his own, basing himself in Los Angeles. Ironically, when Hollywood came calling for *The Benny Goodman Story* Elman, who played himself, was too ill to recreate his famous solo on "Angels"; his trumpet part was dubbed by Mannie Klein.

BIBLIOGRAPHY: J. Chilton, "Ziggy Elman," in: *Who's Who of Jazz: Storyville to Swing Street* (1978); D. Fairweather, "Ziggy Elman," in: *Jazz: The Rough Guide* (1995); O. Ferguson, "The Boy from the Back Row," in: *The New Republic* (May 17, 1939).

[George Robinson (2nd ed.)]

EL MELEKH NE'EMAN (Heb. אֵל מֶלֶךְ נֶאֱמָן; "God, faithful King"), an affirmation of faith pronounced before the recital of the **Shema*. The rabbis interpreted the word *Amen as being composed of the initial letters of *El Melekh Ne'eman* (Shab. 119b). The phrase, however, is pronounced only in private prayer and not at public services where an interposition (even Amen) between *Shema* and the preceding benediction is omitted (according to some opinions) as an unlawful "interruption." A midrashic interpretation (Tanḥ, B., Lev. 74ff.) derives the custom of reciting *El Melekh Ne'eman* from the fact that the *Shema* consists of 245 words, and the phrase *El Melekh Ne'eman* brings the number up to 248, corresponding to that of the human limbs (cf. Ps. 35:10 "All my bones shall say: Lord, who is like unto Thee"). At public synagogue services where the *ḥazzan* repeats the last three words of the *Shema* aloud, the number of the words comes to 248 and the recital of *El Melekh Ne'eman* is therefore omitted (see Sh. Ar., OḤ 61:3).

BIBLIOGRAPHY: Elbogen, Gottesdienst, 21ff.; Eisenstein, Dinim, 16.

EL MELEKH YOSHEV (Heb. אֵל מֶלֶךְ יוֹשֵׁב; "God, King enthroned"), first words and name of a petitional prayer for the forgiving of sins, with reference to *God's Thirteen Attributes (Ex. 34:6–7). It is the main theme and refrain of the **Seliḥot* services in all rites and is thought to have originated in the sixth century C.E.

BIBLIOGRAPHY: Elbogen, Gottesdienst, 222; Davidson, Oẓar, 1 (1929), 177, no. 3822.

ELNATHAN BEN ACHBOR (Heb. אֶלְנָתָן; "God has given"; Septuagint reads here the semantically equivalent Yehonatan), a minister of King *Jehoiakim (Jer. 36:12). Yeivin identifies him with Elnathan, the father-in-law of King Jehoiakim (II Kings 24:8). At the king's command Elnathan brought the prophet *Uriah from asylum in Egypt to be executed (Jer. 26:20–23). In another episode he begged the king not to burn Jeremiah's scroll of denunciation (Jer. 36:25). Certain scholars feel that these two acts are incompatible. However, human behavior is not always consistent. Indeed, Elnathan's reverence for Jeremiah's scroll may very well have resulted from a guilty conscience because of his role in Uriah's murder.

The *Lachish ostraca mention a prophet of Zedekiah's reign whose words are "not good, making hands weak" (6:2–8), as well as an army officer named C[on]iah b. Elnathan, who went to Egypt (3:13–21). Torczyner (Tur-Sinai) attempted to relate the two references and explained that the ostraca refer to the prophet Uriah's being brought back from Egypt by

Elnathan. The fact remains, however, that Jeremiah speaks of a prophet who fled to Egypt during Jehoiakim's reign, while the ostraca refer to a prophet of Zedekiah's time. In addition, according to the biblical text, the minister who goes to Egypt is Elnathan b. Achbor, while in the Lachish ostraca it is C[on]iah b. Elnathan. Therefore it seems that two similar but not identical events took place, the first during Jehoiakim's and the second during Zedekiah's reign. The "true" prophets opposed an Egyptian orientation and preached capitulation to Babylonia ("to weaken our hands"). During the reigns of both kings they were persecuted and forced to flee. Political fugitives had traditionally sought asylum in Egypt. It is almost certain that C[on]iah mentioned in the ostraca was the son of the Elnathan in the biblical text, and that he performed a mission in the time of Zedekiah similar to his father's during Jehoiakim's reign.

BIBLIOGRAPHY: H. Torczyner (Tur-Sinai) et al., *The Lachish Letters* (1938), 63–67; idem, *Te'udot Lakhish* (1940), 93–103; Yeivin, in: *Tarbiz*, 12 (1940/41), 255–9; Malamat, in: BJPES, 14 (1948), 871. **ADD. BIBLIOGRAPHY:** W. Holladay, *Jeremiah 2* (1989), 252.

[Jacob Elbaum]

ELNECAVÉ, DAVID (1882–1963), journalist and writer. Born in Istanbul, Turkey, he studied at the Rabbinical Seminar of Istanbul and in 1909 founded the Sephardi Zionist daily *El Djudio*. Political persecution in Turkey for his Zionist activities motivated his immigration to Sofia, Bulgaria, where he continued to publish *El Djudio* between 1925 and 1930. In 1930 he immigrated to Argentina and was the correspondent of the JTA. In 1931 he founded the Spanish bi-weekly *La Luz*, which fulfilled a central role in spreading the Zionist ideology among the Sephardim in Argentina during the 1930s and 1940s. After his death *La Luz* was directed by his son Nissim and subsequently by his grandson David. Elnecavé was the author of a number of books on biblical and Jewish topics, including *El buen pastor* and *Introducción a la Biblia*.

[Efraim Zadoff (2nd ed.)]

EL NORA ALILAH (Heb. אֵל נוֹרָא עֲלִילָה; "God that doest wondrously"), name of a solemn hymn for the **Ne'ilah* service of the Day of Atonement. The initial letters of the stanzas (משה חזק) form the name of its author, Moses b. Jacob *Ibn Ezra of Spain. The motive of this hymn is expressed in the refrain of each of its eight stanzas: "Pardon at Thy people's cry,/ As the closing hour draws nigh," referring to the last hours of the Day of Atonement. The hymn (which is to be found in the prayer books of Aragon, Barcelona, Algiers, Tunisia, Leghorn, Constantine, and Tlemcen) originally formed part only of the Sephardi and Yemenite (*Tiklal*) *Ne'ilah* liturgy, but because of its moving text and solemn melody some Ashkenazi congregations also included it in their liturgy (cf. *High Holiday Prayerbook*, ed. M. Silverman (1954^2), 458).

[Meir Ydit]

ELOESSER, ARTHUR (**Marius Daalmann**; 1870–1938), German literary historian and dramatic critic. Born and educated in Berlin, Eloesser was denied an academic career at the university because of his refusal to convert and thus became a drama critic for the *Vossische Zeitung* and a producer at the Lessing Theatre in Berlin. He published essays and criticism in the *Neue Rundschau* and edited the works of Otto Ludwig, Heinrich von Kleist, Shakespeare, and Frank Wedekind. In 1925 Eloesser wrote the first biography of Thomas Mann. His main achievement was *Die Deutsche Literatur vom Barock bis zur Gegenwart* (2 vols., 1930–31). Its second volume was published in English as *Modern German Literature* (1933) and contained a preface by Eloesser's cousin, Ludwig Lewisohn. He published monographs on French and German literary figures and an autobiographical work, *Die Strasse meiner Jugend* (1919). Eloesser was long indifferent to his Jewishness, but he adopted a positive Jewish attitude after Hitler came to power and was impressed by two visits to Palestine. He became an occasional contributor to the *Juedische Rundschau* and in 1933 published *Judentum and deutsches Geistesleben*. In 1936 Eloesser published *Vom Ghetto nach Europa* on the role of the Jews in 19th-century culture from material he had prepared for *Juden im deutschen Kulturbereich* and whose publication was prohibited by the Nazis. It concentrated on German-Jewish authors such as Moses *Mendelsssohn, Berthold *Auerbach, and Heinrich *Heine. Eloesser promoted the return to Ereẓ Israel; however, on his return from his second journey to Palestine he became severely ill and died in the Jewish hospital in Berlin in 1938.

BIBLIOGRAPHY: A. Terwey, "Arthur Eloesser: der Philologe als Kritiker," in: G. Bey (ed.), *Berliner Universität und deutsche Literaturgeschichte* (1998), 201–14; D. Schaaf, *Der Theaterkritiker Arthur Eloesser* (1962).

[Ann-Kristin Koch (2nd ed.)]

ELON, AMOS (1926–), Israeli journalist and author. Born in Vienna, Elon came to Israel as a young child. He began his career as a journalist for *Ba-Maḥaneh* and in 1948 published his first book, *Yerushalayim Lo Naflah* ("Jerusalem Did Not Fall"). From 1954 he was associated with *Ha'aretz* and from 1961 was a member of the editorial board. He served as foreign correspondent in New York, Washington, Paris, Bonn, and Eastern Europe. His book *A Journey through a Haunted Land* (1967), a reportage on the new Germany, was highly praised. His best-selling *The Israelis: Founders and Sons* (1971) was heralded by *Newsweek* magazine as "the most illuminating, even-handed, candid appraisal of the Jewish condition yet to appear," and his biography *Herzl* (1975) was also widely acclaimed. *Herzl* was later made into a Broadway play by Dore *Schary in collaboration with Elon.

His other books include *Between Enemies* (1974), a dialogue with Egyptian Sana Hassan; the novel *Timetable* (1980); *Flight into Egypt* (1981); *Founder: Meyer Amschel Rothschild and His Time* (1996); and *The Pity of It All: A Portrait of the*

German-Jewish Epoch, 1743–1933 (2002). His works have appeared in English, Hebrew, French, German, Italian, Spanish, Portuguese, and Japanese.

ELON, BINYAMIN (**Benny**; 1954–), Israeli rabbi and politician, member of Knesset since the Fourteenth Knesset. Born in Jerusalem, the son of former Supreme Court justice Menachem *Elon, he studied at Yeshivat Merkaz ha-Rav in Jerusalem and the Idra Kolel in the Golan Heights. He served in the IDF in the artillery corps. He was ordained as a rabbi in 1978. In 1979–82 Elon served as rabbi in Kibbutz Sheluḥot in the Beit She'an Valley. In 1983–85 he was an emissary of the Jewish Agency to the Jewish students organizations in the United States, and after his return taught at the Makhon Meir and Atteret Kohanim yeshivot in Jerusalem. He settled with his family in Bet-El near Ramallah in 1982 and in 1987 founded there, together with his wife, Emuna, the Sifriyat Bet-El publishing house, and the Tov Ro'i Institute, where he published Abraham Isaac *Kook's talmudic commentaries. In 1990 he established the Bet Orot Yeshivah, heading it until 1996, when he was elected to the Knesset.

Elon was an active opponent of the Oslo Accords and consequently founded the Emunim Movement, which fought against the establishment of a Palestinian authority, which he viewed from the start as a terrorist entity. He maintained that it was legitimate to discuss a transfer of the Palestinian population to a Jordanian-Palestinian state in Transjordan, and argued that the refugee camps should be dismantled, and the refugees resettled.

Elon entered the Fourteenth Knesset on the list of Reḥavam *Ze'evi's Moledet party, and despite the extreme views that he represented soon came to be known for his mild manner. He promoted the unification of the various right-wing parties in the Knesset and ran in the elections to the Fifteenth and Sixteenth Knessets on the National Union list. Following the assassination of Ze'evi in October 2001, Elon was appointed minister of tourism, but resigned from Ariel *Sharon's government in March 2002 because of Sharon's agreement that the assassins of Ze'evi be held in prison in Jericho instead of being turned over to Israel. He was again appointed minister of tourism in the government formed by Sharon after the elections to the Sixteenth Knesset. During both his terms in the Ministry of Tourism he contended with the drop in tourism to Israel due to the second *Intifada*, by encouraging Christian tourism to the Holy Land and the development of tourist sites in Judea and Samaria. The National Union objected fundamentally to Sharon's disengagement plan, and the removal of Jewish settlements from parts of Ereẓ Israel, and as a result its ministers were dismissed by Ariel Sharon from the government in June 2004, before the government voted on the issue.

Since his dismissal from the government Elon has been an active member in the Finance Committee.

From 1990 Elon was active in establishing various associations engaged in the purchase of property and buildings in East Jerusalem and the renewal of Jewish settlement in them. He was also active in renewing Jewish settlement in Bethlehem, in the vicinity of Rachel's tomb. He maintained close ties with Jewish communities abroad and communities of Christians who support Israel throughout the world.

His wife, EMUNA, an educator and writer, served as the prime minister's adviser on women in 1996–97, and in this capacity led the establishment of the National Authority for the Advancement of Women. She has written numerous children's books.

[Susan Hattis Rolef (2nd ed.)]

ELON (**Fetter**), **MENACHEM** (1922–), Israeli jurist and Supreme Court justice. Born in Dueseldorf, Germany, Elon immigrated to Palestine in 1935. After eight years of study at the Hebron Yeshivah in Jerusalem, where he was ordained as a rabbi, Elon was awarded an M.A. degree in humanities (*cum laude*), and a doctor of laws degree (*cum laude*) from the Hebrew University of Jerusalem, where he subsequently taught for over 40 years. From 1959 to 1966 Elon was adviser on Jewish Law to the Israel Ministry of Justice. From 1966 he taught Jewish Law at the Hebrew University, where he founded and directed the Institute for Research in Jewish Law.

Elon was appointed to the Supreme Court of Israel in 1977 and was named deputy president of the Court in 1988. He was awarded the Israel Prize in 1979 for his classic work, the authoritative four-volume *Ha-Mishpat ha-Ivri* (Eng. version: *Jewish Law: History, Sources, Principles*, 1994). It compares Jewish legal traditions and modern legal systems, emphasizing both the differences between them and their common denominators. The work became the classic textbook in universities and law schools in Israel and abroad in Jewish Law.

The first part of the work deals with the history and elements of Jewish Law, its scientific study and its impact – as a living legal system – on Jewish history and society. The second section deals systematically with the various legal sources of Jewish Law such as exegesis (*midrash*) and interpretation, legislation, custom (*minhag*), precedent, and legal reasoning. The third section is devoted to a broad description of the literary sources of Jewish Law, from biblical times until the modern era, including the basic sources (Bible, Mishnah, and Talmud) and their interpretation, the commentaries and novellae literature, the codificatory literature, and the vast responsa literature. The fourth part deals extensively with the implementation of Jewish Law in the modern legal system, particularly in Israeli legislation and case law. Elon, together with his predecessors (such as Judges S. *Assaf, M. Zilberg, and H. *Cohen), made a remarkable and most important contribution to the implementation of Jewish Law in hundreds of judgments he wrote while serving as a Supreme Court judge. Amongst his most important and renowned judgments are the decision enabling women to serve as active local religious council members, a decision forbidding active euthanasia, and a decision forbidding imprisonment for civil debt.

Elon's attitude in the study of Jewish Law can be characterized by three main qualities: (1) research into all periods of Jewish Law (unlike his predecessors, who focused on the biblical and talmudic periods) and the intensive use of post-talmudic legal sources, in particular the vast responsa literature; (2) historical-analytical methodology, analytically examining each legal institution while examining at the same time how its development was affected both by time and place; (3) emphasis on the potential of Jewish Law to contribute to the modern legal system and indication of how its principals should be implemented in modern law, legislation, and judgments alike.

Elon published many works on the history and nature of Jewish Law and the relationship between it and the modern State of Israel, including *The Freedom of the Person of the Debtor in Jewish Law* (1964, 2000^2), *Religious Legislation in the Laws of the State of Israel and within the Jurisdiction of the Civil and Rabbinical Courts* (1968), *Jewish Law (Mishpat Ivri): Cases and Materials* (1999), and *The Status of Women: Tradition and Transition* (2004). From 1968 to 1971 he was editor of the Jewish Law section of the *Encyclopaedia Judaica*, whose entries were subsequently collected in his *Principles of Jewish Law.* By 1984 he had edited ten volumes of the *Annual of the Institute for Research in Jewish Law* of the Hebrew University of Jerusalem and also edited *Indices to the Responsa of Jewish Law* (5 vols.).

Elon established Chairs of Jewish Law at the Harvard School of Law, New York University, and McGill University, Montreal, and was the founder of the Institute for Research in Jewish Law of the Hebrew University of Jerusalem (1963) and the Center for the Study and Research of Jewish Law at Sha'arei Mishpat College (1997), where he served as dean until 2003. From 1995 Elon also served as the president of the World Union of Jewish Studies and continued to serve as editor of the Jewish Law section of the second edition of the *Encyclopaedia Judaica.*

[Aviad Hacohen (2nd ed.)]

EL PASO, west Texas city bordering New Mexico and situated on the Rio Grande River across from Juarez, Chihuahua, Mexico; Jewish population (1969) was approximately 4,500 out of a total population of 400,000. Its general population increased significantly with the expansion of the Southwest and numbered 750,000 in the early 2000s but the increase of the Jewish population did not keep pace proportionately. There were approximately 5,000 Jews in El Paso in 2005. The Jewish population was unusual in its low median age range, its large proportion of American-born newcomer families, and its large proportion of third-, fourth- and fifth-generation American Jews. Despite its geographic isolation from important Jewish population centers, the El Paso community maintained organizational counterparts of several Jewish institutions and philanthropic agencies. El Paso was a major crossroad for the east-west and north-south trails of the 1800s. There were Jews in El Paso as early as 1850 and major influxes of Jews occurred after each of the world wars. Many Jewish pioneers were involved in business transactions with Mexican government and anti-government forces, with the U.S. Indian Bureau, and with the U.S. Quartermaster Corps. Many Jewish soldiers were stationed at Fort Bliss and other military installations in the area and a sizable number of these stayed on after discharge. Mount Sinai Temple, the oldest Jewish institution in El Paso, is located in the Mission Hills district of the west side of the Franklin Mountains where most Jews reside. In 2005 this Reform congregation consisted of approximately 480 members. Congregation B'nai Zion (Conservative) is located further west and has a comparable membership. Although there was an Orthodox congregation in El Paso between the world wars, none existed by the 1960s until Chabad came to town.

The El Paso Jewish Federation coordinates Jewish organizational activities and the annual Jewish fundraising appeal which originated in 1935. El Paso also boasts a Jewish Family and Children's Service, housing for the elderly, and a Jewish day school, El Paso Hebrew Academy, with grades 1–8. Each of the congregations has a religious school for children and there is a great deal of informal Jewish learning sponsored by many of the local institutions. El Paso is home to a Holocaust Museum and Study Center that serves the Jewish as well as the non-Jewish community. A sizable collection of Judaica was established in the library of the University of Texas at El Paso by the family of the late Dr. Vincent Ravel.

By the 1960s, El Paso Jews were primarily merchants. As in much of the United States, by the new millennium, El Paso's Jews were increasingly professionalized, including lawyers and doctors, accountants, academics, businesspeople, and others.

BIBLIOGRAPHY: Broddy, in: *Southwestern Studies*, 3 (1965); Freudenthal, *ibid.*, no. 3; L.M. Friedman, *Jewish Pioneers and Patriots* (1942), 367–74; F.S. Fierman, *The Impact of the Frontier on a Jewish Family: the Bibos* (1961); idem, in: El Paso County Historical Society, *Password*, 8 (1963), 43–54; idem, *Some Early Jewish Settlers on the Southwestern Frontier* (1960); idem, in: AJA, 16 (1964), 135–60; W.V. D'Antonio and W.H. Form, *Influentials in Two Border Cities: A Study in Community Decision Making* (1965); R. Segalman, "A Test of the Lewinian Hypothesis on Self-Hatred Among the Jews" (Thesis, N.Y. University, 1966).

[Ralph Segalman / Anne Schwartz Schaechner (2nd ed.)]

EL SALVADOR, republic of Central America; population, 6,704,932 (2005); Jewish population, 120.

El Salvador is one of the smallest communities in Latin America. A few Crypto-Jews from Portugal passed through El Salvador in colonial times. The recorded existence of Jews in El Salvador dates back to the first half of the 19th century, when some French-Sephardi Jews settled in the small town of Chalchuapa. More French and German Jews, most of them Alsatians, settled in the capital, San Salvador, during the second half of the 19th century. Alfredo Widawer, arriving in 1909, was the first to organize the services of the High Holidays. East European and some Oriental Jews came during the 1920s and a few German Jews arrived as a consequence of World

War II. During that period, El Salvador granted Salvadoran documents of citizenship to 10,000 Jews, most of them from Hungary, thus rescuing them from deportation to Auschwitz. This operation was carried out by George Mandel-Mantello, a Romanian Jew, who was appointed as first secretary in the Salvadoran Consulate in Geneva, Switzerland. Mandel-Mantello was supported by José Castellanos, consul general of El Salvador in Switzerland, by José Gustavo Guerrero, former president of El Salvador, and by the foreign minister of El Salvador, Julio Enrique.

The communal organization La Comunidad Israelita de El Salvador was founded in 1944, as the representative organ of the Jewish community and the provider of its social and religious needs. A year later it inaugurated its cemetery and in 1950 it opened a synagogue that conducts services on Sabbaths and holidays. The Zionist Organization was established in 1945 and an affiliate of *WIZO somewhat later. There is no regular Jewish school, but some classes in Hebrew and religion are conducted by the rabbi. The Jewish community of El Salvador is affiliated to FEDECO – Federación de Comunidades Judías de Centro América that was founded in 1956. The Liebes and De Sola families were the most prominent in philanthropic, cultural, and business activities of the community. Alexander Freund was for many years the spiritual leader of the community.

Prior to the civil war of 1979–91 there were around 300 Jews in El Salvador, most of them in the capital. A census of the community carried out in 1971 recorded 268 affiliated Jews and 43 non-affiliated; 277 were Ashkenazim and 34 Sephardim; 53 couples were Jewish and 60 were of mixed marriages, with most of the children considered as non-Jews.

The signing of peace treaties in 1991 led to the return of several Jewish couples with children who had moved elsewhere during the civil war, and, as of 2000, the Jewish population in El Salvador was approximately 120. A new community center and synagogue were inaugurated in the 1990s. There are two synagogues, and the community is divided between adherents to Conservative and Reform Judaism. At the Conservative synagogue, Sabbath services are held on Friday evenings only; however, the Comunidad Israelita de El Salvador holds services on Friday, Shabbat morning, and on holidays. University students have a Jewish students association, ejes (Estudiantes Judíos de El Salvador), and a Zionist group, fusla (Federación de Universitarios Sionistas de Latinoamérica), both of which are active throughout the year. For adults, the community offers different educational classes in Hebrew and other topics of interest. The "Chevra of Women" offers a course in Jewish cooking, and there is a monthly Jewish bulletin called *El Kehilatón*, which advertises synagogue events. The Noar Shelanu youth movement, with about 30 children age 8–18 and a kindergarten for young children, meets weekly.

Relations with Israel

El Salvador abstained in the debate about the Partition of Palestine in the UN General Assembly session of November 29, 1947, but was one of the first countries which recognized the State of Israel (on Sept. 11, 1948). The Instituto Cultural El Salvador-Israel was founded in 1956. El Salvador is one of only two countries (Costa Rica is the other) to maintain its embassy in Jerusalem. One of the only times of tension between the two countries was during the civil war, when the Israeli Honorary Consul was kidnapped and murdered by guerillas.

BIBLIOGRAPHY: J. Beller, *Jews in Latin America* (1969), 42–45. **ADD. BIBLIOGRAPHY:** Y. Govrin, *Bi-Tefuẓot ha-Golah*, 16 (1975), 130–32; D. Kranzler, *The Man Who Stopped the Trains to Auschwitz* (2000). **WEBSITE:** http://www.ujcl.org/espanol/elsalvador/.

[Alfred Joseph / Margalit Bejarano (2nd ed.)]

ELTE, HARRY (1880–1944), Dutch architect of buildings with a Jewish (ritual) function in the interwar years; also active as a restorer and project developer. He came to prominence when he won a design competition for a stadium that opened in Amsterdam in 1914. His work was influenced by three architectural styles. His early work, including villas and residential complexes in Amsterdam, reflects the influence of the Berlage School (1900–25). Examples of his Amsterdam School style (1910–30) include the Second Synagogue in The Hague, demolished in 1981, and the Amsterdam nursing home De Joodsche Invalide (Jewish Invalid), both dating from 1924–25. International Expressionism (1920–30) influenced his design for the monumental synagogue on Amsterdam's Jacob Obrechtplein (1927–28), considered Elte's finest achievement. Its Cubist architecture, featuring characteristic colors and use of daylight, reflects the influence of American architect Frank Lloyd Wright. The interior decoration is Art Deco, with beautiful materials and warm colors. While most of the 12 synagogues Elte completed between 1904 and 1932 have since been demolished or converted for some other purpose, the Obrecht Shul continues to serve as a synagogue. It was granted historical monument status and completely restored in 1997. Elte was deported to Theresienstadt in February 1944, where he died on April 1, 1944.

BIBLIOGRAPHY: L. van Grieken a.o., in: *Negentigste Jaarboek van het Genootschap Amstelodamum* (1998), 159–95; R. Wischnitzer, *Architecture of the European Synagogue* (1964), 99, 232–36, 262.

[Julie-Marthe Cohen (2nd ed.)]

ELTEKEH (Heb. אֶלְתְּקֵא, אֶלְתְּקֵה), levitical city in the territory of Dan (Josh. 19:44; 21:23; but according to TJ, Sanh. 1:2, 18c "of Judah"). It was in the "plain of Eltekeh (written: Altaqû)" that *Sennacherib in 701 B.C.E. defeated the Egyptians who had come to the aid of the rebelling king of Judah Hezekiah and his allies. The battle is described in Sennacherib's annals (1:76–79). *Albright proposed identifying Eltekeh with Khirbet al-Muqanna', 6 mi. (10 km.) S.E. of 'Āqir, but recent surveys have shown that this was the largest fortified city in the area and probably the site of *Ekron. Mazar has consequently suggested Tell al Shallāf, about 2½ mi. (4 km.) N.E. of Jabneh, where potsherds from the Early and Late Iron Age have been found.

BIBLIOGRAPHY: Albright, in: BASOR, 15 (1924), 8; 17 (1925), 5f.; Mazar, in: IEJ, 10 (1960), 73–77; Pritchard, Texts, 287f.; EM, 1 (1950), 419f.; Press, Ereẓ, 1 (1951²), 23. **ADD. BIBLIOGRAPHY:** S. Ahituv, *Joshua* (1995), 322.

[Michael Avi-Yonah]

ELTON, SIR GEOFFREY RUDOLPH (1921–1994), British historian. Elton, a son of Victor *Ehrenberg, was born in Tuebingen, Germany, and went to England in 1939. He began teaching at Cambridge University in 1949, and in 1967 was appointed professor of constitutional history. From 1983 to 1988 Elton was Regius Professor of Modern History at Cambridge.

Elton's interpretation of the political and constitutional history of 16th-century England has brought about a major reassessment of the Tudor period. His most important work, *The Tudor Revolution in Government* (1953), portrays the 1530s as a revolutionary decade, when Henry VIII's minister, Thomas Cromwell, reshaped England's government. Elton later extended and consolidated his insights in *England under the Tudors* (1955), and in a collection of documents, *The Tudor Constitution* (1960). His other books include *Reformation Europe* (1963), which is a basic introduction to the subject, and *The Practice of History* (1967). He edited a number of volumes of the *New Cambridge Modern History.*

Elton was one of the most distinguished historians of early modern Britain, although many of his theories about Tudor government were widely disputed. He received innumerable honors, including honorary degrees from six universities, while no fewer than five *Festschriften* were published in his honor. He was knighted in 1986.

ADD. BIBLIOGRAPHY: ODNB online.

[Theodore K. Rabb / William D. Rubinstein (2nd ed.)]

ELUL, the post-Exilic name of the sixth month in the Jewish year. The name is Babylonian and was subsequently adopted in Hebrew, Aramaic, and Arabic. Its first occurrence in a Hebrew text is in Nehemiah 6:15. The zodiacal sign of this month is *Virgo.* In the present fixed calendar, it invariably consists of 29 days, and the first of Elul never falls on a Tuesday, a Thursday, or a Sabbath. In the 20th century, Elul in its earliest occurrence extended from Aug. 8 to Sept. 5 and in its latest from Sept. 6 to Oct. 4. The talmudic rule that Elul invariably consists of 29 days reflects the early endeavor to facilitate the prior calculation of the date of Rosh Ha-Shanah, i.e., the *New Moon of Tishri (the seventh month, which followed Elul, and was therefore directly determined by the length of Elul), and consequently also the dates of the other festivals occurring in that month. For the same reason, the New Moon of Elul was announced to Jewish communities by the messengers of the Sanhedrin (RH 1:3). Witnesses to the sighting of the New Moon of Elul were not permitted to travel on the Sabbath to report their sighting to the court in Jerusalem; the witnesses to the new crescent of Nisan and Tishri were so permitted (RH 1:4; cf. EJ). In Temple times traveling on Sabbath was permitted to report the new crescent of all the months because of the Temple sacrifices (*ibid.*). According to some *tannaim* the first of Elul was to be considered a Rosh Ha-Shanah (beginning of a new year) in respect of the tithing of animals (RH 1:1; Bek. 9:5–6). There is a tradition that the seventh or 17th of Elul had once been observed as a fast, commemorating the death of those spies whom Moses had sent to Canaan and who brought back an evil report of the land (Num. 14:37; Tar. Jon., *ibid.;* Meg. Ta'an. 13, ed. Neubauer; Sh. Ar., OḤ 580:2, et al.).

As it precedes the *Ten Days of Penitence, Elul became a month of repentance and of special ascetic and devotional practices. A rabbinic homily derives an allusion to the name of the month from the initial letters of *Ani le-Dodi ve-Dodi Li* (Heb. אֲנִי לְדוֹדִי וְדוֹדִי לִי; "I am my beloved's, and my beloved is mine," Song 6:3), as describing the relationship between God and His people. The **shofar* is sounded daily at the morning service (except on the Sabbath), and Psalm 27 is recited. In the Sephardi rituals **Seliḥot* are also recited daily throughout Elul, whereas in the Ashkenazi ritual, they are recited only during the last four to nine days of Elul (Sh. Ar., OḤ 581). A similar liturgical divergence existed already in the geonic age (Tur., *ibid.*, citing R. Hai Gaon). Rabbinic *aggadah* connects the special significance of Elul with the 40 days of Moses' stay on Mount Sinai (Ex. 34:28) which was calculated to have commenced on the first of Elul and ended on the tenth of Tishri (the Day of *Atonement, PdRE 46).

BIBLIOGRAPHY: S. Dominitz, *Sefer Ramzei Elul…*, 1 (1928).

[Ephraim Jehudah Wiesenberg]

ELUSA (Gr. Ελουσα), Nabatean city in the Negev, now the ruins of Ḥaluẓa (Ar. al-Khalaṣa), 12 mi. (20 km.) S.W. of Beersheba. Elusa was the starting point of the roads leading from Palestine to Egypt and Sinai in the Roman and Byzantine periods (Ptolemy, *Geography*, 5:15, 7; cf. *Peutinger Map*, where it is located 71 Roman miles from Jerusalem, 24 from Eboda, and 53 from Thamara) and especially of the pilgrim road to Sinai (Theodore, *Itinera Hierosolymitana*, 78). Elusa was colonized by the Nabateans in the last decades of the first century C.E. In the fourth century C.E. Elusa was the seat of a school of rhetoric and had its own police chief; the city's area extended as far as Nessana (Nessana Papyri). In Targum Jonathan (Gen. 16:14) Elusa is identified with Bered. The monk Hilarion visited Elusa and was served wine from the local plantations; the inhabitants of the city apparently spoke Aramaic (Jerome, *Vita Hilarionis*, 25). Its bishops participated in the church councils from 431 onward. In Arab times Elusa was the seat of a district governor who was under the jurisdiction of the governor of Gaza. The site was surveyed by E. Robinson (1838), E.H. Palmer (1869/1870), A. Musil (1897), A. Jaussen, R. Savignac and H. Vincent (1905), and C.L. Woolley and T.E. Lawrence (1914). Although the ruins of the city are extensive, they were greatly damaged by the builders of Gaza during Turkish and British Mandate times. Some of the city's dumps were excavated in 1936 by the archaeologist H. Dunscombe Colt. Excavations were conducted at Elusa by A. Negev in 1973, 1979, and 1980, revealing fortifications (represented by a tower), an area of dwellings, a theater that had been repaired in the fifth century C.E. (based on the evidence of an inscription which speaks of a new floor made for the "old theater"), and a Byzantine period church, one of the largest known in the Negev Desert. Additional, smaller, churches are known at Elusa. A Nabatean cemetery was also discerned near the settlement. New excavations were conducted at the site in 1997 by H. Goldfuss and P. Fabian in the area of the Roman theater, the construction of which can now be shown to date from the late second or early third century C.E., with its abandonment taking place in the sixth century C.E. Additional work was done in an area of pottery workshops on the edge of the settlement.

BIBLIOGRAPHY: C.L. Woolley and T.E. Lawrence, *The Wilderness of Zin* (1915), 113, 145; A. Musil, *Arabia Petraea*, 2 (Ger., 1907), 67–77; M. Schwabe, in: *Zion*, 2 (1937), 106–20; idem, in: BJPES, 4 (1936/37), 61–66; C.J. Kraemer, *Excavations at Nessana*, 3 (1958), geographical index, s.v. *Elousa*. **ADD. BIBLIOGRAPHY:** Y. Tsafrir, L. Di Segni, and J. Green, *Tabula Imperii Romani. Iudaea – Palaestina. Maps and Gazetteer* (1994), 119; H. Goldfuss and P. Fabian, "Haluza (Elusa)," in: *Excavations and Surveys in Israel*, 111 (2000), 93–94; A. Negev and S. Gibson (eds.), *Archaeological Encyclopedia of the Holy Land* (2001), 156–58; P. Fabian and Y. Goren, "A New Type of Late Roman Storage Jar from the Negev," in: J.H. Humphrey (ed.), *The Roman and Byzantine Near East;* JRA Supplement No. 49 (2002), 145–55; R. Rosenthal-Heginbottom (ed.), *The Nabateans in the Negev* (2003).

[Michael Avi-Yonah / Shimon Gibson (2nd ed.)]

ELVIRA (Eliberis, Illiberis), town in Andalusia, Spain, near Granada. The church council convened in Elvira in 300–303 (or 309) issued canons forbidding marriage between Christian women and Jews unless the Jew first adopted Christianity (§16); prohibiting Jews from keeping Christian concubines (§78); from entertaining at their tables Christian clergy or laymen (§50); and from blessing fields belonging to Christians (§49): Christians who turned to Jews for such blessings were to be excommunicated. These were the earliest canons of any church council directed against the Jews. A Jewish community still existed in Elvira at the time of the Muslim conquest. Its scholars corresponded with Saadiah Gaon in the tenth century, as attested by Abraham *Ibn Daud in *Sefer ha-Kabbalah* (ed., G.D. Cohen (1967), 79). In the course of time the Elvira community became merged in that of Granada.

BIBLIOGRAPHY: J. Parkes, *Conflict of the Church and the Synagogue* (1930), 174ff.; C.G. Goldaraz, *El Códice Lucense* (1954), 377–93; J. Vives, *Concilios Visigóticos e Hispano-Romanos* (1963), 1–15.

[Haim Beinart]

EL-YAM, Israeli merchant shipping company. Cargo Ships El-Yam Ltd. was founded in 1949 by a subsidiary of the Israel Discount Bank and started operations in 1953 with three 10,800-ton vessels. It developed rapidly and in 1977 its fleet (owned through affiliated and subsidiary companies), consisting of bulk carriers and refrigerated vessels for the transport of fruit, meat, and dairy products, exceeded 1.75 million tons deadweight, representing an investment of $200,000,000.

ELYAN, SIR ISADORE VICTOR (1909–), chief justice of Swaziland. Born in Dublin, Ireland, Elyan qualified as a lawyer and from 1946 was a magistrate in the British Colony of Gold Coast (Ghana) until his appointment as judge of the Basutoland Court of Appeal in 1955. From 1965 to 1970 he was chief justice of Swaziland and from 1966 also served as judge of the Court of Appeal for newly independent Botswana.

ELYASHAR, JACOB BEN ḤAYYIM JOSEPH (after 1720–1788), rabbi and communal leader in Ereẓ Israel. Elyashar was born in Hebron. He was a grandson, through his mother, of Jacob Vilna, a member of the group of *Judah he-Ḥasid. He acted as an emissary of the Hebron community to various countries, visiting Italy, Germany, and Poland after 1751, Baghdad in 1763, and Sofia and other Turkish towns in 1768, returning in about 1770 to Hebron, where he became one of its notables. He was included there among the pupils of Ḥ.J.D. *Azulai and the two became very close friends. He helped Azulai in his literary activities, copying on his behalf various manuscripts. In 1773 Elyashar again visited Baghdad as an emissary of the Hebron community, and in 1774 went to Basra where he stayed until 1781. During that time the Persian army in 1775 captured the town, ruling over it until 1779.

Elyashar, who was a composer of *piyyutim* and poems, commemorated the day the Persians left Basra by composing a poem, "*Megillat Paras,*" in which he described events in Basra during the siege and its capture by the Persians. It was first published by his grandson, Jacob Saul *Elyashar, at the beginning of the latter's *Ish Emunim* (1888). A critical version with a commentary was published by M. *Benayahu in his book *Rabbi Ya'akov Elyashar* (1960). Jacob also composed poems in honor of that day, which the Jews of Basra continued to recite annually amid great celebrations for about 100 years after the event. In 1781, through the influence of the well-known Farḥi family, he reached Safed. There he served as *av bet din* and one of the leaders of the community. He devoted himself to the rebuilding of *Safed, whose Jewish settlement began to develop anew in the years 1778–79. He wrote several books which were lost as a result of his wanderings and the persecutions he suffered.

BIBLIOGRAPHY: M. Benayahu, *Rabbi Ya'akov Elyashar* (Heb. 1960); idem, *Rabbi Ḥayyim Yosef David Azulai* (Heb. 1959), index, s.v.; Yaari, Sheluḥei, 591f. and index, s.v.; A. Ben-Jacob, *Yehudei Bavel* (1965), 123, 139, 282, 335f.

[A'hron Oppenheimer]

ELYASHAR, JACOB SAUL BEN ELIEZER JEROHAM (1817–1906), Sephardi chief rabbi of Ereẓ Israel (*rishon le-Ẓion*). A grandson of Jacob ben Ḥayyim *Elyashar, he was born in Safed. His father, a *dayyan, shoḥet*, and cantor there, was arrested by the Turkish authorities, but succeeded in escaping and settled with his family in Jerusalem. When Jacob Saul was seven, he lost his father, and his mother remarried in 1828. His stepfather, Benjamin Mordecai *Navon, became his teacher and supported him for many years. Elyashar married the daughter of *ḥakham bashi, Raphael Meir *Panigel. He was appointed a *dayyan* in Jerusalem in 1853, and in 1869 head of the *bet din*. He succeeded his father-in-law as *ḥakham bashi* and *rishon le-Zion* in 1893.

A cultured scholar and a fluent linguist, Elyashar wrote thousands of responsa in answer to questions from both Ashkenazim and Sephardim all over the world. He was respected by the authorities and the heads of other religious communities, and received orders of merit from the Turkish sultan, Abdul Hamid, in 1893, and the German kaiser, William II, in 1898. He was accepted by both the Sephardi and Ashkenazi communities and worked hard to put religious institutions in Jerusalem on a solid foundation. The affection in which he was held is reflected in the fact that he was referred to as "*Yissa Berakhah*" ("conferring a blessing"), the word *Yissa* (יִשָּׂא) being derived from the Hebrew initials of his name. He enjoyed marked success as an emissary to Smyrna (1845), Damascus (1854), Alexandria (1856), and Leghorn (1873).

In 1888 when a controversy arose as to the permissibility of working on the land during the following year, a sabbatical year, Elyashar decided that such work could be permitted by selling the land formally to a non-Jew, but suggested that each Jewish agricultural settlement leave a small portion of land uncultivated as a symbol and reminder of the commandment. Elyashar died in Jerusalem, where the Givat Sha'ul district is named after him.

He was the author of the following works, all published in Jerusalem (some by his son, Ḥayyim Moshe) and all bearing the word "Ish," the initials of his name, in their title: (1) *Yikrav Ish* (1876–81), 2 parts, novellae and responsa, which were included in the *Benei Binyamin* of his stepfather; (2) *Ish Emunim* (1888), homilies for festivals and various special occasions; (3) *Ma'aseh Ish* (1892), responsa; (4) *Derekh Ish*, homilies; (5) *Divrei Ish*, 2 parts (1892–96), homilies; (6) *Simḥah le-Ish* (1888), novellae, responsa, and *piyyutim;* (7) *Yissa Ish* (1896), responsa; (8) *Olat Ish*, responsa, as well as a number of sermons entitled *Penei Ish* (1899); (9) *Sha'al ha-Ish* (1909), responsa and rulings, together with responsa by his son, Ḥayyim Moshe, entitled *Penei ḤaMA;* (10) *Kavod le-Ish* (1910), responsa, including the eulogies in his honor. Elyashar possessed a large collection of manuscripts, some of which are in the Jerusalem National Library.

His eldest son, Rabbi ḤAYYIM MOSHE ELYASHAR (1845–1924), a merchant and businessman, represented the Jewish community on the council of heads of religious communities established by the Turkish authorities, and, in the early days of the Mandate, served as *rishon le-Ẓion*. He was one of the initiators of the combined rabbinical committee which was the forerunner of the chief rabbinate of Ereẓ Israel. His son ISAAC ELIACHAR (1873–1933), the first chairman of the United (Sephardi and Ashkenazi) Jewish Community Council of Jerusalem, was appointed to the Jerusalem municipality in 1917. His grandson ELIYAHU ELIACHAR (1898–1981) was chairman of the United Community Council of Jerusalem from 1938 until 1949. He headed for many years the Committee of the Sephardi Community of Jerusalem and served during the mandatory period as a member of the Asefat ha-Nivḥarim and the Va'ad Le'ummi. He was a member of the First and Second Knesset.

BIBLIOGRAPHY: J.S. Elyashar, *Toledot ve-Zikhronot* (autobiography), in: *Lu'aḥ Ereẓ Yisrael*, 6 (1900), 39–61, ed. and annot. by A.M. Luncz; Frumkin-Rivlin, 3 (1929), 310–1; M.D. Gaon, *Yehudei ha-Mizraḥ be-Ereẓ Yisrael*, 2 (1937), 59–60, 62–68; Yaari, Sheluḥei, index; Benayahu, in: *Yerushalayim*, 4 (1953), 212; EẒD.

[Geulah Bat Yehuda (Raphael)]

ELYASHIV (Heb. אֶלְיָשִׁיב), moshav in central Israel, in the Ḥefer Plain, affiliated to Tenu'at ha-Moshavim. One of the first Yemenite agricultural settlements in Israel, it was founded in 1933. Its economy was based on intensive farming including citrus orchards as well as outside employment. In 2002 the population of Elyashiv was 436.

[Efraim Orni / Shaked Gilboa (2nd ed.)]

ELZAS, BARNETT ABRAHAM (1867–1939), U.S. Reform rabbi and historian. Elzas was born in Germany, the son of a Hebrew teacher, and moved with his parents to Holland and then to London where he was educated at Jews' College and the University of London. In 1890 he went to America and served congregations in Toronto, Canada and Sacramento, California, being eventually appointed to the pulpit of Congregation Beth Elohim in Charleston, South Carolina (1894). Elzas became keenly interested in local Jewish history and made an exhaustive study of records of Charleston Jewry and of the older smaller communities of the state. After writing a number of studies on the subject, he produced the comprehensive *Jews of South Carolina: From Earliest Times to the Present Day* (1905), which still ranks as one of the best historical studies of an American Jewish community. While in Charleston, Elzas also qualified at the Medical College of South Carolina (1900), although he never practiced. In 1910 he moved to New York City where he ministered to the Hebrew Congregation of the Deaf and served as Jewish chaplain to the City Department of Correction and the State Mental Hygiene Department. He also served as president of the New York Board of Rabbis. In 1912 Elzas became rabbi of Beth Miriam Congregation, Long Branch, N.J.

BIBLIOGRAPHY: Bloch, in: CCARY, 47 (1937), 225–9; C. Reznikoff and U.Z. Engelman, *The Jews of Charleston* (1950), index.

[Thomas J. Tobias]

EMANATION, a theory describing the origin of the material universe from a transcendent first principle. According to this theory, the universe, which is multiple, is generated from the One, which is unitary, through the medium of a hierarchy of immaterial substances. The ultimate source is undiminished, while the beings which are emanated are progressively less perfect as they are further removed from the first principle. The process is conceived as being atemporal. In neoplatonic emanationism the ultimate product, the material universe, is not regarded as evil, as in gnostic systems of emanation. A variety of models are used to describe emanation. For example, it is compared to the efflux of light from a luminous body, or to water flowing from a spring. The emanationist theory was given its classical formulation by Plotinus in the *Enneads*, in which the typical fourfold scheme of the One, Intellect, Soul, and Nature is found. Emanationism tends to be combined with an eschatology (or soteriology) that envisions the soul's return to its ultimate source of being by *epostrophē* or "reversion" (see A. Altmann, *Studies in Religious Philosophy and Mysticism* (1969), 41ff.). The theory of emanation was developed further by Plotinus' successors, particularly Proclus, who systematized the scheme of *monēproodos-epistrophē* (immanence, procession, reversion) to account for the process of emanation.

In Jewish Philosophy

The Hebrew terms used for emanation are *aẓilut* or *aẓilah* (cf. Num. 11:17), *hishtalshelut, meshekh, shefa;* the verbs *shalaḥ* and *sadar* (in the pu'al) are also used (see J. Klatzkin, *Thesaurus Philosophicus* (1930), 96; 4 (1933), 112). The theory of emanation was known to medieval Arabic and Jewish philosophers from several sources. Plotinus was known from the *Theology of Aristotle* (in both a vulgate and long recension), a paraphrase of texts from the *Enneads*, as well as from Plotinian material ascribed to "al-Sheikh al-Yūnānī" ("The Greek Sage," probably Porphyry, editor of the Enneads), and a work titled *al-ʿIlm al-Ilāhī* ("The Divine Science"), falsely ascribed to al-*Fārābī (translations of this material are in Plotinus, *Opera*, ed. by H. Schwyzer (1959), vol. 2). Proclus was known from the *Liber de causis* (*Kitāb al-Idāh fī al-Khayr al-Maḥḍ*) ascribed to Aristotle but actually based on Proclus' Elements *of Theology* (ed. and tr. by E.R. Dodds, 1963). One must also take into account neoplatonic texts such as the pseudo-Aristotelian source utilized by Isaac *Israeli and Abraham *Ibn Ḥasdai (see S.M. Stern, in *Oriens*, 13–14 (1960–61), 58ff.) and the pseudo-Empedoclean *Book of Five Substances* (ed. by D. Kaufmann, *Studien ueber Salomo Ibn Gabirol* (1899), 17ff.). Jewish philosophers also relied on the appropriation and development of emanationism by Arabic philosophers such as al-*Kindī, al-Fārābī, *Avicenna, and the Sincere *Brethren (Ikhwān al-Ṣafā'). In medieval Arabic and Jewish neo-Aristotelianism, the neoplatonic theory of emanation was applied to the Aristotelian-Ptolemaic cosmology which posited a series of nine concentric spheres encompassing the earth, each endowed with an intelligence. Thus, Aristotle's active intellect (*De Anima*, 3) was identified either with Plotinus' universal intellect in the neoplatonic hierarchy, or with the intelligence of the lowest sphere (of the moon) in the Aristotelian-Ptolemaic cosmology. Emanation is a necessary (natural) and eternal process, and is thus thought to imply the absence of will and design on the part of the ultimate source. Thus, the theory of emanation is in conflict with the biblical concept of temporal creation by divine volition. Also, emanationism sees the divine source as somehow omnipresently immanent in the world, and it therefore tends toward pantheistic expressions.

In their discussions of cosmology, Jewish philosophers sometimes tried to harmonize emanation with biblical concepts of *creation and *providence. Isaac Israeli, for example, postulates an initial act of creation by "the will and power" of God which results in the first two substances, which are in his system prime matter and form (or wisdom), while the subsequent entities are generated by a process of emanation. These are the typical hierarchy of intellect, soul, and nature of Plotinus, but the universal soul, like the individual soul, is tripartite (rational, animal, vegetable; as in Ibn *Gabirol), and nature is identified with the first or outer sphere. Each emanated being is derived from "the shadow" of its anterior cause. Ibn Gabirol injected an element of voluntarism into an emanationist system with his notion of "will," which mediates between the first essence and primary matter and form, which together constitute the hypostasis of intellect. Will thus appears not as a function of the creator (cf. Israeli), but as a distinct hypostasis. Gabirol often appeals to the metaphors of a spring of water, light from the sun, the reflection in a mirror, and human speech to explain emanation. There is a pronounced tendency toward pantheism (see *Mekor Ḥayyim* 5:39, 3:16).

Pseudo-*Baḥya's *Kitāb Maʿanī al-Nafs* ("On the Essence of the Soul") combines creation and emanation. The entire chain of being hinges on God's will and wisdom. Intellect is called *Shekhinah* and soul is called *Kevod Elohei Yisrael* (see Guttmann, Philosophies, 110). *Abraham bar Ḥiyya posits five worlds above the celestial spheres, which he correlates with the five days of creation, giving each a theological interpretation. The lower three (the worlds of knowledge, soul, and creation) seem to correspond to the neoplatonic hypostases. Above them are the world of light (*ha-olam ha-nurani*) and the world of dominion (*olam ha-ravrevanut*), probably derived from an Arabic neoplatonic work (*Megillat ha-Megalleh*, ed. by A. Posnanski (1924), 21ff.; see also, G. Scholem, in MGWJ, 75 (1931), 172ff.; and Guttmann, Philosophies, 112ff.). Like Ibn Gabirol, Abraham bar Ḥiyya uses expressions which are tantamount to pantheism. God is essentially identical with the universe insofar as He gives it the power of being.

The emanation theory of Arabic and Jewish Aristotelians, an intricate system explaining the derivation of the spheres and their intelligences, was rejected by *Judah Halevi as an unproven claim (*Kuzari*, 4:25). Abraham *Ibn Daud also rejected the emanationist explanation of the derivation of the spheres and their intelligences, but without denying the order itself (*Emunah Ramah*, ed. by S. Weil (1852), 67). The position of *Maimonides is complex. He was keenly aware of the opposition between eternal necessary emanation of the world from God and the free act of creation. Nevertheless he wrote: "It has been said that the world derives from the overflow (*fayḍ*) of God and that He has caused to overflow to it everything in it that is produced in time." In the same context he compares the derivation of the world from God to a spring of water which, he says, is "the most fitting simile for the action of one who is separate from matter" (*Guide of the Perplexed*, 2:12). Divine emanation also accounts for cognition and prophecy (*ibid.*, 2:37). The governance of the lower world is perfected by means of forces emanating from the spheres (*ibid.*, 2:5). Still, this emanation is said to be unlike that of heat from fire and light from the sun in that it constantly assures duration and order for the existents that emanate from God by "wisely contrived governance" (*ibid.*, 1:59). Maimonides' insistence on creation in time and insertion of intention and wisdom into a scheme of emanation appear to contradict the presuppositions of the latter. *Levi b. Gershom found several difficulties with the theory of emanation which postulates an eternal procession from God (*Milḥamot Adonai*, 6:1, 7; see also Guttmann, Philosophies, 211ff.). He maintained, for example, that it was impossible for existence to flow constantly from God to the heavenly bodies (as opposed to their being brought into being at once), for the heavens would thus exist only potentially.

[Joel Kraemer]

In Kabbalah

Though the term *aẓilut* has many meanings in Hebrew, the Jewish philosophers and kabbalists used it to describe different forms of emanation. The Hebrew term is understood as pointing to both the process of emanation and to the realm that is emanated. The major concept that is conveyed by this term is the prolongation of a spiritual entity into a hypostasis that does not separate itself essentially from its source. According to such a view, the Infinity, *Ein-Sof*, underwent a process of autogenesis that produced a realm of ten divine powers which, different as they are from each other, nevertheless constitute together the divine zone. In this mode of understanding the process of emanation is conceived of as remaining within God, offering a pseudo-etymology of *aẓilut* as if related to the Hebrew word *eẓlo*, "with him," namely with God. Though articulated since the 13th century, this view has much earlier Jewish sources, as early as second century, according to which some angels are extensions of the divine glory and return to it after completing their mission. This view is known in Kabbalah as the doctrine of essence, which means that the divine emanated powers are identical with the divine essence. According to another view, the emanation is constituted as the shadow of the higher plane of being. This view understands *aẓilut* as if derived from the Hebrew *ẓel*, "shadow," and points to a concept of efflux that somehow leaves its source. This view is more consonant with the kabbalistic theory according to which the first emanated powers are the instruments used by the Infinite to create the world and to interact with it, or the vessels which contain the divine energy, which pour themselves out. The instrumental view of emanation is closer to, and derived and adapted by, the kabbalists from Neoplatonic sources which reached them via Arabic and Latin translations. In some few cases, the astrological theory of emanations descending from stars and other celestial bodies was represented by the term *aẓilut*.

Though emanation explains the gradual descent from the Infinity to the lower world as part of a great chain of being, in two important cases there is a direct emanation from the divinity: both the Torah and the soul are described as circumventing the great chain of being, and having a special relationship with the divine. In these cases, evident in Naḥmanides and Cordovero, the special emanation is described as a cord that allows the kabbalist to have a theurgical impact on the divine sphere.

In many forms of theosophies, the first world is described as the world of emanation, *olam ha-aẓilut*, as part of the fourfold distinction ABYA (*Aẓilut, Beri'ah, Yeẓirah, Asiyyah*). During the Renaissance period, kabbalists in Italy like Johanan *Alemanno or David Messer *Leon paid special attention to the processes of the emanation of the *Sefirot*, and this development influenced the Safedian kabbalists.

[Moshe Idel (2nd ed.)]

BIBLIOGRAPHY: Guttman, Philosophies, index; D. Neumark, *Geschichte der juedischen Philosophie des Mittelalters* 1 (1907), 503ff.; Scholem, Mysticism, s.v. *emanation;* idem, in: *Tarbiz*, 2 (1931/32), 415–42; 3 (1932/33), 33–66; J. Ben-Shlomo, *Torat ha-Elohut shel R. Moshe Cordovero* (1965), 170–82. **ADD. BIBLIOGRAPHY:** E. Gottlieb, *Studies in Kabbalah Literature* (1978), 11–17, 397–476; E. Gottlieb and M. Idel, *Enchanted Chains* (2005); M. Idel, "Between the View of Sefirot as Essence and Instruments in the Renaissance Period," in: *Italia*, 3 (1982), 89–111 (Heb.).

EMANCIPATION.

Definitions and Dialectics

Emancipation of the Jews in modern times stands alongside such other emancipatory movements as those of the serfs, women, slaves in the United States, and Catholics in England. The term "emancipation" is derived from Latin (*emancipatio*), and originally meant in ancient Rome the liberation of a son from the authority of his father and his attainment of independent legal status. It has come to mean the liberation of individuals or groups from servitude, legal restrictions, and political and social disabilities. Jewish emancipation denotes the abolition of disabilities and inequities applied specially to Jews, the recognition of Jews as equal to other citizens, and the formal granting of the rights and duties of citizenship. Essentially the legal act of emancipation should have been simply the expression of the diminution of social hostility and psychological aversion toward Jews in the host nation. Indeed, Jewish emancipation was related to the weakening of the general social antipathy toward Jews; but the antipathy was not obliterated, and constantly hampered the realization of equality even after it had been proclaimed by the state and included in the law. Emancipation was achieved by ideological and social change and political and psychological strife. Before achieving full emancipation the Jews in many countries passed through several transitional stages. They had to overcome the barriers of vested interests and such ancient prejudices as the hateful image of the Jew as alien, his religion odious, and his economics unscrupulous. Ideologically, emancipation stemmed from the utopian political and social thought since the 18th century. Emancipation was, however, dependent on actual political and social conditions in each country and on the residential, cultural, and social characteristics of the Jewish population. Stages in the history of emancipation have been marked by the strength or weakness of egalitarian ideology and the corresponding interaction with existing laws, institutions, and relationships.

The Three Periods in the History of Jewish Emancipation

The first period, "heralding emancipation," covered the 50 years preceding the *French Revolution (1740–89). The second period, the 90 years from the French Revolution until the Congress of *Berlin (1789–1878), comprised emancipation in Western and Central Europe. Finally, the third period extended from the Congress of Berlin to the Nazis' rise to power (1878–1933) and saw in an atmosphere charged with newly inflamed hatred and racial animosity the achievement of Jewish emancipation in Eastern Europe, and the struggle in many countries to maintain civic equality and the right to national definition.

During the first period, demands for alleviating the lot of the Jews, with a view to their ultimate emancipation, were based on a theory of the "civic improvement of the Jews." The proponents of this idea, men like John *Toland, Christian Wilhelm von *Dohm, Comte de *Mirabeau, and their supporters, argued that existing legislation disabling the Jews was motivated primarily by religious intolerance, hence contrary to the enlightened "spirit of the times." They pointed out, moreover, the economic advantages which would accrue to the state as a result of permitting Jews to function in society with the same rights and obligations as other groups. Admitting the faults of the Jews pointed out by opponents, enlightened thinkers showed the defects to be the natural result of the degrading status in which Jews were compelled to live when all decent ways of life were closed to them. Such considerations were expressed in the deliberations on the Jewish question in prerevolutionary *France. Their influence is reflected in the announcement of an essay competition set by the Société Royale des Arts et Sciences in 1785 on the question: "Are there any ways of making the Jews of France happier and more useful?" and the entry of Abbé Henri *Grégoire which gained the prize. New legislation ameliorating the status of Jews was inspired by this idea. Notable examples were the 1740 law enabling the Jews to become naturalized in the British colonies if they had lived there for at least seven years, and the law passed by the British Parliament in May 1753, according the Jews of *England the right of naturalization. The British government, however, was compelled to revoke the latter law on Dec. 20, 1753, because of vigorous public opposition. For the first time Jews were also given the right, in several places (Leghorn [Italy] and Belorussia), to elect representatives to municipalities and other institutions, like merchant and burgher organizations, although with some educational limitations. The *Toleranz-Patent* (1781–82) of *Joseph II of Austria aimed at encouraging the integration of the Jews into Christian society, and is thereby a law "heralding emancipation," as were the laws abolishing the "body tax" (see *taxation) in Austria in 1781 and in the France of Louis XVI in 1784. The declarations and laws issued on freedom of conscience and religion at the time of the American Revolution were radical in their egalitarianism (see below).

Among the Jewish initiatives toward obtaining civic liberation, the literary activity of Moses *Mendelssohn is of historic importance, and the demands of Zalkind *Hourwitz are worth noting. The petitions for equal rights and "equality in religious rights," presented by U.S. Jews in 1784 and 1787, set an example which was later widely followed.

The second period opens with the principles and wars of the French Revolution and ends with the resolutions and tactics of the Congress of Berlin. In the intervening 90 years, Jewish emancipation became a political and legal fact in all European countries where revolution and liberalism were in the ascendancy: France, *Belgium, the *Netherlands, *Italy, *Germany, and *Austria-Hungary. The revolutionary peaks of 1789–91, 1830–31, 1848–49, and times of fundamental change in the structure of European states (e.g., unification of Germany and of Italy, and national independence in Hungary) were periods of progress in Jewish emancipation. Even where the emancipation evolved from legislation created within the permanent framework of the existing order (England and Scandinavia), or as the result of international circumstances (*Switzerland), or international pressure (*Serbia; *Bulgaria), the relation between the new liberal political climate and the emancipation of the Jews was decisive. The ideals of the Enlightenment were also evident in the numerous arguments and lengthy literary and political deliberations on Jewish emancipation which took place during this period. It was stressed that keeping the Jews in a politically limited and socially inferior status was incompatible with the principle of civic equality. Such deprivation would be a contradiction of the principle of "natural rights" of man, and, therefore, would undermine the civic equality of all who had attained it by revolution and the application of this principle. Emphasis was placed on the belief that "it is the objective of every political organization to protect the natural rights of man," hence "all citizens have the right to all the liberties and advantages of citizens, without exception."

As men, Jews should be guaranteed political rights in the countries in which they reside. Their ethnic origin and messianic hopes notwithstanding, the Jews had adopted the language and the culture of their environment; they were loyal to the state and identified themselves with the national feelings of their fellow countrymen. The activity of Jews in the struggle for their rights was bound up with their energetic participation in the general striving toward political liberty and egalitarianism as exemplified by Heinrich *Heine, Ludwig *Boerne, Johann *Jacoby, Ignaz *Kuranda; by the journalists and parliamentarians Gabriel *Riesser, Berr Isaac *Berr, Moritz *Veit, Sir David *Salomons, and Lionel Nathan

*Rothschild; and by the statesman Adolphe *Crémieux, who in 1870 issued in the name of the French government the law which conferred French citizenship on the Jews of *Algeria. Jewish society fought for its emancipation not only through general institutions (the *Board of Deputies of British Jews, the Central *Consistory of Paris, individual communities), but also through organizations specifically devoted to this aim. The *Alliance Israélite Universelle worked energetically for its declared goal "of striving universally for the freedom of the Jews."

The third period (1878–1933) witnessed a reaction to Jewish emancipation, and in Europe was marked with the prevalence of rabid *antisemitism. Intense opposition brought many Jews to realize that the state's legal recognition of Jewish civic and political equality does not automatically bring social recognition of this equality. The controversy over Jewish emancipation intensified and became embittered in almost every European country. Racism and nationalism were the bases for anti-emancipation agitation. Opponents claimed that emancipation was granted under the false pretenses that Judaism is only a religion, and that emancipated Jews would give up all Jewish national identity and assimilate into the host nations. The "price of admittance" had not been paid by most Jews, who continued to form a separate national group. Even in the view of many liberals, the claim of Jews for participation in the government of the nation in which they were not an organic part was unjustified. Racists added that Jews should not be granted civil rights or become assimilated because their racial inferiority could only harm the "superior race." Throughout its difficult and complex history, Jewish emancipation was a touchstone of freedom and social openness in European culture. Support came from those who cherished liberalism in life, thought, and politics, while bitter opposition came mostly from the reactionary camp. In Jewish life the fight for emancipation at first went hand in hand with a readiness to assimilate, and then, in the late 19th century, became associated with national Jewish loyalty and *autonomy.

Emancipation in Various Countries

UNITED STATES. The first country to emancipate the Jews was the United States. Jewish political inferiority during the colonial period before 1776, however, was not the result of a peculiar legal status. It derived rather from the Jews' belonging to the non-Protestant portion of the population, or in some colonies their nonmembership in one privileged Protestant denomination. Before the period of the American Revolution, Jews living in the colonies were generally ineligible for public office, owing to a Protestant form of oath which operated to exclude Catholics as well. There are instances where Jews entered public life nevertheless, perhaps by disregarding such forms. Jews were not limited in the rights of domicile, economic activity, or the practice of Judaism. Their full enjoyment of civil rights, together with the newness, foreignness, and minuscule numbers of colonial Jews, probably did not encourage them to seek the full political rights which they lacked.

The American Revolution and the Federal Constitution brought emancipation in the political realm to Jews and other disadvantaged white minorities. Most of the newly enacted state constitutions abolished Christian oath formularies and separated church and state. The Virginia Statute of Religious Liberty, long promoted by Thomas Jefferson and enacted in 1786, not only guaranteed freedom of worship and prohibited public support of religious institutions, but provided that "religious opinions and beliefs shall in no wise diminish, enlarge, or affect civil capacities." This law influenced the Federal Constitution of 1787. The latter's clause that "no religious test shall ever be required as a qualification for any office or public trust under the United States" is the closest the United States ever came to a definitive act of religious emancipation, including Jews. The First Amendment, enacted in 1791 within the Bill of Rights, completed the process by disestablishing all religions. Such Federal constitutional law did not, however, supersede the rights of individual states, although virtually all of them emulated the Federal model. The right of Jews to hold public office was actually sharply debated in Maryland between 1816 and the abolition of the Christian oath requirement in 1824. Vestigial oath clauses remained on the statute books of North Carolina until 1868 and New Hampshire until 1877, but they were generally disregarded. Both states had only a handful of Jews.

For emancipation in Latin America see *Latin America.

ENGLAND. Jewish emancipation in England came through the gradual change in the climate of social opinion rather than through revolution, although the ideas of the American and French revolutions, and the emancipation of English Catholics in 1829, were influential in changing English attitudes. Jews had participated with Catholic leaders in planning the strategy for achieving Catholic emancipation. Jewish emancipation in England was accomplished by laws specifically relating to the Jews. These laws were passed only after some social equality had become an accomplished fact and the state was required to give it legal expression. Literature, as well as law, did much to shape and reflect public opinion. Byron, for example, expressed sympathy for the suffering Jew; Richard *Cumberland in *The Jew* (1794) created a complimentary portrait of the Jew as a man. In addition, there were English translations of the literature written in defense of the Jews by such men as *Lessing, Mendelssohn, and Grégoire; publication of books and essays by various English authors calling for emancipation of Jews; and the defense of the rights of Jews in other countries by English diplomacy (e.g., at the Congresses of Vienna and Aix-la-Chapelle; support of Moses *Montefiore's interventions in the *Damascus Affair; Morocco; Russia). The change in public attitude toward Jews was largely due to their civic and economic progress. In practice, neither the right of the Jews to reside in England, nor their choice of profession or commercial opportunity were restricted after their return in the 17th century, the Jews being gradually allowed to improve their economic and social status to a great extent. Jewish civic and political inequality was bound up with the formula of the oath of loyalty, "according to the usages of the Anglican Church," to be taken in order to hold any office. In the deliberations on the emancipation of the Catholics (1828), one of the bishops proposed the new formula, "on the true faith of a Christian," which would then only discriminate against Jews. Thereafter, Jews and their public sympathizers and parliamentary supporters demanded the abolition of this formula for Jews. An attempt in 1830 by a Liberal member, Sir Robert Grant, to change the oath, was carried at first by a majority of 18, but was defeated in second reading. In 1833 after the reform of the British Parliament, Grant proposed "that it is expedient to remove all civil disabilities at present affecting His Majesty's subjects of the Jewish religion, with the like exceptions as are provided with reference to His Majesty's subjects professing the Roman Catholic religion." During the discussion following this motion, speeches were made which have become classics in the polemics of Jewish emancipation, including one by the English historian Macaulay (see *Apologetics). The motion was finally carried by a great majority in all three readings. The House of Lords, however, rejected it, as it was to do again in 1834. During this time, nevertheless, Jews were being elected to various honorary positions. After David Salomons, a banker and communal worker, was elected sheriff in 1835, the government passed a law in Parliament which enabled Jews to hold this position. Similarly, after Salomons was elected to the court of aldermen in 1841 and again in 1844, a law was passed in 1845 enabling a Jew elected to municipal office to substitute an oath which was acceptable to his conscience for the prejudicial declaration ordinarily demanded. In 1835 a law was enacted which exempted voters from taking any oath. The Jews were enabled in 1837 to receive degrees from the University of London (a secular university), and in 1841, the Jew Isaac Lyon *Goldsmid was knighted. Admission of Jews to Parliament and university was gradual, changes coming through compromises occasioned by the election of two Jews, Lionel Nathan Rothschild and David Salomons, to Parliament and their struggle to take their seats from 1841 to 1858; a compromise law of 1858; the deletion by law in 1866 of the Christological portion of the oath; and a further abolition of limitations for Jews in 1871.

BRITISH COMMONWEALTH. The later development of the major countries of the British Commonwealth and their colonization by the English (and to a far lesser extent by Europeans) created a situation in which the problems of political emancipation did not present themselves either at all or to any great degree. This development became effective only toward the middle of the 19th century or later, and by this time the climate of opinion and political thinking was characterized by liberal concepts averse to legal discrimination for reasons of religion. Originally administered as colonies direct from London through a local representative of the central government, they achieved or were granted self-government when these liberal concepts were dominant. The social stratification of the settlers also had an influence in the same direction. These were frontier societies engaged in promoting and establishing themselves, in which there was no room for religious discrimination. And in that frontier society, Jews themselves occupied a prominent position and played an important role as entrepreneurs of various kinds. The generally superior educational attainment of Jews also helped. A further element was the very small percentage of the total European population that Jews constituted, in New Zealand never more than about a quarter percent and in Australia one-half percent. The problem confronting the Jews in these Commonwealth countries was not "legalized" religious discrimination and restrictions but the absence thereof and the prevalence of measures of social freedom which brought quite different problems manifested in a trend to intermarriage and complete assimilation.

SCANDINAVIAN COUNTRIES. Emancipation was not an acute problem in the Scandinavian countries in which Jewish settlements were comparatively recent (17th and 18th centuries) and few in number. There Jewish emancipation came as the legal expression of the quiet victory of a sociopolitical principle natural to civilized states, developing in a conservative mode. On March 29, 1814, the king of Denmark authorized all "the believers in the Mosaic faith" born in Denmark, or living there legally, to engage in all professions, obliged them to keep their books in Danish or in German, and narrowed community autonomy. In 1837 Jews became eligible for municipal election, and in 1843, the special Jewish *oath was abrogated. In the constitution of June 5, 1849, article 84 was tantamount to a grant of emancipation in refusing to recognize the inequality of "any person on the basis of religious grounds." In Sweden the government abolished discrimination against Jews by an administrative decree on June 30, 1838, but was compelled to rescind it under pressure of public opinion. Some disabilities were abolished by general laws on freedom in the choice of profession. In 1860 Jews were permitted to acquire real estate. Marriage between Jews and Christians was legalized in 1863, and in 1873 it was also permitted to give a Jewish education to children born of such marriages. In 1865 Jews were granted the active right to vote and in 1870, the passive right. In Norway, the 1814 prohibition against the entrance of Jews was abrogated in 1851, after several unsuccessful previous attempts in 1842, 1845, and 1848. It was only in 1891 that the Jews were authorized to enter government service.

FRANCE. The emancipation of the Jews of France was linked to the French Revolution and its principles. Jewish equality was implied in the Declaration of the Rights of Man (Aug. 27, 1789), where it states that no man ought to be molested because of his opinions, including his religious opinions. Equality was gradually implemented through various national laws amid a continual, and sometimes fierce, discussion of the applicability of full equality to Jews, but full emancipation was granted on Sept. 27, 1791. Various features in the composition and distribution of the Jewish population, and in the traditional French attitude toward Jews, caused this acrimonious two-year struggle (see also *France, *French Revolution, *Alsace). During the debate in the National Assembly Comte de *Clermont-Tonnerre, an advocate of emancipation, explicitly formulated the assimilationist assumptions of the emancipation when he declared on Dec. 23, 1789: "The Jews should be denied everything as a nation, but granted everything as individuals…" and that "it should not be tolerated that the Jews become a separate political formation or class in the country. Every one of them must individually become a citizen; if they do not want this, they must inform us and we shall then be compelled to expel them. The existence of a nation within a nation is unacceptable to our country." Indeed, Jews striving for emancipation abandoned all demands for autonomy, especially those of the Portuguese communities in the south of France (see *Avignon; *Bordeaux; *Berr Isaac Berr), who were emancipated somewhat earlier than the Ashkenazi Jews of Alsace. The law of September 1791 (ratified by the king on November 13) emancipating all Jews as a matter of principle was considered by Jews as an historic turn in their fate, "a tremendous revolution which heralded happiness," and a victory of revolutionary principles, while the clergy and the royalists considered it a "further insult" to the Church and French historic tradition.

Every territory conquered by the French revolutionary armies, or placed under their rule, and where the laws of France were introduced, saw the proclamation of Jewish equality (e.g., Belgium, the Netherlands, Italy, southern Germany). Jews in these countries considered the French "friends of the Jews," and *Napoleon Bonaparte was admired by most, even though he later (from 1806 publicly) restricted full emancipation (see France, *Assembly of Jewish Notables, French *Sanhedrin). Napoleon's restrictions lapsed in 1818, and ironically were not renewed by the reinstituted reactionary Bourbon regime; civic equality of the Jews in France became an established fact. Jewish legal equality was renewed by the law of Feb. 8, 1831 (passed in the French Parliament after numerous discussions), which recognized the Jewish religion as equal in rights to the Christian churches, and provided for the salaries of its religious officials to be paid by the state. In 1846 the *oath *more Judaico* was abolished by a decision of the court of appeal.

THE NETHERLANDS. The French revolutionary conquest of the Netherlands precipitated Jewish emancipation. It was declared legally on Sept. 2, 1796, by the Batavian National Assembly, which stated that "it is impossible to deprive any Jew of the rights and privileges which are attached to Batavian citizenship, if he wishes to employ them, on condition that the Jew answers to all the requirements and fulfills all the obligations to which every citizen is bound." Both the basis of this law and the discussion about it centered on the definition of Jews and their aims. Neither party to the discussion was inimical to Jews. The opponents of emancipation emphasized the political nature of the Jewish people, who, although deprived of a state, considered Ereẓ Israel to be its country and the Torah its law. One of the debaters, Van Hamelsveld, claimed that since the Jews anticipate a messiah, bringing political revival, to grant them political rights in Batavia would cause the Jews to deviate from their correct historic path, which was similar to that of the Greeks, who stood on the verge of a political revival. All Jews, the argument continued, should have civic rights, which are encompassed by human rights, while political rights should only be given to those who explicitly declare their wish to become Batavian citizens. This conception was supported by the majority of Dutch Jews and their communal leaders, both noted for loyalty to the monarchy (the princes of Orange) and the desire not to cooperate with the revolutionaries who relied on the French conquest.

The opponents of equality claimed that by their religion the Jews were monarchists and thus opposed to any republican regime. They argued, in addition, that Jews are opposed to the abolition of their autonomy and feared that active participation of the Jewish masses in the affairs of state would finally bring misfortune to the Jewish population. In practice, emancipation in the Netherlands did not encounter much difficulty (see the *Netherlands), and the change of regime in the Netherlands did not change the law of equality. In the constitution, redrafted in 1848, the article on equality was even more clearly formulated: "The members of the various religions are to benefit from the same rights as the citizens of the state and the citizens of the communities, and they have an equal right to hold honorary, clerical, and public service positions."

With the conquest of Belgium by the French armies, the laws of France were applied. Emancipation continued through the time of union with the Netherlands (1815–30), and was incorporated into the Belgian constitution of 1831, which proclaimed the equality of all citizens.

ITALY. The beginnings of emancipation in *Italy were also connected with the victories of the French revolutionary armies. Opening the gates of the ghetto and the destruction of their walls symbolized the new regime. The government of the Cisalpine Republic invited the Jews to send their delegates to its founding assembly, and declared in its first proclamation that "the Jews are citizens and society must recognize them as citizens." One of the first steps of the government of the Republic in Rome was to publish in February 1798 the following decree: "The Jews answering to all the conditions required for the obtention of the rights of Roman citizens shall become subject to the laws which have been decreed for all the citizens of the Republic. Therefore, from this day, all the special laws and decrees concerning the Jews are declared to be null and void." The grounds for this decree were the "sanctified principles of the Constitution of the Roman Republic," according to which "the laws must equally apply to every Roman citizen." Support of Italian patriotism, unification, and revolutionary aims became characteristic of traditional Jewish community leaders (rabbis, *parnasim*, etc.), as well as Italian Jewry in general during the 19th century.

The first emancipation in Italy was of short duration, being repealed with the return of the "ancient order." The rhythm of repeal varied in the different Italian states. The renewed animation of the Italian liberation movement in the 1840s helped to bring about a considerable shift in public opinion in favor of the Jews. During the Revolution of 1848, the equality of the Jews was proclaimed in almost all the states of Italy: the duchy of Tuscany in its founding constitution of Feb. 17, 1848; Sardinia (which granted Jews civic rights on Mar. 29, 1848) on July 8, 1848; and Rome at the beginning of 1849. The general reaction which followed the year of the Revolution especially affected the Jews of the Papal States, where the period of reaction was also of longer duration. Only with the unification of Italy in 1870 did emancipation also come to the Jews of Rome when all restrictions connected with religion were abolished by the decree of Oct. 13, 1870, and by the parliamentary decision of Dec. 15, 1870. Liberation of parts of Italy during the process of unification also accomplished Jewish emancipation: in Modena, June 14, 1859; Lombardy, July 4, 1859; Romagna, Aug. 10, 1859; Umbria, Feb. 27, 1860; Sicily, Feb. 12, 1861; Naples, Feb. 16, 1861; and Venice, Aug. 4, 1866. Jewish emancipation in Italy was an expression of both social reality and public opinion, until the conclusion of the alliance between Benito *Mussolini and Adolf *Hitler.

GERMANY. Jewish emancipation in Germany prior to unification was related, as in Italy, to aspirations for the reform of the state along liberal and democratic lines, and to the desire for unifying the nation, as well as to the revolutionary movement. But after 1848 Germany was controlled by conservative, "historic," elements, which shaped the form of German unity and the nature of its political life. The process of emancipation in Germany was, therefore, a prolonged and bitter struggle, complicated by *assimilation on the one hand, and the power of the German "tradition of hatred" of Jews on the other (see G.E. Lessing; Ch. W. von Dohm). The struggle was to last from the 1780s until the passing of the law on Jewish equality in the North German Confederation on July 3, 1869, and its extension, with the ratification of the Constitution, to the whole of the German Empire on April 14, 1871. Emancipation in Germany also came first to those regions conquered by the French (see *Westphalia; *Frankfurt on the Main; *Hamburg). In the German states which retained their independence, "improvements and concessions" in the situation of the Jews were introduced (e.g., the abolition of the body tax, etc.).

The most important initial law in the emancipation of German Jews during the French revolutionary period was the edict issued in *Prussia on March 11, 1812, with its various modifications and limitations. It recognized all Jews already resident in Prussia by virtue of privileges and "special concessions" as citizens of Prussia, and abrogated all limitations on their rights of residence and commerce, all special taxes, and in general, all special laws relating to the Jews. It imposed on Jews all civic duties, including army service, and entitled them to serve in municipal and academic offices. However it did not give them the right of appointment in the civil service and army, and did not regulate communal affairs and Jewish religious education. After liberation of the "free cities" in Germany from French domination, stringent measures were taken to return the "ancient order," i.e., they endeavored to deprive the Jews of their civic rights (Frankfurt; Hamburg) and even of their right of residence (*Bremen; *Luebeck). The Jews appealed to the Congress of Vienna for assistance, thus making Jewish emancipation in Germany an international question. A result of the German-Jewish conflict was the wording of article 16 of the credentials of the German Confederation (June 10, 1815), which stated that only rights granted Jews "by the states" will be continued and not rights granted "in the states," thus eviscerating, through the change of one word, the rights granted under French dominion. The states did indeed use this opportunity to restrict the freedom of the Jews (see Bremen, Luebeck, Hamburg, Frankfurt, *Mecklenburg). Only during the 1830s was the movement for Jewish emancipation revived, a movement in which the literary and political activities of Gabriel Riesser played a central role. He succeeded in founding societies for the obtention of equality which influenced the governments and public opinion. Riesser considered himself a German nationalist, but he gave a distinctly Jewish communal character to the Jewish fight for their rights in Germany. The most prominent and talented members of the Jewish community aided Riesser in the battle, as did all of the Jewish communities in the German states. By the 1840s the results of this campaign were evident in public opinion in Prussia, expressed by the demands of the provincial assemblies (*Landtage*), and in the "law on the reform of the Jews" (July 23, 1847). The law resulted in a certain improvement in the organization of the Jewish communities, especially in southern Germany.

The Revolution of 1848 caused all the German states to proclaim emancipation. "The fundamental rights of the German people" (published on Dec. 27, 1848), which were to serve as the norm for every constitution of the German states, declared that "civil and political rights are not conditioned by religion or restricted as a result of it" and that "religion must not diminish civic obligations." This article was included, in one form or another, in the basic constitutions of most German states (Prussia, April 6, 1848, Dec. 5, 1848; Wuerttemberg, Dec. 21, 1848, Jan. 14, 1849; *Baden, Nov. 17, 1849) and was even preserved in the "constitutions" of the early reactionary period. Article 12 of the Prussian Constitution (Jan. 31, 1850) declared "freedom of religion and the freedom of organization of religious societies," and, further, that "the use of civic and political rights is not dependent on religion," nor does the "use of religious freedom impair civic and political obligations." This article appeared to be a firm guarantee for the emancipation of Jews.

Serious attempts were made during the 1850s to challenge the emancipation as a matter of principle and to abolish it in fact. Friedrich Julius *Stahl stressed the Christian character of the state and the resultant impossibility of granting equality to the Jews. In 1856 a motion was even introduced for the abolition of article 12 of the constitution. But the Jewish communities, led by Ludwig *Philippson, raised a storm of protest and the motion was dismissed. However, through its interpretation of the "amended" constitution's article 14, an article which dealt with the Christian religion, a means was found to bar Jews from government service. In other states, too (e.g., *Bavaria) many discriminatory laws were revived or remained in force.

On Nov. 1, 1867, all restrictions on the Jews' right of residence, acquisition of real estate, and choice of profession were abolished in the states of the North German Confederation. These restrictions were similarly abolished in the states of southern Germany (Bavaria in 1861; Wuerttemberg in 1862; Baden in 1864). The law of equality was passed by the Parliament of the North German Confederation on July 3, 1869. With the extension of this law to the states united within the German Empire (Bavaria, April 22, 1871), the struggle of Germany's Jews for emancipation achieved success.

AUSTRIA AND HUNGARY. The first period of emancipation in Austria made no change in the status of the Jews. But on the basis of the general constitution of the empire (March 4, 1849), which contained an article on "civic and political rights" being "not dependent on religion," all restrictions on Jews were abolished. With the abrogation of this constitution on Dec. 31, 1851, however, the ancient disabilities were renewed in aspects of life ranging from the acquisition of real estate (Oct. 20, 1853) to the employment of male and female Christian domestics. It was only during the 1860s that emancipatory laws were reinstituted. On Dec. 21, 1867, emancipation was achieved in Austria with the promulgation of the new fundamental laws in which article 14 assured "complete freedom of religion and conscience for all" and that "the benefits derived from civic and political rights were not dependent on faith and religion." "In any event," the article continued, "religious faith should not collide with the fulfillment of civic obligations."

In Hungary the townspeople tended to oppose granting rights to the Jews, whose numbers were constantly increasing. However, the lower aristocracy, whose economic progress was connected with the commercial activity of the Jews, and who were generally the standard-bearers of national liberalism, actively supported the Jews. As a result of their influence the demand "to give to the Jews all those rights from which the non-aristocratic population benefits" was included in the instructions of the provincial assemblies to their delegates in parliament. These instructions resulted in the law making the Jewish religion a "government-recognized religion," abolishing the "tolerance-tax," and declaring "the Jews equal in their civic rights to the other citizens who were not of the nobility." Therefore, public and government offices, including positions in the war ministry, which were not reserved for the nobility, could be occupied by Jews (1840). The Upper House however did not ratify the law, and the king would not even agree to the abolition of the "tolerance-tax." The Austrian government consented only to the extension of the right of residence to the Jews. Magyarization was made a prerequisite for Hungarian Jewry before it could achieve emancipation. The Jews have "to speak the language of Hungary and to sing its songs" so as "to cleave to the fatherland, which we have acquired for ourselves." But *Orthodoxy, in the words of Moṣes *Sofer, claimed that emancipation – i.e., "having all the same rights as the other inhabitants of our country" – proves that it is the Will of God to maintain His people in the Exile for a prolonged period, therefore the Jews should be roused to ask for mercy and pray for Redemption. The assimilationists and reformers claimed that declarations of the Orthodox had "strengthened the opponents of equality" and had caused the Upper House in 1844 to deny even the abolition of the "tolerance-tax" (abolished two years later by the Austrian government, after exacting "compensation" from the Jews for losses anticipated as a result of the abolition). Direct negotiations conducted by the Jews with the Austrian government, without taking into consideration the national rule in Hungary, angered the Hungarian nationalists and brought about a deterioration in their relations with the Jews. During the first days of the Revolution in 1848, the Hungarian Parliament deliberated on the issue of equality for the Jews. Even the Liberals, who in principle demanded it, were mostly of the opinion that such equality must be gradual and conditional to preliminary "reform" of the Jews. The Parliamentary Assembly, on March 14, 1848, decided to grant to the Jews the right to vote, but had to rescind this decision because of demonstrations and riots against Jews in several Hungarian towns (in most cases in connection with the admission of the Jews into the National Guard). The riots were not suppressed by the government, which even exerted pressure on the Jews to relinquish their rights "of their own free will." The patriotic activity, however, of many Jews during Hungary's war of independence created a bond between the Hungarian national cause and the Jews, strengthened by severe fines imposed on the Jewish communities by the victorious Austrians. On July 28, 1849, the government presented a motion to the Founding Assembly in Szegedin (Szeged) stating that "every believer in the Mosaic faith born on the soil of Hungary, or who has settled on it legally, shall benefit from all those civic and political rights which the believers of other religions enjoy." This emancipation turned out to be only a gesture, because the rule of the Hungarian government was rapidly disintegrating. Jewish emancipation was to become legal only with the establishment of Austria-Hungary as a dual monarchy. The two Hungarian houses of parliament, on Dec. 20/27, 1867, declared one of the fundamental laws of Hungary to be that "the Israelite inhabitants are equal to the Christian inhabitants in their civic and political rights" (art. 1) and that "all the laws, usages, and decrees which are in contradiction with these are hereby abrogated" (art. 2).

SWITZERLAND. The struggle for emancipation in Switzerland was drawn out over more than 75 years. It developed from nine

French demands imposed upon Switzerland (1797) to exempt French Jews visiting the country from special customs duties and taxes. The Helvetic Republic, established in 1798, passed general resolutions on emancipation. Special taxes on Jews were abrogated on July 1, 1798, as "a disgrace to the honor of mankind." This problem only concerned *Aargau, the one canton in which Jews were living legally. Full emancipation was rejected in 1799. The constitution of 1848 declared the theoretical equality of all Swiss citizens (art. 4), but, in effect, reserved full rights of citizenship only for members of one of the recognized Christian churches (art. 41). In 1856 the National Council decided that Jews living in the cantons permanently were to benefit from civic and political rights in their places of residence, and guaranteed their right to move freely within Switzerland. These resolutions, however, met with strong opposition from both the public and the authorities of Aargau. Only on Aug. 27, 1863, was the vote granted to the Jews of Canton Aargau. The emancipation of Switzerland's Jews concluded as it had begun by pressure from the outside. Many countries (France, the Netherlands, the U.S.A.) requested that Switzerland not discriminate against their Jewish citizens visiting there. Threats to cancel commercial treaties were made by France in 1835 and 1864, and the Netherlands in 1863, if the rights of their Jewish citizens were not guaranteed. Switzerland's consent to such demands created the anomaly of giving preference to Jews of other countries over Jews of Swiss nationality, which strengthened the case of those who demanded full emancipation. On Jan. 14, 1866, all restrictions concerning the right of Jews to establish residence were abolished, and on April 19, 1874, article 49 of the new constitution declared full emancipation in Switzerland.

THE BALKANS. In the Balkan countries (*Greece, *Bulgaria, *Serbia, and *Romania), which gained their independence from the *Ottoman Empire with the support of Russia, the question of the status of Jews was raised as soon as each country became independent. The Jews were generally loyal to *Turkey. The Christian insurgents were imbued with religious fanaticism, and Russia's hostility toward the Jews was notorious.

The question of Jewish emancipation became connected with the fate of Muslim minorities. From the time of establishment of the Balkan countries, these factors brought about the intervention of the great powers to help determine the status of minorities. In the protocol of the Conference of London (Nov. 30, 1830), which recognized the independence of Greece, the powers agreed that "all the subjects of the new state, without distinction of religion, shall be eligible for appointment in public service, government, and honorary positions, and their treatment should be based on complete equality in all religious, civic and political matters."

In the *irade* (a decree on governmental organization), which the sultan gave to Serbia on Dec. 24, 1838, the obligation of the government to "protect the property, the freedom, and the honor" of all the inhabitants was emphasized. After the Crimean War, the protocol of the Council of Constantinople (Feb. 11, 1856) declared that in the principalities of the Danube (Moldavia and Wallachia, which by their union formed the Kingdom of Romania) "freedom would be given to all the members of the various religions, and all of them, without distinction of religion, would be accorded the protection of the law, would be eligible for employment in the service of the public and society, and would be authorized to acquire lands and real estate." The Treaty of Paris (Aug. 19, 1858), however, stated in article 46 that "those belonging to the Christian Churches would benefit from political equality, while the extension of political rights to other elements of the population was the concern of the legislature." Agreeing in principle with the non-equality practiced in Serbia and Romania, the article continued to be the source of discrimination and expulsions (in Serbia, 1856 and 1869; in Romania, 1867–70, etc.), and even riots (in Romania, 1866–68).

It was only in Greece that emancipation gradually materialized (1870–72) without any additional outside pressure. In the other Balkan countries, emancipation was guaranteed by the Congress of Berlin, where, as a result of the numerous intercessions of the Alliance Israélite Universelle, it was decided that special articles on equality in Bulgaria, Serbia, and Romania would be a condition for international recognition of their independence. The article on Bulgaria declared that "no person should be deprived of his civic or political rights because of his religious beliefs," and that "all the inhabitants of the Bulgarian Principality, without distinction of religion or race, may be accepted into every public office, government service, and honorary position." With respect to Serbia, the Congress decided to consent to Serbian independence on the condition that religious freedom be recognized. The kingdoms of Bulgaria and Serbia included the articles on emancipation in their constitutions.

ROMANIA. The situation developed differently in Romania. Article 44, ratified at the Congress of Berlin, dealt with emancipation in Romania, and although not explicitly mentioning the Jews, reflected an understanding of their oppressed position in that country and was directed toward ameliorating it. The article declared "the differences between the religious faiths, or the credo of any person, cannot serve as a pretext for exclusion from the society which enjoys civic and political rights, or from certain professions, categories of crafts or industry, in any place." "Freedom of worship," the article continued, "shall be guaranteed to members of all religions in Romania, as well as to all foreigners, and no obstacles shall be laid in the way of the hierarchic organization of the various communities or their relations with their spiritual leaders. The treatment of the subjects of all the powers, businessmen, or others, when in Romania, shall be on the basis of complete equality." In actual practice, the Romanian government found a way to nullify this article. Although formally drafting the seventh article of its constitution according to the demands of the Congress of Berlin (the difference in religions and faiths in

Romania shall not entail any limitations in the acquisition of civic and political rights), the Romanian authorities included articles on "aliens" which permitted civic rights to be given to only 885 Jews while enabling the government to withhold these rights from more than 250,000 Jews (1885) who were declared aliens and required to undergo naturalization.

The peace treaty concluded with Romania after World War I (Dec. 9, 1919) included an article stating that "all those born in Romania, who are not subjects of another country by birth, shall become Romanian citizens on the strength of their birth in the country." In addition, a special article (7) was drafted into the treaty according to which Romania "commits herself to recognize as Romanian citizens the Jews living on Romanian territory who do not have any other nationality, by the actual fact of their living in the country, without requiring any formal demands of them." Another article (8) declared that "all Romanian subjects shall be equal before the law and shall benefit from the same civic rights without any distinction based on race, religion, or language." However, the motion to include article 7 in the constitution of 1923 was rejected, and the Jews were again required to provide documents attesting their right of citizenship causing about 10% of the Jewish population to remain without rights.

POLAND. Demands for Jewish emancipation in *Poland were presented at the end of the 18th century, amid the social and spiritual agitation resulting from the collapse of the regime and the state. During the interim period between its second and third partition, Poland's struggle for existence compelled it to seek ways of exploiting all available resources, including the increased economic resources which would accrue from "reform of the Jews." Thus "reform" was proposed by Mateusz *Butrymowicz, Tadeusz *Czacki, Kołłątaj, and others, mainly in the spirit of mercantilist exploitation of Jewish economic activity and their "improvement" through assimilation into Polish culture rather than as the natural result of a liberal regime in which Jews would be permitted civic equality and access to Polish cultural life. The Jewish population in Poland, which was the largest and most specifically Jewish in the Diaspora, could not be considered a mere collectivity of individuals. Influenced by Western political liberalism, Polish theorists formulating the methods for Jewish "reform" believed that the state should be based on the principles of civic equality legislated systematically and implemented with persistence by the state. It was the conflict between the theoretical liberal and the practical mercantilist orientations which caused the complete failure of the projects to "reform the Jews." The constitution of May 3, 1791, did not mention the Jews, and the law on the municipalities was based on the principle that municipal citizenship could be granted only to Christians. After the dismemberment of Poland, Polish legislation concerning Jews was applied only within those territories which enjoyed intermittent independence: the Grand Duchy of Warsaw, 1807–13; Kingdom of Poland, 1815–30; and Republic of *Cracow, 1815–46. Polish attitudes continued to influence the status of the Jews under alien rule, especially during the Polish uprisings, and in autonomous Galicia from 1848 to 1918.

The Grand Duchy of Warsaw tortuously followed Napoleon Bonaparte's policy toward the Jews. On Oct. 17, 1808, the duke decreed that "the inhabitants of the Grand Duchy of Warsaw of the Mosaic faith" could not make use of their political rights for a period of ten years, though "this law will not prevent us from authorizing individual members of this religion to benefit from political rights even before the lapse of the said period, should they be found meritorious and suitable." However, all petitions presented by a group of individuals, who considered themselves deserving of full equality, were dismissed by the government which emphasized that "equality before the law does not transform the inhabitants of the country into citizens." The government also took pains to issue special laws against the Jews, such as prohibiting the acquisition of estates, and restricting residence in Warsaw.

The Kingdom of Poland followed a similar but simpler course: it promised and did even less to emancipate Jews. In its draft constitution presented at the Congress of Vienna, an article promised that "all the civic rights, which are guaranteed in the present laws and regulations, shall also be reserved for Jewish people; special reforms should also be introduced in order to facilitate a larger Jewish participation in the rights of citizens." During the same year (1815), however, the Jewish question was studied by a reforms commission, headed by Prince Adam *Czartoryski, which endorsed the principle of emancipation only in theory, withholding it in practice until the Jews took up agriculture, abolished their community organization, acquired modern Polish education, and refrained from trading in and sale of alcoholic beverage (see *Wine and Liquor Trade). The decree which abrogated the equality of the Jews was prolonged by the Sejm (parliament). All suggestions advanced by "progressive," wealthy, or enlightened Jews (*maskilim*) to be considered "reformed" and separate from Jewish society as a whole and, therefore, worthy of civic rights brought no legal change in the condition of the Jews. An extensive polemical literature emerged, which was overwhelmingly and violently opposed to the Jews.

During the Polish uprising of 1830, there were those who favored the equality of the Jews, and there were some Jews, especially among the youth and the masses, who openly manifested their sympathy for the uprising and wished to participate in it. The leaders of the uprising and the Sejm generally adopted a negative attitude toward the desires of the Jews. A step toward Jewish emancipation was made later by Marquis Wielopolski who obtained from Czar *Alexander II permission to grant the Jews "partial civic equality." As a result, Jews were allowed to acquire land, and residence restrictions in several towns and regions were abolished, as were the Jewish oath and other limitations. But the use of Hebrew or Yiddish in bookkeeping or documents was forbidden on May 24, 1862. The national revolutionary government of 1863 addressed itself to "the Polish brothers of the Mosaic faith" in a special manifesto in which it promised that "the people's government would not ask about religion and race, only the place of birth," and that the Jews would be granted "all civic rights without restrictions" (see Dov Berush *Meisels).

The Sejm in Galicia ratified on Dec. 21, 1867, the abolition of restrictions on Jews' participation in municipal elections. The recognition of Jewish emancipation in principle was widespread among Polish progressives in the 1860s and 1870s. The belief was based on the assumption that after emancipation the Jews were bound to identify themselves nationally and politically with Poland and assimilate its culture. However, the increase in Jewish population and its social and cultural cohesiveness convinced the Poles that this assumption was illusory. The Poles argued that although the Jews fulfilled their civic obligations and were loyal to the state, they did not accept assimilation. Opposition to the Jews grew continually in intensity. It was encouraged by the Russian government's policy of "divide and rule," and by the Christian urban classes' enmity toward the Jews as rivals in commerce and in the liberal professions.

At the beginning of the 20th century Jewish participation in revolutionary activity (1905), the development of their own press, public schools, and economic institutions, the rise of modern Jewish nationalism (*Zionism, the *Bund, etc.), and the weight of their increasing numbers in municipal and *Duma elections sharpened Polish opposition to emancipation for the Jews. Only the Polish socialist movements demanded Jewish civic and political equality. During the German conquest of Poland in World War I, many laws and regulations directed against the Jews were actually abolished, and the organization of the communities received a more democratic character. Between the two World Wars the Jewish fight for equality in independent Poland was influenced by these developments. Emancipation of the Jews in Poland had been guaranteed by the Treaty of Versailles (arts. 86 and 93), and, in particular, by the "additional Treaty of Versailles" (June 28, 1919) signed by Poland, which provided for *minority rights in Poland. After numerous delays, the Polish government was compelled to sign the treaty. Although the Polish constitution of March 17, 1921, included the "additional Treaty of Versailles" and promised "complete equality in civic rights" (art. 9), there was also included an article stating that "in order to execute the constitution, the preparation of suitable legislation would be required." In other words, until the publication of new laws, it was possible – perhaps even necessary – to apply the ancient laws and restrictions. It was only in 1931 that several of these laws and restrictions were abrogated. In the new Polish constitution of April 23, 1935, the principle of equality was outlined in article 7 according to which "the rights of a citizen would not be restricted because of his origin, religion, sex, or nationality," and that "the right of the citizen to determine the course of public affairs would be considered in respect to the value of his efforts in the service of public welfare." Yet the violent opposition of Polish authorities and society to Jewish emancipation did not cease. The law of equality and the law concerning the rights of minorities were successfully emptied of their contents, remaining merely a political and judicial framework for Jewish complaints against the oppressive injustice and perverted laws under which they were compelled to live.

RUSSIA. The beginnings of the struggle for emancipation in Russia took place after the first partition of Poland (1772), when Russia annexed Polish provinces which contained large Jewish populations (Belorussia). On May 7, 1780, Catherine II accepted the "requests of the Jews living in the districts of *Mogilev and *Polotsk to register among the merchants." She ratified the rights of the Jews who had registered with the merchant class and who had been elected to public positions in the self-governing institutions of the burghers, ordering officials not to prevent the Jews from exercising this right (May 13, 1733). This episode is the beginning of the difficult fight for Jewish emancipation in Russia. Emancipation conflicted with the ideology of the czarist regime, which was built on a system of special privileges in all areas of life, and on rigid social classes legally separated. Under such a regime, every attempt to attain Jewish civic equality was doomed to failure from the start. The promptings of theory and pretensions toward principle often resulted in decrees which were supposedly intended to "reform" the Jews in order to render them suitable "for admission into civil society." On Dec. 23, 1791, the *Pale of Settlement was set up for the Jews, with further discriminations and impositions following suit. The Commission for the Reform of the Jews, at first inclined toward the liberal opinion that "prohibitions should be reduced and liberties increased" (Sept. 20, 1803), in the end issued the "Jewish Statute" of 1804 which determined the limits of the Pale of Settlement and imposed further domiciliary and economic disabilities. The commission, however, encouraged Jews to enter agriculture by recommending that the government allocate land and subsidies for their agricultural settlements. Also, Jews were to be permitted to attend general schools of all standards. In 1847 Czar Nicholas I replied to Moses Montefiore's plea for Jewish emancipation by saying that "such a thing is inconceivable, and as long as I live, such a thing shall not take place." Yet Nicholas supposedly believed in the principle of "betterment of the Jews," which meant that "if the experiment to direct the Jews toward useful work should succeed, time will gradually bring about automatically the abolition of those restrictions, which in the meantime are still indispensable." The czar's *Cantonist decree was occasionally "explained" by reasons of "reform in order to achieve citizenship."

During the reign of Alexander II, the situation remained basically unchanged. He ordered the appointment of a special commission to "examine all the existing regulations concerning the Jews in order to adapt them toward the general objective of the integration of this nation within the country, as far as the moral condition of the Jews renders them suitable for this" (March 31, 1856). The czar, however, shared with some members of the commission their opposition to Minister of the Interior Lanskoy's belief that the civic equality of the Jews was a preliminary condition for their assimilation. Alexander II held the view that "the emancipation of the Jews of Russia must be graduated in accordance with their intellectual progress and their adaptation to useful occupations." He only consented to the extension of the rights to certain classes in the Jewish population who had proven their usefulness to the state (see *Russia). He rejected any "far-reaching" suggestions, such as the abolition of the Pale of Settlement, or even less dramatic but immediate alleviation of the Jewish plight. During the reign of *Alexander III the Supreme Commission for the Study of the Current Laws Concerning the Jews was set up on Feb. 4, 1883, under the presidency of Count K. von Pahlen. On May 24, 1888, a report was presented whose majority opinion suggested "changing the system of laws and restrictions for a system of graduated laws of freedom and equality," because "from the governmental point of view, the Jew should benefit from all the rights available." Alexander III, however, rejected the opinion of the majority, accepting the minority viewpoint which accentuated the policy of discrimination. Convinced that there was no hope for an improvement in their conditions within the framework of the existing political regime, many Jews became active participants in the revolutionary movement.

While previous generations of Jews had presented their demands for reform to the authorities through the intermediary of *shtadlanim* (Nathan Note *Notkin, Lippman Selzer), *deputies of the Jewish people, or delegations of the wealthy and intellectual (Baron Horace *Guenzburg, Samuel *Poliakoff, Alexander *Passover, and others), the generation prior to the Russian Revolution expressed their demands for civic equality through increased numbers of Jewish political parties and movements (see *Bund; *Jewish Socialist Workers' Party ("Sejmists"); *Po'alei Zion). All of these parties approved of the "political struggle" within Russia in general and the struggle for the rights of the Jews in particular. At the beginning of 1906, political activism within Russia was included in the program of the Zionist Organization, largely for the purpose of obtaining civic, political, and national rights for the Jews. With the rise of the revolutionary movement (1904–05), and the appointment of Prince Svjatopolk-Mirski as minister of the interior (succeeding V.K. *Plehve who was assassinated by a revolutionary) to "appease" the public, many groups of Russian Jews presented demands for civic equality to the government. In April 1905 the *Society for the Attainment of Equal Rights for the Jewish People in Russia was established. As a protest against the 1892 law which deprived Jews of the right to vote in local elections, the league encouraged Jewish members of the municipalities appointed by the government to resign. It also organized a protest movement against the intention of the government to deprive Jews of the right to vote for members of the Duma.

Jewish revolutionary activities, especially participation in revolutionary parties and in the Bund, led the government to intensify its persecutions (see *Pogroms; *Minsk; *Kishinev; *Gomel; *Zhitomir) and actually to declare "war on the Jews" to "protect the Russian state and people." The czar's decree issued on the eve of the first revolution, Dec. 12, 1904, which was intended to appease the public, promised an "investigation into the laws which restrict the rights of aliens," and that "the restrictions which are necessary for the welfare of the state and the Russian people are not to be abolished." To the government manifesto of Oct. 17, 1905, Count *Witte appended a declaration which discriminated against Jews in the application of "civic freedom." Dealing with the "civic equality of all citizens without distinction of religion and nationality," the declaration stated "this would be executed through the channels of ordinary legislation," while the application of the other articles (freedom of the press and assembly) would be carried out immediately. And to article 76 in the basic laws issued on May 6, 1906, guaranteeing "to every Russian citizen the right to freely choose his place of residence," the Russian government added that "the restrictions to these laws are to be defined in special laws."

The first Duma did not deal specifically with the "Jewish question"; yet in answer to the opening speech of the czar it undertook to prepare "a law on the complete equality of rights of all citizens and to abolish all the restrictions and privileges which are conditioned on class, nationality, religion, or sex." A motion to this effect was introduced and supported by 151 delegates. A special commission was appointed to draft the bill, but the first Duma was dissolved before the work was completed. The government introduced a motion in the second Duma for the abolition of all restrictions based on faith or religion, "with the exception of the restrictions concerning the Jews." The Duma commission decided to delete this limitation, but it did not succeed in bringing the revised law to the plenum before the second Duma was also dissolved. In the third Duma, which was not a liberal one, the Jewish deputy L.N. *Nisselovich introduced (May 31, 1910) a bill, supported by 166 deputies, for the abolition of the Pale of Settlement. The bill was transferred (Feb. 9, 1911) to the commission on "personal liberties," but it, too, failed to reach the plenum. The government removed the issue of Jewish equality from the agenda as a matter of principle. During World War I the partial abolition of the Pale of Settlement by a circular of the minister of the interior (August 1915) was actually forced by the pressure of Jewish refugees expelled by the Russian authorities from the front area.

After the overthrow of the czarist regime the decree of the Russian Provisional Government (March–October, 1917), although not formulated only for Jews, was the most complete of all the laws of civic equality enacted with respect to the status of the Jews. In its preamble the decree stated that "according to our firm inner consciousness, in a free country, all citizens must be equal before the law, and the conscience of the nation cannot consent to the restriction of the rights of individual citizens because of their religion or race." On the basis of this ideology the Provisional Government decreed that "all the restrictions in the rights of Russian citizens because of their attachment to any faith, religion, or nation – such restrictions as are in force according to existing laws – shall be abolished." The first article of the decree enumerated in nine subsections the categories of restrictions to be abolished – both those in force throughout Russia and those limited to localities or regions. In six articles (2–7), the decree specified in great detail, giving dates of publication and numbers in the legal codes, all the numerous laws discriminating against Jews and members of other religions and nations. Article 8 declared invalid all prior administrative orders issued by civil or military authorities "which contained restrictions in rights because of affiliation with any faith, religion, or nation." Inclusion of an itemization of anti-Jewish legislation in the equality decree, reflecting the extent of Russian discrimination and the struggle for emancipation, resulted from the initiative and counsel of the Jewish Political Committee (delegates of the Jewish parties and Jewish representatives in the Duma), which provided this material for the government. The policy of the antisemitic czarist Russian govern-ment had compelled the Jews to act for themselves in every sphere of life: legal defense, self-defense against pogroms, founding schools and educating the masses, mutual credit, professional training, emigration arrangements, and political organization. The resulting "strengthening" of the Jews' ability to solve the problems of everyday life, together with the widespread appeal of the Zionist movement, increased Jewish cohesion to the point where it became a powerful instrument in the fight for survival. A basic political demand of Jewish political parties was "national *autonomy," expressing the collective character of Russian Jewry's struggle for emancipation.

THE BALTIC STATES. *Finland, *Estonia, *Latvia, and *Lithuania, which all became independent after World War I, included Jewish civic equality in their constitutions, because the *League of Nations accepted them as members only after committing themselves to providing for minority rights.

On Jan. 12, 1918, by granting emancipation in its constitution, Finland abolished the prohibition against Jewish settlement in force from 1806. This prohibition had been relaxed only for a few Jewish soldiers, whose other rights were nevertheless restricted, after their demobilization in 1865. The constitution permitted all Jews living in the country for at least five years prior to 1918 to become naturalized citizens.

Estonia's constitution of 1919 promised the Jews full equality. The law concerning cultural autonomy (Feb. 5, 1925) granted the Jews the right to elect a national council to administer their own schools, provide for their cultural needs, and supervise the communal organizations.

In Latvia civic equality was promised in its constitution. A special law on minorities (Oct. 8, 1919) granted the Jews, among other minorities, extensive cultural autonomy. An official appointed by the minority group was placed at the head of its school network. With the abrogation of the constitution in May 1934, the autonomous institutions of minorities were also dissolved.

The leader of the Lithuanian Paris peace delegation, Prof. Voldemaras, informed the *Comité des Délégations, in a letter of Aug. 5, 1919, that Lithuania would now promise the Jews representation in the country's legislative institutions, complete autonomy in their internal affairs, legal status for their autonomous institutions, recognition of the right to use their mother tongue, and the appointment of a special minister for Jewish affairs. The promises were ratified in the constitution of 1922 and, to a large extent, in the constitution of 1928, even though autonomous Jewish institutions in the meantime were dissolved. With the dissolution of the Jewish National Council and the Jewish Ministry in 1924, the Jewish community again became merely a religious community.

MUSLIM STATES. In the Islamic world there was no emancipation in the Western sense, neither as a public movement to which was linked the Jewish desire for civic equality and participation in the life of the state, nor as a reform movement holding civic equality to be a sign of a new order. To a certain extent, however, the civic equality granted to the Jews in the Ottoman Empire may be considered "emancipation." During the 19th century the sultan twice, in 1839 and 1856, proclaimed the civic equality of Jews and Christians, which represented a great change in the attitude of the Islamic countries toward "infidels." The revolution incited by the Young Turks in 1908 resulted in the ratification of this equality. The number of Jews who participated in the organizations of the Young Turks, and in the political life of Turkey, was not inconsiderable. After World I, Turkey signed a minorities treaty (1923), but, in the letter of the Jewish notables to *Kemal Pasha of Feb. 6, 1926, the Jews officially waived these rights for fear that they be accused of separatism. *Yemen, which won its independence between the two World Wars, never granted legal emancipation to Jews. Other Arab states (*Egypt, *Iraq, *Syria, *Libya, *Morocco, *Algeria, *Tunisia) granted Jewish emancipation officially, but took it away in reality after the Israel War of Independence through restrictions, persecutions, and humiliations as Jew-hatred became part of the fight against Zionism and Israel.

BIBLIOGRAPHY: Graetz, Hist; Dubnow, Hist; J. Katz, *Jewish Emancipation and Self-Emancipation* (1986); idem, *Out of the Ghetto: The Social Background of Jewish Emancipation, 1770–1870* (1973); S.W. Baron, *The Modern Age*, in: L. Schwarz (ed.), *Great Ages and Ideas of the Jewish People* (1956), 315–484; Baron, Social, 2 and 3 (1937); idem, *Die Judenfrage auf dem Wiener Kongress* (1920); idem, in: *Journal of Modern History*, 10 (1938); idem, in: *Diogenes*, 29 (1960), 56–81; R. Mahler, *Jewish Emancipation – A Selection of Documents* (1941); B. Dinur, *Be-Mifneh ha-Dorot* (1955), 9–68, 231–354; H.M. Sachar, *Course of Modern Jewish History* (1958); D. Rudavsky, *Emancipation and Adjustment* (1967); M.A. Meyer, *The Origins of the Modern Jew* (1967); S. Ettinger, in: *Scripta Hierosolymitana*, 7 (1961), 193–219; idem, in: H.H. Ben-Sasson (ed.), *Toledot Am Yisrael*, 3 (1969), 30–51, 86–110, 157–77, 223–72, 297–302, 340–53; A. Gorali, *She'elat ha-Mi'ut ha-Yehudi be-Ḥevver ha-Le'ummim* (1952); E. Silberner, *Ha-Sozyalizm ha-Ma'aravi u-She'elat ha-Yehudim* (1956); Y. Toury, *Mehumah u-Mevukhah be-Mahpekhat 1848* (1968); M.U. Schappes (ed.), *Documentary History of the Jews in the United States 1654–1875* (1950); J.L. Blau and S.W.

Baron, *Jews of the United States, 1790–1840*, 3 vols. (1963); C. Stember, et al., *Jews in the Mind of America* (1966); H.S.Q. Henriques, *Jews and English Law* (1908); I. Finestein, in: JHSET, 20 (1954–61), 113–44; Roth, England; V.D. Lipman, *Social History of the Jews in England 1850–1950* (1954); A. Cohen, in: REJ, 1 (1880), 83–104; N. Leven, *Cinquante ans d'histoire: L'Alliance Israélite Universelle 1860–1910*, 2 vols. (1911–20); B. Hagani, *L'Emancipation des Juifs* (1928); R. Anchel, *Napoléon et les Juifs* (1928); S. Posener, in: JSOS, 1 (1939), 271–326; E. Tcherikower, *Yidn in Frankraykh*, 2 vols. (1942); A.Z. Aescoly, *Ha-Emanẓipaẓyah ha-Yehudit, ha-Mahpekhah ha-Ẓarefatit u-Malkhut Napoleon* (1952); Z. Szajkowski, *Economic Status of the Jews in Alsace, Metz and Lorraine, 1648–1789* (1954); A. Hertzberg, *French Enlightenment and the Jews* (1968); I. Freund, *Die Emanzipation der Juden in Preussen*, 2 vols. (1912); N. Rotenstreich, in: YLBI, 4 (1959), 3–36; U. Tal, *Ha-Antishemiyyut ba-Reich ha-Germani ha-Sheni* (1963); F. Friedmann, *Die galizischen Juden im Kampfe um ihre Gleichberechtigung* (1929); Y. Gruenbaum, *Milḥemet Yehudei Polin* (1941); R. Mahler, *Toledot ha-Yehudim be-Polin (ad la-Me'ah ha-Tesha Esreh)* (1946), 216ff.; N.M. Gelber, in: *Zion*, 13–14 (1948–49), 106–43; idem, in: I. Halpern (ed.), *Beit Yisrael be-Polin*, 1 (1948), 110–27; A. Hartglas, *ibid.*, 128–51; B. Bernstein, in: *Gedenkbuch … David Kaufmann* (1900), 599–628; N. Katzburg, *Antishemiyyut be-Hungaryah, 1867–1914* (1969); idem, in: *Zion*, 22 (1957), 119–48; PK Romanyah; Dubnow, Hist Russ; Y. Maor, *She'elat ha-Yehudim ba-Tenu'ah ha-Liberalit ve-ha-Mahpekhanit be-Rusyah, 1890–1914* (1964); L. Greenberg, *Jews in Russia* (1965); S. Ullmann, *Histoire des Juifs en Belgique jusqu'au 19e siècle (1700–1830)* (1934); Z.H. Ilfeld, *Divrei Negidim* (Amsterdam, 1799); S. Seeligman, *De emancipatie der Joden in Nederland* (1913); Roth, Italy, 421–536; Milano, Italia, 338–419; HM Koritzinsky, *Jødernes historie i Norge* (1922); H. Valentin, *Judarnas Historia i Sverige* (1924); A. Linwald, *Die daenische Regierung und die Juden* (1928); L. Wolf, *Notes on the Diplomatic History of the Jewish Question* (1919); O.I. Janowsky, *Jews and the Minority Rights, 1898–1919* (1933). **ADD. BIBLIOGRAPHY:** P. Birnbaum and I. Katznelson (eds.), *Paths of Emancipation: Jews, States, and Citizenship* (1995); R. Liedtke and S. Wendehorst (eds.), *The Emancipation of Catholics, Jews and Protestants: Minorities and the Nation-State in Nineteenth-Century Europe* (1999).

[Benzion Dinur (Dinaburg)]

EMANUEL, a man of Jewish origin mentioned in a letter of the Austrian envoy in Istanbul in 1591 as the Turkish sultan's nominee for the *gospodar* of the principality of Moldavia. According to the envoy the man came from Poland and owed his appointment to the efforts of the physician Solomon *Ashkenazi, and even more to the large sums (half a million ducats) which he had paid to the sultan and his courtiers. The envoy states that Emanuel had many enemies and that his appointment might be nullified even before he left Turkey. Some identify Emanuel with Prince Aron Vodă, ruler of Moldavia from 1591 to 1595, who rebelled in 1594 against the Turks; 19 Jews from Turkey who were in Jassy at that time were then killed along with the Turks. This identification has no grounds; according to some Romanian historians, Aron belonged to a princely Moldavian family. Emanuel could have been one of those who tried to buy the Moldavian throne but did not succeed, as the Austrian envoy indeed says.

BIBLIOGRAPHY: E. Schwarzfeld, in: *Anuar pentru Israeliți*, 7 (1885), 113–6; JC (Jan. 2, 1885), 5.

[Eliyahu Feldman]

EMANUEL, WALTER LEWIS (1869–1915), humorist. A London lawyer, Emanuel contributed to *Punch* and wrote amusing books such as *A Dog Day* (1902), *The Snob* (1904), *The Dog World and Anti-Cat Review* (1909), and *One Hundred Years Hence* (1911). His father and brother both served as secretary to the Board of Deputies of British Jews and Emanuel himself was active in communal affairs.

EMAR, ancient city in the Near East. The cuneiform finds from Emar, at modern Meskeneh, must be understood in relation to those from *Ugarit. They are contemporary, spanning the 13th and early 12th centuries B.C.E.. Emar is directly inland from Ugarit, on the great bend of the Euphrates River. Both populations were dominated by Semitic speakers, whose dialects appear to have been distinct, though both western. Both towns were ruled in this period by their own local kings, with a circle of dependent towns and villages. For our understanding of the indigenous culture, it is unfortunate that Emar did not share Ugarit's alphabetic cuneiform alternative. Like much of Ugarit's cuneiform, the texts from Emar are mostly written in Akkadian, the language of the eastern Mesopotamians who were the system's first users. Emar's most striking textual discovery is the archive of a scribal school that was run by the man who oversaw the main body of public religious life in the town. As a whole, the cuneiform finds from Emar offer a counterpoint to Ugarit, that adds variety and nuance to our picture of Syria at the time of Israel's emergence. Politically and socially, Emar was in some ways more like Israel than was Ugarit (see below).

Excavations at Emar have taken place in two phases, the second of which is still in progress as of 2006. When Lake el-Assad was created by a new dam in the 1970s, a French team led by Jean-Claude Margueron explored much of the Late Bronze II town. All of the cuneiform finds came from this phase of work and belong to this period, including the tablets from the illicit antiquities market. Tablets were uncovered in a pair of temples, a public building of modest size, and several houses. The major discovery, however, was the building M_1, both the residence and shrine of an official who called himself "the diviner of the gods of Emar." Roughly a thousand tablets and fragments were found here, mostly written in Akkadian, but also including two Hittite letters, scribal lore in Sumerian, and divination manuals in Sumerian and in Hurrian. The diviner was a well-educated man.

Margueron did not uncover any strata from earlier periods, even though texts from other sites make clear that Emar already existed in the third millennium, at the time of the *Ebla archives. He concluded that the town was completely rebuilt under Hittite sponsorship at the end of the 14th century. New excavations by a joint German-Syrian team led by Uwe Finkbeiner, Shawki Sha'ath, and Farouk Ismail, beginning in 1996, have now demonstrated that the older town occupied the same site, suggesting greater cultural continuity in the society depicted in the texts. Perhaps the most fascinating feature of the Emar excavations, in vivid contrast to Ugarit, is the lack of a proper palace. The texts prove that the town had a king and palace, but no royal archives were unearthed, and the small public building that Margueron identified as the palace is far from convincing. It appears that the palace did not occupy either of the two main high points of the tell, both of which have been explored. Without palace finds, other buildings and their contents take center stage. Beyond the building M_1, three temples were found, one pair at the western summit of the town and another just above the diviner's residence, near the middle of the site. Several houses were excavated, proving that unlike some administrative and religious enclosures, these city walls protected a substantial population. The texts from the temple include only lists, and those from the houses are private legal documents.

The real novelty at Emar is the diviner's building, which has a temple-shaped hall and entrance, modified by rooms along one side. Cuneiform tablets were found jumbled across its main level, badly broken and suggesting collapse from a second story. The archive is diverse, with various threads indicating the diviner's personal interest. A large collection of lexical tablets includes colophon signatures for this diviner and his associates or students. Some of the divination lists include similar signatures, and the nature of the texts by itself suits the "diviner" title. The Hittite letters involve the financial interests of the first in the family of diviners, a man named Zu-Ba'la. Many of the tablets reflect everyday affairs at Emar rather than standard professional texts. These are divided into two main groups, both of which carry Emar's main interest for the Bible because they reflect the particular life of this Syrian site. There are many private legal documents of the same type as those from Emar's houses. One part of these record the affairs of Zu-Ba'la's family through four generations. A larger number of tablets and fragments pertains to the administration of Emar's religious institutions, apparently including the activity of the building M_1 itself. To our benefit, some of this administration was tied to prominent rites and festivals that are described in considerable detail. A few of the ritual texts were even copied as exercises. Throughout the rituals, "the diviner" receives various portions and payments, evidently for his services, and he surfaces occasionally with other roles.

The longer ritual texts form two natural groups. One set is defined by the calendar, for rites defined by the sacred year, generally celebrated once a year. Most prominent is the *zukru* for the turn of the year every fall, which survives in two versions. The simpler rite was understood to be annual. One tablet presents a special event focused on a certain seventh year, first anticipated by ritual preparations a year in advance. Nothing defines the *zukru* itself, a local Semitic word that makes best sense as something spoken. The central event of the *zukru* in both annual and seventh-year forms is a procession outside the town walls that has the god Dagan (see *Dagon) pass between upright stones. Dagan is the most important god of this part of the Euphrates valley. At Emar, he is invoked by far most often in personal names, and the *zukru* festival presents him as the explicit head of the pantheon. This is a major event for a preeminent god, gathering all the people and including offerings for all the town's gods. Removed from Dagan's temple in favor of the external site and simple stones, the whole thing has an old-fashioned feel to it. Neither the king nor any temple servant has any active role. Somehow, the rite is central to Emar's identity as a single community.

Another small set of festivals is defined by special events not tied to the calendar. The two most impressive are rites to install in office two leading priestesses, one for the storm god, and the other for the goddess Ashtartu. In the first rite, the priestess of the storm god is prepared in stages to move from her father's house to the house of the god. She takes up residence in the temple, a privilege that may be shared only by the priestess of Ashtartu. These installations take place only upon the death of a sitting priestess.

As a whole, the collection of ritual administration is dominated by local concerns, and this allows us a view of longstanding religious practices at Emar in western Syria. With cuneiform archives, local origin cannot be taken for granted, because the scribal lore is often learned from distant sources, ultimately founded in eastern Mesopotamia. For those interested in the Bible, the distinction is crucial. Western Syrian culture shared much more with ancient Israel than did eastern Mesopotamia, and this explains the many continuities in religious practice.

By any measure but the most traditional, however, the Bible is a product of the first millennium, the periods of the kingdoms, the ends of Israel and Judah, and the early survival of Judah's people. Many would challenge the very relevance of a Late Bronze site to the Bible, and the application merits conscious explanation. First of all, Emar must be considered in combination with Ugarit, the more famous city on the Mediterranean coast. The archives of Ugarit date to the same period and are also cuneiform based. Because a subset of the Ugarit tablets is written in an alphabetic cuneiform with the local West Semitic dialect, this site has attracted special interest, and it presents unique comparative possibilities. In a larger sense, however, Ugarit and Emar should be treated in combination, with the same argument for their relevance to the Bible. This is especially true for questions about religion.

Together, Ugarit and Emar provide a baseline from written evidence for understanding what is ancient and indigenous in the Bible, as opposed to late borrowings from outside contacts with distant empires. Both sites are far north of Israel and Judah, and they represent distinct expressions of Syrian culture. Both reflect many contrasts with the peoples of the Bible. Where we find points of continuity, these probably reflect deep lines of cultural likeness between these northern and southern societies. Little if anything can be treated as borrowed, because there is no reason to imagine any contact between these populations, either directly or through intermediaries. The comparisons are then all the more valuable for the independence of the writings on both sides. By the nature of this comparison across cultures, in no case does it date any biblical text or tradition. Common ground between early Syrian writing and the Bible may undermine certain arguments for late foreign influence or uniquely late and Judahite developments. Where similar features appear, the biblical expression appears then to be in long continuity with regional patterns.

Before addressing the specific possibilities of how Emar texts may illuminate the Bible, it is worth distinguishing the applications from Emar and Ugarit. Ugarit is essential for good reason. The West Semitic dialect of Ugarit by itself offers the primary point of reference for the earliest development of Hebrew. Emar's tablets are entirely cuneiform, and the local West Semitic language is only visible in personal names, terms that pass into the texts without translation, occasional glosses for Emar vocabulary, and grammar that does not fit proper Akkadian. In spite of these limitations, it still seems that the dialect of coastal Ugarit had more in common with ancient Hebrew than did that of Emar. More precisely, an adequate grammatical comparison is impossible for Emar Semitic, but the vocabulary of Ugarit overlaps substantially with Biblical Hebrew, much more than that of Emar.

In a way, religion presents a similar situation. With El (Ilu), Baal (Ba'lu), and Asherah (Athiratu) among the leading deities, even the vocabulary of Ugarit's pantheon coincides more with the Bible's divine names than does the pantheon of Emar. Of course, the name of Israel's particular god YHWH appears in neither, a detail not to be missed. Like the vocabulary of the languages as a whole, the religious vocabulary of Ugarit matches that of the Bible in significant ways, including sacred personnel (e.g. the *khn* "priest"). Ugarit's religious poetry displays themes and language that have echoes in the Bible, especially in the poetry of Jerusalem. Emar's ritual texts offer comparisons based less on vocabulary than on procedure, but the degree of ritual similarity is striking.

As we consider various individual comparisons between Emar documents and the Bible, we must keep in mind at least two dimensions of the Emar component: its inland geography, and its political heritage. Like Ugarit's, Emar's archives are earlier than biblical writing, from what would be the first stages of Israel's existence in the land and before. Both are far north of Israel, though closer than the origins of cuneiform in eastern Mesopotamia. Cultural proximity must be distinguished from physical distance and decided by the actual characteristics of the peoples involved. Egypt is physically closer to Israel and Judah than either of these two northern sites, but its language and religion are much more sharply separated. It appears that the peoples of the Bible shared much with those of the lands directly to the north, to an extent measured by the specific continuities found between their writings, even across centuries of chronological distance. Especially in the case of Emar, we must remember that this evidence precedes the spread of the *Arameans across Syria at the beginning of the Iron Age.

In spite of the fact that both Emar and Ugarit are roughly the same distance north of Israel, their geographical relationship both to each other and to Israel requires precision. According to various biblical lore, confirmed by the 9th-century Mesha Inscription from Moab, Israel straddled the Jordan River valley, with a sizable population on the east side. In Genesis 31, the tradition of Jacob's return from Syria has Laban chase him south along an inland route, from the vicinity of the Euphrates into this territory east of the Jordan River. On the southwestern elbow of the Euphrates, Emar participated in currents of exchange that moved north and south without ever entering the coastal regions or the land more properly called Canaan.

The other large factor to keep in mind as context for any Emar comparisons is political tradition. During the 13th century, Emar did have a king whose power is visible even though no royal archive was discovered. Because most of the Emar texts were not composed in the palace, however, including the whole output of the building M_1's diviner, we have an unusually good view of life outside royal circles. At Emar, kings struggled to establish true dominance in a town that for centuries had maintained a stubborn tradition of collective decision-making, defined by "elders" or a governing council. The public ritual life of Emar, as depicted in the diviner's archive, gives the king no active role, in radical contrast to the ritual found at Ugarit. In this respect, the Emar evidence stands in closer continuity to the world of the Bible than does that of Ugarit. The Bible also leaves much of the world of kings opaque. We learn almost nothing about royal and palace ritual and religion. In the Torah, Israel is presented as celebrating its festivals as a gathered people, without kings.

The tablets from the authorized excavations at Emar were only published in the mid-1980s, and their study has barely passed its first phase. Because the author both took part in this early research and maintained a continuing interest in the Bible, he has pursued several separate applications, and this article follows his personal work. There remains much to be done, however, especially to take advantage of the social context offered by Emar. Very soon after the publication of the main Emar volumes, Ben-Barak incorporated Emar into her discussions of women's inheritance, as with Zelophehad's daughters. Hundreds of legal documents from private households can be identified with Emar, whether or not from the authorized excavations. These offer a rich and varied portrait of family affairs in Late Bronze Syria, as a backdrop to the portrayal of family life and law in the Bible.

A second category of broad comparison that has not yet attracted attention is political. In broad terms, the Bible presents Israel as a people that maintained a political identity for some long period without having a king. Emar represents a very different setting in that its political identity is defined by the town and whatever surrounding population depends on it. Nevertheless, the combination of evidence from Late Bronze Emar itself and about Emar (written Imar) in the Middle Bronze archives of *Mari suggests that a strong monarchy only emerged in the 13th century. Kings may have existed during earlier periods, but their leadership was always balanced by a vigorous collective alternative. During the Middle Bronze Age, this took the form of a council called the *tahtamum*, known only at Emar and Tuttul. Even at the time of the Late Bronze archives, elders retained important legal and ritual responsibilities. Israel's monarchy also had to build its power in a political environment with long-established traditions for collective governance, in this case rooted in populations spread across a much larger region. Aside from any direct political comparison, the strength of collective political life at Emar gives its public religious celebrations a flavor more like what the Bible portrays for Israel than much Near Eastern public ritual, which tends to revolve around the king.

The most striking specific comparisons between Emar texts and the Bible have to do with religion, and public ritual life in particular. One preoccupation of the biblical Torah is the definition of a collective Jewish religious practice by reference to Israel in its life before kings, before Jerusalem and its temple, even before settlement in the land. This religious practice includes a major public component, with the ark and its tent shrine, priests for all Israel, and festivals to be celebrated in the name of Israel.

Although Emar religion belongs to a Late Bronze Age town, far to Israel's north, the cultural framework has points in common with Israel, beyond the collective political traditions. Most telling is the foundation of a shared temple architecture. In broad Near Eastern terms, the temples of Syria-Palestine, drawn north-south to include what become the lands of Israel and Judah, stand out from many other types. Even in the central cities of significant states, Syrian temples are most often constructed along one axis, with a doorway that opens directly onto the main sanctuary room. Four Emar temples, including the sacred room of the diviner's building M_1, share this form. The only descriptions of temple form in the Bible apply to Solomon's structure at Jerusalem and the mobile tent of *Exodus. Both of these share the simple axial layout of the regional type. Together with these simple sanctuary forms we find a lack of large temple-based communities, in contrast to the major sacred centers of the southern Mesopotamian cities, for one. Only a small number of priests enter the temple, and it is rare that the temple serves as the home for sacred personnel. At Emar, it is possible that only the storm god's (NIN.DINGIR) priestess and perhaps the neighboring *mash'artu* priestess of Ashtartu lived in the temples they served.

The most provocative comparisons between Emar and biblical religion relate to ritual procedure. Two clusters merit special attention, one related to the calendrical structure of festivals and the other to the technique of anointing. Both clusters are embedded in the public ritual life of the people on both sides of the comparison. On the biblical side, the closest comparisons appear in the priestly lore of the Torah. Although the finished versions of this lore may date to the exile of Judah or later, the similarities to Emar practice suggest that these traits do not derive from external contacts unique to such late times. They appear to be deeply indigenous, never borrowed, arising and developing in the local setting.

Three of Emar's all-town festivals are constructed around seven-day blocks, like the Bible's seven-day festivals of Pesah/Massot (Passover/Unleavened Bread) and Sukkot (Booths). Two of the Emar events are the installation rites for the priestesses of the storm god and Ashtartu, which were evidently performed after the death of the previous officeholder. Only one was celebrated according to the annual calendar, and the similarities are striking. Emar's *zukru* festival was focused on the full moon of the first month, with a seven-day period of feasting to follow. Emar counted the new year from the fall. At least once, a special version took place in the seventh year, and this event was by far the most expensive rite recorded in the archive. The *zukru* was an all-town festival during which the whole population brought all the gods outside the walls to pay special honor to Dagan as head of Emar's pantheon. The word *zukru* is West Semitic, not Akkadian, and probably represents an act defined by speech, a prayer or oath that renewed devotion to Dagan in this leading role.

Emar's *zukru* has more in common with the major calendar festivals than does any one rite found at Ugarit. Pesah/Massot and Sukkot are celebrated at the two axes of the ancient year, in spring and fall, and in the Holiness Code and Priestly versions of Leviticus 23 and Numbers 28–29, both incorporate a seven-day block and are focused on the full moon. The autumn new year at Emar matches the timing of Sukkot, in particular. Although this feast came to give came to give pride of place to the spring event in later tradition, the importance of the autumn equinox is visible in several aspects of the biblical calendar. In spite of the count of numbered months from the spring in priestly writing and the eventual borrowing of the Babylonian calendar with its spring new year, Exodus 23:16 and 34:22 indicate a turn of the year in the fall. This tradition is preserved in Rosh Hashanah, celebrated at the new moon of the first autumn month. A late note at the end of Deuteronomy preserves the most striking comparison with Emar's *zukru* (31:10–11). Every seventh year, at the feast of Sukkot, the written instruction of Moses was to be read aloud to the assembled population. The calendar is exactly like that of Emar's'special event, and the centrality of speech also offers an impressive continuity. How can we explain these similarities? The contents of each religious tradition are surely distinct. Deuteronomy's choice of this timing for such a major rite must, however, reflect ancient practices in Israel or Judah, even if they are transformed here to fit the notion of a Mosaic text. Somehow, the *zukru* at Emar belongs to a stream of ritual custom in which the biblical festivals participate at a later date. Where the calendar of biblical ritual corresponds with that of Emar's *zukru*, it is unlikely that the biblical timing was first created or borrowed at the date of textual composition, even if that may finally be exilic or later. The priestly calendar for the spring and fall festivals, along with the fall rite of Deuteronomy 31, appear to be much older than the texts in which they are embedded.

Aside from the calendar, Emar's festival accounts resemble the Torah instructions for Israel in at least one more important respect. They share an emphasis on the assembly of the people, without differentiation, and without leadership by any special individual, whether priest or king. In the Bible, Moses and Aaron have leading ritual roles, depending on the context, but the spring and fall festivals never specify the role of a priest, even in the Holiness and Priestly versions of Leviticus 23 and Numbers 28–29. All the accounts of Israel's primary festivals emphasize the gathering of the populace. At Emar, the most striking comparison again is found in the *zukru*, "given" by "the sons of the land of Emar" together and with feasting by "the people" as a whole. The feasting takes place outside the city walls, where all the gods of the town have gathered to witness Dagan's procession between sacred stones. Although the king's financial commitment to the festival is impressive, no ritual role is attributed to him. Likewise, the diviner is absent. Only the gods have individual roles, and we are never told who moves them or manipulates their statues. What is important is the participation of all the people and all their gods, the human and divine population of Emar. The same full participation characterizes the ideal of the Torah festivals.

The continuities between the worlds of Emar and of the Bible have more to do with the structures of their societies. At the same time, the ritual calendar and emphasis on the collective at the ritual expense of the king, for example, are not universal Near Eastern traits. Somehow, both Ugarit and Emar show different expressions of a cultural kinship that reached north and south along the Mediterranean and inland. The overlapping preoccupations of Torah instruction and the Emar ritual texts allow glimpses of this common cultural foundation beneath the superstructures of their separate developments. These glimpses warn us neither to treat the Bible and its religion as a world unto itself nor to explain points of similarity by the notion of borrowing, especially by contacts with conquering Mesopotamian powers. Rather, these similarities are hints of a massive commonality, from which the distinct features of particular peoples developed. The commonality itself is not uniform across the ancient world, and the north-south axis is striking, even as lines of distinction will not often be sharp. Emar, like Ugarit and other Syrian sites with cuneiform archives from the Bronze Age, suggests a depth to the cultural traditions embedded in the Bible that is too easily neglected. Evaluation of the stories and the events they describe is a problem that requires other comparative evidence.

BIBLIOGRAPHY: M. Adamthwaite, *Late Hittite Emar* (2001); D. Arnaud, *Recherches au pays d'Astata, Emar VI. 1–4* (1985–87); idem, *Textes syriens de l'âge du Bronze Recent* (1991); G. Beckman, *Texts from the Vicinity of Emar in the Collection of Jonathan Rose.* 1996; Z. Ben-Barak, in, M. Heltzer and E. Lipinski (ed.), *Society and Economy in the Eastern Mediterranean (c. 1500–1000 B.C.)* (1988), 87–97; D. Beyer, *Emar IV. Les sceau.* (2001); M. Chavalas, (ed.). *Emar: The History, Religion, and Culture of a Syrian Town in the Late Bronze Age* (1996); U. Finkbeiner, et al. in: *Baghdader Mitteilungen*, 32 (2001) 41–110; ibid, 33 (2002), 109–46; ibid, 34 (2003) 9–100; D. Fleming, *The Installation of Baal's High Priestess at Emar* (1992); idem, in, *Ugarit-Forschungen* 24 (1992) 59–71; idem, in, RB 106 (1999) 8–35; 161–74; idem; *Time at Emar* (2000); J.-C. Margueron, (ed.), *Le Moyen-Euphrate* (1980); Articles by Arnaud, Laroche, and Margueron; idem, in, BA, 58 (1995) 126–38; E. Pentiuc, *West Semitic Vocabulary in the Akkadian Texts from Emar* (2001); R. Pruzsinszky, *Die Personennamen der Texte aus Emar* (2003); S. Stephano, *L'accadico di Emar.* (1998); A. Tsukimoto, in, *Acta Sumerologica*, 12 (1990) 177–259; (II), 13 (1991) 275–333; (III) 14 (1992) 311–15; (IV) 16 (1994) 231–36; J. Westenholz, *Cuneiform Inscriptions in the Collection of the Bible Lands Museum: The Emar Tablets* (2000).

[Daniel Fleming (2nd ed.)]

EMBALMING. The natural drying out of the body by solar heat (mummification) is the oldest method of preserving a corpse. The ancient Egyptians may have simply tried to dry corpses in the hot desert sands, or as in one of the chambers found at Thebes, in rooms which were artificially heated. Embalming is the artificial treatment of a corpse to prevent or delay its putrefaction. In ancient Egypt the technique consisted, according to Herodotus, of using an iron hook to draw out the brain through the nostrils, and then making a cut along the flank to remove the abdominal contents, which were washed and soaked in palm wine and infusions of spices, and then stored in "canopic" jars. The heart, as seat of intelligence, was removed, wrapped in linen, and replaced into the chest cavity. The cavity was filled with myrrh, cassia, and other spices before being sewn up; the body was then washed and wrapped from head to foot in fine linen. The Bible describes embalmers as "physicians" (Gen. 50:2), and mentions it (perhaps to provide local color) only with reference to Jacob and Joseph (Gen. 50:2–3, 26), who both died in Egypt. The statement that the process required 40 days (Gen. 50:3) is at variance with Herodotus' statement that it required 70, the period which the Bible assigns to the Egyptians' mourning for Jacob. In actuality, the mummification process might range between 30 and 200 days. The strong belief in an afterlife was what made preservation of the body so important in Egypt, in marked contrast to the situation in ancient Israel.

Today embalming before burial is widely practiced in the United States by undertakers, who inject a formalin solution into the blood vessels; but in Israel it is rare, being confined entirely to bodies being sent abroad for burial (in conformity with international regulations).

BIBLIOGRAPHY: H.E. Sigerist, *A History of Medicine* (1951), 353–54; I. Thorwald, *Science and Secrets of Early Medicine* (1962), index. **ADD. BIBLIOGRAPHY:** L. Lesko, in: CANE III, 1764–66.

[Heinrich Karplus]

EMBDEN, GUSTAV (1874–1933), German biochemist. Born in Hamburg, Embden was appointed professor of physiology at Frankfurt University in 1914, where he carried on his productive investigations into the chemistry of muscular contraction. Recognizing that muscle glycogen is not directly oxidized for energy, he helped to elaborate the metabolic pathways by which carbohydrate is degraded within the cell. This biochemical pattern, which bears his name, is characteristic of most living cells. Embden also stressed the significance of phosphoric acid in the intracellular metabolism of sugars. Other research contributions were in the area of fat metabolism. He contributed, with G. Schmidt, to *Handbuch der biologischen Arbeitsmethoden* (1921–39) and edited, with others, *Handbuch der normalen undpathologischen Physiologie* (6 vols., 1925–29).

[George H. Fried]

EMBER, AARON (1878–1926), U.S. Orientalist and Egyptologist. Born in Kovno, Lithuania, Ember migrated to the U.S. in 1891. From 1904 to 1910 he worked as a fellow of Semitics at Johns Hopkins University and from 1911 was assistant professor (professor 1924) in its Semitics department. His studies in Ancient Egyptian, Assyrian, Arabic, and Ethiopic led him to seek an earlier form of proto-Semitic in Egyptian, which he came to regard as the oldest Semitic language. He died as a result of a fire in his house in which his wife and child also perished. His papers, which were partially destroyed, were partly published by Cyrus Adler in the *Paul Haupt Anniversary Volume* (1926), in a chapter entitled "Partial Assimilation in Old Egyptian" (pp. 300–12), where Ember discussed the phonological relationship of Egyptian to Semitic languages and his theory that abstract terms developed from a concrete basis. The book also includes a biographical sketch of Ember. In 1930 a manuscript that survived the fire was published as A. Ember, *Egypto-Semitic Studies*. Its publication was due in large part to the efforts of Ember's former teacher, the great Egyptologist Kurt Sethe of Berlin. Ember took an active part in the Jewish community of Baltimore. For many years he was a director of the Baltimore Talmud Torah and of the Isaac Davidson School and helped to found the Jewish Public Library there. He was also an ardent Zionist and assisted the Hebrew University Library, Jerusalem.

BIBLIOGRAPHY: H. Loewe, *Aaron Ember* (Ger., 1926); K. Sethe, in: *Zeitschrift fuer aegyptische Sprache und Altertumskunde*, 4 (1926), 130–1. **ADD. BIBLIOGRAPHY:** O. Sellers, in: AJSL, 50 (1934), 109–10.

EMBRYO (Heb. עֻבָּר, *ubbar*), a child in the womb of its mother before its head emerges (Sanh. 72b; Sh. Ar., ḤM 425:2), the Hebrew *ubbar* meaning the unborn child in both the embryonic and fetal stages. Generally speaking, an embryo is incapable of having legal rights or duties, although there are various rules intended to protect its rights when born, and to prevent uncertainty with regard to its status.

Determining the Identity of the Embryo

A widow or divorced woman must not remarry until 90 days after the death of her husband or after her divorce (Sh. Ar., EH 13:1; see *Marriages, Prohibited). The reason for this prohibition is to remove any doubt should she immediately become pregnant from her second husband, as to whether the child she bears is a nine-month child of the first, or a seven-month child of the second, a doubt which might seriously affect its personal status (Yev. 41a–42a; and Codes).

Mother or Embryo

Who Takes Precedence? On the question of whether an embryo may be killed in order to save its mother in the case of a difficult confinement, see *Abortion.

Parentage

Generally, the same laws that apply in determining the parentage of a born child and the capacity of the mother or her husband to deprive it of its status apply to the embryo; see **Mamzer*; Parent and *Child.

Levirate Marriage or *Ḥlizah* of a Pregnant Woman

If a woman was pregnant when her husband died and the child is subsequently born alive, she is exempt from levirate marriage or *ḥalizah* (Sh. Ar., EH 156:4; see *Levirate Marriage and *Ḥalizah*).

Proselytization

For the status of a child born after its mother became a proselyte while pregnant with it see *Proselyte.

Succession

An embryo is incapable of acquiring rights, for only a person born can possess rights. Accordingly, if an embryo dies in its mother's womb, it does not leave the right of succession, to which it would have been entitled had it been alive when the deceased died, to those who would have been its heirs had it been born alive when the deceased died. Instead, such right of succession passes to the heirs of the deceased as if the embryo had never existed (BB 142a; Nid. 44a; and Codes, Rif to Yev. 67a). There is a contrary opinion, however, to the effect that intestate succession being automatic, the embryo does acquire it (*Piskei ha-Rosh* to Yev. 67a; see Tur, ḤM 210). All agree, however, that a child born alive after the death of its father inherits its father as though it had been alive when he died (Rif, Ritba, to Yev. 67a, *Beit Yosef* and Bah to Tur and Sh. Ar. loc. cit.; see *Ḥiddushei Ḥayyim ha-Levi* to Yad, Terumot 8:4). Hence, an embryo that is born after the death of the deceased, even if it dies the day it is born, leaves the right of succession (after its mother) to its heirs on its father's side, but not to those on its mother's side – who would have inherited had the embryo died in her womb (Tur and Sh. Ar., ḤM 276:5). Only in respect of the special rights due to a firstborn son is a child born after the death of his father not of equal status with one already born when the father dies. Thus, if twins are born, the first one will not be entitled to the additional share in the father's estate due to the firstborn (see *Firstborn), since the Torah states of the primogenitary right, "If they have borne him children …" (Deut. 21:15), i.e., only a firstborn alive when the father dies, but not an embryo, is entitled to the (additional) primogenitary share (BB 142b, and Codes).

A will in favor of the embryo of another has no validity, even if the embryo is born alive, since no rights can be conferred upon one not yet born (BB 141b–142; *Piskei ha-Rosh* to Yev. 67a; Sh. Ar., ḤM 210:1). However, when a man whose wife is pregnant makes a will in favor of his own embryo whether it be a will of a person being on his deathbed (*shekhiv me-ra*) or of a person regarded as being in health (*bari*) (see *Wills) –

it is valid, because a person is favorably disposed toward his own child and wholeheartedly wishes to transfer ownership to him (Sh. Ar., ḤM 253:26–27). Some are of the opinion that this law applies only to a will made by a person on his deathbed and not to one made by a healthy person (*Beit Yosef* to Tur, ḤM 210:3; Sh. Ar., ḤM 210:1).

Contractual Obligations to an Embryo

According to some authorities although transfer of rights cannot be made to an embryo, a contractual obligation can be undertaken in his favor (see *Contract). A guardian can be appointed to protect the rights of an embryo (Sh. Ar., ḤM 290:1).

The State of Israel

In general, Jewish law is followed. With regard to succession, however, section 3 of the law of succession (1965) provides that a person born within 300 days after the death of the deceased is deemed to have been living when the deceased died, unless it is proved that he was conceived thereafter. In terms of section 33 (b) of the Capacity and Guardianship Law, 5722–1962, the court may appoint a guardian for a child *en ventre de sa mére.*

BIBLIOGRAPHY: Gulak, Yesodei, 1 (1922), 33; 3 (1922), 82, 116, 147; ET, 7 (1956), 50–53; 8 (1957), 102–20; 11 (1965), 255f.; Miklishanski, in: *Sefer ha-Yovel... Federbush* (1960), 251–60; G. Ellinson, in: *Sinai*, 66 (1969/70), 20–49; Elon, *Ha-Mishpat Ha-Ivri* (1988), I, 496; idem. *Jewish Law* (1994), II, 604.

[Ben-Zion (Benno) Schereschewsky]

EMDEN, city in Germany. The first authentic reference to Jews in Emden dates from the first half of the 16th century. David *Gans mentions Jews of Emden in his *Ẓemaḥ David.* A Jewish cemetery is mentioned in 1586. In 1590 the citizens of Emden complained to the representative of the emperor that the Jews were permitted to follow their religious precepts openly and were exempted from wearing the Jewish *badge. Marranos from Portugal passed through Emden on their way to Amsterdam, and a few settled in Emden and returned to Judaism. Moses Uri ha-Levy (1594–1620), a former rabbi of Emden who settled in Amsterdam, officiated there as the first *ḥakham* of the Portuguese community. The city council of Emden discriminated between the local Jews and the Portuguese, encouraging the latter to settle in the city, while attempting to expel the former. Their attempts, however, were unsuccessful, since the duke intervened in their favor. The judicial rights of the Portuguese Jews were defined in a grant of privilege issued by the city council in 1649, and renewed in 1703. In 1744, when Emden was annexed to *Prussia, the Jews there came under Prussian law. In 1762 there was an outbreak of anti-Jewish riots in Emden. In 1808, during the rule of Louis Bonaparte, the Jews in Emden were granted equal civic rights. There were then 500 Jews living in Emden. The rights of the Emden Jews were abolished under Hanoverian rule in 1815, and they did not obtain emancipation until 1842. Noted rabbis of Emden were Jacob *Emden (1728–33), and Samson Raphael *Hirsch (1841–47).

The community numbered 900 in 1905, and 1,000 in 1930. Nearly half left with the advent of Nazi rule and another quarter through 1938. The synagogue was burned down on *Kristallnacht* and most of those remaining were later deported and perished, including at least 150 on October 23, 1941. Community life was not resumed after the Holocaust.

BIBLIOGRAPHY: Lewin, in: MGWJ, 2 (1890), 27–32; H. Kellenbenz, *Sephardim an der unteren Elbe* (1958), index; M. Markreich, in: *Jahrbuch der juedischen Gemeinden Schleswig-Holsteins*, 5 (1933/34), 24–36; PK Germanyah; Germ Jud, 2 (1968), 208–9; A. Cassuto, in: *Juedische Familien-Forschung*, 2 (1926), 289. **ADD. BIBLIOGRAPHY:** J. Lokers, *Die Juden in Emden 1530–1906* (1990); M. Claudi, *Die wir verloren haben. Lebensgeschichten Emder Juden* (1991); M. Studemund-Halévy, in: *Aschkenas*, 7 (1997), 389–439.

[Zvi Avneri]

EMDEN, JACOB (pen name **Yaveẓ**; derived from **Ya'akov Ben Ẓevi**; 1697–1776), rabbi, halakhic authority, kabbalist, and anti-Shabbatean polemicist. Emden was regarded as one of the outstanding scholars of his generation. Emden's teacher was his father Ẓevi Hirsch *Ashkenazi (Ḥakham Ẓevi). He inherited his father's interest in secular studies, his dissociation from the Ashkenazi method of study (*pilpul*) and customs, his stormy, independent, and uncompromising character, and his devotion to the campaign against the Shabbateans and their sympathizers. In addition, he possessed a fine literary talent, a critical tendency, and a knowledge unusual for his age of general non-halakhic Jewish literature. He was also familiar with sciences and languages (German, Dutch, Latin). Despite his distinguished descent and his remarkable talmudic attainments, Emden occupied no official position, with the exception of a few years as rabbi of Emden (1728–33). This made it possible for him to be exceptionally critical toward the society and the tradition of his time. He was more on guard about anything that he considered *ḥillul ha-Shem* (bringing the name of the Jew into disrepute) than for the good name of the rabbinate and of the community. He made extensive use of the private printing press he founded in *Altona to disseminate his views. As a result, because of his views on a number of issues, both personal and communal, he became a figure of contention. His important halakhic works are *Leḥem Shamayim*, on the Mishnah (pt. 1, 1728; pt. 2, 1768); a letter of criticism against R. Ezekiel Katzenellenbogen, rabbi of Altona (1736); responsa, *She'elat Yaveẓ* (2 pts., 1738–59); *Mor u-Keẓi'ah*, on the Shulḥan Arukh, OḤ (2 pts., 1761–68). In addition, he published an important edition of the prayer book (whose parts had different names) with a valuable commentary (1745–48). This prayer book was reprinted several times. His main historical importance lies in his campaigns against the Shabbateans to which he dedicated many years. He relentlessly examined and investigated every suspicious phenomenon pertaining to the sect. He called upon the contemporary rabbis to publish excommunications and mercilessly attacked anyone suspected of supporting or showing sympathy to the Shabbateans. The Shabbateans were accustomed to introduce hints of their secret doctrine into their literary works, particularly in the field of Kabbalah. Consequently, Emden became an expert in uncovering such allusions and hidden meanings, and developed an extraordinarily sharp critical faculty by which he could recognize any suggestion of the Shabbatean heresy. Many books in which no one saw anything to which objection could be taken, were condemned by him as heretical. Though at times he was at fault and suspected the innocent without cause, his judgment in general was sound (F. Lachover and I. Tishby (eds.) *Mishnat ha-Zohar*, 1 (1957^2), 52–56).

His most famous controversy was with Jonathan *Eybeschuetz, rabbi of the "Three Communities" (Altona, Hamburg, Wandsbek) from 1750 until he died in 1764. It commenced in 1751 soon after Eybeschuetz came to Altona and did not cease even with the latter's death. It divided German Jewry, particularly rabbinic circles, into two camps, and undermined the prestige of rabbinical institutions.

The conflict at first centered around several amulets which Eybeschuetz circulated in Metz and Hamburg. Emden published their content in his work *Sefat Emet u-Leshon Zehorit* (1751) and interpreted them rather convincingly as Shabbatean amulets. As a result of this publication, Emden was compelled to escape to Amsterdam for some time and there he published in *Torat ha-Kena'ot* (1752) an anthology of documents on Shabbateanism. Eybeschuetz too was a great scholar; he had devoted disciples but also many enemies. He was suspected of adhering secretly to the Shabbatean groups or at least of affinity to them. His son was a declared Shabbatean. Eybeschuetz denied the accusation, which in any case could not be proved with certainty. The majority of the greatest rabbis in Poland, Moravia, and Bohemia, as well as the leaders of the Three Communities supported him, either because the accusation was utterly incredible, or because condemnation of a rabbi who enjoyed such an enormous prestige as Eybeschuetz would cause inestimable damage to the communal organizations as a whole. Emden disregarded these considerations vehemently. He fought his opponent and his numerous supporters by means of books and pamphlets which came out in unabated succession.

Emden's major works in this dispute, apart from several small pamphlets and leaflets, are *Edut be-Ya'akov* (1756); *Shevirat Luḥot ha-Even* (1756–59), a detailed critique of the defense of Eybeschuetz; *Luḥot Edut, Sefer Hitabbekut* (1762–67), which also includes important protocols on the Shabbatean propaganda activities in the yeshivah of Eybeschuetz in Hamburg and in the great yeshivah in Pressburg. In addition, Emden dedicated his *Sefer Shimmush* as "a special weapon for every Jew to use in order to know what to answer to the Shabbatean groups" (1758–62) and to fight Frankism, which arose in his time. The two opposing camps in Altona requested the intervention of the authorities and it was only through this intervention that the conflict subsided.

From this campaign, Emden went on to criticize the Zohar, the bastion of the Shabbateans (see *Kabbalah). The Zohar was regarded by many as second only to the Bible in sanctity. Emden had questioned its antiquity, and consequently its sanctity in *Mitpaḥat Sefarim* (1768), which provoked opposition. His piety and profound attachment to tradition would not permit him to condemn the work as a whole. Nevertheless, he did not hesitate to state his conclusion that later and forged additions had been interpolated into an ancient and sacred book. His critical attitude toward accepted ideas and beliefs is revealed also in his criticism of the *Guide of the Perplexed*, the major work of Jewish philosophy, which he found to contain heretical tendencies; he did not believe that *Maimonides was its author. His activity in many directions as well as his general approach which he based on the use of grammar, philology, and history and the like, his brilliant and scholarly style, his tolerant attitude to Christians and his deprecation of Polish Jews, created a certain affinity between him and the first proponents of Haskalah, who had already emerged in his day, and most of whom were opposed to the Kabbalah and its influence. Although in fact Emden rejected philosophy and scientific criticism in the sphere of Judaism, permitting only the study of the natural sciences, he was friendly with Israel of Zamosc and his disciple, Moses *Mendelssohn. He held discussions with them on halakhic topics, customs, and principles of religion. From the correspondence between Emden and Mendelssohn, the difference between the *maskil* of the old school such as Emden and the new type such as Mendelssohn emerges clearly.

The independence, originality, and stormy temperament of Emden are noticeable in his halakhic works. In certain subjects he takes up an extreme view against the majority opinion, and in others he is outstandingly lenient (e.g., with regard to concubinage and eating legumes during Passover). In a dispute with Israel of Zamosc on the authority of the Shulḥan Arukh, it was precisely Emden who upheld the principle of the freedom of the *posek* (halakhic authority), from dependence on this code. Emden's autobiography, *Megillat Sefer* (first published from an Oxford Ms. in 1896), is unique in the rabbinic world. In addition to its historical importance it is of no small belletristic value.

Emden's ability as a grammarian is evident in his commentary on the prayers (*Siddur Beit Ya'akov*), where he combines grammatical comments and kabbalistic commentary. He explains, for example, that *barukh* is not a passive past participle but a noun like *raḥum*, the *kamaẓ* compensating for the lack of a *dagesh* in the letter *resh*. In consequence he arrives at the explanation that God is the source of blessings. He also discusses mishnaic Hebrew (e.g., the word "*Nishtannah*" as a conflation of *nif'al* and *hitpa'el*). In his commentary on the Mishnah *Leḥem Shamayim*, he discusses variant readings, determining the correct one by linguistic considerations. *Em la-Binah*, his commentary on Scripture, abounds in inferences drawn from differences between synonyms, and *Gal Ed* contains discussions on correct vocalization.

BIBLIOGRAPHY: M.J. Cohen, *Jacob Emden, a Man of Controversy* (1937); G. Scholem, in: KS, 16 (1939/40), 320–38; Y. Raphael, in *Aresheth*, 3 (1961), 231–76; B.-Z. Katz, *Rabbanut, Ḥasidut, Haskalah*, 1 (1957); A. Shochat, *Im Ḥillufei Tekufot* (1960), index; J. Katz, *Exclusiveness and Tolerance* (1961), index; M.A. Wagenaar, *Toledot Yaveẓ* (1868);

D. Kogan, *Toledot ha-Mekubalim ha-Shabbeta'im ve-ha-Ḥasidim*, 2 (1913), 27–64; A.R. Malakhi, in: *Hadoar*, 18 (1938–39), 155–6; M. Grunwald, *Hamburgs deutsche Juden* (1904), 89–124.

[Moshe Shraga Samet]

°**EMERY, RICHARD WILDER** (1912–1989), U.S. historian. Emery was professor of history at Queens College, New York. A non-Jew interested in medieval French history, Emery began detailed research on the rich notarial records of Perpignan in southern France. The amount of material of Jewish interest was so great that he devoted a separate volume to this subject, *The Jews of Perpignan in the Thirteenth Century: An Economic Study Based on Notarial Records* (1959), which was followed by other monographs. This is the most detailed study of certain aspects of the history of a medieval Jewish community that has ever appeared, and it reveals the existence of vast untapped sources of information. In addition, his studies have thrown much light on the real extent and consequences of the forced conversions that began in 1391 and on eminent personalities, such as Menahem *Meiri and Profiat *Duran. He also wrote *The Friars in Medieval France: A Catalogue of French Mendicant Convents 1200–1550* (1962) and *Heresy and Inquisition in Narbonne* (1967).

[Cecil Roth]

EMESA (now **Homs**), city in Syria. It was ruled by a dynasty which enjoyed friendly political relations in the first century C.E. with Agrippa I (Jos., Ant., 18:135; 19:338) and with Agrippa II (*ibid.*, 20:139). The marriages contracted between members of the two royal families were apparently dictated by political expedience. It is likely, although evidence is lacking, that at this period Jews were living in Emesa. Azizus king of Emesa consented to be circumcised in order to marry Drusilla the sister of Agrippa II, and it may be that he was not the only proselyte in his kingdom at this time. There is reference to other proselytes in Emesa at a later period, in about the third century (TJ, Yev. 11:2, 11d, et. al.). Several Palestinian *amoraim* visited Emesa: Ḥiyya b. Abba received money for orphans and widows from the local Jews (TJ, Meg. 3:1, 74a). R. Yose was asked there about the laws concerning a levirate marriage and proselytes (TJ, Yev. 11:2, 11d), and R. Haggai about those concerning the tithe from fields rented to non-Jews (TJ, Dem. 6:1, 25b; TJ, Av. Zar. 1:9, 40b). Still in existence at the time of the Arab conquest (635–40), members of the community assisted the conquerors. With the fall of the *Umayyad caliphate and the Byzantine invasions of the region, the town was impoverished and the Jews abandoned it. *Benjamin of Tudela, the 12th century traveler, found about 20 families there. After a short period of prosperity during the 13th century, there is no further information on Jews in the town.

BIBLIOGRAPHY: Neubauer, Géogr, 299–300; Domaszewski, in: ARW, 11 (1908), 223–42; R. Dussaud, Topographie historique de la Syrie … (1927), index; Al-Balādhurī, *Futūḥ al-Buldān* (Cairo, 1932), 143; M.N. Adler, *The Itinerary of Benjamin of Tudela* (1907), 31. **ADD. BIBLIOGRAPHY:** "Ḥimṣ," in: EIS², 3, 397–402 (incl. bibl.)

[Lea Roth / Aryeh Shmuelevitz]

EMIN PASHA (**Eduard Schnitzer**; 1840–1892), Austrian traveler and explorer. Born of Jewish parents in Silesia, he was baptized as a child. He served as a quarantine doctor in Albania, and from 1870–74 as private physician to the governor of Albania. He adopted a Turkish name, Emin Effendi, and entered the services of General Gordon, who was then governor of the Equatorial Province of Egypt. When Gordon was made governor general of the Sudan in 1878, he appointed Emin to succeed him. They were both determined to stamp out the slave trade, and Emin traveled the length and breadth of his province continuously on the watch. When the Mahdi revolution broke out in 1881, Emin Pasha (as he now called himself) held his province although he was completely surrounded and isolated. The Germans and the British made various plans to relieve him but the British explorer H.M. Stanley was the first to reach him and with great difficulty persuaded him to leave the province. In 1880 Emin entered the service of the Germans and led an expedition along the coast of Lake Victoria to Lake Albert. The aim was to acquire certain lands for the German government but while he was traveling, the Anglo-German agreement was signed excluding these territories. He was ordered to return but quarreled with the Germans and refused. Disease now broke out among the men of his expedition and Emin went into the Congo, sending the able members to the coast while he stayed inland with the stricken. In 1892 Emin was murdered by slave traders against whom he had never stopped fighting. Emin was a good governor, a great linguist, and his contributions to the ornithology, ethnography, and meteorology of Central Africa were important. He published a number of treatises and diaries. Emin Pasha Gulf, the Southern Bay of Lake Victoria, was named after him.

BIBLIOGRAPHY: F. Stuhlmann, *Mit Emin Pascha ins Herz von Afrika* (1894), contains bibliography p. 59–60; G. Schweinfurt et al. (eds.), *Emin Pasha in Central Africa* (1888); B. Schweitzer, *Emin Pasha, his Life and Work* (1898); A.F.A. Symons, *Emin, Governor of Equatoria* (1950). **ADD. BIBLIOGRAPHY:** C. Edel and J.P. Sicre, *Vers les montagnes de la lune – Sur les traces d'Emin Pasha* (1993); I.R. Smith, *The Emin Pasha Relief Expedition 1886–1890* (1972); S. White, *The Lost Empire on the Nile – H.M. Stanley, Emin Pasha and the Imperialists* (1969).

EMIOT, ISRAEL (pseudonym of **I. Goldwasser**; 1909–1978), Yiddish poet. Influenced by the Warsaw Jewish Writers' Club, Emiot moved in the years 1932–36 from ḥasidic to worldly themes and published several collections containing ballads on Jewish history, pastoral lyrics, and innovative triolets that reflect the somber interwar mood (*Mit Zikh Aleyn*, "Alone with Self"; *Tropen in Yam*, "Drops in the Ocean"; *Bay Zayt*, "Beside Me"; *Iber Makhitses*, "Over Partitions"). In 1939 he fled to Russia, where *Lider* ("Songs," 1940) contained lamentations about family, homeland, and war. While he was a correspondent in Birobidzhan (1944–8), he published *Oyfgang* ("Rising," 1947), with Sovietized content. When the Jewish *Anti-Fascist Committee was liquidated (1948), he was arrested and imprisoned for seven years in Siberia. Repatriated to Poland, he published *Benkshaft* ("Yearning," 1957), before immigrating to the

U.S. (1958), where he republished and augmented his previous work during the years 1960–69: *In Nign Ayngehert* ("In Melody Absorbed"), *Fardekte Spiglen* ("Covered Mirrors"), *In Mitele Yorn* ("In Middle Years"), *Eyder Du Leshst Mikh Oys* ("Before You Extinguish Me"), and *Tsulib Di Tsen Umshuldike* ("For the Sake of Ten Innocents"). His prose memoir *Der Birobidzhaner Inyen* ("The Birobidzhan Affair," 1960) provides a dispassionate account of his Siberian experience, retained in the author's 1981 translation, while his verse translation, *Siberia* (1991), reveals a more anguished personal account. Emiot edited the trilingual journal *Roots*. His work after 1958 includes sonnets, addresses to God, free verse, lyrics of alienation and love, and reflections on the U.S. in prose and poetry. He expanded his interest in musical themes and modernist poetry, but maintained his use of traditional Jewish imagery.

BIBLIOGRAPHY: LNYL, 6 (1965), 601–6; J. Glatsteyn, *Mit Mayne Fartog-Bikher* (1963), 523–35.

[Leah Zazulyer (2nd ed.)]

EMMA LAZARUS FEDERATION OF JEWISH WOMEN'S CLUBS, U.S. progressive women's group, founded in 1944 by the Women's Division of the Jewish People's Fraternal Order (JPFO) of the International Workers Order (IWO). Formed to combat antisemitism and racism and to nurture positive Jewish identification through a broad program of Jewish education, the Emma Lazarus Division attracted a membership of left-wing, largely Yiddish-speaking women of the immigrant generation. One founder was labor leader, Clara Lemlich *Shavelson.

In 1951, when New York State's attorney general initiated proceedings against the IWO as a subversive institution, the Women's Division reorganized as the Emma Lazarus Federation of Jewish Women's Clubs. Despite revelations about Stalinist terrors and antisemitism, ELF Executive Director June Croll Gordon and her successor, Rose Reynes, called for coexistence with the U.S.S.R. ELF's public disregard of Soviet antisemitism remained a conspicuous blind spot.

At home, the ELF commissioned writer Eve Merriam to write a biography of poet and essayist Emma *Lazarus, and in 1954 published Yuri Suhl's biography of Ernestine *Rose, who was seen to combine Jewish patriotism with broad humanism. The Federation wrote study outlines of other Jewish women, including Rebecca *Gratz, Lillian *Wald, Sophie Loeb, and Penina *Moise. The ELF also developed curricula on working women, dissident women (from Anne Hutchinson to Ethel Rosenberg), and black women, and joined in a statement of principle with the Sojourners for Truth and Justice, an African-American women's group. In the 1950s and 1960s, it sent food and clothing to the South and joined boycotts and sit-ins. In 1963, the ELF initiated a petition campaign for the U.S. to ratify the Genocide Convention, adopted by the UN General Assembly in 1948; it considered this campaign its most important political project.

With chapters in Brooklyn, the Bronx, Boston, Los Angeles, San Francisco, Chicago, Philadelphia, Detroit, Miami, Rochester, Newark, Jersey City, Lakewood, and Toms River, New Jersey, the ELF maintained its educational and political activism for almost 40 years, attracting approximately 4,000–5,000 members in 100 clubs at its peak. Affected by the aging of the membership, the transformation of women's work, and the women's movement, ELF disbanded in 1989, though some individual clubs remained.

BIBLIOGRAPHY: J. Antler, "Between Culture and Politics: The Emma Lazarus Federation of Jewish Women's Clubs and the Promulgation of Women's History, 1944–1989," in: A. Kessler-Harris and K.K. Sklar (eds.), *U.S. History as Women's History* (1995); idem, "Emma Lazarus Federation," in: P.E. Hyman and D.D. Moore (eds.), *Jewish Women in America*, vol. 1 (1997), 375–77.

[Joyce Antler (2nd ed.)]

EMMANUEL, ISAAC SAMUEL (1899–1972), Greek-born rabbi and historian. Emmanuel was born in Salonika, the son of Samuel Emmanuel, a rabbi. He studied at the rabbinical seminary there and was ordained at the Jewish Theological Seminary of Breslau. Thereafter he held pulpits in Curaçao, Panama, Rio de Janeiro, and Cincinnati. His works include *Histoire de l'industrie des israelites de Salonique* (1935); *Gedolei Saloniki le-Dorotam* (1936), 500 epitaphs of the Jewish cemetery of Salonika with biographical notes; *Precious Stones of the Jews of Curaçao* (1957); *Maẓẓevot Saloniki* (2 vols., 1963–68); and with his wife Suzanne A. Emmanuel (1912–1969), *History of the Jews of The Netherlands Antilles* (2 vols., 1970).

EMMAUS, ancient town in the Judean Shephelah, 20 mi. (33 km.) N.W. of Jerusalem. It is first mentioned as the site of the camp of the Seleucid army under Georgias, which Judah Maccabee routed in 166 B.C.E. (I Macc. 3:40). Six years later it was fortified by Bacchides (Jos., Ant., 13:15; I Macc. 9:50). In 43 B.C.E. the Roman general Cassius sold its inhabitants into slavery for failure to pay taxes (Jos., Ant., 14:275; Wars, 1:222).

When Zealot activity was intensified in the area immediately after the death of Herod in 4 B.C.E., Varus burnt down the city in reprisal (Jos., Wars, 17:29). During the Jewish War, Vespasian established a fortified camp at Emmaus (in 68 C.E.) and stationed the Fifth Macedonian Legion there (*ibid.*, 4:444–5); during the Bar Kokhba War (132–135 C.E.), Roman detachments were posted there to encircle the rebels (Lam. R. 1:16, no. 45). In talmudic sources the city was considered the boundary between the Central Mountain Range and the Shephelah (TJ, Shev. 9:2, 38d). Described as a place of "fair waters and healthy climate" (ARN[1] 14, 59), it apparently possessed hot springs and public baths, which is possibly the reason for its Hebrew name Hammat (*ḥam*, "hot"; Song Zuta, 6:9). Eleazar b. Arak settled in Emmaus after the death of his teacher Johanan b. Zakkai, and there, far removed from his colleagues, he is said to have forgotten his learning (Eccl. R. 7:7, no. 2; Shab. 147b). The city was also the home of *Neḥunya b. ha-Kanah (Mid. Tan. to 26:13). Archaeological remains indicate that a Samaritan community had lived there. According to

Christian tradition, Jesus appeared before his disciples at Emmaus after his crucifixion and resurrection (Luke 24:13–16). In the third century, the Christian writer Julius Africanus lived there. In 221 he headed a deputation that induced the emperor Elagabalus to confer on Emmaus the status of a city enjoying Roman rights, and it was henceforth called Nicopolis. There was a Christian community there from very early times and Jews continued to live in the city until the Arab conquest in 639 (J. Moschos, in: *Patrologia graeca*, ed. by Migne, vol. 87, pt. 3 (1863), 3032). A plague broke out in the city after the Arabs took it (the "Plague of Emmaus") and it decimated the conquerors. After the founding of Ramleh, the town (see *Latrun) declined in importance. It became the Arab village 'Imwās on the Jerusalem–Tel Aviv highway which before 1948 had a population of 1,420 Muslims and was destroyed during the Six-Day War (1967). Excavations conducted there in 1924–25 by the Ecole biblique et archéologique française uncovered remains of a Roman villa and a Christian basilica that was destroyed during the Samaritan revolt in the sixth century and later rebuilt. The Crusaders also erected a small church there. Today the excavations are part of Ayalon-Canada park.

BIBLIOGRAPHY: L.H. Vincent and F.M. Abel, *Emmaüs* (Fr., 1932); Neubauer, Géogr, 100–2.

[Michael Avi-Yonah]

EMŐD, TAMAS (Ernő Fleischer; 1888–1938), Hungarian poet. Emőd was born at Berekböszörmény and graduated in law at Oradea (then Nagyvárad) Law Faculty. He worked as a journalist but mainly devoted himself to literature. Emőd's first poems, influenced by the great Hungarian poet E. Ady, appeared in the avant-garde anthology *Holnap* ("Tomorrow"). The poems he wrote during World War I were particularly well-known. Emőd chose Jewish subjects for a number of his works, including *Temetés* ("Funeral"), *Falusi zsidó* ("The Village Jew"), and *Vox Humana*. Of his plays, the most important are *A vándor katona* ("The Wandering Soldier"), written in collaboration with F. Karinthy, and *Ferenc Jóska ládájából* ("From Ferenc Jóska's Box"). Emőd was one of the originators of the *chanson*, which was at one time a feature of Hungarian literary cabarets.

BIBLIOGRAPHY: *Magyar Irodalmi Lexikon*, 1 (1963), 290.

[Baruch Yaron]

EMOTIONS. Jewish tradition has shown a positive interest in human emotions, and they are portrayed and discussed in the Bible, Talmud, Jewish philosophy, and mysticism.

Bible

Biblical figures are frequently emotional, and in this lies much of their human appeal and credibility. Genesis introduces feelings of *Love, *Joy, Fear, and their opposites (in, e.g., 3:6; 4:5; 29:18; and 37:3) that are later found in such figures as Saul and David, the psalmist, and the lovers of the Song of Songs. Similarly, in His initial appearances God is portrayed as a deity who acts out of deep feelings of compassion and anger (Gen. 4:10; 15; 6:5; 8:21; 18:17; 29:31), emotions which are revealed at Sinai as essential to His nature (Ex. 20:5, 6; 34:6). The Israelites encountered God's fearsome, possessive love, frequently expressed in jealous wrath and moral indignation, in their desert wanderings, and the prophets tended to identify with these same emotions (see Ex. 19:3; 32:9; Num. 14:11; 17:8; Isa. 65:3; Jer. 7:19; Ezek. 16:36). However, the Torah advocates a different set of relationships and emotions as an ideal, one in which God loves His people and wishes them to respond in love as well as fear (Deut. 6:5; 10:12, 15), and in which man is exhorted to rid himself of hatred and lust, relate to his fellow man in love and kindness, and joyfully observe God's commandments (Ex. 20:14; Lev. 14:17, 18; Deut. 16:11). Then God will bless men both materially and spiritually, meaning with emotional peace and happiness (Num. 6:24–26; Isa., 65:17ff.).

Talmud

Prophetic and rabbinic Judaism also appeal, in particular, to such emotions, as in Micah's terse summary of the religious ethic (6:8: "to do justice, to love kindness (*ḥesed*), and to walk humbly with your God"; and in Hillel's paraphrase of Lev. 19:18: "what is hateful to you, do not do to your fellow man" (Shab. 31a)). Anger, jealousy, lust, and pride are all condemned by the rabbis (see, e.g., Avot 2:11; 4:21); the Talmud even blames the destruction of the Second Temple on the Jews for the sin of unjustified hatred, *Sinat ḥinnam* (Yoma 9b). The ideal emotional type, according to the rabbis, is one who controls his passions and is good-hearted, humble, and peace loving (Avot 1:12; 2:9; 4:1; 5:11). Such a man finds emotional gratification in the study and observance of the law, enjoying a happiness (*simḥah shel mitzvah*) that, while itself a reward, is an intimation of future bliss as well. Prayer (as well as devotional, i.e., *musar*, literature, and most poetry), study, and ritual increasingly became outlets for the Jewish psyche in exile, and deeply felt personal and national emotions were formalized in such holidays as Simḥat Torah and such commemorations as the Ninth of Av.

Medieval Jewish Philosophy

Medieval Jewish philosophy resumed the attempt of Hellenistic Jewish thought to subjugate the emotions to the intellect, and attempted, even more than rabbinic exegesis did, to rationalize away the biblical depiction of God's emotions (see *Allegorical Interpretation and *God, Attributes of). Using Arabic mediated Greek models, Jewish philosophers analyzed emotions in terms of both the humors and organs of the body and the faculties, or parts, of the soul. Whatever the variation in details (for which see *Soul), however, the philosophers generally agreed with Aristotle that moderation should be observed in expressing emotion (see, e.g., Solomon ibn Gabirol, *The Improvement of the Moral Qualities* (1901), pt. 4, 84–86; and *The Eight Chapters of Maimonides on Ethics* (1966), 54ff.). Yet for all its rational emphasis, like that of its Arabic and late Greek predecessors, Jewish philosophy views the dispassionate, analytical search for Truth as a religious quest, beginning in anxious doubt and culminating in feelings of certitude and the bliss of divine love (Saadiah Gaon, *The Book of Beliefs and Opinions*, trans. by S. Rosenblatt (1948), introduction, 6ff.; Maimonides, *The Guide of the Perplexed*, trans. by S. Pines (1963), introduction, 5ff., 51, 618ff.).

Mysticism and Hasidism

Jewish mysticism seeks to lead man from a state of psychic alienation to one of ecstatic intimacy with God. Mostly, however, it attempts to reach this emotional goal through an intellectual process and a discipline parallel to that of philosophy. It is mainly *Ḥasidism, with its suggestion of antinomianism and its anti-intellectual direction, that emphasizes the emotions – particularly joy, trust, and gratitude – as a primary means to the religious life.

BIBLIOGRAPHY: S. Schechter, *Some Aspects of Rabbinic Theology* (1909), 148–69; S. Belkin, *In his Image* (1960), 185–93.

[Alfred L. Ivry]

°**EMPEDOCLES** (fifth century B.C.E.), Greek poet, prophet, and natural philosopher who set forth the doctrine of the four elements, which dominated Arabic, Hebrew, and Latin thought in the Middle Ages. Empedocles is known in medieval Jewish circles through stray references to him and his work, mainly found in the works of Aristotle, which were translated into Arabic and then into Hebrew. The form of his name in the Hebrew translations from the Arabic follows the Arabic form, that is, Abnduqlīs, Abīduqlīs, and others. In translations from the Latin, the Latin form is found. Empedocles' name was taken over by late Greek neoplatonic circles and affixed to treatises later translated into Arabic, which became known to medieval Jewish thinkers. The main representative of this literature is the *Book of the Five Substances*. The Arabic version is lost but it is partially preserved in a Hebrew translation, published by D. Kaufmann as an appendix to his *Studien ueber Salomon ibn Gabirol* (1899).

Among medieval Jewish philosophers, Shem Tov ibn Falaquera mentions that Solomon ibn Gabirol's *Source of Life* was influenced by the *Book of the Five Substances* (S. Munk, Mélanges, 1). Joseph ibn Zaddik refers to the true conception of the will as a secret whose true meaning may be derived from the *Book of Empedocles* or works by other philosophers written on these subjects. Judah Halevi twice refers to Empedocles as the head of a philosophic school, in his *Kuzari* (4:25 and 5:14). Maimonides, in his famous letter to Samuel ibn Tibbon, states that one should not waste one's time studying the works of Empedocles, which form a part of ancient (pre-Aristotelian) philosophy (A. Marx, in: JQR, 25 (1935), 380).

BIBLIOGRAPHY: Stern, in: EI[2], s.v. *Anbadukīs;* Steinschneider, Uebersetzungen, index; D. Kaufmann, *Geschichte der Attributenlehre* (repr. 1967), index; A. Altmann and S.M. Stern, *Isaac Israeli, A Neoplatonic Philosopher…* (1958), index.

[Lawrence V. Berman]

°**EMPEREUR, CONSTANTIJN L'** (1591–1648), Dutch Calvinist theologian and Christian Hebraist. L'Empereur pursued an academic career as a theologian. Only following his appointment to the professorship of Hebrew at the University of Leiden (1627) did he start to study rabbinical literature seriously. Within six years he published several (fairly competent) editions of rabbinical works, most of them with a parallel Latin translation and annotations, meant to facilitate the study and use of Jewish literature. He paid *Menasseh ben Israel and Isaac *Aboab da Fonseca to assist him in his studies. His books did not sell well. His emphasis on rabbinical literature in his lectures was not well received by the students and professors of the theological faculty, and he was ordered to focus on biblical Hebrew. In 1633 he was passed over in a fiercely contested appointment to a professorship in the faculty of theology. To compensate him, the board of the university raised his salary, and justified this unusual generosity by appointing him to a spurious professorship of Jewish controversies, which did not entail any duties. In 1637 he published an edition, translation, and commentary on the tractate *Bava Kamma*, a highly original (although implicitly antisemitic) work in which he compared its rulings with the corresponding legislations of Roman Law. In 1647 he was, finally, appointed to a professorship in the faculty of theology.

BIBLIOGRAPHY: P. van Rooden, *Theology, Biblical Scholarship and Rabbinical Studies in the Seventeenth Century* (1989).

[Peter van Rooden (2nd ed.)]

EMPEROR WORSHIP, the Roman cult established during the reign of Augustus, first in the provinces but not in Italy, and practiced throughout the Roman Empire. It is the direct continuation of the Hellenistic worship of the ruler. Emperor worship first appeared in Palestine during the reign of *Herod the Great. Although it was completely unacceptable to the Jewish population, Herod could nevertheless not afford to lag behind other vassal princes in establishing the cult. Thus although a temple was not erected in Jerusalem to honor the emperor, these rites were adopted in the cities of Sebaste and Caesarea, both predominantly non-Jewish. The Jewish population, though not the Christian, was everywhere exempted from the loyal duty of emperor worship and only one attempt was made to compel the Jewish nation to accept emperor worship, when *Caligula issued a decree to erect a statue of himself in the sanctuary at Jerusalem (Jos., Ant., 18:262; Jos., Wars, 2:184; Philo, *De Legatione ad Gaium*, 188, 207–8; Tacitus, *Historiae*, 5:9). The decree was never carried out, however, due to the death of Caligula in January 41 C.E.

Following the destruction of the Second Temple there was a tendency among the rabbis to mitigate various laws concerning idolatry, which was no longer considered a threat to the Jewish community. Nevertheless these same rabbis continued to reject any compliance with the imperial cult.

BIBLIOGRAPHY: C.R. Taylor, *The Divinity of the Roman Emperor* (1931); CAH, 10 (1934), 481–9 (bibliography: 951f.); Urbach, in: *Eretz Israel*, 5 (1958), 189–205 (English summary: 94f.); A. Schalit, *Koenig Herodes* (1969), 421–3.

[Isaiah Gafni]

EMRĀNI (**Imrāni**; probably a pen name; 1454–after 1536), Judeo-Persian poet. Emrāni was born in Isfahan and died in Kashan. He is considered the second greatest Judeo-Persian poet after *Shāhin. Emrāni produced the following Judeo-Persian works, the majority of which were discovered after 1960.

1. *Fath-Nāmeh* ("Book of Victory") is an epic poetic paraphrase of the biblical books of Joshua, I and II Samuel, part of I Kings, and the Book of Ruth. This is Emrāni's longest composition. It was composed in 1474 and consists of about 10,000 couplets. In some *Fath-Nāmeh* mss. one may find other poetic compositions such as *Shofetim-Nāmeh* and *Pilegesh al ha-Giva* with interpolations which do not belong to Emrāni.

2. *Ganj-Nāmeh* ("Book of Treasure") is a poetic paraphrase of *Pirkei Avot*. Composed in 1536, this is apparently Emrāni's last important work and consists of about 5,000 couplets.

3. The following are relatively short poems by Emrāni found in collections of mss: (a) *Vājebāt-e Sizdahgāneh....* a poetic paraphrase of Maimonides' Thirteen Principles; (b) *Hanukkah-Nāmeh* ("Book of Hanukkah") narrates the historical events of Hanukkah; (c) *Entekhāb-e Nakhlestān* ("Choice of the Palm Grove") is a didactic poetic work; (d) *Sāqi-Nāmeh* ("Book of the Cupbearer") is a mystical-lyrical poem; (e) *Qesse-ye Haft Barādarān* ("Story of the Seven Brothers"), written in prose and verse, narrates the story of Hannah and her seven sons who were murdered because they refused to worship the Greek idols; (f) *Asarah harugei ha-malkhut* ("The Ten Martyrs of the Kingdom"), in prose and verse, relates the torture and death suffered by ten Jewish sages of Mishnaic times; (g) a few other short poems mostly of didactic nature; (h) a few short prose works such as the story of the *Akedah (Binding of Isaac) and *tafsir* of *Pirkei Avot*.

Some selections of Emrāni's works have been published in Persian transliteration (Netzer, 1973). The manuscripts of Emrāni's works are kept in the libraries of the Hebrew University of Jerusalem, the Ben-Zvi Institute, JTS in New York, HUC in Cincinnati, and the British Library in London.

BIBLIOGRAPHY: A. Netzer, *Montakhab-e ashʿār-e farsi az āsār-e yahudiyān-e Irān* (Teheran, 1973); idem, *Oẓar Kitvei Yad shel Yehudei Paras be-Makhon Ben-Zvi* (1985); D. Yeroushalmi, *The Judeo-Persian Poet ʿEmrāni and His Book of Treasure* (1995).

[Amnon Netzer (2nd ed.)]

EMSHEIMER, ERNST (1904–1989), Swedish musicologist of German birth. Born in Frankfurt on the Main, Germany, Emsheimer studied piano and music theory, and thereafter musicology, at the universities of Vienna and Freiburg, where he received his doctorate in 1927. After concluding his studies he went to Soviet Russia, where he began his research on folk and non-European musical traditions. He was research assistant at the Russian Academy of Sciences in Leningrad from 1932 until 1937, and accompanied a music research expedition in northern Caucasia in 1936. In 1937 he joined a scientific expedition to the northwestern provinces of China. In 1937 Emsheimer immigrated to Sweden, where he intensified the ethnomusicological tradition. From 1949 until his retirement in 1973 he was the curator of the music history museum in Stockholm. After War World II he investigated Georgian folk polyphony. In 1962, he created jointly with Erik Stockmann the first study group on European instruments under the auspices of the International Folk Music Council and founded the famous series of studies dedicated to popular European and non-European instruments under the title *Studia Instrumentorum Musicae Popularis*, of which the first volume appeared in 1969. His writings include *Musikethnographische Bibliographie der nichtslavischen Voelker in Russland* (1943); *Preliminary Remarks on Mongolian Music and Instruments* (1943); *Music of Eastern Mongolia* (1943); and *Lappischer Kultgesang* (1950).

BIBLIOGRAPHY: MGG², S.V; NG², S.V.

[Amnon Shiloah (2nd ed.)]

EMUNAH, World Religious Zionist Women's Organization, the third largest women's movement in Israel. Founded in Jerusalem in 1925, Emunah was incorporated as a worldwide movement in 1977. World Emunah combines the Israel National Religious Women's Movement and its sister organizations in 28 countries with a membership of over 150,000. This voluntary organization is devoted to educational and social service programs. Emunah is unique in that it is rooted in Jewish tradition and emphasizes the spiritual and moral heritage of the Jewish people within a Zionist framework. In Israel, Emunah has around 100,000 members.

The Israeli programs include a network of 120 day care centers, six residential homes for deprived children, six high schools, an arts and technology college for girls, and Emunah's teachers college. Its social-welfare projects in Israel range from literacy programs to group dynamics and family counseling. The organization runs an emergency center for abused children. In Israel, Emunah volunteers' activities in the absorption of new immigrants have been noted with distinction by the awarding to them of municipal and national awards. In the field of women's rights, Emunah is active in promoting legislation and representing women in such bodies as the rabbinical courts. The organization also runs a club for business and career women.

In addition to supporting the Israeli projects, the member organizations worldwide conduct adult education outreach programs within their own countries to strengthen their commitment to Jewish values and Jewish living. Emunah worldwide is actively involved in community programs relating to religious education, support for Israel, and pressing contemporary issues affecting world Jewry. Emunah is represented on major Zionist and Jewish bodies in its member countries as well as in international forums.

WEBSITE: www.emunah.org.il.

ENCYCLOPEDIAS.

Encyclopedias of General Content in Hebrew and Yiddish Outside of Israel

The first Hebrew encyclopedias were translations or adaptations of Arabic works, which were intended as systematic presentations of the sciences in the medieval Aristotelian scheme, not usually arranged in alphabetical order. The first of these was *Yesodei ha-Tevunah u-Migdal ha-Emunah* by *Abraham b. Ḥiyya ha-Nasi of Barcelona (in the early 12th century), which included sections on mathematics, geometry, astronomy, optics, and music. Only the preface and the beginning of this work have been preserved in manuscript. In 1247 Judah b. Solomon ibn Matka, a native of Toledo, Spain, wrote an Arabic work that he later translated into Hebrew as *Midrash ha-Ḥokhmah.* The first part deals with logic, physics, and metaphysics, in addition to commentaries on passages in Genesis, Psalms, and Proverbs; the second, with mathematics, in addition to a kabbalistic study of the letters of the Hebrew alphabet; there is also an enumeration of Bible passages that are to be interpreted philosophically. Again, only fragments of this encyclopedia have been preserved.

Shem Tov b. Joseph *Falaquera, another Spanish scholar of the 13th century, wrote *De'ot ha-Filosofim*, dealing with physics and metaphysics, based mainly on Averroes. Although the two extant manuscripts of this work ascribe its authorship to Samuel ibn *Tibbon, Zunz and Steinschneider identify Falaquera as its author. *Gershon b. Solomon of Arles presents a vivid picture of the scientific works available in Hebrew in the late 13th century in his *Sha'ar ha-Shamayim.* In the introduction he states that he used only Hebrew sources or works in Hebrew translation; thus, it is known that at this time some of the works of the major writers of classic antiquity had become part of the Jewish cultural background. His book is divided into three parts: physics, subdivided into a discussion of the four elements, minerals, plants, and animals; astronomy, according to Almagest (see *Ptolemy), *Avicenna, *Averroes, *Aristotle, and others; and theology or metaphysics, according to Averroes and Maimonides. This work is the oldest medieval encyclopedia to be printed, although in abridged form, first in Venice in 1547 and several times in the 19th century, as a part of the program of the East European Haskalah to broaden the horizon of the masses. Based in part on *Sha'ar ha-Shamayim* is the *Shevilei Emunah* by the 14th-century Spanish scholar Meir ben Isaac *Aldabi, whose intent was to combine natural sciences and Jewish religious tradition (Riva di Trento, 1518). Between the 15th and 18th centuries no major encyclopedia was written by Jews, as their interest in the general sciences declined. In 1530–32 the Sephardi physician Solomon b. Jacob *Almoli published a plan for such a work, *Me'assef le-Khol ha-Maḥanot*, in Constantinople. Another small work was *Kelal Kaẓer mi-Kol ha-Rashum bi-Khetav* by Judah ibn Bulat, another exile from Spain in Constantinople, who attempted to organize the sciences systematically (Constantinople, 1531–32; reprint Jerusalem, 1936).

Jacob b. Isaac *Zahalon, a physician in Ferrara, Italy, had prepared a large work to be called "*Oẓar ha-Hokhmot,*" but only the third part, devoted to medicine, appeared, *Oẓar ha-Hayyim* (Venice, 1683). In the 17th century physicians were the only Jews in Central and Eastern Europe who had an opportunity for secular education. Thus, another representative of that profession, Tobias *Cohn (Tobias b. Moses Narol of Metz), compiled an encyclopedic work, *Ma'ase Toviyyah* (Venice, 1707), covering metaphysics, physics, astronomy, geography, medicine, and pharmacology.

With the rise of the Haskalah, an interest in publishing a general encyclopedia in Hebrew developed. In particular David *Franco-Mendes, a Jewish community leader and Hebrew poet in Holland, formulated such a suggestion in *Ha-Me'assef* (1785), but except for a prospectus, *Ahavat David*, nothing came of it. A pupil of the Gaon of Vilna, Phinehas Elijah b. Meir Horowitz, tried to present the general sciences from the point of view of Jewish tradition in his *Sefer ha-Berit* (Bruenn, 1797). This work became quite popular, as is evidenced by the publication of several editions in the 19th century. In 1856 Julius *Barasch, a Romanian physician, published the philosophical part of a general encyclopedia under the title *Oẓar ha-Ḥokhmah.* The first alphabetically arranged general encyclopedia in Hebrew was attempted by Isaac Goldmann in Warsaw in 1888; it was called *Ha-Eshkol*, but only six parts came out, and even the first letter of the Hebrew alphabet was not completed.

Joseph *Lurie and Ḥayyim Dov *Horowitz began the first general encyclopedia in Yiddish, *Di Algemeyne Yidishe Entsiklopedye*, in St. Petersburg, Russia, in 1904, but only three parts were published before the venture failed. In 1917 the well-known Yiddish writer and journalist Hillel *Zeitlin began *Di Ershte Algemeyne un Yudishe Hand-Entsiklopedye* with similar abortive results. David Goldblatt's *Algemeyne Ilustrirte Entsiklopedye* (2 vols., New York, 1920–23) was more successful, but it did not get beyond *alef* either (it should be remembered that an initial *alef* for transliterated words is equivalent in the Latin alphabet to *a*, *e*, *i*, *o*, and *u*).

The most ambitious attempt in Yiddish encyclopedias was *Algemeyne Entsiklopedye*, published by the Dubnow Fund from 1931, first in Paris and then in New York. After the first five volumes, devoted to general subjects, seven more on Jews and Judaism, arranged according to topic, were published by 1966.

Encyclopedias of Jewish Content Only

The first large Jewish encyclopedia in alphabetical arrangement was *Paḥad Yiẓḥak* (13 vols., 1750–1888) by Isaac ben Samuel *Lampronti, a physician in Ferrara, who worked on this reference book covering Talmud, rabbinics, and responsa throughout his life, part of it being published posthumously. It was the first such enterprise to be completed to the last letter of the alphabet. In each entry the history of the topic is traced through Mishnah, Talmud, and the responsa up to Lampronti's day.

With the development of the study of Judaism and Jewish history on a scientific basis in the 19th century, the Jews sought to emulate others in promoting encyclopedias devoted to their interests alone. The Jewish historian Isaac Marcus *Jost suggested such a project in his journal *Israelitische Annalen* in 1840. In 1844 the prestigious scholars Moritz Steinschneider and David Cassel published *Plan der Real-Enzyklopaedie des Judenthums, zunaechstfuer die Mitarbeiter.* Some of the articles intended for this work found their way into the general encyclopedia edited by Ersch and Gruber, *Allgemeine Enzyklopaedie der Wissenschaften und Kuenste*, into other journals, or into separate monographs. Another talmudic dictionary was begun by the Prague chief rabbi, Solomon Judah Leib *Rapoport, under the title *Erekh Millin* (Prague, 1852), but it did not go beyond the letter *alef.*

The first Jewish encyclopedia in German was the *Real-Encyclopaedie fuer Bibel und Talmud* by Jacob *Hamburger, chief rabbi of the German principality of Mecklenburg-Strelitz. It treated biblical and talmudic subjects in two separate volumes with a six-part supplement and appeared in three editions, the latest between 1896 and 1901. In spite of many defects, it was considered an achievement for its time, since it was helpful in tracing Jewish religious ideas in the Bible and Talmud.

Aḥad Ha-Am's suggestion to publish a Jewish encyclopedia in Hebrew did not gain much support. He had wanted to present the salient areas of Judaism and Jewish history and literature in a systematic, rather than an alphabetical scheme. There were objections that Hebrew literature was in its beginnings and could not sustain such an ambitious venture. Others believed that a general encyclopedia in Hebrew was needed more urgently than one devoted to Jewish subjects only. On Aḥad Ha-Am's suggestion, a sample of the *Oẓar ha-Yahadut* was published in Warsaw in 1906, containing four articles by four young scholars who later made their mark in Jewish learning, David *Neumark, Hirsch (Ẓevi) Perez *Chajes, Ismar *Elbogen, and Joseph *Klausner.

Despite the great accomplishments in Jewish studies in Europe during the 19th century, it was not granted to European Jewry to publish the first synthesis of its rich harvest. Instead, it was the American Jewish community, which at the turn of the century consisted of a population less than half its present size, a large proportion of whom were new immigrants, that published this basic work, *The Jewish Encyclopedia* (12 vols., 1901–06). Under the editorship of Isidore *Singer and with the participation of hundreds of scholars in the United States and abroad, the attempt was made to bring all Jewish knowledge within the scope of this work. Naturally it, too, had weaknesses, as in its treatment of modern Hebrew literature and the history of East European Jewry, but many of its entries (e.g., those by Louis Ginzberg) have remained unsurpassed statements. Shortly thereafter, Judah David *Eisenstein prepared a ten-volume encyclopedia in Hebrew, *Oẓar Yisrael* (New York, 1906–13). Unlike the *Jewish Encyclopedia*, which took account both of the traditional and the modernist viewpoints, its approach was more traditional, but it was considered inadequate in many respects.

Also influenced by the *Jewish Encyclopedia* was the Russian *Yevreyskaya Entsiklopediya* (16 vols., St. Petersburg, 1906–13) under the editorship of such outstanding scholars as Judah Leib *Katzenelson (Buki ben Yogli), Simon *Dubnow, David *Guenzburg, and Albert (Abraham) *Harkavy. Yet, while omitting some of the material about Jewish life in America that figured so prominently in the *Jewish Encyclopedia*, it concentrated on Eastern Europe and gave full scope to modern Hebrew literature. Its ideology was that of the *Galut* ("Diaspora") nationalism advocated by Dubnow, but the Zionist point of view was also presented. Thus, it was in a way a complement to the *Jewish Encyclopedia.*

Under the leadership of George *Herlitz and Bruno Kirschner, the *Juedisches Lexikon* (Berlin, 1927–30), a five-volume work in German, was published. Because of its size it had to be more limited in scope than the *Jewish Encyclopedia* and concentrated more on contemporary Jewish life than had the other major Jewish encyclopedias published earlier in the century. A more ambitious project was the *Encyclopaedia Judaica* (10 vols., Berlin, 1928–34) in German under the editorship of Jacob *Klatzkin, Nahum *Goldmann, and Ismar Elbogen. It was intended to present a new synthesis of Jewish knowledge some 20 years after the appearance of the *Jewish Encyclopedia* and to include all those areas neglected in the earlier pioneering work. However, because of the establishment of the Hitler regime in Germany, the plan could not be completed; only ten volumes appeared, through the article "Lyra." Of its Hebrew companion, *Eshkol, Enẓiklopedyah Yisre'elit* (Berlin, 1929–32), only two volumes were printed, not completing even the first letter. An oddity among encyclopedias with Jewish content published in Germany was the *Sigilla Veri* (4 vols., Erfurt, 1929–31), a work with antisemitic sponsorship in four volumes through the article "Polak."

The need for a more up-to-date and popular encyclopedia in English in the mid-20th century was met by a number of one-volume works, which are noted below in the bibliography, and by the *Universal Jewish Encyclopedia* in ten volumes (New York, 1939–43). Similar in purpose to the *Juedisches Lexikon* (whose English translation rights the editors Isaac *Landman and others had secured at the time of its publication), it concentrated on the more recent past and on the history of American Jewry.

The growth of the Latin American Jewish community is reflected in the *Enciclopedia Judaica Castellana* (10 vols., Mexico, 1948–51), based largely on the *Universal Jewish Encyclopedia* but containing original material for Latin America.

Encyclopedias in Israel

The first general encyclopedia in Palestine on a large scale was the *Enẓiklopedyah Kelalit* (6 vols., 1935–37). It was conceived and planned by Joseph Klausner. A work on a larger scale is the *Enẓiklopedyah Kelalit Yizre'el* (16 vols., 1950–61). Another popular work is the *Enẓiklopedyah Kelalit Massadah*

(6 vols., 1960–61) with a supplementary volume (1966). The most ambitious Jewish encyclopedia ever attempted is *Ha-Enẓiklopedyah ha-Ivrit* (*Encyclopaedia Hebraica*; (1949–1981); first supplementary volume, covering volumes 1–16, 1967; second supplementary volume, 1983), a general, Jewish, and Israel reference work.

The special needs of Israel require, in addition to general and Jewish encyclopedias, specialized ones devoted to such fields as the social sciences, agriculture, and education, as well as Bible and Talmud. The young State of Israel has already met the need to a considerable extent.

Jews and Judaism in General Encyclopedias

Until the 19th century the treatment of Jews and Judaism in encyclopedias as well as in all other reference works was determined by the Christian point of view. Primary attention was paid to the biblical period as a background to Christianity, but very little interest was shown in the period that followed.

Among the first general encyclopedias to depart from this pattern was the Ersch-Gruber Allgemeine *Enzyklopaedie der Wissenschaften und Kuenste* (1818–89), when it included Moritz *Steinschneider among its contributors. His article on Jewish literature in its volume in 1850 and published separately in English translation in 1857 is considered a classic.

Since that time post-biblical Jewish history and Judaism have generally received more comprehensive and fairer treatment. It is now customary to assign such topics to recognized Jewish scholars. Notable among such encyclopedias are Hastings' Encyclopedia *of Religion and Ethics* (1908–26), *Religion in Geschichte und Gegenwart* (1927–31², 1957–65³), *Encyclopedia of the Social Sciences* (1930–35; repr. 1948–49), and *New Catholic Encyclopedia* (1967).

Quite striking is the difference between the earlier and more recent editions of the *Encyclopaedia Britannica*. In its third edition of 1797 the detailed history of the Jews ended with the destruction of the Second Temple in the year 70. The laws of rabbinic Judaism that followed are dismissed as mere "absurdities" deserving no consideration. In a concluding paragraph the history of the following 16 centuries is summarized with persecutions and massacres duly noted, the more tolerant attitude of the present day emphasized, and mentioning the recent emancipation of the Jews in France in 1791.

In the ninth edition of 1881 the history is divided into two articles, "Israel," dealing with antiquity and the medieval period, until the emancipation, written by the German Protestant Bible scholar Julius *Wellhausen, who gave a fair presentation, also referring to Jewish scholars, such as Jost, Graetz, and Herzfeld, in his bibliography, and "Jews," the period beginning with Mendelssohn, written by Israel Davis, a Jewish lay leader in England. More recent editions have had contributions by Isidore *Epstein, Norman *Bentwich, Jacob R. *Marcus, and other well known Jewish scholars.

Jewish Encyclopedias

ENGLISH. Major works: *Jewish Encyclopedia*, 12 vols. (1901–06; 1925²; repr., 1963); *Universal Jewish Encyclopedia*, 10 vols. (1939–43); *Encyclopaedia Judaica* (1971, 2006²).

Other works: J. De Haas (ed.), *Encyclopedia of Jewish Knowledge* (1934); A.M. Hyamson and A.M. Silbermann (eds.), *Vallentine's Jewish Encyclopedia* (1938); *American Jewish Cyclopedia* (1943); D.D. Runes, *Concise Dictionary of Judaism* (1959); P. Birnbaum, *A Book of Jewish Concepts* (1964); S. Glustrom, *Language of Judaism* (1966); Z. Werblowsky and G. Wigoder, *Encyclopedia of the Jewish Religion* (1990²); J. Neusner, *Encyclopedia of Judaism*, 3 vols. with supplements (1999, 2003); G. Wigoder et al., *New Encyclopedia of Judaism* (2002²).

Special encyclopedias: *Interpreter's Dictionary of the Bible*, 4 vols. (1962); G. Wigoder, S. Paul, et al., *Illustrated Dictionary and Concordance of the Bible* (2005²); A. Negev and S. Gibson, *Archeological Encyclopedia of the Holy Land* (2001); S. Spector and G. Wigoder, *Encyclopedia of Jewish Life Before and During the Holocaust*, 3 vols. (2001); R. Rozett and S. Spector, *Encyclopedia of the Holocaust* (2000); *Yad Vashem Encyclopedia of the Righteous Among the Nations* (vols. 1–6, 2003–5), in progress; P. Hyman and D.D. Moore, *Jewish Women in America: An Historical Encyclopedia*, 2 vols. (1997); M.D. Sherman, *Orthodox Judaism in America: A Bibliographical Dictionary and Sourcebook* (1996); P.S. Nadell, *Conservative Judaism in America: A Biographical Dictionary and Sourcebook* (1988); K.M. Olitzky, L.J. Sussman, and M.H. Stern, *Reform Judaism in America: A Biographical Dictionary and Sourcebook* (1993); A. Steinberg, *Encyclopedia of Jewish Medical Ethics*, tr. F. Rosner (2003); R. Slater, *Great Jews in Sports* (2000²); R. Posner, *Junior Judaica* (1994²); G. Wigoder et al., *Student's Encyclopedia of Judaism* (2004).

DUTCH. J. Meijer, *Encyclopaedia Sefardica Neerlandica* (deals with the Sephardi community in Holland).

GERMAN. Major works: *Juedisches Lexikon*, 5 vols. (1927–30), *Encyclopaedia Judaica*, 10 vols. (1928–34), incomplete (*Aachen* to *Lyra* only).

Other works: E.B. Cohn, *Das juedische* ABC (1935); E. Bin Gorion, et al. (eds.), *Philo-Lexikon; Handbuch des juedischen Wissens* (1937⁴); *Philo-Atlas; Handbuch fuer die juedische Auswanderung* (1938); J.F. Oppenheimer (ed.), *Lexikon des Judentums* (1967; a revision and up-dating of the *Philo-Lexikon*).

Special encyclopedias: J.L. Hamburger, *Real-Encyclopaediefuer Bibel und Talmud*, 2 vols. (1896–1901³), Supplement 6 vols.

HEBREW. J.D. Eisenstein (ed.), *Oẓar Yisrael*, 10 vols. (1907–13); *Eshkol, Enẓiklopedyah Yisre'elit*, 2 vols. (1929–32), incomplete – *A-Antipas* only (Hebrew edition of *Encyclopaedia Judaica*); I. Press, *Ereẓ Yisrael, Enẓiklopedyah Topografit Historit*, 4 vols. (1951–55²); S.Z. Ariel, *Enẓiklopedyah Me'ir Nativ le-Halakhot, Minhagim, Darkhei Musar u-Ma'asim Tovim* (1960); J. Pevsner, *Enẓiklopedyah Yehudit* (1966); idem, *Enẓiklopedyah Yuda'ikah* (1961); C. Roth and G. Wigoder (eds.), *Enẓiklopedyah shelha-Yahadut*, 2 vols. (1969; revised Hebrew edition of *Standard*

Jewish Encyclopedia); Y.T. Lewinsky, *Enẓiklopedyah shel Havai u-Masoret ba-Yahadut*, 2 vols. (1970).

Bible: B. Natanson, *Ma'arekhet Sifrei Kodesh* (1870); A.H. Rosenberg, *Oẓar ha-Shemot Asher be-Khitvei ha-Kodesh*, 10 vols. (1898–1922); *Enẓiklopedyah Mikra'it*, 8 vols. (1950–82); P. Ne'eman, *Enẓiklopedyah le-Geografyah Mikra'it*, 4 vols. (1962–65); D. Kimḥi, *Enẓiklopedyah le-Ishim ba-Tanakh*, 2 vols. (1964?); M. Solieli and M. Berkooz (eds.), *Leksikon Mikra'i*, 2 vols. (1964/65); G. Cornfeld and B. Lurie (eds.), *Enẓiklopedyah shel ha-Mikra vi-ymei Bayit Sheni* (1967); Talmud and Rabbinics: I. Lampronti, *Paḥad Yiẓḥak*, 13 vols. (1750–1888; repr. 1998); M. Guttman, *Mafte'aḥ ha-Talmud*, 4 vols. (1906–30), incomplete; H.Z. Medini, *Sedei Ḥemed*, 16 vols. (1896–1911); *Enẓiklopedyah Talmudit*, 28 vols. (1947–2005); M. Wulliger, *Koveẓ ha-Tosafot, Oẓar Nehmad*, 3 vols. (1952); I.M. Fishleder, *Mivẓar Yisrael* (1958); A.N. Orenstein, *Enẓiklopedyah le-To'orei-Kavod be-Yisrael*, 4 vols. (1958–63) (encyclopedia on honorific titles in the Bible and Rabbinic literature); A. Maged, *Beit Aharon* (encyclopedia of talmudic principles and personalities), 11 vols. (1962–78).

HUNGARIAN. *Magyar Zsidó Lexikon* (1930), 1929 edition published as *Zsidó Lexikon.*

PORTUGUESE. F. Levisky, *Enciclopédia Judaica Resumida* (1961); C. Roth, *Enciclopédia Judaica*, 3 vols. (1967).

RUSSIAN. *Yevreyskaya entsiklopediya*, 16 vols. (1906–13); "Shorter Jewish Encyclopedia," 11 vols. (1976–2005).

SPANISH. P. Link, *Manual Enciclopédico Judío* (1950); *Enciclopedia Judaica Castellana*, 10 vols. (1948-51); E. Weinfeld, *Judaismo Contemprano* (1961).

YIDDISH. *Algemeyne Entsiklopedye: Yidn*, 7 vols. (1939–66); H.B. Bass (ed.), *Dertsiungs-Entsiklopedye*, 3 vols. (1957–59), in progress; S. Petrushka, *Yidishe Folks-Entsiklopedye*, 2 vols. (1943, 1949^2).

SERBO-CROATIAN. O. Mandić, *Leksikon judaizma i krscanstva* (1969).

ISRAEL ENCYCLOPEDIAS

General and Jewish Content

J. Klausner (ed.), *Enẓiklopedyah Kelalit*, 6 vols. (1935–37); *Ha-Enẓiklopedyah ha-Ivrit*, 21 vols. (1949–81); *Enẓiklopedyah Kelalit Yizre'el*, 16 vols. (1950–61); D. Pines (ed.), *Enẓiklopedyah la-Am*, 3 vols. (1956–57); *Enẓiklopedyah Kelalit Massadah*, 6 vols. and supplement (1958–66).

Junior Encyclopedias

S.Z. Ariel (ed.), *Enẓiklopedyah Ma'yan*, 12 vols. (1950–62); Y. Safra (ed.), *Margaliyyot, Enẓiklopedyah li-Yladim*, 9 vols. (1954–66); I. Avnon (ed.), *Mikhlal, Enziklopedyah la-No'ar*, 15 vols. (1963^2).

Special Encyclopedias

Agriculture: *Ha-Enẓiklopedyah le-Ḥakla'ut* (vol. 1, 1966), in progress; Education: *Enẓiklopedyah Ḥinnukhit*, 5 vols. (1959–69); History: M. Timor, *Enziklopedyah-le Historyah*; H. Messing, *Enẓiklopedyah Historit shel Medinot ha-Olam* (1966); Literature: B. Karou (ed.), *Enẓiklopedyah le-Safrut Yisraelit u-Khelalit*, 4 vols. (1961^2); J. Twersky, *Sifrut ha-Olam, Leksikon*, 4 vols. (1962/63–1963/64); Music: I. Shalita, *Enẓiklopedyah le-Musikah*, 2 vols (1965); Social sciences: *Enẓiklopedyah le-Madda'ei ha-Ḥevrah*, 6 vols. (1962–70); Sports and physical education: Y. Abiram, *Enẓiklopedyah li-Sport u-le-Tarbut ha-Guf*, 2 vols. (1966^2).

[Theodore Wiener]

ENDECJA (so called after the pronunciation of N.D., abbr. of Polish "Narodowa Demokracja," National Democracy; also Endeks), right-wing political party which became a focus for Polish antisemitism in the first half of the 20th century. The party was active in all parts of partitioned Poland. It originated from the "National League," established at the end of the 19th century, to unite Poles of various political allegiance to work for the resurrection of Poland. At first the liberal and right-wing tendencies in the party were balanced, but from 1903 the chauvinist tendency gained in strength, finding expression in struggle against the Jews and a stand against liberalism, among other objectives. It also adopted a pro-Russian and anti-German policy. In Galicia, Endecja was set up in 1905, where it was anti-Ukrainian, and in 1907 won a victory in the elections to the Austrian parliament in which its representative was elected president of the "Polish club" of all Polish deputies in the parliament. Between 1907 and 1911 Endecja was split and weakened by an internal crisis over its pro-Russian policy. During the elections to the fourth Duma in 1912 in Warsaw, when the Jewish vote tipped the balance in favor of a Socialist candidate against the Polish majority, the occasion was used by Endecja as a springboard to strengthen the party. Under the leadership of Roman *Dmowski, Endecja proclaimed an anti-Jewish economic boycott, which was carried out by the mass of Poles. During World War I, the party supported Russia and the Allies and achieved its maximum influence on the future of Poland through the establishment of the National Polish Committee, in which Dmowski played a decisive role as chairman. This committee was recognized as the official representative of the Polish nation at the Versailles Peace Conference. The Endecja-led delegation took part in the coalition government of 1919 headed by I. Paderewski. Endecja became the dominant party in the first elected Polish parliament (Sejm), and took a share in several governments until Pilsudski's coup in 1926. Active mainly on behalf of the interests of the petty bourgeois urban classes, the party was adept in making political capital out of emotionally charged issues, such as a chauvinistic attitude toward the national minorities. Endecja continued its extreme antisemitic stand in its struggle to preserve the Polish character of the towns in Poland against Jewish influence and economic competition. Its connections with capitalist circles and the clergy determined its objectives in domestic policy. Endecja was instrumental in the passing of various laws intended to curtail Jewish influence on the Polish economy and culture. It was active in the numerus clausus case of 1923, and later influenced the youth in the universities to demonstrate against the Jewish students, leading to bloody incidents. Concerning discrimination in commercial taxation Endecja found it difficult to remain consistent, since the party largely represented the urban element in Poland. However it acted energetically regarding the extension of the government monopoly, and in support of Polish cooperatives – all in an anti-Jewish direction – and in the economic restriction of Jews, even if the aims did not correspond with the party's basic principles concerning the sanctity of private property and free enterprise. Through the economic boycott Endecja inspired the *Rozwoj organization. The party's antisemitic influence was strong in military circles, particularly among the Polish volunteers who returned after the war from France and the United States, led by General *Haller. With Hitler's rise to power and the spread of Nazism in Europe, Endecja changed its traditional attitude toward Germany, which it had always considered Poland's principal enemy. The party's youth faction, influenced by Fascist ideas, founded a new body, *NARA, that saw in the Nazi regime a desirable example for Poland. After the outbreak of World War II and the collapse of the Pilsudski regime, which had been Endecja's political opponent, the party's influence increased among Polish émigré circles, both among the army reorganizing abroad and the government-in-exile, established first in France and later in England. During the Nazi occupation Endecja was also active in the nationalist underground movement "Armja Krajowa," which in many cases acted against Jews. In 1970 it still had adherents among Poles outside the country.

BIBLIOGRAPHY: S. Segal, *The New Poland and the Jews* (1938); R.L. Buell, *Poland, Key to Europe* (1939), index, s.v. *Endeks;* A. Bełcikowska, *Stronnictwa i związki polityczne w Polsce* (1925); L. Oberlaender, *Opatrznośiowy żyd* (1932); A. Micewski, *Z geografii politycznej II Reczypospolitej* (1964). **ADD. BIBLIOGRAPHY:** R. Wapinski, *Narodowa Demokracja;* S. Rudnicki, *Oboz narodowo radykalny, geneza i dzialalnosc* (1985).

[Moshe Landau]

ENDELMAN, TODD M. (1946–), scholar of Jewish history. Born in Fresno, Calif., he was educated at the University of California at Berkeley, and at Warwick University, Coventry, England, and the Hebrew Union College-Jewish Institute of Religion. He received his doctorate from Harvard University in 1976. He was an assistant professor of Jewish history at the Bernard Revel Graduate School of Yeshiva University in New York from 1976 to 1979 and a lecturer in history at Hebrew Union College-Jewish Institute of Religion in 1979. From 1979 to 1985 Endelman was an associate professor of modern Jewish and European history at Indiana University, Bloomington. He became the William Haber Professor of Modern Jewish History at the University of Michigan, Ann Arbor, in 1985, and the director of the university's Jean and Samuel Frankel Center for Judaic Studies. In 1982 and 1999 he was a visiting scholar at the Oxford Centre for Postgraduate Hebrew Studies.

Endelman is known as a specialist in the social history of the Jews of Western Europe, particularly Anglo-Jewish history, and his work examines conversion and other forms of radical assimilation. His 1979 work, *The Jews of Georgian England, 1714–1830: Tradition and Change in a Liberal Society*, received the National Jewish Book Award for History and the A.S. Diamond Memorial Prize of the Jewish Historical Society of England. His other works include *Radical Assimilation in English Jewish History, 1656–1945* (1990) and *The Jews of Britain, 1656–2000* (2002). He served as editor of (and contributor to) *Jewish Apostasy in the Modern World* (1987) and *Comparing Jewish Societies* (1997). He was coeditor, with Tony Kushner, of *Disraeli's Jewishness* (2002). He has written extensively for academic journals and has contributed to many works, including *The Legacy of Jewish Migration: 1881 and Its Impact* (1983), *History and Hate: The Dimensions of Anti-Semitism* (1986), *Living with Anti-Semitism: Modern Jewish Responses* (1987), and *The Self-Fashioning of Disraeli, 1818–1851* (2000).

A fellow of the American Academy for Jewish Research, he is also a member of the American Historical Association, the Association for Jewish Studies, and the Jewish Historical Society of England. He has received fellowships from the National Endowment for the Humanities, the Memorial Foundation for Jewish Culture, the Lucius N. Littauer Foundation, and the Lilly Endowment. Endelman's later research involves the study of Jewish apostasy in Europe and America from the Enlightenment to the present.

[Dorothy Bauhoff (2nd ed.)]

ENDINGEN, town in Baden, Germany, site of a notorious *blood libel. Jews are first mentioned there in 1331; in 1349 they were affected by the *Black Death persecutions. When the headless corpses of two adults and two children were found in the grounds of the cemetery in March 1470, Rabbi Elias and his two brothers (granduncles of *Joseph b. Gershon of Rosheim) were accused of ritual murder, tortured, put on trial, and burned at the stake on April 8, 1470. On May 5, Emperor Frederick III condemned the executions on the grounds that the Jews were under imperial protection and ordered the release of other imprisoned Jews, repeating this demand on June 22 and stressing papal prohibitions of the blood libel. In consequence of the libel, the Jews were expelled from Endingen. Despite imperial and papal disapproval, the blood libel story was kept alive; the remains of the supposed victims were enshrined in the altar of the Church of St. Peter. The story was reenacted in the *Endinger Judenspiel*, first performed before huge crowds in 1616. A church bell cast in 1714 bears reliefs of the headless children. Carrying the children's relics in church processions was prohibited under Emperor *Joseph II (1765–90). By 1871 some Jews were living in the town once more. Their number reached 43 in 1888, but declined to ten in 1925, and five in 1933. The remaining couple was deported in 1940. In 1967 the remains of the "martyred" children were removed from the church.

BIBLIOGRAPHY: K.V. Amira, *Das Endinger Judenspiel* (1883); I. Kracauer, in: REJ, 16 (1888), 236–45; Baron, (1967), 177, 372; K.J. Baum, in: *Miscellanea Mediaevalia*, 4 (1966), 337–49; Germ. Jud., 2 (1968), 209–10; F. Hundschnurscher and G. Taddey, *Die Juedischen Gemeinden in Baden* (1968); K. Kurrus, in: Schau-ins-Land, *83. Jahresheft des Breisgauer Geschichtsvereins* (1965), 133–48; T. Oelsner, in: *Aufbau* (Dec. 18, 1966 and July 31, 1970); *New York Times* (Oct. 1, 1967). **ADD. BIBLIOGRAPHY:** W. Frey, in: R. Erb (ed.), *Die Legende vom Ritualmord* (1993), 201–21.

ENDINGEN AND LENGNAU, villages in the Swiss canton of *Aargau, in the Surbtal near the German border. A few Jewish families are known to have lived there during the Middle Ages, when the villages were in the county of Baden, but organized communities were not formed until early in the 17th century. Around 1650 Marharam (Meir) Guggenheim was their leader. The legal status of the Jews was based on letters of protection, which had to be renewed (and paid for) periodically. From 1696 these letters were renewed every 16 years, the last dating from 1792. The letters authorized them to trade in the whole Baden region, though not in real estate, but for the most part they engaged in the sale of livestock. They were authorized to grant loans against movable property only. The number of Jewish houses was limited and a Jew and non-Jew were forbidden to live under the same roof. The Jews were subject to the bailiff, but they had recourse to their rabbis in civil and religious affairs. The 1776 letter of protection limited Jewish residence in the county of Baden to Endingen and Lengnau only. From 20 households in the entire county in 1634, the number grew to 35 in 1702, 94 in 1761, 108 in 1774, and 240 in 1890.

A cemetery was leased to the Jews in 1603 on a small island in the Rhine, called the *Judenaeule* or *Judeninsel*. In 1750 they were allowed to acquire another cemetery (*Waldfriedhof*), halfway between the two villages. In the same year a permanent synagogue was dedicated in Lengnau (which had no church!), and in Endingen in 1764; both communities shared the services of a rabbi from around the same date. The synagogues were rebuilt in 1848 and 1852 respectively.

The French Revolution and the formation of the Helvetic Republic brought the Jews of Endingen and Lengnau no nearer to civic and political emancipation. By a law of 1798 they at least achieved the status of other aliens in the republic. When the French left in 1803, the Christian population of the district rioted, plundering Jewish homes, as had already happened in 1729 and recurred in 1861. The Jews' Law of 1809 was a retrograde move, and like the laws of 1824 (*Organisationsgesetz*) and 1835 (*Schulgesetz*) led to increased interference in the autonomy of the communities, which by then had achieved the legal status of public corporations. The struggle for full equality continued and was successful only in 1878. The Reform movement led to sharp controversies within the communities, but the majority remained loyal to tradition. The Jewish scholars J. *Fuerst and M. *Kayserling served as rabbis of the communities from 1854 to 1858 and 1861 to 1870 respectively. The Jewish population of Endingen and Lengnau, around 1,500 in 1850, had decreased to less than 100 by 1950, and in 1962 the combined community had only 17 members. The Swiss-Jewish Home for the Aged was established in Lengnau in 1903.

BIBLIOGRAPHY: A. Weldler-Steinberg, *Geschichte der Juden in der Schweiz* (1966), index; F. Guggenheim-Gruenberg, *Die Sprache der Schweizer Juden von Endingen und Lengnau* (1950); idem, *Aus einem alten Endingen Gemeindebuch* (1952); idem, *Die aeltesten juedischen Familien in Lengnau und Endingen* (1954); idem, *Der Friedhof auf der Judeninselim Rhein …* (1956).

°ENDLICH, QUIRIN (d. 1888), antisemitic journalist in Vienna called the "Judenfresser" ("Jew-eater"), particularly prominent during the revolution of 1848. Endlich first contributed to S. *Ebersberg's *Zuschauer*, later founding *Schild und Schwert* ("Shield and Sword"), with a column entitled "Judenkontrolle" which heaped denunciations and obscenities upon the Jews. Taking advantage of the newly proclaimed freedom of the press, Endlich called the Jews "Austria's greatest disaster" and asserted that all their activities were destructive. His book, *Der Einfluss der Juden auf unsere Civilisation*, was published in 1848. According to Endlich, the Jews had instigated all the unrest of March 1848 in order to achieve their emancipation. To divert public resentment, they stimulated hatred against the real benefactors of the people, i.e., the aristocracy and the army. By building railways the Jews ruined the innkeepers and carters, and their factories ruined the artisans. His style and methods were later adopted by the Austrian *Christian Social Party.

BIBLIOGRAPHY: Y. Smotricz, *Mahpekhat 1848 be-Austria* (1957), 15–24; J.A. von Helfert, *Die Wiener Journalistik im Jahre 1848* (1877), index.

[Israel Smotricz]

EN-DOR (Heb. עֵין דּוֹר, עֵין דֹּאר).

(1) A city in the territory of Issachar that was occupied by the strong Manasseh tribe (Josh. 17:11). The biblical statement that Gideon's triumph over the Midianites took place at En-Dor (Ps. 83:11) corresponds well with its location north of the hill of Moreh (Gibeath-Moreh, Judg. 7:1). The city's notoriety is mainly due to Saul's visit to "the woman that divineth by a ghost" – the famous witch of En-Dor (1 Sam. 28:7). Saul disguised himself because he and his army were then at Gilboa and the Philistines at Shunem and he had to pass near the enemy camp to reach En-Dor. Eusebius describes it as a very large village 4 m. (6½ km.) south of Mount Tabor and north of the Little Hermon (al-Nabī Daḥī), and also mentions its proximity to Na'im, near Scythopolis (Onom. 34:8; 94:20). En-Dor seems to have been originally part of the district of Sepphoris and was detached from it with Na'im to form a separate district. The name is preserved in ʿIndūr, east of Na'im and north of the hill of Moreh. Tell al-ʿAjjūl or Khirbat al-Ṣafṣāfa, two tells in the vicinity of Na'im containing Iron Age remains, have been suggested as possible sites of the ancient city.

[Michael Avi-Yonah]

(2) The modern kibbutz of En Dor, S.E. of Mt. Tabor, was founded on June 16, 1948, a few days after the region was secured by Israel forces in the War of Independence. It is affiliated to Kibbutz Arẓi ha-Shomer ha-Ẓa'ir. Its settlers include Israel-born pioneers and immigrants from the United States, Bulgaria, Turkey, Germany, and South America. Its economy was based on field crops, poultry, dairy cattle, and a factory for modern electronic equipment. The kibbutz also operated a station for seed development. In the mid-1990s the population was approximately 635, rising to 783 in 2002.

[Efraim Orni / Shaked Gilboa (2nd ed.)]

BIBLIOGRAPHY: Zafrir, in: BJPES, 14 (1948/49), 93; Abel, Geog, 2 (1938), 316; Zori, in: PEQ, 84 (1952), 114ff.; Aharoni, in: JNES, 26 (1967), 213., n. 9.

EN-DOR, WITCH OF, the popular designation of a medium from the town of En-Dor in Manasseh, who was consulted by King *Saul (1 Sam. 28:7–25). (The woman is not designated "witch," Heb. *mekašepah*.) The narrative begins with a report of the Philistine advance; their superiority is so great that Saul, seized with terror, vainly seeks ways of discovering the will of God. In desperation, he resorts to necromancy, which he himself has outlawed (*ibid.* 28:3; cf. Deut. 18:11). Saul finds the necromancer of En-Dor, who is persuaded to accede to his request to conjure up *Samuel. The prophet rebukes Saul and predicts his defeat at the hands of the Philistines. The woman, who had recognized Saul, solicitously provides him with a meal before he departs.

[Shlomo Balter]

In the *Aggadah*

According to the *aggadah*, the witch of En-Dor was the mother of *Abner and was called Zephaniah (the hidden one; PdRE 33), while Pseudo-Philo calls her Sedecla (unrighteous) and tells that she deceived Israel with her sorcery for 40 years (Pseudo-Philo 64:3–5). The rabbis state that the evocation of Samuel took place within 12 months of his death when the body has not yet decomposed and the soul still hovers near it (Shab. 152b). The witch knew it was Saul who called upon her because the ghost appeared face upward, while for an ordinary person it comes face downward (Lev. R. 26:7). From the details given in this story, the rabbis concluded that the necromancer sees the spirit but does not hear it, while the person that evokes the spirit hears its voice but does not see it. Others present neither see nor hear it (Lev. R. 26:7).

Two interpretations are given of the words "*Elohim Olim*" (1 Sam. 28:13). One is that Samuel was evoked like a god and thus told Saul, "Do you not know that just as punishment is inflicted upon the worshiper so it is inflicted upon the worshipped?" The other is that the word "*elohim*" refers to Moses (Ex. 7:1). Samuel, fearing that the Day of Judgment had come, brought Moses up with him to act as his advocate.

BIBLIOGRAPHY: Ginzberg, Legends, 4 (1913), 70, 73; 6 (1928), 235–8.

°**ENDRE, LÁSZLÓ** (1895–1946), Hungarian antisemite. After World War I Endre joined various antisemitic organizations and published anti-Jewish pamphlets, including a booklet in 1936 on the *Protocols of the *Elders of Zion*. In 1937 he organized the "Socialist Party for the Defense of the Race," which merged with Szalasi's party in August of that year. His administrative career started in the White Terror period; he served as county sheriff in various places and from 1923 on in Gödöllő. In 1937, as deputy prefect of the Pest district, he became known for his brutal orders against the Jews. In 1940, in a memorandum to Prime Minister Teleky, he proposed the sterilization of the Jews serving in forced labor units. He maintained close ties with the German Nazi party and attended several of its conventions.

Shortly after the formation of the puppet government under Sztójay (March 1944), he became director-general of the Ministry of Interior, with the special assignment of dealing with the "Jewish problem." He then issued various orders for the concentration of the Jews in ghettos, including the secret order of April 14, 1944, providing for the establishment of ghettos in Hungary. In his statement to the Israeli Police, Adolf *Eichmann described Endre as a very clever man who needed no urging to act against the Jews; on the contrary, he was sometimes forced to restrain Endre. In his negotiations with (Israel) Rezsö *Kasztner, Eichmann on one occasion hesitated to agree to one of Kasztner's requests, wondering "What will Endre say?" During the Soviet advance into Hungary in 1945, Endre fled to Austria, where he was caught by an American unit, turned over to Hungary, sentenced to death, and executed in Budapest.

BIBLIOGRAPHY: E. Landau (ed.), *Kastner Bericht* … (1961); M. Himler, *Igy néztek ki a magyar nemzet sirásói* (1958), 174–84; J. Robinson and P. Friedman, *Guide to Jewish History under Nazi Impact* (1960), 328; R. Hilberg, *Destruction of the European Jews* (1961), index.

[Yehouda Marton]

ENELOW, HYMAN (**Hillel Gershom**; 1877–1934), U.S. Reform rabbi, scholar, and writer. Enelow, who was born in Kovno, Lithuania, went to the U.S. as a young man, age 16, and was ordained by Hebrew Union College in 1898. Enelow served as rabbi of Temple Israel, Paducah, Kentucky (1898–1901), Temple Adath Israel, Louisville, Kentucky (1901–12), and Temple Emanu-El, New York (1912–34). During World War I, Enelow served in France with the Jewish Welfare Board. He was vice president of the Central Conference of American Rabbis (1925–27), its president (1927–29), and a member of both the American Historical Association and the American Jewish Historical Society. Enelow was instrumental in having chairs for Jewish studies established at Harvard (with the aid of his friend Lucius *Littauer) and Columbia (aided by Mrs. Nathan Miller). His numerous books on Jewish religion include the following: *The Synagogue in Modern Life* (1916); *The Faith of Israel* (1917); and *A Jewish View of Jesus* (1920). His *Selected Works* were published in four volumes by F. Levy in 1935.

Enelow's four-volume edition of Israel *Al-Nakawa's *Menorat ha-Maʾor* (1929–32) was an important contribution to Jewish scholarship. His thesis that this work served as the model for Isaac *Aboab's work of the same name was widely discussed though not universally accepted. Of equal importance is Enelow's edition of *Mishnat Eliezer* (or *Midrash of 32 Hermeneutic Rules*, with an English introduction and full apparatus, 1933). A collection of manuscripts was presented in his memory to the Jewish Theological Seminary, New York, by his friend Mrs. Nathan Miller. His private library of over 20,000 volumes was also willed to the Seminary.

BIBLIOGRAPHY: Philipson, in: AJYB, 36 (1934), 25–53; Rivkind, in: *Essays ... L.R. Miller* (1938), 69–83 (Heb. sect.); Kressel, Leksikon, 1 (1965), 127–8.

EN-GANNIM (Heb. עֵין גַּנִּים).

(1) A locality in the territory of Judah, about 2 mi. (3 km.) south of Beth-Shemesh, that is mentioned in the Bible together with Zanoah (Josh. 15:34). Its identification with ʿAyn Faṭīr near Beit Jimal has been proposed.

(2) A levitical city in the territory of Issachar (Josh. 19:21; 21:29). This has been identified by various scholars with the modern Jenin on the southern extremity of the Jezreel Valley, which Josephus mentions (Wars, 3:48) as Ginaea, on the northern border of Samaria. Jenin, however, is probably the biblical Beth-ha-Gan ("gardenhouse," II Kings 9:27), and a more plausible identification is Khirbat Beit (Bayt) Jann near Jabneel on the northern border of Issachar.

BIBLIOGRAPHY: G. Dalman, *Sacred Sites and Ways* (1935), 211; Abel, Geog, 2 (1938), 317; Albright, in: ZAW, 44 (1926), 231f.; A. Saarisalo, in: *Boundary between Issachar and Naphtali* (1927), 37–39.

[Michael Avi-Yonah]

EN-GEDI (Heb. עֵין גֶּדִי).

(1) An oasis on the western shore of the Dead Sea and one of the most important archaeological sites in the Judean Desert. En-Gedi (En-Gaddi in Greek and Latin; ʿAyn Jiddī in Arabic) is actually the name of the perennial spring which flows from a height of 656 ft. (200 m.) above the Dead Sea. In the Bible, the wasteland near the spring where David sought refuge from Saul is called "the wilderness of En-Gedi" and the enclosed camps at the top of the mountains, the "strongholds of En-Gedi" (I Sam. 24:1–2). En-Gedi is also mentioned among the cities of the tribe of Judah in the Judean Desert (Josh. 15:62). A later biblical source (II Chron. 20:2) identifies En-Gedi with Hazazon-Tamar but this is rejected by most scholars. In the Song of Songs 1:14 the beloved is compared to "a cluster of henna in the vineyards of En-Gedi"; the "fishers" of En-Gedi are mentioned in Ezekiel 47:10.

In later literary sources, Josephus speaks of En-Gedi as the capital of a Judean toparchy and tells of its destruction during the Jewish War (Wars, 3:55; 4:402). From documents found in the "Cave of the Letters" in Naḥal Ḥever, it appears that in the period before the Bar Kokhba War (132–135), the Jewish village of En-Gedi was imperial property and Roman garrison troops were stationed there. But in the time of Bar Kokhba, it was under his control, and was one of his military and administrative centers (see *Judean Desert Caves). In the Roman-Byzantine period, the settlement of En-Gedi is mentioned by the Church Fathers; Eusebius describes it as a very large Jewish village (Onom. 86:18). En-Gedi was then famous for its fine dates and rare spices, and for its balsam.

After surveys of the area, five seasons of excavations were conducted at En-Gedi by B. Mazar, T. Dothan, and I. Dunayevsky between the years 1961–62 and 1964–65. The settlement of En-Gedi was found to have been established only in the seventh century B.C.E. with no evidence of occupation in the time of David (tenth century B.C.E.). Excavations showed that Tell Goren (Tell el-Jurn), a small hill above the southwestern part of the plain near Naḥal Arugot, was one of the main centers in the oasis beginning with the Israelite and especially in the Iron II, Hellenistic, and Roman-Byzantine periods. Surveys of the area revealed that the inhabitants of En-Gedi had developed an efficient irrigation system and engaged in intensive agriculture. The combination of abundant water and warm climate made it possible for them to cultivate the palm trees and balsam plants for which En-Gedi was renowned. The settlement was apparently administered by a central authority which was responsible for building terraces, aqueducts, and reservoirs, as well as a network of strongholds and watchtowers along the road linking En-Gedi with Teqoa.

Five periods of occupation were uncovered on Tell Goren. The earliest settlement, Stratum V, was a flourishing town which had spread down the slopes of the tell dating from the Judean kingdom (c. 630–582 B.C.E.). Various installations, especially a series of large clay "barrels" fixed in the ground, together with pottery, metal tools, and ovens indicated that workshops had been set up for some special industry. This discovery conforms with various literary sources (Josephus and others) which mention En-Gedi as a center for the production of opobalsamon ("balsam"). It can thus be assumed that En-Gedi was a royal estate which ran this costly industry in the service of the king. This first settlement was apparently destroyed and burned by Nebuchadnezzar in 582/1 B.C.E.

The next town on the tell (Stratum IV) belongs to the Persian period (fifth–fourth centuries B.C.E.). Its area was more extensive than the Israelite one and its buildings were larger and well-built. A very large house, part of it two-storied, which contained 23 rooms, was found on the northern slope of the tell. En-Gedi at this time was part of the province of Judah as attested by the many sherds inscribed "Yehud," the official name of the province.

Stratum III belongs to the Hasmonean period. Its famous dates are mentioned in this period by Ben Sira (Ecclus. 24:14). En-Gedi flourished, especially at the time of Alexander *Yannai and his successors (103–37 B.C.E.). A large fortress on the tell was probably destroyed in the period of the Parthian invasion and the last war of the Hasmoneans against Herod.

The next occupation (Stratum II) contains a strong fortress on the top of the tell surrounded by a thick stone wall with a rectangular tower. This settlement is attributed to the time of Herod's successors (4–68 C.E.); it was destroyed and burned apparently during the Jewish War in 68 C.E. Coins from the "Year Two" of the war were found in the area of the conflagration.

During the Roman-Byzantine period (Stratum I) the inhabitants of the tell lived in temporary structures and cultivated the slopes of the hill (third–fifth centuries C.E.). It appears that at least from the time of the Herodian period the main settlement at En-Gedi moved down to the plain, east and northeast of Tell Goren between Naḥal David and Naḥal Arugot.

A Roman bath was found in the center of this plain about 660 ft. (200 m.) west of the shore of the Dead Sea. It is dated by finds, especially six bronze coins, to the period between the fall of the Second Temple and the Bar Kokhba War.

A sacred enclosure from the Chalcolithic period was found on a terrace above the spring. It consists of a group of stone structures of a very high architectural standard. The main building was apparently a temple which served as the central sanctuary for the inhabitants of the region.

Excavations (1970) brought to light the remains of a Jewish settlement dating from the Byzantine period. The synagogue had a beautiful mosaic floor depicting peacocks eating grapes, and the words "Peace on Israel," as well as a unique inscription consisting of 18 lines which, inter alia, calls down a curse on "anyone causing a controversy between a man and his fellows or who (says) slanders his friends before the gentiles or steals the property of his friends, or anyone revealing the secret of the town to the gentiles. …" (According to Lieberman, it was designed against those revealing the secrets of the balsam industry.) A seven branched menorah of bronze and more than 5,000 coins (found in the synagogue's cash box by the ark) were also uncovered.

[Benjamin Mazar]

Since the writing of the entry above by Benjamin Mazar, new archaeological work and historical studies concerning En-Gedi have been made. En-Gedi is an oasis on the fringe of the Judean Desert, situated in the middle of the western shore of the Dead Sea, in the rift valley, the lowest place on earth. The climate of the rift valley is arid and climatic changes have in the past influenced the flow of the springs as well as the levels of the Dead Sea. The source of the springs is in the aquifer of the Judaean Group of the Cenoman-Touron Formation. In the past, there were ten springs, but only four are active today: 'Arugot, David, En-Gedi, and Shulamit.

En-Gedi is mentioned for the first time in the Bible as Hazazon Tamar (Gen. 14:7), which was identified as En-Gedi (II Chron. 20: 2). In I Samuel 23:29; 24:2–3, David took refuge in the wilderness of En-Gedi. En-Gedi is mentioned once in each of the Talmudic writings (TJ, Shevi'it 9:2, 38d; TB, Shabbat 26a). The inhabitants of En-Gedi made their living from agriculture. They cultivated a very poor marl and stony soil with irrigation channels from the waters of the springs. They also collected salt and asphalt (bitumen) from the shores of the Dead Sea, as well as chunks of sulfur from the marl plains for the production of medicines. The main cultivations in this oasis were palm trees and barley; balsam, a cash crop, was also grown in the region. Writers from the Roman period praised the excellent dates that grew in En-Gedi and Judaea (Pliny, *Hist. Nat.* 13:6, 26; Josephus, Ant., 9: 7). The palm tree, a symbol of Judaea, was used as a motif on Jewish coins and Flavian victory coins. Transportation between En-Gedi and other parts of the country was dictated by geographical and political conditions. During ancient times En-Gedi had a strong connection with Jerusalem. During the First Temple period, En-Gedi was first established as a military outpost on the western shores of the Dead Sea over against Moab and Edom. Later maritime transportation was undertaken on the Dead Sea, as has been proven by the discovery of wooden and stone anchors, as well as of anchorages near En-Gedi and at other locations around the Dead Sea. Although sailing vessels have not yet been found underwater, drawings and graffiti of sailing ships are known from Masada and on the mosaic map of Madaba. The connection between En-Gedi and Nabataea, and later with Arabia, is attested by ancient historians, on the one hand, as well as in the Judean Desert Documents, on the other. Nabatean coins have also been found in archaeological excavations.

During the 1980s–90s a systematic archaeological survey was conducted in the area, and a number of intact burials of the Second Temple period were revealed and excavated. These were family tombs and the bodies were wrapped with linen shrouds and interred in wooden coffins, usually without funerary objects (Hadas, 1994). In the late 1990s a large area of the Byzantine village adjacent to the synagogue was excavated and many dwellings were revealed, all of which supports Eusebius' description of En-Gedi as "a large village of Jews" (Hirschfeld, in press). During this project the irrigated agricultural systems were also investigated and excavated (Hadas, 2002). In recent years (2003–5), a new suburb of En-Gedi dating from the Second Temple period has been revealed to the northwest of the synagogue (Hadas, forthcoming). Caves in the cliffs behind En-Gedi have also been surveyed, revealing Bar-Kochba coins and papyri in some of them, and much earlier Persian period ornaments in another. Additional excavations conducted in the area of the synagogue area (Hadas, in press) have shown that the Byzantine village was destroyed and burnt in the sixth century C.E. This was the end of the Jewish settlement, which had existed here almost continuously for about one thousand years. A gap in the occupation of En-Gedi existed until the 13th–14th centuries C.E., when a Mamluke village was founded at the spot and existed there for about a century. Remains of this period were found above the synagogue site and in the general vicinity. A water mill was also built at this time (Hadas, 2001–2) and it still exists near the En-Gedi spring. En-Gedi remained in ruins until the establishment of the State of Israel in 1948.

[Gideon Hadas (2nd ed.)]

(2) Settlement in the Judean Desert on the west bank of the Dead Sea, founded by Israeli-born youth first as a *Naḥal military outpost in 1953 and later in 1956 as a civilian kibbutz affiliated to the Iḥud ha-Kevuẓot ve-ha-Kibbutzim. Its primary functions were, initially, those of defense; but it also successfully developed farming methods adapted to the local conditions of a hot desert climate and an abundance of fresh water from the En-Gedi Springs. These are fed by an underground flow (from the rain-rich intake area on the western slopes of the Hebron Hills), which emerges on a fault line. An area surrounding the Springs has been declared a nature reserve because of the small enclave of Sudano-Deccanian flora existing there. A field school of the Society for the Preservation of Nature, a youth hostel (Bet Sara), and a recreation home are all situated there. Until 1967 the means of transportation to En-Gedi were by land or sea from Sodom, on the south side of the Dead Sea. In 1962 a narrow asphalt road was built and it replaced the 50 km. dirt road that was frequently destroyed by flash floods in the winter months. At that time there was a motorboat that sailed from Sodom to En-Gedi, and a medical doctor used to arrive once a week by light plane (Piper) from Beer Sheva. In 1971 an asphalt road was built northwards and connected En-Gedi to Jerusalem, shortening the travel time from En-Gedi to Tel Aviv, from 5 to 2 hours. The kibbutz economy was based mainly on tourism, including a guest house and medicinal waters. Farming was based on mango plantations, date palms, and herbs. The kibbutz had a 25-acre botanical garden with 900 plant species from all over the world. In 2002 the population of En-Gedi was 603.

[Efraim Orni / Shaked Gilboa and Gideon Hadas (2nd ed.)]

BIBLIOGRAPHY: B. Mazar et al., *En-Gedi, Ḥafirot…* (1963); B. Mazar, in: BIES, 30 (1966), 183ff.; idem, in: *Archaeology*, 16 (1963), 99ff.; idem, in: *Archaeology and Old Testament Study*, ed. by D. Winton Thomas (1967), 223ff.; idem, in: IEJ, 14 (1964), 121–30; 17 (1967), 133–43; Y. Aharoni, in: *Atiqot*, 5 (1961–62), En-Gedi; ibid., 3 (1961), 148–62; idem, in: IEJ, 12 (1962), 186–99; B. Mazar, S. Lieberman, and E.E. Urbach, in: Tarbiz, 40 (Oct. 1970), 18–30. **ADD. BIBLIOGRAPHY:** G. Hadas, "Stone Anchors," in: *Atiqot*, 21 (1992), 55–57; idem, "Nine Tombs," in: *Atiqot*, 24 (Hebrew; 1994); idem, "Water Mills," in: BAIAS, 19–20 (2001–2), 71–93; idem, "Ancient Irrigation Agriculture in the Oasis of Ein Gedi" (Doctoral Thesis, 2002); idem, "Excavations by the Synagogue," in: *Atiqot*, 49 (in press); G. Hadas et al., "Two Ancient Wooden Anchors," in: JNA, 34:2 (2005), 307–15; Y. Hirschfeld, Excavations (forthcoming).

ENGEL, ELIOT L. (1947–), U.S. congressman. Engel was born and raised in New York. His family lived in a third floor Bronx tenement and around the time of his bar mitzvah moved to middle-class public housing. During the summers of his teenage years, he worked as an actor. In 1969, he graduated from Hunter-Lehman College with a B.A. in history and received a master's degree in guidance and counseling in 1973 from Herbert H. Lehman College of the City University of New York. In 1987, he received a law degree from New York Law School. After graduation from college he was a teacher and guidance counselor in the New York school system before entering politics.

He began his political career as a member of the New York Assembly (1977–88) where he chaired the Committee on Alcoholism and Substance Abuse as well as the Subcommittee on Mitchell-Lama Housing. After six terms in the Assembly, he challenged ten-term incumbent Mario Biaggi, who had been convicted of bribery and extortion. He beat him in a Democratic primary, which was paramount to election in the district. He served in Congress from 1989. In Congress he was a member of the Energy Committee and a member of the International Relations Committee. In typical New York fashion he pursued the three I's strategy: Israel, Ireland, and Italy. He was outspoken in his defense of Israel, and a prime mover of the bill to move the American Embassy from Tel Aviv to Jerusalem. He also pressed the issue of American participation in Bosnia during the crisis of the mid-1990s. Engel was a member of the Congressional Human Rights Caucus, the Democratic Study Group on Health, and the Long Island Sound Caucus. He co-chaired the Albanian Issues Caucus and was an Executive Board Member of the Congressional Ad Hoc Committee on Irish Affairs.

BIBLIOGRAPHY: L.S. Maisel and I. Forman, *Jews in American Politics* (2001); K.F. Stone, *The Congressional Minyan: The Jews of Capitol Hill* (2002).

[Michael Berenbaum (2nd ed.)]

ENGEL, JOEL (**Yuli Dimitriyevich**; 1868–1927), composer and music editor, a pioneer of music in Ereẓ Israel. Born in Berdyansk, Russia, he studied at Kharkov and the Moscow Conservatory. He was music critic of the journal *Russkiye Vedomosti* for 20 years and in 1911 he published a collection of criticism, *At the Opera*. The turning point in Engel's work came in 1900, when he began to adapt Jewish folk songs and to organize concerts for their performance. His activity attracted young Jewish musicians and the Society for Jewish Folk Music was founded in 1908. In 1912 Engel took part with S. *An-Ski in an ethnographical expedition to South Russia, and collected many folk songs among the Jewish population. Engel found in the Ḥasidic wordless *niggunim* manifestations of an original Hebrew melos. He believed that folk songs sung for years by the Jewish people, even though containing alien elements, reflected the Jewish spirit. He applied this idea in his most important composition, the music to An-Ski's play *The Dybbuk* (published as a suite for orchestra, 1926). He also set Hebrew poems of *Bialik and *Tchernichowsky to music. In 1924 he settled in Tel Aviv and devoted himself to the creation of original Hebrew-Palestinian songs. His music for Peretz's works was performed at the Peretz Festival in the Ohel Theater in 1926. He also wrote children's songs. In 1916 in Moscow he published *Fifty Children's Songs* (in Yiddish). More songs appeared in the booklets *Yaldei Sadeh* (1923) and *Shirei Yeladim*, and in a posthumous collection *Be-Keren Za-*

vit (1927). The Tel Aviv municipality named a prize for Israel composers after Engel.

BIBLIOGRAPHY: Sendrey, Music, index; A. Weisser, *Modern Renaissance of Jewish Music* (1954), 71–80; M. Ravina, *Yo'el Engel, Ḥayyav vi-Yẓirato* (1937), includes bibliography; idem, *Yo'el Engel ve-ha-Musikah ha-Yehudit* (1947), includes list of compositions and books written by J. Engel.

[Simha Katz]

ENGEL, JOSEPH BEN JUDAH (1859–1920), Polish rabbi and halakhist. Born in Tarnow, after his marriage he settled in Bendin, where his father-in-law lived, and there became famous as one of the greatest of Polish rabbis. In 1906 he was elected *av bet din* of Cracow and was the virtual chief rabbi of the city, no one being appointed to the position during his tenure of office. At the outbreak of World War I he moved to Vienna where he died.

Engel wrote more than 100 works on *halakhah, aggadah*, and Kabbalah. His works comprise a sort of (mostly alphabetic) encyclopedia and include 30 volumes on Talmud; more than 20 volumes on Kabbalah; and five of responsa, novellae on talmudic themes and on the Shulḥan Arukh, and sermons. During his lifetime about 20 of his works were published, but the rest have remained in manuscript. After his death a committee of the friends of Engel was formed in Vienna, with the name "Ohavei Torah," for the purpose of collecting and publishing all his manuscripts. Some of them are in the process of publication, but many others were lost as a consequence of the Holocaust.

The following of his published works are noteworthy: *Atvan de-Oraita* (1891), giving 27 fundamental principles on talmudic methodology; *Beit ha-Oẓar* (Pt. 1, 1903; Pt. 2, 1907), on biblical themes, arranged in alphabetical order; *Bet Porat*, responsa (Pt. 1, 1907; Pt. 2, 1912); *Oẓerot Yosef* (1921), comprising eight sermons; halakhic novellae on the laws of the sabbatical year as they apply at the present time (1928); and novellae to Shulḥan Arukh *Yoreh De'ah* (1929). His revolutionary interpretation concerning the sabbatical year is noteworthy: even if the sabbatical year applies to modern times, it has only the force of a rabbinical enactment, whereas the *mitzvah* of settling in Ereẓ Israel is a commandment ordained by the Torah and hence completely abrogates the laws of the sabbatical year, thus making it unnecessary, in order to permit cultivation of the land, to have recourse to the expedient of selling it temporarily to a non-Jew. Other published works of his are *Gilyonei ha-Shas*, marginal notes on the Babylonian and Jerusalem Talmuds in three volumes (1924–37), containing source references, novellae, and comparisons. They testify to Engel's great erudition. He reveals points of similarity with the subject under discussion in apparently unconnected passages. Additional works are *Hoshen Yosef* (1945), novellae on the Maharit, and on the *Avnei Millu'im* of Aryeh Leib ha-Kohen; *Gevurot Shemonim* (1903), containing 80 solutions to a single problem; and *Ẓiyyunim la-Torah* (1904), consisting of 40 pilpulistic discourses. These last works in particular reflect Engel's keen and penetrating intellect. His approach to the Kabbalah is interesting in that he finds a parallel in the Talmud for every kabbalistic idea, and endeavors to demonstrate the close connection between Jewish mysticism and the rational part of the talmudic *halakhah* and *aggadah*. Recognized as an outstanding halakhist, he was consulted on halakhic problems by hundreds of rabbis.

BIBLIOGRAPHY: J.L. in: *Der Israelit* (1930), no. 15–16, p. 3f.; S.J. Zevin, *Soferim u-Sefarim-Pesakim/Perushim ve-Ḥiddushim* (1959), 150–56; Gashuri, in: *Pinkas Bendin* (1959), 329.

[Itzhak Alfassi]

ENGEL, JÓZSEF (1815–1901), Hungarian sculptor, born at Sátoraljaujhely, Hungary. Intended for the rabbinate, he was sent to study at the yeshivah of Moses *Sofer at Pressburg. While still studying, Engel began to practice sculpture, and his father asked the rabbi whether this was permissible according to rabbinic law. On his receiving a negative reply, Engel was forced to stop. When his father died, however, Engel left for Vienna and became apprentice to a wood-carver. In 1840 he moved to England, where he made his name and executed busts of Queen Victoria and of Prince Albert, who commissioned several works from him. He also executed a bust of Sir David *Salomons, the first Jewish lord mayor of London. In 1847 he went to Rome, remaining there for nearly 20 years before returning to Hungary.

BIBLIOGRAPHY: Roth, Art, 868.

ENGELBERG, ḤAYYIM OF (Ferdinand Franz Engelberger; d. 1642), apostate who converted to Christianity in 1636 to evade the penalty for stealing. After publishing a missionary pamphlet, he went to Vienna where he won the favor of *Ferdinand III. When he and two Jewish accomplices were caught pilfering gems from the treasury and sentenced to death, he assumed that the emperor would pardon him and accepted the last sacraments peacefully. Becoming aware that the sentence was to be carried out, he smashed a crucifix, rejected Christianity, and asked to die a Jew, also announcing that he had desecrated the *Host. This admission spurred the mob to kill a number of Jews and plunder their homes. After being tortured and maimed, Ḥayyim was burned at the stake on the Sabbath, Aug. 26, 1642, and was heard mumbling: "May my death be my atonement." The incident was commemorated on two marble tablets in Vienna. His wife and children, whom he had persuaded to accept baptism, escaped to Poland and reverted to Judaism.

BIBLIOGRAPHY: D. Kaufmann, *Die letzte Vertreibung der Juden aus Wien* (1889), 36–38; H. Gold, *Geschichte der Juden in Wien* (1966), 18–19; Glanz, in: JSOS, 5 (1943), 8–9; Baron, 14 (1969), 239f., 392.

ENGELMANN, GABRIEL (d. 1850), Hungarian talmudist and *rosh yeshivah*. Engelmann was born in Vaguihely. For 15 years he served as *dayyan* in his native town and later was appointed rabbi and *av bet din* of Rohonc, Hungary, where he remained until his death. He devoted most of his life to his yeshivah and in the introduction to his *Einei Yisrael* (pt. 1) relates that he chose for himself the way trodden by most Jewish scholars to devote himself to study and teaching. His contemporaries esteemed him highly and those who gave their approbations to his books included Moses *Sofer. Engelmann's *Einei Yisrael* is in two parts, the first (Vienna, 1822) on tractates *Shevu'ot* and *Bava Batra*, the second (*ibid.*, 1824) on *Ḥullin*. Some erroneously attributed to him the *Gevurat ha-Shem* (1838), a commentary on the Passover *Haggadah*, but its author is Gabriel b. Jacob Katz of Szamotuly.

BIBLIOGRAPHY: Fuenn, Keneset, 206; J.J. (L.) Greenwald (Grunwald), *Pe'erei Ḥakhmei Medinatenu* (1910), 61 no. 6; P.Z. Schwartz, *Shem ha-Gedolim me-Ereẓ Hagar*, 1 (1914), 22b no. 7; M. Stein, *Magyar Rabbik*, 2 (1906), 152.

[Naphtali Ben-Menahem]

ENGELMANN, SUSANNE CHARLOTTE (1886–?), educator. Born in Germany, she was recognized during the Weimar period as an influential educator of girls, as well as the author of significant works on education, including *Die Krise der heutigen Maedchenerziehung* (1929) and *Methodik des deutschen Unterrichts* (1929). From 1933 on, she was deprived of the right to pursue her professional work, but she did not leave Berlin until 1940, when she migrated to the U.S. She was a guest scholar at Wilson College, Chambersburg, Pa., and lectured at other institutions. Her writings after 1940 stressed the educational changes in Germany of the 1930s and the war period. As author of *German Education and Reeducation* (1945), she was characterized as one of the most competent writers to assess the effectiveness of Nazi methods of indoctrination and the necessity of reeducating the German mind.

[William W. Brickman]

ENGELSBERG, LEON (1919–1998), Israel painter. Born in E. Europe, Engelsberg studied at the Warsaw Academy of Art. He settled in Israel after World War II in Jerusalem, in 1955. He painted expressionist landscapes of the Jerusalem countryside, but did not exhibit. His landscapes describe the hills and valleys of the Jerusalem area, so that landmarks like the Temple Mount and other religious sites are absent from his paintings. He won the Yad Vashem and Sussman prizes.

ENGLAND. The British Isles were unknown to the Jews until a late date, and the settlement of the Jews in medieval England was among the latest in Europe. It is possible that a small nucleus was to be found there under the Romans and that in the Saxon period, isolated Jews extended their commercial activities as far as the British Isles. But the slender evidence formerly adduced in support of this (e.g., the references in the *Liber Poenitentialis* ascribed to Archbishop Theodore of Canterbury, 669) has no validity.

The Medieval Period

Jews were settled in some numbers in the continental possessions of William the Conqueror. With the Norman Conquest in 1066, it was inevitable that some should follow him to England, even if (as sometimes reported) he did not specifically invite them. The new community thus had a comparatively artificial origin, and possessed a remarkable homogeneity, being composed almost entirely of financiers and their dependents. It may thus be regarded as a type of late medieval Jewry in composition and in occupation as well as in its close subjection to royal control.

The community originated in the main in northern France, of which it was to some extent a cultural, linguistic, and economic offshoot. A minority came from Germany, Italy, and Spain, while one or two came even from Russia and the Muslim countries. By the mid-12th century, communities were to be found in most of the greater cities of the country, in *Lincoln, *Winchester, *York, *Oxford, *Norwich, and *Bristol. However, the *London community was always the most important. Until 1177 the only cemetery allowed was in London. No communities were found west of *Exeter or north of York. The Jews were treated tolerantly by the Norman monarchs. William Rufus (1087–1100) is even said to have encouraged them to enter into disputations with Christian clerics. Under Henry I (1100–35), an exemplary charter of liberties, the text of which is no longer preserved, was probably granted to the Jews.

In the course of the 12th century, anti-Jewish feeling began to manifest itself. In 1130 the Jews of London were fined the then enormous sum of £2,000 on the charge that one of their number had killed a sick man. The first recorded *blood libel took place at Norwich in 1144 and was imitated at *Gloucester in 1168, before the precedent came to be followed outside England. Similar accusations were made before the end of the century at *Bury St. Edmunds (1181), Bristol (before 1183), and Winchester (1192). Nevertheless, the community grew in wealth and numbers, and its financial importance became increasingly recognized and exploited by the Crown. In 1168 a tallage (an arbitrary tax, theoretically levied only in emergency) of 5,000 marks (a mark was two-thirds of a £) was imposed by Henry II. In 1188 a tax of one-fourth of the value of their movable property was levied upon London Jewry. The amount raised, according to the rough contemporary estimate, was £60,000, as against only £70,000 raised from the general population. The annual revenue obtained by the state from the Jews is conjectured to have averaged at this time £3,000. *Aaron of Lincoln (c. 1125–1186) was the greatest English capitalist of his day. His financial aid made possible the completion of several English monasteries and abbeys, besides secular buildings. On his death, his property and credits were claimed by the Exchequer, where a special department was set up to deal with them.

The period of relative tranquility ended with the spread of crusading enthusiasm under Richard I. At his coronation, a riot began at the doors of Westminster Hall, which ended in the sack of London's Jewry and the murder of many of its inhabitants (September 1189). The example spread throughout the country in the following spring. The leaders were in many cases members of the lesser baronage whose religious ardor was heightened by their financial indebtedness to the Jews. At Dunstable, the handful of Jews saved themselves by accepting Christianity. At Lynn (later *King's Lynn), foreign sailors exterminated the entire little community. At *Stamford and Norwich, all who did not take refuge in the royal castle perished. The most tragic episode occurred in York. There, the community, headed by R. *Yom-Tov b. Isaac of Joigny, escaped massacre by voluntary death (March 16–17, 1190).

These outrages had been accompanied everywhere by the burning of the deeds of debts due to the Jews. The Crown, which derived much revenue from the profits of the moneylenders, thus suffered considerable loss. Accordingly, after his return from captivity (to supply ransom the Jews of the country had been made to contribute three times as much as the citizens of London) Richard, by his "Ordinance of the Jewry" (1194), ordered the establishment of an **archa* or chirograph chest in principal cities, under the charge of Jewish and Christian "chirographers," in which duplicate records of all debts contracted with the Jews were to be deposited. Thus, whatever disorders might occur, the Crown's dues were henceforth secure. As coordinating authority over these provincial centers, ultimately some 26 in number, there came into being the *Scaccarium Judaeorum* or "*Exchequer of the Jews" – an institution with both judicial and financial functions. Closely connected with it was the office of *Presbyter Judaeorum* or *archpresbyter – not a chief rabbi, as once believed, but official representative and expert on Jewish matters appointed by the Crown. Of the occupants of this post, the names of Jacob of London (appointed 1199), Josce (1207), *Aaron (fil' (i.e., son of) Josce) of York (1236), *Elias le Eveske (1243), Hagin (Ḥayyim) fil' Moses of Lincoln (1258), and Cok Hagin fil' Deulecresse (1281) are known. In the Exchequer, the Jews of England had an organization acting in the royal interest equaled in no other European country. Its records, preserved in unparalleled completeness, yield minute information as to their condition.

The English communities never fully recovered from the blow they received at the time of the accession of Richard I. John indeed favored them at first and in 1201 confirmed their charter of liberties. However, later in his reign he began to squeeze money out of them by a succession of desperate expedients culminating in 1210 in the harshly-exacted Bristol Tallage of 60,000 or 66,000 marks (though this figure may have been used merely to describe a vast sum) which reduced them to the verge of ruin. Nevertheless, the barons viewed the Jews with aversion, as instruments of royal oppression; in the course of armed baronial resistance to the Crown, the Jewry of London was sacked. A clause in the Magna Carta (omitted in subsequent reconfirmations) restricted the claims of Jewish creditors against the estates of landowners who had died in their debt.

During the minority of Henry III, the Jews recovered some degree of prosperity. This was, however, counterbalanced by the introduction at the Council of Oxford (1222) of the discriminatory legislation of the Fourth *Lateran Council of 1215, which was enforced in England earlier and more consistently than in any other part of Europe. The most important of these provisions was the wearing of the Jewish *Badge which here took the form of the two tablets of stone.

From the beginning of the personal rule of Henry III in 1232, the condition of the Jews rapidly deteriorated. Tallage succeeded tallage with disastrous regularity. A "Parliament of Jews," consisting of six representatives from each of the major communities and two from the smaller centers, was held at *Worcester in 1241 in order to apportion one such levy. When nothing further could be extorted from the Jews directly, Henry exercised his rights as suzerain by mortgaging them to his brother, Richard of Cornwall. They were subsequently made over to Edward, the heir to the throne, who in turn consigned them to their competitors, the Cahorsins. The Crown, however, resumed its rights before the expiration of the period.

Meanwhile, ecclesiastical enactments against the Jews were enforced with unprecedented severity. A new synagogue built at London was confiscated on a frivolous pretext (1232). There was a whole series of ritual murder accusations, culminating in the classical case of Hugh of *Lincoln in 1255. In 1253 a decree was issued forbidding the Jews to live henceforward except in towns with established communities. With the outbreak of the Barons' Wars in 1263, the Jews found themselves exposed to the animosity of the insurgents who regarded them as the instruments of royal oppression. From 1263 to 1266, one Jewish community after another was sacked, with considerable loss of life, including those of London (which suffered twice, in 1263 and 1264), *Cambridge, *Canterbury, Worcester, and Lincoln.

The Expulsion

On his accession in 1272, Edward I found the Jews so impoverished that their importance to the treasury had become negligible. Moreover, foreign bankers who enjoyed a higher patronage had begun to render the services for which the Jews had formerly been indispensable. By the *Statutum de Judaismo* of 1275, the king endeavored to effect a radical change in the occupations and mode of life of his Jewish subjects. The practice of usury was forbidden. On the other hand, they were empowered to engage in commerce and (for an experimental period) to rent farms on short leases. They were not, however, permitted to enter the Gild Merchant, without which the privilege to engage in trade was virtually useless; nor were they given the security of tenure necessary for agricultural pursuits. The *Statutum* failed in its purpose. A few of the wealthier began to trade in wool and corn (though this was in many cases a mask for moneylending) but others continued to carry on clandestinely the petty usury now prohibited by law; while some eked out a living from their capital by clipping the coinage. This led

Jewish settlement in Britain before the expulsion of 1290, and communities existing in the late 20th century.

in 1278 to widespread arrests and hangings, in many cases on the flimsiest pretexts.

Edward may have contemplated a relaxation of the situation by permitting a resumption of usury but for a variety of economic and political reasons, and from sheer rapacity, he finally decided to resolve the problem drastically. On July 18, 1290, he issued an edict for the banishment of the Jews from England – the first of the great general expulsions of the Middle Ages – by All Saints' Day (November 1). Most of the refugees made their way to France, Flanders, and Germany.

The English Jews of the Middle Ages perhaps numbered fewer than 4,000, though contemporary chroniclers put the figure far higher. They formed, intellectually as well as politically, an offshoot of the neighboring Franco-German center, even speaking French among themselves. Their interests were accordingly halakhic rather than literary, though no name of the first importance figures among them. Outstanding scholars included *Jacob b. Judah of London, author of the ritual compendium *Ez Ḥayyim*; the grammarian Benjamin of *Cambridge; Isaac b. Perez of Northampton; *Moses b. Ha-Nesi'ah of London who wrote the grammatical work *Sefer ha-Shoham*; *Meir of Norwich, a liturgical poet; *Moses b. Yom-Tov of London, halakhist and grammarian; and his sons *Benedict of Lincoln (Berechiah of Nicole) and *Elijah Menahem of London, physician, scholar, and financier, the greatest luminary of medieval English Jewry.

Their expulsion in 1290 cleared England of the Jews more completely than was the case in any other European country. The **Domus Conversorum* founded by Henry III in London in 1232 continued indeed to function until the beginning of the 17th century, but ultimately its few inmates were in every case foreigners. The only professing Jews known to have come to the country were half a dozen individuals in 1310 (perhaps to negotiate conditions for readmission), one or two physicians who were invited professionally, and occasional wandering adventurers.

The Resettlement Period

This almost absolute isolation was broken by the repercussions of the expulsions from Spain and Portugal and of the activities of the Inquisition in the Iberian Peninsula, which drove refugees throughout Western Europe. A small *Marrano settlement was established in London in the reigns of Henry VIII and Edward VI but broke up on the accession of Mary in 1553 and the Catholic reaction which ensued. In the reign of Elizabeth, a semi-overt congregation existed for some years in London and Bristol, comprising among others Dr. Hector *Nunez whose commercial connections were found useful by the government in Spanish affairs, and Roderigo *Lopez, the queen's physician, who was executed in 1594 on a charge of having plotted against her life. The latter was connected by marriage with Alvaro Mendes (Solomon *Abenaes), duke of Mytilene, who sent diplomatic missions to the English court on more than one occasion. Although this Marrano community at one time numbered approximately 100 persons, it had no legal guarantee of existence. With a change in political and economic conditions in 1609, it disappeared.

Toward the middle of the 17th century, a new Marrano colony grew up in London, partly of refugees who had been settled for a time at Rouen and the Canary Islands. The revolution and the spread of extreme Puritan doctrine among the English people led to the development of a spirit more favorable to the Jews, which increased proportionately with the importance attached to the Old Testament. Sir Henry *Finch, Roger Williams, Edward *Nicholas, and John Sadler were among the notables who joined in the agitation for the formal readmission of the Jews into England, whether as a measure of humanity or in the hopes of securing their conversion. The economic revival under *Cromwell, coupled with his anti-Spanish policy, combined to create an atmosphere more and more favorable to the Marrano merchants, some of whom, such as Antonio Fernandez *Carvajal, rendered the government valuable service in obtaining intelligence from the continent.

Meanwhile, the reported discovery of Jews in America by Antonio (Aaron) de *Montezinos had led *Manasseh Ben Israel, the Amsterdam rabbi and mystic, to look forward to the millennium which would be ushered in by the completion of the dispersion through the official introduction of the Jews to the "end of the earth" (*Kezeh ha-Arez* = Angle-Terre). Negotiations with him, which had been going on fitfully since 1650, came to a head with his arrival in England in the autumn of 1655. A petition presented on behalf of the Jews was backed up by his eloquent plea in the "Humble Addresses" (Amsterdam, 1655), presented to the Lord Protector. On December 4, 1655, a conference of notables met at Whitehall to consider the whole question. The judges present decided that there was no statute which excluded the Jews from the country. On the other hand, a large body of theological and mercantile opinion manifested itself, which would consent to readmission only on the severest terms. After four sessions, Cromwell dissolved the conference before it arrived at a positive conclusion. In the following March, the London Marranos presented a fresh petition, merely asking for permission to have their own burial ground and to be protected from disturbance in the performance of their religious ceremonies. Their position was meanwhile strengthened by a judicial ruling which restored the property of Antonio *Robles (seized on the outbreak of war with Spain because of his Spanish nationality), mainly on the grounds that he was a Jew. In July, as it seems, the petition of the previous March was at last taken into consideration and assented to by the Council of State. Although the relevant pages were subsequently torn out of the minute book, the settlement of the Jews in England was never thereafter seriously questioned. This was far from the formal recall for which Manasseh Ben Israel had hoped, but its very informality secured its continuance even after the restoration of the monarchy in 1660 and saved English Jewry from that special and inferior status which was the rule elsewhere in Europe.

The easygoing King Charles II was indeed little disposed, on his return to England, to reverse the arrangement which had become established under the Protectorate, in spite of anti-Jewish agitation fostered by Thomas Violet and embodied in a petition by the City of London. In 1664, in consequence of an attempt at blackmail made by the Earl of Berkshire and Paul Ricaut, the community received from the Crown a formal promise of protection, and in 1673, after another petty persecution, a guarantee of freedom of worship, which was confirmed in similar circumstances in 1685. This pragmatic policy of protection for the Jews was continued throughout the reigns of the later Stuarts. Suggestions for special taxation (which must inevitably have led to special status) were not implemented. The legality of the practice of Judaism in England at last received indirect parliamentary recognition in the Act for Suppressing Blasphemy of 1698.

The community henceforth grew in wealth and in importance. Its numbers were increased by immigrants, principally from Amsterdam, or else directly from Spain and Portugal. Its position was consistently favorable, despite certain vexatious restrictions – e.g., the obligation to support their children even after conversion to Christianity and the limitation of the number of "Jew Brokers" in the City of London to 12. The only other community in the British Isles was a small Sephardi group in *Dublin. Nevertheless Jews figured in an increasing proportion in the growing colonial empire – at *Tangier, *New York, *Bombay, and in the West Indies – especially *Jamaica and *Barbados. Numbers rapidly grew in the final years of the 17th century, particularly during the period of the close connection with Holland under William of Orange, when several families came over from Amsterdam. A new synagogue, now classified as an historic monument, was erected in Bevis Marks in London in 1701. The upper class of the community was composed of brokers and foreign traders; the lucrative coral trade, for example, was almost entirely in their hands. Jews entered gradually into various aspects of the country's life. Mention may be made of city magnates, such as Samson *Gideon and Joseph *Salvador, whose financial advice was sought by successive ministries, and of Jacob de *Castro Sarmento, a notable physician and scientist, of Moses *Mendes, the poet, and of Emanuel *Mendes da Costa, clerk and librarian of the Royal Society and a prolific writer.

Meanwhile, an influx of Ashkenazim had followed upon the Sephardi pioneers. The forerunners came principally from Amsterdam and Hamburg, but they were followed by others from other parts of Germany and elsewhere, and later in increasing numbers from Eastern Europe. About 1690, a small Ashkenazi community was formed in London. In 1706, as the result of a communal dispute, a second was formed, and in 1761, a third. The newcomers were, for the most part, distinctly lower in social and commercial status than their Sephardi precursors. A large number of them were occupied in itinerant trading in country areas where the Jewish peddler became a familiar figure. They generally returned to pass the Sabbath in some provincial center. Thus congregations, several of which have since disappeared, grew up in the course of the second half of the 18th century in many country towns – Canterbury, Norwich, Exeter, and others, as well as ports such as *Portsmouth, *Liverpool, Bristol, *Plymouth, King's Lynn, *Penzance, and Falmouth, and manufacturing centers such as *Birmingham and *Manchester. London remained, however, the only considerable center.

The external history of the Jews in England was meanwhile tranquil. In 1753 the introduction to Parliament of the Jewish Naturalization Bill ("The Jew Bill"), giving foreign-born Jews facilities for acquiring the privileges enjoyed by their native-born children, resulted in an anti-Jewish agitation so virulent that the government withdrew the measure; but it was not accompanied by physical violence. Political opposition, on the other hand, led to greater solidarity among the various sections of the community. From 1760 representatives of the Ashkenazi congregations began to act intermittently with the *deputados* of the Sephardim as a watch-committee in matters of common interest. This gradually developed into the London Committee of Deputies of British Jews (usually known as the *Board of Deputies), ultimately comprising representatives also of provincial and (in a minor degree) "colonial" congregations, which assumed its present form in the middle of the 19th century.

The 19th Century

The Napoleonic Wars marked an epoch in the history of the Jews in England. Ashkenazi families, notably the *Goldsmids and *Rothschilds, began to occupy an increasingly important place in English finance and society. A generation of native-born Jews had meanwhile grown up, who were stimulated by the example of Jewish emancipation in France and elsewhere to desire similar rights for themselves. The civic and political disabilities from which they suffered did not in fact amount to very much, for they had enjoyed a great measure of social emancipation almost from the beginning, and commercial restrictions were confined to a few galling limitations in the city of London. In 1829, on the triumph of the movement for Catholic emancipation, agitation began for similar legislation on behalf of the Jews. It was championed in the Commons by Robert Grant and Thomas Babington *Macaulay, the great Whig historian, and in the Lords by the Duke of Sussex, son of George III, a keen Hebraist. On its second introduction in 1833, the Jewish Emancipation Bill was passed by the recently reformed House of Commons, but it was consistently rejected by the Lords in one session after the other. Meanwhile, the Jews were admitted to the office of sheriff (1835) and other municipal offices (1845). Minor disabilities were removed by the Religious Opinions Relief Bill (1846), which left their exclusion from Parliament the only serious grievance of which the English Jews could complain. Lionel de *Rothschild was elected by the city of London as its parliamentary representative time after time from 1847, but the continued opposition of the Lords blocked the legislation which could have enabled him to take the required oaths. In 1858, however, a compromise was reached, and each house of Parliament was allowed to settle its own form of oath. In 1885 Nathaniel de *Rothschild (Lionel's son) was raised to the peerage – the first professing Jew to receive that honor. The example of Benjamin *Disraeli, one of the most brilliant of modern English statesmen, who made no effort to disguise his Jewish origin and sympathies, did much to improve the general social and political position of the Jews. Sir George *Jessel was made solicitor general in 1871, and several Jews subsequently received government appointments. Herbert (later Viscount) *Samuel became a cabinet minister in 1909. Sir David *Salomons, who had been the first Jewish sheriff in 1835 and the first Jewish alderman in 1847, became lord mayor of London in 1855 – a position in which

Shavuot—festival of the first fruits—celebrated in a kibbutz in Israel with the presentation of first fruits. In the Temple period, Shavuot was the time when the individual farmer would set out with his neighbors in joyous procession to Jerusalem, bringing a selection of his ripe first fruits (*bikkurim*) as a thanksgiving offering. *Photo: Z. Radovan, Jerusalem.*

The Jewish holy days and festivals fall into two categories: those commanded by the Pentateuch, such as Sabbath, Rosh Ha-Shanah, Day of Atonement (Yom Kippur), and the Pilgrim Festivals (Passover, Shavuot, and Sukkot), and those added later, such as Purim (1st–2nd century C.E.) and Ḥanukkah (2nd century). All these are observed in various ways by Jews around the world.

SABBATH AND FESTIVALS

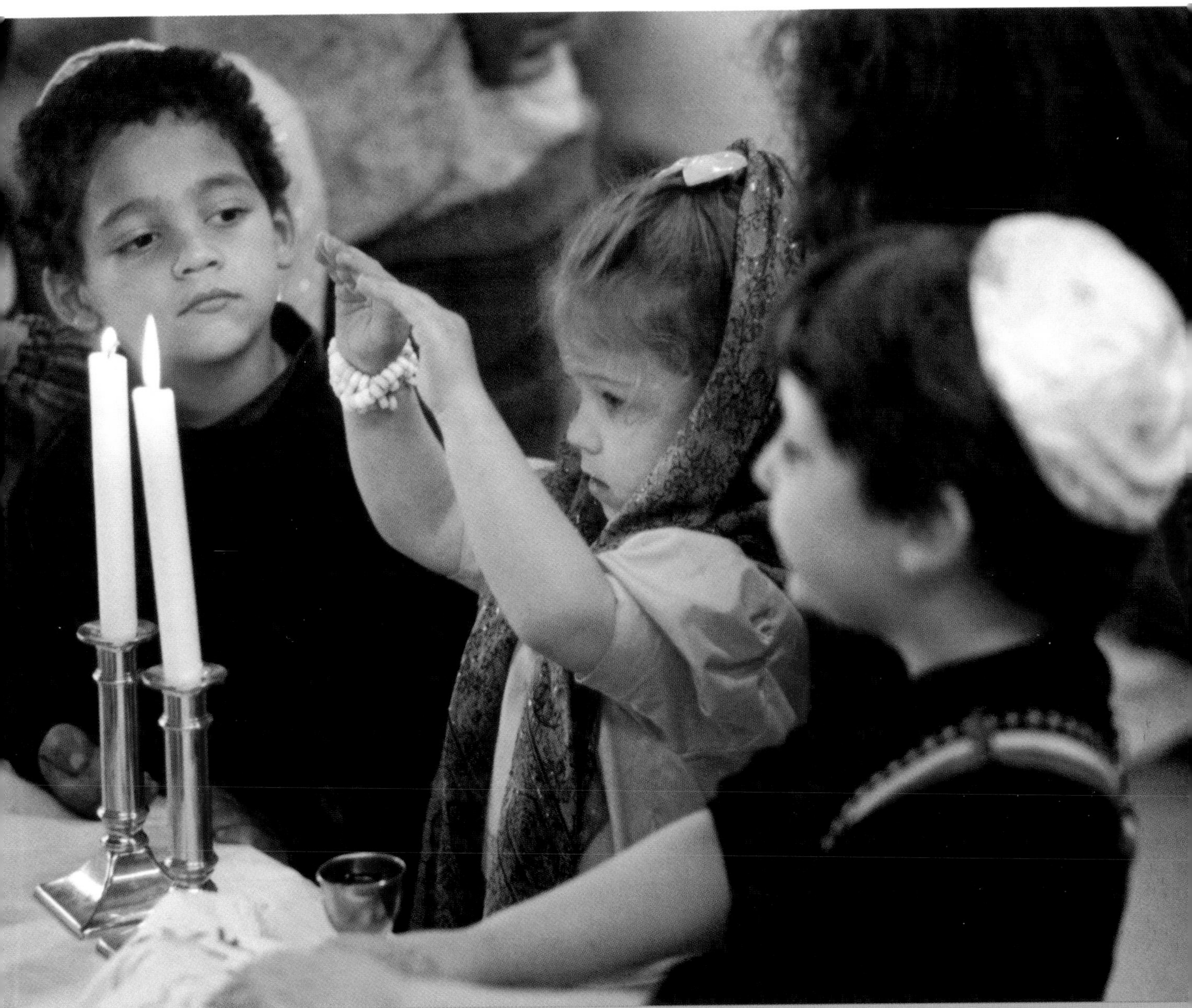

(opposite page) TOP: Yemenite Jews celebrate the last day of Ḥanukkah. The traditional stone-made *hanukkiyyah*, also called a *menorah*, is fully lit. *Photo: Z. Radovan, Jerusalem.*

(opposite page) BOTTOM: A Jewish family from Bukhara celebrating their first Ḥanukkah in Israel. *Photo: Z. Radovan, Jerusalem.*

(this page): Three young children practice Sabbath candle lighting at a day school in Berlin. *© David H. Wells/Corbis.*

ABOVE: An Israeli man and his daughters burn food containing leavening as part of their preparation for Passover. © *Ronen Zvulun/Reuters/Corbis.*

RIGHT: A young boy pats down the soil around a sapling he has just planted for the Tu Bi-Shevat holiday—the "New Year for Trees"—Herzliyya, Israel, 2000. © *Hanan Isachar/Corbis.*

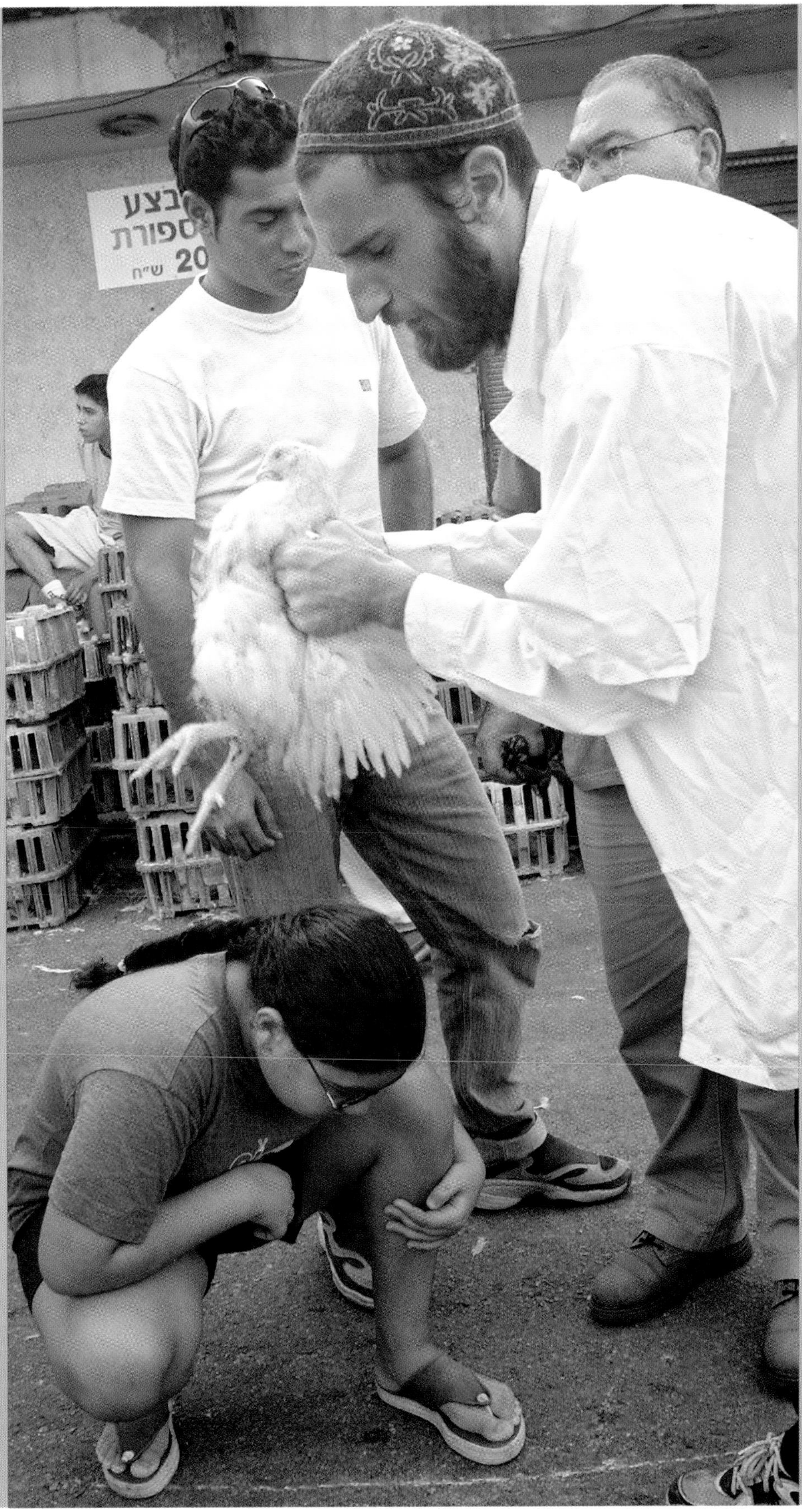

An Israeli girl kneels as a man waves a chicken over her head during a *kaparot* ceremony in Bnei Brak, Israel, 2005. *Kaparot* is performed before Yom Kippur, and it is believed that sins from the past year are transferred to the chicken. The bird is then slaughtered and given to the poor. *Photo by David Silverman/Getty Images.*

ABOVE: Laden table at the Maimuna festival—a celebration held by all Maghrebi Jews and many Eastern communities after the closing of the last day of Passover, which, according to tradition, is the anniversary of the death of Maimonides' father Maimon ben Joseph. *Photo: Nathan Alpert, Israel Government Press Office.*

(opposite page): The Deller Family Sukkah. Permanently at the Israel Museum Jerusalem, painted wood with traditional symbolic pictures, Fischach, Southern Germany, c. 1837. Wood, oil paint. 196/1. *Gift of the Deller family with the help of Dr. Heinrich Feuchtwanger. Photo © The Israel Museum, Jerusalem, by Avraham Hay.*

Israeli youth carry a Torah scroll during the celebration of Simḥat Torah (Rejoicing over the Law) at Rabin's square in Tel Aviv, 2005. © *Eyal Ofer/Corbis.*

Purim, Adloyada festival, Tel Aviv. *Photo: David Harris.*

several Jews have since followed him. In 1890 religious restrictions on virtually every political position and dignity were removed and Jewish emancipation became complete.

Considerable changes had meanwhile been taking place within the community. There was a gradual movement toward greater cohesion. The Sephardi community had to yield pride of place to the Ashkenazim before the end of the 18th century. Solomon *Hirschel, son of R. Hirschel *Levin (Hart Lyon), was appointed rabbi of the Great Synagogue in London in 1802, in succession to David Tevele *Schiff of Frankfurt. His authority was recognized by the other Ashkenazi congregations in London, who were induced by him to enter into a closer union. His successor, Nathan Marcus *Adler, who was elected to office by the delegates of the London congregations in association with those of the major provincial communities, may be considered the first chief rabbi. The extension of his authority is indicated in the *Laws and Regulations for all the Synagogues in the British Empire* which he issued in 1847. He was followed as chief rabbi in 1891 by his son, Hermann *Adler, who had been acting as his father's delegate for some years. He was succeeded by Joseph Herman *Hertz.

COMMUNAL EXPANSION. During the 19th century Anglo-Jewry took the lead in measures for the protection of the Jews and the amelioration of their position in every part of the world. In this they were assured of the assistance of the British government, which was now identified with a strikingly protective policy toward the Jews, especially of Palestine and the Muslim countries of the Middle East – partly because of the absence of closely allied Christian bodies on whose behalf the exertion of political influence could ostensibly be based, as was the case with the rival Russian and French governments. The Board of Deputies increased in scope of activity and in importance. Sir Moses *Montefiore, backed up by the British government, acted as the ambassador for the whole of Jewry, in the event of persecution, from the *Damascus Affair of 1840 onward. In 1871 the *Anglo-Jewish Association was founded to collaborate in the work of the *Alliance Israélite Universelle, prejudiced by the enmities aroused through the Franco-Prussian War; and in 1878 the Joint (Conjoint) Foreign Committee, which it formed in conjunction with the Board of Deputies, came into being as an agency for safeguarding Jewish interests abroad. The **Jewish Chronicle*, the first permanent Anglo-Jewish periodical (now the oldest continuing Jewish publication in the world), was established in 1841. In 1855 *Jews' College was founded in London – the first theological seminary for the training of Anglo-Jewish ministers of religion. It was followed four years later by the Jewish Board of Guardians (since 1964 known as the Jewish Welfare Board), a model London organization for the relief of the poor, which was widely imitated in provincial centers. The loose union for certain charitable and other purposes of the Ashkenazi synagogues in London, which had been in existence since the beginning of the century, became consolidated in 1870 by the establishment, under authority of an act of Parliament, of the United Synagogue which is today one of the most powerful Jewish religious organizations of its sort in the world.

The basis of the community had meanwhile been broadening, though it remained overwhelmingly centered in London. The industrial developments of the 19th century led to a widening of the area of Jewish settlement, important communities based largely on German immigration being formed or expanded in provincial centers such as Manchester, *Bradford, etc. All were Ashkenazi, except at Manchester, where a Sephardi community was also organized in the second half of the century, mostly composed of newcomers from the Levant. With the recrudescence of persecution in Russia in 1881, immigration increased immensely. A majority of the refugees settled in London; the communities of Manchester, Birmingham, and other places were similarly reinforced while that of *Leeds, wholly based on the tailoring industry, proportionately attracted the greatest number of all. The congregations in all the more important industrial towns and seaports throughout the country – including *Scotland, *Wales, and *Ireland – now grew to important dimensions. However, at the same time, some of the older country centers, such as Canterbury or Penzance, were decaying. The newcomers largely settled in urban districts and entered one or two specific trades; the ready-made clothing industry was virtually created as a result of their efforts. The characteristically English Trade Union and Friendly Society movements rapidly acquired a stronghold. The tide of immigration was, however, checked by the Aliens Immigration Act of 1905, passed after a long agitation which at one time assumed something of an antisemitic complexion.

The Federation of Synagogues was established in London by the first Lord *Swaythling in 1887 to coordinate the many small congregations set up by the Russian-Polish immigrant elements – partly in rivalry with the "aristocratic" United Synagogue. The Reform movement had been introduced into England, in spite of strenuous opposition, in 1840, when the West London Synagogue of British Jews was founded. It was long confined almost entirely to the capital. Branch congregations were set up before the end of the 19th century only in Manchester and in Bradford. A more radical movement was begun by the foundation at the beginning of the 20th century, under the auspices of C.G. *Montefiore, of the Jewish Religious Union, which in 1910 established the Liberal Jewish Synagogue. This also showed in the mid-century a considerable measure of expansion. The vast mass of English Jewry, however, remained attached to the compromising Orthodoxy represented by the United Synagogue.

SCHOLARSHIP AND CULTURE. The most eminent Jewish scholars associated with England have been immigrants from abroad, such as David *Nieto, Ephraim *Luzzatto, Michael *Friedlaender, Solomon *Schechter, and Adolf *Buechler. The most eminent native-born scholars have been humanists rather than talmudists, such as David *Levi, an able polemicist and translator of the liturgy, and (in more recent years)

Israel *Abrahams, H.M.J. *Loewe, and C.G. Montefiore. On the other hand, through the building up of the superb collections of Hebrew printed books and manuscripts at the British Museum, the *Bodleian Library at Oxford, and the Library of the University of Cambridge (the last predominating in the **Genizah* Mss.), England has become in many ways the Mecca of the Jewish student throughout the world.

The *Disraelis, father and son, are noteworthy figures in the English literature of the 19th century. Grace *Aguilar and Amy *Levy are among the earliest names in a series of Anglo-Jewish novelists which culminated with Israel *Zangwill, Louis *Golding, etc. Joseph *Jacobs was an eminent figure in English as well as in Jewish letters. Sir Sidney *Lee, editor of the *Dictionary of National Biography* and the foremost Shakespearian scholar of his day, and Sir Israel *Gollancz, secretary of the British Academy, illustrated the Jewish contribution to English literary studies. In art, Simeon *Solomon, Solomon J. *Solomon, Sir Jacob *Epstein, and Sir William *Rothenstein were notable figures. Sir Landon Ronald occupied an important position in the world of music. Alfred *Sutro was among the most popular English dramatists of the Edwardian era, while in the middle of the 20th century Arnold *Wesker, Harold *Pinter, Wolf *Mankowitz, Peter *Shaffer and others have attracted considerable attention. In politics, the Jewish representation in Parliament is considerable. Jews have been identified with all parties (since World War II, especially the Labour Party), and individuals have risen to high rank under governments of every complexion.

[Cecil Roth]

Modern Period

MASS IMMIGRATION. The mass immigration from Eastern Europe that began in 1881 opened a new epoch in Anglo-Jewish history. The Anglo-Jewish community was affected not only by the sheer size of the migration, which increased the population of the community from 65,000 in 1880 to 300,000 in 1914, but also by the differences it imposed on the character of the community. The immigration injected into what was by then an increasingly middle-class, anglicized, mainly latitudinarian body, a mass of proletarian, Yiddish-speaking, predominantly Orthodox immigrants. Whereas the existing community had begun to disperse from the old Jewish quarters into the suburbs, the immigrants formed compact, overcrowded ghettos in East London, Manchester, Leeds, Liverpool, and Glasgow. Furthermore, while the earlier English Jews had tended to seek an increasing diversity of occupations in the 19th century, the immigrants were concentrated in a limited number of trades: in 1901, about 40% of the gainfully employed Russo-Polish immigrant males were tailors, about 12–13% were in the boot and shoe trade, and about 10% were in the furniture trade, mainly as cabinetmakers. The immigrants created a network of institutions such as Yiddish and a few Hebrew newspapers and fraternal societies and trade unions, although the Jewish trade-union movement had no lasting history in Britain. They also created many small synagogues (*ḥevrot*) and joined in the London Federation of Synagogues – albeit under the leadership of English Jews – headed by Sir Samuel Montagu, later Lord Swaythling.

The communal leadership sought to "anglicize" the immigrants by encouraging their participation in classes in English, the state-aided Jewish schools, such as the Jews' Free School, and clubs and youth movements, like the *Jewish Lads Brigade. The London *United Synagogue tried to found a large synagogue in the Jewish quarter with associated community services (the "East End Scheme"), but this plan was frustrated largely by opposition from the *ḥevrot* it was intended to replace. The immigrants themselves generally sought anglicization, as British prestige was high in the world and the British libertarian tradition was appreciated among Jews. While some stalwarts, such as the Machzike Hadath community, remained aloof, many immigrants joined the United Synagogue, since its rite was broadly traditional. The instance of social mobility was high among the immigrants: they sought economic independence, moved to the suburbs, and joined the Anglo-Jewish middle class. Leaving aside minorities of Orthodox, secularists, Yiddishists, socialists, and anarchists, the Anglo-Jewish community that evolved was probably more integrated than any other in the western lands of immigration.

The influx of so many aliens, at a time when there was no effective control over immigration, produced considerable reaction among the native population. Charges were made that aliens working for low wages on piecework in small workshops would depress wages generally and cause unemployment; pressure on housing accommodation would cause overcrowding, raise rents, and introduce "key money" (premiums for grant of tenancies); the English or "Christian" character of whole neighborhoods would be altered, and immigrants would bring disease and crime. Strong sections of the trade unions were hostile to immigration. Organizations such as the British Brothers' League were formed to combat it, and, unfortunately, the peak years of immigration occurred during a period of economic depression.

The charges against the aliens were investigated by several official inquiries, culminating in the Royal Commission on Aliens in 1903, which declared all the charges unfounded, except, in part, that relating to overcrowded housing conditions. A majority of the commission recommended measures to prevent the concentration of immigrants in particular areas. This move proved impracticable, but the government reacted by introducing the 1905 Aliens Act to restrict immigration. The act had some effect at first, but, since it contained appeal provisions for genuine refugees from racial or religious persecution, the number of immigrants increased again to the former annual average. Many opponents of immigration sought to distinguish between the immigrant population and the established Jewish community. The latter had at first displayed an ambivalent attitude toward the immigrants. Although they recognized the humanitarian problem, some leaders feared that the communal institutions would be swamped by the helpless, and at first it was not generally appreciated that

Russian persecution was more than a temporary check on the progress of liberalization. In the earlier years, therefore, attempts were made to dissuade immigrants from coming to England and even to "repatriate" them to Eastern Europe. After the 1903–04 pogroms, however, there was no longer any doubt about the nature of the situation in Eastern Europe and the support of the Jewish communal leadership for immigration was unquestioned.

PARTICIPATION IN PUBLIC LIFE. Meanwhile, political emancipation for British Jews reached its climax when the first peerage was conferred upon a Jew, Lord *Rothschild (1885). The attainment of social acceptance was expressed by the presence of a number of Jews in the "Marlborough House set" centered around the Prince of Wales (later Edward VII); Lord Rothschild and his brothers, Alfred and Leopold, the Reuben brothers, Arthur and Albert *Sassoon, Sir Ernest *Cassel, Baron de *Hirsch, and others, were members of this group. Jews had also become prominent in politics as Conservative members of Parliament (such as the communal leaders Lionel Louis and Benjamin *Cohen), although as a group they still belonged primarily to the Liberal Party which had fostered Jewish emancipation. Notable in the Asquith administration, which began in 1906, were Sir Rufus Isaacs (who became lord chief justice as Lord *Reading in 1913) and the young Herbert Samuel. The prominence of Jews in Liberal politics, the Marconi case (in which both Isaacs and Samuel were, however unfairly, involved), the wealth of Jewish financiers, and even the friendship of Jews with royalty were all ingredients in the literary antisemitism of the Edwardian period, in which Hilaire Belloc, G.K. Chesterton, and Rudyard Kipling all attacked the allegedly alien influences in high places.

WORLD WAR I. The outbreak of World War I (1914) ended the great immigration, although the refugees from Belgium included a considerable number of Jews of East European origin. The high-strung xenophobia of the early war years, in which everything related to Germany was attacked, created some antisemitism and some curious anti-German reactions in the Anglo-Jewish community. The demand for uniform clothing produced an economic boom which benefited small Jewish entrepreneurs. On the other hand, because their civilian occupations were generally not essential enough to defer them from military service in the national interest, the proportion of Jews in the armed forces was higher than in the general population. Genuine loyalty, however, was also responsible for this factor: there were 10,000 casualties among the 50,000 Jews serving, and 1,596 were decorated (including six recipients of the highest award, the Victoria Cross), which was also probably above the general average. Of special significance was the raising of Jewish battalions of the Royal Fusiliers to serve in the campaign to liberate Palestine from the Turks.

The outstanding event of the war, however, was the attainment of the *Balfour Declaration in 1917. Zionism in England originated with the *Ḥovevei Zion in 1887, led by Elim d'Avigdor and Colonel Albert *Goldsmid. Although some of the older members of Anglo-Jewry were interested in the Jewish national movement, the recent immigrants provided the mass of support, particularly after the development of political Zionism in 1897. *Herzl visited England on a number of occasions and the offer of *Uganda was made to him by Joseph *Chamberlain, then colonial secretary. Although Sir Francis Montefiore became president of the English Zionist Federation, formed in 1899, many leading figures of the established community, notably the first Lord Rothschild, Sir Samuel *Montagu (Lord Swaythling), and Hermann *Adler, the chief rabbi, opposed it. The turmoil World War I brought to the Middle East and the desire to influence American Jewry on behalf of the Western allies provided Chaim *Weizmann with the opportunity to persuade the British government to issue the Balfour Declaration. To some extent, Weizmann had been anticipated by Herbert Samuel, a member of the government until 1916, in a pro-Zionist memorandum to the prime minister. The official leadership of the community was now much more disposed to Zionism: the new chief rabbi, Joseph Hertz, the Haham of the Sephardim, Moses *Gaster, and the second Lord Rothschild (who succeeded his father in 1915) were all actively associated with Zionism. The issue of the declaration had been preceded by a letter to the *Times* from the presidents of the Board of Deputies (D.L. Alexander) and the Anglo-Jewish Association (Claude Montefiore) dissociating themselves from Jewish nationalism. The declaration precipitated the resignation of Alexander and the victory of the pro-Zionists, whose views were henceforth the official policy of the Anglo-Jewish establishment. The events of 1917 thus served as a catalyst within the Anglo-Jewish community and promoted it into a new role in world Jewry, since Britain was to become the administering power for the Jewish National Home.

RELIGIOUS AND SOCIAL TRENDS. Although Russo-Jewish immigrants had exercised a decisive influence in the religious and intellectual spheres, they were not alone. A group of British- or Empire-born scholars and writers grew up in the 1880s with the Romanian-born Solomon *Schechter as their mentor. The Anglo-Jewish Historical Exhibition of 1887 (with whose organization the art connoisseur Sir Isidore Spielmann was associated) was visited by Heinrich *Graetz, who urged the formation of a body to study Anglo-Jewish history. This suggestion was implemented in 1893 by the foundation of the *Jewish Historical Society of England, with whose work Lucien *Wolf, equally celebrated as an expert on international affairs, was associated for over 35 years. Apart from the continuation of historical studies, the specifically Anglo-Jewish renaissance was short; Schechter and Jacobs moved to America, as did the *Jewish Quarterly Review (begun by Claude Montefiore and Israel Abrahams in 1888).

The main body of religious Anglo-Jewry continued its latitudinarian way. While small congregations of German or East European origin maintained a separate existence on the extreme right of the religious spectrum, the immigrants increasingly joined the United Synagogue in London and its provincial counterparts. Some changes in liturgical usage had been sanctioned by the aged chief rabbi, Nathan Marcus Adler, in 1880 and may have led to his retirement from active office. His son, Hermann, who succeeded him sanctioned further changes in 1892. But these changes were in detail rather than substance and followed what the United Synagogue then described as its principle of progressive Conservatism, an attitude confirmed by the next chief rabbi, Hertz.

In contrast to this trend was a movement in the 1890s for more radical change that soon broke from the Orthodox ranks, although several of those originally concerned, such as Simeon *Singer, the translator of the prayer book, remained in the Orthodox community. As a result, in 1902, Claude Montefiore formed the Jewish Religious Union, which soon developed into the Liberal Jewish Synagogue.

The 1920s was a period of deceptive political calm and relative intellectual stagnation for Anglo-Jewry. Socially, the decade saw the progressive anglicization of the community and its increasing upward mobility from the working to the middle class. Small businesses prospered; the new generation turned to professional callings as lawyers, doctors, dentists, and accountants; and university education, even in the established institutions, began to be the practice for the middle class, instead of the prerogative of virtually the upper class alone. Social change was reflected in the steady exodus from the crowded Jewish quarters in London and the main provincial centers as middle-class families acquired a house and garden in the expanding residential suburbs. A distinctively Anglo-Jewish, middle-class way of life began to develop there, and Golders Green became as characteristic a milieu of interwar Anglo-Jewry as Maida Vale had been in the 1880s.

An attempt to finance a massive education renaissance as the Jewish memorial to World War I fell far short of achievement, but the United Synagogue, under the effective paternalism of the industrialist Sir Robert Waley-*Cohen, continued to expand as an efficiently run religious organization and founded new synagogues in the developing districts of London. During this period, the Board of Deputies was led by Sir Osmond d'Avigdor-Goldsmid, a founder of the "mixed" *Jewish Agency, on which both Zionists and non-Zionists served. Although the Zionist victory of 1917 had changed the community's political trend, it had not yet effected a social revolution and removed control from members of the older establishment.

THE SHADOW OF NAZISM. The 1930s were overshadowed by the rise of fascism, which produced an immigration of 90,000 refugees (73,000 from Germany and Austria, 10,000 from Czechoslovakia, 4,000–5,000 from Poland, and 2,000 from Italy and elsewhere). Of this number, 10,000–12,000 left Britain in 1940, 2,000–2,500 were transferred as internees to Australia and Canada and did not return, and 15,000–20,000 left after 1945 or died during the period, so that some 40,000–55,000 prewar refugees, mostly but not exclusively Jewish, were counted in Britain by 1950. Quantitatively, this was a substantial intake for a community of between 300,000 and 400,000, though a much smaller one than the Russo-Jewish immigration of 1881–1914. Qualitatively, its impact was almost as great. The Central European immigrants were essentially from the middle class, unlike the originally proletarian Russo-Jewish ones. Before drastic restrictions were imposed on the export of property from Germany, the refugees of the 1930s brought considerable capital: it is estimated that up to mid-1938, £12,000,000 were transferred from Germany to Britain. The immigrants created or transplanted many businesses, particularly in the fashion trades, pharmaceutical production, and light engineering, and made London the European center of the fur trade in place of Leipzig. Equally important was the influence of the many professionals, intellectuals, and artists upon British scientific, literary, and cultural life.

The effect of this immigration upon Anglo-Jewry was even more dramatic. Both branches of religious life were strengthened. Ministers and scholars trained in the German Reform movement revitalized progressive Judaism; the Frankfurt-inspired Orthodox expanded the separatist Orthodox movement in England and also produced a shift to the right in the United Synagogue. The Jewish day-school movement, the *Gateshead yeshivah (founded in 1927) and associated institutions and, after 1945, a number of other educational institutions (especially in North and North-West London) were strengthened by German and Hungarian Jews. The Central European immigrants virtually created a cultural revival in the academic sphere. They took part in every aspect of activity from rabbinic studies to Anglo-Jewish historiography, and postwar institutions like the Department of Hebrew and Jewish Studies at University College, London, would have been unthinkable without them.

Continental fascism was imitated in England on a smaller scale and fostered by the economic depression of the early 1930s. Attacks on Jews and Jewish property by the "blackshirts" led by the English fascist leader Sir Oswald Mosley, provocative processions through the Jewish areas, and street clashes with left-wing elements followed, but were checked by the 1936 Public Order Act, which, inter alia, banned the wearing of political uniforms. The need to defend the community against these attacks induced a feeling of solidarity that was intensified by the need to raise funds for the relief of refugees and the work of settlement in Palestine. Fund raising again became a primary communal commitment that served as a unifying force as well as an engrossing organizational and social activity.

WORLD WAR II. The outbreak of war in 1939 had a centrifugal effect on Anglo-Jewry. At first schoolchildren and some mothers were evacuated from London and other large centers of population; the heavy bombing which began in the autumn of 1940 brought about a more general dispersal. Service in the armed forces took away women as well as men, and in 1940 refugees were subjected to large-scale, though temporary, internment. Religious and communal life in London continued on a smaller scale, and the dispersal of the population was followed by a regrouping in new communities in the evacuation areas. The countryside and small towns, which had hardly known a Jew, became the homes of thriving communities for the duration of the war, and some of these new communities maintained their existence even after the war. The main effect of the war on the distribution of the Jewish population, however, is seen in the East End of London and in some of the other Jewish quarters in the main provincial cities, where the bombing destroyed the physical environment. The Ashkenazi Great Synagogue in Duke's Place, London, was only one of the Jewish monuments and institutions that was lost. In the East End of London, the old Jewish residential area was never rebuilt though some of the older people remained or returned and many others continued to come in daily to work.

ENGLAND AND PALESTINE. The relations of the developing Jewish community in Palestine with the British government as a mandatory power increasingly concerned the Anglo-Jewish community, which expressed opposition to the policy set down in the White Paper of 1939, limiting Jewish immigration to Palestine. Support for a Jewish state was the policy of the Zionist bodies and the *World Jewish Congress, but not of the *Anglo-Jewish Association nor of its splinter group, the anti-Zionist Jewish Fellowship, headed by Sir Basil *Henriques (which dissolved in 1948). The Anglo-Jewish Association enjoyed great prestige for its distinguished membership and 70 years of concern with foreign affairs. The wish to mobilize the support in the representative body of Anglo-Jewry for Zionist policies was combined with a desire to make its leadership reflect the changing character of the community as a whole. These aspirations were symbolized by the 1939 election of Selig *Brodetsky, a first generation Russo-Jewish immigrant, educated in Britain, as president of the Board of Deputies. They were realized in 1943 by a carefully planned campaign to secure the election to the board of a majority committed to the creation of a Jewish state in Palestine. The newly elected board dissolved its joint Foreign Committee with the Anglo-Jewish Association. As in World War I, the problems of Palestine effected a polarization in the Anglo-Jewish community between those who put primary emphasis on Jewish national ideals and those who stressed the overriding claims of British citizenship.

Although this dichotomy was unrealistic in many respects, it sharpened communal tensions. After the creation of the State of Israel, the Anglo-Jewish Association adopted a policy of goodwill toward the new state, but stressed the responsibilities of Anglo-Jews as citizens of Britain who were identified with its national life. Communal tensions were also heightened by some antisemitism, which resulted from the conflict between the mandatory administration and the *yishuv*, beginning with the assassination of Lord Moyne in 1944 and culminating in the hanging of two British army sergeants in August 1947. The latter was followed by minor disorders in some provincial cities and some attacks on Jewish property. Normalcy was restored after the establishment of diplomatic relations between the British government and the new state.

EDUCATION. The need to provide for the education of children dispersed in the 1939–45 evacuation led to the formation of a joint emergency organization. In 1945 Jewish education was substantially reorganized on this basis with a central council for the whole country and an executive board for London, representing the United Synagogue and other Orthodox institutions. Jewish education during the evacuation had been limited to an average of one hour a week, and improvement of standards after the war was slow. The new organization was responsible for the reconstitution of the Jews' Free School and two other of the prewar private schools that were closed during the war, one of which was a secondary comprehensive school in a central location with a planned complement of 1,500 pupils. As Jewish education regained importance, the schools took various forms: the Jewish secondary schools movement, begun in 1929 by Victor Schonfeld; the day schools begun in the 1950s under Zionist auspices; independent Orthodox day schools with Yiddish as a language of instruction; the long-standing provincial day schools; and Carmel College, a private school in the country, founded by Kopul Rosen.

Early Postwar Period

Chief Rabbi Hertz died in January 1946 and Israel *Brodie succeeded him in May 1948. The first chief rabbi to be both born and educated in Britain, Brodie found the religious spectrum of Anglo-Jewry not only growing stronger at either end but also tending to disintegrate in the middle. Orthodoxy, combining strict observance and exact learning with secular culture, had been strengthened by the Central European refugees of the Frankfurt school and, particularly after 1945, was also increased by refugees from Poland and Hungary, many of whom were Ḥasidim. The Reform and Liberal congregations, while still a minority, probably increased their membership at a greater rate than the United Synagogue, opening numerous new congregations and founding the Leo Baeck College to train their own ministers. Although their leadership was clearly strengthened by the Central European immigration of 1933–39, much of their postwar membership could only have come from the ranks of the nominally Orthodox. The Spanish and Portuguese Congregation also increased with the immigration of Jews from Egypt, Iraq, and Aden.

In 1956, Anglo-Jewry celebrated the tercentenary of the resettlement, with a more or less united service at the historic Bevis Marks Synagogue and a dinner at London's Guildhall, in the presence of the Duke of Edinburgh. But the sentiments of communal solidarity – and of self-congratulation on communal self-discipline – engendered by these celebrations were short-lived. There had already been considerable changes within the main synagogal bodies. The character of the Federation of Synagogues changed as its membership, while hardly increasing, moved from the small *ḥevrot* of the

East End to live in the suburbs. There they often attended local synagogues but retained membership in the federation for sentiment and burial rights. The old-fashioned minister (and even his clerical collar) had disappeared in the United Synagogue in favor of younger rabbis, often pupils of Jews' College under the direction of Isidore *Epstein, who strove to remodel it as a rabbinical seminary. The *bet din*, under the influence above all of the great scholar Yehezkel *Abramsky, steadily kept the religious orientation of the United Synagogue to the right; at the same time, however, the old lay leadership, under the presidency of Frank Samuel and Ewen Montagu, tended toward religious flexibility. The influence of members of the older families must not be exaggerated, however. As early as the 1950s, a new generation of laymen – second-generation citizens, Zionist, and traditionally Orthodox – was maturing in the United Synagogue.

In all these changes lay the seeds of conflict, which crystallized around Louis *Jacobs, a rabbi of Orthodox practice who held certain modernist views. Minister of the fashionable New West End Synagogue (London), Jacobs was appointed tutor of Jews' College in 1959 with the consent of the chief rabbi. The latter, however, vetoed Jacobs' appointment as college principal and then in 1964 his reappointment to his former synagogue, because he held that Jacobs maintained parts of the Torah were not of divine origin and human reason should select which parts were divine. The local management of the synagogue persisted in their desire to have Jacobs as minister and permitted him to preach, although the requisite certificate or special sanction had not been issued by the chief rabbi. The central body of the United Synagogue then constitutionally deposed Jacobs' supporters, who founded a new congregation in another area with Jacobs as minister. The "Jacobs Affair" received wide publicity in the non-Jewish press, but its significance may have been exaggerated. Since the formation of the Reform Synagogue in 1840, Anglo-Jewry has not been very interested in theology or biblical criticism, as distinct from ritual or liturgy. There were personal and social factors underlying the controversy, and a shift took place in the leadership of the United Synagogue in 1962, when the presidency was first filled from outside the circle of older families by the financier and industrialist Sir Isaac *Wolfson. The incident that led to the formation of a new synagogue was over a disciplinary issue, not a theological one (preaching without the chief rabbi's certificate), and the new congregation has not yet inspired a wider movement. The issues involved in the "Jacobs Affair" and its consequences could, however, be regarded as marginal to the much more important problem of Jewish religious life, i.e., the progressive alienation of growing sections of the Anglo-Jewish community from Jewish religious affiliation of any kind.

The main countervailing factor to the trend away from Jewish identification was the influence of the State of Israel. Mobilizing support for Israel was a major communal and social activity and, to some extent, a substitute for the organized religious life of earlier times. But it actively affected only a minority of the community until the *Six-Day War (1967), when the danger to and triumph of Israel produced an emotional reaction unprecedented in intensity and affecting even many who were previously estranged from Jewish life. It was not clear, however, how lasting the effect would be or whether it might weaken Anglo-Jewry still further by adding to those numbers, previously inconsiderable, who have gone to settle in Israel. Anglo-Jewry made little impact on world scholarship in the second third of the 20th century.

[Vivian David Lipman]

DEMOGRAPHY. The number of Jews in Britain, which was estimated to be 410,000 in 1967, is declining in absolute terms. World Jewish population figures show that during the 1960s Britain's Jewish community has slipped numerically from fourth to sixth place. This decline is being felt acutely in the provinces, in both very small communities and larger centers. Greater London, on the other hand, has maintained its level of 280,000 Jewish inhabitants (61% of the total Jewish population of the country). Close to 75% of the Jewish population of Britain is concentrated in the country's five largest cities. The most significant trend in the last two decades has been the migration of the Jewish population from the urban central areas – the old ghetto quarters – to the new suburban districts surrounding big conurbations. The exodus from the older districts has not, however, been characterized as a transplantation of old communities in new areas. A concomitant phenomenon has been the wider distribution of the Jewish population in places more distant from urban centers and settlement in a more scattered fashion among a predominantly non-Jewish population. In these areas Jews lack effective community organization and are isolated from the more developed forms of Jewish life found nearer the cities, exposing them to the potent forces of assimilation. The influence of assimilation must be regarded as one of the factors contributing to the numerical decline of the community. In purely demographic terms, the most visible symptom of this decline, and one reflecting the speed with which it is taking place, is the drop in Jewish marriages, and the intermarriage rate has been estimated to be between 12% and 25%. The drastic change can be seen when the synagogue marriage rate of 4.0 per thousand in the period 1961–65 is compared with the marriage rate in the general population, which was 7.5 in the same period. This very substantial difference may be attributed to two main causes:

(a) the rise in the number of Jews who marry by civil ceremony only, a phenomenon which might also signify a rise in the rate of intermarriage;

(b) the decline in the Jewish birthrate over the last few decades. In the second half of the 20th century a strong tendency had set in among Jews in Britain not to go through a religious ceremony in the synagogue, the causal factor for which might be the increase in the intermarriage rate.

OCCUPATIONS. The occupational trends in the second quarter of the 20th century (up to the 1960s) have been as follows:

large numbers have abandoned the semi-skilled and manual occupations; increasing proportions have entered occupations with opportunities for self-employment, such as shopkeeping, hairdressing, and taxi driving; and there has been a continuous rise in the number of Jews entering the professions. The number of economically active persons in the community has declined, but one explanation for this turn is the greater number of Jewish students who remain in school after age 15 and proceed into the professions. The disproportionate Jewish interest in finance has drastically decreased and preoccupation with manufacturing has increased substantially. Since the beginning of the 20th century, the predominance of Jewish-owned merchant banks has declined, while Jews have become more prominent in enterprises of large-scale production, particularly of consumer goods. On the whole, information concerning industrial distribution shows that remarkable similarities exist between Jews in Britain, the United States, Canada, and continental Europe. In all cases large concentrations of Jews are found in the clothing and textile trades, distributive trades, and light industries, and to an increasing degree in professional and administrative services. There is an under-representation of Jews, however, in agriculture and heavy industries. The fact that the younger generation has largely avoided the traditional Jewish industrial setting of tailoring and furniture making in the last three decades has resulted in a decline of the Jewish labor and trade-union movements that flourished at the turn of the century. The Jewish worker in the 1950s exhibited a strong tendency to leave the ranks of the working class and become self-employed. It has been estimated that Jewish students compose 3% of the total student population of Britain, whereas Jews account for less than 1% of the population of the country. In addition, only 11.4% of the Jewish women were economically active, compared to 33.9% in the general population.

COMMUNITY LIFE. Organization life in Britain boasts a wide array of charitable, religious, educational, recreational, and political groups. These often overlap both in function and membership, which makes it difficult to estimate the proportions of Jews associated with particular types of organizations. Some figures are available, however; in London 61% of the Jews are members of synagogues, as are 75% in Liverpool; in Leeds more than 43% contribute to charitable organizations, and over 63% contribute to the *Jewish National Fund; in the Willesden district of London, 72% of the boys and 53% of the girls are members of Jewish youth groups. Youth organizations are divided into the following categories: various clubs offering social and sports activities, the best example of which is *Maccabi; Zionist organizations offering educational and recreational programs and strengthening cultural and personal ties with Israel, such as *Habonim and *Bnei Akiva; organizations providing study courses and the Jewish Youth Study Group movement; and societies for Jewish students at universities and colleges. The larger representative youth organizations are the Jewish Youth Council, on which nearly 40 organizations are represented; the Association of Jewish Youth, with some 15,000 members; and the Inter-University Jewish Federation, with some 30 affiliated societies in most universities and in many other higher educational establishments.

Some of the basic constituents of religious identification seem to have remained stable since the 1930s. Thus, in 1934 there were 310 registered synagogues in England and Wales and 400 in 1962; however, considering that there were fewer than 300,000 Jews in the country in 1934, the number of synagogues per thousand Jews had not changed. In London more than a third of the Jewish population is not affiliated with any synagogue, while in Leeds and Liverpool less than a quarter of the Jews were found to be similarly unaffiliated. All the surveys taken in this area point to the fact that the vast majority of Jews still ascribe to religious burial. Synagogue attendance compared with prewar years has been low, except for the High Holidays; however, fragmentary statistics on this point suggest that attendance runs parallel to church attendance among the general population, i.e., between 13–15% of the population attend services weekly. Some religious practices, such as bar-mitzvahs, are observed by a substantial majority, and other practices, such as circumcision, are almost universally maintained. There can be no doubt, however, that on the whole the influence of religion on Anglo-Jewry has declined. Immanuel *Jakobovits, who was elected chief rabbi in 1966, declared after taking office in 1967 that the survival of Judaism was the primary challenge, in view of "staggering losses by defections, assimilation and intermarriage." He drew particular attention to the estimate that 85% of the students and 90% of the 2,000 academics were outside organized Jewish religious life.

EDUCATION AND CULTURE. The leadership of the community agrees that the key to the preservation of Jewish identification in general, and religious practice in particular, is education, although Jewish education in and of itself will not insure identification without the maintenance of a Jewish atmosphere in the home. Statistics also reveal a continuing desire on the part of Jews to associate mainly with fellow-Jews. Education has been constantly highlighted, therefore, and in the past 15 years much effort has gone into the establishment of Jewish day schools, especially after it became evident that Jewish education imparted through *talmud torah* classes after school hours was becoming less and less satisfactory. In 1962 it was estimated that in London and the provinces, at any one time, only about 57% of Jewish children of school age were receiving Jewish instruction. Despite the efforts to extend day-school programs to larger numbers, the achievement is less impressive than it might at first appear. In the whole of Britain in 1963 there were some 8,800 children in the 48 Jewish day schools (of which only 12 were secondary schools), a figure that represented a doubling of students compared with the situation ten years before. Progress since 1963 has been rather slow, although a certain amount of consolidation in the day-school movement has taken place. (See also *Education, Great Britain.)

Higher Jewish and Hebrew *education can be obtained in yeshivot and colleges with specialized departments in these fields. A survey published in 1962 showed that in the eight yeshivot in Britain, there were 392 full-time students (many of whom were from overseas). Jews' College had 31 students in its combined degree and minister's-diploma course during the 1959–60 session. Similarly, the numbers associated with cultural bodies such as the Jewish Historical Society or the Friends of Yiddish are relatively small. The larger Jewish public is reached, however, by the Jewish press, which has a strong influence on the measure of individual identification. The leading position is taken by the *Jewish Chronicle*, which has the widest circulation in the community. A number of smaller newspapers also cater to some of the provincial towns and to some sections of the community more actively connected with Israel and its specific political parties. Two leading academic journals, *The Jewish Journal of Sociology* (1959–) and *The Journal of Jewish Studies* (1949–), are published, and two social science units, one at the Board of Deputies and the other at the Institute of Jewish Affairs, are specifically engaged in research on Jews. There is no regular Hebrew publication in the form of a journal or a newspaper, and the almost total decline of Yiddish is reflected in the closing of the last weekly Yiddish newspaper in 1967. The trend in Britain toward an open society and the existence of equal citizenship rights has closed the social distance between the Jewish minority and British society, and in turn has been eroding Jewish identification. There can be no doubt that progressive emancipation has been leading to a greater degree of assimilation. The persistence of prejudice and some degree of discrimination against Jews has worked, however, in the opposite direction. During the 1950s and 1960s Britain was not free of such anti-Jewish prejudices. They have been promoted by tiny antisemitic groups, who in 1959 and again in 1965 engaged in desecration and arson against synagogues and have spasmodically disseminated virulent antisemitic literature. Less extreme or overt prejudice has also been evident in the business world; for example, in some insurance firms and other commercial enterprises. Quotas exist for Jewish pupils in some elite schools, and Jews have been excluded from the membership of some recreational clubs. At the same time forces more favorable to gentile-Jewish relations have been growing in the postwar period. Special efforts made by the Council of Christians and Jews, established in 1942 and functioning through its 20 branches, have succeeded in fostering better Jewish-gentile relations in the 1960s.

[Ernest Krausz]

Later Developments

DEMOGRAPHY. A conference in March 1977, organized by the Board of Deputies of British Jews and the Institute of Jewish Affairs, surveyed Jewish life in modern Britain and reviewed trends since a previous conference in 1962, basing itself on the social and demographic data produced by the Board's Research Unit, established in 1965. Generally, the conference found a trend towards polarization in Anglo-Jewry: a growing minority were intensifying their commitment to Jewish religion and education, but there was also an increasing general drift towards intermarriage and assimilation. No official estimates of the Jewish population had been published since the estimate of the Research Unit in 1965 of 410,000, but informed observers now put the number of those identified with the Anglo-Jewish community at considerably below 400,000. While between 1960 and 1979 the annual number of burials (and cremations) under Jewish auspices remained in the range between 4,600 and 4,900, the number of persons married under Jewish religious auspices fell from an annual average of 3,664 for 1960–65 to 2,782 for 1975–79 and 2,606 in 1979. Local community surveys carried out indicated households of sizes varying from 2.4 to 2.98 according to the age structure and character of the local Jewish community, and data on children per marriage in the 1970s reinforced the conclusion that Anglo-Jewry was not replacing itself by natural increase: nor was this deficiency being made up by net immigration.

The surveys confirmed the picture of organized Anglo-Jewry as consisting of increasingly middle class, and increasingly aging, communities; with a high proportion of home- and car-ownership, and a wide range of occupations; and with a tendency well above the national average towards self-employment. Geographically, there remained pockets of elderly and often poorer residents in the inner cities but the trends were towards dispersal from the larger conurbations into the suburbs and countryside, combined with the decline or extinction of established smaller provincial communities.

Synagogue affiliation showed 110,000 members of synagogues in 1977, a decline of 6% since 1970; the Central Orthodox (e.g., United Synagogue and Federation of Synagogues) appeared to be losing ground to the Progressives (Reform and Liberal) with over 20% of the membership and to the small but growing right-wing Orthodox (3.5%). This apparent trend towards religious polarization was also found in the marriage figures for 1979, with the Progressives responsible for 22.5% (compared with 18.6% in 1960–65) and the right-wing Orthodox for 8.4% of the total number of synagogue marriages. The overall decline in synagogue affiliation continued into the 21st century, dropping to a membership of 88,000 in 362 congregations in 2001. The United Synagogue and Federation of Synagogues accounted for half the congregations, with the United Synagogue accounting for 57 percent of overall membership, the Progressives next with 25,000 members (28 percent), and the Ḥaredim with 7,500 (8.5 percent).

The Jewish population continued to decline in the 1980s, from 336,000 (plus or minus 10%) in 1983 to around 300,000 in 1990, a level which it maintained into the 21st century, making it the fifth largest Jewish community in the world. The percentage of Jews who were members of synagogues in the central Orthodox stream fell from 70.5% in 1983 to 64% in 1990. The percentage of those affiliated to the right-wing Orthodox community increased from 4.4% in 1983 to 10% in 1984, falling to 6.9% in 1990. Only the Progressive movements showed signs of consistent growth. In 1983, 22.4% of Jews affiliated to synagogues belonged to Reform and Liberal congregations. According to 1990 figures, the Reform Synagogues of Great Britain accounted for 17%, the Union of Liberal and Progressive Synagogues claimed 7%, with the Masorti movement taking a small, but growing share. The Sephardi community held steady at just under 3% of the total.

The geographical and social distribution of British Jews barely altered. Two-thirds continued to inhabit the capital. The only growth areas were the "sun-belt" towns on the South Coast such as Brighton, the largest with 10,000. Manchester Jewry maintained its numbers at around 30,000, but Leeds had seen a fall from around 14,000 to about 11,000. A similar drop was estimated for Glasgow. Within each metropolitan center, Jews remain concentrated in a small number of prosperous, suburban, middle-class districts: Bury in Manchester, Moortown in Leeds, northwest London and Redbridge, an eastern suburb of the capital. The first centers of settlement are now almost bereft of Jewish residents or institutions.

In the mid-1990s the Board of Deputies Community Research Unit estimated the total number of Israelis in the UK to be at least 27,000. Their distribution reflected that of the Jewish population. Over two-thirds live in Greater London, with the majority concentrated in the northwestern boroughs. The highest concentration of Israelis outside London, 7% of the total, is in the northwest of England. The Israelis had a different age profile than British Jews. Over 25% were aged under 16 and only 2% were over 65 years, as compared to 17% and 25% respectively for British Jews. There have been no significant changes in the geographical or occupational distribution of British Jews.

POLITICAL DEVELOPMENTS. The General Election of 1979 returned to the new House of Commons 21 Labour and 11 Conservative Jewish members. The new Conservative Government included one Jewish cabinet minister, Sir Keith Joseph, responsible for industry and regarded as a strong influence on the economic thinking of Prime Minister Thatcher, and senior ministers outside the cabinet including Nigel Lawson (Financial Secretary, Treasury), Leon Brittan (Home Office), Mrs. Sally Oppenheim (Consumer Affairs), as well as junior ministers such as Malcolm Rifkind (Scotland) and Geoffrey Finsberg and Lord Bellwin (Environment). In spite of the prime minister's personal commitment to Israel and the strong Jewish vote in her constituency (Finchley), concern was expressed at the pro-Arab record of influential Foreign Office ministers and some evidence of Britain modifying her attitude towards Israel in line with developing EEC policies on the Middle East.

In 1980, earlier discussion of the question whether there was a specifically Jewish pattern of voting crystallized in a debate between the political scientist, Dr. Geoffrey Alderman, who maintained that Jews voted according to their communal interests and could exercise a key influence in important marginal constituencies, and Dr. Barry Kosmin, director of the Board of Deputies' Research Unit, who showed that the trend of Jewish voters to support the Conservative Party merely reflected their increasingly middle class status; and even if Jews did vote to support a particular policy, they could not affect the outcome in more than a very few constituencies.

A disturbing change during the later 1970s was that of the extreme right-wing National Front from latent to overt antisemitism; and their obtaining 75,000 votes, with some high percentages locally, in the 1976 district council elections. In the 1979 general election, however, when the turnout was much higher, their 301 candidates polled a total of only 191,000 votes with the highest vote for any of their candidates just over 2000; nor did any National Front candidate win even one local council seat. However, in late 1980 Anglo-Jewry shared the unease caused in European Jewry generally by the violence of right-wing movements, notably the Paris synagogue bombing; and the recurrence of anti-Jewish incidents, albeit scattered and unpublicized, combined with deepening economic recession, gave cause for concern.

The principal manifestation of anti-Jewish activity was however associated with the Arab and overwhelmingly left-wing propaganda against Israel, particularly on university campuses. With some 12,000 Arab students in British universities and higher technical institutions, outnumbering Jewish students, especially in engineering and other vocational faculties, anti-Israel propaganda in student organizations had been rife for some years, and it developed into overt anti-Jewish discrimination in 1977. The (British) National Union of Students had voted in 1974 to "refuse any assistance (financial or otherwise) to openly racist and fascist organizations … and to prevent, by whatever means are necessary," any members of these organizations from speaking in colleges. The resolution of the UN Assembly in November 1975, equating Zionism with racism, thus gave a welcome opportunity to the Socialist Workers Party and the General Union of Palestinian Students. Student unions at some eight universities and five polytechnics voted to withdraw recognition from local university Jewish societies. Decisions at such meetings are usually taken by a small minority of the total number of students in the institution, and several were subsequently reversed. In 1980, however, the exclusion of Israeli scholars from an Arab-sponsored colloquium at Exeter University was widely criticized as an infringement of academic (and tax-payer supported) freedom of discussion.

Support for Israel continued to be possibly the most socially unifying factor in Anglo-Jewry with the organizational framework complementing, even to some extent replacing, more traditional patterns of organization. The advent of the Begin Likud government in 1977 evoked at first a detached, even critical, attitude, from personalities accustomed to dealing with the previous governments in Israel. The peace initiative of Prime Minister Begin and the Camp David agreement which followed, however, produced a much more sympathetic attitude within Anglo-Jewry. The Likud government's settlement policy in the administered territories, however, evoked controversy within Anglo-Jewry, in which Chief Rabbi Jakobovits became involved, when he argued that the retention of occupied territory in the Holy Land had to be considered in the light of the possibility of advancing the cause of peace and the saving of life. While there was not unqualified support for his views within Anglo-Jewry, there was condemnation of attempts to impugn the integrity of his commitment to the cause of Israel. Organizationally, the union of the Zionist Federation of Great Britain with the Mizrachi as the United Zionists was announced but not consummated as of 1981.

The 1980s saw a shift of political allegiances among British Jews from the left to the right. Affluence and self-interest have underpinned the trend, but it was abetted by the perceived anti-Zionism of the Labour Party and the appeal of Mrs. Thatcher, prime minister for most of the period, who was seen as "strong" on Jewish issues. Yet the same period saw manifestations of a stubborn prejudice against Jews within Conservative political circles.

In the June 1983 General Election, 28 Jewish MPs were elected of whom 17 were Conservative and 11 Labour. Three Jews were appointed to serve in the new cabinet, rising to four in 1984 and briefly five in 1986. The General Election of June 1987 saw 63 Jewish candidates. Of these, 16 Conservative and 7 Labour candidates were elected. This marked the second highest ever number of Jewish Tory MPs and a big fall in the number of Jewish Labourites. In the June 1992 General Election out of 43 Jewish Parliamentary candidates, 11 Tory, 8 Labour, and 1 Liberal Democrat were successful. The unsuccessful candidates included 4 Jewish Greens, a new phenomenon. Three Jewish Conservative MPs retired and two others were defeated. Among the appointments to the new cabinet made by the prime minister, John Major, were two Jews: Michael Howard, secretary of state for the environment (home secretary in 1993) and Malcolm Rifkind, secretary of state for defense.

Unlike the rest of Europe, the far-right has been conspicuously unsuccessful in British electoral politics at either a local or national level. In April 1992, the British National Party obtained a mere 7,000 votes for the 13 candidates it fielded. The National Front did even worse, winning under 5,000 votes in 13 constituencies. A visit to Britain by M. Le Pen in December 1991 was met by Jewish protests and anti-fascist demonstrations.

The government's stand on immigration and asylum issues throughout the decade has aroused disquiet among sections of the Jewish population. In February 1992, a delegation from the Jewish Council for Community Relations saw the then home secretary, Kenneth Baker, to protest against the Asylum Bill. The Board of Deputies also expressed its concern. The Jewish historical experience was alluded to several times by Jewish speakers in the debates accompanying the Asylum Bill's passage through Parliament during 1991–93.

Another long-running Parliamentary issue of Jewish concern was the punishment of alleged Nazi war criminals and collaborators domiciled in the United Kingdom. An All Party Parliamentary War Crimes Group was formed in November 1986 to press first for a government investigation and, subsequently, for action against suspected war criminals. Intense lobbying and media revelations caused the government to announce an inquiry in February 1988. Its report in July 1989 called for legislation to enable the trial in Britain of men suspected of committing war crimes in Nazi-occupied Europe at a time when they were not of British nationality. Legislation was introduced into Parliament in November 1989, but opposition by a minority of MPs and a majority of Peers delayed its passage into law until May 1991. The debates about the bill exposed the persistence of many negative stereotypes about the Jews. By April 1992, around £10 million had been spent on the investigations being conducted by the Metropolitan War Crimes Unit and its Scottish counterpart. Over 90 cases were being looked into, but there was still no indication of any case coming to trial.

In July 1992, Antony Gecas, a former member of the 11th Lithuanian Police Battalion who had lived in Scotland since 1946, lost his libel case against Scottish TV for a program which had accused him of being a war criminal. The hearing lasted four months and cost £650,000. In his ruling, the presiding judge, Lord Milligan, concluded that Gecas had "participated in many operations involving the killing of innocent Soviet citizens including Jews in particular." Despite this, Gecas has not been charged with war crimes under the 1991 Act.

Anti-Jewish prejudice surfaced in politics and society. Leon Brittan, the trade and industry secretary who resigned from the cabinet over the "Westland Affair" in 1986, Lord Young, secretary of state for trade and industry who Mrs. Thatcher wanted to take over the chairmanship of the Conservative Party, and Edwina Currie (née Cohen), a junior health minister who resigned in December 1988 over her pronouncements on salmonella in eggs, were all thought to have been victims of a "whispering campaign" among Tory backbenchers.

A series of criminal cases involving Jews attracted much attention and discussion during the late 1980s. The Jewishness of those involved was mentioned sometimes directly, sometimes obliquely, and efforts were made to find a link between this and the malfeasance in question. Such commentary could be open and well-intentioned, but at other times it was insidious and malevolent.

In August 1990, the first trial in the Guinness fraud case, which had lasted 113 days, resulted in the conviction of Gerald Ronson, Sir Jack Lyons, Anthony Parnes, and Ernest Saunders. Parnes, Ronson, and Lyons were Jews, the last two being notable donors to Jewish causes. Saunders was Viennese-born of Jewish parents, but raised as a Christian. In the two subsequent trials connected with the Guinness affair, none of the defendants was Jewish and none was convicted. This fostered the sense that the defendants in the first case had been at best "fall-guys" or, at worst, victimized.

The sensational death of Robert Maxwell in November 1991 was followed rapidly by the collapse of his business empire and the revelation that he had stolen hundreds of millions of pounds from his employees' pension fund in order to prop up the share value of his companies. His sons were subsequently arrested for abetting this fraud and await trial. Although Maxwell's ostentatious burial on the Mount of Olives could not help but draw attention to his Jewish roots, media commentary was relatively restrained. However, it was widely considered that Maxwell and the Jewish entrepreneurs in the Guinness case were outsiders in the City. This denied them protection by the "old boys" network when their schemes, in no way unique, ran foul of the law.

British Jews were, on the whole, spared violent forms of antisemitism. The exception was 1990 when, over a 12-month period there were 29 cases of vandalism against Jewish cemeteries, synagogues, and Holocaust memorials in the London area alone and seven reported cases of physical assault on Jewish persons. This violence is miniscule compared to the assault on non-white minorities, but the attacks provoked media comment and provoked reassuring statements from the prime minister in May 1990.

The most prevalent form of anti-Jewish action in Britain has been the distribution of antisemitic literature. In November 1990, Greville Janner, MP, sponsored an early day motion in the House of Commons which attracted the names of 100 MPs in support of suppressing the circulation of Holocaust Denial material. In March 1991, Dowager Lady Birdwood was charged under the Public Order Act (1986) for distributing the ritual murder accusation against the Jews. She was subsequently found guilty and given a two-year unconditional discharge. In December 1992, glossily produced pseudo-Ḥanukkah cards containing doggerel that embraced antisemitic libels were sent to hundreds of Jewish organizations and prominent individuals. Police investigations failed to identify the source of this "hate mail" and the Government has consistently rebuffed pleas by the Board of Deputies, most recently in October 1992, for a community libel law.

The announcement that a gathering of Holocaust Denial practitioners would be held in London in November 1991 led to demands that the home secretary ban the entry of Robert Faurrison and Fred Leuchter. Leuchter actually entered the country illegally and was deported after showing up at a "conference" that was heavily-picketed by anti-fascist groups. David *Irving, sometime British historian and now a propagandist well known for addressing neo-Nazi rallies in Germany, had become a linchpin in this shadowy global network.

Jews and the Holocaust figured in several historical controversies. In 1987 Jim Allen's anti-Zionist play *Perdition* deployed the canard that Zionists collaborated with the Nazis. Production was canceled after expressions of outrage from the Jewish community and intense media scrutiny, but this only inflamed the debate. The War Crimes Bill occasioned many reflections on the Holocaust, often yoked disturbingly to Jewish terrorism in Palestine in 1946–47. In January 1992, when Irving claimed to have discovered new Eichmann papers the press treated him as a right-wing historian whose views merited serious reportage. In July 1992, the *Sunday Times* caused a storm of controversy by employing him to transcribe and comment on newly revealed portions of Goebbels' diary.

Alan Clark, junior defense minister, was widely condemned in December 1991 for attending a party to launch the revised version of Irving's book *Hitler's War* in which Irving states that Hitler was innocent of the Final Solution and denies the existence of gas chambers for killing Jews. Clark later endorsed a political biography of Churchill by John Charmley, which appeared in January 1993, that suggested Britain should have made peace with Hitler in 1940 or 1941. Clark and Charmley agreed that there was little to choose between Stalinism and Nazism, and that the plight of the Jews under Nazism was a marginal issue. The exposure in the *Guardian* newspaper in May and December 1992 of war crimes in the Nazi-occupied Channel Islands, and the concurrence of the local authorities in the deportation of Jews, shed a different light on the matter. The Irving affair reached a head when Irving filed a libel suit in 1996 against Deborah Lipstadt and her British publisher, Penguin Books, claiming that Lipstadt's *Denying the Holocaust* had accused him of being a Nazi apologist, Holocaust denier, racist, and antisemite. Lipstadt contended that this was precisely what he was, and the Court agreed in its 2001 verdict denying his suit.

Controversy also surrounded efforts to set up an *eruv* in the London borough of Barnet. The project was launched by the United Synagogue "*Eruv* Committee" in 1987. In June 1992 it was passed by the Public Works Committee of Barnet Council. It was then considered by the Hampstead Garden Suburb Trust, which manages this architecturally unique suburban area. At a stormy meeting in September 1992, the Trust's chairman, Lord MacGregor, was censured for approving a letter to Barnet Council advising it to reject the plan and calling the *eruv* "a very unpleasant exhibition of fundamentalism." He subsequently resigned. This fracas made the *eruv* into a heated issue locally and in the national newspapers. On February 24, 1993, the council's planning committee defeated the *eruv* proposal by 11 to 7 votes. Jewish councilors were split and it generated fierce opposition from both Orthodox and "assimilationist" Jews. It was also attacked by non-Jews unable to accept the public expression of Jewish difference.

In June 1992 the prime minister, John Major, appointed two Jews to his new government: Michael Howard became secretary of state for the environment and Malcolm Rifkind was appointed secretary of state for defense. After a cabinet reshuffle in March 1993, Howard was made home secretary. In November 2003, however, Howard was elected leader of the British Conservative Party, the first Jewish leader of a government or opposition party in Britain in the 20th century. Howard stepped down after the 2005 elections. Another reshuffle in September 1995 led to Rifkind's appointment as foreign secretary. He was the first Jew to hold this office since the brief tenure of Rufus Isaacs, the Marquess of Reading, in 1931.

After the death of John Smith MP, in April 1994 the Labour Party chose Tony Blair MP, as its new leader. He actively sought to heal the breach between British Jews and the Labour Party so marked in the 1980s. Blair promoted a number of Jewish MPs and political activists. Blair's closest advisers include Peter Mandelson MP, and David Miliband. In October 1995, Barbara Roche MP, a former headgirl of the Jews' Free School, was elevated to the ranks of the Labour shadow government. The veteran Jewish Labour MP, Greville Janner, former president of the Board of Deputies and chairman of the House of Commons Employment Select Committee, announced that he would not stand again for Parliament at the next general election.

The far-Right enjoyed a modest revival in September 1993, when Derek Beackon, an unemployed 47-year-old former steward for the neo-Nazi British National Party (BNP), won a local council by-election in the Milwall ward of the Isle of Dogs in London's docklands. However, the election of the first BNP councilor proved to be a local quirk. Beackon took 34% of the vote, winning by seven votes, in a contest with a disorganized Labour Party opposition. The vote was more of a protest gesture than an endorsement of neo-Nazi ideology. The BNP "triumph" was universally deplored by mainstream politicians and triggered the revival of a national anti-racism campaign. In the May 1994 local council elections, Beackon increased his vote by 500. But he polled only 30% of the total vote on a much higher turnout that resulted in a Labour victory. The BNP won over 25% in two other east London constituencies, but failed to elect a single councilor.

The Board of Deputies reported that antisemitic incidents numbered 346 in 1993 (as against 292 in 1992) and 327 in 1994. In 2000 the number was 405 and in 2002, 350. Jewish cemeteries were desecrated in Newport in May 1993; Southampton in August 1993; East Ham, London, in December 1993, January 1994 and June 1995; Bournemouth in July 1995. A Manchester synagogue was daubed with swastikas in August 1993 and the following month a Jewish nursery school in Stamford Hill, London, was destroyed in an arson attack. There were mailings of antisemitic literature in September and December 1993. In April 1994, 80-year-old Lady Birdwood was found guilty of distributing material liable to incite racial hatred. Upsurges in antisemitic incidents were generally related to events reflecting the conflict in the Middle East, like 9/11 or the 2002 Israeli military action against Jenin. In this context, in a particularly outrageous act, Britain's 48,000-member Association of University Teachers decided in April 2005 to boycott Israel's Bar-Ilan and Haifa universities. In the face of international pressure it rescinded its decision a month later.

Jewish leaders made numerous representations to the government for stronger legislation against racism. In December 1993, the Board of Deputies gave evidence of escalating anti-Jewish activity to the House of Commons Home Affairs Select Committee. The Board assisted the drafting of a private members bill, introduced into the House of Commons by the Conservative MP Hartley Booth, to impose tougher penalties on criminals convicted of racial crimes and outlaw group defamation. In January 1994 the Runnymede Trust published a report, "A Very Light Sleeper: The Persistence and Dangers of Anti-Semitism," charting the increase of anti-Jewish attacks and urging that religious discrimination be outlawed. The Home Affairs Select Committee report in April 1994 recommended making "racial harassment" an offense and tightening the penalties for racial crimes.

Michael Howard promised to clamp down on racial violence, but rebuffed calls for tougher legislative action made by a Board delegation in February 1994. The government refused to support Booth's widely backed bill, and in June 1994 rejected the recommendations of the Home Affairs Select Committee. However, in October 1995, the minister of state at the Home Office gave instructions to the police and the courts to be as harsh as possible within the existing legal framework when dealing with racial crimes. Meanwhile, Howard flagged new measures to reduce illegal immigration and curb the number of "bogus" asylum seekers. His proposals were regretted by Jewish representatives.

Following the Washington Peace Accords in September 1993, anxiety about communal security focused on militant Islamic groups allowed to operate in the UK. In February 1994 the Board complained to the Home Office about Hizb ut-Tahrir, an association of mainly overseas Muslim students attending British universities. After the March 1994 Hebron massacre, which was condemned by the chief rabbi and president of the Board of Deputies, there were attacks on Jewish targets in London, Birmingham, and Oxford. After the bombing of the Israeli Embassy and JIA offices, in London on July 26–27, 1994 (see below), Jewish organizations reiterated their concern about radical Islamic groups. The Board unsuccessfully called on the Home Office to ban a rally organized by Hizb ut-Tahrir at Wembley Conference Centre in August 1994. After much prevarication, in November 1994, the governing body of the London School of Oriental and Asian Studies (SOAS) banned Hizb ut-Tahrir from holding meetings on SOAS premises. Hizb ut-Tahrir held a mass meeting in Trafalgar Square in August 1995 at which speakers called for the destruction of Israel and denied that the Holocaust had taken place. British Jews have also been concerned by the growing influence of the Chicago-based Nation of Islam among British blacks. In 2002 Sheik Abdullah al-Faisal was arrested for incitement to murder Jews.

War crimes cases continued to cause controversy. In February 1994 the Scottish police war crimes unit was wound up and the Crown Office later announced that there was insufficient evidence to charge Antony Gecas, the sole subject of investigations, under the 1991 War Crimes Act. In December 1994, Lord Campbell of Alloway introduced into the House of Lords a bill to stop war crimes trials in England, basing his case on the need to harmonize English with Scottish practice. It was opposed by the government. In July 1995, Simeon Serafimovicz, an 84-year-old former carpenter, was charged with the murder of four Jews in Belorussia in 1941–42. He is the first person in England ever to be charged with war crimes under the Act. However, British efforts to prosecute war criminals, from the passage of the Act through the early years of the 21st century, have been, on the whole, tepid.

The bid by the United Synagogue Eruv Committee, launched in 1987, to establish an *eruv* with a circumference of 6.5 miles in Golders Green, Hendon, and Hempstead Garden Suburb finally met with success. In February 1992, Barnet Council planning committee had rejected the proposal. An appeal was lodged with the Department of the Environment and a revised plan was put to the planning committee in October 1993. It was again rejected, but the Department of the Environment ordered a public inquiry which took evidence in December 1993. Much of the rhetoric at the inquiry by opponents of the *eruv* was lurid and inflammatory. In September 1994 the government inspector conducting the inquiry issued his report. It refuted the arguments of *eruv* protesters and the following month, during Sukkot, John Gummer, Secretary of State for the Environment, gave his sanction for its erection.

THE ANGLO-JEWISH HERITAGE. The introduction of government aid for historic places of worship in use assisted the restoration of the third oldest surviving synagogue, Exeter, established in 1763/4 and re-opened in October 1980, its use as a synagogue being combined with the provision of a center for Jewish students at Exeter University. This highlighted the problem of architecturally and historically important Jewish buildings no longer viable because of the movement of Jewish population from provincial towns or city centers, which was exemplified by the appeal to convert the former Sephardi synagogue in Manchester established in 1874 to a Jewish museum.

A unique commemoration took place on October 31, 1978 when on the initiative of the Jewish Historical Society of England, and in the presence of the chief rabbi and the archbishop of York, the massacre of the Jews of *York in 1190 was commemorated by the unveiling of a plaque at Clifford's Tower, the site of the massacre. The inscription in English reads: "On the night of Friday, 16 March 1190, some 150 Jews and Jewesses of York, having sought protection in the royal castle on this site from a mob incited by Richard Malebisse and others, chose to die at each other's hands rather than renounce their faith," and concludes with the verses in Hebrew: "They ascribe glory to the Lord and his praise in the isles" (Isaiah 42:12); the word *ha-iy*, "the island," being the name used for England in medieval Hebrew.

COMMUNITY LIFE. In mid-1979, Lord Fisher of Camden retired as president of the Board of Deputies. His six years of office saw the affiliation of the Board to the World Jewish Congress, changes in the organization and representational basis of the board, and the growth of a sense of communal purpose in support for Israel and Soviet Jewry, and in opposition to threats against civil liberties from extremes of the left and right. He was succeeded by Greville Janner, QC, MP, son of a former president (Lord Janner) and, at 50, the Board's youngest president. On taking office, he declared that his policy would be to emphasize working with youth and with provincial communities.

The 1980s also saw the first visit of a prime minister, Mr. James Callaghan, to the Board as well as that of the foreign secretary, Lord Carrington, at his own request, to explain British policy in relation to Israel.

The community was increasingly concerned with the problems of meeting the welfare needs of its increasingly aging membership. The London Jewish Welfare Board devoted the greater proportion of its expenditure to homes and flatlets, day centers and home visits to the aged. Coordination of social work was advanced by cooperation between organizations and professional workers, and shared use of accommodation in buildings like the Golders Green Sobell House or the Redbridge Jewish Centre.

The Board of Deputies acquired a new chief executive in February 1991 when Neville Nagler, a senior civil servant, succeeded Hayyim Pinner, holder of the position for 14 years. In June 1991, Judge Israel Finestein, QC, won the election for the presidency of the Board of Deputies and succeeded the outgoing Dr. Lionel Kopelowitz who had held office since 1985. Rosalind Preston was elected the first woman vice president of the Board. Finestein announced that he intended to increase democracy in Anglo-Jewry and secure greater participation in communal governance by the young, women, regional communities, and academics.

Chief Rabbi Dr. Immanuel Jakobovits was elevated to the House of Lords in January 1988 and in March 1991 was awarded the prestigious Templeton Prize for progress in religion. In May 1991 he was criticized by figures in the Joint Israel Appeal because of an interview in the *Evening Standard* newspaper in which he expressed reservations concerning Israeli conduct in the Administered Territories. He was succeeded in September 1991 by Rabbi Dr. Jonathan Sacks. As principal of Jews' College, in 1989 Sacks organized two important conferences on "traditional alternatives" in Judaism, one on general and another on specifically women's issues.

In February 1992, the new chief rabbi unveiled his review of women's role in Jewish life and named Rosalind Preston as its head. This followed a bitter struggle over women's services in Stanmore Synagogue. Although in April 1991 he resigned from a Jewish education "think tank" because it included a Reform rabbi, in April 1992 Chief Rabbi Dr. Sacks led a delegation that embraced Reform and Liberal rabbis (including a woman) to a major interfaith conference.

In September 1992 a report on the United Synagogue, conducted under the guidance of Stanley Kalms, found "mistakes, miscalculations, poor management, and financial errors" and revealed a debt of £9 million. The report also noted that a majority of members felt alienated by the rightward trend of the rabbinate and recommended an "inclusivist" position. It precipitated the resignation of Sidney Frosh, the president. In December 1992, the United Synagogue announced £0.8 million of cuts and a freeze on rabbis' salaries. It wound up its three-year old *sheḥitah* operation, established as a result of the bitter "*sheḥitah* wars" in the 1980s, with a loss of £0.7 million.

The search for economies underlay the amalgamation of the Jewish Blind Society and the Jewish Welfare Board to form Jewish Care in December 1988. In the recession of the early 1980s and again in the slump of 1990–92, Jewish welfare organizations had to cater for Jewish unemployed persons, too, despite a shrinking income base. The second recession saw many of the fortunes built up by Jewish entrepreneurs in the 1980s crumble. Grodzinski, the *kasher* baker, went into receivership in February 1991 after trading for 102 years. The famous *kasher* caterer Schaverin suffered a similar fate in November 1991. In June 1992, the Glasgow *Jewish Echo* closed down after 64 years of publication.

Nor was Anglo-Jewry immune to the social problems afflicting the rest of society. In July 1991 David Rubin, son of an eminent rabbi, absconded after allegedly defrauding fellow-Jews of millions of pounds. A few weeks later, a child-abuse case in the Orthodox community of Stamford Hill led to violent demonstrations by members of the community against the family that had taken the matter to the police.

Jewish communal institutions have been dogged by poor finances, while attempts at reorganization have had uneven success. In March 1993 the highly effective and inexpensive Association of Jewish 6th Formers (AJ6), which prepares Jewish teenagers for university, faced closure due to lack of funds. AJ6 received a last-minute reprieve, but the affair showed the need for a strategic funding policy. In April 1993, Lord Young, former Tory cabinet minister and businessman, initiated the Central Council of Jewish Social Services (CCJSS) which he envisaged as a directorate for British Jewry. In July 1993 he was elected chairman of the CCJSS, now embracing over 40 Jewish organizations.

Lord Young dismissed the Board of Deputies as inefficient and incapable of providing either policies or leadership. His view appeared to be confirmed when plans for its reform were stymied. In December 1993, the Board failed to give a two-thirds majority to measures to decrease the size of the executive, the number of Deputies, and the frequency of plenary meetings. The election of Eldred Tabachnik, QC, as president in June 1994 revived hopes of reform.

The United Synagogue (US), which announced that it had lost £1 million on a disastrous *sheḥitah* operation in June 1993, pulled itself back into the black by means of draconian economies. A series of institutional reforms failed to placate women who demanded a greater say in its affairs (see below). The Rix Report on Jewish youth in September 1994 called for greater investment in youth work which was met with alacrity by the CJCS and other funding bodies. After a series of poor appeal results, the JIA was relaunched in October 1995.

The most important communal initiative was the inauguration of Jewish Continuity in April 1993. Jewish Continuity was intended to raise money to fund new and existing educational projects, invest in people to "champion" Judaism, and provide advice and guidance across the whole Jewish community. However, Continuity immediately aroused the suspicions of Progressive Jews because of the absence of any but Orthodox Jews from its directorate and staff. In May 1994 an allocations board was set up that included members of the Reform and Liberal movements. Continuity hoped to avoid Orthodox criticism of this move by making the allocations board semi-detached, dispensing moneys given it for the purpose by Continuity. In July 1994, Continuity reached an agreement with the JIA that £12 million of the money raised by the JIA in Britain would go to educational projects identified by Continuity. In September 1994 it announced its first grants, totaling £435,000. The largest number and amount of grants went to Orthodox causes.

During 1995, critics continued to charge Jewish Continuity with bias and a lack of strategy. In October 1995 it announced a major review of its operations, to determine what its role should be and end the confusion between its functions as grant giver and service provider. The review would also deal with the antagonism which had built up between it and the JIA and Progressive Jews in Britain.

The fortunes of Jewish Continuity were inextricably linked with those of its progenitor, Rabbi Dr. Sacks. He appeared increasingly beleaguered by an intractable rabbinate, an assertive Jewish women's movement and confident Masorti, Reform, and Progressive movements. In February 1993 a Jewish women's prayer group held the first women's Sabbath service in a manner authorized by Rabbi Dr. Sacks: in a private house and without use of a *Sefer Torah* or prayers requiring a male quorum. But there was pressure for more radical, and according to many authorities permissible, steps such as use of a *Sefer Torah* and praying in a synagogue. In March 1994, a women's prayer group defied Rabbi Dr. Sacks and held a service using a *Sefer Torah* on a Sunday at Yakar, an independent Orthodox study center in London.

In July 1993, Rabbi Dr. Sacks issued guidelines to the US on how to accommodate women's demands for greater involvement. He ruled that women could become members of the US council and sit on synagogue boards of management, but only by co-option not election. This did not satisfy the women of the US. In October 1993, Rabbi Dr. Sacks announced his solution to the problem of *agunot*. He recommended mandatory prenuptial contracts entitling the wife to support from her husband until divorced by a *get*, and mutual cooperation to achieve that end. Enforcement of this recommendation was stymied by members of his Beth Din.

The inquiry into women in the community, initiated by Rabbi Dr. Sacks and headed by Rosalind Preston, announced its findings in June 1994. It revealed that women wanted more spiritual involvement, more rituals in recognition of female life-cycle events, the right to say *kaddish*, greater recognition of the needs of single women and single mothers, urgent reform of the *get* system, and greater sensitivity by *Batei Din* to women's issues including domestic violence. Yet Sacks found it difficult to deliver anything meaningful and his hands were still tied even on prenuptial agreements. Acting out of frustration, on October 28, 1995, "chained" Jewish women demonstrated outside the office of the United Synagogue Chief Rabbinate. The debate about Jewish women's rights under *halakhah* has consistently attracted national press and television coverage.

In January 1995 Sacks launched an attack on the Masorti movement in England. The pretext was an article in the Masorti magazine insinuating that he had recognized marriages conducted by Masorti rabbis. He responded with an article in the ultra-Orthodox *Jewish Tribune* in which he declared that the Masorti were guilty of "intellectual dishonesty"; using the term "*ganavim*" (thieves) to describe them. He stated that a follower of Masorti had "severed his links with the faith of his ancestors." Masorti, Reform, and Liberal rabbis, as well as lay leaders upbraided Sacks for the violence of his outburst. It put the future of Jewish Continuity into doubt since non-Orthodox Jews could not see how a body under Sacks' influence could fund their work or merit their support and Rabbi Dr. Sacks struggled to contain the damage.

The cultural agenda has been dominated by the anniversaries connected with World War II and the Holocaust. The 50th anniversary of the Warsaw Ghetto Uprising, the liberation of Auschwitz, the liberation of Belsen, and the end of the war were all marked by commemorative events, academic conferences, and a spate of publications. Media coverage of these events was intense and raised public awareness of the Holocaust. In November 1994, the Imperial War Museum announced that it was considering the construction of a permanent exhibit on genocide in the 20th century, focused on the Holocaust. Plans for a Holocaust Museum were unveiled in Manchester, too. Beit Shalom, the first Holocaust Museum in Britain, a private initiative originated, funded, and developed by a non-Jewish family in rural Nottinghamshire, opened in September 1995.

The Board of Deputies considered legal action against the Jewish authors, producers, and director of a TV fictional film, "Wall of Silence," about murders in the ḥasidic community of North London. First screened at the 9th Jewish Film Festival and then transmitted on BBC on October 17, 1993, the film was widely criticized for presenting negative stereotypes of Orthodox Judaism.

A Center for Jewish Studies was inaugurated at SOAS in December 1993, for German-Jewish Studies at Sussex University, and Sephardi Studies in London, under the auspices of the Sephardi community, in 1994. In November 1994, Dr. Dovid Katz started the Oxford Institute for Yiddish Studies, incurring the wrath of the Oxford Center for Hebrew and Jewish Studies, from which he subsequently resigned. New positions in Jewish studies were created at professorial level at Manchester University and at lecturer level at Bristol University. The Institute for Jewish Affairs transferred to a new home in April 1993 and broke away from the World Jewish Congress, forming instead close ties with the American Jewish Committee. Jewish Book Week moved to a new venue and attracted bigger literary figures and audiences than ever before. A specially designed building to house the London Jewish Museum was opened in Camden in 1995. In 1994 the *Jewish Quarterly* was invigorated by a new editor, Elena Lappin.

EDUCATION AND CULTURE. While estimates of the Jewish child population (and of those receiving part-time Jewish education) fell with the decline of the general child population in Britain, the number enrolled in Jewish day schools reached some 13,000 at the end of the 1970s, representing over 20% of the estimated Jewish child population. New Jewish day schools continued to be founded and there were positive developments in Jewish adult education in various aspects involving synagogues of different religious affiliation, the Lubavitch movement, and courses for younger Jewish leaders. Enrollment continued to rise through the 1980s and 1990s reaching 30% in 1992 and 51% in 1999. The United Synagogue Agency for Jewish Education operated 14 primary and nursery schools and five secondary schools in the early 2000s and had trained over 150 teachers since 1997. The Leo Baeck College Center for Jewish Education offered an M.A. program in Jewish education from 2002.

In 1984, Jews' College moved to new accommodations and the Manor House Sternberg Center for Reform Judaism was set up. Jewish museums were founded in London and Manchester. In 1990–92 there were several conferences and publications on the preservation of the documents, artifacts, and buildings that constitute the Jewish heritage in Britain. Sadly, Bevis Marks synagogue suffered collateral damage from an IRA bomb attack in London in August 1992. In 1991, Immanuel College was opened and the Jewish Chronicle Chair in Modern Jewish History was established at University College London to mark the paper's 150th anniversary and a chair in Modern Jewish Studies was dedicated at the University of Manchester. During 1992–93, lectureships in Modern Jewish History were established at Warwick and Leicester universities. In 1992, Dr. David Paterson was succeeded by Professor Phillip Alexander as head of the Oxford Center for Postgraduate Hebrew Studies, having secured its future. Jewish schools topped the national league for the award of "A" Levels in August 1992. Less happy publicity was created by the decision of state-aided Jewish schools in Liverpool and Manchester in September 1991 not to admit Jewish children from a Reform Jewish background.

Jewish culture found diverse expression in the courses of the Spiro Institute throughout the decade. There were festivals of Yiddish culture on the South Bank, an annual Jewish Film Festival, and Jewish music festival. In December 1991, *Leon the Pig Farmer*, an independent film funded largely by Jews and on a Jewish subject, won awards at the Edinburgh and Venice Film Festivals. In 1988, the conference "Remembering for the Future" inquired into the Holocaust. The anniversary of the massacre at Clifford's Tower in York in 1090 occasioned several solemn events. The 50th anniversary of the 1942 Wannsee Conference was the subject of an international conference in London organized principally by the Wiener Library. During 1992 there were many celebrations of the Sephardi experience to mark the anniversary of the expulsion from Spain.

[Vivian David Lipman and David Cesarani]

Relations with Israel

Britain's relations with Israel should be viewed in the perspective of half a century, beginning with the closing phases of World War I. In November 1917, with the war against Germany and her allies still at its height, the British government issued a statement of policy, the *Balfour Declaration, favoring the establishment of a Jewish national home in Palestine. The near euphoria and sense of gratitude to Britain that this announcement aroused among Jews everywhere was to give way a generation later to an atmosphere of bitterness and mutual recrimination, in which the British Mandate over Palestine finally came to an end (1948). But in the intervening years, despite all the frictions and difficulties, the foundations of Jewish statehood had in fact been laid. The period immediately following Israel's Declaration of Independence in May 1948 was a somber one in the relations between the new state and the former mandatory power. Unlike the United States and the Soviet Union, Britain refused to recognize the newly established state for many months. At the United Nations General Assembly in Paris in the latter part of 1948, the British delegation was the principal, though ultimately unsuccessful, protagonist of the so-called *Bernadotte Plan, a central feature of which was the proposal to transfer the Negev from Israel to the Arabs. Relations between Britain and what it termed "the Jewish authorities in Tel Aviv" reached an acute point when, on Jan. 7, 1949, in the course of renewed fighting between Israel and Egypt, the Israelis shot down five British planes that had been sent on a reconnaissance mission from the Suez Canal Zone. At this time, however, a strong reaction against the policy of Foreign Secretary Ernest *Bevin began to assert itself in Britain. The debate in the House of Commons on January 28 was a damaging one to the government. Three days later Bevin announced the *de facto* recognition of Israel and, shortly thereafter, the appointment of Britain's first diplomatic representative to Israel, Sir Knox Helm.

Gradually a new pattern of relations evolved between the two countries. The period of Bevin's influence had not been forgotten by the people of Israel, but Britain's initial role in having made the development of Jewish nationhood in Palestine politically and physically possible was increasingly recalled and recognized. Steady progress was made in day-to-day contacts through trade, tourism, and cultural relations. But despite these positive developments, British policy toward Israel continued to be markedly reserved, for reasons connected with Britain's interests and commitments in the Arab world. As late as 1955, the British government still harbored ideas about the transfer of at least a part of the Negev to Egypt. This attitude was reflected in Prime Minister Anthony Eden's speech at the Guildhall on Nov. 9, 1955, in which he suggested a compromise on the frontiers set by the Partition Resolution of 1947 and those established under the Armistice Agreements as a way out of the Arab-Israel impasse. This proposal was unequivocally rejected by Israel and eventually abandoned. Less than a year later, Britain and Israel found themselves in unlikely association in military action against Egypt–Israel in Sinai, Britain in Suez. The events leading to this development were President Nasser's nationalization of the Suez Canal on the one hand, and his active sponsorship of the *fedayeen* terror gangs, organized on Arab territory for acts of murder and sabotage within Israel, on the other.

For more than a century, the preservation of Britain's communications with India, the keystone of her empire, had been a dominant factor in Britain's interest in the Middle East. In 1947, India achieved independence almost contemporaneously with Israel. The strategic and political implications of this event for Britain's status in the world were not immediately obvious. Britain remained the paramount power in the Middle East with military bases in Iraq, Egypt, and Jordan, and with a vital financial stake in the ever-increasing oil wealth that was being uncovered not only in Iran but in the Arab lands bordering on the Gulf, including Iraq, Kuwait, Bahrain, and the sheikhdoms. In the mid-1950s a revolutionary change occurred: the collapse of British power and prestige that accompanied the Suez debacle of 1956 was followed two years later by the murder of the king of Iraq and the lynching of his premier, Nuri Said, Britain's faithful friend and ally. The last British base in the Arab Middle East other than one in Aden was now relinquished. By 1968, as Britain's policy of withdrawal from direct military commitment to areas east of Suez began to be extended even to the Persian Gulf; Aden too was abandoned. Middle East oil, so vital to the European economy, continued to flow more or less uninterruptedly because of the mutual interests of the Arab governments on the one hand and of Western purchasers on the other. But the old power relationship, including its implications for Israel, had dissolved.

Nevertheless, Britain's role in the area in the 1960s must not be underestimated. As a great world financial and trading community, with the support of experienced and effective diplomats, Britain continued to exert extensive influence. The decline of Britain's authority in the Arab world significantly affected British-Israel relations. Although the traditional sensitivity of the Foreign Office to possible Arab reactions persisted, a more relaxed, less inhibited attitude toward Israel began to assert itself. This was manifested not only in official contacts and public statements, but also in willingness to sell Israel such major items of military equipment as Centurion tanks, naval vessels, and submarines. Within the aggregate of Britain's overseas trade, Israel occupied a modest but increasingly significant place in 1968. The total bilateral trade between the two countries in 1967 amounted to about $215,000,000, an increase of nearly 75% compared with 1957. In fact, the value of Britain's exports to Israel exceeded that to any of the Arab countries. Britain constituted Israel's most important overseas market, with agricultural products (notably citrus) and polished diamonds predominating. Israel–British economic relations have long been a target of the Arab boycott offices, but, as trade figures reveal, their success has been marginal. The Suez Canal – blocked as a result of the *Six-Day War – remained closed. The resultant loss to British trade and shipping, although eventually much reduced, undoubtedly contributed to Britain's active interest in seeking a solution to the Middle East crisis. British diplomats at the United Nations thus took a leading part in sponsoring and securing the passage of the Security Council resolution of Nov. 22, 1967. The war brought about a rupture in relations between Britain and a number of Arab countries, but these were reestablished, and Britain's policy ostensibly aimed at seeking to maintain a balance of friendship with both the Arab states and Israel.

Although there is not always an identity of views between Israel and Britain on the problems of the Middle East, there was a broad base of common understanding in the late 1960s. The interest of the British people in Israel is not a passing phenomenon but rests on deep religious and spiritual foundations and was impressively demonstrated at the time of the Six-Day War. Attitudes and suspicions on the part of both countries survive from a more troubled period in their relationship. But the dominant motive was one of mutual regard that found its expression not only in political and economic spheres, but also in cultural relations and public opinion.

[Arthur Lourie]

For most of the 1980s British foreign policy was conducted by Sir Geoffrey Howe. Britain urged the PLO to recognize Israel and renounce terrorism, while calling on Israel to halt settlements in the occupied territories as a *quid pro quo*. Between 1984 and 1987 there were several friendly high-level exchange visits, but British unease about conditions in the Gaza Strip were forcefully expressed by junior Foreign Office Minister David Mellor during a visit in January 1988. After Yasser Arafat announced acceptance of UN resolutions 242 and 338 and renounced the armed struggle, William Waldegrave, Mellor's successor, met with Abu Bassam Sharrif of the PLO.

The outbreak of the *intifada* in 1989 led to the revival of the propaganda war in the media and in student politics. British Government officials repeatedly expressed concern at Israeli handling of the disturbances. In March 1990, the new foreign secretary, Douglas Hurd, met with Abu Bassam Sharrif, although the Palestinian terrorist attack on Israel in May 1990 led to demands to sever links with the PLO. Hurd issued a call to the Palestinians to curb terrorism, but contacts with the PLO continued. The situation was transformed by Iraq's invasion of Kuwait in August 1990. The British Government deplored PLO support for Saddam Hussein and rejected any "linkage" between Iraq's invasion and the Palestinian problem, although in October 1990 it said that Israeli policy towards the Palestinians could not go unchanged. In November 1991, Britain resumed diplomatic ties with Syria, severed after the 1988 Lockerbie disaster, which was now a member of the anti-Iraq coalition.

When the war started, hundreds of British Jews, including the chief rabbi, went to Israel on solidarity missions. Prime Minister John Major congratulated Israel on its "admirable restraint" following Iraqi missile attacks. Popular attitudes towards Israel and the Palestinians changed radically, although British official policy soon reverted to type. In January 1992 Mr. Major addressed a letter to the Zionist Federation of Great Britain calling on Anglo-Jewish leaders to intervene with the Israel Government against the deportation of 12 Palestinian activists. On July 30, 1992, Mr. Major addressed the annual dinner of the Conservative Friends of Israel. He called the settlements "a major impediment to the peace process," denounced the Arab boycott as "iniquitous" and said it should be ended in return for freezing the settlements.

In March 1993, Douglas Hogg, the minister of state at the Foreign Office, met with Faisal Husseini and PLO officials, thus ending the ban on official ministerial contacts with the PLO. On July 2, 1993, the Foreign Secretary met Husseini along with Nabil Shaath and Afif Safieh, the PLO's London representative. Following the White House Accords, which were welcomed by the government and opposition parties, Douglas Hogg visited Yasser Arafat in Tunisia and the status of the PLO office in London was upgraded to a "delegation." The Foreign Secretary, Douglas Hurd, visited Israel during a Middle East tour in December 1994. A visit to London by Israeli prime minister Yiẓhak Rabin was curtailed by a terrorist bombing in Israel.

On October 30, 1994, Prince Philip made the first royal visit to Israel. During his 25-hour stay he attended a ceremony at Yad Vashem to honor his mother for rescuing Jews in Greece during the war, and dined with President Ezer Weizman. In March 1995, Prime Minister John Major became the second serving British premier to go to Israel. The accent of his visit was firmly on strengthening trade links between the two countries. However, British diplomats avoided the Jerusalem 3000 celebrations.

The peace accords divided British Jews. While welcomed by Israel Finestein, president of the Board of Deputies, and Chief Rabbi Dr. Jonathan Sacks, they were anathematized by British Mizrachi and Ḥerut, including many rabbis. On December 15, 1993, during an official visit to London, Yasser Arafat met British Jewish leaders including Israel Finestein, Lord Rothschild, Greville Janner MP, and Sir Sigmund Sternberg. But 60 rabbis and prominent *dayyanim* issued a statement condemning the meeting. On August 6, 1995, businessman and JIA leader Cyril Stein and Rabbi Alan Kimche, the outreach director of Jewish Continuity (see below), joined a demonstration outside the Israeli Embassy in London against the peace negotiations. It was organized by the New York Rabbi Avi Weiss. In October 1995, Rabbi Dr. Sacks was again attacked by his own rabbinate for endorsing the peace process and the principle of withdrawal from the West Bank.

The peace process had a more dangerous and tragic impact. On July 26–27, 1994 bombs exploded outside the Israeli Embassy at Palace Green, Kensington, and Balfour House in North Finchley, which houses the offices of the Joint Israel Appeal (JIA) and the Zionist Federation. Nineteen people were injured in the first attack, none seriously, but the embassy was badly damaged. The Jewish community was aggrieved that its warnings to the authorities had been ignored. Armed police guards were subsequently posted at potential Jewish targets and communal security stepped up, but the government refused to help fund the installation of surveillance systems. In December 1994, Israeli police minister Moshe Shaḥal held talks with Scotland Yard in London to discuss measures to counter the threat posed by radical Islamic groups operating in London. On September 5, 1995, Danny Frei, a former pupil of Hasmonean school in London, was murdered in Israel on the West Bank where he lived.

During the Blair years, Israel's relations with England were fairly smooth. Blair himself exhibited warmth and support while maintaining what England considers an even-handed approach to the Middle East conflict. In a meeting with Shimon Peres in October 2005 he called Israel's disengagement from Gaza a "crucial and courageous act," reaffirming his commitment to a secure Israel as well as a viable Palestinian state. The British media, on the other hand, and particularly the BBC, is perceived as hostile in Israel and in effect as encouraging terrorism through its biased reporting.

[Vivian David Lipman and David Ceserani]

BIBLIOGRAPHY: GENERAL: Roth, Mag Bibl; Lehmann, Nova Bibl (include detailed bibliography on Anglo-Jewish history up to 1961); Roth, England; J. Finestein, *Short History of Anglo-Jewry* (1957); A.M. Hyamson, *History of the Jews in England* (1928[2]); D.S. Katz, *The Jews in the History of England, 1485–1850* (1994); H.S.Q. Henriques, *Jews and the English Law* (1908). MIDDLE AGES: M. Adler, *Jews of Medieval England* (1939); J. Jacobs, *Jews of Angevin England* (1893); H.G. Richardson, *English Jewry under Angevin Kings* (1960); B.L. Abrahams, *Expulsion of the Jews from England in 1290* (1895); G. Caro, *Sozial-und Wirtschaftsgeschichte der Juden*, 1 (1909), 313–51; 2 (1920), 3–68; Rigg-Jenkinson, Exchequer; M.D. Davis, *Hebrew Deeds of English Jews before 1290* (1888). MODERN PERIOD (FROM 17th CENTURY): V.D. Lipman, *Social History of the Jews in England 1850–1950* (1954); idem (ed.), *Three Centuries of Anglo-Jewish History* (1961); idem, *A Century of Social Service 1859–1959* (1959); idem, *A History of the Jews in Britain since 1858* (1990); idem, in: JHSET, 21 (1968), 78–103; T. Endelman, *The Jews of Georgian England, 1714–1830: Tradition in a Liberal Society* (1979); D. Englander (ed.), *A Documentary History of the Jews in Britain, 1840–1920* (1993); G. Alderman, *Modern British Jewry* (1992); J. Gould and S. Esh (ed.), *Jewish Life in Modern Britain* (1964); M. Freedman (ed.), *A Minority in Britain* (1955); A.M. Hyamson, *Sephardim of England* (1951); L.P. Gartner, *The Jewish Immigrant in England, 1870–1914* (1960); N. Bentwich, *They Found Refuge* (1956); C. Roth, *Rise of Provincial Jewry* (1950); idem, *Life of Menasseh ben Israel* (1934); idem, *Essays and Portraits in Anglo-Jewish History* (1962); idem, *The Great Synagogue, London 1890–1940* (1950); J. Shaftesley (ed.), *Remember the Days* (1966); L. Wolf, *Menasseh ben Israel's Mission to Oliver Cromwell* (1901); idem, *Essays in Jewish History* (1932); C.H.L. Emanuel, *A Century and a Half of Jewish History, Extracted from the Minute Books of the London Committee of Deputies of the British Jews* (1910); S. Salomon, *The Jews of Britain* (1938); *Gesher*, 3 (Oct. 1961); P.H. Emden, *Jews of Britain* (1943); I. Finestein, *A Short History of Anglo-Jewry* (1957); E. Krausz, *Leeds Jewry: Its History and Social Structure* (1964); B. Litvinoff, *A Peculiar People* (1969), 168–70; Temkin, in: AJYB, 58 (1957), 3–63; Prais and Schmool, in: JJSO, 10 (1968), 5–34; 9 (1967), 149–74; H. Brotz, *ibid.*, 1 (1959), 94–113; Bentwich, *ibid.*, 2 (1960), 16–24; Krausz, *ibid.*, 4 (1962), 82–90; idem, in: *In the Dispersion*, no. 3 (1963–64), 80–89; N. Cohen, in: *Tradition*, 8 (1966), 40–57; C. Bermant, *Troubled Eden* (1969); B. Wasserstein, *Britain and the Jews of Europe, 1939–1945* (1979); V.D. and S. Lipman (eds.), *Jewish Life in Britain 1962–77* (1981); *Jewish Journal of Sociology* 19, 228; House of Commons Official Report (November 25, 1977), cols. 2058ff; IJA Research Reports, Western Europe 2, 3 G.B. 7, 8, Western Europe 77/1, 2; August 1980, No. 10; *Sunday Telegraph* (December 3, 1977); "The Jews of Britain," *Jewish Chronicle Supplement* (November 24, 1978); Research Unit, Board of Deputies, *Steel City Jews* (1976); idem, *Jews in an Inner London Borough* (1975); *Social Demography of Redbridge Jewry* (1979). **ADD. BIBLIOGRAPHY:** T. Endelman, *The Jews of Britain, 1656–2000* (2002); W.D. Rubinstein, *A History of the Jews in the English-Speaking World: Great Britain* (1996); AJYB 2003. RELATIONS WITH ISRAEL: W. Eytan, *The First Ten Years* (1958); E.H. Samuel, *British Traditions in Administration of Israel* (1957).

ENGLARD, YITZHAK (1933–), Israeli jurist. Englard was born in Frankfurt, Germany. He received his Magister Juris (cum laude) at the Hebrew University of Jerusalem in 1956 and his Diploma d'Etudes Superieures at the Faculte de Droit, Paris. Admitted to the Israeli Bar in 1960, he served in the Israel Defense Forces (as judge advocate) in 1962–63. Subsequently he became professor and later dean of the Hebrew University Law Faculty and director of the university's Institute for Research in Jewish Law. He was also a visiting professor at the University of Zurich, Switzerland; the University of Grenbole, France; and the University of Toronto, Canada. He was also an honorary member of the World Jewish Academy of Sciences.

In 1997 Englard was awarded the Israel Prize for law and in 1997–2003 he served as a justice of the Israel Supreme Court, occupying the "Orthodox seat." He wrote numerous books and articles on torts and Jewish law, state and religion, legal capacity and comparative law. Englard has been a critic of Menachem *Elon's dogmatic-historic approach to **Mishpat Ivri*, preferring to place the emphasis on spiritual input rather than legal doctrine in assessing the desired relationship between *halakhah* and Israeli law.

[Leon Fine (2nd ed.)]

ENGLISH LITERATURE.

Biblical and Hebraic Influences

The Bible has generally been found to be congenial to the English spirit. Indeed, the earliest English poetry consists of the seventh-century metrical paraphrases of Genesis and Exodus attributed to Caedmon (died c. 680). Here the emphasis is on the military prowess of the ancient Hebrew warriors. Abraham in his fight against the five kings (Gen. 14) takes on the character of an Anglo-Saxon tribal chief leading his thanes into battle. One early biblical work was *Jacob and Josep*, an anonymous early 13th-century poem written in the Midlands dialect. As in France, biblical figures also appear in the medieval miracle or mystery plays staged in York and other towns. A more religious understanding of the Old Testament was achieved later, in the period of the Reformation, with works such as the Greek academic drama about Jephthah written in 1544 by the Catholic Christopherson. This Hebrew judge inspired several dramatic works, notably the ballad "Jephthah Judge of Israel," quoted by William *Shakespeare (*Hamlet*, Act 2, Scene 2) and included in Bishop Thomas Percy's *Reliques of Ancient English Poetry* (1765); and *Jephthes Sive Votum* (1554), by the Scottish poet George Buchanan, who also wrote a Latin paraphrase of the Psalms (1566). Other biblical works of the 16th century were *God's Promises* (1547–48) by John Bale; *The Historie of Jacob and Esau* (1557), a comedy by Nicholas Udall in which Esau represents the Catholics and Jacob the faithful Protestants; the anonymous *New Enterlude of Godly Queene Hester* (1560), which had strong political undertones; Thomas Garber's *The Commody of the most vertuous and Godlye Susanna* (1578); and *The Love of King David and Fair Bethsabe* (1599) by George Peele mainly about Absalom. From the Middle Ages, biblical and Hebraic influences had a profound impact on English culture. Works inspired by the Bible were especially prominent in the 17th century, first during the era of Puritanism, and later when the undogmatic, practical temper of Anglican piety led to a new evaluation both of the Jews and of the Hebrew scriptures. The Puritans were particularly drawn to the Psalms and to the records of the Judges of Israel, with whom they were apt to identify themselves. John *Milton, their greatest representative, knew Hebrew, and his epic *Paradise Lost* (1667) and *Samson Agonistes* (1671) are steeped in biblical and Judaic lore. The Puritans' doctrine of election and covenant also derived to a great extent from Hebrew sources. They made the "Covenant" a central feature of their theological system and also of their social life, often undertaking their religious and political obligations to one another on the basis of a formal covenant, as recorded in Genesis. There are interesting developments of the covenant idea in the philosophies of Thomas Hobbes (1588–1679) and John Locke (1632–1704), and also in Milton and the 17th-century religious radicals known as the Levellers. The same period saw the publication of other works based on the Bible or Jewish history, such as the *Davideis* (1656), an anti-royalist epic poem by Abraham Cowley, and *Titus and Berenice* (1677), a play by Thomas Otway based on the tragedy *Bérénice* by Jean *Racine. John Dryden dramatized Milton's *Paradise Lost* unconvincingly as *The State of Innocence and Fall of Man* (1677). His famous satire *Absalom and Achitophel* (1681), in which David represents Charles II, reflects the contemporary political scene. In the 18th century, various minor writers provided the librettos for Handel's oratorios, over a dozen of which deal with Old Testament themes ranging from *Israel in Egypt* (1738) to *Judas Maccabaeus* (1747). Hannah More, who wrote *Belshazzar* (one of her *Sacred Dramas*, 1782), was one of several English writers who paid attention to this figure. Others were Henry Hart Milman (*Belshazzar*, 1822); Robert Eyres Landor, who wrote *The Impious Feast* (1828); and Lord *Byron, whose *Hebrew Melodies* (1815) contains a poem on this subject. William Wordsworth revealed an imagination shaped by biblical forms and patterns, and in "Michael" the dramatic focus of the whole poem is the picture of an old man setting up a heap of stones as a covenant between himself and his son at their parting. In a more scholarly field, the Christian Hebraist Robert *Lowth devoted much time to the study of Hebrew poetry in the Bible. One novelist in whom a fairly strong Hebraic background can be discerned is Henry Fielding, whose *Joseph Andrews* (1742) was intended to recall the lives of Joseph and Abraham.

BIBLICAL MOTIFS IN LATER WRITERS. During the third decade of the 19th century, the biblical figure of Cain was the center of some literary controversy and interest. The publication of an English translation of Salomon Gessner's German prose epic *Der Tod Abels* (1758) in 1761 set a fashion, and Coleridge's "Gothic" work on this theme was one of many. Byron's attempt to transform the first murderer into a hero in his *Cain* (1821) roused a storm of protest, provoking *The Ghost of Abel* (1822), a riposte by William *Blake. A less revolutionary side of Byron is seen in his *Hebrew Melodies*, which includes poems on Jephthah's daughter, Sennacherib, and the Babylonian Exile. The 19th century produced many other works of biblical inspiration by English writers. One which had a great vogue in its day was *Joseph and His Brethren* (1824), a grandiose epic poem written under a pen name by Charles Jeremiah Wells. In his *Poems* (1870), Dante Gabriel Rossetti used Midrashic and legendary material for his treatment of the conflict between Satan and Lilith and Adam and Eve in "Eden Bower." Alfred Austin wrote *The Tower of Babel* (1874); and in defiance of the censors Oscar Wilde first published his daring comedy *Salomé* in French (1893), the English version only being allowed on to the British stage in 1931. A number of leading 20th-century writers maintained this interest in the personalities and themes of the Old Testament. They include C.M. Doughty, with the dramatic poem *Adam Cast Forth* (1908); George Bernard Shaw, in his play *Back to Methuselah* (1921); Thomas Sturge Moore, author of the plays *Absalom* (1903), *Mariamne* (1911), and *Judith* (1911); the poet John Masefield who wrote *A King's Daughter* (1923) on Jezebel; D.H. Lawrence, with his play *David* (1926); Arnold Bennett, whose *Judith* had a brief, sensational run in 1919; and Sir James Barrie, who wrote the imaginative but unsuccessful play *The Boy David* (1936). The works of the Scots playwright James Bridie include *Tobias and the Angel* (1930), *Jonah and the Whale* (1932), and *Susannah and the Elders* (1937). A number of anti-biblical *Old Testament Plays* were published in 1950 by Laurence Housman. Figures from the Bible are also introduced in *A Sleep of Prisoners* (1951), a symbolic play written by Christopher Fry, whose *The Firstborn* (1946) transformed Moses into a superman. Curiously enough, most of the Jewish writers who emerged in Britain during the 19th and 20th centuries avoided biblical subjects and devoted their attention to social and historical themes. However, Isaac *Rosenberg wrote a Nietzschean drama, *Moses* (1916).

IMPACT OF JEWISH PHILOSOPHY AND MYSTICISM. In the general abandonment of medieval Christian authorities during the Reformation, there was a certain tendency to look to the medieval Jewish philosophers and exegetes for guidance. The thinking of writers like John, Jeremy Taylor (1613–1667), and the "Cambridge Platonists" was in part shaped by the Bible and by Maimonides. The Platonist poet Henry More (1614–1687) drew heavily on both Philo and Maimonides, and made frequent reference to the Kabbalah. Like many other English writers of his time, More had, however, only a very imperfect idea of what the Kabbalah contained. Two earlier writers whose works contain kabbalistic allusions are the Rabelaisian satirist Thomas Nash and Francis Bacon. Nash's *Pierce Pennilesse His Supplication to the Divell* (1592), a humorous discourse on the vices and customs of the day, draws from the Christian Kabbalah; while Bacon's *The New Atlantis* (1627) describes the utopian Pacific island of Bensalem, where the Jewish colonists have a college of natural philosophy called "Solomon's House" and are governed by rules of kabbalistic antiquity. Genuine kabbalistic motifs, admittedly obtained at second hand, are to be found in the late 18th century in the works of William Blake. His notion of the sexual inner life of his divine "Emanations" and "Specters" is at least partially kabbalistic, while his portrait of the "Giant Albion" is explicitly derived from the kabbalistic notion of the *Adam Kadmon* ("Primal Man"). Kabbalistic notions and images later played a part in the occult system employed by W.B. Yeats (1865–1939) in his poetry; and in the mid-20th century the Kabbalah acquired a considerable vogue, exemplified by the poetry of Nathaniel *Tarn and by *Riders in the Chariot* (1961), a novel by the Australian writer Patrick White.

The Figure of the Jew

Jews were expelled from England in 1290, and the great medieval English works in which Jews were portrayed, notably John Gower's *Confessio Amantis* (c. 1390), William Langland's *The Vision of Piers Plowman* (three versions c. 1360–1400), and Geoffrey *Chaucer's *Prioress's Tale* (one of the *Canterbury Tales*, c. 1390) were all composed about a century later. The figure of the Jew was therefore almost certainly not drawn from life, but rather from imagination and popular tradition, the latter a mixture of prejudice and idealization. This approach is not untypical of medieval writing generally, which often used stereotypes and symbols and gave them concrete shape. The evil stereotype of the Jew is clearly based on the Christian account of the crucifixion of Jesus, including his betrayal by Judas (identified with the Jew in general) and his often-stated enmity toward the Jewish scribes and Pharisees. This provided the basis for the image of the Jew in the early mystery or "miracle" plays, current from the 13th century, which presented the Bible records in dramatic form. A contemporary touch was sometimes added by representing Judas as a Jewish usurer. There is an historical link between the dramatizing of the Crucifixion and the rise of the *blood libel, which reached its culmination in the notorious case of *Hugh of Lincoln (1255). This accusation became the subject of several horrific early poems, including the old Scottish ballad of "The Jew's Daughter," reproduced in Percy's *Reliques*. In this ballad the story is slightly varied, the ritual murder being committed by a young Jewess. Chaucer's *Prioress's Tale*, a story of child murder committed by Jews, explicitly refers the reader to the case of Hugh of Lincoln a hundred years earlier, the suggestion being that the killing of Christian children by Jews was habitual. Echoes of these medieval fantasies continue to be heard down the centuries, and they provide the starting point for Christopher *Marlowe's *The Jew of Malta* (c. 1589) and for Shakespeare's *The Merchant of Venice* (c. 1596). Both Marlowe's Barabas and Shakespeare's Shylock obviously delight in the murder of Christians either by knife or by poison, a partial reflection of the charges leveled at the trial of the unfortunate Marrano physician Roderigo *Lopez. The stage Jew down to the Elizabethan period looked rather like the Devil in the old mystery plays, and was very often dressed in a similar costume: this explains why, in Shakespeare's play, Launcelot Gobbo describes Shylock as "the very devil incarnation," while Solanio sees him as the devil come "in the likeness of a Jew."

THE DUAL IMAGE. The Jew, however, aroused not only fear and hatred but also awe, and even admiration. Thus the medieval imagination had room not only for Judas, but also for heroic Old Testament figures such as Isaac and Moses. There is no doubt that the Israelites at the Red Sea in the old mysteries were also clearly identified as Jews. *Judah Maccabee (another Judas) was one of the famous Nine Worthies of early legend, along with David and Joshua. Shakespeare, who refers to the Jews in seven of his plays, draws on this tradition in the closing scene of his comedy, *Love's Labour's Lost*. Another early Christian tradition which carries undertones of admiration and awe is that of the *Wandering Jew. Ahasuerus, as he is sometimes called, in the early ballads was a "cursed shoemaker" who churlishly refused to allow Jesus to rest on a stone when he was on his way to Golgotha, and for this was made to wander the world forever. As the Jew who lives on eternally to testify to the salvation offered to the world, he is by no means an unsympathetic figure. In later romantic literature, particularly in poems by Percy Bysshe Shelley (*Queen Mab*, 1813) and Wordsworth ("Song for the Wandering Jew," 1800), he finally symbolizes universal wisdom and experience. The anonymous interlude *Jacob and Esau* (first published in 1568) includes acting directions which state that the players "are to be considered to be Hebrews, and so should be apparalled with attire." Thus, both Jacob the saint and his brother Esau, the lewd ruffian, are clearly Jews. The portrait of the Jew therefore becomes ambiguous: he is both hero and villain, angel and devil. There is more of the devil than the angel in the early portraits, but the balance varies. What is lacking is the middle, neutral ground of everyday reality, for little attempt is made to visualize the Jew in his ordinary environment. It is, however, worth noting certain speeches in *The Merchant of Venice*, especially Shylock's famous lines beginning, "I am a Jew. Hath not a Jew eyes? hath not a Jew hands, organs, dimensions, senses, affections, passions?" Here, there is at least a glimmer of realism. Jews are usually referred to by writers of the Elizabethan and succeeding periods in derogatory terms, the very word Jew invariably suggesting extortioner, beggar, thief, or devil's accomplice. But the resettlement of the Jews in England after 1656 and the new undogmatic character of 17th-century Anglicanism led to some change. George Herbert's poem "The Jews" (in *The Temple*, 1633) breathes a strain of devout love for Israel as the exiled people of God. Herbert was imitated a few years later by Henry Vaughan who, in an equally passionate poem of the same title, prays that he "might live to see the Olive bear her proper branches." The reference is to the metaphor of the olive used by the apostle Paul (N.T. Rom., 11), when he speaks of Israel as destined one day to be restored to flourishing growth. William Hemings based his drama, *The Jewes Tragedy* (1662), on the Jewish revolt against Rome, as described by *Josephus and *Josippon. Milton's *Samson Agonistes* presents a picture which is in part that of the heroic Jew of the Bible, in part a self-portrait of the poet himself. This marks a new phenomenon: the subjective projection of the author into the portrait of the Jew, and it was not to be repeated until much later, by such 19th-century poets as Byron and Coleridge, and by James Joyce in the figure of Leopold Bloom in *Ulysses* (1922).

LATER DRAMA AND FICTION. In 18th-century drama the Jew continued to be portrayed as either utterly evil and depraved or else completely virtuous. One dramatist might often produce both types, as did Charles Dibdin in *The Jew and the Doctor* (1788) and *The School for Prejudice* (1801). Richard Brinsley Sheridan introduces an unpleasant Jew, Isaac, in his comic opera, *The Duenna* (1775), balanced by a virtuous Jew, Moses, in *The School for Scandal* (1777). The hero of an anonymous play, *The Israelites* (1785), is a Mr. Israel, who practices all the virtues that the Christians only profess. The most sympathetic portrayal of all is that of the Jew Sheva in Richard *Cumberland's play, *The Jew* (1794). A kind of Shylock in reverse, Sheva is the English counterpart of the hero of the German dramatist *Lessing's *Nathan der Weise* (1779). In fiction there was a similar tendency to extremes. The vicious and criminal Jew painted by Daniel Defoe in *Roxana* (1724) is balanced in Tobias Smollett's novel *The Adventures of Ferdinand Count Fathom* (1753), where the benevolent Joshuah Manasseh insists on lending the hero money without interest. Yet Smollett himself had a few years earlier (in *The Adventures of Roderick Random*, 1748) drawn a no less exaggerated portrait of the Jewish usurer in Isaac Rapine, whose name suggests his character. The same duality in the portrait of the Jew is noticeable in the 19th century. Maria Edgeworth, having produced a gallery of rascally Jews in her early *Moral Tales* (1801), compensated for those in *Harrington* (1816), a novel largely devoted to the rehabilitation of the Jews, whom she represents as noble, generous, and worthy of respect and affection. All this was part of the new liberal attitude generated by the French Revolution and the spread of the belief in human equality and perfectibility. To entertain anti-Jewish prejudices was to subscribe to outmoded social and ethical forms. Thus, "Imperfect Sympathies," one of the *Essays of Elia* (1823–33) by Charles Lamb, expresses mild reservations about "Jews Christianizing, Christians Judaizing," Lamb having little time for Jewish conversion or assimilation. The novel *Ivanhoe* (1819) by Sir Walter Scott introduces Isaac of York, the medieval usurer who, though described as "mean and unamiable," is in fact radically humanized in line with the new conceptions. He has become grey rather than black, and his daughter Rebecca is entirely white, good, and beautiful. Scott has come a long way from the earlier stereotypes, and the Jews, far from being murderers, preach peace and respect for human life to the murderous Christian knights. In later 19th-century English novels there are many Jewish portraits. William Makepeace Thackeray always pictures his Jews as given to deceit and as suitable objects for social satire. In his *Notes of a Journey from Cornhill to Grand Cairo …* (1846), which includes the record of a visit to the Holy Land, Thackeray indulges in a rather more emphatic strain of antisemitism. Charles Kingsley and Charles *Dickens, on the other hand, both have sympathetic as well as unfavorable portraits. Kingsley's bad Jews are to be found in *Alton Locke* (1850), and his good Jew in *Hypatia* (1853), while Dickens introduces Fagin, the corrupter of youth and receiver of stolen goods, in *Oliver Twist* (1837–38), and Mr. Riah, the benefactor of society and ally of the innocent, in *Our Mutual Friend* (1864–65). Charles Reade has as the central character of his novel *It is Never too Late to Mend* (1856) a Jew, Isaac Levi, who initially more sinned against than sinning, ends by taking a terrible revenge on his rascally foe. George Henry Borrow, an agent of the British and Foreign Bible Society, was obsessed with Jewish exoticism, but disliked Jews as people. He used a Hebrew title for *Targum* (1835), a collection of translations, and in his most famous work, *The Bible in Spain* (1843), recorded his encounter with the alleged leader of Spain's surviving Marranos and included his own verse translation of *Adon Olam*. In his novel *The Way We Live Now* (1875), Anthony Trollope drew the fantastically wicked Jew Augustus Melmotte on a melodramatic scale and with no real attempt at verisimilitude. But in the following year, the ultimately noble Jew makes his appearance in George *Eliot's Zionist novel, *Daniel Deronda* (1876). This shows the Jews not merely as worthy of sympathy, but as having within them a spiritual energy through which mankind may one day be saved and made whole. The 19th-century belief in race and nationality as a source of vital inspiration has here combined with a certain moral idealism to produce a remarkable vision of the Jewish renaissance, in some measure prophetic of what was to come after the rise of Herzlian Zionism. Something similar is to be found in the novelist and statesman Benjamin *Disraeli, who never tired of vaunting the superiority of the Jewish race as a storehouse of energy and vision. In *Tancred* (1847) and his biography of

Lord George Bentinck (1852) he maintained his belief that the Jews were "the aristocrats of mankind." George du Maurier propagated a Jewish caricature nourished by the new Nietzschean philosophy of race. Svengali, the evil Jew in his novel *Trilby* (1894), is the eternal alien, mysterious and sinister, a sorcerer whose occult powers give the novel the character of a Gothic thriller. Svengali belongs, of course, to an "inferior race," and his exploits are ultimately designed to corrupt the "pure white race" personified in the novel's heroine, Trilby. On the other hand, George Meredith, in *The Tragic Comedians* (1880), presents a romantically attractive Jew, Alvan, who is actually a portrait of the German-Jewish socialist Ferdinand *Lassalle. Sir Thomas Henry Hall Caine also showed unstinted sympathy and admiration for the Jew in his novel of Jewish life in Morocco, *The Scapegoat* (1891), although his account is not without some inner contradictions. The non-Jewish Anglo-American Henry Harland, using the pen name Sidney Luska, published three novels – *As It Was Written* (1885), *Mrs. Peixada* (1886), and *The Yoke of Thorah* (1887) – in the guise of an immigrant of Jewish background describing the life of the German Jews of New York. The poets Wordsworth and Byron were drawn to the romantic glamour of the Jewish past, the former in a touching descriptive lyric, "A Jewish Family" (1828), the latter in the more famous *Hebrew Melodies.* Like Blake, Shelley was repelled by the Old Testament's stress on the Law and the Commandments – his instinct being toward free love and anarchism – but was drawn to the figure of the Wandering Jew. Samuel Taylor Coleridge, too, in his "Rime of the Ancient Mariner" (in *Lyrical Ballads*, 1798) shows an interest in the same theme evidently derived from his reading of M.G. Lewis' gruesome novel *The Monk* (1796). Coleridge translated *Kinat Jeshurun*, a Hebrew dirge on the death of Queen Charlotte by his friend Hyman *Hurwitz, calling it *Israel's Lament* (1817). The warmest and most detailed accounts of Jews are to be found in the poetry of Robert *Browning, who seemed determined to show that even post-biblical Jews, such as the medieval Rabbi Ben Ezra and the Jews of the Roman ghetto, could be given sympathetic, even noble, treatment. Browning tried to do in poetry what *Rembrandt had done in paint – suggest the mixture of everyday realism and sublimity in the lives of Jews. Matthew Arnold, the most "Hebraic" of 19th-century English writers, paid tribute to Hebrew culture in his elegy "On Heine's Grave" (*New Poems*, 1867), while Algernon Charles Swinburne gave expression to great indignation in his poem "On the Russian Persecution of the Jews" (1882).

THE 20TH CENTURY. English poets of the 20th century have shown less interest in Jews. T.S. Eliot makes a return to the medieval stereotype of avaricious extortioner in his phrase: "My house is a decayed house,/and the jew squats on the window sill, the owner/spawned in some estaminet of Antwerp/…" (*Gerontion* and other references), although elsewhere he speaks with veneration of Nehemiah, the prophet who "grieved for the broken city Jerusalem." In Catholic writers such as Hilaire Belloc, G.K. Chesterton, and Graham Greene, there is a similar rendering of the dark image of the Jew. Belloc, an anti-capitalist, held that the Jews and Protestants were the arch-enemies of civilization and evolved a belief in a "Jewish conspiracy" (*The Jews*, 1922). Greene revived the medieval connection between Judas and the Devil in *A Gun for Sale* (1936) and *Orient Express* (1933), and in *Brighton Rock* (1938), where the Jewish gang-leader Colleoni – one of the most sinister villains in English literature – leads the hero, Pinkie, to damnation. Frankly antisemitic portraits can also be found in the writings of D.H. Lawrence and Wyndham Lewis. A more mild and benevolent portraiture emerges from the biblical dramas of James Bridie, Laurence Housman, and Christopher Fry. George Bernard Shaw brought back the Jew-Devil stage tradition in burlesque form in *Man and Superman* (1903); and various characters in *Major Barbara* (1905), *Saint Joan* (1923), and *The Doctor's Dilemma* (1906) express Shaw's not unkindly view of the Jew in modern society. An important development in the 20th century was the attempt to abandon the old stereotype and depict Jews in natural, human terms. John Galsworthy took the lead in his novels and more particularly in his play *Loyalties* (1922). Here the Jew, Ferdinand de Levis, is the victim of a robbery at a country-house party. The other guests band together to defend the thief because he is one of them, whereas the Jew is an alien. Galsworthy has carefully purged his imagination of the kind of emotional attitudes that determined the reaction of Shakespeare and his audience to the basically similar situation in *The Merchant of Venice*, and the result is an objective study in social psychology. A similarly unemotional approach is to be found in James Joyce's *Ulysses*, where the central character, Leopold Bloom, is neither exactly hero nor anti-hero but something in between. Less flamboyant Jewish characters appear in novels by E.M. Forster, *The Longest Journey* (1907); and C.P. Snow. The latter's *The Conscience of the Rich* (1958) is devoted to the affairs of a Jewish family who differ from the English upper class around them only in an extra touch of gregariousness and more tenacious adherence to tradition.

Palestine and Israel in English Literature

Ever since medieval times English writers have recorded impressions of their visits to the Holy Land or written imaginative works based on Jewish historical themes. One of the earliest books of this kind was the *Voiage* (1357–71) of the 14th-century Anglo-French traveler Sir John Mandeville. Outstanding works over the centuries were Henry Maundrell's *A Journey from Aleppo to Jerusalem at Easter 1697* (1703); *The Fall of Jerusalem* (1820), a play by Henry Hart Milman, dean of St. Paul's, who also wrote a *History of the Jews* (1829); *Eothen* (1844), travel impressions by Alexander William Kinglake; *The Brook Kerith* (1916), a novel by the Irish writer George Moore; and *Oriental Encounters. Palestine and Syria 1894–1896* (1918) by Marmaduke William Pickthall. Britain's Mandate in Palestine, which led to a political confrontation with the *yishuv*, and the State of Israel found wide reflection in English fiction, generally of inferior merit. G.K. Chesterton, an antisemite who condoned massacres of Jews during the First Crusade as "a form of democratic violence," was nevertheless attracted to the Zionist ideal of emancipation through physical toil, recording his impressions of a visit to the Holy Land in *The New Jerusalem* (1920). A thinly disguised account of Jewish-British relations in Ereẓ Israel is combined with an accurate description of Palestine under the Romans in W.P. Crozier's *The Letters of Pontius Pilate* (1928). Some writers were intensely pro-Zionist, others violently hostile and pro-Arab. Muriel Spark's *The Mandelbaum Gate* (1965) was a tale of divided Jerusalem with an anti-Israel bias, but another non-Jewish novelist, Lynne Reid Banks, who wrote *An End to Running* (1962; U.S. ed., *House of Hope*) and *Children at the Gate* (1968), settled at kibbutz Yasur. Of the many books about Palestine and Israel written by English Jews outstanding was Arthur *Koestler's dramatic *Thieves in the Night* (1946).

The Jewish Contribution

Before the Expulsion of 1290, the Jews of England were culturally an integral part of medieval French Jewry, speaking Norman French, and conducting their business affairs in Hebrew or Latin and their literary activities almost exclusively in Hebrew. *Berechiah ben Natronai ha-Nakdan, the 12th–13th-century author of *Mishlei Shu'alim* ("Fox Fables"), is probably identical with Benedict le Poinctur (i.e., punctuator, Hebrew *Nakdan*), who is known to have been living in Oxford in 1194. Berechiah's "Fox Fables" compiled from a variety of Jewish, Oriental, and other medieval sources, were both popular and influential, partly determining the shape of later medieval bestiaries. Their influence may also be seen in the Latin *Gesta Romanorum*, first compiled in England (c. 1330; first printed c. 1472). An important literary figure of the Elizabethan period, John Florio (1553?–1625), was descended from converted Italian Jews. A friend of Ben Jonson and Sir Philip Sidney, he influenced Shakespeare, whose *Hamlet* and *The Tempest* echo Florio's pioneering translation of the *Essays* of Montaigne (1603). It was not until nearly a hundred years after the readmission of the Jews in 1665 that they began to play any significant part in English literary affairs. Moses *Mendes, the grandson of a Marrano physician, was a well-known poetaster and minor playwright. His ballad-opera, *The Double Disappointment* (1746), was the first work written for the theater by an English Jew. He also wrote *The Battiad* (1751), a satire, in collaboration with Dr. Isaac *Schomberg. Jael (Mendes) Pye (d. 1782), a convert like Mendes, made a brief but significant entry into English literature with poems and a novel; while another early poet, Emma (Lyon) Henry (1788–1870), a staunch Jewess, received the patronage of the Prince Regent in the early 19th century. Many of the Anglo-Jewish writers of the 18th and 19th centuries were either remote from Jewish life or actually abandoned Judaism. They include Isaac *D'Israeli, father of Benjamin Disraeli, Earl of Beaconsfield; the half-Jew John Leycester *Adolphus, the first person to deduce Sir Walter Scott's authorship of the *Waverley Novels;* members of the *Palgrave dynasty, notably Sir Francis (Cohen) Palgrave and his son, Francis Turner Palgrave, editor of the famous *Golden Treasury* of English Verse (1861); and Sir Arthur Wing Pinero (1855–1934), the most successful dramatist of his time, who was also of Jewish origin. Late writers included Stephen Hudson (Sydney Schiff); Naomi Jacob; Ada *Leverson; Benn Levy; Lewis Melville; Leonard *Merrick; E.H.W. *Meyerstein; Siegfried *Sassoon; Humbert *Wolfe; and Leonard *Woolf.

JEWISH THEMES. From the early 19th century onward, many Anglo-Jewish writers devoted a large part of their talent to Jewish themes. Several of these committed authors were women. The sisters Celia (Moss) Levetus (1819–1873) and Marion (Moss) Hartog (1821–1907), who ran a private school for 40 years, together published a collection of poems, *Early Efforts* (1838[1], 1839[2]); a three-volume *Romance of Jewish History* (1840); *Tales of Jewish History* (1843); and a short-lived *Jewish Sabbath Journal* (1855). Better known was Grace *Aguilar, a vigorous champion of Judaism, who wrote the first significant Anglo-Jewish novel, *The Vale of Cedars* (1850). Two other women writers were Alice Lucas (1851–1935) and Nina (Davis) Salaman (1877–1925), both of whom wrote poetry; Nina Salaman also translated medieval Hebrew verse. Novels on Jewish themes proliferated from the latter half of the 19th century. Benjamin *Farjeon, a writer of North African Sephardi origin, really created this new genre with works such as *Solomon Isaacs* (1877), *Aaron the Jew* (1894), and *Pride of Race* (1900), which described the London-Jewish scene and especially the growing populace of the East End. This was the main location for the more famous novels of Israel *Zangwill, who remains the greatest single figure in England's Jewish literary history. Although Zangwill wrote many books on non-Jewish themes, he is best remembered for his "ghetto" stories – *Children of the Ghetto* (1892), *Ghetto Tragedies* (1893), *The King of Schnorrers* (1894), and *Dreamers of the Ghetto* (1899). At about the same time, Jewish middle-class life was being faithfully described by three women novelists, Amy *Levy; Julia (Davis) *Frankau ("Frank Danby"); and Mrs. Alfred Sidgwick (Cecily Ullman, 1855–1934), whose works include *Scenes of Jewish Life* (1904), *In Other Days* (1915), and *Refugee* (1934). Their books had little impact outside the Jewish community, but their common central theme – mixed marriage – became increasingly popular. This was the case with the novelist G.B. *Stern, but the most sentimental, and obsessive, use of the motif occurs in the works of Louis *Golding, whose *Magnolia Street* (1932) and "Doomington" novels enshrine this aspect of Jewish assimilation with an archetypal repetitiveness that suggests a permanent solution of the "Jewish problem" through wholesale extra-marriage. The outstanding Jewish poet of the 20th century was Isaac *Rosenberg, whose feeling for the sufferings of the soldiers in the trenches of World War I was in part nourished by the Bible. Izak *Goller, originally a preacher, was a more intensely Jewish poet, whose passionate Zionist sympathies and outspoken manner brought him both fame and notoriety during the 1930s. Other Jewish writers included S.L. *Bensusan; the biographer and historian, Philip *Guedalla;

and M.J. Landa. A number of Jewish writers also became eminent as literary scholars and critics. They include Sir Sidney *Lee; F.S. Boas; Sir Israel *Gollancz; Laurie *Magnus; V. de Sola Pinto; Jacob Isaacs (d. 1973), first professor of English at the Hebrew University of Jerusalem; David *Daiches; and George Steiner. The left-wing publisher, author, and pacifist, Victor *Gollancz, attempted to synthesize his conception of Judaism with a liberalized Christianity. Joseph *Leftwich, J.M. Cohen (d. 1989), and Jacob Sonntag (d. 1984) were prominent editors, anthologists, and translators.

NEW IMPULSES. In the mid-20th century a new dimension was given to the problem of Jewish existence both by the European Holocaust and its aftermath and by the birth and consolidation of the State of Israel. These momentous events, shattering old illusions, in time created a new sense of tragedy and peril, in which the Jew became the focus of a universal situation. This feeling can be detected in several Anglo-Jewish writers, although none of them was as significant as such U.S. authors as Saul *Bellow, Bernard *Malamud, and Philip *Roth. In poetry the outstanding names were Dannie *Abse, Karen Gershon, Michael Hamburger, Emanuel *Litvinoff, Rudolf Nassauer, Jon *Silkin, and Nathaniel Tarn. A writer whose novels, essays, and political and philosophical works commanded wide attention from the 1930s onward was the Hungarian-born Arthur Koestler. Like Koestler, Stephen Spender (1909–1995), a leading poet and critic of partly Jewish origin, was a disillusioned leftist. His works include impressions of Israel, *Learning Laughter* (1952). Elias *Canetti was a refugee playwright who continued to write in German, his works being translated into English. Harold *Pinter, Peter *Shaffer, and Arnold *Wesker were leading playwrights of the post-World War II era. In 2005 Pinter was awarded the Nobel Prize for literature. Janina David (1930–) described her childhood experiences in pre-war Poland and the Warsaw ghetto in *A Square of Sky* (1964); its sequel, *A Touch of Earth* (1966), tells of her postwar move to Australia. *The Quick and the Dead* (1969), a novel by Thomas Wiseman (1930–), reflects early memories of Vienna during the 1930s and the *Anschluss* era. A few writers attempted to demythologize the Jewish image by presenting Jews as basically similar to their fellows. The novelist Alexander Baron, the novelist and playwright Wolf *Mankowitz, and Arnold Wesker all belong to this category, although Mankowitz later reassessed his commitment to Judaism. Popular novelists included the Socialist member of parliament Maurice Edelman, whose book *The Fratricides* (1963) has a Jewish doctor as its hero; and Henry Cecil (Judge Henry Cecil Leon), who specialized in legal themes. From the late 1950s a "new wave" of Anglo-Jewish writers appeared following the publication of *The Bankrupts* (1958), a novel by Brian *Glanville harshly criticizing Jewish family life and social forms. Works of similar inspiration were written by Dan *Jacobson, Frederic Raphael, and Bernard *Kops. Following the general inclination to reject or debunk the inheritance of an older generation – these writers were not, however, entirely destructive, their aim being to strip Jewish life in England of its complacency and hypocrisy. Other writers were more firmly committed to Jewish values and ideals. They include the humorist Chaim Bermant; the novelists Gerda Charles, Lionel Davidson, William Goldman (1910–), Chaim Raphael, and Bernice Rubens; and the Welsh-born poet Jeremy Robson (1939–), who edited *Letters to Israel* (1969) and an *Anthology of Young British Poets* (1968).

Another member of this group was the critic John Jacob Gross (1935–), assistant editor of *Encounter*. The Six-Day War of June 1967 galvanized many Jewish writers in England into a sudden awareness of a common destiny shared with the Israelis in their hour of peril. This found expression in a forthright letter to the London *Sunday Times* (June 4) signed by more than 30 Anglo-Jewish authors.

[Harold Harel Fisch]

Later Developments

The trends which had characterized Anglo-Jewish literature during the 1960s continued to manifest themselves in the 1970s. New books were published by virtually all of the better-known writers, including the novelists Gerda *Charles, Frederic *Raphael, Chaim *Raphael, Nadine *Gordimer, Bernard *Kops, Barnet *Litvinoff, Chaim *Bermant, Bernice *Rubens, the last of whom was awarded the Booker Prize for Fiction in 1970 for *The Elected Member* (1970), the story of a drug addict and his Jewish family set against the background of London's East End.

One of the new trends in the years under review was a growing closeness to the Hebrew tradition. Dan *Jacobson's *The Rape of Tamar* (1970) brought King David, his family, and court to life in a searching and brilliant retelling of biblical narrative. His drama, *The Caves of Adullam* (1972), treated the David-Saul relationship no less interestingly. Later heroism was described in David *Kossoff's *Voices of Masada* (1973), the story of the siege as it might have been told by the two women who, according to Josephus, were the only Jewish survivors. In another historical novel, *Another Time, Another Voice* (1971), Barnet Litvinoff deals with Shabbetai Ẓevi, while against the background of present-day Israel Lionel *Davidson's detective story, *Smith's Gazelle* (1971), deftly wove together kibbutz and Bedouin and the Israel love for nature.

Davidson, who settled in Israel after the Six-Day War, in 1972 became the first writer in English to win the Shazar Prize of the Israel Government for the encouragement of immigrant authors. Another English writer who settled in Israel was Karen *Gershon, the German-born poet, whose poems on Jerusalem were the heart of her volume of verse, *Legacies and Encounters, Poems 1966–1971* (1972). A cycle of the Jerusalem poems appeared in Israel with Hebrew translations facing each page.

The new, sometimes even personal, relation of Anglo-Jewish writers to Israel is paralleled by a deeper involvement with the Jewish past in England itself. Thus, Gerda Charles' novel, *The Destiny Waltz* (1971), grew out of the life of Isaac

*Rosenberg, the East End poet who died in World War I, while Maurice *Edelman went further back to write *Disraeli in Love* (1972), a portrait of the statesman in his youth. The largely interrelated aristocratic families that dominated the Anglo-Jewish community in the 19th century and even later were vividly described in *The Cousinhood* (1971) by Chaim Bermant.

The nearer past continued to be reflected in literature, Emanuel *Litvinoff's *Journey through a Small Planet* (1972) depicting an East End childhood in the 1930s and Arnold *Wesker in his play, *The Old Ones* (1973), evoking ideologies and eccentricities of an older East End generation that is now vanishing. The second part of David *Daiches' autobiography, *A Third World* (1971), describes the author's years in the United States, while *Mist of Memory* (1973) by the South African writer Bernard Sachs portrayed a Lithuanian childhood and full, contemplative years in South Africa – its politics, racial conflicts, trade unionism, and Jewish attitudes.

Another book on South Africa, Dan Jacobson's novel on interracial marriage, *Evidence of Love* (1960), was translated and published in the Soviet Union. Both Jacobson and Sachs, like other South African Jewish writers, in recent years made their home in England. Similarly, Canadians like Norman Levine and Mordecai *Richler, though continuing to write about Canada, became resident in England, and Richler's *St. Urbain's Horseman* (1971) sharply described expatriates in the film and television industry.

[Shulamit Nardi]

Starting in the 1980s Anglo-Jewish literature has undergone something of a transformation. Instead of specifically English concerns and forms of expression, many recent Anglo-Jewish novelists are influenced by the American Jewish novel and incorporate European Jewish history and the contemporary State of Israel into their fiction. This marked lack of parochialism is reflected in novels, often first novels, published in the 1980s by Elaine *Feinstein, Howard *Jacobson, Emanuel *Litvinoff, Simon Louvish, Bernice *Rubens, and Clive *Sinclair.

In 1985, the London *Times Literary Supplement* indicated a serious general interest in Anglo-Jewish literature by organizing a symposium for English and American Jewish writers on the role of Hebrew and Yiddish culture in the writer's life and work. In general, national British radio, television, and press have devoted a significant amount of time to Anglo-Jewish literature which, in recent years, has included many individual profiles of Jewish novelists in England. Clive Sinclair and Howard Jacobson, in particular, have achieved national prominence with Sinclair, in 1983, designated one of the 20 "Best of Young British Novelists" and Jacobson's *Peeping Tom* (1984), his second novel, winning a special *Guardian* fiction prize. Since 1984, the Institute of Jewish Affairs, the London-based research arm of the World Jewish Congress, has organized a regular Jewish writers' circle which has brought together many Anglo-Jewish writers for the first time. This group has grown out of a colloquium in 1984 on Literature and the Contemporary Jewish Experience which included the participation of the Israeli writer Aharon *Appelfeld and the literary critic George *Steiner.

In contrast to Anglo-Jewish literature which includes explicitly Jewish concerns, many Jewish writers in England continue to abstain from overt expression of their Jewishness in a fictional context. Prominent examples, in these terms, include Anita *Brookner's *Hotel du Lac* (1984), which won the Booker McConnel Prize for Fiction in 1984, Gabriel *Josipovici's *Conversations in Another Room* (1984), and Russell Hoban's *Pilgermann* (1983). Against this trend, however, Anita Brookner's *Family and Friends* (1985), for the first time in her fiction, obliquely refers to the author's European Jewish background and her *The Latecomers* (1988) makes explicit her grief for a lost European past as well as her Central European Jewish antecedents. Gabriel Josipovici's literary criticism reveals a profound interest and knowledge of Jewish literature. Two of Josipovici's novels, *The Big Glass* (1991) and *In a Hotel Garden* (1993), are concerned, respectively, with a Hebraic understanding of art and the continued European dialogue with Jewish history. Josipovici has also published his much acclaimed *The Book of God: A Response to the Bible* (1988) which has had a considerable impact on his fiction. Josipovici has also written the introduction to the English translation of Aharon Appelfeld's *The Retreat* (1985).

A young Anglo-Jewish playwright, who has emerged in the last decade, is Stephen Poliakoff, whose plays have been regularly produced in both London and New York. Older playwrights, Bernard *Kops and Arnold *Wesker, continue to produce drama of interest, especially Bernard Kops' *Ezra* (1980) and Arnold Wesker's *The Merchant* (1977). Between 1977 and 1981 Harold *Pinter's collected *Plays* were published to much acclaim and Peter *Shaffer, the author of *Amadeus* (1980), staged *Yonadab* (1985), a play based on Dan *Jacobson's *The Rape of Tamar* (1970), which played in a West End London theater. Jacobson, who was born in South Africa and has lived in England for nearly three decades, continues to produce fiction of high quality as demonstrated by his autobiographical set of short stories, *Time and Time Again* (1985) and his novel *The God-Fearer.* The poet Dannie *Abse has published *A Strong Dose of Myself* (1983), the third volume of his autobiography, and his *Collected Poems: 1945–1976* appeared in 1977.

Much Anglo-Jewish literature continues to situate Jewish characters in a specifically English context. In a comic tour de force, Howard Jacobson contrasts Englishness and Jewishness in his popular campus novel, *Coming From Behind* (1983). Jacobson's *Peeping Tom* (1984) is a brilliant and lasting comic treatment of the same theme. His *The Very Model of a Man* (1992) and *Roots Shmoots: Journeys among Jews* (1993) are explorations of his Jewishness.

Frederic *Raphael's *Heaven and Earth* (1985) examines Anglo-Jewishness in the political context of an amoral English conservatism. A more conventional account of middle class Jewish life in England – and its relationship to the State of Israel – is provided by Rosemary Friedman's trilogy, *Proofs* *of Affection* (1982), *Rose of Jericho* (1984), and *To Live in Peace* (1986). Friedman's fiction demonstrates that the family saga continues to be a popular form of Anglo-Jewish self-expression. Chaim *Bermant's *The Patriarch: A Jewish Family Saga* (1981) is another example of this genre, as is Maisie Mosco's bestselling *Almonds and Raisins* trilogy (1979–81). Judith Summers' first novel, *Dear Sister* (1985), is a woman-centered Jewish family saga.

While much Anglo-Jewish literature continues to be set in an English milieu, many Jewish novelists have begun to reveal a fruitful interest in European Jewish history and the contemporary State of Israel. Emanuel Litvinoff's *Falls The Shadow* (1983), using the form of a detective novel, examines the Jewishness of modern-day Israel and the relationship of the Jewish State to the Holocaust. A more controversial account of these themes is found in George Steiner's *The Portage to San Cristobal of A.H.* (1981). The 1982 West End stage version of this novella excited a prolonged exchange of articles and letters in the London *Times* and the *Jewish Chronicle*. Steiner also published an interesting work of fiction, *Proofs and Three Fables* (1992). Other works of fiction by Jewish critics include Al Alvarez's *Day of Atonement* (1991) and Harold Pinter's autobiographical novel *The Dwarfs* (1990 but mainly written in the 1950s). Pinter, like Steven *Berkoff in his challenging plays, was deeply influenced by his poor London East End Jewish background. Provocative fictional accounts of contemporary Israel are found in Simon Louvish's novels, *The Therapy of Avram Blok* (1985), *The Death of Moishe-Ganel* (1986), *City of Blok* (1988), *The Last Trump of Avram Blok* (1990), and *The Silencer* (1991). Louvish, who lives London, was raised in Jerusalem and served in the Six-Day War. His fiction is an iconoclastic, deliberately grotesque, portrait of the State of Israel. Clive Sinclair's *Blood Libels* (1985), his second novel, also utilizes Israeli history, especially the Lebanon War, and combines such history with a haunting imagination. In fact, Sinclair epitomizes the explicitly Jewish self-assertion and maturity of a new generation of Anglo-Jewish writers that has emerged in the 1980s. He describes himself as a Jewish writer "in a national sense" and so situates his fiction in Eastern Europe, America, and Israel. In this way, he eschews the usual self-referring, parochial concerns of the Anglo-Jewish novel. This is especially true in his collection of short stories, *Hearts of Gold* (1979) – which won the Somerset Maugham Award in 1981 – and *Bedbugs* (1982). His later works are *Cosmetic Effects* (1989), *Augustus Rex* (1992), and *Diaspora Blues: A View of Israel* (1987).

Elaine Feinstein is another Anglo-Jewish writer who, over the last decade, has consistently produced fiction of the highest literary excellence and has demonstrated a profound engagement with European history. Her fiction, especially *Children of the Rose* (1975), *The Ecstasy of Dr. Miriam Gardner* (1976), *The Shadow Master* (1978), *The Survivors* (1982), and *The Border* (1984), all demonstrate the persistence of the past in her characters' lives. Apart from *The Survivors*, all of these novels have a continental European setting. That is, Feinstein's fiction has successfully drawn on European Jewish history in a bid to understand her own sense of Jewishness. In recent years this has been clearly focused in her autobiographical *The Survivors*, set in England, and her less overtly autobiographical *The Border* which is set in Central Europe in 1938. *The Border* received high critical acclaim. The novel, using the form of a collection of letters and diaries, enacts the irrevocable march of history leading up to the outbreak of World War II. In juxtaposition to this historical backdrop, Feinstein's rare lucidity evokes her characters' passionately differing sense of reality. Bernice Rubens' *Brothers* (1983) utilizes modern Jewish history in more expansive terms than Feinstein, but, perhaps because of this, with less success.

The growing strength of British-Jewish writing is further indicated by a younger generation of Jewish novelists which is now emerging. Work by them includes Jenny Diski's *Like Mother* (1988), Will Self's *Cock and Bull* (1992), and Jonathan Wilson's *Schoom* (1993). When this writing is coupled with the plays of a number of young Jewish dramatists such as Diane Samuels, Julia Pascall, and Gavin Kostick, then the future of British-Jewish literature looks particularly healthy.

The last decade has demonstrated that there is a coincidence of interests between English literature in general and the concerns of the Anglo-Jewish novel. In recent years, much of the best English fiction looks to Asia, the Americas, and continental Europe for its subject matter and sense of history. It is not uncommon, therefore, for non-Jewish writers to incorporate Jewish history into their novels. With regard to the Holocaust, two of the most prominent examples of this phenomena are Thomas Keneally's Booker Prize winning *Schindler's Ark* (1982) – based on the life of the righteous gentile Oskar *Schindler – and D.M. Thomas' controversial *The White Hotel* (1981).

[Bryan Cheyette]

BIBLIOGRAPHY: E.N. Calisch, *The Jew in English Literature* (1909), includes bibliography; D. Philipson, *The Jew in English Fiction* (1911); M.J. Landa, *The Jew in Drama* (1926; repr. 1969); H. Michelson, *The Jew in Early English Literature* (1926), includes bibliography; L. Magnus, in: E.R. Bevan and C. Singer (eds.), *The Legacy of Israel* (1927), 483–505; W.B. Selbie, *ibid.*, 407–33; E.D. Coleman, *The Bible in English Drama* (1931), a bibliography; idem, *The Jew in English Drama* (1943; repr. 1970), a bibliography; H.R.S. van der Veen, *Jewish Characters in Eighteenth Century English Fiction and Drama* (1935), includes bibliography; M.F. Modder, *The Jew in the Literature of England* (1939), includes bibliography; J. Trachtenberg, *The Devil and the Jews* (1961), includes bibliography; J.L. Blau, *The Christian Interpretation of the Cabala in the Renaissance* (1944); A.M. Hyamson, in: *Anglo-Jewish Notabilities* (1949), 4–73; J. Leftwich, in: *Jewish Quarterly* (Spring 1953), 14–24; A. Baron, *ibid.* (Spring 1955); H. Fisch, *The Dual Image* (1959); idem, *Jerusalem and Albion* (1964), includes bibliographical references; D. Daiches, in: L. Finkelstein (ed.), *The Jews* …, 2 (1960^3), 1452–71; E. Rosenberg, *From Shylock to Svengali* (1960), includes bibliography; G.K. Anderson, *The Legend of the Wandering Jew* (1965); M. Roston, *Biblical Drama in England* (1968), includes bibliography; D.J. DeLaura, *Hebrew and Hellene in Victorian England* (1969), includes bibliography; Shunami, Bibl, 248ff.

EN-HAROD (Heb. עֵין חֲרֹד).

Ancient

Spring where Gideon and his people camped during his war against the Midianites and the place where he selected the men for his night ambush (Judg. 7:1). It is identified with a spring on a northwestern spur of Mt. Gilboa, and may also be the unnamed fountain where Saul camped against the Philistines (I Sam. 29:1). From Byzantine times it was believed that the battle between David and Goliath took place at En-Harod. The Arabs thus called it Ain Jalud ("Spring of Goliath"), by which name it became famous as the site of the Mongol defeat by the Mamluk sultan Kotuz in 1260.

En-Harod is also an unidentified locality which was the home of Shammah and Elika, two of David's warriors (II Sam. 23:25; cf. I Chron. 11:27).

[Michael Avi-Yonah]

Modern

En-Harod is the name of two kibbutzim in the Harod Valley, one affiliated with Ha-Kibbutz ha-Me'uḥad and the other with Iḥud ha-Kevuẓot ve-ha-Kibbutzim. The original En-Harod was founded in 1921 at the foot of Mt. Gilboa near Harod Spring by a pioneer group of *Gedud ha-Avodah. They set up two tent camps and started draining the malarial swamps of the "Nuris Bloc" recently acquired by the *Jewish National Fund. At En-Harod, the principles of the "large and growing kibbutz" were worked out in its first years and laid down by Shelomo *Lavi. At the same time, fierce discussions were held between members accepting the Gedud ha-Avodah doctrine of a countrywide commune of kibbutzim and others who demanded that every village constitute a separate economic unit. The former concentrated at neighboring *Tel Yosef, and the latter at En-Harod. When the Gedud declined, most of its groups associated themselves with En-Harod, eventually forming Ha-Kibbutz ha-Me'uḥad. In 1929 the En-Harod settlement was transferred to the northern rim of the valley, on the slope of the Ẓeva'im (Qūmī) Ridge. In the 1930s, the kibbutz quickly increased in membership, intensified its farming, and opened manufacturing enterprises. Exposed to frequent attacks during the 1936–39 Arab riots, special night squads of the Haganah were set up and trained at En-Harod, under Orde *Wingate. In the Israeli War of Independence (1948), a Palmaḥ group from En-Harod dislodged the Arab Legion from its positions menacing the Harod Valley at Zirʿīn (Yizre'el) and al-Mazar on Mt. Gilboa. In the 1951–52 split in the Kibbutz Me'uḥad movement, members of En-Harod were about equally divided between Mapai and the *Aḥdut-Avodah faction of Mapam, causing the settlement to be split between Iḥud ha-Kevuẓot ve-ha-Kibbutzim and Ha-Kibbutz ha-Me'uḥad, the latter setting up a new kibbutz adjoining the veteran settlement in the northwest. Both kibbutzim developed highly intensive farming (beehives, dairy cattle, poultry, fishery, fields crops, and orchards) and each had a number of industrial enterprises (at En-Harod "Iḥud," stainless steel sanitary equipment, other metal products, a printing press, and a guest house, and at En-Harod "Me'uḥad," steel works, a furniture factory, medical and industrial recording equipment, and software). Tel Yosef and En-Harod maintained the Bet Sturman Museum and Study Center containing collections and documents on the region's nature, history, and settlement history; nearby, a large open-air stage for art performances was set up. There was also a museum for contemporary art, Mishkan la-Ommanut (see *Museums, Israel). In 1968 En-Harod "Me'uḥad" had 760 inhabitants, and En-Harod "Iḥud" had 690. In the mid-1990s the population of En-Harod "Me'uḥad" was approximately 875, and the population of En-Harod "Iḥud" was approximately 720. At the end of 2002 the population of En-Harod "Me'uḥad" was 809 and the population of En-Harod "Iḥud" was 559.

WEBSITE: www.einharodm.co.il (for Me'uḥad).

[Efraim Orni]

ENNERY, JONAS D' (1801–1863), French politician, geographer, and educationalist. Ennery, who was born in Nancy, was principal of the school of the Jewish community in Strasbourg. In 1849, despite the anti-Jewish disorders in Alsace, he was elected to the constituent assembly, where he sat among the members of the "Mountain" (left wing). After Napoleon III's coup d'état in 1852, Ennery was exiled to Belgium. His works include *Dictionnaire général de géographie universelle* (4 vols., 1839–41) and *Prières d'un coeur israélite* (1848).

ENOCH (Heb. חֲנוֹךְ). (1) Son of Cain, father of Irad. The world's first city was named after Enoch (Gen. 4:17f.). It has been suggested that the writer is punning on the root *ḥnk*, "to found," "initiate." (2) Son of Jared, father of Methuselah, seventh generation of the human race (Gen. 5:18–24; I Chron. 1:3). Sasson (in Bibliography) has suggested that as seventh in the line of Adam, Enoch's life of piety is in contrast with the seventh in the line of Cain, who is associated with bloodshed. In comparison with the life-span of his ancestors and descendants, his life is short and corresponds in years with the number of days in the solar year. It is further said of him that he "walked with God; then he was no more for God took him" (Gen. 5:23). This cryptic statement implies the existence of some fuller narrative about Enoch, now lost, perhaps connecting him with the sun god (see below). Legend has stepped in to fill the gap. Some scholars have pointed to a similarity with the Mesopotamian story of Enmeduranna, the seventh king before the flood, who was very close to the sun-god to whom his capital city was dedicated. Hess follows Borger (Bibliography) in suggesting that a better Mesopotamian counterpart of Enoch would be Utuabzu, adviser to Enmeduranki. Utuabzu, seventh in a list of sages before the Mesopotamian flood, like Enoch ascended into heaven.

[Nahum M. Sarna / S. David Sperling (2nd ed.)]

In the Apocrypha

In Jewish apocryphal literature of the Second Temple period similar motifs to those of Enmeduranna are connected with Enoch (seventh in Seth's line); he too learned God's mysteries and had access to the heavenly tablets. It is therefore probable that the similarity between the later legends about Enoch and the figure of the Babylonian legendary king can be explained by the fact that Genesis preserves a partly expurgated narrative about Enoch and that some of the original mythological motifs continued to exist in oral tradition until they reached their present form in Jewish pseudepigrapha and medieval legends and mystical literature. Enoch became a hero in Jewish apocalyptic literature and two Jewish apocalyptic books are ascribed to him: the so-called Ethiopic and Slavonic Books of Enoch. The figure of Enoch was especially significant in the spiritual movement from which the *Dead Sea Sect originated. Thus his story and his writings are treated in the Book of *Jubilees, his prophecies are hinted at in the Testament of the Twelve Patriarchs, and he plays an active role in the Genesis Apocryphon, one of the *Dead Sea Scrolls. Cave 4 at Qumran yielded Aramaic fragments many of which correspond to the apocalyptic I Enoch. The importance attached to Enoch in some Jewish circles in the Second Temple period aroused the opposition of the more rationalistic Jewish sages. Therefore in rabbinic literature Enoch is sometimes presented as evil and the biblical statement that he was taken by God is simply explained as a reference to his death. The first to claim that Enoch merely died was Ben Sira (Ecclus. 44:16; 49:14–16) – even Joseph, Shem, Seth, Enoch, and Adam had to die. It is interesting to note that all these biblical personages (with the exception of Joseph, but note "The Prayer of Joseph") became heroes of Jewish, Gnostic, and Christian mystical speculations. It is also important that while the Hebrew text of Ben Sira presents Enoch as a "sign of knowledge to all generations" – a hint at his mystical wisdom – by the time of the Greek translation (135 B.C.E.) Enoch had become "an example of repentance for all generations," reflecting the legend that there was repentance before the Flood. This legend, in a curious form, occurs even in Mormon holy scriptures (Moses 6:27–7:19).

[David Flusser]

In the *Aggadah*

Enoch was among the nine righteous men who entered paradise without suffering the pangs of death (DEZ 1, end). "He ascended to heaven on God's command, and was given the name *Metatron the Great Scribe" (Targ. Yer. to Gen. 5:4). During his lifetime Enoch was the guardian of the "secret of intercalation" and of the "miraculous rod" with which Moses later performed the miracles in Egypt (PdRE 7:40). He is the central figure in some late Midrashim, such as *Sefer Ḥanokh* and *Ḥayyei Ḥanokh* (which are related to the legends found in the various pseudepigraphic Books of Enoch and other apocryphic works). Enoch lived in a secret place as a hidden righteous man and was called by an angel to leave his retreat to go to teach men to walk in the ways of God. He taught for 243 years, during which peace and prosperity reigned in the world. He made a powerful impression on all he taught, including kings and princes, and they acclaimed him as their king. As a reward for instructing mankind, God resolved to install him as king over the angels in heaven too. He ascended to heaven in a fiery chariot drawn by fiery chargers. When Enoch arrived in heaven the angels exclaimed: "How comes a man born of a woman amid the fire-consuming angels?" To which God replied: "Be not offended, for all mankind denied Me and My dominion and paid homage to the idols; I therefore transferred the *Shekhinah* ['Divine Presence'] from earth to heaven, and this man Enoch is the elect of men." God arrayed him in a magnificent garment and a luminous crown, opened to him all the gates of wisdom, gave him the name "Metatron," prince and chief of all heavenly hosts, transformed his body into a flame, and engirdled him by storm, whirlwind, and thundering (*Sefer ha-Yashar* to Genesis, p. 11a–13a). Notwithstanding these legends, third-century Palestinian rabbis deny the miraculous translation of Enoch, and state that he vacillated all his life between righteousness and sinfulness, whereupon God removed him from the world before he relapsed again into sin (Gen. R. 25:1). This derogatory evaluation of Enoch was, at least in part, a reaction against the use made by Christians of the legend of Enoch's ascension to heaven.

In Islam

A prophet named Idrīs is mentioned in the Koran in Suras 19:57–58 and 21:85. The commentators identify him with Enoch, whom God "took" (Gen. 5:22–25), namely, that he did not die. The Muslims shaped the character of Idrīs, the brother of "Noah," in keeping with Jewish *aggadah*, as already found in Ben Sira, Josephus, and the books of the Pseudepigrapha, in various languages, which are attributed to Enoch. The brother of "Noah" was well versed in books and was therefore named Idrīs ("the expounder of books"). Like the Jews, the Muslims occasionally identify him with Elijah, as well as with al-Khaḍir (see *Mūsā).

[Haïm Z'ew Hirschberg]

BIBLIOGRAPHY: U. Cassuto, *A Commentary on the Book of Genesis*, 1 (1961), 263, 281–6; E.A. Speiser, in: *The Anchor Bible*, Genesis (1964), 41–43; Ginzberg, Legends, 1 (1925), 125–40; 5 (1925), 156–64. IN APOCRYPHA AND AGGADAH: Ginzberg, Legends, 1 (1925), 125–40; 6 (1928), 157–65; N. Avigad and Y. Yadin, *Genesis Apocryphon* (1956), 16–19, 40; Y. Yadin, *The Ben Sira Scroll from Massada* (1965), 38; E.E. Urbach, *Ḥazal* (1969), 295. IN ISLAM: Tha'labī, *Qiṣaṣ* (Cairo, A.H. 1348), 32; A.J. Wensinck, in: EIS, 2 (1927), 449–50, s.v. *Idrīs*, incl. bibl.; G. Weil, *Biblische Legenden der Muselmaenner* (1845), 62. **ADD. BIBLIOGRAPHY:** R. Borger, in: JNES, 33 (1974), 183–96; J. Milik, *Books of Enoch: Aramaic Fragments of Qumran Cave 4* (1976); J. Sasson, in: ZAW, 90 (1978), 171–85; R. Hess, in: ABD II, 508; J. Fitzmyer, *The Genesis Apocryphon of Qumran Cave 1* (2004^{3}); C. Rowland, in: DDD, 301–5.

ENOCH, ETHIOPIC BOOK OF (known as **I Enoch**; abbr. **I En.**), one of the most important of the apocalyptic works, dating from the period of the Second Temple. It is named after the biblical Enoch, son of Jared, about whom it is stated in Genesis 5:24 that he "walked with God; then he was no more, for God took him," which was understood to mean that he ascended to heaven during his lifetime. The work consists of different sections, which are generally clearly indicated.

In its present form it is divided into five parts, consisting of some nine separate sections, as follows:

(1) 1–5: An introduction, in which Enoch relates the good in store for the "elect" after the final "day of judgment"; 6–11 describes Shamḥazai and his cohorts, the chiefs of the watchers (cf. Dan. 4:10–14); they are "sons of God … the Nephilim" of Genesis 6:4, who lust after the daughters of men and sire children (cf. the Greek *gigantes*), who consume the labor of others, and teach mankind the arts of magic and the art of fashioning weapons of destruction. Uriel, one of the angels of the "Heavenly Presence," is sent by God to apprise Noah of the impending flood, destined to come upon the earth because of this wickedness. The angel Gabriel is sent to destroy the children of the "watchers" and the angel Michael to bind the "watchers" in *Sheol until the day of the last judgment; 12–36 continues the foregoing except for the fact that here the leader of the Nephilim is called Azael, and Enoch the "righteous scribe" acts as the intermediary between them and God. It continues with Enoch's journey through the universe, during which he is granted a view of all the elements of creation (hills of darkness, rivers of fire, the abode of the spirits, the place of the great future "judgment," the garden of Eden, Gehenna, the sun, the stars, etc.) and among them also "the seat of glory," upon which sits "the great glory" (God).

(2) 37–71: This section deals with the "last day." The Messiah, who is here called the "Elect One," is envisioned as a preexistent being who has, from time immemorial, been "under the wings of the Lord of the spirits" and who, on the last day of judgment, is destined to act as the judge of all mortal beings (41). The ministering angels, who lift their voices in song in the morning, first greet the "Lord of spirits" (or the "ancient of days" of Dan. 7:9) and then the "Elect One."

(3) 72–82: The Book of the Courses of the Heavenly Luminaries. This book is entirely separate and distinct from the preceding one. It gives a detailed description of the course of the sun, of the moon and of the stars, of the falling of dew and of rain, of the recurring seasons of the year, etc. The nature of the "true" calendar of 364 days per year, i.e., 52 weeks, is also explained (by means of a description of the procession of the sun through the "gates" and "windows" of the heavens).

(4) 83–90: This part is similar in content to section (2). In it are related, by means of dream-visions and symbols, the deluge and the history of the children of Israel down to the beginning of the Hasmonean era.

(5) 91–108, which may be subdivided as follows: (a) 91–105: another survey of the history of man and of the children of Israel. History is divided into ten periods, seven of which have already occurred (the creation, the flood, Abraham, the revelation at Sinai, the Temple, the destruction of the Temple, the time of the election of "the righteous shoot") and three which belong to the future. In them the righteous shall triumph, the Temple will be rebuilt, and the day of the last judgment come; (b) 106–107: The Book of Noah, the story of Noah's birth, similar in content to the Genesis Apocryphon and to the Book of Noah found at Qumran; (c) 108: Enoch's instructions to mankind.

The different parts of the work are not merely a compilation of various heterogeneous elements, but apparently also reflect different periods in the life of the community in which these "books" arose. In its view of the role of Enoch and in its solar calendar it has affinities with the Book of *Jubilees (which mentions it – 4:17–23 et al. – and is dependent upon it), as well as with other apocalyptic literature (cf. the Testament of Levi, 10:5; 14:1 et al.). These books are also familiar with the Noah story, as apparently with chapters 80–93. On the other hand chapters 37–71 reflect the views of esoteric circles. In the Talmud, R. Akiva, who was among the sages who delved into such lore (*ma'aseh merkavah*; see Tosef., Ḥag. 2:4), expressed similar ideas concerning a preexistent Messiah who sits on a seat next to the "Divine Presence" (*Shekhinah*; Sanh. 38b; Ḥag. 14a), and similar ideas are found in the later "pseudepigraphic" midrashic literature (ed. by A. Jellinek in his *Beit ha-Midrash* and in PR 36–46). One passage in this section (67:6–8), which speaks about mineral waters used medicinally by mighty and wicked monarchs, apparently alludes to Herod (cf. Jos., Ant., 17:171) and hence dates from after his reign (or possibly the days of the early *procurators). The belief in a Temple which will descend from heaven (91–105) also stems from separatist circles, such as those represented by the authors of the Dead Sea Manual of *Discipline who did not consider the Second Temple to be sacred and dissociated themselves from it. The final chapter is both ideologically and linguistically close to the *Dead Sea Scrolls, and the term "righteous shoot" is also common in the writings of this sect.

The Book of Enoch had tremendous influence. From it, or at any rate, through it the Manual of Discipline received the solar calendar and it also served as an exemplar for the composition of the burgeoning apocalyptic literary genre. From it too comes the concept of a preexistent Messiah, which influenced early Christianity and prepared the way for the belief in the divinity of Jesus (see later). It was this influence which was apparently responsible for the negative attitude of some of the talmudic sages of the third century C.E. who regarded Enoch as a wicked and hypocritical figure (Gen. R. 25:1). Only later, at the beginning of the Middle Ages, did the rabbis deal with the mystical knowledge traditionally vouchsafed Enoch. Some early Church Fathers (like Tertullian) considered the book to be part of the canon. However, from the fourth century on, it gradually lost importance in the Western Church and only in the Ethiopic Church is it still considered canonical. The Book of Enoch became known again in Europe only in the 18th century when James Bruce brought parts of it from Ethiopia. In the 19th century, Dalman (who is also responsible for the chapter divisions), and later Charles, disseminated it in the world of Western scholarship.

The original language of the Book of Enoch was, according to Joseph Halévy, Hebrew, but the fragments of the book found in Qumran are all in Aramaic. Charles' hypothesis is that the book consists of Hebrew and Aramaic portions indiscriminately combined. The book was translated into Greek and from Greek into Ethiopic. Only part of the Greek translation is extant. The Book of Enoch is quoted in the Epistle of Jude (14–15) in the New Testament and its influence has been discovered at many other points in the New Testament and in the Church Fathers (cf. Charles, Apocrypha, 2 (1913), 180–5). Of the Greek translation, chapters 1–32 were found in Egypt in 1886–7 and were published by Bouriant in 1892. In 1930 the University of Michigan purchased this manuscript, as well as the manuscript of chapters 97:6–104, 106–107, which were published by Bonner (*The Last Chapters of Enoch in Greek*, 1937). The most complete Ethiopic version was published by R.H. Charles as *The Ethiopic Version of the Book of Enoch edited from 23 Mss.* (1906). There are the following translations of the Ethiopic text into modern languages: English, Charles, Apocrypha, 2 (1913), 163–28; German, G. Beer, in: E. Kautsch (ed.), *Apocryphen und Pseudepigraphen*, 2 (1900), 236–310; French, F. Martin, *Le livre d'Hénoch* (1906); Hebrew, A. Kahana, *Ha-Sefarim ha-Ḥizonim*, 1 (1936), 19–101.

BIBLIOGRAPHY: J. Flemming and L. Radermacher, *Das Buch Henoch* (1901); H.B. Swete, *Old Testament in Greek* (1912^4), 789–809; P. Volz, *Eschatologie der juedischen Gemeinde im neutestamentlichen Zeitalter* (1934), 16–25; H.H. Rowley, *Relevance of Apocalyptic* (1947), 54–60, incl. bibl.; idem, *Jewish Apocalyptic and the Dead Sea Scrolls* (1957); J.T. Milik, in: *Biblica*, 32 (1951), 393–400; idem, in: RB, 65 (1958), 70–77; N. Avigad and Y. Yadin, *Megillah Ḥizonit li-Vereshit* (1957), 13–15, 31, 34 (Heb. section); Y.M. Grintz, *Perakim be-Toledot Bayit Sheni* (1969), 105–42.

[Yehoshua M. Grintz]

ENOCH, SLAVONIC BOOK OF (known as **II Enoch**; abbr. **II En.**; also entitled the **Book of the Secrets of Enoch**, or several variations on this), apocryphal work translated in the tenth or 11th century from Greek into Slavonic. The dating is deduced from the evidence of certain linguistic peculiarities. The first complete edition of the work was published by A. Popov in 1880. It was edited and studied by M. Sokolov (1899 and 1910) who made a special examination of the quotations from Old Russian literature it contains. An edition and translation of the work into French was made by A. Vaillant (1952). There are considerable differences between the two recensions (one long and one short) found in the manuscripts. Vaillant and other scholars maintain that the short recension is closer to the original text than the long one, which in their view contains many interpolations made by two revisers. Nonetheless the long recension seems to contain some material belonging to the original text omitted from the short recension.

The Slavonic Book of Enoch begins with *Enoch's account of his journey on the wings of angels through the seven heavens. This account, which contains astronomical information and descriptions of various classes of obedient and rebellious angels, recalls, despite considerable differences in detail, similar passages in the Ethiopic Book of *Enoch. In the seventh heaven Enoch sees from afar the Lord, who speaks to him and orders the angel Vreveil to describe to him the workings of heaven and earth, as well as disquisitions on various other topics, and commands Enoch to record these in 360 books. This is followed by an account of the creation given to Enoch which is succeeded in turn by Enoch's exhortations to his sons. These exhortations include moral admonitions, injunctions concerning sacrifices, a description of what Enoch has seen in the heavens, and an eschatology. The tale continues with Enoch being carried away by angels. His son Methuselah is ordained as a priest, offers animal sacrifices, and at the end of his life sees in a vision the Lord, who announces the deluge and commands him to choose Nir, the second son of Lamech (i.e., Noah's brother), as his successor in the priestly office. After the death of Methuselah, Nir offers animal sacrifices. After more than 200 years, when people have changed for the worse, Sophonim, Nir's wife, becomes pregnant in her old age. Rebuked by her husband who believes her unfaithful, she dies. A child comes forth from her corpse. He has the distinctive signs of priesthood and is named Melchizedek. When the time of the deluge approaches, the Lord informs Nir that Melchizedek will be taken to Eden by the archangel Michael and will be forever the priest of priests, or, as Nir puts it, the head of the priests of the "other" people (those who will live after the deluge).

In the long recension the Lord refers to the 13 priests headed by Melchizedek's son Nir who precede the Melchizedek known from the Bible and to 12 priests who follow the second Melchizedek; after them will come the great high priest, the Word of God, who created all things visible and invisible. This allusion to the Christian concept of the Christ has no counterpart in the short recension. The latter, which ends with the removal of the first Melchizedek, is possibly cut short, and in this case the long recension may have preserved some original materials.

Various hypotheses have been put forward on the origin of the Slavonic Book of Enoch and the influences discernible in it. There are unmistakable echoes of Christian doctrine in the long recension, but only doubtful ones, or none at all, in the short. If, as seems probable, the latter text is comparatively free from interpolation, there does not appear to be any firm ground for maintaining, as Vaillant does, that the work originated in a Christian milieu. It is possible that it reflects tendencies of one or even several Jewish groups; there are many quotations from biblical texts and allusions to them and to Ben Sira. It is reasonably likely that the original work, which is more or less represented by the short recension, was an amalgam of two or more texts of differing provenance. A significant clue may be provided by the fact that in two passages – in Enoch's exhortations to his sons (Vaillant, p. 58–59) and in the account of the sacrifice offered by Methuselah (p. 66–67) – the text makes it clear that the four legs of the sacrificial animals should be tied together. A passage in the Babylonian Talmud (Tam. 31b) characterizes this way of tying sacrificial animals as a custom of the sectarians (*minim*). It is therefore a possibility that some portions of the Slavonic Book of Enoch, or the whole of it, reflect the views of a Jewish sect which was heterodox in rabbinic eyes. In this connection, it may be asked if the story of Melchizedek recounted in this work also belongs to the lore of this sect.

Some portions of the Slavonic Book of Enoch show Iranian influences. A passage in the exhortations of Enoch (Vaillant, p. 56–57) referring to the souls of animals accusing man certainly derives, as W. Otto noted, from the Zoroastrian scriptures; its ultimate source may be found in the Avestic Gathas (Yasna 29). The reference in the same passage to the habitation assigned to the souls of the animals in the Great Aeon may also reflect Zoroastrian views. It may be significant that these passages immediately precede the sectarian passage of sacrificial animals (Vaillant, p. 58–59). A passage in the exhortations of Enoch (p. 60–63) in which he refers to God having established the division of time in the Aeon of Creation and to these divisions (the years, months, days, and hours) disappearing in the eschatological Great Aeon is also reminiscent of Iranian doctrines on the creation of the Time of Long Dominion (which has the ordinary divisions of time) and to its merging at the end with Infinite Time (which has none). It has been claimed, with good reason, that the account of the creation the Lord gives to Enoch (Vaillant, p. 28–31) also contains some Iranian elements. The book also shows an Egyptian influence. The Greek original of the Slavonic text appears to have been full of Hebraisms; it may be supposed that the author was familiar with the language of the Septuagint. However, in at least one case (Vaillant, p. 10) a post-biblical Hebrew expression, *porkei ʿol*, seems to have been translated.

Chronologically the Slavonic Book of Enoch comes after the Ethiopic Book of Enoch. *A terminus a quo* is suggested (though not established) by the hypothesis that the Mishnah may include a reference to the sacrificial usages of a sect within which at least some portions of this text may have originated. There are some not wholly conclusive indications that the Greek original of the work may have still existed in the 13th century.

BIBLIOGRAPHY: Charles, Apocrypha, 2 (1913), 425–69; G.N. Bonwetsch, *Die Buecher der Geheimnisse Hennochs* (1922); R. Otto, *Reich Gottes und Menschensohn* (1934), 160–4; G. Scholem, *Ursprung und Anfaenge der Kabbala* (1962), 62ff.; D. Winston, in: *History of Religions*, 5 (1965), 198f.; A. Rubinstein, in: JJS, 13 (1962), 1–21.

[Shlomo Pines]

ENOCH BEN ABRAHAM (d. after 1662), talmudist and preacher. In 1649, after having served as preacher in Cracow, he left for Gnesen where he was appointed rabbi. He afterward became *dayyan* at Posen. As a result of the suffering and poverty caused by the Chmielnicki rebellion (1648–49), Enoch left Poland and settled at Oettingen (Germany) where he was appointed rabbi, remaining there, probably until his death. His works, published posthumously, are *Vikkuʾaḥ Yosef ve-ha-Shevatim* (Amsterdam, 1680), an attempt to exonerate Joseph's brothers; *Reshit Bikkurim* (1708), three sermons on God's existence, revelation, and reward and punishment, published as part one of his grandson Enoch b. Judah's book of the same title. The introduction mentions his commentaries on Psalms, Proverbs, and Esther; *Berit Olam*, homilies on the Bible; and novellae on the *Tur Oraḥ Ḥayyim*. Some of his responsa, together with those of his son Judah and his grandson, appear in *Ḥinnukh Beit Yehudah* (1708).

BIBLIOGRAPHY: J. Perles, *Geschichte der Juden in Posen* (1865), 82, 83; J.E. Sokolow, *Gan Peraḥim* (1890), 120.

[Jacob Hirsch Haberman]

ENOSH (Heb. אֱנוֹשׁ; "man, mankind"), eldest son of *Seth and the father of Kenan (Gen. 4:26; 5:6, 9; I Chron. 1:1–2). He lived 905 years (Gen. 5:11). It was in his day that the name YHWH was first invoked (*ibid.* 4:26).

In the *Aggadah*

The generation of Enosh is the "counsel of the ungodly" of Ps. 1:1. Enosh and his contemporaries studied and practiced the arts of divination and control of heavenly forces, thereby making way for the generation of the flood (Zohar 1:56a), and were also the first to practice idolatry (Sif. Deut. 43; see also Shab. 118b). Four revolutions in nature occurred during the days of Enosh: the mountains became barren; corpses began to putrefy; the faces of men became apelike (rather than Godlike); and demons lost their fear of men (Gen. R. 23:6).

BIBLIOGRAPHY: Cassuto, in: EM, 1 (1965), 450; E.A. Speiser, *Genesis* (1964), 37–38. IN THE AGGADAH: I. Ḥasida, *Ishei ha-Tanakh* (1964), 73.

EN-RIMMON (Heb. עֵין רִמּוֹן), ancient town in the northern Negev. Originally part of the territory of Simeon (Josh. 19:7), it was absorbed by the tribe of Judah in the time of David (*ibid.* 15:32; I Chron. 4:32). It was resettled by Jews in the Persian period (Neh. 11:29). In the masoretic text of the Books of Joshua and Chronicles, En-Rimmon appears as two separate cities (Ain and Rimmon) but as one city in the Book of Nehemiah and the Septuagint. In the fourth century C.E. Eusebius refers to it as a large Jewish village (Onom. 88:17; 146:25). The name may be preserved in the Arabic Khirbat Umm al-Ramāmīn, about 8 mi. (13 km.) north of Beersheba.

BIBLIOGRAPHY: Abel, Geog, 2 (1938), 318; Avi-Yonah, Geog, 114. **ADD. BIBLIOGRAPHY:** S. Ahituv, *Joshua* (1995), 303.

[Michael Avi-Yonah]

ENRIQUES, PAOLO (1878–1932), Italian zoologist. Born at Leghorn, he became director of the Institute of Zoology at Padua in 1921 and remained there until his death. His zoological studies dealt with comparative physiology and protozoology. Among works of wider scope were his *La teoria cellulare* (1911), in which he attempted a synthesis of modern biological problems; *Riproduzione nei protozoi* (1924); and a series of monographs on genetics and evolution in which Enriques attempted to reconcile Mendelian heredity with the Darwinian theory of evolution.

[Mordecai L. Gabriel]

ENRÍQUEZ (Henríques), ISABEL (fl. 1660), Spanish poet. According to Miguel de *Barrios, she was "famous in the Academies of Madrid for her rare talent." In 1636 Isaac *Cardozo dedicated to her his *Panegýrieo... del color verde.* At some date after this she fled to Amsterdam, where she openly professed Judaism. It was here that she was befriended by Barrios, who dedicated two poems to her in his *Aplauso métrico* (1673). In his *Relación de los poetas*, Barrios cites a *décima* of hers and describes her as the author of a volume of verse. Together with Isabel *Correa, Isabel Enríquez is reputed to have been a member of Belmonte's Academia de los Sitibundos in Amsterdam.

BIBLIOGRAPHY: M. de Barrios, *Relación de los Poetas y Escriptores Españoles de la Nación Judayca* (1683), 56; Kayserling, Bibl, 52; Brugmans-Frank, 455.

[Kenneth R. Scholberg]

ENRÍQUEZ (Henriquez) BASURTO, DIEGO (b. 1621), *Marrano poet, son of Antonio Enríquez *Gomez. Probably born in Spain, he lived with his father in Rouen, France, and later moved to the Low Countries. Apparently while in Antwerp, Enríquez was the target of a vicious lampoon written in 1664. Enríquez wrote a sonnet in praise of his father's *Siglo pitagórico.* A longer poem, *El Triunpho de la Virtud y Paciencia de Job*, dedicated to Anne of Austria, employs a variety of verse forms and is divided into six "visions," with intercalated portions of the Psalms (Rouen, 1649).

BIBLIOGRAPHY: Roth, Marranos, 246, 333; Kayserling, Bibl, 26; Barrera, *Catálogo del teatro antiguo español* (1860), 136; I.S. Revah, *Spinoza et le Dr. Juan de Prado* (1959), 24, 74–76.

[Kenneth R. Scholberg]

ENRÍQUEZ (or **Henríquez**) **GÓMEZ, ANTONIO** (pseudonym of **Enrique Enriquez de Paz**; 1601–1663), Spanish playwright and poet. Born in Segovia Cuenca, he was the son of a Portuguese Converso family that had been persecuted by the Inquisition for several generations. From 1577 the family began to practice Judaism in secret. They kept the Sabbath and festivals, observed some of the laws and customs pertaining to *kashrut*, and performed certain acts that were distinctly Jewish. His grandfather Diego de Mora was arrested for judaizing in 1588 and died in an Inquisition prison. Some members of the family escaped to France where they openly practiced Judaism. His father Diego Enríquez de Mora was arrested and tried in 1624 and then left for France. Once his Christian wife died, his father married a second wife, this time from a Converso family. Antonio lived in Cuenca, Seville, and Madrid. Together with other Converso writers and poets, Antonio was at the court of Felipe IV. Antonio, whose mother was an old Christian, also married an old Christian but raised his children as Jews. His literary career was a great success. He wrote about 40 plays and many prose and poetry pieces. For purely racist reasons his literary work was almost totally ignored until recent times. His works bear clear testimony of his "Jewish" identity. Gómez had a distinguished military career, rising to the rank of captain and receiving the decoration of Knight of the Order of San Miguel. Together with his son, Diego Enríquez Basurto (who also became a well-known author), Enríquez Gómez left Spain in about 1636 and lived for a time in France, in Bordeaux and Rouen, where most of his books were published. He later moved to Holland, where he reverted openly to Judaism; he was symbolically punished in absentia at an auto-da-fé in Seville on April 13, 1660. Enríquez Gómez felt very bitter that he had to live away in a country where his mother tongue, in which he produced masterpieces, was not spoken. For some unknown reason, he returned to Spain in around 1649 and lived in Seville under a false name. He intended to continue to live as a Jew and had plans to move to Naples. He continued to write using a pen name Fernando de Zárato y Castronovo. For more than ten years he was able to remain incognito. His real identity was discovered because of the drama he wrote. The Inquisition examined the background of the playwright whose work aroused its suspicion. In 1660 he was burnt in effigy. He was arrested in 1661 and was thrown into prison where his life ended in 1663.

Enríquez Gómez was a lyric, dramatic, and epic poet, as well as a noted satirist. His major works include the *Academias morales de las musas*, dedicated to Anne of Austria (Bordeaux, 1642), and *El siglo pitagórico y vida de don Gregorio Guadaña* (Rouen, 1644). The latter, a novel in verse and prose, presents a series of 14 transformations of a soul in different bodies, satirizing various classes of society. Enríquez Góez also wrote *Luis dado de Dios a Luis y Ana* (Paris, 1645), dedicated to Louis XIII of France; *Torre de Babilonia* (Rouen, 1649); and a biblical epic about Samson, *El Sansón nazareno* (Rouen, 1656). In the prologue to this last work, Gómez refers to his authorship of 22 plays. These are mainly concerned with themes of honor, love, and friendship and half are based on biblical subjects. In many of his works Enríquez Gómez very strongly criticized the Inquisition. Enríquez Gómez composed a ballad dedicated to the martyr Lope de Vega (Juda el Creyente), who was burned at Valladolid on July 25, 1644.

Revah's research has clarified many dark points in Gómez's biography and introduced his literary creation to the wider academic and literary world.

BIBLIOGRAPHY: Kayserling, Bibl, 49; J. Caro Baroja, *Judíos en la España moderna y contemporánea*, 3 (1961), index; H.V. Besso, *Dramatic Literature of the Sephardic Jews of Amsterdam in the XVIIth and XVIIIth Centuries* (1947), index; C.A. de la Barrera y Leirado, *Catálogo bibliográfico y biográfico del teatro antiguo español* (1860), 134–42; Roth, Marranos, 246, 333; Revah, in: REJ, 118 (1959–60), 50–51, 71–72; idem, in: REJ, 131 (1962), 83–168; M. Gendreau-Massaloux, in: REJ, 136 (1977), 368–87; J. Antonio Cid, in: *Homenaje a Julio Caro Baroja* (1978), 271–300; L.R. Torgal, in: *Biblos*, 55 (1979), 197–232; J. Rauchwarger, in: REJ, 138 (1979), 69–87; A. Márquez, in: *Nueva Revista de Filología Hispánica*, 30 (1881), 513–33; G.F. Dille, in: *Papers on Language and Literature*, 14 (1978), 11–21; idem, *Antonio Enríquez Gómez* (1988); idem, in: *Pe'amim*, 46–47 (1991), 222–34; A. Márquez, *Literatura e Inquisición en España (1478–1834)* (1980), 113–20; T. Oelman, in: *Bulletin of Hispanic Studies*, 60 (1983), 201–9; idem, *Marrano Poets of the Seventeenth Century: An Anthology of the Poetry of João Pinto Delgado, Antonio Enríquez Gómez, and Miguel de Barrios* (1982); C.H.

Rose, in: *The Spanish Inquisition and the Inquisitorial Mind* (1987), 53–71; M. McGaha, in: *Sefarad*, 48 (1988), 59–92; idem, in: *Bulletin of Hispanic Studies*, 69 (1992), 127–39; P.G. Martínez Domene and M. Ángeles Pérez Sánchez, in: *Letras de Deusto*, 46 (1990), 65–80; C.L. Wilke, in: REJ, 150 (1991), 203–8 [Review]; M. Harris, in: *Bulletin of the Comediantes*, 43 (1991), 147–61; N. Kramer-Hellinx, in: *Pe'amim*, 46–47 (1991), 196–221.

[Kenneth R. Scholberg / Yom Tov Assis (2nd ed.)]

EN-ROGEL (Heb. עֵין רֹגֵל), a spring or well southeast of Jerusalem on the border between the tribes of Judah and Benjamin, between En-Shemesh and the *Hinnom Valley (Josh. 15:7; 18:16). Jonathan and Ahimaaz, who acted as spies and runners for David when he was fleeing from Absalom, waited there for news from Jerusalem (II Sam. 17:17). Adonijah's aborted attempt to succeed David as king took place at En-Rogel (I Kings 1:9) and it is probably identical with the "dragon's well" (Ein ha-Tannim) mentioned in Nehemiah 2:13. En-Rogel has been identified with a well, 60 ft. (18 m.) deep, called Bīr (Bi'r) Ayyūb ("Job's Well"; perhaps a corruption of "Joab's well" [Ahituv]), situated at the convergence of the Hinnom and *Kidron valleys, some 500 meters south of the city of David outside the walls of the Old City of Jerusalem. It sometimes overflows in rainy winters, justifying its definition as a spring. Alternatively, the well was dug on the site of the ancient spring that had been stopped up.

BIBLIOGRAPHY: Hecker, in: M. Avi-Yonah (ed.), *Sefer Yerushalayim*, 1 (1956), 199–200; H. Vincent, *Jérusalem antique*, 1 (1912), 134–8; idem, *Jérusalem de l'Ancien Testament*, 1 (1954), 284–8; G.A. Smith, *Jerusalem*, 1 (1907), 108–11; G. Dalman, *Jerusalem und sein Gelaende* (1930), 163–7; A.S. Marmardji, *Textes géographiques arabes sur la Palestine* (1951), 14; J. Simons, *Jerusalem in the Old Testament* (1952), 158–63. **ADD. BIBLIOGRAPHY:** S. Ahituv, *Joshua* (1995), 246; M. Cogan, *I Kings* (2000), 159.

[Michael Avi-Yonah]

ENSHEIM, MOSES (also known as **Brisac** and **Moses Metz**; 1750–1839), mathematician and Hebrew versifier. Ensheim left his native Metz in order to avoid having to become a rabbi, and for many years led a wandering life. From 1782 to 1785 he was employed as a tutor in the home of Moses *Mendelssohn in Berlin. He then returned to Metz, where he gave private lessons in mathematics since, as a Jew, he was precluded from teaching in the new central school in the city. He also started working with the Hebrew journal *Ha-Me'assef* in which (vol. 6 (1790), 69–72) he published his *Shalosh Ḥidot*, a satire against billiards and card games, and two hymns: *Al-ha-Va'ad ha-Gadol asher bi-Medinat Ẓarefat* (6 (1790), 33–37), addressed to the National Assembly in Versailles; and *La-Menaẓe'aḥ Shir*, a hymn on the occasion of the Metz civic fete of 1792. The latter was sung in the Metz synagogue to the tune of the *Marseillaise*. Ensheim was a friend of Abbé *Grégoire, and helped him with the preparation of his essay on the Jews (1788). He was also acquainted with several French mathematicians of note, and his *Recherches sur les calculs différentiels et intégrals* (1799) was highly regarded by Lagrange and Laplace. Ensheim spent the last years of his life in Bayonne as a tutor in the home of Abraham *Furtado. He bequeathed a quarter of his estate, amounting to 12,000 francs, to the Jewish elementary school in Metz.

BIBLIOGRAPHY: Steinschneider, Cat Bod, 972; Klausner, Sifrut, 1 (1952), 320–1. **ADD. BIBLIOGRAPHY:** P.A. Meyer, *La communauté juive de Metz au XVIII siècle* (1993).

[Jefim (Hayyim) Schirmann]

ENSISHEIM, town in Haut-Rhin department, Alsace, E. France, about 19 mi. (30 km.) S. of *Colmar. R. *Meir of Rothenburg was held prisoner there from 1286. The first evidence that Jews were living in the town dates from 1291. They were among the victims of the *Armleder persecutions in 1338. The community had hardly been reconstituted when it suffered from the persecutions accompanying the *Black Death in 1348–49. A few Jews again settled there from 1371. The small community welcomed the Jews expelled from Kaysersberg and *Mulhouse at the beginning of the 16th century. After an ordinance of 1547, only one Jewish family was allowed to reside in Ensisheim and the surrounding localities, and the synagogue was closed for worship. In 1689, some Jews were again admitted for a short while on payment of a high protection fee. It was not until 1824 that some Jews again settled there. Only a few Jews were still living there in 1936. At an unknown date there was a *blood libel in Ensisheim and the Jews there were put on trial.

BIBLIOGRAPHY: Germ Jud, 2 (1968), 211ff.; E. Scheid, *Histoire des Juifs d'Alsace* (1887), 78, 107, 118, 135; F.J. Merklen, *Histoire d'Ensisheim*, 1 (1840), 185ff, 348; 2 (1840), 286 and passim; Z. Szajkowski, *Franco-Judaica* (1962), nos. 21, 1429.

[Bernhard Blumenkranz]

ENTEBBE RAID. On Sunday, June 27, 1976, an Air France jet plane en route from Tel Aviv to Paris with over 200 passengers on board, including 80 Israelis, was hijacked after it took off from Athens where it had made an interim landing. The hijackers claimed to belong to the Popular Front for the Liberation of Palestine. The plane landed at Benghazi Airport in Libya later the same day, and after refueling there (although Libyan authorities denied this), it took off in the direction of Amman and ultimately landed at Entebbe Airport near Kampala, Uganda, in complete darkness.

On Wednesday, June 30, the terrorists – after releasing 47 of the passengers, including elderly women, children, and the sick – issued their demands for the release of 53 Palestinian terrorists imprisoned in various countries, 40 of them in Israel, setting the following Thursday at noon as the deadline, and threatening to kill all the remaining passengers and blow up the plane if their demands were not met. Later, they extended the deadline for another 24 hours.

Meanwhile, on the previous two days the hijackers released 148 passengers, most of them Jews who were not Israelis, leaving 102 hostages, mostly Israelis, plus the crew of the airline.

On July 1, the Israeli government announced that it would submit to the demands of the hijackers and officially asked France to negotiate on its behalf for the return of the hostages.

It later transpired, however, that from the moment that the hijack took place a rescue plan was drawn up, and on July 4, Israel and the whole world thrilled at the news of an attack by an Israeli commando unit at Entebbe, which effected the release of the hostages. The operation was rightly described as the most daring and incredible rescue mission in military history, taking place as it did, in a hostile country, 2,500 miles distant and with minimal time for planning its complicated details. The operation, which had been kept a guarded secret, was under the command of Brigadier-General Dan Shomron and was carried out with giant American Hercules transport planes.

The rescuers landed at the airport with orders only to return fire directed at them and did so at Ugandan soldiers who fired at them from the control tower. Storming the place where the hostages had been housed, they shouted to them to keep their heads down, with the result that the rescue was thus effected with a minimum of loss of life.

Three of the civilians lost their lives, two in the actual operation and one succumbing to wounds in Nairobi Hospital. There was a single military casualty – Lt.-Col. Jonathan ("Yoni") Netanyahu, commander of the strike force, the 30-year-old son of Professor Ben-Zion Netanyahu. He was buried with full military honors in the Military Cemetery on Mt. Herzl. Among those present were President Katzir, Prime Minister Rabin, and Chief of Staff Mordecai Gur.

One hostage, Mrs. Dora Bloch, was left behind, since she had earlier been taken to a hospital in Kampala and it transpired that she was later brutally murdered.

Kurt Waldheim, secretary-general of the UN, described the rescue operation as a violation of Ugandan sovereignty and claimed that the situation created by it was likely to have serious international repercussions, especially as far as Africa was concerned. (It was in fact condemned at a summit meeting of the Organization of African Unity.) This, however, was the only discordant note in a flood of congratulations which poured in, including one from President Ford – a message which was declared to be "unprecedented," since no American president had ever congratulated Israel on a military action.

[Louis Isaac Rabinowitz (2nd ed.)]

ENTIN, JOEL (1875–1959), Yiddish editor, educator, and translator. Entin was born in Pohost, Russia, where he received a traditional religious and secular education. He became active in Ḥibbat Zion and in 1890 moved to Moscow to work for Bnei Zion. He arrived in New York in 1891 where he audited classes at Columbia University. Although he wrote chiefly in Yiddish, his first publication was an English poem. With Jacob *Gordin he organized in 1896 the Fraye Yidishe Folksbine. Entin was a journalist and commentator on current events and literature for the Yiddish daily *Varhayt* (1905–15). He co-edited the second volume of the literary almanac *Yugend* (1908) and *Der Yidisher Kemfer*, the Labor Zionist weekly (1916–20). He translated novels, plays, and stories into Yiddish and was a founder of Yiddish secular schools, the Jewish Teachers' Seminary (1919), and the People's Relief Committee during World War I. He was active in the American Jewish Congress and the Farband Labor Zionist Order. His *Gezamlte Shriftn* ("Collected Works"), edited by S. Shapiro, appeared posthumously in New York in 1960.

BIBLIOGRAPHY: Rejzen, Leksikon, 2 (1927), 780–7; Z. Zilbertsvayg, *Leksikon fun Yidishn Teater* (1934), 1577–79; E. Shulman, *Geshikhte fun der Yidisher Literatur in Amerike* (1943), 136f.; LNYL, 7 (1968), 3–8. **ADD. BIBLIOGRAPHY:** R.R. Wisse, *A Little Love in Big Manhattan* (1988).

[Elias Schulman / Marc Miller (2nd ed.)]

ENTRE RÍOS, province in the Argentine Republic and one of the most important centers of Jewish agricultural settlement. In 2005 the Jewish population was estimated at 1,200 families, 550 of them in the capital city of Paraná. Entre Ríos has been the focal point of Jewish settlement in Argentina since the beginning of Jewish immigration to the country. The Jewish Colonization Association (ICA) first purchased land in the province in 1892 and the first settlers came during the same year. Argentina's national census of 1895 indicated that of the 6,085 people who declared their Jewish affiliation 3,880, or about 64%, lived in Entre Ríos. The amount of land in Entre Ríos owned by the Jewish agricultural settlements continued to increase until 1940, when it reached its peak of 571,988 acres.

On the perimeter of the agricultural settlements, Jewish communities began to develop in the towns and later in distant principal cities. A 1909 survey found Jews in seven cities and towns and their number at that time was estimated at 585 in contrast to 9,948 who lived in the Jewish agricultural settlements. Another poll, conducted in 1943, estimated the number of Jews in Entre Ríos at 20,803, of whom 9,266 were engaged in agriculture in the Jewish settlements, 4,695 lived in 17 adjacent villages, and the remainder – 6,842 persons – were settled in 76 towns, villages, and hamlets in the province. As a result of the Jewish agricultural colonization in the province Entre Ríos has such Hebrew and Jewish place names as Carmel, Baron Ginzburg, and Avigdor. Jews in Entre Ríos have had local political importance, a rare circumstance within Argentinian Jewry as a whole. During the first years of settlement the Jewish colonies established in Colón, Uruguay, and Villaguay increased the population of these regions by about 55%. This relative numerical importance, however, was not maintained. The settlements were arenas for Argentinian political struggles which had tragic consequences in 1916–17 when synagogues were destroyed and Torah scrolls desecrated in the Clara colony. In 1921 the Jews of Entre Ríos suffered violent antisemitism – camouflaged as anti-Communism – a phenomenon which increased particularly during the 1930s and 1940s.

The concentration of Jews in rural areas helped to preserve Jewish life especially where Jews constituted a majority. Jewish economic organizations – such as Sociedad Agrícola Lucienville, which was possibly the first agricultural cooperative in Argentina, and the Fondo Comunal, among the largest in the province – remained of economic importance. Nevertheless, the diminishing number of Jewish agricultural settlements and the general migration to Buenos Aires and its environs have had severe consequences for the Jews of Entre Ríos. The 1947 census recorded 11,876 Jews who declared their Jewish affiliation, i.e., 4.9% of all avowed Jews in Argentina; the 1960 census indicated the number had declined to 9,000. According to data provided in 1968 by the Va'ad ha-Kehillot (Central Committee of Jewish Communities), the number of Jews had decreased to 8,000, of whom about 3,050 lived in Paraná, the capital of the province. The same data refers to some 30 congregations in the province, but only nine of them, with 442 students (141 in Paraná), maintained any kind of Jewish education and there were only five youth centers. Nevertheless, these congregations provide a framework for activities and their membership in the regional branches of the Va'ad ha-Kehillot and of the *DAIA brings them assistance in providing communal services and constitutes a mutual defense against antisemitism. Other local and regional committees allow the Jews of Entre Ríos to contribute to central welfare projects in Buenos Aires – such as the Jewish hospital, and the national and Israel funds.

BIBLIOGRAPHY: H. Avni, "*Mifalo ha-Hityashevuti shel ha-Baron Hirsch be-Argentinah*" (Dissertation, Jerusalem, 1969), includes English summary and bibliography; Jewish Colonization Association, *Rapport ...* (1909).

[Haim Avni]

ENVIRONMENTAL SCIENCES.

> The Holy Blessed One took the first human, and passing before all the trees of the Garden of Eden, said, "See my works, how fine and excellent they are! All that I created, I created for you. Reflect on this, and do not corrupt or desolate my world; for if you do, there will be no one to repair it after you" (Midrash Ecclesiastes Rabbah 7:13).

The philosophy of materialism and humanity's right to dominate its environment has led to man's rapid development. This attitude further developed during the Middle Ages and the Enlightenment in Western Europe on the basis of biblical interpretation. Western society embraced man's dominance of nature, and technological advances through the ages enabled people to overcome the environment and attain a higher standard of living. Technological innovations, such as plowing, harvesting, forest clearing, and animal husbandry, helped overcome natural obstacles and tame nature.

Ecological and environmental concern can be found in Jewish sources from the Bible onward. In Genesis 2:15 man is given stewardship of the earth – *le-ovedah u-le-shomerah*. Man is to preserve the earth, to look after it, and to tend it. He is not the owner, nor the master. The earth was not given to man in absolute ownership to use (or abuse) as he saw fit; but rather it was given to him to maintain and to preserve for his benefit and for that of future generations. Some of the many topics dealt with in Jewish sources include *shemittah* – the fallow year; *bal tashḥit* – the prohibition of purposeless waste; felling of fruit-bearing trees; raising small cattle in Ereẓ Israel; sanitary disposal of human waste; air pollution; water quality; noise; and many more. For a comprehensive discussion of this topic see *Ecology.

The Mishnah and Talmud elaborate and expound on biblical passages that deal with nature and its preservation in order to curtail environmental damage. The approach taken by the rabbis to limit the harmful effects of different environmental sources was to treat them not as absolutes but according to prevailing conditions, and this is still applicable today. Injury to the environment included not only cases of proximate causation but also those in which conditions were created that might reasonably give rise to nuisance.

The Coalition on the Environment and Jewish Life was founded in 1993 to promote environmental education, scholarship, advocacy, and action in the American Jewish community. COEJL is sponsored by a broad coalition of national Jewish organizations and has organized regional affiliates in communities across North America. COEJL is the Jewish member of the National Religious Partnership for the Environment (www.coejl.org/about/).

Environmental studies (environmental sciences) is a relatively new field that gained recognition after the publication of Rachel Carson's *Silent Spring*. It crosses the boundaries of traditional disciplines, challenging us to look at the relationship between humans and their environment from a variety of perspectives. It is closely related to ecology and draws heavily on the physical sciences (chemistry and physics) as well as on biology and mathematics. Furthermore, due to globalization the careful integration of natural and social science data and information is vital to scientific research and societal decision-making related to a wide range of pressing environmental issues.

Complex interactions in the air, on land, underground, and in rivers, bays, and oceans are intricately linked to one another – and to our well-being. Below we shall briefly review the contributions made to the various disciplines comprising environmental sciences.

Atmospheric Sciences

Atmospheric sciences deal with environmental issues such as acid deposition, air pollution and quality, and stratospheric ozone. One of its goals is to identify and quantify the natural and anthropogenic processes that regulate the chemical composition of the troposphere and middle atmosphere and to assess future changes brought about by human activities. They deal with topics as varied as the role of the biosphere in producing and consuming trace gases; the importance of the chemical and photochemical processes occurring in different atmospheric environments; and the role of transport processes connecting these environments (e.g., large-scale advection, convection, stratosphere/troposphere exchanges, and continental export).

By the mid-1980s there was undeniable evidence that our planet was getting hotter, a massive 10% shift in only 30 years, so the idea of reduced solar radiation just did not fit and was not widely accepted in the scientific community. This began to change in 2001, when G. Stanhill and a colleague at the Volcani Center in Bet Dagan, Israel, collected all the available evidence together and proved that, on the average, records showed that the amount of solar radiation reaching the Earth's surface had gone down by between 0.23 and 0.32% each year from 1958 to 1992 (solar dimming).

Theoretical and experimental research in atmospheric radiative transfer and remote sensing of aerosol, their interaction with clouds and radiation, and impact on climate, with emphasis on biomass burning in the tropics was being conducted by Yoram J. Kaufman at the Goddard Space Flight Center. Joseph M. Prospero at the University of Miami was a specialist in the global-scale properties of aerosols focusing on the aerosol chemistry of the marine atmosphere and the biogeochemical effects of the long-range atmospheric transport of materials from the continents to the ocean environment. He pioneered in the study of mineral aerosol (soil dust) transport, showing that huge quantities of dust were carried by winds from arid regions to the oceans.

Richard Siegmund Lindzen at MIT was renowned for his research in dynamic meteorology on topics such as the atmospheric transport of heat and momentum from the tropics to higher latitudes. He developed models for the Earth's climate with specific concern for the stability of the ice caps, the sensitivity to increases in CO_2, the origin of the 100,000 year cycle in glaciation, and the maintenance of regional variations in climate. Alan Robock, at Rutgers University, was involved in many aspects of climate change. He conducted both observational analyses and climate model simulations and his current research focuses on soil moisture variations, the effects of volcanic eruptions on climate, detection and attribution of human effects on the climate system, and the impacts of climate change on human activities. In the 1980s much of his work addressed the problem of nuclear winter, the climatic effects of nuclear war, demonstrating long-term (several-year) effects with a computer model, disproving the dirty snow effect, and discovering observational evidence of surface cooling due to forest fire smoke plumes in the atmosphere.

Research on cloud physics and dynamics, atmospheric radiative transfer, atmospheric dynamics, and satellite remote sensing of the Earth's climate and other planetary atmospheres was being conducted by Dr. Rossow of NASA. His early work focused on the clouds and dynamics of the atmospheres of Venus and Jupiter and he served on the Science Teams for the Pioneer Venus and Galileo (to Jupiter) space missions. Eli Tziperman of Harvard University worked on climate dynamics, trying to understand physical processes that affect the Earth's climate on time scales of a few years to millions of years.

The first numerical model able to simulate El Niño and the Southern Oscillation (ENSO), a pattern of interannual climate variability centered in the tropical Pacific but with global consequences, was devised by Mark Cane of Columbia University. In 1985 this model was used to make the first physically based forecasts of El Niño. Dr. Cane also worked extensively on the impact of El Niño on human activity, especially agriculture.

Oceanography

Oceanography is the science that studies the world's oceans, its waters and depths, how they move and how they play a part in the whole of our planet. The sea is not just salty water, but a living system that controls many aspects of this planet. Limnology is the scientific study of the physical, geographical, chemical, and biological aspects of inland freshwater systems. The factors studied in such bodies of water as lakes, rivers, swamps, and reservoirs include productivity, interactions among organisms and between organisms and their environment, characteristics of the water and of the water bottom, and pollution problems. Structure, function, and long-term changes in these water bodies are also of importance.

Global studies of freshwater lakes with emphasis on biological, chemical, and physical interactions between the surrounding watersheds and lakes are the fields of interest of Charles Goldman of UC Davis with particular emphasis on eutrophication of lakes, nutrient limiting factors, the impact of climate and weather, and the use and importance of long-term data sets in environmental research. The core research has been directed towards a better understanding of lake processes and measures to preserve the water quality of lakes.

The research efforts of Paul G. Falkowski of Rutgers University were directed towards understanding the co-evolution of biological physical systems, evolution, paleoecology, photosynthesis, biophysics, biogeochemical cycles, and symbiosis. The cycling of nutrients and energy transfer in the microbial food chain, the dynamics of nutrient uptake by marine phytoplankton, the interaction of chemical-biological processes at the microbial level, and the impact of physical-biological processes on marine primary productivity were the major interests of Joel Goldman, UC SC.

Daniel P. Schrag of Harvard University applied geochemistry to problems in paleoclimatology and oceanography on a variety of timescales. A large portion of his current research effort used corals as recorders of information on past and present climates. Modern corals from the Pacific were being used to reconstruct El Niño variability over the last few centuries, and to assess the reliability of coral records. He also used geochemistry of corals to understand recent patterns of ocean circulation.

Understanding major biogeochemical cycles in the marine environment, as they operate today and in the past, were the main research interests of Mark A. Altabet, University of Massachusetts. He specialized in nitrogen cycling in the marine environment; nitrogen isotope biogeochemistry; particle fluxes in the open ocean; marine productivity; oceanic paleochemistry and paleoproductivity. Much of this research relates to the Earth's carbon cycle and control of atmospheric CO_2 concentration. Related work involved studies of N_2O and carbon isotopes.

Soil Microbiology

Soil microbiology deals with the improvement of knowledge and understanding of the microbial processes involved in geochemical cycles (e.g., carbon and nitrogen cycles) and in the factors contributing to the quality of our environment and our foods, in order to understand them and to eventually control them. These objectives require improved knowledge of microbial populations and their activities. They also require improved knowledge of how terrestrial ecosystems work, using integrated methods for research of the processes.

Over and above improved knowledge of soil micro-flora and their activities, and more generally the biological functioning of soils, soil microbiology is concerned with the identification of the bio-indicators of soil quality, and the management of native micro-flora (sustainable agriculture) and/or introduction of selected strains (microbial inoculation) in order to improve soil quality (bio-remediation) and/or reduce the use of synthetic inputs (pesticides and nitrogen fertilizers) thus contributing to the improvement of food quality (residue reduction).

Selman Abraham *Waksman was born in the Ukraine in 1888 and immigrated to the United States in 1910. In 1915 he graduated from Rutgers University. His decision to enter agriculture was guided by Jacob G. Lipman, a bacteriologist who was dean of the College of Agriculture and himself an immigrant from Russia.

In 1939 Waksman and his colleagues undertook a systematic effort to identify soil organisms producing soluble substances that might be useful in the control of infectious diseases, what are now known as antibiotics. He developed simple screening techniques and applied these to a variety of samples of soil and other natural materials. Within a decade ten antibiotics were isolated and characterized, three of them with important clinical applications: actinomycin in 1940, streptomycin (with A. Schatz) in 1944, and neomycin in 1949. Eighteen antibiotics were discovered under his general direction. The many awards and honors that were showered on Waksman after 1940 culminated in the Nobel Prize.

M. Alexander, of Cornell University, focused his research in the areas of soil and environmental microbiology, bioavailability and aging of chemical pollutants, and microbial transformations that are of environmental or agricultural importance in natural environments. His research dealt with the bioavailability and biodegradation of a variety of toxic organic chemicals and pesticides in soils, subsoils, groundwaters, and surface waters. A variety of different issues are dealt with, including the biodegradation of sorbed chemicals, interaction between species during transformations of chemicals, finding means to enhance microbial destruction of pollutants, exploring bioremediation methodologies to promote the use of introduced microorganisms to rid natural environments of toxicants, and unique problems arising because of persistence of low concentrations of organic compounds.

Hydrology

Hydrology is the study of all waters in and upon the Earth. It includes groundwater, surface water, and rainfall. It embraces the concept of hydrological cycle.

The large volume of research in the last several decades has shown an increasing frequency of many chemical and microbial constituents that have not historically been considered as contaminants being present in the environment on a global scale. The sources of these emerging contaminants are from municipal, agricultural, and industrial wastewater sources.

Environmental hydrology aims to provide information on these compounds for evaluation of their potential threat to environmental and human health. To accomplish this goal researchers need to develop analytical methods to measure chemicals and microorganisms in a variety of matrices (e.g., water, sediment, waste); determine the environmental occurrence of these potential contaminants; characterize the myriad of sources and source pathways that determine contaminant release to the environment; define and quantify processes that determine their transport and fate through the environment; and identify potential ecologic effects from exposure to these chemicals or microorganisms. Environmental hydrology seeks to combine models of the atmosphere, land surface, or rivers, for example, into full-fledged simulated ecosystems. These simulations are critical throughout the physical and natural sciences.

Gedeon Dagan, Tel Aviv University, is a hydrologist whose main interests are the theory of flow through porous media; groundwater hydrology and water waves; and naval hydrodynamics. His research has led to the application of effective strategies for protecting and restoring groundwater, which constitutes 97% of the world's useable freshwater.

He contributed greatly in aquifer characterization and monitoring. This research is important because groundwater protection is hindered by difficulties in observing and characterizing the subsurface. Therefore, effective strategies for protecting and restoring groundwater require realistic predictions of the effects of different management options. He was awarded the Stockholm Water Prize for having established the basis of a new field within geohydrology, where contaminant spreading in the subsurface environment is determined in such a way that it accounts for heterogeneity and for biochemical processes.

Jacob Bear is professor emeritus of the Technion-Israel Institute of Technology. His teaching, research, and consulting covered the areas of groundwater hydrology and hydraulics, management of water resources, subsurface contamination and remediation, and the general theory of transport phenomena in porous media.

Biological Plant Protection

Biological plant protection, or biological control, is concerned with the identification, screening, release, and monitoring of biological agents for long-term, cost-effective control of invading plant pests. Effective biological control is an essential element in the sustainable management of invading alien pests. Main research areas in this field include studies on the role played by insects, spider mites, nematodes, and microorganisms in reduction of plant pests and improvement of their strains and application methods for biological and integrated programs of plant protection. The goal is environmentally safe control of pests of open-field, greenhouse, mushroom house, and orchard cultures, as well as urban forest and park trees.

Ilan *Chet, president of the Weizmann Institute of Science, Israel, was a member of the UN Panel for Applied Microbiology and Biotechnology. His research dealt with the biological control of plant disease using environment-friendly microorganisms, focusing on the basic, applied, and biotechnological aspects of this field. Prof. Chet was awarded the Israel Prize (1996) and the Wolf Prize (1998).

Desertification and Afforestation

Desertification is a worldwide phenomenon. Land deterioration into desert-like conditions occurs in the world at the rate of 6 million hectares a year as the result both of climatic conditions and man's destructive use of the soil: failure to arrest this process endangers the vital infrastructure of a country. Combating desertification is essential to ensuring the long-term productivity of inhabited lands in arid and semi-arid regions. Desertification occurs at the transition zones between true deserts and cultivated lands. These transition zones have very fragile, delicately balanced ecosystems. In these marginal areas, human activity may stress the ecosystem beyond its tolerance limit, resulting in degradation of the land.

JNF activities are aimed at arresting the spread of the desert and improving the ecology of the area. One of the central questions troubling people concerned with the quality of life is the maintenance of a reasonable level of environment preservation in these dense urban areas. The JNF deals with this problem through planting forests around urban settlements. Through this afforestation work, Israel will be the only country to have more trees at the conclusion of the century than at the beginning! These forests enable the town dweller to have contact with nature, improve his quality of life, and create green lungs which absorb pollutants and emit carbon dioxide.

Savanization is another strategy for halting the desertification process. In the desertification process, the ecological system is controlled by sparse vegetation of bushes and green growth. In the savanization process the bushes are replaced with trees and the inferior vegetation with herbaceous growth. This involves sophisticated measures for collection of water, preservation of soil, planting of trees, and increasing natural vegetation and animal life in the area. Forests contribute to soil conservation, prevent soil erosion, act as a barrier against dust, noise and air pollution, create shade and comfortable miniclimates, halt desertification on the border of arid zones, and contribute ecologically and globally to reducing the greenhouse effect by releasing oxygen into the atmosphere and absorbing carbon dioxide.

One of the most important agrotechnological innovations of modern times is probably the Israeli invention of drip irrigation by Simcha Blass and his son (the father conceived the idea, the son developed the dripper). Drip irrigation has many advantages over other irrigation methods and is especially suited for arid and semi-arid regions.

Blass developed a drip irrigation system for greenhouse use and in the 1960s began drip irrigation experiments in the Negev Desert. Development in capillary tubes, self-filtering systems, fertilizer injectors, and improved emitter bodies has increased the usage of these systems at an exponential rate. From 1974 to 1984, the worldwide acreage under these systems quadrupled.

Ecological responses to global climate change; the interactions between biodiversity, desertification, and climate change; and the role of individual species in the provision of ecosystem services are topics studied by Uriel Safriel. He worked on projects carried out jointly by Israel, Jordan, and the Palestine Authority, for example, as regional expert for Israel on the "Initiative for Collaboration to Control Natural Resource Degradation (Desertification) of Arid Lands in the Middle East," a joint project of Israel, the Palestinian Authority, Jordan, Egypt, and Tunisia, facilitated by the World Bank. He was head of the delegation of Israel to the Intergovernmental Negotiating Committee on Desertification.

Environmental Law

Environmental law uses sustainability as an organizing principle to develop new strategies for the protection of land, water, and biological resources by integrating environmental laws, tax laws, development laws, and other tools. Environmental law aims to solve environmental problems and promote sustainable societies through the use of law, to incorporate fundamental principles of ecology and justice into international law, to strengthen national environmental law systems and support public interest movements around the world, and to educate and train public-interest-minded environmental lawyers.

Topics of concern in environmental law include climate change, biodiversity and wildlife, biotechnology, sustainable development, persistent organic pollutants, and human rights and the environment.

Joel B. Eisen, director of the Robert R. Merhige, Jr., Center of Environmental Law, served as counsel to the U.S. House of Representatives. He taught courses on environmental law, urban environmental law, international environmental law, environmental dispute resolution, property, and energy law and policy.

Robert J. Goldstein was director of environmental programs, Pace Law School. His publications include *Environmental Ethics and Ecology: Green Wood in the Bundle of Sticks*; *Environmental Ethics and Law*; *Environmental Ethics and Posi-*

tive Law; Only Who Can Prevent Forest Fires?: Considering Environmental Context in Fire Suppression and Land Use; Putting Environmental Law on the Map: A Spatial Approach to Environmental Law Using GIS and Forestry Law.

Howard Latin, of the Rutgers Law School, was involved in environmental law, international environmental law, tort law, and products liability law. Latin was an advisor to a three-year Congressional Office of Technology assessment study on "Rethinking Environmental Regulation." He is among the most widely read scholars in the environmental law field and served as a consultant for environmental groups advocating marine conservation and pollution control. He engaged in political lobbying efforts to protect ocean wildlife in the Bahamas, Western Australia, the Galapagos Islands, and the United States.

Dan Mandelker is one of the U.S.'s leading scholars and teachers in land use law. He was also a pioneer in the teaching of environmental law and state and local government law. In environmental law, Mandelker is best known for his widely used treatise, *NEPA Law and Litigation.*

Sustainable Development

From conferences at Stockholm in 1972, to Rio de Janeiro in 1992, and finally to Johannesburg in 2002, the global community has embarked on a three-decade journey aimed at furthering progress towards broad global sustainable development objectives. During the course of this 30-year period, a manifold range of sustainable development issues has been discussed, debated, deliberated, and negotiated, serving as a critical call for action of individuals, voluntary organizations, businesses, institutions, and governments.

Sustainable development is defined as "development that meets the needs of the present without compromising the ability of future generations to meet their own needs" (Brundtland Report, 1987). For development to be sustainable it must integrate environmental stewardship, economic development, and the well-being of all people – not just for today but for generations to come.

The Rio conference was also known as the United Nations Conference on Environment and Development, or more simply the Earth Summit, bringing together nearly 150 representatives of states including Israel who negotiated, signed, and agreed to a global action plan for sustainable development which they called Agenda 21. In addition, four new international treaties – on climate change, biological diversity, desertification, and high-seas fishing – were signed in the official sessions. Further, a United Nations Commission on Sustainable Development was established to monitor the implementation of these agreements and to act as a forum for the ongoing negotiation of international policies on environment and development.

Agenda 21 has been the basis for action by many national and local governments. Many countries have set up national advisory councils to promote dialogue between government, environmentalists, the private sector, and the general community and include nearly 2,000 cities worldwide with their own local plans. They have also established programs for monitoring national progress on sustainable development indicators. Within this framework, one of the most successful programs which has been adopted by governments all over the world is the Man and Biosphere program. Biosphere Reserves are areas of terrestrial and coastal ecosystems promoting solutions to reconcile the conservation of biodiversity with its sustainable use. They are internationally recognized, nominated by national governments, and remain under sovereign jurisdiction of the states where they are located. The Israel National Commission for UNESCO has formed a MAB committee, though with just one Biosphere Reserve in Israel so far, Mount Carmel, these issues are receiving broader attention.

ISRAEL'S COMMITMENT. Israel established environmental institutions after the Stockholm conference in 1973 with the Environmental Protection Service as part of the Prime Minister's Office, in 1976 within the Ministry of Interior, and finally in December 1988 a full-fledged Ministry of Environment with district and local offices. The program was initiated by Uri Marinov, while physical planning and development was guided by Valerie Brachya as deputy director-general. In the mid-1990s the Ministry of Environment, aided by the Mediterranean Action Plan of the United Nations Environment Program, initiated a strategy for sustainable development in Israel.

The Israeli government's decision of August 4, 2002, calls for the minister of environment to report to the government on the Johannesburg Summit and on ways to incorporate the conclusions of the conference in government policy. As Agenda 21 calls for including environmental and development issues in all government decisions that have to do with economy, social policy, energy, agriculture, transportation, and commerce, it was decided that every government office would prepare its own strategy for sustainable development. Integrating environmental issues within policy decision-making calls for the gathering of information and using efficient ways to evaluate dangers and profits for the environment.

In August 2004, the Ministry of Environment presented the government with a report on the implementation of government decisions on sustainable development. The report shows that all government offices began the process of assimilating sustainable development issues, with the Ministries of Finance and Commerce first to present their strategies. Current guidelines and programs were being developed for ecotourism, educational programs for schools, and general strategies for sustainability.

Non-Government Organizations (NGO) concerned with environmental issues have played an important role in contributing to public awareness and pressure on the government to allocate more resources for these issues. Among these are the Society for the Protection of Nature in Israel (SPNI), Friends of the Earth/Middle East, Adam Teva VaDin, the Heschel Center, and local initiatives like Sustainable Jerusalem. There are a number of private foundations supporting issues related to environment, sustainability, and education. These organizations continue to work together in promoting sustainable development policies in Israel, assisting in professional knowledge and experience. The Knesset established a Commission for Future Generations, whose responsibility is the coordination of programs at the parliamentary level.

University courses and research including sustainability are developing rapidly from the esoteric programs of the 1970s in Environmental Health at the Hebrew University to exclusive degrees in environmental sciences at all the universities attached to a variety of subjects like economics, geography, and earth sciences.

ENVIRONMENT AND SUSTAINABLE DEVELOPMENT IN JUDAISM. Essentially an agrarian society, certain concepts in Judaism relate more specifically to sustainability. The commandment to plant fruit-bearing trees on entering the Holy Land relates to the consideration and investment that is made for future generations. This is paralleled with the commandment of *bal tashḥit* ("do not destroy") used in the Bible with reference to the proper behavior with regard to trees during wartime (only non-fruit-bearing trees may be chopped down). The talmudic sages expanded this to forbid the destruction or damaging of anything potentially useful to man.

Another set of laws that apply in the Holy Land are those concerning sabbatical and jubilee years: *shemittah* and *yovel*. *Shemittah* refers to the seventh year, when one must refrain from working the land in order to enrich the soil and prevent exhaustion of the land. Through keeping this commandment the fields rest for one year, and products that might be produced during that time are not used. *Yovel* refers to the fiftieth year, adding the cancellation of debts to the *shemittah* regulations. It also involves the reversion of land to the original tribal structure, thus preventing large-scale concentration of land and looking after local and individual interests and maintaining sustainability.

Finally, urban laws fall under "doing good" and "preventing bad," i.e., laws that instruct in the right way and those that relate to tort. The city had defined borders and could be extended only through a decision of the Sanhedrin. Perhaps the rebuilding of cities in the layered tel is the epitome of recycling urban land and preventing the deterioration of the immediate agricultural hinterland. The maintenance of public monuments was part of the joint responsibility of the public and private domain.

See also *Conservation; *Ecology.

[Miriam Waldman, Zev Gerstl and Michael Turner (2nd ed.)]

°**EÖTVÖS, BARON JÓZSEF** (1813–1871), Hungarian statesman, author, and jurist; he fought for and brought in the legislation granting *emancipation to the Jews in Hungary. Eötvös became a member of the Hungarian diet in the Liberal opposition. In 1840 he published his classic work *A zsidók emancipatiója* ("Emancipation of the Jews") where he refuted the arguments of those who rejected emancipation of the Jews unconditionally, as well as of those who first required the "betterment of the Jews" before they attained emancipation. Only emancipation without any prior conditions, Eötvös claimed, would improve the way of life of the Jews whose defects he did not deny, and whose assimilation he advocated in this as well as in his other writings. Eötvös was a member of the revolutionary government (1848) as minister of public instruction and religious affairs. After the failure of the revolution, he fled to Germany, from where he returned in 1851. He retired from political life and was elected president of the Hungarian Academy. With the formation of the independent Hungarian government in 1867, he once more held the same ministerial position and succeeded in having the bill on the emancipation of the Jews passed during that year. Eötvös also sought to organize the structure of Hungarian Jewry upon the principle of a unified community, without any intervention in its internal affairs. To this end, he convened a national congress of the Jews of Hungary in 1868, but his project did not materialize. Eötvös was a talented writer of fiction and in his fictional works also expressed his ideas concerning the Jews (*A falu jegyzöje*, 1845; *The Village Notary*, 1850).

BIBLIOGRAPHY: B. Heller, in: IMIT, 36 (1913), 7–55 (Hung.); J. Bánóczi, in: J. Eötvös, *A zsidók emancipatiója* (1922), 3–8; N. Katzburg, in: *Bar-Ilan, Sefer ha-Shanah*, 1 (1963), 282–301 (Heb.), 56–57 (Eng. summary); idem, in: *Aresheth*, 4 (1966), 322–6 (Heb.); idem, *Antishemiyyut be-Hungaryah 1867–1914* (1969), 19–24; idem, in: R.L. Braham (ed.), *Hungarian Jewish Studies*, 2 (1969), 1–33 (Eng.).

[Baruch Yaron]

EPERNAY, town in the Marne department, northern France, approximately 19 mi. (about 30 km.) E. of Châlons-sur-Marne. During the Middle Ages, the Jewish community there was sufficiently large to occupy three streets, the Rue Juiverie, Rue Haute, and Basse Juiverie. On the eve of World War II, a small community, which was to be cruelly tried during the persecutions, existed in Epernay. In 1969, the community numbered fewer than 200.

BIBLIOGRAPHY: Gross, Gal Jud, 66; H.H.B. Poterlet, *Notice historique ... d'Epernay* (1837), 33–34; Z. Szajkowski, *Analytical Franco-Jewish Gazetteer* (1966), 224.

[Bernhard Blumenkranz]

EPHESUS, Greek city on the W. coast of Asia Minor, at the mouth of the River Cayster. Ephesus had an important Jewish community in the first century and its beginning apparently goes back to the early Hellenistic era. Information about it is found chiefly in Josephus, but also in Philo, in inscriptions, and Acts. What is perhaps the earliest information about the Jews of Ephesus appears in Josephus (Apion, 2:39) referring to *Antiochus II. Josephus also mentions a decree of the consul Lentulus in 49 B.C.E. concerning the Jews. Ephesus played an exceptionally important role in the history of early Christianity, and its main importance in Jewish history is in the opposition of the Jewish community to Paul's missionary activity there. Paul laid the foundation of the first Christian community in Ephesus against the vehement opposition of the local Jews and the non-Jews who were worshipers of Artemis (Acts 19, and the Epistle to the Ephesians). Paul disputed his critics in the hall of Tyrannus within the city (Acts 19:9), but the whereabouts of this location have not been discovered during excavations at the site. With the rise of Christianity throughout the Roman Empire, Ephesus became one of the most important centers of the new religion. The third Ecumenical Council was held there in 431 C.E. With the political change during the sixth and seventh centuries in Asia Minor, Ephesus ceased to exist. Close to the ruins of Ephesus is the modern town of Selçuk.

BIBLIOGRAPHY: Schuerer, Gesch, 3 (1909[4]), 15f.; Juster, Juifs, 1 (1914), 190; E. Stein, *Histoire du Bas-Empire* (1949), 309f.; J. Klausner, *Mi-Yeshu ad Paulus*, 2 (1951[2]), 87, 91–97. **ADD. BIBLIOGRAPHY:** C. Foss, *Ephesus After Antiquity* (1978); R.E. Oster, *A Bibliography of Ancient Ephesus* (1987); A. Bammer, *Ephesos: Stadt an Fluss und Meer* (1988); E.C. Blake and A.C. Edmonds, *Biblical Sites in Turkey* (1998).

[Abraham Schalit / Shimon Gibson (2nd ed.)]

EPHOD (Heb. אֵפוֹד). The term ephod occurs several times in the Bible, where it appears to describe different cultic objects. In Exodus 28 the ephod is a garment made of expensive materials. In I Samuel 2:18; 22:18; II Samuel 6:14 the ephod is made of linen (Heb. *bad*). In Judges 17:5; 18:14–20 the ephod is mentioned along with a sculpted image (Heb *pesel*) of the kind outlawed by the Decalogue. In Judges 8:24–27 Gideon makes an ephod out of captured Midianite metals, which he sets up (*wayaṣṣeg*) in Oprah, which Israel "whored after," i.e., worshipped. Another biblical form of the word ephod is *ʾafuddah* (Heb. אֲפֻדָּה: Ex. 28:8; 39:5; Isa. 30:22), to which the verb *ʾafad* (Ex. 29:5; Lev. 8:7), with the meaning "gird" or "adorn," is related. In its broader sense in what appear to be early texts, ephod includes the entire mantic instrument (e.g., I Sam. 2:28; 23:6, 9; 30:7; cf. I Sam. 21:10). It is possible that the robe worn by the priest (see below) from which the golden bells were suspended may also be included in the term ephod. (The bells were necessary to alert Yahweh that the priest, and not some intruder, was entering the sanctuary so that the priest would not be killed for entering the holy place (Ex. 28:31–35).) Biblical religion prohibited many forms of soothsaying and divination by means of auguries, but did permit, side by side with prophecy, the priestly ephod (see *Divination). Both prophecy and the ephod were seen as a means of seeking the counsel of God and of obtaining a revelation of His will. The technical term for consulting the ephod and the Urim and Thummim is "to come before the Lord" (Ex. 28:30; cf. Num. 27:21), that is, either in the Tabernacle or before the ark (Judg. 20:27; cf. Judg. 20:18, 23, 27; I Sam. 14:18, 41 et al.). Some biblical references indicate that in ancient Israel use was made of an ephod, together with *teraphim (Hos. 3:4) and a graven image, for approaching God (Judg. 17:4–5; 18:14, 17, 20; Isa. 30:22; cf. Judg. 8:27). The Pentateuch contains no clear description of the shape of the ephod, nor does the Hebrew root of the word furnish any additional clues. The Hebrew word seems related to the Akkadian *epattu*, plural *epadātu*, which signifies a costly garment in the Cappadocian tablets, and to Ugaritic *ʾipd* (KTU 4. 707:13; 4. 780:1, 3, 4, 7); plural *ʾiptt* (KTU 4. 707:11); dual *ʾipdm* (KTU 1. 136:10) with the same meaning. The ephod has an apparent analogue in Greek *ependytēs* (overgarment). A similar word is found in Aquila's translation of ephod. According to H. Thiersch (see bibliography), the *ependytēs* originated in Syria, spreading from there through Asia Minor and Greece. But while correct about the Oriental origin of the *ependytēs* and its physical resemblance to the ephod, Tiersch seems to have erred about the cultic use of the Greek garment. It seems instead to have served as a luxury item for Orientalizing Greeks. (See Muller in Bibliography.) The pentateuchal ephod was engraved with the names of the Twelve Tribes, apparently to signify the totality of the nation (Ex. 28:9–12). It is not stated how the ephod was made in the days of the Judges (*Gideon: Judg. 8:27; *Micah: Judg. 17:5), nor the ephod at Shiloh (e.g., I Sam. 2:18; and Nob: *ibid.* 22:18), and that used in connection with Saul's campaign against the Philistines (*ibid.* 14:3). The Pentateuch contains a description of the ephod of Aaron (Ex. 28). The most common occurrences refer to an upper garment, the ornamented vestment which the high priest wore over the blue robe ("the robe of the ephod"). To this he bound the *breastplate together with the principal vehicle for enquiring of God, the *Urim and Thummim. All of these attestations are confined to Exodus 25, 28, 35, 39 and Leviticus 8 in settings that describe Aaron as a priest, with him and his sons wearing breeches (Ex. 28:42), an invention of the Persian period, and must be dated to post-exilic times. According to this description, the ephod was an embroidered work "of gold, of blue, purple, and crimson yarns, and of fine twisted linen, worked into designs." To its two ends were attached two straps which fastened over the shoulders, and on each of the shoulder straps was set a *shoham* stone (identification uncertain), engraved with the names of the tribes of Israel. The breastpiece (Heb. *ḥoshen* חֹשֶׁן) was bound to the ephod at the top by rings and chains and at the bottom by a cord of blue, while in the middle it was encircled by "the decorated band" which was also made "in the style of the ephod" and of the same combination of gold thread and four yarns. The ephod seems to have been a square, sleeveless garment, falling from just below the armpits to the heels ("like a sort of horsewoman's surcoat," according to Rashi (to Ex. 28:6)). According to this view, it enveloped the entire body. According to the commentary of R. Samuel ben Meir (to Ex. 28:7), however, the ephod enclosed the body from the waist downward, the upper part of the body being covered by the breastpiece. Josephus (Ant., 3:162; Wars, 5:231–236) states that the ephod had sleeves and resembled a type of waistcoat ("the *epomis*" of the Greeks – used by the LXX in translating "ephod" of the Pentateuch); it was variegated and had "the middle of the breast uncovered" for the insertion of the breastplate. The high priest used the ephod along with the breastplate and the Urim and Thummim as a means of divination. Lesser priests, as well as others engaged in sacred ministrations, Samuel (I Sam. 2:18), and once even David (II Sam. 6:14) wore a simple ephod of linen, apparently during sacred service or at special celebrations (I Sam. 22:18).

According to the Talmud, each thread of the ephod consisted of six blue strands, six of purple, six of scarlet, and six of fine twisted linen, with a thread of gold in each twist of six strands, making a total of 28 strands (Yoma 71b, 72a). The names of the tribes were engraved on the onyx stones with the *shamir* (Sot. 48b; Git. 68a). The ephod was one of the eight vestments worn by the high priest (Yoma 7:5; Maim., Yad, Kelei ha-Mikdash, ch. 8–10) and, together with the onyx stones, was used in the Second Temple. The ephod was believed to atone for the sin of idolatry (Zev. 88b). Gideon was said to have made an ephod because the name of his tribe, Manasseh, was not included on the stones of the ephod (Yal., Judg. 64).

BIBLIOGRAPHY: Foote, in: JBL, 21 (1902), 1–47; Sellin, in: *Orientalische Studien … Th. Noeldeke*, 2 (1906), 699–717; idem, in: JPOS, 14 (1934), 185–94; 17 (1937), 236–51; idem, in: ZAW, 55 (1937), 296–8; Elhorst, in: JBL, 30 (1910), 254–76; W.R. Arnold, *Ephod and the Ark* (1917); Budde, in: ZAW, 39 (1921), 1–47; J. Gabriel, *Untersuchungen ueber das alttestamentliche Priestertum* (1933), 44–70; H. Thiersch, *Ependytes und Ephod* (1936); J. Lewy, in: JAOS, 57 (1937), 436; de Vaux, Anc Isr, 349–51; idem, in: RB, 47 (1938), 108–11 (Fr.); H.G. May, in: AJSLL, 56 (1939), 44ff.; W.F. Albright, in: BASOR, 83 (1941), 39ff.; idem, *Yahweh and the Gods of Canaan* (1968), 171, 174–7, 179; J. Morgenstern, *The Ark, the Ephod and the "Tent of Meeting"* (1945); M. Haran, in: *Tarbiz*, 24 (1954/55), 380–91; idem, in: *Sefer N.H. Tur-Sinai* (1960), 36ff.; idem, in: *Scripta Hierosolymitana*, 8 (1961), 279–84 (Eng.); Elliger, in: VT, 8 (1958), 19–35 (Ger.); Kaufmann Y., Toledot, 1 (1960), 486–502. **ADD. BIBLIOGRAPHY:** V. Muller, in: AJA, 42 (1938), 314–15; J. Durham, *Exodus* (Word; 1987), 385–86; C. Meyers, in: ABD II, 550; M. Miller, in: *Hesperia*, 58 (1989), 313–29; N. Sarna, *JPS Torah Commentary Exodus* (1991), 178–79; C. van Dam, *The Urim and Thummim …* (1997); J. Tropper, *Ugaritische Grammatik* (2000), 183, 286.

[Yehoshua M. Grintz / S. David Sperling (2nd ed.)]

EPHRAIM (Heb. אֶפְרַיִם), younger son of *Joseph, born to him in Egypt by his wife *Asenath daughter of Poti-Phera (Gen. 41:50–52); the eponymous ancestor of one of the two tribes descended from Joseph. Before his death, Jacob adopted both Ephraim and his older brother *Manasseh as his sons on a par with Reuben and Simeon, thereby ensuring that each would become the ancestor of an entire Israelite tribe, rather than of half a tribe (48:5, 16). He made Ephraim the recipient of a greater blessing than his older brother (48:13–20), thus giving greater prominence and importance to the tribe of Ephraim. The story is an etiological explanation of the prominence of the Ephraimites in historical times. In contrast to the pentateuchal tradition, I Chr. 7:20–29 maintains that Ephraim and his family remained in Canaan and says nothing about Ephraim's birth in Egypt.

The Name

From about 745 B.C.E. onward, the name Ephraim also served as a popular alternative to Israel to designate the people of

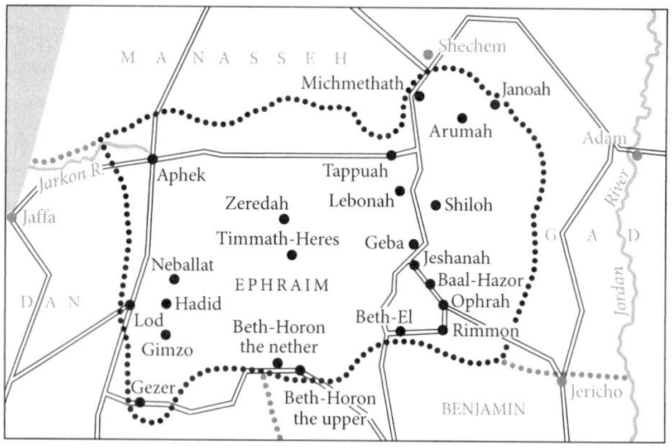

Territory of the tribe of Ephraim.

the shrunken northern kingdom or their descendants (Isa. 7:5, 8; Jer. 31:17, 20; Hos. 5:3, 5, et al.). The origin of the name Ephraim is not clear. According to Genesis 41:52, Joseph, in so naming his son, made a wordplay based on the root פרי ("to be fruitful"). Most scholars consider this to be the correct derivation, and hold that the name means "fertile land," with the addition of an old locative suffix – *aim* (*-ayim*). However, some view the name as a derivative of the post-biblical אָפָר ("a place of pasture"). In both theories the name is geographical, the tribe having been called after the region it occupied, "the land of Ephraim," "the country of Ephraim" (Obad. 19), or "the hill country (Heb. *har*) of Ephraim." Least likely is the suggested connection with Akkadian *eperu*, "dust," "region," cognate with Heb. *ʿapar*, that would have resulted in spelling Ephraim with initial *ayin*.

The Land of Ephraim

This area comprises the hill country of central Palestine. In this region there is no watershed plateau as in Judah, but a complex of ridges, spurs, and valleys surrounding the central valley, el-Makhnah, which is apparently to be identified with Michmethath (Josh. 16:6; 17:7). Shechem stands at the northwest extremity of this valley. On the east, two long spurs descend to the Jordan plain: Qarn as-Sarṭabah (RH 2:4) and Rās al-Kharrubueh. Wādi esh-shaʿīr, which falls into the Alexander River, continues northwest from the central plain of Shechem. To the northeast is the plain of Sychar (al-ʿAskar), which is formed by Wādi Beidān falling into Wādi Fāri, which in turn flows into the Jordan. The Shalem Plain, linked to the Jordan Valley by Wādi Ifjīm, extends to the east. The plain of Michmethath stretches southward until it reaches the Lebonah Ridge (Khān Lubbān), which hems it in on the south. The hill country of Ephraim is one of the most fertile areas in Palestine and at present is planted with such fruit trees as vine, olive, pomegranate, carob, etc. Prior to Israelite settlement, it was wooded (Josh. 17:18), and during the monarchy, beasts of prey still roamed there (II Kings 2:24). The coastal strip parallel to the hill country of Ephraim is extremely narrow; it is unsuitable for anchorage and ships found shelter in the river estuaries (Alexander, Ḥaderah; see Sharon in *Israel, Land of: Geographical Survey). It is widely accepted that the lists of tribal territories in Joshua 13–19 reflect the situation before the period of the monarchy. It is difficult, however, to determine the exact limits of the territory of Ephraim, since it is only indicated as part of the wider unit, the house of Joseph (which included Manasseh), and the biblical data are variously interpreted by scholars (see Yeivin, bibliography).

The Tribe

From the genealogical lists of the tribe of Ephraim (Num. 26:35ff.; I Chron. 7:20ff.), it is known that its families intermingled with other tribes, especially *Asher, *Benjamin, and *Judah. The central position of the Ephraimites' area of settlement and their militant spirit led them to encroach upon Manasseh, whose power declined with the passage of time. After the migration of the *Danites (Judg. 18) to the north, and the defeat of the *Benjaminites (Judg. 19), the Ephraimites spread both south and southwest, coming into conflict and mingling with Judah in areas severed from the Jebusites of *Jerusalem (see *Jebus) during the period of the Judges. This explains why, in various biblical lists, certain families, places, and areas are sometimes attributed to Judah, Benjamin, or Dan, and sometimes to Ephraim. According to the Bible, the conquest of Canaan was led by *Joshua of the tribe of Ephraim. In the ensuing period of the Judges, the accounts of the disputes with *Gideon (Judg. 8) and *Jephthah (Judg. 12) illustrate the pride of the Ephraimites, who claimed seniority among the tribes and precedence over the fraternal tribe of Manasseh (cf. Gen. 48:13–20). This was doubtless due not only to the political independence that they achieved in the period of the Judges, but also to the location of the religious center of *Shiloh in their territory. The military and political importance of the Ephraimites is reflected in some ancient biblical poems, such as the Song of Deborah (Judg. 5:14). Jacob's blessing (Gen. 49) praises Joseph for his prowess and his hegemony over the other tribes, but contains no reference to Joseph's sons Ephraim and Manasseh, perhaps because it dates from a time when Joseph still counted as only one tribe in the league of Israelite tribes. In the blessing of Moses, however, the sons of Joseph are referred to as "the myriads of Ephraim," and "the thousands of Manasseh" (Deut. 33:17), which probably reflects the later date, on the whole, of the pronouncements on the tribes in Deuteronomy 33, as compared with those in Genesis 49. The self-aggrandizement of the Ephraimites over the other tribes and their tendency to isolation, inherent in such self-aggrandizement, ultimately proved fatal to themselves and to the entire nation, since it brought about the end of the united kingdom of David and Solomon and the diminution of the state's prestige. The man held responsible in the Bible for the breakup was an Ephraimite – *Jeroboam son of Nebat, from Zeredah in the land of Ephraim (I Kings 11:26).

[*Encyclopaedia Hebraica*]

In the *Aggadah*

The preference shown by Jacob toward Ephraim, in placing his right hand on his head instead of on Manasseh's and in twice mentioning Ephraim before Manasseh (Gen. 48:14–20), was interpreted by the rabbis as an all-inclusive nullification of Manasseh's prerogatives as the firstborn. Thus Ephraim was granted precedence to Manasseh in the distribution of the Holy Land (Josh. 16:5); in the order of the banners during the wandering and camping in the desert (Num. 2:18, 20); and in the consecration of the Tabernacle (Num. 7:48, 54). Likewise, the descendants of Ephraim ruled before those of Manasseh, i.e., Joshua before Gideon, Jeroboam before Jehu (Gen. R. 97:5; Num. R. 14:4). Jacob instructed Ephraim for 17 years, yet when he came with Joseph, together with his brother Manasseh, to receive Jacob's blessings, Jacob did not recognize him, for upon seeing Jeroboam and Ahab as issuing from Ephraim, the prophetic spirit left him. Only after Joseph's prayer did it return, whereupon seeing that Joshua too would descend from Ephraim, he blessed him, giving him precedence over Manasseh (Tanḥ., Va-Yeḥi 6). R. Aḥa in the name of R. Levi explains Jeremiah 31:19 to mean that Jacob blessed Ephraim thus: "You shall be the head of the tribes and the head of the academies; and the best and most prominent of my children shall be called after thy name" (Lev. R. 2:3). Moreover, one of the two future Messiahs will originate from Ephraim; he will prepare the way for the Messiah, son of David, and defeat Gog and Magog and the kingdom of Edom; according to some sources he will be killed in battle (Targ. Yer. Ex. 40:11; Suk. 52a). Ephraim's standard was black and bore the emblem of a bullock in accordance with Deuteronomy 33:17 (Num. R. 2:7). The tribe of Ephraim camped to the west, whence came snow, hail, cold, and heat, since Ephraim had the strength to withstand them, as stated in Psalms 80:3 (Num. R. 2:10). The archangel Raphael was appointed to assist at God's throne to heal the breach wrought by Ephraim's descendant, Jeroboam the idol worshiper (*ibid.*). According to the Midrash, the tribe of Ephraim erred in their calculation of the termination of the Egyptian bondage and left the country 30 years before the date ordained for redemption. On their way to Canaan the Philistines waged war against them, killing 300,000 of their number. Their bones were heaped up along the road. In order that the children of Israel would not see these bleached bones and consequently take fright and return to Egypt, God did not lead them on the straight road from Egypt to the Land of Israel, but led them by a circuitous route. According to the Palestinian Targum (Ezek. 37) and the Talmud (Sanh. 92b) it was these bones which were resuscitated by Ezekiel (in the "Vision of the Dry Bones," cf. Ezek.).

BIBLIOGRAPHY: Abel, Geog, 1 (1933), 359; 2 (1938), 56, 81; S. Yeivin, in: EM, 1 (1950), 505–12 (incl. bibl.); Aharoni, Land, 236–37; Ginzberg, Legends, index. **ADD. BIBLIOGRAPHY:** S. Japhet, *I & II Chronicles* (1993), 178–87; S. Ahituv, *Joshua* (1995), 275–80.

EPHRAIM, family mainly active in Berlin. Its first member to settle there was HEINE (ḤAYYIM) EPHRAIM (1665–1748), born in Altona, who rose to be court jeweler and head of the Berlin Jewish community (1726–32). His son was Veitel Heine *Ephraim, most of whose great-grandsons embraced

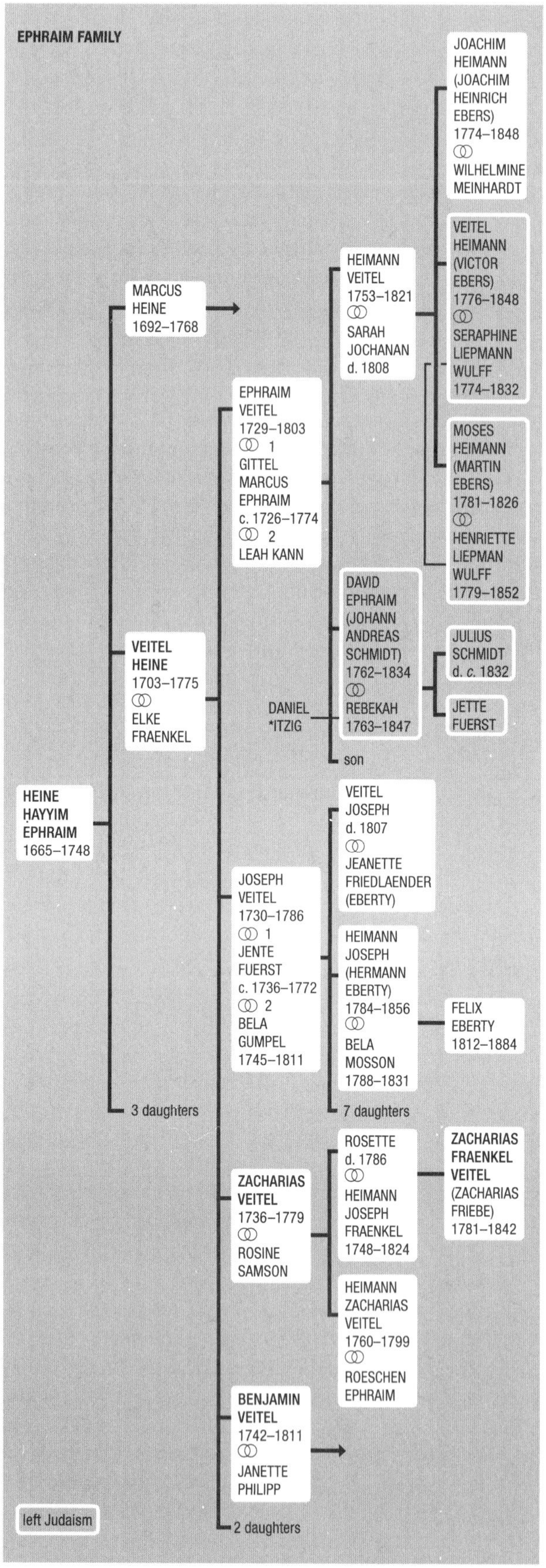

Christianity and changed their names to Ebers; some of their descendants were ennobled. Veitel Heine's grandson, DAVID (1762–1834), married a daughter of Daniel *Itzig; following a financial scandal he fled to Vienna, embraced Catholicism, and changed his family name to Schmidt. ZACHARIAS (1736–1779), son of Veitel Heine, showed marked business ability. His grandson ZACHARIAS FRAENKEL (1781–1842) was an influential banker. As representative of the Berlin community, he demanded conscription of the Jews in 1812.

Veitel Heine's youngest son BENJAMIN (1742–1811) was a businessman and government confidential agent. After varying success in questionable business transactions, he reorganized the family lace factory in Potsdam, opening a school for his girl workers, which was highly commended. In 1779 he took on in his factory unemployed Jewish girls and women from the recently annexed Polish territory. He successfully averted the expulsion orders of Frederick William II by stressing the usefulness of his 700 to 1,500 workers to the state. In Berlin, Benjamin maintained a leading salon, was the first Jew to own an art collection, and had access to ruling circles, having loaned the king large sums before his accession. In 1787 he was sent on a secret mission to Brussels to assure the anti-Austrian rebels of Prussian support. In 1790 the king entrusted him with the mission of contacting the French government to arrange a treaty, with a government post promised as his reward. His expenditure of large sums of his own fortune in Paris aroused suspicions against him in Berlin; at the same time Prussia changed her diplomatic course. Discredited and impoverished, Benjamin demanded recognition and reimbursement. An advocate of close French-Prussian ties, he was entrusted with minor diplomatic roles in negotiations with France. His pro-French attitude led to his arrest in 1806; he was later released by the victorious French. He died in relative poverty.

BIBLIOGRAPHY: H. Rachel et al., *Berliner Grosskaufleute*, 2 (1938), index; H. Schnee, *Die Hoffinanz und der moderne Staat*, 1 (1953), 145–68; J. Jacobson, *Die Judenbuergerbuecher der Stadt Berlin 1809–1851* (1962), index; Kuehn, in: *Deutsche Rundschau*, 166 (1916), 171–91; L. Geiger, *Geschichte der Juden in Berlin*, 1 (1871), 140–4; S. Stern, *The Court Jew* (1950), index; J. Meisl (ed.), *Protokollbuch der juedischen Gemeinde Berlin (1723–1854)* (Heb. and Ger., 1962), 473; M. Stern, in: *Juedische Familien-Forschung*, 1 (1925), 6–10, 31–32, 82–86; B.V. Ephraim, *Ueber meine Verhaftung* (1907); Gelber, in: MGWJ, 71 (1927), 62–66; Jacobson, in: ZGJD, 1 (1929), 152–62.

[Henry Wasserman]

EPHRAIM, VEITEL HEINE (1703–1775), court jeweler and head of the Berlin community. From 1730 he regularly attended the Leipzig fairs, and supplied jewels to the Prussian court and silver to the mint, strengthening his position by furnishing loans to the crown prince. The wedding of two orphans in his home in 1740 was attended by the court. In 1745 Ephraim was officially appointed court jeweler to the king of Prussia. After the death of his father in 1748 Ephraim was elected head of the Berlin Jewish community, continuing in this office until his death. He proved a benevolent though despotic leader, enjoying the continued support of *Frederick II. In 1743 Ephraim appointed his brother-in-law, David *Fraenkel, the teacher of Moses *Mendelssohn, rabbi of Berlin. He also forced a personal enemy, Abraham Posner, a *maskil*, who wanted to shave off his beard in demonstration of his unorthodox convictions, to retain his beard. Ephraim built a school for the children employed in his factories and an educational foundation bearing his name. During the Seven Years' War (1756–63) Ephraim organized a consortium (including Daniel *Itzig and other financiers) for the mint farming rights in Prussia and the conquered territories, especially Saxony. The consortium bought up all the precious metals and good coinage and issued a series of debased coins, which became known as "Ephraimiten." Through these government-authorized inflationary measures about one-sixth of Prussia's war expenditures were defrayed, but the general populace became impoverished and Ephraim was attacked from the pulpit and in pamphlets. Frederick II issued a formal discharge to Ephraim although refusing to have it made public. After the war Ephraim was active in measures taken to improve the coinage. Having amassed great wealth during the war, Ephraim invested it in building a castle-type residence and in manufacturing ventures. He leased the Potsdam orphanage factory for fine gold and silver thread, over which he was granted a monopoly, and owned a Brussels lace factory, employing 200 workers. He died one of the richest men in Berlin.

BIBLIOGRAPHY: H. Rachel et al., *Berliner Grosskaufleute*, 2 (1938); H. Schnee, *Die Hoffinanz und der moderne Staat*, 1 (1953), 145–68; 5 (1965), 25, 26; H. Rachel, in: ZGJD, 2 (1930), 188ff; L. Geiger, *Geschichte der Juden in Berlin*, 1 (1871), 82, 84, 86f.; 2 (1871), 140ff.; M. Stern, *Beitraege zur Geschichte der Juden in Berlin* (1909); idem, in: *Juedische Familien-Forschung*, 1 (1925), 6, 82; J. Jacobson, *Die Judenbuergerbuecher der Stadt Berlin 1809–1851* (1962), index; S. Stern, *The Court Jew* (1950), index.

EPHRAIM BEN ISAAC (of Regensburg; 1110–1175), tosafist, member of the *bet din* of Regensburg, and the greatest of the *paytanim* (liturgical poets) of Germany. Among his teachers were *Isaac b. Asher ha-Levi and *Isaac b. Mordecai of Regensburg. He was held in great esteem by his contemporaries, being referred to as "the great Rabbi Ephraim" and as "Ben Yakir" (an allusion to Jer. 31:20). His youth was spent in France, where he was among the first pupils of Jacob b. Meir *Tam (Rabbenu Tam). Ephraim was uncompromising in his pursuit of truth; his intransigence often brought him into conflict with other scholars, even with Jacob Tam himself. Once, after a particularly heated dispute with the rabbis of Speyer, Rabbenu Tam answered him sharply: "From the day I have known you, I have never heard you concede a point" (*Sefer ha-Yashar*, no. 64). Rabbenu Tam, however, appreciating Ephraim's selfless motives, bore him no ill will, even referring to him affectionately as "my brother Rabbi Ephraim" (*ibid.*, n. 80).

When the rabbis of Speyer complained to Rabbenu Tam that Ephraim was overly lenient, a literary controversy arose, in which Ephraim's letters to Rabbenu Tam evidenced undeviating adherence to Jewish law and custom. Ephraim remained in Speyer for a short while after the dispute, then moved on to Worms, and finally to Regensburg. Ephraim is the author of *Tosafot* (cited in early works); a commentary on *Avot;* and halakhic decisions. He also apparently wrote *Arba Panim* ("Four Aspects"), a commentary to *Seder Nezikin*. Thirty-two of his *piyyutim* are extant. They reflect the severe hardships which the Jews of Germany suffered in the Regensburg massacre of 1137 and the Second Crusade (1146–47). Zunz regarded Ephraim's poems as superior to all other contemporary Hebrew poetry written in Germany. They are distinctive in form and content, and powerful in expression. Ephraim also employed the metric forms of Sephardi poetry and one of his *seliḥot* is in the Sephardi festival liturgy.

BIBLIOGRAPHY: Zunz, Lit Poesie, 274–80; idem, *Nachtrag zur Literaturgeschichte* … (1867), 16–17; Davidson, Oẓar, 4 (1933), 369, index; Germ Jud, 1 (1934), 289–90; V. Aptowitzer, *Mavo le-Sefer Ravyah* (1938), 321–3; A.M. Habermann, in: YMḤSI, 4 (1938), 121–95; Urbach, Tosafot, 72–73, 170–7; Weinberg, in: *Hadorom*, 23 (1965/66), 31–53; Ta-Shema, in: KS, 42 (1966/67), 507–8.

[Abraham Meir Habermann]

EPHRAIM BEN JACOB HA-KOHEN (1616–1678), rabbinic authority. Ephraim served as a judge in Vilna together with *Shabbetai Kohen and Aaron Samuel *Koidanover in the *bet din* of his teacher, Moses Ben Isaac Judah *Lima. During the Swedish War (1655), Ephraim fled from Vilna to Velke Mezerici in Moravia. From there he went to Prague, where he established a yeshivah. He then moved to Vienna, remaining there until 1666, when he was appointed head of the *bet din* in Ofen (Buda). There he established a famous yeshivah and corresponded with some of the most prominent rabbis of his time, including those of Turkey and Ereẓ Israel, among them Moses *Galante and Moses ibn *Ḥabib. Toward the end of his life he was invited to the rabbinate of the Ashkenazi congregation of Jerusalem, a position which, 80 years earlier, his grandfather R. Ephraim ha-Kohen had held. He died, however, before he could take up the position. Ephraim was one of the great legal authorities of his generation. His decisions on many questions, civil, domestic, and religious, helped influence Jewish life in several countries for a number of generations. His only published work is his responsa, *Sha'ar Efrayim* on the Shulḥan Arukh, published by his son Aryeh Loeb (Sulzbach, 1689). Other works have remained in manuscript. Ephraim was the grandfather of Ẓevi Hirsch *Ashkenazi, the "Ḥakham Ẓevi."

BIBLIOGRAPHY: D. Kaufmann, *Die letzte Vertreibung der Juden aus Wien* … (1889), 62; *Even ha-Me'ir*, 2 (1907), 27f., no. 148; J.J. (L.) Greenwald (Grunwald), *Sefer Toledot Ḥakhmei Yisrael, Kolel Toledot R. Efrayim ha-Kohen mi-Vilna* (1924); Frumkin-Rivlin, 1 (1929), 107f.; H. Gold (ed.), *Juden und Judengemeinden Maehrens* (1929), 227f.

[Aharon Fuerst]

EPHRAIM BEN JACOB OF BONN (b. 1132), liturgical poet and commentator. When his teacher Joel b. Isaac ha-Levi left Bonn, Ephraim succeeded him as *av bet din*. He also taught for some time in Mainz and Speyer. In 1197, he resided in Bonn and Neuss, leaving the latter town only three days before its Jews were massacred. He appears to have died shortly thereafter. Ephraim wrote the *Sefer Zekhirah* ("Book of Remembrance") and dirges on the sufferings of the Jews during the Second Crusade. He also composed *piyyutim* for the festivals, 27 of which (two in Aramaic) have been published. His commentary on *piyyutim* still exists in manuscript; it contains many traditional details concerning the early liturgical poets, poems, and liturgical customs (Hamburg, Ms. no. 152). The well-known legend describing the martyrdom of *Amnon of Mainz, as well as the legend concerning the early *paytan* R. *Yannai, who out of jealousy of his pupil R. Eleazar *Kallir put a scorpion in his shoe, are attributed to him. He also wrote *tosafot* and commentaries to the treatises of *Eruvin, Ketubbot*, and *Avot*, besides halakhic responsa and commentaries to benedictions and various customs. R. Ephraim is also referred to in his hymns as "Shalom"; it was possibly an additional name. The meaning of the word יְלִיבַּייה added to his name has not yet been clarified. It has been suggested that he had a German name such as *Geliebter* ("beloved") which was commonly pronounced *"yelība."*

BIBLIOGRAPHY: A.M. Habermann (ed.), *Gezerot Ashkenaz ve-Ẓarefat* (1945), 115–36; Davidson, Oẓar, 4 (1933), 369, s.v. *Efrayim mi-Bona (b. Ya'akov);* Zunz, Lit Poesie, 288–93; Germ Jud, 1 (1934), 49–50, no. 6; V. Aptowitzer, *Mavo le-Sefer Ravyah* (1938), 319–21; Habermann, in: YMḤSI, 7 (1958), 215–96; Baron, Social, index.

[Abraham Meir Habermann]

EPHRAIM BEN SHEMARIAH (c. 980–c. 1060), leader of the Palestinian community in *Cairo during the first half of the 11th century. Ephraim's father, Shemariah, was born in *Gaza and later moved to *Egypt with his family. Ephraim himself studied in the Palestinian yeshivah, where he received the title *ḥaver* ("scholar") from the *gaon* Josiah. He was engaged in commerce, but in about 1020 became the rabbi of the Palestinian community. Although he came into conflict with an opposing faction from time to time, he held his position for more than 30 years. Ephraim supported the Jews in Palestine and, especially, the Palestinian yeshivah. He was a close friend of the *gaon* R. *Solomon b. Judah, with whom he corresponded for many years.

BIBLIOGRAPHY: S. Poznański, in: REJ, 48 (1904), 145–75; A. Cowley, in: JQR, 19 (1906/07), 107–8; M. Schwab, in: REJ, 70 (1920), 63; Mann, Egypt, index; Mann, Texts, 1 (1931), 314; Hirschberg, Afrikah, 1 (1965), 131, 159–60, 175, 260.

[Eliyahu Ashtor]

EPHRAIM IBN AVI ALRAGAN (late 11 and early 12th centuries), North African halakhist. He is referred to in halakhic literature as "Rabbenu Ephraim," "Ephraim of Kaleah," "Ephraim the Sephardi," "Ephraim, pupil of the Rif" (i.e., Isaac *Alfasi), "Ephraim the Elder," etc. He lived in *Qalʿat Ḥammād (Algeria). Ephraim was an outstanding disciple of Alfasi, with whom he discussed halakhic problems and Alfasi at times accepted his view. The "*Mahadura Batra*" (second recension of the *halakhot* of Alfasi) contains Ephraim's amendments. He was the first to write a commentary on the *halakhot* of Alfasi, and this is referred to in the works of *rishonim* under various names: *haggahot* ("glosses"), *hassagot* ("critiques"), *teshuvot* ("responsa"), *tosafot* ("addenda"), and *tashlum halakhot* ("complement to the *halakhot*"). The work has not survived, but quotations from it appear in the works of the *rishonim*, and a substantial part of it, on *Bava Kamma*, was published in the *Temim De'im*, no. 68, margin in the Romm Vilna (1882) edition of Alfasi. The quotations indicate that the book covered the whole of the *halakhot* and possibly also the Mishnah of tractates which Alfasi did not include in his work. The book consists of supplements to the *halakhot* ("additional *halakhot* omitted by Alfasi"), explanations of passages from the *Gemara* which Alfasi quoted without comment, explanations of the text itself, and refutations of Alfasi's critics. It also contains criticism of Alfasi, mainly where he disagrees with the decisions of the Babylonian *geonim* and North African scholars, and with their customs. The criticisms are presented vigorously but respectfully. Sometimes, when an opinion attributed to Alfasi is not acceptable to Ephraim, he, like other admirers of Alfasi, questions the attribution. Ephraim's purpose was to secure universal acceptance for the *halakhot;* even his criticisms were directed to this end, for by citing the views of earlier scholars which conflict with those of Alfasi, those who disagreed with him could still use the work as a whole as an authoritative code. Because the *rishonim* quoted mainly the criticisms of Ephraim, it was thought that the whole work was critical. Ephraim exercised an influence particularly on the early scholars of Provence and Catalonia, such as *Abraham b. David of Posquiéres, *Zerahiah ha-Levi, *Jonathan ha-Kohen of Lunel, *Isaac b. Abba Mari of Marseilles, and *Naḥmanides. Much of his teachings are contained in their works, sometimes without attribution. In some cases his glosses in the margins were incorporated in error by copyists into the text of the *halakhot* itself. Solomon b. Parḥon was one of Ephraim's pupils.

BIBLIOGRAPHY: Benedikt, in: KS, 25 (1948/49), 164–9, 229–30; 26 (1949/50), 216, 322–38; 31 (1955 /56), 264; Ta-Shema, *ibid.*, 42 (1966/67), 507–8.

[Binyamin Zeev Benedikt]

EPHRAIM SOLOMON BEN AARON OF LUNTSHITS (Leczyca; 1550–1619), rabbi and renowned preacher. He was known as "Ephraim of Luntshits," the popular pronunciation of Leczyca among Polish Jews. The name "Solomon" was added some time after 1601. In his youth Ephraim was sent to study in the yeshivah of Solomon *Luria. At an early age he had already gained a reputation as a preacher, in which capacity he traveled to Lublin, Lemberg, Jaroslaw, and other towns. It is not known whether he ever held a regular communal post before he became head of a yeshivah in Lemberg when he was already past fifty. In 1604, he arrived in Prague where he served as president of the rabbinical court and head of the yeshivah, but he relinquished his rabbinical post in the last year of his life. As a preacher he was distinguished for his lucid and fascinating sermons. He addressed the heads of the *Council of Four Lands when they met in Lublin and was apparently on friendly terms with the leaders of that council on whose recommendation he was appointed *rosh yeshivah* in Lemberg. Ephraim's sermons shed much light on the religious and communal life of the Polish-Jewish community of his time. He railed against the wealthy members of the congregation whose passion for money and luxury caused them to withhold assistance from their needy brethren and he criticized their pretensions to spiritual and religious status on the basis of their commercial success. He said that wealth corrupts and destroys the character of men when they do not appreciate its purpose. At the same time, he complained about the poor who wished to enjoy the charity of the rich without making any effort to provide for their needs. In addition, he attacked certain casuistic methods of talmudic study (*pilpul*) which often neglected the truth, and the desire for personal aggrandizement among communal leaders.

Ephraim's sermons were collected and published in various books: *Ir Gibborim* (Basle, 1580); *Olelot Efrayim* (Lublin, 1590); *Oraḥ le-Ḥayyim* (*ibid.*, 1595); *Keli Yakar* (*ibid.*, 1602), commentary on the Pentateuch in homiletic style that was subsequently included in various editions of the rabbinical Bible (*Mikra'ot Gedolot*); *Siftei Da'at* (Prague, 1610); *Ammudei Shesh* (*ibid.*, 1617); *Petiḥot u-She'arim* (Zolkiew, 1799). He also compiled a book of sermons entitled *Rivevot Efrayim*, which is occasionally mentioned in his other works. He composed three *seliḥot* in connection with the invasion of Prague in 1611 by the army of the bishop of Passau.

BIBLIOGRAPHY: M. Gruenwald, *Rabbi Salomo Efraim Luntschitz* (Ger., 1892); I. Bettan, *Studies in Jewish Preaching* (1939), 273–316; idem, in: HUCA, 8–9 (1931/32), 443–80; Halpern, Pinkas, 607, index; H.H. Ben-Sasson, *Hagut ve-Hanhagah* (1959), 263, index; idem, in: *Zion*, 19 (1954), 142–66; H.R. Rabinowitz, *Deyokena'ot shel Darshanim* (1967), 137–49; G. Klemperer, in: HJ, 12 (1950), 38ff.

[Abraham David]

EPHRATH (Heb. אֶפְרָת), an additional name for *Bethlehem of Judah: "Ephrath – the same is Bethlehem" (Gen. 35:19; 48:7; LXX, Josh. 15:59b; cf. Micah 5:1). In the genealogical tables in the Bible, which provide information on the distribution of the clans and the places occupied by them, Ephrath appears as the wife of Caleb and the mother of "Hur the first-born of Ephrath, the father of Bethlehem" (I Chron. 2:19, 50; 4:4). The various biblical references apparently indicate that in addition to the Calebite clans, originating from the south, the Ephrathites, who possibly were of a different origin, also penetrated into the Bethlehem district, and their influence there was so great that the chief city of the district was named for them. Jesse, David's father, was called "Ephrathite" (I Sam. 17:12) and so were Naomi's sons (Ruth 1:2).

[Moshe Kochavi]

EPHRATI, DAVID TEVELE BEN ABRAHAM (1849–1884), talmudic scholar. Born in Merits (near Vilna), he showed exceptional talent as a child and at the age of 14 had already written his *Daltot Zahav* on the Shulḥan Arukh *Oraḥ Ḥayyim* and *Yoreh De'ah*. At 15, his articles and studies began to appear in the periodical *Ha-Levanon*, and he continued to write regularly. At the age of 22 he wrote a halakhic work, *Migdal David*. Ephrati was one of the most active leaders of the Ḥibbat Zion movement, and was on intimate terms with Elijah *Guttmacher and Ẓevi Hirsch *Kalischer. In 1873 he was sentenced to a year's imprisonment for his Zionist activities. He refused invitations to rabbinic posts and, from 1868 lived alternately in Mogilev and Gorodok, later moving to Vitebsk where he engaged in business. Toward the end of his life he moved to Berlin, where he became friendly with Azriel *Hildesheimer. He died in Frankfurt on the Main. Ephrati was also the author of *Toledot Anshei Shem* (1875), biographical sketches of great Jewish scholars, with an appendix, *Divrei David*, consisting of homilies and novellae; this work is of considerable historical importance. Other works are *Yad David* (1880), *halakhah* and *aggadah; Matta Efrati* (1882), novellae and responsa; *Kohelet David ha-Efrati* (1884), a commentary on Ecclesiastes; *Sha'ar ha-Zekenim* (1884), a collection of manuscripts of early authorities with his own commentary, *Mevo Efrati*. Ephrati was also editor of a monthly periodical called *Eẓ Ḥayyim*. Many of his works have remained unpublished.

BIBLIOGRAPHY: *Ha-Asif*, 2 (1885), 754; *Oẓar ha-Sifrut*, 1 (1887), 129–32 (2nd pagination), contains an autobiography.

[Itzhak Alfassi]

EPHRON (Heb. עֶפְרוֹן).

(1) Mountain on the northern boundary between Judah and Benjamin 8 mi. (13 km.) west of Jerusalem between Nephtoah (Liftā) and *Balaah-Kiriath-Jearim (Tell Deir al-Azhar; Josh. 15:9). Ephron probably constituted the mountainous area extending from Har ha-Menuḥot to Qaryat al-ʿInab.

(2) A town in Transjordan captured by *Judah Maccabee during his retreat from Gilead in the direction of *Beth-Shean (I Macc. 5:46–52; II Macc. 12:27–29; Jos., Ant., 12:346). It appears in the account of the conquest of Ptolemaic Palestine by *Antiochus III in 218 B.C.E. as Gephrous (Polybius, 5:70, 12). It is identified with al-Ṭayyiba, 7½ mi. (12 km.) north-east of Pella.

BIBLIOGRAPHY: Aharoni, Land, index; Avi-Yonah, 176; C. Steuernagel, *Der Adschlun* (1927), 447f.; Abel, in: RB, 32 (1923), 520.

[Michael Avi-Yonah]

EPHRON (Heb. עֶפְרוֹן, עֶפְרֹן), son of Zohar, from whom *Abraham purchased the cave of *Machpelah and the field east of Mamre (Gen. 23; 25:9; 49:29–30; 50:13). Abraham sought a burial site for Sarah, but as he was a "resident alien," he did not own land. He therefore sought to purchase the cave belonging to Ephron, who, after much bargaining, agreed to accept 400 shekels of silver. Ephron is described as a "Hittite," though the form of his name and that of his father is West Semitic. While "Hittite" in the Bible may sometimes refer to Canaan's pre-Israelite inhabitants (cf. Gen. 26:34 with Gen 27:46), and not to the Hittites of Anatolia in the second millennium B.C.E., the first millennium Arameo-Hittites were within the orbit of the biblical writers. Some scholars interpret the name Ephron as being related to *ʿofer* ("gazelle"); S. Yeivin's explanation that Ephron is not a personal name but an indication that the man was an ʿApiru (see *Habiru) of Hittite origin is ingenious but unlikely.

BIBLIOGRAPHY: S. Yeivin, in: *Beth Mikra*, 7 (1963), 44–45 and note 281; E.A. Speiser, *Genesis* (*The Anchor Bible*, 1964), 172; N. Sarna, *Understanding Genesis* (1967), 168ff. **ADD. BIBLIOGRAPHY:** J. van Seters, in: VT, 22 (1972), 64–81; N. Sarna, *Genesis* (JPS; 1989), 396.

EPHRON, NORA (1941–), U.S. writer, film director. Ephron was born on Manhattan's Upper West Side, but her family moved to Beverly Hills by the time she turned three. Her parents, screenwriting duo Pheobe and Henry Ephron, wrote such classics as *Carousel* (1956) and *There's No Business Like Show Business* (1954). They based their script *Take Her, She's Mine* on the letters their daughter wrote home while she was attending Wellesley College. In 1962, after finishing school, Ephron moved to New York City, launching a career in journalism. She worked for the *New York Post* and, later, for publications such as *Esquire*, the *New York Times Magazine*, and *New York Magazine*. Her work is collected in such books as *Wallflower at the Orgy* (1970), *Crazy Salad* (1975), and *Scribble, Scribble* (1978). After a brief marriage to writer Dan Greenburg, Ephron married Carl *Bernstein, the journalist who, along with Bob Woodward, first brought the Watergate scandal to the country's attention in the pages of the *Washington Post*. The marriage broke up while Ephron was pregnant with their second son, Max, and the breakup became the basis for her semiautobiographical novel, *Heartburn*. With two young children to support, Ephron turned to her family trade – screenwriting. Her scripts frequently focus on strong, independent women struggling to achieve their ambitions. Ephron wrote such films as *Silkwood* (1983), *When Harry Met Sally* (1989), and *Sleepless in Seattle* (1993). She made her directorial debut with the comedy *This is My Life* (1992), which she co-wrote with her sister Delia. She continued to write and direct movies, including the box office smash *You've Got Mail* (1998) and *Bewitched* (2005).

[Casey Schwartz (2nd ed.)]

EPHROS, GERSHON (1890–1978), *ḥazzan*. Born in Poland, he went to Palestine at 20, and studied under the musicologist A.Z. *Idelsohn, for whom he also conducted a choir. Later he immigrated to the U.S. where he received appointments as *ḥazzan* and taught singing in schools. Ephros composed liturgical music for soloists, choir, and organ, and arranged Ḥasidic dances and Israel songs. His main work is his *Cantorial Anthology* in five volumes (1929–57), a practical collection of older and recent works for all the synagogue services of the year, which also contains some of Ephros' own compositions.

In 1976 the Gershon Ephros Cantorial Anthology Foundation was established for the purpose of continuing the publication of his Anthology, of which 6 volumes have now been published. In 1979 the American Society for Jewish Music published an index to them. Two records of his liturgical songs and songs for children have appeared.

[Akiva Zimmerman (2nd ed.)]

EPHRUSSI, BORIS (1901–1977), geneticist. Ephrussi was born in Moscow but moved to Paris after the 1917 Revolution, where he graduated in zoology (1922) and obtained his doctorate in experimental embryology (1932) from the University of Paris. A Rockefeller fellowship with George Beadle at California Institute of Technology (1934) determined Ephrussi's career as a geneticist. The German occupation of France forced him into exile in the United States, where he worked mainly at Johns Hopkins University, Baltimore. He became professor of genetics at the Sorbonne, Paris (1945), and director of the newly established Laboratory of Physiological Genetics in Gif-sur-Yvette near Paris (1956). After a period of major organizational difficulties, he moved to the U.S. as professor at Western Reserve University, Cleveland (1962), until he returned to direct the same institute near Paris, now renamed the Center of Molecular Genetics, until 1972. Before 1945 Ephrussi was one of the few internationally recognized French geneticists in France and he largely directed the reorganization of the field after World War II. His collaboration with Beadle helped establish the concept that genes control cellular events. Subsequently he pursued the then highly contentious concept that cytoplasmic factors influenced by external factors are genetically transmitted independently of conventional genes. The experimental validity of his work was subsequently vindicated by the discovery of mitochondrial DNA. His many honors included election to the French Academy of Sciences (1978).

[Michael Denman (2nd ed.)]

°**EPICTETUS** (c. 100 C.E.), Greek Stoic philosopher, who made several noncommittal observations on the Jews. Epictetus wrote no books; the sole source of his teachings is the *Discourses* of Arrian. Here (1:11, 12–13) it is related that Epictetus indicated the differences between the dietary concepts of the Jews, Syrians, Egyptians, and Romans, noting their incompatibility; and later (1:22, 4) he is reported as classifying these four peoples as in agreement on the substance of the principle of sanctification, though differing on details, such as the eating of pork. A third passage (2:9, 19–22) shows that Epictetus knew of the importance of ritual immersion for proselytism. The Galileans mentioned by him (4:7, 6) cannot be identified with the Zealots; here, the more usual explanation – that Epictetus was referring to Christians – is preferable.

BIBLIOGRAPHY: Reinach, Textes, 154–5.

[Menahem Stern]

EPICUREANISM, a philosophy of adjustment to the social changes after *Alexander the Great (336–323), founded by Epicurus, 342/1–270 B.C.E., "the most revered and the most reviled of all founders of thought in the Greco-Roman world" (De Witt). Recent scholarship sees in it a "bridge" to certain rabbinic and Christian moods. Epicurus taught freedom from fear and desire through knowledge as the natural and pleasurable life. He endorsed religious observance but denied earthly involvement of the perfect gods and with it providence, presage, punishment, and penitential prayer. The transformation of Epicureanism into a competitive sect celebrating Epicurus as "savior" increased the already existing opposition to it. Rhetorical literature falsely accused Epicurus of materialistic hedonism. Complaints of Epicurean dogmatism, "beguiling speech" (Col. 2:4), and compelling argumentation (of Avot 2:14 "…[know] what to answer the Epicurean") are frequently heard. Rabbinic condemnation reflects knowledge of Greco-Roman rhetoric, experiences with individuals and centers (Gadara, Gaza, Caesarea), and, possibly, the favoritism shown to Epicureanism by *Antiochus Epiphanes and *Hadrian. "Epicurean" became thus a byword for "deviance" – ranging from disrespect to atheism – in Philo, Josephus, and rabbinism alike (see **Apikoros*). An early unexpanded version of the "four who entered 'Paradise'" (Ḥag. 14b) may once have signified Epicurus' school ("the garden"), since it fits Akiva's past, Ben Azzai's celibacy and many Epicurean sayings, Elisha b. Avuyah's heterodoxy, and Ben Zoma's gnosticism (Epicureanism and Gnosticism were equated also by the Church Fathers). Akiva's "mystical" admonition (Ḥag. 14b) could easily have been a parody on the "apocalyptic"-enthusiastic style of the Epicureans (parallel parody H. Usener, *Epicurea*, fragm. 364; Gen. R. 1:5, Theodor-Albeck, p. 2 mentions "nothing from nothing"; Mid. Ps. to 1:22 the "automatic" universe; cf. Jos., Ant., 10:280).

Agreements, however, both in content and literary form, between rabbinism and Epicureanism are striking: study for its own sake (Vatican fragment 45 and Avot 6:1); removal of doubt (*Life* 121b, *Doctr.* 22 and Avot 1:16); mortality and urgency (Vat. fr. 10 and Avot 2:15); acquisition of a companion (*To Menoeceus*, end, and Avot 1:6); diet of bread and water (Bailey, fr. 37 and Avot 6:4); satisfaction with one's lot (Bailey, fr. 69–70 and Avot 4:1); and avoidance of public office (Bailey, fr. 85–87; Vat. fr. 58; *Doctr.* 7 and Avot 1:10–11; 2:3; etc.). Epicurus anticipated Judaism's denial of astral divinity and rule. With the general rise of the lower classes he accorded human dignity even to the prostitute, an evaluation continued in the Midrash (Sif. Num. 78; Gen. R. 85:8) and the Gospels (Matt. 1:3; 5, etc.). In Hellenism and Christianity, too, denunciation of Epicurus together with partial adoption of his ethics is frequent. The centrality of the sage in post-Socratic ethics and rhetoric facilitated such developments.

BIBLIOGRAPHY: C. Bailey, *Epicurus* (Greek and Eng., 1926); N.W. De Witt, *Epicurus and his Philosophy* (1954); A.M.J. Festugiére, *Epicurus and his Gods* (1956); S. Lieberman, in: A. Altmann (ed.), *Biblical and Other Studies* (1963), 123–41; *Reallexikon fuer Antike und Christentum*, 5 (1962), 681–819, s.v. *Epikur* (contains bibliography).

[Henry Albert Fischel]

EPIRUS, province in N.W. Greece. Epirus was an independent despotate between c. 1214 and 1340. Under the first and strongest of its despots, Theodore Ducas Angelus, the Jews (see *Durazzo, *Arta, *Ioannina) were subjected to a persecution in which Jewish property was confiscated and Judaism probably prohibited. This was subsequently extended to Salonika, captured by Theodore in 1224, and continued even after Salonika was retaken from Epirus in 1246. With the strengthening of the empire under *Michael VIII Palaeologus, parts of Epirus reverted to the empire and the persecutions came to an end. His son Andronicus II Palaeologus placed the Jews of Ioannina (Janina), the most important of the Epirote communities, under his direct protection and angered the Church by favoring the Jews.

BIBLIOGRAPHY: J. Starr, *Romania* (Eng., 1949), 20–23; J. Mann, in: REJ, 82 (1926), 372–3; P. Charanis, in: *Speculum*, 22 (1947), 75–76.

[Andrew Sharf]

EPISCOPUS JUDAEORUM (Lat. "bishop of the Jews"), title given by the Christian authorities in the Middle Ages to the head of the Jewish community or its rabbi. The significance of the title, which is much disputed, is sometimes clarified when Hebrew and Latin forms are found side by side. In Germany the title is mentioned in the privilege granted to the Jews of Worms in 1090, addressed to Salman the "Jews' bishop," a distinguished scholar. The "bishop" of the Jews in Worms, later called the *hegmon parnas*, was the permanent chairman of the community board; the last man to hold the title, Michael Gernstein, died in 1792. In Cologne the first "bishop" of the Jews is mentioned from 1135 to 1159. His successors were in office for long terms, although elections were held annually; some of them were rabbis. In Silesia, the "Jews' bishop" held the offices of rabbi, ritual slaughterer, cantor, and religious teacher in 1315. Found in England in the 12th century, the term (*Eveske* in Anglo-French) was sometimes equivalent to the Hebrew *kohen*. It is therefore impossible to maintain that in England it denoted an official rabbinical position.

BIBLIOGRAPHY: Baron, Community, 1 (1942), index; R. Hoeniger and M. Stern (eds.), *Das Judenschreinsbuch der Laurenzpfarre zu Koeln*, 1 (1888), nos. 234–40; J. Jacobs, *Jews of Angevin England* (1893), 202–4, 372–3; Aronius, *Regesten*, nos. 171, 581; H. Stokes, *Studies in Anglo-Jewish History* (1913), 18–43; Roth, England, 94–95; H.G. Richardson, *English Jewry under Angevin Kings* (1960), 124–9.

[Isaac Levitats]

EPITAPHS. Commemorative inscriptions marking the place of burial were known at the time of the First Temple following the custom of the other Oriental nations, in particular the Phoenicians. The most elaborate as yet discovered is a rock-carved inscription over a burial cave in the Kidron Valley outside Jerusalem apparently referred to explicitly in Isaiah 22:15–16, indicating the grave of the royal steward Shebna: "This is (the sepulcher of) … yahu who is over the House. There is no silver and no gold here but (his bones) and the bones of his slave-wife with him. Cursed be the man who will open this." In the Second Temple period, there grew up the practice of burial in sarcophagi or secondary burial in *ossuaries: these generally bore at the most the names of the persons whose bones had been brought together in them. On the other hand, more elaborate inscriptions were placed over some burial places, such as the tomb of the priestly family of Benei *Hezir in the Kidron Valley. From the period of Roman-Byzantine domination, after the fall of Jerusalem in 70 C.E., many epitaphs are preserved, brought together by J.B. Frey in the second volume of his *Corpus Inscriptionum Judaicarum*, the largest number being from the *catacombs of *Bet She'arim in Galilee. Normally these bear only the name of the deceased, whether in Hebrew or in Greek: in two cases the epitaph is a lengthy poem in Greek verses.

To the same period belong the very large number of epitaphs found in the Roman catacombs, collected with others from Europe in Frey's first volume. Of these, the great majority (approximately 75 percent) are in Greek: most of the remaining 25 percent are in Latin. Only a small minority include any Hebrew, and these, mainly stereotyped phrases ("Peace" or "Peace upon his resting place"). On the other hand, a very large number are distinguished by Jewish symbols such as the seven-branched candelabrum, or *menorah*. The Roman epitaphs are on the whole brief, giving little more detail than the name of the deceased, sometimes with the addition of the communal position he held (e.g., *grammateus*, "secretary"; *archon*, "warden"); one of them includes a poem in Latin hexameters. Contemporary with and similar to the Roman Jewish catacombs are some of *Venosa in south Italy. Here, however, there was a tendency for the epitaphs to be longer, more elaborate and more descriptive, as in the case of that of a girl of 14 who, it is related, in a remarkable inscription in curious Late Latin, was the only child of her distinguished parents, was conveyed to her grave amid universal lamentation, and was commemorated by two rabbis and two messengers from the Holy Land (Frey, no. 611).

From Venosa and the neighboring region of south Italy a series of *tombstones also have been preserved which demonstrate how, from about the year 800, Hebrew displaced Latin and Greek in funerary epitaphs. These are now relatively long, mention Jewish schools and "scholars of the academy" (e.g., Nathan b. Ephraim of Venosa, who died in 846), and in one case incorporate poetical passages from a funerary prayer. In other lands of Europe (Greece, Gaul, Spain, Pannonia) epitaphs of the late classical period in Latin and Greek are similarly preserved: the Mérida (Spain) inscription is trilingual, in Greek, Latin, and Hebrew.

In due course, however, as knowledge of Hebrew spread and Latin came to be considered the language of the Church, the use of Hebrew became universal. From the 11th century, tombstones with epitaphs in Hebrew are preserved in Spain, France, Germany, and elsewhere. These are generally at the beginning very brief, containing little more than the name of the deceased. Later they tend to become more elaborate. The Spanish epitaphs of the 13th–14th century (collected by F. Cantera), written sometimes on all sides of raised horizontal tombstones, are veritable literary documents. The French medieval inscriptions are collected by M. Schwab. Similar collections for some other countries remain a desideratum. In Italy, from the 16th century, it became usual to incorporate in the epitaph a short poem in a stereotyped lilting meter: a very large number of those composed by R. Leone *Modena of Venice have been published by A. Berliner and R. Pacifici. Less literary, but historically of great importance, are the funerary inscriptions from such places as Prague (published by S. Hock), Frankfurt on the Main (published by M. Horovitz), Salonika (published by I.S. Emmanuel). No epitaphs are preserved from the Papal States in Italy or France (Avignon, Carpentras) during the age of the ghetto, when commemorative inscriptions over the dead were sternly forbidden.

In the 17th century, the communities established in Western Europe by the ex-Marranos reintroduced the use of vernacular on tombstones, as instanced in the epitaphs from Amsterdam (published by D. Henriques de Castro), Hamburg (collected by M. Gruenwald), Curaçao (published by I.S. Emmanuel), Barbados (published by E.M. Shilstone), Jamaica (included by J.A.P.M. Andrade in his *A record of the Jews in Jamaica*, 1941), New York (published by David de Sola Pool), London, Venice, Leghorn, Bordeaux, Bayonne, etc. Many of the Spanish epitaphs end with the valedictory abbreviation "SBAGDG" (*Sua bendita alma goze de gloria*, "May his blessed soul enjoy glory"), or something similar. Sometimes these inscriptions are bilingual (Spanish/Portuguese, and Hebrew). English (though not Dutch, German, etc., elsewhere) began to appear already in the 17th century: in 1684 the epitaph of the English court jeweler, Isaac Alvarez Nunes, in London, incorporates an English poem in Alexandrine couplets. The cemeteries of the Ashkenazi communities on the other hand did not as yet admit the vernacular. The inscriptions were here now longer and more elaborate, sometimes incorporating crude verses giving the name of the deceased in acrostic form. The inscription in the case of a man was generally headed פ"נ for פֹּה נִקְבַּר ("here lies"), for a woman, פ"ט, for פֹּה טְמוּנָה ("here is interred"). At the close, the abbreviation תנצב"ה for תְּהִי נַפְשׁוֹ צְרוּרָה בִּצְרוֹר הַחַיִּים ("May his soul be bound up in the bond of eternal life"; cf. I Sam. 25:29) was usual. This has remained the case down to the present time, and in recent times is sometimes the only Hebrew element that remains.

In the course of the 19th century in most of the countries of the Western world the vernacular began to encroach more and more in epitaphs. At the beginning the secular name of the deceased alone figured together with the Hebrew; later a fairly lengthy vernacular (e.g., English) inscription paralleled and repeated the details of the Hebrew: in due course often the Hebrew name alone figured, or sometimes not even this. In some cemeteries (e.g., in England) the use of some Hebrew has been made obligatory; in others, belonging to strongly Orthodox groups, no English whatsoever is allowed. In Israel, the tendency is now for simple epitaphs in which Hebrew alone figures.

BIBLIOGRAPHY: Cantera-Millás, Inscripciones; M. Schwab, *Rapport sur les inscriptions hébraïques de la France (= Nouvelles Archives des Missions Scientifiques*, 12 (1904), 143–402); A. Berliner, *Luḥot Avanim, hebraeische Grabinschriften in Italien*, 1 (1881); R. Pacifici, *Le iscrizioni dell'antico cimetero ebraico a Venezia* (1936); S. Hock, *Die Familien Prags* (1892); M. Horovitz, *Die Inschriften des alten Friedhofs … Frankfurt a. M.* (1901); I.S. Emmanuel, *Maẓẓevot Saloniki* (1963–68); D.H. de Castro, *Keur van Grafsteenen …* (1883); M. Gruenwald, *Portugiesengraeber auf deutscher Erde* (1902); I.S. Emmanuel, *Precious Stones of the Jews of Curaçao* (1957); E.M. Shilstone, *Monumental Inscriptions in the Burial Ground of the Jewish Synagogue at Bridgetown, Barbados* (1956); J.A.P.M. Andrade, *A Record of the Jews in Jamaica* (1941); D. de Sola Pool, *Portraits Etched in Stone* (1952).

[Cecil Roth]

EPPENSTEIN, SIMON

EPPENSTEIN, SIMON (1864–1920), German rabbi and scholar. Eppenstein was born in Krotoszyn, Poland, and served as rabbi at Briesen (West Prussia) 1889–1911, and thereafter was lecturer in Jewish history and Bible exegesis at the Berlin Rabbinical Seminary. As an early supporter of religious Zionism (Mizrachi), he conducted some of his lectures at the Seminary in Hebrew.

Eppenstein's main fields of study were the geonic period, on which he wrote *Beitraege zur Geschichte und Literatur im geonaeischen Zeitalter* (1913), and medieval Bible exegesis, such as publishing *Astruc's Midrash ha-Torah* (1899), Joseph *Kara's commentaries on the Bible, as well as *Saadiah Gaon's introduction to his commentary on the Psalms (publ. in *Festschrift A. Harkavy*). He also made Hebrew translations of Joseph b. Judah ibn *Aknin's *Marpeh Nefashot* (in *Festschrift N. Sokolow*) and *Abraham b. Moses b. Maimon's *Kifāyat al-ʿĀbidin* (in *Festschrift J. Lewy*). Eppenstein also wrote a biography of Maimonides (for W. *Bacher's work on him), as well as one on his son Abraham (in *Jahres-Bericht des Rabbiner-Seminars zu Berlin fuer 1912/13*). He also edited and annotated the fourth edition of the fifth volume of *Graetz's *Geschichte der Juden* (1909) and the *Festschrift D. Hoffmann* (1914).

BIBLIOGRAPHY: X.N. Simchoni, in: *Ha-Tekufah*, 9 (1921), 488–90; A.B. Posner, in: *Festschrift… J. Freimann* (1937), 172–9 (incl. bibl.); E. Ben-Reshef, in: S. Federbush (ed.), *Ḥokhmat Yisrael be-Maʿarav Eiropah*, 1 (1958), 37–39; Kressel, *Leksikon*, 1 (1965), 134–5.

[Akiva Posner]

EPPLER, SANDOR

EPPLER, SANDOR (1890–1942), Hungarian communal worker. Eppler, the son of an Orthodox rabbi, was born in Budapest and despite his association with the Neolog movement maintained an Orthodox way of life. After completing his studies in a business academy, he entered the service of the Neolog community of Budapest and as a result of his outstanding organizational and administrative ability became its general secretary.

His abilities, however, found full scope following the anti-Jewish discrimination in Hungary, which began in 1938, and the consequent impoverishment of the Jews of the country. He undertook negotiations with the government and participated, initially as an observer, at the Evian Conference in 1938. He established contact with the Jewish welfare organizations of France and England, and in 1939 proceeded for that purpose – with Samuel Stern, chairman of the National Council of Hungarian Communities (Neolog) – to Paris and London, where he pleaded unsuccessfully with Lord Winterton, the chairman of the Inter-Government Commission for Refugees in London, to include Hungarian Jewry in Germany and Austria among those granted priority in emigration.

As a result Eppler devoted himself energetically to the problem of the rehabilitation of the Jews of Hungary, especially after the annexation to Hungary in 1939–40 of territory which had belonged to it before World War I and contained the largest Jewish population, and the arrival of Jewish refugees from Germany, Slovakia, and Poland. He established welfare organizations, educational and trade institutions, reopening schools which had been closed.

His greatest achievement was the Jewish Hospital which gave employment to Jewish doctors whose qualifications, received outside Hungary, were not recognized. In opposition to the leadership of the community he assisted in the *hakhsharah* of *ḥalutzim* who intended on immigrating to Ereẓ Israel.

Eppler published a number of works on social service: *A budapesti zsidóság szociális munkàja* ("Social Work of the Jews of Budapest," 1937); *A zsidóság helyzete, kulturàlis és szociàlis munkàja Europa tizenkét àllamàban* ("The Position of the Jews, Their Cultural and Social Activities in Twelve European Countries," 1938); *A rabbik szerepe a hitközségi ügyintézésben* ("The Function of Rabbis in Communal Activities," 1940); *Zsidó segitöszervezetek* ("Jewish Welfare Organizations," 1942).

Eppler died a natural death in 1942.

BIBLIOGRAPHY: P. Ujvari (ed.), *Magyar Zsidó Lexikon* (1929); B. Vihar (ed.), *Sàrga könyv* (1946); F. Karsai, in: *Evkonyv* (1971/72), 162–180.

[Baruch Yaron]

EPPSTEIN, PAUL

EPPSTEIN, PAUL (1901–1944), sociologist and German-Jewish community leader, "elder" of *Theresienstadt. Eppstein, born in Mannheim, was lecturer in sociology at the university there from 1926 until 1933. After the *Kristallnacht* pogrom of November 1938, he was invited to England as a sociology lecturer but refused to go. As a prominent Jewish youth leader, organizer, and speaker he was one of the founders of the Reichsausschus der juedischen Jugend-Verbaende (National Board of Jewish Youth Organizations) and of the

Reichsvertretung der deutschen Juden; he was the head of its welfare department, retaining the position when it became the Nazi-imposed *Reichsvereinigung, until his deportation to Theresienstadt in January 1943. Upon his arrival he was, on *Eichmann's orders, nominated "*Judenaeltester*" ("Jewish Elder") in place of Jacob *Edelstein. On September 27, 1944, he was arrested by the *Gestapo, apparently for having helped to organize clandestinely self-defense among the inmates, and immediately shot.

BIBLIOGRAPHY: J. Robinson, *And the Crooked Shall be Made Straight* (1965), index; H.G. Adler, *Theresienstadt, 1941–45* (Ger., 1960²); idem, *Die Verheimlichte Wahrheit* (1958); *Juedische Sozialarbeit*, 4 (1959), no. 3–4, 23–26 (*Gedenkblatt fuer Dr. Paul Eppstein*); S. Kaznelson (ed.), *Juden im deutschen Kulturbereich* (1959²), 693. **ADD. BIBLIOGRAPHY:** E. Meixner-Wülker, *Zwiespalt – Jugend zwischen* NS*-Erziehung und – Verfolgung* (1988); T. Simonsohn, *Errinnerungen an Paul Eppsteinin: Theresienstädter Studien und Dokumente* (1996), 127–29.

[Yehuda Reshef / Bjoern Siegel (2nd ed.)]

EPSTEIN, ABRAHAM (1841–1918), rabbinic scholar and historian. Epstein was born in Staro-Konstantinov, Russia, to a wealthy family. Epstein leased some land near Kozmin in 1865 and worked it himself for many years, trying to persuade some of the local Jewish poor to do the same. During that period he developed an interest in natural sciences and built a laboratory, where he carried out various experiments. After his father's death Epstein left his farm and took over the family business. In 1861 he traveled to Western Europe, where he met some of the leading figures in Jewish scholarship (S.J.L. *Rapoport, Z. *Frankel, and M. *Sachs) who greatly stimulated his interest in Jewish studies. Gradually, he liquidated his shares in the family business and devoted himself to research. In 1876 he settled in Vienna, where he pursued his studies and contributed articles to learned Hebrew periodicals. Among Epstein's Midrash and Targum studies are *Kadmut ha-Tanḥuma* (1886), on the antiquity and origin of *Midrash Tanḥuma*; and a critical edition of *Eldad ha-Dani* (1891) with a comprehensive introduction, notes, and appendices, including a note on *Beta Israel and their customs. On the Franco-German school he wrote "Der Gerschom Meor-ha-Golah zugeschriebene Talmud-Kommentar" (in *Festschrift ... Steinschneider* (1896), 115–43), an article which aroused much interest and revolutionized the study of pre-Rashi Talmud commentaries; *Schemaja, der Schueler und Sekretaer Raschis* (1897); a critical edition of *Ma'asei ha-Ge'onim* (1901), a collection of responsa of the Franco-German school; and *Das talmudische Lexikon Jechuse Tannaim we-Amoraim und Jehuda b. Kalonimos aus Speier* (1895). Epstein's historical studies on the same period include *Juedische Altertuemer in Worms und Speyer* (1896) and *Mishpaḥat Lurie* (1901). In the controversy between Rapoport and I. *Weiss, Epstein defended the former in *Divrei Bikkoret* (1896). Epstein's works manifest his vast knowledge and painstaking research: he combined the best of Eastern scholarship with Western method and is recognized as an outstanding scholar in his fields. A collection of some of his writings appeared under the title *Mi-Kadmoniyyot ha-Yehudim* (1887), of which the second volume of *Kitvei R. Avraham Epstein* (1950–57), edited by A.M. Habermann, is an enlarged version. An autobiographical sketch was published in N. Sokolow, *Sefer Zikkaron le-Sifrei Yisrael* (1889, 162–6), and is reproduced in *Kitvei R. Avraham Epstein* (1, 1950, 14–19). Epstein willed his large and valuable library to the Vienna Jewish Theological Seminary.

BIBLIOGRAPHY: V. Aptowitzer, in: AZDJ, 82 (1918), 246–7; S. Poznański, in: ZHB, 21 (1918), 18–25 (includes bibliography); idem, in: *Ost und West*, 18 (1918), 207–12; S. Federbush (ed.), *Ḥokhmat Yisrael be-Ma'arav Eiropah*, 1 (1958), 40–46; Kressel, Leksikon, 1 (1965), 136–7.

[Zvi Avneri]

EPSTEIN, ABRAHAM (1880–1952), Hebrew literary critic. Born in Slutsk, Russia, he started his teaching profession on the faculty of the Hebrew Teachers' Seminary in Odessa and taught later at the Herzliah Hebrew Teachers' Institute in New York City, where he settled in 1925.

Epstein's first creative works were published in *Ha-Ẓofeh*, but he began his career as a literary critic with an essay in *Ereẓ* (1918). Although he was impressionistic rather than analytical in his approach, Epstein was a sensitive and earnest critic. *Soferim* ("Writers," 1934), his first volume of criticism, deals mainly with non-American Hebrew authors but it also discusses four Hebrew writers in America: Yitẓhak Dov *Berkowitz, Benjamin *Silkiner, Shalom Dov Ber *Maximon, and Israel Zev Frishberg. *Mi-Karov u-me-Raḥok* ("From Near and Far," 1943) is devoted mostly to Hebrew literature in America, but included are also critical essays on other leading Hebrew writers. Some of the essays in the book are devoted to Yiddish literature in America and to the biblical books Song of Songs and Ruth. *Soferim Ivrim ba-Amerikah* (2 vols., 1952) is a critical work on the major Hebrew poets and novelists in the United States.

BIBLIOGRAPHY: *Hadoar*, 32 (1952), 128; Waxman, Literature 4 (1960²), 1076.

[Eisig Silberschlag]

EPSTEIN, ABRAHAM (1892–1942), U.S. economist and sociologist. Born in Russia, Epstein immigrated to the United States in 1910. He specialized in the problems of the aged and their economic maintenance, and became a leading advocate of publicly financed old age pensions. Through publications, research, legislative drafting, and political activity, Epstein was instrumental in preparing the ground for the 1935 Social Security Act, but remained critical of the principles adopted by the federal legislation and their implementation. In 1939, the federal government incorporated many of Epstein's recommendations through major amendments. In 1927 Epstein organized the American Association for Old Age Security which in 1933 became the American Association for Social Security. From 1934 to 1937 Epstein served as United States representative on the social insurance committee of the League of Nations' International Labor Office, and as a consultant for the Social Security Board. He also taught at Brooklyn College and New York University. Epstein's major publications include *The Negro Migrant in Pittsburgh* (1918), *The Problem of Old Age Pensions in Industry* (1926), *Facing Old Age* (1922), *The Challenge of the Aged* (1928), and *Insecurity, a Challenge to America* (1938).

[Roy Lubove]

EPSTEIN, ABRAHAM MEIR BEN ARYEH LEIB, also called **Meir Harif** ("sharpwitted"; 1726–1772), talmudist. Epstein was born in Grodno. He studied under his father, the kabbalist Aryeh Leib *Epstein, with whom he later also pursued halakhic studies. The results of their joint work appear in the talmudic glosses *Divrei Ḥiddud*. In 1750 he was appointed rabbi of Lyskovo, and in 1752 of Nowy-Mysz. In the dispute between *Eybeschuetz and *Emden on the use of amulets, Epstein, like his father, supported the former. He leaned toward *Ḥasidism and received Israel of Plotsk, a pupil of *Dov Baer of Mezhirech, with great respect. The added name Abraham was given to him during a serious illness in 1756. He was held in great esteem by his contemporaries and was frequently consulted on halakhic problems. He was the author of novellae to the Talmud and to Maimonides' *Mishneh Torah* (*Shevil Nahar, Divrei Yedidim, Mahadura Batra*); a collection of sermons, *Vikku'aḥ Ger ve-Toshav*; an ethical treatise in the form of a dialogue; responsa; glosses and novellae to the Shulḥan Arukh, *Yoreh De'ah*, together with contributions by his father. Some of his novellae are contained in the works of his contemporaries. His ethical will was published as an appendix to the *Gevurot ha-Ari* of Ephraim Mordecai Epstein (1888^2).

BIBLIOGRAPHY: Ephraim Mordecai Epstein, *Gevurot ha-Ari* (1888^2), 27–29; *Yahadut Lita*, 3 (1967), 30.

[Samuel Abba Horodezky]

EPSTEIN, ALVIN (1925–), U.S. actor. Born in the Bronx, New York, Epstein acted with a U.S. Army company in Europe after World War II, then joined the French Mime Theater and toured Europe. He joined the Habimah Theater, Israel, in 1953. He spent three years in Israel – the first one devoted to learning Hebrew. During the following two years he played 11 roles, gaining invaluable experience working with many well-trained actors who had come from the Moscow Art Theater School. He subsequently played in New York and on tour, his roles including Lucky in *Waiting for Godot*, Feste in *Twelfth Night*, the title role in Pirandello's *Henry IV*, Shabelsky in *Ivanov*, and Lee Strasberg in *Nobody Dies on Friday*.

Epstein served as artistic director of the Guthrie Theater and, for almost 25 years, he was the associate director of the Yale Repertory Theater. He also taught acting at the ART/MXAT Institute (Institute for Advanced Theater Training).

Epstein performed throughout the United States, staging over 20 productions and performing in over 100. His Broadway and off-Broadway credits include his debut with former fellow student Marcel *Marceau, as well as roles in Orson Welles' *King Lear*, *The Threepenny Opera* (co-starring with rock star Sting), the world premiere of *When the World Was Green* (*A Chef's Fable*), and *Tuesdays with Morrie*. For 20 years Epstein and Martha Schlamme performed *A Kurt Weill Cabaret* on tour in the U.S. and South America, with a year's run on Broadway.

Epstein reprised the role of Lucky in the 1961 TV movie version of *Waiting for Godot*. He also played in the TV series *The Doctors* (1981) and appeared in the TV movie *Doing Life* (1986). On the big screen, he had a role in *Never Met Picasso* (1996) and *Alma Mater* (2002). Epstein also lent his voice to the films *Everybody Rides the Carousel* (1975) and *Beauty and the Beast* (1991).

In 2004 he became involved with the Colleagues Theater Company in New York. Founded in 1996 by Catherine Wolf, its aim is to "identify and develop performance opportunities for the mature and seasoned actor and to provide training opportunities in theatrical craftsmanship for gifted high school graduates from underserved communities." Epstein appeared in the CTC's productions of *The Mad Woman of Chaillot; 24 Evenings of Wit and Wisdom;* and *Tasting Memories.*

[Ruth Beloff (2nd ed.)]

EPSTEIN, ARYEH LEIB BEN MORDECAI (1705–1775), rabbi and kabbalist. Epstein was born in Grodno and was a pupil of Isaac of Grodno, Poland, and Aryeh Leib b. Nathan of Slutsk. After a brief period as a merchant he took up the position of preacher in Grodno and in 1741 became rabbi in Berestovitsa and Golynka. In 1745 he went to Koenigsberg, where he developed an extensive educational system. He sided with Jonathan *Eybeschuetz in the latter's dispute with Jacob *Emden, sharply criticizing the bickering in rabbinical circles. Two inquiries which he sent to Eybeschuetz in 1758 are extant, the one dealing with a halakhic matter, the other with the liturgy. Epstein was responsible for the introduction of a number of important *takkanot* in the Koenigsberg community and also for the establishment of the Great Synagogue there.

His works include *Or ha-Shanim*, on the 613 commandments (Frankfurt on the Oder, 1754); *Sefer ha-Pardes*, consisting of novellae to tractate *Shabbat*; sermons; funeral orations; a treatise on positive and negative commandments called *Yalkut Sakhar va-Onesh*, with an appendix entitled *Kunteres ha-Re'ayot* on Shulḥan Arukh, *Oraḥ Ḥayyim* (Koenigsberg, 1764); and *Mishnat Gur-Aryeh*, a commentary on Isaac *Luria's prayer book (published in part only, Koenigsberg, 1765). He also published his responsa under the title *Teshuvot Maharal* (Morenu ha-Rav R. Aryeh Leib; *ibid.*, 1769); wrote glosses to the Talmud (together with his son Abraham Meir); glosses and novellae to Shulḥan Arukh, *Yoreh De'ah*, to which his son also contributed (Vilna, 1883); and several other works.

BIBLIOGRAPHY: J. Emden, *Mitpaḥat Sefarim* (Lemberg, 1870), 119; D. Kahana, *Toledot ha-Shabbeta'im ve-ha-Ḥasidim*, 2 (1914), 57; S.A. Friedenstein, *Ir Gibborim* (1880), 41, 44ff., 47–50; E.M. Epstein, *Gevurot ha-Ari* (1888^2); H.N. Maggid (Steinschneider), *Ir Vilna* (1900), 44; *Sefer Yahadut Lita*, 3 (1967), 30.

[Samuel Abba Horodezky]

EPSTEIN, BARUCH HA-LEVI (1860–1942), Russian talmudic scholar. Born in Bobruisk, Epstein received his early education from his father, R. Jehiel Michal *Epstein, author of *Arukh ha-Shulḥan*. In his youth he distinguished himself by his unusual diligence and his phenomenal memory. He continued his studies under his uncle, Naphtali Ẓevi Judah *Berlin, who, recognizing his outstanding abilities, devoted special attention to him. Berlin later married Baruch's sister. Epstein declined offers to occupy rabbinical positions in such great communities as Pinsk, Moscow, and Petrograd, preferring to work in a bank and to devote all his spare time to his studies. His correspondence with many leading scholars brought him wide recognition. Epstein is best known for his *Torah Temimah*, a compilation of quotations from the oral law arranged according to the scriptural verses to which they refer and annotated by a brilliant commentary which attests to his vast and profound knowledge of Talmud.

BIBLIOGRAPHY: B. Epstein, *Mekor Barukh* (1928); H. Seidman, *Elleh Ezkerah*, 1 (1956), 142–9; *Sefer Yahadut Lita*, 1 (1959), 293, no. 5; 3 (1967), 31, under his father's name; A.Z. Tarshish, *R. Barukh ha-Levi Epstein* (1967).

[Mordechai Hacohen]

EPSTEIN, BRIAN SAMUEL (Shmuel; 1934–1967), British impresario, one of history's most successful show business entrepreneurs whose success in managing the Beatles changed the world of music. Epstein was born on Yom Kippur to Harry (Tzvi) and Malka ("Queenie") in Liverpool, where the family owned a furniture store and where Epstein became manager of the store's record department. When his father opened an NEMS music store on Whitechapel Street, Brian was put in charge, becoming fully engrossed in the world of music and writing a music column for *Mersey Beat* beginning August 3, 1961. The store was down the street and around the corner from a basement nightclub called The Cavern, and it was there on November 9, 1961, that Epstein first met and saw the Beatles perform. Three weeks later he approached John Lennon and offered to become the Beatles' manager. Paul McCartney's father – who had once bought a piano at the Epstein furniture store – immediately approved, telling Paul that Epstein would make a good manager. "He thought Jewish people were very good with money," McCartney said years later. "That was the common wisdom. He thought Brian would be very good for us.... And he was right.... If anyone was the fifth Beatle, it was Brian."

Epstein immediately changed the Beatles' appearance from their unpolished, jeans and leather-jacket greaser look to one of neatly tailored matching suits; and he ordered them not to eat, smoke, or swear on stage and to bow to the audience after each number. After getting rejected by all the major British record companies, Epstein landed the Beatles a recording contract in June 1962 with EMI's smallest labels, Parlophone, headed by Sir George Martin. Drummer Pete Best was fired and replaced by Ringo Starr, and the elements for success were now in place. Indeed, in little more than a year under Epstein's direction, the Beatles began enjoying the greatest success that any popular artists had ever achieved.

Epstein's homosexuality, and his alleged infatuation with Lennon, were the subject of many articles and books. It was extensively rumored that in the Beatles' song "Baby You're A Rich Man," Lennon sang "Baby you're a rich fag Jew" as a slur against Epstein. The audible ambiguity of the recording fueled the rumor into a worldwide urban legend, though it was never authoritatively confirmed.

Epstein died of a drug overdose, likely from some sort of sleeping pills, at age 32. Once he died the Beatles became embroiled in a tangle of conflicts, money squabbles, and personal jealousies, and their business affairs began to unravel. Within three more years the group disbanded.

In addition to managing the Beatles, Epstein also managed Gerry & the Pacemakers, Billy J. Kramer & The Dakotas, The Fourmost, and Cilla Black. He wrote an autobiography, *A Cellarful of Noise* (1964).

[Elli Wohlgelernter (2nd ed.)]

EPSTEIN, CHAIM FISCHEL (1874–1942), Orthodox rabbi. Born in Taurogen, Lithuania, Epstein was recognized for his brilliance at an early age. After studying Talmud at the famed Telshe Yeshiva, Epstein wrote his first book, *Ḥinukh le-Na'ar* (a commentary on Aaron Ha-Levi's *Sefer ha-Ḥinukh*), at age 16. That same year, he entered the Volozhin yeshivah, studying under its famed leaders, Rabbi Naphtali Ẓevi Judah *Berlin and Rabbi Ḥayyim *Soloveitchik. At only 18 years of age, Epstein was ordained as a rabbi by Rabbi Soloveitchik and Rabbi Shelomo Cohen of Vilna.

Notably, Epstein also studied secular subjects, which many other Orthodox rabbis of his time did not, earning the equivalent of a high school diploma at a gymnasium in Shedlitz. Epstein also displayed an energetic interest in the fledgling Zionist movement. He wrote poetry about the Land of Israel, was affiliated with the *Ḥibbat Zion movement, and attended a Zionist conference in Minsk in 1902. Eventually, he became a founder of the Mizrachi movement of religious Zionists, and continued to endorse Zionism after immigrating to the U.S.

At age 24 Epstein began a series of rabbinical positions, including Grosowa (near Minsk) and Sainee, where he remained until the outbreak of World War I. Toward the end of the war, Epstein was named chief rabbi of an Estonian Jewish region. During this time, Epstein completed a Ph.D. degree and taught Jewish philosophy at the local university.

Epstein declined invitations to serve congregations in London and Liverpool, instead immigrating to the U.S. in 1923. He served many communities, including in Bayonne, New Jersey; Cleveland; Cincinnati; and Brooklyn. Like many of his colleagues from Eastern Europe, he faced resistance from more liberal lay leaders and congregants regarding standards of Jewish practice, particularly *kashrut*. Yet Epstein's reputation as a scholar assured that many rabbinical colleagues and lay leaders came to him to adjudicate matters of Jewish law.

In 1923, he served as a rabbinical judge in a *kashrut* dispute between two prominent Canadian rabbis. Epstein wrote several volumes of highly regarded responsa, including *Teshuvah Shelemah*. A second volume addressing matters of American concern was published in 1940 in the U.S.

Epstein lived his later years in St. Louis, serving as chief rabbi of the United Orthodox community and head of the city's newly established Va'ad ha-Ir. He remained the leading Orthodox rabbi in St. Louis until his death.

BIBLIOGRAPHY: M. Sherman, *Orthodox Judaism in America* (1996).

[Michael Berenbaum (2nd ed.)]

EPSTEIN, CHARLOTTE (1884–1938), U.S. swimmer and champion of U.S. women's participation in the Olympic Games; known as the "Mother of Women's Swimming in America." The daughter of Moritz H. and Sara Epstein, Charlotte was born in New York City and educated at the Ethical Culture School. She became a court stenographer. Epstein, who enjoyed swimming competitively, joined the recently formed National Women's Life-Saving League in 1911; in 1913, she served as chair of the Athletic Branch of the National Women's Life-Saving League in which role she and colleagues campaigned to reform gender constraints in aquatic sports and to convince the Amateur Athletic Union (AAU) to allow women to compete in Olympic aquatic events.

In October 1917 Epstein founded the New York City Women's Swimming Association (WSA), a non-profit club, to advance the sport of women's swimming. "Eppie," as she was known, launched the swimming careers of many American and Olympic swimming champions when she became team manager of WSA, chairman of its Sports Committee and, in 1929, president. She successfully battled the U.S. Olympic Committee to enable American female swimmers and divers to compete in the 1920 Olympics in Antwerp, Belgium, the first time women participated in aquatic Olympic events. As U.S. Olympic Women's Swimming Team Manager in 1920, 1924, and 1932, Epstein's WSA members won Olympic championships and set numerous world records. Epstein served as chair of the national AAU women's swimming committee.

Eppie worked with Jewish organizations with suitable swimming pools. The WSA team of Olympians swam at the Young Women's Hebrew Association of New York for national championship meets in the 1920s. In 1935 Epstein served as chair of the Swimming Committee of the Second Maccabiah Games where WSA swimmer Janice Lifson triumphed. In 1936 Epstein refused to attend the Berlin Olympic Games and withdrew from the American Olympic Committee in protest at U.S. participation in the "Nazi Olympics." Epstein's major influence on swimming continued until her death. She was inducted into the International Swimming Hall of Fame and the International Jewish Sport Hall of Fame.

BIBLIOGRAPHY: L.J. Borish, "'The Cradle of American Champions, Women Champions … Swim Champions': Charlotte Epstein, Gender and Jewish Identity, and the Physical Emancipation of Women in Aquatic Sports," in: *The International Journal of the History of Sport*, 21 (March 2004), 197–235; idem, "Epstein, Charlotte," in: P.E. Hyman and D. Dash Moore, *Jewish Women in America: An Historical Encyclopedia*, vol. 1 (1997), 380–82.

[Linda J. Borish (2nd ed.)]

EPSTEIN, CLAIRE (1911–2000), Israeli archaeologist, expert on the Chalcolithic culture of the Golan Heights. Born in London, Epstein was the only daughter and oldest of three children of German immigrants, Olga and Mortimer Epstein. Educated at the University of London in English and Italian literature, Epstein became active in Zionist circles, studying Hebrew and helping to found the local branch of the Habonim youth movement. She also translated material from Hebrew for the Peel Commission. In 1937 Epstein immigrated to British Mandate Palestine, settling in Tel Aviv where she worked as liaison to the Mandate Government until 1942. Answering a call to help with the war effort, she joined the Women's Corps of the British army, serving four and a half years in Egypt. Shortly after returning to Tel Aviv, Epstein became a member of the newly established kibbutz En Gev on the S.E. shore of the Sea of Galilee. In 1955 Epstein joined kibbutz Ginnosar and remained one of its members for the rest of her life. Epstein's first digging experience was as a field supervisor on the Tel Hazor under the direction of Yigael Yadin. It was only at the age of 50 that Epstein embarked on her formal studies at the Institute of Archaeology of University College, London, eventually earning her Ph.D. under Kathleen Kenyon in 1962 on the subject of "Palestinian Bichrome" pottery. As a full-time archaeologist, working for the Israel Department of Antiquities (later the Israel Antiquities Authority), Epstein conducted numerous surveys and excavations in Israel, notably the Golan emergency archaeological survey in 1967. Subsequently Epstein excavated numerous Chalcolithic sites on the Golan Heights, and the results of her work were eventually published in a monograph titled *The Chalcolithic Culture of the Golan* (1998). Epstein was the author of numerous articles on the late prehistory of Israel, including excavation reports, and research papers, one of which was on her interpretation of the stratigraphy of the sacred area at Megiddo. Epstein was the recipient of numerous prizes: the Percy Schimmel Award, the prestigious Israel Prize, and the Irene Levy-Sala Award.

BIBLIOGRAPHY: "Obituaries: Claire Epstein (1911–2000)," in: *Bulletin of the Anglo-Israel Archaeological Society*, 18 (2000), 111–14.

[Eliot Braun (2nd ed.)]

EPSTEIN, GILBERT (1927–), U.S. Conservative rabbi. Epstein was born in New York City, educated at Yeshiva University (1948), and then moved to the Jewish Theological Seminary, where he was ordained in 1952. He then served in congregations in the New York suburbs of Woodmere (1952–55) and Hewlitt (1955–61) before moving to the Conservative synagogue on Fifth Avenue. He was among the first to lead teen tours to Israel and was the first director of Kefar Silver's summer camp in Israel (1962–64).

In 1965 Epstein joined the *Rabbinical Assembly and headed its Joint Commission on Rabbinic Placement, the very sensitive job and highly political position of matching rabbis with congregations, thus enabling young rabbis to advance, successful rabbis to move to larger and ever larger congregations, and those whose careers have been difficult to find additional employment. It was a position that he handled with grace and tact. His task was to deal with rabbis and congregations in times of crisis and transition. During the years of major growth of the Conservative movement, the job was exceedingly demanding because there were so many positions to fill. As the rate of expansion declined and the need for rabbis settled down, his work became difficult in a different sense as he had to redirect rabbis to positions where they could succeed. He helped Wolfe *Kelman and represented the Conservative Rabbinate in many national organizations including the National Conference of Soviet Jewry, the New York Board of Rabbis, and the Conference of Presidents of Major American Jewish Organizations.

[Michael Berenbaum (2nd ed.)]

EPSTEIN, HARRY H. (1903–2003), U.S. rabbi. Epstein was born in Plunge, Lithuania, and raised in New York and especially Chicago. He attended the Rabbi Isaac Elchanan Theological Seminary, where Bernard *Revel became a mentor. Epstein continued his education at the famed Slobodka Yeshivah and its branch in Hebron, Palestine, both of which were headed by his uncle, Moses Mordecai *Epstein. He obtained traditional *semikhah* (ordination) from three rabbis, including Abraham Isaac *Kook, later the first Ashkenazi chief rabbi of Israel. He also obtained B.Ph. and M.A. degrees from Emory University, a Ph.D. from the School of Law of the University of Illinois, and a D.D. (honorus causa) from the Jewish Theological Seminary.

Epstein's was a surprisingly eclectic education given the dominant influence of his traditionalist father, Ephraim, an Orthodox rabbi who helped launch what became Chicago's Hebrew Theological College. The Slobodka Yeshivah was noted for the **Musar* approach, which fostered modern Jewish character through piety and faith alongside talmudic study. RIETS provided American Orthodox training but the remainder of his education, including public school in Chicago, was secular. His background prepared him well for an evolving East European-American Judaism and rabbinical career.

After a year filling a pulpit at Tulsa's B'nai Emunah, Revel's father-in-law's congregation, where Epstein advised oil-rich members on philanthropy, in 1928 he became the rabbi at Ahavath Achim, the more affluent of Atlanta's four Orthodox synagogues. Fluent in Yiddish and English, and mixing learned Talmud classes for the old guard with early Friday night services for their acculturating children, Epstein offered a trans-generational, gradual accommodation to middle-class Jewish life in America by becoming an exemplar of the Modern Orthodoxy championed by Joseph *Lookstein and Leo *Jung during the interwar years. Traditional observance was coupled with modern education in a synagogue-center environment hosting a variety of activities. Epstein, who lost a brother in the 1929 Hebron massacre, also led his congregation as an ardent Zionist. He headed regional Zionist efforts, participated in national conferences during World War II to aid European Jewry, co-chaired Atlanta Jewish Federation campaigns with Reform Rabbi Jacob Rothschild after the war, and served as a model for modern, traditional rabbis throughout the South. Following national trends he drew his congregation into the Conservative fold in 1954, something he later regretted when his successor, Arnold Goodman, allowed women to read from the Torah and he realized that Orthodoxy could have survived.

Epstein wrote *Judaism and Progress: Sermons and Addresses* (1934).

BIBLIOGRAPHY: M.K. Bauman, *Harry H. Epstein and the Rabbinate as Conduit for Change* (1994); K.W. Stein, *A History of Ahavath Achim Synagogue, 1887–1987* (1987).

[Mark K. Bauman (2nd ed.)]

EPSTEIN, ISAAC BEN MORDECAI (c. 1780–1857), talmudist and kabbalist. Epstein, who had already written halakhic works in his youth, attached himself against the will of his grandfather to *Chabad Ḥasidism, and thenceforth devoted himself to the study of Kabbalah and Chabad teaching, burning his previous halakhic writings. He felt that only *Shneur Zalman of Lyady, whose favorite pupil he became, was capable of revealing the innermost secrets of the divine Law. Epstein served as rabbi of Gomel. In his old age he himself made his debut as a *ẓaddik*. In the handling of halakhic problems he took pains to write in an unpretentious and clear style. He left ten studies on Chabad teaching including *Ma'amar ha-Shiflut ve-ha-Simḥah* (1864) and *Ma'amar Yeẓi'at Miẓrayim* (1877); the others are in manuscript. He also wrote homilies for the weekly portions of the Law and the festivals, some of which were published with his *Ma'amar Yeẓi'at Miẓrayim*.

BIBLIOGRAPHY: Bermann, in: *Keneset ha-Gedolah*, ed. by S. Suwalski, 1 pt. 3 (1890), 18–22; I. Heilmann, *Beit-Rabbi*, 1 (1965, photogr. reprint of 1902), 136, 165–6, 174–5.

[Samuel Abba Horodezky]

EPSTEIN, ISIDORE (1894–1962), English rabbi and scholar. Epstein was born in Kovno, Lithuania, and immigrated with his parents first to France and then in 1911 to England. He later studied in Hungarian yeshivot, particularly at Pressburg, and at London University until 1926. From 1921 to 1928 he served as rabbi in Middlesborough. In 1928 Epstein began teaching Semitics at Jews' College where he was also librarian; in 1945 he became director of studies; and in 1948, principal. Epstein expanded the activities of Jews' College by introducing a *ḥazzanut* department, a rabbinical diploma class, and an institute for training teachers.

Epstein's first publications were in history as reflected in responsa: *Responsa of Rabbi Solomon b. Adreth of Barcelona (1235–1310) as a Source of the History of Spain* (1925) and *The*

Responsa of Rabbi Simon b. Zemah Duran as a Source of the History of the Jews in North Africa (1930); they were published together in their second editions as *Studies in the Communal Life of the Jews of Spain, as Reflected in the Responsa of Rabbi Solomon ben Adreth and Rabbi Simeon ben Zemach Duran* (1968). His *Faith of Judaism* (1954) is an important theological statement of the Orthodox position in the light of modern philosophy and science. While this work addressed itself chiefly to the believing Jew, Epstein's *Judaism* (1954), "a historical presentation," spoke to the non-Jewish world. Epstein contributed the article on Judaism to the *Encyclopaedia Britannica* (from the 1958 edition onward). He was the first Jewish scholar to be given this assignment and the first to present Judaism in its entirety, not merely as a forerunner of Christianity. Articles on Jewish subjects in *Chambers' Encyclopedia*, too, were either written or edited by him (1950 and subsequent editions). Epstein's major achievement in Jewish scholarship was supervising the English translation of the Babylonian Talmud (Soncino, 35 vols., 1935–52; 18 vols., 1961). This monumental work made the Talmud accessible to the English-speaking world. Epstein also edited *Moses Maimonides, 1135–1204; Anglo-Jewish Papers in Connection with the Eighth Century of His Birth* (1935) and coedited *Essays in Honor of the Very Rev. Dr. J.H. Hertz* (1943); he had assisted *Hertz with many of his publications. Apart from contributions to learned periodicals and Festschriften, Epstein also published a variety of theological and historical studies for educational purposes. As a scholar, writer, and educator, Epstein played a significant role in modern Anglo-Jewish scholarship.

BIBLIOGRAPHY: H. Zeidman, in: S. Federbush (ed.), *Ḥokhmat Yisrael be-Eiropah* (1965), 18–26; C. Roth and R.P. Lehman, in: JHSET, 21 (1968), 327–36.

[Hirsch Jacob Zimmels]

EPSTEIN, IZHAC (1862–1943), Hebrew writer and linguist, and a pioneer in modern Hebrew education in Ereẓ Israel and in the Diaspora. The brother of the writer Zalman *Epstein, he was born in Luban, Belorussia. In 1886 he (together with five others) was sent to Palestine for training in agricultural colonies at the expense of Baron Edmond de Rothschild. After working for four years in Zikhron Ya'akov and Rosh Pinnah, he became a teacher. In 1891 he was appointed principal of a public school which had just been opened in Safed and later taught in public schools in Metullah and Rosh Pinnah. He studied at the University of Lausanne from 1902 to 1908 and directed the Alliance school in Salonika from 1908 to 1915. Influenced by the psychophysiological school of T.A. Ribot, Epstein pioneered in the new method (the "natural" method) of teaching Hebrew. According to this system explanations are made only in the language that is being taught. Epstein expounded the new method in *"Ivrit be-Ivrit"* (*Ha-Shilo'aḥ*, 4 (1898), 385–96), which was later published as an introduction to his textbook of that name in 1900. The work had a fundamental influence on Hebrew teaching. The subject was also treated by Epstein in his doctoral thesis "La Pensée et la Polyglossie" (1915). In *"She'elah Ne'lamah"* ("The Obscure Question," *Ha-Shilo'aḥ*, 17 (1907), 193–206), he discussed Jewish-Arab relationships in Ereẓ Israel and urged Zionists to adopt a more compromising attitude.

After World War I, Epstein returned to Ereẓ Israel where he served for a short time as principal of the Lewinsky Teachers' Seminary in Jaffa and then as supervisor of the schools under the auspices of the Zionist movement. Upon resigning from his official duties, he devoted himself to the study of Hebrew linguistics, concentrating especially on problems of phonetics. He coined many new words and phrases, particularly in pedagogy and psychology. Among his other books are *Hegyonei Lashon* (1947) and *Meḥkarim ba-Psikhologyah shel ha-Lashon ve-ha-Ḥinnukh ha-Ivri* (1947).

BIBLIOGRAPHY: "Yiẓḥak Epstein," in: *Sifriyyat Rishonim*, 8:1, 1943; *Tidhar*, 2 (1947), 822f.

EPSTEIN, SIR JACOB (1880–1959), English sculptor, considered one of the greatest sculptors of the 20th century, and probably the most famous Anglo-Jewish artist of his time. He was born on New York's Lower East Side into a family of Polish Jewish immigrants and studied at the Art Students League. His first assignment came from the non-Jewish writer, Hutchins Hapgood, who asked him to illustrate a book about the Jewish quarter of New York, *The Spirit of the Ghetto* (1902, reissued 1967). He used the fee to go to Paris, where he studied at the Ecole des Beaux-Arts. In 1905 he went to London, which became his home for the rest of his life; he was naturalized in 1910. In 1907 he was commissioned to decorate the facade of the British Medical Association in the Strand. His series of 18 figures, *The Birth of Energy*, shocked the British public because he had refused to disguise sexual characteristics, and because one figure was of a woman in advanced pregnancy. The nationwide protest made him famous. Epstein remained the subject of heated moral and aesthetic criticism almost to the end of his career.

Epstein was an admirer of the prehistoric carvers, the archaic Greek sculptors, the African, Polynesian, and pre-Columbian image-makers. In creating his works he drew on his vast knowledge of the sculpture of all places and periods, yet always retained the powerful imprint of his own style. His style passed through several successive phases. *The Birth of Energy* was executed in a naturalistic classical tradition. *The Tomb of Oscar Wilde in Paris* (1912) is in a very different style. It consists of a strange figure with a human face and swept-back wings reminiscent of the hieratic winged bulls of Assyrian sculpture. The face is surmounted by a crown decorated with representations of the Seven Deadly Sins.

Epstein's only abstract sculptures were executed during the years 1913–15. *Rock Drill* (1913) is a sculpture romanticizing the power of the machine; *Venus I* and *Venus II* are also experiments in abstraction. In later years Epstein felt that abstract sculpture was of no value in itself, but that it had helped him to develop his sense of form.

In the monumental works executed after World War I, Epstein aroused hostile criticism by his expressionist distortion of form and by his treatment of sacred themes in a deliberately crude and primitive style. By this means he endeavored to express elemental forces. *Genesis* (1931) is the solid, heavy figure of a pregnant woman with a brooding head like an African mask. The dynamic, advancing figure of *Adam* (1939) is even more "primitive." *Jacob and the Angel* (1941) is more naturalistic. His sculptures on Christian themes also gave rise to controversy owing to his unorthodox treatment of traditional subjects. In his day Epstein was probably the most controversial artist in Britain, arousing fierce hostility, often laced with overt or covert antisemitism, from conservatives, but also great praise from many experts.

Throughout his life Epstein cast portraits in bronze, and many critics believe that as a portraitist he was second only to Rodin. Executed in a naturalistic, renaissance style, these works aimed at expressing the personality rather than the mere physical features of the sitter. Characteristic of these bronzes is the pitting and furrowing of the surface to suggest the clay from which they were cast. Among the many eminent figures Epstein portrayed were Albert Einstein, Chaim Weizmann, and Yehudi Menuhin. He was also an excellent draftsman; his drawings included illustrations of the Old Testament, and a series inspired by Baudelaire's *Les Fleurs du Mal.*

By the end of World War II Epstein had become acceptable to the British art establishment, and in 1954 he was knighted. Although he had no organizational links with Judaism, he always recalled with great warmth his origins in the New York ghetto, and never lost his broad Lower East Side accent. He said in his memoirs (*Let there be Sculpture*, 1942): "I imagine that the feeling I have for expressing a human point of view, giving human rather than abstract implications to my work, comes from these early formative years." In his late period, Epstein executed a number of religious works. These are in a sense more conservative than his earlier works and though elements of abstraction and distortion still exist they are no longer so dominant. They include *Lazarus* in the chapel of New College, Oxford (1947), the *Madonna and Child* in Cavendish Square, London (1953), the *Christ in Majesty* (1957) at Llandaff Cathedral, and the *St. Michael and the Devil* (1959) at Coventry. After his death, 105 of his clay models were donated to the Israel Museum, Jerusalem, by Lady Epstein. He wrote an autobiography, *Let There Be Sculpture* (1940), which he published in revised form in 1955 as *Epstein: An Autobiography.*

BIBLIOGRAPHY: R. Buckle, *Jacob Epstein, Sculptor* (1963). **ADD. BIBLIOGRAPHY:** ODNB online; S. Gardiner, *Epstein: Artist Against the Establishment* (1992); J. Rose, *Daemons and Angels: A Life of Jacob Epstein* (2002).

[Alfred Werner]

EPSTEIN, JACOB NAHUM (1878–1952), Talmud scholar. Born in Brest-Litovsk, Epstein studied at home with his father, at the Mir yeshivah, and at the universities in Vienna and Berne, receiving his doctorate from the latter. In 1923 he became lecturer at the Hochschule fuer die Wissenschaft des Judentums in Berlin and in 1925 professor of talmudic philology at the newly founded Hebrew University. He formulated the basis for a new approach to talmudic studies in which he trained generations of scholars, and such outstanding individuals as S. Lieberman, G. Alon, S. Abramson, M. Margaliot, and E.Z. Melammed. On the occasion of his 70th birthday, pupils and fellow scholars presented him with a jubilee volume. Early in his career Epstein devoted studies to books of the Bible and the Elephantine papyri, but the major portion of his life's work was dedicated to rabbinical literature, particularly to the Mishnah text about which he wrote *Mavo le-Nusaḥ ha-Mishnah* (2 vols., 1948). This work is considered to be the most authoritative study of the original text of the Mishnah. The author displays great erudition and critical acumen in attempting to establish the correct version of the Mishnah and its development. He clarifies many difficult passages in the Mishnah and the Talmudim. Two works were published posthumously, edited by E.Z. Melammed: *Mevo'ot le-Sifrut ha-Tanna'im* (1957, containing an introduction to the Mishnah and Tosefta, introductions to the 18 *masekhtot* of the Mishnah, and an introduction to halakhic Midrashim) and *Mevo'ot le-Sifrut ha-Amora'im* (1962, including introductions to nine tractates of the Babylonian Talmud, an introduction to the Jerusalem Talmud, and alternate versions of the latter, down to the end of tractate *Shabbat*). These works, together with the preliminary studies such as *Dikduk Aramit Bavlit* ("Babylonian Aramaic Grammar," ed. by E.Z. Melammed, 1960), were actually preparatory to a critical edition of the Mishnah text, which unfortunately remained an unfulfilled dream. Epstein was also concerned with establishing a correct version of the Jerusalem Talmud, a problem connected with the relationship between the *editio princeps* and the Leiden manuscript. He also initiated the ambitious plan of translating the Babylonian Talmud into Hebrew, accompanied by variant texts and a short commentary. Three tractates (*Bava Kamma, Bava Meẓia*, and *Bava Batra*) were published (1952–60).

It was natural that other early rabbinic texts should similarly engage Epstein's attention. He defined the Tosefta to be a supplement to the Mishnah recording older materials, omitting controversies and traditions, and commenting on established (Mishnah) texts. He also wrote studies on the halakhic Midrashim and prepared a new edition of the *Mekhilta de-R. Simeon ben Yoḥai* (ed. by E.Z. Melammed, 1955) which, in addition to being reconstructed from materials embodied in such other works as D. Hoffmann's edition of 1905, used fragments of this lost Midrash found in the Cairo *Genizah.*

In the field of geonic literature, Epstein edited the geonic commentary to the sixth order of the Mishnah (*Tohorot*, 1921–24; supplement, 1945), the introduction to which had studies on the **She'iltot* of R. Aḥa Gaon. He devoted other studies to such medieval talmudic commentators as Rashi and his son-in-law and pupil, the early tosafist, Judah b. Nathan; Elijah b. Menahem of London; Yom Tov b. Abraham and others. His contribution to the modern study of rabbinical literature was of far-reaching importance. Epstein's essays and reviews appeared in many learned periodicals, and he was cofounder and coeditor of the quarterly *Devir* (1923–24), and edited the first 23 volumes of the quarterly *Tarbiz* (1930–52). He was an active member of the Vaad ha-Lashon and presided over several of its committees.

BIBLIOGRAPHY: *Sefer ha-Yovel... J.N. Epstein* (= *Tarbiz*, 20, 1950); S. Abramson, *J.N. Epstein, Reshimah Bibliografit ... ve-Toledot Ḥayyav* (1942); M. Schwabe, et al., *Le-Zikhro shel J.N. Epstein* (1952); Loewinger, in: S. Federbush (ed.), *Ḥokhmat Yisra'el be-Ma'arav Eiropah*, 2 (1963), 49ff.

EPSTEIN, JEAN (1897–1953), French director. Epstein was born in Warsaw but lived and worked in France. As a young man the experimental cinema attracted him, and he directed his first film, *Pasteur*, when he was 25, thereafter working largely in the realistic mode, using outdoor settings and everyday scenes in such films as *La Belle Nivernaise* and *Finis Terrae* (1928), a documentary-style tale of Bannec island fishermen. In *La Chute de la Maison Usher* (1928) he created notable indoor atmospheric effects as well, introducing the use of slow motion. One of his last films was *Les Feux de la Mer* (1948). His sister MARIE EPSTEIN (1899–1995) worked with him and also with Jean Benoît-Lévy, writing the screenplay for and sharing direction of the classic *La Maternelle* (1933) with Benoît-Lévy.

EPSTEIN, JEHIEL MICHAL BEN AARON ISAAC HALEVI (1829–1908), rabbi and halakhic authority. Epstein was born in Bobruisk, Belorussia. He studied in Volozhin under R. Isaac of Volozhin from 1842. At first unwilling to enter the rabbinate, he was persuaded to do so by the rabbi of his native town, R. Elijah Goldberg, who formally ordained him, and c. 1862 he was appointed to his first rabbinate in Novosybkov where there were many *Chabad Ḥasidim. During that period he visited R. Menahem Mendel of Lyubavich, author of *Ẓemaḥ Ẓedek*, from whom he also received *semikhah*. In 1874 he was appointed rabbi of Novogrudok, Belorussia, where he remained until his death.

Epstein's fame rests upon his *Arukh ha-Shulḥan*, consisting of novellae and halakhic rulings on the four parts of the Shulḥan Arukh: *Oraḥ Ḥayyim* (1903–07), *Yoreh De'ah* (1894–98), *Even ha-Ezer* (1905–06), and *Ḥoshen Mishpat* (1884–93). In the introduction to the volume on *Ḥoshen Mishpat*, Epstein explains that just as Maimonides saw the need to compose the *Mishneh Torah* and Joseph Caro the Shulḥan Arukh, in order to codify the halakhah in their times, there was now a need to bring the Shulḥan Arukh up to date by giving the halakhic rulings which had been promulgated by authorities subsequent to Caro, both in works devoted to that purpose and in responsa. He said that "great anxiety and confusion" had resulted from those new rulings and his work was intended to give the final halakhic summation up to his day. Although in its external arrangement the work follows the chapters of the Shulḥan Arukh, in its internal arrangements he conforms to that of the *Mishneh Torah* of Maimonides. According to Epstein the principal aim of the study of Torah is not dialectical and casuistic exercise, the "uprooting of mountains"; but to arrive at a definite knowledge of the *halakhah*. He showed a marked tendency toward leniency in his rulings, and he gave expression to this tendency in a statement to Rabbi J.L. *Maimon who obtained *semikhah* from him. "When any problem in connection with the prohibitions of the Torah comes before you, you must first presume it is permitted, and only after you have carefully studied the *rishonim* and can find no possibility of leniency are you obliged to rule that it is forbidden" (Maimon, *Sarei ha-Me'ah*, p. 112).

The *Arukh ha-Shulḥan* has become an authoritative work. Like the Shulḥan Arukh on which it is based, it deals only with the laws which have a practical importance. After Epstein completed it, however, he undertook the writing of additional works dealing with such laws as are not applicable at the present time, to which he gave the suggestive title *Arukh ha-Shulḥan le-Atid* ("Arukh ha-Shulḥan for the Future"), which were published posthumously. They deal with agricultural laws (*Zera'im*, 3 pts., 1938–46); *Sanhedrin, Mamrim, Melakhim, Shekalim*, and *Kiddush ha-Ḥodesh* (1962); and *Kodashim* (1969). In them he takes especial care to indicate his sources, tracing the development of each law from its first source to its latest form. His son Baruch *Epstein gives an attractive picture of the manner in which his father would encourage candidates to the rabbinate. He would exhort them always to consider the pros and cons before giving a halakhic decision, and to show every consideration to the person putting the problem, so as not to confuse him.

Among his other works are *Or la-Yesharim* (1869), a commentary on the *Sefer ha-Yashar* of Jacob *Tam in which he defends Tam against the criticisms leveled against him by later authorities. Only two of his responsa have been published (in the *Even Me'ir* of M. Gordon, 1909).

BIBLIOGRAPHY: B. Epstein, *Mekor Barukh*, 3 (1928), 1163–75; H. Tchernowitz, *Toledot ha-Posekim*, 3 (1947), 299–305; J.L. Maimon (Fishman), *Anashim shel Ẓurah* (1947), 133–79; S.Y. Zevin, *Soferim u-Sefarim* (1959), 30–35; A.Z. Tarshish, *R. Barukh ha-Levi Epstein* (1967), 41–69.

[Yehoshua Horowitz]

EPSTEIN, JEHIEL MICHAL BEN ABRAHAM HALEVI (d. 1706), German rabbi and author. Epstein is principally known for his *Kiẓẓur Shelah* (Fuerth, 1683, 1696) and for a *siddur* which he issued with a translation of the prayers, laws, and customs in Yiddish, entitled *Derekh Yesharah* (Frankfurt, 1697). These he wrote largely for the benefit of Jews living in isolated villages that were without the guidance of rabbis and teachers. *Kiẓẓur Shelah*, mainly an abbreviated version of Isaiah *Horowitz' *Shenei Luḥot ha-Berit* (*Shelah*), also contains glosses as well as new laws and customs which Epstein extracted from works appearing after the publication of Horowitz' book. In addition, the author deals with Jewish education, its organization and syllabus. Criticizing the prevailing system, he proposed that the pupils be first taught the Bible and the four *sedarim* of the Mishnah relevant to the times (an approach reminiscent of that of *Judah Loew b. Bezalel of Prague) and only subsequently the Talmud and the codes. He opposed the form of casuistry known as *ḥillukim* on the basis of its being largely forced. The proposed educational reform could, he maintained, only be achieved through cooperation between the *ḥeder*, the home, and the *bet midrash*. *Kiẓẓur Shelah* was translated into Yiddish by Wolf Gershels of Prague under the title of *Eẓ Ḥayyim* (Frankfurt, 1720), 39 editions of which have appeared. It is very doubtful whether he had any associations with the Shabbatean movement, although he was suspected of it because of the wording of a certain passage in his *siddur*. He was also the author of *Derekh ha-Yashar la-Olam ha-Ba* (Frankfurt, 1703), an ethical work written in Yiddish, which language, he contended, had become a religious and cultural necessity in Jewish life; since it had acquired a sacred character, the gulf between it and Hebrew, the holy tongue, was progressively diminishing. His works provide an insight into the contemporary life of the smaller Jewish communities of Germany.

BIBLIOGRAPHY: M. Horovitz, *Avnei Zikkaron* (1901), 158; J. Freimann, in: JJLG, 15 (1923), 37; B. Wachstein, *ibid.*, 16 (1924), 169–71; S. Noble, in: *Yivo Bleter*, 35 (1951), 121–38; H. Liberman, *ibid.*, 36 (1952), 305–21; Zinberg, Sifrut, 4 (1958), 108–10, 257–9.

[Yehoshua Horowitz]

EPSTEIN, JUDITH (1895–1988), U.S. Hadassah leader. Epstein was born in Worcester, Massachusetts. She became involved in Jewish communal activity while at Hunter College, from which she graduated in 1916. Epstein served Hadassah in many capacities from 1928 when she was national secretary. She was chairman of various national departments, including membership and Zionist public relations, and was editor of *Hadassah Magazine*. Named vice president in 1934, Epstein served as national president of Hadassah during 1937–39 and 1943–47. From 1947 she was an honorary vice president. She traveled to virtually every Jewish community in the country, and for many years she played a prominent role at sessions of the Zionist General Council in the United States and abroad.

Dedicated to the needs and the future of the Jewish state, Epstein was largely responsible for funding the Rothschild-Hadassah-University Hospital in Jerusalem.

During her lifetime, she was an ardent advocate for young women. In her name and to honor her legacy, the Judith Epstein Memorial Award was created in 1991 to recognize the achievements of National Young Leaders Advisory Council (NYLAC) representatives, who are responsible for initiating activities and events that will bring visibility to Hadassah as well as bringing other young women into the organization. Each year the award is presented to a young leader whose community project was the most successful in promoting Hadassah in a meaningful way.

[Gladys Rosen / Ruth Beloff (2nd ed.)]

EPSTEIN, JULIUS J. (1909–2000), **AND PHILIP G.** (1909–1952), U.S. screenwriters. New York-born identical twins, Julius and Philip Epstein graduated from Pennsylvania State University in 1931. They had their first play, *And Stars Remain*, produced by the Theatre Guild in 1936. After working separately for two years, they joined Warner Brothers and became the best-known screenwriting team of the 1940s. Their films included *Daughters Courageous* (1939), *Four Wives* (1939), *No Time for Comedy* (1940), *Casablanca* (1942), *The Bride Came C.O.D.* (1941), *The Strawberry Blonde* (1941), *The Man Who Came to Dinner* (1941), *Yankee Doodle Dandy* (1942), *The Male Animal* (1942), *The Battle of Britain* (1943), *Arsenic and Old Lace* (1944), *Mr. Skeffington* (1944), *Saturday's Children* (1946), *Romance on the High Seas* (1948), *My Foolish Heart* (1949), *Take Care of My Little Girl* (1951), *Forever Female* (1953), *The Last Time I Saw Paris* (1954), and *The Brothers Karamazov* (1958).

In 1943, the Epstein brothers won a Best Screenplay Academy Award for *Casablanca*, which they had adapted from an unproduced play with the forgettable title "Everybody Comes to Rick's."

After Philip's death, Julius continued to work alone. Among his screenplays were his Oscar-nominated *Four Daughters* (1938), *The Tender Trap* (1955), *The Reluctant Debutante* (1958), *Take a Giant Step* (1959), *Tall Story* (1960), *Light in the Piazza* (1962), *Fanny* (1964), *Send Me No Flowers* (1964), *Any Wednesday* (1966), his Oscar-nominated *Pete 'n' Tillie* (1972), *Cross of Iron* (1977), *House Calls* (1978), and his Oscar-nominated *Reuben, Reuben* (1983).

In 1956 Julius won a Laurel Award for Screenwriting Achievement. In 1998, some 15 years after he had retired, Julius received the Los Angeles Film Critics Association Career Achievement Award.

[Jonathan Licht / Ruth Beloff (2nd ed.)]

EPSTEIN, KALONYMUS KALMAN OF CRACOW (d. 1823), ḥasidic *ẓaddik*. A disciple of *Elimelech of Lyzhansk and *Jacob Isaac ha-Ḥozeh ("the Seer") of Lublin, he became noted for the ecstatic mode of prayer he adopted. In 1785 he organized groups of Ḥasidim in Cracow, and arranged *minyanim* where they prayed with *devekut* ("devotion") employing pronounced bodily movements. They were strongly opposed by the Cracow community, this opposition resulting in excommunications issued by Isaac Ha-Levi of Cracow and his *bet din* in 1786 and 1787. Epstein, however, withstood his opponents and actively propagated Ḥasidism throughout western Galicia. His main work, *Ma'or va-Shemesh* (Breslau, 1842), a commentary on the Pentateuch, is one of the fundamental works of Ḥasidism, and includes information on the activities and the personalities of *ẓaddikim*. It was published in many editions. His son, Aaron (d. 1883), succeeded Epstein as the leading propagator of Ḥasidism in western Galicia and founded the first *kloiz* (ḥasidic synagogue) in Cracow, called after him R. Aaron's *kloiz*. Another son, Joseph Baruch of Neustadt (d. 1867), became known as a miracle worker. He was known as "the good Jew" of Neustadt, for the simplicity of his life and conduct.

BIBLIOGRAPHY: A. Markus, *Ha-Ḥasidut* (1954), index; B. Friedberg, *Luḥot Zikkaron* (1969), 39–45, 95; A. Bauminger, in: *Sefer Kraka* (1959), 33; M.S. Geshuri, *ibid.*, 167–8; L. Grossman, *Shem u-She'erit* (1943), 65; Dubnow, Ḥasidut, 167–8, 450–2.

EPSTEIN, LESLIE (1938–), U.S. writer. Born in Los Angeles and having a father as well as an uncle who were screenwriters (Julius J. and Philip G. *Epstein), Leslie Epstein was no outsider to Hollywood life: his *San Remo Drive: A Novel from Memory* (2003) is a recounting of his childhood as well as its repossession by the novel's protagonist. Its writing must have been cathartic yet this act of purgation runs throughout much of Epstein's work, which deals with those who are powerless or deluded or both, and who are presented to us in a tight narrative line that offers dark satire as a way of recounting the horrific. *The King of the Jews* (1986), a meditation upon the uses of power and self-deception, explores the nature of Trumpelman (based on Rumkowski, the ruler of the Lodz ghetto). Though the book is a controversial one, Epstein being charged with trivializing the Holocaust, the novel has also won much praise for its strongly controlled tone that veers between pathos and comedy. His most endearing character is Leib Goldkorn, a former Viennese musician, who undergoes a series of mishaps yet whose reflections are by turns chilling, sweet, and astonished by the chaos and destruction that he sees. He threads his way through *The Steinway Quintet* (1976), *Goldkorn Tales* (1985), and *Ice Fire Water* (1999).

Epstein attended Yale and Oxford and served as the director of the Creative Writing Program at Boston University for over 20 years.

[Lewis Fried (2nd ed.)]

EPSTEIN, LOUIS M. (1887–1949), U.S. Conservative rabbi and authority on Jewish marriage law. Epstein was born in Anyksciai, Lithuania. When his father, Rabbi Ezriel Epstein, went to the United States to accept a pulpit, he left his son behind to study at the yeshivah in Slobodka. He graduated from Columbia University (1911) and was ordained at the Jewish Theological Seminary in New York in 1913. He served in various congregations in Dallas, Texas, and Toledo, Ohio, before assuming the leadership of Beth Hamedrosh Hagdol in Roxbury, Massachusetts, in 1918 and then becoming rabbi of Kehilath Israel in Brookline, Massachusetts, where he served for the remainder of his career. Epstein was president of the Rabbinical Assembly (1922–25) and chairman of its committee on Jewish Law (1936–40). Epstein wrote *The Jewish Marriage Contract* (1927), *Marriage Laws in the Bible and Talmud* (1942), and *Sex Laws and Customs in Judaism* (1948). His scholarly attainments made him a leading figure in the Conservative movement. He was instrumental in framing various proposals in Jewish law, the best known being a method of solving the *agunah problem published in his *Li-She'elat ha-Agunah* (1940). Under Epstein's proposal, the husband would authorize the wife to act as his agent for the purpose of a *get*. This innovation was accepted by his colleagues but was abandoned by the Rabbinical Assembly because of the opposition of the Orthodox rabbinate and of some members of the faculty of the Jewish Theological Seminary.

[Benjamin Z. Kreitman]

EPSTEIN, MELECH (1889–1979), Yiddish journalist and editor. Born in Ruzhany, Belorussia, Epstein received a traditional Jewish education but left home at the age of 13 and became involved in socialist activities in Russia and Poland. In 1913 he immigrated to the U.S., where he joined the Communist Party in 1921. Epstein was one of the founders of the Yiddish daily *Morgn Frayhayt* and its chief editor from 1925 to 1928. He also served on the editorial board of the Communist monthly *Der Hamer*. He left the Communist Party in 1939 in protest against the Hitler-Stalin pact. Thereafter he contributed to the *Forverts* and *Tsukunft* as well as to the English-language Jewish press. He wrote *Sacco un Vanzetti* ("Sacco and Vanzetti," 1927), *Sovyetn Farband Boyt Sotsyalizm* ("The Soviet Union Builds Socialism," 1935), and *The Jew and Communism … in the Jewish Community, U.S.A., 1919–1941* (1959).

BIBLIOGRAPHY: A. Rejzen, Leksikon, 2 (1927), 798–800; LYNL, 7 (1968), 21–2; S. Bickel (ed.), *Pinkes far der Forshung fun der Yidisher Literatur un Prese*, 1 (1965), 325, 327, 331–2; *Sefer Yahadut Lita*, 3 (1967), 31. **ADD. BIBLIOGRAPHY:** B. Kohen (ed.), *Leksikon fun Yidish-Shraybers* (1986), 419.

[Israel Ch. Biletzky / Lily O. Kahn (2nd ed.)]

EPSTEIN, MORRIS (1921–1973), U.S. author and editor. Epstein was born in Newark, N.J., and studied at Yeshiva University and Columbia, receiving his doctorate from New York University in 1957. In his early years he wrote a number of children's books. In 1940 Epstein, together with Sigmund Laufer and Ezekiel Schloss, established the bi-monthly youth magazine *World Over* (1940–83) under the auspices of the Bureau of Jewish Education and published with the support of the New York Jewish Board of Education. The 16-page English-language magazine served as a learning tool to challenge Jewish youth and reinforce the ideas they learned at Hebrew school and in the home, but with a non-academic bent. While the three founders produced most of the text and artwork for the magazine themselves, they also included stories and essays submitted from the U.S. and abroad. Epstein was also the managing editor of the *Jewish Education Magazine*. He edited and translated the tales of *Sindabar (*Tales of Sendebar*, 1967) and in 1970 published a book on the *Sefer *Minhagim*, an illustrated collection of Jewish customs (Venice, 1593). In 1955 he joined Stern College for Women of Yeshiva University and was appointed full professor and chairman of the English Department in 1966. He wrote radio plays, drama reviews, and scholarly essays, and broadcasted and lectured extensively.

Books by Epstein include *My Holiday Story Book* (1958), *A Pictorial Treasury of Jewish Holidays and Customs* (1959), *A Picture Parade of Jewish History* (1963), *The New World Over*

Story Book: An Illustrated Anthology for Jewish Youth (1968), *More World Over Stories: An Illustrated Anthology for Jewish Youth* (1968), and *All about Jewish Holidays and Customs* (1970).

[Ruth Beloff (2nd ed.)]

EPSTEIN, MOSES MORDECAI (1866–1933), talmudist and *rosh yeshivah* in Lithuania and Ereẓ Israel. Born in Bakst, Moses studied in his youth at the Volozhin yeshivah where he was known as the "*illui* ("prodigy") of Bakst." At Volozhin he supported the Ḥovevei Zion group, founded by students of the yeshivah and in 1891 was a member of a Ḥovevei Zion delegation, which bought the land for the settlement of Ḥaderah. In 1893 he was appointed head of the Keneset Israel yeshivah of Slobodka, a position he filled until his death. During World War I he wandered from town to town in Russia at the head of his yeshivah and after the war became one of the leaders of religious Jewry in Lithuania and a cofounder of its rabbinical council. In 1923 at the conference of the Agudat Israel held in Vienna, he was elected a member of the *Kenesiyyah ha-Gedolah*, the supreme body of the organization, and the *Mo'ezet Gedolei ha-Torah*, its rabbinical council, established on that occasion. In 1924 he transferred most of the Keneset Israel student body to their sister yeshivah in *Hebron, which he had established. After the 1929 riots in Hebron in which many of the students were killed, he moved the yeshivah to Jerusalem. His method of studying Jewish law was to seek an understanding of the structure of individual laws as a means of comprehending the system of talmudic law in general. To this end he made a special study of Maimonides, whose method of halakhic commentary he sought to elucidate. In his teaching, likewise, he stressed the understanding of the underlying principles of individual laws more than expertise in wider areas. Epstein's method was adopted in numerous yeshivot. A collection of his lectures, entitled *Levush Mordekhai*, was published in four volumes: on tractate *Bava Kamma* (1901); on *Bava Meẓia* (1929); on the four parts of the Shulḥan Arukh (1946); and on *Yevamot* and *Gittin* (1948).

BIBLIOGRAPHY: S.J. Zevin, *Ishim ve-Shitot* (1958²), 275–91.

[David Tamar]

EPSTEIN, PAUL SOPHUS (1883–1966), theoretical physicist. Epstein was born in Warsaw. After his studies in Russia he went on to take a degree in optics in Germany. He left Russia in 1919 and lectured for two years at the Technische Hochschule in Zurich, Switzerland. In 1921 he went to the U.S. and became a professor at the California Institute of Technology at Pasadena. Epstein's scientific output was very impressive, and his studies covered wide fields which included applications of the quantum theory (in a series of papers in the Berlin periodical *Zeitschrift fuer Physik*), spectroscopy, radiation pressure, Stark effect, thermodynamics, fluid mechanics, theory of elasticity, and earth magnetism. In 1937 he published a *Textbook of Thermodynamics*.

[Arthur Beer]

EPSTEIN, SEYMOUR (1917–), U.S. author. Epstein's novels, *Pillar of Salt* (1960), *The Successor* (1961), *Leah* (1964), and *Caught in that Music* (1967), and his collection of short stories, *A Penny for Charity* (1965), are mostly about first-generation immigrants no longer bound by traditional commitments. Perhaps his most powerful novel, *Looking for Fred Schmidt*, was published in 1973.

EPSTEIN, ZALMAN (1860–1936), Hebrew essayist and critic. Epstein was born in Luban, Belorussia, and he received his early education at the Volozhin yeshivah. At the age of 16 he moved to Odessa where he lived for 30 years. He served on the central committee of Ḥovevei Zion from 1890 to 1900 in Odessa. Later Epstein lived in St. Petersburg, Warsaw, and Moscow, and settled in Palestine in 1925. In 1879 he began to publish letters and articles in the Hebrew press, some under the pen-names of "Shelomo ha-Elkoshi" and "Ben Azzai." His article, "The Spirit of Nationalism and its Results in Modern Times," which appeared in *Ha-Meliẓ* in 1882, brought him a measure of recognition. He became a regular contributor to *Ha-Meliẓ* and later to *Ha-Ẓefirah*, *Ha-Shilo'aḥ*, and other journals, writing primarily about Jewish problems, particularly the settlement of Palestine and Zionism. He contributed a series of articles in Yiddish to the St. Petersburg paper *Der Tog*. Epstein also commented on Hebrew and general literature, and published a number of poetic sketches, the best known of which are the series *Mi-Sefer ha-Zikhronot shel Shelomo ha-Elkoshi* ("From Shelomo ha-Elkoshi's Book of Reminiscences"). In his article "*Ha-Sefer ve-ha-Ḥayyim*" ("Books and Life"), in: *Lu'aḥ Aḥi'asaf*, 1 (1894), he called upon Hebrew writers not to concern themselves solely with Jewish problems. Epstein was a romantic who respected and admired Jewish traditions and sought to blend Judaism and humanism. He was the first to publish articles in Hebrew on Dostoyevski, Tolstoy, and Turgenev (in *Ha-Boker Or*, *Ben-Ammi*, and *Ha-Zeman*). His style was biblical and ornate. Only a few of his hundreds of articles and sketches were collected in the two volumes of his work, one of which appeared in St. Petersburg in 1905, the other in Tel Aviv in 1938. His monograph *Moshe Leib Lilienblum* was published in 1935.

BIBLIOGRAPHY: Autobiographical note in the preface to J. Fichmann (ed.), *Kitvei Zalman Epstein* (1938).

[Gedalyah Elkoshi]

EPSTEIN HA-LEVI, MOSES JEHIEL (1890–1971), rabbi and *admor*. Epstein was born in Ozarow, Poland, where he received his rabbinic education. In 1913 he was appointed rabbi there and in 1918 *admor*. Epstein immigrated to the U.S. in 1927 and in 1953 came to Israel and settled in Tel Aviv. He was a leader of Agudat Israel and a member of the *Mo'ezet Gedolei ha-Torah* and also active in educational and charity affairs. His works are *Esh Dat* (11 vols.) and *Be'er Moshe*. He was awarded the Israel Prize for rabbinical literature in 1968.

ER (Heb. עֵר; "watcher, watchful"), the name of two biblical figures. (1) The eldest son of Judah and the daughter of Shua, a Canaanite (Gen. 38:2–3). He married *Tamar but died childless because of his wickedness (Gen. 38:6–7; 46:12; Num. 26:19; I Chron. 2:3). The nature of his offense is not specified. (2) The son of Shelah, the grandson of Judah, and the father of Lecah (I Chron. 4:21).

BIBLIOGRAPHY: W.F. Albright, *Yahweh and the Gods of Canaan* (1968), 69–70, 233p.

°**ERASMUS OF ROTTERDAM** (**Desiderius Erasmus Roterodamus**; 1469–1536), European humanist, theologian, and writer. Netherlands-born Erasmus lived and worked in all major countries of Europe and wrote only in Latin.

Erasmus' view of Judaism as a religion was fully determined by traditions of the New Testament (especially by the epistles ascribed to Paul) and of the Early Church (in the first place, Jerome, to a lesser extent, Augustine). An original aspect of this position is that he regularly used the words *Judaismus, Judaeus*, etc., to stigmatize bad Christians, "for whom religion consists of rituals and observations of corporeal things" (a letter of December 1504). In another writing, he says, "Judaism I call not Jewish impiety, but prescriptions about external things, such as food, fasting, clothes, which to a certain degree resemble the rituals of the Jews" (*Declarationes ad censuras Lutetiae*, 1532). In fact, the majority of Erasmus' anti-Mosaic attacks are directed against this "new Judaism."

As far as the Jewish Bible (the Old Testament) is concerned, it is only natural that a Christian humanist professing "the philosophy of Christ" placed the New Testament higher than the Old. But on many occasions he insisted on the importance for Christians of the Old Testament in its entirety and, even more significantly, on the complete inadmissibility of contrasting the two Testaments.

As a humanist (in the strict and specific sense of the word) Erasmus highly appreciated Hebrew and demanded thorough knowledge of the original language of the Bible. "Who does not master all three holy tongues [i.e., Hebrew, Greek, and Latin], is not a theologian, but a violator of the holy Theology" (*Adagiae*, 1515). But Erasmus' own knowledge of Hebrew was rudimentary and he was completely dependent on other scholars' commentaries and upon their direct, personal help (in his New Testament commentaries and paraphrases of Psalms). Hence numerous mistakes, "anti-philological" interpretations (discrediting Erasmus' general method), and even a kind of irritation against "ambiguities" of Hebrew can be found in his writings.

Erasmus' attitude toward Jewry of his day should be evaluated against a background of the universal hatred of Jews, intolerance, and missionary zeal in the 15th and 16th centuries, especially in Germany. This sinister background is often apparent, much more in private correspondence than in writings intended for print. In some of the latter we find remarks that are comparatively moderate and reasonable. Thus, Erasmus thinks that the number of Jews, their force, and influence are insignificant, and, consequently, they are of no danger to Christianity; that forced conversion of Jews is absolutely inadmissible, and even that Christian missionary activity among Jews is perhaps useless; that the expulsion of Jews from Spain should be condemned, and that the Marranos should be treated mercifully, etc. Such remarks spring organically from the deepest principles of Erasmus' understanding of the world and must be considered as really "erasmian." But the "erasmian spirit," expressing itself in a well-known line from a letter (January 30, 1523 (4)), "I have a temperament such that I could love even a Jew, if only he were well-mannered and friendly, and did not mouth blasphemy on Christ in my presence," was far from always being uppermost. In fact, he never met a real Jew all his life, never sought out such a meeting, and never wrote anything especially devoted to Jews or Judaism. He was, in fact, indifferent to the living "remnant of Israel"; the flesh-and-blood Jew was simply not within his field of vision. This indifference, in a time of catastrophic sharpening of religious and national fanaticism, could have been an initial step toward true tolerance. Erasmus' position could be qualified as asemitism; suggesting that he was an antisemite seems to be as unhistorical as claiming he was sympathetic toward Jews.

BIBLIOGRAPHY: G. Kisch, *Erasmus' Stellung zu Juden and Judentum* (1969)[Kisch considers Erasmus a rabid antisemite, equal to Luther]; S. Markish, *Erasmus and the Jews*, with an Afterword by Arthur A. Cohen (1986); G.B. Winkler, "Erasmus und die Juden," in: *Festschrift Franz Loidl zum 65 Geburstag* (1970), 381–392; C. Augustijn, "Erasmus und die Juden," in: *Nederlands Archief voor Kerkengeschiedenis*, 60:1 (1980), 22–38.

[Shimon Markish]

°**ERATOSTHENES OF CYRENE** (c. 275–194 B.C.E.), polymath, author of *Geographica*, a first-rate geography much used by *Strabo, who cites his description of Arabia (16:4, 2), commenting upon the occupations of the inhabitants (including the Judeans), soil, flora, water supply, and distances. Strabo elsewhere (16:2, 44) cites Eratosthenes' theory that the region around Edom was once a lake and that the land came into existence as a result of volcanic eruptions.

ERECH (Sum. **Unug**; Akk. **Uruk**; modern **Warka** in Iraq), city mentioned as one of the mainstays of the kingdom of *Nimrod (Gen. 10:10), and perhaps referred to in Ezra 4:9. In ancient times Uruk lay on the bank of the Euphrates, approximately 40 mi. (65 km.) N.W. of Ur; the river has now shifted far to the west, leaving the city in the desert. The site was occupied in the fifth millennium B.C.E., and experienced its first peak of prosperity in about 3300–3100 B.C.E., when it was probably the largest religious center of Sumer, with large temples and the earliest written documents so far known. The legendary hero Gilgamesh was probably an historical king of Uruk in about 2700 B.C.E. Uruk played a part in the rise of the Neo-Sumerian kings of Ur, and was the seat of a dynasty of West Semitic rulers shortly before the time of Hammurapi. Thereafter, it was politically unimportant, but remained a seat of learning until Seleucid times. It was the cult center of Anu, the sky god, and of Inanna-Ishtar, the goddess of love and war. In 1912 the German Oriental Society began to excavate the site and allowing for the interruptions caused by wars continued until the end of the 20th century.

ADD. BIBLIOGRAPHY: J-C. Margueron, in: ABD II, 570–73; CANE, 4, 2960 (index); M. Powell, in: JAOS, 117 (1997), 608; S. Dunham, in: JAOS, 119 (1999), 139.

[Richard S. Ellis]

EREẒ ISRAEL (Heb. אֶרֶץ יִשְׂרָאֵל), Hebrew name of Land of Israel. The term Ereẓ Israel is biblical, although its meaning varies, designating both the territory actually inhabited by the Israelites (I Sam. 13:19) and the Northern Kingdom (II Kings 5:2). It was, however, only from the Second Temple period onward that Ereẓ Israel became the current appellation of the Promised Land. It was the official Hebrew designation of the area governed by British mandate after World War I until 1948. For further details, see *Canaan, Land of; *Israel, Land of (Geographical Survey).

ERFURT, city in Thuringia, Germany. Jews are first mentioned there in the 12th century. At first under the protection of the king, by the second half of the 12th century they had passed to the jurisdiction of the archbishop of Mainz, who composed an *oath formula for them in German. In 1209 the king also relinquished his right to collect taxes from the Jews, which in 1212 was explicitly granted to the archbishop. In 1221 anti-Jewish riots broke out in Erfurt: the synagogue was burned down, and a number of Jews were murdered while some threw themselves into the flames. Among the martyrs was the *paytan* and cantor Samuel b. Kalonymus. Nevertheless, the Jewish community of Erfurt continued to exist and even to expand. After some time a new synagogue was built and well-known rabbis chose Erfurt as their seat. Between 1286 and 1293 Asher b. *Jehiel probably lived there, and at about the same time Kalonymus b. Eliezer ha-Nakdan composed his *Masorah Ketannah*, still preserved in manuscript in Erfurt. During the Middle Ages the Jews of Erfurt followed the Saxony prayer rite. The community's Book of Ritual is preserved at Jews' College, London (Ms. 104, 4). At the beginning of the 14th century protection over the Jews passed to the municipality; this, however, was unable to save them from massacre during the Black *Death: at the beginning of March 1349 over 100 Jews were murdered by the populace, and many set fire to their homes and perished in the flames. Those who survived were driven from the city. Among the martyrs was Alexander Suslin ha-Kohen, author of *Sefer ha-Aguddah*. Israel b. Joel *Susslin mentions the Erfurt martyrs in an elegy (*Sefer ha-Dema'ot*, 2, 126–7). The city council again permitted Jews to settle within the city walls and build a new synagogue in 1357. During the following century the Erfurt community became one of the largest and most important in Germany, some of the most celebrated rabbis officiating there. Meir b. Baruch *ha-Levi served there for some time; a disciple of his was Hillel of *Erfurt. In the middle of the 15th century Jacob b. Judah *Weil taught there. During this period, Erfurt Jews played an important role in banking in Thuringia. In 1391 the king canceled all the debts owed by Christians to the Erfurt Jews and handed them over to the municipality for 2,000 gulden; the municipality claimed this sum from the Jews but promised them to return part of the debts. Subsequently the Jews had to pay a special tax to the king's treasury. In 1418 they were compelled to declare the amount of their property on oath, in the synagogue, and the king collected new taxes from them on this basis. In 1451 and 1452 Nicolas of *Cusa and John of *Capistrano visited Erfurt. Their anti-Jewish sermons greatly agitated the populace, and in 1453 the city council withdrew protection from the Jews, who subsequently left Erfurt.

Around 1820 the Prussian authorities used the tombstones in the Jewish cemetery for the fortification of the city. At that time Jews again began to settle in Erfurt, numbering some 144 in 1840 when a new synagogue was dedicated. The communal archives from 1855 to 1936 have been transferred to the Central Archives for the History of the Jewish People in Jerusalem. The community numbered 546 in 1880 (1.03% of the total population); 795 in 1910 (0.72%); and 831 in 1933 (0.6%). After the advent of the Nazis the majority left Erfurt, 263 remaining in 1939. The synagogue was burned down on Nov. 9, 1938. The community was compelled to pay for the benzene used for igniting the synagogue and for clearing the ruins. The men were detained in the local school, where they were mistreated, and subsequently deported to *Buchenwald. Of the 188 Jews remaining in Erfurt in September 1941, 152 were deported to the East in four transports between May 1942 and January 1944.

A few Jews returned to Erfurt after the war, and there were 40 in 1951. A new synagogue was opened in 1952, and the community numbered 120 in 1961. As a result of the immigration of Jews from the former Soviet Union, the number of community members rose to 550 in 2003. One of the famous manuscripts of the Tosefta was found in Erfurt after which it is named (S. Leibman, intr. *Tosefta bi-Feshuto*).

BIBLIOGRAPHY: A. Jaraczewsky, *Geschichte der Juden in Erfurt* (1868); Wiener, in: MGWJ, 17 (1868), 313–17, 352–59, 385–95; Th. Kronner, *Festschrift zur Einweihung der neuen Synagoge in Erfurt* (1884); Suessmann, in: MGADJ, 5 (1914), 1–126; Germ Jud, 1 (1963), 97–102; 2 (1968), 215–25; PKG; Baron, 9 (1965), 223–26. **ADD. BIBLIOGRAPHY:** E. Menzel, in: *Beitraege zur Geschichte juedischen Lebens in Thueringen* (1996), 117–132; O. Zucht, *Die Geschichte der Juden in Erfurt …* (2001).

[Zvi Avneri / Stefan Rohrbacher (2nd ed.)]

ERGAS, JOSEPH BEN EMANUEL (1685–1730), rabbi, kabbalist, and author of books on halakhic and kabbalistic matters. Ergas, who was of Marrano descent, was born in Leghorn. The headdress of a knight engraved on his tomb in Leghorn perhaps indicates descent from a noble Spanish family. Samuel of Fez was his teacher of *halakhah* and *Benjamin ha-Kohen Vitale of Reggio taught him Kabbalah. As a young man, he traveled throughout Italy and preached public sermons, urging repentance. For a while he stayed in Pisa where he founded a yeshivah, Neveh Shalom. Later, he was appointed rabbi in Leghorn, and remained there until his death. Ergas became famous for his pamphlet *Tokhaḥat Megullah*, the polemic against the Shabbatean Nehemiah *Ḥayon, and an addition to it called *Ha-Ẓad Naḥash* (London, 1715). His kabbalistic works include *Shomer Emunim* (Amsterdam, 1736), in which he explains the principles of the Kabbalah in the form of a dialogue between Shaltiel, who believes only in the revealed Torah, and Jehoiada, the victor in this argument, who believes also in the esoteric aspect of the Torah; *Shomer Emunim* includes *Mevo Petaḥim*, an appendix to the former, a selection from *Luria's doctrine, and an introduction to the Kabbalah, and *Minḥat Yosef*, an ethical-religious anthology and the rules for the study of the kabbalistic doctrines. A selection of his responsa was published by his disciple Malachi Ha-Kohen as *Divrei Yosef* (Leghorn, 1742). The publisher's introduction mentions several *piyyutim* written by Ergas. Ergas was an enthusiastic believer in the importance and sanctity of the Kabbalah in general and of the *Zohar in particular, despite his view that marginal annotations had been introduced into the proper text of the Zohar. He opposed philosophy, which he considered alien to Judaism and an invention of heretics. He opposed *Maimonides' explanations of the stories of the Creation and the visions of Ezekiel in the spirit of Aristotle's natural philosophy. Ergas' style is distinguished by its clarity.

Ergas' Kabbalah evinces affinities with that of Moses Ḥayyim *Luzzatto, and tension over this issue developed between the two kabbalists.

BIBLIOGRAPHY: Joseph ben Emanuel Ergas, *Shomer Emunim*, ed. by S.A. Horodezky (repr. 1927), introd. **ADD. BIBLIOGRAPHY:** R. Goetschel, "La justification de la kabbale dans le 'Shômer Emûnîm' of Joseph Ergas (1685–1730)," in: U. Haxen, H. Trautner-Kromann, and K.L. Goldschmidt Salamon (eds.), *Jewish Studies in a New Europe; Proceedings of the Fifth Congress of Jewish Studies in Copenhagen* (1994), 269–81.

[Azriel Shochat]

ERIK, MAX (pseudonym of **Zalmen Merkin**; 1898–1937), Yiddish literary critic and literary historian. Born in Sosnowiec (Poland), Erik was educated privately (among his tutors was Ḥayyim Naḥman *Bialik) and in a traditional *ḥeder*. He later studied at a Russian-language high school and at a Polish officers' training school from which he graduated as a reserve officer. His uncle was Yitzkhak Peysekzon, a founder of the Jewish Labor Bund. In 1922 he settled in Vilna where he taught Yiddish and Polish literature in Yiddish-language high schools. Erik published his first essays in 1920 on neo-Romanism and Hugo Tsukerman in I.M. Weissenberg's *Yudishe Zamelbikher* and then contributed studies, essays, and critical articles to various Yiddish periodicals including *Ringen*, *Literarishe Bleter*, *Bikher Velt*, and the *Vilner Tog*. His first works on Yiddish literature were *Konstruktsiye Shtudiyen: tsu der Konstruktsye fun der Goldene Keyt* ("Construction Studies: On the Construction of the Golden Chain," 1924), an analysis of the variants of I.L. *Peretz's plays; *Vegn Alt-Yidishn Roman un Novele – 14ter–16ter Yorhundert* ("On the Old Yiddish Novel – 14th–16th Centuries," 1926); and *Di Geshikhte fun der Yidisher Literatur fun di Eltste Tsaytn biz der Haskole Tekufe* ("History of Yiddish Literature – from the Beginning to the Haskalah Period," 1928). Erik's work helped found the field of Old Yiddish studies. He also formulated the long-dominant but now disproven theory of Yiddish *shpilmener* ("troubadours") who composed, or adapted from other languages, the extant Old Yiddish epics. In 1929 Erik settled in the Soviet Union. He lived in Minsk and Kiev and taught Yiddish literature at various Jewish institutions of higher learning. Increasingly, his works in this period were written from the official party-line point of view and include a study of Sholem *Asch (1931); *Etyudn tsu der Geshikhte fun der Haskole* ("Studies in the History of the Haskalah," 1934); and *Di Yidishe Literatur in XIX Yorhundert*, vol. 1, coauthored with A. Rosenzweig ("A History of Yiddish Literature in the 19th century," 1935). He also edited *Di Komedies fun der Berliner Ufklerung* ("The Comedies of the Berlin Haskalah," 1933) and a selection of the works of Solomon *Ettinger (1935). Upon the liquidation of the Institute for Jewish Proletarian Culture of the Ukrainian Academy of Science in May 1936, Erik was arrested and exiled to the Vietlosian prison camp in Siberia, where he died.

BIBLIOGRAPHY: Rejzen, *Leksikon*, 2 (1927), 815–8; J. Shatzky, in: J. Opatoshu and H. Leivick (eds.), *Zamlbikher*, 8 (1952), 41–54. **ADD. BIBLIOGRAPHY:** LNYL, 7 (1968), 37–41; A.A. Greenbaum, *Jewish Scholarship and Scholarly Institutions in Soviet Russia, 1918–1953* (1978); C. Shmeruk, in: *Studies in Yiddish Literature and Folklore*, 7 (1986) 1–36.

[Elias Schulman / Barry Trachtenberg (2nd ed.)]

ERIKSON, ERIK HOMBERGER (1902–1994), U.S. psychoanalyst. Born in Frankfurt, Germany, Erikson immigrated to the U.S. in 1933. He taught and did research at Harvard, Yale, and the University of California until 1951, when he joined the senior staff of the Austen Riggs Center at Stockbridge, Mass. In 1960 he was appointed professor of human development and psychiatry at Harvard. Erikson's research into the cultures of the Yurok and Sioux Indians resulted in *Childhood and Society* (1950, 1963^2), in which he discussed childbearing methods and human development. In the same book he dealt with the evolution of identity and character, including the American and German, and with antisemitism and the role of Jews in changing culture. In *Young Man Luther* (1958), Erikson related the reformer's adolescent crisis of identity (identity versus identity diffusion) and the historical crisis of his age. He later clarified his concept of the synthesis of the ego through successive identifications by the child with individuals, group ideals, and goals. His *Insight and Responsibility* (1966) discusses the ethical implications of psychoanalytic insight and the responsibility of each generation to succeeding generations.

Other books by Erikson include *Identity: Youth and Crisis* (1968), *Gandhi's Truth on the Origins of Militant Nonviolence* (1969), *The Twentieth-century Sciences: Studies in the Biography of Ideas* (1972), *Dimensions of a New Identity* (1974), *Life History and the Historical Moment* (1975), *Toys and Reasons:*

Stages in the Ritualization of Experience (1977), *Adulthood: Essays* (1978), *Themes of Work and Love in Adulthood* (1980), *St. George and the Dandelion: Forty Years of Practice As a Jungian Analyst* (1982), *Vital Involvement in Old Age: The Experience of Old Age in Our Time* (1986), *Identity and the Life Cycle* (1988), *The Life Cycle Completed* (1995), and *The Erik Erikson Reader* (2000).

For *Gandhi's Truth* (1969), Erikson was awarded the Pulitzer Prize and National Book Award.

Erikson is labeled an ego-psychologist in that he built on Freud's early work on the ego, though with emphasis on social rather than sexual factors. He is best known for his work in expanding Freud's theory of stages. Often referred to as the "father of psychosocial development" and "the architect of identity," and the man who coined the term "identity crisis," Erikson believed that development functions by what he called the "epigenetic principle." According to this principle, we develop through a predetermined unfolding of our personalities in eight stages. Each person's progress through each stage is in part determined by his/her success, or lack of it, in the previous stages. If one interferes with any stage of that natural order of development or does not manage a stage well, one could develop maladaptations and malignancies as well as jeopardize one's future development.

Erikson also theorized about the interaction of generations, which he called "mutuality": not only do parents influence their children's development, as Freud suggested, but children also influence their parents' development, Erikson contended.

BIBLIOGRAPHY: E. Pumpian-Mindlin, in: F.G. Alexander et al. (eds.), *Psychoanalytic Pioneers* (1966), 524–33; H.W. Maier, *Three Theories of Child Development* (1965), 12–74 (bibliography 297–300); B. Kaplan (ed.), *Studying Personality Cross-Culturally* (1961), index. **ADD. BIBLIOGRAPHY:** R. Evans, *Dialogue with Erik Erikson* (1967); R. Coles, *Erik H. Erikson, the Growth of his Work* (1970); P. Roazen, *Erik H. Erikson: The Power and Limits of a Vision* (1976); J.E. Wright, *Erikson, Identity and Religion* (1982); F. Gross, *Introducing Erik Erikson* (1987); H. Zock, *A Psychology of Ultimate Concern: Erik H. Erikson's Contribution to the Psychology of Religion* (1990); R. Wallerstein and L. Goldberger (eds.), *Ideas and Identities: The Life and Work of Erik Erikson* (1999); K. Welchman, *Erik Erikson* (2000).

[Louis Miller / Ruth Beloff (2nd ed.)]

ERLANGER (D'Erlanger), family of German bankers, originating in Frankfurt. RAPHAEL ERLANGER (1806–1878) learned banking with the Rothschilds and eventually established in Frankfurt his own bank, Erlanger and Sons, which was mainly concerned with the formation of German provincial banks and existed until 1904. Raphael received titles from the rulers of Portugal, Saxe-Meiningen, and Austria. Three of his sons expanded the banking operations. VICTOR (1840–1894) managed the Vienna branch which went into liquidation in the 1890s. FREDERIC-EMILE (1832–1911) established the London house. LUDWIG (1836–1898) headed the original bank in Frankfurt, which was absorbed by the Dresdner Bank in 1904. In Paris and London the Erlangers became part of Europe's banking elite, although their attempt to float a Confederate loan during the American Civil War miscarried.

ADD. BIBLIOGRAPHY: G. Mendelsohn, *Die Familie Erlanger – Bankiers, Mäzene, Künstler* (2005).

[Joachim O. Ronall]

ERLANGER, CAMILLE (1863–1919), composer. Born in Paris of an Alsatian family, Erlanger studied composition at the Paris Conservatoire with Delibes and Massenet, and received the Rome Prize in 1888 for his cantata *Velléda*. Erlanger wrote nine operas. His first opera, *Kermaria*, produced in 1897 by the Opéra-Comique, made little impression. However, his next attempt – *Le Juif Polonais* (1900), based on the story by Erckman-Chatrian – was very popular and remained in the operatic repertoire until 1933. His most popular opera was an opéra-comique – *Aphorodite* (1906), adapted from Pierre Louÿs' novel and performed over 180 times in 20 years. Erlanger was particularly influenced by Weber, whom he greatly admired, and to a much lesser extent by Wagner. Other operas of his are *Bacchus triomphant* (1909) and *Hannele Mattern* (1911). He also wrote the symphonic poem *Maître et Serviteur*, based on Tolstoy's story, which remained in manuscript; *La Chasse fantastique* (1893); *Le fils de l'étoile* (drame musical, 1904), and many songs.

ADD. BIBLIOGRAPHY: Grove online; C. Mendès, "Le Juif polonais," *Le journal* (April 11, 1900); A. Bachelet, "Camille Erlanger," in: *Monde musical*, v (1919).

[Israela Stein (2nd ed.)]

ERLANGER, JOSEPH (1874–1965), U.S. physiologist and Nobel Prize winner. Erlanger, who was born in San Francisco, graduated from Johns Hopkins University in 1899. From 1906 to 1910 he was professor of physiology at Wisconsin Medical School and from 1910 held the chair of physiology at Washington University School of Medicine in St. Louis. He and Herbert Spencer Gasser received the 1944 Nobel Prize for physiology and medicine, for their work on the functional differentiation of nerves and on the influence of pulse pressure on kidney secretion. Erlanger made fundamental contributions to the knowledge of the cardiovascular and nervous system and to methods of physiological investigation. He invented a graphic method for measuring blood pressure and studied the mechanism of production of sounds used in measuring blood pressure by the auscultatory method. He studied nerve action potentials by cathode ray oscillograph; induction shocks as stimuli; traumatic shock and impulse initiation and conduction in the heart.

BIBLIOGRAPHY: S.R. Kagan, *Jewish Medicine* (1952).

[Suessmann Muntner]

ERLANGER, MICHEL (1828–1892), French communal worker. Son of the rabbi in Wissenbourg, Alsace, he had a traditional Jewish education. Erlanger was among the founders of the *Alliance Israélite Universelle and a member of its central committee. He helped Charles *Netter to establish the *Mikveh Israel agricultural school, and accompanied Baron Edmond de *Rothschild's representative, Albert *Cohn, on his visits to Ereẓ Israel. Erlanger advised Rothschild on his philanthropic activities and acted as his liaison with the *Hibbat Zion movement and colonists in Ereẓ Israel. He was vice president of the Jewish *Consistoire in Paris, a member of the board, and treasurer of the Société des Etudes Juives.

BIBLIOGRAPHY: A. Druyanow (ed.), *Ketavim le-Toledot Ḥibbat-Ẓiyyon*, 3 vols. (1919–32), index; *Bulletin de l'Alliance Israélite Universelle*, 5:17 (1892), 10–15.

[Yehuda Slutsky]

ERLANGER, PHILIPPE (1903–1987), French writer and art critic, son of Camille *Erlanger and related on his mother's side to the Comte de *Camondo. Born in Paris, Erlanger wished to become a diplomat but worked principally at the Ministry of Education, where for 40 years he headed the cultural-exchange office. In this position he organized hundreds of exhibitions and was one of the founders of the Cannes film festival. Erlanger was also a prolific journalist and art critic (*Les Peintres de la réalité*, 1946; *Les Gisants*, 1947) and wrote more than 30 books. He began as a novelist, but from the 1930s his main work was biographical, falling midway between scientific historical research and literary psychological studies. Among his subjects have been the French kings Charles VII (1945), Henri III (1933), Louis XIII (1946), Louis XIV (1961, 1965), and their entourage: Diane de Poitiers, Henri II's favorite (1955), the two antagonistic advisers of Louis XIII, Cinq-Mars (1962) and Richelieu (3 vols., 1967–1970), Gaston d'Orléans, Louis XIV's brother (1953), and the "Régent" Philippe d'Orléans (1938), as well as Marguerite d'Anjou, queen of England (1932), the Duke of Buckingham (1951), and the Borgia family (1934). The only contemporary subject of his biographies was Georges Clemenceau (1968). Erlanger received many prizes and honors.

BIBLIOGRAPHY: *Biblio*, 24 (June/July 1966), 6.

ERLICH, HENRYK (Wolf Hersh; 1882–1941), journalist; leader of the *Bund in Poland. Erlich was born of a well-to-do family in Lublin; his father was a Ḥasid who became a *maskil* and a Ḥovev Zion. Having joined the Bund in 1903 while a student at the University of Warsaw, Erlich was arrested several times for revolutionary activities and expelled from the university. Later he graduated in law from the University of St. Petersburg and became a member of the central committee of the Bund. After the 1917 revolution he was a leading figure in the Petrograd (Leningrad) Workers' Soviet. In October 1918 he returned to Warsaw, becoming prominent in the Bund, and editor of the party's Yiddish daily *Di Folkstsaytung*. He was a member of the Warsaw city council and the *kehillah* board, and participated in numerous international socialist congresses. On the German invasion of Poland in September 1939 Erlich left Warsaw with his family, and in October was arrested by the Soviet authorities. With Victor *Alter he was accused of active subversion and helping Polish intelligence, and was condemned to death; the sentence was later commuted to ten years' hard labor. In September 1941, following the amnesty for all convicted Polish citizens in Soviet Russia, Erlich and Alter were set free. After their release they were approached by Soviet representatives to join a Jewish anti-Fascist committee. However, in the early morning of Dec. 4, 1941, they were again arrested in Kuibyshev. According to a communication of Feb. 23, 1943, from Maxim *Litvinov, then Soviet ambassador to the United States, addressed to William Green, president of the American Federation of Labor, Erlich and Alter were executed shortly after their arrest "for hostile activities, including appeals to the Soviet troops to stop bloodshed and immediately conclude peace with Germany." The executions aroused worldwide protests by Labor and Liberal organizations. His wife, whom he married in 1911, was SOPHIA *DUBNOW-ERLICH (1885–1986), the daughter of the historian Simon *Dubnow.

BIBLIOGRAPHY: *American Representation of General Jewish Worker's Union of Poland, The Case of Henryk Erlich and Victor Alter* (1943); Chamberlain, in: *New Leader* (March 13, 1943); *The Militant* (March 20, 1943); *Henryk Erlich und Victor Alter* (Yid., 1951), includes bibl. 459–72. **ADD. BIBLIOGRAPHY:** H. Erlich, *The Struggle for Revolutionary Socialism* (1934); G. Pickhan, "*Gegen dem Strom*," in: *Der Algemeiner Juedische Arbeiterbund "Bund" in Polen 1918–1939* (2001), index.

[Ezekiel Lifschutz]

ERLICH, VERA STEIN (1897–1980), Yugoslav social-cultural anthropologist and psychologist. Vera Erlich devoted many years to the study of family relationships in rural areas. She managed to save her material on the eve of World War II, and it eventually formed the basis of her book *Porodica u transformaciji* (1964; *Family in Transition: A study of 300 Yugoslav villages*, 1966). From 1945 to 1950 Vera Erlich was a United Nations Relief and Rehabilitation Administration (UNRRA) psychiatric social worker with displaced persons in Italy. She then went to the United States, and for ten years acted as lecturer in Slavic languages and literature and a research fellow in anthropology at Berkeley University. In 1960 she returned to Yugoslavia and became a professor in anthropology at the University of Zagreb. Her published works include *Savremeno dijete* ("The Contemporary Child," 1936) and *U društvu sa čovekom* ("In the Company of Man," 1968). In her capacity of professional consultant, she was helpful to the operations of UNRRA (the United Nations Relief and Rehabilitation Administration) and the IRO.

She was married to Dr. Benno Stein, a noted psychologist of Zagreb, murdered in the Jasenovac death camp.

[Zdenko Lowenthal]

ERLIK, DAVID (1909–1995), Israeli physician, one of the founders of modern surgery in Israel. Erlik was born in Pinsk, Russia, in 1909. His family came to Palestine in 1924 and settled in Haifa. From 1928 to 1935 he studied medicine in Strasbourg, France. In 1936 Erlik was accepted for a residency in

Jerusalem's Hadassah Hospital, where he spent the next dozen years training in general surgical techniques. In 1948 he was asked by Israel's Ministry of Health to put together the surgical department at the abandoned British Mandatory Hospital in Haifa, by then renamed Rambam Hospital. As its chief of surgery for over 30 years, Erlik was instrumental in making Rambam the major medical center in northern Israel, including the successful association between the Haifa Technion and Rambam's medical school, which opened its doors in 1969.

Erlik was a pioneer and innovator of surgical procedures involving the blood vessels in the abdomen and kidneys. In 1966 he carried out the first kidney transplant in Israel, and under his stewardship Rambam became the leading transplant center in the country. Erlik created a surgical standard of excellence with which he imbued the next generations of surgeons in Israel.

Erlik was awarded the Israel Prize in life sciences in 1992.

BIBLIOGRAPHY: M. Hashmonai, "David Erlik (1909–1995) – A Founder of Surgery in Modern Israel," in: *Digestive Surgery*, 21 (2004), 447–51.

[Ruth Rossing (2nd ed.)]

ERMAN, JOHANN PETER ADOLF (1854–1937), German Egyptologist, usually cited as Adolf Erman, or A. Erman. Erman studied at Leipzig and Berlin under Georg *Ebers, and then became director of the Egyptian Section of the Berlin Museum and professor of Egyptology (1884–1923). Primarily a philologist, his work established a solid foundation for all subsequent philological study in ancient Egyptian. At the turn of the 20th century, under the auspices of the Prussian Academy of Science, he began work on the great dictionary of the Egyptian language, the *Woerterbuch der aegyptischen Sprache* (vol. 1, 1926). The second revised edition of his *Neuaegyptische Grammatik* (1933^2), dictated from memory when he was virtually blind, still remains the standard grammar of Late Egyptian. In addition to numerous philological, technical works, he wrote popular books on Egyptian literature, culture, and art. In an article "Eine aegyptische Quelle der Sprueche Salomos" (in *Sitzungsberichte der Deutschen (Preussischen) Akademie der Wissenschaften*, 15 (1924), 86–93), Erman maintained the direct relationship of Proverbs 22:17–24:22 to the Instruction of Amen-em-opet. This had considerable repercussions in biblical studies, for scholars began to see the close, sometimes direct, relationship of biblical wisdom literature to ancient Near Eastern wisdom literature. Erman, himself a Protestant, was of Jewish descent, and although not actively persecuted, suffered indignity and humiliation under the Nazis until his death in Berlin. His autobiography *Mein Werden und mein Wirken* appeared in 1929.

BIBLIOGRAPHY: *Journal of Egyptian Archaeology*, 23 (1937), 81; 24 (1938), 231.

[Alan Richard Schulman and Michael Fox]

ERNAKULAM (formerly **Angicaymal**), town in Kerala, India, about 5 mi. (8 km.) from *Cochin. A community of "black Jews" is known to have existed there since the 15th century. Moses *Pereira de Paiva (1687) lists it as the second largest Jewish settlement on the Malabar Coast after Cochin, with 150 families. In 1970 "Jew Street" contained two large synagogues, Theckoobagam (said to have been built in 1625) and Kadvoobhagam (1150), formerly containing valuable liturgical objects; services were held in them alternately on the Sabbath and festivals. Two old cemeteries lie some distance from this street. In 1922, the elders of the synagogues wrote to the British Zionist Federation expressing their desire to settle in Palestine. In recent years the community has declined, mainly because of emigration to Israel. None of the Ernakulam synagogues function any more.

BIBLIOGRAPHY: Bar-Giora, in: *Sefunot*, 2 (1958), 214–45; Fischel, in: *Herzl Yearbook*, 4 (1961/62), 324–8. **ADD. BIBLIOGRAPHY:** J.B. Segal, *A History of the Jews of Cochin* (1993).

[Walter Joseph Fischel]

°**ERPENIUS (van Erpe), THOMAS** (1584–1624), Dutch Orientalist. Erpenius traveled (1608–12) extensively through the libraries of Europe, availing himself while at Venice of Jewish instruction. In Leiden, where in 1613 he was appointed professor of Oriental languages (initially excluding but from 1619 on including Hebrew), he ran an Oriental press. Erpenius' own work covers various Oriental languages, such as his *Orationes tres de Linguarum Ebreae et Arabicae Dignitate* (Leiden, 1621). His works include grammars of Hebrew (Leiden, 1621; Geneva, 1627; Leiden, 1659); of Aramaic and Syriac (Amsterdam, 1628); the books of Samuel and Kings edited and translated into Hebrew and Latin; the Pentateuch in Arabic (Leiden, 1621); Psalms in Syriac (1628); and a treatise on the punctuation of the divine name (Rostock, 1626). After Erpenius' death his Oriental manuscripts were purchased and donated to Cambridge University (a.o. Hebrew Mss. Ee. 5.8–10, Mm. 6.26.1–2).

BIBLIOGRAPHY: Nouvelle Biographie Universelle, 13 (1815), 372–6, includes bibliography.

[Raphael Loewe]

ERRERA, CARLO (1867–1936), Italian geographer and historian of exploration. Errera, who was born in Trieste, and originally trained as a geographer, became interested in the Italian explorers and cartographers of the 15th and 16th centuries, and produced numerous monographs on their activities. These detailed analyses were synthesized in *L'Epoca delle grandi scoperte geografiche* (1902, 1926^3). An "Irredentist" with a particular interest in the Adriatic region, Errera wrote a number of books and pamphlets on this subject. He was vice president of the Italian National Research Council.

[Frank D. Grande]

ERRERA, LÉO (1858–1905), Belgian botanist and Jewish leader. Errera studied in Brussels, Strasbourg, and at the Botanical Institute of Wuerzburg. In 1884 he was appointed lecturer at the University of Brussels (professor, 1895), where he founded the Botanical Institute in 1891. In 1898 he was elected to the Royal Academy of Belgium. Errera's research included discovery of glycogen as the reserve carbohydrate of fungi, studies on the role of alkaloids in plants, and pioneer studies on the physical laws governing the shape of cells. His collected works were published in five volumes between 1908 and 1922. Errera was prominent in local and international Jewish activities. He was connected with the Alliance Israélite Universelle and he participated in many international conferences on Jewish questions. In 1893 he published a pamphlet protesting the persecution of Russian Jews, *Les Juifs russes: extermination ou émancipation* (English ed. 1894; German ed., together with the author's study on the Kishinev pogrom, 1903). His brother was Paul Joseph *Errera.

BIBLIOGRAPHY: Massart, in: *Annuaire de la Société Royale des Sciences naturelles et médicales de Bruxelles* (1905); Fredericq and Mossart, in: *Annuaire de l'Académie Royale de Belgique* (1908), 131–279; A. Errera, in: *Commemoration Léo Errera*, ed. by Université libre de Bruxelles (1960), 17–37 (includes bibliography); Pelseneer, in: *Bulletin de la Société Royale de Botanique de Belgique*, 92 (1960), 269–70.

ERRERA, PAUL JOSEPH (1860–1922), Belgian jurist. Born in Brussels, son of the banker Jacques Errera, Paul Errera became professor of constitutional law at Brussels, was rector of the university from 1908 to 1911, and its administrative vice president in 1919. He was a member of the Royal Academy of Belgium. Errera published several works on Belgian law, including *Les Masuirs* (1891), *Les Warechaix* (1894), and *Traité de Droit publie belge* (1918^2). He was active in Jewish affairs and a member of both the Jewish Colonization Association and the central committee of the Alliance Israélite Universelle.

[Rose Bieber]

ERTER, ISAAC (1791–1851), Hebrew satirist of the Haskalah. Born in Koniuszek near Przemysl, Erter, during the earlier part of his life, lived in various places including Lvov, where he, together with a group of young *maskilim*, was excommunicated in 1816 by Rabbi Jacob Ornstein; Budapest, where he studied medicine (1825–29); and Brody, then an important commercial and cultural center for Galician Jewry, where he settled in 1831 and remained for the rest of his life. In addition to his literary work, Erter was also active communally among Haskalah circles, showing special interest in the plans for a reform of contemporary Jewish society. Toward the end of his life, he collaborated with his friend Y.H. *Schorr in the early stages of the founding of *He-Ḥalutz*, a Hebrew periodical dedicated to the study of Judaica in the spirit of religious reform, and distinguished by a boldly critical treatment of problems relating to Jewish tradition.

Erter's only book, *Ha-Ẓofeh le-Veit Yisrael* ("The Watchman of the House of Israel," 1858), consists of five satires, all of which had been published separately (between 1823 and 1851) with the addition of some personal correspondence relevant to his literary career. Noteworthy among the satires are the following: *Ḥasidut ve-Ḥokhmah* ("Ḥasidism and Wisdom"), *Tashlikh* (the ceremony of symbolically casting one's sins into the water on Rosh Ha-Shanah), and *Gilgul Nefesh* ("Transmigration of the Soul"). Written in the form of epistles, several of the satires seem to have been modeled on the work of Lucian, the second-century Greek satirist, whose writings were very popular in European Rationalist literature and which Erter came to know in Wieland's German translation. Lucian's satiric and ironic treatment of Greek mythology and of ignorant and boorish antiquity during its decline was adapted by Erter in his fight against the traditionalist Jewish society of his day. The recurring character – a type of "*persona satirae*" – "the watchman of the House of Israel," has its source in the prophet-castigator of Ezekiel 3:17 (whence also the title); by virtue of the authority of the biblical figure, Erter's watchman reviews the reality of Jewish society in Galicia and Poland in the first half of the 19th century. In this narrative, written in an autobiographical manner, the "observer" gathers evidence and confronts the reader with confessions of figures belonging to an imaginary, fanciful world, confessions made in a dream state or after death. Having endowed them with a keen rhetoric ability, Erter enables these figures to explain their character and experience by ironic exaggeration, coupled with the idealistic pathos characteristic of the Haskalah movement.

The subjects treated in the satires are the hypocrisy, ignorance, and superstition, which in Erter's view characterize the world of Ḥasidism; the rabbis, who are accused of pedantry, pursuit of personal glory, and literary plagiarism; and the leaders of the Jewish community, condemned for their corruption. The irony is likewise directed, although to a lesser extent, at the *maskilim*, who ignore the plight of their brethren, and at Erter's colleagues, the physicians, who abuse their profession out of either ignorance or the pursuit of gain and glory. These facts are presented in an extremely satiric form with Erter's frequent use of not only conventional personifications of human qualities, in the tradition of satirical allegory, but also demonic figures drawn from the Jewish legends, such as angels, Samael, and reincarnated souls. The satirist pretends to be an objective reporter of empirical facts who, in his experimental approach, employs such satiric devices as scales which expose the true value of human qualities, nets which catch the sins of persons regarded by all as above reproach, and the cynical confessions of deceased sinners. He even has recourse to the pseudo-magical devices of a miraculous shortening of a journey and instantaneous flight to distant places so as to keep track of events in all areas of Jewish sojourn. The number of observations made is basic to his method, for in describing as many facets as possible of Jewish life which to him seem disgraceful, Erter seeks to stress his accusations by way of irony. Assuming an air of innocence, he is apparently surprised and shocked at the various reports of deceit and ignorance which are conveyed to him by the characters which inhabit the shadow of his sketches. His style is most important in the shaping of his satire. Using biblical phraseology extensively, he highlights the disparity between the sublime and the ideal in the original biblical source from which that phraseology is drawn and the ugly and the ridiculous state of the contemporary world which it describes. He also parodies traditional legal sources and adapts for his purpose some traditional sayings and proverbs. His idiom reflects the elaborate Hebrew style of the period and does not lack a certain rhetorical symmetry. A new edition of *Ha-Ẓofeh le-Veit Yisrael* was published in 1996.

BIBLIOGRAPHY: J. Chotzmen, in: JQR, 3 (1891), 106–119; idem, *Hebrew Humour and other Essays* (1905), 127–39; M. Lovitch, in: HUCA (1904), 224–34; M. Weissberg, in: MGWJ, 62 (1928), 184–92; Waxman, Literature, 3 (1960²), 187–94; S. Bernfeld, *Sefer ha-Shanah*, 2 (1935), 134–42; Klausner, Sifrut (1952²), 321–49. **ADD. BIBLIOGRAPHY:** M. Peli, *Darkhei ha-Sippur shel Erter ba-Satirah Gilglul Nefesh* (1973); N. Orland, "Aufklaerung, Emanzipation und Zionismus," in: *Veröffentlichungen aus dem Institut Kirche und Judentum*, 5 (1977), 36–41; J. Vilian, "*Ḥasidut ve-Ḥokhmah le-Yiẓḥak Erter,*" in: *Dappim le-Meḥkar be-Sifrut*, 5–6 (1989), 277–86; S. Werses, "*Gilgul Nefesh shel Erter be-Tirgumo le-Yiddish,*" in: *Ḥuliot,* 2 (1994), 29–49; S. Werses, "*Tofa'ot shel Magiyah ve-Demonologiyah ba-Aspaklariyah ha-Satirit shel Maskilei Galiẓiya,*" in: *Meḥkarei Yerushalayim ba-Folklor ha-Yehudi*, 17 (1995), 33–62; Y. Friedlander, Introduction to *Ha-Ẓofeh le-Veit Yisrael* (1996).

[Samuel Werses]

ERUV (pl. **Eruvin**; Heb. עֵרוּב), term applied to various symbolical acts which facilitate the accomplishment of otherwise forbidden acts on the Sabbath and festivals. The literal meaning of *eruv* is "mixing" and it probably connotes the insertion of the forbidden into the sphere of the permissible (cf. Maim., Yad, Eruvin, 1:6). Thus, though it is forbidden (biblically, according to some authorities, rabbinically, according to others) to walk further than 2,000 cubits from one's town on the Sabbath or festivals, one may "mix" the forbidden and permitted areas by establishing an *eruv teḥumim* (boundary *eruv*). This is accomplished by placing sufficient food for two meals (also called *eruv teḥumim*) less than 2,000 cubits from the town, thus establishing another "residence" from which one can again walk the permissible distance in any direction. This ordinance is evidently ancient since its existence is assumed in tannaitic sources (cf. Er. 3–5; Tosef. Er. 3–7; et al). It is discussed extensively in the Talmud (cf. Er. 26b–61b; TJ, Er. 3–5) and by later authorities (e.g., Tur, Sh. Ar., OḤ 408–16).

A similarly old statute (attributed to Solomon in Er. 21b) is that of *eruv ḥaẓerot* (domain *eruv*). While carrying between private and public domains is forbidden on the Sabbath, the rabbis also forbade carrying between two private domains. For example, if several houses opened onto one courtyard, an object could not be removed from one house to another, nor from a house to the courtyard (the latter is considered private property, owned by all the residents, if it is surrounded by a wall at least ten handbreadths high). To facilitate such carrying, a loaf of bread (called *eruv ḥaẓerot*) owned by all the residents is placed in one of the houses, thereby symbolically creating mutual ownership of all the dwellings. The houses and courtyard are thereby "mixed" together into one private domain. The sources indicate that *eruv ḥaẓerot* was already practiced in the time of the Second Temple; the details are elaborated in rabbinic literature from tannaitic times (Er. 1:10; 2:6, et al.; see also Er. 17b; 61b–82a, et al.) down to the later codes (cf. Tur, Sh. Ar., OḤ 366–95).

To "mix" private and public domains in order that an individual may carry from one to the other or within the latter, an *eruv* is erected around a given settled district. According to most early authorities, this *eruv* consists of a minimum of four poles at least ten handbreadths high, connected by other poles from top to top, forming the shape of a gate. The accepted practice among Jewish communities for generations has been to erect such an *eruv* by connecting poles (of the required height) with iron wires. A minority opinion among the authorities, based on a disagreement of interpretation of a talmudic section (Er. 11a–b; cf. Tur, Sh. Ar., OḤ 362), holds that the poles must also be no more than ten cubits apart.

No *eruv*, however, can permit carrying within what rabbinic law considers as falling under the biblical definition of public domain (cf. Shab. 6b; Er. 6). According to most authorities, such a domain is defined as an area crossed by at least 600,000 people (the number of Jews who fled Egypt) every day, and this definition is accepted in law. Since such public domains exist only in the largest cities, an *eruv* is effective in most areas. Some consider the minority opinion, which finds a biblically defined public domain in most settlements. While individuals refrain from carrying in such areas, the authorities admit that this practice is not required of everyone by law (cf. Shab. 6b; Tos. to Shab., s.v. *Kan;* Tur, Sh. Ar., OḤ 303, 345).]

According to rabbinical decree, in order to cook for the Sabbath during a festival immediately preceding it, one must establish an *eruv tavshilin* (cooking *eruv*). Before the festival, bread and a cooked food (some feel the former is unnecessary) are put aside for the Sabbath. Since the preparation of food for the Sabbath begins before the festival, it may be continued during the holidays. The preparation of food for the festival and that for the Sabbath are thus "mixed." The food prepared before the holiday is "mixed" with that prepared within the day, and the use of both is permitted. The term *eruv tavshilin* is applied both to the act of setting aside the food and to the food itself. This practice also evidently dates from an early period, since a controversy is recorded between the schools of Shammai and Hillel regarding one detail: Bet Shammai held that not one but two cooked dishes must be set aside. *Eruv tavshilin* is made by every householder, although, in principle, one man's *eruv* (e.g., that of the rabbi) can dispense the whole congregation or city. The making of the *eruv* is preceded by the standard benediction "Blessed art Thou … Who hast sanctified us with Thy commandments and hast commanded us concerning the ordinance of the *eruv*" followed by an Aramaic sentence to the effect that "by virtue of this *eruv* it is permitted to bake, to cook, and to kindle light as well as to provide for our necessary wants on this festival day for the succeeding Sabbath; for us and for all the Israelites living in this town." In some congregations it is customary to announce before the evening service of the festival that those who have forgotten to make *eruv tavshilin* are dispensed by the rabbi's *eruv*. In the Portuguese rite of Amsterdam the congregation was reminded by the *ḥazzan* on the day preceding the eve of the festival of the obligation to make *eruv* (*Vosses tens obrigaçao de fazer Hirub*). The rules regarding *eruv tavshilin* are discussed in the Talmud (cf. Mishnah Beẓah 2:1; TB, Beẓah 16a–17b; TJ, Beẓah 2:1) and the codes (Sh. Ar., OḤ 527).

BIBLIOGRAPHY: S. Ganzfried, *Code of Jewish Law*, tr. by H.E. Goldin, 2 (1928), 135–45; 3 (1928), 14–16; H. Tchernowitz, *Tikkun Shabbat* (1900); N.Z. Nobel, *Porat Yosef* (1914); Eisenstein, Dinim, 326–8.

[Zvi Kaplan]

ERUVIN (Heb. עֵרוּבִין), the second tractate of the order *Mo'ed* in the Mishnah, Tosefta, and in both the Babylonian and Jerusalem Talmuds. It deals with all aspects of the Sabbath *eruv*: *eruv* of Sabbath boundaries, the *eruv* of courtyards, and the *eruv* of the partnership of alleys (see *Eruv). It is thus a continuation of the tractate *Shabbat*, and in fact, it appears that originally the two tractates were one, but in view of its length (24 and 10 chapters) it was divided into two. This is evidenced by the fact that the last chapter, the Mishnah of *Eruvin*, is a kind of supplement to both *Shabbat* and *Eruvin* and deals with several details of the law of the Sabbath. The Tosefta of *Eruvin* also concludes with a statement which applies to the Sabbath: "The *halakhot* of the Sabbath … are like mountains hanging by a hair, having few biblical verses and many *halakhot* that have nothing upon which they can be supported" (cf. Ḥag. 1:8). *Eruvin* contains traditions which relate to the realia of the Second Temple period. Thus chapter 1:10 states that soldiers proceeding to battle are exempted from four things: they are permitted to collect wood for fuel from any place – and it is not regarded as theft; they are exempt from washing hands before touching food; they do not have to tithe **demai* produce; and they are permitted to carry things from tent to tent and from the tent into the camp without an *eruv*. Chapter 10:11–15 similarly gives a collection of *halakhot* regarding activities generally forbidden because they conflict with the spirit of Sabbath rest but permitted in the Temple. The chief sources of the Mishnah of *Eruvin* in its present form are, as usual, the pupils of Akiva-Meir, Judah, Yose, Simeon, and Eleazar. It is said of Judah that wherever he teaches a Mishnah in *Eruvin*, the *halakhah* goes according to his teaching (Er. 81b).

The first two chapters deal with the alley and with domains of a semi-private nature (*karmelit*), where the sages permitted carrying after minor modifications had been made. Chapters three to five deal with the limits of travel on the Sabbath and their extension by *eruv*. The next three chapters deal with the *eruv* of courtyards and of entrances owned jointly, and, as stated, chapter ten discusses various details of the *halakhot* of the Sabbath. According to Mishnah 6:1, if a Jew shares a courtyard with a non-Jew or with one who does not admit the validity of the *eruv* (such as a Samaritan or a Sadducee), he is thereby precluded from carrying articles from his house into the common alley on the Sabbath. The effect of this law was to limit joint residence with a gentile or sectarian in a building served by a common courtyard, or using the courtyard on Sabbaths (cf. Er. 62b: "lest he learn from his actions"). In the Jerusalem Talmud (Er. 7:9, 24c), however, Joshua b. Levi states: Why are *eruvin* made in courtyards? For the sake of peace, i.e., the carrying of the food before the Sabbath into the house of one of the neighbors for the *eruv* of courtyards promotes peace among the neighbors. The Jerusalem Talmud goes on to relate the case of a woman who was hated by her neighbor and sent her *eruv* through her son. When the neighbor saw the son she embraced and kissed him; on his return home he told his mother, who said, "She loves me so much and I did not know it," and as a result they were reconciled.

The order of the chapters in the manuscripts differs from that in the printed text. In the Munich manuscript chapter five precedes chapter three, and in the Oxford manuscript chapter four follows chapter two and chapter five follows six, but the order of the Tosefta accords more with that of the printed texts even though in many *halakhot* its order is different from that of the Mishnah. The Tosefta in the printed texts and in the Vienna manuscript of *Eruvin* has eight chapters – in the Erfurt manuscript (Zuckermandel's edition) it is divided into 11 chapters – and supplements the topics dealt with in the Mishnah. Worthy of note are the collection of *halakhot* in chapter 4 (3): 5–9 which discuss war on the Sabbath. If gentiles come to attack Jewish cities, it is permitted to go out with arms and desecrate the Sabbath; this applies only if they are bent on hostilities which endanger lives, but if their purpose is only to take spoil, it is forbidden. If, however, they move against towns near the border, even if only to take chaff or stubble, it is permitted to go out against them with arms and desecrate the Sabbath. In the Babylonian Talmud tractate *Eruvin* is considered one of the most difficult tractates, apparently because of the mathematical calculations (see, e.g., 14a–b or 76a–b) as well as because of the difficulty in understanding the various designs of the domains and their mutual relationship, despite the fact that sketches are provided in order to illustrate them (starting with the later printed versions).

Many scholars conclude from the discussion in Eruvin 32b, where there occurs the phrase, "Did you embody it in your *Gemara*?" that the *amoraim* already possessed a *Gemara* on the Mishnah which was methodically arranged (see the epistle of Sherira Gaon, ed. by B.M. Levin (1921), 63; Halevi, *Dorot*, 3 (1923), 117, et al.). It can also be seen from *Eruvin* 72a–b that there was an early editing of various discussions in the Talmud which preceded its final editing (see C. Albeck, *Mavo la-Talmudim* (1969), p. 578). Scattered throughout

Eruvin are many *aggadot* and ethical dicta. One tells how "for three years Bet Hillel and Bet Shammai disagreed, one school saying, 'the *halakhah* follows us,' and the other, 'the *halakhah* follows us.' A heavenly voice [**bat kol*] was heard to say, 'Both are the words of the living God but the *halakhah* follows Bet Hillel.' Since, however, 'both are the words of the living God,' why did Bet Hillel merit to have the *halakhah* established according to them – Because they were genial and modest, and taught their own sayings and those of Bet Shammai. Furthermore, they put Bet Shammai's words before their own.... This teaches you that whosoever humbles himself the Holy One exalts, and whosoever exalts himself, the Holy One humbles" (Er. 13b). The method of learning and memorizing in the academy of Rabban Gamaliel of Jabneh and of Simeon b. Gamaliel is reflected in an anachronistic aggadic *baraita*, quoted in *Eruvin* 54b, that describes the "order of the Mishnah" which Moses received from the Almighty and its teaching to the elders and the nation (cf. Epstein, *Tanna'im*, 187). Among the many apothegms to be found in *Eruvin* are the following: "The numerical value of the word *yayin* ["wine"] is 70 and that of *sod* ["secret"] also 70, to teach that when wine enters, secrets are divulged" (65a); "A man's character can be recognized by three things; by his cup [*kos*], by his purse [*kis*], and by his anger [*ka'as*]; some say also by his mirth" (65b). In addition to the many commentaries, editions, and translations available today, Abraham Goldberg has published a critical edition and commentary to Mishnah *Eruvin*, which discusses the historical levels in this tractate of the Mishnah, its relation to the Tosefta, and many of the traditions and interpretations found in the two Talmudim.

BIBLIOGRAPHY: Epstein, Tanna'im, 300–22; C. Albeck (ed.), *Shishah Sidrei Mishnah*, 2 (1958), 77ff. **ADD. BIBLIOGRAPHY:** Goldberg, *The Mishnah Treatise Eruvin* (1986).

[Yitzhak Dov Gilat]

ERWITT, ELLIOTT (1928–), U.S. photographer. Born in Paris to Russian parents, Erwitt immigrated to the United States with them in 1939. The family settled in Los Angeles, where Erwitt studied photography from 1942 to 1944 at Los Angeles City College. He worked as a photographic assistant in the U.S. Army before going to New York to study film. There, his work gained the regard of three influential figures in photography: Edward *Steichen of the Museum of Modern Art; Robert *Capa at Magnum, the photo agency; and Roy Stryker at the Standard Oil Company photo library. Steichen included several of Erwitt's pictures in the Modern's monumental 1955 "Family of Man" show, Stryker hired him as a staff photographer, and Capa promised a membership at Magnum after Erwitt's two-year army hitch. He remained with Magnum for more than 50 years. Erwitt's photography has often reflected his sense of humor: a quiet sense of the ridiculous, sometimes punctuated with visual puns, sometimes with hilariously candid juxtapositions. Most of his images, in black and white, were candids, taken with a small Leica, which he carried constantly. Some familiar photographs included Richard M. Nixon and Nikita S. Khrushchev at the famous "kitchen debate" in the Soviet Union; a bored-looking dog lifting his leg during a political speech by Nelson A. Rockefeller; and Jacqueline Kennedy in Arlington National Cemetery, clutching the flag that covered her husband's coffin. Other memorable pictures are of unknown people at unknown places and times. The cover of one of his books, *Personal Exposures*, for example, shows a photograph, taken at a beach in California in 1955, of a parked car whose side-view mirror reflects a couple kissing.

[Stewart Kampel (2nd ed.)]

ESARHADDON (Akk. *Aššur-aḫ(a)-iddina*, "Ashur has given me a brother" (for the other siblings); Heb. אֵסַר־חַדּוֹן), king of Assyria from 680 to 669 B.C.E., third ruler of the Sargonid dynasty. Though a younger son, he was preferred for the succession because of the influence of his mother Naqiʿa-Zakutu. His reign is characterized by three main policies. The first was the reconciliation of Babylonia by the rebuilding of Babylon, which his father Sennacherib had destroyed in 689 B.C.E. The second was the maintenance of Assyrian rule and influence in the northern and eastern marches of the empire, especially in the face of the Scythian invasion of 679 B.C.E. and its consequences in the north, and the gradual political and military consolidation of the Medes on the Iranian plateau. With some of the latter he concluded vassal treaties in 672 B.C.E. to ensure the orderly succession of his son Ashurbanipal to the throne. The terminology of these treaties bears comparison in structure and detail with various parts of the contemporaneous Book of *Deuteronomy, especially the final section of curses in Deuteronomy 28:15ff. The third aspect of Assyrian imperial policy during the reign of Esarhaddon was the response to the danger of increasing Egyptian influence and intrigue among the vassal states of Syria, Phoenicia, and Palestine, involving punitive campaigns against insurgent cities in 677 and 675 B.C.E. and an expedition to the Arabian desert in 676 B.C.E., and culminating in the defeat and conquest of Egypt in 671 B.C.E. Esarhaddon relates that he made 22 western vassals, including *Manasseh of Judah, drag beams and timber for the construction of his palace in Nineveh and stone statues of protective deities (see Pritchard, Texts, 291). This may be the historical nucleus of II Chronicles 33:11–12, according to which Manasseh was taken in chains to Babylonia by the army officers of the king of Assyria but was later allowed to return to his kingdom. But the political orientation of Judah in those years is obscure and Manasseh may have steered a national course for a time. Assyrian cultural influence in Judah was strong in the reign of Esarhaddon, and according to Ezra 4:2 he continued the colonization of Samaria with foreign settlers.

BIBLIOGRAPHY: CAH, 3 (1925), 79–80, 393; R. Borger, in: AFO Beiheft, 9 (1956); D.J. Wiseman, in: *Iraq*, 20 (1958); D.R. Hillers, *Treaty Curses and the Old Testament Prophets* (1964); M. Weinfeld, in: *Biblica*, 46 (1965), 417–27. **ADD. BIBLIOGRAPHY:** A.Grayson, in: ABD II, 574; S. Parpola and K. Watanabe, *Neo-Assyrian Treaties and Loyalty Oaths*

(SAA II; 1988); M. Luukko and G. van Buylaere, *The Political Correspondence of Esarhaddon* (SAA XVI; 2002); F. Reynolds, *The Babylonian Correspondence of Esarhaddon* (SAA 17; 2003).

[Aaron Shaffer]

ESAU (Heb. עֵשָׂו; meaning uncertain; see below), the firstborn son of *Isaac and *Rebekah, the twin brother of *Jacob (Gen. 25:24–26). Esau is also called Edom (25:30) and is the ancestor of the Edomites (Gen. 36; Mal. 1:2–3; see *Edom). The Bible does not describe Esau at great length; but he is featured as a hairy man, "a skillful hunter, a man of the outdoors," and the favored son of Isaac, in sharp contrast to Jacob, a mild man, "smooth-skinned," and the favored son of Rebekah (Gen. 25:25, 27–28; 27:11). According to the biblical narrative, while Rebekah was pregnant with the twins, "the children struggled in her womb" and in her anxiety Rebekah "went to inquire of the Lord." The oracle she received in reply describes, in fact, not so much the relationship between Jacob and Esau as that between the Israelites and the Edomites: each of the boys would become the progenitor of a nation, and "One people [would] be mightier than the other, and the older would serve the younger." In a sense, the prophecy began to be fulfilled in the lifetime of the two ancestors, through two episodes in which Jacob gains the upper hand. First a starving Esau took an oath whereby he agreed to relinquish his birthright to his brother in exchange for a meal (25:29–34). The oath, it should be noted, was as binding as a written document. The narrative at this point contrasts with pentateuchal law, which guarantees certain privileges to the firstborn (Deut. 21:15–17), and reflects an earlier state of affairs in which the transfer of the birthright was possible. The socio-legal situation behind this incident is clarified in the finds of *Nuzi (see *Patriarchs). The second event which gives the struggle between the two brothers special significance is the loss by Esau of the patriarchal blessing (Gen. 27). Jacob, following the advice of his mother, disguised himself as Esau and received the blessing promised by Isaac to his brother. When Esau discovered the deception and implored his father for a blessing, he was told, "See, your abode shall enjoy the fat of the earth and the dew of heaven above. Yet by your sword you shall live, and you shall serve your brother; but when you grow restive, you shall break his yoke from your neck." This "blessing" contains echoes of the oracle which Rebekah had received, the supremacy of the younger brother over the firstborn being emphasized in both cases. However, at the end of Isaac's blessing there is a hint of Edom's recovery of her independence in the days of Solomon (I Kings 11:21–22, 25) and Jehoram (II Kings 8:20–22). Incensed by Jacob's deception, Esau intended to kill Jacob once Isaac was dead (Gen. 27:41). When Rebekah became aware of this, she advised Jacob to flee to her brother *Laban in *Haran, where he stayed for 20 years. Meanwhile Esau, having taken two wives from among the indigenous peoples of Canaan and a third from among the daughters of his uncle, Ishmael (regarding their names, and the parentages of the Canaanite ones, there are two different traditions: Gen. 26:34; 28:9; and Gen. 36:2), and having begotten children, migrated with all his household and his belongings "to another land because of his brother Jacob. For their possessions were too many and the land where they sojourned could not support them because of their livestock" (Gen. 36:6–7). Esau settled in the land of Seir, alongside the descendants of Seir the Horite, who were already living there (36:20). When Jacob, on his way home from Haran, had advanced into *Gilead as far south as *Penuel, he decided to try to appease his brother by sending messengers with greetings. Esau set out to meet him with a band of 400 stalwarts; and when his messengers returned and made this known to Jacob, he was frightened and sent ahead some herds of livestock as gifts (32:4–22; 33:1–2). As it turned out, however, Jacob's fears proved to be unfounded; for Esau came with 400 of his men to welcome his brother just south of the *Jabbok, greeted him with every sign of affection, and refused to accept the gifts. He wished to escort Jacob and his company southward through Transjordan to his home in Seir where he would no doubt act the older, if not unkind, brother; but Jacob persuaded him to go ahead, and then proceeded westward to the land of Canaan (33:4–16). In this incident as in the sale of the birthright Esau is a good but simple fellow, easily manipulated by his wily brother.

Three popular etymologies are connected with Esau. In the description given of him at his birth – "red, like a hairy mantle all over" (Gen. 25:25) – at most only the second part can have anything to do with the name Esau (Heb. Esav, ʿEsaw), which may be related to the Arabic root *ġšw*, "to cover." The redness, in contrast, can only explain his other name, Edom (Heb. ʾEdom), connected with the word *ʾadom* ("red"). In verse 30, the same name is explained by his impatient plea, when he came home hungry, for some of the "red stuff" (i.e., lentils) that Jacob was cooking. The red down ("hairy mantle," Heb. *ʾadderet seʿar*) with which he is said to have been covered at birth may originally have served to explain the name Seir (Heb. *seʿir*).

[Yuval Kamrat]

In the *Aggadah*

The personality of Esau is discussed in the *aggadah* from three different aspects, the differentiation between which causes difficulties. He is discussed as the brother of Jacob, as identical with *Edom, and sometimes with *Rome, with whom Edom was identified.

JACOB'S BROTHER. Esau's relations with *Jacob were a favored theme for many homilies and *aggadot*. Generally the *aggadah* follows the biblical account, and so do the pseudepigraphic works of the Second Temple period (particularly the Book of *Jubilees and the *Testament of the Twelve Patriarchs), but they aim at describing Esau as completely wicked. However, there are also descriptions aimed at finding some redeeming features in him, such as the dictum of Simeon b. Gamaliel: "All my days I attended upon my father but I did not attain to one hundredth of the attention Esau gave his father, for I attended him in soiled garments and when I went out to the market-place I went with clean clothes. When Esau, however, attended his father, he waited upon him in regal garments, saying, 'Father's honor is to be respected only in regal garments'" (Gen. R. 65:16). So too the homily: "And Esau saw that the daughters of Canaan pleased not Isaac his father; so Esau went unto Ishmael and took Mahalath [Gen. 28:8–9]; Joshua b. Levi said: he intended to mend his ways [*Maḥalat*, root: "to forgive"] because the Holy One pardoned his iniquities" (Gen. R. 66:13). The aggadists also find some merit in his relations with Jacob. Thus Simeon b. Yoḥai says: "It is a well-known fact that Esau hated Jacob, yet at that moment his compassion was turned to him and he kissed him wholeheartedly" (Sif. Num. 69, cf. a similar saying of Simeon b. Eleazar in Gen. R. 78:9). Here too, however, the opposite opinion is expressed that he did not kiss him "with his whole heart" or that he even "intended to bite him" (*ibid.*). The homilies which portray the wickedness of Esau are many and very diversified. He is said to have committed the most heinous sins – idolatry, adultery, and bloodshed (Gen. R. 63:12) – and he was hypocritical, asking questions like "how does one tithe salt ... how does one tithe straw?" (Gen. R. 63:10).

ESAU AS EDOM. The identification of Esau with Edom (cf. Gen. 36:1, 43) is often referred to in the Bible and is found in all the apocrypha and pseudepigrapha of the Second Temple period and naturally in talmudic and midrashic sources too. *Amalek, the eternal enemy of Israel, is one of his descendants. Since the end of the Second Temple, the identification of *Haman the Agagite (Esth. 3:1; 8:3, 5; 9:24) as "a descendant of the seed of Amalek" (an identification first found explicitly in Jos., Ant., 11:20, apparently on the basis of the connection between the name "Agagite" and *Agag, king of Amalek: I Sam. 15:8–9, 20, 32–33, and cf. Num. 24:7) served as a fertile source for many homilies connecting the stories of the Book of Esther with Esau. Most of these homilies are naturally condemnatory, but there occur some with a slightly different tone, such as "R. Ḥanina said, whoever says that the Holy One is indulgent will be punished. The truth is that He is patient but ultimately claims His due; Jacob caused Esau to utter one cry [Gen. 27:34], and where was he requited? In Shushan the capital, as it is stated [Esth. 4:1] 'and he cried with a loud and a bitter cry'" (Gen. R. 67:4).

ESAU AS ROME. The identification of Esau with Rome is not found in the literature of the Second Temple period; attempts at detecting it in the Ezra Apocalypse (IV Ezra 6:7–8 and in Jos. Ant.) and in the Targum of *Onkelos to the Pentateuch have no real basis. The identification appears first, apparently, in an *aggadah* of the period following the *Bar Kokhba War (132–135 C.E.): "It has been taught: Judah b. Ilai said: My teacher Baruch (or, "blessed be he" – see later) used to say 'The voice is the voice of Jacob, but the hands are the hands of Esau [Gen. 27:22]; the voice of Jacob cries out at what the hands of Esau did to him at Bethar'" (TJ, Ta'an. 4:8, 68d; Gen. R. 65:21, et al. – "Baruch my teacher" may be a cryptic reference to *Akiva). The identification is also found in a conversation between Akiva and *Tinneius Rufus (Tanḥ. Terumah, 3) and is common in the mouths of the scholars of the age following the Hadrianic persecutions (Gen. R. 67:7 – Yose b. Ḥalafta; Tanh. B., Deut. supplement 5 (p.5) – Simeon b. Gamaliel). Thereafter it became very widespread (see the anonymous homily in Sif. Deut. 41, ed. Finkelstein, p. 85). In general Esau is referred to in a derogatory vein but here too there are exceptions such as: "For the three tears that Esau shed [Gen. 27:38], Israel suffered in three wars, as it says [Ps. 80:6]: Thou hast fed them with the bread of tears, and given them tears to drink in large measure" (*shalish*, ARN^2 47, 130).

[Moshe David Herr]

BIBLIOGRAPHY: C.H. Gordon, in: BA, 3 (1940), 5; R. de Vaux, in: RB, 56 (1949), 22ff.; E.A. Speiser, in: JBL, 74 (1955), 252–56; idem, in: IEJ, 17 (1957), 212–13; idem, *Genesis* (1964), 193–213, 258–61; V. Maag in: *Theologische Zeitschrift*, 13 (1957), 418–29; H.L. Ginsberg, in: JBL, 80 (1961), 342; N.M. Sarna, *Understanding Genesis* (1966), 181–88; Y. Heinemann, *Darkhei ha-Aggadah* (1954^2), index. **ADD. BIBLIOGRAPHY:** N. Sarna, *Genesis* (JPS; 1989), 177–82.

ESCALONA, town in Castile, central Spain. A Jewish community existed in Escalona during the Muslim period and remained in the town after the Christian conquest in 1083. The rights of the Jews in Escalona were established by the *fuero* ("municipal charter") of 1130. This gave them equal status with Christians and Moors, although a Jew was not permitted to act as judge in Christian lawsuits. Jews in Escalona owned vineyards and real estate throughout the existence of the settlement there. In the 1290 tax distribution among the Jewish communities, the Jews of Escalona were not included specifically, probably due to their small number. The community was destroyed during the persecutions of 1391, but was renewed in the 15th century, when it was fairly small. In 1453 real estate in the city was given to R. Salamon, the physician of Countess Juana Pimentel, in appreciation of his services. The list of the taxes levied on the community is an important source of information, showing that it paid 1,000 maravedis in 1474, and 2,000 maravedis in 1482. The levy for the war against Granada amounted to 38 gold castellanos in 1485. The community paid 5,040 maravedis in 1489, 6,570 maravedis in 1490, and 4,000 maravedis in 1491. From a source preserved in the municipal archives we know that a Jewish quarter existed between 1477 and 1489. There is a reference to a Jewish slaughterhouse. Following the segregation of the Jews in 1483 the mosque of the Muslims was included within the Jewish quarter. Thus the community apparently continued to exist until the expulsion of the Jews from Spain in 1492. Don Isaac *Abrabanel had business interests in the town. There was a group of *Conversos living in Escalona, and those suspected of secretly practicing Judaism were tried by the Inquisition of Toledo.

BIBLIOGRAPHY: Baer, Urkunden, index; Suárez Fernández, Documentos, 67, 80, 405; Beinart, in: *Tarbiz*, 26 (1956/57), 77, 82; Ashtor, Korot, 2 (1966), 143. **ADD. BIBLIOGRAPHY:** P. León Tello, *Judíos de Toledo*, 1 (1979), 291–4; A. Malalana Ureña, *Escalona medieval (1083–1400)* (1987), 195–7; J.L. Lacave, *Juderías y sinagogas*, (1992), 314.

[Haim Beinart / Yom Tov Assis (2nd ed.)]

ESCAPA, JOSEPH BEN SAUL (1570–1662), Turkish rabbi and author. Escapa was the descendant of a family from Castile which settled in *Salonika. He served there as head of a yeshivah, and was a colleague of Ḥayyim *Shabbetai. From about 1620 he was rabbi of the Salonikan community in Smyrna, and in 1648 was appointed rabbi of all the congregations of the city. Under his leadership, the united Smyrna community became one of the most important in Turkey. Gifted with administrative ability, he introduced regulations concerning the collection of taxes and the supervision of communal affairs; these practices are followed to the present day by the community of Smyrna and surrounding territory. Escapa's enactments were collected by R. Joshua Judah and published in his *Avodat Massa* (Salonika, 1846). Escapa was one of the most vehement opponents of *Shabbetai Ẓevi, who was his disciple and whom he had ordained, and proclaimed it a religious duty to put Shabbetai Ẓevi to death. Escapa wrote a commentary on the Shulḥan Arukh, called *Rosh Yosef*, of which only sections – on *Oraḥ Ḥayyim* (Smyrna, 1657), and *Ḥoshen Mishpat* (*ibid.*, 1659) – were published. He also wrote responsa (Frankfurt on the Oder, 1709), and a work on *Maimonides which has remained in manuscript.

BIBLIOGRAPHY: J. Sasportas, *Ẓiẓat Novel Ẓevi*, ed. by I. Tishbi (1954), 378, index; Conforte, Kore, 46a; Rosanes, Togarmah, 2 (1938), 208–10; Werses, in: *Yavneh*, 3 (1942), 101ff.; Scholem, Shabbetai Ẓevi, 89–90, 113, 119–20, 140, 304–5.

ESCHATOLOGY. In general, the term "eschatology" designates the doctrine concerning "the last things." The word "last" can be understood either absolutely as referring to the ultimate destiny of mankind in general or of each individual man, or relatively as referring to the end of a certain period in the history of mankind or of a nation that is followed by another, entirely different, historical period.

INTRODUCTION

The Bible has no word for the abstract idea of eschatology. It does, however, have a term – *ʾaḥarit ha-yamim* – that often has eschatological connotations, at least in the broad sense mentioned above. It means literally "the end of the days," i.e., "the end of time." Just as the cognate Akkadian term, *ina aḥrât ūmī* (from the older *ina aḥriāt ūmī*), often shortened to *ina aḥrâti*, means simply "in the future" or "for [all] the future," so also the Hebrew term *be-ʾaḥarit ha-yamim* can sometimes mean merely "in the future, in time to come," without necessarily having any eschatological connotation (thus, e.g., Deut. 4:30; 31:29; cf. *ʾaḥarit*, "a future," in Jer. 29:11; et al.). In the Prophets, however, *be-ʾaḥarit ha-yamim* generally has an eschatological connotation (see below).

In the last few centuries before the destruction of the Second Temple, a new term with a strictly eschatological meaning in the absolute sense appears. This term, *keẓ* (*qeẓ*) *ha-yamim*, means literally "the term of the days" (Dan. 12:13b; cf. the similar term, *ʿet qeẓ* "the time of the term," Dan. 8:17; 11:35, 40; 12:4, 9).

Some scholars have sought to derive Israelite eschatological ideas from similar concepts of its ancient neighbors, Egypt and Babylonia. At most, there may have been some borrowings from these sources by the Prophets in the secondary details of their descriptions dealing with the horrendous conditions of the eschatological period. More likely, the features for which there are early extra-Israelite parallels were concepts common to the entire ancient Near East. Essentially, eschatology in Israel is an inner-Israelite development. Only in the very later period, i.e., in Daniel and the so-called intertestamental literature of the Jews, can a certain amount of borrowing from Persian sources be shown as probable.

It is difficult to date several eschatological oracles. In certain cases where, for instance, reference is made in a pre-Exilic prophet to Jerusalem as already destroyed and the people of Judah as already in exile, it is legitimate to suggest that such passages are later insertions into the pre-Exilic Prophets. However, when such criteria are lacking, the supposition should normally be that the eschatological oracles in question belong to the pre-Exilic prophet to whom they are attributed.

IN THE BIBLE

For the sake of showing how eschatological ideas evolved in ancient Israel, it is useful to consider the preprophetic period, the early prophetic oracles, the later pre-Exilic Prophets, and the Exilic and post-Exilic Prophets.

Pre-Prophetic Period

In the age of the Patriarchs, of Moses and Joshua, and of the Judges, and in the first few centuries of the monarchy there is little evidence of true eschatology. Yet the basis of later Israelite eschatology was really laid down in that early age. From the time of Abraham on, those descendants of his who later called themselves *bene Yisrael*, "the Israelites," venerated their one and only God as a "living God," i.e., as one who took an active part in the history of His people. They were conscious of the fact that He had made them His "*chosen people." Since He was not only the special God of Israel but also the sole Lord of the entire world, Israelite religion combined a certain "particularism" as the "chosen people" with a certain universalism, which looked forward to their God's reign over all mankind. They regarded Him as a just God, who would reward or punish all men according to their morally good or evil lives. Because of His *covenant with His chosen people, He proves Himself to be faithful and loyal to His promises (thus showing His frequently praised *ʾemet* or *ʾemunah*, "faithfulness," and *ḥesed*, "mercy"); therefore in times of need He sends His people "saviors," such as Moses and Joshua, the various "Judges," and especially David, the ideal *mashiʾaḥ*, "anointed" (see *Messiah) king, who was promised an everlasting dynasty (II Sam. 7:11–16). The hope and expectation that this relationship between the God of Israel and His people would continue in the future led to the genuine eschatology that is found in the books of the so-called "writing" Prophets (as distinct from such earlier prophets as Elijah and Elisha). The essential origin of Israel's eschatology lay in Israel's belief in its election by God as the means by which He would establish His universal reign over all mankind, combined with His promise to Israel of its own land, "the Promised Land," "the land of Canaan," as His pledge guaranteeing this promise.

Early Pre-Exilic Prophets

Among all the prophets of Israel, only the recorded oracles of Amos and Hosea were uttered before the destruction of the Northern kingdom of Israel (722 B.C.E.).

AMOS. The prophetic activity of *Amos took place in approximately 750 B.C.E., during the brief period of peace and prosperity that both Israel and Judah enjoyed after Jeroboam II, king of Israel (786–746), inflicted a decisive defeat (at an uncertain date) on the Arameans of Damascus (II Kings 14:25–27). This prosperity led to various forms of social injustice, whereby the relatively small class of rich landowners and government officials oppressed the poor, as well as to an indulgence by many of the people of both kingdoms in the degrading practices of their pagan neighbors. With divinely inspired foresight, Amos knew that these evils would bring about a time of crisis when the wrath of God would condemn to inevitable doom (Amos 1:3, 6, 9; et al.) not only the pagan nations (1:3–2:3) but also Judah and especially Israel (2:4–6:14). The prophet based his prediction of Israel's and Judah's punishment on the much older concept of their election by God as His "Chosen People": "You only have I known of all the families of the earth; therefore I will punish you for all your iniquities" (3:2).

In designating the time of God's future punishment, Amos was the first to call it "the *Day of the Lord" (*yom* YHWH), a term that was taken up, with further developments of the concept, by many of the later prophets (Isa. 13:6, 9; Ezek. 13:5; Joel 1:15; 2:1, 11; 3:4; 4:14; Obad. 15; Zeph. 1:7, 14; Mal. 3:23), with variations such as "the day of the Lord's fury" (Zeph. 1:18), "that Day" (*ha-yom ha-hu'*, Isa. 2:11; Zeph. 1:15), or simply "the Day" (*ha-yom*, Mal. 3:19; cf. Ezek. 7:7). However, Amos did not invent the term; it is clear from his reference to it that it was already in popular use. Its origin is obscure, and at first it may have had a military connotation, "the day of the Lord's victory over the enemies of His people" (cf. the expression "the day of Midian" in Isa. 9:3, where, however, it refers to Israel's victory over the Midianites). In any case, at the time of Amos the common people were using the term to designate the time when their God would bring them complete victory over their enemies and thus lead them into the "light" of lasting peace and prosperity. The prophet turned this expectation of theirs directly against them: "Woe to you that desire the day of the Lord! Wherefore would you have the day of the Lord (YHWH)? It is darkness, not light.... No, the day of the Lord shall be darkness, not light, gloomy, devoid of brightness" (5:18, 20). In 8:9–10 Amos enlarges on this theme: "And on that day, says the Lord God, I will make the sun go down at noon, and darken the earth in the clear day. And I will turn your feasts into mourning and all your songs into lamentation; I will bring sackcloth upon all loins, and baldness on every head; and I will make it like the mourning for an only son, and the end of it like a bitter day." While Amos used the image of a midday eclipse of the sun merely in a figurative sense, the eschatological oracles of later prophets (e.g., Isa. 13:10) developed this image into vast cosmic disturbances, seemingly to be understood literally, that would accompany the Day of the Lord.

Although for Amos the event initiating the new historical era would be primarily one of punishment and destruction, he includes, because he is aware of God's fidelity to His promises, the hope that for those who "seek the Lord" (5:4–6) "it may be that the Lord, the God of hosts, will be gracious to the remnant of Joseph" (5:14–15). Here again there occurs the earliest use of a term, "the remnant" (*she'erit*; see *Remnant of Israel), that was reused and at times received a different connotation in later eschatological writings (Jer. 6:9; 31:7; Ezek. 9:8; et al.; sometimes also in the form *she'ar*, Isa. 10:20–21; 11:11, 16; et al.). For Amos it designates those who will survive the destruction of the Northern Kingdom.

In order that the Book of Amos might end on a more positive note of hope, the last verses of the book (9:11–15), concerning the restoration of Israel, were apparently added by a post-Exilic editor. The later origin of this passage seems probable because it presupposes that the Davidic dynasty has come to an end and that the walls of Jerusalem have "breaches" and the city is in "ruins" (9:11).

HOSEA. It is generally agreed that *Hosea, the only "writing" prophet who was a native of the Northern Kingdom, was a contemporary of Amos, although apparently a younger one, for some of his oracles were probably delivered shortly before the fall of Samaria, although none after that date (722 B.C.E.). Like Amos, Hosea inveighed vigorously against the moral evils in Israel. Yet his vehement threats of terrible punishments (Hos. 2:3–7, 16–25; 5:14; 10:14–15; 13:7–8; et al.) are mingled with generous promises of forgiveness and future happiness (2:16–23; 6:1–3; 11:8–9; 12:6; 14:2–9; et al.); this is done with such sudden and confusing transitions that some scholars regard the book as a rather haphazard collection of Hosea's short oracles strung together by some later editor in complete disorder, while others see in this a reflection on the Lord's part of the prophet's own experience with his faithless wife (1:2–9; 3:1–3; cf. McKenzie, in CBQ, 17 (1955), 287–289).

If eschatology is understood in the broad sense of a dramatic change from one historical period to an entirely different one in the future, Hosea no doubt shows genuine eschatological concepts. Some of these, which are original with him, played an important role in later eschatological writings. Such, for instance, is Hosea's concept of renewal of God's love for and covenant with Israel as in the days following the Exodus from Egypt (2:14–15; 11:1). The notable – and seminal – feature of this new covenant is that it has a built-in guarantee against Israel's ever giving cause for its dissolution as it did with the original covenant. With the covenant, Israel will receive a new nature which will render it incapable of breaking it (Hos. 2:21–22; see Jeremiah below). Another notable eschatological concept is the view of a future in which Israel will never again be attacked by human enemies from without and will live in peaceful harmony with all living creatures within its border.

Later Pre-Exilic Prophets

In the second half of the eighth century B.C.E. two prophets, Isaiah and Micah, were active in Judah, and some of their oracles are eschatological in the broad sense described above. Similar eschatological oracles are found in Zephaniah, Nahum, and Jeremiah, who lived about a century later.

ISAIAH. The authentic prophecies of *Isaiah, who was active as a prophet from approximately 740 to at least 701 B.C.E., are found in the first 39 chapters ("Proto-Isaiah") of the long book (66 chapters) that is attributed to him; even in the first 39 chapters there are several sections, some rather long (e.g., the eschatologically important "Apocalypse of Isaiah" in 24:1–27:13), that are later additions to the Book of Isaiah. These, as well as "Deutero-Isaiah" (40:1–55:13) and "Trito-Isaiah" (56:1–66:24) – the question of a Trito-Isaiah is still, however, disputed – will be considered below for their eschatological import. Only those oracles with eschatological bearing that are clearly or at least probably from Isaiah or his disciples are treated here.

Isaiah lived at a time of national crisis for Judah: the Assyrians under Tiglath-Pileser III (745–727) ravaged and annexed Syria and most of the northern kingdom of Israel, and under Shalmaneser V (727–722) and Sargon (722–705) subdued the rest of Israel and most of the Philistine plain; meanwhile the wicked Ahaz (735–715) and even the pious Hezekiah (715–687), kings of Judah, played the game of international politics rather than trust in help from the Lord. Filled with a deep sense of God's utter holiness by his call to prophesy, Isaiah fulminated against idolatry and general wickedness in Israel and Judah. Many of his vehement threats of the punishment that would come on "the Day of the Lord" have a genuine eschatological ring: they predict universal destruction, not only for Israel and Judah, but also for the pagan nations, especially those who were the "rod of His wrath," and these oracles often have the overtones of cosmic disturbances that became characteristic of later Jewish eschatology. Thus, for instance: "For the Lord of hosts has a day against all that is proud and lofty.... And the haughtiness of man shall be humbled, and the pride of men shall be brought low; and the Lord alone will be exalted on that day" (2:12, 17); "You will be visited by the Lord of hosts with thunder, and with earthquake, and great noise, with whirlwind and tempest, and the flame of a devouring fire. And the multitude of all the nations that fight against Ariel ... shall be like a dream, a vision of the night" (29:6–7).

A recurring theme with eschatological implications in Isaiah is that of the "remnant of Israel" (10:21–22; 11:11, 16; 14:30; 28:5; 37:32). To some extent this term implies a threat, as in Amos 5:15 (cf. "only a remnant" in Isa. 10:22), but usually it includes a consoling promise that at least a remnant of the people will be left with whom the Lord will be pleased (cf. "to recover the remnant of His people" in 11:11, and similar phrases in 4:3; 11:16; 28:5). There is no good reason for rejecting these passages as not authentic or for placing them in the Exilic or post-Exilic period, since there is mention of a son of the prophet with the symbolic name of Shear-Jashub (7:3), which means "a remnant shall return." (This, however, occurs in a third person story about the prophet, and its historicity is therefore not technically assured; but see Isa. 6:11–13.)

A new theme in Isaiah is the prospect of a future ideal king of Judah. This occurs in the so-called Immanuel passages, although, apart from its use as an exclamation in 8:8, the name Immanuel, meaning "God is with us," occurs only in 7:14, and the literary form of third person narrative, among other things, raises doubts as to its historicity (see *Immanuel). When King Ahaz of Jerusalem is threatened with war by a coalition of the kings of Israel and Damascus if he does not enter into an anti-Assyrian league, Isaiah urges him to trust solely in the Lord and gives him this sign: "Therefore the Lord Himself will give you a sign: behold, a young woman shall conceive, and bear a son, and shall call his name Immanuel.... Before the child knows how to refuse the evil, and choose the good, the land before whose two kings you are in dread will be deserted" (7:14, 16). Although the exact meaning of this passage is disputed, it is usually understood as referring directly to Ahaz' son and successor Hezekiah, who is here given the symbolic name "God is with us." Probably 9:5–6 is to be connected with this passage. Here, after singing of joyful peace following a great victory that the Lord has wrought for His people, the prophet continues: "For to us a child is born, to us a son is given; and the government will be upon his shoulder; and his name will be called Pele-Joez-El-Gibbor-Abi-Ad-Sar-Shalom ["Wonderful Counselor, Mighty God, Everlasting Father, Prince of Peace"]; of the increase of his government and of peace there be no end, upon the throne of David, and over his kingdom, to establish it, and to uphold it with justice and with righteousness from this time forth and for evermore. The zeal of the Lord of hosts will do this." Finally, connected with these two prophecies is that of 11:1–5: "There shall come forth a shoot from the stump of Jesse, and a branch shall grow forth out of his roots. And the Spirit of the Lord shall rest upon him, the spirit of wisdom and understanding, the spirit of counsel and might, the spirit of knowledge and the fear of the Lord. And his delight shall be in the fear of the Lord. He shall not judge by what his eyes see, or decide by what his ears hear; but with righteousness he shall judge the poor, and decide with equity for the meek of the earth; and he shall smite the earth with the rod of his mouth, and with the breath of his lips he shall slay the wicked. Righteousness shall be the girdle of his waist and faithfulness the girdle of his loins." These passages are quoted here at length because in their description of the future ideal king of Judah, they laid the foundation for the so-called Royal Messianism in the post-Exilic period, an important element in late Jewish eschatology. There is no solid reason for denying the Isaian authorship of these prophecies; even though the pre-Exilic prophets may not have held the kingship of Judah, as they knew it, in high esteem, they must have been aware of the constant tradition based on Nathan's oracle concerning the perpetual endurance of the Davidic dynasty (II Sam. 7:12–16; Ps. 89:20–38; see *Messiah).

Like Hosea 2:20, 23–25, Isaiah describes the peace of the Messianic age as a return to the happiness of the Garden of Eden, where all creatures, wild beasts as well as men, would live in tranquil harmony; "for the earth shall be full of the knowledge of the Lord, as the waters cover the sea" (11:6–9).

MICAH. Contemporaneous with Isaiah, *Micah, a native of Moresheth in Judah, apparently had a much shorter prophetic ministry. Like Isaiah, he looked forward, in a broader eschatological sense, to an ideal ruler (the basis of Royal Messianism) who would be of the Davidic dynasty, coming from David's native town of Beth-Lehem (5:1–3).

The theme of Mount Zion's eventually becoming the religious center of all mankind, which is further developed in later Jewish eschatology, is first enunciated in a prophecy that is given, in almost identical words, in both Micah 4:1–4 and Isaiah 2:2–4. Some scholars hold that this prophecy is not original in either Micah or Isaiah, but that it was inserted in both books from some common source by a later editor. Yet there is no solid reason for assigning a post-Exilic date to it. Interestingly enough, in the post-Exilic book of Joel, where there is a description of the eschatological war that will be waged between the Lord and His pagan enemies, the classical words of the earlier oracle describing universal peace are turned into the directly opposite sense: "Beat your plowshares into swords, and your pruning-hooks into spears" (Joel 4:10).

ZEPHANIAH. The prophet *Zephaniah probably uttered his oracles at about 640–603 B.C.E., in the first decade of the reign of King Josiah of Judah, a turbulent period when the idolatry and general wickedness of the people of Judah, combined with the political folly of Jerusalem's leaders in favoring the declining power of Assyria, led him to believe that "the great day of the Lord is near" (Zeph. 1:14). The bold imagery he used in describing this terrible "day" had much influence on later Jewish eschatological writings. After depicting the destruction of all the wicked on this day of doom (1:2–14), he cries out: "A day of wrath is that day, a day of distress and anguish, a day of ruin and devastation, a day of darkness and gloom, a day of clouds and thick darkness, a day of trumpet blast and battle cry against the fortified cities and against the lofty battlements. I will bring distress on men, so that they shall walk like the blind, because they have sinned against the Lord; their blood shall be poured out like dust, and their flesh like dung. Neither their silver nor their gold shall be able to deliver them on the day of the wrath of the Lord. In the fire of his jealous wrath, all the earth shall be consumed; for a full, yea, sudden end he will make of all the inhabitants of the earth" (1:15–18).

In genuine prophetic tradition, Zephaniah ascribes to the Lord phrases such as "the remnant of My people" and "the survivors of My nation" (2:9), adding "For I will leave in the midst of you a people humble and lowly. They shall take refuge in the name of the Lord, those who are left in Israel; they shall do no wrong and utter no lies, nor shall there be found in their mouth a deceitful tongue. For they shall pasture and lie down, and none shall make them afraid" (3:12–13). However, the final verses of the book (3:14–20) were probably added to it in the Exile or in the post-Exilic period since they speak of the gathering in of the scattered exiles of Zion.

NAHUM. Although the short Book of *Nahum, as such, consists essentially of a hymn of victory over the fall of Nineveh (612 B.C.E.), this hymn is introduced by an incomplete "alphabetic" psalm (Nah. 1:2–8), in which God's wrath is portrayed in the vivid colors that are later employed in describing the cosmic disturbances accompanying the great and terrible Day of the Lord.

JEREMIAH. In the broad sense of eschatology as the "end" of a given historical period that would be followed by a very different one, the Book of *Jeremiah, despite its seemingly disturbed sequence of poetic oracles and prose narratives combined with later scribal accretions, can be considered as practically eschatological throughout. Jeremiah clearly foresaw that the kingdom of Judah was doomed, because most of its people refused to give up their evil ways and their political leaders resisted the Babylonians whom God had sent to punish His people. One can almost speak of "realized eschatology" in Jeremiah, since for the prophet the doom was so imminent as to be felt as already present. Sixteen of his oracles begin with the expression *hinneh yamim ba'im* ("Behold, the days are coming when…"; 7:32; 9:24; 16:14; 19:6; et al.), which for Jeremiah is almost the equivalent of the eschatological term "at the end of days," when the imminent and actual invasion of the Babylonians under Nebuchadnezzar (cf. 15:1–4; 34:8–22; 37:3–10; et al.) will take place.

Yet even when the situation looked utterly hopeless for Judah, the prophet still believed that in God's mercy a remnant would survive the Babylonian destruction of Jerusalem (32:1–15), just as he had expected a reprieve for the remnant left in the Northern Kingdom (3:11–18) and a restoration of Judah's exiles taken to Babylonia in the first deportation of 597 B.C.E. (24:1–10). Like Isaiah and Micah a century before his time, Jeremiah looked forward to the continuity of the Davidic dynasty in an ideal king of the future (23:5–6). (In the symbolic name that the prophet gives to the new, ideal king, YHWH *ẓidekenu* (*ẓideqenu*) (Heb. יהוה צִדְקֵנוּ), there is most likely an intentional allusion – with obvious inversion – to the name of the last, wicked king of Judah, Zedekiah (Heb. צִדְקִיָּהוּ).) Moreover, Jeremiah, obviously inspired by Hosea 2:21–22, foresaw that Israel's reestablishment would entail a renewal of the ancient Sinaitic covenant in such a way that it would bring about a true change of heart, a new, interior spirituality (31:31–34).

Exilic and Post-Exilic Prophets

During the Babylonian exile and in the centuries that followed the gradual return of the Jewish exiles to the land of

Israel until the latest writings in the Bible, important developments took place in Jewish eschatological thought. This can be seen especially in the writings of Ezekiel, the so-called Deutero-Isaiah (Isa. 40:1–55:13), the so-called Trito-Isaiah (Isa. 56:1–66:24), Haggai, Zechariah, and Malachi, Joel, the so-called Deutero-Zechariah (Zech. 9:1–14:21), the author of the so-called Apocalypse of Isaiah (Isa. 24:1–27:13), and finally in the Book of Daniel.

EZEKIEL. Since it can rightly be said that the Babylonian destruction of Jerusalem in 587 B.C.E. formed the climactic turning point, not only in the political history of ancient Israel but also in its religious orientation, the prophet *Ezekiel is unique in many ways, particularly as he prophesied before that destruction (although already in Babylonia), as well as during the first few decades of the Jewish exile in Babylonia, where he had been taken in the first deportation of Jews by Nebuchadnezzar in 597 B.C.E. He shows a more intense sense than the older prophets both of the imminence of God's punitive judgment on the pagan nations (Ezek. 25:1–32:32) and of the restoration of God's chosen people to a holier state than before.

For Ezekiel, Judah's restoration would be almost as miraculous as the resurrection of the dead to life, which is illustrated in his well-known vision of the valley filled with dead men's bones that took on flesh and came back to life (37:1–14). Although the new religious life of Judah would be essentially based on a sincere inner conversion to the Lord (11:19–20; 36:26–27), it would be centered on an elaborately described worship in a rebuilt temple in Jerusalem; this holy city, with its new symbolic name of "The-Lord-Is-There," would be in the center of the new land of Israel, with six of the twelve tribes of Israel living in parallel geographic strips to the north of it, and the other six in similar strips to the south (40:1–48:35).

Now that Judah no longer had its own king, Ezekiel kept alive the ancient expectation of a continuance of the Davidic dynasty – the basis of later messianism. However, for this prophet, Judah's future ruler as the Lord's viceroy would have the title of only "prince" (*nasi*, anciently "a tribal chief"), not "king" (44:3; 45:17; et al). He would be a true shepherd of the Lord's flock (34:11–24). Chastened Israel, though now scattered throughout the world, would be the Lord's means of establishing His reign over all the earth, and would thus fulfill the promise He made to the Patriarchs (36:1–38). A diligent elaborator of Jeremiah motifs, he conceived in his own way the motif of a change in Israel's nature – "a new heart and a new spirit," with variations (11:17–20; 16:60; 36:24–28) – which would guarantee the new covenant against dissolution as in the case of the first. However, he stresses in his inimitable manner (36:20–23, 29–31) the principle first clearly enunciated in I Samuel 12:22, according to which God's motive is not compassion for undeserving Israel, but His own prestige, since His name, because it is associated with Israel, is discredited in the eyes of the nations by Israel's misfortunes. That is why, even after proving that he is able to restore Israel to its land, He will further "prove Himself great and holy" in the eyes of the nations (38:23) by demonstrating through Gog and Magog that He is able to prevent their being subjugated again (39:22–29).

The fantastic word pictures drawn by Ezekiel, which he used directly only for describing eschatology in the broad sense, e.g., that of *Gog and Magog who represented for the prophet the hostile pagan nations of his time (38:1–39:20), were destined to find many echoes in later Jewish writers, who reused them in depicting their eschatology in the strict sense – the "end" of the world as men knew it.

DEUTERO-ISAIAH. The anonymous writer who composed Isaiah 40:1–55:13 and to whom modern scholars have given the name "Deutero-Isaiah" (the "Second Isaiah") is generally believed to have prophesied in the last years preceding the conquest of Babylon by the Persians under Cyrus the Great in 539 B.C.E. Just as the prophet knew that the Lord had used the pagan kings of Assyria and Babylon to punish His sinful people according to the predictions of the earlier prophets (Isa. 1:21–31; Jer. 7:1–15; Ezek. 22:1–22), so he foresaw that the Lord would use the pagan king of Persia as His "anointed one" (cf. Isa. 44:28; 45:1 with Jer. 25:9; 27:6; 43:10) to liberate repentant Judah from its captivity. The prophet's preaching, therefore, is almost entirely one of consolation for his afflicted fellow exiles. From an eschatological viewpoint, Deutero-Isaiah is important for his clear perception of God's plan in directing man's history on earth; the Lord alone prearranged this history from beginning to end (Isa. 41:22–23; 42:8–9; 46:8–13; et al.). The prophet treats this history of man on a cosmic scale; the restoration of Judah is to be a "new creation" for all mankind as well as for the Jews (41:17–20; 42:5–7; 43:1; 45:8). This plan of God for the world's salvation would be carried out by the *Servant of the Lord (*ʿeved YHWH*), who both personifies Israel (49:3) and has a mission for Israel (49:5–6); his sufferings atone for man's sins, but his glorious exaltation brings peace and salvation to the world (52:13–53:12). With Deutero-Isaiah there begins a more transcendent concept of eschatology; climactic events in history are viewed not so much as the beginning of a new historical era brought about by human means, but rather as a transformation of the world on a cosmic scale produced by God's extraordinary intervention in man's history.

HAGGAI, ZECHARIAH, AND MALACHI. When Zerubbabel, the grandson of King Jehoiachin of Judah, was appointed governor of the small Persian province of Judah, the prophets *Haggai and *Zechariah temporarily saw him as the one who could continue the Davidic dynasty (Hag. 2:20–23; Zech. 4:6–7; 6:9–14 (emending "Joshua son of Jehozadak, the high priest," to "Zerubbabel" in v. 11; cf. "the Shoot" in 3:8)); thus they kept alive the messianic expectation in Judah. Moreover, the strange type of symbolism that first appears in Zechariah 1:7–2:13 and 5:1–6:8, connected with the concept of an incredibly enlarged Jerusalem (Zech. 2:5–9), was later reechoed in the eschatological imagery of Daniel and the later Jewish writers.

The book that bears the title *Malachi ("my messenger"), apparently borrowed from Malachi 3:1, was probably written about the time of Ezra and Nehemiah (second half of the fifth century B.C.E.). This prophet predicts that the Lord will come to His temple preceded by His messenger, and will hold His Day of Judgment against the wicked (Mal. 3:1–6). In what is generally considered to be a later addition to the book, this messenger is identified with "Elijah the prophet [coming] before the great and terrible day of the Lord" (3:23). Since on the basis of II Kings 2:11 it was commonly assumed that Elijah never died, a popular belief, later elaborated on in Jewish writings, held that he would return to earth as the precursor of the *Messiah (cf. Matt. 11:14; 16:14; Mark 9:11–13; Luke 1:17; John 1:21; et al.).

JOEL. A terrible plague of locusts (Joel 1:2–20) was seen by the prophet *Joel, who probably prophesied between 400 and 350 B.C.E., to have eschatological significance in that it symbolized the forces hostile to God on "the day of the Lord…, a day of darkness and gloom, a day of clouds and thick darkness! Like blackness there is spread upon the mountains …" (2:1–17). Yet the Lord would be victorious over His enemies (4:1–16) and bring salvation and blessings to His chosen people (2:18–3:5). This is eschatology in the strict sense, involving cosmic disturbances as the initiation of the new, transcendent era (3:1–4).

In the verse in which Joel has God say: "I will gather all the nations, and bring them down to the valley of Jehoshaphat, and I will enter into judgment with them there, on account of My people and My heritage Israel…" (4:2), the term "valley of Jehoshaphat" has no geographic significance; it merely means "the place where the Lord judges." Later tradition identified it with the Kidron Valley to the east of Jerusalem, and consequently this valley and the Mount of Olives to the east of it became a favorite burial place, where one would be at hand at the resurrection of the dead for general judgment on the Last Day.

DEUTERO-ZECHARIAH. The last six chapters of the Book of Zechariah (9:1–14:21) differ in so many respects from the first eight chapters that many modern scholars attribute them to a later writer (or even to two later writers – one for 9:1–11:17, and another for 12:1–14:21), who apparently lived some time between Joel (c. 400–350 B.C.E.) and Ben Sira (c. 180 B.C.E.). Rejoicing over the fall of Syria and the coastal cities of Palestine (9:1–8), perhaps as the victorious army of Alexander the Great advanced toward Egypt in 332 B.C.E., the prophet saw in their fall a sign of the imminent coming of the Messiah as a prince of peace: "Rejoice greatly, O daughter of Zion, shout aloud, O daughter of Jerusalem; Lo, your king comes to you; triumphant and victorious is he, humble, and riding on an ass …" (Zech. 9:9). In describing the new, transcendent era, the prophet develops the symbolic language of the older prophets, especially that of Ezekiel, but it already has more of the fantastic imagery that is characteristic of *apocalyptic literature. A theme that later receives further development is that of the sufferings that God's people must still endure (14:1–2, 13–14a) before "the Lord will become King over all the earth" (14:9).

TRITO-ISAIAH. Many scholars hold that the last 11 chapters of the Book of Isaiah (56:1–66:24) form a unit quite distinct from both Proto-Isaiah (1:1–39:8) and Deutero-Isaiah (40:1–55:13). This section probably consists of a collection of writings composed by different men at various times in the post-Exilic period (even though 57:3–13a may possibly be of pre-Exilic origin). From an eschatological viewpoint, the passages in Isaiah 60:1–62:12; 65:17–25; 66:7–17, depicting the glory of the new Jerusalem and the joy of all the earth, and the passage in 66:18–21, describing the gathering of all the nations of the earth for God's final judgment on mankind, are of particular importance. (On the bearing of the "unquenchable fire" (66:24), together with Jer. 7:30–8:3; 19:6; 31:40, for the later eschatological concept of the eternal fire of Gehenna, see below.)

"APOCALYPSE OF ISAIAH." Isaiah 24:1–27:13 is so different from the rest of Isaiah that it seems to have been written by some anonymous prophet distinct from all the other prophets whose prophecies have been gathered together in the large compilation now known as the Book of Isaiah. The hymns of praise (24:14–16a), thanksgiving (25:1–12), and supplication (26:1–19) that are interspersed among the various prophecies of doom and blessing suggest that this section once formed a sort of "liturgy." Nowhere in the section is there any reference or even allusion to an historical event that could be used for dating the composition. Yet in the descriptions of the devastation of the entire world (24:1–13), of the concomitant cosmic disturbances (24:19–23a), and the salvation of the "remnant" (26:20–21), the style and language are so similar to later apocalyptic writings that this section is commonly called "the Apocalypse of Isaiah," and the date of its composition is generally placed not long before the composition of the genuinely apocalyptic chapters in the Book of Daniel. Concepts that play a large role in the later apocalyptic writings, such as the eschatological banquet (Isa. 25:6) and the resurrection of the dead (26:19, perhaps to be understood here in the literal sense as distinct from the symbolic resurrection of the dead, signifying national resurrection, in Ezek. 37:1–14) appear here for the first time (see the Book of *Isaiah).

DANIEL. The first section of the Book of *Daniel is a compilation of six (or five, the first being merely introductory) aggadic stories about Daniel and his three companions, who are presented as living in Babylon in the sixth century B.C.E., toward the end of the Neo-Babylonian empire and the beginning of the empire of the Medes and Persians (Dan. 1:1–6:29); the second section contains four visions or revelations (7:1–12:13) that Daniel is said to have received and which foretell the history of the Near East from the time of Nebuchadnezzar, king of Babylon (605–562 B.C.E.), to that of Antiochus IV Epiphanes, king of Syria (175–164 B.C.E.). This compilation was made in its present form shortly before the death of Epiphanes, at a time when Judaism in Palestine was suffering a severe crisis both from defection toward pagan Hellenism from within, and from violent persecution from without by Epiphanes to make the Jews forsake their ancient religion.

The older aggadic stories were retold in the book for the sake of encouraging faithful Jews to withstand persecution; as the Lord had come to the rescue of Daniel and his companions, so also would He intervene in the present crisis by putting an end to the pagan empires and establishing His reign over all the earth by means of His chosen people, for He is the Lord of history, who "changes times and seasons; he removes kings, and sets up kings" (2:21).

The second half of the book (7:1–12:13) contains the earliest preserved form of apocalyptic literature in the strict sense, a type of writing that was frequently imitated and developed by Jews at least until the destruction of the Second Temple. This type of writing, in brief, purports to be a revelation (Greek *apocalypsis*, literally an "uncovering") of the future, especially the final destiny of the world, which was given to some ancient worthy centuries or even millennia earlier, but was left "hidden" (Gr. *apocryphon* – hence many of these writings are called "*apocrypha") until the present time of crisis.

Persian influence on the apocalyptic writings can be seen, not only, e.g., in their more elaborate *angelology, but especially in their division of history into various distinct eras or "monarchies." The Persians divided their history of the world into three "monarchies": the Assyrian, the Median, and the Persian. In the Hellenistic period a fourth "monarchy" was added – their own Greek "kingdom," which as far as Palestine was concerned, consisted of the Ptolemaic dynasty in Egypt and the Seleucid dynasty in Syria, with the capital at Antioch. The Jews adapted this four-monarchy theory of history to their own situation by substituting the Babylonian empire (as better known to them) for the Assyrian empire, and by adding a fifth "kingdom" – the universal reign of God on earth, based on His chosen people, Israel. This last kingdom would be "an everlasting kingdom" (3:33) – a concept that is eschatology in the strict sense. In Daniel this view of world history is presented in two places: first, in the aggadic story of Nebuchadnezzar's dream of the gigantic statue made of four different materials (symbolizing the four successive pagan empires), that was smashed by a rock hewn without hands from a mountain, which itself "became a great mountain and filled the whole earth," the kingdom of God, "which shall never be destroyed…, and it shall stand for ever" (2:31–45); secondly, in the apocalypse of chapter 7, where four beasts (each with a characteristic number to show the number of rulers) representing the four successive pagan empires are destroyed by God, and in their place "one like a son of man" receives from the Lord "dominion, and glory, and kingdom, that all peoples, nations, and languages should serve him; his dominion is an everlasting dominion, which shall not pass away, and his kingdom one that shall not be destroyed" (7:13–14).

In Daniel, the "one like a son of man" (a Semitism meaning simply "one like a human being") is a symbol, as stated explicitly, representing "the people of the saints of the Most High" (7:27); that he "came with the clouds of heaven" (7:13), i.e., had his origin from God, is said primarily to contrast him with the four great beasts that "came up from the sea" (7:3), i.e., from the realms of chaos (cf. Gen. 1:2). However, as will be shown below, this purely symbolic figure of "one like a son of man" was soon regarded as a real person, the Messiah.

Daniel contains the first unequivocal affirmation of a belief in the eschatological resurrection of the dead: "There shall be a time of trouble…; and at that time your people shall be delivered, every one whose name shall be found written in the book. And many of those who sleep in the dust of the earth shall awake, some to everlasting life, and some to shame and everlasting contempt" (12:1–2). This does not necessarily imply a universal resurrection of all mankind at "the end of the world"; the expression "many of those" hardly means "all men, numerous as they are." But it does offer a solution to the age-old problem of divine retribution, why the just suffer and the wicked seem to prosper in this life. The Book of Job struggled in vain with this problem; yet even the well-known passage in Job 19:25–27, where the text itself is not clear, seems merely to have the sufferer reassert his firm belief that God would some day vindicate Job's righteousness. Belief in the resurrection of the dead may have been adumbrated in the "Apocalypse of Isaiah" (Isa. 26:19; see above) and in the pious hope of the Psalmist (Ps. 73:23–26), yet it appears in Daniel 12:1–2 with startling suddenness. Perhaps there is some influence here from the Zoroastrian religion of the Persians, which had such a belief. However, the occasion for the expression of this belief in Israel was apparently due to Israel's conviction, on the one hand, of God's justice in rewarding the good, and on the other hand the martyrdom of so many innocent Jews in Antiochus Epiphanes' persecution.

Another important trait in the eschatology of Daniel is the attempt by the author of the apocalypse contained in chapter 9 to show that "the end" was to come in the near future; he does this by interpreting the 70 years of exile that had been foretold by Jeremiah (Jer. 25:11; 29:10) to mean 70 weeks of years or 490 years, and to argue from this by his own strange chronology that only three and a half years still remained before the end would come. The author may well have been the compiler of the entire book, for the references to the remaining three and a half years before "the end" in the other apocalypses (7:25b; 8:14; 12:7) seem to be insertions made by him. Later on, additions were made to the book in 12:11 and 12:12, in order to lengthen the period of waiting when the earlier predictions failed to be fulfilled.

IN THE INTERTESTAMENTAL LITERATURE

Apocrypha and Pseudepigrapha

Certain Jewish writings that were composed after the completion of the latest book of the Hebrew Bible (probably Daniel, c. 165 B.C.E.) and before the completion of the books of the New Testament are commonly referred to as the "intertestamental literature." With the exception of some fragments that have been found at *Qumran, these writings have been preserved in Greek (or in secondary translations made from the Greek), although most of them were originally written not in Greek but in Hebrew or Aramaic. None of these books is included in the Jewish or Protestant canon; but seven of them, which are found in the *Septuagint, are included in the Bible of Roman Catholics and Orthodox Christians. These seven books – Tobit, Judith, Baruch, I and II Maccabees, the Wisdom of Ben Sira, and the Wisdom of Solomon – are called "deuterocanonical" (i.e., belonging to the "second canon") by the Catholics; Protestants call them "the *Apocrypha," and the rest, "the Pseudepigrapha." Some of these books – the Ethiopic and the Slavonic Books of Enoch, the Apocalypse of Ezra, the Syriac and the Greek Apocalypses of Baruch, the Jewish Sibylline Oracles, etc. – are primarily apocalyptic and of prime importance for the eschatological concepts of the period in question. However, even the pseudohistorical writings (Jubilees, Life of Adam and Eve, Ascension of Isaiah, etc.) and the moral-didactic writings (Wisdom of Solomon, Testaments of the Twelve Patriarchs, Psalms of Solomon, etc.) provide much information concerning eschatological ideas of the Jews in the last two centuries before, and the first century after, the destruction of the Second Temple. Almost all the intertestamental writings have come down in copies or translations made by Christian scribes, who often interpolated new passages containing Christian concepts into the older original Jewish compositions. However, it is generally not difficult to discern which passages are Christian interpolations.

MESSIANISM. Although Jewish eschatology, including that of the intertestamental literature, was always theocentric, i.e., concerned basically with the ultimate triumph of God and His justice, it combined this with certain preliminary events that would precede the establishment of God's universal reign over all mankind on "the Day of the Lord." Chief among these preliminary events would be the reign of the *Messiah (I En. 45:3; 105:2; 28:29; 13:32–35; 14:9). Not only from the intertestamental writings but also from Josephus (Wars, 2:6, 12; Ant., 13:9) and the New Testament (Matt. 23:23–24; etc.), it is clear that in the last two centuries before the destruction of the Second Temple and even in the succeeding generations, e.g., at the time of the revolt of Bar Kokhba (132–135 C.E.), belief in the imminent coming of the Messiah was widespread in Judaism. During that period more than one contender arose to claim the title of Messiah (cf. Acts 5:36; 12:38). The intertestamental literature naturally reflects this belief, but not always in a uniform fashion.

Some of these writings speak of certain personages who would precede the coming of the Messiah. On the basis of Deuteronomy 18:15 ("A prophet will the Lord thy God raise up into thee…, like unto me; unto him ye shall hearken"), some of the apocalyptic writers of this period predicted that a special prophet, or even Moses himself, would come to prepare the way for the Messiah. Jeremiah, "a friend of his brethren, who prays much for his people and for the holy city" (II Macc. 15:14) and highly respected by the Jews of the period, was sometimes identified with this precursor of the Messiah. However, the chief candidate for the office of the precursor of the Messiah was the prophet Elijah, in keeping with the oracle of Malachi 3:23–24; by his miracles and his preaching he would reform the people and make them ready to receive the Messiah (cf. e.g., Ecclus. 48:10–11).

Reckoning Eschatological Times. In imitation of the attempts made in Daniel to calculate the time remaining before "the end of time" (cf. Ass. Mos. 1:18; IV Ezra 3:14), the apocalyptic writers of the intertestamental period devised various methods for reckoning "the times of the Messiah," *Yemot ha-Mashiaḥ*. Jubilees, for instance, divided the history of the world into a great number of "jubilees" (period of 50 years each) in order to establish when "the end" would come. Other writings divided the history of the world into 12 periods of 400 years apiece (IV Ezra 14:11; Test. Patr., Abraham A 19, B 7; Life of Adam and Eve 42). Some reckoned by millennia and maintained that the reign of the Messiah itself would last for a thousand years, referring to "the Messianic millennium," a period of peace and happiness on earth before the final Day of the Lord.

Birth Pangs of the Messiah. In general, the intertestamental literature depicts the period preceding the coming of the Messiah as one of terrible distress: plagues and famine, floods and earthquakes, wars and revolutions, accompanied by such cosmic disturbances as the darkening of the sun and the moon and the falling of the stars from the sky. In part, these ideas were derived from contemporary events, such as the dispersion and persecutions suffered by the people of Israel, and in part from the descriptions of the Day of the Lord found in the writings of the earlier prophets. The purpose of these terrifying pictures was to encourage the faithful in Israel to bear their afflictions patiently as God's will for them, for only when the cup of evil was filled to the brim would the Messiah come to bring salvation. These sufferings, therefore, are commonly called "the pangs of the Messiah," *ḥevlo shel Mashiaḥ*, meaning that Israel, like a mother, was to bring forth the Messiah in the pangs of childbirth.

On the basis of Ezekiel 38:1–39:20, the pre-messianic wars are presented as the Lord's fight against Gog and Magog, symbols of the powers of evil in the world. The leader of these evil forces bears such names as Satan, Belial (or Beliar), Maste Din (or Mastema), and (in the Greek versions) the Anti-Christ. However, it should be noted that this pre-messianic warfare is to be understood primarily as a spiritual, not a military, one; and the Lord's use of Israel in establishing His reign over all mankind is not intended to imply an Israelite political empire.

Son of Man. Besides such titles as "savior" and "redeemer," which are given to the expected Messiah in the intertestamental writings, a special title is given to him in the (Ethiopic) Book of Enoch (I En.; written shortly after Daniel) and in the Apocalypse of *Ezra (IV Ezra; written c. 30 years after the destruction of the Second Temple), that of the "son of man." This title is clearly borrowed from Daniel 7:13. Although in Daniel the term is purely symbolic (see above), the intertestamental books use it in reference to an actual person, the Messiah. According to these writings, the "son of man," who stands "at the throne of God" in heaven, existed "before the sun and the stars were created" (I En. 46:1–3); he will bring salvation at the end of the ages, when he will be enthroned as king of the world (IV Ezra 13:26).

4TH WORLD TO COME. The apocalyptic writings after Daniel (though in this book the terms themselves are not used) divide the time after God's great eschatological interventions as "this (present) time" (*olam ha-zeh*) and "the time to come" (*olam ha-ba*, lit. "the coming time"; cf. I En. 23:1; IV Ezra 7:30, 43; Test. Patr., Abraham 19, B 7). It is only in the latter period – the eschatological period in the strict sense – that full retribution for good and evil is meted out by God to every man.

Retribution. Israel always had firm faith in the Lord's justice, in His rewarding the good and punishing the wicked. However, in Israel there was a definite development of this concept in two important points: (1) from collective responsibility and retribution to individual responsibility and retribution, and (2) from full retribution in man's mortal life to full retribution only "in the world to come (**olam ha-ba*)," i.e., after man's death.

Although even in the oldest periods of biblical theology Israel often expressed the belief that God rewards and punishes each man according to his own deeds (cf. e.g., I Sam. 26:23), as can be seen in the numerous cases of divine punishment meted out to individual sinners (Cain, Lot's wife, Miriam, Er and Onan, etc.) and as frequently stressed in the wisdom literature, in pre-Exilic Israel the emphasis was placed primarily on collective retribution; the whole group (family, tribe, nation) was responsible for the deeds of its members. It was Ezekiel in particular who shifted the concept of divine retribution from a collective to an individual one (cf. especially Ezek. 18; Jer. 31:29–30 is probably a later addition, borrowed from Ezek. 18:2–3). However, the principle that every man is rewarded or punished in this life for his good or evil deeds seemed to be contradicted by ordinary experience; and the problem of why the innocent suffer and the wicked prosper in this life, as presented especially in *Job, appeared to be an insoluble mystery, best left to God's wisdom.

Resurrection of the Dead. A solution to this problem was finally found in the belief of the resurrection of the dead (*teḥiyyat ha-metim*), i.e., in the notion that the dead would come back to life, both in body and in soul, on the Day of the Lord. The earliest clear expression of this belief is in Daniel 12:12, and subsequently it was often expressed by many writers of the intertestamental literature (II Macc. 7:9, 11, 14, 23; 12:43; 14:46; Jub. 23:30; Test. Patr., Men. 98:10; IV Ezra 7:29–33; etc.). Some of these writings speak of all men, good and bad alike, rising from the dead for judgment on the Day of the Lord; others maintain that only the just will rise to life, since the condemnation that the wicked receive at God's tribunal can scarcely be called "life" (so apparently even in Dan. 12:2). Moreover, some of the apocalyptic writings (e.g., II En. 66:5) speak of two resurrections: the first only of the just, at the beginning of the Messianic millennium; the second of the wicked, at the final Day of the Lord, which is for the wicked a "second death."

A special concept of a future life immediately after death is seemingly found in the Wisdom of *Solomon, a Greek composition (c. 75 B.C.E.) by an Alexandrian Jew, who was influenced by the Greek philosophical concept of the immortality of the human soul (cf. Wisd. 3:1–9). Yet the author of this work really follows the common Hebrew concept of life as truly human only when man's body and soul are united.

In the last two centuries before the destruction of the Second Temple the *Pharisees believed in the resurrection of the dead, whereas the *Sadducees did not (Jos., Ant., 18:14; Wars, 2:14; cf. also Mark 12:18; Acts 23:8).

Until the last two centuries before the destruction of the Second Temple the Jews retained the ancient Israelite concept of *Sheol, the dark abode in the nether world of all the dead, good and bad alike (thus still Ben Sira: e.g., Ecclus. 14:16; 28:21; 51:6, 9). However, when the concept of individual retribution after death developed in Judaism during this period, the concept of Sheol underwent various changes in the different intertestamental writings. According to some of these writings there are various levels in Sheol (e.g., six: IV Ezra 7:36–37), so that even before the resurrection of the dead the wicked are tormented in various degrees in Sheol's lower levels, whereas the good enjoy bliss in its highest level. According to other writings Sheol is replaced by **Gehinnom* (Gehenna), the place where the damned are in torment, whereas the just, either immediately after death or only at the resurrection, have the delights of an eschatological *Garden of Eden or Paradise.

Gehenna. The word "Gehenna" is the Greek form of the Aramaic *Gehinnom* for the Hebrew *Ge* (*Bene*) *Hinnom* ("the Valley of (the sons of) Hinnom"), the ravine in the south of ancient Jerusalem (Josh. 15:8; 18:16). Since it had been defiled by being the site of the Topheth worship of Molech (II Kings 23:10; Jer. 32:35; etc.), Jeremiah cursed the place and predicted that, at the Babylonian destruction of Jerusalem, this valley would be filled with the corpses of the city's inhabitants, to be burned there and rot like "dung upon the face of the earth" (Jer. 7:32–8:3; 19:6; 31:40). Trito-Isaiah (Isa. 66:24) clearly alludes to these sayings in Jeremiah, even though he does not use the word "Gehenna," when he speaks of the eschatological punishments of the wicked: "And they shall go forth, and look upon the carcasses of the men that have rebelled against me; for their worm shall not die, neither shall their fire be quenched; and they shall be an abhorrence unto all flesh."

The intertestamental writings add further gruesome details to the torments suffered by the wicked in this fiery pit, where their bodies burn eternally, although, incongruously, they are, at the same time, rotting away with worms and maggots (cf. IV Ezra 7:36; I En. 27:2; 48:9; 54:1; 90:26–27; 103:8; Ass. Mos. 10:19; II Bar. 85:12–13).

Eschatological Paradise. The term "paradise" is from the Greek word that the Septuagint uses to translate the Hebrew term, Gan Eden ("the Garden of Eden"). Since the earlier prophets had depicted, in figurative terms, the eschatological bliss of "the new earth" as a return to the original peace and joy of the Garden of Eden before Adam's sin (cf. Isa. 11:6–9; 51:3; Ezek. 36:35), the intertestamental writers call the place where the righteous are to enjoy endless bliss "the Garden of Eden" (IV Ezra 4:7; 7:36, 123; 8:52; II En. 42:3; 65:10). It is not identical with "heaven" as God's abode. But just as Gehenna is pictured as having several levels, one lower than the other, so the eschatological paradise has at least three levels (I En. 8), one higher than the other, the uppermost being nearest to God's abode in heaven. As in the case of Gehenna, so also in regard to the eschatological paradise there is inconsistency in these writings concerning the time when the just enter this place of paradisiacal bliss, whether immediately after death, or only at the resurrection.

One of the features of the eschatological paradise, at least during the "messianic millennium," is the participation in the messianic banquet (based on Isa. 25:6; cf. the Qumran literature below, and Matt. 8:11). A special privilege at this banquet in the world to come is to be seated at the side of Abraham (Test. Patr., Abraham 20; cf. Luke 16:26; the poor man Lazarus in "Abraham's bosom").

Dead Sea Scrolls

The writings composed by the *Essene community that lived at Qumran from approximately 150 B.C.E. to 68 or 70 C.E., generally called "the *Dead Sea Scrolls," can from a merely chronological viewpoint be classified with the intertestamental literature; yet, because of their unique importance for revealing the specifically Essene concepts of eschatology, they are here given separate treatment.

IMMINENCE OF THE END OF DAYS. The presumably Essene community of Jews that had its headquarters at the site now known as Khirbat Qumrān, near the northwestern shore of the Dead Sea, was very concerned with eschatology. Its life was organized by austere rules, especially by an exact observance of the various precepts of the Torah, particularly those concerning ritual purity, so that this would hasten the coming Day of the Lord and, at the same time, make the members of the community ready to stand at God's awesome tribunal on that day. They lived in the barren Desert of Judah, not merely because they had fled from Jerusalem and its Temple on account of what they considered the illegitimacy of the Hasmonean high priests and their successors who were appointed by the conquering Romans, but more particularly because they thus sought to carry out literally the command (originally intended merely in a metaphorical sense) of Isaiah 40:3: "Clear ye in the wilderness the way of the Lord" (cf. 1QS 8:12–14; 9:19). They were convinced that they were living "at the end of the era of wickedness" (CD 6:10, 14; 12:23; 14:19), which was soon to be followed by "the era of (divine) favor" (1QH 15:5). They believed that they were living in the "last days" foretold long ago by the ancient prophets; and, therefore, they held that their anonymous founder, whom they called the *Moreh Ẓedek* "Teacher of Righteousness" (probably to be understood as "the right teacher," i.e., the one who explained the Torah correctly), had been raised up by God "to make known to the later generations what He would do in the last generation" (CD 11:12). Their *pesher* ("commentary") on Habakkuk 2:1–2 says: "Its interpretation concerns the Teacher of Righteousness, to whom God made known all the secrets of the words of His servants the prophets" (1QpHab 7:4–5). The Qumran community apparently expected "the end" to come 40 years after the death of their founder (CD 20:14–15), during which period the wicked in Israel would be destroyed by God (CD 20:15–16). However, when the members of the community were disappointed in the nonfulfillment of this expectation, they admitted that only God knows when the end will come. So the writer of the *pesher* on Habakkuk 2:3a says: "Its interpretation is that the final end may be prolonged, indeed longer than anything of which the prophets spoke, for the secrets (or mysteries) of God are for wondrous fulfillment" (1QpHab 7:7–8). The interpreter, therefore, says on Habakkuk 2:3b: "Its meaning concerns the men of truth, who carry out the Law (Torah) and do not let their hands grow too weak to serve the truth, despite the final end being long drawn out; for all the limits set by God will come in their due time, as He has set for them in His mysterious wisdom" (1QpHab 7:10–14).

ESCHATOLOGICAL WAR. Before "the end" there will be, according to the Qumranites, a great eschatological war, waged not only against the powers of evil but also against all wicked men, not excluding the wicked of Israel. In fact, the Qumranites placed in the latter class all the Jews who did not belong to their community. They alone were "the remnant of Israel" (CD 1:4–5), God's "chosen ones" (1QM 8:6). They called themselves "the Sons of Light"; all others were "the Sons of Darkness." This ethical dualism, perhaps influenced by Persian thought (though not foreign to the older Hebrew Scriptures), is typical of Qumran theology: "He [God] created man to rule the world, and He set for him two spirits by which he would walk until the appointed time of His visitation; these are the spirits of truth and perversity" (1QS 3:17–19).

The eschatological war, besides being referred to in other Qumran writings, is described at great length and in great detail in a fairly well-preserved scroll of 19 columns to which the title "The War of the Sons of Light against the Sons of Darkness" has been given. This document is a strange mixture of sound military tactics combined with idealistic warfare, in which God and His angels fight on the side of the Sons of Light against Belial (Satan) and his evil spirits, who come to the aid of the Sons of Darkness. The good fight is waged also against Gog and Magog (cf. Ezek. 38:1–39:20), here merely symbols of the powers of evil. It seems, therefore, that this eschatological war is to be viewed as waged on a transcendental plane, despite the elaborate rules based on mundane battles; the Essenes of Qumran, like their predecessors the Hassideans of Hasmonean times (cf. I Macc. 7:13–17; and perhaps Dan. 11:34), were not militarists. They trusted more in the power of God than in the force of arms. In the end God would be victorious, and then the messianic age would begin.

MESSIANISM. The "Teacher of Righteousness" did not regard himself, nor did his disciples regard him, as a Messiah. In fact, there is little messianism in the earliest Qumran documents. However, when the 40 years had elapsed after the death of their founder and "the end" had not yet come, the Qumran writers speak more often of the ultimate salvation that would come with the appearance of the Messiah: "the coming of the prophet and the Messiahs (*meshiḥe* – note the plural) of Aaron and Israel" (1QS 9:11; cf. 4QTestimonia).

For the Jews of that time the Hebrew term, *ha-Mashi'aḥ*, "The Messiah" (lit. "the Anointed One"), did not have the same connotations that its Greek translation, *Christos*, had for Christians. From certain other passages, in the Qumran writings it appears quite certain that this community, which was fundamentally a priestly one, expected an especially anointed high priest ("the Messiah of Aaron") as well as an especially anointed lay ruler ("the Messiah of Israel"). It should be noted that in the Cairo Damascus Document (CD 7:20) the royal Messiah is not called a "king," but a "prince" (*nasi*, in keeping with Ezek. 34:24; 37:25; etc.). The concept of two Messiahs, one royal and one priestly, probably goes back to Zechariah 4:14: "These are the two anointed ones that stand by the Lord of the whole earth" (said of Zerubbabel of the Davidic line and of the priest Joshua). On the presence and precedence of the royal Messiah and the priestly Messiah at the eschatological "messianic banquet," see below.

It is not clear what the Qumranites meant by the "prophet" who precedes these two Messiahs. He may be the "prophet like Moses" foretold in Deuteronomy 18:15, 18, since the Qumranites believed they were living or were to live under a "new covenant" (CD 8:35 – the term, no doubt, borrowed from Jer. 31:31); or he may be Elijah (on the basis of Mal. 3:23), in whom the Qumranites were interested.

FUTURE LIFE. Although the Qumran community possessed and, therefore, apparently prized several of the books of the so-called intertestamental literature mentioned above – Jubilees, Enoch, Testaments of Levi and Naphtali, etc. – its own compositions, at least as far as now known, betray relatively little concern with the future world after death. They do not use the terms, "this world," and "the coming world," to designate the present and the future eras. There is no explicit mention of the resurrection of the bodies of their deceased members, but neither is there any denial of such a belief. Perhaps it was taken for granted, or it was left as one of God's mysteries about which they should not speculate. However, they do say the righteous "will share the lot of God's Holy Ones," i.e., the angels (1QH 11:11–12), and they are to enjoy "everlasting" bliss (see below).

The Qumran writings often speak of "the end" (*Keẓ*), i.e., of the present era (1QS 3:23; 4:18, 25; CD 4:9–10; 20:15; 1QpHab 7:2; etc.). The end will be preceded by the "pangs" of the premessianic era (1QH passim), by cosmic storms (1QH 3:13–16), and by a cosmic conflagration (1QH 3:29–31; cf. 1QM 14:17). At "an appointed time of decisive judgment" (*mo'ed mishpat neḥerashah*: 1QS 4:20) God will judge both angels and men (1QH 7:28–29), for in the present era there are both good and evil spirits (1QS 3:20–22).

RETRIBUTION. Whereas the writings of the Qumran community do not mention either a "Gehenna" for the wicked or a "Garden of Eden" for the just in the afterlife, they do, apparently, speak of the punishment of the wicked as an everlasting death, and reward of the just as an eternity of bliss: "The doors of the Pit will be closed upon those who are pregnant with wickedness, and the bars of eternity upon all the spirits of worthlessness" (1QH 3:18). "But the reward of all those who walk in it [the way of truth] will be a healing remedy and abundant well-being in a long life and a fruitfulness of seed, together with all the blessings of eternity and everlasting bliss in life forever, and a crown of glory with a recompense of majesty in light everlasting" (1QS 4:6–8).

NEW TEMPLE. Because of God's promise of "new heavens and a new earth" (Isa. 65:17), the apocalyptic writings sometimes speak of a new Jerusalem with its new temple as coming down from heaven to the earth. Since the Qumran community was basically a priestly one, it was naturally interested in a new temple for the messianic age of bliss on earth. Even the so-called War Scroll gives instructions on how the priests and levites are to function in the new temple (1QM 2:1–6). But, surprisingly, the new temple of the Qumranites is not thought of as coming down ready-made from heaven, but as built by themselves according to a new plan revealed by God.

The *Temple Scroll, like the Torah, is written as if dictated by God to Moses. Besides giving various precepts concerning ritual purity, festivals, sacrifices, etc., it presents detailed prescriptions for the construction of the new temple and its surrounding courts. The resulting construction differs from all the previous temples – of Solomon, of Zerubbabel, and of Herod, and even from the idealistic temple of Ezekiel 40:1–42:20.

To understand the relationship between this proposed man-made temple and "the house that He [God] will make for you at the end of days," as mentioned in certain Qumran *pesharim*, one must remember that the Qumran community lived a quasi-sacramental life: their cultic acts both prepared for, and symbolized, the full reality that would come to pass in the messianic age. This is likewise the case in regard to the so-called messianic banquet at Qumran.

MESSIANIC BANQUET. The midday and evening meals at Qumran were cultic acts. Those who were ritually unclean or who were penalized for various faults could not be present at them. The Davidic Messiah and the Priest (or Aaronic Messiah) are depicted as already present at these repasts, even though this would not be actually true until "the end of days."

The protocol of these eschatological meals is described in 1QSa 2:11–22: "This is the (order of the) seating of 'the Men of the Name who are invited to the Feast' (a phrase based on Num. 16:2, but with Qumranite interpretation) for the council of the community, if … [?] the Messiah with them. The priest shall come in at the head of the whole assembly of Israel, and all the ancestral leaders of the Aaronide priests…; and they shall take their seats, each one according to his rank. After that, the Messiah of Israel shall come in; and the head of the thousands of Israel shall take their seats, each one according to his rank." The text then continues with instructions on the blessing of the bread and wine by the priest, who is the first to partake of them, followed by the Messiah of Israel, and finally by "all the assembly of the community." This rite is to be observed when at least ten men are present. One striking element in this ritual is the precedence given to the priestly Messiah over the royal (lay) Messiah – which would be expected in such a sacerdotally oriented community. Another important feature is that this ceremony is to be observed even when only a *minyan* is present. This ritual meal, therefore, is both a foreshadowing and a quasi-sacramental anticipation of the great eschatological messianic banquet that is often referred to in other religious writings of the period (e.g., the New Testament).

From its earliest beginnings in God's promises to the patriarchs until the dispersion of the Jews after the destruction of the Second Temple, Israel always kept alive its eschatological hopes and expectations, based both on a belief in God's justice and on an optimism that, with God's help, good would ultimately triumph over evil in the world.

[Louis F. Hartman]

IN THE TALMUDIC PERIOD

The eschatology of the Talmud and the Midrash is based upon that of the Bible and is very similar to that of the Apocrypha. A distinction is generally made between "the days of the Messiah" and "the world to come." The former is regarded as the transition stage to the world to come, and various periods are mentioned for it: 40, 70 ("those generations"), 365 ("as the days of the solar year"), and 400 years (Sanh. 99a; Sif. Deut. 310) as in Esdras (IV Ezra). A late *baraita* states that this world will exist for "6,000 years, of which the first 2,000 will be a period of desolation, 2,000 of Torah, and the last 2,000 the messianic era" (Sanh. 97a–b; Av. Zar. 9a). There is also a view that "4,291 years after the creation, the world will be orphaned"; when there will break out "the war of the great sea-monsters" (almost certainly referring to the civil wars of the Roman Empire during the period of its decline and fall), "the war of Gog and Magog," etc.; "And the Holy One Blessed Be He will renew his world only after 7,000 years" (Sanh. 97b). Not only the year of redemption but even the very month and day was fixed by those "who calculated the end" (*ibid.*) – the 14th day of Nisan, according to R. Joshua (Mekh., Pisḥa 14) whose view is accepted in preference to that of R. Eliezer.

Since, however, these calculations did not prove true, the scholars proceeded to enumerate among "the seven things hidden from men" "when the Davidic dynasty will return, and when the guilty kingdom will fall" (Pes. 54b; Mekh., Va-Yassa 5). Moreover the Messiah was included among the "three things that will come unawares" (Sanh. 97a). When Jonathan b. Uzziel wanted to reveal the "messianic end" in his translation of the Hagiographa "a heavenly voice was heard to say 'enough!'" (Meg. 3a). There is an even more striking saying from a period later than that of the early *tannaim*: "May the bones of those who calculate the end rot. For they say: Since the time has arrived and he has not come, he will never come" (Sanh. 97b). At a still later period it was enunciated that: "All the calculated times have gone and everything depends upon repentance and good deeds" (*ibid.*). Moreover the children of Israel were even placed under an oath "not to make known the end, and not forcibly to hasten the advent of the end" (Ket. 111a).

[Joseph Gedaliah Klausner]

IN KABBALAH

Introduction

Apart from basic ideas concerning reward and punishment, life after death, the *Messiah, redemption, and resurrection, there is hardly a commonly held belief among the Jews regarding eschatological details. This lacuna provided an obvious opportunity for free play for the imaginative, the visionary, and the superstitious, and so became the field in which the kabbalists left their mark: for they dealt extensively with just these concepts. It is understandable that with such scope they could never arrive at a decision which was acceptable to all, and thus various trends developed. From fairly simple beginnings, eschatological teaching developed in the *Zohar, and in the kabbalistic works which followed it, and it had many ramifications.

Life after Death

Of great importance here are the views of *Naḥmanides in *Sha'ar ha-Gemul* on the Zohar, and of the Lurianic school as they are crystallized in the great summary of Aaron Berechiah b. Moses of Modena, *Ma'avar Yabbok*. Generally speaking, they stress, after the time of Naḥmanides, the differing fates of the three parts of the soul, which are separated from one another after death. The *nefesh* (the lowest part) remains below by the grave, and suffers punishment for transgressions after the first judgment, which is called *ḥibbut ha-kever* ("punishment of the grave") or *din ha-kever* ("judgment of the grave"). The *ru'aḥ* is also punished for its sins, but after 12 months, it enters the earthly Garden of Eden, or "the Garden of Eden below." The *neshamah* returns to its source in "the Garden of Eden above"; for, according to the Zohar, the *neshamah* is not liable to sin, and punishment falls only upon the *nefesh* and the *ru'aḥ* (although other opinions exist in early Kabbalah). In certain cases the *nefashot* ascend to the category of *ruḥot*, and *ruḥot* to the category of *neshamot*. The *ẓeror ha-ḥayyim* ("the bond of life"), in which the *neshamot* are stored, is interpreted in various ways. It is the concealed Eden, prepared for the delight of the *neshamot;* it is the "treasury" beneath the throne of glory in which the *neshamot* are stored until the resurrection; or it is one of the *sefirot*, or even their totality, into which the *neshamah* is gathered when it is in communion and bound up with God. There are a large number of descriptions in kabbalistic literature of the details and the various degrees of punishment in the abodes of *Gehinnom*, and of pleasure in the Garden of Eden and its various standards. They dealt with the problem of how the *ruḥot* or the *neshamot* could have any experience without physical faculties; what kind of garment the *ruḥot* wore, and the method of their survival. (According to some, the garment of the *ruḥot* was woven of the commandments and good deeds, and was called *ḥaluka de-rabbanan* ("the garment of the rabbis").) Naḥmanides called the domain of pleasure after death *olam ha-neshamot* ("the world of souls"), and distinguished it absolutely from the *olam ha-ba* ("the world to come"), which would be after the resurrection. This distinction was generally accepted by the Kabbalah. In the "world of souls," the *neshamot* are not incorporated into the Divine, but preserve their individual existence. The idea of punishment in *Gehinnom* (which was envisaged as a subtle spiritual fire which burned and purified the souls) conflicted to no uncertain way with the idea of atonement through transmigration (**Gilgul*). There was no settled opinion on the question of which sin was punished by *Gehinnom*, and which by transmigration. One can only say that with the development of the Kabbalah transmigration took on an ever more important role in this context. Both the Garden of Eden and *Gehinnom* were beyond this world, or on the borders of it, whereas the theory of transmigration ensured reward and punishment in large measure in this world. Kabbalists sought various compromises between these two paths, but they came to no agreed solution. Attempts were also made to remove the whole subject of *Gehinnom* from its literal sense and to interpret it either according to the view of *Maimonides, or metaphorically as referring to transmigration. The eschatology of the Kabbalah, and particularly that of the Zohar, was greatly influenced by the idea of the preexistence of souls. The existence of the soul in "the world of souls" is nothing more than its return to its original existence before its descent into the body.

The Messiah and Redemption

The Messiah receives a special emanation from the *sefirah malkhut* ("kingship"), the last of the *sefirot*. However, there is no trace of the concept of the divinity of the Messiah. The picture of the personal Messiah is pale and shadowy and does not add much to the descriptions of him in the Midrashim of redemption which were composed before the growth of the Kabbalah. In the Zohar, there are a few new elements. According to the Zohar, the Messiah dwells in the Garden of Eden in a special palace, called *kan ẓippor* ("the bird's nest"), and he will first be revealed in Upper Galilee. Some believed that the soul of the Messiah had not suffered transmigration, but was "new," while others contended that it was the soul of Adam (the first man) which had previously transmigrated to King David. The letters of Adam (*alef, dalet, mem*) refer to Adam, David, and the Messiah – a *notarikon* found from the end of the 13th century. There is possibly some Christian influence here because, according to Paul, Adam, the first man, corresponds to Jesus, "the last man" (Rom. 5:17). Descriptions of redemption in the Zohar follow in the footsteps of the Midrashim with the addition of some points and certain changes in theme. The redemption will be a miracle, and all that accompanies it miraculous (the stars sparkling and falling, the wars of the end of time, the fall of the Pope, who is called symbolically in the Zohar "the priest of On"). The idea of the pangs of redemption is greatly stressed, and the condition of Israel on the eve of redemption is pictured in terms which reflect the historical conditions of the 13th century. Descriptions of the redemption became more numerous at times of crisis, and particularly after the expulsion from Spain. However, in the later Kabbalah (Moses of *Cordovero and Isaac *Luria), their importance declined. On the other hand, the mystical basis of redemption was emphasized – the basis that developed from the time of Naḥmanides and his school and which centered on the midrashic view that redemption would be a return to that perfection which was sullied by the sin of Adam and Eve. It would not be something entirely new, but a restoration, or a renewal. Creation at the time of redemption would assume the form that was intended from the beginning by the eternal intellect. Only at the redemption would there be a revelation of the original nature of Creation which has become obscured or impaired in this world. Hence, the extreme utopian character of these ideas. In the Divine realm, the state of redemption is expressed as the end of the "exile of the *Shekhinah*," the restoration of the divine unity throughout all areas of existence. ("In that day the Lord shall be One, and His name One" – hence the view that the true unity of God will be revealed only in the time to come, while during the years of exile it is as if sin had rendered His unity imperfect.) At the time of redemption there will be a continuous union of king and queen, or of the *sefirot Tiferet* and *Shekhinah*; that is to say that there will be an unceasing stream of Divine influence through all worlds, and this will bind them eternally together. The hidden secrets of the Torah will be revealed, and the Kabbalah will be the literal sense of the Torah. The messianic age will last approximately a thousand years, but many believed that these years would not be identical with human years, for the planets and the stars would move more slowly, so that time would be prolonged (this view was particularly current in the circle of the *Sefer ha-*Temunah* ("Book of the Image"), and it has origins in the Apocryphal books). It is obvious, on the basis of these theories, that the kabbalists believed that the natural order would change in the messianic era (unlike the view of Maimonides). As to the problem of whether the redemption would be a miracle or the logical result of a process already immanent, kabbalistic opinion was divided. After the expulsion from Spain, the view gradually prevailed that the appearance of the Messiah would be a symbolic event. Redemption depended on the deeds of Israel, and on the fulfillment of its historic destiny. The coming of the redeemer would testify to the completion of the "restoration," but would not cause it.

Resurrection at the End of the World

The Kabbalah does not cast any doubt on the physical resurrection of the dead, which will take place at the end of the days of redemption, "on the great day of judgment." The novel expositions of the kabbalists revolved round the question of the fate of those who were to be resurrected. Naḥmanides taught that after a normal physical life the resurrected body would be purified, and be clothed in *malakhut* ("the garments of the angels"), and, thereby, pass into the future spiritual world, which would come into being after the destruction of this world; and this new world would appear after the resurrection. In the world to come the souls and their "spiritualized" bodies would be gathered together in the ranks of the *sefirot*, in the true "bond of life." According to Naḥmanides, the souls, even in this state, would preserve their individual identity. But afterward other views emerged. The author of the Zohar speaks of "holy bodies" after the resurrection, but does not state his specific view of their future except by allusion. One widespread view identified the world to come with the *sefirah Binah* and its manifestations. After the life of pleasure experienced by the resurrected, this world would be destroyed, and some say that it would return to chaos ("waste and void") in order to be recreated in a new form. Perhaps the world to come would be the creation of another link in the chain of "creations" or *shemitot* ("sabbaticals"; according to the view of the author of *Sefer ha-Temunah*) or even the creation of a spiritual existence through which all existing things ascend to reach the world of the *sefirot*, and return to their primeval being, or their "higher source." In the "Great Jubilee," after 50,000 years, everything will return to the bosom of the *sefirah Binah*, which is also called the "mother of the world." Even the other *sefirot*, through which God guides creation, will be destroyed with the destruction of creation. In contrast to the teaching of the author of *Sefer ha-Temunah* concerning the creation of worlds according to a fixed cycle (*Baḥya ben Asher speaks of 18,000 jubilees), most of the kabbalists maintained that there would be only one creation, and, correspondingly, only one eternal "world to come." The contradiction of having two judgments on man's fate, one after death, and the other after resurrection, one of which would appear to be superfluous, caused some kabbalists to restrict the great Day of Judgment to the nations of the world, while the souls of Israel, in their view, would be judged immediately after death.

[Gershom Scholem]

IN ISLAM

Introduction

From the beginning of Muhammad's prophetic career, he was impressed with eschatological ideas about the descriptions of the occurrences which were to take place on the last day. Contending that the "insured children of Abraham [the Jews]" did not feel the crushing terror of God's last judgment, J. Wellhausen concluded that Muhammad must have been greatly influenced by Christian eschatological ideas, especially the descriptions of the punishment of the sinners as they were spread in Arabia by monks and hermits who lived in the deserts of the Arabian peninsula. However after a thorough examination of Koranic material, T. Andrae concluded that Wellhausen's assumption has no foundation in the Koran. No decisive judgment can be made as to which religion – Judaism or Christianity – was more influential in Muhammad's formulation of an eschatology. In any event, it may be added that the same ideas are to be found in the poems of Jews in Arabia, and the works of the *ḥanīfs* and contemporary pagan poets. The texts found among the Dead Sea Scrolls show that these ideas were familiar to Jewish circles in pre-Christian times. Thus, it is probable that the beliefs about resurrection, the last judgment, paradise, and hell were current in Arabia among Jews, Christians, and Arabs alike. It is therefore not astonishing that Koranic eschatological descriptions and beliefs have parallels in the Apocrypha, the *aggadah*, and the apocalypses.

The Day of Judgment

On many occasions Muhammad repeats the descriptions of *yawm al-qiyāma* ("the day of resurrection"), an expression which occurs 70 times (e.g., 2:79, 107; 16:125; 58:19; 75:1–35), and *al-sāʿa* ("the hour"), 40 times (e.g., 6:31, 40; 79:42). He also uses many other names for that day, e.g., *yawm al-ḥisāb* ("day of reckoning"; 38:15, 25, 53), and describes it in many different fashions. On that day all men come back to life to be judged (28:85; 77:13–14); it will be a day of great calamity, when everyone will try to flee, so that "the leg shall be bared" (68:42; i.e., the loins will be girded for flight); on that day the trumpets (of resurrection) shall be blown (6:73). According to Sura 69:13, "the trumpet shall be blown with one blast," but Sura 39:68 states that the trumpet shall be blown twice: at the first sound "those who are in the heavens and in the earth shall swoon, save whom God pleases. Then it shall be blown again and, lo! they shall stand up and look on." This *āya* ("verse") was of great importance for later descriptions of the last judgment: the sound of the trumpet will be followed by an earthquake (78:18); all this will occur "as the twinkling of an eye, or nigher still!" (16:79); at the second sound all the dead will return to life and gather at the *al-maḥshar* ("the gathering place"). Later Muslim tradition states that this gathering will take place in Jerusalem (see below): Allah will come to the judgment with a host of angels; the scales will be set up for the exact weighing of the good deeds (7:7–8) and "no soul shall be wronged at all" (21:48); the books of the deeds of every individual will be opened and the reckoning made (10:62; 80:11–15; 89:7–12); Allah himself will judge or every sinner will bear witness against himself (17:14–15; 36:65; 69:19, 25–27; 89:13, 23); the *ṣirāṭ* (37:23), the way to hell, will lead the sinners to their place of punishment. The prevailing opinion in the Koran is that intercession (*shafāʿa*) will not avail the sinner (2:45, 255; 74:49; cf. Ps. 49:8) because man must face his Judge alone. Nevertheless, the Judge, Allah, the Merciful, can allow intercession (2:256; 19:90). According to the **ḥadīth* Muhammad can intercede for the believers and his intercession will be helpful.

Retribution

Descriptions of the last day are related to those dealing with the lot of the sinners and the righteous: on that "overwhelming day" the sinners shall be "humble, laboring, toiling – shall broil upon a burning fire; shall be given to drink from a boiling spring! no food shall they have save from the foul thorn, which shall not fatten nor avail against hunger! [But the faithful] shall be comfortable … in a lofty garden wherein they shall hear no foolish word; wherein is a flowing fountain; wherein are couches raised on high, and goblets set down, and cushions arranged, and carpets spread" (88:1–16; cf. also 67:7–8). In some suras the bright and large-eyed virgin maids (the *houri*) are mentioned. They take part in the banquets arranged in paradise and some are wedded to the pious (e.g., 44:54; 55:70–74; 56:15–22).

Muhammad was greatly concerned with the concept of hell (*jahannam*; Heb. *gei-hinnom*, cf. Josh. 15:8; 18:16), but his descriptions of it are not clearly defined. *Jahannam* is seen as something mobile, possibly a monster which swallows the sinners (cf. 67:8; 89:23–24). Muhammad's conception of paradise (usually called *janna* ("garden"), but twice named *firdaws* or *jannat al-firdaws*, 18:107; 23:11) is much clearer, and is of a very material nature. Later Muslim traditionalists and theologians found in his descriptions many difficulties which had to be elaborated, explained, and adapted to philosophical and ethical trends.

Resurrection

Among the signs of the resurrection the *ḥadīth* mentions the appearance of the *Dajjāl* – the arch foe of the true Believers – and the descent of ʿĪsa (Jesus Christ) at the "hour" (cf. Sura 43:61). Later eschatological descriptions assign a special role to the Temple Mount, the Valley of Hinnom, and the Mount of Olives. According to ʿAbdallah ibn Salām, a Jew from Medina who embraced Islam after Muhammad's arrival in that city, the *ṣirāṭ* – the narrow bridge over the Valley of Hinnom which all creatures must cross on judgment day – extends between the Mount of Olives and the Temple area (where the Lord will take His stand on that day); according to the basic writings of Islam it is a real bridge, which a Muslim is required to believe in. A certain area of the Mount of Olives is called *sāhira*, where men will assemble at the hour of resurrection – its soil is white and no blood has ever been shed on it. Obviously, these places are particularly suitable as burial places of prophets, as they relieve them of the necessity of performing the "subterranean journey" to Jerusalem and enable them to be the first to be resurrected. According to Islamic tradition, many Muslim mystics, saints, and heroes were buried near the Temple Mount or on the Mount of Olives, evidently so that they, too, might be among the first to rise on the day of resurrection. A special place in eschatological descriptions is reserved for the *Dajjāl*, Allah's enemy (the *Armilus of the Jewish legend and the *Antichrist of Christianity), and for the War of Yājūj and Mājūj (*Gog and Magog). These legends embody many reminiscences of Jewish and Christian stories. The *Dajjāl* will wage war and conquer the entire world, except three cities – Mecca, Medina, and Jerusalem; the battles of the *Dajjāl* will be similar to the battles of Yājūj, which will be fought in the neighborhood of Jerusalem. In eschatological descriptions, Muslim writers created many new legends. Though devoting a great deal of space to this subject, the Koran never mentions any definite place. Tradition filled the gap by assigning the locale to Jerusalem and its surroundings. Books are extant – outstanding among them are the *Kitāb al-Zuhd* ("Book of Asceticism") and the *Kitāb Aḥwāl al-Qiyāma* ("Book of the Phases of Resurrection") – which mainly consist of descriptions of the resurrection: the angel Isrāfīl will sound three trumpet blasts, whereupon all mankind will assemble at the gathering place on the Mount of Olives. Gabriel will move paradise to the right side of Allah's Throne and hell to the left side. Abraham, Moses, Jesus, and Muhammad will stand to the right of the scales of justice; the angel Raḍwān will open the gates of paradise and the angel Malik will open the gates of hell. The bridge (*ṣirāṭ*) which all men must cross is long and slippery and narrower than a hair, sharper than a sword, and blacker than night; it has seven arches, and on each arch men are questioned about their deeds. Particularly interesting – in view of parallels in later midrashic literature – are the four mountains associated with the day of resurrection: Khalīl (i.e., Hebron), Lebanon, Ṭūr (the Mount of Olives), and Jūdī (Ararat), each of which will shine like a white pearl, with incomparable splendor, between heaven and earth. They will stand at the four corners of the Temple. With the exception of those concerning the *ṣirāṭ*, which seems to be of Persian origin, these legends are based on Jewish or Christian conceptions (e.g., I En. 26–27; Av. Zar. 2b).

[Haïm Z'ew Hirschberg]

BIBLIOGRAPHY: GENERAL: J. Klausner, *The Messianic Idea in Israel* (1956); A.H. Silver, *A History of Messianic Speculation in Israel* (1959²). IN THE BIBLE: L. Černý, *The Day of Yahweh and Some Relevant Problems* (1948); C. Steuernagel, in: *Festschrift fuer Alfred Bertholet* (1950), 479–87; G.A.F. Knight, in: *Scottish Journal of Theology*, 4 (1951), 355–62; T.C. Vriezen, in: VT Supplement 1 (1953), 199–229; idem, *An Outline of Old Testament Theology* (1958), index; G.W. Buchanan, in: JNES, 20 (1961), 188–93; G. von Rad, *Old Testament Theology* (1962), index; R.H. Charles, *Eschatology* (1963); W. Eichrodt, *Theology of the Old Testament* (1964), index; H.P. Mueller, in: VT, 14 (1964), 276–93; O. Ploeger, *Theocracy and Eschatology* (1968); Scholem, Mysticism, index. IN THE TALMUD: G.F. Moore, *Judaism in the First Centuries of the Christian Era*, 2 (1927), 275–395; A. Kohut, in: ZDMG 21 (1867), 552ff.; R.H. Charles, *A Critical History of the Doctrine of a Future Life…* (1899); W. Bousset, *Der Antichrist in der Ueberlief-*

erung des Judentums (1895). IN THE INTERTESTAMENTAL LITERATURE: D.S. Russell, *The Method and Message of Jewish Apocalyptic* (1964), with very good bibliography; B. Vawter, in: CBQ, 22 (1960), 33–46; S. Mowinkel, *He That Cometh: The Messianic Concept in the Old Testament and Later Judaism* (1956); J. Bloch, *On the Apocalyptic in Judaism* (1952). IN THE DEAD SEA SCROLLS: H. Ringgren, *The Faith of Qumran* (1963); E.F. Sutcliffe, *The Monks of Qumran* (1960), 83–90; R.E. Brown, in: CBQ, 19 (1957), 53–82; P. Grelot, in: *Revue de Qumran*, 1 (1958–59), 113–31; A.M. Habermann, *Megillot Midbar Yehudah* (1959). IN ISLAM: Tor Andrae, *Der Ursprung des Islams und das Christentum* (1926), 83ff.; J. Wellhausen, *Reste arabischen Heidentums* (1897^2), 240; K. Ahrens, *Muhammed als Religionsstifter* (1935), 23, 59; J.W. Hirschberg, *Der Dīwān des as-Samauʾal ibn Ādija* (1931), 10, 19, 24, 48, 54–56, 58–59; idem, *Juedische und christliche Lehren…* (1939), 73–78, 139–62; idem, *Yisrael be-Arav* (1946), 208–14, 240–1; idem, in: *Rocznik Orientalistyczny*, 17 (1952), 342–8; M. Wolff, *Muhammedanische Eschatologie* (1872; containing K. Ahwāl al-Quiyama); R. Leszynsky, *Mohammedanische Traditionen vom juengsten Gericht* (1909; containing K. al Zuhd); J. Horovitz, *Das koranische Paradies* (1923); A. Eichler, *Die Dschinn, Teufel und Engel im Koran* (1928); I. Goldziher, *Muhammedanische Studien*, 2 (1890), 308ff.

ESCHELBACHER, JOSEPH (1848–1916), author and rabbi in Bruchsal, Baden (1870–1900), and Berlin. His main work, *Das Judentum und das Wesen des Christentums*, was written in answer to Adolf von Harnack; others include a biography of Jehiel Michael Sachs and a work on the attitude to the Jews revealed by contemporary Protestant theology. His son MAX (1880–1964), rabbi in Bruchsal, Freiburg, and Duesseldorf (1913–39), published comparative studies on Jewish law and a book on the Duesseldorf community. In 1939 he escaped to England, where he remained until his death.

ESCUDERO, LORENZO (d. apparently in 1682), convert to Judaism and polemist. He was born in Córdoba (Spain) to Old Christian parents. He left his wife in Seville when he was 40 years old and apparently married an English woman who converted later on to Judaism. Later, he went to Amsterdam, studied Judaism, and in due course was converted, being known henceforth as Abraham Israel Peregrino (i.e., "the convert") or Abraham Guer (Ger) de Cordova. After the Portuguese community in Amsterdam refused to convert him, he applied to the Ashkenazi community, which agreed to do so. He was circumcised in 1658. Subsequently, the Portuguese community changed its attitude towards the new convert. Although a skilled fencer and able musician, he spent the rest of his life in penury. Perhaps he served as *shamash* in the Portuguese synagogue. After his conversion, he was invited to the wedding of Emperor Leopold and Marguarita Maria in Brussels, despite the prohibition of Philip IV, Margarita's father, of Jews to dwell in his Flemish territory. It is astonishing that a convert to Judaism was invited to Spanish-ruled Flanders. Attempts in Brussels to bring him back to Christianity failed. He adopted a very daring attitude towards Christian lay and religious leaders and he challenged Alonso de Cepeda to participate in the debate with Isaac Orobio de Castro. He lived in London from 1655 to 1659, when he was denounced to the Lisbon Inquisition. Abraham Guer was converted out of conviction, but he was not the author of *Fortaleza del Judaismo y confusion del estraño* as suggested by some scholars, including Cecil Roth (prob. Amsterdam, c. 1680), of which manuscript translations exist in Italian and in Hebrew (under the title *Ẓeriʾaḥ Bet El*). According to his own testimony he was attracted to Judaism under the influence of the Dominican Fray Luis de Granada, whose spiritualism and attack against Christian "physical ritual" attracted both old and new Christians. *Copia da vida do bemaventurado Abraham Pelengrino* (sic; formerly in the D. Henriques de Castro collection, no. 534), contrary to what Roth wrote, was written by another convert, Manuel Cardoso de Macedo, who also took the name Abraham Peregrino, who died in 1652. Daniel Levi (Miguel) de *Barrios wrote a sonnet in his honor. Escudero was not an isolated case of a Jewish convert in 17th-century Amsterdam.

BIBLIOGRAPHY: G.B. de' Rossi, *Bibliotheca Judaica Antichristiana* (1800), 5–7, 128; P. de Azevedo, in: Academia das Sciencias de Lisboa, *Boletim da segumeha classe*, 9 (1915), 464; L. Wolf, *Jews in The Canary Islands* (1926), 203n; A. Marx, in: *Studies in Jewish Bibliography in Memory of A.S. Freidus* (1929), 259, 264; I.S. Revah, *Spinoza et le Dr Juan de Prado* (1959), 31n. **ADD. BIBLIOGRAPHY:** Y. Kaplan, in: *Proceedings of the 7th WCJS*, vol. 4 (1981), 87–101 (Heb. section).

[Cecil Roth / Yom Tov Assis (2nd ed.)]

ESHEL, YITZḤAK (1912–), *ḥazzan*. Yitzḥak Eshel was born in Debrecen, Hungary. He studied in a *ḥeder* and in yeshivot, among them the Ḥatam Sofer Yeshivah in Bratislava (Pressburg). At the age of 19 he was appointed chief cantor in Munich, where he also continued to practice music and studied in the Conservatory. He served as cantor in Manchester and in his birthplace, Debrecen. In 1938 he was appointed cantor in the famous Nozyck Synagogue in Warsaw, but because of the antisemitic atmosphere he decided not to accept the position. In 1949 he immigrated to Israel where he became the cantor in the Great Synagogue in Ramat Gan. He became known throughout the country, officiating at prayer services and appearing in concerts in different parts of the country. He served as chief cantor of the Beth-El Synagogue in Tel Aviv, and in 1956 for a year was chief cantor of the Shomrei Hadass congregation in Antwerp. He moved to the United States and was appointed chief cantor of the Poʾale Zedeck Synagogue in Pittsburgh. When he returned to Israel in 1961 he was chief cantor of the central Hekhal Meir Synagogue in Tel Aviv, where he served until 1970. He founded a choir, which was led by the English-born director, Martin White. From 1970 he appeared in various synagogues in Israel and in the Diaspora and trained many young cantors. Yitzḥak Eshel has produced records of cantorial music and Yiddish songs. He is considered one of the creative cantors, while his original compositions are written in a traditional spirit. He published articles on cantorial music and other Jewish music in the journal of the Shaʾarey Zedek Synagogue in Pittsburgh.

[Akiva Zimmerman]

ESHET ḤAYIL (Heb. אֵשֶׁת חַיִל; "a woman of valor"), opening words praising the virtuous woman in Proverbs 31:10–31. This poem enumerates the qualities of the ideal wife in a sequential alphabetic acrostic of 22 verses, one for each of the letters of the Hebrew alphabet. She is lauded as provident, economically successful, working hard for husband and household, and charitable to the needy. She possesses optimism, faces life with confidence, and speaks in wisdom and kindness. Her efforts enable her husband to function as a prominent communal leader, "As he sits among the elders of the land." The conclusion of the passage celebrates a woman's domestic and spiritual strengths: "Grace is deceitful, and beauty is vain, But a woman that fears the Lord, she shall be praised ... and let her works praise her in the (city) gates."

In many Jewish families the song is recited or chanted on Friday evenings before the *Kiddush*. This custom originated in kabbalistic circles and initially referred to the *Shekhinah* ("Divine presence") as the mystical mother and wife. Later this devotion became a domestic ceremony in which the family paid homage to its wife and mother. Other sources maintain that *Eshet Ḥayil* refers to the Sabbath or the Torah. In some places this song was chanted at Jewish weddings. Its verses have often been used as inscriptions on tombstones of the pious; in Sephardi rituals the first verse is recited before the **Ashkavah* ("laying to rest") prayer at women's funerals.

Derashot to some of the singular verses of *Eshet Ḥayil* appear in tannaitic, talmudic, and midrashic literature. Several smaller Midrashim expound the poem in sequence, a genre which has assumed the rubric *Midreshei Eshet Ḥayil*. Some of these Midrashim interpret the entire poem as referring to Sarah. One such text appears in *Tanḥuma*, Ḥayei Sarah 4. Two additional versions, which interpret the poem until the verse "Her husband is prominent in the gates" (Prov. 31:23), appear in *Tanḥuma*, ed. Buber, Ḥayei Sarah 3, pp. 116–18, and in *Aggadat Bereshit*, ed. Buber (Cracow, 1893), ch. 34, pp. 66–69. Several *Midreshei Eshet Ḥayil* interpret each of the verses of *Eshet Ḥayil* as referring to a different biblical female personality.

The earliest surviving manuscript of *Midrash Eshet Ḥayil* was copied in 1270. This text, which was erroneously appended to the end of *Midrash Proverbs*, is actually an independent Midrash. It contains *derashot* to the first 20 verses only. The women in the first eight verses, all mentioned in the Pentateuch, are presented in chronological order: the wife of Noah, Sarah, Rebekah, Leah, Rachel, Bithiah the daughter of Pharaoh, Jocheved, and Miriam. The remaining women appear in non-chronological order. With the exception of Elisheba, the women mentioned in the latter group appear in the Prophets and Hagiographa. A critical edition of this Midrash has been prepared by Y. Levine (*Midreshei Eshet Ḥayil*, pp. 1–151).

Several *Genizah* fragments of *Midrash Eshet Ḥayil* survive. One such text was published by L. Ginzberg (*Ginzei Schechter*, 1 (1928), 163–68). Other versions have been annotated by Y. Levine (*Midreshei Eshet Ḥayil*, pp. 254–83) and M.B. Lerner (*Sefer Zikaron le-Tirzah Lifshitz*). Additionally, four Yemenite editions of *Midrash Eshet Ḥayil* containing *derashot* to the entire poem exist in their entirety. The version in *Midrash ha-Gadol*, by R. David ha-Adani, refers to the verse beginning "And the lifespan of Sarah" (Gen. 23:1) (ed. Margulies, pp. 368–74). Another edition, based on *Midrash ha-Gadol*, appears in *Midrash ha-Ḥefez*, by R. Zechariah ha-Rofeh (*Midrash ha-Ḥefeẓ al Ḥamishah Ḥumshei Torah*, Bereishit–Shemot, Jerusalem, 1991, Gen. 23:1–2, pp. 163–64). An additional edition is attributed to R. Moses Albalidah and was published by Z.M. Rabinowitz in *Mi-Ẓefunot Yehudei Teiman* (1962), pp. 209–22. However, this ascription is questionable (*Midreshei Eshet Ḥayil*, p. 244).

The *Eshet Ḥayil* poem also served as the basis for many post-medieval *derashot*, in which traditional sources concerning women, primarily talmudic and midrashic, were expounded. This external form was particularly prevalent and common among Sephardi rabbis as eulogies for women. Contemporary Jewish feminists have sought to reclaim this poem and have offered new insights and interpretations.

BIBLIOGRAPHY: A. Bardack, "Praising the Work of Valiant Women: A Feminist Endorsement of *Eshet Hayil*," in: D. Orenstein (ed.), *Lifecycles*, 1 (1994), 136–40, 395, 415; Y. Levine, "*Eshet Ḥayil (Mishlei 31:10–31) ba-Pulḥan ha-Yehudi*," in: *Beit Mikra*, 31:4 (1986), 339–47; Y. Levine Katz, "*Midreshei Eshet Ḥayil*," Dissertation, Bar-Ilan University (1993); M.B. Lerner, "*Keta Ḥadash mi-Midrash Eshet Ḥayil u-Tehilato shel Ma'amar Yud-Bet Nashim*," in: *Sefer Zikaron le-Tirzah Lifshitz* (2005); S. Valler, "Who is *eset hayil* in Rabbinic Literature?" in: A. Brenner (ed.), *A Feminist Companion to Wisdom Literature* (The Feminist Companion to the Bible, 9) (1995), 85–97.

[Yael Levine (2nd ed.)]

ESHKOL (Shkolnik), LEVI (1895–1969), Israeli statesman and third prime minister of Israel, member of the Second to Sixth Knessets. Eshkol was born in Oratova, in the Kiev district in the Ukraine, into a prosperous ḥasidic family. As a child he studied at a *ḥeder* and with private tutors up to the age of 16, when he entered the Hebrew high school in Vilna. Eshkol joined the Ẓe'irei Zion movement in Vilna. He settled in Ereẓ Israel in 1913 and began his career as an agricultural worker and watchman. He was one of the founders of a workers' commune called *Ha-Avodah* in Petaḥ Tikvah, which then moved to a plot of land near Kalandia, north of Jerusalem, and from there to Rishon le-Zion. In 1918–20 he served in the *Jewish Legion, and after World War I was one of the founders of kevuẓat *Deganyah Bet, soon becoming its treasurer and economic planner, securing funds for its development from central labor and Zionist institutions. In later years he became active in initiating and managing various institutions within the framework of the *Histadrut. In 1921 he served on the Defense Committee of the Histadrut, and in 1922, while on a mission to Europe to acquire arms, he was arrested and detained for several weeks by the Vienna police for allegedly purchasing arms illegally. Eshkol was one of the first leaders of the *yishuv to* recognize the importance of securing an adequate supply of water for agricultural development, and was one of the founders of the *Mekorot Water Company, which he directed in the years 1937–51. In 1934 he was also one of the initiators and implementers of the *Haavarah project for transferring Jewish capital from Nazi Germany to Palestine in the form of capital goods and was sent to Berlin to oversee the arrangement. In 1940 he became a member of the National Command of the Haganah, where he was in charge of finances and played a major role in organizing illicit arms manufacturing activities. In 1942–45 Eshkol served as secretary of *Mapai, and in 1944–48 secretary of the Workers' Council of Tel Aviv. In 1947, he was among those in charge of registration in the *yishuv* for national military service in anticipation of the approaching armed struggle. He was simultaneously a member of the Negev Committee, which prepared the defense of the Negev settlements.

Eshkol was a member of the Jewish Agency Executive, its treasurer in the years 1949–51, and head of the Settlement Department in the years 1948–63, simultaneously holding ministerial posts in the governments of David *Ben-Gurion and Moshe *Sharett. As head of the Settlement Department he oversaw the establishment of 371 new settlements and the expansion of an additional 60.

In 1948–49 Eshkol served as director general of the Ministry of Defense (he was referred to as deputy minister), helping Ben-Gurion set up and organize the ministry. He was elected to the Second Knesset in 1951, serving as minister of agriculture and development in 1951–52. In 1952 he replaced Eliezer *Kaplan, who had passed away, as minister of finance, a position he held until replacing Ben-Gurion as prime minister in 1963, overseeing the implementation of the New Economic Plan introduced by Kaplan and reaping the economic benefits of the Restitution Agreement signed with West Germany in September 1952 – three months after he became minister of finance. Under his direction the Israeli economy entered two decades of rapid economic growth, with GDP rising by an average of 10 percent annually. In 1953–55, Eshkol headed Israel's delegation in negotiations with President Eisenhower's special envoy, Eric Johnston, on the allocation of water resources between Israel and its neighbors. After the Arabs rejected the Johnston Plan that emerged from these negotiations, Israel embarked on the construction of the National Water Carrier, involving the channeling of water from the Jordan River to the Negev, which Eshkol strongly supported. In 1954, when Ben-Gurion temporarily retired to Sedeh Boker, he designated Eshkol as his successor, but the Mapai institutions elected Moshe Sharett, and Eshkol continued to serve as minister of finance.

In 1960 Eshkol was a member of the cabinet committee that exonerated Pinḥas *Lavon from responsibility in the Lavon Affair, but several months later he supported Lavon's dismissal from his post as secretary-general of the Histadrut. In the following years Eshkol used all his patience, equanimity, and skill to resolve the crisis as amicably as possible. When in 1963 Ben-Gurion was finally obliged to resign as a result of the crisis, it was Eshkol who was chosen to succeed him as prime minister and minister of defense. Despite pressure by Ben-Gurion, after becoming prime minister Eshkol refused to reopen the Lavon Affair. This refusal, plus Eshkol's success in getting Mapai and *Aḥdut ha-Avodah-Po'alei Zion to form a single list – the Alignment – in the elections to the Sixth Knesset in 1965, finally caused Ben-Gurion and his supporters in Mapai to leave the party and form *Rafi, which ran independently.

Soon after becoming prime minister Eshkol reversed Ben-Gurion's policy and agreed to bring the remains of Ze'ev *Jabotinsky for burial in Israel. Eshkol was the first Israeli prime minister to visit the United States, at the invitation of U.S. president Lyndon *Johnson, and during his premiership the U.S. started selling Israel significant quantities of arms, though until the Six-Day War France remained its main source of arms. It was also Eshkol who decided to establish formal diplomatic relations with West Germany in 1965. His attempts to improve relations with the Soviet Union failed, and these relations were broken by the latter in the aftermath of the Six-Day War.

The National Water Carrier was inaugurated about a year after Eshkol became prime minister. The Arabs responded by initiating a project to divert the headwaters of the Jordan and repeatedly shelling settlements in northern Israel. In November 1964, Eshkol approved air operations (for the first time since the *Sinai Campaign) against Syrian artillery positions and the Arab diversion works. In the following two and a half years the security situation became increasingly tense, and the IDF undertook numerous operations in reaction to Syrian and Jordanian attacks and to acts of sabotage by infiltrators. A further deterioration took place in May 1967, when President Gamal Abdel *Nasser closed the Straits of Tiran to shipping bound for Eilat, called for the withdrawal of UN peacekeeping forces from the Gaza Strip, and started to amass troops in the Sinai Peninsula. Eshkol's policy was to try to avert war at any cost, but when all his efforts failed he approved preemptive action by the IDF. On the eve of the outbreak of the war, and due to growing public pressure, he invited Rafi and *Gaḥal to join a government of national unity, and handed over the defense portfolio to Moshe *Dayan, even though he had wanted to appoint Yigal *Allon to the post. After the war Eshkol did not object to Israel's returning most captured territories in return for a comprehensive peace, and in December 1967 accepted Security Council Resolution 242, which spoke of Israeli withdrawal from territories in return for recognition of its right to live in peace within secure and recognized borders. However, the Arab Summit at Khartoum in 1968 rejected any prospect of negotiations with Israel. Eshkol paid a second visit to the United States in January 1968 when President Johnson agreed to upgrade U.S. arms sales to Israel.

In the aftermath of the Six-Day War Eshkol actively supported the establishment of the Israel Labor Party, through the merging of Mapai, Aḥdut ha-Avodah-Po'alei Zion, and Rafi. The Labor Party was established in January 1968, and Levi Eshkol stood at its head until his sudden death in February 1969.

BIBLIOGRAPHY: H. Laufbahn, *Levi Eshkol* (Heb., 1965); T. Prittie, *Eshkol the Man and the Nation* (1969); H.M. Christman (ed.), *The State Papers of Levi Eshkol* (1969); Y. Shapiro, *Levi Eshkol: Be-Ma'a lot ha-Sheliḥut* (1969); S. Perla, *Levi Eshkol: Unifier of a Nation* (1970); D. Giladi, *Levi Eshkol – Kevarnit ha-Hityashvut ha-Hamonit 1948–1952* (1993); A.Gluska, *Ha-Imut bein ha-Mateh ha-Kelali u-vein Memshelet Eshkol bi-Tekufat ha-Hamtanah* (2001); A. Lamfrum and H. Zoref, *Levi Eshkol: Rosh ha-Memshalah ha-Shelishi: Mivḥar Te'udot mi-Pirkei Ḥayyav 1895–1969* (2002); Y. Goldstein, *Eshkol: Biografiyah* (2003).

[Susan Hattis Rolef (2nd ed.)]

ESHTAOL (Heb. אֶשְׁתָּאוֹל), biblical town in the Judean Shephelah, in the territory of the tribe of Dan, usually mentioned together with nearby Zorah (Josh. 15:33; 19:41). The Danites set out on their march to Laish from these towns (Judg. 18:2) and somewhere between were the tombs of Samson and his father Manoah (Judg. 13:25; 16:31). The *aggadah* describes the two towns as mountains facing each other (Sot. 9b). In the fourth century C.E. Eusebius mentions a village called Eshtaol in the Eleutheropolis (Bet Guvrin) district, 10 mi. (16 km.) north of the city; its location is not clear (Onom. 88:12–14). Estori ha-Parḥi (14th century) was the first to identify Eshtaol with Ishwaʿ, north of Zorah and 16½ mi. (27 km.) west of Jerusalem (*Kaftor va-Feraḥ*, 302). The ancient city was perhaps located at Tell Abu-al-Qābūs, on the hill above the village of Ishwaʿ, where remains of the Iron Age have been found. In the War of Independence (1948), the village (pop. 600) was taken during the building of the "Burma road" to Jerusalem; it had been abandoned by its inhabitants.

[Michael Avi-Yonah]

The name Eshtaol was renewed when a moshav, affiliated with Tenu'at ha-Moshavim, was founded by newcomers from Yemen, at the site of Ishwaʿ in the Judean Foothills north of Beth-Shemesh. Initially this was a work village whose settlers were employed at reclaiming the terrain for farming. Gradually, the main branches – deciduous fruit orchards, vineyards, garden crops, etc. – were developed. Near the village a forest tree nursery of the Jewish National Fund offered further employment to the settlers who also worked in nearby forests, e.g. the President's Forest commemorating Chaim *Weizmann, which served as a recreation ground. The crossroads near Eshtaol bears the name Ẓomet Shimshon ("Samson Junction"). In 1968, Eshtaol numbered 320 inhabitants, rising to 480 in the mid-1990s and 702 in 2002 as the moshav underwent expansion.

[Efraim Orni]

BIBLIOGRAPHY: J. Garstang, *Joshua, Judges* (1931), 375; Montgomery, in: JBL, 54 (1935), 61; Malky, in: JPOS, 20 (1946), 43ff.; Aharoni, Land, index; Avi-Yonah, Geog, 111.

ESHTEMOA (Heb. אֶשְׁתְּמוֹעַ, אֶשְׁתְּמֹה, אֶשְׁתְּמֹעַ), levitical city in the territory of Judah, south of Hebron (Josh. 15:50; 21:14; I Sam. 30:28; I Chron. 6:42) that belonged to the family of Caleb (I Chron. 4:17, 19). According to Eusebius, in the fourth century C.E. it was still a large Jewish village in the district of Bet Guvrin (Eleutheropolis; Onom. 26:11; 82:20). The site is occupied by the Arab village of al-Samūʿ where many fragments of synagogue ornamentation, such as reliefs of candelabra, have been found. Remains of an ancient synagogue were uncovered by excavations conducted by L.A. Mayer and A. Reifenberg in 1935–36.

On November 13, 1966, the Israeli army attacked the Arab village – then in Jordan with a population of about 2,500 Muslims – which was serving as the base of terrorist raiders who had committed a number of outrages in Israeli territory. The village fell into Israeli hands as a result of the *Six-Day War in 1967. Excavations by Z. Yeivin in 1969–70 led to the discovery of a mosaic pavement with an Aramaic inscription at the synagogue site. The synagogue differs in plan and details from the type common in Galilee in the third and fourth centuries C.E. It measures 40 ft. (12 m.) by 65 ft. (20 m.). Iron Age jewelry and ingots were found beneath the floor.

BIBLIOGRAPHY: Mayer and Reifenberg, in: BJPES, 9 (1941–42), 41–44; 10 (1942–43), 10–11; idem, in: JPOS, 19 (1939), 314–26. **ADD. BIBLIOGRAPHY:** A. Negev and S. Gibson, *Archaeological Encyclopedia of the Holy Land* (2001²), s.v.

[Michael Avi-Yonah]

ESKELES, family in Vienna. The name is derived from Elkesh, i.e., Olkusz, town in Krakow province. The first noted member, GABRIEL BEN JUDAH LOEW ESKELES (d. 1718), was born in Cracow. A pupil of Samuel *Koidanover, he became rabbi of Olkusz in 1684. The rabbinate of Prague was offered to him in 1683 but it is not clear if he accepted it. He became rabbi of Metz in 1695, and in 1708/9 *Landesrabbiner* ("chief rabbi") of Moravia and head of the yeshivah in Nikolsburg (Mikulov), sharing his office with David *Oppenheim. In 1712 he banned the kabbalist and Shabbatean Nehemiah *Ḥayon. Gabriel left unpublished novellae on the Talmud tractates *Shabbat* and *Megillah,* a commentary on *Avot*, and a collection of responsa (now lost), known mainly from quotations in Meir *Eisenstadt's *Panim Me'irot*.

His son ISSACHAR BERUSH (Bernard Gabriel, 1692–1753) married a daughter of Samson *Wertheimer, and, as written on his tombstone, "wrapped in a gold-trimmed cloak" became rabbi of Kremsier (Kromeriz) at the age of 18. As he absented himself frequently on business, he appointed a substitute rabbi. In 1717 he is mentioned as rabbi of Mainz. Around 1719 he settled in Vienna as court purveyor (see *Court Jews), supplying arms and other commodities. He succeeded his father as chief rabbi of Moravia and in 1725 followed Samson Wertheimer as chief rabbi of Hungary, administering both offices from Vienna. When consulted by the Moravian authorities in 1727, he suggested that they enforce the precept forbidding Jews from shaving with a razor, and advocated distinctive dress for Jews except for traveling. He translated into German the Moravian *takkanot* (published in 1880 by Gerson Wolf) for the Austrian government. His novellae on

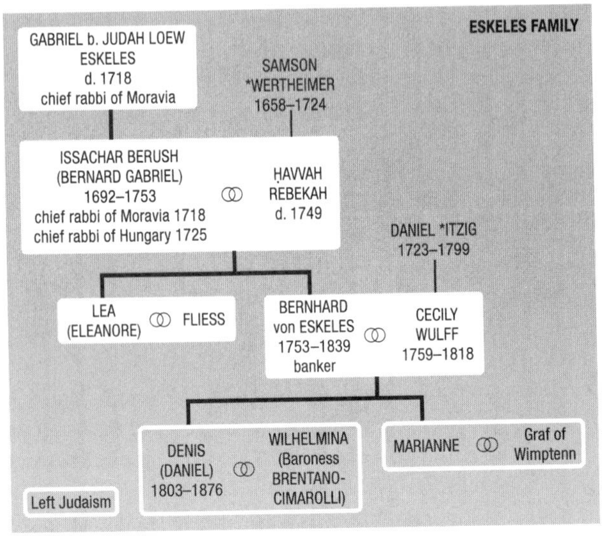

tractate *Berakhot* remain unpublished. Using his influence at court, he supported Diego *d'Aguilar's efforts to prevent the expulsion of the Jews from Moravia in 1742, and from Prague and Bohemia in 1744–45. Four days before his death, he established the Eskeles-Stiftung (see below).

Issachar's son BERNHARD (1753–1839), born after his father's death, became one of the outstanding financiers in Austria at the beginning of the 19th century. After an unsuccessful start in Amsterdam, where he lost his father's legacy (over 400,000 florins), he returned in 1774 to Vienna, married Cecily Wulff (née *Itzig), and went into partnership with her brother-in-law Nathan von *Arnstein. Following the rise of his banking house and his uncovering of a banking forgery (1795), he was entrusted with government financial tasks and his advice was sought by *Joseph II and *Francis I. He founded the Austrian National Bank in 1816, and, competing with Salomon Mayer *Rothschild, promoted railway construction. Ennobled in 1797, he became a baron in 1822. It is assumed that he was the author of an anonymous exposé of the Jewish situation used by Joseph II for his *Toleranzpatent*. In 1815, he was one of the signatories of a petition for Jewish rights (see *Austria). The only Austrian Jew invited to the Napoleonic *Sanhedrin in 1806, he informed the police out of loyalty to Austria. In an obituary (AZJ, 1839, 518–9) he was attacked for failing to make sufficient use of his influence and wealth for the benefit of the Jews. Bernhard's wife CECILY (1759–1818), a daughter of Daniel Itzig, made their house a meeting place for high society (see *Salons), mainly during the Congress of *Vienna. Her parties rivaled those of her sister Fanny von *Arnstein. *Goethe made her acquaintance at Carlsbad. Bernhard and Cecily's children were baptized in 1824. DENIS (Daniel) inherited the firm, which went bankrupt in 1859, as a result of his connection with the French Crédit Mobilier. Issachar's elder daughter LEA (Eleanore) was involved in a Prussian spy scandal. Because of this Valentin Guenther (with whom she had had two children), who had played an important part in the formulation of the *Toleranzpatent*, was banished from court. In later years Goethe corresponded with her.

The Eskeles-Stiftung

Issachar established a foundation for Torah teaching to children and providing dowries for poor brides. Endowed with 50,000 florins, the foundation was one of the largest in the Hapsburg empire. When in 1782 the government ordered that it should be used for the newly founded *Normalschulen* (see *Austria, education) Bernhard sued the government, and it was agreed that the foundation should be used for its original aims as well as for the new ones. As its income had decreased considerably, Bernhard doubled the capital in 1811. In 1839 he altered the statute, adding a donation for five Moravian university-trained rabbis and ten students. The latter were required to be of Jewish faith when granted the scholarship, but they were not to lose it if they were baptized. Of the two trustees one was to be a member of the Eskeles family of any religion, who was to propose the second, a Moravian resident of Jewish religion, who could be replaced if he were baptized. The foundation's committee still existed in Brno in the 1930s.

BIBLIOGRAPHY: Wiener, in: *Illustrierte Monatshefte fuer die gesamten Interessen des Judenthums*, 1 (1865), 387–94; W. Mueller, *Urkundliche Beitraege…* (1903), 68–92; B. Wachstein, *Die Inschriften des alten Judenfriedhofes in Wien*, 2 (1917), 350–70; H. Gold (ed.), *Die Juden und Judengemeinden Maehrens in Vergangenheit und Gegenwart* (1929), index; Michael, Or, no. 657; M. Grunwald, *Vienna* (1936), index; H. Spiel, *Fanny von Arnstein* (1962), index; H. Schnee, *Die Hoffinanz und der moderne Staat*, 4 (1963), 331; M. Friedman, in: *Sefunot*, 10 (1966), 508, 532–5; K. Grunwald, in: YLBI, 12 (1967), 168; L. Singer, in: JGGJČ, 5 (1933), 295–7; T. Jakabovits, in JGGJČ, 5 (1933), 79–136 passim.

[Meir Lamed]

ESPINOSA, EDOUARD (1872–1950), British ballet dancer and teacher. Espinosa belonged to a renowned family of dancers and teachers, originally of Sephardi extraction. His father Léon E. (1825–1904) studied at the Paris Opera school, danced at the Théâtre de la Porte-Saint-Martin, and toured the U.S. before joining the Bolshoi Ballet in Moscow as premier danseur de contrast. He settled in London in 1872, where he opened a school. Edouard was born in London and trained by his father. He danced under Henry Irving at Lyceum Theatre, London (1891–96) and for a season (1893) under Charles *Frohman, New York. From 1896 to 1939 he was ballet master at Covent Garden and other London theaters, producing dances for numerous shows, including *Chu Chin Chow* (1916), *Maid of the Mountains* (1917), and *The Last Waltz* (1922). He was one of the founders of the Royal Academy of Dancing in 1920 and of the British Ballet Company in 1930. After his death the latter was directed by his son Eduard Kelly Espinosa (d. 1991) and daughter Ivette (d. 1992). He also wrote manuals on dance technique.

[Amnon Shiloah (2nd ed.)]

ESPINOZA, ENRIQUE (pseudonym of **Samuel Glusberg**; 1898–1987), Argentine author, publisher, and, journalist. His pseudonym combines the names of Henrich Heine and Baruch Spinoza. Born in Kishinev, Espinoza arrived in Argentina at the age of seven. He founded and edited the literary reviews *Cuadernos Americanos* (1919) and *Babel* (1921–51), first in Buenos Aires and later in Santiago de Chile, where he settled in 1935 for health and political reasons, and also founded the Babel publishing house, which launched books by new Argentinian writers. In 1945 he conducted a symposium on "the Jewish Question" among prominent Latin American intellectuals, published in *Babel* 26. He was co-founder and first secretary of the Argentine Writers' Association, and a member of avant-garde movements in literature and the arts. His short stories and articles deal with Jewish identity, immigration, antisemitism, and the Holocaust, as well as ethical and universal social issues. His contemporaries saw him as the perfect intellectual blend of cosmopolitanism and Jewishness. His best-known stories appeared in *La levita gris: cuentos judíos de ambiente porteño* (1924); and *Ruth y Noemí* (1934). His essays were collected in *De un lado y otro* (1956), *Heine, el ángel y el león* (1953), and *Spinoza, ángel y paloma* (1978).

BIBLIOGRAPHY: R. Gardiol, *Argentina's Jewish Short Story Writers* (1986); N. Lindstrom, *Jewish Issues in Argentine Literature* (1989); D.B. Lockhart, *Jewish Writers of Latin America. A Dictionary* (1997).

[Florinda Goldberg (2nd ed.)]

ESRA, organization founded January 26, 1884, with its headquarters in Berlin and its major objective to support Jewish agricultural settlers in Ereẓ Israel and Syria without the traditional **Ḥalukkah* system. At the end of 1886 a group of young Berlin Jews produced a manifesto prompted by the movement of Russian Jews to Ereẓ Israel to establish agricultural settlements, proclaiming: "These Russian Jews, who have been continually tortured and persecuted, were able to initiate this excellent project out of their intense need. Shall German Jewry, which enjoys the full protection of an impartial government, stand idly by and merely watch their efforts? We, who have had intellectual hegemony since the days of Mendelssohn, stand ashamed before Russian Jewry." The founding assembly of the Verein zur Unterstuetzung ackerbautreibender Juden in Palaestina und Syrien ("Association for the Support of Jewish Farmers in Palestine and Syria") took place in Berlin in 1884. Its early leaders were Willy *Bambus and Hirsch *Hildesheimer, the son of Rabbi Esriel Hildesheimer, who coopted the Orthodox camp into the organization. At its peak, the leaders of the organization included Otto *Warburg and Eugen *Mittwoch. The association, which had branches throughout Germany, published the newspapers *Serubabel* and **Selbstemanzipation*, pamphlets about agricultural settlement by Bambus, and the periodical, *Zion*. In 1891, the association succeeded in forming an umbrella organization for all European associations supporting settlement in Ereẓ Israel. Esra supported individual settlers in almost all agricultural villages, devoting special attention to the Qastina settlement (later Be'er Toviyyah), the Benei Yehudah colony in the Golan, Yemenite immigrants, and educational projects. When political Zionism gained momentum, the association emphasized the value of practical settlement in Palestine, while opposing Zionist political activity. Even at the end of World War I, it stated firmly that despite the "Charter" (i.e, the Balfour Declaration, to which they would not refer by name), supreme value must still be attached to settlement, without which there is no real basis for "national rights." Since the Zionist organization now began its large-scale settlement projects (inter alia, in the Jezreel Valley), the activities of Esra became superfluous. The association disappeared in the early 1920s.

BIBLIOGRAPHY: *Esra, Festschrift zum 25-jaehrigen Jubilaeum* (1909); 35 *Jahre Verein Esra* (1919). **ADD. BIBLIOGRAPHY:** J. Reinharz, "The Esra Verein and Jewish Colonization in Palestine," in: LBIYB, 24 (1979), 261–90.

[Getzel Kressel / Bjoern Siegel (2nd ed.)]

ESSELIN, ALTER (**Artur Eselin**; pseudonym of **Ore Serebrenik**; 1889–1974), Yiddish poet. Born in Chernigov, Ukraine, Esselin immigrated to the U.S. at the age of 16, worked as a carpenter in various cities, and settled in 1925 in Milwaukee, Wisconsin. His first poems appeared in 1919 in local Yiddish newspapers (*Der Veg*, Detroit; *Kundes*, New York). In a few years, he received significant literary recognition. His poetry volumes, *Knoytn* ("Candlewicks," 1927), *Unter der Last* ("Under the Yoke," 1936), and *Lider fun a Midbernik* ("Poems of a Hermit," 1954), are marked by their sadness. He often laments his lonely vigil far from Yiddish centers and voices his pride that he earns his living with saw and hammer. Death is a frequent theme, and in a poetic epitaph he describes himself as a poet who poisoned himself with songs in which honey and arsenic were mixed. A selection of his poems, translated into English, with an introduction by his son, Joseph Esselin, appeared in 1968.

BIBLIOGRAPHY: Y. Bronshteyn, *Fun Eygn Hoyz* (1963), 267–74. **ADD. BIBLIOGRAPHY:** LNYL, 7 (1968), 9–10.

[Sol Liptzin / Eliezer Niborski (2nd ed.)]

ESSEN (in Jewish sources: עסא), city in North Rhine-Westphalia, Germany. Jews are first mentioned there in the 13th century. During the *Black Death (1349) they were expelled from the city, but subsequently allowed to return. Jews are mentioned in a list of taxpayers of 1399. Between 1545 and 1578 there were no Jews in Essen. The first municipal law concerning the trades open to Jews was passed in 1598. Jurisdiction over Essen Jewry was disputed between the monastery and the municipality during the period 1662 to 1686. Although there were only seven Jews living in Essen in 1652 and 13 in 1791, a synagogue was built there in 1683 and a cemetery consecrated in 1716. Several Jewish physicians were living in Essen in this period. With the city's expansion in the mid-19th century the number of Jews rose from 19 in 1805 to 750 in 1869.

There were approximately 5,000 Jewish residents in 1930 and 4,500 (0.7% of the total population) in 1933. Jewish businesses were Aryanized and Jewish workers, no matter how prominent, were fired, including Benno Schmidt who invented stainless steel and was dismissed by Krupp and Company. The synagogue built in 1913 was desecrated by the Nazis in 1938. Seven hundred Jewish men aged 16–60 were arrested and deported to Dachau. Among the Jews not arrested were Ingo Freed and his father; Freed went on to serve as the architect of the United States Holocaust Memorial Museum. By May 17, 1939, 1,636 Jews remained in Essen. Those who had not already left were deported between 1941 and 1943. Deportations commenced when 247 Jews were sent to Lodz on October 27, 1941; 121 were sent to Minsk in November; an unknown number were deported to Riga in December; and in April 1942, 355 were sent to Izbica and from there presumably to Belzec. According to ration cards issued in 1942, there were 527 Jews left in May who were confined to the Holbeckshof camp in Essen-Steele and from there were deported to concentration camps. Two hundred ninety-four were sent to Theresienstadt on July 21. In April 1944, 39 Jews still lived in Essen, mostly people in mixed marriages. In the fall the Jewish population grew as an acute labor shortage at Krupp led to the arrival of 520 young Jews. Many later died in Bergen-Belsen. About 100 survivors returned after the war. A community was again established in Essen after the war and a synagogue was opened in 1959. There were 170 Jews living in Essen in 1970 (0.03% of the total population) and 130 in 1989. As a result of the immigration of Jews from the Former Soviet Union, their number rose to 667 in 2003.

BIBLIOGRAPHY: S. Samuel, *Geschichte der Juden in Stadt und Stift Essen … 1291–1802* (1905); Baron, 14 (1969), 209ff.; idem, *Geschichte der Juden in Stadt und Synagogenbezirk Essen 1802–1913* (1913); Germ Jud, 2 (1968), 227; H.J. Steinberg, *Widerstand und Verfolgung in Essen 1933–1945* (1969). **ADD. BIBLIOGRAPHY:** M. Zimmermann, *Juedisches Leben in Essen 1800–1933* (1993).

[Azriel Shochat]

ESSENES, a religious communalistic Jewish sect or association in the latter half of the Second Temple period, from the second century B.C.E. to the end of the first century C.E. Contemporary or near-contemporary descriptions are found in *Philo (*Every Good Man is Free*, *Hypothetica*), *Josephus (*Antiquities* and *War*, including references to individual Essenes), and Pliny the Elder (*Natural History*). Brief references from later authors are in Hegesippus (2nd century, who merely lists them, with other Jewish sects), Hippolytus (2nd–3rd century B.C.E., who seems dependent on neither Josephus nor Philo), and Synesius (4th–5th century C.E., apparently based on Pliny). Epiphanius (4th century C.E.) refers to both *Essenoi* (as a Samaritan sect) and *Ossaioi/Ossenoi*, whom he locates near the Dead Sea. The information in these sources is not always consistent. Josephus, who (improbably) claims to have been a member of the Essenes for a while, is probably less idealistic or fanciful than either Philo or Pliny, though he is relying on more than one source himself, while the latter preserve some probably reliable information. Josephus names them as one of his three main Jewish parties (*hairesis*), and according to Philo, they numbered about 4,000. According to both authors, their members lived in monastic communities; Josephus states that some married and some did not, while Philo is unclear, stating that they had children but did not "take women." Pliny says they lived "without women … or money" but seems to consider them as living in one place only, "above En-Gedi." The *Dead Sea Scrolls are widely regarded as belonging to the Essenes and if so they extend our knowledge of them considerably. There is no reference to the Essenes in the rabbinic literature, or in the New Testament, though it has frequently been suggested that *John the Baptist was influenced by Essenism since he lived, preached, and baptized beside the Jordan River only a few miles from Qumran. Some New Testament scholars also believe that the early Church may have incorporated Essene elements into its structure. The very existence of a pre-Christian Jewish quasi-monastic (and celibate) community is important for the understanding of subsequent Christian ascetic practices. A gateway and nearby district near Mt. Zion in Jerusalem has been excavated and plausibly identified as an Essene quarter (Pixner, following a suggestion from Yadin), but no absolute proof exists. Qumran is widely identified as an Essene settlement (see below); two other possible Essene locations have been proposed near the Dead Sea at Ain al-Ghuweir (by P. Bar-Adon) and above En-Gedi (by Y. Hirschfeld).

Their origins are unclear. They seem to have emerged as a distinct party, along with Sadducees and Pharisees, in the wake of the Hasmonean revolt, though all three probably have earlier roots. Some scholars regard both the Essenes and Pharisees as originating from the *ḥasidim* mentioned in connection with the Maccabean revolt; but the different *halakhah* and calendar, as well as strong criticism of apparently Pharisaic beliefs and practices, make this unlikely. It has also been suggested (Murphy-O'Connor) that they had immigrated from Babylonia at about this time or, alternatively (García Martínez), that they arose out of the Palestinian Jewish "apocalyptic movement."

The Essenes and the Dead Sea Scrolls

The Qumran scrolls have generally been interpreted as belonging to the Essenes, and their descriptions of sectarian communities cohere well with the classical sources, especially once the difference between the descriptions of the Damascus Document and the Community Rule is observed, since these differences can partly explain the discrepancies in the classical sources as well as control our interpretation of them. Thus, for instance, Josephus' account fits rather well with the many settlements (called "camps" and "cities") of the "Damascus" community, and with the existence of marrying and non-marrying orders, with the lengthy initiation procedures, attitudes towards women, limited participation in the Temple cult, and strict adherence to Torah and Sabbath; while Pliny seems to allude to the *yaḥad* described in the Community Rule, which is represented as a single and entirely celibate community – most likely that living at Qumran. Although the interpretation of the Qumran settlement is currently controversial, the site has generally been regarded as according well with the accounts of Essene lifestyle reported in the ancient sources, and this settlement has been understood either as a headquarters or a retreat center for the wider movement (Stegemann), or the home of a group that split off from the main body under the leadership of a figure named in the Qumran scrolls as the "Teacher of Righteousness." This figure is unnamed in the scrolls, but has been variously identified with known Essene figures mentioned by Josephus, in particular "Judah the Essene."

Meaning and Origin of the Name

There is a wide diversity of opinion as to the etymology of the name "Essene." Greek writers refer to them by names of which the most common are Ἐσσηνοί and Ἐσσαῖοι. The English "Essene" comes from the first form through the Latin. Philo invariably uses the second, and explains the name with reference to the Greek *hosioi*, while *Josephus uses both forms. Among the numerous theories that have been proposed are the following: (1) the most popular is a derivation from חסידים (*ḥasidim*, "pious"), a name used in I and II Maccabees of those especially loyal to the Torah (there are also references in rabbinic literature). Alternatively, the basis may be the Aramaic form חסיא, the plural of חסא ("pious") (the same derivation, but from Syriac, has also been proposed); (2) from Aramaic אסא, "heal," based on Josephus's account of their interest in medicinal herbs and the possible connection between Essenes and Therapeutae made by Philo. (Whether the Therapeutae should be regarded as linked to the Essenes, rather than just compared by Philo, is dubious); (3) from חשאים or חשאין ("the silent ones"), based on a passage from the Mishnah which mentions two rooms in the Temple of Jerusalem, one called the "chamber of utensils," and the other, the "chamber of חשאים" (chamber of "secrets" in H. Danby's translation). In the chamber of חשאים, the "sin-fearing ones" used to depose their gifts "in secret" and impoverished gentlefolk could help themselves to these gifts, equally in secret. This is now discarded, though it possibly fits with Josephus' statement that the Essenes sent offerings to the Temple, but offered sacrifices "by themselves" (εφ' αὑτων). Less probable are (4) from Heb. עשׂים or עשׂין "doers (of Torah)"; (5) from חשן "breastplate": Josephus uses *essen* to refer to this item, and it also figures in the liturgy of the Qumran "Songs of the Sabbath Sacrifice"; and (6) from the celibate priestly *Essenas* who ministered to Artemis at Ephesus (reported by Pausanius).

Rites, Practices, and Doctrines

By critically combining the evidence of the Qumran scrolls and the classical sources, the following description can be offered. The Essenes lived frugal, usually celibate, lives, supporting themselves by manual labor, generally agricultural, and practicing common ownership. They were also devoted to study of the Torah in its minutest details and performed frequent washing to maintain ritual purity (Josephus says they avoided oil, which was often used for cleaning the body). They had a rigorous and lengthy system of initiation. Unlike the Pharisees and Sadducees, they lived a segregated lifestyle with very limited contact with those outside. On the evidence of the Dead Sea Scrolls, they deemed themselves the only true Israel and regarded the religious observances of other Israelites, and especially in the Temple, as corrupt. On all these grounds they qualify to be called a "sect." Like the Pharisees, they stressed the need for personal piety and separation from the impurities of daily life, imposing on themselves levitical rules of purity: but while the Essenes (so Josephus) believed in the immortality of the soul, they rejected the Pharisaic doctrine of bodily resurrection. It has recently been proposed that the *halakhah* of the Scrolls is similar to that ascribed to Sadducees in the rabbinic literature.

The Essenes laid a strong emphasis on scrupulous obedience to the Torah, as they interpreted it. They emphasized observance of the Sabbath and the observance of festivals on the appropriate days, according to their own 364-day calendar, based on the solar year – which may explain Josephus' statement that they prayed towards the sun every morning. According to Josephus, they then worked through the greater part of the morning, then having gathered they girded themselves in white linen garments, and bathed in cold water (Jos., War, 2:129). They had their midday meal together, with a grace recited by a priest before and after the meal. The meal, eaten in a state of purity, seems to have played a very important role in sustaining the corporate identity of the sect. After working until the evening, they again ate together, in total silence. In all its activities, each Essene community was governed by rank and learning; the leaders directed the procedure, and named the persons to officiate. The Essenes zealously studied the sacred books and had an interest in medicinal herbs. They abstained from oaths, and blasphemy against God was punishable by death.

Initiation and Organization

New members of the community were recruited by adopting candidates after a probationary period. Those wishing to enter had to wait before being given the emblems – a belt, a white garment, and a hatchet for digging holes in the earth (whenever they wished to relieve themselves; *ibid.*, 2:127; 148). Then they were allowed to follow their routine and receive "more purifying washings for holiness" but were not yet permitted to take part in the common meals. After a probationary period of two more years the new member was admitted to the society, but not until he had taken oaths to observe the rules. Some form of communal ownership of goods was allowed, apparently more complete in the *yaḥad*, which, as the name ("union") implies, may have seen itself as a corporate unit, whose holiness depended on the individual holiness of all its members who worked, ate, and studied in communion. The Damascus Document describes a looser social structure, with an "overseer" (*mevakker*) in charge of each "camp" and ideology: corporate activity is less intense, but also subject to similar disciplinary rules. The settlements of married members were organized on the basis of individual households, with wives and children included in the sect automatically. This community also had dealings with non-Jews and owned slaves, though detailed accounts of such aspects are not provided. While the classical sources say little about priestly leadership, the Scrolls accord a very important role to the priesthood in matters of law and of course liturgy; how far they were responsible for the wider governance of the sect is unclear.

Essene participation in wider Jewish affairs is hard to assess. Apart from the mention of individual Essenes, however, Josephus states that they participated bravely in the war against Rome, and the discovery at Masada of some manuscripts that may have originated at Qumran, together with evidence of the Roman destruction of Qumran in about 68 B.C.E. and the many copies of a "War Rule" in the caves, in which the Romans appear as a thinly disguised enemy, support this claim. After the end of this war, the Essenes seem either to have disappeared or fled or dispersed: but the existence of copies of the Damascus Document in the Cairo *Genizah* may suggest that some of their traditions continued and influenced, among others, the *Karaites.

ADD. BIBLIOGRAPHY: G. Vermes and M.D. Goodman, *The Essenes According to the Classical Sources* (1989); T.S. Beall, *Josephus' Description of the Essenes illustrated by the Dead Sea Scrolls* (1988); P. Bar-Adon, "Another Settlement of the Judean Desert Sect at En e-Ghuweir on the Dead Sea," in: *Bulletin of the American School of Archaeological Research*, 227:1–26 (1977); Y. Hirschfeld, *Qumran in Context: Reassessing the Archaeological Evidence* (2004); J. Murphy-O'Connor, "The Essenes and Their History," in: *Revue Biblique*, 81: 215–44 (1974); J. Kampen, "A Reconsideration of the Name 'Essene'," in: HUCA, 57 (1986), 61–81; S. Goranson, "Essenes. Etymology from *'sh*," in: *Revue de Qumrân*, 11 (1984), 483–98; "Posidonius, Strabo and Marcus Vipsanius Agrippa as Sources on Essenes," in: JJS, 45 (1994), 295–98; A.H. Jones, *Essenes* (1985); R. Bergmeier, *Die Essener-Berichte des Flavius Josephus* (1993); F. García Martínez and J. Trebolle Barrera, *The People of the Dead Sea Scrolls* (1995); B. Pixner, "Jerusalem's Essene Gateway: Where the Community Lived in Jesus' Time," in: *Biblical Archaeology Review*, 23:3 (1997), 22–31, 64–66; H. Stegemann, *The Library of Qumran: On the Essenes, Qumran, John the Baptist, and Jesus* (1998).

[Menahem Mansoor / Philip Davies (2nd ed.)]

ESSEX COUNTY, county in New Jersey, U.S. Located in northern New Jersey, Essex County has an area of 127 sq. miles (330 sq. km.) and in 2005 was the second largest county in New Jersey by population. Essex County is part of the United Jewish Communities of MetroWest, which encompasses Essex, *Morris, Sussex, and northern *Union counties and serves a Jewish population of approximately 120,000.

Early History

The Jewish history of Essex County is rooted in the city of Newark. Records indicate that a small number of Sephardi Jews were among the earliest Jewish settlers in the Newark area, but, with few records and no synagogues to document their stay in the area, the growth of Newark's Jewish community is attributed to the arrival of German Jews in the 1840s. Conventional wisdom has it that the first recorded Jewish settler in Newark was Louis Trier in 1844. Trier had six children, among them Abraham, who in 1845 became the first Jewish child to be officially registered as born in Newark.

Prince Street and the Third Ward

Of the many memories associated with Jewish Newark, none engenders more enthusiasm than stories about life on Prince Street and the six blocks of Yiddish-speaking neighborhoods that bordered and surrounded Prince Street. This was Newark's Third Ward. The boundaries at the eastern end were High Street (now Martin Luther King Boulevard) from Clinton Avenue to Springfield Avenue. The western boundaries were Belmont Avenue (now Irving Turner Boulevard) from Clinton Avenue to South Orange Avenue. This is where Newark's Jews, some 50,000 of them by 1911, lived and worked. First there were peddlers who came to the area, then came the pushcarts, followed by Jewish merchants who opened storefronts on Prince Street. Prince Street was described as "Baghdad on the Passaic" by one of the founders of the Jewish Historical Society of MetroWest, Saul Schwarz. Residents kept to the neighborhood. For entertainment, old and young attended Yiddish plays and operettas at Elving's Metropolitan Theater (1922–44). This first generation of Jewish immigrants also maintained memberships in mutual benefit and burial societies. For German Jews there was the KUV, Kranken Untersteutzung Verein, or Chronic Benefits Society, and for East European Jews, these societies, or "landsmanschaften," helped ease their adjustment to life in America. Two of the most popular occupations at this time were that of the saloonkeeper and the pharmacist. For sons of Jewish immigrants, boxing was a way to make a living. The starting place for Newark's Jewish fighters was the High Street YMHA. Noted amateurs were Newark's only Jewish mayor, Meyer Ellenstein, and Newark's bagel king Sonny Amster. Professional boxing sites were Laurel Garden or the Newark Veledrome. Newark's Jewish boxers were also recruited into an organization designed to counter pro-Nazi activities in the Newark area in 1933 and were called "The Minutemen."

Synagogues

By 1855, the number of Jewish families living in Newark was estimated at 200. The steady increase of Jewish families had already manifested itself when, in 1848, as many as 60 families joined the newly incorporated "Jewish Religious Congregation B'nai Jeshurun." This was Newark's first synagogue and New Jersey's oldest Reform congregation. Isaac Schwarz was its first rabbi. Newark's second oldest congregation, Temple B'nai Abraham, founded in 1855, was followed by Congregation Oheb Shalom in 1860. Oheb Shalom was one of the seven charter members of the *United Synagogue of America. These synagogues continue to host large congregations but are now located in the Essex County towns of Short Hills, Livingston, and South Orange respectively. In its heyday, however, Newark was home to as many as 43 synagogues. After numerous mergers and relocations, Essex County is currently home to 27 synagogues. There is one neighborhood synagogue with member services still located in downtown Newark, Ahavas Sholom, and one continuously operating synagogue, Mount Sinai Congregation, located at the Ivy Hill Apartments in suburban Newark. Of the many distinguished rabbis that served the greater Newark community, one in particular earned national and international recognition. Rabbi Dr. Joachim *Prinz, who fled Nazi Germany, became chief rabbi of Temple B'nai Abraham in 1939. Prinz used his pulpit to rally support for America's civil rights movement and counted civil rights leader, Dr. Martin Luther King, Jr., as one of his close friends.

Business, Industry, and Philanthropy

Louis *Bamberger and Felix Fuld established what became, by 1920, the nation's fourth largest department store, L. Bamberger and Company. Bamberger and Fuld were Essex County's, and possibly New Jersey's, greatest philanthropists of all time. The two men were the largest donors for Newark's Beth Israel Hospital, the YM-YWHA building on High Street, the building that houses the world-renowned Newark Museum, and the lasting legacy of an annual cherry blossom festival (more cherry trees than Washington, D.C.) at Branch Brook Park courtesy of Carrie Bamberger Fuld. Bamberger and Fuld donated some $18 million dollars to found the world famous Institute for Advanced Study located in Princeton, New Jersey, which offered world renowned scientist, Albert *Einstein, a position as the first head of its mathematics department. Einstein's connection to Newark's Jewish community is well documented.

Newark's Jews owned manufacturing businesses in industries such as leather, trunk, and harness manufacturing as well as jewelry manufacturing. Prominent industries such as Louis Aronson's Ronson Lighter Company and A. Hollander Sons, which grew into the largest fur dressing and dyeing operation in the world, earned Newark the name "workshop of the nation." New Jersey's premier supermarkets, Kings, ShopRite, Pathmark, and Wakefern Food Corporation were founded by members of the MetroWest community following World War II. Jewish businessmen with family roots in Newark continue to play a role in the renaissance of Newark. Jewish landmarks from the past are finding new uses.

Charitable Institutions

The collective accomplishments of Newark's Jewry include the founding and funding of Newark's Jewish hospital, Beth Israel Hospital (1901), which merged into St. Barnabas Healthcare System in 1996, and whose profits from the sale of the hospital are managed by the Jewish community as the Healthcare Foundation of New Jersey, and New Jersey's first Jewish home for the aged, Daughters of Israel Geriatric Center, founded in 1906, and located in West Orange. The first YM-YWHA was located on Newark's High Street in 1924. MetroWest now maintains two "Y" buildings, one in West Orange and the other at its Whippany Campus in Morris County. The community's social service agencies are distributed around the greater MetroWest area.

Educational Institutions

A congregational Hebrew school was established at B'nai Jeshurun in 1863; the Plaut Free Memorial Hebrew School followed in 1888. A *talmud torah* was established in 1899 in a store on Newark's Broome Street. Michael Stavistsky spearheaded the movement to establish the JEA, or Jewish Education Association, in 1937. Not well known is the Bet Yeled Jewish Folk School organized in 1950. The first major day school, Yeshiva of Newark, merged with the *talmud torah*, and was renamed the Hebrew Academy of Essex County in 1943; it subsequently merged with the Hebrew Youth Institute, and was renamed the Hebrew Youth Academy in 1962. Currently, it is the Joseph Kushner Hebrew Academy located in Livingston. Two individuals, Professor Nathan Winter and Horace Bier, were responsible for most of the Solomon Schechter Day Schools founded in New Jersey.

The newspaper-of-record, the *Jewish News*, began publishing in 1947. This paper is now the *New Jersey Jewish News*, and has the distinction of being the nation's second largest Jewish newspaper.

Shift to the Suburbs

In 1948, Newark was home to as many as 65,000 Jewish residents with an additional 21,000 Jews living in its suburbs. In the decades after World War II, there was a large-scale movement to the suburbs to towns such as South Orange, West Orange, Livingston, and more recently, Millburn-Short Hills. Flight was intensified by the Newark riots of 1967 and paralleled similar movements by Jewish communities elsewhere into the suburbs. In the mid-1990s the Jewish population of Essex County, including Newark, numbered approximately 76,200. The Jewish population of Livingston was approximately 12,600, and the Jewish population of West Orange was approximately 16,900.

Mergers of Institutions and Agencies

In 1923, an agreement to merge 13 Jewish agencies resulted in Essex County's Conference of Jewish Charities. The Essex County Council of Jewish Agencies was formed in 1936. The Jewish Community Council of Essex County, established in 1944, went one step further and incorporated the community's welfare services, fundraising, and community relations programs within one central federation. The 1973 merger of towns in the greater Summit area with the Jewish Community Council of Essex County reflected the movement of Jews west to towns in Morris County. The last significant merger occurred in 1983 between the Jewish Community Federation of Metropolitan New Jersey (Essex County) and the Jewish Federation of Morris and Sussex to create the United Jewish Communities of MetroWest.

MetroWest in Footlights

Essex County's greatest contributions to Jewish life in America are in the broad field of entertainment. Theater owner Morris Schlesinger is credited with discovering singer/film star Al *Jolson; Dore *Schary, executive producer at MGM studios, produced as many as 350 movies and also wrote the Pulitzer Prize-winning play *Sunrise at Campobello*; Essex County claims world-famous comedian Joseph Levitch, a.k.a. Jerry *Lewis; composer Jerome *Kern attended Barringer High School; Broadway producer Burton Shevelove produced *A Funny Thing Happened on the Way to the Forum;* choreographer Dean Collins gave us the steps to the West Coast Swing; there was children's poet Ilo Orleans; Beat Generation poet Allen *Ginsberg; and Newark's Jewish neighborhoods, mom and pop merchants, synagogues, rabbis, and institutions have been immortalized on the pages of American literature by Pulitzer Prize-winning author and Weequahic High School graduate Philip *Roth, who depicts Newark time and again in his novels.

[Linda Forgosh (2nd ed.)]

ESSLINGEN, city in Baden-Wuerttemberg, Germany. The sum levied on Esslingen Jewry in the tax list of 1241 indicates that it was one of the largest communities in Swabia, comprising more than 10% of the town's population. In the 13th century the community owned a synagogue, a drinking (or dance) hall, and a cemetery. The "Jews' Street" is first mentioned in 1308, but Jewish residence was not confined to it. Jews were allowed to join the guild on payment; the main Jewish occupation was moneylending. When attacked during the *Black Death persecutions in 1349, the Jews in Esslingen set fire to their synagogue; some committed suicide and others fled. However, in 1366 Jews are again mentioned in Esslingen. There were 14 in 1387, 21 in 1391. Esslingen Jewry loaned 84 hellers to the city in 1384; a Jew named Saecklin lent money to Duke Leopold III of Austria some time before 1385. By 1439 there were no Jews left in Esslingen. In the 16th century several Jews were admitted for short periods at high rents and taxes. However, the city expelled this group in 1543. Later it admitted two Jewish physicians. In 1806 Frederick I of Wuerttemberg allowed five Jewish families to settle in Esslingen, who founded a hardware factory and organized a community. A synagogue was built in 1817–19, a Jewish elementary school opened in 1825, and an orphanage was established in 1842. The Jewish population numbered 88 in 1823; 101 in 1831; 160 in 1860; 145 (1% of the total) in 1892; and 128 in 1930. During the Nazi regime the interior of the synagogue was destroyed (1938) and the building later used as a center for training Hitler youth. The last 34 Jews remaining in Esslingen were deported in 1941–42, including some of the children of the orphanage and the headmaster. There were 12 Jews living in Esslingen in 1965. After 1992 Jews from the Former Soviet Union settled in Esslingen. About 230 Jews who belonged to the Jewish community in Stuttgart were living in and around Esslingen in 2004.

BIBLIOGRAPHY: Germ. Jud, 2, s.v.; P. Sauer, *Die juedischen Gemeinden in Wuerttemberg und Hohenzollern* (1966), 173–78, incl. bibliog.; FJW, 341; R. Overdick, *Die rechtliche und wirtschaftliche Stellung der Juden in Suedwestdeutschland* (1965), 69–92, 144–150, 169–184. **ADD. BIBLIOGRAPHY:** H. Hoerburger, *Judenvertreibungen im Spaetmittelalter* (1981); J. Hahn, *Juedisches Leben in Esslingen* (1994).

ESTE, JOÃO BAPTISTA DE (17th century), Italian-Portuguese convert to Catholicism and anti-Jewish polemist. Born in Ferrara, he was baptized in Évora and became a consultant in Jewish matters to the Portuguese Inquisition. His works include a "Dialogue Between a Pupil and his Catechizing Teacher, Resolving All the Doubts that the Obstinate Jews are Wont to Make Against the Catholic Faith, with Cogent Arguments both from the Holy Prophets and from their Own Rabbis" (*Dialogo entre discipulo e Mestre catechizante*, Lisbon, 1621, 1674), and a "Summary of All the Festivals, Holidays, and Ceremonies, both from the Written Law and from their Talmud and Other Rabbis" (unpublished).

BIBLIOGRAPHY: M. Kayserling, *Geschichte der Juden in Portugal* (1867), 291f.; Kayserling, Bibl, 115; J.L. D'Azevedo, *Historia dos Christaõs Novos Portugueses* (1921), index; J. Mendes dos Remedios, *Os Judeus em Portugal*, 2 (1928), 302–10.

[Martin A. Cohen]

ESTELLA (Stella), city in northern Spain. The Jewish community there was one of the most important in the kingdom of Navarre, the third after Tudela and Pamplona. The earliest information concerning the settlement dates from the 11th century. The Jews lived in the citadel and in the adjacent unwalled area. Because of the privileges granted to the Jews there, the city attracted other Jews from many parts of Spain during the 12th century. The growth of the Jewish community in Estella was also due to the city's location on the route of the pilgrims to Santiago. There were Jews from Andalusia who fled from the Almoravid invaders and Jews from France who were attracted to the city. These included the poet Moses *Ibn Ezra, who was warned by *Judah Halevi against residing in so remote a town, which he compared to living among wolves, bears, and lions. In 1144 King García Ramirez transferred the synagogue to the bishop of Pamplona to be converted into a church. A *fuero* ("municipal charter") granted to Estella in 1164 contained a series of articles regulating relations between Jews and Gentiles. A responsum of Solomon b. Abraham *Adret (4:268) deals with problems of the sewage and the water conduit in the Jewish quarter. In 1265 there were 29 Jewish householders in Estella paying land tax and rent to the king. Following the death of Carlos IV in 1328 the Jews of Estella were particularly hard hit by anti-Jewish rioters. Many were killed. The Jewish quarter in Estella was destroyed and most of its inhabitants perished in 1328 during the French invasion, as recorded by *Menahem b. Aaron ibn Zeraḥ in his introduction to his code *Ẓeidah la-Derekh*. The community began to revive in the second half of the 14th century. There were 85 Jewish families in Estella in 1366. In 1365 Charles II appointed Judah b. Samuel ha-Levi of Estella to act as high commissioner for the crown for collecting the money in services and taxes owed by Jews and in 1390 sent him on a diplomatic mission. Jews of Estella engaged in tax farming throughout the 15th century. The city opened its doors to the exiles from Aragon and Castile but the Jews in Estella suffered the same fate, with the rest of those of Navarre, in 1498.

BIBLIOGRAPHY: M. Kayserling, *Geschichte Portugal*, 1 (1861), index; Baer, Spain, index; Baer, Urkunden, index; Cantera-Millás, Inscripciones, 291–2. **ADD. BIBLIOGRAPHY:** J. Carrasco Pérez, in: MEAH, 30:2 (1981), 109–20; idem, in: *En la España medieval*, 2–3; *Estudios en memoria del Profesor D. Salvador de Moxó*, vol. 1 (1982), 275–95; B. Leroy, in: *Archives Juives*, 17:1 (1981), 1–6.

[Haim Beinart / Yom Tov Assis (2nd ed.)]

ESTERKE, Jewish woman from the village of Opoczno, Poland, said to have been a mistress of the Polish King *Casimir the Great (1310–1370). Reports claim that her outstanding beauty caught the king's eye while he was passing through her town. Her two sons, Pelka and Niemera, were given grants of land from their father and were raised as Christians. The names of her daughter (or daughters) were never recorded, but with the king's approval, they supposedly remained Jewish. Alternate endings to Esterke's story include the king's severing his relationship with her; Esterke's death while they are still together; and Esterke's suicide either immediately after the king's death or several years later. Although a house in Opoczno was designated as her family home, and her grave was believed to be in Lobzow Park, near Cracow, there is no historical basis for any of the Esterke legends, and there is no mention of her either in court documents or in Jewish sources. Written mention of Esterke appears in the late 15th century in a history by Polish cleric Jan Dlugosz (1415–1480). The first Jewish source to mention Esterke is *Ẓemaḥ David* by David Gans, written in 1595. Gans believed in the historicity of the report and gave a Christian source for it. The relationship of Esterke and Casimir, with its obvious parallel to the Book of Esther, was appealing; the theme was used by Jewish writers as late as the 19th century. Versions of Esterke's story in Polish antisemitic literature attempted to undermine customary Jewish privileges granted to Jews by King *Boleslav V (1221–1279) and continued by King Casimir, suggesting that they were promulgated to please a lover rather than for the good of the nation. A 16th-century priest alluded to Esterke in his book *Jewish Cruelties*, claiming that her "gentle words induced him [Casimir] to devise by scheme this loathsome law under the name of the Prince Boleslav.…" Such negative allusions to Esterke continued in Christian writings until the 19th century; the belief that this Jewish woman actively interceded for her people gave Casimir the nickname "the Polish Ahasuarus." Despite confirmations by modern historians that Esterke is best regarded as an example of a literary trope of the seductive Jewish woman, popular from the early Middle Ages, and despite the fact that her name was used to further antisemitic claims, her sentimental appeal persists among Jews.

BIBLIOGRAPHY: E. Aizenberg, "Una Judia Muy Fermosa: The Jewess as Sex Object in Medieval Spanish Literature and Lore," in: *La Corónica*, 12 (Spring 1984), 187–94; Ch. Shmeruk, *The Esterke Story in Yiddish and Polish Literature* (1985); E. Taitz, S. Henry, and C.I. Tallan (eds.), *The JPS Guide to Jewish Women: 600 B.C.E.–1900 C.E.* (2003), 84.

[Emily Taitz (2nd ed.)]

ESTERMANN, IMMANUEL (1900–1973), U.S. physicist. Estermann, born in Berlin, was educated and worked at Hamburg University until 1933 when he immigrated to the U.S.A. For the next 20 years he was professor at the Carnegie Institute of Technology, and a consultant on the Manhattan (atomic bomb) Project. From 1951 he was with the Office of Naval Research, and in 1959 became its scientific director in London. From 1964 onward he had a visiting professorship at the Technion in Haifa. Estermann's main fields of work were on molecular beams, low temperatures, solid state physics, and semiconductors. Among his books was *Recent Research in Molecular Beams* (1959). He edited *Methods of Experimental Physics* (vol. 1, 1959) and coedited *Advances in Atomic and Molecular Physics* (3 vols., 1965–68).

[Samuel Aaron Miller]

ESTEVENS, DAVID (born before 1670–died after 1715), Jewish artist of Spanish (Marrano) origin. He lived in Denmark, studying in Copenhagen under the French artist Jacques d'Agar; he also spent some time in England. His best-known work is a portrait executed in London of Rabbi David *Nieto which was afterward engraved by James McArdell (1727). He may also have been the artist of the well-known portrait of Ẓevi Hirsch *Ashkenazi (the Ḥakham Ẓevi).

BIBLIOGRAPHY: F. Landsberger, in: HUCA, 16 (1941), 387–8.

[Cecil Roth]

ESTHER (Heb. אֶסְתֵּר), daughter of Abihail, an exile at *Susa, and heroine of the Book of Esther. The name Esther is probably from Old Persian *star* (well attested in the later Persian dialects), with the same meaning as English "star." She is once called Hadassah (Esth. 2:7), a testimony to the practice of Jews having double names, as do the heroes in *Daniel. She was orphaned as a child, and her cousin *Mordecai adopted her and brought her up.

When Queen *Vashti fell into disgrace because of her disobedience to King *Ahasuerus, Esther was among the beautiful virgins chosen to be presented to the king (1:19–2:8). Ahasuerus was struck by her beauty, and made her queen instead of Vashti (2:17). Esther, however, did not reveal the fact that she was a Jew.

Later, when *Haman, the prime minister, persuaded the king to issue an edict of extermination of all the Jews of the empire, Esther, on Mordecai's advice, endangered her own life by appearing before the king without being invited, in order to intercede for her people (4:16–17). Seeing that the king was well disposed toward her, she invited him and Haman to a private banquet, during which she did not reveal her desire, however, but invited them to another banquet, thus misleading Haman by making him think that he was in the queen's good graces. Her real intention, however, was to take revenge on him. During the second banquet, Queen Esther revealed her origin to the king, begged for her life and the life of her people, and named her enemy (7:3–6). Angry with Haman, Ahasuerus went into the palace garden. Haman, in great fear, remained to plead for his life from the queen. While imploring, he fell on Esther's couch and was found in this compromising situation on the king's return. He was immediately condemned to be hanged on the gallows he had prepared for Mordecai. The king complied with Esther's request, and the edict of destruction was changed into permission given to the Jews to avenge themselves on their enemies.

See also *Scroll of Esther.

In the *Aggadah*

Esther was a descendant of King Saul. Her father died soon after her conception and her mother when she was born (Meg. 13a), and she was brought up by Mordecai as his daughter. Her real name was Hadassah, but she was called Esther by non-Jews, this being the Persian name for Venus (*ibid.*). Esther was one of the four most beautiful women in the world (*ibid.* 15a), though some say that she was of sallow complexion but endowed with great charm. Like the myrtle (Heb. *hadassah*) she was of ideal height, neither too short nor too tall (*ibid.* 13a). All who beheld her were struck by her beauty: she was more beautiful than either Median or Persian women (Esth. R. 6:9). In addition, everyone took her to be one of his own people (Meg. 13a). Before Esther was made queen, Ahasuerus would compare women who entered with a statue of Vashti that stood near his bed. After his marriage the statue was replaced by one of Esther (*Midrash Abba Guryon*, Parashah 2). When Esther became queen she refused to disclose her lineage to Ahasuerus though she claimed that like him she was of royal descent. She also criticized him for killing Vashti and for following the brutish advice of the Persian and Median nobles, pointing out that the earlier kings (Nebuchadnezzar and Belshazzar) had followed the counsel of prophets (Daniel). At her suggestion he sought out Mordecai whose advice he requested on how to induce Esther to reveal her ancestry, complaining that neither giving banquets and reducing taxation in her honor nor showering gifts upon her had been of any avail. Mordecai suggested that maidens be again assembled as if the king wished to remarry and that Esther, aroused by jealousy, would comply with his wishes. But this too was in vain (Meg. 13a).

Mordecai was appointed to the king's gate, the same appointment that Hananiah and his companions had received from Nebuchadnezzar (Dan. 2:49). His task was to inform Ahasuerus of any conspiracy against him. Bigthan and Teresh, who had previously kept the gate, became incensed, saying: "The king has removed two officials and replaced them by this single barbarian." To prove the superiority of their guardianship over that of the Jew, they decided to kill the king. Not realizing that Mordecai as a member of the Sanhedrin knew 70 languages, they conversed together in their native Tarsean. In Mordecai's name Esther informed the king, who ordered the two to be hanged. All affairs of state were entered into the king's chronicles and whenever the king wanted to be reminded of past events they would be read out to him. The information given by Mordecai was written in the book, and this was the beginning of Haman's downfall (Esth. 6). This was why the sages said: "whoever repeats something in the name of one who said it brings redemption to the world" (Perek Kinyan Torah = Avot 6:6 in the prayer book version; Esth. R. 6:13; Meg. 15a; PdRE 50). The three days appointed by Esther as fast days (Esth. 4:16) were the 13th, 14th, and 15th of Nisan. Mordecai sent back word complaining that these days included the first day of Passover! To which she replied: "Jewish elder! Without an Israel, why should there be Passover?" Mordecai understood and canceled the Passover festivity, replacing it with a fast (Esth. R. 8:6). Esther's motive in inviting Haman to the banquet was that he should not discover that she was Jewish, and that the Jews should not say: "We have a sister in the king's palace," and so neglect to pray for God's mercy. She also thought that by being friendly to Haman she would rouse the king's jealousy to such an extent that he would kill both of them (Meg. 15b). Haman thought that Esther prepared the banquet in his honor, little realizing that she had set a trap for him (Mid. Prov. 9:2). With the revocation of the evil decree, Esther sent to the sages and asked them to perpetuate her name by the reading of the book of Esther and by the institution of a feast. When they answered that this would incite the ill-will of the nations, she replied: "I am already recorded in the chronicles of the kings of Media and Persia (Meg. 7a)."

[Elimelech Epstein Halevy]

In the Arts

Of all the biblical heroines Esther has enjoyed greatest popularity among writers, artists, and musicians, representing feminine modesty, courage, and self-sacrifice. From the Renaissance era onward she figured in a vast array of dramas, including many Jewish plays intended for presentation on the *Purim festival. Two early works on this theme were *La Representatione della Reina Hester* (c. 1500), an Italian verse mystery that went through several editions during the 16th century, and the last of the 43 plays of the French *Mistére du Viel Testament*, a work of the later Middle Ages. These were followed by the German Meistersinger Hans Sachs' *Esther* (1530) and an English verse play, *A New Enterlude of Godly Queene Hester,* published anonymously in 1561. The latter, which entirely omitted the character of Vashti and muted the role of Mordecai, contained marked political undertones reflecting popular dissatisfaction with King Henry VIII and his ministers of state. A work of the same period was Solomon *Usque's *Esther,* first staged in Venice in 1558. This Portuguese play, later revised by Leone *Modena, was remarkably successful and attracted many non-Jews to its performances.

The subject gave rise to a series of dramatic interpretations in France, beginning with the Huguenot playwright Antoine de Montchrétien's three verse tragedies, *Esther* (1585), *Vashti* (1589), and *Aman* (1601). During the 17th century a drama, *Esther* (1644), was written by Pierre Du Ryer and a long epic poem of the same name (1673) by Jean Desmarets de Saint-Sorlin, both in the austere religious manner of the period. The major French literary treatment of the theme was *Racine's epic tragedy *Esther* (1689), written for presentation at the Saint-Cyr girls' school supervised by Madame de Maintenon, the morganatic wife of Louis XIV, and first performed with choruses by J.-B. Moreau. Esther herself, a model of Christian womanly virtues, evidently represented the sponsor, while Vasthi (Vashti) represented the king's former mistress, Madame de Montespan, heightening the political implications of the play. Other 17th-century works on the subject include *Aman y Mardoqueo o la reina Ester*, a play by the Spanish New Christian Felipe *Godínez; the refugee Portuguese Marrano João *Pinto Delgado's *Poema de la Reyna Ester* (Rouen, 1627), part of a volume dedicated to Cardinal Richelieu; Mardochée Astruc's Judeo-Provençal *Tragediou de la Reine Esther;* and Isaac Cohen de *Lara's *Comedia famosa de Aman y Mordochay* (1699).

Interest in the theme was maintained during the 18th–20th centuries, beginning with Manuel Joseph Martin's *La Soberbia castigada. Historia … de Esther y Mardocheo* (1781). A Yiddish play, *Esther, oder di belonte Tugend* (1827, 1854³), was written by J. Herz, and Hebrew adaptations of Racine's classic drama made by S.J.L. *Rapoport (in *She'erit Judah*, 1827) and, in complete form, by Meir Ha-Levi *Letteris (*Shelom Esther*, 1843). The virtues of the Jewish heroine were emphasized in the Austrian dramatist Franz Grillparzer's unfinished play *Esther* (1848), and other treatments included J.A. Vaillant's Romanian *Legenda lui Aman și Mardoheu* (1868), Joseph Shabbetai Farḥi's Italian *Alegria di Purim* (1875), and the U.S. writer Frank C. Bliss' verse drama *Queen Esther* (1881). Almost the only biblical play to escape censorship in 19th-century England was *Esther the Royal Jewess: or the Death of Haman*, a lavishly produced melodrama by Elisabeth Polack, which was staged in London in 1835. There have been numerous plays about Esther from the early 20th century onward: *Esther, princesse d'Israël* (1912) by André Dumas and S.C. Leconte; H. Pereira *Mendes' *Esther and Harbonah* (1917); Max *Brod's *Esther* (1918); John Masefield's *Esther* (1922), a pastiche of Racine; and other works of the same name by Felix *Braun (1925), Sammy *Gronemann (1926), and the U.S. dramatist Sonia V. Daugherty (1929). Three other modern treatments are Izak *Goller's fantasy *A Purim-Night's Dream* (1931) and James Bridie's *What Say They?* (1939); and a rare biblical novel on the subject, Maria Poggel-Degenhardt's *Koenigin Vasthi; Roman aus der Zeit Esthers* (1928). Most successful were the satiric Megilla-Lieder of the Yiddish poet Itzik *Manger adapted for the stage in Israel in 1965.

In art the Book of Esther is represented in the cycle of paintings from the third-century synagogue at *Dura-Europos and also in the ninth-century mural in the basilica of San Clemente in Rome. The scenes depicted at Dura-Europos were Esther and Ahasuerus enthroned and Mordecai riding in triumph on a regal white horse. They could be seen clearly from the women's benches, and it has been suggested that they were placed there because women normally came to synagogue to attend the reading of the Scroll of Esther which, according to *Joshua bar Levi (Meg. 4a), they were obliged to hear. In medieval Christian iconography, Esther was associated with the cult of the Virgin Mary. Her intercession with Ahasuerus on behalf of the Jews was interpreted as a prefiguration of the Virgin's mediation on behalf of mankind. After the Middle Ages the story of Esther was treated in a less symbolic manner and was used instead as a storehouse of picturesque episodes. The story was sometimes presented in a narrative cycle of varying length or in individual episodes. Examples of the cycle form may be found on an arch over the north portal of the Chartres Cathedral (13th century), a 17th-century Belgian tapestry in the cathedral of Saragosa, and an 18th-century set of Gobelin tapestries. Popular single subjects were the toilet of Esther, the triumph of Mordecai, and the punishment of Haman. Renaissance artists such as Botticelli, Filippino Lippi, Mantegna, Tintoretto, and Paolo Veronese painted subjects from the Book of Esther. Botticelli (or Filippino Lippi) decorated two marriage-caskets (1428) with scenes from the biblical story, including the long misinterpreted figure *La Derelitta*, now supposed to represent Mordecai lamenting before the palace at Shushan. The Venetian painters Tintoretto and Veronese treated the Esther story as an occasion for pomp and pageantry, Tintoretto painting the *Swooning of Esther* (1545), a subject later treated by Poussin. The Book of Esther was also popular with 17th-century artists in the Netherlands. Rubens and Jan Steen painted *Esther Before Ahasuerus*, and Jan Steen also executed a spirited, almost farcical, *Wrath of Ahasuerus* (1660). Rembrandt painted *Mordecai pleading with Esther* (1655), *Ahasuerus and Haman at Esther's Feast* (1660), and *Haman in Disgrace* (1660). A charming *Toilet of Esther* was executed by Théodore Chassériau in 1841.

An early musical treatment of the subject is a 14th-century motet for three voices, *Quoniam novi probatur*, in which Haman, or someone whose fate he symbolizes, voices his complaint (see C. Parrish, *The Notation of Mediaeval Music* (1957), 138–40). Palestrina wrote a five-voiced motet, *Quid habes Hester?* (publ. 1575), the text of which is the dialogue between Esther and Ahasuerus in the apocryphal additions to Esther (15:9–14). From the late 17th century onward the Esther story attracted the attention of many serious composers. Some 17th- and early 18th-century works were A. Stradella's oratorio *Ester, liberatrice dell' popolo ebreo* (c. 1670); M.-A. Charpentier's quasi-oratorio *Historia Esther* (date unknown); G. Legrenzi's oratorio *Gli sponsali d'Ester* (1676); J.-B. Moreau's choruses for Racine's *Esther*; A. Lotti's oratorio *L 'umilità coronata in Esther* (1712); and A. Caldara's oratorio *Ester* (1723). Handel's masque *Haman and Mordecai*, with a text by John Arbuthnot and (probably) Alexander Pope based on Racine's drama, was first performed at the Duke of Chandos' palace near Edgware in 1720, and was Handel's first English composition in oratorio form. Worked into a full oratorio 12 years later, with additional words by Samuel Humphreys, it had a triumphant reception at the King's Theater in London in 1732. The libretto was translated into Hebrew by the Venetian rabbi Jacob Raphael Saraval (1707–1782), and two copies of it – with the scenic indications in English and Italian respectively – are in the *Ets Haim* Library, Amsterdam; no evidence of a performance has yet been discovered (see Adler, Prat Mus, 1 (1966), 123–4, 212). One of the few works on the subject in the second half of the 18th century was K. Ditters von Dittersdorf's oratorio *La liberatrice del popolo giudaico nella Persia o sia l'Esther* (1773).

The 19th century saw a few operatic variants of the story, such as Guidi's *Ester d'Engaddi*, set by A. Peri (1843) and G. Pacini (1847), while Eugen d'Albert wrote an overture to Grillparzer's *Esther* (1888). For performances of Racine's play at the Comédie Française during this period the choruses were composed by several undistinguished musicians; later contributions include those by Reynaldo *Hahn (1905) and Marcel Samuel-Rousseau (1912). The most notable modern work on the subject is Darius *Milhaud's opera *Esther de Carpentras*, which dramatized the staging of an old Provençal Purim play with the threat posed by a conversionist bishop of Carpentras. *Esther*, an opera by Jan Meyerowitz with text by Langston Hughes, was written in 1956. Meyerowitz also wrote a choral work, *Midrash Esther* (premiere, 1957).

The music of the Jewish Purim plays has not survived in notation, except for a few songs collected by 20th-century folklorists from surviving practitioners. Some Yiddish and Hebrew poems of the early 18th century were published with the indication "to be sung to the tune of Haman in the Aḥashverosh play" (see Idelsohn, Music, 437), but this tune has not yet been recovered. However, the tradition is evident in Isaac Offenbach's play *Koenigin Esther* (manuscript dated 1833, at the Jewish Institute of Religion, New York), which includes some "couplets" and in which the court jester seems a more important figure than the biblical personages. Hermann Cohn's five-act parody *Der Barbier von Schuschan* (1894) was an imitation of P. Cornelius' *Barbier von Bagdad*; Abraham *Goldfaden's *Kenig Akhashverosh* (c. 1885) produced no memorable tune; and M. Gelbart wrote *Akhashverosh*, a Purim play in New York (1916). For the production of K.J. *Silman's *Megillat Esther* by the *Ohel theater, the music was written by Y. *Admon (Gorochow). The music for the production of Itzik Manger's *Di Megille* was written by Dov Seltzer in a "revival style" reminiscent of the East European Jewish song tradition in general and of the Yiddish theater tradition in particular. Nahum *Nardi's songs to Levin *Kipnis' kindergarten Purim play *Misḥak Purim*, written in the early 1930s, have become Israel folksongs.

See also *Purim-Shpil.

BIBLIOGRAPHY: BIBLE: See bibliography to *Scroll of Esther. IN THE AGGADAH: Ginzberg, Legends, index. IN THE ARTS: R. Schwartz, *Esther im deutschen und neulateinischen Drama des Reformations-Zeitalters* (1894); E. Wind, in: *Journal of the Warburg Institute*, 4 (1940), 114–7; M. Roston, *Biblical Drama in England From the Middle Ages to the Present Day* (1968), 72–74; L. Réau, *Iconographie de l'art chrétien*, 2, pt. 1 (1956), 335–42, includes bibliography; E. Kirschbaum (ed.), *Lexikon der christlichen Ikonographie*, 1 (1968), 683–7; F. Rosenberg, in: *Festschrift… Adolf Tobler* (1905), 335–54; P. Goodman, *Purim Anthology* (1960).

ESTHER (pseudonym of **Malkah Lifschitz**, whose names by marriage were **Frumkin** and **Wichmann**; 1880–1943), communist leader, writer, and educator, born in Minsk; one of the most original women in the Jewish labor movement. She acquired a wide Jewish knowledge in childhood, including Hebrew and Bible studies, and studied in St. Petersburg and Berlin. From 1896 Esther was active in Social Democrat circles in Minsk influenced by A. *Liessin, and from 1901 in the *Bund. She edited Bundist periodicals after the 1905 revolution. A representative of the extreme Yiddishists at the *Czernowitz Yiddish Conference, Esther was one of the main promoters in the Bund of Jewish education in Yiddish. She published two books on the subject in Yiddish: "On the Question of the Jewish National School" (1910) and "What Kind of National School Do We Need" (1917). She was imprisoned several times for revolutionary activities and went to Switzerland, where she became a member of the foreign committee of the Bund. After the 1917 February Revolution, she became a member of the central committee of the Bund, and was elected to the Minsk municipal and community councils. She took an active part in founding a network of Yiddish schools, courses for teachers, and other educational institutions. At first violently opposed to the Bolsheviks, she later became a leader of the Kombund, and in May 1921 voted for the self-liquidation of the Bund and joined the Communist Party. From 1921 to 1930 she was a member of the education department of the *Yevsektsiya. With M. *Litvakov she brought out a Yiddish edition of Lenin's writings in eight volumes, and wrote a biography of Lenin in Yiddish (3 eds., 1925–26). She also edited the Moscow Yiddish daily, *Emes*. She was rector of the Jewish section of the "Communist University of the National Minorities of the West" (KUNMZ) from 1925 to 1936. In January 1938 she was arrested and imprisoned but refused to admit to the false charges proffered against her. In August 1940 she was sentenced to eight years in detention and died in the detention camp in Karaganda.

BIBLIOGRAPHY: S. Schwarz, *The Jews in the Soviet Union* (1951), index; LNYL, 1 (1956), 141–3.

[Moshe Mishkinsky / Shmuel Spector (2nd ed.)]

ESTHER, ADDITIONS TO THE BOOK OF. The Book of Esther in the Septuagint, followed by the Old Latin version, contains six passages comprising 107 verses that are not found in the Hebrew text. In the fourth century C.E., *Jerome, when compiling the Latin Vulgate Bible, removed all these additions and grouped them as an appendix at the end of the Book of Esther. Although Jerome had provided notes to indicate where each addition belonged within the canonical book, subsequent scribes sometimes neglected to copy the explanatory notes, resulting in a meaningless combination of separate portions. The confusion was compounded in the 13th century when Stephen Langton, having divided the text of the Vulgate into chapters, numbered the chapters of the canonical and the apocryphal portions of Esther consecutively. Rearranged in their proper order and with chapter and verse numbering according to Jerome's sequence, the six additions are as follows: A (11:2–12:6), Mordecai saves King Artaxerxes' life; B (13:1–7), the edict of Artaxerxes ordering the massacre of the Jews; C (13:8–14:19), the prayers of Mordecai and Esther; D (15:1–6), Esther risks her life to appeal to the king; E (16:1–24), Artaxerxes' second edict, denouncing Haman and supporting the Jews; F (10:4–11:1), the interpretation of Mordecai's dream. These additions belong within the sequence of the canonical text as follows: A before 1:1; B after 3:13; C and D after 4:17; E after 7:12; F after 10:3.

The author (or authors) of the additions is unknown, but probably at least some of them were composed by Lysimachus, an Alexandrian Jew who lived in Jerusalem and who translated the canonical Hebrew text of Esther into Greek about 114 B.C.E. (11:1). Although the name of God does not appear in the canonical Book of Esther, all but one of the additions contain it. Likewise, although prayer is not mentioned in the canonical text, addition C includes two devout prayers. Thus it appears that one of the purposes of the expansions is to introduce into the book certain religious elements that are conspicuously absent from the Hebrew narrative. Occasionally the additions contradict statements in the canonical text. For example, according to the Hebrew, Mordecai discovered the plot against the king sometime after the seventh year of the reign of Ahasuerus (Esther 2:16–21), whereas addition A suggests that this occurred in the second year of the king's reign; in 16:10 Haman is called a Macedonian, whereas in Esther 3:1 he is called the Agagite (= Amalekite); and in 13:6 the date set for the massacre of the Jews is the fourteenth of Adar, whereas in Esther 3:13 it is the thirteenth of Adar.

BIBLIOGRAPHY: Schuerer, Gesch, 3 (1909), 449–52; J.A.F. Gregg, in: Charles, Apocrypha, 1 (1913), 665–84; R.H. Pfeiffer, *History of New Testament Times, with an Introduction to the Apocrypha* (1949), 304–12; B.M. Metzger, *Introduction to the Apocrypha* (1957), 55–63.

[Bruce M. Metzger]

ESTHER, FAST OF (Heb. תַּעֲנִית אֶסְתֵּר, *Ta'anit Esther*), the day before *Purim on which it is customary to fast (unless that day falls on the Sabbath; see below). The *She'iltot* of R. Aḥa of Shabḥa (eighth century; ed. by S.K. Mirsky, 3 (1964), 222, no. 69) has the earliest record of the custom of fasting on the 13th of Adar. It quotes the declaration of R. Samuel b. Isaac (Meg. 2a), "The 13th day of Adar is the time for public gathering," and refers to the words of Esther (9:18) "The other Jews in the king's provinces gathered together and stood up for themselves on the 13th day of the month of Adar"; explaining that the purpose of the gathering was for public prayer and fasting (cf. *Asher b. Jehiel on Meg. 2a, who quotes R. Tam in a similar vein). Maimonides accepts the custom of public fasting on this day finding his scriptural authority in the words "Regarding the fasting and the crying" (Esth. 9:31). Comparing it with other public fasts he declares, "Whereas the other fasts are postponed to the following day if they would otherwise fall on the Sabbath the Fast of Esther is anticipated to the Thursday, since fasting here must precede the celebration" (Maim., Yad, Ta'anit 5:5). An earlier tradition of fasting in connection with Purim is preserved in the Talmud (Sof. 14:4), which specifically excludes fasting on the 13th of Adar, "because of Nicanor and his men." This is in accordance with the prohibition of *Megillat Ta'anit* against fasting on those days on which the Maccabean victories over *Nicanor and their other enemies were celebrated. Elsewhere tractate *Soferim* asserts: "Our Rabbis in the West [i.e., Ereẓ Israel] are accustomed to fast at intervals after Purim [i.e., on the three subsequent days: Monday, Thursday, and Monday] in commemoration of the three days fasted by Esther and Mordecai and those who joined them" (Sof. 21:1). Although *Jacob b. Asher's Tur (OḤ 686) refers to this ancient custom, there is no historical indication of its preservation. It was probably falling into desuetude at the very time that the tractate *Soferim* was being edited, as the contemporaneous composition of the *She'iltot* indicates. In his gloss on the reference to the fast in the Shulḥan Arukh (OḤ 686:2), Isserles considers the Fast of Esther as less obligatory than other statutory public fasts. He allows concessions to nursing mothers and pregnant women, and even to those with an eye-ache. He advocates, nevertheless, its continued observance. Special *seliḥot* are recited in addition to those of a regular fast-day, and the fast-day portion of the Torah is read (Ex. 32:11–14; 34:1–10). The day is especially observed by Persian Jews. The afternoon *Taḥanun* is omitted in anticipation of Purim joy.

BIBLIOGRAPHY: Eisenstein, Dinim, 440–1; Schwarz, in: *Festschrift... Simonsen* (1923), 188–205; N.S. Doniach, *Purim or the Feast of Esther* (1933), 65–67; Hilevitz, in: *Sinai*, 64 (1969), 215–42; Pearl, *Guide to the Minor Festivals and Fasts* (1963), 73–76.

[Isaac Newman]

ESTHER RABBAH (Heb. אֶסְתֵּר רַבָּה), *Midrash Aggadah* on the *Scroll of Esther. In the *editio princeps* (Constantinople, 1517?) the work is referred to as "*Midrash *Ahasuerus*" while in the second edition (Pesaro, 1519) it is called "*Midrash Megillat Esther*" and the title "Ahasueros." On the origin of the name "*Esther Rabbah*," see **Ruth Rabbah*.

The Structure

In the *editio princeps*, *Esther Rabbah* is divided into six sections. However, subsequent editions have ten, the last section being subdivided into five smaller ones. In fact, the work consists of two different Midrashim: *Esther Rabbah* 1 (sections 1–6) and *Esther Rabbah* 2 (sections 7–10).

Esther Rabbah 1

This is an exegetical Midrash which expounds the first two chapters of the Scroll of Esther verse by verse. The sections are introduced by proems of the classical type characteristic of amoraic Midrashim, opening with an extraneous verse which is interpreted and then connected with that expounded at the beginning of the section. There are 16 proems, the majority in the name of an *amora*, the rest anonymous. Most of them commence with a verse from the Prophets or the Hagiographa, only a small number with one from the Pentateuch. Section 2 concludes with a message of consolation. The language of *Esther Rabbah* 1, like that of the Jerusalem Talmud, is mishnaic Hebrew with an admixture of Galilean *Aramaic and a liberal sprinkling of Greek words. The work, which contains much original tannaitic and early amoraic material, quotes Aquila's translation, and draws upon tannaitic literature, the Jerusalem Talmud, **Genesis Rabbah*, and **Leviticus Rabbah*, but was apparently unaware of the Aramaic translation of the Scroll of Esther, some passages of which are even cited as statements of *amoraim*. The Babylonian *Talmud is also not utilized. On the other hand, **Targum Sheni*, **Ecclesiastes Rabbah*, **Midrash Tehillim*, *Midrash Abba Guryon*, and *Midrash Panim Aḥerim* to Esther, Version 2 (see smaller *Midrashim) all draw upon *Esther Rabbah* 1. It is thus apparently an amoraic Midrash, redacted in Ereẓ Israel not later than the beginning of the sixth century C.E.

Esther Rabbah 2

This, likewise an exegetical Midrash, covers Esther 3:1–8:15, but with many omissions. Its few proems are not of the classical type in that they do not conclude with the verse expounded at the beginning of the section. It quotes the Septuagint Additions to the Scroll of Esther: Mordecai's dream about the two sea monsters (8:5); the prayers of Mordecai and Esther (8:7); and the conversation of Esther and Ahasuerus (9:1). It borrowed these additions as well as other *aggadot* from *Josippon (chap. 4). Alongside later material, however, it also contains older homilies. Early medieval scholars cite expositions from part of a Midrash on Esther parallel to *Esther Rabbah* 2, which, however, do not occur in the present text. The redactors of *Ecclesiastes Rabbah*, *Midrash Tehillim*, **Midrash Samuel*, and **Genesis Rabbati* were unacquainted with *Esther Rabbah* 2. All these Midrashim, as well as *Midrash Abba Guryon*, drew upon an earlier midrashic work on Esther 3ff. which apparently constituted the original second part of *Esther Rabbah* 1. On the other hand, *Midrash Panim Aḥerim* to Esther, Version 1, **Yalkut Shimoni*, and perhaps also **Midrash Lekaḥ Tov*, draw upon *Esther Rabbah* 2. All this would seem to make *Esther Rabbah* 2 a composite work containing remnants of the original second part of *Esther Rabbah* 1 with later additions in the style and language of the later aggadic works (see *Midrash). *Esther Rabbah* 2, which contains valuable information on anti-Jewish manifestations in the late Roman empire, was redacted about the 11th century. After it was attached to *Esther Rabbah* 1 the original second half of the latter was lost.

Esther Rabbah is thus composed of two different Midrashim which were apparently combined by a copyist in the 12th or 13th century C.E. The earliest extant manuscripts date from the beginning of the 15th century C.E.

Editions

Esther Rabbah was first published at Pesaro in 1519 together with Midrashim on the other four scrolls, which, however, are completely unrelated to it. This edition has often been reprinted. There is as yet no critical edition of the work based on manuscripts. An English translation by Maurice Simon appeared in the Soncino Midrash (1939).

BIBLIOGRAPHY: Zunz-Albeck, Derashot, 128–30, 423–5; B. Lerner, "The First edition of 'Midrash Hamesh hamegillot…", Yad leHeiman: Studies in Hebrew culture in Memory of A.M. Haberman (ed. Z. Malachi), Lydda, 1984, pp. 289–311 (Hebrew); J. Tabory, "The Division of Midrash Esther Rabbah," Teuda, 11 (1996), pp. 191–204 (Hebrew); idem, "The Proems to the Seventh Chapter of Esther Rabbah and Midrash Abba Guryon," *Mehkerei Yerushalayim be-sifrut Ivrit*, 15 (1997), pp. 171–182 (Hebrew).

[Moshe David Herr]

ESTONIA (Est. **Esti**), independent state from the 1990s, after the breakup of the Soviet Union, bordering on the gulfs of Finland and Riga. Estonia was an independent republic from 1918 to 1940. From 1940 to the dissolution of the U.S.S.R., with an interval of German occupation (1941–44), Estonia was a Soviet Socialist Republic. Until 1918 part of Russia (Estland and the northern part of Livland), the area of Estonia was not included in the Pale of Settlement. In 1897 some 4,000 Jews lived on this territory, including about 1,200 in *Tallinn (then Revel). The nucleus of this community was founded by Jewish soldiers after their demobilization from the army of Czar Nicholas I (see *Cantonists), who established a Jewish cemetery in the town in 1856. There were approximately 1,800 Jews living in the university town of *Tartu (known among Jews by its German name Dorpat), about 480 in Narva (then belonging to the district of St. Petersburg), and about 400 in Pärnu, on the Gulf of Riga. (See Map: Jews in Estonia.) Jews took part in the struggle for Estonian independence. In independent Estonia, the Jews numbered 4,566 in 1922 and 4,381 in 1934 (about 0.4% of the total population), of whom 2,203 lived in Tallinn, the capital, and 920 in Tartu; 923 (57.4% of those supporting families) were occupied in commerce, 484 (30.1%) in industry and crafts, 159 (9.9%) in the liberal professions, 26 (1.6%) were house owners, and 16 (1.0%) were religious officials. About 642 of the total were employees (officials and laborers) and the remainder were self-employed.

Estonia was the only country in Eastern Europe to fulfill its obligations toward its national minorities according to the concepts of the Minorities Treaties (see *Minority Rights), even though it had refused to become a signatory. The law on national-cultural autonomy was confirmed by the Estonian parliament on Feb. 5, 1925, and four minorities – Russian, German, Swedish, and Jewish – were accordingly recognized. The Jewish autonomous institutions, headed by a Cultural Council, were established in 1926. However, only 75% of Estonian Jewry (about 3,252 persons in 1939) registered with the Jewish minority list; the remainder ranged themselves with other nationalities, in particular Russian. The first Cultural Council was composed of 12 Zionist representatives, nine Yiddishists,

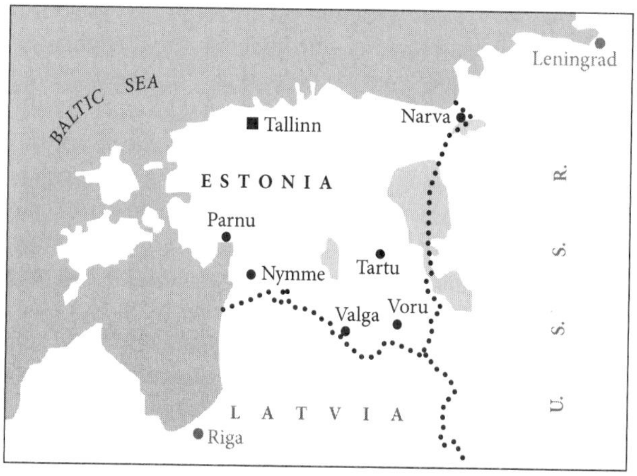

Major Jewish communities in Estonia, 1918–1940.

and six Independents. Subsequently the Zionists gained in strength, and by 1939 held 20 of the Council's 27 seats. After a severe struggle within the Council on the issue whether the language of instruction in Jewish schools should be Hebrew or Yiddish, the supporters of Hebrew finally prevailed, and most of the Jewish schools were affiliated to the Hebrew Tarbut educational network, including the two secondary schools of Tallinn and Tartu. About 75% of the Jewish children attended Jewish schools. A chair for Hebrew language and literature was established at the University of Tartu. There were three Jewish cooperative banks in Tallinn, Tartu, and Narva, with a total of 625 members in 1935. Estonian Jewry attained important national achievements, but because of its small numbers remained culturally dependent on the neighboring Jewish populations of Latvia and Lithuania. During the 1930s, a Fascist movement was formed in Estonia which launched an antisemitic propaganda campaign. The hardening anti-Jewish attitude was reflected in the decrease of the number of students at the University of Tartu, from 188 in 1926 to 96 in 1934.

After the annexation of Estonia to the Soviet Union in 1940, the Jewish institutions were liquidated and the political and social organizations disbanded. On the eve of the German invasion of the Soviet Union, some 500 communal leaders and affluent members of the congregation were arrested and deported to the Russian interior. Due to the efforts of the Soviet army to halt the German advance on Leningrad, the conquest of Estonia took about two months. Tallinn was not occupied until Sept. 3, 1941, and about 3,000 Estonian Jews succeeded in escaping to the Russian interior. All the Jews remaining in the zone of German occupation were murdered by the end of 1941 by the *Einsatzkommando* 1a with the active help of Estonian nationalist Omakaitse units. On October 12 all men aged 16 and above, about 440, were murdered, and in the last weeks of 1941 the others were liquidated – in all, 936 Jews according to the report of *Einsatzgruppe* A, from January 1942. This left Estonia *"judenfrei,"* a fact which was reported in the Wannsee Conference at the same time. In 1942 and early 1943 about 3,000 Jews, mainly from Germany, were sent to the extermination camp in Kalevi Liiva. By May 1943 Heinrich *Himmler had ordered the cessation of mass shooting and the erection of forced labor camps. The main camp in Estonia was Vaivara, commanded by Hans Aumeier (sentenced and executed in 1947). About 20,000 Jewish prisoners, mainly from Vilna and Kaunas (Kovno), passed through its gates to labor camps at Klooga, Lagedi, Ereda, and others. The inmates were employed in mining slate and building fortifications. The successful advance of the Soviet army led to the evacuation of the camps to Tallinn and from there to *Stutthof from where a "death march" of 10,000 took place along the Baltic coast. Other camps were also liquidated (2,400 killed at Klooga and 426 at Lagedi). On Sept. 22, 1944, Estonia was finally liberated. The Germans attempted to burn the bodies of their victims to conceal their crimes.

After the war, Jews from all parts of Russia gathered in Estonia. The Jewish population numbered 5,436 in 1959 (0.5% of the total) of whom 1,350 (25%) declared Yiddish as their mother tongue, about 400 Estonian, and the remainder Russian; 3,714 Jews (1.3% of the total population) lived in Tallinn. As in the rest of the Soviet Union, there was no organized Jewish life in the Estonian S.S.R.

[Yehuda Slutsky / Shmuel Spector (2nd ed.)]

Revival of Jewish Life

There were an estimated 3,200 Jews in Estonia at the end of 1993 and 1,800 in 2001.

Jewish communal life was renewed in 1988 with the creation of the Jewish Cultural Society in Tallinn, the first of its kind in the Soviet Union. The Society organized concerts and lectures, and a Jewish school going up to the ninth grade was opened in 1990. Jewish culture clubs were also started in Tartu, Narva, and Kohtla-Järve. Other organizations followed, like the Maccabi sports club and the Jewish Veterans Union. Courses in Hebrew were offered. The Jewish Community was established in 1992 as a voluntary umbrella organization; its charter was approved on April 11, 1992. The community published a Jewish newspaper, *Hashakhar* ("Dawn"), and the radio program "Shalom Aleichem" was broadcast monthly. A synagogue was also reopened, attended mostly by the elderly.

In November 1993, an Estonian translation of the *Protocols of the Elders of Zion*, giving no details of the publisher, appeared in Tallinn bookshops. After the protests of the Jewish community and the Estonia-Israel Friendship Society, the book was withdrawn by the bookshop owners. However, in August 1994 the nationalist weekly *Eesti* published an article by Juri Lina, an Estonian émigré in Sweden, claiming that the *Protocols* were authentic and demanding to lift restrictions on their publication.

A more serious danger for the future of the small Jewish community in the country lay in the activities of Russian extremists in Estonia. An antigovernment demonstration, organized by ethnic Russians in Narva (North East) in December 1993, displayed anti-Jewish placards; two parties which are counterparts to Zhirinovsky's LDPR in Russia – the harshly antisemitic Ruskii Sobor Estonii [Russian Council of Estonia] and Liberal Demokraatiik Partei, led by Piotr Rozhok – continued to operate.

Another potentially dangerous phenomenon in Estonia was the continuing romanticization of the Estonian military units which, during World War II, fought together with Nazi troops, some of them in the SS; many of them were guilty of murderous acts against Jews.

BIBLIOGRAPHY: K. Jokton, *Di Geshikhte fun di Yidn in Estland* (1927); N. Geuss, *Zur Geschichte der Juden in Eesti*, 2 vols. (1933–37); idem, *Bibliografie fun Yidishe Druk-Oysgabn in Esti* (1937); *Yahadut Latviyyah* (1953), 310–1; *Ershter Yidisher Kultur Kongres, Paris* (1937), 65–66, 196–200; I. Garr, in: *Algemeyne Yidishe Entsiklopedie*, 6 (1963), 395–401; M. Dworzecki, *Maḥanot ha-Yehudim be-Estonyah* (1970), with Eng. summ.; U. Schmelz and S. DellaPergola, in: AJYB, 1995, 478; *Supplement to the Monthly Bulletin of Statistics*, 2, 1995, Jerusalem; *Antisemitism World Report 1994*, London: Institute of Jewish Affairs, 139; *Antisemitism World Report 1995*, London: Institute of Jewish Affairs, 112–113; *Mezhdunarodnaia Evreiskaia Gazeta* (MEG), 1993. **ADD. BIBLIOGRAPHY:** PK. **WEBSITE:** www.jewishvirtuallibrary.org.

ESTORI (Isaac ben Moses) HA-PARḤI (1280–1355?), first topographer of Ereẓ Israel. The family was originally from Florenza, Andalusia, Spain – hence, the name ha-Parḥi, a Hebrew translation of the Spanish *flor* ("flower"). In the introduction to his main work Estori refers to himself as *Ish Tori* ("Man of Tours") in Touraine, France. It appears that he was born in Provence. He studied in Montpellier with his relative Jacob b. Makhir *Ibn Tibbon and with *Asher b. Jehiel. He obtained a broad general education, including the study of medicine as well. When the Jews were expelled from France in 1306, Estori went to Perpignan and Barcelona and then to Toledo. He stopped in Cairo in 1313 on his way to Ereẓ Israel. He studied with Baruch Ashkenazi in Jerusalem but left because of the negative attitude to Maimonides among the scholars of the city. Estori then settled in Beisan (Beth-Shean), where he was respected as a physician. He continued to earn his livelihood as a physician wherever he went. From Beisan he traveled throughout the land investigating ancient sites. He spent two years studying the Galilee and five years, other parts of the country. In Beisan he wrote *Sefer Kaftor va-Feraḥ* (Venice, 1549), which was completed in 1322. In this book he delineated the names of the towns and villages in the land. He also presented a complete discussion of the topographic principle that applied to the land. The book, based upon first hand visits to the sites, is rich in information. The book gives the borders of Ereẓ Israel as presented in the Bible and in the *halakhah*. It describes Jerusalem and the various regions of the country and presents a list of the biblical, talmudic, and Arabic names of the sites. Most of the 180 identifications of ancient sites that he made were correct. He was the first person to identify the sites of *Usha, *Modi'in, *Bethar, and others. His ruling that the biblical and talmudic names of villages and rivers are preserved in the Arabic, with only slight changes, is accepted by modern scholarship. Especially important is his study of ancient coins, which he compared with contemporary coins. He also compared the weights and measures of the Bible and the Talmud with contemporary weights and measures. He investigated plants, noting their Arabic names and attempting to determine their Hebrew names according to the Mishnah and Talmud. He also described the appearance of Jewish dress in Ereẓ Israel and in those countries of the Diaspora with which he was acquainted. He discovered the ruins of an ancient synagogue in Beisan and also described the remnants of an ancient synagogue in Hukok. He also provides information about the different religions and religious sects: Muslims, Christians, Jews, *Samaritans (whom he calls Sadducees), and Karaites. He gives valuable information on the Jewish settlements in Israel during his time. He mentions 11 Jewish communities, three of which were in Transjordan. A.M. *Luncz published a critical edition of *Kaftor va-Feraḥ* (Jerusalem, 1897), in which he mentions a number of other books that Estori wrote, though most of them are not extant. Estori's books include a translation of the book of medicine *De Remediis* by the physician Armengaud (Eremenganus) of Montpellier; a translation of the book *Hakabusim* containing articles and notes on medical matters, probably collected by the physician Elijah b. Judah; an exposition of some chapters from the Canon of Avicenna; *Battei ha-Nefesh*, words of admonition and moral rebuke; *Shoshannat ha-Melekh*, on the humanities and the sciences in the Talmud; and *Sha'ar ha-Shamayim*, expositions and novellae on the Talmud.

BIBLIOGRAPHY: Steinschneider, Uebersetzungen, 778, 835; A.M. Luncz (ed.), *Lu'aḥ Ereẓ Yisrael*, 3 (1897), 108–30; idem, in: *Ha-Me'ammer*, 3 (1919), 69–76; Gruenhut, in: ZDPV, 31 (1908), 281–96; Klein, in: HHY, 7 (1923), 103–32; S. Klein, *Toledot ha-Yishuv ha-Yehudi be-Ereẓ Yisrael* (1952²), 156–61; A. Yaari, *Masot Ereẓ Yisrael* (1946), 98–105; Zinberg, Sifrut, 2 (1960), 133, 415; J. Braslavski (Braslavi), *Le-Ḥeker Arẓenu* (1954), 263–8; idem, in: *Bikat Beit She'an* (1962), 80–95; Mirsky, in: *Torah she-be-al-Peh*, 8 (1966), 51–59.

[Jacob Elbaum]

ESTRAIKH, GENNADY (1952–), Yiddish scholar, writer, and journalist. Born in Zaporizhzhia, Ukraine, into a Yiddish-speaking family from a Jewish agricultural colony, he received his first degree in electronics and lived in Moscow (1976–91). In 1979 his family's application for an exit visa to Israel was rejected. In 1981 he joined the Jewish Historical and Ethnographical Commission, an independent scholarly body that sought to revive Jewish scholarship in the Soviet Union. From 1985 he regularly published short stories about contemporary Jewish life and essays on Jewish culture in the Moscow Yiddish monthly *Sovetish Heymland*, which he joined in 1988 as managing editor. His collection of stories *Di Royte Balke* ("The Red Ravine," 1988) and two editions of *Kratkiĭ Idish-Russish Slovar'* ("Concise Yiddish-Russian Dictionary," 1989/1990) appeared as supplements to that journal. In 1991 he moved to Oxford to pursue a doctorate, resulting in the book *Soviet Yiddish: Language Planning and Linguistic Development* (1999). In 1994–2002 he edited the Yiddish literary monthly *Di Pen*, worked at the Oxford Institute for Yiddish Studies, and taught Yiddish language and culture at London University's School of Oriental and African Studies. In 2003 he was appointed visiting professor of Yiddish studies at New York University. He is a regular columnist for the New York weekly *Forverts* (also under the pseudonyms G. Yakobi and Yakov London). He has published numerous scholarly articles on 20th century Yiddish culture in English and Yiddish. Other books include *Moskver Purim-Shpiln* ("Moscow Purim Plays," 1993), *Intensive Yiddish* (1996), and *In Harness: Yiddish Writers' Romance With Communism* (2005).

[Mikhail Krutikov (2nd ed.)]

ESTROSA (or **Istrumsa**), **DANIEL** (1582?–1653), Salonikan rabbi and halakhist. Estrosa was born in Salonika and studied under Isaac Franco and Mordecai *Kalai. He was apparently appointed as head of the famous yeshivah of the community known as "Portugala Yaḥya" during the latter years of Kalai's life. Among his pupils were David *Conforte, Gershon b. Abraham Motal, and Gabriel Esperanza. He died in Salonika during a plague. The only one of Estrosa's works published under his own name is *Magen Gibborim* (Salonika, 1754), responsa. It contains valuable glosses on the readings of Maimonides' *Yad* and of Jacob b. Asher's *Tur*. Other known works by him are included in the publications of others: his *Kunteres Shemot ha-Gittin* in the *Yerekh Avraham*, pt. 1 (Salonika, 1815), 1a–4b, of his grandson, Ḥayyim Abraham Estrosa, who also included his grandfather's novellae on chapter three of tractate *Avodah Zarah* in his *Ben Avraham* (Salonika, 1826); glosses on the *Tur*, *Ḥoshen Mishpat*, in the *Doresh Mishpat* (Salonika, 1655) of Solomon b. Samuel Florentin; and his halakhic decisions in the works of his colleagues and disciples.

BIBLIOGRAPHY: Conforte, Kore, s.v.; Rosanes, Togarmah, 3 (1938), 178; I.S. Emmanuel, *Gedolei Saloniki le-Dorotam*, 1 (1936), 309–11, no. 467; idem, *Maẓẓevot Saloniki*, 1 (1963), 313f., no. 717.

ESZTERGOM (Ger. **Gran**), city in N. Hungary, on the Danube; it had the oldest Jewish community in Hungary. This is mentioned for the first time during the 11th century, when Kalonymus b. Shabbetai lived in Esztergom; he is known for the severe legal decision which he pronounced against two merchants of Regensburg who arrived in Esztergom after the beginning of the Sabbath (Zedekiah Anav, *Shibbolei ha-Leket, Hilkhot Shabbat*, para. 60; see also Rashi to Beẓah 24b). The community lived in a closed Jewish quarter under the protection of the archbishop, granted by him in 1294, and the royal court, and had grown to 1,000 persons before the expulsion of the Jews from Esztergom in 1526. Jews resettled in Esztergom during the 18th century, and numbered 870 in 1850, 1,540 in 1910, 1,300 in 1930, and 450 in 1941, attached to a labor camp in 1942 along with thousands of other Jews. On June 13–16, 1944, they were deported to Auschwitz via Farkan. Only 52 survivors returned and there were only ten Jews living in Esztergom in 1970.

BIBLIOGRAPHY: F. Knauz and L.C. Dedek, *Monumenta Ecclesiae Strigoniensis*, 3 vols. (1874–1924); V.E. László, in: R.L. Braham (ed.), *Hungarian Jewish Studies*, 2 (1969), 137–82.

[*Encyclopaedia Hebraica*]

ETAM (Heb. עֵיטָם).

(1) The cleft in the rock where 3,000 men of Judah came to speak with Samson after he had slaughtered the Philistines (Judg. 15:8, 11). Some scholars identify it with ʿIrāq Ismāʿīn, 2½ mi. (4 km.) southeast of Zorah.

(2) A village in the northern Negev, mentioned together with En-Rimmon (I Chron. 4:32) and identified with the prominent Tell Beit Mirsim, where remains of the Israelite period, including walls, have been found.

(3) A city in the territory of Judah, located in the Bethlehem district according to a Septuagint addition to Joshua 15:59. It was fortified by Rehoboam together with Bethlehem and Tekoa (II Chron. 11:6). Josephus relates that it was one of Solomon's pleasure resorts and describes it as "delightful for, and abounding in, parks and flowing streams" (Ant., 8:186). It is most likely to be identified with Khirbat al-Ḥūḥ, a large tell with Iron Age remains, near Ein-Atan in the vicinity of the Pools of Solomon. According to the Talmud, the waters of its spring were brought to the Temple (TJ, Yoma 3:8, 41a), probably a reference to the aqueduct built by Pilate to catch the waters of the spring of Etam (Jos., Wars, 2:175; Ant., 18:60). A Kefar Etam is mentioned in the Mishnah (Yev. 12:6).

BIBLIOGRAPHY: Kraus, in: ZDPV, 72 (1956), 152–62; Aharoni, Land, index; Press, Ereẓ, 4 (1955^2), s.v.

[Michael Avi-Yonah]

ÉTAMPES (Heb. איטנפש), town in the Seine et Oise department, S. of Paris. At the time of the expulsion of 1182, King Philip Augustus gave the synagogue to the canons of Étampes to be converted into the collegiate church of Sainte-Croix (destroyed during the Revolution). There is still a rue de la Juiverie in Étampes, near the Place de l'Hôtel de Ville. One house in this square is still called the "synagogue," a name also given to the vast cellar (since filled in) under 39 and 41, rue Ste-Croix. Local tradition holds that Jews took refuge in the cellars of the quarter to escape persecutions and expulsions and that they buried their treasures there. Until 1182, R. Nathan b. Meshulam, great-grandfather of Joseph b. Nathan *Official, author of *Yosef ha-Mekanne*, lived in Étampes.

BIBLIOGRAPHY: Gross, Gal Jud, 44–45; B. Fleureau, *Les antiquitez... d'Etampes* (1683), 380f.; M. de Mont-Rond, *Essais historiques sur... Etampes* (1836), 1, 136ff.; M. Legrand, *Etampes pittoresque* (1897), passim.

[Bernhard Blumenkranz]

ETHAN (Heb. אֵיתָן; "permanent, enduring"? or "one consecrated [to a temple]"?). The Bible ostensibly mentions four individuals named Ethan: (1) Ethan the Ezrahite, a sage (along with *Heman, Calcol, and Darda, "sons of Mahol") whom Solomon surpassed in wisdom (I Kings 5:11). Psalm 89 is ascribed to him. (2) A son of Zerah son of Judah (I Chron. 2:6, 8). His brothers are Zimri, Heman, Calcol, and "Dara." (3) A levite Temple musician in the time of David, colleague of the levites Heman and Asaph (I Chron. 6:29; 15:17, 19; in some lists Ethan's name is replaced by Jeduthun (*ibid.* 16:41; 25:1–2; II Chron. 5:12; 35:15). (4) An ancestor of Asaph (I Chron. 6:27). In view of their common association with Heman, Calcol, and Dar(d)a, the first two Ethans are undoubtedly identical. The descent from Judah alleged in I Chronicles 2 probably represents a (pre-Chronicles) midrashic attempt to explain the epithet "Ezrahite" on the basis of the name of Zerah, Judah's son. The epithet is usually understood today to mean a member or descendant of the native pre-Israelite population of Palestine. (*'Ezraḥ* may be a loan from Akkadian *um/nzarḫu*, "homeborn" (Deller apud Cogan in Bibliography).) Ethan (and Heman, cf. Ps. 88:1) was thus descended from the latter. Since both Ethan and Heman are credited with psalms, it is hard not to identify them with the musicians of the same names in David's time ((3), above; note, too, that the epithet applied to Heman, Calcol, and Darda in I Kings 5:11, "sons of Mahol," is interpreted by W.F. Albright as "members of an orchestral guild"). As "Ezrahites" they may thus have been among the several non-Israelites holding prominent positions in David's time. The levite ancestry ascribed to them in Chronicles is typical of that book's treatment of cultic personnel (cf. the levite lineage it gives the Ephraimite Samuel, I Chron. 6:13; contrast I Sam. 1:1). Thus the first three Ethans appear to be one: one of the eponymous ancestors (cf. I Chron. 6:18ff.) of the guilds of Temple musicians (cf. to Calcol the Temple musician named *Krkr* on one of the 14–12th centuries B.C.E. ivories from Megiddo; in Pritchard, Texts, 263), living (according to Chron.) in the time of David, and of pre-Israelite Palestinian ancestry. His wisdom apparently was his psalmodic skill.

BIBLIOGRAPHY: Albright, Arch Rel, 126–7, 205; W.F. Albright, *Yahweh and the Gods of Canaan* (1968), 217–8; Maisler (Mazar), in: EM, 1 (1950), 276–7 (incl. bibl.); Sarna, in: JBL (1955), 272ff. **ADD. BIBLIOGRAPHY:** M. Cogan, *I Kings* (2000), 222.

[Jeffrey Howard Tigay]

ETHBAAL (Heb. אֶתְבַּעַל; "Baal is with him" – pronounced *Ittoba'al*?), a name borne by several kings of city-states in the area that classical sources call *Phoenicia, corresponding in the main to present-day Lebanon and Northwest Israel. Akkadian transcriptions indicate that the initial *alef* of Itobaal might be elided in pronunciation. (1) King of Tyre and Sidon, ca. 887–856 B.C.E., father of Jezebel (I Kings 16:31; Jos., Ant., 8:317). According to Menander of Ephesus, the historian of Phoenicia quoted by Josephus, Ethbaal (Ithobalos) was a priest of Astarte (as is attested of later kings of Sidon), who became king by murdering his predecessor, and ruled for 32 years (Jos., Apion, 1:123). A year-long drought in his reign (identified by Josephus as that in Ahab's reign, cf. I Kings 17) ended, according to Menander, when Ethbaal "made supplications to the gods, whereupon a heavy thunderstorm broke out" (Jos., Ant., 8:324). He founded the Phoenician city Botrys and the Libyan city Auza (*ibid.*). (2) Son of *Hiram (Ahiram), a tenth-century B.C.E. king of Byblos (Pritchard, Texts, 2, 504; *ibid.*, 3, 661). (3) An eighth-century king of Tyre who paid tribute to Tiglath-Pileser III ca. 740 B.C.E., whose existence was unknown before 1972. (4) A king of Sidon installed by Sennacherib in 701 as a replacement for the rebellious Lulli. (5) A sixth-century B.C.E. king of Tyre (Jos., Apion, 1:156).

BIBLIOGRAPHY: Z.S. Harris, *A Grammar of the Phoenician Language* (1936), 85; J.A. Montgomery, *The Book of Kings* (ICC, 1951), 286; J.M. Grintz, in: EM, 1 (1965), 790–1 (includes bibl.). **ADD. BIBLIOGRAPHY:** B. Peckham, in: ABD V, 349–57; H. Katzenstein, in: ABD VI, 686–90; J. Friedrich, W. Röllig, and M. Guzzo, *Phönizisch-Punische Grammatik* (1999), 13; H. Tadmor, *The Inscriptions of Tiglath-Pileser III King of Assyria* (1994), 266–67; M. Cogan, *I Kings* (2000), 421; COS II, 181–83, 287, 302–3.

[Jeffrey Howard Tigay / S. David Sperling (2nd ed.)]

°**ETHERIDGE, JOHN WESLEY** (1804–1866), English student of Judaica. Etheridge, who was a Methodist minister, held no academic position. His published works deal with both the Syriac Bible and the Targum, of which he did English translations of Onkelos and Pseudo-Jonathan to the Pentateuch, *The Targum of Onkelos and Jonathan ben Uzziel on the Pentateuch* (2 vols., 1862, 1865). He also published *Horae Aramaicae: Outlines of the Semitic Language* (London, 1843) and in 1856 a survey of Jewish learning entitled *Jerusalem and Tiberias: Sora and Cordova.* As a pioneering introduction to the various departments of Jewish learning, the work is not without significance.

ADD. BIBLIOGRAPHY: ODNB online.

[Raphael Loewe]

ETHICAL CULTURE, an American nontheistic movement based on a humanist ideology. From the time of its establishment in 1876, the Ethical Culture movement has appealed to a relatively well-educated, middle- and upper-class, socially idealistic public. Originally and until about 1945, the people attracted to this movement were residents of major urban centers: New York, Chicago, Philadelphia, St. Louis. Felix *Adler (1851–1933), the leading figure of the first half century of the movement, was deeply influenced in his idealism by both the American transcendentalist Ralph Waldo Emerson and the German transcendentalist Immanuel Kant. Adler's personal variation of Kant's ethic was developed into a "religion of duty," purportedly neutral on theological and metaphysical questions.

Among the comparatively small number of followers of Adler (never more than about 5,000), Jews of German background were prominent in New York City; outside of New York, Germans of Christian background outnumbered the Jews. Again, as the social service activities of the New York group entered the Lower East Side, some of the young Jews of Eastern European backgrounds joined the movement; nothing comparable occurred in other urban centers. Thus it is possible to describe the New York Society for Ethical Culture as largely an offshoot of German Reform Judaism, while describing the other Ethical Culture societies as largely offshoots of liberal German Protestantism.

The later philosophical orientation of the Ethical Culture movement was influenced by American humanistic and naturalistic ideas, and its audience became increasingly a Jewish and non-Jewish suburban public. The suburban societies have also served as compromise religious "homes" for couples of mixed background.

In keeping with the movement's mandate to affirm the importance of working to make people's lives and the world at large more humane, the American Ethical Union takes positions on specific issues at delegated national assemblies and meetings, striving to apply its ideals to current concerns. Local Ethical Societies engage in a wide range of service, humanitarian, and social change projects. An affiliate of the AEU, the National Service Conference, works with other non-governmental organizations at the United Nations and within the AEU on ethical peace-building and other programs. The Washington Ethical Action Office works toward achieving its selected goals by activities such as lobbying and disseminating information through the Washington Ethical Action Report.

Since 1990, some of the resolutions passed by the American Ethical Union include opposing capital punishment, seeking a peaceful solution to the Middle East conflict by ensuring a Palestinian state and a secure Israel, supporting the legalization of gay marriages, and advocating free choice regarding abortion.

On the international front, the International Humanist and Ethical Union has special consultative status with the UN, general consultative status at UNICEF and the Council of Europe, and maintains operational relations with UNESCO.

Succeeding Adler, David Algernon *Black led the movement into the 1980s.

BIBLIOGRAPHY: American Ethical Union, *Ethical Religion* (1940); D.S. Muzzey, *Ethical Religion* (1943); idem, *Ethical Imperatives* (1946); H. Neumann, *Spokesman for Ethical Religion* (1951); H. Radest, *Toward Common Ground: The Story of the Ethical Societies in the United States* (1969). **ADD. BIBLIOGRAPHY:** C. Neuhaus, *A Lively Connection: Intimate Encounters with the Ethical Movement in America* (1978); H. Friess, *Felix Adler & Ethical Culture: Memories & Studies* (1981); E. Ericson (ed.), *The Humanist Way: An Introduction to Ethical Humanist Religion* (1988); H. Radest, *Can We Teach Ethics?* (1989); H. Radest, *Felix Adler: An Ethical Culture* (1998).

[Joseph L. Blau / Ruth Beloff (2nd ed.)]

ETHICAL LITERATURE (Heb. סִפְרוּת הַמּוּסָר, *sifrut ha-musar*). There is no specific ethical literature as such in the biblical and talmudic period insofar as a systematic formulation of Jewish *ethics is concerned. Even the Wisdom *literature of the Bible, though entirely ethical in content, does not aim at giving a systematic exposition of this science of morals and human duties, but confines itself to apothegms and unconnected moral sayings. The same is true of the tractate **Avot*, the only wholly ethical tractate of the Mishnah, which consists largely of the favorite ethical maxims of individual rabbis, and later works, such as **Derekh Ereẓ* and **Kallah*. The ethical principles and concepts of Judaism are scattered throughout the vast area of rabbinic literature and it was only in the Middle Ages that this data was used as the basis of ethical works and from this time ethical literature becomes a specific genre of Jewish literature.

The term "ethical literature," applied to a type of Hebrew literature, has two different meanings. Both refer to an important part of Hebrew literature in medieval and early modern times, but while one denotes a literary form which encompasses a group of works closely resembling each other structurally, the other denotes a literary purpose expressed in various literary forms. Traditional authors generally use the term in the first sense, while the latter sense is preferred by modern scholars.

Literary Form

"CLASSICAL" ETHICAL LITERATURE. These writings are in book form and aim at instructing the Jew in religious and moral behavior. Structurally, the books are uniform: each is divided according to the component parts of the ideal righteous way of life; the material is treated methodically – analyzing, explaining, and demonstrating how to achieve each moral virtue (usually treated in a separate chapter or section) in the author's ethical system.

The first major work in "classical" ethical literature, *Ḥovot ha-Levavot*, by Baḥya b. Joseph ibn *Paquda (written in the 11th century), postulates ten religious and moral virtues, each forming the subject of a separate chapter. In *Ma'alot ha-Middot*, Jehiel b. Jekuthiel *Anav of Rome expounds 24 ethical principles of perfect moral conduct (positive and negative – the latter to be avoided). Baḥya b. Asher, one of the most prominent kabbalists in Spain, lists and analyzes the components of moral perfection in alphabetical order in *Kad ha-Kemah*, while Moses Ḥayyim *Luzzatto's major ethical work *Mesillat Yesharim*, constructed in the tradition of the *baraita* of R. *Phinehas b. Jair, enumerates the main steps to perfection and holiness. Writings falling into this structural category form the main body of the traditional ethical literature.

ETHICAL MONOGRAPHS. Closely following the formalistic pattern of "classical" ethical literature, ethical monographs concentrate on one particular stage in the journey to religious perfection. The first major work of this kind was the *Sha'arei Teshuvah* by *Jonah b. Abraham Gerondi. In this work the author analyzes every situation and problem that might possibly confront a repentant sinner and advises him how to purge himself completely of the effects of sin. Jonah Gerondi paved the way for what was to become one of the major literary forms in medieval Hebrew literature.

Literary Purpose

The second meaning of the term ethical literature includes, besides the two categories mentioned (the classical ethical writing and the ethical monograph), nine literary forms, which, though structurally very different, have the same objective – to posit ethical and religious principles. The search for moral and spiritual perfection is the purpose of ethical literature just as practical observance of *mitzvot* is the purpose of halakhic literature.

HOMILETIC LITERATURE. Hebrew medieval *homiletic literature is didactic and, in this sense, does not differ from "classical" ethical writings. The difference between the two is in their methods. Homiletic literature forms the bulk of ethical literature and for centuries influenced Jewish life more than any of the other ethical literary writings. Except for halakhic literature, no other type of Hebrew literature has achieved such a variety in content and form, has inspired authors over such a long period, and has reached such wide audiences.

ETHICAL WILLS. Developed in Germany, France, and Spain from the 11th to the 13th centuries, writers have used this literary form until modern times. *Ethical "wills" usually refer to short, concise works in which the main principles of moral behavior are expounded and which are written in the form of a father's last words to his children. Frequently, the "will" is nothing but a literary cliché, and quite often was applied to short ethical works not really intended as "wills." Many of the works in this category are pseudepigraphic and are later compilations attributed to early scholars.

ETHICAL LETTERS. This form includes actual letters in which the writer instructs either his son or another person, who was far away, to live a moral life; and short ethical treatises, called "a letter" ("*iggeret*"), which is also the conventional name applied to any short work. *Naḥmanides' letters to his sons belong to the first category, whereas the work "*Iggeret ha-Musar*" by R. Shem Tov *Falaquera is typical of the second.

MORALISTIC STORYBOOKS. One of the earliest literary forms used by writers of ethical literature, the first moralistic storybook, **Midrash Aseret ha-Dibberot*, a collection of moralistic tales in the form of exempla and short homilies, was probably written in the geonic period. Structurally, the work is a series of stories which exemplify the way to achieve complete devotion to each one of the Ten Commandments. *Nissim b. Jacob b. Nissim ibn Shahin's *Sefer ha-Ma'asiyyot* ("Book of Tales"), better known as *Ḥibbur Yafeh me-ha-Yeshu'ah*, is also an early work (11th century) expressed in this form. Originally written in Arabic, it was translated into Hebrew and as such influenced later Jewish writers. After the 15th century, moralistic-storybook writing became more common in Yiddish literature than in Hebrew.

HANHAGOT LITERATURE. Unlike the genres described above, which usually strive to teach the most basic and essential principles of ethical behavior, *hanhagot* literature concentrates on small practical details and not on general spiritual fundaments. The objective – to instruct the individual in the minutest details of daily behavior – makes use both of halakhic laws and of ethical principles. *Hanhagot* literature began to develop in the 13th-century *Sefer ha-Yirah* by R. Jonah Gerondi, and later *Ẓeidah la-Derekh by* *Menahem b. Aaron ibn Zeraḥ, but it was still popular, mainly in Eastern Europe, in the 17th and 18th centuries.

EULOGIES. This type of ethical literature belongs to homiletics because eulogies – written obituaries at least – were considered homilies. Eulogies are usually didactic with the virtues of the mourned dead serving as emulative qualities. Hundreds were printed, either as separate booklets or forming parts of a more general homiletic work.

COLLECTIONS OF ETHICAL FABLES AND EPIGRAMS. The first collections were influenced by Arabic works; sometimes these compilations were translations from the Arabic (e.g., *Musrei ha-Pilosofim*, attributed to Isḥaq ibn Hunayn or **Mivhar ha-Peninim*, attributed to R. Solomon b. Judah ibn *Gabirol, or **Kalila and Dimna*).

ETHICAL POETRY. Ethical treatises were sometimes written in verse. Structurally, many of them follow biblical examples, especially the Proverbs, and list the commandments in poetical form. One of the earliest works in this literary form, *Shirei Musar Haskel* (1505), was attributed to *Hai Gaon. Some of the *maqāma* literature should also be included (*Beḥinat Olam* by *Jedaiah ha-Penini, and *Iggeret ha-Musar* and *Sefer Mevakkesh* by Falaquera).

INTERPRETATIONS OF THE BOOK OF PROVERBS AND OF THE TRACTATE AVOT. The Book of Proverbs and *Avot*, mainly concerned with ethics, formed the basis of many medieval ethical writings. The interpretation served as a vehicle for the author's own concepts of Jewish ethics. Popular in medieval literature, these commentaries were usually regarded as independent works of ethics, and not part of the literature of exegesis and interpretation.

The objective of all these literary forms is to give workable and practical answers to the moral problems of the times. Their answers however were derived from theological considerations which lie outside the scope of ethical literature. Conceptually, ethical literature is not original in any of the disciplines it draws upon: theology, anthropology, philosophy, or psychology. The new concepts which originated in theological and theosophical literature were adapted to everyday religious life by ethical literature. It expressed them in different literary forms to make them acceptable to the public at large and it is thus, in form rather than in content, that ethical literature was original. Forms of expression usually do not interest theological innovators who mainly address themselves to the intellectual elite of the community, but a writer of an ethical work cannot disregard them. Since his main objective is to influence the life and religious behavior of the community as a whole, the ethical writer cannot afford to address only a segment of the public; consequently structural considerations play an important role.

Two unrelated processes have thus shaped the history of ethical literature: (a) the development of the literary forms as such; (b) the general development of Jewish religious thought on which ethical literature drew for its content and which it popularized. The merger of these two processes is the reason why ethical literature tends to be more conservative, less radical and innovative, than the theological movements in which the concepts it used originated. This phenomenon is apparent at every stage of the history of ethical literature, excluding perhaps the first period in Spain (see below). Ethical literature, in adapting new ideas, couched them in traditional literary genres for which it drew on aggadic lore. All the ethical writers used the aggadic form. The fusion of the old and the new, in form and content, made ethical literature the catalytic agent that preserved the new ideas and introduced them into the bloodstream of Judaism. Ethical literature modified the more radical implications of these concepts, and made them acceptable to the traditional community at large.

Since the ideas that ethical literature propounded originated with the ideological and theological movements in medieval Judaism, its history also reflects the development of these movements. Consequently there are four types of Hebrew medieval ethical literature: philosophical, rabbinic, Ashkenazi-ḥasidic (see *Hasidei Ashkenaz), and kabbalistic; the last greatly influenced modern ḥasidic ethical literature. These testify to four distinct ideological movements. The development of each of these types will be briefly studied.

Philosophical-Ethical Literature

The beginnings of Jewish ethical literature in the Middle Ages are rooted in the development of Jewish philosophy of that period. The last chapter of *Emunot ve-De'ot* by Saadiah Gaon (ninth century), which is on human behavior, may be regarded as the first Jewish medieval work in ethics. Distinct from the body of the book, both because of its form and because of its contents, it seems to be a separate work on ethics. The philosophical basis of Saadiah's ethical concepts did not develop out of earlier Jewish thought, and this might be the reason why this part of his work did not have a lasting influence on later Jewish ethical writings. *Tikkun Middot ha-Nefesh* (11th century) by Solomon ibn Gabirol suffered a similar fate, probably because the ethical system developed in the work was also alien to Jewish thought and did not fit into the accepted morals and ethics of the talmudic *aggadah*. Ibn Gabirol tried to show that the fusion of the four essential elements in medieval thought and the five senses formed the bases of all human characteristics.

Both works are written in Arabic, and both were translated (early 12th century) into Hebrew by R. Judah ibn Tibbon. They are an attempt at introducing a "pure ethic" into Jewish philosophy – a direct application of alien philosophical ideas to the field of Jewish ethics, without either blending them with, or using, the wealth of random ethical material already existing in Jewish tradition. In *Sefer ha-Ma'asiyyot*, a book of ethics which appeared at about the same time (11th century), also written in Arabic, but which was early translated into Hebrew, the author, R. Nissim b. Jacob b. Nissim ibn Shahin, used the opposite approach to that of Saadiah Gaon's and Ibn Gabirol's. He collected ethical stories and sayings from the Talmud to which he added medieval tales and concepts scarcely using philosophical ideas and applying no ethical system. It came to be widely used and accepted in its Hebrew version by all later writers of the ethical tale.

These works were precursory to the body of Jewish philosophical writings and it was *Ḥovot ha-Levavot* of Baḥya ibn Paquda, one of the most penetrating works in medieval literature, which gave impetus to this literature. The first medieval Jewish work to evolve an ethical system rooted in Jewish thought, it tried to come to grips with the fundamental spiritual problems that troubled the medieval Jewish mind. While the influence of contemporary medieval philosophy can easily be detected, especially in the first section which is a philosophical treatise on the unity of God, Baḥya ibn Paquda also culled from such sources as biblical and rabbinic literatures, and Arabic proverbs, tales, and epigrams to create what is primarily an ethical guide. The most influential single Jewish work in ethics in a period of over 600 years, its impact may be partly attributed to the author's profound and fundamental treatment of what was probably the most challenging question to Judaism at the time – the inner quality of religious life.

All major medieval ethical works came to grapple with this basic and crucial problem which essentially grew out of an age that had adopted the Platonic concept of matter and spirit being antagonistic elements and consequently creating a rift within man. The ethical and spiritual teachings in the Talmud had come to be relegated to a secondary position and Judaism thus came to be seen as a materialistic religion, based on practical deeds and actions, and not on spiritual attitudes which, to the medieval scholars, seemed the essence of religious life. Jewish moralists were therefore confronted with the problem of reconciling the contemporary Jewish concept of religious life which was practically orientated and consequently seen as inferior, with the new ideas which saw religion almost exclusively in a spiritual light. While this question was also considered from a purely philosophical point of view, and thus formed the basis of many medieval philosophical writings, it most needed to be answered in the sphere of morals and ethics to which the community at large turned for guidance.

The conflict was resolved in ethical literature through a reinterpretation of the ancient Jewish heritage in which its spiritual values were stressed in the light of the moral and ethical concepts of the age. Nowhere was the problem more sharply and clearly stated than in the introduction to *Ḥovot ha-Levavot*. Baḥya ibn Paquda's ethical system, except for minor changes and variations, was generally accepted by philosophical-ethical literature. He stressed: (a) the idea of *kavvanah* – any ritual act as such does not represent spiritual fulfillment, unless it is performed with the right *kavvanah* (awareness and intention); the deed becomes a means in the fulfillment of a religious duty. Religious value thus also came to be attached to the spiritual attitude of the doer, and not to the deed alone; (b) a whole system of purely spiritual commandments – the *ḥovot ha-levavot*, which gave the title to the work. Spiritual commandments, according to Baḥya ibn Paquda, are those that are completely detached from any physical act, and they, therefore, do not include the traditionally "spiritual" religious acts of prayer and study, because the mouth or the eyes (physical organs) are required in their performance. These commandments he set out as: reaffirmation of God's unity, recognition of His workings in the world, divine worship, trust in God, sincerity of purpose, humanity, repentance, self-examination, asceticism, and the love of God.

With variations in emphasis, this double or triple system of commandments (practical commandments, *kavvanah*, and *ḥovot ha-levavot*) is found in other philosophical-ethical writings: *Hegyon ha-Nefesh* by *Abraham b. Ḥiyya ha-Nasi of Barcelona, in which the spiritual meaning of repentance is described; *Yesod Mora* in which Abraham *Ibn Ezra gave a spiritual foundation to the commandments; and especially in the works of *Maimonides. The latter, sometimes orientated toward "purely philosophical ethics" as in *Shemonah Perakim*, are also invested with philosophical and spiritual-moral commandments which complement the practical laws, as in *Sefer ha-Madda* of the *Mishneh Torah*. These works ushered in a new period in ethical literature: writings were now in Hebrew and the need to establish a link between the new philosophical-ethical ideas, directed toward the spiritualization and immanence of religious life, and the older more traditional Jewish concepts, became more pronounced. For the Jewish philosophers it had been easier to express "pure philosophy" in Arabic rather than in Hebrew. Henceforth however, even philosophers based their ethical works on biblical passages and talmudic sayings, and thus integrated more closely the ancient Jewish ethical teachings with the new philosophical-ethical ideas.

The relationship between moral perfection and maximum religious fulfillment was one of the main problems that confronted Hebrew philosophers. Maximum fulfillment was usually understood as philosophical contemplation, which had nothing to do with social life and ethical behavior. Was ethics, therefore, to be considered only as a means toward attaining this religious fulfillment, or was ethics an end in itself? Maimonides' writings contain both contradictory concepts; in most places Maimonides subordinates ethics to philosophy but there are places where he sees ethical behavior as the best possible approach to God which man can achieve. Most of the followers of Maimonides tended to see ethics as a means and not as a religious end, e.g., Shem Tov Falaquera's *Sefer ha-Ma'alot*. This approach to ethics possibly contributed to the fact that philosophical-ethical literature after the 13th century ceased to be a vehicle of expression of the ethician.

The search for the inner religious quality of life had found expression in ethical literature before Maimonides, but especially after him philosophers tried to give rational and spiritual reasons for the practical commandments. The commandments were thus considered only seemingly materialistic, and their true essence was seen as spiritual. During the 13th century Jewish thought used allegorization as a means to reveal the hidden spiritual meaning of the commandments and the Torah, thus breaking with the Maimonidean rationale. *Malmad ha-Talmidim*, by Jacob b. Abba Mari b. Samson *Anatoli, and the polemic and exegetic writings of Zerahiah b. Isaac b. Sheal-tiel *Gracian (Ḥen) demonstrate this trend. This development within philosophical-ethical literature was later blamed for the conversion of so many Jews during the Spanish persecutions of the late 14th and the 15th centuries: the contention of these Jews had been that if the true meaning of the commandments was a hidden spiritual one, why sacrifice one's life in order to preserve the outer meaningless, material shell?

Rabbinic-Ethical Literature

The rise of rabbinic-ethical literature, especially in 13th-century Spain, Provence, and Italy, came as a reaction to such trends and was a revolt against Jewish philosophy influenced by Aristotelian concepts. Rabbinic-ethical literature was receptive to organized ethical thought; its aim, however, was to show that a moral system was already existent in the *aggadah* and in the Talmud. Jonah Gerondi, one of the first Hebrew ethicians, dedicated his major ethical work *Sha'arei Teshuvah* ("The Gates of Repentance") to the problem of repentance, much as Abraham b. Hiyya had done a hundred years earlier. According to him, a systematic arrangement of the old talmudic sayings together with a suitable exegetical commentary would present a complete and satisfactory system. Jonah and the other writers of this literature tried especially to emphasize the spiritual dicta found in older Jewish tradition, thus minimizing and possibly reconciling the antithesis between medieval beliefs and this older tradition.

It is significant that many of the writers of rabbinic-ethical literature were kabbalists, though they did not reveal their mystic ideas in their popular ethical works. Naḥmanides' ethical treatise, *Sha'ar ha-Gemul*, discusses the various categories of the just and the wicked and their retribution in the world to come. Baḥya b. Asher wrote a very popular rabbinic-ethical work, *Kad ha-Kemaḥ*, in which, following the rabbinic-spiritualistic method, he enumerates alphabetically and studies different ethical problems. These and other ethicians (some modern scholars even maintain that Jonah Gerondi had been a kabbalist) presented the public with a rabbinic-ethical system, while in their closed mystical circles they resolved the antithesis between the spirituality of religion and the material aspect of the Torah through mystic speculation.

There were, however, some rabbinic-ethical writers who merely tried to compile and systematize the different talmudic-ethical writings. Thus, most of *Ma'alot ha-Middot* by Jehiel b. Jekuthiel Anav is a collection of talmudic and midrashic sayings arranged according to theme and content. The objective of later works, e.g., the two versions of *Menorat ha-Ma'or*, one by Israel *Al-Nakawa b. Joseph of Toledo, the other by Isaac *Aboab, was similar. Rabbinic-ethical literature, therefore, did not try to innovate, but to apply traditional Jewish ethics to the medieval world. In the process, it even revived some of the old forms of aggadic literature which came to serve as vehicles of expression.

Ashkenazi-Ḥasidic Literature

The creative verve of the Ḥasidei Ashkenaz movement in Germany expressed itself in a body of ethical writings (see *Sefer* **Ḥasidim* (first published 1538, Bologna), *Judah b. Samuel he-Ḥasid of Regensburg, *Samuel b. Kalonymus he-Ḥasid of Speyer, and *Eleazar b. Judah b. Kalonymus of Worms) that deviate in character from the philosophical-ethical literature and rabbinic-ethical literature of the time. (The former, however, had already reached its zenith when Ashkenazi ḥasidic literature started to develop, while the latter began at the same time.) While *Sefer Ḥasidim*, a work of major scope, epitomizes Ashkenazi-ḥasidic literature, writings of lesser range and reputation are equally representative, e.g., the introductory chapters to the halakhic work *Sefer ha-Roke'aḥ* by *Eleazar of Worms and the ethical works *Sefer ha-Gan* (1899) by Isaac b. Eliezer and *Sefer Ḥasidim Katan* (1866) by Moses b. Eleazar ha-Kohen (14th and 15th centuries) are almost exclusively based on Ashkenazi-ḥasidic moral teachings. The problems which faced the Ashkenazi ethician, essentially the same as those that confronted the Hebrew thinkers of Spain, Italy, and Provence, were approached differently and were expressed neither in the variety of forms nor given the systematic treatment of the philosophical-ethical and rabbinic-ethical literatures of the south. The teachings of Greco-Arabic philosophy had not reached and therefore had not influenced the Jewish communities in Germany and in northern France. Thus while medieval European thinkers were essentially confronted by the same challenge, their response grew out of their immediate cultural environment.

Ashkenazi-ḥasidic literature is basically less abstract (less consideration is given to principles and fundamentals and more attention is paid to actual situations and concrete problems) than the literatures of the south. Structurally, the two types of literary writings also differ widely. *Sefer Ḥasidim* is not patterned on the methodical division of *Ḥovot ha-Levavot.* It is comprised of 2,000 short random passages in which every situation and every phase of moral and religious life is discussed. Thus Ashkenazi-ethical thinking was much more concerned with the specific problems to which local historical conditions gave rise than were their southern counterparts.

The approach of the Ḥasidei Ashkenaz to the concept of the spiritual essence of religious and moral behavior and their interpretation of the practical commandments of the old teachings became the classical solution to all such questions in rabbinic literature. They contended that all commandments and ethical demands made upon man by God are a test in order to examine man's devotion to his creator. The religious value of certain deeds therefore does not lie in the actual performance but in the spiritual and religious effort that constitutes the action, e.g., a rich man who paid the ransom for a captured Jew and released him does not attain the spiritual height of the poor man who, with much effort, collected the ransom from many people, but upon paying the money found that the Jew had already been released. It is not the deed alone that counts, but the effort and devotion which God expects of man in following His will. Thus the reasons for (and even the meaning of) the commandments become negligible and even irrelevant: God in His infinite wisdom chose certain deeds by which to try man; they could be any deeds. What is important is that God's will was revealed through certain commandments and through certain ethical standards; it is not for man to ask why.

Ashkenazi Ḥasidim thus arrived at a certain scale of religious and ethical values and of commandments which ranged from the most difficult and trying precepts to acts which everybody could easily perform; the latter were therefore considered secondary. The religious value in the study of the talmudic tractate *Mo'ed Katan*, which deals with death and mourning, is higher than that of the study of other tractates. The more a commandment contradicts average human desires and instincts, the more religious value is attached to it. Thus, the greatest sacrifice that man can possibly make – to die for **kiddush ha-Shem* (be martyred in the sanctification of God's name) – is man's supreme religious fulfillment. This view, prevalent during the times of the *Crusades, was able to take root in an age when thousands of Jews in Germany and northern France died for *kiddush ha-Shem.*

The Ashkenazi-ḥasidic movement thus gave new relevance and new spiritual meaning even to the simplest and most practical of the religious and moral commandments. A more radical principle which also directly affected a whole pattern of behavior was the distinction made between *din Torah* (the "earthly law") and *din shamayim* (the "heavenly law"). Strict observance of the Torah precepts does not necessarily lead to the highest religious fulfillment; for this a higher moral law – *din shamayim*, the law of conscience – is necessary. According to the Torah, a thief is a thief; but according to *din shamayim* a clear distinction must be made between a man who steals bread out of hunger and a rich man who steals in order to further enrich himself. This does not mean that the laws of the Torah should be abandoned; a pious man however should try to transcend them and follow a higher spiritual and moral law.

During the 12th and 13th centuries, when Ashkenazi-ḥasidic theology and ethics flourished, Jewish life and thought of southern and northern Europe were clearly distinct: they were almost two separate cultures. The 13th century saw the slow bridging of the gulf – Ashkenazi ideas spread to southern Europe where they influenced rabbinic-ethical writers, and after the expulsion from Spain in 1492, Ashkenazi-ḥasidic ethics were a bulwark on which Judaism drew, to reorientate itself ideologically after the great tragedy.

Creativity in philosophical-ethical thought came to an end with the expulsion from Spain, mainly because philosophy was seen as a contributory factor to the conversion of hundreds of thousands of Spanish Jews. Writers like Joseph b. Ḥayyim *Jabez and Isaac Abrabanel clearly denounced current Jewish philosophical thinking. It was a time when Judaism seemed to have fallen into a theological void – the old beliefs were shattered by the tragedy, and for a time nothing, at least nothing systematic and of embracing scope, seemed to replace philosophical thinking. A new theological outlook, the *Kabbalah, which came to form the largest body of ethical writings in Jewish literature, finally gave literary expression to Jewish life and its aspirations in the aftermath of the expulsion. Ashkenazi-ḥasidic ethical thought had been only a temporary moral and spiritual support to the Jews of southern Europe and it was integrated into the *Kabbalah which began to develop during the 16th century.

Kabbalistic-Ethical Literature

The early European kabbalists usually tended to confine themselves to their closed circles and did not want to turn the Kabbalah into a popular literature. The center of kabbalistic learning established in Safed during the 16th century, however, created a body of moral writings which were directed toward the Jewish community at large and which started the 300-year period of kabbalistic-ethical literature.

This literature drew on earlier kabbalistic works, especially the *Zohar, as well as on Ashkenazi-ḥasidic ethics and rabbinic-ethical thought. Using the Kabbalah and its mystical system as a basis, kabbalistic-ethical teachings were formulated along the same strong systematic lines. Central to kabbalistic-ethical literature are two closely related concepts: (1) an ethical dogma in which the commandments are conceived symbolically; (2) the idea that the temporal world reflects the eternal world and vice versa and that there is an interdependence between the performance of deeds on this earth and processes in the divine mystical world. The symbolic approach to the commandments demanded of man to adhere to them with all his might because they reflect divine mystical actions. Through the idea of reflective worlds, man's deeds formed part of the divine drama, and enabled man by means of his action to influence the mystical powers. Moses b. Jacob *Cordovero's *Tomer Devorah*, one of the first kabbalistic ethical works of this period, is a detailed guide to moral behavior and how such conduct could and should reflect divine essences and satisfy divine requirements. His pupil and follower, *Elijah b. Moses de Vidas, the author of *Reshit Ḥokhmah*, developed the idea that man's moral deeds are reflected in the heavenly struggle between good and evil. The *Kabbalah of Isaac *Luria, which developed in the last part of the 16th century, strengthened this concept by stressing even more man's responsibility in the war raging in the mystical spheres.

The kabbalistic-ethical literature, which, from the 17th century onward continued to develop in Eastern Europe, was based almost exclusively on Lurianic teachings. It emphasized more strongly the power of Satan and the consequences that sin has in the divine world. Works like Ẓevi Hirsch *Koidonover's *Kav ha-Yashar*, which was very popular, used kabbalistic-Lurianic teachings to warn the reader against the havoc which sin might wreak on the sinner as such, and on the world as a whole.

Kabbalistic theosophy firmly rooted this literature in systematic mystical reasoning and gave it a theological structure. The actual teachings, the positive and negative precepts, did not, however (with a few exceptions, like the custom of *tikkun*, see *Kabbalah), originate with the kabbalist but were culled from older ethical literature: rabbinic and Ashkenazi-ḥasidic.

The Shabbatean movement, which deeply influenced all of Judaism in the second half of the 17th century, did not use ethical literature as a vehicle of expression (see *Shabbetai Zevi). Despite the ethical work *Tikkunei Teshuvah* (published by I. Tishby) by *Nathan of Gaza, most of the Shabbatean literature was theosophical in nature. Some of the Shabbateans who wrote popular ethical works tended to conceal their theological views and only occasional allusions can be found.

During the 18th century two converging trends in Jewish thought – kabbalism and messianism – gave rise to the kabbalistic-ethical works of Moses Ḥayyim *Luzzatto: *Mesillat Yesharim*, *Da'at Tevunot*, and *Derekh ha-Shem*. The controversy that raged around Luzzatto, one of the major ethicians in Jewish literature, forced him to conceal the kabbalistic elements in his works through the use of pseudo-philosophical language and terms. His works, which became popular toward the end of the century, are read to this day.

Ḥasidic literature of the late 18th century and throughout the 19th century is almost exclusively ethical. Most of it is comprised of homilies in which moral behavior is strongly stressed; some of the writings, however, are purely ethical in nature, e.g., *Sefer ha-Middot* by R. *Naḥman of Bratslav or *Tanya* by R. *Shneur Zalman of Lyady. The collections of ḥasidic stories and fables are usually didactic and have an ethical theme. The *Mitnaggedim*, opponents of Ḥasidism, also based their teachings on Lurianic ethical literature. From their ranks sprang the *Musar movement which tried to introduce the study of major ethical works into the yeshivot and for whom moral behavior became the greatest religious fulfillment man could aspire to. Haskalah literature at the end of the 18th and the beginning of the 19th centuries also used the traditions of ethical literature in its didactic endeavors.

Hebrew ethical literature, a diversified corpus of writings, is characterized by an underlying unity which cuts across not only the divergent ideological movements out of which the literature grew and which it represents, but also subsumes the various vehicles of expression used by ethicians. Hebrew ethical writers were primarily concerned with a number of elemental universal problems. The solutions they presented, while reflecting the various ideologies, are basically a response to the most crucial point at hand – man and the human condition, his position in the cosmos, and his attitude to the ways of God. They thus transcended the specific dogma to which they adhered and considered the dilemma of man in its universal aspects. Fundamental to this literature are such questions as: the ill fate suffered by the just and the success enjoyed by the wicked in this life; the ways of divine judgment; God's knowledge and active management of the temporal world;

why the wicked were created; freedom of choice in ethical and religious matters and the boundaries of that freedom; the meaning of sin and in what relation does the repentant sinner stand to the just who has never sinned; the relation between fear of God motivated by the thought of retributive justice and fear of God aroused by God's greatness; the relationship between the worship of God through fear and the worship of God through love; the meaning of *devekut* (communion with God) and the ways to achieve it; the essence of *kavvanah* and its place in ethical life; the right attitude to Gentiles; the fate of the just and the wicked after death; the essence of the soul; existence after the resurrection; social behavior in and toward the family; and similar questions which transcend time and space to create one unifying body of literary writings. Some of the answers are dictated by the special character and inclinations of the writer more so than by the movement to which he belonged.

Unlike the philosopher and theologian, the ethician is faced with concrete situations, actual people; his responses are therefore more pragmatic and less dogmatic – he tackles the questions practically and in human terms. Ethical literature thus, through the uniqueness of this aspect of its character – the specific moral confrontation with man's universal dilemma – has carved out for itself an independent place in Hebrew literature and it is not merely another branch of theological literature.

Form as much as content was a unifying factor in the corpus of ethical writings that classified it into a literature. Ethicians were obliged to use different literary means in order that their works might be accepted by a wide and sometimes uneducated public. This unavoidable emphasis on form, and not only on content, placed ethical literature into a separate category and set it apart from the other branches of religious thinking. The constant use of fables, stories, epigrams, jokes, and hagiography as vehicles of expression created a distinct literature which was read not only for didactic purposes but also to be enjoyed. The literary and didactic role played by literature during the Middle Ages is comparable to that of fiction in modern times.

BIBLIOGRAPHY: S.D. Breslauer, *Contemporary Jewish Ethics: A Bibliographical Survey* (1985); S.D. Breslauer, *Modern Jewish Morality: A Bibliographical Survey* (1986); I. Bettan, *Studies in Jewish Preaching* (1939); Werblowsky, in: *Annual of Jewish Studies*, 1 (1964), 95–139; L. Roth (ed.), *Likkut ha-De'ot ve-ha-Middot…* (1946²); I. Heinemann, *Ta'amei ha-Mitzvot be-Sifrut Yisrael*, 1 (1959); idem, in HUCA, 23 pt. 1 (1950/51), 611–43; I. Tishby, *Mishnat ha-Zohar*, 2 (1961), 247–362, 581–606, 655–761; idem, *Mivḥar Sifrut ha-Musar* (in press); G. Scholem, *On Kabbalah and its Symbolism* (1965), passim; idem, *Von der mystischen Gestalt der Gottheit* (1962), passim; G. Vajda, *La Théologie ascétique de Baḥya Ibn Paquda* (1947); idem, *L'amour de Dieu dans la théologie juive du Moyen Age* (1957); Dan, in: Molad, 22 (1964), 82–84; S. Shalem, *Rabbi Moshe Alsheikh* (1966); I. Abrahams (ed.), *Hebrew Ethical Wills*, 2 vols. (1948), includes bibl.; Waxman, Literature, 1 (1960²), 355–71, 459–62; 2 (1960²), 271–300, 643–49; 3 (1960²), 640–704; 4 (1960²) sects. 121–7, and index.

[Joseph Dan]

ETHICS.

IN THE BIBLE

There is no abstract, comprehensive concept in the Bible which parallels the modern concept of "ethics." The term *musar* designates "ethics" in later Hebrew, but in the Bible it indicates merely the educational function fulfilled by the father (Prov. 1:8) and is close in meaning to "rebuke." In the Bible ethical demands are considered an essential part of the demands God places upon man. This close connection between the ethical and religious realms (although the two are not completely identified) is one of the principal characteristics of the Bible; hence, the central position of ethics throughout the Bible. Accordingly, the Bible had a decisive influence upon the molding of ethics in European culture in general, both directly and indirectly through the ethical teachings in apocryphal literature (see *Apocrypha and Pseudepigrapha) and the New Testament which are based on biblical ethics.

Social Ethics

The command to refrain from harming one's fellow man and to avoid doing evil to the weak is fundamental to biblical ethics. Most of the ethical commands specified in the Bible belong to this category: due justice (Ex. 23:1–2; Deut. 16:18–20); avoidance of bribery (e.g., Ex. 23:8), robbery, and oppression (Ex. 22:20; Deut. 24:14); defense of the *widow and the *orphan; compassionate behavior toward the *slave; and the prohibition of gossip. Added to these were the commands to sustain the poor (Deut. 15:7–11), feed the hungry, and clothe the naked (Isa. 58:7; Ezek. 18:7). The radical but logical conclusion derived from this is that man is obliged to suppress his desires and feed even his enemy (Prov. 25:21), return his enemy's lost property, and help him raise his ass which is prostrate under its burden (Ex. 23:4–5). Biblical ethics, which cautions man to love and respect his fellow man, reaches its highest level in the commandment: "You shall not hate your kinsman in your heart, reprove your neighbor," which concludes with "Love your neighbor as yourself. I am the Lord" (Lev. 19:17–18). The principle aim of this commandment, as of others, is the avoidance of unfounded hatred which destroys the life of the society.

The general trend of social ethics was summed up by the prophets who said: "Hate evil and love good and establish justice in the gate" (Amos 5:15); and similarly: "He has told you, O man, what is good; and what does the Lord require of you but to do justice and love kindness, and to walk humbly with your God" (Micah 6:8). These passages and their like not only summarize the teaching of ethics, but also place it at the center of the Israelite faith. A summation of biblical ethical teachings is contained in the well-known saying of Hillel: "What is hateful to you do not unto another" (Shab. 31a).

The Ethical Perfection of the Individual

Unlike the ethical system of Greek philosophy, which seeks to define the various virtues (who is courageous, generous, or just, etc.), the Bible demands of every human being that he perform the good deed, and behave virtuously toward his fellow man, and is not concerned with abstract definitions. This attitude is almost explicitly expressed in Jeremiah 9:22–23: "Let not the wise man glory in his wisdom, let not the strong man glory in his strength, let not the rich man glory in his riches. Only in this should one glory: in his earnest devotion to me. For I am the Lord who exercises kindness, justice, and equity in the world; for in these I delight – declares the Lord." From this it follows that doing what is right and just is the essence of biblical ethics. The personal ethical ideal is the *ẓaddik* (the good man; see *Righteousness). Ezekiel defines him in detail for the purpose of explaining the doctrine of reward and *punishment, and his definition is nothing but an enumeration of the deeds performed by the good man and of those from which he refrains (Ezek. 18:5–9). The essence of all of these acts is the proper relationship between man and man, except for one commandment, to shun idolatry, which is solely a duty of man to God. A similar definition of the good man appears in Isaiah 33:15 and in Psalm 15. Added to the ideal of the righteous man in Psalms is the Godfearing man who finds happiness in the teachings of God and in the worship of Him and who shuns the life devoid of ethical earnestness (e.g., Ps. 1). The personal ethical ideal received further expression in the character of *Abraham, who was credited with several especially fine and noble qualities. He was complaisant in his relationship with Lot, hospitable, compassionate toward the evil inhabitants of Sodom, humble and generous in his dealings with the people of Heth, and he refused to profit from the booty of the war with Amraphel.

Distinguishing Feature of Social Ethics in the Bible

The lofty level of biblical ethics which is evident in the command to love one's neighbor, in the character of Abraham, and in the first Psalm, is peculiar to the Bible, and it is difficult to find its like in any other source; however, the general ethical commandments in the Bible, which are based on the principle of refraining from harming others, are a matter of general human concern and constitute the fundamentals of ethics. Some characteristic features of biblical ethics, such as due justice and the rights of the widow and the orphan, are prevalent in the ancient Near East (see below). Therefore the generalization that the Bible is unique among religious works in the content of its ethical teachings cannot be made. However, the Bible does differ from every other religious or ethical work in the importance which it assigns to the simple and fundamental ethical demand. The other nations of the ancient Near East reveal their ethical sense in compositions that are marginal to their culture: in a few proverbs dispersed throughout the wisdom literature, in prologues to collections of laws, in various specific laws, and in confessions (see below). The connection between ethical teachings and primary cultural creations – the images of the gods, the cult, the major corpus of law – is weak. The ethical aspirations of these cultures are sometimes, but not always, expressed in their religion and social organization, while the Bible places the ethical demand at the focus of the religion and the national culture. The ethical demand is of primary concern to the prophets, who state explicitly that this is the essence of their religious teaching. Basic sections of biblical law – the Ten Commandments, Leviticus 19, the blessings and curses of Mount Gerizim and Mount Ebal (Deut. 27:15–26) – contain many important ethical commandments. Biblical law itself testifies to its ethical aim: "Or what great nation has laws and norms as just (*ẓaddikim*) as all this Teaching…" (Deut. 4:8). While the wisdom literature of Israel is similar to that of the neighboring cultures, it is distinctive in the greater stress it places upon ethical education (see below). The assumption that God is – or should be – just, and the question of reward and punishment which follows from that assumption, are the bases of the religious experiences found in Psalms, Job, and some prophetic passages. The opinion of Hillel the Elder that the ethical demand is the essence of the Torah may be questioned, for it can hardly be said to be the only pillar of the biblical faith. However, there is certainly a clear tendency in the Bible to place the ethical demand at the focus of the faith, even if it does share it with other concerns such as monotheism (see biblical view of *God).

Biblical ethics teachings, though clear and forceful, are not extraordinary in content, for the Bible requires nothing other than the proper behavior which is necessary for the existence of society. Biblical ethics does not demand, as do certain other systems of ethics (Christianity, Buddhism, and even some systems in later Judaism), that man withdraw completely or even partially from everyday life to attain perfection. Asceticism, which views the normal human situation as the root of evil, is foreign to the Bible and to the cultures of the Near East in general. The Bible approves of life as it is, and, accordingly, makes its ethical demand compatible with social reality. However, the degree of justice which it is possible to achieve within the bounds of reality is demanded with a clear forcefulness which allows for no compromise. This makes the Bible more radical than most ethical systems. The ethical teachings of the Bible, like the Bible generally, are addressed first and foremost to Israel. But some biblical passages extend the ethical demand to encompass all mankind, such as the *Noachide laws (Gen. 9:1–7), the story of Sodom (Gen. 19:20ff.), or the rebuke of Amos against the neighboring kingdoms for their cruelty (Amos 1:3–2:3). The setting of the Book of Job is also outside the Israelite realm.

Sexual Ethics

What has been said up to here applies only to social ethics, in view of the fact that in the realm of sexual morality the biblical outlook differs from that of neighboring cultures. The Bible abhors any sexual perversion such as *homosexuality or copulation with animals, prescribing severe punishments for offenders (Lev. 18:22–23; 20:13, 15–16). The adulteress sins not only against her husband, but also against God (e.g., Ex. 20:14; Lev. 20:10; Mal. 3:5). Fornication is generally frowned upon, severely condemned by *Hosea, and legally punishable by death in some cases (Lev. 21:9; Deut. 22:21). The other peoples of the ancient Near East did not treat these offenses with such severity. They regarded *adultery as essentially an infringement upon the rights of the husband – damage done to his property, like robbery or theft – and not as an abominable act sinful to God. Society was reconciled to prostitution, although a certain stigma was attached to it. Therefore Babylonian law, for example, defines the legal status of the various types of prostitution and treats it as it treats other phenomena in society (e.g., Code of Hammurapi, 145, 181, in: Pritchard, Texts, 172, 174; Middle Assyrian Laws, 40, in: *ibid.*, 183). There is little opposition to sexual perversions: homosexuality is numbered among the sins in the Egyptian "Book of the Dead" (see below); Hittite law punishes copulation only with certain animals, and even these not very severely (see below). This opposition, which is occasionally expressed, does not declare these acts to be an outright abomination. Fornication and more serious sexual offenses are ascribed to the gods in *mythology, and possibly played a role in the cult (see *Kedeshah*). Therefore, it is clear that the biblical stand on these matters is unique. The biblical sexual ethic was imposed by Christianity on most of the civilized world in theory if not in practice but in the ancient world it was unique to Israel.

Ethical Teaching in the Bible

MEANS OF INSTRUCTION. The orientation of biblical ethics is uniform in content, but is expressed in different ways, according to the viewpoint of the particular book of the Bible. The strongest and most radical expression of the goal of biblical ethics is found in the rebukes of the prophets, who chastise the people relentlessly for ethical transgressions and demand ethical perfection (especially in the realm of social ethics) without compromise. But their rebukes do not really constitute instruction, for they do not always teach one how to behave in particular situations.

Biblical law is concerned with providing ethical instruction in particular acts. The legal sections of the Torah explicitly and in detail forbid various offenses such as murder, robbery, and bribery, and explicitly demand support of the poor, love of one's neighbor, and the like (see below).

Both prophecy and law demand of man in the name of God that he behave properly. Their ethical outlook is a fundamental element in their demand that man do God's will, and therefore is not practical utilitarianism, even though they teach the doctrine of reward and punishment. This ethical attitude is given added depth in the Psalms, where it becomes a matter of religious feeling that throbs in the heart of the righteous man who seeks closeness with his God (see Ps. 1; 15, especially verses 2, 4, 24:4; 34:13–15). The Book of Job also stresses the commandment of righteousness to which the individual is subject, but from another aspect. Job is not content to protest that he did not commit transgressions of robbery, oppression, or bribery, but asserts that he actually observed positive ethical commandments and was strict with himself beyond the requirements of the law. For example, he claims he did much to support those in need of his help: "Because I delivered the poor who cried, and the fatherless who had none to help him. The blessing of the destitutes came upon me, and I gladdened the heart of the widow" (Job 29:12–13). Job 31 contains a series of oaths concerning his righteousness, all beginning with *ʾim*, "if," which is often equivalent to "I swear": "(I swear) I have not rejected the cause of my man servant …" (verse 13); "(I swear) I have not made gold my trust …" (verse 24). Job is careful to be above suspicion not only in social ethics, but also in sexual ethics, for he claims: "If I have been enticed by a woman, and have lain in wait at the door of another man, may my wife be used by another …" (31:9–10).

The ethical teachings in all the biblical books so far surveyed are considered an essential element of God's demands of man. In this respect, the attitude of *Proverbs is different. Most of the proverbs aim at proving to man that it is worthwhile for him to follow the good path from the consideration of simple worldly wisdom. For example, Proverbs does not declare that adultery is prohibited but points out the dangers in it (6:24–35). In a similar vein are the following verses: "Do not slander a servant to his master, lest he curse you, and you be made to feel your guilt" (Prov. 30:10), and "If your enemy is hungry, give him bread to eat … for you will heap coals of fire on his head, and the Lord will reward you" (25:21–22). Although there is also a reference to God here, man is placed at the center of ethical instruction. This approach is more practical and utilitarian than the approach of the Bible in general, due to the practical educational orientation of the Book of Proverbs. While Proverbs belongs to the category of general wisdom literature which was prevalent in the ancient Near East, it nevertheless differs from other works of this type in the prominence it gives to ethical instruction; in Proverbs it is of prime importance, while in the wisdom literature of the peoples of the ancient Near East, it is of secondary importance. There are two reasons for this: first, Proverbs aims at the education of the young citizen while the works of Ahikar and Egyptian didactic literature place more emphasis on the training of the official; second, Israelite wisdom literature identified the righteous man with the sage on the one hand, and the evil man with the fool on the other (e.g., Prov. 10:21, 23).

*Ecclesiastes, in those sections that deviate from stereotyped wisdom literature, casts doubt on the benefit of wisdom in general, and on the simple utilitarian ethical instruction contained in Proverbs. He knows that "there is not one good man on earth who does what is best (i.e., leads to the most desirable results, 6:12) and does not err" (7:20). In his despair he says: "don't overdo goodness …" (7:16–18).

ETHICAL INSTRUCTION IN THE BIBLICAL NARRATIVE. Narrative is the one literary form in the Bible which is not entirely infused with an ethical orientation. In biblical narratives ethical instruction is presented indirectly in the form of words of praise for noble deeds, and even this praise is, for the most part, not explicit. Deeds which are represented as noble include Joseph's fleeing from adultery (Gen. 39:7–18), the mercy shown by David in not killing Saul (I Sam. 24; 26:3–25), and the story of Rizpah, daughter of Aiah (II Sam. 21:10). Abraham is the only biblical character who can truly be described as an ethical model. The other heroes in biblical narrative (Judah, Joseph, Moses, Caleb, Joshua), although blessed with fine qualities, are not described as models of ethical perfection. The Bible portrays their shortcomings clearly (though implicitly; Isaac's weakness of character, Jacob's cunning, the sins of Saul and David) and does not make the slightest attempt to whitewash the ethical defects of its heroes. However, it is the rule in biblical narrative that appropriate punishment follows specific transgressions: Jacob, who bought the birthright by deception, is himself deceived by Laban; David is punished for his sin with Bath-Sheba, and so on. Yet these features are not especially emphasized and thus do not give biblical narrative a prominent ethical orientation. It has been said that biblical narrative takes no clear moral stance, but rather rejoices in the success of its heroes even when they act immorally (Jacob, when he bought the birthright; Rachel, when she stole the household idols; Jael, when she killed Sisera). It is true that the main intent of biblical narrative is to make known the greatness of God, whose acts are the only ones that are perfect. Thus the narrator can afford to see human beings as they are. He does not force himself to moralize overmuch, or to make his heroes model men, but introduces the ethical aspect only where it suits the story. Thus in the narrator's attitude to his heroes one observes a kind of tolerant, knowledgeable understanding of human nature: it is this which makes most biblical stories great, both as literature and as ethics.

LAW AND ETHICS. The Bible does not make a formal distinction between those commandments which could be classified as ethical, those which are concerned with ritual (circumcision, sacrifices, the prohibition against eating blood), and those which deal with common legal matters. Scholarship is obligated to differentiate between these categories and to see where the ethical aim appears. The ethical aim can be distinguished by recognizing the difference between the basic, general commandment "Thou shalt not murder" and the laws concerning the punishment of the murderer (e.g., Num. 35). Thus ethical commandments, in the strict sense, are laws without sanctions, to be obeyed but not enforced, e.g., the commandments of gleanings, the forgotten sheaf, and the corner of the field (Lev. 19:9–10, see **Leket, Shikhḥah, and Pe'ah*); the prohibition against harming the orphan and the widow (e.g., Ex. 22:21–23); the prohibition against delaying payment of wages (Lev. 19:13). Aside from the clearly ethical commandments, there is a general tendency in biblical law to emphasize the aspiration for justice which is the basis for every law. To be sure, every law is based upon the ethical viewpoint of the legislator and attempts, through the power of practical regulations, to enforce the ethics accepted by the existing society; however, biblical law aspires to this end clearly and consistently, as for example, "Justice, justice shall you pursue" (as the summary of practical regulations concerning the establishment of courts, Deut. 16:18–20), the laws of the Bible are defined explicitly as "just laws and statutes" (Deut. 4:8). Accordingly ethical and social reasons were attached to several laws, such as the commandment for the Sabbath: "So that your male and female slave may rest as you do. Remember that you were a slave …" (Deut. 5:14–15). This tendency is revealed in laws whose purpose was to defend the weak and to limit the power of the oppressor, such as the laws governing the Hebrew slave (Ex. 21:2; Deut. 15:12) or the relatively lenient punishment of the thief. Yet it must be remembered that law is based not only on the abstract viewpoint of the legislator, but also on the needs of the society according to its particular structure and customs. Therefore an evaluation of biblical law is incomplete if only the ethical aspect is considered; however, the discussion of the aim of law is not essential to the definition of biblical ethics.

ETHICAL INSTRUCTION AMONG THE PEOPLES OF THE ANCIENT NEAR EAST

Egypt

The Egyptian attitude toward ethics is expressed in literary works of different types. Among these works it is worth noting the books of proverbs (wisdom literature) which teach practical wisdom and proper behavior and include basic ethical principles such as not to covet, rob, or trespass, to be diligent in the performance of justice, and the like. Along with these principles, the books of proverbs include advice on practical knowledge which goes beyond the foundations of pure ethics; there is even the impression that the Egyptian sages advised their students to act justly because in this way they would succeed and achieve their goals, and not because justice is an ethical principle in its own right. According to Frankfort, however, this impression is the product of insufficient understanding of the Egyptian world view.

Another type of literature similar to wisdom literature in its ethical orientation and termed "ideal biography" by scholars is seen in the compositions which were engraved on the walls of tombstones and monuments to the dead. In them, the deceased tells what he did and how he conducted himself throughout his life, as for example: "I spoke the truth, I acted honestly … I judged both sides to the satisfaction of both. I rescued, with all my power, the weak from the strong. I gave bread to the hungry, and clothing to the poor, etc."

Another aspect of Egyptian ethics is revealed in the collection of writings called the "Book of the Dead." This is a collection of documents from various ancient sources, whose purpose is to assure the passage of the dead into eternal life. It contains statements which the deceased must make when he stands in judgment upon entering the world of the dead, such as: "I did not do evil to any man … I did not revile the name of the god, I did not slander the servant in front of his master … I did not murder, I did not cause a death … I did not sin by homosexuality, etc." (ch. 125). The deceased announces that he did not commit ethical offenses or transgressions of the cult, without distinguishing between the two. The list is arranged in a stereotyped manner, but it does contain certain ethical principles. On the other hand, the negative confession is close in purpose to a magical incantation, a kind of amulet which is helpful to every man after death even if he was not righteous during his life.

There is yet another basic concept in Egyptian culture which has, without doubt, ethical significance, namely, the concept of *maʿat* which means truth, justice, honesty, or proper order. It is said that the gods live in *maʿat*; the king who sets aright the order of the country and establishes just rules is setting *maʿat* upon its foundation; the way of an honest man – and especially the way of an official who must judge a just case – is *maʿat*; and also the order according to which nature behaves is *maʿat*.

It is difficult to discuss the meaning of the Egyptian doctrine of ethics, because the Egyptian world view in general is beyond reach; the reason being, in Bonnet's opinion, that the Egyptian ethics was not specifically related to the teachings and practices of the religion. Ethical qualities are not characteristic of the gods, and there are cases where Egyptian religion expresses a viewpoint which is not ethical. In Frankfort's opinion, one should not claim that the Egyptians did not have a highly developed ethical doctrine, but one should deal with what is particular to their outlook. The Egyptian saw his world as secure and orderly and nature as behaving always according to *maʿat*. The duty of man is to act according to the same secure and eternal law, to be congenial, not to be ambitious and bad-tempered, and to enjoy the good things in life without anxiety. The Egyptian does not know the fear of sin because his god does not demand that he observe positive and negative precepts. Instead, he helps those who generally behave according to *maʿat*, and corrects the sinner by means of punishment. According to Frankfort, the confession of the dead is not characteristic of the Egyptian ethical outlook; it originates in fear in the face of death, but does not directly affect the way of life.

Mesopotamia

The Sumerian legislator king Lipit-Ishtar announces in the prologue and epilogue of his law code that he acted lawfully and justly during his kingship and diligently guarded the freedom of the people of Sumer and Akkad, and insured that the father helped his sons and the sons their father. Hammurapi too, in the prologue to his law code, states that he ruled justly in his land, suppressed wickedness and evil, and prevented the strong from oppressing the weak; in his epilogue he commands that justice be done to the orphan and the widow so that the oppressed will find salvation in his just laws and will bless him before the gods. Thus, there was an ethical basis to law in Sumer and Akkad. Babylonian wisdom literature is not as abundant as that of Egypt, but the extant literature contains ethical instructions such as not to requite evil to one's enemy, not to gossip, and the like; there is also a warning not to marry a prostitute because she will not be faithful to her husband. In atonement rites, which were intended to save the sick and atone for injuries likely to be done to one's fellow man, the magico-cultic aspect is more important than the ethical aspect (see *Atonement). A type of ethical instruction is also included in the plentiful "omen" literature. Among the collections of omens of all types, which usually have no ethical content, are also omens which contain ethical teachings such as: "if one renders good, good will be rendered to him." The gods are, to a certain extent, considered to be the guardians of ethics and the dispensers of retribution to the evil. However, there is also a Babylonian document which expresses man's despair over the lack of justice in the rule of the gods. The author of this document clearly sees how society oppresses the just, the honest, and the poor and praises the wicked man who succeeds. Mesopotamian myth shows that the gods of Sumer and Akkad were not ethical. The religious Babylonian believed that man was created so that the gods could benefit from his labor, and was not certain that the rule of the gods was just and beneficent. The fear of sin was well-known to him, but the sin itself – if he sinned, how he sinned, when he sinned – was hidden from him.

Documents devoted to ethical instruction have not been preserved from the remaining civilizations of the ancient Near East, but there is some indirect information on this subject. For example, in *Ugarit it was the king's duty to pursue justice for the widow and to protect the weak (II Keret, 46:50; cf. also II Aqhat, V. 7–8). In Hittite law (188), punishment was decreed for copulation with some animals (Pritchard, Texts, 196), and in this legal collection, as well as several other Mesopotamian ones, there were laws concerning incest.

[Jacob Licht]

IN LATER JEWISH THOUGHT

The Jewish religion has essentially an ethical character. From its biblical origins to its present stage of development, the ethical element has always been central to the Jewish religion, both as a principle and as a goal. However the intimate connection between religion and ethics was differently interpreted in different periods of Jewish thought. At least two principal trends can be distinguished, the first identifying Jewish ethics with moderation (the middle way), the second insisting on the extreme demands of an absolute ethic. Many thinkers emphasize that Judaism transcends the ethical framework of religion, thereby assuming a metaethical character. Examples of this trend are divine demands, made in prophetic revelations, which seem to conflict with moral norms, and the existence of human suffering.

In talmudic literature, legislative concerns are never the last word. Not only does the *aggadah*, by means of moral lessons, complete and temper the autonomy of the *halakhah*, and not only is the tractate *Avot* an anthology of moral thought; but, more obviously, in every conflict between the legal rigidity of the law and the criteria of ethics, the latter hold sway. Fear of God is superior to wisdom; actions surpass ideas; man is called upon to take a stand in favor not of reason but of the good. Ethics appear not as speculative principles but in terms of human experience; the talmudic sages are presented as moral exemplars and the ideal of holiness is identified with a scrupulously honest and pure life.

Medieval and modern literature testify to the dual tendency to formulate an ethic which is both theoretical and practical. Some medieval Jewish philosophers developed systematic formulations of Jewish ethical ideas, as for example *Saadiah Gaon and Solomon ibn *Gabirol, whose *Tikkun Middot ha-Nefesh* is unusual in that it expounds an autonomous ethic which has no connection with religious doctrine. *Maimonides' *Shemonah Perakim* is a classical work of Jewish ethics which shows similarities to the *Ethics* of Aristotle. There is scarcely a Jewish philosopher or exegete of the Middle Ages who does not devote at least some portion of his work to showing that the body of Jewish thought and its biblical or talmudic sources revolved around ethics. This trend continues to modern times when Jewish philosophers, since Moses *Mendelssohn, place ethics at the center of their description of the universe. For example, Moritz *Lazarus and Elijah *Benamozegh, in the 19th century, give this tendency a classical expression, one composing a standard work entitled *Die Ethik des Judentums* ("Ethics of Judaism"), the other by comparing Jewish and Christian ethics (*Morale juive et morale chrétienne*). It would be out of place to mention *Spinoza in this connection, for while his *Tractatus Theologico-Politicus* shows Jewish influences, the same is not true of his *Ethics*.

In addition to the literature mentioned there are a number of works which are important for the development of medieval and modern Jewish ethics because they reflect an individual or collective experience. The Kabbalah and other mystical currents contributed greatly to the emergence of these works. Examples of this type of literature are *Baḥya ibn Paquda's *Ḥovot ha-Levavot*, the *Sefer Ḥasidim* (see *Ethical Literature), and M.Ḥ. *Luzzatto's *Mesillat Yesharim*. These works have become very popular and have been adopted by such opposing Jewish circles as the *Ḥasidim and **Mitnaggedim*. In the 19th century, under the influence of R. Israel *Lipkin (Salanter), the *Musar movement reintroduced the primacy of ethics into the highly intellectual talmudic academies.

The Middle Way and the Absolute

The intimate connection between religion and ethics was interpreted differently in different periods of Jewish life and thought. At least two principal tendencies can be distinguished. In line with the ideal set down in Proverbs and various Psalms, and also in the Jewish Hellenistic writings and Palestinian teachings in the rabbinic period, Jewish ethics strives for moderation. It condemns excess, obviously in the sense of evil but also in the sense of good, and condemns equally greed and waste, debauchery and abstinence, pleasure and asceticism, impiety and bigotry. Maimonides developed this identification of Jewish ethics with the middle way (*Shemonah Perakim;* Yad, De'ot) though, at times, he tends toward a more ascetic position. The majority of medieval and modern Jewish philosophers follow Maimonides' general view and the theme of moderation in Jewish ethics. Consequently, they were opposed to ethical extremism such as that of Christianity, and this view became a commonplace in Jewish apologetics.

Nevertheless, the notion of moderation is not the only facet of Jewish ethics. The biblical books of Job and Ecclesiastes strongly criticize the middle way. In the Book of Job especially, where the middle way is recommended by the friends of Job, this approach is ultimately rejected by God. The Talmud goes further in its declaration that the attitude of moderation is the attitude of Sodom: "He that says, 'What is mine is mine and what is thine is thine' – this is the middle way, and some say that this is the way of Sodom" (Avot 5:13). It is not surprising, therefore, that the Talmud praises well-known sages who, going beyond the strict letter of the law (*li-fenim mi-shurat ha-din*), gave their entire fortune to the poor (R. Yeshevav), practiced celibacy (Ben Azzai), spent many hours of the day and night in prayer (R. Ḥanina b. Dosa), and, altogether, seemed generally to conform to the monastic ideals of the *Essenes. Asceticism is central to the works of Baḥya and Luzzatto, the *Sefer ha-Ḥasidism*, and, in a way even to 18th century Ḥasidism. It is true that in this mystical movement, whose influence is still being felt today, asceticism was transformed into joy, but the ethic of this joy was as extreme and absolute as was the ascetic ethic.

It would therefore be incorrect to associate Jewish ethics with a uniform and moderate attitude. This attitude, which is often presented as a contrast to Christian ethics, is actually only one aspect of Jewish ethics. The other aspect, with its extreme and absolute demands, is equally typical of Jewish thought.

The Ethical and the Metaethical

By the implications of certain of its teachings, Judaism goes beyond the limits of the ethical, and enters the domain of the metaethical, "beyond good and evil." Already in the Bible, the concept of holiness is affirmed much more often as a category which transcends ethical considerations, rather than as an ethical postulate. The transcendence of God elevates holiness above the moral equity guaranteed by the Covenant. The well-known verse of Isaiah, "For My thoughts are not your thoughts, neither are your ways My ways" (55:8), is often employed by medieval and modern Jewish thinkers as a key for interpreting certain problems which escaped all ethical definition, most notably the problems of freedom and suffering.

How should one accept, from the point of view of ethics, the unusual conduct of certain prophets (Hosea's association with a prostitute; the nudity of Isaiah; the celibacy of Jeremiah)? Unless they resorted to allegorical exegesis, the biblical commentators were forced to admit, and they did so willingly, that there operated here a certain arbitrary divine will which transcended ethical categories. Maimonides expounded this theme in stating that God remains the supreme arbiter of the gift of prophecy. Prophecy is not intrinsically bound to ethical qualities. Of course, only an ethical person can become a prophet, but the man of the highest ethical qualities cannot become a prophet without God's charismatic and transcendent will.

Similarly, the midrashic interpretations of the sacrifice of Isaac, of the dramas of Saul or of Job, are much closer to the existentialist point of view of Kierkegaard or of Kafka than to the systems of Maimonides or of Kant. The conflict between Saul and David was not a matter of ethics but of good or bad fortune. Abraham, ultimately, should have disobeyed the divine command to sacrifice his son, which was inspired more by Satan than by God. Job was perfectly innocent, and his inexplicable sufferings could generate nothing but tears. These, and similar themes, which are scattered throughout talmudic and ḥasidic literature, were often taken up by the Jewish existentialists of the 20th century such as Martin *Buber and Franz *Rosenzweig. They culminate in the doctrine of radical insecurity, whose sources one may find in the Bible, but which finds a more cohesive expression in a talmudic formulation: *Kulei hai ve-ulai* ("All this and perhaps?"). Even while the most apparently perfect conditions can be gathered together to weigh the balance in favor of good or evil, there yet remains a coefficient of uncertainty which is beyond good and evil. It is possible that events will follow the ethical expectations. It is also possible, however, that these expectations will not be fulfilled. It is true that this disorder is interpreted as a voluntary (and temporary) weakness of God which permits man to exercise his will. Thus, this metaethical Jewish view remains ultimately ethical and never leads to a passive pessimism. The divine transcendence does not disturb the ethical equilibrium except in order to call upon man to reestablish, together with God, an equilibrium which has been disrupted. The metaethical is the price for the inalienable moral essence of the Covenant.

[Andre Neher]

BIBLIOGRAPHY: BIBLIOGRAPHIES AND ENCYCLOPAEDIAS: N. Amsel, *Jewish Encyclopedia of Moral and Ethical Issues* (1994); S.D. Breslauer, *Contemporary Jewish Ethics: A Bibliographical Survey* (1985); S.D. Breslauer, *Modern Jewish Morality: A Bibliographical Survey* (1986). IN THE BIBLE: F. Wagner, *Geschichte des Sittlichkeitsbegriffs* (1928–36); A. Weiser, *Religion und Sittlichkeit der Genesis* (1928); W.I. Baumgartner, *Israelitische und altorientalische Weisheit* (1933), 4–7, 24–30; F.R. Kraus, in: ZA, 43 (1936), 77–113; Kaufmann Y., Toledot, 1 (1937), 27ff., 31ff., 431–3; 2 (1945), 68–70, 557–628; J. Hempel, *Das Ethos des Alten Testaments* (1938); H. Duesberg, *Les scribes inspirés*, 1 (1938), 92–126, 481–500; H. Frankfort, *Ancient Egyptian Religion* (1948), 56–80; N.W. Porteous, in: H.H. Rowley (ed.), *Studies in Old Testament Prophecy* (1950), 143–56; E. Neufeld, *The Hittite Laws* (1951), 53; A. Gelin, *Morale et l'Ancient Testament* (1952), 71–92; H. Kruse, in: *Verbum Domini*, 30 (1952), 3–13, 65–80, 143–53; H. Bonnet, *Reallexikon der aegyptischen Religionsgeschichte* (1952); W.G. Lambert, in: *Ex Oriente Lux*, 15 (1957–58), 184–96; idem, *Babylonian Wisdom Literature* (1960); S.E. Loewenstamm, in: *Sefer S. Dim* (1958), 124–5; idem, in: BM, 13 (1962), 55–59; E. Jacob, in; VT *Supplement*, 7 (1960), 39–51; E. Hammershaimb, *ibid.*, 73–101; M. Greenberg, in: *Y. Kaufmann Jubilee Volume* (1960), 5–28. IN LATER JEWISH THOUGHT: M. Lazarus, *Ethics of Judaism* (1900); G.F. Moore, *Judaism*, 2 (1927, repr. 1958), 79–111; C.G. Montefiore and H. Loewe, *Rabbinic Anthology* (1963), 490–9; Guttmann, Philosophies, index; M. Kadushin, *Worship and Ethics* (1964); S. Bernfeld, *Foundations of Jewish Ethics* (1967); B. Herring, *Jewish Ethics and Halakhah for Our Times: Sources and Commentary*, 2 vol. (1984–89); L. Finkelstein (ed.), *The Jews*, 2 (1960³), 1010–42; M.J. Routtenberg, in: F.E. Johnson (ed.), *Patterns of Ethics in America Today* (1960), 7–27.

ETHIOPIA (Abyssinia), Christian kingdom in N.E. Africa. Under Egyptian rule from 2000 B.C.E. to about 1000 B.C.E., Ethiopia (Heb. *Kush*) appears alongside Egypt in the Bible, sharing its prophesied doom (e.g., Isa. 20:3); Tirhakah, the pharaoh, is mentioned as king of Ethiopia during the Assyrian conquest of the Northern kingdom (II Kings 19:9 and Isa. 37:9). The wealth of Ethiopia and Seba are also cited (Isa. 43:3; 45:14). However, Ethiopia figures most prominently as an example of a remote place, cf. Amos 9:7, where God rebukes Israel saying, "Are you not like the Ethiopians to me, O people of Israel?" Independent of Egypt, Ethiopia was ruled by a dynasty of Arabian origin which invaded the country in the second century B.C.E., ruled from the city of Axum, and determined the Semitic quality of the customs and language of the Hamitic people. The kings at Axum called themselves *negus-nagast* ("king of kings"). They traced their descent to Menelik whom they claimed to have been the son of King Solomon and the queen of Sheba. This legend finds expression in the classic Ethiopian chronicle of the 14th century C.E., the *Kebra Negast* ("Glory of Kings"). Among other stories, the latter describes Solomon's seduction of and contract with the queen of Sheba, whose son brought Judaic customs and civil law to Ethiopia. The Holy Ark was also conveyed to Ethiopia to be returned to Zion only when Christ would reappear in Jerusalem and the Ethiopian Christians would reign triumphant in the Holy City. Indeed, the Coptic Monophysite Christianity accepted by the Ethiopians, probably in the fifth century, retained certain Jewish elements derived from the contact and influence of local Jews or from early Christianity itself. It is also possible that they were influenced by South Arabian Jews in pre-Islamic times. In the eighth century, the capital of the kingdom was moved from Axum as a result of Muslim expansion into Ethiopia. The Christian kings of the Zague dynasty who strove to restore their hegemony from the 13th century claimed descent from Solomon and maintained that the Ethiopian aristocracy was taken from Jerusalem to Axum. The lion of Judah has remained the symbol of the emperor of Ethiopia. The literary language of Ethiopia is Ge'ez, a Semitic tongue, which was replaced by Amharic. All holy works are written in Ge'ez, including the Bible (probably translated from Greek or Syriac) and the only complete extant versions of the apocryphal books of Enoch and Jubilees, which were translated from the lost Greek and included in the canon. During the Middle Ages, most works were translated from Arabic, including the major Jewish history, *Josippon*, called in Ge'ez, *Zena Ayhud* ("History of the Jews"), and other Jewish chronicles and religious works gleaned from Arabic sources.

Ethiopian Church in Jerusalem

The Ethiopian Church is one of the oldest churches in the Holy Land. An Ethiopian convert is mentioned in the Acts of the Apostles (8:27–28) and Ethiopian monks and pilgrims are referred to in early pilgrim records. In 1172, in the crusader kingdom of Jerusalem, they possessed altars in the holy places, in the vicinity of which they had established monasteries. Under the Muslim rulers, after the downfall of the crusader kingdom, the Ethiopians obtained more extensive rights. They are mentioned in connection with the Church of the Tomb of the Virgin, and the chapel of St. Mary of Egypt (14th century), and as having chapels in the Church of the Holy Sepulcher (15th century). Toward the end of the 17th century, however, unable to meet the exactions of the Turkish pashas, they lost most of their holdings in the Holy Sepulcher. From an early date until the beginning of the 19th century, the Ethiopians had important rights in the Deir el-Sultan Monastery near the Holy Sepulcher, which have since been claimed by the Coptic Church. The Ethiopians were left with hovels on the roof of the chapel of St. Helena which is part of the church of the Holy Sepulcher. In the New City of Jerusalem there is an Ethiopian church with an adjoining monastery. There are also two monasteries in the Old City and one on the western bank of the Jordan River.

Relations with Israel

Direct contacts between Ethiopia and the *yishuv* started in 1936, when Emperor Haile Selassie, his family, and officers found refuge in Jerusalem after the Italian conquest of Ethiopia. The emperor lived there for about one year, but numerous Ethiopian notables spent the whole period of their exile in Palestine. During World War II, a number of Jewish soldiers from Palestine served with the British forces in the reconquest of Ethiopia, both under the command of Orde *Wingate, whose personal ADC during the Ethiopian campaign was a Palestinian Jewish officer, and in the regular East-African Command, particularly in the commando units that fought in Eritrea. After his return to Addis Ababa the emperor called a number of Palestinian Jews to serve in various capacities within the Ethiopian government. The first beginnings of economic ties between the two countries also developed at that time. Palestinian-manufactured goods reached Ethiopia, and some Jewish experts worked in Ethiopia.

From 1948

Ethiopia abstained in the crucial UN vote on Nov. 29, 1947 on the partition of Palestine, in view of her cautious line of neutrality in most of her dealings with the problems of the Middle East. In 1948 Ethiopia extended only de facto recognition to Israel; however, it continued to maintain its consulate general in West Jerusalem, thereby maintaining close contacts with Israel. In 1955, when an Israeli mission took part in Haile Selassie's Silver Jubilee celebrations in Addis Ababa, an agreement was reached to establish an Israeli consulate general in Addis Ababa, which began to function in the summer of 1956. In September 1961 Ethiopia extended de jure recognition to Israel and diplomatic relations at ambassadorial level were established.

In international forums, Ethiopia maintained her traditional neutrality in the Arab-Israel conflict; repeatedly refused to join anti-Israel initiatives; and tried to urge reconciliation, negotiations, and peace, often in the face of an opposite stand adopted by the Afro-Asian and nonaligned groups in which Ethiopia became an ever more active member. The formal relations between the two countries steadily normalized and bilateral relations began to reflect the relatively close geographical proximity of the two countries. Numerous personalities of both countries paid mutual official and semi-official visits. In 1960 the Empress Menem went on a pilgrimage to Jerusalem. In the same year the Israel minister of agriculture, Moshe *Dayan, paid an official visit to Ethiopia. Israel's foreign minister, Golda Meir, visited Addis Ababa in 1962, and her successor Abba *Eban visited there. It was particularly in economic and technical cooperation, however, that mutual ties found expression.

With the opening of the Straits of Tiran to unhampered Israel shipping and the recognition of the Gulf of Akaba as an international waterway following the Sinai Campaign of 1956, Eilat and Massawa, and later on also Assab and Djibouti, became major ports of call for the ships of both nations. With the introduction of more modern ships, the time required for the trip from Eilat to Massawa steadily decreased, so that by 1970 this run was made in just over 48 hours. In 1970 a regular air link between Lydda and Addis Ababa was inaugurated by El Al Airlines, cutting flying time between Israel and Ethiopia to just over three hours. Commerce between the two countries developed steadily, with Israel selling mainly manufactured goods and buying primary products from Ethiopia. Economic cooperation between the two countries started early in the 1950s with the establishment of an Israeli meat-packing plant in Asmara, but it received particular impetus in the 1960s. A large Ethiopian-Israel cotton farm exists in the Awash Valley, an Ethiopian-Israel pharmaceutical plant in Addis Ababa, and a number of other enterprises. During the 1960s Israeli experts served in various fields in Ethiopia, from public transportation through fishing and agriculture to Ethiopian geological surveys. Numerous Ethiopian students studied in various institutions in Israel in widely diverse fields, e.g., agriculture and communications.

Cultural ties occupy a special place in the relations between the two countries, particularly those between the institutions of higher learning. In 1959 the Haifa Technion entered into close relations with the Engineering College in Addis Ababa, which later became part of the Haile Selassie I University, in which Israeli professors subsequently served. In 1970 an agreement was reached between the Haile Selassie I University and the Hebrew University for the joint development of a microbiology institute in Addis Ababa. Close collaboration existed also in medicine, town planning, water development, and related fields.

[Hanan Bar-On]

Starting in the 1960s Israel was a major supplier of military aid to Ethiopia, which continued even after Ethiopia broke off diplomatic relations with Israel in 1973 in the wake of the

Yom Kippur War and also after the Marxist Mengistru regime replaced Haile Selassie in 1974. From the 1980s such assistance was linked to Ethiopia's agreement to allow Ethiopian Jews, the so-called Falashas (see *Beta Israel), to immigrate to Israel, a condition that was fulfilled in two dramatic airlifts in 1984 and 1991. Diplomatic relations were renewed in 1989 at embassy level.

BIBLIOGRAPHY: I. Ben-Zvi, *The Exiled and the Redeemed* (1967); index, also s.v. *Falashas*; A.Z. Aescoly, in: *Tarbiz*, 5 (1934), 341–9; E.W. Budge (tr.), *Kebra Negast, Queen of Sheba and Her Only Son...* (1932); idem, *A History of Ethiopia, Nubia and Abyssinia* (1938); E. Littmann, *Legend of the Queen of Sheba in the Tradition of Axum* (Bibliotheca Abbisinica no. 1, 1904); R. Pankhurst, *An Introduction to the Ethiopian Economic History* (1961); J. Harden, *An Introduction to Ethiopic Christian Literature* (1926); Colbi, *Christianity in the Holy Land* (1969), 107–108, 139, 156–57.

ETHNARCH (Gr. ἐθνάρχος), title given to John *Hyrcanus II and his sons by official decree of Julius Caesar in 47 B.C.E. in addition to the office of high priest (Jos., Ant., 14:192ff.). The meaning of ethnarch – head of the people – excluded the title or the rights of a king, and Josephus comments that whereas "Pompey restored the high priesthood to Hyrcanus and permitted him to have the leadership of the nation," he nevertheless "forbade him to wear a diadem" (*ibid.*, 20:244). This distinction is apparent again in the description by Josephus of the appointment of Herod's son Archelaus. Augustus "appointed Archelaus not king indeed, but ethnarch of half of the territory that had been subject to Herod, and promised to reward him with the title of king if he really proved able to act in that capacity" (*ibid.*, 17:317).

The title ethnarch was also used to designate the head of the Jewish community at Alexandria. Strabo, quoted by Josephus (*ibid.*, 14:117), describes the Alexandrian ethnarch as one "who governs the people and adjudicates suits and supervises contracts and ordinances, just as if he were the head of a sovereign state." Philo, however, relates that Augustus replaced that ethnarch with a *gerousia* or Council of Elders (*In Flaccum*, 74ff.). Certain scholars have attempted to identify the term Σαραμέλ in I Maccabees 14:28 with ethnarch (see *Asaramel). The term ethnarch was not confined to Jewish rulers. Thus there is mention of an ethnarch at Damascus under the king Aretas (II Cor. 11:32).

BIBLIOGRAPHY: Schuerer, Hist, 107ff.; Schuerer, Gesch, 3 (1909[4]), 76–78; A. Schalit, *Koenig Herodes* (1969), 224ff.; Baron, Community, index.

[Isaiah Gafni]

ETIQUETTE (Heb. דֶּרֶךְ־אֶרֶץ, *derekh ereẓ*), the proper conduct of man at home and in society. The sages demanded of the Jew, particularly the scholar, good manners in all his activities. The rules of *derekh ereẓ are assembled in the tractates *Avot, Derekh Ereẓ Rabbah*, and *Derekh Ereẓ Zuta*, and are scattered throughout the Talmud and the Midrashim. A substantial number of them are set forth in Maimonides' *Mishneh Torah, Hilkhot De'ot*.

The rules of etiquette covered every aspect of man's conduct, including the most seemingly insignificant. Only a few of the most important rules are given here.

Speech

A man should speak pleasantly with everyone (Yoma 86a) and, Maimonides adds: "When speaking he should neither shout nor scream nor raise his voice excessively." When he meets his fellow he should be the first to extend greetings. As an example the Talmud cites the instance of Johanan b. Zakkai, whom no one ever preceded in extending greeting (Ber. 17a). Since, in the heat of argument, a man is liable to interrupt his fellow and stubbornly assert his own opinion, even after being convinced that the other is right, the sages laid down rules for the conduct of an argument: not to speak before one who is greater in wisdom, nor to interrupt the speech of another, not to be hasty in answering, to ask only relevant questions and to answer appropriately, to speak on the first point first and on the last point last, to say "I have not heard" when he has no tradition to that effect, to acknowledge the truth (Avot 5:7).

Walking

A scholar should not carry himself stiffly, with his neck outstretched... nor walk mincingly as do women and haughty people... nor run in a public place like a madman, nor bend his body as if he is a hunchback, but he should look downward, as when standing in prayer, and walk in the street like a man going about his business (Maim., Yad, De'ot 5:8).

Clothing

The Talmud regularizes expenditure on food and clothing by the principle: A man should always spend on food less than his means allow, and clothe himself in accordance with his means (Ḥul. 84b). The sages were most particular that their clothing should be becoming and clean, even to the extent of declaring that any scholar upon whose garment a stain is found is worthy of death (Shab. 114a). Maimonides applies the doctrine of the Golden Mean to clothing: "He should not wear clothes, of gold and purple, for instance, fit for a king, and at which everyone stares, nor clothes worn by the poor that put to shame those wearing them, but he should wear modest dress" (De'ot 5:9).

Eating and Drinking

In eating and drinking, too, he should not indulge in extremes, but content himself with the minimum necessary for health. He should eat only in his own home, at his table, but not in the market place, for "he who eats in the market place is like a dog" (Kid. 40b). A scholar should not eat standing, nor lick his fingers, for this is the way of gluttons (DEZ 5). Gulping one's drink in a single draught is a sign of greediness (Beẓah 25b). One should not drink out of a cup and then give it to his fellow, for not all people are alike, and sensitive people are particular about this (Tosef., Ber. 5:9).

Treatment of Wife and Children

The rabbis were extremely particular about conduct in the family circle. The responsibility for this was placed primarily on the husband and father, to whom they gave the following directives: "A man should always observe the honor due to his wife, because blessings rest on a man's home only on account of his wife." "A man should always be careful not to wrong his wife (with words), for being given to tears, she is easily hurt." He should consult his wife in all matters affecting the home: If your wife is short, bend down and listen to her words (BM 59a). They enjoined the head of the household to be indulgent, not to take offense, and not to terrorize his household, so as to avoid quarrels (Ta'an. 20b; Git. 6b).

Personal Relations

Most controversies are due to the tendency to ascribe bad motives to the words and actions of others. As a result the sages urged: "Let the honor of your neighbor be as dear to you as your own" (Avot 2:10), and "Love all men and honor them, and forgo your will for that of your neighbor" (DEZ 1). Good and worthy intentions may fail if they are implemented at the wrong moment. Hence, the rabbis counseled: "Do not pacify your fellow in the hour of his anger; nor comfort him when his dead one lies before him" (Avot 4:18). One should not present oneself to one's friend, or even to the members of his household, at an inconvenient time: "Do not enter your own house suddenly, and all the more, your neighbor's house" (Pes. 112a) counseled Akiva. The concern of the rabbis in this matter is reflected in the statement, "Let all men learn good manners from the Omnipresent, who stood at the entrance to Eden and called out to Adam, as it says, 'The Lord God called to Adam, saying, "Where art thou"'" (DER 5). Many modern and medieval ethical works praise *Derekh Erez*, adherence to its precepts, and, at the same time, stress the duty of other strictures to those mentioned in the Talmud.

BIBLIOGRAPHY: Krauss, Tal Arch, 3 (1912), 2ff.; A. Kohn, in: *Ben-Chananja*, 2 (1859), 66–67, 167–8, 210–1, 258–64 (Ger.); J. Friedmann, *Der gesellschaftliche Verkehr und die Umgangsformen in talmudischer Zeit* (1914); M. Higger, *Massekhtot Ze'irot* (1929), 1–7; idem, *Massekhtot Derekh Erez* (1935), 11–18 (English section); A. Cohen, *Everyman's Talmud* (1932), 168–266; C.G. Montefiore and H. Loewe, *A Rabbinical Anthology* (1938), 451–523; G. Friedlander, *Laws and Customs of Israel* (1927), passim.

[Abraham Arzi]

ETROG (Heb. אֶתְרוֹג), citrus fruit among the Four Species used on Sukkot. The Bible describes what is usually rendered as "the fruit of a goodly tree" (*peri ez hadar*; Lev. 23:40), traditionally interpreted as being the *etrog* (*Citrus medica*). The word *etrog*, the name by which this fruit is known in talmudic literature, derives, according to one view, from the Persian *torong*, according to another, from the Sanskrit *suranga*, meaning "beautifully colored." Some maintain that the *etrog* tree, along with its name, reached Erez Israel only during the Second Temple period, even as it was brought to Greece from its native land, India, only after the campaigns of Alexander the Great. Others contend that "the fruit of a goodly tree" is to be identified with the *Pinus* or *Cedrus*, called *dar* in Sanskrit; others say that what is meant is simply any beautiful (*hadur*) fruit. There is evidence that the *etrog* was known in ancient Egypt; its use as one of the Four Species on Sukkot was probably responsible for its wider cultivation in Erez Israel in olden days, for neighboring countries set no great store upon its fruit, which is not particularly good. Indeed, even during the Hasmonean period, which abounds in evidence of its cultivation in Erez Israel, the *etrog* was not grown in Italy and is not mentioned by Pliny (23–79 C.E.) among the products of that country.

The *etrog* was formerly unique among the fruit trees of Erez Israel in requiring constant irrigation for its growth, whereas the others were only occasionally irrigated, and then only to increase their yield of fruit. This fact is adduced among the various proofs that "the fruit of a goodly tree" (*peri ez hadar*) is to be identified with the *etrog*, *ez hadar* being interpreted as *ez hiddur*, that is, the tree which requires water. Since the *etrog* was the only *citrus known in Erez Israel in the mishnaic and talmudic period, the question of the permissibility of an *etrog* from a grafted tree for the performance of the religious rite did not arise until comparatively recent times.

The *etrog* was a conspicuous ornamental motif among Jews during the Second Temple period, appearing on coins of Simeon and other Hasmoneans, and it is often depicted on the walls of synagogues and in mosaics. When Alexander Yannai once acted contrary to the *halakhah* in the Temple, "all the people pelted him with their *etrogim*" (Suk. 4:9; Tosef., *ibid.* 3:16; Jos., Ant., 13:372). In the mishnaic and talmudic period, when the *etrog* was widely cultivated in Erez Israel, it was comparatively cheap, a large *etrog* selling for two perutot (Me'il. 6:4). An especially beautiful *etrog*, which was in great demand for the festival, cost very much more, at times as much as the price of three meals (TJ, Suk. 3:12, 54a). There were periods (for example during the Hadrianic persecutions) when *etrogim* had to be brought from far-flung places in Erez Israel (Tosef., Dem. 3:14). Various uses were made of the *etrog*; its thick skin was eaten either pickled in vinegar or boiled to a pulp (Suk. 36b; Ma'as. 1:4), and a perfume was extracted from its peel (Suk. 37b), which was also highly valued as an antidote against snake-bite (Shab. 109b).

Today, the *etrog* is not extensively cultivated in the world, and is grown primarily for the citronate that is extracted from its peel. There are many strains of *etrog*. In Israel the small strain is predominant; the large strain was brought to the country by the Yemenites (cf. Suk. 36b, about a large *etrog* which was carried on the shoulder). In addition to the sour *etrog*, there is also the sweet strain (cf. Shab. 109b). With the increase in the species of the genus citrus, the *etrog* was crossed with other citrus plants, which probably accounts for the present difficulty of growing an *etrog* which has not been grafted on a lemon or hushhash stock, the ungrafted variety being vulnerable to pests and diseases, and its *pittam* (the protuberance, the pistil) usually being atrophied. Whereas in ancient times the *pittam* was a conspicuous mark of the *etrog's* excellence, there are those today who are particularly anxious to obtain only an ungrafted *etrog*, which usually has no *pittam*. There are several distinguishing signs by which the grafted and the ungrafted *etrog* can be distinguished. The skin of the latter is generally rougher than that of the former, and, according to some halakhic authorities, the seed of the latter lies longitudinally within the fruit, and that of the former, latitudinally. Until the end of the 19th century the center for the cultivation of *etrogim* was the island of *Corfu, from where they were exported to Jewish communities in Europe. Later these began to use the *etrogim* of Ereẓ Israel. Today the *etrog* groves in Israel supply local needs and also export many *etrogim* abroad.

BIBLIOGRAPHY: V. Loret, *Le cédratier dans l'antiquité* (1891); Loew, Flora, 3 (1924), 285ff.; S. Tolkowski, in: JPOS, 8 (1928), 17–23; J. Feliks, *Olam ha-Ẓome'aḥ ha-Mikra'i* (1957), 66–70.

[Jehuda Feliks]

ETROG, SOREL (1933–), sculptor, painter, poet, filmmaker. Etrog was born in Jassy, Romania. In 1950, he immigrated with his family to Israel. He studied at the Israel Institute of Painting and Sculpture in Tel Aviv (1953–55). From 1955 to 1958, he was a member of the Ein Hod artists' colony. Etrog held his first solo show in Tel Aviv (1958). Awarded a scholarship to the Brooklyn Museum Art School/Institute, he studied in New York in 1958–59 and established a studio there.

In the summer of 1959, Etrog was invited to work in Canada by prominent art collector Samuel Zacks. That year, he held a solo exhibition at Toronto's Gallery Moos and in 1963 he moved permanently to Toronto. From 1964 to 1984 he worked in his studios in both Toronto and Florence, Italy. Etrog was one of three artists representing Canada at the 1966 Venice Biennale, where his reputation as a leading contemporary sculptor was confirmed.

Etrog is best known for his large public sculptures which range from the biomorphic to monumental bronze and steel structures. Marshall McLuhan described his "hinge" and "link" work as a drama of dialogue and interchange that reflects the "transformation of the old machine and its consumer products into new vital images of primal art and perception." Etrog also began as a painter in Israel. His "painted constructions" investigate the interdependency of painting and relief. He also realized a significant body of drawings, including studies and large-scale works on paper and canvas. His art is a process of exploration into the nature of human consciousness and the human condition. A poet himself, Etrog worked collaboratively with writers such as McLuhan, Claudio Aveline, Samuel Beckett, and Eugene *Ionesco.

The subject of numerous exhibitions, Etrog's art is widely represented in major museums and collections around the world, including the Tate Museum, London; the Museum of Modern Art, New York; the Guggenheim Museum, New York; the Hirshhorn Museum, Washington, D.C.; the Israel Museum, Jerusalem; the Kroeller-Mueller Museum, Otterlo; the Musée d'Arte Moderne, Paris; and the National Gallery of Canada, Ottawa. Among his many public and private commissions is *Powersoul*, which he created for the 1988 Olympics in Seoul, Korea. In 1968, Etrog designed the Canadian film award statuette (called "the Etrog" until 1980, when it was renamed the "Genie").

In recognition of his contributions to contemporary art, Etrog was named a Member of the Order of Canada in 1995 and a Chevalier dans l'Ordre des Arts et des Lettres by France in 1996.

BIBLIOGRAPHY: T.A. Heinrich, *The Painted Constructions 1952–1960 of Sorel Etrog* (1968); C. Ragghianti, *Sorel Etrog Sculptures Engravings Lithographs Documents* (1968); P. Restany, *Sorel Etrog* (2001); W. Withrow, *Sorel Etrog* (1967).

[Joyce Zemans (2nd ed.)]

ETTELSON, HARRY WILLIAM (1883–1975), U.S. Reform rabbi. Ettelson was born in Mobile, Alabama, and received his B.A. with Phi Beta Kappa honors from the University of Cincinnati in 1900, at the age of 17. He was ordained at Hebrew Union College, where he was valedictorian of his class, in 1904. Ettelson earned his M.A. from the University of Chicago while serving as rabbi of Temple Achduth Vesholom in Fort Wayne, Indiana (1904–10), and his Ph.D. from Yale University in 1916 while serving as rabbi of Congregation Beth Israel in Hartford, Connecticut (1911–19). He served as a Navy chaplain at Pelham Bay Training Station during World War I, then became rabbi of Temple Rodeph Shalom in Philadelphia (1919–24), where he also served as president of the Philadelphia Board of Jewish Ministers, vice chancellor of the Jewish Chautauqua Society, and a member of the editorial board of the Jewish Publication Society.

In 1925, he moved to Memphis to assume the pulpit of Congregation Children of Israel (later, Temple Israel), where he remained until his death, serving his final 21 years as rabbi emeritus. He was both a religious and civic leader in Memphis, where he was founder and first president of the Cross-Cut Club, an organization of Memphis clergymen of all faiths that formed the nucleus of that city's chapter of the *National Conference of Christians and Jews (NCCJ). He also instituted several citywide interfaith initiatives, including Peace Heroes Day; Good Will and Brotherhood Day (later expanded by the NCCJ to Brotherhood Week); and non-sectarian Union Civic Thanksgiving Day services.

Ettelson's reputation as both a scholar and an orator reached its zenith in 1932, when he engaged in a public debate on religion with Clarence Darrow, the noted attorney of Scopes trial fame, who traveled around the country debating clergymen. Although there was no official decision as to a winner, according to the *Memphis Press-Scimitar*, "by and large, the majority sided with Dr. Ettelson's masterly approach" to the question, "Is Religion Necessary?" That same year, his congregation awarded him the Joseph Newberger Memorial Cup, in recognition of his service to the Memphis Jewish community. In 1940, Southwestern University awarded him an honorary doctorate.

As chairman of the CCAR-UAHC Joint Commission on Information on Judaism in the 1940s, Ettelson developed the

"Popular Studies in Judaism" program. He also served as president of the Hebrew Union College Alumni Association and was a member of the HUC Board of Governors as well as of the Executive Board of the Central Conference of American Rabbis (1912). A frequent contributor to Jewish literary periodicals and a translator of poetry into Hebrew and Yiddish, he also wrote the book, *The Integrity of I Maccabees* (1925), and published a translation of the epigrams of Shem Tov ben Joseph *Falaquera, a 13th-century Jewish scholar and physician from Spain.

BIBLIOGRAPHY: *Journal of the 87th Annual Convention of the Central Conference of American Rabbis* (1976).

[Bezalel Gordon (2nd ed.)]

ETTENBERG, SYLVIA CUTLER (1917–), U.S. Jewish educator, particularly within the Conservative movement. Born in Brooklyn, she received a B.A. from Brooklyn College and a Bachelor of Pedagogy from the Jewish Theological Seminary of America (JTS). In 1940 she married Moshe Ettenberg, an engineering professor; the couple had two children.

Although her career was spent almost exclusively at the Jewish Theological Seminary of America, her influence was felt in a wide range of institutions and settings. Ettenberg, the first female senior administrator at JTS, played a leading role in some of the most important and innovative projects of Conservative Jewish education. She was directly involved in the founding of the Seminary's supplementary high school (the Prozdor) in 1951, the creation of the Melton Research Center in 1959, and the eventual establishment of the William Davidson Graduate School of Jewish Education in 1996. She worked on the creation of a joint undergraduate degree program between JTS and Columbia University and helped supervise the Department of Jewish Education at the Seminary as it developed its M.A. and doctoral programs.

Arguably, her most notable achievement was Camp Ramah, a summer educational camping program that grew into an international network of camps. Ramah was first launched in Wisconsin in 1947 by a group of community leaders from Chicago. But it was Ettenberg and Moshe Davis who brought Ramah inside the world of JTS itself, creating an infrastructure for the camping system that developed over time and nurtured the powerful educational vision embodied in the camps. The Ramah camps had a profound impact on Jewish education and provided a large percentage of the future academic, lay, and professional leadership of Conservative Judaism.

Ettenberg received an honorary doctorate from JTS, the Behrman House Books – Jewish Educators Assembly lifetime achievement award, and the Samuel Rothberg Prize in Jewish education from the Hebrew University of Jerusalem.

[Barry W. Holtz (2nd ed.)]

ETTENDORF, township in the Bas-Rhin department, France. Two Jewish families were recorded in the town in 1449. In 1784 the Jewish population of Ettendorf reached its peak of 124, but from the Revolution, it steadily declined; there were 37 Jews there in 1868 and only one family in 1926. The Ettendorf community, though small, possessed two important institutions, which also served about 20 other communities in Lower Alsace: a cemetery opened during the late 15th century and a talmudical school established in the middle of the 18th century.

BIBLIOGRAPHY: D. Fischer, *Ein geschichtlicher Blick auf… Ettendorf* (1868); U. Ginsburg, in: *Souvenir et Science*, 2:1 (1931), 14ff.

[Bernhard Blumenkranz]

ETTING, pioneer Jewish family in Baltimore, Maryland. ELIJAH ETTING (1724–1778), progenitor of the family in the U.S., arrived in the U.S. from Germany in 1758, settling in York, Pennsylvania, where he became an important Indian trader. After his death his widow, SHINAH (née Solomon), moved to Baltimore with five of her seven children. Her two sons Reuben and Solomon also settled there eventually. REUBEN ETTING (1762–1848), Maryland political figure, was born in York, Pa. During a period when Jews still lived in Maryland by license rather than by right, Reuben assumed the duties of a full citizen in 1798 when a war between the United States and France seemed imminent and became captain of a militia company. Reuben was long involved in politics as a Jeffersonian Republican and was appointed U.S. marshal for Maryland in 1801 by President Jefferson. He was thus the first Jew in Maryland to hold public office, a quarter of a century before the Jews gained civic equality in the state. SOLOMON ETTING (1764–1847), businessman, political figure, and Jewish civic rights leader, also born in York, Pa., became a *shoḥet* at the age of 18, the first American Jew to serve in this capacity. At first a hardware storekeeper, Solomon subsequently became a banker, a shipper, a founder of the Baltimore and Ohio Railroad, and an important businessman. He was prominent in the Baltimore Republican Society, a Jeffersonian political club. He was a leader in the defense of Baltimore against the British in the War of 1812, during which his 18-year-old son Samuel was wounded in the battle at nearby Fort McHenry. Etting was a "manager" of the Maryland State Colonization Society, which sought to promote the resettlement of blacks in Africa. Etting was active in the Baltimore German Society and served as its vice president from 1820 to 1840. Although he was not involved in any Jewish organization in Baltimore, he supported the synagogue of his youth, Mikveh Israel, in Philadelphia. In 1801 he purchased land for a Jewish cemetery in Baltimore. He also led in the struggle for Jewish civic rights, opposing the Maryland law requiring of officeholders a Christian oath. As early as 1797 he appealed to the State Legislature on behalf of a "sect of people called Jews, deprived of invaluable rights of citizenship and praying to be placed on the same footing as other good citizens." This petition initiated a three-decade struggle, which ended successfully in 1826. Soon thereafter, Etting served as a Baltimore councilman. Solomon Etting's second wife was the daughter of the prominent leader Barnard *Gratz.

BIBLIOGRAPHY: Rosenbloom, Biog Dict, 35–36; AJHS, 2 (1894), 33–44; 17 (1909), 81–88; 34 (1937), 66–69; Baroway, in: *Mary-*

land Historical Magazine, 15 (1920), 1–20; E.M. Altfeld, *Jews Struggle for Religious and Civil Liberty in Maryland* (1924), index; A.J.M. Pedley (ed.), *Manuscript Collections of the Maryland Historical Society* (1968), index.

[Isaac M. Fein]

ETTINGER, family noted for its scholars and community leaders, originally from *Oettingen, Bavaria, from which the name derives. It is probably related to families named Oettingen or Ettingen: members of its East European branch were prominent in Jewish life in modern times. First of note was Ḥayyim Judah Leib Ettinger who in 1717 moved from Holesov (Holleschau), Moravia, to head a yeshivah in Lemberg, Poland. His brother, JOSEPH, served as a preacher in Glogau, Silesia, and wrote commentaries on the Torah, *Edut bi-Yehosef* (Sulzbach, 1741). Ḥayyim's son AARON (1720–1769), rabbi in Jaworow and Rzeszow, fought the spread of Ḥasidism in Galicia. Well-known in the 19th century were Mordecai Ze'ev *Ettinger and his brother-in-law, Joseph Saul ha-Levi *Nathanson. Mordecai's son, Isaac Aaron Ettinger (1827–1891), served as rabbi in Przemysl and Lemberg. With BARUCH MORDECAI, rabbi of *Bobruisk in *Belorussia for about 50 years until he settled in Ereẓ Israel in 1851, the family assumed a leading position in *Chabad ḥasidic circles; Baruch Mordecai was a close disciple of *Shneur Zalman of Lyady. In the 20th century many members of the family, such as Akiva *Ettinger, took a prominent part in the economic and cultural life of East European Jewry and Ereẓ Israel. SAMUEL ETTINGER (1919–1988), who was born in Kiev, became professor of Jewish history at the Hebrew University, Jerusalem. He wrote *Toledot Yisrael ba-Et ha-Ḥadashah* ("Jewish History in Modern Times," 1970) and edited a volume of essays by H. Graetz in Hebrew (*Darkhei ha-Historiyah ha-Yehudit*, 1969).

BIBLIOGRAPHY: S. Buber, *Anshei Shem* (1895), 25, 67–69, 123–4, 151–2; Ch. N. Dembitzer, *Kelilat Yofi*, 1 (1960), 116–27, 146–9; J. Slutzky (ed.), *Sefer Bobruisk* (1967), 269. **ADD. BIBLIOGRAPHY:** "Devarim le-Zikhroh shel Shemuel Ettinger," in: *Zion*, 53:4 (1988), 423–40.

[Yehuda Slutsky]

ETTINGER, AKIVA JACOB (1872–1945), agricultural expert; founder and administrator of Jewish settlements in Ereẓ Israel. Ettinger, born in Vitebsk, Belorussia, came from a distinguished family (his mother was descended from R. Akiva *Eger). He studied agriculture at the University of St. Petersburg and in West European countries. Representing the *Jewish Colonization Association (ICA), he took part in 1898 in an investigation of the situation of Jewish farmers in southern Russia, and was then asked to establish a Jewish model farm in Bessarabia. In 1911 he served as agricultural adviser to ICA in South America. Ettinger, together with *Aḥad Ha-Am, was sent to Ereẓ Israel in 1902 by the *Odessa Committee of Ḥovevei Zion to investigate the state of the Jewish settlements. In 1914 he was asked by the Zionist Organization and the Jewish National Fund to serve as adviser and inspector for Jewish agricultural settlement in Ereẓ Israel, but because of the outbreak of war he went to The Hague, where the Jewish National Fund had its temporary head office. There he wrote a programmatic booklet, *Jewish Colonization in Palestine: Methods, Plans and Capital* (1916^2, published in English, German, and Russian).

During the negotiations over the *Balfour Declaration, Ettinger was invited by Chaim *Weizmann to London as adviser on settlement matters, and composed a comprehensive memorandum, *Palestine after the War: Proposals for Administration and Development* (1918). Ettinger settled in Palestine in 1918, serving as director of the agricultural settlement department of the Zionist Organization until 1924. In 1919, after the purchase of land for *Kiryat Anavim on the rocky Judean hills, he founded the village which became a model for hill settlements. His most important achievement involved the vast settlement project of the Jezreel Valley during 1921–24. From 1924 to 1932 Ettinger played a prominent role on behalf of the Jewish National Fund in the purchase of land and the drafting and implementation of settlement (the kevuẓah, kibbutz, and moshav) and aided their development on a mixed farming basis with emphasis on dairy farming and orchards. He also introduced new afforestation methods. From 1932 until his death Ettinger was adviser to the agricultural Yakhin Company of the Histadrut.

Ettinger wrote many articles on agriculture in Ereẓ Israel. His booklets include *Nahalal* (1924), *Emek Yizre'el* (1926), and *Ha-Karmel* (1931). His memoirs are titled *Im Ḥakla'im Yehudim ba-Tefuẓot* ("With Jewish Farmers in the Diaspora," 1942), and *Im Ḥakla'im Ivriyyim be-Arẓenu* ("With Hebrew Farmers in our Country," 1945).

BIBLIOGRAPHY: A. Bein, *Return to the Soil* (1952), index.

[Alexander Bein]

ETTINGER, MORDECAI ZE'EV BEN ISAAC AARON SEGAL (1804–1863), Polish rabbinical scholar, and scion of a long line of rabbis (see *Ettinger family). He studied under Naphtali Hirsch Sohastov, rabbi of Lemberg, and under his own uncle, Jacob *Ornstein. Although renowned for his great scholarship, he never occupied a rabbinical position, his considerable personal fortune rendering him independent. In 1857 he was chosen rabbi of Cracow and its environs and indicated his acceptance but changed his mind. He served as "*nasi* of the Holy Land" of the Austrian *kolel*, an honorable position always given to the greatest of the rabbis. In this capacity he did much to help consolidate the position of the Jewish community in Ereẓ Israel. He studied together with his brother-in-law, Joseph Saul ha-Levi *Nathanson, many joint works resulting from their 25 years of collaboration.

First and foremost of them was *Mefareshei ha-Yam* (Lemberg, 1827), novellae and elucidation appended to the *Yam ha-Talmud* on the tractate *Bava Kamma*, by their uncle, Moses Joshua Heshel Ornstein of Tarnogrod; at the end of this work is included their halakhic correspondence with such contemporaries as Moses *Sofer, Mordecai *Banet, and Akiva *Eger. Their remaining joint works to be noted are *Me'irat Einayim*

(Vilna, 1839), a work in seven sections on the inspection of animals' lungs; *Magen Gibborim*, 1 (Lemberg, 1834), 2 (Zolkieve, 1839); two commentaries on the first 235 chapters of the Shulḥan Arukh, *Oraḥ Ḥayyim;* glosses to and emendations of the glosses of Mordecai *Jaffe on the Talmud (published in the Romm Vilna edition of the Talmud); *Ma'aseh Alfas* (in the Romm Vilna edition of Alfasi), glosses on the *halakhot* of Isaac Alfasi and the Mordecai; *Ner Ma'aravi*. a commentary on the Jerusalem Talmud which includes references under the title *Ein Mishpat* and glosses thereto entitled *Gilyon ha-Shas* (published in the Piotrkow 1859–60 edition of the Jerusalem Talmud).

This fruitful partnership ended in 1859, Ettinger having published in Solomon *Kluger of Brod's booklet *Moda'ah le-Veit Yisrael* (1859), which contained a ban against machine-baked *mazzot*, whereupon Nathanson published a contrary opinion in a booklet called *Bittul Moda'ah* (1859). After the rift with his brother-in-law, Ettinger devoted himself to study together with his son Isaac Aaron *(Ma'amar Mordekhai*, no. 58), and decided to publish responsa and novellae independently. To this period belong his important responsa *Ma'amar Mordekhai* (1852), which deal to a great extent with the laws of **agunah*. A collection of his responsa, *Shevet Aḥim*, has remained in manuscript.

His most famous son was ISAAC AARON (1827–1891) who served as rabbi in Przemysl and in 1888 succeeded Ẓevi Hirsch Ornstein as rabbi of Lemberg, remaining there until his death. Like his father, he at first refused all rabbinical offers, including the rabbinate of Przemysl, and like him also served as "*nasi* of the Holy Land." His novellae were published together with his father's *Ma'amar Mordekhai*, and his responsa are found in his *Maharya ha-Levi* (2 vols., 1893), as well as in various works of contemporary rabbis.

BIBLIOGRAPHY: S. Buber, *Anshei Shem* (1895), 151f.; I.T. Eisenstadt and S. Wiener, *Da'at Kedoshim* (1897–98), 178; H.N. Dembitzer, *Kelilat Yofi*, 1 (1888), 146a–49b, 156a–b; L. Ginzberg, *Perushim ve-Ḥiddushim ba-Yerushalmi*, 1 (1941), LXI (Eng. introd.); EG.

[Itzhak Alfassi]

ETTINGER, SHMUEL (1919–1988), Israeli historian. Born in Kiev, U.S.S.R., Ettinger immigrated to Ereẓ Israel in 1936 and studied at the Hebrew University of Jerusalem, where he received his doctorate in 1956 for his study "The Jewish Colonization of the Ukraine, 1569–1648." In 1952, while still a research student, he joined the teaching staff of the Hebrew University, and in 1965 he became professor of modern Jewish history. He was a visiting professor at Oxford University in 1969–70.

Ettinger's major fields of research include Russian Jewish history (from its beginnings until the Soviet era), the attitude of 17th- and 18th-century European thought toward Judaism and Jews, modern Jewish historiography, and the roots and development of modern antisemitism.

His research on the Muscovite state and its attitude toward the Jews and on the Jewish settlement in the Ukraine constituted a basic contribution to the critical study of the history of the Jews in Russia. In his study of the ḥasidic movement and its historical influence he emphasized the role of the ḥasidic leadership as a powerful formative factor in the continued existence of Jewish autonomy under the centralist regimes of Russia and Austria after the partitions of Poland. The importance of his methodical contribution to the study of the origins of modern antisemitism lies in his unmasking the inherent nature of the critical, and even antagonistic attitude toward Judaism in the major trends of modern European social thought: from the English deism and French rationalism of the 17th and 18th centuries to the romanticism, nationalism, social Darwinism, and even liberalism and socialism of the 19th century. As a representative of the Jerusalem school of Jewish studies, Ettinger emphasized a conceptual framework revolving around the unity and continuity of Jewish history. Within this framework he regarded the centrality of the redemptive principle as an historical motive force even in its secular manifestations, especially in the social and national radicalism of modern Jewish history. His research method, in which he regarded himself as continuing along the path of B.Z. Dinur and Y. Baer, was characterized by the tension between a broad teleological view of Jewish history and its central tendencies, and a rare command of critical investigative methods directed toward detailed elements of historical reality in a wide variety of areas.

Ettinger's studies were published mainly in the journals *Zion, He-Avar, Molad, Gesher, Scripta Hierosolymitana, Cahiers d'Histoire Mondiale*, and the publications of the Israel Historical Society. He published two works of a general nature on modern Jewish history: a volume of his university lectures, *Toledot Am Yisrael mi-Yemei ha-Absolutism ad La-Hakamat Medinat Yisrael* ("History of the Jewish People from the Era of Absolutism until the Establishment of the State of Israel," last edition 1968), and *Toledot Am Yisrael ba-Zeman he-Ḥadash* ("History of the Jewish People in Modern Times," 1969), the latter being the third volume of a series on Jewish history by teachers of the Hebrew University. The latter volume is aimed at a broader reading public and deals in greater detail with the period from the 1880s until after the Six-Day War. During the 1960s, a parallel series in Russian was prepared and published under his editorship (*Ocherki po Istorii Yevreiskogo Naroda*, last edition 1972). He also published a volume of theoretical essays, excerpts from the diary and correspondence of the historian Graetz (*Ẓvi Graetz, Darkhei ha-Historiah ha-Yehudit*, 1969), and a history textbook for Israeli high schools.

Ettinger served on the editorial board of *Zion*, the journal for Jewish history (editorial secretary 1955–59, and editor from 1960) and on the executive board of the Israeli Historical Society and the Central Archives for the History of the Jewish People. He was among the initiators and directors of many research projects, among them the Center for Eastern European Jewish Studies, which he headed.

Closely related to his scientific work was his intensive public activity, devoted mainly to two areas: the educational system of Israel, at every level, and the national awakening of the Jews in Soviet Russia and their spiritual and social integration in Israel.

[Otto Dov Kulka]

ETTINGER, SOLOMON (**Shloyme**; 1803–1856), Yiddish poet and dramatist. Born in Warsaw, orphaned, and then raised in Leczna by his paternal uncle, Ettinger moved to Zamosc after marrying Golda, the daughter of magnate Judah Leib Wolf, where he was influenced by the Haskalah. He studied pharmacy and medicine in Lemberg (Lvov) – where he discovered the writer in himself – and practiced medicine, despite difficulties with certification in Poland. Although he knew both Hebrew and German, he chose to write in Yiddish, attempting to create his own literary style. The influence of Lessing, Buerger, and other German writers can be traced in his works, and he was also influenced by the Yiddish comedies of Isaac *Euchel and Aaron *Wolfsohn-Halle. Ettinger wrote satirical and witty ballads, epigrams, poems, and dramas. His fables (*mesholim*) reflect an influence by the Maggid of Dubno (see Jacob ben Wolf *Kranz), who left his imprint on Zamosc with this genre in the early 19th century. Ettinger concentrated on individual problems rather than on the contemporary ones with which Haskalah literature generally concerned itself. He influenced not only Abraham *Goldfaden but also Sholem Yankev *Abramovitsh and later writers. In his play, *Serkele*, he portrays an ambitious woman who pursues wealth and power and gives a vivid picture of the local environment and customs. He starkly outlines the foibles and passions of the fledgling urban Jewish bourgeoisie, foreshadowing his great heir in this genre, Isaac Bashevis *Singer. He also wrote two unfinished plays: *Der Feter fun Amerika* ("The American Uncle") and *Di Freylekhe Yungelayt* ("The Jolly Young People").

Because of censorship, the only piece to appear in his lifetime was a short Hebrew poem (1837); but some of his fables and poems were posthumously published. His son, W. Ettinger, a well-known Russian publisher, brought out his *Mesholim* in St. Petersburg (1889, 1890²). The definitive edition of his works, *Ale Ksovim fun Dr. Shloyme Ettinger* ("Collected Works of Dr. Shloyme Ettinger"), in two volumes, edited by Max Weinreich, was published in Vilna in 1925; and his *Geklibene Verk* ("Selected Works"), edited by Max Erik, appeared in Kiev in 1935. In 1957 another selection, *Oysgeklibene Shriften* edited by S. Rollanski (Rozhansky), was published in Buenos Aires.

BIBLIOGRAPHY: J. Leftwich, *The Golden Peacock* (1961), 693f.; Bloch, in: *Journal of Jewish Bibliography*, 1 (1938), 21f.; Rejzen, *Leksikon*, 2 (1927), 725–39; M. Weinreich, *Bilder fun der Yidisher Literatur-Geshikhte* (1928), 280–91; S. Niger, *Yiddish Literature in the Past Two Hundred Years* 3 (1952), 174–6; I. Zinberg, *Geshikhte fun der Literatur bay Yidn*, 8:2 (1937), 233–48.

[Elias Schulman / Jack S. Berger (2nd ed.)]

ETTINGHAUSEN, RICHARD (1906–1979), historian of Islamic art. Ettinghausen was born in Germany and studied in Frankfurt, where he received his doctorate in Islamic studies in 1931, from which time he devoted himself to the study of, and research into, Islamic art. In 1934 he immigrated to the United States. His extensive contributions to Islamic art were in academic teaching, museum activities, and scholarly publications. From 1934 to 1937 he was research associate of the American Institute of Persian Art and Archaeology and from 1938 to 1949 he taught Islamic art at the University of Michigan, Ann Arbor. In 1944, he also began to work in the Near Eastern Section of the Freer Gallery of Art at the Smithsonian Institution, where he acted as head curator from 1961 to 1967. Continuing to combine university and museum work, he taught at the Institute of Fine Arts at New York University from 1961, was appointed Hagop Kevorkian Professor of Islamic Art in 1967, and consultative chairman of the Islamic Department of the Metropolitan Museum of Art in New York in 1969, at the same time acting as trustee of various galleries and museums, such as the Phillips Gallery and the Textile Museum, Washington, and was the main promoter of the L.A. Mayer Memorial Institute, dedicated to Islamic art, opened in 1974 in Jerusalem.

He was the author of numerous scholarly publications, covering a very wide range of subjects, but particularly studies dedicated to Islamic painting. These are again extremely varied with much attention paid to Persian, Turkish, Muslim, Indian, and of course Arab, painting. They include studies in Muslim iconography – *The Unicorn* (1950), *Paintings of the Sultans and Emperors of India in American Collections* (1961), *Persian Paintings in the Bernard Berenson Collection* (1961), and *Arab Painting* (1962). He initiated and organized many exhibitions which dealt with problems of Islamic art for which he compiled the catalogs. He was the editor of *Ars Islamica*, the first periodical dedicated to Islamic arts (1938–50); he then became a member of the editorial board of *Ars Orientalis* (1954–67), as well as of *Artibus Asiae*; he was co-editor of *Kunst des Orients*.

[Miriam Rosen-Ayalon]

ETTLINGEN, town in Baden, Germany. The Jews living there at the time of the *Black Death, 1348–49, suffered from persecution. At assemblies of the regional Estates held in 1588, 1589, and 1591, the representatives of Ettlingen pressed for the expulsion of the Jews from the city. There were two Jewish families living in Ettlingen in 1683. In 1729 a "protected" Jew, Mayer (originally from Malsch), had to leave his home near the castle and was permitted to build a house of medium size near the town square. The Jews of Ettlingen paid a protection tax of 16 florins in the 18th century, which was reduced to 8 florins in 1812. A prayer hall was opened in 1812 and a synagogue in 1849; it was replaced by a building in Renaissance style in 1889. The community numbered 33 in 1825 and 70 in 1900. In 1933 there were 48 Jews in the city, joined later by 31 from other locales. About two-thirds emigrated or left for other German cities during the Nazi era and the rest were deported. On Nov. 10, 1939, the synagogue was demolished.

R. Jacob *Ettlinger and other Jews bearing the name probably originated from Ettlingen.

BIBLIOGRAPHY: *Fuehrer durch die juedische Wohlfahrtspflege* (1932/33), 348; Germ Jud, 2 (1968), 232–3; F.M. Hundsnurscher and G. Taddey, *Die juedischen Gemeinden in Baden* (1967), index.

ETTLINGER, JACOB (1798–1871), German rabbi and champion of neo-Orthodoxy. After receiving preliminary instruction from his father, Aaron Ettlinger, *Klausrabbiner*, a local rabbi in Karlsruhe, Jacob continued his studies under three eminent rabbis: Asher Wallerstein, Abraham Bing, and Wolf Hamburger. He was one of the first Jews admitted to the University of Wuerzburg, but was forced to leave because of an antisemitic outbreak. In 1826, he was appointed *Kreisrabbiner* ("district rabbi") for the districts of Ladenburg and Ingolstadt and settled in Mannheim, where he founded a yeshivah that attracted numerous students including Samson Raphael *Hirsch. Ten years later, he was appointed chief rabbi of Altona, a post which he retained until his death. The yeshivah which he established in that city was attended by Israel (Azriel) *Hildesheimer.

An unswerving traditionalist, Ettlinger reacted to the conference of Reform rabbis in Brunswick (1844) by rallying many of his colleagues in protest against what they considered the gravest threat to Judaism's future. A notable result of this move was Ettlinger's decision to publish works reflecting the stand of Jewish Orthodoxy, among them his pamphlet, *Shelomei Emunei Yisrael*, and *Der Zionswaechter*, a journal of traditionalist thought, with a Hebrew supplement, *Shomer Ẓiyyon ha-Ne'eman*, edited by S.J. Enoch (1845). He was the last rabbi to preside over the Altona *bet din* before its jurisdiction in civil matters was revoked by the Danish authorities in 1863. In the following year, Denmark ceded Altona with Schleswig-Holstein to Prussia and Ettlinger made such a favorable impression on the Prussian king, William, during his visit to Altona in 1865, that the rights previously enjoyed by the Jewish community under the Danes were reconfirmed by royal decree. An outstanding halakhist, Ettlinger published the following works (all printed at Altona, unless otherwise indicated): *Bikkurei Ya'akov*, on the laws concerning the festival of Tabernacles (1836; 2nd ed. with the addition *Tosefot Bikkurim*, 1858); *Arukh la-Ner*, glosses on various talmudic treatises (on *Yevamot* 1850; 2nd ed. Piotrkow 1914; on *Makkot* and *Keritot* 1855; on *Sukkah* 1858; on *Niddah* 1864; on *Rosh ha-Shanah* and *Sanhedrin*, Warsaw, 1873); *Binyan Ẓiyyon*, responsa (1868), and its sequel, *She'elot u-Teshuvot Binyan Ẓiyyon ha-Hadashot* (Vilna, 1874); *Minḥat Ani*, homilies (1874; 2nd ed. Frankfurt, 1924) and a number of sermons in German. A collection of his articles and addresses was published by L.M. Bamberger (Schildberg, 1899). Through Hirsch and Hildesheimer, Ettlinger exerted an incalculable influence on the course of neo-Orthodoxy in Germany. His great modesty is reflected in his will which stipulates that only the barest details be inscribed on his tombstone.

BIBLIOGRAPHY: A. Posner and E. Freimann, in: L. Jung (ed.), *Guardians of our Heritage* (1958).

[Shlomo Eidelberg]

ETTLINGER, MARION (1949–), U.S. photographer. Ettlinger, the daughter of German Jews who fled the Nazis in December 1938, grew up in Queens, N.Y., and was educated at Cooper Union in Manhattan, where she studied painting. She discovered photography then but it was not until 1983, when she got an assignment from *Esquire* magazine, that she found her calling and her career. *Esquire*, celebrating its 50th birthday, asked Ettlinger to photograph authors who had contributed to a special issue of the magazine. Her photograph of the writer Truman Capote, in striking profile, proved memorable, and in more than 20 years Ettlinger photographed more than 600 authors for book jackets. She worked exclusively in black and white, using only natural light. More than 200 of her author photos were collected in *Author Photo: Portraits, 1983–2002*, a coffee-table volume that includes well-known writers as well as her own image. Previously, authors often tended to appear on the covers of their books in relaxed, un-self-conscious moods and settings. But Ettlinger made portraits for the book jackets, the authors posed and orchestrated as objects in their own right, and her name entered the language as a verb. To be "Ettlingered," according to an article in the *New York Times*, means to have imparted to you an aura of distinction and renown. Publishers considered these photos as assets to help sell their books.

[Stewart Kampel (2nd ed.)]

ETZIONI, AMITAI WERNER (1929–), sociologist. Etzioni was born in Cologne, West Germany, but immigrated at an early age to Ereẓ Israel, studying at the Hebrew University and later at the University of California at Berkeley, where he received his doctorate in sociology in 1958. He was on the faculty of Columbia University from 1958, and chairman of the department of sociology from 1969. From 1979 to 1980 he served as senior adviser to the White House and in the latter year was University Professor at George Washington University. In 1987–89, he served as the Thomas Henry Carroll Ford Foundation Professor at the Harvard Business School. In 1989–90 he was the founding president of the International Society for the Advancement of Socio-Economics, and in 1990 he founded the Communitarian Network, a nonprofit, nonpartisan organization dedicated to shoring up the moral, social, and political foundations of society. He was the editor of *The Responsive Community: Rights and Responsibilities*, the organization's quarterly journal, from 1991 to 2004. Etzioni also served as the president of the American Sociological Association in 1994–95. His primary areas of interest are political sociology and organizational analysis. Etzioni is a member of the Science Information Council of the National Science Foundation and a member of the Social Problems Research Committee of the National Institute of Mental Health, as well as a consultant to many organizations, including the President's Advisory Committee on Campus Unrest and Change.

He contributed over 80 articles to various professional journals and books and wrote numerous books, of which the most important is *The Active Society: A Theory of Societal and*

Political Processes (1968). Among the others are *A Diary of a Commando Soldier* (1952), *The Moon-Doogle: Domestic and International Implications of the Space Race* (1964), *Political Unification: A Comparative Study of Leaders and Forces* (1965), *Demonstration Democracy* (1971), *The Moral Dimension: Toward a New Economics* (1988), *The Spirit of Community* (1993), *The New Golden Rule* (1996), *The Limits of Privacy* (1999), *The Monochrome Society* (2001), *My Brother's Keeper: A Memoir and a Message* (2003), and *From Empire to Community: A New Approach to International Relations* (2004).

Etzioni has been the recipient of a Guggenheim Fellowship and the William Mosher Award for the most distinguished academic article in the *Public Administration Review* in 1967. In 2001 he was named one of the top 100 American intellectuals. At the same year he was awarded the John P. McGovern Award in Behavioral Sciences as well as the Officer's Cross of the Order of Merit of the Federal Republic of Germany. He was also the recipient of the Seventh James Wilbur Award for Extraordinary Contributions to the Appreciation and Advancement of Human Values by the Conference on Value Inquiry as well as the Sociological Practice Association's Outstanding Contribution Award.

[Jacob Jay Lindenthal]

EUCHEL, ISAAC ABRAHAM (1756–1804), Hebrew author, Bible commentator, and one of the leaders of the *Haskalah in Germany. Born in Copenhagen, Euchel, having received a traditional education, moved in 1773 to Koenigsberg, where he earned his living as a tutor in the home of the wealthy *Friedlaender family. In 1781 he attended Kant's lectures at the University of Koenigsberg. He was recommended for a lectureship in Hebrew at the university but was rejected because he was Jewish. In 1787, Euchel moved to Berlin, where he managed the printing press of the Juedische Freischule (Ḥinnukh Ne'arim School). Later he worked as a bookkeeper for a commercial firm.

Euchel's literary and communal activity began in 1782 (in Koenigsberg) with the publication of his pamphlet *Sefat Emet*, in which he called for the establishment of a school in Koenigsberg, based on the principles of the Enlightenment. In 1782 he was one of the founders of *Ḥevrat Doreshei Leshon Ever* (The Society of Advocates of the Hebrew Language), which started to publish *Ha-Me'assef*, and, with Menahem Mendel Breslau, published *Naḥal ha-Besor*, the prospectus of *Ha-Me'assef*. He served as one of the editors of *Ha-Me'assef* as long as he was in Koenigsberg (till 1790), and published several articles in that periodical, including the first monograph on Moses Mendelssohn, entitled *Toledot Rabbenu he-Ḥakham Moshe ben Menaḥem* (published in book form in Berlin, 1789). He also prepared a free translation of the prayer book into German (1786) and wrote a commentary on Proverbs, with a German translation in Hebrew characters (Berlin, 1790). In addition, he is credited with the authorship of *Iggerot Meshullam Ben Uriyyah ha-Eshtemo'i* which started to appear in *Ha-Me'assef* in the autumn of 1789, and which seemed in some respects to imitate Montesquieu's *Persian Letters*. In 1797 he published in Breslau a pamphlet (German in Hebrew characters) entitled *Ist nach dem juedischen Gesetze das Uebernachten der Todten wirklieh verboten?* To combat the influence of the Orthodox, Euchel wrote (about 1792) a satirical comedy in colloquial Yiddish, called *Reb Henekh, Oder Vos Tut Men Damit*. No copies are extant of this edition, which apparently was published after Euchel's death. A new edition in Gothic characters (*Reb Henoch; oder Was thut men damit*) appeared in Berlin in 1846; and in 1933, Z. Rejzen republished it in his *Arkhiv far der Geshikhte fun Yidishen Teater un Drama*, from the manuscript preserved in the Rosenthaliana library in Amsterdam. The play, sharply satirical, especially in the portrayal of the Orthodox, reflects the relations between Jews and non-Jews in Prussia during the period of the struggle for emancipation.

BIBLIOGRAPHY: Klausner, Sifrut, 1 (1952^2), 131–43; M. Erik, *Di Komedies fun der Berliner Oyfklerung* (1933), 42–61; J.L. Landau, *Short Lectures on Modern Hebrew Literature* (1938^2), index; N. Slouschz, *Renascence of Hebrew Literature* (1909), 41.

[Gedalyah Elkoshi]

°**EUGENIUS**, name of four popes. They include the following:

EUGENIUS III (1145–53). At the time of Eugenius' solemn entry into Rome in 1145, the Jews of the city formed part of the procession which welcomed him. Probably as a result of the anti-Jewish persecutions following the preaching of the Second Crusade, Eugenius renewed the *Sicut Judaeis*, Pope Calixtus II's bull of protection for the Jews (see papal *bulls). In doing this, he may have acted on the advice of *Bernard of Clairvaux, his former teacher, with whom he maintained close relations. In one of a series of letters to Pope Eugenius written between 1149 and 1152, Bernard pointed out that the concern of the pope should also go out to the Jews.

EUGENIUS IV (1431–47). The greater part of his reign was especially favorable for the Jews. In 1432, soon after his ascent to the papal throne, Eugenius IV ratified the privileges of the Jewish communities of Lombardy, the Marches, and Sardinia. He retained his predecessor's Jewish personal physician, Elia di Sabato, and in 1433 confirmed his freedom of the city and his salary. On Feb. 6, 1434, he assured the German Jewish communities of his protection, particularly against attempts at forced conversion, any interference with the practice of their religion, and desecration of their cemeteries. Eugenius ordered the lay and ecclesiastical authorities to assist the Jewish communities in the payment of their taxes.

The change in his attitude probably followed on the deliberations of the Council of Basle (1431–37), which also adopted a severe attitude toward Christian heresies. In order not to appear dilatory in his strictness toward the Jews, in 1442 Eugenius forbade Christians in Leon and Castile to have any relationships with them as maids or menservants. The Jews were forbidden to erect any new synagogues, to lend money on interest, and to work on Sundays and Christian holidays;

they were to be excluded from public office and could not testify against Christians. The provisions of this bull were soon extended to Italy, where the Jews were also prohibited from studying any book but the Pentateuch. As a result many Jews left the Papal States, taking refuge especially in Mantua, where the ruler, Giovanni Francesco Gonzaga, offered them fairly liberal conditions. After large sums of money had changed hands, the restrictive measures were rescinded in December 1443. From then on, Eugenius once more extended his protection to the Jews. Only a few days before his death, he issued a bull against forced baptisms in Spain.

BIBLIOGRAPHY: Vogelstein-Rieger, 1 (1895), 222–3; 2 (1896), 9–13; Milano, Italia, 154–6; Roth, Italy, 162–4 and passim; J. Gill, *Eugenius IV* (Eng., 1961); M.A. Dimier, in: *Dictionnaire d'histoire et de géographie ecclesiastiques*, 15 (1963), 1349ff.; S. Grayzel, *Church and the Jews...* (1966^2), 76.

[Bernhard Blumenkranz]

°**EUHEMERUS** (fourth century B.C.E.), writer. In his *Hiera Anagraphe* ("Sacred History"), Euhemerus suggested that the gods had originally been benefactors of mankind who were subsequently worshipped because of their great deeds. Josephus cites him as establishing the antiquity of the Jews (Apion, 1:216).

EULAU, HEINZ (1915–2004), U.S. political scientist. Born in Offenbach, Germany, Eulau went to the U.S. as a young man in 1935. He earned his bachelor's, master's, and doctoral degrees in political science from the University of California-Berkeley from 1937 to 1941. During 1946–47 he was assistant editor of the *New Republic* and then taught at Antioch College. He worked in the Library of Congress in Washington and later in the Department of Justice, and in 1958 became professor of political science at Stanford University and served as chair from 1969–74 and 1981–84. Eulau was one of the leading exponents of the behaviorist trend in American political science, which attempted to transform the study of political science into a scientifically oriented discipline based on empirical research and a wide interdisciplinary frame of reference. A path-breaking scholar in the field of legislative research, he specialized in the theory and practice of political representation and electoral behavior. The behavioral movement, which he brought to Stanford, introduced psychology and sociology to study the linkages between political institutions and citizens. He was also instrumental in creating a new field of research focusing on the systematic quantitative analysis of citizens' attitudes and choices. His thesis was set out in his work *The Behavioral Persuasion in Politics* (1963), which followed *Political Behavior* (1956) and *Legislative Behavior* (1959), both of which he co-authored with J.C. Wahlke. In 1961 he became general editor of the *International Yearbook of Political Behavior Research* and was also associate editor for political science of the *International Encyclopaedia of the Social Sciences* (1968).

Eulau was president of the American Political Science Association from 1971 to 1972. In 1976, he helped found *Legislative Studies Quarterly*, a journal published at the University of Iowa. He retired from Stanford in 1986 but remained active as the William Bennett Munro Professor Emeritus of Political Science. He also wrote *The Legislative System* (1962), *Class and Party in the Eisenhower Years* (1962), *Lawyers in Politics* (1964), *Political Science* (1969), *Labyrinths of Democracy* (with K. Prewitt, 1973), *Technology and Civility* (1977), *The Politics of Representation* (1978), *Politics, Self and Society* (1986), and *Micro-Macro Dilemmas in Political Science* (1996). In 1998, he took a light-hearted swipe at university life in *The Politics of Academic Culture: Foibles, Fables and Facts,* and in 2001 co-authored a family history, *The Mishpokhe from Eulau-Jilove.*

In 1986, the American Political Science Association established the Heinz Eulau Award to honor his contributions to political science. In 2002, the Heinz Eulau Political Behavior Fellowship was established by the Stanford Institute for the Quantitative Study of Society. In 1999 he was awarded the Warren E. Miller Award for meritorious service to the social sciences, one of the country's highest honors in the social sciences.

His wife, CLEO MISHKIN EULAU (1923–2004), died five days after her husband. She was the Stanford University adjunct clinical professor in the department of psychiatry and behavioral sciences. In 1994, the Cleo Eulau Center was founded as a service and study center dedicated to developing innovative solutions to helping at-risk children and teens. In 2002, she was the first woman and first non-psychiatrist to receive the Lifetime Achievement Award from Stanford's department of psychiatry.

[Edwin Emanuel Gutmann / Ruth Beloff (2nd ed.)]

EULENBURG, ERNST (1847–1926), music publisher. The Musikverlag Eulenburg, founded by Eulenburg in Leipzig in 1874, at first published mainly educational literature, but was gradually extended to include scores and especially miniature scores of orchestral and chamber music. His son KURT transferred the firm to London in 1939. He enlarged the number of miniature scores and also increased the output of modern music. In 1957 the shares of the Eulenburg Edition were taken over by Schott of London.

EULENBURG, ISAAC BEN ABRAHAM MOSES ISRAEL (d. 1657), rabbi and author, also known as Isaac Przybyslawa. Isaac's father, who died in 1605, was the cantor and scribe of the old synagogue of Cracow. Isaac studied under Joel *Sirkes and from 1640 to 1647 served as *dayyan* and preacher in Cracow. Moses Jekuthiel Kaufman, in *Leḥem ha-Panim*, quotes one of his halakhic decisions given during his stay in Cracow. In 1648 Isaac became rabbi of Lissa and, finally, of Leipnik (Moravia), where he died. He is incorrectly held by some to have occupied a rabbinical position in Brest-Litovsk (Brisk), Lithuania, and in Nikolsburg. Eulenburg's novellae on the Shulḥan Arukh, *Even ha-Ezer* and *Ḥoshen Mishpat*, a work on marriage and divorce, and his responsa, have remained in manuscript. He is sometimes identified with the "Isaac ha-Darshan" frequently referred to by Michael Jospes in his *Birkat ha-Mayim* (1861), and has also been identified by several scholars (Zunz and Landshut) with Isaac b. Abraham Moses Israel, the author of a *seliḥah* bewailing the massacre of the Jews of Podolia and Ukraine in 1648–49. Lewin, however, maintains the author to have been a rabbi of Posen who bore the same name.

BIBLIOGRAPHY: Landshuth, Ammudet, xiii–xv, no. 7; H.N. Dembitzer, *Kelilat Yofi*, 2 (1893), 97b; S. Buber, *Anshei Shem* (1895), 114, no. 271; Wettstein, in: *Sefer ha-Yovel… N. Sokolow* (1904), 297f., no. 21; L. Lewin, *Geschichte der Juden in Lissa* (1904), 173f., 372f. (no. 18), 378.

[Itzhak Alfassi]

EUNUCH. The Hebrew word *sārīs* (Heb. סָרִיס), a loanword from Akkadian, has two meanings in the Bible: the first and most common is "eunuch" (e.g. II Kings 8:6; 9:32; 20:18 (= Isa. 39:7); Isa. 56:3–5; and Jer. 39:7) (*ʾīš sārīs* and all the instances in the Book of Esther (2:3 passim)); and second, a government official or officer, not necessarily a eunuch (I Sam. 8:14–15; I Kings 22:9). Inasmuch as eunuchs in some cultures were married, it is not impossible that Potiphar (Gen. 37:36; 39:1) was a eunuch, which could account for the notorious actions of his wife (Tadmor, apud Zevit in Bibliography). Daniel and his companions, though not specifically called "eunuchs," are supervised by the chief of the eunuchs (Dan. 1:3, 7, 10, 18), in apparent fulfillment of the prophecy (II Kgs. 20:18 = Isa. 39:7) that some of Hezekiah's offspring would be eunuchs in the palace of the king of Babylonia. As was the case in Assyria (see Grayson in Bibliography, 98), eunuchs could rise to high positions, as shown by the place they occupy in the list in Jeremiah 29:2, where the hierarchical order of the captives is given as the king, his mother, the *sarisim*, the *sarim* ("leaders"), and the craftsmen (but cf. II Kings 24:12, 15). The Akkadian *ša rēši*, elliptical for *ša rēš šarri izuzzū*, "the one who stands by the head of the king," was pronounced *sa rēsi* in Middle and Late Assyrian, resulting in the Hebrew and Aramaic forms with *samekh*. There are clear attestations of Akkadian *ša rēši* in the meaning "eunuch." In court circles the *ša rēši* is sometimes opposed to *ša ziqni*, "the one of the beard." Middle Assyrian royal ordinances regulating women's quarters prescribed examination of the *ša rēši* to assure his status of eunuch, and subsequent castration if he failed the examination. Being turned into a *ša rēši* (*ana ša rēšēn turrû*) was a punishment for adultery in the Middle Assyrian laws (A15) and for sodomy (A20). There are attestations of *ša rēši* that do not demand the sense "eunuch" (See CAD R, 289–97) and that is true for the Hebrew loan as well. The law excluding eunuchs from the Israelite community (Deut. 23:2) describes the eunuch as the one with crushed testicles (the normal form of childhood castration) rather than by the ambivalent term *sārīs*. II Kings 18:17 mentions *Rab-saris* (mistakenly treated by the Hebrew writer as a proper name) together with other high-ranking officials in the Assyrian kingdom. The reference to *Rab-saris* in Jeremiah 39:3, 13 testifies to the existence of this class in the Neo-Babylonian kingdom as well. The date of a bilingual Akkadian-Aramaic inscription from Nineveh is indicated by the *limmu* (i.e., eponym) of a *rab ša rēši*. Since the office of *limmu* was held only by high officials, it is evident that the office of *Rab-saris* was of high rank. Isaiah 56:3–5, comforts the eunuchs who keep the Sabbath and observe the covenant; they are promised "a *yad*, either a memorial stele (Talmon) or a share (Japhet) in the temple precincts, and a name, better than sons and daughters."

BIBLIOGRAPHY: M. Springling, in: AJSLL, 49 (1932), 53–54; E. Weidner, in: AFO, 17 (1955–56), 264–5; H.G. Gueterbock, in: *Oriens*, 10 (1957), 361; A. Goetze, in: *Journal of Cuneiform Studies*, 13 (1959), 66; M. and H. Tadmor, in: BIES, 31 (1967), 77–78. **ADD. BIBLIOGRAPHY:** S. Talmon, in: H. Beinart and S. Loewenstamm (eds.), *Studies… Cassuto*, 1987, 137–41; S. Japhet, in: MAARAV, 8 (FS Gevirtz; 1992), 65–80; M. Cogan and H. Tadmor, *II Kings* (1988), 112; A.K. Grayson, in: M. Dietrich and O. Loretz (eds.), *Von Alten Orient zum Alten Testament FS von Soden* (1995), 85–97; H. Tadmor, in: Z. Zevit et al. (eds.), *Solving Riddles… Studies J.C. Greenfield* (1995), 317–25; idem, in: S. Parpola and R. Whiting (eds.), *Papers XLVII Recontre Assyriologique Internationale* (2002), 1–9; R. Mattila, *The King's Magnates* (2000), 61–76, 163–64; N. Fox, *In the Service of the King* (2000), 196–203; P. Mankowski, *Akkadian Loanwords in Biblical Hebrew* (2000), 123–25; COS 2, 355.

[S. David Sperling (2nd ed.)]

EUPHEMISM AND DYSPHEMISM.

Euphemism

Euphemism is the substitution of an agreeable or inoffensive word or term for one that is indelicate, blasphemous, or taboo. Various types of euphemisms are found in the Bible, including (1) avoidance of direct implication of the speaker – "Should you gouge out these men's eyes" rather than "our eyes" (Num. 16:14; similarly, I Sam. 29:4); (2) avoidance of direct implication in an oath – "God do so to the enemies of David" rather than "my enemies," David being the speaker (I Sam. 25:22; similarly, I Sam. 20:16); (3) avoidance of the expression "to die": several different euphemistic expressions are employed, e.g., (a) "I am about to go the way of all the earth" (I Kings 2:2); (b) "I shall go the way whence I shall not return" (Job 16:22); (c) "Enoch walked with God; then he was no more, for God took him" (Gen. 5:24; cf. II Kings 2:3); and (d) "They shall sleep a perpetual sleep and not wake" (Jer. 51:39, 57); (4) avoidance of "cursing" (or rather, "blaspheming") God: the Hebrew verb *barakh* ברך ("bless" or "praise") is employed (I Kings 21:10, 13; Job 1:5, 11; 2:5, 9), or, instead of the verb, the object is changed from "YHWH" to "the enemies of YHWH" (II Sam. 12:14); and (5) avoidance of indelicate and offensive expressions: (a) the expression "to cover one's legs" (Heb. *hasekh raglayim*) is substituted for "to defecate" (Judg. 3:24; I Sam. 24:3); "the bread he eats" (Gen. 39:6) for "the woman with whom he has sexual relations" (cf. Prov. 30:20); (b) the following are changed by the *keri* (*qeri*) of the masoretic text: the verb *shagal* ("to rape") to *shakhav* (Deut. 28:30; Isa. 13:16; Jer. 3:2; Zech. 14:2); *ʿafolim* ("hemorrhoids") to *teḥorim* (Deut. 28:27; I Sam. 5:6, 9, 12; 6:4, 5); *ḥare(ʾe)hem* ("their excrement") to *ẓoʾatam* (II Kings 18:27;

Isa. 36:12; cf. also II Kings 10:27 where *Le-maḥaraʾot* is read *le-moẓaʾot*); and *sheineihem* ("their urine") to *memei ragleihem* (II Kings 18:27; Isa. 36:12).

Lists of euphemistic expressions in the Bible are found in early tannaitic collections of halakhic Midrash. Eleven examples are given in the *Mekhilta* (Shirah 6) and seven in the *Sifrei* (Num. 84). The technical term employed is *kinnah ha-katuv*, "Scripture used a euphemistic expression." Later collections of Midrash (Tanḥ. Be-Shalah 16; Gen. R. 49:7; Ex. R. 13:1) employed the phrase **tikkun soferim* ("emendation of the scribes") and record additional examples of this phenomenon. Though the difference in terminology reflects two different schools of thought, namely those holding that the Bible itself originally employed euphemistic expressions and those holding that the change was first made by the *soferim*, both agree that the changes were made in deference to the honor of the Lord (Lieberman). Examples of one such list follow: (1) "Abraham remained standing before the Lord" for "The Lord remained standing before Abraham" (Gen. 18:22); (2) "For his sons were blaspheming themselves" for "blaspheming God" (I Sam. 3:13); (3) "But my people have changed their glory for that which does not profit" for "My glory" (Jer. 2:11); (4) "Are you not from everlasting, O Lord my God, my Holy One? We shall not die" for "You shall not die" (Hab. 1:12); and (5) "For he who touches you touches the apple of his eye" for "my eye" (Zech. 2:12). Another kind of substitution resulting from religious scruples is found in the change of the vocalization of the verb *raʾah* (ראה; "to see") from the active to the passive, "to be seen" (Luzzatto). It is used when referring to the three appointed times during the year that the Israelite was obliged to make a pilgrimage to Jerusalem in order "to see," i.e., to be in the presence of God (e.g., Ex. 23:15; 34:20, 23; Deut. 16:16).

Dysphemism

Dysphemism is the substitution of an offensive or disparaging term for an inoffensive one. The biblical examples pertain to idolatry: (1) *ʾElil* ("idol"), whose etymology is uncertain (it may be the diminutive of *ʾel* ("god") or derived from *ʾal* ("non-entity")), means worthlessness, nothingness (e.g., Jer. 14:14; Job 13:4); (2) *shikkuẓ* ("abomination") is found in the expression, "Chemosh, the abomination of Moab and Molech, the abomination of the Ammonites" (I Kings 11:7; cf. also II Kings 23:13; cf. also the dysphemistic use of *shikkuẓ meshomem* ("abomination of desolation"; e.g., Dan. 11:31)). The plurals *shikkuzim* (e.g., Deut. 29:16; II Kings 23:24) and *gillulim* (literally, "dung-pellets"; "fetishes"; e.g., Lev. 26:30), and *toʿevah* ("abomination"; e.g., II Kings 23:13, "Milcom, the abomination of the Ammonites"), are comparable terms; (3) the word *boshet* ("shame") is substituted for *baʿal* ("lord"; originally a title for the God of Israel, but later interpreted as the name of the Canaanite god, Baal, in several personal names: the names of Saul's son, Eshbaal (I Chron. 8:33; 9:39), and grandson (Jonathan's son), Merib-Baal (I Chron. 8:34; 9:40), are changed to Ish-Bosheth (II Sam. 2:8) and Mephibosheth (II Sam. 4:4); the name of the "judge" Jerubbaal (Gideon; Judg. 6:32) later appears as Jerubbesheth (II Sam. 11:21)); (4) the vocalization of "Ashtoreth, the goddess of the Sidonites" may be a dysphemism alluding to *boshet*, "shame" (e.g., I Kings 11:5, 33), Ashtoreth for Ashtereth (cf. Gr. Astarte).

A. Geiger thought the same was true of the pointing of *Molech, the god of the Ammonites (e.g., I Kings 11:7), but since O. Eissfeldt's study of this term, the word *molekh*, which may have originally meant "vow" or "sacrifice," and its pointing, which may be original to a West Semitic dialect, have been subject to debate. Some scholars have also assumed a similar pointing for the Hebrew word, *tofet*, *tefet* (cf. Gr. Thappeth, Thapheth, Tapheth). The substitution of the place name Beth-Aven ("house of iniquity") for Beth-El ("house of God"; Hos. 4:15; 5:8) is also a kind of dysphemism which was employed because of the idolatrous worship in that place.

[Shalom M. Paul]

In the Talmud

Euphemisms are extensively used in the Talmud and Midrash. The recourse to them is based upon various considerations. The first is the insistence on the need for pure and refined speech and the avoidance of all gross and vulgar expressions. This is explicitly stated in the Talmud: "One should not utter a gross expression" and examples are given of the manner in which the Bible itself employs circumlocutions to avoid the use of the word "unclean." Actual examples are given: two disciples of Rav were discussing how the discourse in the academy had exhausted them. One of them said that he was as exhausted as a pig ("*davar aḥer*," see later), while the other said "as a kid." Rav refused to speak to the former. Similarly it is stated that Hillel foretold of Johanan b. Zakkai (or Judah ha-Nasi of R. Johanan) that he would be an outstanding teacher in Israel because, instead of saying, as his colleague did, "we may gather olives in uncleanness," he said "we may not gather olives in cleanness," and the forecast was fulfilled (Pes. 3b). The rabbis even regard the use of the phrase "eating bread" in Genesis 39:6 (Gen. R. 86:6) and in Exodus 2:20 (Tanḥ. 1:11) as a euphemism for sexual intercourse (that they are probably right with regard to the former seems clear from a comparison between Gen. 39:6 and 9).

This delicacy is particularly evident in the euphemisms used for the privy parts of the body and their functions. The male genital organ is referred to as "the organ" (*ever*: BM 84a) and the female as "that place" (Nid. 20a). The toilet is called "the house of water" (Meg. 3:2) or "the house of the chair" (Tam. 1:1; Ber. 25a). Urine is called "the water of the feet" (Ker. 6a) or "the jet" (*silon*: Ber. 25a) and defecation "having need of his apertures" (Git. 70a) or "turning aside" (*ponim*: Toh. 10:2; *nifneh*: Ber. 62a). Sexual intercourse is "the usage of the bed" (*tashmish ha-mittah*: Yoma 8:1) or simply *tashmish* (Ket. 65b) and so on.

A special euphemism is the use of the phrase *davar aḥer* ("another thing") for anything repulsive. It is generally used for the *pig, but is variously employed also for leprosy (Pes.

76b, 112b), sexual intercourse (Ber. 8b), immorality (Ket. 7:5), and idolatry (Men. 13:10; Shab. 17b).

The second reason for euphemisms is in order to avoid phrases which would wound susceptibilities. The most common euphemism in this category is the phrase *sagi nahor* ("with excess of light," cf. T. Gray on Milton's blindness "but blasted with excess of light") for a blind man (Ber. 56a; TJ, Pe'ah 8:9, 21b) and in fact it is regarded as so characteristic that a euphemism is called "*sagi nahor* language" (TJ, Pe'ah 5:5, 19a; Lev. R. 34:13). Various euphemisms such as "departed" (*niftar:* BB 16b), "his soul rested" (*naḥ nafsho:* MK 25a/b; Ket., 104a), and "left life for the living" (*shavak ḥayyim le-kol ḥai*) are used for death, and a cemetery is called "the house of life" (cf. Eccles. 12:5).

The third reason is based on the injunction "a man should not open his mouth to Satan" (Ber. 19a), i.e., one should not invite misfortune by ominous statements. The rabbis detect such a euphemism in the use of the third person "and it [the people of Israel] shall go up from the land" (Ex. 1:10). According to the Talmud Pharaoh actually meant to say "and we shall [be forced to] go up from the land," and they will possess it, "but it is like a man who curses himself and hangs the curse on someone else" (Sot. 11a). To this category belongs the use of the phrase "the enemies of Israel" for Israel when it speaks of calamity overtaking the Jewish people (Suk. 29a; Lev. R. 25:1) or "the enemies of the Sages" (Ta'an. 7a) and the forecast of calamities is couched in the words "and every trouble which shall *not* come on Israel" (Pes. 117a).

Dysphemisms or cacophysms are usually employed with regard to idolatry and idolatrous sites and practices. The Talmud (Av. Zar. 2a) discusses whether the word *ed* used for the heathen festival (Av. Zar. 1:1) should be written correctly with an *ayyin* ("testimony") or with an *alef* ("calamity") – a dysphemism. Idolatrous worship is called *tumah* ("uncleanness": Tosef. Av. Zar. 7:2), the festive day "a day of repulsion" (*yom nibbul*: Gen. R. 87:7), and the verse "ye shall destroy their name" (Deut. 12:3) is interpreted as meaning that a dysphemistic name is to be given for its correct one: "where its name is Bet Galya ["the house of revelation"] it should be called Bet Karya ["the house of concealment"]; where its name is Ein Kol ["the all-seeing eye"] it should be called Ein Koẓ ["the eye of a thorn"]" (Av. Zar. 46a). It should, however, be pointed out that the rabbis are not always consistent in their avoidance of unpleasant expressions (cf. Lieberman).

During the Middle Ages and until recent times dysphemisms became common in Yiddish when referring to the non-Jewish equivalents of Jewish ceremonies and institutions. They usually took the form of a disparaging, assonantal word. Thus a non-Jewish wedding (*ḥatunnah*, Yid. *khasene*) was contemptuously referred to as a "*hashlereh*'" a word without meaning, and for *bet tefillah* ("a house of prayer"), *bet tiflah* ("a house of abomination") was used. Those phrases, however, belong to the common and even vulgar vernacular.

For euphemisms to avoid using the Divine Name see *Names of God. To those given there may be added a peculiar one which became current in the Middle Ages, the *Kiveyakhol* ("as though to say").

BIBLIOGRAPHY: IN THE BIBLE: A. Geiger, *Ha-Mikra ve-Targumav* (1959), 172ff., 193ff., 199ff.; O. Eissfeldt, *Molk als Opferbegriff* (1935); S. Lieberman, *Hellenism in Jewish Palestine* (1950), 28–37; T. Noeldeke, *Neue Beitraege zur semitischen Sprachwissenschaft* (1910), 87ff.; H.C. Brichto, *The Problem of 'Curse' in the Hebrew Bible* (1963), 160ff., 170–2 (examples in Arabic). IN THE TALMUD: S. Lieberman, *Hellenism in Jewish Palestine* (1950), 34; E.Z. Melammed, in: *Sefer Zikkaron… Benjamin de Vries* (1968), 119ff. **ADD. BIBLIOGRAPHY:** B. Landsberger, "Das 'gute Wort,'" in: MAOG, 4 (1929), 294–321; M. Held, in: H. Beinart (ed.), *Studies in Bible …Cassuto* (1987), 104–14; D. Marcus, in: JANES, 11 (1979), 81–84; idem, JAOS, 103 (1980), 307–10; A. Cooper, in: JJS, 32 (1981), 56–64: M. Pope, ABD I, 720–25; G. Rendsburg, in: VT, 45 (1995), 513–23; S. Storch, *Euphemismen in der Hebräischen Bibel* (2000).

[Louis Isaac Rabinowitz]

EUPHRATES (Heb. פְּרָת; Dead Sea Scrolls *Pwrt;* from Akk. *Purattu* and Sumerian *Buranun*), the longest river (c. 1,700 mi., 2,700 km.) in Western Asia. In texts from the third millennium B.C.E. from Mari the river occurs as a deity. From its sources in northeast Turkey the river takes a southerly course into northern Syria, where it turns southeast and flows into the Persian Gulf after joining the *Tigris. According to Genesis 2:14, the Euphrates was one of the four branches of the river which rises in Eden to water the *garden of Eden. The Euphrates – also called "The River" or "The Great River" (see below) – forms the northern boundary of the ideal land promised to Israel (Gen. 15:18; Deut. 11:24; Josh. 1:4). The river is also referred to in Jeremiah 51:60–64, when Jeremiah instructed Seraiah upon reaching Babylon to read the prophecies of Jeremiah, bind them with a stone, and cast them into the Euphrates as a sign of the imminent destruction of that city. The Greek name *Mesopotamia, like the Hebrew Aram-Naharaim ("Aram of the [Two] Rivers"; e.g., Gen. 24:10), originally designated only the northwest corner of Mesopotamia which is bordered by the Euphrates on the north, west, and south. Later, however, the name was interpreted as the land between the Tigris and the Euphrates, i.e., Assyria and Babylonia. Since Mesopotamia is poor in rainfall, its inhabitants have always had to depend on the two rivers for irrigation. Water was brought to the individual fields through an elaborate system of canals. Naturally, a great many cities were built on or near the banks of the Euphrates; among the best known are Carchemish, Mari, Babylon, Erech, and Ur, known from biblical and cuneiform sources, and Pumbedita, Nehardea, Mata Meḥasya, and Sura, known from the Babylonian Talmud.

[Raphael Kutscher]

The term "beyond the river" (*ever ha-nahar*) denotes the region along the Euphrates, but the exact region referred to changes according to the geographical viewpoint or to the emerging geopolitical and administrative situation. The term "beyond the river" in Joshua 24:2–3 refers to the region east of the Euphrates, the place of origin of the patriarchs. In contrast, in I Kings 5:4 it describes the empire of Solomon from a viewpoint east of the Euphrates: from Tiphsah (missing in Septuagint and probably a gloss; Greek Thapsakos; modern Dibseh, on the western bend of the Euphrates) to Gaza. The area thus described is designated in Assyrian royal inscriptions and documents by the term *eber nāri*, i.e., Hebrew *ever ha-nahar*. This term in its wider geographical connotation is identical with the geopolitical Hebrew term. Thus Esarhaddon, king of Assyria, includes in the expression "the kings of northern Syria and *eber nāri*" the kings of Tyre, Judah, Edom, Moab, Gaza, Ashkelon, Ekron, Byblos, Arvad, Samsimuruna, Ammon, and Ashdod, and he sums them up as: "12 kings of the sea coast" (I.J. Gelb et al., *The Assyrian Dictionary*, 4 (1958), 8).

In Sumerian and Old Babylonian documents, the Euphrates River was already a geographical demarcation. In the Old Babylonian *Mari documents, two West Semitic terms describe the regions on either side of the river: *aḫarātum* ("the far land") and *aqdamātum* ("the near land"). The first is perhaps "west," and the second "east." At the time of the Persian Empire, a later, second official term for the area was *Athurā* (Assyria), but the original official-geographical term prevailed in Neo- and Late Babylonian documents and in contemporary Hebrew and Aramaic sources (Ezra 8:36 (Heb.); Ezra 4:10, 11 (Aram. *ʿabar naharah*)). The Perath mentioned in Jeremiah 13:4–7 is not the river Euphrates, but most probably Parah (cf. Josh. 18:23), near Anathoth (today ʿAin Farah).

[Pinhas Artzi]

BIBLIOGRAPHY: J. Obermeyer, *Die Landschaft Babylonien…* (1929), 52–61; E.Y. Kutscher, in: *Scripta Hierosolymitana*, 4 (1957), 12; J.J. Finkelstein, in: JNES, 21 (1962), 73–92; *The Oxford Atlas* (1963), map 56–57; EB, 8 (1967), 825–7. **ADD. BIBLIOGRAPHY:** W. Holladay, *Jeremiah 1* (Heremeneia; 1986), 396; M. Stolper, in: JNES, 48 (1989), 283–305; K. van der Toorn, in: DDD, 314–16; J. Hull, in: ABD VI, 572; S.D. Sperling, in: G. Knoppers and J. McConville (eds.), *Reconsidering Israel and Judah* (2000), 244–45; P. Briant, *From Cyrus to Alexander* (2002), index, 1165, s.v. *Ebir Nāri*.

EUPOLEMUS (Gr. Ἐυπόλεμος), first significant Greco-Jewish historian. His name, the time when he lived, and the content of the remaining fragments of his work combine to make it likely that he is identical with Eupolemus, son of John, son of Hakkoz, who in 161–60 B.C.E. brought back from Rome a promise of assistance for *Judah Maccabee (I Macc. 8:17–32). His father John is mentioned as having gained concessions for Jerusalem from Antiochus III after the Seleucid conquest of Coele-Syria (II Macc. 4:11). Six passages from Eupolemus' writings survive in the works of Eusebius and Clement of Alexandria, who found them in the monograph *On the Jews* by *Alexander Polyhistor (85–35 B.C.E.). Because of its Samaritan bias and its incompatibility with other remnants, it is customary to label the fragment dealing with Abraham as *Pseudo-Eupolemus*.

Eupolemus entitled his book *On the Kings of Judah*. Another title, *On the Prophecy of Elijah*, is either a subtitle or a chapter of the former. Eupolemus' history covered the period from Moses (perhaps from the creation) to his own day. He reckoned 5,149 years from Adam to the fifth year of Demetrius Soter (158–157 B.C.E.), evidently the year in which he completed his chronicle (Clement, *Stromata* 1. 141, 4).

Fragment 1, though brief, was extensively quoted, because it summed up the Jewish and, later, the Christian response to Greek philosophy and science: "Moses was the first wise man, the first who imparted the alphabet to the Jews; the Phoenicians received it from the Jews, and the Greeks from the Phoenicians; also laws were first written by Moses for the Jews."

Fragment 2 is the longest single remnant of a Greco-Jewish text prior to *Philo. The reigns of Joshua, Samuel, and Saul and his son (*sic*) David are all mentioned briefly. The text becomes more detailed in its description of David's campaign. Eupolemus was a priest himself, and it is natural that he should have chosen as his central theme the Temple of Jerusalem. An angel hovered above to show David the site of the future Temple, which he himself was forbidden to build. When Solomon became king at the age of 12, he ordered the client-kings, Vaphres of Egypt and Suron (Hiram) of Tyre, to supply him with labor, and each sent 80,000 men. The exchange of letters between the kings concocted by Eupolemus is reproduced verbatim. Eupolemus' account of the dimensions of the Temple and its furnishings is, as a rule, inconsistent with that of the Septuagint and the Hebrew Bible. Also, Eupolemus' Temple, the gold surplus of which was sent to Suron, is more gilded than the traditional one (see *Theophilus). Solomon died at the age of 52, after transferring the tabernacle's furnishings from Shiloh with great pomp (cf. LXX, I Kings 2:12; SOR 14). In the last fragment, the authenticity of which is sometimes erroneously questioned, Eupolemus describes the conquest of Jerusalem by Nebuchadnezzar, assisted by the Median king, Astibares, and an allied force of 300,000 men. The invasion followed Jeremiah's discovery that the king was worshipping the golden Baal. The Temple and its furnishings were shipped to Babylon. However, the prophet salvaged the tablets of the Law (II Macc. 2:1ff.).

Eupolemus' history was not a mere restatement of the biblical version. He changed or invented the names of men and locations and dealt freely with other facts. He continued the chronicler's method of rewriting the past in the light of the contemporary scene. Thus he contributes a scarecrow to Solomon's Temple and gives the dimensions of that Temple as similar to those of the Second Temple, which was standing in his day. The Mosaic account of the Tabernacle is a significant element in Eupolemus' description of the Temple. Though his Greek vocabulary is narrow and his syntax atrocious, Eupolemus' texts are valuable as the only confirmed remnants of the Greek used in Jerusalem.

He was indebted to the Septuagint for the Hexateuch, but there is no evidence (contrary to Freudenthal) that Eupolemus made use of the Greek versions of Kings and Chronicles. Technical terms transliterated in the Septuagint are rendered by Eupolemus into Greek. He is the first Jewish historian who borrowed from nonbiblical sources. He drew upon Herodotus, Ctesias, and Greco-Phoenician and Greco-Egyptian historians. There is no evidence that Eupolemus directly influenced Josephus or the rabbinic literature, though parallels, such as the age of Solomon and the king's request for Egyptian workers, need an explanation. In contrast to Eupolemus' devotion to Jerusalem and its Temple, Pseudo-Eupolemus follows a syncretistic Samaritan tradition. According to him, the Tower of Babel was built by the giants who had escaped the flood. Abraham was born in the Babylonian city of Camarina, called by some Urie. This patriarch surpassed all men in nobility and wisdom. He taught astronomy and astrology, first to the Phoenicians, and later to the Egyptians, tipping the balance in favor of the Phoenicians, who were later bested by the invading Armenians. He was then entertained by Melchizedek, the king and priest of the Temple of "*Argarizin*," which may be translated as "Mount of Most High." He mentions the visit Abraham's wife made to the Egyptian king, and mentions the miracle of the king being unable to have intercourse with her (cf. *Genesis Apocryphon* 20:17). After his wife was restored to him, Abraham lived in Heliopolis, where he instructed the Egyptian priests. The discovery of the sciences and astrology is attributed to Enoch, who, according to Pseudo-Eupolemus, was identical with the Greek Atlas. He identifies the Babylonian Belus with Noah, and the father of Ham with Kronos.

A passage dealing with Abraham, attributed by Alexander Polyhistor to an anonymous writer (Eusebius, *Praeparatio Evangelica*, 9:18, 2), is now ascribed by Freudenthal and Jacoby to Pseudo-Eupolemus on the basis of similarity of content. Walter, however, questions the identification. The apparent pro-Seleucid and anti-Egyptian bias of Pseudo-Eupolemus, the link with the Enochite texts, such as the Book of Enoch, Jubilees, and Genesis Apocryphon, and the fact that the passage is evidently criticized in *Sibylline Oracles* (3:218ff.) suggests a pre-Maccabean dating for Pseudo-Eupolemus. If this dating is warranted, Pseudo-Eupolemus would then be the oldest syncretic presentation of a biblical text.

BIBLIOGRAPHY: FRAGMENTS: F. Jacoby, *Fragmente der griechischen Historiker*, 3c, 2 (1958), 671–9, nos. 723–4; Eusebius, *Praeparatio Evangelica*, 9:17; 9:30–34; 9:39. COMMENTARIES: J. Freudenthal, *Hellenistische Studien* (1874–75), 82–130; Wacholder, in: HUCA, 34 (1963), 83–113; Pauly-Wissowa, 11 (1907), 1227–29, no. 11; Walter, in: *Klio*, 43–45 (1965), 282–90.

[Ben Zion Wacholder]

EUROPA PLAN, code name for a large scale rescue plan to exchange European Jews for money, developed in the autumn of 1942 by the "Working Group" in Slovakia, an unusual alliance between Zionists and ultra-Orthodox Jews headed by a Zionist and a woman, Gisi *Fleishmann, at the suggestion of Rabbi Michael *Weissmandel, the ultra-Orthodox leader who was the son-in-law of the spiritual leader of Slovakian Jewry, Rabbi Samuel David Halevi Ungar, the rabbi of Nitra, and a cousin of Fleishmann. Between March 26 and the end of July 1942 some 50,000 Jews had been deported to Poland. Another 7,000–8,000 Jews had escaped to Hungary, which was an indication that the Jews had internalized their peril even before they had become aware of the *Final Solution. At Weissmandel's initiative but with the group's support an offer was made to Dieter *Wisliceny, Eichmann's emissary to Slovakia, to ransom Jews for money and an initial bribe, whose sum total is still a matter of historical dispute but was between $20,000 and $55,000, was accepted. Soon thereafter the deportation of Slovakian Jews was halted. The Working Group believed that the bribe had brought the deportations to a halt and that larger sums would indeed save a larger number of Jews. They had few options and this desperate action was perceived to be effective. It certainly had the sanction of Jewish tradition with its detailed teachings regarding the redemption of captives. In his posthumous memoirs edited by his brother and disciples Weissmandel bitterly criticizes the Jewish leadership in the West for not being forthcoming with the required sums of money and for their unwillingness to support such unusual, nonlegal actions. It was part of his attack against the Zionists and against assimilated, Westernized, secularized Jews. However, no evidence has been uncovered that link the bribe to the halt in deportations. Contemporary historians agree that internal Slovakian concerns over the impact of the deportation of Jews on the economy was the reason for halting the deportations. Even the Vatican had protested, which had additional impact, since Jozef Tiso, the president of Slovakia, was a priest. Wisliceny was a secondary official and could not have stopped the deportations on his own accord. It is known that Wisliceny, who received an advance payment from the Working Group, forwarded $20,000 to the WVHA (Main Economy Administration Office of the SS). The negotiations dragged on until August 1943 with Himmler's consent, perhaps as a way of feeling out Jewish power, but then broke off on Himmler's order (according to Wisliceny). Why did Germany consent to the halt in deportations? From the German perspective, Slovakia was an ally of Germany and the Slovakian Jews were comparatively small in number and could be dealt with after the massive deportations from Poland were completed. Indeed, they were deported to Auschwitz in 1944.

The financial means, fixed at $2–3 million, were to be provided by Jewish organizations in the free world, and mainly by the *American Jewish Joint Distribution Committee (JDC). Saly Mayer, the JDC representative in Geneva, proposed to deposit the money in blocked accounts in Switzerland until the end of the war, according to the transfer regulations of the Allied countries, because the Joint was unwilling to break the Allied transfer regulations and to send money directly to the enemy, which clearly would have jeopardized its legal standing in the United States. The Germans were well aware of the difficulties that the Jews had in raising the promised sums though the Jews did not know that the Germans were informed about their communications with Switzerland. It is assumed that the main idea behind the apparent German willingness to discuss the plan lay in Nazi counterpropaganda. The Europa Plan served later as a basis for the negotiations between *Eichmann and the "Relief and Rescue Committee" headed by

Rezsö *Kasztner in Budapest in the summer of 1944 and the so-called offer of one million Jews for 10,000 trucks.

BIBLIOGRAPHY: L. Rothkirchen, *Ḥurban Yahadut Slovakia* (1961), includes Eng. summary, passim; O.J. Neumann, *Be-Ẓel ha-Mavet* (1958), 160–5; M.D. Weissmandel, *Min ha-Meẓar* (1960), passim; A. Weissberg, *Desperate Mission: Joel Brand's Story* (1958) passim; N. Levin, *The Holocaust* (1968), 535–40; Y. Bauer, *Jews for Sale: Nazi Jewish Negotiations 1933–45* (1994); S. Aronson, "The 'Europa Plan,'" in: W. Laqueur (ed.), *Yale Encyclopedia of the Holocaust* (2001).

[Michael Berenbaum (2nd ed.)]

EUROPE.

Antiquity

The earliest contacts of the ancient Hebrews with Europe and Europeans were probably through the Greek traders who were familiar figures all over the eastern Mediterranean littoral as early as the eighth century B.C.E. It must however be borne in mind that the Hebrews were settled mainly in the uplands of Ereẓ Israel away from the coastal area, while the Greeks were at this time almost as much Asiatics as Europeans geographically. It was probably at the time of the First Exile after the fall of Jerusalem in 586 B.C.E. that Jews first penetrated into Europe. The Hebrew prophets, for instance Isaiah, speak more than once of the future redemption of the Jewish exiles from the "isles of the sea," by which presumably the Greek coastlands were implied, and it is likely enough that at this period Greek slave dealers purchased Jewish captives for sale on their domestic markets. Although their absorption in the Persian Empire confirmed the Asiatic nature of the Jewish people for a long period, that empire's expansionist ambitions westward to some extent opened it and its Jewish population to Western and European ideas and influences. After the return from Exile, Greek influences on the trading cities of the Palestinian littoral were becoming strong, and some later books of the Bible (e.g., Ecclesiastes) seem to show a distinct Hellenic coloring. It was, however, the conquests by *Alexander the Great in the fourth century B.C.E. that definitely changed the character of this area. Hitherto, Ereẓ Israel had been part of the Near Eastern Afro-Asiatic nexus, looking to, and influenced by, Syria, Assyria, and Babylonia to the north, the Arabian tribes to the east, and Egypt to the south. Alexander the Great broke down as it were the barrier that had hitherto divided this region from Europe. Henceforth, Ereẓ Israel looked west, not east, and, with the surrounding area, was part of the European nexus and sphere of influence, more or less sharply divided from Asia and the Asiatic powers. Insofar as it continued to be affected by the neighboring land areas, it was by those (Syria, Egypt) that had largely succumbed to Greek influences and could now be regarded almost as extensions of Europe. Although great masses of Jews remained under Partho-Persian rule in *Mesopotamia, the most important settlement outside Ereẓ Israel was in Greek-speaking *Alexandria, which had constant and intimate contacts with the centers of European life. It was here in fact in the ensuing period that the Jews produced their great Hellenistic literature, reaching its climax in *Philo and constituting their first literary expression in the language of European culture. From certain points of view, the *Hasmonean revolt in the second century B.C.E. could be considered a reaction against the tendency that has been described – an attempt to stem the inroads of European culture and to reassert Asiatic values. However, its success was only temporary. The Hasmonean monarchs, while asserting political independence, ultimately succumbed to some extent to European cultural influences. The Roman conquest of 63 B.C.E. brought Ereẓ Israel and its population – still the largest and most creative part of the Jewish people – under European rule and within the European cultural orbit. It is hardly an exaggeration to say that from now on, down to the Arab conquest in 640, Ereẓ Israel and its population constituted in effect part of Europe; and the European influences on the Jewish population there – and hence on Judaism itself – became increasingly strong.

Meanwhile the actual Jewish settlement in Europe was growing. From the third century B.C.E. Jews are mentioned in inscriptions, etc., on the mainland of *Greece. The early Hasmonean rulers had entered into diplomatic relations with *Rome, necessitating the dispatch of envoys thither, and there is a somewhat obscure reference to the expulsion of Jewish religious propagandists thence in 139 B.C.E. Thereafter, the wars of the Romans in Asia Minor and their conquest of Ereẓ Israel inevitably resulted in the arrival on the Roman slave market of Jewish captives (many of whom would win their freedom or else be ransomed by their coreligionists), while the capital of the empire inevitably attracted visitors, emissaries, and merchants. Rabbinic sources, the New Testament, and *Josephus all confirm the impression of a solid Jewish community there in the first century C.E., the subsequent importance of which is attested by several series of *catacombs and hundreds of inscriptions. As early as 59 B.C.E. *Cicero, in his oration in defense of Flaccus who had raided the Jewish temple offerings in the Greek islands, could assert that the Jews were present at the trial in Rome in such numbers as to overawe the court. Jews were also present at this period in many other places throughout *Italy, especially along the trade routes leading to the ports commanding trade with the East. The existence of Jewish settlements all over the Roman Empire in its heyday is recorded in Gaul (see *France), *Spain, Pannonia, even in the Rhineland (see *Germany), and it is probable that there was no Roman province without a Jewish settlement, even if no definite evidence is preserved. The total number involved was far from insignificant. The Jewish population of Rome has been estimated (with some exaggeration) at as many as 50,000, and it has been asserted that they constituted something like one-tenth of the population of the empire as a whole. The Jews of Europe, by the time of the breakup of the Roman Empire, were probably to be reckoned at some hundreds of thousands. On the other hand, their cultural significance was slight. They made barely the slightest contribution to rabbinic or Hebrew culture in the talmudic age, nor is any work of this period extant in Latin which is certainly of Jewish authorship.

Rise of Christianity and Islam

Under the Roman Empire, to the fourth century, the position of the Jews was on the whole good. Although looked down upon, both because of the "superstitions" to which they adhered and their lowly economic status, their religion was tolerated, and from 212 they enjoyed Roman citizenship with all its advantages and responsibilities along with the other free inhabitants of the empire. With the Christianization of the empire, however, their position deteriorated, though at first socially more than juridically, the ground being prepared for their systematic degradation which was to become the rule in Christian Europe in the Middle Ages. The Barbarian invasions probably affected the Jews, as a mainly urban element, more than the rest of the population, so that it seems their numbers were drastically reduced in this period. Moreover, the new rulers, once they adopted Christianity – especially in its Catholic form – were unable to preserve the delicate balance between sufferance and intolerance that had been achieved under the earlier Christian emperors – all the more so since this period witnessed the periodical triumph of religious fanaticism in the *Byzantine Empire, setting a baneful example to the rest of the Western world. Restrictions were imposed by the Church at an early date; from 305 successive *Church Councils repeatedly reissued discriminatory legislation. Hence the period between the fifth and eighth centuries was punctuated all over Europe by religious riots, coercion, compulsory baptisms, and widespread expulsions, culminating in the great disaster to the Jewish community of Spain under the Visigoths, about which we are particularly well informed. The Jewish population of Western Europe was now, it seems, reduced to relative unimportance, except perhaps in some parts of Italy.

Conditions changed for the better in the eighth century. The Arab conquests opened up Spain to new colonization which seems to have attained significant proportions – at first, it is true, in a quasi-Asiatic cultural setting – but this was destined to be temporary, waning with the Reconquest and the expansion of the Christian kingdoms. Simultaneously, and apparently with the sedulous encouragement of the Carolingian rulers in France, Italy, and Germany, Jewish merchants and traders (typified in the *Radanites who had their base in the Rhone delta) became active in Western, then in Central Europe, establishing a fresh nexus of Jewish communities or reinforcing the old. In Eastern Europe – an outlet for their exports of the manufactured products of the West, a source of their purchases of raw materials and slaves – they presumably joined up with older Jewish settlements that had spread northward from the Black Sea and Crimea or along the Danube valley. This period moreover coincided with that of the near-extinction of the old settlement in Ereẓ Israel and the drastic dwindling of that of Mesopotamia and the neighboring lands, due in part to political and in part to economic causes. The result was that in this period, approximately between 800 and 1050, there took place either a mass transference of the Jewish population from East to West, or else a phenomenal expansion of the one and dwindling of the other which had much the same effect. From the 11th century, in any case, the center of Jewry and of Jewish intellectual life was transferred to Europe, where it was to remain for nearly 1,000 years. The new settlers were moreover of a different type in many respects from the old. They (especially those of Northern Europe) might be termed "Talmud Jews" who guided their lives in every respect according to the detailed prescriptions that had become evolved recently in Ereẓ Israel and especially Mesopotamia, and considered that the study of the Talmud was the greatest of religious duties and of personal pleasures. Hence, when the great talmudic academies of Mesopotamia decayed in the 11th century, those of Northern Europe – especially France and the Rhineland – were ready to take their place; and the former rabbinic traditions were perpetuated there for centuries. In the south of Europe, particularly in Spain, a somewhat different intellectual tradition prevailed, literature, belles lettres, philosophy, and poetry attaining new heights. At the same time, the position of the Jews, straddling the Latin-Christian and the Arab-Islamic cultures, qualified them in a unique degree to perform the function of middlemen in intellectual as well as economic activities; and while on the one hand they participated in the scientific and philosophical activities of the Islamic world, on the other they were to a great extent responsible for the transference of the superb fruits of these activities to the 12th-century Christian world, and so helped to bring about the Latin renaissance and the revival of learning in Europe.

Medieval Position

It is possible to exaggerate the well-being of the Jews in Europe in the Dark Ages, but there can be no question as to the great and tragic difference that resulted from the *Crusades. Hitherto, attacks on the Jews had been sporadic and occasional, but from the onslaught on the Jewish communities in France and the Rhineland in 1096 they became commonplace during any period of religious excitement or incitement; not only when the Christian forces marched against the infidels or heretics, but when such preposterous charges as that of the *blood libel (from 1141) or of the desecration of the *Host (after 1215) were brought up against the Jews. The stimulus given to European trade by the Crusades and the expansion of the Italian trading republics undermined the position of the Jewish international merchants. As a result of this, combined with the fact that at this period the Church's attack on the practice of usury reached its climax, the Jews of Northern Europe especially were now driven into the profession of *moneylending – encouraged and protected by their rulers, whose systematic and rapacious system of taxation converted this into a primary source of revenue for themselves. On the other hand, the profession of moneylending, besides affording ample leisure for the talmudic study that had become the all-pervading passion of Northern European Jewry, endowed them temporarily, in the intervals of spoliation, with a remarkable degree of economic well-being, so that the Jews of France, Germany, and *England in the Middle Ages constituted one of the most affluent nonnobiliary societies of the contemporary world. Thus, economic resentment was now added to the ever-increasing religious hatred. It was under the influence of this atmosphere that the fourth *Lateran Council of 1215 codified and reenacted the former anti-Jewish discriminatory legislation with innovations such as the enforcement of the wearing by the Jews of a distinctive humiliating *badge to distinguish them from other men. This henceforth remained a standard of conduct, to be enforced whenever the spirit of reaction triumphed. Such an attitude was increasingly intensified by the constant activity of the Christian mendicant orders, especially the *Dominicans, founded at this period precisely to combat heresy and unbelief. It was partly due to their influence that the Jews were expelled from England in 1290 and from France in 1306, their now diminished utility to the royal treasury being outweighed by the immediate profit of a single confiscatory measure. The Jews were absent from England henceforth until well after the end of the Middle Ages, and feeble attempts at reestablishment in France were unsuccessful.

Most of the refugees from these countries probably found their way ultimately to Germany, where political fragmentation prevented any similar wholesale measure, although the outbreaks of massacre, particularly at the time of the *Black Death of 1348–49, far outdid in scale and horror anything else of the sort known in medieval Jewish history. Hence it was only a feeble remnant that maintained the Jewish connection here unbroken. On the other hand, the greater security, and opportunities for profitable activity in an economically undeveloped area, drew Jews (as well as non-Jews) at this time to *Poland, now struggling for revival after the devastation wrought by Tatar invasions of the 13th century. With the close of the Middle Ages this country became the essential bulwark of Jewish life in Europe, perpetuating the intellectual traditions of France and the Rhineland, still maintaining the colloquial German of their ancestors as their *Yiddish vernacular, and developing in the *Council of the [Four] Lands and the sister-bodies autonomous institutions hardly paralleled elsewhere in Diaspora history. Poland therefore became the center of "*Ashkenazi" Jewry, i.e., those of (Franco-) German origin.

Meanwhile, the condition of the Jews of Spain too, after reaching unprecedented heights of culture as well as of political influence even under the Christian kings, began to deteriorate owing to the constant propaganda of the friars. A wave of massacres in 1391 initiated the problem of the *Conversos or *Marranos or *New Christians, which inexorably led in due course to the establishment of the *Inquisition in 1484, and the Expulsion from Spain in 1492 and from *Portugal (leaving behind however a compact body of Marranos) in 1497. The refugees made their way in great numbers eastward, where they revived the flagging communities that had survived from Byzantine times. Turkey-in-Europe (see *Ottoman Empire; apart from Turkey-in-Asia, where the same occurred) thus became the great center of *Sephardi (or Spanish and Portuguese) Jewry, as Poland was of Ashkenazi Jewry, and the communities in *Constantinople, *Salonika, and other places preserved the ancient traditions of Spanish-speaking Jewry in islands of western Mediterranean culture transplanted to Eastern Europe.

Renaissance and Counter-Reformation

In the first half of the 16th century, the Italian mainland (the Jews had been expelled from *Sicily and *Sardinia, with the rest of the Aragonese dominions, in 1492) had witnessed a remarkable development in Jewish cultural life and activity, in the spirit of the Renaissance. But this was changed by the Counter-Reformation. The Jews were expelled from the Kingdom of *Naples by its Spanish rulers in 1542; the old anti-Jewish code with new extensions was rigidly enforced in northern Italy (especially the papal dominions) from 1555 onward, accompanied by the institution of the *ghetto and heartless enforcement of the ghetto system henceforth invariable in Catholic Europe. Although Jewish communities continued to exist in the famous ghettos of *Rome, *Venice, *Mantua, etc., which, though not numerically large, played a great part in Jewish cultural life, a considerable proportion of Italian Jewry (especially from the center and south of the peninsula) was now absorbed in the Sephardi communities of the Near East. It is important, however, to note that these newly reestablished centers, under Muslim rule, whether or not in the geographical bounds of Europe, were henceforth basically European in culture, outlook, and language: segments as it were of medieval Europe embedded fossilwise in Asiatic or African soil.

The Renaissance and the accompanying movements established for centuries the predominance of Europe in the world politically, culturally, and scientifically. It hence confirmed the predominance of European Jewry over its coreligionists in other continents, most paradoxically, precisely at the time when most of Europe rejected, ejected, and excluded the Jews. Though European Jewry had led in every aspect of Jewish creativity since the beginning of the millennium, there had been solid collaboration hitherto from elements in other continents; from now on, the lead of Europe was overwhelmingly great, and so far as Jewish life in the other continents was concerned it was on the whole as protractions of European Jewish life. The development of *printing confirmed and accentuated this cultural hegemony. For four and a half centuries at least, almost all Hebrew printing was done in Europe – with the inevitable result that the European Hebrew texts in particular were accepted as classical, and new works by European Jewish scholars became universally accepted while others of perhaps equal merit might remain in manuscript and almost unknown in wider circles.

The culmination of the age of degradation was accompanied, however, by the glimmer of a new dawn. Marranos mainly from Portugal rather than Spain, settling at this period in Northern Europe for the sake of business more than freedom of conscience, ventured little by little to throw off the disguise of Christianity. By the end of the 16th century, a number of new Jewish communities, hovering as yet on the borders of clandestinity, began to establish themselves in this area, where for generations no Jews had been known; and by the middle of the 17th century there were at *Amsterdam, *Hamburg, and other cities (a little later in *London also) open Jewish communities of a new "modern" type, socially assimilated to the world around them.

In Eastern Europe, by this time, the Jews had become involved in the hatreds that had been engendered between the Roman Catholic Poles and their persecuted Greek Catholic subjects in the *Ukraine. In consequence, when the latter rose in revolt under the Cossack hetman *Chmielnicki in 1648–49, Jews as well as Poles suffered, the Jews even more than the Poles, the ensuing wave of massacres ending the days of tranquility that had hitherto been the rule there. Henceforth, the tide of emigration set in the reverse direction, from east to west, the communities of Germany, and thereafter of Western Europe, being considerably reinforced. This was intensified as generations passed and the condition of Polish Jewry constantly deteriorated. Conversely, at this period the emergence in Germany after the Peace of Westphalia (1648) of competing states and would-be resplendent courts gave opportunities such as had never existed before for lucrative activities for Jewish factors and *Court Jews, new Jewish communities often developing around them. Thus here too a new type of socially assimilated Jew began to emerge in the 17th century, culminating in the 18th in the remarkable figure of Moses *Mendelssohn, almost the first Jew to play a role of real importance in European cultural life.

Emancipation

Thus by the end of the 18th century a new type of Jew had emerged in Western Europe. After the outbreak of the French Revolution it was hence inevitable that the new doctrine of Liberty, Equality, and Fraternity should be applied, at first reluctantly, to the Jews as well – that is, that they should be given the same rights, receive the same treatment, and have the same duties as other men. Or, to put it another way, they were now formally recognized as Europeans, differentiated from other Europeans by adherence to another faith. These new doctrines were moreover imposed by or imitated from the French almost all over the continent of Europe where Jews were to be found. A reaction followed the fall of Napoleon in 1815; but henceforth Jewish political equality was part of the liberal creed, and it was accepted almost everywhere by the

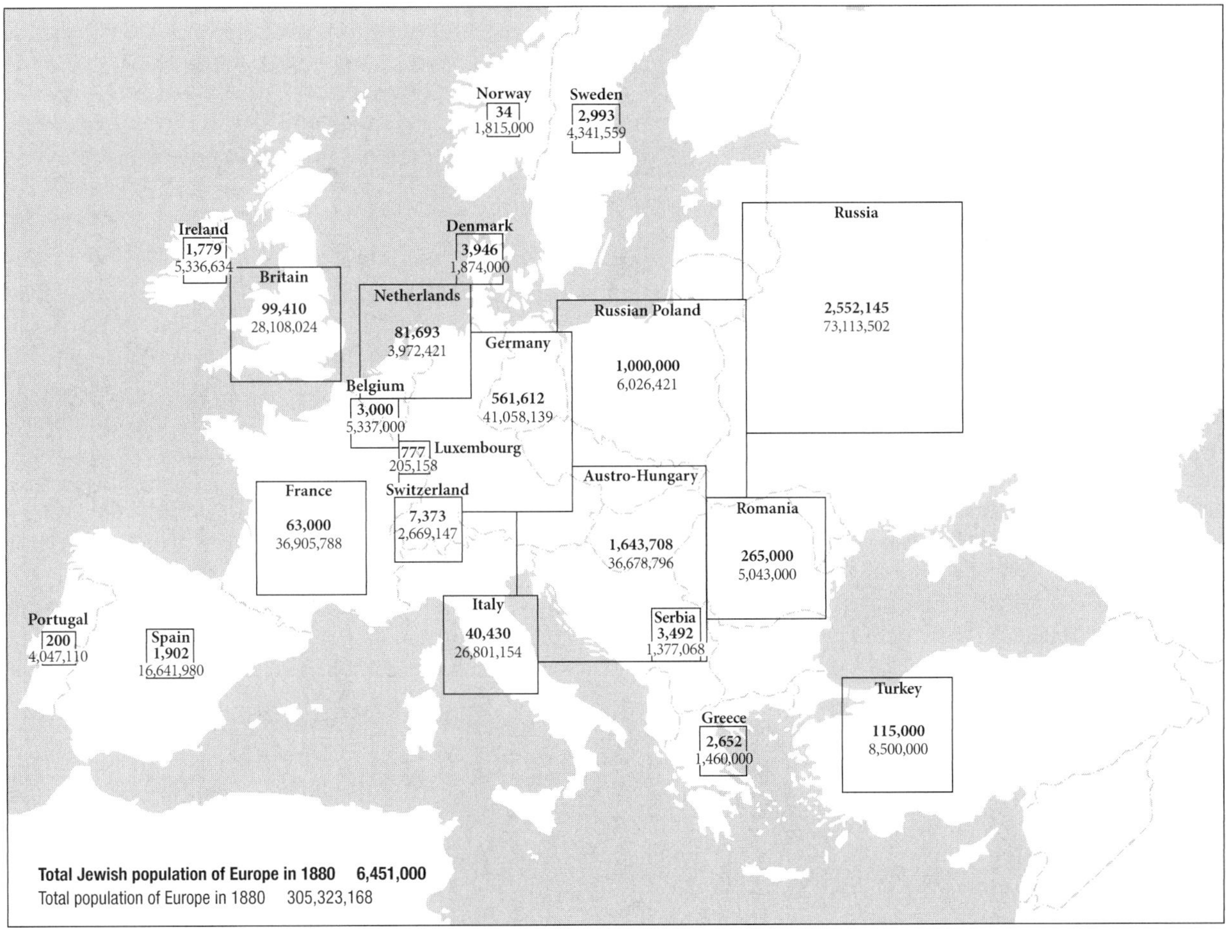

Jewish population of Europe, 1880. Jewish figures based on American Jewish Yearbook.

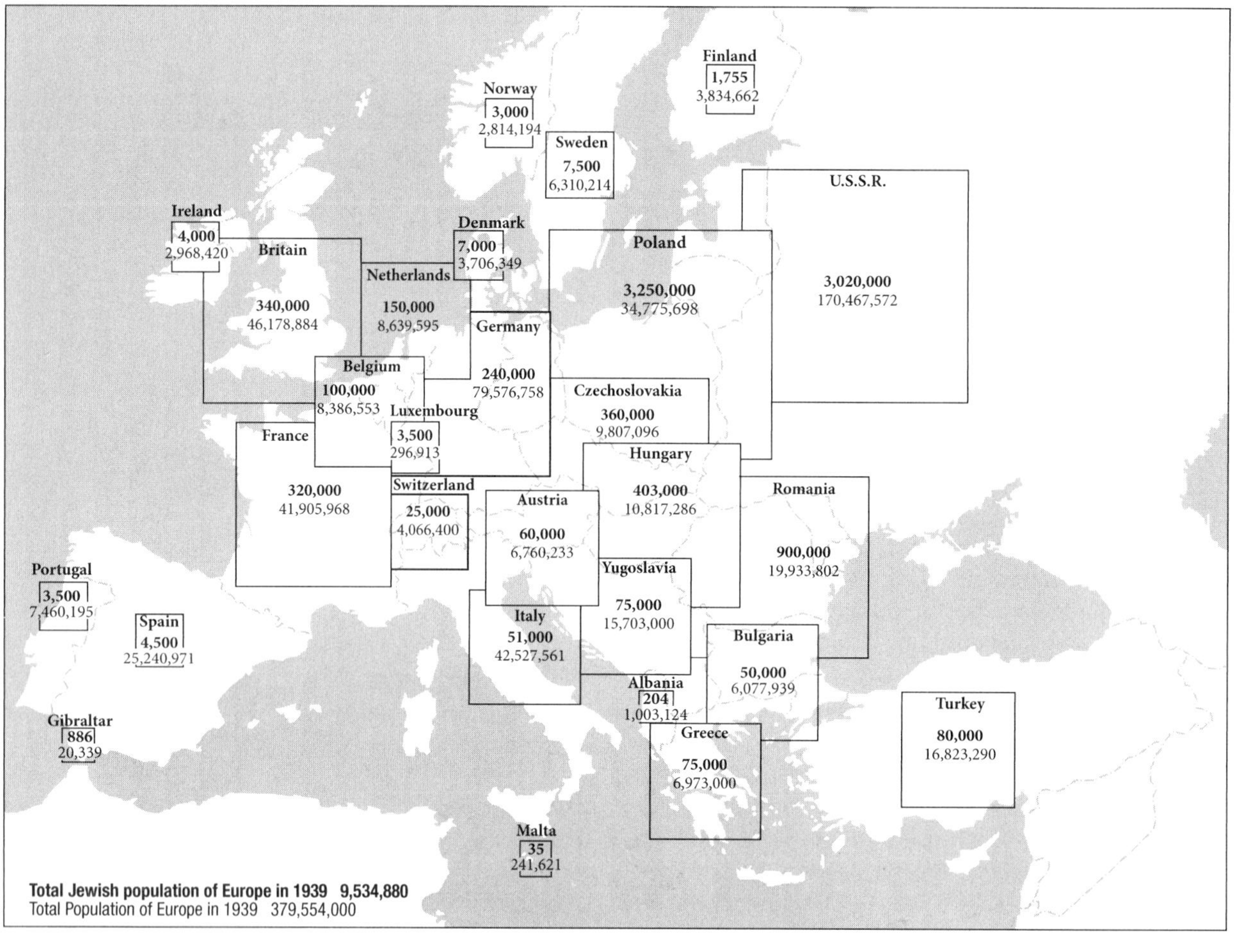

Population in 1939, before the outbreak of World War II. Jewish figures based on American Jewish Yearbook.

third quarter of the 19th century (the crucial year may be fixed at 1870), Jewish *emancipation being henceforth the rule. Jews now began to play a role of increasing importance in European cultural, literary, scientific, social, and even political activity. At the same time, Jewish *assimilation became accelerated, both in the extreme form of conversion to the dominant faith, and in the more loyal form of the representation of Judaism simply as a divergent European religion – that is, *Reform Judaism, in all its branches and aspects (including *neo-Orthodoxy). The development of a Hebrew secular literature along European models (*Haskalah) and of vernacular literature on Hebrew scholarly themes (Wissenschaft des Judentums) were other aspects of this same tendency.

There was however one area where this new attitude did not apply, and the exception was numerically more important, and in its way more significant, than the rule. In *Russia (where there was no important Jewish settlement until the annexation of those areas of the old Polish kingdom which had the largest Jewish population) these were years not of progress but (with rare intervals) of reaction, and in 1881 a wave of massacres (*pogroms) began on a scale and of a type which recalled the Middle Ages, to be followed by economic and social restrictions of unprecedented scope (the *"May Laws"). A wave of emigration (see *migration) followed on a vast scale. This entirely changed the face of European Jewry within very few years. It greatly reinforced the Jewish communities of Western Europe, in particular that of England, and even changed their character. But far more important than this was the transatlantic migration. Emigration largely from Germany in the first three-quarters of the 19th century had relieved the pressure of population in that country and at the same time greatly developed the Jewish community in the *United States of America. Now, within a few years, as a result of immigration from Eastern Europe, it was to be reinforced in fantastic proportions. The results were all-important. For eight centuries after approximately the year 1000, the essential center of Jewish life and creativity had been in Europe. Outside the European area there had been only relatively unimportant offshoots, and this applied in particular to Ashkenazi Jewry. After the 1880s the United States was to be the second, and in due course the first, center of Jewish life in the world, from the point of view of population, and the relative role of European Jewry correspondingly diminished. From the early Victorian era the Western European Jewish communities had taken the lead in political and charitable activities on behalf of their depressed coreligionists elsewhere. From now on, their preponderance waned, passing in an increasing degree to America. The process of emigration was paralleled in *Romania and *Galicia (then under Austrian rule). Between 1880 and 1914, about two million Jews from Eastern Europe transferred themselves to the New World. It is true that natural increase kept the total population level actually unchanged, but had it not been for the emigration it would have continued to rise enormously.

During this period, the ancient Sephardi communities of the Mediterranean area had been affected by quasi-lethargy. Although under the rule of Turkey and the Balkan successor states their material and political condition was on the whole not adverse, the spirit of creativity that had been so marked in Spain had now passed from them almost entirely.

World War I

World War I marked the beginning of a cataclysm in European Jewish life. The revolutions of 1917 brought the Russian Jews emancipation, but at the same time ushered in the Bolshevik regime which in the long run severed the mass of Russian Jews from their coreligionists abroad, and indeed from Judaism. On the other hand, the removal of the traditional residence restrictions, which had hitherto confined the Jews to the *Pale of Settlement, implied that henceforth they were spread more evenly throughout the vast Russian territories, in Asia as well as Europe. Although the rights of the Jews in the Succession States, which were severed mainly from Russia (especially Poland with a very large Jewish population), were nominally guaranteed by the Versailles treaties, the actuality fell short of this. The ensuing period was hence one of strain and perplexity, and emigration continued – though on a smaller scale than hitherto. Owing to restrictions in North America it was now largely directed to South America, and in part to Ereẓ Israel, as a result of the *Balfour Declaration which was specifically intended to help solve the problems of European Jewry.

Rise of Antisemitism and Nazism

In Germany, the dazzling progress of persons of Jewish extraction after Emancipation had given rise at the close of the 19th century to the new racial *antisemitism. For a long while this had remained an annoyance rather than a menace, although in France the *Dreyfus case from 1894 to 1896 had caused a major political convulsion and convinced Theodor *Herzl that

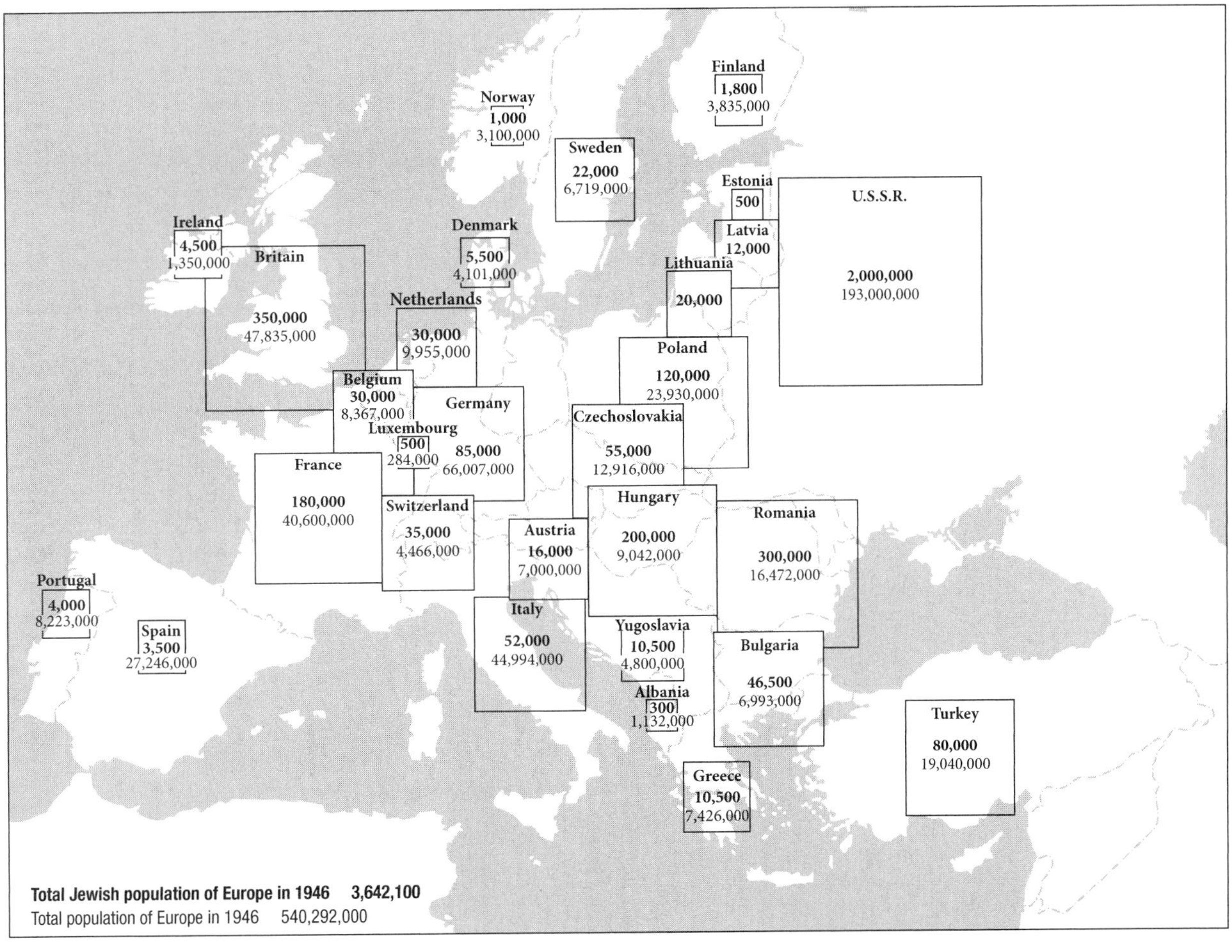

Population after World War II. Jewish figures based on American Jewish Yearbook.

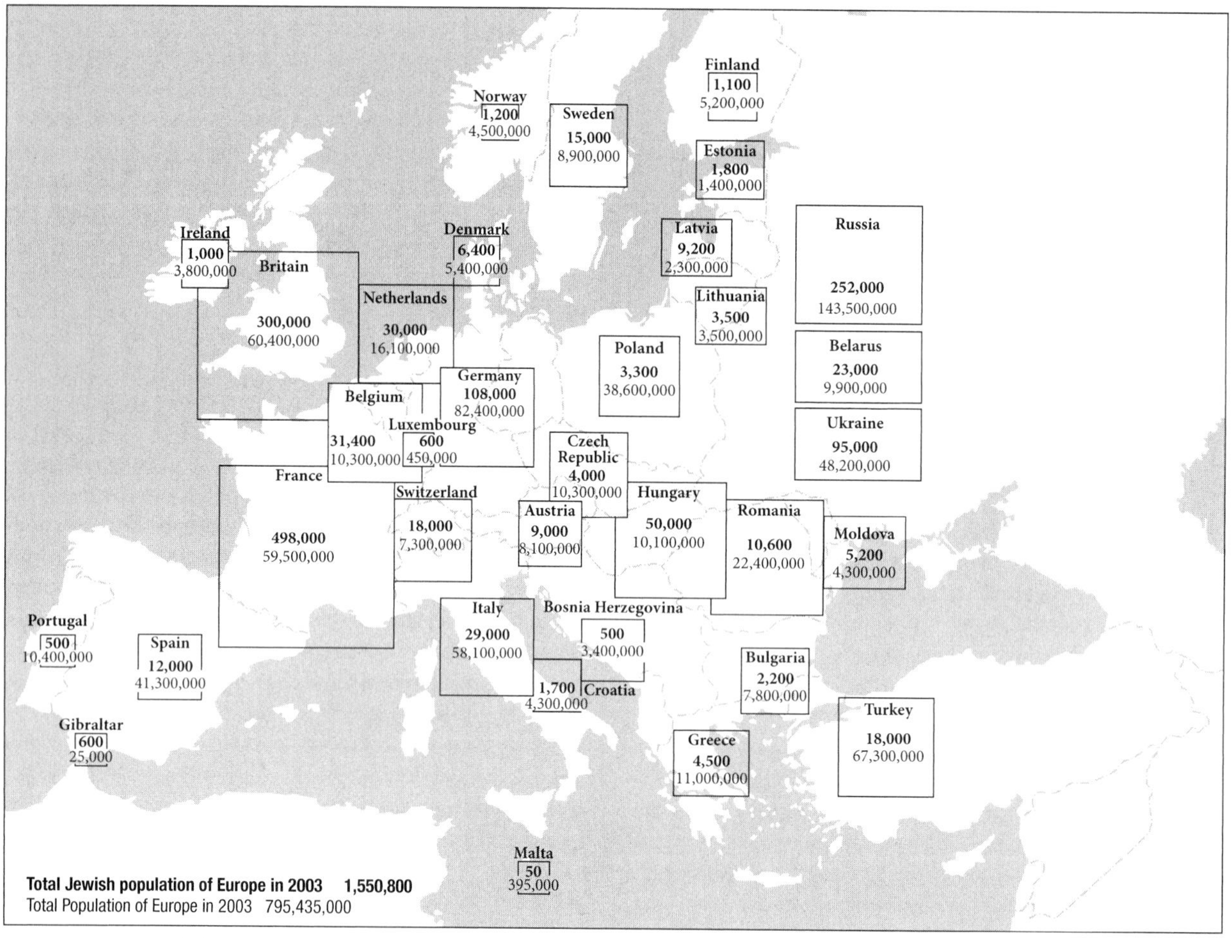

Population 2003. Jewish figures based on American Jewish Yearbook.

the solution to the Jewish problem must be sought outside the setting of European life. The German defeat in World War I and the physical as well as moral distress that ensued gave the antisemitic movement in that country an enormous impetus, and it became a cardinal principle of the Nazi Party (see *National Socialism) which attained power in 1933. The persecution that ensued drove very large numbers of Jews from Germany and *Austria into exile, to other parts of Europe, to Ereẓ Israel, and to other continents. This, however, proved to be only a beginning. During World War II, in the course of which the German armies overran almost all those parts of continental Europe in which Jewish communities existed, a systematic campaign of extermination was carried out. By the conclusion of hostilities in 1945, some 6,000,000 had perished in the *Holocaust out of the 9,000,000 who had lived in Europe in 1933, apart from the hundreds of thousands who had gone into exile; most of the greatest Jewish communities of the Continent – *Vienna, *Berlin, *Warsaw, *Lodz – had been annihilated. Many lands – including *Poland, *Yugoslavia, *Czechoslovakia, and even *Holland, as well as Germany and Austria – had become almost empty of Jews, most of the handful of survivors preferring to leave the blood-soaked soil. The great talmudic academies of Eastern Europe had been destroyed, as well as the center of Sephardi culture in the Balkans. Moreover, the Russian Jewish remnant seemed to be cut off from Jewish life even more completely than before, henceforth having no creative role to play.

The proportion of European Jewry in the world Jewish population declined in the course of half a century from 87.2% in 1880 to 58.05% in 1939, and then to 30% in 1968 and 12% in 2003. After approximately a thousand years, the European dominance in Jewish life has ended. It has on the one hand reverted to the ancestral soil in Asia; on the other, been transferred to the New World beyond the Atlantic Ocean.

For bibliography see *History, and individual countries and communities.

[Cecil Roth]

EUROPEAN COMMUNITY, THE.

The Beginning of the European Economic Community

After World War II, Europe was suffering from the wide destruction caused by the war and the deep separation between two different camps: one which had struggled for freedom and the other which had tried to subdue Europe under Nazi dictatorship and coldly organized the massacre of six million Jews.

Winston Churchill, who had been British prime minister during the war, launched an appeal for European unity on September 19, 1946, in Zurich. The first concrete example of European economic integration was the customs union among Belgium, the Netherlands, and Luxembourg, called "Benelux" which started on January 1, 1948.

U.S. Secretary of State George Marshall was ready to promise American aid for the reconstruction of Europe, on condition that European countries would pool their efforts and would agree among themselves on the distribution of American aid. Thus in 1948 was established the first post-war European organization, the OEEC (Organization for European Economic Cooperation). Many other organizations were created, and like NATO, the Atlantic Alliance, in 1949, the Council of Europe in 1949, an instrument of inter-governmental cooperation with no transfer of national sovereignty.

Robert Schuman, the French minister for foreign affairs, declared on May 9, 1950:

> The contribution which an organized and active Europe can make to civilization is indispensable for the maintenance of peaceful relations. Because Europe was not united, we have had war. The uniting of the European nations requires that the age-old opposition between France and Germany be eliminated. The action to be taken must first of all concern France and Germany.

On April 19, 1951, six countries (Belgium, the Federal Republic of Germany, France, Italy, Luxembourg, and the Netherlands) signed the Treaty establishing the European Coal and Steel Community (ECSC). It was thought that by pooling coal and steel, two of the most important raw materials for heavy industry, new military conflicts could be avoided and industrialization could be promoted. This sectorial approach very soon proved itself too narrow, and it was decided to make a bold step forward to full economic integration; on March 25, 1957, the six countries signed the Rome Treaty establishing the European Economic Community (EEC), which entered into force on January 1, 1958.

The creation of a vast common market was the first objective with the aim of reaching higher living standards, full employment, and economic expansion. After some years of a transitional period goods were to flow freely among the six member states thanks to the gradual disappearance of tariffs; a common agricultural policy was established as well. The Commission in Brussels was to coordinate the work and prepare specific proposals to be submitted to the Council of Ministers which alone had the power of decision, thus keeping it in the hands of the member countries; the Commission would then have to implement the decisions taken by the Council.

Israel and the EEC

The French scholar Dominique Moisy divides the relations between Israel and Western Europe into three periods: the first 20 years, in the 1950s and 1960s when "Israel was perceived by Europeans as a courageous and small pioneer state symbolized by the kibbutz"; "the virtual ostracism of the 1970s and the turn of the decade, when Israel was seen mainly as an ambitious imperialist power bent on expansion"; and the new third phase "characterized by a more neutral and less emotional approach to Israel."

The ink of the signatures on the Treaty of Rome was not yet dry when the Israeli government tried to establish contacts with the Community. It submitted a memorandum to the Commission of the EEC in Brussels on October 30, 1958, and a year later Israel was the third country to seek the accreditation of an ambassador as Chief of the Israeli Mission to the EEC, the ECSC, and Euratom. On June 20, 1960, David Ben-Gurion, the Israeli prime minister, met at Val Duchesse in Brussels with Prof. Hallstein, president of the Commission, and with Mr. Rey, member of the Commission in charge of external relations. Ben-Gurion expressed the wish of the Israeli government to sign an association agreement with the EEC.

The Commission submitted a detailed questionnaire to Israel and the Israeli Ministry of Foreign Affairs answered in a memorandum of September 27, 1960, explaining that it was seeking an Association Agreement with the EEC according to Article 238 of the Treaty of Rome; this would entail the creation of a customs union and would lead to the establishment of the clauses for Israeli participation in the framework of the Common Agricultural Policy envisaged by the EEC, as well as the harmonization of the economic and social policies.

During the following years the Israeli Ministry of Foreign Affairs developed extensive diplomatic activity at the Commission in Brussels and in each of the six capitals of the member states as well as in the European Parliament in Strasbourg.

On July 7, 1961, the diplomatic representatives of Israel brought to the attention of the governments in each of the six member countries an identical Note Verbale in which it asked for the opening of negotiations with the EEC on all the outstanding problems without defining beforehand their possible solution.

The Council of Ministers of the EEC decided on July 28, 1961, to invite the Commission to start a study of the relations between Israel and the EEC. Again the Israeli government, in a memorandum of November 24, 1961 to the Commission, expressed its wish to reach a global and preferential agreement, reiterating the same point of view in a note of February 1962 to the six governments. The first parliamentary delegation of the political groups of the European Parliament, headed by Alain Poher, arrived in Israel in February 1962.

In April 1962 the Council of Ministers of the EEC decided to open exploratory talks with Israel, which started in Brussels in May 1962; following these talks the Council of Ministers decided on September 24, 1962, to open negotiations between the EEC and Israel "in order to seek solutions to problems of commercial relations between Israel and the Community." These negotiations started in Brussels on September 26, 1962; the head of the Israel delegation was Mr. Levi Eshkol, then minister of finance, while M. Jean Rey, member of the Commission, headed the delegation of the EEC.

Israeli representatives explained the repercussions of the Common Agricultural Policy on third-party countries and put forward some original proposals like the idea of "trafic de perfectionnement passif" according to which European raw material included in an Israeli industrial product and reexported to the EEC should not be subject to the payment of custom duties.

The negotiations were held in three subsequent meetings in Brussels, on November 1962, June 1963, and March–April 1964; they reached a first non-preferential commercial agreement.

The Israeli government had to decide whether to accept this first agreement, limited as it was in its scope, or reject it in order to obtain a larger agreement more suitable to the solution of Israeli foreign trade problems. It was decided to sign the first agreement while at the same time endeavoring to enlarge it. Ambassador Amiel Najar said during the last phase of the negotiations:

> Even if all the considerations which I have expressed bring us necessarily and logically to the need for a global agreement between the European Community and Israel, my Government responding to the friendly advice and suggestions made to it in various capitals, has accepted the request of the EEC to follow what is called a pragmatic way.

Thus the commercial agreement was signed in Brussels by Golda Meir, minister of foreign affairs, on June 4, 1964; it allowed a temporary and partial suspension of the Common External Tariff (CET) on about 20 products of interest to Israel and the removal of quantitative restrictions. Since it was not a preferential agreement, the reduction had to be "erga omnes," i.e., for all members of GATT (the General Agreement on Tariffs and Trade); since Israel was not a major supplier to the EEC for any item, it was very difficult to find products which could benefit Israel without causing an excessive loss to the EEC. Generally it was granted a 20% reduction, reaching 40% for grapefruits, 35% for avocados, and 10% only for grapefruit juice; moreover an acceleration of national tariffs to the CET was decided for some other products, providing a concession of temporary and decreasing value since CET had to be progressively implemented anyway.

The economic value of this commercial agreement was very limited, yet it was the first institutional link with the EEC, establishing a joint committee, and had attached to it an important protocol according to which if the EEC were to give any new concession on oranges to any third country in the future, a review of the commercial agreement with Israel would become possible.

This was a very important principle since it was understood that even without naming the North African countries, they were the first ones to be considered. The North African countries enjoyed a privileged status in the Rome Treaty as previous French colonies, and it was of great importance to avoid the discrimination of Israel vis-à-vis these countries, especially Morocco, in the trade of oranges, a major Israeli export at that time to Europe.

The European Parliament was of great help in that period because even if it had no competence, it gave moral support to the Israeli demands; before the Parliament M. Rey said on January 24, 1964 that the commercial agreement would permit the various problems not yet settled in its framework to be reexamined periodically with the Israeli friends; "we will strive thus progressively to strengthen it and enlarge it."

A report was submitted by M. Blaisse in the name of the Commission for the external trade of the EP in 1964, in favor of "a first agreement giving satisfaction to both parties." An official delegation of the European Parliament came to Israel in November 1964 headed by President Duvieusart. The following year, 1965, Mr. G.L. Moro presented a provisional report proposing a resolution, later approved by the EP, in which Article 1 read:

> Reaffirms that only the association of Israel to the European Community, according to Article 238 of the Treaty establishing the EEC, will allow the complete satisfactions of the reciprocal interest.

Thus the principle of an association was reaffirmed by the EP, while Israeli representatives stressed in the meetings of the Mixed Commission in April 1965 and in June 1966 that a global agreement remained the aim of the Israeli government. This goal was stressed in a formal diplomatic note and a memorandum on October 4, 1966, to the Commission and the Governments of the Six in which a demand was put forward to substitute the commercial agreement expiring on July 1, 1967, by an association agreement. In this memorandum it was said inter alia:

> Be it in the domain of commercial exchanges and industrial organization, in that of international cooperation or in that of science and technology, if Europe of the Six would conclude a large association agreement with Israel, it would find in it a loyal and efficient partner.

The Council of Ministers invited the Commission in December 1966 to start exploratory talks with Israel on the problems raised in this note; thus for the first time the Council was authorizing the Commission to discuss a new agreement with Israel.

In June 1967 the Six-Day War started and on June 7, while the Israeli people were engaged in a struggle for their security, the Commission decided to recommend to the Council of Ministers the conclusion of an Association Agreement with Israel, taking into account the special links existing between Europe and Israel. Undoubtedly this was a decision of great political importance even if it could not be implemented without the consent of the Six at the Council.

A special Committee of the Permanent Representatives of the Six in Brussels envisaged in January 1968 either a preferential agreement with Israel for all industrial products at zero custom duty, or a more limited preferential agreement including most industrial products and a reduction of custom duties of 25% to 60% or only an acceleration of the custom reductions due in the framework of the "Kennedy Round," the GATT multilateral negotiation. It seems that at the time only the Federal Republic of Germany and the Netherlands supported the first solution, while Italy, Belgium, and Luxembourg preferred the second and France was against any kind of preferential agreement. In October 1968 the Commission stated again that a preferential agreement was the most suitable means to solve the problem of Israel in its relations with the EEC.

The stand of the member states was divided; in March 1968 the government of the Netherlands declared that the Community should treat in a uniform way all the states of the Mediterranean and therefore they could not accept a preferential agreement with Spain and the North African countries while refusing Israel the same chance. On December 10, 1968, Mr. Luns, then Netherlands minister of foreign affairs, declared:

> The Netherlands can not accept the fact that no progress was accomplished with Israel while important decisions were taken for other Mediterranean countries such as Morocco, Tunisia, Spain.

At the Council meeting of January 27, 1969, Mr. Lahr said that it was necessary to establish a double link in the concessions to be made to the Mediterranean countries: a link in timing concerning the simultaneous conclusion of the agreements and a link concerning the content of these agreements. The idea of parallelism between Israel and the North African countries was raised again in February 1969 at the European Parliament in a resolution in which the Commission was asked to prepare at the same time the association agreements with Tunisia and Morocco and the agreement with Israel.

France, according to the press, in May 1969 still refused to consider a preferential agreement with Israel because of the political situation prevailing in the Middle East. This meant simply that the protests of the Arab states against any further preference to Israel were carefully heard in Paris.

Israel on its side was interested in stronger ties with the EEC both for political and economic reasons; Western Europe was an important market for its exports since its agricultural products were suited to the countries of a continental temperate climate, while its industrial products were most suited for sophisticated countries with a high standard of living. An association would entail a structural change in Israeli industry, probably imposing the closure of the least efficient factories, but the process would enhance productivity and would therefore be a healthy one. One could also hope that the association would encourage European investments in the Israeli economy, which had a level of import of goods similar to that of other Mediterranean countries with a population ten times bigger.

On September 1, 1969, the Commission applied a reduction of 40% on the custom duty on oranges; however, the system of reference prices remained unchanged.

France, probably anxious to make progress with the North African countries, changed its stand and at the meeting of the Council of Ministers of July 22, 1969, Foreign Minister Schuman stated that whoever was in favor of a preferential agreement with Israel must at the same time accept the same principle for any Arab country asking for it as well. This idea was accepted by the other members of the Community and the way was open for a decision. On October 17, 1969, the Council issued the mandate for the negotiations "within the general framework of its Mediterranean policy and in expectation of a balanced development in its relations with the countries of the region."

Finally a preferential agreement with Israel was signed on June 29, 1970, in Luxembourg; on the same day a similar treaty was signed with Spain: the Netherlands would have opposed the signature of an agreement with Spain, because of the Franco regime, and made it conditional on a simultaneous signature with Israel.

An association under Article 238 was refused to Israel mainly on political grounds, but a new interpretation was given to Article 113, on which also this agreement was based, in order to give it a preferential nature. Under the clause of the agreement, which entered into force on October 1, 1970, with a duration of five years, more than 850 Israeli industrial products exported to the EEC benefited from a reduction in custom duties which progressively reached 50%. Some sensitive products were put on a special list and given a smaller reduction or a quota ceiling (cotton fabrics); other Israeli products were totally excluded. It was then that the important principle of some reciprocal treatment was established by Israel for goods originating in the EEC; these goods were divided in four categories and a reduction of between 30% and 10% was granted by Israel. The value of custom reduction given by Israel was equal to 40% of that granted by the EEC to Israel.

Israeli agricultural products were granted a 40% reduction in customs duties for citrus, bananas, and avocados; a 30% reduction for fresh vegetables and 40% on fruit preserves. No modification was introduced in the system of reference price.

Some Arab states opposed the conclusion of the new agreement with Israel fearing that it would weaken the Arab boycott; the secretariat of the Arab League sent a memorandum to the Commission threatening to impose a boycott on the EEC members. There was also a hint that Arab oil producers would reconsider their policy if Israel were to be linked to the Community.

The Enlargement of the Community

The accession of Great Britain, Denmark, and Ireland to the Community on January 1, 1973, created a completely new situation that could deeply affect the Israeli economy. Israel was worried mainly by the changes that would occur in Great Britain because of the great weight of this country in Israeli exports (especially of agricultural products) as well as the fact that the British would raise their custom duties up to the level of CET. The British market had been for years traditionally the most important outlet for Israeli fresh oranges and citrus juices; the British government had a very liberal policy on food imports since its agriculture could not supply more than a small part of local consumption. Entering the Community meant a major change for Great Britain since the Community had a huge surplus of food and the EC would impose the Common Agricultural Policy. Custom duties on fresh oranges and orange juice, for example, would rise steeply; Morocco and Tunisia would enjoy a 4% reduction and therefore there was a danger of diversion of trade in favor of the oranges of these countries against Israeli fruit. Plywood and bromine were among the Israeli industrial products that would have to pay higher custom duties because of the British adhesion to the EEC.

The Mediterranean Policy

On February 9, 1971, the European Parliament adopted a resolution inviting the member states to draw up a common policy towards the Mediterranean countries. At the meeting of the EEC Council of Ministers on June 26–27, 1972, Maurice Schuman, French foreign minister, presented a completely new idea: that a "global solution for manufactured products" be found to solve most of the problems of Spain, Israel, and other Mediterranean countries.

The official Israeli reaction to the French proposal was stated by Foreign Minister Abba Eban in a press conference given on August 7, 1972:

> I was asked about an idea, proposed by M. Schuman, of a Mediterranean free-trade area including Israel. I think it is a positive idea. It responds to Israel's desire to be associated with a large market and a large community into which its exports would have free entry. We must understand, and our industrialists too, that reciprocity is involved. We would have to open our market, which is a large one for Europe, much more widely…

On November 6 and 7, 1972, the Community Council of Ministers set out the guidelines of the global approach which was to include all the countries of the Mediterranean plus Jordan, with the aim of creating free-trade areas progressively covering also the main agricultural products, as well as organizing financial cooperation for some countries.

On January 30, 1973, a protocol was signed by the Community with Israel and a formal promise was given that a new agreement should be negotiated and would enter into force before January 1974, when the first adjustment to CET was due to take place in Great Britain.

The Council gave a first mandate to the Commission on June 25/26, 1973, but it was not possible to respect the timetable and to complete the package deal with Israel, Spain, Morocco, Tunisia, Algeria, and Malta before the end of the year. At the very last moment the British government decided unilaterally to apply a "standstill," not raising duties on imports from the six Mediterranean countries. The danger of a negative repercussion on the Israeli economy deriving from the British adhesion was thus temporarily avoided.

A wide range of opinions appeared once more among the member states of the Community. France gave all its support to Spain and the North African countries and stressed its friendship for the Arab countries. Italy was torn between the necessity of paying for most of the concessions to be made on agricultural products of other Mediterranean countries, often in competition with its own, and the desire to play fully its role of a Mediterranean power. Germany, the main commercial partner of the Mediterranean countries, had a moral obligation to Israel and the will to reach an understanding with the Arab states, while generally helping in removing obstacles in the way of the Israeli agreement. In the Benelux countries the business community was eager for closer links with Spain, while public opinion and Parliaments were against Spain for political reasons and in favor of closer links with Israel. A compromise was found enabling each member state to foster its political and economic goals in accordance with its sympathies and interests. In order to avoid United States' opposition to the Mediterranean policy, Great Britain asked and obtained the assurance that no reverse preferences should be given by the southern Mediterranean countries, with the exception of Israel, to the EEC.

After a first round of negotiations, the Commission sent back its proposals to the Council, accepting most of the Israeli requests, in order to obtain a "supplementary mandate." The Council met again and in its session of July 22/23, 1974, gave the general guidelines for a new mandate.

In December 1974 a new round of negotiations led, after a non-stop meeting from 3 P.M. till 7:25 A.M. next morning, to an agreed text of the new treaty establishing a free trade area for industrial products. The new agreement was signed in Brussels on May 11, 1975, by Foreign Minister Yigal Allon for Israel and by the Irish foreign minister, Garrett Fitzgerald, for the EEC. The agreement, which came into force on July 1, 1975, has no time limit and is therefore still in force; it is of a much wider scope than the two previous ones as it establishes a free trade area although limited to industrial products; Israel gave full reciprocity but with a delay of some years. Thus, while the EEC completed tariff dismantling on Israeli goods already on July 1, 1977, the gradual implementation of the same dismantling by Israel on EEC goods was completed on January 1, 1989, simultaneously to goods originating in the United States thanks to the Free Trade Agreement between Israel and that country.

The Israeli industrialist could now look at the whole Community as its potential market and should be able to produce on a much bigger scale well above the needs of the Israeli domestic market. On the other hand the competition with European goods was now felt inside Israel itself and this implied the need to reach higher productivity, better quality, and in general a more competitive product.

Political Cooperation

The first aim of the EEC was political although at first it was easier to build the economic side; in November 1970 the foreign ministers of the Six discussed for the first time in Munich a common stand on Middle Eastern problems. Immediately after the Yom Kippur War of October 1973, an oil boycott was declared by OAPEC, the Arab Oil Producers Organization, against the Netherlands and Denmark. This provoked the Declaration of the Nine of November 6, 1973, a kind of total surrender to the Arabs in which four principles were established as the basis for the common European policy: the inadmissibility of acquisition of territories by force; the necessity for Israel to end the territorial occupation in place since 1967; the respect for suzerainty, territorial integrity, and independence of every state of the region and their rights to live in peace within secure and recognized borders; the recognition that due account should be taken of the legitimate rights of the Palestinians.

The beginning of the Euro-Arab dialogue at the end of December 1973 in Copenhagen and its subsequent evolution was a factor for a change to a growingly pro-Arab stand. The Declaration of the Nine in Venice was given on June 13, 1980, after the historic meeting of President Anwar Sadat with Prime Minister Menachem Begin in Jerusalem and the subsequent signature of the Peace Treaty between Israel and Egypt in 1979. In December 1979 the Soviet Union invaded Afghanistan. Some believe that the strategic aim of Europe was to use the outraged feelings of Third World countries regarding the invasion in order to reinforce the European presence in the Islamic world. To this purpose the price of supporting the Arab thesis, the PLO, and the right to self-determination of the Palestinians did not seem too high. According to the Venice declaration of June 13, 1980, the countries of the European Community would be ready to participate in "a system of concrete and obligatory guaranties including in the field" (Art. 5), the Palestinian people should be able "to exercise fully its right to self-determination" (Art. 6), the PLO "must be associated with the negotiations" (Art. 7), the Jewish settlements in the administered territories are considered to be illegal and "a grave obstacle to the peace process" (Art. 9), Israel should put an end to its territorial occupation (Art. 9). Israel did not agree to the text and the spirit of the Venice declaration which ignored the Camp David peace treaty between Israel and Egypt and was considered to be unbalanced and pro-Arab.

The Israeli invasion of Lebanon in 1982 brought the relations with the states of the EEC to their lowest ebb; the Ten at Luxembourg in their declaration of June 29, 1982, maintained "their vigorous condemnation of the Israeli invasion of Lebanon," demanded "an immediate withdrawal of Israeli forces," and "a simultaneous withdrawal of the Palestinian forces in West Beirut" and admonished that:

> Israel will not obtain the security to which it has a right by using force and creating "faits accomplis" but it can find this security by satisfying the legitimate aspirations of the Palestinian people, who should have the opportunity to exercise their right to self-determination with all that this implies.

The Council of Ministers also decided to suspend the signature of the second Financial Protocol already initialed. Israel was even accused by Mr. Pisani, member of the EC Commission, to have blocked European humanitarian aid to Lebanon – which had never been sent in the first place.

At the beginning of September 1982 the massacre at Sabra and Shatila provoked the "profound shock and revulsion" of the Ten; they also welcomed the American initiative contained in President Reagan's speech of September 1, 1982, and underlined "the importance of the statement adopted by Arab heads of state and governments at Fez on September 9" calling "for a similar expression of a will of peace on the part of Israel" (Declaration of the Ten of September 20, 1982).

At the European Council of Stuttgart (June 17–19, 1983) the Ten, under the presidency of Germany, took a positive view of the Israeli-Lebanese Peace Treaty and decided to resume normal relations with Israel allowing for the signature of the second financial protocol and the meeting of the Council of Cooperation. In the Dublin summit of December 3–4, 1984, the Ten reiterated that the PLO must be associated with negotiations but refrained from any new Middle Eastern initiative. Bettino Craxi was the first European prime minister to go and meet Yasser Arafat, in Tunisia on December 7, 1984. The Ten had mixed feelings about American initiatives; they considered Arafat as a moderate who could be convinced to state publicly the abandonment of terror; they felt that if Arafat disappeared any successor might be much more radical. The huge economic interest of many European companies in the Arab countries seemed best assured by intimate contact with Arafat.

In the year 1985 two events showed how wide the gap between the Europeans and Israel had remained: the Israeli raid on the PLO headquarters near Tunis on October 1, and the hijacking of the Italian boat *Achille Lauro* some days later. The first was compared by an Italian minister to the Nazi killing of innocent hostages, among them Jews, by the Nazis in Fosse Ardeatine near Rome in March 1944; the second gave rise in the Italian media to the idea that Israel could avoid Palestinian terrorism if it only agreed to make concessions to the PLO.

The Israeli prime minister, Shimon Peres, launched a peace plan at the General Assembly of the United Nations in New York in October 1985, with the idea of an international conference that would accompany direct negotiations among the parties. Peres presented an Israeli scheme for peace at the Council of Cooperation in Brussels in January 1987. The declaration of the Twelve of February 23, 1987, reasserted that a negotiated solution in the Middle East should be based on the Venice Declaration; the Twelve were in favor of an international conference under the auspices of the United Nations and they expressed the wish "to see an improvement in the living conditions of the inhabitants of the occupied territories."

The entrance of Spain and Portugal into the European Community on January 1, 1986, worried Israeli farmers because 70% of their total production is exported and about

70% of total agricultural exports go to the EC countries; their exports could be endangered by preferential treatment given to Spain, their main competitor.

At a very early stage, in 1982, the Israeli Mission in Brussels voiced its concerns about the possible negative repercussions of the entry of Spain; the EC decided that traditional currents of trade should be allowed to continue unhampered. In this spirit a protocol was signed on December 8, 1986, that was aimed at solving some of the problems of Israeli agricultural exports during the transitional period of the Spanish accession. At the end of July 1987 the additional protocols of adaptation between Israel, Spain, and Portugal were initialed.

A problem which gave rise to some tension between Israel and the EC Commission was the sudden decision by the Council of Ministers to unilaterally grant the same preferences enjoyed by Israeli products entering the EC to Palestinian products originating in the territories. The decision was published on December 31, 1986; the Israeli authorities felt that the Twelve had more in mind to help the Palestinian entity evolve into a state than merely economic matters.

After months of negotiations Israel accepted the EC decision for the direct export of agricultural products from the West Bank and Gaza Strip to the EC. Subsequently the Council of Ministers approved on December 15, 1987, the signature of three additional protocols, including one on Israeli agricultural exports, which was long overdue, since it had to give Israel some defense against damages caused by the Spanish adhesion of January 1, 1986. The European Parliament, in an unprecedented move, decided on March 9, 1988, not to approve the ratification of the Protocols because of Israeli repression of the Intifada and the obstruction of Palestinian exports, which had been settled by then. This was a *de facto* political sanction using economic means; eventually the European Parliament ratified the three protocols on October 12, 1988.

On December 30, 1989, there was a demonstration in Jerusalem organized by the Peace Now movement. Excessive force was used by the Israeli police and on January 18, 1990, the European Parliament condemned "the brutal intervention of the Israeli police during the demonstration" and recalled a previous resolution concerning the closing down of Palestinian universities. The EP called on the Commission "to freeze immediately budget heading 7394 allocated to scientific cooperation with Israel." The EC Commission on February 7 quickly complied with this resolution and suspended the scientific cooperation; it took more than a year to restore those joint projects unilaterally brought to an end by the Commission.

Financial aid to the Palestinians started in 1982 with a small sum of 3 million ECU yearly; in the year 1991 after the Gulf War, an emergency aid of 60 millions ECU was decided upon but again the Commission made it conditional on the nomination of its representative for the distribution of this aid in the territories: a request considered by the Israelis to be political.

In a meeting which took place in Paris in June 1991 between Foreign Minister David Levy and the European "troika" a wide agreement was reached: Israel would be admitted to the European Economic Space, the Community would participate in the future Peace Conference on the Middle East, and the Commission would appoint its representative to the territories. No timetable or technical details were given and the entrance of Israel to the European Economic Space was never implemented.

[Sergio I. Minerbi]

Later Developments

Relations between Israel and the European Union (EU) are now formally governed by the Euro-Mediterranean Partnership, established through the EU-Israel Association Agreement and the regional dimension of the Barcelona Process.

Israel was keen on becoming a part of the Barcelona Process, initiated in 1995, between the EU and 12 Mediterranean partners. This initiative was conceived by the EU mainly with a view to the Maghreb countries. These countries, which had historical ties with France, were sending thousands of emigrants to Europe. The EU felt that raising the standard of life in the Maghreb countries and creating new jobs would bring less pressure to immigrate to the EU. The situation was radically different for Israel.

Ten years later, the achievements of the Barcelona Process are rather modest. Mediterranean countries need to create 5 million jobs a year, a target which seems impossible to attain. The EU also hoped that through the Euro-Mediterranean Partnership it would have a say in the Middle East peace process.

The major development which took place since the early 1990s in the relations between Israel and the EU has been the signature of the Association Agreement, which was signed on November 20, 1995, and replaced the earlier Cooperation Agreement of 1975. The Association Agreement went into force on June 1, 2000, following ratification by the 15 Member State Parliaments, the European Parliament, and the Knesset.

The principles outlined in the treaty were not always fully implemented. According to the treaty, regional cooperation should be encouraged, a regular political dialogue should be established, as well as a dialogue on scientific, technological, and cultural matters. The regular political dialogue has taken place on rare occasions, probably because the EU was constantly taking sides in the ongoing conflict between Israel and the Palestinians, in favor of the latter.

The situation has been rather better in the field of economic cooperation. In trade relations, the EU is Israel's major trading partner, with about 40% of Israeli imports coming from the EU and about 33% of Israeli exports directed to the EU. In the year 2004, total imports from the EU reached $16,813 million, while total exports reached $10,721 million. The figures excluding diamonds are respectively $7,611 million for the imports and $7,435 million for the exports. One could jump to the conclusion that the huge deficit of about $4 billion a year is due mainly to the trade in diamonds.

Cooperation has been the best in the field of science and technology. Israel is highly advanced in technological innovation, especially in the electronics industry and biotechnology. Many achievements in the electronics industry are due to fall-out from military research.

On March 8, 1999, the Agreement for Scientific and Technical Cooperation between the European Community and Israel went into force. Thus Israel has been fully associated with the 5th Framework Programme (FP5) for Community RTD (1999–2002). Later, Israel became fully associated in the 6th Framework Programme (2002–06) as of December 16, 2002.

With the access granted to Israel to the Framework Programme for Community RTD, the financial flow was reversed. Instead of the about $20 million a year received by Israeli bodies from the EU, $36.6 million were paid by Israel as its participation fee. Israel's share is calculated on the basis of the percentage of its GNP compared to the total GNP of all contributing countries. Israel's status of "Associated Country" requires financial participation in the FP budget, which reached Euro 150 million for FP5 and Euro 192 million for FP6. In return Israeli organizations, which take part in selected joint EU-Israel projects, can receive a financial contribution from the Commission consisting of the reimbursement of some of the costs incurred. The Israeli contributions are very substantial in comparison with the total expenditure of the Israeli government in support of industrial-scientific research.

The main advantage of working with European bodies is to share risks and costs. On the other hand, about 40 percent of the groups working in the framework program do not envisage any product at all. In September 2003, there were 623 joint research projects associating Israeli groups to the FP5; out of them, 143 were under Israeli coordination. Total estimated European funds to Israeli research reached Euro 163 million in FP5.

At the end of September 2000, the Palestinians started a new Intifada. Five years later, in September 2005, the Palestinians counted more than 3,000 victims, while the Israelis lost more than 1,000 people, mainly civilians. The Palestinians perpetrated many terrorist actions, but obtained no political results, notwithstanding the support they received from the EU.

On April 30, 2003, the U.S. State Department released the text of the "roadmap" to a permanent solution to the Israeli-Palestinian conflict. The roadmap specifies the steps for the two parties to take to reach a settlement, and a timeline for doing so, under the auspices of the Quartet – the United States, the European Union, the United Nations, and Russia.

On June 4, 2003, a meeting took place at Aqaba, with President George Bush, King Abdullah of Jordan, Israeli Prime Minister Ariel Sharon, and Palestinian Prime Minister Mahmoud Abbas. In his statement Prime Minister Ariel Sharon referred to the possibility of establishing a Palestinian state within temporary borders, if the conditions for this were met. The Palestinian state will, inter alia, be completely demilitarized. This state will be the home of the Palestinian diaspora; no Palestinian refugees will be permitted to enter the territory of the State of Israel.

On May 1, 2004, the EU was enlarged to 25 Member States and established a new "European Neighborhood Policy" designed to offer its neighbors greater political, security, economic, and cultural cooperation. Policy negotiations with partner countries are meant to bring upon an agreed Action Plan.

On the political level, the discrepancies between the European stand and Israeli policy were most intense during the year 2004 and, sometimes, Israel felt that the Europeans went further than criticizing a policy, but were casting doubt on the legitimacy of the existence of the State of Israel. The European Council of March 25–6, 2004 declared:

> The European Council expressed its deep concern at the situation in the Middle East ... following in particular the extra-judicial killing of Hamas leader Sheikh Ahmed Yassin. While having repeatedly condemned terrorist atrocities against Israelis and recognized Israel's right to protect its citizens against terrorist attacks, the European Union has consistently opposed extra-judicial killings, which are contrary to international law.

In July 2004, Javier Solana, the chief representative for foreign policy and security of EU, met Prime Minister Ariel Sharon, who said: "Israel is interested in integrating the international community, mainly Europe, in the peace process with the Palestinians, but without a radical modification of the European stand, mainly regarding the security of Israel and its need of defending itself, it will be very difficult to do so." Solana said on this occasion: "The EU has a role in Middle East peace talks, like it or not."

The EU asked Israel to dismantle its security fence, to freeze the settlements in the territories, to stop extrajudicial executions ("targeted killings"), to guarantee human rights and better living conditions for the Palestinians.

The EU is one of the main contributors of financial aid to the Palestinian Authority and Israel has expressed doubts that a part of its disbursement is not being used for terrorist activities. The European Anti-Fraud Office, OLAF, made an investigation, but did not find enough proof to substantiate the accusation, while at the same time it did not exclude the possibility altogether.

Among the possible causes of the negative stand taken by the EU the following may be indicated: the success of Palestinian propaganda depicting Israel as a demon comparable to the Nazis; the success of the Intifada in influencing public opinion, especially through television; the enormous economic interests of most of the European countries in the Arab countries and their desire to go on selling them huge quantities of arms.

After the death of Yasser Arafat, chairman of the PLO, in November 2004, a new Palestinian leadership agreed to and implemented a kind of truce. Israel, for its part, decided unilaterally to dismantle all 21 of its settlements in the Gaza Strip (*Gush Katif) and from four more settlements in northern

Samaria. Disengagement from the Gaza Strip was completed on September 12, 2005.

The Action Plan with Israel was concluded on December 13, 2004. It allows the possibility for Israel to participate progressively in key aspects of EU policies and programs, to upgrade the scope and intensity of political cooperation, to encourage Israeli legislation as a means to open the EU internal market to Israel, and to achieve greater liberalization of trade, services, and agriculture. The Action Plan identifies, inter alia, as priorities cooperation in the Middle East conflict and other areas, counter-terrorism, non-proliferation of weapons of mass destruction, human rights, improved dialogue between cultures and religions, migration issues, the fight against organized crime and human trafficking and police and judicial cooperation, transport, energy, environment, science and technology, and people-to-people contacts.

On September 15, 2005, Israeli Foreign Minister Silvan Shalom met in New York with Benita Ferrero-Waldner, the European Commissioner for External Relations and European Neighborhood Policy. She said:

> I have also reiterated to Minister Shalom that disengagement has to bring tangible and immediate improvement to the lives of ordinary Palestinians. It has to offer hope to both sides. We are working closely with James Wolfensohn, the Quartet Special Envoy, on ways to revitalize the Palestinian economy. We have offered our help and support to resolve crucial issues such as border crossing, customs and links between West Bank and Gaza.

The Israeli authorities have been very satisfied with the new Action Plan, which extends cooperation to new fields. But it is doubtful that the Israelis really understand that this increased cooperation has a price: to accept the involvement of the EU in the peace process with the Palestinians. Vice Prime Minister Shimon Peres said that eventually a larger Europe will incorporate the Middle East. Then, Israel will certainly ask to be included in the economic network of Europe.

Main Agreements between Israel and the EEC

4 June 1964 Commercial Agreement

29 June 1970 (Preferential) Agreement

11 May 1975 Agreement (Industrial Free Trade Area); *Kitvei Amana*, n. 882.

8 February 1977 Additional Protocol to the Agreement (on Scientific Cooperation); *Kitvei Amana*, n. 924.

18 March 1981 Second Additional Protocol to the Agreement (relating to Greece); *Kitvei Amana*, n. 965.

24 June 1983 Second Financial Protocol, *Kitvei Amana*, n. 966.

18 December 1984 Third Additional Protocol to the Agreement, *Kitvei Amana*, n. 986.

15 December 1987 Fourth Additional Agreement to the Agreement (relating to Portugal and Spain), *Official Journal of the European Communities*, L 327 of 30.11.1988.

15 December 1987 Third Financial Protocol, *Ibidem.*

20 November 1995 Signature of the Association Agreement

1 June 2000 The Association Agreement entered into force

8 March 1999 Agreement for Scientific and Technical Co-operation between the EC and Israel, entered into force

16 December 2002 Israel associated to the 6th Framework Programme

13 December 2004 Action Plan with Israel concluded

[Sergio I. Minerbi (2nd ed.)]

°**EUSEBIUS PAMPHILI** (c. 260–339 C.E.), Church Father and archbishop of Caesarea. Eusebius was born in Caesarea Maritima, where he was a pupil of the priest Pamphilus (c. 240–309), who had studied with Origen. Eusebius was appointed bishop in c. 313. He was associated with imperial court circles and was a devoted admirer of the emperor *Constantine. A scholar in a wide range of fields, Eusebius was a prolific writer on exegesis, history, apologetics, and dogmatics. Especially important is his *Chronicle*, a summary of world history based partly on the Bible. *Historia Ecclesiastica* is a study of Church history in ten volumes (completed in 324) up to the time of the victory of Christianity under Constantine. Important for Church history is his small work on the Christian martyrs of Palestine. He also wrote a biography of Constantine, a panegyric to the emperor who built the first churches in Palestine (notably those at Bethlehem and at Golgotha in Jerusalem).

Eusebius' theological position is reflected in his two great works:

(1) *Praeparatio Evangelica* ("Preparation for Christianity"), in which he proves the Greek views on religion to be baseless, Judaism alone providing the proper foundation for the establishment of religion;

(2) *Demonstratio Evangelica* ("Proof of the Truth of Christianity"), in which he severely criticizes Judaism for failing to perceive that the revelation of God in the Bible was merely a prelude to "the glad tidings [the gospel] of the kingdom of God" and that only in the New Testament do these "glad tidings" appear.

The *Onomasticon* of Eusebius, written between 313 and early 325, contains more than 1,000 place-names mentioned in the Bible and gospels which he arranged alphabetically by books of the Bible, following the Septuagint spelling of the names. The primary aim was for it to be used as a sourcebook to facilitate the reading of the Old Testament with the topography of the Holy Land as its backdrop. At the time of Eusebius, the proper veneration of the places associated with Jesus had still not been fully established and so he would not have deemed it necessary to list such sites in his *Onomasticon*. One assumes that when Eusebius wrote in Greek "one can see this place to this very day…," it meant that he had actually visited the place himself, or that he acquired some reliable first-hand information about it. He was particularly good when it came to places in the hill country and along the coast, but less reliable about far-flung places. There is also information in his work about provinces and administrative districts, about the ethnic makeup of settlements, topography and holy places, and references to roads. The distances, taken from Roman road maps (e.g., the Peutinger Map) and stated in Roman miles, help determine urban boundaries and the course of highways, and they also provide information on the physical geography of the country. Eusebius also consulted the writings of Josephus. He reports that in his time Jews, Christians, and pagans coexisted in the country, with a large number of Jewish villages in his day but only four Christian ones. The *Onomasticon* was also a major source of inspiration for the *Madaba mosaic map of the Holy Land, which is dated to the second half of the sixth century. The mosaicist in some cases even copied Eusebius' mistakes. While this was not in any way a comprehensive listing of all the places in the Bible – a feat Eusebius may very well have intended but never succeeded to do – his work serves as an important source of information on the country in the early fourth century.

In c. 420 the *Onomasticon* was translated into Latin by Jerome who made several additions reflecting the changes that had meanwhile occurred. Extracts from the Syriac version appeared in 1924. Klostermann's edition from 1904 *Das Onomastikon der biblischen Ortsnamen* was until recently the version most frequently referred to by scholars. A translation into Hebrew was made by Ezra Zion Melamed in 1933 and published with a commentary in *Tarbiz* (reprinted as a separate publication in 1966). A translation into English was made by G.S.P. Freeman-Grenville (2003).

BIBLIOGRAPHY: J.P. Migne (ed.), *Patrologia Graeca*, vols. XIX–XXIV (complete works); R. Laqueur, *Eusebius als Historiker seiner Zeit* (1929); H. Berkhof, *Die Theologie des Eusebius* (1939); 4 (1932/33), 78–96, 248–84; Thomsen, in: ZDPV, 26 (1903), 97ff. **ADD. BIBLIOGRAPHY:** D.S. Wallace-Hadrill, *Eusebius of Caesarea* (1960); R.M. Grant, *Eusebius as Church Historian* (1980); T.D. Barnes, *Constantine and Eusebius* (1981); E.Z. Melamed, "Onomasticon," in: *Encyclopedia Biblica* (1955), 151–54; E.Z. Melamed (transl. with notes), *The Onomastikon of Eusebius* (1966); D. Groh, "The Onomasticon of Eusebius and the Rise of Christian Palestine," in: *Studia Patristica*, 18 (1985), 23–31; L. Di Segni, "The 'Onomasticon' of Eusebius and the Madaba Map," in: M. Piccirillo and E. Alliata (eds.), *The Madaba Map Centenary, 1897–1997* (1999), 115–20; G.P. Grenville, R.L. Chapman, and J.E. Taylor, *Palestine in the Fourth Century. The Onomasticon by Eusebius of Caesarea* (2003).

[Michael Avi-Yonah / Shimon Gibson (2nd ed.)]

EUTHANASIA, term denoting "the action of inducing gentle and easy death," first used by the British moral historian W.E.H. Lecky in 1869. Among advocates of this measure to terminate the life of sufferers from incurable or painful disease are many earlier philosophers, Christian as well as pagan, including Plato in his *Republic* (3:405ff.) and Sir Thomas More in his *Utopia* (2:7). The precise Hebrew equivalent for euthanasia, *mitah yafah* ("pleasant death"), occurs several times in the Talmud, though always in connection with the duty to reduce to a minimum the anguish of capital criminals before their execution (e.g., Sanh. 45a), and never in the sense of deliberately hastening the end of persons dying from natural causes. In the Jewish view, life being of infinite worth, any fraction of it is of equally infinite value, and the relief from suffering cannot be purchased at the cost of life itself, whatever other concessions Jewish law may make or urge for the mitigation of pain. Hence, "a patient on his deathbed is considered as a living person in every respect ... and it is forbidden to cause him to die quickly ... or to move him from his place (lest this hasten his death);... and whoever closes his eyes with the onset of death is regarded as shedding blood" (Sh. Ar., YD 339:1 and gloss). Indeed, killing any innocent person, "whether he is healthy or about to die from natural causes," is legally codified as murder (Maim. Yad, Roẓe'aḥ 2:7). Some recent rabbinical responsa, however, are inclined to sanction the cessation of "heroic" methods to prolong a lingering life without hope of recovery. The withdrawal of treatment under such circumstances might be justified on the basis of the permission to remove from a dying person an extraneous impediment, such as "a clattering noise or salt on his tongue, delaying the departure of his soul" (Sh. Ar., loc. cit., gloss).

The otherwise uncompromising opposition to euthanasia no doubt springs from the life-affirming attitude of Judaism in which, nationally as well as individually, life in misery is to be preferred to death with glory or dignity, a sentiment which stirred the Psalmist to exclaim gratefully: "The Lord hath chastened me sore; but He hath not given me over unto death" (Ps. 118:18). For the same reason, martyrdom is permitted only in the most exceptional circumstances; to lay down one's life, even for the fulfillment of divine laws, when such sacrifice is not required by law, is regarded as a mortal offense (Maim. Yad, Yesodei ha-Torah 5:4).

[Immanuel Jakobovits]

In Nazi Germany

Euthanasia was also a euphemism used by the Nazi regime for the murder of the disabled, a group of human beings defamed as "life unworthy of life." Although Adolf Hitler and his associates talked about "mercy death" their aim was not to shorten the lives of persons with painful terminal diseases but to kill those they considered inferior, who could otherwise have lived for many years.

The belief that mentally and physically disabled human beings should be excluded from a nation's gene pool was a staple argument of the international eugenic movement, in Germany known as racial hygiene, and had led to widespread sterilization of the disabled in various countries, including the United States. The Nazis incorporated the goals of the eugenicists into their racial world view, and on July 14, 1933, only four and a half months after Hitler became chancellor, the German government enacted the Law for the Prevention of Offspring with Hereditary Diseases, the so-called sterilization law mandating the compulsory sterilization of the disabled. This law led to the sterilization of three to four hundred thousand disabled German nationals, representing about 0.5 percent of the German population.

The attack on patients with disabilities in state hospitals and nursing homes during the 1930s had involved sterilization and a reduced standard of care. But this was only the beginning. In 1935 Adolf Hitler told Gerhard Wagner, the Reich physicians' leader, that once war began he would implement the killing of the disabled. As Germany unleashed World War II and Nazi policy became more radical, the regime crossed the line separating traditional eugenic policies from killing operations. Although this radical decision had been initiated by the political leadership, the scientific and medical community did not oppose it, because the idea had circulated since at least 1920, the year the jurist Karl Binding and the psychiatrist Alfred Hoche published *The Authorization for the Destruction of Life Unworthy of Life.*

The first Nazi killing operation was directed against institutionalized disabled patients. It started with the killing of infants and young children born with mental or physical disabilities. Hitler appointed Dr. Karl Brandt, his escorting physician, and Philipp Bouhler, who headed the Chancellery of the Fuehrer (*Kanzlei des Fuehrers*, or KdF), to direct the killing operation, and they in turn designated Viktor Brack, chief of Office II in the KdF, as the person to implement the Fuehrer's order. The so-called children's euthanasia was top-secret and was carried out in various hospitals. There the children were placed in so-called special children's wards; they were killed with an overdose of common barbiturates, and sometimes also through starvation diets.

In September 1939, the killing operation was expanded to include adults. Hitler first appointed Leonardo Conti, state secretary for health in the Reich Ministry of Interior, to direct adult euthanasia, telling him in the presence of Hans Heinrich Lammers and Martin Bormann "that he considered it appropriate that life unfit for living of severely insane patients should be ended by intervention that would result in death." Conti accepted the assignment, but he did not remain in charge long; within a few weeks, Hitler replaced him, turning once again to Brandt and Bouhler as his plenipotentiaries, so that Brack and the KdF could administer adult euthanasia alongside that for children. To avoid implicating the Chancellery, the staff administering the euthanasia killings moved from the KdF into a confiscated Jewish villa at Tiergarten Street number 4 and euthanasia was thus soon known as Operation T4, or simply as T4.

The method used to kill the children could not be used to kill the far larger number of adults. To accomplish its task, T4 therefore constructed killing centers, including gas chambers and crematoria, and developed a killing technique to select, transport, and "process" the victims. And always the killers robbed the corpses of their victims, taking gold teeth and bridge work to enrich the state as well as internal organs to enrich "scientific research." For this purpose, T4 established six killing centers – Brandenburg, Grafeneck, Hartheim, Sonnenstein, Bernburg, and Hadamar – but only four were ever operational at the same time. To hide the killings, T4 used subterfuge to fool the relatives; the killing centers camouflaged as hospitals wrote letters of condolence and issued fraudulent death certificates.

In their 1920 book, Binding and Hoche had argued that euthanasia could only function if the act of this kind of mercy death would be decriminalized, so that physicians would not have to fear prosecution under the murder statute, paragraph 212 of the German penal code, which remained in force throughout the Nazi period. Since Hitler absolutely refused to consider promulgating a euthanasia law, the KdF decided to ask Hitler for written orders, so that they could convince physicians to collaborate. In October 1939, Hitler finally signed a document, more an authorization than an order, that had been prepared by the KdF. But to emphasize that war would not only alter the international status of the Reich but also herald "domestic purification," he predated it to September 1, 1939, the day World War II began. Prepared on Hitler's personal stationery, as if mass murder was his "private affair," but never promulgated or published in any legal gazette, this authorization did not actually have the force of law, but served, nevertheless, as the "legal" basis for the killing operation.

The imposed secrecy did not prevent news of the murder of the disabled to reach the general population. The unrest of victims' relatives posed a danger to the regime, and in August 1941 Hitler therefore ordered a stop to the gassing of the disabled. This order did not, however, end the killing of the disabled; only their gassing in killing centers stopped. Children's euthanasia continued without interruption; adults were murdered in regular hospitals spread throughout the Reich. The T4 killing centers also continued to operate for several years; they were used to kill concentration camp inmates under a killing enterprise known as Operation 14 f13. The Austrian killing center Hartheim near Linz continued in operation until late in 1944 for the killings under 14f13 and later for the murder of prisoners from the nearby Mauthausen concentration camp. Furthermore, a selected number of T4 male staff members were dispatched to Lublin to operate the killing centers of Operation Reinhard: Belzec, Sobibor, and Treblinka. One of those was the Austrian physician Irmfried Eberl, medical director of the T4 killing centers in Brandenburg and Bernburg, who served as the first commandant of Treblinka.

After the war, the perpetrators argued that Jews were never killed in Operation T4, since they did not "deserve" mercy death, and this was believed at the Nuremberg and later trials. But this was not true. Jewish institutionalized disabled patients were included alongside non-Jewish victims from the beginning. In the spring of 1940, however, a decision was made on the highest level to kill Jewish patients as a group. They were concentrated in a number of central institutions, and killed in the closest killing center. But for the Jews there were no letters of condolence; the Jews were supposed to disappear without a trace. In the end, however, T4 did issue fraudulent death certificates long after the victims had been killed; this permitted T4 to extort money for weeks, even months, for upkeep of the already murdered Jewish patients. To accomplish this, T4 claimed the patients had been deported to a non-existent hospital in Cholm in Poland, and issued fraudulent death certificates with that non-existent address.

[Henry Friedlander (2nd ed.)]

BIBLIOGRAPHY: I. Jakobovits, *Jewish Medical Ethics* (1959²), 123–5; idem, *Journal of a Rabbi* (1967²), 165f. (= *Essays... I. Brodie* (1967), 195, Eng. pt.). **ADD. BIBLIOGRAPHY:** L. Alexander, "Medical Science under Dictatorship," in: *New England Journal of Medicine*, 241:2 (1949), 39–47; G.E. Allen, "The Eugenics Record Office at Cold Spring Harbor, 1910–1940: An Essay in Institutional History," in: *Osiris*, 2d ser., 2 (1986), 225–64; G. Aly, "Medizin gegen Unbrauchbare," in: *Beiträge zur nationalsozialistischen Gesundheits- und Sozialpolitik*, 1 (1985), 9–74; idem, "Der saubere und der schmutzige Fortschritt," in: *Beiträge zur nationalsozialistischen Gesundheits- und Sozialpolitik*, 2 (1985), 9–78; I. Arndt and W. Scheffler, "Organisierter Massenmord an Juden in nationalsozialistischen Vernichtungslagern," in: *Vierteljahrshefte für Zeitgeschichte*, 24 (1976), 105–35; G. Bock, *Zwangssterilisation im Nationalsozialismus: Studien zur Rassenpolitik und Frauenpolitik* (1986); M. Burleigh, *Death and Deliverance: "Euthanasia" in Germany, c. 1900–1945* (1995); P. Chroust (ed.), *Friedrich Mennecke, Innenansichten eines medizinischen Täters im Nationalsozialismus. Eine Edition seiner Briefe, 1935–1947*, 2 vols. paginated throughout (1987); K. Doerner, "Nationalsozialismus und Lebensvernichtung," in: *Vierteljahrshefte fuer Zeitgeschichte*, 15 (1967), 121–52; H. Friedlander, *The Origins of Nazi Genocide: From Euthanasia to the Final Solution* (1995); S.J. Gould, *The Mismeasure of Man* (1981); M.H. Kater, *Doctors Under Hitler* (1989); F.K. Kaul, *Nazimordaktion T4: Ein Bericht ueber die erste industriemässig durchgeführte Mordaktion des Naziregimes* (1973); E. Klee, *"Euthanasie" im NS-Staat: Die "Vernichtung lebensunwerten Lebens"* (1983); D.J. Kevles, *In the Name of Eugenics: Genetics and the Uses of Human Heredity* (1985); S. Kühl, *The Nazi Connection: Eugenics, American Racism, and German National Socialism* (1994); R.J. Lifton, *The Nazi Doctors: Medical Killing and the Psychology of Genocide* (1986); A. Mitscherlich and F. Mielke (eds.), *Medizin ohne Menschlichkeit: Dokumente des Nuernberger Aerzteprozesses* (1960); B. Mueller-Hill, *Murderous Science: Elimination by Scientific Selection of Jews, Gypsies, and Others, Germany, 1933–1945*, trans. G.R. Fraser (1988); K. Nowak, *"Euthanasie" und Sterilisierung im "Dritten Reich"* (1980²); A. Platen-Hallermund, *Die Tötung Geisteskranker in Deutschland: Aus der deutschen Aerztekommission beim amerikanischen Militaergericht* (1948); A. Rueckerl, *NS-Vernichtungslager im Spiegel deutscher Strafprozesse* (1977); H.W. Schmuhl, *Rassenhygiene, Nationalsozialismus, Euthanasie: Von der Verhütung zur Vernichtung "lebensunwerten Lebens," 1890–1945* (1987); G. Sereny, *Into that Darkness: From Mercy Killing to Mass Murder* (1974); S.F. Weiss, "The Race Hygiene Movement in Germany," in: *Osiris*, 2d ser., 3 (1987), 193–236.

°**EUTROPIUS** (fourth century C.E.), author of a compendium of Roman history. He mentions *Pompey's Judean campaign in 63 B.C.E. and the subjugation of the Jews by *Vespasian (*Breviarium*, 6:14, 16; 7:19).

[Jacob Petroff]

EVANS, ELI (1936–), U.S. administrator and Jewish historian. Evans was born in Durham, North Carolina, where his father served six terms as mayor from 1950 to 1962. His grandmother founded the first southern chapter of the Hadassah organization in the pre-World War I period.

After graduating from the University of North Carolina in 1958, he took a law degree at Yale University in 1963. He worked in various branches of government, state and national, as a speechwriter for President Lyndon Johnson, and as a White House assistant.

In 1973, he published *The Provincials: A Personal History of Jews in the South.* The book provided an insight into the Jewry of the southern United States, which had never been studied in depth previously. One of Evans' most revealing statistics was that more than 45 Jews held mayorships and other leading government positions in southern communities. The book generated a new field of study of southern Jewry.

Turning his focus to philanthropy, in 1977 Evans became the first president of the Revson Foundation, the charitable organization started by Charles Revson, the founder of Revlon. He guided the foundation in four specific areas: urban affairs, with special emphasis on New York City; education; bio-medical research policy; and Jewish philanthropy and education.

In the Jewish field, the foundation made a number of significant gifts. The first major grant helped to underwrite the ten-part television series *Civilization and the Jews*, narrated by Abba Eban. A second gift made possible the production of *Sesame Street* in Hebrew by Israel Education Television. A further large gift was allocated to the Jewish Museum, New York, for its remodeling and expansion to provide an electronics education center on all aspects of Judaism.

In 1988 Evans published a biography of the Civil War secretary of state *Judah P. Benjamin: The Jewish Confederate.* Evans mined previously untapped sources and demonstrated aspects of Benjamin's personality that reflected the continuing strain of his Judaism even though the well-known southerner did not practice his faith. In 1993 he published a collection of essays entitled *The Lonely Days Were Sundays: Reflections of a Jewish Southerner.*

Evans retired from the Revson Foundation in 2003. In 2004 the foundation honored its president emeritus with a substantial financial gift to the Carolina Center for Jewish Studies at the University of North Carolina at Chapel Hill to establish a program in Evans' name to support outreach activities on campus and in communities across North Carolina. The center, which was established at UNC's College of Arts and Sciences in 2003, engages in teaching and research to explore Jewish history, culture, and religion in the United States and abroad. Involved with the center for Jewish studies since its inception, Evans serves as chairman of the advisory board.

Often referred to as "the poet laureate of southern Jews," Evans has served as the voice, as well as the heart and soul, of both his fellow southerners and fellow Americans.

[David Geffen / Ruth Beloff (2nd ed.)]

EVANS, JANE (1907–2004), U.S. Jewish communal leader. Born in New York City, Evans was raised as a Reform Jew in Brooklyn, beginning her lifelong affiliation with the Reform movement. She received her B.A. from Xavier University in Cincinnati and moved to St. Louis in 1928 where she began to work as a designer and taught at the local YM/YWHA. She was recruited from there to become the executive director of the National Federation of Temple Sisterhoods for the *Union of American Hebrew Congregations in 1951. She developed its program on Jewish education and on world peace and through the *World Union of Progressive Judaism expanded the work of the NFTS overseas. She brought the energy and leadership of the NFTS to the Jewish Braille Institute, whose board she had joined in 1933, only two years after it was founded. Under her leadership the Jewish Braille Institute provided resources to the Jewish blind in 40 countries. She eventually became president of the JBI in 1979, three years after her retirement from the UAHC, until 1993 when at the spry age of 86 she stepped down.

A woman of great intellect, integrity, and energy, Evans taught at the New School for Social Research in New York and devoted herself to Jewish and philanthropic causes throughout her long and active life. Widely known as a distinguished national leader, a religious pacifist, and an advocate for human rights, she was a founder and former president of the Jewish Peace Fellowship and former president of the National Peace Conference. She was awarded the Abraham Joshua Heschel Award for peace work in the Jewish tradition. She served on the Commission on Displaced Persons of the American Jewish Conference after World War II.

BIBLIOGRAPHY: K.M. Olitzsky, L.J. Sussman, and M.H. Stern, *Reform Judaism in America: A Biographical Dictionary and Sourcebook* (1993).

[Michael Berenbaum (2nd ed.)]

EVANS, ROBERT (1930–), U.S. film producer and actor. Born Robert Shapera in New York, Evans decided to become an actor in elementary school, and at 12 was cast in *Radio Mystery Theater* as a Nazi colonel. At 14 he was a regular talent on the radio program *Let's Pretend.* He changed his name to Evans in middle school, and began to find roles on television. He ventured out to Hollywood, but returned home to work in his brother's women's clothing company, Evan Picone. By 25 he was a millionaire, and at 26 he was rediscovered at a Beverly Hills hotel swimming pool and cast in the Lon Chaney biopic *The Man of a Thousand Faces* (1957) as studio head Irving *Thalberg opposite James Cagney. When the actors, writer, and director disliked working with him on his next film, the adaptation of Earnest Hemingway's *The Sun Also Rises* (1957), 20th Century Fox producer Darryl *Zanuck paid a visit to the Mexican set and said, "The kid stays in the picture. And anybody who doesn't like it can quit!" Evans was inspired by Zanuck's power and decided he wanted to become a producer. He was hired by 20th Century Fox but left Fox before ever making a picture. Tycoon Charles Bludhorn made Evans an offer he couldn't refuse, putting him in charge of Paramount Pictures. Under his leadership, Paramount had a string of hits: *The Odd Couple* (1968), *Rosemary's Baby* (1968), *Goodbye, Columbus* (1969), *Love Story* (1970), and *The Godfather* (1972), which won the Academy Award for best picture. Evans became enamored of actress Ali MacGraw; the couple married in 1969, and had a son, Joshua, before divorcing in 1972 (she left him for Steve McQueen whom she had met on the set of the Evans production *The Getaway*). Evans left Paramount to produce his own films, most notably *Chinatown* (1974), *Marathon Man* (1976), *Black Sunday* (1977), and *Urban Cowboy* (1980). Drug abuse, drug charges, and other scandals as well as two box-office bombs, *The Cotton Club* (1984) and *The Two Jakes* (1990), sunk his career. Broke but unbowed, Evans wrote his memoir *The Kid Stays in the Picture* in 1994, which became a bestseller and a cult favorite audio classic, later adopted by the Library of Congress. Evans was rewarded by a renewed deal at Paramount Studios. In 2003, he provided the voice for an animated cartoon, *Kid Notorious*, based on his exploits. Later film projects include producing the film *How to Lose a Guy in 10 Days* (2003).

[Adam Wills (2nd ed.)]

EVE (Heb. חַוָּה, Ḥavvah), the first woman, wife of *Adam, and mother of the human race. After Adam had reviewed and assigned names to the animals, but had not found a suitable mate among them, God put him to sleep, removed one of his ribs, and formed it into a woman. Adam immediately recognized this being as an integral part of himself, his own bone and flesh, and called her "Woman" (Heb. *ʾishah*) because she was taken "from Man" (Heb. *ʾish*). (Unlike the two English words, the Hebrew ones are completely unrelated etymologically, despite their outward resemblance.) For this reason, a man leaves his father and mother and clings to his wife so that two become one (Gen. 2:23–24).

It was the woman whom the serpent induced to eat the forbidden fruit of the tree of knowledge of good and evil, and she in turn gave some to her husband to eat. It brought them intellectual maturity (some say also sexual awareness, but this was more likely born with the first recognition of physical kinship; see above), and earned for the woman the pain of childbirth and subjection to her husband, and for the man drudgery. After this incident, Adam named his wife Eve Ḥavvah because she was "the Mother of all Living" (Gen. 3:20), an epithet with strong mythical overtones suggesting that Eve was originally a goddess who was demythologized by the biblical writer. The Greek translates the name as *Zōē* ("life"), in keeping with the wordplay. Rabbinic exegesis, however, connected the name with Aramaic *ḥewyā* ("serpent"), and observed that the serpent was her undoing and that she was her husband's "serpent." This etymology has been revived in recent times by the connection of the name with a *ḥwt*, probably Hawwat, a Phoenician deity attested in a stela from Carthage in North Africa, and on urns from Cagliari in Italy. That she was a serpent-goddess is based only on the Aramaic etymology.

In biblical Hebrew (Job 18:12) *ṣēlāʿ* is an epithet meaning "wife." Eve's creation from Adam's rib or side (Heb. *ṣēlāʿ*) provides the epithet with an etiology. The Sumerian Paradise Myth of Enki and Ninḫursag provides another possible sidelight on the role of the rib in the biblical story. When Enki had a pain in his rib, Ninḫursag caused the goddess Nin-ti, "Lady of the Rib," to be born from him. The Sumerian logogram *ti* means both "rib" and "life," and it may be that the Mesopotamian "Rib Lady" lies behind the rib/life motif in the biblical story.

Eve gave birth to Cain and Abel (Gen. 4:1–2), and after Abel was murdered, she gave birth to Seth as a replacement (Gen. 4:25). The etiology of women's sexual subjugation to their husbands (Gen 4:16) is extended in the New Testament. According to I Tim. 2:14, the story of Eve's creation after Adam and the fact that she, not he, was deceived justify female subjection to men and their exclusion from speaking roles in the church. Although nothing further is related of Eve in the Bible, her figure continues to generate an enormous amount of feminist and theological literature.

[Marvin H. Pope / S. David Sperling (2nd ed.)]

In the *Aggadah*

Eve was created from the 13th rib on Adam's right side (Targ. Jon., Gen. 2:21) after Adam's first wife, *Lilith, left him. God chose not to create her from Adam's head, lest she be swell-headed; nor from his eye, lest she be a flirt; nor from his ear, lest she be an eavesdropper; nor from his mouth, lest she be a gossip; nor from his heart, lest she be prone to jealousy; nor from his hand, lest she be thievish; nor from his foot, lest she be a gadabout (Gen. R. 18:2). As soon as Adam beheld Eve, who was exceedingly beautiful (BB 58a), he embraced and kissed her. He called her *Ishah* (אישה), and himself *Ish* (איש), the addition of the letter *yod* to his name and the letter *he* to hers indicating that as long as they walked in a godly path, the Divine Name (Yod-He) would protect them against all harm. However, if they went astray, His Name would be withdrawn, and there would remain only *esh* (אש, "fire"), which would consume them. Ten resplendent bridal canopies, studded with gems, pearls, and gold, were erected for Eve by God, who Himself gave her away in marriage and pronounced the blessings, while angels danced and beat timbrels and stood guard over the bridal chamber (PdRE 12).

*Samael (Satan), prompted by jealousy, chose the serpent to mislead Eve (PdRE 13). According to another tradition, the serpent itself wished to lead Eve to sin since it desired her (Sot. 9b; Shab. 196a). The serpent approached Eve rather than Adam since it knew that women are more readily persuaded (ARN[1] 1:4). Initially, Eve hesitated to eat the fruit itself, and only did so after touching the tree and discovering that no harm befell her (Yal., Gen. 26). Immediately she saw the Angel of Death before her. Expecting her end to be imminent, she resolved to make Adam also eat of the forbidden fruit lest he take another wife after her death (PdRE 13). Nine curses and death were pronounced on Eve in consequence of her disobedience (PdRE 1). Eve conceived and bore Cain and Abel, according to one view, on the day of her expulsion from Eden (Gen. R. 22:2). Afterward Adam and Eve lived apart for 130 years (Er. 18b). After they were reunited, she bore Seth (Gen. R. 23:5). When Eve died, she was interred beside Adam in the cave of Machpelah in Hebron (PdRE 20).

In Christian Tradition

The New Testament mentions the deception of Eve as a warning to Christians (II Cor. 11:3), and stresses Adam's precedence in support of the view that women ought to be submissive and find their fulfillment in childbearing (I Tim. 2:11–15; cf. I Cor. 11:8–12). While Eve does not figure as a type in the New Testament, Paul's doctrine of the "New Adam" (i.e., Jesus) and his implicit comparison of Eve and the Church (Eph. 5:22–23) anticipate the development of later Christian typology according to which the creation of Eve from Adam's rib represents the emergence of the Church from the open wound in the side of Jesus upon the cross.

Justin, Irenaeus, and other Church Fathers compared and contrasted Eve, the first woman, and Mary, the mother of Jesus. Mary is seen as "new Eve," a title which Paul assigned to the Church collectively. The disobedience and the infidelity of the first (who, like Mary, was married and a virgin at the time of sin) is contrasted with and followed by the obedience and faith of the second. Eve is thus restored to wholeness in the Virgin Mary as Adam is in Jesus. Protestants, in their opposition to the Catholic veneration of Mary, did not develop this typology (see *Adam in Christianity).

In Islam

Eve (Ar. Ḥawwāʾ), the name of Adam's wife, is not mentioned expressly in the Koran; she is called the "spouse" in the tale of their sinning against Allah, having been influenced by Iblīs, the Satan (7:18, 20:115). Nevertheless, this name is found in three poems of the old-Arabic poetry, one of *Umayya ibn Abī-al-Ṣalt and two of ʿAdī ibn Zayd, a Christian living in the times of Muhammad. (The third poem is suspected to be a falsification.)

For Eve in the arts, see *Adam, In the Arts.

[Haïm Z'ew Hirschberg]

BIBLIOGRAPHY: H. Gressmann, in: ARW, 10 (1907), 358ff.; S. Reinach, in: RHR, 78 (1918), 185ff.; A.H. Krappe, in: *Gaster Anniversary Volume* (1936), 312–22; T.C. Vriezen, *Onderzoek naar de Paradijsvoorstelling* (1937); S.N. Kramer, *Enki and Ninhursag* (1945); idem, *History Begins at Sumer* (1958), 195–6; J. Heller, in: *Archiv Orientalni*, 26 (1958), 636–58 (Ger.). IN THE AGGADAH: Ginzberg, Legends, index. IN CHRISTIAN TRADITION: *New Catholic Encyclopedia*, 5 (1967), 655–7; *Dictionnaire de Théologie Catholique*, 5 (1913), 1640–55; Dubarle, in: *Recherches de Science Religieuse*, 39 (1951), 49–64. IN ISLAM: J. Horovitz, *Koranische Untersuchungen* (1926), 108–9; Hirschberg, in: *Rocznik Orientalistyczny*, 9 (1933), 22–36; J. Eisenberg and G. Vajda, in: EIS[2] (1966). **ADD. BIBLIOGRAPHY:** KAI II, 102–3; E. Pagels, *Adam, Eve and the Serpent* (1988); H. Wallace, in: ABD II, 666–67; N. Wyatt, in: DDD, 316–17.

EVENARI, MICHAEL (originally **Walter Schwarz**; 1904–1989), Israel botanist. Born in France, Evenari went to Ereẓ Israel in 1933, having carried out plant research in universities in France, Czechoslovakia, and Germany. He joined the Hebrew University in 1934. During World War II he served in the Jewish Brigade and after returning to civilian life, lectured at several U.S. and South American universities. From 1952 to 1957 Evenari was dean of the faculty of science at the Hebrew University and headed the botany department as professor of plant physiology. He served as vice president of the Hebrew University from 1953 to 1959. Evenari's main fields of research were the study of the influence of red and infra-red light on the germination of seeds, and the determination of the food value of algae for livestock and their large-scale cultivation. With a grant from the Rockefeller Foundation, Evenari carried out research on the methods used by *Nabateans, Romans, and Byzantines to maintain a thriving agricultural existence in the northern Negev in spite of the low annual rainfall of the area. He set up experimental farms at *Shivta and *Avedat based on archaeological findings in the area. Evenari served on several UNESCO bodies, dealing with arid zone development.

EVEN HA-TO'IM (Heb. אֶבֶן הַטּוֹעִים or הַטּעַן), a stone in Jerusalem, It is mentioned once in the Mishnah (Ta'an. 3:8) in the story of *Onias (Ḥoni) the circle drawer. When asked to pray that the rains cease, he answered: "Go and see if the *even ha-to'im* has been washed away," indicating that just as it was impossible for it to be washed away so was it impossible to pray for the rain to cease. This picturesque reply is reminiscent of one in the Jerusalem Talmud showing that praying for the cessation of rain is unnecessary (Ta'an. 3:11, 67a). An anonymous Aramaic passage in the Jerusalem Talmud (Ta'anit 3:11, 66d) interprets the *even ha-to'im* as a place where "one who lost an item would receive it from there, and one who found an item would bring it to there." A similar tradition is reflected in a *baraita* found in the Babylonian Talmud (BM 28b) which mentions the *even ha-to'an* in connection with the return of lost property during the Second Temple period. People who had lost or found objects in Jerusalem and on the road to the capital met by the side of this stone: "The one stood and announced his find and the other submitted evidence of ownership and received it." According to these traditions, the name is to be interpreted as "the stone for those wandering," i.e., in search of someone or something. The reading *even ha-to'an* ("the claimant's stone") is faulty (Dik. Sof., *ibid.*), and any conclusions deriving from it are therefore invalid.

BIBLIOGRAPHY: Krauss, Tal Arch, 362; Sepp, in: ZDPV, 2 (1879), 48–51.

[Jacob Eliahu Ephrathi]

EVEN-OR, MARY (1939–1989), Israeli composer. Even-Or studied at the Music Teachers' Seminary in Tel Aviv in 1959, the Oranim Seminary in 1960–62, and with Yehezkel *Braun. She studied law at Tel Aviv University and music in 1976–80 at the Rubin Academy of Music in Tel Aviv and Tel Aviv University. Even-Or was a member of the Israel Composers' League from 1980; from 1981 she was a member of ACUM and of the International Association of Women Composers. Her works include *Dances* for flute, clarinet, violin, bass, and percussion (1961); *Dreams* for flute, clarinet, and guitar (1977); *Music for Strings* (1979); *Espressioni Musicali* for choir a cappella (1981); *Cardioyada* for brass quintet (1981); *Musikinesis* for symphony orchestra (1983).

[Ury Eppstein (2nd ed.)]

EVEN SHEMUEL (Kaufmann), JUDAH (1886–1976), Israel educator, lexicographer, and writer. Even Shemuel was born in Balta, Ukraine, and received a yeshivah education. He studied in various countries and his thesis at Dropsie College, Philadelphia, "Rabbi Yomtov Lipman Muelhausen…" (1927), contained his edition of *Muelhausen's *Sefer ha-Eshkol.* From 1913 he was active in the Zionist Labor movement in Montreal, Canada, and became the first principal of its teachers training college. As a contributor to *Ha-Toren* and the *Zukunft* and a lecturer on Jewish philosophy and sociology, he gained a reputation as a spiritual guide of the movement. He also tried to reconcile the Hebraists with the Yiddishists.

Even Shemuel settled in Palestine in 1926 at the invitation of the Devir publishing house to edit, with Ḥ.N. *Bialik, I. *Efros, and B. *Silkiner, an English-Hebrew dictionary (1929; 29th and revised repr. 1963). He continued his cultural activities in the Histadrut and became the first general secretary of the Friends of the Hebrew University. When the *Va'ad Le'ummi established a cultural division, Even Shemuel was appointed its head, remaining there until 1947. He received the Israel Prize in Jewish studies in 1973.

His principal scholarly work is a vocalized edition of Maimonides' *Guide of the Perplexed* in Samuel ibn Tibbon's Hebrew translation (3 vols., 1935–60), with introductions, extensive commentary, and notes. A one-volume edition of the whole work with a short introduction appeared in 1946. Even Shemuel also published *Midreshei Ge'ullah* (1943, 1954^2), an anthology of messianic and apocalyptic literature from the conclusion of the Talmud to the 13th century. He edited various volumes in fields of Jewish scholarship.

BIBLIOGRAPHY: Kressel, Leksikon, 1 (1965), 14–15; P. Birnbaum, in: *Hadoar*, 47 (1968), 587–9.

EVEN SHETIYYAH (Heb. אֶבֶן שְׁתִיָּה), tannaitic term which was understood in two ways in talmudic times: "the rock from which the world was woven, and "the foundation rock." Both meanings presuppose the belief that the world was created from the rock which, placed at the center of the world in the Holy of Holies (*Devir*) of the Temple in Jerusalem, constitutes the focal point of the world. The Holy Ark was placed upon this rock, and during the Second Temple period the high priest rested the fire-pan on it when he entered the Holy of Holies on the Day of Atonement. The Mishnah (Yoma 5:2) states that the rock had been at the site of the *Devir* since "the time of the early prophets" (i.e., David and Solomon); that it was three finger breadths higher than the ground; and that it was called *shetiyyah*. However, R. *Yose b. Halafta (Tosef., Yoma 3:6) explains the term as having cosmogonic significance and the subsequent Midrash is based on this view. The Mishnah clearly dates the placing of the stone to the time of the Temple's construction and ignores the mythological dimension; other tannaitic views similarly deny that the creation was initiated at Zion (Yoma 54b). The mishnaic source may have antedated the cosmogonic belief; it may have postdated it and rejected it; or it may have assumed that it was the cosmogenetic rock that was brought to the Temple site. The later Midrash states that the entire Temple was founded upon the rock, and that the stone was possessed of magical properties.

The relationship of the *even shetiyyah* to the rock presently housed under the Dome of the Rock (the "Mosque of Omar") built on the Temple Mount is not fully clear. Muslim tradition identifies the two, and this is the view most widely held today. The major difficulty here is the size: the rock housed in the Dome of the Rock measures approximately 58 by 51 feet, an area larger than the entire Holy of Holies in which the *even shetiyyah* was found. The later Midrash does state, though, that the entire Temple was based on this rock, which, it implies, merely broke through in the Holy of Holies. In medieval times it was thought that the ground around the rock had been worn away by violence and the erosion of centuries, revealing it in its present magnitude (cf. Radbaz, Responsa, 2 (1882), nos. 639, 691). A second theory states that the rock under the Dome is not the *even shetiyyah* but the foundation-rock of the great altar of holocausts; the cave under the rock would then have served to collect ashes and other sacrificial refuse. In that case, the Holy of Holies would have stood to the west of the present Dome of the Rock, which presents architectural and topographical difficulties.

BIBLIOGRAPHY: Ginzberg, Legends, 5 (1925), 14–16; H. Albeck, *Shishah Sidrei Mishnah*, 2 (1958), 469; S. Lieberman, *Tosefta ki-Feshutah*, 4 (1962), 772–3; de Vaux, Anc Isr, 318–9; H.H. Rowley, *Worship in the Bible* (1967), 76n. (bibl.); D. Noy, in: G. Elkoshi et al. (eds.), *Ve-li-Yrushalayim* (1968), 360–94.

[Gerald Y. Blidstein]

EVEN-SHOSHAN, AVRAHAM (1906–1984), Hebrew educator, writer, and editor. His father, Chaim David Rosenstein (1871–1934), was an educator and Zionist leader, who was imprisoned by the Soviet government for his activities. Avraham was born in Minsk, and went to Palestine in 1925. He served as teacher and principal in a number of schools, and from 1954 until 1968 was director of the Bet ha-Kerem Teachers Institute in Jerusalem. His first literary efforts appeared in a children's magazine (*Ittonenu*) which he helped edit (1932–36). Subsequently he published stories, poems, and plays for children, and translated children's books into Hebrew. He is best known for a monumental Hebrew dictionary which he compiled, *Millon Ḥadash Menukkad u-Mezuyyar* ("New Vocalized and Illustrated Dictionary"), which originally appeared in five volumes and a supplementary volume (1947–58); a seven-volume edition subsequently appeared, which is now also available in other formats. His *Concordance to the Bible* listing and explaining the words and expressions of the Bible appeared between 1977 and 1979. Even-Shoshan was awarded the Israel Prize in 1978 and the Bialik Prize in 1981. His brother SHELOMO EVEN-SHOSHAN (1910–) was one of the founders of kibbutz Sedeh Naḥum. He contributed poems, stories, and articles to the labor press and from 1944 was one of the editors at the Kibbutz ha-Me'uḥad publishing house. His books include an appreciation of Yiẓḥak *Katzenelson and translations from Soviet Russian literature.

[Getzel Kressel]

EVENTOV, YAKIR (**Drago Steiner**; 1901–1984), journalist and historian.

Born in Koprivnica, Yugoslavia, he lived and worked in Zagreb until his immigration to Palestine. A Zionist activist from his youth in the Ha-Po'el ha-Ẓa'ir branch in Yugoslavia, he edited the Zionist weekly *Židov* and an "Anthology of Hebrew Literature," to which he contributed his own translations.

Arriving in Palestine in 1934, he spent a year in kibbutz Merḥavyah; the next year he joined the staff of the Haifa Electric Corporation and worked there until his retirement. He devoted all his spare time to the study of Jewish history, producing with the assistance of C. *Rotem a volume entitled "History of the Jews in Yugoslavia" (1979), the first work in Hebrew on the subject.

With his wife, Ethel, he initiated in 1955, and directed from his home in Haifa, an archival collection of documents and materials on Jewish life in all parts of Yugoslavia. It was called the Museum and Historical Section of the Association of Immigrants from Yugoslavia. After the Eventovs' death, the collection was renamed in their honor the Eventov Archives, and in 1986 it was transferred to Jerusalem, where it became part of the Central Archives for the History of the Jewish People.

[Zvi Loker (2nd ed.)]

EVEN YEHUDAH (Heb. אֶבֶן יְהוּדָה), rural settlement in central Israel, 4⅓ mi. (7 km.) southeast of Netanyah. The settlement area consists of 3.2 sq. mi. (8.3 sq. km.). It was founded in 1932 by the members of the *Benei Binyamin movement. Two neighboring villages, Be'er Gannim and Tel Ẓur, later merged with it. In 1950 it received municipal council status. The youth village Hadassim was also included in its boundaries. Citrus orchards constituted the principal branch of its economy. In the early 1970s the settlement began to decline. However, after the Yom Kippur War there was an influx of new residents, so that the population grew from 4,000 in 1968 to 8,480 in 2002, with income much higher than the national average. It is named after Eliezer *Ben-Yehuda.

WEBSITE: www.even-yehuda.mumi.il.

[Efraim Orni / Shaked Gilboa (2nd ed.)]

EVEN YIẒḤAK (Heb. אֶבֶן יִצְחָק), kibbutz in Israel, in the Manasseh Hills of Samaria, affiliated with Iḥud ha-Kibbutzim, founded on March 11, 1945, by pioneers from Germany, many of whom had been hiding in Holland under Nazi occupation from 1940. They were joined by Jews from other countries.

Farming was based on field crops, fruit, and livestock. The kibbutz owned two factories: a plastics plant in partnership with Kibbutz Mishmar ha-Emek, and a biochemical plant. In 2002 the population was 393. The settlement, named after the South African Zionist Isaac Ochberg, is generally known as "Gal Ed" (Monument"), a memorial to the settlers' comrades who perished in the Holocaust.

WEBSITE: www.megido.org.il.

[Efraim Orni]

EVER HADANI (pseudonym of **Aharon Feldman**; 1899–1972), Hebrew writer. Born near Pinsk, he immigrated to Palestine in 1913, and after serving with the Jewish Legion during World War I, lived in the kibbutzim Maḥanayim and Kefar Giladi. He edited agricultural publications and from 1948 worked in the Israel Ministry of Agriculture. Apart from his publications in many newspapers, he wrote several novels, including *Ẓerif ha-Eẓ* ("The Wood Hut," 1930), an early romantic novel about Israel's pioneers, and the trilogy *Nahalolim* ("Brambles," 1935); but the bulk of his writing was devoted to the history of Jewish settlement in Galilee and Samaria. Among his dozen books on this subject are *Ha-Shomer* (1931) and *Ḥakla'ut ve-Hityashevut be-Yisrael* (1958). His collected works appeared in seven volumes (1968).

BIBLIOGRAPHY: J. Ovray (Ovasi), *Ma'amarim u-Reshimot* (1947), 251–8; S. Ginzburg, *Be-Massekhet ha-Sifrut* (1945), 251–8.

[Getzel Kressel]

EVER MIN HA-HAI (Heb. אֵבֶר מִן הַחַי; "a limb from a living animal"), designation of the biblical injunction against removal of a limb or of a piece of flesh from a living animal and its consumption. Deuteronomy 12:23 states "and thou shalt not eat the life with the flesh." The prohibition forms part of the Jewish *dietary laws and is one of the seven Noachian Laws (derived from Gen. 9:4), which, according to rabbinic view, are incumbent on non-Jews as well (Sanh. 56a–b; see also Ḥul. 101b–102a; Maim., Yad, Ma'akhalot Asurot 5:1–15; Sh. Ar., YD 62).

BIBLIOGRAPHY: ET, 1 (1947), 48–51; Eisenstein, Dinim, 7.

EVIAN CONFERENCE, conference of 32 nations convened but not attended by President Franklin Delano Roosevelt on July 6–14, 1938, at the Hôtel Royal in Evian on the French side of Lake Geneva to consider the plight of refugees – the euphemistic way of referring to the Jewish question. The conference was convened against the backdrop of the German incorporation of Austria in March 1938, which sparked a massive exodus of Jews to any country willing to receive them. Convening the conference was the first American government initiative regarding refugees.

The Evian Conference was conceived by President Roosevelt as a grand gesture in response to mounting pressure in the United States to do something about the refugee problem. The call for the conference was greeted warmly by the American Jewish community but it also triggered a hostile reaction from American isolationist and anti-immigration forces. Thomas Jenkins, one of those who wanted to restrict immigration, accused the president of going "on a visionary excursion into the warm fields of altruism. He forgets the cold winds of poverty and penury that are sweeping over the one third of our people who are ill clothed, ill housed, ill fed." American Jews and their allies were pressing the admission of greater numbers of immigrants. Restrictionist forces kept reminding the president of the Depression, of the domestic agenda, and of the need to put America first. Roosevelt sought to balance both concerns, to assuage but also not to provoke. Walking such a political tightrope hampered any effort to pressure the international community. Internationally, Romania flatly refused to attend; it wanted to get rid of its Jews, not to import new ones, and Switzerland spurned an invitation to host the conference.

The very invitation to the conference gave an indication of its reluctance to act. Attending countries were assured that "no country would be expected to receive more immigrants than were permitted under existing laws." Nor would any government be expected to subsidize refugees: all new programs would have to be funded by private agencies. American isolationists were assuaged by the understanding that U.S. quota system for immigrants would not be touched. Britain was told that Palestine would not be on the agenda. Two days after Roosevelt's announcement of the Evian Conference, Hitler issued a characteristic statement:

> I can only hope that the other world which has such deep sympathy for these criminals [Jews] will at least be generous enough to convert this sympathy into practical aid. We on our part are ready to put all these criminals at the disposal of these countries, for all I care, even on luxury ships.

The United States delegation was not headed by the president or the vice president, nor by Secretary of State Cordell Hull or Undersecretary Summer Welles. Instead, Roosevelt nominated Myron C. Taylor, a businessman who was one of his close friends. Great Britain also sent a special delegation. The other nations used their diplomats in the region. Foreign leaders got the message. The French premier told his British counterpart that the American president was acting to soothe public opinion. Under these circumstances, little was expected or accomplished.

For nine days the delegates met at the Hôtel Royal, along with representatives of 39 private relief agencies, 21 of them Jewish. The world press gave the event extensive coverage.

Delegates from each country rose in turn to profess their sympathy with the plight of the refugees. They also offered plausible excuses for declining to open their countries' doors. Britain had no room on its small island and refused to open Palestine to Jewish refugees. The United States spoke abstractly about "political" refugees, using the euphemism to glide over the fact that most of the refugees were Jewish. It would fill its quota, but do no more.

The Australian delegate was more candid. "We don't have a racial problem and we don't want to import one," he said. For Canada, still in the midst of the Depression, "none was too many." Canada would, however, accept farmers – small comfort for the urbanized Jews seeking to leave Germany. Colombia's delegate could not resign himself to believe "that two thousand years of Christian civilization must lead to this terrible catastrophe." In any case, his country could offer nothing. The Venezuelan delegate was reluctant to disturb the "demographic equilibrium" of his country. No Jewish merchants, peddlers, or intellectuals were wanted in Venezuela.

Holland and Denmark were ready to extend temporary asylum to a few refugees. Only the Dominican Republic made a generous offer to receive Jews. In the end, however, few came. Even though an inter-governmental group was established at Evian to coordinate policy, the tidal wave of refugees soon overwhelmed the few offers of assistance. The German Foreign Office viewed the conference with considerable interest and sensed in it a vindication of its own attitudes toward the Jews:

> Since in many countries it was recently regarded as wholly incomprehensible why Germany did not wish to preserve in its population an element like the Jews … it appears astounding that countries seem in no way anxious to make use of these elements themselves now that the opportunity offers.

At that point in time, the announced policy of Nazi Germany was the emigration – forced or otherwise – of the Jews. The Evian Conference demonstrated that forced emigration would not work since no country – or groups of countries – were willing to receive the Jews in numbers adequate to make Germany "*judenrein*." As events unfolded, the Jewish problem became more acute but four months later when the events of the November pogrom of **Kristallnacht* triggered a tidal wave of Jewish emigration and over the course of the next two years as Germany invaded country after country, more and more Jews came under its control and the problem of what to do with the Jews became ever more acute, ever less solvable by means of emigration.

BIBLIOGRAPHY: H. Feingold, *The Politics of Compromise: The Roosevelt Administration and the Holocaust* (1970); H. Feingold, *Bearing Witness, How America and Its Jews Responded to the Holocaust* (1995); D. Wyman, *The Abandonment of the Jews* (1984); D. Wyman, *Paper Walls: America and the Refugee Crisis* (1985).

[Michael Berenbaum (2nd ed.)]

EVIDENCE.

Non-Evidentiary Proceedings in Biblical Law

The revelation of divine law is found not only in legislation but also in adjudication in particular cases (cf. Lev. 24:12–13; Num. 15:32–34; 27:1–8; Deut. 1:17), whether through Moses or judges or priests (Ex. 28:30; Num. 27:21; Deut. 17:9–12; 21:5; 33:8–10), and God requires no evidence: He is all knowing and His decision is infallible (cf. Gen. 31:50). That adjudications without evidence continued to survive in judicial, nondivine proceedings is demonstrated by the report of the trial held by King Solomon between the two women each claiming the same child (I Kings 3:24–25) and by contemporaneous trial reports from other civilizations. Judges appear to have devised their own tests of credibility.

Evidentiary Proceedings in Biblical Law

The existence and availability of human witnesses and other modes of proof seem from earliest times to have been part of judicial proceedings (cf. Ex. 22:9, 12). Witnesses appear to have testified to the facts prior to God being asked to pronounce the law (Num. 15:32–35); and eventually it came about that a person "able to testify, as one who has either seen or known of the matter," was guilty of an offense if he failed to come forward and testify (Lev. 5:1).

Evidence in Criminal Cases

PROOF OF GUILT. Biblical law had already established that in criminal cases the evidence of at least two witnesses is a *sine qua non* of any conviction and punishment (Deut. 17:6; 19:15). This rule appears to have applied both in judicial and in priestly adjudications (cf. Deut. 19:17), and was interpreted as prescribing a minimum burden of proof, from which no later legal development could in any way derogate.

Post-biblical law thus concentrated on devising measures to assure the greatest possible reliability of witnesses' testimony: they were cautioned by the court that they would be rigorously cross-examined, that they must not rely on hearsay or on opinions, and that they must be conscious of their grave responsibility – since a human life was at stake (Sanh. 4:5). They were in fact subjected to cross-examination by the court – each witness separately – and their evidence would not be accepted unless their respective testimonies were found to be consistent with each other in all relevant particulars (Sanh. 5:1–4; Maim. Yad, Sanh. 12:1–3; for particulars of the cross-examination of witnesses and their qualifications, see *Witness).

The further rule was evolved that it was not sufficient for witnesses to testify to the commission of the offense by the accused: they also had to testify that the accused had been warned by them beforehand against committing that particular offense (*hatra'ah*) – that is, that the accused knew that in committing the act he was violating the law (Tosef. Sanh. 11, 1; Sanh. 8b; et al.). Elaborate rules were laid down for the identification of the accused by the witnesses, and where the court was not satisfied beyond any doubt as to such identification, the accused was discharged even before the witnesses were examined on the merits of the case (Maim. *ibid.*). According to some scholars, he was also thus discharged where the victim of the offense had not been identified by the witnesses to the satisfaction of the court (see *Leḥem Mishneh, ibid.*).

EVIDENCE IN DEFENSE. Whereas a witness testifying in a criminal case was not allowed to raise a point in defense of or against the accused (Maim. Yad, Edut 5:8) – a witness being disqualified from performing the function of a judge – when the evidence of the prosecuting witnesses had been found admissible and *prima facie* conclusive, public announcements had to be made inviting any person able to raise a point in favor (*zekhut*) of the accused, to come forward and speak (Sanh. 6:1). While the charge against the accused could be proved only by the *viva voce* evidence of witnesses, any shred of evidence from which a defense could be inferred would be used in his favor (Rashi, Sanh. 42b). For this purpose, a favorable point is not necessarily a rebuttal of the testimony of the prosecuting witnesses, but merely any fact or circumstance likely to arouse in the mind of the court a doubt as to the guilt of the accused; hence such points did not automatically result in an acquittal, but they were sufficient justification for the case to be remitted to the court for reconsideration – even four or five times. There is no explicit presumption of innocence in Jewish law; the requirements of proof of guilt are, however, so stringent and rigorous, and the possibilities of establishing a valid defense so wide and flexible, that a conviction is much more difficult and an acquittal much easier to obtain than under a rebuttable presumption of innocence.

POST-TALMUDIC LAW. In talmudic law the standards of proof required, even in criminal cases, were largely reduced where the jurisdiction rested on considerations of the "emergency" (*hora'at sha'ah;* see *Extraordinary Remedies). After the virtual cessation of jurisdiction in capital cases (see *Capital Punishment), and particularly in post-talmudic law, all criminal jurisdiction rested on considerations of "emergency" to which the provisions relating to the dispensation from the normal rules of evidence and procedure were held to apply. The rules of evidence prevailing in the Sanhedrin were held inapplicable in the courts of the Diaspora, when they were called upon to enforce public order by the imposition of *fines or *flogging (Resp. Rashba, vol. 4, no. 311).

Evidence in Civil Cases

BURDEN OF PROOF. It was in the law of evidence in civil cases in which the genius of the talmudic jurists, unfettered by scriptural restrictions, could develop fully. The obstacle that there was to be "one manner of law" (Lev. 24:22) in criminal and civil cases alike (Sanh. 4:1) was overcome with the assertion that the Torah takes pity on the money (property) of the people of Israel, and if the standards of proof in civil cases were as strict and rigorous as in criminal cases, nobody would lend his neighbor any money anymore, for fear the borrower would deny his debt or the memory of a witness would fail him (TJ, Sanh. 4:1). Accordingly, a balance had to be struck between the exigencies of formal justice which required the burden of proof to be on the initiator of the proceedings (Sif. Deut. 16; BK 46b) and commercial and judicial convenience which required the greatest possible elasticity in handling and discharging that burden.

PRESUMPTION OF RIGHTFUL POSSESSION. The fundamental rule that the plaintiff has the burden of proving his claim (*ha-mozi mi-ḥavero alav ha-re'ayah*) is based on the presumption (*ḥazakah*) of the rightful possession by the defendant of the chose in action – i.e., the thing (or money) claimed (*ḥezkat mamon*): so long as the defendant's possession was not proved to be unrightful, it will not be disturbed – hence a defendant in possession is always in a better position than the plaintiff (Shevu'ot 46; Maim. Yad, To'en ve-Nitan, 8:1; Sh. Ar., ḤM 133:1). But in order to raise the presumption of title, the possession must be accompanied by a claim of right (BB 3:3 and Codes); where the defendant in possession does not claim a specific right thereto, the burden is shifted to him to prove a right to retain the chose in action. Or where a claim is made according to custom, and the defense (that is, the possession) is contrary to custom, such as in a claim for workmen's wages (TJ, BM 7:1, 11b), the presumption of rightfulness operates in favor of the plaintiff and shifts the burden of proof onto the defendant. In an action between heirs, where the defendant has seized part of the estate, his claim of right is not any better than that of the plaintiff, and he will have to prove that his possession is rightful (Yev. 37b and Tos. *ibid.*). Where a man was seen to take a chattel out of a house, it was held to be on him to prove that he took it rightfully (BB 33b; Hai Gaon, *Sefer ha-Mikkaḥ ve-ha-Mimkar*, ch. 40), presumably because his possession was too recent to give rise to any presumption to that effect. Conversely, past possession which had meanwhile ceased (*ḥezkat mara kamma*) would give rise to a presumption of title only where the other party was not in possession either (BM 100a). These rules do not apply to possession of land and houses but only of money and chattels – for lands and other immovables there must be an uninterrupted possession of three years (BB 3:1), coupled with a claim of right (BB 3:3), in order to give rise to a presumption of title.

PRESUMPTIONS AND QUASI-PRESUMPTIONS OF CONDUCT. In order to mitigate the burden of proof and to simplify the judicial process, the sages have, presumably from their own accumulated judicial experience, established a vast number of quasi-presumptions, rooted in the psychology of human conduct, which apply to every litigant before the court, unless and until the contrary is proved. To give a few examples: a man does not waste his words or his money in vain without good cause (Ket. 58b, 10a); nor will he stand by inactive when his money is taken or his property endangered (Shab. 117b, 120b, 153a; Sanh. 72b) or when a wrong is being done or threatened to him (BB 60a). A man does not pay a debt before it falls due (BB 5a–b); nor does a man tolerate defects in a thing sold to him (Ket. 75b–76a). On the other hand, no man buys a chattel without having first seen and examined it *(ibid.)*. A debtor will not easily lie in the face of his creditor (BM 3a), nor a wife in the face of her husband (Ket. 22b), nor anybody in the face of a man who must know the truth (Tos. Ket. 18a; BK 107a). A man is not expected to remember things which do not concern him (Shevu. 34b). A man will not leave his house empty and his household unprovided for (Ket. 107a). However, he is apt to understate his fortune so as not to appear rich (BB 174b–175a), and will rather have one ounce of his own than nine ounces of his neighbor's (BM 38a); nor will he sell and dispose of any of his goods unless he has to (BB 47b). No man commits a wrong unless for his own benefit (BM 5b) and the purpose of an act is its normal consequence ("everybody knows why the bride gets married"; Shab. 33a). No person is lighthearted in the hour of his death (BB 175a), or defrauds the Temple treasury (*hekdesh;* Shevu. 42b; Ar. 23a). Apart from such general presumptions, there are special ones relating to particular contracts or offices, as for example the presumption that an agent has duly performed the duties of his agency (Git. 64a), or that a priest has duly performed the duties of his office (TJ, Shek. 7:2, 50c).

PRESUMPTIONS OF CREDIBILITY (*NE'EMANUT*). Much stronger than these general and special presumptions of conduct are two further categories of presumptions, which are – theoretically at least – irrebuttable (comparable to, but not identical with, the Roman *praesumptiones iuris et de iure*). One is the presumption of credibility (*ne'emanut*) and the other is the presumption of common sense (*umdana mukhaḥat*).

The presumption of credibility is primarily based on the notion that the party or witness concerned has an intimate knowledge of the matter in issue and has no reason to distort it. Thus, where a man says he has divorced his wife, his word is taken as conclusive for the court to permit her remarriage – because the matter is within his own knowledge, and he has no reason to distort it, as he could even now divorce her any time (BB 134b–135a, but see Maim. Gerushin 12:5; Sh. Ar., EH 152:1; see also *Divorce). Or, a woman is believed when she says that her first husband has divorced her – because the matter is within her own knowledge and she need not have disclosed her previous marriage at all (*ha-peh she-asar hu ha-peh she-hittir;* Ket. 2:5). Or, an action will not lie for land which the defendant had told the plaintiff he had bought from the plaintiff's father, although the defendant could not prove the purchase: he will be believed that he bought it, because he need not have disclosed that it had ever belonged to the plaintiff's father in the first place (Ket. 2:2). The law would be different where the ownership of the plaintiff's father could be proved by witnesses (*ibid.*).

Some of these irrebuttable presumptions of credibility are based on Scripture, e.g., where a father says he has given his daughter in marriage (Deut. 22:16: "I gave this man my daughter to wife"; Ket. 22a), or a father's nomination of his firstborn son (BB 127b, following Deut. 21:17). There are, however, also presumptions of credibility which rank in weight with the rebuttable presumptions of conduct – that is, they are capable of being displaced by express evidence to the contrary. A man is presumed not to lie about matters which are easily ascertainable (Yev. 115a); and a man is presumed to remember matters which are extraordinary and astonishing (Hul. 75b). Conversely, a man whose words were proved false on one point, will no longer be believed on other points in the same case; notwithstanding any presumption in his favor, he will be required to adduce express proof for the other points (BM 17a; Maim. Yad, Gerushin 13:1). Credibility is also presumed for statements made for purposes unconnected with the litigation (*mesi'aḥ lefi tummo:* Git. 28b; cf. BK 114f.). A man is believed where his statement (e.g., that he had become a convert on his own, without a *bet din*) disqualifies him (Yev. 47a), but no such statement is accepted as proof of disqualification of anybody else, even his wife or children (*ibid.*).

PRESUMPTIONS OF COMMON SENSE (*UMDANA MUKHAHAT*). The presumption of common sense applies to bring acts or conduct into conformity with reason or propriety: the presumption is that a person acts reasonably and properly, notwithstanding any outward appearance to the contrary; and his acts will therefore be judged not according to appearances, but according to what, in reason and propriety, they ought to have been. Thus, a man is presumed not to give away the whole of his property during his lifetime; hence where a dying person disposed of all his property and then recovered, his act will not be enforced by the courts, and he is regarded as having acted in the mistaken belief that he was going to die (BB 146b). The same applies to transactions made for an ulterior motive; where a woman had given away her property in order to deprive her future husband of his legal rights thereto, and on divorce reclaimed the property, the court is reported to have torn the deed of gift into pieces (Ket. 78b; Maim. Zekhiyyah u-Mattanah 6:12). A husband giving his property to his wife is irrebuttably presumed to have made her only his trustee and not to have deprived himself and his children of all his property (BB 131b; for a list of these presumptions see *Piskei ha-Rosh* Ket. 11:9).

PRESUMPTIONS OF CONDITIONS (*UMDANA BE-GILLUI DA'AT*). While these presumptions apply whether or not the mistake or motive was expressed or admitted, there are other cases in which these or similar presumptions apply only where such mistake or motive can be inferred from express statements made at the time of the transaction (*umdanot be-gillui da'at*). Thus, where a man disposed of his property, mentioning that he had decided to emigrate, and then he did not in fact emigrate, he will be presumed to have disposed of his property only conditional on his emigration (Kid. 49b). Or, where a man had made a will bequeathing his property to strangers, because he had heard that his sons had died, and then it appeared that they had not died, his will was set aside as having been made by mistake (BB 132a). Even where a vendor had stated, at the time of the sale, that he sold in order to have the money for a certain purpose, and that purpose could not afterward be effected, he was held entitled to have the sale set aside (Ket. 97a). It has been said that reservations giving rise to such presumptions must, however, always be reasonable: the man desiring to emigrate, for instance, could have the sale or gift of his landed properties set aside if the emigration did not transpire, but not the sale of his personal effects which he would be assumed to take with him on his emigration (Tos., Ket. 97a).

JUDICIAL NOTICE (*ANAN SAHADEI*). All these presumptions and quasi-presumptions are being taken notice of by the court *ex officio (anan sahadei*; Resp. Rosh 34:1; 81:1), and in this respect they are similar to matters of custom and usage (cf. TJ, Pe'ah 7:6, 20b). Not unlike the concept of "judicial notice" in modern law, they replace formal evidence which would otherwise have to be adduced by the party on whom the burden of proof lies: in the language of the Mishnah, the disputant of a presumption of credibility in a given case would say, "we do not live from his mouth," but he has to adduce proof to verify his words (cf. Ket. 1:6–9). In some cases, especially those involving marital status, courts will take notice also of common repute or rumor (*kol*; Git. 89a; Ket. 36b; et al.; on presumptions see also **Ḥazakah*).

MODES OF PROOF. Where neither presumption nor custom avails the party on whom the burden of proof lies, he may discharge it by adducing evidence, either in the form of an *oath, or in the form of a *shetar*, or in the form of the testimony of *witnesses.

EVALUATION OF EVIDENCE. Notwithstanding the formal and apparent sufficiency of the evidence adduced, however, the court is not bound by it, but has to weigh its reliability and satisfy itself of its truth before deciding the case in accordance therewith: it is a matter for the mind and heart of the individual judge, and no hard-and-fast rules can be laid down (Maim. Yad, Sanh. 24:1–2).

FRAUD ON THE COURT. Where the judge has gained the impression that the case before him, though duly proven, is a fraud (*din merummeh*), Maimonides holds that he ought to disqualify himself and leave the case to be decided by some other judge (*ibid*. 3); but the better opinion appears to be that he ought to dismiss the case there and then (Resp. Rosh 68:20; ḤM 15:3). Where it was the defendant who had deceived the court, judgment would be given in favor of the plaintiff, so as not to let "the sinner reap the fruits of his sin" (Resp. Rosh 107:6). The same rule would apply where a party sought to prevent the court from discovering the whole truth, whether by refusing to submit to cross-examination, or by suppressing evidence, or by any other means (*ibid*.).

ADDITIONAL EVIDENCE. Even though a case has been duly proved and decided, any party claiming that new evidence has been discovered, which might change the outcome of the proceedings, is entitled to have the case reopened (Sanh. 4:1). The only exceptions to this rule are, first, where the court has fixed a time limit for the adducing of additional evidence and that time has expired; and second, where the party has expressly declared in court that there is no additional evidence available to him (Sanh. 3:8) – in these cases it is apprehended that the additional evidence might have been fabricated (Rashi, Sanh. 31a).

FORMAL EVIDENCE (*GILLUI MILTA BE-ALMA*). It is not only by vesting a wide discretion in the judge but also by legislatively relaxing the rules of evidence in proper cases that the law seeks to avoid any possible hardships which may arise from the objective difficulties of obtaining evidence. Such legislative relaxations are to be found particularly in respect of routine matters. Thus no formal evidence is required for the identification of litigants who identify themselves; even a relative or a minor can identify a brother-in-law for the purpose of *ḥaliẓah* (Yev. 39b; see *Levirate Marriage) or the evidence of one witness (who would nowadays be called a "formal" witness) is sufficient to establish matters of physical examination, such as the appearance of signs of puberty or the symptoms of a disease – matters which have to be proved, not because they can be seriously contested but in order "that judgment may be rendered without a stammer" (Rashi, Ket. 28a).

LEGISLATIVE RELAXATION OF RULES OF EVIDENCE. In matters of marital status, there are many situations where the law contents itself with the evidence of a disqualified or a single witness, or hearsay, or other generally inadmissible modes of proof, because, in the language of Maimonides, these are generally matters which can be verified by other means and on which a man will not normally lie, as e.g., the death of another man; "and while the Torah insists on the testimony of two witnesses and all the other rules of evidence in cases which cannot be proved otherwise, as e.g., whether A killed B or A lent money to B, in these matters in which it is unlikely that any witness would lie, have the sages seen fit to relax the rules and to accept the evidence of bondswomen, and in writing, and without cross-examination, so that the daughters of Israel may not lose their remedy" (Gerushin 13, 29).

[Haim Hermann Cohn]

Circumstantial Evidence

The above discussion concerned various *legal* presumptions – based on conduct, on credibility, on common sense, presumptions of the existence of a given condition, and "judicial notice" – all of which involve interpretation of and legal consequences derived from known facts. There remains, however, a basic question, as to whether facts may be determined in reliance on circumstantial evidence. Circumstantial evidence is evidence that does not directly prove the specific fact for which proof is required, but necessitates a deductive process of drawing conclusions to prove that fact.

In *dinei mamonot* (monetary cases), as stated above, it is undisputed that a presumption may be relied upon for the determination of an actor's intent. However, regarding the commission of an act itself or the actor's identity, the *rishonim* take varying approaches: Maimonides (Yad, Sanhedrin 24:1) adopts the view that in such monetary cases facts can be determined on the basis of circumstantial evidence, provided that the evidence offers good and convincing proof. For example, if a person claims that he left a specific article as a deposit with a decedent and presents signs which prove that the article is his, and a judge is persuaded that the article is not the decedent's property – the article will be taken from the heirs and given to the claimant, even if there is no will directing that this be done. An opposite view appears in the responsum of R. Yosef Colon (Responsa Maharik, §129; Italy, 15th century), which provides that a presumption can only be relied upon to determine the intention of an actor, but cannot be used as proof of the actual commission of the act or the actor's identity, regarding which judges only rely on direct evidence.

Regarding personal status, marriages and divorces, testimony that an act of divorce or marriage actually took place is required to confirm its validity; regarding marriage, all authorities agree that circumstantial evidence is sufficient to prove commission of the act. However, with respect to divorce, there is a need for constitutive evidence – supporting witnesses who witnessed the act of divorce – and the authorities are divided as to whether circumstantial evidence is sufficient for this. Rabbenu Tam (Tosafot at Gittin 4a) takes the view that actual witnesses are necessary and that circumstantial evidence is insufficient, while R. Alfasi (TB Gittin 47b–48a and Rabbenu Nissim, ad loc) reasons that circumstantial evidence can take the place of witnesses who confer validity to the *get*.

In penal law as well there are disputes about the status of circumstantial evidence. The accepted view is that capital cases may not be decided and punishments may not be imposed except on the basis of clear and direct proofs (see Maimonides, Yad, Sanhedrin 20:1), and there is a clear distinction in this context between monetary cases and capital cases (*dinei mamonot* and *dinei nefashot*).

However, the Tosafists (Shevuot 34a) take a different view, postulating that a person may also be convicted of murder in reliance on circumstantial evidence, when such evidence is absolute and incontrovertible – just as the same evidence would have substantiated the defendant's liability for monetary damages had he not actually killed the victim but only injured him.

According to some authorities, even Maimonides would agree that the prohibition against reliance on circumstantial evidence applies exclusively to actual capital cases, but that in other types of penal cases, such as *malkot* (lashes), circumstantial evidence can be relied upon in the same manner as in *dinei mamonot* (monetary cases) (Responsum Maharik, Part 87).

An exception to the rule with regard to capital cases is that of adultery, in which the basic rule is that circumstantial evidence is sufficient. The view of the *amora* Samuel in the Talmud (Makkot 7a) is that to convict a man and a woman of adultery, it is sufficient that the witnesses testify that they appeared to be engaged in an act of adultery, and there is no requirement that witnesses testify to having witnessed the actual sexual act. This opinion was accepted as the binding halakhic rule by most authorities (Yad, Issurei Bi'ah 1:19; Sh. Ar., EH 20:1). The main explanation for this divergence from the strict evidentiary requirements of criminal law, especially in capital matters, is that the sages considered it unreasonable to assume that biblical law required witnesses who witnessed the actual sexual act, both because of the technical difficulty and the indecency involved, and they therefore assumed that under biblical law it was sufficient that there be testimony that they were seen behaving "like adulterers" (see *Adultery).

LESSENING THE BURDEN OF PROOF IN CRIMINAL LAW – PUNISHMENT IN DEVIATION FROM THE LAW. Another category of cases which deviates from the rule that capital cases may only be decided in reliance upon direct evidence are those decided in accordance with the doctrine allowing the imposition of punishment in deviation from the strictures of criminal and evidentiary law when the exigencies of the times necessitate such punishment (*le-migdar milta*, i.e., to provide "a fence around the words" of Torah). This category was discussed at length in the Israeli Supreme Court decision in the *Nagar* case (Cr.A. 543/79 *Nagar v. State of Israel*, PD 35(1) 163–170, opinion of Justice Elon). We will review some of this discussion.

> Toward the end of the Tanna'itic era, we read of the establishment of a principle – followed for many years beforehand – which constituted a significant change in Jewish criminal law, with respect to both penal law and the rules of procedure and evidence in criminal trials:
>
> R. Eleazar b. Jacob stated, "I heard that even without any Torah [authority for their rulings], *beth din* may administer flogging and [death] penalties; not, however, for the purpose of transgressing the words of the Torah but in order to make a fence around the Torah" (TB Yevamot 90b; Sanhedrin 46a). In TJ Yerushalmi, Ḥagigah 2.2, the text is "I heard that they administer penalties not in accordance with the *halakhah* and they administer penalties not in accordance with the Torah" (page 165 of the *Nagar* decision).

On the basis of this fundamental provision, which enabled the courts to deviate from the original law of the Torah in criminal and evidentiary law, in accordance with the needs of the time and the place, both the courts and the communal leaders utilized their authority to enact communal regulations (see ***Takkanot*):

> Detailed legislation by way of regulations which were enacted during all of the periods against the background of variegated religious, societal, economic and moral circumstances.... This legislation granted broad power to determine criminal penalties and litigation procedures which conformed to the needs of the time and of society, and was accompanied by a serious warning not to infringe a person's stature as a human being, and his dignity more than necessary. After determining the scope of this extended authority given to the halakhic authorities in the area of criminal law Maimonides gives the following summary of the Sages' obligation when exercising these powers: "All these matters are carried out in accordance with what the judge deems necessary under the exigencies of that time, and his acts should always be for the sake of heaven and he should not take a frivolous attitude to human dignity" (Maimonides, Yad., Sanhedrin, ch. 24., 10) (*ibid.*, pp. 165–66).

Formally, such regulations are defined as "temporary provisions," but they have become part of substantive Jewish law in practice. At various times, Jewish courts throughout the Diaspora have exercised this authority even in imposing death sentences without requiring a court of 23, and without the stringent rules of evidence imposed by the original Jewish Law (see Elon, Jewish Law, pp. 515–19, and notes 100, 104–108).

As noted, in its original format, Jewish Law was strict in its requirements for direct evidence. Maimonides makes the following illuminating observations on the strict evidentiary requirements of Jewish Law (*Sefer ha-Mitzvot*, Negative Commandments, §290): "Even if A pursues B with intent to kill, and B takes refuge in a house, and the pursuer follows him, and we enter after them and find B in his last gasp and his enemy, A, standing over him with a knife in his hand, and both of them are covered with blood, the Sanhedrin may not find the pursuer A liable for capital punishment, since there are no direct witnesses who actually saw the murder …" The reason given by Maimonides is that if the court was permitted to convict a suspect of a criminal offense on the basis of other than the unequivocal testimony of witnesses to the actual act, the court might soon find itself convicting of criminal offences on the basis of a "speculative evaluation of the evidence." He completes his comments with the observation, that "it is better and more desirable that a thousand guilty persons go free than that a single innocent person be put to death."

In contrast with the stringency that characterized the original Jewish Law, the authority to impose punishment in a manner that deviated from Torah law enabled the courts in numerous Jewish communities to be content with circumstantial evidence alone, even for purposes of conviction for serious offenses such as murder. R. Isaac b. Sheshet of Perfet (Spain and North Africa; late 14th century) ruled that defendants accused of murder could be convicted relying on circumstantial evidence alone, provided there are convincing proofs and plausible reasons.

> In any event, in order to "create a safeguard," since someone from among you has died, if you decide that the death penalty is called for because a crime has been committed heinously, violently and deliberately (it appears that they lay in wait for him [the victim] at night and during day, and openly brandished weapons against him in the presence of the communal leaders), then you may [impose the death penalty]… even when there are no eyewitnesses, if there are convincing proofs and plausible reasons.

In another responsum, the Ribash ruled that for the same reason it is also possible to rely on the confession of a litigant supplemented by circumstantial evidence (similar to the provision in the law of evidence practiced in the State of Israel, allowing conviction of the accused on the basis of a confession given outside court, with the addition of "something extra"):

> Jewish courts [at this time] impose flogging and punishment not prescribed by the law, for capital jurisdiction was abrogated, but in accordance with the needs of the time, and even without unequivocal testimony, so long as there are clear grounds to show that he [the accused] committed the offense. In such a case, it is the practice to accept the defendant's confession even in a capital case, even where there is no clear proof, in order that what he says, together with some measure of corroboration, may shed light on what happened (*ibid.*, 234).

Not every part of the Jewish Diaspora enjoyed such broad autonomous criminal jurisdiction, and the extent of juridical authority differed according to the period and the location. However, jurisdiction similar to that enjoyed by the Spanish center in the Middle Ages also existed at a later period in the Jewish community of Poland. It was during this period that we hear of Polish communities exercising the power of "imposing punishment not prescribed in the Torah," in order to convict defendants on the basis of circumstantial evidence (*Nagar, ibid.*, pp. 167–169).

It is important to emphasize that, where convictions were based on circumstantial evidence, it was constantly reiterated that such evidence, even if not clear and direct, must be of a kind that the judges "believe to be the truth" (*Resp. Rashba*, attributed to Naḥmanides, §279), and that this kind of adjudication is only possible where "the accusation is proven to be well grounded"; and that "the sole intention is to pursue justice and truth and there is no other motive (*Resp. Zikhron Yehudah* § 79, *Nagar, ibid.* 170).

As noted above, these principles constituted the basis of the ruling of the Israeli Supreme Court in *Nagar*, under which one suspected of murder could be convicted relying on incontrovertible circumstantial evidence, even though the court had no direct evidence of his having committed the offense, and even though the body itself had not been found (see *Capital Punishment).

DOCUMENTS AS EVIDENCE. There is evidence of written documents serving as legally valid proof in the Bible itself: "and written in the books and sealed, and witnesses called" (Jer. 32:44).

The talmudic rule is that deeds constitute valid proof in a court. "Resh Lakish said: If witnesses are signed on a deed it is as if their testimony had been examined in court" (TB Ketubbot 18b). Several reasons are given for this ruling: first, because the deeds are drawn up with the debtor's consent and he has mentally resolved to agree to their contents since he derives some benefit or profit thereby; second, because the texts of the deeds are uniform and everyone understands their import; and third, because people customarily rely on them, since otherwise they would be unable to do business with one another. The *rishonim* therefore ruled that, in order for a deed to be binding, it must be written with the debtor's consent and at his request; a deed which was written by witnesses of their own initiative is not binding (Tosafot, Ketubot 18b; Naḥmanides, Bava Bathra 171a; Hame'iri, Ketubot 20a).

Under biblical law, the authenticity of a deed is presumed, "a person does not dare to forge" (Rashi, at Gittin 3a). However, the changing times and different moral and social attitudes precluded continued adjudication of deeds on the basis of simple authentication by way of the witnesses' signature, on the presumption that this excluded the possibility of forgery. The Rabbis henceforth enacted that all deeds would require substantiation. Thus, a person making a claim based on a deed, or relying on it as evidence, bore the burden of proof of demonstrating that the witnesses' signature was genuine. Substantiating evidence for a deed could consist of additional testimony on the signature, comparison of the signatures to other recognized signatures of the witnesses who signed, or the summoning of the signing witnesses to testify that the signature on the deed was indeed theirs.

Maimonides took a different view regarding the nature of a deed. Maimonides contended (Hilkhot Edut 3:4) that under Biblical law oral testimony is sufficient in all areas of law, including *dinei mamonot* (monetary civil cases). According to Maimonides, the requirement and acceptance of the signature of witnesses as proof of a deed is rooted in a rabbinic regulation, enacted so as not to "lock the door against borrowers" – i.e., economic life would be impossible if it were necessary to confirm every loan by way of oral testimony in court. In Maimonides' view, the requirement of substantiation of a deed is an offshoot of this rabbinic regulation, intended to prevent forgery of deeds.

In addition to requiring that witnesses' signatures be substantiated in order to prevent forgery of a deed, the Talmud prescribes that deeds are not to be written on paper (on which the original text could be erased) or untanned animal skin, because writing on this kind of paper can be easily forged (TB Gittin 21a–22b). Similarly, deeds cannot be written in a manner that enables the forging of their concluding section, or the addition of words that did not appear in the original text; a deed written in such a manner is inadmissible as evidence (Tb BB 160a f.; cf. *Shetar*).

OBJECTION TO EVIDENCE BY RIVAL LITIGANT. The litigants are allowed to make conditions regarding the rules of evidence in a civil case, in which they agree to admit otherwise inadmissible evidence. Nevertheless, so long as a trial has not yet finished, either litigant can object to the hearing of inadmissible evidence (Sh. Ar., ḤM 22:1). Moreover, if the agreement between the parties was not made in the court, the litigant can renege on his consent to accept such evidence even after the trial's conclusion (*Siftei Kohen.*, ad loc.). In order for a litigant to submit evidence that is otherwise inadmissible and deny the other litigant the right to object to such, he must make an agreement with the other litigant through an act of *kinyan*.

EVIDENCE THAT INFRINGES PRIVACY AND VIOLATES HUMAN DIGNITY. *Human dignity and the right to privacy are extensively protected in Jewish law. Nevertheless, at times the search for the truth necessitates the violation of a suspect's dignity or privacy. The conflict between the value of determining the truth (even by prohibited means) and that of preserving human dignity was discussed in the Israeli Supreme Court's decision in the rehearing of the Vaknin case (FH 9/83 *Military Appeals Court v. Vaknin*, PD 42(3) 837). In that case, the police obtained incriminating evidence against a defendant suspected of possessing dangerous drugs by forcing him to drink salt water, as a result of which he vomited up the drug packages that he had swallowed. The Court was requested to decide on whether the police action fell within the ambit of section 2 of the Protection of Privacy Law, 5741–1981. An affirmative ruling on this point could disqualify the illegally procured evidence, precluding reliance thereon for a conviction. On the other hand, if the conclusion was that the police action was not proscribed by the Protection of Privacy Law, then, even though the act itself was improper, the evidence obtained thereby would be admissible. (In general, under Israel law only evidence obtained through infringement of privacy as defined by the Protection of Privacy Law is rendered inadmissible.)

The Court ruled that this case did not involve an infringement of privacy, and the evidence was therefore admissible. Justice Elon held that the Protection of Privacy Law should be interpreted in accordance with Jewish law, and therefore adduced sources in Jewish law concerning the prohibition of disclosing secrets, the prohibition on opening another person's letters without permission, and others. Nevertheless, Elon indicated a number of specific cases in which the need to obtain evidence prevails over the need to protect privacy or human dignity – both with regard to penal law and monetary law:

> Eavesdropping is an affirmative precept (*mitzvah*) in certain circumstances as for example in order to obtain evidence in a case involving grave criminal activity (such as incitement). In such a case, "they may hide witnesses [against] him behind a fence" (Mishnah Sanhedrin 7.10), and it is permitted to do so in order to obtain evidence regarding any manner of criminal activity. (See R. Joseph Babad's *Minḥat Ḥinukh* – Commandment §462: "This is evidently not the simple meaning of the Mishnah in Sanhedrin ad loc: 'Witnesses are not hidden against any who are subject to the death penalty according to the Torah law, other than these' – and the matter requires clarification.") Similarly, it was permitted to open a letter addressed to another person where there are grounds for suspecting that the letter's author intends to commit a wrongdoing with the addressee's money and the matter can be clarified by opening the letter and reading it (see Responsa Hikekei Lev, Part I, *Yoreh De'ah*, 49, responsa of R. Hayyim Palache, rabbi of Izmir in the mid-19th century and one of the outstanding respondents during the period of the *aḥaronim*. See also *Responsa Maharik*, n. 110, of R. Joseph *Colon, one of the great halakhic sages in Italy during the 15th century, and Sh. Ar. YD, 228.33 Rema).

In addition to the principles elucidated in the *Vaknin* decision, there is also the issue of investigating the adulterous wife (*sotah*; see *Ordeal). Although this is a procedure based upon the occurrence of a miracle, which is not practiced in our time, it is intended to clarify guilt, and involves the humiliation of the woman being investigated.

An additional case raising the question of the clash between the need for evidence and the right to privacy came before the High Rabbinical Court of Appeals (Appeal 5733/216, R.D. 9, 331). The case concerned a husband who claimed that his wife was mentally ill, and therefore requested that the Court order her to undergo psychological treatment in order to restore "domestic peace." In the event of her refusal, he requested that she be declared "a rebellious wife" (*moredet*). The husband requested to summon her doctor as witness to her mental condition, but the latter conditioned his testimony on the wife's agreement to waiving medical confidentiality, which the wife refused to do. The president of the Court, Rabbi Shlomo Goren, and Rabbi Mordechai Eliyahu both held that the suspicion regarding a mental impairment was firmly based and that the doctor should therefore be compelled to testify to the court. On the other hand, Rabbi Yosef Kafah ruled that the probative value of the doctor's testimony was minimal, as he would only testify on her medical condition as it had been many years back. On the other hand, the testimony was liable to cause her serious damage, given that she was engaged in education and would be derided by her students. Rabbi Kafah therefore ruled that the doctor's testimony should not be required.

ACCEPTING EVIDENCE AFTER THE CONCLUSION OF THE TRIAL. The Mishnah (Sanhedrin 3:8) states that "whenever evidence is brought – it can contradict the ruling." In other words, after the trial's conclusion, even if the obligation ruled upon was discharged, the ruling can be annulled if new evidence was brought before the court. In such a case, a new trial must be held. The *tannaim* (*ibid.)* disputed the issue of whether the Court can place a time limitation on the period during which a litigant can proffer new evidence. The law was decided according to R. Simeon b. Gamaliel – namely, that the court cannot impose a time limit on a litigant's submission of new evidence which, irrespective of when it was submitted, will be accepted. A limitation on the submission of new evidence is only effective if the litigant himself declared that he has no further evidence; in such a case he is prevented from bringing further evidence at a later stage (Maimonides,Yad, Sanhedrin 7:6–9; Sh. Ar., ḤM 20).

[Menachem Elon (2nd ed.)]

BIBLIOGRAPHY: Z. Frankel, *Der gerichtliche Beweis nach mosaisch-talmudischem Rechte* (1846); J. Freudenthal, in: MGWJ, 9 (1860), 161–75; N. Hirsch, in: *Jeschurun*, 12 (Ger., 1865/66), 80–88, 109–22, 147–65, 249–58, 382–94; J. Klein, *Das Gesetz ueber das gerichtliche Beweisverfahren nach mosaisch-thalmudischem Rechte* (1885); Gulak, Yesodei, 4 (1922), passim; S. Assaf, *Battei Din ve-Sidreihem* (1924), 102ff.; S. Rosenbaum, in: *Ha-Mishpat*, 1 (1927), 280–90; S. Kaatz, in: *Jeschurun*, 15 (Ger., 1928), 89–98, 179–87; Z. Karl, in: *Ha-Mishpat ha-Ivri*, 3 (1928), 89–127; A. Gulak, *Le-Ḥeker Toledot ha-Mishpat ha-Ivri bi-Tekufat ha-Talmud*, 1 (*Dinei Karka'ot*, 1929), 66f.; D.M. Shohet, *The Jewish Court in the Middle Ages* (1931), 171–85 (contains bibliography); P. Dickstein, in: *Ha-Mishpat ha-Ivri*, 4 (1932/33), 212–20; Herzog, Institutions, 1 (1936), 233, 255ff., 367ff.; 2 (1939), 185–8; ET, 1 (1951³), 137–41; 2 (1949), 70f.; 3 (1951); 106–10; 4 (1952), 199–208; 6 (1954), 85, 106, 705–14; 7 (1956), 290–5; 8 (1957), 404–44, 609–23, 722–43; 9 (1959), 64–103, 156–7, 448–9, 722–46; 12 (1967), 307–13; A. Karlin, in: *Ha-Peraklit*, 11 (1954/55), 49–57, 154–61, 247–54; 12 (1955/56), 185–91; J. Ginzberg, *Mishpatim le-Yisrael* (1956), passim; S. Fischer, in: *No'am*, 2 (1959), 211–22; E.E. Urbach, in: *Mazkeret... Herzog* (1962), 395–7, 402–8; Jaeger, in: *Recueils de la Société Jean Bodin*, 16 (1965); Ch. S. Hefez, in: *Mishpatim*, 1 (1969), 67ff.; Elon, Mafte'aḥ, 279–302; J.S. Zuri, *Mishpat ha-Talmud* (1921), 38–64. **ADD. BIBLIOGRAPHY:** M. Elon, *Ha-Mishpat ha-Ivri* (1988), 1: 423, 502–504, 649, 800f., 827; 3: 1377f., 1442, 1486f.; idem, *Jewish Law* (1994), 2:516, 610f., 803, 981f., 1013; 4: 1646f., 1715, 1767f.; idem, *Jewish Law* (Cases and Materials) (1999), 200ff; M. Elon and B. Lifshitz, *Mafte'aḥ ha-She'elot ve-ha-Teshuvot shel Ḥakhmei Sefarad u-Ẓefon Afrikah* (1986), 1:135–42; 2:440–47; B. Lifshitz and E. Shohetman, *Mafte'aḥ ha-She'elot ve-ha-Teshuvot shel Ḥakhmei Ashkenaz, Ẓarefat ve-Italyah* (1997), 90–91, 298–304; S. Albeck, *Ha-Re'ayot de-Dinei ha-Talmud* (1987); E. Shochetman, *Seder ha-Din* (1988), 269–317; D. Frimer, "*Kevi'at Abbahut al-yedei Bedikat Dam ba-Mishpat ha-Yisraeli u-va-Mishpat ha-Ivri*," in: *Shenaton ha-Mishpat ha-Ivri*, 5 (5738), 219–42; Y. Ben Meir, "*Re'ayot Nesibatiyyot ba-Mishpat ha-Ivri*," in: *Dinei Yisrael*, 18 (5755–5756); Y. Ungar and A. Rachnitz (eds.), *Mishpatei Ereẓ*, 2 (2004); I. Warhaftig, "*Beirur Uvdot ba-Mishpat toch Pegi'a be-Ẓeni'ut ha-Perat*," in: *Mishpatei Ereẓ*, 2 (2004), 220–21.

EVIL EYE (Heb. עַיִן הָרַע, *ayin ha-ra*; lit., "the eye of the evil"; Aram. עֵינָא בִּישָׁא, *eina bisha*), a widespread belief that some persons may produce malevolent effects on others by looking at them, based on the supposed power of some eyes to bewitch or harm by glance. In early Jewish literature the acceptance of the existence of the evil eye as fact precluded any theoretical explanation of this phenomenon and discussion of its origin. In post-talmudic literature, however, one of the following two explanations is generally found: (1) the evil eye contains the element of fire, and so spreads destruction (Judah Loew b. Bezalel ("Maharal") in *Netivot Olam*, 107d); (2) the angry glance of a man's eye calls into being an evil angel who takes vengeance on the cause of wrath (Manasseh Ben Israel in *Nishmat Ḥayyim*, 3:27; cf. *Sefer Ḥasidim*, ed. by J. Wistinetzki (1924^2), 242 no. 981).

As both explanations imply magic, folk beliefs governing magic and countermagic are evidenced in beliefs connected with casting and averting the evil eye.

Casting the Evil Eye

Whereas a "good-eyed" person is generous and good-hearted, the "evil eye," in biblical (cf. I Sam. 18:9; Prov. 28:22) and tannaitic (cf. Avot 2:9, 11; 5:13, 19) sources, denotes stinginess, selfishness, and jealousy; in the *aggadah* of Palestinian *amoraim* the evil eye is a prevalent motif. Furthermore, jealousy was linked with magic and with fatal consequences. Hence, talmudic and midrashic elaborations of biblical narratives represent Sarah as casting the evil eye on Hagar (Gen. R. 4.45:5), Joseph's brothers on Joseph (*ibid.* 84:10), Og the giant on Jacob (Ber. 54b). Likewise, the evil eye caused the breaking of the first tablets of the Law (Num. R. 12:4) and the death of Daniel's three companions (Sanh. 93a).

This magical power of the eye was not confined to biblical evildoers; folk heroes, regarded as sacred wonder-workers, were believed to have exercised it as well, but for benevolent purposes. So R. *Simeon b. Yoḥai transforms an evil person into "a heap of bones" by means of his magic endowment (Shab. 34a; PdRK ed. by S. Buber (1868), 90a–b), and, with a look, R. Johanan, the *amora*, kills a man who calumniated

Jerusalem (BB 75a). The magical aspect of the deed is stressed in killing by transformation (Ber. 58a).

Averting the Evil Eye

Folk beliefs and folk customs are especially evident in the attitude toward the aversion of the evil eye. All measures taken against it are either (1) preventive or (2) counteractive.

(1) The belief that the evil eye is activated by arousing the jealousy and malice of the "jettatori" (i.e., the endowed people) calls for preventive measures of self-restraint, e.g., the avoidance of any expression of praise, approbation, and of beauty, domestic or socioeconomic success, or happiness. For this reason Abraham sent his son Isaac home at night after the **Akedah* (Gen. R. 56:11); Jacob advised his handsome and strong sons not to enter the same gate all together "on account of the eye" (*ibid.* 91:6); similarly, Joshua advised Ephraim and Manasseh to hide in a forest (Josh. 17:15; BB 118a–b). Prominent men, beautiful women, and newborn babies – all of whom are likely to attract special attention – are especially susceptible to the evil eye. If, however, the beauty is veiled, riches not exhibited, and a child covered with a dirty bag or given an ugly name, the happy event may pass unnoticed, and the evil eye thus remains passive. Therefore, a costly garment should not be spread over the bed when guests are visiting the house as "it will be burned by the eye of the guests" (BM 30a), and precious glass should be broken at a wedding. The idea that "blessing comes only upon those things which are hidden from the eye" (Ta'an. 8b) is undoubtedly connected with such preventive measures.

(2) Once the evil eye has been activated, and the threat of danger and harm is close to realization, there is no need for preventive measures: only confrontation and war measures based on countermagic which deceive or defeat the evil eye can then save the endangered person. The use of a mirror (ornament) or a specific color (red, blue) may blight its source by reflecting the glance; an obscene gesture or a holy verse (*amulet) may avert the evil eye by frightening it; and an outstretched hand may stop its rays. According to the Talmud (Ber. 55b), whoever is afraid of the evil eye should stick his right thumb in his left hand and his left thumb in his right hand, proclaiming: "I, so and so, son of so and so, am of the seed of Joseph, whom the evil eye may not affect." The gesture (a "fig") – universally used to avert the evil eye by putting it to shame (this original meaning was probably unknown to sages who prescribed it) – took on a Jewish character by the pronouncement of the aggadic sentence that the descendants of Joseph are immune from the evil eye (Ber. 20a).

Other means of fighting and subduing the activated evil eye stem from attempts to absorb the devastating glance, and so to neutralize it. To divert the glance from the intended target, "interesting" objects may be hung between the eyes of the endangered person, e.g., precious stones, or as strange and unexpected an object as a tail of a fox between the eyes of a horse in need of protection (Tosef., Shab. 4:5).

The belief in the evil eye and the various means, both sacred and profane, of averting it, were very prevalent among East European Jews; to this day they exist in many Oriental Jewish communities. In modern times the use of blue paint and a metal amulet in the form of an open palm of the hand are still widespread in Oriental communities, and among Yiddish-speaking Ashkenazi Jews, it is customary to "qualify" any praise with the phrase *keyn ayen hore* ("may there be no evil eye" often shortened to *kaynahora*). The custom of tying a red band around the wrist or neck of a newborn child also derives from a fear of the evil eye. In Yiddish, even the name "evil eye" is euphemistically called *git-oyg* ("good eye"). R. Lilienthal (see bibl.) lists over 80 anti-evil eye practices recorded among East European Jews. The striking resemblance to those listed in monographs on Oriental Jewish communities (cf. Ḥ. Mizraḥi, *Yehudei Paras* (1959), 115–7) can be explained by the universality of the motif of the evil eye, on the one hand, and its particular Jewish expression, on the other.

BIBLIOGRAPHY: L. Blau, *Das altjuedische Zauberwesen* (in: *Jahresbericht der Landes-Rabbinerschule in Budapest fuer das Schuljahr 1897–98*), 152–6; F.T. Elworthy, *The Evil Eye* (1895); Ginzberg, Legends, index; M. Grunwald, in: MGJV, 5 (1900), 40f., 47f.; A. Loewinger, in: *Menorah* (Vienna), 4 (1926), 551–69; R. Lilienthal, in: *Yidishe Filologye*, 1 (1924); S. Seligmann, *Der boese Blick und Verwandtes* (1910); idem, *Die Zauberkraft des Auges* (1922); S. Thompson, *Motif-Index of Folk-Literature*, 2 (1956), 121 (D 993), 364ff. (D 2071); J. Trachtenberg, *Jewish Magic and Superstition* (1939), 54–56, 283.

[Dov Noy]

EVIL-MERODACH (Heb. אֱוִיל מְרֹדַךְ), son of *Nebuchadnezzar, king of Babylonia from 562–560 B.C.E. The Babylonian form of the name is Amēl Marduk ("man of Marduk"). During Evil-Merodach's reign, the stability of the royal court of Babylon was undermined and there appeared the first signs of the decline of the neo-Babylonian Empire. After two years as king, he was assassinated, probably by his brother-in-law Nergal-šar-uṣur (Nergal Sarezer), who succeeded him on the throne (Jer. 39:3, 13). It is related in the Bible (II Kings 25:27–30; Jer. 52:31–34) that Evil-Merodach freed *Jehoiachin, king of Judah, from prison in the 37th year of Jehoiachin's exile in Babylon and that he accorded him a food allotment for life and treated him better than his other vassals. His motives can only be guessed at. He may have contemplated a far-reaching reverse of his father's policies.

BIBLIOGRAPHY: Weisbach, in: E. Ebeling and B. Meissner (eds.), *Reallexikon der Assyriologie*, 1 (1932), 94; Bright, Hist, 334; EM, 1 (1965), 138–9, incl. bibl. **ADD. BIBLIOGRAPHY:** R. Sack, *Amēl-Marduk 562–560* B.C. (1972); idem, in: ABD II, 679; W. Holladay, *Jeremiah 2* (1989), 291.

[Bustanay Oded]

EVOLUTION. Although evolutionary ideas are very old, being found in the works of Greek philosophers and echoed in the *aggadah* and the Midrash, the main stimulus to evolutionary thought came from the theory developed at the end of the

18th century, according to which life on earth has existed for millions of years, and not for less than 6,000, as held by the biblical tradition current in the civilized world. The theory of evolution produced a sharp reaction on the part of those intellectuals and scholars who subscribed to the assumption of the stability of the species from the six days of creation. Besides scientists who cast doubts on the validity of the theory, its chief opponents were (and still are) religious people who accept the creation story in Genesis literally. There are, however, religious thinkers who see in the principle of evolution a concept that accords with the idea of divine providence, some of them not only regarding the account of creation in Genesis as a simple explanation "in ordinary language" of the actual process of creation, but seeing in it a deeper significance. Some point to aggadic and midrashic statements which contain allusions to evolution and to the fact that life existed on earth in epochs preceding the accepted reckoning in Judaism. When discussing the Greek philosophers' views on "the eternity of the universe," a similar problem confronted Maimonides, who says (*Guide*, 2:25):

> We do not reject the eternity of the universe because certain passages in Scripture confirm the creation; for such passages are not more numerous than those in which God is represented as a corporeal being. Nor is it impossible or difficult to find for them a suitable interpretation. We might have explained them in the same manner as we did in respect to the incorporeality of God and this might have been easier … However, we have not done so … for the eternity of the universe has not been proved and there is no need of scriptural passages to reject it … If we were to accept the eternity of the universe as taught by Plato, we should not be in opposition to the fundamental principles of our religion … The scriptural text might have been explained accordingly … But there is no necessity for this expedient, so long as the theory has not been proved. As there is no proof sufficient to convince us … we take the text of the Bible literally.

Applying this to the subject under discussion and stating it in contemporary terms, it may be said that if proofs were forthcoming for the theory of evolution (on the assumption that there exists One who directs creation), a way would be found of explaining the biblical passages accordingly.

Although Judah Halevi clearly recognized the need to accept the Scriptures literally, he nevertheless stated in his *Kuzari* (1:67): "If, after all, a believer in the Law finds himself compelled to admit an eternal matter and the existence of many worlds prior to this one, this would not impair his belief." In the latter part of this sentence Judah Halevi alludes to the statement of R. Abbahu (Gen. R. 3:7) that God "created worlds and destroyed them," while according to R. Judah b. Simon there was "a succession of times (days and nights) before that," that is, before the first day of creation (*ibid.*). To this province belong also such statements as: "'And there was evening and there was morning, the sixth day' (Gen. 1:31). R. Simon b. Marta said, 'Up to this point we count according to the reckoning of the world, after it according to another reckoning'" (Gen. R. 9:16), that is, time before the final creation of the world has a different meaning from that after it, which is the reckoning that we follow. The relativity of time in the term "day" is referred to in the statement (Gen. R. 19:8) which distinguishes between the human and the divine day, the latter being a thousand years in duration, as it is said (Ps. 90:4): "For a thousand years in Thy sight are but as yesterday." Alongside these notions there are homiletical interpretations of biblical passages according to which all organisms were fully created in the six days of creation, after which no changes have occurred in them (Hul. 60a). In contrast to those who extended the period of creation, a *tanna* curtailed it by stating that "on the first day the entire world was created," this being the view of R. Nehemiah, who disagreed with R. Judah's opinion that "the world was created in six days" (Tanḥ. B., Gen. 7). All these sages based their views on biblical verses, which could be interpreted either way. In this connection Rabbi A.I. *Kook has remarked that "everyone knows that the creation is one of the mysteries of the Torah, and if all the statements are merely to be taken literally, what mystery is there?" (*Iggerot ha-Re'iyyah* (1961^{2}), no. 91). The literature of the sages is pluralistic in its world outlook, especially in the spheres of cosmology and biology. The *tannaim* and *amoraim* absorbed legends and "factual" stories, the views of Greco-Roman science, and the folklore of ancient peoples. Among these were ideas which have no basis in fact nor any support in biblical passages and are even in conflict with the creation story. There was, for example, the view about the development of living organisms from nonliving substances which, known as spontaneous generation and accepted until the 19th century, penetrated into the *halakhah*. There was also the "assumption that a mouse does not breed" (Sifra, *Shemini*, Parashah 5; Ḥul. 127a), and hence the halakhic discussion on the question of the uncleanness of "a mouse which is half flesh and half earth" (Ḥul. 9:6. As late as in 1652 Helmont, a Dutch chemist, still suggested a method of producing mice by putting rags into a heap of grain). There was similarly the prevailing view that vermin originate from perspiration or from dirt. Thus the Talmud (Shab. 107b) declared that "vermin do not breed," against which an objection was raised from the reference made to "eggs of vermin" (see Ḥul. 9:6). The salamander, too, was thought to originate from a fire which burnt continuously for several years (see Ḥag. 27a). In the belief that some organisms develop on food itself, it was permitted to eat certain foods on which maggots develop.

The folklore of various nations tells of organisms, such as *mandrakes, that are half plant and half human. There was also the belief that some birds grow on trees in the form of fruit, and R. Tam (12th century) was asked whether they require *sheḥitah*, to which he replied that they do (see Loew, Flora, 4 (1934), 348). The *halakhah* mentions an organism called אַבְנֵי הַשָּׂדֶה or אַדְנֵי הַשָּׂדֶה, whose corpse, like that of a human being, communicates uncleanness (Sifra, *Shemini*, ch. 6; Kil. 8:5). Explained by some as referring to the chimpanzee, it is said in the Jerusalem Talmud (Kil. 8:5, 31c) to be "a man of the mountains who lives from his navel; if the navel is severed, he does not live," the reference being to a manlike organism joined by its navel like a plant to the ground. Legends about such an organism were current among various nations (see R. Patai, *Adam ve-Adamah*, 1 (1942), 216ff.). Mermaids, the legendary half-human, half-fish beings, also figure in the *halakhah*, the unclean "living creatures that are in the waters" (Lev. 11:10) being interpreted as "including mermaids," which however, unlike a human corpse, do not communicate uncleanness when dead (Sifra, *Shemini*, Parashah 3). The sages who quoted these *halakhot* or statements were influenced by the leading scientists of the time, such as Aristotle, Galen, and others, who had confirmed these "facts" and to whom there undoubtedly applied the principle that "if someone tells you that there is wisdom among the non-Jews, believe him" (Lam. R. 2:13). As it deals with all spheres of life and with theoretical subjects, the *halakhah* also on occasion incorporated legendary, fictitious ideas. In the field of "science" the sages were ready to accept various views current among their contemporaries (but proved in our day to be without foundation) and did not hesitate to give expression to them even if they were contrary to their accepted views.

To this province belong *halakhot* relating to *mixed species (*kilayim*). Despite the assumption inherent in the Bible that in the six days of creation all organisms were fully formed, statements of the sages in the *aggadah* and the *halakhah* refer to the production of new species by hybridization and grafting. The Tosefta and the Jerusalem Talmud of tractate *Kilayim* cite many "facts" about the formation of a third species by grafting two species of flora, some systematically very remote from each other (see *Biology; it is now evident that no new species can be produced by grafting). Thus, for example, it is asserted that, by sowing together the seeds of an apple and a watermelon a third species, the *melon (called in Greek *melopepon*, the apple-melon), is obtained (TJ, Kil. 1:2, 27a), even as a dangerous creature called *arvad* is produced by mating a snake with a species of *lizard (Ḥul. 127a). Another tradition holds that after Anah the son of Zibeon had produced a *mule, which is a dangerous animal, by crossing a stallion and a she-ass (יֵמִם, a *hemi-onos*, i.e., a half-ass; cf. Gen. 36:24), "the Holy One blessed be He appointed a *ḥakhina* [a poisonous snake] which He mated with a *ḥardon* [a species of lizard] to produce a *ḥavarbar*," a species of noxious animal whose bite proved fatal to Anah (TJ, Ber. 8:6, 12b). This story is mentioned in a discussion on whether mixed species originated during the six days of creation (*ibid.;* Tosef. Ber. 6:11). On this subject there is the view of the *tanna* R. Yose (Pes. 54a) that "two things God originally planned to create on the eve of the Sabbath [of the creation] but were not created until the termination of the Sabbath, and at the termination of the Sabbath the Holy One blessed be He granted Adam knowledge of a kind like the divine, whereupon he took two stones, rubbed them together, and fire issued from them [cf. the tale of Prometheus]; he also took two [heterogeneous] animals and crossed them, and from them came forth the mule." Thus R. Yose held that hybridization represents a remarkable wisdom granted to man, who is prone to produce new organisms, "like the divine creator."

Another *aggadah*, which declares that God Himself "changes His world once every seven years," mentions various animals, one of which is replaced by the other (TJ, Shab. 1:3, 3b). The reference here may be to seven years of God, one of whose days is a thousand years (see above; although there is a statement (BK 16b) that "the male hyena (צבוע) becomes a bat after seven years," etc.).

Proofs of Evolution

The existence in prehistoric times of gigantic animals, then extinct, is alluded to in biblical verses referring to the dragon, the *leviathan, the Rahab, and others. Having perhaps found traces of the footprints of primeval animals or remains of their skeletons (footprints of prehistoric reptiles have been discovered near Jerusalem in recent times), the ancients had their imaginations stirred to describe these huge animals and explain the reasons for their extinction.

One of the crucial problems confronting the evolutionists was the question of the transition from ape to man. In the literature of the sages there are allusions to a connection between man and ape. Thus the *amoraim* Rav and Samuel held divergent views on the nature of the rib from which woman was created, the one holding that it was a tail (Ber. 61a). In the opinion of R. Judah: "[God] made him [i.e., man] a tail like an animal and then removed it from him for his honor" (Gen. R. 14:12). Even Adam was not the first man, for "974 generations preceded the creation of the world and they were swept away in a trice because they were evil" (Mid. Ps. to 90:13; cf. Shab. 88b). Nor was Adam anatomically perfect, since he was a hermaphrodite (Gen. R. 8:1); the fingers of his hands were joined together, and it was only from Noah onward that people were born with separated fingers (Mid. *Avkir* to Gen. 5:29; and similarly in Tanh. to *ibid.*). In the days of Enosh there took place a moral degeneration; human beings changed, and "their faces became like apes" (Gen. R. 23:6; cf. Sanh. 109b). All these statements are based on a homiletical interpretation of biblical verses, but underlying them was probably the view of the *tanna* or *amora* which he expressed in this manner. Finally there is a statement that attests to an observation and a conclusion drawn from the realm of comparative anatomy: the *amora* R. Samuel of Cappadocia concluded from a common feature in fishes and birds that the latter, too, were created "out of alluvial mud": this can be proved "from the fact that birds have on their legs scales like those of fishes" (Ḥul. 27b).

At the beginning of the 20th century the naturalist De Vries (1848–1935) drew attention to the fact that in some flora and fauna characteristics suddenly appear which, though not present in their progenitors, are transmitted by heredity to the progeny. These changes, known as mutations, for the most part small and fortuitous, are in the view of scholars the basis of the evolutionary processes. Through the accumulation of these mutations, organisms were separated during millions of years of evolution into strains, species, and higher systematic groups. According to Neo-Darwinism the fortuitous mutations and the operation of natural selection were responsible for evolution, whereas according to Neo-Lamarckism, development cannot be accounted for without assuming that there is something in the living substance which guides it toward development. In this sense there is a statement of the rabbis: "There is no herb which has not a guardian angel in heaven that strikes it and says, Grow!" (Gen. R. 10:6). Other scholars maintain that there are metaphysical factors that guide and direct the existence and development of the organism. This theory, known as teleology, approximates to the religious view of the Creator's providence over His creatures. Some leading evolutionists, although dissociating themselves from the teleological approach, nevertheless agreed that it was impossible to explain evolution on the basis only of known forces. Thus G.L. Stebbins, who made a study of evolution in flora, argued that evolution can be explained by mutations, hybridization, and natural selection directed by a certain force of unknown nature. Certain embryologists, too, assumed that in ontogeny – the development of the individual during the embryonic period – there is an unknown or nonrational force directing it toward its development, and in this there is a parallel between phylogeny, the development of the species, and ontogeny, the development of the individual.

However much these views fall out of fashion as molecular biology progresses and the fossil record is clarified, these assumptions have an indubitable religious significance, and in this connection mention should be made of the words of Rabbi Kook: "The theory of evolution, which is at present increasingly conquering the world, is more in harmony with the mysteries of Kabbalah than all other philosophical theories" (*Orot ha-Kodesh*, ii, 558). On the other hand there are many evolutionists who are not prepared to include in the scheme of creation and evolution a nonrational force and hold that these "unknown" forces, responsible for the evolutionary process, will be revealed and defined as known chemical or physical forces. There are numerous theories to explain the mechanism of evolution, but the doubts exceed the certainties. When Rabbi Kook was asked about the problem of evolution, he summed it up as follows: "Nothing in the Torah is contradicted by any knowledge in the world that emerges from research. But we must not accept hypotheses as certainties, even if there is a wide agreement about them" (*Iggerot ha-Re'iyyah*, no. 91).

BIBLIOGRAPHY: S.B. Ulman, *Madda'ei ha-Teva u-Veri' at ha-Olam* (1944); M.M. Kasher, in: *Sefer Yovel... Samuel K. Mirsky* (1958), 256–84; idem, in: *Sinai*, 48 (1960), 21–33; J. Feliks, *Kilei Zera'im ve-Harkavah* (1967), 7–12, 112–5; idem, in: *Teva va-Areẓ*, 7 (1965), 330–7; O. Wolfsberg, in: L. Jung (ed.), *Jewish Library*, 2 (1968), 145–70.

[Jehuda Feliks]

ÉVORA, capital of Alto Alentejo province, S. central Portugal. It had one of the most important Jewish communities in the country. Regulations defining the powers of the *Arraby Moor issued during the reign of King Alfonso III (1248–79) laid down that the chief rabbi of the Jewish communities in Alentejo (Alemtejo) should reside in Évora. In 1360, 1388, and 1434, the Évora community was given privileges by the king defining the limits of its autonomy. In 1325 the Jews of Évora were compelled by a special decree to wear a yellow shield of David on their hats (see Jewish *badge). On several occasions the kings of Portugal intervened in favor of the Jews of Évora who engaged in varied economic activities. In 1392 John I ordered the town authorities to desist from further confiscation of Jewish property in the synagogues of Évora, and in 1408 he granted the Jews a privilege permitting them to enlarge their quarter. The old Jewish quarter can still be visited. On the doorposts of stone-made houses three slots for *mezzuzot* were found. In 1478 the community paid a sum of 264,430 cruzados to the crown. After the decree of expulsion and forced conversions of 1496/7, Évora continued to be an important center of **anusim*. In April 1505 these were set upon by bands of rioters, who manhandled them and set the synagogue on fire. From 1542, the year in which Luis *Dias of Setúbal was burned at the stake there, a tribunal of the Inquisition was active in Évora. Numerous *anusim* were condemned to the stake from the 16th to 18th centuries.

BIBLIOGRAPHY: M. Kayserling, *Geschichte der Juden in Portugal* (1867), index; J. Mendes dos Remedios, *Os Judeus em Portugal*, 1 (1895), 226, 362, 382; L. Wolf, *Reports on the Marranos or Crypto-Jews of Portugal* (1926), 6–7; N. Slouschz, *Ha-Anusim be-Portugal* (1932), 10–12, 16, 21, 24, 69; B. Roth, in: REJ, 126 (1957), 94–95; Roth, Marranos, index; J. dos Santos Ramalho Coelho, in: *A Cidade de Évora*, 63/64 (1980/81), 267–84; M.J.P. Ferro Tavares, in: *Anuario de Estudios Medievales*, 17 (1987), 551–58; A.B. Coelho, *Inquisicío de Évora dos promórdios a 1668*, 2 vols. (1987); M. do Carmo Teixeira and L.M.L. Ferreira Runa, in: *Revista de História Económica e Social*, 22 (1988), 51–76; L.M.L. Ferreira Runa, in: *Arqueologia do estado*, vol. 1 (1988), 375–86; M.B.A. Araújo, in: *Inquisicío*, vol. 1 (1989–90), 49–72.

ÉVREUX, capital of the Eure department, N.W. France. During the Middle Ages, Évreux was renowned as a center of Jewish scholarship. Most famous of its scholars was the tosafist *Samuel (b. Sheneor) of Évreux, known as the "Prince of Évreux"; his elder brother, *Moses of Évreux, was also a tosafist, and his two other brothers, the liturgical poet Judah and the commentator *Isaac of Évreux, are also well known. The Jewish community lived in the "rue aux Juifs," later known as Rue de la Bove. The synagogue was situated on the eastern side of the street. After the expulsion of 1306, no community existed in Évreux. In the 1950s, a community was established by Jews from North Africa. In 1968 it had about 250 members.

BIBLIOGRAPHY: Gross, Gal Jud, 38–43; U. Lamiray, *Promenades... dans Evreux* (1927), 162f.

[Bernhard Blumenkranz]

EVRON (Heb. עֶבְרוֹן), kibbutz in the Plain of Acre, Israel, near Nahariyyah, affiliated with Kibbutz Arẓi ha-Shomer ha-Ẓa'ir. Evron was founded in 1945 by immigrants from Poland and Romania. In addition to intensive farming (cotton and avocado plantations), the kibbutz had a factory for irrigation equipment and a quarry. In 2002 the population was 686. Ebron (Evron) was a town of the tribe of Asher (Josh. 19:28).

WEBSITE: www.matte-asher-region.muni.il.

[Efraim Orni]

EVRON, EPHRAIM (1920–1995), Israel diplomat. Evron was born in Haifa and was educated at the Reali High School there, continuing his studies at the Hebrew University, and graduating in history in 1940. He served in the British army during World War II from 1941 to 1946 and in the Israel Defense Forces in 1948. In the same year he entered the Foreign Office, and in 1950 was appointed director, but the following year was transferred to the Office of the Prime Minister. He served as personal assistant to Moshe Sharett, David Ben-Gurion, and Pinḥas Lavon, and his close involvement with the last in the "Lavon Affair" brought him into conflict with Moshe Dayan, then chief of staff, and nearly wrecked his political career. He left government service and took up a position representing the Histadrut in the U.S.A., rejoining the Foreign Office in 1961 when he was appointed counselor, and subsequently minister, at the Israeli Embassy in London.

In 1965 he was appointed minister to the Israeli Embassy in Washington and served in that capacity until 1968 when he was appointed ambassador to Sweden; in 1969 he became ambassador to Canada where he served until 1971. On his return to Israel he was appointed deputy to the director-general of the Foreign Office and in 1977 director-general.

In October 1978 he was appointed ambassador to the U.S., in succession of Simcha *Dinitz, taking up his appointment in December of that year and serving until 1982.

EWALD, HEINRICH GEORG AUGUST (1803–1875), Protestant theologian; scholar of the Bible, Israelite history, and Semitic languages. Ewald was a pupil of J.G. *Eichhorn. He served as professor at Goettingen (1827–37, 1848–67) and Tuebingen (1838–48). He was twice dismissed from his post – once in 1837 for protesting against the abolition of the Hanoverian constitution by the king, and again in 1867 for refusing to swear allegiance to the king of Prussia. Ewald viewed historical criticism not as a religious threat but as a means of reconstructing the process by which divine providence had chosen to reveal the true faith to humanity. He believed that the stories of the patriarchs could be used to reconstruct ancient Israelite tribal history, but that the patriarchs themselves were "ideal types." Ewald was more positive in his historical assessment of Moses. As for the Hebrew prophets, it was through them that God gave the most important truths to humanity. Ewald also did research on Hebrew and Arabic grammar and on the medieval works of Hebrew grammar, which were written in Arabic. He is considered the father of the theory of Hebrew syntax. In his *Kritische Grammatik der hebraeischen Sprache* (1827–80^{8}; pt. 3 trans. as *Syntax of the Hebrew of the Old Testament*, 1879), he attempted to discover the principles which determine linguistic forms and explain them. J. *Wellhausen, T. *Noeldeke, and *A.Dillmann, were among his pupils. His books include *Die Komposition der Genesis kritisch untersucht* (1823); *Grammatica critica linguae arabicae…* (2 vols., Leipzig, 1831–33); *Die Dichter des Alten Bundes erklaert* (2 vols., 1966–67); *Die Propheten des Alten Bundes erklaert* (3 vols., 1867–68^{2}); *Geschichte des Volkes Israel bis Christus* (5 vols., 1843–55; 7 vols., 1851–59); *The History of Israel* (8 vols., 1883–), according to H. Graetz a turning point in the treatment of Jewish history by Christian scholars; *Ausfuehrliches Lehrbuch der hebraeischen Sprache des Alten Bundes* (1870); and *Theologie des Alten und Neuen Bundes* (1871–78).

BIBLIOGRAPHY: T.W. Davies, *Heinrich Ewald, Orientalist and Theologian* (1903), incl. bibl.; H.J. Kraus, *Geschichte der historisch-kritischen Erforschung des Alten Testaments* (1956), 182–90; RGG^{3}, 2 (1927), 453–5. **ADD. BIBLIOGRAPHY:** J. Rogerson, in: DBI, 1, 363–64.

[Samuel Ephraim Loewenstamm / S. David Sperling (2nd ed.)]

EXCERPTA VALESIANA, historical work, written c. 550 and treating the reigns of Odoacer and Theodoric (474–526). It notes a conflict between Jews and Christians, probably over baptism, at Ravenna, after which the Christians burned the synagogues. The author, bitterly anti-Arian, is sharply critical of Theodoric, the Arian Ostrogoth ruler of Italy, who imposed the contribution of funds necessary to rebuild the synagogues.

[Jacob Petroff]

EXCHEQUER OF THE JEWS, department of medieval English government for Jewish affairs. The squared tablecloth (12th century, Fr. *eschequier*) used like an abacus for counting money in settling the sheriffs' accounts gave its name to the Exchequer, a branch of the royal administration in which accounts were rendered and revenue questions decided. A separate Jewish department (subordinate to the main Exchequer) may have originated in the Exchequer of Aaron, established for the affairs of *Aaron of Lincoln, whose assets passed to the Crown on his death (1186). By 1194 there were already justices or keepers of the Jews. Benedict of Talmont may have served as a Jewish Justice of the Jews in the last years of the 12th century. After 1199 only Christians, varying in number from two to five, were appointed. Other Jewish "officials," the most important being the *archpresbyter (*Presbyter Judeorum*), were associated with the Exchequer of the Jews in the 13th century.

Its functions were both administrative and judicial. It controlled the system of *archae* (or chests), at first six or seven, later over 20, in towns with established Jewish communities: appointing and dismissing their officials, ordering the withdrawal and restoration of chirographs. All moneylending transactions (other than the lending of money against pawned movables) had to be registered in these *archae*. When the debt became due, the Exchequer of the Jews would issue an authorization for the levying of the debt at the request of the creditor; only if the debtor had died would this need to be preceded by legal proceedings. The Exchequer of the Jews also exercised a jurisdiction over cases involving Jewish debts which had passed into the hands of the Crown or had been transferred to other Christian creditors. At certain periods in the 13th century Crown revenue from Jewish sources was handled by the ordinary Exchequer, but in others the Exchequer of the Jews collected such revenue, retained it in a separate treasury, and disbursed it on the king's instructions. The Plea Rolls of the Exchequer of the Jews survive for 1219–20, 1244, 1253, and in a virtually continuous series from 1266 to 1287 (in course of publication).

BIBLIOGRAPHY: Roth, England, index; H.G. Richardson, *English Jewry under Angevin Kings* (1960); A.B. Cramer, in: *American Historical Review*, 45 (1939–40), 327–37; idem, in: *Speculum*, 16 (1941), 226–9; Meekings, in: *Bulletin, Institute of Historical Research*, 28 (1955), 173–88; Rigg-Jenkinson-Cohen-Brand, Exchequer.

[Vivian David Lipman]

EXECUTION (Civil), laws concerning methods of recovering a debt.

Definition and Substance of the Concept

In Jewish law, a debt or obligation (*ḥiyyuv*) creates in favor of the creditor not only a personal right of action against the debtor, but also a right *in rem* in the form of a lien over the latter's property (termed *aḥarayut nekhasim*; see *Lien; Law of *Obligation). Hence, many of the laws concerning the methods of satisfying a debt out of the debtor's property also apply to the recovery of a debt with the consent of the debtor, and not merely to recovery of a debt by court action; e.g., such matters as the distinction between the different categories of assets out of which the debt must be satisfied, the distinction between free and "encumbered and alienated assets" (*nekhasim benei ḥorin* and *meshu'badim*, respectively), or the matter of preferential rights as between several creditors, etc.

Recovery of debt will here be dealt with from two main aspects: (1) methods of recovery involving the exercise of constraint against the person or liberty of the debtor; and (2) methods of recovery from the debtor's assets.

Execution in Jewish Law and in Other Legal Systems – Fundamental Principles

There are detailed instructions under biblical law governing the relationship between the lender (creditor) and borrower (debtor; Ex. 22:24–26; Deut. 24:6; 10–13), the essence of which is to enjoin the creditor not to prejudice the debtor's basic necessities of life or his personal honor and freedom. This is in contrast to the right given the creditor in the laws of Hammurapi to enslave the debtor as well as the debtor's wife, children, and slaves (secs. 114–6, 151–2, also 117–9) and in further contrast with similar provisions in the laws of Assyria, Ashnunna, Sumer, etc. (see Elon, *Ḥerut ha-Perat* 3–8). In biblical law the institution of slavery is limited to two cases only: (1) the thief who does not have the means to make restitution and is "sold for his theft" (Ex. 22:2); and (2) the person who voluntarily "sells himself" because of his extreme poverty (Lev. 25:39). Scriptural references indicate, however, that in practice bondage for debt was customary at times (II Kings 4:1; Isa. 50:1 and see I Sam. 22:2) – presumably under the influence of the surrounding legal systems; but the practice was strongly criticized by the prophets (Amos 2:6; 8:4–6; Micah 2:1–2) and after Nehemiah's sharp condemnation of the "nobles and rulers" for indulging in this practice (Neh. 5:1–13) bondage for debt was abolished in practice as well as in theory. The Bible makes no mention of imprisonment for debt and, indeed, Jewish law has given only the most limited recognition to *imprisonment, even in the field of criminal law.

Accordingly, methods of execution in Jewish law were in direct contradistinction to execution procedures under the Roman Twelve Tables. By the *legis actio per manus iniectionem*, the creditor was entitled – on the expiration of the 30 days' grace given the debtor to repay his debt and a further 60 days within which someone could redeem him from imprisonment and pay the debt on his behalf – to put the debtor to death or to sell him "*trans tiberim*"; if there were several creditors, each was entitled to a share of the debtor's corpse. The underlying motive of execution in Roman law was not only to satisfy the creditor's legitimate and material claim, but also to extract vengeance and to punish the debtor for not fulfilling his obligation (see H.F. Jolowicz, *Historical Introduction to the Study of Roman Law* (1952^2), 192; Elon, *Ḥerut ha-Perat* 11f.). In the course of time the harshness of these provisions were modified and the creditor's right to sell or to put the debtor to death was abolished by the *Lex Poetelia* in 313 (326?) B.C.E., but it still remained possible to imprison the debtor until he repaid the debt or made adequate compensation for it by his own labor (Elon, *ibid.*). The basic attitude toward the creditor-debtor relationship as laid down in biblical law, with the later further requirement that the debtor make repayment by the due date, has, throughout the ages, remained at the root of the rules of execution in Jewish law (see Yad, Malveh, chs. 1 and 2; Tur and Sh. Ar., ḤM 97–98), although certain changes and modifications were, at various times, introduced in keeping with the social and ethical realities prevailing in the different centers of Jewish life (see below).

Distinguishing between a Pauper and a Man of Means

The biblical passages mentioned above already delineated the basic concept of protecting the poor against the obduracy of their creditors. Talmudic scholars emphasized the distinction in unequivocal terms: "To the poor of your people you shall not be as a creditor, but to the rich" (Mekh., ed. Horowitz-Rabin, Mishpatim; 19, p. 316), and "You shall not be as a creditor to him – do not harass and demand from him when you know he has no means" (Mekh. SbY to 22:24; BM 75b and Codes). In post-talmudic times the distinction acquired a particular significance, especially in relation to imprisonment for debt.

Entry into the Debtor's Home

Entering the home of the debtor, in order to remove his assets in satisfaction of a debt, was prohibited in the Torah (Deut. 24:10–11). According to one opinion, entry for this purpose was forbidden to both the creditor and the debtor – so that the former might not remove assets of the best kind and so that the latter might not take out assets of the worst kind – only the officer of the court being permitted to enter in order to remove assets of a median kind (see below TJ, BM 9:14,12b). The majority of the scholars, however, interpreted the prohibition as directed only against the creditor, to prevent him from violating the borrower's private domain and conspiring against his person or property (TJ, BM 9:14,12b; Git. 50a and Codes). To avoid the danger of this happening to even the slightest degree, some of the scholars were of the opinion that it was also forbidden for the creditor forcibly to seize a pledge from the debtor, even if it was found outside his home and even if the court had sanctioned a distraint on him. According to these scholars it was only permissible for the officer of the court forcibly to extract from the debtor security for his debt (Sif. Deut. 276; Tosef., BM 10:8; BM 31b; 113 a–b). Some scholars expressed the opinion that, in principle, the prohibition against entering the debtor's home only applied to the creditor personally and that the officer of the court was even permitted to enter the debtor's home for the purpose of recovering assets in satisfaction of the debt; other scholars also prohibited the officer of the court from entering the debtor's house and the *halakhah* was so decided (BM 113b and Codes). Similarly, a further dispute between the scholars as to whether the prohibition against entry applied in respect of all debts or only to debts arising from loans, was decided in accordance with the latter view (Sif. Deut. 276; BM 115a and Codes).

The prohibition against entering the debtor's home hindered the effective recovery of a debt if the debtor pleaded that he had no assets and if no assets were found outside his home, since it was impossible to search his home so as to ascertain the truth of his plea. The post-talmudic scholars sought to overcome this difficulty in various ways. For example, Alfasi decided that entry is permissible if the debtor is "given to violent and evil ways and is arrogant" (i.e., in refusing to pay – quoted in *Sefer ha-Terumot*, 1:3), but Maimonides did not accept this view and regarded any permission to enter the debtor's home as against biblical law (Yad, Malveh, 2:2), and other scholars also rejected any permit of this nature (*Sefer ha-Terumot*, 1:3; Resp. Rashba, vol. 1, no. 909; vol. 2, no. 225). Some scholars sought to overcome the problem by giving a restricted interpretation to the biblical prohibition. Thus, for example, Meir ha-Levi *Abulafia argued that the officer of the court is only prohibited from entering the debtor's home when the debt can be recovered from other assets outside his home; if no such other assets are found and the creditor contends – even doubtfully – that the debtor has assets inside his home, the court officer may enter the latter's home and seek assets on which to levy execution (quoted in Tur, ḤM 97:26). Jacob b. Meir Tam and Asher b. Jehiel offered a solution based on the following reasoning: the biblical prohibition refers only to the case of the creditor attempting to take a pledge from the debtor's property as security for repayment of the loan at some time after the debt was created; but not to the case of the creditor seeking entry in order to collect payment of the debt, after the lapse of the due date (see also *Pledge). It follows therefore that entry into the debtor's home in the latter circumstances had never in fact been prohibited and was permissible (*Sefer ha-Yashar*, Nov. no. 602); *Piskei ha-Rosh*, BM 9:46–47), and this distinction was accepted by the majority of the *posekim* (Sh. Ar., ḤM 97:6,15 and standard commentaries); but such entry was nevertheless still restricted to the court officer (Tur, ḤM 97:26; Sh. Ar., ḤM 97:6,15; *Keẓot ha-Ḥoshen*, ḤM 97, n. 2; Elon, *Ḥerut ha-Perat* (60, n. 35)). When it is clear that the debtor is impoverished and has no property, entry into his home is prohibited since "this can only cause him shame and suffering" (Sma, ḤM 99–13).

Compulsory Labor

The possibility of compelling satisfaction of a debt by means of the debtor's own labor was recognized in various legal systems during the Middle Ages. This form of compulsion represented a temporizing with the institution of enslavement for debt – all the recognized characteristics of this sometimes being manifest, while at other times and places the debtor was merely required to cover the principal and interest of the debt with his own labor (see Elon, *Ḥerut ha-Perat* 68ff.).

There was in Jewish law no trace of this kind of compulsion until the 11th century (except for the contents of one of the *aggadot* concerning the destruction of the Temple: Git. 58a). From this time onward, however, the question was discussed in the light of the surrounding legal realities and the need for more efficient methods of debt collection. On the one hand, the halakhic scholars regarded compulsory labor as prejudicial to the debtor's personal liberty – particularly in view of the general attitude of Jewish law toward any kind of labor – hire as a restraint on personal freedom, for which reason it has afforded the laborer special privileges, such as the right of retracing, etc. (BM 10a, 77a; see also *Labor Law). On the other hand, compulsory labor involved no actual deprivation of the debtor's liberty – such as resulted from a sale into slavery – if its object was merely to give the creditor due satisfaction for his debt. Alfasi, and other scholars following him, decided that the debtor should labor – hire himself in order to repay his debt (quoted in Resp. Maharam of Rothenburg, ed. Cremona, no. 146). Some scholars distinguished between different kinds of obligations, and thus, for example, it was decided that in the case of a debt arising from the debtor's obligation to maintain his wife, he could be compelled to work in order to maintain her, since he expressly undertook to do so in the *ketubbah* – a factor not present in any other obligation and thus precluding compulsory labor (Elijah of Paris, Tos., Ket. 63a). Other scholars were of the opinion that compulsory labor was precluded in all cases, including even that of a wife's maintenance (Jacob *Tam quoted in *Haggahot Maimoniyyot;* Yad, Ishut, 12: s.s. 8), and this view was accepted by the majority of the *posekim* (Rosh, Resp. no. 78:2; Tur, EH, 70; Tur, ḤM 97:28–30; 99:18–19; Sh. Ar., EH 70:3; 154:3; HM 97:15), although some of the latter did recognize the exception in respect of a wife's maintenance (*Rema*, EH 70:3; *Ḥelkat Meḥokek*, Beit Shemu'el and *Yeshu'ot Ya'akov*, ibid.). A further opinion that compulsory labor could be imposed in respect of other obligations, if the debtor was accustomed to labor and to hiring himself (the opinion of Radbaz, quoted in *Erekh Lehem*, HM 97:15), was later rejected by most of the scholars (*Tal Orot*, Parashat Kedoshim; Mishkenot ha-Ro'im, "Beth," no. 39).

Imprisonment for Debt

In talmudic times and for a long time afterward, Jewish law completely excluded the possibility of imprisonment for debt. In the course of time, however, and because of the surrounding legal realities as well as internal social and economic changes, the question of imprisonment for debt came to the surface in Jewish law, and a number of basic halakhic rules were laid down on this subject. For greater detail see *Imprisonment for Debt.

Execution Procedure

Execution procedure in Jewish law is based upon talmudic and post-talmudic sources and may be briefly summarized as follows: when it is sought to execute a judgment of the court ("if the borrower fails to give of his own accord, payment is levied through the court": Yad, Malveh 18:1), the court will grant a stay of execution – if so requested by the debtor in order to give him the chance of raising money to repay the debt – for a period of 30 days; during this period the debtor is not obliged to provide any pledge or surety, unless the court sees grounds for suspecting that he will place his assets beyond reach or in some other manner evade payment of the debt (Sh. Ar., ḤM 100:1; Resp. Maharik, sec. 14); the period of the stay may be increased or reduced by the court, depending on the circumstances (Tur ḤM 100:1; *Rema* ḤM 100:1), but no stay will be granted in respect of certain debts arising from tort (Yad, Ḥovel u-Mazzik, 2:20; see also Sh. Ar., ḤM 420:27; for further details concerning the stay, see *Arukh ha-Shulḥan*, ḤM 100:2). No stay of execution will be granted when an appeal is lodged against the judgment, unless so warranted by special circumstances (*Rema* ḤM 14:4; *Bah* ḤM 14:4; see also *Takkanot ha-Diyyun be-Vattei ha-Din ha-Rabbaniyyim be-Yisrael*, 5720 – 1959/60, Rule 132, and *Taxation). The creditor may also demand that the court impose a general ban on anyone who has money or chattels and refuses, without reasonable cause, to repay a debt (Yad, Malveh, 22:1; Sh. Ar., ḤM 100:1). Upon the debtor's failure to repay within the period of the stay, the court will issue a writ of *adrakhta* (see below, Yad, *ibid.*; ḤM 100:3), which is followed by various other procedural steps until the actual sale of the debtor's property or the creditor's "going down" to the property (*horadat ba'al ḥov la-nekhasim*), in satisfaction of the debt. If a stay of execution is not sought by the debtor and he declares that he will not pay the debt, the writ of *adrakhta* is issued forthwith (BK 112b; Yad and Sh. Ar., *ibid.*). If the debtor is found to have no property he is "warned" by the court three times – on a consecutive Monday, Thursday, and Monday – and then the lesser ban (*niddui) is pronounced against him until he pays the debt or pleads that he has no means of doing so and delivers a solemn oath accordingly (the oath of *ein li*; see below). If he suffers the ban for 30 days without seeking its retraction, it will be extended for a further 30 days and thereafter the full ban (*ḥerem*, "excommunication") is pronounced against him (ḤM, *ibid.*).

Adrakhta and Tirpa

The word *adrakhta* means "to pursue and overtake" (cf. Judg. 20:43; Ket. 60b), hence it is the term used for a document empowering a creditor to "pursue" his debtor's property and levy payment thereon, wherever found (Rashi to BM 16b and 35b). Other scholars gave the term the meaning of the word *dorekh* ("treading upon"), i.e., by virtue of the writ of *adrakhta*, the creditor becomes master over and "treads upon" the debtor's property for the purpose of recovering the debt therefrom (*Rashbam* to BB 169a and see *Yad Ramah*, ibid.). The writ is issued for the recovery payment out of both the free prospect, and the "encumbered and alienated" property (*nekhasim benei ḥorin* and *meshu'badim*; see *lien). The *adrakhta* in respect of free property is written as follows: "X was adjudged to be indebted to Y in such and such an amount and, he not having paid voluntarily, we have written out this *adrakhta* on such and such a field of his." Thereupon the bond of indebtedness is torn up, and according to one opinion, this fact must be stated in the writ of *adrakhta* to prevent any possibility of the creditor recovering a second time on the same bond (Yad, Malveh, 22:13; Sh. Ar., ḤM 98:9–10; Meiri, in: *Shitah Mekubbezet* BK 111b).

If the debtor has no free property, the *adrakhta* on the "encumbered and alienated" property is written thus: "X was adjudged to be indebted to Y in such and such an amount by virtue of a bond in the latter's hands; since he has not paid the debt and whereas we have not found any free property of his and have already torn up Y's bond, we therefore give Y the power to investigate and seek out and lay hands on all the property of X that he can find, including all the lands sold by X from such and such a time on, and Y is hereby authorized to recover the debt and levy payment on all such property" (Yad, Malveh, 22:6; Sh. Ar., ḤM 98:9; for the *adrakhta* version as to orphans' property, see Yad, Malveh, 12:9; ḤM 109:2). If the creditor finds any encumbered property which he is entitled to seize for the purpose of recovering payment, he will do so and thereupon the *adrakhta* is torn up (for the same reasons as the bond is torn up) and a writ of *tirpa* ("tearing apart," seizure) is issued (in which the tearing up of the *adrakhta* is recited: for the text see Yad, Malveh, 22:8; Sh. Ar., ḤM 98:9; for a different order of procedure concerning the *adrakhta* and *tirpa*, see commentaries to BK and BB, *ibid.*). A creditor executing a *tirpa* against encumbered property is required to take a solemn oath that he has not yet recovered payment of the debt, nor granted a release from or sold his claim (Shevu. 45a; Yad, Malveh, 22:10; ḤM 114:4).

Appraisement and Related Procedures

After the creditor finds free property of the debtor and also in the case of recovering payment from encumbered property, following upon a writ of *tirpa*, an appraisement (*shuma*) of the property is made (at the instance of the court) by three persons possessing the necessary expertise (Codes, *ibid.*; according to some scholars the appraisement is made before the *adrakhta* or *tirpa* is written, *Yad Ramah*, BB 169a). The appraisement is made according to the value for which the property can be sold at the particular time and place, without any need for the creditor to sell it somewhere else or wait until the price might rise (HM 101:9). If the appraisers disagree, the majority opinion is accepted and if each gives a different estimate, the average of the three estimates is taken (ḤM 103:1–3). The appraisement document is headed by the words *iggeret shum* ("letter of appraisement"), by which name it is known (MK 3:3, BM 1:8; for other interpretations of the term *iggeret shum* see commentaries on BM 20a and MK 18b).

After the appraisement has been approved by the court, there is a public announcement or advertisement (*hakhrazah*) in which the judges announce: "whoever wishes to buy may come and do so," in order to find the highest bidder. In origin, the law of *hakhrazah* applied in respect of consecrated property and the property of *orphans (Ar. 2lb and Codes), but was extended also to property sold in execution (Ket. 100b; Tos. to Ar. 2lb and Codes). The scholars disputed the question whether the sale of orphans' property should be so advertised for 30 or 60 days and the *halakhah* was decided that the period should be 30 days where the announcement is made daily and 60 days where it is made on Mondays and Thursdays only (Ar. 2lb and Codes.). According to some of the *posekim*, an announcement for 30 days is made even in matters not concerned with orphans' property (*Rema* ḤM 103:1), but another opinion is that in the case of recovering payment out of free property, an announcement is made "as may be deemed necessary, until there are no higher bids" (*ibid.*).

The announcement is made in the morning and evening, when the "workmen set out and return home," and is only made for the sale of land, not for the sale of chattels, nor, if the sale is for urgent purposes, such as maintenance, funeral expenses, or polltax (Ket. 100b and Codes). The property is sold to the person paying the highest price beyond the appraised value or – if there be no one to raise the price – to the person paying the appraised value. The purchaser is given a *shetar hakhrazah* or *iggeret bikkoret* ("letter of examination," Ket. 99b and see Rashi ad loc.; cf. also *Tosefot Yom Tov*, Ket. 11:5; for the text see *Sefer ha-Terumot*, 3:2; Beit Yosef ḤM 103:17; cf. also other interpretations in *A rukh ha-Shalem*, s.v. *iggeret bikkoret*). The creditor is given a preferential right of acquiring the property for himself if no one offers more than the appraised value or if he equals any other offers (Sh. Ar., ḤM 103:1). In this event the creditor is given a *shetar horadah* (i.e., he "goes down" to the property, it is "appraised" to him; for the text see Tur ḤM 103:17 where it is called a *shetar shuma;* cf. BM 16b, where it is called a *shetar aḥaletata* Yad, Malveh, 22:10–11) where it is also called a *shetar horadah* but a different version of the text is given; see also the standard commentaries and Gulak, *ibid.*).

One opinion is that once the *adrakhta* has reached the hands of the creditor, he may also enjoy the fruits of the property, but another opinion is that he may do so only after the appraisement and the announcement (BM 35b) – the *halakhah* was decided in accordance with the latter view (Malveh, 22:12). The execution proceedings are completed when the property is sold and the proceeds paid to the creditor or the property itself transferred to him.

Restoration of Property Transferred to the Creditor

In strict law the creditor to whom the debtor's land is transferred is not thereafter obliged to return the land if the debtor subsequently acquired the means to repay the debt in cash; but the scholars enacted, in a *takkanah* referred to in the Talmud as *shuma hadar* (BM 16b and Codes; cf. Gulak, *Ha-Hiyyuv ve-Shi'budav*, 125, on the use of the term *shuma* in this connection), that this should be done for the sake of "Do what is right and good in the sight of the Lord" (Deut. 6:18 and see *Takkanot). Chattels recovered by the creditor, however, are not returnable to the debtor (*Rema* ḤM 103:9). According to one view, land is returnable to the debtor if he repays the debt within 12 months but the *halakhah* was decided according to the view that land is always returnable to the debtor (i.e., upon repayment of the debt, BM 16b. and 35a, Codes). Land recovered by the creditor and then sold by him, or given in gift, or inherited upon his death, is however not returnable to the debtor (*ibid.*). According to some scholars, the land must always be returned to a debtor, even if given by him voluntarily in satisfaction of the debt and not as a result of execution proceedings; but other scholars hold that his voluntary surrender of the land is a bar to its ever being returned to him against payment of the debt (*ibid.*). Similarly, a stipulation between the creditor and debtor and effected by way of a formal *kinyan* (see *Acquisition, Modes of), to the effect that the former shall not be obliged to return the land to the latter, holds good even when the land is turned over to the creditor as a result of execution proceedings (Sh. Ar., ḤM 103:9).

Categories of Assets for Recovery of Debt

If the debtor owns cash (coins), chattels, and land, he must pay in cash and cannot refer the creditor to other property (Sh. Ar., ḤM 101:1); if the debtor wishes to pay in cash but the creditor wants land or chattels, some scholars give the creditor the right to choose, but the *halakhah* was decided according to the view that the choice is the debtor's (Tur and Sh. Ar., ḤM 101:3). If the debtor owns land only, the creditor may refuse to accept it and choose to wait until the debtor is able to pay him in cash (ḤM 101:4). If the debtor has chattels and land but no cash, the creditor recovers payment out of the chattels, but the debtor has the right to choose the chattels for this purpose (ḤM 101:2); the creditor cannot demand land if the debtor offers chattels in payment.

If the debtor has no chattels or such chattels do not satisfy the debt, payment is extracted from his land (Malveh 22:4 and ḤM 101:10) and – when such land consists of fields of different quality – in this order: a debt arising from tort is satisfied from the *idit* or best land; a wife's jointure (*Ketubbah*) from the *zibburit* (the poorest or worst land); and all other obligations from the *beinonit* or land of medium quality (Git. 48b; Yad, Malveh 19:1; ḤM 102:1). In strict law, according to some scholars, all obligations except those in tort can be satisfied from the *zibburit*, but the scholars prescribed that all obligations except for the wife's jointure should be satisfied from the *beinonit* so as not to close the door before a borrower; other scholars hold the opinion that in strict law, all obligations except those in tort and the wife's jointure must be satisfied from the *beinonit* (Git. 49b and Codes; TJ, Git. 5:1,26c; and see above entry into the debtor's home; above, on the question of levying payment on chattels or land sold by the debtor to a third party see *Lien).

In many places it was customarily stipulated in bond agreements that the debtor had to pay the debt in cash, without putting the creditor to the trouble of execution proceedings and for this purpose the debtor was obliged personally to deal with the sale of his property and to pay the creditor in cash (Resp. Rashba, quoted in *Beit Yosef* ḤM 101:5).

"Arrangement" for the Benefit of Impoverished Debtors (*siddur le-ba'al ḥov*). The Pentateuch lays down various provisions concerning the taking of a pledge from a borrower and the duty to restore it in case the borrower is impoverished and requires the pledge for the elementary necessities of life. The scholars have interpreted these laws as applying to the taking of a pledge other than at the time of the loan and for purposes of securing the loan, but not when it is taken in satisfaction of the loan (see *Pledge). The scholars laid down that when the creditor seeks to levy on the debtor's property – i.e., after due date of payment and in satisfaction of the debt – certain property serving the debtor's elementary needs is to be entirely beyond the reach of the levy. This exclusion of a part of the debtor's property from the creditor's grasp is termed *mesaredin le-va'al ḥov;* i.e., an assessment is made of how much to leave the debtor for his vital necessities (Rashi, BM 113b), or an "arrangement" is made for his necessities, as laid down by the scholars (Rashi to Ned. 65b); the version of some scholars is *mesaredin le-va'al ḥov,* from the word שָׂרִיד = a remnant, i.e., leaving the debtor a shred or remnant (Rashi, 113b).

The basic idea of an "arrangement" is found in a *baraita* which lays down that a creditor may demand that an expensive suit of clothing belonging to the debtor be sold in satisfaction of the debt, but the latter must be left with some other ordinary clothing. In the opinion of R. Ishmael and R. Akiva, "all Israelites are entitled to the same robe," and even an expensive suit must be left to the debtor (BM 113b). However, the detailed laws of "arrangement" laid down by Judah ha-Nasi in the Mishnah (Ar. 6:3), relate only to *arakhin* obligations (to the Temple) and not ordinary debts and only in the *baraita* cited is mention made of "arrangement" in relation to all debts (BM 113b). According to some of the *amoraim*, no "arrangement" of this nature is ever made (BM 114a) and this view is followed by some of the *posekim* (*Sefer ha-Yashar*, Nov. no. 602), but the majority of the *posekim* confirm the institution (Yad, Malveh, 1:7; 2:1–2; Sh. Ar., ḤM 97:6ff, 23). There is also an opinion that "arrangement" is only made in the case of a debt originating from loan (and not, for example, from hire; ḤM 97:29; *Arukh ha-Shulḥan* 97:35).

Within the framework of the arrangement the debtor is left with the following: food for a period of 30 days – according to the normal requirements of the average townsman, even though the debtor may have lived as a pauper; clothing for a period of 12 months ("he does not require to wear silken apparel or a head-covering of gold – these shall be taken from him and he shall be given what is due to him"; see above); a bed and other requirements for sleeping; essential home furniture, such as a table and chair (*Arukh ha-Shulḥan* 97:26); his shoes; an artisan is left with two of each kind of tool used by him (Yad, Malveh 1:7 and ḤM 97:23); according to R. Eliezer a farmer is left with a pair of working animals, and the owner of an ass or a boat is left with the ass or boat respectively, but the majority opinion of the scholars, according to which the *halakhah* was decided, is that these are regular assets and not artisans' utensils (Ar. 23b; and Codes). The debtor retains his **tefillin* but not his books (*ibid.*), but some scholars say that if the debtor is a *talmid ḥakham*, his books are not taken from him (the opinion of Judah Barzillai, quoted in *Sefer ha-Terumot* 1:1,8). An interesting innovation is the decision of Moses *Sofer (at the beginning of 19th century) that a shopkeeper's stock of goods is not to be sold in execution, "since in these times the essence of their livelihood is to buy and sell on credit, it would amount to taking their lives in pledge (Deut. 24:6) if their stock is taken from their shops; therefore the practice is to take payment in installments at fixed times … so that the shopkeeper shall not fail completely" (Nov. Hatam Sofer ḤM 97).

The laws of the "arrangement" are not concerned with the needs of the debtor's wife and children, even though they are the debtor's responsibility (Ar. 6:3f., and Codes). Hai Gaon held the view, however, that the debtor's needs for his household and children, for whose maintenance he is responsible, come within the arrangement – and this was the practice in Kairouan (see Elon, *Ḥerut ha-Perat* 47, n. 43). The creditor does not, however – but for an entirely different reason – levy payment on the clothing of the debtor's wife and children, even if it was bought by the debtor with his own money. In the opinion of some of the *posekim*, this includes their Sabbath and festival garments, even if they are very expensive. The reason is that it is presumed that such garments are given by the debtor to his wife and children with the intention that the garments become their own property and the law precludes the creditor from levying payment on chattels that have passed out of the debtor's ownership (Yad, Malveh, 1:5; ḤM 97:25,26 and Isserles ad loc; and see *Lien). Some scholars hold, on the strength of this view, that a wife's jewelry given to her by her husband, the debtor, is also excluded from the creditor's levy (and see Sma, ḤM 97 n. 62). Garments or jewelry owned by the debtor's wife prior to their marriage or acquired thereafter with her own private funds, as well as garments or jewelry expressly purchased by the husband for his wife, are clearly excluded from the levy (ḤM 97:26 and Sma 63).

Plurality of Creditors – Preferential Rights

In the case of a written obligation (*shetar* or deed), the creditor in whose favor the obligation was first established takes preference in levying payment on the debtor's land, whether still in the latter's possession (i.e., the free property) or whether already acquired from the debtor by a third party (i.e., "encumbered and alienated" property; Ket. 94a; Yad, Malveh, 20:1; Sh. Ar., ḤM 104:1). This preferential right upon recovery of a debt is the result of an attitude of Jewish law which gives the creditor, upon the creation of the debt and over and above his personal right of recourse against the debtor, a lien on the latter's land. This lien, which is in the nature of a right, takes precedence over any similar right acquired by a subsequent creditor. If a later creditor forestalls an earlier one in levying on the debtor's land, some scholars hold that what he succeeds in recovering cannot be taken from him by an earlier creditor despite the right of a creditor by deed to seize a debtor's "encumbered and alienated" assets – since a later creditor still takes precedence over a regular purchaser, so that "the door shall not be bolted before a borrower" (Ket. 94a and Tos. to *ibid.*). Other scholars (*ibid*), followed by the majority of the *posekim* (Alfasi and Asheri to Ket. 94a; and Codes), hold that in these circumstances the levy of the later creditor is not valid and the earlier creditor may seize from the later one whatever the later may have recovered. However, if the later creditor forestalls the earlier one and levies on the beinonit land, but leaves the debtor with *zibburit*, the levy will be valid since the earlier creditor is still able to recover his debt from the *zibburit* (Sh. Ar., ḤM 104:1).

So far as the debtor's chattels are concerned, the earlier creditor takes no precedence in recovering his debt from such chattels, since there is no lien over movable property. In the case of two creditors simultaneously claiming the debtor's chattels, some scholars hold that the earlier creditor takes precedence but the majority opinion of the *posekim* is that there is no preferential right and the debtor's assets are shared between the two creditors (see below; Ket. 94a; and Codes). Even in respect of land there is no preferential right unless the land was in the debtor's possession prior to establishment of the debt; and if the debtor, at the time the debt was established, charges in favor of two or more creditors any land which he may acquire in the future (see *Lien), the earlier creditor will have no preferential right in respect of such land, since when the debtor acquires the land it is automatically charged in favor of both creditors (BB 157b; and Codes).

In the case of a mere oral obligation there is no preferential right between creditors, neither over land nor chattels, and two creditors seeking to levy payment at the same time must share the debtor's property (Rif. Resp. no. 197; see also Sma to Sh. Ar., ḤM 104 no. 3 and 31). According to some scholars, however, there is an order of preference in respect of land in the debtor's possession (ḤM 104:13 and Sma), even in the case of oral debt.

The *posekim* dispute the method of dividing the debtor's property amongst his creditors when there is no preferential right. One opinion is that each creditor takes a share of the property in proportion to the size of his debt, since it would be inequitable to divide the property equally in proportion to the number of creditors (Rabennu Hananel, in Tur ḤM 104:11; Yad, Malveh 20:4 quoting the Geonim); whereas others hold that the debtor's property is shared equally amongst the creditors according to their number, provided that no creditor receives more than the due amount of his debt, since the small creditor is thereby afforded greater protection (Ket. 94a; Alfasi and Rashi ad loc.; and Codes).

Preferential Rights and Insolvency

A consequence of the law of preference as described above is that Jewish law does not recognize some of the laws of insolvency customary in other legal systems. Thus, it does not recognize a concurrence with regard to division of an insolvent estate, whereby all the debtor's assets – save for those specifically charged in favor of a particular creditor or creditors – are divided among his creditors on a concurrent basis in proportion to the size of each creditor's claim. Because of the lien over the debtor's land afforded in Jewish law to each of the creditors, the order of precedence in recovering a debt follows the order of the establishment of the various liens, in similar manner to the order of preference in other legal systems regarding specifically charged assets. Even in cases where there is no prescribed order of preference, for example, in respect of the debtor's chattels or land acquired by him after the establishment of the debt, the assets are distributed amongst the creditors in proportion to the number of creditors and not to the size of each claim.

In post-talmudic times the law was supplemented, within the above-mentioned framework, by a number of rules very similar to the familiar insolvency laws. Some of these rules were aimed at protecting all the creditors. Thus, for example, it was laid down that in cases where the law afforded no preferential right, a proportional share of the debtor's estate had to be reserved for those creditors who had not yet claimed repayment and even for those creditors holding claims that were not yet due for payment. (*Teshuvot Maimoniyyot*, Mishp. no. 41; Rashba, Resp. vol. 1, no. 1111; *Keẓot ha-Ḥoshen* ḤM 104, s.s. 2). It also became customary to announce in public that anyone failing to lodge his claim against a particular insolvent within a specified period would lose his right (Rashba, Resp. vol. 1, no. 893).

In different periods, when economic crises led to an increase in cases of insolvency, various *takkanot* were enacted to deal with the situation (see Elon, *Ḥerut ha-Perat* 172 ff.). These provided for the appointment of a trustee (*ne'eman*) over the property of an insolvent (a *boreaḥ* or "fugitive" as he is called in the halakhic literature and *takkanot* of Poland, Germany, and Lithuania in the 17th and 18th centuries: see Elon, *Ḥerut ha-*

Perat 180, no. 265). The trustee's task was to collect and receive all the debtor's property – which thus became vested in him – and to sell the same and distribute the proceeds amongst the creditors; the *takkanot* prescribed a punishment of a year's imprisonment for a debtor who willfully squandered his property, and could not pay his debts (Halpern, Pinkas Takk. 112, 128; Elon, *Ḥerut ha-Perat* 180–3).

Execution in the Absence of the Debtor

The scholars of the Talmud express conflicting opinions on the question of levying payment on the debtor's property when he is absent and there is no reasonable prospect of reaching him. One opinion is that in these circumstances, payment is not levied, even if the creditor should take an oath that the debt has not yet been paid; another opinion is that a debt is not recovered in the debtor's absence except with regard to a debt on which interest is payable; third opinion is that payment is not levied unless the debtor had faced trial and thereafter taken flight; a further view is that payment is levied in the debtor's absence and the possibility that he may have paid the debt and received a release from his bond is disregarded, in order that "a person shall not take his neighbor's money and then go and sit abroad, which would cause the door to be bolted before borrowers" (Ket. 88a, TJ, Ket. 9:9,33b, 8). Some of the *posekim* follow the third of these opinions (Hai Gaon, quoted in *Sefer ha-Terumot*, 15:1; Rabbenu Ḥananel, quoted by Alfasi, Asheri, and in Tos. to Ket. 88a); the majority of the *posekim*, however, hold the opinion that payment is levied in the debtor's absence, on both his land and chattels, after the creditor has presented his bond of indebtedness and taken an oath that the debt had not yet been paid (Alfasi and Asheri, Ket. 88a; Yad, Malveh, 13:1; Sh. Ar., ḤM 106:1). In the event that the debtor goes abroad before the debt falls due for payment, some scholars hold that by virtue of the presumption that no person pays a debt before its due date, the creditor may levy payment without taking the oath of non-payment – even though the debt may meanwhile have fallen due – since the fact that the creditor holds the bond of indebtedness obviates the fear that the debtor may meanwhile have paid the debt through an agent. Other scholars hold that in these circumstances the creditor is required to take the prescribed oath just because of the fear that the debtor may have paid the debt through an agent (*Sefer ah-Terumot*, 15:1; Tur, ḤM 106:3).

At no time is payment levied in the debtor's absence, unless the latter cannot be reached by an agent in a return journey lasting not more than 30 days (some scholars fix a longer and others a shorter period); if the debtor is somewhere where he can be reached in less than the stated period, the court will dispatch an agent to notify the debtor of the proposed levy on his assets. The expenses involved are paid by the creditor, but these may be recovered in turn from the debtor (Yad, Malveh, 13:1 and ḤM 106:1); expenses incurred by the creditor for his own benefit, such as those connected with the issue of a writ of *adrakhta*, etc. are not recoverable from the debtor (Sma n. 2 and *Siftei Kohen* ḤM 106). Execution in the debtor's absence is conditional upon the prior fulfillment of three requirements by the creditor: (1) probate of the bond of indebtedness held by him; (2) proof that the debtor is abroad and is not available to face trial; and (3) proof that the assets on which it is sought to levy payment belong to the debtor (Malveh 13:2; ḤM 106:2). In order to obviate the difficulties attending an execution in the debtor's absence, the creditor may request the court to restrain the debtor from leaving the country unless he provides a surety for the payment of the debt (Sh. Ar., ḤM 73:10; see also Elon, *Ḥerut ha-Perat* 218, n. 409; PDR 2:65ff.).

Impoverished Debtors and the Plea of Ein li

"It is the law of the Torah that when the lender comes to recover payment of the debt, and it is found that the borrower has property, then an assessment ["arrangement"] for his vital needs is made and the remainder is given to his creditor …; if it is found that the debtor has no property, or that he only has objects which fall within the assessment – the debtor is allowed to go his way (and he is not imprisoned, neither is he asked to produce evidence that he is a pauper, nor is an oath taken from him in the manner that an idolator is adjudged, as it is written: 'you shall not be as a creditor unto him.'" (Yad, Malveh, 2:1). This was the law as it prevailed until geonic times. The advent of the geonic period was accompanied by material changes in the economic life of Babylonian Jewry. Commerce, extending to the North African and other countries, came increasingly to replace agriculture and the crafts as the mainstay of Jewish existence. Whereas formerly loans were taken primarily for the borrower's daily needs, they now came to be employed mainly for profit-making purposes, and the growing capital flow and development of external trade made it difficult to keep a check on the assets of a debtor, all of which encouraged the phenomenon of concealing assets. In the course of time this led to the adoption of far-reaching changes in the means of recovering a debt (see above; and also Imprisonment for *Debt.). These changes only partially asserted themselves in the geonic period, but two developments from this period may be mentioned, both aimed at a more effective process of debt recovery from a debtor pleading a lack of means.

One development was to place the debtor under a strict ban for a predetermined period, as a means of compelling payment. Thus it was decided by Hai Gaon, the first to mention this practice, that because of the adoption of various subterfuges by people of means seeking to evade payment of their debts – including those falsely swearing to their lack of means – any debtor pleading a lack of means to pay a debt shall have the ban imposed on him for a period of 90 days, during which time he is "severed" from Israel – so as to induce the disclosure of his assets and payment of the debt. Upon the expiry of this period he is made to take an oath that he has no means (for the terms of the oath, see below). Only a debtor who is reputed to be a pauper and known as such by the people is exempt from the ban when pleading no means of paying his debt (see A. Harkavy, *Zikkaron la-Rishonim*, no. 182). The ban for 90 days is also mentioned in the Talmud (BK

112b), but there it is imposed on a debtor who has means and pleads in court that the bond of indebtedness is a forgery; if, after being given a respite in order to prove his plea, he fails to appear in court, the ban will be imposed on him for 90 days and thereafter an *adrakhta* issued on his assets. This drastic innovation was not generally accepted as part of Jewish law. It was rejected by Alfasi and Raviah as contrary to the law (their statements quoted by way of the Mordecai in *Baḥ* ḤM 99:5) and it is not mentioned at all by later *posekim*. Only in the 16th and 17th centuries is it mentioned again – in various communal *takkanot* – as the imposition of a ban for a period of three days, thirty days, etc., with reference to a debtor pleading that he has no means (see Elon, *Ḥerut ha-Perat* 44, n. 25).

A second development in the geonic period toward more efficient debt collection was a *takkanah* providing for the administration of the oath of *ein li* ("I have no means") or *shevu'at ha-ḥashad* (oath taken when "suspected" of having means) to a debtor pleading a lack of means to repay his debt: "After the redaction of the *Gemara*, when the early geonim saw the swindlers increase in number and the door bolted before a borrower, they regulated that a solemn oath – having the stringency of biblical law – be taken from a borrower to the effect that he has nothing beyond the assessment that is made for him and that he has not concealed anything with others and has given no returnable gifts; the oath shall include that whatever he may earn or that may come into his hand or possession, in any manner whatever, shall not be used at all to feed or clothe either his wife or children or be given to anyone as a gift, save that he shall take from it sustenance for 30 days and raiment for 12 months – such as is due to him; neither the sustenance of gluttons nor of the nobility nor the raiment of high officials, but such as he has accustomed to – and the remainder he shall give to his creditors, in due order of preference, until the whole of his debt is collected" (Yad, Malveh, 2:2). Unlike the case of the ban imposed for 90 days, the pauper was also subjected to this oath, but was later exempted from it by Maimonides, on the grounds that the oath was designed "to deal with swindlers and not with those generally accepted to be paupers" (Yad, Malveh, 2:4). The administration of this oath, as qualified by Maimonides, was accepted by the *posekim* (Tur and Sh. Ar., ḤM 99:4).

A similar oath can be traced in the legal systems of various European countries, commencing from the 12th century onward; thus for example, in the *Offenbarungseid* of German and Austrian law, the debtor is also committed to make over all his future earnings to his creditor (see Elon, *Ḥerut ha-Perat* 49, n. 52).

The underlying purport of the Jewish laws of execution is to ensure the existence of an effective debt-collection procedure, so as not to "bolt the door before a borrower," while maintaining adequate safeguards against the violation of a debtor's personal freedom and dignity. The pursuit of this twofold objective has ensured that the laws of execution at all times recognize a material distinction between a genuinely impoverished debtor and a debtor of means seeking to evade fulfillment of his obligations towards the creditor, a distinction lucidly enunciated in the statements of Maimonides already cited.

[Menachem Elon]

In the State of Israel

The laws and proceedings for the execution of judgments in the State of Israel in general, particularly with respect to the imprisonment of debtors, were significantly changed by the Supreme Court's decision in the *Perah* case (HCJ 5304/92, *Perah v.* Minister of Justice, 47(4) PD 715). This decision, written by the deputy-president of the Court (Justice Menachem Elon), relied on the position adopted by Jewish law regarding imprisonment for the enforcement of debts. The Perah organization had petitioned the court to nullify one of the regulations that allowed for the excessively easy imprisonment of debtors, without the debtor even having to be brought before the head of the Execution of Judgments Office.

The decision begins by noting that "the central issue of this complaint is the fundamental right of a person to freedom and dignity in the context of imprisonment for debt." In the ruling, Justice Elon presents a detailed description of the position of Jewish law and its development as attested by a broad range of sources dealing with the execution of judgments in general, and imprisonment for debt in particular, from the biblical era through the contemporary period. In focusing on the detailed process that lead to the Knesset enacting the Execution of Judgments Law, he noted that support for the proposed bill was based on principles of Jewish law that reject the view that collection measures also serve as a punishment of the debtor. Justice Elon also relied on the fact that the Basic Law: Human Dignity and Liberty establishes the values of the State of Israel as a Jewish and democratic state.

In wake of this decision, a number of amendments were made to the Execution of Judgments Law, allowing imprisonment for debt only in certain particular instances. (See also the detailed discussion of the decision in the entry *Imprisonment for Debt.)

The *Negola* decision (LCA 7700/95, *Negola v.* Hazan, 50 (1) PD 338) was another Supreme Court decision in which the Court relied upon the "ancient social sources of Jewish law" regarding the rules of execution of judgments. In that case, in the framework of proceedings to enforce collection of a debt, attachment proceedings were instituted for the sale of the petitioners/debtor's residential apartment, and an alternative arrangement was established in accordance with the provisions of the Execution of Judgments Law. These provisions require that, prior to ordering the sale of a residential apartment, the head of the Execution of Judgments Office must be shown that "the debtor and his family members who live with him will have a reasonable place to live, or that there is an alternative arrangement for them." Justice Strassbourg-Cohen's decision discusses the nature of such an "alternative arrangement," and analyzes in detail the criteria and the considerations for striking a balance between the creditor's right to collect his debt, on the one hand, and the special personal circumstances of the creditors, on the other. Justice Tirkel added that the alternative residence must also be appropriate in terms of the time that the debtor is able to stay there. Accordingly, if the debtor had been entitled to live his entire life in the apartment that he owned, he is entitled to an alternative arrangement that assure him a lifelong residence. This determination stems from the interpretation of the law in light of its purpose – namely, that it mandates the protection of the debtor's basic living needs, as expressed in the prohibition against attaching part of a debtor's salary, his clothing, beds, tools, etc. Judge Tirkel pointed out that this arrangement is based on ancient principles of social welfare within Jewish law: "No man shall take the mill or the upper millstone to pledge; for he takes a man's life to pledge," (Deut 24:6); and "And if he be a poor man, thou shall not sleep with his pledge, you shall surely return him the pledge when the sun goes down, that he may sleep in his garment" (Deut 24:12–13), these being concepts that continued to develop over generations. Justice Tal concurred with the opinions of Justices Strassbourg-Cohen and Turkel, but added that in certain cases, where "the debtor … lives in a house that he had built for himself with the money of others," the verse "he who builds his house with unfairness and his upper chambers with injustice" (Jer 22:13) is applicable and he is not entitled to the same protection.

Extensive use of Jewish law was made in this regard in a decision of the Petah Tikvah Magistrate's Court regarding the imposition of liens on a debtor's assets. The Court relied on the writings of the Rosh (*Piskei Ha-Rosh*, BK 1.5) and of Rabbi Israel Isserlein (*Terumat ha-Deshen*, §305), from which it emerged that, prior to imposing a temporary lien on assets in order to prevent the debtor from hiding them, there must also be proof of the grounds of the action, and it must be shown that there is a likelihood that the defendant will attempt to hide these assets. The reason is that the purpose of imposing a lien on the assets is not to punish the defendant, but to prevent a situation which would encumber enforcement of the judgment (Maharshal, *Yam Shel Shlomo*, BK 1.20; Civil Application 4804/02, *NMC v.* Ben Chalouche, Registrar Zvi Weitzmann). The same Court also discussed the issue of what situation is considered to be one that encumbers the execution of judgment and concluded, on the basis of Jewish legal sources (Sh. Ar., HM, 73.10; *Shakh* on Shulhan Arukh, op.cit.; Maharshal, op. cit.), that, in order to obtain temporary relief, it is necessary to prove an active attempt on the part of the defendant to conceal his assets and to frustrate the execution of a judgment, and it is not sufficient to prove his inability to discharge the debt. (Civil Application 2264/04, *Rosenthal v.* Shinterko).

Another decision handed down by the same court, also dealing with liens, reviewed the developments in Jewish law regarding the ability to enter a debtor's house to collect a debt, in accordance with the *Perah* decision, while taking care to maintain the debtor's dignity and not to harm him. In light of this review, the Court examined the proper balance between the defendant's rights and the plaintiff's rights, and the degree of harm that can legitimately be caused to the defendant in order to secure the plaintiff's rights (Civil Petition 2621/04, *Shinterko v.* Rosenthal, Judge Zvi Weitzmann).

Regarding this matter, see also FF 24891/03, *A.N. v.* A.T.; Civil Application 743/02 *G.A. v.* G.A., regarding an injunction against leaving the country; Execution of Judgment File 17-09642-96-8 – re foreclosure on a secured asset.

Concerning the use of Jewish law, see also Civil Petition 18702/02 *Polaski v.* Galaxy Electronics (Haifa District Court, Judge Yakovshvili), regarding an arrangement of the debtor's assets and a lien on sacred objects; and 3403/01 *Ziva v.* Yaakov, 5761(1) PDM, 756 (Jerusalem District Court, Judge Moshe Drori), regarding the execution of an act without a signature of the creditor.)

[Menachem Elon (2nd ed.)]

BIBLIOGRAPHY: M. Bloch, *Die Civilprocess-Ordnung nach mosaiich-rabbinischen Rechte* (1882), 90–106; Gulak, Yesodei, 107–9; 4 (1922), 184–96; Gulak, Oẓar, 314–36; idem, *Toledot ha-Mishpat be-Yisrael bi-Tekufat ha-Talmud*, 1 (1939) (*Ha-Hiyyuv ve-Shi'budav*), 118–40; Herzog, Instit 1 (1936) 4f; 386; S.J. Zevin, in: *Sinai*, 3 (1938),55–71, 246; ET, 5 (1953), 92–132; 9 (1959), 143–55; B. Cohen, in: *Louis Ginsberg Jubilee Volume* (1945), 113–32, republished in his *Jewish and Roman Law* (1966), 159–78; addenda ibid. 772–75. **ADD. BIBLIOGRAPHY:** M. Elon, *Kevod ha-Adam ve-Ḥeruto be-Darkei ha-Hoẓa'ah la-Po'al* (2000), idem, *Ha-Mishpat ha-Ivri* (1988), I:105, 194, 486, 515, 535, 601, 633; 2:885, 1284f; 3:1319, 1370f; idem, *Jewish Law* (1994), 1:117, 218; 2:591, 627, 651f, 744, 784; 3:1079, 1533f., 1576, 1635; ibid., *Jewish Law (Cases and Materials)* (1999), 455–75; M. Elon and B. Lifshitz, *Mafte'aḥ ha-She'elot ve-ha-Teshuvot shel Ḥakhmei Sefarad u-Ẓefon Afrikah* (1986), (1), 89–103; B. Lifshitz and E. Shohetman, *Mafte'aḥ ha-She'elot ve-ha-Teshuvot shel Ḥakhmei Ashkenaz, Ẓarefat ve-Italyah* (1997), 61–67.

EXEMPLA OF THE RABBIS, a collection of more than 300 Hebrew stories – the largest collection of its kind compiled in the Middle Ages – so entitled by M. Gaster, who discovered them in manuscript and published them (1924). Most of the stories, especially in the beginning of the book, are similar to, or identical with, those in the talmudic-midrashic literature, although in the latter part, there are some longer, more developed, stories, not found in the Talmud or Midrash. While the manuscript is undoubtedly of medieval times, Gaster maintains that the collection itself is a very early one, predating the Talmud. Furthermore, he tries to prove that for their stories the talmudic sages did not use oral sources, but rather a narrative Hebrew literature, of which the only extant specimen is this collection. This he concludes on the basis of the organization of the work in accordance with literary principles. No proof, however, exists for Gaster's conclusions. It is much more logical to suppose that the compiler of the *Exempla* collected stories from the talmudic-midrashic literature, adding to them medieval stories, with which he became acquainted through oral or written sources. All this material he organized together according to strict literary principles. The existence of two other medieval compilations of this sort –*Mi-

drash Aseret ha-Dibberot and Rabbenu *Nissim of Kairouan's *Sefer ha-Ma'asiyyot* (which was written in Arabic) – seems to corroborate the theory that Gaster's manuscript belongs to a medieval tradition, according to which later authors tried to provide their contemporaries with a selection of narrative material in the talmudic-midrashic literature. Although the exact date of this collection is unknown, it may be assumed that it was not compiled before the 11th or the 12th century. Literarily the collection presents a unified structure, in that every story opens with either *Ma'aseh* ("A story") or *Tanu rabbanan* ("The sages taught"). More important, however, is the purposeful arrangement of the stories: each is related, in content and ideas, with those preceding and following it, thus forming an interconnected chain of stories. Abraham's search for the true God, for instance, is preceded by the story of his destruction of the idols and subsequent trial by Nimrod and is followed by the account of Hadrian's attempt to present himself as a god. The book, a collection of stories of many types, contains only a few which properly belong to the literary type known as the *exemplum.

See also *Fiction, the Hebrew Story in the Middle Ages.

BIBLIOGRAPHY: M. Gaster, *The Exempla of the Rabbis* (1924, repr. 1968). **ADD. BIBLIOGRAPHY:** J. Dan, *Ha-Sippur ha-Ivri bi-Yemei ha-Beinayim: Iyyunim be-Yoldotav* (1974); A. Alba, *Cuentos de los rabinos* (1991).

[Joseph Dan]

EXEMPLUM, legend or anecdote from the lives of the sages to suggest emulation as instruction. In medieval Hebrew literature it is very difficult to distinguish between the legend and *hagiography, historical fiction, and various kinds of fables. The exemplum is not defined by its own, intrinsic literary character, but rather by the intent of the author which is not always known and not always clearly expressed in the story. An anecdote is an exemplum only if it is known that its purpose was to serve as an ethical model to be followed. To discover this purpose, however, is not always possible.

Talmudic-midrashic literature, for example, preserved hundreds of stories and anecdotes describing the lives of the *tannaim* and the *amoraim*. Many of these were related by pupils in admiration of their teachers after the latter's death; others out of pure historical interest to preserve the fame of the great rabbis for posterity. The rabbis themselves told autobiographical anecdotes and some parables served only to prove a halakhic or midrashic point. The Middle Ages used the corpus of these stories, whatever the original character or intent of the tales, as exempla: that is to say, a pious Jew had to learn how the old sages behaved so that he might emulate them and achieve the same high moral and religious standards. In the late Middle Ages, this process of turning biographies and hagiographies into exempla continued. In the 16th century, the pupils of the kabbalist Isaac *Luria of Safed evolved a cycle of hagiographies about him which became very popular in Eastern Europe in the 17th and 18th centuries, and were included in many ethical and kabbalistic works. When the Ḥasidim evolved their own cycle of legends around their leader *Israel Baal Shem Tov, they used many of the tales woven around Luria, giving them a sometimes factual basis. It is evident, therefore, that both in fact and in popular tradition the Baal Shem Tov used legends about Luria as exempla for emulation, or at least he was described by his pupils as following in the ways of Luria. Medieval literature produced a few works which used talmudic-midrashic narrative material as exempla for their own generations. This was the purpose of collections like *The *Exempla of the Rabbis*, a large collection of talmudic stories and medieval additions, and *Sefer ha-Ma'asiyyot* of R. *Nissim of Kairouan. The latter was originally written in Arabic, in order that the general public, not familiar with talmudic literature, could read the stories and benefit from them. Another example is the early **Midrash Aseret ha-Dibberot* (see *Fiction, the Hebrew Story in the Middle Ages). Most of the stories included in these works, especially in the last one, are not exempla in the ordinary sense. Though their intention is to teach ethical and religious behavior to the average Jew, the examples they set forth are often so extreme that no one would be expected to follow their teachings exactly. In *Midrash Aseret ha-Dibberot*, for instance, a story which is intended to demonstrate the importance of observing the Sabbath relates how a cow that had belonged to a Jew refused to work on the Sabbath, and only when the Jew explained to the cow that gentiles may work on the Sabbath did the animal comply. Another story illustrates the commandment not to give a false oath in the name of God. It describes the misfortunes which befell a man who refused to swear under any circumstances, even to the truth. R. Nissim, in his collection, tells the story of a man who, using most of his income to help the poor, was told by Heaven that he still was not perfect. He then sold his wife into slavery and gave the money to the poor. These tales have an extreme, unrealistic standard of moral behavior which is more closely connected with Muslim fanatic sects than with talmudic Jewish ethics. They are exempla in the sense that they demonstrate the extent to which a saintly person has gone in order to fulfill one of the commandments; they are not exempla intended to teach moderate, everyday behavior to the wider public.

A large body of exempla, short anecdotes, and more developed stories was introduced into Hebrew literature in Spain through Arabic sources, and was included in Jewish philosophical and ethical-philosophical works, as well as in more narrative form in the **maqamat* and romances of the time. Most of these exempla are of Indian origin, transmitted, by way of Persian and Arabic literature, into Jewish works. They are models of wisdom and not only of ethics. There is also a strong Sufi element in those found in the works of *Baḥya ibn Paquda or Shem Tov ibn *Falaquera. Some medieval writings served as exempla without having been written for that purpose, specifically the Jewish martyrologies; "The Ten Martyrs" (A. Jellinek, *Beit ha-Midrash*, 2 (1938²), 64–72, under the title *Midrash Elleh Ezkerah*), a medieval work describing the death of the *Ten Martyrs in Roman time, became a model of behavior for Jews in the Middle Ages. The corpus of historical chronicles describing the massacres in Germany and northern France during the Crusades, though written primarily as historical works, served for centuries as exempla to any Jewish community under threat of conversion or death. Contemporaries of the expulsion from Spain repeatedly complain of those who did not follow the example set by their Ashkenazi brothers during the Crusades, but preferred conversion to exile. History itself, or historical chronicles, served in this case as exempla in the full sense of the term.

The largest body of exempla in medieval Hebrew literature is to be found in *Sefer Ḥasidim* (see bibliography), the main ethical work of the *Ḥasidei Ashkenaz in the 12th and 13th centuries. The book includes hundreds of exempla; however, where generally the exempla tend to specify men whose undoubted virtue should prompt emulation of their deeds, the exempla in *Sefer Ḥasidim* are always anonymous. Where the name is mentioned (e.g., "a certain Joseph or Mordecai"), it has no associative meaning. Most of the exempla start with: "There was a Jew who…" or "It is told about a Ḥasid who…" The tendency toward anonymity was part of the ethical ideology of *Judah he-Ḥasid, the author of most of the book. The ideology based itself on the concept that if great deeds are told about a person, he, or his family, might take sinful pride in the fact (pride being regarded by the Ḥasidim as one of the cardinal sins). Unlike the exempla influenced by Islam, the exempla of *Sefer Ḥasidim* are concrete, reflecting everyday life and everyday ethical problems. It is possible that many of the episodes actually happened, the author using true anecdotes to illustrate his ethical standards. Many of the exempla describe the behavior of Jews during the persecutions of the Crusades; these served as models of behavior to many communities. Most of the exempla, however, describe the right, ethical way to behave when tempted by pride, by the evil powers lurking in man, how to conduct oneself toward women, gentiles, etc.

In the Ashkenazi ḥasidic exempla there is a class of anecdotes which expound ways of repentance involving the use of extreme self-mortification. Exempla of the same sort are found 300 years later in 16th-century Safed when mystic sages (some of them tried to remain anonymous) used the same type of mortification as a means to repent for their own sins and for the sins of the people of Israel.

In a sense, modern ḥasidic narrative literature served also as exempla, but its purpose was different. The wonderful stories told about the *ẓaddikim* were not models of conduct to be followed implicitly by Ḥasidim. The *ẓaddikim* had a different code of behavior from their believers, and the stories of their behavior were intended to provoke meditation, to bring the ḥasid into deeper understanding of the ways of the *ẓaddikim* and the ways of God, and thereby to some extent to influence the ḥasid's own ethical behavior.

BIBLIOGRAPHY: M. Gaster, *The Exempla of the Rabbis* (Eng. and Heb., 1924, 1968² with introd. by Braude); J. Meitlis, *Das Ma'assebuch* (1933); J. Wistinetzki and J. Freiman (eds.), *Sefer Ḥasidim* (1924, repr. 1955); A. Jellinek (ed.), *Beit ha-Midrash*, 6 vols. (1938²); J.R. Marcus, *Jew in the Medieval World* (1960), 225–83. **ADD. BIBLIOGRAPHY:** J. Dan, *Ha-Sippur ha-Ivri bi-Yemei ha-Beinayim: Iyyunim be-Toldotav* (1974); A. Alba, *Midrás de los Diez Mandamientos y Libro precioso de la Salvación* (1989); idem, *Cuentos de los rabinos* (1991).

[Joseph Dan]

EXETER, town in S.W. England. Before the expulsion of the Jews in 1290, Exeter was the most westerly Jewish community in England. The first mention of Jews there is in 1181. Only one Exeter Jew, Amiot, is mentioned as contributing to the *Northampton Donum of 1194, but subsequently Exeter became the seat of one of the **archae* for the registration of Jewish debts. In 1275 the local chirographers, both Jewish and Christian, were accused of forgery but were acquitted. At an ecclesiastical synod held at Exeter in 1287, the church restrictions regarding the Jews were reenacted. On the eve of the expulsion of 1290, the community numbered nearly 40 householders, who possessed considerable debts and a large quantity of corn. At the beginning of the 18th century some Italian Jews were living at Exeter, including Gabriel Treves and Joseph Ottolenghi (later of South Carolina). The conversion of Ottolenghi to Christianity about 1735 caused considerable controversy. Exeter subsequently became a center of peddling activities. The synagogue still standing was built in 1763. In 1968, 20 Jews lived in Exeter, apart from a number of Jewish students at the university. In the mid-1990s and 2000s the Jewish population numbered approximately 150. There is an Orthodox synagogue, which today holds monthly services.

BIBLIOGRAPHY: Adler, in: *Transactions of the Devonshire Association for the Advancement of Science, Literature and Art*, 63 (1931), 221–40; Rigg, Exchequer, index; Roth, Mag Bibl, index; idem, *Rise of Provincial Jewry* (1950), 59–61. **ADD. BIBLIOGRAPHY:** JYB, 2004.

[Cecil Roth]

EXILARCH (Aram. רֵישׁ גָּלוּתָא, *resh galuta*), lay head of the Jewish community in Babylon. (See Chart: Exilarchs of Parthian and Sasanid Periods and Chart: Babylonian Exilarchs.)

Until the Arab Conquest

The government of Babylonian Jewry for the first 12 centuries C.E. lay in the hands of the exilarch. Rabbinic traditions incorporated in the **Seder Olam Zuta*, trace the origin of the institution to the last years of the exile of Jehoiachin, on the basis of II Kings 25:27. Further data were derived from I Chronicles 3:17ff. Whether such an institution actually existed before Parthian times is not known, and certainty is impossible. Sources on Jewish life in first-century Parthian Babylonia, however, leave little ground to suppose there was an exilarch then. Josephus' account of the Jewish "state" of *Anilaeus and Asinaeus suggests, to the contrary, that no state-sanctioned Jewish government functioned at that time. Whatever the earlier situation, Neusner has put forward the conjecture that the Parthian government under Vologases I (d. 79 C.E.) probably established a feudal regime to govern Jewry as part of its

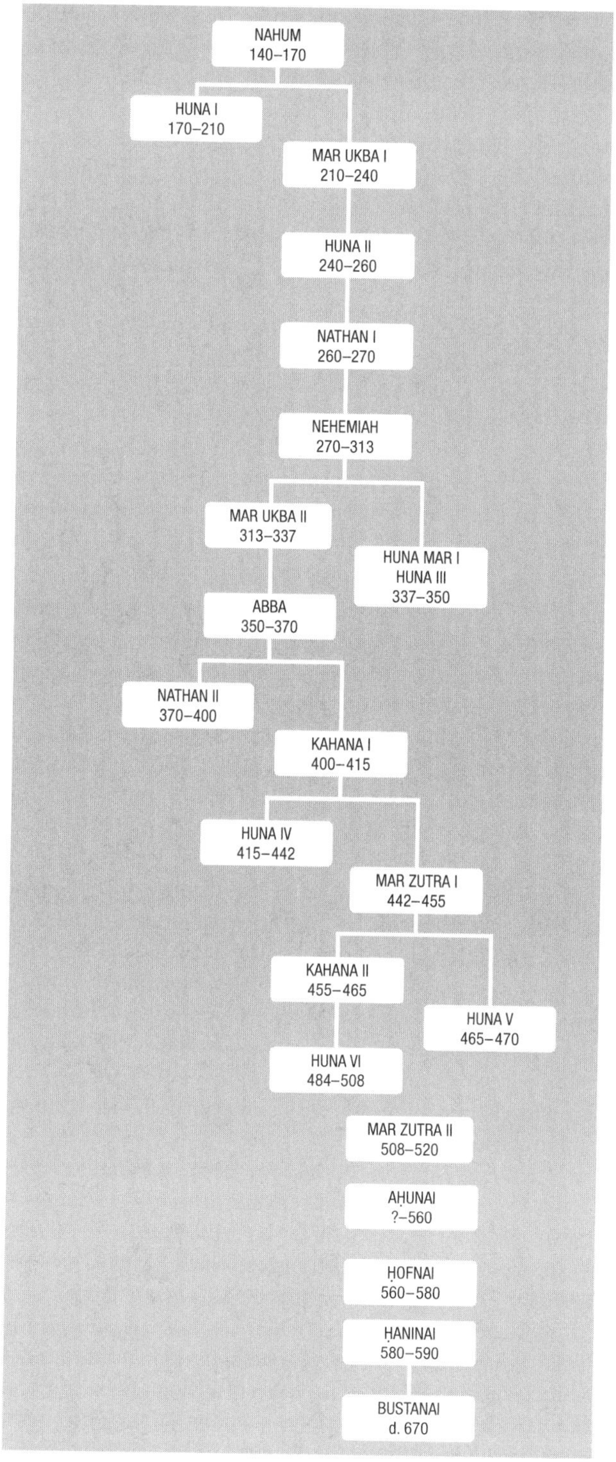

List of exilarchs of the Parthian and Sasanid periods (based on F. Lazarus; see bibl.).

reorganization of the Arsacid administration (see *Babylonia). Jews played an important part in first-century Middle Eastern politics, not only in Palestine, but also in *Armenia, *Adiabene, Charax Spasinu, and Babylonia itself. It was important to organize a loyal administration for Jewry, both for the stability of the empire, and for the purposes of foreign affairs. The Jews, living on both sides of the contested frontier between Rome and Parthia, could prove useful to either party able to enlist their support. Furthermore, the destruction of Jerusalem and, with it, the Temple administration which had formerly issued religious instruction to the Diaspora, necessitated Parthian consideration. The Romans, supporting the new rabbinical authority in Jabneh (see *Johanan b. Zakkai), exerted substantially more control than before.

The Parthians, perhaps earlier contented to allow local Jewry to receive instruction from Jerusalem, certainly took advantage of the change in Palestinian politics and the anti-Roman turn in world Jewish opinion, to establish local control of Jewry under close supervision. The result was highly beneficial. In the next century, Jews were the most loyal supporters of the Parthian cause against *Trajan, Septimius *Severus, and Alexander *Severus. In Palestine, circles of Jewish messianists were prepared to cooperate with the Parthians against Rome.

The first clear evidence of the existence of the exilarch comes in the middle of the second century C.E. Some Jewish authority certainly existed about 145 C.E. when *Hananiah the nephew of Joshua b. Hananiah intercalated the calendar in Babylonia (Eccles. R. 7, 8, no. 4, 7:26, for his exile to Babylonia; Ber. 63a; TJ, Sanh. 1:2, 19a; TJ, Ned. 6:13, 40a, for the intercalation). The accounts of the intercalation contain the name of a local official, given variously as Ahijah and Neḥunyon. At about the same time, moreover, Rabban *Simeon b. Gamaliel II rebuked R. Nathan, of Babylonia, for his part in a conspiracy against the former's rule, saying "Granted that the sash of office (*kamara*) of your father has indeed helped you to become *av bet din*, shall we therefore make you also *nasi?*" (Hor. 13b). Since the *kamara*, mentioned in various Iranian inscriptions, was one of the significations of office in Iran, it stands to reason that R. Nathan was the son of the Jewish ruler of Babylonia. The first talmudic mention of the title of *resh galuta*, however, occurs with reference to Huna the exilarch (TJ, Ket. 12:3, 35a; TJ, Kil. 9:3, 32b; Gen. R. 33:3). *Judah ha-Nasi stated that if Huna were to come to Palestine he would give precedence to him, for Huna was descended from the male line of the Davidic household, while the patriarch, from the female line. Ḥiyya and his nephew *Rav may have been related to the exilarch, for both Babylonians claimed Davidic ancestry. Ḥiyya came from the same town as the exilarch, and called his nephew Rav *bar Paḥti*. The title *paḥat* was used in the Parthian documents from Nisa for satrap, and if Rav was son of a Jewish *paḥat*, then his father must have held high rank within the Parthian feudal structure. Other Jewish authorities, earlier in the same period, were reported by Palestinian rabbinic messengers to have Parthian names, wear Parthian dress, enjoy the perquisites of a retinue, and execute capital punishment, and yet to be knowledgeable in the law (Git. 14a–b; TJ, Kid. 3:4, 64a; TJ, Git. 1:5, 43c–d). So it is reasonable to suppose that a Jewish government did exist through the last century and a half of Parthian rule in Babylonia.

1. **Bustanai** d. 670
2. **Ḥisdai I b. Bustanai**
3. **Bar Adai b. Bustanai**
4. **Ḥisdai II b. Bar Adai**
5. **Solomon b. Ḥisdai II** *c.* 733–759
6. **Isaac Iskoi b. Solomon**
7. **Judah (Zakkai b. Aḥunai)** d. before 771
8. **Natronai b. Ḥavivai** 771
9. **Moses**
10. **Isaac Iskoi b. Moses**
11. **David b. Judah** *c.* 820–857
12. **Judah I b. David** *c.* 857
13. **Natronai** after 857
14. **Ḥisdai III b. Natronia**
15. **Ukba** *c.* 900–915
16. **David b. Zakkai** *c.* 918–940
17. **Josiah (Hasan) b. Zakkai** 930–933 (?)
18. **Judah II b. David** 940
19. **Solomon b. Josiah** *c.* 951–953
20. **Azariah b. Solomon**
21. **Hezekiah I b. Hezekiah I** ?
22. **David I b. Hezekiah I** ?
23. **Hezekiah II b. David I** before 1021–1058
24. **David II b. Hezekiah II** 1058–d. *c.* 1090
25. **Hezekiah III b. David II** from *c.* 1090
26. **David III b. Hezekiah III**
27. **Ḥisdai IV b. David III** d. before 1135
28. **Daniel b. Ḥisdai IV** *c.* 1150–1174
29. **Samuel of Mosul?** 1174 (?)–*c.* 1195
30. **David (b. Samuel ?)** d. after 1201
31. **Daniel**
32. **Samuel (b. Azariah ?)** 1240 (?)–1270 (?)

1, 2–6	H. Tykocinski, in: *Devir*, 1 (1923), 178, 179.
7	*Iggeret Rav Sherira Gaon*, ed. by B.M. Lewin (1921) 104.
8	*ibid.*, L. Ginsberg, Geonica, 1 (1909), 16 ff.
9, 10	A. Harkavy ed. *Teshuvot ha-Geonim* (1887), 378.
11, 12	S. Abramson, *Ba-Merkazim u-va Tefuẓot* (1965), 11–14.
13	Harkavy, loc. cit.
14	Abramson, op. cit., 10.
15, 16	J. Mann, in: *Tarbiẓ*, 5 (1934), 150 ff.
17	*ibid.*, 164; *Iggeret Rav Sherira Gaon*, 117.
18–22	Mann, in: *Sefer Zikkaron... S. Poznański* (1927), 19, 20, 21.
23	*ibid.*, 21–22, S. Assaf, in: *Tarbiẓ*, 11 (1940), 152 ff.
24–25	Mann, in: *Sefer... Poznański*, 22–23.
26	Mann, Texts, 1 (1931), 208.
27	Abramson, in: KS, 26 (1950), 93.
28	*ibid.*, 93, idem, in: *Perakim*, 1 (1967/68), 14.
29–32	Mann, in: *Sefer... Poznański*, 24–25.
	Abramson, in: *Perakim*, 1 (1967/68), 16.

[Abraham David]

List of Babylonian exilarchs during the Middle Ages.

The advent of the Sassanids, in 226 C.E., necessitated the provision of a new political foundation for Jewish self-government. At first, the Jewish administrators continued as before, hoping to hoodwink the Sassanids and forcibly to keep the Jews in line. R. Shila, for example, administered lashes to a man who had intercourse with a gentile woman; the man informed against him, whereupon a government agent (*parastak*) investigated the case. Shila persuaded the agent that he was loyal, and then murdered the informant (Ber. 58a). But in a similar situation, R. *Kahana had to flee to Palestine (BK 117a), for, Rav told him, "Until now the Greeks [Parthians] were here, who did not punish bloodshed, but now the Persians are here, and they will certainly cry, 'Rebellion, rebellion!'" For their part, the Sassanids under Ardashir I (226–42), who were closely associated with the cult of Ormuzd and Ānahīta, thought they could forcibly convert the various peoples of Babylonia and Mesopotamia to their religion. So for the first two decades of Sassanian rule, no modus vivendi could be reached. *Shapur I (242–272) chose a different, more tolerant policy, encouraging Mani to preach a syncretistic religion of Buddha, Zoroaster, and Jesus (but not Moses!) to appeal to the several major groups of the empire, and seeking to conciliate the Jewish community as well. The Jewish government was given a legitimate role in administering Jewish affairs, when it promised to abide by state law in matters of concern to the state, specifically rules of land tenure and payment of taxes. The agreement of *Samuel and Shapur I, summarized by Samuel's teaching that "the law of the government is law," was closely adhered to by the Jewish regime, which enjoyed a secure position, with few, brief interruptions, for the next four centuries. It is not known what role, if any, the exilarch played in the negotiations preceding this agreement. If there was one Jewish government in Babylonia, as seems plausible, then Samuel must have been acting in its behalf. But rabbinic traditions, which are the only ones to survive, do not mention the participation of the contemporary exilarch, Mar *Ukba I, in the matter.

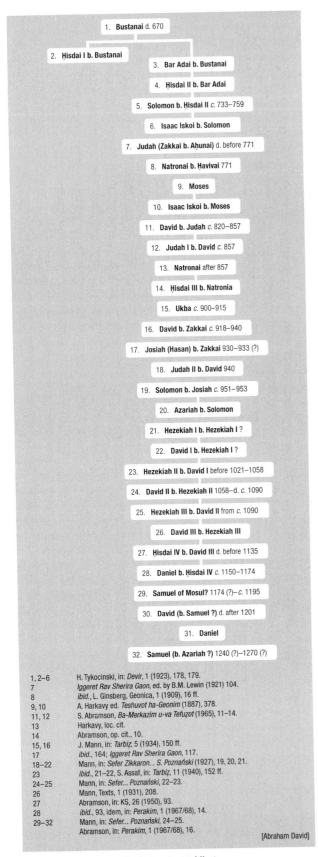

Rabbinic opinion on the third-century exilarchate was divided. In the early part of the century, it is clear that the leading rabbis were subordinate to the exilarch. Rav was forced by him to administer market prices, which Rav held was not a proper function of the *agoranomos*, or market supervisor. Samuel deferred to the exilarch Mar Ukba. It was, after all, the exilarch who had earlier employed rabbinically trained functionaries in the courts and bureaus of Babylonia in late Arsacid times. He had done so probably to circumvent the local Jewish strongmen, typified by Anilaeus and Asinaeus in the first century, and the Parthianized Jewish nobility referred to above, in the second century. The rabbis appealed to the people on the basis of their knowledge of Mosaic revelation, which, they held, was unique to their schools, and they moreover affirmed the exilarch's claim to Davidic origin. At the outset, therefore, the rabbinate and the exilarchate were closely allied against the centripetal forces of feudal autonomy represented by local Jewish upper-class landholders. By the last third of the third century, however, tension developed between the exilarchate and certain rabbinical circles. The exilarch justified his rule over Jewry as an heir of the Davidic household, just as did the Maccabeans, the Herodians, Jesus, and others who claimed the right to govern "Israel." That claim did not depend upon study in the rabbinical academies or conformity to rabbinical rules. Whether or not the exilarch was a "good Jew" by rabbinic standards is ultimately irrelevant to the issue. The rabbis saw themselves as the sole bearers of Mosaic revelation in its complete, dual form. They alone possessed the Oral Law, which completed the written one and determined its interpretation. About 275, Geniva, a disciple of Rav, caused so much trouble for the exilarch that the latter sought the advice of the Palestinian *Eleazar b. Pedat. He was counseled to forebear. Geniva was shortly thereafter executed by the state. It is not known what Geniva did to irritate the exilarch. The only clue to his doctrine is his teaching that rabbis should be called kings, the proof-text for which was Proverbs 8:15, "By me kings reign." The eighth chapter of Proverbs was consistently interpreted by the rabbis as the message of the Torah personified. If by "me," meaning "Torah," kings rule, then those not qualified by "Torah" should subordinate themselves to those who are, namely the rabbis. If Geniva made such an assertion of rabbinical superiority, the exilarch would wisely have handed him over to the Sassanids, for subversion of the exilarch was subversion, likewise, of the Sassanid system of millet-government. At the end of the century, Judah b. Ezekiel founded the school at Pumbedita and, for the next 50 years, the heads of the school kept a fund for its support, thus attempting to remain independent of the exilarchic treasury. At the same time, leading rabbis asserted that rabbis should not have to pay the *karga*, or head tax, imposed by the Sassanid regime on minority communities. They held that Scriptures, tradition, and even Artaxerxes of Achemenid times, had all freed them of that obligation. Since taxes were apportioned by communities, the exilarch would have had to collect funds from other Jews in order to exempt the rabbis. This he did not attempt, and a further irritant in the relations of the two groups was the consequence. By the middle of the fourth century, the academy at Pumbedita, now headed by Rava, was subject to close exilarchic supervision, and moved to the exilarchic capital at *Maḥoza.

When, under Pērōz (459–84), Jews and Christians were persecuted, the exilarch Huna V was executed, according to the letter of R. Sherira, in the year 470. The office of exilarch remained vacant for some time. The virtual chaos of the reigns before Khusro I (531–79) combined with the anti-Jewish activities of the Mazdakites supported by the throne in the time of Kavadh (488–531), and the economic depression of the period, produced a lapse in orderly government for Jewry as well. For a time (c. 510–20) the exilarch Mar *Zutra II threw off fealty to the throne, probably provoked by Kavadh's support of Mazdak. From Khusro onward, the situation was restored to its former favorable condition.

[Jacob Neusner]

During the Arab Period

The first exilarch of the Arab period was *Bustanai, who founded a new dynasty of exilarchs from the descendants of his Jewish wife and his other wife, the daughter of the king of *Persia who was given to him, according to the sources, by *Omar ibn al-Khaṭṭāb. Some opinions doubt the authenticity of the latter detail, because Omar did not visit *Iraq, but the texts possibly refer to one of his generals. This fact expresses the recognition granted by the Arab rule to the scion of the House of David who stood at the head of the Jewish community. The children of his Jewish wife disqualified the children of the Persian wife from acting as exilarchs with the argument that since the mother had not been converted, her children had the status of non-Jews. The polemics and the halakhic discussion have been preserved in a series of sources. The *ḥakhamim* of the academies decided in favor of the Persian branch. In spite of the protests, which were also voiced after this decision, the descendants of the Persian wife were appointed as exilarchs.

Relations with the *Rashei Yeshivot*

The exilarchs maintained close ties with the heads of the Sura and Pumbedita academies. They also concerned themselves with the incomes of these academies which were raised throughout the Diaspora. One of the exilarchs, *Solomon b. Ḥisdai, the great-grandson of Bustanai from the Jewish branch (reigned 733–59), was himself a scholar and distinguished himself with his concern for the academy of Sura and its aggrandizement. He took Mar Samuel out of the Pumbedita academy and appointed him head of the Sura academy (*Iggeret R. Sherira Ga'on*, ed. by B.M. Lewin (1921), 106). Twenty-six years later he appointed Rav *Yehudai, who was also a disciple of the Pumbedita academy, to the same position. Although the position of exilarch was hereditary, it was not always the firstborn who was chosen, but rather the member of the family who was most suitable and accepted by the academy heads and the important merchants who wielded influence in the court of the caliph. The exilarchs and the heads of the Sura and Pumbedita academies were dependent on each other, because the election of each of them required the confirmation of the other party. Against this background, there were examples of self-assertion. *Anan b. David, the nephew of Solomon b. Ḥisdai, was worthy of being elected as exilarch because of his erudition, but the *ḥakhamim* found a "disqualifying blemish" in him because of his negation of the Oral Law. His younger brother Hananiah was elected in his place. The leaders of the Karaite community, who were known as *nesi'im*, were descended from Anan.

The split between the *Rabbanites and the *Karaites appears to have been the cause of the decline in the status of the exilarchs and the limitation of their authority. Caliph al-Ma'mūn (ruled 813–33) granted the request of the Karaites that their leader be recognized as the *nasi* of their community. In 825 he issued an order according to which any ten men – Jews, Christians, or Zoroastrians – were authorized to organize themselves into an independent community and were at liberty to elect a leader. After the death of the exilarch Iskoy II, there were two rivals to his position, *David b. Judah and Daniel. The dispute was brought before the caliph for arbitration by the supporters of both parties. It is possible that the above-mentioned order was also a result of this situation and R. *Sherira hints that the decline in the status of the exilarchs was due to this contention. From then onward they were compelled to share the spheres of their influence and their incomes with the academy heads. Another change which occurred was that the gatherings of the *ḥakhamim* which took place on fast days and on the Sabbaths of the weekly portion of *Lekh Lekha*, which were known as *Shabbeta de-Rigla* and which had until then been held in the home of the exilarch, were from then on held in the academies. The penalization powers of the exilarch were also restricted.

A dispute over the incomes of the exilarch and the academy head resulted in a crisis in which the latter gained the upper hand. The exilarch *Ukba attempted to appropriate the incomes of Khurāsān from which the Pumbedita academy had until then benefited. According to *Seder Olam Zuta* (Neubauer, Chronicles, 2 (1895), 78), *Kohen Ẓedek, the *gaon* of Pumbedita, was supported by the bankers and merchants *Joseph b. Phinehas, *Aaron b. Amram, and *Netira, and in 913 Ukba was expelled by the caliph al-Muqtadir (908–32), at first to Kermanshah and later to Kairouan, where he was received with much respect and the *Sefer Torah* was lowered before him (see below). The office of exilarch was vacant for three to four years until, under public pressure, *David b. Zakkai, the nephew of Ukba, was elected. David b. Zakkai (918–40) was a powerful personality and he insisted upon his right of appointing the academy head according to his own discretion. His candidate for the position of *gaon* of Pumbedita was Kohen Zedek, while that of his rivals was *Kubashshir b. Kimoi. The latter refused to confirm the appointment of David as exilarch and he ostracized him until they reconciled themselves in 922. David endeavored to raise the status of the Sura academy, and in 928 he appointed R. *Saadiah Gaon as its head, having recognized his vast Torah erudition. When he appointed him, he adjured R. Saadiah Gaon "not to appoint any other exilarch beside himself, not to associate himself with those who plotted against him, and not to deviate from his words in any direction." It appears that R. Saadiah Gaon desired to be independent of the exilarch and also to intervene in secular affairs. The crisis finally erupted between them when R. Saadiah Gaon refused to ratify a legal decision of the exilarch after it had already been ratified by the *gaon* of Pumbedita. David b. Zakkai issued a *ḥerem* ("ban") against R. Saadiah Gaon and appointed *Joseph b. Jacob ibn Satia in his place. R. Saadiah Gaon, in turn, issued a *ḥerem* against David b. Zakkai and appointed Josiah (Hasan), the brother of David b. Zakkai, as exilarch. Masʿūdī relates that the dispute was brought before the vizier ʿAlī ibn ʿIsā. On Purim of 937, an agreement was concluded between the opponents. David b. Zakkai attained a respected position in the court of the Abbasid caliph al-Muqtadir, who supported him against those communities which refused to pay their taxes to him; the caliph also assisted him in his feud with R. Saadiah Gaon.

In general, the separation between the various functions of the exilarchs and the *geonim* was maintained: *Hezekiah (II) b. David, a descendant of David b. Zakkai, was an exception; he combined the exilarchate with the position of academy head. He was exilarch for over 40 years, and from 1038 he succeeded *Hai as head of the Pumbedita academy until his death in 1058. As a result of the conflict between the exilarch *Daniel b. Ḥasdai (1150–74) and the *gaon* *Samuel b. Ali, the exilarch opened an academy in Baghdad which was independent of that of the *gaon*. When he died childless, two candidates of the Josiah b. Zakkai branch, David and Samuel, sought his position. The latter, who benefited from the support of the *gaon* Samuel b. Ali, was compelled to yield several of his powers to the *gaon*. From then onward most of the powers of the exilarchs were transferred to the heads of the academies.

The Induction Ceremony

The appointment of the exilarch was the occasion for a glorious ceremony, the description of which has come down to us from *Nathan b. Isaac ha-Bavli (Neubauer, Chronicles, 2 (1895), 83–85). It was accompanied by a popular festivity, the climax of which was the gathering in the synagogue on the Sabbath, when hymns were recited in honor of the exilarch and he was blessed with special blessings and *piyyutim*. His name was mentioned in the *Kaddish* and he delivered a sermon or authorized the head of the academy to do so. The *ḥazzan* lowered the *Sefer Torah* before him while the congregation stood on its feet. The people sent him presents. The festivities were extended over seven days, during which he was host to the people in his home. The Arab chroniclers who mention this office point out that descent from the House of David was an indispensable condition to election. The aristocratic origin and the heredity of the exilarchate made a strong impression on the Shi'ites already during the early history of Islam, to the point that they compared it to the imamate and their theory on the subject of the legitimate caliphate. In their writings they describe meetings between exilarchs and caliphs and imams as equals, with the former reproving the Muslims. Bīrūnī (d. 1048) and others in his wake regarded the exilarch as the lord of all the world's Jews, who were subordinated to him.

Official Status, Powers, and Functions

The status of the exilarch became one of the subjects in the discussion held between the Muslim researcher of religions Ibn Ḥazm (994–1064) and *Samuel ibn Nagrela ha-Nagid in Spain. The latter pointed out the honor and the powers of the exilarch of the House of David and considered this to be the fulfillment of the verse: "The scepter shall not depart from Judah, Nor the ruler's staff from between his feet" (Gen 49:10). Ibn Ḥazm rejected his words and claimed that the exilarch did not wield any influence, neither over the Jews nor over any others, that he lacked authority, and that his title was merely an honorary one and devoid of any actual meaning. A similar discussion was held in Jerusalem between a Jewish *ḥakham* and a Christian clergyman named Abraham di Tibériade. G. *Vajda, whose writings on this subject are based on a manuscript of 1689, assumes that this event occurred during the tenth century and possibly even later. The Jew points to the existence of the exilarchate as a proof that the sovereignty of the House of David has not been interrupted and that the Messiah has not yet come. He also refers to the above verse of Genesis. The clergyman mocks and denigrates that status of the exilarch who is not endowed with the title of king, lives in an outlying town of Iraq and not in the Promised Land, and lacks any punitive powers.

The Muslim rule granted the exilarch the same recognition as the Katholikos, the head of the Nestorian community. A letter of appointment of the exilarch is not available, but there is reason to assume that his powers and functions were of a similar character. In the letter of appointment which was granted to the Nestorian Katholikos in Baghdad during the 12th century it is said that he is authorized to intervene and mediate in the disputes between the various sects of his community and to dispense justice and that he is also responsible for the supervision of their charitable funds. Anyone disobeying him or interfering in his affairs will be liable to punishment. He shall organize the collection of the poll tax and its transfer to the government which, in exchange, will guarantee the lives of the people of his community and protect its property. The receipt of this letter of appointment was accompanied by a ceremony in which a delegate of the government participated. In addition to the duty of the exilarch to transfer the poll tax of his community to the authorities, he was also responsible for the execution of the Covenant of *Omar, the discriminatory laws which affected protected subjects. The Arab author Ibn al-Jawzī (d. 1200) relates that in 1031 the Katholikos and the Jewish exilarch were requested to assure that the members of their communities wear the special garb of protected subjects.

Benjamin of Tudela, the traveler who visited Baghdad in about 1168, writes of the exilarch Daniel b. Ḥisdai that his function had the confirmation of the caliph, who had ordered both Jews and Muslims to stand in the exilarch's presence. The caliph received him in his palace every Thursday, and on his way his carriage was preceded by horsemen who called for the clearing of the way before the son of David. "He has been invested with authority over all the congregations of Israel at the hands of the Amīr al-Muʾminīn, the Lord of Islam. For thus Muhammad commanded concerning him and his descendants" (*Masot Binyamin*, ed. by M.N. Adler (1902), 39–40, Eng. part). From the end of the 12th century the Baghdad academy heads assumed most of the powers of the exilarchs; from then onward they were the delegates of the community before the government. The letters of appointment which were granted to the academy heads in 1209, 1247, and 1250 by the Abbasid government, and which have been preserved, shed light on the functions of the exilarchs and their powers during this period when their leadership was a real one. These letters state that the members of their communities were to obey the exilarch's instructions and were to pay him the accepted taxes; the exilarch was to judge them and it was his duty to enforce the protection conditions and heed the orders of the caliph.

There is a divergence of opinions among scholars as to the appointment of judges (*dayyanim*) by the exilarch and its dependence on the academy heads. It appears that this matter varied with the authority exerted by the exilarchs. It can be divided into five periods: (a) until the reign of al-Maʾmūn appointments were made by the exilarch; (b) until after David b. Zakkai, when authority was divided between the exilarchs and the academy heads, the appointment by each party was restricted to its own domain; (c) during the days of Hai Gaon appointments were made by the supreme *bet din* of the academy heads; (d) in the 11th and 12th centuries appointments were made by the exilarchs; and (e) after 1175 (the year of the death of the exilarch Daniel) it was only the academy heads who appointed the *dayyanim*. Also, when the exilarchs appointed the *dayyanim*, the *pitka de-dinuta* ("judicial authorization") was granted by the academy heads, while the exilarch merely gave formal permission. The exilarch disposed of a tribunal known as *bet dina de-nasi* ("*bet din* of the *nasi*") or *bava de-maruta* ("gate of the master"). If the exilarch was a *ḥakham*, he headed the *bet din* himself. On most occasions, however, it was a distinguished *ḥakham*, the *dayyana de-bava* ("judge of the gate"), who headed the tribunal. R. Ẓemaḥ b. Solomon is mentioned as head of the tribunal of the exilarch Ḥisdai b. Natronai during the middle of the ninth century.

The exilarch had the following means of penalization at his disposal: bans, fines, imprisonment, and flogging. During the reign of the caliph al-Maʾmūn his penal authority was restricted so that the only remaining instrument was the ban. During a later period his powers were, however, once more extended and R. *Pethahiah of Regensburg, who visited Mosul during the 1170s, relates that the exilarch was authorized to sentence offenders, even if the second party was a Muslim, and that he had a prison in which he detained offenders.

The exilarch participated in the institution of halakhic *takkanot*, such as the one in connection with the collection of debts and the *ketubbah* from movable property instead of from real estate, a *takkanah* which was circulated throughout the Diaspora with the signature of the exilarch in collaboration with his *dayyanim*, the academy heads, and their *battei din*. A letter has been found from the exilarch, dated from 835, concerning the fixation of the intercalation – the exclusive right of the Palestinian academy. His incomes were derived from the taxes which were paid by the communities under his jurisdiction and which received government protection. According to the report of Nathan ha-Bavli (Neubauer, Chronicles, 2 (1895), 85) every Jew aged 20 years or older paid an annual tax of two *zuzim*. Butchers paid ¼ dinar as a fixed annual sum. The exilarch also derived incomes from *ketubbot*, *gittin* ("divorce bills"), bills, and gifts. These details are also confirmed by an Arab source which adds that the Jews paid him one-fifth of their income, as well as redemption fees for male children and animals. At the close of the 12th century the exilarch of Mosul owned fields and vineyards, in addition to half of the poll tax which he collected from his community for the authorities. The exilarchs bestowed honorary titles upon personalities who supported them. These included: "Friend of the *Nesi'ut* (Exilarchate)," "Favorable to the *Nesi'ut*," and "Supporter of the *Nesi'ut*."

The Exilarchate Outside Baghdad

From the 11th century, the period of the decline of the Abbasida caliphate when independent governments were formed in Mosul, Damascus, and Aleppo, descendants of the Babylonian exilarch's family also arrived in these places. As a result of their descent from the House of David the communities appointed them as *nesi'im* over themselves, while they also obtained their recognition by the authorities as the delegates of the Jewish community. They appointed officials and *dayyanim*, judged the people, collected the poll tax, and received tithes.

YEMEN. During the 12th century the Jews of Yemen were placed under the formal "authority" of the exilarch of Babylonia and the Palestinian *rosh yeshivah* of Egypt. This was expressed by the fact that the above personalities were mentioned by the *ḥakham* before his sermon, the interpreter before the reading of the Torah, and the person who recited the blessing at meals. In a document of 1134 concerning Maḍmūn b. Japheth Hasan Bendar of Aden (d. 1151) there is the expression: *nagid* of the Jews of Yemen "appointed by the exilarch and the academy heads." It, is however, possible that this refers to members of the Babylonian exilarch's household who came to Yemen. During the 1130s the cousin of the Babylonian exilarch, who had come from Persia, was in Yemen. "He promoted himself to [a leading] position and the local people gave him permission to make decisions in religious law in the synagogues of all Israel" (S.D. Goitein, in *Sinai*, 33 (1953), 232). The latter struck the minister who mentioned the "authority" of *Maẓli'aḥ, the Palestinian *gaon* of Egypt, in his prayer. Benjamin of Tudela relates that in his time the Yemenite community was led by Shalmon ha-Nasi and his brother Hanan, descendants of David, who "divided up" the country between themselves. They corresponded with their relative, the Babylonian exilarch, and addressed their religious questions to him. It should be noted that during subsequent periods the *nesi'im* of Yemen were referred to as *resh galuta*, although they had no connections with the Babylonian exilarch or the House of David.

PALESTINE AND EGYPT. The members of the family of the Babylonian exilarch who came to Palestine and Egypt were received with deference, but their status was merely a formal one without any practical basis in administration. As a result of the abortive rebellion of the exilarch Zutra against the Persian king Kavadh I (488–531) and the hanging of the rebel at the beginning of the sixth century, his wife fled to Palestine. When his son Zutra II, who was born after the death of his father, reached the age of 18, he was appointed *rosh pirka* or head of the Sanhedrin in Tiberias (520 C.E.). Eight or ten generations of his descendants succeeded him in this position. At the close of the tenth and during the 11th centuries members of the Babylonian exilarch's household appeared in Palestine and Egypt. The only one of these who rose to power in Palestine and combined the functions of *nasi* and *gaon* during the years from 1051 to 1062 was *Daniel b. Azariah of the family of Josiah b. Zakkai. He left Babylonia because his family had been deposed by the exilarch *Hezekiah II. Daniel succeeded the *gaon* *Solomon b. Judah and supplanted Joseph b. Solomon ha-Kohen, who was *av bet din* and to whom the position of *gaon* was due. From his seat in Ramleh and Jerusalem he ruled over the whole of Palestine and Syria, where he was the judge; he also appointed *dayyanim*. Even the communities of Egypt were subordinated to him. After his death the position of *gaon* reverted to *Elijah b. Solomon ha-Kohen.

David, the son of Daniel, would not reconcile himself to the loss of the sovereignty of the House of David over Palestine and Egypt. He attempted to undermine the Palestinian academy which had been exiled to Tyre because of the invasion of the Seljuks in 1071. In 1081 he went to Egypt, where he was received with respect and his needs were provided for. However, when he desired to dominate the Egyptian communities and the coastal towns of Palestine, he clashed with Mevorakh ha-Nagid. He imposed taxes and ruled with tyranny. The Fatimid caliph al-Mustanṣir bi-Allah (1036–1094), who claimed descent from the "Prophet" and favored the descendants of David, supported him. David was finally deposed in 1094. The Jews of Egypt accepted the formal authority of the Babylonian exilarch. In 1162 Daniel b. Ḥisdai ordained *Nethanel b. Moses ha-Levi in Baghdad as *gaon* and appointed him to the "*bet din ha-gadol* in all the provinces of Egypt." Even several years later, the name of the exilarch appeared in legal documents which were traditionally written with the "authorization" of the *nasi*. During Maimonides' time a *nasi* named Judah b. Josiah lived in Egypt; he ratified the legal decisions of Maimonides. There were *nesi'im* who demanded judicial powers for themselves, but the community and its leaders rejected these requests.

During the first half of the 13th century the *nasi* Solomon b. Jesse and his brother Hodayah, who had come from Damascus, lived in Egypt. The latter came into conflict with a *dayyan* from France named Joseph b. Gershom, who lived in Alexandria in the days of *Abraham b. David Maimuni (1205–1237), over a question of authority. The *nasi* issued a ban against the *dayyan* and anyone who would materially assist the Frenchman. In the reply of the *nagid* to the appeal of the *dayyan*, which was also ratified by other *ḥakhamim*, the tendency to restrict the authority of the *nasi* and to reduce it to a merely formal ratification is evident. Even though the exilarchs considered themselves as the appointees over the Jews of the lands of dispersion and even though they signed themselves "the head of all Israel's exiles," their intervention was not viewed favorably in all places and practical powers were not entrusted to them. This opposition was particularly outspoken in Palestine, which was not part of the Diaspora, and in those places in the Orient where the Jewish communities were led by *negidim*.

Hulagu, the Mongolian khan who liquidated the Abbasid caliphate with the conquest of Baghdad in 1258, did not harm the Jewish community and its exilarch Samuel b. David. The exilarchs maintained their positions during subsequent years and some opinions assume that their status was improved. There is no information available on their activities and only the names of some of them are known. The exilarchate was brought to an end by Tamerlane in 1401. Until the beginning of the 18th century it was the practice of the governors of the important towns of Iraq to appoint a wealthy Jew as *ṣarrāf bāshī* ("chief banker"); he also acted as *nasi* of the local Jews. His powers were almost identical to those of the Babylonian exilarch during the Middle Ages. The *nasi* of Baghdad was the "*nasi* of the state" and his authority also extended to distant communities. This office was the patrimony of the descendants of the House of David and was passed down from father to son. From the 18th century until 1849 the *nesi'im* who were appointed were not from the House of David. From then onward the functions of *nesi'im* were transferred to the **ḥakhām bāshī*.

[Eliezer Bashan (Sternberg)]

BIBLIOGRAPHY: UNTIL THE ARAB CONQUEST: F. Lazarus, in: Bruell, Jahrbuecher, 10 (1890), 1–181; A.D. Goode, in: JQR, 31 (1940/41), 149–69; J. Liver, *Toledot Beit David* (1959), 37–46; M. Beer, in: *Zion*, 28 (1963), 3–33; idem, in: PAAJR, 35 (1967), 43–74; Neusner, Babylonia, 1 (1965), 50–58, 97–112; 2 (1966), 92–125; 3 (1968), 41–94; 4 (1968), 73–124; J. Gafni, in: *Niv ha-Midrashiyyah* (1968/69), 221–3; M. Beer, *Rashut ha-Golah be-Bavel bi-Ymei ha-Mishnah ve-ha-Talmud* (1970). FROM THE ARAB CONQUEST ON: Neubauer, Chronicles, 1 (1887), 63–67; 2 (1895), 78–87; Ibn Daud, Tradition, index; H. Tykocinski, in: *Devir*, 1 (1923), 145–79; J. Mann, in: *Sefer Zikkaron… S. Poznański* (1927), 18–32; Mann, Texts, index; idem, in: *Tarbiz*, 5 (1934), 148–61; I. Goldziher, in: *Jeschurun* (ed. by J. Kobak), 8 (1871), 76–78; idem, in: REJ, 8 (1884), 121–5; S. Pines, *ibid.*, 100 (1936), 71–73; F. Lazarus, in: MGWJ, 78 (1934), 279–88; W. Fischel, *ibid.*, 79 (1935), 302–22; idem, in: *Sefer Magnes* (1938), 181–7; A.D. Goode, in: JQR, 31 (1940/41), 149–69; S. Assaf, Geonim, 24–41; S.D. Goitein, in: *Sefer ha-Yovel… M.M. Kaplan* (1953), 51–53; idem, in: *Bo'i Teiman*, ed. by Y. Ratzaby (1967), 15–25; Abramson, Merkazim, 9–24; G. Vajda, in: *Bulletin de l'Institut de Recherche et d'Histoire des Textes*, 15 (1967/68), 137–50.

EXILE, ASSYRIAN. The mass deportation of population groups from conquered nations, as a measure to prevent these nations from rebelling, was introduced as a general policy by Tiglath-Pileser III in the second half of the eighth century B.C.E. Although deportation by Assyrian kings is well attested in the ninth century, it was Tiglath-Pileser's innovation to practice deportation on a vast scale and to accompany it with population exchange; a practice continued by his successors in Assyria. (The Babylonians did not accompany deportation with population exchange.) The first deportation of peoples from the northern Israelite kingdom took place when Tiglath-Pileser III campaigned against Syria and Palestine (734–732 B.C.E.), at which time *Pekah son of Remaliah joined the rebellion led by the king of *Aram-Damascus against Assyria. In the course of this campaign the Assyrians conquered Gilead and deported the heads of the Israelite clans that inhabited Transjordan (I Chron. 5:6, 26). One of Tiglath-Pileser III's fragmentary inscriptions lists several thousand captives, apparently only males, whom he exiled from eight cities in Galilee (among which were biblical Hannathon, Jotbah, Rumah, and Merom).

When *Hoshea son of Elah revolted against Assyria, Shalmaneser V besieged and conquered Samaria. His successor, Sargon II, states that 27,290 people (variant 27,280) were exiled from the city of Samaria. In place of the Israelite deportees, Sargon settled residents of other defeated nations in the Assyrian province of Samaria. In this connection the Bible mentions exiles from Babylon, Cuthah, Avva, Hamath, and Sepharvaim (II Kings 17:24), while an inscription of Sargon II specifies members of four Arab tribes who were settled in "Omriland" (Bīt Ḫumri) in 716/5 B.C.E. Finally, according to Ezra 4:1–2, forbears of the later Samaritans were brought into the province of Samaria by Esarhaddon, and, according to Ezra 4:9–10, "the great glorious Asenappar" – probably to be identified with Ashurbanipal – settled people from *Erech, *Babylon, *Shushan, and other localities in the city of Samaria and elsewhere in Syria-Palestine. However, it cannot be determined whether these seventh-century colonists were brought in to replace Israelites, who may have revolted again and been deported. The foreign elements that were brought to Samaria assimilated into the remaining Israelite population; the outcome of this lengthy process was a distinct cultural-national group which became known as the *Samaritans, i.e., the population of the province of Samaria. The Assyrians also exiled inhabitants of Judah (see *Sennacherib, *Hezekiah).

The Israelite exiles were settled mainly in the Assyrian provinces in Upper Mesopotamia (biblical Aram-Naharaim), along the Habor River in the vicinity of Gozan (Tell-Ḥalāf). After 716 when some "cities of the Medes" came under Assyrian control, some Israelites were resettled in Media (II Kings 17:6; 18:11; probably in the province of Ḫarḫar (Diakonoff in Bibliography)). In I Chronicles 5:26 there is the addition "and Hara" (הרא: LXX, Lucian recension *kai harran*, possibly referring to Haran (cf. Isa. 11:11)).

Notwithstanding the manifold legends fabricated about the exile of the so-called "*Ten Lost Tribes," there is no certain information about the fate of the Israelite exiles in Mesopotamia during the Assyrian empire or at a later period. Only a few extant allusions in the Bible and in epigraphic sources testify to their existence. Of the latter sources, the onomastic evidence from Mesopotamia contained in Assyrian documents dated to the end of the eighth and to the seventh centuries is of particular significance, since it presents names which are known from the Bible to be Israelite. However, with the exception of personal names composed of the Israelite theophoric element *yau* (YHWH), it is not always certain that the reference is to Israelite exiles, since these names are common Northwest Semitic ones and may also designate either Phoenicians or Arameans.

The documents dealing with or discovered at Gozan, which is mentioned in the Bible in relation to the exile of Israel (see above), are particularly instructive in this respect. One letter (ABL 633) actually mentions one Ḫalabišu (or less likely, Haldu) from Samaria living in Gozan, although he may not have been an Israelite. The same document, however, names two officials called Palṭiyau and Niriyau (= biblical Pelatiah and Neriah respectively) who almost certainly were. Another Assyrian letter (ABL 1009), dated to the seventh century B.C.E., mentions Samaritans among the troops of the Assyrian king who were serving in Mesopotamia. In a commercial contract from Gozan (JADD 234 = SAA 6:34) dated to the end of the eighth century, the signatory witnesses are two high-ranking officials in the Assyrian administration whose names are Nādbiyau (biblical Nedabiah), who bore the title "chariot driver," and Paqaha (identical with the Israelite royal name Pekah), whose title was "village manager." In a document discovered at Gozan (No. 111) two typical Hebrew names are mentioned – Usi'a (*Hosea) and Dayana (Dinah), as well as Yaseme'il. In B. Mazar's opinion, this document concerns Hosea's redemption of an Israelite woman (Dinah) from an Aramean. In a legal document from Nineveh (SAA 14:50) one Il-yau (= אליהו) sells a girl.

Traces of Israelite captives (and possibly even Judeans) seem to appear from the end of the eighth century at Calah (present-day Nimrud) on the Tigris, then capital of Assyria. An Aramaic ostracon discovered there lists Northwest Semitic personal names, some of which are common in Israel, such as Elisha, Haggai, Hananel, and Menahem. This document possibly concerns a group of Israelites who lived in Calah alongside Phoenician and Aramean elements, and who worked as craftsmen in one of the enterprises of the Assyrian kingdom. Among the Nimrud ivories which bear inscriptions in Phoenician-Aramaic script, one is clearly a Hebrew inscription (ND. 10150). Some bronze bowls also found there were engraved with West Semitic names, such as Yibḫar-ʾel, El-heli, and Aḥiyô (Ahio), the last name being unmistakably Hebrew. It cannot be ascertained how these objects, dating from the second half of the eighth century, reached Calah, but they may have been taken as spoil from Samaria when the city fell.

Various Assyrian documents contain additional names of an ordinary Hebrew type, such as Menahem, Amram, Naboth, and Abram, but it is difficult to determine beyond doubt that they belong to descendants of the Israelite exiles. In an Assyrian administrative document from the second half of the eighth century B.C.E., the name Aḫiyaqāma appears in relation to the Assyrian city of Halah (Ḫalaḫḫa), which is mentioned in the Bible as one of the places to which the Israelite exiles were deported (II Kings 17:6; 18:11). The text could be interpreted as referring to an Israelite deportee named Ahikam. In the view of Tur-Sinai (Torczyner), the inscription on an amulet discovered at Arslan Tash (ancient Hadatta), east of the Euphrates, is written in Hebrew (though this is doubtful; see Sperling in Bibliography), and he attributes it to an Israelite deportee from Samaria. The existence of an Israelite exile is also alluded to in legendary tradition, such as that embodied in the book of Tobit. The hero claims descent from the tribe of Naphtali, supposedly deported in the days of Shalmaneser.

From the documents that presumably refer to the Israelites, or for that matter to any other exiles, it is evident that as a rule they did not possess the status of slaves or of an oppressed population. The exiles were first settled in Mesopotamia as land tenants of the king (cf. the words of Rab-Shakeh in II Kings 18:32), while the craftsmen among them were employed in state enterprises. Eventually, some of the exiles achieved economic and social status and even occupied high-ranking positions in the Assyrian administration. They were given the right to agricultural holdings and to observe the customs of their forefathers, and enjoyed a certain measure of internal autonomy. The striking of roots in Mesopotamian society by a large part of the descendants of the Israelite exiles resulted in their eventual absorption into the foreign milieu. Nevertheless, part of the Israelite community undoubtedly preserved its distinct national character and maintained connections with the homeland (cf. II Kings 17:28), later merging with the Judean exile. The return to Zion apparently included remnants of the ten tribes, as alluded to in the Bible (see the prophecies concerning national unification in Ezek. 16:53ff.; 37:16ff.; and cf. Zech. 8:13; 10:6ff.) and as indicated in the genealogical lists of Ezra and Nehemiah (cf., e.g., Ezra 2:2; Neh. 7:7).

BIBLIOGRAPHY: S. Schiffer, *Keilinschriftliche Spuren...* (OLZ 10, Beiheft 1, 1907); W. Rosenau, in: HUCA, 1 (1925), 79ff.; A. Ungnad, in: J. Friedrich et al., *Die Inschriften vom Tell Halaf* (1940); H.J. May, in: BA, 6 (1943), 55ff.; H. Torczyner, in: JNES, 6 (1947), 18ff.; B. Maisler (Mazar), in: BIES, 15 (1949–50), 83ff.; EM, 2 (1954), 500–3 (incl. bibl.); J.B. Segal, in: *Iraq*, 19 (1957), 139ff.; W.F. Albright, in: BASOR, 149 (1958), 33–36; A.R. Millard, in: *Iraq*, 24 (1962), 41ff.; R.D. Barnett, in: *Eretz Israel*, 8 (1967), 1*–7*; S.M. Paul, in: JBL, 88 (1969), 73–74. **ADD. BIBLIOGRAPHY:** B. Oded, *Mass Deportations and Deportees in the Neo-Assyrian Empire* (1979); idem, in: K. van Lerberghe and A. Schoors (eds.), *Immigration and Emigration within the Ancient Near East* (FS Lipiński, 1995), 205–12; S.D. Sperling, in: HUCA, 53 (1982), 1–10; H. Tadmor and M. Cogan, *II Kings* (1988), 176–80, 198–201, 336–37; M. Diakonoff, in: *Scripta Hierosolymitana*, 33 (FS Tadmor; 1991), 13–20; I. Ephʿal, *ibid.*, 36–45; B. Becking, *The Fall of Samaria* (1992); H. Tadmor, *Tiglath-Pileser III* (1994), 82–3; G. Knoppers, *I Chronicles 1–9* (AB; 2003), 382.

[Abraham Malamat]

EXILE, BABYLONIAN, exiles of Judah to Babylonia, sixth–fifth centuries B.C.E. Although Babylonia was not the only destination of former Judahites, it was the Babylonian deportees and their descendants whose perspectives inform the Hebrew Bible. Modern scholarship has adopted their perspective in dividing Israelite/Jewish history into "pre-exilic," "exilic," and "post-exilic" periods. The destruction of the Assyrian empire brought only temporary respite to the kingdom of Judah. The newly established Chaldean (Neo-Babylonian) dynasty

(626 B.C.E.), which together with Media and the Umman-manda (Scythians?) destroyed Nineveh (612), quickly established its own rule (604) in "the land of Hatti" (Syro-Palestine). Although the prophet *Nahum rejoiced over Nineveh's fall and Habakkuk was stunned by Babylon's rise (Hab. 1:1ff.), Jeremiah foretold that Babylonian rule would last "70 years" (Jer. 25:12; 29:10) and counseled submission. The setback that Babylon suffered at the hands of Egypt (601), however, encouraged King *Jehoiakim to rebel (II Kings 24:1). The uprising was crushed by Nebuchadnezzar himself (598–597), but the statement that Jehoiakim was led into exile (Dan. 1:1ff.; I Esd. 1:39ff.; cf. II Chron. 36:5–6) is probably unhistorical. It is likely that he died in Jerusalem, reviled by Jeremiah (cf. II Kings 24:6; Jer. 22:13–19; 36:30–31), and that the city was surrendered by his son Jehoiachin on March 16, 597 B.C.E. (II Kings 24:8ff.; II Chron. 36:9ff.). As punishment for the rebellion, Nebuchadnezzar sent into exile the young king and his family, royal officials, warriors, artisans, and other distinguished people from Jerusalem and Judah, and took much spoil from the Temple and palace (II Kings 24:12ff.; Jer. 13:18–19; II Chron. 36:9–10). The number of exiles is reported in round numbers once as 10,000 exclusive of artisans (II Kings 24:14) and once as 7,000 "mighty men" and 1,000 artisans (II Kings 24:16). Probably because Jehoiachin surrendered in time, Nebuchadnezzar did not destroy Jerusalem. He took the exiled king's uncle Mattaniah, made him a vassal king, and changed his name to Zedekiah (II Kings 24:17; Ezek. 17:11ff.). Jehoiachin, however, retained his royal status, and a Babylonian tablet of 592 reports that he and his five sons, along with other exiles, were allotted rations by Nebuchadnezzar. The seal impressions "Eliakim steward of Yaukin," discovered at Tell Beit Mirsim, Beth-Shemesh, and Ramat Raḥel, may indicate that his royal estates were preserved intact.

In the eyes of Jeremiah, the exilic community was, metaphorically, a basket of excellent figs and would ultimately be restored to the land, while the remaining population were bad figs and would experience further destruction (Jer. 24:1–10). Ezekiel, settled among the exiles, provides evidence that events were dated according "to the exile of King Jehoiachin" (Ezek. 1:2). Despite the continuous preaching of Jeremiah and Ezekiel, prophets in Judah such as Hananiah son of Azzur (Jer. 28:1ff.) and in Babylonia such as Ahab son of Kolaiah, Zedekiah son of Maaseiah, and Shemaiah the Nehelamite (Jer. 29:21ff.) encouraged the rump state of Judah to believe that deliverance was at hand. Relying upon Egypt (Jer. 37:5; Ezek. 17:15; 29:6–7), Zedekiah rebelled. This time the city was destroyed (586 or 587) and the Temple burned. For breaking his oath of allegiance Zedekiah was blinded, exiled to Babylon, and his sons were executed. Other leading officials were likewise put to death. The Temple vessels were taken as booty, and all but the poorest were sent into exile (II Kings 25:1–21; Jer. 39:1–10; 52:1–27; II Chron. 36:11–21; cf. also Dan. 5). Whereas excavation shows clear evidence of destruction at this time in several Judahite sites, e.g., Tell Beit Mirsim, Lachish, Beth-Shemesh, Beth-Zur, etc., the evidence thus far is that Benjamin remained untouched. (On the archaeological situation see C. Carter, O. Lipschits, A. Zertal, and J. Zorn, apud Lipschits and Blenkinsopp in Bibliography.) Appointed governor by the conquerors, *Gedaliah son of Ahikam resided in the Benjaminite town of Mizpah until he was assassinated by *Ishmael son of Nethaniah of the royal family (II Kings 25:22–25; Jer. 40:7ff.). The people then fled to Egypt, taking Jeremiah with them (Jer. 41–43), and in 582 a third group was carried off into Babylonian exile (Jer. 52:30). The same source which reports this last small exile of 745 Judahites gives figures of 3,023 and 832 for the exiles of Jehoiachin and Zedekiah respectively (Jer. 52:28–30). It is not clear how these figures are to be reconciled with those cited earlier.

The destruction of the state and the Temple and the exile to Babylonia were traumatic experiences that concomitantly brought forth desires for revenge and stirrings of repentance. Feelings ran strong not only against Babylon (Isa. 47; Jer. 51; Ps. 137) but also against neighboring Edom, which rejoiced at, and benefited from, the destruction (Ezek. 25:12–14; 35:1ff; Obad.; Mal. 1:3–5; Ps. 137:7; Lam. 4:21–22). Although Jeremiah and Ezekiel explained the impending destruction as punishment for moral and cultic sins, the actual destruction was a shock. It aroused strong lament (Book of Lamentations) and regular commemorative fasts (Zech. 7:1ff.; 8:18–19) and a yearning to be reconciled with God and restored to the land of Judah (Ps. 137; Lam. 3:39ff.; 5:19–21). The Sabbath and festivals continued to be observed, and names such as Shabbethai (Ezra 10:15; Neh. 8:7; 11:16; *Murashu Tablets) and *Haggai (the prophet; and a personal name in the Murashu Tablets) made their appearance. The contrast between monotheism and polytheism became sharpened (e.g., Isa. 44:6ff.), and gentiles attracted to the God of Israel were promised a share in the restored Temple if they observed the Sabbath and the Covenant, probably of circumcision (Isa. 65:1ff.). Except for the leaders who had contact with Babylonian officials – *Sheshbazzar/Shenazzar (Ezra 1:8ff.; 5:14; 6:5; I Chron. 3:18), *Zerubbabel son of Shaltiel (Ezra 3:2), Mordecai (Ezra 2:2), Bilshan (Ezra 2:2) – and were therefore given, or adopted, Babylonian names (cf. Esth. 2:5, 7; Dan. 1:5ff.), the majority of exiles in Babylonia, as in Egypt, preserved the practice of giving Hebrew names.

Economically, the exiles did not fare badly, and socially they succeeded in preserving their clan and family structure intact. A prominent position was held by King Jehoiachin, who in 561 was exalted by King Amel-Marduk (*Evil-Merodach) over the other exiled kings. The communal leaders, "the elders of Judah/Israel" (Ezek. 8:1; 14:1; 20:1, 3), maintained their traditional authority and were known as "elders of the exile (Jer. 29:1). Craftsmen and builders were engaged in the royal building projects in Babylon, and clay tablets record rations distributed in 592 to such as Semachiah, Gaddiel, and Urimelech. Many were settled on "mounds" (*tel*), i.e., sites that had formerly been destroyed and needed to be rebuilt, such as Tel-Melah and Tel-Harsha (Ezra 2:59; Neh. 7:61). Ezekiel had a house in Tel-Abib (Akkadian for "mound caused by the deluge"), which lay along the Chebar Canal (Ezek. 1:1; 3:15, 23;

8:1) in the vicinity of Nippur. Jeremiah had encouraged the exiles to settle down, build houses and plant gardens, lead a normal life, and preserve public security (Jer. 29:4ff.). One of the Jews receiving royal rations in 592 was "Shelemiah the gardener." The best evidence of continuity in the cultural sphere is the activity of the prophets Ezekiel, Deutero-Isaiah, Haggai, and *Zechariah. The first was born in Judah and was exiled with Jehoiachin. He relentlessly prophesied the destruction of Temple and state and with equal certainty delineated its reconstruction. The last two, who were doubtlessly born in exile, returned to Judah to inspire the reconstruction. The great unknown prophet who goes by the name Deutero-Isaiah (Isa. 40–66) probably knew only exile and yet foretold the restoration in the most lyric of biblical poetry.

Return from Exile

Just as the greatest tragedy of the destruction of Jerusalem by the Babylonians in 586 B.C.E. was the loss of the Temple, so the first task after the return from exile was its reconstruction. As Cyrus embarked upon his conquest of Babylon, Deutero-Isaiah looked upon him as the Lord's shepherd and anointed, called upon to release the exiled Jews, rebuild the city, and reestablish the Temple (Isa. 44:28; 45:1, 13). A policy of restoration and reconstruction was pursued by Cyrus throughout the conquered territories, and he announced it proudly in his Akkadian-language cylinder inscription (COS 2:314–16). The specific permission granted the Jews was proclaimed orally throughout the Diaspora and put down in writing. As his victories and policy of restoration were attributed to Marduk in the Babylonian inscription, so in the proclamation to the Jews they were attributed to the God of Heaven, the title by which the God of Israel was generally known at that time (cf. Ezra 5:12; 7:12). No decree specifically granting permission to the exiles to return or to rebuild the city of Jerusalem has come down. Permission is granted simply to rebuild the Temple and for the exiles to return to Jerusalem for that purpose. Those not returning are encouraged to assist the repatriates financially (Ezra 1:2–4). An Aramaic memorandum deposited in the treasury archives in Median Ecbatana (Heb. Achmetha; modern Hamadan), Cyrus' summer residence, gives the dimensions and certain architectural features of the Temple, and states that expenses are to be met by the royal treasury (Ezra 6:1–5). The Temple vessels were released by the treasurer Mithredath, at Cyrus' order, to Sheshbazzar/Shenazzar, prince of Judah, who restored them to Jerusalem (Ezra 1:7–11; 5:14–15; 6:5). Sheshbazzar was given the title of governor (*peḥah*) and entrusted with the task of rebuilding the Temple (Ezra 16–17). Although the sources are not clear on the subject, he was apparently succeeded in this assignment by his nephew Zerubbabel, who likewise bore the title "governor" (Ezra 3:1–13; 5:1–23; Haggai 1:1; 2:1–2, 21).

Zerubbabel son of Shealtiel and *Joshua son of Jehozadak, who was descended from a family of high priests, appear at the beginning of a list of 12 leaders, symbolizing the unity of Israel, who headed the groups returning from exile (Neh. 7:7; one name has accidentally been left out from the parallel list in Ezra 2:2). Besides Zerubbabel ("Seed-of-Babylon") at least three other leaders bear non-Hebrew names – Mordecai (related to a name compounded with Marduk), Bilshan (= Bab. Belšunu, "Their Lord"), and Bigvai. The last name is from Persian *bagāvahyah*, "through God, the better," and recurs in the first list of 17 or 18 returning families, along with such unusual names as Pahath-Moab ("Governor of Moab") and Elam (Ezra 2:6–7, 14; Neh. 7:11–12, 19). Perhaps these names refer to Israelites exiled from Transjordan (I Chron. 5:26) and to those who settled in Media (II Kings 17:6), hence the Persian name, and in Elam (Isa. 11:11). Since most, if not all, of the place-names in the second list are located in Benjamin (Ezra 2:20 or 21–35; Neh. 7:25–38), it is likely that these 17 (18) families settled in Judah. Interestingly, exactly 17 settlements are cited for Judah in the time of Nehemiah (Neh. 11:25–30). The subsequent lists enumerate families of priests, levites, singers, gatekeepers, temple servants (*Nethinim*), and "sons of Solomon's servants" (Ezra 2:36–58; Neh. 7:39–60). In addition to these families, whose genealogical records were in order, there were other repatriates whose records were not. The priests among them were disqualified from the priesthood (Ezra 2:59–63; Neh. 7:61–65). At least one of these families, however, that of Hakkoz, was apparently reinstated at a later date (Ezra 8:33; Neh. 3:4). The number of members of each family and town often varies between the two parallel lists, while the total of all the figures falls far below the recorded total sum. While the difference could be made up by adding women and children, it should also be noted that the given totals are schematic numbers, formed of various combinations of seven and three: 42,360 plus 7,337 slaves (Ezra 2:64–65; Neh. 7:66–67). Despite the list's title indicating that it numbers "the members of the province who returned from exile … with Zerubbabel" (Ezra 2:1–2; Neh. 7:6–7), the origin, nature, and purpose of the list has been much debated. The first recorded act of the newly established community was the reinstitution of the regular daily ritual on the first of Tishri, and later the celebration of the festival of Tabernacles "as prescribed in the Torah of Moses." It was at the time of this festival that Solomon's Temple had been dedicated (I Kings 8:62ff.). Like that structure, the Second Temple was to be built with cedars from Lebanon, and at the foundation ceremonies, priestly and levitical choirs chanted psalms of praise and thanksgiving, "according to the order of David" and as was prophesied by Jeremiah (Jer. 33:10–11). The link with tradition is evident from the fact that while the young rejoiced, the elders, who remembered the First Temple, wept (Ezra 3:10–12).

The repatriates' ties with the past took on a strong ethnic coloring. In the neighboring provinces, particularly in Samaria, the Assyrian kings had earlier introduced an alien population which, in the course of time, came to worship the God of Israel (II Kings 17). They now wanted to participate in the erection of the Jerusalem Temple. The repatriates felt no kinship with these elements and claimed that Cyrus' decree was for themselves alone. Rebuffed, these "opponents of Judah and Benjamin," this new "people of the land," succeeded in thwarting by one means or another the efforts of the Jews to rebuild the Temple during the reign of Cyrus and *Cambyses (Ezra 4:1–5). Years of famine followed and a certain demoralization set in. The rebellions and wars that took place in the Persian Empire after the death of Cambyses reverberated in Judah, and the prophets Haggai and Zechariah rose in 520 to encourage the Jewish leaders to resume construction of the Temple. They did so with enthusiasm and Haggai prophesied to Zerubbabel in messianic terms. The son of the same Jehoiachin, whom Jeremiah had likened to a signet which the Lord deliberately pulled off his hand and cast away (Jer. 22:24), would become just such a signet on the Lord's hand (Haggai 2:23), and the righteous Davidic "shoot" foreseen by Jeremiah (Jer. 23:5–6) was to sprout up and rule alongside the high priest (Zech. 6:12–13). The actual building was again called into question, this time by Tattenai, governor of Trans-Euphrates. The Jews could produce no document granting them permission to build the Temple, but they reported that such a document was on file in the royal archives. When the memorandum of Cyrus was located in Ecbatana, Darius reconfirmed the decree with its provision for covering expenses and agreed to pay the expenses of a daily sacrifice on behalf of the royal family. Building subsequently proceeded and the dedication was held on Adar 3, 515, "as prescribed in the Book of Moses"; Passover was then celebrated by all those "who had separated themselves from the impurity of the nations of the land… to seek the Lord God of Israel" (Ezra 5–6). The Temple was rebuilt and the enemies of Judah were foiled, but Zerubbabel did not ascend the throne of David. No more is heard of him, and upon the death of Darius, the opponents of Judah sought to stir up King Xerxes against Judah (Ezra 4:7ff.). The restored community only became firmly established during the 40-year reign of Artaxerxes I, when *Ezra and *Nehemiah undertook the twin tasks of the codification of the law and the fortification of Jerusalem.

BIBLIOGRAPHY: E.F. Weidner, in: *Mélanges Syriens Offorts à M. Bâné Dussaud*, 2 (1939), 923ff.; W.F. Albright, in: BA, 5 (1942), 49ff.; D.J. Wiseman, *Chronicles of the Chaldean Kings* (1956); Bright, Hist. 302ff.; *Return from Exile*; E. Bickerman, in: JBL, 65 (1946), 249–75; J. Liver, *Yemei Ezra ve-Neḥemyah* (1953); idem, *Toledot Beit David* (1959), 64ff.; idem, in: *Eretz Israel*, 5 (1959), 114–9; Bright, Hist. 341ff.; H. Tadmor, in: *Oz le-David Ben Gurion* (1964), 470–73; M. Myers, *Ezra-Nehemiah* (Eng., 1965); F.M. Cross, in: HTR, 59 (1966), 201–11. **ADD. BIBLIOGRAPHY:** W. Hinz, in: ASN, 59–60; M. Coogan, *West Semitic Personal Names in the Murašû Documents* (1976), 23; A. Kuhrt, in: JSOT, 25 (1983), 83–97; P. Dion, in: ZAW 95 (1983), 111–12; J. Blenkinsopp, *Ezra-Nehemiah* (1988); M. Dandamayev, in: JAOS, 112 (1992), 163–64; S. Ahituv, *Handbook of Ancient Hebrew Inscriptions* (1992), 128; B. Oded, in: K. van Leberghe and A. Schoors (eds.), *Immigration and Emigration within the Ancient Near East* (1995), 205–12; R. Albertz, in: idem and B. Becking (eds.), *Yahwism after the Exile* (2003), 1–17; O. Lipschits and J. Blenkinsopp (eds.), *Judah and the Judeans in the Neo-Babylonian Period* (2003); R. Zadok, *ibid.*, 471–589.

[Bezalel Porten]

EXISTENTIALISM, a modern philosophical movement, which intends to elucidate concrete human existence. To the movement belong such people as S. Kierkegaard, A. Schopenhauer, M. Heidegger, J.-P. Sartre, G. Marcel, M. Buber, F. Rosenzweig, and J.B. Soloveitchik.

Embracing a number of disparate philosophical positions, existentialism can be described as a reaction to traditional philosophy with its emphasis on the static, the abstract, the objective, and the purely rational. In its reaction, existentialism emphasizes the dynamic, the concrete, the subjective, and the personal. More specifically, existentialism opposes Idealism, which gave priority to the idea over factuality and largely neglected the part of the philosopher himself in the construction of his philosophy. Existentialism stresses personal involvement and "engagement," action, choice, and commitment, and regards the actual situation of the existential subject as the starting point of thought. Revolting against the Cartesian view of the self as a thinking entity, existentialism is concerned with the existential subject in his wholeness and concreteness – the willing, feeling, thinking person, who decides and acts from the perspective of his particular life situation rather than from some universal vantage point provided by reason or history. One of the important influences on existentialism was phenomenology, which attempts to understand the world and man not through causal formulae and analysis, but through openness to the whole range of phenomena that are manifest, without asking whether they are "real" in some metaphysical sense. Yet, whereas E. Husserl's phenomenology investigated human consciousness and its intentionality, existentialists themselves were rather interested in existential situations as insecurity, anguish, depression, shame, tragedy, hope, solidarity, and love. Both Husserl's phenomenology and existentialism did not relate to the Kantian *Ding an sich*, reality in itself, but in the way reality appears to the subject that is open to it: they do not explain phenomena, they rather describe them.

Existentialism in Jewish Thought

Existentialist motifs are central to the writings of many modern Jewish thinkers. One may for instance find existential motifs in the thinking of Rabbi Nahman of Breslav (Meir, 37–54).

According to F. Rosenzweig, Hermann Cohen's thought prepared his own existential thinking (F. Rosenzweig and S.H. Bergman highlighted the dichotomy between the neo-Kantian Cohen of Marburg and the neo-Cohen of Berlin, whereas A. Altmann thought that there was one great continuity in Cohen's neo-Kantian thinking). It was the concern for the individual which led Cohen to accord religion an independent place in his philosophic system. He argued that religion is necessary insofar as it posits the categories of sin, repentance, and salvation to deal with the problems of the individual, which Kantian ethics overlooks in its concern with man in general. Cohen emphasizes the relation between God and man, rather than theoretical speculation concerning God. With his notion of "correlation" Cohen maintains that the relationship between

God and man is characterized by the holy spirit. Through his relation to God and his acknowledging God as the model and source of holiness, man strives to attain holiness for himself. Man and God are partners in bringing the work of creation to completion, i.e., in bringing about the messianic era. Both the deeds of man and the divine grace are necessary for the salvation of mankind.

Jewish existentialism proper begins with Franz Rosenzweig. Following Cohen, Rosenzweig attaches a great importance to the individual. In *Das neue Denken* ("The New Thinking," 1925) he criticizes traditional philosophical categories, instead making the personal experience of the individual the starting point of philosophy. Because God, the world, and man are experienced as three distinct entities, Rosenzweig rejects the approach of philosophy from the pre-Socratics until Hegel which reduced in a monistic manner these three "substances" to one basic essence, to God (in pantheism), to man (in anthropology), or to the world (in materialism). The separation and interrelationship of God, man, and the world is central to his New Thinking. He explains that the relation between God and the world is cognized as creation; between God and man, as revelation; and between man and the world, as redemption. As a result, the I is less a Cartesian *cogito* than a relating being, called upon to respond.

All of Martin Buber's mature thought bears the stamp of a closely similar existentialism of dialogue reflected in his notion of the I-you relationship, and his insistence on the concrete, on the unique, on the everyday, on the situation rather than the "-ism," on response with one's whole being and the personal wholeness that comes into being in that response. At the center of Buber's existentialism stands "holy insecurity" or the "narrow ridge" – the trust that meaning is open and accessible in the lived concrete, that transcendence addresses us in the events of everyday life, that man's true concern is not unraveling the divine mysteries, but the way of man in partnership with God. The partnership with "the eternal You" comes into expression in the meeting and encounter with a you. The living presence of God is felt when one is present to the other and makes the other present.

For Abraham Joshua Heschel religious reality does not begin with the essence of God but with His presence, not with dogma or metaphysics but with that sense of wonder and the ineffable which is experienced by every man. Through this sense of wonder man is led toward that transcendent reality to which each finite thing alludes through its own unique reality. Heschel approaches philosophy of religion as "situational thinking" and "depth theology" which endeavor to "rediscover the questions to which religion is an answer" (A.J. Heschel, *God in Search of Man* [1955], 3).

Basic existentialist themes are also found in the thought of Rabbi Joseph B. Soloveitchik. His thinking is pervaded by such themes as loneliness and alienation, but also heroic readiness of obeying the divine commandments. Soloveitchik's halakhic hero lives through the normative prism of *halakhah*. He is the ideal type who orients his life to halakhic discipline and develops an indifference toward the chaotic, death, and the absurd.

Although the existential Jewish writer F. Kafka has his own anti-hero, who is the object of circumstances, of misunderstandings, and alienation and who possesses a total lack of communication, one may sense Kafka's longing for a fuller life in his description of alienated modern man (Meir, 129–145). In their various writings, all Jewish existentialists proposed that their readers adopt an "authentic" lifestyle, the content of which differed from author to author.

BIBLIOGRAPHY: E.B. Borowitz, *A Layman's Introduction to Religious Existentialism* (1965); M. Friedman, *The Worlds of Existentialism; A Critical Reader* (1964); idem, *To Deny Our Nothingness: Contemporary Images of Man* (1967). **ADD. BIBLIOGRAPHY:** D. Hartman, "The Halakhic Hero: Rabbi Joseph Soloveitchik, Halakhic Man," in: *Judaism*, 9 (1989), 249–73; E. Meir, *Jewish Existential Philosophers in Dialogue* (Hebrew; 2004).

[Maurice Friedman / Ephraim Meir (2nd ed.)]

EXODUS, BOOK OF (Heb. title) שְׁמוֹת [וְאֵלֶּה] "[And these are] the names of" – the first words of the book; Gk. *exodos ton wion Israel ex aigyptou*], "departure [of the children of Israel from Egypt]"; (cf. Sefer *Yeẓi'at Miẓrayim* ("book of the departure from Egypt"), *Dikdukei Te'amim*, 57) the second book of the Pentateuch. The masoretic notice at the end of Exodus (C.D. Ginsburg's edition) gives it 1,209 verses (middle verse: 22:27), 16,713 words, and 33,529 letters; 33 (or 29) triennial sections (*sedarim*), 11 annual ones (*parashiyyot*). According to the traditional chronology, the book's narrative embraces 129 years, from the death of Joseph (A.M. 2320) to the erection of the Tabernacle in the second year after the Exodus (A.M. 2449). The book itself is the end-product of centuries of composition. It has 40 chapters (adopted from the Vulgate in the 14th century).

Book of Exodus – Contents

Chs. 1:1–18:27	**The Liberation.**
1:1–2:25	The enslavement of Israel and the advent of Moses.
3:1–7:13	The call and commissioning of Moses.
7:14–11:10	The plagues.
12:1–13:16	Firstborn plague and Passover rite.
13:17–15:21	The miracle at the sea.
15:22–17:16	Trouble and deliverance on the way to Sinai.
18:1–27	Jethro's visit and the organization of the people.
Chs. 19:1–24:18	**The Covenant.**
19:1–20:21	The theophany at Mt. Sinai and the Decalogue.
20:22–23:33	Rules and admonitions.
24:1–18	The Covenant ceremony.
Chs. 25:1–40:38	**The Tabernacle and the Golden Calf.**
25:1–27:19	Orders to build the Tabernacle.
27:20–31:18	Activities and actors in the Sanctuary.
32:1–34:35	The Golden Calf.
35:1–40:38	Building the Tabernacle.

Structure and Content

Although it is part of a continuous narrative that runs through the *Pentateuch, the Book of Exodus shows signs of having been intended as a distinct unit. (See Table: Analysis of the Book of Exodus.) The opening verses of the book do not continue Genesis 50:26, but briefly recapitulate the genealogy of Genesis 46:8–27 as a background for the story of Israel's proliferation, which sets in motion events leading to the departure from Egypt. Similarly the last verses of the book (40:36 ff.) look ahead to (and epitomize) Numbers 9:15–23 to round out the account of the Tabernacle; Exodus 40:35 has its proper sequel only in Leviticus 1:1. Beginning with a backward glance and ending with a forward one, the book gives the appearance of a (to be sure, secondary) literary entity unto itself.

Genesis describes Israel's antecedents and God's promises of progeny and land to the patriarchs. Exodus relates the fulfillment of these promises in three great divisions:

(1) The liberation – God redeems Israel from slavery and demonstrates His faithfulness, His compassion, and His power (Ex. 1–17);

(2) The covenant – God establishes a covenant with Israel and gives them rules to make them His kingdom of priests, a holy nation (Ex. 19–24);

(3) The Tabernacle – God ordains the building of a sanctuary for Himself in the midst of His people, so that He might dwell among them, care for, and guide them (Ex. 25–31, 35–40).

The visit of *Jethro (Ex. 18) shows signs of being out of chronological order (see below). In the third division, the sequence of command and execution is interrupted by the *Golden Calf episode (Ex. 32–34), the people's travesty of God's provision for securing His presence among them.

The contents of the book may be divided as follows:

A. THE ENSLAVEMENT OF ISRAEL AND THE ADVENT OF MOSES (1:1–2:25). Israel's proliferation (described in terms employed in the primeval history (Gen. 1:28; 9:7) and the patriarchal promises (Gen. 17:2, 6; 28:14)) provokes the king of Egypt to employ increasingly brutal measures in an effort to reduce it: forced labor proving to be inadequate, he resorts first to a clandestine, and when that fails to a public, order to put to death all male infants of the Hebrews. In this evil time, a boy is born to Levite parents, and to save him, his mother hides him in the Nile's canebrake. Pharaoh's daughter retrieves the infant and connives with his sister (who stands watch close-by) to restore it to his family. Later the child is brought back to the princess; she names him *Moses (probably of Egyptian derivation; cf. the final element of such royal names as Thutmose "born of [the god] Thut") and adopts him as her son.

Three acts of rescue by the young man Moses (adumbrations of his future role) are related: he rescues a Hebrew from an Egyptian taskmaster, one Hebrew from the unjust attack of another, and finally, as a fugitive in Midian, he rescues the daughters of the local priest from bullies (note the rising scale of disinterest). Moses takes up with the priest and marries his daughter who gives birth to a son. His retreat from the struggle of his people in Egypt is temporary, however, for God has taken note of their misery and resolves to act.

Well-knit as the narrative is, inconsistencies occur, suggesting a separate provenance of its elements; e.g., though prodigiously prolific, the Israelites have only two midwives; and though Moses seems to be the first child of his parents, he turns out to have an older sister (cf. Ex. R. 1:19 according to which the marriage is really a remarriage). The theme of fertility (a veritable refrain in ch. 1) and birth dominates and unites this whole section, giving the impression of a distinct design.

The birth story of Moses has been compared with that of Sargon of Agade (Pritchard, Texts, 119; COS I, 461) and Cyrus (Herodotus, 1:107 ff.). However, an Egyptian myth telling how Isis concealed her infant child in a delta papyrus thicket to save him from the predator Seth offers a closer analogue, and points to local Egyptian color in the Moses story (W. Helck).

B. THE CALL AND COMMISSIONING OF MOSES (3:1–7:13). While shepherding his father-in-law's flock deep in the wilderness, Moses comes upon the mountain of God (unknown to him as such). The wonderful apparition of a bush that burns without being burnt draws him into the presence of God, who calls him to lead Israel out of Egypt. Moses' repeated objections of inadequacy finally impel God to appoint his brother *Aaron as his spokesman (an etiology of how Levite-priests became the spokesmen and mediators of prophecy in Israel (Lev. 10:11; Deut. 24:8; 33:10; II Chron. 17:8–9)). The two bring God's message to the grateful people. Speaking to Pharaoh, however, they disguise their demand (upon God's instruction) as a request for leave to worship God in the wilderness at a three-day's march from Egypt. Pharaoh rebuffs them contemptuously: "Who is YHWH that I should heed him and let Israel go – I do not know YHWH, nor will I let Israel go" (Ex. 5:2). He then orders that the Israelites' toil be intensified, which sends Moses back with a bitter complaint to God. God responds with a renewed charge and vow to liberate Israel in fulfillment of His promise to the Patriarchs. However, neither the people nor Pharaoh are moved by Moses' report of this transaction, so God prepares Moses and Aaron to act against the Egyptians.

The *burning bush story includes the revelation of the proper divine name, YHWH, and its interpretation – the enigmatic "I am/shall be what I am/shall be" (3:13–15). Moses' supposition that the people would ask God's name is itself unclear – all the more so since the contingency fails to materialize in the sequel. The coherence of the fragments in 4:18–26 is problematic (Naḥmanides supposes that verses 22–23 belong to the story of the last plague; in the Samaritan Pentateuch they are in fact repeated in 11:4), and the meaning of the night encounter with YHWH in which Zipporah saves the life of one of her family by circumcising her son is wholly obscure (Jacob's nocturnal struggle with a "man" at Jabbok (Gen.

32:25ff.) may be aptly compared to this incident). An adumbration of the plague of the firstborn on the paschal night, from which Israel's firstborn are saved through a blood rite, has been seen here.

The most salient problem of this complex section is the repetition in 6:2–7:13 of the main outline of 3:1–6:1 – the revelation to Moses of God's plan to save Israel; Moses' mission to Pharaoh and Israel; his objection that he is clumsy of speech and the consequent appointment of Aaron as his spokesman; and Pharaoh's rebuff of the brothers. The medieval French exegete Joseph Bekhor Shor suggests that at least part of the second narrative recapitulates the first (at 6:13, 29); in fact, it appears that these are variant narrations of Moses' call and commissioning. The contribution of the second narrative is its stress on God's involvement in Israel's liberation: Pharaoh's rebuff challenges God's reputation, and He must teach the arrogant Egyptian who He is. Thus the major motive of the plague story is introduced (cf. 7:5 with 7:17; 8:6, 18; 9:14, 16, 29).

C. THE PLAGUES (7:14–11:10). After Pharaoh spurns the credentials of Moses and Aaron as God's messengers because his magicians imitated them, the brothers are instructed to bring on *plagues of blood, frogs, and lice. The first two are again imitated by the magicians, but the third is beyond them, and they confess it to be "the finger of God." Six more plagues follow, with Pharaoh oscillating between obduracy and concession. When, with the eighth plague (locusts) he engages in real negotiation with Moses, it is Moses' turn to be difficult. He so exasperates the king that after the ninth plague (darkness) he is expelled from the palace with a warning never to show his face there again. Moses stalks out in a rage after warning Pharaoh of the final plague of the firstborn.

The plague narrative is constructed on a 3.3.3. (plus 1) pattern – reflected in the tannaitic mnemonic *Deẓakh ʿAdash Be'aḥav* and expressly noted by medieval exegetes (Samuel b. Meir, Levi b. Gershom, Abrabanel). This pattern is imposed on heterogeneous materials whose inconsistencies have troubled readers from earliest times (for details, see *Plagues of Egypt). Despite this, the effect of the narrative is achieved: human arrogance toward God is not only futile; in the end it overmasters its subject and leads him to his destruction.

D. FIRSTBORN PLAGUE AND PASSOVER RITE (12:1–13:16). A fortnight earlier, on the first of the spring month (later, Nisan), God had prescribed the protective rite and sacrificial meal that Israel was to carry out on the night of the final plague – namely, the slaughter of the Pesaḥ (protective/pass-over (Mekh.)) lamb, the daubing of its blood on doorposts and lintels, strict confinement indoors, and consuming of the roast flesh in haste and readiness to leave (see *Passover).

The text moves on to link the Pesaḥ with the future week-long festival of *maẓẓot*, whose onset coincides with the Pesaḥ night (14 Nisan), and whose main feature – unleavened bread – accompanies the Pesaḥ meal as well. The two, evidently distinct, holy days are henceforth to be celebrated as memorials of the Exodus – their coincidence on the same date being the basis of their combination. (Only in 12:39 is an etiology of the *Maẓẓot* Festival associating it directly with the events of the Exodus given – the inability of the Israelites to tarry in Egypt long enough for their dough to rise.)

Moses passes on to the people only the injunction concerning the Pesaḥ. However, his message too has a part that looks to the future. This time the link with the future is the Pesaḥ rite itself: in time to come it is to be reenacted (annually) as a memorial to the sparing of Israel's firstborn during the plague that struck Egypt. (The Samaritan mode of celebrating the rite, preserving all its dramatic and apotropaic features, appears closer to the intention of the text than the Jewish mode, deliberately emptied of them (cf. *National Geographic Magazine*, 37:1 [1920], 34–35, 44–45; Pes. 9:5; Abraham Ibn Ezra on 12:24).

On the fateful night, the bereaved Egyptians press the Israelites to leave. The latter had already fulfilled (*ʿaśu* (12:35), pluperfect) Moses' order to ask the Egyptians for valuables (and thus get some return for their unrequited labor and suffering (Sanh. 91a; Ḥezkuni on 3:21f.; B. Jacob, in: MGWJ, 32 (1924), 285ff.). (The notice (Ex. 3:20) that the valuables are worn by children is probably an etiology of a festive practice of Jews in the Egyptian diaspora of the later first millennium.) Verses 37–42 of chapter 12 are notes on the departure: the first station; the size of the host (conceived as an army: *ragli*, "footmen," *ẓiv'ot* YHWH, "the troops of YHWH"); the large admixture of non-Israelites; the etiology of *maẓẓot*; "the night of vigil."

Further regulations concerning the Pesaḥ in verses 43–49 continue verses 1–20, and belong (in the light of verse 50) before verse 29. They appear here owing to their assumption of settled conditions and the presence of foreigners among the celebrants. A passage enjoining the commemoration of the Exodus with the *Maẓẓot* Festival (a variant of verses 15–20) and the dedication of firstlings follows. Notable is the conception of both as pedagogic measures – vehicles for the transmission of God's mighty deeds to future generations. A large agglomeration of ritual materials of quite varied character and provenance has thus been attracted to this point in the narrative. The reason is clearly to link the rites and holy days in question – doubtless pre-Israelite in origin – with their meaning in Israel.

E. THE MIRACLE AT THE SEA (13:17–15:21). A report of God's providential guidance of the departing Israelites is followed by a prose and poetic account of the miracle at the *yam suf*, usually rendered "Sea of Reeds" or "Red Sea." (On the problematic term see Vervenne in Bibliography; location unknown; every body of marsh and water from Lake Sirbonis in the north, across the Isthmus of Suez, to the Gulf of Suez in the south has been proposed.) The theme of teaching Egypt who YHWH is reaches its culmination in God's assertion of authority against Pharaoh and his whole army (14:4). God's design having been abetted by Pharaoh's change of heart and pursuit of Israel, Moses bids the frightened people to "stand fast and see the salvation of YHWH...YHWH will fight for you and you be still!" God displays His sovereign control of the sea, which he first blows apart so that Israel can pass through it on dry land and then allows to close on the pursuing Egyptians. The prose of chapter 14 is elevated: refrain-like clauses (cf. 14:6–7, 9, 17, 23, 26, 28) and phrases (cf. 14:16, 22, 29) summed up in 15:19 and climaxed by a strongly cadenced five-clause coda (14:30–31).

The "Song of the *Sea" – a paean to God the warrior (15:3) – follows. Its junctures are marked by three verses in "staircase parallelism" (a b c d / a b e f) – verses 6, 11, 16b – dividing it into four parts: (a) a declaration of intent to hymn God's victory and a summary of its essence – the drowning of Pharaoh's army; (b) the piling up of waters by God's wind, the greedy pursuit by the enemy, and the drowning of the enemy; (c) God's guidance of the people to His holy abode (the Land of Canaan), inspiring terror in all the neighboring countries; (d) coda: God's implanting His people in His own mountain, His dwelling-place, His sanctuary in the Land of Canaan; acclamation of God as eternal king.

As the celebration of a specific event, the song is comparable only to Deborah's hymn (Judg. 5), although from verse 12 on it moves on to Israel's journey to its land and its settlement therein. A hymn to the victor at the sea has apparently been expanded into a larger celebration of God's deeds for Israel from the Exodus to the settlement, incorporated here because of its first half. The language displays several early features (*-emo* suffixes; retention of radical *y* in *yekhasyumu*; staircase parallelism; echoes of the primeval battle with Yam (the Canaanite god of the sea), cf. Cassuto in bibl.); the mention of Philistia, the references to cavalry, and the sanctuary on God's mountain, however, indicate a date no earlier than the tenth century for the present form of the song.

F. TROUBLE AND DELIVERANCE ON THE WAY TO SINAI (15:22–17:16). The interval between the crossing of the sea and the arrival at Sinai is filled with four episodes relating trials and tribulations (catchwords: *nissah* "try, test" and the assonant *nes* "(en)sign" (15:25; 16:4; 17:2, 7, 15)). (a) Marah, where a miraculous healing of brackish water is connected with an obscure law giving, a trial, and an admonition evocative of epilogues to law collections. (b) The *manna story – an only partly fused composite (note the allusion to quail that has no sequel here) – teaching God's capacity to provide food even in the wilderness. It also illustrates the holiness of the Sabbath: just as God ceased providing manna on the Sabbath, so must Israel rest from procuring and preparing food on that day; 16:35 notes that the manna ceased only when Israel arrived in Canaan (cf. Josh. 5:12). (c) Massah and Meribah: the people complain of thirst, Moses strikes "a rock at Horeb" (but the camp is at Rephidim, a station away from the holy mountain; 17:1 and 19:1–2) and water gushes forth. (d) The encounter with *Amalek: by virtue of Moses' raised hands and the force mustered by Joshua Amalek is defeated; God's oath to wipe out Amalek is memorialized by an altar named "YHWH is my ensign."

These stories are more or less paralleled by post-Sinai narratives: the third story, by the "Waters of Meribah" episode in Numbers 20:2–13, in which Moses and Aaron are denied entry into Canaan; the second, by the story of Numbers 11 – chiefly about the quail – which ends with the people's being punished for their complaint (Joseph Bekhor Shor identifies the Exodus with the Numbers story in his comment to Ex. 16:13); the fourth, by the encounter with Amalek and others in Numbers 14:45, in which Israel is defeated. Nor are they free of occasional post-Sinai allusions: e.g., "before YHWH" of 16:9, a commonplace reference to the tent-sanctuary; the "rock at Horeb" (17:6); the Negebite nomads of Amalek. Notwithstanding their shaky anchorage in time and place, these episodes are thematically fitting here. They display God's providence and His capacity to deliver Israel from distress, thus paving the way for His claim upon them based on their experience of Him ("You have seen what I did to the Egyptians, how I bore you on eagles' wings and brought you to me"; 19:4). Punishment would be out of place here, but not so in the post-Sinai narrative, where the credit established by God and the covenant obligation of loyal devotion to Him count against the people.

G. JETHRO'S VISIT AND THE ORGANIZATION OF THE PEOPLE (EX. 18). Drawn by the wonders done for Israel, and accompanied by Moses' divorced wife, and children (but cf. 4:20), Jethro comes to the encampment at the mountain of God. He confesses YHWH's superiority to all other gods and offers sacrifice to him. On the morrow, seeing how Moses is overwhelmed by the charge of the people, Jethro proposes a division of labor between Moses – who should retain only the functions of mediating between God and the people – and a hierarchy of officers who would care for all other needs. (The text speaks of judicial functions, but the terminology (cf. e.g., I Sam. 8:12; II Sam. 18:1; II Kings 1:9ff.; 11:10) is military, in line with the conception of the Israelites as an army.) Whether Jethro's visit occurred before or after the Sinai law giving has long divided exegetes (see Mekh., Ibn Ezra, Naḥmanides on 18:1). The argument for a later visit is based on (a) the location of the camp at the holy mountain (cf. 19:1–2); (b) the allusion to an already present cult site (18:12); (c) Moses' teaching of God's laws and statutes (18:20); (d) the representation in Deuteronomy 1:9–10 of the administrative organization here ascribed to Jethro as having occurred just before the people left Sinai; and, finally (e) the notice of Numbers 10:29ff. that Moses' father-in-law was in the camp at that time.

Thematically, the episode suits its context: its first half relates a foreigner's appreciation of the great acts of God told in the preceding chapters; its second half foreshadows Moses' mediatory and legislative function – the topic of the rest of the book. Rabbinic exegesis, for its part, found the contrast in attitude to Israel between Amalek and the equally foreign Jethro to be the point of the juxtaposition of chapter 18 to chapter 17 – a contrast whose historical consequences are depicted in I Samuel 15:6 (see at length David Kimḥi on Judg. 1:16).

H. THE THEOPHANY AT MT. SINAI AND THE DECALOGUE (19:1–20:21 (18)). On the first of the third month after the Exodus (i.e., 1 Sivan, in later terms) Israel arrives at Sinai. Moses ascends to the mountaintop where God descends, and messages concerning God's proposal to contract a covenant with Israel are carried by Moses to and from the people. Upon their acceptance in principle of God's proposal, Moses prepares the people for the theophany (divine manifestation). On the third day, amid lightning and thunder, God manifests Himself on the mountain and speaks the *Decalogue. Terrified, the people fall back and beg Moses to be their intermediary with God. Moses approaches the cloud "where God was" to receive the rest of the commandments.

The details and order of the narrative in chapters 19 and 20 are perplexing. Weighty matters crowd together in a barely intelligible sequence. The number of Moses' ascents and descents is unclear. The stated aim of the theophany in 19:9 (to let the people overhear God's dialogue with Moses so that they might believe him forever) has no sequel – except perhaps in the unspecified dialogue alluded to in verse 19b. The people are strictly barred from approaching the mountain – a wholly unnecessary precaution. The order to return with Aaron (verse 24) has no sequel (unless it be 24:1); and what Moses said to the people (19:25) is left unsaid.

The Decalogue – a self-contained entity – is only loosely related to the context (see *Decalogue). The terror of the people (19:18–20) seems to follow upon God's speaking the Decalogue (as in Deut. 5:20ff.), but it has long been felt (especially since no reference to God's speech occurs in the passage) that it belongs properly to the pre-Decalogue situation described in 19:16ff. (cf. Naḥmanides).

The extraordinary complexity is best explained as the result of the interweaving of parallel narrations; the author appears to have been reluctant to exclude any scrap of data relevant to this momentous occasion.

I. RULES AND ADMONITIONS (20:22 (19)–23:33). The further stipulations of the covenant are told to Moses, to be transmitted by him to Israel. These consist of cultic regulations, civil and criminal laws, and socio-moral exhortations, arranged as follows: (a) rules concerning access to God in worship (20:22 (19)–26 (23)); (b) the emancipation of Hebrew slaves (21:1–11); (c) homicide and assault (21:12–27); (d) the homicidal ox (21:28–32); (e) injury to property, i.e., to animals (including theft; 21:33–22:3) and to crops (22:4–5); the responsibility of bailees and borrowers (22:6–14); seduction (22:15–16 – from the vantage point of the father's interest, i.e., the bride-price); (f) a miscellany of religio-moral admonitions and commandments (22:17–23:13); (g) a cultic calendar (23:14–19). Admonitions to obey the accompanying angel of God and to keep strictly apart from the society and worship of the Canaanites serve as the epilogue to the section (contrast Lev. 26 and Deut. 28 with their clear-cut blessings and curses, the formally proper epilogue to a law collection; cf. Hammurapi's Laws, Pritchard, Texts, 178ff; COS II:335–53). These "utterances of YHWH" and "rules" (usually understood as the categorical and casuistic statements, respectively (cf. Ibn Ezra on 21:1)) appear to constitute the "*Book of the Covenant" that Moses is said (24:7) to have written down and read to the people; hence the section is conventionally named "the (larger) Book of the Covenant" (to distinguish it from the "smaller": 34:11–26, on which see below). It is made up of heterogeneous elements, including prior entities – note the title of 21:1; or the interrupted series of participial clauses concerning capital crimes in 21:12, 15–17. Sets of five clauses are discernible: the slave laws, the homicidal ox, theft. A general design is evident: the section begins and ends with cultic-religious admonitions and commands; in between these the impersonal casuistic laws appear (note the transition in 21:2, "If you buy") – their environment bestowing on them its character of a divine address and commandment. A fairly clear principle of association and gradation is discernible from (c) through (e); the precedence given to (b) is conditioned by the situation – limitation of slavery among Hebrews being the chief boon that their liberator conferred upon them. Indeed the very gradation referred to betrays a clear hierarchy of values (contrast the arrangement of laws in the Babylonian collections of Eshnunna and Hammurapi (Pritchard, Texts, 161–177; COS II (332–53)). Notable is the recognition of the slave as a person in his own right in 21:20, 26–27, unparalleled in ancient law (though still holding him less than a free man; cf. 21:21, 32). Ibn Ezra's summary of the section merits quotation:

> The essence [of the laws] is that one should not do violence to or coerce a weaker man. First, subjugation of the person is taken up – namely, enslavement… Assault is dealt with for the sake of the law on injuring slaves… And talion is dealt with in order to distinguish the case of maiming a free man from that of a slave… The goring ox is mentioned to stipulate the rule in the case of the killing of a slave… Violence to property is the next topic. First field and vineyard are taken up, for they constitute the essence of property; next, crops – produced by the earth; and then bailees and the borrower. And next, the seducer who coerces a minor… The resident alien is mentioned because he is helpless, and similarly the widow and orphan and the poor debtor.
>
> Afterward the violence that may be perpetrated covertly is taken up: cursing God, which one would fear to do openly; or delaying payment of the sacred dues of wine and oil… and… purveying false reports… Judges are addressed in the injunction against perverting justice – which is violence that can be done covertly… And the reason for mentioning the fallow year is to declare the yield forfeit to the poor, and the Sabbath, so that servant and alien may rest… The intention of 23:13 is to reinforce the second commandment [against worship of other gods]; and that is the reason for the three pilgrimage festivals, namely, the assemblage of all Israel to worship God…

This ingenious, if somewhat one-sided, view of the continuity of the section has the merit of highlighting the extraordinary preoccupation of the rulings and admonitions with socio-moral values. Especially noteworthy is the fact that although the laws have numerous parallels to other Near Eastern legal collections, the notion of their divine origin appears unique to Israel.

J. THE COVENANT CEREMONY (EX. 24). Moses relates the rules and admonitions to the people, who accept them. He then writes them down, and, after a second reading and acceptance, performs a sacrifice and blood-sprinkling ceremony to conclude the pact. Moses and Israel's notables ascend the mountain for the sacrificial meal, consecrated by a vision of God. Afterward, Moses takes leave of the notables and enters the cloud on the mountaintop to receive the stone tablets and the laws which God is to give him.

The chronology and interrelation of the elements of this chapter have long puzzled exegetes. The first two verses of chapter 24, not picked up until verse 9, are vaguely evocative of 19:24. Some rabbinic opinion places all of the events of 24:1–11 before the pronouncement of the Decalogue (Yoma 4b; Rashi to 24:1) going so far as to identify the people's acceptance reported in 19:8 with that reported in 24:3 (or 7; Saadiah, cited by Ibn Ezra on 20:21). There is discontinuity between 24:11 and 12: in between, Moses and the elders must have descended the mountain. The relation of the six and seven days of 24:16 to prior events is again obscure, rabbinic opinion being divided as to whether they preceded or followed the Decalogue speech (see Rashi). The impression is unavoidable that heterogeneous matter has been combined.

K. ORDERS TO BUILD THE TABERNACLE (TENT OF MEETING, 25:1–27:19). God commands that materials be assembled for making Him a dwelling place amid the people (see *Tabernacle). A vision of the tent-sanctuary that God intends in all its detail is shown to Moses (25:9, 40; 26:30; 27:8; cf. I Chron. 28:12, 19 with reference to Solomon's Temple, and the dream of Gudea, the neo-Sumerian ruler of Lagash, summarized in H. Frankfort, *Kingship and the Gods* (1955²), 255–8; COS II, 417–33). First in importance and first described is the ark – the receptacle of the "tablets of the pact" that Moses is to receive – and the cherubim on its cover, where God will "meet with" Moses and give him his orders concerning Israel (25:22). Next, the table and lampstand, the furnishings of the outer room of the sanctuary. All these articles are of gold or wood overlaid with gold, as befits the holiest part of the sanctuary.

The inner tent is to be of richest cloths: linen of several plies, and blue, purple, and crimson wool, on which figures of cherubim are woven; gold clasps connect the cloths. A cover of goatskin, on which yet another of ram and dolphin skins lies, protects the inner cloths of the tent.

Planks of acacia wood, set in silver sockets and secured by horizontal poles, form the walls of the Sanctuary – all the wood overlaid with gold. A curtain of finest cloth separates the ark from the outer sanctuary; in the entrance to the latter, a similar curtain (but with embroidered rather than woven designs) is hung.

A square wooden altar overlaid with copper and having copper service vessels stands in the courtyard. The linen curtains forming the rectangular court are attached to poles set in copper sockets. The materials of the sanctuary are clearly graded in accord with the sanctity of the objects made of them (M. Haran).

L. ACTIVITIES AND ACTORS IN THE SANCTUARY (27:20–31:18). Reference to the light which is to be lit nightly in the Tabernacle and tended by Aaron and his sons leads to a description of their investiture. The gorgeous sacred vestments of Aaron, the high priest, are described, then the simpler attire of his sons. There follows a week-long ritual to be carried out by Moses to consecrate Aaron and his sons as priests. Linked to this account of the consecration ritual, through reference to the altar, is a prescription for the modest daily sacrifices that are to be made in the Sanctuary (one sheep in the morning, one in the afternoon). The peroration of this section (29:42b–46) would be a fitting close to the entire description of the Tabernacle and its personnel.

However, there is more to come: a gold-plated wooden incense altar for the outer sanctuary; an injunction to collect a half-shekel personal ransom from each Israelite to protect him ("make expiation for him") against the evil effects of a census – the money to be assigned to the sanctuary; a description of the bronze laver and its use by the priests. The references to the incense altar and the laver include descriptions of the priestly use of them, which may be the reason for their location after the section on the priesthood rather than before it, together with the other furniture. (On the problem see Meyers in Bibliography. The Samaritan text indeed transposes the description of the incense altar to follow 26:35.) Recipes for the anointing oil and the incense conclude the uses for which the materials listed at the start of the section have been collected. God then names the craftsmen responsible for executing all these instructions.

Finally, a Sabbath law, prescribing death for its violation, is promulgated. The link with the foregoing is the term "labor" (31:5), the sense of the juxtaposition (as correctly inferred by the rabbinic exegetes (cf. Rashi, Samuel b. Meir, Ibn Ezra)) being to establish the priority of the Sabbath rest even over the building of the Tabernacle.

SECTIONS K. AND L. are not a natural sequel to 24:12–13, and the notice of 31:18 (God gave Moses the stone tablets when He had finished speaking with him on the mountain) only underscores the foreignness of the Tabernacle sections to the narrative framework that surrounds them. To be sure, there is an associative link between the announcement of a delivery of stone tablets to Moses and the order to prepare an ark to receive them (cf. the identical sequence of ideas in Deut. 10:1–3); and since the ark passage was but a part of the detailed description of the desert sanctuary, its inclusion entailed the rest of the passage. Rashi (following Tanhuma Ki Tissa 31 (181), cf. Elijah Mizrahi's comment to Rashi on 31:18) frankly removes all of 25:1–31:17 from the present order of the narrative, and places it after the golden calf episode, i.e., he makes the story of the execution of the orders to build the Tabernacle follow immediately upon the giving of the orders. As we shall see, however, the present order has its logic.

M. THE *GOLDEN CALF (EX. 32–34). Not knowing how Moses could have survived 40 days on the mountain and fearing the worst, the people implore Aaron to "make them a god" to lead them. Aaron fashions a calf out of their golden earrings, which the people acknowledge as their redeeming god; Aaron then proclaims the morrow a festival for YHWH whom the calf must therefore symbolize; the calf – in essence an unauthorized (indeed a forbidden (20:2ff.) and hence "apostate") means of securing the divine presence – thus travesties the Tabernacle (cf. Judah Halevi's trenchant interpretation in Kuzari, 1:97, and David Kimḥi on the related "apostasy" of Jeroboam, at I Kings 12:28). Meanwhile, on the mountain, God wrathfully dismisses Moses, threatening to destroy the people. Moses' plea on their behalf is successful, and he descends, bearing the stone tablets, to the festive throng. At the sight of their revel, Moses breaks the tablets (signifying the rupture of the covenant, in accord with standard ancient custom), and, having ground the calf into powder, makes the people drink its remains (rabbinic exegetes interpret this, in accord with Num. 5:16ff., as an ordeal to discover the guilty; cf. Av. Zar. 44a; Targ. Jon. on 32:20). The Levites rally to Moses and put to death about 3,000 offenders, in return for which they are consecrated to God's service (an etiology of the tribe's conversion to clerical status). Moses now undertakes to obtain remission of Israel's sin and restoration of the covenant. At first he is ordered to lead the people onward under the guidance of an angel; God's presence amid the stiff-necked people will be too dangerous for them (33:1–5, a reflective gloss on 32:34). There follows a barely integrated passage telling how Moses pitched his tent outside the camp as an oracle site for himself and the people, and how he there held intimate conversations with God; in the present context, this appears as a result of God's refusal to be amid the people. Moses now strives to move God to rescind His decision (He rescinds in 33:14), and at the same time to secure the people against God's wrath should they sin in His presence. Banking on his favor with God, Moses extracts from Him a revelation – both visual ("I will make all My goodness pass before you" (33:19)) and conceptual ("and I will proclaim before you the name of YHWH" (*ibid*)) of His compassionate attributes (34:6–7), whereupon Moses entreats God to show this compassion and forgive offenses of the stiff-necked people He made His own. (Moses again successfully implores God by appealing to His compassionate attributes in his intercession on Israel's behalf after the incident of the spies (Num. 14:18); partial citations of these "thirteen attributes of God," as they are traditionally styled, occur in Joel 2:13; Jonah 4:2; Nah. 1:3; Ps. 86:15; 103:8; 145:8; Neh. 9:17. For the subsequent use of the passage in public intercessory prayers, see RH 17b.)

God's abrupt response is to conclude a covenant – in the present context, to renew the broken covenant (though it is not so expressed) – with stipulations that prove to be a variant repetition of 23:12, 14–33, beginning with the topic dealt with last in the earlier passage. The two main concerns of these stipulations are the prohibition of apostasy and the cultic calendar – against both of which Israel offended when they worshipped the golden calf in an invented festival (Joseph Bekhor Shor). Moses is commanded to write down the covenant terms (34:27). The sequel in verse 28 says that he wrote down "the ten words" on stone tablets (and thus renewed the broken relationship with God). However, this contradicts 34:1, in which God Himself undertakes to rewrite on the new set of tablets the same words that had been on the first set, namely, the Decalogue of chapter 20. The understanding of 34:28 has been traditionally governed by verse one (the subject of "he wrote" being taken as God) no doubt correctly (cf. the unequivocal sense of "the ten words" in Deut. 4:13; 10:4); but this means that in 34: (10–) 27 and 28 two different conceptions of the covenant terms have been crudely juxtaposed (see further, *Decalogue).

A fitting conclusion to this episode in which Moses confronted God resolutely, staking all on the special relationship between them, is the notice (34:29ff.) that Moses' face had become uncannily radiant through his intimate converse with God. The golden calf narrative rivals that of the Sinai theophany in its complexity, and for the same reason: charged with intense significance, both were subject to reflections and elaborations that tradition carefully gathered and preserved.

N. BUILDING THE TABERNACLE (EX. 35–40). Having reconciled God to Israel, Moses can proceed to build His dwelling place amid the people. Starting with the last, first, Moses admonishes the people concerning the Sabbath rest, then collects the materials and appoints the craftsmen, who set about building. The order of execution differs from the order of the commands: degree of sanctity determined the order of items in chapters 25ff., common practice determined the order of construction ("The rule is that a man builds his house first and only afterward brings furniture into it," Ber. 55a; cf. Naḥmanides on 25:1). The tent structure is built first, then its contents, finally the accouterments of the court. An itemization of materials used follows. Then the priests' accouterments are made.

The completed work is presented to Moses, who, at the command of God, sets it up on the first day of the first month of the second year after the Exodus. Immediately the Divine Presence fills it, and its exterior sign, the cloud (fire by night), covers the tent. (Previously, the Presence and the cloud and fire had rested on the top of Mt. Sinai 24:16–17.) Thus, even though Israel should depart from Sinai, the presence of God would accompany them. The book ends with an anticipation of Numbers 9:15–23, relating how the Divine Presence, attached to the Tabernacle, guided Israel throughout its desert sojourn. (See Table: Analysis of the Book of Exodus.)

ANALYSIS OF THE BOOK OF EXODUS (after S.R. Driver, *Introduction* (1913[3]), 22–42)

P	1–5 7 13–14 23*b*–25		
J	**1** 6 8–12 20*b* **2** 15–23*a*		
E	15–20*a* 21–22 1–14		
P			
J	**3** 2–4*a* 5 7–8 16–18 **4** 1–16 19–20*a*		
E	1 4*b* 6 9–15 19–22 17–18		
P	2–30		
J	22–26 29–31 **5** 3 5–23 **6** 1		
E	20*b*–21 27–28 1–2 4		
P	1–13 19–20*a* 21*b*–22		
J	**7** 14–15*a* 16.17.18 20c–21*a*		
E	15*b* 17 20*b*		
P	1–3 11*b*–15 8–12		
J	23–29 **8** 4–11a 16–28 **9** 1–7 13–21		
E	22–23*a*		
P			
J	23*b* 24*b* 25*b*–34 **10** 1–11 13*b*		
E	24*a* 25*a* 35 12–13*a* 14*a*		
P			
J	14*b*–15*a* 15*c*–19 24–26 28–29		
E	15*b* 20–23 27		
P	9–10 1–20 28 37*a*		
J	**11** 4–8 **12** } 21–27 29–30		
E	1–3 31–36		
P	40–41 1–2 20		
J	**13** } 3–16 21–22		
E	37*b*–39 42*a* 17–19		
P	1–4 8–9 15–18 21*a*		
J	**14** 5–7 10*a* 11–14 19*b*–20 21*b*		
E	10*b* 19*a*		
P	21*c*–23 26–27*a* 28–29		
J	24–25 27*b* 30–31 **15**		
E	1–18		
P	19 1–3 6–24 31–36		
J	22–27 **16** 4–5 25–30		
E	20–21		
P	1*a* 7		1–2*a*
J	**17** 1*b*–2		**18** **19**
E	3–6 8–16		1–27
P			
J	3*b*–9 11*b*–13		18 20–25
E	2*b*–3*a* 10–11*a* 14–17		19
E	**20–23**	P	
		J	**24** 1–2 9–11
		E	3–8 12–14
P	15–18*a*		
J		P	**25–31** 18*a*
E	18*b*		
P			
J	**31** **32** } 9–14 25–34		
E	18b 1–8 15–24 35		
P	29–35		
J	**33** 1–4 12–23 **34** 1–28		
E	5–11		
P	**35–40**		

Text and Composition

Like the rest of the Pentateuch, Exodus is textually among the best preserved books of the Bible. Very few passages appear corrupt (e.g., 17:16a), and the versions offer little improvement over the received Hebrew (though there are hundreds of variants (see the apparatus in *Biblia Hebraica Stuttgartensia*) some of which have appeared in Exodus-fragments of the Dead Sea Scrolls; see bibl.). Remarkable for its extensiveness and appealing in substance is the Samaritan Hebrew and Septuagint insertion in 22:4, indicated by brackets below:

> "If a man uses his field or vineyard for grazing, and lets his beast loose so that it grazes in another man's field [he shall make restitution out of his own field according to the yield expected; but if it consumed the whole field (שלם ישלם משדהו כתבואתה ואם כל השדה יבעה)] he shall make restitution from the best part of his own field or vineyard."

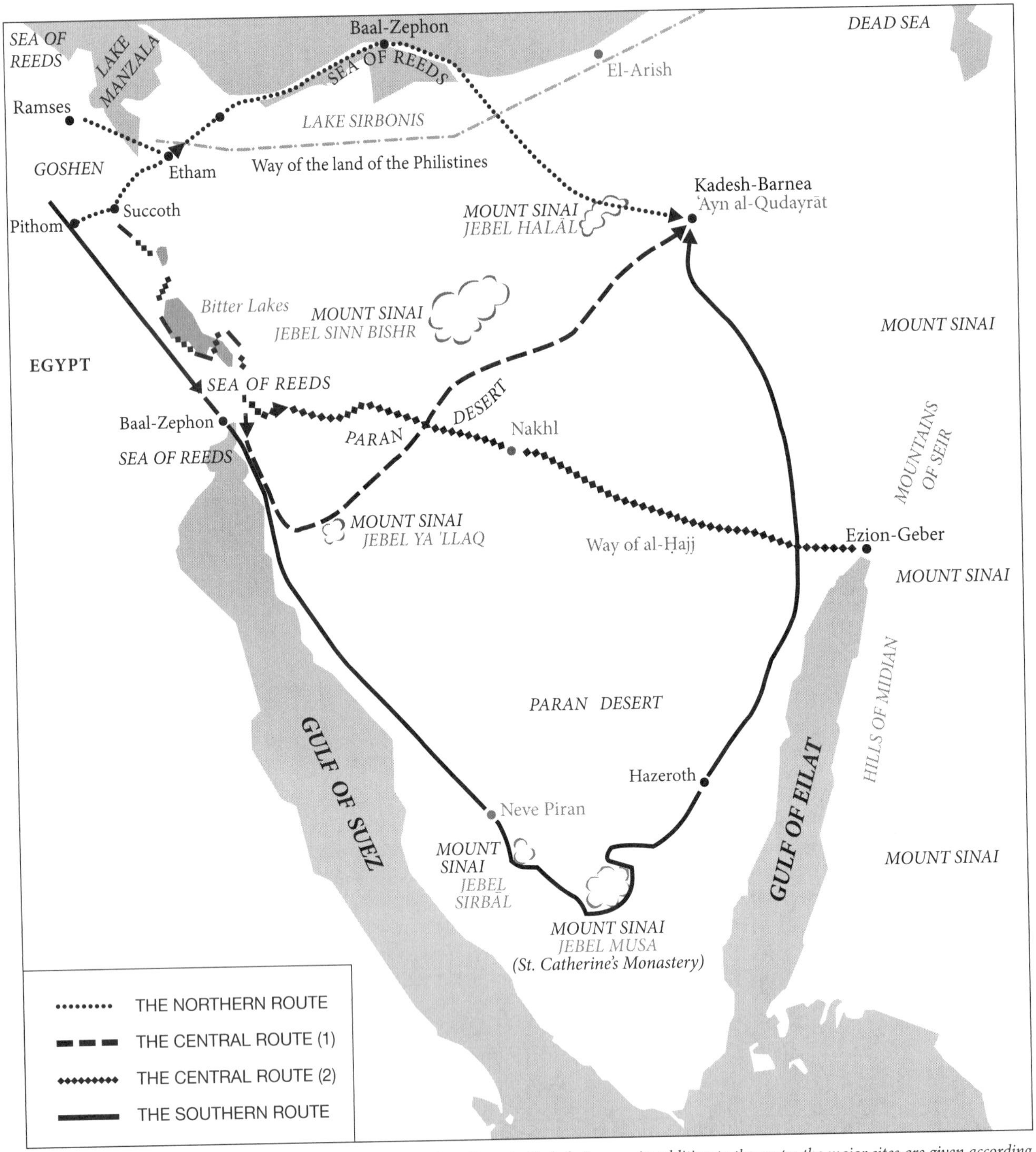

Map 1. Map illustrating major theories on the Israelites' route from Egypt to Kadesh-Barnea; in addition to the routes the major sites are given according to various theories.

This reading obviates the legal difficulty inherent in the plain sense of the received Hebrew that was troublesome to Rava in BK 6b. The Septuagint of the last six chapters (which virtually repeat the orders for building the Tabernacle merely substituting past tenses for future) is abbreviated in places and follows a different order from the received Hebrew. D.W. Gooding has argued, however, that far from throwing a cloud over the antiquity and primacy of the Hebrew, these changes betray the impatience of the translators and the ineptness of later editors. The Greek's incompleteness and absurdity in spots speaks against its priority over the sensible and consistent account of the Hebrew. That the book is composed of heterogeneous materials of varied provenance is a plausible inference from the repetitions, inconsistencies, and incoherence that have been indicated in the survey of its contents given above. The assumption of a few tradition strands that have been woven together or sometimes merely juxtaposed, recognizable by characteristic conceptual and linguistic constants, has proven to give the most satisfactory solution to the question of the book's composition. Conventional criticism reckons with three such strands, styled J, E, and P (Priestly Source), that were combined in stages by editors. There is much controversy over details, some scholars denying the existence of E, others finding it necessary to postulate yet a fourth strand (variously identified and styled J^1, N, or L). More recently, controversy has broken out over the standing of P as an independent document – for details see *Pentateuch and Schwartz in Bibliography. The three conventional strands, however, remain the starting point of critical assessment of the book's composition. They are set forth in the accompanying table according to the analysis of S.R. Driver (1913). It must be borne in mind that such schematic representation cannot do justice to the careful, qualified arguments that underlie the analysis, nor can it indicate where preexistent entities and editorial work are postulated.

Subsequent study has focused on the earlier stages of the tradition, recognizing behind the narrative strands individual tales, or themes, or a ground form of the traditional sequence of events; and behind the law collection, smaller series (e.g., decalogues) of admonitions or categorical statements, or casuistically formulated rules. The ultimate provenance of the material and the manner of its transmission can only be speculated upon. It is reasonable to suppose that the narrative of the liberation from Egypt was utilized in the celebration of the Passover, especially in view of the pedagogic purpose of the celebration (13:8); less secure is the assumption of a covenant festival in which the Sinai law giving and covenant-making were celebrated, or rather dramatized in accord with the "libretto" of chapter 19–20: bereft of any plausible liturgical use is the golden calf episode. As a vehicle of transmission the liturgy may thus have played a considerable, but not exclusive role; as the original well-spring of the traditions, it is wholly inadequate. The theory that the present narrative has a poetic substratum is commended by traces of poetic language, and not infrequent patches of elevated style

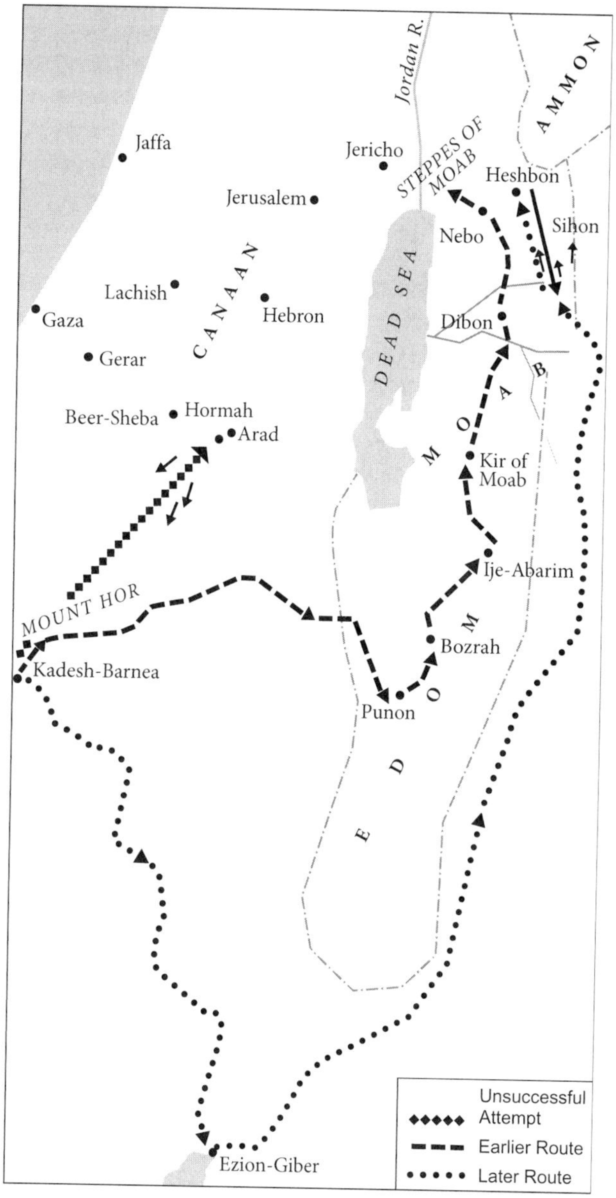

Map 2. Map illustrating earlier and later traditions regarding the route of the Israelites from Kadesh-Barnea to the Moabite Plateau.

in which parallelism and refrain appear (e.g., 3:15b; 9:23–24; 14 (see above, E); 19:3–6). That the narrative is to be comprehended as saga – the enthusiastic relation of events under the impact of their significance – has been persuasively put forward by M. Buber.

Attention is being focused increasingly upon the editorial contribution to the shaping of the traditions. The disposition of the material must have been dictated in the main by the order of events as related in the individual strands. Indications are that all strands shared a common ground form; the variants that appear are, therefore, to be regarded as maximal. Two forms of the covenant document were preserved – "the smaller Book of the Covenant" (the "cultic Decalogue" in 34:10–26) and the other incorporated now in the "Book of the

Covenant" (23:12, 14–33). Two versions of the "accompanying angel" theme were preserved: one in 23:20ff. – non-pejorative, the other in 33:2ff. – pejorative. Widely diverging blocks of material laid claim to having been delivered to Moses on Sinai during his 40-day stay with God; the result is the obscure chronology that frames the "Book of the Covenant" and the block of the Tabernacle plans – the editor(s) being hard put to find a place for all the legitimate claimants. However, alongside the evidence of embarrassment and perplexity stands the grand design of the material and its generally skillful composition as a testimony to the intelligence and spiritual vitality of the editors. Through their labor, at once conservative and creative, the traditions of ancient Israel have reached us in a form richer, more problematic – and therefore more suggestive – than they had ever been in their primary state.

Historical Reflexes

Current scholarly consensus based on archaeology holds the enslavement and exodus traditions to be unhistorical. Indeed, the Book of Exodus itself underlines its unhistoricity by its abundance of miracle tales and by not bothering to name either the Pharaoh of the enslavement or of the exodus. (The popular identification of the oppressor as *Ramses II is based (a) on the mention of the city name *Ramses (2) (Ex. 1:11; 12:37; Num. 33:3, 5) and the "land of Ramses" (Gen. 47:11), but the royal name Ramses itself was borne by 11 pharaohs of the 19th and 20th Egyptian dynasties; (b) on the attestation of a people "Israel" in Asia Minor on the stela of *Merneptah, son of Ramses II.) What may be attempted is the dating of the material of the book, which is bound up with the larger question of the dating of the Pentateuch as a whole. Here, the following indications, taken from the Book of Exodus alone, may be collected:

a) The latter half of the "Song of the Sea," particularly the mention of Philistia, points to a post-settlement date (see E. above).

b) 16:35 is connected with Joshua 5:12 and, like it, has a post-settlement perspective.

c) The laws reflect a non-monarchic, tribal society of villagers living on the soil. Blood revenge and self-help are recognized. Neither the judicial system of the monarchy nor the new categories of crime that arose under it are visible.

d) It has been proposed to see in the Exodus Tabernacle a reflection of the Davidic tent-shrine (II Sam. 6:17), in which the gorgeous cloths and lavish gold overlay would be more credible as well (Cross, in bibl.). Alternatively, the Shiloh sanctuary has been suggested as the ultimate model of the Tabernacle (I Sam. 2:22; Ps. 78:60; cf. esp. II Sam. 7:6 on the pre-Davidic home of YHWH), though the present description shows strong affinities to the plan and furniture of the Solomonic Temple (M. Haran). Most recently, affinities have been sought with the Jewish temple at *Elephantine in Egypt destroyed in the fifth century (Rosenberg in Bibliography).

e) The correspondence between the story of the Golden Calf and that of the two golden calves set up by Jeroboam I in Bethel and Dan (cf. esp. Ex. 32:4b, 8b; I Kings 12:28b) indicates a genetic connection between the two. Since the Jeroboam narrative evidently expresses the view of the Jerusalemite orthodoxy (whose estimate of the calves is not attested in north-Israelite literature before Hosea (8:5f.; 13:2), it may be inferred that the present form of the Golden Calf story reflects their polemic against the calves of the north. It can therefore not be earlier than the division of the monarchy after Solomon's death.

f) Pithom, "house of (the god) Atum," named along with Ramses as one of the two "store cities/garrison cities" built by the Israelites (Ex.. 1:11), does not appear as a city name before the late sixth century B.C.E. As for Ramses, it is now known that the great monuments from this ancient city (Egyptian Piramesse) built at Qantir by the pharaohs of the 18th and 19th dynasties were transported to Tanis and Bubastis centuries later. The addition of these two names to Exodus 1:11 is an attempt by Egyptian Jews in the sixth century or later to relate the enslavement traditions to their own environment (Redford, Wente in Bibliography).

g) In Exodus 28:42 priests are required to wear breeches in order to protect against inadvertent self-exposure at the altar. Breeches or trousers are a Persian invention. The earlier pre-Exilic law (Ex. 20:23) required the more difficult elimination of stepped altars to achieve the same goal of modesty (Sperling in Bibliography).

The lower limits of the historical allusions and the inferable backgrounds of the material in Exodus thus range from post-settlement times to the earlier Persian period (sixth to fifth centuries).

Main Themes

The Book of Exodus contains the final form of Israelite traditions concerning the birth of the nation and the founding of its main institutions (excepting the monarchy).

a. The birth of the nation was a revelation of God's trustworthiness, compassion, and power that was to serve for all time as a ground for hope in Him in time of trouble (Isa. 11:15–16; Micah 7:15; Ps. 77:16ff.). In the burning bush narrative, God's compassion is the sole motive of His rescue of Israel: He heard their cry and took note of their misery. What is peculiar in this instance of rescue is not its motive (cf. the Sodom and Gomorrah story) but its result – the bringing of a people to its promised land. Thus the trustworthiness of God is manifest. In the second commissioning narrative (Ex. 6), God's mindfulness of His promise to the Patriarchs is on a par with His compassion as a motive of His action. His redemption of Israel from Egypt thus attests to His faithfulness. Again, the circumstances of the redemption – God's "taking one nation from the midst of another by prodigious acts" (Deut. 4:34) – show the measureless power at His disposal. Egypt's Pharaoh is the paradigm of heathen might and arrogance. However, the plagues and the drowning of his army in the sea demonstrate the nullity of all earthly power in the face of God (cf. Isa. 31).

The episodes in the wilderness further delineate God's nature: He is revealed as the reliable provider of all His people's vital needs (cf. Deut. 8:3ff.).

b. These deeds establish God's capacity to be the protector of Israel, His right to possess Israel as His redeemed property, and His claim on their obedience and loyalty (cf. the association of ideas in Deut. 6:20–25, and Ibn Ezra thereon). They are the basis of His proposing His covenant to Israel at Sinai.

The Sinai covenant differs essentially from that made with the Patriarchs. The latter is an unconditional promise, the grant of a sovereign to his loyal servants (M. Weinfeld); the former is a sovereign's rule for his subjects, similar in form and spirit to ancient vassal treaties. At Sinai, obligations were laid upon the people, the express will of their lord, the fulfillment of which was the condition of their happiness.

The terms of the covenant – in every form in which they have been transmitted – are couched as an address by God to the people. Their publicity is essential. Since Israel is to be a holy order (19:6), the entire nation must know its sacred regimen. This distinguishes the convenant rules from the laws of other ancient civilizations; they are not ensurers of domestic tranquillity through justice and defense of the weak (e.g., Hammurapi's laws; Pritchard, Texts, 178; COS II, 336) – no system of law so conceived was made the vehicle of public education – but a discipline whereby holiness and righteousness before God are achieved (cf. Ex. 22:30).

c. The people's response to God is a major concern of the book. They have no militant role in their own liberation, but must merely carry out various instructions. At the sea, when they panic, they are commanded to "stand fast and see the salvation of YHWH"; and when it comes "they had faith in YHWH and in Moses His servant" (14:31). This is clearly a spiritual peak.

On the way to Sinai, they repeatedly fall to complaining about their wants, unable to rise above their cares to a quiet trust in God. He supplies their need time and again, giving them every reason to have faith in Him, yet they cannot learn to be trustful. The terror He inspires in them at Sinai is not enough to keep them from recourse to an idol when they despair. Experience of His deliverances fails to instill in them permanently the faith that "nothing is too wonderful for YHWH" (cf. Ps. 78).

d. Exodus depicts the founding of all the main institutions of Israel excepting the monarchy: the human agency through which God acts on and speaks to humanity – the archetype of the prophet; the priest and the consecrated tribe of defenders of the faith, the Levites; the sanctuary – God's dwelling place amid His people, where He is accessible to them for worship and oracle, and by which He guides them along the way; forms of worship – daily sacrifice and annual memorial festivals; and, above all, the covenant, through which God and people are bound to each other: "I will take you to be My people, and I will be your God" – a veritable marriage formula.

These themes remained at the heart of biblical thought. The complex structure of the Book of Exodus, the effect of ages of reflection and elaboration on each of them, bespeaks their continuous vitality throughout the biblical period.

BIBLIOGRAPHY: COMMENTARIES: A. Knobel and A. Dillmann, *Kurzgefasstes exegetisches Handbuch zum Alten Testament* (1880); A.H. Mc-Neile, *Westminster Commentaries* (1908); S.R. Driver, *Cambridge Bible* (1911); A. Kahana, *Torah, Nevi'im u-Khetuvim*..., 2 (1913); G. Beer and K. Galling, *Handbuch zum Alten Testament*, Reihe I, 3 (1939); M.D. Cassuto, *A Commentary on the Book of Exodus* (1968); M. Noth, *The Book of Exodus* (1962); M. Greenberg, *Understanding Exodus*, 1 (1969); J.C. Rylaarsdam, in: *The Interpreter's Bible*, 1 (1952); S. Goldman, *From Slavery to Freedom* (1958). GENERAL STUDIES: W. Rudolph, *Der "Elohist" von Exodus bis Josua* (1938); M. Noth, Ueberlief (1948); G. von Rad, *The Problem of the Hexateuch and Other Essays* (1966); F.V. Winnet, *The Mosaic Tradition* (1949). MOSES: H. Gressmann, *Mose und seine Zeit* (1913); M. Buber, *Moses* (1946); P. Déman et al. in: *Cahiers Sioniens*, 8 (1954); E. Osswald, *Das Bild des Mose* (1962); S. Loewenstamm, in: EM, 5 (1968), 482–95. CHAPTERS 1–18: W. Helck, in: VT, 15 (1965), 35ff.; B.S. Childs, in: JBL, 84 (1965), 109ff.; B. Jacob, in: *Essays... J.H. Hertz* (1944), 245ff.; M.D. Cassuto, in: *Eretz Israel*, 1 (1953), 85ff.; S. Mowinckel, in: HUCA, 32 (1961), 121ff.; H. Kosmala, in: VT, 12 (1962), 14ff.; M. Greenberg, in: *Papers of the Fourth World Congress of Jewish Studies*, 1 (1967), 151ff.; J. Pedersen, *Israel, Its Life and Culture*, 3–4 (1940), 728ff.; F.M. Cross, *Studies in Ancient Yahwistic Poetry* (1950), 83ff.; M.D. Cassuto, in: *Keneset le-Zekher Ḥ.N. Bialik*, 8 (1944), 121ff.; J. Muilenburg, in: *Studia Biblica et Semitica* (in honor of Th. C. Vriezen; 1966), 233ff. LITERARY CRITICISM: G. Fohrer, *Ueberlieferung und Geschichte des Exodus* (1964); S. Loewenstamm, *Masoret Yeẓi'at Miẓrayim* (1965). CHAPTERS 19–24: W. Beyerlin, *Origins and History of the Oldest Sinaitic Traditions* (1965); H.H. Rowley, *Men of God* (1963), 1–36; A. Alt, *Essays on Old Testament History and Religion* (1966), 79ff.; M. Noth, *The Laws in the Pentateuch and Other Studies* (1966), 1ff.; H. Cazelles, *Etudes sur le Code de l'Alliance* (1946); G. Mendenhall, in: BA, 17 (1954), 26ff., 49ff.; M. David, in: *Oudtestamentische Studiën*, 7 (1950), 149ff.; D.J. McCarthy, *Treaty and Covenant* (1963); M. Greenberg, in: IDB, 1 (1962), 733ff.; M. Weinfeld, in: JAOS, 90 (1970), 184ff. THE TABERNACLE, ETC.: F.M. Cross, Jr., in: BA, 10 (1947), 45ff.; H. Haran, in: JSS, 5 (1960), 50ff.; idem, in: *Scripta Hierosolymitana*, 7 (1961), 272ff.; idem, in: JBL, 81 (1962), 14ff.; idem, in: HUCA, 36 (1965), 191ff.; S. Loewenstamm, in: EM, 5 (1968), 532–48. TEXTUAL CRITICISM AND DEAD SEA SCROLL FRAGMENTS: D.W. Gooding, *The Account of the Tabernacle* (1959); P.W. Skehan, in: JBL, 74 (1955), 182ff.; F.M. Cross, Jr., *The Ancient Library of Qumran* (1961), 184ff.; M. Baillet et al., *Discoveries in the Judean Desert*, 3 (1962), 49ff., 142. **ADD. BIBLIOGRAPHY:** J. Sanderson, *An Exodus Scroll from Qumran* (1986); J. Durham, *Exodus* (Word; 1987); N. Sarna, *Exodus* (JPS; 1991); idem, in: ABD II, 689–700, with bibl.; K. Kitchen, ibid., 700–8; A. Wente, in: ABD V, 617–18; Y. Hoffman, *The Doctrine of the Exodus in the Bible* (1983); E. Blum, *Studien zur Komposition des Pentateuch* (1990); D. Redford, in: VT, 13 (1963), 401–13; idem, *Egypt, Canaan and Israel in Ancient Times* (1992), 451; A. Cooper and B. Goldstein, in: MAARAV, 8 (1992), 15–37; J. van Seters, *The Life of Moses* ... (1994); M. Vervenne, in: K. van Lerberghe and A. Schoors (eds.), *Immigration and Emigration within the Ancient Near East* (1995), 403–29; C. Meyers, in: M. Fox et al (eds.), *Texts, Temples ... FS Haran* (1996), 33–46; G. Davies, *ibid.*, 71–85; B. Schwartz, *ibid.*, 103–34; C. Houtman, *Exodus* (HCOT, 4 vols. (1993–2002); E. Frerichs and L. Lesko (eds.), *Exodus: The Egyptian Evidence* (1997); W. Propp, *Exodus 1–18* (AB; 1998); S.D. Sperling, in: R. Chazan et al., *Ki Baruch Hu* (Studies Levine; 1999), 373–85; S. Rosenberg, in: NEA, 67 (2004), 4–13.

[Moshe Greenberg / S. David Sperling (2nd ed.)]

EXODUS RABBAH (Heb. שְׁמוֹת רַבָּה, *Shemot Rabbah*), aggadic Midrash on the Book of Exodus (for the designation "*Rabbah*," see **Ruth Rabbah*).

The Structure

Exodus Rabbah, which is divided into 52 sections, consists of two different Midrashim (see *Esther Rabbah*; and *Numbers Rabbah*): *Exodus Rabbah I* (sections 1–14) and *Exodus Rabbah II* (sections 15–52).

Exodus Rabbah I

An exegetical Midrash to Exodus 1–10, *Exodus Rabbah I* interprets successively, each chapter, verse, and, at times, each word. The division into sections generally follows the early Ereẓ Israel triennial cycle (see *Torah, Reading of the). Each section begins with one or more proems (**Derashah*; **Midrash*), of which there are more than 20 in *Exodus Rabbah*. Except for one which opens with the name of an *amora* and a verse from Isaiah, all the proems are anonymous and begin with a verse from the Hagiographa (mainly from Psalms, Proverbs, and Job). The structure of some proems is defective, particularly in their ending and in their connection with the beginning of the section. The sections have no epilogues. *Exodus Rabbah I* is written for the most part in Hebrew, in part mishnaic, and in part Hebrew of the early Middle Ages. *Aramaic (also Babylonian Aramaic) is only sparingly used and there is a sprinkling of Greek and Latin words. In style and content *Exodus Rabbah I* often resembles later medieval Midrashim and *aggadot*, such as *Sefer ha-Yashar*. The redactor of *Exodus Rabbah* drew upon tannaitic literature, the Jerusalem Talmud, **Genesis Rabbah*, **Leviticus Rabbah*, **Lamentations Rabbah*, and other early aggadic Midrashim of the amoraic period, and he made extensive use of the Babylonian Talmud and of Midrashim of the **Yelammedenu-Tanḥuma* type. Such Midrashim were the chief source of the work, and many of its homilies occur in the various editions of the *Tanḥuma*, mostly in the printed one. The redactor of *Exodus Rabbah* broke the lengthy expositions of the *Yelammedenu-Tanḥuma* type, which included halakhic material as well, linking the shorter units to appropriate biblical verses, at the same time incorporating additional material from numerous other sources. In using legends of the Babylonian Talmud, the redactor tried, often not very successfully, to change their language from Babylonian to Galilean Aramaic. His intention apparently was to compile a Midrash, in continuation of *Genesis Rabbah*, on the Book of Exodus up to the point where the **Mekhilta* begins. The redaction of *Exodus Rabbah I* took place, it seems, not earlier than the tenth century C.E.

Exodus Rabbah II

Exodus 12–40 is a homiletical *Midrash of the *Yelammedenu-Tanḥuma* type. The division into sections is based on the triennial cycle. Introduced by proems characteristic of the *Yelammedenu-Tanḥuma* Midrashim, some of which are quoted in the name of R. *Tanḥuma, the sections frequently conclude with epilogues referring to redemption and the promise of a happier future. *Exodus Rabbah II*, which contains some Greek and Latin words, is mainly in mishnaic Hebrew, with an admixture of Galilean Aramaic – the original language from which some of the *aggadot*, taken from an earlier Midrash, were translated into Hebrew. *Exodus Rabbah II* makes use of tannaitic literature, the Jerusalem Talmud, and early amoraic Midrashim, but not entire themes from the Babylonian Talmud. Many of its homilies also occur in the known editions of the *Tanḥuma*. It contains several halakhic expositions, numerous parables, and some *aggadot* of a comparatively late type. For the most part, however, it exhibits features which place it earlier than *Exodus Rabbah I*, and it was apparently compiled in the ninth century C.E. It is probably the second part of a Midrash, the first part of which, no longer extant, served as the main source of *Exodus Rabbah I*. *Exodus Rabbah I* and *II* were apparently combined by a copyist in the 11th or 12th century C.E. The first scholar known to have been acquainted with the entire work in its present form was *Naḥmanides, who quotes it in his commentary on the Pentateuch.

Editions

Exodus Rabbah was first printed in Constantinople, together with the four other Midrashim on the Pentateuch (see **Genesis Rabbah*) in 1512. This edition, on which all subsequent ones are based, contains many mistakes and often gives only abbreviated texts of other Midrashim where a parallel homily occurs in full. Several manuscripts of the work are extant but have not yet been fully investigated. Until a scholarly edition is published, no thorough study of *Exodus Rabbah* is possible.

BIBLIOGRAPHY: Zunz-Albeck, Derashot, 124f.; Lehrman, in: *Soncino Midrash* (1939), Eng.; J. Mann, *The Bible as Read and Preached in the Old Synagogue*, 1 (1940); S. Lieberman, *Midrash Devarim Rabbah* (1964^2), xxii. **ADD. BIBLIOGRAPHY:** Shinan, Midrash Shemot Rabbah, Chapters I–XIV (1984); M. Bregman, *The Tanḥuma-Yelammedenu Literature* (2003).

[Moshe David Herr]

EXPULSIONS, The Jews underwent expulsions during the time of the Assyrian and Babylonian kingdoms (see Assyrian *Exile; Babylonian *Exile). Pagan *Rome also adopted on rare occasions a policy of removing the Jews from the capital, considering them an undesirable element: there is some vague information on the expulsion of the Jews from Rome in 139 B.C.E. among the other "Chaldeans." In 19 C.E. Tiberius ordered the expulsion of all the Jews in Italy if they would not abandon their faith. In 50 C.E. Claudius expelled them from Rome. From the end of the Bar Kokhba Revolt (135 C.E.) until the capture of Jerusalem by the Muslims (638), the Jews were prohibited from entering that city and its boundaries. The policy of expelling Jews was however only adopted by victorious Christianity from the fourth century C.E., in implementation of its objectives to separate the Jews from the rest of society, and degrade and oppress them so that they would convert to Christianity. Individual expulsions from Islamic countries, such as the expulsion from *Tlemcen (N. Africa), are also recorded during the tenth century (see J. Miller (ed.), *Teshu-*

vot Ge'onei Mizrahò u-Ma'arav (1888), 31a, no. 133). The phenomenon of expulsions is, however, overwhelmingly found in Christian lands. Some of these were "general expulsions" which removed the Jews from the territory of a whole country for an extended period. The expulsion from *England in 1290 (the number of expelled has been estimated at 16,000) removed the Jews from its borders until after 1650. The expulsions from *France, especially those of 1306 and 1394, evicted the Jews from most of the territory within the borders of France until 1789. The expulsions from *Spain and *Portugal, 1492–97 (where the number of victims has been assessed by historians from 100,000 to several hundreds of thousands), removed the Jews from the Iberian peninsula almost until the present day and brought about a series of expulsions of Jews from lands within the sphere of influence of these countries. At the time of the *Black Death (1348–50), the Jews were expelled from many places in Europe, but in most localities, especially in *Germany, they were readmitted after a short while. The presence of Jews was rigorously prohibited in *Russia from the 15th century until 1772, when masses of Jews accrued to Russia from the annexed Polish-Lithuanian territories. Even after this date, there was an attempt to maintain this prohibition in the form of the *Pale of Settlement until 1917. Within the framework of its enforcement numerous expulsions of both groups of Jews and entire communities from towns and villages which were "out of bounds" (such as the expulsion from *Moscow in 1891) were carried out. There were also expulsions of short duration from the boundaries of entire countries, such as the expulsion from *Lithuania in 1495. Expulsions from specific regions and towns were frequent and regular occurrences in Germany and northern *Italy during the 14th to 16th centuries, but in certain cases they were also ordered down to the 18th century (the expulsion from *Prague, 1744–52). The political fragmentation of these countries during the Middle Ages usually enabled the Jews to settle within the proximity of the baronage or town from which they had been expelled and to return there after a short interval. During World War I, the Russian authorities evacuated about 600,000 Jews from Poland, Lithuania, and the Baltic countries to the interior of Russia, an act regarded as an expulsion.

While the motives for the expulsions fall into differing and variegated categories, the root of them all was hatred of the Jew. This hatred was at times exploited by fiscal considerations of the rulers responsible for the expulsions.

Socio-economic factors contributed to the hostility of the Christian merchants and craftsmen toward their Jewish rivals, the hatred of Christian debtors for the Jewish moneylenders, and, on the other hand, the occasional feeling that there was no need for the Jews as moneylenders for interest and that they did not fulfill any other economic-social function. Tendencies and sentiments of national and political consolidation also played their part. In Spain, the desire to isolate the *New Christians from Jewish influence was also a factor in the expulsion. In an epoch when the menace of death hovered continually over the Jews, especially in places where they had grown accustomed to expulsion and rapid readmission, expulsion was considered the lightest of possible evils. *Judah Loew b. Bezalel (the Maharal of Prague) thought that the era of exile in which he lived was more tolerable because its principal sufferings consisted of expulsions, which he described as the divorce of a woman by her husband. The Jews of *Frankfurt, when they were actually expelled, also felt that "we went in joy and in sorrow; because of the destruction and the disgrace, we grieved for our community and we rejoiced that we had escaped with so many survivors" (poem by R. Elhanan b. Abraham Helin, at end of pt. 3 of *Ẓemaḥ David*, 1692). The general expulsions were however considered disasters, and the expulsion from Spain in particular became a fearful memory for the nation. The expulsions always resulted in losses to property and damage to body and spirit. In addition to the losses caused by forced sales – when the buyer realized that the Jew was compelled to abandon all his real property, and at times many of his movable goods – insecurity and vagrancy left their imprint on the social and economic life of the Jews, especially in the German and Italian states. Highway robberies and losses suffered during the enforced travels also increased the damage to property. Much information is available on attacks and murders committed against expelled Jews who left their country and the protection of the authorities. Even in those expulsions where instructions were given to protect the departing Jews, such as the expulsions from England and Spain, there were numerous attacks. The wanderings were the cause of many diseases and also reduced the natural increase. A shocking description of the sufferings of the exiles from Spain and Portugal is given in the writings of the kabbalist Judah b. Jacob *Ḥayyat. He relates of himself and his companions after they had reached the safety of Muslim Tunis: "We ate the grass of the fields, and every day I ground with my own hands in the house of the Ishmaelites for the thinnest slice of bread not even fit for a dog. During the nights, my stomach was close to the ground – and my belly my cushion. Because of the great cold of the autumn – we had no garments in the frost and no houses to lodge in – we dug trenches in the refuse heaps of the town and put our bodies therein" (introduction to *Minḥat Yehudah* (Mantua, 1558), 3a).

The expulsions left their impress on the entire nation and its history, both materially and spiritually. They maintained and constantly intensified the feeling of foreignness of the Jews in the Diaspora. The consecutive expulsions from England, France, and Spain resulted in a situation where after 1492 there were no Jews living openly on the European coast of the Atlantic Ocean in a period when this had become the center of world traffic. The expulsions of the late 15th century resulted in the return of many Jews to the Islamic countries, in particular to the Ottoman Empire. The Jews were also driven into *Poland-Lithuania. Frequently, the expulsions caused the centers of gravity of Jewish life to be removed from one place to another, the creation of new centers of settlement, messianic movements, and a renewed relationship with Ereẓ Israel; it was no coincidence that the kabbalists of *Safed were Spanish exiles. The expulsions also caused the Jews of Spain to come into contact with those of Italy, the Balkans, Asia Minor, North Africa, and many Middle Eastern countries, where they influenced and fashioned the social-spiritual character of many communities in these regions. The expulsions may be considered one of the decisive factors shaping the map of Jewish settlement and one of the forces which molded the thinking of Jews both in relation to themselves and to the world of nations and states which surrounded them.

For expulsion by the Nazis, see *Holocaust.

BIBLIOGRAPHY: S.P. Rabinowitz, *Moza'ei Golah* (1894); B.L. Abrahams, in: JQR, 7 (1894/95), 75–100, 236–58, 428–58; A. Marx, *ibid.*, 20 (1907/08), 240–71; R. Straus, *Die Judengemeinde Regensburg im ausgehenden Mittelalter* (1932); idem (ed.), *Urkunden und Aktenstuecke zur Geschichte der Juden in Regensburg* (1960); E.M. Kulisher, *Europe on the Move* (1948), index, s.v. *Jews;* I. Sonne, *Mi-Paulo ha-Revi'i ad Pi'us ha-Ḥamishi* (1954); Baer, Spain, index; JSOS, index.

[Haim Hillel Ben-Sasson]

EXTRADITION.

Biblical Sources

EXTRADITION OF SLAVES. The Torah relates directly to the issue of extradition in the context of a slave who flees from his slavery, prohibiting a person from returning to his master an escaped slave who is now in his custody: "Do not deliver to his master a slave who has escaped from his master. He shall dwell in your midst with you, in the place he shall choose in one of your gates, where it is good for him; you shall not oppress him" (Deut 23:16–17). Some Biblical commentators have interpreted this passage on the basis of the context in which it appears, viz. as referring to a slave who during battle escapes from the enemy camp to the Israelite camp, the reason for the prohibition on his extradition being that it is better for the slave to remain in the Israelite camp than to return to worshipping idolatry. An additional reason proposed is a practical one, deriving from the aforesaid battle context – namely, the danger that the slave will "learn the way into the city," so that to return him to his master would constitute a danger to the security of the city (Naḥmanides. *ad loc.*; Ibn Ezra, *ad loc.*). A case in which the question of extraditing a slave at a time of battle arose in I Samuel 30:11–16: David and his men, in pursuit of the Amalekites, found an Egyptian slave who had been forsaken by his Amalekite masters. The slave agreed to show David and his men the location of the Amalekite troop, in return for David's promise that he would not return him to his masters.

According to the Talmud, the prohibition against extradition applies to a Canaanite slave who has fled from Jewish masters outside the Land of Israel into the Land of Israel (Bavli, Gittin 45a; Maim., Yad, Avadim 8.10). Rabbi Judah the Prince is of the opinion that the prohibition applies to a person who purchases a slave on condition that he emancipate him, and later regrets his act and seeks the slave for himself.

EXTRADITION OF AN ESCAPED CRIMINAL. The Torah rejects the possibility that an escaped criminal may acquire refuge from punishment by entering sacred grounds: "If a person shall maliciously kill another with guile, he shall be taken to die (even) from my altar" (Exod 21:14). In this manner, the Torah abrogated the rule, widespread at that time and even later (I Kings 2: 29–32), that entry upon sacred ground can spare a murderer from his just punishment. Biblical commentators emphasized that this law is intended to serve as a contrast to the law of one who committed inadvertent manslaughter, who is given a special place to live and guaranteed protection from persecution by the blood avenger (see *City of Refuge). A murderer with malice aforethought has nowhere to seek refuge, not even the altar. Maimonides (*Guide* 3.39) emphasizes the difference between the Torah's command against delivering an escaped slave, regarding whom we are commanded to have mercy and to grant protection and care for all his needs, and a malicious person, whom we are commanded not to pity and not to protect, and who must be turned over to the officer of justice even if he grasps hold of the altar.

INSTANCES OF EXTRADITION IN THE TORAH. The Book of Judges (15:9–13) relates that, after Samson smote the Philistines, the Philistines retaliated against Israel, in order to capture Samson and to take revenge for his deeds. The men of Judah went to Samson and told him that they had come to take him so as to extradite him to the Philistines. Samson asked the men of Judah to swear to him that they themselves would not harm him but would only extradite him to the Philistines. They duly did so, binding Samson with ropes; however, as soon as he was delivered to the Philistines he flung off the ropes with which he had been bound and once again struck down a thousand Philistines. Some halakhic authorities classified Samson's extradition as performed under duress, for had the men of Judah not given Samson to the Philistines, the Philistines would have killed them (*Or Sameah* on Maim., Yad, Yesodei ha-Torah 5.5). From the commentary of Radak (II Samuel 20:22), it follows that extradition was only possible due to Samson's consent, but that they would not have been entitled to extradite him against his will.

Following the incident involving the concubine at Gibeah (Judges 19–21), during which people from the town of Gibeah in the territory of Benjamin perpetrated an act of rape and murder, the other tribes of Israel gathered together and demanded that the clans of Benjamin turn over the perpetrators of the atrocity, in order to "eliminate the evil from Israel" (*ibid.* 20:12–14). The Benjaminites refused to extradite the men and went to war against the other tribes of Israel. Nahmanides, in his Torah Commentary (Gen. 19:8) states that the Benjaminites were not obligated to deliver the sinners from Gibeah into the hands of the other tribes of Israel, because the responsibility to take action lay exclusively in the hands of the tribal court of Benjamin, each tribe having jurisdiction over its own members.

Another incident relating to extradition appears in I Samuel 23:10–12, when David, fleeing from Saul, together with his followers, came to the aid of the townsfolk of Keilah, saving them from the Philistines. After David had smitten the Philistines at Keilah, Saul heard that David was situated there, and went with his army in order to capture him. David inquired of God, through the ephod (sacred oracle) held by the Abiathar the priest, as to whether the heads of Keilah would deliver him into the hands of Saul. God responded that they would extradite him, whereupon David left the city. The text implies that, in this case as well, the delivery of David into the hands of Saul by the people of Keilah, had it occurred, would have been one of extradition under duress, as had they not turned David over to Saul, Saul would have destroyed the town.

Talmudic Period

Following the era of the Talmud and thereafter, in periods during which Jewish communities found themselves under the suzerainty of a heathen ruler, whether in Israel or in the various Diaspora communities, the issue of extradition was considered from various angles: the criminal justice aspect of the offender's acts; the relationship between Israel and the other nations of the world; the relationship between the Jewish legal system and the non-Jewish legal system; and the relationship of the Jewish community towards its own members who had deviated from the right path. Jewish legal autonomy, while containing a not-insignificant measure of juridical competence even in the field of criminal law, was nevertheless restricted with respect to the majority of cases concerning serious offenses and offenses of interest to the authorities, in which areas the authorities retained the right of adjudication and the right to punish. We will now deal with the main problems and questions discussed in the talmudic literature in this regard.

THE SEIZURE AND EXTRADITION OF JEWISH THIEVES AND ROBBERS. During the talmudic period, the Sages encountered cases in which they were requested by the Roman administration to hand over Jewish criminals. We find differing opinions among the Sages regarding the question as to whether such extradition is prohibited or permitted, or possibly even desirable. The Talmud relates how R. Eleazar b. Simeon seized thieves and robbers on behalf of the Roman administration, and the dispute that arose in this regard with R. Joshua b. Korha. R. Joshua b. Korha reacted to R. Eleazar b. Simeon's acts with the words: "Vinegar son of wine: how long will you continue to deliver the people of God to death?" R. Eleazar b. Simeon answered by way of a parable: "I am eliminating thorns from the vineyard" to which R. Joshua b. Korha retorted: "Let the owner of the vineyard [i.e., God] come and eliminate his thorns" (TB, BM 83b). A further discussion of the same issue appears in the sequel to this talmudic passage, which records that R. Ishmael b. Yose would also apprehend offenders at the bidding of the authorities. These controversies reflect the aversion to turning over a Jew to the Roman government, which was suspected of not conducting fair trials, hostility to Jews, and persecution of their persons and property.

SAVING JEWS SUSPECTED OF SERIOUS CRIMES. An additional incident discussed by the Talmud and its commentaries (Bavli, Niddah 61a) reflects the divergent approaches to the issue of granting asylum to a murderer. In this case, certain persons who were suspected of murder approached R. Tarfon with the request that he hide them from the authorities. R. Tarfon's response was that he could not hide them, for the Sages had stated that one should take heed of an evil rumor, viz. that they were in fact murderers. Talmudic commentators are divided as to the reason for R. Tarfon's refusal to hide them. According to Rashi (*ad loc.*), R. Tarfon suspected there might be truth to the rumor that they had murdered, in which case it would be forbidden to save them. According to R. Aḥa Gaon (*She'iltot de-Rav Aḥa* §129; Tosafot, *ad loc.*), R. Tarfon's suspicion did not emanate from the fact that he was forbidden to save them, but rather from the danger to which he would be exposed were he to save them. R. Asher b. Jehiel (Rosh, on *Niddah* 9.5) adopts the *She'iltot's* explanation and rejects that of Rashi, because, according to his view, it cannot be forbidden to save a person's life merely because of a rumor that he has sinned. From Asheri's words, it follows that, when it is clear that the person has indeed committed a crime, it would be forbidden to save him even according to Rashi's disputants. R. Solomon Luria (*Yam shel Shelomo* on TB Nid. 61a) states unequivocally that a distinction must be made between the case of one who has *definitely* murdered, whom it is forbidden to save and who must be handed over to the authorities to judge, and the case of a rumor, which gives rise to a mere *suspicion*, in which case the individual, who is presumed innocent until proven guilty, must be saved, provided there is no danger to the savior in doing so.

Post-Talmudic Period

Over the centuries during which Jews were in various Diasporas and subject to the whims of foreign rulers, many and varied questions arose concerning the interrelationship between the Jewish community and the Jewish legal system and between the authorities and the local legal system. Within this reality, and in view of the need to grapple with the phenomenon of criminality that existed within the Jewish community, the question often arose as to the need to hand over Jewish criminal offenders to the authorities. In post-ralmudic and responsa literature, various aspects of this topic are considered.

DELIVERING A CRIMINAL WHO ENDANGERS THE COMMUNITY. When a given individual's criminal conduct constituted a danger to the entire Jewish community, such as when the non-Jewish authorities are liable to harm the entire Jewish community on account of the acts of an individual offender, or when only the non-Jewish authorities have the power to prevent the offender continuing in his socially unacceptable conduct, he may be extradited to the non-Jewish authorities. Thus, already in the 13th century it was ruled that the non-Jewish authorities could be informed, and extradition was permissible, in the case of a violent man who regularly assaulted others, or a person whose criminal acts encouraged gentiles to contrive plots against the Jewish community, in order to remove the danger from the entire Jewish community (*Maharah Or Zaru'a*, #142). The Shulḥan Arukh rules (ḤM 388) that a Jew who harasses the community, and not merely one individual, could be delivered into the hands of the non-Jews in order "to beat, imprison or fine him." R. Moshe Isserles adds, in his glosses to the Shulḥan Arukh (*ad loc.*) that even a Jew who is engaged in forgery – if there is a danger that the Jewish community will be harmed by his activities, and he fails to take heed of the warnings made to him – may be delivered to the authorities, in order to demonstrate that only he, the offender, engages in forgery, and no other member of the community does so. Elsewhere, Isserles writes that the permission to deliver such offenders to the non-Jewish authorities is based upon the principle of "*rodef*" – i.e., that any Jew is permitted, if necessary, to kill a person who is pursuing his fellow with the aim of killing him, in order to save the life of the pursued: "One who endangers the community, e.g., if he engages in forgery in a locality where the authorities forbid it, has the status of a *rodef* and it is permitted to deliver him to the authorities" (*Rema*, ḤM 425.1). R. David Halevi, in his commentary *Turei Zahav* on the Shulḥan Arukh (ḤM 157.8) similarly rules that anyone who transgresses and rebels against the local law in a manner that endangers the Jewish community may be turned into the authorities, even if the authorities do not demand that he be handed over.

WHEN THE COMMUNITY IS THREATENED IF THE WANTED PERSON IIS NOT DELIVERED. The Tosefta (*Terumot* 7.20) deals with a case in which non-Jews demanded that a group of Jews hand over one of their number to be killed, or else they would all be killed. The Tosefta rules that it is forbidden to deliver a single Jewish soul; rather, they should all be killed. However, if a specific person was designated to be handed over, they should deliver that individual rather than allow all of them to be killed. The Jerusalem Talmud records an amoraic controversy as to whether such a person can only be delivered if he is in fact deserving of death, as was Sheba son of Bichri who rebelled against King David's rule (2 Samuel 20). In other words the story of Sheba is seen as the source of the ruling by the Tosefta. The alternative view is that he should be handed over request, even if he is not liable to the death penalty. It is noteworthy that the case of the Tosefta does not discuss the issue of extradition – i.e. deliverance of a suspected criminal for the purpose of trying him – but only (translating it into the contemporary context) the case of a terrorist group which threatens to kill many people unless an individual is handed over to them. Nonetheless, the halakhic authorities relied on it in cases where the non-Jewish authorities required the handing over of a specific individual and threatened the lives of other Jews in the event that he was not delivered. Maimonides (Yad, Yesodei ha-Torah 5.5) ruled that, if the wanted person is deserving of death, he may be handed over in order to prevent the killing of the remainder of the group; however, "we avoid ruling this way where possible." In a case brought before R. Joel Sirkis (*Responsa Ba"ḥ ha-Yeshanot* §43), the leaders of the Jewish community were asked to deliver to the Christian authorities for trial a Jew who, according to the authorities, had collaborated in the desecration of Christian religious artifacts. The authorities demanded his extradition, stipulating that, if he was not extradited, the community leaders would have to take his place for any punishment that was decreed. Sirkis ruled that the words of Maimonides – that a person who is liable for the death penalty may be extradited – apply even where the non-Jewish authorities have grounds to kill him under their laws, even if he is not deserving of death according to Jewish law. In such a case, it was not certain that handing over the Jew would result in his death, because the authorities intended to conduct a trial, and the possibility existed that he would be proven innocent. Hence, R. Sirkis ruled that his delivery to the non-Jewish authorities was permitted even *de jure*, in contrast to Maimonides' ruling that we avoid ruling that way where possible. Furthermore, in this case too permission to deliver the accused was given only because there was prima facie evidence of his guilt, and that the grounds for which the non-Jews sought to judge him were thereby substantiated; hence, the accused himself was considered responsible for the allegations made against him.

SAVING JEWS SUSPECTED OF SERIOUS CRIMES FROM THE LAWS OF THE AUTHORITIES. R. Jair Ḥayyim Bacharach (*Resp. Ḥavvot Yair* §146) was asked about a case involving a Jewish youth, a fugitive murderer, who was later caught by the authorities. R. Bacharach rejected the possibility that he could be delivered to the non-Jewish court, even by the relatives of the murder victim (by virtue of the *a fortiori* argument that they could in any event deliver him to the authorities based on the law of the blood avenger; see *Blood Avenger). At the same time, based on Rashi's interpretation of the talmudic passage about R. Tarfon, he rules that it is forbidden to save the youth from the authorities, because of the duty to "eradicate all evil from your midst." He then raises the possibility that, even though it is forbidden to save him, it may be permitted to give him advice on how to escape. In suggesting this possibility, R. Bacharach relies on the words of R. Tarfon in the talmudic story, who told those people who sought refuge with him that they should hide themselves – what may have amounted to advice on the part of R. Tarfon. R. Jacob Emden (*Resp.* She'ilat Ya'avetz II. 9) rejects this possibility out of hand, ruling that it is forbidden to give advice to a murderer on how to evade the judgment against him. In the case brought before him, after one Jew who had murdered another Jew was arrested by the authorities, he was given the possibility of acquitting himself by swearing a solemn oath that another person killed the victim and he was not the murderer. The local rabbi ruled that the murderer should save himself from death by swearing falsely. R. Emden vehemently rejects this advice and states that "it is forbidden to save him from death through any means, even an [otherwise permissible one]," and certainly not through making a false oath.

EXTRADITION BASED ON THE PRINCIPLE THAT "THE LAW OF THE LAND IS LAW". In the rulings of the great halakhic authorities of Spain from the 13th century onward, the authority of the local non-Jewish government is accepted also in matters of penal law, by virtue of the principle that "the law of the land is law" (see **dina de-malkhuta dina*), and not only regarding matters of local administration and civil law. The Rashba, in a responsum cited by the *Beit Yosef* on the Tur (ḤM 388), discusses a case in which the Jewish community was asked by the non-Jewish authorities to determine whether a particular Jew had transgressed a criminal offense; if so, he would be punished by the authorities. The Rashba, relying upon the principle of "*dina de-malkhuta dina*," sets forth the following rule that, when a Jewish court operates under the government's authority, there is no need to insist on all the normal evidential strictures of the Torah – warning, valid witnesses, etc. – even in capital matters for, were the Jewish court to insist on such requirements, the world would be desolate, as murderers and their companions would multiply. The Rashba proceeds to rule, relying on the above-mentioned talmudic cases involving R. Eleazar Simeon and R. Ishmael b. Yose, that anyone who is appointed by the king is permitted to turn in Jewish criminals to the king. The Ritva, a disciple of the Rashba, also explained the acts of the aforesaid *tannaim* on the basis of the principle of "*dina de-malhuta dina*," which applies even in the realm of criminal law (*Ḥiddushei ha-Ritva ha-Ḥadashim*, at BM 83b).

R. Samuel de Modena (Salonika, 16th century; *Resp.* Maharshdam ḤM 55), relying on a responsum of the Rabad, rules, on the basis of the principle of "*dina de-malkhuta dina*" that acts of the government concerning the punishment of criminals are legally binding just as the government has authority to enact laws in the city.

In the 19th century, R. Moses Schick (Resp. *Maharam Schick*, HM 50) utilized the above-cited rulings of Rashba and Ritva in relation to a case in which the Jewish community suspected, albeit without any conclusive evidence, that a woman had murdered her husband. The question was asked whether there was any obligation to report the case to the authorities. Maharam Schick determines, in relation to the legitimacy of governmental enactments in punishing criminals, that "…anything they do whose purpose is to benefit society, their law is law," and that the woman could be reported to the authorities, albeit he concludes that great scholars should not initiate this matter, but rather do nothing – neither save nor extradite the suspect.

The State of Israel

The Extradition Law, 5714 – 1954, determines the ways and means by which a person can be extradited from the State of Israel to another country that requests his extradition. Amongst the provisions set down in the Law, compliance with which is essential to perform the extradition, are the following: the existence of a reciprocal agreement between Israel and the requesting state; that the offense concerned not be of a political nature; that the extradition be to a state, the fairness of whose judicial proceedings the State of Israel acknowledges; and, that no person shall be extradited who has already been brought to trial in the State of Israel for the same offense.

In the Aloni affair (HCJ 852/86 Aloni v. Minister of Justice, PD 41(2)1) the issue of extradition was heard by the Supreme Court of the State of Israel, together with an examination of the existing legal framework in Israel in light of the principles of Jewish law. The Court was asked to decide the issue of whether the State should be ordered to extradite to the French authorities a man who was wanted in France for murder. The accused was declared extraditable according to the Israeli Extradition Law, pursuant to a treaty between the two states, but the justice minister decided not to execute the extradition order, due to fear of danger to the life of the defendant by prisoners in the French prison in the event of his extradition. Justice Menachem Elon analyzed the position of Jewish law on the topic of extradition at length and in great detail, based on the above-cited and other sources. His conclusion was that the provisions of the Extradition Law accord, first and foremost, with the categorical stand of Jewish law, which negates the possibility that a suspect in the commission of an offense evade accountability for his acts, particularly if the alleged crime is murder. Justice Elon relies on the justifications in favor of extradition approved by the great halakhic authorities, even where extradition was forced on the Jewish community by the non-Jewish authorities. These justifications were based either on substantive Jewish law itself, or on the principle of "*dina de-malkhuta dina*" – i.e., in order to establish social order and the rule of law. According to Elon, the sources of Jewish law indicate that throughout Jewish history extradition was permitted in specific cases, even when no supervision of the judicial system or the penalty prescribed was performed by the Jewish community. Therefore, it is all the more justified today when it is executed freely by a sovereign Jewish State, with rights equal to those of the state requesting the extradition, and when the Jewish State has the ability to monitor the integrity of the judicial system in the other state and to annul the extradition treaty with it in the event that the said judicial system lacks such integrity. Elon suggests that this view would be concurred with even by the authorities who opposed cooperation with non-Jewish courts unless the crime posed a danger to the Jewish community. This opposition was based on their fear of a miscarriage of justice being caused by the extradition, a fear that was regarded as more significant than the benefit gained in punishing the criminal. These being the reasons for their opposition to extradition based on cooperation with non-Jewish courts, the same authorities would not object to extradition performed by and with the advantages afforded by a sovereign Jewish State.

From the above-cited rulings of *Ḥavvot Yair* and *She'ilat Ya'avetz*, which set forth a prohibition on shielding the criminal in cases of serious crimes, Justice Elon derives that, in a sovereign Jewish state, their rulings should be understood as indicating a duty to extradite. According to Elon, in a small

Jewish community the argument may be made that, while it is forbidden to conceal the offender from the authorities, there is no obligation to hand him over, and if the authorities so desire they can come and search for him. By contrast, in a sovereign state, it is impossible to simply turn a blind eye, because such is not the way of a Jewish state, which has a duty either to try the offender, if this is possible according to its laws, or to extradite him to a state which has the ability to try him, subject to the restrictions stipulated in the law. According to the aforementioned arguments, when it is impossible to try the offender in Israel, the State of Israel must extradite the offender in order to eliminate the evil from its midst.

In the same judgment, Justice Elon ruled that, in the event of a *reasonable probability* of danger to the life of the accused were he to serve his sentence in a foreign country, he should not be extradited. This was in contradistinction to the majority of the Court, who ruled that extradition should only be avoided in the event of a *high probability* of danger to his life. Justice Elon also ruled that the execution of the extradition be delayed until arrangements are put in place to ensure that the accused's wife will not find herself in a state of abandonment (*iggun*). It should also be noted that, in this judgment, Justice Elon recommended that the Extradition Law be amended so as to allow a criminal sentenced by a foreign court to serve his sentence in an Israeli jail; indeed, in 1999 the law was amended in this spirit.

The position adopted by Justice Elon aroused controversy. Amongst his disputants was R. Shaul Yisraeli (see bibliography), who emphasized the prohibition of litigating before non-Jewish courts. According to R. Yisraeli, the possibility of delivering a Jew to the authorities by virtue of the Law of the King and "*dina de-malkhuta dina*" only exists where there is no autonomous government in Israel and no possibility of trying the criminal under Jewish law. In addition, he states that the authority of government law, by virtue of the principle of "*dina de-malkhuta dina*," only applies to those citizens who live within the borders of that state. It does not extend to validate an extradition agreement between states, and it is therefore forbidden for the State to enter into an extradition treaty which, according to R. Yisraeli, has no validity from the halakhic point of view even *post factum*. R. Yisraeli also emphasizes the merits of the Land of Israel, by whose virtue arguments (for his innocence) may be found in his favor (Makkot 7a). The solution suggested by R. Yisraeli to ensure that the State of Israel does not become a "sanctuary for criminals" is for the State to enact a law according extra-territorial status to Israeli criminal law, enabling all Jewish criminals to be tried in Israel.

It should be noted that the Jerusalem Rabbinical Court, in considering the issue dealt with by the aforesaid Supreme Court judgment, determined that an extradition treaty made by the State of Israel with another state has halakhic validity by virtue of the principle of "*dina de-malkhuta dina*" because "it is a matter of good governance that the State of Israel not become a refuge for Israeli criminals and that we should be able to punish criminals who are located in other countries – in Israel" (File 8384/5747, pp. 27–28, given on 12 Tishrei 5748, 5/10/87).

ADD. BIBLIOGRAPHY: M. Elon, *Jewish Law* (1994), 4:1861, 1862; idem, *Jewish Law* (*Cases and Materials*) (1999), 369–88; idem., "Laws of Extradition in Jewish Law," in: *Teḥumin*, 8 (1986/7) 263–86; 304–9 (in Hebrew); S. Yisraeli, "Extradition of an Offender to a Foreign Jurisdiction," in: *ibid.*, 287–96 (in Hebrew); J.D. Bleich, "Extradition of an Offender to a Non-Jewish People," in: *ibid.*, 297–303 (in Hebrew); idem, "Extradition of an Offender Who Has Fled to Ereẓ Yisrael," in: *Or ha-Mizraḥ*, 35 (1986/7), 247–69; Y. Gershuni, "Is it Permitted for the Government of Israel to Extradite a Criminal to Another Nation?" in: *Or ha-Mizraḥ*, 21 (1971/2), 69–77 (in Hebrew); B. Rabinowitz, "Teomim, Extradition For Imprisonment by Non-Jews" in: *No'am*, 7 (1963/4), 336–60 (in Hebrew).

[Menachem Elon (2nd ed.)]

EXTRAORDINARY REMEDIES.

Extrajudicial Remedies

As in other ancient civilizations, the earliest method of vindicating violated rights under biblical law was self-redress. A burglar at night may be killed on the spot (Ex. 22:1), life may be taken for life (see *Blood-Avenger) and limb for limb (see *Talion). Even when another man's rights were violated, one was exhorted not to stand idly by, but to interfere actively to vindicate them (Lev. 19:16; and cf. Ex. 23:4–5; Deut. 22:1–4). Again, as in other systems of law, self-redress was largely superseded by judicial redress – firstly because of unavoidable excesses on the part of avengers, secondly because the effectiveness of self-redress always depended upon the injured party being stronger than the wrongdoer and the weak victim was in, the danger of being left without a remedy, and thirdly because an injured party ought not to be the judge in his own cause. The right to self-help survived in the criminal law mainly in the form of self-defense or the defense of others; but in civil law self-redress is in talmudic law much more in evidence than in most other systems, and was a well-established legal remedy.

The biblical license to kill the nocturnal burglar (Ex.) is retained in talmudic law for the reason that such a burglar presumably knows beforehand that, if caught, he might be killed by the irate landlord and is therefore presumed to come with the intention to kill the landlord first, and: "whoever comes to kill you, better forestall him and kill him first" (Yoma 85b; Maim. Yad, Genevah, 9:7–9). There is no restriction in law as to the mode of killing such a burglar: "you may kill him in whatever way you can" (Sanh. 72b). But if the thief is caught alive, no harm may be done to him; nor may the landlord lay hands on him if he knows that the thief comes for money only and has no murderous designs, or where there are people around who would hinder him (*ibid.*; Maim. *ibid.*, 10–12). Similarly, the biblical allusion to the duty of saving the girl in danger (Deut. 22:27) led to the rule that a man was allowed to kill the persecutor in order to save the persecuted girl from death or rape (Maim. Yad, Roẓe'ah u-Shemirat Nefesh, 1:10). While efforts must be made to avert the danger by means other than killing, a man is not to be charged with culpable homicide if he did kill even though the danger could have been averted by other means (*ibid.*, 13). A person is under a duty to save another from death or rape even by killing the offender, and his failure to do so, while not a punishable offense (*ibid.*, 15–16), is considered a grave sin (Lev. 19:16; Deut. 25:12).

The general right of self-redress in civil cases has been stated by Maimonides as follows: "A man may take the law into his own hands, if he had the power to do so, since he acts in conformity with the law and he is not obliged to take the trouble and go to court, even though he would lose nothing by the delay involved in court proceedings; and where his adversary complained and brought him to court, and the court found that he had acted lawfully and had judged for himself truthfully according to law, his act cannot be challenged" (Yad., Sanhedrin, 2:12). This final rule was preceded by a dispute between talmudic jurists, some of whom held that a man may take the law into his own hands only where otherwise, i.e., by going to court, he would suffer monetary damage (BK 27b). This view was rejected because there could be nothing wrong in doing what the law had laid down as right in the first place (*Piskei ha-Rosh* 3:3). The party taking the law into his own hands only took the risk that the court might, on the complaint of the other party, overrule him; so that in cases of any doubt it was always safer to go to court at the outset.

There were, however, cases of doubt as to what the law actually was, and as to where the respective rights of the parties lay – in which instance the court would uphold the title of that party who had already taken the law into his own hands and put the court, so to speak, before a fait accompli (*kol de-allim gaver*: BB 34b). The reason for this rule – "a very startling phenomenon indeed" (Herzog) – is stated by Asheri to be that it would be unreasonable to leave the parties quarreling all the time – one trying to outwit the other – so it was laid down that once one of them had possessed himself of the chose in action, he was to prevail; the presumption being that the better and truer one's right is, the better and more unrelenting effort one will make to vindicate it, while a man with a doubtful right will not go to the trouble of vindicating it at the risk of being again deprived of it in court (*Piskei ha-Rosh* 3:22). This reasoning appears to be both legally and psychologically unsatisfactory; a better explanation might be that where the other party did not establish any better title to the chose in action, he could not succeed as against the party in possession, such possession being for this purpose recognized as accompanied by a claim of right (see *Evidence).

The rule applied not only to land but also to movables and money. Although courts are no longer competent to award *fines, where a person entitled in law to a fine has taken it from the wrongdoer, *tefisah*, he may retain it (BK 15b; Sh. Ar., HM 1:5); and where he had taken more than was due to him, the wrongdoer may sue only for the return of the balance (Tur and *Rema*, *ibid.*). A wife who had succeeded in collecting her *ketubbah* from her husband is allowed to retain it notwithstanding the husband's contention that only half of it is due to her (Ket. 16b). The holder of a bill which was unenforceable because of formal defects may retain the amount of the bill if he succeeded in collecting it (the numerous and rather complicated rules of *tefisah* were compiled by Jacob Lissa and are appended to ch. 25 of the standard editions of Sh. Ar., ḤM). But there is a notable exception to this rule; namely, no creditor may enter the debtor's house against his will, for it is written, "Thou shalt stand without" (Deut. 24:11); nor may the debtor's property be attached or sold in satisfaction of a debt otherwise than by process of the court (BM 9:13). Even where the debtor had agreed, by contract in writing, that the creditor may satisfy himself by seizing the debtor's property in case of default, the creditor was not allowed to do so except where no court was available to award him a legal judgment (Sh. Ar., ḤM 61,6; see *Execution; *Pledge).

Two instances of extrajudicial authority in inflicting punishments for crime may be mentioned. One is the prerogative of the king to kill any person disobeying or slandering him (Maim. Yad., Melakhim, 3:8) – not only is the king not bound by the rules of law and procedure, but he may lawfully execute murderers acquitted for lack of evidence or other formal grounds if he considers it necessary for the public good (*ibid.*, 10). The other is the right of zealots (*kanna'im*) to kill thieves of Temple utensils, idolatrous blasphemers, and men cohabiting with idolatresses, without legal process, if they are caught *inflagrante delicto* (Sanh. 9:6): this rule derives its justification from the praise God heaped on Phinehas for his impassioned act in stabbing the man whom he found cohabiting with the Midianite woman (Num. 25:6–13).

Extralegal Remedies

Instances are already reported in the Bible of punishments being inflicted, mostly drastic and wholesale, and sometimes at the express command of God, but outside the framework of the law and without legal process (e.g., Gen. 34:25–29; Ex. 32:27–28; Judg. 20:13). With the elaboration of talmudic criminal law and procedure and rules of evidence, and the consequential complication of the criminal process, the necessity soon arose for extraordinary procedures in cases of emergency (*Hora'at Sha'ah*): it was in such an emergency that Simeon b. Shetaḥ is reported to have sentenced and executed 80 witches in Ashkelon on one day (Sanh. 6:4). Extralegal punishments such as these were stated to be justified or even mandatory whenever the court considered their infliction necessary for upholding the authority and enforcing the observance of the law (Yev. 90b; TJ, Hag. 2:2,78a). With the lapse of capital jurisdiction (see *bet din*) – but not previously, as some scholars wrongly hold – this emergency power was called in aid to enable courts to administer the criminal law and uphold law and order generally, the very lapsing of the jurisdiction creating the "emergency" which necessitated the recourse to such emergency powers. Thus, courts were empowered to inflict corporal and even capital punishment on offenders who were not, under the law, liable to be so punished (Maim. Yad, Sanhedrin, 24:4); and there are instances already in talmudic times of illegal punishments being administered – such as cutting off the hand of a recidivist offender (Sanh. 58b), or burning an adulteress alive (Sanh. 52b; the Talmud (*ibid.*), however, adds: "That was done because the *bet din* at that time was not learned in the law."), or piercing the eyes of a murderer (Sanh. 27a). In post-talmudic times, new forms of *capital punishment were advisedly introduced, not only for penological reasons but also to demonstrate that these courts were not administering the regular law. Justification for such innovations was found in the biblical reference to "the judges that shall be in those days" (Deut. 17:9), the nature and content of the *Hora'at Sha'ah*, as the term indicates, depending on the circumstances and requirements of the time (*Bet ha-Beḥirah* Sanh. 52b; Resp. Rashba vol. 5, no. 238). The same considerations led to a general dispensation with formal requirements of the law of evidence and *procedure (Resp. Rashba vol. 4, no. 311). Conversely, prior deviations from such law, as, e.g., executions on the strength of *confessions only, were retrospectively explained as exceptional emergencies (Maim., loc. cit. 18:6).

A peculiar instance of an extra-legal remedy is the rule that where a litigant has a dangerously violent man for his adversary, he may be allowed to sue him in non-Jewish courts under non-Jewish law (Maim. *ibid.*, 26:7; Resp.Rosh 6:27; Tur, ḤM 2; see *Judicial Autonomy; **Mishpat Ivri*). In civil cases, courts are vested with proprietary powers so as to be able to do justice and grant remedies even contrary to the letter of the law (Maim. loc. cit., 24:6; and see *Confiscation and Expropriation; **Takkanot*).

[Haim Hermann Cohn]

The fundamental provision referred to above allowed the *Bet Din* to deviate from original Biblical and Talmudic law in matters of evidence, procedure and penal policy, guided by the needs of the time and the place. Based on this provision, both the courts and the communal leaders utilized their authority to enact communal regulations (see entry: **Takkanot ha-Kahal*) with detailed legislation concerning penal policy. Formally, such regulations are defined as "emergency provisions" (*hora'at sha'ah*), but they were in fact incorporated into substantive Jewish law. Indeed, Jewish courts throughout the Jewish Diaspora occasionally exercised their extra-legal punitive powers to adjudicate capital cases, and even to impose death sentences, without requiring a court of 23, and without being bound by the stringent rules of evidence imposed by the original Jewish law.

The Israeli Supreme Court discussed this issue at length in the *Nagar* case (Cr.A 543/79 *Nagar v.* State of Israel 35 (1) PD 113. Based on this principle, Justice Elon ruled that suspects could be convicted for the commission of murder even where the Court had no direct evidence of their commission of the crime, and even where the dead body had not been found.

For a broad discussion of this topic, see entries: *Capital Punishment; *Evidence.

[Menachem Elon (2nd ed.)]

BIBLIOGRAPHY: Vogelstein, in: MGWJ, 48 (1904), 513–53; H. Cohen, in: *Jeschurun*, 9 (1922), 272–99; S. Assaf, *Ha-Onshin Aḥarei Ḥatimat ha-Talmud* (1922), passim; Gulak, Yesodei, 1 (1922), 171; 2 (1922), 17, 18; A. Gulak, *Toledot ha-Mishpat be-Yisrael*, 1 (1939), *Ha-Ḥiyyuv ve-Shi'budav*, 112 n. 41, 113–6; Herzog, Instit, 1 (1936), 226–8, 264f., 272f.; B. Cohen, *Jewish and Roman Law*, 2 (1966), 624–50, addenda 793–6; ET, 2 (1949), 11–13, 7 (1956), 385f.; 8 (1957), 512–27; Z. Wahrhaftig, *Ha-Ḥazakah ba-Mishpat ha-Ivri* (1964), 51–77. **ADD. BIBLIOGRAPHY:** M. Elon, *Ha-Mishpat ha-Ivri* (1988), 1:15f, 49ff., 421ff., 436ff., 1324ff.; idem, *Jewish Law* (1994), 1:15ff, 55ff.; 2:515ff., 533ff.; 4:1582; idem, *Jewish Law (Cases and Materials)* (1999), 200ff.; M. Elon and B. Lifshitz, *Mafte'aḥ ha-She-elot ve-ha-Teshuvot shel Ḥakhmei Sefarad u-Ẓefon Afrikah* (1986), 2:332, 337, 343; B. Lifshitz and E. Shohetman, *Mafte'aḥ ha-She'elot ve-ha-Teshuvot shel Ḥakhmei Ashkenaz, Ẓarefat ve-Italyah* (1997), 230.

EYAL (Heb. אֱיָל; "strength"), kibbutz in central Israel, on the eastern border of the Sharon, northeast of the Arab town Qalqilya, affiliated with Ha-Kibbutz ha-Me'uḥad. Eyal was originally founded on July 3, 1947 as a *Palmaḥ outpost near the Syrian border east of Lake Huleh, where it fulfilled a vital function during the Israel War of Independence (1948). After the war, the settlement was transferred (Nov. 1, 1948) to its present site, which was also vulnerable to attack until the Six-Day War of 1967. Its farming was based on field crops, orchards including organic farming and milch cattle. The kibbutz operates two factories: Eyal Microwave for microwave components and one for optical lenses (in partnership with kibbutz *Shamir). In 2002 the population was 385.

WEBSITE: www.eyal.org.il.

[Efraim Orni / Shaked Gilboa (2nd ed.)]

EYBESCHUETZ, JONATHAN (ben Nathan Nata; 1690/95–1764), talmudist and kabbalist. Eybeschuetz, a child prodigy, studied in Poland, Moravia, and Prague. In his youth, after the death of his father, he studied in Prossnitz under Meir Eisenstadt and Eliezer ha-Levi Ettinger, his uncle, and in Vienna under Samson Wertheimer. He married the daughter of Isaac Spira, the *av bet din* of Bunzlau. After traveling for some time he settled in Prague in 1715, and in time became head of the yeshivah and a famous preacher. When he was in Prague he had many contacts with priests and the intelligentsia, debating religious topics and matters of faith with them. He became friendly with Cardinal Hassebauer and also discussed religious questions with him. Through the help of the cardinal, Eybeschuetz received permission to print the Talmud with the omission of all passages contradicting the principles of Christianity. Aroused to anger by this, David *Oppenheim and the rabbis of Frankfurt had the license to print revoked.

The people of Prague held Eybeschuetz in high esteem and he was considered second only to David Oppenheim. In 1725 he was among the Prague rabbis who excommunicated the Shabbatean sect. After the death of David Oppenheim (1736), he was appointed *dayyan* of Prague. Elected rabbi of Metz in 1741, he subsequently became rabbi of the "Three Communities," Altona, Hamburg, and Wandsbek (1750). Both in Metz and in Altona he had many disciples and was considered a great preacher.

His position in the Three Communities, however, was undermined when the dispute broke out concerning his suspected leanings toward Shabbateanism. This controversy accompanied Eybeschuetz throughout his life, and the quarrel had repercussions in every community from Holland to Poland. His main opponent was Jacob *Emden, also a famous talmudist and his rival in the candidature to the rabbinate of the Three Communities. The quarrel developed into a great public dispute which divided the rabbis of the day. While most of the German rabbis opposed Eybeschuetz, his support came from the rabbis of Poland and Moravia. A fruitless attempt at mediation was made by Ezekiel *Landau, rabbi of Prague. Most of Eybeschuetz' own community was loyal to him and confidently accepted his refutation of the charges made by his opponent, but dissension reached such a pitch that both sides appealed to the authorities in Hamburg and the government of Denmark for a judicial ruling. The king favored Eybeschuetz and ordered new elections, which resulted in his reappointment. Yet the literary polemic continued, even prompting several Christian scholars to participate, some of whom, thinking that Eybeschuetz was a secret Christian, came to his defense. After his reelection as rabbi of the Three Communities, some rabbis of Frankfurt, Amsterdam, and Metz challenged him to appear before them to reply to the suspicions raised against him. Eybeschuetz refused, and when the matter was brought before the Council of the Four Lands in 1753, the council issued a ruling in his favor. In 1760 the quarrel broke out once more when some Shabbatean elements were discovered among the students of Eybeschuetz' yeshivah. At the same time his younger son, Wolf, presented himself as a Shabbatean prophet, with the result that the yeshivah was closed. When Moses Mendelssohn was in Hamburg in 1761, Eybeschuetz treated him with great respect, even publishing a letter on him (*Kerem Ḥemed*, 3 (1838), 224–5), incontrovertible testimony to Eybeschuetz' awareness of Mendelssohn's ideological approach.

Eybeschuetz was considered not only one of the greatest preachers of his time but also one of the giants of the Talmud, acclaimed for his acumen and particularly incisive intellect. Thirty of his works in the field of *halakhah* have been published. His method of teaching aroused great enthusiasm among the pilpulists, and his works, *Urim ve-Tummim* on *Ḥoshen Mishpat* (1775–77), *Kereti u-Feleti* on *Yoreh De'ah* (1763), and *Benei Ahuvah* on Maimonides (1819), were considered masterpieces of pilpulistic literature. To the present day they are regarded as classics by students of the Talmud. They are unique in that the many *pilpulim* they include are in most cases based on clear, logical principles that give them their permanent value. His homiletic works, *Ya'arot Devash* (1779–82), *Tiferet Yonatan* (1819), and *Ahavat Yonatan* (1766), also found many admirers. In succeeding generations his reputation was sustained by these works. Since (apart from *Kereti u-Feleti*) his works were not printed in his lifetime, it is clear that his great influence among his contemporaries must have derived from the power of his oral teaching and from his personality, both of which were highly praised by many writers. Of his books on the Kabbalah, only one was printed, *Shem Olam* (1891), but during his lifetime Eybeschuetz was considered a great kabbalist.

Opinions are still divided on the assessment of this striking personality, his supporters and detractors vying with one another with an extraordinary intensity. The great bitterness surrounding the controversies on the question of his secret relationship with the Shabbateans stems precisely from his being recognized as a true master of the Torah. It was hard to believe that a man who had himself signed a *ḥerem* against the Shabbateans could have secretly held their beliefs. Suspicions were aroused against him on two occasions: in 1724, with the appearance of a manuscript entitled *Va-Avo ha-Yom el ha-Ayin*, which the Shabbateans, and also several of his own students, ascribed to him. This book (preserved in Ms.) is indisputably a Shabbatean work. Even after he had signed the *ḥerem* against the Shabbateans, suspicion was not allayed and it prevented his election to the rabbinate of Prague. In 1751, the dispute grew more virulent when some amulets written by Eybeschuetz in Metz and Altona were opened. Jacob Emden deciphered them and found that they contained unmistakable Shabbatean formulae (*Sefat Emet*, 1752). Eybeschuetz denied that the amulets had any continuous logical meaning, maintaining that they consisted simply of "Holy Names" (*Luḥot Edut*, 1755), and he even put forward an interpretation of them based on his system. His opponents retorted that the real interpretation of the amulets could be discovered from the work attributed to him, *Va-Avo ha-Yom el ha-Ayin*, and that they could and should be interpreted as having a meaningful content. Scholarly historical research has advanced three views concerning Eybeschuetz' relationship with Shabbateanism: that he was never a Shabbatean and that suspicions on this score were completely unfounded (Zinz, Mortimer, Cohen, Klemperer); that he was a Shabbatean in his youth but turned his back on the sect around the time of the *ḥerem* of 1725 (Bernhard Baer, Saul Pinhas Rabinowitz); that he was a crypto-Shabbatean from the time he studied in Prossnitz and Prague until the end of his life (Graetz, David Kahana, Scholem, Perlmutter). An interpretation of his kabbalistic beliefs must also depend on his relationship with Shabbateanism. Some believe that the book *Shem Olam*, which deals with the philosophical explanation of the nature of God, is a work whose kabbalistic teaching only confirms generally accepted kabbalistic teaching (Mieses); others consider that the book is undoubtedly Shabbatean in its conception of God (Perlmutter). Still others believe that the work is a forgery or was erroneously attributed to Eybeschuetz (Margulies). Recent research has demonstrated a close relationship between *Shem Olam* and *Va-Avo ha-Yom el ha-Ayin*.

BIBLIOGRAPHY: B. Brilling, in: HUCA, 34 (1963), 217–28; 35 (1964), 255–73; D.L. Zinz, *Gedulat Yehonatan* (1930); M.J. Cohen, *Jacob Emden, a Man of Controversy* (1937); G. Scholem in; KS, 16

(1939–40), 320–38; idem, in: *Zion*, 6 (1940–1), 96–100; idem, *Leket Margaliyyot* (1941); R. Margulies, *Sibbat Hitnahaguto shel Rabbenu Ya'akov me-Emden le-Rabbenu Yehonatan Eybeschuetz* (1941); A. Ha-Shiloni (I. Raphael), *La-Pulmus ha-Meḥuddash al Shabbeta'uto shel R. Yehonatan Eybeschuetz* (1942); M.A. Perlmutter, *R. Yehonatan Eybeschuetz ve-Yaḥaso la-Shabbeta'ut* (1947); Mifal ha-Bibliografyah ha-Ivrit, *Ḥoveret le-Dugmah* (1964), 13–24.

[Gershom Scholem]

EYDOUX, EMMANUEL, pen name of **Roger Eisinger** (1913–), French author. Descended from Alsatian Jews, he was born in Marseilles, where he engaged in business until 1965. He then abandoned commerce and taught Jewish history and thought in an ORT school. He was active in the cultural life of the Marseilles Jewish community. Eydoux began publishing poems in 1945, under the pen name of "Catapulte." He then wrote plays and books on the history of Judaism. The main poetic works of Eydoux were *Le Chant de l'Exil* (1945–47), *Abraham l'Hébreu et Samuelle Voyant* (1946), *L'Evangile selon les Hébreux* (1954), and *Elégies inachevées* (1959). He wrote a play, *Ghetto à Varsovie* (1960), and a tetralogy including *Pogrom* (1963) and *Eliezer ben Yehouda* (1966). Eydoux was also the author of *Le dernier Pourimspiel des orphelins du docteur Janusz Korczak* (1967), which has its setting in the Warsaw ghetto under the Nazis. His didactic works include *La Science de l'Être* (1949) and *Introduction à l'histoire de la civilisation d'Israël* (1961).

[Moshe Catane]

EYLENBURG, ISSACHAR BAER BEN ISRAEL LEISER PARNAS (1550–1623), talmudist. Eylenburg was born in Posen and studied under Mordecai *Jaffe, *Judah Loew b. Bezalel (the "Maharal") of Prague, and Joshua *Falk. He served as rabbi and *av bet din* of Gorizia, Italy. In his *Be'er Sheva* (Frankfurt, 1709), he attempts to provide *tosafot* for those tractates which do not possess them. His halakhic method is original. Taking the actual talmudic *halakhah* as the basis of his discussion, he adopts a critical attitude to the commentaries of such *rishonim* as Isaac *Alfasi, *Rashi, and *Maimonides, not hesitating to disagree with them or even to reject them. He is opposed to philosophy, condemning Maimonides and others who "arrogated to themselves the right to read the works of sectarians." The work follows to a considerable extent the method of Judah Loew b. Bezalel in *halakhah*. Eylenburg also wrote *Ẓeidah la-Derekh* (Prague, 1623), a supercommentary to Rashi's commentary on the Pentateuch, with glosses to other supercommentaries on Rashi, including that of Elijah *Mizraḥi. His halakhic work was highly regarded by the scholars of Safed, who invited him in 1621 to serve as rabbi of the Ashkenazi community of that city, in place of Moses Da *Castellazzo whom they wished to dismiss. Eylenburg declined the invitation, only to be invited again upon Castellazzo's death, when he accepted. He died in Austerlitz on his way to Safed.

BIBLIOGRAPHY: Azulai, 1 (1852), 115, no. 427; Perles, in: MGWJ, 14 (1865), 123; S.M. Chones, *Toledot ha-Posekim* (1910), 59, 93–95; Gottesdiener, in: *Azkarah... Kook*, 4 (1937), 344; M.A. Shulvas, *Roma vi-Yrushalayim* (1944), 96; Benayahu, in: *Tarbiz*, 29 (1959/60), 73.

[Isaac Ze'ev Kahane]

EYNIKEYT ("Unity"), official organ of the Jewish *Anti-Fascist Committee in the Soviet Union. *Eynikeyt* began to appear in Kuibyshev in June 1942 once every ten days under the editorship of Shakhne Epstein. The editorial board consisted of: D. *Bergelson, Y. *Dobrushin, S. *Halkin, S. *Mikhoels, L. Strongin, I. *Fefer, L. *Kvitko, and A. *Kushnirov. After Epstein died, G. Shitz was named chief editor. In July 1943 *Eynikeyt* moved to Moscow and became a weekly magazine. By February 1945 it began to come out three times a week, but publication was stopped on Nov. 20, 1948, with the liquidation of all Jewish cultural institutions in the U.S.S.R. Altogether, about 700 issues of *Eynikeyt* were published, and its contributors included all the Yiddish writers of the Soviet Union. Some of their contributions were first published there, like Fefer's famous poem "Ich bin a Yid" ("I Am a Jew"). The newspaper was devoted entirely to the war effort, carrying stories on the atrocities perpetrated against Jews in the countries occupied by the Germans and emphasizing the contribution and the bravery of Jews in the war against the Nazis. There was a column called "Jewish Life Abroad," with reports on Jewish events outside the U.S.S.R., Jews in the anti-Nazi underground, and also events in the *yishuv* of Palestine. The paper reported the visit of Mikhoels and Fefer to the U.S., Canada, Mexico, and Great Britain, and also the visit of the Americans Goldberg and Novik. These visits later served the KGB in drawing up its accusations of espionage for the West in the case of the Jewish Anti-Fascist Committee. After the war *Eynikeyt* continued to appear under the guidance and supervision of the Soviet authorities. This control was especially noticeable in the paper's editorial policy toward the struggle of the *yishuv* in Palestine. In the first half of 1948, in conformity with official Soviet policy, the paper supported Israel's *War of Independence and the establishment of the State of Israel. But from September 1948 until its dissolution, it published attacks on Zionism. The employees of *Eynikeyt* shared the fate of other Jewish cultural activists.

BIBLIOGRAPHY: Ben-Yosef, in: *Yad Vashem Studies*, 4 (1960), 135–61; Litvak, in: *Gesher* (1966), 218–32.

[Yehuda Slutsky / Shmuel Spector (2nd ed.)]

EYTAN, RACHEL (1931–1987), Hebrew author. Eytan spent part of her childhood in children's homes and later lived in a kibbutz. She was trained as a teacher and worked with children of new immigrants. Her first novel, *Ha-Raki'a ha-Ḥamishi* (1962; *The Fifth Heaven*, 1985) depicts in realistic style the life of abandoned children living in an orphanage in Ereẓ Israel during World War II. The novel, which was awarded the prestigious Brenner Prize, was one of the early attempts of Israeli literature to deal with the underprivileged "inferior" groups of the new Jewish society. In 1967 Eytan moved to New York and was appointed professor of Hebrew and Yiddish at Hofstra

University. Her second novel, *Shidah ve-Shidot* ("Pleasures of Man," 1974) is the story of a young married woman who has a passionate affair with a member of the Israel Philharmonic Orchestra, told against the background of the urban, hedonistic society of Tel Aviv following the Six-Day War.

BIBLIOGRAPHY: Y. Oren, in: *Yedioth Aharonoth* (Dec. 6, 1974); E. Ben Ezer, in: *Al ha-Mishmar* (Dec. 6, 1974); A. Zehavi, in: *Yedioth Aharonoth* (Dec. 20, 1974); G. Shaked, *Ha-Sipporet ha-Ivrit*, 4 (1993), 161–62, 383; T. Mishmar, *"Ein Osim Leḥem mi-Ideologyot"* (on *The Fifth Heaven*), in: *Te'oriyah u-Vikkoret*, 7 (1995), 147–58.

[Anat Feinberg (2nd ed.)]

EYTAN (Ettinghausen), WALTER (1910–2001), Israel diplomat. He was the son of Maurice L. Ettinghausen (1882–1974), bibliophile and antiquarian bookseller. Eytan, born in Munich, was educated in England and taught German language and literature in Oxford from 1934. Eytan served in the British army from 1940 to 1945. Settling in Palestine in 1946, he served as director of the Civil Service and Diplomatic College of the *Jewish Agency in Jerusalem. In this capacity, and particularly as first general director of the Ministry for Foreign Affairs under Moshe *Sharett and Golda *Meir (1948–59), he greatly influenced the structure and character of Israel's foreign service. In 1949 he headed the Israel delegation both to the Rhodes armistice negotiations and to the Lausanne Conference with the Arab states (see State of *Israel: Historical Survey). In 1955 Eytan headed the Israel delegation to the Atomic Energy Conference in Geneva. He served as Israel ambassador to France from 1959 until 1970. In March 1972, Eytan was appointed head of the Board of Governors of the Israel Broadcasting Authority, in succession to Chaim *Yahil, and held the position until his retirement in 1978. He wrote *The First Ten Years: Diplomatic History of Israel* (1958).

[Netanel Lorch]

EZEKIEL, a major prophet who is said to have begun prophesying in the fifth year of Jehoiachin's exile in Babylonia, seven years before the final fall of Jerusalem; his prophecies are recorded in the book that bears his name. The name Ezekiel (Heb. יְחֶזְקֵאל; Gk. *Iezkiēl;* Vulg. *Ezechiel* [cf., in I Chron. 24:16, and for (י)חִזְקִיָּה(וּ)], = יְחִזְקֵאל?) seems to be derived from יְחַזֵּק אֵל "may God strengthen" (namely, "the child" (so Noth, Personennamen, 202; others cf., Ezek. 3:8f., 14)).

LOCATION OF THE BOOK IN THE CANON

The talmudic arrangement of the major prophets is Jeremiah, Ezekiel, and Isaiah, the departure from the true historical order being justified thus: "The Book of Kings ends with doom, Jeremiah is all doom, Ezekiel begins with doom but ends with consolation, while Isaiah is all consolation, so we place doom alongside doom and consolation alongside consolation" (BB 14b). This arrangement appears in some early Bible manuscripts (Ginsburg, *Introduction*, 5), but manuscripts of the Ben Asher tradition (e.g., Leningrad, Aleppo) and the early printings follow the proper chronological order (Isaiah, Jeremiah, and Ezekiel) as in present texts (cf. Kimḥi's introduction to Jeremiah; *Minḥat Shai's* introduction to Isaiah).

Book of Ezekiel – Contents

Chs. 1:1–3:21	**The call of the prophet.**
Chs. 3:22–24:27	**The doom of Judah and Jerusalem.**
3:22–5:17	House arrest and dramatic representation of siege and punishment.
6:1–7:27	Prophecies against the mountains of Israel and the populations of the land.
8:1–11:25	A visionary transportation to Jerusalem.
12:1–20	Dramatic representation of the exile of Judah and its king.
12:21–14:11	On false prophets and the popular attitude towards prophecy.
14:12–23	No salvation through vicarious merit.
15:1–8	Parable of the vine wood.
16:1–63	Parable of the nymphomaniacal adulteress.
17:1–24	Parable of the two eagles.
18:1–32	God's absolute justice.
19:1–14	A dirge over the monarchy.
20:1–44	The compulsory new exodus.
21:1–37	The punishing sword: three oracles.
22:1–31	Unclean Jerusalem: three oracles.
23:1–49	The dissolute sisters, Oholah and Oholibah.
24:1–14	The filthy pot: a parable of Jerusalem.
24:15–27	Death of the prophet's wife.
Chs. 25:1–32:32	**Dooms against foreign nations.**
25:1–17	Brief dooms against Ammon, Moab, Edom, and Philistia.
26:1–28:26	Doom against Phoenicia.
29:1–32:32	Seven oracles against Egypt.
Ch. 33:1–33	**A miscellany from the time of the fall.**
Chs. 34:1–39:29	**Prophecies of Israel's restoration.**
34:1–31	Renovation of the leadership of Israel.
35:1–36:15	Renovation of the mountains of Israel.
36:16–38	A new heart and spirit: the condition of lasting possession of the land.
37:1–28	The revival of the dead bones of Israel and the unification of its two scepters.
38:1–39:29	The invasion of Gog and his fall.
Chs. 40:1–48:35	**A messianic priestly code.**
40:1–43:12	A visionary transportation to the future temple.
43:13–46:24	Ordinances of the cult and its personnel.
47:1–12	The life-giving stream issuing from the temple.
47:13–48:35	Allocation of the land.

STRUCTURE AND CONTENTS

The talmudic bipartition of the book recalls Josephus' statement that Ezekiel "left behind two books" (Jos., Ant., 10:79) –

The Dates in the Book of Ezekiel

Text	Year	Month	Day	B.C.E.[1]	Event
1:1	30	4	5	Note[2]	Vision of heavenly beings.
1:2f.	5	–	5	July[2] 593	Vision of God's vehicle and call of the prophet.
3:16	A week later				Appointment as lookout.
8:1	6	6	5	Sept. 592	Vision of temple abominations.
20:1	7	5	10	Aug. 591	Prophecy of compulsory exodus.
24:1	9	10	10[3]	Jan. 588	Beginning of Jerusalem's siege.
26:1	11	–	1	587–6	Prophecy of Tyre's destruction.
29:1	10	10	12	Jan. 587	Prophecy of Egypt's destruction.
29:17	27	1	1	April 571	Tyre's doom amended, substituting Egypt therefor.
30:20	11	1	7	April 587	Prophecy of Pharaoh's destruction.
31:1	11	3	1	June 587	Parable of Pharaoh as a fallen tree.
32:1	12[4]	12	1	March 585[4]	Dirge over Pharaoh.
32:17	12	–[5]	15	March 585[5]	Lament over Pharaoh in Sheol.
33:21	12	10	5	Jan. 585	Arrival of fugitive with news of Jerusalem's fall[6].
40:1	25	1/7[7]	10	April/Oct. 573[7]	Vision of future temple.

1 The year-count in the dates starts from the exile of King Jehoiachin (1:2; 33:21; 40:1), datable by a Babylonian chronicle to 2 Adar (mid-March) 597. However, II Chron. 36:10 has the exile beginning at "the turn of the year" – i.e., the next month, Nisan, the start of Nebuchadnezzar's 8th year (II Kings 24:12). The era of the exile thus began in Nisan (April) 597, and its years, like Babylonian regnal years, ran from Nisan to Adar.
2 The date formula in vs. 2 is manifestly an editorial gloss on that of vs. 1 (hence the third person and the absence of the month); the era of the 30th year is enigmatic (traditionally: from the discovery of the Torah in Josiah's reign [622 B.C.E.], or the jubilee year [see note 7 below]). Some take 30 to be the age of the prophet at his call (cf. Gen. 8:13).
3 Not the usual data formula: = II Kings 25:1 and perhaps taken from there.
4 LXX: 11th year, i.e. 586.
5 Month to be supplied from 32:1; LXX: 1st month (April 586).
6 About five months after Jerusalem's fall, in the summer of 586 (Tammuz [July]–Ab [August], Jer. 39:2; 52:6f., 12), the 19th (Nisan–Adar) year of Nebuchadnezzar and the 11th (Tishri–Elul) year of Zedekiah.
7 Heb. Rosh Ha-Shanah; LXX: first month (Nisan [April]); tradition, comparing Lev. 25:9: seventh month (Tishri [Oct.]). Tradition thus makes the 25th year of exile a jubilee year; since 20 years before is called the 30th year (1:1, taking 1:2 as its gloss), tradition interprets it as counting to a jubilee that coincided with the discovery of the Torah in the reign of Zedekiah (see Targum and Kimḥi at 1:1).

possibly (cf. R. Marcus) a reference to the fact that chapters 1–24 are, on the whole, prophecies of Israel's doom, while chapters 25–48 are prophecies of consolation. The contents of the book may be subsumed under these two major rubrics, with further specification by subject and date. (See Table: Book of Ezekiel – Contents and Table: Dates in the Book of Ezekiel.)

The marking of certain prophecies (or events) by dates possibly signifies their evidential value to the prophet (cf. his concern over being vindicated by events: 2:5; 12:26ff.; 29:21; 33:33) and may adumbrate the Second Isaiah's argument from prophecy (Isa. 41:26f.; 42:9; 44:8; 45:21; 46:10f.; 48:3ff.). First practiced by Jeremiah's biographer, the custom of dating is at its height in Ezekiel, and is followed by Haggai (1:1, 15; 2:1; 10; 20) and Zechariah (1:1; 7:1) – though Ezekiel's formula is unique.

From the prophet's call to the start of Jerusalem's siege the dated prophecies are condemnatory, and this is true of the great bulk of chapters 1–24 (cf. the scroll of "laments and moaning and woe" that the prophet eats in 2:10–3:3). During the siege years and briefly thereafter, the dated prophecies condemn Israel's neighbors – the subjects of chapters 25–32 (note the clustering of dates in the Egypt oracles, perhaps signifying an expectation of Egypt's imminent fall). The news of Jerusalem's fall is embedded in a miscellany of brief oracles related to the first part of the book (ch. 33), and is followed by consolatory prophecies of Israel's restoration (chs. 34–48). The sole dated prophecy among these opens the detailed program of the future theocracy's institutions in chapters 40–48.

The division of the book into pre-fall doom prophecies and post-fall consolations must thus be at once qualified by recognition of the intermediate status of the oracles against foreign nations; both thematically and chronologically they straddle the two major divisions. Moreover, the two divisions are not strictly homogeneous thematically (nor is it likely they ever were). Besides prophecies of doom, the first half of the book contains both calls to repentance (14:6; 18) and a few consolations (e.g., 17:22–24), of which 11:14–21 is palpably pre-fall (though intruded into its present context by association with what precedes it). Similarly, condemnation appears in the post-fall prophecies (e.g., 34:1–10; 36:3ff.) – entirely appropriate to its context. Nor is the block of foreign-nation oracles exhaustive: a veiled anti-Babylonian oracle comes earlier (21:33–37) and an explicit anti-Edomite oracle comes later (ch. 35), both integrated into their contexts. Nor is the dating strictly followed in the face of a good countervailing reason.

Grouping the Egyptian oracles entailed an overlap between the last-dated of them and the arrival of the fugitive from Jerusalem. And the eventual substitution of Egypt for Tyre as Nebuchadnezzar's prey (in the dated appendix to ch. 29) advised setting the Tyrian prophecies ahead of the Egyptian, though the latter set in first.

The book thus shows signs of a deliberate editing and arrangement along thematic-chronological lines. Occasional erratic entities are not enough to destroy this overall impression.

The stylistic consistency of the book is striking. Excepting 1:2ff. (an editorial gloss to 1:1), it is couched in the form of a first-person report by the prophet of God's communications to him or the visions he was shown. Only five statements in the book are his own (4:14; 9:8; 11:13; 21:5). His reactions to popular sayings, even his complaints, are clothed as oracles of encouragement or exhortation (contrast, e.g., 33:30–33 with Jer. 15:10ff.). Oracle-reports begin with: וַיְהִי (הָיָה) דְבַר ה׳ אֵלַי ("This word of the Lord came to me"). The prophet is addressed בֶּן אָדָם ("O man!" or "mortal!") often followed by an imperative to say or do something (the prophet rarely reports that he executed the order). The message proper is introduced by כֹּה אָמַר ה׳ ("Thus said the Lord"), whose frequency is explained by 2:4; 10:11; 3:27. Doom-prophecies regularly state the ground of the punishment, introducing it with יַעַן ("inasmuch as"), followed by the sentence of punishment, introduced by לכן ("so then" or "assuredly"). The characteristically Ezekelian concluding phrase is וְיָדְעוּ (וידַעְתֶּם) כִּי אֲנִי ה׳ ("then they [you] shall know that I am the Lord") – with minor variations. A penchant for formulas is one of several affinities of Ezekiel to the priestly writings of the Pentateuch (see *Holiness Code).

ANALYSIS OF THE CONTENTS

The Call of the Prophet

(1:1–3:21). By the Chebar River (Akk. *nār Kabari*, a large canal that left the Euphrates near Babylon and passed through Nippur), the prophet is accosted and overwhelmed by a cloud-and-fire apparition of the divine vehicle – a wheeled platform, borne by four hybrid creatures – on which was enthroned the fiery Majesty (*kavod*) of the Lord. Fortified to face his defiant audience, the prophet is sent to announce to them God's coming punishment (cf. Jer. 1:7ff.; 18f.). He is fed a scroll on which the doom is inscribed (cf. Jer. 15:16). Afterward a wind bears him to the exile community of Tel Abib (Akk. *til abūbi*, "mound [abandoned since the time] of the Flood"), where he recovers from shock. Again he is addressed and appointed to be a lookout to warn Israel of the catastrophic consequences of their wickedness. This role delimits his responsibility: as a lookout, he is not accountable for the reaction of his audience – an important release for a prophet anticipating an indifferent or hostile reception.

The appearance of the fiery presence of God to stand by his devotees (Ex. 16:10; Num. 14:10; 16:19), and His coming on a cherub to their aid (Ps. 18:8ff.) were elements of tradition. The Chebar River – like the Ulai and the Tigris of Daniel 8:2; 10:4 – may, as a "clean place" of running water (Lev. 14:5), have served as a revelation site (cf. Mekhilta, *Petiḥta*), in which case the theophany was not wholly unexpected. (The presence of prophets among the exiles seems not to have been unusual; cf. Jer. 29:15; Ezek. 13:9.)

Appointment as a lookout recurs in 33:1–21 in association with its natural concomitant, a call to repentance. Such calls are found otherwise only in 14:6 and chapter 18. Hence the common assumption that the role of a lookout calling for repentance belongs to the latter part of the prophet's career is to be rejected as baselessly shifting a theme attested only before the fall to the post-fall prophecy. (Equally baseless is the notion that as a lookout the prophet addressed the individual rather than the nation; cf. the explicit addresses in 18:31; 33:11.) To be sure, the prophet did not have in mind any but the exilic remnant of the "house of Israel" when he called for repentance – the Jerusalemites were inexorably doomed – but he regarded them as a nucleus of a new Israel, not as discrete individuals. Nonetheless, 3: 16b–21 is intrusive in its context; it may well have sprung from the prophet's later reflection upon his role and responsibility toward his audience during the first part of his career, which was dominated by a "negative" message. Its incorporation into the account of the call bespeaks a desire to collect here all the components of the prophet's first (and principal) role.

The Doom of Judah and Jerusalem (3:22–24:27)

HOUSE ARREST AND DRAMATIC REPRESENTATION OF SIEGE AND PUNISHMENT (3:22–5:17). The prophet is ordered to shut himself up, "bound," in his house, and to refrain from speaking and publicly censuring the people (cf. Amos 5:10; Isa. 29:21); he can speak only to deliver God's messages. The prophet's withdrawal is borne out by every notice of his contact with others (8:1; 14:1; 20:1; 33:30ff.). He is visited at home; he is never on the street or in the market, no reflex of daily life outside makes its way into his utterances. "For the most part Ezekiel lives in a separate world. Other people drift in and out of the book, but there is little direct contact" (Freedman). The only conversation recorded with other human beings is by the command of God (24:18ff.). Except for dramatic representations, the prophet does nothing. "Though told in story form, Ezekiel's account is more a spiritual diary of personal experience of God and his inner reaction to it than a record of objective occurrences" (*ibid.*). In accordance with his tendency to extremes, he carries Jeremiah's gloomy unsociability (Jer. 15:17; 16:2, 5, 8) to its last degree (an analogy from Second Temple times occurs in Jos., Wars, 6:300ff.). Release from his "dumbness" came only with the arrival of the fugitive bearing news of Jerusalem's fall (24:26f.; 33:2ff.).

Orders for a complex series of acts representing the coming doom follow: (a) a model of the siege of Jerusalem is to be built and prophesied against; (b) through lying motionless on his sides, the prophet is to "bear the punishment" (cf. Num. 14:34; this is the usual meaning of the phrase, see especially Ezek. 14:6–10) of Judah and Israel for a number of days equivalent to the years of their punishment; (c) he is to consume scant rations of a loaf of mixed grains and water to show the siege-famine; (d) he is to bake a cake (*'ugah*, in direct contact with fuel or ashes, see *Bread) on human excrement (later exchanged for cattle dung) to symbolize the "unclean" food of exiles (cf. Hos. 9:3f.); (e) he is, finally, to shave his head and dispose of the hair in thirds to symbolize the annihilation of the population (cf. Isa. 7:20; Zech 13:8f.). Act (d) is intrusive and belongs thematically with the acts of chapter 12; it was attracted to this section by the food prescription of 4:10ff.

PROPHECIES DIRECTED AGAINST THE MOUNTAINS (= the land; vs. 1) OF ISRAEL AND THEIR HEATHEN CULT INSTALLATIONS (chs. 6 and 7; cf. Lev. 6:30) AND AGAINST THE POPULATION. Chapter seven proclaims that "the end has come" (Amos 8:2; Gen. 6:13) for all classes of the populace.

A VISIONARY TRANSPORTATION TO JERUSALEM (chs. 8–11). In a trance-vision, the prophet is taken to see the abominations in the Temple (ch. 8) and the destruction of Jerusalem by heavenly executioners (9:1–10:7). While he prophesies against a cabal of 25 leading men, one Pelatiah drops dead. A thematically associated denunciation of the Jerusalemites' design to supplant the exiles and a promise of the latter's restoration follows. In the course of the vision, the stages of the departure of God's Majesty from the Temple and the city are recounted (10:18f. (referring to vs. 4?); 11:22f.). The historical implications of this vision are discussed below.

DRAMATIC REPRESENTATION OF THE EXILE OF JUDAH AND ITS KING (12:1–16). After the event, the original references to the king's disguise in verses 6 and 12 were interpretatively adjusted to conform with the blinding of King Zedekiah (II Kings 25:7). Verses 17–20 order the prophet to represent, as he eats, the fright of the Jerusalemites.

ON PROPHECY (12:21–14:11). Two denunciations of the popular dismissal of doom prophecies precede a long diatribe against false prophets of weal (= Jer. 23:25ff.), and sorceresses. Another oracle declares God inaccessible to the heathenish Israelites for normal oracular consultation (under the dispensation of wrath, only one-way communications from God to man obtained).

NO SALVATION THROUGH VICARIOUS MERIT (14:12–23; against Gen. 18:24, etc.). The legendary worthies Noah, Daniel (apparently akin to the Ugaritic righteous ruler Dnil; Pritchard, Texts, 149ff.; COS I, 343–56), and Job could save themselves alone – not even their own children – from God's judgment. (This theme is related to the intercessory function of prophecy (cf. 13:5 with 22:30) and is thus linked to the preceding oracles.) Yet with Jerusalem, an exception will be made: some unworthies will escape with their children to Babylonia to justify God's dooming the city to Ezekiel's hearers who will thus be able to see for themselves what a depraved lot the Jerusalemites are.

THREE PARABLES (chs. 15–17). Chapter 15 contains the parable of the vine wood. Not the useful vine (Hos. 10:1; Jer. 2:21; Ps. 80:9, 15) but the useless vine wood is the fit image of Israel – good only for fuel, and hence consigned to destruction.

Chapter 16 contains the parable of the nymphomaniacal adulteress. This lurid, even pornographic, parable, immoderate in its language and its historical judgments, combines these elements: the image of marriage for the covenant relation of God and Israel (Hos. 1–3; Jer. 2:2; 3:1); Jerusalem's Jebusite origin – used to argue the genetic depravity of Israel; the view that political alliances (whether voluntary or coerced) are equivalent to apostasy – both expressing reliance on powers other than God. At verse 44, the figure is skewed and loses its form. Jerusalem is unfavorably compared to her "sisters" Samaria and Sodom. Undeserving as she is, God will, out of faithfulness to His ancient covenant, yet redeem her and let her rule her sisters. Then she will be ashamed of her past.

It is likely that verses 44ff. are secondary; but to consider them post-fall because of the concluding promise of restoration is to miss the prevailingly condemnatory context of the promise. Contrast the reversed proportions of the same elements in the restoration prophecy of 36:16 –7.

Chapter 17 concerns the parable of the two eagles (Nebuchadnezzar and Psammetichus II, see below), a cedar (Jehoiachin), and a vine (Zedekiah): a denunciation of Zedekiah for seeking Egyptian aid to rebel against, and thus break his vassal oath to, Nebuchadnezzar. An oath by YHWH is inviolable even if coerced (II Chron. 36:13). A consolatory appendix (vss. 22ff.) predicting the replanting of a sprig of the cedar, and in no way part of the denunciation, evidently stems from the last period of the prophet.

GOD'S ABSOLUTE JUSTICE (ch. 18). In this chapter Ezekiel maintains that there will be no vicarious suffering of one generation for another's sins (vss. 1–20), or condemnation of a presently good man for his wicked past (21–28); hence to repent is to live in God's grace. The argument was provoked by the current epigram (Jer. 31:28): "Fathers have eaten unripe grapes and the children's teeth are set on edge?," charging God with punishing the innocent descendants of wicked forefathers (cf. indeed II Kings 23:26; 24:3f.; Jer. 15:4; Lam. 5:7), an "inequitable" procedure (vss. 25, 29). The prophet is at pains to deny any "vertical" bequeathal of guilt, either between generations (as in Ex. 20:5), or within a single generation. Thus only the guilty are punished, and even they may be reconciled with God by repentance.

The presentation is systematic and couched in casuistic-legal terms – the idiom of abstract expression familiar to the priest-prophet (cf. 14; 33:1–20). For the sake of symmetry, the argument is carried beyond the immediate issue to its obverse – the denial too of "vertical" bequeathal of merit. The form shows theology comprehended as law – specifically, God's rule of justice brought into line with Deuteronomy

24:16's directive to earthly judges. Notable too is Ezekiel's catalogue of righteous traits; its linguistic and substantive affinity with pentateuchal law is highlighted by contrast with other such catalogues in Isaiah 33:15 ff. and Psalms 15.

A DIRGE OVER THE MONARCHY (ch. 19). In this dirge Ezekiel employs two images: that of a lioness and her cubs, and that of a vine and its branches.

THE COMPULSORY NEW EXODUS (ch. 20). This is a review of Israel's past as a series of refusals to accept God's laws and concludes with an affirmation by God to balk its present intention of assimilation to the pagans. God will force His kingship upon them, restore them by force to their land, and there receive their worship.

A plan to normalize the religious life of the exiles by renewing the sacrificial cult in Babylonia has been hypothesized as the provocation of this message. This chapter reveals important aspects of the prophet's theology of history: the predetermination of the exile (cf. Ps. 106:26); Israel's child-sacrifice as a punitive divine ordinance; concern for His reputation among humankind as the primary motive of God's dealings with Israel. The idea that Israel's restoration is a divine necessity which, if need be, will be forced upon Israel is developed less vehemently later in chapter 36.

THE PUNISHING SWORD: THREE ORACLES (ch. 21). The first of these announces the indiscriminate work of God's sword "from the south northward" (such "horizontal" involvement of innocent with guilty contemporaries is not covered in ch. 18; contrast 9:4); the second is a song to a sharpened sword; the third, a dramatic picture of Nebuchadnezzar taking omens at the crossroad to determine whether his sword should strike Rabbath Ammon or Jerusalem. Verses 33 ff., misleadingly addressed to Ammon, warn that ultimately the instrument of God's punishment (Babylonia) would itself be struck down by barbarians (cf. Isa. 10:12 ff.). This is the only anti-Babylonian oracle in the book.

UNCLEAN JERUSALEM: THREE ORACLES (ch. 22). The first is an arraignment of the "bloody city" (Nah. 3:1) – of Nineveh, whose terms recall Leviticus 18–20; the second, a reminiscence of Isaiah 1:20 – once silver, the city is now all dross; the third oracle, a variation of Zephaniah 3:1–8 – all the classes of the city are corrupt. The prophet's avowal that not a soul could be found to redeem the city in God's sight is a hyperbole similar to I Kings 19:14, Jeremiah 5:1 ff., and Lamentations 2:14. It does not mean that Ezekiel and Jeremiah could not have been contemporaries (as Torrey argued).

THE DISSOLUTE SISTERS, OHOLAH (Samaria, i.e., "her own tent") AND OHOLIBAH (Jerusalem, i.e., "my tent is in her") (ch. 23). The relations of the two Israelite kingdoms with Egypt, Assyria, and Babylonia are represented – in the extravagant manner of chapter 16 – as the shameless sexual frenzies of two harlot sisters. From verse 36 on, the apostasy motif of chapter 16 appears in a disordered epilogue.

THE FILTHY POT: A PARABLE OF JERUSALEM (24:1–14; cf. 11:3 ff.), dating to the start of the siege, anticipating its purgation through fire.

THE DEATH OF THE PROPHET'S WIFE (24:15–27). The prophet must dramatically represent, by his abstention from mourning, the paralyzing shock that will engulf the exiles at hearing of the city's fall (cf. Jer. 16:5–7). However, for the prophet, the arrival of that news will end his dumbness (i.e., release him from obsession with Jerusalem's fall).

Doom Pronounced Against Foreign Nations (chs. 25–32)
These chapters consist of prophecies of doom pronounced against seven foreign nations involved in Judah's revolt (Jer. 27:3). Excepting Egypt, they failed to support Judah; they all survived her. The dating of these prophecies shows that their location is approximately chronological. Condemnatory of Israel's enemies, they are a preliminary to prophecies of Israel's restoration.

BRIEF PROPHECIES OF DOOM AGAINST AMMON, MOAB, EDOM, AND PHILISTIA (ch. 25; cf. Jer. 47–49). PROPHECY OF DOOM AGAINST PHOENICIA (chs. 26–28). Four prophecies are directed against Tyre and one last against Sidon. Noteworthy is the representation of the island city as a ship loaded with merchandise (the amazing itemization of which is a prime source of information on east Mediterranean commerce of the time (see Bondi, Bartoloni in Bibliography); Ezekiel might have come by this from Phoenician traders and artisans known to have been pensioners of the Babylonian king; Pritchard, Texts, 308). Also remarkable is the image of the king of Tyre as an expelled denizen of God's garden (28:12–19) – a tantalizingly obscure variant of the Eden myth.

EPILOGUE TO CHAPTERS 25–28 (28:24–26). The epilogue contains the promise that after its restoration, Israel will never again suffer the contempt of these neighbors, since they will all have been destroyed. Excepting Edom and Philistia who are vaguely charged with "taking revenge," the charges against these nations are their hubris and their contempt of Israel (both offensive to God). Why Tyre receives such a measure of wrath is unclear.

SEVEN ORACLES AGAINST EGYPT (chs. 29–32). The unusual clustering of dated prophecies may signify the prophet's expectation of Egypt's imminent fall to Nebuchadnezzar after the defeat of Apries (see below), and his concern for establishing the priority of his prophecies to that event. Egypt's offense is its unreliability as an ally (29:6 = Isa. 36:6), or Pharaoh's hubris. However, because Egypt tried to help Judah, it is promised a restoration (29:13 ff.). The latest passage in the book is an appendix to the first Egyptian oracle. Nebuchadnezzar, having failed to reduce Tyre, is promised Egypt as his wages (on the historical background, see below). The presence of this amendment to the Tyre prophecies alongside the untouched – and by then confuted – original prophecies attests to the inviolate status of Ezekiel's oracles in his own (and subsequent age's) estimation. It is a warning against the easy assumption of later tampering with the prophet's words.

The standpoint of the prophecies against the nations is one of sensitivity to the diminution suffered by God owing to Israel's humiliation. Israel's fall gave occasion to its neighbors to gloat and aggrandize themselves. Heathen arrogance reached its limit; God must now act to assert his authority on earth. This necessarily entails the restoration of Israel, which is indeed anticipated several times in this section (25:14; 28:25; 29:16, 21). The interconnection of the doom of the nations and Israel's restoration is seen also in the sequence of chapters 35–36, on which see below.

A Miscellany From the Time of the Fall (ch. 33)

Verses 1–20: The kernel of this piece is the despairing cry of the people: How can we live, immersed as we are in sin (vs. 10)? It stimulates a clarification of the constructive aspect of the doom prophecy – the prophet's role as a lookout, warning his hearers of the consequence of their sin and urging them to repent and live. Previously isolated elements (3:16b–19; 14:6; 18:21ff.) are woven into a new whole, meeting the need of the hour. As in 18, a legal-casuistic style is the vehicle of doctrinal statement.

Verses 21ff.: The arrival of the fugitive with news of Jerusalem's fall brings an end to the prophet's dumbness – to what effect, remains obscure.

Verses 23–33, in form a single prophecy, comprise two heterogeneous pieces. Verses 23–29 are a scornful rejection of claims on the part of those dwelling in the land of Israel after the fall to retain title to the land despite their fewness (a later, pathetic version of 11:15b). Verses 30–33 promise the prophet that, although he is now no more than an entertainer to the people who flock to hear him, the imminent advent of doom will make them take his words seriously. Why this pre-fall piece is placed here is unclear.

All of chapter 33 belongs to the doom prophecy, but it reflects a situation just before and after the fall – later than that of chapter 24. It is dated later than the first dated foreign-nation prophecies (which themselves straddle the fall). The arrangement of chapter 33 after the block of foreign-nation prophecies is therefore reasonable.

Prophecies of Israel's Restoration (chs. 34–39)

RENOVATION OF THE LEADERSHIP OF ISRAEL (ch. 34). In a new tone of compassion, God inveighs against the bad shepherds who misguided his flock and promises personally to take it in charge (vss. 1–16; cf. Jer. 23:1ff.). The image is then skewed, and bucks and rams within the flock are blamed for having bullied the rest. A new David will be their shepherd, and under him they will enjoy all the covenant blessings of Leviticus 26:4–12.

THE RENOVATION OF THE MOUNTAINS OF ISRAEL (countering ch. 6; 35:1–36:15). For encroaching upon Judah, the hill country of Seir will be desolated (cf. III Ezra 4:50) – along with all others who dared lay hands on God's land (vs. 5). Then the hill country of Israel will prosper as never before, and reproaches of infertility, famine, and "bereaving its inhabitants" (through conquest by foreigners and deportations) will be removed forever.

A NEW HEART AND SPIRIT: THE CONDITION OF LASTING POSSESSION OF THE LAND (36:16–38). With inexorable logic the theology of Israel's career is expounded: exiled for its sins, Israel brought the Lord into disrepute among the nations. In order to establish His authority on earth, God must restore and glorify Israel. But to prevent a repetition of the disaster, God will alter the moral nature of the people, giving them a new heart and spirit and thus insuring that they will be faithful to him (cf. Jer. 32:39 [Ezek. 11:19]; Jer. 31:32f.). That the benefactions to Israel are merely incidental to God's concern for His reputation is repeatedly insisted upon (vss. 22, 32).

Though the gentle conclusion of the prophecy (vss. 33–38) mitigates it somewhat, it emerges as even more thoroughly theocentric than the related doctrine of the compulsory exodus in chapter 20.

THE REVIVAL OF THE DEAD BONES OF ISRAEL AND THE UNIFICATION OF ITS TWO SCEPTERS (ch. 37). Once again a popular saying ("Our bones are dried up, our hope is lost ...") provides the stimulus for a prophecy, this time a prophetic vision. With the prophet's participation (as in the vision of Jerusalem's destruction, 11:4–13) "all the house of Israel," by now reduced to "very many and very dry bones," are miraculously reconstituted.

The imagery of the second oracle is related: Ezekiel is ordered to represent symbolically the reunification of the monarchy by joining two sticks, inscribed, respectively, "Judah's" and "Joseph's." The happiness of the future kingdom under God is summed up in four everlasting boons: possession of the promised land, rule by David, God's covenant of well-being, God's presence in His sanctuary among them.

The conclusion of chapter 37 brings to an end the account of Israel's restoration and renovation, and the last verse adumbrates the theme of the program of chapters 40–48. Between the two, however, appear the prophecies on Gog, presupposing the situation arrived at by the end of chapter 37.

THE INVASION OF GOG AND HIS FALL (chs. 38–39). Lured by the prospect of loot, Gog (whose name is modeled on that of King Gyges of Lydia, but who is not, here, a historical personage) and his barbarian allies will march down from the north against defenseless Israel. God, however, will destroy his great host on the mountains of Israel, thus demonstrating to Israel that He is their God, and to the nations that Israel's former misfortune resulted from God's wrath, not His weakness.

Influence of earlier prophecies on this depiction of Gog's fall is acknowledged in 38:17. The menace of a nameless northern nation occurs in Jeremiah 1:14; 4:6; and other passages; and a concerted assault of pagans, in Isaiah 29:1ff.; Micah 8:11ff.

According to Isaiah, Assyria was to perish on the mountains of Israel, not by the sword of man (14:24ff.; 31:8). In pre-exilic prophecy, however, the assault of the heathen was punishment for Israel's sins, and their collapse must precede Israel's redemption. Ezekiel adapted these unfulfilled prophecies to the exilic situation. A heathen assault could come now only against a restored Israel, and it could not be punitive. Inspired by the ancient model of Pharaoh's fall at the sea, Ezekiel conceives the motive of the assault to be the prospect of pillaging a defenseless people (Ex. 15:9); the significance of the heathen's fall is derived from the same model: to shed glory on God (Ex. 14:4; cf. Ezek. 39:13).

A Messianic Priestly Code (Kaufmann; chs. 40–48)

Following the general topical order of the priestly writings in the Pentateuch, a description of the future sanctuary, regulations for the cult and its personnel, and provisions for settlement in the land are set out in detail. Modernization and rectification of past wrongs are pervasive motives.

A VISIONARY TRANSPORTATION TO THE FUTURE TEMPLE (40:1–43:12; a counterpart to chs. 8–11). A blueprint of the Temple area is narrated as a tour through its courts, gates, and rooms, the prophet being guided by an angelic "man" with a measuring rod and line. The design appears to follow the latest form of the Solomonic Temple, with some schematization (e.g., the preference for the number 25; cf. the 25th year, 40:1). The prophet witnesses the return of the divine Majesty through the east gate, by which it had exited in 11:1, into the inner sanctum. Thence an oracle issues, condemning the past contiguity of the palace and the Temple as a defilement of the latter, and banning it for the future.

ORDINANCES OF THE CULT AND ITS PERSONNEL (43:13–46:24). These sections deal with the altar, the reorganization of the clergy (Zadokites alone to remain full priests, the rest to be degraded to menials for having served at the "idolatrous" rural sanctuaries), their regulations and perquisites, the territorial "sacred oblation" which is to be set aside for them and the temple, a brief cultic calendar. Mention of the "oblation" attracts regulations concerning the "chieftain" (king), to whom holdings on each side of the oblation are assigned (in consequence, his ancient right [or abuse] of expropriation (I Sam. 8:14) is abolished). Besides his role in the cult, his responsibility for maintaining justice is touched upon (45:9ff.).

The discontinuity and loose order of this section suggest that it is a composite that took shape piecemeal.

THE LIFE-GIVING STREAM ISSUING FROM THE TEMPLE (47:1–12). The vision of this marvelous stream, through which the prophet is led by his angelic guide, bridges the topic of the Temple and cult and that of the land, which follows.

THE ALLOCATION OF THE LAND (7:13–48:35). The boundaries of the future Land of Israel are essentially those of Numbers 34:1–12, and consequently exclude Transjordan, historically Israelite. Another rectification is the right extended to permanently resident aliens to share in tribal holdings. Yet another is the equalization of the tribal holdings: all receive equal latitudinal strips of land with some coastal plain, some highlands, and some bit of the Jordan-Dead Sea depression. Jerusalem will bear the new name "YHWH is there" (cf. 37:26–28).

THE TEXT AND ITS INTEGRITY

According to critical scholars, the text of Ezekiel is among the most corrupt of the Bible. That technical passages (e.g., the account of the divine vehicle, the list of Tyre's merchandise, the Temple blueprint) – at best difficult to understand – should have suffered in transmission is not surprising. However, poetry too has been garbled (cf. chs. 7; 21). The Greek ("Septuagint") often provides a remedy, but at the same time raises new questions because of its frequently shorter text. In the light of the Greek, the received Hebrew text appears conflate – i.e., it exhibits variants, synonymous readings, and tags that have been collected from several versions of the prophet's words. The texts of Ezekiel and Jeremiah were peculiarly susceptible to expansion and the addition of tags owing to the fact that they are very formulaic, their idiom being modeled upon the two most highly stylized and formulaic works of early Israelite tradition – the pentateuchal priestly writings and Deuteronomy respectively.

On occasion, allusions to events later than the prophecies that contain them indicate post-event touching up (see, e.g., on ch. 12, above). Since none reflects events later than the last-dated item in the book (see below), the assumption that someone other than the prophet is responsible for them is unnecessary.

Recurrently, a piece will show a juncture at which a breakdown in form (20), a skewing of theme (16; 23; 34), or change of mood (17) appears. Repetitions (see on ch. 33), discontinuities, and erratic blocks (38–39; 40–48) argue against the originality and integrity of a piece. But whether such phenomena point to another hand rather than to later reflections or editorial activity of the prophet himself is a matter of dispute among critics. The common assumption that a circle of disciple-transmitters existed who had a large part in the shaping of the present text and its disjunctures lacks any evidential basis.

LOCALE AND HISTORICAL BACKGROUND

Information supplied by contemporary records suffices to test the claim of the book that its contents fall between July 593 and April 571 B.C.E.

Just before breaking off, the Babylonian Chronicle reports that in December 594 Nebuchadnezzar called out his army against Syria – for the first time since his conquest of Jerusalem in 597. It seems hardly coincidental that (a) just at that time a new king, Psammetichus II, came to the throne of Egypt, who showed a lively interest in Syria, and (b) an anti-Babylonian conspiracy of Phoenicians and Palestinians was formed in Jerusalem in Zedekiah's fourth year – 594/3 (Jer. 27).

In the same year Jeremiah had his altercation with Hananiah ben Azzur, who prophesied the imminent fall of Babylon and the return, within two years, of King Jehoiachin and his exiles (Jer. 28).

The situation of the exiles can be gathered from Jeremiah's letter to them, which was sent about this time (Jer. 29). There, too, prophets (whom Jeremiah brands as false) encouraged in the people expectations of a speedy end to their exile – which Jeremiah was at pains to quash. He not only exhorts them to be reconciled to their captivity, he communicates to them an oracle (ch. 24) unconditionally condemning Jerusalem to a horrible end. Hope in the future of Jerusalem is futile and wrong; the future belongs to the exiles from whom the nation will be regenerated (so 24:6 f.).

In 591 Psammetichus made a state visit to some shrines on the Syrian coast, probably not without political overtones. About two years later, evidently in collaboration with Egypt and its Palestinian allies, Judah revolted. Nebuchadnezzar called out a powerful army which laid siege to Jerusalem in January 588. Shortly afterward, Psammetichus died, but his successor, Apries, maintained his policy. An Egyptian force marched into Palestine, giving Jerusalem temporary relief (Jer. 37:5; 34:21). But it was soon beaten back, and the siege resumed until famine brought Jerusalem to its knees in the summer of 586.

None of the neighbors of Judah was destroyed in the revolt; Tyre and Egypt are known to have preserved their independence. During or directly after Jerusalem's ordeal, Tyre was besieged by Nebuchadnezzar for 13 years (Jos., Apion, 1.21), the end being reckoned between 575–72. The city came under Babylonian control, but was not sacked. Only in 568/7 did Nebuchadnezzar finally move against Egypt (Pritchard, Texts, 308d); the outcome of that campaign is unknown, but Egypt remained independent until its conquest by Cambyses of Persia in 525.

The whole span of Ezekiel's dates falls within the reign of Nebuchadnezzar (605/4–562). He and he alone appears in the book as the conqueror of Judah and the appointed scourge of God for the nations. Every clear historical allusion in the book is to this, or some preceding, period. Especially significant is the book's ignorance of events later than its last date. Its author lived to see the failure of his Tyre prophecy, and emended it in 571. However he did not know that not Nebuchadnezzar, but Cambyses, would conquer Egypt (525) – which would not then go into a 40-year exile; and that Babylon's end would not be sanguinary and fiery (21:36 ff.) but virtually bloodless (539). Persia is mentioned only as an exotic adjunct to the forces of Tyre and Gog – indicating that the author was ignorant of what happened from 550 on, when Cyrus united Media and Persia into the nucleus of the Persian Empire. If the author(s?) of 34–48 lived later than 538, they would have seen the confuting of all their restoration prophecies and programs by events. In sum: no post-571 anachronism has left its mark in the book to necessitate the assumption of another hand than Ezekiel's.

That the locale of the prophecy is Babylonia is said several times (1:1; 3:11; 15; 11:24) and implied by the era of "our exile" (33:21; 40:1). Several prophecies have an explicitly exilic standpoint or audience (11:15 ff.; 12:11ff.; 13:9; 14:22; 20:34 ff.; 24:21b; note also the peculiarly Ezekelian usage of "on the soil of Israel," unnatural for someone living in the land of Israel, 12:22; 18:2; 21:7; 33:24).

At the same time, the almost exclusive focus on Jerusalem in the doom prophecies and the passionate addresses to her have given rise to the view that at least part of the prophecy originated in Jerusalem – the present exilic cast of the whole being editorial (so Rashi at 1:3, combining statements in the Mekhilta to Ex. 12:1 and 15:9). However, the lack of a convincing explanation for such an alleged editorial transfer of originally Jerusalem prophecies to Babylonia leads one to ask whether the anomaly of Ezekiel's prophecy, given its Babylonian setting, is really so implausible.

Ezekiel fails to discriminate between exiles and homelanders in his diatribes; his audience is an undifferentiated "rebellious house," i.e., they are unconscious of any deep-dyed guilt and expect shortly a turn for the better in their fortunes; and they are encouraged in this by their prophets (ch. 13). The situation corresponds to what is known from Jeremiah to have obtained in Jerusalem the year prior to Ezekiel's call (see above). However, Jeremiah's letter reveals that precisely the same situation obtained among the Babylonian exiles. So much so that Jeremiah's major concern is to create a cleavage between the exiles and the Jerusalemites with regard to their hopes for the immediate future. Both his exhortation to become reconciled to a long captivity and his prediction of an inexorable and total doom for Jerusalem are intended to make the exiles despair of Jerusalem's survival, to tear them from the hopes they attached to the city. Only so could they be brought to repentance and the realization of their destiny as the "good figs" (Jer. 24:7).

The implications of Jerusalem's fate were thus hardly less profound for the exiles than for the Jerusalemites themselves (indeed most of the exiles were from Jerusalem, II Kings 24:14 ff.). Had Jeremiah been in Tel Abib he would have found no topic of more absorbing concern to his audience than the future of the city; and his letter shows what the tenor of his message to them would have been: "laments, and moaning, and woe."

An exiled Ezekiel's preoccupation with Jerusalem (not quite exclusive; his calls to repentance are directed at the exiles, cf. Jer. 24:7, end) is unexceptionable. Anomalous among prophets is his continuously addressing an audience that is apparently hundreds of miles away. But the appearance is misleading. Prophecies against foreign nations, an established genre, always involve an incongruity between the ostensible audience (the foreign nations) and the real one – the Israelites for whose ears the prophecies are really meant and for whom they bear a vital message. Similarly an exiled prophet's address to Jerusalem would have been meant for the ears of his immediate environment. Since in fact and spirit that environment was thoroughly Jerusalemite, the prophet would not have sensed any incongruity between his ostensible and his real audience. Whatever anomaly attaches to an exiled Ezekiel's prophecy arises out of the anomalous coexistence of two Jerusalemite communities hundreds of miles apart at this juncture of history.

That Ezekiel was far from Jerusalem during his career as a prophet is the most plausible explanation of his Temple vision in chapters 8–11. This congeries of strange cults and sinister plotting going on all at once at different locations in the temple precinct is evidently a montage whose elements are drawn principally, but not exclusively, from the syncretistic cult fostered by Manasseh and eradicated by Josiah (cf. II Chron. 33:7; II Kings 23:11; we do not know whether Josiah's reforms completely survived his death). As the report of a divine vision, the account had powerful significance even to an audience removed from its scene.

INFLUENCES UPON THE PROPHET

Of the man Ezekiel all that is known is that he was a priest (1:3), married to a woman who died during the siege of Jerusalem (24:15ff.). He was, presumably, among the aristocrats who were deported with King Jehoiachin in 597. By then he had acquired the priestly learning and attitudes that characterize his prophecy: knowledge of the layout of the Temple and its regimen; of the historico-religious traditions of Israel, and of the idiom of priestly writing of the Pentateuch that dominates his prose (critics dispute the direction of the influence: some attributing to Ezekiel the invention of certain priestly idioms; most allowing the influence at least of the Holiness Code (Lev. 17–26) upon the prophet – the issue is a pivot of pentateuchal criticism); and sensitivity to the "clean" and the "unclean" (e.g., his frequent allusion to menstrual uncleanness, *niddah*), and, above all, to the awesome holiness of God.

Passion and a fertile imagination, tending to the baroque, shine through his writings. He is the master of the dramatic, representational action (which has a portentous, mysteriously causal character; in 24:24 the prophet is called a prefiguring "sign," *mofet*). He was famous for his (often lurid) imagery (21:5). His actions and his images are more numerous and more complex than those of any of his predecessors. As a visionary too he has no peer; indeed he innovated a genre: the transportation-and-tour vision, so common in later apocalypse. It is no wonder that people flocked to his "entertainments" (33:32).

Ezekiel was immersed in the whole range of Israel's prophetic tradition. Archaic models inspire him – prophesying under seizure by "the hand of YHWH" (cf. Elijah [I Kings 18:46] and Elisha [II Kings 3:5]), transportation by the "wind of YHWH" (cf. Elijah, I Kings 18:12; II Kings 2:16). He is the only prophet after Moses who not only envisions the future but lays down a blueprint and a law for it. He reflects nothing of the eschatological vision of the unity of humankind under God introduced into Judahite prophecy by Isaiah (2:2ff.; 18:7; 19:24f.; Mic. 4:1ff.; Hab. 2:14; Zeph. 3:9; Jer. 3:17), but holds on to the earlier view that, while God rules over all, His special grace and holiness are, and will be, confined to Israel.

Yet Ezekiel was deeply indebted to classical, literary prophecy as well. Instances of this have been pointed out in the analysis of the contents of the book. It need be remarked here only that by far the most striking affinities of Ezekiel's prophecy are with Jeremiah. The two have in common a vocabulary and a stock of concepts and figures (eating God's words (Jer. 15:16), the harlot sisters (3:6ff.), the bad shepherds (23:1ff.), the lookout (6:17), and many more) beyond what may be explained by mere contemporaneity. That Ezekiel had heard (of) Jeremiah before 597 is to be assumed (cf. Ezek 9:4); that he continued to receive word of his prophecies afterward is likely, since such word did reach the exiles (Jer. 29:24ff.).

EZEKIEL'S MESSAGE AND ITS EFFECTS

For Ezekiel the key to the agony of Judah was to be found in the curses attached to God's covenant (as in Lev. 26; Deut. 28), which, since the age of Manasseh, had cast a pall over Judahite religious thought (cf. II Kings 21:10ff.; 22:19ff.; 24:3). As Ezekiel saw it, the entire history of Israel was one continuous breach of covenant, for which the fall was the just and predicted punishment. In the face of nihilistic cynicism (18:1, 25), he insisted on the justice, the reasonableness, and the regularity of God's dealings with men. That is the ground of his denunciation and of his call to repentance as well.

What was not anticipated in the early curses was the aspersion cast on God's power by their operation. It had been assumed that with punishment would come contrition (Lev. 26:41) and repentance (Deut. 30:1ff.), to be followed by reconciliation and restoration. That seems to be the presupposition of Ezekiel's call (to the exiles) to repent (18:30ff.). But in view of the injury to God's reputation (cf. 36:20, a projection onto others of an inner-Israelite reaction?), the idea took hold of the prophet that Israel's rehabilitation could not depend on the gamble that Israel would indeed repent. Frustrated by the people's obduracy, the prophet announced a compulsory new exodus (20:32ff.), underlying which was the necessity of vindicating God's power. Contrition would come later (20:43; cf. 16:61; 36:31) and was no longer a precondition of redemption. As for repentance, God would see to it that after the people were restored they would remain permanently reconciled with, and obedient to, God; not they, but He would make them a new heart (contrast 36:26 (= 11:19) with 18:31). Then they could enjoy eternal blessedness that would serve as a witness of the power of their God to the world.

The doctrine of God's stake in the preservation and restoration of Israel appears in the Second Isaiah (43:25; 48:9, 11); it must have contributed to the exile's will to resist assimilation to their environment and to their faith in a national future.

The effect of Ezekiel's denunciation may be detected in his audience's acknowledgment of their sin in 33:10 at the time of the fall (contrast 18:1), and even more clearly in the version given by the Chronicler of Zedekiah's reign (II Chron. 36:11ff.). II Kings 24:18ff. knows nothing of the defilement of the temple, nor does it charge the king with violating his vassal oath (Ezek. 8; 17).

Ezekiel's visions and his angelic actors in them inaugurated a literary category that flourished in post-exilic prophecy and apocalyptic (cf. Zech., Dan.). The visionary transportation-tour became the standard vehicle for apocalyptic revelations of the secrets of the cosmos.

The least influential part of Ezekiel's prophecy was his program for the future (chs. 40–48). Medieval exegetes were painfully aware of the contradictions in detail between what Ezekiel laid down and what the community of the Restoration did; they "saved" Ezekiel by declaring his program to be purely messianic (which indeed it is; see, e.g., the conflicting positions of Rashi and Kimḥi on 43:11; cf. Rashi on vss. 21ff. and Kimḥi on vs. 25 and 45:21ff.). The authorities of Second Temple times may also have thought so; in practice, they made the Torah their rule, and ignored Ezekiel's program entirely.

LATER DOUBTS ABOUT THE CIRCULATION OF THE BOOK

The divergence in moral theology between Ezekiel 18:4 and Exodus 20:5b did not embarrass later authorities; it was but one of several matters of doctrine that Moses ordained and a later prophet abrogated (so Mak. 24a). Divergences in law were another matter, and by the first century C.E. the many conflicts between the Torah and laws in Ezekiel's program had become so worrisome that withdrawal of the book from circulation was being considered (*bikkeshu lignoz et Sefer Yeḥezkel*). Only Ḥananiah ben Hezekiah's demonstration that the conflicts could be reconciled kept the book available (Shab. 13b). The possibility was evidently more important than the specific reconciliations, for barely a trace of Ḥananiah's efforts was transmitted (Sifre to Deut. 25:15; cf. Men. 45a).

Another argument for withdrawing the book was the danger surrounding inquiry into the divine vehicle described in chapters 1 and 10. A ramified theosophical doctrine, taught only to a select few, was anchored in that vision (*Ma'aseh Merkavah*; "account of the chariot"; Ḥag. 2:1). The risk inherent in it of overstepping proper bounds is illustrated by a report of a child who "was looking into *ḥashmal* (Ḥag. 13a), when fire leaped forth from *hashmal* and consumed him." Once again the book was saved from withdrawal by Ḥananiah who pointed out that such children were very rare (Ḥag. 13a). The first chapter of the book remained problematic, and the anonymous opinion of the Mishnah is that it is not to be recited as a *haftarah* (Meg. 4:10). There is a similar stricture upon Ezekiel 16, because of its insult to Jerusalem. Neither is normative and chapter 1 is customarily the *haftarah* of (the first day of) Shavuot. Ezekiel is not referred to by name in the New Testament but the influence of the book on the book of Revelation is unmistakable.

[Moshe Greenberg]

EZEKIEL IN THE *AGGADAH*

Four aspects of Ezekiel's prophetic career figure most prominently in rabbinic literature:

(1) The divine chariot revelation (chap. 1), which became the basis not only of Jewish mysticism but also of various kinds of esoteric speculations (see *Merkabah Mysticism), and its study was therefore restricted within the rabbinic school curriculum (Ḥag. 2:1; Tosef., Ḥag. 2:1), and excluded from the synagogue *haftarah* reading (Meg. 4:10); but according to Tosef., Meg. 4:34, it could be recited to the public, though apparently without the Aramaic translation; subsequently it was introduced as the prophetical reading for (the first day of) Shavuot.

(2) The fierce denunciations of Israel which might be exploited by the Church for anti-Jewish polemical purposes and were therefore partly unacceptable to the rabbis.

(3) The resurrection of the dry bones (chap. 37), which was a potentially favorite theme for sectarian speculations and was therefore played down by a number of rabbis.

(4) Ezekiel's vision of the future temple and his priestly laws, which appear to contradict the pentateuchal rules and very nearly led to the exclusion of the Book of Ezekiel from the canon (Shab. 13b, and parallels).

The general popularity of Ezekiel's revelation in non-rabbinic circles was bound to dampen rabbinic enthusiasm. Although many of the leading talmudic scholars, from the first through fourth centuries, continued to study and expound mystical concepts based on Ezekiel's *Ma'aseh Merkavah* (cf. Tosef., Ḥag. 2:1ff.; TJ, Ḥag. 2:1, 77a), there was a sharp reaction in Palestine from the second century onward regarding certain kinds of esoteric speculations of an apocalyptic nature. Of four rabbis who entered the heavenly "garden" only one, R. *Akiva, "ascended in peace and descended in peace." The other three were spiritually harmed by their spiritual adventures, which were henceforth strongly, though not always successfully, discouraged (Tosef., Ḥag. 2:3ff., and parallels; cf. Hag. 2:1). It is interesting to note that Ezekiel's detailed description of the heavenly chariot was contrasted unfavorably not only with the prophecies of Moses and Samuel – "whatever he saw he related; hence Scripture calls him (disparagingly) 'son of man'" (Tanḥ., Ẓav 13) – but also with Isaiah's restrained revelation (Isa. 6:1ff.). Ezekiel was therefore likened to "a villager who saw the king," while Isaiah resembled "a townsman who saw the king" (Ḥag. 13b).

Although the Midrash emphasizes that God had commanded the heavens to open before Ezekiel (Gen. R. 5:5) – perhaps as a counterweight to similar claims on behalf of Jesus – according to R. Eliezer, "a maidservant saw at the [Red] Sea what Ezekiel and all the other prophets never saw" (Mekh., *Shirah*, 3; cf. Mekh., *Yitro, Ba-hodesh*, 3). R. Eliezer, whose early contacts with Jesus' disciples made him especially wary of sectarian ideas (Av. Zar. 16b–17a; et al.), was anxious to emphasize the immense revelation to all Israel rather than to a select few. In line with his "nationalistic" tendency, he prohibited the *haftarah* reading of chapter 16 (on Jerusalem's "abominations"), sharply rebuking a student who had ignored his interdict (Meg. 4:10; Tosef Meg. 4:34; et al.).

R. Eliezer somewhat reduced the significance of Ezekiel's resurrection of the dry bones, pointing out that "the dead whom Ezekiel revived stood up, recited a song [i.e., of praise], and [immediately] died" (Sanh. 92b). R. Judah apparently regarded the story as an allegorical vision; but other rabbis fully accepted the resurrection miracle.

In later midrashic literature, Ezekiel is praised for his love of Israel; hence he was deemed worthy to perform the resuscitation miracle (SER 5:23). He was criticized, however, for his initial doubting of the possibility of such a miracle. Because of his lack of faith, he was doomed to die on foreign soil (PdRE 33).

The *halakhah* of the Book of Ezekiel deviates on a number of points from the Torah. Although attempts were made to reconcile the contradictions (most notably by Hananiah b. Hezekiah who saved the canonicity of the book), a number of cases were left to be "interpreted by Elijah in the future" (Men. 45a, and parallels). R. Yose b. Hanina, a third century *amora*, frankly conceded that Ezekiel's doctrine of personal responsibility (Ezek. 18:3–4) was irreconcilable with Moses' teaching concerning "visiting the iniquity of the father upon the children and upon the children's children" (Ex. 34:7, et al.; Mak. 24a).

According to R. *Simeon b. Yoḥai, Ezekiel was consulted by Ḥananiah, Mishael, and Azariah whether to bow down to Nebuchadnezzar's idol. He referred them to Isaiah 26:20, in effect advising them to hide and flee. They refused to accept his counsel and prepared to die for the sanctification of God's name. Despite Ezekiel's tearful pleading, God refused to promise His aid, though saving them in the end (Song. R. 7:8). The Midrash reflects the conflicting opinions on the preferable Jewish reaction to the Hadrianic persecution. Ezekiel represents' the moderate compromising view such as that of R. Yose b. Kisma (cf. Av. Zar. 18a), while the course of martyrdom followed by R. Akiva and R. Ḥanina b. Teradyon, among others (Ber. 61b; Av. Zar. 18a), was preferred by R. Simeon (a disciple of R. Akiva), who fearlessly braved death when he demanded to be instructed by his imprisoned master (Pes. 112a), and risked his life again when he openly denounced the Romans (Shab. 33b).

[Moses Aberbach / Stephen G. Wald (2nd ed.)]

EZEKIEL'S TOMB

According to a tradition this was located at a village 20 miles (32 km.) south of the town of Ḥilla in central Iraq. The Arabs refer to Ezekiel as to other prophets as "Dhū al-Kifl" (various etymologies have been suggested such as "doubly rewarded"; "guarantor"?) for the responsibility that he bore for the people of Israel. The tomb is mentioned for the first time in the epistle of R. *Sherira Gaon (c. 986), and a detailed description is given by *Benjamin of Tudela about 1170, *Pethahiah of Regensburg (about the same time), and later by other travelers, Jewish and non-Jewish. It is situated in a man-made cave, covered by a cupola. Over the cupola a magnificent outer tomb is built, coinciding in its linear dimensions with the lower tomb, and it is at this outer tomb that the pilgrims pray. In the room adjoining Ezekiel's tomb there are five tombs purported to contain the remains of five *geonim*. Another room, with a window, is referred to as "Elijah's Cave," and a third room contains the tomb of Menahem Ṣāliḥ *Daniel, a well-known philanthropist whose family was entrusted with guarding the tomb. The walls bear various inscriptions, including three poems in the Arab-Spanish meter composed by the Babylonian poet R. Abdallah Khuḍayr and in honor of donors. Pilgrimages to the tomb were usually made in the late spring, especially on Shavuot. A special parchment scroll, "the Scroll of Ezekiel," was read, containing passages from the Book of Ezekiel and written on behalf of the ascent to heaven of the souls of the departed. In 1860 the Muslims made an attempt to wrest ownership of the tomb from the Jews, but a government emissary from Constantinople decided in favor of the Jews.

[Abraham Ben-Yaacob]

IN ISLAM

The name of the prophet Ezekiel (Ḥizqīl) is not mentioned in the *Koran. However Sura 2:244 ("Dost thou not look at those who left their homes by thousands, for fear of death; and God said to them 'Die,' and then He quickened them again …") alludes to Ezekiel 37:1–10. According to *Qiṣaṣ al-Anbiyā'* (Legends of the Prophets), the mother of Ḥizqīl ibn Būdhī was barren (an allusion to Hannah, the mother of Samuel the prophet), and he is therefore referred to as "the son of the old woman." It was he who resuscitated the dead who were killed by the plague (al-ṭā'ūn).

[Haïm Z'ew Hirschberg]

IN THE ARTS

Ezekiel and his prophetic vision have not inspired many works of literary importance. Apart from Barbara Macandrew's *Ezekiel and Other Poems* (1871), a lyric by Emma *Lazarus, "The New Ezekiel" (in *Songs of a Semite*, 1882), predicting the Jewish people's national revival in Ereẓ Israel, works on the theme include a poem by Franz *Werfel, *Ezechiel, der Prophet* (1953), a tale of the Babylonian captivity by Lieselotte Hoffmann, and Albert *Cohen's one-act play *Ezéchiel* (1933), a dialogue representing the struggle between prophetic vision and reality.

In art the important subjects drawn from the Book of Ezekiel are the apocalyptic visions – the Chariot (Merkavah) with fiery wheels, the resurrection of the dry bones, and the locked gate. There are also some scenes showing Ezekiel undergoing various ordeals – eating a scroll, lying prostrate in expiation of the sins of Israel and Judah, and cutting his hair and beard and weighing them in the balance. The prophet is usually shown with the fiery chariot or the double wheel, taken as a symbol of the two Testaments. Sometimes he also holds a scroll reading "Porta clausa est, non aperietur" (44:2). In the third-century frescoes of the synagogue at *Dura-Europos there is an outstanding cycle of scenes from the Book of Ezekiel. There are representations of the men slaughtering the people of Jerusalem (9:1–6), the prophet taken up by the hair and transported to the Valley of the Dry Bones, and the winds breathing life into the bones. The sixth-century Rabbula Gospels (Laurentiana, Florence) portray Ezekiel in conjunction with Jesus and David. In Oriental art he appears in frescoes in Greece (Hosios David, Salonika, fifth century), and in the church of Bachkovo, Bulgaria (12th century), and frequently in icons in those lands influenced by the Byzantine tradition. In the West, Ezekiel is first encountered in illumination, as in the ninth-century Bible of San Paolo Fuori le Mura. The earliest Western monastic example is the fresco in San Vicenzo de Galliano (c. 1007). There is a 12th-century statue by Benedetto Antelami on the facade of Borgo San Donnino, Fidenza, and a cycle in the lower church of Schwarzheindorf, near Bonn, Germany. Thirteenth-century portrayals in French churches are on the portal of Saint-Firmin, Amiens, on a window, at Bourges, and in La Sainte-Chapelle, Paris. The vision of the divine chariot also appears in Lesnovo, Serbia (14th century), and in the Pitti Palace, Florence. The Valley of the Dry Bones appears in miniature painting from the ninth to the 14th centuries in both East and West; it culminates in the Signorelli fresco in the cathedral of Orvieto and the Tintoretto painting in the Scuola di San Rocco, Venice. Michelangelo's famous representation of Ezekiel among other prophets of Israel appears on the ceiling of the Sistine Chapel (1508–10). In the early 19th century the English poet and artist William *Blake produced a fine engraving and a painting of the prophet.

Ezekiel's vision, in contrast to that of Isaiah, mentions only "sounds" and "voices," but even this unspecific conception would seem to call for some musical embodiment which, however, must inevitably fall short of the sublime suggestions in the biblical source. This is, for example, true of cantorial interpretations of the *Ve-ha-Ofanim* prayer and of the many *ofan* poems (see **Piyyut*). In art music the major composers have generally avoided the subject of Ezekiel's vision, whereas that of Isaiah (with its explicit "tonal" description and established place in Christian liturgy) offers far more promising material to the composer. The two visions, combined in the Prologue to Goethe's *Faust*, have an ambitious setting in the prologue act of Arrigo Boito's *Mefistofele* (1868, 1875[3]). The Valley of the Dry Bones is described by Franz Liszt in his *Ossa arida* for choir and organ (1879) and a symphonic work, *The Valley of Dry Bones*, was composed by A.W. *Binder (1935). The biblical text has also been set by several Israel composers, generally for choir. In a very different musical tradition the Afro-American spiritual "Ezekiel Saw the Wheel," with its simple rhythmic tune, is interesting for its text: this swiftly turns from the description of "a wheel in a wheel – way up in the middle of the sky" to criticism of the behavior of certain members of the congregation. Another popular spiritual, "Dry Bones," which has often been effectively arranged for vocal or instrumental ensembles, transforms the terrifying biblical scene into a syncopated, jocular description of the gradual joining together of the bones and of their subsequent separation in reverse order.

BIBLIOGRAPHY: COMMENTARIES: A.B. Davidson and A.W. Streane (Eng., 1916); G.A. Cooke (ICC, 1937); G. Fohrer and K. Galling (Ger., 1955); W. Zimmerli (Ger., 1955–69); J.W. Wevers (Eng., 1969); R. Eliezer of Beaugency, ed. by S. Poznański (Heb., 1910); S.D. Luzzatto (Heb., 1876). OTHER WORKS: Kaufmann, Y., Religion, 401–46; Kaufmann, Y., Toledot, 3:475–583; J. Lindblom, *Prophecy in Ancient Israel* (1962), index; G. von Rad, *Old Testament Theology*, 2 (1965), 220–37; M. Buber, *Torat-ha-Nevi'im* (1942), 168–72. SPECIAL STUDIES: C.C. Torrey, *Pseudo-Ezekiel and the Original Prophecy* (1930); S. Spiegel, in: *Harvard Theological Review*, 24 (1931), 245–321; idem, in: JBL, 54 (1935), 145–71; V. Herntrich, *Ezechielprobleme* (1932); C.G. Howie, *The Date and Composition of Ezekiel* (1950); G. Fohrer, *Die Hauptprobleme des Buches Ezechiel* (1952); H.H. Rowley, *Men of God* (1963), 169–210; S. Krauss, in: *Ha-Shilo'aḥ*, 8 (1901), 109–18, 300–6; Y.N. Simḥoni, in: *He-Atid*, 4 (1912), 209–34; 5 (1912), 47–74; M.H. Segal, in: F.I. Baer et al. (ed.), *Magnes Anniversary Book* (1938), 168–77; A. Margolioth, in: *Tarbiz*, 22 (1950/51), 21–27; D.N. Freedman, in: *Interpretation*, 8 (1954), 446–71; K.S. Freedy and D.B. Redford, *Journal of the American Oriental Society*, 90 (1970), 462–85. IN THE AGGADAH: Ginzberg, Legends, index. TOMB OF EZEKIEL: R. Joseph Hayyim Alhakam, *Mamlekhet Kohanim* (Bagdad, 1873). EZEKIEL IN ISLAM: "*Ḥizkīl*," in: EIS², 3, 535 (incl. bibl.); H. Speyer, *Die biblischen Erzaehlungen im Qoran* (1961), 412–3. IN THE ARTS: L. Réau, *Iconographie de l'art chrétien*, 2 pt. 1 (1956), 373–8, incl. bibl. **ADD. BIBLIOGRAPHY:** W. Eichrodt, *Ezekiel* (OTL; 1970); J. Levenson, *Theology of the Program of Restoration of Ezekiel 40–48* (1976); W. Zimmerli, *A Commentary on the Book of the Prophet Ezekiel 1–24* (Hermeneia; 1979); idem … *Ezekiel 24–48* (Hermeneia; 1983); A. Hurvitz, *A Linguistic Study …Priestly Source…and Ezekiel* (1982); M. Greenberg, *Ezekiel 1–20* (AB; 1983); idem, *Ezekiel 21–37* (AB; 1997); R. Klein, *Ezekiel* (1988); L. Boadt, in: ABD, 2, 711–22; L. Allen, *Ezekiel 1–19* (Word; 1994); idem, *Ezekiel 20–48* (Word; 1990); J. Galambush, *Jerusalem in the Book of Ezekiel: The City as Yahweh's Wife* (1992); S. Bondì, in: V. Krings (ed), *La civilsation phénicienne et punique* (1995), 268–81; P. Bartoloni, *ibid.*, 282–89; D. Block, *The Book of Ezekiel 1–24* (NICOT; 1997); *Ezekiel 25–48* (NICOT; 1998); M. Cohen (ed.), *Mikra'ot Gedolot 'Haketer' Ezekiel* (2000); R.L. Kohn, *A New Heart and a New Soul: Ezekiel, the Exile and Torah* (2002); M. Goshen-Gottstein and S. Talmon (eds.), *Hebrew University Bible: The Book of Ezekiel* (critical text-edition; 2004).

EZEKIEL, ABRAHAM EZEKIEL (1757–1806), English artist, son of the silversmith Abraham Ezekiel (d. 1799) who helped to build the synagogue in Exeter in 1763 together with his brother Benjamin. The son, practicing as a silversmith, watchmaker, and scientific optician, was a successful miniature and portrait painter enjoying a high reputation locally. He also engraved portraits by Opie (1783), Reynolds (1795), and others and executed several bookplates.

His son, SOLOMON (Isaac) EZEKIEL (1781–1867), a plumber and tinsmith by trade, settled in Penzance in Cornwall. He founded "The Penzance Hebrew Society for Promoting the Diffusion of Religious Knowledge," printed (1844–47) the lectures on Abraham and Isaac which he gave before it, and published an incisive letter (1820) which prevented the establishment of a Conversionist Society in Penzance.

BIBLIOGRAPHY: Rubens, in: JHSET, 14 (1935–39), 104–6; C. Roth, *Rise of Provincial Jewry* (1950), 60; JC (March 22, 1867), and supplement (May–June 1933). **ADD. BIBLIOGRAPHY:** ODNB online.

[Cecil Roth]

EZEKIEL, APOCRYPHAL BOOKS OF. Josephus (Ant., 10:79) appears to refer to two books of Ezekiel, one of which was presumably an apocryphal work. Reference to such a work is also made in the stichometry of Nicephorus, patriarch of Constantinople (806–15), and the pseudo-Athanasian canon list. Fragments of an Ezekiel book are preserved in various ancient sources. The longest is the story of the blind man and the lame found in Epiphanius (c. 315–402; *Adversus Haereses*, 64:70, 5, ed. Hall). It is a parable designed to prove the resurrection of both body and soul by demonstrating their interdependence. A lame and a blind man conspired together to rob a king's orchard, the blind man using his legs to transport the lame man who guided his steps. An almost identical story serves a similar function in rabbinic sources (Sanh. 91a–b; cf. Mekh. Shirata, 2; Lev. R. 4:5). A second fragment is to be found in Clement of Rome's (Pope Clement I 92?–100) *Epistula ad Corinthios*, 83 (PG, 1 (1886), 226), opening "Repent, House of Israel, of your lawlessnesses." This fragment is of a strongly prophetic character based on the language of biblical prophecy. It is also quoted in part by Church Father Clement of Alexandria (*Paedagogus* 1:91, 2; PG, vol. 7, 357). A third tiny fragment is preserved in Clement of Alexandria's *Quis dives salvetur?* (40:2; PG, 9 (1890), 645) and it may belong to the same "prophetic" Ezekiel apocryphon. It seems to be difficult, however, to conceive of the story of the lame and the blind as belonging to the same work, and either an addition or two Ezekiel apocrypha are involved. Another short sentence attributed to Ezekiel occurs in various forms. In Epiphanius, *Adversus Haereses* (30:30, 1; PG, 41 (1863), 458), the form is found "and the heifer shall bear and they shall say, 'She has not borne.'" This is employed in Christological contexts and it is difficult to discern its original import. Various scholars also assign the above quotation in Clement of Rome *Epistula ad Corinthios* (1:23; PG, vol. 1, p. 260) to an Ezekiel book. Some fragments of a Greek Ezekiel apocryphon were discovered on a papyrus and published by Campbell Bonner in 1940. These fragments include one passage which is quoted by Clement of Alexandria (*Paedagogus*, 1:84, 2–4; PG, 8 (1891), 512) as from Ezekiel, which confirms their identification. This document too bears the prophetic stamp observed in some of the above quotations and it may derive from the same work.

BIBLIOGRAPHY: M.R. James, *Lost Apocrypha of the Old Testament* (1920), 64–70; Holl, in: *Aus Schrift und Geschichte, Theologische Abhandlungen Adolf Schlatter* (1922), 85–98; C. Bonner, *Studies and Documents*, 12 (1940), 183ff.

[Michael E. Stone]

EZEKIEL, JACOB (1812–1899), U.S. communal leader. Ezekiel was born in Philadelphia, Pennsylvania, and was apprenticed as a bookbinder. In 1833 he moved to Baltimore, where he helped to establish the Hebrew Benevolent Society. The next year he moved to Richmond, Virginia, where he entered the dry goods business, and became active in Jewish affairs. In 1841 Ezekiel took issue with President Tyler's reference to Americans as a "Christian" people, and Tyler acknowledged Ezekiel's protest as well founded. In 1845 Ezekiel protested local ordinances that severely punished violators of the Sunday blue laws and brought about their repeal. A revised code adopted in Virginia in 1849, as a result of Ezekiel's campaigning, protected citizens who observed the Jewish Sabbath from incurring penalties for violating Sunday laws. Ezekiel was a leading protester against seeming U.S. acquiescence to Swiss anti-Jewish discrimination which helped to bring about a modification of the U.S.-Swiss treaty in 1857. Moving to Cincinnati in 1869, Ezekiel served as secretary to the board of governors of Hebrew Union College from 1876 to 1896. His son was the sculptor Moses Jacob *Ezekiel, whose *Ecce Homo*, a bronze sculpture of a suffering Christ, done about 1899, was included in the exhibition "The Hand and the Spirit; Religious Art in America, 1700–1900," which was shown at the University Art Museum, Berkeley, in 1972.

BIBLIOGRAPHY: H.T. Ezekiel and G. Lichtenstein, *Jews of Richmond* (1917), 117–8; AJHSP, 9 (1901), 160–3.

EZEKIEL, MORDECAI JOSEPH BRILL (1899–1974), U.S. agricultural economist. Ezekiel, who was born in Richmond, Virginia, received a bachelor of science degree in agriculture from Maryland Agricultural College (1918), a master of science degree from the University of Minnesota (1923), and a Ph.D. in economics from the Robert Brookings Graduate School of Economics and Government (1926).

Ezekiel spent his career in federal government and United Nations service. He was statistical assistant in agriculture to the U.S. Census Bureau from 1919 to 1922, when he joined the farm management division of the Department of Agriculture. From 1930 to 1933 he was assistant chief economist of the Federal Farm Board. In 1932 he formulated the details of what was to become the Agriculture Adjustment Administration and helped prepare a draft of the Agricultural Adjustment Act. Ezekiel was also involved with the founding conferences and early activities of what was to become the United Nations Food and Agriculture Organization. From 1933 to 1944 he was economic adviser to the secretary of agriculture. He returned to the Department of Agriculture for two years and then spent 15 years in the economic division of the Food and Agriculture Organization of the UN (1947–62), the final year as assistant director-general. In 1962 he became chief of the UN division of program control staff in the State Department's agency for international development. He retired from the FAO in 1962 to take a position with the United States Agency for International Development. He served as chief of the United Nations Division of this agency until his retirement in 1967. During the last years of his life, Ezekiel took occasional assignments as consultant. In 1969 he worked for several months with the FAO, helping to prepare a report entitled "Indicative Plan for World Agricultural Development."

Ezekiel's major interests besides agricultural economics were economic development and econometrics, subjects on which he contributed many articles to professional periodicals and wrote a number of books. Among his published works are *Methods of Correlation Analysis* (1930, 1941²); *$2,500 a Year – from Scarcity to Abundance* (1936); *Jobs for All Through Industrial Expansion* (1939); and the F.A.O. publication *Uses of Agricultural Surpluses to Finance Economic Development in Underdeveloped Countries – A Pilot Study in India* (1955). He was also co-author and editor of *Towards World Prosperity* (1947).

[Joachim O. Ronall / Ruth Beloff (2nd ed.)]

EZEKIEL, MOSES (1891–1969), Indian botanist. Born in Nagpur, Ezekiel was economic botanist to the government of Gwalior (1918–22), professor of botany at Wilson College, Bombay, and later principal of the College of Science at Nadiad, Gujarat (1947–50). From 1952 he headed the biology department at Petlad College. His works include *Animal Histology* (1927), *A Handbook of Plant Sociology* (1947), and *Three Great Evils – Contamination, Adulteration and Poisoning of Foodstuffs* (1947). Ezekiel, who was active in Jewish life, also wrote *The History and Culture of the Bene-Israel in India* (1948).

[Mordecai L. Gabriel]

EZEKIEL, MOSES JACOB (1844–1917), U.S. sculptor. Ezekiel was born in Richmond, Virginia, and his sculpture is imbued with elements of his Southern and Jewish roots. As a youth he modeled *Cain Receiving the Curse of the Almighty* and *Moses Receiving the Law on Mount Sinai*, both of which are now lost. He attended the Virginia Military Institute, and served in the Confederate army during the American Civil War. After the war, he studied art in Cincinnati and Berlin in the late 1860s.

His bas-relief *Israel* (1873), in which Israel is represented allegorically, won the Michael Beer Prix de Rome. A 1904 replica of the lost original resides at the Skirball Museum Cincinnati at Hebrew Union College. The first foreigner to receive the prize, Ezekiel embarked on two years of study in Rome beginning in 1874, where he then settled permanently. His studio in the Baths of Diocletian became a fashionable gathering place for artisans of all persuasions as well as royalty and politicians. The B'nai B'rith commissioned his enormous marble group *Religious Liberty* for the Centennial Exposition of 1876 (National Museum of American Jewish History, Philadelphia). This was one of the earliest of several monuments he made for the United States as well as for European countries. In 1888 he designed the seal for the recently established Jewish Publication Society of America. Inscribed in the seal, which shows Jerusalem with a Shield of David, is the motto "Israel's mission is peace." He also executed portrait busts, including bronze heads of Robert E. Lee (c. 1886, Virginia Military Institute Museum, Lexington) and Rabbi Isaac Mayer *Wise (1899, Hebrew Union College, Cincinnati). The king of Italy knighted Ezekiel in 1907. Although he lived most of his adult life in Rome, his will specified that his body return to America after his death. He was buried at the foot of a Confederate memorial he designed for Arlington National Cemetery (1914). His autobiography, *Memoirs from the Baths of Diocletian*, was published posthumously in 1975.

BIBLIOGRAPHY: D. Philipson, "Moses Jacob Ezekiel," in: *Publications of the American Jewish Historical Society*, 28 (1922), 1–62.

[Samantha Baskind (2nd ed.)]

EZEKIEL, NISSIM (1924–2004), Indian poet, critic, social commentator, and editor. Ezekiel was a member of Bombay's *Bene Israel community. His father was a distinguished editor, professor of botany and zoology at Bombay University, and principal of a number of colleges. Nissim Ezekiel was the father of post-Independence Indian poetry. Born in Bombay (Mumbai) he studied first at Bombay University, taking his M.A. in 1947, and then at Birkbeck College, London. He later worked on *The Illustrated Weekly of India* (1952–54) and later headed the English department of the Bombay College of Arts, where he was professor of English and reader in American literature. Ezekiel published literary reviews and verse collections, including *A Time to Change and Other Poems* (1957), *The Third* (1958), and *The Unfinished Man* (1960). Some of his verse appeared in British poetry journals. He was brought up in a secular milieu and even as a child preferred the poetry of T.S. Eliot, W.B. Yeats, and Ezra Pound to the English poetry being written in India. His poetic engagements paralleled those of Ted Hughes, Philip Larkin, and other postwar British poets but he developed his own voice marked by tenderness and irony. His use of Indian English vernacular after the 1960s gave his poetic language a rich humorous seam to draw on. Ezekiel received the Sahitya Akademi award in 1983 and the Padma-Shri, India's highest civilian honor, in 1988.

[Tudor Parfitt (2nd ed.)]

EZEKIEL BEN REUBEN MANASSEH (d. 1851), Baghdad philanthropist who distributed large amounts of money for charitable purposes in Iraq and Ereẓ Israel. In 1840 Ezekiel established the Baghdad rabbinical academy, named Bet Zilkha and also Midrash Abi Manshi after its benefactor. The yeshivah was first headed by R. Abdallah *Somekh and provided the students with all their needs. Ezekiel also built in Baghdad the "new synagogue" in 1847, the "small synagogue" in 1849, and Kneset Yeḥezkel in Safed, which was named after him (it now bears the name of R. Moses *Alshekh). He also donated half of the construction costs of the Bet Ya'akov synagogue, better known as Hurbat R. Yehudah he-Ḥasid, in the Old City of Jerusalem. After his death, his sons Manasseh and Sason continued his philanthropic work.

BIBLIOGRAPHY: A. Ben-Jacob, *Toledot ha-Rav Abdallah Somekh* (1949), 15–20; idem, *Yehudei Bavel* (1965), 175–7.

[Abraham Ben-Yaacob]

EZEKIEL FEIVEL BEN ZE'EV WOLF (1755–1833), Lithuanian preacher, known as the "*maggid* of Deretschin." Ezekiel was born in Planaga, Lithuania. In his youth he was appointed preacher in his native town and, subsequently, in Deretschin. At the age of 19 he was an itinerant preacher in the Jewish communities of Galicia, Hungary, and Germany (where he remained for some time in Breslau). In Vilna he made the acquaintance of Elijah b. Solomon (the Gaon of Vilna) and through him, of Solomon Zalman of Volozhin, brother of *Ḥayyim b. Isaac of Volozhin. Solomon made a deep impression upon Ezekiel, who wrote his biography (*Toledot Adam*, in 2 parts (Dyhernfurth, 1801–09); frequently reprinted). This contains details of Solomon's life and his teachings as well as stories current about him, and is a unique work for its period, reflecting the widening of the horizons of Hebrew literature in Lithuania at the end of the 18th century. Ezekiel sharply censures those rabbis who neglect study of the Scriptures as a result of their preoccupation with the Talmud and codes. In 1811 Ezekiel accepted an invitation to become the "*maggid*" (official preacher) of Vilna, a post in which he served until his death.

Other works by Ezekiel are *Musar Haskel* (Dyhernfurth, 1790), an exposition of *Hilkhot De'ot* and *Teshuvah* of Maimonides, and a commentary *Be'urei Maharif* (i.e., Morenu ha-Rav Ezekiel Feivel) on the *Midrash Rabbah* to Genesis, Exodus, and Leviticus, which was published in Vilna together with the text in 1878. A third volume of *Toledot Adam* remains unpublished.

BIBLIOGRAPHY: H.N. Maggid-Steinschneider, *Ir Vilna*, 1 (1990), 87–90; S.J. Fuenn, *Kiryah Ne'emanah* (1915[2]), 241–4; *Yahadut Lita*, 3 (1967), 54.

[Abraham David]

EZEKIEL THE POET, Hellenistic Jewish writer of tragedies. *Eusebius quotes from a unique Greek tragedy on a biblical theme, entitled *Exagoge* ("The Exodus"), written by Ezekiel "the writer of tragedies" (*Praeparatio Evangelica* 9:28), giving *Alexander Polyhistor as his source. The fragments are the only surviving example of a Jewish drama in antiquity that is consciously patterned after Greek drama.

The play begins with a long soliloquy by Moses containing an exposition of the events that have led up to the first scene. Moses tells how the Jews came to Egypt, how they were oppressed, and how Moses was cast into the water and saved by Pharaoh's daughter (1–31). He then tells how he learned about his childhood, avenged a kinsman who was being beaten by an Egyptian, and fled from Egypt for fear of Pharaoh's retaliation (32–58). The action of the play apparently begins with Moses watching the seven fair daughters of Raquel ("Reuel" – Jethro, cf. Ex. 2:18, 18:1) and with Zipporah telling him that he is in the land of Libya, which "is held by Ethiopians" but ruled by her father (59–65). Later, in reply to a question of a certain Chum, Zipporah says that she is wedded to the stranger (66ff.). Moses tells of a dream in which he saw a kingly person seated on Mount Sinai. In his dream, the throne was offered to Moses and he accepted it (68–82). Moses' father-in-law interprets this dream to mean that Moses will be a leader and a judge, who will know all things past, present, and future (83–89). Moses then sees the burning bush and inquires about it (90–95). God tells Moses to remove his shoes and have no fear, for He is God. He then appoints Moses His messenger to Pharaoh to tell him that he will lead the people of Israel out of Egypt (96–112). Moses complains that he lacks the eloquence for the task (113–5), at which God says that Aaron will speak for him (116–9). God then tells Moses to cast down his rod and turns it into a snake. He tells him to put his hand into his bosom and it (his hand) becomes leprous (120–31). There is a description by God of the plagues that He intends to send on the Egyptians and He tells Moses to instruct the Hebrew people about the Passover (132–92). A messenger relates the destruction of the Egyptians and how the Hebrews were saved (193–242). The last two fragments depict the oasis at Elim with its 12 springs of water and its 70 palm trees (243–53) and the wonderful bird that appeared there (254–69). This latter description is probably in the voice of a messenger sent by Moses to find a resting place.

From this summary it can be seen how closely the author follows the biblical account in the Book of Exodus. The vocabulary, too, reflects the Septuagint. Some elements, however, seem to be original to the author, or else derive from aggadic material, as, for example, the character of Chum in line 66ff.; the dream of Moses in line 68–82; the details of the destruction of the Egyptians, line 193–242; and the appearance of the bird (the Phoenix?) in lines 254–69.

The 269 verses of iambic trimeters that have been preserved represent a considerable portion of the play. This indicates that the author, influenced directly or indirectly by Euripides, was fluent in Greek and adept at writing verse. Aside from being a late example of ancient Greek tragedy, the play may be seen as an anticipation of the later medieval passion plays. Like these its primary function was probably to exploit the existing profane form as a vehicle toward familiarizing its audience with sacred history. The dependence of the work on the Septuagint means that it was written not earlier than the beginning of the second century B.C.E., while the latest date is the middle of the first century B.C.E., when it is mentioned by Alexander Polyhistor. Eusebius' reference to Ezekiel "the writer of tragedies" (an epithet also found in Clement of Alexandria) suggests the existence of more examples of this genre by the same author.

BIBLIOGRAPHY: Clement of Alexandria, *Stromata* 1:23, 155ff.; J. Wieneke (ed.), *Ezechielis Judaei poetae Alexandrini…* (Lat., 1931); J. Gutmann, *Ha-Sifrut ha-Yehudit ha-Hellenistit…* (1963), 9–69; G.M. Sifakis, *Studies in the History of Hellenistic Drama* (1967), 122–4; Pauly-Wissowa, 12 (1909), 1701–02.

[Marshall S. Hurwitz]

EẒ ḤAYYIM, an Orthodox educational institution in Jerusalem, including a kindergarten, a *talmud torah*, a preparatory yeshivah ("*yeshivah ketanah*"), a yeshivah, and a **kolel*. During the Turkish period Eẓ Ḥayyim served as the central Ashkenazi educational institution of the old *yishuv*, particularly for the youth of the Perushim community (the descendants of the disciples of Elijah, Gaon of Vilna), the ḥasidim having established the Ḥayyei Olam Yeshivah.

Eẓ Ḥayyim was established as a *talmud torah* for orphans in the early 1850s at a meeting held in the women's gallery of the "Menahem Zion" Bet Midrash in the courtyard of the Ḥurvah Synagogue, and reflected the growth of the Ashkenazi community, particularly with regard to children. Its budget was originally entirely dependent upon direct allocations from the Kolel Jerusalem in Vilna and R. Samuel *Salant was appointed its head. In 1855, a "Ḥevrat Talmud Torah" was founded in Jerusalem which assumed responsibility for the institution under the leadership of R. Salant and R. Isaiah *Bardaki. The Ḥevrah imposed indirect taxes on the Ashkenazi community, in the form of a fixed percentage from weddings, circumcisions, and synagogue offerings, to augment those funds which were received from abroad.

The regulations provided inter alia that if a pupil showed no learning ability by the time he reached the age of 13 he was to be taught a trade, the leaders of the *yishuv* thus accepting, at least in principle, the idea of occupational training.

In 1858 there arrived in Jerusalem R. Saul Benjamin Ha-Kohen Radzkowitz, a man of considerable organizational ability and imagination, who took upon himself the task of establishing Eẓ Ḥayyim on a firm footing and extending its activities. His unconventional activities, however, gave rise to fears on the part of the conservative leadership that the institution might collapse and he was dismissed, a step which gave rise to an unusually violent controversy.

At first the curriculum was strictly confined to religious subjects, which led to considerable criticism, as a result of which two hours daily were devoted to writing and arithmetic, in 1867. The critics were still not satisfied. Eẓ Ḥayyim came to be regarded as the symbol of old-fashioned conservatism and in response to its opposition to changes in the curriculum the first modern schools in Jerusalem were opened (Lemel, the Alliance Israélite, and Evelina de Rothschild, etc.).

World War I cut off the sources of income from abroad and the British occupation in 1917 found the institution in a perilous state. Funds from the United States were in the hands of the Zionists, who opposed its educational approach in principle. The Committee of Delegates, which had control of the distribution of aid to the Jews of Ereẓ Israel, applied great pressure on Eẓ Ḥayyim to institute comprehensive reforms in methods and curriculum, including Hebrew as the language of instruction. The pressure was resisted, and after much effort Eẓ Ḥayyim succeeded in establishing anew its connections with the Diaspora, thus ensuring its continuation.

Up to and including the beginning of the Mandatory period Eẓ Ḥayyim was one of the three institutions which had the deciding voice in the election of the leadership of the old *yishuv*, the other two being the Kolelim Committee and the Bikkur Ḥolim Hospital. In 1919 it was one of the deciding factors in the election of Rabbi A.I. *Kook as chief rabbi of Jerusalem.

During the Mandatory period the prestige of Eẓ Ḥayyim diminished even among the old Ashkenazi *yishuv* with the founding of new schools and yeshivot. Nevertheless the energetic leadership of R. Jehiel Michel *Tykocinski ensured not only its survival but even its expansion. In 1929 its center moved to a new and spacious building adjacent to the Maḥaneh Yehudah market while branches were established in all the old suburbs of Jerusalem.

Despite its curriculum certain changes have taken place, the most outstanding of which is the use of Hebrew in the branches in non-religious subjects, although in the main building Yiddish is still the language of instruction even in non-religious subjects.

As of June 2005, Eẓ Ḥayyim had some 1,000 pupils, ages three to seventeen. Located on three campuses around Jerusalem, including the original building near the Maḥaneh Yehudah market, Eẓ Ḥayyim also had a *kolel* of approximately 150 young married men (*avrekhim*) who received financial support. It had a dining room, an aid fund for the needy, and a library of some 20,000 volumes.

BIBLIOGRAPHY: J.M. Tykocinski, in: *Lu'aḥ Ereẓ Yisrael*, 9 (1904), 121–67; A.R. Malachi, in: *Talpiyyot* 9, nos. 1–2 (1965).

[Menachem Friedman]

EZINE, district of Çanakkale, Turkey. Ezine was situated in the vicinity of many important cities like Troy, Neadria, and Alexandria Troas. The Ottoman domination in this region began in the 1350s. Ezine became an important settlement point owing to its fertile land and trade routes. The first Jewish presence in Ezine can be traced back to 1845 when five "alien" (*yabanciyan*) Jews were reported. Overpopulation of the Jews in Çanakkale brought same families to Ezine Centrum as well as to other parts of the district, such as Bayramiç, Kumkale, and Yenişehir in the late 19th century. The Jews lived in a small quarter composed of 40 households and today known as *Yahudi Sokağı*. In 1894 there were 130 Jews in Ezine, 60 in Bayramiç, 24 in Kumkale, and 13 in Yenişehir. During the Gallipoli Campaign of World War I, the Jewish population in Ezine temporarily increased due to mass flight from the battlefields. The Jewish community in Ezine was attached to Çanakkale for religious purposes until the Gallipoli Campaign. Thus, it had neither a synagogue nor a private cemetery. Ezine Jews were engaged in peddling, export of grain, bonito, leather, and cotton, butchery, jewelry, green groceries, money-changing, and viniculture. The Hakim, Kohen, Yuday, Ruso, and Elinda families were the best known Jewish families in Ezine. After the establishment of the Turkish Republic, the Jewish population in Ezine began to diminish. Official records show that in 1927 there were only 31 Jews. The small Jewish presence lasted until the 1960s. Among the Jewish cultural heritage are a few Jewish houses and one synagogue whose building later served as a place to remove seeds from cotton and today is abandoned.

BIBLIOGRAPHY: *Cezair-i Bahr-i Sefid Vilayet Salnamesi* (1293), 86; *Karasi Vilayet Salnamesi* (H.1305), 141; *Ezine Nüfus Müdürlüğü, 3 Sıra Numaralı Esas Defteri*, 105–52; A. Galanté, *Histoire des Juifs d'Anatolie*, 4 (İstanbul, 1987), 223; J.M. Cook, *The Troas: the Archeo-*

logical and Topographical Study (1973), 316, 374–82; V. Cuinet, *La Turquie d'Asie*, 3 (1894), 696, 763–70.

[M. Mustafa Kulu (2nd ed.)]

EZION-GEBER (Heb. (גָּבֶר) עֶצְיוֹן גֶּבֶר), first mentioned in the Bible as one of the camping sites of the Israelite tribes on their way to Canaan (Num. 33:35–36).

As such, it is mentioned next to Elath in Deuteronomy 2:8. From the biblical narrative of the Exodus (Num. 21:4), it may be deduced that Ezion-Geber was somewhere on the Gulf of Elath. Its location on the Gulf of Elath and function as a port and shipyard during the reign of Solomon is clearly stated in I Kings 9:26. II Chronicles 8:17 indicates that it was not Solomon who founded Ezion-Geber and Elath. According to archaeological evidence it was most probably the Edomites or Midianites as early as the end of the Late Bronze Age (see *Timna). The port and shipyard of Ezion-Geber are again mentioned in connection with the unsuccessful attempt by Jehoshaphat in the ninth century B.C.E. to renew the gold route to Ophir (I Kings 22:49). After this, it disappears from the biblical annals, and in the eighth century B.C.E., there is mention only of the struggle between the kings of Judah and Edom for the possession of the city of Elath.

In 1934 F. Frank discovered Tell al-Khalayfa, a low mound approximately ⅓ mi. (c. 0.6 km.) north of the shores of the Gulf of Elath, between modern Eilat and Akaba, and he identified it with Ezion-Geber. N. Glueck subsequently excavated the site (1938–40) and identified it with Ezion-Geber and Elath, assuming a change of the former name to Elath in the days of the kings of Judah. According to him, the site was not only the Solomonic port, but also an important industrial center for the manufacture of copper and iron tools, which served as export goods for the trading ventures of Solomon. Recent excavations in the Arabah and the discovery of an early Iron Age I port installation in the bay and on the island Jazīrat Farʿūn, 7½ mi. (12 km.) south of modern Eilat, have suggested a reconsideration of the date and character of the ruins of Tell al-Khalayfa, and consequently of the location of Ezion-Geber. It has become clear that the site was fortified, perhaps serving as a caravanserai, and not a copper smelting plant, and an identification with the ancient city of Elath has been suggested. It has been proposed that the port and shipyard of Ezion-Geber should be identified with the island of Jazīrat Farʿūn, the only natural anchorage in the Gulf of Elath. Extensive casemate walls and a well-built port testify to its maritime use in early biblical days. From archaeological discoveries in the southern Arabah (1969), it can be deduced that long before Solomon's ships were assembled at Ezion-Geber–Jazīrat Farʿūn, Egyptian mining expeditions on their way to the Arabah copper mines used Ezion-Geber as their harbor.

BIBLIOGRAPHY: F. Frank, in; ZDPV, 57 (1934), 191–280, esp. 244; N. Glueck, *The Other Side of the Jordan* (1940), 89–113; idem, *Rivers in the Desert* (1959), index; idem, in: BA, 28 (1965), 70–87, incl. bibl.; B. Rothenberg, in: PEQ, 94 (1962), 5–71; 101 (1969), 57–59; idem, *Ẓefunot Negev* (1967), 189–213; idem, in: *Illustrated London News*, 255 (Nov. 15, 1969), 32–33; 255 (Nov. 29, 1969), 28–29.

[Beno Rothenberg]

EZOBI, JEHOSEPH BEN HANAN BEN NATHAN (13th century), *paytan*. Ezobi was born and lived in Provence (his name signifies that his family came from the town of Orange, close to Avignon) and probably taught in Perpignan. Abraham *Bedersi praises him as his master and as a talented poet (*Ḥerev ha-Mithappekhet*, verse 148), and Todros b. Judah Abulafia in a hymn in his honor writes: "He is known as Ezov [hyssop]; how pleasant is the hyssop – even the cedars cannot obscure him" (*Gan ha-Meshalim ve-ha-Ḥidot*, 2 pt. 1 (1931), 46). "*Ka'arat ha-Kesef*" ("The Silver Plate"), an educational, ethical, and religious poem, is Ezobi's best-known hymn (printed by Steinschneider, 1860, and in Joseph Ḥayyim ben Elijah al-Ḥakam, *Nifla'im Ma'aśekh… Ma'aśiyot*, 1989), dedicated to his son on the day of his wedding. The name derives from its 130 verses – equal in numbers to the 130 *shekels, the weight of the silver plates offered by the princes of the tribes to the Tabernacle (Num. 7:13ff.). In this poem, Ezobi appeals to his son to follow the ways of the Torah. He warns him not to be misled by Greek philosophy, and encourages him to learn grammar and poetics, to study the Talmud and its commentators, such as Alfasi and Maimonides, and to follow his own example and become a liturgist. He also enjoins his son not to favor the wealthy over the poor. In an appended note, he requests his son to read this poem every week. The poem was translated into Latin by *Reuchlin (Tuebingen, 1512–14). Another translation was published by Jean Mercier (Paris, 1561). I. Freedman published an English translation (1895/6); M. Forcano translated it into Catalan (1997). Other poems by him include "*Aromem El Ram*," a strophic hymn (*zulat*) for the seventh day of Passover on the splitting of the Red Sea; "*Aggid Ḥasdei ha-El*," a strophic hymn for Shavuot; "*Az me-Rosh Mikdemei Ereẓ*," another *zulat* on the death of Moses, for Simḥat Torah; "*Ezkor Yamim mi-Kedem*," in commemoration of the *Ten Martyrs; a *seliḥah*, "*Ayeh Na Ḥasadekha Adonai?*" (of uncertain authorship), etc. Some of his poems have not been published, for example a *bakkashah* studied by B. Bar-Tikva that includes the letter *mem* in every word. Ezobi plays skillfully with motifs taken from the Midrashim, adding some irony and personal humor. Schirmann compares the qualities of his poems with the best works of the early *paytanim*. *Sefer Millu'im* ("Book of Addenda"), known only from a quotation in the responsa of R. Solomon b. Abraham *Adret (Constantinople, 1516, no. 25), is a homiletic commentary, in prose, on the 613 commandments.

His brother Eleazar, also a poet, exchanged poems with Abraham Bedersi; he was born in Carpentras and lived in Béziers. Another brother, Meshullam, settled in Segovia, Castile, where he wrote in 1279 a short work on Hebrew grammar, *Aguddat Ezob* (Ms. Hebr. 992 of the Bibl. Nat., Paris, unpublished, see C. del Valle, in: *Helmántica*, 163 (2003), 191–205), based in the grammars of Jonah ibn Janaḥ and David Kimḥi.

It is probable that he also wrote the commentary on the Torah, *Sefer ha-Ezobi*, still in manuscript.

BIBLIOGRAPHY: Zunz, Lit Poesie, 351, 480; Davidson, Oẓar, 4 (1933), 397; Schirmann, Sefarad, 2 (1956), 343–8; I. Freedman, in: JQR, 8 (1895/96), 534–40; J. Reuchlin, Ezobi, Jehoseph ben Hanan ben Nathan, *Rabi Ioseph Hyssopaeus Parpinianensis iudaeorum poeta dulcissimus ex hebraica lingua in latina[m]traductus* (1512); M. Steinschneider, *Musar Haskel ve-Shir ha-Keara* (1860); Weinberger, in: HUCA, 37 (1966), 1ff. (Heb.); B. Bar-Tikva, in: *Sefer Aviad* (1986), 185–94; idem, in: *Jewish Studies in a New Europe* (1998), 54–63; idem, in: *Talpiyot*, 10 (1998), 397–405; Schirmann-Fleischer, *The History of Hebrew Poetry in Christian Spain and Southern France* (1997), 464–67, 469 n. 2; M. Forcano, in: *Anuari de Filologia, Estudis Hebreus I Arameus*, 20 (1997), 67–79.

[Angel Sáenz-Badillos (2nd ed.)]

EZRA (Heb. עֶזְרָא; "[YHWH] helps"), priest and scribe who played a major role in the rebuilding of the Temple, after the return from the Babylonian exile.

The Man and His Mission

Ezra whose name means "help" (possibly a shortened form for עֲזַרְיָה "The Lord has helped," the name of two of his ancestors (7:1, 3)) was, along with Nehemiah, one of the two notable figures of the post-exilic community in Judah (sixth–fifth century B.C.E.). His work is known from the last three chapters (7–10) of the book that bears his name, and from chapter 8 of the book of Nehemiah (see *Ezra and Nehemiah, Book of). Ezra was both a priest, whose ancestry is traced back to Aaron (7:1–5), and a scribe "well versed in the law of Moses" (v. 6, 11). Just as another Persian king, *Cyrus, had done in his time (538), so also one of his successors, *Artaxerxes I (465–424), issued a royal edict to Ezra granting permission for Jews to go with him to Jerusalem. Ezra was permitted to bring with him gold and silver donations from other Jews, and regular maintenance expenses of the Temple were to be provided from the royal treasury. Ezra's mission was "to expound the law of the Lord" and "to teach laws and rules to Israel" (v. 10). For this purpose he was granted not only a royal subsidy, but he was also empowered to appoint judges, enforce religious law, and even to apply the death penalty. In response to critics who argue that such a concern by a Persian king for a foreign cult would be unlikely, the Passover papyrus issued by *Darius II in 419/18 to the Jews at Elephantine in Egypt regarding the date and method for celebrating the Passover (Porten) has often been cited. Nevertheless, the question of imperial authorization of Jewish law by the Persian Empire continues to be a subject of debate (Watts).

Date

The date of Ezra is problematic as is his relationship with Nehemiah, because apart from Neh. 8:9, and two other minor references (Neh. 12:26, 36), the two are never mentioned together. According to their respective books, Ezra assumed his mission in the seventh year of Artaxerxes (458) and Nehemiah came in the 20th year of the same king (445). This would mean that Ezra, who came at the express command of Artaxerxes to implement and teach the law, did not conduct his first public reading of the Law until 13 years later. Another problem for the biblical chronology is that Ezra found many people in Jerusalem but, according to Nehemiah, in his time, Jerusalem was unpopulated. For these reasons and others, some scholars believe Ezra came to Jerusalem much later, either in the 37th year of Artaxerxes I (428) or in the seventh year of Artaxerxes II (397) (see discussion in Klein).

His Journey to Jerusalem

Ezra's four month journey to Jerusalem is described by Ezra in a first-person memoir. After listing the names of the leaders returning with him, Ezra discovers there were no Levites in his party so he had to muster up 38 Levites from some Levitical families. Another problem was security. Because Ezra had originally made a declaration of trust in God before the king, he felt it inappropriate to request from him the customary escort. Thus he accounted the party's safe arrival in Jerusalem with all its treasure intact as a mark of divine benevolence.

Ezra's Reaction to Reports of Intermarriage

When Ezra arrived in Jerusalem he was informed that some people, including members of the clergy and aristocracy, had contracted foreign marriages. Immediately upon hearing this news Ezra engaged in mourning rites, tore his garments, and fasted and, on behalf of the people, confessed their sins and uttered a prayer of contrition. At the initiative of one of the leaders of the community Ezra was urged to take immediate action. An emergency national assembly was convened, and Ezra addressed the crowd in a winter rainstorm calling upon the people to divorce their foreign wives. The assembled crowd agreed to Ezra's plea, but because of the heavy rains and the complexity of the matter (Ezra's extension of legal prohibitions of marriages that had previously been permitted), they requested that a commission of investigation be set up. After three months the commission reported back with a list of priests, Levites, and Israelites who had intermarried. It is often thought that Ezra's action insisting on the divorce of foreign wives and their children, together with Nehemiah's concern that the children of these foreign women could not speak the language of Judah (Neh. 13:24), represented a shift in Israelite matrimonial law. Previously offspring of intermarriage was judged patrilineally; now it was to be on the matrilineal principle (for a different view, see Cohen).

The Reading of the Torah

Chapter 8 of the book of Nehemiah records that Ezra publicly read the Torah on the first day of the seventh month (Rosh Ha-Shanah). He stood upon a platform with dignitaries standing on his right and left. The ceremony began with an invocation by Ezra and a response by the people saying "Amen, Amen" (v. 6). During the reading the people stood while the text was made clear to them (or translated for them (into Aramaic)) by the Levites (van der Kooij). The people were emotionally overcome by the occasion and wept. However, they were enjoined not to be sad rather to celebrate the day joyously with eating, drinking, and gift giving. The day after the public reading, a group of priests and Levites continued to study the Torah with Ezra and came across the regulations for observing the feast of Tabernacles on that very month. A proclamation was issued to celebrate the festival which was done with great joy, and the Torah was again read publicly during the entire eight days of the festival.

Significance of Ezra's Torah Reading

Ezra's reading of the Torah inaugurated a new element in Jewish life whereby the Torah was read and explicated on regular occasions in public. This public reading also led to the democratization of knowledge of the Torah among Jews, since prior to this event most parts of the Torah were under the exclusive provenance and control of the priests (Knohl).

[David Marcus (2nd ed.)]

In the *Aggadah*

Ezra was still studying under *Baruch b. Neriah in Babylonia when Daniel and his companions left for Palestine. He regarded the study of the Torah as of greater importance than the task of reconstructing the Temple. Therefore it was only after his master's death that Ezra decided to gather the exiles who had not gone up earlier with Daniel and who desired to return to the Holy Land and rebuild the Temple in Jerusalem (Song R. 5:5). Ezra had another reason for remaining in Babylon after Daniel's departure: he was considerate of the feelings of Joshua the son of Jehozadak, of the high-priestly family of Zadok. Joshua would have been embarrassed by Ezra's presence in the Land of Israel, in view of the latter's greater qualification for the office of high priest. Ezra, therefore, remained in Babylon until Joshua's death. After Ezra went to the Land of Israel, he was appointed high priest. He had carefully worked out his own pedigree before he left Babylonia (BB 15a) and in order to insure the purity of those remaining there he took with him all those of doubtful or impure descent (Kid. 69b). He was so zealous in spreading the Torah, that rabbis said of him, "If Moses had not anticipated him, Ezra would have received the Torah" (Tosef., Sanh. 4:7). He restored and reestablished the Torah that had been almost completely forgotten (Suk. 20a). He ordained that public readings from the Torah take place not only on Sabbaths, but also on Mondays and Thursdays (Meg. 31b; TJ, Meg. 4:1, 75a). He also had the Bible rewritten in "Assyrian" characters, leaving the old Hebrew characters to the Samaritans (Sanh. 21b). He established schools everywhere to fill the existing needs and in the hope that the rivalry between the institutions would redound to the benefit of the pupils (BB 21b–22a). He also enacted the ordinances known as "the ten regulations of Ezra" (see BK 82a–b; TJ, Meg. loc. cit.) and together with five of his companions, compiled the Mishnah (tractate *Kelim*, in A. Jellinek, *Beit ha-Midrash*, 2 (1853), 88). Aside from the book which bears his name, Ezra wrote the genealogies of the Book of Chronicles up to his own time (BB 15a) and had a hand in writing the Book of Psalms (Song R. 4:19). The rabbis identify him with the prophet Malachi (Meg. 15a). He is one of the five men whose piety is especially extolled by the rabbis (Mid. Ps. to 105:2).

In Islam

Muhammad claims (Sura 9:30) that in the opinion of the Jews, ʿUzayr (Ezra) is the son of God. These words are an enigma because no such opinion is to be found among the Jews, even though Ezra was singled out for special appreciation (see Sanh. 21b; Yev. 86b). The Muslim traditionalists attempt to explain the words of Muhammad with a Muslim legend, whose origin appears to stem from IV Ezra 14:18–19. The people of Israel sinned, they were punished by God, the Holy Ark was removed, and the Torah was forgotten. It was due, however, to Ezra's merit that his heart was filled with the Torah of God, which he taught to the people of Israel. When the Holy Ark was returned to them and they compared that which Ezra taught them with the text of the *Sefer Torah* in the Holy Ark, the words they found were identical. They deduced from this that Ezra was the son of Allah. Ṭabarī cites another version of this legend: the Jewish scholars themselves hid the Ark, after they were beaten by the Amalekites. H.Z. Hirschberg proposed another assumption, based on the words of Ibn Ḥazm (I, 99), namely, that the "righteous" who live in Yemen believe that ʿUzayr was indeed the son of Allah. According to other Muslim sources, there were some Yemenite Jews who had converted to Islam who believed that Ezra was the messiah. For Muhammad, Ezra, the apostle (!) of the messiah, can be seen in the same light as the Christians saw Jesus, the messiah, the son of Allah. An allusion to the figure of Ezra as the apostle of the messiah is found in a tale which is widespread among the Jews of Yemen, according to which Ezra requested that they immigrate to Ereẓ Israel, and because they did not, he cursed them. Yemenite Jews have therefore refrained from naming their children Ezra. According to some Muslim commentators, ʿUzayr is the man who passed by the destroyed city (of Jerusalem; Sura 2:261) and did not believe that it could be rebuilt (see *Jeremiah).

[Haïm Z'ew Hirschberg]

Tomb of Ezra

There are a number of traditions concerning the site of Ezra's tomb. According to Josephus it is in Jerusalem; others hold that he was buried in Urta or in Zunzumu on the Tigris; but the general accepted version is that his tomb is situated at ʿUzēr, a village near Basra. This tradition is mentioned by *Benjamin of Tudela, *Pethahiah of Regensburg, Judah *Al-Ḥarizi, and other travelers, Jewish and non-Jewish, who visited Babylonia. The tomb is in a building covered by a cupola and on its walls are written a variety of inscriptions. Nearby, there is a *khan* in which the visitors to the tomb gather, and which also contains shops where Arab and Jewish merchants offered their wares in the period between Passover and Shavuot, the time of pilgrimages to the tomb. The visitors lit candles and made solemn vows. Special prayers were said (e.g., one was that composed by R. *Joseph Ḥayyim Al-Ḥakam, contained in his book *Mamlekhet Kohanim*, Baghdad, 1873). The Muslims fear the tomb and ascribe to it supernatural powers, and many legends are linked to it.

[Abraham Ben-Yaacob]

BIBLIOGRAPHY: J.M. Myers, *Ezra, Nehemiah* (1965); D.J. Clines, *Ezra, Nehemiah, Esther* (1984); H.G.M.Williamson, *Ezra, Nehemiah* (1985); J. Blenkinsopp, *Ezra-Nehemiah* (1988); A. van der Kooij, "Nehemiah 8:8 and the Question of the 'Targum'-Tradition," in: G.J. Norton and S. Pisano (eds.), *Tradition of the Text: Studies Offered to Dominique Barthélemy in Celebration of his 70th Birthday* (1991), 79–90; R.W. Klein, "Ezra-Nehemiah, Books of," in: D.N. Freedman (ed.), *Anchor Bible Dictionary*, 2 (1992), 731–42; S.J.D. Cohen, *The Beginnings of Jewishness* (1999); J.W. Watts (ed), *Persia and Torah: The Theory of Imperial Authorization of the Pentateuch* (2001); B. Porten, "The Passover Letter (3.46)," in: W.W. Hallo (ed.), *The Context of Scripture*, 3 (2002), 116–17; I. Knohl, *The Divine Symphony: The Bible's Many Voices* (2003). IN THE AGGADAH: Ginzberg, Legends, 4 (1913), 354–9; 6 (1928), 441–7. IN ISLAM: Ṭabarī, *Tafsīr*, 10 (1327 A.H.), 78–79; Nīsābūrī, *ibid.*, 68–69; Ṭabarī, *Tafsīr*, 3 (1323 A.H.), 19–20 (to Sura 2:261); Thaʿlabī, Qiṣaṣ (1356 A.H.), 291–3; H. Speyer, *Biblische Erzaehlungen…* (1961), 413; H.Z. Hirschberg, in: *Leshonenu*, 15 (1947), 130–3. TOMB: Ben-Jacob, in: *Edoth*, 1:1 (1945), 37–40. **ADD. BIBLIOGRAPHY:** EIS^2, 10, 960, s.v. *ʿUzayr* (incl. bibl.).

EZRA, family prominent in India in the 19th and 20th centuries. JOSEPH BEN EZRA BEN JOSEPH KHLEF (d. 1855), one of the notables of the Jewish community in Baghdad, traveled to India at the beginning of the 19th century. Together with his sons Ezekiel and David, he settled in Calcutta, engaging in commerce and becoming very wealthy. After some time, he returned to Baghdad, where he died. The family was known as Baḥer (Ar. "sea"), possibly because they were among the first to cross the sea to India. The traveler *Benjamin II first mentioned Joseph as among the most distinguished personalities of Calcutta in 1849. Joseph's son DAVID (1797–1882) was president of the Calcutta Jewish community and one of the outstanding Oriental philanthropists. Contributing generously to charitable institutions in India and Iraq, he assisted the Palestinian *sheluḥim* ("emissaries") who often visited India, and also provided funds for the ransoming of captives. A street was named after him in Calcutta, where he built two magnificent synagogues: Neweh Shalom (1856) and Bet El (1870).

His son ELIAS DAVID (1830–1886) was also a wealthy philanthropist. In 1882 he opened a school for the poor in Calcutta and in 1883/84 built a synagogue named Maghen David after his father. He contributed 12,000 rupees toward the establishment of a zoological garden which became known as "Ezra House." In 1870, he married Mozelle (Mazal-Tov; 1850–1921), the daughter of Sir Albert *Sassoon. She founded a large hospital for the poor in Calcutta, named Ezra Hospital after her husband, and two yeshivot: Mazal Ẓome'aḥ and Knesset Eliahu in Jerusalem. Their son SIR DAVID (1871–1947), president of the Jewish community of Calcutta, was also a noted philanthropist. In 1912 he married Rachel (1877–1952), daughter of Solomon David Sassoon. Both were active in many spheres of public life: David was president of a scientific society for the study of nature in India; Rachel founded the League of Jewish Women in 1913 and administered two hospitals. In recognition of their services to India, David was knighted in 1927. During World War II, they gave generous relief to refugees from Europe.

BIBLIOGRAPHY: D.S. Sassoon, *History of the Jews in Baghdad* (1949), index.

[Abraham Ben-Yaacob]

EZRA, APOCALYPSE OF (also known as **Ezra IV**), book of visions ascribed to Ezra the Scribe, written between 95–100 C.E., probably in Ereẓ Israel. It is extant in some Greek fragments, Latin, Syriac, Ethiopic, two separate Arabic versions, Armenian, Georgian, and a Coptic fragment.

The book is composed of seven visions. The first three, in the form of dialogues between Ezra and the angel Uriel, deal primarily with the destruction of the Temple and Jerusalem and with theodicy. Each of these three visions concludes with a brief eschatological revelation. The fourth vision is of a weeping, bereaved woman who is transformed into the heavenly Jerusalem, the promise of redemption for Zion. Next, Ezra sees an eagle with 12 wings, eight "little wings," and three heads. This, he is told, is the fourth beast which appeared to Daniel (Dan. 7), the fourth wicked world empire, its heads and wings representing kings and emperors. Ezra witnesses its judgment and destruction at the hands of a lion, a symbol of the Messiah, after which the righteous rejoice in the messianic kingdom. The sixth vision sees one "as the form of a man," rising from the sea, who is attacked by innumerable hosts, which he destroys to be greeted by a joyous multitude – another vision of the Messiah's victory over the evil nations. In the last vision, Ezra receives the Torah, the 24 books of the Bible, and the 70 books of secret, apocalyptic lore, and then prepares for his assumption to heaven.

IV Ezra is considered one of the high points of Jewish apocalyptic literature, combining sensitive perception with profound and daring analysis. The author is deeply concerned with the theological problems arising from the destruction of Jerusalem: "Is Israel any worse than Babylon, that they rule over us?" he asks (IV Ezra 3:27ff.). This question brings him to grips with some basic problems concerning the nature of man. How could God create man with an "evil heart" and, when giving him the Torah, not remove this evil heart, which causes him to transgress its laws? Further, why is man given understanding, so that sinning, he knows that he sins and is destined for Gehenna? To these and other such questions raised in the first three visions, no real solution is offered. Ultimately, the angel can only say that God's ways are inscrutable, that He rejoices in the righteous few, and that Ezra and those like him are assured of their salvation. But the author's real answer is perhaps to be sought elsewhere, in the eschatological sections which conclude each of these visions, and in the three eschatological visions which follow, the solution to these problems residing in the eschatological occurrences themselves.

The book is preserved in the Latin Church and is included by Protestants in the Apocrypha. It did not survive in the Eastern Church, however, and except for a few patristic quotations (e.g., Clement of Alexandria, *Stromata*, 3:16, 10) and the reuse of the text in the late "Esdras Apocalypse," the Greek text is no longer extant. There is much debate as to whether the original was Hebrew or Aramaic, the former seeming the more likely possibility. In the Latin, two additional chapters (sometimes called III Ezra and V Ezra respectively; see Greek Book of *Ezra) occur at the beginning and at the end of the book. The book is included in many Ethiopic and Armenian biblical manuscripts, but has survived in only one Syriac manuscript (Cod. Ambrosianus) and in two incomplete Georgian copies.

A large portion of ch. 7 does not appear in the Vulgate Latin manuscripts, the publication of which in 1875 from *Codex Ambianensis* by R. Bensly was followed by the discovery of a series of Latin codices containing this section. Kabisch, with the subsequent support of de Faye and Box, maintained the book to be composed of a series of five separate source documents: a Salathiel apocalypse (cf. IV Ezra 3:2) covering substantially the first four visions; the Eagle vision (A); the Son of Man vision (M); the final Ezra vision (E^1); and a second Ezra source which included the apocalyptic sections of Visions 1–4. This hypothesis was strongly attacked by Clemen and Gunkel, who were followed by Violet and, later, Keulers. These emphasize the basic structural unity of the work, pointing to its division into seven visions separated by prayer and fast, the appearance of the same technical terminology throughout, and the questionable nature of many of the so-called "inconsistencies" or "contradictions" between the sources. They thus accept the basic unity of the work, at the same time not denying the possibility that the author employed existing written or oral sources. The book contains no traces of sectarian or Essene ideas and sometimes follows the line of traditional rabbinic exegesis (cf. IV Ezra 6:7–10 and Gen. R. 63:9, Mid. Hag. to Gen. 25:26 et al.). It also includes a fragment of a Midrash on the 13 Attributes (IV Ezra 123ff.) and similar material. The date is established primarily by the identification of the three heads of the eagle in chapters 11–12 with the Flavian emperors.

BIBLIOGRAPHY: H. Gunkel, in: E. Kautzsch (ed.), *Apokryphen und Pseudepigraphen des Alten Testaments*, 2 (1900), 331–401; L. Vaganay, *Le problème eschatologique dans le IVe livre d'Esdras* (1906); Schuerer, Gesch, 3 (1909[4]), 315–35; B. Violet, *Die Esra-Apokalypse* (1910–24); G.H. Box, *The Ezra-Apocalypse* (1912); J. Keulers, *Die eschatologische Lehre des vierten Esrabuches* (1922); R.P. Blake, in: HTR, 19 (1926), 299–320; 22 (1929), 57–105; L. Gry, *Les dires prophetiques d'Esdras* (1938); M. Stone, in: HTR, 60 (1967), 107–15; idem, in: *Le Muséon*, 79 (1966), 387–400.

[Michael E. Stone]

EZRA, DEREK, BARON (1919–), British industrial administrator. Ezra was educated at Magdalene College, Cambridge, and served in the British army during World War II, being appointed a member of the Order of the British Empire and awarded the United States Bronze Star. In 1947 he joined the newly nationalized coal industry. After holding posts in sales and marketing on the National Coal Board, he became a member of the board in 1965 and deputy chairman in 1967, and was chairman, the highest position in the industry, from 1971 to 1982. His period of office included the 1974 miners' strike, but he was generally characterized by a conciliatory attitude in industrial relations. Ezra was knighted in 1974 and created a life peer in 1983. After retirement from the coal board, he joined the Social Democratic Party in the House of Lords and held numerous British and European directorships and advisory posts in industry and commerce. He was appointed a Grand Officer of the Italian Order of Merit and held French and Luxembourg decorations.

[Vivian David Lipman]

EZRA, GREEK BOOK OF (also called the **Apocryphal Ezra, First Esdras**, or **Third Esdras**), a Greek translation of the last two chapters of II Chronicles, the entire Book of Ezra (except for 1:6), and Nehemiah 7:73–8:13. It differs from the canonical version in that a section of Ezra is transposed, Nehemiah 1 does not follow Ezra, and a noncanonical story is introduced. The following summary illustrates these changes.

The first chapter corresponds to II Chronicles 35 and 36 (omitting the last two verses since they appear in Ezra 1:1 and 2, which corresponds to Greek Ezra 2:1 and 2); Josiah celebrates Passover, battles with the Egyptians, and dies of his wounds; his successors; the sack of Jerusalem; the destruction of the Temple; the Babylonian exile. Chapter 2 corresponds to Ezra 1; 4:7 to end of 4 (2–4:6 being transposed to chapter 5); Cyrus permits the Jews to return and rebuild the Temple; the Temple vessels are returned; the correspondence between a certain Artaxerxes and the Jews' antagonists (Jos., Ant., 11:26, changes this to, or understands it as, Cambyses); interruption of the construction of the Temple until the reign of Darius. Chapters 3 and 4: each of three guardsmen of Darius suggests what is most powerful – wine, royal power, or womankind – and the third, Zerubbabel, answers "womankind" but adds "truth," thereby winning the contest; as a reward he requests permission to rebuild the Temple; Darius complies. Chapters 5:1–6: preparations for Zerubbabel's expedition. Chapters 5:6–9:36 correspond to Ezra 2:1–4:5 and to Ezra 6 to the end: catalog of those who returned; erection of the Altar; reference to the earlier troubles from Cyrus' reign to Darius' second year; the Temple rebuilt; Ezra's expedition. Chapter 9:37 to end, corresponding to Nehemiah 7:73–8:13: Ezra reads the Torah at a public gathering.

The canonical version tells of Zerubbabel's return, breaks off the narrative at the halt of the Temple construction, records letters between the Jews' enemies and the king, and returns to the narrative. By noting that the interruption lasted until the time of Darius before the correspondence (4:5) and at its close, the author indicates that, for him, the documents are earlier than Darius' reign. The Greek Ezra, placing these documents after Cyrus' proclamation, before Zerubbabel's return, conveys this same picture of a poison-pen correspondence prior to Darius (Kaufmann Y., Toledot, 4 (1956), 522–7 upholds this view, as do Josephus and traditional commentators). It differs from the canonical version in that Zerubbabel's expedition occurs under Darius rather than Cyrus.

Josephus used the work as a source for his discussion of the post-Exilic Return (Ant., 11:1–56); little else can be said about it with assurance. To some the work is complete and the concluding conjunction and verb – "and they were gathered" – are a formal close. If the work is a unit, the Nehemiah passage may have been introduced to underscore Ezra's emphasis on the Law. Others see the conjunction-verb endings as evidence that the work is incomplete; it belongs to the next verse (Neh. 8:14). If the author's starting point and closing are unknown, so is his purpose. The translated material has been seen as a version based on the Septuagint, a revision of a translation older than the Septuagint, or an independent translation from the Hebrew and Aramaic. And the "guardsmen" episode has been variously labeled as a Greek, Oriental, or more specifically, Aramaic or Persian folk-tale. The story may be an originally non-Jewish story that was reworked. Scholars think the answer "Truth" is an addition and the contest was limited to one answer per guardsman. Furthermore, Truth is praised; the force of the other elements is proved by example. However, womankind's power is shown in two ways. Woman is presented as the life-giving mother and clother of man (an important ancillary function of woman in antiquity). Without a mother there can be no king or vine-cultivator to produce wine. This sufficiently proves womankind's superiority over the others. At this point a new motif is introduced – woman as temptress for whose favor man dares all; here biblical sounding phrases appear – "beautiful to look at," 4:18 (cf. Gen. 29:17); and "leave one's father and cleave to one's wife," 4:20 (cf. Gen. 2:24) – which may reflect Jewish influence. The guardsman mentions an incident showing Darius' subservience to a concubine. Darius and his nobles exchange glances (shocked at the temerity?); immediately Truth is eulogized. This second motif on woman provides an opening for introducing Truth and placing an *aggadah*-like moral lesson within the framework of the Return.

BIBLIOGRAPHY: Cook, in: Charles, Apocrypha, 1 (1913), 1–58 (translation and discussion); Thackeray, in: J. Hasting, *A Dictionary of the Bible*, 1 (1898), 758–63 (lists early literature); O. Eissfeldt, *Einleitung in das Alte Testament* (1964^{3}) 777–81; S. Jellicoe, *The Septuagint and Modern Study* (1968), 290–4.

[Jacob Petroff]

EZRA AND NEHEMIAH, BOOKS OF, two books in the Hagiographa (i.e., the Book of Ezra and the Book of Nehemiah), which were originally a single work.

The Masoretic tradition regarded the books of Ezra and Nehemiah as one book and referred to it as the Book of Ezra. This was also the Greek tradition, and the same Greek name, Esdras, was given to both books (see below). The division into separate books does not occur until the time of Origen (fourth century C.E.) and this division was transferred into the Vulgate where the books are called I Esdras (Ezra) and II Esdras (Nehemiah). It was not until the 15th century that Hebrew manuscripts, and subsequently all modern printed Hebrew editions, followed this practice of dividing the books. However, there are good reasons (linguistic, literary, and thematic) for the argument that the two books were originally separate works (Kraemer), which were brought together by a later compiler, and are now to be read as a single unit (Grabbe).

Place in the Canon

There are two traditions regarding the place of Ezra-Nehemiah in the Hebrew Bible. The more dominant Babylonian tradition, which is followed by all modern printed editions, places Ezra-Nehemiah immediately before Chronicles, the last book of the Writings. However, the Palestinian tradition, which is found in major Tiberian manuscripts, such as Aleppo and Leningrad, places Chronicles first in the Writings (before the Psalms), and places Ezra-Nehemiah last. In the Protestant Old Testament (e.g., the NRSV version), Ezra-Nehemiah is placed among the historical books, after Chronicles and before Esther. In the Roman Catholic Old Testament (e.g., the Douay-Rheims version), the books are similarly placed after Chronicles but before Tobit, Judith, and Esther.

Text and Versions

Some Hebrew fragments from the Book of Ezra (4QEzra) were found in Cave 4 at Qumran (Ulrich). The fragments contain part of the text of Ezra 4:2–6, 9–11, and 5:17–6:5 and exhibit two orthographic variants (e.g., at Ezra 4:10, 4QEzra reads נַהֲרָא for MT's נַהֲרָה), and two minor grammatical variants concerning singular and plural forms of verbs (e.g., at Ezra 6:1 where 4QEzra reads the singular ובקר "he searched" for MT's וּבַקַּרוּ "they searched"). The Greek tradition knew of two versions of Ezra-Nehemiah, one of which is known as II Esdras, and is a very literal translation of the Hebrew. This version numbers Ezra-Nehemiah consecutively so that chapters 1–10 of II Esdras represent the Book of Ezra, and chapters 11–23 represent the Book of Nehemiah. However, the other version, known as I Esdras, is wholly concerned with Ezra and not Nehemiah. It offers a rendering of the entire Book of Ezra but translates only that portion of the Book of Nehemiah (7:72–8:13) which deals with Ezra. This additional section is attached directly to what is chapter 10 in the Masoretic version.

Languages of the Books

The language of Ezra-Nehemiah is late biblical Hebrew (Polzin) and the text exhibits features which are characteristic of this later language. These include use of the -ו consecutive with the cohortative (וָאֶשְׁלְחָה), increased use of pronominal suffixes to the verb (וַיִּתְּנֵם) and of הָיָה with the participle (הָיוּ אֹמְרִים), many Akkadian and Persian loan words (such as אִגֶּרֶת "letter" = Akk. *egirtu*; פַּרְדֵּס "garden" = Pers. *pairidaeza*), and many Aramaisms (Naveh and Greenfield). Parts of Ezra are written in Aramaic (4:8–6:18, 7:11–26), and it has been suggested that originally the entire book of Ezra-Nehemiah was written in Aramaic and was subsequently translated (Marcus). In support of this theory is the fact that there is no extant Targum for Ezra-Nehemiah.

Book of Ezra: Outline

(1) Edict of Cyrus and rebuilding of the Temple (chapters 1–6)
Edict of Cyrus (1:1–11)
List of those returning with Zerubbabel (2:1–3:1)
Restoration of worship and laying foundations of the Temple (3:2–13)
Opposition to the Temple building (4:1–24)
Appeal to Darius and favorable response (5:1–6:14)
Completion of the Temple (6:15–22)
(2) Work of Ezra (chapters 7–10)
Edict of Artaxerxes to Ezra (7:1–28)
List of those going back with Ezra (8:1–14)
Return to Jerusalem (8:15–36)
Ezra reaction to news of intermarriage (9:1–10:14)
List of those who had intermarried (10:15–44)

Book of Nehemiah: Outline

(1) Nehemiah's mission (chapters 1–7)
Nehemiah's response to news from Jerusalem (1:1–11)
Permission to go to Jerusalem granted (2:1–9)
Arrival at Jerusalem and secret inspection of walls at night (2:10–20)
Reconstruction of the city's wall (3:1–38)
Threats against the workers (4:1–17)
Economic problems (5:1–13)
Nehemiah's administration (5:14–19)
Intrigues against Nehemiah (6:1–19)
More defensive measures (7:1–4)
List of the exiles with Zerubbabel (7:5–8:1a = Ezra 2:1–3:1)
(2) Ezra's reading of the Torah and religious celebrations (chapters 8–9)
The reading of the Torah (8:1b-12)
Celebration of the Feast of Tabernacles (8:13–18)
Day of penance and prayer of the Levites (9:1–37)
(3) Nehemiah's reforms (chapters 10–13)
Code of Nehemiah (10:1–40)
The population of Jerusalem and Judah (11:1–36)
Clerical genealogies (12:1–26)
Dedication of the wall (12:27–43)
Provision made for Temple services (12:44–47)
Expulsion of foreigners (13:1–9)
Renewal of Levitical support (13:10–14)
Enforcing Sabbath regulations (13:15–22)
Problem of mixed marriages (13:23–29)
Summary of other reforms (13:30–31)

Authorship and Date

The question of the authorship of Ezra-Nehemiah is bound up with its relation with the book of Chronicles. Since the time of Zunz (1832), the consensus of modern scholarship has been that the author of Chronicles was also the author of Ezra-Nehemiah, and this view still has its adherents (Blenkinsopp, Clines (1984)). Arguments for joint authorship include common vocabulary, style, uniformity of theological conceptions, similar description of religious ceremonies, penchant for occupational and genealogical lists, and, most importantly, the fact that the first few verses of Ezra (1:1–3a) are identical to the last two verses of Chronicles (II Chron 36:22–23), thus indicating that Chronicles leads in by means of catchlines to the following Book of Ezra (Haran). The position of Ezra-Nehemiah before Chronicles in the Protestant and Catholic Old Testament canons would seem to lend support for this point of view. In recent times, however, the independent authorship of both works has been argued on the basis of the following perceived contrasts: that Chronicles glorifies David, highly regards prophecy, has a conciliatory view of Northerners, and a miraculous view of history, whereas Ezra-Nehemiah emphasizes Moses and the Exodus, is forceful about its opposition to the Northerners (Samaritans), and has a different view of history. Ezra-Nehemiah ought then to be dated to the end of the fifth century B.C.E. whereas Chronicles is a later book composed at the end of the fourth century B.C.E. (Japhet). The catchlines at the end of Chronicles were borrowed from Ezra to give the book of Chronicles an "upbeat" ending heralding Cyrus' decree, and so not ending with the exile of the people in Babylon (Williamson).

Contents of the Books

Ezra-Nehemiah deals with the period of the restoration of the Jewish community in Judah, then the Persian province of Yehud, in the sixth–fifth centuries B.C.E. during the approximately 100 years between the time of the edict of *Cyrus (538) permitting the Jews to go back to Jerusalem and the 32nd year of the reign of *Artaxerxes I (433). Three different periods are represented in the books, each with different leaders and different royal missions. The first period (Ezra, chaps. 1–6) goes from the time of the edict of Cyrus (538) until the rebuilding of the temple (516), when the leaders of the Jews were Sheshbazzar and Zerubbabel. The second period (Ezra, chaps. 7–10 and Neh., chap. 8) commences in the seventh year of the reign of Artaxerxes (458), when Ezra is given a royal mandate to lead a group of exiles back to Jerusalem. The third period (Neh., chaps. 1–7 and 9–13) encompasses a 12-year period from the 20th year of the reign of Artaxerxes (445) until his 32nd year (433), and deals with the work of Nehemiah.

THE FIRST PERIOD (EZRA, CHAPS. 1–6). The first period, embracing 22 years from 538 to 516, includes an account of (1) the edict of Cyrus; (2) a list of the first returnees; (3) restoration of worship and laying foundations of the Temple; (4) opposition to the Temple building; (5) the appeal to *Darius and his favorable response; and (6) the completion of the Temple. In this period the leaders were *Sheshbazzar and *Zerubbabel. Sheshbazzar is thought to be identical with Senanazzar (the fourth son of Jeconiah (Jehoiachin), I Chron. 3:18), and is termed both prince (נָשִׂיא) and governor (פֶּחָה). Zerubbabel is one of the leaders of the first émigrés (2:2), and probably succeeded Sheshbazzar (4:2), though both are said to have laid foundations of the Temple (Sheshbazzar in Ezra 5:16 and Zerubbabel in Zech. 4:9).

The Edict of Cyrus (1:1–11). There are two accounts given in the Book of Ezra of the edict of Cyrus: a Jewish version in Hebrew, and a Persian version in Aramaic. The Jewish/Hebrew version has Cyrus declare that God has given him "all the kingdoms of the earth," that He has ordered the reconstruction of the Temple, and that any of God's people who so wish may return to assist in the carrying out of the order (1:1–3). The Persian/Aramaic version gives extra details detailing the specifications of the Temple to be built (e.g., its height and width should be 60 cubits, emulating the Temple destroyed by the Babylonians), that expenses for the Temple will be paid by the state, and that precious utensils captured by *Nebuchadnezzar and brought to Babylon will be returned (6:3–5). This last fact is actually mentioned in the first chapter of Ezra (v. 7). Cyrus released the cult objects and delivered them to Sheshbazzar, the governor of Judah, via Mithredath, the state treasurer. The Cyrus cylinder records similar acts of amnesty and favor shown to the peoples and deities of other countries following his conquest of Babylon in 539 (Cogan).

A List of the First Returnees (2:1–3:1). The list of the returning exiles with Zerubbabel is itemized by family, place of origin, occupation (e.g., priests, Levites, singers, gatekeepers, etc.). Because this list is repeated in its entirety in Nehemiah (Neh. 7:6–8:1a) there has been much discussion of the list's purpose, and where the list originally belonged. Most likely, the writer in the Book of Ezra was using a later list compiled for other uses, and its purpose at the beginning of Ezra is to magnify the first response of the exiles to Cyrus' edict. However, in the Book of Nehemiah, the list is used for a different purpose, as a starting point of a campaign to induce those who had settled elsewhere in Judah to move to Jerusalem, which needed repopulation.

Restoration of Worship and Laying Foundations of the Temple (3:2–13). Among the first activities of the returning exiles in 538 were to erect an altar on the site of the Temple, renew sacrificial worship, and celebrate the festival of Tabernacles. Preparations were then made for the rebuilding of the Temple, parallel to the preparations made for Solomon's Temple. The laying of the foundations was performed with a special service: prayer and song. The people's response was enthusiastic and they wept out of joy. However, there were a number of the returned exiles who had seen the first Temple, and these people wept in memory of this destroyed Temple to such an extent that the weeping for joy could not be distinguished from those weeping in memory of the destroyed Temple.

Opposition to the Temple Building (4:1–24). Work on the Temple did not proceed smoothly and, although it was started in the second year after the return (537), work was not continued on it until the second year of Darius I (521). The long delay of some 21 years between the laying of the Temple's foundations in 537 and its completion in 516 is explained as due to opposition by the local population. The opposition arose primarily as a result of the exclusionary policy of the returnees about permitting the indigenous population to participate in the rebuilding effort. The returnees believed that they were the true representatives of the people of God who had gone into exile, and that those who had not gone into exile but remained in the land, or were descendants of displaced peoples who had subsequently adopted Israel's religion, were not entitled to join in this project. The opponents are called צָרֵי יְהוּדָה וּבִנְיָמִן "adversaries of Judah and Benjamin" and עַם־הָאָרֶץ "people of the land," and they attempted to thwart the rebuilding effort by various means including writing accusatory letters to the Persian kings. These accusatory letters contained in 4:6–23 are problematic on two counts: first, because they do not deal with the rebuilding of the Temple but with the rebuilding of the city, and second because these letters are addressed to Persian kings who reigned long after the Temple was actually completed (516). These letters are sent to *Xerxes I (486–465) and *Artaxerxes I (465–424). That the section containing these letters is misplaced is clear from the fact that it is put in a different place in I Esdras, where these letters occur in chapter 2, and not in chapter 4 as in the Masoretic text.

Appeal to Darius and Favorable Response (5:1–6:14). The end of chapter 4 reverts back to the proper chronology, that of the second year of Darius (521), at which time the prophets *Haggai and *Zechariah encouraged the Jews to persist in the building of the Temple. The renewed activity led to an investigation by local Persian authorities, and a letter of inquiry (not a complaint like the preceding communications) was sent to Darius. The Persian authorities reported that they had gone to Jerusalem, observed the state of building operations, and had requested information on the authorization of the project. They were informed by the Jewish leaders of the edict of Cyrus granting the Jews permission to rebuild the Temple, and the letter asked the king to verify whether or not Cyrus did issue this edict. Darius then ordered a search in the royal archives, and the edict was found and is reproduced in his reply to the local authorities (see above). Darius issues instruction that the Cyrus decree be honored, and that expenses for the project be defrayed from the tax income accruing to the royal treasury from the province. Moreover, provisions were to be made for daily religious observances so that prayers could be made for the welfare of the king and his family. The aforementioned Cyrus Cylinder is often pointed to as an example of a Persian monarch who requested prayer from other peoples for his own and his son's welfare.

Completion of the Temple (6:15–22). The reconstruction on the Temple was completed in the sixth year of the reign of Darius I (516); the work had taken 21 years since the foundation was laid in the second year of Cyrus (537). A joyful dedication ceremony took place with enormous amounts of sacrifices, "one hundred bulls, two hundred rams, four hundred lambs, and twelve goats." Shortly afterwards the returned exiles celebrated the Passover, together with those of the indigenous population who had "separated themselves from the uncleanliness of the nations of the lands," a hint that the returnees were open to permitting others into their fold (see also Neh. 10:29).

THE SECOND PERIOD (EZRA, CHAPS. 7–10 AND NEH., CHAPS. 8–9). The second period dated in the seventh year of the reign of Artaxerxes I (458) deals with the work of *Ezra, after whom the book was named, and includes (1) the edict of Artaxerxes to Ezra; (2) Ezra's return to Jerusalem; (3) his reaction to news of intermarriage; (4) his reading of the Torah; and (5) a day of penance and a prayer of the Levites. In this period, the leader is Ezra, a priest whose ancestry is traced back to Aaron (7:1–5), and a scribe "well versed in the law of Moses" (7:6, 11). The date of Ezra is problematic as is his relationship with *Nehemiah, because apart from Nehemiah 8:9, and two other minor references (Neh. 12:26, 36), the two are never mentioned together. According to their respective books, Ezra assumed his mission in the seventh year of Artaxerxes (458) and Nehemiah came in the 20th year of the same king (445). This would mean that Ezra, who came at the express command of Artaxerxes to implement and teach the law, did not conduct his first public reading of the Law until 13 years later. Another problem for the biblical chronology is that Ezra found many people in Jerusalem but, according to Nehemiah, in his time, Jerusalem was unpopulated. For these reasons and others, some scholars believe Ezra came to Jerusalem much later, either in the 37th year of Artaxerxes I (428) or in the seventh year of Artaxerxes II (397) (see discussion in Klein).

The Edict of Artaxerxes to Ezra (7:1–28). In the seventh year of his reign (458), Artaxerxes I (465–424) issued a royal edict granting permission for Jews to go to Jerusalem with Ezra. Ezra was permitted to bring with him gold and silver donations from other Jews. Regular maintenance expenses of the Temple were to be provided from the royal treasury and there was to be release of taxes for Temple personnel. Ezra's mission was "to expound the law of the Lord" and "to teach laws and rules to Israel" (v. 10). For this purpose he was granted, not only a royal subsidy, but he was also empowered to appoint judges, enforce religious law, and even to apply the death penalty. In response to critics who argue that such a concern by a Persian king for a foreign cult would be unlikely, the Passover papyrus issued by Darius II in 419/18 to the Jews at Elephantine in Egypt regarding the date and method for celebrating the Passover (Porten) has often been cited. Nevertheless, the question of imperial authorization of Jewish law by the Persian Empire continues to be a subject of debate (Watts).

Ezra's Return to Jerusalem (8:1–36). Ezra's four-month journey to Jerusalem is described by Ezra in a first-person memoir. After listing the names of the leaders returning with him, Ezra discovers there were no *Levites in his party so he had to muster up 38 Levites from some Levitical families. Another problem was security. Because Ezra had originally made a declaration of trust in God before the king, he felt it inappropriate to request from him the customary escort. Thus he accounted the party's safe arrival in Jerusalem with all its treasure intact as a mark of divine benevolence.

Ezra's Reaction to News of Intermarriage (9:1–10:44). When Ezra arrived in Jerusalem he was informed that some people, including members of the clergy and aristocracy, had contracted foreign marriages. Immediately upon hearing this news Ezra engaged in mourning rites, tore his garments and fasted, and, on behalf of the people, confessed their sins and uttered a prayer of contrition. He is joined by a group of supporters who are also disturbed by this news. At the initiative of a certain Shecaniah son of Jehiel, Ezra was urged to take immediate action. An emergency national assembly was convened, and Ezra addressed the crowd in a winter rainstorm calling upon the people to divorce their foreign wives. The assembled crowd agreed to Ezra's plea, but because of the heavy rains and the complexity of the matter (Ezra's extension of legal prohibitions of marriages that had previously been permitted), they requested that a commission of investigation be set up. After three months the commission reported back with a list of priests, Levites, and Israelites who had intermarried.

Ezra's Reading of the Torah (Neh 8:1–12). Seemingly out of order, Ezra reappears in chapter 8 of the Book of Nehemiah where it is recounted that he publicly read the Torah on the first day of the seventh month (Rosh Ha-Shanah). He stood upon a platform with dignitaries standing on his right and left. The ceremony began with an invocation by Ezra and a response by the people saying "Amen, Amen." During the reading the people stood while the text was made clear to them (or translated for them (into Aramaic)) by the Levites (van der Kooij). The people were emotionally overcome by the occasion and wept. However, they were enjoined not to be sad, rather to celebrate the day joyously with eating, drinking, and gift giving. The day after the public reading, a group of priests and Levites continued to study the Torah with Ezra and came across the regulations for observing the feast of Tabernacles on that very month. A proclamation was issued to celebrate the festival which was done with great joy, and the Torah was again read publicly during the entire eight days of the festival. It has often been pointed out that the feast of Tabernacles which is described as being discovered anew from the Torah reading and had not been observed since the days of Joshua, had already been observed not too much earlier by the first returnees (Ezra 3:4). Furthermore, the materials said to be collected for the festival (branches of olive, pine, myrtle, palm, and leafy trees) differ from those mandated for the festival in Leviticus 23:40 (where the materials are the fruit of הָדָר trees (later interpreted as the citron), willows of the brook, palms, and bough of leafy trees (later interpreted as the myrtle)). Most strikingly, these materials are said to be used to construct סֻכֹּת "tabernacles," and not to be used for making of the לוּלָב and אֶתְרוֹג in accordance with the later rabbinic interpretation.

Day of Penance and Prayer of the Levites (Neh. 9:1–37). On the 24th day of the month, immediately after the celebration of the feast of Tabernacles, a fast day was announced. The identification and purpose of this fast day is unknown. Most commentators believe that this fast and following prayer of the Levites should come after the events described in Ezra 10, which was concerned with problems of intermarriage. The long prayer of the Levites (v. 5–37) is akin to one of the historical hymns in the Psalter (cf., Ps. 105, 106, 135, 136) (Fensham). The hymn contains stereotypical Psalm language, and contains references to the creation, the covenant with Abraham, the acts of God in Egypt, the wanderings in the desert, Sinai, the conquest, the Judges, and to later periods. Many of the sections are divided by the independent pronoun וְאַתָּה (v. 6, 7, 19, 27, 33). The hymn is noteworthy in not mentioning David and Solomon, two of Judah's glorious rulers, nor is there any mention of the exile and the current restoration, events central to Ezra and Nehemiah. Verses 6–11 of this hymn are included in the Jewish morning prayer service (פְּסוּקֵי דְזִמְרָא).

THE THIRD PERIOD (NEH., CHAPS. 1–7 AND 9–13). The third period encompasses 12 years from the 20th year of the reign of Artaxerxes I (445) until his 32nd year (433), and deals with the work of Nehemiah, who had held an important office (termed a "cupbearer") in the royal household of the Persian king Artaxerxes I (465–424). The work of Nehemiah described in the form of a first-person memoir includes his rebuilding of the walls of Jerusalem and his economic and religious reforms. One of the characteristics of Nehemiah's memoirs is that he intersperses short direct prayers within his narrative usually starting with זָכְרָה לִּי אֱלֹהַי or with slight variations (5:19, 6:14, 13:14, 22, 29, 31) but once with שְׁמַע אֱלֹהֵינוּ (3:36–37). In particular, this period deals with (1) Nehemiah's response to the news from Jerusalem; (2) Nehemiah's efforts at reconstructing and fortifying Jerusalem; (3) intrigues against Nehemiah; (4) the dedication of the wall; (5) Nehemiah's resolution of economic problems; (6) Nehemiah's religious reforms.

Nehemiah's Response to News from Jerusalem (1:1–2:9). In the 20th year of the Persian king Artaxerxes I (445), a delegation of Jews arrived from Jerusalem at Susa, the king's winter residence, and informed Nehemiah of the deteriorating conditions back in Judah. The walls of Jerusalem were in a precarious state and repairs could not be undertaken (since they were specifically forbidden by an earlier decree of the same Artaxerxes (Ezra 4:21)). The news about Jerusalem upset Nehemiah, and he sought and was granted permission from the king to go to Jerusalem as governor and rebuild the city. This change in Persian policy is thought to have come after the Egyptian revolt of 448 when it was believed that a relatively strong and friendly Judah could better serve Persia's strategic interests (Myers). Nehemiah was also granted much material assistance including supplies of wood for the rebuilding effort. However, unlike Ezra, Nehemiah requested a military escort for safe conduct throughout the provinces of the western satrapies.

Nehemiah's Efforts at Reconstructing and Fortifying Jerusalem (2:10–4:17, 7:1–4). A short time after his arrival in Jerusalem Nehemiah made a nocturnal inspection tour of the city walls riding on a donkey. He relates that he could not continue riding, but had to dismount, because of the massive stones left by the overthrow of the city by the Babylonians. After his tour of inspection, Nehemiah disclosed to the local Jewish officials his mission to rebuild the walls. Nehemiah set to the task of rebuilding the wall by dividing the work into some 40 sections. Nearly all social classes (priests, Levites, Temple functionaries, and laypeople) participated in the building effort. Throughout the time of the building, Nehemiah encountered opposition and harassment from the leaders of the Persian provinces, who had previously administered the affairs of Judah, especially from one *Sanballat, a Horonite (from Beth Horon), also termed the Samarian/Samaritan. Sanballat resorted to mockery and ridicule, stating: "that stone wall they are building – if a fox climbed it he would breach it" (3:33–35). To counter the opposition, Nehemiah provided a guard for the workmen, and the masons and their helpers also carried swords. Because of the magnitude of the project, the workmen were separated from each other by large distances, so a trumpeter was provided ready to sound the alarm, the idea being that should one group be attacked the others would come to their aid. Nehemiah ordered the workers to remain in Jerusalem partly for self-protection and partly to assist in guarding the city. After the wall was rebuilt, Nehemiah appointed Hanani his brother and a similar-named individual, Hananiah, to be in charge of security. He also gave an order that the gates to the city should be closed before the guards went off duty and that they should be opened only when the sun was high (at midmorning). In addition to the security police, there was a citizen patrol whose duty it was to keep watch around their own houses. The central problem was the small population of Jerusalem: the city was extensive and spacious, but the people it in were few, and the houses were not yet built. Nehemiah decided to bring one of ten people from the surrounding population into Jerusalem (11:1–2).

Intrigues against Nehemiah (6:1–19). One of Nehemiah's enemies, Tobiah, an Ammonite, had intermarried with a prominent family in Judah. He had tried unsuccessfully to subvert Nehemiah's work by enlisting their aid, but without success. Since Nehemiah's enemies could not prevent the rebuilding and fortification of the city they made desperate attempts to capture him. One plan was to lure him away from Jerusalem to some unspecified place. Four times they attempted to invite him to "meetings," and each time Nehemiah, knowing their harmful intentions, refused their invitation. When these attempts failed, a fifth attempt was made to hurt Nehemiah by framing him before the Persian authorities with a false report that he planned to have himself proclaimed king in Judah. A sixth attempt to damage Nehemiah was to pay a false prophet, Shemaiah, to lure Nehemiah into the Temple, but Nehemiah, realizing that this was a plot, refused to go. Despite these threats, Nehemiah reports that the wall was completed in just 52 days, which seems to be an incredibly short time for such a monumental task. According to Josephus, the project took two years and four months.

Dedication of the Wall (12:27–43). A large gathering of priests, Levites, musicians, and notables assembled from all over Judah for the dedication of the wall in Jerusalem. Nehemiah divided the participants into two processions each commencing from the same point; one procession marched south towards the Dung Gate and then around the right side of the wall, the other marched north along the top of the left side, and both groups joined up together at the Temple square. Each procession was led by a choir, and musicians with trumpets, cymbals, harps, and lyres brought up the rear. Ezra is said to have marched in one procession (though his presence in the text is probably an editorial addition), and Nehemiah in the other. The two joyful processions met up in the Temple square where the dedication was concluded with many sacrifices.

Nehemiah's Resolution of Economic Problems (5:1–19). During the period of the rebuilding, the people complained about the scarcity of food and the burden of high taxes. To meet their basic needs, the poor were required to pledge their possessions, even to sell sons and daughters into slavery. Nehemiah reacted angrily against the creditors accusing them of violating the covenant of brotherhood. When his appeal to the creditors voluntarily to take remedial action failed, Nehemiah forced them to take an oath, reinforced by a symbolic act of shaking out his garment, to restore property taken in pledge, as well as to forgive claims for loans. Nehemiah himself alleviated the people's tax burden by refusing to accept the very liberal household allowance for his official retinue which amounted to some 40 shekels of silver a day.

Nehemiah's Religious Reforms (10:1–40, 12:44–47, 13:1–29). Nehemiah's religious reforms are found (a) in the so-called Code of Nehemiah; and (b) in the regulations he enacted upon embarking on his second term as governor in the 32nd year of Artaxerxes I (433).

Code of Nehemiah (10:1–40). The Code of Nehemiah represents pledges made by the community to observe the Torah, its commandments and regulations. It is preceded by a list of signers including Nehemiah, his officials, the priests, Levites, and prominent family members (1–28). In the Code, the community promised to do seven things: (1) to avoid mixed marriages with the peoples of the land; (2) not to buy from foreigners on Sabbaths and holy days; (3) to observe the sabbatical year; (4) to pay a new annual third shekel temple tax; (5) to supply offerings for the services and wood for the Temple altar; (6) to supply the first fruits, firstlings, tithes, and other contributions to the Temple; (7) to bring the tithes due to the priests and Levites to local storehouses.

Regulations Enacted by Nehemiah during his Second Term as Governor (13:1–31). Expulsion of Foreigners (13:1–9). In their continued reading of the Torah the community came across a law (possibly referring to Deut 23:4–6) that Ammonites and Moabites were prohibited from becoming Israelites, and so they resolved to separate from foreigners (עֵרֶב). When Nehemiah returned from an official visit to the Persian court in the 32nd year of Artaxerxes (433) he discovered that the high priest Eliashib had given living quarters in a former storage room of the Temple to one of his old enemies Tobiah, the Ammonite (see above). When Nehemiah returned he evicted Tobiah, discarded all his belongings, and had the chambers purified and restored to their original use.

Renewal of Levitical Support (13:10–14). Another consequence of Nehemiah's absence at the Persian court was that the people had stopped giving tithes to the Levites forcing them to return to their villages. Nehemiah took steps to bring back the Levites to Jerusalem by ensuring that outstanding payments, which had not been collected during his absence, would be paid and that future tithes would be regularly given.

Enforcing Sabbath Regulations (13:15–22). Nehemiah reports that in his day the Sabbath had been utterly commercialized. People were working in vineyards and on the farms, and Phoenician traders set up shops in Jerusalem on the Sabbath. Nehemiah attempted to put a stop to this Sabbath activity by ordering the gates of the city closed during the Sabbath. Despite his orders, the Phoenician traders camped outside the walls hoping to entice customers to come outside.

Problem of Mixed Marriages (13:23–29). As in Ezra's day, Nehemiah had to deal with problems arising from marriages with foreign women. A major concern of his was the fact that the children of these marriages could no longer speak the language of Judah. Nehemiah ordered an end to further intermarriage, but he did not go as far as Ezra who demanded divorce from foreign wives.

Significance of the Books for Later Judaism

Ezra and Nehemiah's actions and decrees may be seen as the beginning of an ongoing reinterpretation of tradition in its application to changing circumstances (Talmon). Ezra's reading of the Torah inaugurated a new element in Jewish life whereby the Torah was read and explicated on regular occasions in public. This public reading also led to the democratization of knowledge of the Torah among Jews, since prior to this event most parts of the Torah were under the exclusive provenance and control of the priests (Knohl). The differences between the formulation of regulations in the Book of Nehemiah and their counterparts in the Torah illustrate the process of legal elaboration necessary to meet contemporary exigencies (Clines, 1981). These differences can be seen in at least three areas: contributions to the Temple, regulations regarding Sabbath observance, and new intermarriage prohibitions.

TEMPLE CONTRIBUTIONS. Some examples of modifications to Pentateuchal laws introduced in the Code of Nehemiah involve upkeep of the Temple. In Exodus 30:11–16, mention is made of a one-time half-shekel tax. The Code of Nehemiah, however, establishes an annual Temple tax, that of one-third of a shekel. In Leviticus 6:1–6, it is stated that fire should burn continuously on the altar but it does not prescribe the mechanism by which this ought to be done. The Code of Nehemiah does this by stipulating how the wood for the altar is to be obtained. In Deuteronomy 14:23–26, it is enjoined that tithes for the Levites are to be brought to the Temple. The Code of Nehemiah modifies this regulation by permitting an alternate collection system in provincial depots. All these stipulations for the Temple maintenance represent an innovation in ancient Israel, since now the upkeep of the Temple is made the responsibility of the entire community, not just of the king or the governor (Eskenazi).

SABBATH OBSERVANCE. In the Pentateuch, the Sabbath law enjoins rest from work (e.g., Ex. 20:8–11; 23:12; and *passim*), but nowhere defines buying food as work, yet buying food from foreigners on the Sabbath is prohibited in the Code of Nehemiah. According to Amos 8:5, pre-exilic Israelites did not trade on the Sabbath, but the new conditions in Nehemiah's time of foreign merchants coming into Jerusalem on the Sabbath led to this new interpretation of the law.

NEW INTERMARRIAGE PROHIBITIONS. The stipulations against intermarriage in Exodus 34:11–16 and Deuteronomy 7:1–4 prohibit intermarriage with Canaanites (Hittites, Perizzites, Hivites, and Jebusites). Both Ezra and Nehemiah redefine these old Canaanites (who had long disappeared) as the new Canaanites, the current Ashdodites, Ammonites, and Moabites. It is often thought that Ezra's action insisting on the divorce of foreign wives and their children, together with Nehemiah's concern that the children of these foreign women could not speak the language of Judah, represented a shift in Israelite matrimonial law. Previously offspring of intermarriage was judged patrilineally; now it was to be on the matrilineal principle (for a different view, see Cohen).

BIBLIOGRAPHY: J.M. Myers, *Ezra, Nehemiah* (1965); S. Japhet, "The Supposed Common Authorship of Chronicles and Ezra-Nehemiah Investigated Anew," in: VT, 18 (1968), 330–71; R. Polzin, *Late Biblical Hebrew: Toward an Historical Typology of Biblical Hebrew Prose* (1976); S. Talmon, "Ezra, Nehemiah," in: L.K. Crim (ed.), *The Interpreter's Dictionary of the Bible. Supplementary Volume* (1976), 317–28; F.C. Fensham, "Neh. 9 and Pss. 105, 106, 135 and 136. Post-Exilic Historical Traditions in Poetic Form," in: JNSL, 9 (1981), 35–51; D.J.C. Clines, "Nehemiah 10 as an Example of Early Jewish Biblical Exegesis," in: JSOT, 21 (1981), 11–17; J. Naveh and J.C. Greenfield, "Hebrew and Aramaic in the Persian Period," in: W.D. Davies and L. Finkelstein (eds.), *Introduction; The Persian Period*; The Cambridge History of Judaism, 1 (1984), 115–29; D.J.C. Clines, *Ezra, Nehemiah, Esther* (1984); M. Haran, "Explaining the Identical Lines at the End of Chronicles and the Beginning of Ezra," in: BR, 2 (1986), 18–20; H.G.M. Williamson, "Did the Author of Chronicles Also Write the Books of Ezra and Nehemiah? Clutching at Catchlines," in: BR, 3 (1987), 56–59; J. Blenkinsopp, *Ezra-Nehemiah* (1988); T.C. Eskenazi, *In An Age of Prose: A Literary Approach to Ezra-Nehemiah* (1988); A. van der Kooij, "Nehemiah 8:8 and the Question of the 'Targum'-Tradition," in: G.J. Norton and S. Pisano (eds.), *Tradition of the Text: Studies Offered to Dominique Barthélemy in Celebration of his 70th Birthday* (1991), 79–90; R.W. Klein, "Ezra-Nehemiah, Books of," in: D.N. Freedman (ed.), *Anchor Bible Dictionary* (1992), 2:731–42; E. Ulrich, "Ezra and Qoheleth Manuscripts from Qumran (4QEzra, 4QQoh^{a,b})," in: E. Ulrich et al. (eds.), *Priests, Prophets, and Scribes: Essays on the Formation and Heritage of Second Temple Judaism in Honour of Joseph Blenkinsopp* (1992), 139–57; S. Japhet, *I & II Chronicles* (1993); D. Kraemer, "On the Relationship of the Books of Ezra and Nehemiah," in: JSOT, 59 (1993), 73–92; L.L. Grabbe, *Ezra-Nehemiah* (1998); D. Marcus, "Is the Book of Nehemiah a Translation from Aramaic?" in: M. Lubetski et al. (eds.), *Boundaries of the Ancient Near Eastern World: A Tribute to Cyrus H. Gordon* (1998), 103–10; M. Cogan, "Cyrus Cylinder (2.124)," in: W.W. Hallo (ed.), *The Context of Scripture* (2000), 2:314–16; J.W. Watts (ed.), *Persia and Torah: The Theory of Imperial Authorization of the Pentateuch* (2001); B. Porten, "The Passover Letter (3.46)," in: W.W. Hallo (ed.), *The Context of Scripture* (2002), 3:116–17; S.J.D. Cohen, *The Beginnings of Jewishness* (1999); I. Knohl, *The Divine Symphony: The Bible's Many Voices* (2003).

[David Marcus (2nd ed.)]

EZRA BEN ABRAHAM BEN MAZHIR (c. 12th century), *rosh yeshivah* in *Damascus. *Benjamin of Tudela, who met Ezra, lists the officials of the yeshivah, the leader being Ezra's brother Sar Shalom, who bore the title of "father" of the yeshivah. Like his father, who had preceded him, Ezra assumed the title of *gaon* and laid claim to all the privileges which had previously been accorded to the yeshivah in Ereẓ Israel, of which the Damascus yeshivah was regarded as a continuation. These claims were disputed by the heads of the Fostat Yeshivah, and the controversy between the two institutions developed into a rivalry between the strongminded R. *Samuel b. Ali, head of the Baghdad Yeshivah, who supported Ezra, and *Daniel b. Hasdai, the Babylonian exilarch, who championed Fostat. The rivalry continued for many years.

BIBLIOGRAPHY: Mann, Texts, 1 (1931), 230, 232, 251–2, 257; Assaf, in: *Tarbiz*, 1:1 (1930), 105; 1:2 (1930), 80–81; 1:3 (1930), 67, 77.

[Eliyahu Ashtor]

EZRA BEN EZEKIEL HA-BAVLI (1660–after 1742), rabbi and poet in *Baghdad. Ezra was vehement in his criticism of the Jews of Baghdad. In his *Tokheḥot Musar* ("Moral Reproofs," 1735), written in rhymed prose, both in Hebrew and Aramaic, he severely took them to task for their low moral standards. He reproved them for wasting time on drink and frivolity, for their lack of support of the poor, and for their disregard of Torah. The sharpness of his criticism led to his persecution by the community and he was either imprisoned or expelled from the community. Ezra also wrote *Netivot Shalom* (1742), homilies on the Pentateuch.

BIBLIOGRAPHY: Benjacob, Oẓar, 617; A. Ben-Jacob, *Yehudei Bavel* (1965), 97, 309.

EZRA BEN NISAN (1595–1666), *Karaite scholar and physician, leader of the community of Troki, Lithuania. In 1634 he fulfilled the duties of *dayyan*, and in 1640–43 held the position of *shofet* (judge). Ezra came in contact with the famous Jewish scholar and kabbalist Joseph Solomon *Delmedigo of Candia, who spent five years in Lithuania as a physician of Prince Krzysztof Radziwiłł. It may be that Delmedigo imparted his knowledge of medicine to him, but he probably taught him Rashi's commentary to the Pentateuch with Elijah *Mizraḥi's and *Ibn Ezra's commentaries. Ezra had a large library, which supposedly was burnt in the course of the Russian invasion in 1655. According to A. *Firkovich, Delmedigo taught him medicine, introduced him to the prince, and even to King Jan Casimir (1648–68), and Ezra occupied Delmedigo's position after he left. Accordingly, Ezra cured a daughter of the king, who granted him lands in Troki that were seized after his demise by local Dominicans, because Ezra had only two daughters who never married. There is no evidence from other sources confirming this information. Ezra also became a hero of Karaite folklore. Ezra composed some liturgical poems, some of them included in the Karaite *Siddur* (IV, Vilna 1890).

BIBLIOGRAPHY: G. Akhiezer and I. Dvorkin, in: *Pe'amim*, 98–99 (2004), 243–34; A. Firkovich, *Avnei Zikkaron* (1872), 251–53; M. Kizilov, *Leipziger Beiträge zur jüdische Geschichte und Kultur I* (2003), 83–103; Mann, Texts, 2 (1935), 1545, index.

[Golda Akhiezer (2nd ed.)]

EZRA BEN SOLOMON (d. 1238 or 1245), one of the leading kabbalists of his day in Gerona, Spain. For a long time scholars thought him identical with *Azriel b. Menahem of Gerona, since various authors attributed to Azriel works written by Ezra and vice versa. However, the poems of Meshullam b. Solomon da *Piera, a contemporary of the two and also a native of Gerona, make it possible definitely to determine that Ezra and Azriel were two different individuals who lived in Gerona at the same time. This fact is also confirmed by testimonies of kabbalists from the late 13th and early 14th centuries. G. *Scholem's discovery of several of their works and I. Tishby's studies have established that the two men represented different kabbalistic trends.

According to Abraham *Abulafia, Ezra wrote a commentary to the *Sefer *Yezirah* (see A. *Jellinek, *Beit ha-Midrash*, 3 (1938), 43) which has not survived. His commentary on the Song of Songs, attributed to *Naḥmanides, was first published in Altona in 1764, with many errors repeated in all subsequent editions. It was republished by H.D. Chavel in *Kitvei Rabbenu Moshe ben Naḥman* (2, 1964, 474–548), but this edition too contains all the errors of its predecessors. It has been translated into French and commented upon by G. Vajda (see bibl.). Both Ezra and Azriel wrote commentaries on talmudic legends. Several fragments of Ezra's commentary appear in *Likkutei Shikhḥah u-Fe'ah* (Ferrara, 1556); however, the publisher, Abraham b. Judah Elmaleh, concealed the author's name. The work exists in several manuscripts, especially Vatican 441. Two of Ezra's letters which have survived were published by G. Scholem (in *Sefer Bialik* (1934), 155–62).

Ezra's works show the influence of his teacher *Isaac the Blind. In his turn, Ezra greatly influenced his contemporaries and the kabbalists of the 13th and 14th centuries. His colleague and contemporary Jacob b. Sheshet *Gerondi, who cites him several times, sometimes in agreement and often in dispute, in *Meshiv Devarim Nekhoḥim* and *Ha-Emunah ve-ha-Bittaḥon*, calls him "the sage (*ha-ḥakham*) Rabbi Ezra." Azriel follows in Ezra's footsteps in his commentary on talmudic legends, although he changes the meaning and the outlook. The greatest scholar of the period, Naḥmanides, cites Ezra's writings on at least one occasion. As noted by I. Tishby, his influence can also be discerned in the works of other noteworthy personalities, especially *Baḥya b. Asher, who mentions him by name only twice but uses his writings many times; Joshua *Ibn Shu'ayb, who cites Ezra on many occasions in his *Derashot al ha-Torah* (the printed copy often confuses Ezra with Abraham *Ibn Ezra); and *Isaac b. Samuel of Acre, who cites Ezra in his book *Me'irat Einayim* (in Ms.). Traces of Ezra's commentary on the Song of Songs appear in the *Zohar.

BIBLIOGRAPHY: G. Scholem, *Reshit ha-Kabbalah* (1948), 127–30; idem, in: *Sefer Bialik* (1934), 141–62; idem, *Kitvei Yad be-Kabbalah* (1930), 1–3; idem, *Ursprung und Anfaenge der Kabbala* (1962), 328–32; I. Tishby, *Perush ha-Aggadot le-R. Azri'el* (1945); idem, in: *Zion*, 9 (1944), 178–85; idem, in: *Sinai*, 16 (1945), 159–78; E. Gottlieb, *Ha-Kabbalah be-Khitvei R. Baḥya ben Asher* (1970), 38–73; idem, in: *Tarbiz*, 37 (1967/68), 294–317; idem, in; KS, 40 (1964/65), 1–9; G. Vajda, *Le Commentaire d'Ezra de Gérone sur le Cantique des Cantiques* (1969).

[Efraim Gottlieb]

EZRA OF MONTCONTOUR (late 12th and early 13th century), French tosafist. Ezra studied under *Judah b. Isaac Sir Leon of Paris. *Meir b. Baruch of Rothenburg studied under Ezra (see his responsum, Cremona, 312). Ezra was head of a yeshivah at Montcontour. He was generally referred to as "the prophet" by the *rishonim* and this is how he is mentioned in the *tosafot* (Git. 88a; Shev. 25a; Tos. R. Perez to BK 23b, etc.). However, mention of "Ezra" without any title might also refer to him. The epithet might stem from his connections with the kabbalists. Traditions handed down by his contemporaries relate that Ezra, like his friend *Jacob of Marvege, attained an "ascent of the soul." There is no evidence, however, that he himself was a kabbalist. According to these same traditions, Ezra was the grandson of Abraham *Ibn Ezra.

BIBLIOGRAPHY: Weiss, in: HHY, 5 (1921), 46–47; Marx, *ibid.*, 197; Scholem, in: *Tarbiz*, 2 (1930/31), 244f., 514; Fried, *ibid.*, 514; Urbach, Tosafot, 278f.

[Israel Moses Ta-Shma]

EZRIN, HERSHELL (1947–), Canadian diplomat, public servant, businessman, Jewish community leader. Ezrin was born in Toronto to Sydney and Marcia Ezrin, both the children of immigrants from Russia and Poland. After graduating from Hebrew day school, he earned his B.A. and M.A. degrees in history from the University of Toronto and Carleton University before joining the Canadian Department of External Affairs in 1969, shortly after Pierre Elliot Trudeau was elected Canada's prime minister. Ezrin's foreign postings included Los Angeles, New York, and New Delhi. During the 1980s he served in high positions in the federal and Ontario governments before entering the private sector in 1988. Subsequently Ezrin held a series of top executive posts, including chairman and CEO of GPC Canada, a public affairs and strategic communications firm. He also served as a senior counselor and political adviser to several government officials.

Ezrin was active on behalf of a number of Toronto Jewish organizations, including the Holy Blossom Temple Foundation, the Baycrest Centre for Geriatric Care, and Mount Sinai Hospital. He also served as an adviser to both the State of Israel Bonds and the Canada-Israel Committee. He also served the broader community in numerous capacities, most notably as chair of the Board of the Toronto Symphony Orchestra, and wrote widely on public affairs.

In 2004 Ezrin became CEO of the Canadian Council for Israel and Jewish Advocacy (CIJA), an organization established by the Jewish federations in 2004 to lobby on behalf of the organized Jewish community on both domestic and Israel-related matters. As the first CEO of CIJA, which includes oversight of both the Canada-Israel Committee and the Canadian Jewish Congress, Ezrin had the task of giving the Canadian Jewish community effective direction and a strong and effective voice in the larger Canadian community.

[Harold M. Waller (2nd ed.)]

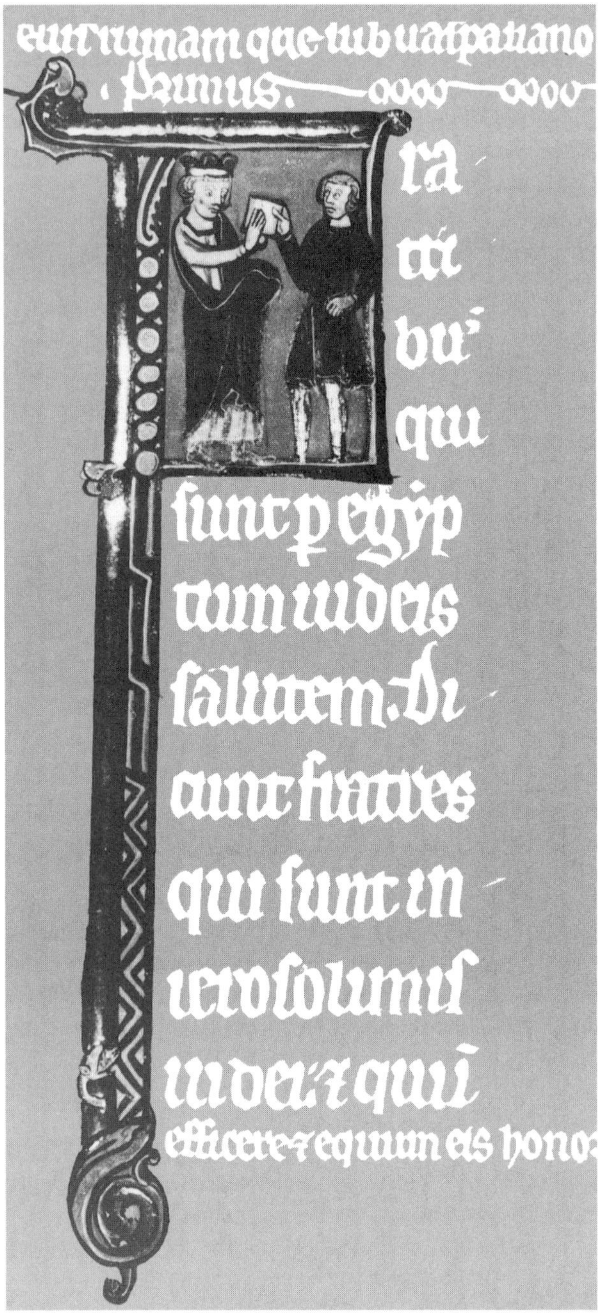

Historiated initial letter "F" of the word Fratribus *at the beginning of II Maccabees in a 12th-century manuscript from France. It illustrates the sending of the letter from the Jews of Jerusalem to their brethren in Egypt calling on them to observe the feast of Ḥannukah. Bordeaux, Bibliothèque Municipale, Ms. 21, fol. 256v.*

FA–FEU

FABIUS, LAURENT (1946–), French politician – the youngest premier in the history of the Republic. Fabius was born in France to a Jewish family which converted to Catholicism during World War II. After completing his studies in political science and humanities, he became active in the Socialist party. In 1978 he was elected deputé to the French Assembly. When François Mitterrand was elected president of the Republic in 1981, Fabius joined the government, first as minister in charge of the budget (1981–83) and then as minister for industry and research (1983–84). In 1984, with the collapse of the alliance between the Socialists and the Communists and the generally poor showing of the government in the public opinion polls, Mitterrand called in Fabius, as a representative of the new technocratic trend in the Socialist party, to lead the new government. With the appointment of the young, articulate politician, polls took an upswing. "Modernization and unity – these will be the priorities of my government," stated Fabius when taking office.

In 1986 the Socialists were ousted by a right-wing government and Fabius ceased to be prime minister. When the Socialists returned to power in 1988, Fabius was elected president of the National Assembly, a position he held until he became first secretary of the Socialist party in 1992. He had the difficult task of pulling the party out of a slump but support for the Socialists continued to plummet. At the end of 1992, the party agreed to send him and two former health ministers to trial for their ministerial responsibility for a 1985 scandal when HIV-contaminated blood had been knowingly distributed by high officials; over 1,000 people had acquired the HIV virus and 200 died. The National Assembly and the Senate endorsed the decision to send the three to trial. Fabius had asked to be brought to trial, saying to the Senate "Innocent and recognized as such, I come before you to ask you to charge me with errors I did not commit," and was eventually found not guilty. Reelected a member of the National Assembly in 1993, he became, its president for the second time two years later when the left came back to power. In 2000 he was appointed minister of economy, finances and industry in the government led by Socialist premier Lionel Jospin, but the electoral defeat of the left in the 2002 general elections sent him back to the opposition benches of the National Assembly. In 2004 Fabius took a strong stand against the European constitutional treaty, a rather unexpected move that surprised political commentators, who viewed him as a moderate, center-to-left politician. Defying the leadership of the Socialist Party, which endorsed the constitutional treaty, Fabius followed the mood of the public, which overwhelmingly dismissed the treaty in the referendum of May 2005, thereby conceivably improving his chances in the presidential elections of 2007.

Fabius wrote *La France inégale* (1975), *Le cœur du futur* (1985), *C'est en allant vers la mer* (1990), *Les blessures de la vérité* (1995), *Cela commence par une ballade* (2003), and *Une certaine idée de l'Europe* (2004).

BIBLIOGRAPHY: J.-G. Fredet, *Fabius, les brûlures d'une ambition* (2001).

[Gideon Kouts / Dror Franck Sullaper (2nd ed.)]

FABLE, an animal tale (according to the most general and hence most widely accepted definition), i.e., a tale in which the characters are animals, and which contains a moral lesson. The genre also includes tales in which plants or inanimate objects act and talk.

Introduction

Definitions vary according to the importance ascribed to the thematic factor (the animal story) or the functional factor (its didactic tendency). As a literary creation, the fable developed out of oral folklore, and it can thus be asserted that the thematic element is closely related to those popular origins, while the didactic quality is the product of a more sophisticated cultural level, usually of an individual whose specific aim is to educate (e.g., the Greek pedagogues, the rabbis of the Mishnah and the Talmud, the *darshanim*, and the priests of the various churches during the Middle Ages). Because the earliest sources of the European literary fable and the oldest known collection are connected with the name of the Greek Aesop, the animal fable has often been called the Aesopian fable.

While the animal society of the fable operates very similarly to its human analogue, the activity, in general, remains exclusively within the realm of the animal world. Some fables, however, do depict interaction between humans and animals. A similarity between the fable and the fairy tale (*maerchen*, Heb. *ma'asiyyah*) is seen in this fanciful conception of animals functioning as human beings. Yet within the fable itself, the plot is usually realistic and seldom contains magical elements, such as metamorphoses, revivals of the dead, and ghosts. The fable further differs from the fairy tale in its being mono-episodic. A series of episodes related or written together have developed into the beast epic, but each of those episodes can be isolated from its wider context. Like the fairy tale, though, the fable too uses universal motifs and stock characters. The latter are either stereotyped or endowed with conventional functions within the animal society.

The source of the fable lies in the observation of animals in their natural setting, and the tale often remains etiological. More sophisticated plots and the didactic application of the concrete story to the realm of ethics result from the tendency to draw obvious parallels and to develop potential analogies. In these cases, the two possible narrative forms are the metaphorical and generalizing fables.

Among various conjectures as to the origin of the fable, the 19th-century scholar, Julius Landsberger, maintained that the fable originated with the Jews (*Hebraeer*), pointing out the similarity between the names Aesop and Asaph. While this theory has been contradicted (by Joseph *Jacobs and others), some of the Hebrew fables are nevertheless among the most ancient that are extant in literary form. These are traced back to the 15th–14th centuries B.C.E., and a still earlier oral tradition can be assumed.

The Hebrew term for fable, *mashal* (מָשָׁל), is linked, in popular etymology, to the two homonymic roots *mshl*, meaning respectively "to liken," and "to rule." This is explained by the fact that *meshalim* were narrated by rulers or related to future rulers in order to instruct them in just ways.

In the Bible

The biblical term refers to the proverb, aphorism, and to allegorical prophecy. Later interpretation applied the term to allegory (Ezek. 17:3–12), to the parable (II Sam. 12:1–4), and to the fable. Of the latter there are two prime examples: Jotham's fable told to the citizens of Shechem on Mount Gerizim (Judg. 9:8–15), in which he likens their king, Abimelech, to the bramble which became the king of the trees; and the fable of the thistle and the cedar of Lebanon in the answer given by Jehoash, the king of Israel, to Amaziah, the king of

Judah (II Kings 14:9; II Chron. 25:18). One interpretation of I Kings 5:13 (where Solomon is said to have spoken of trees and animals) is that it refers to Solomon's writing of fables, a field in which the Semitic wise man (e.g., *Ahikar) characteristically engaged.

In the Talmud and Midrash

A much richer source of fables is the talmudic-midrashic literature, which mentions several outstanding fabulists, notably *Hillel (Sof. 16:7), and his pupil, *Johanan b. Zakkai (Suk. 28a; BB 134a; Sof. 16:6). Johanan mastered three genres: fox tales, palm tales (lit., "the talk of palm trees"), and washerman tales. (The last, *mishlei kovesim*, has been interpreted by Landsberger (see bibl.) as referring to the first century C.E. Libyan fabulist, Kybisses, a view rejected by D. Noy (see bibl. *Maḥanayim*, 91), and others.) According to the Talmud, the most prolific of the fabulists was R. *Meir, a *tanna* in the last generation (Sanh. 38b–39b); he was reputed to have known 300 fables, but only three were transmitted to his students. (The numbers are formulistic and perhaps exaggerated.) It is even said that when he died "the composers of fables ceased" (Sot. 49a). J.L. *Gordon argues that R. Meir's fables were Aesopian and that he had heard them from his teacher, *Elisha b. Avuyah, who was acquainted with Greek culture. *Bar Kappara, in the following generation, is said to have known as many fables as R. Meir (Eccles. R. 1:3). It is interesting to note that the fox, the hero of a great number of European fables, is a central figure in the talmudic tradition of animal fables. In the Midrash, the fox himself is depicted as a teller of fables (Gen. R. 78:7).

The same period reflects an increased affinity with the Aesopian tradition and the Indian animal tales (as they are known from the Jatakas and the *Panchatantra*). According to Jacobs, of 30 talmudic fables only six lack Greek or Indian parallels; many show both. I. *Ziegler maintains that the fables as taught by the rabbis were adapted to their audience more than their Greek counterparts: the insistence on moral and theological teaching is stronger with the rabbis, as seen in the following comparison of *epimythia* (i.e., the proverb-like statements concluding the narrative). In the fable of the fox who ate too many grapes and was required to fast before he was able to leave the vineyard, the Aesopian version concludes that time takes care of everything, whereas *Ecclesiastes Rabbah* brings a moralizing quotation from Ecclesiastes (5:14): "As he came forth of his mother's womb, naked shall he return."

In the Middle Ages

THE ALPHABET OF *BEN SIRA. Among the stories in this work are the fable of Leviathan and the fox, an etiological fable about the enmity between cat and mouse; and other stories containing motifs from international folklore and possibly based on folktales. The 1698 Amsterdam edition was printed with "*Musar al-pi ha-Ḥidah*," a fragment of a collection of fables, printed in the early 16th century under the name *Ḥidot Isopeto*. ("The Riddles of Isopet"). The name Isopeto, for Aesop, appears in other Jewish writings, and parallels the name Ysopet in the Romance languages.

ḤIBBUR YAFEH MIN HA-YESHU'AH ("The Book of Redemption"). In the 11th century Rabbenu Nissim, from Kairouan (see *Nissim b. Jacob b. Nissim ibn Shahin), wrote this book of tales, which also includes two fables. The work, originally written in Arabic, was discovered in 1896; prior to that, only the Hebrew translation (*Ma'asiyyot she-ba-Talmud*, Constantinople, 1519) was known.

KALILA AND DIMNA. Translated into Latin as *Directorium Vitae by* the apostate *John of Capua, this composition was of great importance to European fable literature; it became the basis of all translations. According to A.S. Rappoport, the Greek translation of *Kalila and Dimna* (ed. by J. Derenbourg, 1881) was also made by a Jew, Simeon, in 1080. The original is to be traced back through the eighth-century Arabic translation to an origin in the Indian *Panchatantra*. This line of influence from India nourished the prose fiction of the Jews of Muslim and later of Christian Spain and of Provence.

SEFER SHA'ASHU'IM ("Book of Delights"). Written at the end of the 12th century by Joseph b. Meir *Ibn Zabara – whose cultural environment was clearly Muslim – this work bears some relation to the *Taḥkemoni* of Judah *Al-Ḥarizi, and to the *maqamat* of the Arabic poet Al-Ḥariri. It contains a fable which deals with a conflict between the strong leopard and the sly fox and which in turn forms the framework for another fable and for four other stories, describing faithless women (one of them the widow of Ephesus, which also appears in Petronius' *Satyricon*). One of the stories is a version of the fable of the fox in the vineyard, completely devoid, however, of the homiletic bent of the Midrash. The book shows traces of Arabic, Greek, and Indian culture, and has parallels in collections of medieval exempla literature. It was translated into English by M. Hadas as *The Book of Delight* (1960).

BEN HA-MELEKH VE-HA-NAZIR ("The Prince and the Hermit"). Translated into Hebrew by Abraham ibn Ḥisdai in Spain at the end of the 12th or beginning of the 13th century (first printed edition, Constantinople, 1518), this work was discovered by Steinschneider to be a translation and adaptation of the Greek "Barlaam and Joasaph." Indian in origin (c. eighth century), it is a typical example of Indian wisdom literature, in which the stories are told by a wise man as he tutors a young prince.

MISHLEI SHU'ALIM ("Fox Fables"). This work was written by R. *Berechiah b. Natronai ha-Nakdan who lived during the creative period of Jewish fable literature (end of the 12th and beginning of the 13th century), and was printed in Mantua in 1557. The use of the name *Mishlei Shu'alim*, identical with a genre of fables mentioned in the Talmud (Suk. 28a; Sanh. 38b), is explained on the title page by the statement that the fox is the most cunning of animals, and therefore the cleverest. The number of fables included in this collection varies between 107 and 115 with the different manuscripts. They are written in the form of *maqamat*, in a clear, lively style; structurally each has an *epimythium*, the first two lines of which comprise the *pro-*

mythium as well (i.e., a proverb-like statement at the opening of the narrative). The religious tendency of the Midrash, totally absent in *Sefer Sha'ashu'im*, appears vaguely in Berechiah's composition. Its tone is clearly Jewish: biblical references are numerous, other sources are echoed in it, mythological creatures are changed to men. A talmudic reference to R. *Akiva (Ber. 61) is the source of Berechiah's story of the fox and the fish. On the other hand, the work also displays many parallels to the West-European Aesopian tradition, including the Old-French compilation of Marie de France and the *Directorium Vitae*. Some parallels also appear in the popular late-medieval beast epic *Roman de Renart* (High German, *Reinhart Fuchs*; Low German, *Reynke de Vos*). It is possible that Marie de France and Berechiah had common sources in the West European Isopet traditions, in which case the title and the printer's remark can be explained by the immense popularity of fox fables at that period.

Mishlei Shu'alim became part of European Jewish culture: a Yiddish translation by Jacob Koppelman appeared as early as 1588 in Freiburg, and was reprinted several times in Prague, Vilna, and Warsaw, Several reprints in Hebrew were also rendered in different parts of Europe. Popular among non-Jews as well, it appeared in a Latin translation by Melchior Hanel (Prague, 1661), and the German author, G.E. Lessing, translated seven of the fables into German (*Abhandlung ueber die Fabel*, 1759). M. Hadas published an English translation, *Fables of a Jewish Aesop* (1967).

MESHAL HA-KADMONI ("The Fable of the Ancient"). The Spanish Hebrew writer, Isaac ben Solomon ibn *Sahula, aspired to create a Hebrew fable independent of foreign influences, and titled his book *Meshal ha-Kadmoni*, so as to stress the fact that its sources were in the Talmud and Midrash. In fact, however, he did not succeed in completely eliminating foreign influences. Written in the form of a *maqama*, the fables are cast in dialogue. Their moral lessons are Jewish, and the animals, well versed in Jewish learning: the deer is an expert in Talmud, the rooster, a Bible scholar, and the hare knows the *posekim*. They are also knowledgeable in such fields as logic, grammar, and biology. Neither characterization nor plots are fabular in the popular or traditional sense, which, according to Heller, renders Sahula's fables less important than those of Ibn Zabara or of Berechiah. *Meshal ha-Kadmoni* was first printed in 1480. The Venetian edition of 1546 is amply and imaginatively illustrated with pictures of the disputing animals. The book, which gained popularity, was translated into Yiddish by Gershon Wiener (Frankfurt, 1693).

SEFER HA-MESHALIM ("The Book of Riddles"). The 13th-century kabbalist Joseph *Gikatilla compiled this non-kabbalistic collection of approximately 140 riddles, essentially didactic in nature, and often lacking the ingenuity of a genuine riddle. (Some manuscripts, however, include only about half the number of riddles.) The basis of comparison in these riddles varies among plants, animals, and inanimate objects. It was published by I. Davidson in 1927.

IGGERET BA'ALEI ḤAYYIM ("The Animals' Collection"). A translation by *Kalonymus b. Kalonymus (Arles, 1316, in seven days) of the end of the 25th book of a Muslim encyclopedia, its first printed edition appeared in Mantua in 1557 (ed. by J. Landsberger, 1882). Its sources include Greek and Arabic but are primarily Indian. Several elements of this work are not characteristic of the fable: the animals, for instance, dispute throughout the book with human beings before the king of ghosts, and the plot is not mono-episodic. On the other hand, the context of law courts and the depiction of animals functioning like human beings do resemble the fable. The Jewish element in the translation is the addition of a Jew to the Muslim who represents men in the trial. There is clearly a relationship between *Iggeret Ba'alei Ḥayyim* and the Bidpai literature, and parallels to some of its "characters" are found in *Kalila and Dimna*. The popularity of this work is evidenced by the fact that it was printed several times and translated into Yiddish.

MISHLEI SENDABAR ("The Tales of Sendabar," Sindbad). Translated into Hebrew the same year as *Iggeret Ba'alei Ḥayyim* (1316), these tales exist in eight Oriental versions (Greek, Syriac, Old Spanish, three Persian ones, Arabic, and Hebrew), all under the same name. (In all the major Western languages they appear as *The Seven Sages*.) M. Epstein suggests the possibility of a Hebrew origin on the basis of a similarity to Vashti the Queen in the Book of Esther. The wickedness of women is the central theme of both the frame tale and those told by the sages. One of the sages of the Hebrew version, Lokman, is, according to tradition, the Arabic Aesop. The distinctive feature of the Hebrew *Mishlei Sendabar* is the freeing of the woman at the end; in other versions she is killed or otherwise severely punished. The intermediary between the Indian and the Arabic versions is generally held to be Pahlevi. Epstein points out, however, that the Hebrew alone bears some features which distinguish the Western from the Eastern version. According to others, the bridge is either the Byzantine Empire or the Crusaders. A.M. *Habermann's view is that the book was translated to Hebrew from Arabic, although this has not been proved to be the only possibility. Modern editions include M. Epstein's (*Tales of Sendebar*, 1967) and A.M. Habermann's (*Mishlei Sindbad*, 1946). (See *Sindabar.)

MISHLEI IRASTO ("Tales of Irasto"). Translated by the early 16th century rabbi of Amsterdam, Isaac *Uziel, this work is very similar to *Mishlei Sindabar*, but the coarse elements have been excluded. It was translated, according to Habermann, from Italian; according to A. *Elmaleh (editor of *Mishlei Irasto*, 1945), from Latin.

In the Post-Medieval Period

THE KUHBUCH. This most popular collection of Yiddish fables in Europe is known only in Moses Wallich's edition (Frankfurt, 1687). Its name is taken from an earlier compilation of the same name, no longer extant, which was printed in 1555 by Abraham b. Mattathias. While it apparently included parts of *Mishlei Shu'alim* and *Meshal ha-Kadmoni*, its fables are not direct translations; it also includes stories in the typical Renaissance style of Decameron. A modern German translation by R. Beatus was published by A. Freimann in 1926.

DARSHANIM. The various ideological schools of medieval Jewry employed fables as religious exempla. The rationalists, the Hasidei Ashkenaz, and the representatives of the Kabbalah in its various stages all used fables allegorically or metaphorically to support and to exemplify their ideas. It is quite likely that fables were used by *darshanim* after the Middle Ages as well, although few examples are extant. Fables with a clear homiletical tendency appear among the *meshalim* of Jacob of Dubno (Jacob *Kranz, better known as the Dubno Maggid), one of the outstanding *darshanim* of the Musar Movement. It is somewhat exaggerated, however, to call him "the Jewish Aesop," as M. *Mendelssohn did, since he drew the background material for his fables primarily from everyday life; as H. Glatt (*He Spoke in Parables*, 1957) has said, "he was more of a parablist than a fabler." One of his fables is the Aesopian "One Donkey for Two People." Other classical fables in his repertoire include "The Crafty Woodcock" (i.e., the Aesopian "The Fox, the Cock, and the Dog") and "The Utensils that Gave Birth" (cf. *Kalila and Dimna* and *Panchatantra*). The stories in his commentary to *Pirkei Avot* also contain fables.

In Modern Hebrew Literature

EARLY PERIOD. Modern Hebrew literature, highly didactic in its early stages (late 18th–early 19th centuries), found the fable a useful literary device. Isaac ha-Levi *Satanow wrote the pseudepigraphic *Mishlei Asaf* (2 vols., Berlin, 1788–91). Imaginatively attributed to Asaph b. Berechiah (1 Chron. 6:24), the work is stylistically imitative of Proverbs and the Wisdom of *Ben Sira. Its animal fables, which tend to be allegorical, are composed in the talmudic and the Aesopian traditions. In the same period, such writers as Joel *Loewe and Isaac Euchel dealt with the fable from a theoretical standpoint.

Shalom ben Jacob *Cohen's *Mishlei Agur* (Berlin, 1799; 1911) includes verses and verse-dramas, which sometimes have fabular characteristics. The Yiddish satirist Solomon *Ettinger, who associated with the Zamosc *maskilim*, differed from most of his contemporaries in stressing style more than ideology. Influenced by German drama and fable literature (Lessing, Gellert), Ettinger added Jewish content to the foreign themes. Many of his fables are essentially epigrammatic.

LATE 19TH CENTURY. Later in the 19th century, the poet J.L. Gordon published *Mishlei Yehudah* (1860), a collection mainly of translations of La Fontaine's fables. In the preface to this work, he gave a history of the Hebrew fable. *Gam Elleh Mishlei Yehudah*, another collection of fables, appeared in 1871. While Gordon essentially collected and transmitted fables from the European tradition to Hebrew, A. *Paperna wrote a book of fables *Mishlei ha-Zeman* (1894), essentially a long discourse among various animals on the question of who was the happiest of them all. Irony is the dominating tone of the work, and amusement apparently its primary purpose, although it may also have some practical implications. In verging on the comic, this work resembles the 18th-century German fables. In 1893 Joshua *Steinberg published his *Mishlei Yehoshu'a* which are mainly epigrams. Collections of East European Jewish fables such as these were published as far east as Baghdad.

HEBREW TRANSLATIONS OF FABLES. A number of (Hebrew) translations of fables appeared in the 19th century, including: I.L. *Jeiteles' translation of Lessing's fables; Solomon Pundy's (b. 1812) of the German folklorist Pfeffel's fables; Benjamin Kewall's (1806–1880) adaptation of 52 of Aesop's fables *Pirḥei Kedem* (1843). The Italian Jewish writer S.D. *Luzzatto in *Kinnor Na'im* (Vienna, 1825), translated fables by Aesop and Lessing. Krylov's fables were translated by Meir Wolf Singer (1885) and by Chayim Susskind (1891). In the beginning of the 20th century a new translation of Lessing's fables was made by Moses *Reicherson (1902), and a translation of Krylov by S.L. *Gordon (1907). More than 400 years after its translation into Hebrew, *Kalila and Dimna* was retranslated by Elmaleh (1926).

THE 20TH CENTURY. Few literary fables have been written in the 20th century. Among Jewish works, the most important is probably that written by Eliezer *Steinbarg and published in Romania (*Shriftn*, 2 vols., 1932–33), shortly after the death of the author. The two volumes, written in rich, rhythmic Yiddish verse, include 150 fables of animals and inanimate objects alike. (His fables were published earlier (1928) with wood-cuts by A. *Kolnik.) Some of the fables have *epimythia*; others convey the moral lesson through the tale itself.

Hananiah Reichman, who translated the fables of Krylov (1950), includes in his epigrammatic collections much fabular material, adapted to his own concise and ironic verse form. His books include *Mi-Mishlei ha-Ammim u-mi-Pi Ḥakhamim* (1941), *Pitgamim u-Mikhtamim* (1955), and *Devash va-Okeẓ* (1960). He also translated Steinbarg's fables into Hebrew (1954). An interesting contribution is E. *Fleischer's *Meshalim* (1957), a book of fables which was sent to Ereẓ Israel from a prison camp in Eastern Europe. The author used the pseudonym Bar-Abba. Written basically in the classical vein of La Fontaine and Krylov, these fables have new themes and combine humor with bitter social satire.

The religious fables (a minority among parables, as *Yalkut Meshalim* (ed. S. Sheinfold) generally in the case of exempla) of the Ḥafez Ḥayyim (R. *Israel Meir ha-Kohen from Radin) were published in Tel Aviv in 1952. From the oral tradition, Naphtali Gross' *Mayselekh un Mesholim* (1955, 1968²) shows a low percentage of fables in the East European Jewish tradition. Less than five percent (27 of the 540 fables) in the collection are fables. H. Schwarzbaum's commentary shows that these few have a great affinity to both the European Aesopian tradition and to the traditional Jewish sources. The percentage of animal fables is still lower (less than two percent) in the collections of the Israel Folktale Archives.

Summary
The fable in general, and Jewish fable in particular, has almost disappeared from the oral tradition. The largest number of Jewish fables is found in the talmudic-midrashic literature in the Near East, and in the medieval European Jewish collections. Foreign influences upon these fables are decisive, but it is clear to both reader and scholar that some of the early stages of the history of the fable, as far as it can be reconstructed at the present, point to Ereẓ Israel.

BIBLIOGRAPHY: B. Heller, in: J. Bolte and G. Polivka (eds.), *Anmerkung zu den Kinder-und Hausmaerchen der Brueder Grimm*, 4 (1930), 315–64; J. Landsberger, *Die Fabeln des Sophos* (1859); D. Noy, in: *Maḥanayim*, 56 (1961); 69 (1962); 79 (1963); 84, 91, and 92 (1964); 111 (1967); idem, in: *Yeda-Am*, 1–8 (1948–63); I. Ziegler, *Die Koenigsgleichnisse des Midrasch beleuchtet durch die roemische Kaiserzeit* (1963); H. Schwarzbaum, *Talmudic-Midrashic Affinities of some Aesopic Fables* (1965), incl. bibl.; M. Buber (ed.), *Tales of Hasidim*, 2 vols. (1947–48); idem (ed.), *The Tales of Rabbi Nachman* (1962); Zinberg, Sifrut, 5 (1959); 6 (1960); A.S. Rappaport, *The Folklore of the Jews* (1937); Waxman, Literature, index; Steinschneider, Uebersetzungen, index.

[Galit Hasan-Rockem]

°**FABRI, FELIX** (15th century), Dominican monk in Ulm (Germany). In 1480 he accompanied the German noble Georg von Stein on a pilgrimage to Palestine. Landing at Jaffa, Fabri proceeded by way of Ramleh to Jerusalem. From there he visited Jericho and Bethlehem, and a longer journey took him through Hebron and Gaza to Mount Sinai. He returned to Ulm in 1483. Fabri noted many remarkable details in the countries he visited and wrote an account of his travels that has been translated in the Palestine Pilgrims' Texts.

BIBLIOGRAPHY: *The Wanderings of Felix Fabri*, tr. by A. Steward, 2 vols., 1893–97.

[Michael Avi-Yonah]

FABRICANT, SOLOMON (1906–1989), U.S. economist. Fabricant, who was born in Brooklyn, New York, received his B.A. from New York University and his M.A. (1930) and Ph.D. in economics from Columbia University (1938). In 1930 he joined the National Bureau of Economic Research as a research assistant. He was connected with the Bureau throughout his career, and from 1953 to 1965 was director of research. In 1947, after World War II service with the War Production Board and the European regional office of the United Nations Relief and Rehabilitation Agency (UNRRA), he became an associate professor of economics at New York University and a year later a full professor. In 1955 he became a member of the NBER board of directors, and a director emeritus in 1981. During his 50 years with the Bureau, he produced research on such topics as manufacturing output and employment, business cycles, government employment, and changes in productivity.

Regarded as the world authority on the characteristics of business cycles and the "father" of current productivity measures, Fabricant devoted himself to research and writing on developmental economics, business fluctuations, and macroeconomic theory.

His numerous publications include *Output of Manufacturing Industries, 1899–1937* (1940), *Employment in Manufacturing, 1899–1939* (1942), *The Trend of Government Activity in the United States since 1900* (1952), *Basic Facts on Productivity Change* (1959), *Measurement of Technological Change* (1965), *A Primer on Productivity* (1969), *Five Monographs on Business Income* (with C. Warburton, 1973), and *The Economic Growth of the United States: Perspective and Prospective* (1979).

[Joachim O. Ronall / Ruth Beloff (2nd ed.)]

FACING HISTORY AND OURSELVES, Holocaust education program begun in 1976 just as consciousness of the Holocaust was moving beyond the survivor community, when two Brookline, Massachusetts, teachers integrated a unit on the Holocaust and Human Behavior into their 8th grade social studies course. Throughout the next decade, it expanded its outreach, first in Massachusetts with support from that state's Department of Education, and then across the country as one of the model programs designated by the National Diffusion Network of the Office of Education.

In 1990, Facing History opened its first regional office in Chicago, to be followed by offices in six other regions and one in Europe. The organization has now evolved into a program of teacher training, resource preparation, and ongoing research and development that now reaches more than 21,000 educators and over 1.6 million students in 90 countries around the world.

Faithful to its name, there are two dimensions to Facing History and Ourselves, the historical material and the individual student – the self. Facing History's intellectual and pedagogic framework was built upon a synthesis of history and ethics for effective history education. It included a language and a vocabulary for studying difficult and complicated history. It conveyed an understanding that such history did not have to happen but instead was the culmination of a series of ongoing choices (or lack of choosing) and decisions at every level of society. It further engaged students with a sense of the connection of that history to their present and future worlds. The model was interdisciplinary, and built upon the methods of the humanities – inquiry, analysis, interpretation, and judgment. Facing History engaged students in confronting, as distinct from simply studying, the past. Its pedagogy insisted on going beyond the simple answer and response to grapple with complexity and uncertainty in order to come to informed choice which recognized an ethical imperative while rejecting helpless relativism.

From the beginning the core case study of Facing History and Ourselves has been an in-depth study of the failure of democracy in Germany and the events leading to the Holocaust. Studying the unique and universal lessons of the Holocaust helps students to think morally about their own behavior and to reflect on the moral nature of the decisions they have made. By examining the circumstances of this piece of history, students explore fundamental issues of citizenship, responsibility, and decision-making in a democracy.

In Facing History classrooms, middle and high school students learn to think about individual decision-making and to exercise the faculty of making judgments. By illuminating common themes of justice, law, and morality in the past and present, Facing History offers students a framework and a vocabulary for examining the meaning and responsibility of citizenship and the tools to recognize bigotry and indifference in their own worlds. Through a rigorous examination of the steps and events that led to the Holocaust, along with other case studies of collective violence and genocide, Facing History teaches one of the most significant and necessary lessons for adolescents to understand: prevention of collective violence is possible. The mass violence and genocide in the past were not inevitable but rather were shaped by choices made by individuals and groups – choices that at the time may have seemed ordinary and unimportant, but taken together, led to extraordinary, unimaginable consequences.

Facing History encourages adolescents to draw connections among events in the past, choices in the present, and the possibilities of the future. It began with the study of the Holocaust and the Armenian Genocide but it gradually expanded its concerns. The Facing History program offers teachers and students vocabulary, concepts, and materials to confront the mass violations of human rights and human dignity in recent history, whether they be in the breakdown of democracy in Germany in the 1920s and 1930s, or in South Africa, or the Armenian Genocide, or the more recent genocides in Rwanda, Bosnia, or the Sudan.

Students learn to recognize universal themes of prejudice, discrimination, and de-humanization, as well as courage, caring, responsible participation, and steps that can be taken toward prevention.

The Facing History framework is also built upon the notion that democracies are fragile enterprises and can only remain vital through the active, thoughtful, and responsible participation of its citizens. Education for democratic citizenship means encouraging students to recognize that participation can make a difference and is integral to the ethical choices and decisions that we all face. Very often, those decisions are influenced by labeling and stereotyping, and by how we define group identities and who belongs and who does not. Facing History courses embody a sequence of study which begins with identity – first individual identity and then group identities with their definitions of membership. From there the study examines the failure of democracy and the steps leading to the Holocaust – the most documented case of 20th century indifference, de-humanization, hatred, racism, and antisemitism. It goes on to explore difficult questions of judgment, memory, and legacy, and the necessity for responsible participation to prevent injustice. The program ends with a section called "Choosing to Participate" with examples of individuals who have taken small steps to build just and inclusive communities and whose stories illuminate the courage and compassion that is needed to protect democracy today and in generations to come.

Facing History is often described as a journey, back and forth between past, present, and future. Its language and vocabulary are tools for entry into history – terms like perpetrator, victim, defender, bystander, rescuer, collaborator, and opportunist. Students learn that terms like identity, membership, legacy, denial, memory, and judgment can help them understand complicated history, but that an authentic use of that language needs to be rooted in the constellation of individual and group choices, decisions, and behaviors that Facing History has called "Ourselves."

The Facing History journey further embraces a pedagogy that is rooted in the concerns and issues of adolescence: the overarching interest in individual and group identity; in acceptance or rejection, in conformity or non-conformity, in labeling, ostracism, loyalty, fairness, and peer group pressure. It speaks to the adolescent's newly discovered ideas of subjectivity, competing truths, and differing perspectives, along with the growing capacity to think hypothetically and the inclination to find personal meaning in newly introduced phenomena.

The elements of Facing History pedagogy have been demonstrated in hundreds of institutes and workshops and have characterized teaching and learning in thousands of classrooms. These institutes are given in both face-to-face and online environments, and include an online campus with modules and lesson plans to extend the program. Since the examination of difficult and complex issues of human behavior in critical moments in past and present requires careful thinking and reflection, Facing History teachers employ effective strategies to encourage students to listen, to take another's perspective, to understand differing points of view, and to undertake intellectual risks in their analysis and discussion. Meaningful intellectual growth is a process of confronting imbalance and dissonance as students grapple with new ideas and different perspectives that contradict unexamined premises, so these teachers carefully challenge generalizations and push for clear distinctions in language and explication. Building upon the increasing ability to think hypothetically and imagine options, Facing History teachers stretch the historical imagination by urging delineation of what might have been done, choices that could have been made, and alternative scenarios that could have come about.

Equally important, Facing History pedagogy embodies teaching the skills of in-depth historical thinking and understanding. These include knowledge of chronology, causality, and point of view; along with the ability to analyze evidence, take different perspectives, make distinctions and understand relationships. Facing History teachers make these skills explicit and provide opportunities for continual demonstration and practice. They further believe that all students are capable of attaining the high standards necessary to engage deeply in the resource materials of the program. Yet students learn differently, so it is essential to use multiple assessments in their classrooms to honor the complexity of their thinking.

Evaluation of Facing History has been a priority of the program since its inception. Researchers have studied the impact of the program in such areas as adolescent psychosocial and moral development and education, violence and violence prevention, historical understanding, citizenship education, empathy, self-concept and social interest, academic achievement, teacher professional development, and school climate. In a major study funded by the Carnegie Corporation of New York, Facing History classes were shown to be significantly successful in expanding adolescents' capacities for interpersonal understanding, and in enhancing the ability to reflect upon the personal meaning of issues of social justice.

As Facing History completes three decades of teaching about the Holocaust and other examples of collective violence and looks ahead to the 21st century, its impetus is to go beyond memory and legacy and ask how those perspectives can lead to prevention. Its content and pedagogy is helping students become more global and giving them tools and concepts to build bridges and relationships for global understanding and participation. Thus, the global outreach to educators has become critical. Through its website (www.facinghistory.org) Facing History has facilitated online forums for scholars and educators on such issues as the impact of religion on identity, the nature of transitional justice in societies which have undergone mass violence, and the role of education in creating a civil society. Through its power to engage teachers and students, Facing History can facilitate thoughtful and positive change in a school community and convey that while participation can make a difference in sustaining democracy. Such participation, including judgments of right and wrong, needs to be informed, as opposed to constrained by history.

Major Facing History Publications

Included are *Facing History and Ourselves: Holocaust and Human Behavior* (primary resource book); *Crime Against Humanity and Civilization: The Genocide of the Armenians; I Promised I Would Tell* (Holocaust Survivor Memoir); *Elements of Time* (companion guide to Facing History's videotape collection of Holocaust survivor testimonies); *Facing History and Ourselves: Jews of Poland; Race and Membership in American History; The Eugenics Movement.*

BIBLIOGRAPHY: D. Barr, "Early Adolescents' Reflections on Social Justice: Facing History and Ourselves in Practice and Assessment," in: *Intercultural Education* (May 2005); M. Sleeper and M.S. Strom, "Facing History and Ourselves," in: M. Elias and H. Arnold (eds.), *The Educator's Guide to Emotional Intelligence and Academic Learning: Social-Emotional Learning in the Classroom* (2006); M. Sleeper, A. Strom, and M.S. Strom, "Goals of Universal Primary and Secondary Education," paper delivered at American Academy of Arts and Sciences workshop (Cambridge, 2004); M.S. Strom, M. Sleeper, and M. Johnson, "Facing History and Ourselves: A Synthesis of History and Ethics in Effective History Education," in: A. Garrod (ed.), *Learning for Life Moral Education Theory and Practice* (1992); T. Tollefson, "Facing History and Ourselves," paper delivered at Conference on Education and the Civic Purposes of Schools" (San Jose, Costa Rica, 2005).

[Martin Sleeper (2nd ed.)]

FACKENHEIM, EMIL (1916–2003), philosopher. Fackenheim was born in Halle, Germany. After graduating from the Stadtgymnasium in 1935, and despite the encouragement of his classics teacher, Adolph Loercher, to study classical philology, he chose to move to Berlin and enter the rabbinical program at the Hochschule fuer die Wissenschaft des Judentums. For three years, he studied Midrash, Bible, history, and philosophy; he also began a degree in philosophy at the University of Halle. His academic career in Germany was interrupted by *Kristallnacht* and internment for several months in Sachsenhausen. In the spring of 1940 he fled to Aberdeen, Scotland, and matriculated in a degree program in philosophy at the university. A year later, he and other refugees were gathered in camps and dispersed throughout the British Empire. Fackenheim traveled by ship to Canada, was interned in a camp in Sherbrooke, Ontario, and eventually released. He was accepted into the doctoral program in philosophy at the University of Toronto and received his degree in 1945 with a dissertation on Medieval Arabic philosophy and its classical antecedents. From 1943 to 1948 he served as rabbi for congregation Anshe Shalom in Hamilton, Ontario. Invited to teach philosophy at the University of Toronto in 1948, he remained there until 1983, when he retired as university professor. He and his family immigrated to Israel in 1983. He taught at the Institute for Contemporary Jewry at the Hebrew University for several years. In the 1980s he taught German theological students in Israel and in the 1990s traveled several times to Germany, receiving various degrees and honors.

In the postwar period Fackenheim pursued two intellectual interests. First, he examined the tension between faith and reason from Kant to Kierkegaard, writing important essays on Kant on evil and on history and essays on Schelling. Second, he explored the role of revelation in modern culture, in particular Jewish faith, autonomy, the challenge of naturalism and secularism, and the defense of revelation in the thought of Martin Buber and Franz Rosenzweig. Fackenheim developed an existential account of historically situated agency and self-constitution, which he articulated and defended in his short book, *Metaphysics and Historicity*, based on his Aquinas Lecture at Marquette University. His philosophical project on faith and reason, for which he received a Guggenheim Fellowship in 1956–57, became a book on Hegel, *The Religious Dimension in Hegel's Thought*, published in 1968. In the course of the decade that he worked on Hegel, Fackenheim's existential thinking took the shape of a distinctly dialectical style of argumentation and analysis, indebted to his interpretive work on Hegel and to his understanding of the early works of Kierkegaard.

Until 1966 Fackenheim had largely avoided dealing with the Nazi assault on Jews and Judaism and the atrocities of the death camps. In the summer of 1966 he delivered a paper on the "death of God" movement and the "self-exposure of faith to the modern secular world," in which he ended by acknowledging the centrality of facing the horrors of Auschwitz. At the end of that paper, he acknowledged the role that Elie *Wiesel's autobiographical, fictional reflections might play in showing how Jewish faith could be exposed to those horrors and yet survive. The next spring, on March 24, 1967, at a symposium convened by the American Jewish Committee and organized by the editor of its journal *Judaism*, Steven Schwarzchild, "Jewish Values in a Post-Holocaust Future," Fackenheim first formulated and presented his imperative for authentic Jewish response to the Holocaust, what he called the 614th commandment, "Jews are forbidden to give Hitler any posthumous victories." He elaborated the reasoning that led to this imperative and its hermeneutical content in "Jewish Faith and the Holocaust," which appeared in *Commentary* and, in a slightly different form, in the introduction to his book of essays, *Quest for Past and Future*. Its argument received its most developed form in the third chapter of *God's Presence in History*, published in 1970 and based on his 1968 Deems Lectures at New York University.

In these central writings, Fackenheim argued that no intellectual understanding – historical, political, theological, or psychological – of the evil of Auschwitz is possible; the event has no "meaning" or "purpose." Even the most comprehensive philosophical systems, the Hegelian system most of all, founder on the rock of radical evil. But while no such intellectual comprehension is satisfying and hence no intellectual response acceptable, an existential response is necessary. No theoretical, philosophical, or theological source, however, is capable of framing what a genuine response should be. At this point, thought must go to school with life; one can and must turn to actual lived experience, during and after the event, to grasp how Jews have responded and hence how one ought to respond. Ongoing Jewish life, Fackenheim claims, can be interpreted as a response to a sense of obligation or duty, and this duty is a duty to oppose all that Nazism sought to accomplish in its hatred of Jews and Judaism and in its rejection of human dignity and worth. While for secular Jews, such a duty has no ground but is accepted as binding without one, for believing Jews, the only ground that is possible is the Voice of a Commanding God. Hence, for them, it has the status of a divine command, alongside but not superseding the other, traditional 613 Biblical commandments. It is, in his famous formulation, a 614th commandment.

Fackenheim had arrived at this imperative of resistance to Nazi purposes, this duty of genuine post-Holocaust Jewish existence, alongside an ongoing reflection on revelation and modernity and as an expression of a newly appreciated necessity of exposing faith and obligation to a post-Holocaust situation. His journey had capitalized on several crucial insights. One was that after Auschwitz, as he put it, even Hegel would not be a Hegelian, i.e., that Auschwitz was a case of evil for evil's sake and was therefore unassimilable to any prior conceptual system. Even the most systematic philosophic thought was historically situated and was ruptured by the horrors of the death camps. Second was the commitment to existential-dialectical thinking about the human condition and to its hermeneutical character. Third was the recognition that while Auschwitz threatened all prior systems, ways of life, and beliefs, Judaism must and could survive exposure to it. The work of Elie Wiesel and Wiesel's life itself confirmed this hope and this realization.

In the 1970s Fackenheim's thought extended the lines of thinking that we have summarized. First, in his book *Encounters Between Judaism and Modern Philosophy* he explored how modern philosophy had ignored or distorted Judaism and had exposed its own inadequacies in so doing. Second, he applied the framework just described to a variety of themes – most notably to the State of Israel, its reestablishment and defense, but also to the belief in God, the relationship between Jews and Christians, and the necessity of struggling against all attempts to diminish human dignity and the value of human life. These efforts continued throughout his life and in effect amount to a ramification of the interpretation of the 614th commandment, for Jews, Christians, philosophers, historians, Germans, and others. Finally, he turned to important philosophical problems with his existential and hermeneutical argument. The crucial problem had to do with the possibility of performing the imperative of resistance or, as one might put it, the possibility of confronting the radical threat of rupture and not giving way to total despair. This was to become the central problem of his magnum opus, *To Mend the World*, published in 1983 (with new introductory material in 1987 and again in 1993).

In the earlier period, culminating in 1970, Fackenheim had argued from the necessity of the commandment or imperative to its possibility, either on Kantian grounds, that duty entails the freedom to perform it, or on Rosenzweigian grounds, that along with the commandments that God grants in an act of grace, He also gives humankind out of the same love the freedom to perform them. By the late 1970s Fackenheim had come to see the extent to which both responses failed to respect the victims of the Nazi horrors. In the crucial chapter of *To Mend the World*, he systematically and dialectically explores the agency of evil and its victims, in order to arrive at a moment when the victim's lucid understanding grasps the whole of horror, and yet reacts to it and in opposition to it with surprise. He confirms this intellectual grasp with an emblematic case of victims of the camps and the atrocities, who both see clearly what they are being subjected to, what the evil is, and sense a duty to oppose it in their life. He then goes on to claim that this episode constitutes an ontological ground of resistance, and that Judaism, through the idea of a cosmic rupture and a human act that respects and yet opposes it, what is called in the Jewish mystical tradition (Kabbalah) *tikkun olam*, provides philosophy with a concept essential to grasp the possibility of genuine post-Holocaust life. *To Mend the World* proceeds to apply these lessons in three domains – philosophy, Christianity, and Jewish existence, in each case locating an emblematic case of *tikkun* (mending or repair) that respects the evil of Auschwitz as a total and unqualified rupture and yet finds a route to hope and recovery. Hegel, he remarks, had said that the wounds of Spirit heal without leaving scars. Hegel was wrong – while healing is necessary (and hence recovery as a hermeneutical and existential activity), the scars of the Holocaust will and must remain.

This line of argument was not without its difficulties, and challenges have been made to it. Fackenheim, in the last two decades of his life, once more extended its lines – with a book on the Bible and how it ought to be read by Jews and Christians, together, in a post-Holocaust world, with a survey of Jewish belief and practice in the 1980s, and with a number of essays on the State of Israel as a paradigmatically genuine response to the Nazi assault, i.e., as a unique blending of religious purposes and secular self-reliance, combining a commitment to a homeland for Jews against the most extreme assault and to its defense. Philosophically, in his last years, Fackenheim focused on two issues that were connected in his mind, one the radicality of the Nazi evil and the question "why they did it," and secondly the character of the type of victim called the *Musselmanner*, which Primo Levi famously called the "drowned" and identified as the characteristic product of the death camps. These two issues also continue themes of Fackenheim's earlier work, the nature of the radical evil that was Auschwitz and the question whether there is not a type of victim of the Nazi horrors that must be respected and not dishonored, and yet that is outside the bounds of the ontological ground of resistance itself.

Fackenheim's philosophical commitments were deeply immersed in existential and concrete realities, most notably the historicity of philosophical and religious thought, the hermeneutical and situated character of human existence, and the unprecedented evil of Nazis and the death camps. Auschwitz led him to expose philosophy, culture, and religion unconditionally to historical refutation; yet his deepest yearnings were to find continued hope and to avoid despair, to appreciate the necessity of Jewish life and the defense of human value and dignity. These dispositions, however, were what we might call "rationally defended yearnings" and hence necessities (duties and obligations) only in a deeply contextual sense. He wanted them to be objective and absolute duties, but in the context of his developed thinking, after the 1960s, there are no such duties, or, if we think there are, they are ones that carry no global or general authority. What force they bear must be defended one by one and situation by situation, within the larger context of a commitment to face the utter rupture of Auschwitz and still go on with life, to heal and recover while nonetheless not expecting the scars of history to disappear.

BIBLIOGRAPHY: L. Greenspan, and G. Nicholson (eds.), *Fackenheim: German Philosophy & Jewish Thought* (1992); M.L. Morgan (ed.), *The Jewish Thought of Emil Fackenheim* (1987); idem, *Emil Fackenheim: Jewish Philosophers and Jewish Philosophy* (1996); idem, *Beyond Auschwitz: Post-Holocaust Jewish Thought in America* (2001).

[Michael L. Morgan (2nd ed.)]

FACTOR, MAX (1877–1938), U.S. cosmetics manufacturer. Factor was born in Lodz, Poland, where at the age of eight he served an apprenticeship to a dentist-pharmacist. Years of mixing potions instilled in him a fascination with the human form. Factor opened his own shop in Moscow, where he sold hand-made rouges, creams, fragrances, and wigs. A traveling theatrical troupe wore Factor's makeup while performing for Russian nobility. Appreciating his handiwork, the Russian aristocrats appointed Factor the official cosmetic expert for the royal family and the Imperial Russian Grand Opera. Factor emigrated to the United States in 1904, and opened a cosmetics booth at the World's Fair in St. Louis. He moved his family to Los Angeles, where, in 1909, he opened a cosmetics and perfume shop in the center of the city's theatrical district. The business subsequently developed into Max Factor & Co., the largest cosmetics firm in California for decades.

In 1914, Factor created a makeup specifically for movie actors which, unlike theatrical makeup, would not crack or cake. Film stars rushed to his makeup studio, anxious to try out his "flexible greasepaint," while producers headed for the wigs that Factor made from human hair. In 1938 he developed pancake makeup, a new type of material to be used by actors in Technicolor films, which soon became the standard makeup for all color motion pictures.

In the 1920s Factor introduced cosmetics to the public, promoting the idea that every girl could look like a movie star by using Max Factor Makeup. When pancake was launched, it became one of the fastest-growing, largest-selling, single makeup items in the history of cosmetics. Factor was responsible for countless other cosmetic innovations, including the word "makeup" itself, which he coined. He and his company created such mainstays as lip gloss, the eyebrow pencil, false eyelashes, waterproof makeup, and the concept of cosmetic "color harmony." He also developed numerous makeup techniques for movie special effects, as well as personal application.

Much of his work has been preserved at the Hollywood History Museum in Hollywood, California. The exhibits include the lobby and various makeup rooms from his studio, as well as thousands of rare Hollywood costumes, props, sets, and memorabilia.

Factor co-authored the book *The Technique of Stage Make-up: A Practical Manual for the Use of Max Factor's Theatrical Make-up* (with J. Knapp, 1942).

Each of his four sons joined the business. DAVIS FACTOR (1902–1991), who was born in Russia, became chairman of the board. MAX FACTOR, JR. (1904–1996), born in St. Louis, became vice chairman of the board. A specialist in cosmetic chemistry, he received awards from the motion picture and television industry for designing special makeup to go before the cameras. LOUIS FACTOR (1907–1975), also born in St. Louis, became vice president and assistant secretary of the firm. Los Angeles-born SIDNEY FACTOR (1916–) was a member of the board. Max Factor's son-in-law, MAX FIRESTEIN (1894–?) of Denver, became chairman of the board's executive committee. Active in Jewish organizational life, he was president of the Los Angeles Jewish Community Council and served on the national campaign cabinet of the United Jewish Appeal. His sons ALFRED FIRESTEIN (1924–) and CHESTER FIRESTEIN (1930–) became president and executive vice president, respectively, of Max Factor Co. DAVIS FACTOR (1935–) of the third generation was director of marketing in the international division. By the end of the 1960s Max Factor had become the third-largest U.S. cosmetics manufacturer, and the largest in the international field.

Max Factor became a division of Procter & Gamble in Hunt Valley, Maryland.

BIBLIOGRAPHY: F. Basten, R. Salvatore, and P. Hoffman (eds.), *Max Factor's Hollywood: Glamour, Movies and Make-Up* (1995).

[Ruth Beloff (2nd ed.)]

FADENHECHT, YEHOSHUA (1846–1910), religious Zionist and a founder of the *Mizrachi movement in Galicia. Born in Berezhany, Galicia, he moved to Kolomea, where he was registrar of births and deaths for the local Jewish community throughout his life. In the early 1880s, he founded one of the first Zionist associations in Galicia, and struggled against extremely Orthodox anti-Zionist circles. One of Herzl's earliest religious supporters, Fadenhecht published suggestions regarding *aliyah* to Ereẓ Israel in the second issue of the newspaper *Die Welt*. For many years he contributed articles on current affairs to the Hebrew press in Galicia. After the First Zionist Congress at Basle (1897), he published *Yizre'el*, intended to be a Hebrew periodical; its sole issue was entirely filled with his own contributions devoted to explaining political Zionism, Herzl's beliefs, and the value of the Zionist Congress – all in the frame of reference of his controversy with ultra-Orthodox opponents.

BIBLIOGRAPHY: *Ha-Miẓpeh*, 7 no. 2 (1910); *Ba-Mishor*, 5 no. 203 (1944).

[Getzel Kressel]

FADIMAN, CLIFTON (1904–1999), U.S. literary critic. Fadiman was born in New York and graduated from Columbia University in 1925. He became editor in chief at Simon & Schuster and then book editor of the *New Yorker* (1933–43) and was widely known for his weekly radio program *Information Please* (1938–48). His collected essays were published in *Party of One: Selected Writings* (1955). He was a familiar figure offering suggestions to readers in the Book-of-the Month Club and guiding the selections of The Reader's Club. An editor and anthologist, he helped put together the multivolume *Great Books of the Western World* (1990) and also edited *The Treasury of the Encyclopedia Britannica* (1992). He was awarded, in 1993, the National Book Foundation Medal for Distinguished Contribution to American Letters. He was remembered by Carolyn Heilbrun in *When Men Were the Only Models We Had: My Teachers Barzun, Fadiman, and Trilling* (2002).

BIBLIOGRAPHY: R. Severo, "Clifton Fadiman," in: *New York Times* (June 21, 1999).

[Lewis Fried (2nd ed.)]

°**FADUS, CUSPIUS,** Roman procurator of Judea 44–46 C.E. Fadus was appointed by the emperor Claudius after the short period of Jewish government which ended with the death of *Agrippa I. He had specific instructions to punish the inhabitants of Caesarea and Sebaste, mostly soldiers, who had shown disrespect to the dead king. Upon arrival he found the Jews in Perea in Transjordan engaged in a border dispute with the inhabitants of Philadelphia (Rabbath Ammon). The Jews asserted themselves and killed many of their opponents, thereby arousing the anger of Fadus, who sentenced one of their leaders to death and banished two others. He also took action against the false prophet *Theudas (Acts 5:36), whom he killed together with many of his followers. According to Josephus, one of his major concerns was to rid Judea of its many robbers. In matters not involving state security he apparently ruled with moderation and generally did not interfere with Jewish customs. In one instance, however, he demanded that the sacred vestments of the high priest be handed over to the Romans for safekeeping, a practice once before adopted by the Romans but abandoned a few years earlier. The Jews protested and obtained his leave to send an embassy to Rome. Claudius, influenced in part by the intervention of the young Agrippa II, revoked the decision. Fadus was succeeded by *Tiberius Julius Alexander.

BIBLIOGRAPHY: Jos., Ant., 15:406; 19:363–4; 20:2–14, 97–100; Jos., Wars, 2:220; Schuerer, Gesch, 1 (1901), 565–6; Pauly-Wissowa, 8 (1901), 1895, no. 2.

[Lea Roth]

FAENZA, city in N. central Italy. In the 14th century the Jews of Faenza were moneylenders. As a result of the sermons of *Bernardino da Feltre, the celebrated physician Lazzaro da Pavia was expelled from the city in c. 1480. The liturgical poet Raphael ben Isaac da Faenza also lived in the city in the mid-15th century. There is also documented evidence of the presence of a rabbinate of Faenza in the same years. Isaac *Azulai, who manufactured majolica *seder* plates, worked here in 1575. From the 16th century until the Napoleon era there is no evidence that Jews lived in Faenza.

BIBLIOGRAPHY: Milano, Italia, 127, 358; Roth, Italy, 199, 202, 445. **ADD. BIBLIOGRAPHY:** G. Caravita, *Ebrei in Romagna: 1938–1945: dalle leggi razziali allo sterminio* (1991); L. Picciotto, *Il libro della memoria: gli ebrei deportati dall'Italia, 1943–1945* (2001).

[Attilio Milano / Federica Francesconi (2nd ed.)]

FAGARAS (Rom. **Făgăraş**; Hung. **Fogaras**), town in Transylvania, Romania; until 1918 in Hungary. Jews were not permitted to settle there until the beginning of the 19th century. In the 17th century, however, they occasionally visited the fortress at Fagaras to present petitions to the prince of Transylvania. The settlement of Jews 12 miles (20 km.) from the town in the village of Porumbak, today known by the Romanian name of Porumbacul de Sus, was of special interest. From the judicial aspect, this village belonged to the owners of the town Fagaras. In 1697, two Sephardi Jews, Avigdor b. Abraham and Naphtali b. Abraham, leased a workshop there for the manufacture of glass articles. They signed the contract of tenancy in Hebrew characters; this document is preserved in the community archives in Budapest. They were followed by other lessees as well as by Jews who leased the local tavern. A community was organized and a cemetery acquired in Fagaras in 1827. At the beginning of the community's existence its members used mostly the German language, only later going over to Hungarian. After 1919 many of them started to teach their children the language of the new country – Romanian. The synagogue was erected in 1859. There were 286 Jews living in Fagaras in 1856; 485 in 1891; 514 in 1910; 457 in 1920; 390 in 1930; and 267 in 1941. The Jewish contribution to the economic development of the town and the region was very important during the entire existence of the local community. A Jewish school was founded in 1867; the language of instruction was German until 1903, Hungarian until the end of World War I, and subsequently Romanian. It was closed down in 1938. The community joined the neologist organization (see *Neology) in 1869 and became Orthodox in 1926. The rabbi of Fagaras, Adolf Keleman (1861–1917), visited Ereẓ Israel in 1905 and subsequently published his impressions of the journey in Hungarian.

For long periods of time the relations between the Jews and the Romanian and Hungarian population of the region was more or less normal, with relatively few antisemitic incidents.

During the Romanian Fascist regime (1940–44), Jewish possessions and communal property were confiscated. Some of the men were conscripted for forced labor and others (mostly those accused for Communist activities) were deported to *Transnistria. The Jews from the surrounding villages were concentrated in the town. There were 360 Jews living in Fagaras in 1947. Subsequently many left, first for the bigger cities in Romania, and after that abroad (mostly to Israel), and 20 remained by 1970.

BIBLIOGRAPHY: *Sitzungs-Protokoll fuer die Beschluesse der Fogaraser israelitischen Kultusgemeinde*, 1861–1874; *Grundbuch der Sitze und deren Inhaber in Fogaraser Tempel*, in: the Central Archives for the History of the Jewish People (RM 189); *Pinkas Ḥevrah Kaddisha 1827–61* (*ibid.*, RM 190); MHJ, 5 pt. 1 (1959), no. 716, 808, 864, 868, 887; 8 (1965), no. 360; *Magyar Zsid Lexikon* (1929), 284.

[Yehouda Marton / Paul Schveiger (2nd ed.)]

°**FAGIUS, PAULUS** (**Paul Buechelin**; 1504–1549), Hebraist. Born at Rheinzabern, in the Rhineland-Palatinate, Germany, he was professor of theology at Strasbourg and later of Hebrew at Cambridge. He studied Hebrew with Wolfgang Capito and with Elijah Levita, whom he invited to supervise the Hebrew press he established in Isny (Bavaria). He translated the following Hebrew books into Latin: Elijah Levita's *Tishbi* (Isny, 1541; Basle, 1557) and *Meturgeman* (Isny, 1542); the Talmud tractate *Avot* (Isny, 1541). He edited a Hebrew version of the book of Tobit with a Latin translation (Isny, 1542); the *Alphabet of Ben Sira* (Isny, 1542), and David Kimhi's commentary to Psalms 1–10 (Constance, 1544). He edited several chapters of Targum Onkelos (Strasbourg, 1546) and wrote an exegetic treatise on the first four chapters of Genesis. ("*Exegesis sive expositio dictionum hebraicarum literalis et simplex in quatuor capita Geneseos*," Isny, 1542). He was the author of an elementary Hebrew grammar (Constance, 1543) and translated an anonymous booklet by a converted Jew, who endeavored, with reference to Jewish sources, to prove the truth of Christianity (*Liber Fidei*, Isny, 1542; a short extract, under the title *Parvus Tractatulus*, appeared in the same year in the Hebrew Prayers edited by Fagius). Some parts of the same text had been already published and translated by Sebastian Münster in 1537. He began the republication of a revised edition of the concordance *Me'ir Nativ*. After his migration to England, where he died, this work was completed by Antonius Reuchlin (Basle, 1556).

BIBLIOGRAPHY: L. Geiger, *Das Studium der hebraeischen Sprache in Deutschland* (1870), 66; Steinschneider, Cat Bod, 977, no. 5048; 3080, no. 9397; idem, in: REJ, 4 (1882), 78–87; 5 (1882), 57–67; idem, in: ZHB, 2 (1897), 149–50, no. 178; Perles, Beitraege, index; M. Stern, *Urkundliche Beitraege ueber die Stellung der Paepste zu den Juden* (1893), no. 159; J.-B. Prijs, *Die Basler hebräischen Drucke* (1964), 82–83, 500; A.M. Habermann, in: *Alei Sefer*, 2 (1976), 97–104; R. Peter, in: *Revue d'Histoire et de Philosophie Religieuses*, 59 (1979), 385–390; L.T. Stuckenbruck, in: G.G. Xeravits and J. Zsengeller (eds.), *The Book of Tobit* (2005), 194–219.

[Giulio Busi (2nd ed.)]

FAHN, ABRAHAM (1916–), botanist. Fahn was born in Vienna but grew up in Halicz and went to school there and in Stanislawow (Poland). He immigrated to Ereẓ Israel in 1935. Fahn studied biology at the Hebrew University, where he obtained his doctorate in 1948. In 1952–53 he did research at the Jodrell Laboratory, Kew, and in the school of Botany at Cambridge, England. In 1956 he was a research fellow at Harvard University and in 1965 he was appointed full professor at the Hebrew University. Fahn published a number of scientific books: *Plant Anatomy* (in Hebrew, 1962; translated into English, Spanish, Indonesian, and Chinese); *Secretory Tissues in Plants* (in English, 1979); and, with coauthors, *Wood Anatomy and the Identification of Trees and Shrubs of Israel and Adjacent Regions* (in English, 1986); *Xerophytes* (in English, 1992); and *The Cultivated Plants of Israel* (in Hebrew, 1998). Fahn was dean of the Faculty of Science in 1963–66. He is an honorary member of leading scientific societies, foreign member of the Linnaean Society of London, and corresponding member of the Botanical Society of America. He was awarded the Israel Prize for science in 1963.

[Bracha Rager (2nd ed.)]

FAHN, REUBEN (1878–1939?), Hebrew writer and investigator of Karaism. Born in eastern Galicia, he became a prosperous merchant in Halicz and developed an interest in the town's Karaites. He settled in Stanislav in 1918 and became secretary of the National Council of Galician Jewry in the short-lived West Ukrainian Republic (1918–19). On the outbreak of World War II he was put on trial by the Russians for Zionist activities and taken to Russia where he disappeared without trace. A regular contributor to the Hebrew press from his youth, Fahn wrote poetry, articles, and stories, particularly on the Karaites, and studies of Haskalah literature. Two volumes of his collected works were published: *Sefer ha-Kara'im* (1929) and *Pirkei Haskalah* (1937). A book of his essays, *Massot*, appeared in Jerusalem in 1943 (preface by Dov Sadan). His *Mivḥar Ketavim* (selected works), ed. by N. Govrin, appeared in 1969.

BIBLIOGRAPHY: *Genazim*, 1 (1961), 115–8, includes bibliography; Kressel, Leksikon, 2 (1967), 571f.; *Arim ve-Immahot be-Yisrael; Stanislav*, 5 (1952), s.v.

[Getzel Kressel]

FAIN, SAMMY (1902–1989), U.S. songwriter. Born in New York and named Samuel Feinberg, Fain was a trained pianist who worked in vaudeville and in the music-publishing business before achieving success as a composer in the mid-1920s. In a six-decade career, he wrote the music for such well-loved popular songs as "I'll Be Seeing You," "That Old Feeling," "Secret Love," and "Love Is a Many-Splendored Thing." He won Academy Awards for the latter two and his songs received eight other Academy Award nominations. Among his other major songs were "I Can Dream, Can't I?" with his frequent lyricist-partner, Irving Kahal, "Dear Hearts and Gentle People," and the title song from the film *April Love*. Earlier, he had hits with "Let a Smile Be Your Umbrella on a Rainy (Rainy) Day," "Wedding Bells Are Breaking Up That Old Gang of Mine," and "When I Take My Sugar to Tea." Called to Hollywood, the team of Fain and Kahal wrote songs for a number of movie musicals. One of their most successful movie songs, "You Brought a New Kind of Love to Me," was introduced by Maurice Chevalier. "That Old Feeling," one of the great torch ballads, was introduced in the movie *Vogues of 1938*. Perhaps his most famous song was "I'll Be Seeing You," which was popularized in nightclubs in the 1940s and went on to become one of the most romantic signature songs of World War II. During the 1950s, with the lyricist Bob Hilliard, Fain composed the songs for the 1951 Disney film *Alice in Wonderland*, including "I'm Late." With Paul Francis Webster, he wrote the music for the films *A Certain Smile* (1958) and *Tender Is the Night* (1961). Some of the other movies for which he wrote the music include *Call Me Mister* (1951) and a remake of *The Jazz Singer* (1953).

[Stewart Kampel (2nd ed.)]

FAIRSTEIN, LINDA A. (1943–), U.S. prosecutor and author. Fairstein grew up in Mount Vernon, N.Y., a suburb of New York City. She went to Vassar College and the University of Virginia Law School. In 1972 she began working in the office of Frank Hogan, the Manhattan district attorney. At the time, the office had seven women among 170 prosecutors. By 2001, when she left, half of the office's 600 prosecutors were women. In a 30-year career of major cases, legislative reforms, and best-selling books that explored the legal and emotional realities of rape, Fairstein became the nation's best-known prosecutor of sex crimes. She became chief of the sex-crimes unit in 1976, two years after it was created as the first such unit in the country. It had four prosecutors at the time; when she left it had 40. In 1977 Fairstein was a principal advocate of New York's so-called rape shield law, which prohibited, in most cases, what had long been a common defense practice in rape and sexual assault cases: exploring the sexual history of victims to suggest promiscuity. Later she lobbied successfully for a similar law in rape-homicide prosecutions. Fairstein was also credited with a major role in the passage of a law in 1983 that struck down a requirement that victims of rape and other sex crimes prove that they had offered "earnest resistance." She also was a principal advocate of the Sexual Assault Reform Act of 2001, which facilitated the prosecution of date rape and of rapes involving the use of drugs.

As chief of the sex-crimes unit in the district attorney's office, she oversaw the disposition of 500 to 700 cases a year involving rape and other sexual abuses. Between 125 and 175 of those cases were prosecuted as felonies. Fairstein played a key role in a notorious 1986 case involving Robert E. Chambers Jr., who killed Jennifer Levin in Central Park after an evening in a "preppie bar." Fairstein doggedly prosecuted the case and used the defense's own witness to demonstrate that Chambers's choke hold on the victim could have been intentionally lethal.

Fairstein served as the model for several no-nonsense prosecutors in the movies *Farrell for the People* (1982) and *Presumed Innocent* (2001). The author Robert Daley dedicated his 1985 novel, *Hands of a Stranger*, to Fairstein, and fictionalized many of her well-known cases. It was made into a television movie.

In 1996, Fairstein published her first novel, *Final Jeopardy*, which introduced the character Alexandra Cooper, who bore a striking resemblance to the author. The book was a critical and commercial success and was followed the next year by *Likely to Die*, which was an international bestseller. By 2005 she had published six novels. Her nonfiction book, *Sexual Violence: Our War Against Rape*, published in 1994, was a *New York Times* notable book.

[Stewart Kampel (2nd ed.)]

FAÏTLOVITCH, JACQUES (1881–1955), Orientalist, devoted to *Beta Israel (Falasha) research and relief work. Faïtlovitch was born in Lodz. He studied Oriental languages at the Ecole des Hautes Etudes in Paris, particularly Ethiopic and Amharic under Joseph *Halévy, who aroused his interest in the Beta Israel. He made 11 missions to Ethiopia (1904–5, 1908–9, 1913, 1920–21, 1923–24, 1926, 1928–29, 1934, 1942–43, 1943–44, 1946). In 1904 he went to Ethiopia for the first time and spent 18 months among the Beta Israel, studying their beliefs and customs. The results were published in his *Notes d'un voyage chez les Falachas* (1905). In his view the Beta Israel were Jews needing help to resist Christian missionary activity, which threatened their survival as a Jewish community. He promised them to enlist world Jewry on their behalf and took two young Beta Israel with him to Europe to be educated as future teachers. Having failed to win the support of the Alliance Israélite Universelle, he organized "pro-Falasha" committees in Italy and Germany to raise funds for Jewish education for the Beta Israel in Abyssinia and abroad. In 1908–09 Faïtlovitch spent 15 months in Abyssinia; he was received by Emperor Menelik II and pleaded for equitable treatment for the Beta Israel. This voyage is described in his book *Quer durch Abessinien* (1910; *Massa el ha-Falashim*, 1959). Finally, he established one school in Dembea during his third voyage in 1913. After World War I Faïtlovitch, who had lectured at Geneva University (1915–19), transferred the center of pro-Falasha activity to the United States, and with the aid of the New York Committee a boarding school for Beta Israel children was opened in Addis Ababa in May 1923. Starting from 1927 Faïtlovitch settled in Tel Aviv but he had a nomadic life and spent many years in the United States. The Italian conquest in 1935–36 hampered the expanding activity and World War II stopped it entirely. After the establishment of the State of Israel he was able to persuade the Jewish Agency to take up educational work among the Beta Israel. Faïtlovich was an indefatigable lecturer, everywhere trying to stir active interest in the "Black Jews of Abyssinia." He considered the Beta Israel ethnologically the descendants of genuine Jews and an integral part of the Jewish people. An observant Jew himself, he felt that it was not enough to study the Beta Israel, but that it was an obligation to save them from extinction and lead them through education into the fold of traditional Judaism. He took out of Ethiopia to study in Europe, Egypt and Palestine 25 young boys. He was interested in the quest for the *nidḥei Israel* and in *proselytism; he created committees for the conversion of people from Asia and Africa. In addition to the books mentioned above, he published *Mota Mus* (Heb., Fr., 1906), *Proverbes Abyssins* (1907), "Nouveaux Proverbes Abyssins" (in *Rivista degli Studi Orientali*, 2 (1909), 757–66), *Les Falachas d'après les Explorateurs* (1907), *Versi Abissini* (It., 1910), and *Falascha-Briefe* (1913). He wrote numerous articles and pamphlets and a series of tracts in Amharic intended for distribution among the Beta Israel. The only article that he wrote in English is entitled "Falashas" (in AJYB, 22 (1920), 80–100). Faïtlovitch bequeathed his valuable library to the Tel Aviv Municipality, with the collection now located in Tel Aviv University.

ADD. BIBLIOGRAPHY: J. Quirin, *The Evolution of the Ethiopian Jews* (1992), 193–200; D. Summerfield, *From Falashas to Ethiopian Jews* (2003), 39–90; E. Trevisan Semi, "De Lodz à Addis Abeba, Faitlovitch et les Juifs d'Ethiopie," in: *Les Cahiers du Judaïsme* 10 (2001), 60–71; idem, "Faitlovitch," in: *Pe'amim* 100 (2004) (Heb); idem, *The "Ingathering of the Exiles": Jacques Faitlovitch, "Father of the Beta Israel" (1881–1955)* (2005).

[Max Wurmbrand / Emanuela Trevisan Semi (2nd ed.)]

FAITUSI, JACOB BEN ABRAHAM (d. 1812), Jerusalem emissary and talmudist. Faitusi was born in *Tunis and immigrated to *Jerusalem around 1800. In 1806 he became an emissary of Jerusalem to *Tripoli, *Tunisia, and *Algeria. He published: *Berit Ya'akov* (Leghorn, 1800), including the *Shitah Mekubbeẓet* of Bezalel *Ashkenazi to tractate *Sotah*, the *Likkutei Ge'onim* of various authors on tractates *Nedarim* and *Nazir*, and *Likkutim* on tractate *Nazir* by Abraham ibn Musa, to which he appended *Sha'arei Ẓedek* by *Levi b. Gershom on the 13 hermeneutical principles and an original work on the subject entitled *Yagel Ya'akov; Mizbaḥ Kapparah* (*ibid.*, 1810), containing the *Shitah Mekubbeẓet* to *Menaḥot, Zevaḥim*, and *Bekhorot*, novellae on *Ḥullin* attributed to *Naḥmanides and *Ronu le-Ya'akov*, his own commentary on tractates *Ḥullin* and *Temurah*. Appended to the work are homilies in praise of the Land of Israel; *Mareh ha-Ofanim* (*ibid.*, 1810) including the novellae of *Asher b. Jehiel on *Sotah* and his own commentary, *Yagel Ya'akov*, on *Pesaḥim, Beẓah, Rosh Ha-Shanah, Avodah Zarah*, and *Makkot*. Faitusi died in Algeria, while on a mission there. His son, ḤAYYIM DAVID, published Jacob's *Yerekh Ya'akov* (*ibid.*, 1842), homilies on the Pentateuch and the Five Scrolls, together with *Kokhav mi-Ya'akov*, novellae on the Talmud and responsa.

BIBLIOGRAPHY: Frumkin-Rivlin, 3 (1929), 127–8; Rosanes, Togarmah, 5 (1938), 279; Yaari, Sheluḥei, 707–8; Hirschberg, Afrikah, 2 (1965), 160, 347 n. 33.

[Simon Marcus]

FAIVOVICH HITZCOVICH, ANGEL (1901–1990), Chilean politician. Born in Santiago, he received the title of agronomical engineer in 1922 and was appointed assistant in the zootechnic section of the University of Chile. In 1930 he graduated in law and in 1935 was elected councilor of the Municipality of Santiago. In 1937 he was elected from the Radical Party as a member of Parliament for Santiago and in 1945 as senator. He served several terms. Faivovich was professor of International Law and Juridic and Social Studies at the University of Chile. He was president of the Radical Party between 1946 and 1952, during the administration of Gabriel Gonzalez Videla, exercising considerable political influence in government circles. He opposed the candidacy of Allende, dividing the Radical Party and founding the Party of Radical Democracy. He bequeathed his fortune to beneficial causes in Chile and Israel, particularly to the Weizmann Institute of Science in Reḥovot.

[Moshe Nes El (2nd ed.)]

FAIYŪM (Fayyūm), district and city in Upper Egypt, southwest of *Cairo. In the early Middle Ages flourishing Jewish communities seem to have existed there, since *Saadiah Gaon was born there, in approximately 882, received his basic education in the city of Dilas of the Faiyūm district, and wrote his first two books there. Benjamin of Tudela, the 12th-century traveler, found 200 Jews there according to one of his manuscripts, and 20 Jews according to another. Since the former number appears in most of his writings, it would be possible to assume that the figure applies to the Jewish population of the entire district. In any case, the number of the Jews in the Faiyūm district declined in that period as the whole of its population decreased formidably; its depopulation was progressive. Jacob *Saphir, the 19th-century traveler, reported in his book (*Even Sappir* (1866), 259) that only a single Jew lived in Faiyūm, and that he was a newcomer to the town. In 1907 there were 43 Jews in the town and district, but the community later dissolved.

ADD. BIBLIOGRAPHY: E. Strauss (Ashtor), *Toldot ha-Yehudim be-Miẓrayim ve-Suriya*, vol. 1 (1944), 31–32; N. Golb, "The Topography of the Jews in Medieval Egypt," in: JNES, 24 (1965), 125–26, 127–28; E. Ashtor, "The Number of Jews in Medieval Egypt," in: JJS, 18–19 (1967/8), 16–17; J.M. Landau, *Jews in Nineteenth-Century Egypt* (1969), 8, 50, 255.

[Eliyahu Ashtor]

FAJANS, KASIMIR (1887–1975), U.S. physical chemist who did pioneering work on radioactivity and isotopes. Fajans was born in Warsaw, and after studying in Leipzig, Heidelberg, and Zurich, worked with Rutherford in Manchester. After a period on the staff of the Technische Hochschule at Karlsruhe, Fajans went to the University of Munich, where in 1923 he became full professor of physical chemistry. In 1932 he secured support from the Rockefeller Foundation for the establishment of an institute of physical chemistry in Munich, of which he became director, but in 1935 he was forced by the Nazis to leave the institute. He emigrated to the U.S. and in 1936 became professor of chemistry at the University of Michigan at Ann Arbor. Fajans, with Goehring, discovered the element 91 (uranium X2 or brevium), the more stable isotope of which (called protoactinium) was discovered independently a little later by Hahn and Meitner and also by Soddy and Cranston. Of Fajans' contributions to scientific journals, many are concerned with brevium, other work on radioactive transformations, and the chemistry of the radioactive elements. But he was also active in numerous other fields of physical chemistry. For some time he was coeditor of *Zeitschrift für Kristallographie* and associate editor of the *Journal of Physical and Colloid Chemistry*. He wrote *Radioaktivität und die neueste Entwicklung der Lehre von den chemischen Elementen* (1920^2), *Physikalisch-chemisches Praktikum* (1929, with J. Wuest), *Radioelements and Isotopes; Chemical Forces and Optical Properties of Substances* (1931), and *Quanticule Theory of Chemical Bonding* (1960).

BIBLIOGRAPHY: Lange, in: *Zeitschrift fuer Elektrochemie*, 61 (1957), 773–4.

[Samuel Aaron Miller]

FALAISE, town in the Calvados department, France. During the 12th and 13th centuries there was a Jewish community in Falaise, which was still remembered until 1890 in the name "Rue aux Juifs." Among the scholars there were the tosafists *Samson b. Joseph of Falaise and *Samuel b. Solomon of Falaise (also known as Sir Morel), who was one of the leading French tosafists and also a successful financier. He took part in the *disputation on the Talmud in 1240, but appears to have died before 1247. His son Jean may have been converted to Christianity.

BIBLIOGRAPHY: Gross, Gal Jud 476–83; P.G. Langevin, *Recherches Historiques sur Falaise* (1814), 39; L. Musset in: *Bulletin de la Société Antiquaire de Normandie*, 50 (1946), 305ff.

[Bernhard Blumenkranz]

FALAQUERA (also **Falaguera**, **Falaquero**, **Palquera**), family in Spain; one of the most aristocratic and wealthy families of the Jewish community of *Tudela. The Falaqueras ranked among "the great of the community," i.e., the eight families in whose hands the administration of the community was concentrated, according to the communal regulations of 1305, and whose consent and signatures were required to authorize every such regulation. A certain R. Joseph b. Shem Tov ibn Falaquera was appointed in 1287 head of the *dayyanim* empowered to try informers. Other members of this family, Joseph b. Judah, Joseph b. Isaac, and Solomon b. Moses, are mentioned as *muqaddimūn* (leaders) of the community of Tudela at the close of the 13th and early 14th century. Nathan b. Falaquera (also mentioned by the name Naçan del Gabay) held important positions in the financial administration of Navarre at the close of the 14th century. The philosopher and poet Shem Tov b. Joseph ibn *Falaquera was also a member of this family. A branch of the Falaquera family lived in the town of Huesca.

BIBLIOGRAPHY: Baer, Spain, 1 (1961), 425; Baer, Urkunden, index. **ADD. BIBLIOGRAPHY:** M. de la E. Marín Padilla, in: *Anuario de Estudios Medievales*, 15 (1985), 497–512.

[Joseph Kaplan]

FALAQUERA, NATHAN BEN JOEL (late 13th century), Spanish physician. He may be identical with Nathan of Montpellier, the teacher of the anonymous author of *Sefer ha-Yashar*. Falaquera is the author of a book on medicine, *Ẓori ha-Guf* ("Balm for the Body"), written in Hebrew; however, although he uses medical and botanic terms taken from talmudic literature, his sources are mainly Arabic. The opinions of Hippocrates, Galen, Averroes, Avicenna, and Maimonides are given. Three manuscripts of the book are still extant and it was quoted by Joseph b. Eliezer ha-Sephardi, author of *Ohel Yosef* on Abraham ibn Ezra's commentary on the Torah.

BIBLIOGRAPHY: H. Friedenwald, *Jews and Medicine* (1944), 661; G. Sarton, *Introduction to the History of Science*, 2 pt. 2 (1931), 1096–97.

[David Margalith]

FALAQUERA, SHEM TOV BEN JOSEPH IBN (1223/8–after 1290), philosopher, translator, commentator, poet, and encyclopedist. Falaquera was born in Spain between 1223 and 1228; his last known work refers to events in 1290. Various etymologies have been suggested for his name, which was the name of a prominent Jewish family in Tudela. Hebrew spellings include פלקירא, פלקירה, פלכרה, בלקירה, פלאקיר, פלקריי.

European spellings include Falaquera, Palquera, Palaquera, Palquira, Palqira, Palkira, Palkera, Phalkira, Phalchera.

Most of Falaquera's prose works survive, many in multiple editions or manuscripts, but Falaquera testifies that half of his prolific youthful poetry (totaling some 20,000 verses) was lost, and in later life, although he abandoned his poetic career, he continued to intersperse poetry with his prose works. Some of this poetry was humorous. "Time said to the fool: Be a doctor / You can kill people and take their money / You'll have an advantage over the angels of death / For they kill a man, but for free." His prose is also marked by occasional humor. His last known work, in defense of *Maimonides' *Guide of the Perplexed*, plays on the name of the philosopher's opponent Solomon Petit and calls him *peti* (fool).

We do not know how Falaquera supported himself. Repeated references to poverty in some of his writings may indicate personal indigence. We also have no evidence whether he ever married or had a family. With only a few exceptions, Falaquera's references to women were generally quite negative and even misogynist. In one of his poems he aims his barbs at women: "Let your soul not trust in a woman / A woman is a spread net and pit (Proverbs 1:17, 22:14) / How can we still believe that she is honest [straight] / For woman was taken from a rib?" If the "Seeker" in his *Book of the Seeker* represents Falaquera himself (since the Seeker's curriculum would have made him approximately Falaquera's age at the time he composed the book), and if the "Seeker" is patterned after the character Kalkol in his earlier *Epistle on Ethics*, we may be able to infer from Kalkol's never marrying (because he did not want to waste his time or strength on women, or to become entrapped by them) that Falaquera himself never married for similar reasons.

Modern scholarly interest in Falaquera, going back to the early stages of **Wissenschaft des Judentums*, began with Leopold *Zunz's doctoral disseration, "De Schemtob Palkira" (Halle University, December 21, 1820) on the life, times, and doctrines of Falaquera. In 1857 Solomon *Munk published Falaquera's Hebrew paraphrase of selections from the lost Arabic original of the *Fons Vitae*, on the basis of which Munk determined that the previously unknown and presumably Arab author was actually the Hebrew poet and philosopher Solomon ibn *Gabirol. Over the next century most of Falaquera's works were published (some with translations into European languages). The latter decades of the 20th century saw a resurgence of interest in Falaquera, with books, major studies, and doctoral dissertations by R.K. Barkan, G. Dahan, S. Harvey, M.H. Levine, A. Melamed, D. Schwartz, Y. Shiffman, L. Stitskin, M. Zonta. R. Jospe's *Torah and Sophia: The Life and Thought of Shem Tov ibn Falaquera* (Cincinnati, 1988) includes a biography, descriptions of Falaquera's works, and systematic survey of his philosophy, with a special study of his psychology.

Works

We know of eighteen works by Falaquera, all written in Hebrew, in line with Falaquera's aim of spreading philosophy among the Jewish people. Based on internal evidence, in their probable chronological order they are the following:

1. *Battei Hanhagat ha-Nefesh – Batei Hanhagat Guf ha-Bari* (Verses on the Regimen of the Healthy Body and Soul), a composite of two works on health and ethics, published by S. Munter (Tel Aviv, 1950).

2. *Iggeret ha-Musar* (Epistle on Ethics), a **maqama* (prose narrative interspersed with verse), replete with Jewish and Arabic ethical maxims, recounting the adventures of a youth, Kalkol, in search of wisdom. Edited by A.M. Haberman (Jerusalem, 1936), this early work forms a model for Falaquera's later and larger *Book of the Seeker*.

3. *Ẓori ha-Yagon* (The Balm for Sorrow), also a *maqama*, containing rabbinic and philosophic consolations, in several editions; critical edition with annotated English translation and a survey of the consolation genre of literature by R.K. Barkan (Ph.D. dissertation, Columbia University, 1971).

4. *Megillat ha-Zikkaron* (The Scroll of Remembrance). The work, of which Falaquera says elsewhere "in which I discuss times past, for at this time hordes of troubles come upon us daily," probably chronicling Jewish sufferings, is not extant.

5. *Iggeret ha-Vikku'aḥ* (The Epistle of the Debate). The subtitle of the book is *Be-Ve'ur ha-Haskamah asher bein ha-Torah ve-ha-Ḥokhmah* (Explaining the Harmony Between the Torah and Philosophy). A popular work, much of it written in rhymed prose, the book describes a debate between a *ḥasid*, a pious traditionalist Jew and a *ḥakham*, a philosopher, and is deeply indebted to Ibn Rushd's *Faṣl al-Maqal* (Decisive Treatise). S. Harvey's *Falaquera's Epistle of the Debate: An Introduction to Jewish Philosophy* (Cambridge, MA, 1987; Italian: Genova, 2005) includes a critical edition of the Hebrew text with annotated English translation and valuable appendices. Harvey (1992) has also suggested persuasively that the debate is patterned on the Maimonidean controversy of the 1230s. A Latin translation of the *Epistle* with French notes and introduction was published by G. Dahan (in *Sefarad*, 39 (1979), 1–112).

6. *Reshit Ḥokhmah* (The Beginning of Wisdom), an encyclopedic introduction to the sciences in three parts: I – On the moral qualities necessary for the study of science; II – The enumeration of the sciences; III – The necessity of philosophy for the attainment of felicity; the philosophy of Plato and the philosophy of Aristotle. Major portions of the book, which was edited by M. David (Berlin, 1902), are paraphrases of Arabic philosophers, especially Al-Farabi.

7. *Sefer ha-Ma'alot* (The Book of Degrees), an ethical work describing the corporeal, spiritual, and divine degrees of human perfection. The term *ma'alot*, degrees, also means virtues. Those of the divine rank are the most perfect people, namely the prophets, who no longer exist. Those of the spiritual rank are the true philosophers. Most people are of the corporeal rank, enslaved to their bodily needs. The book, a sequel to *Reshit Ḥokhmah*, but unlike the former an original work of Falaquera's own ideas, was one of three Hebrew books in the

library of the 15th century Italian Christian philosopher Pico della Mirandola. Leopold *Zunz first wished to publish this book, but found only one manuscript, and it was eventually published by L. Venetianer (Berlin, 1894).

8. *Sefer ha-Mevakkesh* (The Book of the Seeker). The book was composed in Ḥeshvan, 5024 (= Oct.–Nov. 1263) when Falaquera was past 35 and approaching 40 years of age. A *maqama* expanding on the theme of the youthful seeker of wisdom (like his earlier *Epistle on Ethics*), the book surveys the arts and professions, as well as the sciences (only the sciences had been presented in his *Reshit Ḥokhmah*), culminating in philosophy. Several 19th- and early 20th-century editions of the book exist. M.H. Levine prepared a critical edition and translation of Part I in his Ph.D. thesis (Columbia University, 1954), and his translation was revised and published separately (New York, 1976).

9. *De'ot ha-Philosofim* (The Opinions of the Philosophers). This voluminous work, only minor sections of which have been published, is a major encyclopedia of the sciences, extending over some 600 pages in ms. Parma – De Rossi 164 (= Jewish National and Hebrew University Library microfilm 13897) and ms. Leyden 20 (= Jewish National and Hebrew University Library microfilm 17368). It was written to propagate philosophy and science among the Jews, and quotes extensively from Arabic sources. R. Jospe (1988) published a table of contents of the work, aspects of which were analyzed by S. Harvey, G. Freudenthal, A. Ivry, and M. Zonta in *The Medieval Hebrew Encyclopedias of Science and Philosophy*, ed. S. Harvey, (Dordrecht, 2000). Falaquera states that his purpose in composing the work was to teach true philosophy to the Jews, distinguishing true opinions from those which have not been demonstrated and are mere conjecture; and to provide a convenient and systematic collection of the opinions of the philosophers in accurate Hebrew translation, which would also serve as "a review book for me in old age."

10. *Sefer ha-Nefesh* (The Book of the Soul). The first systematic Hebrew work of psychology, the book was published in several 19th- and early 20th-century editions. A critical edition with annotated English translation and extensive discussion was published by R. Jospe (1988). The book, which frequently reviews material earlier discussed in *De'ot ha-Philosophim*, reflects (and in places paraphrases) classical and Arabic sources, prominent among them Ibn Rushd, Ibn Sina, and Isḥaq ibn Ḥunain.

11. *Shelemut ha-Ma'asim* (The Perfection of Actions). An annotated edition of this work on ethics in ten chapters was published by R. Jospe (1988). The first six chapters of the book, as B. Chiesa has shown (in A. Vivian, ed., *Biblische und judaistische Studien, Festschrift fuer Paolo Sacchi* [Frankfurt am Main, 1990], 583–612), are for the most part an abridged translation of the *Summa Alexandrinorum*, an epitome of Aristotle's *Nicomachean Ethics*. The last four chapters reflect Arabic ethical literature, especially Ḥunain ibn Isḥaq's *Adab al-Falasifah* (Aphorisms of the Philosophers). Typically, Falaquera translated anew or paraphrased those Arabic passages he was interested in citing – as he also did in his other works – and did not take advantage of existing Hebrew translations, such as Judah Al-Ḥarizi's translation of the *Adab*, the *Musarei ha-Filosofim*.

12. *Iggeret ha-Ḥalom* (The Treatise of the Dream). Edited by H. Malter (in JQR, n.s. 1, 1910/11, 451–501), this treatise does not deal with dreams (as some scholars thought), but derives its name from a superscription by a copyist about the author: "He said that he saw in a dream that he was composing this treatise, and when he awoke, he engaged in it, and this is its beginning." The treatise begins: "A treatise [literally: epistle] collecting words of peace and truth." Maimonides had understood Zechariah 8:19 ("Love truth and peace") as referring to intellectual and moral perfection, and Falaquera's division of Part I (Peace), dealing with physical and spiritual well-being, and Part II (Truth), dealing with truth in speech and actions, and speculative truth, reflects Maimonides' interpretation.

13. *Sefer ha-Derash* (The Book of Interpretation). The work is not extant. It was probably a rationalistic commentary on aggadic passages in the Talmud or Midrash. Fragmentary citations in later authors (published by R. Jospe and D. Schwartz, 1993) may be taken from this work. (See below, *Perush*).

14. *Perush* (Bible Commentary). Falaquera's Bible Commentary is no longer extant. However, Samuel ibn Seneh Zarza's commentary on the Torah, *Mekor Ḥayyim*, which frequently deals with the commentaries of Abraham Ibn Ezra, also cites Falaquera in twenty-six passages; these citations, presumably taken from Falaquera's Bible commentary, were published with English translation by R. Jospe (1988). Nineteen additional citations to Falaquera are found in Zarza's *Mikhlol Yofi*, a commentary to rabbinic *derashot* (homilies) and *aggadot* (lore). Of these nineteen, seven are identical with passages cited in *Mekor Ḥayyim*. Since the *Mikhlol Yofi* is a commentary on rabbinic texts, and since eight of the remaining twelve citations make no reference to a biblical verse, it may well be that the twelve, or at least these eight, citations are not from Falaquera's Bible Commentary but from his Book of Interpretation. The twelve passages in question were published with English translation and discussion by R. Jospe and D. Schwartz (1993). The surviving fragmentary citations support the view that both commentaries, on the Bible and on rabbinic texts, were frequently philosophical in approach.

15. *Moreh ha-Moreh* (The Guide to the Guide). One of the very first commentaries to Maimonides' *Guide of the Perplexed*, Falaquera's work is unusual in its philosophic precision and breadth; in its extensive citations of Arabic sources and comparisons of Maimonides' opinions with those sources; and in its new and precise translation of those sections of the *Guide* discussed by Falaquera. The title is usually understood as a play on the title of Maimonides' book, but based on Falaquera's own explanation of the name in the Introduction, it could also be called "The Guide of the Rebellious," namely as correcting the opinions of those who oppose and misinterpret Maimonides' *Guide*. It was first published by M.S. Bis-

liches (Pressburg, 1837); an annotated, critical edition with commentary and extensive research into Falaquera's Arabic sources was published by Y. Shiffman (Jerusalem, 2001). Falaquera cites Ibn Rushd so frequently throughout the book that he does not refer to him by name, but simply refers to him as *ha-ḥakham ha-nizkar* ("the mentioned philosopher"). The third appendix to the book entails a detailed and careful critique of Samuel ibn Tibbon's Hebrew translation of the *Guide of the Perplexed*.

16. *Likkutim mi-Sefer Mekor Ḥayyim* (Selections from [Solomon ibn Gabirol's] *Fons Vitae*). This text is extant in two manuscripts. The Paris manuscript was published with an annotated French translation by S. Munk in his *Mélanges de Philosophie Juive et Arabe* (Paris, 1857; reprinted 1927); the Parma manuscript was edited with an annotated Italian translation by R. Gatti (Genova, 2001). The Selections eliminate the dialogical form of Solomon ibn Gabirol's original, and may reflect agreement with Abraham ibn Daud's criticism that Gabirol's "words could be included in less than one tenth of that book," and that he had substituted many untrue arguments for one true demonstration. The Selections also occasionally rearrange the order of the original, perhaps in accordance with what Gabirol himself said (3:1), that he had not followed any specific order and that the student should reorder the arguments as appropriate. Occasionally the Selections are nearly identical with the original, and sometimes even longer, including examples or illustrations not found in Gabirol's work.

17. *Likkutim mi-Sefer ha-Aẓamim ha-Ḥamishah* (Selections from the Book of the Five Substances). Also an abridged Hebrew translation or paraphrase of passages from a Neo-Platonic, Pseudo-Empedoclean work, this work was published by David Kaufmann in *Studien ueber Salomon ibn Gabirol* (Budapest, 1899).

18. *Mikhtav al Devar ha-Moreh* (Letter Concerning the *Guide* [*of the Perplexed*]). Falaquera's last known work, the letter in defense of Maimonides' *Guide of the Perplexed* against opponents of philosophy was written in 5050 (= 1290 C.E.). Falaquera mocks Maimonides' opponents, comparing them to Korah's rebellion against Moses. Part of the problem results from the anti-rationalists' ignorance of philosophy and Arabic, and the inadequacy of the two Hebrew translations of the *Guide*, especially the second translation, by Judah Al-Harizi. The letter is included anonymously at the end of Abba Mari ben Moses Ha-Yarḥi's *Minḥat Kena'ot*, ed. M.L. Bisliches (Pressburg, 1838), pp. 182–185, and at the end of *Iggerot Kena'ot*, pp. 23–24 (Part 3 of *Kovez̧ Teshuvot ha-Rambam ve-Iggerotav*, 1859).

Philosophy

Since Falaquera considered philosophy to be necessary for attaining ultimate human felicity, and believed in the harmony of revealed and rational truth, he wrote many of his works with the explicit aim of propagating the study of philosophy among the Jewish people by making it available in Hebrew translation. These works, which can be characterized as text-books, encyclopedic surveys or introductions to philosophy, were often replete with new Hebrew translations or paraphrases (typically abridged) from Arabic philosophical literature, even in cases like the *Guide of the Perplexed* and the *Aphorisms of the Philosophers* for which Hebrew translations already existed, because of Falaquera's insistence on accuracy, terminological consistency and stylistic clarity.

His competence in philosophy and his critical sense for nuance led him to juxtapose, compare and contrast diverse philosophical opinions. Since true human perfection is intellectual, dissemination of philosophy in Hebrew and rebuttal of its opponents serve a religious as well as a cultural need.

A consistent theme in Falaquera's works is the harmony of faith and reason. The Torah and philosophy, when both are properly understood, are "sisters" and "twins." The rabbinic saying, "Rabbi Meir found a pomegranate; he ate what was within and discarded the peel" (BT Ḥagigah 15b) means that one should accept in philosophy what is true and in accord with the Torah. Reason can verify religious truth, and faith perfects reason.

To reject philosophy because some philosophers have erred is (in an image borrowed from Ibn Rushd) like denying water to a person dying of thirst, just because some people have drowned. A Jew should learn the truth from any source, as one takes honey from a bee. For "all nations share in the sciences; they are not peculiar to one people;" and "Accept the truth from whoever utters it; look at the content, not at the speaker" (*Sefer ha-Ma'alot*).

Falaquera's rationalism is manifest throughout his works, including his Bible exegesis and his specific treatises. He equates the Platonic doctrine of creation with that of Genesis, and he reads his intellectualism into Biblical ethics, to derive an extreme asceticism with misogynic overtones. Falaquera's position (*Shelemut ha-Ma'asim*, ch. 6, following the *Summa Alexandrinorum*, an epitome of Aristotle's *Nicomachean Ethics*) emphasizing the priority of contemplation and rejecting ethics as the ultimate human end, is more extreme than that of Aristotle himself, for whom the external causes or goods required for ethics can become an impediment to perfection and contemplation (*theoria*), whereas for Falaquera the ethical involvement and social commitments themselves impede contemplation (Hebrew: *eẓah*; Arabic: *ra'y*). Despite Falaquera's clear concern for the philosophic education of his people, he believed that genuine felicity is attained by the "solitary" (*mitboded*) individual, who is isolated not physically but spiritually from the external distractions of society and the internal interference of the appetites.

Knowledge of God begins, for Falaquera, with self-knowledge, i.e., knowledge of one's soul. We find throughout his works statements reflecting the Delphic Maxim, "Know yourself." Thus: "Know your soul, O Man, and you will know your Creator." By the science of psychology, a person "will know his soul and his Creator." Psychology is, therefore, prior to all the other sciences: "Knowledge of the soul is prior to the knowledge of God, and … is the most excellent form of knowledge after the knowledge of God" (*Sefer ha-Nefesh*, Introduction; *De'ot ha-Philosofim* VI:A:1).

Falaquera was not an original thinker of the first order, nor did he claim to be original; but the breadth and depth of his knowledge of Judaism, philosophy, and science make him an important figure in the history of Jewish philosophy. The pioneering philosophical efforts of earlier luminaries attained an enduring impact through their consolidation and popularization by philosophers like Falaquera, whose contribution is no less important for the fact that their light was often a reflected one.

BIBLIOGRAPHY: I. Efros, "Palquera's *Reshit Hokmah* and Alfarabi's *Ihsa al 'Ulum*," in: JQR, n.s. 25 (1934–35), 227–35; P. Fenton, "Shem Tov ibn Falaquera ve-ha-Te'ologiyah shel Aristo," in: *Da'at* (1992), 27–39; S. Harvey, "Falaquera's *Epistle of the Debate* and the Maimonidean Controversy of the 1230s," in: R. Link-Salinger (ed.), *Torah and Wisdom: Studies in Jewish Philosophy, Kabbalah and Halacha: Essays in Honor of Arthur Hyman* (1992), 75–86; S. Harvey, "*Mekoran shel ha-Muva'ot min ha-Etica le-Aristo ba-*Moreh *u-ve-*Moreh ha-Moreh," in: A. Ravitzky (ed.), *From Rome to Jerusalem: J. Sermonetta Memorial Volume* (1998), 87–102; R. Jospe, "Rejecting Moral Virtue as the Ultimate Human End," in: W.M. Brinner and S.D. Ricks (eds.), *Studies in Islamic and Judaic Traditions* (1986), 185–204; idem, "Ikkarei ha-Yahadut shel R. Shem Tov ibn Falaquera," in: S. Heller-Willensky and M. Idel (eds.), *Studies in Jewish Thought* (1989), 291–301; R. Jospe and D. Schwartz, "Shem Tov ibn Falaquera's Lost Bible Commentary," in: HUCA, 64 (1993), 167–200; H. Malter, "Shem Tob ben Joseph Palquera: A Thinker of the Thirteenth Century," in: JQR, n.s. 1 (1910–11), 151–81; A. Melamed, *The Philosopher-King in Medieval and Renaissance Jewish Political Thought* (2003); S. Munk, *Melanges de Philosophie Juive et Arabe* (1857; reprint, 1927); M. Steinschneider, Uebersetzungen, 5ff., 37ff., 356, 380, 422ff., 989; Y. Shiffman, "*Shem Tov Falaquera ke-Farshan* Moreh Nevukhim *la-Rambam: Kavim le-Haguto*," in: *Maimonidean Studies* 3 (1992–3), 1–29; L. Stitskin, *Eight Jewish Philosophers in the Tradition of Personalism* (1979), 134–40; M. Zonta, *Un Dizionario Filosofico Ebraico del XIII Secolo: L'introduzione al "Sefer De'ot ha-Filosofim" di Shem Tob ibn Falaquera* (1992); M. Zonta, *Un Interprete Ebreo della Filosofia di Galeno: Gli Scritti Filosofici di Galeno Nell'opera di Shem Tob ibn Falaquera* (1995); idem, *La Filosofia antica nel Medioevo Ebraico* (Brescia, 1996), 204–12.

[Raphael Jospe (2nd ed.)]

FALCO, MARIO (1884–1943), Italian jurist. Born in Turin, Falco specialized in canon and ecclesiastical law. He became lecturer in law at the universities of Macerata (1910) and Parma (1912) and was appointed to the chair at the University of Milan on its foundation in 1924. He held this post until the promulgation of the antisemitic laws in 1938. Most of Falco's extensive legal writings are concerned with canon law. They include *Il Concetto Giuridico di Separazione della Chiesa dallo Stato* (1913), *La Codificazione del Diritto Canonico* (1921), and *Corso di Diritto Ecclesiastico* (1938). An active Zionist, he participated in Jewish affairs both locally and nationally and was a member of a government committee which prepared the draft law on the Italian Jewish community in 1930.

[Giorgio Romano]

FALESHTY (Rom. **Făleşti**), town in Bessarabia, today Republic of Moldova. In 1817, the community numbered 176 families (out of a total of 364 families) and 4,518 persons (68% of the total population) in 1897. As the czarist legislation restricting Jewish settlement in border areas (see *Russia) applied to Faleshty, the Jews were frequently expelled from the town on the grounds that they were living there illegally. In 1887 a society for settlement in Ereẓ Israel was established in Faleshty, and with the assistance of funds provided by Baron Edmond de *Rothschild, 25 families settled in 1887 in Kastina (*Be'er Toviyyah). In 1925, 106 Jewish families in Faleshty were occupied in agriculture, farming an area of 1,025 hectares. The Jewish population numbered 3,258 in 1930 (51.7% of the total).

Holocaust Period

The Romanian withdrawal in 1940 took place without incident. The incoming Soviet authorities established a Yiddish-language secondary school, but on June 19, 1941, exiled all Zionists and businessmen to Siberia. Most of the exiles survived the war; some returned and settled in the larger towns or went to Israel, while others remained in Siberia.

An aerial bombardment at the beginning of the war (June 21, 1941) caused the first Jewish casualties. Those who had horses at their disposal quickly fled the town, while others followed on foot. A few succeeded in crossing the Dniester with Russian help and escaped from there into the interior of the U.S.S.R. Most of the fleeing Jews, however, were caught on the way by Romanian-German forces and put to death. On June 27 Faleshty was taken over by German troops, who were also joined by Italian forces. The local population and peasants from the surrounding villages collaborated with the occupying forces in robbing and burning Jewish property and murdering the Jews. Romanian troops arrived at a later date and stepped up the murderous campaign. The Jews were concentrated in a ghetto raised at the town's entrance, to which the Jews of other places in the vicinity were brought. The young people were put on forced labor; at night they were imprisoned in the great synagogue and there German and Romanian troops assaulted the women among them. The others were driven out of the ghetto and forced to walk to a nearby village, Limbenii Noui, where many died of disease and starvation. In September the survivors were again deported, this time to the Mărculeşti camp. In October those who were still able to walk were expelled to *Transnistria, where practically all of them either succumbed to the inhuman conditions or were murdered by soldiers. One group of Faleshty Jews, including the town's rabbi, Ihiel Flam, were taken to a river in mid-winter, forced to break the ice, strip, and throw themselves into the freezing waters. Only a very small number of Faleshty's Jews survived the war.

BIBLIOGRAPHY: *Eynikeyt* (March 6, 1945).

[Jean Ancel]

FALK, family of U.S. industrialists and philanthropists. MAURICE FALK (1866–1946) was born in Pittsburgh, Pennsylvania, where his father worked as a tailor. At the age of 27 he obtained a controlling interest in a small smelting concern, the Duquesne Reduction Company, which in subsequent years expanded its operations to include many sizeable steel and refining holdings. One of the founders of the Federation of Jewish Philanthropies in Pittsburgh, he and his younger brother Leon gave ten million dollars in 1929 to establish the Maurice and Laura Falk Foundation, whose beneficiaries have included many educational institutions. A branch foundation, the Maurice Falk Institute for Economic Research in Israel, was established at the Hebrew University in Jerusalem. The bulk of his large estate was willed to the Foundation for the purpose of studying social problems "for the benefit of mankind."

LEON FALK (1870–1928) was associated with his brother in most of his business and charitable undertakings, joining with him in 1928 to establish the Falk Medical Clinic at the University of Pittsburgh. He also served as director of the Pittsburgh Federation of Jewish Philanthropies and donated considerable sums to Pittsburgh's Montefiore Hospital and YM-YWHA. His son, LEON FALK JR. (1901–1988), served as president of the Federation of Jewish Philanthropies in Pittsburgh and in 1939 as vice chairman of the *American Jewish Joint Distribution Committee. When Maurice Falk granted money in 1939–40 to study the possibility of resettling Jewish refugees in the Caribbean, Leon Jr. traveled to the Dominican Republic to investigate conditions there and acted as chairman of the Dominican Republic Settlement Association. He became treasurer of Falk and Company in 1928 and was chairman of the board from 1948 to 1952.

The Falk Medical Fund is a grant-making foundation incorporated in 1960 as an outgrowth of the Maurice and Laura Falk Foundation.. The fund focuses on social policy related to mental health, community health, and civil rights and minorities issues. Since its inception, the fund has awarded grants targeted to the elimination of racism and the creation of programs that combine research in psychiatry and mental health with issues of racism, prejudice, violence, and bigotry. The Falk Foundation was a major contributor to the Brookings Institution, one of Washington's oldest think tanks, which named its auditorium after the Falk family.

SIGO FALK served as chairman of the Maurice Falk Fund as well as the Leon Falk Family Trust. He was also a director of Duquesne Light Holdings, Allegheny Land Trust, and the Pittsburgh Symphony. He was a trustee of Chatham College, where he served as board chair from 1995 to 2002, and the Historical Society of Western Pennsylvania. Falk was formerly the associate director of Health Systems Agency of Southwestern Pennsylvania and president of Cranberry Emergency and Diagnostic Center. In 2001, he was honored as the Outstanding Philanthropist by the Association of Fund-raising Professionals.

[Hillel Halkin / Ruth Beloff (2nd ed.)]

FALK, BERNARD (1882–1960), British author. Falk began his career on the *Daily Dispatch* in his home town, Manchester, and went to London to become news editor of the *Evening News*. He edited the weekly *Reynolds News* and the *Sunday Dispatch* (1919–32). He then retired from newspapers and wrote books on life in Fleet Street. He also wrote *The Naked Lady* (1934), a life of Adah Isaacs *Menken: *Rachel the Immortal* (1936), the life of the famous French actress *Rachel; *The Way of the Montagues* (1947); and books on Turner and Rowlandson. Falk published an autobiography, *He Laughed in Fleet Street* (1933).

FALK, JACOB JOSHUA BEN ẒEVI HIRSCH (1680–1756), rabbi and halakhic authority. Falk was born in Cracow and was a descendant of Joshua Heschel b. Joseph of *Cracow, the author of *Meginnei Shelomo*. He studied in Polish yeshivot and took up residence in Lemberg after his marriage to the daughter of Solomon Segal Landau, an important member of that community. There he was appointed inspector of the *talmud torah*. He became wealthy and was a leader of the community. In 1702 his wife, daughter, mother-in-law, and her father were killed by the explosion of a gunpowder storehouse, and he himself was miraculously saved. As a result he vowed "to apply himself diligently to the study of the Talmud and the Codes" (Introduction to the *Penei Yehoshu'a*). He left Lemberg and served as rabbi in the communities of Tarlow, Kurow, and Lesko (Lisko) successively. In 1717 he was invited to become rabbi of Lemberg, succeeding Ẓevi Hirsch Ashkenazi (the Ḥakham Ẓevi). His yeshivah became the central yeshivah of Poland. Falk was one of the most extreme opponents of the *Shabbatean movement, then gaining ground in Poland, and he excommunicated the Shabbateans in 1722. In consequence of the opposition he had aroused, he was compelled to leave Lemberg in 1724 and went to Buczacz where he lived for some years. Between 1730 and 1734 he served as rabbi of Berlin. He then accepted an invitation to succeed Jacob *Reischer as rabbi of Metz and remained there until 1741.

From Metz he went to Frankfurt where he was rabbi until 1751. The hostile attitude of the town authorities and internal communal quarrels following his intervention in the controversy around Jonathan *Eybeschuetz, in which he sided with Jacob *Emden, caused his resignation and departure from the city, and he lived for a time in Mannheim and Worms. He continued his campaign against Eybeschuetz, sending him a letter entitled "the final warning" on Sivan 11, 1751 and in 1752 excommunicated him. In response to the demands of the Altona community that he rescind the ban, Falk demanded that Eybeschuetz appear before a *bet din* of three ordained rabbis to answer for his actions. Ḥ.J.D. *Azulai, who repeatedly praised Falk's wide knowledge (as well as that of his second wife), visited him in Worms in 1754. Falk told him some "dismaying details" about the affair, and Azulai expressed his shock at the "desecration of the Torah and the defamation of the Divine Name" as a result of the publication of the dispute between the Jewish scholars. From Worms Falk went to Offenbach, where he died. He was buried in Frankfurt and although he requested that no eulogy should be said after his death he was eulogized by Ezekiel *Landau (see Frankfurt Memorbuch, National Library, Jerusalem).

Falk became renowned through his *Penei Yehoshu'a*, regarded as one of the outstanding works of novellae on the Talmud. Since Falk's grandfather published responsa under the same title ("The Face of Joshua"), the grandson called his work *Appei Zutrei* ("The Small Face") to distinguish it from *Ravrevei* ("The Large Face") of his grandfather. The work is distinguished by its penetrating explanation of difficult talmudic themes. Originally published in separate parts – *Berakhot* and the order *Mo'ed* (Frankfurt, 1752); *Ketubbot, Gittin*, and *Kiddushin*, with *Kunteres Aḥaron* (Amsterdam, 1739); *Bava Kamma* and *Bava Meẓia* (Frankfurt, 1756), *Ḥullin, Makkot*, and *Shevu'ot* and a second edition on *Mo'ed* and the Tur, *Ḥoshen Mishpat* (Fuerth, 1780) – it was published together for the first time in Lemberg in 1809. Among his other works still in manuscript the following may be noted: *Sefer Minḥat Ani*, novellae to *Eruvin, Niddah*, and *Yevamot; Kelal Gadol*, on the problem of "*rov* and **ḥazakah*" (i.e., where the principle of following the majority, *rov*, conflicts with that of a previous presumption, *ḥazakah*), and responsa. Only a few of his responsa have been published (in various collections). His purpose was "to explain most of the difficulties raised by the tosafists on Rashi's commentary … as well as such points as the tosafists leave unsolved, or for which they admit that their solution is unsatisfactory, or where their answer appears forced." In his introduction to the *Penei Yehoshu'a* he asserts that he always took care that his conclusions should be in conformity with the *halakhah* of the Talmud and the Codes and was careful not to commit to writing any novellae which did not conform with the truth, "but whenever something new occurred to me on a talmudic topic or in explanation of Rashi and *tosafot* and it appeared to me to approximate to the truth, according to the method of our predecessors and teachers, I accepted it." He also stresses that his sole purpose was "to stimulate the scholar and to bring about a more profound analysis on the part of those who already know how to arrive at halakhic decisions." These features of the work explain its constant popularity among students, and its frequent reprints. He emphasizes that Kabbalah is sometimes of help in explaining the *aggadot*; but despite his reliance on the Zohar and on the works of kabbalists (*Penei Yehoshu'a* to Ber. 10a) he declares "we have no dealings with esoteric lore."

Falk had three sons, two of whom are mainly of note. ISSACHAR DOV (1712–1744), who was born at Lesko, Galicia, studied under his father and Ẓevi Hirsch Ashkenazi of Halberstadt. He became the rabbi of Podhajce, Galicia, and in 1744 he was appointed head of the yeshivah at Metz, but died on the way there, in Berlin, before being able to take up the appointment. Four of his responsa were published in *Kiryat Ḥannah* of R. Gershon b. Isaac Moses Coblenz (Metz, 1785; nos. 41–44). His decision in the case of a *get* (bill of divorce), in which he disagreed with R. Jacob Yokel *Horowitz, is preserved in *She'elat Ḥakham*, and was published at the end of the responsa of R. Ḥayyim Kohen Rapoport (1957, pp. 243–4). Issachar Dov's novellae appear under the title of *Ḥezkat Avahata* in the book *Tesha Shitot* (1800, pp. 53b–80b) of his son Ẓevi Hirsch Rosanes.

His brother ARYEH LEIB (1715–1789) accompanied his father to Germany. He was appointed *rosh yeshivah* in Frankfurt during his father's incumbency, and held the position from 1745 to 1750. When his father left Frankfurt, Aryeh Leib was appointed rabbi of Sokal, then in Poland. In 1754 he signed the excommunication against the *Frankists in Brody. From 1761 to 1789 he was rabbi of Hanover. In the affair of the Cleves *get he supported Israel *Lipschuetz. He published the fourth part of his father's *Penei Yehoshu'a*, adding to it his own novellae to *Bava Kamma* under the title *Penei Aryeh* (Fuerth, 1780). He was succeeded as rabbi of Hanover by his son ISSACHAR BERISH (1747–1807). Issachar's son, SAMUEL, was appointed rabbi of Groningen, Holland, in 1802. After about seven years he succeeded his brother-in-law, Jehiel Aryeh Leib *Loewenstamm, as rabbi of Leeuwarden, Holland. In 1815 he succeeded his father-in-law as rabbi of the Ashkenazi community of Amsterdam, and finally served as rabbi of Amersfoort. He supported the *Haskalah movement among the Jews of Holland, approved the translation of the Bible into Dutch, and was the first rabbi in Holland to preach in the vernacular. Moses *Sofer refers to him in respectful terms (*Ḥatam Sofer*, pt. 2, EH, no. 139). He also encouraged the foundation of a general fund known as *Kolel Hod*, i.e., "H-olland and (Heb. ו) D-eutschland (Germany)," for the support of the poor of the Holy Land. Samuel's son ISSACHAR BAER BERENSTEIN (1808–1893) was born in Leeuwarden and died in The Hague. From the death of his father until 1848 he served in Amsterdam as a *dayyan*. He was then appointed chief rabbi of The Hague, succeeding Joseph Asher Lehmann, and served there 45 years. He was highly esteemed by the Dutch government for his activities in organizing various communal institutions.

BIBLIOGRAPHY: E.L. Landshuth, *Toledot Anshei ha-Shem u-Fe'ulatam ba-Adat Berlin* (1884), 27–34, 111; Bruell, Jahrbuecher, 7 (1885), 163–6; H.N. Dembitzer, *Kelilat Yofi*, 1 (1888), 108b–115b; 2 (1893), 77b; M. Horovitz, *Frankfurter Rabbinen*, 3 (1884), 5–61; S. Buber, *Anshei Shem* (1895), 43f. (on Aryeh Leib), 104–9, 125; J. Loewenstein, in: *Ha-Peles*, 2 (1902), 3 (1903); J.H. Simchovitz, in: MGWJ, 54 (1910), 608–21; D. Kahana, *Toledot ha-Mekubbalim…*, 2 (1927[3]), 23, 37–39, 44–52; Z.(H.) Horowitz (ed.), *Kitvei ha-Ge'onim* (1928), 28ff. (on Jacob Joshua), 67, 97–100 (on Issachar Berish); D. Wachstein, in: *Studies in Jewish Bibliography … A.S. Freidus* (1929), 15–31 (Heb. pt.); J.A. Kamelhar, *Dor De'ah*, 2 (1935), 19–26; D.A.L. Zins, *Ateret Yehoshu'a* (1936); N.M. Gelber, in: *Arim ve-Immahot be-Yisrael*, 6 (1955), 108 n. 8 (on Aryeh Leib); J. Meisel, *Pinkas Kehillat Berlin* (1962), 502 (index s.v. *Joshua Falk*).

[Yehoshua Horowitz]

FALK, JOSHUA (1799–1864), U.S. Orthodox rabbi, scholar, and author. Joshua ben Mordechai Hakohen Falk was born in Poland and immigrated to America in 1854. He served as rabbi of two communities in New York, Newburgh and Poughkeepsie, before becoming an itinerant preacher and then retiring from the active rabbinate. Known as "the father of American

Hebrew literature," Falk wrote the first book in the Hebrew language to be published in America (aside from the Bible and prayer books): *Avnei Yehoshua* ("The Stones of Joshua"), a commentary on the Ethics of the Fathers (1860). The interesting colophon to the book reads: "I give thanks that it was my good fortune to be the typesetter of this scholarly book, the first of its kind in America. Blessed be the God of Israel, who surely will not deny us the Redeemer." Falk also wrote *Binyan Yehoshua* ("The Edifice of Joshua"), novellæ on the Talmud, and *Homat Yehoshua* ("The Wall of Joshua"), an anthology of sermons.

WEBSITE: The Jewish Virtual Library; Jewish Encyclopedia.com.

[Bezalel Gordon (2nd ed.)]

FALK, JOSHUA BEN ALEXANDER HA-KOHEN (c. 1555–1614), Polish yeshivah head and halakhist commonly referred to as "Sma" from the initials of the title of his major work. Falk was born in Lublin and studied under Moses Isserles and Solomon Luria, but refused to serve as rabbi of the community. He devoted his life to teaching, receiving financial support from his father-in-law, Israel b. Joseph Edels, the communal leader of Lemberg, who also maintained the yeshivah conducted by Falk. The yeshivah attracted many pupils, some of whom later achieved fame as rabbis. Famed as a halakhic authority, Falk took an active part in the Council of the Four Lands and was one of the signatories in 1587 to the decree against purchasing rabbinical positions. In 1607 he presided over a session of the Council which passed a decree on the subject of interest, which the intensified financial activity among East European Jewry had rendered an urgent halakhic problem. Falk's resolute refusal to change his view on a *get* ("bill of divorce") which he had issued for a seriously ill man, and which Meir ben Gedaliah *Lublin and Mordecai *Jaffe had declared invalid, led to a vehement clash of opinions among contemporary rabbis, Falk being upheld by those assembled at Jaroslaw in 1611.

Falk's most celebrated work is *Sefer Me'irat Einayim*, a commentary on the Shulḥan Arukh, *Ḥoshen Mishpat*, published in all editions of the Shulḥan Arukh. He was moved to write the commentary because of the large number of halakhists and exponents of the laws who, in his opinion, "have rent the Torah, which is our garment, into 12 pieces, and because of the many scholars who, content to base their halakhic decisions on the Shulḥan Arukh alone without investigating the sources (especially *Jacob b. Asher's Tur together with Joseph *Caro's *Beit Yosef* and Moses Isserles' *Darkhei Moshe*), remained ignorant of the sources and rationale of the law and rendered incorrect halakhic decisions."

Sefer Me'irat Einayim is the fourth part of a more extensive commentary on the Tur and Shulḥan Arukh, the first three parts entitled *Perishah, Derishah*, and *Be'urim*. The whole commentary is entitled *Beit Yisrael* (after Falk's father-in-law). Because *Me'irat Einayim* was based on the first three parts of his commentary, it was essential for the reader first to study the Tur and the other three parts of his commentary. Though Falk apparently intended to write a work on the whole Shulḥan Arukh, he succeeded in covering only the *Ḥoshen Mishpat*. The *Me'irat Einayim* is an extensive exposition and elaboration upon that work, especially upon Moses Isserles' glosses, Falk often acting as the intermediary between Joseph Caro and Isserles where they disagreed. Falk's work contributed greatly in making the Shulḥan Arukh an authoritative source of codified Jewish law. Falk also wrote *Kunteres al ha-Ribbit* (1692) on the laws of interest promulgated by the Council of the Four Lands in 1607. Several of his numerous responsa have been published in various collections (*Ge'onei Batra'ei, Bayit Ḥadash, Masot Binyamin*). He wrote novellae on 14 tractates of Isaac Alfasi (the Rif) and on the commentary to it by Nissim b. Reuben Gerondi (the Ran), expositions on the Kabbalah and philosophy, and several other works, all of which were destroyed in a fire in Lemberg.

[Shlomo Eidelberg]

His great grandson ḤAYYIM (ABRAHAM) BEN SAMUEL FEIVUSH (PHOEBUS; late 17th century), was also a rabbi. After the expulsion of the Jews from Vienna (1670), Ḥayyim went to Jerusalem with his father, author of *Leket Shemu'el* and *Derush Shemu'el*, and in his old age he settled in Hebron, where he died. He wrote a commentary to the Book of Psalms, under the title *Ereẓ ha-Ḥayyim* (Constantinople, 1750?). Ḥ.J.D. Azulai mentions Ḥayyim's commentary to nearly all of the Bible.

BIBLIOGRAPHY: S. Buber, *Anshei Shem* (1895), 80–82 (no. 197), 129, 238; Rav Zair (H. Tchernowitz), in: *Ha-Shilo'aḥ*, 6 (1899), 233–40; idem, *Toledot ha-Posekim*, 2 (1947), 231ff.; 3 (1947), 112–20; Halpern, Pinkas, index 588, s.v. *Yeshu'a b. Aleksander*; H.H. Ben-Sasson, *Hagut ve-Hanhagah* (1959), index, s.v. *Yehoshu'a Falk*.

FALK, KAUFMAN GEORGE (1880–1953), U.S. physical chemist and biochemist. Born in New York, Falk taught physical chemistry at Columbia University. He wrote on ignition temperatures, refractive index, chemical equilibria, the electronic theory of valency, and on biochemical topics. His books were *Chemical Reactions, their Theory and Mechanism* (1920), *Chemistry of Enzyme Action* (1921), and *Catalytic Action* (1922). He was president of the Hebrew Technical Institute in New York from 1924.

FALK, MARCIA (1946–), U.S. poet, translator, and liturgist. Falk was born in New York City and grew up in New Hyde Park, N.Y. During her childhood, she began painting (becoming a life member of the Art Students League in Manhattan), writing poetry, and studying Hebrew. She received her B.A. in philosophy, *magna cum laude*, Phi Beta Kappa, from Brandeis University and both her M.A. in English and her Ph.D. in English and comparative literature from Stanford University. Falk was a Fulbright Scholar and a postdoctoral fellow in Bible and Hebrew literature at the Hebrew University of Jerusalem, and has taught at Stanford, the State University of New York at Binghamton, and the Claremont Colleges. In

2001 she held the Priesand Chair in Jewish Women's Studies at HUC-JIR in Cincinnati.

Falk won international acclaim for her translation of the Song of Songs, originally published in 1977 and subsequently released in several editions, most recently as *The Song of Songs: Love Lyrics from the Bible* (2004). Her translation, which made lavish use of assonance and alliteration and interpreted obscure images for modern readers, represented a radical departure from earlier translations. In 1996 Falk published *The Book of Blessings: New Jewish Prayers for Daily Life, the Sabbath, and the New Moon Festival*, a groundbreaking prayer book. *The Book of Blessings* contains new, egalitarian Hebrew and English blessings, along with poems and meditations, as alternatives to the traditional Jewish liturgy. Falk offers nongendered non-anthropomorphic epithets of the divine, such as "source of life" and "breath of all living things."

Falk translated the Yiddish poet Malka *Tussman, *With Teeth in the Earth: Selected Poems of Malka Heifetz Tussman* (1992), and the Israeli mystical poet *Zelda, *The Spectacular Difference* (2004). Falk's own vision, characterized by clarity and quietude, is evident in her two published poetry collections, *It Is July in Virginia: A Poem Sequence* (1985) and *This Year in Jerusalem* (1986).

BIBLIOGRAPHY: L. Day, "In the Hidden Garden: Two Translations of the Song of Songs," in: *The Hudson Review*, 48/2 (1995), 259–69; D. Ellenson, "Marcia Falk's *The Book of Blessings*: The Issue Is Theological," in: *CCAR Journal* (Spring 2000), 18–23; L. Hoffman, "Marcia Falk's *The Book of Blessings*," in: *Prooftexts: A Journal of Jewish Literary History*, 19/1 (1999), 87–93.

[Lucille Lang Day (2nd ed.)]

FALK, MIKSA (1828–1908), Hungarian journalist and politician. Born in Budapest, Falk contributed early in his life to leading newspapers. From 1858 he was one of Count Széchenyi's close friends – in spite of the fact that this Hungarian statesman was antisemitic – and Falk published Széchenyi's political writings. In 1861 Falk was prosecuted for printing an article demanding the restoration of the Hungarian constitution and was sentenced to six months imprisonment. In the same year Falk was sponsored by the liberal leader Ferenc Deák for membership in the National Academy of Sciences. In 1866 he became a tutor in Magyar of the empress Elizabeth, wife of Francis Joseph. After the "compromise" of 1867 in which he had played a considerable part, and by which Hungary recovered its independence within the Hapsburg monarchy, Falk became chief editor of the government German-language newspaper *Pester Lloyd*. Falk converted to Christianity, sat in parliament for ten years, and wrote on Hungarian history.

BIBLIOGRAPHY: *Magyar Irodalmi Lexikon*, 1 (1963), 324.

[Baruch Yaron]

FALK, PETER (1927–), U.S. actor. Born in New York, Falk worked for the Budget Bureau of the state of Connecticut as an efficiency expert after receiving his M.B.A. in public administration in 1953. Bored with his job, he turned first to theater and television and then to film, eventually receiving Oscar nominations for his performances in *Murder Inc.* (1960) and *Pocketful of Miracles* (1961). In the 1970s Falk made a convincing impression in the films *Husbands* and *A Woman under the Influence* and starred in his own popular television detective series *Columbo*, new episodes of which were filmed after more than a 20-year break. As perhaps an illustration of the concept that life imitates art, his daughter Catherine Falk became a private detective.

In 1972 he appeared on Broadway in *The Prisoner of Second Avenue*. In 1987, he starred in Wim Wenders' Cannes Award-winning film *Der Himmel ueber Berlin/Wings of Desire*, and Rob Reiner's *The Princess Bride*. Other film roles include *The Balcony* (1963), *Robin and the 7 Hoods* (1964), *The Great Race* (1965), *Luv* (1967), *Mikey and Nicky* (1976), *Murder by Death* (1976), *The Cheap Detective* (1978), *The In-Laws* (1979), *Big Trouble* (1986), *Happy New Year* (1987), *In the Spirit* (1990), *Roommates* (1995), *Lakeboat* (2000), *Enemies of Laughter* (2001), *Corky Romano* (2001), *Three Days of Rain* (2002), *Undisputed* (2002), *The Thing about My Folks* (2004), and *Checking Out* (2004).

In addition to winning five Emmy awards, Falk has been nominated for seven other Emmys for his television performances. His memorable TV portrayals have also earned him a Golden Globe award and eight other GG nominations.

[Jonathan Licht / Ruth Beloff (2nd ed.)]

FALK, SAMUEL JACOB ḤAYYIM (c. 1710–1782), kabbalist and adventurer, known as the "Ba'al Shem of London." Falk, who was born in Galicia, was intimately connected with leaders of the Shabbatean sectarians for many years, e.g., Moses David of Podhajce. He became known early as a magician, escaped burning as a sorcerer in Westphalia, was banished by the archbishop elector of Cologne, and about 1742 made his way to England. Here he achieved notoriety in both Jewish and non-Jewish circles for his kabbalistic practices based on the use of the mysterious Name of God, hence becoming known as a *Ba'al Shem ("Master of the [Divine] Name"). He had a private synagogue in his house in Wellclose Square, and also established a kabbalistic laboratory on London Bridge where he carried out alchemical experiments which aroused some notice. Among those who were attracted to him, was the international adventurer Theodore De Stein, who claimed to be king of Corsica and hoped to obtain through Falk's alchemical experiments sufficient gold to enable him to "regain" his throne. He was also in touch with, among others, the Duke of Orleans, the Polish Prince Czartoryski, and the Marquise de la Croix. On one occasion, Falk is said to have saved the Great Synagogue from destruction by fire by means of a magical inscription which he inscribed on the doorposts. On the other hand, he was denounced as a Shabbatean heretic and fraud by his embittered contemporary Jacob *Emden. He was, at the outset, on the worst possible terms with the official London community. However, in the end he became reconciled with it and received the support of the Goldsmid family. As a result of this, or possibly of success in a lottery, he died in relatively affluent circumstances, leaving a considerable legacy to Jewish charities and an annual payment for the upkeep of the chief rabbinate in London. Much light is thrown on his personality and activities in the semi-literate diary of his henchman Hirsch Kalish, preserved in manuscript in the Adler Collection in the Jewish Theological Seminary of America, N.Y.; one of his own kabbalistic notebooks is in the library of the *bet ha-midrash* in London. Toward the end of his life, his portrait was painted by the distinguished Anglo-American artist John Copley. This is now frequently reproduced erroneously as the portrait of the famous *Israel Ba'al Shem Tov, founder of Ḥasidism.

BIBLIOGRAPHY: C. Roth, *Essays and Portraits in Anglo-Jewish History* (1962), 139–64; idem., Mag Bibl, 124–5; Wirszubski, in: *Zion*, 7 (1942), 73–93.

[Cecil Roth]

FALKOWITSCH, JOEL BAERISCH (19th century), Hebrew and Yiddish essayist. Falkowitsch was born in Dubno and lived in Odessa. In addition to a free Hebrew translation of Lessing's *Philotas* under the title *Amminadav* (1868), he published two successfully produced plays in Yiddish: *Reb Khayml der Kotsin* ("Reb Khayml the Judge," 1866) and *Rokhele di Zingerin* ("Rokhele the Singer," 1868). Although baptized a few years before his death, he remained well disposed to Judaism. Falkowitsch appeared at blood-libel trials where he argued against the antisemitic charges. When anti-Jewish attacks appeared in the Warsaw Russian newspaper, *Varshavsky Dnevnik*, he wrote a defense in German, called *Wort zur Zeit* ("A Timely Word," Hebrew transl. "*Davar be-Itto*" in the weekly Ha-Kol (1877), 8–21).

BIBLIOGRAPHY: *Ha-Boker-Or*, 4 (1879), 844; S. Wiener, *Kohelet Moshe* (1893–1936), 3 no. 25; Zeitlin, *Bibliotheca*, 81, 467; Rejzen, *Leksikon*, 3 (1929), 13–16.

[Jefim (Hayyim) Schirmann / Marc Miller (2nd ed.)]

FALL, LEO (1873–1925), composer. Born in Olomouc, Moravia, Fall, the son of a military bandmaster, was educated at the Vienna Conservatory and served as a theater conductor. His first three successful operettas, *Der fidele Bauer* (1907), *Die Dollarprinzessin* (1907), and *Die geschiedene Frau* (1908), placed him among the masters of the "second period of the operetta," with Franz Lehar and Oscar *Straus. His most popular works were *Die Rose von Stambul* (1916) and *Madame Pompadour* (1922). Fall's music was distinguished for its charm of melody and clever orchestration.

FALL RIVER, city in S.E. Massachusetts near Rhode Island border. The Jewish population of Fall River has been declining for the past 35 years and now numbers less than 1,000, a decrease from the 1970 population of 4,000 Jews. Attracted by the early cotton-manufacturing industries, the first Jews settled in Fall River during the 1860s and 1870s. Formal religious services were first held in 1874. These first settlers were German Jews; the community and its religious, social, and welfare institutions were soon changed considerably by the influx of Russian immigrants in the 1880s and 1890s. Two of the three congregations serving the community in 1970 – American Brothers of Israel and Congregation Adas Israel – were established in this era. Adas Israel, originally the Adas Israel Society, was founded in 1885; dissidents from Adas Israel established the American Brothers of Israel about 1892. At the beginning of the 20th century a third synagogue, Aguda B'nai Jacob, was founded. Abraham Lipshitz began ministering to these three congregations, which made up the Orthodox community, about 1910, serving them for over 30 years. In the decade 1910–20 Congregation Beth David was founded, Hebrew schools were established, and in 1924 a Conservative synagogue, Temple Beth El, was founded. Morton Goldberg served the congregation from 1925 to 1937, when Jacob Freedman replaced him as spiritual leader. Rabbi Freedman helped found the Fall River Jewish Community Council (1938), which in 1970 included about 25 societies and organizations. The other major communal institution is the Fall River United Jewish Appeal.

Jews prominent in Fall River life have included David L. Gourse, clothier and commissioner of public welfare; Albert Rubin, a state legislator for many years; H. William Radovsky, finance commissioner; and Rabbi Samuel Ruderman, long considered the spokesman for the Jewish community. David H. Radovsky and Moses Entin both played important roles in fraternal organizations and in the Zionist movement. Two nationally known businessmen and philanthropists, Jacob Ziskind and Albert A. List, were from Fall River. Another resident, Dr. Irving Fradkin, inaugurated Dollars for Scholars, an educational funding program which has been adopted by communities throughout the United States.

From their arrival in Fall River, Jews were involved in peddling and in operating small retail establishments. Many Jewish-owned businesses suffered as a result of the 1904 textile strike. Later, large furniture and retail clothing stores were established, and Jews engaged in finance and in operating textile mills. Although textile production has decreased, many Jews are involved in garment contracting; others are professionals, small retailers, and landlords. The declining Jewish population in Fall River can be attributed to a high rate of intermarriage as well as to increased social and physical mobility; Somerset and Highlands are new areas of Jewish residence.

[Bernard Wax]

FALTICENI (Rom. **Fălticeni**), town in Moldavia, N.E. Romania. The first Jews settled there between 1772 and 1774, and an organized community existed from 1780, when the town was officially founded under the name of Şoldăneşti, later changed to Fălticeni, as a commercial center between Austrian Bukovina and Moldavia. In 1781 the landowner permitted the building of a synagogue in the form of a regular house and put a plot for a cemetery at the disposal of the community. Many of the Jews were Sadgora ḥasidim or belonged to Chabad. Several leaders of the community were killed by Greek revolutionaries in 1821, because the Jews were unable to pay them the money they demanded. The community numbered 1,500 in 1803, 5,767 in 1859 (63.5% of the total), 5.499 in 1899, 4,751 in 1910 and 4,216 in 1930 (36.6%). Up to World War I the majority of the Jews in Falticeni were occupied in crafts, and the rest in commerce. Jewish traders held an annual fair there. The community had a hospital, an old age home, 11 synagogues, a *talmud* torah and two schools (for boys and girls). Among the rabbis were Joshua Falik (1835–1915), author of Torah studies; Aryeh Leib Rosen (d. 1950), author of responsa published in *Eitan Aryeh*; and Alter Dorf. The Jewish scholar Solomon Zalman *Schechter also lived in Falticeni, where he studied Torah. Other prominent figures were the Hebrew writer Mattitiyahu Simḥah Rabener, director of the Israelite-Romanian school (in the 1860s and 1870s); the traveler Israel Joseph Benjamin (*Benjamin II); the painter Rubin Zelicovici (Reuven *Rubin; later emigrated to Israel); the mathematician David Rimer (later emigrated to Israel); and the journalist Ḥayyim Rimer, former director of the Jewish periodical of Romania *Revista Cultului Mozaic* (1980–94) At the end of the 19th and beginning of the 20th centuries a Zionist organization led by Shulem Mayer was active. After World War I, when Bukovina was incorporated within Romania, Falticeni ceased to be a border town and the economic situation of the Jews deteriorated. In the 1930s members of the antisemitic parties organized the looting of Jewish shops and forcibly prevented Jews from attending the annual fair.

Holocaust Period

There were 4,020 Jews living in Falticeni in 1941, about one-third of the total population. Under the Fascist regime (September 1940–January 1941) a "Green House" was set up in the center of town, where Jewish merchants were brought and tortured until they agreed to pay for their release. On the eve of war with the Soviet Union (June 1941), a German headquarters was set up in the town and the synagogues were expropriated to be used as military barracks. All male Jews were concentrated in camps, from which 1,000 were sent on to Bessarabia for forced labor; those wealthy enough were able to ransom themselves. More Jews were sent on forced labor far from their homes, where a number perished in the harsh conditions. Falticeni was evacuated in the spring of 1944, at the approach of the Soviet Army. The Jews took refuge in Suceava and Botosani and returned six months later to find their houses stripped of all their possessions. By the time the other inhabitants had returned, the Jews had succeeded in restoring public services both in the town itself and throughout the district.

The Jewish population numbered 4,700 in 1947, but decreased to 3,000 in 1950. In 1944–48 a Jewish secondary school functioned. In 1969 there were about 150 families with one synagogue. In 1994, 51 Jews lived in Falticeni. In Israel there is an organization of Jews from Falticeni.

BIBLIOGRAPHY: A. Gorovei, *Folticeni* (1938); PK Romanyah, 188–92; E. Schwarzfeld, in: *Egalitatea*, 22 (1911), 162–3, 170–1, 178–9, 186–7, 194–5; idem, *Împopularea, reîmpopularea şi întemeierea tîrgurilor şi tîrguşoarelor din Moldova* (1914), 24–26; M. Schwarzfeld, in: *Analele Societății Istorice Iuliu Barasch*, 2, pt. 1 (1888), 65, 73; W. Filderman, in: *Sliha*, 1 no. 3(1956), 3; 1 no. 4 (1956), 3. **ADD. BIBLIOGRAPHY:** O. Bacalu, D. Rimer, and N. Vaintraub (eds.), *Fălticeni* (1995).

[Theodor Lavi / Lucian-Zeev Herscovici (2nd ed.)]

FALUDY, GYÖRGY (1913–2006), Hungarian poet and author; born in Budapest. He translated François Villon's poetry into Hungarian (*Villon balladái*, 1937). In 1939 Faludy fled to France and eventually settled in the United States, where he volunteered for service in the U.S. Army. He returned to Hungary in 1946 and devoted himself to writing and journalism. Five years later he was arrested on a political charge, and was released from prison in 1953. Faludy then joined the editorial board of the literary journal *Irodalmi Ujság*. It was in this paper that in 1956 he published a poem about his experiences in prison. At the time, the publication of the poem was regarded as an indication of the liberalization of the regime. Almost immediately, however, the failure of the revolution forced him to flee the country once again. This time he went to England, where he resumed publication of *Irodalmi Ujság*. Faludy's works include *A pompéji strázsán* ("On the Guard at Pompei," 1938); *Európai költők antológiája* ("An Anthology of European Poets," 1938); and the prose works *Tragoedie eines Volkes* (1958) and *Emlékkönyv a rót Bizáncról* ("Memories of Red Byzantium," 1961). In 1962 he published his autobiography, *My Happy Days in Hell*, in English. Faludy's works in Hungarian were burned by the Nazis and in later years confiscated by the Communists.

BIBLIOGRAPHY: *Magvar Irodalmi Lexikon*, 1 (1963), 327.

[Baruch Yaron]

FAMILIANTS LAWS (*Familiantengesetze*; Heb. *Gezerat ha-Sheniyyot* in allusion to Yev. 2:4 (20a)), legislation regulating the number of Jews in Bohemia, Moravia, and Silesia entitled to found families. The laws were introduced by *Charles VI in 1726–27 to curtail the number of the Jewish population. The number of families fixed was 8,451 for Bohemia, 5,106 for Moravia, and 119 for Silesia. The laws were expressly confirmed, with certain modifications (see below), by Joseph II in his Toleranzpatent of 1781. The structure of the Familiants system was basically the same for all three regions. In Bohemia the apportionment of the number of families was allotted to the *Kreis* (district) authorities, while in Moravia the communities themselves, which were more compact and exercised a relatively strong autonomy, had more influence in the apportionment. The regulations remained, with some alleviations, in force until 1848. According to this system no Jew could marry and found a family unless he possessed one of the "family numbers" (*Familiennummern*). This could only be transferred to the eldest son (at the age of 24) after the death of the Familiant. A younger son (but not a daughter) could inherit the number only after the death of an older brother. The family numbers were carefully registered by the district authorities in the *Familiantenbuch* (register of Familiants), and candidates for obtaining one in the *Kompetentenbuch*. If a Familiant had daughters only, his Familiant "number" (*Familiantenstelle*) expired. In addition, Jews were permitted to reside only in places to which they had been admitted before 1726, and within these they were limited to special quarters, streets, and even houses (*Judenhaeuser-židovny*). Violations of the regulations could be punished by flogging and expulsion.

The Toleranzpatents and other laws, such as the Systemalpatent (see *Bohemia) of 1797, introduced various changes in the Familiants system. The numbers were increased to 8,600 for Bohemia and 5,400 for Moravia. Alleviations were introduced which tended to favor the upper or professional strata in Jewish society, marriage permits being granted for second or third sons against high payments. On request for a marriage permit the applicant had to prove that he possessed 300 florins (in Prague 500). From 1786 a certificate to prove that he had attended a German or Jewish-German school was required, and from 1812 he had to take an examination in the catechism *Benei Ẓiyyon*, drawn up by Naphtali Herz *Homberg. Marriage permits could also be given to those taking up agriculture or a guild craft, or after military service. Communal employees were generally permitted to marry as "supernumeraries," but they were not allowed to transfer their permits to their eldest sons.

The Familiants system forced many Jews to marry secretly ("*Bodenchassines*," "attic weddings") or "*pod pokličkou*" ("under cover"). The children of such couples were considered illegitimate by the authorities and had to bear their mothers' names. It was not until 1847 that the fathers were permitted to acknowledge their fatherhood in the records and thus a quasi-legitimacy was established. In one instance, in Prostejov (Prossnitz) in 1841, some women who had "illegitimate" children were sentenced to forced labor and only released by special favor.

Because of the Familiants system a large number of Jews were not able to settle anywhere permanently; they wandered about the country, and contributed largely to developing a Jewish beggar group (see *Begging and Beggars). People in this category lived virtually outside the law, deprived of any economic status or regular means of livelihood. The system gave rise to conflicts within the communities, and led to tensions in Jewish society, which had before been relatively homogeneous despite the social differences. Lawsuits before secular authorities, denunciations, bribery, and sale of expired family numbers to higher bidders from outside the community instead of transfer to candidates within it were frequent occurrences. In disrupting Jewish family life the Familiants system became one of the causes of *assimilation. It also led to large-scale emigration from these areas. Many of the communities in Hungary (Slovakia) were founded by the younger sons of Moravian Jewish families.

It is significant that although in movements of Jewish enlightenment (see *Haskalah) the Familiants Laws were occasionally referred to as "pharaonic laws," no attempts were made to protest against them, and only in the 1840s, and even then anonymously, were thoughts in that strain raised in journals and poems.

With the March Revolution of 1848 the Familiants system ceased to be effective, although formal abolition was only decreed in 1859. The numerus clausus on marriage and closure of areas to Jews ceased. The corpus of legal enactments on Jews in Bohemia and Moravia is collected in H. Kopetz, *Versuch einer systematischen Darstellung der in Boehmen bezueglich der Juden bestehenden Gesetze und Verordnungen* (1846) and H. Scari, *Systematische Darstellung der in Betreff der Juden in Maehren und im K.K. Antheile Schlesiens erlassenen Gesetze und Verordnungen* (1835), index; see also *Bavaria and *Prussia.

Echoes of the Familiants system are found in belletristic writings by Jewish authors, such as Leopold *Kompert's "*Ohne Bewilligung*" ("Without Permit") and Vojtěch *Rakous' *Na rozcesti* ("On the Crossroads").

BIBLIOGRAPHY: A. Frankl-Gruen, *Geschichte der Juden in Kremsier*, 1 (1896), 29–30; Th. Haas, *Die Juden in Maehren* (1908), 5–11, 58–64; A. Stein, *Geschichte der Juden in Boehmen* (1904), 108–10; A.F. Pribram, *Urkunden und Akten zur Geschichte der Juden in Wien*, 1–2 (1918), index; H. Flesch, in: MGJW, 71 (1927), 267–74; R. Rosenzweig, in: ZGJT, 2 (1931), 38–44; 3 (1932/33), 61–71; A. Grotte, *ibid.*, 209–12; I. Herrisch, in: JGGJC, 4 (1932), 497–99; R. Mahler, *Divrei Yemei Yisrael*, 1 pt. 2 (1954^2), 207–15; Y. Z Kahana, in: *Zion*, 8 (1943), 203–6; R. Kestenberg-Gladstein, *Neuere Geschichte der Juden in den boehmischen Laendern*, 1 (1969), index; idem, in: *Tarbiz*, 29 (1960), 293–4; idem, in: *Jews of Czechoslovakia*, 1 (1968), 21–22, 29, 30; idem, in: *Field of Yiddish*, 3 (1969), 305–9.

[Ruth Kestenberg-Gladstein]

FAMILY.

In the Bible

An accurate sociological description of the family and its legal status in biblical times is virtually impossible because the relevant evidence is not of a strictly socio-descriptive nature.

SOURCES. Some of the most often quoted examples of family life and its functions come from literary passages in the epic tradition. Thus, one finds considerable attention given to the interaction of various members in the patriarchal community. The history of the Israelite people is predicated on the Divine promise made to its eponymous ancestor Israel and his progenitors. The different branches of the tribal league are traced back to the sons born to Israel by his four wives, and neighboring peoples are judged according to their ancestral relationship to the Hebrew patriarchs. The framework of these relationships is literary, taking the form of stories about the family life of Abraham and his descendants. Other important figures such as Moses and Aaron are also identified by their family ties with the Levitical tribe. Another focal point for tales of family life is the period of occupation and settlement in the land. Family glimpses are afforded of such heroic figures as Caleb and his daughter, Gideon, and Samson. The prophet Samuel and the first Israelite monarchs are also cast in vivid family portraits.

The lack of suitable documents dealing with everyday life (see below) makes it necessary to utilize these literary allusions to family life in developing a picture of the family in biblical times. It should be noted, however, that there are sometimes discrepancies between the situation reflected in biblical narratives and that reflected in legal texts (e.g., marriage to a half-sister, while forbidden in Lev. 18:9, 20:17, and Deut. 27:22, is recorded in Gen. 20:12, in connection with Abraham and Sarah, and the possibility is indicated in II Sam. 13:13, in connection with Amnon and Tamar). A gap between law and practice would not be surprising, and perhaps it is this which is reflected in the divergence between the legal and narrative traditions.

A second source of information is genealogies, found especially in Genesis (pertaining to the patriarchs and other ancient figures) and in I Chronicles (giving the family trees of the main tribal leaders and groups), but also scattered throughout the epic passages of the Pentateuch (e.g., the genealogies of Moses and Aaron).

In poetical compositions, too, one sometimes finds allusions to marriage or to marital relationships (e.g., the prophetic allegory of Ezek. 16 and the depiction of the ideal wife in Prov. 31:10–31).

Strictly legislative materials are unfortunately few and of limited scope. Leviticus 18 and 20 gives the "forbidden degrees," i.e., a list of those relationships which are consanguineous and therefore make marriage forbidden (see below). Numbers 5:11–31 describes the ritual process for testing a woman suspected by her husband of infidelity. A case in the epic tradition is cited as a precedent for the inheritance rights of daughters in the absence of sons (Num. 26:28–34; 27:1–11; 36:10–12; Josh. 17:1–6). Social legislation pertaining specifically to the family is found primarily in Deuteronomy. The legal responsibility of the bride to be a virgin (if advertised as such) when entering into marriage and certain subsidiary matters, such as intercourse with a marriageable girl before marriage, are dealt with in Deuteronomy 22:13–23:1. The process of *divorce is outlined (in only the briefest form) in Deuteronomy 24:1–4, while military exemption for a new bridegroom is prescribed in verse 5 of the same chapter. The laws relating to *levirate marriage appear in Deuteronomy 25:5–10. Apart from scattered verses on miscellaneous aspects of family status, these are the main legal passages on the subject of family law. It is obvious from this brief survey that many basic themes are neglected entirely.

Unlike the discoveries from other cultures in the ancient Near East, the discoveries from ancient Israel have yielded no strictly legal documents pertaining to marriage. Mesopotamia has yielded hundreds of contracts and other types of documents, many of which are marriage arrangements. Much has been learned from such documents found at Nuzi, and the *Elephantine papyri include a marriage contract. That such documents were used by the Israelites is clear: it is known, for example, that a marriage was dissolved by giving the wife a *sefer keritut* ("writ of separation," Deut. 24:1, 3; Isa. 50:1; Jer. 3:8). The earliest direct reference to a Jewish marriage contract (apart from the one in the Elephantine papyri) is in the apocryphal Book of Tobit, where it is written that Raguel "… took a scroll and wrote out the contract and they affixed their seals to it" (Tob. 7:14). These scattered allusions seem to confirm that marriage contracts were used in ancient Israel; the lack of direct evidence is apparently accidental.

THE FAMILY UNIT. The Israelite family as reflected in all genealogical and narrative sources is patriarchical. Attempts have been made to find traces of matriarchy and fratriarchy in the earliest stages of Israel's history, but none of the arguments is convincing (see below).

The family was aptly termed *bet av* ("house of a father"; e.g., Gen. 24:38; 46:31). To found a family was "to build a house" (Deut. 25:10). The *bayit* ("house") was a subdivision of the *mishpaḥah* ("clan, family [in the larger sense]," Josh. 7:14). The criterion for membership in a family (in the wider sense) was blood relationship, legal ties (e.g., marriage), or geographical proximity. The genealogies of I Chronicles sometimes speak of the clan leader as the "father" of a town, or towns, in his district (e.g., I Chron. 2:51, 52). A common livelihood or profession was probably a major factor in family and clan solidarity. Besides those families who engaged primarily in agriculture (conducted on their own lands), there were others who practiced some specific trade (e.g., they were linen workers, I Chron. 4:21, or potters, I Chron. 4:23). The sacerdotal functions of the Levites and the sons of Aaron are the most striking case in point.

Family solidarity is reflected in customs such as blood revenge (Num. 35:9–34; Deut. 19:1–13). Not only was this vengeance exacted upon members of another clan who had killed a kinsman (II Sam. 3:22–27, 30), but even within the framework of a clan, the members of a particular family were responsible for exacting the death penalty when another member of their family was killed in an intra-family murder (II Sam. 14:4–11). The avenger (*go'el*) also had other responsibilities. A near kinsman was required to redeem a relative who had been forced by penury to sell himself into slavery (Lev. 25:47–49). The same obligation held true for family property that had been sold because of poverty (Lev. 25:25; cf. Jer. 32:7). The Book of Ruth refers to this custom but is complicated by the requirement that the surviving widow also be taken (more or less in line with the Levirate practice (Deut. 15:5–10)). The family was a religious as well as a social unit (Ex. 12:3; I Sam. 20:6, 29; Job. 1:5; see *Education).

CONSANGUINITY. The ties of blood relationship that forbade sexual relations are spelled out in order to prevent ritual violations (Lev. 18:6–18; 20:11–14, 17, 19–21). One's consanguineous relatives, "near kin" (*she'er besaro*), as thus defined, were the father (*av*), mother (*em*), father's wife (*eshet av*), sister (*aḥot*) –

whether the daughter of the father or the mother, granddaughter – whether the daughter of a son or of a daughter, daughter of the wife of one's father (*bat-eshet av*), the father's sister, the mother's sister, the father's brother and his wife – the aunt (*dodah*), the son's wife (*kallah*) – in biblical terms, the "bride" in relation to the parents of her husband, and the brother's wife (*eshet a*). It was forbidden to take a woman and her daughter (Lev. 18:17; stated conversely, a woman and her mother, Lev. 20:14) or granddaughter; likewise a man was prohibited from taking his wife's sister (called *ẓarah*, a "rival") while his wife was still alive (Lev. 18:18; contrast Jacob's marriage to Leah and Rachel).

FUNCTIONS OF FAMILY MEMBERS. The respective functions and status of these persons are reflected in scattered passages. The father was the head of the family unit and owner of its property (Num. 26:54–55). He was the chief authority and, as such, is portrayed as commanding (Gen. 50:16; Jer. 35:6–10; Prov. 6:20) and rebuking (Gen. 37:10; Num. 12:14). Ideally he was expected to be benevolent, to show love to his family (Gen. 25:28; 37:4; 44:20) and also pity (Ps. 103:13). The patriarchal blessing (Gen. 27) evidently carried legal force with regard to the distribution of the patrimony and other attendant privileges.

The mother, if she were the senior wife of a harem or the sole wife of a monogamous marriage, occupied a place of honor and authority in spite of her subordination to her husband (see below). At his death she might become the actual, and probably the legal, head of the household (II Kings 8:1–6) if there were no sons of responsible age. As a widow, she was especially vulnerable to oppression; concern for her welfare was deemed a measure of good government and wholesome society (e.g., Deut. 24:17). The influence of famous mothers in epic tradition, e.g., Sarah (Gen. 21:12) and the wife of Manoah (Judg. 13:23), is illustrative of the significance attached to their role. Not all of their power was exercised openly; often the motherly stratagem is deemed worthy of special notice in the epic tradition, e.g., the stratagems of Rebekah (Gen. 27:5–17), Leah (Gen. 30:16), and Rachel (Gen. 31:34). The mother naturally displayed care and love (Gen. 25:28; Isa. 49:15; 66:13; Prov. 4:3).

The role of the queen mother (*gevirah*) stands out in several instances (e.g., I Kings 2:19; 15:13; cf. II Chron. 15:16). The almost uniform practice of naming the mother of the newly crowned Judahite king (e.g., I Kings 14:21) may be a reflection of her special status, but not necessarily. The biblical narrative was evidently concerned with keeping track of the royal heirs by this means, perhaps in order to stress the particular family or region whose daughter had gained the distinction of having her son rise to the throne (cf. II Kings 21:19 and 23:36 where the Galilean origin of the kings' mothers is indicated). It is not certain that in every case the son of the chief wife gained the succession.

The greatest misfortune that could befall a woman was childlessness (Gen. 30:23; I Sam. 1). Children were a blessing from the Almighty (Ps. 127:3–5); they assured the continuance of the family name (Num. 27:4, 8; 36:8b). The mother was more directly involved in the early training of the children than was the father (Prov. 1:8). When the children grew older, the father assumed responsibility for instructing the son (Gen. 18:19; Ex. 12:26–27; 13:8, 14, 15; Deut. 6:7), while the mother evidently kept charge of the daughter until marriage (Micah 7:6). Children were exhorted to honor both parents (Ex. 20:12; Deut. 5:16), and the inclusion of this command in the Decalogue probably accounts for the threatened death penalty to offenders (Ex. 21:15; Lev. 20:9; Deut. 27:16). The decline in respect for parents was symptomatic of the dissolution of society (Ezek. 22:7; Micah 7:6; Prov. 20:20). The demonstration of this respect was primarily through obedience (Gen. 28:7; Lev. 19:3; Deut. 21:18–21; Prov. 1:8; 30:17). Parental control included the right to sell daughters in marriage, although there were limitations on selling her into slavery (Ex. 21:7–11; cf. 22:15–16; Neh. 5:5), and an absolute ban on selling her for prostitution (Lev. 19:29). The father could annul his daughter's vows (Num. 30:4–6), and damages were paid to him for a wrong done to her (Ex. 22:15–16; Deut. 22:28–29). A daughter who was widowed or divorced might return to her father's household (Gen. 38:11, Lev. 22:13; Ruth 1:15).

The terms "brother" (*aḥ*) and "sister" (*aḥot*) applied both to offspring of the same father and mother (Gen. 4:2) as well as to offspring who had only one common parent, either a father (Gen. 20:12) or mother (Gen. 43:7; Lev. 18:9; 20:17). Attempts have been made to find traces of a fratriarchal system in the most ancient Israelite traditions; e.g., in Laban's role (Gen. 24) as head of the family when his sister Rebekah was sent to marry Isaac. Laban's role, however, can be explained without recourse to fratriarchy; Laban, as the direct descendant of Nahor (Gen. 24:15, 29; 29:5), certainly was slated to become head of the family after his own father's demise. Another biblical incident, the concern of Jacob's sons after the humiliation of their sister, whom they called their "daughter" (Gen. 34:17), can also be understood in this way.

Brotherly solidarity is frequently stressed (e.g., Prov. 17:17), and harmony among brothers was held up as an ideal (Ps. 133:1). Brothers were obligated to avenge each other's murder (II Sam. 3:27) as part of their duty as *go'el* ("defender" or "redeemer"; Num. 35:19–28; Deut. 19:6; Josh. 20:3; II Sam. 14:11). Another aspect of this responsibility was the requirement that one ransom a brother who had been taken captive or had gone into servitude as the result of financial adversity (Lev. 25:48; Ps. 49:8; cf. Neh. 5:8).

The term "brother" is often extended to more distant relatives, e.g., nephews (e.g., Gen. 13:8; 14:14), fellow tribesmen (Lev. 21:10), and others (Deut. 2:4, 8; 23:8).

Other members of the immediate family were the paternal uncle (*dod*; e.g., Lev. 10:4; 20:20) and the paternal aunt (*dodah*; the father's sister, Ex. 6:20; and the wife of the father's brother, Lev. 18:14; 20:20); also cousins (male, *ben-dod*, Lev. 25:49; Num. 36:11; female, *bat-dod*, Esth. 2:7).

MARRIAGE AND ADOPTION. Though a man left his parents when he married (Gen. 2:24), he normally remained a member of his father's family. In relation to his wife, he was "master" (*ba'al*; e.g., Gen. 20:3; Ex. 21:3, 22; Lev. 21:4; Deut. 24:4). He "took" her from her parents, or she was "given" to him by her father, or by her master or mistress, if she was a slave (Gen. 2:22; 16:3; 34:9, 21). The marriage agreement, which, judging from neighboring cultures, was probably set down in a written contract, was made between the husband and either the bride's father alone (Gen. 29; 34:16; Ex. 22:16; Deut. 22:29; Ruth 4:10) or both her parents (Gen. 21:21; 24). The marriage negotiations might result from an attraction that had already developed between two young people (e.g., Samson and the Philistine girl, Judg. 14), but generally the father must have taken the initiative since evidently he had the right to determine who would be his daughter's spouse (Caleb, Josh. 15:16; Saul, I Sam. 18:17, 19, 21, 27; 25:44). If a man seduced a virgin, he had to pay her bride-price to her father, who could, at his own discretion, give his daughter to this man in marriage or withhold her from him (Ex. 22:15). However, if he forced her, he was obligated to marry her and pay her price, and had no right ever to divorce her (Deut. 22:28–29).

Generally, prior to the consummation of the marriage a *betrothal was entered into; under this arrangement the bride-price (*mohar*) was established (Gen. 34:12; Ex. 22:16; I Sam. 18:25), accompanied by a gift (*mattan*; Gen. 34:12). A time limit was set by which the payments were to be completed and the marriage put into effect (I Sam. 18:17–19, 26:27). The engagement was a legal transaction in the fullest sense. An engaged man was exempt from military service (Deut. 20:7). The legal status of a betrothed virgin was such that she was prohibited to other men. If someone besides her fiancé had intercourse with her, she was held guilty of adultery. If the act took place in town, where she could have cried for help, the woman was equally guilty; but if it happened in the country she was exonerated by the benefit of the doubt – perhaps she did cry out and was not heard (Deut. 22:23–27).

The essence of the *marriage ceremony seems to have been the transfer of the bride to the house of the groom. He would don a turban (Isa. 61:10) and proceed with his companions to the house of the bride. There the bride, richly attired (Isa. 61:10; Ps. 45:14–15) and veiled (Song 4:1, 3; 6:7; cf. Gen. 24:65; 29:23–25), awaited him. She was then conducted to the house of the bridegroom (Gen. 24:67; Ps. 45:15–16). The festivities included songs extolling the virtues of the bridal pair (Jer. 16:9) – Psalms 45 and Song of Songs evidently represent such compositions – and a feast of seven days (Gen. 29:22–27; Judg. 14:10–12) or even a fortnight (Tob. 8:20). Unusual circumstances might require that the feast be at the home of the bride's parents, but under normal circumstances it must have taken place at the home of the groom. The marriage was consummated on the first night (Gen. 29:23), and the bride's nuptial attire (*simlah*) was kept afterward as evidence of her virginity (*betulim*; Deut. 22:13–21).

The modern definitions of *monogamy and polygamy are not strictly applicable to the ancient world. It was normal for the head of a household to have only one legal, full-fledged wife (Heb. *ishshah*; Akk. *aššatu*); if she were barren, the husband had the right to take a concubine who was often the handmaiden of his wife (Gen. 16:1–2; 29:15–30; 30:1ff.). However, a man might take two wives of equal standing (Gen. 26:34; 28:9; 29:15–30; 36:2–5; I Sam. 1:2). In that case the law forbade his depriving his firstborn son of his legitimate double portion in the interests of the son of the other wife, should she be the favorite (Deut. 21:15–17). Royal polygamy (Deut. 17:17; I Kings 11:1–8) was partly a reflection of foreign policy, each new addition to the harem representing a new or renewed treaty relationship. Heroic leaders would also be expected to have numerous wives and to father many offspring (Judg. 8:30–31; I Sam. 25:42–43).

Living with her husband, the wife was normally close to her husband's father (*ḥam*; I Sam. 4:19, 21) and mother (*ḥamot*; Ruth passim; Micah 7:6). Occasions when the groom stayed with the bride's parents (*ḥoten*, e.g., Ex. 18:1; *ḥotenet*, Deut. 27:23) are noted in the Bible precisely because they were not the norm. Heroic figures such as Moses and Jacob (cf. also Sinuhe, the hero of an Egyptian historical novel) were forced because of unusual circumstances to spend long periods with their in-laws.

When her father died, a woman's brother would perform all the duties of the *ḥoten* (Gen. 24:50, 55). Brothers- and sisters-in-law were considered too closely related to marry (Lev. 18:16, 18; 20:21), except in the case of the husband's brother (*yavam*), who was expected to fulfill the Levirate responsibility.

*Adoption is clearly demonstrated in the case of Jacob's accepting Manasseh and Ephraim as sons (Gen. 48:5); parallels from other ancient Near Eastern cultures have been noted. The absorption of various clans, e.g., the *Calebites and Jerahmeelites into the tribe of Judah, suggests that adoption may have been more widespread in Israelite society. Divine adoption of the king seems to be reflected in certain passages (II Sam. 7:14; Ps. 2:7). It has been suggested, on the basis of parallel customs from Nuzi, that Abraham had adopted Eliezer, his chief servant (Gen. 15:2), and that Laban had also adopted Jacob before sons of his own were born (Gen. 31:1–2). The evidence is too scanty for firm conclusions, but one would be surprised if no adoption whatever was practiced (cf. the metaphorical use of adoption symbolism (Ezek. 16:1–7; Hos. 11:1–4)).

[Anson Rainey]

Post-Biblical

The subject of the family in the post-biblical period is considered here under two aspects:

(a) family in its wider sense of individuals related by marriage or consanguinity, and

(b) the smaller unit consisting of parents and children.

THE LARGER FAMILY UNIT. There is no doubt that the word "family" was used in this sense, i.e., the descendants of an eponymous ancestor, and various families are referred to in the Talmud, such as the families of Bet Zerifa (Kid. 71a), Bet Zevaim and Bet Kupai (Yev. 15b), and Bet Dorkati (Ket. 10b). Among the priestly families, a completely pure and unsullied genealogy was rigidly insisted upon. It took the most extreme forms, and it was laid down that "they set a higher standard in matters of priestly descent" (Ket. 13a). Josephus, who prided himself on his priestly descent (Life, 1:1), states that the genealogies of the priests were carefully preserved in the archives of the Temple. The attempt of the Pharisees to remove John Hyrcanus (I) from his office of high priesthood (Kid. 66a; cf. Jos., Ant., 13:10, 288–92) and the pathetic incident of R. Zechariah b. ha-Kaẓav, a priest, who was forced to divorce his wife, despite his oath that he had not left her for a moment during their capture by enemy soldiery (Ket. 2:9), are both based on the law that a woman who had been taken captive by non-Jewish soldiers was forbidden to marry a *kohen*.

What was obligatory and mandatory for priestly families was regarded as desirable for non-priestly families. Most of the last chapter of the talmudic tractate *Kiddushin* deals with this question, with the aim of ensuring the purity of the family. Both purity of descent and eugenic considerations were regarded as important: "A man should not marry into a family which has a recurrent history of epilepsy or leprosy" (Yev. 64b). The responsibility of the individual member of a family toward the good name of the family as a whole is constantly stressed: "A family is like a heap of stones. Remove one, and the whole structure can collapse" (Gen. R. 100:7). "Woe unto him who sullies his children and his family" (Kid. 70a) and "whosoever brings disrepute upon himself brings disrepute upon his whole family" (Num. R. 21:3). This regard for the good name of the family as a whole gave rise to the impressive ceremony of *Keẓaẓah in which "all the members of the family" participated when one of them "married a woman who was not worthy of them" (Ket. 28b).

There were "aristocratic families of Israel" on whom alone "the Holy One, blessed be He, causes his Divine Spirit to rest" (Kid. 70b). They alone were regarded as worthy of marrying into the priestly families. The status of certain families as "pure and impure" and as "sullied and unsullied" was well known (Ket. 28b.). It was regarded as a meritorious act to marry the daughter of a scholar (Pes. 49a), and genealogical lists were drawn up, and carefully preserved (Pes. 62b; Yev. 49b). The last *mishnah* of Ta'anit (4:8) records an ancient custom that on the 15th of Av and on the Day of Atonement the young men of Jerusalem used to go out in the vineyards to choose their brides, and the maidens adjured them saying; "Young man, lift up thine eyes and see what thou art choosing for thyself. Set not thine eyes on beauty; set thine eyes on family." On the other hand, a blind eye was turned to a family in which it was known that there had been an undesirable admixture which could not be traced (Kid. 71a). During the talmudic period, the marked tendency of descendants to continue the calling or the profession of their forebears is referred to in a statement justifying the fact that retribution is taken in the case of the worshiper of Moloch "from the man and his family" (Lev. 20:5). "If he sinned, in what did his family sin? Because there is not a family containing a publican of which all the members are not publicans or containing a thief in which they are not all thieves" (Shev. 39a). Mention is also made of "families of scribes, which produce scribes, of scholars who produce scholars, and of plutocrats who produce plutocrats" (Eccl. R. 4:9). This emphasis on the worthiness of the families as a prime consideration in choosing one's life partner has persisted throughout the social life of the Jews. It was commonplace among East European Jews for the parents of the potential bride or bridegroom to ensure that the parents should be such as "one could sit down with them at table." It is an interesting fact that in Hebrew and in Yiddish there is a word (*mechutan*) to designate the relationship established between the parents of the bride and the parents of the bridegroom, or between the respective families.

THE SMALLER FAMILY UNIT. In Jewish social life and tradition the family constitutes perhaps the most closely knit unit in any society. All members of the family, husband and wife, parents and children, are bound by mutual ties of responsibility.

Although in theory polygamy is permitted by both Bible and Talmud, the ideal set forward is always of husband, wife, and children forming one unit. The passage from Psalms, "it shall be well with thee, thy wife shall be a fruitful vine in the innermost part of thy house; thy children like olive plants round about thy table" (Ps. 128:2–3), formed the basis of innumerable homilies on the part of the rabbis extolling the virtue of domestic bliss (cf. Tanh. Va-Yishlaḥ; ser 18, etc.). The family was regarded as the smallest social unit through which the cultural and religious heritage of Judaism can be transmitted.

Where Christianity glorified celibacy and monasticism as the highest ideal and a means of extolling the virtue of chastity, Judaism extolled the institution of marriage and the family. It is significant of the difference in outlook that whereas Paul regarded celibacy as the highest virtue and only reluctantly gave permission to marry, "But if they cannot contain, let them marry; for it is better to marry than burn" (i.e., incur the death penalty of burning for incest and adultery; I Cor. 7:9), a Midrash attributes the death of Nadab and Abihu, the two sons of Aaron, "from a fire from the Lord" (Lev. 10:2) to the fact that in their arrogance they refused to marry (Lev. R. 20:10). The rabbis pointed to the verse "He created it [the world] not a waste, he formed it to be inhabited" (Is. 45:18) as a justification for the religious duty not only of marrying but of setting up a family. R. Eliezer went so far as to regard the man who does not marry and shirks the duty of rearing children as equivalent to a murderer (Tosef., Yev. 8:4). The Mishnah (Yev. 6:6) lays it down as a duty to procreate, in accordance with Gen. 1:28 "Be fruitful and multiply," the minimum number of children for its fulfillment being two (according to Bet Shammai two male children; according to Bet Hillel one male and one female). So essentially was this regarded as the purpose of marriage that according to the same Mishnah not only was a man permitted, but even enjoined, to divorce his wife after ten years of barrenness.

The discussion in the Babylonian Talmud to this Mishnah (60b–63a) is replete with statements emphasizing the sacred nature of this duty and the joy, beauty, and sanctity of the Jewish home. It includes such statements as "He who has no wife lives without joy, without blessing, and without goodness"; "of that man who loves his wife as himself, honors her more than himself, who guides his sons and daughters in the right way, and arranges for their early marriage, Scripture says 'and thou shalt know that thy tent is peace' (Job. 5:24)."

The family unit was regarded as a closed one. The spontaneous blessing of Balaam "How goodly are thy tents, O Jacob" (Num. 24:5) was inspired by the fact that he saw that "the doors [of their houses] were not opened opposite those of their neighbors" (cf. Rashi *ad loc.*). The wife was supposed largely to confine herself to her household duties and strangers were somewhat discouraged, despite the emphasis placed upon the duty of hospitality. The wife and mother was the undisputed mistress of the home.

Children are a divine trust (cf. the story of the death of R. Meir's two children, Yal. Prov. 964). It was the father's duty to teach his child religion, to teach him a trade, even to teach him to swim (Kid. 40a), and it was strictly forbidden to a parent to show favoritism to any of his children (Shab. 10b). No duty ranked higher than the fifth commandment, "honor thy father and thy mother" (Ex. 20:12). Domestic harmony was enjoined in the injunction "a man should spend less than his means on food, up to his means on clothes, beyond his means in honoring wife and children, because they are dependent on him" (Ḥul. 84b).

This constant insistence upon the value of the family as a social unit for the propagation of domestic and religious virtues and the significant fact that the accepted Hebrew word for marriage is *kiddushin*, "sanctification," had the result of making the Jewish home the most vital factor in the survival of Judaism and the preservation of the Jewish way of life, much more than the synagogue or school. It was also a major factor for moral purity.

The traditional Jewish home exemplified the maxim "where there is peace and harmony between husband and wife the **Shekhinah* dwells between them." A religious spirit of practical observance pervades it, from the **mezuzah* on the doorpost to the strict observance of the dietary laws in the kitchen. The home was the center of religious practice and ceremonial. Its outstanding expression was the festive meal on Sabbaths and festivals with the kindled candles on the table, the **Kiddush*, **Zemirot*, and Grace before and after Meals. The outstanding such occasion is the *seder* on Passover eve. But there was also the *Sukkah, the morning and night prayers, the blessing of the children by their father on the eve of Sabbath and Festivals, and the blessing of the parents (significantly called "my father, my teacher," and "my mother, my teacher") in the Grace after Meals.

Nor were the social and humane virtues overlooked. The placing of a coin in the charity box (usually for the poor of the Holy Land, the "Meir Ba'al Ha-Nes Fund") initiated the duty of charity; Deut. 11:15 was interpreted to mean that one should feed one's domestic animals before sitting down to one's meal.

Perhaps in nothing was the strength of the family bond more seen than in the paradox that whereas in theory divorce among Jews is the easiest of all processes, in practice it was, until recent times, a comparative and even absolute rarity. The powerful bond which united parents and children in one bond with mutual responsibilities and mutual consideration made it a bulwark of Judaism able to withstand all stresses from without and from within.

See also: Marriage, Husband and Wife, Parent and Child.

[Louis Isaac Rabinowitz]

BIBLIOGRAPHY: BIBLICAL PERIOD: The most important treatment of recent times is that of de Vaux, Anc Isr, 19–55 (incl. bibl., pp. 520–3); see also I. Mendelsohn, in: BA, 11 (1948), 24–40; idem, in: IEJ, 9 (1959), 180–3; R. Patai, *Sex and Family in the Bible and the Middle East* (1959); A.F. Rainey, in: *Orientalia*, 34 (1965), 10–22. POST-BIBLICAL PERIOD: D. Aronson, *The Jewish Way of Life* (1946), 104–123; I. Epstein, *The Jewish Way of Life* (1946), 196–9, 203–5; M.M. Kaplan, *Judaism as a Civilization* (1935), 416–22; I. Maybaum, *The Jewish Home* (1945).

FAMILY, AMERICAN JEWISH.

Introduction

Any discussion of American Jewish family life as an institution must view it within the context of contemporary American social, economic, and political life. All contemporary American Jews are "Jews by choice" in that their relationship with the Jewish people, Judaism, and its institutions is voluntary. They have freedom and feel part of mainstream American life.

The experience of the Jewish family in the United States over the past century has been one of acculturation and accommodation to the norms and values of American society. The diversity within Jewish life precludes a description of an archetypal contemporary American Jewish family. In contrast, according to Glatzer the historic Jewish family – at least in theory (1959) – was (1) patriarchal, (2) three generational, (3) home oriented, (4) pious, and (5) devoted to study, particularly the Bible, Talmud and other Jewish texts. As in all other modern Jewish societies, the majority of Jewish families in the United States today, and perhaps the majority of Jewish families in the typology suggested bear scant resemblance to Glatzer's model of the premodern European Jewish family.

Many Jewish families still share certain distinctive socioeconomic characteristics, i.e., they are middle or upper middle class, are politically to the left of center, and socialize often with other Jews. But many, from day to day, are hardly distinguishable from their non-Jewish neighbors. In a profound way, the religion most practiced by American Jewish families has been America itself, its freedoms, democracy, openness, and unprecedented opportunities.

The transition from tradition and self-segregation characterizes the development of the American Jewish family in the United States. These processes affected virtually every aspect of family life, from size and residential patterns to marriage and career choices. There are some who see this process as having weakened the Jewish family, leading it in the direction of ultimate extinction as a distinctive type; others see evidence of surprising strength and the maintenance of tradition in a world of dramatic change. Often citing the same evidence, they perceive the Jewish family as having successfully transformed itself in response to the conditions of its environment, requiring, perhaps, only some redefinition. The process of change which the Jewish family underwent in America may be divided into four eras: (1) the years defined by mass immigration or its consequences, beginning in 1881 and lasting until the late 1920s, (2) the mid-century era, lasting from about 1930 to the mid-1960s, (3) the decades of the 1970s and 1980s, and (4) the end of the 20th century and the beginning of the 21st.

Immigration

The majority of Jews living in the United States today are third-, fourth-, and fifth-generation descendants of the families of some 2,650,000 immigrants who arrived in America between the last two decades of the 19th century and the first quarter of the 20th century as part of the mass transplantation of peoples from Eastern and Southern Europe. Howe (1976) points out that for Jews, more than for any other European group, this historic migration was a movement of families, signified by the great proportion of females and children who took part in it. Mass migration, which is usually set in motion by an economic or political crisis, war, or natural disaster, disrupts the normal development of family life. "Yet, it was the ferocious loyalty of the Jews to the idea of the family as they knew it, the family both as locus of experience and as fulfillment of their obligation to perpetuate their line, that enabled them to survive (the immigration experience)" (p. 20). However, immigration put an enormous strain on the family. The older generation was often left behind, never to be seen again. Husbands came before their wives and children thus beginning the process of Americanization earlier. Family reunions were often joyous but seldom without problems as both husband and wife had changed in the intervening years; the husband had become more American, the wife had become used to handling family matters. There were also problems of abandonment, of husbands who had disappeared into the great abyss of America.

The majority of Eastern European Jewish families who came to the United States were nominally Orthodox; they were not, though, among the most learned or pious of that generation. Those who were well established in Europe stayed in Europe. "There is little recognition [today] of the fact that a significant group of the post-1905 immigrants had [already] moved away from Jewish culture …" (Sklare, 1971, p. 17). Nevertheless, they held on to a distinctive Jewish ethos and way of life brought from their towns and villages. Within their world, molded by centuries of Jewish tradition, arranged marriages were common, and large families were desirable, if not always achievable. With a high infant mortality rate and the death of young children by disease, for some children to survive, many more had to be born. The husband was the dominant spouse, the primary breadwinner, and the master of the house, at least in theory. Yet, quite often, the wife was forced to work or in business both husband and wife often worked together. The needs of the group, especially one's family, generally took precedence over any one of its members. Personal achievement of boys and men was encouraged, knowing that the rewards would benefit the entire family. The boundaries of family loyalty and commitment generally extended beyond the immediate household to include a wider circle of relatives.

During this period, economic survival was the immediate concern of each family. "Between 1900 and 1920, it can be argued, more American Jews were engaged in a really difficult struggle for existence than at any time before or since" (Glazer, 1965, p. 23). Despite this, when family members assisted one another the difficulties of resettlement were eased. Countless veteran families legally undertook responsibility for new immigrant relatives, helping them find housing and employment, and, when necessary, sharing food, shelter, and clothing, until the newest arrivals were securely settled.

The many hardships of starting life in a new society put great pressures on the functioning of the family. For example, in the lore of the old country the Jewish father was the natural and unchallenged head of the household, respected and feared by all family members. The Jewish mother was revered for her dedication to her husband and the responsibility she assumed for her young children. Upon reaching America these relationships often changed. The difficulty of adult immigrants in parting with the ways of the old country, in learning to read English and speak it without an accent, in finding gainful employment, and in general, mastering the new environment, in many cases led to the reversal of roles between parents and children. "'Green' parents turned to their Americanized children for succor. Parents became children, and children were unwillingly pressed into the role of parents" (Feingold, 1992, p. 38). Young children learned English more readily and it was not uncommon for them to serve as family spokesman when dealing with the school teacher, principal, policemen and other non-Jewish authorities. In addition, thousands of children were removed from school to work in sweatshops or to perform other menial labor in order to guarantee their family's subsistence income. Inevitably, many children, feeling more American than their parents, were embarrassed by the latter's foreignness and derided them for being "greenhorns" – and then often felt guilty for it. Many immigrant families, perhaps those who were initially less stable, experienced various levels of dysfunction in response to these pressures.

A primary source that reflects the struggles and vicissitudes of first generation Jewish families in America is the letters to the editor column of the then popular Yiddish daily, the *Forverts*, a collection known as *A Bintel Brief*. The thousands of letters sent to this column by immigrants, beginning in 1906, bear testimony to the family arguments, difficulties with raising children, infidelity, divorce, and particularly, cases of paternal desertion experienced by many Jewish families. "The number of [Jewish] men who left their families became so great at one time that the *Forverts*, in cooperation with the National Desertion Bureau, established a special column to trace them" (Metzker, 1972, p. 10).

Another source on Jewish family life from this period, *The Jewish Communal Register* (1918), is a compendium of socio-economic and demographic data on approximately a million and a half New York Jews, one-half of all the Jews in the United States at that time. One table, covering the period from 1901 to 1916, compiled by the United Hebrew Charities, indicates a steady decrease, from 11,447 to 6,014, in the number of Jewish families receiving community assistance. As Morris Waldman, at the time the executive director of the Federated Jewish Charities of Boston, pointed out:

> [T]he striking thing is, that in spite of the rapid increase of the Jewish population, due to immigration as well as to natural causes, the number of dependent families has steadily diminished year by year, not only proportionately, but actually… This is particularly gratifying in the light of the fact that the number of dependent families among other elements in the city, judging by the experience of other private relief agencies, has increased in proportion to the increase of their population. This proves that the Jews from eastern European countries are not willing dependents. On the contrary, they make every effort to care for themselves and thus remain self-respecting as well as self-supporting (pp. 991–92).

These words portend the successful social and economic integration of the American Jewish family into American society during the coming decades. America was expanding, jobs were available and workers were needed.

The Mid-Century

Although the challenges of resettlement seemed overwhelming at the time, the Jewish family, in retrospect, stood up to them rather well. The evidence for this is the remarkably rapid social mobility of second-generation American Jews whose parents, in spite of their struggles, saw to their education and general welfare. This second era encompasses approximately 40 years divisible, into two periods. The first began roughly around 1925 and lasted until 1945; the second commenced with the end of World War II and continued until the mid-1960s. During the first 20 years immigrant Jewish families underwent a remarkable social metamorphosis. After World War II they emerged thoroughly Americanized and ready to reap the benefits of the country's post-war economic upsurge.

Quota legislation adopted by Congress in 1921 and 1924, known as the Johnson Acts, effectively ended 40 years of continuous immigration to the United States. With the abatement of mass immigration, the problems of resettlement faded, and the tenor of Jewish community life changed. Those who came in the 1880s and 1890s had been here for decades; their children were American born and American educated. After the mid-1920s, integration into the American mainstream became the most important issue on the Jewish community's agenda.

With impressive speed, masses of Jewish families in cities throughout the United States found the means to relocate from the area of first settlement to a second, more desirable, community. As early as 1925, for example, Brownsville had become the largest center of Jewish population in all of New York City, more populous than the Lower East Side of Manhattan, which many of its inhabitants had left in search of cleaner, healthier, and more spacious living (Landesman, 1969). Geographic mobility, usually the move from a small apartment in an older, run down quarter, to a larger apartment or home in a newer, more prestigious section, was the by-product of social and economic success. The *Menorah Journal* of April 1928 points out:

> In the United States the benefits of equality have now been attained for all practical purposes. Every number of every Jewish weekly in the land points with pride to some Jewish judge or governor, to Jewish bankers, real estate operators and merchants, to members of the faith who are actors and authors and editors, or who have been honored for some success dear to the hearts of their fellow Americans (*ibid.*, p. 361).

Ironically, the process of becoming established took place against a backdrop of significant antisemitism and discrimination which only peaked towards the end of the 1930s. During these years, "gangs attacked Jews on the streets of Brooklyn and other eastern cities with little interference from the police, while organizations calling themselves the Christian Front of the Christian Mobilizers conducted 'Buy Christian' campaigns, cheered the Fuehrer and denounced prominent American Jews" (O'Brien, 1967, p. 271). If nothing else, the effect of antisemitic street violence was reason enough for Jewish families to leave the working class neighborhoods of the Lower East Side of Manhattan, the Bronx, and Brooklyn where older Jewish enclaves bordered the neighborhoods of other immigrant groups. Both intergroup conflict and increasing prosperity stimulated geographic mobility.

By 1920, first-generation Jewish immigrants were outnumbered by their American-born Jewish children who began "asserting themselves in the Jewish community" (Hutchinson, 1956). "As members of the second generation began to strive for the values of the dominant society, they introduced the seeds of conflict into the … community" (Kramer and Leventman, 1961). By the beginning of the 1940s, it was clear that younger Jewish families, by then virtually all second generation Americans, bore the values and cultural patterns of their native land. One observer from that era writes: "Today in America, Jewry, like a chameleon, has taken on the color of its new surroundings. Its soul remains divided between the memory of its Eastern heritage – of traditions nursed through centuries of ghetto life – and the interests of the community, which has received it. Its thought has been cast increasingly in the American vernacular …" (*ibid.*). Typically, second-generation families attenuated the Orthodox rituals, which were the only form of religious Judaism their parents and grandparents had known in Eastern Europe, even if these had not been consistently observed. Kramer and Leventman note that upon becoming adults, the children of immigrants "acquired a middle-class inclination to make distinctions between the sacred and the secular unknown in the ghetto … What the second generation required were religious institutions adapted to the norms of its new status" (*ibid.*, p. 11). Sklare (1972) thus attributes the success of Conservative Judaism during the period 1920–1950 to "its appeal to young marrieds who were in the process of establishing independent households and developing a pattern of Jewish living that would be distinctive to their generation.… Younger Jews who wished to retain continuity with their past and at the same time integrate into American middle-class culture found Conservative Judaism to be the perfect solution to their dilemma" (Sklare, *ibid.*). Both Conservative and Reform Judaism represented a restructuring of European Orthodox religious patterns that appealed more to American Jewish sensibilities. In particular, they sanctioned shorter, mixed-pew Sabbath worship services with greater decorum. For families of both movements, the weekly synagogue service became the main, and for many the only, even if infrequent, family religious activity, with the exception of the Passover seder, Hanukkah candles, or celebrating a family life cycle event, such as a bar or bat mitzvah. The synagogue was used for life cycle events: birth and bar-mitzvah, marriage and death, times of crisis and illness as well as on the High Holidays. One observer spoke of it as a Judaism of "hatch em, match em, patch em and dispatch em."

To be sure, many family traditions brought from Europe endured and were passed on to the first American-born generation. "Certain deeply felt attitudes, well adapted to the conditions of the *shtetl*, were brought … by East European immigrants and transplanted in American soil. If this soil had been completely uncongenial to them, they would be dead and forgotten by now; but the soil was partly congenial, partly inimical" (Yaffe, p. 278). Jewish families saw in the pluralistic nature of American society a tolerance for non-native customs that did not exist in the more highly structured and traditional societies of Europe. This openness helped foster a kind of biculturalism – Jewish and American. Even while seeking to emulate the ways of their new surroundings, most immigrants could not divest themselves of their old country values and norms. As a result, many never felt fully at home in America. By contrast, their children, born in the United States, though only one generation removed from Eastern Europe, saw themselves as American in all respects.

Structural acculturation among second generation Jewish families began as early as the 1920s, says Feingold, and was expressed through:

> A loosening of the ties of kinship, and ultimately the large extended family was replaced by a small nuclear one. Family clans that had settled in the same neighborhood dispersed. The nuclear family was compelled to bear alone the stress of rapid change or decline in fortune. Occasionally families cracked under the strain, but most often the changed Jewish family survived and continued to live as before – or as much as was possible (*ibid.*, p. 37).

The dispersion to which Feingold refers was not universal. Second generation families, in fact, often continued to live in the same community, and sometimes even in the same apartment building or complex. This was also true in certain cities more than others. Pittsburgh for example, has had a stable Jewish upper-middle-class neighborhood since the 1930s and is still using the infrastructure created more than three quarters of a century ago. During this era, three generation households, consisting of grandparents, parents, and children, were not as uncommon as they were to become. Grandparents often maintained an active role in managing the family. No doubt this helped many young couples by reducing their child-rearing responsibilities, affording them additional time for work or schooling. In spite of discrimination, many children of immigrants succeeded in entering American colleges and universities. They trained for the "free" professions of law, medicine, dentistry, pharmacy and accounting (Glazer 1965, p. 33). It was during this period that large numbers of American Jewish families improved their socio-economic status, becoming solidly middle class.

According to Glazer, in the mid-1930s almost one-half of young Jewish adults came from homes where their fathers were blue-collar workers, and about one-third from homes where their fathers owned their own businesses or were managers and officials in other enterprises. In one-tenth of the homes the fathers were clerks, and in fewer than one-twentieth they were professionals. In contrast, some 60 percent of the younger generation was engaged in "clerical and kindred" work, and many headed for an independent business career or profession. In smaller cities during the 1930s, such as Detroit, Buffalo, and San Francisco, an even larger percentage of young Jews, including women, were becoming teachers, white-collar clerks, and salespeople (*ibid.*, pp. 30–32). Their solid penetration of the middle class during this period set the stage for even greater socio-economic advancement during the next two decades.

Even before reaching the middle class economically, American Jewish families displayed many of the social patterns of this group. A prime example of this is the decline in the birth rate. "The process of family limitation among American Jews," says Sklare, "has its roots in the fertility behavior of the first generation. But it was not until the second generation that newer conceptions of family size made deep inroads" (*ibid.*, 1971, p. 79). In 11 community-wide studies carried out between 1930 and 1940 Seligman (see Glazer, p. 34) reports on Jewish fertility ratios (the proportion of children under 5 per 1,000 persons aged 20–54) ranging from 81 to 122. Among non-Jewish Caucasians in 1940 from across the United States, the ratio is 154. Glazer comments that "in the late 'Thirties, it seem[s] fair to conclude that a modicum of relative prosperity had been accompanied by a very rapid drop in the size of the Jewish family" (*ibid.*, p. 35). "By 1938," notes Feingold, "50 percent of Jewish families produced two or fewer children. Jews were on their way to becoming America's most efficient contraceptors" (p. 48). Sociologists and others at that time who were sensitive to these trends predicted a decline in the size of the American Jewish community.

By 1940 American Jews had adopted the model of the middle-class American family more successfully than any other immigrant group. This status is portrayed in a number of popular wartime- and postwar-period novels, including *A Tree Grows in Brooklyn* (Betty Smith, 1943), *A Walker in the City* (Alfred Kazin, 1951), *Marjorie Morningstar* (Herman Wouk, 1955), and *Good-bye Columbus* (Philip Roth, 1959). Jewish families portrayed in earlier works, such as Abraham Cahan's *The Rise of David Levinsky* (1917) and Henry Roth's *Call It Sleep* (1934), are, by comparison, preoccupied with the more fundamental issues of resettlement and becoming "real" Americans. After 1940, these themes are no longer relevant. Fictional Jewish families as portrayed by Jewish authors in the 1940s are unmistakably, middle-class American families who also happen to be Jewish.

Glazer asserts that "the fifteen years of prosperity from the end of the thirties to the mid-fifties ... wrought great changes, and created the Jewish community we know today.... This community of businessmen and professional men is better educated and wealthier than most of the population – probably as well educated and as wealthy as some of the oldest and longest established elements in the United States" (*ibid.*, p. 3). Glazer attributes this success to the fact that Jews, more than other immigrant groups, had for generations engaged in various urban, middle-class occupations, and in spirit had long belonged to the middle class.

Upon its rise to the middle class, the Jewish family began exhibiting additional signs of modernization. Strodbeck (1957) offers evidence which demonstrates that after World War II, Jews, as compared to Italians, place less stress on "familism," i.e., they are more willing to leave home and live independently. This suggests that certain values, which helped American Jews achieve higher social rank, might have had a negative impact on family solidarity. Balswick (1966) concludes on the basis of "writings and research material of the last twenty years," that "the American Jewish family is closely knit. It is more closely knit than non-Jewish families with which it has been compared" (p. 166). However, this conclusion is challenged by Westerman (1967), who cites various methodological problems with Balswick's analysis, particularly a failure to compare contemporary Jewish families with those of previous generations.

America's economic boom following World War II helped to usher in a golden age for the American Jewish family. The G.I. Bill of Rights helped American Jewish veterans get an education and universities expanded to meet growing needs. Veterans' benefits also enabled them to purchase homes. Social integration was advanced by the relocation of second- and third-generation Jewish families from urban areas of second settlement to the periphery of the city and its suburbs. This migration brought about a paradigm shift in American Jewish life whose effect on the family, in particular, was fundamental and far reaching.

Shapiro (1992) cites the reasons for the unprecedented growth of the suburbs after 1945 as follows, including:

> the increased use of automobiles, postwar prosperity, the pent-up demand for housing created by the depression and the war, the desire of veterans to resume a normal family life after the dislocations of wartime, the baby boom of the late 1940s and 1950s, government programs that encouraged the building and purchase of houses by veterans ... (p. 43)

Many Jewish families found the means to abandon the crowded and deteriorating conditions of the city for the newness and openness of the suburbs. Gordon (1959) specifically cites the shortage of urban living space as a key factor in their migration.

> The depression years of the 1930s were followed closely by World War II. During that fifteen-year period, few, if any, new homes were built, and even fewer families could afford to purchase them, whatever their cost. Families "doubled up": sons or daughters who were recently married moved in with their parents until conditions improved.... The builders of mass-produced homes, such as those in Levittown, provided "low-cost housing." Prices were reasonable enough to satisfy young people who were determined to establish their own family life, independent of parents and in-laws.

But not all young, upwardly mobile Jewish families in the period were so determined, and pockets of urban Jewish life remained. Dawidowicz describes one postwar group that chose to stay in the city.

> After years of housing starvation (during the Depression and the war years), many young families in New York found that the great Queens building boom of 1948–1951 offered them a wide choice of modest apartments at modest monthly rentals from $75 to $140. Besides wanting a place to live at rents they could afford, these young people were fleeing from the changes in their old neighborhoods in Manhattan, the Bronx, and Brooklyn. They were looking for an inexpensive facsimile of the suburbs a half hour from Times Square. (p. 68)

The experience of suburban living influenced the dynamics of Jewish family life. The new environment engendered a process of social change reminiscent of the experience of immigrant families two generations earlier. This is described by Mary Antin in her autobiography *The Promised Land* (1912), in which she notes how:

> In Polotzk we had been trained and watched, our days had been regulated, our conduct prescribed. In America, suddenly we were let loose on the street. Why? Because my father having renounced his faith, and my mother being uncertain of hers, they had no particular creed to hold us to... My parents knew only that they desired us to be like American children; and seeing how their neighbors gave their children boundless liberty, they turned us also loose, never doubting but that the American way was the best way (pp. 270–1).

Gordon (1959) observes that "the suburb is helping to produce marked changes in the basic structures of the Jewish family and its educational, political, religious, cultural and social life" (p. 19). Life in suburbia was so different from life in the city that changes in family life were inevitable.

One important consequence of these changes was the virtual full acceptance and social integration of the Jewish family into American society. This development was discussed in Will Herberg's classic book *Protestant, Catholic, Jew: A Study in Religious Sociology* (1955), one of the most influential works in the postwar sociology of American religion. Herberg posits that by the mid-twentieth century, Judaism was no longer considered marginal to American society. Affiliation with a major religious faith was important to Americans, and Judaism, as the seminal creed of America's Judeo-Christian tradition, duly qualified. Jews, as individuals, might still encounter discrimination, but the Jewish tradition, especially as manifest within the home and family, was seen as consonant with the highest of American values (Herberg, *ibid.*, and Kramer and Levantman, p. 153). In Herberg's typology Jews, who were three percent of the American population, constituted one third of its religious experience. Of course, the Judaism of the suburbs was not the pseudo-Orthodoxy of the immigrant generation. Reform, Reconstructionist, and Conservative Judaism, at least until the 1970s, were the only streams of Judaism to successfully take root there. The modern and often lavish temples and synagogues erected in the 1950s and 1960s conveyed the message that the Jewish family felt self-assured and at home in America (Sklare and Greenblum, 1967). Some were designed by prominent architects, Jewish and non-Jewish – they manifested the sense that Jews had arrived and were taking root.

Synagogue affiliation was altogether a different experience in the suburbs. The distances characteristic of suburban living made regular synagogue participation, for those so inclined, more difficult. Whereas in the city, the synagogue was classically a neighborhood institution, in the suburbs it served a widely dispersed population often accessible only by car. Thus, synagogue attendance could no longer be an informal and spontaneous affair. The increased distance between home and synagogue was but one of the postwar changes in Jewish family life. The Conservative movement responded by permitting travel to and from synagogue by car on the Sabbath. Orthodoxy, which continued to prohibit travel felt more at home in the city or turned a blind eye to those who traveled to synagogue. Living within walking distance of the synagogue was later to be a boon to the sense of community among Orthodox and traditional Jews.

The transplanting of Jewish community life from the city to the suburbs contributed to (1) the long range decline of the Jewish neighborhood, (2) an increase in formal affiliation as a means of community attachment, (3) the child-centered family, (4) the transformation of gender roles, and (5) increased geographic mobility.

According to Shapiro:

> The diffusion of Jewish population into the suburbs and exurbs diluted Jewish identity. In the compacted Jewish neighborhoods of the cities, Jewish identity was absorbed through osmosis. In suburbia, it had to be nurtured. Jewish suburbanites lived [mostly] in localities where, in contrast to the city, most of the people were not Jews, the local store did not sell Jewish [especially Yiddish language] newspapers, there were no kosher butchers, synagogues were not numerous, and corned beef sandwiches were not readily available. (p. 147)

In the old neighborhood, grandchildren often lived within proximity of their grandparents, which naturally facilitated more frequent contact. This intimacy made it more likely that family traditions were passed on. Suburban living distanced these generations. The Yiddish of immigrant grandparents, which was understood and spoken, albeit typically unused, by the second generation, seemed foreign and arcane to their suburban grandchildren. A Sunday visit to *bubbie* and *zaidie* in the city might take in shopping at the Jewish bakery, bookstore, or kosher butcher. Such casual activities were the most intensive Jewish cultural encounters some third- and fourth-generation children would experience.

While this scenario partly reflects an overall distancing from tradition, it also points to the diminuition of intense Jewish family activity in the suburbs. Such activity is a source of mimetic norms, i.e., knowledge that is "imbibed from parents and friends, and patterned on conduct regularly observed in home and street, synagogue and school" (Soloveitchik, 1994). This form of learning emerges naturally in the traditional Jewish neighborhood. The Jewish neighborhood, much like the *shtetl* of prewar Europe, is an example of *gemeinschaft*, an informal, corporate form of community life. In contrast, suburban Jewish life is likened to *gesellschaft*, a form of community organization wherein social interaction is more disparate and the transmission of culture more formalized. It has become more common for suburban Jewish families who do not live near one another to meet and interact only within the context of formal activities. These scheduled Jewish experiences, such as attendance at synagogue services, school meetings, youth group programs, adult learning courses, holiday celebrations and cultural events, compete for time with a miscellany of other activities. (See Sklare; Gans; Blau; Gordon; and Kramer and Leventman, *op. cit.*)

The suburban synagogue is the central, even if not the sole, focus of public Jewish life. Synagogue membership entitles a family, or any one of its members: to celebrate the Jewish holidays as part of the congregation; to the services of the rabbi and his assistant; to attend synagogue-run classes and lectures; to receive Jewish news and information through the in-house newsletter, and to use the synagogue's facilities for the celebration of family life-cycle events. For the newly suburbanized Jews, this reflected the dependency of the family on the Jewish skills and knowledge of community professionals. In many instances for that generation, even such classic family rites as lighting Hanukkah candles or participating in a

Passover *seder* no longer took place at home, but in the synagogue, under the direction of a rabbi, or teacher.

Observers note the extent to which the contemporary American Jewish family, particularly in suburbia, became child centered. While concern for the well-being and education of children is basic to Jewish tradition, the child-oriented behavior of American Jewish families is a more recent phenomenon. This generation of American Jews was often characterized by a Judaism that was for the young – children attending Hebrew school at least until bar and bat mitzvah – and the old – grandparents attending regularly as a routine part of their lives.

Having acquired the economic means to provide more than basic food, clothing and shelter, Jewish parents developed a tendency to indulge their children with a surfeit of material goods. This behavior is reflected, says Sklare (1971, p. 88), in the expression "'they gave their son everything.' 'Everything' means the best of everything from the necessities to the luxuries: it includes clothing, medical attention, entertainment, vacations, schools and myriad other items." In this same context, observed Gordon, "The financial burdens that Jewish parents in suburbia gladly bear for what they regard as the best interests of their children is often astonishing [and sometimes disturbing] to persons who are aware of the sacrifices these entail" (Gordon, *ibid.*, p. 65). Many second- and third-generation American Jewish parents acknowledged that the very move to suburbia was "for the sake of the children."

Another example of child-focused family behavior was reflected in the attitude towards ritual observance and Jewish education. According to Sklare, any ritual that is centered on the child is more likely to be retained by the family (*ibid.*, pp. 115, 116). This means that (1) the ritual activity must provide an opportunity to directly involve the child, and (2) it should convey "optimism, fun, and gratification." The Passover *seder* and the lighting of candles at Hanukkah are two often-cited examples. Toward the end of the 20th century, Sukkot experienced an increase in the percentage of observance as Jews had land and backyards where they could build a *sukkah* and it was a family centered, do-it-yourself activity, a perfect suburban project. This understanding of ritual correlates religious practice with the interests of children. Consequently, within the year of their youngest child's bar or bat mitzvah, many parents discontinued their child's formal Jewish education, choosing not to renew their synagogue membership, to curtail their other Jewish communal activities, and sometimes to reduce the family's observance of home rituals.

In their respective analyses of Jewish suburban life, Gans (*ibid.*, p. 233) and Gordon (*ibid.*, pp. 19, 59–60) discuss changes in the family that developed with respect to both males and females in the mid 20th Century. According to Gans:

> In the suburb… the men's daytime absence shifts a much greater role in its affairs to the women, except in functions requiring business skills, and aspirations such as power…[Women's'] concern with Jewish education seems also to be stronger than that of the men…This is a major shift from the traditional Jewish family organization in which the father, as religious leader of the household, supervised the children's education for an adult community in which he himself was playing a role.

In response to their husbands' preoccupation with earning a living, claims Gordon, suburban Jewish women in the postwar era began to take responsibility for matters for which their husbands were once considered the sole authority in theory if not in practice. This mirrored the responsibility that other American women assumed for the transmission of culture.

> My observation…, and particularly this intensive study of suburban Jewish family life, leads to the conclusion that.… "all major decisions are made by the husband while all the minor ones are made by the wife." The major decisions… deal with such matters as war and peace, sputnik and satellites. The minor issues include rearing the children and choosing their schools, the particular synagogue with which to affiliate, the neighborhood into which to move and the kind of home to buy.
>
> The Jewish woman has acquired her new position of… leadership by default… So completely engrossed in business affairs… [the husband] generally gives little attention to spiritual and cultural matters that involve his home and family. The husband's failure has led inevitably to the wife's new status.

The geographic mobility among Jewish families in the postwar era primarily reflects their relocation to the local suburbs, not inter-state or cross country migration. It is true that from the 1950s it became increasingly common for the corporate breadwinner to be transferred great distances. However, since many Jews remained excluded from the corporate sector during these years, the voluntary move to the nearby suburbs was far more common. Jewish families moved not only from the city to the suburbs, but in time they also moved within and between suburbs. As its income rose, it was not uncommon for a family to sell its home in a less expensive section of one suburb and move to a higher status area within the same suburb. Naturally, families also moved from lower to higher status suburbs. Kramer and Levantman note that the "securely American status of the third generation and its increasing mobility have released it from old ties and community sentiments…."

The Mid-1960s to the 1980s

By the middle of the 1960s Jewish family life in America appeared to have reached the zenith of prosperity and security. From a historical perspective, few, if any other Jewish communities could claim to feel so well integrated into surrounding society. Sklare (1971) contends that this very success resulted in "[a] paucity of substantial research studies on the American-Jewish family…The Jewish family constellation has not created social problems in the general society. In fact it has done just the opposite: the Jewish family seems to have solved problems rather than caused them" (p. 73).

But all was not perfect. Acculturation and integration came with a price. "As upward mobility pushed immigrants' children to the suburbs, their parents were linked to memories of dark stairways, stale smells, cramped apartments, loud voices, and barbarous accents. In comparison, blending into a bland mainstream was a big step forward. With so much discarded, little remained to give their distinctiveness purpose except sentimental leftovers fed by kitsch, Broadway shows, and self-righteousness...This mix of ethnic remnants and carbon-copy assimilation left such parents little to pass on" (Rubin, 1995, pp. 93–94). The poignancy of this transformation became more evident towards the end of the 1960s when traditional notions about family life were confronted by the popularization of values that were more liberal and individual oriented. Many of the assumptions regarding what constitutes a "sound and healthy" family were challenged. Questions were raised about the structure and purpose of the family, as well as the obligations of family members towards each other. "Since 1970, or thereabouts," says Cohen (1983, pp. 114–15) "the American family has undergone such dramatic changes as to spark a popular and scholarly debate about whether it is in fact disintegrating."

The mythic portrayal of the American family is prevalent in the way Jewish institutions are structured. The family is defined as two parents and children. A fixed division of labor is presumed and children are seen as the focus of the family. Membership costs are often defined by family. Synagogue membership is usually stated in family units. Meeting are scheduled as if the family defined above is the norm; so too, programming and fees. These institutions have been slow to change even as women have become officers, major donors and decision makers. It is as if the sisterhood continued to serve Friday evening tea at the *Oneg Shabbat* even though the rabbi, cantor, president and principal supporters may now be women.

Rela Mintz Geffen reports that according to the 1990 National Jewish Population Survey the most common household in the Jewish community comprises one adult Jew living alone; the next most common is two adults Jews; and only then two adult Jews with at least one child under the age of 18 living at home. Only 14% of Jewish households in the survey were comprised of two Jewish adults and with at least one child under 18 living at home. In contemporary parlance, the "conventional Jewish family" is two Jews, one male, one female – whether born Jewish or not – with one child under the age of 18 living at home.

Contemporary Jews live not only in the traditional family but also as singles of all ages; empty nest couples whose children have left home and will not again return; senior adults living alone or in communities and facilities, widowed or married; dual-career spouses; single parents, whether by death of one's spouse, loss or divorce; and non-traditional couples, gay men and lesbian women. These people, constituting a majority of all Jews, often feel unacknowledged by contemporary American Jewish institutions. Programming and normative language of the community often excludes them and many respond accordingly. There may be an asymmetry between the definition of family embodied in community institutions and the actual configuration of the way Jews in America live.

"For American Jews," says Fishman (1994), "as for other Americans today, there is no one model of 'the family.' Jewish families reflect, in somewhat less extreme profile, an America in which less than 15 percent of households conform to the model of father, mother-at-home, and children living together...[Thus t]he 'typical' American Jewish household today is more likely than not to be atypical in some way. Proportions of older, single, divorced, remarried, or dual-career households make up more of the Jewish population than intact young families with children" (pp. 5, 33). As a result of these changes, social scientists no longer study American families, per se; instead, surveys are conducted among "households," such as in the Council of Jewish Federations (CJF) 1990 National Jewish Population Survey (p. 33). The term "household" accommodates a more flexible and wider range of domestic living arrangements than those associated with the conventional western family.

Trends which first emerged some 25–30 years ago continue to have an impact upon Jewish family life. These include: a decrease in the rate of marriage; the postponement of first time marriage; an increase in the number of marriages that end in divorce; an increase in the rate of intermarriage, particularly non-conversionary marriages; a decrease in the birth rate to a level lower than replacement; an increase in geographic mobility; an increase in cohabitation, and single motherhood; and an increase in substance abuse. Some have argued that there is an increase in domestic violence and in homosexuality but they may be mistaken. It is certainly the case that there is an increase in *acknowledgement* of domestic violence and or homosexuality. It was commonplace to link these phenomena with a decrease in Jewish education and the practice of Jewish ritual, but the evidence is mixed. The number of children receiving a day school education is at all-time high and the measurement of Jewish ritual observance does not necessarily indicate a decline. There is no doubt that Jewish values must compete in the open marketplace of ideas in a multicultural United States, where exposure to other value systems is commonplace.

Fishman (*ibid.*) examines a number of these trends by comparing data from the 1970 National Jewish Population Study (NJPS) and the CJF 1990 National Jewish Population Study with data drawn throughout the 1980s from some two dozen Jewish communities. Regarding marriage, her analysis indicates that while in 1970 nearly four-fifths of all adult American Jews were married, by 1990 this figure had decreased to about two-thirds. A parallel decrease was recorded for all adults in the United States. Over the last 30 years being single in America has developed into a lifestyle. Whereas in 1970–1 17 percent of Jewish men were still single at ages 25–34, this figure increased to about 50 percent in 1990. An even greater increase applies to Jewish women ages 25–34; only 10 percent of this group was not married in 1970–1, in comparison to about half in 1990. By age 45, however, over 90 percent of all Jews are reported to have been married at least one time.

"The delay or avoidance of marriage is but one of many factors which may lower Jewish birthrates" (Cohen, 1983, p. 117). Still, another factor is higher education; the more education a couple has completed, the less likely it is to produce more than one or two children. It is understandable then, that Jewish couples, who in comparison with the rest of the population complete more years of education and also marry late, often raise smaller families. This tendency was observed among Jewish families by Seligman and Antonovsky, even in the midst of America's baby boom. Orthodox Jews are the exception. Seligman and Antonovsku cautioned that "[t]he high proportion of two-person and three-person [Jewish] families may be indicative of a declining reproductive rate…" (in Sklare, 1958, p. 66). The impact of this trend was noted over a decade later. "[I]n the second generation," says Sklare, "the birth rate dropped so precipitously as to have serious implications for Jewish population size as well as for group continuity" (1971, p. 79).

A low birth rate has continued into the third and fourth generations. In 1990, 93 percent of Jewish women ages 18 to 24 and 55 percent of those ages 25 to 34 had not yet had children (Fishman, *ibid.*, p. 31). As a result, with the exception of the Orthodox community, the Jewish birth rate in America presently stands at significant less than replacement level of 2.1. Averting the presumed consequences of what appears to be a looming demographic crisis currently occupies a high position on the organized Jewish community's national agenda. A significantly attenuated Jewish population would weaken the Jewish community's standing at large, including its ability to act on behalf of its own interests. It would jeopardize the existence of a range of local Jewish institutions, from family services to community centers and schools, as well as the Jewish community's fundraising efforts on behalf of Israel and distressed Jews in other countries. Finally, some have presumed that it would sap the vitality of American Jewish culture and creativity. Others who study American Judaism believe that the intensity of Jewish life and the freedom of Jews to create as Jews, to act publicly as Jews and feel free even in their seemingly secular pursuits to act as Jews will offset the loss of numbers. Many who point to the problem of intermarriage are slow to acknowledge the tremendous contribution, energy and vitality brought to all institutions and all denominations of Judaism by Jews by choice, those not born as Jews.

The significance of this low birth rate is compounded by the high outmarriage rate – the rate is subject to dispute ranging between 45–52%. Just as the intermarriage [rate] has increased dramatically among younger American Jews, rates of conversion have fallen, especially after the introduction by Reform Judaism's acceptance of patrilineal descent. Mixed marriage is five times higher among Jews 18 to 34 than it is among those over age 55" (Fishman in Bayme and Rosen, p. 26). Ironically, the rise in intermarriage is not unrelated to a decline in antisemitism. Jews are now regarded as acceptable partners for non-Jews and the opposition from the non-Jewish family has declined markedly. Intermarriage also has less to do with one's Jewish identity and allegiance to the Jewish people than it did a generation or two ago. During the mid-1950s, according to Rosenthal (1963), the overall community intermarriage rate for the Greater Washington, D.C., area, a mid-sized yet highly cosmopolitan Jewish community, was 13 percent. In larger Jewish communities, the rate was between 6–10 percent. By the 1970s, intermarriage rates in many American communities had risen to approximately 30 percent. Whereas, according to Medding, et al. (1992), Jewish identification tends to be passed on to the next generation in conversionary marriages, especially Orthodox and Conservative conversionary marriages, this is not true of mixed marriages. "Jewish identification in mixed marriages is accompanied by the presence of symbols of Christian identification, resulting in dual-identity households at all levels of Jewish identification" (p. 39). Daniel Elazar called this the permeability of contemporary boundaries. So long as mixed marriages constitute the great majority of outmarriages, intermarriage poses a major challenge to transmission of Judaism through Jewish family life in America.

Divorce, like outmarriage, was once relatively rare among American Jews. This is no longer the case. Divorce, especially that which results in long-term single parent households, has increased over the last three decades. Data from the CJF 1990 NJPS reveals "18 divorces for every 100 ever-married men and 19 for every 100 ever-married women [indicating that] divorce has become relatively common among American Jews." "Rising rates of divorce," says Fishman, "have created a situation in which one-third of Jewish children live in homes which have been touched by divorce: about ten percent of Jewish children live in single parent homes and twenty percent live in households in which at least one spouse has been divorced" (1994, p. 34). Clearly, the traditional notion of a two parent family with mother and father raising their own children together is not the only form that contemporary Jewish family life has taken.

Active extended kin relations continued to characterize American Jewish family life until the 1970s. Yet there too the picture may be a bit overdone. Children left for college and left for jobs; grandparents migrated to the South and also to the West. It was presumed that grandparents would be the major repository of Jewish values and yet in the contemporary family it is often the grandparents who are most removed from Jewish education. And because of immigration, because of the Holocaust, many grandparents grew up without grandparents and do not have an image of what grandparenting involved. And American culture, which does not revere the elderly, certainly offers few models to teach them.

On the other hand, the increase in geographic mobility during the last quarter century has enhanced extended family ties. Greater family resources, the ease of travel, the lowering of long distance phone rates, and ubiquity of the internet have increased the involvement of grandparents with their grandchildren. At the same time divorce and intermarriage pose unique challenges. Especially perplexing is the relationship of grandparents to their grandchildren when the custodial parent is not their child. According to the CJF 1990 NJPS, between the years 1985–1990, 25 percent of adults surveyed changed residence, at least once, between cities within the same state. Another 24 percent changed residence, at least once, between states. Frequent mobility makes it more difficult to develop long-term social relationships within a community. Three generation relationships, as well as active ties between cousins, have become rarer but also more cherished in recent years. There is a tendency for extended family events to be limited to infrequent holiday gatherings or major life-cycle celebrations.

No doubt an added challenge to Jewish family life has been the development of the dual career family. According to the CJF 1990 NJPS about three-fourths of women aged 25–44 and two-thirds of women aged 45–64 are members of the labor force. "Today the labor force participation of Jewish women departs radically from patterns of the recent past. In most cities the majority of Jewish mothers continue to work even while their children are quite young. In Boston, Baltimore, San Francisco, and Washington, three out of every five Jewish mothers with pre-school children are working" (Fishman, *ibid*., p. 17). Nearly 40 percent of working Jewish women under the age of 44 in 1990 are reported to work in some professional capacity, as compared to 24 percent in 1970. In 1957, says Goldstein, only about 30 percent of Jewish women aged 25–44 were employed at all (*ibid*., p. 113). Remaining at home to raise children was a more common practice. The increased availability of professional day care services, many under Jewish auspices, aided the growth of dual career families in recent decades. It also should be noted that contrary to many historical recollections women in the traditional Jewish home often worked outside of the home; their labor was necessary for the survival of the family. When the husband studied the wife was responsible for providing for the family and in the immigrant family, the working mother was also essential for survival. Stay at home mothers may have reflected the mid-century American middle class ideal rather than actual practice. In fact, the wife not having to work was a status symbol in mid-century America. The empowerment of women, the increasing professionalization of and opportunity for women pose challenges to the Jewish family but is not unprecedented in the Jewish experience. Substance abuse, domestic violence and incest, pathologies long considered to exist at strictly marginal levels among Jewish families, began to receive increased attention in the 1970s. It is not clear whether earlier instances of these problems were more common but went largely unreported, or whether more acculturated third- and fourth-generation Jewish families in fact have been more susceptible. The training of *mikveh* ladies to recognize signs of physical abuse by a husband is a clear indication that these problems are not confined to the secular family alone.

As late as the end of the 1960s, alcoholism was not seen as a problem that affected many Jewish families. Franzblau (1967) cited findings by the Yale Center of Alcoholic Studies indicating that first-time admissions to New York State Hospitals are fifty times as numerous among Irish as among Jews, fifteen times as numerous among Scandinavians, ten times as numerous among Italians, nine times as numerous among the English and eight times as numerous among the Germans. According to Franzblau, Jewish families of the period compared favorably to non-Jewish families "whether the factual material presented be on juvenile delinquency, adult criminality, prison populations, family desertion and non-support, separation and divorce rates, commitments to mental hospitals for the tertiary manifestations of syphilis…" (p. 59). He suggested then that "Jewish home and Jewish family life are…endowed with some mysterious extra safeguards against the disintegrative forces of the environment" (*ibid*.).

More recent estimates of alcoholism among Jewish adults range from five to fifteen percent. Since about 92 percent of all Jews marry by age 45, alcoholism among Jews is both a family and a personal problem. Increased recognition of alcoholism and drug addiction within the Jewish community has led to the establishment of Jewish support groups as alternatives to groups like Alcoholics Anonymous which have a Christian orientation.

Domestic violence, including the sexual abuse of children, was considered, for all intents and purposes, absent from the consciousness among American Jews during the middle part of the century, but certainly not during the immigrant experience. The winter 1991–2 *Journal of Jewish Communal Service*, poignantly entitled "Family Violence IS a Jewish Issue," offers five articles that examine both spousal and elderly abuse, as well as describe abuse treatment programs operated by various local Jewish communal agencies. The April 1990 issue of *Moment* features an article entitled "Confronting Sexual Abuse in Jewish Families" in which the author describes her own and others' victimization and offers other victims' advice. She rejects "[t]he myth that Jewish families and incestuous families are a contradiction in terms…" and confronts an issue formerly never associated with Jews.

Conventional family values have been decidedly challenged by the liberal atmosphere which prevails on most American university campuses. In the 1960s, questions about the typical western family, a topic generally relegated to sociology and anthropology lectures, spilled over from the lecture hall to the streets. The counterculture experience, in which so many young Jews participated, encouraged alternative family forms and lifestyles. This partially explains the disproportionate number of Jews who affiliated with communes and cults. Although the experiment with communal living more or less ended by the mid-1970s, Jewish involvement in cults has continued to this day but is now regarded as a much more marginal phenomenon, except to those whose children are within the cults. The Baal Teshuvah movement, in which children become more observant than their parents – and often unable to eat in their homes or to spend Shabbat and holidays with them – is also a challenge to the family structure. It is also present within Orthodoxy where Modern Orthodox parents have *ḥaredi* children who find their parents' Orthodoxy not sufficiently devout. The attractiveness of cults to young Jews is explained by some observers as a reaction to low self-esteem among those who cannot meet the high expectations of their parents or community. Others see it as a response to the spiritual emptiness found in so many contemporary Jewish families and synagogues. The ḥavurah and programs that educate the Jewish family, both of which initially gained wider popularity in the early 1970s, reflect the efforts of the Jewish community to combat these problems.

The community ḥavurah is modeled after the student organized Havurah that "originated in the late 1960s [in New York and Boston] with young Jews who were unhappy with the Conservative and Reform congregations in which they had been raised. Influenced by the counterculture, they were dissatisfied with contemporary Jewish institutions, both religious and communal, which they regarded as "sterile, impersonal, hierarchical, and divorced from Jewish tradition" (Weissler, p. 200). Both the independent ḥavurah, which is unaffiliated with any community institution, and the synagogue or community center ḥavurah, whose participants are generally affiliated with these institutions, typically consists of a small number (10–20) of singles, couples, or sometimes both. The typical ḥavurah holds Sabbath and holiday services, celebrates life-cycle events, organizes study groups, and undertakes one or more social action causes. The particular activities of each ḥavurah reflect the interests of its membership. It is an attempt to establish community and to retain a personal dimension to institutional Jewish life.

The small and intimate setting of the ḥavurah compares favorably to the vast and formal surroundings of many American synagogues to those seeking fellowship and spirituality in their worship. The ḥavurah experience is an "opportunity to have a continuing intimate association – to feel a sense of belonging, to be linked with people they know personally and who care about them, and to have people with whom to share happiness and sorrow – bar mitzvahs, Passover *seders*, sickness, death, etc." (Reisman, p. 207). The ḥavurah experience is used by many singles, couples, and families, as a substitute for the natural family and community network that was once much more prevalent within American Jewish life.

Economic considerations also play a role in Jewish affiliation. The higher one's economic status, the more likely one is to affiliate with the Jewish community and the less likely one is to intermarry. Rates of intermarriage are consistently higher among those of lesser socioeconomic achievement as measured by education, occupation and income, especially for those under 45. In 1990 one in two of those Jews with an income of more than $100,000 were Jewishly affiliated; the rate of affiliation was one in three for those earning less than $60,000. Lower income Jews also feel disaffiliated from Jewish life.

Jewish education programs for families have existed in the United States for decades, but it is only since the 1970s that this approach has been developed as a sub-specialty (Schiff, p. 262). Jewish family education is based on the premise that, although "the attitudes and behavior patterns [of most American Jewish families presently]…resemble those of the non-Jewish, white middle-class (Rosenman, p. 153)," a percentage of these families are willing, or can be induced, to be tutored in basic Jewish knowledge, skills and values and helped to integrate these into their lives." Programs in Jewish family education exist at the local level where they are sponsored by community centers, synagogues, day schools, [and] family service agencies. At the national level, the William Petschek National Jewish Family Center established in 1981 by the American Jewish Committee, the Whizin Institute for Jewish Family Life at the University of Judaism in Los Angeles, Brandeis University in Waltham, MA, Yeshiva University in New York, and other universities, are among those institutions that offer research opportunities, professional and lay seminars, personnel training, and produce and disseminate educational materials. Although the proliferation of these institutions reflects the growing importance of this field in the eyes of community educators and leaders, it is also indicative of the sense of urgency which surrounds the present condition of the American Jewish family.

Two important studies in the 1970s (Himmelfarb, 1974 and Bock, 1976) found that the most salient influence on adult Jewish identification was the family. Yet, most synagogues, schools and community centers focused their programming exclusively on children, leaving the family to its own devices. Wolfson (1983) called the family's reliance on the institution to provide opportunities for Jewish celebration a "dependency cycle." He called on synagogues and schools to empower families with the skills and resources to create a home filled with Jewish celebration, content and values. In 1989, Wolfson gathered a group of pioneering Jewish family educators to establish the Whizin Institute for Jewish Family Life to further the field of practice in Jewish family education. Hundreds of Jewish professionals and laity attended Whizin seminars to learn the latest strategies for "reaching and teaching" the Jewish family. By the end of the century, virtually every synagogue, school and JCC had a full range of Jewish family education programming (Wolfson and Bank, 1998).

End of the 20th Century

At the end of the 20th century, the American Jewish family more strongly resembled its non-Jewish neighbor than its own forebear of a hundred years ago. Goldstein and other "survivalists" insist that Jewish families continue to maintain sufficient distinctive collectivist socio-economic and socio-cultural characteristics to guarantee continuity, at least for the foreseeable future. Cohen (1994) argues that current intermarriage and birth rates will result in a smaller, but qualitatively stronger American Jewish community "[O]n the family level, rather than the group level, for the vast majority of families, intermarriage eventually severs the link of future generations with the Jewish people." While Cohen remains optimistic about the overall long range survival of the American Jewish community, he foresees the disappearance of many presently existing Jewish family lines.

The only variance to the observations above lies within the Orthodox sector. Orthodox families, who constitute some ten percent of the American Jewish population, do not reflect the trends of the wider Jewish community. Although domestic problems of all stripes do occur within Orthodox circles, their incidence appears limited because it is less reported and certainly less acknowledged. Characteristically, the more religiously observant the family and the more segregated it is from the general society, the less likely it is to experience intermarriage, a low birth rate, and other elements accompanying assimilation.

Among the main purposes and functions of the family, says Bayme (1989), is the transmission of culture and heritage, the basis of group identity. In the middle decades of the past century, this task, he contends, has been transferred to the Jewish school. "We today ask of Jewish schools not only to transmit knowledge and cultural literacy of Judaism but also to transmit Jewish identity and consciousness. Conversely, research has demonstrated that without the cooperation and involvement of families Jewish schools can achieve very little." Recent trends in education emphasize family participation and recent life cycle and calendar ritual behavior also demonstrate an increase in activities that are family centered, albeit with a broadened definition of family.

Can Jewish families continue to fulfill their historical function? Can the definition of Jewish family accommodate all alternative household forms, including cohabiting couples and groups, singles, lesbians and gays, and still guarantee long range Jewish survival? These serious questions are currently being asked by individuals, such as Bayme, as well as other concerned academicians and social scientists, community lay leaders and professionals. The Jewish family is not about to disappear from the American scene; however, it clearly will have undergone significant transformations.

Social policy planners and senior educators who wish to strengthen the Jewish family are presently busy at both the national and community level. Among their objectives is to guarantee the affordability of quality Jewish family education, for children as well as adults, and affordable rates for community center, synagogue, and summer camp participation. For those who chose maximal Jewish life, day school education, Jewish summer camps and synagogue membership along with their ancillary activities pose a heavy financial burden. (One important commentator has joked that day school tuition is "Jewish birth control.") They stress that programming for the Jewish family should be appealing, of high quality, marketed vigorously, and supported by community funds. Maximum and efficient use of communal resources, they contend, would help provide affordable day care and other vital services to assist dual income and financially distressed families. A cogent community strategy can help minimize the additional costs of Jewish living, making affiliation and participation affordable to many more families.

The family is the nexus between the individual and society. The welfare of both is dependent upon the success of the family as an institution in fulfilling its primary goals of socializing and educating its members. Similarly, individual Jewish identity and the viability of Jewish communal life in the United States are tied to the cultural integrity of the American Jewish family. The historic Jewish family, in various countries and in various periods, has demonstrated great resilience in the face of physical, spiritual and economic pressures. Ironically, it is the relative absence of these pressures in America, which presents a challenge to Jewish survival. External antisemitism is not forcing Jews to remain together. They are comfortably accepted and acceptable within American culture. A low birth rate, high intermarriage, and the diverse forms of family life present new and different challenges to the American Jewish family. "Given the inexorably integrative forces of American society and the resultant parallel trends among Jews," note Lipset and Rabb (1995) "it is reasonable to predict that the Jewish community as a whole will be severely reduced in numbers by the middle of the next century." In an attempt to forestall this outcome, the organized Jewish community is developing policies and programs aimed at supporting and strengthening the family. The next few decades are sure to reveal the results of these efforts.

BIBLIOGRAPHY: "The Workshop of Israel," in: *The Menorah Journal* (April 1928), 361; M. Antin, *The Promised Land* (1912); C. Baum, P. Hyman, and S. Michel, *The Jewish Women in America* (1975); J. Balswick, "Are American Jewish Families Closely Knit?" in: *Jewish Social Studies*, 28:3 (1966), 159–167; S. Bayme, "The Jewish Family in American Culture," paper presented at the Institute for American Values Conference: *What Do Families Do?*, Stanford University, Nov. 1989; B. Cohen, *Sociocultural Changes in American Jewish Life as Reflected in Selected Jewish Literature* (1972); S.M. Cohen, *American Modernity and Jewish Identity* (1983); idem, "Why Intermarriage May Not Threaten Jewish Continuity," in: *Moment*, 19:6 (1994), 54–57; L. Dawidowicz, *The Jewish Presence: Essays on Identity and History* (1977); H.L. Feingold, *A Time for Searching: Entering the Mainstream 1920–1945* (1992); S. Barack Fishman, "The Changing American Jewish Family Faces the 1990s," in: S. Bayme and G. Rosen (eds.), *The Jewish Family and Jewish Continuity* (1994), 3–52; A.N. Franzblau, "A New Look at the Psychodynamics of Jewish Family Living," in: N. Kiell, *The Psychodynamics of American Jewish Life* (1967); N. Glatzer, "The Jewish Family and Humanistic Values," in: *Journal of Jewish Communal Service*, 36 (1969), 269–73; N. Glazer, "Social Characteristics of American Jews," in: J.L. Blau, N.G. Glazer, O. and M.F. Handlin, and H. Stein (eds.), *The Characteristics of American Jews* (1965), first published as "Social Characteristics of American Jews, 1654–1954," in: AJYB, 56 (1955); S. Goldstein, *Highlights of the CJF 1990 National Jewish Population Survey* (1991); A.I. Gordon, *Jews in Transition* (1949); idem, *Jews in Suburbia* (1959); S.C. Heilman, *Synagogue Life: A Study in Symbolic Interaction* (1973); W. Herberg, *Protestant, Catholic, Jews: An Essay in American Religious Sociology* (1955); I. Howe, *World of Our Fathers* (1976); E.P. Hutchinson, *Immigrants and Their Children, 1850–1950* (1956), 13–15; *The Jewish Communal Register*, Kehillah (Jewish Community of New York; 1918); *Journal of Jewish Communal Service*, 68:2 (1991–92), 114–39; D. Katz, *Home Fires: An Intimate Portrait* (1992); J.R. Kramer and S. Levantman, *Children of the Gilded Ghetto: Conflict Resolutions of Three Generations of American Jews* (1961); A.E. Landesman, *Brownsville: The Birth, Development and Passing of a Jewish Community in New York* (1969); S.M. Lipset and E. Raab, *Jews and the New American Scene* (1995); N. Linzer, *The Jewish Family: Authority and Tradition in Modern Perspective* (1984); S.R. Lowenstein, "Confronting Sexual Abuse in Jewish Families," in: *Moment*,

15:2 (1990), 48–53: A. Markowitz, "Jews in Cults: Why We're Vulnerable and How They Snare Our Children," in: *Moment*, 18:4 (1993), 22–55; I. Metzker (ed.), *A Bintel Brief: Sixty Years of Letters from the Lower East Side to the Jewish Daily Forward* (1971); D.D. Moore, *At Home in America: Second Generation New York Jews* (1981); D.J. O'Brien, "American Catholics and Anti-Semitism in the 1930's," in: *Catholic World*, 204 (1967), 270–276; B. Reisman, "The Havurah: An Approach to Humanizing Jewish Organizational Life," in: *Journal of Jewish Communal Service*, 52 (1985), 202–9; E. Rosenthal, "Studies of Jewish Intermarriage in the United States," in: AJYB, 64 (1963), 3–53; B. Rubin, *Assimilation and Its Discontents* (1995); A.I. Schiff, "Trends and Challenges in Jewish Family Life Education," in: *Journal of Jewish Communal Service*, 67 (1991), 262–68; C. Selengut, "American Jewish Converts to New Religious Movements," *Jewish Journal of Sociology*, 30:2 (1988); B.B. Seligman and A. Antonovsky, "Some Aspects of Jewish Demography," in: Sklare (ed.), *The Jews: Social Patterns of an American Group* (1958); E.S. Shapiro, *A Time for Healing: American Jewry Since World War II* (1992); C.B. Sherman, "Demographic and Social Aspects," in: O.I. Janowsky (ed.), *The American Jew: A Reappraisal* (1964); M. Sklare, *Conservative Judaism: An American Religious Movement* (1972); idem, *America's Jews* (1971); M. Sklare and J. Greenblum, *Jewish Identity on the Suburban Frontier: A Study of Group Survival in the Open Society* (1967); H. Soloveitchik, "Rupture and Reconstruction: The Transformation of Contemporary Orthodoxy," in: *Tradition*, 24:4 (1994), 64–130; F.L. Strodbeck, in: *Report of the Social Science Research Council's Committee on Identification of Talent*, by D.C. McClelland and others, 1957; J. Westerman, "Notes on Balswick's Article – A Response," in: *Jewish Social Studies*, 29:4 (1967), 241–44; C. Weissler, "Coming of Age in the Havurah Movement: Bar Mitzvah in the Havurah Family," in: S.M. Cohen and P.E. Hyman (eds.), *The Jewish Family: Myths and Reality* (1986), 200–17; J. Yaffe, *The American Jews: Portrait of a Split Personality* (1968). **ADD. BIBLIOGRAPHY:** G. Bock, "The Jewish Schooling of American Jews: A Study of Non-cognitive Educational Effects" (Doctoral dissertation, Harvard University; 1976); H. Himmelfarb, "The Impact of Religious Schooling: The Effects of Jewish Education on Adult Religious Involvement" (Doctoral dissertation, University of Chicago; 1974); R.G. Wolfson, "Shall You Teach Them Diligently?" University Papers, University of Judaism (1983); A. Bank, and R.G. Wolfson, *First Fruit: A Whizin Anthology of Jewish Family Education,* Whizin Institute for Jewish Family Life, University of Judaism (1998).

[Arden J. Geldman and Rela Mintz Geffen (2nd ed.)]

FAMINE AND DROUGHT. Agriculture in Ereẓ Israel was dependent on irregular rainfall, but drought and consequent famine were of frequent occurrence. The paradoxical appreciation by Deuteronomy 11:10ff. of this disadvantage (as involving God in constant attention to the land) puts a good face upon what Ezekiel 36:30 bluntly calls the land's "reproach among the nations for its famine." Kimḥi comments on this as follows: "The land of Israel stands in greater need of rain than other lands [being mountainous in contrast, e.g., to the great river valleys of Mesopotamia and Egypt]; hence famine is more common in it than elsewhere. And when one has to leave his land for another because of famine – as witness Abraham, Isaac, and Elimelech – it is a reproach to it." Another cause of famine through natural causes was the failure of the crop through pests and disease. In addition to these two "acts of God," famine was caused by siege in time of war. Of the famines in Ereẓ Israel mentioned in the Bible (the most famous, the seven years' famine predicted by Joseph in Egypt, included also the Land of Israel – Gen. 41:54, 43:1) most were due to drought (Gen. 12:10; 26:1; 41:54; Ruth 1:1; II Sam. 21:1; I Kings 18:1–2; II Kings 8:1; and apparently Amos 4:6 (cf. verses 7ff.), two to the result of siege – that of Samaria by Ben-Hadad (II Kings 6:24–29) and of Jerusalem by Nebuchadnezzar (*ibid.* 25:3) – and one the result of a visitation of locusts (Joel 1:4–20). A vivid description of the effects of drought occurs in Jeremiah 14:1–6. The same conditions, both natural and man-made (cf. Jos., Wars, 5:424–35), continued during the period of the Second Temple, but to them were added famine, or at least shortage of food, which resulted from the strict adherence to the law requiring that land should remain untilled during the Sabbatical year, to which there is no historical reference in the Bible. The frequency of famine is reflected in the fact that of the seven calamities said in the Mishnah to afflict the world because of sin, three are famines of various degrees of intensity: the "famine of drought," which does not affect the whole population, the "famine of panic," which affects all, and the "famine of utter destruction" (Avot 5:8). The traditional triad of major catastrophes consists of "pestilence, sword, and famine" (cf. Jer. 14:12; 21:7, 9; 24:10; Ezek. 6:11, etc.; compare the *Hashkivenu* and the *Avinu Malkenu* prayers). The fact that, given a choice of one of these three, David chose pestilence suggests that it was the least of them (II Sam. 24:14f.). Lamentations gives a preference in the scale of suffering to famine over the sword (4:9). This would indicate that famine was the greatest evil of all: it is in fact difficult to envisage the terrible suffering endured through famine in ancient times. The grim picture, given by R. Johanan, imaginative though it is, of the consequences of the seven-year famine predicted by *Elisha (II Kings 8:1) – that in the fourth year people would be reduced to eating unclean animals, in the fifth reptiles and insects, in the sixth their children, and in the seventh their own flesh (Ta'an. 5a) – is probably not so exaggerated as may appear. Both during the famine caused by the siege of Samaria by *Ben-Hadad and of Jerusalem by Nebuchadnezzar, the eating of human flesh is mentioned (II Kings 6:29; Lam. 2:20–31; 4:10). Ashurbanipal, king of Assyria (669–27) claims that the Babylonians under siege by him ate their children. Similarly, Assyrian treaties threaten potential violators that they will be reduced to eating their children. Josephus mentions the eating of children in Jerusalem during the Roman War (Wars 6:201–13, cf. I Bar. 2:2ff.). A pathetic story is told of one of the wealthiest women of Jerusalem picking out grain from animal dung after the Roman War (Git. 56a). There are at least three historical references to famine caused by the observance of the Sabbatical year, one during the siege of Jerusalem by the forces of Antiochus IV (Ant. 12:378 = I Macc. 6:49–54), one in the war of Herod against Antigonus (*ibid.*, 14:476) and one during Herod's reign (*ibid.*, 15:7 – see also *Shemittah). The Midrash (Ruth Rabbah 1:4) enumerates ten famines which visited the world. It includes only seven of those mentioned in the Bible as due to drought, and makes up the complement by one ascribed to the time of Adam, one to the time of Lamech and a spiritual famine for lack of God's word (Amos 8:11, usually taken as eschatological). This midrashic passage also differentiates between the famine of Elijah which was a sporadic "famine of drought" and that of Elisha which was one "of [economic] panic." One of the three things "which the Holy One, blessed be He, proclaims in person" (Ber. 55a), famine was regarded as the direct result of transgressions. This is, of course, specifically mentioned in the Bible where the rule is that famine and drought are either threatened (Lev. 26:19f., 26; Deut. 11:17; 28:23; I Kings 17:1; Zech. 14:17) or suffered for sins. Amos (4:6ff.) interprets occurrences of these calamities as prods to repentance – warning notices of God's wrath aimed to bring the people to contrition and thus avert final destruction. The tendency of the rabbis was to make famine the punishment for specific transgressions – the failure to give the tithes and other dues from one's produce, as a kind of quid pro quo (Avot 5:8; Shab. 32b; for the contrary promise of abundance as a reward for bringing tithes – cf. Mal. 3:10–11). As a result, fasting and supplicatory prayers and fasts were instituted (see *Fasting and *Ta'anit – for biblical examples cf. Jer. 14:12 and Joel 2:14–15 for famine caused through pestilence) and the prayers of both pious individuals and people possessing special virtues were regarded as effective in bringing the drought to an end (BM 85b; TJ, Ta'an. 1:2, 65b). The rabbis permitted emigration from Ereẓ Israel in the case of famine, but only when it reached serious proportions (BB 91b; Gen. R. 25 end). Basing themselves on Genesis 41:50 the rabbis (Taan. 11a) forbade procreation during the years of famine.

See also *Rain.

ADD. BIBLIOGRAPHY: A.L. Oppenheim, in: *Iraq*, 17 (1955), 77–8; W. Shea, in: ABD II, 769–73; A. Berlin, *Lamentations* (OTL; 2002), 75–76.

[Louis Isaac Rabinowitz]

FANO, town on the Adriatic coast of Italy. Jews lived in Fano from the 14th century under special protection. In 1332 they were prosperous enough to lend 1,000 ducats to the lord of the city, Galeotto Malatesta. When all heretics were exiled in 1367, the Jewish community was unaffected. Besides moneylenders, it included customs farmers, physicians, and merchants and the Jews are said to have paid half the town taxes. In 1464 the Jewish *badge was imposed. In 1492 a friar raised a *blood libel against the Jews but the municipal council protected them. Between 1502 and 1517 Gershom *Soncino set up his press in Fano, printing books in Hebrew as well as in other languages. Altogether 15 Hebrew books came from his press here, the earliest being the *Me'ah Berakhot* after the Roman rite (1503), and possibly *Ibn Sahula's *Mashal ha-Kadmoni* (second edition with illustrations) which Soncino may have begun before 1500 while still in Brescia. Later appeared the *Rokeaḥ*, a *maḥzor* according to the Roman rite, a *siddur* in *Judeo-Italian, the *Kuzari*, and Albo's *Sefer ha-Ikkarim*. After his return from Pesaro in 1516, he printed during that year and the next the *Arba'ah Turim* of Jacob ben Asher. In 1542 Fano received many of the Jews who had fled from Sicily. With the expulsion from the Papal States, to which Fano now belonged, the Jews had to leave it; 25 loan bankers returned temporarily in 1587/88 in consequence of the liberal policies of Pope Sixtus V, but with the reaction of 1593 the community ceased to exist. In 1901 only three Jews lived in Fano.

BIBLIOGRAPHY: Milano, Italia, index; Roth, Italy, index; Loevinson, in: REJ, 93 (1932), 169–71; D.W. Amram, *Makers of Hebrew Books in Italy* (1909), index; H.D.B. Friedberg, *Toledot ha-Defus ha-Ivri bi-Medinot Italyah...* (1956^2), 28, 30, 50, 52–53.

[Attilio Milano]

FANO, Italian family name, in use from about 1400. Noted are AVIGDOR FANO (second half of 15th century), poet. His short poem *Ozer Nashim* was composed in reply to *Sone ha-Nashim*, an attack on the feminine sex by Abraham of Sarteano; MENAHEM AZARIAH DA *FANO, rabbi and kabbalist; Ezra BEN ISAAC FANO (16th–17th centuries), scribe, rabbi, and kabbalist living in Venice and Mantua. The last copied and owned valuable Hebrew manuscripts, some of which he personally annotated and published. He probably visited Safed in the 1580s, and together with his friends and students R. Mordechai Dato and Menahem Azariah da Fano and his Safed teacher R. Israel Saruk helped disseminate the Safed Kabbalah in Italy. He also wrote works on Kabbalah; JACOB BEN JOAB ELIJAH DA FANO (16th century), scholar and poet in Cento, Ferrara, and Bologna. He composed an elegy on the Marrano martyrs of Ancona of 1555, which he published somewhat incongruously with a satire against women in his *Shiltei ha-Gibborim* (Ferrara, 1556). On papal instructions, the duke of Ferrara ordered the punishment of the author and burning of the volume, which is now very rare. Fano also wrote *Petaḥ Tikvah* on the Ten Commandments, being the first part of a work *Zokher ha-Berit* (unpublished); JOSEPH (Ippolito) DA FANO (c. 1550–1630), communal leader. A notable figure in the Jewish community, he was on familiar terms with the dukes of Mantua and of Ferrara and was sometimes employed by them as an intermediary. Some time before 1628, he is said to have been raised to the rank of Marquis of Villimpenta, in which case he was the first Jew to be ennobled in Europe. The facts, however, require further elucidation; ISAAC BERECHIAH BEN JUDAH ARYEH FANO (17th century), rabbi and kabbalist in Lugo. He composed liturgical poems and homilies.

BIBLIOGRAPHY: Milano, Italia, index; Ghirondi-Neppi, index; Ravà, in: *Educatore israelita*, 22 (1874), 172–7; Kaufmann, in: REJ, 35 (1897), 84–90; 36 (1898), 108–11; Roth, in: JJS, 1 (1948/49), 144–6. **ADD. BIBLIOGRAPHY:** Benayahu, in: *Soloveitchik Jubilee Volume* (1984), 786–855.

[Attilio Milano / Moti Benmelech (2nd ed.)]

FANO, GUIDO ALBERTO (1875–1961), composer, pianist, conductor, teacher, and writer on music. Fano studied in Padua with Vittorio Orefice and Cesare Pollini (piano). He took a composition diploma at the Bologna Liceo Musicale (1897) and a law degree at the university (1901). He taught piano at the Liceo Musicale in Bologna and became director of the conservatories of Parma (1905–11), Naples (1912–16), and Palermo (1916–22). He ended his career at the Milan Conservatory (1922–38, 1945–47) as a piano teacher. His works include an opera, *Iuturna* (1903), *La tentazione di Gesù* (1909), and *Impressioni sinfoniche da Napoleone* (1949) for orchestra; *Andante appassionato* for violin and piano (1908); piano music: Sonatina op.5 (1906) and four fantasies, op.6 (1906), Sonata, E (1920), *Imago, Solitudo* (1933) and *Rimembranze* (1950); and songs. Among his writings are *Pensieri sulla musica* (Bologna, 1903), *I regi istituti musicali d'Italia e il disegno di ruolo per il Conservatorio di Milano* (Parma, 1908), *Le Studio del Pianoforte* (3 vols., 1923–24), and Introduction to F. Fano: *Giuseppe Martucci: saggio biografico-critico* (Milan, 1950), 7–13.

BIBLIOGRAPHY: Grove online; MGG; *Dizionario biografico degli italiani* (1960–); *Dizionario enciclopedico universale della musica e dei musicisti.*

[Israela Stein (2nd ed.)]

FANO, MENAHEM AZARIAH DA (1548–1620), Italian rabbi and kabbalist. The scion of a wealthy family and a prolific author, he was a recognized authority on rabbinic law and the foremost exponent in the West of the kabbalistic system of Moses *Cordovero. Under the influence of Israel *Sarug, who during his stay in Italy spread the knowledge of the mystical system of Isaac *Luria, Menahem Azariah became an admirer of the latter, though without departing from the system of Moses Cordovero. A pupil of R. Ishmael Ḥanina of Valmontone in Ferrara, he was active in Ferrara, Venice, Reggio, and Mantua. Together with his brothers he aided the victims of the earthquake of 1570. He was a patron of Jewish learning, contributing funds for the publication of such works as Cordovero's *Pardes Rimmonim* (Salonika, 1584) and Joseph Caro's commentary *Kesef Mishneh* (Venice, 1574–76) on Maimonides' *Code*.

Fano's fame as a talmudist is borne out by the collection of 130 responsa bearing his name which was published in 1600 in Venice and in 1788 in Dyhernfurth. His style of writing was precise and he displayed considerable originality in the views he expressed. He enjoyed great popularity as a teacher, attracting students from far and wide, from Germany as well as Italy. One of his disciples compared him to an angel of God in appearance. His gentleness and humility showed themselves in his refusal to answer adverse criticism leveled against him by a contemporary scholar on account of certain statements he made with regard to the ritual of the *lulav* on the festival of Tabernacles. Amadeo Recanati dedicated to him his Italian translation of Maimonides' *Guide of the Perplexed*; Isaiah *Horowitz praised his theological treatise *Yonat Elem* (Amsterdam, 1648) saying of it, "the overwhelming majority of his words, and perhaps all of them, are true, and his Torah is true" (introduction to *Novelot Ḥokhmah* (Basle, 1631) by Joseph *Delmedigo). Seventeen of his works have been published. These include a summary of the legal decisions of Isaac *Alfasi and his own major work on the Kabbalah, entitled *Asarah Ma'amarot* (only parts have been printed, Venice, 1597); *Kanfei Yonah* (Korzec, 1786), a kabbalistic work on prayer; and *Gilgulei Neshamot* (Prague, 1688) on the transmigration of the soul. Many of his kabbalistic interpretations must have been made for the first time in the course of sermons delivered by him. Extant in manuscript are liturgical poems, elegies, comments on the teachings of Isaac Luria, and a voluminous correspondence. He died in Mantua.

BIBLIOGRAPHY: L. Woidislawski, *Toledot Rabbenu Menaḥem Azaryah mi-Fano* (1903); S. Simonsohn, *Toledot ha-Yehudim be-Dukkasut Mantovah* (1964), 665, index, s.v.; M.A. Szulwas, *Ḥayyei ha-Yehudim be-Italyah bi-Tekufat ha-Renaissance* (1955) 196, 220.

[Samuel Rosenblatt]

°**FĀRĀBĪ, ABŪ NAṢR MUḤAMMAD, AL-** (c. 870–c. 950), one of the greatest philosophers of the medieval Islamic world. Al-Fārābī had considerable influence on Jewish philosophers, particularly *Maimonides. Having spent most of his life in *Baghdad, he became associated in 942 with the illustrious court of Sayf al-Dawla, the Ḥamdānid ruler of Syria, residing mainly in *Aleppo.

Al-Fārābī played a major role in the dissemination of ancient philosophy in the Islamic world. His teacher was the Nestorian Yuḥannā ibn Ḥaylān (see M. Meyerhof, *Von Alexandrien nach Bagdad* (1930), 405, 414, 416ff.). He was thus familiar with the Christian tradition of Aristotelian studies initially cultivated in *Alexandria and transmitted by Syriac-speaking Christians to the Islamic world. While in Baghdad, al-Fārābī apparently had contacts with the Christian Baghdad school of Aristotelian studies, the leading member of which was Mattā ibn Yūnus. Aristotle was studied together with his commentators, *Alexander of Aphrodisias and *Themistius, as well as with commentators of the neoplatonic school of Alexandria (Ammonius son of Hermias and his pupils). The paramount philosophical task al-Fārābī faced was to naturalize the pagan philosophic tradition of antiquity within the confines of a society structured by a revealed law.

His Philosophy

The bulk of al-Fārābī's teaching and writing was devoted to interpreting Aristotle, particularly the logical works. He wrote commentaries and paraphrases on the entire *Organon*. In natural philosophy he followed the *Physics* closely. His metaphysics is a blend of the *Metaphysics* and neoplatonism. Creation is viewed by him as an atemporal process of emanation which flows from the unique, unqualified First Being. Al-Fārābī combines the neoplatonic theory of emanation with the Aristotelian-Ptolemaic *cosmology which posits a system of celestial spheres and their intelligences encompassing the sublunar world. The intelligence of the last sphere (the moon) presides over the sublunar world and is called the active *intellect. Al-Fārābī thus follows that interpretation of the *nous poietikós* ("active intellect"; *De anima*, 3), which regards it as a cosmic entity. The active intellect is "the Giver of Forms" (*wāhib al-ṣuwar*; *dator formarum*): it conveys forms to the world, thus constituting the rational structure of the universe. It also actualizes the potential intellect of the individual. Al-Fārābī's theory of intellection is complicated and his various discussions of the subject, mainly in the treatises "On the Intellect" and *Arā' Ahl al-Madīna al-Fāḍila* ("The Opinion of the Citizens of the Virtuous City," ed. by A. Nader, 1959) are not entirely consistent. The individual potential (or material) intellect, influenced by the active intellect, becomes the intellect in act. When it achieves perfection, it becomes what is termed the acquired intellect, which is said to be close to the active intellect. The one who achieves this perfection thereby becomes intelligizer (*ʿāqil*), intelligized (*maʿqūl*), and intellect (*ʿaql*), free from matter, and "divine" (see *al-Siyāsa al-Madaniyya* ("The Political Regime," ed. by F. Najjar (1964), 36). In "The Virtuous City" (p. 31), this threefold identity is posited of God.

Al-Fārābī equates intellectual perfection with supreme happiness. The individual who achieves this perfection and happiness is considered to be the philosopher or sage. If such a person has the additional quality of a perfect imagination, so that intelligible forms flow from the intellect to the imagination becoming embodied in sensible forms, he is more than a sage: he is a *prophet. The process by which the forms flow from the First Being through the active intellect to the particular intellect and then the imagination is called "revelation" (*waḥī*). To become a statesman, in addition to being a prophet, he needs also the power of persuasion in order to lead men to the correct actions that bring happiness ("The Virtuous City," 104). The prophet is thus essentially a philosopher, one who is capable of conveying philosophical truth (theoretical and practical) to the unreflective masses on the level of the imagination, in myths and symbols. The philosopher, lawgiver (i.e., prophet), and imām (head of the community) are ideally one and the same person (*Taḥṣīl al-Saʿāda*, "The Attainment of Happiness," tr. by M. Mahdi, in *Alfarabi's Philosophy of Plato and Aristotle* (1962), paras. 57, 58). Religion is thus "an imitation of philosophy" (*ibid.*, para. 55). This concept of prophecy is traced by R. Walzer to certain ideas in middle Platonism (*Greek into Arabic* (1962), 206ff.). The identity of the philosopher and ruler is, of course, rooted ultimately in Plato's concept of the philosopher-king in the *Republic*.

Political Theory

Al-Fārābī's political theory depends mainly on Plato, principally on the *Republic* and *Laws*. The *Republic* inspired his typology of the corrupt and perfect political regimes in "The Virtuous City" and "The Political Regime." The elaboration of a theory concerning the perfect city, the perfect nation, and the perfect world state in the whole of the inhabited world (*maʿmūra; oikoumene*) is traced by Walzer to middle Platonic developments (see *Oriens*, 16 (1963), 46ff.). Plato's *Laws* was of crucial importance for al-Fārābī (and Islamic philosophy in general), for it envisioned a society based on a single divine law comprehending both religious and civil aspects of life (see L. Strauss, in REJ, 100 (1936), 2). Aristotle's dictum, "man is by nature a political animal," played an important role in al-Fārābī's political theory, but he apparently did not utilize the *Politics* to an appreciable extent. Al-Fārābī's choice of Plato's political philosophy had a determining effect upon the later development of Islamic, as well as Jewish philosophy. In ethical theory Aristotle's *Nicomachean Ethics* was of decisive influence (along with Porphyry's now lost commentary).

Al-Fārābī's political theory thus posits a fundamental distinction in society between the elite (the sages who know by reason) and the masses (the believers who apprehend by imagination). Philosophical truth is universal. It is adapted by the prophets to the requirements of various groups and nations in the guise of religion. There are many religions; each is an approximation (of greater or lesser validity) of the single truth of reason (see, e.g., "The Political Regime," 85ff.). While giving priority to philosophy, al-Fārābī recognized the role of religion in human life as an instrument for the welfare of society and the edification of the unphilosophical masses. He was interested in preserving the masses from the possible pernicious effects of the truths of reason. Consequently, he wrote esoterically so as not to disturb unreflective commitment to religion and morality, as well as to evade persecution by religious and state authorities (L. Strauss, in *Louis Ginzberg Jubilee Volume*, 1 (1945), 357ff.).

Influence on Jewish Thought

Al-Fārābī's impact on medieval Jewish thought was considerable. In Hebrew texts he is called either by his Arabic name (Abū Naṣr or al-Fārābī) or by the Hebrew equivalent of the former (Abū Yeshaʿ). Abū Bakr is sometimes erroneously substituted for Abū Naṣr.

Strauss (loc. cit.) first demonstrated the dominating influence of al-Fārābī's political philosophy on *Maimonides. Maimonides' esteem for al-Fārābī, which no doubt encouraged the acceptance of the latter within Jewish philosophical circles, is clear from a letter he wrote to Samuel ibn Tibbon (see JQR, 25 (1934/35), 379). Maimonides recommended exclusively al-Fārābī's works on logic and praised all his writings, especially "The Book of Principles" ("The Political Regime"), as impeccably excellent and worthy of study, adding, "for he is a great man." In the introduction to his translation of *The Guide of the Perplexed* (1963), S. Pines states that in theoretical and political science Maimonides followed al-Fārābī on all points (p. lxxviii). The main lines of influence are traced by Pines: Maimonides' esoteric style and the tendency to embed "outrageously unorthodox statements" in a cryptic, veiled context are fashioned according to the model of al-Fārābī (see also Strauss, in *Essays on Maimonides*, ed. by S.W. Baron (1941), 37ff.). Maimonides was also influenced by al-Fārābī's negative assessment of the Kalām, as well as his treatment of such crucial issues as creation, intellection, prophecy, and providence.

Extensive quotations in Maimonides' *Shemonah Perakim* are taken from al-Fārābī's *Fuṣūl al-Madanī* (*Aphorisms of the Statesman*, ed. and tr. by D.M. Dunlop, 1961), as was shown by H. Davidson (in PAAJR, 31 (1963), 33–50). Al-Fārābī's influence may also be discerned in Maimonides' code of Jewish law. A passage in *Mishneh Torah* (Deʿot, 6:1), to the effect that one who lives in an evil city should immigrate to a place where the people are righteous or, if this is impossible, live in isolation, seems to reflect a similar statement in al-Fārābī's *Aphorisms of the Statesman* (para. 88). The comparison of those who are physically infirm, and whose sense of taste is consequently impaired, with those who are psychologically infirm and morally corrupt (Deʿot, 2:1) is virtually a verbatim translation of a similar comparison by al-Fārābī in "The Political Regime" (p. 83). It is possible that al-Fārābī's specification and ordering of the ideas that should be taught in the virtuous religious community (*al-milla al-fāḍila*) influenced the choice of subjects treated and their sequence in *Mishneh Torah* (Yesodei ha-Torah; cf. *Kitāb al-Milla*, "The Book of Religion," ed. by M. Mahdi (1968), 44ff.).

Hebrew Translations

Many of al-Fārābī's works were translated into Hebrew. M. Steinschneider (Uebersetzungen, para. 158) lists eight. The microfilm collection of the Institute of Hebrew Manuscripts at the Hebrew University in Jerusalem contains about 25 works, including some interesting logical works not mentioned by Steinschneider. A partial translation of the tripartite work that comprises "The Attainment of Happiness," "The Philosophy of Plato," and "The Philosophy of Aristotle," together with the music part of *Iḥṣā' al-ʿUlūm* ("The Register of the Sciences"), is contained in Shem Tov ibn *Falaquera's *Reshit Ḥokhmah* (see M. Steinschneider, *Al-Farabi* (1896), 176ff., 224ff.; Strauss, in MGWJ, 80 (1936), 96ff.). "The Political Regime" was translated in part under the title *Sefer ha-Hathalot* (ed. by Z. Filipowski in *Sefer ha-Asif*, 1849). Falaquera often cites al-Fārābī in his commentary on the *Guide, Moreh ha-Moreh*. According to S.O. Heller-Wilensky, Isaac ibn *Latīf quotes two whole chapters of "The Virtuous City" in his *Shaʿar ha-Shamayim* (in *Jewish Medieval and Renaissance Studies*, ed. by A. Altmann (1967), 196).

[Joel Kraemer]

As Musician

Al-Fārābī was one of the outstanding theorists of Arabic music and several Arabic sources extol his musical talent and his excellence as an *ʿūd* player. He wrote several treatises on music of which the most famous are *Kitāb al-Mūsīqī al-Kabīr* ("The Grand Book of Music") and *Iḥṣā' al-ʿUlūm* ("The Classification of the Sciences") in which he enumerates all the known sciences and defines their nature and object; part of the third chapter deals with the science of music. This work became known in Medieval Europe through its several Latin translations (see H.G. Farmer, *Arabic-Latin Writings on Music*, 1934) and was translated into Hebrew by Kalonymus b. Kalonymus of Arles in 1314 under the title: *Ma'amar be-Mispar ha-Ḥokhmot* (see A. Shiloah, *Yuval*, 2 (1971), 115–27). Among Jewish writers who used the section on music in their works are Shem Tov ibn *Falaquera in his *Reshit Ḥokhma* and Joseph ibn *Aknin in chapter VII of his *Ṭibb al-Nufūs*. The section on music as well as several passages compiled in the "Grand Book of Music" is included in the Hebrew version of Ibn Salt's treatise on music and occurs in a Genizah fragment (British Museum, Ms. Or.5565c).

[Amnon Shiloah (2nd ed.)]

BIBLIOGRAPHY: Brockelmann, Arab Lit., 1 (1943), 232ff.; supplement, 1 (1937), 375ff., 957ff.; N. Rescher, *Al Farabi. An Annotated Bibliography* (1962); R. Walzer, in: EIS² s.v. *al-Farabi*; H.G. Farmer, *Al-Fārābī's Arabic Latin Writings on Music* (1960²), 3–16; H. Avenary, in *Tatzlil*, 3 (1963), 163.

FARAJ, MURAD (1866–1956), Egyptian Karaite author and theologian. Born in *Cairo and trained as a lawyer, Faraj was a government official during the reign of the khedive ʿAbbās Ḥilmī (1892–1914). He took a keen interest in the problems of the Egyptian Jewish community and was particularly active among the *Karaites, whom he served for a time as *dayyan*. After resigning this post, he practiced law until 1932, when he turned exclusively to literary pursuits.

Faraj, who wrote in Hebrew and Arabic, published some 30 volumes of poetry, religious works, and books on law. Two books of verse, highly praised by the great Egyptian poet Aḥmad Shawqī, were *Dīwān Murād* ("Murad's Poetical Works," 5 vols., 1912–29) and *Al-Shuʿarā' al-Yahūd al-ʿArab* ("The Jewish Poets in Arabic," 1929; 1939²). He also published *Shir ʿIvri mi-Meshorer ʿAravi* ("A Hebrew Song of an Arab Poet," 1945) in both Hebrew and Arabic. In his verse he was a meticulous craftsman with a fondness for difficult and unusual expressions.

All but one of Faraj's theological works were written in Arabic. They include *Al-Qarā'ūn wa-al-Rabbānūn* ("The Karaites and the Rabbanites," 1918); *Al-Yahūdiyya* ("Judaism," 1920); *Tafsīr al-Tawrā* ("Torah Commentary," 1928); *Al-Qudsiyyāt* ("Holy Offerings," translated into Hebrew by the author in 1923); *Amthāl Sulaimān* ("The Proverbs of Solomon," 1938), an Arabic translation of and commentary on the Book of Proverbs; and *Ayyūb* ("Job," 1950), an Arabic translation of several chapters of the Book of Job. Two books on linguistics were *Ustādh al-ʿIbriyya* ("The Hebrew Teacher," 1925) and *Multaqā al-Lughatayn al-ʿIbriyya wa-al-ʿArabiyya* ("The Crossroads of the Hebrew and Arabic Languages," 5 vols., 1930–50). Faraj also wrote *Al-Furūq al-Qānūniyya* ("On Legal Differences," 1917) which, from 1928, became a standard textbook at Cairo University. In addition to all of these works, Faraj published several legal dissertations and many articles and reviews. In 1936 he was elected a member of the Egyptian Academy for the Arabic Language.

ADD. BIBLIOGRAPHY: J.M. Landau, *Jews in Nineteenth-Century Egypt* (1969), index.

[Hayyim J. Cohen]

FARAJ (Moses) BEN SOLOMON DA AGRIGENTO (Girgenti), also known as **Ferragut** and **Faraj ben Salim** (13th century), physician, translator, and author. Faraj was personal physician and official translator to Charles I of Anjou, king of Sicily, for whom he translated several medical treatises from Arabic into Latin. Among these are *Liber Continens* (Ar. *Al-Ḥāwī*), a medical encyclopedia in 20 parts by Rhazes (al-Rāzī), which he finished translating in 1279 and which was printed five times between 1486 and 1542; *Tacuini Aegritudinum ac Morborum Corporis…*, a translation made in 1280 of the *Taqwīm al-Abdān* by Abū ʿAlī ibn Jazla; and *De Medicis Expertis* by Pseudo-Galen. Faraj's authorship of other books cannot definitely be authenticated. However, if, as seems likely, Faraj is the same person as Moses b. Solomon of Salerno, he is also the author of a commentary on the *Guide* by *Maimonides. A picture of Faraj receiving the *Al-Ḥāwī* for translation from Charles I appears in a 13th-century illuminated manuscript.

BIBLIOGRAPHY: Roth, Italy, 93–94.

[Attilio Milano]

FARBAND, American Jewish Labor Zionist fraternal order. The establishment of the Farband was first conceived in Philadelphia in 1908 by a small group headed by Meyer L. Brown which sought to build a fraternal order in which Labor Zionists would feel at home – one that would combine fraternal benefits and mutual aid with a Labor Zionist outlook and program. In the succeeding two years groups were formed in several cities, and on June 10–16 a founding conference of the national Farband took place in Rochester, New York. It adopted the name Yiddish Natzionaler Arbeiter Farband (Jewish National Workers Alliance) and formulated the following program:

The JNWA strives to organize all Jewish workers on the following principles:

1. Mutual help in case of need, sickness, and death.

2. Education of Jewish workers to full awareness of their national and social interests.

3. Support of all endeavors which lead to the national liberation and renascence of the Jewish people… support of all activities which lead to the strengthening and liberation of the working class.

With the then existing Jewish fraternal orders largely devoid of ideological content, and with the only other Jewish workers order – the *Workmen's Circle (Arbeiter Ring) – adopting an anti-Zionist position, Farband, with its socialist-Zionist viewpoint and program in Israel and America, grew in number from 1,000 in 1911 to 25,000 in 1946 and 40,000 in 1972.

In 1911 Farband developed the first modern insurance and mutual benefit system for Jewish workers. The organization received its official charter, licensing it to sell various insurance and medical plans, from the State of New York on January 6, 1913, and from Canada in 1921. The main mutual benefits of Farband include: life, accident, health, hospitalization, and juvenile insurance; a major medical plan; and savings and loan groups.

From its inception Farband was involved in Jewish communal affairs at home and abroad. In 1913 it fought against the "literacy test" given to immigrants and protested against the *Beilis Trial. During World War I Farband participated in the establishment of the American Jewish Congress and the People's Relief Committee, and sent many volunteers to fight in the ranks of the Jewish Legion. During World War II Farband campaigned actively to raise funds for the Labor Zionist Committee for Relief and Rehabilitation. It also energetically supported the founding of the American Jewish Conference in 1944. Farband has also been active in the civil rights struggle and has espoused many other liberal causes both in the United States and Canada.

Farband concentrates much of its energies on cultural activities. In addition to maintaining a network of day and evening schools, Farband established "educational bureaus" in the 1920s to encourage Jewish cultural activities by promoting "Onegei Shabbat," musical and drama presentations, seminars, study groups, and lectures throughout the United States and Canada. Farband encourages its members to use Hebrew and Yiddish and in cooperation with the Hillel Foundation has since 1966 promoted the study of the Yiddish language and literature on many campuses throughout the United States. Farband supports the Jewish Teachers' Seminary, the People's University in New York, the Farband Book Publishing Association, and a number of newspapers and periodicals in Yiddish, Hebrew, and English. It provides educational programs during the summer months through its network of summer camps: in 1926 Unser Camp (for adults) and Kinderwelt (for youth) were created in New York. The educational and financial success of these camps stimulated the creation of similar camps throughout the United States and Canada. Habonim is the youth movement of the Farband, as well as of Po'alei Zion and Pioneer Women.

As a Labor Zionist organization Farband has always maintained strong ties with Ereẓ Israel and the State of Israel, especially the workers' groups there. At its founding conference, it resolved to institute obligatory taxes for the benefit of workers in Ereẓ Israel. Important Israeli leaders, among them David Ben-Gurion, Izhak Ben-Zvi, Golda Meir, and Zalman Shazar, have frequently come to the United States to address its conventions and leaders. In 1919 Farband opened a branch in Ereẓ Israel, and during the Mandatory period and after World War II it campaigned energetically and assisted with funds and manpower in the creation of the Jewish State. After the birth of Israel, Farband continued its work on behalf of the cooperative, pioneering sector through support of the Histadrut. It consistently invested a part of its insurance funds in bodies which promote its ideals and today is the largest investor in Ampal, the American investment arm associated with the Histadrut.

Since the 1930s the possibility of the unification of Po'alei Zion and Farband has been discussed frequently, since both share the same Labor Zionist philosophy, the same goals in America and Israel, and have cooperated on the most important national and international projects. In 1954, during Farband's Montreal convention, Zalman Shazar, subsequently president of the State of Israel, personally offered his services in this direction. However, only after the New York convention in 1967 did Farband seriously negotiate the unification of Labor Zionist forces in America. The 22nd national convention, held in New York December 23–26, 1971, finally brought this about by bringing into the legal framework of Farband the members and branches of Poalei Zion and the American Habonim Association, the latter comprising the alumni of the Labor Zionist youth movement. The name was changed to Labor Zionist Alliance. The national offices are in Farband House, New York City, and regional offices are maintained in principal cities throughout the United States and Canada.

[Jehuda Reinharz]

The 22nd national convention, held in New York December 232–6, 1971, finally brought about the merger of Farband, Poalei Zion, and the American Habonim Association, comprising the alumni of the Labor Zionist youth movement. The name was changed to Labor Zionist Alliance and was changed once again in 2004 to Ameinu.

[Daniel Mann (2nd ed.)]

FARBER, MARVIN (1901–1980), U.S. philosopher, founder of the International Phenomenological Society in 1939 and editor of the journal *Philosophy and Phenomenological Research* from 1940 and, from 1951, *American Lectures in Philosophy.* Farber was born in Buffalo, New York, and educated at Harvard University and in Germany. He taught at Ohio State University, State University of New York at Buffalo, and at the University of Pennsylvania. Starting as an instructor in philosophy at the University of Buffalo in 1927, he became successively assistant professor, professor, department chairman, acting dean of the graduate school, distinguished professor and, in 1964, distinguished service professor.

Farber was the first to bring Husserl's phenomenology to the attention of American philosophers. In 1928 he published *Phenomenology as a Method and as a Philosophical Discipline*, and in 1943 *The Foundation of Phenomenology.* He edited *Philosophical Essays in Memory of Edmund Husserl* (1940). Though Farber was a follower of Husserl and expositor of contemporary German and French thought, he criticized the anti-scientific attitude of Husserl, Max Scheler, and others, as well as the anti-rationalist tendencies in other contemporary European thinkers such as Heidegger. His views tended toward naturalism and pragmatism, as expressed in his volume *Naturalism and Subjectivism* (1959) and in his many articles.

Other books by Farber include *The Aims of Phenomenology: The Motives, Methods, and Impact of Husserl's Thought* (1966), *Phenomenology and Existence: Toward a Philosophy within Nature* (1967), *Foundation of Phenomenology: Edmund Husserl & the Quest for a Rigorous Science of Philosophy* (1967), *Basic Issues of Philosophy: Experience, Reality, and Human Values* (1968), and *The Search for an Alternative: Philosophical Perspectives of Subjectivism & Marxism* (with R. Chisholm, 1984).

Farber was a member of philosophy societies around the world, such as the Institut Philosophe, Paris; International Phenomenological Society (past president); American Philosophical Association (president of the Eastern Division), C.S. Pierce Society, Symbolic Logic Association (executive committee), and American Association of University Professors, Phi Beta Kappa.

BIBLIOGRAPHY: H. Spiegelberg, *The Phenomenological Movement*, 2 (1960), 627–9; **ADD. BIBLIOGRAPHY:** D. Mathur, *Naturalistic Philosophies of Experience: Studies in James, Dewey and Farber against the Background of Husserl's Phenomenology* (1971).

[Richard H. Popkin / Ruth Beloff (2nd ed.)]

FARBER, VIOLA (1931–1998), U.S. dancer, choreographer, and teacher. Of German birth, Farber arrived in the U.S. at the age of seven and became a citizen in 1944. She studied modern dance with Katherine Litz, and Merce Cunningham and also took ballet classes with Alfredo Corvino. In 1953, she became a founding member of Cunningham's company as a dancer and choreographed some of its works until 1968. Among her works from this period are *Crises, Paired*, and *Nocturne.* To the Cunningham technique Farber, as a passionate dancer, added her personal contribution of human warmth. Dense, demanding movement and a humorous, bounding enthusiasm characterized her style. In 1968, she founded her own company and began choreographing her own works. Most of her work has been either set to original music or danced in silence. However, in one case her *Dune and Nightshade* was choreographed to Beethoven's Moonlight Sonata. She also taught in Salt Lake City and Columbus, Ohio, and served on the faculty of the New York School of the Arts. In 1981–82, the French government appointed her director of the Centre National de Danse Contemporaine at Angers, for which she created nine works, including *Nuage* and *Oiseaux-Pierres*, continuing to maintain close ties to France. Her choreographed piece *Ainsi de suite* was performed at the Avignon Festival.

[Amnon Shiloah (2nd ed.)]

FARBSTEIN, DAVID ẒEVI (1868–1953), Zionist Swiss politician. Farbstein was born in Warsaw and grew up in a traditional family. He worked at a bank in Warsaw to finance his studies, distancing himself from his Orthodox upbringing. During his studies in Berlin (1892–94) he joined the Russian Jewish Scientific Association and met with N. *Syrkin. He continued his studies at the universities of Zurich and Berne (1894–97), graduating with a thesis on "the legal status of the free and unfree worker in talmudic law." In 1897 he received Swiss citizenship, became a member of the Cultusgemeinde and joined the Social Democratic Party. He protested against the expulsion of Russian-Jewish peddlers from Zurich (1905/06) and led the opposition in the Cultusgemeinde against the well-to-do Swiss-Jewish establishment. As a lawyer, he defended women who had had abortions. In 1902 he was elected to the cantonal parliament, after 1904 to the city parliament. Here he fought against the introduction of a 15-

year waiting period for Orthodox East European Jews to apply for Swiss citizenship, but he did not convince the bourgeois majority (1920). He was the first Jewish member of the Swiss parliament (the Nationalrat," 1922–38). As a Zionist, he helped *Herzl set up the First Zionist Congress in Basle and drafted the statutes of the *Jewish National Fund (Keren Kayemet le-Israel). Already in 1897 he founded the first Zionist group in Zurich. After 1933 he fought Swiss fascism and opposed the policies of the leaders of the Swiss Federation of Jewish Communities as too compromising. He was instrumental in the resignation of Saly Mayer from the presidency of the federation in 1943. He refuted the anti-Jewish allegations of Zurich pastor Walter Hoch.

BIBLIOGRAPHY: H. Strauss-Zweig, *David Farbstein. Juedischer Sozialist – sozialistischer Jude* (2002); *Davar* (June 22, 1953); *Festschrift zum 50-jaehrigen Bestehen des Schweizerischen Israelitischen Gemeindebundes* (1954), 197ff. (his autobiography).

[Uri Kaufmann (2nd ed.)]

FARBSTEIN, JOSHUA HESCHEL (1870–1948), leader of the *Mizrachi movement, head of the Warsaw Jewish community, and of the Jewish Community Council (Va'ad ha-Kehillah) in Jerusalem (see Israel, Communal *Governance). Born in Warsaw, Farbstein was active in the Ḥibbat Zion movement, and, with the emergence of Herzl, joined the political Zionist movement. Together with his brother, David Ẓevi *Farbstein, he attended the First Zionist Congress and was the first to discuss the religious problems of the Zionist movement in pre-Congress talks with Herzl. Farbstein participated in subsequent Congresses, representing Mizrachi after its formation in 1902. He was president of the Zionist Organization in Poland from 1915 to 1918 and was active during these years in obtaining extensive aid for war victims. A founder of Mizrachi in Poland, he was its president between 1918 and 1931, president of the Keren Hayesod in Poland, a member of the Polish Sejm and of the city council of Warsaw, and, between 1926 and 1931, president of the Warsaw Jewish community. Farbstein settled in Jerusalem in 1931 and was a member of the Zionist Executive between 1931 and 1933. Together with Emanuel *Neumann, he devised the abortive plan to lease 70,000 dunams in Transjordan for Jewish settlement. In Jerusalem he was active in the Community Council, which he headed between 1938 and 1945 (ultimately, as honorary president). Throughout his life he held leading posts in the world Mizrachi movement.

BIBLIOGRAPHY: *Askan le-Mofet* (1945), anthology of articles on J. Farbstein; L. Jaffe (ed.), *Sefer ha-Congress* (1950^2), 191–2, 343–4.

[Getzel Kressel]

FARḤI, family of financiers in *Damascus of Sephardi origin during the 18th and 19th centuries. The family arrived at Damascus from *Aleppo in mid-18th century. Members of this family held the position of **ṣarrāf* ("banker") in the province of Damascus during the 1740s and possibly even earlier. It appears that members of this family also served as officials in the financial administration of the province and during the 1790s the bookkeeping of the provincial treasury was entrusted to them. The status and power of this family reached its climax during the 19th century, when the responsibility for the affairs of the treasury of the provinces of Damascus and Sidon – the center of which was in *Acre – was handed over to one of its members. The family could then undertake the financing of large-scale projects, including participation in the financing of the *ḥajj* (pilgrimage to Mecca) expenses, which was within the domain of the governor of the Damascus Province as the organizer of the *ḥajj* caravan.

The first member of this family to consolidate his position in Damascus was SAUL (Shihada) FARḤI who lived there in the second half of the 18th century. His position in the financial administration of the province enabled him to intervene with the governor of Damascus in favor of the Christians. In 1770 he was a very wealthy man and had good connections with prominent people in Istanbul. Solomon Farḥi, probably the father of Saul, died after torture in 1794.

The sons of Saul were RAPHAEL (died in Damascus, 1845), MOSES (died in Damascus, c. 1830), MENAḤEM (died in Damascus, c. 1830), JOSEPH (died in Damascus, c. 1830), and ḤAYYIM (died in Acre, 1820). RAPHAEL and JOSEPH inherited his position in Damascus and their cousin SOLOMON (Salmon) FARḤI also shared their importance. The third son, ḤAYYIM, entered the service of Aḥmad al-Jazzār Pasha, the governor of the province of Sidon who had fixed his residence in Acre in about 1790. He held the position of *ṣarrāf* and was responsible for the treasury affairs during most of al-Jazzār's rule (until 1804). He distinguished himself during the stand of Acre against Napoleon's armies in 1799. His brother MOSES was his assistant. In 1804 Ḥayyim was imprisoned, but on the death of al-Jazzār he was set free. He immediately joined in the struggle for al-Jazzār's succession as a supporter of Suleiman Pasha. Suleiman achieved the position of governor in 1805 due to the assistance of Ḥayyim who intervened in his favor in Constantinople. Suleiman had complete confidence in Ḥayyim, and he gave him a free hand in the administration and its finances. The Suleiman period (until 1818) was one of consolidation for Ḥayyim and the family in general, especially after Suleiman was also appointed governor of Damascus. Ḥayyim Farḥi also chose Suleiman Pasha's successor, ʿAbdallah Pasha, whom he had helped rise to the position of *ketkhudā* (or **kaḥya*; administrative director) under Suleiman from 1814. In practice, Ḥayyim was the governor of the province from 1818. However, the thirst for power of ʿAbdallah and the presence of men who slandered Ḥayyim before ʿAbdallah brought about his downfall and he was executed (1820) at the height of his glory. This was the first blow to strike the family. Ḥayyim's brothers attempted to avenge him and they participated in the war waged against ʿAbdallah by the governor of Damascus. Because of its financial power, the family nevertheless continued to hold on to its firm position in Damascus, and Raphael Farḥi was the chief sherif in Damascus. Raphael's children were David (died in Damascus, 1907), Aslan (born in 1828), Polica, and Meir. Meir had three sons: Moses, Solomon, and Jacob. The son of Aslan was Joseph Farḥi who died in Beirut in 1840. There is a letter from the Farḥi family to Moses *Montefiore from 1849 signed by Menaḥem Farhi; Judah, Meir, and David, the sons of Raphael Farḥi; Ezekiel, Nathaniel, and Aaron, the sons of Joseph Farḥi; and Solomon, the son of Joseph Farḥi. In that year Montefiore lodged in the house of Isaac Ḥayyim Farḥi. The Egyptian conquest of Syria at the beginning of the 1830s struck a decisive blow at the family, both in relation to its financial matters and its influence in the town. In 1834 the family lost its positions in the financial administration and that of *ṣarrāf*, and only a few of its members remained on the staff of the treasury and in the leadership of the Jewish millet. However, with the return of Ottoman rule in Syria in 1840, one of the members was again appointed to the direction of the treasury administration, even though the family could not regain its former financial power. During the 18th and 19th centuries the family members were the rivals and opponents of powerful Christian families and sometimes found themselves in a perilous situation because Muslim governors wanted to dismiss them from their positions. The new rivals of the Farḥi family in Damascus were the members of Albaḥri family. At the time of the *Damascus Affair the family lost its political influence and some of its members were imprisoned. Aslan Farḥi confessed because he was afraid of torture.

As was the case with other wealthy Jewish families, the Farḥis also played a role in fostering spiritual life and financial support of the needy. Ḥayyim Farḥi was a particularly generous donor to synagogues both in Damascus and in Acre. He owned the magnificent *Farḥi Bible*, which was named after him. After his execution it came into the possession of the British consul in Damascus, and it was only restored to the family nearly a century later. They established family religious trusts for the benefit of yeshivot and **kolelim*, supported scholars, assisted the needy, and arranged for employment in their offices. They also initiated relations between the Jews of Damascus and Palestine and those of Constantinople. As for the relations between the Jews and the government, there is no definite evidence of their intervention, except for some vague evidence concerning a tax exemption for the Jews of *Safed. After the death of Ḥayyim, there was a quarrel over his estate in the Farḥi family, which began in 1833 and continued for many years. The struggle was between the sons of Raphael and their cousins Joseph Hai and Nissim Farḥi, the sons of Menaḥem. Rabbi Jacob Antebi, the chief rabbi of Damascus, wrote a decision in 1833, but Moses, the brother of Hayyim Farhi, and, after the death of Moses, who lived in Acre, his sons Mordecai and Menaḥem rejected the decision. They were supported by Rabbi Ḥayyim Nissim *Abulafia of Tiberias. Rabbi Abraham Ḥayyim *Gagin, the chief rabbi of Jerusalem, defended the decision of Rabbi Antebi. Moses Montefiore and Ẓevi Hirsch Lehren also intervened. In 1847 the rabbis of Damascus wrote about the activity of Judah and David, the sons of Raphael Farḥi, against Isaac Ḥayyim Farḥi, the son of Solomon, who was the translator of the French consul in Damascus. His relative David Farḥi became the Turkish scribe of the French consul, and Nathaniel Farḥi was the treasurer of the consulate. Meir, the brother of Ḥayyim Farḥi, was murdered in 1822. He had married his second wife in 1818 and she bore him his only son, Isaac Ḥayyim. The interior of the house of the Farḥi family in Damascus was very elegant. In later generations the Farḥi family settled in Beirut, Paris, Italy, South America, and Israel. In 1854 Meir Farḥi was appointed sherif in Damascus, but was later dismissed. Also in 1854 Nissan Farḥi was appointed the representative of the Jews in the Mejlis of Damascus.

[Aryeh Shmuelevitz/ Leah Bornstein-Makovetsky (2nd ed.)]

HILLEL BEN JACOB FARHI (1868–1940) poet, translator, and physician, also belonged to this family. Farḥi, who was born in Damascus, studied medicine in *Beirut and London and became a government doctor in *Cairo. In his spare time, he pursued research into Hebrew and Arabic and translated many Jewish religious works into Arabic. These include his *Siddur Farḥi* (1917), which contains an introduction to the history of prayer; *Al-Urjūzah al-Fārḥiyah* ("Farḥi's Poem," 1914), comprising the 613 *Commandments in the form of an Arabic poem; and *Majmūʿat Farḥi* ("Farḥi's Collection," 1922), which contains the Passover *Haggadah, the *Pirkei *Avot*, and the *Azharot* of Solomon ibn *Gabirol. Farḥi's verse translations and his own poetry are marked by lucidity and simplicity. He published a Hebrew version of the *Rubáiyát* of Omar Khayyām (1931) and, with Nissim Mallul, produced an Arabic translation of the *Zikhronot le-Beit David* by A.S. *Friedberg.

A well-known member of this family was ISAAC B. SOLOMON FARḤI, the author of *Tuv Yerushalayim* (Jerusalem, 1842), *Zekhut ha-Rabbim* (Constantinople, 1829), *Imrei Binah* (Belgrade, 1837), *Zekhut u-Mishor* (Smyrna, 1850), *Ẓuf Devash* (Leghorn, 1849), *Shevet Mishor* (Belgrade, 1837), *Matok la-Nefesh* (Constantinople, 1828), *Marpe la-Eẓem* (Constantinople, 1830), *Matok mi-Devash* (Jerusalem, 1842), *Musar Haskel* (Constantinople, 1830), and *Minei Metikah* (Leghorn, 1848), sermons for the Sabbath. NURI FARḤI, a native of Damascus, settled in *Alexandria after having studied in Paris. In Alexandria he engaged in commerce and wrote a history of the Jews in the town from its foundation until his own time, *La Communauté Juive d'Alexandrie de l'Antiquité à nos Jours* (1945). Another member of this family, JOSEPH DAVID FARḤI (1878–1945), became the president of the Jewish community of Beirut.

[Hayyim J. Cohen]

BIBLIOGRAPHY: Ben Zvi, Ereẓ Yisrael, index. **ADD. BIBLIOGRAPHY:** F. Librecht, in: *Magazin fuer die Literatur des Auslandes* (1850), 461–63, 503–4; T. Philipp, in: *Cathedra*, 34 (1985), 97–114; E. Shochetman, in: *Asufot*, 6 (1993), 161–209; idem, in: *Asufot* 11 (1998), 281–308; Y. Harel, *Bisfinot shel Esh la-Ma'arav, Temurot be-Yahadut Surya bi-Tekufat ha-Reformot ha-Ottomaniot 1840–1880* (2003), index; J.M. Landau, *Jews in Nineteenth-Century Egypt* (1969), 101, 338.

FARHI, DANIEL (1941–), French reform rabbi. Farhi was born in Paris to a Jewish family of Turkish descent. He was hidden and protected by a Protestant family during the war, began rabbinical studies in 1959, and was ordained a rabbi in 1966. He chose to join the reform Union Libérale Israélite de France, France's first liberal Jewish congregation, located in Paris and known as "rue Copernic," the street where its main synagogue is located. In 1970, he became first rabbi at the Copernic synagogue, a position that he left in 1977 to create a new liberal movement, the Mouvement Juif Libéral de France (MJLF), originally comprised of just 50 families and subsequently growing to a few hundred. Dedicated to the promotion of Reform Judaism, Farhi also emphasized in his rabbinical activity the importance of inter-religious dialogue, especially with Islam and Christianity. Another main axis of Farhi's concerns was the memory of the Shoah and its transmission, being himself an "*enfant caché*" (hidden child). Farhi was the first to introduce in France the celebration of Yom Ha-Shoah in 1990, with a 24-hour-long recitation of the names of French Jewish deportees and Holocaust victims. He worked in close association with Serge and Beate *Klarsfeld to foster public awareness of the Shoah. Farhi was imprisoned in Germany for trying to pursue Nazi criminals but managed to organize a number of pilgrimages to Auschwitz. He was eventually able to merge his two main concerns – religious dialogue and transmission of the Shoah – when he joined the inter-religious pilgrimage set up by Emile Shoufani, an Arab-Israeli priest from Nazareth, which brought together at Auschwitz Muslims, Christians, and Jews, Israeli and French. Farhi wrote several books on Israel and the transmission of Judaism (*Parler aux enfants d'Israël*), the problematics of liberal Judaism (*Un judaïsme dans le siècle*), and the Shoah (*Au dernier survivant*), as well as two prayer books for Reform communities, *Siddour Taher Libénou* and *Mahzor Anénou*. Fahri also served on the editorial board of the MJLF review, *Tenou'a-Le Mouvement*. He was awarded several prestigious honors, including *chevalier de l'ordre national du Mérite* and *chevalier de l'ordre national de la Légion d'honneur*, a distinction that he received in 1993 from Simone *Veil, state minister and Holocaust survivor.

[Dror Franck Sullaper (2nd ed.)]

FARHI, GABRIEL (1968–), French reform rabbi. Son of leading reform rabbi, Daniel *Farhi, Gabriel completed liberal rabbinical studies in London (Leo Baeck College), where he was ordained in 1996. Subsequently he was the rabbi of the MJLF-Est synagogue, an offshoot of the movement's main congregation. An advisor to the BBC for Jewish affairs, Farhi also serves as the Israelite chaplain at the Georges Pompidou European hospital and headed there a think tank on medical ethics. He was the first non-Orthodox rabbi to be appointed as a chaplain in a French hospital. His keen interest for bioethics, his intimate knowledge of the medical world, and his proximity to the sick and suffering also led him to promote a liberal Jewish viewpoint on bioethics as a teacher at the Faculties of Medicine in Reims and Paris.

[Dror Franck Sullaper (2nd ed.)]

FARHI, MORIS (1935–), writer, poet, and artist. Born in *Ankara, Farhi graduated from Robert College in *Istanbul in 1954 and from the Royal Academy of Dramatic Art in London in 1956. A British subject since 1964, he pursued an acting career for several years and began writing in the 1960s. Between 1960 and 1983 he worked primarily in television, writing numerous scripts for both the BBC and ITV. Many of his poems have appeared in various U.S. and international publications. He became a member of English PEN in the mid-1970s and joined its Writers in Prison Committee in 1988. In 2001 he was made a member of the Order of the British Empire in the Queen's Birthday Honours List for "services to literature." In November 2001 he was elected a vice president of International PEN. He is a fellow of both the Royal Society of Literature and the Royal Geographical Society. His published works include *The Pleasure of Your Death* (1972); *The Last of Days* (1983), a thriller played out in the Middle East against the backdrop of Arab terrorism; *Journey Through the Wilderness* (1989), dealing with a Holocaust survivor's search in South America for the Nazi who murdered his father; *Children of the Rainbow* (1999), about a gypsy survivor of Auschwitz; and *Young Turk* (2004), a series of interrelated stories set in *Turkey.

[Rifat Bali (2nd ed.)]

FARIA, FRANCISCO DE (b. c. 1650), Marrano adventurer. Faria, who was born in Brazil, lived subsequently in Antwerp as an artist, in Holland as an officer in the army, and in England as an interpreter to the Portuguese embassy. In 1680, at the time of the so-called "Popish Plot," he made some startling but unfounded disclosures accusing the Portuguese ambassador of having attempted to bribe him to murder the Earl of Shaftesbury and others. He was rewarded for his revelations, but subsequently disappeared from view.

BIBLIOGRAPHY: Friedman, in: AJHSP, 20 (1911), 115–32 (= his *Early American Jews* (1934), 127–45, 205–9); Roth, Mag Bibl, 125, 248.

[Cecil Roth]

°**FARINACCI, ROBERTO** (1892–1945), leading antisemite in the Italian Fascist regime. A socialist until 1914, Farinacci became one of the founders of the Fascist movement in March 1919. He served as a member of the Gran Consiglio del Fascismo, as a member of parliament, and, between 1925 and 1926, as Fascist Party secretary. Farinacci represented the fanatic and extremist element in the Fascist leadership. In 1921 he founded a daily newspaper, *Cremona Nuova*, later renamed *Il Regime Fascista*, which he edited until 1945. In this newspaper he advocated a strong line against the opponents of the regime, closer relations with Nazi Germany, and the adoption of a racist, antisemitic policy. From 1938 he was one of those who directed the Fascist government's racist policy. His antisemitic book, *La Chiesa e gli Ebrei*, was published in 1938. He also wrote *Storia della rivoluzione fascista* (3 vols., 1940). In July 1943 he fled to Germany, but later returned to Italy, where he was executed by Italian partisans in April 1945.

BIBLIOGRAPHY: R. de Felice, *Storia degli ebrei italiani sotto il fascismo* (1961); Roth, Italy, 522, 525; Milano, Italia, 691; P. Pellicano, *Ecco il diavolo, Israele!* (1938); Starr, in: JSOS, 1 (1939), 105–24. **ADD. BIBLIOGRAPHY:** H. Fornari, *Mussolini's Gadfly: Roberto Farinacci* (1971); U.A. Grimaldi, *Farinacci, il piu fascista* (1972); R.A. Rozzi, *I cremonesi e Farinacci* (1991).

[Daniel Carpi]

FARISSOL, ABRAHAM BEN MORDECAI (c. 1451–c. 1525), Bible commentator, geographer, and polemicist. Born in Avignon, Abraham spent most of his life in Ferrara, Italy, where he did most of his work, and in Mantua. He served as a cantor, and for many years as a copyist, a task he performed with great devotion and care. It seems that he was highly regarded by the Jews of Ferrara, for they chose him to represent Judaism before the duke of Ferrara in a religious dispute with two Dominican monks. Farissol's main works are (1) *Pirḥei Shoshannim*, a short commentary on the Torah, which was never printed but is extant in manuscript; a commentary on Ecclesiastes, also in manuscript; and a commentary on the Book of Job, printed in the Bomberg Bible (Venice 1516–17). (2) *Magen Avraham*, a work dedicated to the defense of Judaism in religious disputes, and containing in two separate chapters, polemical attacks against Christianity and Islam. Most of the work is based upon the writings of earlier medieval Hebrew polemicists, but parts were influenced by the author's own experience in the dispute in Ferrara. The work is still extant in manuscript. (3) *Iggeret Orḥot Olam*, his most famous and most important work, is the first modern Hebrew work on geography (Ferrara 1524; Venice 1586; and many subsequent printings). Each of its 30 chapters deals with a certain geographical area or subject. In addition, many cosmological and historical matters are also treated. The author collected all the evidence he could regarding Jewish settlements in each country. The inclusion of a description of the New World makes Farissol the first Hebrew writer to deal in detail with the newly-discovered America. The 14th chapter of *Iggeret Orḥot Olam*, which deals mainly with the settlements of the *Ten Lost Tribes, is of special interest. According to Farissol's introduction to this chapter, it is clear that what moved him to undertake this investigation was the appearance in Italy in 1523 of David *Reuveni, many of whose descriptions are included in this work.

BIBLIOGRAPHY: Steinschneider, Cat Bod, 689–90; Benjacob, Oẓar, 9 no. 189, 296 no. 490; Graetz, Hist, 4 (1894), 411–3; Waxman, Literature, 2 (1960^2), 485–7, 556.

FARISSOL, JACOB BEN ḤAYYIM (Comprat [Comprado], Vidal Farissol; b. 1405?), Provençal Hebrew poet and philosophical commentator. At the age of 17 Farissol wrote *Beit Ya'akov* (Ms.), a commentary to Judah Halevi's *Kuzari*, based on the lectures of his teacher Solomon b. Menahem Frat Maimon; this commentary is in many ways similar to those of his fellow students, Solomon b. Judah (Solomon Vivas) and Nethanel Caspi. His commentary, like those of his fellow students, is important for the understanding and establishing of the Hebrew text of the *Kuzari*. In the summer of 1453 Farissol was in Avignon and is apparently identical with the poet Jacob who, in a *piyyut* (*Mi Kamokha*) for *Hoshana Rabba*, tells of a thwarted Jewish persecution on Sept. 15, 1443. He also is the author of a liturgical poem (*Tamid*) for the eve of the Day of Atonement.

BIBLIOGRAPHY: Zunz, Lit Poesie, 525; *Literaturblatt des Orients*, 10 (1849), 343; HB, 7 (1864), 27; 16 (1876), 127, no. 2; Steinschneider, *Katalog ... Berlin*, 2 pt. 1 (1878), 110–5, no. 124, 141 (specimen of text); idem, *Polemische und apologetische Literatur...* (1877), 351; Gross, Gal Jud, 6–7; ZHB, 13 (1909), 30.

[Jefim (Hayyim) Schirmann]

FARJEON, BENJAMIN LEOPOLD (1838–1903), English novelist. Farjeon, who was born in London into an Orthodox family of North African origin, went to Australia at the age of 17. He eventually became editor and part owner of the first daily newspaper in New Zealand, the *Otago Daily Times*. Returning to England in 1868, he published his first novel, *Grif* (1870), a story of Australian life, which became his best-known work. Farjeon modeled his work on Dickens and later on Wilkie Collins, first writing Christmas pieces and then mystery stories. His 40 novels included several with Jewish subjects, among them *Solomon Isaacs* (1877), *Fair Jewess* and *Aaron the Jew* (1894), *Miriam Rozella* (1897), and *Pride of Race* (1900). He portrayed Jews sympathetically, but was inclined to sentimentality. Farjeon married Margaret Jefferson, daughter of a famous American actor, and three of their children – who had no connection with the Jewish community – were well-known writers. JOSEPH JEFFERSON FARJEON (1883–1955) wrote novels, plays, and *The Compleat Smuggler* (1938). HERBERT FARJEON (1887–1945) was drama critic for several London papers and wrote light verse and revues. ELEANOR FARJEON (1881–1965) wrote fiction, verse for children and, with her brother Herbert, a comedy, *The Two Bouquets* (1936). She was the author of the famous hymn, "Morning Has Broken," which has in recent years become a popular hit song. Her depiction of her early life, *A Nursery in the Nineties*, gives a warm portrayal of her father. On her death, the Children's Book Circle of England established an annual award in her honor. Her brother, HARRY FARJEON (1878–1948), was a well-known composer of light classical music.

BIBLIOGRAPHY: M.F. Modder, *Jew in the Literature of England* (1939), 311–7. **ADD. BIBLIOGRAPHY:** B. Cheyette, "From Apology to Revolt: Benjamin Farjeon, Amt Levy, and the Post-Emacipation Jewish Novel, " in: JHSET, 29 (1982–86), 253–66; A. l. Farjeon, *Morning Has Broken: A Biography of Eleanor Farjeon* (1986); D.M. Blakelock, *Eleanor: Portrait of a Farjeon* (1966); ODNB online for Benjamin Farjeon and Eleanor Frajeon.

FARKAS, LADISLAUS (Wilhelm; 1904–1948), Israel physical chemist. Farkas was born in Dunaszerdahely, Slovakia, the son of a pharmacist. From 1928 he worked at the Kaiser

Wilhelm Institute for Physical Chemistry in Berlin-Dahlem as assistant to Fritz Haber. On the advent of Nazism in 1933, Farkas moved to Cambridge and in 1934 joined the staff of the Sieff Institute in Reḥovot and of the Hebrew University of Jerusalem, where he was subsequently appointed professor of physical chemistry. He was killed in an air crash while on his way to the U.S. to buy scientific equipment. He left his mark on a generation of students who were later among Israel's outstanding chemists. Farkas' research covered photochemistry, gas reactions, combustion, the chemistry of parahydrogen and heavy hydrogen, and the recovery of bromine and the reactions of its compounds. During World War II, he acted as secretary of the Scientific Advisory Committee of the Palestine War Supply Board and was instrumental in developing local production methods for essential chemicals from the resources of the Dead Sea. He laid the foundations for the establishment of the Research Council of Israel.

BIBLIOGRAPHY: I. Farkas and E.P. Wigner, *L. Farkas Memorial Volume* (1952).

[Samuel Aaron Miller]

FARKAS, RUTH (née **Lewis**; 1906–1996), U.S. sociologist and diplomat. Farkas was born in New York and gained degrees in education from New York University (B.A. and Ed.D.) and Columbia (M.A. in sociology, 1932). She was a sociology instructor at the New York University School of Education from 1945 to 1955, and in 1962, she was appointed director of the William Allison White Psychoanalytical Institute, and became chairman of President's Advisory Council of the New York University Graduate School of Social Work.

As a sociologist and educator she came to the attention of Secretary of State Dean Rusk and was appointed a member of the Executive Committee of the U.S. National Commission for UNESCO and of the Department of State Foreign Service Selection Board. She was also consultant sociologist to the U.S. delegations to the International Conference on Eradication of Illiteracy in Iran (1965) and the International Conference of the Status and Rights of Women in Helsinki (1967). She served as chief delegate to the Conference of the Pan-Pacific Southeast Asia Women's Association in Australia in 1961 and in New Zealand in 1972. Farkas was a member of the President's Special Education committee for Dissemination of Human Rights and of the President's Committee for the Handicapped. She served on Governor Rockefeller's New York State Women's Advisory Council and on the Council of the Child Study Association of America, and was the recipient of a number of awards for work with the handicapped and the aged. From 1965 she served as Consultant for Personnel and Public Relations of Alexander's Incorporated, founded by her husband, George Farkas.

She was involved in many philanthropic activities through the Role Foundation, which she established in 1967. Farkas served as United States ambassador to Luxembourg from 1973 to 1976. In 1982 she was honored by Columbia University's Teachers College with a Distinguished Alumni Award.

ADD. BIBLIOGRAPHY: A. Morin, *Her Excellency* (1995).

FARMERS' FEDERATION OF ISRAEL (Hitaḥadut ha-Ikkarim be-Yisrael), an association of private farmers in Israel. It grew out of the Union of Moshavot in Judea and Samaria, which was founded in 1920 with a membership of seven villages. The Federation is concerned with the professional, economic, cultural and social problems of its members and represents them vis-à-vis government agencies on marketing, taxation, transportation, and similar questions. By 1970 it had local branches in the form of agricultural committees or cooperatives in 42 villages, and members in some 60 other villages were assisted through its institutions; its total membership was over 8,000 families. The Federation worked through 14 associations for specific branches of agriculture and a number of affiliated companies, including mortgage and benefit funds, and companies for supply, marketing, and transportation. Also affiliated were 80 agricultural, 10 citrus-growing, and 11 transportation cooperatives, the Pardess citrus-growers' syndicate and the wine-growers' association of Rishon le-Zion and Zikhron Ya'akov. The Federation maintained an agricultural secondary school at Pardes Ḥannah and supported youth and sports clubs. It was among the founders of Kuppat Ḥolim Ammamit (People's Sick Fund; now Kuppat Ḥolim Me'uḥedet) which provides medical care for its members. It took the initiative in expanding a number of older moshavot through the absorption of new settlers and assisted in founding several new moshavim.

BIBLIOGRAPHY: *Bustenai* (weekly, 1929–39); *Ikkarei Yisrael* (monthly, 1959–); *Ikkarei Yisrael-Sefer ha-Shanah* (Yearbook, 1950–).

[Gedalyah Elkoshi]

FARO, city in S. Portugal, Algrave province. Jews were organized there as a community in the 15th century. The first book to be printed in Portugal, the Hebrew Pentateuch, in square type and vocalized, was published in Faro in 1487 by Don Samuel Porteira (see *Incunabula). By 1494 (or 1496?) the Porteiras had printed at least 14 Talmud tractates, of which fragments only have survived. At the expulsion from Portugal in 1497 David Porteira went to Pesaro (Italy) where he continued printing Talmud tractates. Traces of the Farense type can also be found in Fez. Members of a Faro family (Marranos?) lived in Bayonne, London, Dublin, and Jamaica in the 17th and 18th centuries. At the beginning of the 19th century Jews again settled in Faro; a cemetery was opened in 1820, and a synagogue in 1850. Early in the 20th century the community comprised about 50 families. In 1970 there were no more than five Jews living in the whole province, and the two synagogues were in disuse.

BIBLIOGRAPHY: M. Kayserling, *Geschichte der Juden in Portugal* (1867), index; J. Mendes dos Remedios, *Os judeus em Portugal* (1895), index; S. Seligmann, in: ZHB, 12 (1908), 16–19; M.B. Amzalak,

Tipografia Hebraica em Portugal… (1922), 19–21; J. Bloch, in: *Bulletin of the New York Public Library*, 42 (1938), 26ff. **ADD. BIBLIOGRAPHY:** J.F. Mascarenhas, *Dos documentos arqueológicos recentemente achados sobre os judeus no Algarve*, (1980); J.M. Abecassis, in: *Anais do Municipio de Faro; Boletim Cultural*, 15 (1985), 45–74; idem, in: *Memórias da Academia das Ciências de Lisboa*, 25 (1986), 439–534; A. Iria, in: *Memórias da Academia das Ciências*, 25 (1986), 293–438.

FASSŪTA, Christian-Arab village in western Upper Galilee, Israel, 3 mi. (5 km.) northeast of Maʿalot, identified with Mifshata where the priestly family of Harim settled after the destruction of the Second Temple. In the Middle Ages, the village is mentioned by the poet Eliezer ha-Kallir. Cave tombs, parts of ancient buildings, and cisterns have been found at the site. Its inhabitants, most of whom belong to the Greek-Catholic (Uniate) faith, are engaged principally in growing olives, deciduous fruit, and tobacco. The village's jurisdiction extends over 0.3 sq. mi. (0.785 sq. km.). In 2002 its population was 2,860.

BIBLIOGRAPHY: I. Ben Zvi, *She'ar Yashuv* (1927), 140ff.

[Efraim Orni]

FAST, HOWARD MELVIN (1914–2003), U.S. author, best known for his imaginative historical novels as well as detective fiction published under the name E.V. Cunningham. *Fallen Angel* (1951) was published under the name of Walter Ericson. Born and educated in New York City, Fast spent the Depression years of the 1930s working in many parts of the U.S. at various jobs. Some early novels had no success, but in 1937 his story *The Children* attracted favorable notice when it appeared in *Story* magazine. When his *Place in the City* was published in the same year, Fast quickly gained recognition. A number of his works deal with American history, notably *Conceived in Liberty* (1939), *The Unvanquished* (1942), *Citizen Tom Paine* (1943), *Freedom Road* (1944), and *April Morning* (1961). Fast also wrote on themes involving injustice, as in *The Passion of Sacco and Vanzetti* (1953), and on oppression as in *The Last Frontier* (1942), an epic account of an American Indian tribe's attempted flight to Canada and in *Spartacus* (1952). During the years 1943–56 Fast was an active member of the American Communist Party, and in 1950 he was jailed for contempt of Congress. One of the leading American leftist writers of the 1950s, he was awarded the Stalin Peace Prize in 1953. The later excesses of the Stalin regime disillusioned him, however, and he explained his break with Communism in *The Naked God* (1957). Despite his political activities, Fast wrote a number of books on Jewish themes, including *Haym Salomon: Son of Liberty* (1941), a young people's biography of the American Revolution's financier. Two other historical works were *Romance of a People* (1941) and a *Picture-Book History of the Jews* (1942), written in collaboration with his wife. *My Glorious Brothers* (1949), generally considered one of Fast's outstanding novels, retells the story of the Maccabean revolt, while *Moses, Prince of Egypt* (1958) was planned as the first of a series of works on the life of the great lawgiver. In his "Immigrants" novels, Fast studies, against a vast sweep of modern American history, beginning with the last part of the 19th century, the interweaving destinies and social mobility of immigrant families, one of them being the Levy progeny. Fast's television scriptwriting resulted in his receiving an Emmy award from the U.S. National Academy of Television Arts and Sciences in 1977. His autobiography, *Being Red*, appeared in 1990. His novel *The Bridge Builder's Story* (1995) traces a young gentile man's acceptance of his own life as he finds understanding through identification with both the suffering and survival of Jews in the Holocaust. Scott Waring's maturation, achieved through analysis, is a liberation from the past and an ability to create a life that comports with this new-found freedom.

BIBLIOGRAPHY: *Current Biography* (April, 1943) s.v. **ADD. BIBLIOGRAPHY:** A. Macdonald, *Howard Fast: A Criticial Companion* (1996).

[Harold U. Ribalow / Rohan Saxena and Lewis Fried (2nd ed.)]

FASTING AND FAST DAYS, the precept (or custom) of refraining from eating and drinking.

In the Bible

Although the origins of the ritual of fasting are obscure, several current theories claim that it originated as (1) a spiritual preparation for partaking of a sacred meal (W.R. Smith); (2) a method for inducing a state of susceptibility to visions (E.B. Tylor); and (3) a means of providing new vitality during periods of human or natural infertility (T.H. Gaster). Scriptural citations have been adduced to support all these theories, but fasting in the Bible clearly emerged in response to more spiritual needs. The Hebrew root for fasting, *ẓwm* (צום), can be used both as a verb and a noun, e.g., "David fasted a fast" (II Sam. 12:16), a meaning verified in the next verse: "he ate no food." A synonymous idiom *ʿinnah nefesh* (lit. "afflict the body") includes fasting as part of a general regimen of abstinence, a broader meaning confirmed by the following:

(a) laws annulling women's vows and oaths that contain the phrase "all self-denying oaths to afflict her body" (Num. 30:14, cf. verses 3, 7, 10–13), referring to all forms of abstinence, not just fasting; (b) Daniel, who expressly "afflicts himself" (Dan. 10:12) not only by abstaining from choice food, meat, and wine (in biblical terminology, he is not actually fasting) but also from anointing himself (10:3); and (c) the example of King David, who, in addition to fasting, sleeps on the ground, does not change his clothes, and refrains from anointing and washing (II Sam. 12:16–20, though the term *ʿinnah nefesh* is absent). In biblical poetry *ẓwm* and *ʿinnah nefesh* are parallel but not synonymous. Indeed, one verse (Isa. 58:5) indicates that it is rather the root *ẓwm* which has taken on the broader sense of *ʿinnah nefesh*: "…that a man should bow his head like a bulrush and make his bed on sackcloth and ashes, is this what you call a fast…?" Thus, the rabbis declare that *ʿinnah nefesh*, enjoined for the *Day of Atonement (Lev. 16:29, 31; 23:27–32), consists not only of fasting but of other forms of self-denial such as abstention from "washing, anointing, wearing shoes, and cohabitation" (Yoma 8:1; cf. Targ. Jon., Lev. 16:29).

Fasting is attested in the oldest strata of biblical literature and there can be no doubt that spontaneous fasting was widespread from earliest times both among individuals and groups. In the ritual practiced in the First Temple, fasting was clearly a permanent feature (Isa. 1:13, lxx; Jer. 36:9, "before the Lord"; cf. Joel 1:14; 2:15–17). The death of a national leader (e.g., King Saul) could initiate a day-long fast (II Sam. 1:12), or, alternatively, the fast might be observed for seven days (I Sam. 31:13). The authority to proclaim a public fast was vested in the elders of the local community, who, however, could be pressured by the royal palace to proclaim a fast (e.g., for Naboth's undoing, I Kings 21:8–12).

The purposes of fasting are various. Its most widely attested function, for the community as well as the individual, is to avert or terminate a calamity by eliciting God's compassion. For example, God mitigates Ahab's punishment because he fasted and humbled himself (I Kings 21:27–29). King David fasted in the hope that "the Lord will be gracious to me and the boy will live. But now that he is dead why should I fast?" (II Sam. 12:22–23). Many other passages also indicate the use of fasting as a means of winning divine forgiveness (e.g., Ps. 35:13; 69:11; Ezra 10:6), implying that fasting is basically an act of penance, a ritual expression of remorse, submission, and supplication.

Fasting was practiced as a preparation for communing with the spirits of the dead or with the Deity, as when Saul fasted the day before the appearance of Samuel's apparition (I Sam. 28:20). To be vouchsafed a theophany, Moses fasted for as long as 40 days (Ex. 34:28 [twice, according to Deut. 9:9, 18]; Elijah, I Kings 19:8). On the two occasions when Daniel's prayers were answered by means of a vision (Dan. 9:20ff.; 10:7ff.), his preparatory rituals included fasting (Dan. 9:3; 10:3). That death occasioned a fast is implied by the couriers' surprise when King David refused to fast after the death of the infant son born to him by Bath-Sheba (II Sam. 12:21).

When a calamity, human or natural, threatened or struck a whole community, a public fast was proclaimed. Thus, Israel observed fasts in its wars against Benjamin (Judg. 20:26), the Philistines (I Sam. 7:6; 14:24), and its Transjordanian enemies (II Chron. 20:3); similarly fasts were observed in the hope of averting annihilation by the Babylonians (Jer. 36:3, 9; see below) and by the Persians (Esth. 4:3, 16). The purpose of fasts during wartime was to seek God's direct intervention (e.g., I Sam. 7:9ff.) or advice as transmitted through an oracle (e.g., Judg. 20:26–28). Fasting served as a means of supplicating God to end a famine caused by a plague of locusts (Joel 1:14; 2:12, 15), and to alleviate the oppression of foreign rule (Neh. 9:1). As a preventive or intercessory measure, fasting was used to avert the threat of divine punishment, exemplified by the fast declared for Naboth's alleged cursing of God (I Kings 21:9) and after Jonah's prophecy of Nineveh's doom (3:5).

The biblical evidence thus far cited indicates that fasting, both individual and collective, was a spontaneous reaction to exigencies. In the pre-exilic period there is no record of specific fast days in the annual calendar (except the Day of Atonement), although some Bible critics even conjecture that this, too, was originally an emergency rite and was fixed on the tenth of Tishri only at the end of the First Temple. There is a record of a fast day in Jeremiah's time (Jer. 36:3ff.), but this too originated as an emergency rite ("a fast day was proclaimed," verse 9) and was not repeated. That portion of Deutero-Isaiah which describes a fast (Isa. 58:3ff.) became the *haftarah* reading for the Day of Atonement morning service, but the text can hardly be speaking of an observance of the Day of Atonement (cf. v. 4).

Fixed fast days are first mentioned by the post-Exilic prophet Zechariah who proclaims the word of the Lord thus: "The fast of the fourth month, the fast of the fifth, the fast of the seventh and the fast of the tenth…" (Zech. 8:19; cf. 7:3, 5). Jewish tradition has it that these fasts commemorate the critical events which culminated in the destruction of the Temple: the tenth of Tevet (the tenth month), the beginning of the siege of Jerusalem; the 17th of Tammuz (the fourth month), the breaching of the walls; the ninth of Av (the fifth month), when the Temple was destroyed; and the third of Tishri (the seventh month), when Gedaliah, the Babylonian-appointed governor of Judah, was assassinated. Some scholars maintain that these fast days are much older, marking the beginning of a Lenten period which preceded the seasonal festivals, and to which only later tradition affixed the events of the national catastrophe. It is argued that the historical basis for the four fast days coinciding with the events ascribed to them is weak in the light of present knowledge. Jeremiah dates the destruction of the First Temple to the tenth of Av (52:12ff.), whereas II Kings claims the seventh (25:8ff.); there is, however, no biblical witness for the ninth. It is surprising that a permanent fast day was proclaimed for the murder of Gedaliah, who was a Babylonian puppet and not a member of the House of David. Lastly, there is no scriptural authority for the 17th of Tammuz as the date for the breaching of the walls of Jerusalem.

Nevertheless, the claim of the Book of Zechariah (e.g., 7:5) that the four fasts were instituted upon the destruction of the state cannot be discounted. If, as it is now suggested, the fast recorded in Jeremiah was prompted by the sacking of Ashkelon (November/December 604 B.C.E.) and by the similar fate which threatened Jerusalem, it is then conceivable that four different fast days sprang up simultaneously as a reaction to the trauma of destruction and exile. Moreover, would Zechariah have been asked whether the fasts should be abolished if the historical reality of the Second Temple had not rendered them meaningless? Indeed, the people consulted the prophet Zechariah about abolishing the fasts only when the Second Temple was approaching completion (Zech. 7:1; cf. Ezra 6:15), a time which coincided with the end of the 70 years of exile predicted by Jeremiah (Zech. 7:5; cf. Jer. 25:12). There is no need to look for other reasons to account for the proclamation of the fasts than the destruction of Jerusalem and the Temple.

Thus, fasting, a spontaneous phenomenon in the days of the First Temple, may have entered the calendar as a regular and recurring event only after the exile. Finally, fasting as a discipline, a routine for the pious, is attested only in post-biblical times in the Apocrypha, Pseudepigrapha, and Qumran literature.

[Jacob Milgrom]

Second Temple Period

During the Second Temple period, daily or biweekly fastings were practiced for reasons of *asceticism, especially among women (Judith 8:6; Luke 2:37; TJ, Ḥag 2:2, 77d), but also among men (Luke 18:12; Mark 2:18), or in preparation for an apocalyptic revelation (Dan. 10:3, 12; ii Bar. 12:5; 20:5–21:1; 43:3; iv Ezra 5:13–20; 6:35; Sanh. 65b; TJ, Kil. 9:4, 32b). The Jewish literature of the Second Temple period also advocates fasting as a way of atonement for sins committed either unintentionally (Ps. of Sol. 3:9) or even deliberately (Test. Patr., Sim. 3:4), or to prevent them (*ibid.*, Joseph 3:4; 4:8; 10:1–2). These reasons for fasting were strengthened by the destruction of the Second Temple and even more by the repression of the *Bar Kokhba revolt and the subsequent religious persecutions.

Fasting Laws and Customs

The laws of fasting detailed in talmudic literature and by halakhic authorities (Maim. Yad, Ta'aniyyot, 4; Tur and Sh. Ar., OḤ, 579) have basically not changed from the biblical period. Founded on very ancient popular and spontaneous customs, they were, in the main, like the reasons for fasting, not peculiar to the Jewish people, but current in the whole of the ancient Near East. The description of a public fast held by the Phoenicians of Carthage, at the end of the second century b.c.e. (Tertullian, *De jejuniis* 16), is almost identical to descriptions of fasts in the Bible, in Second Temple literature, and in rabbinic sources.

The fast was accompanied by prayer (during the First Temple period sacrifices were offered) and confession of sins (Judg. 20:26; I Sam. 7:6; Ezra 10:1). From the Second Temple period onward, the public fast was also accompanied by the reading of the Torah (Neh. 9:3). On solemn fasts (Ta'an. 4:1; Tosef. Ta'an. 4:1), four prayers – *Shaḥarit, Ḥaẓot* ("noon"), *Minḥah*, and *Ne'ilat She'arim* – were recited as well as *Ma'ariv*. The *Amidah of the fast day consisted of 24 benedictions – "the eighteen of every day, to which another six were added" (Ta'an. 2:2–4; *Ḥemdah Genuzah* (1863), nos. 160–1; Tur, OḤ, 579) – and the liturgy was elaborated with special passages of supplication (*Anenu* – "Answer us!," Ta'an. 14a), *seliḥot*, and prayers for mercy. The central part of the service was the sounding of the *shofar* (Joel 2:1) or the *ḥaẓoẓerot* ("trumpets"; I Macc. 3:54), trumpets (as main instruments) accompanied by horns (RH 3:4; Tosef. to RH 3:3). The blowing of *shofarot* and trumpets was performed in a different manner in the Temple and on the Temple Mount from the other localities (RH 27a; Ta'an. 16b); the exact procedure, however, is not known. (According to one opinion, there was no blowing outside the Temple area at all; see Ta'an. 2:4–5.) During the Middle Ages, in some Jewish communities, *shofarot* were sounded, in others, trumpets (see Beit Yosef to Tur, OḤ, 579).

Prayers were generally held in the open (II Chron. 20:5; Judith 4:11) and all the people humiliated themselves publicly by tearing their clothes, wearing sackcloth (I Kings 21:27; Joel 2:13; Ps. 35:13; Judith 4:10, 8:5), and putting ashes or earth on their heads (Isa. 58:5; Neh. 9:1; *Joseph and Asenath*, 10). The cemetery was also visited. (For the various ways in which these customs were understood see TJ, Ta'an. 2:1, 65a; Ta'an. 16a.) The humiliation was applied even to the most holy objects; at times also the priests (Joel 1:13; Judith 4:14–15), the king (Jonah 3:6), or the *nasi* (Ta'an. 2:1) wore sackcloth and ashes. There were those who covered even the altar with sackcloth (Judith 4:12), and the ark, containing the Torah scrolls, was taken into the street and covered with ashes (Ta'an. 2:1). During the mass assembly (Joel 2:16; Judith 4:11), one of the elders would rebuke the people and the affairs of the community were investigated in order to determine who was the cause of the evil (I Kings 21:9–13; Ta'an. 2:1; Ta'an. 12b).

In many places young children and animals were obliged to fast – a practice which prevailed not only among other nations (Jonah 3:5, 7; TJ, Ta'an. 2:1, 65b) but even in Israel (Judith 4:9–11; Pseudo-Philo's *Liber Antiquitatum Biblicarum* 30:4–5; concerning the participation of the young children cf. II Chron. 20:13; Joel 2:16). The sages, however, exempted young children (and animals), the sick, those obliged to preserve their strength, and, in most cases, pregnant and nursing women (Tosef. to Ta'an. 2:12; 3:2).

There is some similarity, especially in the case of the solemn fasts, between the customs of fasting and those of *mourning. On ordinary fast days only food and drink were prohibited, while on the important ones washing (for pleasure), anointing, the wearing of shoes (for pleasure), and cohabitation were also forbidden. People also refrained from work on these days (some, who were stricter, considered work to be absolutely prohibited (TJ, Ta'an. 1:6, 64c)) and shops were closed (Ta'an. 1:5–6). It was also customary for some to sleep on the ground (II Sam. 12:16).

Ordinary fast days lasted for the duration of the daylight hours; the important fasts were a full 24 hours. Fasts were held either for one day or sometimes for a series of three or seven days; occasionally even daily for a continued period. (Ta'an. 1:5–6; cf. also e.g., Judith 4:13). In exceptional cases, fasts were also held on the Sabbath and the festivals, but it was usually forbidden to fast on those days; some authorities also forbade fasting on the eve of the Sabbath, of festivals, and of the New Moon. In order not to mar the celebration of joyful events in Jewish history, Hananiah b. Hezekiah b. Garon (first century C.E.) compiled the **Megillat Ta'anit* ("Scroll of Fasting") which lists 35 commemorative dates on which a public fast could not be proclaimed. In time, however, the *Megillat Ta'anit* was abrogated. It was customary to hold public fast days on Mondays and Thursdays (Tosef. to Ta'an. 2:4); individuals, however, especially after the destruction of the Temple, took upon themselves to fast every Monday and Thursday (Ta'an. 12a).

The *halakhah* is that in such cases the individual, in contrast to the community, has to commit himself to fast during the afternoon of the preceding day (*ibid.*). It was also possible to fast for a specific number of hours (Ta'an. 11b–12a). On some occasions, the fast was not a total one, but people refrained only from meat, wine, anointment with oil, and other pleasures (Cowley, Aramaic, no. 30; Dan. 10:3; Test. Patr., Reu. 1:10; Judah 15:4; iv Ezra 9:24; as well as generally in talmudic literature and in that of the Middle Ages).

The Purpose and Conception of Fasting

In the ancient Near East, prayer and fasting were advocated as a means to have one's requests fulfilled by the gods (Ahikar, Armenian version, 2:49, from where, it appears, the idea was derived in Tobit, short version, 2:8; cf. also Test. Patr., Ben. 1:4). The Bible emphasizes that the fast is not an end in itself but only a means through which man can humble his heart and repent for his sins; his repentance must manifest itself in his deeds (Joel 2:13; Jonah 3:8). The idea is especially stressed in Isaiah (58:3ff.) where the contrast is made between a fast which is not accompanied by any real repentance, and which is therefore unacceptable to God, and the true fast which leads to God's merciful forgiveness: "Is not this the fast that I have chosen? To loose the fetters of wickedness, To undo the bands of the yoke, and to let the oppressed go free… Is it not to deal thy bread to the hungry, and that thou bring the poor that are cast out to thy house? When thou seest the naked, that thou cover him… Then shalt thou call, and the Lord will answer."

The Second Temple period literature also stressed that a fast without sincere repentance is valueless and senseless (Test. Patr., Ash. 2:8; 4:3; cf. *ibid.*, Joseph 3:5 – in addition to the fast, Joseph gave his food to the poor and the sick). In the Second Temple period fasting was also seen as an "ascetic exercise" which serves to purify man and bring him closer to God. This appears to have been the original significance of the fasts of the members of the **ma'amadot* (Ta'an. 4:2–3 (supplement); cf. *Theophrastus on the Jews who fasted during the offering of the sacrifices, and Philo on the Day of Atonement). This conception of fasting closely resembles the concept of complete abstinence and asceticism whose purpose is to induce ecstasy and apocalyptic visions and is found not only in the apocalyptic literature of the Second Temple period (the *Qumran sect seems to have held a "fast" day of which little is known), but also among certain circles of talmudic rabbis, especially after the destruction of the Temple. This "philosophy" led to an exaggerated propagation of fasting which, in turn, aroused a sharp counteraction in general rabbinic literature; the rabbis condemned ascetic women, especially widows and "fasting maids" (TJ, Sot. 3:4, 19a). R. *Yose even went further and declared: "The individual has no right to afflict himself by fasting, lest he become a burden on the community which will then have to provide for him" (Tosef. Ta'an. 2:12); as did *Samuel, according to whose opinion "Whoever fasts is called a sinner" (Ta'an. 11a).

The study of the Torah is of greater importance than fasting and therefore "a scholar has no right to fast because, in doing so, he decreases the work of heaven" (Ta'an. 11a–b). This led to a trend in the *halakhah* which sought to limit even public fasts and their severity, emphasizing however at the same time the original significance of fasting – good deeds and repentance. It found expression in *Saadiah Gaon's opinion (*Ketav ha-Tokhehah ve-ha-Hazharah* – "Letter of Reproach and Warning") that rather than keep a voluntary (or vowed) fast, it is preferable for a person to desist from committing a sin. Fasting was widely practiced by the mystics and the kabbalists, especially by *Ḥasidei Ashkenaz, but the latter-day Ḥasidim were opposed to the idea.

In modern times, except for the Day of Atonement and the Ninth of *Av, which are the two major fast days, other statutory fasts seem to lack general appeal. Orthodox authorities have, therefore, tried to reinvest some fast days with more relevant meaning (e.g., declaring the Tenth of *Tevet as a fast day to commemorate those who perished during the Nazi persecutions and whose *yahrzeit is unknown) but to no great avail. The extension of Jewish sovereignty over the entire city of Jerusalem (1967) has increased the tendency to abolish the fast days of the Third of Tishri (Fast of Gedaliah), the Tenth of Tevet, and the 17th of *Tammuz (but not the Ninth of *Av). Reform Judaism recognizes only one mandatory fast – the Day of Atonement. Its general attitude toward other fast days (public or private) is negative, based upon Isaiah 58:3–8.

[Moshe David Herr]

Classification of Fasts

Fast days fall into three main categories: (1) fasts decreed in the Bible or instituted to commemorate biblical events; (2) fasts decreed by the rabbis; (3) private fasts.

(1) FASTS DECREED OR MENTIONED IN THE BIBLE. The Day of Atonement (Yom Kippur) on which it is commanded "Ye shall afflict your souls" so that the individual may be cleansed from sins (Lev. 16:29–31; 23:27–32; Num. 29:7ff.); this is the only fast ordained in the Pentateuch.

The Ninth of Av (*Tishah be-Av*), a day of mourning for the destruction of the First and Second Temples (see Jer. 52:12–13 where, however, the date is given as the Tenth), and other calamitous occasions.

The 17th of Tammuz, in commemoration of the breaching of the walls of Jerusalem in the First Temple period (Jer. 39:2 where the date is the 9th) and *Titus breaching the walls of Jerusalem, and of other calamities which befell the Jewish people (Ta'an. 4:6, Ta'an. 28b, also Sh. Ar., OḤ, 549:2).

The Tenth of Tevet, in memory of the siege of Jerusalem by *Nebuchadnezzar, king of Babylon (II Kings 25:1–2, Jer. 52:4ff.; Ezek. 24:1–2).

The Third of Tishri, called *Ẓom Gedalyah* (the Fast of Gedaliah), in memory of the slaying of Gedaliah and his associates (Jer. 41:1–2; II Kings 25:25).

The Fast of *Esther (*Ta'anit Ester*) on the 13th of Adar, the day before *Purim (Esth. 4:16).

Besides the Day of Atonement, which is a pentateuchal fast, the other four fast days were also already observed in the period of the Second Temple. *Zechariah prophesied that they would be transformed into days of joy and gladness (Zech. 8:19).

On the Day of Atonement and on the Ninth of Av, fasting is observed by total abstention from food and drink from sunset until nightfall of the following day; on the other fast days, the fast lasts only from before dawn until nightfall of the same day. All fasts may be broken if danger to health is involved. Pregnant and nursing women are, under certain circumstances, exempt from observance (Sh. Ar., OḤ, 50:1 (Isserles) and 554:5).

If one of the above occurs on a Sabbath, the fasting is delayed until Sunday (Meg. 1:3 and Meg. 5a); only in the case of the Day of Atonement is the fast observed even on Sabbath. In the case of the Fast of Esther, observance is on the preceding Thursday (Sh. Ar., OḤ, 686:2).

(2) FASTS DECREED BY THE RABBIS. It has become customary for the especially pious to fast from morning until evening on the following days:

During the Ten Days of *Penitence (i.e., between Rosh Ha-Shanah and the Day of Atonement) and as many days as possible during the month of Elul (Sh. Ar., OḤ, 581:2).

The first Monday and Thursday, and the following Monday after *Passover and *Sukkot (Tur and Sh. Ar., OḤ, 492). This fast was interpreted as an atonement for possible sins committed while in a state of drunkenness and gluttony during the holidays (see Tos. to Kid. 81a s.v. *Sekava*).

*ShOVaVIM TaT (initial letters of eight consecutive weekly Pentateuch portions starting with *Shemot* which are eight Thursdays of the winter months of an intercalated year).

During the *Three Weeks of Mourning between the 17th of Tammuz and the Ninth of Av (Tur. and Sh. Ar., OḤ, 551:16). This fast was motivated by a profound grief for the destruction of Jerusalem.

The Seventh of *Adar, traditional date of the death of Moses observed in many communities by the members of the **ḥevra kaddisha* ("burial society") who fasted prior to their annual banquet held on the evening of that same day.

Yom Kippur Katan ("Minor Yom Kippur"), the last day of each month, on which many communities fasted and recited a special liturgy.

The eve of Passover, firstborn males' fast. This fast is a symbol of the sanctification of the Jewish firstborn who were saved during the tenth plague in Egypt (Ex. 13:1ff.). It is also kept in order to stimulate the appetite for the **maẓẓah* ("unleavened bread") at the festive meal (Sof. 21:3).

Days commemorating disastrous events in Jewish history (full list in Tur and Sh. Ar., OḤ, 580:2).

PRIVATE FASTS. In addition to the fixed days listed above, fasts are held on the following private occasions:

The anniversary (**yahrzeit*) of a parent's death or of that of a teacher (Ned. 12a).

The groom and the bride fast on their wedding day until the ceremony (Isserles to Sh. Ar., EH, 61:1), unless it is Rosh Ḥodesh (Isserles to Sh. Ar., OḤ, 573:1).

To avert the evil consequences of nightmares (*Ta'anit Ḥalom*). In talmudic times, it was believed that bad dreams could have pernicious effects (Shab. 11a). This fast was regarded as of such urgency that the rabbis permitted it even on the Sabbath, but advocated fasting on a weekday as well as a repentance for having dishonored the Sabbath joy through fasting (Ta'an. 12b; Ber. 31b). In later centuries, however, the obligatory nature of this fast was mitigated by halakhic authorities (see Sh. Ar., OḤ, 288, 5).

If a Torah scroll is dropped, it is customary for those present to fast a day.

In the mishnaic period, the members of the *Sanhedrin fasted on the day on which they sentenced a person to death (Sanh. 63a).

BIBLIOGRAPHY: A. Buechler, *Types of Jewish-Palestinian Piety* (1922), 128–264; idem, *Studies in Sin and Atonement* (1928), 441–56; M.S. Freiberger, *Das Fasten im alten Israel* (1927); G.F. Moore, *Judaism* (1927), index; M. Grintz, *Sefer Yehudit* (1957), index s.v. *Ẓom*; Allon, Meḥkarim, 2 (1958), 120–7; E. Samuel, in: *Turei Yeshurun*, 16 (1970), 17–22. In the Bible: W.R. Smith, *Lectures on the Religion of the Semites*, ed. by S.A. Cook (1927[3]), 434, 673; J.A. Montgomery, in: jbl, 51 (1932), 183–213; T.H. Gaster, *Festivals of the Jewish Year* (1955), 190–211; Kaufmann, Y., Toledot, 4 (1956), 266–8; A. Malamat, in: IEJ 6 (1956), 251ff.; E.B. Tylor, in: EB, s.v. *Fast.* Post-biblical Period: Urbach, in: *Sefer Yovel... Y. Baer* (1960), 48–68; Lowy, in: JJS, 9 (1958), 19–38; Elbogen, Gottesdienst, index s.v. *Fasttage.*

FASTLICHT, ADOLFO (1905–1964), Mexican Zionist leader. Born in Galicia, then part of Austria, he studied in traditional and public schools there. He was also active in the Zionist youth organizations. In 1925 he emigrated to Mexico, where he opened a dental workshop together with his brother. He continued his studies and graduated as a dentist. Fastlicht was involved in the establishment of the Organización Sionista Unida "Kadima" (the Zionist Federation) in 1925 and acted as its vice president in 1929. In 1933 he traveled to Ereẓ Israel, where he stayed a year. After his return he served as president of B'nai B'rith, Maccabi, the Zionist Federation, the Anti Defamation League, and the Comité Central – the umbrella organization of the Jewish community that acted as its political representative. Fastlicht was the first honorary consul of the State of Israel in Mexico, promoted the organization of the Instituto de Intercambio Cultural México-Israel, and was the honorary president of the Israeli-Mexican Commerce Chamber.

[Efraim Zadoff (2nd ed.)]

FATIMIDS, Shi'ite Muslim dynasty which ruled in *Egypt (969–1171), and in other parts of North Africa (*Tunisia, 909–

1051), and the Near East (*Syria, 969–1076 and *Palestine, 969–1099). The Fatimids traced their ancestry to Fāṭima, the daughter of Muhammad, and ʿAlī, her husband, who, in their opinion, was his only rightful successor. The Jews enjoyed a reasonable degree of tolerance, security, and prosperity during their reign.

The establishment of the Fatimid dynasty resulted from the efforts of the Ismāʿīli branch of the Shi'a, which sought to restore the caliphate to the direct descendants of the Prophet and to reconcile Islamic religion, based on divine revelation, with Greek philosophy, in order that the ideas of other religions could merge with their own. Hence, the members of this Islamic sect were inclined to be tolerant. Their liberal attitude toward non-Muslim subjects also stemmed from the fact that the great majority of their Muslim subjects remained faithful to orthodox Sunni Islam and hostile to the Shi'ite caliphs who therefore were forced to appoint Christian and Jewish intellectuals as officials and ministers. Christians could build new churches without difficulty and celebrate their holidays with solemn processions, sometimes attended by the caliphs themselves. The second Fatimid caliph of Egypt, al-ʿAzīz (975–996), appointed two brothers of his Christian wife to the posts of patriarch of *Jerusalem and *Alexandria respectively. While Jews did not attain such exalted positions, they mostly enjoyed religious freedom and their civil rights were not curtailed. Usually the authorities did not enforce the repressive laws of the Covenant of *Omar, which demanded that distinctive signs be worn by non-Muslims, and the duties of Jewish merchants were less than those required by Islamic law. Recent research on *genizah* documents has revealed considerable data on non-Jews, some from Christian countries, who went to Egypt in the 11th century in order to convert to Judaism (see N. Golb, in *Sefunot*, 8 (1964), 85ff.; E. Ashtor, in *Zion*, 30 (1965), 69ff.)

The third caliph, al-Ḥākim (996–1020), however, persecuted non-Muslims during the latter part of his reign. In 1012, he took decisive action to humiliate non-Muslims and segregate them from the "true believers" – the two aims of the Covenant of Omar. Jews and Christians were forbidden to ride horses and to keep Muslim servants. Christian sources indicate that many churches were destroyed, including the Church of the Holy Sepulcher in Jerusalem. Many Christians and some Jews embraced Islam or left the country to escape the persecutions. Al-Ḥākim's measures served as the model for Muslim zealots in the future. His successor al-Ẓāhir (1020–34) and the later Fatimids returned to the traditional policy of tolerance. But *genizah* documents show that on occasion Jews were victims of the hatred of viziers and other dignitaries. Some were Christians who attempted to harass the Jews and bring about their dismissal from government posts. The Jewish officials, called *sar* ("commander") in Hebrew documents, protected their coreligionists, appointed them to various posts, and gave them government commissariat orders. They never rose to the position of vizier, as some Christians did, but some held important posts at court, thus enhancing the social standing of the community. The first of these dignitaries was the Jewish court physician of Caliph al-Muʿizz, the first Fatimid of Egypt. Some scholars have identified him with the general Jawhar or with Yaʿqūb *Ibn Killis, a Jewish convert to Islam, who became vizier in Cairo. However, B. *Lewis has proved that the Italian Jew Paltiel of Oria who appears in *Megillat Aḥimaʿaẓ* was Mūsā b. Eleazar, the court physician of al-Muʿizz. In about 994, Manasseh b. Ibrāhīm al-Qazzāz, praised as a benefactor of Syrian Jewry in Hebrew poems found in the *genizah*, became head of the administration in Syria when the Christian ʿĪsā b. Nestorius was appointed vizier of the caliph al-ʿAzīz. The brothers Abū Saʿd and Abū Naṣr (Hebr. Abraham and Ḥesed) b. Sahl (Yashar; possibly Karaites) who were merchants from *Tustar, southwestern Persia, and influential at the court in *Cairo in the second quarter of the 11th century, were murdered in 1047. In the early 12th century, the Jew Abu al-Munajjā Shaʿyā, chief minister of agriculture, ordered the digging of a canal which still bears his name.

For various reasons, the economic policy of the Fatimids was very advantageous for the Jews. The caliphs' interest in increasing trade between Egypt and other countries stemmed partly from a belief that they could thus win converts to their religious persuasion. They succeeded in diverting the trade between India and the Near East from the Persian Gulf to the Red Sea which became the main artery of a great international trade. Many Jewish merchants, of varying degrees of wealth, participated in the India trade, as the Fatimids neither created monopolies nor harassed small merchants and industrialists in other ways in the manner of other Muslim rulers.

The Jewish communities of Egypt and Syria were headed by a *nagid*, who was appointed by the Fatimid caliph (see *Nagid).

Medieval Jewish tradition ascribes the creation of this position to the Fatimids' desire to remove the influence of the *exilarch on Egyptian Jewry. This view has been accepted by modern scholars. S.D. *Goitein, however, holds that the office of the *nagid* developed independent of the aspirations and the policies of the Fatimids. Apparently the first of the *negidim* was Paltiel of Oria. Later on other court physicians held this post, including Judah b. Saadiah (1065–79), his brother Mevorakh (1079–1110), and *Samuel b. Hananiah (c. 1140–59).

BIBLIOGRAPHY: Mann, Egypt; Fischel, Islam, 44ff.; S.D. Goitein, *A Mediterranean Society*, 1 (1967), index; idem, in: JQR, 53 (1962/63), 117ff.; E. Ashtor, in: *Zion*, 30 (1965), 143ff.; B. Lewis, in: *Bulletin of the School of Oriental and African Studies*, 30 (1967), 177–81. **ADD. BIBLIOGRAPHY:** M. Gil, *A History of Palestine (634–1099)* (1992); M.R. Cohen, *Jewish Self-Government in Medieval Egypt* (1980).

[Eliyahu Ashtor]

FEARING, KENNETH (1902–1961), U.S. poet and novelist. Fearing was born in Chicago and graduated from the University of Wisconsin and later settled in New York. He is regarded as a significant voice in 20th-century American poetry. His verse, mainly satirical, was written in the vernacular and gave expression to the nightmarish quality of urban life during the late 1930s and 1940s. His first volume of poetry, *Angel Arms*, was published in 1929. This was followed by *Poems* (1935), *Dead Reckoning* (1938), *Collected Poems* (1940), *Afternoon of a Pawnbroker* (1943), *Stranger at Coney Island* (1948), and *New and Selected Poems* (1956). The movies, newspapers, comic strips, radio, and advertising were all targets for his mordant attacks, as was the American faith in success and wealth. Fearing's effects are achieved by a mastery of objective presentation, which anticipated the surrealist manner, pop poetry, and concrete trends of a later generation of American poets. Fearing's first novel, *The Hospital* (1939) was followed by *The Dagger in the Mind* (1941); *Clark Gifford's Body* (1942); *The Big Clock* (1946), the story of a manhunt; *The Loneliest Girl in the World* (1951); *The Generous Heart* (1954); and *The Crozart Story* (1960).

BIBLIOGRAPHY: S.J. Kunitz (ed.), *Twentieth Century Authors (First Supplement)* (1955), 319. **ADD. BIBLIOGRAPHY:** R. Barnard, *The Great Depression and the Culture of Abundance: Kenneth Fearing, Nathanael West and Mass Culture in the 1930s* (1995); A. Anderson, *Fear Ruled Them All: Kenneth Fearing's Literature of Corporate Conspiracy* (2003).

[David Ignatow]

FEAR OF GOD (Heb. *yirat elohim*, but in the Talmud *yirat shamayim*, lit. "fear of Heaven"), ethical religious concept, sometimes confused with *yirat ḥet*, "the fear of sin," but in fact quite distinct from it. The daily private prayer of Rav (Ber. 16a), which has been incorporated in the Ashkenazi liturgy in the Blessing for the New Moon, speaks of "a life of fear of Heaven and of fear of sin." In the latter, "fear" is to be understood in the sense of apprehension of the consequences of sin but in the former in the sense of "reverence"; as such it refers to an ethical outlook and a religious attitude, which is distinct from the actual performance of the commandments. "Fear of God" frequently occurs in the Bible, particularly with regard to Abraham's willingness to sacrifice Isaac (Gen. 22:12), and it is mentioned as that which God primarily desires of man (Deut. 10:12). Nevertheless it does not seem to have an exact connotation in the Bible (see *Love and Fear of God), and it was the rabbis who formulated the doctrine of Fear of God with some precision. Basing itself on Leviticus 19:14 (and similar verses, e.g., 19:32, 25:17, 36:43), the *Sifra* (in loc. cf. Kid. 32b) maintains that the phrase "thou shalt fear thy God" is used only for those commandments which "are known to the heart" ("the sin is known to the heart of the person who commits it, but other men cannot detect it" – Rashi in loc.) i.e., there are no social sanctions attached to it, and the impulse behind its performance is reverence for God. This is, in fact, reflected in Exodus 1:17 and it is emphasized, from a slightly different aspect, in the famous maxim of Antigonus of *Sokho, "Be as servants who serve their master without thought of reward, but let the fear of heaven be upon thee" (Avot 1:3). It was spelled out by Johanan b. Zakkai, when on his deathbed he enjoined his disciples: "Let the fear of Heaven be upon you as the fear of flesh and blood." In answer to their surprised query "and not more?" he answered, "If only it were as much! When a person wishes to commit a transgression he says, 'I hope no man will see me'" (Ber. 28b). The characteristic of the God-fearing man is that he "speaketh truth in his heart" (Ps. 15:2; BB 88a).

The fear of God complements knowledge of the Torah. According to one opinion it is only through fear of heaven that one can arrive at true knowledge of the Torah: "He who possesses learning without the fear of heaven is like a treasurer who is entrusted with the inner keys but not with the outer. How is he to enter?" Another opinion is: "Woe to him who has no courtyard yet makes a gate for it," since it is through knowledge that one attains fear of God (Shab. 31a–b). Since fear of God is a state of mind and an ethical attitude, it can best be acquired by considering and following the example of one's teacher by waiting on him, with the result that one of the consequences of depriving a disciple of the privilege of waiting upon his master is that he deprives him of the fear of God (Ket. 96a). The quality and practice of fear of God depend upon man alone. The statement upon which is based the fundamental Jewish doctrine of the absolute free *will of man is couched in the words "Everything is in the hands of heaven except the fear of heaven." The proof verse for this statement is "what doth the Lord thy God require of thee, but to fear the Lord" (Deut. 10:12), and, countering this, the Talmud asks, "Is then fear of heaven such a small thing?" answering that it was only Moses who so regarded it (Ber. 33b).

For the relationship between fear of God and love of God see *Love and Fear of God.

[Louis Isaac Rabinowitz]

The traditional attitude toward the fear (*yir'ah*) of God was thus ambivalent: it was highly valued, but at the same time was regarded as inferior to the love of God. (Cf. "Love and Fear of God; see TB Sota 31a). Later Jewish thought attempted to resolve this ambivalence by positing the fear of God as an equivocal term. *Bahya ibn Paquda (11th century), in his *Duties of the Heart* 10:6, characterized two different types of fear as a lower "fear of punishment" and a higher "fear of [divine] glory." Abraham *Ibn Daud (early 12th century) differentiated between "fear of harm" (analogous to the fear of a snake bite or of a king's punishment) and "fear of greatness," analogous to respect for an exalted person, such as a prophet, who would not harm a person (*The Exalted Faith* VI). Maimonides (late 12th century) categorized the fear of God as a positive commandment. Nevertheless, the halakhic status he accorded to the fear of God did not prevent it from being presented in diverse ways. In his *Book of the Commandments* (commandment #4), Maimonides characterized it as "the fear of punishment," whereas in his *Code* he characterized it as the feeling of human insignificance deriving from contemplation of God's "great and wonderful actions and creations" (Foundations of the Torah 2:1). Nevertheless, later in the *Code* Maimonides presents "service based on fear" as a religiously inferior type of behavior of "the ignorant (*'amei ha-arez*), women and children," deriving from their hope for reward and fear of punishment (Laws of Repentance 10:1). At the end of his *Guide of the*

Perplexed (3:52), Maimonides characterizes fear as resulting from the entire system of commandments, and as expressing a sense of shame in the presence of God. Isaac Arama (15th century) differentiates among three types of fear in his *Binding of Isaac* (ch. 92): in addition to the sublime fear of greatness and inferior "fear not for its own sake" he posits a fear which is the fruit of belief in the divine will, which makes possible undetermined events. In another work (*Ḥazut Kashah*, ch. 3) Arama characterizes this third type of fear as a supra-philosophical rank, because, in his view, although the philosophers recognized God's supreme greatness, they did not fear God, since in their view God could not harm people.

The fear of God was also characterized in diverse ways in the Kabbalah by means of the different **sefirot*: fear was symbolized by the *sefirot* "wisdom" (*ḥokhmah*) (based on Job 28:28), "understanding (*binah*) (based on Proverbs 1:7), "power" (*gevurah*), which has the same *gematria* (numerical value) as *yir'ah* (fear), or "kingdom" (*malkhut*) (based on Mishnah Sanhedrin 2:5).

[Hannah Kasher (2nd ed.)]

BIBLIOGRAPHY: *Urbach, Ḥazal*, 348–370. **ADD. BIBLIOGRAPHY:** H. Kreisel, *Maimonides' Political Thought: Studies in Ethics, Law and the Human Ideal* (1999), ch. 7.

FEATHER, LEONARD (1914–1994), jazz critic, producer, composer, lyricist, and instrumentalist. Feather was born into an upper-middle-class Jewish family in the London suburbs and was supposed to follow his father into the family garment business, but after a friend played Louis Armstrong's "West Side Blues" for him in a local record store, young Leonard decided on another career path. He had already been studying piano and clarinet, so his musical knowledge was greater than many of his early competitors. At the urging of the American record producer and critic John Hammond, Feather made his way to the United States in 1935 and never looked back. He quickly became an influential critic at *Esquire* and *Metronome*, eventually landing the job of jazz critic at the *Los Angeles Times*. More important, Feather was a prolific author, responsible for several key texts including *The Encyclopedia of Jazz* (co-edited with Ira Gitler) and the pioneering volume *Inside Bebop* (1949), his first book, and countless liner notes. From his pulpit at the *LA Times*, Feather was also a tireless opponent of segregation and racism in jazz at a time when few regular jobs were open to African-American musicians.

BIBLIOGRAPHY: G. Giddins, "Leonard Feather, 1914–1980," in: *The Village Voice* (Sept. 29, 1980); "The Leonard Feather Scrapbooks," at: www.leonardfeather.com; P. Watrous, "Leonard Feather, 80, Composer and the Dean of Jazz Critics," in: *New York Times* (Sept. 24, 1994).

[George Robinson (2nd ed.)]

FEDER, ERNST (**Ernesto A.**, pseudonym: **Spectator**; 1881–1964), German lawyer and journalist. Born into a liberal German-Jewish family in Berlin, Feder studied law, economics, and history, completing his Ph.D. with a prize-winning thesis (*Verantwortlichkeit fuer fremdes Verschulden nach dem Buergerlichen Gesetzbuche*) at Berlin University in 1902. From 1907, he worked as an independent lawyer in Berlin, joined by Arthur Loewe in 1911. He also contributed to several legal and economic journals. In 1918, together with Theodor *Wolff and others, he founded the German Democratic Party (DDP) and was elected its chairman. From 1919 to 1931, he was domestic politics editor of the *Berliner Tageblatt*, the leading democratic-liberal paper of the Weimar Republic (edited by Wolff from 1907 to 1933). Owing to a dispute with the publisher, Feder resigned in 1931 and resumed private law practice besides working as a freelance writer and journalist. He was elected a member of several press associations and judicial bodies, including the Tribunal d'Honneur International des Journalists in The Hague (1931–33). An ardent supporter of post-imperial democratic Germany, Feder rejected Zionism and was active in Jewish communal organizations like the *Central-Verein. He was a close friend of leading German-Jewish figures like Paul *Nathan and James *Simon (cf. LBI YB, 10 (1965), 3–23).

In 1933, Feder managed to flee via Switzerland to Paris where he gave lectures at the Collège libre des Sciences Sociales and the Institut de Droit International, contributed to various papers like *Mass und Wert* (est. by Thomas *Mann) and *Aufbau*, and frequently traveled to Denmark, Finland, and Tunisia. After being interned at the Camp de la Braconne, he fled to Brazil in July 1941. In Rio de Janeiro, he continued lecturing and writing well over 40 papers in Brazil and abroad. After he was awarded the *Bundesverdienstkreuz* in 1952, he was personally invited by Theodor Heuss and others to return to West Berlin, where he lived from 1957 until his death in 1964. His literary papers were donated to the Leo Baeck Institute New York. Among his published works are numerous legal and economic studies (cf. ABJ, 6 (1998), 509–513), several biographies, and historical studies: *Theodor Barth und der demokratische Gedanke* (1919); *Hugo Preuss. Ein Lebensbild* (1926); *Politik und Humanitaet. Paul Nathan. Ein Lebensbild* (1929; cf. LBI YB, 3 (1958), 60–80); *Bismarcks grosses Spiel. Die geheimen Tagebuecher Ludwig Bambergers* (1932); and *Les Huguenots en Allemagne* (1935). Feder's memoirs, *Encontros / Encuentros* (1944/45), originally appeared in Portuguese and Spanish (German edition: *Begegnungen. Die Großen der Welt im Zwiegespräch*, 1950). His diaries were first published by A. Paucker, "Searchlight on the Decline of the Weimar Republic – The Diaries of Ernst Feder," in: LBI YB, 13 (1968), 161–234; *Heute sprach ich mit … Tagebuecher eines Berliner Publizisten 1926–1932*, ed. C. Lowenthal-Hensel / A. Paucker (1971).

BIBLIOGRAPHY: *Aufbau*, no. 12 (1956); *MB* (April 17, 1964 and 1965); W. Roeder (ed.), *International Biographical Dictionary of Central European Emigrés 1933–1945*, vol. I (1980), 168; H. Schmuck (ed.), *Jewish Biographical Archive*, F. 237 (1995), 140–45; Series II, F. II/145 (2003), 197–204; R. Heuer (ed.), *Archiv Bibliographia Judaica*, vol. VI (1998), 505–13 (incl. bibl.).

[Johannes Valentin Schwarz (2nd ed.)]

FEDER, RICHARD (1875–1970), Czech rabbi; from 1953 chief rabbi of Moravia residing in Brno, and from 1961 also chief rabbi of Bohemia. After graduating at the Vienna rabbinical seminary, he officiated in Kojetin and other communities, where the preaching was conducted in Czech (Louny, Roudnice nad Labem, and Kolin). During the war he was sent to the concentration camp of Theresienstadt where he was active as a rabbi. A prolific writer, Feder wrote popular works on Jewish lore and conducted research on the history of the communities of Roudnice nad Labem and Kolin. His main works are *Židovská tragedie* ("Jewish Tragedy," 1947), one of the first books published on the Holocaust; *Židovské besídky* ("Jewish Tales"; several volumes) for children; *Hebrejská učebnice* (1923), a textbook of Hebrew, also in German; *Židé a kreštáné* ("Jews and Christians," 1919); *Židovství a židé* ("Jews and Judaism," 1955); and *Sinai* (1955), a textbook of Jewish religious instruction. In 1965 the state conferred on Feder a medal in recognition of his part in reconstruction and his "uncompromising stand in the fight against fascism and for peace."

BIBLIOGRAPHY: *Věstnik židovských náboženskýchobci v československu*, 27, no. 8 (1965), 1–2; 27, no. 11 (1965), 2–3; A. Charim, *Die toten Gemeinden* (1966), 29–36; R. Iltis, in: *Židovská ročenka* (1965/66), 78; R. Feder, *ibid.*, 31–38; (1960/61), 28–37.

FEDER, TOBIAS (pseudonym of **Tobias Gutman**; c. 1760–1817), Haskalah writer, poet, and grammarian, born in Przedborz, near Cracow. Supporting himself by teaching, proofreading, and commerce, he wandered through Galicia, Poland, and Russia. In Galicia he associated himself with the leading Haskalah writers, differing from them in his sharp polemic style directed against all those whose views on science and literature differed from his own. He was a versatile writer and wrote plays, satires, and studies in linguistics and grammar, seeking to synthesize Haskalah and tradition. However, the major part of his work was apparently lost and only a small fraction ever published, most of it posthumously. His works include: *Kol Nehi* (Warsaw, 1798), an elegy on *Elijah b. Solomon, the Vilna Gaon – and *Shem u-She'erit* (first published in Lemberg, 1877), a collection of poems. He also wrote poems in honor of Czar Alexander I's victory over Napoleon, *Shir Haẓlaḥat Aleksander be-Ḥaẓoto et Mitkomemav* (1814) and *Simḥah ve-Sason la-Yehudim* (Berdichev, 1814). Several of his smaller works were published in the Hebrew newspaper *Ḥavaẓẓelet*. His early grammatical work *Beit Toviyyah* (no longer extant) formed the basis for the introduction to Hebrew grammar in his *Mevasser Tov* (Mohilev, 1820?), which included a work on the Masorah, *Menorat Shelomo* of R. Phoebus of Dubrovno, as well as poems and novellae. Feder was also the author of the first anti-Yiddish polemic work in Hebrew *Kol Meḥaẓeẓim* (Berdichev, 1816; Lemberg, 1853) which was directed against Mendel *Levin's Yiddish translation of the biblical book of Proverbs. Publication of this polemic was, however, withheld, at the request of Levin's friends, until after the death of both men.

BIBLIOGRAPHY: Klausner, Sifrut, 1 (1952²), 239ff., and see bibliography for Mendel *Levin.

[Getzel Kressel]

FEDERATIONS OF COMMUNITIES, TERRITORIAL. Throughout the Middle Ages and early modern times individual Jewish communities, though jealous of their independence, formed on occasion federations on a district, regional, or countrywide basis. These were prompted in the Middle Ages in many instances by external needs, principally the obligation imposed by the government to collect state and other taxes on a corporate basis, and in others by internal need and trends. Such consolidations were largely sporadic and came into being for a specific purpose. In some countries, however, they were of long duration. *Synods in France and other countries brought communities together to consult on matters of mutual interest and to adopt regulations, mainly on the internal social, moral, judicial, and political affairs of the communities. Frequently conferences were convened for such purposes.

In Aragon communities of entire districts formed into *collecta* for tax collection. In other countries also the insistence of the state authorities to bargain on taxes with the communities of the entire domain, or at least of a wide region, resulted in the formation of federations, some ephemeral, and some more lasting; some were formed on Jewish initiative and others ordered by the state. Many of these federations of communities, once engaged in a common enterprise, utilized their mutual contacts to further their internal needs. Such were the *Councils of the Lands of Poland-Lithuania, and Bohemia and Moravia in the late Middle Ages as well as the *Landjudenschaft of German principalities up to the 18th century.

In modern times much of the organization of the new-type Orthodox, Conservative, and Reform congregations has been based on territorial federation. Freed from the task of tax collection they serve on a voluntary basis the religious requirements, social needs, and aims of the trend to which they adhere within the boundaries of the state. The formation of such federations received considerable stimulus through the growing sense of patriotism to the state, the break-up of the old local community, the wish of opponent religious camps to secure a countrywide framework to strengthen their positions, and the rapid development of modern communications systems. The movements to *autonomism and the implementation of *minority rights also considerably influenced the formation of federations between the two world wars.

See also history of individual countries in Europe; *United States; *Va'ad Le'ummi, *Takkanot.

BIBLIOGRAPHY: Baron, Community, 3 (1942), index; O.I. Janowsky, *Change and Challenge, a History of 50 years of JWB* (1966).

[Isaac Levitats]

FEDERBUSCH, SIMON (1892–1969), rabbi, author, and Zionist leader. Federbusch was born in Narol, Galicia. He was ordained by prominent rabbis in Poland before World War I and also received a rabbinical degree from the Vienna *Israelitisch-Theologische Lehranstalt in 1923. He settled in Lvov (Lemberg) and was a member of the Polish Sejm (parliament) from 1922 to 1928, and vigorously supported legislation for Jewish education and for the rehabilitation of Jewish war victims. Active in the Mizrachi movement from his student days, Federbusch helped found Ha-Po'el ha-Mizrachi and was president of the Mizrachi Organization of Galicia from 1924 to 1930. During those years he edited *Gilyonot*, a Hebrew weekly, and *Mizraḥah*, a Hebrew monthly. In 1930 he became rabbi of the United Hebrew Congregation of Helsinki, Finland, and the following year was elected chief rabbi of Finland. In this position he promoted interfaith understanding, helped defeat a bill banning *sheḥitah*, and helped secure Finnish entry visas for many Jewish refugees from Nazi Germany.

In 1940 he moved to New York City, where he was rabbi and principal of the Yeshiva Rabbi Israel Salanter (Bronx), a position he held until his death. He was president of Ha-Po'el Ha-Mizrachi of America from 1942 to 1948. From 1944 he was chairman of the *Histadrut Ivrit. He was a member of the executive of *Brit Ivrit Olamit ("The World Hebrew Union"), the executive of the World Jewish Congress, the World Zionist Actions Committee, the World Mizrachi Council, and the presidium of the World Federation of Polish Jews.

Federbusch was the author of many articles and scholarly works in Hebrew, German, Yiddish, English, Polish, and Swedish on rabbinical literature, Jewish philosophy and ethics, and religious Zionist thought. He tried to clarify contemporary problems in the light of classical Jewish sources. Among his works are *Shelemut ha-Yahadut* (1929), *Iyyunim* (1929), *Ha-Musar ve-ha-Mishpat be-Yisrael* (1943, 1947^2), *Mishpat ha-Melukhah be-Yisrael* (1952), *Ha-Lashon ha-Ivrit be-Yisrael u-ve-Ammim* (1967), *World Jewry Today* (1959), and *Ḥikrei Yahadut* (1965). He also edited a number of books, such as *Maimonides, His Teachings and Personality* (1956), *Rashi, His Teachings and Personality* (1958), and *Ḥokhmat Yisrael be-Ma'arav Eiropah* (3 vols., 1958–1965; vol. 3 entitled *Ḥokhmat Yisrael be-Eiropah*) on modern European Jewish scholars.

BIBLIOGRAPHY: D. Telsner, in: J.L. Maimon (ed.), *Sefer Yovel… S. Federbush* (1960), 9–40 (incl. bibl.).

[Gershon Hadas]

FEDERMAN, MAX (1902–1991), Canadian labor leader and Zionist. Federman was born in Dzialoszyce, Poland, and in 1920 joined his father, who had previously immigrated to Toronto. Federman found work in the fur industry and became active in the International Union of Fur and Leather Workers. A committed Socialist and strident anti-Communist, he spent 20 years battling Communist infiltration of his union and was regularly denounced as a class renegade in the *Vochenblatt*, the Yiddish Communist weekly in Toronto. In 1935, his union split along ideological lines and finally dissolved in 1955. The union's members joined the Amalgamated Meat Cutters of the AFL/CIO. Federman eventually became manager of the union's Fur and Leather Department in Toronto.

Federman was also active on behalf of the Toronto Jewish community. In the aftermath of World War II he helped win labor support for the reopening of Canadian immigration and, especially, the removal of barriers to Jewish immigration. He represented labor in fur industry negotiations with the Canadian government regarding the postwar admission of Jewish furriers to Canada from Europe. When the government agreed to the admission of 500 fur workers and their families, Federman was part of the Canadian team that visited Displaced Persons camps in Germany, Austria, and Italy to select the workers.

An ardent Zionist, Federman was chairman of *Aḥdut ha-Avodah-Poalei Zion and instrumental in establishing a vocational training school in Upper Galilee in 1961. In addition, he was active in numerous labor and communal organizations in Toronto, including the Trades and Labour Council, the Executive Trade Union Committee, the Histadrut, the Jewish Labour Committee, the Borochov School, the Co-Operative Commonwealth Federation (CCF) and its successor, the New Democratic Party. Following an upsurge in antisemitic hate activity in Toronto in the early 1960s, Federman joined the Community Anti-Nazi Committee of the Canadian Jewish Congress.

[Frank Bialystok (2nd ed.)]

FEDERN, PAUL (1871–1950), Austrian psychoanalyst. Federn, the son of a distinguished Viennese physician, graduated from the medical school in Vienna. In 1904 he joined Freud's inner circle, being preceded only by three physicians: Adler, Stekel, and Reitler. His initial studies and publications combined the viewpoints of biology and psychology. In 1912 he contributed papers on sexual subjects and night fears and in 1913–14 papers on sadism, masochism, and dream interpretation, stressing the ego psychological point of view. He also wrote on telepathy and extrasensory perception. During World War I he was a doctor in the Austrian army. Federn devoted himself to the training of analysts and was the chairman of the education committee of the Vienna Society. His interest in social psychology led to a major work, a study of the psychology of revolution, *Zur Psychologie der Revolution: Die vaterlose Gesellschaft* (1919). In the 1920s he wrote papers on many psychoanalytic issues. After Freud's illness in 1924 Federn became his deputy, and continued that function until 1938, when he immigrated to the United States. Federn's most original findings were in the field of ego psychology and the psychoses. He contributed greatly to the understanding of the manifestations of the ego, the sources of its feeling, and the nature of its attachments to objects. His study of the ego, especially in dreams, neuroses, and schizophrenia, permitted him to develop important concepts – at times at variance with those of Freud – which came to be applied in new methods to the therapy of the psychoses. From 1940 the dynamics of the psychosis became clearer to him, and he published papers on the analysis of psychosis (1943) and on the psychotherapy of latent schizophrenia (1949). In his will, Federn entrusted Eduardo Weiss with editing his works on ego psychology, which appeared as *Ego Psychology and the Psychoses* (1953).

BIBLIOGRAPHY: E. Weiss, in: F.G. Alexander et al. (eds.), *Psychoanalytic Pioneers* (1966), 142–59. **ADD. BIBLIOGRAPHY:** M.T. Melo de Carvalho, *Paul Federn – une autre voie pour la théorie du moi* (1996); E. Federn, "Thirty- five Years with Freud – 100th Anniversary of Paul Federn, October 13, 1971," in: *Psyche*, 10 (1971), 721–37.

[Louis Miller]

FEFER, ITZIK (1900–1952), Soviet Yiddish poet. Fefer was born in the Ukrainian *shtetl* of Shpola. He first joined the Jewish Labor Bund but, in 1919, became a member of the Communist Party. Soon after his debut as a Yiddish poet (1920), he became prominent in Soviet-Yiddish literature. In 1922 he formulated his literary credo of *proste reyd* ("simple speech"). By nature lyrical and even sentimental, his Yiddish was rich and idiomatic and his verses rhythmic and musical. He harnessed himself to the party line, and played a central role in the Soviet-Yiddish literary hierarchy. His works, which appeared in Soviet-Yiddish magazines, were often collected and published. Though he wrote the well-known poem "Stalin," he also wrote "*Ikh bin a Yid*" ("I Am a Jew") during World War II when the party permitted such poems. His poems *Shotens fun Varshever Geto* ("Shadows of the Warsaw Ghetto") are a valuable contribution to the literature of the Holocaust. He also wrote poems about Birobidzhan, the Jewish autonomous region in the Russian Far East, as well as nature poetry and poems for children.

In 1943 Fefer visited the U.S., Canada, Mexico, and the U.K. with Shloyme *Mikhoels, as a representative of the Jewish *Anti-Fascist Committee. Arrested in the Stalinist anti-Jewish purges in 1948, he was killed on August 12, 1952. In the 1990s, the publication of archival materials revealed his role as an informer for the Soviet secret police.

BIBLIOGRAPHY: S. Niger, *Yidishe Shrayber in Sovet-Rusland* (1958); J. Glatstein, *In Tokh Genumen* (1960); I. Yonasovitch, *Mit Yidishe Shrayber in Rusland* (1949); S. Bickel, *Shrayber fun Mayn Dor* (1964); Y.Y. Cohen (ed.), *Pirsumim Yehudiyyim bi-Verit ha-Mo'aẓot (1917–1960)* (1961); M. Basok, *Mivḥar Shirat Yidish* (1963); S. Meltzer (ed. and tr.), *Al Naharot* (1956); J. Leftwich, *The Golden Peacock* (1939, 1961); B.Z. Goldberg, *The Jewish Problem in the Soviet Union* (1961), index. **ADD. BIBLIOGRAPHY:** I. Howe et al. (eds.), *The Penguin Book of Modern Yiddish Verse* (1988); J. Rubenstein and V.P. Naumov (eds.), *Stalin's Secret Pogrom: The Postwar Inquisition of the Jewish Anti-Fascist Committee* (2001); G. Estraikh, in: *Shofar*, 3 (2002), 14–31.

[Melech Ravitch / Gennady Estraikh (2nd ed.)]

FEIBELMAN, JULIAN BECK (1897–1980), U.S. Reform rabbi. Feibelman was born in Jackson, Mississippi. After serving in the army during World War I, he was ordained at Hebrew Union College (1926). Feibelman served as assistant rabbi of Reform Congregation Keneseth Israel in Philadelphia, and from 1936 he was rabbi of Temple Sinai in New Orleans, Louisiana. Active in New Orleans community life, he was the spokesman for the Jewish community and a central figure in ecumenism in the area. Feibelman was a lecturer at Tulane University. He served as president of the Louisiana Society for Social Hygiene and the New Orleans Family Service Society. His book *The Making of a Rabbi* appeared in 1980.

ADD. BIBLIOGRAPHY: B. Klein, *An Oral History of the Jewish Community in the South: interview with Julian Feidelman* (1968).

[Abram Vossen Goodman]

FEIBUSCH, HANS (1898–1998), English painter, sculptor, and lithographer. Born in Frankfurt, Germany, the son of a dentist, he served in World War I and in 1930 was awarded the German state prize for painters. His early work was destroyed by the Nazis. Feibusch came to England in 1933 and was naturalized in 1940. He is especially well known for his murals in churches – including Chichester Cathedral – public buildings, and private houses. These depict classical mythology as well as religious subjects. Emphasizing the human figure, they are elegant and decorative, with a feeling for gesture and rhythm. He also executed colored lithographs and wrote *Mural Painting* and *The Revelation of St. John* (both 1946), and produced Old Testament figures as well for Stern Hall, London. For much of his life in Britain Feibusch was closely associated with Anglicanism; at the end of his long life he returned to Judaism, and died three weeks short of his hundredth birthday.

ADD. BIBLIOGRAPHY: P. Foster (ed.), *Feibusch Murals: Chichester and Beyond* (1997); ODNB online.

FEIDMAN, GIORA (1936–) clarinetist, fourth generation of a klezmer dynasty. Born in Argentina, he studied clarinet with his father, a well-known Klezmer, and from age 14 played with his father at Jewish weddings. He studied at the Buenos Aires conservatory and at 18 was leading clarinetist of the Colon theater orchestra. On the recommendation of Paul *Kletzki, Feidman joined the Israel Philharmonic Orchestra in 1957, playing with it until 1974. During this period he taught at the Tel Aviv Academy of Music and participated in radio recordings of Israeli folk music. Feidman turned to Klezmer music only in the mid-1960s. When recording for Kol Israel, he decided spontaneously to record the popular tune "Silk Pyjamas" in Klezmer style; it was received so well that Feidman repeated his initiative several times. Feidman concluded that "this is what the Israeli public yearns for."

In 1969 Feidman was a soloist at the first ḥasidic music festival. There he met the well-known, self-taught Klezmer Moshe (Musa) Berlin, who invited him to play at Meron, where Giora was introduced to Israeli Klezmers and encountered a repertoire influenced by Greek, Turkish and Arab music, new to him. From the outset his playing was distinguished by two styles of performance: one, the familiar eastern European enriched by Feidman's restrained, gentle style with which he performed Ḥasidic tunes, and improvisatory pieces which he termed "*tefillah*" (prayer); the other, his innovative use of a bass-clarinet in addition to clarinet, in the course of a single tune. He toured abroad popularizing Klezmer music among Jewish and non-Jewish audiences, bringing it to concert halls and even to churches and monasteries. His Master classes in Israel and abroad helped entice young musicians, Jewish and gentile, to this type of music and Klezmer bands began to sprout in Israel and Europe. Feidman did not hesitate to infuse his "Klezmer music" (which included traditional Ḥasidic *niggunim*, Yiddish songs and a few select Israeli tunes) with artistic music, both classical and modern, fitting Klezmer's openness. Feidman's publications include dozens of recorded albums and about fifteen anthologies from his repertoire. His music was featured in many films, among them *Schindler's List* and *Love Story*.

His father LEVI FEIDMAN (1903–1980) was born in Kishinev, to a Klezmorim family. His father Gedaliah and his grandfather both played the trombone. Gedaliah's band, which included Gypsy musicians, played at both Jewish and non-Jewish events, with a repertoire based mainly on Jewish material and its style Jewish-Bessarabian, with Gypsy influences. After World War I, Levi moved to Argentina. In Buenos Aires he supported himself playing the saxophone but also learned the clarinet and bass-clarinet. By 21 he had already mastered the clarinets, all the saxophones, flute and piccolo and played with different bands. After immigrating to Israel in 1965, he quickly integrated into the Israeli music scene, playing in the opera orchestra and at weddings with various Klezmorim. The Klezmer convention in his memory led to the annual convention at Elkana led by the Klezmer Musa Berlin.

[Y. Mazor]

FEIERBERG, MORDECAI ZE'EV (1874–1899), Hebrew writer. Born in Novograd-Volynsk (Volhynia, Russia) into a family of devout Ḥasidim, Feierberg spent his childhood in a village, where he was tutored by his father, a *shoḥet*. The family returned to the city when Feierberg was about ten. His studies, while concentrating mainly on *Gemara* and *posekim*, since he was expected to become a *shoḥet*, also included medieval religious philosophy (*Maimonides, *Judah Halevi), Kabbalah, and ḥasidic works. Subsequently, he came under the influence of the Haskalah and began reading the Bible and modern Hebrew literature. His secular studies led to a serious conflict between him and his strict father who beat him mercilessly and repeatedly drove him out of the house. Feierberg, however, was not deterred. In a final attempt to bring him back to the traditional fold, his father betrothed him to the daughter of the *shoḥet* of an adjoining town and set him up as a grocer. The store however, became a center for the *maskilim* and Ḥovevei Zion of Novograd-Volynsk and the engagement was broken because Feierberg, always sickly, contracted tuberculosis. Feierberg's literary career began in 1896 when he went to Warsaw, then a center of the Hebrew press and modern Hebrew literature, and submitted a collection of poems and stories to Nahum *Sokolow, the editor of *Ha-Ẓefirah. Sokolow advised the novice writer to give up poetry and concentrate on fiction. His first story, "*Ya'akov ha-Shomer*" ("Jacob the Watchman," in: *Ha-Ẓefirah*, 1897), appeared a year later. His other five short stories were published in 1897 and 1898; three of them – "*Ha-Egel*" ("The Calf," 1899), "*Ha-Kame'a*" ("The Amulet," 1897), and "*Ba-Erev*" ("In the Evening," 1898) – in the prestigious monthly *Ha-Shilo'aḥ*, founded by *Aḥad Ha-Am; and the other two – "*Ha-Ẓelalim*" ("The Shadows") and "*Leil Aviv*" ("A Spring Night") – in *Lu'aḥ Aḥi'asaf* (1898). Turning to journalism for a short period, Feierberg also wrote feature articles on Jewish life in Novograd-Volynsk for the daily *Ha-Meliẓ*. Aḥad Ha-Am, who had befriended and thought highly of him, obtained a stipend for him from the well-known tea merchant K. *Wissotzky. Free from economic dependence on his hostile father, Feierberg, at long last, could give vent to his creative powers. They found expression in his major work "*Le'an?*" ("Whither?"). While it was being prepared for press in *Ha-Shilo'aḥ* (Aḥad Ha-Am made substantial alterations with the author's assent), Feierberg was planning to compose an extensive historical narrative on Israel Ba'al Shem Tov, the founder of Ḥasidism. The work, as well as other of his literary projects, was never written. He died of tuberculosis in the spring of 1899, before "*Le'an?*" appeared in print. Two polemical articles on Hebrew literature and on the contemporaneous Jewish intelligentsia were printed posthumously. The first edition of his collected works appeared in 1904. Further editions have appeared since; the most extensive one was edited by E. Steinman (Tel Aviv, 1941).

Feierberg's stories, articles, journalistic reports, and letters barely comprise a single thin volume and while most of his works lack artistic maturity, his contemporaries and modern critics have recognized in him an original literary mind. His stories, among the most important landmarks in modern Hebrew fiction, express the spiritual-cultural conflict between adherence to traditional Jewish life and the aspiration toward a secular, modern, "European" cultural existence. The theme, expressed earlier by Haskalah authors who considered it their duty to inculcate secular-humanistic values into Jewish life in the 1890s, with such writers as Feierberg, Ḥ.N. *Bialik, and M.J. *Berdyczewski, was exposed in all its tragic depth.

Feierberg's greatness as a writer can be attributed not only to his sensitive aesthetic intuitiveness but, in spite of his youth and inexperience, to an original literary ideology whose basic principles he crystallized. Feierberg thought that the function of Hebrew literature was to describe authentically "the image of our (Jewish) innermost world"; that is, to express the particular outlook of the contemporary East European Jew as conditioned by his education, traditions, and environment. He also believed in a particular Jewish "view of the world," stating that "The air a Jew breathes, the sky he sees, the earth he treads, and all the external sights revealed to him acquire a different form and shape in his soul from what they really are or how they are perceived by other people." Though he conceded that this special "form and shape" stemmed from a distortion of the national Jewish life by the "poison" that had tainted the national existence of the Jewish people for generations, he demanded that the Hebrew author (and he for one fulfilled this demand) express it. Only in this way could Hebrew literature make a valuable contribution to world literature. "Indeed the Hebrew tragedy can drown out the tumult of Rome." Feierberg felt that Hebrew literature should have remained rooted within the East European Jewish ghetto; it should not have tried to detach its themes and physical, as well as mental landscapes, from their environment; and should not have turned toward the "wide world" of Europe, as was the cry of many contemporaneous influential Hebrew authors. It should not depict the Jewish world from the outside, nor criticize its defects in the light of foreign values, nor emphasize the physical-external aspects of Jewish life specifying its economic and cultural structure; but through the artistic and aesthetic power of the narrative as such, Hebrew literature should directly express the "Jewish situation" from within. To develop this literary art, the young Feierberg had to break with the tradition of the Hebrew fiction, especially the literature of the Haskalah and the trend followed by most of the contemporaneous Hebrew writers of his day. He had to evolve the genre of the lyrical story which focuses on personal situations, usually of a distressing nature, that are symbolic of the "Jewish condition" as a whole. Feierberg thus introduced into Hebrew fiction the genre of the confessional lyrical short story in which the deep personal distress of an individual becomes a symbol. The genre also greatly influenced Berdyczewski, Brenner, and Gnessin and became a basic literary form of 20th-century Hebrew fiction.

Feierberg was but a trailblazer in a genre whose development demanded rigid literary and mental discipline. His tendency toward the use of affected language, hyperboles, and sentimental clichés was one of a number of his shortcomings. Another was his failure at times to achieve a viable synthesis between form and content and the idea to be expressed, i.e., direct lyrical expression of his turbulent world and the literary-descriptive frameworks in which he wanted to cast it. The artistic quality of his works is in direct relation to the success with which he achieved this synthesis.

"*Ya'akov ha-Shomer,*" a weak groping toward this aesthetic synthesis, has for protagonist a Jewish soldier of the days of Czar Nicholas II who had been impressed into the Russian Army. Taken from his parents' home at a tender age he returns to the margins of Jewish society after years in a distant gentile environment. The life of such a Jew (then extensively described in Hebrew and Yiddish literature) symbolized for Feierberg the theme that was to form the core of all his works: the relationship ("the border-state") between life in the traditional Jewish community and life outside of it, between loyalty to the spiritual ascetic tradition and the yearning for nature and the life of the senses. He saw himself and his generation torn between these opposing polarities. In "*Ya'akov ha-Shomer*" the tension in Feierberg the man in giving personal expression to his innermost belief prevented the writer from portraying the protagonist convincingly. A certain discrepancy also exists between the significance with which Feierberg invested the hero's experience and the experience as such. Estrangement from Judaism was forced on Ya'akov the watchman externally and his experience is therefore not a valid representation of the spiritual state of the Jew wavering between two worlds. The Jewish czarist soldier, too weak a vehicle to carry the symbol, only partly answers the author's needs of emotional and mental expression and the synthesis between content and self-expression is therefore not realized.

In two of his later stories, "*Ha-Ẓelalim*" and "*Leil Aviv,*" Feierberg broke almost completely with the traditional concepts of plot and character and composed poetic-prose fragments through which he gave direct, bare, and discursive-lyrical expression to the "border-state." Despite the literary sincerity and passages of great beauty and power (especially in "*Leil Aviv*"), the desired synthesis is only partially achieved. In the absence of the rigors of a narrative framework, the stories became infused with sentimentalism expressed in undisciplined language.

The three short stories, "*Ba-Erev,*" "*Ha-Kame'a,*" and "*Ha-Egel,*" were written as childhood reminiscences of Ḥofni Ba'al-Dimyon ("Hophni the Imaginative"), the hero-narrator. As Feierberg had written to Aḥad Ha-Am, in the Ḥofni stories he intended to create a "complete world of the Jew" who would be a kind of "hero of the times." He wanted to develop the idea and proceed from Ḥofni's childhood to later periods in his life. He died, however, before he had time to complete the project. In the tales of Ḥofni's childhood, Feierberg used a narrative-reminiscing expository style which, while restraining his language and his sentimental temperament, fully expressed his personality. Artistically, "*Ba-Erev*" is considered his best work. The story is divided into two parts: in the first, Ḥofni reminisces about his *ḥeder* studies during the long winter nights; in the second, he reconstructs a legend told by his mother on coming home from the *ḥeder.* A seemingly popular ḥasidic tale, the legend serves Feierberg as a symbol through which he could clearly and most effectively express the spiritual "border state" in which Ḥofni would have found himself as a young man. Both parts form a single "world" of oppression and gloom conveying a struggle between loyalty to an ancient and ascetic culture, absolute in its demands of adherence, and a powerful yearning toward a different world. Life in this world of great tension is an endless "trial"; failure lurks everywhere and the burden of responsibility oppresses to the breaking point.

In "*Ha-Kame'a,*" in which Ḥofni recalls his childhood nightmares, this view is sharply expressed, though in a more discursive and less narrative symbolic manner. During these nights of terror he senses the distress and tension that lay in store for him. The talisman, a "weapon" with which Ḥofni's father and the old kabbalist from the *Klaus* equipped him, is from the start seen as insufficient protection and too light an arm for the fierce battle ahead of him. In "*Ha-Egel*" Feierberg deviates from his regular themes. Ḥofni reminisces on his love for a calf. The description of the child's terrible shock at his parents' indifference toward the young calf they intended for slaughter portends the depression and isolation of a man whose moral sensitivity would make him lose his sense of identity with his environment. It presages the "border state" of suspension between being within and without, belonging and revolt.

In *"Le'an?"* Feierberg dwells in minute detail on the sensitive, thinking individual who detaches himself and is cut off from the historical Jewish community. The hero, Naḥman, is the leader prototype, but he has lost contact with his community. His character and education makes him an "aristocrat", an "elected" Jew. The scion of a rabbinical dynasty, his father educates him to be a "soldier" (the same idea also appears in *"Ha-Kame'a"*) and to assume a life of responsibility in the unceasing battle to protect Judaism from secular inroads. His detachment from the community begins at a very early age when he was taught to regard the "normal" Jewish existence around him as a frivolity which he himself morally could not afford to lead. At this stage one type of alienation is apparent – a detachment between the community and its representative, between the public and the individual who is able to personify ideally the values in which all believe. Naḥman, the ideal, wants to perform great deeds: he wants to heal the historical schism in the fate of the Jewish people by hastening the coming of the Messiah. In his search for a way, he steeps himself in the holy books; years pass and he despairs of messianic redemption. He then becomes interested in the Haskalah, thus alienating himself completely. Naḥman's loss of faith in Divine Providence is sudden and swift and his position in the Jewish community becomes a "border state" of unbearable tension which finds concrete expression in the synagogue on the Ninth of *Av: "The whole congregation is praying, it has one heart now, and he – the other heart – is lonely and separated from the community, cut off from his people … And how he would have liked to rejoin his people! He would have given his life for the bond. But how could he? No, he had undone the knot of his own free will and could not tie it again …." This sense of separation is like a hidden disease within Naḥman, but at last the rift between him and his father and the community breaks out in the open with his symbolic act of extinguishing the candle in the synagogue on the Day of Atonement. Naḥman now lapses into a mental state which the community interprets as madness. Toward the end of the story he makes a final attempt at rejoining his people. In a speech at a Ḥibbat Zion gathering, he propounds the idea of national renaissance and a return to the East. This speech is Naḥman's last call and outcry, he then fades away and dies.

Structurally weak, because Feierberg tried to incorporate the Naḥman story into a narrative of reminiscences (as a continuation of the Ḥofni stories), *"Le'an?"* is nevertheless one of the great literary achievements in Hebrew fiction. The tragic proportions of its hero have been attained by few figures in Hebrew literature. The story gives full expression to the torment of the Jew who is torn between the temporal historical moment and his sense of responsibility toward the Jewish heritage of the ages and toward Jewish history. By grappling sincerely and honestly with the tragic problem of the Diaspora Jew in a modern world, Feierberg left an indelible imprint on modern Hebrew literature.

An English translation of *Whither and Other Stories* appeared in 1973 and *"The Calf"* was included in G. Abramson (ed.), *The Oxford Book of Hebrew Short Stories* (1996). For other works which have been translated into English see Goell, Bibliography.

BIBLIOGRAPHY: M.J. Berdyczewski, *Ma'amarim* (1922), 266f.; J.H. Brenner, *Ketavim*, 2 (1953²), 241–3; J. Fichmann, *Ruḥot Menaggenot* (1953), 277–83; S. Ẓemaḥ, *Massah u-Vikkoret* (1954), 9–26; B. Kurzweil, *Sifrutenu ha-Ḥadashah-Hemshekh o Mahpekhah?* (1965), 149–71; J. Klausner, *Yoẓerim u-Vonim*, 2 (1929), 165–82; S. Rawidowitz, in: *Ha-Tekufah*, 11 (1921), 399–419; E. Steinman, *Be-Ma'gal ha-Dorot* (1944), 87–112; A. Sha'anan, *Ha-Sifrut ha-Ivrit ha-Ḥadashah li-Zeramehah*. 2 (1962), 249–66; Waxman, Literature, 4 (1960), 54–62. **ADD. BIBLIOGRAPHY:** E. Avisar, *"Samkhut ha-Av u-Ze'akat ha-Ben be-'Le'an,'"* in: *Hadoar*, 53 (1974), 372–74; A.L. Mintz, "Mordecai Zev Feierberg and the Reveries of Redemption," in: AJSR, 2 (1977), 171–99; S. Werses, in: *Moznayim*, 48:5–6 (1979), 280–91; M. Bosak, *"Rabbi Naḥman mi-Braslav ke-Model le-Gibboro shel 'Le'an,'"* in: *Mabu'a*, 15 (1980); D. Steinhart, "Figures of Thought; Psycho-Narration in the Fiction of Berdichewsky, Bershadsky and Feierberg," in: *Prooftexts*, 8:2 (1988), 197–217; H. Bar Yosef, *"Eyzeh min Romantikan Haya Feierberg?"* in: *Bikoret u-Farshanut*, 23 (1988) 87–116; G.Shaked, *Ha-Sipporet ha-Ivrit*, 1 (1997), 206–13; Aberbach, "David, Mordecai Ze'ev Feierberg," in: *Jewish Quarterly*, 46:2 (1999), 51–52.

[Dan Miron]

FEIERSTEIN, RICARDO (1942–), Argentinian writer. Feierstein was born in Buenos Aires. In his youth he joined Zionist and socialist movements; later he lived for some years on a kibbutz. His literary writings, his achievements as editor of the journal *Raíces* and director of the Milá and Acervo Cultural publishing houses, and his contributions to periodicals reflect his continuous involvement with Jewish cultural life in Argentina. In his writing, Feierstein seeks to close the gap between ideologically oriented and aesthetic literature. His poetry, narratives, and essays seek to build a harmonious individual identity as an Argentinian, a Jew, and a socialist, and the successes and failures of such attempts lie at the core of his writing. His poem "Nosotros, la generación del desierto" ("We, the Generation of the Wilderness," 1984, tr. 1989) speaks for a whole generation that lives between historical events and conflicting trends, unable to establish its own ground. The trilogy of novels *Sinfonía inocente* exposes the unrealized coming-of-age of an Argentinian Jew from adolescence (*Entre la izquierda y la pared*, 1983), to his kibbutz experience (*El caramelo descompuesto*, 1979), to his search for reintegration in a politically shattered Argentina (*Escala uno en cincuenta*. 1984). In *Mestizo* (1988; tr. 2000), a murder mystery frames the search for a fullly realized Argentinian-Jewish identity, while his later novel, *La logia del umbral* (2002), exposes the painful collective failure of such a project (especially in the shadow of the AMIA terrorist bombing in 1994). His views of Argentinian Jewry and their existential experience as a dynamic cultural *mestizaje* (a term meaning racial but also cultural mix in Latin America) are discussed in his books *Judaísmo 2000* (1988) and *Contraexilio y mestizaje: Ser judío en la Argentina* (1990). He also edited *Historia de los judíos argentinos* (1993); *Cuentos judíos latinoamericanos* (1989); *Cien años de narrativa judeo-argentina 1889–1989* (1990). His poems and stories have been translated into English, French, German, and Hebrew. Feierstein was visiting lecturer at American and German universities, and received awards in Argentina and Mexico.

BIBLIOGRAPHY: R. DiAntonio and N. Glickman, *Tradition and Innovation: Reflections on Latin American Jewish Writing* (1993); R. Gardiol, *The Silver Candelabra and Other Stories – A Century of Jewish Argentine Literature* (1997); N. Lindstrom, *Jewish Issues in Argentine Literature* (1989); D.B. Lockhart, *Jewish Writers of Latin America. A Dictionary* (1997); L. Senkman, *La identidad judía en la literatura argentina* (1983); S.A. Sadow and J. Kates, *We, the Generation in the Wilderness* (1989).

[Florinda Goldberg (2nd ed.)]

FEIFFER, JULES (1929–), U.S. cartoonist and writer. Born in the Bronx, New York, Feiffer studied at James Monroe High School and entered the Art Students' League. From 1947 to 1951 he studied at the Pratt Institute while working as an assistant on the comic *The Spirit*. Growing up, he had always assumed that *The Spirit* was Jewish. In 1949 he created his first Sunday cartoon page feature, *Clifford.* He served in the U.S. Army from 1951 to 1953, working with a cartoon animation unit. Upon leaving the army, Feiffer worked in a number of jobs until in 1956, the New York weekly magazine *The Village Voice* began to publish his cartoons. His comic strip, which was simply called *Feiffer*, was an immediate success and appeared regularly in *The Village Voice* and was also internationally syndicated. His satirical cartoons made moral and political statements on a wide range of contemporary issues, both political and personal – from nuclear holocaust, the arms race, and presidential politics to male-female relationships and human fears, and neuroses – and were characterized by the revelation of the private thoughts of his characters. After appearing weekly for 43 years, Feiffer's last syndicated cartoon strip was published on June 18, 2000.

Although known primarily for his cartoons, Feiffer has also achieved success as a playwright, screenwriter, and novelist. His plays of the late 1960s, *Little Murders* (1967), *God Bless* (1968), and *The White House Murder Case* (1969), were all highly political. *Little Murders,* which depicted the horrors of urban life, was later made into a film. In 1963, he came out against the Vietnam War, subsequently speaking at peace demonstrations in Washington.

His screenplay for the 1971 movie *Carnal Knowledge* and his play *Knock Knock* (1976) dealt with more personal issues, the former with middle-age crisis and the latter with social values. His play *Grownups* (1981) focused on interfamily relationships and conflicts. He also wrote the screenplay for the film comedy *I Want to Go Home* (1989), directed by Alan Resnais and starring Adolph Green, as well as the script for the 1991 TV series *The Nudnik Show.*

In 1986 Feiffer received the Pulitzer Prize in editorial cartooning, and in 2004 was honored with the Ian McLellan Hunter Award by the Writers Guild of America.

Among Feiffer's many published works are *Sick Sick Sick: A Guide to Non-Confident Living* (1958); *Great Comic Book Heroes* (1965), a critical history of the comic book superheroes of the late 1930s and early 1940s; *Jules Feiffer's America, from Eisenhower to Reagan* (1982); *Marriage Is an invasion of Privacy, and Other Dangerous Views* (1984); *Ronald Reagan in Movie America: A Jules Feiffer Production* (1988); and *President Bill: A Graphic Epic* (with W. Brown, 1990). Some of his many books for children include *The Man in the Ceiling* (1993); *A Barrel of Laughs, a Vale of Tears* (1995); *Tantrum* (1997); *Meanwhile* (1997); *I Lost My Bear* (1998); and *Bark, George* (1999).

ADD. BIBLIOGRAPHY: K. McAuliffe, *The Great American Newspaper: The Rise and Fall of the Village Voice* (1978); S. Heller (ed.), *Man Bites Man: Two Decades of Satiric Art – 1960–1980* (1981).

[Susan Strul / Ruth Beloff (2nd ed.)]

FEIGEL, SIGI (1921–2004), Swiss Jewish community leader. Born into a Russian-Jewish family, Feigel grew up in the central Swiss Catholic village of Hergiswil (Nidwalden), isolated from any organized Jewish community. In his youth, he experienced much Catholic anti-Judaism. After serving in the Swiss army (1939–45), he studied law at Zurich University and graduated with a doctoral degree in law. He entered the textile firm of his father-in-law, serving as its director until 1977. He was president of the Jewish community of Zurich in 1972–86, initiating a program of lectures by prominent figures and thus getting the Jewish community much publicity. Among the lecturers were Bruno *Kreisky, Axel Springer, and Willy *Brandt. He fought for the enlargement of the Jewish Oberer Friesenberg cemetery in Zurich, meeting opposition in right-wing circles. As a prominent media figure, he helped win popular support for the Anti-Racism Law (1993). With his colleague Rolf *Bloch, he tried to mediate between American-Jewish demands and Swiss politicians and bankers in the 1995–96 Swiss bank account affair. He seems to have coined the phrase, "Justice for the victims, fairness for Switzerland." He founded several foundations to fight racism, xenophobia, and antisemitism, and for the housing of homeless young people. He also initiated the re-writing of textbooks on Jewish history and religion in Switzerland. After selling the textile firm (1977), he returned to law studies and received the Zurich lawyer's diploma at the age of 62. He wrote the standard commentary on the Swiss Anti-Racism Law. The Jewish community chose him as its honorary president.

BIBLIOGRAPHY: K. Obermueller, *Schweizer auf Bewaehrung* (1998); *Antisemitismus: Umgang mit einer Herausforderung: Festschrift zum 70. Geburtstag* (1991); S. Feigel, *Der Erziehungszweck im schweiz. Strafvollzug* (1949).

[Uri Kaufmann (2nd ed.)]

FEIGENBAUM, ARYEH (1885–1981), Israel ophthalmologist. Born in Lemberg, Feigenbaum trained in Vienna and emigrated to Ereẓ Israel in 1913. He became head of the eye department of the Straus Health Center, Jerusalem, and conducted a vigorous campaign against trachoma, serving hundreds of Arabs and Jews a day in his clinics. In 1914 he organized a trachoma conference, the first of its kind, in Palestine and wrote and published the report and recommendations.

From 1922 to 1954 Feigenbaum was head of the ophthalmological department of the Hadassah Hospital and in 1938 first chairman of the pre-faculty of medicine. He was a founder and editor of the first Hebrew medical journal *Harefuah* (1920) and of *Acta Medica Orientalia* (1942). In 1927 he wrote the first Hebrew textbook on ophthalmology, *Ha-Ayin*.

BIBLIOGRAPHY: *Harefuah*, 70 (1966), 473–7.

[Lucien Harris]

FEIGENBAUM, BENJAMIN (1860–1932), Yiddish journalist, essayist, editor, and pamphleteer. Born in Warsaw, the son of ḥasidic parents, he rejected the religious traditions in which he had been brought up and developed into a militant atheist and agitator for socialism. Leaving home, he proceeded in 1884 to Antwerp, in 1887 to London, where he wrote for Yiddish and Hebrew periodicals and published pamphlets on socialism, reaching the United States in 1891. In America, he joined the United Hebrew Trades, writing tracts to win the support of Jewish laborers for socialism and atheism. He also wrote for the *Forverts* and *Arbeter-Tsaytung*, and for the literary monthly *Tsukunft*, of which he was editor for a time. He wrote his essays under several pseudonyms including Shabbes, Shabsovitch, and Sh. Peshes. In 1900 he became general secretary of the newly formed Arbeter Ring (*Workmen's Circle), which he established firmly before resigning in 1903. In 1909 he served as chairman of the mass meeting which sanctioned the general strike of the waist and dress trade, the so-called "uprising of 20,000." His publications include *Vi Kumt a Yid tsu Sotsyalizmus* (1889); *Kosher un Treyfe un Andere Mitsves* (1909); *Yidishkayt un Sotsyalizm* (1942).

BIBLIOGRAPHY: Rejzen, Leksikon, 3 (1929), 44–49; L. Kobrin, *Mayne Fuftsik Yor in Amerike* (1966), 64–75. **ADD. BIBLIOGRAPHY:** Bal-Makhshoves, *Populere Visnshaftlekhe Literatur* (1910), 76–83; M. Shtarkman, in: *YIVO Bleter*, 4 (1932), 354–87; M. Osherovitch, *Geshikhte fun Forverts* (1947), 43–56.

[Melvyn Dubofsky / Marc Miller (2nd ed.)]

FEIGENBAUM, ISAAC HA-KOHEN (1826–1911), Polish rabbi and *posek*. Feigenbaum studied under R. Isaac Meir Alter of Gur (*Gora Kalwaria). In 1893 he founded the first periodical devoted to rabbinic studies, the monthly *Sha'arei Torah*, to which leading contemporary rabbis contributed, and in which he himself wrote the leading article. The journal was continued after his death by his son, Israel Isser Feigenbaum, and ceased publication only at the outbreak of World War II. Among Feigenbaum's works are a critical edition of the *Urim ve-Tummim* of Jonathan *Eybeschuetz with his own commentary (Warsaw, 1881). Feigenbaum was one of the few Polish rabbis, particularly among the Ḥasidim (he was an adherent of the *Kotsk dynasty), who was an ardent supporter of the Ḥibbat Zion movement. He was a member of the Menuḥah ve-Naḥalah Society of Warsaw which founded *Reḥovot, and he himself purchased land under the aegis of the society.

BIBLIOGRAPHY: J.J. Feigenbaum, *Or Penei Yizḥak* (1939, reprint 1966).

[Louis Isaac Rabinowitz]

FEIGENBERG, MEÏR (1923–), Danish theater manager. After academic studies in Stockholm and practical theater work in Copenhagen, Feigenberg became director of the Riddersalen Theater from 1947 to 1950 and of the Frederiksberg Theatre (now Dr. Dantes Aveny) in 1950–52 with a repertoire ranging from Ibsen and Chekhov to Kjell Abell and Tennessee Williams. Feigenberg was director of the New Theatre in 1966–69 and the Danish Theater in 1974–91, which he led with a sure sense of balance between the highbrow and the popular, between the classical and the modern, sometimes in collaboration with the Royal Theater.

[Bent Lexner (2nd ed.)]

FEIGIN, DOV (1907–2000), Israel sculptor. Feigin was born in Lugansk, Russia, and immigrated to Palestine in 1927. He studied in Paris between 1933 and 1937, and in 1947–48 was one of the founders of the New Horizons Group which tried to introduce modernism to Israel art. In 1962, he created a monumental sculpture in stone at Mizpeh Ramon in the Negev. Before 1950, Feigin worked in stone and concrete, and produced massive human forms, in post-cubist style. An example is the monument at Reḥovot *In Memory of Our Warriors*, a relief characterized by its sharply defined contours. His later work became abstract and he composed linear forms in bronze, copper, and iron. Feigin won several prizes: in 1945–46 the Dizengoff prize, in 1953 the Haifa Municipality prize, and in 1985 the Sandberg prize from the Israel Museum.

BIBLIOGRAPHY: B. Tammuz and M. Wykes-Joyce, *Art in Israel* (1966), 152–3; H. Gamzu, *Painting and Sculpture in Israel* (1951), 113–5.

[Yona Fischer]

FEIGIN, SAMUEL ISAAC (1893–1950), Orientalist and biblical scholar. Feigin was born in Krichev. As a youth he went to Palestine; he completed his studies at the Hebrew Teachers' College in Jerusalem and fought in the Ottoman Army during World War I. Feigin emigrated to the United States in 1920 and studied at Yale University until 1923. He held several teaching posts and then in 1932 joined the staff of the Oriental Institute of the University of Chicago. He also taught at the College of Jewish Studies and the Hebrew Theological College (both in Chicago). Feigin's main interest was ancient Babylonian civilization and its relation to biblical life and literature. He wrote *Mi-Sitrei he-ʿAvar* ("From the Secrets of the Past," 1943), a collection of scholarly studies on biblical themes, and *Anshei Sefer* (1950), a collection of biographical essays. He also contributed important articles to scholarly journals.

BIBLIOGRAPHY: Irwin, in: JNES, 9 (1950), 121–3.

[Samuel Sandmel]

FEIGL, BEDRICH (**Friedrich**; 1884–1966), Czech painter and graphic artist. In 1907, he was a founder of the Osma group

("The Eight") which, with Emil Filla as its leading personality, marked the break of Czech art with traditional classicism. This break profoundly influenced modern Czech painting. Feigl created the best work of his expressionistic period with his landscapes of Copenhagen, Berlin, and the fishing villages on the French Riviera. He is, however, best known for his sketches of Prague ghetto life. Feigl also did book illustrations (H. Politzer, ed., *Sippurim*, 1937). After escaping from Nazi-occupied Prague, Feigl spent World War II in London. Here, he prepared the plates for the first Czechoslovak postwar banknotes.

BIBLIOGRAPHY: G. Marzynski, *Friedrich Feigl* (Ger., 1921); *Příruční slovník naučný*, 1 (1962), 711.

[Avigdor Dagan]

FEIGL, FRITZ (1891–1971), analytical chemist and a leader of the Brazilian Jewish community. Feigl was born in Vienna and served as an officer in the Austrian Army in World War I. He joined the staff of the Technische Hochschule in Vienna in the early 1920s and became professor of chemistry there in 1935. The *Anschluss* of 1938 forced him out of his position and he emigrated to Brazil, where in 1941 he became head of the Ministry of Agriculture's mineral production laboratory. In 1953 he was appointed professor of chemistry at the University of Brazil. In his work on chemical analysis and microanalysis Feigl specialized mainly in spot tests, on which he became a world authority. He was the main pioneer of new procedures in this field. His books include *Spot Test Analysis* (2 vols., 1934), *Theory, Practice, and Uses of Spot Tests in Qualitative Analysis* (1938), *Laboratory Manual of Spot Tests* (1944), and *Chemistry of Specific Selective and Sensitive Reactions* (1949). Feigl was active in communal and Zionist activities in Brazil, where he served as president of the Confederation of Jewish Federations. In 1951 he became a member of the world executive of the World Jewish Congress. He was a member of the board of governors of the Hebrew University of Jerusalem and of the Weizmann Institute of Science in Reḥovot.

[Samuel Aaron Miller]

FEIGL, HERBERT (1902–1988), U.S. philosopher and one of the founders of the Vienna Circle discussion group, which espoused the doctrine of logical positivism. He was born in Reichenberg, Bohemia. In 1922, antisemitism in German universities led Feigl to the University of Vienna, where he received his Ph.D. in philosophy in 1927. At the university Feigl, influenced by Moritz Schlick, became interested in philosophical problems in the foundations of physics. In 1924, with Schlick and Friedrich Waissman, he assembled a discussion group that was later called the "Vienna Circle."

Feigl emigrated to the United States late in 1930 on an International Rockefeller Fellowship and spent nine months at Harvard University, whose faculty he regarded as the American equivalent of the Vienna Circle. He taught at the University of Iowa (1931–40), and in 1940 became professor of philosophy at the University of Minnesota, where he remained until he retired in 1971. He was appointed regents professor of the University of Minnesota in 1967.

In 1949 he and his colleague Wilfrid Sellars edited *Readings in Philosophical Analysis*, which became a standard text of analytic philosophy and logical empiricism. That year they and several other colleagues founded the *Philosophical Studies* journal. In 1953 he and May Brodbeck edited *Readings in the Philosophy of Science*, which became the standard anthology in the field.

In 1953 Feigl obtained a grant to establish the Minnesota Center for Philosophy of Science. The first such institution of its kind in the country, if not the world, it drew philosophers of science from around the globe to participate in workshops and collaborative research.

Feigl served on the governing board of the Philosophy of Science Association and was a founding member (1934) of the editorial board of *Philosophy of Science*, which later became the official journal of the Association. He was president of the Western Division of the American Philosophical Association (1961–62). His first book, *Theorie und Erfahrung in der Physik* ("Theory and Experience in Physics"), was published in 1929. In his writings, Feigl attempted to formulate and defend the principles of the doctrine of logical positivism (also called "consistent empiricism" and "logical empiricism" – the latter name by Feigl). The main tenet of this theory is that meaningful statements must be empirically verified. Feigl gradually moved away from a strict interpretation of this principle to a position that allows for different categories of meaningfulness.

Other books by Feigl include *The "Mental" and the "Physical": The Essay and a Postscript* (1967) and *The Foundations of Science and the Concepts of Psychology and Psychoanalysis* (with M. Scriven, 1976). He also edited *Concepts, Theories & the Mind-Body Problem* (1972).

BIBLIOGRAPHY: H. Feigl and W. Sellars (eds.), *Readings in Philosophical Analysis* (1949); P. Feyerabend and G. Maxwell (eds.), *Mind, Matter, and Method; Essays in Philosophy and Science in Honor of Herbert Feigl* (1966), contains a bibliography of his work. **ADD. BIBLIOGRAPHY:** R. Cohen (ed.), *Herbert Feigl: Inquiries & Provocations, Selected Writings 1929 to 1974* (2001).

[Avrum Stroll / Ruth Beloff (2nd ed.)]

FEILER, ARTHUR (1879–1942), economist. Born in Breslau, he was a contributor to the financial section of the *Frankfurter Zeitung*, from 1903 to 1910, and from 1910 to 1930 was a senior editor of the paper. He taught at the University of Frankfurt for some time during the late 1920s, and at the Graduate Business School in Koenigsberg from 1932 to 1933. In 1933 he emigrated to the United States where he worked at the graduate faculty of the New School for Social Research in New York. His numerous publications include *Die Konjunkturperiode 1907–13 in Deutschland* (1914); *Amerika-Europa: Erfahrungen einer Reise* (1926); *America Seen Through German Eyes* (1928); *Das Experiment des Bolschewismus* (1930[3]); and (with M. Ascoli) *Fascism for Whom?* (1938).

[Edith Hirsch]

FEINBERG, family of pioneer settlers in Ereẓ Israel.

YOSEF FEINBERG (1855–1902) was born in Simferopol in the Crimea, the son of wealthy parents, and studied chemistry at Swiss and German universities. Aroused by the 1881 pogroms, he went to Ereẓ Israel in the spring of 1882, taking a large sum of money. He joined Zalman *Levontin in founding *Rishon le-Zion on land which he helped to buy. Feinberg went to Western Europe and succeeded in gaining Baron Edmond de *Rothschild's support for the idea of Jewish settlement in Ereẓ Israel. However, Feinberg opposed the Baron's paternalistic system of management, and after a dispute in 1887 with the Baron's representative, Yehoshua *Ossowetzky, he was forced to sell his property and leave the settlement, together with other founding members. He bought an oil press in Lydda, but was forced to sell it because of financial straits. He then opened a pharmacy in Jaffa. He was among those who received Theodor *Herzl in Ereẓ Israel in 1898.

ISRAEL ("Lotik"; 1865–1911) younger brother of Yosef, was born in Sebastopol, Crimea. In the early 1880s Israel settled in Rishon le-Zion, where he married Fania Belkind, a member of *Bilu. Leaving Rishon le-Zion with his brother, Feinberg settled in Gederah, where he was one of the settlement's first watchmen (1891) and organized the planting of eucalyptus groves to drain the swamps. In 1898 he moved with his family to *Ḥaderah, but, contracting malaria, was forced to move to Jerusalem. The family returned to Ḥaderah a few years later, and Feinberg tried to reestablish his farm there but died as a result of the debilitating effects of malaria and hard labor.

AVSHALOM (1889–1917) cofounder of *Nili, son of Israel. He was born in Gederah and as a young man he studied in France. Upon his return he worked at the agricultural station set up by Aharon *Aaronsohn at Athlit. A few months after the outbreak of World War I, he and Aaronsohn founded the anti-Turkish intelligence network, Nili. In 1915 Feinberg reached Egypt on an American ship, establishing contact with British naval intelligence, who returned him to Athlit. When Aaronsohn went to England to negotiate with the government, Feinberg, Sarah *Aaronsohn, and Joseph *Lishansky continued to develop the intelligence ring, impatiently awaiting the results of Aaronsohn's mission. In 1917 Feinberg again set out for Egypt, this time on foot, along with Lishansky, but was shot and killed by Bedouin near the British front in Sinai. In 1967, after the Six-Day War, Feinberg's remains were discovered near Rafa under a palm tree which had sprung from date seeds he carried with him on his journey. He was reburied on Mount Herzl in Jerusalem and given a state funeral. Feinberg was one of the romantic figures of his time. His letters and memoirs, preserved in the Nili archives at *Zikhron Ya'akov, offer an insight into the world of the first generation born in the new Jewish settlements. His letters and memoirs were published under the title *Avshalom* (1971) by A. Amir.

BIBLIOGRAPHY: A. Yaari, *Goodly Heritage* (1958), index; A. Engle, *Nili Spies* (1959), index; D. Idelevitch (ed.), *Rishon le-Ẓiyyon* (1941), 41–47,507; M. Smilansky, *Mishpaḥat ha-Adamah*, 1 (1954²), 159–62; 2 (1954), 72–77; Dinur, Haganah, 1 pt. 1 (1954), 80f., 279, 354–62; 1, pt. 2 (1956), 730–3; J. Yaari-Poleskin, *Ḥolemim ve-Loḥamim* (1964³), 103–9; E. Livneh (ed.), *Nili: Toledoteha shel He'azah Medinit* (1961).

[Yehuda Slutsky]

FEINBERG, ABRAHAM (1908–1998), U.S. businessman and organization leader. Feinberg, who was born in New York City, received his law degrees from Fordham and New York University. He occupied a number of prominent executive positions, among them chairmanship of the board of the Kayser-Roth Corporation until 1964 and chairmanship of the executive committee of the American Bank and Trust Company. He served for several years on the New York City Board of Education. Feinberg was highly active in American Jewish life and on behalf of the State of Israel. He helped to organize Jewish support for Democratic presidential candidates (e.g., John F. Kennedy). He had a long relationship with Brandeis University, serving as a trustee in 1953; chairman of the board of trustees from 1954 to 1961; a Brandeis Fellow in 1953; and was awarded an honorary doctorate in 1961. And through his generous donation, the International Center for Ethics, Justice and Public Life was established at Brandeis University. Feinberg and his family also endowed the Feinberg Graduate School at the Weizmann Institute in Israel.

Feinberg was the founder and first president of Americans for Haganah, a group formed in the early 1940s to help provide arms and other critical materials to the *yishuv* in Palestine. He offered his home to Zionist leaders who were trying to gain support of the U.S. government, and he aided European Jews seeking refuge. He accompanied Chaim *Weizmann, Israel's first president, to his first meeting with President Harry Truman. Active in American politics, Feinberg worked informally with the United States and Israeli governments during Middle East crises, led many Democratic fundraisers, and served as a confidant to U.S. presidents Harry Truman, John Kennedy, and Lyndon Johnson.

In 1960 Feinberg was named B'nai B'rith's Man of the Year, an event that was attended by Harry Truman.

Feinberg served as president of the Development Corporation for Israel, which conducts the worldwide sale of Israel Bonds, and as president of the American Committee for the Weizmann Institute of Science. In 1966 he led a syndicate of American Jewish businessmen that successfully bid for a franchise to produce and sell Coca-Cola in Israel, thus breaking the company's long-standing acquiescence to the Arab boycott.

In 1983 Feinberg established three scholarships at the Weizmann Institute (The Belle and Philip Feinberg Scholarship; The Lillian Feinberg Scholarship; and The Shirley and Judge Wilfred Feinberg Scholarship). Feinberg also supported numerous medical causes, including schizophrenia research in both New York and Israel. He endowed the psychiatric wing at Schneider Children's Medical Center for Israel.

[Ruth Beloff (2nd ed.)]

FEINBERG, ABRAHAM L. (1899–1986), Reform rabbi and activist. Feinberg was born in Bellaire, Ohio, to immigrant parents from Grinkishok (Grinkiskis), Lithuania, which Feinberg referred to as "the birthplace of my spirit." He earned a B.A. from the University of Cincinnati and was ordained at Hebrew Union College in 1924. After ordination he served in a number of American pulpits but left the rabbinate in 1929 to embark on a singing career as Arthur Frome. He returned to the pulpit in 1935 in response to Hitler's growing strength and attacks on the Jews. In 1943 he accepted a position at Toronto's Holy Blossom Temple, the premier Reform congregation in Canada. During his tenure, the Holy Blossom grew rapidly, a testimony to Feinberg's skills as religious leader, and especially as a preacher. He extended his influence by being a highly successful radio orator.

A firm believer in the prophetic ethic as emphasized in Reform Judaism, Feinberg had supported various left-wing causes while in the United States, and threw himself into the Canadian scene with energy. Holding that Canada should be free of all forms of prejudice, he spoke out against antisemitism and racism including Canada's wartime treatment of the Japanese and discrimination against blacks in Canada. He was a crucial presence on the Joint Public Relations Committee of the Canadian Jewish Congress and B'nai B'rith, pressing the committee to protest mandatory prayers and Christmas carols in Ontario public schools and to lobby for fair employment and housing practices in Ontario. Feinberg became an outspoken advocate of nuclear disarmament and chaired the Toronto Committee for Disarmament while he continued his advocacy of civil rights as the vice president of the Toronto Association for Civil Rights. Feinberg's political activism led to surveillance by Royal Canadian Mounted Police intelligence officers. An RCMP file eventually released to his daughter contained 1,100 pages, with even more devoured by the RCMP's shredder.

Feinberg retired from Holy Blossom in 1961 and was named rabbi emeritus. He continued his activism, protesting the war in Vietnam, and in late 1966 and early 1967 led a delegation to meet with Ho Chi Minh. In 1972 he moved to Berkeley, California, to be near his son Jonathan but relocated across the Bay to be the rabbi for Glide Memorial Church, which catered to "the outcasts of our social system." He also became a spokesman for "gray lib," fighting oppression of the elderly. He subsequently moved to Reno, Nevada, where he continued his advocacy for the elderly. At age 70 Feinberg resumed his singing career and released 10 songs, but his most famous performance was singing "Give Peace a Chance," with John Lennon and Yoko Ono in their Montreal hotel room in 1969.

Feinberg was the author of three books, *Storm the Gates of Jericho* (1964); *Rabbi Feinberg's Hanoi Diary* (1968); *Sex and the Pulpit* (1981). He also wrote numerous magazine and newspaper articles.

[Richard Menkis (2nd ed.)]

FEINBERG, DAVID (1840–1916), Russian communal leader. Born in Kovno (Kaunas), Lithuania, Feinberg studied law at St. Petersburg University. While in his twenties he attained a responsible position in the St. Petersburg-Warsaw railroad company and was active in promoting the organization of a community in St. Petersburg. Feinberg was instrumental in obtaining, with the support of Baron Horace Guenzburg, Samuel *Poliakoff, and others, authorization for building the first synagogue as well as for the establishment of a Jewish cemetery there. He enlisted the support of Adolphe Crémieux, Baron Maurice de Hirsch, and Sir Moses Montefiore in the struggle of Russian Jewry for rights. When the *Jewish Colonization Association (ICA) was founded in 1891 Feinberg became its secretary-general and was active in promoting Jewish agricultural settlement in *Argentina, where one of the settlements was named after him. During World War I he did much to relieve the sufferings of refugees.

BIBLIOGRAPHY: S. Ginsburg, *Amolike Peterburg* (1944), 111–24; Feinberg, in: *He-Avar*, 4 (1956), 20–36; I. Halpern, *Yehudim ve-Yahadut be-Mizraḥ Eiropah* (1969), 372–3.

FEINBERG, KENNETH (1945–), U.S. attorney, expert in mediation and alternative dispute resolution. Born and raised in Brockton, Mass., Feinberg graduated cum laude from the University of Massachusetts in 1967 and from New York University School of Law, where he was articles editor of the *Law Review*, in 1970. He served as law clerk to Chief Judge Stanley H. Fuld, New York State Court of Appeals, from 1970 to 1972. He was assistant U.S. attorney, Southern District of New York, from 1972 to 1975 and special counsel, U.S. Senate Committee on the Judiciary, from 1975 to 1980. Feinberg served as administrative assistant to Senator Edward M. Kennedy from 1977 to 1979. He was a partner in the firm of Kaye, Scholer, Fierman, Hays & Handler from 1980 to 1992, then founded The Feinberg Group in Washington, D.C., in 1993. He was also a lecturer at the University of Pennsylvania Law School, New York University School of Law, University of Virginia Law School, and Columbia Law School.

Feinberg served as mediator and arbiter in thousands of disputes, involving such issues as breach of contract, product liability, civil fraud, and various environmental matters. He served as court-appointed special settlement master in several high-profile cases, including the Agent Orange product liability litigation, the RICO class action concerning the Shoreham Nuclear Facility, and many asbestos personal injury litigations. He was the first trustee of the Dalkon Shield Claimants' Trust. Feinberg was one of three arbitrators chosen to determine the fair market value of the Zapruder film of the John F. Kennedy assassination, and he was one of two arbitrators selected to determine the allocation of legal fees in the Holocaust slave labor litigation.

In 2001 Feinberg was appointed Special Master of the Federal September 11th Victim Compensation Fund by Attorney General John Ashcroft. The Fund was created by federal legislation to compensate victims and families of victims injured or killed in the terrorist attacks of September 11, 2001, provided they relinquished their right to sue. Working for 33 months entirely pro bono, Feinberg developed the preliminary regulations governing the administration of the fund and solicited comments and criticism, which were often harsh. He held more than two dozen "town hall meetings" with families, in addition to personal meetings. Feinberg administered all aspects of the program, which awarded $7 billion. Families who were dissatisfied with an award could appeal through an informal hearing; Feinberg personally presided over more than 900 of the 1,600 hearings. At the end of the process, he won the admiration of many of his former critics, who praised his fairness and his willingness to adjust some aspects of both the procedure and the awards.

In 2005 Feinberg published his book *What Is Life Worth? The Unprecedented Effort to Compensate the Victims of 9/11*, in which he details the immense challenges and difficult emotional components of his work with victims' families. A member of the National Judicial Panel and the recipient of numerous honors, he was named Lawyer of the Year by the *National Law Journal* in 2004.

[Dorothy Bauhoff (2nd ed.)]

FEINBERG, LEON (**Yehude-Arye-Leyb / Leonid Grebniov**; 1897–1969), Yiddish journalist, novelist, and poet. Born in Kodyma (Ukraine), he studied at the University of Moscow, fought as a Red Guard in the Civil War, immigrated to Palestine, and traveled the world as a sailor, before settling in the U.S. His first volume of Russian poetry (1914) was influenced by Symbolism. Although he continued writing in Russian (further volumes 1919, 1923, 1947), he also began writing in Yiddish. He was on the staff of the Yiddish daily *Frayhayt*, and the monthly *Der Hamer*. A feature writer (and later city editor) for *Der Tog*, he served as president of the New York Yiddish PEN Club. His fifteen novels include the verse novels *Der Farmishpeter Dor* ("The Condemned Generation," 1954) and *Der Gebentshter Dor* ("The Blessed Generation," 1962) which depict the lives of two generations of Jews who were caught in the net of the Russian Revolution but succeeded in immigrating to America and Palestine. *Der Khorever Dor* ("The Ruined Generation," 1967) describes the lives of those who remained in Russia and faced the realities of Soviet life. English translations of his work are to be found in J. Leftwich, *The Golden Peacock* (1940), and J.B. Cooperman, *America in Yiddish Poetry* (1967).

BIBLIOGRAPHY: Rejzen, Leksikon, 3 (1929), 57–60. **ADD. BIBLIOGRAPHY:** LNYL 7 (1968), 349–53; G.G. Branover (ed.), *Rossiĭskaia evreĭskaia entsiklopediia*, 3 (1997), 189–90; G. Estraikh, *In Harness: Yiddish Writers' Romance with Communism* (2005), 96–8.

[Israel Ch. Biletzky / Jerold C. Frakes (2nd ed.)]

FEINBERG, LOUIS (1887–1949), U.S. Conservative rabbi and community leader. Born in Rossieny, Lithuania, Feinberg was brought to the United States in 1903. He was educated in the public schools of Philadelphia and graduated from the University of Pennsylvania with a B.A. His Jewish education was received at the Talmud Torah, Gratz and Dropsie Colleges, and Yeshivah Mishkan Israel. He entered the Jewish Theological Seminary, was ordained in 1916, graduating with honors and serving as valedictorian of his class. He served two years as rabbi of Congregation Ohel Jacob in Philadelphia. In 1918, he came to Cincinnati as rabbi of Adath Israel (organized in 1847). He was the first of the modern American rabbis to come to Cincinnati. He emphasized the Saturday morning service, introducing weekly sermons in English and congregational singing. He organized the Adathean Society to involve young men and women in congregational activity. He established a congregational school when it became apparent that many members' children were not attending the local Talmud Torah schools. In 1933, he introduced a combined graduation and confirmation service and thus, for the first time in a traditional synagogue, girls became eligible for confirmation. In 1947, the congregation adopted an amendment to the constitution which provided for representation of women on the Board of Trustees.

As the congregation grew, he advocated for the enlargement of the synagogue, eventually undertaking a significant building fund campaign. In 1927, a magnificent stone building was erected at a cost of $450,000. Several of its features exhibited Rabbi Feinberg's influence: the interior decoration developed by Dr. Boris *Schatz of the *Bezalel School of Arts and Crafts in Palestine, and the monumental dome comprising the ceiling of the sanctuary, its rim inscribed with Hebrew inscriptions from the Pentateuch, prophets, medieval philosophers, and the modern poet Ḥayyim Naḥman *Bialik, selected and arranged by Rabbi Feinberg.

In addition to his activity within the congregation, Feinberg took a prominent role in the larger community. He served as president of the local Board of Rabbis and on the boards of the Bureau of Jewish Education, United Jewish Social Agencies, and Jewish Community Council. He was active in Mizrachi and in the Zionist Organization of America. A passionate Zionist, he helped establish a Palestine Scholarship Program in the community, which enabled five young members of his congregation to spend an entire year in Israel. He was a founder of the *Young Judea movement, and an editor of *Our Jewish Youth* which later became *Young Judean*. In 1937, at the age of 50, he visited Palestine himself for the first time. He called Zionism "the newest development of the Messianic idea."

Feinberg was a member of the Law Committee of the Jewish Theological Seminary and was a founder of the Menorah Society at the University of Pennsylvania. He translated the Laws of Charity from the *Shulḥan Arukh* for the New York School of Philanthropy, published articles on Jewish law in Hebrew, Yiddish, and English, and wrote short stories about Jewish life under the pseudonym Yishuvnik. A graduate fellowship at JTS was created in his memory, and the congregation sponsored the publication of a posthumous collection of his essays, *The Spiritual Foundations of Judaism*, edited by Emanual Gamoran.

[Nancy Klein (2nd ed.)]

FEINBERG, NATHAN (1895–?), international jurist. Born in Kovno (Kaunas), Lithuania, Feinberg studied international law in Zurich and Geneva. In 1919–21 he was departmental head of the Ministry of Jewish Affairs in Lithuania; 1922–24 secretary of the *Comité des Délégations Juives at Paris; and he conducted a private law practice in Palestine in 1925–27 and again in 1934–35. From 1931–33 he lectured at Geneva University. In 1945 he was appointed lecturer in international relations at the Hebrew University, in 1947 also in international law, and professor in 1949; he was the first dean of the university's Faculty of Law (1949–51). Feinberg served from 1962 as one of Israel's representatives on the International Court of Arbitration in the Hague. His published work is mainly concerned with Jewish minority status in post-World War I Europe (*La question des minorités à la Conférence de la Paix 1919–20*, 1929); with the Palestine mandate in international law (*Some Problems of the Palestine Mandate*, 1936; *Ereẓ Yisrael bi-Tekufat ha-Mandat u-Medinat Yisrael*, 1963); with the Jewish defense against Hitler and the Nazis (*Ha-Ma'arakhah ha-Yehudit neged Hitler…*, 1957); as well as with the Arab-Jewish conflict (*Arab-Israel Conflict in International Law*, 1970). Feinberg was co-editor of the *Jewish Year Book of International Law* (1949) and edited a volume of studies in public international law in memory of Sir Hersh Lauterpacht (1962).

FEINBERG, ROBERT (1912–1975), U.S. labor lawyer and arbitrator. He was labor counsel of the United Jewish Appeal, the Federation of Jewish Philanthropies of New York, the National Jewish Welfare Board, the Development Corporation for Israel, the Jewish Child Care Association of New York, the Jewish Board of Guardians, the National Council of Jewish Women, the Jewish Family Service, the Jewish Association for Service, and other philanthropic agencies and organizations. Feinberg was senior partner in the law firm of Guggenheimer and Untermyer, and held positions with the National War Labor Board and the National Wage Stabilization Board.

[Milton Ridvas Konvitz]

FEINBERG, SAMUEL YEVGENYEVICH (1890–1962), pianist and composer. Born in Odessa, Feinberg graduated from the Moscow Conservatory in 1911 (as a pianist, class of Goldenveizer) and was appointed professor of piano (from 1922) and director of the piano faculty from 1936 until his death. As a composer he studied with Zhilyaev and was a member of the ASM (Association of Contemporary Music). His music was modernist and influenced by Scriabin, although it frequently contained folklore elements. Among his compositions were three piano concertos: 1931, 1944 (awarded the Stalin Prize), and 1947; 12 piano sonatas; and a sonata for violin and piano. He wrote *Sudba muzykalnoy formy* ("The Future Musical Form," 1968) and *Pianizm kak iskusstvo* ("The Art of Piano Playing," 1968).

ADD. BIBLIOGRAPHY: NG[2]; V. Belyayev, *Samuil Feinberg* (1927); L. Sabaneyev, *Modern Russian Composers* (1927); I. Likhacheva (ed.), *S. Ye. Feinberg: Pianist, kompozitor, issledovatel'* (1984); C. Sirodeau, "Sur Samuil Feinberg," in: *Cycle Scalkottas, Paris 1998–1999* (1999), incl. catalogue of works.

[Marina Rizarev (2nd ed.)]

FEINBRUN-DOTHAN, NAOMI (1900–1995), Israel botanist. Born in Moscow and raised in Kishinev, Feinbrun-Dothan immigrated to Palestine in 1924. Working with Alexander *Eig, she helped gather the plants which formed the basis for the Hebrew University's herbarium. She was part of the Hebrew University from its establishment, becoming a full professor in botany in 1966. She was instrumental in preparation and publishing of *Flora Palaestina*. In 1991 she was awarded the Israel Prize for knowledge of the Land of Israel.

[Fern Lee Seckbach (2nd ed.)]

FEINGOLD, DAVID SIDNEY (1922–), chemist. Feingold was born in the United States and studied at the Massachusetts Institute of Technology and the University of Zurich. He immigrated to Israel in 1949 and obtained his Ph.D. at the Hebrew University of Jerusalem before joining the department of microbiological chemistry at the Hadassah Medical School. He received the Israel Prize for exact sciences (1957) jointly with his colleagues Gad Avigad and Shlomo Hestrin. He returned to the University of California (1956) and was appointed professor of microbiology at the University of Pittsburgh School of Medicine (1966). Feingold's research concerned sugar metabolism in bacteria and the bean sprout *phaseolus aureus* and in particular the synthesis of polysaccharides in bacterial cell walls. He also studied the implications for clinical infections, particularly by pseudomonas, and anti-bacterial chemotherapy.

FEINGOLD, RUSSELL (1953–), U.S. senator. Feingold was born in Janeville, Wisc., which had a small Jewish community and no synagogue, so Feingold and his sister were taken on a 90-mile round trip to attend Hebrew school at a Reform congregation. As a high school student he won the state debating championship and then went on to earn his B.A. with honors from the University of Wisconsin in Madison, where he was elected to Phi Betta Kappa. He then attended Oxford on a Rhodes Scholarship (1976) and then Harvard Law School (LL.B., 1979). His interest in politics was intense and after a few years in private practice, at the age of 29 he was elected to the Wisconsin State Senate, where he served for 10 years, earning his spurs as chair of the Committee on Aging, Banking, and Communication.

He challenged incumbent Senator Robert Kasten (R-WI) who had heavy support from the Jewish community because of his chairmanship of the influential Foreign Operations Sub-Committee of the Appropriations Committee, the sub-committee where foreign aid is allocated. Despite Feingold's clear Jewish identity, under the incumbency rule, pro-Israel PACS and politically active Jews supported Kasten. If an incumbent had a strong pro-Israel record, Jewish political activists continued their support regardless of whom the challenger was. Thus, Feingold was widely outspent. Characteristically, he made light of his lack of Jewish support, expressing shock that his support for Israel and Jewish bona-fides were called into question. "I am the only candidate for the Senate whose sister is a rabbi living in Israel," he would say. Feingold made his modest support a badge of honor. He won a surprising victory.

In the Senate Feingold was a fiscal hawk, attacking unwarranted expenditures in the federal budget. His national prominence came from his co-sponsorship with Senator John McCain of the McCain-Feingold bill that attempted to limit campaign spending and soft-money contributions. They did not succeed in passing their bill during his first term. Feingold placed stringent restrictions on his own fundraising for reelection. Caught in a close race, he refused an offer of $500,000 from the Democratic National Committee and voters gave him a narrow victory. McCain-Feingold finally became law early in the Bush Administration. And once again in his reelection bid of 2004, Feingold held fast to his own standards despite serious political opposition.

His positions were generally liberal. Feingold voted against an antiterrorism measure because he objected to its provisions regarding inmates on death row. He fought a constitutional amendment to prohibit flag burning in keeping with Wisconsin's progressive tradition. He was an early and consistent opponent of the war in Iraq, believing that it diverted attention from the fight against terrorism. Though Wisconsin had fewer than 30,000 Jews it was represented by a second Jewish senator as well, Herbert *Kohl.

BIBLIOGRAPHY: L.S. Maisel and I. Forman, *Jews in American Politics* (2001); K.F. Stone, *The Congressional Minyan: The Jews of Capitol Hill* (2002).

[Michael Berenbaum (2nd ed.)]

FEINMAN, SIGMUND (1862–1909), Yiddish actor-manager. Born near Kishinev, Feinman acted in Bessarabia and Romania, went to New York in 1886, and worked with *Adler, *Mogulesko, and *Kessler, doing his best work in Jacob Gordin's plays. Returning to Europe in 1906, he and his wife Dinah (formerly married to Jacob Adler) established a reputation in London and on the Continent. He played Othello in Romania, 1909, and died while rehearsing in Lodz. Manuscripts of Feinman's own plays and translations were acquired by the *YIVO Institute. His wife DINAH FEINMAN (1862–1946) acted in *A Doll's House, Mirele Efros*, and *La Dame aux Camélias*.

FEINSINGER, JOSHUA (**Shaye**; 1839–1872), Russian *ḥazzan*. Born in Lithuania, Feinsinger was taught singing by his father, himself a *ḥazzan*. After completing his musical training, he became chief *ḥazzan* in the Polish town of Leczyca. In 1868 he was appointed chief *ḥazzan* in Vilna. Possessing a phenomenal voice and originality of expression, Feinsinger became famous as one of the greatest *ḥazzanim* of the mid-19th century. His most notable compositions were for the *Yoẓer prayers for the *Sefirah* Sabbaths.

FEINSTEIN, ARYEH LOEB (1821–1903), Lithuanian scholar and writer. Feinstein was born in Damachev near Brest-Litovsk. He was a successful businessman in that city, active in communal affairs, and wrote a history of its Jewish community, *Ir Tehillah* (1886, repr. 1968). He also published a Passover *Haggadah* with commentary, *Talpiyyot* (1870), and a commentary on Psalms under the same title (1896). Among his other works are *Migdal David* (1895), on talmudic discussions of David and his dynasty; *Divrei Ḥakhamim ve-Ḥidotam* (1895), on the *Rabbah b. Bar Ḥana tales; and *Elef ha-Magen* (1900), linguistic studies.

BIBLIOGRAPHY: Kressel, Leksikon, 2 (1967), 626–7; EG, 2 (1955), index.

FEINSTEIN, DIANNE GOLDMAN (1933–), U.S. Democratic senator from California. Feinstein was a centrist legislator and a pioneering politician. She was the first woman to be elected president of San Francisco's Board of Supervisors (1969), mayor of San Francisco (1978), nominated by a major party for governor of California (1990), elected U.S. senator from California (1992), and appointed to the Senate Judiciary Committee (1993).

The daughter of Dr. Leon Goldman, a prominent surgeon, and his wife Betty (Rosenburg), Feinstein started a public service career at a young age. Born and raised in San Francisco, she attended Stanford University where she won her first election as vice president of the Student Body. Upon graduation in 1955 she was awarded a Coro Foundation fellowship to study public policy. Five years later the governor appointed her to the California Women's Board of Terms and Parole, where she served until 1966. Elected to the San Francisco Board of Supervisors in 1969, Feinstein served for nine years, five years as Board president. She was serving in this capacity in 1978 when Mayor George Moscone was assassinated in his city hall office. Feinstein became the acting mayor. A year later, she was elected in her own right, serving the city from 1978 to 1988 when term limits forced her from office. In 1990 the Democratic Party nominated Feinstein for governor, she was narrowly defeated. Two years later, California voters sent her to the U.S. Senate to fill two years of a vacated seat; she was subsequently elected to full six-year terms in 1994 and 2000.

For much of her career Feinstein focused on crime prevention. As mayor of San Francisco she cut the crime rate 27 percent. A successful advocate for victims of crime and crime prevention, she was instrumental in passing the Gun-Free Schools Act (1994); the Hate Crimes Sentencing Enforcement Act (1993); the Comprehensive Methamphetamine Control Act (1996); and the Assault Weapons Ban 1994–2004. Supportive of the Jewish community, Feinstein was a member of Congregation Emanu-El in San Francisco, California, where she was confirmed.

BIBLIOGRAPHY: A.F. Kahn and G. Matthews, "120 Years of Women's Activism," in: A.F. Kahn and M. Dollinger (eds.), *California Jews* (2003).

[Ava F. Kahn (2nd ed.)]

FEINSTEIN, ELAINE (1930–), English novelist, poet, and translator. Born in Bootle, Feinstein was educated at Cambridge University. She has worked as an editor for the Cambridge University Press and lectured in English at Bishop's Stortford Training College and the University of Essex until 1970. She is now a full-time writer. Feinstein published her first novel, *The Circle,* in 1970. She also translated *The Selected Poems of Marina Tsvetayeva* (1971) and *Three Russian Poets: Margarita Aliger, Yunna Moritz, Bella Akhmadulina,* (1978). As an editor she chose the *Selected Poems of John Clare* (1968) and, with Fay Weldon, *New Stories 4* (1979). She has also published volumes of short stories and plays, *Breath* (1975) and *Echoes* (1980). The Holocaust is central to *Children of the Rose* (1975) and *The Border* (1984). She also wrote a book on the blues singer Bessie Smith (1985).

Her prodigious literary output includes volumes of poetry such as *The Magic Apple Tree* (1971), *At The Edge* (1972) and *The Celebrants and Other Poems* (1973). Feinstein is regarded as an important English novelist. She has described her early fiction as an "extension" of her poetry as her novels combine the poetic with a larger historical canvas. Her fiction, therefore, has ranged through European history and, at the same time, has retained a poetic use of language and myth. With remarkable economy, several of Feinstein's novels, *Children of the Rose* (1975), *The Ecstasy of Dr. Miriam Garner* (1976), *The Shadow Master* (1978), and *The Border* (1984), incorporate the violence, fanaticism, and pseudoapocalyptic character of modern history. The ever-present themes of exile and betrayal in Feinstein's novels are given a wider historical dimension which shapes the lives of her cosmopolitan characters. *The Survivors* (1982), an autobiographical novel, has an exclusively English setting and uses the compressed form of a conventional family saga. Feinstein is also a biographer of note, having written lives of Pushkin (1998), Ted Hughes (2001), and *Lawrence's Women* (1993), about the love life of D.H. Lawrence.

Feinstein consciously writes in a Central European literary tradition. She is the first post-war English-Jewish novelist to successfully eschew the parochial concerns and forms of expression of the Anglo-Jewish novel and has located her sense of Jewishness in a wider European context. *The Border* is a representative example of Feinstein's ability to express in an exciting love story a multifarious vision of the world made up of history and autobiography, poetry and myth, literature and science. In this way, Feinstein has managed to broaden the concerns of the Anglo-Jewish novel and develop a lasting poetic voice in a distinct and imaginative manner.

[Bryan Cheyette]

FEINSTEIN, ḤAYYIM JACOB HA-KOHEN (second half of the 19th century), emissary from Safed who visited the Jewish communities in the Orient, including Aden, Yemen, and India. He was in the last country three times, in 1866, 1873, and 1887. While in Calcutta, he noted disapprovingly the practice of the Jews of using the trolley on the Sabbath, and wrote a treatise, *Imrei Shabbat* (1874), in which he vehemently opposed this custom. He published *Torat Immekha* (1886), in which he opposed other practices of Baghdadi Jews. In *Cochin (which he visited twice) he took the side of the "Non-White Jews," as he called the "Black Jews," and fought for their emancipation, maintaining that they were actually the early settlers while the "White Jews" were newcomers. He expressed these views in his *Mashbit Milḥamot* (1889) which he submitted to the Cochin Jews and to the chief rabbi of Jerusalem, Meir Panigel. His report appeared as a supplement to the second edition of his *Imrei Shabbat* (1889).

BIBLIOGRAPHY: A. Yaari, *Ha-Defus ha-Ivri be-Arẓot ha-Mizraḥ*, 2 (1940), 29, 30; idem, in: *Sinai*, 4 (1939), 416–21; 26 (1950), 342–4; D.S. Sassoon, *Ohel Dawid*, 2 (1932), 966–7; Bar-Giora, in: *Sefunot*, 1 (1947), 265–6.

[Walter Joseph Fischel]

FEINSTEIN, MEIR (1927–1947), Jew condemned to death by the British in Palestine. Feinstein was born in the Old City of Jerusalem. In his youth he went to work in the kibbutz of Negbah, where he joined the *Palmaḥ, and at the age of 16 volunteered for service in the British army. In 1946 he joined the I.Ẓ.L. and on Oct. 30 took part in an attack on the railway station of Jerusalem. During his get-away, fire was opened on him from a passing car and he was badly wounded in his left hand. As a result, whereas his companions managed to escape, he took refuge in a house and the bloodstains enabled his pursuers to find him. After his left hand was amputated he was put on trial and sentenced to death on Apr. 3, 1947. He shared the condemned cell with Moshe *Barazani, and the date of their execution was fixed for the morning of the 21st. At 9 P.M. on the previous evening, they placed an explosive charge, which had been smuggled into the cell, between their hearts and set it off, thus cheating the gallows.

BIBLIOGRAPHY: Y. Nedava, *Olei-ha-Gardom* (1966); Y. Gurion, *Ha-Nizzaḥon Olei Gardom* (1971).

FEINSTEIN, MOSES (1895–1986), rabbi and leader of American Orthodoxy. Feinstein was born in Uzda, near Minsk, Belorussia, where his father, from whom he received his early education, was rabbi. In 1921 he became rabbi of Luban, near Minsk, where he served until he immigrated to the United States in 1937. There Feinstein was appointed *rosh yeshivah* of New York's Metivta Tiferet Jerusalem. Under his guidance, it became one of the leading American yeshivot. Feinstein arrived in America with three children: Faye Gittel, who married a distinguished rabbi, Moses Shisgal; Shifra, who married Rabbi Dr. Moses Tendler, long-time rabbi in Monsey, New York, as well as teacher of Talmud and professor of biology at Yeshiva University; and David, who succeeded his father as the head of Metivta Tiferet Jerusalem. A son, Reuven, was born in America. He became the head of the Metivta Tiferet Jerusalem branch in Staten Island, New York City.

After World War II, Feinstein became one of the leading figures in Orthodox Jewry in America. After the death of the *rosh yeshivah* of the Lakewood Yeshiva, Rabbi Aaron *Kotler, Feinstein became the acknowledged leader of Orthodoxy. While he did address broader, communal issues throughout his lifetime, his major impact was in the realm of Halakhah. His reputation grew rapidly to the point that his rulings were accepted as authoritative by Orthodox Jews throughout the world. Feinstein's responsa are entitled *Iggerot Moshe*, the first four volumes follow the Shulḥan Arukh: *Oraḥ Ḥayyim* (1959), *Yoreh De'ah* (1959), *Even ha-Ezer* (1961), and *Ḥoshen Mishpat* (1963), while subsequent volumes (1973, 2 vols. in 1981, 1996) contain responsa from different sections of the Shulḥan Arukh. A detailed index to *Iggerot Moshe*, entitled *Yad Moshe* was published in 1987. He also published his talmudic novellae entitled *Dibrot Moshe* to *Bava Kamma* in two volumes (1946, 1953), to *Bava Meẓia* (1966), to *Shabbat* in two volumes (1971, 1976), to *Kiddushin* and *Yevamot* (1979), to *Gittin* (1982), to *Ḥulin* and *Nedarim* (1983), and to *Ketubbot* and *Pesaḥim* (1984). *Darash Moshe*, his sermons on the weekly Torah reading and the holidays, were published posthumously in 1988.

Feinstein's world view encompassed the world of Torah. "My entire world view," he wrote (*Iggerot Moshe* 2:11), "stems only from knowledge of Torah without any mixture of outside ideas, whose judgment is truth whether it is strict or lenient. Arguments derived from foreign outlooks or false opinions of the heart are nothing." Nevertheless, Feinstein was keenly aware of the world around him, constantly applying the principles of Torah law to new situations and circumstances. Indeed, when he dealt with medical problems, he always consulted with leading physicians, often asking for a second opinion. He demanded to understand the medical issues in depth. Feinstein served as the *posek* (halakhic decisor) for many medical students and doctors as well as for the Association of Orthodox Jewish Scientists.

Feinstein's responsa deal with a very broad range of issues and topics. He devoted a great deal of time to grappling with problems in Jewish education. He had little tolerance for the teaching of secular studies; however, he permitted it because of government regulations (ibid. 3:83). He demanded that science textbooks agree with the idea that God created the world (ibid. 3:73). He was unyielding in his opposition to coed classes, but he did allow women to teach boys, acknowledging the reality of the educational world in America. He required fathers to pay for the tuition for their daughters' education.

The Modern Orthodox community in America also looked to Rabbi Feinstein for halakhic guidance. At times, his answers to their questions exhibited a flexibility he did not show to the ultra-Orthodox community. For instance, Feinstein permitted fathers to be present at school performances where girls under the age of 11 sang, even though he frowned upon the practice (ibid. 1:26).

Other topics that received his attention include the height of the *meḥiẓah* (partition) in the synagogue, the use of glass in constructing a *meḥiẓah*, renting a hotel ballroom for High Holy Day services, allowing an American owner of an Israeli factory to keep his factory open on the second day of Yom Tov, the status of children conceived through artificial insemination, and allowing *shoḥatim* (ritual slaughterers) to form their own union.

Feinstein, highly regarded for his dedication and selflessness, was elected to positions of importance in the Orthodox Jewish world. He was president of the *Union of Orthodox Rabbis and chairman of the American branch of the Mo'eẓet Gedolei ha-Torah of Agudat Israel. He was also active in guiding and obtaining support for Orthodox Israeli educational institutions, particularly the Ḥinnukh Aẓma'i school system of Agudat Israel. Despite his public, communal involvement and his role as the leading *posek* of the second half of the 20th century, Feinstein was renowned for his simple lifestyle, his piety, and his humility.

Feinstein passed away during the night before the Fast of Esther, March 23, 1986. Over 150,000 people attended the funeral services in New York. Eulogies were given by rabbis from the entire spectrum of Orthodoxy, from a representative of the Satmar ḥasidic community to two speakers from Yeshiva University. He was buried three days later in Jerusalem. An obituary notice appeared in the "Milestones" section of *Time* magazine (April 7, 1986, p. 42). Perhaps the most telling indication of his impact on Orthodox Jewry in the 20th century is the saying that every rabbi receiving Orthodox ordination in America needed two things upon graduation: A *lu'aḥ*, a calendar that lists all the changes in the prayer services, and Rabbi Moses Feinstein's telephone number.

BIBLIOGRAPHY: O. Rand (ed.), *Toledot Anshei Shem* (1950), 98. A. Rakefet (Rothkoff), in: *Niv ha-Midrashia* (Spring-Summer 1971), 58–71; I. Robinson, in: *Judaism*, 35 (1986), 35–46; M.D. Angel, in: *Tradition*, 23:3 (1988), 41–52; N. Baumel Joseph, in: *American Jewish History*, 83:2 (1995), 205–22; W. Kelman, in: *Survey of Jewish Affairs 1987* (1988), 173–87; M.D. Tendler, in: *Pioneers in Jewish Medical Ethics* (1997), 55–68; F. Rosner, in: *Pioneers in Jewish Medical Ethics* (1997), 47–75; N. Sherman, in: *Jewish Observer*, 19:7 (1986), 8–30; S. Finkelman, *Reb Moshe: The Life and Ideals of HaGaon Rabbi Moshe Feinstein* (1986); D. Hartman, "*Setiyah u-Gevulot ba-Halakhah ha-Ortodoxit be-Et ha-Ḥadashah*," dissertation (2003).

[David Derovan (2nd ed.)]

FEINSTEIN, MOSES (1896–1964), Hebrew poet and educator. Born in Russia, Feinstein arrived in the United States in 1912. He devoted his life to Herzliah – the Hebrew Academy and Teachers' Institute which he founded in New York in 1921. His volumes of poetry are the lyrical *Shirim ve-Sonettot* ("Poems and Sonnets," 1935); *Ḥalom ve-Goral* ("Dream and Destiny," 1937), a description of a journey to Palestine; and *Abraham Abulafia* (1957), a philosophical poem about the 13th-century mystic. Feinstein's collected poems appeared posthumously in a volume called *Al Saf ha-Sof* ("At the Threshold of the End," 1964).

BIBLIOGRAPHY: Silberschlag, in: JBA, 23 (1965/66), 70–76; A. Epstein, *Soferim Ivrim ba-Amerikah*, 1 (1952), 125–41; R. Wallenrod, *The Literature of Modern Israel* (1956), index; Waxman, Literature, 4 (1960^2), 1072–73; 5 (1960^2), 192–4.

[Eisig Silberschlag]

FEINSTONE, MORRIS (1878–1945), U.S. labor leader. Feinstone, born in Warsaw, was trained as a woodcarver there. After completing school he emigrated to England where he became president of a woodcarvers' union in London (1895). Later in Birmingham he was active in the beginnings of the British Labour Party. In 1910 Feinstone emigrated to the U.S. where he found employment in various skilled trades, securing permanent work in the umbrella industry. He soon became an official of the Umbrella Handle and Stick Makers' Union and an important figure in the United Hebrew Trades, an organization which sheltered the smaller and weaker American Jewish trade unions. Feinstone was a close associate of the organization's outstanding leader, Max Pine, whom he succeeded as United Hebrew Trades' secretary in 1928. Feinstone continued Pine's policy of supporting the socialist labor sector in Jewish Palestine through the Histadrut. He also represented the United Hebrew Trades on the executive board of the Central Trades and Labor Council of Greater New York, wrote articles in the New York *Call* and the Yiddish *Jewish Daily Forward* endorsing socialism and labor Zionism, and worked for the establishment of an independent labor party. With the advent of the New Deal, Feinstone's socialist teachings were incorporated by the American Labor Party, which satisfied his desire for a working class political organization. Thereafter, until his death he concentrated on obtaining support for Jewish labor in Palestine.

[Melvyn Dubofsky]

FEIS, HERBERT (1893–1972), U.S. economic historian. Feis, who was born in New York City, was an instructor in economics at Harvard (1920–21), associate professor at the University of Kansas (1922–25), and professor and head of the department of economics at the University of Cincinnati (1926–29). Between 1922 and 1927 he was U.S. adviser to the International Labor Office of the League of Nations. In 1930, he became a member of the staff of the Council on Foreign Relations, in 1931 economic adviser to the U.S. State Department, and from 1937 to 1943 he was adviser on international economics.

Feis was a special adviser to the U.S. secretary of war from 1944 to 1946, and during that period was chief technical adviser to the World Economic and Monetary Conference in London. From 1948 he was a member of the Institute for Advanced Study at Princeton. His many publications include *Europe, The World's Banker 1870–1914* (1930, 1965^3), *The Spanish Story* (1948, 1966^2), *The Road to Pearl Harbor* (1950, 1964^2), *The Diplomacy of the Dollar* (1950, 1965^2), *The China Tangle* (1953, 1965^3), *Churchill, Roosevelt, Stalin* (1957, 1966^2), *Between War and Peace – the Potsdam Conference* (1960, 1967^2), *Japan Subdued* (1961), *Foreign Aid and Foreign Policy* (1964, 1966^2), *1933: Characters in Crisis* (1966), *The Atomic Bomb & the End of World War II* (1966), and *The Birth of Israel: The Tousled Diplomatic Bed* (1969). Feis was awarded the Pulitzer Prize in 1961 for *Between War and Peace*, which dealt with the origins of the Cold War.

In 1982 the American Historical Association established the Herbert Feis Award, which is offered annually to recognize the scholarly interests of historians outside academe and the importance of the work of independent scholars in the United States.

Feis' wife, Ruth, was the granddaughter of James Garfield, the 20th president of the United States.

BIBLIOGRAPHY: *Current Biography Yearbook, 1961* (1962), 156–8. **ADD. BIBLIOGRAPHY:** D. Yergler, *Herbert Feis, Wilsonian Internationalism, and America's Technological-Democracy* (1993).

[Joachim O. Ronall / Ruth Beloff (2nd ed.)]

FEITELSON, MENAHEM MENDEL (1870–1912), Hebrew writer and critic. Feitelson, who was born in Mikhailovka, Crimea, taught in Melitopol, and was active in the Hebrew Language Association in that city. A contributor to the Hebrew press from his youth, he later published articles of topical interest and literary criticism. He wrote for *Ha-Meliẓ* (a comprehensive study of Mendele Mokher Seforim), *Ha-Ẓefirah*, and other journals. After publishing *Meḥkarim be-Korot Yisrael* (1890), he gave up writing for a time, taught in Sebastopol, and at the turn of the century settled in Yekaterinoslav. There he wrote a series of articles on Hebrew writers for *Ha-Shiloʾah* and also contributed to other periodicals. Unable to find employment in the literary centers of Eastern Europe, he grew increasingly depressed and committed suicide in 1912. The immediate reason for Feitelson's suicide is believed to be Mendele's insulting remarks to him regarding the essay he had written on Mendele. I. Cohen edited a collection of Feitelson's prose, *Beḥinot ve-Haʾarakhot* (1970), which includes an essay on the writer by A.B. Jaffe.

BIBLIOGRAPHY: F. Lachower, in: M.M. Feitelson, *Ketavim* (1914); N. Goren, *Mevakkerim be-Sifrutenu* (1944), 59–68; Waxman, Literature, 4 (1960^2), 412–3; J. Barzilai, *Ha-Shiloʾaḥ* 1896–1927 (1964), [index to *Ha-Shiloʾaḥ*], 41.

[Getzel Kressel]

FEITH, DOUGLAS J. (1953–), U.S. government adviser. Born and reared in Philadelphia, where his father, Dalck Feith, a Holocaust survivor, was a prominent businessman and philanthropist. Feith was educated at Harvard College (*magna cum laude* 1975) and Georgetown University Law Center (*magna cum laude* 1978). He began his public career in 1975, working as an intern on Senator Henry M. ("Scoop") Jackson's Subcommittee on Investigations. Feith then served in the Reagan Administration as a National Security Council Middle East specialist and as Richard Perle's deputy at the Pentagon. Throughout the 1990s, he advised Republican members of Congress on a range of national security matters, including the Gulf War, arms control, and Bosnia. Feith has written numerous newspaper and journal articles on national security issues such as terrorism, missile defenses, chemical weapons, U.S.-Soviet relations, and the Middle East

In July 2001 Feith was appointed by President George W. Bush as under secretary of defense for policy, effectively the third-ranking civilian position in the U.S. Department of Defense. Following the September 11, 2001, attack on the World Trade Center and the Pentagon, Feith played an important role in developing U.S. government strategy for the war on terrorism, advising Secretary of Defense Rumsfeld on policy issues relating to Afghanistan, Iraq, and other aspects of the war. Feith was instrumental also in other defense initiatives, including realigning the U.S. global defense posture, adding new members to the North Atlantic Treaty Organization and reforming NATO's military and civilian structures, creating new U.S. defense ties in South Asia, launching of the Global Peace Operations Initiative to increase the capacity of various countries to send forces abroad to keep or enforce the peace and negotiating with Russia the Moscow Treaty on offensive nuclear weapons.

Like a number of Jewish intellectuals who grew up in liberal, pro-Franklin Delano Roosevelt homes, Feith came to identify himself with a group of "neo-conservatives" serving in or supporting the Reagan Administration who viewed the Cold War as a clash of basic philosophical principles, not just a great power contest. Feith also staked out contrarian views on such issues as the "oil weapon" (he thought its power exaggerated and the financial costs would be high for whatever state tried to use it), arms control treaties (he thought their benefits were illusory), and the Oslo peace process (he predicted it would fail as a result of Arafat's deficient statesmanship and lack of commitment to peace). Those views generated controversy and helped make him a lightning rod later for critics of the Iraq War of 2003. While rejecting the label of Wilsonian idealism, Feith, along with Natan *Sharansky and Paul Wolfowitz, has helped elaborate the idea, which President George W. Bush has made central to U.S. foreign policy, that democratic institutions are the route to peace and prosperity and that peoples in the Middle East, as elsewhere, will choose freedom and democratic political institutions if given the chance.

Feith's community work included service as president of the Charles E. Smith Jewish Day School.

[Mark Feldman (2nd ed.)]

FEIWEL, BERTHOLD (1875–1937), Zionist leader and poet. Born in Pohrlitz, Moravia, Feiwel began his higher education in Brno, where he founded the Zionist student organization Veritas. In 1893 he studied law at Vienna University and became Herzl's close associate, helping to organize the First Zionist Congress in 1897. He contributed to the central organ of the Zionist Organization, *Die Welt*, and became its editor-in-chief in 1901. In his articles he emphasized that Zionism cannot content itself with the political and diplomatic activity of its leaders; it must also bring about the renewal of Jewish spiritual and social life in the Diaspora. At the first Conference of Austrian Zionists at Olmuetz (1901), Feiwel introduced a program of Zionist Diaspora activity, arguing that Zionism means not only the Jewish people seeking refuge in Ereẓ Israel, but also preparing itself (in the Diaspora) for its future commonwealth. Diaspora work covered the whole range of Jewish life in the countries of dispersion: political, economic, cultural, and sporting activities. When his program was rejected by the Zionist Executive, Feiwel resigned as editor of *Die Welt* and, together with Martin Buber, Chaim Weizmann, and others, created the Democratic Fraction as an opposition group at the Fifth Zionist Congress. Together with Martin Buber, Davis Trietsch, and the painter E.M. Lilien, Feiwel founded the *Juedischer Verlag, a publishing house that distributed mainly German translations of Hebrew and Yiddish literature.

In 1903, after the *Kishinev pogrom, Feiwel published *Die Judenmassacres in Kischinew* under the pseudonym Told. Based on an on-the-spot investigation, this book shocked public opinion. Feiwel had close contacts with Jewish authors in Eastern Europe and became a gifted translator of their works. In the book *Junge Harfen* (1914) he presented their modern poetry. The *Juedischer Almanach* (1902), an anthology edited by Feiwel, as well as *Lieder des Ghetto* (1902, 1920), translations of poems of the Yiddish poet Morris Rosenfeld with drawings by E.M. Lilien, also had considerable literary influence. After World War I (1919), Feiwel's friend Weizmann summoned him to London to become his political and economic adviser. When Keren Hayesod was founded (1920), Feiwel became one of its first directors. In 1933 he settled in Jerusalem.

BIBLIOGRAPHY: *Berthold Feiwel ha-Ish u-Fo'alo* (1959); Ch. Weizmann, *Trial and Error* (1949), index. **ADD. BIBLIOGRAPHY:** A. Schenker, *Der juedische Verlag 1902–1938 – Zwischen Aufbruch, Bluete und Vernichtung* (2003).

[Samuel Hugo Bergman]

FEJÉR, LEOPOLD (1880–1959), Hungarian mathematician. Fejér was educated in Budapest and Berlin. He spent a year in Berlin where he met H.A. Schwarz who had a decisive influence on his mathematical career. He was appointed professor at Budapest in 1911 and elected to full membership in the Hungarian Academy of Sciences in 1930. After being dismissed from his chair during World War II he narrowly escaped being killed by the fascist regime. Fejér's Ph.D. thesis contained the classic result now known as Fejér's theorem that "a Fourier series is Cesàro summable (C,1) to the value of the function at each point of continuity." This key result gave great impetus to further developments in Fourier and divergent series. A complete list of his publications is given in *Matematikai Lapok* (vol. 1 (1950), 267–72).

BIBLIOGRAPHY: G. Pólya, in: *Journal of the London Mathematical Society*, 36 (1961), 501–6.

[Barry Spain]

FEJTÖ, FRANÇOIS (**Ferenc**; 1906–), author, critic, and journalist. Fejtö was born in Zagreb. Together with P. Ignotus and A. József, he was a founder of the Hungarian literary journal *Szép Szó* (Budapest, 1935). In 1938 he was accused by the Budapest police of being a Communist and fled from Hungary, settling in Paris. An expert on Eastern European politics, Fejtö was a prominent socialist and an independent thinker. Both in his political writings and in his fiction he was preoccupied with the Jewish question, particularly the relationship of Jews and Communists. His works include *Érzelmes utazás* ("Sentimental Journey," 1937), *Chine–URSS, la fin d'une hégémonie* (1964), *Henri Heine* (1946), and *Le printemps des peuples dans les pays communistes* (1960).

BIBLIOGRAPHY: *Magyar Irodalmi Lexikon*, 1 (1963), 341.

[Baruch Yaron]

FEKETE, MICHAEL (1886–1957), Israel mathematician. Born at Zenta, Hungary, Fekete was associated with the Hungarian School of Mathematics and was assistant at Budapest University from 1912 to 1919. In 1928 he accepted a position as lecturer at the Institute of Mathematics in the Hebrew University, Jerusalem, becoming professor in the following year. From 1946 to 1948 he was rector of the university. A dedicated teacher, he laid the foundations of mathematical studies and research there, and played an important part in the development of his department.

Fekete's many and varied contributions included the theory of numbers, algebraic equations, and above all the theory of functions. He considered his greatest achievement to have been the discovery of the transfinite diameter, which won him the Israel Prize for the exact sciences in 1955.

BIBLIOGRAPHY: J.C. Poggendorf, *Biographisch-literarisches Handwoerterbuch*, 2 (1937), s.v. (incls. list of his works).

[David Maisel]

FELD, ISAAC (1862–1922), poet who wrote in German. Born in Lvov, Feld studied and practiced law, in addition to teaching throughout his life. One of the members of Ḥovevei Zion in Galicia, his *Dort wo die Zeder* was a very popular Zionist song. It first appeared in the journal *Selbstemanzipation* in the early 1880s, and was later included in many German, Yiddish, and Hebrew anthologies of Jewish songs. It was published with music in the *Blauweiss Liederbuch* (1914).

ADD. BIBLIOGRAPHY: N.M. Gelber, *Toledot ha-Tenu'ah ha-Ẓiyyonit be-Galicia*, index.

[Getzel Kressel]

FELD, JACOB (1899–1975), U.S. civil engineer. Born in Austria, Feld was taken to the U.S. in 1906. He was a graduate of City College, N.Y., and got his Ph.D. from the University of Cincinnati. His engineering designs and constructions include the New York Coliseum, Guggenheim Museum, Yonkers Raceway, Sixth Avenue Subway of N.Y.C., airfields, and a naval training station. He was a special consultant to the U.S. Air Force and in 1959 became chairman of the engineering division, New York Academy of Science and later became president of the academy and a fellow of the American Society of Civil Engineers (ASCE), which cited him in 1969 as Metropolitan Engineer of the Year. Feld was active in Jewish community affairs.

FELDBERG, LEON (1910–), South African newspaper publisher and editor. Son of the rabbi of Krok, Lithuania, he went to yeshivot in Ponevezh and Slobodka, and received a rabbinical diploma. He started his journalistic career in Riga, working for Yiddish newspapers. In 1929, he emigrated to South Africa and, after serving as a minister and teacher, went into business. In 1936 he established the weekly *South African Jewish Times*, which he edited until 1969. He also set up a printing and publishing plant and issued the *South African Jewish Year Book* (1960, 1961) and *South African Jewry* (1965, 1967).

[Lewis Sowden]

FELDER, GEDALIA (1921/2–1991), Canadian rabbi and halakhic authority. Felder was born in Iczuki-dolne in Galicia and studied in the local yeshivah and with other rabbis in Poland, including Yeshivat Keter Torah Radomsk in Cracow. His father, Hersch, immigrated to Canada in 1930, living briefly in Winnipeg and then in Montreal before bringing his family to Canada in 1937. Felder continued his studies in Montreal and then in Toronto under Rabbi Abraham Price at his Yeshivat Torat Chaim. Felder received his ordination from Price in 1940.

Between 1940 and 1949 Felder served as rabbi for several small Jewish communities in southern Ontario: Sarnia (1941–43), Belleville (1943–45), and Brantford (1945–49). One of his students in the last town spoke of the *menschlichkeit* of Felder and the warm reception students received in his household. Between 1943 and 1945 Felder was a part-time chaplain with the Royal Canadian Air Force for Trenton and District. In 1949 Felder moved to Toronto, where he remained for the rest of his life. Upon his arrival, Felder assumed the pulpit of Shomrei Shabbos, a synagogue founded by Galician Jews in the late 19th century. He taught at Price's Yeshivat Torat Chaim and was a staunch supporter of the Eitz Chaim Talmud Torah, the school established by Polish Jews several decades earlier. In Toronto, he also served for years as the chairman of the Va'ad ha-Kashrut of the Central Region (i.e., Ontario) of the Canadian Jewish Congress, and was a supporter of the Mizrachi organization. Felder did not cut himself off from non-Orthodox Jews, participating in the Toronto Rabbinical Fellowship, which brought together for discussion rabbis of various denominations, including, among others, Walter Wurzberger (Orthodox), Stuart *Rosenberg (Conservative), and Gunther *Plaut (Reform).

Felder achieved an international reputation on the basis of his halakhic works: the *Yesodei Yeshurun* (6 vols., 1954–70), which deals with laws regarding the liturgy, the Sabbath, and Passover; the two-volume *Naḥalat Ẓevi* (1952–72) in which he grapples with the thorny issues of adoption, proselytes, and divorce; some of his early responsa are collected in *She'elot u-Teshuvot She'elat Yeshurun* (1964); and in 1977 Felder published an edition of *Sefer Tanya Rabbati*, a work attributed to Jehiel ben Jekuthiel ha-Rofe Anav of 13th century Italy. Felder also published in a host of journals devoted to halakhic issues. In recognition of Felder's erudition, he was appointed one of the five members of the Beth Din of the Rabbinical Council of America.

[Richard Menkis (2nd ed.)]

FELDHEIM, PHILIPP (1901–1990), U.S. publisher of sacred books and translations in English translation. Born in Vienna, Feldheim was sent away to a series of yeshivot in Europe where he studied under the direction of Rabbi Joseph Ẓevi *Duschinksy. He returned to Vienna, where he was active in communal affairs, most especially Agudat Israel. Arrested on **Kristallnacht* Feldheim resolved to leave Austria and immigrated to the United States with thirty dollars in his pocket. He settled in Williamsburg, where he first sold books from his apartment and received shipments of Jewish sacred books from Europe. From his apartment he moved to rented quarters and then decided to publish books instead of only importing them.

He was involved in printing the first Talmud to be printed in the United States. He moved to Washington Heights in 1950, where he came under the influence of Rabbi Joseph *Breuer, who encouraged him to translate important Jewish books into English, much as the community in Germany had made sacred works available in German. Feldheim undertook the publication of the English translation of the writings of Rabbi Samson Raphael Hirsch and Rabbi Elie Monk, and such works as *The Path of the Just* and the *Gates of Repentance* and Irving Bunim's *Ethics from Sinai*. He was both a distributor and publisher and spearheaded the creation of an English-language ultra-Orthodox corpus of works, essential for reaching a new generation of Jews comfortable in the English language.

[Michael Berenbaum (2nd ed.)]

FELDMAN, ABRAHAM JEHIEL (1893–1977), U.S. Reform rabbi and a Zionist leader. Feldman was born in Kiev, Ukraine, immigrating to New York in 1906 and settling in the lower East Side. He went to college at the University of Cincinatti where he received his B.A. (1917) and he was ordained at Hebrew Union College (1918). He then served in pulpits at the Free Synagogue in Flushing, the Congregation Children of Israel in Athens, Georgia, and Keneseth Israel in Philadelphia, where the illness of the senior rabbi forced him to assume responsibilities ordinarily not given to a younger rabbi. In 1925, he moved to Beth Israel of Hartford, Conn., where he served as rabbi until his retirement in 1968, setting a tradition of longevity that was to mark the religious leadership of Connecticut's capital. In the New Deal, he served as education director for the National Recovery Administration in Connecticut and later was State Chairman of the National Recovery Administration Adjustment Board. He was a founder with Samuel Neusner of the *Connecticut Jewish Ledger* and served as editor until 1977. He was a master orator, who felt that the sermon may not only inform the mind but shape the heart. He perceived himself as the Jewish ambassador to the non-Jewish world and taught a course at the Hartford Theological Seminary. A distinguished leader in state and communal affairs, he has also been prominent in rabbinical circles and was president of the Central Conference of American Rabbis during 1947–49, President of the interdenominational Synagogue Council of America (1955–57). A prolific author and journalist, activist rabbi and communal Rabbi Feldman wrote 26 books and many scholarly articles as well as literally thousands of journalistic pieces. Among his books are *Why I am a Zionist* (1945) and *American Reform Rabbi* (1965), as well as many articles.

BIBLIOGRAPHY: L. Karol, "Rabbinic Leadership in the Reform Movement as Reflected in the Life and Writings of Abraham Jehiel Feldman" (Rabbinic Thesis, Hebrew Union College); A.J. Feldman, *The American Jew* (1964).

[Abram Vossen Goodman]

FELDMAN, HERMAN (1889–1969), U.S. army officer. Born in New York, Feldman joined the army as a private in the field artillery. During World War I he was sent to France and was commissioned in the field artillery. During World War II Feldman again served in the quartermaster corps, eventually being promoted to major general. At the end of the war, Feldman was awarded the Legion of Merit for outstanding services in England and North Africa. A second Legion of Merit was awarded by Admiral Nimitz for outstanding service in the Pacific. He also earned the Distinguished Service Medal and Army Commendation Medal for his service in World War II. In 1949 Feldman was nominated by President Truman as quartermaster general. He retired in 1951 after a distinguished 43-year army career.

[Ruth Beloff (2nd ed.)]

FELDMAN, IRVING (1928–), U.S. poet. Feldman taught at Kenyon College from 1958 to 1964, and subsequently at the New York State University in Buffalo. His poetry, including *The Pripet Marshes* (1965), is frequently on Jewish themes. In his reading of Feldman's poetry, found in *The Hollins Critic* of February 1997, David Slavitt has called the poem "The Pripet Marches" "one of the dozen or so most interesting and powerful poems of our generation." Feldman's poems are found, as well, in his *Collected Poems, 1954–2004* (2004).

BIBLIOGRAPHY: H. Schweizer (ed.), *The Poetry of Irving Feldman* (1992).

[Lewis Fried (2nd ed.)]

FELDMAN, LOUIS H. (1926–), U.S. professor of classics and literature. Born in Hartford, Connecticut, Feldman received his undergraduate degree from Trinity College in 1946, and his master's degree in 1947; his doctoral degree in classical philology is from Harvard University (1951). He was a teaching fellow at Trinity in 1951 and 1952, then an instructor in classics in 1952 and 1953. He was an instructor at Hobart and William Smith Colleges from 1953 to 1955, then joined Yeshiva University of New York as an instructor in humanities and history. He was an assistant professor at Yeshiva University from 1956 to 1961, an associate professor from 1961, and he was appointed a professor of classics in 1966. He subsequently became the

Abraham Wouk Family Professor of Classics and Literature. Feldman served as associate editor of *Classical Weekly* from 1955 to 1957 and as managing editor of *Classical World* from 1957 to 1959.

Feldman is renowned as a scholar of Hellenistic civilization, specifically of the works of Josephus. A fellow of the American Academy for Jewish Research, he received numerous fellowships and awards, including a Ford Foundation fellowship (1951–52), a Guggenheim fellowship (1963), a grant from the Memorial Foundation for Jewish Culture (1969), and a grant from the American Philosophical Association (1972). He was named a senior fellow of the American Council of Learned Societies in 1971, a Littauer Foundation fellow in 1973, and a Wurzweiler Foundation fellow in 1974.

Feldman's works include *Scholarship on Philo and Josephus, 1937–1962* (1963), *Josephus and Modern Scholarship, 1937–1980* (1984), *Jew and Gentile in the Ancient World: Attitudes and Interactions from Alexander to Justinian* (1993), *Studies in Hellenistic Judaism* (1998), and *Studies in Josephus' Rewritten Bible* (1998). He was editor and translator of *Jewish Antiquities, Books 18–20* (1965) and editor of *Jewish Life and Thought among Greeks and Romans: Primary Readings* (1996). He coedited, with Gohei Hata, *Josephus, Judaism, and Christianity* (1987) and *Josephus, the Bible, and History* (1989). Feldman contributed extensively to journals in his field, and he was departmental editor of Hellenistic literature for the first edition of the *Encyclopaedia Judaica* and a contributor to the *Encyclopaedia Brittanica*.

[Dorothy Bauhoff (2nd ed.)]

FELDMAN, MARTIN ("Marty"; 1934–1982), British comedian and scriptwriter. Born in London to Orthodox Jewish parents, Marty Feldman left school at 15 and, in 1957, joined the BBC as a staff writer, continuing for ten years as a television and radio comedy scriptwriter for such shows as BBC radio's *Round the Horne*. From 1967 he was chiefly an actor, his trademark bulging eyes and gangling frame being instantly recognizable. He became internationally famous in the five years after he moved to Hollywood in 1974, co-starring with Gene *Wilder in such cult comedies as *Young Frankenstein* (1974), in which he played "Igor," and *Silent Movie* (1976). Like many clowns, in private life Feldman was a sad, unhappy man. His bulging eyes were caused by a chronic thyroid deficiency, and his manic-depressive personality led to dependence on drugs and alcohol. He died of a heart attack at the age of 48.

BIBLIOGRAPHY: ODNB.

[William D. Rubinstein (2nd ed.)]

FELDMAN, MIROSLAV (1899–1976), Yugoslav poet and playwright. A practicing physician, Feldman was born in Virovitica. His first poems appeared in 1920. Later collections included *Ratna lirika* ("War Lyrics," 1947) and *Pitat će kako je bilo* ("They Will Ask How It Was," 1959). Among his successful dramas were *Zec* ("Rabbit," 1932), *Profesor Žić* (1934), *U pozadini* ("Behind the Lines," 1939, 1953²), and *Doći će dan* ("The Day Will Come," 1951). Feldman, who dealt mainly with war and love themes, was president of the Croatian Writers' Association (1955). He also wrote theatrical pieces and in 1976 was awarded the AVNOJ prize (the highest literary award). At first a Zionist, he later embraced Communism.

FELDMAN, MORTON (1926–1987), U.S. composer. Born in New York City, Feldman began studying the piano with Vera Maurina-Press at the age of 12 (the work *Madame Press Died Last Week at Ninety* was written in 1970 in her memory), and later studied composition and counterpoint with Wallingford Riegger and Stefan *Wolpe. With composers John Cage, Earle Brown, and Christian Wolff and pianist David Tudor, he became part of an American avant-garde group interested in bringing to music the same aesthetic concepts of art and expression that had marked the abstract expressionist American painters (such as de Kooning and Pollock) of the early 1950s. His earliest works, *Projections* (1950–51), explored the field of indeterminacy in music and the use of graphic notation. Although Feldman later varied and combined his methods of notating works, he was always concerned with examining the extreme limits of slowness (in durations and tempi) and softness (of dynamic range) of which music is capable, and with timbres created by non-traditional methods, e.g., piano sounds produced without traditional forms of attack. His output was large: many piano pieces for soloist and combinations of two and three pianos, notably *Last Pieces*; and orchestral and ensemble works – *Numbers*, for nine instruments; *Atlantis* (1958); *Structures for Orchestra* (1960–62); *Out of Last Pieces; For Franz Kline*, for soprano and four other players; *Rabbi Akiba*, for soprano and ten instruments; *On Time and the Instrumental Factor*, for small orchestra (1969); and the series of pieces for solo viola and various groupings of accompanying instruments entitled *The Viola in My Life*. He worked on films, and collaborated on the ballet *Summerspace* (1966) with choreographer Merce Cunningham and painter Robert Rauschenberg. In 1971 Feldman wrote *Rothko Chapel* for soloists, chorus, and instrumental ensemble which was commissioned as a tribute to the painter, who had died a year before. Some of the composer's late works reflected his interest in the woven patterns in Anatolian rugs and in Jasper John's crosshatch paintings (*Why Patterns*, 1978, *Crippled Symmetry*, 1983). *Coptic Light* (1986), Feldman's last orchestral work, was inspired by the early Coptic textiles at the Louvre. Feldman defended his aesthetics in a number of essays (*Essays*, ed. W. Zimmermann, Kerpen, 1985).

ADD. BIBLIOGRAPHY: NG²; MGG²; T. DeLio (ed.), *The Music of Morton Feldman* (1985).

[Max Loppert / Yulia Kreinin (2nd ed.)]

FELDMAN, SANDRA (1939–), U.S. teacher, trade union activist, and labor union executive. Born in New York City to Milton and Frances Abramowitz, Feldman earned an M.A. degree in English literature from New York University. Active in the civil rights movement of the 1960s, she also taught elementary school on the Lower East Side of Manhattan. In 1966 Feldman became a full-time field representative for New York City's United Federation of Teachers. She worked her way through the ranks following in the footsteps of her mentor, Albert *Shanker. In 1986, she became the first woman president of the largest local union in the United States. She served until 1997, when on May 6, the national American Federation of Teacher's executive council unanimously elected her the 15th president of the national organization. In the same month, she was also elected a vice president of the American Federation of Labor-Congress of Industrial Organizations (AFL-CIO).

As a public school educator, Feldman devoted herself to improving the working conditions of teachers, promoting higher educational standards for students, and strengthening curricula in the schools. During her tenure as president of the American Federation of Teachers, the organization experienced record growth, representing more than one million educators, healthcare professionals, public employees, and retirees. Feldman's second husband was Arthur Barnes, former president of the New York Urban Coalition.

Feldman supported the rights and concerns of children, women, and workers on local, national, and global levels through her association with the Council on Competitiveness, the International Rescue Committee, the A. Philip Randolph Institute, the Jewish Labor Committee, the Coalition of Labor Women, the New York Urban League, Women's Forum, Women's Committee on Refugee Children, Child Labor Coalition, the United States Committee for UNICEF, and the National Council of Americans to Prevent Handgun Violence.

BIBLIOGRAPHY: R. Holub. "Feldman, Sandra," in: P.E. Hyman and D. Dash Moore (eds.), *Jewish Women in America: An Historical Encyclopedia*, vol. 1 (1997), 404–5; "Feldman, Sandra," in: *Who's Who in America 2004*, vol. 1, 1568–69. **WEBSITE:** www.aft.org.

[Peggy K. Pearlstein (2nd ed.)]

FELDMAN, SHIMSHON SIMON (1909–1995), leader of the Jewish Ashkenazi community of Mexico. He was born in Skvira, Ukraine, and studied in a *talmud torah*, and in a Russian public school. His mother died before his 13th birthday, and in 1924 he immigrated alone to Mexico. During his first years there he worked as a peddler. In 1928 he opened his first shop and brought his father and brothers to Mexico. In the 1930s he prospered and at the end of World War II owned a number of factories. In 1942 he joined the Board of the Ashkenazi Nidhei Isroel congregation. In 1942 he became its president – a position he held for 50 years. In this role he dedicated himself to the strengthening of Jewish education and to the development of Jewish schools, to religious community life, to supplying Jewish and non-Jewish needs, and to giving moral and material support to the State of Israel.

[Efraim Zadoff (2nd ed.)]

FELDMAN, WILHELM (1868–1919), Polish author and critic. Born in Zbaraz, Galicia, he was of ḥasidic origin, but advocated assimilation and was in fact converted before his death. As editor of the Cracow monthly *Krytyka* (1901–14) and as a literary critic, Feldman was prominent in the progressive literary movement, Mloda Polska ("Young Poland"). His critical works include *Współczesna literatura polska* ("Contemporary Polish Literature," 1903, 1930[8]), a study which roused considerable controversy owing to his radical opinions; and *Współczesna krytyka literacka w Polsce* ("Contemporary Literary Criticism in Poland," 1905). Among Feldman's political books are *Stronnictwa i programy polityczne w Galicji, 1846–1906* ("Political Parties and Programs in Galicia 1846–1906," 2 vols., 1907); and *Dzieje polskiej myśli politycznej w okresie porozbiorowym* ("History of Polish Political Thought since the Partitions," 3 vols., 1920). Although Feldman wrote novels on Jewish themes, his unsympathetic attitude became increasingly evident. Two works on Jewish problems were *Asymilatorzy syoniści i polacy* ("Assimilationists, Zionists and Poles," 1893); and *Stosunek Adama Mickiewicza do Żydów* ("Mickiewicz's Attitude to the Jews," 1890).

Wilhelm Feldman's son JÓZEF (1899–1946), historian, was professor at the Jagellonian University of Cracow. His books include *Polska i sprawa wschodnia 1709–1714* ("Poland and the Eastern Question 1709–1714," 1926) and *Problem polsko-niemiecki w dziejach* (1946, tr. of previous version *Polish-German Antagonism in History*, 1935).

BIBLIOGRAPHY: *Pamęci Wilhelma Feldmana* (1927), incls. bibl.; E. Mendlesohn, in: *Slavic Review*, 18 (1969), 577–90; *Księga Pamiątkowa ku czci Józefa Feldmana* (= K. Tymieniecki and Z. Woyciechowski (eds.), *Roczniki Historyczne*, no. 18, 1949), incls. French summaries; *Polski Słownik Biograficzny*, 6 (1948), 396–404. **ADD. BIBLIOGRAPHY:** E. Mendelsohn, "*Wilhelm Feldman ve-Alfred Nosig, Hitbollut ve-Ẓiyyonut be-Lvov*," in: *Galed* 11, 89–111.

[Moshe Altbauer]

FELDSHUH, TOVAH (1952–), U.S. actress. Born Terri Sue Feldshuh in New York, she attended Scarsdale High School, Sarah Lawrence College, and the University of Minnesota, studying drama under Uta Hagen. She switched to using her Hebrew name Tovah when a boyfriend in college complained that Terri Sue sounded too Southern, in marked contrast to generations of Jewish actors who changed their names. She made her stage debut in July 1971 playing small parts in *Cyrano de Bergerac* at the Guthrie in Minneapolis. Her Broadway debut followed in 1973, when she played two parts in the musical *Cyrano*. In 1974 Feldshuh appeared as Myriam in the comedy *Dreyfus in Rehearsal* on Broadway, in the title role in *Yentl* at the Brooklyn Academy of Music Playhouse, and in the musical revue *Rodgers & Hart* at the beginning of 1975. In October 1975, she reprised her role in *Yentl* on Broadway at the Eugene O'Neill Theater, which earned her a Tony nomination and a Theater World Award. Feldshuh's extensive and acclaimed film and television career includes appearances on the soap opera *Ryan's Hope* (1975) and in the made-for-TV movie *The Amazing Howard Hughes* (1977) as Katharine Hepburn, followed by her role as Czech freedom fighter Helena Slomova in the 1978 TV mini-series *Holocaust*. Years later, Feldshuh would also narrate the film testimony at the U.S. Holocaust Museum. From 1991, she had a repeat role as defense attorney Danielle Melnick on the crime drama *Law & Order*. Her feature film roles include *The Idolmaker* (1980), *Daniel* (1983), *Brewster's Millions* (1985), *Saying Kaddish* (1991), *Citizen Cohn* (1992), *A Walk On the Moon* (1999), and *Kissing Jessica Stein* (2001). In 1989, Feldshuh returned to Broadway as Maria in *Lend Me a Tenor* at the Royale Theater, which earned her a third Tony nomination. Her fourth Tony nomination came in 2004 for her one-woman show about the life of Golda Meir, *Golda's Balcony*. Other awards and nominations include four Drama Desk awards, four Outer Critics Circle awards, the Obie, the Emmy, the Eleanor Roosevelt Humanities Award, Hadassah's Myrtle Wreath, and the Israel Peace Medal. Married to attorney Andrew Harris-Levy, Feldshuh has two children. Pulitzer Prize-nominated playwright David Feldshuh is her brother.

[Adam Wills (2nd ed.)]

FELEKY, GÉZA (1890–1936), Hungarian journalist, author, and art critic. Born in Budapest, he wrote on art for *Nyugat* ("West") and later joined the liberal newspapers, *Pesti Napló* ("Budapest Daily") and *Világ* ("World"). He was editor in chief of *Világ* (1920–25), and later became a director of *Magyar Hirlap* ("Hungarian News"). He strove to regain Jewish rights lost under the Horthy regency and was author of historical essays, including *Kaiser und Krieg* (1933).

°FELIX, ANTONIUS, procurator of Judea 52–60 C.E. He was a brother of the freedman Pallas, who was influential in Rome. Felix, appointed to the procuratorship by the emperor Claudius, married Drusilla, daughter of Agrippa I (cf. Acts 24:24). Felix's period of office was one of constant unrest. Tacitus (Historiae 5:9; Annales 12:54) states scathingly that "with all manner of cruelty and lust he exercised royal function in the spirit of a slave." Immediately on his arrival in Judea he seized Eleazar b. Dinai, the leader of the *Sicarii, together with a number of his men, and sent them in chains to Rome; he crucified many more. Taking advantage of the hostility of the Sicarii toward certain classes among the Jews, Felix encouraged them to assassinate the high priest Jonathan, who had presumed to advise him on how to conduct affairs in Judea. He ruthlessly crushed any real or imaginary attempt at rebellion. Believing an exhortation by a prophet to go into the wilderness to be an incitement to insurrection, he dispatched a force which killed many who had been persuaded to go there (Jos., Ant., 20:166). An Egyptian prophet promised to demonstrate to the masses his power to make the walls of Jerusalem fall at a simple command. When he arrived at the Mount of Olives with his followers, Felix attacked them and killed many, although the prophet himself escaped (cf. Acts 21:38). In Caesarea, the residence of the procurator, a civic dispute between the Syrians and the Jews erupted into violence. When the Jews refused to desist, Felix sent soldiers against them. During Felix's term of office, the apostle Paul was imprisoned. According to the New Testament, he was kept in custody to please the Jews (Acts 23:24; 24:27), but this motive is difficult to accept in view of all that transpired during Felix's procuratorship. The more probable explanation is that Paul's being a Roman citizen prevented Felix from treating him as he had others. In 60 C.E. Felix was succeeded by *Festus Porcius, under whom the conflict in Caesarea continued.

BIBLIOGRAPHY: Jos., Loeb (ed.), vol. 9, index; Pauly-Wissowa, 2 (1894), 2616–18, no. 54; Schuerer, Hist, 180, 228–34.

[Lea Roth]

FELIX LIBERTATE (Lat. "Happy through Freedom"), name of a society founded in Amsterdam in February 1795 with the object of attaining Jewish emancipation in the Netherlands and spreading enlightened ideas among Amsterdam Jewry. The society was sponsored by a number of prominent – mainly Ashkenazi – Jews, including M.S. *Asser and Dr. H. de H. Lemon, who wanted to enlist opinion both inside and outside the Jewish community for obtaining full civic rights for the Jews. Leaders of Amsterdam Jewry, who did not allow them to spread their views in the synagogue, opposed their activities. Contrary to the Orangist majority of the Jewish community, the members of Felix Libertate were sympathizers of the party of the Radical Patriots. Attempts by the municipal council to intervene in the dispute were unsuccessful. One of the first acts of Felix Libertate was the translation of the Declaration of the Rights of Man and the Citizen into Yiddish. Felix Libertate failed to win general approval from other revolutionary societies, although one-third of the membership was not Jewish. They therefore conducted an active campaign both verbally and in print to have their resolution for Jewish emancipation accepted. Pamphlets were published by M.S. Asser and David *Friedrichsfeld, among others, stressing the competence of Jews as active citizens and a republican universalist outlook. On September 2, 1796, the National Assembly declared complete emancipation. Subsequently, Felix Libertate demanded a revision of the statutes of the Amsterdam Ashkenazi community, especially those regulating its governing body and care of the poor. When the *parnasim* rejected these claims, 21 members seceded from the community and founded the Adath Jessurun congregation, whose members were excommunicated by the existing *parnasim*. The two communities engaged in bitter controversy and both published a Yiddish journal entitled "Discourse" (Yid. דישקורש), one issued by the older body, the so-called "*Alte Kehile*" and the other by the "*Naye Kehile*" (1797–98). When two members of Felix Libertate, Bromet and Lemon, were elected to the National Assembly, they dismissed the *parnasim* with the help of the government in March 1798. However, the *parnasim* succeeded in having the dismissal annulled when a less extreme group came to power (June 1798). Subsequently, Felix Libertate discontinued its activities. The Adath Jessurun congregation existed until it was reunited with the old *kehillah* by a decree of King Louis Bonaparte in 1808.

BIBLIOGRAPHY: Bloom, in: *Essays ... Salo Wittmayer Baron* (1959), 105–22; M.E. Bolle, *De opheffing van de autonomie der Kehilloth* *in Nederland 1796* (1960); Bloemgarten, in: *Studia Rosenthaliana*, 1 pt. 1 (1967), 66–99, pt. 2, 45–70; 2 pt. 1 (1968), 42–65. **ADD. BIBLIOGRAPHY:** J. Michman, *Dutch Jewry during the Emancipation Period 1787–1815. Gothic Turrets on a Corinthian Building* (1995); J. Michman and M. Aptroot, *Storm in the Community. Yiddish Polemical Pamphlets of Amsterdam Jewry 1797–1798* (2002).

[Jozeph Michman (Melkman) / Bart Wallet (2nd ed.)]

FELLER, ABRAHAM HOWARD (1905–1952), U.S. lawyer and government official. Feller was born in New York City. He taught at Harvard from 1931 to 1934, specializing in international law. Entering government service in Washington, Feller worked in a variety of federal agencies for the next 12 years, as special assistant to the U.S. Attorney General's Office, as legal consultant to the Office of Lend-Lease Administration, and during World War II as general counsel of the Office of War Information and general counsel of the UN Relief and Rehabilitation Administration. In 1946 he was appointed general counsel to the United Nations, a position in which he functioned as chief legal adviser to Secretary-General Trygve Lie. Several days after Lie's resignation in 1952, Feller leaped to his death from his New York apartment. Although he himself had made no such declaration, his suicide was widely interpreted both nationally and internationally as a protest against the Senate Internal Security Committee's investigation of alleged "Communist penetration" of the American delegation to the UN. His book *The United Nations and the World Community* (1952) appeared shortly before his death.

FELLER, SHNEYUR ZALMAN (1913–), lawyer. He was born in Botosani (North Moldavia) and studied law at the University of Jassy. In 1944, as a refugee in the Soviet Union, Feller was appointed public prosecutor in Kishinev. He returned to Romania in 1946 and worked as a lawyer in Botosani where he was also deputy mayor and president of the Jewish community. From 1948 he was successively judge and public prosecutor. He held other high offices in the Ministry of Justice and in 1951 was appointed professor of jurisprudence at the University of Bucharest. Between 1949 and 1961 he published many articles and notes on criminal law and drafted the Romanian penal code. Feller, who emigrated to Israel in 1963, joined the Hebrew University in 1965, and became professor of criminal law in 1968. In 1971 he was named dean of the Law Faculty and in 1972 he became a full professor. In 1981 he retired from the Hebrew University, but continued to teach voluntarily at the Faculty and at the Ramat Gan Law College. In 1994 he was awarded the Israel Prize.

FELLNER, WILLIAM JOHN (1905–1983), U.S. economist. Fellner was born in Budapest and studied at the university there. Fellner's main interests lay in economic analysis and monetary policies. He was a partner in an industrial enterprise and lectured in economics in Budapest before going to the U.S. in 1938. He taught economics first at the University of California at Berkeley and, beginning in 1952, at Yale University, where he was appointed professor of economics and subsequently chairman of the department. Regarded as one of America's premier economists, Fellner served the United States government as consulting expert to the U.S. Treasury Department and the National Securities Board. In 1973 he was appointed by President Nixon to the U.S. Council of Economic Advisers. That year he was also appointed one of the first resident scholars of the American Enterprise Institute for Public Policy Research. He also served as a policy adviser to the *European Community.

His major publications include a treatise on *War Inflation* (1942), *Monetary Policies and Full Employment* (1946), *Competition among the Few* (1949), *Trends and Cycles in Economic Activity* (1956), *Emergence and Content of Modern Economic Analysis* (1960), *Probability and Profit* (1965), *Maintaining and Restoring Balance in International Payments* (1966), *Ten Economic Studies in the Tradition of Irving Fisher* (1967), *Towards a Reconstruction of Macroeconomics* (1976), *Contemporary Economic Problems* (1978–81), and *Economic Theory Amidst Political Currents: The Spreading Interest in Monetarism and in the Theory of Market* (1982).

BIBLIOGRAPHY: B. Balassa, *Economic Progress, Private Values, and Public Policy: Essays in Honor of William Fellner* (1972); J. Marshall, *William J. Fellner: A Bio-Bibliography* (1992).

[Joachim O. Ronall / Ruth Beloff (2nd ed.)]

FELMAN, AHARON LEIB (1867–1893), pioneer in citrus culture in Ereẓ Israel and author of the first Hebrew book on the subject. Felman was born in Mezhirech and in 1884 he settled in Ereẓ Israel with his family. He worked in his father's orchard near Jaffa, learning citrus culture from the Arabs. Felman saw the future of Jewish settlement in Ereẓ Israel in the planting of groves on the Coastal Plain, and to train future settlers he wrote a short book on citrus culture entitled *Ma'yan Gannim* ("Spring of the Gardens"), printed in Jerusalem in 1891. It is written in the language of the Mishnah and deals with many aspects of citrus culture, from the purchase of land to the planting of trees, their care, and the cure for various diseases. He died in Petaḥ Tikvah.

BIBLIOGRAPHY: A. Felman, *Ḥaluẓei ha-Pardesanut ha-Ivrit be-Ereẓ Yisrael* (19401, 115–7; Tolkowsky, *Peri Eẓ Hadar* (1966), 253f.

[Avraham Yaari]

FELS, U.S. family of manufacturers and philanthropists.

JOSEPH FELS (1853–1914) was born in Halifax County, Virginia. After living in North Carolina, the Fels family moved to Baltimore, where Joseph left school at 15 to join his father's soap manufacturing business. In 1875 he went into the soap business on his own in Philadelphia. He began manufacturing soap and washing powders by the naphtha process in 1893, and by 1896 the Fels-Naphtha Company's products were so successful that Fels was able to devote most of his time to philanthropic causes. He came to believe that his fortune had been amassed by robbing society, and sought to spend it on causes that would end the unregulated free enterprise system which allowed some men to accumulate great wealth at the expense of others. In 1905 he was converted to Henry George's "single tax" philosophy, which Fels preferred to call "Christianity." Fels believed that God had given land to all the people of the earth, and tax on the unearned increments of landowners would enable all society's members to share the land's bounties. Substantial financial contributions by Fels helped the single tax movement throughout the world, especially in England, where he and his wife lived during 1901–11. He proselytized for the single tax wherever he traveled, as well as for various political reform movements. Fels financed colonies in the United States and England that provided work for the unemployed; he supported the women's suffrage movement in the Western world, and helped social welfare agencies in England. Fels organized the first mass deputation of English women to present petitions to Parliament describing the plight of the poor in London's East End. He was one of the first American manufacturers to institute profit sharing for his workers. Fels backed the Zionist movement and was active in the Jewish Territorial Organization.

MARY FELS (1863–1953). a distant cousin of her husband Joseph, was born in Sembach, Bavaria, and was taken to the U.S. in 1869. She helped her husband with his projects until his death, after which she concentrated her efforts on Zionist activities. She organized the Joseph Fels Foundation in 1925 to advance human welfare through education and to promote the exchange of culture and ideas, especially between the United States and Ereẓ Israel. Mary Fels edited the magazine *The Public* (1917–19) and wrote a biography of her husband (1916).

SAMUEL SIMEON FELS (1869–1950), Joseph's younger brother, was born in Yanceyville, N.C. A partner in the Fels-Naphtha Company, he funded the Fels Planetarium in Philadelphia (1934). In 1936 he established the Samuel S. Fels Fund to promote research in the natural and physical sciences. He also created the Fels Institute of Local and State Government at the University of Pennsylvania.

BIBLIOGRAPHY: Steffens, in: *American Magazine* (Oct. 1910), 744–6; M. Fels, *Joseph Fels, His Life-Work* (1916); Howe, in: *Survey* (March 28, 1914), 812–3; Zangwill, in: *Voice of Jerusalem* (1921), 337–49; *New York Times* (May 17, 1953), 88; Kellogg, in: *Survey*, 86 (1950), 135.

[Robert Asher]

FELSENTHAL, BERNHARD (1822–1908), U.S. Reform rabbi. Felsenthal was born in Munchweile, Germany. He intended to enter the Bavarian civil service, but seeing no prospect of being admitted, he attended a teachers' seminary at *Kaiserslautern and taught in Jewish schools before settling in the U.S. in 1854. There Felsenthal served a congregation in Madison, Indiana, as officiant and teacher; then in 1858 he moved to Chicago as clerk in a banking house, while also devoting himself to rabbinical and theological study. Deeply influenced by David *Einhorn, Felsenthal became one of the first protagonists of Reform Judaism in the Midwest. He was a strong opponent of slavery and refused to accept a pulpit in Mobile, Alabama. He was a founder and secretary of the Chicago Juedisches Reformverein. A statement of Reform views which he published in 1859, *Kol Kore ba-Midbar: Ueber Juedische Reform*, attracted some attention, and when the Reformverein developed into the Sinai Congregation, he became its first rabbi (1861). He was ordained by Einhorn and Samuel Adler. In 1864 Felsenthal became rabbi of the newly formed Zion Congregation, which he headed until his retirement in 1887. Felsenthal was a constant student and, though he wrote no books, wielded a ready pen. When questions on ritual came to him, he generally took an advanced Reform view. In several instances he dissented from the proposals of Isaac M. *Wise. Thus, he strongly opposed the establishment of a rabbinical seminary, believing that conditions in America did not provide a satisfactory foundation. On the other hand, he advocated Jewish day schools. In 1879 he declined a professorship at Hebrew Union College. In later years Felsenthal became concerned with the threat to the Jews in America posed by religious indifference, and feeling that the course taken by Reform was preparing a "beautiful death" for Judaism, became an enthusiastic supporter of the Zionist movement. Felsenthal was a founder of the Jewish Publication Society of America and of the American Jewish Historical Society.

BIBLIOGRAPHY: E. Felsenthal (ed.), *Bernhard Felsenthal, Teacher in Israel* (1924), includes extracts from his writings and bibliography; Stolz, in: CCARY, 18 (1908), 161; idem, in: AJHSP, 17 (1909), 218–22. *Universal Jewish Encyclopedia* (1941) 4: 273–274. **ADD. BIBLIOGRAPHY:** K. Olitzky, L. Sussman, and M.H. Stern, *Reform Judaism in America: A Biographical Dictionary and Sourcebook* (1993).

[Sefton D. Temkin]

FELZENBAUM, MICHAEL (**Mikhoel**; 1951–), Yiddish writer. Born in Vassilkoe (Ukraine), Felzenbaum studied drama in Leningrad (1968–74) and then founded the Yiddish Cultural Society in Belz, where he was active in the theater and the Pedagogical Institute (1974–88). In 1991 he immigrated to Israel. As co-founder and later editor of the annual *Naye Vegn* (1992), executive director of the Yiddish Culture Center in Tel Aviv, and head of the H. Leyvik Publishing House, he won the Dovid Hofshteyn Prize (1999) for his multifaceted and socially provocative work. His dramatic and narrative œuvre, which unites the Jewish, modern Yiddish, and European and American literary traditions, is marked by a postmodern, "post-Yiddish" character. An antithetical process operates in his improvised intertextual world that strives toward primordial chaos, where nothing begins at the beginning, but everything is revealed in its grotesque and absurd dimensions. Traditional myths and fairy tales function as empty, anachronistic vessels without creative-metaphorical significance in the post-Holocaust world. While the prose works display earthy and mordant qualities, his poems exhibit a sensitivity and thoroughly developed spontaneity characteristic of folk songs. His works appeared in the most important Yiddish literary journals; his book publications are *Es Kumt der Tog* ("Day Arrives," 1992), *A Libe Regn* ("Rain of Love," 1994), *Der Nakht-Malekh* ("Angel of the Night," 1997), *Un Itst Ikh Bin Dayn Nign* ("And Now I Am Your Melody," 1998), and *Shabesdike Shvebelekh* ("Sabbath Matches," 2003).

BIBLIOGRAPHY: A. Starck, "Interview with Mikhoel Felsenbaum," in: *The Mendele Review* (Feb. 15, 2004); idem, "A Critical Study of Mikhoel Felsenbaum's 'Shabesdike shvebelekh,'" ibid. (shakti.trincoll.edu/~mendele/tmrarc.htm); idem, "*Shabesdike Shvebelekh*: A Postmodernist Novel by Mikhoel Felsenbaum," in: J. Sherman (ed.), *Yiddish after the Holocaust* (2004), 300–18; V. Tchernin, in: *Shabesdike Shvebelekh* (2003), 9–12.

[Astrid Starck (2nd ed.)]

FEMINISM, both a political movement seeking social equities for women and an ideological movement analyzing a wide range of phenomena in terms of gender politics. Jewish feminism in the modern era has played a significant and transformative role in virtually every area of Jewish religious, social, and intellectual life.

Jewish Feminism and its Impact Prior to the 1960s

Although modern Jewish feminist movements were inspired in large measure by Enlightenment claims regarding human equality and dignity, proto-feminist efforts to raise women's social and religious position can be found in many Jewish communities prior to the 19th century. Tracing shifts in gender ideology and in women's actual status is difficult, however, because of the paucity of sources written by women prior to the 17th-century memoir by *Glueckel of Hameln. References to women in male-authored documents, particularly responsa literature and legal documents, give some evidence of sporadic agitations for change in women's status in Jewish communal life and religious life. For example, numerous sources indicate that in Germany and France between 1000 and 1300, a time of high economic and social status for Jewish women, women demanded increased involvement in religious life, including the voluntary assumption of commandments from which they were exempt in talmudic Judaism (Grossman).

Critical evaluation of the position of women within Judaism also appears as part of Christian traditions of anti-Judaism. In the *Nizzaḥon Vetus*, an anthology of 12th- and 13th-century Jewish-Christian polemic in northern France and Germany, Christians criticized Jews for not including women within the covenant: "We baptize both males and females and in that way we accept our faith, but in your case only men and not women can be circumcised." In the *Juden Buchlein* (1519), Victor von Karben mocks the refusal of Jews to include women in a prayer quorum. This critique continued in the notorious anti-Jewish text, Johann Eisenmenger's *Entdecktes Judentum* (1700), and women's inferior status within Judaism became a major theme among German (and some American) Protestant (and some Catholic) theologians in the 19th and early 20th centuries (J. Plaskow, K. von Kellenbach, S. Heschel). The inferior status of women within Judaism was presented in order to denigrate Judaism as "Oriental" and "primitive" and to challenge whether Jews should be accorded emancipation into European society. Jewish women's inferiority was also cited in Christian theological writings to argue that Jesus treated women as equals whereas other rabbis of his day did not, a claim with little historical grounding. Jewish apologetic responses to such charges began in 19th-century Germany with arguments that Judaism honors and elevates women's status in the home and community by exempting them from the religious obligations of study and public prayer incumbent on men. The nature of these charges and counter-charges made it difficult to articulate Jewish feminist criticisms of sexism.

Jewish enlightenment and, later, socialist critics of Jewish communal and religious structures often fought for women's rights, but feminists did not always ally themselves with secularism and against religion as a means to improve women's status. With modern pressures to reshape both gender roles and the status of minority groups, Jewish women had to await emancipation as both Jews and as women to enter secular society. While Jews were permitted entry into German universities in the early 19th century, women were excluded until the 1890s. At the same time, some European feminist organizations did not admit Jews. Rather, early efforts at redressing gender imbalance attempted to enhance women's educational opportunities and position within the Jewish community, creating social service and charitable organizations run by women. The *Juedischer Frauenbund (Jewish Women's Organization) was founded in Germany in 1904 by Bertha *Pappenheim and strove to win voting rights for women within Jewish communal affairs. Within the United States, Rebecca *Gratz founded the 19th-century Sunday school movement that created new roles for women in Jewish education. The tradition of Jewish women's *salons was significant not only as a new, neutral space for Christians and Jews to meet, but as an emerging culture of conversation and reflection on gender and Jewish identity. Indeed, Jewish women intellectuals, from the 18th to the 20th centuries, frequently found greater resonance within Christian society, and were sometimes only reluctantly admitted to Jewish intellectual circles; Martin *Buber, for example, initially did not want to admit women to the Juedisches Lehrhaus, the adult Jewish educational center he founded in Frankfurt am Main in 1920 (Friedman).

Changes in women's status within the synagogue came slowly. In mid-19th century Germany, teenage girls were given ceremonies of *confirmation along with boys in Reform congregations, similar to ceremonies prevalent in churches, but women still sat separately from men in the synagogue. Mixed seating in the synagogue was first introduced in the United States in 1851 in Albany, New York, and in 1854 at Temple Emanu-El in New York City. It became common in the United States after 1869 when many new post-Civil War synagogues opened but did not spread to European Reform synagogues until much later and then only tentatively (Goldman).

Conversely, modernity also saw the distinct spheres of women's traditional expressions of Judaism minimized or eliminated by non-Orthodox Jews, such as **mikveh* observance (immersion in the ritual bath following menstruation and childbirth), which declined radically in the modern era, though revived in the late 20th century. Since the *mikveh* served as a gathering place for women to socialize and also to exert authority in the absence of men, its decline undermined women's opportunities to assemble away from male presence. Further, the falloff in adherence to Jewish law weakened women's status as sources of domestic and gendered legal expertise, particularly concerning laws of *kashrut*. Traditionally entrusted with responsibility for the laws of **niddah* and *kashrut*, women had been viewed with the moral trust, intellectual ability, and religious commitment necessary for their strict adherence to those often complex laws. Still, male authorities, whether fathers, husbands, or rabbis, always retained ultimate control over adherence to laws within women's domain.

The modern era opened new public and communal religious and educational opportunities for women. Pressure from the changes in secular society that encouraged women and men to take advantage of equalizing educational and vocational opportunities affected the Jewish world, too. Educational reforms in the Orthodox and ḥasidic communities of Eastern Europe in the early 20th century, led by Sara *Schnirer, established a network of schools for religious girls, *Beth Jacob, and the liberal rabbinical seminaries established in Europe and the United States in the late 19th century permitted some women to attend courses, although not to receive rabbinic ordination.

The United States had a small and relatively uneducated Jewish community prior to the 1880s. Women received only minimal Jewish education and were not voting members of the community. The demography quickly shifted at the turn of the century, as over two million Jews from Eastern Europe arrived as immigrants between 1881 and 1924. They included women who had been exposed to political organizing and analysis, and who soon became major forces in the nascent labor, socialist, anarchist, and communist movements in New York and other cities in the early years of the 20th century. Rose *Schneiderman, for example, was a leader of the *Women's Trade Union League, the campaign for women's suffrage, and the *International Ladies Garment Workers Union. However, once those movements were institutionalized – as labor unions and political parties – women were removed from leadership positions. Separate women's organizations also played an important role within Jewish communal life in the United States; the *National Council of Jewish Women, founded by Hannah Greenebaum *Solomon at the 1893 World Parliament of Religions in Chicago, initially provided educational and vocational training for immigrants through a series of *"settlement houses" established in impoverished urban areas.

The Impact of Feminism Since the 1960s

Jewish women, including Betty *Friedan, Gloria *Steinem, and Letty Cottin *Pogrebin, have been in the forefront of the Second Wave feminist movement in the United States that began in the late 1960s. The re-emergence of a Jewish feminist movement, as part of the Second Feminist wave, led to major changes in women's status in Judaism and to a flourishing of Jewish feminist scholarship and theology. The most dramatic change in Judaism for many centuries came with the equality of women in synagogue worship, a movement led by American Jewish feminists and which has gradually extended to Jewish communities elsewhere in the world. The public honoring of young women in the synagogue, the Bat Mitzvah, became widespread by the late 1960s, followed by decisions by Reform, Reconstructionist, and Conservative denominations of Judaism to include women in the prayer quorum, call women to the Torah, and allow women to lead synagogue worship services. Perhaps the most striking transformation from previous Jewish practice has been the ordination of women as rabbis (see **Semikhah*).

The first ordination of a woman as a Reform rabbi took place in Germany in 1935; she was Regina *Jonas, murdered at Auschwitz in 1944. Ordination of women as rabbis and cantors was initiated in the United States in the 1970s by Reform Judaism (1972) and was subsequently adopted by the Reconstructionist (1974) and Conservative (1984 for rabbis, 1986 for cantors) movements. Several hundred women rabbis and cantors have been ordained thus far in the United States, and in Britain. Commissions within the Reform, Reconstructionist, and Conservative movements have revised the prayer book *liturgy to use inclusive or gender-neutral language and include references to the biblical matriarchs as well as patriarchs. Feminist biblical commentaries, written from a range of religious perspectives, have also been published (Frankel; Goldstein; Kates and Reimer). Numerous collections of feminist rituals and blessings to mark occasions in women's lives have been developed, including feminist Passover liturgies, prayers for the birth and weaning of a baby, and ceremonies for naming baby girls (see *Birth), egalitarian wedding services for hetero- and homosexual couples (see *Marriage), and celebration of *Rosh Ḥodesh, the New Moon, as a women's holiday.

Within Orthodoxy at the beginning of the 21st century, women now have opportunities for studying rabbinic texts, heretofore limited to men. With training in particular areas of Jewish law, women serve as legal advisors to Orthodox women regarding issues connected with divorce and *niddah* observance. Orthodox women have established women-only prayer groups and institutions for studying rabbinic texts, and a few Orthodox synagogues have started to permit women to read from the Torah under certain circumstances and conditions, deliver a sermon, and even lead the service. Several clauses have been proposed for inclusion in the **ketubbah* (religious marriage contract) that would provide recourse for a woman whose husband refuses to grant her a Jewish divorce, though none has yet attained universal approval by Orthodox rabbis. The problem of the **agunah* remains a central issue for Orthodox feminists, particularly in Israel, where the Orthodox rabbinate has exclusive control over Jewish marriage and divorce. Organizations of Orthodox women attempting to address the problem of the *agunah* include the Jewish Orthodox Feminist Alliance, and Getting Equitable Treatment.

By contrast, the Reform movement has entirely eliminated the *get, the divorce decree given by a man to his wife, while the Conservative movement has developed a clause that can be inserted into a *ketubbah* that allows a *bet din* (court of Jewish law) to issue a *get* to a woman if her husband refuses to do so. Since 1980, the Reconstructionist movement has used an egalitarian *get* that can be issued by either spouse.

Feminism, Zionism, and the State of Israel

During its early years, the political Zionist movement, centered in Europe in the late 19th and early 20th centuries, harbored considerable ambivalence toward women. Although *Zionism presented itself as an emancipatory movement for Jews, positions of political leadership were firmly maintained in men's hands. The Zionist negation of the Diaspora was linked to a negation of piety, and overcoming the Diaspora meant "becoming a man" (*le-hitgaber*). During the early waves of immigration to Palestine prior to statehood, women worked alongside men in the cultivation of farmland; they have also served with men in Jewish self-defense forces prior to and after the foundation of the state. Yet with the establishment of the State of Israel, women were not granted proportional roles of power within the government, even though Israel's Declaration of Independence proclaimed full equality (Herzog; Hazelton). Instead, a myth of gender equality within the State was promoted to disguise the reality of women's subservience. Thus, while women held traditionally male positions within the kibbutz system, few men took on traditionally female positions, such as childcare, and while women are drafted into the Israeli army, they are generally assigned subordinate tasks and are not given combat duty. Most problematic, since the Orthodox rabbinate holds full legal control over marriage and divorce, women's freedom to initiate and control marital relationships is impeded and women rabbis are disempowered. Women are also prohibited from public communal prayer at Jewish holy sites, such as the Western Wall in Jerusalem, despite years of court challenges by feminist groups.

Although a woman, Golda *Meir served as Israel's prime minister from 1969 to 1974; few women have held senior positions within the Israeli cabinet or parliament. Given the central role of army service in establishing careers within the political and financial arenas, the unequal position of women in the Israeli military has had long-term career consequences. Racial discrimination within Israel against Jews from non-European backgrounds and the Israeli emphasis on large families has also affected women's ability to acquire an education, escape poverty, and achieve career success. Nevertheless, women are increasingly educated and constitute a high percentage of the Israeli workforce. The Israel Women's Network, founded by Alice Shalvi in 1984, is an advocacy group for women's rights that concentrates on legislative and political efforts to overcome discrimination against women in the workplace, military, religious courts, and in the healthcare and educational arenas. With particular attention to violence and sexual harassment, the IWN helped secure passage in 1998 of legislation criminalizing sexual harassment and holding both the harasser and employer responsible for civil damages.

Throughout the modern era women managed to retain some influence in Zionist social service organizations within the Jewish communities of North America and Europe, collecting and distributing funds and goods, and running schools and vocational training programs. Those activities, a central feature of maintaining Jewish communal cohesion, became the basis for modern women's organizations, such as *Hadassah, the National Council of Jewish Women, *WIZO, *Na'amat, and Women's *ORT (Organization for Rehabilitation and Training), which became wealthy and powerful institutions during the course of the 20th century.

In the aftermath of the 1967 Arab-Israeli war that left Israel with control of the West Bank and Gaza, several feminist organizations emerged that called for return of the occupied territories to Palestinian control, and condemned the violence and impoverishment in those territories. Women in Black, founded in 1988 to hold weekly silent vigils of Israeli and Palestinian women calling for an end to the occupation, soon became an international peace network and has been nominated for the Nobel Peace Prize. New Profile is a feminist organization that seeks to change Israel from a militarized to a peace-seeking culture, and works especially on educating children for peace (see essays in Fuchs, *Israeli Women's Studies*).

Feminist Scholarship

Historical study of Jews, which began in the 19th century, was initially seen as a manly endeavor and women's lives and contributions were virtually ignored in chronicles of the Jewish experience. The growth of the field of women's studies, particularly in the United States, helped establish a counterpart within Jewish Studies. Feminist analysis has criticized masculinist biases in describing the Jewish past, but has also used historicism to justify feminist innovations (see *Historians, Women). Feminist analyses of rabbinic literature have uncovered legal precedents for changing halakhic prescriptions regarding women (Hauptman) and interpretive patterns of leniency in establishing Jewish law (Biale), as well as patterns of gendered rhetoric in rabbinic literature that create the masculinity of men and of God (Boyarin; Baskin; Eilberg-Schwartz).

Feminist attention to gender has also exposed the male biases in describing Jewish experience (Koltun; Heschel; Rutenberg). Modernity has been elevated as rational, progressive, and male by describing pre-modern Judaism via tropes of nostalgia using female metaphors. Modern Judaism was described as both positively masculine, in seeking political and religious emancipation, and negatively feminine, as in Haskalah literature in which leaving the Jewish fold and associating with Christians was described as a kind of prostitution (Feiner). In early 20th century debates over which language was more appropriate for Jews, Yiddish or Hebrew, the former was viewed as an effeminate, women's language, while Hebrew was valorized as male. Few women writing modern Hebrew or Yiddish literature were accorded the same recognition for their work as their male colleagues by a literary establishment dominated by men, and few writings by women have been included in the "canon" (Seidman; Fuchs).

In the early years of women's studies, the task seemed to be fairly straightforward. Textual expressions of misogyny and male-centeredness were demonstrated, and even if the thinker had been dead for centuries, his influence was generally said to continue to this day, as part of a long chain of patriarchal tradition. More recently, however, feminist scholars have developed more complex analyses, demonstrating ambivalences toward women within the same thinker and text, and also turning to metaphorical uses of masculine and feminine imagery in matters not explicitly related to men and women. Male privilege is not always a straightforward matter. For instance, classical and modern Jewish texts evoke an identification between men and the male God, yet undermine that identification by depicting all Jews, including men, as female in relationship to God.

Feminists differ in how to interpret women's experience and power in patriarchal structures. Some find ways in which women turned their exclusion from aspects of Judaism into a positive experience. C. Weissler has discovered numerous prayers traditionally recited by early modern women as they undertook various domestic duties, such as baking *ḥallah* and kindling Sabbath lights (*Voices of the Matriarchs* (1998); see **Tkhines*; *Liturgy). S. Sered has found that women respond to the male-oriented religious system by becoming ritual experts within the female sphere, sacralizing and holding authority over the domestic sphere and the laws of *niddah* and *mikveh*. Excluded from the realm of men, she argues, women redefine their realm as normative and meaningful. J. Bahloul's study of Algerian Jewish women delineated a strong social network of women. Still other feminists argue that finding women's empowerment in female spheres mandated by men undermines arguments for gender equality and may romanticize women's experience unjustifiably.

Perhaps the most controversial field of feminist scholarship is study of gender and the Holocaust (Ofer and Weitzman, eds.). Women were more likely than men to be chosen by the Judenraete for deportation from ghettos to death camps, and women were more likely than men to be selected for immediate gassing upon arrival at the death camps. J. Ringelheim suggests that women and children made up 60 to 70 percent of those gassed in the initial selections. Based on deportation and death figures as well as the numbers of Jews in DP camps at the end of the war, Ringelheim concludes that more Jewish women were deported and killed than Jewish men, a disparity due to Nazi policies of killing pregnant women and those who arrived at camps with children, as well as the far larger percentage of elderly women than men among Jewish deportees.

Feminist Analyses of Judaism

During the 1970s feminist critics began to expose the absence of women's voices within the male-dominated structures promoted by Judaism's exclusively male-authored texts. Feminists also strove to reconstruct the lost voices of women, trying to recover evidence of women's history and self-understanding that would allow a more diversified picture of the multiple Judaisms that have flourished throughout the Jewish past. While Judaism traditionally defines itself as a divinely revealed religion, its beliefs and practices have been interpreted and regulated almost exclusively by male authorities until the modern period. Feminist analysis has pointed out that men have created the legal systems articulated in the Mishnah, Talmud, and codes of Jewish law, and acted as supreme arbiters of its interpretation by reserving the rabbinate for men. Courts of Jewish law were historically run by male rabbis, and women were excluded as witnesses in most court cases. In rabbinic law, men may contract a marriage or divorce a wife, but women can neither acquire a husband nor divorce him. Women enter into rabbinic discourse as objects of discussion, when their ritual purity, sexual control, or marital status impinges upon men's lives.

Many Jewish feminists have suggested that the insistence on overwhelmingly male imagery for God was a deliberate effort to strengthen the male-dominated institutional arrangements of Jewish life and undergird male authority over women in the religious and societal realms. As a result, feminist analysis views Jewish texts with suspicion for their collusion with societal patriarchy in silencing women's voices, or, even worse, as creating patriarchal oppression and endowing it with the aura of divine sanction. At the same time, some feminists have culled biblical and rabbinic texts to find counter-patriarchal traditions that support principles of justice and equality, or voices of trickster women seeking to correct halakhic inequities (Pardes; Adler). Even as D. Setel argued that the prophet Hosea's metaphor of Israel as God's adulterous wife was pornographic, R. Adler noted that God's reunion with the adulterous Israel, which violates Deuteronomic law (20:4) mandating a husband's divorce of an adulterous wife, might be understood as a "constructive violation" of Jewish law – "the metaphor that preserves the covenant breaks the law" (Adler, 163–64).

By the 1980s, Jewish feminist theology (see *Theology, Feminist) began redefining classical, male-authored Jewish understandings of God, as well as associated concepts, such as revelation, the problem of evil, and the nature of prayer. Basing their critique of Judaism on the premise that all experience is gender-based, theologians like J. Plaskow and R. Adler demanded a reconsideration of theological and ethical categories assumed to be universal, but which, they argued, reify men's experience and have little relevance to women. Jewish feminist theology flourished in particular in the United States, supported by the growth of the academic field of women's studies at American universities and by the theoretical insights of Christian feminist theology.

Under the influence of postmodernism, feminist thought has attempted to denaturalize assumptions regarding women, emphasizing the social rather than biological creation of "woman" and the attendant assumptions regarding heteronormativity. An ideology of compulsory heterosexuality, not innate inclination, feminists argue, has pressured women into marriage with men and defined homosexuality as sinful. Feminist analysis has noted that in contrast to male homosexuality, lesbianism was never clearly defined in biblical literature, and never condemned with the severity of male homosexuality in rabbinic literature. Similarly, the condemnation of male masturbation in rabbinic texts finds no female counterpart, and the genital self-examination by women that is mandated in rabbinic laws regulating the laws of *niddah* replicates masturbatory acts. Freedom of sexual expression for women and men is considered central to women's rights but also essential to reclaiming women's control over their bodies after centuries in which fathers, husbands, and male rabbis regulated women's lives (Schneer and Aviv; Magonet).

*Lesbian Jewish identity as both homosocial and homosexual has been marginalized in the recent efflorescence of queer Jewish studies and its attention to the (male) body as a site of Jewish cultural, sexual, and religious identity. Lesbian thinkers have emphasized the body as a source of the spiritual, celebrating manifestations of women's sexuality and arguing the centrality of eroticism to religiosity (Plaskow, *Standing Again at Sinai*). Although numerous gay and lesbian synagogues, as well as a World Congregation of Gay and Lesbian Jewish Organizations have been founded in recent decades, only the Reform and Reconstructionist rabbinical seminaries ordain openly gay and lesbian rabbis (R. Alpart, S.L. Elwell, and S. Idelson, eds. *Lesbian Rabbis: The First Generation* (2001)).

Adler has argued that the traditional male-only environments of rabbinic study not only fostered homoeroticism, but was dominated by a "methodolatry" that revolved around male concerns, omitting those of women. Responding to a husband's post-World War II query, asking a rabbi if he is halakhically obligated to divorce his wife because her incarceration in a concentration camp may have included forced intercourse, Adler notes that only the man's requirements form the question and not those of his wife. In responding to the absence of women from the formative practices and exegeses of rabbinic Judaism, Plaskow insists that women as well as men stood at Sinai and received God's revelation, and that their experiences and interpretations should be included as equally normative as the rabbinic law developed by men in response to the revelation.

Other feminist analyses of *halakhah* proceed differently. Both R. Biale and Hauptman have pointed to halakhic interpretations that have been favorable to women, and to sociological processes of analyzing *halakhah* that result in lenient conclusions. These scholars explain certain traditional practices, such as excluding women from being called to the Torah for an *aliyah*, as reflections of particular social settings, not as eternal legal dicta.

Changes in Feminist Theory

Postmodernism, which has had a strong influence on feminist theory, has changed the modes of understanding power and analyzing language. Instead of viewing power solely as hierarchical domination, feminist theory, influenced by M. Foucault, has come to understand power as capillary, a disciplinary regime maintaining its force not only through conventional sources of domination, but also through the unconventional, including language itself. Complementing Foucault's understanding of the exercise of power are studies by Gramsci and Althusser of the consent of the disempowered to regimens that maintain their subjugation. Changing the understanding of power opens new ways to interpret women's position within Judaism. T. El-Or's study of *ḥaredi* (ultra-Orthodox) women demonstrates that their education is designed to keep them in a state of ignorance and subordination to men. By contrast, Sered's studies argue that women's piety and rituals create a sense of personal self-worth and permit female religious leadership within women-only domains, such as the *mikveh* and *ezrat nashim*. L. Levitt has challenged classical liberalism as a tool of feminist empowerment, and M. Peskowitz has called for greater attention to the ideological function of rabbinic texts in creating power structures and the adherence to them. Surprisingly little attention has been given by Jewish feminism to theorizing race and class, in contrast to other feminisms. E. Shohat has written on Arab-Jewish identity and the biases toward Europe in Jewish self-understanding, and K. Brodkin has described *How Jews Became White Folks* (1999) in the United States. Feminist efforts to address antisemitism as part of a larger critique of racism are notable within a multicultural atmosphere that has tended to ignore Jewish experience (Biale, Galchinsky, and Heschel, eds.; M. Brettschneider, ed.; Bulkin, Pratt, and Smith, eds.).

Contemporary attention to the ways Jewish women's experiences have differed from those of men has led to both internal and external critiques of Judaism. While countless Jewish theologians in previous generations proclaimed the moral superiority of Jewish law, most disregarded the ethical significance of the inferior status of women in Jewish law. Written in apologetic terms for a wider Christian readership, traditional Jewish theology tended to defend the traditional, subordinate role of women as an expression of respect for a femininity that is considered intrinsic and not culturally produced. Jewish feminism has struggled with the fine line between its critique of Judaism's sexism and antisemitic attacks on Judaism.

BIBLIOGRAPHY: A. Grossman, *Pious and Rebellious: Jewish Women in Medieval Europe* (2004); J. Plaskow, "Feminist Anti-Judaism and the Christian God," in: *Journal of Feminist Studies in Religion*, 7:2 (1991), 99–108; K. von Kellenbach. *Anti-Judaism in Feminist Religious Writings* (1994); S. Heschel, "Configurations of Patriarchy, Judaism and Nazism in German Feminist Thought," in: T. Rudavsky (ed.), *Gender and Judaism* (1995); idem, "Jüdische-feministische Theologie und Antijudaismus in christlich-feministischer Theologie," in L. Siegele-Wenschkewitz (ed.), *Feministische Theologie und die Verantwortung für die Geschitchte* (1988); M. Friedman, *Martin Buber's Life and Work: The Early Years 1878–1923* (1981); K. Goldman, *Beyond the Synagogue Gallery: Finding a Place for Women in American Ju-*

daism (2000); E. Frankel, *The Five Books of Miriam* (1998); E. Goldstein, *The Women's Torah Commentary* (2000); J.A. Kates and G.T. Reimer, *Reading Ruth* (1994); L. Hazelton, *Israeli Women* (1977); H. Herzog, *Gendering Politics: Women in Israel* (1999); E. Fuchs, *Israeli Women's Studies: A Reader* (2005); J. Hauptman, *Rereading the Rabbis* (1998); R. Biale, *Women and Jewish Law* (1984); D. Boyarin, *Carnal Israel: Reading Sex in Talmudic Culture* (1993); J.R. Baskin, *Midrashic Women: Formations of the Feminine in Rabbinic Literature* (2002); H. Eilberg-Schwartz. *God's Phallus and Other Problems for Men and Monotheism* (1994); E. Koltun, *The Jewish Woman: New Perspectives* (1976); S. Heschel (ed.), *On Being a Jewish Feminist* (1983; rep. 1995); D. Rutenberg (ed.), *Yentl's Revenge: The Next Generation of Jewish Feminism* (2003); S. Feiner, *The Jewish Enlightenment* (2003); N. Seidman, *A Marriage Made in Heaven: The Sexual Politics of Hebrew and Yiddish* (1997); E. Fuchs, *Israeli Mythogenies* (1987); S.S. Sered, *Women as Ritual Experts* (1992); J. Bahloul, *The Architecture of Memory* (1996); D. Ofer and L. Weitzman (eds.), *Women in the Holocaust* (1999); J. Ringelheim, in: T. Wobbe (ed.), *Nach Osten nationalsozialistisher Verbrechen* (1992); I. Pardes, *Countertraditions in the Bible: A Feminist Approach* (1992); R. Adler, *Engendering Judaism: An Inclusive Theology and Ethics* (1997); J. Plaskow, *Standing Again at Sinai* (1990); D. Schneer and C. Aviv, *Queer Jews* (2002); J. Magonet (ed.), *Jewish Explorations of Sexuality* (1995); T. El-Or, *Educated and Ignorant: Ultraorthodox Jewish Women and their World* (1994); L. Levitt, *Jews and Feminism: The Ambivalent Search for Home* (1997); M. Peskowitz, *Spinning Fantasies: Rabbis, Gender and History* (1997); D. Biale, M. Galchinsky, and S. Heschel (eds.), *Insider, Outsider: American Jews and Multiculturalism* (1998); M. Brettschneider (ed.), *The Narrow Bridge: Jewish Views on Multiculturalism* (1996); E. Bulkin, M.B. Pratt, and B. Smith (eds.), *Yours in Struggle: Three Feminist Perspectives on Anti-Semitism and Racism* (1984).

[Susannah Heschel (2nd ed.)]

FENICHEL, OTTO (1897–1946), Austrian psychoanalyst. Born in Vienna, he moved to Berlin in 1922 and studied at the Psycho-Analytic Institute under Max *Eitingon and in 1926 joined the staff. With the coming of the Nazi regime he left Berlin in 1933 and went to Norway and Prague, where he taught. In 1938 he went to the U.S. and taught in Los Angeles. He wrote two important textbooks on psychoanalysis, *The Outline of Clinical Psychoanalysis* (1934) and *The Psychoanalytic Theory of Neurosis* (1945). Some of these contributions have become classics in their field, for example, "Elements of a psychoanalytic theory of anti-Semitism" in which he tried to trace the sources of anti-Jewish prejudice. *The Psychoanalytic Theory of Neurosis* is a systematic, comprehensive, and detailed study of every major form of neurosis from a psychoanalytic point of view. The theoretical formulations are painstakingly worked out along with old, new, and controversial points of view. Freud's thinking is followed historically on each issue, along with the major contributions of Karl Abraham, Sándor Ferenczi, and Ernest Jones. In addition, there is an encyclopedic bibliography containing more than 1,600 items. Fenichel also wrote a short monograph, *Problems of Psychoanalytic Technique* (1941), which is a classic in its systematic clarity and scientific discipline. His collected papers were published in two series in 1953–54.

[Hilel Klein]

FENICHEL, SAMUEL (d. 1893), Hungarian scientific explorer. Fenichel was born in Nagyenyed. Although he was a frail young man, he had by the age of 20 explored the Dobruja swamps of Romania for zoological specimens. Then, in spite of his health, he spent 14 months exploring New Guinea, where he collected hundreds of specimens of birds, many of them unknown species. He also gathered more than 10,000 specimens of butterflies. The variety of his collection and its careful documentation make it of special scientific significance. He died in New Guinea.

BIBLIOGRAPHY: Wininger, Biog.

FENNEL (Heb. קֶצַח, *kezah*), an herb, the sowing and threshing of which are described by Isaiah (28:25, 27). Fennel is the plant *Nigella sativa,* whose black seeds are used as a condiment. It was used as a condiment in talmudic times, being sprinkled on dough before it was baked (Tosef., TY 1:2; Men. 23b). Different views were expressed on its medicinal and nutritional value, one being that it is good for the heart (Ber. 40a), another that too much of it is injurious to the heart (Kal., ch. 1), and yet another that its pungent smell is harmful (Ber., *ibid*). Galen, and following him Asaph ha-Rofe, recommended fennel for nasal inflammation (L. Venetianer, *Asaf Judaeus*, 1 (1915), 172). In Israel three species of fennel grow wild, a cultivated species being raised to a limited extent for use as a condiment.

BIBLIOGRAPHY: Loew, Flora, 3 (1924), 120–3; J. Feliks, *Olam ha-Ẓome'aḥ ha-Mikra'i* (1968[2]), 184. **ADD BIBLIOGRAPHY:** Feliks, Ha-Ẓome'aḥ, 147.

[Jehuda Feliks]

FÉNYES, ADOLF (1867–1945), Hungarian painter. He was born in Budapest, where he studied law and painting. Fényes participated in the establishment of the Hungarian association of painters and sculptors. In his early work there is evidence of the influence of naturalism, but later there is a strong impressionist influence, especially in his somber scenes of poverty. His work reflects his considerable development and includes biblical subjects. Fényes painted monumental scenes from nature. He represented Hungarian painting in many international exhibitions and his name was well known outside Hungary. He died in Budapest of starvation and suffering shortly after the Holocaust.

BIBLIOGRAPHY: *Magyar Zsidó Lexikon* (1929), 274–5; uje, 4 (1941), 274.

[Baruch Yaron]

FENYŐ, LÁSZLÓ (1902–1945), Hungarian poet. Born into poverty, Fenyő wrote pessimistic verse protesting against the cruelty of the world. His first collection, *Épites orgonája* ("Organ of the Building," 1922), was banned, and a volume of selected poems, *Elitélt* ("The Judged," 1959), appeared 14 years after his murder by the Nazis.

FENYŐ (formerly **Fleischman**), **MIKSA** (1877–1972), Hungarian author and literary critic. Fenyő, who was born in

Mélykút, was secretary of the Union of Industrialists for 40 years until he left Hungary for New York in 1948. Fenyő was a founder and an editor of the periodical *Nyugat*. He sought to raise the standards of Hungarian literature and education to those of Western Europe, and his scholarly researches and essays did much to contribute to such an improvement. Fenyő became a convert to Christianity. However, in his memoirs, he includes an important description of contemporary Jewish society. He did the same in the diary *Az elsodort ország* ("The Destroyed Country," 1964), written secretly during the Holocaust while hiding among "Aryans" in Hungary. His main works are *Casanova* (1912); *Bethlen István* ("Count István Bethlen," 1937); and his recollections of *Nyugat, Följegyzések a "Nyugat" folyóiratról és környékéről* (1960).

BIBLIOGRAPHY: A. Szerb, *Magyar Irodalmtörténet* (1943), 447–8; Irodalmi Lexikon (1927), 310; *Magyar Zsidó Lexikon* (1929), 275; Magyar Irodalmi Lexikon, 1 (1963), 347.

[Baruch Yaron]

FEODOSIYA (**Theodosia**; Black Sea port in Crimea, Ukraine; one of the most ancient towns). Founded during the Hellenistic period as the Greek colony of Theodosia, it was called Kaffa (Caffa) until the Russian conquest (1783). The Jewish settlement was also one of the oldest on Russian territory, its beginnings dating from the Hellenistic period. The old synagogue of Feodosiya, thought to be the most ancient in Russia, had an inscription which testified to its construction in 909. Under the rule of the Republic of Genoa from 1266, Feodosiya became the center of the Genoese colonies on the Black Sea. In order to attract merchants from all nations there, freedom of religion was granted for all Christian sects, Muslims, and Jews. The traveler Schiltberg, who visited Feodosiya at the beginning of the 15th century, relates of the existence of two communities in the town – a *Rabbanite and a *Karaite one. The Jews engaged in commerce and maintained relations with the Near East and Poland. The constitution of the town, proclaimed in Genoa in 1449, called on the consul and city elders to protect the Jews as all members of other religions, "from any robbery, from scheming against their property when one of them died intestate, and from other molestations of the bishop."

The situation of the Jews remained unchanged when the government of the town was transferred to the Bank of San Giorgio, a powerful financial company that administered the eastern colonies of Genoa (1453–75). The community continued to develop under Turkish rule also (1475–1783). At the beginning of the 16th century *Moses b. Jacob of Kiev, of Lithuanian origin, held rabbinical office in Feodosiya. He composed a uniform *siddur* for all the Jews of Crimea (the Kaffa rite) and instituted 18 *takkanot* for the community.

After annexation by Russia, Feodosiya was incorporated in the *Pale of Settlement. In 1897 there were 3,109 Jews in the town (12.9% of the total population), mainly Ashkenazim who had emigrated from Lithuania and Ukraine. On Oct. 17, 1905, pogroms accompanied by murder and looting broke out. The Jewish population of Feodosiya numbered 3,248 (11.3% of the total) in 1926 and 2,922 (6.5%) in 1939. After the February Revolution (1917) three Jews (Zionists) served on the local council. Between the wars there was a Yiddish school and a Jewish section in the local Teachers College. Feodosiya was occupied by the Germans on November 2, 1941. A ghetto was organized, and on December 4, 1941 *Einsatzkommando 10b* murdered 1,700 Jews (according to another document, 2,500). In February-May 1942 the last 200 Jews were killed. In 1970 the Jewish population of Feodosiya consisted of Crimean and Russian Jews and Karaites. There was no synagogue. Many left during the mass emigration of the 1990s.

BIBLIOGRAPHY: I. Markon, in: *Zikkaron le-Avraham Eliyahu Harkavy* (1908), 449–69; E. Farfel, *Beit Keneset ha-Attik ha-Nimẓa be-Ir Feodosiya* (1912).

[Yehuda Slutsky / Shmuel Spector (2nd ed.)]

FERARU, LEON (originally **Otto Enselberg**; 1887–1961), Romanian poet. Born in Braila, Feraru took his penname from his father's occupation as a blacksmith (Rom. *fierar*). As a schoolboy he was a Jewish socialist. Upon completing high school he began to study medicine in Bucharest, but had to leave because of antisemitic persecution. In 1907 he emigrated to France, where he studied literature in Montpellier, receiving a degree in 1913, when he emigrated to the United States. Before emigrating, Feraru published poems on social themes (among them the fate of the working woman) and articles in Romanian literary periodicals, among them *Viata Romaneasca* (Romanian Life) and the Jewish periodicals *Lumea Israelita* and *Egalitatea*. After emigrating to the U.S. he continued to compose Romanian verse on social themes, on the landscape of his native country, and on his Jewish family. He published two volumes of poems in Romanian, both in Bucharest, *Maghernita veche si alte versuri din anii tineri* ("The Old Hovel and Other Poems of My Youth," 1926) and *Arabescuri* ("Arabesques," 1937), being considered a universalist poet. Feraru taught Romanian language and literature at Canadian and American universities: Toronto; Columbia (1917–26); Long Island (1927–47). He also published scholarly studies in English, among them *The Development of Romanian Poetry* (1929) and edited the periodicals *Romanian Literary News* and *The Romanian Review*.

BIBLIOGRAPHY: D. Safran, *Completare la judaismul roman* (1981), 74–9; A.B. Joffe, *Bi-Sedot Zarim* (1996), 160–2, 459; A. Mirodan, *Dictionar neconventional*, 2 (1997), 268–72.

[Lucian-Zeev Herscovici (2nd ed.)]

FERBER, EDNA (1887–1968), U.S. novelist and playwright. She was born into a middle-class family in Kalamazoo, Michigan, and at the age of 17 became a newspaper reporter in Appleton, Wisconsin. Later she went to the *Milwaukee Journal* and the *Chicago Tribune*. Her first novel, *Dawn O'Hara*, appeared in 1911, but it was a series of short stories collected under the title *Emma Mc-Chesney and Co.* (1915) that established her as a professional writer. Edna Ferber wrote more than a score of novels, some superficial, some serious, but all smoothly and persuasively written. They deal with the life of ordinary Americans and in many the central character is a woman. *Fanny Herself* (1917) is the story of a small-town Jewish girl; *So Big* (1924), the story of a woman's struggle for independence, won the Pulitzer Prize in 1924. *Show Boat* (1926) became a successful musical; *Cimarron* (1930), *Saratoga Trunk* (1941), and *Giant* (1952) were all best-selling novels which were made into motion pictures. *Dinner at Eight* (1932) and *Stage Door* (1936), both written in collaboration with George S. *Kaufman, were her best-known plays. Edna Ferber wrote comparatively little about Jews and Judaism, but in her first autobiography, *A Peculiar Treasure* (1939), she depicted with humor and understanding her life in a small Jewish community, and she identified herself closely with the Jewish plight during the Nazi years. Her second autobiography, *A Kind of Magic* (1963), includes her impressions of the State of Israel.

BIBLIOGRAPHY: S.I. Kunitz and H. Haycraft (eds.), *Twentieth Century Authors* (1950^2), s.v., and supplement I (1955); Brenn and Spencer, in: *Bulletin of Bibliography*, 22 (1958), 152–6.

[Harold U. Ribalow]

FERBER, HERBERT (**Silvers**; 1906–1991), U.S. sculptor and painter. A native of New York City, Ferber was born Herbert Ferber Silvers. While studying at the City University of New York and Columbia University, where he received a B.S. (1927) and a D.D.S. (1930), Ferber also took classes at the Beaux Arts Institute of Design (1927–30) and the National Academy of Design (1930).

His early direct carvings in wood from the 1930s employed techniques similar to William *Zorach's and Jo *Davidson's. These small figurative sculptures engaged social justice themes, popular with painters such as Raphael *Soyer and Ben *Shahn. The Midtown Galleries mounted Ferber's first solo exhibition in December 1937. In the late 1940s, Ferber eschewed figuration and began welding bronze, lead, copper, and brass as he developed his mature open-form abstract style of sculpture. Akin to Abstract Expressionist painters, Ferber derived inspiration from Surrealist imagery and ancient myth.

Ferber's work was commissioned by B'nai Israel Synagogue, Millburn, New Jersey (1951); Temple Anshe Chesed, Cleveland, Ohio (1956); and Temple of Aaron, St. Paul, Minnesota (1956). An eight by twelve foot abstractly rendered burning bush made of jagged lead-coated copper adorns a wedge-shaped panel projecting from the facade of the B'nai Israel congregation. Titled *And the Bush Was Not Consumed*, this symbolic representation evokes the impression of flames through an open biomorphic style that incorporates snaking vertical and spiral forms. Ferber's textured sculpture identifies the building and serves as a metaphor for the Jewish people. Indeed, the rabbi of the congregation felt that like the Jewish people, the bush was burned but not consumed. This commission was the impetus for several other sculptures designed specifically for walls.

During the 1960s Ferber began a series titled *Homage to Piranesi* in which he enclosed rhythmic forms in wire cages. In March 1961 Ferber's *Sculpture as Environment* was installed in a room at the Whitney Museum of American Art. One of the first sculptures designed to encompass indoor space on a large scale, the work helped to stimulate a larger movement of installation art in the early 1970s. A year later Ferber's first major retrospective was shown at the Walker Art Gallery in Minneapolis. Houston's Museum of Fine Arts held a retrospective in 1981.

Lesser known are Ferber's canvases and works on paper. These abstract images typically show the influence of color field painting, as exemplified by Marc *Rothko and Barnett *Newman.

BIBLIOGRAPHY: E.C. Goossen, R. Goldwater, and I. Sandler, *Three American Sculptors: Ferber, Hare, and Lassaw* (1959); A. Kampf, *Contemporary Synagogue Art: Developments in the United States, 1945–1965* (1966), 75–79; E.C. Goossen, *Herbert Ferber* (1981); W.C. Agee, *Herbert Ferber: Sculpture, Painting, Drawing: 1945–1980* (1983); L. Verderame, *The Founder of Sculpture as Environment: Herbert Ferber (1906–1991)* (1998).

[Samantha Baskind (2nd ed.)]

FERBER, ẒEVI HIRSCH (1879–1966), English rabbi. Ferber was born in Kovno and studied in Lithuanian yeshivot. In 1911 he settled in England and after teaching Talmud in Manchester was appointed rabbi of the West End Talmud Torah Synagogue in London, where he remained until his retirement in 1954. His congregation had its own cemetery, and a number of other small congregations were associated with his, mainly for the benefits of burial. As a result Ferber was able to be independent of the official religious organizations, a situation of which he took full advantage. He was a witty and eloquent preacher in the style of the old-fashioned Lithuanian *maggidim*. Ferber was a prolific writer, mainly on homiletic but also on halakhic subjects; most of his publications were in the form of pamphlets. His most important work was *Kerem ha-Ẓevi*, a halakhic and aggadic commentary on the Pentateuch (1920–38). He also wrote a commentary on the Passover *Haggadah* under the same title (1958).

BIBLIOGRAPHY: *Yahadut Lita*, 3 (1967), 79.

[Louis Isaac Rabinowitz]

°FERDINAND, name of three Holy Roman emperors.

FERDINAND I ruler of Austria; emperor, 1556–64. On his accession to the Austrian throne in 1527 Ferdinand I confirmed the customary Jewish privileges. He opposed the expulsion of *Prague Jewry in 1541, permitting the Jew Hermann to print Hebrew books there and punished the ringleaders of anti-Jewish outbursts in *Litomerice and *Zatec. In 1551 he ordered the Jews within his realm to wear a yellow *badge. Many of his expulsion decrees for Lower Austria, Silesia, Prague, and Vienna, issued in the 1540s and 1550s, were averted or only partially applied after payments by the Jews. In 1557 he canceled the safe conducts granted to Bohemian Jews, granting them later in exceptional cases. He authorized the Jesuits of Prague in 1561 to undertake the *censorship of Hebrew books and forced the Jews to attend their sermons. As emperor he confirmed the privileges accorded to the Jews within the empire.

Ferdinand II king of Bohemia from 1617 and of Hungary from 1621; emperor, 1619–37. A fanatic Catholic and protagonist of the Counter-Reformation in his domains, Ferdinand II was preoccupied for most of his reign with combating Protestantism. The first emperor to employ *court Jews, he was dependent on Jewish financiers, mainly Jacob Bassevi *Treuenberg. For his protection during the Thirty Years' War, the Jews of Bohemia had to pay onerous taxes. Ferdinand ignored the petitions of the city council of *Vienna to expel the Jews, instead granting them successively more favorable privileges (that of 1624 was granted "in perpetuity"). He secured the return of the communities expelled from *Hanau and *Mantua. He allowed the Vienna community to build a synagogue in 1624 (insisting that they settle in a separate quarter), permitted the enlargement of the *Prague Jewish quarter in 1627, and commuted the death sentence on Yom Tov Lippmann *Heller to a heavy fine. For all these benefits, however, the Jews had to pay large emoluments.

Ferdinand III emperor, 1637–57; son of Ferdinand II. Immediately after his accession the Vienna city council urgently petitioned him to expel the Jews; though refusing to do this, Ferdinand III placed them under the jurisdiction of the municipality until 1641, and did not confirm their privileges until Nov. 5, 1638. These were renewed and expanded in 1645 in return for substantial payment. An expulsion order was averted in 1652 on payment of 35,000 florins, and Ferdinand granted the Vienna community broader privileges and internal jurisdiction in return for thrice that sum. In 1650 he ordered that Jews be allowed to remain only in places where they had been in residence in 1618. He gave his court Jew, Hirschel *Mayer, widespread power over the Vienna community.

BIBLIOGRAPHY: Wischnitzer, in: JSOS, 16 (1954), 338–9; G. Wolf, *Geschichte der Juden in Wien* (1876), 21–25; M. Grunwald, *Vienna* (1936), index; H. Tietze, *Die Juden Wiens* (1935), 47; Popper, in: MGWJ, 38 (1894), 371–9; I. Schwarz, *Geschichte der Juden in Wien* (1913), 50–51; Dubnow, Weltgesch, 6 (1927), 219, 222–27; Bondy-Dworský, 1–2 (1906), 348, 371–492, 973 passim; A.F. Pribram, *Urkunden und Akten zur Geschichte der Juden in Wien*, 1 (1918), 123–74; D. Kaufmann, *Die letzte Vertreibung der Juden aus Wien* (1889), 32–65; Wolf, in: MGWJ, 10 (1861), 370–3, 426–30; J. Fraenkel (ed.), *The Jews in Austria* (1967), 320–1.

[Henry Wasserman]

FERDINAND, PHILIP (1556–1599), English Hebraist. Ferdinand, who was born in Poland as a Jew, lived for some time in Constantinople. He became in turn a Roman Catholic and a Protestant, and then went to England, where he taught Hebrew first at Oxford and then at Cambridge. In 1597 he published in Cambridge *Haec sunt verba Dei*, a Latin translation of the 613 Commandments and of other excerpts from rabbinical literature. In 1598 he went to teach Hebrew at Leiden, where the Christian historian and philologist Joseph Scaliger was one of his pupils. He died soon afterwards.

BIBLIOGRAPHY: Stein, in: *Essays… J.H. Hertz* (1942), 397–412; DNB, s.v.; H.P. Stokes, *Studies in Anglo-Jewish History* (1913), 209–11. **ADD. BIBLIOGRAPHY:** ODNB online.

[Cecil Roth]

°**FERDINAND** (1452–1516) and **ISABELLA** (1451–1504), the monarchs whose marriage created the union of Castile and Aragon which formed the Kingdom of *Spain. Because of their religious zeal, they became known as the "Catholic monarchs." A popular tradition, partly corroborated by documents, credits Jewish and *Converso courtiers with a primary role in arranging the marriage contract concluded in 1469 between Isabella, heiress to the crown of Castile, and Ferdinand, prince of Aragon. On the death of Henry IV in 1474, Isabella and Ferdinand began to reign in Castile, then with the accession of Ferdinand to the throne of Aragon in 1479, the two realms were united.

In its first phase their policy adhered to the tradition of relative tolerance which characterized the attitude of the kings of Christian Spain. Generally, this was expressed in their willingness to extend their protection to Jewish communities or individuals whenever they were subjected to outbursts of mob hatred and fury instigated by monks. At the same time the Catholic monarchs employed Jews like Abraham *Seneor, Meir *Melamed, Isaac and Joseph *Abrabanel, and Conversos like Alfonso de la *Cavalleria, Gabriel *Sánchez, and Luis de *Santangel in the administration of the state.

The first sign of deterioration in their attitude toward the Jews can be detected when, at a session of the Cortes held in April 1476 at Madrigal, the monarchs promulgated sweeping edicts for judicial and administrative reforms, including revocation of all the rights of the **aljamas* ("communities") to exercise criminal jurisdiction. Resolving that unified Spain should also be united in faith, they determined to eradicate the sin of heresy which had spread amid the Conversos, namely the tendency to revert to Judaism. In this they were clearly influenced by their desire to win the support of both the clergy and the burghers, who demanded that extreme measures be taken against the Conversos. The outcome of all these pressures was the establishment of the Spanish *Inquisition in 1480. Traditionally, Isabella has been regarded as the living symbol of the religious awakening in Spain, but an examination of the letters exchanged between the king and the queen shows that they acted in perfect accord, moved by the same fanatical urge.

As the Inquisition's investigations in the 1480s proved that the Conversos did indeed tend to revert to Judaism in large numbers, the monarchs concluded that, owing to the close relations between Jews and Conversos, the latter would persist in their heresy. The decision to expel the Jews may have been foreshadowed by the eviction from Andalusia in 1483, but the general expulsion order was promulgated on March 31, 1492. During the three months given to the Jews of Spain to prepare their departure, the royal couple endeavored to ensure that the expulsion took place in accordance with their instructions, lest the Jews be robbed of their property; but this was often to no avail. On July 30, 1493, they issued a letter of protection to all Jewish exiles returning to Spain from Portugal to be baptized, pledging that their property would then be restored to them without loss. It seems that in their decision to expel the Jews from Spain, Ferdinand and Isabella were motivated principally by arguments of a political and religious nature, for the sake of which they were willing to sacrifice every other practical consideration.

BIBLIOGRAPHY: F. Fernández-Armesto, *Ferdinand and Isabella* (1975). For further bibliography see under *Spain.

FERENCZI (Fraenkel), SÁNDOR (1873–1933), Hungarian psychoanalyst and psychiatrist. Born in Miskolc, Hungary, Ferenczi became interested in hypnosis and in 1900 began the practice of neurology and psychiatry in Budapest. Ferenczi was the closest friend of *Freud, whom he first met in 1908, and they exchanged more than 1,000 letters. An inspiring lecturer on psychoanalysis and an outstanding therapist, Ferenczi was the senior member of Freud's group. In 1909 he accompanied Freud to the United States and became a central figure in the psychoanalytic movement. Ferenczi's initial papers (1908) were on psychosexual disturbances, and in papers issued in 1911 he set out for the first time the difference between active and passive homosexuality and its relation to paranoia. In 1913 Ferenczi wrote his classic essay, *Entwicklungsstufen des Wirklichkeitssinnes*, in which he described, on the basis of his analytical experience and observation of children, the child's view of his own omnipotence and the development of his sense of reality. In the works written in this period Ferenczi expanded and checked Freud's findings and indicated new applications and approaches. In 1924 he published a creative and theoretical book: *Versuch einer Genitaltheorie* (*Thalassa: A Theory of Genitality*, 1938). Here he correlated biology with psychology and invented the method of "bioanalysis," relating sexual drives to the act of returning to the womb. Ferenczi developed a technique of active therapy, requesting the patient to act or behave in a certain way. He discussed this technique in an essay (1921) and reviewed it in 1925 with his *Kontraindikazionen der aktiven psychoanalitischen Technik*. In 1926 he published *Further Contributions to the Theory and Technique of Psychoanalysis*, a work which elaborated and systematized his technique and also contained many clinical essays, such as those on hysteria and tics. He was the first to emphasize the great importance of loving bodily contact with the mother for the child's development, as well as the dangers of too intense stimulation of the baby by adults. Freud became highly critical of some of Ferenczi's experiments in technique and by 1931 Ferenczi began to revise some of his methods, as they had not achieved the anticipated results. However, his ideas on the early object relations of the infant and their impact on personality development, and his ideas about the deeper functions of the ego dealt with areas which preoccupy analytical thinking and have produced a number of controversial theories.

BIBLIOGRAPHY: S. Lorand, in: F. Alexander et al. (eds.), *Psychoanalytic Pioneers* (1966), 14–35, incl. bibl.; E. Jones, *The Life and Work of Sigmund Freud*, 2 (1955), index; I. De Forest, *The Leaven of Love* (1954), incl. bibl.; F. Auld, in: IESS, 5 (1968), 367–9, incl. bibl. **ADD. BIBLIOGRAPHY:** E. Falzeder and E. Brabant (eds.), *Correspondence of Sigmund Freud and Sandor Ferenczi*, 3 vols. (1994, 1996, 2000); M. Stanton, *Sandor Ferenczi: Reconsidering Active Intervention* (1993); A.W. Rachman, *Sandor Ferenczi: The Psychotherapist of Tenderness and Passion* (1996); P.L. Rudnytsky, P. Giampieri-Deutsch, and A.Bokay (eds.), *Fernczi's Turn in Psychoanalysis* (1996).

[Louis Miller]

FERKAUF, EUGENE (1921–), U.S. businessman and philanthropist. Born in Brooklyn, N.Y., Ferkauf learned the retailing business from his father, who owned two luggage stores in Manhattan. After serving in World War II, he began his own business career in 1948 with a modest retail discount store in New York. This grew into the E.J. Korvette chain of discount stores, which at the height of its success included 45 department stores and 60 supermarkets. At one point in the early 1960s Korvette was opening one big new store every seven weeks. In 1962 Ferkauf appeared on the cover of *Time* magazine with the banner headline "Discounting Gets Respectable" and a feature story entitled "Everybody Loves a Bargain" (July 6). However, Ferkauf and his executives found it difficult to administer the chain as it grew larger. In 1968 Korvette's merged with Spartans Industries, which abandoned the discount model. Ferkauf resigned from the combine shortly afterward. Five years later the firm was sold to Arlen Realty. Arlen later sold it to a French firm. In 1980, Korvette's ceased operations altogether.

Ferkauf was a prominent contributor to Jewish educational funds in the U.S. and Israel, and endowed a graduate school of social services at Yeshiva University, New York, a high school at Or Yehudah, Israel, and four hospitals to serve underprivileged communities in South America. Ferkauf was also a patron of the arts, as shown by his support of New York's Metropolitan Museum of Modern Art and the Lincoln Center of the Performing Arts. In Israel, he and his wife, Estelle, sponsored the Administration Wing of the Bezalel Academy of Art and Design. Ferkauf was also the main promoter of Atid, a commercial organization set up to stimulate Israel exports to the U.S. He was made an honorary life member of the Board of Governors of the Technion in Haifa. Ferkauf wrote the book *Going into Business: How to Do It, by the Man Who Did It* (1977).

ADD. BIBLIOGRAPHY: R. Sobel, *When Giants Stumble: Classic Business Blunders and How to Avoid Them* (1999); I. Barmash, *The Self-Made Man: Stress and Success American Style* (2003); R. Spector, *Category Killers: The Retail Revolution and Its Impact on Consumer Culture* (2005).

[Joachim O. Ronall / Ruth Beloff (2nd ed.)

FERNANDES VILLAREAL, MANOEL (1608–1652), Portuguese soldier, diplomat, and author. He was a prominent businessman and writer. Born in Lisbon of *Marrano descent, Fernandes Villareal became a captain in the Portuguese Army. He eventually went to live in France, settling in Rouen in about 1638. An agent of the House of Braganza, he was for a time Portuguese consul general in Paris, where he entered the circle of Cardinal Richelieu. Under Richelieu, France welcomed Iberian refugees, many of whom were New Christians. He supported Portugal's efforts to achieve independence and in 1642 he became a close advisor of the Portuguese ambassador, Dom Vasco Luis da Gama. He headed two centers which were in charge of Portuguese propaganda in support of Portuguese independence. As a reward for his services he was appointed to the post of regulating trade between Portugal and France. He prepared some economic programs for the welfare of the newly reestablished Portuguese kingdom and hoped to curtail the power of the Inquisition. He planned the return to Portugal of New Christian merchants. Under his influence an attempt was made to abolish any distinction between Old and New Christians and a pardon was granted in February 1649 to all Portuguese who would return from exile. It was then that Fernandes de Villareal decided to return to Portugal for a visit. While visiting Lisbon in 1649–50, Fernandes Villareal was denounced as a Judaizer by a friar who was a literary rival. The Inquisition uncovered his "New Christian" origin and secret adherence to Judaism, and Fernandes Villareal was condemned to death. He was garroted on Dec. 1, 1652. A few years after his death, some of his relatives officially reverted to Judaism in Leghorn. Fernandes Villareal wrote, in Portuguese and Spanish, works on history, politics, and military techniques. These include his *Epítome genealógico del Duque de Richelieu y discursos políticos* (Pamplona, 1641), a panegyric dedicated to Richelieu. The title of the 1642 edition was *El político cristianíssimo o dicursos políticos sobre algunas acciones de la vida del … Duque de Richelieu.* He was inspired by Machiavelli's *Discorsi* and *Principe.* He also wrote the poem *El color verde a la divina Celia* (Madrid, 1637) and a play, *El Príncipe Vendido* (Paris, 1643). He was destined, however, to be remembered more as a tragic victim of the Inquisition than as a writer. While his works had no influence in Spain, in Portugal they were received with great interest.

BIBLIOGRAPHY: Roth, Marranos, 159–60, 340; J. Caro Baroja, *Judíos en la España moderna y contemporánea*, 2 (1962), 128–9; Kayserling, Bibl, 109. **ADD. BIBLIOGRAPHY:** I.S. Révah, in: *Iberida*, 1 (1959), 181–207; M. Gendreau-Massaloux and C. Hubard Rose, in: REJ, 136 (1977), 368–87; H.P. Salomon, in: *Inquisição*, vol. 2 (1989–90), 765–73.

[Kenneth R. Scholberg / Yom Tov Assis (2nd ed.)]

FERNBERGER, SAMUEL (1887–1956), U.S. psychologist. Born in Pennsylvania, Fernberger received his Ph.D. in psychology from the University of Pennsylvania in 1912. He served as professor at Clark University for eight years, and then at the University of Pennsylvania from 1920. He is best known for his work in psychophysics, sensation, perception, and the history of psychology.

Fernberger wrote an article detailing the early history of the American Psychological Association (APA), a professional organization for psychologists founded in 1892 and incorporated in 1925. Considered a classic in the history of psychology, the article, entitled "The American Psychological Association: A Historical Summary, 1892–1930," was first published in the *Psychological Bulletin* in 1932. In 1937 Fernberger published *Elementary General Psychology.*

[Ruth Beloff (2nd ed.)]

FERNHOF, ISAAC (1868–1919), Hebrew author, editor, and poet. Born in Buchach, Galicia, he was a teacher all his life, first in his native town, then in Zlochow, and finally in Stanislav. During World War I he went to Bohemia, where he taught Galician refugee children. In 1918 he returned to Stanislav, then under Ukrainian rule, and suffered dire poverty and famine. He died there soon after. Fernhof began writing poetry and articles in the late 1880s, and later published *Sifrei Sha'ashu'im* (1896–99), a small literary periodical to which leading writers such as Tchernichowsky, Peretz, Brainin, Klausner, and others contributed. Subsequently he tried unsuccessfully to publish literary journals (*Ha-Ẓa'ir, Ha-Yarden*). A book of his stories, *Me-Aggadot ha-Ḥayyim*, appeared in 1908. He left a series of stories depicting *Mitnaggedim* which were published long after his death as *Sefer ha-Mitnaggedim* (ed. Israel Cohen, 1952). This includes an article published after the appearance of Herzl's *Jewish State* in which Fernhof prophetically refers to the utopian state by the name of "Israel."

BIBLIOGRAPHY: R. Fahn, in: *Ba-Derekh* (March 9, 1934); idem, in: *Haolam*, 32 (1939), 394–5; *Arim ve-Immahot be-Yisrael – Sefer Stanislav* (1952), 182, and index of names; M. Henish, *Mi-Bayit u-mi-Ḥuẓ* (1961), 263–5; Rabbi Binyamin, *Mishpeḥot Soferim* (1960), 136–8; *Sefer Buczacz* (1957), 122–31; I. Cohen, *Sha'ar Soferim* (1962), 397–403.

[Getzel Kressel]

FERRARA, city in N. central Italy, with an ancient and renowned Jewish community. An inscription dating from Roman times and a document of 1088 may relate to local Jewish life. Privileges enjoyed by Jews were recorded in 1275. In the same century two tosafists both named R. Moses b. Meir lived in Ferrara, and perhaps also the philosopher *Hillel b. Samuel of Verona. In the early years of the 14th century some Jews were heavily fined by the Inquisition. Two sonnets by Francesco di Vannozzo (1376) reflect the popular resentment against certain Jews. About 1435 *Elijah of Ferrara settled in Jerusalem. From the middle of the 15th century a period of prosperity began for the community, thanks to the protection of the House of Este. In 1448, on Lionello d' Este's request, Pope Nicholas V curbed the anti-Jewish sermons of the friars; in 1451 Duke Borso declared that he would protect the Jews who entered his lands; in 1473 Ercole I, in opposition to papal demands, protected his Jewish subjects, particularly the moneylenders. In 1481 he authorized Samuel Melli of Rome to buy a mansion in Ferrara and turn it into a synagogue, which is still used. At this time the geographer Abraham Farissol lived in Ferrara, as well as Abraham Sarfati, teacher of Hebrew at the University of Ferrara, and, in 1477, the printer Abraham b. Ḥayyim the Dyer (dei Tintori) of Pesaro (see below).

The policy of giving refuge to persecuted Jews, especially those who could prove useful, was continued by all successive Este dukes. In 1492, when the first refugees from Spain appeared in Italy, Ercole I allowed some of them to settle in Ferrara, promising to let them have their own leaders and judges, permitting them to practice commerce and medicine, and granting them tax reductions. This was the beginning of the Spanish community in Ferrara, which set up its own synagogue and separate administration. In 1532 Ercole II issued another permit allowing Jews from Bohemia and other countries in Central Europe to come and settle in Ferrara. This was the origin of the German group in Ferrara which also established its own synagogue. In 1524 and 1538 the same duke gave encouragement to the Marranos and in 1553 they were specifically allowed to return to the Jewish faith. In 1540 an invitation to settle in Ferrara was extended to the harassed Jews of Milan and one year later to those banished from the kingdom of Naples. In 1569, when the Jews were expelled from the Papal States (except Rome and Ancona), many from Bologna settled in Ferrara. In the middle of the 16th century there were ten synagogues in Ferrara. However, although the dukes spared their Jews from Church oppression, they allowed the Talmud to be burned in 1553. In 1554 a congress of delegates from the Italian communities was held in Ferrara to decide on precautionary measures, including the precensorship of Hebrew books.

Among the outstanding personalities in Ferrara at that time were Don Samuel *Abrabanel, the last leader of Neapolitan Jewry, the Marrano Gracia *Nasi, *Amatus Lusitanus, who taught medicine at the University of Ferrara, the *Usque family, and the engineer Abraham Colorni. In the sphere of Jewish learning there were the poets Jacob *Fano and Abraham dei Galicchi *Jagel, the physicians Moses and Azriel *Alatino, the chronicler Samuel Usque, his kinsman the printer Abraham Usque (see below), and the polymath Azariah dei *Rossi.

[Alexander Carlebach]

When Ferrara passed under the rule of the Church in 1598, the condition of the Jews grew much worse. In the same year the Jewish *badge was introduced. In the following year all real estate had to be sold, synagogues were limited to three, one for each rite, and the loan banks were closed; however this last decree was repealed a short time later, the banks being finally closed only in 1683. In 1624 the construction of a ghetto was decreed and two years later the Jews were confined to it. The Jews were forced to be present at conversionist sermons and Jewish physicians were forbidden to attend to Christians. A similar state of affairs persisted throughout the 17th and 18th centuries; from time to time the situation was exacerbated by mob attacks on the ghetto (1648, 1651, 1705, 1747, 1754) and by a *blood libel charge in 1721. In spite of this the life of Jews in Ferrara was far more tolerable than in Rome.

The Jewish population numbered 1,500 persons in 1601, was at much the same level in 1703 (328 families), and rose to 2,000 in the 19th century. Outstanding personalities included the rabbi and physician Isaac *Lampronti, author of the talmudic encyclopedia *Paḥad Yiẓḥak*, and the rabbis Jacob Daniel *Olmo, poet, and Solomon *Finzi, author of an introduction to the Talmud. In 1796, after the French occupation, Jews were granted equal civil rights and in 1797 the ghetto's gates were removed. The successive alternations in Ferrara of Austrian, French, and finally, in 1814, papal rule were reflected in the vicissitudes of Jewish life. In 1826 the Jews were locked up in the ghetto once more, but in 1859–60 they finally obtained their freedom when Ferrara became part of the Italian kingdom. For the next 80 years there was a new period of prosperity, Jews being appointed to high public offices in the town's administration and taking a prominent part in the affairs of the Italian Jewish community. Renzo Ravenna was *sindaco* ("mayor") before the Fascist crisis, and Felice Ravenna was president of the Union of Jewish Communities from 1933 to 1937. In spite of this the Jewish population dwindled because of steady emigration.

[Attilio Milano]

The Holocaust Period and After

In 1936 the community of Ferrara had 760 members. On Sept. 24, 1941, the synagogue was devastated by the fascists. During the autumn-winter 1943 about 200 Jews were sent to extermination camps, of whom only five returned. Three more Jews were killed in the streets on Nov. 14–15, 1943. The Jewish population in Ferrara was reduced to 200 at the end of the war. The population further dropped to 150 in 1970 and 100 at the beginning of the 21st century.

[Sergio DellaPergola]

Hebrew Printing in Ferrara

Under the enlightened rule of the House of Este, Hebrew printing flourished twice for short periods in Ferrara in the 15th and 16th centuries. In 1477 *Abraham b. Ḥayyim the Dyer (dei Tintori; מִן הַצּוֹבְעִים; *min ha-ẓove'im*), of Pesaro, using Abraham *Conat's type, printed here Levi b. Gerson's commentary on Job, and finished printing the edition of Tur, *Yoreh De'ah* which Conat had begun in Mantua. The second somewhat longer period extended from 1551 to 1558, when first Samuel ibn Askara Ẓarefati of Pesaro and then Abraham Usque, partly with the former's assistance, printed well over 30 books in Ferrara. Among the first was Isaac Abrabanel's *Ma'yenei ha-Yeshu'ah* and Jedaiah ha-Penini's *Beḥinat Olam*. Under Usque, halakhic, theological, and liturgical items were printed, among them the first editions of Menahem ibn Ẓeraḥ's *Ẓedah la-Derekh* (1554), Ḥasdai Crescas' *Or Adonai* (1556), Jonah Gerondi's *Issur ve-Hetter*, and Jacob Fano's *Shiltei ha-Gibborim* (including an elegy on the Marrano martyrs of Ancona), 1556. Apparently complaints by the Church about this publication led to the closing of the press. Usque also printed a number of works mainly, but not exclusively, of Jewish significance in Spanish and Portuguese, including the Ferrara Bible (1553) and the "Consolation for the Tribulations of Israel" by Samuel Usque (1553). Toward the end of the 17th century an attempt at reviving Hebrew printing at Ferrara was made by the non-Jewish printer Girolamo Filoni, who printed in 1693 a handsome small prayer book (*Siddur mi-Berakhah*), compiled by J. Nisim and Abraham Ḥayyim da Fano, printers from Mantua. Filoni also issued a broadsheet primer with the Hebrew alphabet and some basic prayers. Shortly after, Filoni melted down his Hebrew type and converted it into a Latin font. The *takkanot* of the Ferrara community of 1767 provided for less gifted pupils of the Jewish school (*Talmud Torah*) to attend the workshop of the printer Salvador Serri to learn the craft of Hebrew printing, both for their own good and for the preservation of this important craft (see Asaf, *Mekorot* 2 (1930), 206–8). No other evidence of Hebrew printing in Ferrara at that period is available.

BIBLIOGRAPHY: A. Pesaro, *Memorie storiche sulla comunità israelitica ferrarese* (1878); idem, *Appendice alle memorie…* (1880); A. Balleti, *Gli ebrei e gli estensi* (1930²); Milano, Bibliotheca, index; idem, in: RMI, 33 (1967), 364ff.; Kaufmann, in: REJ, 20 (1890), 34–72; Perreau, in: *Vessillo israelitico*, 27 (1879), 108–10, 139–42; Terracini, in: RMI, 18 (1952), 3–11, 63–72, 113–21; G.B. De'Rossi, *De typographia hebraeo-ferrariensi commentarius historicus…* (1780); Magrini, in: RMI, 10 (1935/36), 126–32; Roth, in: HUCA, 10 (1935), 466–8; idem, in: *Modern Language Review*, 38 (1943), 307–17; Ḥ.D. Friedberg, *Toledot ha-Defus ha-Ivri be-Italyah* (1956²), 26ff.

°**FERRER, VICENTE** (c. 1350–1419), Dominican friar, canonized by the Catholic Church. Some scholars consider that he was directly responsible for the anti-Jewish persecutions in Spain of 1391. However, it seems that he was on his way to Avignon at the time. In a Lenten sermon delivered in Valencia after the disorders, he condemned the behavior of the rioters. Ferrer advocated conversion to Christianity from conviction and emphasized more than once the Jewish origin of Jesus. Nevertheless his appearances provoked mass demonstrations accompanied by anti-Jewish outbursts. These took place in particular in the first and second decades of the 15th century. The conversion of *Solomon ha-Levi, rabbi of Burgos, and possibly that of Don Samuel *Abrabanel of Seville, are attributable to Ferrer's direct influence.

After the 1391 persecutions, when the problem of *Conversos arose, Ferrer initiated the policy toward the Jews adopted by the antipope Benedict XIII, by Ferdinand I of Aragon for whose choice as king in 1409 Ferrer was responsible, and by the queen mother Catalina, regent of Castile. This policy was embodied in social and communal, economic and legal restrictions in Aragon and Castile. In 1412, Ferrer collaborated with Pablo de Santa María in formulating the laws of Valladolid directed against the Jews. He used his influence to implement a program to evict the Jews from their quarters lest they should have a bad influence on the Christians, i.e., the Conversos, who still lived in their former homes.

Throughout this period, Ferrer went from place to place preaching. As a result of his sermons, the populace more than once refused to sell the Jews food supplies and other necessities. The Jews of Tamarite de Litera complained to Ferdinand I that they were afraid that anti-Jewish riots would occur as a result of Ferrer's sermons, and the king ordered the city officials to protect them (May 25, 1414). The Jews of Aynsa moved out of town when they heard that Ferrer was coming to preach there, and returned only after he had left (1414). Ferdinand compelled the Jews and Moors to listen to Ferrer's sermons and imposed heavy fines upon those who were absent. At the height of the disputation of *Tortosa (November 1413) Ferdinand wrote to Ferrer in Majorca, asking him to go to Tortosa in order to bring about the conversion of the Jews assembled there. From there he was to proceed to Saragossa, where the conversion of numerous Jews was also anticipated. A vessel was placed at the friar's disposal for this purpose. In May 1414 Ferdinand wrote to Ferrer rejoicing over the conversion of 122 Jews in Guadalajara. Ferrer evidently attempted to persuade the Jews to come to the baptismal font by all means except physical force. In 1408 he was in Italy where *Bernardino da Siena heard him preach in Alessandria and was thereby stimulated to imitate him.

Ferrer wrote several theological tracts but his sermons, numbering over 6,000, form his principal work. These he delivered in Catalan and they were then summarized in Latin.

BIBLIOGRAPHY: Baer, Spain, index s.v. *Vincent Ferrer*; J.E. Martínez Ferrando, *San Vicente Ferrer y la casa Real de Aragón* (1955), incl. bibl.

[Haim Beinart and Zvi Avneri]

FERRIS, IRIS (1910–1970), Indian educator and social worker. Iris Ferris, who was born in Calcutta, became headmistress of one of the city's secondary schools while still in her twenties. She was active in the local Jewish Women's League. A member of the Girl Guide movement from childhood, she rose to become commissioner for training in West Bengal. In 1953 she settled in London and joined the staff of the world bureau of the Girl Guide movement of which she soon became general secretary.

[Flower Elias]

FERRIZUEL, JOSEPH HA-NASI (called **Cidellus**: **"Little Cid"** or **"Chief"**; d.c. 1145), physician of Alfonso VI of Castile. He was allotted property in and around Toledo after its capture in 1085 during the Christian reconquest. Ferrizuel was active on behalf of the Jews of Guadalajara when this town was occupied the same year. His position at court is indicated by the part he played in proposing a marriage for the king's daughter Urraca on behalf of the Castilian nobles. When the proposal was rejected by Alfonso, Ferrizuel lost favor. Ferrizuel gave assistance to the Jews who fled from areas under Muslim rule in Spain to the Christian kingdoms in the north. However, Abraham ibn Daud relates that he treated the Karaites ruthlessly and expelled them from all the citadels in Castile. Judah Halevi dedicated several poems to him and to his nephew Solomon b. Ferrizuel, who was murdered on his return from a successful political mission abroad, and subsequently mourned by the poet. In 1110, a year after Alfonso's death, Ferrizuel was one of the witnesses and signatories to a charter of immunities granted by Queen Urraca. Nothing about Ferrizuel is known after this date. He had probably died by 1145, when Alfonso VII gave his property to the Cathedral of Toledo.

BIBLIOGRAPHY: Baer, Spain, index s.v. *Joseph Ferrizuel*; Baer, Urkunden, 2 (1936), 14, 552 n. l; idem, in: *Zion*, 1 (1936), 17; Abraham ibn Daud, *Book of Tradition – Sefer ha-Qabbalah*, ed. and tr. by G. Cohen (1967), index.

[Haim Beinart]

FESELA (Federación Sefaradí Latinoamericana), roof organization of the Sephardi communities of Latin America, affiliated to the World Sephardi Federation as well as to the World Zionist Organization. FESELA was founded in 1972 in Lima (Peru) during the Conference of Jewish Communities in Latin America by a group of young Sephardi leaders representing the new leadership of Sephardim born in Latin America. They were seeking representation in the World Zionist Organization not through political parties but on the basis of their ethnic identity – as Sephardim.

The executive of FESELA is rotated: every two years a different president and secretary – from a different country – must be elected, and the seat of FESELA moves to their respective country. Membership in FESELA is institutional and not personal, and each country is entitled to one vote. In addition to Argentina, Brazil, Colombia, Chile, Guatemala, Mexico, Panama, Peru, Uruguay, and Venezuela, the Cuban Sephardi community of Miami is also active on the board.

The main objectives of FESELA are to represent the Sephardi communities of Latin America, to strengthen Sephardi identity, to combat assimilation, to promote the Zionist cause. and to support the State of Israel. FESELA promotes cultural activities of Sephardim in Latin America and supports the publication of *Sefardica*, a journal published by CIDICSEF – Centro de Investigación y Difusión de la Cultura Sefaradí (Center for the Study and Diffusion of Sephardi Culture) in Buenos Aires.

[Margalit Bejarano (2nd ed.)]

FESTIVALS (Heb. חַג, *ḥag*; מוֹעֵד, *mo'ed*; or יוֹם טוֹב, *yom tov*).

Introduction

The root of חַג is חָגַג *ḥagog*, to celebrate, or possibly חוּג *ḥug*, to go round. It is related to the Arabic *ḥajja* which means to go on a pilgrimage from which comes ḥajj, the pilgrimage to Mecca. The term *mo'ed* means an appointed place, time, or season.

The festivals can be divided into two main categories each of which can be subdivided: (1) those commanded by the Pentateuch, and (2) those added later.

The Pentateuchal festivals are (a) the *Sabbath (not strictly a festival), (b) the three pilgrim festivals, *Passover, *Shavuot, and *Sukkot, with Shemini Aẓret which is considered in some respects a festival in its own right, (c) the New Year (*Rosh Ha-Shanah) and the Day of *Atonement, (d) *Rosh Ḥodesh, the first day of the lunar month. These divisions can however be still further divided. Rosh Ha-Shanah and the Day of Atonement, while obviously belonging to a single pattern, nevertheless differ from each other completely. The three *pilgrim festivals, too, although similar in many aspects differ in detail. There is, furthermore, a decided difference between the first and last festival days and the middle days termed *ḥol ha-mo'ed* (see below). The second category too can be subdivided: *Purim and *Ḥanukkah; the first being biblical (Book of Esther) and the second from the Hasmonean period; memorial days such as *Lag ba-Omer (medieval) and the 15th of *Av (mishnaic) to which may be added *Tu bi-Shevat; thirdly, certain festival days added in modern times to mark historic events of Jewish importance. Apart from the above are also festival days of individuals or communities to record salvation or a similar event.

A festival is characterized by three factors: (1) rejoicing, which mostly takes the form of ceremonial meals (with the exception of the Day of Atonement), and, on the more important biblical festivals, the prohibition of work; (2) the liturgy (or in Temple times, the special sacrificial service); and (3) special ceremonials of the festival, such as eating of *mazzot* on Passover (biblical injunction), lighting of the candles of Ḥannukah (talmudic), and the planting of saplings on Tu bi-Shevat (custom).

The liturgy is in effect dictated by the type of festival. The main changes from everyday prayer are mainly in (a) the *Amidah, (b) the addition of *Hallel, (c) the reading of the *Torah, (d) the *Musaf service representing the special sacrifices of the day (for details, see below – Liturgy). It can generally be stated that the less important the festival, the less changes are made in the liturgy. On Sabbath, the pilgrim festivals, and the high holidays, it is customary for the woman to light *candles accompanied by a special benediction, and (except Sabbath) also by the *she-heḥeyanu*, whereas the man makes sanctification (*Kiddush*) over wine (except on the Day of Atonement). It is interesting to note that the national day of mourning, Ninth of *Av, is also regarded in a sense as a festival, as it is termed *"mo'ed"* in Lamentations (1:15), and, according to tradition, will be the greatest festival in the time to come (with reference to Jer. 31:13).

In the Bible

The festivals mentioned in the Pentateuch as "feasts" (חַגִּים *ḥaggim*) are Passover (Ex. 12:14), also called "the feast of unleavened bread"; Shavuot, otherwise "the feast of harvest" (Ex. 23:16) or the "day of the first fruits"; and *Sukkot, also known as "the feast of ingathering" (*ibid.*) and sometimes called simply "feast" (*ḥag*) in the Bible. The sages, too, mostly use the term *ḥag* by itself to refer to Sukkot. Common to all three festivals is the pilgrimage to Jerusalem from which the term (שָׁלֹשׁ רְגָלִים "the three pilgrim festivals") is derived. The term "appointed seasons" (*mo'adim*) in the Pentateuch, however, includes also Rosh Ha-Shanah and the Day of Atonement, as in the verse "These are the appointed seasons of the Lord, even holy convocations, which ye shall proclaim in their appointed season" (Lev. 23:4). At times the term "appointed seasons" is used for all the days which are "holy convocations," including the Sabbath. Rosh Ḥodesh, on which work is not forbidden by biblical injunction and which is not mentioned at all with the festivals in Leviticus, is nevertheless included among "the appointed seasons" in the section on sacrifices (Num. 28:11). It seems that the prophets, too, sometimes use "appointed seasons" to refer to the Sabbath and Rosh Ḥodesh though mostly these days are not indicated. In one instance only the three pilgrim festivals are included "on the appointed seasons, three times in the year" (II Chron. 8:13). Thus the term "season" generally has a wider meaning in the Bible than "feast" because only the three pilgrim festivals are called "feast," whereas "season" usually comprises also Rosh Ha-Shanah and the Day of Atonement. A day of feasting and joy, whether fixed by individuals or established by the whole people to be observed by succeeding generations, which does not entail special sacrifices, is called *yom tov* (I Sam. 25:8; Esth. 8:17).

The festivals, like the Sabbath, have their origin in Divine commandments. Leviticus commands not only "it is a Sabbath unto the Lord" (23:3) and "the Sabbaths of the Lord," but also "the appointed seasons of the Lord" (23:4, 44). In the Bible the common expression "feast of the Lord" (see Hos. 9:5) or "a feast to the Lord" refers to Passover as well as to Shavuot and to Sukkot. Similarly, the festival which the children of Israel were to celebrate with sacrifices to the Lord in the wilderness is termed "feast." Aaron, too, at the incident of the golden calf, proclaims "Tomorrow shall be a feast to the Lord" (Ex. 32:5).

The Source of the Festivals

In the pagan religions of the ancient East, the festivals were established by man in order to find favor with the deity and prevent disasters. It was against this concept that the prophets militated (cf. *Sacrifices). The biblical concept, on the other hand, is the exact antithesis, for not only are the festivals commanded by God but the service on these days as well. The festival sacrifices (*Musaf*) are not offered for any material reward, but in obedience to the Divine command. Among the sins of *Jeroboam is mentioned his ordainment of a feast "like unto the feast that is in Judah" on the 15th of the eighth month "in the month which he had devised of his own heart," and his bringing sacrifices on it (I Kings 12:32–33). Apart from this incident, there is no mention in the Bible of alterations to the festivals as stated in the Pentateuch or the creation of new ones; "the feast of the Lord from year to year in Shiloh" (Judg. 21:19) is seemingly one of the festivals mentioned in the Pentateuch. In the Bible various reasons are given for the festivals. Some are specifically connected with the exodus from Egypt. Passover, the feast of unleavened bread, is celebrated on the anniversary of the day that God led the children of Israel out of Egypt. The paschal lamb was commanded for all generations to commemorate "that He passed over the houses of the children of Israel in Egypt" (Ex. 12:27) and the unleavened bread is in memory of the haste with which the Israelites left Egypt. Similarly, the reason for dwelling in tabernacles on Sukkot is "that your generations may know that I made the children of Israel to dwell in booths when I brought them out of the land of Egypt" (Lev. 23:43); and even for Shavuot it is said, "And thou shalt remember that thou wast a bondman in Egypt; and thou shalt observe and do these statutes" (Deut. 16:12; cf. Naḥmanides ad loc.; cf. Deut. 5:15 on Sabbath). The recital on the offering of the first fruits also testifies to the exodus from Egypt (Deut. 26:5–10). Together with their theological-historical sources, the festivals are also connected with the annual agricultural cycle. Shavuot is the festival "of the first fruits of wheat harvest" (Ex. 34:22) on which two loaves made from the new wheat crop were offered; hence its names: "the harvest feast" and "the day of the first fruits." Sukkot is "the feast of the ingathering" at the end of the agricultural year when the ingathering from the threshing floor and the winepress is completed. Even Passover, in the spring, apart from the commemoration of the exodus, has an agricultural basis. The *Omer* sacrifice of the new barley was offered on the second day of the festival and permitted the partaking of the new grain crop.

The festivals thus seem to be rooted in two distinct sources which, according to some scholars, are independent of each other. They claim that the agricultural festivals antedate their theological-historical source, specifically pointing to the fact that Passover and Sukkot are celebrated in seasons when night and day are roughly of equal length. Their contention, however, is unacceptable since each festival in the Pentateuch is based on two distinct types of reasons stated sometimes even in the same paragraph. In the case of Passover, the agricultural motif is added to the clearly historical aspect of the festival, while with Sukkot, the historical aspect of the festival is added to the agricultural although this historical aspect is not specifically connected with the time of the year of Sukkot. At any rate the distinction between "the ancient folk festivals" and the later "theological festivals" is doubtful. Contrary to the three pilgrim festivals which are mentioned in the Bible together with their double motifs, no reason, save it being a Divine precept, is given for the day of "memorial proclaimed with the blast of horns" (i.e., the later Rosh Ha-Shanah), celebrated on the first day of the seventh month. The Day of Atonement, however, was inaugurated for the atonement of sins.

Celebration of the Festival

The Pentateuch cites two specific commandments in connection with the "seasons of the Lord, holy convocations": work is forbidden and, as a remembrance, sacrifices are to be brought to the accompaniment of trumpet blowing before the Lord (Num. 10:10). The Bible also specifically commands rejoicing on Shavuot (Deut. 16:11) and especially on Sukkot (Lev. 23:40; Deut. 16:14–15; cf. Neh. 8:17). Such commandments, however, were common to all the festivals, as is proven for instance by

TISHRI · HESHVAN · KISLEV · TEVET · SHEVAT · ADAR · NISAN · IYYAR · SIVAN · TAMMUZ · AV · ELUL

TISHRI
1 ROSH HASHANAH (New Year)
2 ROSH HASHANAH (New Year)
3 Fast of Gedaliah
Ten Days of Penitence
10 YOM KIPPUR (Day of Atonement)
15 SUKKOT (Tabernacles)
16
17 18 19 ḥol ha-mo'ed
20
21 Hoshanah Rabba
22 SHEMINI AZERET / SIMḤAT TORAH
23 SIMḤAT TORAH

KISLEV
25 26 27 28 29 30 ḤANUKKAH

TEVET
1 2
10 Fast of Tenth of Tevet

SHEVAT
15 Tu bi-Shevat

ADAR
13 Fast of Esther
14 PURIM
15 Shushan Purim

NISAN
14 Fast of the Firstborn
15 PESAḤ (Passover)
16
17 18 19 ḥol ha-mo'ed
20
21 PESAḤ Last Day
22
27 Yom ha-Sho'ah (Day of Holocaust)

IYYAR
5 YOM HAAZMAUT (Independence Day)
18 Lag ba-Omer

SIVAN
6 SHAVUOT (Pentecost)
7

TAMMUZ
17 Fast of Seventeenth of Tamuz
Three Weeks of Mourning

AV
9 Fast of Tishah be-Av
15 Fifteenth of Av
Nine Days

Counting of the Omer: 2, 3, 5, 6, 7, 8, 9, 10, 11, 12, 13, 14, 15, 16, 17, 18, 19, 21, 22, 23, 24, 25, 26, 27, 28, 29, 30, 31, 32, 33, 34, 35, 36, 37, 38, 39, 40, 41, 42, 43, 44, 45, 46, 47, 48, 49

Legend:
JEWISH HOLIDAY
MINOR HOLIDAY
Second day holiday in Diaspora only
✡ Pilgrimage festivals
✳ Counting of the Omer (Sefirah period) begins
○ Seliḥot prayer
† Simḥat Torah in Israel only
For Sephardi and Ashkenazi dates of *Seliḥot* prayer see *Seliḥot*.

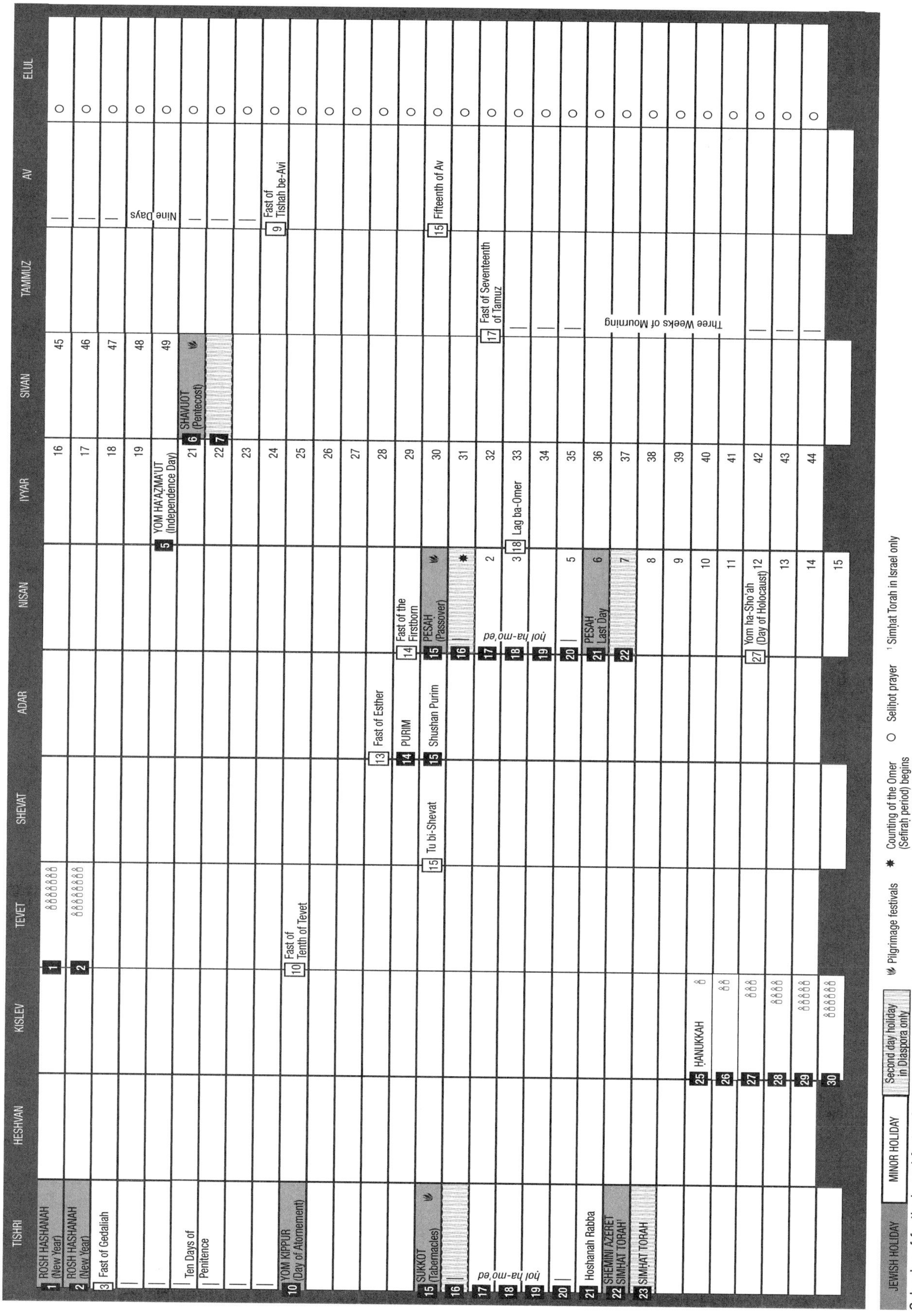

Calendar of festivals and fasts of the Jewish year (for Sephardi and Ashkenazi dates of *Seliḥot* prayer see *Seliḥot*).

the great rejoicings on Passover (Ezra 6:22; II Chron. 30:21ff.) and those "on the first day of the seventh month" (Neh. 8:2, 9ff.). These celebrations, especially when the people gathered in the Temple, are testified to by Isaiah: "Ye shall have a song as in the night when a feast is hallowed; And gladness of heart, as when one goeth with a pipe to come into the mountain of the Lord to the Rock of Israel" (30:29). The festivals are therefore referred to as days of mirth, gladness, and joy. It seems that the rejoicing of the people at the golden calf – "[they] offered burnt offerings, and brought peace offerings and the people sat down to eat and drink and rose up to make merry" (Ex. 32:6) – was typical of all festive celebrations, in which the huge feast as well as dancing occupied a prominent place. The celebrations were, however, limited by the sanctity of the festival, and there is no hint in the Bible of the orgies, wildness, and promiscuous abandon connected with the pagan festivals in the ancient Near East. The Pentateuch even stresses the fact that the rejoicings are of the whole community, including slaves, and commands not to forget the levite, the proselyte, the orphan, or the widow (Deut. 16:11, 14). During the early Second Temple period it was customary to send presents to the needy on the festivals (Neh. 8:10–12).

In the Apocrypha and Hellenistic Jewish Literature

During the early Second Temple period the laws of the Sabbath and festivals came to be very strictly observed. The festivals were celebrated with great rejoicings and it was customary to invite the poor to the feasting (Tob. 2:1–2). Many would go up to Jerusalem on all the festivals. During the persecutions of Antiochus, observance of the Sabbath and festivals was forbidden. *Demetrius, however, declared the Sabbaths, New Moons, and festivals, including three days before and after, to be holidays for all Jews in the Seleucid kingdom (testified to in his letter to Jonathan the Maccabee; I Macc. 10:34).

In contrast to the Greek and Roman festival celebrations which were accompanied by gluttonous, drunken, and bacchanalian revelries, Hellenistic Jewish writers stressed the uniqueness of the Jewish festivals. *Philo claims that the cessation of work on the festival was a possible danger since eating and drinking arouse lust and other low instincts. Giving vent to these feelings without restriction could lead to vice and limitless evil since the festival would serve as a protective means against retribution. The lawgiver therefore did not permit his people to celebrate their festivals in the way of other nations but commanded them first to purify themselves through the restriction of their desires for pleasure at the very time of their celebrations. Then they were to gather at the Temple to participate in the hymns, prayers, and sacrifices so that the place, the sight, and the service would influence their finer senses – sight and hearing – with a spirit of piety. Last but not least, by commanding the sacrifice of a sin-offering, he warned the people to stop sinning; for it seems that a person would not transgress at the very time he asks for forgiveness. Those gathered for the festive banquet do not come to stuff themselves with meat and wine like other nations, but through prayers and psalms follow the tradition of their forefathers. Therefore the Day of Atonement is also a festival though the partaking of food is forbidden and there is no wild rejoicing, merrymaking, and dancing accompanied by song and music which arouse uncontrollable desires. Ignorance of the nature of true happiness leads people to assume that on the festivals joy is to be achieved through physical indulgences (Philo, Spec. 2:193–4). Philo further states that the true significance of the festival is to find pleasure and enjoyment through meditation about the world and the harmony existing in it (*ibid.*, 2:52). Were man's virtue constantly to rule his desires, his whole life, from his birth to the day he dies, would be one long festival (*ibid.*, 2:42).

In Talmudic Literature

The term *ḥaggim*, as referring to Jewish festivals, hardly occurs in rabbinical literature (except in prayers which are in an archaic language). Instead, the festivals mentioned in the Bible are called *mo'adot*. *Mo'ed* (though not *ha-mo'ed*) in the singular is mostly applied to the intermediate days, especially to distinguish them from festival days on which no work at all is allowed. These are usually called *yom tov*. As in the Bible, *yom tov* was also applied in rabbinic literature to days of rejoicing (general or private) not mentioned in the Pentateuch, and on which work was allowed. These were either new festivals ordained for all times or days of rejoicing for certain events. It is doubtful whether the Day of Atonement was included in the term *yom tov* (but see Ta'an. 4:8).

The commandment concerning the feast of unleavened bread, that "… no manner of work shall be done in them…, save that which every man must eat, that only may be done by you" (Ex. 12:16), was interpreted by the sages to mean that work, for purposes of eating, is allowed on all those festivals (Sif. Num. 147) on which "servile work" is prohibited by the Pentateuch. (In contrast to the Sabbath and the Day of Atonement where it is ordained "ye shall do no work.") The types of work forbidden on the Sabbath but allowed on *yom tov* for the purpose of eating (Beẓah 5:2) are kneading, baking, slaughtering, skinning, salting, cutting, burning, and carrying (the last two are also permitted for purposes other than eating; Beẓah 12a–b). Hunting, reaping, sheaf binding, threshing, winnowing, selecting, and grinding are forbidden (as to sifting, opinion is divided). Types of work for the indirect preparation of food (מכשירי אוכל נפש) are permitted. The differentiation between the types of work allowed and those forbidden is apparently based on customs prevalent at the time. Except for the work permitted for the sake of food and some other minor allowances made (see Beẓah 5:1), everything forbidden on the Sabbath is also forbidden on the festivals. Moreover, the prohibition of handling *mukẓeh (non-usable) objects is stricter on the festivals than on the Sabbath so that the festival prohibitions should not be taken lightly (Beẓah 2a–b).

The festivals are also similar to the Sabbath in rejoicing and in honoring the day. All halakhic Midrashim interpret the term "holy convocation" to mean that the festivals are to be sanctified "with food and drink and clean clothes" and "the Day of Atonement, on which there is no food or drink, the Torah states that one must honor it with clean clothes" (Shab. 119a). It was usual to cut one's hair before the festivals. Similarly, it was the custom, later incorporated in the *halakhah*, not to work or eat in the late afternoon preceding the festival. In the Middle Ages, it became customary to light a candle on the eve of the festival and to recite a blessing, as on the Sabbath. Rejoicing on the festival involved eating and drinking (concerning the prohibition of fasting see Judith 8:6; TJ, Ta'an. 2:12) and giving presents to the women and children. During the tannaitic period the sages disputed the question as to how a person should spend the festival: "R. Eliezer says that a person should either eat and drink or sit and study on the festival; R. Joshua declares that a person's time should be divided between eating and drinking and the house of learning." R. Johanan, the *amora*, found support in the Scriptures for both opinions (Pes. 68b; cf. Beẓah 15b; Sif. Deut. 135, is similar to R. Joshua's opinion). The *amoraim* also disagreed on the similar question as to whether the festivals were meant for the study of Torah, or whether eating and drinking was the main reason and permission to study the Torah on them but a secondary consideration (TJ, Shab. 15:3). According to the sources, it seems that it was customary to go to the *bet ha-midrash* both on the eve of the festival as well as in the morning. Prayers, however, were shortened because of the festive meal. The sages, while stating that "the festivals were given to Israel only for their own pleasure" (S. Buber (ed.), *Midrash Tanḥuma* (1885), Mid. Tanḥuma Gen. 4), nevertheless noted the difference between Israel and the nations: "You grant the nations many festivals and they eat, drink, and are wanton, they go to the theater, the circus, and anger You by word and deed; but Israel is not so. You grant them festivals and they eat, drink, and rejoice, and go to the synagogues and *battei midrash* ("houses of learning") and multiply their prayers, their festival offerings, and their sacrifices" (PdRK 340–1). It seems that R. Joshua's opinion ("half to the Lord and half for yourselves") was practiced and became *halakhah*. However, practices of drunkenness and licentiousness are also mentioned (Beẓah 4a; Kid. 81a); R. Abba bar Memel, a Palestinian *amora*, states, "Did they not forbid work on the intermediate days only in order that people should eat, drink, and diligently study the Torah? But they eat, drink, and are wanton" (TJ, MK 2:3) – exactly as the Midrash describes the gentile nations.

Paul opposed the observance of the Sabbath and the festivals (Gal. 4:10; Col. 2:16). Traces of the Jewish-Christian dispute concerning the festivals are found in the Midrash (S. Buber (ed.), *Midrash Tanḥuma* (1885), *Pinḥas*, para. 17). The sharp condemnation by the sages of "he who despises the festivals" (Avot 3:12; Pes. 118a) is probably directed against the Christian heretics, and probably because of them the observance of the Sabbath and the festivals was stressed so strongly in Ereẓ Israel. Later, in the Middle Ages, Judah Halevi states that the festivals were the main factor which upheld Israel in its exile (*Kuzari* 3:10).

The Intermediate Days

Apart from the laws governing the *musaf* sacrifices on the festivals, nothing is stated about the festival days following the first day of Passover and Sukkot, respectively, which the sages called *ḥolo shel mo'ed* or just *mo'ed*. They taught that these days are also to be considered as days of "holy convocation." Only partial work is permitted on them for "the Torah gave the sages the power of determining on which day it is forbidden to do work and on which day it is allowed; which work is forbidden and which allowed" (Sif. Deut. 135). Generally, work which prevents deterioration or loss is permitted on the intermediate days; where this is not the case, work is forbidden. It is forbidden to delay work in order to do it on the intermediate days except for public works. In Ereẓ Israel stringent laws were imposed whereby no work at all was done, even if it was required for the festival itself. The *halakhah*, however, conformed to the Babylonian practice which allowed some work (as mentioned above). All must rejoice on the intermediate days; thus marriage is not permitted on these days as rejoicing should not be mixed, *ein me'arevim simḥah be-simḥah* (MK 8b).

[Moshe David Herr]

Second Days of Festivals

In the Diaspora an extra day (in Heb. *yom tov sheni shel galuyyot*) is added to each of the biblical festival days, except for *ḥol ha-mo'ed* and the Day of Atonement. The practice originated because of the uncertainty in the Diaspora of the day on which the Sanhedrin announced the New Moon. Later, when astronomical calculations were relied upon, the sages declared that the custom should nevertheless be accepted as permanent. Although the Day of Atonement was an exception, as a double fast day was considered too difficult, there were individuals who observed two days. Rosh Ha-Shanah, on the other hand, gradually came to be observed as a two-day festival even in Ereẓ Israel; beginnings of the custom here, too, are to be found in the Second Temple period (RH 4:4), although it became universal only in the Middle Ages. With regard to Passover and Sukkot, the first day of *ḥol ha-mo'ed* was observed as a full festival day in the Diaspora while an additional day was added at the end. Thus on Passover a second *seder* is held on the second night and an eighth day is added. The day following Shemini Aẓeret at the completion of Sukkot became known as Simḥat Torah, the "Rejoicing of the Law." As long as the new moon was determined by visual evidence, there was no fixed date for Shavuot, so that the day of the festival was not in any doubt as it was always on the 50th day counting from the second day of Passover, which day would have been ratified in good time by the Sanhedrin messengers. Despite this, a second day was observed in the Diaspora for Shavuot as well. It would appear that certain sources regard the second day as a punishment and that for its observance no reward is to be expected (TJ, Eruv. 3:9). The only difference in observance between the additional days and regular festival days is in the practice concerning burial, the use of medicine (Sh. Ar., OḤ, 496:2), and laws regarding *nolad* (the appearance or creation of something not previously in existence). An egg, for instance, which was laid on the first day of the festival remains forbidden all that day but may be eaten on the second day (*ibid.* 513:5). On the second day of Rosh Ha-Shanah, however, *nolad* is not permitted to be used because the two days are considered one long day. Certain trends in Conservative Judaism have made the second festival day optional, while the Reform has abolished it altogether, even for Rosh Ha-Shanah.

A person from Ereẓ Israel who temporarily visits the Diaspora has to observe the additional day when in company, so as not to arouse controversy (*ibid.* 496:3, cf. Pes. 4:1; see *Domicile). A visitor to Ereẓ Israel, however, observes only one day if he has any intention of staying. According to Ẓevi Hirsch *Ashkenazi, even without such intention he observes one day only (*Ḥakham Ẓevi*, resp. no. 167).

Liturgy

On the three pilgrim festivals and on the high holidays a special *Amidah is recited while on Rosh Ḥodesh and *ḥol ha-mo'ed* the ordinary weekday *Amidah* is said. In both, the *ya'aleh ve-yavo prayer is included, as also in the Grace after Meals. On Ḥanukkah and Purim *al ha-nissim, recounting the miracles of the particular festival, is said in both *Amidah* and Grace. The *Amidah* is followed by *Hallel, preceded and completed by a benediction. On Shavuot, Sukkot (including *ḥol ha'mo'ed*), Shemini Aẓeret, and Ḥanukkah, *Hallel* is recited in its complete form. On Passover full *Hallel* is recited on the first day(s) only but not on *ḥol ha-mo'ed* or on the last festival day(s) when only "half" *Hallel* is recited. Full *Hallel* is also recited during the *seder* and in many congregations also at the conclusion of the evening service on Passover eve. On Rosh Ha-Shanah and the Day of Atonement, *Hallel* is deleted as these are days of judgment. On Purim, too, *Hallel* is not recited. On Rosh Ḥodesh "half" *Hallel* is recited (a Babylonian custom). The Torah reading on the festivals is from two scrolls: the first portion always contains a reference to the festivals, while the second is from Numbers 28–29 concerning the special sacrifice of the day. On Simḥat Torah three scrolls are read: in the first the Pentateuch is concluded; in the second it is begun again; while from the third the reading is of the sacrifices of the day. Unlike on the Sabbath, there is no reading at the afternoon service, except on the Day of Atonement. On the other hand, in many congregations the Torah is read on Simḥat Torah eve. It is customary to read the Song of Songs on the Sabbath during Passover and Ecclesiastes on the Sabbath of Sukkot. On Shavuot the Book of Ruth is read and on Purim the Book of Esther. Lamentations is read on the Ninth of Av. On all the Pentateuchal festivals, including *ḥol ha-mo'ed* and Rosh Ḥodesh, the **Musaf Amidah* is recited which corresponds to the special sacrifices of the day. On Rosh Ḥodesh the *tefillin are taken off before *Musaf*, while on *ḥol ha-mo'ed tefillin* are not used except according to Ashkenazi practice in the Diaspora, when they are taken off before *Hallel*. In contrast to Ereẓ Israel, the priests recite the *priestly blessing in the Diaspora only during the *Musaf* service of the festivals (excluding Rosh Ḥodesh). When one of the festival days is followed by the Sabbath, a procedure known as **eruv tavshilin* permits the preparation of food on the festival for the Sabbath, which would otherwise be prohibited.

The "good days" mentioned in **Megillat Ta'anit*, of which some are also mentioned in other sources, were all established in the Second Temple period. Save for Ḥanukkah and Purim all have long disappeared, the last one being Nicanor's Day (13th Adar) which was still observed in Ereẓ Israel in the seventh to ninth centuries. During the Middle Ages and in modern times other days became commonly accepted as "good days," some without any official standing. These are Lag ba-Omer, the 15th of Av, and Tu bi-Shevat, and lately Israel *Independence Day, which is also celebrated as a holiday with special prayers and *Hallel*.

Women and the Festivals

Women are responsible for obeying all of Judaism's negative commandments and for observing most of the positive commandments. These positive precepts include celebrating the Sabbath and all of the holy days and festivals of the Jewish year (TB Pes. 109a). However, women are exempt from the following positive *mitzvot* linked to festivals and holy days: hearing the *shofar* on Rosh ha-Shanah, dwelling in a *sukkah* during the Sukkot festival, waving the *lulav* on Sukkot, and counting the *omer*. Since these are all commandments that are to be performed at fixed times of the year, they conform to the exemption of women from time-bound *mitzvot* prescribed in Kid. 1:7. Yet, the Talmud specifically obligates women to other time-bound festival observances, generally rituals that take place in the home. These include *kiddush* (sanctification of wine) on the Sabbath (Ber. 20b), and, according to most authorities, on the festivals as well; kindling Sabbath and festival lights and the Hanukkah lamp (Shab. 23a); listening to the reading of the *megillah* (Scroll of Esther) on Purim (Meg. 4a); and eating *maẓẓah* (Pes. 43b) and drinking four cups of wine at the Passover *seder* (Pes.108a).

A number of rabbinic authorities have held that a woman's voluntary performance of those festival *mitzvot* from which she is halakhically exempt should be understood as a praiseworthy personal *minhag* (custom) or permitted as a fulfillment of an individual *neder* (vow). Authorities have been divided over whether one who observes an optional *mitzvah* may recite the benediction that usually accompanies the performance of that precept. R. Moses *Isserles (the Rema, 1525 or 1530–1572) maintained that a woman could recite the blessing in this case (Sh. Ar., *Oraḥ Ḥayyim* 589:6) and this became the custom among Ashkenazi Jews. Thus, a woman may choose to listen to the *shofar* or may sound it herself, and she may recite the appropriate blessing (OḤ 589:6). A woman may not sound the *shofar* on behalf of others, according to the principle that only one who is obligated to perform a precept may perform it for others (OḤ 589:1).

Two of the three commandments specifically associated with women in rabbinic tradition are connected with Sabbath observance (Shab. 2:6). These are the kindling of Sabbath lights before sunset (*hadlakah*) and removing some of the dough from the Sabbath loaf and burning it in the oven in remembrance of Temple sacrifice (*ḥallah*). These two obligations may also be performed by a man if no woman is present; however, the Shulḥan Arukh rules that a woman takes precedence over a man in kindling the Sabbath lights for her household (OḤ 263:2, 3).

Women, like men, are required to fast and afflict themselves in various ways on the Day of Atonement and to refrain from doing any work (Suk. 28b); they are also obligated to observe all other mandated fast days. Pregnant women are expected to fast (OḤ 617:1). If a pregnant woman says she must eat, she may be given incremental amounts of liquid and then food until she is satisfied (OḤ 617:1). A woman in childbirth, from the onset of labor until three days after the birth of her child, must eat normally (OḤ 617:4). A nursing mother should fast unless her fasting will jeopardize her child's health.

Men have traditionally observed Simḥat Torah with festive celebration, particularly circular processions (*hakafot*) around the synagogue, and joyous dancing, with the Torah scrolls. In recent years many women have initiated separate women's *hakafot* with the Torah scrolls. There is no halakhic objection to this practice since a woman, like a man, is permitted to touch and hold the Torah scroll at all times (YD 282:9). Some contemporary Orthodox authorities, however, oppose this innovation because they link it with their perceptions of feminism as a threat to traditional Jewish life.

Rosh Ḥodesh, the festival marking the New Moon and the start of each month, is strongly associated with women in Jewish tradition. In some eras in the Jewish past, women's abstention from work on *Rosh Ḥodesh* was encouraged; the Shulḥan Arukh says women may work on *Rosh Ḥodesh* but praises Jewish women who refrain from doing so (OḤ 417:1). Women are forbidden to fast on *Rosh Ḥodesh* (OḤ 418:1) and it is a *mitzvah* for them to feast (OḤ 419:1). However, women are exempt from the obligation to bless the New Moon on its appearance, since this is a time-bound positive precept (*Halikhot Betah* 16:10). In recent decades, many Jewish women have reclaimed their traditional association with this day, forming *Rosh Ḥodesh* groups for study and fellowship.

[Judith R. Baskin (2nd ed.)]

BIBLIOGRAPHY: G.F. Moore, *Judaism*, 2 (1927), 40–54; E. Rackman, *Sabbath and Festivals in the Modern Age* (1961); Y. Vainstein, *Cycle of the Jewish Year* (1961^2); H. Schauss, *Guide to Jewish Holy Days* (1962); S.Y. Zevin, *Ha-Mo'adim ba-Halakhah* (1963^{10}); Y.L. Barukh and Y.T. Levinsky (eds.), *Sefer ha-Mo'adim*, 8 vols. ($1963–65^6$); S. Goren, *Torat ha-Mo'adim* (1964); E. Kitov, *Book of Our Heritage*, 1 (1968). See also the bibliographies attached to the articles on the individual festivals. ON SECOND DAYS OF FESTIVALS: *Conservative Judaism*, 24:2 (Winter 1970), 21–59. **ADD. BIBLIOGRAPHY:** P.V. Adelman, *Miriam's Well: Rituals for Jewish Women Around the Year* (1986); S. Cohen Anisfeld, T. Mohr, and C. Spector (eds.), *The Women's Passover Companion: Women's Reflections on the Festival of Freedom* (2003); ibid., *The Women's Seder Sourcebook: Rituals and Readings for Use at the Passover Seder* (2003; R. Biale, *Women in Jewish Law: An Exploration of Women's Issues in Halakhic Sources* (1995); E.M. Broner, *Bringing Home the Light: A Jewish Woman's Handbook of Rituals* (1999); M. Kaufman, *The Woman in Jewish Law and Tradition* (1993); G. Twersky Reimer and J.A. Kates (eds.), *Beginning Anew: A Woman's Companion to the High Holy Days* (1997).

FESTSCHRIFTEN (from German; lit. "festival writings"). A Festschrift is usually a volume of articles by several authors for a celebration, especially a volume of learned essays, by students, colleagues, and admirers to honor a scholar on a special anniversary. The custom of publishing Festschriften became popular in academic circles in Germany in the 19th century and was eagerly adopted by the Jewish scholarly community as well, particularly to honor the birthdays or memory of prominent rabbis, teachers at rabbinical seminaries, and private scholars. An institution, such as a rabbinical seminary, a Jewish school, or a society could also be honored. The contents of these books usually consist of a brief dedication or biographical sketch of the person honored, a list of his writings, and a series of scholarly contributions in the field of his interest.

Early examples of this genre were published in Central Europe when modern Jewish scholarship was striving to achieve recognition within the general community of scholars. At that time formal recognition of scholarship in Jewish subjects was generally denied, except for Bible scholarship; even that field, however, was conceived as an exclusively theological discipline reserved for Christian scholars. Thus the Festschriften served the apologetic tendency prevalent in the early period of modern Jewish learning. With the spread of the methods of modern Jewish scholarship from Germany to other countries, Festschriften also became popular, and this type of literature continues to be published in Israel and the Diaspora. Generally, the main subject of a Festschrift is not the honoree, but in some cases memorial volumes may consist primarily of the literary remains of the person. A related development is the publication of hundreds of memorial volumes dedicated to the Jewish communities that were destroyed during the Holocaust; usually they take the form of reminiscences of the survivors.

Lists and Indexes

A list of Festschriften, "Jubilee, Memorial, and Tribute Volumes" (in: *Universal Jewish Encyclopedia*, 1941), enumerates over a hundred titles for the period 1864–1941. The bibliographical quarterly *Kirjath Sepher* regularly published a list of works under the heading *Kevaẓim* ("collections"), from which a fairly complete bibliography of Jewish Festschriften can be derived. Nearly a hundred Festschriften honoring Jewish educational institutions and published from 1834 on are listed by Leah Y. Mishkin (in: SBB, 5 (1961), 92–101). Many of these, however, have the institutions as their principal subject.

An analytical Festschrift is *An Index to Jewish Festschriften* (1937) by J.R. Marcus and A. Bilgray, which analyzes

54 works by author, title, and subject. A general index to Festschriften that analyzes a substantial number of works of Jewish interest is *Articles on Antiquity in Festschriften, and Index; the Ancient Near East, the Old Testament, Greece, Rome, Roman Law, Byzantium* (1962) by Dorothy Rounds.

I. Joel's *Reshimat Ma'amarim be-Madda'ei ha-Yahadut* (1969, "List of Articles on Jewish Studies"), the first volume of a projected series, analyzes periodicals and collections, including Festschriften published in 1966.

Index to Festschriften in Jewish Studies (1971), compiled and edited by Charles Berlin, gives a comprehensive list of 243 Festschriften with an alphabetical list of authors and articles, and a detailed index. It excludes the Festschriften indexed by Marcus and Bilgray.

[Theodore Wiener]

°**FESTUS, PORCIUS**, Roman procurator of Judea 60–62 C.E. Under his rule the sect of Jewish patriots known as the *Sicarii greatly increased in number, although, according to Josephus, the procurator made every effort to curb their activity. Festus sent his troops to suppress a "deceiver" who led the people into the wilderness promising them victory, and many of them were killed (Jos., Ant., 20:188). Soon after his appointment Nero decided the dispute in *Caesarea between the Syrians and the Jews in such a way as to make the Syrians the masters of the city; this aroused considerable unrest among the Jewish population. Another legacy of the procuratorship of Felix was the trial of the apostle Paul, whom Festus sent to Rome to be tried after a number of hearings. During his procuratorship Agrippa II added an upper story to the former Hasmonean palace in order to be able to overlook the Temple court. The priests countered by erecting a wall screening the Temple from the palace. For military reasons Festus ordered this wall to be demolished but nevertheless permitted the priests to send a delegation to Rome to appeal his decision. Nero was persuaded by his wife, *Poppaea Sabina, to decide in their favor and the wall was allowed to stand. Festus died suddenly in Ereẓ Israel in 62 C.E. and was later succeeded by *Albinus.

BIBLIOGRAPHY: Jos., Wars, 2:271; Jos., Ant. 20:182, 185–8; Acts 24:27; 25:1–26: 32; Schuerer, Hist, 194, 233f., 239f.; Klausner, Bayit Sheni, 5 (1963^5), 36–37; Paul-Wissowa, 43 (1953), 220–7, no. 36.

[Lea Roth]

°**FETTMILCH, VINCENT** (d. 1616), anti-Jewish guild leader in *Frankfurt. In 1612 he presented a petition to the emperor accusing the senate of Frankfurt of corruption and favoring Jews. Though the petition was ignored, he exploited the economic crisis and religious strife to agitate against the senate and the Jews. The populace disregarded two imperial warnings and were unappeased by the expulsion of 60 poor Jewish families. On Aug. 5, 1614, they attacked the ghetto gates, which were forced open after five hours. The Jewish defenders rushed to join their women and children, who were hiding in the cemetery. Two Jews and one Gentile lost their lives and the pillage continued until noon. The cemetery was surrounded by Fettmilch, the self-styled "new Haman," and his followers, and the whole community was forced to leave the city. Meanwhile the emperor had issued an order for Fettmilch's arrest. On March 10, 1616, he and six associates were hanged and quartered; after its return the community commemorated the date annually as the "Purim Winz" ("Purim of Vincent") with the reading of the *Megillat Vinẓ* composed by Elhanan b. Abraham Helin in Hebrew and Yiddish (publ. Frankfurt, 1616).

BIBLIOGRAPHY: A. Freimann and I. Kracauer, *Frankfort* (1929), 73–107 (Eng.); I. Kracauer, *Geschichte der Juden in Frankfurt a.M.*, 1 (1925), 358–410; idem, in: ZGJD, 4 (1890), 127–69, 319–65; 5 (1892), 1–26; D. Gans, *Ẓemaḥ David ha-Shalem* (1966), 228 (introd. in English); Baron, $Social^2$, 14 (1969), 190–7.

FEUCHTWANG, DAVID (1864–1936), rabbi and scholar. After studying in Vienna and Berlin, Feuchtwang succeeded his father Meir as rabbi in *Mikulov, Moravia, in 1892. In 1903 he became rabbi in Vienna and succeeded H.P. *Chajes as chief rabbi (1927). Feuchtwang contributed numerous articles to both Jewish and non-Jewish scholarly journals. Among his published work are *Nachum im Lichte der Assyriologie* (1888), *Das Wasseropfer und die damit verbundenen Zeremonien* (1911), *Der Tierkreis in der Tradition und im synagogalen Ritus* (1913), and *Studien zum Buche Ruth* (1925). He also wrote a study of the Hebrew tombstone inscriptions of Mikulov. Several volumes of his sermons and lectures were published.

FEUCHTWANGER, LION (1884–1958), German historical novelist. Feuchtwanger was born into a Bavarian-Jewish family. Coming from the Jewish community of Fuerth the Feuchtwangers settled in Munich in the mid-1840s, established a successful private bank and a factory for margarine, and were very active in the Orthodox *Synagogenverein Ohel Jakob.* Lion Feuchtwanger studied philosophy at Berlin and Munich; in 1907 he received his doctorate from the University of Munich for a thesis on Heine's *Rabbi of Bacherach.* As a young man he was mainly interested in drama. He wrote about a dozen plays, three of them in collaboration with Brecht. It was after World War I that Feuchtwanger's name first became known. His greatest success came with *Jud Suess* (1925; English edition *Jew Suess*, 1926; U.S. edition *Power*, 1927), a novel about Joseph Suess *Oppenheimer, the 18th-century court Jew, which he had originally written as a play. In 1939 this world best seller, which had already been made into a motion picture in Britain, was used by the Nazis as the basis for a viciously antisemitic film. Feuchtwanger's other big success of the 1920s was *Die haessliche Herzogin Margarete Maultasch* (1923; *The Ugly Duchess*, 1927), a psychological study of an Austrian historical figure. *Erfolg* (1930; *Success*, 1930) daringly exposed the moral corruption of postwar Germany. It was during this period that he began writing his *Josephus trilogy – *Der juedische Krieg* (1932; *Josephus*, 1932), *Die Soehne* (1935; *The Jew of Rome*, 1936), and *Der Tag wird kommen* (1941; *The Day Will Come*, 1942). Lion Feuchtwanger's brother Ludwig was a well-known figure in the cultural life of the Weimar Republic. Until 1933 he was the editor of the Duncker & Humblot publishing house in Munich.

Feuchtwanger spent the winter of 1932/33 on a lecture tour of the U.S. and was there when Hitler came to power. He never returned to Germany, but settled in the south of France. After the French collapse in June 1940, the Vichy regime put him into a concentration camp. With the help of American friends he managed to escape over the Pyrenees and, as a result of the intervention of President Roosevelt, was able to enter the U.S., where he spent the rest of his life. The novel *Die Geschwister Oppenheim* (1933; *The Oppermanns*, 1934) deals with the fate of a German-Jewish family in the early days of Nazi rule. A trip to the U.S.S.R. produced *Moskau 1937*, which included an historic interview with Stalin. The years of exile in France inspired several novels, including *Simone* (1944; Eng. tr., 1944), *Exil* (1939; *Paris Gazette*, 1940), and *Unholdes Frankreich* (1942; *The Devil in France*, 1941). When he was living in Pacific Palisades, California, Feuchtwanger wrote more best sellers, including *Waffen fuer America* (2 vols, 1947–48; *Proud Destiny*, 1947), the story of Benjamin Franklin's activities in France; *Goya* (1951; *This Is the Hour*, 1952); *Narrenweisheit, oder Tod und Verklaerung des Jean-Jacques Rousseau* (1952; *'tis Folly to be Wise…* 1953); *Spanische Ballade* (1955, also published 1955 under the title *Die Juedin von Toledo*; *Raquel the Jewess of Toledo*, 1956), and *Jefta und seine Tochter* (1957; *Jephta and his Daughter*, 1958). Many of these books were translated into more than 30 languages. Feuchtwanger's play *Wahn, oder der Teufel in Boston* (1946) is a penetrating study of Cotton Mather and his times. The 30,000-volume Feuchtwanger Memorial Library, bequeathed to the University of Southern California, was the novelist's third collection; previous libraries were lost in Nazi Germany and occupied France. After World War II, Feuchtwanger received awards and honors from both West and East Germany.

BIBLIOGRAPHY: *Lion Feuchtwanger zum 70. Geburtstag* (1954), contains bibliography; NDB, 5 (1957), 109–10; Zohn, in: *Jewish Quarterly* (Winter 1958/59), 3–4; *Lion Feuchtwanger zum Gedenken* (1959); Yuill, in: *German Men of Letters*, 3 (1964), 179–206. **ADD. BIBLIOGRAPHY:** L. Kahn, *Insight and Action. The Life and Work of Lion Feuchtwanger* (1975); J. Pischel, *Lion Feuchtwanger – Versuch über ein Leben* (1984).

[Harry Zohn / Heike Specht (2nd ed.)]

FEUER, HENRY (1912–), U.S. organic chemist. Born in the Ukraine, Feuer went to U.S. in 1941. He joined Toledo Hospital, Ohio, and subsequently became a faculty member at Purdue University (1946). He was appointed professor of chemistry there in 1961 and professor emeritus in 1979. In 1964–71 he was visiting professor at the Hebrew University of Jerusalem; in 1971 he was visiting professor at the Indian Institute of Technology and in 1979 at the Beijing Institute of Technology. His contributions to scientific journals deal with organic nitrogen compounds, viscosity, absorption of gases, and rocket propellants. From 1962 to 1989 he was president of Organic Electronic Spectral Data, Inc. and managing editor of the Organic Nitro Chemistry Series, Wiley-VCH. He is also a fellow of the American Association for the Advancement of Science, the American Chemical Society, and the Royal Society of Chemistry.

[Sharon Zrachya (2nd ed.)]

FEUER, LEON ISRAEL (1903–1984), U.S. Reform rabbi, orator, and Zionist leader. Feuer was born in Hazleton, Pennsylvania, and ordained at Hebrew Union College in 1927. He received his B.A. from the University of Cincinnati in 1925, an honorary D.D. from HUC-JIR in 1955, and an honorary doctorate from Bowling Green University in 1975. He served his entire rabbinic career in Ohio, first at Temple Tifereth Israel in Cleveland (1927–34) and then at the Collingwood Avenue Temple, Congregation Shomer Emunim in Toledo (1934–74), where he also lectured at the University of Toledo. He gained a reputation as an eloquent and outspoken supporter of liberal social legislation to end racial inequality as well as to protect the rights of workers, the unemployed, women, and children. During the 1930s, Feuer joined forces with Unitarian Minister Rev. Walter Cole to combat the antisemitic radio diatribes of Father Charles Coughlin, raising secret financing to purchase airtime and ghostwriting rebuttal speeches for Cole to broadcast.

Feuer rose to his greatest prominence as an early and influential leader of the Zionist movement in the United States. His book *Why a Jewish State?*, published in 1942, was the first in the English language to advocate an independent Jewish commonwealth in Palestine. In 1943, he became director of the Washington bureau of the American Zionist Emergency Council, obtaining a year's leave of absence from his congregation to head the effort to persuade U.S. political leaders to support the idea of a sovereign Jewish nation. A consummate lobbyist, Feuer convinced representatives and senators in Congress not only to oppose Britain's White Paper restricting Jewish immigration to Palestine but also to pass resolutions calling for the creation of a Jewish state in Palestine after World War II. In 1945, Feuer was elected vice president of the Zionist Organization of America and attended the following year's World Zionist Congress in Basel, Switzerland; as the ZOA delegation's floor whip, he was effective at instilling unity of purpose in achieving the goals of this assembly at such a critical juncture in history.

With the establishment of the State of Israel as the Jewish homeland, Feuer returned to active leadership roles in his community and the Reform movement. He was the organizing chairman of the Jewish Welfare Federation of Toledo and served successively as president of the Toledo Zionist District, the Toledo Lodge of B'nai B'rith, the Jewish Community Council, the United Jewish Fund, and the Toledo United Nations Association. After holding several key CCAR positions, including chairman of the Committee on Justice and Peace and the CCAR-UAHC Joint Social Action Commission, and vice president (1961–63), Feuer was elected president of the *Central Conference of American Rabbis in 1963. He was a proponent of stronger Jewish education requirements in the Reform movement, particularly with regard to customs, ceremonies, and Hebrew. Following his term of office (1963–65), he was appointed a public member of the executive of the American section of the Jewish Agency, the governing body of the World Zionist Organization (1966–71). He also served on an International Commission to study revising the WZO. Upon his retirement from the pulpit in 1974, Feuer joined the faculty of Emory University as a visiting professor. He also co-authored two scholarly works: *The Jew and His Religion* (1935) and *Jewish Literature since the Bible* (2 vols., 1937, 1941).

BIBLIOGRAPHY: K.M. Olitzky, L.J. Sussman, and M.H. Stern, *Reform Judaism in America: A Biographical Dictionary and Sourcebook* (1993).

[Bezalel Gordon (2nd ed.)]

FEUER, LEWIS SAMUEL (1912–2002), U.S. educator. Feuer was born in New York. He taught philosophy and social sciences at City College of New York, Vassar, the University of Vermont, and the University of California at Berkeley from 1957 to 1966. In 1966 he was appointed professor of sociology at the University of Toronto, where he taught sociological theory until 1976. He is the author of *Psychoanalysis and Ethics* (1955), *Spinoza and the Rise of Liberalism* (1958), *The Scientific Intellectual: The Psychological & Sociological Origins of Modern Science* (1963), *The Conflict of Generations: The Character and Significance of Student Movements* (1968), and *Marx and the Intellectuals* (1969). He edited *Marx and Engels: Basic Writings on Politics and Philosophy* (1959). His special interest was in the sociology of ideas. In his study of Spinoza, he related the philosopher's thought to the political and economic currents of his time. In *The Conflict of Generations* and other works, he studied the psychoanalytical and personal factors in social and political thought. He also criticized the theory that the rise of Protestantism has been mainly responsible for scientific inquiry and development. Later books by Feuer include *Einstein and the Generations of Science (1974), Ideology and the Ideologists* (1975), *Philosophy, History, and Social Action: Essays in Honor of Lewis Feuer: With an Autobiographical Essay by Lewis Feuer* (1988), and *Varieties of Scientific Experience: Emotive Aims in Scientific Hypotheses* (1995).

[Ben G. Kayfetz / Ruth Beloff (2nd ed.)

FEUERLICHT, MORRIS MARCUS (1879–1959), U.S. Reform rabbi. Feuerlicht was born in Hungary and ordained at *Hebrew Union College in 1901. He spent his entire rabbinic career in Indiana, first as rabbi of Temple Israel in Lafayette (1901–4) and then of Indianapolis Hebrew Congregation in Indianapolis (1904–51), where he also was a member of the faculty of Butler University. Feuerlicht espoused the philosophy that Judaism's spiritual heritage could contribute much to American life and translated this into respected social activism, to the extent that *The Indianapolis Times* hailed him as "a man in whom the qualities of greatness transcend all the little differences of creed, nationality and sect that divide us." The paper went on to call Feuerlicht "...one of the true assets of the State of Indiana... [a] violent foe of the Ku Klux Klan... [an] orator who bested the famed attorney Clarence Darrow in a [public] debate... [and an effective mediator] who settled many strikes."

In 1927, Feuerlicht was one of the founders of the National Conference of Christians and Jews (renamed the National Conference for Community and Justice in the 1990s). Locally, he was one of the founders of the Marion County chapter of the American Red Cross, as well as the founder and first director of the Indianapolis Family Welfare Society. He served successive terms as president of a number of civic organizations, including the Indiana Conference of Social Work, the Children's Aid Association of Indianapolis, and the Indiana Library and Historical Board. He also served as a civilian chaplain at Fort Benjamin Harrison.

In the realm of scholarship, Feuerlicht, a member of the American Oriental Society, was a contributor to the *Universal Jewish Encyclopedia* and wrote *Judaism's Contribution to the Founding of the Republic,* published by the Jewish Tract Commission.

BIBLIOGRAPHY: K.M. Olitzky, L.J. Sussman, and M.H. Stern, *Reform Judaism in America: A Biographical Dictionary and Sourcebook* (1993).

[Bezalel Gordon (2nd ed.)]

FEUERMANN, EMANUEL (1902–1942), cellist. Born in Kolomea, Galicia, and taken to Vienna at the age of seven, Feuermann gave his first public recitals in 1913. He was a teacher at Cologne Conservatory from 1918 until 1923 and became well known as a soloist. He was on the staff of the Berlin Hochschule fuer Musik (1929–33), but emigrated to the United States in 1938. There he performed as a soloist and made notable appearances in trios with Jascha Heifetz and Artur Rubinstein, and was acclaimed as one of the great cellists of his time.

FEUERRING, MAXIMILIAN (1896–1985), painter. Feuerring worked as an art teacher and art critic in various countries. In World War II he served with the Polish Army and was taken prisoner. In 1948, he organized in Munich the Painters in Exile exhibition, in which he participated with fellow Jewish P.O.W.S. A prolific artist, his paintings reflect the continuous search for problems and conflicts of spiritual or emotional origin. He struggled to integrate the known and the unknown, the formed and the unformed into an organic unity. Feuerring, who lived in Sydney from 1950, twice represented Australia at the São Paulo Biennial and was awarded the Albury Art Prize. He is sometimes known by his Polish surname of Feurring-Emefowicza.

FEUERSTEIN, family of leaders of U.S. Orthodoxy. The Feuersteins, who made their fortune in textiles in Massachusetts, trace their history in the United States to the 1893 arrival in New York of HENRY (Naftali) from Hungary. Instilled with the unyielding Orthodoxy that nurtured such rabbis as Moshe *Teitelbaum, founder of the Satmar ḥasidic dynasty who hailed from the same town, Feuerstein went beyond his modest beginnings as a peddler who plied his wares throughout New York's Hudson Valley to found a sweater mill in Malden, Massachusetts. Soon he became one of a handful of prosperous American businessmen who remained staunchly Orthodox and as such an important supporter of Orthodox institutions. In the 1920s Henry traveled to Palestine, meeting with both Rabbis Abraham I. *Kook, who backed the religious Zionist idea of the emergent "New Yishuv," and Joseph Ḥayyim *Sonnenfeld, the staunchly anti-Zionist leader of Orthodoxy in Jerusalem. He helped sustain Jerusalem's Hungarian community, of which his mother became a member.

SAMUEL (1892–1983), eldest of Henry's three children, all of whom were American-born, expanded both the family concern for Orthodox community needs and the family business, which by the end of World War I as Malden Knitting Mills was worth a then extraordinary million dollars. In the late 1930s and even more after the Holocaust as Orthodoxy in America grew exponentially, the Feuersteins became key figures in helping sustain an expanding number of its institutions – locally, nationally, and internationally. As such they were linked with most of the movement's prominent rabbinic leaders in the 20th century, who looked to them for counsel and economic aid. Feuerstein was close to such rabbis as Leo *Jung, supporting the Vaad Hatzalah (Rescue Committee) in its efforts to save refugees from the Nazis, and Joseph B. *Soloveitchik, helping to found Maimonides, a coeducational Modern Orthodox Jewish day school in Boston (of which he served as board chair). Samuel also helped Shraga Feivel *Mendelowitz found Torah Umesorah (the National Society for Hebrew Day Schools) and served as its president. In 1953 he founded the Young Israel of Brookline, and was instrumental in hiring as its first permanent rabbi, Irving "Yitz" *Greenberg.

MOSES (1916–), eldest of Samuel's five children and educated in Ascher's Institute (Switzerland), Yeshiva College (B.A. 1936), and the Harvard Business School, took on many of the Orthodox communal leadership roles in the next generation. Like his father, he acted as an important link between the traditionalist and modernist wings of Orthodoxy. Most prominently he served as chairman of Torah Umesorah as well as president of the *Union of Orthodox Jewish Congregations of America. Under his presidency from 1954 to 1966, the Union became the largest Orthodox Jewish umbrella organization in the United States. Its certification of foods as kosher as a not-for-profit public service, totally free of the element of personal gain and private vestment, became decisive in making such guarantees reliable and kosher foods widely available. Once the OU seal became the national standard of *kashrut*, companies of high standing seeking acceptance of their products by Jewish consumers began, spontaneously, to turn to the Orthodox Union for that purpose. Moses also mediated between native and European-educated elements in American Orthodoxy, easing tensions between immigrants, who were swelling its ranks, and those who had constituted it in the past.

After Moses' mother, Janette (Kaplan), died, his father married Mitzi Landau. The eldest of their three children, AARON (1926–), educated at Boston Latin School and later Yeshiva College (B.A. 1947), became CEO of the family business. He expanded its products and presided over its growth into a multimillion dollar textile corporation, now called Malden Mills. Famous for the production of the immensely popular and innovative fleece insulation fabrics under the trademark Polartec, Aaron oversaw the opening of new headquarters in Lawrence, Massachusetts. The success of the company helped the family increase its support for countless Jewish institutions. While other textile manufacturers relocated to the Southern United States and later to Latin America or the Far East in search of lower labor costs and higher profits, Malden Mills, under Aaron's leadership, alone remained in the Northeast, loyal to its workers and unwilling to abandon its roots. In December 1995, the Lawrence mill suffered a devastating fire. Confounding expectations that he would relocate where the labor was cheaper, Aaron chose at a cost of $1.5 million per week to continue to pay his idle workers with full benefits for over three months, while he struggled to rebuild and battled with insurance companies who were slow to cover his losses. Explaining his motivation as coming from his Judaism, which taught him that good ethics was good business, Feuerstein often quoted Jeremiah (9:22): "Let the rich man not glory in his riches," but rather show kindness, justice, and righteousness in his actions. He became a national hero, receiving numerous awards and honors as well as an invitation to a joint session of the U.S. Congress. He succeeded in rebuilding, and in 2004 Congress approved $21 million for Polartec garments for the U.S. military in the 2005 Defense Spending Bill.

[Samuel C. Heilman (2nd ed.)]

FEUERSTEIN, BEDŘICH (1892–1934), Czech architect and stage designer. He was responsible for introducing elements of futurism and cubism in Czechoslovakia after World War I, demonstrated in his design for the Institute of Military Geography in Prague (1924). In 1925–27 he was in Tokyo, studying Japanese architecture. His stage designs for many plays produced in the National Theater in Prague, the satirical theater *Osvobozené Divadlo*, and other leading Czech theaters, showed great originality. Best known were his designs for Čapek's *R.U.R.* (1920).

[Avigdor Dagan]

FEUERSTEIN, REUVEN (1921–2005), Israeli psychologist. Born in Botosani, Romania, Feuerstein studied at the University of Geneva under such mentors as Jean Piaget and received his Ph.D. in developmental psychology at the Sorbonne. After qualifying as a teacher, he helped set up a special school for the children of Jews taken to Nazi labor camps. After settling in Israel in 1944, he taught child survivors of the Holocaust and directed Youth Aliyah's psychological service. After directing the psychological services of Youth Aliyah in Europe (1951–55), he was appointed director of the Youth Aliyah child guidance clinic and the Canadian Hadassah-WIZO Research Institute in Jerusalem. His work is set forth in his book (with M. Richelle and the collaboration of Z. Rey) *Children of the Mellah* (*Yaldei ha-Melaḥ*; Jerusalem, 1963).

Feuerstein believes that every human being can be modified to reach a higher level of functioning irrespective of age and regardless of the cause of a problem or the severity of a condition. In 1965 he established his Jerusalem research institute, which has become a mecca for families with problem children. Two of the items he developed are particularly well known: the Learning Potential Assessment Devices, for evaluating learning potential; and the Instrumental Enrichment Program, for improving an individual's way of thinking and functioning. Worldwide, there are more than 1,000 research projects that implement his work, involving all age groups from infants to the elderly, and every ability level from the severely retarded to the highly gifted.

From 1970 Feuerstein served as professor in the School of Education at Bar-Ilan University in Israel. He was director of the Hadassah-WIZO-Canada Research Institute in Jerusalem as well as the Center for Development of Human Potential in Jerusalem. In 1990, France's president François Mitterand honored Feuerstein for his work in training French workers, managers, and executives in the skills of intelligence. In 1992 he was awarded the Israel Prize in social sciences.

Books by Feuerstein include *The Dynamic Assessment of Retarded Performers: The Learning Potential Assessment Device, Theory, Instruments, and Techniques* (with Y. Rand and M. Hoffman, 1979), *Instrumental Enrichment: An Intervention Program for Cognitive Modifiability* (1980), and *Don't Accept Me As I Am: Helping "Retarded" People to Excel* (with Y. Rand and J. Rynders, 1988).

BIBLIOGRAPHY: S. Howard, *Changing Children's Minds: Feuerstein's Revolution in the Teaching of Intelligence* (1993); N. Blagg, *Can We Teach Intelligence? A Comprehensive Evaluation of Feuerstein's Instrumental Enrichment Programme* (1990); A. Kozulin and Y. Rand (eds.), *Experience of Mediated Learning: An Impact of Feuerstein's Theory in Education and Psychology* (2000).

[Ruth Beloff (2nd ed.)]

Abbreviations

•

ABBREVIATIONS

GENERAL ABBREVIATIONS

This list contains abbreviations used in the Encyclopaedia (apart from the standard ones, such as geographical abbreviations, points of compass, etc.). For names of organizations, institutions, etc., in abbreviation, see Index. For bibliographical abbreviations of books and authors in Rabbinical literature, see following lists.

*	Cross reference; i.e., an article is to be found under the word(s) immediately following the asterisk (*).
°	Before the title of an entry, indicates a non-Jew (post-biblical times).
‡	Indicates reconstructed forms.
>	The word following this sign is derived from the preceding one.
<	The word preceding this sign is derived from the following one.

ad loc.	*ad locum*, "at the place"; used in quotations of commentaries.
A.H.	*Anno Hegirae*, "in the year of Hegira," i.e., according to the Muslim calendar.
Akk.	Addadian.
A.M.	*anno mundi*, "in the year (from the creation) of the world."
anon.	anonymous.
Ar.	Arabic.
Aram.	Aramaic.
Ass.	Assyrian.
b.	born; *ben, bar.*
Bab.	Babylonian.
B.C.E.	Before Common Era (= B.C.).
bibl.	bibliography.
Bul.	Bulgarian.
c., ca.	Circa.
C.E.	Common Era (= A.D.).
cf.	*confer*, "compare."
ch., chs.	chapter, chapters.
comp.	compiler, compiled by.
Cz.	Czech.
D	according to the documentary theory, the Deuteronomy document.
d.	died.
Dan.	Danish.
diss., dissert,	dissertation, thesis.
Du.	Dutch.
E.	according to the documentary theory, the Elohist document (i.e., using Elohim as the name of God) of the first five (or six) books of the Bible.
ed.	editor, edited, edition.
eds.	editors.
e.g.	*exempli gratia*, "for example."
Eng.	English.
et al.	*et alibi*, "and elsewhere"; or *et alii*, "and others"; "others."
f., ff.	and following page(s).
fig.	figure.
fl.	flourished.
fol., fols	folio(s).
Fr.	French.
Ger.	German.
Gr.	Greek.
Heb.	Hebrew.
Hg., Hung	Hungarian.
ibid	*Ibidem*, "in the same place."
incl. bibl.	includes bibliography.
introd.	introduction.
It.	Italian.
J	according to the documentary theory, the Jahwist document (i.e., using YHWH as the name of God) of the first five (or six) books of the Bible.
Lat.	Latin.
lit.	literally.
Lith.	Lithuanian.
loc. cit.	*loco citato*, "in the [already] cited place."
Ms., Mss.	Manuscript(s).
n.	note.
n.d.	no date (of publication).
no., nos	number(s).
Nov.	Novellae (Heb. *Ḥiddushim*).
n.p.	place of publication unknown.
op. cit.	*opere citato*, "in the previously mentioned work."
P.	according to the documentary theory, the Priestly document of the first five (or six) books of the Bible.
p., pp.	page(s).
Pers.	Persian.
pl., pls.	plate(s).
Pol.	Polish.
Port.	Potuguese.
pt., pts.	part(s).
publ.	published.
R.	Rabbi or Rav (before names); in Midrash (after an abbreviation) – *Rabbah*.
r.	recto, the first side of a manuscript page.
Resp.	Responsa (Latin "answers," Hebrew *She'elot u-Teshuvot* or *Teshuvot*), collections of rabbinic decisions.
rev.	revised.

Rom.	Romanian.
Rus(s).	Russian.
Slov.	Slovak.
Sp.	Spanish.
s.v.	*sub verbo, sub voce*, "under the (key) word."
Sum	Sumerian.
summ.	Summary.
suppl.	supplement.
Swed.	Swedish.
tr., trans(l).	translator, translated, translation.
Turk.	Turkish.
Ukr.	Ukrainian.
v., vv.	*verso*. The second side of a manuscript page; also verse(s).
Yid.	Yiddish.

ABBREVIATIONS USED IN RABBINICAL LITERATURE

Adderet Eliyahu, Karaite treatise by Elijah b. Moses *Bashyazi.

Admat Kodesh, Resp. by Nissim Ḥayyim Moses b. Joseph |Mizraḥi.

Aguddah, Sefer ha-, Nov. by *Alexander Suslin ha-Kohen.

Ahavat Ḥesed, compilation by *Israel Meir ha-Kohen.

Aliyyot de-Rabbenu Yonah, Nov. by *Jonah b. Avraham Gerondi.

Arukh ha-Shulḥan, codification by Jehiel Michel *Epstein.

Asayin (= positive precepts), subdivision of: (1) *Maimonides, *Sefer ha-Mitzvot;* (2) *Moses b. Jacob of Coucy, *Semag*.

Asefat Dinim, subdivision of *Sedei Ḥemed* by Ḥayyim Hezekiah *Medini, an encyclopaedia of precepts and responsa.

Asheri = *Asher b. Jehiel.

Aeret Ḥakhamim, by Baruch *Frankel-Teomim; pt, 1: Resp. to Sh. Ar.; pt2: Nov. to Talmud.

Ateret Zahav, subdivision of the *Levush*, a codification by Mordecai b. Abraham (Levush) *Jaffe; *Ateret Zahav* parallels Tur. YD.

Ateret Ẓevi, Comm. To Sh. Ar. by Ẓevi Hirsch b. Azriel.

Avir Ya'akov, Resp. by Jacob Avigdor.

Avkat Rokhel, Resp. by Joseph b. Ephraim *Caro.

Avnei Millu'im, Comm. to Sh. Ar., EH, by *Aryeh Loeb b. Joseph ha-Kohen.

Avnei Nezer, Resp. on Sh. Ar. by Abraham b. Ze'ev Nahum Bornstein of *Sochaczew.

Avodat Massa, Compilation of Tax Law by Yoasha Abraham Judah.

Azei ha-Levanon, Resp. by Judah Leib *Zirelson.

Ba'al ha-Tanya – *Shneur Zalman of Lyady.

Ba'ei Ḥayyei, Resp. by Ḥayyim b. Israel *Benveniste.

Ba'er Heitev, Comm. To Sh. Ar. The parts on OḤ and EH are by Judah b. Simeon *Ashkenazi, the parts on YD AND ḤM by *Zechariah Mendel b. Aryeh Leib. Printed in most editions of Sh. Ar.

Baḥ = Joel *Sirkes.

Baḥ, usual abbreviation for *Bayit Ḥadash*, a commentary on Tur by Joel *Sirkes; printed in most editions of Tur.

Bayit Ḥadash, see *Baḥ*.

Berab = Jacob Berab, also called Ri Berav.

Bedek ha-Bayit, by Joseph b. Ephraim *Caro, additions to his *Beit Yosef* (a comm. to Tur). Printed sometimes inside *Beit Yosef*, in smaller type. Appears in most editions of Tur.

Be'er ha-Golah, Commentary to Sh. Ar. By Moses b. Naphtali Hirsch *Rivkes; printed in most editions of Sh. Ar.

Be'er Mayim, Resp. by Raphael b. Abraham Manasseh Jacob.

Be'er Mayim Ḥayyim, Resp. by Samuel b. Ḥayyim *Vital.

Be'er Yiẓḥak, Resp. by Isaac Elhanan *Spector.

Beit ha-Beḥirah, Comm. to Talmud by Menahem b. Solomon *Meiri.

Beit Me'ir, Nov. on Sh. Ar. by Meir b. Judah Leib Posner.

Beit Shelomo, Resp. by Solomon b. Aaron Ḥason (the younger).

Beit Shemu'el, Comm. to Sh. Ar., EH, by *Samuel b. Uri Shraga Phoebus.

Beit Ya'akov, by Jacob b. Jacob Moses *Lorberbaum; pt.1: Nov. to Ket.; pt.2: Comm. to EH.

Beit Yisrael, collective name for the commentaries *Derishah, Perishah*, and *Be'urim* by Joshua b. Alexander ha-Kohen *Falk. See under the names of the commentaries.

Beit Yiẓḥak, Resp. by Isaac *Schmelkes.

Beit Yosef: (1) Comm. on Tur by Joseph b. Ephraim *Caro; printed in most editions of Tur; (2) Resp. by the same.

Ben Yehudah, Resp. by Abraham b. Judah Litsch (ליטש) Rosenbaum.

Bertinoro, Standard commentary to Mishnah by Obadiah *Bertinoro. Printed in most editions of the Mishnah.

[Be'urei] Ha-Gra, Comm. to Bible, Talmud, and Sh. Ar. By *Elijah b. Solomon Zalmon (Gaon of Vilna); printed in major editions of the mentioned works.

Be'urim, Glosses to Isserles *Darkhei Moshe* (a comm. on Tur) by Joshua b. Alexander ha-Kohen *Falk; printed in many editions of Tur.

Binyamin Ze'ev, Resp. by *Benjamin Ze'ev b. Mattathias of Arta.

Birkei Yosef, Nov. by Ḥayyim Joseph David *Azulai.

Ha-Buẓ ve-ha-Argaman, subdivision of the *Levush* (a codification by Mordecai b. Abraham (Levush) *Jaffe); *Ha-Buẓ ve-ha-Argaman* parallels Tur, EH.

Comm. = Commentary

Da'at Kohen, Resp. by Abraham Isaac ha-Kohen. *Kook.

Darkhei Moshe, Comm. on Tur Moses b. Israel *Isserles; printed in most editions of Tur.

Darkhei No'am, Resp. by *Mordecai b. Judah ha-Levi.

Darkhei Teshuvah, Nov. by Ẓevi *Shapiro; printed in the major editions of Sh. Ar.

De'ah ve-Haskel, Resp. by Obadiah Hadaya (see *Yaskil Avdi)*.

Derashot Ran, Sermons by *Nissim b. Reuben Gerondi.
Derekh Ḥayyim, Comm. to *Avot* by *Judah Loew (Lob., Liwa) b. Bezalel (Maharal) of Prague.
Derishah, by Joshua b. Alexander ha-Kohen *Falk; additions to his *Perishah* (comm. on Tur); printed in many editions of Tur.
Derushei ha-Ẓelaḥ, Sermons, by Ezekiel b. Judah Halevi *Landau.
Devar Avraham, Resp. by Abraham *Shapira.
Devar Shemu'el, Resp. by Samuel *Aboab.
Devar Yehoshu'a, Resp. by Joshua Menahem b. Isaac Aryeh Ehrenberg.
Dikdukei Soferim, variae lections of the talmudic text by Raphael Nathan*Rabbinowicz.
Divrei Emet, Resp. by Isaac Bekhor David.
Divrei Ge'onim, Digest of responsa by Ḥayyim Aryeh b. Jeḥiel Ẓevi *Kahana.
Divrei Ḥamudot, Comm. on *Piskei ha-Rosh* by Yom Tov Lipmann b. Nathan ha-Levi *Heller; printed in major editions of the Talmud.
Divrei Ḥayyim several works by Ḥayyim *Halberstamm; if quoted alone refers to his Responsa.
Divrei Malkhi'el, Resp. by Malchiel Tenebaum.
Divrei Rivot, Resp. by Isaac b. Samuel *Adarbi.
Divrei Shemu'el, Resp. by Samuel Raphael Arditi.

Edut be-Ya'akov, Resp. by Jacob b. Abraham *Boton.
Edut bi-Yhosef, Resp. by Joseph b. Isaac *Almosnino.
Ein Ya'akov, Digest of talmudic *aggadot* by Jacob (Ibn) *Habib.
Ein Yiẓḥak, Resp. by Isaac Elhanan *Spector.
Ephraim of Lentshitz = Solomon *Luntschitz.
Erekh Leḥem, Nov. and glosses to Sh. Ar. by Jacob b. Abraham *Castro.
Eshkol, Sefer ha-, Digest of *halakhot* by *Abraham b. Isaac of Narbonne.
Et Sofer, Treatise on Law Court documents by Abraham b. Mordecai *Ankawa, in the 2nd vol. of his Resp. *Kerem Ḥamar.*
Etan ha-Ezraḥi, Resp. by Abraham b. Israel Jehiel (Shrenzl) *Rapaport.
Even ha-Ezel, Nov. to Maimonides' *Yad Ḥazakah* by Isser Zalman *Meltzer.
Even ha-Ezer, also called *Raban* of *Ẓafenat Pa'ne'aḥ,* rabbinical work with varied contents by *Eliezer b. Nathan of Mainz; not identical with the subdivision of Tur, Shulḥan Arukh, etc.
Ezrat Yehudah, Resp. by *Isaar Judah b. Nechemiah of Brisk.

Gan Eden, Karaite treatise by *Aaron b. Elijah of Nicomedia.
Gersonides = *Levi b. Gershom, also called Leo Hebraecus, or Ralbag.
Ginnat Veradim, Resp. by *Abraham b. Mordecai ha-Levi.

Haggahot, another name for *Rema.*
Haggahot Asheri, glosses to *Piskei ha-Rosh* by *Israel of Krems; printed in most Talmud editions.
Haggahot Maimuniyyot, Comm,. to Maimonides' Yad Ḥazakah by *Meir ha-Kohen; printed in most eds. of Yad.
Haggahot Mordekhai, glosses to *Mordekhai* by Samuel *Schlettstadt; printed in most editions of the Talmud after *Mordekhai.*
Haggahot ha-Rashash on Tosafot, annotations of Samuel *Strashun on the Tosafot (printed in major editions of the Talmud).
Ha-Gra = *Elijah b. Solomon Zalman (Gaon of Vilna).
Ha-Gra, Commentaries on Bible, Talmud, and Sh. Ar. respectively, by *Elijah b. Solomon Zalman (Gaon of Vilna); printed in major editions of the mentioned works.
Hai Gaon, Comm. = his comm. on Mishnah.
Ḥakham Ẓevi, Resp. by Ẓevi Hirsch b. Jacob *Ashkenazi.
Halakhot = Rif, *Halakhot.* Compilation and abstract of the Talmud by Isaac b. Jacob ha-Kohen *Alfasi; printed in most editions of the Talmud.
Halakhot Gedolot, compilation of *halakhot* from the Geonic period, arranged acc. to the Talmud. Here cited acc. to ed. Warsaw (1874). Author probably *Simeon Kayyara of Basra.
Halakhot Pesukot le-Rav Yehudai Ga'on compilation of *halakhot.*
Halakhot Pesukot min ha-Ge'onim, compilation of *halakhot* from the geonic period by different authors.
Ḥananel, Comm. to Talmud by *Hananel b. Ḥushi'el; printed in some editions of the Talmud.
Harei Besamim, Resp. by Aryeh Leib b. Isaac *Horowitz.
Ḥassidim, Sefer, Ethical maxims by *Judah b. Samuel he-Ḥasid.
Hassagot Rabad on Rif, Glosses on Rif, *Halakhot,* by *Abraham b. David of Posquières.
Hassagot Rabad [on Yad], Glosses on Maimonides, *Yad Ḥazakah,* by *Abraham b. David of Posquières.
Hassagot Ramban, Glosses by Naḥmanides on Maimonides' *Sefer ha-Mitzvot;* usually printed together with *Sefer ha-Mitzvot.*
Ḥatam Sofer = Moses *Sofer.
Ḥavvot Ya'ir, Resp. and varia by Jair Ḥayyim *Bacharach
Ḥayyim Or Zaru'a = *Ḥayyim (Eliezer) b. Isaac.
Ḥazon Ish = Abraham Isaiah *Karelitz.
Ḥazon Ish, Nov. by Abraham Isaiah *Karelitz
Ḥedvat Ya'akov, Resp. by Aryeh Judah Jacob b. David Dov Meisels (article under his father's name).
Heikhal Yiẓḥak, Resp. by Isaac ha-Levi *Herzog.
Ḥelkat Meḥokek, Comm. to Sh. Ar., by Moses b. Isaac Judah *Lima.
Ḥelkat Ya'akov, Resp. by Mordecai Jacob Breisch.
Ḥemdah Genuzah, , Resp. from the geonic period by different authors.
Ḥemdat Shelomo, Resp. by Solomon Zalman *Lipschitz.
Ḥida = Ḥayyim Joseph David *Azulai.
Ḥiddushei Halakhot ve-Aggadot, Nov. by Samuel Eliezer b. Judah ha-Levi *Edels.
Ḥikekei Lev, Resp. by Ḥayyim *Palaggi.
Ḥikrei Lev, Nov. to Sh. Ar. by Joseph Raphael b. Ḥayyim Joseph Ḥazzan (see article *Ḥazzan Family).
Hil. = Hilkhot … (e.g. *Hilkhot Shabbat).*
Ḥinnukh, Sefer ha-, List and explanation of precepts attributed (probably erroneously) to Aaron ha-Levi of Barcelona (see article **Ha-Ḥinnukh*).
Ḥok Ya'akov, Comm. to Hil. Pesaḥ in Sh. Ar., OḤ, by Jacob b. Joseph *Reicher.
Ḥokhmat Sehlomo (1), Glosses to Talmud, *Rashi* and Tosafot by Solomon b. Jehiel "Maharshal") *Luria; printed in many editions of the Talmud.
Ḥokhmat Sehlomo (2), Glosses and Nov. to Sh. Ar. by Solomon b. Judah Aaron *Kluger printed in many editions of Sh. Ar.
Ḥur, subdivision of the *Levush,* a codification by Mordecai b. Abraham (Levush) *Jaffe; *Hur* (or *Levush ha-Hur)* parallels Tur, OḤ, 242–697.
Ḥut ha-Meshullash, fourth part of the *Tashbeẓ* (Resp.), by Simeon b. Zemaḥ *Duran.

Ibn Ezra, Comm. to the Bible by Abraham *Ibn Ezra; printed in the major editions of the Bible *("Mikra'ot Gedolot").*
Imrei Yosher, Resp. by Meir b. Aaron Judah *Arik.
Ir Shushan, Subdivision of the *Levush,* a codification by Mordecai b. Abraham (Levush) *Jaffe; *Ir Shushan* parallels Tur, ḤM.
Israel of Bruna = Israel b. Ḥayyim *Bruna.
Ittur. Treatise on precepts by *Isaac b. Abba Mari of Marseilles.

Jacob Be Rab = *Be Rab.
Jacob b. Jacob Moses of Lissa = Jacob b. Jacob Moses *Lorberbaum.
Judah B. Simeon = Judah b. Simeon *Ashkenazi.
Judah Minz = Judah b. Eliezer ha-Levi *Minz.

Kappei Aharon, Resp. by Aaron Azriel.
Kehillat Ya'akov, Talmudic methodology, definitions etc. by Israel Jacob b. Yom Tov *Algazi.
Kelei Ḥemdah, Nov. and *pilpulim* by Meir Dan *Plotzki of Ostrova, arranged acc. to the Torah.
Keli Yakar, Annotations to the Torah by Solomon *Luntschitz.
Keneh Ḥokhmah, Sermons by Judah Loeb *Pochwitzer.
Keneset ha-Gedolah, Digest of *halakhot* by Ḥayyim b. Israel *Benveniste; subdivided into annotations to *Beit Yosef* and annotations to Tur.
Keneset Yisrael, Resp. by Ezekiel b. Abraham Katzenellenbogen (see article *Katzenellenbogen Family).
Kerem Ḥamar, Resp. and varia by Abraham b. Mordecai *Ankawa.
Kerem Shelmo. Resp. by Solomon b. Joseph *Amarillo.
Keritut, [Sefer], Methodology of the Talmud by *Samson b. Isaac of Chinon.
Kesef ha-Kedoshim, Comm. to Sh. Ar., ḤM, by Abraham *Wahrmann; printed in major editions of Sh. Ar.
Kesef Mishneh, Comm. to Maimonides, *Yad Ḥazakah,* by Joseph b. Ephraim *Caro; printed in most editions of *Yad Ḥazakah.*
Keẓot ha-Ḥoshen, Comm. to Sh. Ar., ḤM, by *Aryeh Loeb b. Joseph ha-Kohen; printed in major editions of Sh. Ar.
Kol Bo [*Sefer*], Anonymous collection of ritual rules; also called *Sefer ha-Likkutim.*
Kol Mevasser, Resp. by Meshullam *Rath.
Korban Aharon, Comm. to *Sifra* by Aaron b. Abraham *Ibn Ḥayyim; pt. 1 is called: *Middot Aharon.*
Korban Edah, Comm. to Jer. Talmud by David *Fraenkel; with additions: *Shiyyurei Korban;* printed in most editions of Jer. Talmud.
Kunteres ha-Kelalim, subdivision of *Sedei Ḥemed,* an encyclopaedia of precepts and responsa by Ḥayyim Hezekiah *Medini.
Kunteres ha-Semikhah, a treatise by *Levi b. Ḥabib; printed at the end of his responsa.
Kunteres Tikkun Olam, part of *Mispat Shalom* (Nov. by Shalom Mordecai b. Moses *Schwadron).

Lavin (negative precepts), subdivision of: (1) *Maimonides, *Sefer ha-Mitzvot;* (2) *Moses b. Jacob of Coucy, *Semag.*
Leḥem Mishneh, Comm. to Maimonides, *Yad Ḥazakah,* by Abraham [Ḥiyya] b. Moses *Boton; printed in most editions of *Yad Ḥazakah.*
Leḥem Rav, Resp. by Abraham [Ḥiyya] b. Moses *Boton.
Leket Yosher, Resp and varia by Israel b. Pethahiah *Isserlein, collected by *Joseph (Joselein) b. Moses.
Leo Hebraeus = *Levi b. Gershom, also called Ralbag or Gersonides.
Levush = Mordecai b. Abraham *Jaffe.
Levush [Malkhut], Codification by Mordecai b. Abraham (Levush) *Jaffe, with subdivisions: [*Levush ha-] Tekhelet* (parallels Tur OḤ 1–241); [*Levush ha-] Ḥur* (parallels Tur OḤ 242–697); [*Levush] Ateret Zahav* (parallels Tur YD); [*Levush ha-Buẓ ve-ha-Argaman* (parallels Tur EH); [*Levush] Ir Shushan* (parallels Tur ḤM); under the name *Levush* the author wrote also other works.
Li-Leshonot ha-Rambam, fifth part (nos. 1374–1700) of Resp. by *David b. Solomon ibn Abi Zimra (Radbaz).
Likkutim, Sefer ha-, another name for [*Sefer] Kol Bo.*

Ma'adanei Yom Tov, Comm. on *Piskei ha-Rosh* by Yom Tov Lipmann b. Nathan ha-Levi *Heller; printed in many editions of the Talmud.
Mabit = Moses b. Joseph *Trani.
Magen Avot, Comm. to *Avot* by Simeon b. Ẓemaḥ *Duran.
Magen Avraham, Comm. to Sh. Ar., OḤ, by Abraham Abele b. Ḥayyim ha-Levi *Gombiner; printed in many editions of Sh. Ar., OḤ.
Maggid Mishneh, Comm. to Maimonides, *Yad Ḥazakah,* by *Vidal Yom Tov of Tolosa; printed in most editions of the *Yad Ḥazakah.*
Maḥaneh Efrayim, Resp. and Nov., arranged acc. to Maimonides' *Yad Ḥazakah* , by Ephraim b. Aaron *Navon.
Maharai = Israel b. Pethahiah *Isserlein.
Maharal of Prague = *Judah Loew (Lob, Liwa), b. Bezalel.
Maharalbaḥ = *Levi b. Ḥabib.
Maharam Alashkar = Moses b. Isaac *Alashkar.
Maharam Alshekh = Moses b. Ḥayyim *Alashekh.
Maharam Mintz = Moses *Mintz.
Maharam of Lublin = *Meir b. Gedaliah of Lublin.
Maharam of Padua = Meir *Katzenellenbogen.
Maharam of Rothenburg = *Meir b. Baruch of Rothenburg.
Maharam Shik = Moses b. Joseph Schick.
Maharash Engel = Samuel b. Ze'ev Wolf Engel.
Maharashdam = Samuel b. Moses *Medina.
Maharḥash = Ḥayyim (ben) Shabbetai.
Mahari Basan = Jehiel b. Ḥayyim Basan.
Mahari b. Lev = Joseph ibn Lev.
Mahari'az = Jekuthiel Asher Zalman Ensil Zusmir.
Maharibal = *Joseph ibn Lev.
Mahariḥ = Jacob (Israel) *Ḥagiz.
Maharik = Joseph b. Solomon *Colon.
Maharikash = Jacob b. Abraham *Castro.
Maharil = Jacob b. Moses *Moellin.
Maharimat = Joseph b. Moses di Trani (not identical with the Maharit).
Maharit = Joseph b. Moses *Trani.
Maharitaẓ = Yom Tov b. Akiva Ẓahalon. (See article *Ẓahalon Family).
Maharsha = Samuel Eliezer b. Judah ha-Levi *Edels.
Maharshag = Simeon b. Judah Gruenfeld.
Maharshak = Samson b. Isaac of Chinon.
Maharshakh = *Solomon b. Abraham.
Maharshal = Solomon b. Jeḥiel *Luria.
Mahasham = Shalom Mordecai b. Moses *Sschwadron.
Maharyu = Jacob b. Judah *Weil.
Maḥazeh Avraham, Resp. by Abraham Nebagen v. Meir ha-Levi Steinberg.
Maḥazik Berakhah, Nov. by Ḥayyim Joseph David *Azulai.

*Maimonides = Moses b. Maimon, or Rambam.
*Malbim = Meir Loeb b. Jehiel Michael.
Malbim = Malbim's comm. to the Bible; printed in the major editions.
Malbushei Yom Tov, Nov. on *Levush,* OḤ, by Yom Tov Lipmann b. Nathan ha-Levi *Heller.
Mappah, another name for *Rema.*
Mareh ha-Panim, Comm. to Jer. Talmud by Moses b. Simeon *Margolies; printed in most editions of Jer. Talmud.
Margaliyyot ha-Yam, Nov. by Reuben *Margoliot.
Masat Binyamin, Resp. by Benjamin Aaron b. Abraham *Slonik
Mashbir, Ha- = *Joseph Samuel b. Isaac Rodi.
Massa Ḥayyim, Tax *halakhot* by Ḥayyim *Palaggi, with the subdivisions *Missim ve-Arnomiyyot* and *Torat ha-Minhagot.*
Massa Melekh, Compilation of Tax Law by Joseph b. Isaac *Ibn Ezra with concluding part *Ne'ilat She'arim.*
Matteh Asher, Resp. by Asher b. Emanuel Shalem.
Matteh Shimon, Digest of Resp. and Nov. to Tur and *Beit Yosef,* ḤM, by Mordecai Simeon b. Solomon.
Matteh Yosef, Resp. by Joseph b. Moses ha-Levi Nazir (see article under his father's name).
Mayim Amukkim, Resp. by Elijah b. Abraham *Mizraḥi.
Mayim Ḥayyim, Resp. by Ḥayyim b. Dov Beresh Rapaport.
Mayim Rabbim, , Resp. by Raphael *Meldola.
Me-Emek ha-Bakha, , Resp. by Simeon b. Jekuthiel Ephrati.
Me'irat Einayim, usual abbreviation: *Sma* (from: *Sefer Me'irat Einayim*); comm. to Sh. Ar. By Joshua b. Alexander ha-Kohen *Falk; printed in most editions of the Sh. Ar.
Melammed le-Ho'il, Resp. by David Ẓevi *Hoffmann.
Meisharim, [*Sefer*], Rabbinical treatise by *Jeroham b. Meshullam.
Meshiv Davar, Resp. by Naphtali Ẓevi Judah *Berlin.
Mi-Gei ha-Haregah, Resp. by Simeon b. Jekuthiel Ephrati.
Mi-Ma'amakim, Resp. by Ephraim Oshry.
Middot Aharon, first part of *Korban Aharon,* a comm. to *Sifra* by Aaron b. Abraham *Ibn Ḥayyim.
Migdal Oz, Comm. to Maimonides, *Yad Ḥazakah,* by *Ibn Gaon Shem Tov b. Abraham; printed in most editions of the *Yad Ḥazakah.*
Mikhtam le-David, Resp. by David Samuel b. Jacob *Pardo.
Mikkaḥ ve-ha-Mimkar, Sefer ha-, Rabbinical treatise by *Hai Gaon.
Milḥamot ha-Shem, Glosses to Rif, *Halakhot,* by *Naḥmanides.
Minḥat Ḥinnukh, Comm. to *Sefer ha-Ḥinnukh,* by Joseph b. Moses *Babad.
Minḥat Yiẓḥak, Resp. by Isaac Jacob b. Joseph Judah Weiss.
Misgeret ha-Shulḥan, Comm. to Sh. Ar., ḤM, by Benjamin Ze'ev Wolf b. Shabbetai; printed in most editions of Sh. Ar.
Mishkenot ha-Ro'im, Halakhot in alphabetical order by Uzziel Alshekh.
Mishnah Berurah, Comm. to Sh. Ar., OḤ, by *Israel Meir ha-Kohen.
Mishneh le-Melekh, Comm. to Maimonides, *Yad Ḥazakah,* by Judah *Rosanes; printed in most editions of *Yad Ḥazakah.*
Mishpat ha-Kohanim, Nov. to Sh. Ar., ḤM, by Jacob Moses *Lorberbaum, part of his *Netivot ha-Mishpat;* printed in major editions of Sh. Ar.
Mishpat Kohen, Resp. by Abraham Isaac ha-Kohen *Kook.
Mishpat Shalom, Nov. by Shalom Mordecai b. Moses *Schwadron; contains: *Kunteres Tikkun Olam.*
Mishpat u-Ẓedakah be-Ya'akov, Resp. by Jacob b. Reuben *Ibn Ẓur.
Mishpat ha-Urim, Comm. to Sh. Ar., ḤM by Jacob b. Jacob Moses *Lorberbaum, part of his *Netivot ha-Mishpat;* printed in major editons of Sh. Ar.
Mishpat Ẓedek, Resp. by *Melammed Meir b. Shem Tov.
Mishpatim Yesharim, Resp. by Raphael b. Mordecai *Berdugo.
Mishpetei Shemu'el, Resp. by Samuel b. Moses *Kalai (Kal'i).
Mishpetei ha-Tanna'im, Kunteres, Nov on *Levush,* OḤ by Yom Tov Lipmann b. Nathan ha-Levi *Heller.
Mishpetei Uzzi'el (Uziel), Resp. by Ben-Zion Meir Hai *Ouziel.
Missim ve-Arnoniyyot, Tax *halakhot* by Ḥayyim *Palaggi, a subdivision of his work *Massa Ḥayyim* on the same subject.
Mitzvot, Sefer ha-, Elucidation of precepts by *Maimonides; subdivided into *Lavin* (negative precepts) and *Asayin* (positive precepts).
Mitzvot Gadol, Sefer, Elucidation of precepts by *Moses b. Jacob of Coucy, subdivided into *Lavin* (negative precepts) and *Asayin* (positive precepts); the usual abbreviation is *Semag.*
Mitzvot Katan, Sefer, Elucidation of precepts by *Isaac b. Joseph of Corbeil; the usual, abbreviation is *Semak.*
Mo'adim u-Zemannim, Rabbinical treatises by Moses Sternbuch.
Modigliano, Joseph Samuel = *Joseph Samuel b. Isaac, Rodi (Ha-Mashbir).
Mordekhai (Mordecai), halakhic compilation by *Mordecai b. Hillel; printed in most editions of the Talmud after the texts.
Moses b. Maimon = *Maimonides, also called Rambam.
Moses b. Naḥman = Naḥmanides, also called Ramban.
Muram = Isaiah Menahem b. Isaac (from: Morenu R. Mendel).

Naḥal Yiẓḥak, Comm. on Sh. Ar., ḤM, by Isaac Elhanan *Spector.
Naḥalah li-Yhoshu'a, Resp. by Joshua Ẓunẓin.
Naḥalat Shivah, collection of legal forms by *Samuel b. David Moses ha-Levi.
*Naḥmanides = Moses b. Naḥman, also called Ramban.
Naẓiv = Naphtali Ẓevi Judah *Berlin.
Ne'eman Shemu'el, Resp. by Samuel Isaac *Modigilano.
Ne'ilat She'arim, concluding part of *Massa Melekh* (a work on Tax Law) by Joseph b. Isaac *Ibn Ezra, containing an exposition of customary law and subdivided into *Minhagei Issur* and *Minhagei Mamon.*
Ner Ma'aravi, Resp. by Jacob b. Malka.
Netivot ha-Mishpat, by Jacob b. Jacob Moses *Lorberbaum; subdivided into *Mishpat ha-Kohanim,* Nov. to Sh. Ar., ḤM, and *Mishpat ha-Urim,* a comm. on the same; printed in major editions of Sh. Ar.
Netivot Olam, Saying of the Sages by *Judah Loew (Lob, Liwa) b. Bezalel.
Nimmukei Menaḥem of Merseburg, Tax *halakhot* by the same, printed at the end of Resp. Maharyu.
Nimmukei Yosef, Comm. to Rif. *Halakhot,* by Joseph *Ḥabib (Ḥabiba); printed in many editions of the Talmud.
Noda bi-Yhudah, Resp. by Ezekiel b. Judah ha-Levi *Landau; there is a first collection *(Mahadura Kamma)* and a second collection *(Mahadura Tinyana).*
Nov. = Novellae, Ḥiddushim.

Ohel Moshe (1), Notes to Talmud, *Midrash Rabbah,* Yad, *Sifrei* and to several Resp., by Eleazar *Horowitz.

Ohel Moshe (2), Resp. by Moses Jonah Zweig.
Oholei Tam. Resp. by *Tam ibn Yaḥya Jacob b. David; printed in the rabbinical collection *Tummat Yesharim.*
Oholei Ya'akov, Resp. by Jacob de *Castro.
Or ha-Me'ir Resp by Judah Meir b. Jacob Samson Shapiro.
Or Same'aḥ, Comm. to Maimonides, *Yad Ḥazakah,* by *Meir Simḥah ha-Kohen of Dvinsk; printed in many editions of the *Yad Ḥazakah.*
Or Zaru'a [the father] = *Isaac b. Moses of Vienna.
Or Zaru'a [the son] = *Ḥayyim (Eliezer) b. Isaac.
Or Zaru'a, Nov. by *Isaac b. Moses of Vienna.
Orah, Sefer ha-, Compilation of ritual precepts by *Rashi.
Oraḥ la-Ẓaddik, Resp. by Abraham Ḥayyim Rodrigues.
Oẓar ha-Posekim, Digest of Responsa.

Paḥad Yiẓḥak, Rabbinical encyclopaedia by Isaac *Lampronti.
Panim Me'irot, Resp. by Meir b. Isaac *Eisenstadt.
Parashat Mordekhai, Resp. by Mordecai b. Abraham Naphtali *Banet.
Pe'at ha-Sadeh la-Dinim and Pe'at ha-Sadeh la-Kelalim, subdivisions of the *Sedei Ḥemed,* an encyclopaedia of precepts and responsa, by Ḥayyim Hezekaih *Medini.
Penei Moshe (1), Resp. by Moses *Benveniste.
Penei Moshe (2), Comm. to Jer. Talmud by Moses b. Simeon *Margolies; printed in most editions of the Jer. Talmud.
Penei Moshe (3), Comm. on the aggadic passages of 18 treatises of the Bab. and Jer. Talmud, by Moses b. Isaiah Katz.
Penei Yehoshu'a, Nov. by Jacob Joshua b. Ẓevi Hirsch *Falk.
Peri Ḥadash, Comm. on Sh. Ar. By Hezekiah da *Silva.
Perishah, Comm. on Tur by Joshua b. Alexander ha-Kohen *Falk; printed in major edition of Tur; forms together with *Derishah* and *Be'urim* (by the same author) the *Beit Yisrael.*
Pesakim u-Khetavim, 2nd part of the *Terumat ha-Deshen* by Israel b. Pethahiah *Isserlein' also called *Piskei Maharai.*
Pilpula Ḥarifta, Comm. to *Piskei ha-Rosh, Seder Nezikin,* by Yom Tov Lipmann b. Nathan ha-Levi *Heller; printed in major editions of the Talmud.
Piskei Maharai, see *Terumat ha-Deshen,* 2nd part; also called *Pesakim u-Khetavim.*
Piskei ha-Rosh, a compilation of *halakhot,* arranged on the Talmud, by *Asher b. Jehiel (Rosh); printed in major Talmud editions.
Pitḥei Teshuvah, Comm. to Sh. Ar. by Abraham Hirsch b. Jacob *Eisenstadt; printed in major editions of the Sh. Ar.

Rabad = *Abraham b. David of Posquières (Rabad III.).
Raban = *Eliezer b. Nathan of Mainz.
Raban, also called *Ẓafenat Pa'ne'aḥ* or *Even ha-Ezer,* see under the last name.
Rabi Abad = *Abraham b. Isaac of Narbonne.
Radad = David Dov. b. Aryeh Judah Jacob *Meisels.
Radam = Dov Berush b. Isaac Meisels.
Radbaz = *David b Solomon ibn Abi Ziumra.
Radbaz, Comm. to Maimonides, *Yad Ḥazakah,* by *David b. Solomon ibn Abi Zimra.
Ralbag = *Levi b. Gershom, also called Gersonides, or Leo Hebraeus.
Ralbag, Bible comm. by *Levi b. Gershon.
Rama [da Fano] = Menaḥem Azariah *Fano.
Ramah = Meir b. Todros [ha-Levi] *Abulafia.
Ramam = *Menaham of Merseburg.
Rambam = *Maimonides; real name: Moses b. Maimon.
Ramban = *Naḥmanides; real name Moses b. Naḥman.
Ramban, Comm. to Torah by *Naḥmanides; printed in major editions. ("Mikra'ot Gedolot").
Ran = *Nissim b. Reuben Gerondi.
Ran of Rif, Comm. on Rif, *Halakhot,* by Nissim b. Reuben Gerondi.
Ranaḥ = *Elijah b. Ḥayyim.
Rash = *Samson b. Abraham of Sens.
Rash, Comm. to Mishnah, by *Samson b. Abraham of Sens; printed in major Talmud editions.
Rashash = Samuel *Strashun.
Rashba = Solomon b. Abraham *Adret.
Rashba, Resp., see also; *Sefer Teshuvot ha-Rashba ha-Meyuḥasot le-ha-Ramban,* by Solomon b. Abraham *Adret.
Rashbad = Samuel b. David.
Rashbam = *Samuel b. Meir.
Rashbam = Comm. on Bible and Talmud by *Samuel b. Meir; printed in major editions of Bible and most editions of Talmud.
Rashbash = Solomon b. Simeon *Duran.
*Rashi = Solomon b. Isaac of Troyes.
Rashi, Comm. on Bible and Talmud by *Rashi; printed in almost all Bible and Talmud editions.
Raviah = Eliezer b. Joel ha-Levi.
Redak = David *Kimḥi.
Redak, Comm. to Bible by David *Kimḥi.
Redakh = *David b. Ḥayyim ha-Kohen of Corfu.
Re'em = Elijah b. Abraham *Mizraḥi.
Rema = Moses b. Israel *Isserles.
Rema, Glosses to Sh. Ar. by Moses b. Israel *Isserles; printed in almost all editions of the Sh. Ar. inside the text in Rashi type; also called *Mappah* or *Haggahot.*
Remek = Moses Kimḥi.
Remakh = Moses ha-Kohen mi-Lunel.
Reshakh = *Solomon b. Abraham; also called Maharshakh.
Resp. = Responsa, *She'elot u-Teshuvot.*
Ri Berav = *Berab.
Ri Escapa = Joseph b. Saul *Escapa.
Ri Migash = Joseph b. Meir ha-Levi *Ibn Migash.
Riba = Isaac b. Asher ha-Levi; Riba II (Riba ha-Baḥur) = his grandson with the same name.
Ribam = Isaac b. Mordecai (or: Isaac b. Meir).
Ribash = *Isaac b. Sheshet Perfet (or: Barfat).
Rid= *Isaiah b. Mali di Trani the Elder.
Ridbaz = Jacob David b. Ze'ev *Willowski.
Rif = Isaac b. Jacob ha-Kohen *Alfasi.
Rif, *Halakhot,* Compilation and abstract of the Talmud by Isaac b. Jacob ha-Kohen *Alfasi.
Ritba = Yom Tov b. Abraham *Ishbili.
Riẓbam = Isaac b. Mordecai.
Rosh = *Asher b. Jehiel, also called Asheri.
Rosh Mashbir, Resp. by *Joseph Samuel b. Isaac, Rodi.

Sedei Ḥemed, Encyclopaedia of precepts and responsa by Ḥayyim Ḥezekiah *Medini; subdivisions: *Asefat Dinim, Kunteres ha-Kelalim, Pe'at ha-Sadeh la-Dinim, Pe'at ha-Sadeh la-Kelalim.*
Semag, Usual abbreviation of *Sefer Mitzvot Gadol,* elucidation of precepts by *Moses b. Jacob of Coucy; subdivided into *Lavin* (negative precepts) *Asayin* (positive precepts).
Semak, Usual abbreviation of *Sefer Mitzvot Katan,* elucidation of precepts by *Isaac b. Joseph of Corbeil.

Sh. Ar. = *Shulḥan Arukh,* code by Joseph b. Ephraim *Caro.
Sha'ar Mishpat, Comm. to Sh. Ar., ḤM. By Israel Isser b. Ze'ev Wolf.
Sha'arei Shevu'ot, Treatise on the law of oaths by *David b. Saadiah; usually printed together with Rif, *Halakhot;* also called: *She'arim of R. Alfasi.*
Sha'arei Teshuvah, Collection of resp. from Geonic period, by different authors.
Sha'arei Uzzi'el, Rabbinical treatise by Ben-Zion Meir Ha *Ouziel.
Sha'arei Ẓedek, Collection of resp. from Geonic period, by different authors.
Shadal [or Shedal] = Samuel David *Luzzatto.
Shai la-Moreh, Resp. by Shabbetai Jonah.
Shakh, Usual abbreviation of *Siftei Kohen,* a comm. to Sh. Ar., YD and ḤM by *Shabbetai b. Meir ha-Kohen; printed in most editions of Sh. Ar.
Sha'ot-de-Rabbanan, Resp. by *Solomon b. Judah ha-Kohen.
She'arim of R. Alfasi see *Sha'arei Shevu'ot.*
Shedal, see Shadal.
She'elot u-Teshuvot ha-Ge'onim, Collection of resp. by different authors.
She'erit Yisrael, Resp. by Israel Ze'ev Mintzberg.
She'erit Yosef, Resp. by *Joseph b. Mordecai Gershon ha-Kohen.
She'ilat Yaveẓ, Resp. by Jacob *Emden (Yaveẓ).
She'iltot, Compilation arranged acc. to the Torah by *Aḥa (Aḥai) of Shabḥa.
Shem Aryeh, Resp. by Aryeh Leib *Lipschutz.
Shemesh Ẓedakah, Resp. by Samson *Morpurgo.
Shenei ha-Me'orot ha-Gedolim, Resp. by Elijah *Covo.
Shetarot, Sefer ha-, Collection of legal forms by *Judah b. Barzillai al-Bargeloni.
Shevut Ya'akov, Resp. by Jacob b. Joseph Reicher.
Shibbolei ha-Leket Compilation on ritual by Zedekiah b. Avraham *Anav.
Shiltei Gibborim, Comm. to Rif, *Halakhot,* by *Joshua Boaz b. Simeon; printed in major editions of the Talmud.
Shittah Mekubbeẓet, Compilation of talmudical commentaries by Bezalel *Ashkenazi.
Shivat Ẓiyyon, Resp. by Samuel b. Ezekiel *Landau.
Shiyyurei Korban, by David *Fraenkel; additions to his comm. to Jer. Talmud *Korban Edah;* both printed in most editions of Jer. Talmud.
Sho'el u-Meshiv, Resp. by Joseph Saul ha-Levi *Nathanson.
Sh[ulḥan] Ar[ukh] [of Ba'al ha-Tanyal], Code by *Shneur Zalman of Lyady; not identical with the code by Joseph Caro.
Siftei Kohen, Comm. to Sh. Ar., YD and ḤM by *Shabbetai b. Meir ha-Kohen; printed in most editions of Sh. Ar.; usual abbreviation: *Shakh.*
Simḥat Yom Tov, Resp. by Tom Tov b. Jacob *Algazi.
Simlah Ḥadashah, Treatise on *Sheḥitah* by Alexander Sender b. Ephraim Zalman *Schor; see also *Tevu'ot Shor.*
Simeon b. Ẓemaḥ = Simeon b. Ẓemaḥ *Duran.
Sma, Comm. to Sh. Ar. by Joshua b. Alexander ha-Kohen *Falk; the full title is: *Sefer Me'irat Einayim;* printed in most editions of Sh. Ar.
Solomon b. Isaac ha-Levi = Solomon b. Isaac *Levy.
Solomon b. Isaac of Troyes = *Rashi.

Tal Orot, Rabbinical work with various contents, by Joseph ibn Gioia.
Tam, Rabbenu = *Tam Jacob b. Meir.
Tashbaẓ = Samson b. Zadok.
Tashbeẓ = Simeon b. Zemaḥ *Duran, sometimes also abbreviation for Samson b. Zadok, usually known as Tashbaẓ.
Tashbeẓ [Sefer ha-], Resp. by Simeon b. Ẓemaḥ *Duran; the fourth part of this work is called: *Ḥut ha-Meshullash.*
Taz, Usual abbreviation of *Turei Zahav,* comm., to Sh. Ar. by *David b. Samnuel ha-Levi; printed in most editions of Sh. Ar.
(Ha)-Tekhelet, subdivision of the *Levush* (a codification by Mordecai b. Abraham (Levush) *Jaffe); *Ha-Tekhelet* parallels Tur, OḤ 1-241.
Terumat ha-Deshen, by Israel b. Pethahiah *Isserlein; subdivided into a part containing responsa, and a second part called *Pesakim u-Khetavim* or *Piskei Maharai.*
Terumot, Sefer ha-, Compilation of *halakhot* by Samuel b. Isaac *Sardi.
Teshuvot Ba'alei ha-Tosafot, Collection of responsa by the Tosafists.
Teshjvot Ge'onei Mizraḥ u-Ma'aav, Collection of responsa.
Teshuvot ha-Geonim, Collection of responsa from Geonic period.
Teshuvot Ḥakhmei Provinẓyah, Collection of responsa by different Provencal authors.
Teshuvot Ḥakhmei Ẓarefat ve-Loter, Collection of responsa by different French authors.
Teshuvot Maimuniyyot, Resp. pertaining to Maimonides' *Yad Ḥazakah;* printed in major editions of this work after the text; authorship uncertain.
Tevu'ot Shor, by Alexander Sender b. Ephraim Zalman *Schor, a comm. to his *Simlah Ḥadashah,* a work on *Sheḥitah.*
Tiferet Ẓevi, Resp. by Ẓevi Hirsch of the "AHW" Communities (Altona, Hamburg, Wandsbeck).
Tiktin, Judah b. Simeon = Judah b. Simeon *Ashkenazi.
Toledot Adam ve-Ḥavvah, Codification by *Jeroham b. Meshullam.
Torat Emet, Resp. by Aaron b. Joseph *Sasson.
Torat Ḥayyim, , Resp. by Ḥayyim (ben) Shabbetai.
Torat ha-Minhagot, subdivision of the *Massa Ḥayyim* (a work on tax law) by Ḥayyim *Palaggi, containing an exposition of customary law.
Tosafot Rid, Explanations to the Talmud and decisions by *Isaiah b. Mali di Trani the Elder.
Tosefot Yom Tov, comm. to Mishnah by Yom Tov Lipmann b. Nathan ha-Levi *Heller; printed in most editions of the Mishnah.
Tummim, subdivision of the comm. to Sh. Ar., ḤM, *Urim ve-Tummim* by Jonathan *Eybeschuetz; printed in the major editions of Sh. Ar.
Tur, usual abbreviation for the *Arba'ah Turim* of *Jacob b. Asher.
Turei Zahav, Comm. to Sh. Ar. by *David b. Samuel ha-Levi; printed in most editions of Sh. Ar.; usual abbreviation: *Taz.*

Urim, subdivision of the following.
Urim ve-Tummim, Comm. to Sh. Ar., ḤM, by Jonathan *Eybeschuetz; printed in the major editions of Sh. Ar.; subdivided in places into *Urim* and *Tummim.*

Vikku'aḥ Mayim Ḥayyim, Polemics against Isserles and Caro by Ḥayyim b. Bezalel.

Yad Malakhi, Methodological treatise by *Malachi b. Jacob ha-Kohen.

Yad Ramah, Nov. by Meir b. Todros [ha-Levi] *Abulafia.
Yakhin u-Vo'az, Resp. by Ẓemaḥ b. Solomon *Duran.
Yam ha-Gadol, Resp. by Jacob Moses *Toledano.
Yam shel Shelomo, Compilation arranged acc. to Talmud by Solomon b. Jehiel (Maharshal) *Luria.
Yashar, Sefer ha-, by *Tam, Jacob b. Meir (Rabbenu Tam); 1st pt.: Resp.; 2nd pt.: Nov.
Yaskil Avdi, Resp. by Obadiah Hadaya (printed together with his Resp. *De'ah ve-Haskel*).
Yaveẓ = Jacob *Emden.
Yehudah Ya'aleh, Resp. by Judah b. Israel *Aszod.
Yekar Tiferet, Comm. to Maimonides' *Yad Ḥazakah*, by David b. Solomon ibn Zimra, printed in most editions of *Yad Ḥazakah*.
Yere'im [ha-Shalem], *[Sefer]*, Treatise on precepts by *Eliezer b. Samuel of Metz.
Yeshu'ot Ya'akov, Resp. by Jacob Meshullam b. Mordecai Ze'ev *Ornstein.
Yiẓhak Rei'aḥ, Resp. by Isaac b. Samuel Abendanan (see article *Abendanam Family).
Ẓafenat Pa'ne'aḥ (1), also called *Raban* or *Even ha-Ezer*, see under the last name.
Ẓafenat Pa'ne'aḥ (2), Resp. by Joseph *Rozin.
Zayit Ra'anan, Resp. by Moses Judah Leib b. Benjamin Auerbach.
Ẓeidah la-Derekh, Codification by *Menahem b. Aaron ibn Zerah.
Ẓedakah u-Mishpat, Resp. by Ẓedakah b. Saadiah Huẓin.
Zekan Aharon, Resp. by Elijah b. Benjamin ha-Levi.
Zekher Ẓaddik, Sermons by Eliezer *Katzenellenbogen.
Ẓemaḥ Ẓedek (1) Resp. by Menaham Mendel Shneersohn (see under *Shneersohn Family).
Zera Avraham, Resp. by Abraham b. David *Yiẓḥaki.
Zera Emet Resp. by *Ishmael b. Abaham Isaac ha-Kohen.
Ẓevi la-Ẓaddik, Resp. by Ẓevi Elimelech b. David Shapira.
Zikhron Yehudah, Resp. by *Judah b. Asher
Zikhron Yosef, Resp. by Joseph b. Menahem *Steinhardt.
Zikhronot, Sefer ha-, Sermons on several precepts by Samuel *Aboab.
Zikkaron la-Rishonim . . ., by Albert (Abraham Elijah) *Harkavy; contains in vol. 1 pt. 4 (1887) a collection of Geonic responsa.
Ẓiẓ Eliezer, Resp. by Eliezer Judah b. Jacob Gedaliah Waldenberg.

BIBLIOGRAPHICAL ABBREVIATIONS

Bibliographies in English and other languages have been extensively updated, with English translations cited where available. In order to help the reader, the language of books or articles is given where not obvious from titles of books or names of periodicals. Titles of books and periodicals in languages with alphabets other than Latin, are given in transliteration, even where there is a title page in English. Titles of articles in periodicals are not given. Names of Hebrew and Yiddish periodicals well known in English-speaking countries or in Israel under their masthead in Latin characters are given in this form, even when contrary to transliteration rules. Names of authors writing in languages with non-Latin alphabets are given in their Latin alphabet form wherever known; otherwise the names are transliterated. Initials are generally not given for authors of articles in periodicals, except to avoid confusion. Non-abbreviated book titles and names of periodicals are printed in *italics*. Abbreviations are given in the list below.

AASOR	*Annual of the American School of Oriental Research* (1919ff.).
AB	*Analecta Biblica* (1952ff.).
Abel, Géog	F.-M. Abel, *Géographie de la Palestine*, 2 vols. (1933–38).
ABR	*Australian Biblical Review* (1951ff.).
Abr.	Philo, *De Abrahamo*.
Abrahams, Companion	I. Abrahams, *Companion to the Authorised Daily Prayer Book* (rev. ed. 1922).
Abramson, Merkazim	S. Abramson, *Ba-Merkazim u-va-Tefuẓot bi-Tekufat ha-Ge'onim* (1965).
Acts	Acts of the Apostles (New Testament).
ACUM	*Who is who in ACUM [Aguddat Kompozitorim u-Meḥabbrim]*.
ADAJ	*Annual of the Department of Antiquities, Jordan* (1951ff.).
Adam	Adam and Eve (Pseudepigrapha).
ADB	*Allgemeine Deutsche Biographie*, 56 vols. (1875–1912).
Add. Esth.	The Addition to Esther (Apocrypha).
Adler, Prat Mus	1. Adler, *La pratique musicale savante dans quelques communautés juives en Europe au XVIIe et XVIIIe siècles*, 2 vols. (1966).
Adler-Davis	H.M. Adler and A. Davis (ed. and tr.), *Service of the Synagogue, a New Edition of the Festival Prayers with an English Translation in Prose and Verse*, 6 vols. (1905–06).
Aet.	Philo, *De Aeternitate Mundi*.
AFO	*Archiv fuer Orientforschung* (first two volumes under the name *Archiv fuer Keilschriftforschung*) (1923ff.).
Ag. Ber	*Aggadat Bereshit* (ed. Buber, 1902).
Agr.	Philo, *De Agricultura*.
Ag. Sam.	*Aggadat Samuel*.
Ag. Song	*Aggadat Shir ha-Shirim* (Schechter ed., 1896).
Aharoni, Ereẓ	Y. Aharoni, *Ereẓ Yisrael bi-Tekufat ha-Mikra: Geografyah Historit* (1962).
Aharoni, Land	Y. Aharoni, *Land of the Bible* (1966).

Ahikar	Ahikar (Pseudepigrapha).
AI	*Archives Israélites de France* (1840–1936).
AJA	*American Jewish Archives* (1948ff.).
AJHSP	*American Jewish Historical Society – Publications* (after vol. 50 = AJHSQ).
AJHSQ	*American Jewish Historical (Society) Quarterly* (before vol. 50 =AJHSP).
AJSLL	*American Journal of Semitic Languages and Literature* (1884–95 under the title *Hebraica*, since 1942 JNES).
AJYB	*American Jewish Year Book* (1899ff.).
AKM	Abhandlungen fuer die Kunde des Morgenlandes (series).
Albright, Arch	W.F. Albright, *Archaeology of Palestine* (rev. ed. 1960).
Albright, Arch Bib	W.F. Albright, *Archaeology of Palestine and the Bible* (1935^3).
Albright, Arch Rel	W.F. Albright, *Archaeology and the Religion of Israel* (1953^3).
Albright, Stone	W.F. Albright, *From the Stone Age to Christianity* (1957^2).
Alon, Meḥkarim	G. Alon, *Meḥkarim be-Toledot Yisrael bi-Ymei Bayit Sheni u-vi-Tekufat ha-Mishnah ve-ha Talmud*, 2 vols. (1957–58).
Alon, Toledot	G. Alon, *Toledot ha-Yehudim be-Ereẓ Yisrael bi-Tekufat ha-Mishnah ve-ha-Talmud*, I (1958^3), (1961^2).
ALOR	Alter Orient (series).
Alt, Kl Schr	A. Alt, *Kleine Schriften zur Geschichte des Volkes Israel*, 3 vols. (1953–59).
Alt, Landnahme	A. Alt, *Landnahme der Israeliten in Palaestina* (1925); also in Alt, Kl Schr, 1 (1953), 89–125.
Ant.	Josephus, *Jewish Antiquities* (Loeb Classics ed.).
AO	*Acta Orientalia* (1922ff.).
AOR	*Analecta Orientalia* (1931ff.).
AOS	American Oriental Series.
Apion	Josephus, *Against Apion* (Loeb Classics ed.).
Aq.	Aquila's Greek translation of the Bible.
Ar.	*Arakhin* (talmudic tractate).
Artist.	Letter of Aristeas (Pseudepigrapha).
ARN[1]	*Avot de-Rabbi Nathan*, version (1) ed. Schechter, 1887.
ARN[2]	*Avot de-Rabbi Nathan*, version (2) ed. Schechter, 1945^2.
Aronius, Regesten	I. Aronius, *Regesten zur Geschichte der Juden im fraenkischen und deutschen Reiche bis zum Jahre 1273* (1902).
ARW	*Archiv fuer Religionswissenschaft* (1898–1941/42).
AS	*Assyrological Studies* (1931ff.).
Ashtor, Korot	E. Ashtor (Strauss), *Korot ha-Yehudim bi-Sefarad ha-Muslemit*, 1(1966^2), 2(1966).
Ashtor, Toledot	E. Ashtor (Strauss), *Toledot ha-Yehudim be-Miẓrayim ve-Suryah Taḥat Shilton ha-Mamlukim*, 3 vols. (1944–70).
Assaf, Ge'onim	S. Assaf, *Tekufat ha-Ge'onim ve-Sifrutah* (1955).
Assaf, Mekorot	S. Assaf, *Mekorot le-Toledot ha-Ḥinnukh be-Yisrael*, 4 vols. (1925–43).
Ass. Mos.	Assumption of Moses (Pseudepigrapha).
ATA	Alttestamentliche Abhandlungen (series).
ATANT	Abhandlungen zur Theologie des Alten und Neuen Testaments (series).
AUJW	*Allgemeine unabhaengige juedische Wochenzeitung* (till 1966 = AWJD).
AV	Authorized Version of the Bible.
Avad.	*Avadim* (post-talmudic tractate).
Avi-Yonah, Geog	M. Avi-Yonah, *Geografyah Historit shel Ereẓ Yisrael* (1962^3).
Avi-Yonah, Land	M. Avi-Yonah, *The Holy Land from the Persian to the Arab conquest (536 B.C. to A.D. 640)* (1960).
Avot	*Avot* (talmudic tractate).
Av. Zar.	*Avodah Zarah* (talmudic tractate).
AWJD	*Allgemeine Wochenzeitung der Juden in Deutschland* (since 1967 = AUJW).
AZDJ	*Allgemeine Zeitung des Judentums.*
Azulai	Ḥ.Y.D. Azulai, *Shem ha-Gedolim*, ed. by I.E. Benjacob, 2 pts. (1852) (and other editions).
BA	*Biblical Archaeologist* (1938ff.).
Bacher, Bab Amor	W. Bacher, *Agada der babylonischen Amoraeer* (1913^2).
Bacher, Pal Amor	W. Bacher, *Agada der palaestinensischen Amoraeer* (Heb. ed. *Aggadat Amora'ei Ereẓ Yisrael*), 2 vols. (1892–99).
Bacher, Tann	W. Bacher, *Agada der Tannaiten* (Heb. ed. *Aggadot ha-Tanna'im*, vol. 1, pt. 1 and 2 (1903); vol. 2 (1890).
Bacher, Trad	W. Bacher, *Tradition und Tradenten in den Schulen Palaestinas und Babyloniens* (1914).
Baer, Spain	Yitzhak (Fritz) Baer, *History of the Jews in Christian Spain*, 2 vols. (1961–66).
Baer, Studien	Yitzhak (Fritz) Baer, *Studien zur Geschichte der Juden im Koenigreich Aragonien waehrend des 13. und 14. Jahrhunderts* (1913).
Baer, Toledot	Yitzhak (Fritz) Baer, *Toledot ha-Yehudim bi-Sefarad ha-Noẓerit mi-Teḥillatan shel ha-Kehillot ad ha-Gerush*, 2 vols. (1959^2).
Baer, Urkunden	Yitzhak (Fritz) Baer, *Die Juden im christlichen Spanien*, 2 vols. (1929–36).
Baer S., Seder	S.I. Baer, *Seder Avodat Yisrael* (1868 and reprints).
BAIU	*Bulletin de l'Alliance Israélite Universelle* (1861–1913).
Baker, Biog Dict	*Baker's Biographical Dictionary of Musicians*, revised by N. Slonimsky (1958^5; with Supplement 1965).
I Bar.	I Baruch (Apocrypha).
II Bar.	II Baruch (Pseudepigrapha).
III Bar.	III Baruch (Pseudepigrapha).
BAR	*Biblical Archaeology Review.*
Baron, Community	S.W. Baron, *The Jewish Community, its History and Structure to the American Revolution*, 3 vols. (1942).

Baron, Social	S.W. Baron, *Social and Religious History of the Jews,* 3 vols. (1937); enlarged, 1-2(1952^{2}), 3-14 (1957–69).
Barthélemy-Milik	D. Barthélemy and J.T. Milik, *Dead Sea Scrolls: Discoveries in the Judean Desert,* vol. 1 *Qumram Cave* I (1955).
BASOR	*Bulletin of the American School of Oriental Research.*
Bauer-Leander	H. Bauer and P. Leander, *Grammatik des Biblisch-Aramaeischen* (1927; repr. 1962).
BB	(1) *Bava Batra* (talmudic tractate). (2) *Biblische Beitraege* (1943ff.).
BBB	Bonner biblische Beitraege (series).
BBLA	*Beitraege zur biblischen Landes- und Altertumskunde* (until 1949–ZDPV).
BBSAJ	*Bulletin,* British School of Archaeology, Jerusalem (1922–25; after 1927 included in PEFQS).
BDASI	*Alon* (since 1948) or *Hadashot Arkhe'ologiyyot* (since 1961), bulletin of the Department of Antiquities of the State of Israel.
Begrich, Chronologie	J. Begrich, *Chronologie der Koenige von Israel und Juda* (1929).
Bek.	*Bekhorot* (talmudic tractate).
Bel	Bel and the Dragon (Apocrypha).
Benjacob, Oẓar	I.E. Benjacob, *Oẓar ha-Sefarim* (1880; repr. 1956).
Ben Sira	see Ecclus.
Ben-Yehuda, Millon	E. Ben-Yedhuda, *Millon ha-Lashon ha-Ivrit,* 16 vols (1908–59; repr. in 8 vols., 1959).
Benzinger, Archaeologie	I. Benzinger, *Hebraeische Archaeologie* (1927^{3}).
Ben Zvi, Eretz Israel	I. Ben-Zvi, *Eretz Israel under Ottoman Rule* (1960; offprint from L. Finkelstein (ed.), *The Jews, their History, Culture and Religion* (vol. 1).
Ben Zvi, Ereẓ Israel	I. Ben-Zvi, *Ereẓ Israel bi-Ymei ha-Shilton ha-Ottomani (1955).*
Ber.	*Berakhot* (talmudic tractate).
Beẓah	*Beẓah* (talmudic tractate).
BIES	Bulletin of the Israel Exploration Society, see below BJPES.
Bik.	*Bikkurim* (talmudic tractate).
BJCE	Bibliography of Jewish Communities in Europe, catalog at General Archives for the History of the Jewish People, Jerusalem.
BJPES	Bulletin of the Jewish Palestine Exploration Society – English name of the Hebrew periodical known as: 1. *Yedi'ot ha-Ḥevrah ha-Ivrit la-Ḥakirat Ereẓ Yisrael va-Attikoteha* (1933–1954); 2. *Yedi'ot ha-Ḥevrah la-Ḥakirat Ereẓ Yisrael va-Attikoteha* (1954–1962); 3. *Yedi'ot ba-Ḥakirat Ereẓ Yisrael va-Attikoteha* (1962ff.).
BJRL	*Bulletin of the John Rylands Library* (1914ff.).
BK	*Bava Kamma* (talmudic tractate).
BLBI	*Bulletin of the Leo Baeck Institute* (1957ff.).
BM	(1) *Bava Meẓia* (talmudic tractate). (2) *Beit Mikra* (1955/56ff.). (3) British Museum.
BO	*Bibbia e Oriente* (1959ff.).
Bondy-Dworský	G. Bondy and F. Dworský, *Regesten zur Geschichte der Juden in Boehmen, Maehren und Schlesien von 906 bis 1620,* 2 vols. (1906).
BOR	*Bibliotheca Orientalis* (1943ff.).
Borée, Ortsnamen	W. Borée *Die alten Ortsnamen Palaestinas* (1930).
Bousset, Religion	W. Bousset, *Die Religion des Judentums im neutestamentlichen Zeitalter* (1906^{2}).
Bousset-Gressmann	W. Bousset, *Die Religion des Judentums im spaethellenistischen Zeitalter* (1966^{3}).
BR	*Biblical Review* (1916–25).
BRCI	*Bulletin of the Research Council of Israel* (1951/52–1954/55; then divided).
BRE	*Biblical Research* (1956ff.).
BRF	*Bulletin of the Rabinowitz Fund for the Exploration of Ancient Synagogues* (1949ff.).
Briggs, Psalms	Ch. A. and E.G. Briggs, *Critical and Exegetical Commentary on the Book of Psalms,* 2 vols. (ICC, 1906–07).
Bright, Hist	J. Bright, *A History of Israel* (1959).
Brockelmann, Arab Lit	K. Brockelmann, *Geschichte der arabischen Literatur,* 2 vols. 1898–1902), supplement, 3 vols. (1937–42).
Bruell, Jahrbuecher	*Jahrbuecher fuer juedische Geschichte und Litteratur,* ed. by N. Bruell, Frankfurt (1874–90).
Brugmans-Frank	H. Brugmans and A. Frank (eds.), *Geschiedenis der Joden in Nederland* (1940).
BTS	*Bible et Terre Sainte* (1958ff.).
Bull, Index	S. Bull, *Index to Biographies of Contemporary Composers* (1964).
BW	*Biblical World* (1882–1920).
BWANT	*Beitraege zur Wissenschaft vom Alten und Neuen Testament* (1926ff.).
BZ	*Biblische Zeitschrift* (1903ff.).
BZAW	*Beihefte zur Zeitschrift fuer die alttestamentliche Wissenschaft,* supplement to ZAW (1896ff.).
BŻIH	*Biuletyn Zydowskiego Instytutu Historycznego* (1950ff.).
CAB	*Cahiers d'archéologie biblique* (1953ff.).
CAD	*The* [*Chicago*] *Assyrian Dictionary* (1956ff.).
CAH	*Cambridge Ancient History,* 12 vols. (1923–39)
CAH^{2}	*Cambridge Ancient History,* second edition, 14 vols. (1962–2005).
Calwer, Lexikon	*Calwer, Bibellexikon.*
Cant.	Canticles, usually given as Song (= Song of Songs).

Cantera-Millás, Inscripciones	F. Cantera and J.M. Millás, *Las Inscripciones Hebraicas de España* (1956).
CBQ	*Catholic Biblical Quarterly* (1939ff.).
CCARY	Central Conference of American Rabbis, *Yearbook* (1890/91ff.).
CD	*Damascus Document* from the Cairo *Genizah* (published by S. Schechter, *Fragments of a Zadokite Work*, 1910).
Charles, Apocrypha	R.H. Charles, *Apocrypha and Pseudepigrapha . . .*, 2 vols. (1913; repr. 1963–66).
Cher.	Philo, *De Cherubim.*
I (or II) Chron.	Chronicles, book I and II (Bible).
CIG	*Corpus Inscriptionum Graecarum.*
CIJ	*Corpus Inscriptionum Judaicarum,* 2 vols. (1936–52).
CIL	*Corpus Inscriptionum Latinarum.*
CIS	*Corpus Inscriptionum Semiticarum* (1881ff.).
C.J.	Codex Justinianus.
Clermont-Ganneau, Arch	Ch. Clermont-Ganneau, *Archaeological Researches in Palestine*, 2 vols. (1896–99).
CNFI	*Christian News from Israel* (1949ff.).
Cod. Just.	Codex Justinianus.
Cod. Theod.	Codex Theodosinanus.
Col.	Epistle to the Colosssians (New Testament).
Conder, Survey	Palestine Exploration Fund, *Survey of Eastern Palestine*, vol. 1, pt. I (1889) = C.R. Conder, *Memoirs of the . . . Survey.*
Conder-Kitchener	Palestine Exploration Fund, *Survey of Western Palestine*, vol. 1, pts. 1-3 (1881–83) = C.R. Conder and H.H. Kitchener, *Memoirs.*
Conf.	Philo, *De Confusione Linguarum.*
Conforte, Kore	D. Conforte, *Kore ha-Dorot* (1842^{2}).
Cong.	Philo, *De Congressu Quaerendae Eruditionis Gratia.*
Cont.	Philo, *De Vita Contemplativa.*
I (or II) Cor.	Epistles to the Corinthians (New Testament).
Cowley, Aramic	A. Cowley, *Aramaic Papyri of the Fifth Century B.C.* (1923).
Colwey, Cat	A.E. Cowley, *A Concise Catalogue of the Hebrew Printed Books in the Bodleian Library* (1929).
CRB	*Cahiers de la Revue Biblique* (1964ff.).
Crowfoot-Kenyon	J.W. Crowfoot, K.M. Kenyon and E.L. Sukenik, *Buildings of Samaria* (1942).
C.T.	Codex Theodosianus.
DAB	*Dictionary of American Biography* (1928–58).
Daiches, Jews	S. Daiches, *Jews in Babylonia* (1910).
Dalman, Arbeit	G. Dalman, *Arbeit und Sitte in Palaestina*, 7 vols.in 8 (1928–42 repr. 1964).
Dan	Daniel (Bible).
Davidson, Oẓar	I. Davidson, *Oẓar ha-Shirah ve-ha-Piyyut*, 4 vols. (1924–33); Supplement in: HUCA, 12–13 (1937/38), 715–823.
DB	J. Hastings, *Dictionary of the Bible,* 4 vols. (1963^{2}).
DBI	F.G. Vigoureaux et al. (eds.), *Dictionnaire de la Bible*, 5 vols. in 10 (1912); Supplement, 8 vols. (1928–66)
Decal.	Philo, *De Decalogo.*
Dem.	*Demai* (talmudic tractate).
DER	*Derekh Ereẓ Rabbah* (post-talmudic tractate).
Derenbourg, Hist	J. Derenbourg *Essai sur l'histoire et la géographie de la Palestine* (1867).
Det.	Philo, *Quod deterius potiori insidiari solet.*
Deus	Philo, *Quod Deus immutabilis sit.*
Deut.	Deuteronomy (Bible).
Deut. R.	*Deuteronomy Rabbah.*
DEZ	*Derekh Ereẓ Zuta* (post-talmudic tractate).
DHGE	*Dictionnaire d'histoire et de géographie ecclésiastiques,* ed. by A. Baudrillart et al., 17 vols (1912–68).
Dik. Sof	*Dikdukei Soferim,* variae lections of the talmudic text by Raphael Nathan Rabbinovitz (16 vols., 1867–97).
Dinur, Golah	B. Dinur (Dinaburg), *Yisrael ba-Golah,* 2 vols. in 7 (1959–68) = vols. 5 and 6 of his *Toledot Yisrael,* second series.
Dinur, Haganah	B. Dinur (ed.), *Sefer Toledot ha-Haganah* (1954ff.).
Diringer, Iscr	D. Diringer, *Iscrizioni antico-ebraiche palestinesi* (1934).
Discoveries	*Discoveries in the Judean Desert* (1955ff.).
DNB	*Dictionary of National Biography,* 66 vols. (1921–222) with Supplements.
Dubnow, Divrei	S. Dubnow, *Divrei Yemei Am Olam,* 11 vols (1923–38 and further editions).
Dubnow, Ḥasidut	S. Dubnow, *Toledot ha-Ḥasidut* (1960^{2}).
Dubnow, Hist	S. Dubnow, *History of the Jews* (1967).
Dubnow, Hist Russ	S. Dubnow, *History of the Jews in Russia and Poland,* 3 vols. (1916 20).
Dubnow, Outline	S. Dubnow, *An Outline of Jewish History,* 3 vols. (1925–29).
Dubnow, Weltgesch	S. Dubnow, *Weltgeschichte des juedischen Volkes* 10 vols. (1925–29).
Dukes, Poesie	L. Dukes, *Zur Kenntnis der neuhebraeischen religioesen Poesie* (1842).
Dunlop, Khazars	D. H. Dunlop, *History of the Jewish Khazars* (1954).
EA	El Amarna Letters (edited by J.A. Knudtzon), *Die El-Amarna Tafel,* 2 vols. (1907 14).
EB	*Encyclopaedia Britannica.*
EBI	*Estudios biblicos* (1941ff.).
EBIB	T.K. Cheyne and J.S. Black, *Encyclopaedia Biblica,* 4 vols. (1899–1903).
Ebr.	Philo, *De Ebrietate.*
Eccles.	Ecclesiastes (Bible).
Eccles. R.	*Ecclesiastes Rabbah.*
Ecclus.	Ecclesiasticus or Wisdom of Ben Sira (or Sirach; Apocrypha).
Eduy.	*Eduyyot* (mishanic tractate).

EG	*Enziklopedyah shel Galuyyot* (1953ff.).
EH	*Even ha-Ezer.*
EHA	*Enziklopedyah la-Ḥafirot Arkheologiyyot be-Erez Yisrael,* 2 vols. (1970).
EI	*Enzyklopaedie des Islams,* 4 vols. (1905–14). Supplement vol. (1938).
EIS	*Encyclopaedia of Islam,* 4 vols. (1913–36; repr. 1954–68).
EIS^{2}	*Encyclopaedia of Islam, second edition (1960–2000).*
Eisenstein, Dinim	J.D. Eisenstein, *Oẓar Dinim u-Minhagim* (1917; several reprints).
Eisenstein, Yisrael	J.D. Eisenstein, *Oẓar Yisrael* (10 vols, 1907–13; repr. with several additions 1951).
EIV	*Enẓiklopedyah Ivrit* (1949ff.).
EJ	*Encyclopaedia Judaica* (German, A-L only), 10 vols. (1928–34).
EJC	*Enciclopedia Judaica Castellana,* 10 vols. (1948–51).
Elbogen, Century	I Elbogen, *A Century of Jewish Life* (1960^{2}).
Elbogen, Gottesdienst	I Elbogen, *Der juedische Gottesdienst* ... (1931^{3}, repr. 1962).
Elon, Mafte'aḥ	M. Elon (ed.), *Mafte'aḥ ha-She'elot ve-ha-Teshuvot ha-Rosh* (1965).
EM	*Enẓiklopedyah Mikra'it* (1950ff.).
I (or II) En.	I and II Enoch (Pseudepigrapha).
EncRel	*Encyclopedia of Religion,* 15 vols. (1987, 2005^{2}).
Eph.	Epistle to the Ephesians (New Testament).
Ephros, Cant	G. Ephros, *Cantorial Anthology,* 5 vols. (1929–57).
Ep. Jer.	Epistle of Jeremy (Apocrypha).
Epstein, Amora'im	J N. Epstein, *Mevo'ot le-Sifrut ha-Amora'im* (1962).
Epstein, Marriage	L M. Epstein, *Marriage Laws in the Bible and the Talmud* (1942).
Epstein, Mishnah	J. N. Epstein, *Mavo le-Nusaḥ ha-Mishnah,* 2 vols. (1964^{2}).
Epstein, Tanna'im	J. N. Epstein, *Mavo le-Sifruth ha-Tanna'im.* (1947).
ER	*Ecumenical Review.*
Er.	*Eruvin* (talmudic tractate).
ERE	*Encyclopaedia of Religion and Ethics,* 13 vols. (1908–26); reprinted.
ErIsr	*Eretz-Israel,* Israel Exploration Society.
I Esd.	I Esdras (Apocrypha) (= III Ezra).
II Esd.	II Esdras (Apocrypha) (= IV Ezra).
ESE	*Ephemeris fuer semitische Epigraphik,* ed. by M. Lidzbarski.
ESN	*Encyclopaedia Sefaradica Neerlandica,* 2 pts. (1949).
ESS	*Encyclopaedia of the Social Sciences,* 15 vols. (1930–35); reprinted in 8 vols. (1948–49).
Esth.	Esther (Bible).
Est. R.	*Esther Rabbah.*
ET	*Enẓiklopedyah Talmudit* (1947ff.).
Eusebius, Onom.	E. Klostermann (ed.), *Das Onomastikon* (1904), Greek with Hieronymus' Latin translation.
Ex.	Exodus (Bible).
Ex. R.	*Exodus Rabbah.*
Exs	Philo, *De Exsecrationibus.*
EẒD	*Enẓiklopeday shel ha-Ẓiyyonut ha-Datit* (1951ff.).
Ezek.	Ezekiel (Bible).
Ezra	Ezra (Bible).
III Ezra	III Ezra (Pseudepigrapha).
IV Ezra	IV Ezra (Pseudepigrapha).
Feliks, Ha-Ẓome'aḥ	*J. Feliks, Ha-Ẓome'aḥ ve-ha-Ḥai ba-Mishnah* (1983).
Finkelstein, Middle Ages	L. Finkelstein, *Jewish Self-Government in the Middle Ages* (1924).
Fischel, Islam	W.J. Fischel, *Jews in the Economic and Political Life of Mediaeval Islam* (1937; reprint with introduction "The Court Jew in the Islamic World," 1969).
FJW	*Fuehrer durch die juedische Gemeindeverwaltung und Wohlfahrtspflege in Deutschland* (1927/28).
Frankel, Mevo	Z. Frankel, *Mevo ha-Yerushalmi* (1870; reprint 1967).
Frankel, Mishnah	Z. Frankel, *Darkhei ha-Mishnah* (1959^{2}; reprint 1959^{2}).
Frazer, Folk-Lore	J.G. Frazer, *Folk-Lore in the Old Testament,* 3 vols. (1918–19).
Frey, Corpus	J.-B. Frey, *Corpus Inscriptionum Iudaicarum,* 2 vols. (1936–52).
Friedmann, Lebensbilder	A. Friedmann, *Lebensbilder beruehmter Kantoren,* 3 vols. (1918–27).
FRLT	*Forschungen zur Religion und Literatur des Alten und Neuen Testaments* (series) (1950ff.).
Frumkin-Rivlin	A.L. Frumkin and E. Rivlin, *Toledot Ḥakhmei Yerushalayim,* 3 vols. (1928–30), Supplement vol. (1930).
Fuenn, Keneset	S.J. Fuenn, *Keneset Yisrael,* 4 vols. (1887–90).
Fuerst, Bibliotheca	J. Fuerst, *Bibliotheca Judaica,* 2 vols. (1863; repr. 1960).
Fuerst, Karaeertum	J. Fuerst, *Geschichte des Karaeertums,* 3 vols. (1862–69).
Fug.	Philo, *De Fuga et Inventione.*
Gal.	Epistle to the Galatians (New Testament).
Galling, Reallexikon	K. Galling, *Biblisches Reallexikon* (1937).
Gardiner, Onomastica	A.H. Gardiner, *Ancient Egyptian Onomastica,* 3 vols. (1947).
Geiger, Mikra	A. Geiger, *Ha-Mikra ve-Targumav,* tr. by J.L. Baruch (1949).
Geiger, Urschrift	A. Geiger, *Urschrift und Uebersetzungen der Bibel* 1928^{2}).
Gen.	Genesis (Bible).
Gen. R.	*Genesis Rabbah.*
Ger.	*Gerim* (post-talmudic tractate).
Germ Jud	M. Brann, I. Elbogen, A. Freimann, and H. Tykocinski (eds.), *Germania Judaica,* vol. 1 (1917; repr. 1934 and 1963); vol. 2, in 2 pts. (1917–68), ed. by Z. Avneri.

GHAT	*Goettinger Handkommentar zum Alten Testament* (1917–22).
Ghirondi-Neppi	M.S. Ghirondi and G.H. Neppi, *Toledot Gedolei Yisrael u-Ge'onei Italyah ... u-Ve'urim al Sefer Zekher Ẓaddikim li-Verakhah . . .*(1853), index in ZHB, 17 (1914), 171–83.
Gig.	Philo, *De Gigantibus.*
Ginzberg, Legends	L. Ginzberg, *Legends of the Jews,* 7 vols. (1909–38; and many reprints).
Git.	*Gittin* (talmudic tractate).
Glueck, Explorations	N. Glueck, *Explorations in Eastern Palestine,* 2 vols. (1951).
Goell, Bibliography	Y. Goell, *Bibliography of Modern Hebrew Literature in English Translation* (1968).
Goodenough, Symbols	E.R. Goodenough, *Jewish Symbols in the Greco-Roman Period,* 13 vols. (1953–68).
Gordon, Textbook	C.H. Gordon, *Ugaritic Textbook* (1965; repr. 1967).
Graetz, Gesch	H. Graetz, *Geschichte der Juden* (last edition 1874–1908).
Graetz, Hist	H. Graetz, *History of the Jews,* 6 vols. (1891–1902).
Graetz, Psalmen	H. Graetz, *Kritischer Commentar zu den Psalmen,* 2 vols. in 1 (1882–83).
Graetz, Rabbinowitz	H. Graetz, *Divrei Yemei Yisrael,* tr. by S.P. Rabbinowitz. (1928 1929^{2}).
Gray, Names	G.B. Gray, *Studies in Hebrew Proper Names* (1896).
Gressmann, Bilder	H. Gressmann, *Altorientalische Bilder zum Alten Testament* (1927^{2}).
Gressmann, Texte	H. Gressmann, *Altorientalische Texte zum Alten Testament* (1926^{2}).
Gross, Gal Jud	H. Gross, *Gallia Judaica* (1897; repr. with add. 1969).
Grove, Dict	*Grove's Dictionary of Music and Musicians,* ed. by E. Blum 9 vols. (1954^{5}) and suppl. (1961^{5}).
Guedemann, Gesch Erz	M. Guedemann, *Geschichte des Erziehungswesens und der Cultur der abendlaendischen Juden,* 3 vols. (1880–88).
Guedemann, Quellenschr	M. Guedemann, *Quellenschriften zur Geschichte des Unterrichts und der Erziehung bei den deutschen Juden* (1873, 1891).
Guide	Maimonides, *Guide of the Perplexed.*
Gulak, Oẓar	A. Gulak, *Oẓar ha-Shetarot ha-Nehugim be-Yisrael* (1926).
Gulak, Yesodei	A. Gulak, *Yesodei ha-Mishpat ha-Ivri, Seder Dinei Mamonot be-Yisrael, al pi Mekorot ha-Talmud ve-ha-Posekim,* 4 vols. (1922; repr. 1967).
Guttmann, Mafte'aḥ	M. Guttmann, *Mafte'aḥ ha-Talmud,* 3 vols. (1906–30).
Guttmann, Philosophies	J. Guttmann, *Philosophies of Judaism* (1964).
Hab.	*Habakkuk* (Bible).
Ḥag.	*Ḥagigah* (talmudic tractate).
Haggai	*Haggai* (Bible).
Ḥal.	*Ḥallah* (talmudic tractate).
Halevy, Dorot	I. Halevy, *Dorot ha-Rishonim,* 6 vols. (1897–1939).
Halpern, Pinkas	I. Halpern (Halperin), *Pinkas Va'ad Arba Araẓot* (1945).
Hananel-Eškenazi	A. Hananel and Eškenazi (eds.), *Fontes Hebraici ad res oeconomicas socialesque terrarum balcanicarum saeculo XVI pertinentes,* 2 vols, (1958–60; in Bulgarian).
HB	*Hebraeische Bibliographie* (1858–82).
Heb.	Epistle to the Hebrews (New Testament).
Heilprin, Dorot	J. Heilprin (Heilperin), *Seder ha-Dorot,* 3 vols. (1882; repr. 1956).
Her.	Philo, *Quis Rerum Divinarum Heres.*
Hertz, Prayer	J.H. Hertz (ed.), *Authorised Daily Prayer Book* (rev. ed. 1948; repr. 1963).
Herzog, Instit	I. Herzog, *The Main Institutions of Jewish Law,* 2 vols. (1936–39; repr. 1967).
Herzog-Hauck	J.J. Herzog and A. Hauch (eds.), *Real-encyklopaedie fuer protestantische Theologie* (1896–1913^{3}).
HḤY	*Ha-Ẓofeh le-Ḥokhmat Yisrael* (first four volumes under the title *Ha-Ẓofeh me-Ereẓ Hagar)* (1910/11–13).
Hirschberg, Afrikah	H.Z. Hirschberg, *Toledot ha-Yehudim be-Afrikah ha-Ẓofonit,* 2 vols. (1965).
HJ	*Historia Judaica* (1938–61).
HL	*Das Heilige Land* (1857ff.)
ḤM	*Ḥoshen Mishpat.*
Hommel, Ueberliefer.	F. Hommel, *Die altisraelitische Ueberlieferung in inschriftlicher Beleuchtung* (1897).
Hor.	*Horayot* (talmudic tractate).
Horodezky, Ḥasidut	S.A. Horodezky, *Ha-Ḥasidut ve-ha-Ḥasidim,* 4 vols. (1923).
Horowitz, Ereẓ Yis	I.W. Horowitz, *Ereẓ Yisrael u-Shekhenoteha* (1923).
Hos.	Hosea (Bible).
HTR	*Harvard Theological Review* (1908ff.).
HUCA	*Hebrew Union College Annual* (1904; 1924ff.)
Ḥul.	*Ḥullin* (talmudic tractate).
Husik, Philosophy	I. Husik, *History of Medieval Jewish Philosophy* (1932^{2}).
Hyman, Toledot	A. Hyman, *Toledot Tanna'im ve-Amora'im* (1910; repr. 1964).
Ibn Daud, Tradition	Abraham Ibn Daud, *Sefer ha-Qabbalah – The Book of Tradition,* ed. and tr. By G.D. Cohen (1967).
ICC	International Critical Commentary on the Holy Scriptures of the Old and New Testaments (series, 1908ff.).
IDB	*Interpreter's Dictionary of the Bible,* 4 vols. (1962).
Idelsohn, Litugy	A. Z. Idelsohn, *Jewish Liturgy and its Development* (1932; paperback repr. 1967)
Idelsohn, Melodien	A. Z. Idelsohn, *Hebraeisch-orientalischer Melodienschatz,* 10 vols. (1914 32).
Idelsohn, Music	A. Z. Idelsohn, *Jewish Music in its Historical Development* (1929; paperback repr. 1967).

IEJ	*Israel Exploration Journal* (1950ff.).
IESS	*International Encyclopedia of the Social Sciences* (various eds.).
IG	*Inscriptiones Graecae*, ed. by the Prussian Academy.
IGYB	*Israel Government Year Book* (1949/50ff.).
ILR	*Israel Law Review* (1966ff.).
IMIT	*Izraelita Magyar Irodalmi Társulat Évkönyv* (1895 1948).
IMT	International Military Tribunal.
INB	*Israel Numismatic Bulletin* (1962–63).
INJ	*Israel Numismatic Journal* (1963ff.).
Ios	Philo, *De Iosepho.*
Isa.	Isaiah (Bible).
ITHL	Institute for the Translation of Hebrew Literature.
IZBG	*Internationale Zeitschriftenschau fuer Bibelwissenschaft und Grenzgebiete* (1951ff.).
JA	*Journal asiatique* (1822ff.).
James	Epistle of James (New Testament).
JAOS	*Journal of the American Oriental Society* (c. 1850ff.)
Jastrow, Dict	M. Jastrow, *Dictionary of the Targumim, the Talmud Babli and Yerushalmi, and the Midrashic literature*, 2 vols. (1886 1902 and reprints).
JBA	*Jewish Book Annual* (19242ff.).
JBL	*Journal of Biblical Literature* (1881ff.).
JBR	*Journal of Bible and Religion* (1933ff.).
JC	*Jewish Chronicle* (1841ff.).
JCS	*Journal of Cuneiform Studies* (1947ff.).
JE	*Jewish Encyclopedia*, 12 vols. (1901–05 several reprints).
Jer.	Jeremiah (Bible).
Jeremias, Alte Test	A. Jeremias, *Das Alte Testament im Lichte des alten Orients* 1930[4]).
JGGJČ	*Jahrbuch der Gesellschaft fuer Geschichte der Juden in der Čechoslovakischen Republik* (1929–38).
JHSEM	Jewish Historical Society of England, *Miscellanies* (1925ff.).
JHSET	Jewish Historical Society of England, *Transactions* (1893ff.).
JJGL	*Jahrbuch fuer juedische Geschichte und Literatur* (Berlin) (1898–1938).
JJLG	*Jahrbuch der juedische-literarischen Gesellschaft* (Frankfurt) (1903–32).
JJS	*Journal of Jewish Studies* (1948ff.).
JJSO	*Jewish Journal of Sociology* (1959ff.).
JJV	*Jahrbuch fuer juedische Volkskunde* (1898–1924).
JL	*Juedisches Lexikon*, 5 vols. (1927–30).
JMES	*Journal of the Middle East Society* (1947ff.).
JNES	*Journal of Near Eastern Studies* (continuation of AJSLL) (1942ff.).
J.N.U.L.	Jewish National and University Library.
Job	Job (Bible).
Joel	Joel (Bible).
John	Gospel according to John (New Testament).
I, II and III John	Epistles of John (New Testament).
Jos., Ant	Josephus, *Jewish Antiquities* (Loeb Classics ed.).
Jos. Apion	Josephus, *Against Apion* (Loeb Classics ed.).
Jos., index	*Josephus Works*, Loeb Classics ed., index of names.
Jos., Life	Josephus, *Life* (ed. Loeb Classics).
Jos, Wars	Josephus, *The Jewish Wars* (Loeb Classics ed.).
Josh.	Joshua (Bible).
JPESB	Jewish Palestine Exploration Society Bulletin, see BJPES.
JPESJ	Jewish Palestine Exploration Society Journal – Eng. Title of the Hebrew periodical *Kovez ha-Ḥevrah ha-Ivrit la-Ḥakirat Erez Yisrael va-Attikoteha.*
JPOS	*Journal of the Palestine Oriental Society* (1920–48).
JPS	Jewish Publication Society of America, *The Torah* (1962, 1967[2]); *The Holy Scriptures* (1917).
JQR	*Jewish Quarterly Review* (1889ff.).
JR	*Journal of Religion* (1921ff.).
JRAS	*Journal of the Royal Asiatic Society* (1838ff.).
JHR	*Journal of Religious History* (1960/61ff.).
JSOS	*Jewish Social Studies* (1939ff.).
JSS	*Journal of Semitic Studies* (1956ff.).
JTS	*Journal of Theological Studies* (1900ff.).
JTSA	Jewish Theological Seminary of America (also abbreviated as JTS).
Jub.	Jubilees (Pseudepigrapha).
Judg.	Judges (Bible).
Judith	Book of Judith (Apocrypha).
Juster, Juifs	J. Juster, *Les Juifs dans l'Empire Romain*, 2 vols. (1914).
JYB	*Jewish Year Book* (1896ff.).
JZWL	*Juedische Zeitschift fuer Wissenschaft und Leben* (1862–75).
Kal.	*Kallah* (post-talmudic tractate).
Kal. R.	*Kallah Rabbati* (post-talmudic tractate).
Katz, England	*The Jews in the History of England, 1485-1850 (1994).*
Kaufmann, Schriften	D. Kaufmann, *Gesammelte Schriften*, 3 vols. (1908 15).
Kaufmann Y., Religion	Y. Kaufmann, *The Religion of Israel* (1960), abridged tr. of his *Toledot.*
Kaufmann Y., Toledot	Y. Kaufmann, *Toledot ha-Emunah ha-Yisre'elit*, 4 vols. (1937 57).
KAWJ	*Korrespondenzblatt des Vereins zur Gruendung und Erhaltung der Akademie fuer die Wissenschaft des Judentums* (1920 30).
Kayserling, Bibl	M. Kayserling, *Biblioteca Española-Portugueza-Judaica* (1880; repr. 1961).
Kelim	*Kelim* (mishnaic tractate).
Ker.	*Keritot* (talmudic tractate).
Ket.	*Ketubbot* (talmudic tractate).

Kid.	*Kiddushim* (talmudic tractate).
Kil.	*Kilayim* (talmudic tractate).
Kin.	*Kinnim* (mishnaic tractate).
Kisch, Germany	G. Kisch, *Jews in Medieval Germany* (1949).
Kittel, Gesch	R. Kittel, *Geschichte des Volkes Israel,* 3 vols. (1922–28).
Klausner, Bayit Sheni	J. Klausner, *Historyah shel ha-Bayit ha-Sheni,* 5 vols. (1950/512).
Klausner, Sifrut	J. Klausner, *Historyah shel haSifrut ha-Ivrit ha-Ḥadashah,* 6 vols. (1952–582).
Klein, corpus	S. Klein (ed.), *Juedisch-palaestinisches Corpus Inscriptionum* (1920).
Koehler-Baumgartner	L. Koehler and W. Baumgartner, *Lexicon in Veteris Testamenti libros* (1953).
Kohut, Arukh	H.J.A. Kohut (ed.), *Sefer he-Arukh ha-Shalem,* by Nathan b. Jehiel of Rome, 8 vols. (1876–92; Supplement by S. Krauss et al., 1936; repr. 1955).
Krauss, Tal Arch	S. Krauss, *Talmudische Archaeologie,* 3 vols. (1910–12; repr. 1966).
Kressel, Leksikon	G. Kressel, *Leksikon ha-Sifrut ha-Ivrit ba-Dorot ha-Aḥaronim,* 2 vols. (1965–67).
KS	*Kirjath Sepher* (1923/4ff.).
Kut.	*Kuttim* (post-talmudic tractate).
LA	Studium Biblicum Franciscanum, *Liber Annuus* (1951ff.).
L.A.	Philo, *Legum allegoriae.*
Lachower, Sifrut	F. Lachower, *Toledot ha-Sifrut ha-Ivrit ha-Ḥadashah,* 4 vols. (1947–48; several reprints).
Lam.	Lamentations (Bible).
Lam. R.	*Lamentations Rabbah.*
Landshuth, Ammudei	L. Landshuth, *Ammudei ha-Avodah* (1857–62; repr. with index, 1965).
Legat.	Philo, *De Legatione ad Caium.*
Lehmann, Nova Bibl	R.P. Lehmann, *Nova Bibliotheca Anglo-Judaica* (1961).
Lev.	Leviticus (Bible).
Lev. R.	*Leviticus Rabbah.*
Levy, Antologia	I. Levy, *Antologia de liturgia judeo-española* (1965ff.).
Levy J., Chald Targ	J. Levy, *Chaldaeisches Woerterbuch ueber die Targumim,* 2 vols. (1967–68; repr. 1959).
Levy J., Nuehebr Tal	J. Levy, *Neuhebraeisches und chaldaeisches Woerterbuch ueber die Talmudim . . .,* 4 vols. (1875–89; repr. 1963).
Lewin, Oẓar	Lewin, *Oẓar ha-Ge'onim,* 12 vols. (1928–43).
Lewysohn, Zool	L. Lewysohn, *Zoologie des Talmuds* (1858).
Lidzbarski, Handbuch	M. Lidzbarski, *Handbuch der nordsemitischen Epigraphik,* 2 vols (1898).
Life	Josephus, *Life* (Loeb Classis ed.).
LNYL	*Leksikon fun der Nayer Yidisher Literatur* (1956ff.).
Loew, Flora	I. Loew, *Die Flora der Juden,* 4 vols. (1924 34; repr. 1967).
LSI	*Laws of the State of Israel* (1948ff.).
Luckenbill, Records	D.D. Luckenbill, *Ancient Records of Assyria and Babylonia,* 2 vols. (1926).

Luke	Gospel according to Luke (New Testament)
LXX	Septuagint (Greek translation of the Bible).
Ma'as.	*Ma'aserot* (talmudic tractate).
Ma'as. Sh.	*Ma'ase Sheni* (talmudic tractate).
I, II, III, and IVMacc.	Maccabees, I, II, III (Apocrypha), IV (Pseudepigrapha).
Maimonides, Guide	Maimonides, *Guide of the Perplexed.*
Maim., Yad	Maimonides, *Mishneh Torah (Yad Ḥazakah).*
Maisler, Untersuchungen	B. Maisler (Mazar), *Untersuchungen zur alten Geschichte und Ethnographie Syriens und Palaestinas,* 1 (1930).
Mak.	*Makkot* (talmudic tractate).
Makhsh.	*Makhshrin* (mishnaic tractate).
Mal.	Malachi (Bible).
Mann, Egypt	J. Mann, *Jews in Egypt in Palestine under the Fatimid Caliphs,* 2 vols. (1920–22).
Mann, Texts	J. Mann, *Texts and Studies,* 2 vols (1931–35).
Mansi	G.D. Mansi, *Sacrorum Conciliorum nova et amplissima collectio,* 53 vols. in 60 (1901–27; repr. 1960).
Margalioth, Gedolei	M. Margalioth, *Enẓiklopedyah le-Toledot Gedolei Yisrael,* 4 vols. (1946–50).
Margalioth, Ḥakhmei	M. Margalioth, *Enẓiklopedyah le-Ḥakhmei ha-Talmud ve-ha-Ge'onim,* 2 vols. (1945).
Margalioth, Cat	G. Margalioth, *Catalogue of the Hebrew and Samaritan Manuscripts in the British Museum,* 4 vols. (1899–1935).
Mark	Gospel according to Mark (New Testament).
Mart. Isa.	Martyrdom of Isaiah (Pseudepigrapha).
Mas.	Masorah.
Matt.	Gospel according to Matthew (New Testament).
Mayer, Art	L.A. Mayer, *Bibliography of Jewish Art* (1967).
MB	*Wochenzeitung* (formerly *Mitteilungsblatt*) *des Irgun Olej Merkas Europa* (1933ff.).
MEAH	*Miscelánea de estudios drabes y hebraicos* (1952ff.).
Meg.	Megillah (talmudic tractate).
Meg. Ta'an.	*Megillat Ta'anit* (in HUCA, 8 9 (1931–32), 318–51).
Me'il	*Me'ilah* (mishnaic tractate).
MEJ	*Middle East Journal* (1947ff.).
Mehk.	*Mekhilta de-R. Ishmael.*
Mekh. SbY	*Mekhilta de-R. Simeon bar Yoḥai.*
Men.	*Menaḥot* (talmudic tractate).
MER	*Middle East Record* (1960ff.).
Meyer, Gesch	E. Meyer, *Geschichte des Alterums,* 5 vols. in 9 (1925–58).
Meyer, Ursp	E. Meyer, *Urspring und Anfaenge des Christentums* (1921).
Mez.	*Mezuzah* (post-talmudic tractate).
MGADJ	*Mitteilungen des Gesamtarchivs der deutschen Juden* (1909–12).
MGG	*Die Musik in Geschichte und Gegenwart,* 14 vols. (1949–68).

MGG²	*Die Musik in Geschichte und Gegenwart, 2nd edition (1994)*
MGH	*Monumenta Germaniae Historica* (1826ff.).
MGJV	*Mitteilungen der Gesellschaft fuer juedische Volkskunde* (1898–1929); title varies, see also JJV.
MGWJ	*Monatsschrift fuer Geschichte und Wissenschaft des Judentums* (1851–1939).
MHJ	*Monumenta Hungariae Judaica,* 11 vols. (1903–67).
Michael, Or	H.Ḥ. Michael, *Or ha-Ḥayyim: Ḥakhmei Yisrael ve-Sifreihem,* ed. by S.Z. Ḥ. Halberstam and N. Ben-Menahem (1965²).
Mid.	*Middot* (mishnaic tractate).
Mid. Ag.	*Midrash Aggadah.*
Mid. Hag.	*Midrash ha-Gadol.*
Mid. Job.	*Midrash Job.*
Mid. Jonah	*Midrash Jonah.*
Mid. Lek. Tov	*Midrash Lekaḥ Tov.*
Mid. Prov.	*Midrash Proverbs.*
Mid. Ps.	*Midrash Tehillim* (Eng tr. *The Midrash on Psalms* (JPS, 1959).
Mid. Sam.	*Midrash Samuel.*
Mid. Song	*Midrash Shir ha-Shirim.*
Mid. Tan.	*Midrash Tanna'im* on Deuteronomy.
Miége, Maroc	J.L. Miège, *Le Maroc et l'Europe,* 3 vols. (1961 62).
Mig.	Philo, *De Migratione Abrahami.*
Mik.	*Mikva'ot* (mishnaic tractate).
Milano, Bibliotheca	A. Milano, *Bibliotheca Historica Italo-Judaica* (1954); supplement for 1954–63 (1964); supplement for 1964–66 in RMI, 32 (1966).
Milano, Italia	A. Milano, *Storia degli Ebrei in Italia* (1963).
MIO	*Mitteilungen des Instituts fuer Orientforschung* 1953ff.).
Mish.	Mishnah.
MJ	*Le Monde Juif* (1946ff.).
MJC	see Neubauer, Chronicles.
MK	*Mo'ed Katan* (talmudic tractate).
MNDPV	*Mitteilungen und Nachrichten des deutschen Palaestinavereins* (1895–1912).
Mortara, Indice	M. Mortara, *Indice Alfabetico dei Rabbini e Scrittori Israeliti ... in Italia ...* (1886).
Mos	Philo, *De Vita Mosis.*
Moscati, Epig	S, Moscati, *Epigrafia ebraica antica* 1935–1950 (1951).
MT	Masoretic Text of the Bible.
Mueller, Musiker	[E.H. Mueller], *Deutisches Musiker-Lexikon* (1929)
Munk, Mélanges	S. Munk, *Mélanges de philosophie juive et arabe* (1859; repr. 1955).
Mut.	Philo, *De Mutatione Nominum.*
MWJ	*Magazin fuer die Wissenshaft des Judentums* (18745 93).
Nah.	Nahum (Bible).
Naz.	*Nazir* (talmudic tractate).
NDB	*Neue Deutsche Biographie* (1953ff.).
Ned.	*Nedarim* (talmudic tractate).
Neg.	*Nega'im* (mishnaic tractate).
Neh.	Nehemiah (Bible).
NG²	*New Grove Dictionary of Music and Musicians* (2001).
Nuebauer, Cat	A. Neubauer, *Catalogue of the Hebrew Manuscripts in the Bodleian Library ...,* 2 vols. (1886–1906).
Neubauer, Chronicles	A. Neubauer, *Mediaeval Jewish Chronicles,* 2 vols. (Heb., 1887–95; repr. 1965), Eng. title of *Seder ha-Ḥakhamim ve-Korot ha-Yamim.*
Neubauer, Géogr	A. Neubauer, *La géographie du Talmud* (1868).
Neuman, Spain	A.A. Neuman, *The Jews in Spain, their Social, Political, and Cultural Life During the Middle Ages,* 2 vols. (1942).
Neusner, Babylonia	J. Neusner, *History of the Jews in Babylonia,* 5 vols. 1965–70), 2nd revised printing 1969ff.).
Nid.	*Niddah* (talmudic tractate).
Noah	Fragment of Book of Noah (Pseudepigrapha).
Noth, Hist Isr	M. Noth, *History of Israel* (1958).
Noth, Personennamen	M. Noth, *Die israelitischen Personennamen.* ... (1928).
Noth, Ueberlief	M. Noth, *Ueberlieferungsgeschichte des Pentateuchs* (1949).
Noth, Welt	M. Noth, *Die Welt des Alten Testaments* (1957³).
Nowack, Lehrbuch	W. Nowack, *Lehrbuch der hebraeischen Archaeologie,* 2 vols (1894).
NT	New Testament.
Num.	Numbers (Bible).
Num R.	*Numbers Rabbah.*
Obad.	Obadiah (Bible).
ODNB online	*Oxford Dictionary of National Biography.*
OḤ	*Oraḥ Ḥayyim.*
Oho.	*Oholot* (mishnaic tractate).
Olmstead	H.T. Olmstead, *History of Palestine and Syria* (1931; repr. 1965).
OLZ	*Orientalistische Literaturzeitung* (1898ff.)
Onom.	Eusebius, *Onomasticon.*
Op.	Philo, *De Opificio Mundi.*
OPD	*Osef Piskei Din shel ha-Rabbanut ha-Rashit le-Ereẓ Yisrael, Bet ha-Din ha-Gadol le-Irurim* (1950).
Or.	*Orlah* (talmudic tractate).
Or. Sibyll.	Sibylline Oracles (Pseudepigrapha).
OS	*L'Orient Syrien* (1956ff.)
OTS	*Oudtestamentische Studien* (1942ff.).
PAAJR	*Proceedings of the American Academy for Jewish Research* (1930ff.)
Pap 4QS[e]	A papyrus exemplar of IQS.
Par.	*Parah* (mishnaic tractate).
Pauly-Wissowa	A.F. Pauly, *Realencyklopaedie der klassichen Alertumswissenschaft,* ed. by G. Wissowa et al. (1864ff.)

PD	*Piskei Din shel Bet ha-Mishpat ha-Elyon le-Yisrael* (1948ff.)
PDR	*Piskei Din shel Battei ha-Din ha-Rabbaniyyim be-Yisrael.*
PdRE	*Pirkei de-R. Eliezer* (Eng. tr. 1916. (1965^2).
PdRK	*Pesikta de-Rav Kahana.*
Pe'ah	*Pe'ah* (talmudic tractate).
Peake, Commentary	A.J. Peake (ed.), *Commentary on the Bible* (1919; rev. 1962).
Pedersen, Israel	J. Pedersen, *Israel, Its Life and Culture,* 4 vols. in 2 (1926–40).
PEFQS	*Palestine Exploration Fund Quarterly Statement* (1869–1937; since 1938–PEQ).
PEQ	*Palestine Exploration Quarterly* (until 1937 PEFQS; after 1927 includes BBSAJ).
Perles, Beitaege	J. Perles, *Beitraege zur rabbinischen Sprach- und Alterthumskunde* (1893).
Pes.	*Pesaḥim* (talmudic tractate).
Pesh.	Peshitta (Syriac translation of the Bible).
Pesher Hab.	Commentary to Habakkuk from Qumran; see 1Qp Hab.
I and II Pet.	Epistles of Peter (New Testament).
Pfeiffer, Introd	R.H. Pfeiffer, *Introduction to the Old Testament* (1948).
PG	J.P. Migne (ed.), *Patrologia Graeca,* 161 vols. (1866–86).
Phil.	Epistle to the Philippians (New Testament).
Philem.	Epistle to the Philemon (New Testament).
PIASH	*Proceedings of the Israel Academy of Sciences and Humanities* (1963/7ff.).
PJB	*Palaestinajahrbuch des deutschen evangelischen Institutes fuer Altertumswissenschaft,* Jerusalem (1905–1933).
PK	*Pinkas ha-Kehillot,* encyclopedia of Jewish communities, published in over 30 volumes by Yad Vashem from 1970 and arranged by countries, regions and localities. For 3-vol. English edition see Spector, *Jewish Life.*
PL	J.P. Migne (ed.), *Patrologia Latina* 221 vols. (1844–64).
Plant	Philo, *De Plantatione.*
PO	R. Graffin and F. Nau (eds.), *Patrologia Orientalis* (1903ff.)
Pool, Prayer	D. de Sola Pool, *Traditional Prayer Book for Sabbath and Festivals* (1960).
Post	Philo, *De Posteritate Caini.*
PR	*Pesikta Rabbati.*
Praem.	Philo, *De Praemiis et Poenis.*
Prawer, Ẓalbanim	J. Prawer, *Toledot Mamlekhet ha-Ẓalbanim be-Ereẓ Yisrael,* 2 vols. (1963).
Press, Ereẓ	I. Press, *Ereẓ-Yisrael, Enẓiklopedyah Topografit-Historit,* 4 vols. (1951–55).
Pritchard, Pictures	J.B. Pritchard (ed.), *Ancient Near East in Pictures* (1954, 1970).
Pritchard, Texts	J.B. Pritchard (ed.), *Ancient Near East Texts* ... (1970^3).
Pr. Man.	Prayer of Manasses (Apocrypha).
Prob.	Philo, *Quod Omnis Probus Liber Sit.*
Prov.	Proverbs (Bible).
PS	*Palestinsky Sbornik* (Russ. (1881 1916, 1954ff).
Ps.	Psalms (Bible).
PSBA	*Proceedings of the Society of Biblical Archaeology* (1878–1918).
Ps. of Sol	Psalms of Solomon (Pseudepigrapha).

IQ Apoc	The *Genesis Apocryphon* from Qumran, cave one, ed. by N. Avigad and Y. Yadin (1956).
6QD	*Damascus Document* or *Sefer Berit Dammesk* from Qumran, cave six, ed. by M. Baillet, in RB, 63 (1956), 513–23 (see also CD).
QDAP	*Quarterly of the Department of Antiquities in Palestine* (1932ff.).
4QDeut. 32	Manuscript of Deuteronomy 32 from Qumran, cave four (ed. by P.W. Skehan, in BASOR, 136 (1954), 12–15).
4QEx^a	Exodus manuscript in Jewish script from Qumran, cave four.
4QEx$^\alpha$	Exodus manuscript in Paleo-Hebrew script from Qumran, cave four (partially ed. by P.W. Skehan, in JBL, 74 (1955), 182–7).
4QFlor	*Florilegium,* a miscellany from Qumran, cave four (ed. by J.M. Allegro, in JBL, 75 (1956), 176–77 and 77 (1958), 350–54).).
QGJD	*Quellen zur Geschichte der Juden in Deutschland* 1888–98).
IQH	*Thanksgiving Psalms* of *Hodayot* from Qumran, cave one (ed. by E.L. Sukenik and N. Avigad, *Oẓar ha-Megillot ha-Genuzot* (1954).
IQIs^a	Scroll of Isaiah from Qumran, cave one (ed. by N. Burrows et al., *Dead Sea Scrolls* ..., 1 (1950).
IQIs^b	Scroll of Isaiah from Qumran, cave one (ed. E.L. Sukenik and N. Avigad, *Oẓar ha-Megillot ha-Genuzot* (1954).
IQM	The *War Scroll* or *Serekh ha-Milḥamah* (ed. by E.L. Sukenik and N. Avigad, *Oẓar ha-Megillot ha-Genuzot* (1954).
4QpNah	Commentary on Nahum from Qumran, cave four (partially ed. by J.M. Allegro, in JBL, 75 (1956), 89–95).
IQphyl	Phylacteries *(tefillin)* from Qumran, cave one (ed. by Y. Yadin, in *Eretz Israel,* 9 (1969), 60–85).
4Q Prayer of Nabonidus	A document from Qumran, cave four, belonging to a lost Daniel literature (ed. by J.T. Milik, in RB, 63 (1956), 407–15).
IQS	*Manual of Discipline* or *Serekh ha-Yaḥad* from Qumran, cave one (ed. by M. Burrows et al., *Dead Sea Scrolls* ..., 2, pt. 2 (1951).

IQS^{a}	The *Rule of the Congregation or Serekh ha-Edah* from Qumran, cave one (ed. by Burrows et al., *Dead Sea Scrolls* ..., 1 (1950), under the abbreviation IQ28a).
IQS^{b}	*Blessings* or *Divrei Berakhot* from Qumran, cave one (ed. by Burrows et al., *Dead Sea Scrolls* ..., 1 (1950), under the abbreviation IQ28b).
4QSam^{a}	Manuscript of I and II Samuel from Qumran, cave four (partially ed. by F.M. Cross, in BASOR, 132 (1953), 15–26).
4QSam^{b}	Manuscript of I and II Samuel from Qumran, cave four (partially ed. by F.M. Cross, in JBL, 74 (1955), 147–72).
4QTestimonia	Sheet of Testimony from Qumran, cave four (ed. by J.M. Allegro, in JBL, 75 (1956), 174–87).).
4QT.Levi	*Testament of Levi* from Qumran, cave four (partially ed. by J.T. Milik, in RB, 62 (1955), 398–406).
Rabinovitz, Dik Sof	See Dik Sof.
RB	*Revue biblique* (1892ff.)
RBI	*Recherches bibliques* (1954ff.)
RCB	*Revista de cultura biblica* (São Paulo) (1957ff.)
Régné, Cat	J. Régné, *Catalogue des actes . . . des rois d'Aragon, concernant les Juifs* (1213–1327), in: REJ, vols. 60 70, 73, 75–78 (1910–24).
Reinach, Textes	T. Reinach, *Textes d'auteurs Grecs et Romains relatifs au Judaïsme* (1895; repr. 1963).
REJ	*Revue des études juives* (1880ff.).
Rejzen, Leksikon	Z. Rejzen, *Leksikon fun der Yidisher Literature,* 4 vols. (1927–29).
Renan, Ecrivains	A. Neubauer and E. Renan, *Les écrivains juifs français* ... (1893).
Renan, Rabbins	A. Neubauer and E. Renan, *Les rabbins français* (1877).
RES	*Revue des étude sémitiques et Babyloniaca* (1934–45).
Rev.	Revelation (New Testament).
RGG^{3}	*Die Religion in Geschichte und Gegenwart,* 7 vols. (1957–65^{3}).
RH	*Rosh Ha-Shanah* (talmudic tractate).
RHJE	*Revue de l'histoire juive en Egypte* (1947ff.).
RHMH	*Revue d'histoire de la médecine hébraïque* (1948ff.).
RHPR	*Revue d'histoire et de philosophie religieuses* (1921ff.).
RHR	*Revue d'histoire des religions* (1880ff.).
RI	*Rivista Israelitica* (1904–12).
Riemann-Einstein	*Hugo Riemanns Musiklexikon,* ed. by A. Einstein (1929^{11}).
Riemann-Gurlitt	*Hugo Riemanns Musiklexikon,* ed. by W. Gurlitt (1959–67^{12}), Personenteil.
Rigg-Jenkinson, Exchequer	J.M. Rigg, H. Jenkinson and H.G. Richardson (eds.), *Calendar of the Pleas Rolls of the Exchequer of the Jews,* 4 vols. (1905–1970); cf. in each instance also J.M. Rigg (ed.), *Select Pleas* ... (1902).
RMI	*Rassegna Mensile di Israel* (1925ff.).
Rom.	Epistle to the Romans (New Testament).
Rosanes, Togarmah	S.A. Rosanes, *Divrei Yemei Yisrael be-Togarmah,* 6 vols. (1907–45), and in 3 vols. (1930–38^{2}).
Rosenbloom, Biogr Dict	J.R. Rosenbloom, *Biographical Dictionary of Early American Jews* (1960).
Roth, Art	C. Roth, *Jewish Art* (1961).
Roth, Dark Ages	C. Roth (ed.), *World History of the Jewish People,* second series, vol. 2, *Dark Ages* (1966).
Roth, England	C. Roth, *History of the Jews in England* (1964^{3}).
Roth, Italy	C. Roth, *History of the Jews in Italy* (1946).
Roth, Mag Bibl	C. Roth, *Magna Bibliotheca Anglo-Judaica* (1937).
Roth, Marranos	C. Roth, *History of the Marranos* (2nd rev. ed 1959; reprint 1966).
Rowley, Old Test	H.H. Rowley, *Old Testament and Modern Study* (1951; repr. 1961).
RS	*Revue sémitiques d'épigraphie et d'histoire ancienne* (1893/94ff.).
RSO	*Rivista degli studi orientali* (1907ff.).
RSV	Revised Standard Version of the Bible.
Rubinstein, Australia I	*H.L. Rubinstein, The Jews in Australia, A Thematic History, Vol. I (1991).*
Rubinstein, Australia II	*W.D. Rubinstein, The Jews in Australia, A Thematic History, Vol. II (1991).*
Ruth	Ruth (Bible).
Ruth R.	*Ruth Rabbah.*
RV	Revised Version of the Bible.
Sac.	Philo, *De Sacrificiis Abelis et Caini.*
Salfeld, Martyrol	S. Salfeld, *Martyrologium des Nuernberger Memorbuches* (1898).
I and II Sam.	Samuel, book I and II (Bible).
Sanh.	*Sanhedrin* (talmudic tractate).
SBA	Society of Biblical Archaeology.
SBB	*Studies in Bibliography and Booklore* (1953ff.).
SBE	*Semana Biblica Española.*
SBT	*Studies in Biblical Theology* (1951ff.).
SBU	*Svenkst Bibliskt Uppslogsvesk,* 2 vols. (1962–63^{2}).
Schirmann, Italyah	J.Ḥ. Schirmann, *Ha-Shirah ha-Ivrit be-Italyah* (1934).
Schirmann, Sefarad	J.Ḥ. Schirmann, *Ha-Shirah ha-Ivrit bi-Sefarad u-vi-Provence,* 2 vols. (1954–56).
Scholem, Mysticism	G. Scholem, *Major Trends in Jewish Mysticism* (rev. ed. 1946; paperback ed. with additional bibliography 1961).
Scholem, Shabbetai Ẓevi	G. Scholem, *Shabbetai Ẓevi ve-ha-Tenu'ah ha-Shabbeta'it bi-Ymei Ḥayyav,* 2 vols. (1967).
Schrader, Keilinschr	E. Schrader, *Keilinschriften und das Alte Testament* (1903^{3}).
Schuerer, Gesch	E. Schuerer, *Geschichte des juedischen Volkes im Zeitalter Jesu Christi,* 3 vols. and index-vol. (1901–11^{4}).

Schuerer, Hist	E. Schuerer, *History of the Jewish People in the Time of Jesus*, ed. by N.N. Glatzer, abridged paperback edition (1961).
Set. T.	*Sefer Torah* (post-talmudic tractate).
Sem.	*Semaḥot* (post-talmudic tractate).
Sendrey, Music	A. Sendrey, *Bibliography of Jewish Music* (1951).
SER	*Seder Eliyahu Rabbah.*
SEZ	*Seder Eliyahu Zuta.*
Shab	*Shabbat* (talmudic tractate).
Sh. Ar.	J. Caro Shulḥan Arukh. OḤ – *Oraḥ Ḥayyim* YD – *Yoreh De'ah* EH – *Even ha-Ezer* ḤM – *Ḥoshen Mishpat.*
Shek.	*Shekalim* (talmudic tractate).
Shev.	*Shevi'it* (talmudic tractate).
Shevu.	*Shevu'ot* (talmudic tractate).
Shunami, Bibl	S. Shunami, *Bibliography of Jewish Bibliographies* (1965²).
Sif.	*Sifrei Deuteronomy.*
Sif. Num.	*Sifrei Numbers.*
Sifra	*Sifra* on Leviticus.
Sif. Zut.	*Sifrei Zuta.*
SIHM	Sources inédites de l'histoire du Maroc (series).
Silverman, Prayer	M. Silverman (ed.), *Sabbath and Festival Prayer Book* (1946).
Singer, Prayer	S. Singer *Authorised Daily Prayer Book* (1943¹⁷).
Sob.	Philo, *De Sobrietate.*
Sof.	*Soferim* (post-talmudic tractate).
Som.	Philo, *De Somniis.*
Song	Song of Songs (Bible).
Song. Ch.	Song of the Three Children (Apocrypha).
Song R.	*Song of Songs Rabbah.*
SOR	*Seder Olam Rabbah.*
Sot.	*Sotah* (talmudic tractate).
SOZ	*Seder Olam Zuta.*
Spec.	Philo, *De Specialibus Legibus.*
Spector, Jewish Life	*S. Spector (ed.), Encyclopedia of Jewish Life Before and After the Holocaust (2001).*
Steinschneider, Arab lit	M. Steinschneider, *Die arabische Literatur der Juden* (1902).
Steinschneider, Cat Bod	M. Steinschneider, *Catalogus Librorum Hebraeorum in Bibliotheca Bodleiana*, 3 vols. (1852–60; reprints 1931 and 1964).
Steinschneider, Hanbuch	M. Steinschneider, *Bibliographisches Handbuch ueber die . . . Literatur fuer hebraeische Sprachkunde* (1859; repr. with additions 1937).
Steinschneider, Uebersetzungen	M. Steinschneider, *Die hebraeischen Uebersetzungen des Mittelalters* (1893).
Stern, Americans	M.H. Stern, *Americans of Jewish Descent* (1960).
van Straalen, Cat	S. van Straalen, *Catalogue of Hebrew Books in the British Museum Acquired During the Years 1868–1892* (1894).
Suárez Fernández, Docmentos	L. Suárez Fernández, *Documentos acerca de la expulsion de los Judíos de España* (1964).
Suk.	*Sukkah* (talmudic tractate).
Sus.	Susanna (Apocrypha).
SY	*Sefer Yeẓirah.*
Sym.	Symmachus' Greek translation of the Bible.
SZNG	*Studien zur neueren Geschichte.*
Ta'an.	*Ta'anit* (talmudic tractate).
Tam.	*Tamid* (mishnaic tractate).
Tanḥ.	*Tanḥuma.*
Tanḥ. B.	*Tanḥuma.* Buber ed (1885).
Targ. Jon	Targum Jonathan (Aramaic version of the Prophets).
Targ. Onk.	Targum Onkelos (Aramaic version of the Pentateuch).
Targ. Yer.	Targum Yerushalmi.
TB	Babylonian Talmud or Talmud Bavli.
Tcherikover, Corpus	V. Tcherikover, A. Fuks, and M. Stern, *Corpus Papyrorum Judaicorum*, 3 vols. (1957–60).
Tef.	*Tefillin* (post-talmudic tractate).
Tem.	*Temurah* (mishnaic tractate).
Ter.	*Terumah* (talmudic tractate).
Test. Patr.	Testament of the Twelve Patriarchs (Pseudepigrapha). Ash. – Asher Ben. – Benjamin Dan – Dan Gad – Gad Iss. – Issachar Joseph – Joseph Judah – Judah Levi – Levi Naph. – Naphtali Reu. – Reuben Sim. – Simeon Zeb. – Zebulun.
I and II	Epistle to the Thessalonians (New Testament).
Thieme-Becker	U. Thieme and F. Becker (eds.), *Allgemeines Lexikon der bildenden Kuenstler von der Antike bis zur Gegenwart*, 37 vols. (1907–50).
Tidhar	D. Tidhar (ed.), *Enẓiklopedyah la-Ḥalutẓei ha-Yishuv u-Vonav* (1947ff.).
I and II Timothy	Epistles to Timothy (New Testament).
Tit.	Epistle to Titus (New Testament).
TJ	Jerusalem Talmud or Talmud Yerushalmi.
Tob.	Tobit (Apocrypha).
Toh.	*Tohorot* (mishnaic tractate).
Torczyner, Bundeslade	H. Torczyner, *Die Bundeslade und die Anfaenge der Religion Israels* (1930³).
Tos.	*Tosafot.*
Tosef.	Tosefta.
Tristram, Nat Hist	H.B. Tristram, *Natural History of the Bible* (1877⁵).
Tristram, Survey	Palestine Exploration Fund, *Survey of Western Palestine*, vol. 4 (1884) = *Fauna and Flora* by H.B. Tristram.
TS	*Terra Santa* (1943ff.).

TSBA	*Transactions of the Society of Biblical Archaeology* (1872–93).
TY	*Tevul Yom* (mishnaic tractate).
UBSB	United Bible Society, *Bulletin.*
UJE	*Universal Jewish Encyclopedia*, 10 vols. (1939–43).
Uk.	*Ukẓin* (mishnaic tractate).
Urbach, Tosafot	E.E. Urbach, *Ba'alei ha-Tosafot* (1957²).
de Vaux, Anc Isr	R. de Vaux, *Ancient Israel: its Life and Institutions* (1961; paperback 1965).
de Vaux, Instit	R. de Vaux, *Institutions de l'Ancien Testament,* 2 vols. (1958 60).
Virt.	Philo, *De Virtutibus.*
Vogelstein, Chronology	M. Volgelstein, *Biblical Chronology (1944).*
Vogelstein-Rieger	H. Vogelstein and P. Rieger, *Geschichte der Juden in Rom,* 2 vols. (1895–96).
VT	*Vetus Testamentum* (1951ff.).
VTS	*Vetus Testamentum* Supplements (1953ff.).
Vulg.	Vulgate (Latin translation of the Bible).
Wars	Josephus, *The Jewish Wars.*
Watzinger, Denkmaeler	K. Watzinger, *Denkmaeler Palaestinas,* 2 vols. (1933–35).
Waxman, Literature	M. Waxman, *History of Jewish Literature,* 5 vols. (1960²).
Weiss, Dor	I.H. Weiss, *Dor, Dor ve-Doreshav,* 5 vols. (1904⁴).
Wellhausen, Proleg	J. Wellhausen, *Prolegomena zur Geschichte Israels* (1927⁶).
WI	*Die Welt des Islams* (1913ff.).
Winniger, Biog	S. Wininger, *Grosse juedische National-Biographie ...,* 7 vols. (1925–36).
Wisd.	Wisdom of Solomon (Apocrypha)
WLB	*Wiener Library Bulletin* (1958ff.).
Wolf, Bibliotheca	J.C. Wolf, *Bibliotheca Hebraea*, 4 vols. (1715–33).
Wright, Bible	G.E. Wright, *Westminster Historical Atlas to the Bible* (1945).
Wright, Atlas	G.E. Wright, *The Bible and the Ancient Near East* (1961).
WWWJ	*Who's Who in the World Jewry* (New York, 1955, 1965²).
WZJT	*Wissenschaftliche Zeitschrift fuer juedische Theologie* (1835–37).
WZKM	*Wiener Zeitschrift fuer die Kunde des Morgenlandes* (1887ff.).
Yaari, Sheluḥei	A. Yaari, *Sheluḥei Ereẓ Yisrael* (1951).
Yad	Maimonides, *Mishneh Torah (Yad Ḥazakah).*
Yad	*Yadayim* (mishnaic tractate).
Yal.	*Yalkut Shimoni.*
Yal. Mak.	*Yalkut Makhiri.*
Yal. Reub.	*Yalkut Reubeni.*
YD	*Yoreh De'ah.*
YE	*Yevreyskaya Entsiklopediya,* 14 vols. (c. 1910).
Yev.	*Yevamot* (talmudic tractate).
YIVOA	*YIVO Annual of Jewish Social Studies* (1946ff.).
YLBI	*Year Book of the Leo Baeck Institute* (1956ff.).
YMḤEY	See BJPES.
YMḤSI	*Yedi'ot ha-Makhon le-Ḥeker ha-Shirah ha-Ivrit* (1935/36ff.).
YMMY	*Yedi'ot ha-Makhon le-Madda'ei ha-Yahadut* (1924/25ff.).
Yoma	*Yoma* (talmudic tractate).
ZA	*Zeitschrift fuer Assyriologie* (1886/87ff.).
Zav.	*Zavim* (mishnaic tractate).
ZAW	*Zeitschrift fuer die alttestamentliche Wissenschaft und die Kunde des nachbiblishchen Judentums* (1881ff.).
ZAWB	*Beihefte* (supplements) to ZAW.
ZDMG	*Zeitschrift der Deutschen Morgenlaendischen Gesellschaft* (1846ff.).
ZDPV	*Zeitschrift des Deutschen Palaestina-Vereins* (1878–1949; from 1949 = BBLA).
Zech.	Zechariah (Bible).
Zedner, Cat	J. Zedner, *Catalogue of Hebrew Books in the Library of the British Museum* (1867; repr. 1964).
Zeitlin, Bibliotheca	W. Zeitlin, *Bibliotheca Hebraica Post-Mendelssohniana* (1891–95).
Zeph.	Zephaniah (Bible).
Zev.	*Zevaḥim* (talmudic tractate).
ZGGJT	*Zeitschrift der Gesellschaft fuer die Geschichte der Juden in der Tschechoslowakei* (1930–38).
ZGJD	*Zeitschrift fuer die Geschichte der Juden in Deutschland* (1887–92).
ZHB	*Zeitschrift fuer hebraeische Bibliographie* (1896–1920).
Zinberg, Sifrut	I. Zinberg, *Toledot Sifrut Yisrael,* 6 vols. (1955–60).
Ẓiẓ.	*Ẓiẓit* (post-talmudic tractate).
ZNW	*Zeitschrift fuer die neutestamentliche Wissenschaft* (1901ff.).
ZS	*Zeitschrift fuer Semitistik und verwandte Gebiete* (1922ff.).
Zunz, Gesch	L. Zunz, *Zur Geschichte und Literatur* (1845).
Zunz, Gesch	L. Zunz, *Literaturgeschichte der synagogalen Poesie* (1865; Supplement, 1867; repr. 1966).
Zunz, Poesie	L. Zunz, *Synogogale Posie des Mittelalters,* ed. by Freimann (1920²; repr. 1967).
Zunz, Ritus	L. Zunz, *Ritus des synagogalen Gottesdienstes* (1859; repr. 1967).
Zunz, Schr	L. Zunz, *Gesammelte Schriften,* 3 vols. (1875–76).
Zunz, Vortraege	L. Zunz, *Gottesdienstliche vortraege der Juden ...* 1892²; repr. 1966).
Zunz-Albeck, Derashot	L. Zunz, *Ha-Derashot be-Yisrael*, Heb. Tr. of Zunz Vortraege by H. Albeck (1954²).

TRANSLITERATION RULES

HEBREW AND SEMITIC LANGUAGES:

	General	*Scientific*
א	not transliterated[1]	ʾ
בּ	b	b
ב	v	v, <u>b</u>
גּ	g	g
ג		ḡ
דּ	d	d
ד		<u>d</u>
ה	h	h
ו	v – when not a vowel	w
ז	z	z
ח	ḥ	ḥ
ט	t	ṭ, t
י	y – when vowel and at end of words – i	y
כּ	k	k
כ, ך	kh	kh, <u>k</u>
ל	l	<u>l</u>
מ, ם	m	m
נ, ן	n	n
ס	s	s
ע	not transliterated[1]	ʿ
פּ	p	p
פ, ף	f	p, f, ph
צ, ץ	ẓ	ṣ, ẓ
ק	k	q, k
ר	r	r
שׁ	sh[2]	š
שׂ	s	ś, s
תּ	t	t
ת		<u>t</u>
ג׳	dzh, J	ğ
ז׳	zh, J	ž
צ׳	ch	č
◌ָ		å, o, ǒ (short) â, ā (long)
◌ַ	a	a
◌ֲ		a, ^{a}
◌ֵ		e, ẹ, ē
◌ֶ	e	æ, ä, ę
◌ֱ		œ, ĕ, ^{e}
◌ְ	only *sheva na* is transliterated	ə, ĕ, e; only *sheva na* transliterated
◌ִ, ◌ִי	i	i
◌ֹ, וֹ	o	o, o, o
◌ֻ, וּ	u	u, ŭ û, ū
◌ֵי	ei; biblical e	
‡		reconstructed forms of words

1. The letters א and ע are not transliterated.
   An apostrophe (') between vowels indicates that they do not form a diphthong and are to be pronounced separately.
2. *Dagesh ḥazak* (forte) is indicated by doubling of the letter, except for the letter שׁ.
3. Names. Biblical names and biblical place names are rendered according to the Bible translation of the Jewish Publication Society of America. Post-biblical Hebrew names are transliterated; contemporary names are transliterated or rendered as used by the person. Place names are transliterated or rendered by the accepted spelling. Names and some words with an accepted English form are usually not transliterated.

YIDDISH

א	not transliterated
אַ	a
אָ	o
בּ	b
בֿ	v
ג	g
ד	d
ה	h
ו, וּ	u
וו	v
וי	oy
ז	z
זש	zh
ח	kh
ט	t
טש	tsh, ch
י	(consonant) y (vowel) i
יִ	i
יי	ey
ײַ	ay
כּ	k
כ, ך	kh
ל	l
מ, ם	m
נ, ן	n
ס	s
ע	e
פּ	p
פֿ, ף	f
צ, ץ	ts
ק	k
ר	r
שׁ	sh
שׂ	s
תּ	t
ת	s

1. Yiddish transliteration rendered according to U. Weinreich's Modern *English-Yiddish Yiddish-English* Dictionary.
2. Hebrew words in Yiddish are usually transliterated according to standard Yiddish pronunciation, e.g., חזנות = *khazones*.

LADINO

Ladino and Judeo-Spanish words written in Hebrew characters are transliterated phonetically, following the General Rules of Hebrew transliteration (see above) whenever the accepted spelling in Latin characters could not be ascertained.

ARABIC

ا ء	a[1]	ض	ḍ
ب	b	ط	ṭ
ت	t	ظ	ẓ
ث	th	ع	c
ج	j	غ	gh
ح	ḥ	ف	f
خ	kh	ق	q
د	d	ك	k
ذ	dh	ل	l
ر	r	م	m
ز	z	ن	n
س	s	ه	h
ش	sh	و	w
ص	ṣ	ي	y
ـَ	a	ـَا ى	ā
ـِ	i	ـِي	ī
ـُ	u	ـُو	ū
ـَو	aw	ـِيّ	iyy[2]
ـَي	ay	ـُوّ	uww[2]

1. not indicated when initial
2. see note (f)

a) The EJ follows the *Columbia Lippincott Gazetteer* and the *Times Atlas* in transliteration of Arabic place names. Sites that appear in neither are transliterated according to the table above, and subject to the following notes.

b) The EJ follows the *Columbia Encyclopedia* in transliteration of Arabic names. Personal names that do not therein appear are transliterated according to the table above and subject to the following notes (e.g., Ali rather than ᶜAlī, Suleiman rather than Sulayman).

c) The EJ follows the *Webster's Third International Dictionary, Unabridged* in transliteration of Arabic terms that have been integrated into the English language.

d) The term "Abu" will thus appear, usually in disregard of inflection.

e) Nunnation (end vowels, *tanwīn*) are dropped in transliteration.

f) Gemination (*tashdīd*) is indicated by the doubling of the geminated letter, unless an end letter, in which case the gemination is dropped.

g) The definitive article *al-* will always be thus transliterated, unless subject to one of the modifying notes (e.g., El-Arish rather than al-ᶜArīsh; modification according to note (a)).

h) The Arabic transliteration disregards the Sun Letters (the antero-palatals (*al-Ḥurūf al-Shamsiyya*).

i) The *tā-marbūṭa* (ο) is omitted in transliteration, unless in construct-stage (e.g., *Khirba* but *Khirbat Mishmish*).

These modifying notes may lead to various inconsistencies in the Arabic transliteration, but this policy has deliberately been adopted to gain smoother reading of Arabic terms and names.

GREEK

Ancient Greek	*Modern Greek*	*Greek Letters*
a	a	*Α; α; ᾳ*
b	v	*Β; β*
g	gh; g	*Γ; γ*
d	dh	*Δ; δ*
e	e	*Ε; ε*
z	z	*Ζ; ζ*
e; e	i	*Η; η; ῃ*
th	th	*Θ; θ*
i	i	*Ι; ι*
k	k; ky	*Κ; κ*
l	l	*Λ; λ*
m	m	*Μ; μ*
n	n	*Ν; ν*
x	x	*Ξ; ξ*
o	o	*Ο; ο*
p	p	*Π; π*
r; rh	r	*Ρ; ρ; ῥ*
s	s	*Σ; σ; ς*
t	t	*Τ; τ*
u; y	i	*Υ; υ*
ph	f	*Φ; φ*
ch	kh	*Χ; χ*
ps	ps	*Ψ; ψ*
o; ō	o	*Ω; ω; ῳ*
ai	e	*αι*
ei	i	*ει*
oi	i	*οι*
ui	i	*υι*
ou	ou	*ου*
eu	ev	*ευ*
eu; ēu	iv	*ηυ*
–	j	*τζ*
nt	d; nd	*ντ*
mp	b; mb	*μπ*
ngk	g	*γκ*
ng	ng	*νγ*
h	–	ʽ
–	–	ʼ
w	–	*ϝ*

RUSSIAN

А	A
Б	B
В	V
Г	G
Д	D
Е	E, Ye[1]
Ё	Yo, O[2]
Ж	Zh
З	Z
И	I
Й	Y[3]
К	K
Л	L
М	M
Н	N
О	O
П	P
Р	R
С	S
Т	T
У	U
Ф	F
Х	Kh
Ц	Ts
Ч	Ch
Ш	Sh
Щ	Shch
Ъ	omitted; see note [1]
Ы	Y
Ь	omitted; see note [1]
Э	E
Ю	Yu
Я	Ya

1. Ye at the beginning of a word; after all vowels except ***Ы***; and after ***Ъ*** and ***Ь***.
2. O after **Ч**, ***Ш*** and ***Щ***.
3. Omitted after ***Ы***, and in names of people after ***И***.

A. Many first names have an accepted English or quasi-English form which has been preferred to transliteration.
B. Place names have been given according to the *Columbia Lippincott Gazeteer*.
C. Pre-revolutionary spelling has been ignored.
D. Other languages using the Cyrillic alphabet (e.g., Bulgarian, Ukrainian), inasmuch as they appear, have been phonetically transliterated in conformity with the principles of this table.

GLOSSARY

Asterisked terms have separate entries in the Encyclopaedia.

Actions Committee, early name of the Zionist General Council, the supreme institution of the World Zionist Organization in the interim between Congresses. The Zionist Executive's name was then the "Small Actions Committee."

*__Adar__, twelfth month of the Jewish religious year, sixth of the civil, approximating to February–March.

*__Aggadah__, name given to those sections of Talmud and Midrash containing homiletic expositions of the Bible, stories, legends, folklore, anecdotes, or maxims. In contradistinction to **halakhah.*

*__Agunah__, woman unable to remarry according to Jewish law, because of desertion by her husband or inability to accept presumption of death.

*__Aharonim__, later rabbinic authorities. In contradistinction to **rishonim* ("early ones").

Ahavah, liturgical poem inserted in the second benediction of the morning prayer *(*Ahavah Rabbah)* of the festivals and/or special Sabbaths.

Aktion (Ger.), operation involving the mass assembly, deportation, and murder of Jews by the Nazis during the *Holocaust.

*__Aliyah__, (1) being called to Reading of the Law in synagogue; (2) immigration to Ereẓ Israel; (3) one of the waves of immigration to Ereẓ Israel from the early 1880s.

*__Amidah__, main prayer recited at all services; also known as *Shemoneh Esreh* and *Tefillah.*

*__Amora__ (pl. **amoraim**), title given to the Jewish scholars in Ereẓ Israel and Babylonia in the third to sixth centuries who were responsible for the **Gemara.*

Aravah, the *willow; one of the *Four Species used on *Sukkot ("festival of Tabernacles") together with the **etrog, hadas*, and **lulav.*

*__Arvit__, evening prayer.

Asarah be-Tevet, fast on the 10th of Tevet commemorating the commencement of the siege of Jerusalem by Nebuchadnezzar.

Asefat ha-Nivḥarim, representative assembly elected by Jews in Palestine during the period of the British Mandate (1920–48).

*__Ashkenaz__, name applied generally in medieval rabbinical literature to Germany.

*__Ashkenazi__ (pl. **Ashkenazim**), German or West-, Central-, or East-European Jew(s), as contrasted with *Sephardi(m).

*__Av__, fifth month of the Jewish religious year, eleventh of the civil, approximating to July–August.

*__Av bet din__, vice president of the supreme court (*bet din ha-gadol*) in Jerusalem during the Second Temple period; later, title given to communal rabbis as heads of the religious courts (see **bet din*).

*__Badḥan__, jester, particularly at traditional Jewish weddings in Eastern Europe.

*__Bakkashah__ (Heb. "supplication"), type of petitionary prayer, mainly recited in the Sephardi rite on Rosh Ha-Shanah and the Day of Atonement.

Bar, "son of . . . "; frequently appearing in personal names.

*__Baraita__ (pl. **beraitot**), statement of **tanna* not found in *Mishnah.

*__Bar mitzvah__, ceremony marking the initiation of a boy at the age of 13 into the Jewish religious community.

Ben, "son of . . . ", frequently appearing in personal names.

Berakhah (pl. **berakhot**), *benediction, blessing; formula of praise and thanksgiving.

*__Bet din__ (pl. **battei din**), rabbinic court of law.

*__Bet ha-midrash__, school for higher rabbinic learning; often attached to or serving as a synagogue.

*__Bilu__, first modern movement for pioneering and agricultural settlement in Ereẓ Israel, founded in 1882 at Kharkov, Russia.

*__Bund__, Jewish socialist party founded in Vilna in 1897, supporting Jewish national rights; Yiddishist, and anti-Zionist.

Cohen (pl. **Cohanim**), see Kohen.

*__Conservative Judaism__, trend in Judaism developed in the United States in the 20th century which, while opposing extreme changes in traditional observances, permits certain modifications of *halakhah* in response to the changing needs of the Jewish people.

*__Consistory__ (Fr. *consistoire*), governing body of a Jewish communal district in France and certain other countries.

*__Converso(s)__, term applied in Spain and Portugal to converted Jew(s), and sometimes more loosely to their descendants.

*__Crypto-Jew__, term applied to a person who although observing outwardly Christianity (or some other religion) was at heart a Jew and maintained Jewish observances as far as possible (see Converso; Marrano; Neofiti; New Christian; Jadīd al-Islām).

*__Dayyan__, member of rabbinic court.

Decisor, equivalent to the Hebrew *posek* (pl. **posekim*), the rabbi who gives the decision (*halakhah*) in Jewish law or practice.

*__Devekut__, "devotion"; attachment or adhesion to God; communion with God.

*__Diaspora__, Jews living in the "dispersion" outside Ereẓ Israel; area of Jewish settlement outside Ereẓ Israel.

Din, a law (both secular and religious), legal decision, or lawsuit.

Divan, diwan, collection of poems, especially in Hebrew, Arabic, or Persian.

Dunam, unit of land area (1,000 sq. m., c. ¼ acre), used in Israel.

Einsatzgruppen, mobile units of Nazi S.S. and S.D.; in U.S.S.R. and Serbia, mobile killing units.

*__Ein-Sof__, "without end"; "the infinite"; hidden, impersonal aspect of God; also used as a Divine Name.

*__Elul__, sixth month of the Jewish religious calendar, 12th of the civil, precedes the High Holiday season in the fall.

Endloesung, see *Final Solution.

*__Ereẓ Israel__, Land of Israel; Palestine.

*__Eruv__, technical term for rabbinical provision permitting the alleviation of certain restrictions.

*__Etrog__, citron; one of the *Four Species used on *Sukkot together with the **lulav, hadas*, and *aravah.*

Even ha-Ezer, see Shulḥan Arukh.

*__Exilarch__, lay head of Jewish community in Babylonia (see also *resh galuta*), and elsewhere.

*__Final Solution__ (Ger. *Endloesung*), in Nazi terminology, the Nazi-planned mass murder and total annihilation of the Jews.

*__Gabbai__, official of a Jewish congregation; originally a charity collector.

*__Galut__, "exile"; the condition of the Jewish people in dispersion.

*__Gaon__ (pl. **geonim**), head of academy in post-talmudic period, especially in Babylonia.
Gaonate, office of *gaon.
*__Gemara__, traditions, discussions, and rulings of the *amoraim*, commenting on and supplementing the *Mishnah, and forming part of the Babylonian and Palestinian Talmuds (see Talmud).
*__Gematria__, interpretation of Hebrew word according to the numerical value of its letters.
General Government, territory in Poland administered by a German civilian governor-general with headquarters in Cracow after the German occupation in World War II.
*__Genizah__, depository for sacred books. The best known was discovered in the synagogue of Fostat (old Cairo).
Get, bill of *divorce.
*__Ge'ullah__, hymn inserted after the **Shema* into the benediction of the morning prayer of the festivals and special Sabbaths.
*__Gilgul__, metempsychosis; transmigration of souls.
*__Golem__, automaton, especially in human form, created by magical means and endowed with life.
*__Ḥabad__, initials of *ḥokhmah, binah, da'at*: "wisdom, understanding, knowledge"; ḥasidic movement founded in Belorussia by *Shneur Zalman of Lyady.
Hadas, *myrtle; one of the *Four Species used on Sukkot together with the **etrog*, **lulav*, and *aravah*.
*__Haftarah__ (pl. **haftarot**), designation of the portion from the prophetical books of the Bible recited after the synagogue reading from the Pentateuch on Sabbaths and holidays.
*__Haganah__, clandestine Jewish organization for armed self-defense in Ereẓ Israel under the British Mandate, which eventually evolved into a people's militia and became the basis for the Israel army.
*__Haggadah__, ritual recited in the home on *Passover eve at seder table.
Haham, title of chief rabbi of the Spanish and Portuguese congregations in London, England.
*__Hakham__, title of rabbi of *Sephardi congregation.
*__Hakham bashi__, title in the 15th century and modern times of the chief rabbi in the Ottoman Empire, residing in Constantinople (Istanbul), also applied to principal rabbis in provincial towns.
Hakhsharah ("preparation"), organized training in the Diaspora of pioneers for agricultural settlement in Ereẓ Israel.
*__Halakhah__ (pl. **halakhot**), an accepted decision in rabbinic law. Also refers to those parts of the *Talmud concerned with legal matters. In contradistinction to **aggadah*.
Ḥaliẓah, biblically prescribed ceremony (Deut. 25:9–10) performed when a man refuses to marry his brother's childless widow, enabling her to remarry.
*__Hallel__, term referring to Psalms 113-18 in liturgical use.
*__Ḥalukkah__, system of financing the maintenance of Jewish communities in the holy cities of Ereẓ Israel by collections made abroad, mainly in the pre-Zionist era (see *kolel*).
Ḥalutz (pl. **ḥalutzim**), pioneer, especially in agriculture, in Ereẓ Israel.
Ḥalutziyyut, pioneering.
*__Ḥanukkah__, eight-day celebration commemorating the victory of *Judah Maccabee over the Syrian king *Antiochus Epiphanes and the subsequent rededication of the Temple.
Ḥasid, adherent of *Ḥasidism.
*__Ḥasidei Ashkenaz__, medieval pietist movement among the Jews of Germany.
*__Ḥasidism__, (1) religious revivalist movement of popular mysticism among Jews of Germany in the Middle Ages; (2) religious movement founded by *Israel ben Eliezer Ba'al Shem Tov in the first half of the 18th century.
*__Haskalah__, "enlightenment"; movement for spreading modern European culture among Jews c. 1750–1880. See *maskil*.
*__Havdalah__, ceremony marking the end of Sabbath or festival.
*__Ḥazzan__, precentor who intones the liturgy and leads the prayers in synagogue; in earlier times a synagogue official.
*__Ḥeder__ (lit. "room"), school for teaching children Jewish religious observance.
Heikhalot, "palaces"; tradition in Jewish mysticism centering on mystical journeys through the heavenly spheres and palaces to the Divine Chariot (see Merkabah).
*__Ḥerem__, excommunication, imposed by rabbinical authorities for purposes of religious and/or communal discipline; originally, in biblical times, that which is separated from common use either because it was an abomination or because it was consecrated to God.
Ḥeshvan, see Marḥeshvan.
*__Ḥevra kaddisha__, title applied to charitable confraternity (**ḥevrah*), now generally limited to associations for burial of the dead.
*__Ḥibbat Zion__, see Ḥovevei Zion.
*__Histadrut__ (abbr. For Heb. **Ha-Histadrut ha-Kelalit shel ha-Ovedim ha-Ivriyyim be-Ereẓ Israel**). Ereẓ Israel Jewish Labor Federation, founded in 1920; subsequently renamed Histadrut ha-Ovedim be-Ereẓ Israel.
*__Holocaust__, the organized mass persecution and annihilation of European Jewry by the Nazis (1933–1945).
*__Hoshana Rabba__, the seventh day of *Sukkot on which special observances are held.
Ḥoshen Mishpat, see Shulḥan Arukh.
Ḥovevei Zion, federation of *Ḥibbat Zion, early (pre-*Herzl) Zionist movement in Russia.
Illui, outstanding scholar or genius, especially a young prodigy in talmudic learning.
*__Iyyar__, second month of the Jewish religious year, eighth of the civil, approximating to April-May.
I.Ẓ.L. (initials of Heb. ***Irgun Ẓeva'i Le'ummi**; "National Military Organization"), underground Jewish organization in Ereẓ Israel founded in 1931, which engaged from 1937 in retaliatory acts against Arab attacks and later against the British mandatory authorities.
*__Jadīd al-Islām__ (Ar.), a person practicing the Jewish religion in secret although outwardly observing Islām.
*__Jewish Legion__, Jewish units in British army during World War I.
*__Jihād__ (Ar.), in Muslim religious law, holy war waged against infidels.
*__Judenrat__ (Ger. "Jewish council"), council set up in Jewish communities and ghettos under the Nazis to execute their instructions.
*__Judenrein__ (Ger. "clean of Jews"), in Nazi terminology the condition of a locality from which all Jews had been eliminated.
*__Kabbalah__, the Jewish mystical tradition:
  Kabbala iyyunit, speculative Kabbalah;
  Kabbala ma'asit, practical Kabbalah;
  Kabbala nevu'it, prophetic Kabbalah.
Kabbalist, student of Kabbalah.
*__Kaddish__, liturgical doxology.
Kahal, Jewish congregation; among Ashkenazim, *kehillah*.

***Kalām** (Ar.), science of Muslim theology; adherents of the Kalām are called *mutakallimūn*.

***Karaite**, member of a Jewish sect originating in the eighth century which rejected rabbinic (*Rabbanite) Judaism and claimed to accept only Scripture as authoritative.

***Kasher**, ritually permissible food.

Kashrut, Jewish *dietary laws.

***Kavvanah**, "intention"; term denoting the spiritual concentration accompanying prayer and the performance of ritual or of a commandment.

***Kedushah**, main addition to the third blessing in the reader's repetition of the *Amidah* in which the public responds to the precentor's introduction.

Kefar, village; first part of name of many settlements in Israel.

Kehillah, congregation; see *kahal*.

Kelippah (pl. **kelippot**), "husk(s)"; mystical term denoting force(s) of evil.

***Keneset Yisrael**, comprehensive communal organization of the Jews in Palestine during the British Mandate.

Keri, variants in the masoretic (*masorah) text of the Bible between the spelling (*ketiv*) and its pronunciation (*keri*).

***Kerovah** (collective plural (corrupted) from **kerovez̧**), poem(s) incorporated into the **Amidah*.

Ketiv, see *keri*.

***Ketubbah**, marriage contract, stipulating husband's obligations to wife.

Kevuz̧ah, small commune of pioneers constituting an agricultural settlement in Erez̧ Israel (evolved later into *kibbutz).

***Kibbutz** (pl. **kibbutzim**), larger-size commune constituting a settlement in Erez̧ Israel based mainly on agriculture but engaging also in industry.

***Kiddush**, prayer of sanctification, recited over wine or bread on eve of Sabbaths and festivals.

***Kiddush ha-Shem**, term connoting martyrdom or act of strict integrity in support of Judaic principles.

***Kinah** (pl. **kinot**), lamentation dirge(s) for the Ninth of Av and other fast days.

***Kislev**, ninth month of the Jewish religious year, third of the civil, approximating to November-December.

Klaus, name given in Central and Eastern Europe to an institution, usually with synagogue attached, where *Talmud was studied perpetually by adults; applied by Ḥasidim to their synagogue ("*kloyz*").

***Knesset**, parliament of the State of Israel.

K(c)ohen (pl. **K(c)ohanim**), Jew(s) of priestly (Aaronide) descent.

***Kolel**, (1) community in Erez̧ Israel of persons from a particular country or locality, often supported by their fellow countrymen in the Diaspora; (2) institution for higher Torah study.

Kosher, see *kasher*.

***Kristallnacht** (Ger. "crystal night," meaning "night of broken glass"), organized destruction of synagogues, Jewish houses, and shops, accompanied by mass arrests of Jews, which took place in Germany and Austria under the Nazis on the night of Nov. 9–10, 1938.

***Lag ba-Omer**, 33rd (Heb. **lag**) day of the **Omer* period falling on the 18th of *Iyyar; a semi-holiday.

Leḥi (abbr. For Heb. ***Loḥamei Ḥerut Israel**, "Fighters for the Freedom of Israel"), radically anti-British armed underground organization in Palestine, founded in 1940 by dissidents from *I.Z.L.

Levir, husband's brother.

***Levirate marriage** (Heb. *yibbum*), marriage of childless widow (*yevamah*) by brother (*yavam*) of the deceased husband (in accordance with Deut. 25:5); release from such an obligation is effected through *ḥaliz̧ah*.

LHY, see Leḥi.

***Lulav**, palm branch; one of the *Four Species used on *Sukkot together with the **etrog*, *hadas*, and *aravah*.

***Ma'aravot**, hymns inserted into the evening prayer of the three festivals, Passover, Shavuot, and Sukkot.

Ma'ariv, evening prayer; also called **arvit*.

***Ma'barah**, transition camp; temporary settlement for newcomers in Israel during the period of mass immigration following 1948.

***Maftir**, reader of the concluding portion of the Pentateuchal section on Sabbaths and holidays in synagogue; reader of the portion of the prophetical books of the Bible (**haftarah*).

***Maggid**, popular preacher.

***Maḥzor** (pl. **maḥzorim**), festival prayer book.

***Mamzer**, bastard; according to Jewish law, the offspring of an incestuous relationship.

***Mandate, Palestine**, responsibility for the administration of Palestine conferred on Britain by the League of Nations in 1922; mandatory government: the British administration of Palestine.

***Maqāma** (Ar. pl. **maqamāt**), poetic form (rhymed prose) which, in its classical arrangement, has rigid rules of form and content.

***Marḥeshvan**, popularly called Ḥeshvan; eighth month of the Jewish religious year, second of the civil, approximating to October–November.

***Marrano(s)**, descendant(s) of Jew(s) in Spain and Portugal whose ancestors had been converted to Christianity under pressure but who secretly observed Jewish rituals.

Maskil (pl. **maskilim**), adherent of *Haskalah ("Enlightenment") movement.

***Masorah**, body of traditions regarding the correct spelling, writing, and reading of the Hebrew Bible.

Masorete, scholar of the masoretic tradition.

Masoretic, in accordance with the masorah.

Meliz̧ah, in Middle Ages, elegant style; modern usage, florid style using biblical or talmudic phraseology.

Mellah, *Jewish quarter in North African towns.

***Menorah**, candelabrum; seven-branched oil lamp used in the Tabernacle and Temple; also eight-branched candelabrum used on *Ḥanukkah.

Me'orah, hymn inserted into the first benediction of the morning prayer (*Yoz̧er ha-Me'orot*).

***Merkabah**, *merkavah*, "chariot"; mystical discipline associated with Ezekiel's vision of the Divine Throne-Chariot (Ezek. 1).

Meshullaḥ, emissary sent to conduct propaganda or raise funds for rabbinical academies or charitable institutions.

***Mezuzah** (pl. **mezuzot**), parchment scroll with selected Torah verses placed in container and affixed to gates and doorposts of houses occupied by Jews.

***Midrash**, method of interpreting Scripture to elucidate legal points (*Midrash Halakhah*) or to bring out lessons by stories or homiletics (*Midrash Aggadah*). Also the name for a collection of such rabbinic interpretations.

***Mikveh**, ritual bath.

***Minhag** (pl. **minhagim**), ritual custom(s); synagogal rite(s); especially of a specific sector of Jewry.

***Minḥah**, afternoon prayer; originally meal offering in Temple.

***Minyan**, group of ten male adult Jews, the minimum required for communal prayer.

***Mishnah**, earliest codification of Jewish Oral Law.

Mishnah (pl. **mishnayot**), subdivision of tractates of the Mishnah.

Mitnagged (pl. ***Mitnaggedim**), originally, opponents of *Ḥasidism in Eastern Europe.

***Mitzvah**, biblical or rabbinic injunction; applied also to good or charitable deeds.

Mohel, official performing circumcisions.

***Moshav**, smallholders' cooperative agricultural settlement in Israel, see moshav ovedim.

Moshavah, earliest type of Jewish village in modern Ereẓ Israel in which farming is conducted on individual farms mostly on privately owned land.

Moshav ovedim ("workers' moshav"), agricultural village in Israel whose inhabitants possess individual homes and holdings but cooperate in the purchase of equipment, sale of produce, mutual aid, etc.

***Moshav shittufi** ("collective moshav"), agricultural village in Israel whose members possess individual homesteads but where the agriculture and economy are conducted as a collective unit.

Mostegab (Ar.), poem with biblical verse at beginning of each stanza.

***Muqaddam** (Ar., pl. **muqaddamūn**), "leader," "head of the community."

***Musaf**, additional service on Sabbath and festivals; originally the additional sacrifice offered in the Temple.

Musar, traditional ethical literature.

***Musar movement**, ethical movement developing in the latter part of the 19th century among Orthodox Jewish groups in Lithuania; founded by R. Israel *Lipkin (Salanter).

***Nagid** (pl. **negidim**), title applied in Muslim (and some Christian) countries in the Middle Ages to a leader recognized by the state as head of the Jewish community.

Nakdan (pl. **nakdanim**), "punctuator"; scholar of the 9th to 14th centuries who provided biblical manuscripts with masoretic apparatus, vowels, and accents.

***Nasi** (pl. **nesi'im**), talmudic term for president of the Sanhedrin, who was also the spiritual head and later, political representative of the Jewish people; from second century a descendant of Hillel recognized by the Roman authorities as patriarch of the Jews. Now applied to the president of the State of Israel.

***Negev**, the southern, mostly arid, area of Israel.

***Ne'ilah**, concluding service on the *Day of Atonement.

Neofiti, term applied in southern Italy to converts to Christianity from Judaism and their descendants who were suspected of maintaining secret allegiance to Judaism.

***Neology**; **Neolog**; **Neologism**, trend of *Reform Judaism in Hungary forming separate congregations after 1868.

***Nevelah** (lit. "carcass"), meat forbidden by the *dietary laws on account of the absence of, or defect in, the act of *sheḥitah* (ritual slaughter).

***New Christians**, term applied especially in Spain and Portugal to converts from Judaism (and from Islam) and their descendants; "Half New Christian" designated a person one of whose parents was of full Jewish blood.

***Niddah** ("menstruous woman"), woman during the period of menstruation.

***Nisan**, first month of the Jewish religious year, seventh of the civil, approximating to March-April.

Niẓoẓot, "sparks"; mystical term for sparks of the holy light imprisoned in all matter.

Nosaḥ (**nusaḥ**) "version"; (1) textual variant; (2) term applied to distinguish the various prayer rites, e.g., *nosaḥ Ashkenaz*; (3) the accepted tradition of synagogue melody.

***Notarikon**, method of abbreviating Hebrew works or phrases by acronym.

Novella(e) (Heb. **ḥiddush (im)*), commentary on talmudic and later rabbinic subjects that derives new facts or principles from the implications of the text.

***Nuremberg Laws**, Nazi laws excluding Jews from German citizenship, and imposing other restrictions.

Ofan, hymns inserted into a passage of the morning prayer.

***Omer**, first sheaf cut during the barley harvest, offered in the Temple on the second day of Passover.

Omer, Counting of (Heb. *Sefirat ha-Omer*), 49 days counted from the day on which the *omer* was first offered in the Temple (according to the rabbis the 16th of Nisan, i.e., the second day of Passover) until the festival of Shavuot; now a period of semi-mourning.

Oraḥ Ḥayyim, see Shulḥan Arukh.

***Orthodoxy** (Orthodox Judaism), modern term for the strictly traditional sector of Jewry.

***Pale of Settlement**, 25 provinces of czarist Russia where Jews were permitted permanent residence.

***Palmaḥ** (abbr. for Heb. *peluggot maḥaẓ*; "shock companies"), striking arm of the *Haganah.

***Pardes**, medieval biblical exegesis giving the literal, allegorical, homiletical, and esoteric interpretations.

***Parnas**, chief synagogue functionary, originally vested with both religious and administrative functions; subsequently an elected lay leader.

Partition plan(s), proposals for dividing Ereẓ Israel into autonomous areas.

Paytan, composer of **piyyut* (liturgical poetry).

***Peel Commission**, British Royal Commission appointed by the British government in 1936 to inquire into the Palestine problem and make recommendations for its solution.

Pesaḥ, *Passover.

***Pilpul**, in talmudic and rabbinic literature, a sharp dialectic used particularly by talmudists in Poland from the 16th century.

***Pinkas**, community register or minute-book.

***Piyyut**, (pl. **piyyutim**), Hebrew liturgical poetry.

***Pizmon**, poem with refrain.

Posek (pl. ***posekim**), decisor; codifier or rabbinic scholar who pronounces decisions in disputes and on questions of Jewish law.

***Prosbul**, legal method of overcoming the cancelation of debts with the advent of the *sabbatical year.

***Purim**, festival held on Adar 14 or 15 in commemoration of the delivery of the Jews of Persia in the time of *Esther.

Rabban, honorific title higher than that of rabbi, applied to heads of the *Sanhedrin in mishnaic times.

***Rabbanite**, adherent of rabbinic Judaism. In contradistinction to *Karaite.

Reb, rebbe, Yiddish form for rabbi, applied generally to a teacher or ḥasidic rabbi.

***Reconstructionism**, trend in Jewish thought originating in the United States.

***Reform Judaism**, trend in Judaism advocating modification of *Orthodoxy in conformity with the exigencies of contemporary life and thought.

Resh galuta, lay head of Babylonian Jewry (see exilarch).
Responsum (pl. ***responsa**), written opinion (*teshuvah*) given to question (*she'elah*) on aspects of Jewish law by qualified authorities; pl. collection of such queries and opinions in book form (*she'elot u-teshuvot*).
***Rishonim**, older rabbinical authorities. Distinguished from later authorities (**aḥaronim*).
***Rishon le-Zion**, title given to Sephardi chief rabbi of Ereẓ Israel.
***Rosh Ha-Shanah**, two-day holiday (one day in biblical and early mishnaic times) at the beginning of the month of *Tishri (September–October), traditionally the New Year.
Rosh Hodesh, *New Moon, marking the beginning of the Hebrew month.
Rosh Yeshivah, see *Yeshivah.
***R.S.H.A.** (initials of Ger. *Reichssicherheitshauptamt*: "Reich Security Main Office"), the central security department of the German Reich, formed in 1939, and combining the security police (Gestapo and Kripo) and the S.D.
***Sanhedrin**, the assembly of ordained scholars which functioned both as a supreme court and as a legislature before 70 C.E. In modern times the name was given to the body of representative Jews convoked by Napoleon in 1807.
***Savora** (pl. **savoraim**), name given to the Babylonian scholars of the period between the **amoraim* and the **geonim*, approximately 500–700 C.E.
S.D. (initials of Ger. *Sicherheitsdienst*: "security service"), security service of the *S.S. formed in 1932 as the sole intelligence organization of the Nazi party.
Seder, ceremony observed in the Jewish home on the first night of Passover (outside Ereẓ Israel first two nights), when the *Haggadah is recited.
***Sefer Torah**, manuscript scroll of the Pentateuch for public reading in synagogue.
***Sefirot, the ten**, the ten "Numbers"; mystical term denoting the ten spheres or emanations through which the Divine manifests itself; elements of the world; dimensions, primordial numbers.
Selektion (Ger.), (1) in ghettos and other Jewish settlements, the drawing up by Nazis of lists of deportees; (2) separation of incoming victims to concentration camps into two categories – those destined for immediate killing and those to be sent for forced labor.
Seliḥah (pl. ***seliḥot**), penitential prayer.
***Semikhah**, ordination conferring the title "rabbi" and permission to give decisions in matters of ritual and law.
Sephardi (pl. ***Sephardim**), Jew(s) of Spain and Portugal and their descendants, wherever resident, as contrasted with *Ashkenazi(m).
Shabbatean, adherent of the pseudo-messiah *Shabbetai Ẓevi (17th century).
Shaddai, name of God found frequently in the Bible and commonly translated "Almighty."
***Shaḥarit**, morning service.
Shali'aḥ (pl. **sheliḥim**), in Jewish law, messenger, agent; in modern times, an emissary from Ereẓ Israel to Jewish communities or organizations abroad for the purpose of fund-raising, organizing pioneer immigrants, education, etc.
Shalmonit, poetic meter introduced by the liturgical poet *Solomon ha-Bavli.
***Shammash**, synagogue beadle.
***Shavuot**, Pentecost; Festival of Weeks; second of the three annual pilgrim festivals, commemorating the receiving of the Torah at Mt. Sinai.
***Sheḥitah**, ritual slaughtering of animals.
***Shekhinah**, Divine Presence.
Shelishit, poem with three-line stanzas.
***Sheluḥei Ereẓ Israel** (or **shadarim**), emissaries from Ereẓ Israel.
***Shema** ([Yisrael]; "hear… [O Israel]," Deut. 6:4), Judaism's confession of faith, proclaiming the absolute unity of God.
Shemini Aẓeret, final festal day (in the Diaspora, final two days) at the conclusion of *Sukkot.
Shemittah, *Sabbatical year.
Sheniyyah, poem with two-line stanzas.
***Shephelah**, southern part of the coastal plain of Ereẓ Israel.
***Shevat**, eleventh month of the Jewish religious year, fifth of the civil, approximating to January–February.
***Shi'ur Komah**, Hebrew mystical work (c. eighth century) containing a physical description of God's dimensions; term denoting enormous spacial measurement used in speculations concerning the body of the **Shekhinah*.
Shivah, the "seven days" of *mourning following burial of a relative.
***Shofar**, horn of the ram (or any other ritually clean animal excepting the cow) sounded for the memorial blowing on *Rosh Ha-Shanah, and other occasions.
Shoḥet, person qualified to perform **sheḥitah*.
Shomer, *Ha-Shomer, organization of Jewish workers in Ereẓ Israel founded in 1909 to defend Jewish settlements.
***Shtadlan**, Jewish representative or negotiator with access to dignitaries of state, active at royal courts, etc.
***Shtetl**, Jewish small-town community in Eastern Europe.
***Shulḥan Arukh**, Joseph *Caro's code of Jewish law in four parts:
Oraḥ Ḥayyim, laws relating to prayers, Sabbath, festivals, and fasts;
Yoreh De'ah, dietary laws, etc;
Even ha-Ezer, laws dealing with women, marriage, etc;
Ḥoshen Mishpat, civil, criminal law, court procedure, etc.
Siddur, among Ashkenazim, the volume containing the daily prayers (in distinction to the **maḥzor* containing those for the festivals).
***Simḥat Torah**, holiday marking the completion in the synagogue of the annual cycle of reading the Pentateuch; in Ereẓ Israel observed on Shemini Aẓeret (outside Ereẓ Israel on the following day).
***Sinai Campaign**, brief campaign in October–November 1956 when Israel army reacted to Egyptian terrorist attacks and blockade by occupying the Sinai peninsula.
Sitra aḥra, "the other side" (of God); left side; the demoniac and satanic powers.
***Sivan**, third month of the Jewish religious year, ninth of the civil, approximating to May–June.
***Six-Day War**, rapid war in June 1967 when Israel reacted to Arab threats and blockade by defeating the Egyptian, Jordanian, and Syrian armies.
***S.S.** (initials of Ger. *Schutzstaffel*: "protection detachment"), Nazi formation established in 1925 which later became the "elite" organization of the Nazi Party and carried out central tasks in the "Final Solution."
***Status quo ante** community, community in Hungary retaining the status it had held before the convention of the General Jew-

ish Congress there in 1868 and the resultant split in Hungarian Jewry.
*Sukkah, booth or tabernacle erected for *Sukkot when, for seven days, religious Jews "dwell" or at least eat in the *sukkah* (Lev. 23:42).
*Sukkot, festival of Tabernacles; last of the three pilgrim festivals, beginning on the 15th of Tishri.
Sūra (Ar.), chapter of the Koran.
Ta'anit Esther (Fast of *Esther), fast on the 13th of Adar, the day preceding Purim.
Takkanah (pl. ***takkanot**), regulation supplementing the law of the Torah; regulations governing the internal life of communities and congregations.
***Tallit (gadol)**, four-cornered prayer shawl with fringes (*ẓiẓit*) at each corner.
***Tallit katan**, garment with fringes (*ẓiẓit*) appended, worn by observant male Jews under their outer garments.
***Talmud**, "teaching"; compendium of discussion on the Mishnah by generations of scholars and jurists in many academies over a period of several centuries. The Jerusalem (or Palestinian) Talmud mainly contains the discussions of the Palestinian sages. The Babylonian Talmud incorporates the parallel discussion in the Babylonian academies.
Talmud torah, term generally applied to Jewish religious (and ultimately to talmudic) study; also to traditional Jewish religious public schools.
***Tammuz**, fourth month of the Jewish religious year, tenth of the civil, approximating to June-July.
Tanna (pl. ***tannaim**), rabbinic teacher of mishnaic period.
***Targum**, Aramaic translation of the Bible.
***Tefillin**, phylacteries, small leather cases containing passages from Scripture and affixed on the forehead and arm by male Jews during the recital of morning prayers.
Tell (Ar. "mound," "hillock"), ancient mound in the Middle East composed of remains of successive settlements.
***Terefah**, food that is not **kasher*, owing to a defect on the animal.
***Territorialism**, 20th century movement supporting the creation of an autonomous territory for Jewish mass-settlement outside Ereẓ Israel.
***Tevet**, tenth month of the Jewish religious year, fourth of the civil, approximating to December–January.
Tikkun ("restitution," "reintegration"), (1) order of service for certain occasions, mostly recited at night; (2) mystical term denoting restoration of the right order and true unity after the spiritual "catastrophe" which occurred in the cosmos.
Tishah be-Av, Ninth of *Av, fast day commemorating the destruction of the First and Second Temples.
***Tishri**, seventh month of the Jewish religious year, first of the civil, approximating to September–October.
Tokheḥah, reproof sections of the Pentateuch (Lev. 26 and Deut. 28); poem of reproof.
***Torah**, Pentateuch or the Pentateuchal scroll for reading in synagogue; entire body of traditional Jewish teaching and literature.
Tosafist, talmudic glossator, mainly French (12–14th centuries), bringing additions to the commentary by *Rashi.
***Tosafot**, glosses supplied by tosafist.
***Tosefta**, a collection of teachings and traditions of the *tannaim*, closely related to the Mishnah.
Tradent, person who hands down a talmudic statement on the name of his teacher or other earlier authority.
***Tu bi-Shevat**, the 15th day of Shevat, the New Year for Trees; date marking a dividing line for fruit tithing; in modern Israel celebrated as arbor day.
***Uganda Scheme**, plan suggested by the British government in 1903 to establish an autonomous Jewish settlement area in East Africa.
***Va'ad Le'ummi**, national council of the Jewish community in Ereẓ Israel during the period of the British *Mandate.
***Wannsee Conference**, Nazi conference held on Jan. 20, 1942, at which the planned annihilation of European Jewry was endorsed.
Waqf (Ar.), (1) a Muslim charitable pious foundation; (2) state lands and other property passed to the Muslim community for public welfare.
***War of Independence**, war of 1947–49 when the Jews of Israel fought off Arab invading armies and ensured the establishment of the new State.
***White Paper(s)**, report(s) issued by British government, frequently statements of policy, as issued in connection with Palestine during the *Mandate period.
***Wissenschaft des Judentums** (Ger. "Science of Judaism"), movement in Europe beginning in the 19th century for scientific study of Jewish history, religion, and literature.
***Yad Vashem**, Israel official authority for commemorating the *Holocaust in the Nazi era and Jewish resistance and heroism at that time.
Yeshivah (pl. ***yeshivot**), Jewish traditional academy devoted primarily to study of rabbinic literature; *rosh yeshivah*, head of the yeshivah.
YHWH, the letters of the holy name of God, the Tetragrammaton.
Yibbum, see levirate marriage.
Yiḥud, "union"; mystical term for intention which causes the union of God with the **Shekhinah*.
Yishuv, settlement; more specifically, the Jewish community of Ereẓ Israel in the pre-State period. The pre-Zionist community is generally designated the "old yishuv" and the community evolving from 1880, the "new yishuv."
Yom Kippur, Yom ha-Kippurim, *Day of Atonement, solemn fast day observed on the 10th of Tishri.
Yoreh De'ah, see Shulḥan Arukh.
Yoẓer, hymns inserted in the first benediction (*Yoẓer Or*) of the morning **Shema*.
***Ẓaddik**, person outstanding for his faith and piety; especially a ḥasidic rabbi or leader.
Ẓimẓum, "contraction"; mystical term denoting the process whereby God withdraws or contracts within Himself so leaving a primordial vacuum in which creation can take place; primordial exile or self-limitation of God.
***Zionist Commission (1918)**, commission appointed in 1918 by the British government to advise the British military authorities in Palestine on the implementation of the *Balfour Declaration.
Ẓyyonei Zion, the organized opposition to Herzl in connection with the *Uganda Scheme.
***Ẓiẓit**, fringes attached to the **tallit* and **tallit katan*.
***Zohar**, mystical commentary on the Pentateuch; main textbook of *Kabbalah.
Zulat, hymn inserted after the **Shema* in the morning service.